CHILTON'S
TRUCK AND VAN
MANUAL 1992-96

Publisher & Editor-In-Chief Kerry A. Freeman, S.A.E.
Executive Editors Dean F. Morgantini, S.A.E., W. Calvin Settle, Jr., S.A.E.
Managing Editor Nicholas L. D'Andrea
Senior Editors Debra Gaffney, Jacques Gordon, Michael L. Grady, Kevin M. G. Maher, Richard J. Rivele, S.A.E., Richard T. Smith, Jim Taylor, Ron Webb

Special Products Managers Eric O. Cole, Kenneth J. Grabowski, A.S.E., S.A.E.
Project Managers Larry Braun, S.A.E., A.S.C., Thomas P. Browne III, Joseph DeFrancesco, Robert E. Doughten, Benjamin E. Greisler, S.A.E., Martin J. Gunther, Craig P. Nangle, A.S.E., Richard Schwartz
Editorial Staff Jaffer A. Ahmad, Chris Armenti, Bradley Bower, James Carr, Robert A. Chabot, William C. Cottman, A.S.E., Leonard Davis, A.S.E., Michael DiFurio Jr., S.A.E., Robert F. Dougherty Jr., John J. Ferraro, A.S.E., S.A.E., Sam Fiorani, Matthew E. Frederick, William C. Friedauer, Edward J. Giacomucci, A.S.E., S.A.E., Al Gibbs, Herbert Guie Jr, Dawn M. Hoch, David E. Jester, Lori Johnson, A.S.E., William Kessler, Kenneth F. Konzelman, Neil J. Leonard, A.S.E., James R. Marotta, Robert McAnally, Raymond K. Moore, Norman D. Norville, A.S.E., Christine L. Nuckowski, Eric S. Peterson, A.S.E., Ernest H. Ralph, A.S.E., Charles Ramsey, A.S.E., Roy Ripple, A.S.E., Don Schnell, A.S.E., S.A.E., Paul Shanahan, Larry E. Stiles, Gordon L. Tobias, Anthony Tortorici, A.S.E., S.A.E., Albert A. Wood, A.S.E.

Manager, Product Systems Development Robert E. Maxey
Production Manager Andrea M. Steiger
Assistant Production Manager Marsha Park Herman
Production Specialists Christina Davis, Kimberly T. Hayes, Joseph C. McGinty, Elizabeth E. Thompson
Director of Manufacturing Mike D'Imperio
Asst. Manufacturing Manager Robin Norman
President, Chilton Enterprises David S. Loewith
Senior Vice President Ronald A. Hoxter

CHILTON BOOK COMPANY

**ONE OF THE DIVERSIFIED PUBLISHING COMPANIES,
A PART OF CAPITAL CITIES/ABC, INC.**

Manufactured in
© 1995 Chilton Book Company
Chilton Way, Radnor, PA 19089
ISBN 0-8019-7918-8
ISSN 0742-0315

1234567890   4321098765

TRUCK MODELS

Table of Contents

Truck Sections

HOW TO USE THIS MANUAL

Truck Section

Truck sections are grouped by manufacturer and arranged in alphabetical order. The text and illustrations that comprise the service procedures in each Truck Section are arranged in the following order of systems and components: Engine Mechanical, Engine Lubrication, Engine Cooling, Engine Electrical, Emission Controls, Fuel System, Drive Axle, Manual Transmission/Transaxle, Clutch, Automatic Transmission/Transaxle, Front Suspension, Rear Suspension, Steering, Brakes, Chassis Electrical.

Specification charts are always located at the front of each section. All illustrations are located as close as possible to the pertinent text. Procedures are for all models in the particular section unless specifically noted otherwise.

Locating Information

The Table of Contents, at the front of the book, lists the beginning of each Truck Section in the manual.

To find where a particular Truck Section is located in the book, you need only look in the Table of Contents. Once you have found the proper section, you may wish to find where specific procedures are located in that section. Turn to the Index at the front of the section. At the upper left-hand side is a listing of the main topics within the section and the page number they will be found on. Following the main topics is an alphabetical listing of all the procedures within the section and their page numbers.

Safety Notice

Proper service and repair procedures are vital to the safe, reliable operation of all motor vehicles, as well as the personal safety of those performing repairs. This manual outlines procedures for servicing and repairing vehicles using safe effective methods. The procedures contain many NOTES and CAUTIONS which should be followed along with standard safety procedures to eliminate the possibility of personal injury or improper service which could damage the vehicle or compromise its safety.

It is important to note that repair procedures and techniques, tools and parts for servicing motor vehicles, as well as the skill and experience of the individual performing the work vary widely. It is not possible to anticipate all of the conceivable ways or conditions under which vehicles may be serviced, or to provide cautions as to all of the possible hazards that may result. Standard and accepted safety precautions and equipment should be used when handling toxic or flammable fluids, and safety goggles or other protection should be used during cutting, grinding, chiseling, prying, or any other process that can cause material removal or projectiles.

Some procedures require the use of tools specially designed for a specific purpose. Before substituting another tool or procedure, you must be completely satisfied that neither your personal safety, nor the performance of the vehicle will be endangered.

Part Numbers

Part numbers listed in this book are not recommendations by Chilton for any product by brand name. They are references that can be used with interchange manuals and aftermarket supplier catalogs to locate each brand supplier's discrete part number.

Although information in this manual is based on industry sources and is as complete as possible at the time of publication, the possibility exists that some truck manufacturers made later changes which could not be included here. Information on very late models may not be available in some circumstances. While striving for total accuracy, Chilton Book Company cannot assume responsibility for any errors, changes, or omissions that may occur in the compilation of this data.

Copyright Notice

Chrysler Corporation

1

CHRYSLER—Town & Country **DODGE**—Dakota • Caravan • DW Series (pick-up) • Ramcharger • B Series (van) **PLYMOUTH**—Voyager

FIRING ORDERS

NOTE: To avoid confusion, always replace spark plug wires one at a time.

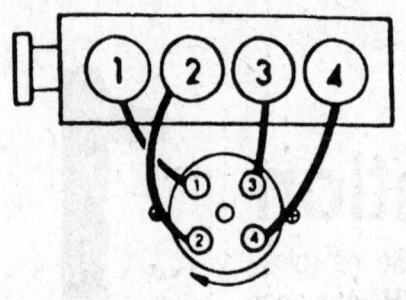

85612004

2.5L engine
Firing order: 1–3–4–2
Distributor rotation: Clockwise

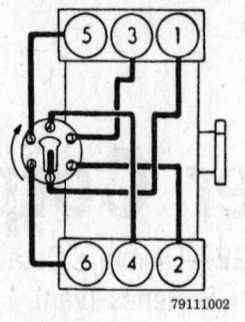

79111002

3.9L Engine
Engine Firing Order:
1–6–5–4–3–2
Distributor Rotation:
Clockwise

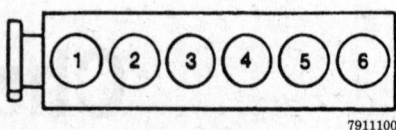

79111003

Cummins 5.9L Turbo-diesel Engine
Engine Firing Order: 1–5–3–6–2–4

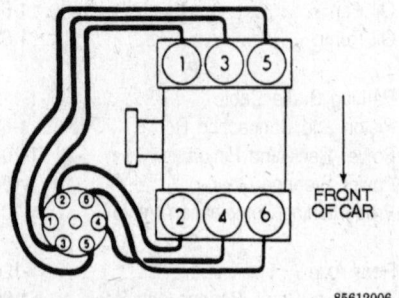

FRONT OF CAR

85612006

3.0L engine
Firing order: 1–2–3–4–5–6
Distributor rotation: Counterclockwise

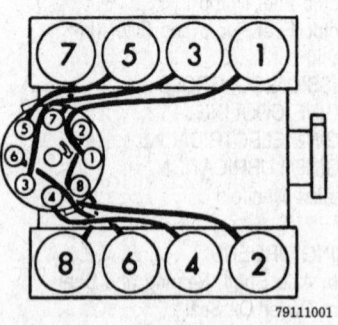

79111001

5.2L and 5.9L Engines
Engine Firing Order: 1–8–4–3–6–5–7–2
Distributor Rotation: Clockwise

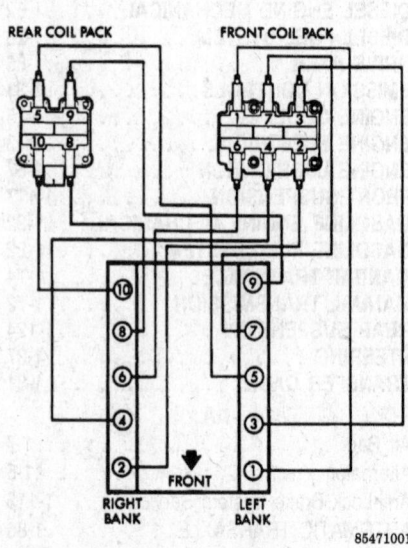

REAR COIL PACK   FRONT COIL PACK

RIGHT BANK   FRONT   LEFT BANK

85471001

8.0L Engine
Engine Firing Order: 1–10–9–4–3–6–5–8–7–2
Distributorless Ignition System

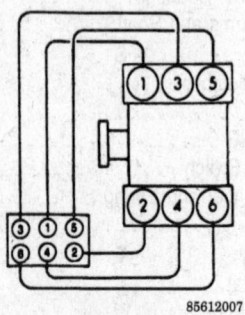

85612007

3.3L and 3.8L engines
Firing order: 1–2–3–4–5–6
Distributorless Ignition
System

ENGINE ELECTRICAL

NOTE: Disconnecting the negative battery cable on some vehicles may interfere with the functions of the on-board computer systems and may require the computer to undergo a relearning process, once the negative battery cable is reconnected.

Distributor

REMOVAL

1. Disconnect the negative battery cable.
2. Disconnect the distributor pickup lead wires and vacuum hose, if equipped.
3. Unfasten the distributor cap retaining clips and lift off the distributor cap with all ignition wires connected. Remove the coil wire, if necessary.
4. Matchmark the rotor to the distributor housing.

NOTE: Do not crank the engine during this procedure. If the engine is cranked, the matchmark must be disregarded.

5. Remove the hold-down bolt and clamp.
6. Remove the distributor from the engine.

INSTALLATION

Timing Not Disturbed

1. Install a new distributor housing O-ring.
2. Install the distributor in the engine so the rotor is aligned with the matchmark on the housing and the housing is aligned with the matchmark on the engine. Make sure the distributor is fully seated and the distributor shaft is fully engaged.
3. Install the hold-down clamp and snug the hold-down bolt.
4. Connect the distributor pickup lead wires.
5. Install the distributor cap and snap the retaining clips into place.
6. Connect the negative battery cable.
7. Adjust the ignition timing and tighten the hold-down bolt.

Timing Disturbed

1. Install a new distributor housing O-ring.
2. Position the engine so the No. 1 piston is at TDC of the compression stroke and the mark on the vibration damper is aligned with **0** on the timing indicator.
3. Install the distributor in the engine so the rotor is aligned with the position of the No. 1 ignition wire on the distributor cap and the housing is aligned with the matchmark on the engine. Make sure the distributor is fully seated and the distributor shaft is fully engaged.
4. Install the hold-down clamp and snug the hold-down bolt.
5. Connect the distributor pickup lead wires.
6. Install the distributor cap and snap the retaining clips into place.
7. Connect the negative battery cable.
8. Adjust the ignition timing and tighten the hold-down nut or bolt.

Distributorless Ignition

REMOVAL AND INSTALLATION

Ignition Coils

3.3L AND 3.8L ENGINES

1. Disconnect the negative battery cable.
2. Remove the electrical connector from the coil assembly. Tag and disconnect the spark plug wires from the coil assembly.
3. Remove the coil mounting bolts and remove the coil assembly from the engine.
4. Mount the coil in position and connect all of the wires. Tighten the coil assembly mounting bolts to 105 inch lbs. (12 Nm).
5. Connect the negative battery cable.

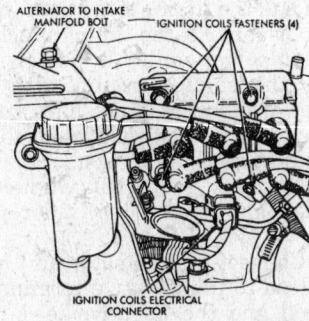

Ignition coil removal — 3.3L and 3.8L engines

8.0L ENGINE

1. The coil packs are located above the right valve cover. The 2 coil packs can be serviced separately.
2. Disconnect the negative battery cable. Disconnect the secondary spark plug cables from the coil packs and label for installation.
3. Disconnect the primary wiring harness from the coil packs. Remove the 4 mounting screws and coil packs.
   To install:
4. Position the coil packs with the wring harness facing down.
5. Install the mounting screws and reconnect the primary and secondary wiring. The 4 wire connect goes to the front pack and the 3 wire to the rear.

Ignition Control Module

The ignition system is controlled through the Powertrain Control Module and does not use a separate ignition control module.

Camshaft Sensor

3.3L AND 3.8L ENGINES

1. The camshaft sensor is located near the right engine mount, in the timing chain case.
2. Disconnect the negative battery cable.
3. Disconnect the sensor electrical connector.
4. Remove the right engine mount support bracket.
5. Loosen the sensor retaining bolt enough to slide the sensor past the bolt. Do not pull on the wiring harness.
   To install:

NOTE: If the removed sensor is reinstalled, clean off the old spacer on the sensor face. A new spacer must be attached to the face before installation

6. Apply engine oil to the O-ring. Install the sensor in the chain case cover and push the sensor down until contact is made with the camshaft gear. While holding the sensor in this position, install and tighten the retaining bolt to 125 inch lbs. (14 Nm).
7. Connect the electrical connector and battery cable, install the engine support bracket, start engine and check operation.

8.0L ENGINE

1. The sensor is located in the timing chain cover on the left side of the engine.
2. Disconnect the negative battery cable and camshaft sensor electrical connector.

3. Remove the sensor bolt and carefully pull the sensor from the timing chain cover in a rocking action with 2 small prybars.

To install:

NOTE: When installing a used camshaft sensor, the sensor depth must be adjusted to prevent contact with the camshaft gear.

4. To install a used camshaft sensor, perform the following:

a. Observe the face of the sensor. If any original rib material remains, it must be cut down flush to the face of the sensor with a razor blade. Remove only enough of the rib material until the face of the sensor is flat. Do not remove more material then necessary or use an electric grinder.

b. From the Dodge/Chrysler/Plymouth dealer, obtain a peel-and-stick paper spacer to provide the proper clearance during sensor installation.

c. Clean the sensor and install the paper spacer.

d. Apply engine oil to the seal and install the sensor to the engine. Do not twist the sensor during installation because the O-ring or paper spacer may be damaged.

e. Scratch a scribe line into the timing chain cover to indicate depth of the sensor. Remove the sensor from the timing cover.

f. Remove the paper spacer from the sensor. This step must be followed to prevent the paper spacer from getting into the engine lubrication system.

g. Install the sensor into the timing case cover with slight rocking motion until the sensor is aligned with the scribe mark. Torque the mounting screw to 50 inch lbs. (6 Nm). Connect the electrical connector and battery cable.

5. Install a new camshaft sensor with a slight rocking motion, without twisting. Push the sensor all the way into the cover until the rib material on the sensor contacts the camshaft gear. Install the mounting screw and torque to 50 inch lbs. (6 Nm). Connect the harness and battery cable.

Crankshaft Sensor

3.3L AND 3.8L ENGINES

1. The crankshaft sensor is located in the transaxle housing.
2. Disconnect the negative battery cable and sensor connector.
3. Remove the retaining bolt and pull the sensor straight out of the transaxle housing.

To install:

NOTE: If the removed sensor is reinstalled, clean off the old spacer on the sensor face. A new spacer must be attached to the face before installation

4. Install the sensor and push down until contact is made with the driveplate. While holding the sensor in place, install the bolt and torque to 105 inch lbs. (12 Nm). Connect the electrical connector and battery cable.

8.0L ENGINE

1. The sensor is located on the right lower side of the cylinder block, forward of the right engine mount, just above the oil pan rail.
2. Disconnect the negative battery cable. Raise the vehicle and support safely.
3. Disconnect the electrical connector and remove the mounting bolt.
4. Carefully pry the sensor from the cylinder block in a rocking motion with 2 small prybars.

To install:

5. Apply engine oil to the sensor O-ring and install with a slight rocking motion. Do not twist.
6. Install the mounting bolt and torque to 70 inch lbs. (8 Nm).
7. Connect the electrical connector and negative battery cable.

Ignition Control Module (ICM)

The 8.0L engine has an ignition control module mounted to the right inner fender, behind the coolant reservoir tank.

Ignition Timing

ADJUSTMENT

2.5L and 3.0L Engines

1. With the engine OFF, clean off the timing marks.
2. Mark the pulley or damper notch and the timing scale with white chalk or paint. If the timing notch on the damper or pulley is not visible, bump the engine around with the starter or turn the crankshaft with a wrench on the front pulley bolt to get it to an accessible position.
3. Connect a suitable inductive timing light to No. 1 cylinder plug wire.
4. Connect a tachometer unit, positive lead to the negative terminal of the coil and the negative lead to a known good engine ground. Select the tachometer appropriate cylinder position.

5. Warm the engine to normal operating temperature.
6. With engine at normal operating temperature, disconnect coolant temperature sensor. Radiator fan and instrument panel check engine lamp should come ON. (See specifications decal under the hood for specific instructions).
7. Read engine rpm on the tachometer 1000 rpm scale, and adjust curb idle to specification noted on the under hood label.
8. Aim the timing light toward timing indicator, and read degree marks. If flash occurs when timing mark is before specification, timing is advanced. If flash occurs when timing mark is after specification, timing is retarded.

NOTE: Models equipped with the 2.5L engine have the timing marks visible through a window on the transaxle housing. Models equipped with the 3.0L engine have the timing marks on the front crankshaft pulley.

9. If adjustment is necessary, loosen the distributor hold down screw. Turn the distributor slowly to specified value, and tighten hold down screw. Recheck ignition timing.
10. Turn the engine OFF and remove the tachometer and timing light.
11. Connect the coolant temperature sensor.

NOTE: Reconnecting the coolant temperature sensor will turn the check engine lamp OFF; however, a fault code will be stored in the SMEC. After 50 to 100 key ON/OFF cycles the SMEC will cancel the fault code. The code can also be canceled by disconnecting the battery.

3.3L, 3.8L and 8.0L Engines

The 3.3L, 3.8L and 8.0L engines use an electronic distributorless ignition system. The ignition timing cannot be changed or set in any way.

3.9L, 5.2L and 5.9L Engines

1. Start the engine, set the parking brake and run the engine until normal operating temperature is reached. Keep all lights and accessories OFF.
2. If a magnetic timing unit is available, insert the probe into the receptacle near the timing scale. The scale is located on the timing chain cover above and to the left of the vibration damper on Pick-Ups or below the damper on Vans.

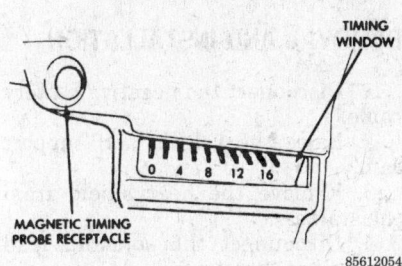

Timing mark — 2.5L engine

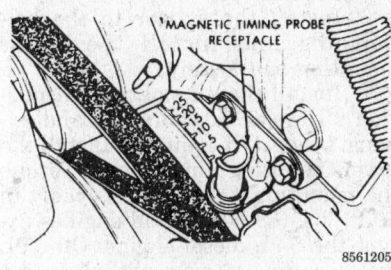

Timing mark — 3.0L engine

3. If a magnetic timing unit is not available, connect a conventional power timing light to the No. 1 cylinder spark plug wire.

4. Connect the red lead of a tachometer to the negative primary terminal of the coil and connect the black lead to a good ground.

5. Set the idle speed according to the Vehicle Emission Control Information (VECI) label. Disconnect and plug the distributor vacuum advance hose at the distributor or computer, if equipped.

6. Connect the Diagnostic Readout Box II (DRBII) and access the Basic Timing Mode. If the DRBII is not available, disconnect the coolant sensor located near the thermostat housing and confirm that the Check Engine light on the instrument panel is **ON**.

7. Aim the timing light at the timing scale or read the magnetic timing unit.

8. If the timing is advanced (higher than the specification on the VECI label), the distributor should be turned clockwise. If the timing is retarded, (lower than the specification on the VECI label), the distributor should be turned counterclockwise.

9. Loosen the distributor hold-down bolt just enough so the distribu-

tor can be rotated. Turn the distributor in the proper direction until the specified timing is reached. Tighten the hold-down bolt and recheck the timing and idle speed.

10. Turn the engine **OFF**. Remove the jumper wire, if used. Connect the vacuum hose or coolant sensor (make sure the Check Engine light does not come ON when started). Disconnect the timing apparatus and tachometer.

11. If the coolant temperature sensor was disconnected, erase the created fault code using the Erase Fault Code mode on the DRBII. If the DRBII is not available, the code can be erased by disconnecting the battery, although it is not recommended.

NOTE: If the battery is disconnected, radio memory will be lost and other fault codes that may have been stored in the computer's memory will be erased. If the coolant sensor code is not erased at this point, it will disappear after 50–100 vehicle key on/off cycles providing there is no problem with that circuit.

Alternator

PRECAUTIONS

Several precautions must be observed when working with the alternator to avoid damaging the unit.

• If the battery is removed for any reason, make sure it is reconnected with the correct polarity. Reversing the battery connections may result in damage to the one-way rectifiers.

• When utilizing a booster battery as a starting aid, always connect the positive to positive terminals and the negative terminal from the booster battery to a good engine ground on the vehicle being started.

• Never use a fast charger as a booster to start vehicles.

• Disconnect the battery cables when charging the battery with a fast charger.

• Never attempt to polarize the alternator.

• Do not use test lights of more than 12 volts when checking diode continuity.

• Do not short across or ground any of the alternator terminals.

• The polarity of the battery, alternator and regulator must be matched and considered before making any electrical connections within the system.

• Never separate the alternator on an open circuit. Make sure all connec-

tions within the circuit are clean and tight.

• Disconnect the battery ground terminal when performing any service on electrical components.

• Disconnect the battery if arc welding is to be done on the vehicle.

BELT TENSION ADJUSTMENT

NOTE: The belt tension is automatically adjusted by the tensioner on the all engines except 2.5L engine. Periodic adjustment is not necessary.

1. Disconnect negative battery cable.

2. Loosen alternator pivot bolt slightly.

3. Loosen the adjuster strap nut or bolt just enough so the alternator can be moved.

4. If the alternator bracket is not equipped with an adjuster bolt, use a prybar and apply tension to the alternator until the belt(s) deflect about $1/4$–$1/2$ in. under a 10 lb. load. Torque the adjuster strap bolt to 200 inch lbs. (23 Nm). Torque the pivot bolt to 30 ft. lbs. (41 Nm).

5. If the bracket is equipped with an adjuster bolt, tighten it until the belts deflect about $1/2$ in. under a 10 lb. load. Torque the adjuster strap nut to 200 inch lbs. (23 Nm). Torque the pivot bolt to 30 ft. lbs. (41 Nm).

6. Reconnect negative battery cable.

REMOVAL AND INSTALLATION

1. Disconnect the negative battery cable.

2. On the all engines except 2.5L engine, use a $3/8$ in. drive breaker bar to lift the belt tensioner and remove the belt. On the 2.5L engine, loosen the mounting bolts, move the alternator toward the engine and remove the drive belt(s).

NOTE: On some Vans, it may be easier to remove the alternator through the right front wheelwell since the fan shroud and possibly air conditioning and heater plumbing under the hood will prevent removal from in front of the vehicle. Raise the vehicle and safely support. Remove the right front wheel and gain access to the alternator on these applications.

3. Remove the mounting bolts, spacers and adjuster bolt. Remove the alternator from the brackets.

4. Remove the battery positive, field and ground terminals from the

rear of the alternator. Remove the wire harness hold-down screw from the alternator.

To install:

5. Connect all wiring to the proper terminals on the rear of the alternator and install the wire harness hold-down screw.

6. Position the alternator in the mounting brackets.

7. Install the spacers, pivot bolt, adjuster strap bolt or nut and adjuster bolt.

8. On the all engines except 2.5L engine, torque the upper bolt to 18 ft. lbs. (24 Nm), the lower bolt to 32 ft. lbs. (43 Nm) and install the belt. On 2.5L engine, install the drive belt(s) and adjust to specification. Torque the adjuster strap nut or bolt to 200 inch lbs. (23 Nm). Torque the pivot bolt to 30 ft. lbs. (41 Nm).

9. Connect the negative battery cable.

Voltage Regulator

REMOVAL AND INSTALLATION

NOTE: The voltage regulator is integrated into the circuitry of the Single Module Engine Con-

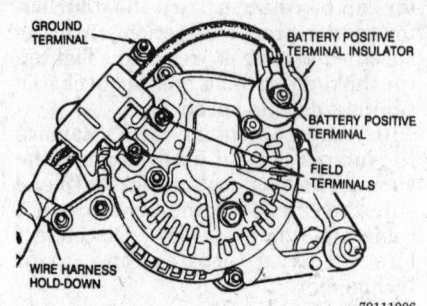

Chrysler 90HS, 120HS and Nippondenso alternator terminals

troller (SMEC) or Single Board Engine Controller (SBEC) on vehicles with EFI and is not serviceable.

1. Disconnect the negative battery cable.

2. Unplug the connector from the voltage regulator.

3. Remove the retaining screws and remove the regulator from the vehicle.

4. The installation is the reversal of the removal procedure. Make sure the connector retainer is properly clipped in place.

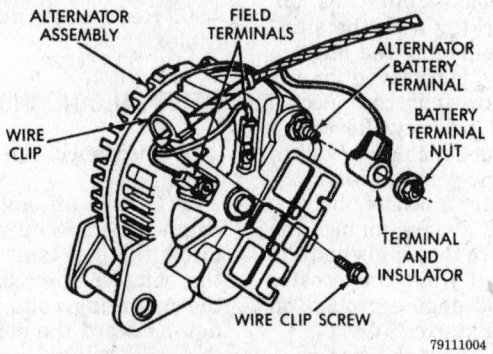

Chrysler 60 and 78 amp alternator terminals

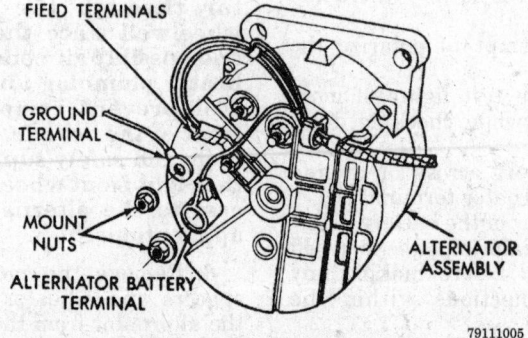

Chrysler 114 amp alternator terminals

Starter

REMOVAL AND INSTALLATION

1. Disconnect the negative battery cable.

2. Raise the vehicle and support safely.

3. Remove the heat shield from the starter.

4. Disconnect the solenoid lead wires from the starter.

5. Unbolt the starter, remove the exhaust bracket and automatic transmission oil cooler tube bracket, if equipped, and remove the starter from the vehicle.

To install:

6. Install the starter to the bellhousing and install the upper mounting bolt loosely.

7. Install the automatic transmission oil cooler tube bracket and exhaust bracket, if equipped. Install the lower mounting nut or bolts. Torque the mounting nut and bolt evenly to 50 ft. lbs. (68 Nm) on all engines except the 5.9L diesel engine. On 5.9L diesel engine, torque the mounting bolts to 32 ft. lbs. (43 Nm).

8. Connect the solenoid lead wires.

9. Install the heat shield.

10. Connect the negative battery cable and check the starter for proper operation.

Intake Manifold Heater

REMOVAL AND INSTALLATION

5.9L Diesel Engine

1. Disconnect the negative battery cable.

2. Remove the intercooler outlet duct from air inlet tube, if equipped.

3. Remove the 4 bolts that attach the air crossover to the intake manifold. Loosen the lower throttle control bracket mounting bolt and move the bracket away from the engine.

4. Loosen the hose clamps on the turbocharger end of the crossover tube and remove the tube and gasket. Cover the turbocharger opening with a clean shop towel.

5. Disconnect the electrical wiring from the intake manifold heater, remove the heater and remove the gasket.

To install:

6. Clean the gasket mounting surface and install a new gasket.

7. Install the intake manifold heater and connect the wiring.

8. Remove the towel from the turbocharger opening and install the air

crossover tube and gasket. Tighten the hose clamps.

9. Rotate the throttle control bracket back into place. Torque all mounting bolts to 18 ft. lbs. (24 Nm).

10. Attach the throttle rod to the throttle lever. Reconnect negative battery cable.

TESTING

1. Disconnect the negative battery cable.

2. Disconnect the wires from the intake manifold heater.

3. Using an ohmmeter, check the resistance from a good ground to each heater terminal.

4. If there is any resistance, or if the circuit is open, inspect the assembly for dirty or corroded connections.

5. If the resistance is 0 ohms, the heater is functioning properly.

6. If the circuit is open, the heater is defective.

79111008

Rotating the throttle bracket away from the engine — 5.9L diesel engine

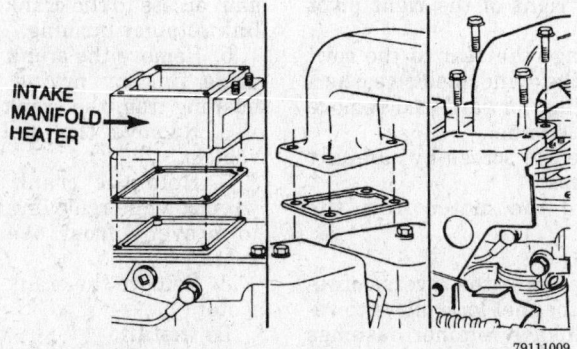

79111009

Intake manifold heater and related parts — 5.9L diesel engine

CHASSIS ELECTRICAL

Air Bag

DISARMING

--------- **WARNING** ---------

Replace air bag system components with Chrysler Mopar specified replacement parts. Substitute parts may visually appear interchangeable, but internal differences may result in inferior occupant protection. The fasteners, screws, and bolts, originally used for the air bag components, have special coatings and are specifically designed for the air bag system. They must never be replaced with any substitutes. Anytime a new fastener is needed, replace with the correct fasteners provided in the service package or fasteners listed in the Chrysler parts books.

Disconnect and isolate the battery negative cable before beginning any airbag system component removal or installation procedure. This will disable the airbag system. Failure to disconnect the battery could result in accidental airbag deployment and possible personal injury. Allow system capacitor to discharge for 2 minutes before removing any airbag components.

Heater Blower Motor

REMOVAL AND INSTALLATION

Dakota

1. Disconnect the negative battery cable.

2. Remove the lower instrument panel module.

3. If equipped with A/C, disconnect the 2 vacuum lines from the recirculating air door actuator.

4. Disconnect the blower motor lead and remove the 2 screws at the top of the blower housing, securing it to the unit cover.

5. Remove the 5 screws from around the blower housing and separate the blower housing from the unit.

6. Remove the 3 screws securing the blower and wheel assembly to the heater A/C unit housing.

7. Using a pair of pliers, remove the spring retaining ring from the center of the blower wheel and remove the wheel.

To install:

8. Install the blower wheel and spring retaining ring.

9. Installation is the reverse of removal. Connect the battery cable and check operation.

Caravan, Voyager and Town & Country

1992–96

1. Disconnect the negative battery cable.

2. Remove the lower right instrument panel assembly.

3. Remove the blower motor screws attaching the the motor to the A/C-heater unit.

4. Allow the blower assembly to drop downward to clear the instrument panel.

5. Install in reverse of removal.

Van

WITHOUT AIR CONDITIONING

1. Disconnect the negative battery cable.

2. Remove the air intake duct and top ½ of the fan shroud, if necessary. Disconnect the blower connector.

3. Remove the 7 screws that fasten the back plate to the heater housing.

4. Remove the blower motor from the vehicle.

5. Remove the spring clip fastening the blower wheel to the blower shaft and pull off the wheel.

6. Remove the vent tube.

7. Remove the nuts fastening the blower motor to the back plate and remove the motor.

To install:

8. Check the seal for breaks or poor adhesion; repair as needed.

9. Install the blower motor to the back plate.

10. Install the vent tube.

11. Install the blower wheel to the shaft and secure the spring clip.

12. Install the assembly to the heater housing and install the 7 screws.

13. Install electrical connector.

14. Install the fan shroud and air duct if removed.

15. Connect the negative battery cable and check the blower motor for proper operation.

WITH AIR CONDITIONING

1. Disconnect the negative battery cable.

2. Remove the air intake duct and top ½ of the fan shroud.

3. Disconnect the blower connector.

4. Remove the blower motor cooling tube.

5. Remove the retaining nuts and washers from the studs holding the blower.

6. Pull the air conditioning lines inboard and upward while removing the blower assembly from the vehicle. Remove the spring clip fastening the blower wheel to the blower shaft and pull off the wheel.

To install:

7. Install the blower wheel to the shaft and install the spring clip. Inspect the blower mounting plate seal and repair as needed. Apply rubber adhesive to the seal to aid in assembly.

8. Install the blower into the housing and install the washers and nuts.

9. Install the cooling tube.

10. Reconnect the electrical connector.

11. Install the fan shroud and air intake duct.

12. Connect the negative battery cable and check the blower motor for proper operation.

Pick-Up and Ramcharger

1. Disconnect the negative battery cable.

2. Disconnect the blower connector.

3. Remove the blower motor cooling tube.

4. Remove the screws or retaining nuts retaining the blower plate to the housing.

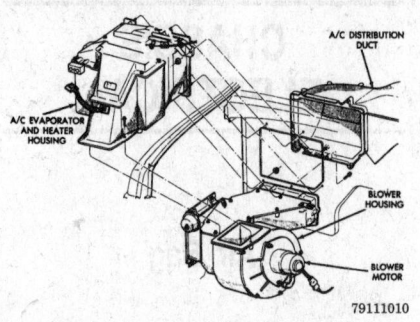

Underhood location of the blower motor — Van with air conditioning

5. Remove the assembly from the housing.

6. Remove the spring clip fastening the blower wheel to the blower shaft and pull off the wheel. Remove the blower from the plate.

To install:

7. Inspect the blower mounting plate seal and repair as necessary.

8. Install the blower to the plate. Install the blower wheel to the shaft and install the spring clip.

9. Install the blower into the housing and install the screws or washers and nuts.

10. Install the cooling tube.

11. Connect the connector.

12. Connect the negative battery cable and check the blower motor for proper operation.

Windshield Wiper Motor

REMOVAL AND INSTALLATION

Dakota

1. Disconnect the negative battery cable.

2. Disconnect the wires from the wiper motor.

3. Remove the mounting bolts and wiper arms.

4. Remove the cowl grill panel. There is a screw in the center of the grille to the right of the right pivot assembly.

5. Disengage the rear of the cowl grille from the windshield weatherstrip by pulling forward and remove the cowl grille panel.

6. Remove the screen by carefully prying up clips.

7. Remove the motor from the vehicle.

To install:

8. Installation is the reverse of removal. Use channel-lock pliers to reinstall the linkage retainer bushings and pins. Torque the motor mounting nuts to 65 inch lbs. (8 Nm) and the

crank arm nut to 96 inch lbs. (11 Nm).

Caravan, Voyager and Town & Country

1. The motor and wiper linkage are serviced as a unit. Disconnect the negative battery cable. Remove the wiper arm and blade assemblies.

2. Open the hood and remove the cowl plenum grille and plastic screen.

3. Remove the hoses from the turret connector. Remove the pivot mounting screws.

4. Disconnect the motor wiring connector from the motor.

5. Remove the retaining nut from the wiper motor shaft to linkage drive crank, and remove the drive crank from the wiper motor shaft.

6. Remove the wiper motor assembly mounting screws and nuts, and remove the wiper motor.

To install:

7. Position the wiper motor against it's mounting surface and secure in position with the mounting screws and nuts Connect the wiring harness.

8. Install the linkage drive crank onto the wiper motor shaft and secure it with the retaining nut. Torque the nut to 95 in. lbs.

9. Install cowl plenum grille plastic screen.

10. Connect hoses to turret connector.

11. Install the cowl plenum grille. Connect the negative battery cable. Close the hood.

12. Install the windshield wiper arm and blade assemblies.

Ramcharger, Van and 1992–93 Pick-Up

1. Disconnect the negative battery cable.

2. Disconnect the wires from the wiper motor.

3. Remove the mounting bolts.

4. Pull the motor out far enough to gain access to the crank arm to motor link retainer bushing.

5. Remove the crank arm from the drive link by prying the retainer bushing from the crank arm.

6. Remove the motor from the vehicle.

7. Hold the crank arm with a wrench while removing the crank nut to prevent from overloading the gears.

8. Remove the crank arm from the motor.

To install:

9. Index the slot correctly and position the crank arm on the motor

shaft. Start the crank nut making sure the crank arm does not move from its slotted position.

10. Hold the crank arm with a wrench and torque the nut to 95 inch lbs. (11 Nm).

11. Lubricate the drive link retainer bushing and install the crank arm pin to the bushing by snapping them together.

12. Install the motor to the vehicle and torque the mounting bolts to 55 inch lbs. (6 Nm).

13. Connect the wires to the motor.

14. Connect the negative battery cable and check the wiper motor for proper operation.

1994–96 Pick-Up

NOTE: This procedure includes the wiper motor linkage.

1. Disconnect the negative battery cable.

2. Remove the wiper arms.

3. Remove the weatherstrip along the front edge of the cowl grille. Release the plastic anchor screws and lift the cowl grille from the vehicle.

4. Remove the washer hoses from the Y-fitting. Remove the wiper linkage mounting bolts.

5. Turn the linkage/motor unit over and unplug the harness and ground connectors.

6. Remove the crank arm from the drive link by prying retainer bushing from the crank arm pin.

7. Remove the 3 retaining screws for the motor-to-linkage bracket.

8. Remove the nut attaching crank arm-to-motor output shaft. Remove the crank arm from the motor.

To install:

9. Position the crank arm on motor drive shaft making sure the slot is indexed properly. Install the crank arm nut to the shaft and torque to 11 ft. lbs. (14 Nm).

10. Install the crank arm pin in the drive link retainer bushing by snap-

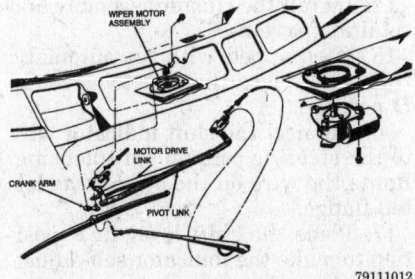

79111012

Typical windshield wiper motor and linkage — Van

ping together with channel-lock pliers.

11. Position the motor on the linkage bracket and torque mounting screws to 55 inch lbs. (6 Nm).

12. Reverse the remaining procedures of removal.

Liftgate Wiper Motor

REMOVAL AND INSTALLATION

1. Disconnect the negative battery cable. Remove the wiper arm and blade assembly.

2. Open the liftgate and remove the trim panel.

3. Remove the 4 mounting screws from liftgate wiper motor and bracket assembly.

4. Disconnect the electrical harness connector and remove the liftgate motor.

To install:

5. Install the liftgate wiper motor and bracket assembly. Secure it with the mounting screws.

6. Connect the wiring harness to the wiper motor.

7. Install the liftgate trim panel and secure it with the mounting screws.

8. Install the liftgate wiper arm and blade assembly.

Windshield Wiper Switch

The windshield wiper switch is a stalk mounted control switch.

REMOVAL AND INSTALLATION

———— WARNING ————

Replace air bag system components with Chrysler Mopar specified replacement parts. Substitute parts may visually appear interchangeable, but internal differences may result in inferior occupant protection. The fasteners, screws, and bolts, originally used for the air bag components, have special coatings and are specifically designed for the air bag system. They must never be replaced with any substitutes. Anytime a new fastener is needed, replace with the correct fasteners provided in the service package or fasteners listed in the Chrysler parts books.

Disconnect and isolate the battery negative cable before beginning any airbag system component removal or installation procedure. This will dis-

able the airbag system. Failure to disconnect the battery could result in accidental airbag deployment and possible personal injury. Allow system capacitor to discharge for 2 minutes before removing any airbag components.

Column Mounted

EXCEPT TILT WHEEL

1. Disconnect the negative battery cable.

2. Remove the lower steering column cover, if equipped.

3. Remove the horn pad mounting screws from behind the steering wheel and remove the horn pad.

4. Remove the steering wheel nut, matchmark the steering wheel to the shaft and remove the steering wheel with a suitable puller.

5. Remove the plastic wiring channel from the underside of the steering column.

6. Disconnect the wiper switch connector, intermittent wipe module connector and cruise control connector, if equipped.

7. Remove the side lock housing cover.

8. Remove the slotted hex-head screw that attaches the wiper switch to the turn signal switch and remove the switch.

9. Remove the control knob from the end of the stalk. Pull the round nylon hider up the control stalk and remove the revealed screws that attach the control stalk sleeve to the wiper switch.

10. Rotate the control stalk shaft to the full clockwise position and remove the shaft from the wiper switch by pulling it straight out.

To install:

11. Install the control shaft to the wiper switch, install the screws, the hider and the control knob.

12. Run the wiring through the opening and down the steering column, position the switch and install the hex-head screw. Make sure the dimmer switch rod is properly engaged.

13. Install the side lock housing cover.

14. Connect the wires and install the wiring channel.

15. Install the steering wheel torque the nut to 45 ft. lbs. (61 Nm).

16. Install the horn pad.

17. Connect the negative battery cable and check the wiper and washer, cruise control, turn signal switch and dimmer switch for proper operation.

18. Install the lower column cover, if equipped.

TILT WHEEL

1. Disconnect the negative battery cable.

2. Remove the lower steering column cover, if equipped and remove the plastic wiring channel from the underside of the steering column.

3. Remove the horn pad mounting screws from behind the steering wheel and remove the horn pad.

4. Remove the steering wheel nut, matchmark the steering wheel to the shaft and remove the steering wheel with a suitable puller.

5. Depress the lock plate with the proper depressing tool, remove the retaining ring from its groove and remove the tool, ring, lock plate, cancelling cam and spring.

6. Remove the switch stalk actuator screw and arm.

7. Remove the hazard switch knob.

8. Disconnect the turn signal switch, wiper switch, intermittent module and cruise control connectors, if equipped.

9. Remove the 3 screws and remove the turn signal switch. Tape the connector to the wires to aid in removal.

10. Remove the ignition key lamp.

11. Place the key in the **LOCK** position and remove the key. Insert a thin tool into the slot next to the switch mounting screw boss, depress the spring latch at the bottom of the slot releasing the lock. Remove the lock cylinder.

12. Remove the buzzer switch and wedge spring.

13. Remove the 3 housing cover screws and remove the housing cover.

14. Remove the wiper switch pivot pin with a punch and remove the switch.

15. Remove the control knob from the end of the stalk. Pull the round nylon hider up the control stalk and remove the revealed screws that attach the control stalk sleeve to the wiper switch.

16. Rotate the control stalk shaft to the full clockwise position and remove the shaft from the wiper switch by pulling it straight out.

To install:

17. Install the control shaft to the wiper switch, install the screws, the hider and the control knob.

18. Run the wiring through the opening and down the steering column, position the switch and install the wiper switch pivot pin.

19. Install the housing cover.

20. Install the buzzer switch and wedge spring.

21. Install the lock cylinder.

22. Install the ignition key lamp.

23. Install the turn signal switch, switch stalk actuator arm and hazard switch knob.

24. Install the spring, cancelling cam, lock plate and ring on the steering shaft. Depress the plate with the depressing tool and install the ring securely in the groove. Remove the tool slowly.

25. Connect the turn signal switch, wiper switch, intermittent module and cruise control connectors, if equipped. Install the trough.

26. Install the steering wheel torque the nut to 45 ft. lbs. (61 Nm).

27. Install the horn pad.

28. Connect the negative battery cable and check the wiper and washer, cruise control, turn signal switch and dimmer switch for proper operation.

29. Install the lower column cover, if equipped.

Instrument Cluster

———— WARNING ————

Replace air bag system components with Chrysler Mopar specified replacement parts. Substitute parts may visually appear interchangeable, but internal differences may result in inferior occupant protection. The fasteners, screws, and bolts, originally used for the air bag components, have special coatings and are specifically designed for the air bag system. They must never be replaced with any substitutes. Anytime a new fastener is needed, replace with the correct fasteners provided in the service package or fasteners listed in the Chrysler parts books.

Disconnect and isolate the battery negative cable before beginning any airbag system component removal or installation procedure. This will disable the airbag system. Failure to disconnect the battery could result in accidental airbag deployment and possible personal injury. Allow system capacitor to discharge for 2 minutes before removing any airbag components.

REMOVAL AND INSTALLATION

Dakota

1. Disconnect the negative battery cable.

2. Remove the cluster bezel and knee blocker.

3. Place the gear selector in the lowest position, if equipped with automatic transmission. Remove the U-shaped retaining clip and disconnect the gear selector indicator cable at the steering column.

4. Remove the cluster retaining screws. Pull the cluster rearward and disconnect the printed circuit connectors.

5. Installation is the reverse of removal. Adjust the gear selector cable.

Caravan, Voyager and Town & Country

1. Disconnect the negative battery cable.

2. Remove the warning indicator grille by prying up with a flat bladed tool.

3. Remove the 3 mounting screws from the warning indicator module assembly and disconnect the wire connector.

4. If equipped with an automatic transaxle, remove the steering column lower cover.

5. If equipped with an automatic transaxle, set the parking brake and shift gear selector into **LOW**.

6. Remove the cluster assembly bezel mounting screws and remove the cluster bezel.

7. Disconnect the shift indicator wire.

8. Remove the cluster assembly retaining screws.

9. Carefully rotate the cluster and disconnect the connector, to access the PRNDL attaching screws.

10. Remove the 2 screws attaching the PRNDL to the cluster.

11. Remove the cluster assembly wiring harness.

To install:

12. Connect the cluster wiring.

13. Connect the speedometer cable.

14. Install the cluster assembly and retaining screws.

15. If equipped with an automatic transaxle, place the selector lever in **D** position.

16. Connect the shift indicator wire to the steering column shift housing. Route the wire on the outside of slotted flange.

17. Place the shift lever in **P** position to make the indicator self-adjust.

18. Connect the shift indicator wire.

19. Install the steering column lower cover.

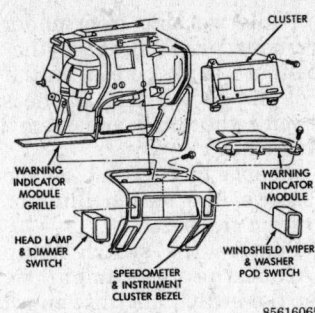

CLUSTER

WARNING INDICATOR MODULE GRILLE

WARNING INDICATOR MODULE

HEAD LAMP & DIMMER SWITCH

WINDSHIELD WIPER & WASHER POD SWITCH

SPEEDOMETER & INSTRUMENT CLUSTER BEZEL

85616065

Instrument panel and cluster mounting — Caravan, Voyager and Town & Country

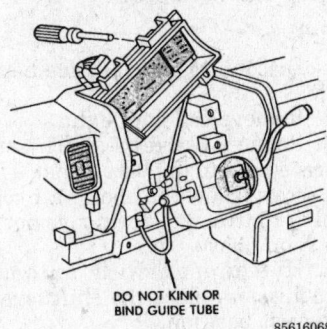

DO NOT KINK OR BIND GUIDE TUBE

85616068

Removal of the PRNDL — Caravan, Voyager and Town & Country

20. Install the cluster assembly bezel. Secure the bezel with the retaining screws.

NOTE: The following instruments can be serviced after removing the instrument cluster mask/lens. Do not completely remove the cluster assembly if only instrument service or cluster bulb replacement is necessary.

Van

1992

1. Disconnect the negative battery cable.

2. Open the glove box. Remove the screws that fasten the hood and bezel assembly. Pull the bezel off the upper retaining clips.

3. Disconnect the gearshift pointer cable from the arm on the steering column, if equipped.

4. Remove the cluster screws. Pull the cluster out far enough to disconnect the speedometer cable by releasing the spring clip.

5. Remove all printed circuit board multiple connectors and the message center connector.

6. Remove the cluster assembly.

7. To remove the speedometer, remove the cluster lens, unplug the Emissions Maintenance Reminder (EMR) timer wires from the speedometer, if equipped, and remove the retaining screws.

To install:

8. Install the speedometer if removed and connect the EMR wiring, if equipped. Position the cluster to the panel and connect the speedometer cable, multiple connectors and message center connector.

9. Push the cluster in place and install the retaining screws.

10. Connect the gearshift pointer cable to the arm on the steering column, if equipped, and adjust if necessary.

11. Install the hood and bezel assembly and install the retaining screws.

12. Connect the negative battery cable.

1993–96

1. Disconnect the negative battery cable.

2. Remove the cluster bezel and knee blocker.

3. Place the gear selector in the **P** position. Disconnect the gear selector indicator cable from the arm on the steering column.

4. Remove the 6 cluster retaining screws. Pull the cluster out and dis-

connect the printed circuit connectors.

5. Installation is the reverse of removal.

Pick-Up and Ramcharger

1992–93

1. Disconnect the negative battery cable.

2. Remove the map light.

3. Remove 6 screws which attach the faceplate to the base panel. There is a screw below the heater/air conditioning control panel which is not visible from above.

4. If equipped with automatic transmission, place the shift lever in its lowest position.

5. Remove the faceplate by pulling the top edge rearward to clear the brow and pulling the bottom out, disengaging the attaching clips. If equipped with 4WD, disconnect the indicator wires.

6. Remove the upper and lower steering column covers. Disconnect the shift indicator actuator cable from the steering column, if equipped.

7. Loosen the heater and air conditioning control and pull it out enough to clear the cluster housing.

8. Remove the screws that retain the cluster and pull the cluster out far enough to disconnect the speedometer cable by releasing the spring clip.

9. Remove all printed circuit board multiple connectors.

10. Remove the cluster assembly.

11. To remove the speedometer, remove the cluster lens, unplug the EMR timer wires from the speedometer, if equipped, and remove the retaining screws.

To install:

12. Install the speedometer, if removed, and connect the EMR wiring, if equipped. Position the cluster to the panel and connect the speedometer cable and multiple connectors.

13. Push the cluster in place and install the retaining screws.

14. Install the heater air conditioning control screws.

15. Connect the shift indicator actuator cable and check for alignment.

16. Install the upper and lower steering column covers.

17. Connect the 4WD indicator, if equipped. Install the cluster faceplate and map light.

18. Connect the negative battery cable.

1994–96

1. Disconnect the negative battery cable.

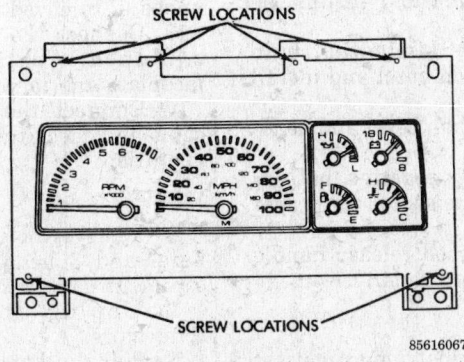

SCREW LOCATIONS

SCREW LOCATIONS

85616067

Instrument cluster mask/lens

2. Remove the cluster bezel and knee blocker.

3. Pull the PRND21 cable and twist to remove from the position arm, if equipped.

4. Push tab on bottom of cable retainer up then squeeze sides to remove retainer from the column.

5. Remove the cluster screws and pull rearward and unplug the electrical connectors.

6. Installation is the reverse of removal. Adjust the PRND21 cable.

Headlight Switch

——— WARNING ———

Replace air bag system components with Chrysler Mopar specified replacement parts. Substitute parts may visually appear interchangeable, but internal differences may result in inferior occupant protection. The fasteners, screws, and bolts, originally used for the air bag components, have special coatings and are specifically designed for the air bag system. They must never be replaced with any substitutes. Anytime a new fastener is needed, replace with the correct fasteners provided in the service package or fasteners listed in the Chrysler parts books.

Disconnect and isolate the battery negative cable before beginning any airbag system component removal or installation procedure. This will disable the airbag system. Failure to disconnect the battery could result in accidental airbag deployment and possible personal injury. Allow system capacitor to discharge for 2 minutes before removing any airbag components.

REMOVAL AND INSTALLATION

Dakota

1. Disconnect the negative battery cable.

2. Remove the steering column cover and remove the instrument panel bezel. Two screws are hidden behind the steering column cover.

3. Remove the screws from the headlight switch bezel, pull the assembly out and disconnect the wiring.

4. Remove the nut retaining the bezel to the bracket. Depress the spring button on the right side of the switch and remove the headlight switch knob and stem.

5. Remove the spanner nut and remove the switch.

6. The installation is the reverse of the removal procedure.

Caravan, Voyager and Town & Country

1992–96

On these models, the left pod switch consists of the headlight, parking lamp and hazard switches.

1. To remove the left POD switch, place a tool in the hole right of the switch in the cluster bezel below the POD switch.

2. Move the tool to the lower tab and depress. Pull the switch out to free the lower tab.

3. Move the tool upward along the right side of the switch to place on the top tab. Pull down on the tab and pull the switch out of the bezel.

4. Disconnect the wire connector.

5. To install, connect the wire connector and push the switch into position until the tab locks in place.

Van

1992–93

1. Disconnect the negative battery cable.

2. Remove the lower steering column cover.

3. Unscrew the hood release handle and lower.

4. Working under the instrument panel, depress the spring button on the headlight switch and pull the stem out.

5. Open the glove box. Remove the screws that fasten the dash bezel assembly. Pull the bezel off the upper retaining clips.

6. Remove the switch bezel and remove the illumination bulb socket.

7. Remove the switch mounting nut from the panel, remove the switch and disconnect the wiring.

To install:

8. Connect the switch, install the switch to the panel and install the mounting nut.

9. Install the illumination bulb socket to the switch bezel and install the bezel.

10. Install the dash bezel and headlight switch stem.

11. Connect the negative battery cable and check the switch for proper operation.

12. Install the hood release handle and lower steering column cover.

1994–96

1. Remove the instrument cluster bezel and knee blocker.

2. While working from under the instrument panel, depress the pull knob stem locking bottom on the bottom of the switch and at the same time, pull the knob and stem from the switch.

3. Remove the switch bezel mounting screws and switch illumination lamp from the bezel.

4. Remove the switch mounting nut from the instrument panel. Lower the switch and disconnect the electrical connector.

5. Installation is the reverse of removal.

Pick-Up and Ramcharger

1992–93

1. Disconnect the negative battery cable.

2. Remove the map light.

3. Remove 6 screws which attach the faceplate to the base panel. There is a screw below the heater/air conditioning control panel which is not visible from above.

4. If equipped with automatic transmission, place the shift lever in its lowest position.

5. Remove the faceplate by pulling the top edge rearward to clear the brow and pulling the bottom out, disengaging the attaching clips. If equipped with 4WD, disconnect the indicator wires.

6. Reach under the instrument panel, depress the spring button and remove the headlight switch knob.

7. Remove the wiper and power mirror switch knobs off their levers, if equipped.

8. Remove the bezel.

9. Remove the switch mounting nut from the panel, remove the switch and disconnect the wiring.

To install:

10. Connect the switch, install the switch to the panel and install the mounting nut.

11. Install the bezel.

12. Install the headlight stem and wiper and power mirror switch knobs, if removed.

13. Connect the 4WD indicator, if equipped. Install the cluster faceplate and map light.

14. Connect the negative battery cable and check the switch for proper operation.

1994–96

1. Remove the instrument cluster bezel and 3 headlight switch-to-instrument panel screws.

2. Unplug the 2 electrical connectors.

3. Pull the knob and stem out to the stop. Depress the button on the

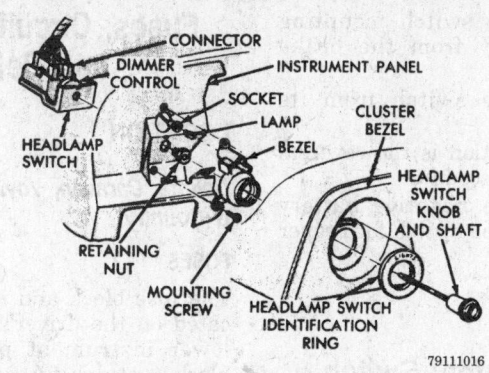

79111016

Headlight switch removal — Van

bottom of the switch and remove the knob/stem assembly. Repeat procedure if does not work the first time.

4. Remove the 2 screws, bezel and housing.

5. Installation is the reverse of removal.

Combination Switch

WARNING

Replace air bag system components with Chrysler Mopar specified replacement parts. Substitute parts may visually appear interchangeable, but internal differences may result in inferior occupant protection. The fasteners, screws, and bolts, originally used for the air bag components, have special coatings and are specifically designed for the air bag system. They must never be replaced with any substitutes. Anytime a new fastener is needed, replace with the correct fasteners provided in the service package or fasteners listed in the Chrysler parts books.

Disconnect and isolate the battery negative cable before beginning any airbag system component removal or installation procedure. This will disable the airbag system. Failure to disconnect the battery could result in accidental airbag deployment and possible personal injury. Allow system capacitor to discharge for 2 minutes before removing any airbag components.

REMOVAL AND INSTALLATION

1. Disconnect the negative battery cable.

2. Remove the tilt lever, if equipped.

3. Remove the steering column covers and knee blockers, if equipped.

4. Remove the combination switch tamper-proof mounting screws and pull the switch away from the steering column.

5. Loosen the connector screw; the screw will remain in the connector.

6. Disconnect the connector from the switch.

7. The installation is the reverse of the removal procedure. Torque the switch connector and retaining screws to 17 inch lbs. (2.0 Nm).

8. Connect the negative battery cable and check all functions of the combination switch for proper operation.

Ignition Lock/Switch

WARNING

Replace air bag system components with Chrysler Mopar specified replacement parts. Substitute parts may visually appear interchangeable, but internal differences may result in inferior occupant protection. The fasteners, screws, and bolts, originally used for the air bag components, have special coatings and are specifically designed for the air bag system. They must never be replaced with any substitutes. Anytime a new fastener is needed, replace with the correct fasteners provided in the service package or fasteners listed in the Chrysler parts books.

Disconnect and isolate the battery negative cable before beginning any airbag system component removal or installation procedure. This will disable the airbag system. Failure to disconnect the battery could result in accidental airbag deployment and possible personal injury. Allow system capacitor to discharge for 2 minutes before removing any airbag components.

REMOVAL AND INSTALLATION

1. Disconnect the negative battery cable.

2. Remove the tilt lever, if equipped.

3. Remove the upper and lower column covers.

4. Remove the 3 ignition switch tamper-proof Torx screws; APEX 440–TX20H or equivalent is required.

5. Pull the switch away from the column. Release the connector locks on the 2 wiring connectors and disconnect them from the switch.

6. Remove the key lock cylinder from the ignition switch by performing the following:

   a. Insert the key and turn the switch in the **LOCK** position. Using a small tool, depress the key cylinder retaining pin flush with the key cylinder surface.

   b. Rotate the key clockwise to the **OFF** position to unseat the key cylinder from the ignition switch assembly. The cylinder bezel should be about ⅛ in. above the ignition switch halo light ring. Do not attempt to remove the key cylinder at this point.

   c. With the key cylinder in the unseated position, rotate the key counterclockwise to the **LOCK** position and remove the key.

   d. Remove the key cylinder from the ignition switch.

To install:

7. Connect the wiring connectors.

8. Mount ignition switch to the column by performing the following:

   a. Position the shifter in **P** position. The park lock dowel pin on the ignition switch assembly must engage with the column park lock slider linkage.

   b. Verify that the ignition switch is in the **LOCK** position. The flag should be parallel to the ignition switch terminals. Apply a small amount of grease to the flag and pin.

   c. Position the park lock link to mid-travel.

   d. Align the locating pin hole and its pin and position the ignition switch against the lock housing face. Make sure the pin is inserted into the park lock link contour slot. Torque the retaining screws to 17 inch lbs.

9. With the key cylinder and ignition switch in the **LOCK** position, key not in cylinder, gently insert the key cylinder into the ignition switch until it bottoms.

10. Insert the key. Simultaneously push in on the cylinder and rotate the

key to the **RUN** position. This action should fully seat the cylinder in the ignition switch.

11. Install the column covers and the tilt lever, if equipped.

12. Connect the negative battery cable and check the push-to-lock and park lock functions, halo lighting and all ignition switch positions for proper operation.

Stoplight Switch

ADJUSTMENT

1. Push the stoplight switch forward in the mounting bracket as far as it will go; the brake pedal should move forward slightly.

2. Pull back on the brake pedal bringing the striker toward the switch until the pedal will not go back any farther. This will cause the switch to ratchet backward into position and automatically adjust.

REMOVAL AND INSTALLATION

1. Disconnect the negative battery cable.

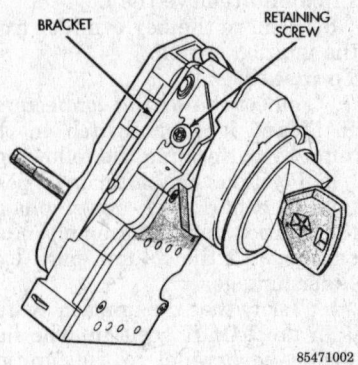

Removing the key lock cylinder retaining screw

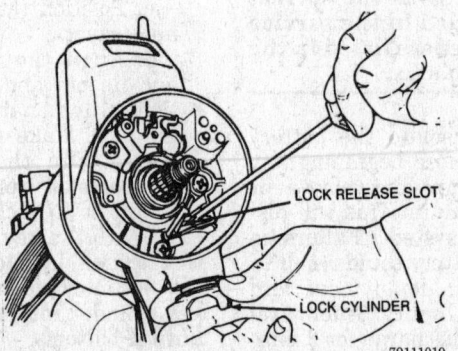

Removing the key lock cylinder

2. Remove the switch mounting bracket assembly from the brake pedal bracket.

3. Remove the switch from its bracket.

4. The installation is the reversal of the removal procedure.

5. Connect the negative battery cable and check the switch for proper operation.

Neutral Safety Switch

REMOVAL AND INSTALLATION

1. The switch is located on the right side of the transmission/transaxle case. It is a 3-pin switch for all except the FWD 4-speed overdrive transaxle. The switch for the FWD is a black 2-pin switch located to the right of the transaxle range switch (white).

2. Disconnect negative battery cable.

3. Raise and safely support the vehicle. Position drain pan under switch.

4. Disconnect switch wiring harness.

5. Remove switch from case.

To install:

6. Verify that switch operating lever fingers are centered in the switch opening in the case when in **P** and **N**.

7. Install new seal on switch and install switch into case. Torque to 25 ft. lbs. (34 Nm).

8. Test continuity of new switch. Connect wire harness and negative battery cable.

9. Add transmission fluid as required to correct level.

Fuses, Circuit Breakers and Relays

LOCATION

Dakota, Caravan, Voyager and Town & Country

FUSES

The fuse block and relay bank is located on the driver's side under the lower instrument panel. The fuse block contains fuses for various circuits as well as circuit breakers, horn relay, ignition lamp thermal time delay, and the turn signal flasher. The hazard warning flasher is mounted into a bracket below the fuse block. The power distribution box is located on the left inner fender.

CIRCUIT BREAKERS

Dakota — 30 amp power window circuit breaker is located in the fuse block

Caravan, Voyager and Town & Country — A/C heater blower motor circuit breaker is located in the fuse block, cavity 26. The headlight circuit breaker is located in the relay bank, near fuse block (location 11)

RELAYS

Dakota — The starter, A/C clutch, auto shut down and radiator fan relays are located in the power distribution center. The time delay, horn and combination buzzer and ABS warning lamp relays are located in the fuse block

Caravan, Voyager and Town & Country — The power window, power seat, ABS, power door lock (lock and unlock) and fog lamp relays are located in the relay bank located in the center of the instrument panel. The low beam, park lamps, name brand speakers, heated rear window, horn, rear A/C and liftgate release relays are located in the fuse bank, located near the fuse block

Pick-Up, Ramcharger and Van

The fuse block and relay bank is located to the left of the glove box on Vans and directly under the steering column on Pick-Ups and Ramchargers. Circuit breakers are also located on the fuse block. The auto shutdown relay, starter relay, A/C cutout relay and part throttle unlock relay are located in the engine compartment near the 50-way bulkhead connector. The power distribution box is located on the left inner fender for Pick-Up and Ramcharger

or on the radiator top support for Van.

Computers

LOCATION

Dakota — 4-wheel ABS control module is located on the left inner fender, behind the power distribution center. The Rear-wheel ABS control module is located at the right kick panel. The Powertrain Control Module is located on the right fender side shield.

Caravan, Voyager and Town & Country — The Powertrain Control Module is located on the left side inner fender, in front of the power distribution box. The daytime running light module is located on the firewall, next to the blower resistor. The ABS control module is located on the left inner fender, below the power distribution box.

1992–93 Pick-Up and Ramcharger — The Rear-wheel ABS control module is located on the right side of the instrument panel, below the heater blower resistor. The Powertrain Control Module is located behind the left headlight (left inner fender).

1994–96 Pick-Up — ABS control unit is located on the left side of the firewall. Air Bag control module (yellow connectors) is located behind the instrument panel. The Powertrain Control Module is located on the right side of the firewall.

Van — The Powertrain Control Module is located in the center of the firewall. The daytime running light control module is located next to the windshield wiper motor. The ABS control module is located next to the windshield washer bottle, behind the ABS hydraulic unit.

Flashers

LOCATION

The turn signal flasher and the hazard flasher are located in the fuse block. Depending on model, the turn signal and hazard flashers are incorporated into a combination flasher and is located in the fuse block.

Cruise Control

ADJUSTMENT

1992–93 Diesel Engine

1. The clearance between the throttle stud and cable clevis should be as small as possible without moving the throttle. If gap is not correct, remove adjustment clip.
2. Push protective sleeve into housing to decrease gap or pull sleeve out of housing to increase gap. Install adjustment clip.

ENGINE COOLING

Radiator

REMOVAL AND INSTALLATION

1. Disconnect the negative battery cable.
2. Drain cooling system. Remove heater hoses from core and cap.
3. Remove the upper hose and coolant reserve tank hose from the radiator.
4. Remove the shroud from the radiator and position aside.
5. Remove the upper radiator mounting screws. On Van, the radiator will be removed from the bottom of the vehicle. Raise and safely support vehicle.
6. Remove the lower hose from the radiator.
7. Disconnect the automatic transmission cooler lines, if equipped, position aside and cap ends.
8. Remove the mounting screws and carefully lift or lower the radiator out of the engine compartment.
   To install:
9. Lift or lower the radiator into position and install the mounting screws.
10. Connect the automatic transmission cooler lines, if removed.
11. Connect the lower hose.
12. Install the upper radiator mounting bolts and shroud.
13. Reconnect negative battery cable.
14. Connect the upper radiator hose and coolant reserve tank hose.
15. Fill the cooling system.
16. Run the vehicle until normal operating temperature is reached. Recheck coolant level and automatic

transmission fluid level and add as required.

Electric Cooling Fan

TESTING

--- **CAUTION** ---
Make sure the key is in the OFF position when checking the electric cooling fan. If not, the fan could turn ON at any time, causing personal injury.

Basic Test

1. Unplug the fan connector.
2. Using a jumper wire, connect the female terminal of the fan connector to the negative battery terminal.
3. The fan should turn ON when the male terminal is connected to the positive battery terminal.
4. If not, the fan is defective and should be replaced.
5. If further testing is required, use a DRBII diagnostic tool.

Electronic Test

1. With the DRBII, activate the radiator fan relay. The radiator fan relay should click. If not, substitute the auto shut down relay in its place. If good relay does not click, check the ignition feed in cavity A of the relay connector and wiring, located in the power distribution box. Wiggle the wiring harnesses from the PCM to the fan relay.
2. Disconnect the PCM wiring harness. With the DRBII in ohmmeter mode, probe cavity C in the radiator fan relay connector. If the resistance is below 5.0 ohms, repair the short to ground. If the resistance is above 5.0 ohms, replace the PCM.
3. If the fan operates on high speed only, check the low speed fan relay and visa-versa.

REMOVAL AND INSTALLATION

NOTE: The cooling fan motor/blade/housing must be serviced as an assembly. No separate service parts are available.

1. Disconnect the negative battery cable and fan motor electrical connector.
2. Remove the upper shroud fasteners and lift the shroud up and out of the attaching clips.
3. Installation is the reverse of removal. Torque the retaining bolts to 105 inch lbs. (12 Nm).

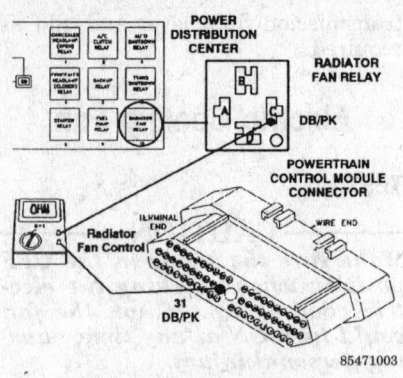

Radiator fan relay terminals

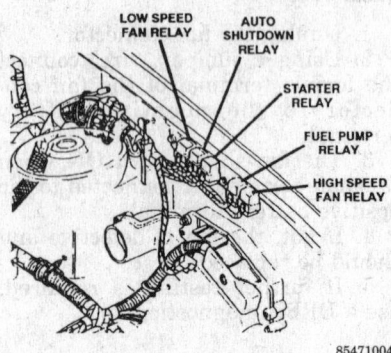

Radiator fan relay locations

Heater Core

REMOVAL AND INSTALLATION

Dakota

1. Disconnect the negative battery cable.

2. Discharge and recover the A/C refrigerant, if equipped.

3. Remove the lower instrument panel module and center air distribution duct.

4. Tape the wiring harness up and out of the way. Disconnect the antenna cable from the retaining clip at the end of the heater housing.

5. Disconnect the blower motor wiring, demister hoses from top of housing and vacuum harness connector from controller.

6. Disconnect the temperature control cable and drain the engine coolant.

7. Disconnect the refrigerant lines and heater hoses and plug open ends. Remove the condensation tube.

8. Remove the 4 housing attaching nuts from the rear engine compartment dash panel. Remove the housing support brace and swing the brace to the left out of the way.

9. Carefully pull the housing rearward until the studs clear the dash panel and allow the unit to drop down. Rotate the unit until the attaching studs are facing downward and remove the housing from the vehicle.

10. Remove the housing top cover. Remove the attaching screws from the heater core retaining bracket and lift the heater core from the housing.

To install:

11. Install the heater core, retaining bracket and retaining screws.

12. Install the housing top cover.

13. Install the heater/air conditioning housing into the vehicle by rotating the housing forward until there attaching studs fit into the dash panel.

14. Install the housing nuts, condensation tube, heater hoses and refrigerant lines.

15. Connect all vacuum lines, cables and electrical connectors to the original locations.

16. Install the remaining components, recharge the A/C system, refill the engine coolant, start the engine and check for leaks.

Caravan, Voyager and Town & Country

1. Disconnect the negative battery cable. Properly discharge the air conditioning system, if equipped. Drain the cooling system.

2. Remove the steering column cover and left and right side under panel silencers.

3. Remove the center bezel by unclipping it from the instrument panel.

4. Remove the accessory switch carrier and the heater/air conditioning control head.

5. Remove storage bin and lower right instrument panel.

6. Disconnect the blower motor lead under the right side of the instrument panel.

7. Remove the right side 40-way connector wiring bracket.

8. Remove the lower right reinforcement, body computer bracket and mid-to-lower reinforcement as an assembly.

9. Disconnect the vacuum lines at the brake booster and water valve.

10. Clamp off the heater hoses near the heater core and remove the hoses from the core tubes. Plug the hose ends and the core tubes to prevent spillage of coolant.

11. If equipped with air conditioning, remove the H-valve and condensation tube.

12. Disconnect the temperature control cable and vacuum harness at the connection at the top of the unit.

13. Remove the retaining nuts from the package mounting studs at the firewall. Disconnect the hanger strap from the package and rotate it aside.

To install:

14. Remove the temperature control door from the unit and clean the unit out with solvent. Lubricate the lower pivot rod and its well and install. Wrap the heater core and/or evaporator with foam tape and place in position. Secure with the screws.

15. Assemble the unit, making sure all vacuum tubes are properly routed.

16. Install the assembly to the vehicle and connect the vacuum harness. Install the nuts to the firewall and install the condensation tube. Fold the carpet back into position.

17. Connect the hanger strap from the package and rotate it aside. Install the 2 brackets supporting the lower edge of the heater housing. Connect the blower motor wiring, resistor wiring and the temperature control cable.

18. Install the retaining screws from the right side to the steering column. Install the instrument panel trim covering and reinforcement.

19. Assemble the unit, making sure all vacuum tubes are properly routed.

20. Install the assembly to the vehicle and connect the vacuum harness. Install the nuts to the firewall and install the condensation tube. Fold the carpet back into position.

21. Connect the hanger strap from the package and rotate it aside. Connect the blower motor wiring and temperature control cable.

22. Install the lower right reinforcement, body computer bracket and mid-to-lower reinforcement as an assembly.

23. Install the right side 40-way connector wiring bracket.

24. Install the lower right instrument panel and storage bin.

25. Install the heater/air conditioning control head and accessory switch carrier.

26. Install the center bezel to the instrument panel.

27. Install the under panel silencers and steering column cover.

28. Install the vacuum lines at the brake booster and water valve.

29. Connect the heater hoses to the core tubes.

30. Using new gaskets, install the H-valve and connect the refrigerant lines. Install the condensation tube.

31. Evacuate and recharge the air conditioning system, if equipped. Add

2 oz. of refrigerant oil during the recharge. Fill the cooling system.

32. Connect the negative battery cable and check the entire climate control system for proper operation and leaks.

33. Connect the negative battery cable and check the entire climate control system for proper operation and leakage.

Van

FRONT HEATER WITHOUT AIR CONDITIONING

1. Disconnect the negative battery cable.

2. Drain the cooling system. Disconnect and plug the heater hoses.

3. Disconnect the temperature control cable from the heater core cover and the blend door crank. Disconnect the vent cable.

4. Disconnect the blower motor power feed and ground wire connector.

5. Remove the screws retaining the heater assembly side cowl and the nuts fastening the heater assembly to the dash panel.

6. Remove the heater unit from the vehicle.

7. Remove the back plate and remove the screws holding the heater

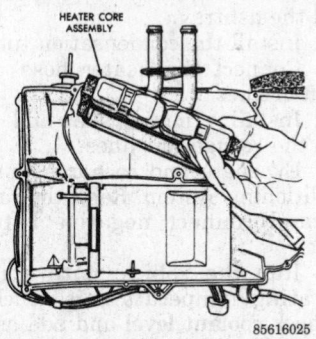

Removing and installing the heater core assembly

core cover to the heater housing. Lift the cover from the housing.

8. Remove the retaining screws from the heater core and remove the core from the heater housing.

To install:

9. Clean out the inside of the housing. Place the heater core into the housing and fasten.

10. Position the blend air door and right vent door in the housing and fasten the heater core cover to the housing.

11. Check the dash panel and side cowl seals for breaks or lack of adhesion and repair as needed.

12. Install the heater assembly to the vehicle.

13. Connect the blower motor power feed and ground wire connector.

14. Position temperature control cable on blend air door crank and attach cable to heater core cover. Connect and adjust vent cable.

15. Connect the heater hoses. Connect negative battery cable.

16. Refill the cooling system.

17. Run the vehicle until normal operating temperature is reached. Recheck coolant level and automatic transmission fluid level and add as required.

FRONT HEATER WITH AIR CONDITIONING

1. Disconnect the negative battery cable. Discharge the air conditioning system.

2. Disconnect the freeze control connector from the wire harness at the H-valve.

3. Drain the cooling system. Place a layer of non-conductive waterproof material over the alternator to prevent coolant from spilling on it when disconnecting the heater hoses. Disconnect and cap the heater hoses.

4. Slowly disconnect the refrigerant plumbing from the H-valve. Remove the 2 screws from the filter drier bracket and swing the plumbing out of the way. Cap open air con-

ditioning lines to prevent contamination of the system.

5. Remove the temperature control cable from the cover.

6. Working from inside the vehicle, remove the glove box, spot cooler bezel and the appearance shield. Working through the glove box opening and under the instrument panel, remove the screws and nuts attaching the evaporator core housing to the dash panel.

7. Remove the 2 screws from the flange connection to the blower housing. Separate the evaporator core housing from the blower housing.

8. Carefully remove the evaporator core housing from the vehicle.

9. Remove the cover from the housing. Remove 1 screw from strap on heater core tubes and pull core out of housing.

To install:

10. Clean the inside of the housing. Place the heater core into the housing and install the retaining strap and screws.

11. Install the housing cover.

12. Attach the blower housing to the evaporator housing.

13. Inspect all air seals and mating surfaces for possible breaks and leaks and repair as needed.

14. Through the glove box opening and under the dash, install the screws and nuts attaching evaporator housing assembly to dash panel.

15. Install the appearance shield, spot cooler bezel and glove box.

16. Attach the temperature control cable to the cover.

17. Position the plumbing and install the 2 screws onto the filter drier bracket.

18. Install a new gasket and connect the refrigerant plumbing to the H-valve.

19. Connect the heater hoses and remove the waterproof material from the alternator. Connect the freeze control wire harness.

20. Evacuate and recharge the air conditioning system.

21. Connect the negative battery cable. Refill the cooling system.

22. Run the vehicle until normal operating temperature is reached. Recheck coolant level and add as required. Check the operation of the entire climate control system.

REAR (AUXILIARY) HEATER

1. Disconnect the negative battery cable.

2. Drain the radiator and disconnect the hoses from the heater. Do this from under the vehicle.

3. Remove the heater assembly-to-floor pan mounting nuts.

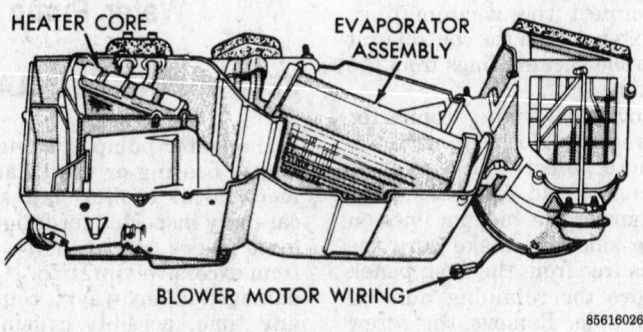

Heater/evaporator assembly components

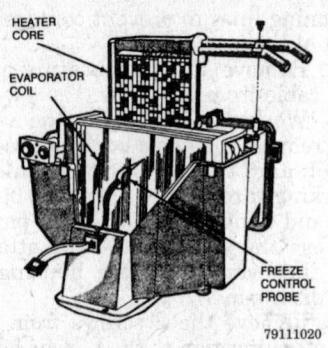

HEATER CORE
EVAPORATOR COIL
FREEZE CONTROL PROBE

79111020

Heater core removal — Van with air conditioning

4. Disconnect the blower motor wiring and remove the heater assembly from the vehicle.

5. Remove the heater core cover and heater core.

To install:

6. Install the heater core and make sure the seals are in place. Install the core cover and heater assembly into the vehicle.

7. Connect the heater hoses and blower wiring. Refill the cooling system, start the engine and check for leaks.

Pick-Up and Ramcharger

WITHOUT AIR CONDITIONING

1. Disconnect the negative battery cable.

2. Drain the cooling system. Remove and plug the heater core hoses.

3. Remove the right side cowl trim panel, if equipped. Remove the glove box assembly. Remove the structural brace through the glovebox opening.

4. Remove the right ½ of the instrument panel lower reinforcement and disconnect the radio ground strap.

5. Disconnect the control cables from the heater housing and the blower motor wires on the engine side.

6. Remove the retaining screw between the package to cowl side sheetmetal.

7. Remove the 6 heater housing retaining nuts on the engine side of the heater assembly and remove the heater housing assembly.

8. Remove the heater housing cover retaining screws and the mode door crank. Separate the cover from the housing.

9. Carefully lift the heater core from the heater housing.

To install:

10. Clean the inside of the housing. Install the heater core into the housing.

11. Install the housing cover.

12. Inspect the dash panel seal for damage and repair as required.

13. Install the assembly to the dash panel and install the retaining nuts.

14. Install the cowl side retaining screws.

15. Connect the blower motor connector.

16. Connect the control cables.

17. Install the right lower instrument panel reinforcement, structural brace, glove box and cowl side trim panel, if equipped.

18. Connect the heater hoses.

19. Refill the radiator.

20. Connect the negative battery cable.

21. Run the vehicle until normal operating temperature is reached. Check coolant level and add as required.

WITH AIR CONDITIONING

1. Disconnect the negative battery cable. Discharge the air condition system. Drain the cooling system. Disconnect and plug the heater hoses and the refrigerant lines.

2. Remove the condensation tube from the housing.

3. Move the transfer case and gear shift levers away from the instrument panel.

4. Remove the right side cowl trim panel, if equipped. Remove the glove box and swing it out from the bottom.

5. Remove the structural brace from the through hole in the glove box opening. Remove the ashtray.

6. Remove the right lower ½ of the dash reinforcement by removing the retaining screws holding it to the instrument panel and to the cowl side trim panel.

7. Disconnect the radio ground strap. Remove the center and floor air distribution ducts.

8. Disconnect the temperature control cable from the assembly and tape it out of the way.

9. Disconnect the vacuum lines from the extension on the control unit and unclip the vacuum lines from the defroster duct.

10. Remove the wiring connector from the resistor block. Remove the blower motor electrical connector from the engine side of the assembly.

11. Disconnect the vacuum lines on the engine side and make sure the grommet is free from the dash panel.

12. Remove the retaining nuts on the engine side. Remove the screw that retains the assembly to the cowl side of the sheetmetal.

13. Remove the assembly from the vehicle.

14. Remove the vacuum actuators, door crank levers, evaporator case cover retaining nuts and screws and the heater core retaining screws. Lift the cover off the assembly and remove the heater core from its mounting.

To install:

15. Clean the inside of the housing. Install the heater core into the housing.

16. Install the housing cover, retaining screws and nuts, levers and actuators.

17. Inspect the dash panel seals for damage and repair as required.

18. Feed the vacuum lines through the hole in the dash panel, install the assembly to the dash panel and install all retaining nuts and screws.

19. Connect the resistor block and blower motor.

20. Connect the vacuum lines to the extension on the control unit and clip the vacuum lines to the defroster duct.

21. Connect the temperature control cable to the assembly.

22. Connect the radio ground strap. Install the center and floor air distribution ducts.

23. Install the dash reinforcement, structural brace, glove box and right side cowl trim panel, if equipped. Install the ashtray.

24. Install the condensation tube.

25. Connect the heater hoses and vacuum lines.

26. Install a new gasket and connect the refrigerant lines.

27. Evacuate and recharge the air conditioning system. Refill the radiator and connect negative battery cable.

28. Run the vehicle until normal operating temperature is reached. Recheck coolant level and add as required. Check operation of the entire climate control system.

Water Pump

REMOVAL AND INSTALLATION

If the water pump is being replaced due to bearing or shaft damage, the mechanical cooling fan should be carefully inspected for fatigue cracks, loose blades or loose rivets resulting from excessive vibration. If the fan is damaged in any way, it could snap at any time, possibly causing serious personal injury or damage to the vehicle.

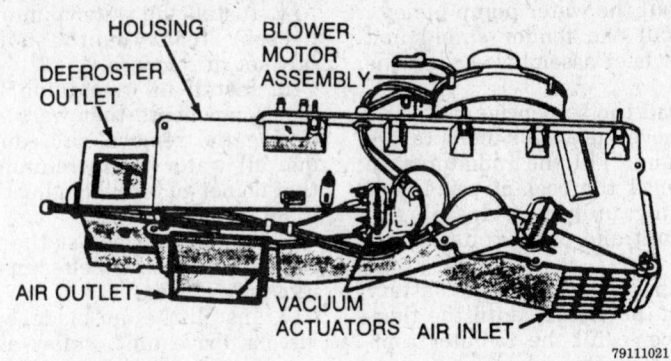

HOUSING · BLOWER MOTOR ASSEMBLY · DEFROSTER OUTLET · AIR OUTLET · VACUUM ACTUATORS · AIR INLET

79111021

Evaporator heater assembly — Pick-Up and Ramcharger with A/C

Dakota

2.5L ENGINE

1. Disconnect the negative battery cable and drain the cooling system.
2. Remove the accessory drive belt and generator.
3. Remove the A/C compressor drive belt idler, compressor solid mount bracket and support the assembly out of the way. The A/C system does not have to be discharged.
4. Disconnect the radiator and heater hoses from the water pump.
5. Remove the water pump retaining bolts, water pump and seal.
6. Remove the water pump pulley and pump from the pump housing.

To install:

7. Clean the gasket mating surfaces.
8. Install the water pump to the housing and torque the bolts to 105 inch lbs. (12 Nm). Install a new O-ring and the assembly to the engine.
9. Torque the upper mounting bolts to 22 ft. lbs. (30 Nm) and the lower bolt to 50 ft. lbs. (68 Nm).
10. Install the heater and radiator hoses.
11. Install the solid mount A/C bracket and compressor. Torque the large bolts to 40 ft. lbs. (54 Nm) and the small bolts to 30 inch lbs. (3 Nm).
12. Install the generator and accessory drive belt. Refill the engine coolant, connect the battery cable, start the engine and check for leaks.

3.9L AND 5.2L ENGINES

1. Disconnect the negative battery cable and drain the engine coolant.
2. Remove the throttle cable from the top of the fan shroud.
3. Remove the upper radiator hoses from the radiator.
4. Use a fan clutch wrench to remove the threaded clutch from the water pump pulley. Turn the nut counterclockwise as viewed from the front. The threads are right hand. Place a suitable bar between the pump pulley bolts to keep the assembly from turning.
5. Remove the fan shroud and clutch fan from the engine at this time. Do not place the clutch fan in a horizontal position because the silicone fluid in the fan drive could drain into the bearing and contaminate the lubricant.
6. Remove the accessory drive belt by relaxing the spring loaded tensioner.
7. Remove the 4 pump pulley retaining bolts and pulley.
8. Remove the lower radiator and heater hoses.
9. Remove the water pump retaining bolts and pump. Be careful not to damage the pump sealing surfaces.

To install:

10. Clean the gasket mating surfaces and install the pump with a new gasket.
11. Install the bolts and torque to 30 ft. lbs. (40 Nm). Install the bypass, heater and radiator hoses.
12. Install the water pump pulley and torque the bolts to 20 ft. lbs. (27 Nm).
13. Install the drive belt and position the fan shroud/clutch fan into place. Using the clutch fan wrench, tighten the clutch fan to the water pump pulley.
14. Install the remaining components, refill the cooling system, start the engine and check for leaks.

Caravan, Voyager and Town & Country

2.5L ENGINE

1. Disconnect the negative battery cable.
2. Drain the cooling system.

NOTE: Raise and safely support the front of the vehicle. Remove the lower splash shield to access to the water pump and drive belts.

3. Remove the drive belts.

4. Remove the upper radiator hose.
5. Without discharging the system, remove the air conditioning compressor from the engine mount and set to one side. If necessary remove the compressor mount (4 bolts) to gain access to the water pump retaining bolts.
6. Remove the alternator and move to one side.
7. Disconnect the lower radiator hose and heater hose.
8. Remove (3) upper screws and (1) lower screw retaining water pump to the engine and remove pump assembly.
9. Remove the 3 screws holding the pulley to the water pump.
10. Remove the 9 screws holding the water pump to the body. Because of the gasket seal a chisel is required to separate the pump from the body.
11. Clean the gasket surfaces on the pump and the body.
12. Remove and discard the O-ring gasket and clean the O-ring groove.

To install:

13. Apply a sealer to the circumference of the new nipple and with a light mallet tap the nipple into the housing.
14. Apply RTV sealant to the body. Assemble the pump to the body and tighten the screws to 105 inch lbs. (12 Nm) and allow the sealant to set before filling and pressurizing the system.
15. Place a new O-ring in the groove.
16. Position the water pump pulley to the water pump and tighten the 3 retaining screws to 105 inch lbs. (12 Nm).
17. Position the replacement pump against the engine and install mounting screws. Tighten the (3) upper screws to 250 inch lbs. (30 Nm) and lower screw to 50 ft. lbs. (68 Nm).
18. Install heater hose and lower radiator hose. Tighten clamps to 16 inch lbs. (1.8 Nm).
19. Install air conditioning compressor and alternator.
20. Install the drive belts and adjust.
21. Fill the cooling system.
22. Connect the negative battery cable.

3.0L ENGINE

1. Disconnect the negative battery cable.
2. Remove the drive belts.
3. Drain the cooling system.
4. Remove the timing case cover and timing belt.
5. Remove the pump assembly mounting bolts.

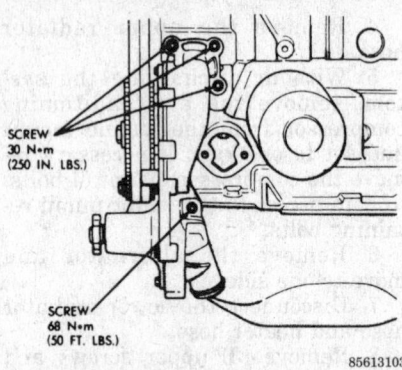

SCREW 30 N·m (250 IN. LBS.)

SCREW 68 N·m (50 FT. LBS.)

85613103

Water pump assembly installation — 2.5l engine

6. Separate the pump assembly from water pipe and remove.
7. Clean gasket and O-ring mounting surfaces.
   To install:
8. Install a new O-ring on water pipe and lubricate with water.
9. Install a new gasket on pump body.
10. Press the water pump assembly into water pipe.
11. Install pump mounting bolts and tighten to 20 ft. lbs. (27 Nm).
12. Install timing belt and cover.
13. Install drive belts.
14. Fill the cooling system.

3.3L AND 3.8L ENGINES

1. Disconnect the negative battery cable.
2. Drain the cooling system.
3. Remove the serpentine belt.
4. Raise the vehicle and support safely. Remove the right front tire and wheel assembly and lower fender shield.
5. Remove the water pump pulley.
6. Remove the 5 mounting screws and remove the pump from the engine.
7. Discard the O-ring.
   To install:
8. Using a new O-ring, install the pump to the engine. Torque the mounting bolts to 21 ft. lbs. (30 Nm).

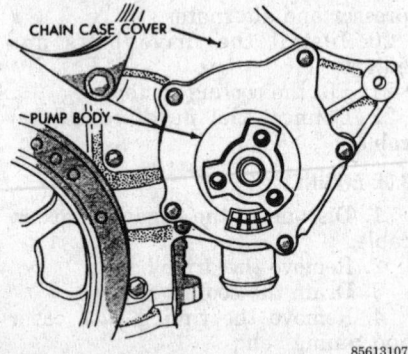

CHAIN CASE COVER

PUMP BODY

85613107

Water pump — 3.3L and 3.8L engines

9. Install the water pump pulley.
10. Install the fender shield and tire and wheel assembly. Lower the vehicle.
11. Install the serpentine belt.
12. Remove the engine temperature sending unit. Fill the radiator with coolant until the coolant comes out the sending unit hole. Install the sending unit and continue to fill the radiator.
13. Connect the negative battery cable, run the vehicle until the thermostat opens, fill the radiator completely and check for leaks.
14. Once the vehicle has cooled, recheck the coolant level.

Pick-Up and Ramcharger

GASOLINE ENGINE

1. Disconnect the negative battery cable. Drain the coolant.
2. Remove the shroud from the radiator and slide it over the fan, if 1-piece.
3. Remove the radiator and lower hose.
4. Remove the fan blade, spacer or viscous drive unit, pulley, bolts and shroud (if it was not removed in Step 2) together. Remove the air pump belt and power steering pump belt.

NOTE: Do not place the viscous fan in an upright position because the silicone fluid in the drive could drain into the bearing and contaminate its lubricant.

5. Loosen the alternator mounting bolts and remove the alternator/air conditioner belts.
6. Remove the alternator bracket. This bracket also supports the air conditioner compressor or idler pulley, which will remain supported by its rear mount.
7. Remove the air pump(s) and the air pump bracket.
8. Unbolt the power steering pump bracket with the pump still attached and position it out of the way.
9. Disconnect the heater and bypass hoses.
10. Remove the remaining pump retaining bolts and remove the pump from the engine.
    To install:
11. Clean and dry the pump mating surfaces. Install a new bypass hose to the engine.
12. Install a new gasket and install the water pump to the engine.
13. Install any bolts that do not retain a bracket. Tighten the bypass hose clamps. Install the heater hose.

14. Install the water pump to compressor front mount bolts and bracket, if removed.
15. Install all remaining brackets and components that were removed during the removal procedure. Torque all water pump retaining bolts that do not go through adjusting slots to 30 ft. lbs. (41 Nm).
16. Install and adjust the alternator/air conditioner belts. Install the remaining belts.
17. Install the fan blade, spacer or viscous drive unit, pulley and bolts along with the shroud (if it is a 1-piece unit) together.
18. Install the radiator, lower hose and shroud.
19. Adjust all belts and torque the remaining water pump retaining bolts to 30 ft. lbs. (41 Nm).
20. Fill the radiator with coolant.
21. Connect the negative battery cable, run the vehicle until the thermostat opens, fill the radiator completely and check for leaks.
22. Once the vehicle has cooled, recheck the coolant level.

5.9L DIESEL ENGINE

1. Disconnect the negative battery cable.
2. Drain the coolant.
3. Use a ⅜ in. drive breaker bar to lift the belt tensioner and remove the belt.
4. Remove the 2 water pump retaining bolts and remove the pump from the engine.
5. Remove the O-ring from the pump groove.
   To install:
6. Clean the O-ring groove and install a new O-ring.
7. Clean the pump mating surfaces and install the pump to the engine.
8. Torque the mounting bolts to 18 ft. lbs. (24 Nm). Fill the radiator with coolant.
9. Install the drive belt.
10. Connect the negative battery cable, run the vehicle until the thermostat opens, fill the radiator completely and check for leaks.
11. Once the vehicle has cooled, recheck the coolant level.

Van

1. Disconnect the negative battery cable and drain the engine coolant.
2. Remove the plastic air cleaner intake tube and radiator fan shroud. Remove the lower ½ first.
3. Remove the upper radiator hose at the radiator.
4. Use a fan clutch wrench to remove the threaded clutch from the

5.9L diesel engine water pump

water pump pulley. Turn the nut counterclockwise as viewed from the front. The threads are right hand. Place a suitable bar between the pump pulley bolts to keep the assembly from turning.

5. Remove the clutch fan from the engine at this time. Do not place the clutch fan in a horizontal position because the silicone fluid in the fan drive could drain into the bearing and contaminate the lubricant.

6. Remove the accessory drive belt by relaxing the spring loaded tensioner.

7. Remove the 4 pump pulley retaining bolts and pulley.

8. Remove the lower radiator and heater hoses.

9. Remove the 7 water pump retaining bolts and pump. Be careful not to damage the pump sealing surfaces.

To install:

10. Clean the gasket mating surfaces and install the pump with a new gasket.

11. Install the bolts and torque to 30 ft. lbs. (40 Nm). Install the bypass, heater and radiator hoses.

12. Install the water pump pulley and torque the bolts to 20 ft. lbs. (27 Nm).

13. Install the drive belt and position the clutch fan into place. Using the clutch fan wrench, tighten the clutch fan to the water pump pulley.

14. Install the remaining components, refill the cooling system, start the engine and check for leaks.

Thermostat

REMOVAL AND INSTALLATION

Caravan, Voyager and Town & Country

The thermostat is located in a water box at the side of the engine (facing grille) 2.5L engine. The thermostat on the 3.0L, 3.3L and 3.8L engines is located in a water box at the timing belt end of the intake manifold.

1. Drain the cooling system to a level below the thermostat.

2. Remove the hoses from the thermostat housing.

3. Remove the thermostat housing.

4. Remove the thermostat and discard the gasket. Clean the gasket surfaces thoroughly.

5. Install a new gasket on water box housing 2.5L engine. Center the thermostat in the water box on gasket surface. Install the thermostat housing on gasket. Make sure thermostat sits in its recess of the housing.

6. Position gasket on water box. Center thermostat in water box and attached housing. Tighten bolts to 15 ft. lbs. (20 Nm). Make sure thermostat flange in seated properly in flange groove of the water box.

7. Connect the radiator hose to the thermostat housing. Tighten the hose clamp to 35 inch lbs. (4.0 Nm).

8. Fill the cooling system.

Dakota, Pick-Up, Ramcharger and Van

EXCEPT 5.9L DIESEL ENGINE

1. Disconnect the negative battery cable. Drain the coolant down to thermostat level or below.

2. Remove the thermostat housing.

3. Remove the thermostat and discard the gasket.

4. Clean the housing mating surfaces and use a new gasket.

5. The installation is the reversal of the removal procedure.

6. Connect the negative battery cable, run the vehicle until the thermostat opens, fill the radiator completely and check for leaks.

7. Once the vehicle has cooled, recheck the coolant level.

5.9L DIESEL ENGINE

1. Disconnect the negative battery cable.

2. Drain the coolant.

3. Use a 3/8 in. drive breaker bar to lift the belt tensioner and remove the belt.

4. Disconnect the upper radiator hose from the thermostat housing.

5. Loosen the alternator mounting bolts and lower the alternator.

6. Unbolt the thermostat housing and remove the housing, engine lifting bracket and thermostat with seal.

To install:

7. Install the new thermostat to the housing, making sure the tang on the thermostat is aligned with the slot in the housing. This will ensure correct positioning of the jiggle pins in the housing. This is important because during cooling system filling. Air vents through the jiggle pin openings, through the upper hose and out the radiator fill neck.

8. Clean the pump mating surfaces.

9. Install the engine lifting bracket, new seal, thermostat and housing. Make sure the seal is installed with the beveled side facing out.

10. Torque the thermostat housing bolts to 18 ft. lbs. (24 Nm). Connect the upper hose to the housing.

11. Reinstall the alternator into position. Torque the upper bolt to 18 ft. lbs. (24 Nm) and the lower bolt to 32 ft. lbs. (43 Nm).

12. Install the drive belt.

13. Connect the negative battery cable, run the vehicle until the thermostat opens, fill the radiator completely and check for leaks.

14. Once the vehicle has cooled, recheck the coolant level.

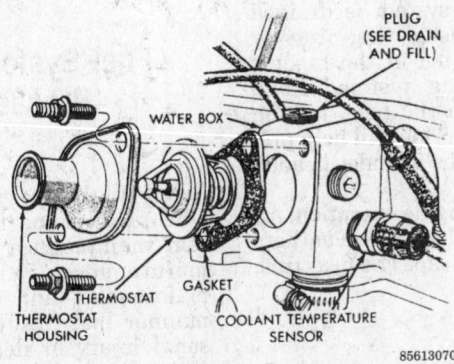

Thermostat installation — 2.5L engine

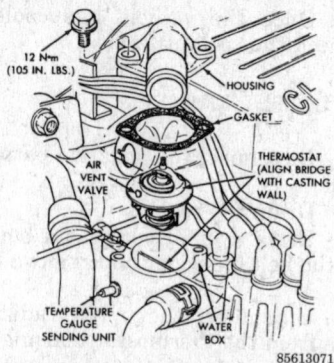

Thermostat installation — 3.0L engine

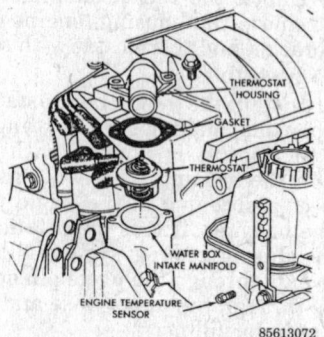

Thermostat installation — 3.3L and 3.8L engines

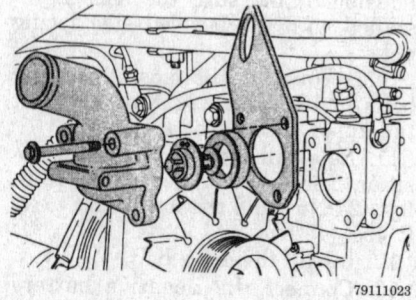

Engine thermostat — 5.9L diesel engine

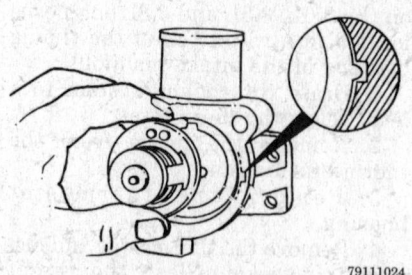

Installing the thermostat in the housing — 5.9L diesel engine

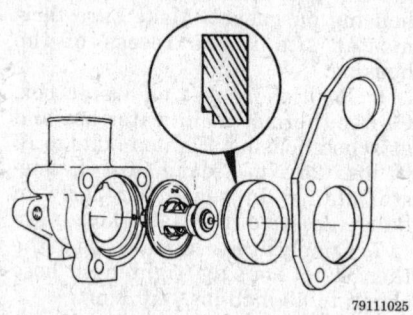

Proper positioning of the rubber seal — 5.9L diesel engine

Cooling System Bleeding

After the cooling system is drained and refilled, loosen the plug or sender/sensor located in the highest part of the cooling system. When coolant spills from the hole, tighten the plug or sensor. This will help prevent hot spots in the cylinder head(s) and overheating.

Under normal engine operation, air trapped in the cooling system gathers under the radiator cap. The next time the engine is operated thermal expansion of coolant will force trapped air past the radiator cap and into the coolant reserve tank where it is vented into the atmosphere. As the engine cools down coolant will be drawn from the reserve tank into the radiator to replace the vented air.

GASOLINE FUEL SYSTEM

Fuel System Service Precautions

Safety is the most important factor when performing not only fuel system maintenance but any type of maintenance. Failure to conduct maintenance and repairs in a safe manner may result in serious personal injury or death. Maintenance and testing of the vehicle's fuel system components can be accomplished safely and effectively by adhering to the following rules and guidelines.

• To avoid the possibility of fire and personal injury, always disconnect the negative battery cable unless the repair or test procedure requires that battery voltage be applied.

• Always relieve the fuel system pressure prior to disconnecting any fuel system component (injector, fuel rail, pressure regulator, etc.), fitting or fuel line connection. Exercise extreme caution whenever relieving fuel system pressure to avoid exposing skin, face and eyes to fuel spray. Please be advised that fuel under pressure may penetrate the skin or any part of the body that it contacts.

• Always place a shop towel or cloth around the fitting or connection prior to loosening to absorb any excess fuel due to spillage. Ensure that all fuel spillage (should it occur) is quickly removed from engine surfaces. Ensure that all fuel soaked cloths or towels are deposited into a suitable waste container.

• Always keep a dry chemical (Class B) fire extinguisher near the work area.

• Do not allow fuel spray or fuel vapors to come into contact with a spark or open flame.

• Always use a backup wrench when loosening and tightening fuel line connection fittings. This will prevent unnecessary stress and torsion to fuel line piping. Always follow the proper torque specifications.

• Always replace worn fuel fitting O-rings with new. Do not substitute fuel hose or equivalent where fuel pipe is installed.

RELIEVING FUEL SYSTEM PRESSURE

Except 3.0L, 3.3L and 3.8L Engines

1. Loosen the fuel filler cap to release fuel tank pressure.
2. Disconnect the injector wiring harness from the engine harness.
3. Connect a jumper wire to ground terminal 1 of the injector harness to engine ground.
4. Being careful not to allow contact between the jumper leads, connect a jumper wire to pin 2 next to the 1 that is grounded and touch the other end of the jumper to the positive battery post for no longer than 5 seconds. This will relieve fuel pressure.
5. Remove the jumper wires and connect the connector.

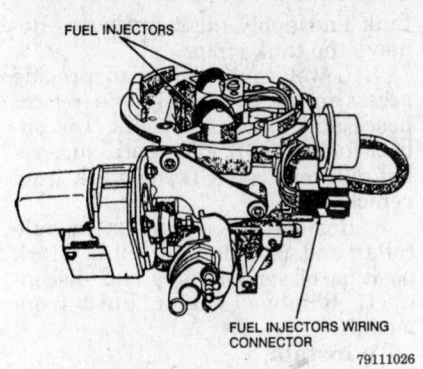

Injector wiring connector location

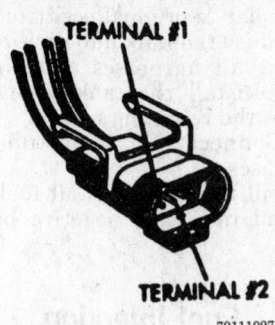

79111027

Fuel injector harness connectors

3.0L Engine

1. Loosen the gas cap to release tank pressure.
2. Disconnect the fuel rail electrical harness from the engine harness.
3. Connect 1 end of a jumper wire to the A142 circuit terminal of the fuel rail harness connector.
4. Connect the other end of the jumper wire to a good ground source.
5. Momentarily ground 1 of the injectors by connecting the other end of the jumper wire to an injector terminal in the harness connector. Repeat the procedure for 2 or 3 injectors.

3.3L and 3.8L Engines

1. Disconnect the negative battery cable.
2. Loosen the gas cap to release tank pressure.
3. Remove the protective cap from the fuel pressure test port on the fuel rail.
4. Place the open end of fuel pressure release hose, tool No. C-4799-1, into an approved gasoline container. Connect the other end of hose C-4799-1 to the fuel pressure test port. Fuel pressure will bleed off through the hose into the gasoline container.

Fuel Tank

REMOVAL AND INSTALLATION

Except Caravan, Voyager and Town & Country

1. Disconnect negative battery cable.
2. Relieve the fuel pressure.
3. Raise the vehicle and support safely.
4. Using the proper equipment, drain the fuel tank.
5. Remove vent hoses from hose routing bracket attacked to the top of the frame rail. Disconnect the electrical connection.
6. Place a transmission jack or equivalent, under the center of the tank and apply slight pressure. Remove the tank straps.
7. Lower tank slightly to provide access to the fuel supply and return hoses, and disconnect hoses. Disconnect fuel vapor line from pressure relief/rollover valve.
8. Lower tank from vehicle.
To install:
9. Raise the tank into position and connect all electrical harnesses and vacuum hoses.
10. Install the tank straps and tighten the retaining nuts.
11. Install vent hoses, if not done, and check all connections.
12. Fill fuel tank, install fuel filler cap and reconnect negative battery cable.

Caravan, Voyager and Town & Country

NOTE: All Wheel Drive vehicles, have a fuel tank that is made of plastic. Care should be taken to avoid damaging this tank. The fuel tank in AWD vehicles is mounted at the side of the vehicle instead of the rear.

1. Release the fuel system pressure. Refer to fuel system pressure release procedure.

—————— CAUTION ——————
Never smoke when working around gasoline! Avoid all sources of sparks or ignition. Gasoline vapors are EXTREMELY volatile!

2. Disconnect battery negative cable.
3. Raise the vehicle and support properly.
4. Remove drain tube rubber cap on left rail and connect a siphon hose

to drain tube. Drain fuel into a safe gasoline container.
5. Remove screws supporting filler tube to inner and outer quarter panel.
6. Disconnect wiring and lines from the tank.
7. Position a transmission jack to support the fuel tank and remove the bolts from fuel tank straps.
8. Lower tank slightly, and carefully work filler tube from tank.
9. Lower tank, disconnect vapor separator rollover valve hose and remove the fuel tank and insulator pad from vehicle.
To install:
10. Support the fuel tank with a transmission jack. Connect the vapor separator rollover valve hose and position insulator pad on fuel tank.

NOTE: Be certain vapor vent hose is clipped to the tank and not pinch between tank and floor pan during installation.

11. Raise tank into position and carefully work filler tube into tank.
12. Install straps and tighten bolts to 40 ft. lbs. (54.2 Nm). Remove transmission jack.
13. Connect lines, drain tube cap and wiring connector, use new hose clamps.
14. Install and tighten filler tube to inner and outer quarter panel. On some models be sure to install the gasket between the filler tube and the inner quarter panel, before installing the mounting screws.
15. Replace cap on drain tube using a new hose clamp.
16. Fill the fuel tank, install the cap, connect battery cable and check operation.

Fuel Filter

REMOVAL AND INSTALLATION

—————— CAUTION ——————
Do not use conventional fuel hoses or clamps when servicing this fuel system. They are not compatible with the injection system and could fail, causing personal injury or damage to the vehicle. Use only hoses and clamps specifically designed for fuel injection.

1. Relieve the fuel pressure.
2. Disconnect the negative battery cable.
3. Remove the filter retaining screw and remove the filter assembly from the mounting plate.

4. Loosen the outlet hose clamp on the filter and inlet hose clamp on the rear fuel tube.

5. Wrap a shop towel around the hoses to absorb fuel. Remove the hoses from the filter and fuel tube and discard the clamps and the filter.

To install:

6. Install the inlet hose on the fuel tube and tighten the new clamp to 10 inch lbs. (1.0 Nm).

7. Install the outlet hose on the filter outlet fitting and tighten the new clamp to 10 inch lbs. (1.0 Nm).

8. Position the filter assembly on the mounting plate and tighten the mounting screw to 75 inch lbs. (8.0 Nm).

9. Connect the negative battery cable, start the engine and check for leaks.

Electric Fuel Pump

PRESSURE TESTING

1. Relieve the fuel pressure.
2. Disconnect the larger diameter fuel supply hose from the engine fuel line assembly.
3. Connect the fuel system pressure tester C–4799B or equivalent, between the fuel supply hose and the engine fuel line assembly.
4. With the key in the **RUN** position, put the DRB I or II in the activate auto shutdown relay mode; this will activate the fuel pump and pressurize the system.
5. The pressure specification is 13.5–15.5 psi. If the pressure is within specifications, reinstall the fuel hose.
6. If fuel pressure is below specifications, install the tester in the fuel supply line between the tank and the filter and repeat the test.
7. If the pressure is 5 psi higher than in Step 5, replace the fuel filter. If no change is observed, squeeze the

return hose. If pressure increases, replace the pressure regulator. If no change is observed, the problem is either a plugged in-tank sock filter or a defective pump.

8. If fuel pressure is above specifications, remove the fuel return line hose from the chassis line at the fuel tank and connect a 3 foot piece of fuel hose to the return line. Put the other end into a 2 gallon minimum capacity approved gasoline container. Repeat the test. If pressure is now correct, check the in-tank return hose for kinking. Replace the fuel pump assembly if the in-tank reservoir check valve or aspirator jet is obstructed.

9. If pressure is still above specifications, remove the fuel return hose from the throttle body. Connect a substitute hose to the throttle body return nipple and place the other end of the hose in a clean container. Repeat the test. If pressure is now correct, check for a restricted fuel return line. If no change is observed, replace the fuel pressure regulator.

REMOVAL AND INSTALLATION

The fuel pump module is installed in the top of the fuel tank. It contains the fuel pump, fuel pump reservoir, pressure relief/rollover valve, electrical connector for the sending unit, fuel filler vent, supply and return tube connections, pressure regulator and the drain tube nipple

1. Disconnect negative battery cable.
2. Relieve the fuel pressure.
3. Raise the vehicle and support safely.
4. Using the proper equipment, drain the fuel tank.
5. Remove vent hoses from hose routing bracket attacked to the top of the frame rail. Disconnect the electrical connection.
6. Place a transmission jack or equivalent, under the center of the

tank and apply slight pressure. Remove the tank straps.

7. Lower tank slightly to provide access to the fuel supply and return hoses and disconnect hoses. Disconnect fuel vapor line from pressure relief/rollover valve. Lower tank from vehicle.

8. Remove the fuel pump module collar and module from tank. Mark position of sender wires and disconnect. Remove sender unit from module.

To install:

9. Replace module and pump assembly as a unit. Reinstall sender to module and reposition into tank. Install collar to original position.

10. Raise the tank into position and connect all harnesses and vacuum hoses. Install the tank straps and tighten the retaining nuts.

11. Connect fuel filler tube and vent hoses.

12. Fill fuel tank, install fuel filler cap and reconnect negative battery cable.

Fuel Injection

IDLE SPEED ADJUSTMENT

1992

1. Start the engine and allow it to reach normal operating temperature. If engine is already hot, run for 2 minutes.

2. Turn the engine OFF and allow 1 minute for the Idle Speed Control (ISC) actuator shaft to fully extend.

3. Disconnect the ISC actuator connector and the coolant temperature sensor.

4. Connect a tachometer to the engine and start the engine.

5. Adjust the extension screw on the actuator shaft until the rpm is within specifications:

3.9L engine — 2500–2600 rpm

5.2L and 5.9L engines — 2750–2850 rpm

6. Turn the engine OFF. Reconnect the ISC actuator connector and the coolant temperature sensor. Remove the tachometer.

1993–96

The idle speed is controlled electronically and cannot be adjusted. If engine idle is not within specifications, remove the throttle body and clean carbon deposits from the idle air control passages. If this does not correct the problem, diagnose the idle air control system.

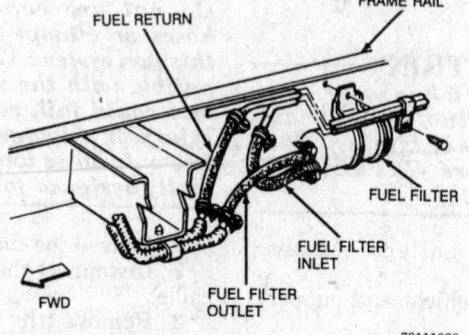

Fuel filter location — fuel injected engine

79111028

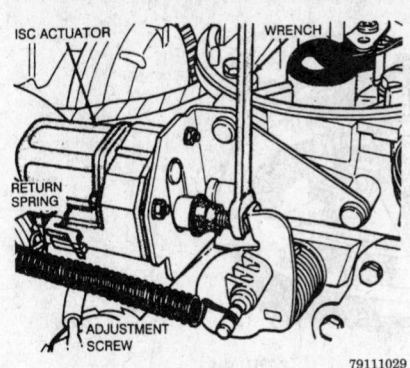

Adjusting the idle speed — 1992 engine

IDLE MIXTURE ADJUSTMENT

There is no idle mixture adjustment provided with the fuel injection system.

Fuel Injector

REMOVAL AND INSTALLATION

2.5L with Single Point Injection

1. Remove air cleaner assembly.
2. Perform fuel system pressure release.
3. Disconnect negative battery cable.
4. Remove fuel pressure regulator.
5. Remove Torx® screw holding down injector cap.
6. With 2 small prying tools, lift cap off injector using slots provided.
7. Using a small prying tool placed in hole in front of electrical connector, gently pry injector from pod.
8. Make sure injector lower O-ring has been removed from pod.
9. To install, place a new lower O-ring on injector and a new O-ring on injector cap. The injector will have upper O-ring already installed.
10. Put injector cap on injector. (Injector and cap are keyed). Cap should sit on injector without interference.

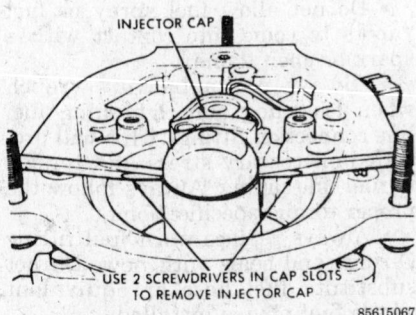

Injector cap removal — 2.5L engine

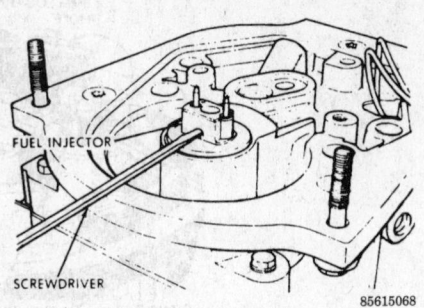

Fuel injector removal — 2.5L engine

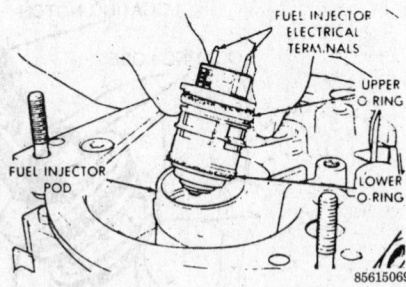

Fuel injector servicing — 2.5L engine

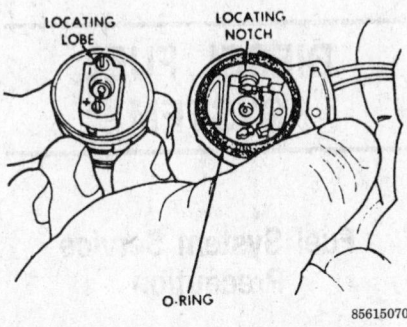

Fuel injector terminal identification — 2.5L engine

Apply a light coating of castor oil or petroleum jelly on O-rings. Place assembly in pod.
11. Rotate cap and injector to align attachment hole.
12. Push down on cap until it contacts injector pod.
13. Install Torx® screw and torque to 35–45 inch lbs. (4–5 Nm).
14. Install fuel pressure regulator.
15. Connect negative battery cable.
16. Test for leaks using ATM tester C–4805 or equivalent. With ignition in the **RUN** position depress ATM button. This will activate pump and

pressurize the system. Check for leaks.
17. Reinstall air cleaner assembly.

Multi-port Fuel Injection

EXCEPT 8.0L ENGINE

1. Remove the air cleaner assembly.
2. Relieve the fuel pressure.
3. Disconnect the negative battery cable.
4. Remove the fuel rail assembly as follows:
   a. Remove the throttle body from the intake manifold.
   b. If equipped with A/C, remove the compressor-to-intake manifold support bracket.
   c. Disconnect the fuel injector connectors. Disconnect the intake air temperature sensor for the 3.9L engine.
   d. Remove the canister purge solenoid bracket assembly.
   e. Disconnect the main fuel line.
   f. Remove the fuel rail bolts and gently rock and pull the left fuel rail until the injectors just start to clear the intake manifold. Repeat this procedure for the right fuel rail. Remove the rail with the injectors still connected.
5. Remove the injector retaining clips and injectors.
To install:
6. Apply engine oil to the seals and push the injector into the fuel rail. Install the retaining clip and fuel rail as follows:
   a. Install the fuel rail/injectors to the intake manifold. Push the right fuel rail down until the injectors have bottomed on the shoulder. Repeat for left side.
   b. Install the rail retaining bolts and remaining components.
7. Connect the negative battery cable, start the engine and check for leaks.

8.0L ENGINE

1. Disconnect the negative battery cable, remove the air cleaner assembly and relieve the fuel pressure.
2. Disconnect the throttle body linkage and remove the throttle body.
3. Remove the ignition coil pack and bracket assembly.
4. Remove the upper intake manifold and disconnect the fuel injector electrical connectors. Label the connectors for installation purposes.
5. Disconnect the fuel lines.
6. Remove the fuel rail retaining bolts.
7. Remove the fuel rail bolts and gently rock and pull the left fuel rail until the injectors just start to clear

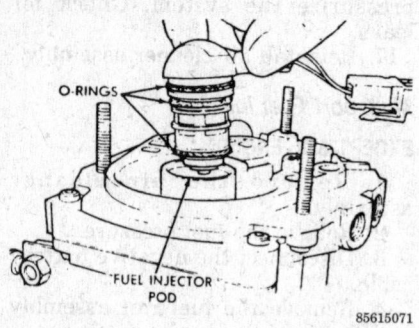

Fuel injector installation — 2.5L engine

85615071

the intake manifold. Repeat this procedure for the right fuel rail. Remove the rail with the injectors still connected.

8. Remove the injector retaining clips and injectors.

To install:

9. Apply engine oil to the seals and push the injector into the fuel rail. Install the retaining clip and fuel rail.

10. Install the fuel rail/injectors to the intake manifold. Push the right fuel rail down until the injectors have bottomed on the shoulder. Repeat for left side.

11. Install the rail retaining bolts and remaining components.

12. Connect the negative battery cable, start the engine and check for leaks.

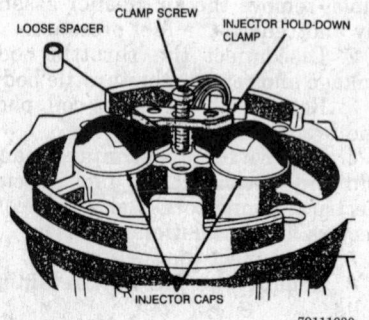

Injector hold-down and spacer — single-point EFI engine

79111030

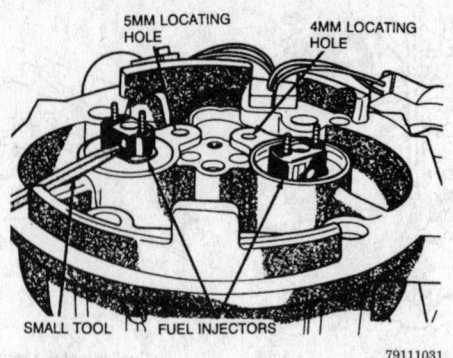

Removing the injector from its pod — single-point EFI engine

79111031

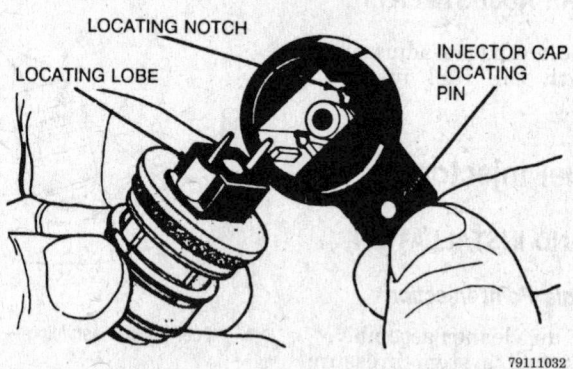

Installing the injector to the cap — single-point EFI engine

79111032

DIESEL FUEL SYSTEM

Fuel System Service Precaution

Safety is the most important factor when performing not only fuel system maintenance but any type of maintenance. Failure to conduct maintenance and repairs in a safe manner may result in serious personal injury or death. Maintenance and testing of the vehicle's fuel system components can be accomplished safely and effectively by adhering to the following rules and guidelines.

• To avoid the possibility of fire and personal injury, always disconnect the negative battery cable unless the repair or test procedure requires that battery voltage be applied.

• Always relieve the fuel system pressure prior to disconnecting any fuel system component (injector, fuel pump, injection pump, etc.), fitting or fuel line connection. Exercise extreme caution whenever relieving fuel system pressure to avoid exposing skin, face and eyes to fuel spray. Please be advised that fuel under pressure may penetrate the skin or any part of the body that it contacts.

• Always place a shop towel or cloth around the fitting or connection prior to loosening to absorb any excess fuel due to spillage. Ensure that all fuel spillage (should it occur) is quickly removed from engine surfaces. Ensure that all fuel soaked cloths or towels are deposited into a suitable waste container.

• Always keep a dry chemical (Class B) fire extinguisher near the work area.

• Do not allow fuel spray or fuel vapors to come into contact with a spark or open flame.

• Always use a backup wrench when loosening and tightening fuel line connection fittings. This will prevent unnecessary stress and torsion to fuel line piping. Always follow the proper torque specifications.

• Always replace worn fuel fitting O-rings and seals with new. Do not substitute fuel hose or equivalent where fuel pipe is installed.

Fuel Filter

REPLACEMENT

Fuel Filter/Water Separator

1. Disconnect the negative battery cable.
2. Disconnect the Water In Filter (WIF) sensor connector.
3. Remove the separator filter assembly from the filter head with a standard oil filter wrench. The filter is located on the left/rear side of the engine.
4. Remove the square cut O-ring from the filter mounting bushing. Remove the WIF sensor from the filter by unscrewing.
5. Drain the fuel/water separator filter and remove the assembly from the fuel filter.

To install:

6. Install a new O-ring to the WIF assembly and install to the new separator filter.
7. Install a new square cut O-ring to the mounting bushing.
8. Fill the fuel/water separator filter with clean diesel fuel.
9. Apply a light coat of oil to the sealing surface of the separator filter.
10. Install the assembly and tighten it ½ turn after the seal contacts the filter head.
11. Reconnect the WIF sensor connector.
12. Connect the negative battery cable, start the engine and check for leaks.

In-Tank Fuel Filter

The in-tank fuel filter is located at the fuel pump/sender module in the top of the fuel tank. Refer to electric fuel pump.

DRAINING WATER FROM THE SYSTEM

The filter should be drained whenever the water-in-fuel warning light remains illuminated. The light will illuminate for about 2 seconds when the ignition is ON and turn should turn OFF. This is a bulb check and is normal.

Filtration and separation of water from the fuel is important for trouble free operation and long life of the fuel system. Regular maintenance, including draining moisture from the fuel/water separator filter is essential to keep water out of the injector pump and injectors. To remove collected water place drain pan under drain tube on separator. Push up on the drain at the bottom filter separator Water-In-Fuel (WIF) sensor. Hold drain open until all water and contaminants have been removed and clean fuel exits the drain.

Electric Fuel Pump and Filter (In-Tank)

REMOVAL AND INSTALLATION

1. Disconnect negative battery cable.
2. Raise the vehicle and support safely.
3. Using the proper equipment, drain the fuel tank.
4. Remove vent hoses from hose routing bracket attacked to the top of the frame rail. Disconnect the electrical connection.
5. Place a transmission jack or equivalent, under the center of the tank and apply slight pressure. Remove the tank straps.
6. Lower tank slightly to provide access to the fuel supply and return hoses and disconnect hoses. Disconnect pressure relief/rollover valve. Lower tank from vehicle.
7. Remove the fuel pump module collar and module from tank. Mark position of sender wires and disconnect. Remove sender unit from module.
8. The in-tank fuel filter is located at the bottom of the pump module and can be removed by prying the mounting tabs back.

To install:

9. If removed, install the in-tank fuel filter into retaining tabs.
10. Replace module and pump assembly as a unit. Reinstall sender to module and reposition into tank. Install collar to original position.
11. Raise the tank into position and connect all harnesses and vacuum hoses. Install the tank straps and tighten the retaining nuts.
12. Connect fuel filler tube and vent hoses.
13. Fill fuel tank, install fuel filler cap and reconnect negative battery cable.

Diesel Injection Pump

The 5.9L engine uses a Bosch VE or P7100 injection pump. The VE pump can be identified by the fuel distributor located on the back side, in a circle. The P7100 pump has the fuel distributor on top, in a straight line.

REMOVAL AND INSTALLATION

NOTE: The Bosch VE lever is indexed to the shaft during pump calibration. Do not remove it from the pump during removal.

1. Disconnect the negative battery cable.
2. Remove the throttle linkage and bracket.
3. Disconnect the fuel drain manifold.
4. Remove the injection pump supply line.
5. Remove the high pressure lines.
6. Disconnect the electrical wire to the fuel shut off valve.
7. Remove the fuel air control tube.
8. Remove the pump support bracket.
9. Remove the oil fill tube bracket and adapter from the front gear cover. The adapter is removed by screwing counterclockwise from the front gear cover.
10. Place a shop towel in the gear cover opening in a position that will prevent the nut and washer from falling into the gear housing. Remove the gear retaining nut and washer.
11. Install the turning tool into the flywheel housing opening on the exhaust side of the engine. Place a ½ in. drive universal joint in the turning tool and attach enough extensions to the joint to make it convenient to turn the tool.
12. Using a ratchet to turn the turning tool, turn the engine until the key way on the fuel pump shaft is pointing approximately in the 6 o'clock position.

NOTE: The built-in timing (TDC) pin is located above the power steering pump, below and to the inside of the fuel injection pump, on the rear of the cam gear housing. The pin will engage into a machined hole in the back of the camshaft gear. It will lock the engine in the TDC position for No. 1 cylinder. Always pull the pin to the resting position before starting the engine after repair procedures.

13. Locate TDC for cylinder No. 1 by turning the engine slowly counterclockwise while pushing in on the TDC pin. Stop turning the engine as soon as the pin engages with the gear timing hole. Disengage the pin after locating TDC and remove the turning equipment.
14. Loosen the lockscrew, remove the special washer from the injection pump and wire it to the line above it so it will not get misplaced. Retighten

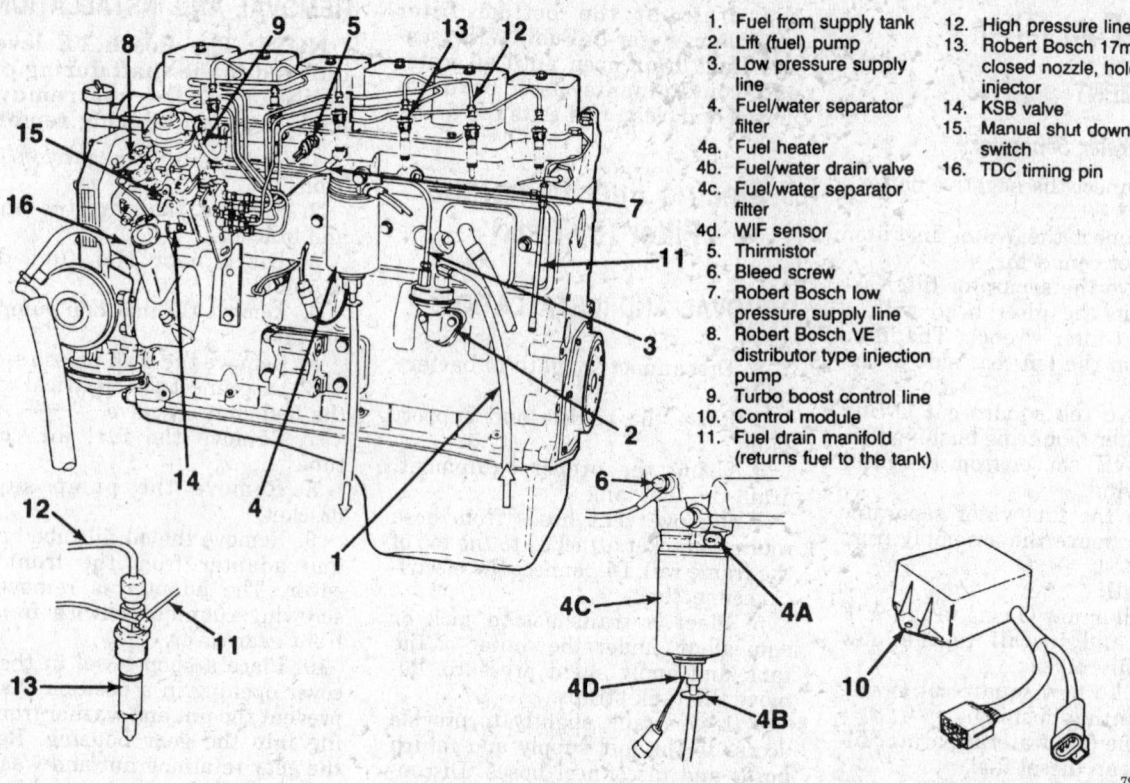

1. Fuel from supply tank
2. Lift (fuel) pump
3. Low pressure supply line
4. Fuel/water separator filter
4a. Fuel heater
4b. Fuel/water drain valve
4c. Fuel/water separator filter
4d. WIF sensor
5. Thirmistor
6. Bleed screw
7. Robert Bosch low pressure supply line
8. Robert Bosch VE distributor type injection pump
9. Turbo boost control line
10. Control module
11. Fuel drain manifold (returns fuel to the tank)
12. High pressure lines
13. Robert Bosch 17mm, closed nozzle, hole type injector
14. KSB valve
15. Manual shut down switch
16. TDC timing pin

79111033

Fuel system components — 5.9L diesel engine

the lockscrew to 22 ft. lbs. (30 Nm) to lock the driveshaft.

15. Using a puller, extract the pump drive gear from the driveshaft.

NOTE: Be careful not to drop the drive gear key into the front cover when removing or installing the pump. If it does drop in, it must be removed before proceeding. Also, pull the cam gear only enough to loosen it from the pump shaft. Pulling too far may damage the gear cover.

16. Remove the mounting nuts and bracket bolts. Remove the injection pump from the vehicle.

17. Remove the gasket and clean the mounting surface.

To install:

18. **To install the Bosch VE injection pump**, proceed as follows:
   a. Install a new gasket.

NOTE: The shaft of a new or reconditioned pump is locked so the key aligns with the drive gear keyway with cylinder No. 1 at TDC.

   b. Install the pump and finger-tighten the mounting nuts; the pump must be free to move in the slots.

   c. Install the pump drive gear, washer and nut to the driveshaft.

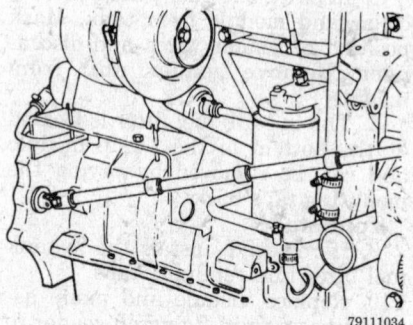

79111034

Installing the turning tool — diesel injection system

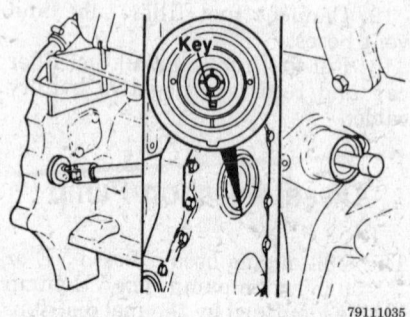

Key

79111035

Locating TDC with the TDC pin — Bosch VE fuel injection

The pump will rotate slightly because of gear helix and clearance. This is acceptable providing the pump is free to move on the flange slots and the crankshaft does not move. Torque the nut to 11–15 ft. lbs. (15–20 Nm). This is not the final torque; do not overtighten.

   d. If installing the original pump, rotate the pump to align the original timing marks and torque the mounting nuts to 18 ft. lbs. (24 Nm).

   e. If installing a replacement pump, take up gear lash by rotating the pump counterclockwise toward the cylinder head and torque the mounting nuts to 18 ft. lbs. (24 Nm). Permanently mark the new injection pump flange to match the mark on the gear housing.

   f. Loosen the lockscrew and install the special washer under the lockscrew. Torque to 19 ft. lbs. (13 Nm). Disengage the TDC pin.

   g. Install the injection pump support bracket. finger-tighten the bolts initially, then torque them to 18 ft. lbs. (24 Nm) in the following sequence: Bracket to block bolts, bracket to injection pump bolts and throttle support bracket bolts.

   h. Now perform the final torque of the pump drive gear retaining nut to 48 ft. lbs. (65 Nm).

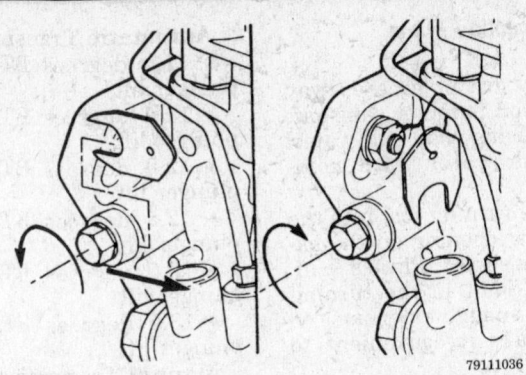

79111036

Removing the special washer from the injection pump

i. Install the oil filler tube assembly and clamp. Torque the bolts to 32 ft. lbs. (43 Nm).

j. Install all fuel lines and the electrical connector to the fuel shut off valve. Tighten the high pressure lines to 18 ft. lbs. (24 Nm).

k. Install the fuel air control tube. Torque the banjo fitting bolt to 9 ft. lbs. (12 Nm).

l. Install the throttle bracket and linkage. When connecting the cable to the control lever, adjust the length so the lever has stop-to-stop movement.

m. Connect the negative battery cable.

19. **To install the Bosch P7100 injection pump**, proceed as follows:

a. Make sure the engine is on TDC of the No. 1 cylinder. Remove the access plug from the side of the pump. Stored behind the the plug is a plastic timing pin tool. This tool is used to align the pump timing tooth to the center of the access hole.

b. If installing the original pump, the pin should already be mounted with the slotted end facing outward. When the position of this tool has been reversed, with the slotted end facing inward, it is used as a pump timing pin tool.

c. If installing a new or rebuilt pump, the pump should have been shipped with the slotted end of the timing pin tool engaged to the timing tooth in the pump.

d. Make sure the timing pin is engaged and loosely install the access plug.

e. Install a new mounting flange O-ring and make sure the mounting area is free of dirt and grease.

f. Position the pump assembly to the mounting flange on the gear cover while aligning the pump shaft through the back of the pump gear. Install the mounting nuts finger-tight.

---WARNING---

Do not attempt to pull the injection pump into the gear cover using the mounting nuts. Damage to the pump and/or the gear cover may occur. The pump must be flat on the mounting before the nuts can be tightened.

g. Torque the mounting and bracket nuts to 18 ft. lbs. (24 Nm). Torque the mounting nuts first.

h. Install the driveshaft gear washer and nut. Preliminary torque should be 7–11 ft. lbs. (10–15 Nm). Overtightening will damage the timing pin. Final torque will be done later.

i. Disengage the timing pin from the rear of the camshaft gear by pulling it straight back. Remove the access plug from the pump and remove the timing pin tool from the pump.

j. Final torque the driveshaft gear nut to 144 ft. lbs. (195 Nm). Use the engine barring tool to prevent the engine from turning.

k. After final torquing, recheck the injection pump timing. Remove the injection pump timing pin tool and bar the engine counterclockwise until all timing marks are in alignment.

l. After timing is correct, remove the timing pin tool from the pump, reverse the position and install the access plug. Torque the plug to 11 ft. lbs. (15 Nm). The timing pin slot should face outward.

m. Install the high pressure fuel lines and torque to 22 ft. lbs. (30 Nm).

---CAUTION---

Do not place any part of the hand near the base of the high pressure line. A fuel leak from a high pressure fuel line has sufficient pressure to penetrate the skin and cause serious bodily harm. Do not bleed the lines if the engine is hot.

Fuel spilling onto a hot exhaust manifold creates the danger of fire.

20. Install the remaining components in the reverse of removal.

21. New or rebuilt P7100 fuel injection pumps must be pre-lubricated before operation. Failure to do so may cause premature governor wear. Prelubricate as follows:

a. Remove the 10mm hex plug on the tip of the injection pump governor.

b. Add 25 oz. (750ml) of clean engine oil through this opening.

c. Install the plug and torque to 18 ft. lbs. (24 Nm).

22. To bleed air from the system, run or crank the engine and carefully loosen the high pressure fitting from each injector 1 at a time. Retighten the fitting after the air has expelled before going on to the next injector fitting. The operation is complete when the engine runs smoothly. If the air cannot be removed, check the pump and supply line for suction leaks.

23. Adjust the idle speed, if necessary.

IDLE SPEED ADJUSTMENT

The high idle speed is factory sealed and cannot be adjusted. The low idle speed adjustment is at the throttle lever stop screw.

1. Start the engine and run until normal operating temperature is reached.

2. An optical tachometer must be used to read engine speed; a conventional tachometer connected to the coil is useless in this instance.

3. Turn the air conditioning **ON**, if equipped.

4. Turn the idle speed screw until the desired idle speed is obtained. The specification for automatic transmission is 700 rpm or for manual transmission is 750 rpm. Tighten the locknut after adjustment.

Injection Pump Timing

ADJUSTMENT

Bosch VE Injection Pump

1. Install the turning tool into the flywheel housing opening on the exhaust side of the engine. Place a ½ in. drive universal joint in the turning tool and attach enough extensions to the joint to make it convenient to turn the tool.

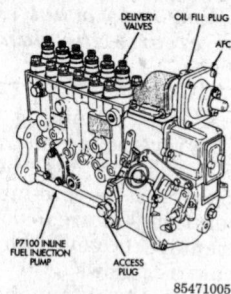

85471005

Timing pin access and
governor fill plug
locations — Bosch P7100
injection pump

2. Using a ratchet to turn the tool, turn the engine until the key way on the fuel pump shaft is pointing approximately in the 6 o'clock position.

3. Locate TDC for cylinder No. 1 by turning the engine slowly while pushing in on the TDC pin. Stop turning the engine as soon as the pin engages with the gear timing hole. Disengage the pin after locating TDC.

4. Remove the plug from the end of the pump.

5. Install the special timing indicator, allowing for adequate indicator pin travel. It may be necessary to disconnect 1 or more fuel lines to properly install the indicator.

NOTE: The indicator is marked in increments of 0.01mm. One revolution of the indicator needle is equal to 0.050mm.

6. Turn the engine counterclockwise until the indicator needle stops moving. Adjust the indicator face to read zero.

7. Rotate the engine back to TDC and count the number of revolutions of the indicator needle. The reading shown when the engine timing pin engages is the amount of plunger lift the pump has at that point.

8. Readjust the indicator face to read zero. Loosen the pump mounting nuts and rotate the pump clockwise toward the cylinder head until the indicator reads the correct value for plunger lift (the reading in Step 7). Torque the mounting nuts to 18 ft. lbs. (24 Nm).

9. Remove the engine turning equipment and timing indicator. Install the timing plug and torque to 7.5 ft. lbs. (10 Nm). Connect any fuel lines that were disconnected.

10. Road test the vehicle.

Bosch P7100 Injection Pump

1. Clean any dirt or grease away from the injection pump or camshaft gear openings using soap and water. Remove excess water with compressed air.

2. Install the turning tool into the flywheel housing opening on the exhaust side of the engine. Place a ½ in. drive universal joint in the turning tool and attach enough extensions to the joint to make it convenient to turn the tool.

3. Remove the No. 6 cylinder valve cover and turn the engine until the intake and exhaust valves are closed.

4. Locate TDC for cylinder No. 1 by turning the engine slowly while pushing in on the TDC pin. Stop turning the engine as soon as the pin engages with the gear timing hole. Disengage the pin after locating TDC. Make sure No. 6 cylinder valves are closed.

5. Place a paint mark on the vibration dampener to indicate TDC.

6. Remove the No. 1 fuel injection line from the pump.

7. With the engine at TDC, loosen but do not remove the front (No. 1) delivery valve holder using special socket 6804. Remove the socket and valve from the injection pump.

8. Remove the delivery valve holder by carefully tipping the holder outboard with 1 hand while using the other hand to hold the spring, fill piece and any shims from slipping out of the holder. Place these parts as an assembly on a clean shop towel.

9. Remove the 2-piece delivery valve and washer from the pump.

10. Install a dial indicator adapter tool 6842 in place of the No. 1 delivery valve holder and tighten finger-tight. Loosen the setscrew on the dial indicator adapter and install the dial indicator 6859 and indicator tip 6843. Position the dial indicator to read 7.0–9.0mm and tighten the setscrew.

11. Make sure all timing pins are removed before barring engine. Use the engine barring tool to rotate the engine in the direction opposite normal. Rotate until the dial indicator reading stops dropping (inner base circle of the injection pump cam).

12. Zero the indicator and note the reading on the small inner dial. Rotate the engine clockwise slowly to TDC and note the pump lift setting on the dial indicator.

13. Note the timing TDC specifications stamped on the engine dataplate (left side timing gear cover) or refer to the following specifications:

Automatic Transmission
- 11.0 degrees BTDC = 5.4mm plunger lift
- 11.5 degrees BTDC = 5.5mm plunger lift
- 12.0 degrees BTDC = 5.6mm plunger lift
- 12.5 degrees BTDC = 5.7mm plunger lift
- 13.0 degrees BTDC = 5.8mm plunger lift
- 13.5 degrees BTDC = 5.9mm plunger lift

Manual Transmission
- 11.0 degrees BTDC = 4.0mm plunger lift
- 11.5 degrees BTDC = 4.05mm plunger lift
- 12.0 degrees BTDC = 4.1mm plunger lift
- 12.5 degrees BTDC = 4.2mm plunger lift
- 13.0 degrees BTDC = 4.3mm plunger lift
- 13.5 degrees BTDC = 4.4mm plunger lift

14. To adjust timing, remove the oil filler tube and adapter from the front of the timing gear cover by turning counterclockwise.

15. Loosen, but do not remove the injection pump shaft nut using the engine barring tool to prevent the engine from timing. Place a magnet on the engine of the shaft to catch the nut and washer from falling into the timing gear case.

16. Position the magnet to the end of the injection pump shaft. Install the special bearing and thrust washer kit 6862 over the pump shaft in the order of 1 thrust washer, 1 bearing, 1 thrust washer. The washer kit is used to keep the pump gear from rotating on the pump shaft when tightening the pump nut.

17. Reinstall the pump shaft nut allowing some clearance between the thrust washers. Do not tighten the nut at this time.

18. Slowly rotate the engine clockwise until reaching the required plunger lift setting on the dial indicator. The injection pump should rotate with the engine since the pump gear is still locked to the pump shaft.

19. At this point, use special gear puller L–4407A to pull the pump gear off the taper of the pump input shaft. Leave the gear puller installed. Make sure the lift setting has not changed.

20. Loosen, but do not remove the gear puller tool bolts. Using the puller, rotate the pump gear counterclockwise by hand, while pushing the gear onto the pump shaft. This will remove the backlash between the pump and camshaft gears.

21. Hand-tighten the shaft nut and remove the gear puller. Torque the shaft nut to 11 ft. lbs. (15 Nm) to seat the shaft taper and remove the nut.

22. Prevent the engine from turning using the barring tool, tighten the shaft nut to 144 ft. lbs. (195 Nm). Repeat timing check sequence and torque sequence to make sure the setting is correct.

23. Remove the dial indicator and adapter. Install a new copper delivery valve washer into the fuel pump and delivery valve assembly. Lubricate the threads of the delivery valve holder with engine oil. Pretorque the valve assembly to 29 ft. lbs. (40 Nm) in 1 motion. Final torque the assembly to 85 ft. lbs. (115 Nm).

24. Install the remaining components, but leave the No. 1 high pressure fuel line loose to facilitate bleeding the air out of the system.

25. Bleed the fuel system and road test the vehicle.

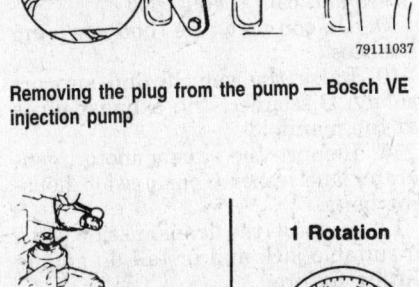

Removing the plug from the pump — Bosch VE injection pump

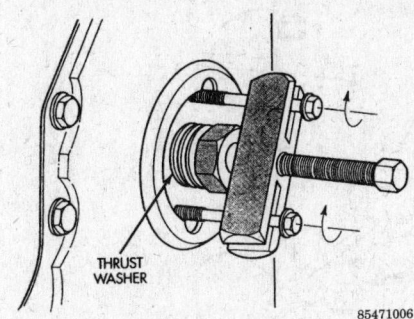

Pump gear puller tool — Bosch P7100 injection pump

Fuel Injector

REMOVAL AND INSTALLATION

1. Disconnect the negative battery cable. Remove the throttle linkage and bracket, if necessary.

2. Disconnect the high pressure fuel supply line to the injector.

3. Disconnect the fuel drain manifold.

4. Clean the area around the injector.

5. Using a 24mm deepwell socket, remove the injector from the cylinder head.

To install:

6. Clean the injector bore with a bore brush.

7. Assemble the injector and 1 new copper sealing washer. Never use more than 1 copper washer.

8. Apply a thin coat of anti-seize compound to the threads of the injector hold-down nut and between the top of the nut and the injector body.

9. Align the protrusion in the injector with the notch in the bore and install the injector. Torque the injector retainer nut to 44 ft. lbs. (60 Nm).

10. Push the O-ring into the groove at the top of the injector.

11. Using new sealing washers, assemble the fuel drain manifold and

high pressure lines. Torque the banjo fitting bolt to 6 ft. lbs. (8 Nm). Leave the high pressure line loose temporarily.

--- **CAUTION** ---

Do not place any part of the hand near the base of the high pressure line. A fuel leak from a high pressure fuel line has sufficient pressure to penetrate the skin and cause serious bodily harm. Do not bleed the lines if the engine is hot. Fuel spilling onto a hot exhaust manifold creates the danger of fire.

12. Reconnect negative battery cable. Install the throttle linkage and bracket, if removed.

13. To bleed air from the system, run or crank the engine and tighten the fitting after the air has expelled. If more than 1 injector was replaced, tighten each fitting after the air has expelled before going on to the next injector fitting. Torque the fittings to 18 ft. lbs. (24 Nm). The operation is complete when the engine runs smoothly. If the air cannot be removed, check the pump and supply line for suction leaks.

EMISSION CONTROLS

Emissions Warning Lamp

RESETTING

Gasoline Heavy Duty Cycle (HDC) Engine

1. Connect the DRBII to the diagnostic connector.

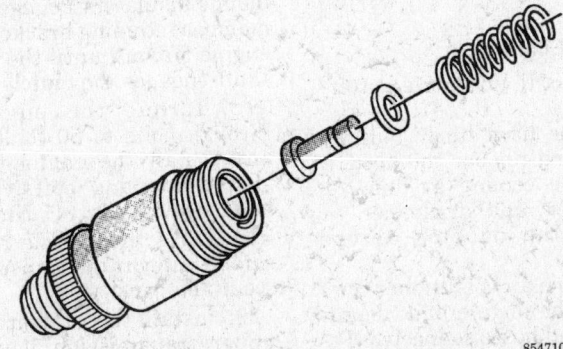

Delivery valve holder — Bosch P7100 injection pump

1 Rotation

0.50 mm

Installing the timing indicator — Bosch VE injection pump

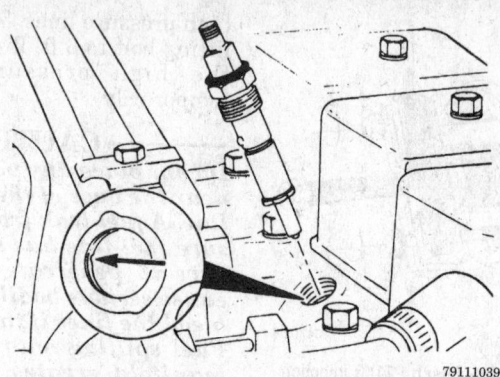

79111039

Installing the fuel injector — diesel fuel system

2. Turn the ignition switch to the **RUN** position and access the Emissions EMR or SRI Tests on the DRBII.

3. Select EMR or SRI Memory Check (Emission Maintenance Reminder EMR/Service Reminder Indicator SRI).

4. Select Reset EMR or SRI Light. This will reset the EMR or SRI timer in the computer and turn the light OFF.

5. Disconnect the DRBII.

GASOLINE ENGINE MECHANICAL

NOTE: Disconnecting the negative battery cable on some vehicles may interfere with the functions of the on-board computer systems and may require the computer to undergo a relearning process, once the negative battery cable is reconnected.

Engine Assembly

REMOVAL AND INSTALLATION

Dakota

4-CYLINDER ENGINE

1. Disconnect the negative battery cable.

2. Scribe the hood hinge outlines on the hood, and remove the hood.

3. Drain the cooling system, remove the battery and air cleaner.

4. Remove the radiator, shroud and cooling fan.

5. Remove the air conditioner compressor from the engine and mounting brackets and hoses connected. Position the assembly to the side and secure out of the way.

6. Disconnect and label the vacuum lines, accelerator cable and speed control cable.

7. Relieve the fuel system pressure and disconnect the fuel lines and brackets.

8. Disconnect the power steering hoses and cap, if equipped.

9. Disconnect the body wiring harness.

10. Raise the vehicle and support safely. Disconnect the exhaust pipe at the manifold.

11. Remove the starter motor and upper transmission housing bolts.

12. Lower the vehicle safely. Support the transmission with a suitable jack and install an engine lifting fixture.

13. Loosen the engine mount through bolts and remove the engine-to-transmission struts and bolts.

14. Raise the engine until the front mount insulators clear the crossmember retaining brackets. Move the engine forward until the drive pinion shaft clears the clutch disc.

15. Remove the engine from the engine compartment and place on an engine stand.

To install:

16. Install the engine into the engine compartment.

17. Lower the engine until the front mount insulators engage with crossmember retaining brackets. Move the engine forward until the drive pinion shaft engages the clutch disc.

18. Torque the engine mount through bolts to 50 ft. lbs. (68 Nm) and install the engine-to-transmission struts and bolts. Torque the bolts to 30 ft. lbs. (41 Nm).

19. Raise the vehicle and support safely. Support the transmission with a suitable jack.

20. Install the starter motor and upper transmission housing bolts. Torque the bolts to 30 ft. lbs. (41 Nm).

21. Lower the vehicle safely. Connect the exhaust pipe at the manifold and torque to 20 ft. lbs. (27 Nm).

22. Connect the body wiring harness.

23. Connect the power steering hoses, if equipped.

24. Connect the vacuum lines, accelerator cable and speed control cable.

25. Connect the vacuum lines, accelerator cable and speed control cable.

26. Install the air conditioner compressor to the engine and mounting brackets with hoses connected.

27. Install the cooling fan, shroud and radiator.

28. Refill the cooling system, install the battery and air cleaner.

29. Install the hood.

30. Connect the negative battery cable, start the engine and check for leaks.

6 AND 8-CYLINDER ENGINES

1. Disconnect the negative battery cable.

2. Scribe the hood hinge outlines on the hood, and remove the hood.

3. Drain the cooling system and remove the air cleaner and battery.

4. Remove the radiator, shroud and cooling fan.

5. Disconnect and label the vacuum lines, accelerator cable and speed control cable.

6. Discharge and recover the A/C system, if equipped. Disconnect the refrigerant lines from the compressor.

7. Relieve the fuel system pressure and disconnect the fuel lines and brackets.

8. Disconnect the power steering hoses and cap, if equipped.

9. Disconnect the body wiring harness.

10. Raise the vehicle and support safely. Disconnect the exhaust pipes at the manifolds.

11. Remove the starter motor, generator and upper transmission housing bolts.

12. Support the transmission with a suitable jack and install an engine lifting fixture.

13. For 4WD vehicles, proceed as follows:

a. Left side: Remove 2 bolts attaching the engine/pinion nose/transmission bracket to transmission bellhousing. Remove the 2 bracket-to-pinion nose adapter bolts. Separate the engine from the insulator by removing the upper nut and washer assembly and bolt from the engine support bracket.

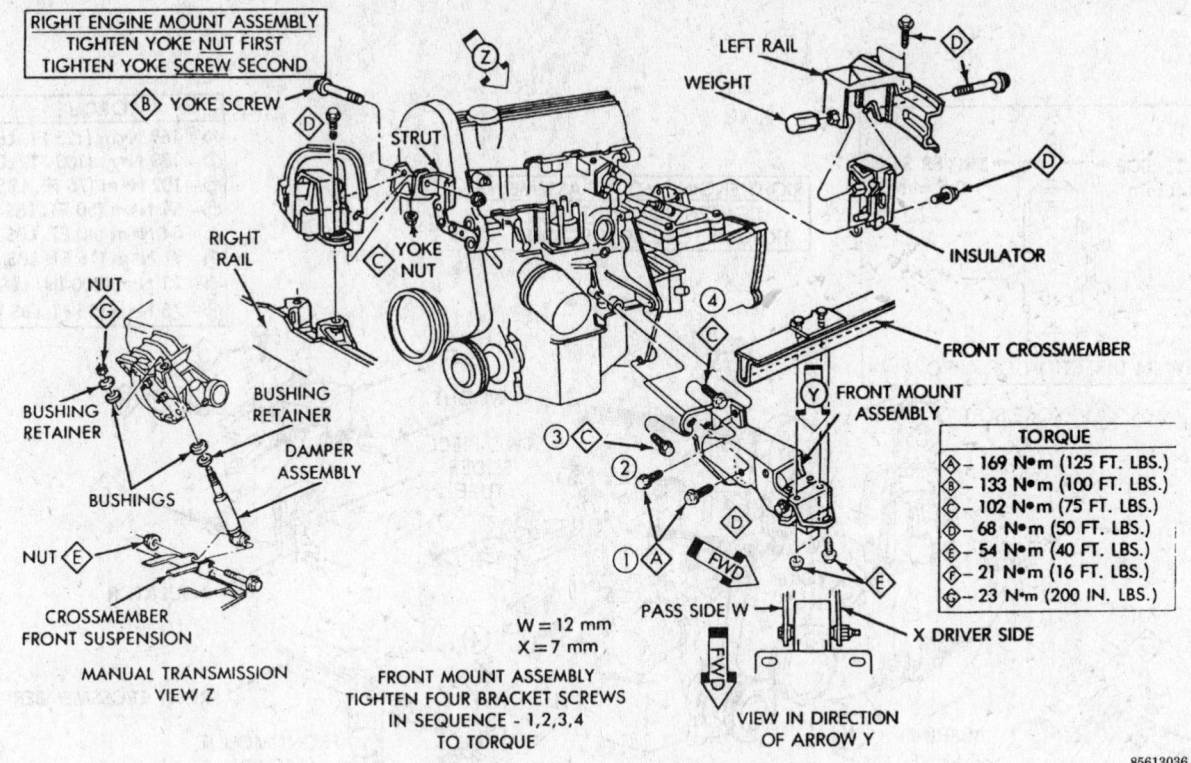

RIGHT ENGINE MOUNT ASSEMBLY
TIGHTEN YOKE NUT FIRST
TIGHTEN YOKE SCREW SECOND

B YOKE SCREW

STRUT

RIGHT RAIL

YOKE NUT

NUT G

BUSHING RETAINER

BUSHING RETAINER

BUSHINGS

DAMPER ASSEMBLY

NUT E

CROSSMEMBER FRONT SUSPENSION

MANUAL TRANSMISSION VIEW Z

LEFT RAIL

WEIGHT

INSULATOR

FRONT CROSSMEMBER

FRONT MOUNT ASSEMBLY

TORQUE	
◇ – 169 N•m (125 FT. LBS.)	
◇ – 133 N•m (100 FT. LBS.)	
◇ – 102 N•m (75 FT. LBS.)	
◇ – 68 N•m (50 FT. LBS.)	
◇ – 54 N•m (40 FT. LBS.)	
◇ – 21 N•m (16 FT. LBS.)	
◇ – 23 N•m (200 IN. LBS.)	

W = 12 mm
X = 7 mm

FRONT MOUNT ASSEMBLY
TIGHTEN FOUR BRACKET SCREWS
IN SEQUENCE - 1,2,3,4
TO TORQUE

PASS SIDE W

X DRIVER SIDE

VIEW IN DIRECTION OF ARROW Y

85613036

Engine mounting — 1992–93 FWD 2.5L engine

b. Right side: Remove the 2 bracket-to-axle bolts and 1 bracket-to-bellhousing bolt. Separate the engine from the insulator by removing the upper nut washer assembly and bolt from the engine support bracket.

14. Lower the vehicle safely.

15. On automatic transmission, remove the torque converter driveplate bolts. On manual transmission, move the engine forward until the drive pinion shaft clears the clutch disc.

16. Loosen the engine mount through bolts and any bellhousing-to-engine bolts.

17. Raise the engine until the front mount insulators clear the crossmember retaining brackets.

18. Remove the engine from the engine compartment and place on an engine stand.

To install:

19. Install the engine lifting device. Raise and safely support the vehicle.

20. Position the engine into the engine compartment and engage the transmission.

21. Install the front engine mounts and lower the vehicle.

22. Remove the engine lifting device.

23. Install the generator, starter motor and power steering hoses.

24. Connect the A/C lines. Evacuate and recharge the A/C system.

25. Using a new gasket, install the throttle body and torque bolts to 200 inch lbs. (23 Nm).

26. Connect the accelerator linkage, starter wires, oil pressure wire, distributor wiring, vacuum lines and fuel lines.

27. Install the radiator and connect the hoses. Refill the cooling system.

28. Install the fan and shroud.

29. Install the air cleaner and battery.

30. Install the hood, connect the battery cables, start the engine and check for leaks.

Caravan, Voyager and Town & Country

1. Disconnect the negative battery cable.

2. Scribe the hood hinge outlines on the hood, and remove the hood.

3. Drain the cooling system. Remove the radiator hoses from the radiator and engine connections.

4. Remove the radiator and fan assembly.

5. Remove the air conditioner compressor from the engine and mounting brackets and hoses connected. Position the assembly to the side and secure out of the way.

6. Remove the power steering pump from the engine with mounting brackets and hoses connected. Position the assembly to the side and secure out of the way.

7. Disconnect all electrical connectors at the alternator, injection unit and engine.

8. Disconnect the fuel line from the gas tank at the fuel pump. Disconnect the heat hoses from the engine.

9. Remove the alternator. Disconnect the clutch cable from the clutch lever, if equipped with a manual transaxle.

10. Remove the transaxle case lower cover.

11. Automatic transaxle, mark the flexplate to torque converter location.

12. Remove the bolts that mount the converter to the flexplate. Attach a small C-clamp to the front bottom of the converter housing to prevent the converter from falling off the transaxle.

13. Disconnect the starter motor wiring and remove the starter motor.

14. Disconnect the exhaust pipe from the exhaust manifold.

15. Remove the right inner engine splash shield. Drain the engine oil and remove the oil filter. Disconnect the engine ground strap.

16. Attach hoist to the engine.

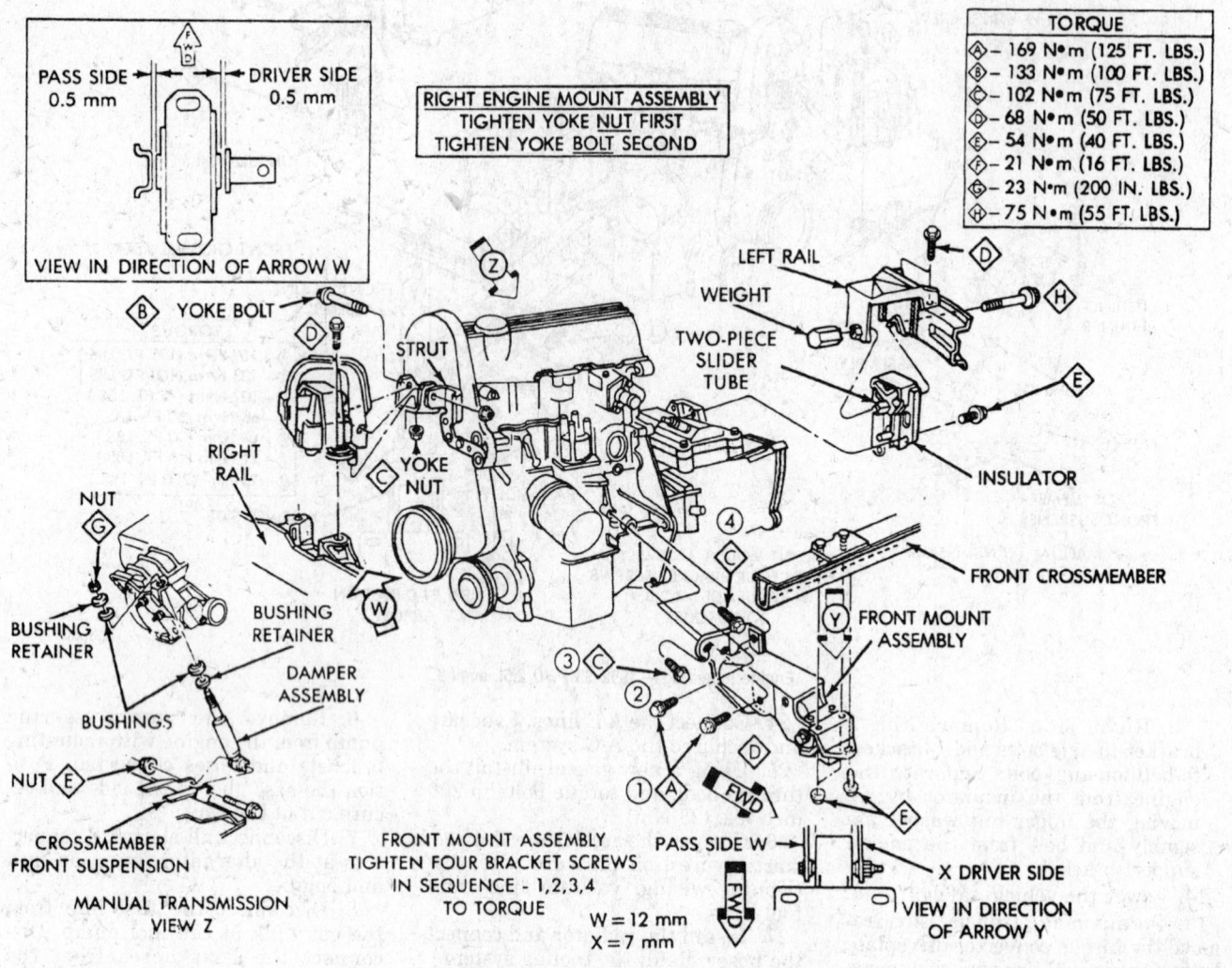

TORQUE	
⟨A⟩ — 169 N•m (125 FT. LBS.)	
⟨B⟩ — 133 N•m (100 FT. LBS.)	
⟨C⟩ — 102 N•m (75 FT. LBS.)	
⟨D⟩ — 68 N•m (50 FT. LBS.)	
⟨E⟩ — 54 N•m (40 FT. LBS.)	
⟨F⟩ — 21 N•m (16 FT. LBS.)	
⟨G⟩ — 23 N•m (200 IN. LBS.)	
⟨H⟩ — 75 N•m (55 FT. LBS.)	

PASS SIDE 0.5 mm — DRIVER SIDE 0.5 mm

VIEW IN DIRECTION OF ARROW W

RIGHT ENGINE MOUNT ASSEMBLY
TIGHTEN YOKE NUT FIRST
TIGHTEN YOKE BOLT SECOND

⟨B⟩ YOKE BOLT
⟨D⟩
Z
STRUT
RIGHT RAIL
⟨C⟩ YOKE NUT
NUT ⟨G⟩
BUSHING RETAINER
BUSHING RETAINER
BUSHINGS
DAMPER ASSEMBLY
NUT ⟨E⟩
W
CROSSMEMBER FRONT SUSPENSION

LEFT RAIL
WEIGHT
TWO-PIECE SLIDER TUBE
⟨D⟩
⟨H⟩
⟨E⟩
INSULATOR

FRONT CROSSMEMBER
Y FRONT MOUNT ASSEMBLY
④
③ ⟨C⟩
② ⟨C⟩
① ⟨A⟩ ⟨D⟩
FWD

MANUAL TRANSMISSION VIEW Z

FRONT MOUNT ASSEMBLY
TIGHTEN FOUR BRACKET SCREWS
IN SEQUENCE - 1,2,3,4
TO TORQUE
W = 12 mm
X = 7 mm

PASS SIDE W
FWD
X DRIVER SIDE
VIEW IN DIRECTION OF ARROW Y

85613037

Engine mounting — 1994–96 FWD 2.5L engine

17. Support the transaxle. Apply slight upward pressure with the chain hoist and remove the through bolt from the right (timing case cover) engine mount.

NOTE: If the complete engine mount is to be removed, mark the insulator position on the side rail to insure exact reinstallation location.

18. Remove the transaxle to cylinder block mounting bolts.
19. Remove the front engine mount through bolt. Remove the manual transaxle anti-roll strut.
20. Remove the insulator through bolt from the inside wheel house mount, or remove the insulator bracket to transaxle mounting bolt.
21. Raise the engine slowly with the hoist (transaxle supported). Separate the engine and transaxle and remove the engine.

To install:

22. With the hoist attached to the engine. Lower the engine into engine compartment.
23. Align the converter to flexplate and the engine mounts. Install all mounting bolts loosely until all are in position, then tighten to 40 ft. lbs.
24. Install the engine to transaxle mounting bolts. Tighten to 70 ft. lbs. (95 Nm) for the 2.5L and 3.0L engines or 75 ft. lbs. (102 Nm) for the 3.3L and 3.8L engines.
25. Remove the engine hoist and transaxle support.
26. Secure the engine ground strap.
27. Install the inner splash shield.
28. Install the starter assembly.
29. Install the exhaust system.
30. Install the transaxle case lower cover for manual transaxle.
31. Remove the C-clamp from the torque converter housing for automatic transaxle.
32. Align flexplate and torque converter with mark previously made for automatic transaxle.

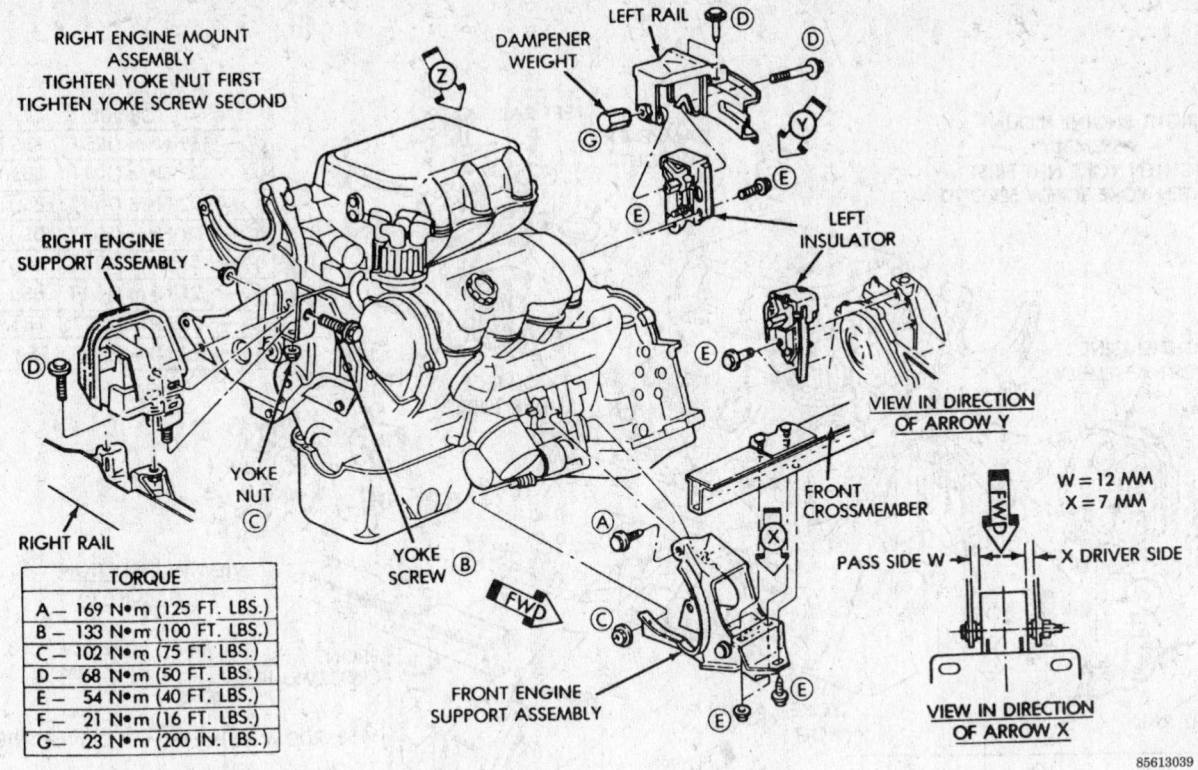

TORQUE	
A —	169 N•m (125 FT. LBS.)
B —	133 N•m (100 FT. LBS.)
C —	102 N•m (75 FT. LBS.)
D —	68 N•m (50 FT. LBS.)
E —	54 N•m (40 FT. LBS.)
F —	21 N•m (16 FT. LBS.)
G —	23 N•m (200 IN. LBS.)

Engine mounting — 1992–93 3.0L engine

33. Install the convertor to flexplate mounting screws. Tighten to 40 ft. lbs. (54 Nm).

34. Install the case lower cover for automatic transaxle.

35. Connect the clutch cable for manual transaxle.

36. Install the power steering pump.

37. Install the air conditioning compressor.

38. Install the alternator.

39. Connect all wiring.

40. Install the radiator, fan and shroud assembly.

41. Connect all cooling system hoses, accelerator cable and fuel lines.

42. Install the engine oil filter. Fill the crankcase to proper oil level.

43. Fill the cooling system.

44. Adjust linkages.

45. Install the air cleaner and hoses.

46. Install the hood.

47. Connect the battery cables, positive cable first.

48. Start the engine and run until normal operation temperature is indicated.

Pick-Up and Ramcharger

1. Relieve the fuel pressure, if equipped with fuel injection. Disconnect the battery cables and remove battery from the vehicle.

2. Scribe hinge position on hood and remove the hood. Remove the oil dipstick and tube. Discharge the air conditioning.

3. Raise the vehicle and support safely. Drain the engine oil and coolant. Remove the lower radiator hose.

4. Remove the starter. Remove the engine to transmission struts, if equipped.

5. Remove the exhaust pipe from the exhaust manifold(s).

6. If equipped with manual transmission, remove the transmission.

7. If equipped with an automatic transmission, remove the inspection plate. Matchmark the flexplate to the converter, remove the torque converter bolts and push the torque converter backwards as far as it will go. Remove the lower bellhousing bolts.

8. Remove the engine mount lower nuts.

9. Disconnect and plug the rubber fuel inlet and return hoses from the fuel lines at the right front of the vehicle. Lower the vehicle.

10. Remove the air cleaner assembly, disconnect all linkages and cables and remove the throttle body. Stuff a clean shop towel into the intake manifold opening to prevent foreign objects from entering.

11. Remove the discharge and suction lines from the air conditioning compressor. Cap the openings on the compressor to prevent foreign objects and moisture from entering the system.

12. Remove the radiator and shroud. Remove the fan and all related parts.

13. Unbolt the power steering pump brackets from the engine and position it aside.

14. Remove the alternator, air pump and all brackets. Disconnect the heater hoses.

15. Remove the distributor cap with all spark plug wires attached.

16. Disconnect all remaining electrical connectors, vacuum hoses and check for any other items preventing engine removal.

17. Attach an engine removal device to the intake manifold or cylinder head.

18. If equipped with an automatic transmission, support the transmission with a floor jack or equivalent. Remove the remaining bellhousing bolts.

19. Remove the engine from the vehicle.

To install:

20. Lower the engine into position and install the upper bellhousing bolts. Remove the engine removal de-

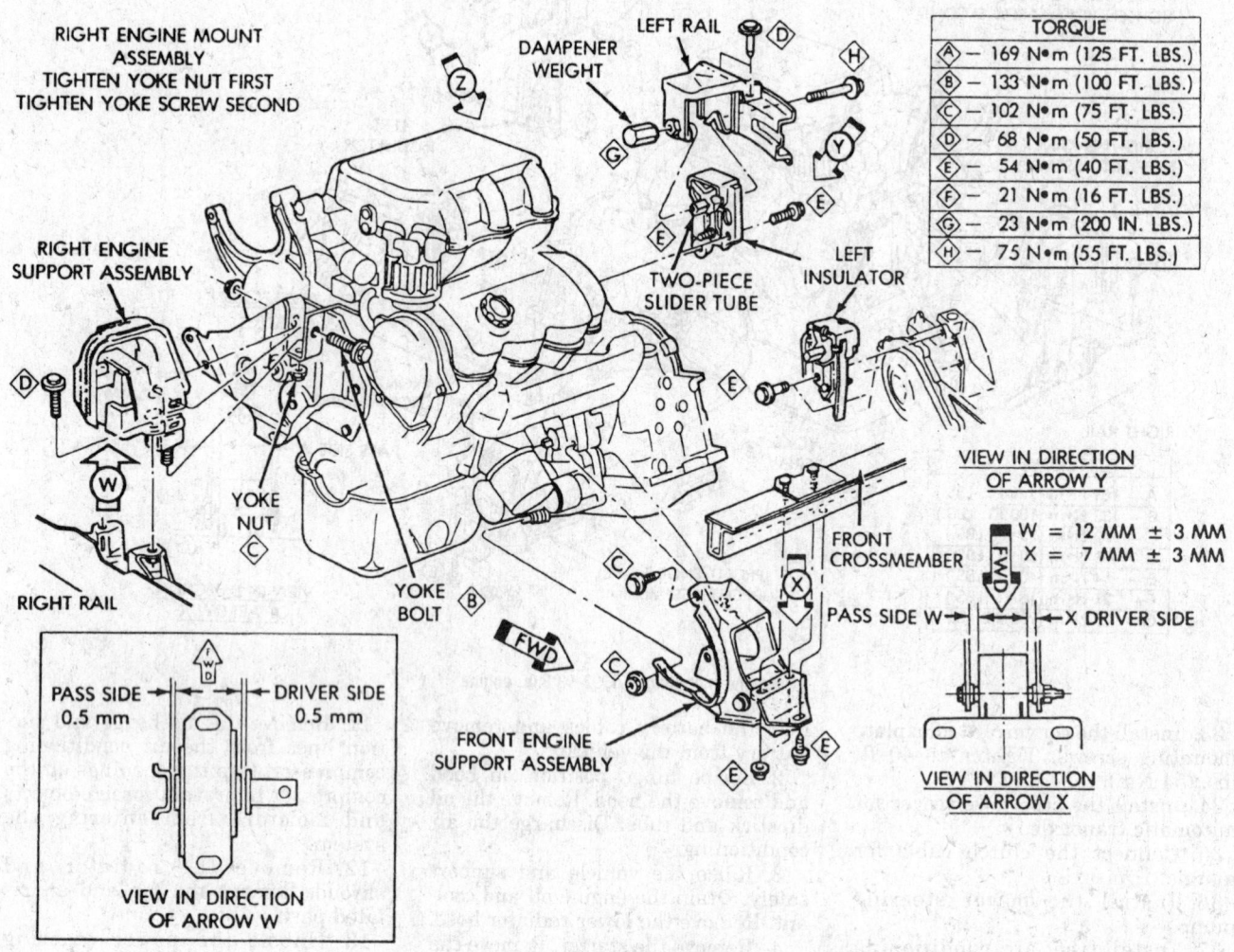

RIGHT ENGINE MOUNT
ASSEMBLY
TIGHTEN YOKE NUT FIRST
TIGHTEN YOKE SCREW SECOND

DAMPENER
WEIGHT

LEFT RAIL

RIGHT ENGINE
SUPPORT ASSEMBLY

TWO-PIECE
SLIDER TUBE

LEFT
INSULATOR

YOKE
NUT

RIGHT RAIL

YOKE
BOLT

FRONT
CROSSMEMBER

FRONT ENGINE
SUPPORT ASSEMBLY

TORQUE	
A — 169 N•m (125 FT. LBS.)	
B — 133 N•m (100 FT. LBS.)	
C — 102 N•m (75 FT. LBS.)	
D — 68 N•m (50 FT. LBS.)	
E — 54 N•m (40 FT. LBS.)	
F — 21 N•m (16 FT. LBS.)	
G — 23 N•m (200 IN. LBS.)	
H — 75 N•m (55 FT. LBS.)	

VIEW IN DIRECTION
OF ARROW Y

W = 12 MM ± 3 MM
X = 7 MM ± 3 MM

PASS SIDE W — X DRIVER SIDE

VIEW IN DIRECTION
OF ARROW X

PASS SIDE
0.5 mm

DRIVER SIDE
0.5 mm

VIEW IN DIRECTION
OF ARROW W

85613040

Engine mounting — 1994–96 3.0L engine

vice. Install the left side exhaust manifold, if it was removed. Install the oil dipstick.

21. Raise the vehicle and support safely.

22. Install the engine mount nuts and the remaining bellhousing bolts.

23. If equipped with a manual transmission, install the transmission and all related parts.

24. If equipped with an automatic transmission, align the torque converter and flexplate and install the bolts. Install the inspection plate, starter and the engine to transmission struts, if equipped.

25. Connect the rubber fuel inlet and return hoses to the fuel lines at the right front of the vehicle.

26. Install the exhaust pipe to the exhaust manifold(s). Install the air pump tube to the exhaust pipe, if equipped. Lower the vehicle.

27. Connect the heater hoses.

28. Install the alternator, air pump, power steering pump and all brackets.

29. Install the air conditioning compressor and connect the lines with new gaskets, if disconnected.

30. Install the throttle body using a new base gasket and connect all linkages and cables. Connect all electrical connectors and vacuum hoses

that were disconnected during the engine removal procedure.

31. Install the lower radiator hose. Install the fan and all related parts. Adjust all belt tensions.

32. Install the radiator and shroud.

33. Install the distributor cap with all spark plug wires attached.

34. Install the air cleaner assembly.

35. Install the hose.

36. Fill the engine with the specified amount of oil and fill the radiator with coolant.

37. Connect the negative battery cable and set all adjustments to specification.

38. Evacuate and recharge the air conditioning system.

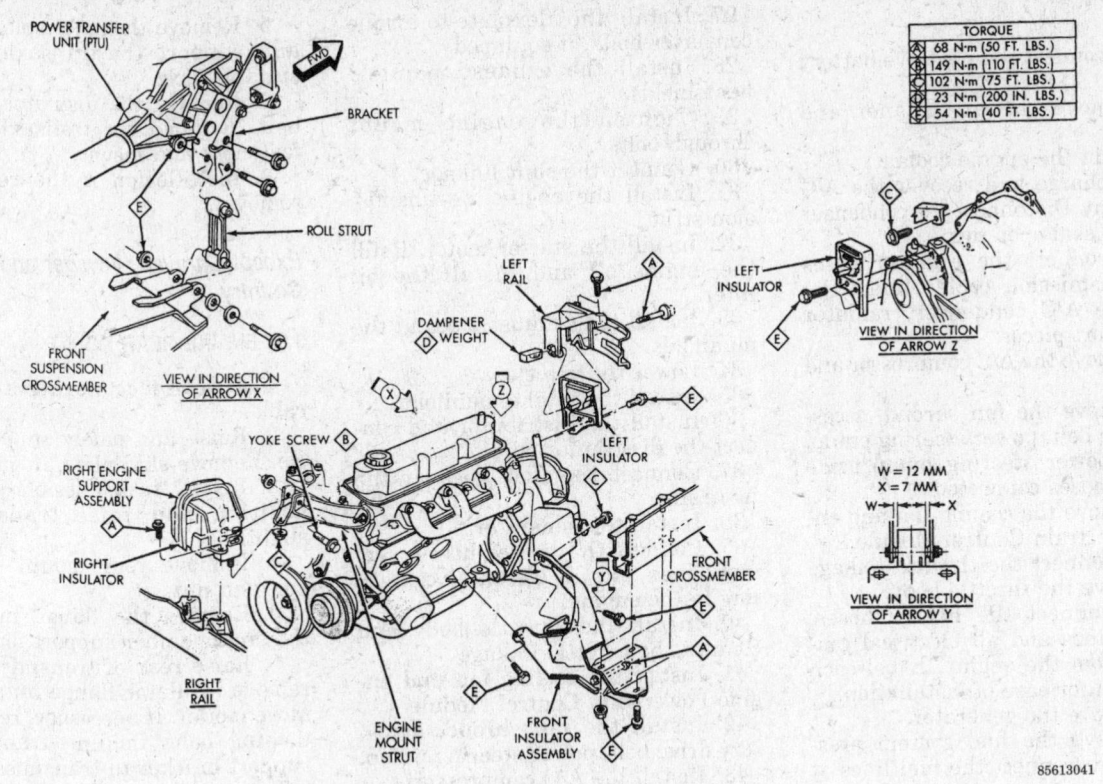

TORQUE	
A	68 N•m (50 FT. LBS.)
B	149 N•m (110 FT. LBS.)
C	102 N•m (75 FT. LBS.)
D	23 N•m (200 IN. LBS.)
E	54 N•m (40 FT. LBS.)

W = 12 MM
X = 7 MM

VIEW IN DIRECTION OF ARROW Y

85613041

Engine mounting — 1992–93 3.3L and 3.8L engines

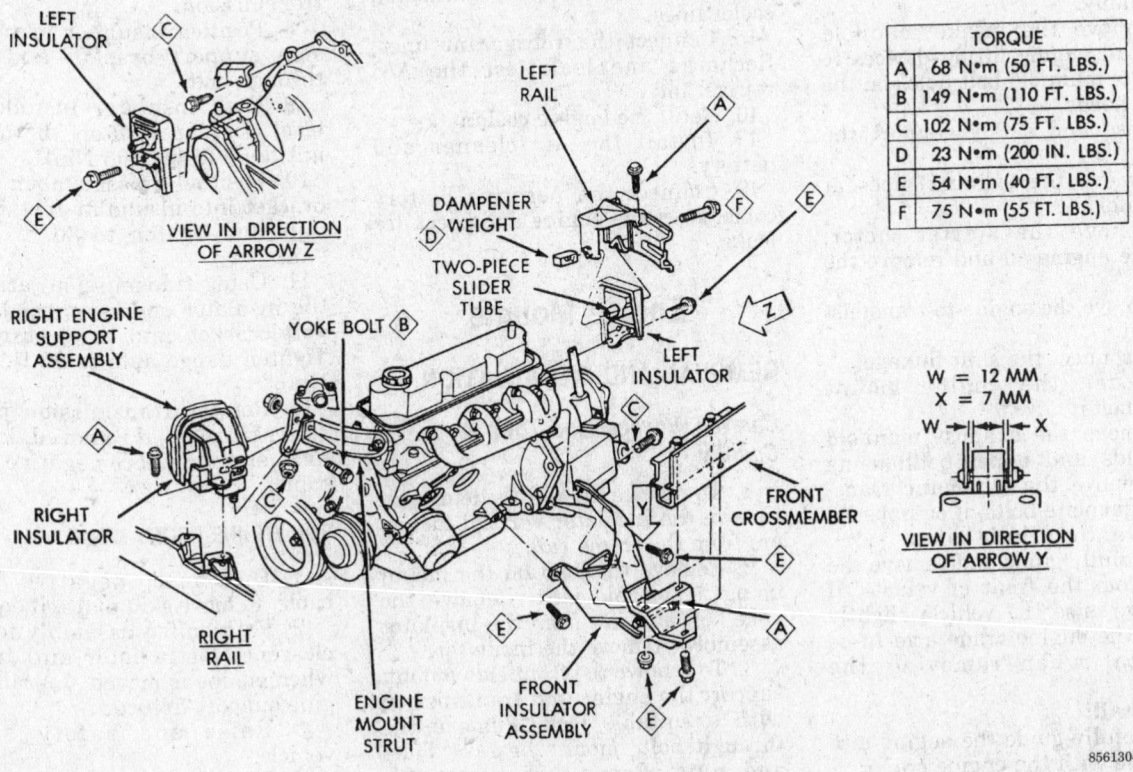

TORQUE	
A	68 N•m (50 FT. LBS.)
B	149 N•m (110 FT. LBS.)
C	102 N•m (75 FT. LBS.)
D	23 N•m (200 IN. LBS.)
E	54 N•m (40 FT. LBS.)
F	75 N•m (55 FT. LBS.)

W = 12 MM
X = 7 MM

VIEW IN DIRECTION OF ARROW Y

85613042

Engine mounting — 1994–96 3.3L and 3.8L engines

Van

1. Disconnect the negative battery cable.
2. Remove the air cleaner and battery.
3. Drain the engine coolant.
4. Discharge and recover the A/C refrigerant. Disconnect the condenser lines and seal openings.
5. Disconnect the radiator hoses and transmission cooler lines. Remove the A/C condenser, radiator and support pieces.
6. Remove the A/C compressor and set aside.
7. Remove the fan shroud, accessory drive belt, power steering pump. Set the power steering pump aside with the hoses connected.
8. Remove the cooling fan and engine Powertrain Control Module.
9. Disconnect the throttle linkage and remove the throttle body.
10. Disconnect the heater hoses, vacuum lines and all electrical connectors from the engine. Label each connection for ease of installation.
11. Remove the generator.
12. Relieve the fuel system pressure and disconnect the fuel lines at the fuel rail.
13. Label and disconnect the distributor wires. Remove the distributor assembly.
14. Remove the intake manifold and install engine lifting devices to the intake manifold bolt holes on the cylinder heads.
15. Raise and safely support the vehicle.
16. Remove the exhaust pipes at the manifolds.
17. Remove the starter motor. Drain the engine oil and remove the oil filter.
18. Remove the engine-to-transmission strut.
19. Disconnect the shift linkage.
20. Loosen the engine mount through bolts.
21. Remove the exhaust manifold heatshields and upper bellhousing bolts. Remove the automatic transmission flexplate bolts, if equipped.
22. Lower the vehicle safely.
23. Carefully guide and remove the engine from the front of vehicle. If necessary, raise the vehicle slightly to allow the engine crane arm to be horizontal when removing the engine.

To install:

24. Carefully guide the engine into the vehicle with the engine crane.
25. Raise the vehicle and support safely.
26. Install the engine mount bolts and bellhousing bolts.

27. Install the flexplate-to-torque converter bolts, if equipped.
28. Install the exhaust manifold heatshields.
29. Tighten the engine mount through bolts.
30. Connect the shift linkage.
31. Install the engine-to-transmission strut.
32. Install the starter motor. Refill the engine oil and install the oil filter.
33. Install the exhaust pipes at the manifolds.
34. Lower the vehicle.
35. Install the intake manifold.
36. Install the distributor and connect the distributor wires.
37. Connect the fuel lines at the fuel rail.
38. Install the generator.
39. Connect the heater hoses, vacuum lines and all electrical connectors to the engine.
40. Install the throttle body and connect the throttle linkage.
41. Install the cooling fan and engine Powertrain Control Module.
42. Install the fan shroud, accessory drive belt, power steering pump.
43. Install the A/C compressor.
44. Install the A/C condenser, radiator and support pieces. Connect the radiator hoses and transmission cooler lines.
45. Connect the refrigerant lines. Recharge and leak test the A/C refrigerant.
46. Refill the engine coolant.
47. Install the air cleaner and battery.
48. Connect the negative battery cable, start the engine and check for leaks.

Engine Mounts

REMOVAL AND INSTALLATION

Caravan, Voyager and Town & Country

1. To remove the right side mount: remove the insulator vertical fasteners from the frame rail.
2. Remove the load on the mount using a suitable jack. Remove the yoke bolt and nut from the insulator assembly. Remove the insulator.
3. To remove the front side mount: support the engine and transmission with a suitable jack. Remove the through bolt, mount bracket bolts and nuts. Remove the insulator assembly.
4. To remove the left side mount: raise the vehicle and support safely. Remove the front left wheel.

5. Remove the inner splash shield and support the transaxle with a suitable jack.
6. Remove the insulator through bolt. Remove the transaxle mount fasteners and mount.
7. Installation is the reverse of removal.

Except Caravan, Voyager and Town & Country

3.9L ENGINE REAR MOUNT

1. Disconnect negative battery cable.
2. Raise and safely support vehicle. Remove skid plate, if equipped.
3. Install transmission jack into position and raise transmission slightly.
4. Remove rear mount through-bolt and nut.
5. Remove the flange nuts from the crossmember support bracket.
6. Raise rear of transmission and remove insulator flange nuts and remove mount. If necessary, remove attaching bolts holding transmission support bracket to transmission.

To install:

7. Install attaching bolts holding transmission support bracket to transmission.
8. Position insulator in transmission support bracket and install through-bolt.
9. With insulator installed in a level position tighten through bolt nut to 50 ft. lbs. (65 Nm).
10. Position crossmember support bracket into insulator. Install flange nuts and tighten to 30 ft. lbs. (41 Nm).
11. Using transmission jack, lower the insulator and crossmember support bracket onto the crossmember. Tighten flange nuts to 30 ft. lbs. (41 Nm).
12. Remove transmission jack, install skid plate, if removed, lower vehicle and reconnect negative battery cable.

3.9L ENGINE FRONT MOUNT

1. Disconnect negative battery cable. Remove skid plate, if equipped.
2. Position fan assembly to insure clearance for radiator and top hose when engine is moved. Install an engine support fixture.
3. Raise and safely support vehicle.
4. Remove nuts from front engine mounting brackets.
5. Raise engine with support fixture far enough to remove mounts, remove remaining bolts and mounts.

To install:

6. Install mounts to engine block.

7. Lower engine to original position and insert bolts through mounting brackets.

8. Install nuts and tighten to 75 ft. lbs. Install skid plate, if removed.

9. Lower vehicle and remove engine support fixture. Reconnect negative battery cable.

2.5L, 5.2L AND 5.9L ENGINES

1. Disconnect negative battery cable.

2. Raise and safely support vehicle.

3. Install transmission jack into position and raise transmission slightly.

4. Remove rear mount through-bolt and nut.

5. Remove U-bracket from frame crossmember and remove insulator from U-bracket.

6. Remove rear engine mount from the bottom face of transmission extension housing.

To install:

7. Install rear mount to bottom of transmission. Torque bolts to 50 ft. lbs. (68 Nm).

8. Install insulator to U-bracket. Tighten nuts to 30 ft. lbs. (41 Nm).

9. Install through-bolt through the U-bracket/insulator assembly and the rear engine support. Tighten to 50 ft. lbs. (68 Nm).

10. Attach U-bracket to crossmember tightening bolts to 30 ft. lbs. (41 Nm). Remove transmission jack and lower vehicle. Connect negative battery cable.

8.0L ENGINE FRONT MOUNT

1. Disconnect the negative battery cable.

2. Position the fan to assure clearance for the radiator top tank and hose.

3. Install an engine lifting device to the engine. Do not lift the engine by the intake manifold.

4. Raise the vehicle and support safely.

5. Lift the engine slightly and remove the through bolt, nut and rubber restrictors.

6. Remove the engine support bracket/cushion bolts and engine support.

To install:

7. Install the engine mount, bracket and heatshield. Install new bolts and torque to 60 ft. lbs. (81 Nm).

8. Install the through bolt, rubber restrictors and nut. Lower the engine and torque the bolt to 50 ft. lbs. (68 Nm).

9. Lower the vehicle and remove the lifting devices.

8.0L ENGINE REAR MOUNT

1. Raise the vehicle and support safely. Position a suitable transmission jack in place.

2. Remove the support cushion stud nuts. Raise the rear of the transmission slightly.

3. Remove the support cushion bolts and remove.

4. Installation is the reverse of removal

Cylinder Head

REMOVAL AND INSTALLATION

2.5L Engine

1. Relieve the fuel pressure if equipped with fuel injection. Disconnect the negative battery cable and unbolt it from the head. Drain the cooling system. Remove the dipstick bracket nut from the thermostat housing.

2. Remove the air cleaner assembly. Remove the upper radiator hose and disconnect the heater hoses.

3. Disconnect and label the vacuum lines, hoses and wiring connectors from the manifold(s), throttle body and cylinder head. Remove the air pump, if equipped.

4. Disconnect the all linkages and the fuel line from the throttle body. Unbolt the cable bracket. Remove the ground strap attaching screw from the fire wall.

5. If equipped with air conditioning, remove the upper compressor mounting bolts. The cylinder head can be remove with the compressor and bracket still mounted. Remove the upper part of the timing belt cover.

6. Raise the vehicle and support safely. Disconnect the converter from the exhaust manifold. Disconnect the water hose and oil drain from the turbocharger, if equipped.

7. Rotate the engine by hand, until the timing marks align (No. 1 piston at TDC). Lower the vehicle.

8. With the timing marks aligned, remove the camshaft sprocket. The camshaft sprocket can be suspended to keep the timing intact. Remove the spark plug wires from the spark plugs.

9. Remove the valve cover and curtain, if equipped. Remove the cylinder head bolts and washers, starting from the middle and working outward.

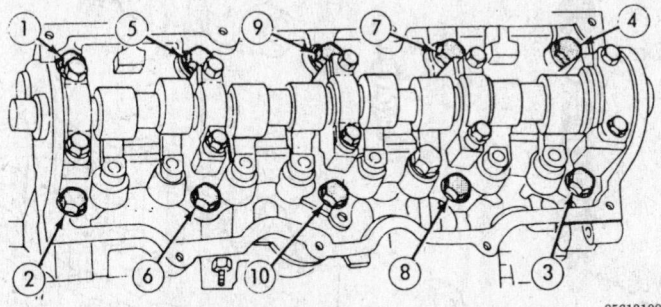

85613108

Cylinder head bolt removal sequence — 2.5L engine

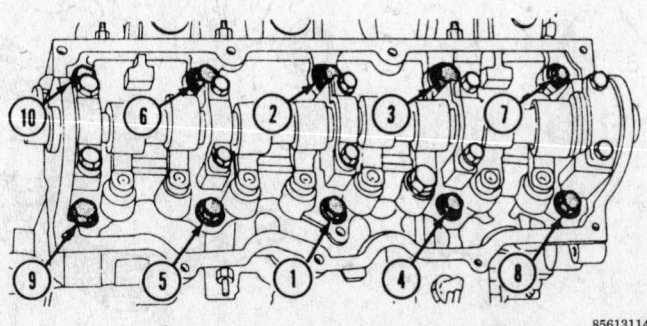

85613114

Cylinder head bolt tightening sequence — 2.5L engine

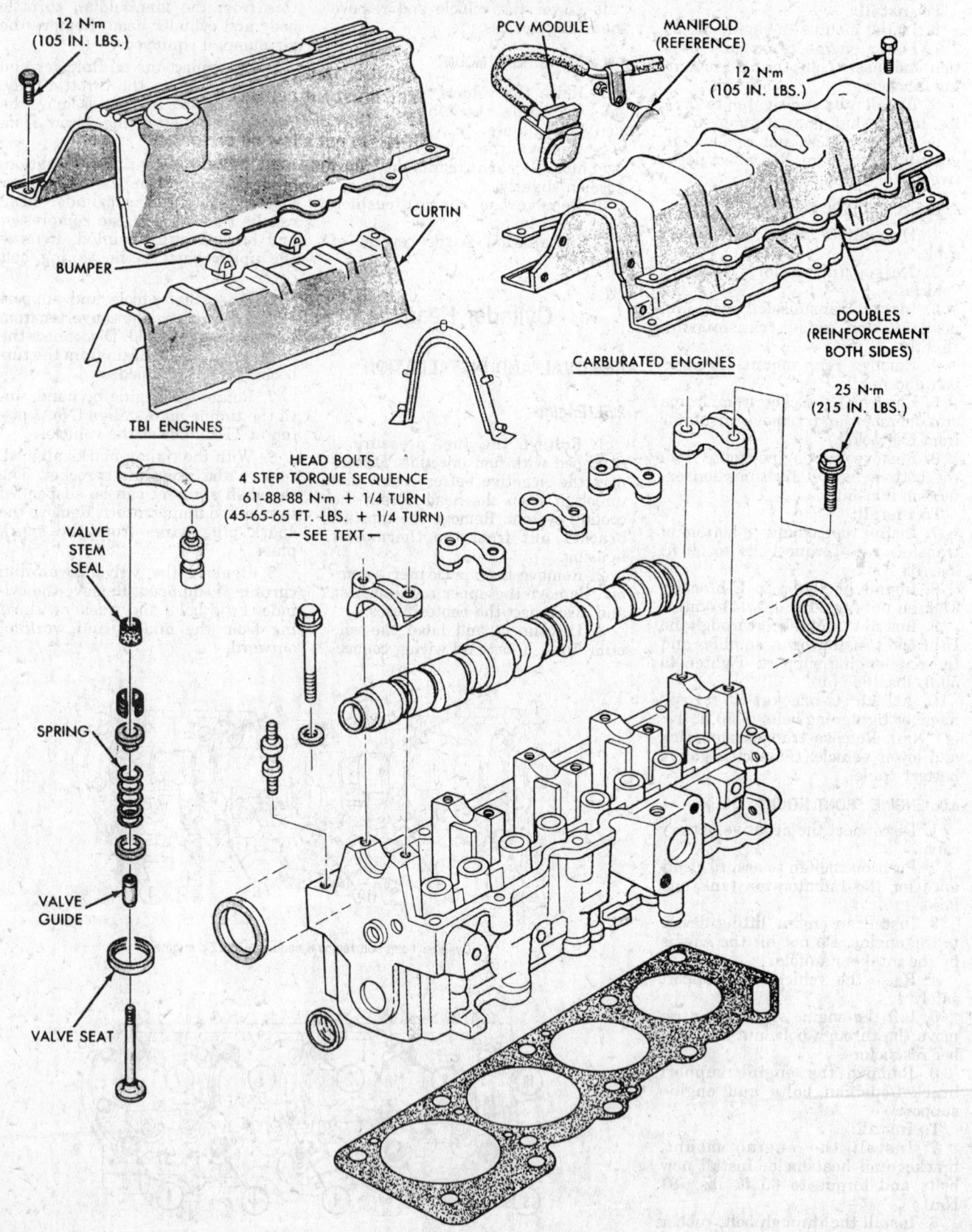

12 N·m
(105 IN. LBS.)

PCV MODULE

MANIFOLD
(REFERENCE)

12 N·m
(105 IN. LBS.)

BUMPER

CURTIN

DOUBLES
(REINFORCEMENT
BOTH SIDES)

CARBURATED ENGINES

25 N·m
(215 IN. LBS.)

TBI ENGINES

HEAD BOLTS
4 STEP TORQUE SEQUENCE
61-88-88 N·m + 1/4 TURN
(45-65-65 FT. LBS. + 1/4 TURN)
—SEE TEXT—

VALVE
STEM
SEAL

SPRING

VALVE
GUIDE

VALVE SEAT

85613115

Cylinder head assembly — 2.5L engine

10. Remove the cylinder head from the engine.

NOTE: Before disassembling or repairing any part of the cylinder head assembly, identify factory installed oversized components. To do so, look for the tops of the bearing caps pained green and O/SJ stamped rearward of the oil gallery plug on the rear of the head. In addition, the barrel of the camshaft is painted green and O/SJ is stamped onto the rear end of the camshaft. Installing standard sized parts in an head equipped with oversized parts or visa-versa will cause severe engine damage.

11. Clean the cylinder head gasket mating surfaces.

To install:

12. Using new gaskets and seals, install the head to the engine. Using new head bolts assembled with the old washers, torque the cylinder head bolts in sequence, to 45 ft. lbs. (61 Nm). Repeating the sequence, torque the bolts to 65 ft. lbs. (88 Nm). With the bolts at 65 ft. lbs. (88 Nm), turn each bolt an additional ¼ turn.

13. Install the timing belt.

14. Install or connect all items that were removed or disconnected during the removal procedures.

15. Refill the cooling system. Connect the negative battery cable. Start the engine and check for leaks.

3.0L Engine

1. Relieve the fuel pressure. Disconnect the negative battery cable. Drain the cooling system.

2. Remove the drive belt and the air conditioning compressor from its mount and support it aside. Using a ½ in. drive breaker bar, insert it into the square hole of the serpentine drive belt tensioner, rotate it counterclockwise (to reduce the belt tension) and remove the belt. Remove the al-

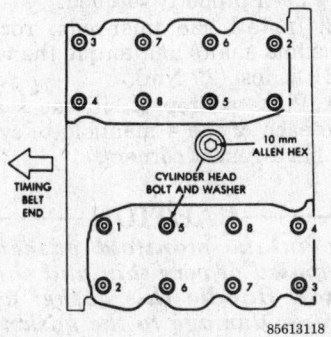

Cylinder head bolt loosing sequence — 3.0L engine

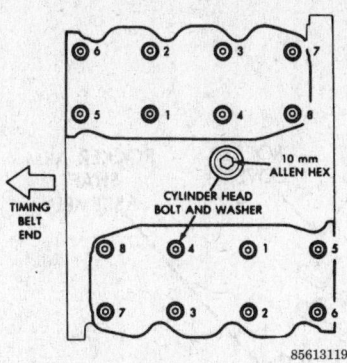

Cylinder head torque sequence — 3.0L engine

ternator and power steering pump from the brackets and move them aside.

3. Raise the vehicle and support safely. Remove the right front wheel assembly and the right inner splash shield.

4. Remove the crankshaft pulleys and the torsional damper.

5. Lower the vehicle. Using a floor jack and a block of wood positioned under the oil pan, raise the engine slightly. Remove the engine mount bracket from the timing cover end of the engine and the timing belt covers.

6. To remove the timing belt, perform the following procedures:

  a. Rotate the crankshaft to position the No. 1 cylinder on the TDC of its compression stroke; the crankshaft sprocket timing mark should align with the oil pan timing indicator and the camshaft sprockets timing marks (triangles) should align with the rear timing belt covers timing marks.

  b. Mark the timing belt in the direction of rotation for reinstallation purposes.

  c. Loosen the timing belt tensioner and remove the timing belt.

NOTE: When removing the timing belt from the camshaft sprocket, make sure the belt does not slip off the other camshaft sprocket. Support extension.

7. Remove the camshaft bearing assembly to cylinder head bolts (do not remove the bolts from the assembly). Remove the rocker arms, rocker shafts and bearing caps as an assembly, as required. Remove the camshafts from the cylinder head and inspect them for damage, if necessary.

8. Remove the intake manifold assembly.

9. Remove the exhaust manifold.

10. Remove the cylinder head bolts starting from the outside and work-

ing inward. Remove the cylinder head from the engine.

11. Clean the gasket mounting surfaces and check the heads for warpage; the maximum warpage allowed is 0.008 in. (0.20mm).

  To install:

12. Install the new cylinder head gaskets over the dowels on the engine block.

13. Install the cylinder heads on the engine and torque the cylinder head bolts in sequence using 3 even steps, to 70 ft. lbs. (95 Nm).

14. Install or connect all items that were removed or disconnected during the removal procedure.

15. When installing the timing belt over the camshaft sprocket, use care not to allow the belt to slip off the opposite camshaft sprocket.

16. Make sure the timing belt is installed on the camshaft sprocket in the same position as when removed.

17. Refill the cooling system. Connect the negative battery cable. Start the engine and check for leaks using the DRB I or II to active the fuel pump. Adjust the timing as required.

3.3L and 3.8L Engines

1. Relieve the fuel pressure. Disconnect the negative battery cable. Drain the cooling system.

2. Remove the intake manifold with throttle body.

3. Disconnect the coil wires, sending unit wire, heater hoses and bypass hose.

4. Remove the closed ventilation system, evaporation control system and cylinder hear cover.

5. Remove the exhaust manifold.

6. Remove the rocker arm and shaft assemblies. Remove the pushrods and identify them in ensure installation in their original positions.

7. Remove the head bolts and remove the cylinder head from the block.

  To install:

8. Clean the gasket mounting surfaces and install a new head gasket to the block.

9. Install the head to the block. Before installing the head bolts, inspect them for stretching. Hold a straight-edge up to the threads. If the threads are not all on line, the bolt is stretched and should be replaced.

10. Torque the bolts in sequence to 45 ft. lbs. (61 Nm). Repeat the sequence and torque the bolts to 65 ft. lbs. (88 Nm). With the bolts at 65 ft. lbs. (88 Nm), turn each bolt an additional ¼ turn.

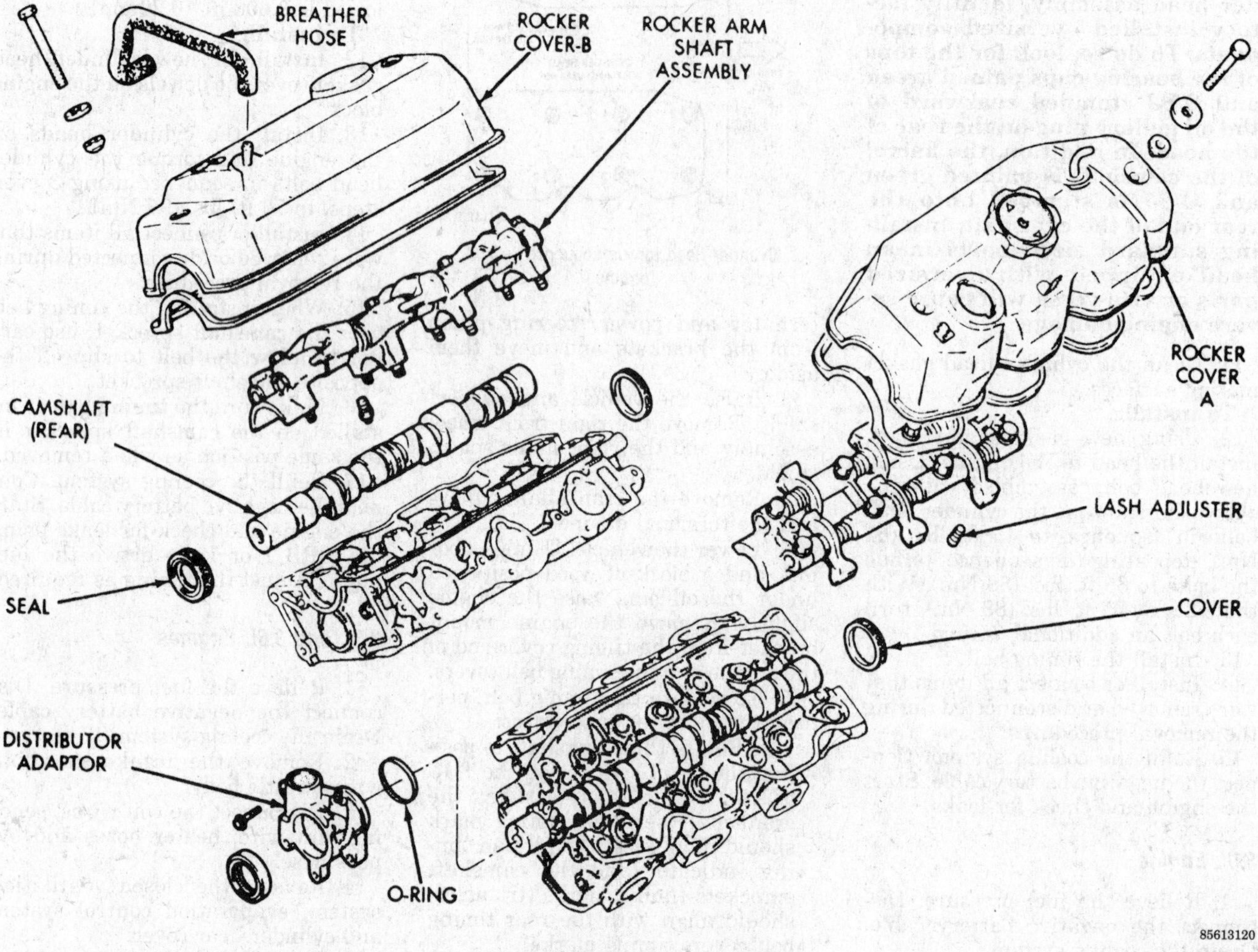

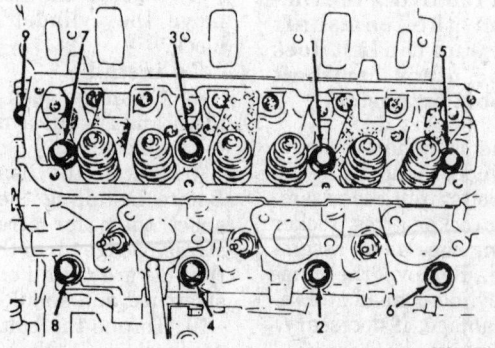

BREATHER HOSE

ROCKER COVER-B

ROCKER ARM SHAFT ASSEMBLY

ROCKER COVER A

CAMSHAFT (REAR)

LASH ADJUSTER

SEAL

COVER

DISTRIBUTOR ADAPTOR

O-RING

85613120

Cylinder head assembly — 3.0L engine

85613121

Cylinder head torque sequence — 3.3L and 3.8L engines

11. Torque the lone head bolt to 25 ft. lbs. (33 Nm) after the other 8 bolts have been properly torqued.

12. Install the pushrods, rocker arms and shafts and torque the bolts to 21 ft. lbs. (29 Nm).

13. Place a drop of silicone sealer onto each of the 4 manifold to cylinder head gasket corners.

CAUTION

The intake manifold gasket is composed of very thin and sharp metal. Handle this gasket with care or damage to the gasket or personal injury could result.

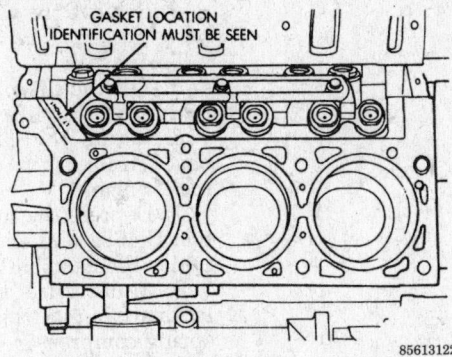

Cylinder head gasket installation — 3.3L and 3.8L engines

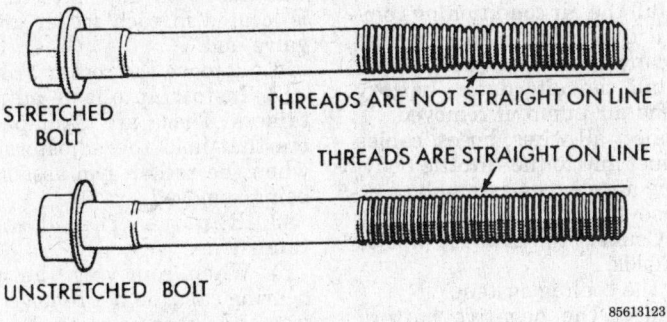

Inspect head bolts for stretch — 3.3L and 3.8L engines

14. Install the intake manifold gasket and torque the end retainers to 105 inch lbs. (12 Nm).

15. Install the intake manifold and torque the bolts in sequence to 10 inch lbs. Repeat the sequence increasing the torque to 17 ft. lbs. (23 Nm) and recheck each bolt for 17 ft. lbs. of torque. After the bolts are torqued, inspect the seals to ensure that they have not become dislodged.

16. Lubricate the injector O-rings with clean oil and position the fuel rail in place. Install the rail retaining bolts.

17. Install the valve cover with a new gasket. Install the exhaust manifold.

18. Install or connect all remaining components that were removed or disconnected during the removal procedures.

19. Refill the cooling system. Connect the negative battery cable. Start the engine and check for leaks.

3.9L, 5.2L, 5.9L and 8.0L Engines

1. Relieve the fuel pressure if equipped with fuel injection. Disconnect the negative battery cable from the battery and drain the cooling system.

2. Raise the vehicle and safely support. Disconnect the exhaust pipe from the manifolds.

3. Remove the alternator, if the right head is being removed, and the air pump and battery ground cable, if the left head is being removed.

4. Remove the air cleaner assembly. Unbolt the air conditioning compressor, if equipped, and lay it aside. Remove the distributor cap with all wires attached.

5. Disconnect all wires, hoses, linkages and cables from the throttle body. Disconnect the fuel line.

6. Disconnect the ignition coil, coolant temperature sending unit wire and all other connectors along the wiring harness connected to items on the intake manifold.

7. Disconnect the heater hose, upper radiator hose and the lower bypass hose clamp.

8. Remove the valve cover(s).

9. Remove the intake manifold assembly. Remove the exhaust manifold(s).

10. Remove the rocker arm and shaft assembly from the head(s). Do not disassemble unless service is required.

11. Remove the pushrods and identify them to ensure installation in their original locations.

12. Remove the head bolts and remove the cylinder head(s).

To install:

13. Clean and dry all gasket surfaces of the cylinder block and head. Inspect all surfaces with a straightedge. If the flatness exceeds 0.0075 times the length of the span measured (in any direction), replace or machine the head gasket surface.

14. Using no sealer, install the new head gasket(s) to the block. Clean, dry and lightly oil all head bolts threads. Install the head(s) and install the head bolts.

15. Torque the head bolts in sequence to 50 ft. lbs. (68 Nm) for all except 8.0L engine. Torque the bolts to 43 ft. lbs. (58 Nm) for the 8.0L engine. Repeat the sequence retightening the bolts to a final torque of 105 ft. lbs. (143 Nm) for all engines. Repeat the second step to ensure all bolts are accurately torqued.

16. Assemble the rocker shaft assembly, if it was serviced. Make sure all rocker arms with a **RH** stamp are installed to the right of those with an **LH**. Install the pushrods, rocker arms and shaft(s) with the notch on the end of the shaft pointing to the engine centerline and to the rear of the right bank or to the front of the left bank. Make sure the long stamped steel retainers are at the No. 2 and 4 positions. Torque the bolts evenly and gradually to 21 ft. lbs. (28 Nm).

17. Clean and dry the intake manifold contact surfaces. Coat the intake manifold side gaskets lightly with sealer and install the gaskets to the heads. Cutouts at the front of the gaskets differentiate the right and left sides.

18. Apply a thin uniform coat of quick dry cement to the front and rear intake manifold gaskets and mounting surfaces on the block and apply a thin bead of sealer to each of 4 the corners. Install the front and rear gaskets engaging the hole in the block and the tangs from the head gaskets. Apply a second thin bead of sealer above the gaskets in the 4 corners.

19. Carefully lower the intake manifold into position engaging the bypass hose. Inspect the gaskets to make sure they have not become dislodged.

20. Install the intake manifold bolts and torque in sequence to 25 ft. lbs. (34 Nm). Repeat the sequence retightening the bolts to a final torque

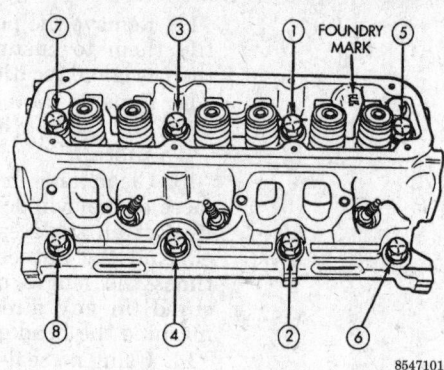

Cylinder head bolt torque sequence — 3.9L engine

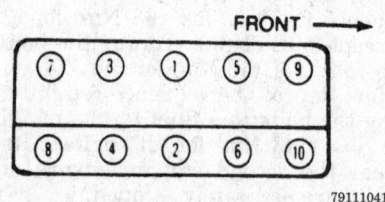

Cylinder head bolt torque sequence — 5.2L and 5.9L engines

of 40 ft. lbs. (54 Nm). Repeat the second step to ensure all bolts are accurately torqued.

21. Install the exhaust manifold(s) and torque the bolts to 20 ft. lbs. (27 Nm). Torque the end nuts to 15 ft. lbs. (20 Nm).

22. Clean and dry the valve cover mating surfaces, bolts and bolt holes. Install the valve cover(s) each with a new gasket.

23. Connect the heater hose, upper radiator hose and the lower bypass hose clamp.

24. Connect the ignition coil, coolant temperature sending unit wire and all other connectors that were

disconnected along the wiring harness.

25. Install the air conditioning compressor, if equipped. Install the distributor cap and all spark plug wires.

26. Install the alternator, battery ground and air pump, if removed.

27. Connect all wires, hoses, cables and the fuel line to the throttle body. Install the air cleaner assembly.

28. Raise the vehicle and safely support. Connect the exhaust pipe to the manifolds.

29. Fill the cooling system.

30. Connect the negative battery cable and set all adjustments to specification.

Valve Lifters

REMOVAL AND INSTALLATION

2.5L Engine

1. Disconnect negative battery cable. Remove air cleaner.

2. Remove the valve cover(s).

3. For each rocker arm, rotate the camshaft until the base circle is in contact with the rocker arm. Depress the valve spring using tool C-4682 or equivalent, and slide the rocker arm out. Keep all components in order for installation.

4. Remove the valve lifter from the bore.

To install:

5. Fill the lifter and bore with oil and install the lifter.

6. Rotate the camshaft until the base circle is in contact with the rocker arm.

7. Depress the rocker arm using to tool C-4682 and slide the rocker arm under the camshaft.

8. Make sure the valve spring locks are in place before releasing the spring compressor.

9. Install the valve cover.

3.0L Engine

The auto-lash adjuster (valve lifter) is located in each rocker arm at the valve end.

1. Remove the rocker arm cover.

2. Install auto-lash adjuster retainers. These are U-shaped retainers that hold the adjusters in place when the rocker arm assemblies are being removed.

3. Remove the distributor extension.

4. When removing the camshaft bearing caps, do not remove the bolts from the bearing caps. Remove the rocker arm, rocker shafts and bearing caps as an assembly.

5. Remove the auto-lash adjuster from the rocker arm.

To install:

6. Install the auto-lash adjuster and retaining tools.

7. Install the rocker arm, shaft and bearing cap assemblies. Torque the bearing caps in 2 steps: 1st step to 85 inch lbs. (10 Nm) and the 2nd step to 180 inch lbs. (20 Nm).

8. Install the remaining components and check operation. The auto-lash adjusters may make noise for short period of time, this is normal. Run the engine at 2000 rpm for 1 minute to bleed air.

3.3L and 3.8L Engines

1. Disconnect the negative battery cable.

2. Remove the cylinder head and intake manifolds.

3. Remove the yoke retainer and aligning yokes.

4. Use tool C-4129 or equivalent to remove the lifters from the bores. If all lifters are being removed, identify each lifter for installation into their original location.

To install:

5. Lubricate the lifters and install into the original position.

6. Install the aligning yokes with yoke retainers.

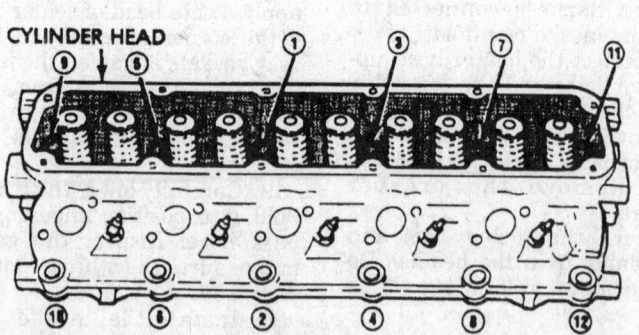

Cylinder head bolt torque sequence — 8.0L engine

SPECIAL TOOL C-4682A

85471013

Removing the rocker arms and valve lifters — 2.5L engine

7. Torque the yoke bolts to 105 inch lbs. (12 Nm).

8. Install the remaining components and check operation. The lifters may make noise for short period of time, this is normal. Run the engine at 2000 rpm for 1 minute to bleed air.

3.9L, 5.2L, 5.9L and 8.0L Engines

1. Disconnect negative battery cable. Remove air cleaner.

2. Relieve the fuel pressure if equipped with fuel injection.

3. Remove the valve cover(s) and rocker arm assembly.

4. Remove the pushrods and identify them to ensure installation in their original locations.

5. Remove the intake manifold assembly, yoke retainer and aligning yokes.

6. Use an appropriate valve lifter removal tool to remove each lifter from its bore. If reinstalling the tappets, identify each upon removal to ensure installation in the original position.

7. If the tappet or bore in cylinder block is scored, scuffed or shows signs of sticking, ream the bore to the next oversize and replace with oversize tappet.

To install:

8. Lubricate the lifter(s) and bore(s) and install. Ensure that the oil feed hole in the side of the tappet body faces up.

9. Install aligning yokes with arrow toward camshaft. Install yoke retainer. Tighten bolts to 200 inch lbs. (23 Nm).

10. Install pushrods to their original positions. Install rocker arm and shaft assembly.

11. Install valve cover(s). Connect negative battery terminal and start vehicle. Check for oil leaks.

Valve Lash

ADJUSTMENT

All gasoline engines are equipped with hydraulic valve lifters. The lifter maintains the correct valve lash and requires no adjustment.

Rocker Arms and Shaft

REMOVAL AND INSTALLATION

2.5L and 3.0L Engines

Refer to the valve lifter procedures for rocker arms and shafts.

Except 2.5L and 3.0L Engines

1. Disconnect the negative battery cable.

2. Remove the valve cover and gasket.

3. Note the positioning of the notch and remove the rocker arms and shaft assembly from the head.

4. Disassemble the assembly as required and replace all worn parts.

NOTE: If equipped with exhaust valve rotators, the exhaust rocker arm must have relief for clearance.

To install:

5. Make sure all rocker arms with an **RH** stamp are installed to the right of those with an **LH**. Install the assembly with the notch on the end of the shaft pointing to the engine centerline and to the rear of the right bank or to the front of the left bank. Make sure the long stamped steel retainers are at the No. 2 and 4 positions. Torque the bolts evenly starting from the center bolts and working outward to 21 ft. lbs. (28 Nm). Allow 20 minutes bleed down time before starting the engine.

6. Clean and dry the valve cover mating surfaces, bolts and bolt holes. Install the valve cover with a new gasket. Torque the screws or nuts to 96 inch lbs. (11 Nm).

7. Connect the negative battery cable and check for leaks.

Intake Manifold

REMOVAL AND INSTALLATION

2.5L Engine

1. Disconnect the negative battery cable and drain the engine coolant.

2. Remove the air cleaner.

3. Label and disconnect all vacuum lines, electrical wiring and fuel lines from the throttle body and intake manifold.

4. Disconnect the throttle linkage. Remove the throttle body from the manifold.

5. Remove the power steering and air pump support bracket, if equipped.

6. Remove the diverter valve assembly and disconnect the air injection tube assembly from the exhaust manifold.

7. Disconnect the water hoses from the water crossover.

8. Raise the vehicle and support safely.

9. Remove the exhaust pipe from the exhaust manifold.

10. Remove the intake manifold strut and intake manifold.

11. Remove the exhaust manifold bolts and manifold.

To install:

12. Install the gaskets, manifolds and bolts. Torque the manifold bolts to 200 inch lbs. (23 Nm).

13. Install the intake manifold strut.

14. Install the exhaust pipe to the exhaust manifold. Connect the EGR tube and torque the bolts to 200 inch lbs. (23 Nm).

15. Lower the vehicle safely.

16. Connect the water hoses and water crossover.

17. Install the diverter valve assembly and disconnect the air injection tube assembly to the exhaust manifold.

18. Install the power steering and air pump support bracket, if equipped.

19. Connect the throttle linkage. Install the throttle body to the manifold.

20. Connect all vacuum lines, electrical wiring and fuel lines to the throttle body and intake manifold.

21. Install the air cleaner.

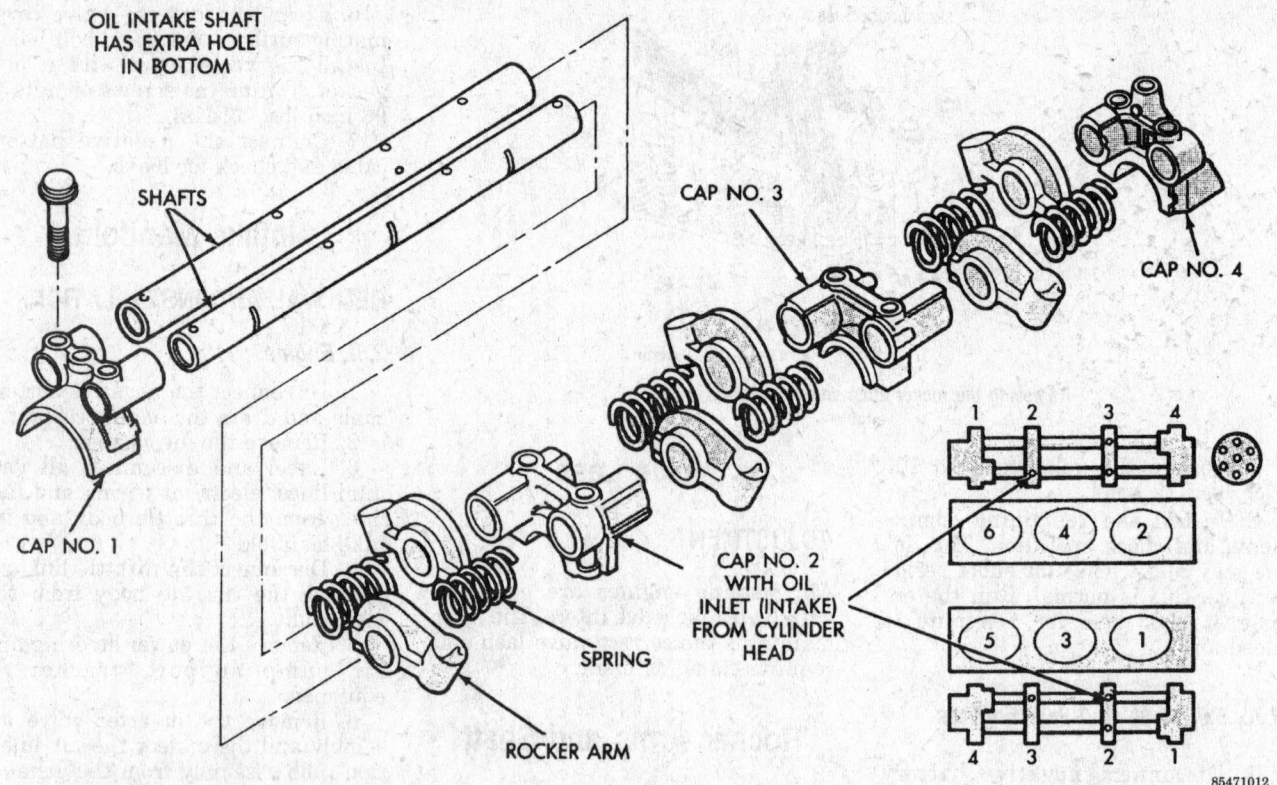

OIL INTAKE SHAFT HAS EXTRA HOLE IN BOTTOM

SHAFTS

CAP NO. 3

CAP NO. 4

CAP NO. 1

CAP NO. 2 WITH OIL INLET (INTAKE) FROM CYLINDER HEAD

SPRING

ROCKER ARM

85471012

Rocker arms, shafts and bearing caps — 3.0L engine

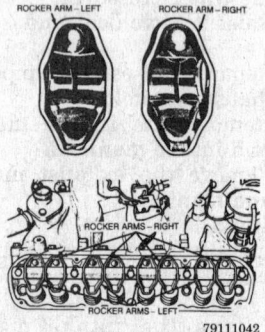

ROCKER ARM – LEFT ROCKER ARM – RIGHT

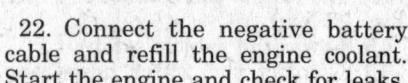

ROCKER ARMS – RIGHT

ROCKER ARMS – LEFT

79111042

Rocker arm/shaft identification — 5.2L and 5.9L engines, 3.9L engine similar

22. Connect the negative battery cable and refill the engine coolant. Start the engine and check for leaks.

3.0L Engine

1. Release fuel system pressure.
2. Disconnect the negative battery cable.
3. Drain the cooling system.
4. Remove the air cleaner.
5. Remove the throttle cable and transaxle kickdown cable.
6. Remove the electrical and vacuum connections from throttle body.

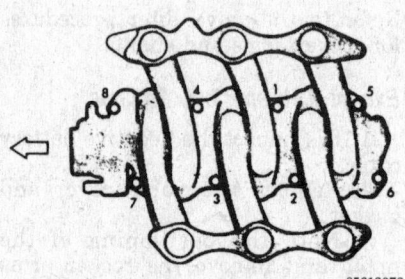

85613078

Intake manifold torque sequence — 3.0L engine

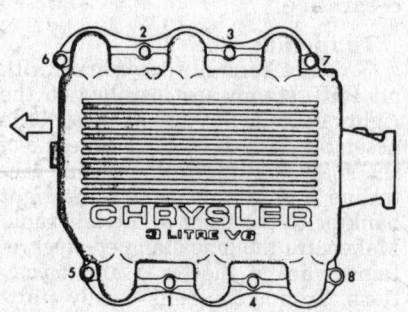

85613079

Intake plenum tightening sequence — 3.0L engine

7. Remove the air intake hose from air cleaner to throttle body.
8. Remove the EGR tube to intake plenum.
9. Remove the electrical connection from charge temperature and coolant temperature sensor.
10. Remove the vacuum connection from the pressure regulator and remove the air intake connection from the manifold.
11. Remove fuel hoses to fuel rail connection.
12. Remove the air intake plenum to manifold bolts (8) and remove air intake plenum and gasket.

WARNING
Whenever the air intake plenum is removed, cover the intake manifold properly to avoid objects from entering cylinder head.

13. Disconnect the fuel injector wiring harness from the engine wiring harness.
14. Remove the pressure regulator attaching bolts and remove pressure regulator from rail.
15. Remove the fuel rail attaching bolts and remove fuel rail.
16. Remove the radiator hose from thermostat housing and heater hose from pipe.

17. Remove the intake manifold attaching nuts and washers and remove intake manifold.

18. Clean the gasket material from cylinder head and manifold gasket surface. Check for cracks or damaged mounting surfaces.

To install:

19. Install a new gasket on the intake surface of the cylinder head and install the intake manifold.

20. Install the intake manifold washers and nuts. Tighten in sequence. Refer to Torque Specification Chart.

21. Clean the injectors and lubricate the injector O-rings with a drop of clean engine oil.

22. Place the tip of each injector into their ports. Push assembly into place until the injectors are seated in their ports.

23. Install rail attaching bolts and tighten to 115 inch lbs. (13 Nm).

24. Install pressure regulator to rail. Install pressure regulator mounting bolts and tighten to 95 inch lbs. (11 Nm).

25. Install fuel supply and return tube hold-down bolt and vacuum crossover tube hold-down bolt. Torque to 95 inch lbs. (11 Nm).

26. Torque fuel pressure regulator hose clamps to 10 inch lbs. (1.3 Nm).

27. Connect injector wiring harness to engine wiring harness.

28. Connect vacuum harness to fuel rail and pressure regulator.

29. Remove covering from intake manifold.

30. Position the intake manifold gasket, beaded side up, on the intake manifold.

31. Put the air intake plenum in place. Install attaching bolts and tighten in sequence to 115 inch lbs. (13 Nm).

32. Connect the fuel line to fuel rail. Tighten clamps to 10 inch lbs. (1.3 Nm).

33. Connect the vacuum hoses to intake plenum.

34. Connect the electrical connection to coolant temperature sensor and charge temperature sensor.

35. Connect the EGR tube flange to intake plenum and torque to 15 ft. lbs. (20 Nm).

36. Connect the throttle body vacuum hoses and electrical connections.

37. Install the throttle cable and transaxle kickdown linkage.

38. Install the radiator and heater hose. Fill the cooling system.

39. Connect the negative battery cable.

3.3L and 3.8L Engines

1. Disconnect the negative battery cable.

2. Relieve the fuel pressure.

3. Drain the cooling system.

4. Remove the air cleaner to throttle body hose assembly.

5. Disconnect the throttle cable and remove the wiring harness from the bracket.

6. Remove AIS motor and TPS wiring connectors from the throttle body.

7. Remove the vacuum hose harness from the throttle body.

8. Remove the PCV and brake booster hoses from the air intake plenum.

9. Disconnect the charge temperature sensor electrical connector. Remove the vacuum harness connectors from the intake plenum.

10. Remove the cylinder head to the intake plenum strut.

11. Disconnect the MAP sensor and oxygen sensor connectors. Remove the engine mounted ground strap.

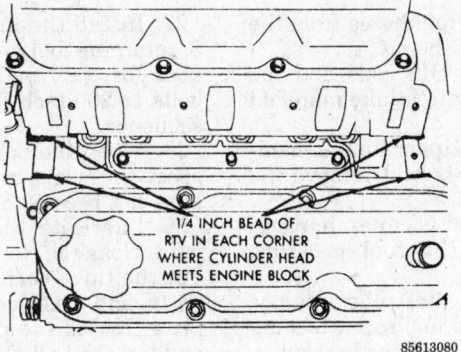

Intake manifold gasket sealing — 3.3L and 3.8L engines

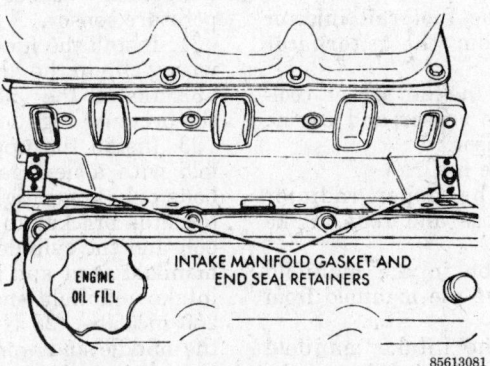

Intake manifold gasket retainers — 3.3L and 3.8L engines

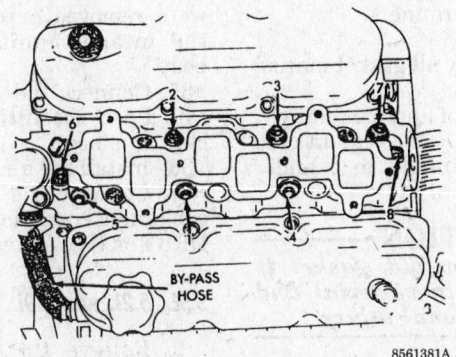

Lower intake manifold torque sequence — 3.3L and 3.8L engines

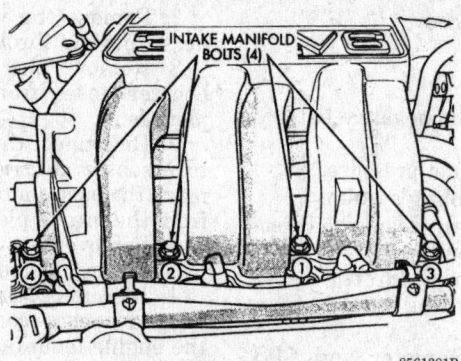

Upper intake manifold torque sequence — 3.3L and 3.8L engines

12. Remove the fuel hoses from the fuel rail and plug them.

13. Remove the DIS coils and the alternator bracket to intake manifold bolt.

14. Remove the upper intake manifold attaching bolts and remove the upper manifold.

15. Remove the vacuum harness connector from the fuel pressure regulator.

16. Remove the fuel tube retainer bracket screw and fuel rail attaching bolts. Spread the retainer bracket to allow for clearance when removing the fuel tube.

17. Remove the fuel rail injector wiring clip from the alternator bracket.

18. Disconnect the cam sensor, coolant temperature sensor and engine temperature sensor.

19. Remove the fuel rail.

20. Remove the upper radiator hose, bypass hose and rear intake manifold hose.

21. Remove the intake manifold bolts and remove the manifold from the engine.

22. Remove the intake manifold seal retaining screws and remove the manifold gasket.

23. Clean out clogged end water passages and fuel runners.

To install:

24. Clean and dry all gasket mating surfaces.

25. Place a drop of approximately ¼ inch diameter of silicone sealant onto each of the 4 manifold to cylinder head gasket corners.

——— CAUTION ———

The intake manifold gasket is made of very thin material and could cause personal injury.

26. Carefully install the intake manifold gasket and torque the end seal retainer screws to 105 inch lbs. (12 Nm).

27. Install the intake manifold and 8 retaining bolts and torque to 10 inch lbs. (1 Nm). Then torque the bolts to 200 inch lbs. (22 Nm) in the sequence.

28. When the bolts are torqued, inspect the seals to ensure that they have not become dislodged.

29. Lubricate the injector O-rings with clean oil to ease installation. Put the tip of each injector into their ports and position the fuel rail in place. Install the rail mounting bolts and tighten to 200 inch lbs. (22 Nm).

30. Connect the cam sensor, coolant temperature sensor and engine temperature sensor.

31. Install the fuel injector harness wiring clip to the alternator bracket.

32. Install the vacuum harness to the pressure regulator.

33. Install the upper intake manifold with a new gasket. Install the bolts only finger tight. Install the alternator bracket to intake manifold bolt and the cylinder head to intake manifold strut and bolts. Torque the intake manifold mounting bolts to 250 inch lbs. (28 Nm) starting from the middle and working inward in the sequence. Torque the bracket and strut bolts to 40 ft. lbs. (54 Nm).

34. Install or connect all items that were removed or disconnected from the intake manifold and throttle body.

35. Connect the fuel hoses to the rail. Push the fittings in until they click in place.

36. Install the air cleaner assembly.

37. Connect the negative battery cable and check for leaks using the DRB I or II to activate the fuel pump.

3.9L, 5.2L and 5.9L Engines

1. Relieve the fuel pressure if equipped with fuel injection. Disconnect the negative battery cable from the battery and drain the cooling system.

2. Remove the air pump and bracket. Removal of the bracket will allow for easier installation of the left front corner of the intake manifold.

3. Remove the air cleaner assembly. Remove the air conditioning compressor or unbolt it and lay it aside, if equipped. Remove the distributor cap with all wires attached.

4. Disconnect all wires, hoses, linkages and cables from the throttle body. Disconnect the fuel line.

5. Disconnect the ignition coil, coolant temperature sending unit wire and all other connectors along the wiring harness connected to items on the intake manifold.

6. Disconnect the heater hose, upper radiator hose and the lower bypass hose clamp.

7. Remove the valve covers.

8. Unbolt the intake manifold from the heads and remove the intake manifold assembly. Disassemble the manifold as required and clean out the exhaust crossover passages.

To install:

9. Clean and dry the intake manifold contact surfaces. Coat the intake manifold side gaskets lightly with sealer and install the gaskets to the heads. Cutouts at the front of the gaskets differentiate the right and left sides.

10. Apply a thin uniform coat of quick dry cement to the front and rear intake manifold gaskets and mounting surfaces on the block and apply a thin bead of sealer to each of 4 the corners. Install the front and rear gaskets engaging the hole in the block and the tangs from the head gaskets. Apply a second thin bead of sealer above the gaskets in the 4 corners.

11. Carefully lower the intake manifold into position engaging the bypass hose. Inspect the gaskets to make sure they have not dislodged.

12. Install the intake manifold bolts with the aspirator tube, air pump bracket and kickdown linkage bracket in place. Torque the bolts in sequence to 25 ft. lbs. (34 Nm). Repeat the sequence retightening the bolts to a final torque of 40 ft. lbs. (54 Nm). Repeat this step to ensure bolts are accurately torqued.

13. Clean and dry the valve cover mating surfaces, bolts and bolt holes. Install the valve covers with a new gasket. Torque the screws or nuts to 95 inch lbs. (11 Nm).

14. Connect the heater hose, upper radiator hose and the lower bypass hose clamp.

15. Connect the ignition coil, coolant temperature sending unit wire

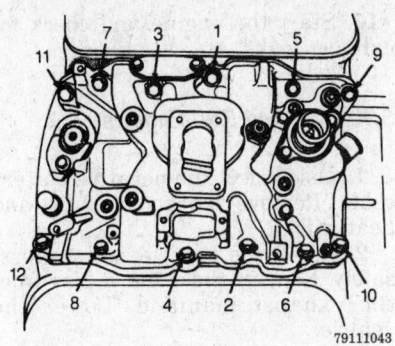

Intake manifold bolt torque sequence — 3.9L engine

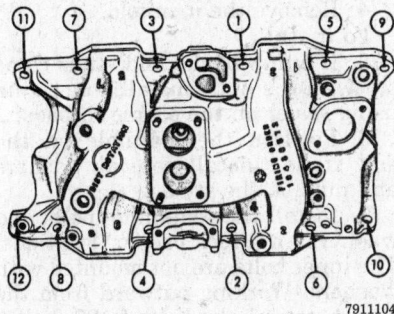

Intake manifold bolt torque sequence — 5.2L and 5.9L engines

and all other connectors that were disconnected along the wiring harness.

16. Install the air conditioning compressor, if equipped. Install the distributor cap and all spark plug wires.

17. Install air pump.

18. Connect all wires, hoses, cables and the fuel line to the throttle body. Install the air cleaner assembly.

19. Fill the cooling system.

20. Connect the negative battery cable and check for leaks.

8.0L Engine

1. Disconnect the negative battery cable and drain the engine coolant.

2. Remove the accessory drive belt, generator and bracket.

3. Remove the A/C compressor and set aside with the hoses still attached. Remove the compressor bracket.

4. Remove the air cleaner assembly.

5. Relief the fuel system pressure and disconnect the fuel lines.

6. Disconnect the accelerator cable, speed control cable and transmission linkage.

7. Remove the ignition coil assemblies.

8. Disconnect and label the vacuum lines, heater hoses, PCV hoses and remove the throttle body.

9. Remove the front upper intake manifold bolts. Retain the 3 rear bolts in the up position with tape or rubber bands.

10. Lift the upper intake manifold out of the engine compartment.

11. Remove the lower intake manifold bolts, manifold and gaskets.

To install:

12. Peel off the protective paper (blue for rear and brown for front) and press firmly onto the block. Make sure the block is free of oil. Insert Mopar® silicone RTV sealer into the 4 corner pockets.

13. Install the lower intake manifold bolts, manifold and gaskets within 3 minutes of sealer application.

14. Torque the bolts in sequence to 40 ft. lbs. (54 Nm).

15. Install the upper intake manifold and gaskets. Torque the bolts to 16 ft. lbs. (22 Nm).

16. Install the throttle body with new gasket and torque to 200 inch lbs. (23 Nm). Connect the vacuum lines, heater hoses, PCV hoses and transmission linkage.

17. Install the ignition coil assemblies.

18. Connect the accelerator cable and speed control cable.

19. Connect the fuel lines.

20. Install the air cleaner assembly.

21. Install the A/C compressor and bracket.

22. Install the accessory drive belt, generator and bracket.

23. Connect the negative battery cable and refill the engine coolant.

Exhaust Manifold

REMOVAL AND INSTALLATION

2.5L Engine

1. Disconnect the negative battery cable and drain the engine coolant.

2. Remove the air cleaner.

3. Label and disconnect all vacuum lines, electrical wiring and fuel lines from the throttle body and intake manifold.

4. Disconnect the throttle linkage. Remove the throttle body from the manifold.

5. Remove the power steering and air pump support bracket, if equipped.

6. Remove the diverter valve assembly and disconnect the air injection tube assembly from the exhaust manifold.

7. Disconnect the water hoses from the water crossover.

8. Raise the vehicle and support safely.

9. Remove the exhaust pipe from the exhaust manifold.

10. Remove the intake manifold strut and intake manifold.

11. Remove the exhaust manifold bolts and manifold.

To install:

12. Install the gaskets, manifolds and bolts. Torque the manifold bolts to 200 inch lbs. (23 Nm).

13. Install the intake manifold strut.

14. Install the exhaust pipe to the exhaust manifold. Connect the EGR tube and torque the bolts to 200 inch lbs. (23 Nm).

15. Lower the vehicle safely.

16. Connect the water hoses and water crossover.

17. Install the diverter valve assembly and disconnect the air injection tube assembly to the exhaust manifold.

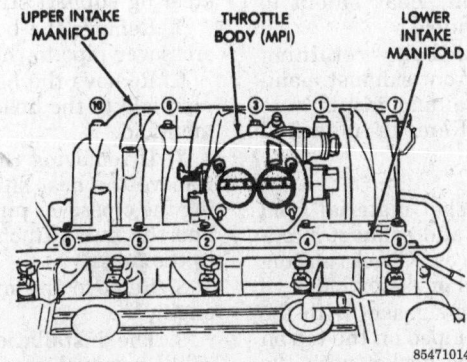

Upper intake manifold bolt torque sequence — 8.0L engine

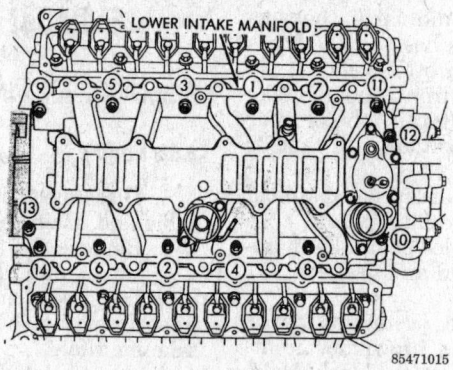

Lower intake manifold bolt torque sequence — 8.0L engine

85471015

18. Install the power steering and air pump support bracket, if equipped.

19. Connect the throttle linkage. Install the throttle body to the manifold.

20. Connect all vacuum lines, electrical wiring and fuel lines to the throttle body and intake manifold.

21. Install the air cleaner.

22. Connect the negative battery cable and refill the engine coolant. Start the engine and check for leaks.

3.0L Engine

1. Disconnect the negative battery cable.

2. Raise vehicle and support properly.

3. Disconnect the exhaust pipe from rear (cowl side) exhaust manifold at articulated joint.

4. Remove the EGR tube from the rear manifold and disconnect oxygen sensor lead.

5. Remove the attaching bolts from crossover pipe to manifold.

6. Remove the attaching nuts which retained manifold to cylinder head and remove manifold.

7. Lower the vehicle and remove bolt securing front heat shield to front exhaust manifold.

8. Remove the bolts retaining crossover pipe to front exhaust manifold and nuts retaining manifold to cylinder head. Remove manifold assembly.

To install:

9. Clean all gasket material from cylinder the head and exhaust manifold gasket surfaces. Check mating surfaces for cracks or distortion.

10. Install the new gasket with the numbers 1-3-5 stamped on the top on the rear bank. The gasket with the numbers 2-4-6 must be installed on the front bank (radiator side).

11. Install rear exhaust manifold and tighten attaching nuts to 15 ft. lbs. (20 Nm).

12. Install exhaust pipe to manifold and tighten shoulder bolts to 20 ft. lbs. (28 Nm).

13. Install crossover pipe to manifold and tighten bolts to 51 ft. lbs. (69 Nm).

14. Install oxygen sensor lead and EGR tube.

15. Install front exhaust manifold and attach exhaust crossover.

16. Install front manifold heat shield and tighten bolts to 10 ft. lbs. (13 Nm).

17. Connect the negative battery cable.

3.3L and 3.8L Engines

1. Disconnect the negative battery cable.

2. If removing the rear manifold, raise the vehicle and support safely. Disconnect the exhaust pipe at the articulated joint from the rear exhaust manifold.

3. Separate the EGR tube from the rear manifold and disconnect the oxygen sensor wire.

4. Remove the alternator/power steering support strut.

5. Remove the bolts attaching the crossover pipe to the manifold.

6. Remove the bolts attaching the manifold to the head and remove the manifold.

7. If removing the front manifold, remove the heat shield, bolts attaching the crossover pipe to the manifold and the nuts attaching the manifold to the head.

8. Remove the manifold from the engine.

9. The installation is the reverse of the removal procedure. Torque all exhaust manifold attaching bolts to 17 ft. lbs. (23 Nm).

10. Start the engine and check for exhaust leaks.

3.9L, 5.2L and 5.9L Engines

1. Disconnect the negative battery cable. Remove the hot air tube and heat shield.

2. Raise the vehicle and support safely. Remove the exhaust pipe from the exhaust manifold. Lower the vehicle.

3. Take note of all conical washer locations and remove the bolts, nuts and washers attaching the manifold to the head.

4. Remove the manifold.

To install:

5. If either of the end studs came out with the nuts, install a new stud using sealer on the coarse threads.

6. Position the manifold on the end studs. Install conical washers and nuts on the studs.

7. Install the remaining bolts and washers in their proper locations. The inner bolts are not mounted with washers. Working outward from the center, torque the bolts to 20 ft. lbs. (27 Nm) and the nuts to 15 ft. lbs. (20 Nm).

8. Install the exhaust pipe to the manifold.

9. Connect the negative battery cable and check for exhaust leaks.

8.0L Engine

1. Disconnect the negative battery cable.

2. Raise the vehicle and support safely.

3. Remove the exhaust pipe from the manifold.

4. Lower the vehicle safely.

5. Remove the exhaust heatshield.

6. Right exhaust manifold: remove the EGR tube and dipstick tube.

7. Remove the exhaust manifold bolts and manifold.

To install:

8. Check the gasket mating surfaces for warpage.

9. Install new gaskets, exhaust manifold and bolts. Torque the bolts to 16 ft. lbs. (22 Nm).

10. Install the EGR tube and dipstick tube for the right manifold.

11. Install the heatshields and torque bolts to 175 inch lbs. (20 Nm).

12. Raise the vehicle and connect the exhaust pipe. Torque the nuts to 25 ft. lbs. (34 Nm).

13. Lower the vehicle, connect the battery cable, start the engine and check for leaks.

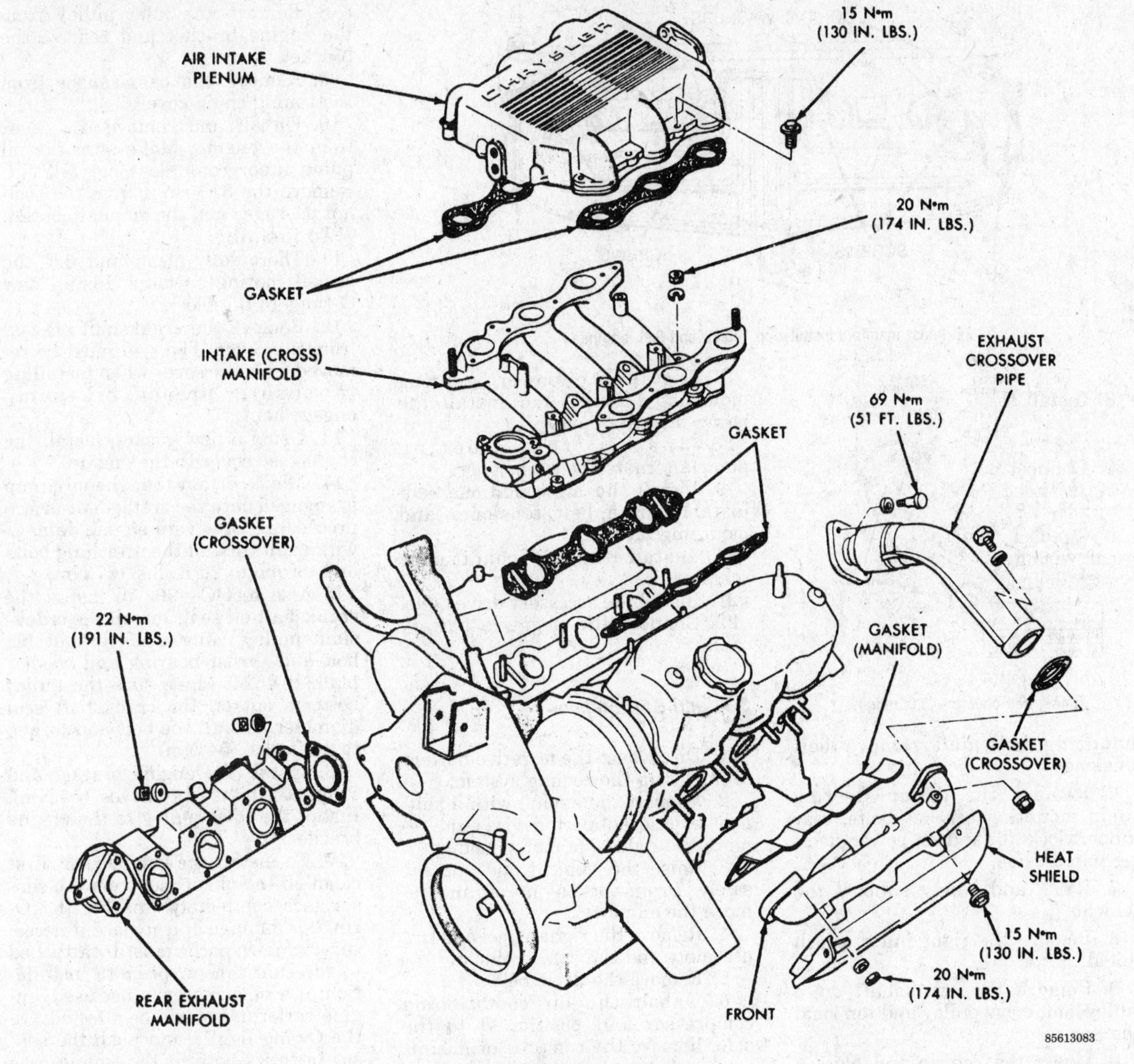

AIR INTAKE PLENUM

15 N•m (130 IN. LBS.)

20 N•m (174 IN. LBS.)

GASKET

INTAKE (CROSS) MANIFOLD

EXHAUST CROSSOVER PIPE

69 N•m (51 FT. LBS.)

GASKET

GASKET (CROSSOVER)

22 N•m (191 IN. LBS.)

GASKET (MANIFOLD)

GASKET (CROSSOVER)

HEAT SHIELD

15 N•m (130 IN. LBS.)

20 N•m (174 IN. LBS.)

REAR EXHAUST MANIFOLD

FRONT

85613083

Manifold assemblies — 3.0L engine

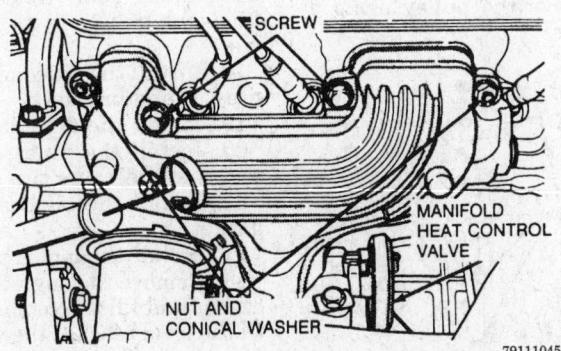

SCREW

MANIFOLD HEAT CONTROL VALVE

NUT AND CONICAL WASHER

79111045

Right exhaust manifold installation — 3.9L engine

Timing Chain Front Cover

REMOVAL AND INSTALLATION

3.0L Engine

1. Disconnect the negative battery cable.
2. Remove the accessory drive belts.
3. Remove the air conditioner compressor mounting bracket bolts and lay compressor aside.
4. Remove the air conditioner mounting bracket and adjustable drive belt tensioner from engine.
5. Remove the steering pump/alternator belt tensioner

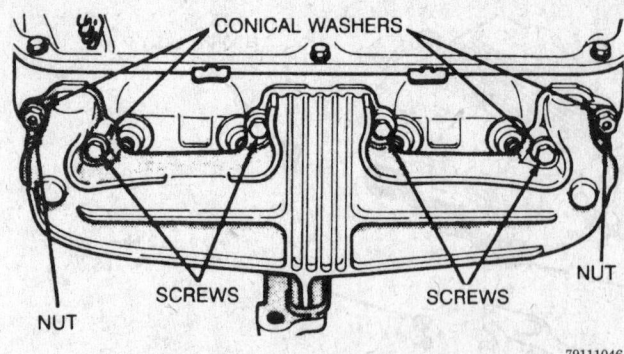

Exhaust manifold installation — 5.2L and 5.9L engines

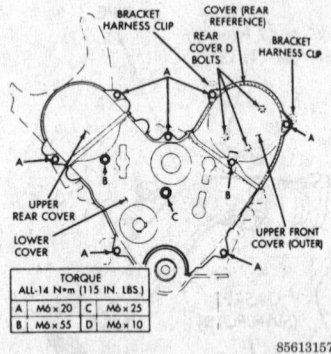

Timing belt covers — 3.0L engine

mounting bolt and remove belt tensioner.

6. Remove the power steering pump mounting bracket bolts, rear support lock nut and set power steering pump aside.

7. Raise and safely support the vehicle.

8. Remove the right inner splash shield.

9. Remove the crankshaft drive pulley bolt, drive pulley and torsional damper.

10. Lower the vehicle and place a floor jack under the engine. Separate engine mount insulator from engine mount bracket.

11. Raise the engine slightly and remove engine mount bracket.

12. Remove the timing belt covers.

To install:

13. Install the timing belt covers and tighten all screws to 10 ft. lbs. (13 Nm).

14. Raise the engine slightly and install engine mount bracket.

15. Install the engine mount insulator into engine mount bracket.

16. Install the torsional damper, drive pulley and drive pulley bolt. Torque bolt to 150 ft. lbs. (110 Nm). Install the right inner splash shield.

17. Install the power steering mounting bracket and install the power steering pump.

18. Install the steering pump/alternator belt tensioner.

19. Install the air conditioner adjustable drive belt tensioner and mounting bracket.

20. Install the air conditioner compressor.

21. Install the accessory drive belts.

22. Connect the negative battery cable.

3.3L and 3.8L Engines

1. Disconnect the negative battery cable. Drain the cooling system.

2. Support the engine with a suitable engine support device and remove the right side motor mount.

3. Raise the vehicle and support safely. Drain the engine oil and remove the oil pan.

4. Remove the right wheel and tire assembly and the splash shield.

5. Remove the drive belt.

6. Unbolt the air conditioning compressor and position it to the side. Remove the compressor mounting bracket.

7. Remove the crankshaft pulley bolt and remove the pulley using a suitable puller.

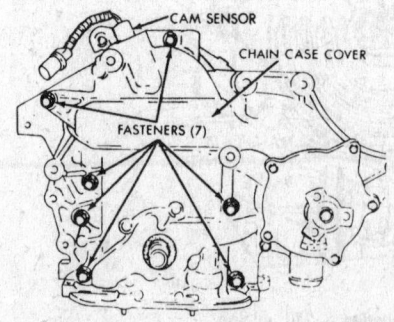

Timing chain case cover bolts — 3.3L and 3.8L engines

8. Remove the idler pulley from the engine bracket and remove the bracket.

9. Remove the cam sensor from the timing chain cover.

10. Unbolt and remove the cover from the engine. Make sure the oil pump inner rotor does not fall out. Remove the 3 O-rings from the coolant passages and the oil pump outlet.

To install:

11. Thoroughly clean and dry the gasket mating surfaces. Install new O-rings to the block.

12. Remove the crankshaft oil seal from the cover. The seal must be removed from the cover when installing to ensure proper oil pump engagement.

13. Using a new gasket, install the chain case cover to the engine.

14. Make certain that the oil pump is engaged onto the crankshaft before proceeding, or severe engine damage will result. Install the attaching bolts and torque to 20 ft. lbs. (27 Nm).

15. Use tool C–4992 to install the crankshaft oil seal. Install the crankshaft pulley using a 5.9 in. suitable bolt and thrust bearing and washer plate L–4524. Make sure the pulley bottoms out on the crankshaft seal diameter. Install the bolt and torque to 40 ft. lbs. (54 Nm).

16. Install the engine bracket and torque the bolts to 40 ft. lbs. (54 Nm). Install the idler pulley to the engine bracket.

17. To install the cam sensor, first clean off the old spacer from the sensor face completely. Inspect the O-ring for damage and replace if necessary. A new spacer must be attached to the cam sensor, prior to installation; if a new spacer is not used, engine performance will be affected. Oil the O-ring lightly and push the sensor in to its bore in the timing case cover until contact is made with the cam timing gear. Hold in this position and tighten it to 9 ft. lbs. (12 Nm).

18. Install the air conditioning compressor and bracket.

19. Install the drive belt.

20. Install the inner splash shield and the wheel and tire assembly.

21. Install the oil pan with a new gasket.

22. Install the motor mount.

23. Remove the engine temperature sensor and fill the cooling system until the level reaches the vacant sensor hole. Install the sensor and continue to fill the radiator. Fill the engine with the proper amount of oil.

24. Connect the negative battery cable and check for leaks.

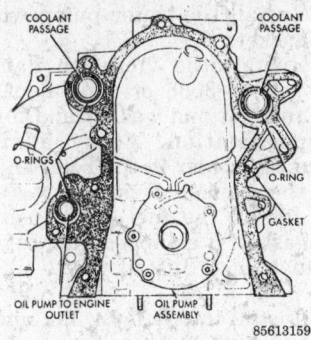

Timing chain cover gaskets and O-rings — 3.3L and 3.8L engines

3.9L, 5.2L and 5.9L Engines

1. Disconnect the negative battery cable.

2. Drain the cooling system.

3. Remove the radiator, fan and all related parts. Remove the water pump from the engine.

4. Remove the crankshaft pulley.

5. Remove the vibration damper using the proper puller.

6. Remove the 2 front bolts from the oil pan.

7. Unbolt the chain cover from the block and remove using caution to avoid damaging the oil pan gasket. Remove the fuel pump from the cover, if equipped.

To install:

8. Clean and dry the mating surfaces of the cover and block. Apply a thin bead of sealer to the oil pan gasket.

9. Install a new cover gasket and install the cover. Torque bolts to 30 ft. lbs. (41 Nm).

10. Install the water pump with a new gasket.

11. Install the damper with tool C–3638 or equivalent. Install the bolt and washer and torque to specification. Apply a small amount of sealer to the bolts and install the crankshaft pulley.

12. Install the mechanical fuel pump using a new gasket, if equipped, and connect the fuel lines. Install the 2 oil pan bolts.

13. Install the radiator, fan and all related parts.

14. Fill the cooling system.

15. Connect the negative battery cable and check for leaks.

8.0L Engine

1. Disconnect the negative battery cable and drain the engine coolant.

2. Remove the serpentine belt, fan shroud and fan.

3. Unbolt the A/C compressor and set on top of the engine without disconnecting the refrigerant lines.

4. Remove the generator, air pump and bracket assembly.

5. Remove the water pump.

6. Remove the vibration damper with a damper puller. Do not use a puller on the outside of the damper.

7. Remove the oil pan bolts with fasten the pan to the cover.

8. Remove the front cover bolts and cover. Be careful not to damage the oil pan gasket.

To install:

9. Lubricate the oil pump rotors with petroleum jelly or lubriplate and install the timing cover with new gasket. Place RTV sealer on the oil pan gasket and corners.

10. Torque the timing cover bolts to 35 ft. lbs. (47 Nm) and the oil pan bolts to 18 ft. lbs. (24 Nm).

11. Install the vibration damper using installation tool C-3688 and torque the bolt to 135 ft. lbs. (183 Nm).

12. Install the water pump, generator, air pump, brackets and A/C compressor.

13. Install the cooling fan, shroud, serpentine belt and refill the cooling system.

14. Connect the battery cable, start the engine and check for leaks.

Front Cover Oil Seal

REPLACEMENT

1. Disconnect the negative battery cable.

2. Remove the belts from the crankshaft pulley.

3. Remove the fan and shroud from the vehicle.

4. Remove the crankshaft pulley.

5. Remove the vibration damper using the proper puller.

6. Using a seal remover pry outward behind the lip of the oil seal. Take care not to damage the crankshaft seal surface of the cover.

To install:

7. Install the new seal by installing the threaded shaft part of the special tool C–4251 into the threads of the crankshaft.

8. Place the seal into the opening with the spring toward the engine. Place the installing adapter C–4251-3 or equivalent, with the thrust bearing and nut on the shaft. Tighten the nut until the tool is flush with the timing chain cover. Remove the tool.

9. Install vibration damper using tool C–3638 or equivalent. Install the bolt and washer and torque to specification.

10. Apply a small amount of sealer to the bolts and install the crankshaft pulley.

11. Install the fan and shroud.

12. Connect the negative battery cable and check for leaks.

Timing Chain and Sprockets

REMOVAL AND INSTALLATION

3.3L and 3.8L Engines

1. If possible, position the engine so the No. 1 piston is at TDC on the compression stroke. Disconnect the negative battery cable. Drain the coolant.

2. Remove the timing chain case cover.

3. Remove the camshaft gear attaching cup washer and remove the timing chain with both gears attached. Remove the timing chain snubber.

To install:

4. Assemble the timing chain and gears.

5. Turn the crankshaft and camshaft to align with the key way locations of the gears.

6. Slide both gears over their respective shafts and use a straightedge to confirm alignment.

7. Install the cup washer and camshaft bolt. Torque the bolt to 35 ft. lbs. (47 Nm).

8. Check camshaft endplay. The specification with a new plate is 0.002–0.006 in. (0.051–0.052mm) or 0.002–0.010 in. (0.51–0.254mm) with a used plate. Replace the thrust plate if not within specifications.

9. Install the timing chain snubber.

10. Thoroughly clean and dry the gasket mating surfaces.

11. Install new O-rings to the block.

12. Remove the crankshaft oil seal from the cover. The seal must be removed from the cover when installing to ensure proper oil pump engagement.

13. Using a new gasket, install the chain case cover to the engine.

14. Make certain the oil pump is engaged onto the crankshaft before proceeding, or severe engine damage will result. Install the attaching bolts and torque to 20 ft. lbs. (27 Nm).

15. Use tool C-4992 to install the crankshaft oil seal. Install the crankshaft pulley using a 5.9 in. suitable bolt and thrust bearing and washer plate L-4524. Make sure the pulley bottoms out on the crankshaft seal

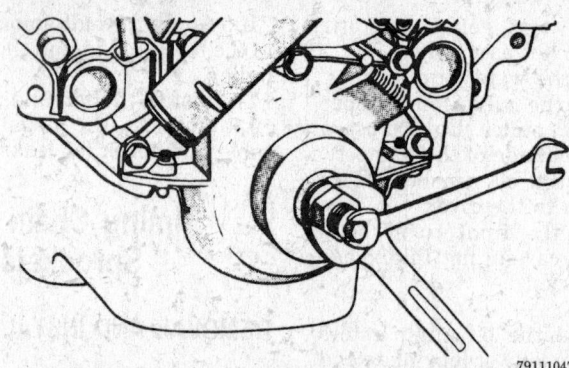

Installing the front cover oil seal — 3.9L, 5.2L and 5.9L engines

79111047

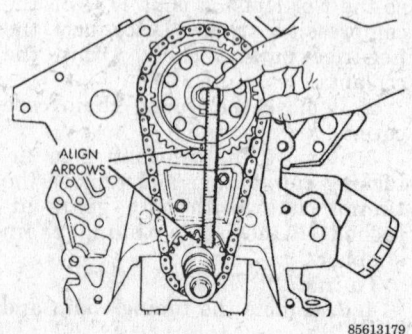

Timing mark alignment — 3.3L and 3.8L engines

85613179

diameter. Install the bolt and torque to 40 ft. lbs. (54 Nm).

16. Install all other parts removed during the chain case cover removal procedure and fill the engine with oil.

17. Connect the negative battery cable, road test the vehicle and check for leaks.

3.9L, 5.2L and 5.9L Engines

1. If possible, crank the engine around so the No. 1 cylinder is at TDC on the compression stroke. Remove the distributor cap to confirm and line the timing mark on the damper pulley with **0** on the timing scale. This will aid in aligning timing marks when installing the timing gears. Disconnect the negative battery cable.

2. Drain the cooling system.

3. Remove the radiator, fan and all related parts. Remove the water pump from the engine.

4. Remove the crankshaft pulley.

5. Remove the vibration damper using the proper puller.

6. Disconnect the fuel lines from the fuel pump, if equipped.

7. Remove the 2 front bolts from the oil pan.

8. Unbolt the chain cover from the block and remove, using caution to avoid damaging the oil pan gasket. Remove the fuel pump from the cover, if equipped.

9. Remove the camshaft gear retaining bolt, cup washer and fuel pump eccentric, if equipped. Remove the timing chain and gears.

To install:

10. Place both camshaft and crankshaft gears on the bench with the timing marks on the exact imaginary center line through both gear bores as they are installed on the engine. Place the timing chain around both sprockets.

11. Turn the crankshaft and camshaft so the keys align with the keyways in the gears when the timing marks are in proper position.

12. Slide both gears over their respective shafts and use a straight-edge to check timing mark alignment.

13. Install the fuel pump eccentric and cup washer, if equipped. Torque the camshaft gear retaining bolt to 35 ft. lbs. (47 Nm).

14. Clean and dry the mating surfaces of the timing chain cover and block. Apply a thin bead of sealer to the oil pan gasket.

15. Install a new cover gasket and install the cover. Torque the bolts to 30 ft. lbs. (41 Nm).

16. Install the water pump with a new gasket.

17. Install the vibration damper with tool C–3638 or equivalent. Install the bolt and washer and torque to specification. Apply a small amount of sealer to the bolts and install the crankshaft pulley.

18. Install the fuel pump using a new gasket, if equipped, and connect the fuel lines. Install the 2 oil pan bolts.

19. Install the radiator, fan and all related parts.

20. Fill the cooling system.

21. Connect the negative battery cable, set all adjustments to specifications and check for leaks.

8.0L Engine

1. Disconnect the negative battery cable and drain the engine coolant.

2. Remove the timing chain front cover.

3. Inspect the timing chain stretch as follows:

a. Place a scale next to the timing chain and place a torque wrench over the camshaft sprocket bolt. Apply torque in the direction of engine rotation to take up the slack. Torque should be 30 ft. lbs. (41 Nm) with the cylinder heads assembled or 15 ft. lbs. (20 Nm) without the cylinder heads.

b. With this torque the crankshaft should be held still.

c. Hold the scale even with the edge of a chain link. Torque in the opposite direction.

d. Note the amount of chain movement. It should not exceed $\frac{1}{8}$ (3.175mm) of movement. If so, replace the timing chain as follows.

4. Remove the camshaft sprocket bolt, camshaft sprocket and chain.

5. Using puller 6444 and jaws 6820, remove the crankshaft sprocket.

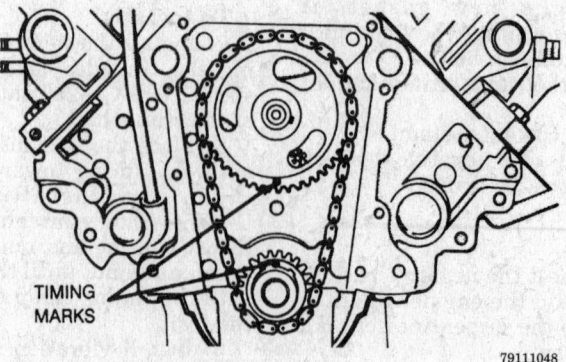

TIMING MARKS

79111048

Timing mark alignment — 3.9L, 5.2L and 5.9L engines

To install:

6. Install the crankshaft sprocket with tools C-3688, C-3718 and MB-990799 until the sprocket rests against the crankshaft shoulder.

7. Align the camshaft sprocket timing mark at the 6 o'clock position and the crankshaft at the 12 o'clock position.

8. Install the camshaft sprocket and chain.

9. Install the camshaft bolt and torque to 45 ft. lbs. (61 Nm).

10. Install the timing chain cover.

11. Connect the battery cable, refill the cooling system, start the engine and check for leaks.

Timing Belt Front Cover and Oil Seal

REMOVAL AND INSTALLATION

2.5L Engine

1. Remove the accessory drive belts.

2. Raise and safely support the vehicle. Remove the right inner splash shield.

3. Loosen and remove the 3 water pump pulley mounting screws and remove the pulley.

4. Remove the 4 crankshaft pulley retaining screws.

5. Remove the nuts at upper portion of timing cover and screws from lower portion and remove both halves of cover.

To install:

6. Install the cover. Secure the upper section to cylinder head with nuts and lower section to cylinder block with screws.

7. Install the crankshaft pulley and tighten the bolt to 20 ft. lbs. (25 Nm), lower vehicle.

8. Install the water pump pulley and tighten screws to 105 inch lbs. (12 Nm).

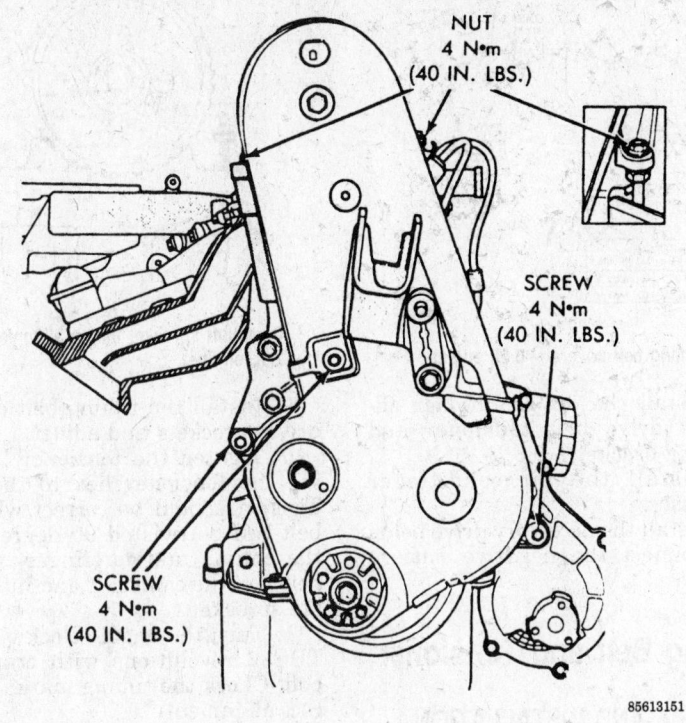

NUT
4 N•m
(40 IN. LBS.)

SCREW
4 N•m
(40 IN. LBS.)

SCREW
4 N•m
(40 IN. LBS.)

85613151

Timing belt cover — 2.5L engine

9. Install the accessory drive belts.

3.0L Engine

1. Disconnect the negative battery cable.

2. Remove the accessory drive belts.

3. Remove the air conditioner compressor mounting bracket bolts and lay compressor aside.

4. Remove the air conditioner mounting bracket and adjustable drive belt tensioner from engine.

5. Remove the steering pump/alternator belt tensioner mounting bolt and remove belt tensioner.

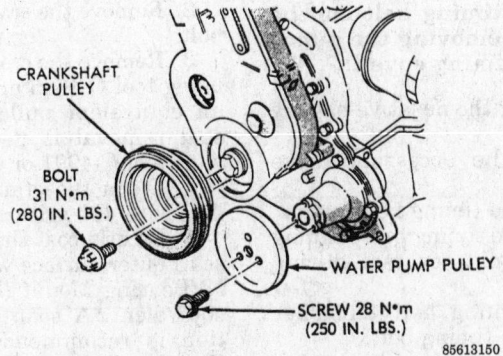

CRANKSHAFT
PULLEY

BOLT
31 N•m
(280 IN. LBS.)

WATER PUMP PULLEY

SCREW 28 N•m
(250 IN. LBS.)

85613150

Crankshaft and water pump pulley — 2.5L engine

6. Remove the power steering pump mounting bracket bolts, rear support lock nut and set power steering pump aside.

7. Raise and safely support the vehicle.

8. Remove the right inner splash shield.

9. Remove the crankshaft drive pulley bolt, drive pulley and torsional damper.

10. Lower the vehicle and place a floor jack under the engine. Separate engine mount insulator from engine mount bracket.

11. Raise the engine slightly and remove engine mount bracket.

12. Remove the timing belt covers.

13. Install the timing belt covers and tighten all screws to 10 ft. lbs.

14. Raise the engine slightly and install engine mount bracket.

15. Install the engine mount insulator into engine mount bracket.

16. Install the torsional damper, drive pulley and drive pulley bolt. Torque bolt to 150 ft. lbs. (110 Nm). Install the right inner splash shield.

17. Install the power steering mounting bracket and install the power steering pump.

18. Install the steering pump/alternator belt tensioner.

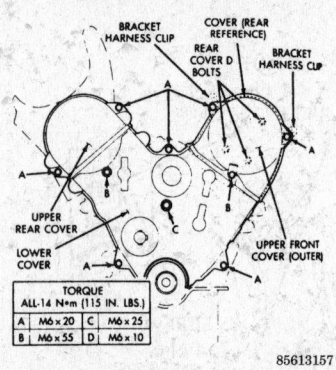

85613157

Timing belt covers — 3.0L engine

19. Install the air conditioner adjustable drive belt tensioner and mounting bracket.
20. Install the air conditioner compressor.
21. Install the accessory drive belts.
22. Connect the negative battery cable.

Timing Belt and Tensioner

REMOVAL AND INSTALLATION

2.5L Engine

1. Remove the solid mount compressor bracket.
2. Remove the accessory drive belts.
3. Remove the timing belt cover.
4. Place a jack under the engine.
5. Separate the right engine mount and raise the engine slightly.
6. Loosen the timing belt tensioner screw, rotate the hex nut, and remove timing belt.
7. Turn the crankshaft and intermediate shaft until markings on both sprockets are aligned.
8. Rotate the camshaft so the arrows on the hub are in line with No. 1 camshaft cap to cylinder head line. Small hole must be in vertical center line.

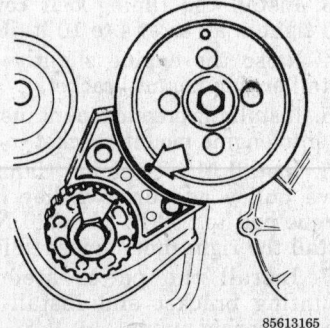

85613165

Crankshaft and intermediate shaft timing mark alignment — 2.5L engine

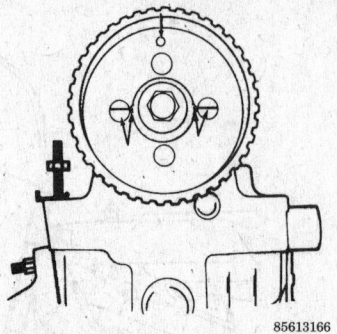

85613166

Camshaft sprocket timing alignment — 2.5L engine

9. Install the timing belt over the drive sprockets and adjust.
10. Tighten the tensioner by turning the tensioner hex to the right. Tension should be correct when the belt can be twisted 90 degrees with the thumb and forefinger, midway between the camshaft and intermediate sprocket.
11. Turn the engine clockwise from TDC 2 revolutions with crankshaft bolt. Check the timing marks for correct alignment.

------- WARNING -------
Do not used the camshaft or intermediate shaft to rotate the engine. Also, do not allow oil or solvent to contact timing belt as they will deteriorate the belt and cause slipping.

12. Tighten lock nut on tensioner while holding weighted wrench in position to 45 ft. lbs. (61 Nm).
13. Install the timing belt cover.
14. Install the accessory drive belts.

NOTE: With timing belt cover installed and No. 1 cylinder at TDC, the small hole in the cam sprocket should be centered in timing belt cover hole.

3.0L Engine

NOTE: The timing belt can be inspected by removing the upper (front outer) timing cover.

1. Disconnect the negative battery cable.
2. Remove the accessory drive belts.
3. Remove the timing belt covers.
4. Identify the timing belt running direction to avoid reversal during installation.
5. Loosen timing belt tensioner bolt and remove timing belt.
6. Remove the crankshaft sprocket flange.

To install:
7. Rotate the crankshaft sprocket until timing mark on crankshaft sprocket is aligned with the oil pump timing mark at 1 o'clock position.
8. Rotate the (inner) camshaft sprocket until mark on (inner) camshaft sprocket is aligned with the timing mark on alternator bracket.
9. Rotate the (outer) camshaft sprocket (radiator side) until mark on the sprocket is aligned with the timing mark on the timing belt inner cover.
10. Install the timing belt on the crankshaft sprocket while maintaining pressure on the tensioner side.
11. Position the timing belt over the camshaft sprocket (radiator side). Next, position the belt under the water pump pulley, then over the (inner) sprocket and finally over the tensioner.
12. Apply rotating force in the opposite direction to the camshaft sprocket (radiator side) to create tension on the timing belt tension side.
13. Rotate the crankshaft in a clockwise direction and recheck engine timing marks.
14. Install the crankshaft sprocket flange.
15. Loosen the tensioner bolt and allow tensioner spring to tension the belt.
16. Again rotate the crankshaft in a clockwise direction (2) full turns. Recheck the engine timing. Tighten the tensioner bolt to 23 ft. lbs. (31 Nm).
17. Install the timing covers.
18. Install the accessory drive belts.
19. Connect battery negative cable.

Timing Sprockets

REMOVAL AND INSTALLATION

2.5L and 3.0L Engines

1. Remove the drive belts, timing belt cover and timing belt.
2. Remove the crankshaft sprocket bolt.
3. Remove the crankshaft sprocket using tool C-4685 and tool L-4524 or an equivalent puller. If crankshaft seal removal is necessary, remove with tool C-4991 or equivalent tool.
4. Clean the crankshaft seal surface with 400 grit paper.
5. Lightly coat the seal (Steel case seal) outer surface with Loctite Stud N' Bearing Mount (P/N 4057987) or equivalent. A soap and water solution is recommended to lubricate (Rubber Coated Case Seal) outer surface.

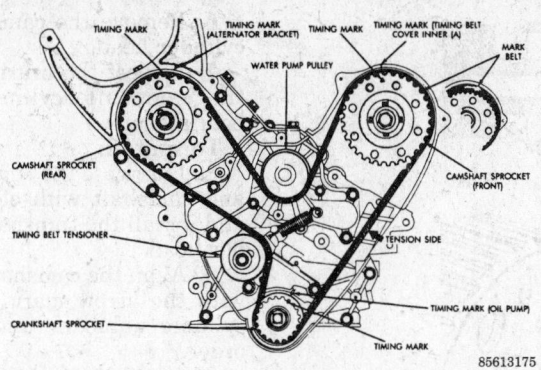

Sprocket timing for belt installation — 3.0L engine

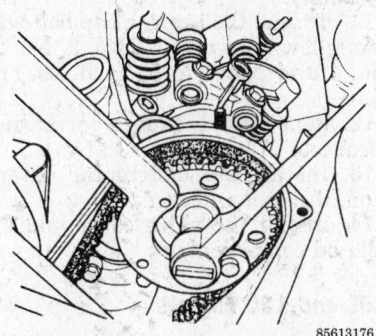

Secure the sprocket when removing or installing the nut — 3.0L engine

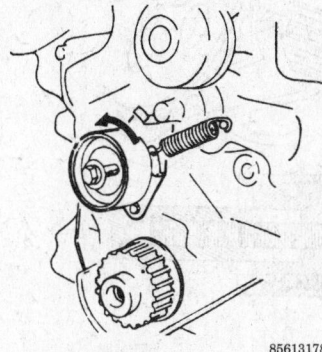

Positioning the tensioner — 3.0L engine

Camshaft

REMOVAL AND INSTALLATION

2.5L Engine

The following procedure is preformed with the engine in the vehicle.

NOTE: Removal of the camshaft requires removal of the camshaft sprocket. To maintain proper engine timing, the timing belt can be left indexed on the sprockets and suspended under light pressure. This will prevent the belt from coming off and maintain timing.

1. Disconnect the negative battery cable. Relieve the fuel pressure, if equipped with fuel injection.
2. Turn the crankshaft so the No. 1 piston is at the TDC of the compression stroke. Remove the upper timing belt cover. Remove the air pump pulley, if equipped.
3. Remove the camshaft sprocket bolt and the sprocket and suspend tightly so the belt does not lose tension. If it does, the belt timing will have to be reset.
4. Remove the valve cover.

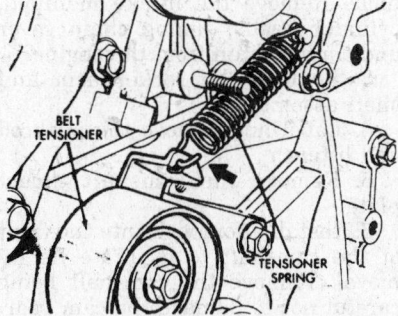

Timing belt tensioner — 3.0L engine

6. Lightly lubricate the seal lip with engine oil.
7. Install seal with tool C-4992.
8. Install the sprocket and install sprocket bolt.
9. Remove and install the camshaft and intermediate shaft sprockets with tool C-4687 and tool C-4687-1 or a similar tool such as a strap wrench.
10. Install the timing belt and timing belt cover.
11. Install the accessory drive belts.

5. Remove the air pump belt from the pulley.
6. If the rocker arms are being reused, mark them for installation identification and loosen the camshaft bearing bolts, evenly and gradually.
7. If the rocker arms are being reused, mark them for installation identification and loosen the camshaft bearing bolts, evenly and gradually.
8. Using a soft mallet, rap the rear of the camshaft a few times to break the bearing caps loose.
9. Remove the bolts, bearing caps and the camshaft with seals.

NOTE: Before replacing the camshaft, identify factory installed oversized components. To do so, look for the tops of the bearing caps pained green and O/SJ stamped rearward of the oil gallery plug on the rear of the head. In addition, the barrel of the camshaft is painted green and O/SJ is stamped onto the rear end of the camshaft. Installing standard sized parts in an head equipped with oversized parts or visa-versa will cause severe engine damage.

10. Check the oil passages for blockage and the parts for damage. Clean all mating surfaces.
   To install:
11. Transfer the sprocket key to the new camshaft. New rocker arms and a new camshaft sprocket bolt are normally included with the camshaft package. Install the rocker arms, lubricate the camshaft and install with end seals installed.
12. Place the bearing caps with No. 1 at the timing belt end and No. 5 at the transaxle end. The camshaft bearing caps are numbered and have arrows facing forward. Torque the camshaft bearing bolts evenly and gradually to 18 ft. lbs. (24 Nm).

NOTE: Apply RTV silicone gasket material to the No. 1 and 5 bearing caps. Install the bearing caps before the seals are installed.

13. Mount a dial indicator to the front of the engine and check the camshaft endplay. Play should not exceed 0.006 in. (0.15mm).
14. Install the camshaft sprocket and the new bolt. Install the air pump pulley, if equipped.
15. Install the valve cover with a new gasket.
16. Connect the negative battery cable and check for leaks.

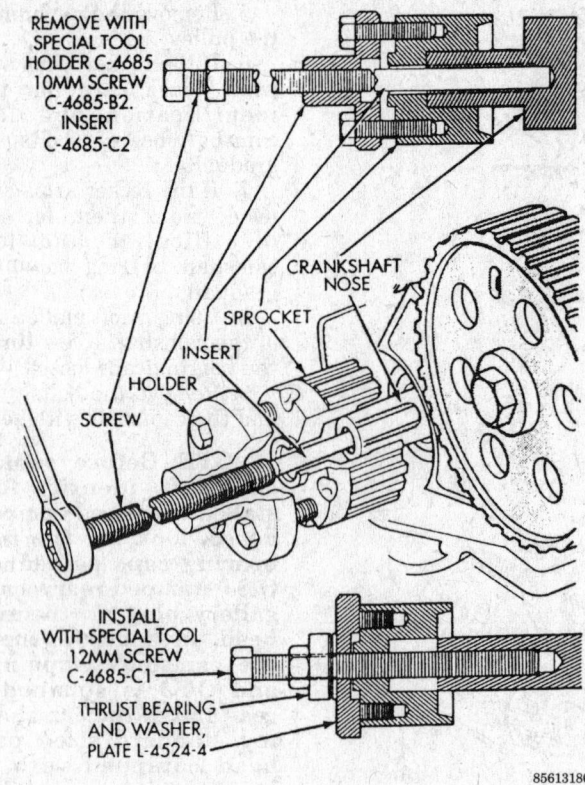

Removing crankshaft sprocket — 2.5L engine

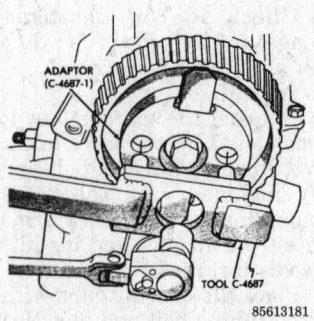

Removing or installing camshaft or intermediate sprocket bolt — 2.5L engine

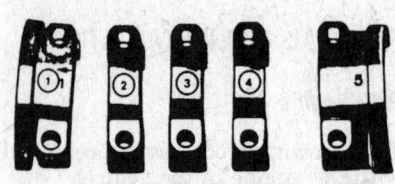

Camshaft bearing caps — 2.5L engine

3.0L Engine

1. Disconnect the negative battery cable. Remove the air cleaner assembly and valve covers.

2. Install auto lash adjuster retainers MD998443 or equivalent on the rocker arms.

3. If removing the right side (front) camshaft, remove the distributor extension.

4. Remove the camshaft bearing caps but do not remove the bolts from the caps.

5. Remove the rocker arms, rocker shafts and bearing caps, as an assembly.

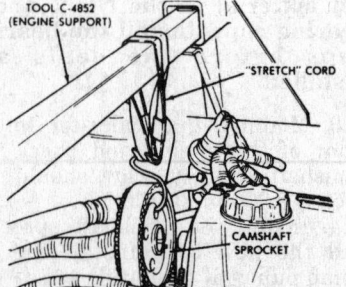

Suspending camshaft sprocket to retain the engine timing — 2.5L engine

6. Remove the camshaft from the cylinder head.

7. Inspect the bearing journals on the camshaft, cylinder head and bearing caps.

To install:

8. Lubricate the camshaft journals and camshaft with clean engine oil and install the camshaft in the cylinder head.

9. Align the camshaft bearing caps with the arrow mark (depending on cylinder numbers) and in numerical order.

10. Apply sealer at the ends of the bearing caps and install the assembly.

11. Torque the bearing cap bolts, in the following sequence: No. 3, No. 2, No. 1 and No. 4 to 85 inch lbs. (10 Nm).

12. Repeat the sequence, increasing torque to 175 inch lbs. (18 Nm).

13. Install the distributor extension, if it was removed.

14. Install the valve cover and all related components.

3.3L and 3.8L Engines

1. Relieve the fuel system pressure. Disconnect the negative battery cable.

2. Remove the engine from the vehicle. Remove the intake manifold, cylinder heads, timing chain cover and timing chain from the engine.

3. Remove the rocker arm and shaft assemblies.

4. Label and remove the pushrod and lifters.

5. Remove the camshaft thrust plate.

6. Install a long bolt into the front of the camshaft to facilitate its removal. Remove the camshaft being careful not to damage the cam bearings with the cam lobes.

To install:

7. Install the camshaft to within 2 in. of its final installation position.

8. Install the camshaft thrust plate and 2 bolts and torque to 10 ft. lbs. (12 Nm).

9. Place both camshaft and crankshaft gears on the bench with the timing marks on the exact imaginary center line through both gear bores as they are installed on the engine. Place the timing chain around both sprockets.

10. Turn the crankshaft and camshaft so the keys align with the key ways in the gears when the timing marks are in proper position.

11. Slide both gears over their respective shafts and use a straight-edge to check timing mark alignment.

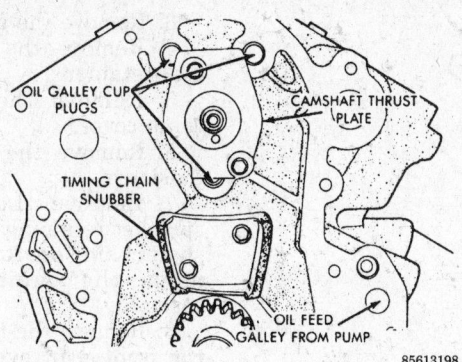

Camshaft thrust plate — 3.3L and 3.8L engines

12. Measure camshaft endplay. If not within specifications, replace the thrust plate.

13. If the camshaft was not replaced, lubricate and install the lifters in their original locations. If the camshaft was replaced, new lifters must be used.

14. Install the pushrods and rocker shaft assemblies.

15. Install the timing chain cover, cylinder heads and intake manifold.

16. Install the engine in the vehicle.

17. When everything is bolted in place, change the engine oil and replace the oil filter.

NOTE: If the camshaft or lifters have been replaced, add 1 pint of Mopar crankcase conditioner, or equivalent when replenishing the oil to aid in break in. This mixture should be left in the engine for a minimum of 500 miles and drained at the next normal oil change.

18. Fill the radiator with coolant.

19. Connect the negative battery cable, set all adjustments to specifications and check for leaks.

3.9L, 5.2L and 5.9L Engines

1. If possible, crank the engine around so the No. 1 cylinder is at TDC on the compression stroke. Remove the distributor cap to confirm and line the timing mark on the damper pulley with **0** on the timing scale. This will aid in aligning timing marks when installing the timing gears. If equipped with fuel injection, relieve the fuel pressure. Disconnect the negative battery cable.

2. Drain the cooling system.

3. Remove the engine from the vehicle.

4. Remove the valve cover(s).

5. Remove the rocker shaft assembly(s). Identify and remove the pushrods.

6. Remove the intake manifold, identify and remove all lifters.

7. Remove the distributor. Lift out the oil pump and distributor driveshaft.

8. Remove the radiator, fan and all related parts.

9. Remove the fuel pump, if equipped. Remove the timing chain cover, timing chain and gears.

10. Note the location of the oil tab and remove the camshaft thrust plate.

11. Install a long bolt into the front of the camshaft to facilitate removal. Remove the camshaft, being careful not to damage any of the cam bearings with the cam lobes.

To install:

12. Install the camshaft to within 2 in. of its final installation position. Install the camshaft Gear Installer tool C–3509 with tongue in back of distributor drive gear. Bolt it in place with the distributor lock plate bolt. This will prevent the camshaft from being pushed in too far and knocking out the welch plug at the rear of the block. This tool should remain in place until the timing chain installation has been completed.

13. Install the camshaft thrust plate and chain oil tab with 3 bolts. Make sure the tang of the oil tab enters the lower right hole in the thrust plate. Torque the bolts to 210 inch lbs. (24 Nm). Make sure the top edge of the oil tab is flat against the thrust plate or it will not feed oil to the chain.

14. Place both camshaft and crankshaft gears on the bench with the timing marks on the exact imaginary center line through both gear bores as they are installed on the engine. Place the timing chain around both sprockets.

15. Turn the crankshaft and camshaft so the keys align with the keyways in the gears when the timing marks are in proper position.

16. Slide both gears over their respective shafts and use a straightedge to check timing mark alignment.

17. Install the fuel pump eccentric and cup washer, if equipped. Torque the camshaft gear retaining bolt to 35 ft. lbs. (47 Nm). Remove the camshaft blocking tool.

18. Measure camshaft endplay. Replace the thrust plate, if not within specifications.

19. Coat the oil pump and distributor driveshaft with oil. Install 3.9L engine shaft so when the gear spirals into place and drops into the oil pump, the slot in the top of the gear is pointing directly to the left front intake manifold bolt hole. Install 5.2L and 5.9L engine shaft in a similar manner, except position it so the slot is parallel with the center line of the camshaft.

20. If the camshaft was not replaced, lubricate and install the lifters in their original locations. If the camshaft was replaced, new lifters must be used.

21. Install the pushrods and rocker shaft assembly.

22. Install the intake manifold. Install the valve cover(s).

23. Install the distributor so the rotor points to the No. 1 spark plug wire position on the cap.

24. Install the timing chain cover and all related parts, fuel pump, if equipped, and radiator.

25. Install the engine into the vehicle.

26. When everything is bolted in place, change the engine oil and replace the oil filter.

NOTE: If the camshaft or lifters have been replaced, add 1 pint of Mopar crankcase conditioner or equivalent, when replenishing the oil to aid in break-in. This mixture should be left in the engine for a minimum of 500 miles and drained at the next normal oil change.

27. Fill the radiator with coolant.

28. Connect the negative battery cable, set all adjustments to specifications and check for leaks.

8.0L Engine

1. Remove the valve covers and rocker arm assemblies. Label each component for installation.

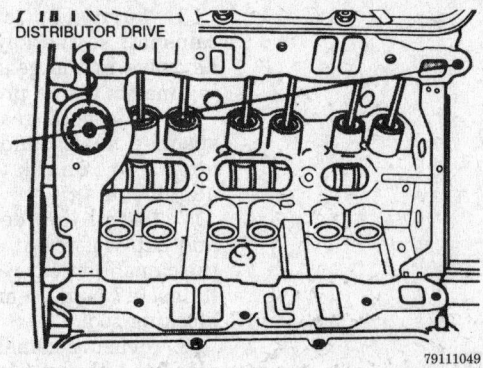

Installed distributor drive gear — 3.9L engine

2. Remove the pushrod and lifters. Label each component for installation.

NOTE: The 4 corner lifters cannot be removed without removing the cylinder heads and gaskets. They can be lifted and retained for camshaft removal.

3. Remove the upper and lower intake manifolds.

4. Remove the timing chain cover and timing chain.

5. Remove the camshaft thrust plate. Install a long bolt into the front of the camshaft to aid in removal. Remove the camshaft being careful not to damage the cam bearings and cam lobes.

To install:

6. Lubricate the cam lobes and journals with assembly lube or equivalent. Install the camshaft with a long bolt in the sprocket hole to help steady the camshaft.

7. Install the camshaft thrust plate and torque the bolts to 16 ft. lbs. (22 Nm).

8. Check the camshaft endplay. It should be 0.002–0.006 in. (0.051–0.152mm). If not, replace the thrust plate.

9. Align the timing marks and install the timing chain/sprockets, front timing cover and remaining components.

10. Add 1 pint of Mopar® Crankcase Conditioner, or equivalent for at least 500 miles.

Intermediate Shaft

REMOVAL AND INSTALLATION

2.5L Engine

The following procedures to be performed with engine removed from vehicle.

1. Remove the distributor assembly.

2. Remove the fuel pump.

3. Remove timing case cover, and timing belt.

4. Remove the intermediate shaft sprocket.

5. Remove the intermediate shaft retainer screws and remove retainer.

6. Remove the intermediate shaft and inspect journals and bushing.

7. When installing the shaft, lubricate the fuel pump eccentric and distributor drive gear. Install the intermediate shaft.

8. Inspect the shaft seal in retainer. Replace if necessary.

9. Lightly lubricate the seal lip with engine oil.

10. Install the intermediate shaft retainer assembly and retainer screws. Tighten screws to 105 inch lbs. On 2.5L engine apply anaerobic (Form-in-Place) gasket material to retainer sealing surface before installing.

11. Install the intermediate shaft sprocket.

12. Check engine timing.

13. Install the timing belt and adjust.

14. Install the timing belt cover.

15. Install the fuel pump.

16. Install the distributor.

Balance Shafts

The 2.5L engine is equipped with 2 balance shafts located in a housing attached to the lower crankcase. These shafts are driven by a chain and 2 gears from the crankshaft at 2 times crankshaft speed. This counterbalance certain engine reciprocating masses.

REMOVAL AND INSTALLATION

1. Remove the engine from vehicle.

2. Remove the timing case cover, timing belt and sprockets.

3. Remove the engine oil pan.

4. Remove the front crankshaft seal retainer.

5. Remove the balance shafts chain cover.

6. Remove the chain guide and tensioner.

7. Remove the balance shafts sprocket retaining screws and crankshaft chain sprocket Torx screws. Remove the chain and sprocket assembly.

8. Remove the balance shafts carrier front gear cover retaining double ended stud. Remove the cover and balance shafts gears.

9. Remove the carrier rear cover and balance shafts.

10. To separate the carrier, remove (6) crankcase to carrier attaching bolts and remove carrier.

11. Take notice of all parts to avoid interchanging.

To install:

12. Install both shafts into carrier the assembly from rear of carrier.

13. Install the rear cover.

14. Install the balance shafts drive and driven gears to shafts.

15. Position the carrier assembly on crankcase and tighten (6) bolts to 40 ft. lbs. (54 Nm).

16. Crankshaft to Balance Shaft Timing must be established. Rotate both balance shafts until the key ways are in the Up position.

17. Install the short hub drive gear on balance shaft driving shaft.

18. Install the long hub gear on the driven shaft.

19. With both gears on the balance shafts and key ways Up, the timing marks should be meshed.

20. Align the balance shaft carrier cover with the carrier housing dowel pin and install double ended stud. Tighten to 105 inch lbs. (12 Nm).

21. Install the crankshaft sprocket and tighten sprocket Torx screw to 11 ft. lbs. (15 Nm).

22. Turn the crankshaft until No. 1 cylinder is at TDC. The timing marks on the chain sprocket should align with the parting line on the left side of No. 1 main bearing cap.

23. Install the chain over the crankshaft sprocket so the nickel plated link of the chain is over the timing mark on the crankshaft sprocket.

24. Install the balance shaft sprocket into the timing chain so the timing mark on the sprocket (yellow dot) mates with the yellow painted link on the chain.

25. With the balance shaft key way in 12 o'clock position slide the balance shaft sprocket on the nose of the balance shaft. The balance shaft may

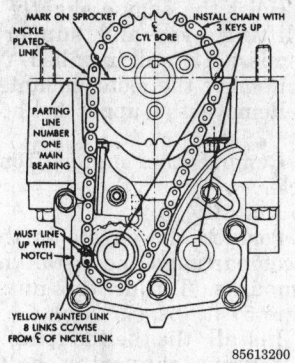

Balance shaft timing — 2.5L engine

85613200

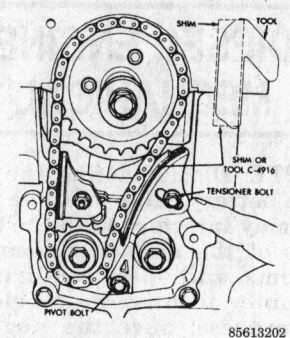

Balance shaft chain tensioner adjustment — 2.5L engine

85613202

have to be pushed in slightly to allow for clearance.

NOTE: The timing mark on the sprocket, the painted link, and the arrow on the side of the gear cover should align if the balance shafts are timed correctly.

26. Install the balance shaft bolt and tighten to 21 ft. lbs. (29 Nm). Placed a wooden block between the crankcase and crankshaft counterbalance to prevent crankshaft from turning.

27. Proper balance shaft Timing Chain Tension must be established.

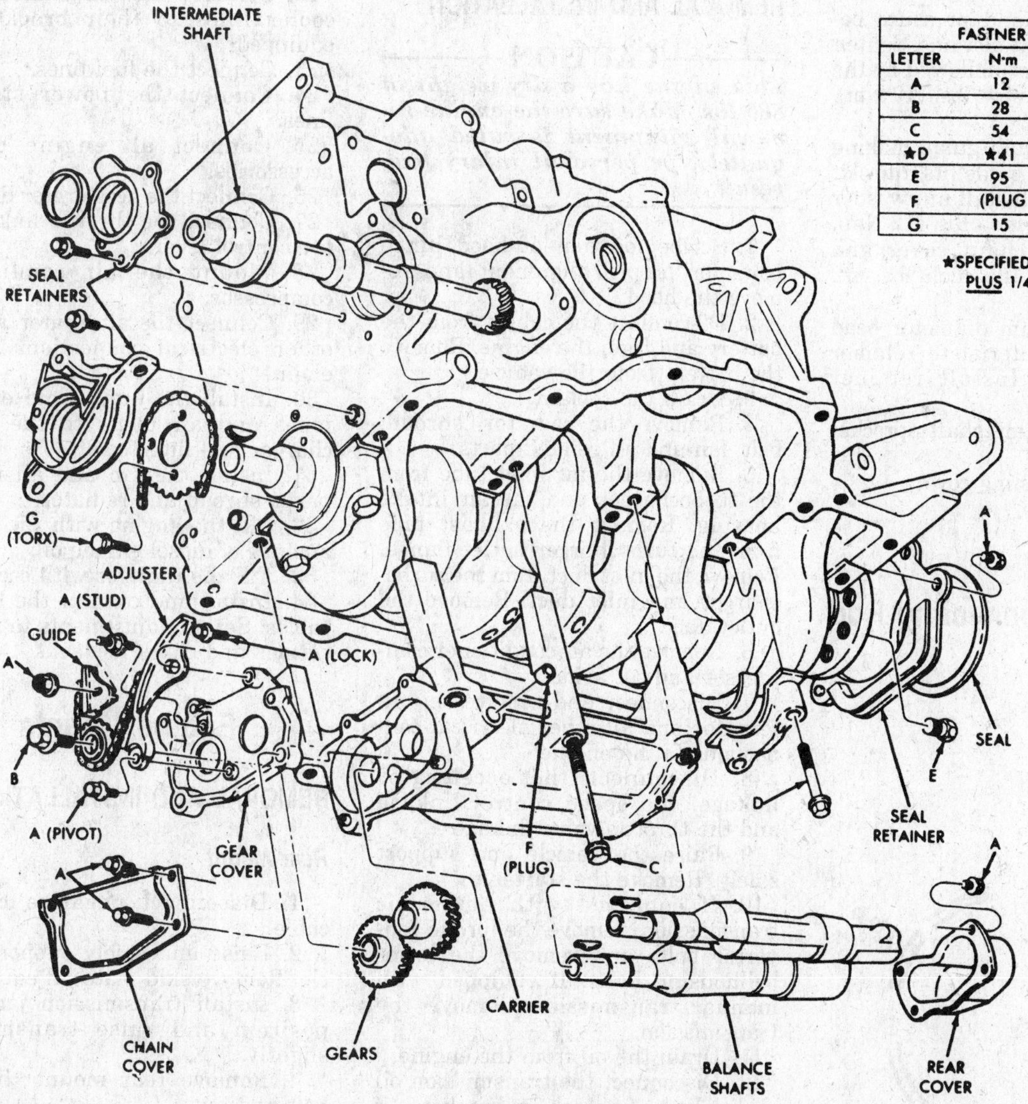

FASTNER TORQUE			
LETTER	N·m	IN. LBS.	FT. LBS.
A	12	105	—
B	28	250	—
C	54	—	40
★D	★41	—	★30
E	95	—	70
F	(PLUG - LOCTITE 277)		
G	15	130	—

★SPECIFIED TORQUE **PLUS** 1/4 TURN

Balance shaft assembly — 2.5L engine

85613201

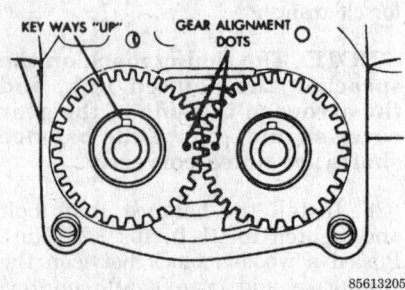

Balance shaft gear timing — 2.5L engine

28. Place a shim 1.0mm thick by 70mm long between the chain and tensioner.

29. Apply firm hand pressure behind the adjustment slot and tighten adjustment bolt first, followed by the pivot screw to 105 inch lbs. (12 Nm). Remove the shim.

30. Install the chain guide making sure the tab on the guide fits into slot on the gear cover. Install nut/washer and tighten to 105 inch lbs. (12 Nm).

31. Install the chain cover and tighten screws to 105 inch lbs. (12 Nm).

32. Apply a 1.5mm diameter bead of RTV gasket material to retainer sealing surface. Install retainer assembly.

33. Install the crankshaft sprocket and timing belt.

34. Install the timing cover.

Piston and Connecting Rod

POSITIONING

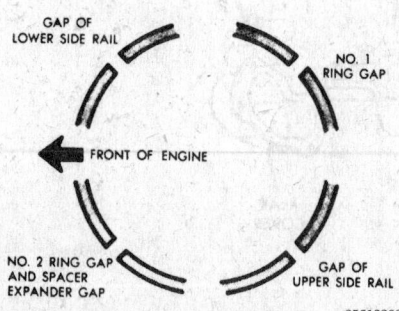

Piston ring positioning

DIESEL ENGINE MECHANICAL

NOTE: Disconnecting the negative battery cable on some vehicles may interfere with the functions of the on-board computer systems and may require the computer to undergo a relearning process, once the negative battery cable is reconnected.

Engine

REMOVAL AND INSTALLATION

——— CAUTION ———
This engine has a dry weight of 880 lbs. Make sure the engine removal equipment is rated adequately, or personal injury may result.

1. Scribe location of hood hinge bolts for proper alignment and remove the hood.

2. Disconnect the cables from the battery and from the engine. Remove the battery from the vehicle.

3. Drain the coolant.

4. Remove the radiator, shroud, belt, fan and all related parts.

5. Remove the air inlet tube from the turbocharger and the air intake housing. Remove the exhaust pipe from the turbocharger outlet flange. Remove the inlet duct from the turbocharger and inlet duct. Remove the outlet duct.

6. Remove the air conditioner compressor and set aside.

7. Disconnect and remove the alternator and all other electrical connections to the engine.

8. Disconnect the accelerator linkage, the speed control linkage and the throttle valve linkage.

9. Raise the vehicle and support safely. Remove the starter.

10. If equipped with automatic transmission, remove the torque converter bolts and remove the lower bellhousing bolts. If equipped with manual transmission, remove the transmission.

11. Drain the oil from the engine.

12. Disconnect the transmission oil cooler lines from their brackets, if equipped.

13. Lower vehicle, disconnect and plug the fuel lines. Disconnect the power steering lines and vacuum pump lines.

14. Hoist the engine slightly using the lifting eyes and support the transmission if still installed.

15. Remove the motor mounts.

16. Remove the upper bellhousing bolts.

17. Remove the engine from the vehicle.

To install:

18. Position the engine in the engine compartment and install the motor mounts. Torque the nuts and bolts to 57 ft. lbs. (77 Nm).

19. Install the bellhousing bolts and torque converter bolts, if equipped. Install the manual transmission, if equipped.

20. Install the starter.

21. Connect the exhaust pipe.

22. Connect the transmission oil cooler lines to their brackets, if equipped.

23. Connect the fuel lines.

24. Connect the power steering lines.

25. Connect all engine driven accessories.

26. Connect the accelerator linkage.

27. Connect the throttle linkage to the control lever.

28. Mount the air conditioner compressor.

29. Connect the alternator and all other electrical connections to the engine.

30. Install the intake and exhaust pipes and air ducts to the turbocharger and intercooler.

31. Install the fan and all related parts, shroud and radiator.

32. Fill the engine with the proper amount of diesel engine oil.

33. Fill the radiator with coolant.

34. Install and connect the battery cables. Set all adjustments to specifications and check for leaks.

Engine Mounts

REMOVAL AND INSTALLATION

Rear Mount

1. Disconnect negative battery cable.

2. Raise and safely support vehicle. Remove skid plate , if equipped.

3. Install transmission jack into position and raise transmission slightly.

4. Remove rear mount throughbolt and nut.

5. Remove the flange nuts from the crossmember support bracket.

6. Raise rear of transmission and remove insulator flange nuts and remove mount. If necessary, remove at-

taching bolts holding transmission support bracket to transmission.

To install:

7. Install attaching bolts holding transmission support bracket to transmission.

8. Position insulator in transmission support bracket and install through-bolt.

9. With insulator installed in a level position tighten through bolt nut to 50 ft. lbs.

10. Position crossmember support bracket into insulator. Install flange nuts and tighten to 30 ft. lbs.

11. Using transmission jack, lower the insulator and crossmember support bracket onto the crossmember. Tighten flange nuts to 30 ft. lbs.

12. Remove transmission jack, install skid plate if removed, lower vehicle and reconnect negative battery cable.

Front Mount

1. Disconnect negative battery cable. Remove skid plate, if equipped.

2. Position fan assembly to insure clearance for radiator and top hose when engine is moved. Install an engine support fixture.

3. Raise and safely support vehicle.

4. Remove nuts from front engine mounting brackets.

5. Raise engine with support fixture far enough to remove mounts, remove remaining bolts and mounts.

To install:

6. Install mounts to engine block.

7. Lower engine to original position and insert bolts through mounting brackets.

8. Install nuts and tighten to 75 ft. lbs. Install skid plate, if removed.

9. Lower vehicle and remove engine support fixture. Reconnect negative battery cable.

Cylinder Head

REMOVAL AND INSTALLATION

1. Disconnect the negative battery cable.

2. Drain the coolant.

3. Disconnect the radiator hose and heater hoses.

4. Remove the turbocharger and air crossover.

5. Remove the exhaust manifold.

6. Remove all fuel lines from the injection pump and remove injector nozzles. Remove the fuel filter.

7. Remove the valve covers.

8. Remove the rocker arms and pushrods.

9. Unbolt the cylinder head from the block. Remove the cylinder head.

10. Inspect the coolant passages. A large accumulation of rust or lime will require service to the block.

11. Inspect the surface of the head for flatness. The maximum variation is 0.0004 in. (0.010mm) within any 2 in. diameter area or 0.012 in. (0.30mm) overall end-to-end or side-to-side.

To install:

12. Thoroughly clean and dry the mating surfaces of the head and block. Position the new head gasket on the dowels.

13. Install the head onto the dowels on the block.

14. Lubricate the pushrod sockets and install the pushrods and rocker arms.

15. Clean, dry and lightly lubricate the head bolts. Install and torque in sequence first to 66 ft. lbs. (90 Nm) and then to 89 ft. lbs. (120 Nm). Tighten an additional 90 degrees. Tighten the 8 mm bolts to 18 ft. lbs. (24 Nm).

16. Install the rocker arm pedestal bolts. Torque to 18 ft. lbs. (24 Nm).

17. Adjust the valve clearance.

18. Install the valve covers with new gaskets. Torque the bolts to 18 ft. lbs. (24 Nm).

19. Install all fuel lines and the fuel filter.

20. Install the exhaust manifold.

21. Install the turbocharger and air crossover.

22. Connect the radiator hose and heater hoses.

23. Fill the radiator with coolant.

24. Connect the negative battery cable, set all adjustments to specifications and check for leaks.

79111052

Cylinder head bolt torque sequence — 5.9L diesel engine

Valve Lifters/Tappet

REMOVAL AND INSTALLATION

1. Disconnect negative battery cable.

2. Remove the valve covers.

3. Drain the cooling system. Remove the rocker lever assemblies and pushrods.

4. Remove the drive belts and fan hub assembly.

5. Remove the vibration damper.

6. Remove the gear housing cover. Remove the lift pump.

7. Insert the dowel tool through the push tube holes and into the top of each tappet. Pull the tappets up and wrap a rubber band around the top of the dowel rods. This will prevent the tappets from dropping into the engine.

8. Align the engine timing marks and remove the bolts in the thrust plate. Remove the camshaft, gear and thrust plate.

9. Insert a trough the full length of the cam bore. Make sure the trough is in the position to catch any falling tappets. Cummins tappet changing tool 3822513 or equivalent, should be used for this procedure.

10. Remove the wooden dowel and catch the tappet in trough. Move the trough so the tappet falls over in the bottom of the trough. Mark each tappet for proper assembly, each tappet must be installed into their original location.

11. Carefully pull the trough and tappet from the cam bore. Repeat as needed to remove each tappet. Inspect the tappet socket, stem and face for excess wear, cracks and other damage. Minimum tappet stem diameter is 0.627 inch (15.925mm). If out of limits, replace tappet.

To install:

12. Install the trough into the cam bore. Feed the installation tool down the tappet bore and into the trough.

13. Feed the installation tool cord through the cam bores. Carefully pull the trough and installation tool out the front.

14. Lubricate the tappets with lubriplate 105 or equivalent.

15. Insert the installation tool into the tappet. Place the tappet and tool in the trough and slide the trough back into the cam bore.

16. Align the tappet below the proper bore and lift the tappet into the bore. After the tappet is in position, rotate the trough 180 degrees to hold tappet in position while the installation tool is removed. Install the dowel and rubber band to hold tappet

in the bore and repeat process as required.

17. Lubricate camshaft lobes, journals and thrust washer and install camshaft into bore. Install lift pump, gear housing cover and vibration damper.

18. Install fan hub assembly and drive belts.

19. Install pushrods, rocker lever assemblies and valve covers.

20. Reconnect negative battery cable, refill coolant and oil as required. Start and check for leaks.

Valve Lash

ADJUSTMENT

1. Perform the adjustment when the engine is below 140°F (60°C).

2. Disconnect the negative battery cable.

3. Use the timing pin to locate TDC for cylinder No. 1. Disengage the pin.

4. Remove the valve covers.

5. With the engine is in this position, the first group of valves may be adjusted:

No. 1 intake: 0.10 in. (0.254mm)
No. 1 exhaust: 0.20 in. (0.508mm)
No. 2 intake: 0.10 in. (0.254mm)
No. 3 exhaust: 0.20 in. (0.508mm)
No. 4 intake: 0.10 in. (0.254mm)
No. 5 exhaust: 0.20 in. (0.508mm)

6. Mark the pulley and rotate the engine 360 degrees.

7. With the engine is in this position, the second group of valves may be adjusted:

No. 2 exhaust: 0.20 in. (0.508mm)
No. 3 intake: 0.10 in. (0.254mm)
No. 4 exhaust: 0.20 in. (0.508mm)
No. 5 intake: 0.10 in. (0.254mm)
No. 6 intake: 0.10 in. (0.254mm)
No. 6 exhaust: 0.20 in. (0.508mm)

8. Torque all locknuts to 18 ft. lbs. (24 Nm).

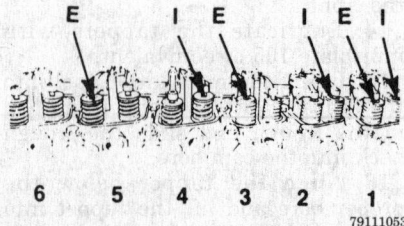

First group of valves to be adjusted — 5.9L diesel engine

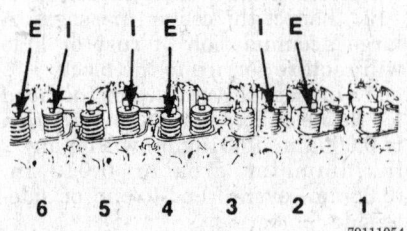

Second group of valves to be adjusted — 5.9L diesel engine

9. Install the valve covers with new gaskets. Torque the bolts to 18 ft. lbs. (24 Nm).

10. Connect the negative battery cable.

Rocker Arm and Pedestal Assembly

REMOVAL AND INSTALLATION

1. Disconnect the negative battery cable. Remove the crossover tube.

2. Remove the valve covers.

3. Loosen the adjusting screw locknuts. Loosen the screws until they stop.

4. Remove the 8mm bolt and 12mm head bolt from the pedestal.

5. Remove the pedestal and rocker arm assembly. Remove the pushrods if necessary.

6. Remove the retaining ring and thrust washer.

7. Remove the rocker arm from the pedestal.

NOTE: Do not disassemble the rocker shaft and pedestal; they must be replaced as an assembly.

8. Remove the locknut and adjusting screw from the rocker arm.

To install:

9. Install the adjusting screw and locknut.

10. Lubricate the shaft with oil and install the rocker arm to the shaft. Install the thrust washer and snapring.

11. Install the pushrods to the engine, if removed.

12. Install the pedestal and rocker arm assembly to the head aligning the dowel in the pedestal with the dowel bore in the head. If the pushrod is holding the pedestal off the head, turn the engine until the pedestal will set on the head without interference.

13. Lubricate the threads of the bolt with oil. Install and torque first to 29 ft. lbs. (40 Nm), then to 62 ft. Lbs. (85 Nm) and finally to 93 ft. lbs. (126 Nm). If all of the pedestals were removed, follow the entire head bolt torque sequence including those head bolts that were not removed in this procedure.

14. Tighten the 8mm bolts to 18 ft. lbs. (24 Nm).

15. Adjust the valves.

16. Install the valve cover with a new gasket. Torque the bolts to 18 ft. lbs. (24 Nm).

17. Connect the negative battery cable.

Intake Manifold Cover

REMOVAL AND INSTALLATION

1. Disconnect negative battery cable.

2. Remove the intercooler outlet duct from air inlet tube, if equipped.

3. Remove the 4 bolts that attach the air crossover to the intake manifold. Loosen the lower throttle control bracket mounting bolt and move the bracket away from the engine.

4. Loosen the hose clamps on the turbocharger end of the crossover tube and remove the tube and gasket. Cover the turbocharger opening with a clean shop towel.

5. Disconnect the electrical wiring from the intake manifold heater, remove the heater and remove the gasket.

6. Disconnect the charge air temperature sensor, fuel heater ground wire and the air temperature switch from the intake manifold cover.

7. Remove the manifold intake cover and gasket. Clean all sealing surfaces.

To install:

8. Using a new gasket install the intake manifold cover.

9. Connect the charge air temperature sensor, fuel heater ground wire and the air temperature switch to the intake manifold cover.

10. Some of the intake manifold bolt holes are drilled through and must be sealed. Apply liquid teflon sealant to the bolts. Install the intake manifold cover bolts and tighten to 18 ft. lbs. (24 Nm).

11. Clean the gasket mounting surface and install a new gasket between the intake manifold cover and the air intake heater.

12. Install the intake manifold heater and connect the wiring.

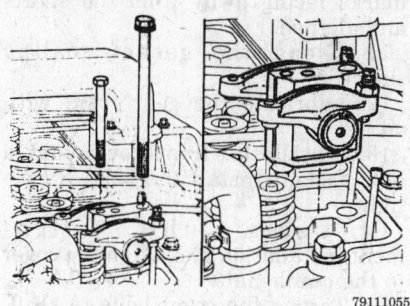

Removing the rocker arm and pedestal assembly — 5.9L diesel engine

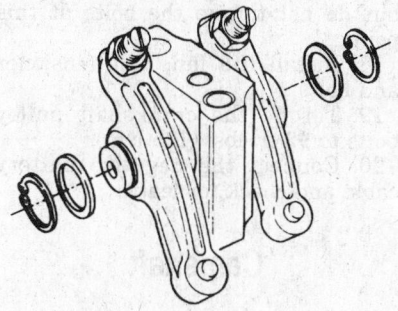

Removing or installing the rocker arm from the pedestal — 5.9L diesel engine

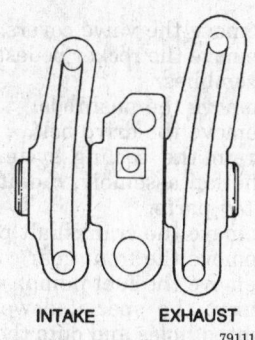

INTAKE   EXHAUST

Proper rocker arm installation — 5.9L diesel engine

13. Remove the towel from the turbocharger opening and install the air crossover tube and gasket. Tighten the hose clamps.

14. Rotate the throttle control bracket back into place. Torque all mounting bolts to 18 ft. lbs. (24 Nm).

15. Attach the throttle rod to the throttle lever.

16. Connect the negative battery cable.

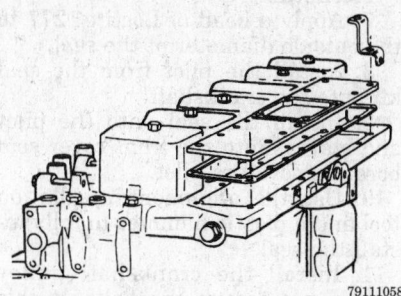

Intake manifold cover and gasket — 5.9L diesel engine

Exhaust Manifold

REMOVAL AND INSTALLATION

1. Disconnect negative battery cable.

2. Disconnect air intake and exhaust pipes.

3. Disconnect the turbocharger oil supply line and the oil drain tube from the turbocharger.

4. Disconnect the intercooler inlet duct from the turbocharger. Remove the turbocharger and gasket.

5. Remove the cab heater supply and return lines. Remove the exhaust manifold and gasket. Clean all sealing surfaces.

To install:

6. Install manifold and new gasket. Tighten bolts in sequence to 32 ft. lbs. (32 Nm).

7. Install turbocharger. Tighten the turbocharger mounting nuts to 24 ft. lbs. (32 Nm).

8. Position the intercooler inlet duct to the turbocharger. Tighten the clamp to 72 inch lbs. (8 Nm).

9. Position the air intake pipe and the exhaust pipe onto the turbocharger and tighten clamps to 72 inch lbs. (8 Nm).

10. Install oil drain tube and oil supply line to the turbocharger.

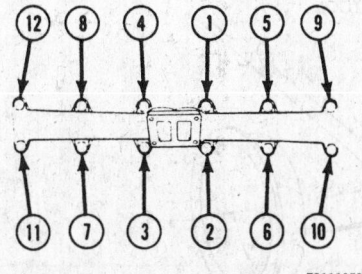

Exhaust manifold torque sequence — 5.9L diesel engine

Tighten the drain tube bolts to 18 ft. lbs. (24 Nm). Tighten the oil supply line fitting to 11 ft. lbs. (15 Nm).

11. Connect the cab heater supply and return lines. Tighten line nuts to 18 ft. lbs. (24 Nm).

12. Reconnect the negative battery cable, start the engine and check for exhaust leaks.

Turbocharger

REMOVAL AND INSTALLATION

1. Disconnect negative battery cable.

2. Disconnect air intake and exhaust pipes.

3. Disconnect the turbocharger oil supply line and the oil drain tube from the turbocharger.

4. Disconnect the intercooler inlet duct from the turbocharger. Remove the turbocharger and gasket.

To install:

5. Inspect the mounting surface for cracks and damage. Install the turbocharger. Apply anti-seize compound to the mounting studs and tighten the turbocharger mounting nuts to 24 ft. lbs. (32 Nm).

6. Position the intercooler inlet duct to the turbocharger. Tighten the clamp to 72 inch lbs. (8 Nm).

7. Position the air intake pipe and the exhaust pipe onto the turbocharger and tighten clamps to 72 inch lbs. (8 Nm).

8. New turbochargers must be prelubricated with fresh engine oil before operation. To do so, poor 2–3 oz. of oil into the supply fitting and rotate the turbine wheel to circulate the oil. Install oil drain tube and oil supply line to the turbocharger. Tighten the drain tube bolts to 18 ft. lbs. (24 Nm). Tighten the oil supply line fitting to 11 ft. lbs. (15 Nm).

9. Connect the cab heater supply and return lines. Tighten line nuts to 18 ft. lbs. (24 Nm).

10. Reconnect the negative battery cable, start the engine and check for leaks.

Timing Gear Front Cover

REMOVAL AND INSTALLATION

1. Disconnect the negative battery cable.

2. Remove the fan drive assembly and belt.

3. Remove the belt tensioner.

4. Remove the oil fill tube and adaptor.

5. Remove the crankshaft pulley.

6. Remove all bolts that attach the cover to the gear housing.

7. Gently pry the gear cover away from the housing and remove from the engine.

To install:

8. Clean the gasket sealing surfaces.

9. Lubricate the gear train with oil.

10. Thoroughly clean and dry the seal area of the crankshaft.

11. Install the front cover and a new gasket. Install the bolts finger-tight.

12. Using the alignment/installation tool, align the cover to the crankshaft.

13. Torque the cover bolts to 18 ft. lbs. (24 Nm). Remove the tool.

14. Install the oil fill tube and adapter.

15. Install the crankshaft pulley but do not torque the bolts at this point.

16. Install the fan, belt tensioner and belt.

17. Torque the crankshaft pulley bolts to 92 ft. lbs. (125 Nm).

18. Connect the negative battery cable and check for leaks.

Front Cover Oil Seal

REPLACEMENT

1. Disconnect the negative battery cable.

2. Remove the drive belt.

3. Remove the crankshaft pulley.

4. Drill two ⅛ in. holes into the seal face, 180 degrees apart.

5. Using a slide hammer with a No. 10 sheetmetal screw, pull the seal out alternating from side to side until the seal is out.

6. Thoroughly clean and dry the crankshaft.

To install:

7. Apply a bead of Loctite®277 to the outside diameter of the seal.

8. Install the pilot from the seal kit onto the crankshaft.

9. Install the seal onto the pilot and start it into the front cover seal bore. Remove the pilot.

10. Use the alignment/installation tool and a plastic hammer to fully install the seal.

11. Install the crankshaft pulley but do not torque the bolts at this point.

12. Install the drive belt.

13. Torque the crankshaft pulley bolts to 92 ft. lbs. (125 Nm).

14. Connect the negative battery cable and check for leaks.

Timing Gears

REMOVAL AND INSTALLATION

1. Disconnect the negative battery cable.

2. Remove the fan drive assembly and belt.

3. Remove the belt tensioner.

4. Remove the oil fill tube and adaptor.

5. Remove the crankshaft pulley.

6. Remove all bolts that attach the cover to the gear housing.

7. Gently pry the gear cover away from the housing and remove from the engine.

8. Using a puller, remove the camshaft gear from the camshaft. Remove the key and replace.

9. Remove the crankshaft gear using heavy duty puller. Remove and install new alignment pin leaving it protrude 0.063 inch above crankshaft surface.

To install:

10. Heat the camshaft gear and crankshaft gear to 250°F (121°C) for 45 minutes. Lubricate the gear mount surface with Lubriplate® 105. Install the gears with the timing

ALIGNMENT/INSTALLATION TOOL

Aligning the cover with the crankshaft — 5.9L diesel engine

marks facing away from the shafts and aligned.

11. Clean the gasket sealing surfaces.

12. Lubricate the gear train with oil.

13. Install the front cover and a new gasket. Install the bolts finger-tight.

14. Using the alignment/installation tool, align the cover to the crankshaft.

15. Torque the cover bolts to 18 ft. lbs. (24 Nm). Remove the tool.

16. Install the oil fill tube and adapter.

17. Install the crankshaft pulley but do not torque the bolts at this point.

18. Install the fan, belt tensioner and belt.

19. Torque the crankshaft pulley bolts to 92 ft. lbs. (125 Nm).

20. Connect the negative battery cable and check for leaks.

Camshaft

REMOVAL AND INSTALLATION

1. Disconnect the negative battery cable.

2. Remove the valve covers.

3. Remove the rocker pedestal and arm assemblies.

4. Remove the pushrods.

5. Remove the drive belt.

6. Drain the cooling system. Remove the fan assembly, radiator and all related parts.

7. Remove the crankshaft pulley.

8. Remove the front gear cover.

9. Remove the fuel pump.

10. Insert the special dowels into the pushrod holes and onto the top of each lifter. When properly installed, the dowels can be use to hold the tappets up securely. Wrap rubber bands around the top of the dowels to prevent them from dropping down.

11. Rotate the crankshaft to align the crankshaft to camshaft timing marks.

12. Remove the bolts from the thrust plate.

13. Remove the camshaft and thrust plate.

14. Press the gear from the camshaft and remove the key.

To install:

15. Install the key on the camshaft.

16. Heat the camshaft gear to 250°F (121°C) for 45 minutes. Lubricate the gear mount surface with Lubriplate® 105. Install the gear to the camshaft with the timing marks facing away from the shaft.

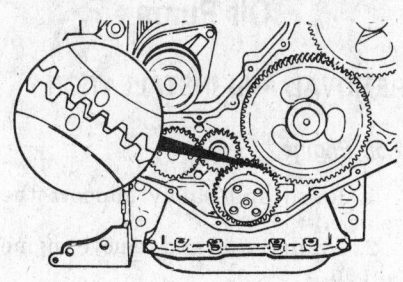

Crankshaft and camshaft gear timing marks — 5.9L diesel engine

17. Lubricate the camshaft bores, lobes, journals and thrust washer with Lubriplate® 105.

NOTE: Do not push the camshaft in too far or it may dislodge the plug in the rear of the camshaft bore, possibly creating a leak.

18. Install the camshaft and thrust washer so the **E** timing mark on the injection pump gear aligns with the **C** timing mark on the camshaft gear and the timing mark on the crankshaft gear align with those on the camshaft gear.

19. Install the thrust washer bolts and torque to 18 ft. lbs. (24 Nm).

20. Check the endplay of the camshaft. The specification is 0.006–0.010 in. (0.152–0.254mm).

21. Check the backlash of the camshaft gear. The specification is 0.003–0.013 in. (0.080–0.330mm).

22. Install the tappets and pushrods.

23. Install the rocker pedestal and arm assemblies.

24. Install the front cover and crankshaft pulley.

25. Install the drive belt and fan assembly.

26. Install the fuel pump.

27. Adjust the valves.

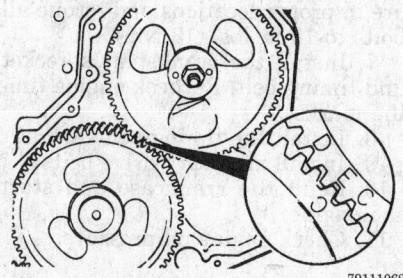

Camshaft and injection pump gear timing marks — 5.9L diesel engine

28. Install the valve covers. Refill cooling system.

29. Connect the negative battery cable and check for leaks.

Piston and Connecting Rod

POSITIONING

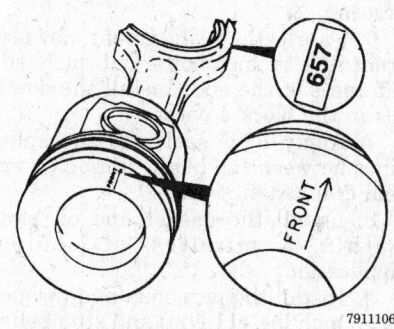

The "FRONT" marking and the number on the rod should be oriented as shown — 5.9L diesel engine

ENGINE LUBRICATION

Oil Pan

REMOVAL AND INSTALLATION

2.5L Engine

1. Raise and safely support the vehicle. Drain the oil pan.

2. Remove the oil pan attaching bolts and remove oil pan.

3. Clean oil pan and engine block gasket surfaces thoroughly.

To install:

4. Apply RTV sealant to oil pan rail at the front seal retainer parting line.

5. Attach the oil pan side gaskets using heavy grease or RTV to hold the gasket in place.

6. Install the new oil pan seals and apply RTV sealant to the ends of the seals at junction where seals and gasket meets.

7. Install oil pan and tighten M8 screws to 15 ft. lbs. (20 Nm), and M6 screws to 105 inch lbs. (12 Nm).

3.0L Engine

1. Raise and safely support the vehicle. Drain the oil pan.

2. Remove the oil pan attaching bolts and remove oil pan.

3. Clean oil pan and engine block gasket surfaces thoroughly.

4. Apply RTV sealant to oil pan.

5. Install oil pan to engine and tighten screws in sequence, working from the center toward the ends, to 50 inch lbs.

3.3L and 3.8L Engines

1. Disconnect the negative battery cable.

2. Raise the vehicle and support safely.

3. Remove the torque converter bolt access cover, if equipped.

4. Drain the engine oil.

5. Remove the oil pan retaining screws and remove the oil pan and gasket.

To install:

6. Thoroughly clean and dry all sealing surfaces, bolts and bolt holes.

7. Apply silicone sealer to the chain cover to block mating seam and the rear main seal retainer to block seam, if equipped.

8. Install a new pan gasket or apply silicone sealer to the sealing surface of the pan and install to the engine.

9. Install the retaining screws and torque to 200 inch lbs. (23 Nm).

10. Install the torque converter bolt access cover, if equipped. Lower the vehicle.

11. Install the dipstick. Fill the engine with the proper amount of oil.

12. Connect the negative battery cable and check for leaks.

3.9L, 5.2L and 5.9L Engines

1. Disconnect the negative battery cable.

2. Remove the engine oil dipstick and engine controller.

3. On Vans, remove the engine cover. Remove the air intake duct.

4. Raise the vehicle and support safely. Drain the engine oil.

5. Remove the transmission support braces.

6. Remove the starter and torque converter inspection cover, if equipped.

7. Remove the oxygen sensor and air injection tube, if equipped.

8. Lower the exhaust crossover pipe.

9. Remove the nut on right engine mount. Loosen nut on left mount. Remove the rear transmission insulator bolts.

10. Using the proper equipment, support the transmission.

11. Raise and safely support the vehicle. Raise the engine and transmis-

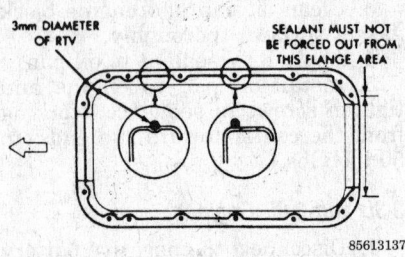

Oil pan RTV sealer application — 3.0L engine

85613137

sion as required to allow for pan removal.

12. Remove the oil pan bolts and remove the pan from the vehicle.

To install:

13. Using a new pan gasket set, apply a thin bead of sealer to the 4 corners where the rubber seals and cork gasket meet.

14. Thoroughly clean and dry all bolts and bolt holes. Install the pan and tighten the bolts to 75 inch lbs. (4 Nm), then retighten to 200 inch lbs. (23 Nm).

15. Lower the engine and transmission and install the engine mount nuts and transmission mount bolts.

16. Install the exhaust crossover pipe. Install the oxygen sensor and air injection tube, if equipped.

17. Install the torque converter inspection cover, if equipped. Install the starter and support braces. Lower the vehicle.

18. Install the dipstick, air intake duct and engine cover, if removed.

19. Fill the engine with the proper amount of oil.

20. Connect the negative battery cable and check for leaks.

8.0L Engine

1. Disconnect the negative battery cable.

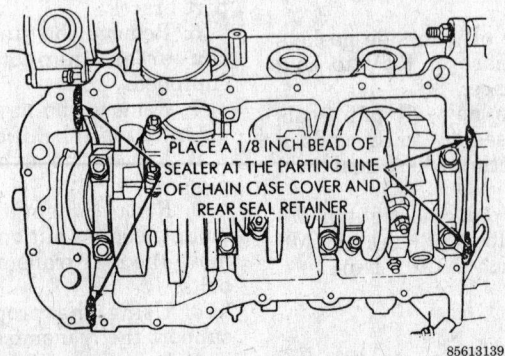

PLACE A 1/8 INCH BEAD OF SEALER AT THE PARTING LINE OF CHAIN CASE COVER AND REAR SEAL RETAINER

85613139

Oil pan sealing — 3.3L and 3.8L engines

2. Raise the vehicle and support safely. Drain the engine oil.

3. Remove the left engine-to-transmission strut.

4. Remove the oil pan and 1-piece gasket. The engine may have to be raised slightly on 2WD vehicles.

To install:

5. Clean the gasket mating surfaces, oil pan and pump pickup screen.

6. Fabricate 4 alignment dowels from $5/16$ x $1\frac{1}{2}$ inch bolts. Cut the head off and slot the end. Install the dowels in the block 4 corners.

7. Apply RTV sealer to the split lines between the block, timing cover and crankshaft seal.

8. Install the gasket and oil pan within 3 minutes of sealer application.

9. Install the pan bolts and torque to 96 inch lbs. (11 Nm) and stud bolts to 144 inch lbs. (16 Nm). Remove the dowel pins and install the correct bolts. Torque the 4 corner bolts to 144 inch lbs. (16 Nm).

5.9L Diesel Engine

1. Remove the engine from the vehicle and place on an engine stand.

2. Drain the engine oil.

3. Remove the oil pan and gasket.

To install:

4. Clean the gasket mating surfaces, oil pan and pump pickup screen.

5. Apply RTV sealer to the split lines between the block, timing cover and crankshaft seal.

6. Install the gasket and oil pan within 3 minutes of sealer application.

7. Install the pan bolts and torque to 18 ft. lbs. (24 Nm). Install the oil drain plug and torque to 60 ft. lbs. (80 Nm).

8. Refill the engine with oil, start the engine and check for leaks.

Oil Pump

REMOVAL AND INSTALLATION

2.5L Engine

1. Raise and safely support the vehicle.

2. Drain the oil and remove engine oil pan.

3. Remove the pump mounting bolts.

4. Pull the pump down and out of the engine.

To install:

5. Prime, by filling pump with fresh oil. Check crankshaft/intermediate shaft timing and oil pump drive alignment. Adjust if necessary.

6. Install pump and rotate back and forth slightly to ensure full surface contact of pump and block.

7. While holding pump in fully seated position, install pump mounting bolts. Torque to 15 ft. lbs. (20 Nm).

8. Install engine oil pan.

9. Refill crankcase, start engine.

10. Check engine oil pressure.

3.0L Engine

The oil pump assembly used on this engine is mounted at the front of the crankshaft. The oil pump also retains the crankshaft front oil seal.

1. Remove accessory drive belts.

2. Remove the timing belt cover and timing belt.

3. Remove the crankshaft sprocket.

4. Remove the oil pump mounting bolts (5), and remove oil pump assembly. Mark mounting bolts for proper installation during reassembly.

To install:

5. Clean the oil pump and engine block gasket surfaces thoroughly.

6. Position a new gasket on pump assembly and install on cylinder block. Make sure correct length bolts are in proper locations and torque all bolts to 10 ft. lbs. (13 Nm).

7. Install the crankshaft sprocket and timing belt. Recheck engine timing marks.

8. Install the timing belt covers.

9. Install accessory drive belts.

10. Refill the crankcase and start the engine.

11. Check engine oil pressure.

3.3L and 3.8L Engines

1. Disconnect the negative battery cable. Remove the dipstick.

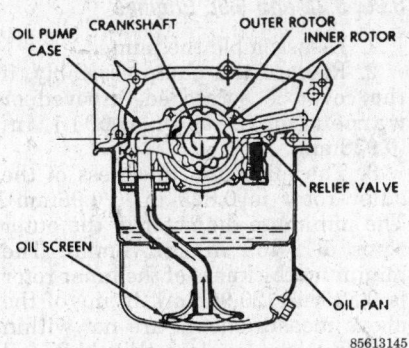

Oil pump components — 3.0L engine

2. Raise the vehicle and support safely. Drain the oil and remove the oil pan.

3. Remove the oil pickup.

4. Remove the chain case cover.

5. Disassemble the oil pump as required.

To install:

6. Assemble the pump. Torque the cover screws to 10 ft. lbs. (12 Nm).

7. Prime the oil pump by filling the rotor cavity with fresh oil and turning the rotors until oil comes out the pressure port. Repeat a few times until no air bubbles are present.

8. Install the chain case cover.

9. Clean out the oil pickup or replace as required. Replace the oil pickup O-ring and install the pickup to the pump.

10. Install the oil pan.

11. Install the dipstick. Fill the engine with the proper amount of oil.

12. Connect the negative battery cable and check the oil pressure.

3.9L, 5.2L and 5.9L Engines

1. Disconnect the negative battery cable.

2. Remove the oil pan.

3. Remove the screen.

4. Unbolt the oil pump from the rear main bearing cap and remove it from the vehicle.

To install:

5. Prime the pump by pouring clean oil into the pump intake and turning the driveshaft until oil comes out the pressure port. Repeat a few times until no air bubbles are present. Install the oil pump with a rotating motion to ensure proper pump driveshaft engagement.

6. Hold the pump flush against the main cap and finger-tighten the attaching bolts.

7. Torque the bolts to 30 ft. lbs. (41 Nm).

8. Install the screen.

9. Install the oil pan with a new gasket.

10. Connect the negative battery cable and check the oil pressure.

8.0L Engine

1. Disconnect the negative battery cable and drain the engine oil.

2. Remove the timing chain cover.

3. Remove the pressure relief plug, gasket, spring and valve.

4. Remove the oil pump cover and pump gears.

To install:

5. Install the pump gears and pack with petroleum jelly or lubriplate. Torque the cover bolts to 125 inch lbs. (14 Nm).

6. Make sure the inner ring moves freely after the cover is installed.

7. Install the timing cover.

8. Lubricate the relief valve with engine oil. Install the valve, spring, gasket and plug. Torque the plug to 15 ft. lbs. (20 Nm).

9. Install a new oil filter, filled with clean engine oil.

10. Install the remaining components, fill with engine oil, start the engine and check for leaks.

5.9L Diesel Engine

1. Disconnect the negative battery cable.

2. Remove the drive belt.

3. Remove the radiator.

4. Remove the fan assembly.

5. Remove the oil fill tube and adaptor.

6. Remove the crankshaft pulley and damper.

7. Remove the front cover.

8. Remove the 4 pump mounting bolts and remove the pump from the block.

To install:

9. Prime the pump by pouring clean oil into the pump intake and turning the driveshaft until oil comes out the pressure port. Repeat a few times until no air bubbles are present. Align the idler gear pin with the locating bore in the block and install the pump.

10. Tighten the mounting bolts in the proper sequence to 44 inch lbs. (5 Nm), then repeat the sequence torquing to 18 ft. lbs. (24 Nm).

NOTE: When the pump is correctly installed, the flange on the pump should not touch the block; the back plate on the pump seats against the bottom of the bore.

11. Measure the backlash of the idler to pump drive gears. The specification is 0.003–0.013 in. (0.08–0.33mm).

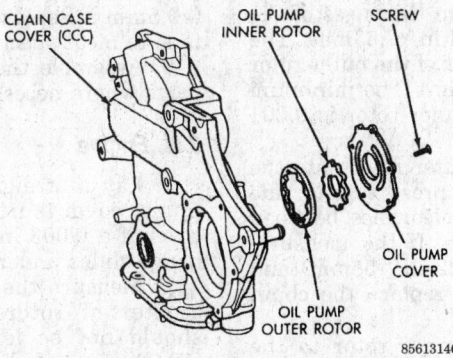

Oil pump assembly — 3.3L and 3.8L engines

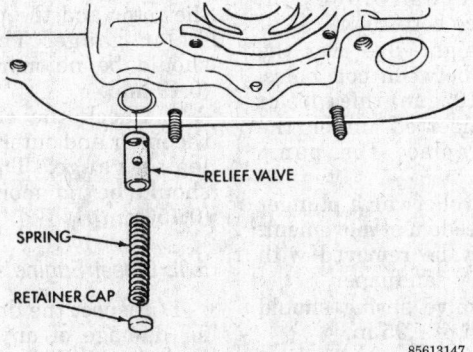

Oil pressure relief valve — 3.3L and 3.8L engines

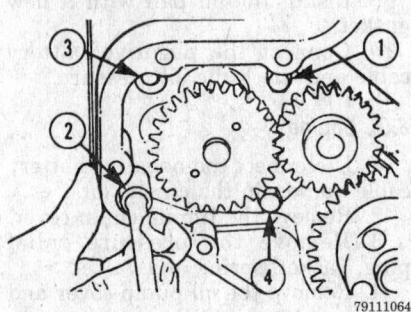

Oil pump torque sequence — 5.9L diesel engine

79111064

12. Measure the backlash of the idler to crankshaft gears. The specification is 0.003–0.013 in. (0.08–0.33mm).

13. Install the front cover, crankshaft damper and pulley.

14. Install the oil fill tube and adaptor.

15. Install the fan assembly, radiator and drive belt.

16. Connect the negative battery cable and check the oil pressure.

CHECKING

2.5L Engine

1. Remove the cover from the oil pump.

2. Check endplay of the inner rotor using a feeler gauge and a straight-edge placed across the pump body. The specification is 0.001–0.004 in. (0.03–0.09mm).

3. Measure the clearance between the inner and outer rotors. The maximum clearance is 0.008 in. (0.20mm).

4. Measure the clearance between the outer rotor and the pump body. The maximum clearance is 0.014 in. (0.35mm).

5. The minimum thickness of the outer rotor is 0.944 in. (23.96mm). The minimum diameter of the outer rotor is 2.77 in. (62.70mm). The minimum thickness of the inner rotor is 0.943 in. (23.95mm).

6. Check the cover for warpage. The maximum allowable is 0.003 in. (0.076mm).

7. Check the pressure relief valve for damage. The spring's free length specification is 1.95 in. (49.50mm).

8. Assemble the outer rotor with the larger chamfered edge in the pump body. Torque the cover screws to 10 ft. lbs. (12 Nm).

3.0L Engine

1. Remove the rear cover.

2. Remove the pump rotors and inspect the case for excessive wear.

3. Measure the diameter of the inner rotor hub that sits in the case. Measure the inside diameter of the inner rotor hub bore. Subtract the first measurement from the second; if the result is over 0.006 in. (0.15mm), replace the oil pump assembly.

4. Measure the clearance between the outer rotor and the case. The specification is 0.004–0.007 in. (0.10–0.18mm).

5. Check the side clearance of the rotors using a feeler gauge and a straight-edge placed across the case. The specification is 0.0015–0.0035 in. (0.04–0.09mm).

6. Check the relief plunger and spring for damage and breakage.

7. Install the rear cover to the case.

3.3L and 3.8L Engines

1. Thoroughly clean and dry all parts. The mating surface of the chain case cover should be smooth. Replace the pump cover if it is scratched or grooved.

2. Lay a straight-edge across the pump cover surface. If a 0.076mm feeler gauge can be inserted between the cover and the straight-edge, the cover should be replaced.

3. The maximum thickness of the outer rotor is 0.301 in. (7.63mm). The minimum diameter of the outer rotor is 3.14 in. (79.78mm). The minimum thickness of the inner rotor is 0.301 in. (7.64m).

4. Install the outer rotor onto the chain case cover, press to one side and measure the clearance between the rotor and case. If the measurement exceeds 0.022 in. (56mm) and the rotor is good, replace the chain case cover.

5. Install the inner rotor to the chain case cover and measure the clearance between the rotors. If the clearance exceeds 0.008 in. (0.203mm), replace both rotors.

6. Place a straight-edge over the chain case cover between bolt holes. If a 0.004 in. (0.102mm) thick feeler gauge can be inserted under the straight-edge, replace the pump assembly.

7. Inspect the relief valve plunger for scoring and freedom of movement. Small marks may be removed with 400-grit wet or dry sandpaper.

8. The relief valve spring should have a free length of 1.95 in.

9. Assemble the pump using new parts where necessary.

3.9L, 5.2L and 5.9L Engines

1. Disassemble the pump.

2. Replace the pump assembly, if the cover is scratched, grooved or warped more than 0.0015 in. (0.038mm).

3. The minimum thickness of the outer rotor is 0.825 in. (20.96mm). The minimum diameter of the outer rotor is 2.469 in. (62.70mm). The minimum thickness of the inner rotor is 0.825 in. (20.96mm). If any of the above measurements are not within specifications, replace the shaft and both rotors.

4. The maximum clearance between the outer rotor and the pump body is 0.014 in. (0.356mm). Replace the pump assembly, if not within specifications.

5. Install the inner rotor and place a straight-edge across the bolt holes. If a feeler gauge of 0.004 in. (0.101mm) or more fits, replace the pump assembly.

6. The maximum clearance between the rotors is 0.080 in. (0.254mm). Replace the shaft and both rotors if not within specifications.

7. Inspect the relief valve plunger for scoring. Small marks may be removed with 400-grit wet of dry sandpaper.

8. The relief valve spring should have a free-length of 1.95 in. (49.5mm). Replace the spring if it fails to meet specifications.

9. Assemble the pump using new parts where necessary.

8.0L Engine

1. Lay a straight-edge across the pump cover surface. Replace the cover if a 0.003 in. (0.076mm) feeler gauge slides under the straight-edge.

2. Measure the thickness and diameter of rotors. The thickness should not be less than 0.744 in. (18.92mm) and diameter should not be less than 3.246 in. (82.45mm).

3. Check the clearance between the rotor and the pump body with a feeler gauge. The measurement should be no more than 0.007 in. (0.19mm).

4. Check the clearance between the inner and outer rotor teeth with a feeler gauge. The measurement should be no more than 0.006 in. (0.150mm).

5.9L Diesel Engine

1. Inspect the drive and idle gears for damage of any type. The maximum backlash between the gears is 0.015 in. (0.38mm).

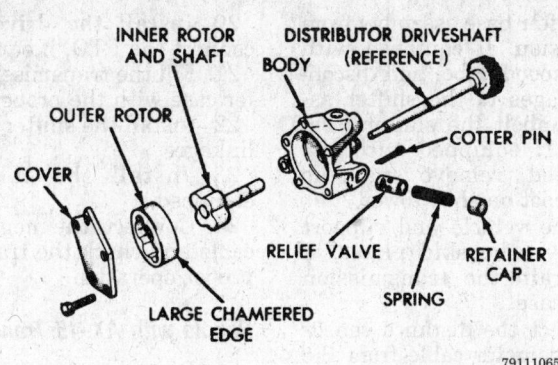

INNER ROTOR
AND SHAFT

DISTRIBUTOR DRIVESHAFT
(REFERENCE)

BODY

OUTER ROTOR

COTTER PIN

COVER

RELIEF VALVE

RETAINER
CAP

LARGE CHAMFERED
EDGE

SPRING

79111065

Exploded view of the oil pump — 5.2L and 5.9L gas engines

2. Remove the back plate.

3. The maximum tip clearance of the rotors is 0.007 in. (0.178mm).

4. Place a straight-edge across the rotors. The maximum clearance is 0.005 in. (0.127mm).

5. The maximum rotor to body clearance is 0.015 in. (0.381mm).

6. Remove the rotor and inspect all parts for visible damage.

7. Assemble the pump using new parts where necessary.

Rear Main Bearing Oil Seal

The 3.9L, 5.2L and 5.9L engines rear main seal may be 2-piece, fitted rope type seal or 2-piece split rubber (Viton) type. In all cases, the upper ½ can be installed with the crankshaft in place. The 2 halves should always be replaced as a set.

REMOVAL AND INSTALLATION

2.5L Engine

1. With the engine or transaxle removed from vehicle, remove the flywheel or flexplate.

2. Pry out rear crankshaft oil seal from seal retainer. Be careful not to nick of damage crankshaft sealing surface or seal retainer.

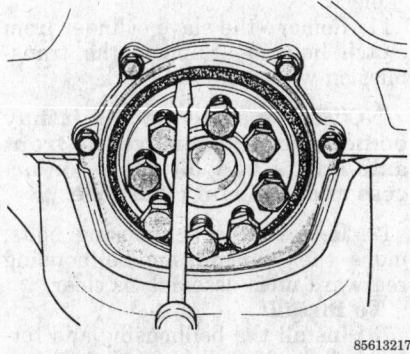

85613217

Removing the 1-piece rear crankshaft seal

3. Place tool C-4681 or equivalent on the crankshaft.

4. Lubricate outer diameter with Loctite Stud N' Bearing Mount (PN. 4057987) or equivalent.

5. Lightly lubricate the seal lip with engine oil and tap in place with a plastic hammer.

6. Install the flywheel/flexplate and tighten bolts to 70 ft. lbs. (95 Nm).

3.0L, 3.3L and 3.8L Engines

1. With the engine or transaxle removed from vehicle, remove the flywheel or flexplate.

2. Pry out the rear crankshaft oil seal from the seal retainer. Be careful not to nick or damage the crankshaft sealing surface or seal retainer.

3. Lightly lubricate the new seal lip with engine oil and install seal in retainer housing using tool MD998718 or equivalent.

4. Install flywheel and tighten the bolts to 70 ft. lbs. (95 Nm).

3.9L, 5.2L and 5.9L Engines

WITH ROPE TYPE SEAL

1. Raise the vehicle and support safely. Drain the engine oil. Remove the oil pan and oil pump.

2. Remove the rear main bearing cap.

3. Remove the lower seal from the cap.

4. To remove the upper rope seal, use oil seal remover and installer kit KD–492 or equivalent, following the instructions provided with the tool.

To install:

5. Wipe the crankshaft surface clean and coat it lightly with oil.

6. Use oil seal remover and installer kit KD–492 or equivalent, to install the upper rope seal. Trim the ends of the upper seal to eliminate frayed ends.

7. Install the lower rope seal in the main cap so both ends protrude.

Use tool C–3511 to seat the seal in its groove. Cut of the portions of the seal that extend above the cap on both sides and install the end seals to the cap.

8. Install the main cap to the block and torque the bolts to 85 ft. lbs. (115 Nm).

9. Install the pan and fill the engine with the proper amount of oil.

10. Connect the negative battery cable and check for leaks.

WITH RUBBER (VITON) TYPE SEAL

1. Raise the vehicle and support safely. Drain the engine oil. Remove the oil pan and oil pump.

2. Remove the rear main bearing cap.

3. Remove the lower seal from the cap.

4. To remove the upper seal, press on one end of the seal with a small blunt tool, rotate the crankshaft slightly and pull out the other end of the seal.

To install:

5. Wipe the crankshaft surface clean and coat it lightly with oil.

6. When installing the upper seal, hold the seal (with the paint stripe to the rear) tightly against the crankshaft and rotate the crankshaft while sliding the seal into the groove. If any rubber has peeled off the back of the new seal, do not use it; it will leak.

7. When installing the lower rubber seal, make sure the paint stripe is positioned to the rear and place a drop of sealer next to both ends of the seal.

8. Install the main cap to the block and torque the bolts to 85 ft. lbs. (115 Nm).

9. Install the oil pump and pan and fill the engine with the proper amount of oil.

10. Connect the negative battery cable and check for leaks.

5.9L Diesel and 8.0L Engines

The rear crankshaft seal is mounted in a housing that is bolted to the rear of the block. A double lipped teflon seal is used.

1. Disconnect the negative battery cable.

2. Remove the transmission.

3. Remove the clutch cover and plate, if equipped.

4. Remove the flywheel.

5. Drill two ⅛ in. holes 180 degrees apart into the seals. Be extremely careful not to drill against the crankshaft.

6. Using a No. 10 sheetmetal screw and a slide hammer, remove the rear seal.

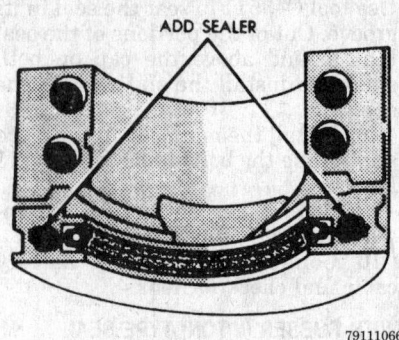

79111066

Lower rear main seal — rubber type seal

To install:

7. Thoroughly clean and dry the crankshaft surface. Do not oil the crankshaft or seal prior to installation or the seal will leak.

8. Install the seal pilot included in the replacement seal kit, on the crankshaft. Push the seal on the pilot and crankshaft. Remove the pilot.

9. If the new seal has a rubber outer diameter, lubricate it with soapy water. If the seal does not have a rubber outer diameter, use Loctite® 277 or equivalent on the outer diameter.

10. Use the alignment tool to install the seal to the proper depth in the housing. Drive the seal in gradually and evenly until the alignment tool stops against the housing.

11. Install flywheel and clutch and cover, if equipped.

12. Install transmission and reconnect negative battery cable. Add oil to correct level, start vehicle and check for leaks.

MANUAL TRANSMISSION

Transmission Assembly

REMOVAL AND INSTALLATION

Except AX–15, NV–3500 and NV–4500 Transmissions

1. Disconnect the negative battery cable.

2. Remove the shift lever. If equipped with the NP–435 4-speed, push the retainer (not the gearshift lever itself) down and rotate it counterclockwise slightly to release. If equipped with the NP–2500 5-speed, unbolt the shifter base assembly from the transmission. If equipped with the A–833 4-speed, label and disconnect the linkages to the shifter assembly and unbolt the shifter from its support. If equipped with the G–360 5-speed, remove snapring under lower boot on shift tower.

3. Raise the vehicle and support safely. Remove the skid plates, if equipped. Drain the transmission and transfer case.

4. Disconnect the distance sensor and the speedometer cable from the transmission or transfer case.

5. Matchmark and remove the driveshaft(s). Disconnect the PTO, if equipped.

6. If equipped with 4WD, disconnect all linkage, electrical connectors and vacuum lines from the transfer case. Using a jack, support the transfer case, unbolt the transfer case from the transmission and slide backward to remove from the vehicle.

7. Disconnect the reverse light switch connector and remove all wiring from any clips on the transmission case.

8. Install an appropriate engine support fixture to hold the engine in place.

9. Support the transmission with a transmission jack.

10. Remove the transmission crossmember.

11. Remove the transmission to bellhousing bolts.

12. Slide the transmission backwards until the input shaft clears the clutch disc. Remove the transmission from the vehicle.

To install:

13. Lubricate the pilot bushing and input shaft splines very lightly with high temperature lubricants.

14. Mount the transmission securely on a transmission jack and lift it in place until the input shaft is centered in the bellhousing opening. Roll the transmission forward until the input shaft splines fully engage with the clutch di

15. Install the transmission to bellhousing bolts. Torque the bolts to 50 ft. lbs. (68 Nm).

16. Install the transmission crossmember. Remove the transmission and engine support fixtures.

17. Install the transfer case and connect all linkage, electrical connectors and vacuum lines to the transfer case.

18. Connect the reverse light switch connector and clip all wiring to the transmission case.

19. Connect speedometer cable and distance sensor, if equipped.

20. Install the driveshaft(s) and connect the PTO, if equipped.

21. Fill the transmission and transfer case with the proper lubricant.

22. Install the shifter assembly and linkages.

23. Install the skid plates, if equipped.

24. Connect the negative battery cable and check the transmission for proper operation.

Dakota with AX–15 Transmission

1. Disconnect the negative battery cable and shift the transmission into Neutral.

2. Raise the vehicle and support safely.

3. Disconnect all cables, electrical connectors and ground wires from the transmission.

4. Drain the transmission fluid and remove the skid plates, if equipped.

5. Mark the driveshaft location and remove at the U-joint.

6. Support the engine with a suitable jack.

7. Remove the transfer case with a suitable jack, if 4WD equipped.

8. Remove the transmission mount nuts and crossmember.

9. Disconnect the exhaust pipes at the manifold and converter. Move the pipes aside to make room for removal.

10. Lower the transmission about 3 inches (7.62mm). Reach up and around the transmission and unseat the shift lever dust boot from the shift tower for the AX–15. Disengage the shift lever for AX–15 transmissions as follows:

  a. Reach up and around the case and press the shift lever retainer downward with a finger.

  b. Turn the retainer counterclockwise to release it.

  c. Lift the lever and retainer out of shift tower. It is not necessary to remove the shift lever from the floorpan boot. Leave the lever in place.

11. Remove the slave cylinder from clutch housing. Support the transmission with a suitable jack.

NOTE: On some models, it may be necessary to remove the front axle struts and oil filter for access and removal clearance.

12. Remove the bellhousing bolts, move the transmission/bellhousing rearward until assembly is clear.

To install:

13. Install the bellhousing and torque bolts to 28 ft. lbs. (38 Nm). Lubricate the release fork pivot ball, re-

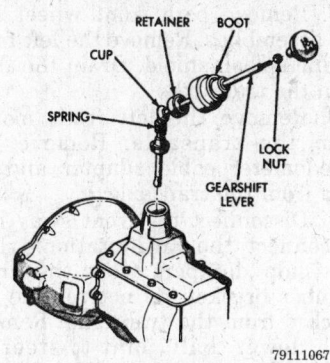

79111067

New Process 435 shifter components

lease fork, bearing hub and bearing retainer with high temperature grease.

14. Install the transmission and align the input shaft with clutch disc. Install the bellhousing bolts and torque to 50 ft. lbs. (68 Nm).

15. Lower the transmission and install the shift lever by pressing the retainer downward and turn clockwise to lock into place. Install the dust boot.

16. Install the transfer case, if 4WD equipped.

17. Refill the transmission with fluid.

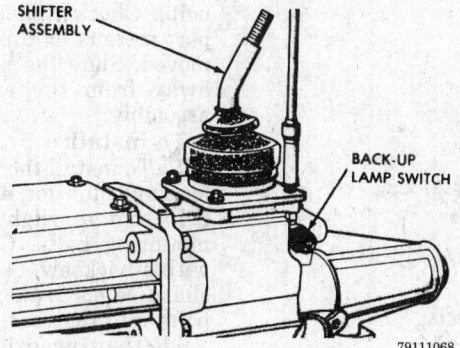

79111068

New Process 2500 transmission

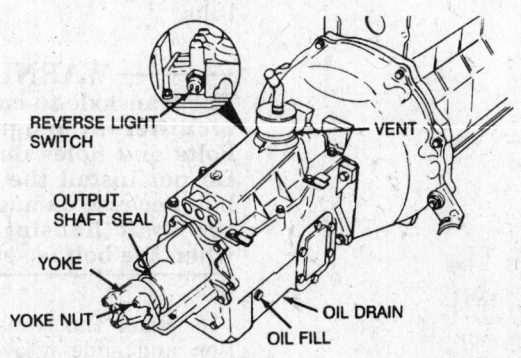

79111069

Getrag G-360 transmission — 5.9L diesel engine

18. Install the crossmember and torque the frame and insulator bolts to 50 ft. lbs. (68 Nm).

19. Install the exhaust pipes, cables, electrical connectors and ground wires.

20. Install the driveshaft to its original position.

21. Install the remaining components, check fluid level and check for leaks.

NV–3500 NV–4500 Transmission

1. Disconnect the negative battery cable, shift the transmission into Neutral and drain the fluid.

2. For the NV–3500, remove the shift boot bezel screws and slide the boot upward on the lever extension. Loosen the extension locknut and unscrew the extension from the shift lever. If the isolator and plate came off during tower removal, remove the assembly from the shift housing. Note that the narrow side of the plate goes toward the driver side of the transmission.

3. For the NV–4500, remove the shift boot-to-floorpan screws and shift lever extension with remover tool 6783 as follows:

    a. Scribe the position of extension on the shank of the shift lever.

    b. Position the notched, lower end of the tool just under the square shank of the shift lever.

    c. Position the tool jaws under the flange on the extension. Tighten the tool and pull the extension off the square shank of the lever.

    d. Remove the extension and tool.

4. Raise the vehicle and support safely.

5. Disconnect all cables, electrical connectors and ground straps.

6. Remove the skid plates, if equipped.

7. Mark the driveshaft(s) and remove.

8. Support the engine with a suitable jackstand.

9. Remove the crossmember by rotating diagonally. Disconnect the exhaust pipe at the manifolds and converter and move out of the way.

10. Remove the slave cylinder and starter motor.

11. Remove the transfer case and linkage, if 4WD equipped.

12. Support the transmission with a suitable jack. Remove the bellhousing-to-engine bolts.

13. Move the transmission rearward until clear of engine.

To install:

14. Move the transmission forward until engaged with clutch plate and engine. Torque the bolts to 45 ft. lbs. (61 Nm).

15. Remove the transmission jack.

16. Install the transfer case and linkage, if 4WD equipped.

17. Install the slave cylinder and starter motor.

18. Install the crossmember by rotating diagonally and torque bolts to 50 ft. lbs. (68 Nm). Connect the exhaust pipes at the manifolds and converter.

19. Install the driveshaft(s) to the original position.

20. Install the skid plates, if equipped.

21. Connect all cables, electrical connectors and ground straps.

22. Lower the vehicle safely.

23. For the NV–3500, apply gasket sealer to the isolator plate and install. Torque the bolts to 7 ft. lbs. (10 Nm).

24. For the NV–3500 and 4500. If the shift lever extension was removed from the shift lever for the NV–3500, install the assembly for both transmissions as follows:

    a. Reposition the upper jaw of the removal/installation tool 6783 above the flange on the lever exten-

sion. Press the extension back into the shift lever.

b. Tighten the tool screw to press onto the lever. Press to the scribe mark done earlier.

c. Remove the special tool.

25. Connect the negative battery cable and refill the transmission fluid.

LINKAGE ADJUSTMENT

A–833 4-Speed Transmission

1. Place the shifter in the neutral position.

2. Raise the vehicle and support safely.

3. Install the fabricated aligning tool to hold the levers in the neutral crossover position.

4. Disconnect the control rods from the levers in the shifter assembly. Make sure the levers are still in the neutral position.

5. Rotate the threaded ends of the shift control rods to adjust the rod length. Starting with the 1/2 rod, adjust it so the fabricated tool does not bind. Repeat with the 3/4 and the reverse rods.

6. Install the rods to their levers with the washers and clips.

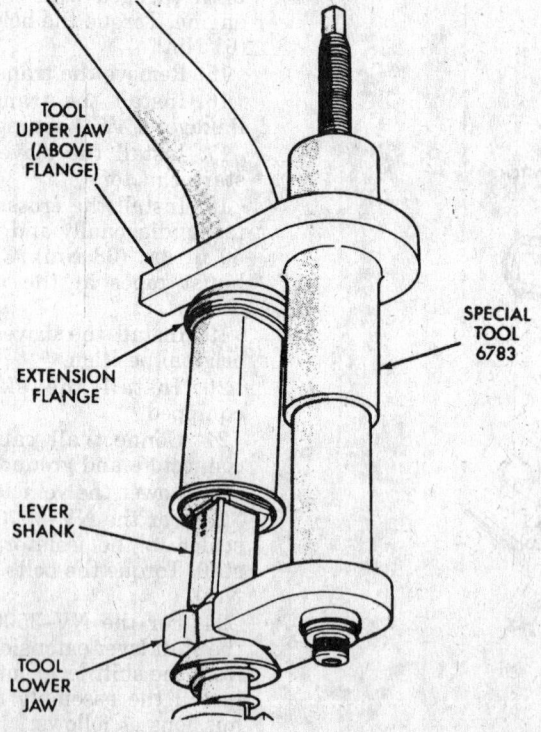

TOOL UPPER JAW (ABOVE FLANGE)

EXTENSION FLANGE

LEVER SHANK

SPECIAL TOOL 6783

TOOL LOWER JAW

85471016

Shift lever extension removal/installation tool 6783 — NV–3500 and 4500 transmissions

7. Remove the alignment tool and check the shifting action for smoothness.

MANUAL TRANSAXLE

Transaxle Assembly

REMOVAL AND INSTALLATION

NOTE: Transaxle removal does not require engine removal.

1. Disconnect the negative battery cable from the battery.

2. Install a sling or lifting bracket to the battery ground strap bolt. Place an engine support device across the engine compartment and connect to the sling. Tighten until slight upward pressure is applied to the engine.

3. Disconnect the gearshift operating control from the transaxle selector lever.

4. Loosen the wheel lug nuts slightly. Raise and support the front of the vehicle.

5. Remove both front wheel and tire assemblies. Remove the left front engine splash shield. Drain the fluid from the transaxle.

6. Remove the left front mount from the transaxle. Remove the speedometer cable adapter and pinion from the transaxle.

7. Disconnect the front sway bar. Disconnect the anti-rotational link (anti-hop damper) from the cross member bracket, do not remove the bracket from the transaxle. Remove both lower ball joint-to-steering knuckle mounting bolts. Pry the ball joint from the steering knuckle. Remove the halfshaft from the drive wheel hub.

8. Remove the halfshafts from the differential.

9. Remove the back-up light switch connector.

10. Remove the engine mount bracket from the front crossover.

11. Remove the front mount insulator through bolt. Place a suitable floor jack or transmission jack under the transaxle and raise to gently support.

12. Remove the top bellhousing bolts.

13. Remove the left engine mount at rear cover plate. Remove the starter motor.

14. Secure the transaxle to the jack and remove the lower bellhousing bolts. Check that all transaxle support mounts or through bolts are removed. Slide the jack and transaxle away from the engine and lower assembly.

To install:

15. To install the transaxle; make 2 locating pins for extra same thread bolts that are slightly longer than the mounting bolts. Cut the heads off with a hacksaw, remove any burrs or sharp edges with a file. Install the bolts into the rear of the engine and guide the transaxle over them. After the transaxle is in position, remove the guide bolts and install mounting bolts.

— WARNING —
The transaxle-to-engine bolts are of different length. Label the bolts and holes during removal. Do not install the wrong length bolt because damage to the selector shaft housing can happen when the bolt is seated.

16. Raise the transaxle into position and slide it over the locating pins. Install the top bellhousing bolts.

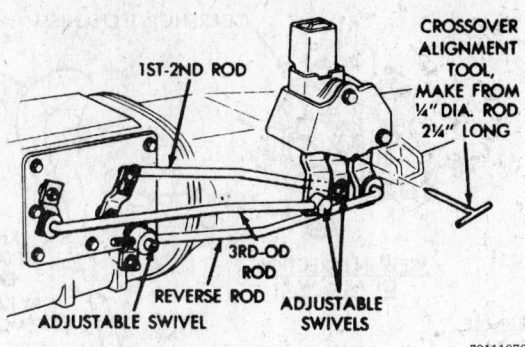

A-833 shifter and linkage

Engine support fixture installed

17. Install the front mount insulator through bolt. Install the left engine mount and the starter motor.

18. Install the halfshafts.

19. Connect the sway bar and anti-hop/rotation link. Install the front wheels and lower the vehicle.

20. Install the speedometer drive and cable. Connect the throttle and shift linkage. Remove the engine support and connect the negative battery cable. Fill the transaxle with the correct lubrication fluid.

SHIFT LINKAGE ADJUSTMENT

NOTE: If a hard shifting situation is experienced, determine if the cables are binding and need replacement, or if a linkage adjustment is necessary. Disconnect both cables at the transaxle and move the selector through the various positions. If the selector moves freely an adjustment may be all that is necessary; if not, cable replacement might be indicated.

1. Working over the left front fender, unscrew the lock pin, from the transaxle selector shaft housing.

2. Reverse the lock pin so the long end faces down and insert into the

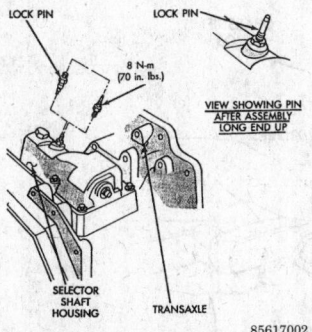

Transaxle pinned in the neutral position

same threaded hole it was removed from. Push the selector shaft into the selector housing while inserting the pin. A hole in the selector shaft will align with the lock pin, allowing the pin to be threaded into the housing. This will lock the selector shaft into the neutral position.

3. From inside the vehicle, remove the gearshift knob by pulling straight up. Remove the reverse pull up ring by first removing the retaining nut and then pull the ring up and off the lever.

4. Remove the shift lever boot. Remove the console.

5. Loosen the selector and crossover cable end adjusting/retainer bolts. Be sure the transaxle end of the cables are connected.

6. Install 1 adjusting lock pin on the side of the lever bracket in hole provided while moving lever slightly to help alignment. Install the other lock pin at the rear of the lever bracket (cross-over cable). Be sure both cable end pieces are free to move.

7. After pins are inserted, the cable ends will be positioned to the correct adjustment point. Tighten the adjustment/retainer bolts to 55 inch lbs.

8. Loosen the selector and crossover cable adjusting screws. Remove the adjusting screw tool and attached spacer block from the shifter support.

9. Install the adjusting screw tool through the attached spacer, and screw the tool into the base of the shifter tower base.

10. Tighten the adjusting screw tool to 20 inch lbs. (2.2 Nm).

11. Tighten the selector/crossover cable retaining screws to 70 inch lbs. (8.0 Nm). Proper torque on the selector/crossover cable bracket is very important for proper operation.

12. Remove the adjusting screw tool and attach it to the bracket.

13. Check the gearshift cables for proper connection to the transaxle.

14. Install console and remainder of the removed parts.

15. Remove the selector housing lock pin at the transaxle and install it in the reversed position. Tighten the lock pin to 105 inch lbs. (12 Nm), check gear shift operation.

CLUTCH

Clutch Assembly

REMOVAL AND INSTALLATION

1. Disconnect the negative battery cable.

2. Raise the vehicle and support safely.

3. Remove the transmission/transaxle and transfer case, if equipped.

4. Remove the clutch housing, release fork and bearing assembly, if equipped.

5. Remove the clutch cover bolts. If cover is to be reused, loosen cover

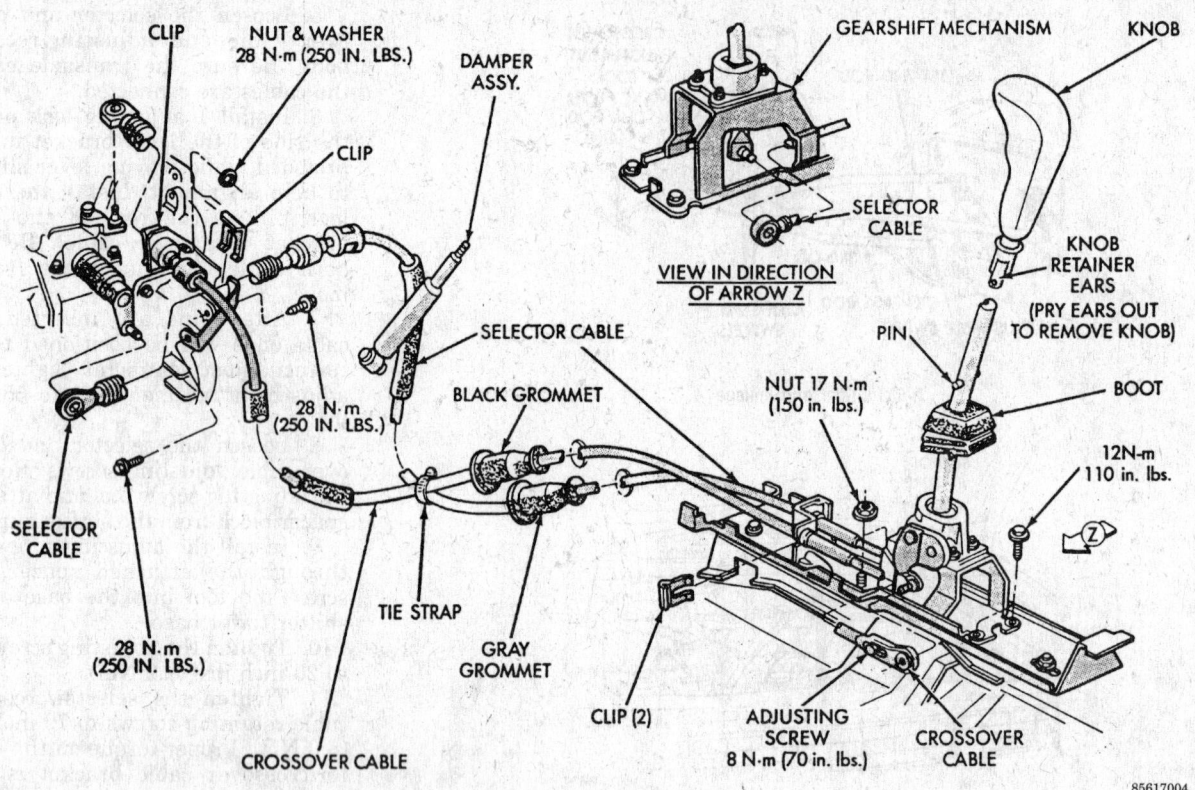

Cable operated gearshift linkage

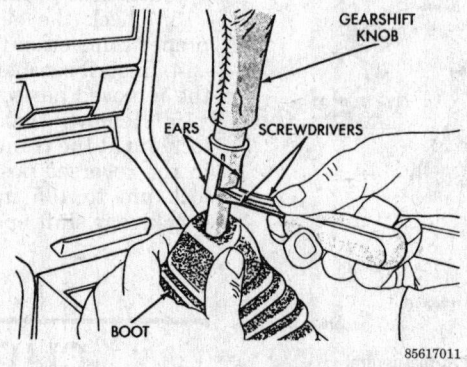

Removing the gearshift knob

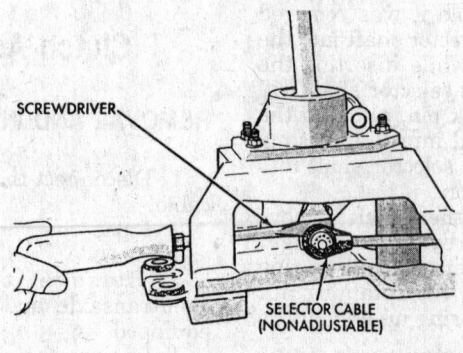

Cable removal

bolts evenly a few threads at a time to avoid warping the cover.

6. Remove the clutch cover and disc.

To install:

7. Install the clutch cover and disc. Use a clutch aligning tool or spare input shaft to center the disc. Tighten all of the bolts finger-tight.

8. The cover bolts must be turned gradually, evenly and to the proper torque to avoid distorting the cover. Torque all bolts except ⅜ in. diameter to 17 ft. lbs. (23 Nm). Torque ⅜ in. diameter bolts similarly to 30 ft. lbs. (41 Nm).

9. Install the transmission/transaxle and transfer case, if equipped.

10. Install the inspection cover.

11. Connect the negative battery cable and check the clutch for proper operation.

PEDAL HEIGHT/FREE-PLAY ADJUSTMENT

NOTE: Chrysler uses a hydraulic clutch release system. There is no adjustment for free-play on vehicles with this system.

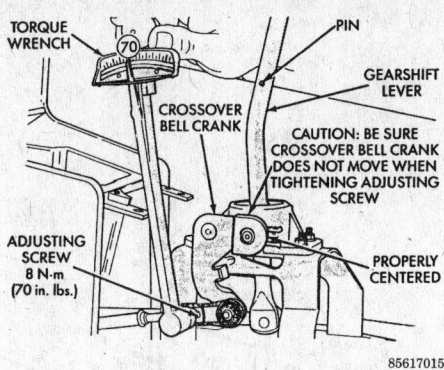

TORQUE WRENCH

PIN

GEARSHIFT LEVER

CROSSOVER BELL CRANK

CAUTION: BE SURE CROSSOVER BELL CRANK DOES NOT MOVE WHEN TIGHTENING ADJUSTING SCREW

ADJUSTING SCREW 8 N·m (70 in. lbs.)

PROPERLY CENTERED

85617015

Crossover cable adjustment

Clutch Master Cylinder and Slave Cylinder

The clutch master cylinder, remote reservoir, slave cylinder and connecting lines are all serviced as a complete assembly. The cylinders and connecting lines are sealed units. They are prefilled with fluid from the factory and cannot be disassembled or serviced separately.

REMOVAL AND INSTALLATION

1. Disconnect the negative battery cable.
2. Raise the vehicle and support safely. On diesel models, remove the slave cylinder shield from the clutch housing.
3. Remove the nuts attaching the slave cylinder to the bellhousing.
4. Remove the slave cylinder and clip from the housing.
5. Lower the vehicle. On diesel models, disconnect the clutch pedal interlock switch wires.
6. Remove the locating clip from the clutch master cylinder mounting bracket.
7. Remove the retaining ring, flat washer and wave washer that attach the clutch master cylinder pushrod to the clutch pedal. Slide the pushrod off the pedal pin. Inspect the bushing on the pedal pin and replace if it is excessively worn.
8. Verify that the cap on the clutch master cylinder reservoir is tight so fluid will not spill during removal.
9. Remove the screws attaching the reservoir and bracket, if equipped, to the dash panel and remove the reservoir.
10. Pull the clutch master cylinder rubber seal from the dash panel.
11. Rotate the clutch master cylinder counterclockwise 45 degrees to unlock it. Remove the cylinder from the dash panel.

12. Remove the clutch master cylinder, remote reservoir, slave cylinder and connecting lines from the vehicle.

To install:

NOTE: The hydraulic clutch system is pre-filled with fluid at the factory and requires no bleeding procedure after installation.

13. Verify that the cap on the fluid reservoir is tight so fluid will not spill during installation.
14. Position the components in the replacement kit in their places on the vehicle.
15. Insert the master cylinder in the dash. Rotate clockwise 45 degrees to lock in place.
16. Lubricate the rubber seal with a lubricant to ease installation. Seat the seal around the cylinder in the dash.
17. Install the fluid reservoir and bracket, if equipped, to the dash panel.
18. Install the master cylinder pushrod to the clutch pedal pin. Secure the rod with the wave washer, flat washer and retaining ring. Install the locating clip. Do not remove the plastic shipping stop from the pushrod until the slave cylinder has been installed.
19. Raise the vehicle and support safely.
20. Insert the slave cylinder pushrod through the opening and make sure the cap on the end of the pushrod is securely engaged in the release lever before tightening the attaching nuts. Torque the nuts to 200 inch lbs. (23 Nm).
21. Install slave cylinder cover, if equipped. Lower the vehicle. Remove the plastic shipping stop from the master cylinder pushrod. Connect clutch pedal interlock switch wires.
22. Operate the clutch pedal a few times to verify proper operation of the system. The system will self-

bleed any air in the system and vent through the reservoir.
23. Connect the negative battery cable and road test the vehicle.

AUTOMATIC TRANSMISSION

Transmission Assembly

REMOVAL AND INSTALLATION

—————— **WARNING** ——————
The transmission and torque converter must be removed as an assembly. If the converter is left on the driveplate, the converter, driveplate, pump bushing and oil seal may be damaged. Also, the driveplate will not support the transmission weight.

Dakota

1. Disconnect the negative battery cable.
2. Remove all necessary exhaust components and move out of the way.
3. Remove the engine-to-transmission struts and skid plates, if equipped.
4. Drain the transmission fluid and disconnect the cooler lines at transmission.
5. Remove the starter and cooler line brackets.
6. Disconnect all cables, electrical connectors and grounds from the transmission.
7. Remove the converter access cover. Mark the converter-to-driveplate for installation purposes and remove the driveplate bolts.
8. Mark the driveshaft and remove from the vehicle.
9. Remove the oil dipstick tube.
10. With the help of an assistant, remove the transfer case, if 4WD equipped.
11. Install an engine support fixture tool C-3487-A with frame hooks to support rear of engine.
12. Raise the transmission slightly and remove the crossmember.
13. Remove the engine-to-transmission bolts. Pull the transmission rearward and put a C-clamp on the bellhousing to keep the torque converter in place during removal.
14. Lower the transmission and remove the torque converter carefully.

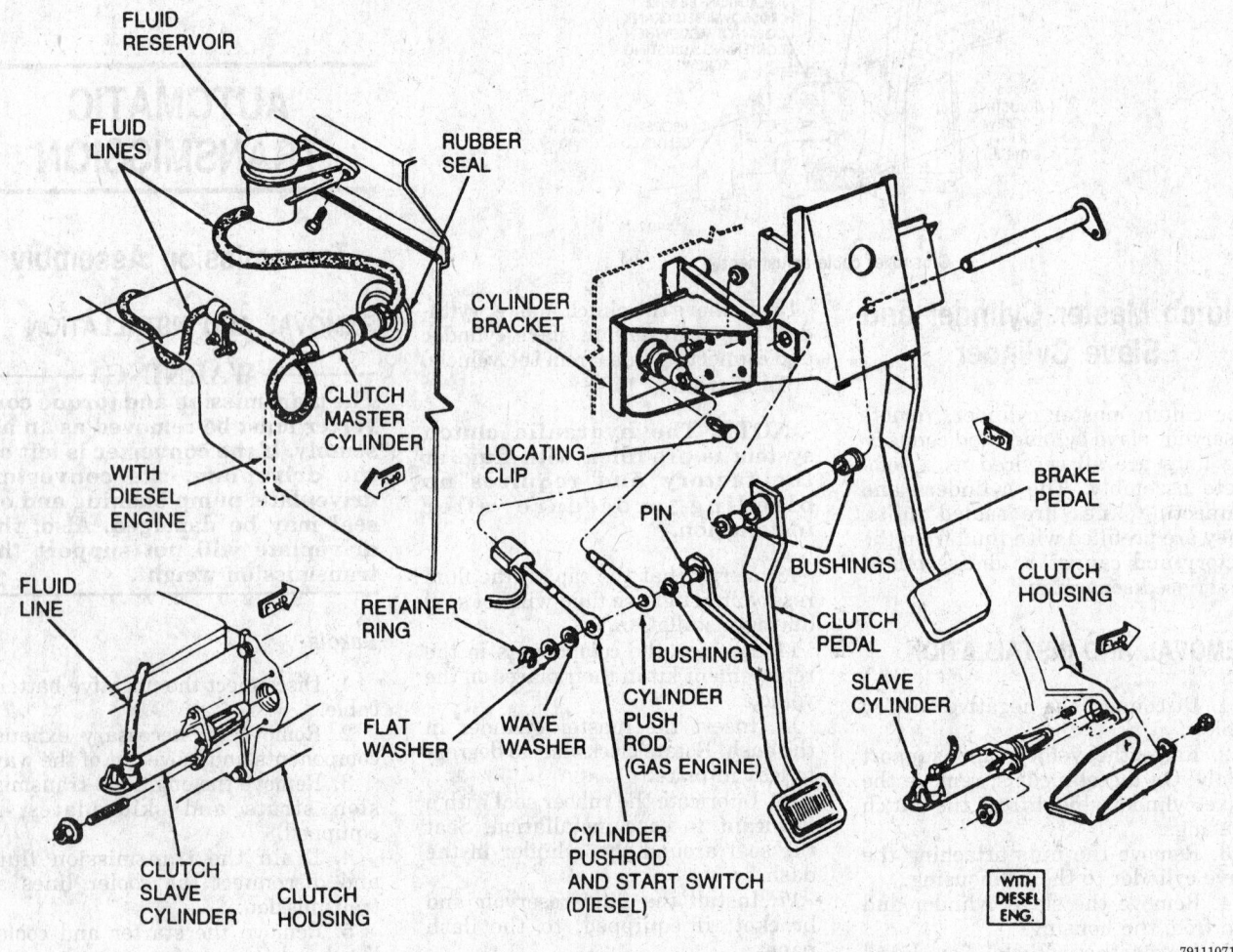

FLUID
RESERVOIR

FLUID
LINES

RUBBER
SEAL

CYLINDER
BRACKET

CLUTCH
MASTER
CYLINDER

LOCATING
CLIP

WITH
DIESEL
ENGINE

PIN

BUSHINGS

BRAKE
PEDAL

CLUTCH
HOUSING

FLUID
LINE

RETAINER
RING

BUSHING

CLUTCH
PEDAL

SLAVE
CYLINDER

CLUTCH
SLAVE
CYLINDER

CLUTCH
HOUSING

FLAT
WASHER

WAVE
WASHER

CYLINDER
PUSH
ROD
(GAS ENGINE)

CYLINDER
PUSHROD
AND START SWITCH
(DIESEL)

WITH
DIESEL
ENG.

79111071

Hydraulic clutch release components — Pick-Up and Ramcharger, Dakota similar

To install:

15. Install the transmission and torque converter carefully.

16. Install the engine-to-transmission bolts and torque to 35–65 ft. lbs. (47–88 Nm).

17. Install the crossmember and torque to 50 ft. lbs. (68 Nm).

18. Lower the engine support fixture tool C-3487-A.

19. With the help of an assistant, install the transfer case, if 4WD equipped.

20. Install the dipstick tube.

21. Install the driveshafts to the original positions.

22. Install the driveplate-to-torque converter bolts and torque to 23 ft. lbs. (31 Nm). Install the cover plate.

23. Connect all cables, electrical connectors and grounds to the transmission.

24. Install the starter motor and connect the cooling lines and brackets.

25. Install the engine-to-transmission struts and skid plates, if equipped.

26. Install all removed exhaust components.

27. Refill the transmission with fluid and connect the battery cable.

Pick-Up, Ramcharger and Van

1. Disconnect the negative battery cable.

2. Raise the vehicle and support safely. Drain the transmission and transfer case, if equipped.

3. Disconnect and lower or remove any exhaust parts as required.

4. Remove the skid plates, if equipped.

5. Matchmark and remove the driveshaft(s).

6. Disconnect the distance sensor, if equipped, and the speedometer cable.

7. If equipped with 4WD, disconnect all linkage, electrical connectors and vacuum lines from the transfer

case. Support the transfer case, unbolt the transfer case from the transmission and slide it backwards to remove from the vehicle.

8. Remove the engine to transmission struts.

9. Remove the starter and the fluid cooler lines bracket.

10. Remove the torque converter inspection cover.

11. Matchmark the converter to the flexplate. Remove the torque converter bolts.

12. Disconnect the wires to the neutral safety switch and lockup solenoid, if equipped.

13. Disconnect the oil cooler lines from the transmission.

14. Disconnect the gearshift rod and torque shaft assembly from the transmission.

15. Disconnect the throttle rod from the lever.

16. Unbolt the oil filler tube brace and lift the oil filler tube out of its bore.

17. Install an appropriate engine support fixture to hold the engine in place when the transmission is out of the vehicle.

18. Raise the transmission slightly.

19. Remove the transmission crossmember.

20. Remove the oil filter, if necessary. Remove all bellhousing bolts and remove the transmission from the vehicle.

To install:

21. Install the transmission securely on the transmission jack. Rotate the converter so it will align with the positioning of the flexplate.

22. Apply a coating of high temperature grease to the torque converter pilot hub.

23. Raise the transmission into place and push it forward until the dowels engage and the bellhousing is flush with the block.

24. Install the bellhousing bolts and torque to 30 ft. lbs. (41 Nm). Install the oil filler tube. Install the oil filter, if removed.

25. Install the transmission crossmember. Remove the engine support fixture and the transmission jack.

26. Install the torque converter bolts and torque as follows:

a. On models with 9.5 inch, 3-lug converter, tighten bolts to 40 ft. lbs. (54 Nm).

b. On models with 9.5 inch, 4-lug converter, tighten bolts to 55 ft. lbs. (74 Nm).

c. On models with 10.75 inch, 4-lug converter, tighten bolts to 270 inch lbs. (31 Nm).

27. Connect the oil cooler lines.

28. Connect the throttle rod to the lever and adjust, if necessary.

29. Connect the gearshift rod and torque shaft assembly to the transmission and adjust if necessary.

30. Connect the wires to the neutral safety switch, and lockup solenoid, if equipped. Make sure all wires are routed correctly and clipped in place.

31. Install the torque converter inspection cover, starter and transmission struts.

32. Install the transfer case, if equipped.

33. Connect the distance sensor, if equipped.

34. Connect the the speedometer cable.

35. Install the driveshaft(s).

36. Install exhaust parts that were removed.

37. Fill the transfer case, if equipped. Lower the vehicle.

38. Connect the negative battery cable.

39. Fill the transmission with the proper amount of Dexron®II.

40. Road test the vehicle, check for leaks and recheck the fluid level.

SHIFT LINKAGE ADJUSTMENT

NOTE: Do not attempt to adjust the linkage if any of the parts are excessively worn. If any rods are removed from the plastic grommets, new grommets should be installed. Pry only where the grommet and rod attach, not on the rod itself. Use pliers to snap the rod into the new grommet.

1. Shift the transmission into **P**.

2. Raise the vehicle and support safely.

3. Loosen the shift rod adjusting swivel lock screw. Make sure the swivel turns freely on the rod.

4. Make sure the valve body is in the **PARK** position by moving lever all the way rearward.

5. Adjust the swivel position on the shift rod to obtain a free pin fit in the torque shaft lever. Tighten the lock screw.

6. If the vehicle starts in any gear other than **P** or **N**, or does not start in both **P** and **N**, then either the adjustment is wrong or another problem exists.

THROTTLE VALVE LINKAGE ADJUSTMENT

42RH and 46RH Transmissions

1. Make sure the ignition switch is **OFF** and remove the air cleaner assembly.

2. Disconnect the cable end from the attaching stud.

3. Verify that the throttle lever is in the fully closed position and throttle lever is at curb idle.

4. Press the cable button inward to release the cable. The button only has to move about 0.070 in. (2.0mm) to release cable.

5. Center the cable end on attachment stud to within 0.039 in. (1.0mm) and release cable button.

6. Recheck the cable adjustment.

Pick-Up and Van with 5.9L Diesel Engine

1. Perform the adjustment with the engine at normal operating temperature.

2. While the throttle lever is seated against the low idle stop screw, the clearance between the actuation pin and the rear end of the slotted cable should be 0.180 inch (4.57 mm).

3. If it is not at specification, lift the locking pawl and slide the cable to the proper position to obtain the specified clearance.

4. Lock the pawl back into place and road test the vehicle.

Pick-Up, Ramcharger and Van with Gasoline Engine

1. Retract the ISC actuator by doing 1 of the following:

a. If the DRBII is available, connect its connector to the diagnostic connector. Start the engine and place the DRBII in the "Throttle Body Minimum Air Flow Test" mode. Disconnect the electrical connector on the ISC actuator. Shut **OFF** the engine and disconnect the DRBII; the actuator is now fully retracted.

b. If the DRBII is not available, 2 jumper wires may be used. With the engine OFF, disconnect the connector to the ISC actuator. Connect a pair of jumper wires to the battery. Connect the negative jumper to the top pin of the ISC actuator and the positive jumper to the other pin. Do not leave the jumpers connected for more than 5 seconds. Disconnect the jumpers and the ISC actuator is fully retracted.

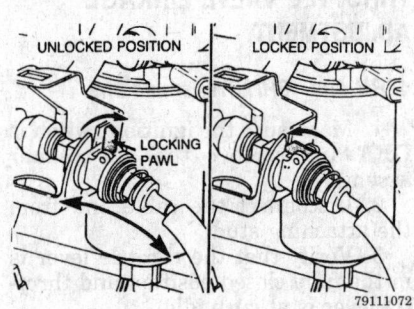

Unlocking and locking the throttle cable pawl

2. Raise the vehicle and support safely.

3. Loosen the adjustable swivel lock screw on the throttle rod enough so the rod travels freely in the swivel.

4. Hold the throttle lever firmly forward against its internal stop and tighten the lock screw. Lower the vehicle.

5. Reconnect the ISC actuator, if equipped.

6. If equipped with fuel injection, turn the ignition key to the **RUN** position for at least 5 seconds but do not start the engine. Turn the key to the **OFF** position.

7. Start the engine and road test the vehicle.

AUTOMATIC TRANSAXLE

Transaxle Assembly

REMOVAL AND INSTALLATION

NOTE: If the vehicle is going to be rolled while the transaxle is out of the vehicle, obtain 2 outer CV-joints to install to the hubs. If the vehicle is rolled without the proper torque applied to the front wheel bearings, the bearings will be destroyed.

1. Disconnect the negative battery cable. If equipped with 3.0L or 3.3L engine, drain the coolant. Remove the dipstick.

2. Install an engine support fixture.

3. Remove the air cleaner assembly if it is preventing access to the upper bellhousing bolts. Remove the upper bellhousing bolts and water tube, where applicable. Unplug all electrical connectors from the transaxle.

4. If equipped with a 2.5L engine, remove the starter attaching nut and bolt at the top of the bellhousing.

5. Raise the vehicle and support safely. Remove the tire and wheel assemblies. Remove the axle end cotter pins, nut locks, spring washers and axle nuts.

6. Remove the ball joint retaining bolts and pry the control arm from the steering knuckle. Position a drain pan under the transaxle where the axles enter the differential or extension housing. Remove the axles from the transaxle or center bearing. Unbolt the center bearing and remove the intermediate axle from the transaxle, if equipped.

7. Drain the transaxle. Disconnect and plug the fluid cooler hoses. Disconnect the shifter and kickdown linkage from the transaxle, if equipped.

8. Remove the speedometer cable adaptor bolt and remove the adaptor from the transaxle.

9. Remove the starter. Remove the torque converter inspection cover, matchmark the torque converter to the flexplate and remove the torque converter bolts.

10. Using the proper equipment, support the weight of the engine.

11. Remove the front motor mount and bracket.

12. If equipped with D.I.S. ignition system, remove the crankshaft position sensor from the bellhousing.

13. Position a suitable jack under the transaxle.

14. Remove the lower bellhousing bolts.

15. Remove the left side splash shield. Remove the transaxle mount bolts.

16. Carefully pry the engine from the transaxle.

17. Slide the transaxle rearward until the locating dowels disengage from the mating holes in the transaxle.

NOTE: Attach a small C-clamp to the edge of the bellhousing. This will hold the torque converter in place during transaxle removal.

18. Pull the transaxle completely away from the engine and remove it from the vehicle.

19. To prepare the vehicle for rolling, support the engine with a suitable support or reinstall the front motor mount to the engine. Then reinstall the ball joints to the steering knuckle and install the retaining bolt. Install the obtained outer CV-joints to the hubs, install the washers and torque the axle nuts to 180 ft. lbs. (244 Nm). The vehicle may now be safely rolled.

To install:

20. Install the transmission securely on the transmission jack. Rotate the converter so it will align with the positioning of the flexplate.

——— WARNING ———
If equipped with a 41TE Transaxle, and the torque converter has been replaced, a Torque Clutch Break-in Procedure must be performed. This procedure will reset the transaxle control module break-in status. Failure to perform this procedure may cause transaxle shutter. To properly do this, a DRB scan tool is required to read or reset the break-in status.

21. Apply a coating of high temperature grease to the torque converter pilot hub.

22. Raise the transaxle into place and push it forward until the dowels engage and the bellhousing is flush with the block.

23. Install the transaxle to bellhousing bolts.

24. Raise the transaxle up and install the left side mount bolts. Install the torque converter bolts and torque to 55 ft. lbs. (74 Nm).

25. Install the front motor mount and bracket. Remove the engine and transaxle support fixtures.

26. Install the starter to the transaxle. Install the bolt finger-tight, if equipped with a 2.5L engine.

27. Install a new O-ring to the speedometer cable adaptor and install to the extension housing; make sure it snaps in place. Install the retaining bolt.

28. Connect the shifter and kickdown linkage to the transaxle, if equipped.

29. Install the axles and center bearing, if equipped. Install the ball joints to the steering knuckles. Torque the axle nuts to 180 ft. lbs. (244 Nm) and install new cotter pins. Install the splash shield and install the wheels. Lower the vehicle. Install the dipstick.

30. Install the upper bellhousing bolts and water pipe, if removed.

31. If equipped with a 2.5L engine, install the starter attaching nut and bolt at the top of the bellhousing. Raise the vehicle again and tighten the starter bolt from underneath the vehicle. Lower the vehicle.

32. Connect all electrical wiring to the transaxle.

33. Install the air cleaner assembly, if it was removed. Fill the transaxle with the proper amount of Dexron®II.

34. Connect the negative battery cable and check the transaxle for proper operation. On the A-604 transaxle perform the upshift and kickdown learn procedure as follows:

a. Maintain constant throttle opening during shifts. Do not move the accelerator pedal during upshifts.

b. Accelerate the vehicle with the throttle 1/8–1/2 open.

c. Make 15–20 1/2, 2/3 and 3/4 upshifts. Accelerating from a full stop to 50 mph each time at the aforementioned throttle opening is sufficient.

d. With the vehicle speed below 25 mph, make 5–8 wide open throttle kick downs to 1st gear from either 2nd or 3rd gear. Allow at least 5 seconds of operation in 2nd or 3rd gear prior to each kickdown.

e. With the vehicle speed greater than 25 mph, make 5 to part throttle to wide open throttle kick downs to either 3rd or 2nd gear from 4th gear. Allow at least 5 seconds of operation in 4th gear, preferably at road load throttle prior to performing the kickdown.

KICKDOWN CABLE ADJUSTMENT

3-speed Transaxle

1. Run the engine until the normal operating temperature is reached. Be sure the choke is fully opened.

2. Loosen the adjustment bracket lock bolt mounted on transaxle to engine flange.

3. Be sure the adjustment bracket can slide freely. Clean as necessary.

4. Slide the bracket toward the engine as far as possible. Release the bracket and move the throttle lever to the right as far as it will go. tighten the adjustment lock bolt to 105 inch lbs.

UPSHIFT AND KICKDOWN LEARNING PROCEDURE

A–604 Ultradrive Transaxle

Since the A–604 is equipped with a learning function, each time the battery cable is disconnected, the ECM memory is lost. In operation, the transaxle must be shifted many times for the learned memory to be re-inputed into the ECM; during this period, the vehicle will experience rough operation. The transaxle must

be at normal operating temperature when learning occurs.

1. Maintain constant throttle opening during shifts. Do not move the accelerator pedal during upshifts.

2. Accelerate the vehicle with the throttle 1/8–1/2 open.

3. Make 15–20 1/2, 2/3 and 3/4 upshifts. Accelerating from a full stop to 50 mph each time at the aforementioned throttle opening is sufficient.

4. With the vehicle speed below 25 mph, make 5–8 wide open throttle kick downs to 1st gear from either 2nd or 3rd gear. Allow at least 5 seconds of operation in 2nd or 3rd gear prior to each kickdown.

5. With the vehicle speed greater than 25 mph, make 5 to part throttle to wide open throttle kick downs to either 3rd or 2nd gear from 4th gear. Allow at least 5 seconds of operation in 4th gear, preferably at road load throttle prior to performing the kickdown.

THROTTLE PRESSURE CABLE ADJUSTMENT

4 Cylinder Engine

1. Run the engine until it reaches normal operating temperature.

2. Loosen the cable mounting bracket lock screw.

3. Position the bracket so both alignment tabs are touching the transaxle case surface and tighten the lock screws.

4. Release the cross lock on the cable assembly by pulling the cross lock up.

5. To ensure proper adjustment, the cable must be free to slide all the way toward the engine against its stop after the cross lock is released.

6. Move the transaxle throttle control lever fully clockwise and press the cross lock down until it snaps into position.

7. Road test the vehicle and check the shift points.

THROTTLE PRESSURE ROD ADJUSTMENT

6 Cylinder Engine

1. Run the engine until it reaches normal operating temperature.

2. Loosen the adjustment swivel lock screw.

3. To ensure proper adjustment, the swivel must be free to slide along the flat end of the throttle rod. Disassembly, clean and lubricate as required.

4. Hold the transaxle throttle control lever firmly toward the engine and tighten the swivel screw.

5. Road test the vehicle and check the shift points.

TRANSFER CASE

Transfer Case Assembly

REMOVAL AND INSTALLATION

AWD Caravan, Voyager and Town & Country

NOTE: Service to the Power Transfer Unit (PTU) is limited to seals, gaskets, end cover bearing and output flange. If any other component fails, the entire unit must be replaced. The transfer unit is sealed from transaxle and has its own oil sump. The unit uses SAE 85W-90 gear lubricant and holds 1.22 qts. (1.15 liters).

1. Raise the vehicle and support safely.

2. Remove the right halfshaft and driveshaft assemblies.

3. Remove the PTU assembly from the transaxle.

4. Installation is the reverse of removal.

4WD Dakota, Pick-Up and Ramcharger

1. Disconnect the negative battery cable.

2. Raise the vehicle and support safely.

3. Remove the skid plates, if equipped. Drain the transfer case fluid.

4. Disconnect the distance sensor, if equipped, and disconnect the speedometer cable or speed sensor from the transfer case.

5. Matchmark and remove front and rear driveshafts.

6. Disconnect the PTO, if equipped.

7. Disconnect the linkage, electrical connectors and vacuum lines from the transfer case. Support the transfer case, unbolt the transfer case from the transmission and slide it backwards to remove it from the vehicle.

To install:

8. Apply silicone sealer to both sides of transfer case-to-transmission gasket and position on transmission.

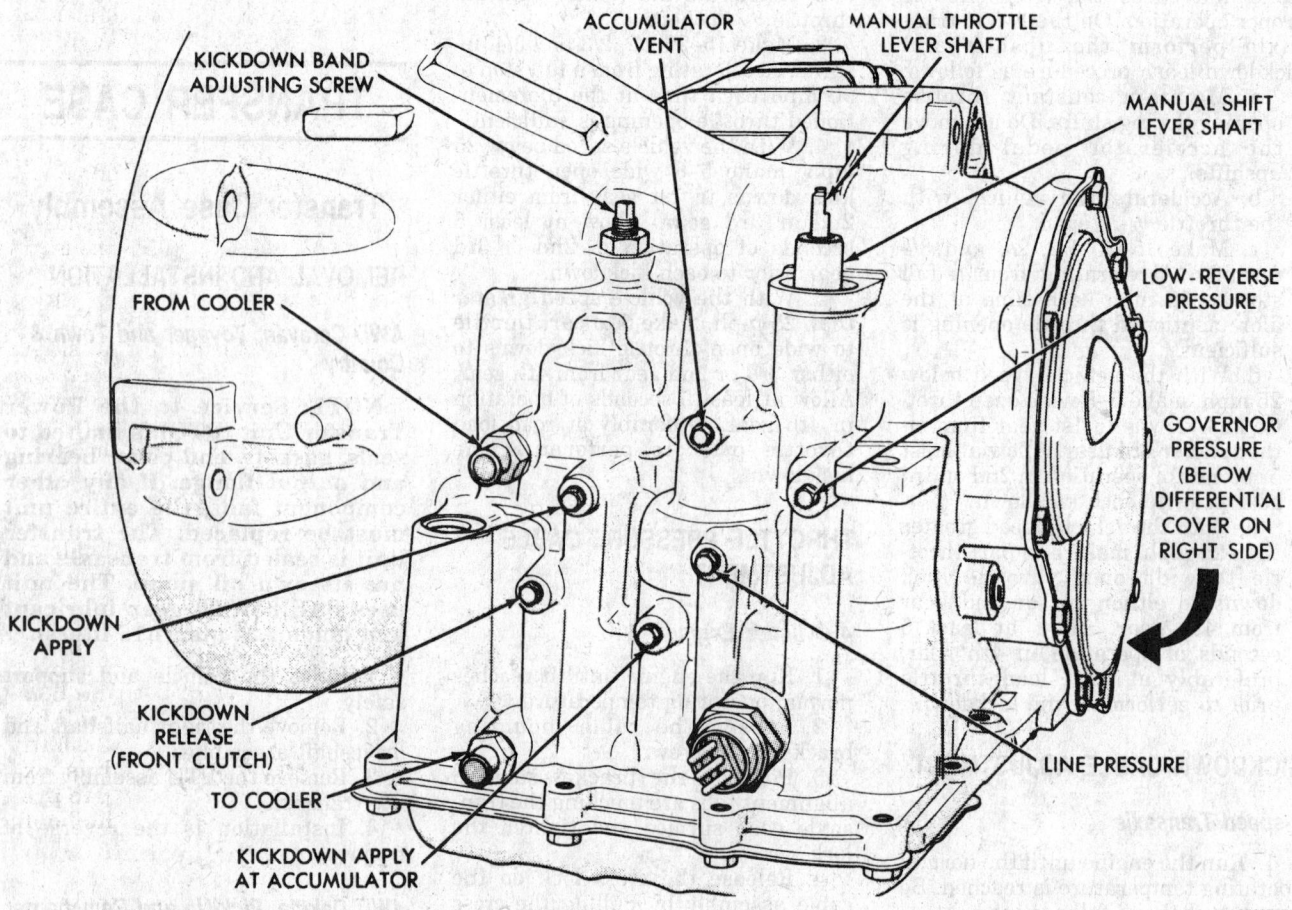

KICKDOWN BAND
ADJUSTING SCREW

ACCUMULATOR
VENT

MANUAL THROTTLE
LEVER SHAFT

MANUAL SHIFT
LEVER SHAFT

FROM COOLER

LOW-REVERSE
PRESSURE

GOVERNOR
PRESSURE
(BELOW
DIFFERENTIAL
COVER ON
RIGHT SIDE)

KICKDOWN
APPLY

KICKDOWN
RELEASE
(FRONT CLUTCH)

TO COOLER

LINE PRESSURE

KICKDOWN APPLY
AT ACCUMULATOR

85617171

Transaxle adjustment and maintenance points — 3-speed Torqueflite transaxle

9. Align and seat transfer case on transmission making sure gear splines are aligned with transmission output shaft. If necessary, align splines by rotating transfer case rear output shaft yoke.

10. Install and tighten attaching nuts to 35 ft. lbs. (47 Nm).

11. Install rear crossmember. Remove transmission support.

12. Align and connect driveshafts.

13. Connect distance sensor wires. Reconnect transfer case shift lever to range lever tightening locknut to 90 inch lbs. (10 Nm).

14. Fill transfer case with lubricant. Install skid plate and lower vehicle.

15. Reconnect negative battery cable and check operation of transfer case.

LINKAGE ADJUSTMENT

New Process 205

1. Shift the transfer case into neutral.

2. Move the shift rod boot upward for access.

3. Loosen the shift bracket bolts and move the bracket as far forward as possible. Tighten the bolts.

4. Check the smoothness of operation of the transfer case.

New Process 231 and 1992–94 NP–241

1. Move the transfer case shift lever boot aside for access to the shift lever and gate.

2. Move the shift lever into the **4H** position. Make sure the lever is against the **4H** gate.

3. Raise the vehicle and support safely.

4. Loosen the shift rod clamp screw until the shift rod is free to slide in the swivel.

5. Verify that the lever is in the **4H** position and correct location if moved out of position.

6. Tighten the clamp screw.

7. Check the smoothness of operation of the transfer case.

1994–96 New Process 231 HD, 241 and 241 HD

1. Move the transfer case shift lever boot aside for access to the shift lever and gate.

2. Move the shift lever into the **2H** position.

3. Raise the vehicle and support safely.

4. Loosen the shift rod lock bolt at trunnion. Check shift rod lock bolt at trunnion.

5. Make sure the rod does not bind in trunnion.

6. Verify that the lever is in the **2H** position and correct location if moved out of position.

7. Tighten the shift rod lock bolt to 90 inch lbs. (10 Nm).

8. Check the smoothness of operation of the transfer case.

DRIVE AXLE

Halfshaft

REMOVAL AND INSTALLATION

Caravan, Voyager and Town & Country

FRONT

1. Remove the cotter pin, lock and spring washer from the front axle ends.

2. Have a helper apply the service brakes and loosen the front axle hub retaining nut.

3. Raise and safely support the vehicle.

4. Remove the hub nut, washer and wheel assembly. Drain transaxle fluid.

NOTE: The speedometer drive pinion must be removed from the transaxle housing before the right halfshaft can be removed. Remove the retaining bolts and lift the pinion with cable connected from the housing.

5. Remove the clamp bolt that secures the ball joint stud with the steering knuckle.

6. Separate the ball joint from the knuckle by prying downward against the knuckle connecting point and the control arm. The knuckle bolt slot may have to be spread with a chisel

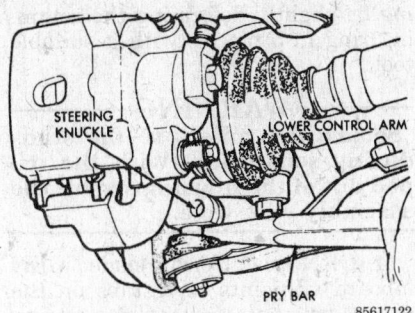

Separating the ball joint from the knuckle

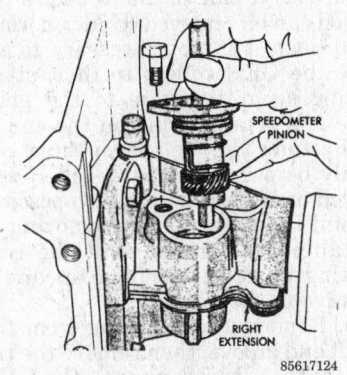

Speedometer pinion removal and installation

to help in removing the ball joint from the knuckle. Take care not to damage the rubber boot.

7. Separate the outer CV (constant velocity) joint splines from the steering knuckle hub by holding the CV housing and pushing the knuckle out and away. If resistance is encountered, use a brass drift and hammer to gently tap the outer hub end of the axle. Do not pry on the outer wear sleeve of the CV-joint.

8. After the outboard end of the drive axle has been removed from the steering knuckle, support the assembly and pull outward on the inner CV-joint housing to remove the assembly from the transaxle.

— **WARNING** —
Do not pull on the shaft or the assembly will disconnect. Pull only on the inner CV-joint housing.

9. Remove the halfshaft from under the vehicle and service as necessary.

To install:

10. To install the halfshaft, hold the inner joint assembly by its housing, align and guide the shaft into the transaxle or intermediate shaft assembly.

11. Lubricate the outer wear sleeve and seal with multi-purpose grease. Push the steering knuckle outward and install the splined outer shaft into the drive hub. Install the steering knuckle assembly. Torque the ball joint clamp bolt to 70 ft. lbs. (95 Nm). Hub nut (splined shaft nut) torque to 180 ft. lbs. (245 Nm). Refill the transaxle with the proper lubrication fluid.

NOTE: If after installing the axle assembly, the inboard boot appears collapsed, vent the boot by inserting a thin round rod between the boot and the shaft. Massage the boot until is expands. Install a new clamp to prevent dirt from entering the boot.

REAR

1. Raise and safely support the rear of the vehicle.

2. Remove the rear wheel.

3. Remove the cotter pin, nut, lock and spring washer from the rear hub.

4. Remove the inner halfshaft retaining bolts.

5. The halfshaft is spring loaded, push it in slightly and then tilt it down to remove it. Pull it out from under the vehicle.

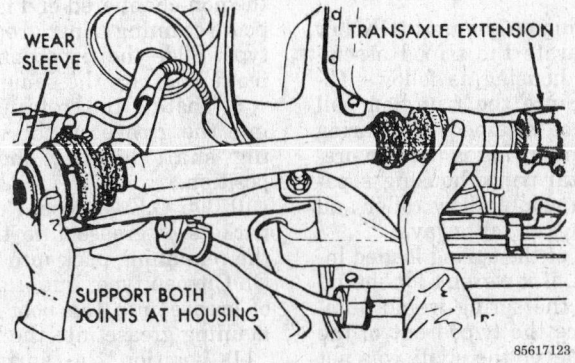

Removing the driveshaft assembly

To install:

6. Insert the end of the halfshaft into the rear hub assembly.

7. Position it on the rear carrier unit and install the retaining bolts.

8. Tighten the retaining bolts to 45 ft. lbs. (61 Nm).

9. Install the hub nut, spring and lock washers, and cotter pin.

10. Install the wheel and tire assembly.

Dakota

FRONT — 4WD

1. With the brakes applied, remove the cotter pin and loosen the halfshaft nut.

2. Raise the vehicle and support safely. Remove the front wheel.

3. Remove the nut, lock and spring washer.

4. Remove the bolts that attach the inner housing flange to the halfshaft flange.

5. Support the halfshaft and separate the stub shaft from the hub bearing and remove. Do not pull on the rubber boot.

To install:

6. Install the halfshaft and torque the inner flange bolts to 65 ft. lbs. (90 Nm).

7. Install the front wheel, lower the vehicle and install the stub shaft washer and nut. With the brakes applied, torque the nut to 190 ft. lbs. (258 Nm). Install the nut lock and cotter pin.

CV–Boot

REMOVAL AND INSTALLATION

Inner Joint

1. With the halfshaft assembly removed from the vehicle, remove the clamps and boot.

2. Remove the inner boot straps using a pliers or side cutter. Pull the boot back.

3. Depending on the unit (GKN or Citroen) separate the tripod assembly from the housing as follows: Citroen type: Since the trunnion ball rollers are not retained on bearing studs a retaining ring is used to prevent accidental tripod/housing separation, which would allow roller and needle bearings to fall away.

In the case of the spring loaded inner CV-joints, if it weren't for the retaining ring, the spring would automatically force the tripod out of the housing whenever the shaft was not installed in the vehicle.

Separate the tripod from the housing by slightly deforming the retaining ring in 3 places, with a suitable tool.

— WARNING —

Secure the rollers to the studs during separation. With the tripod out of the housing secure the assembly with tape.

4. GKN type: Spring loaded GKN inboard CV-joints have tabs on the can cover that prevent the spring from forcing the tripod out of the housing. These tabs must be bent back with a pair of pliers before the tripod can be removed. Under normal conditions it is not necessary to secure the GKN rollers to their studs during separation due to the presence of a retainer ring on the end of each stud. This retention force can easily be overcome if the rollers are pulled or impacted. It is also possible to pull the rollers off by removing or installing the tripod with the connecting shaft at too high an angle, relative to the housing.

5. Remove the snapring from the shaft end groove, then remove the tripod with a brass punch. Coat the splines with tape so not to cut the boot. Remove the boot and excess grease from the shaft.

To install:

6. Remove as much grease as possible from the assembly. Look at the ball housing races and the components for excessive wear.

7. Install the boot and clamps.

NOTE: Do not clean the inner housing with mineral spirits or solvent. Solvents will destroy the rubber seals that are hidden in the housing and permit grease leakage. If wear is excessive, replace as necessary.

8. Fasten the new boot onto the interconnecting shaft. Install the tripod on the shaft as follows: G.K.N. type: Slide the tripod onto the shaft with the non-chamfered end facing the tripod retaining ring groove. Citroen type: Slide the tripod onto the shaft (both sides are the same).

9. Install the retainer snapring into the groove on the interconnecting shaft locking the tripod in position.

10. On G.K.N. type: Put 2 of the 3 packets of grease into the boot and the remaining pack into the housing. On Citroen type: Put ⅔ of the packet of grease into the boot and the remaining grease into the housing.

11. Position the spring into the housing spring pocket with the cup

attached to the exposed end of the spring. Place a small amount of grease in the spring cup.

12. On G.K.N. type: Slip the tripod into the housing and bend down the retaining tabs. Make sure the tabs are holding the housing firmly. On Citroen type: Remove the tape holding the rollers and needle bearings in place. Hold the rollers and needles in place and install the housing. Install the retaining ring into the machined groove in the housing with a punch and plastic hammer. Hold the retaining collar in position with two C-clamps while installing the retainer ring.

— WARNING —

When installing the tripod, the spring must be centered in the housing to insure proper positioning.

13. Position the boot over the retaining groove in the housing and clamp in position.

Outer Joint

1. Remove the boot clamps and discard them.

2. Wipe away the grease to expose the joint.

3. Support the shaft in a vise (Cushion the vise jaws to prevent shaft damage). Hold the outer joint, and using a plastic hammer, give a sharp tap to the top of the joint body to dislodge it from the internal circlip.

4. If the shaft is bent carefully pry the wear sleeve from the CV-joint machined ledge.

5. Remove the circlip from the shaft and discard it.

NOTE: Replacement boot kits will contain this circlip.

6. Unless the shaft is damaged do not remove the heavy spacer ring from the shaft.

7. Place masking tape over the splines to protect the boot from damage.

NOTE: If the shaft must be replaced, care must be taken that the new shaft is of the proper construction, depending on whether the inner joint is spring loaded or not. If the CV-joint was operating satisfactorily, and the grease down not appear contaminated, just replace the boot. If the outer joint is noisy or badly worn, replace the entire unit. The repair kit will include boot, clamps, retaining ring (circlip) and lubricant.

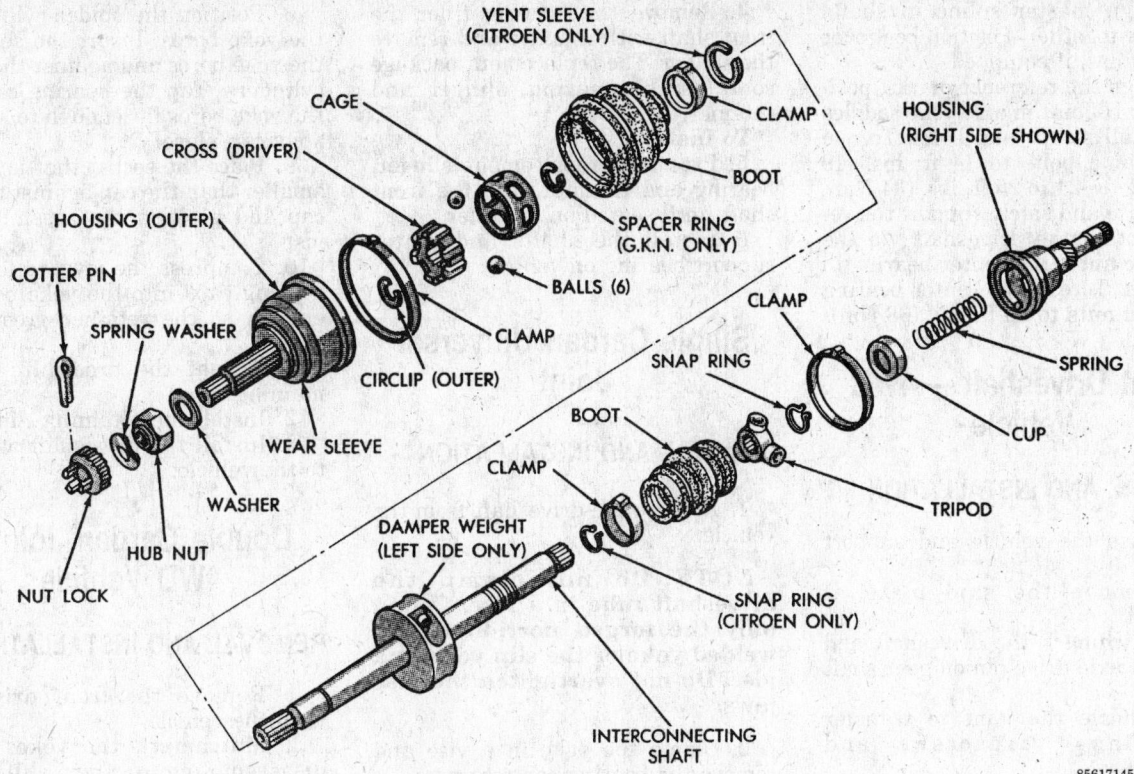

Exploded view of the halfshaft assembly

85617145

8. Remove the boot, clamps and excess grease.

To install:

9. Fasten the boot to the shaft. Install the new retainer circlip provided. Position the outer joint on the splined end of the stub shaft, engage the splines and tap sharply to engage the circlip. Attempt to pull the shafts apart to see if the circlip is properly seated.

10. Position the large end of the boot and secure with a clamp. Install the halfshaft.

Rear Driveshaft

REMOVAL AND INSTALLATION

Caravan, Voyager and Town & Country

1. Raise and safely support the vehicle.

2. Remove the rear driveline module assembly from the vehicle.

3. Remove the viscous coupling, snapring and torque tube bearing shield.

4. Remove torque tube to overrunning clutch case bolts.

5. Slide the torque tube off the torque shaft.

6. Install the torque tube onto the torque shaft. Install the Torque tube to overrunning clutch case bolts, tightening to 250 inch lbs. (28 Nm).

7. Install the bearing shield and snapring. Install the viscous coupling.

8. Install the driveline module into the vehicle. Lower the vehicle.

Except Caravan, Voyager and Town & Country

1–PIECE REAR DRIVESHAFT

1. Raise the vehicle and support safely.

2. Matchmark the driveshaft and the rear axle drive pinion gear shaft yoke.

3. Remove the rear U-joint attaching bolts and both strap clamps from the rear axle drive pinion gear shaft yoke.

4. Fluid may run from the rear of the extension housing or transfer case when the shaft is removed, so position a drain pan under the area.

5. Remove the driveshaft from the transmission or transfer case.

6. The installation is the reversal of the removal procedure. Torque ¼–28 clamp bolts to 14 ft. lbs. (19 Nm) and ⁵/₁₆–24 to 25 ft. lbs. (34 Nm).

2–PIECE REAR DRIVESHAFT

1. Raise the vehicle and support safely.

2. Matchmark the driveshaft and the rear axle drive pinion gear shaft yoke.

3. Remove the rear U-joint attaching bolts and both strap clamps from the rear axle drive pinion gear shaft yoke.

4. Detach the protective boot clamp from the front shaft splines, if equipped, and slide the rear shaft slip yoke from the front shaft at the center bearing. Remove the rear shaft from the vehicle.

5. Matchmark the yokes at the transmission or transfer case and remove the clamp retaining bolts and clamp straps.

6. Remove the center bearing retaining bolts and nuts and remove the front shaft with center bearing from the vehicle.

To install:

7. Lubricate shaft splines. Install front yoke of front shaft to transmission or transfer case and install retaining screws loosely. Loosely install retaining nuts and bolts in center support. As applicable, tighten ¼-inch clamp screws to 14 ft. lbs. (19 Nm). Torque ⁵/₁₆–clamp screw to 25 ft. lbs. (34 Nm).

8. Align master spline in shafts and slide together. Position boot over front splines, if equipped.

9. Align the reference marks, position rear U-Joint in axle yoke saddles and install straps and bolts. Torque ¼–28 clamp bolts to 14 ft. lbs. (19 Nm) and ⁵⁄₁₆–24 to 25 ft. lbs. (34 Nm).

10. Raise and safely support the vehicle. Rotate the driveshaft via the engine to allow the center bearing to self-align. Torque the center bearing bolts and nuts to 50 ft. lbs. (68 Nm).

Front Driveshaft — 4WD Vehicle

REMOVAL AND INSTALLATION

1. Raise the vehicle and support safely.

2. Remove the skid plate, if equipped.

3. Matchmark the driveshaft and the front axle drive pinion gear shaft yoke.

4. Remove the joint to transfer case flange capscrews and lockwashers.

5. Remove the front U-joint attaching bolts and both strap clamps.

6. Remove the front driveshaft from the vehicle.

To install:

7. Install driveshaft and front U-joint attaching bolts and both strap clamps. Torque ¼–28 clamp bolts to 14 ft. lbs. (19 Nm) and ⁵⁄₁₆–24 to 25 ft. lbs. (34 Nm).

8. Install the joint to transfer case flange capscrews and lockwashers and torque to 25 ft. lbs. (34 Nm).

9. Install the skid plate and lower vehicle.

Rear Driveshaft Center Bearing

REMOVAL AND INSTALLATION

1. Remove the shafts and center bearing from the vehicle.

NOTE: Do not clamp the driveshaft tube in a vise. Clamp only the forged portion of the welded yoke in a vise. Do not overtighten the vise jaws.

2. Clamp the front shaft in a vise and remove the bearing support and rubber insulator from the center bearing.

3. Bend the slinger away from the center bearing to provide sufficient clearance for installing a puller.

4. Remove the bearing from the front shaft with a puller and remove the slinger. The replacement package contains the bearing, slinger and retainer.

To install:

5. Press the replacement slinger, bearing and retainer onto the front shaft until seated on shoulder.

6. Install the shafts and center support bearing on vehicle.

Single Cardan Universal Joint

REMOVAL AND INSTALLATION

1. Remove the driveshaft from the vehicle.

NOTE: Do not clamp the driveshaft tube in a vise. Clamp only the forged portion of the welded yoke or the slip yoke in a vise. Do not overtighten the vise jaws.

2. Clamp the yoke in a vise and remove the bearing cap retainers.

3. Place a socket which has an inside diameter larger than the outside diameter of the bearing cap, against the yoke around the perimeter of the first cap to be removed. Place a socket which is slightly smaller than the cap, on the cap opposite the cap to be removed. Then position the yoke in a vise.

4. Compress the jaws until the smaller socket has driven the other cap into the larger socket.

5. Release the jaws and remove the cap that is partially out of the yoke.

6. Repeat the procedure for the remaining cap(s).

To install:

7. Clean and remove any rust from the yoke bores and lubricate lightly with lithium based grease.

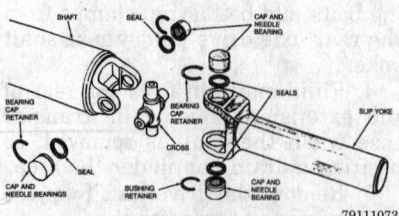

Single Cardan universal joint components

8. Position the spider cylinders in the yoke bores. Insert the seals into the yoke bores and against the spider cylinders. Tap the bearing caps into the yoke bores far enough to keep the spider in place.

9. Place the socket that is slightly smaller than the cap against the first cap and position the assembly in a vise.

10. Compress the jaws to force the bearing caps into the yoke bores far enough so the retainer grooves are visible.

11. Repeat the procedure for remaining caps.

12. Install the retaining clips.

13. Install the driveshaft assembly to the vehicle.

Double Cardan Joint — 4WD Vehicles

REMOVAL AND INSTALLATION

1. Remove the front driveshaft from the vehicle.

2. Matchmark the yokes before disassembling so they will be installed in their original locations to retain driveshaft balance.

3. To expedite removal, remove the bearing caps in the sequence indicated.

4. Support the driveshaft horizontally and aligned with the base plate of the press. Shear the bearing cap plastic retaining ring and position the first link yoke rear arm over a 1⅛ in. socket. Place spider press tool C–4365–1 or equivalent, on the bearing caps in the flange yoke arms. Force the bearing cap out of the yoke with a press.

5. If the bearing cap is not completely removed, insert a spacer between the spider and bearing cap and complete the removal.

6. Rotate the driveshaft 180 degrees and repeat the procedure.

7. Disengage the spider trunnions from the link yoke. Pull the flange yoke and the spider from the centering ball on the ball support tube yoke.

8. To remove the ball socket, separate the joint between the link yoke and the flange yoke by forcing the spider trunnion bushing from the link yoke. Pull the flange yoke and the spider with the ball socket from the centering ball as an assembly.

9. Pry the seal from the ball socket and remove the washers, spring and 3 ball seats.

10. Remove the centering ball from the ball socket using tool set C–4365 or equivalent.

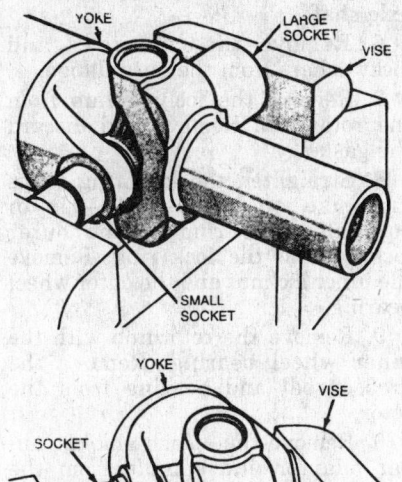

U-joint removal and installation

79111074

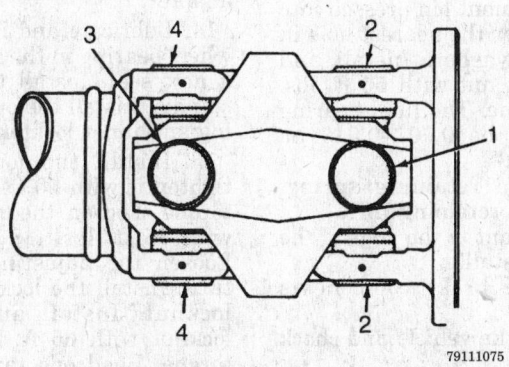

Bearing cap removal sequence

79111075

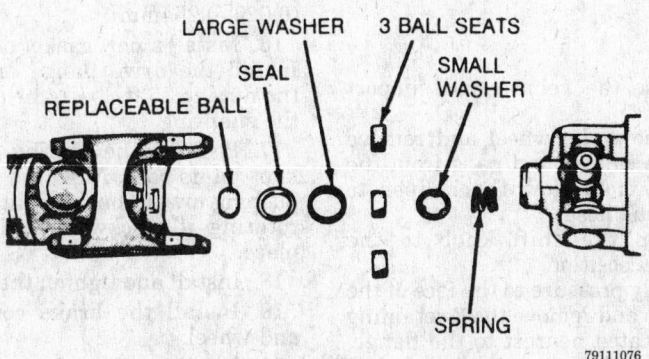

Double Cardan joint components

79111076

To install:

11. Install the centering ball in the socket using special tool C–4365–3. Force the ball into the socket until it is seated firmly against the shoulder at the base of the socket.

12. To install the spider, insert 1 bearing cap partially into 1 of the yoke bores and then rotate the yoke 180 degrees. Insert the spider into the yoke bore and seat the spider trunnion in the bearing cap. Partially insert the opposite bearing cap in the remaining yoke bolt.

13. Force the bearing caps inward while pivoting the spider back and forth to provide free movement of the trunnions in the bearing.

14. When the retainer grooves become visible, install the retainer.

15. Continue to force the caps inward until the opposite retainer can be installed in its groove.

16. Lubricate the centering ball and socket with the lubricant provided in the replacement key.

17. Repeat the installation procedure with the remaining portion of the assembly.

Front Axle Shaft, Bearing and Seal

REMOVAL AND INSTALLATION

Dana 44

RIGHT SIDE SHAFT

1. Raise the vehicle and support safely.

2. Remove the wheel and remove the brake caliper from the rotor. Do not allow the caliper to hang by the hose.

3. Remove the dust cap and driving hub snapring.

4. Remove the driving hub and retaining spring.

5. Remove the wheel bearing nut lock using tool C–4170–A or equivalent. Remove the retaining washer and the wheel bearing adjusting nut.

6. Remove the rotor/hub with wheel bearings and retainer spring plate. Remove the grease seal and bearing from the rotor.

7. Remove the splash shield and spindle from the steering knuckle.

8. Remove the brake caliper adaptor from the knuckle.

9. Remove the axle shaft from the axle housing. Remove the seal and stone guard from the shaft.

To install:

10. Install the seal on the axle shaft stone shield with the lip facing toward the axle shaft splines.

11. Insert the axle assembly into the axle housing making sure not to damage the differential seal.

12. Install the brake caliper adaptor to the knuckle. Install the spindle and splash shield and torque the nuts to 30 ft. lbs. (41 Nm).

13. Lubricate and install the inner wheel bearing in the rotor and install a new seal.

14. Install the assembly to the spindle. Install the adjusting nut and tighten it with 50 ft. lbs. (68 Nm) of torque. Loosen the nut and tighten with 35 ft. lbs. (48 Nm) of torque. Loosen the adjusting nut about 3/8 turn. Position the retaining washer on the adjusting nut by rotating the nut so the alignment pin pressed into the nut will enter the nearest hole in the retaining washer. Install and tighten the nut lock with 50 ft. lbs. (68 Nm) of torque. The final bearing endplay should be 0.001–0.010 in. (0.025–0.254mm).

15. Install the retaining spring, driving hub and retaining ring.

16. Apply sealant to the edge of the dust cap and install.

17. Install the brake components and wheel.

18. Road test the vehicle and check for leaks.

LEFT SIDE SHAFT

1. Raise the vehicle and support safely.

2. Remove the wheel and remove the brake caliper from the rotor. Do not allow the caliper to hang by the hose.

3. Remove the dust cap and driving hub snapring.

4. Remove the driving hub and retaining spring.

5. Remove the wheel bearing nut lock using tool C–4170–A or equivalent. Remove the retaining washer and the wheel bearing adjusting nut.

6. Remove the rotor/hub with wheel bearings and retainer spring plate. Remove the grease seal and bearing from the rotor.

7. Remove the splash shield and spindle from the steering knuckle.

8. Remove the brake caliper adaptor from the knuckle.

9. Disconnect the vacuum hoses and electrical connector from the disconnect housing assembly.

10. Remove the disconnect housing assembly, cover and shield from the axle.

11. Remove the intermediate axle shaft from the axle tube.

12. Remove the shift collar from the disconnect housing.

13. Remove the inner axle shaft seal from the axle tube and remove from the housing. If equipped with a seal guard, discard it; the guard is not used with the replacement seal.

14. Remove the needle bearing from intermediate axle shaft with remover D–354–1. Remove the front differential cover.

15. Force the inner axle shaft toward the center of the vehicle and remove the C–lock from the recessed groove in the shaft.

16. Remove the inner axle shaft using tools D–354–4 and D–354–3 or equivalent.

17. Use tool D–354–1 and puller C–637 or equivalent, to remove the inner axle shaft bearing.

To install:

18. Use tool D–354–4 and C–637 or equivalent, to install the inner axle shaft bearing.

19. Install the inner axle shaft using D–354–4 and D–354–2 or equivalent. Slide the axle shaft into

the side gear and install the C-lock in the groove.

20. Install the replacement seal using the replacing tools.

21. Install the shift collar on the splined end of the inner axle shaft.

22. Install the needle bearing in the end of the intermediate shaft using installer D–328 and driver handle C–4171. Lubricate splined end of shaft with multi-purpose lubricant and install the intermediate axle shaft through the axle tube.

23. Install the disconnect housing assembly and gasket. Make sure the shift fork is properly guided into the shift collar groove. Install the shield.

24. Connect the vacuum hoses and electrical connector to the diaphragm and switch on the disconnect housing assembly.

25. Install the brake caliper adaptor to the knuckle. Install the spindle and splash shield and torque the nuts to 30 ft. lbs. (41 Nm).

26. Lubricate and install the inner wheel bearing in the rotor and install a new seal.

27. Install the assembly to the spindle. Install the adjusting nut and tighten it with 50 ft. lbs. (68 Nm) of torque. Loosen the nut and tighten with 35 ft. lbs. (48 Nm) of torque. Loosen the adjusting nut about ⅜ turn. Position the retaining washer on the adjusting nut by rotating the nut so the alignment pin pressed into the nut will enter the nearest hole in the retaining washer. Install and tighten the lock nut with 50 ft. lbs. (68 Nm) of torque. The final bearing endplay should be 0.001–0.010 in. (0.025–0.254mm).

28. Install the retaining spring, driving hub and retaining ring.

29. Apply sealant to the edge of the dust cap and install.

30. Install the brake components and wheel.

31. Road test the vehicle and check for leaks.

Dana 60

1. Raise the vehicle and support safely.

2. Remove the wheel and remove the brake caliper and pads from the rotor. Do not allow the caliper to hang by the hose.

3. Turn the shift knob to the **ENGAGE** position.

4. Apply pressure to the face of the shift knob and remove the 3 retaining screws located nearest to the flange. Pull outward and remove the shift knob from the base.

5. Remove the snapring from the axle shaft.

6. Remove the capscrews and lockwashers from the base flange.

7. Remove the locking hub from the rotor/hub. Remove and discard the gasket.

8. Straighten the lock ring tangs and use tool DD–1241–JD or equivalent, to remove the outer locknut and the lock ring. Remove the inner locknut and the outer wheel bearing.

9. Remove the rotor/hub with the inner wheel bearing. Remove the grease seal and bearing from the rotor.

10. Remove the splash shield, caliper adaptor and spindle from the steering knuckle.

11. Slide the inner and outer axle shafts with the bronze spacer, seal and slinger from the axle shaft tube and the steering knuckle.

To install:

12. Position the bronze spacer on the axle shaft with the chamfer facing the U–joint. Slide the axle shaft into the steering knuckle and the axle shaft tube.

13. Install the spindle, the brake adaptor and the splash shield. Torque the nuts to 65 ft. lbs. (86 Nm). Position the inner pad on the adapter.

14. Lubricate and install the inner wheel bearing in the rotor and install a new seal. Install the rotor to the spindle. Install the outer wheel bearing and inner locknut.

15. Install the locknut nut and tighten it with 50 ft. lbs. (68 Nm) of torque. Loosen the nut and tighten with 35 ft. lbs. (48 Nm) of torque. Loosen the adjusting nut about ⅜ turn. Install the lock ring and outer locknut. Install and tighten the locknut with 65 ft. lbs. (88 Nm) of torque. Bend one tang over each of the locknuts. The final bearing endplay should be 0.001–0.010 in. (0.025–0.254mm).

16. Install a new gasket on the hub. Install the drive flange and torque the nuts to 35 ft. lbs. (48 Nm). Install the snapring.

17. Position the locking hub shift knob on its base. Align the splines by pushing inward on the shift knob and rotating it clockwise to lock it in place.

18. Install and tighten the 3 screws.

19. Install the brake components and wheel.

20. Road test the vehicle and check for leaks.

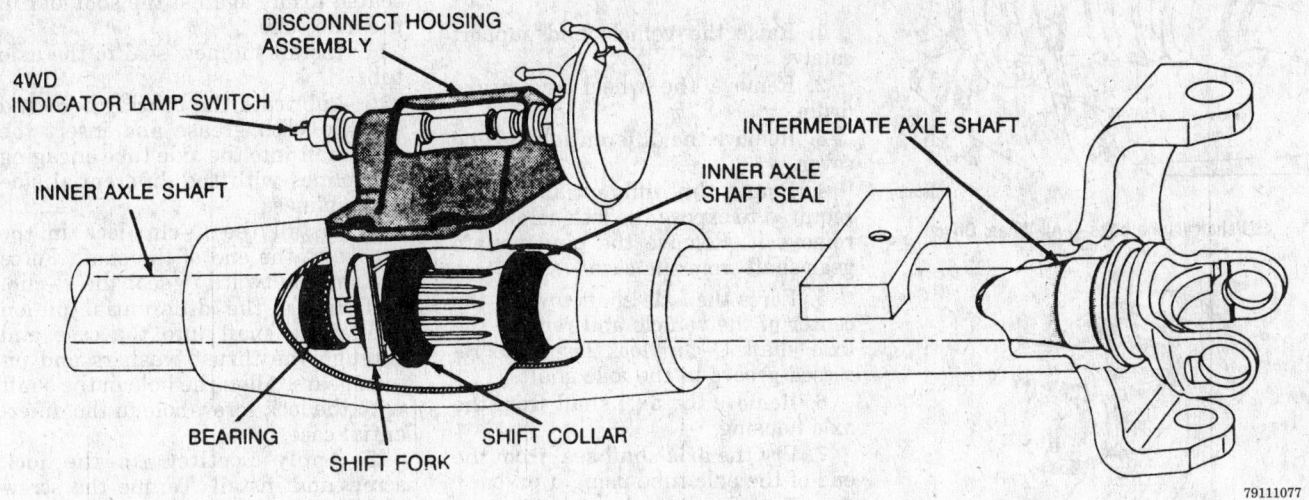

Model 44 left side front axle

79111077

Rear Axle Shaft, Bearing and Seal

REMOVAL AND INSTALLATION

Caravan, Voyager and Town & Country

FRONT WHEEL DRIVE

NOTE: Sodium-based grease is not compatible with lithium-based grease. Read the package labels and be careful not to mix the 2 types. If there is any doubt as to the type of grease used, completely clean the old grease from the bearing and hub before replacing.

1. Raise and support the vehicle with the rear wheels off the floor.
2. Remove the wheel grease cap, cotter pin, nut-lock and bearing adjusting nut.
3. Remove the thrust washer and bearing.
4. Remove the drum from the spindle.
5. Thoroughly clean the old lubricant from the bearings and hub cavity. Inspect the bearing rollers for pitting or other signs of wear. Light discoloration is normal.

To install:

6. Repack the bearings with high temperature multi-purpose EP grease and add a small amount of new grease to the hub cavity. Be sure to force the lubricant between all rollers in the bearing.
7. Install the drum on the spindle after coating the polished spindle surfaces with wheel bearing lubricant.
8. Install the outer bearing cone, thrust washer and adjusting nut.
9. Tighten the adjusting nut to 20–25 ft. lbs. while rotating the wheel.
10. Back off the adjusting nut to completely release the preload from the bearing.
11. Tighten the adjusting nut finger-tight.
12. Position the nut-lock with 1 pair of slots in line with the cotter pin hole. Install the cotter pin.
13. Clean and install the grease cap and wheel.
14. Lower the vehicle.

ALL WHEEL DRIVE

The rear wheel bearings used on these models is a bolt in type unit, this is the same unit that is used on the front knuckle assembly.

1. Raise and support the vehicle.

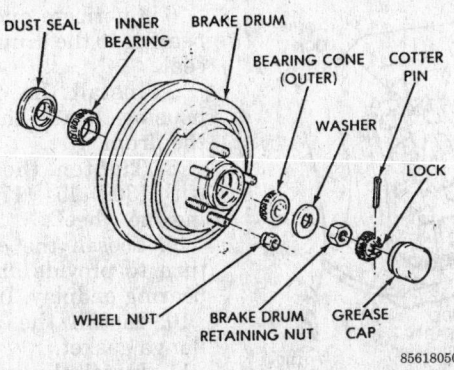

Rear brake drum and bearings — FWD models

85618050

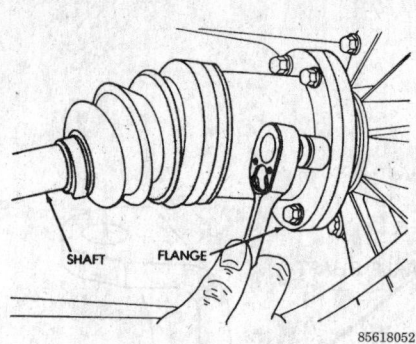

Halfshaft flange bolts — All Wheel Drive

85618052

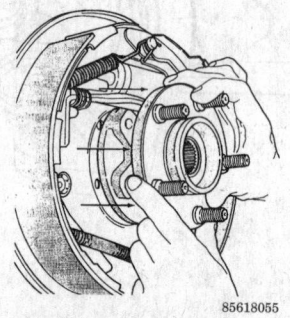

Pull the wheel bearing assembly from the housing — All Wheel Drive

85618055

2. Remove the wheel and tire assembly.

3. Remove the halfshaft flange retaining bolts and remove the halfshaft assembly.

4. Remove the wheel bearing mounting bolts and remove the wheel bearing and hub assembly.

To install:

5. Install the hub and bearing assembly, tighten the bolts to 96 ft. lbs. (130 Nm) in a criss-cross pattern.

NOTE: Thoroughly clean the seal and wear sleeve, lubricate both before installation.

6. Install the halfshaft.

7. Install the washer and hub nut, with the brakes applied tighten the nut to 180 ft. lbs. (244 Nm).

8. Install the spring washer, nut lock and new cotter pin.

9. Install the wheel and tire assembly.

Chrysler 7¼ in., 8¼ in., 8⅜ in. and 9¼ in. Differentials

NOTE: If equipped with a Trac-Loc differential, do not rotate either axle shaft unless both are properly in place. Rotation of 1 axle shaft without the other being installed can result in mis-alignment of the side gears/splines. This will necessitate side gear realignment before the axle shaft can be installed.

1. Raise the vehicle and support safely.

2. Remove the wheel and brake drum.

3. Remove the differential housing cover.

4. Rotate the differential case as required to expose the lock screw and remove it. Remove the pinion mate gear shaft from the case.

5. Force the axle shaft toward the center of the vehicle and remove the axle shaft C–clip lock from the recessed groove in the axle shaft.

6. Remove the axle shaft from the axle housing.

7. Pry the axle shaft seal from the end of the axle tube using a prybar.

8. To remove the bearing from an 7¼ in., 8¼ in. and 8⅜ in. differential, use removal tool C–4167 attached to a slide hammer C–637. To remove the bearing from an 9¼ in. rear, use removal tool C–4828 attached to a slide hammer.

To install:

9. Clean the bearing bore in the axle tube.

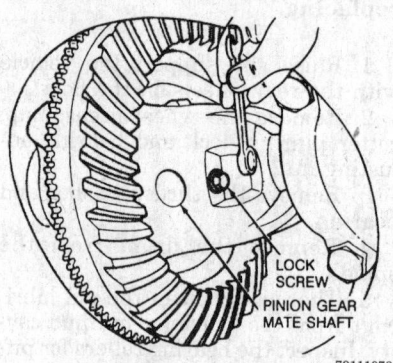

LOCK SCREW

PINION GEAR MATE SHAFT

79111078

Removing the lock screw

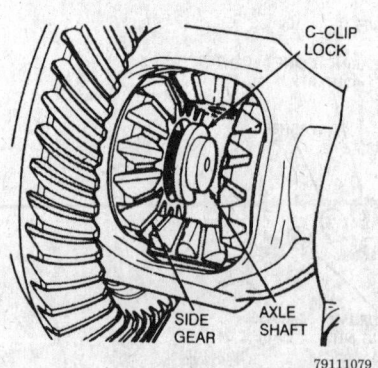

C–CLIP LOCK

SIDE GEAR

AXLE SHAFT

79111079

Removing the C-clip lock

10. Insert the new axle shaft bearing onto the pilot of tool C–4198 for 7¼ in., 8¼ in. and 8⅜ in. differential or tool C–4826 for 9¼ in. rear. The bearing is fully installed when it is seated firmly against the shoulder in the axle tube.

11. Install the new seal to the axle tube.

12. Lubricate the bearing bore and seal lip with grease and insert the axle shaft into the axle tube engaging its splines with the differential side gear splines.

13. Install the C–clip lock in the groove at the end of the shaft. Force the shaft outward to seat the C–clip.

14. Insert the differential pinion gear mate shaft into the case and through the thrust washers and pinion gears. Align the hole in the shaft with the lock screw hole in the differential case.

15. Apply Loctite® to the lock screw and install. Torque the screw to 8 ft. lbs. (11 Nm) for 7¼ in. and 8¼ in. differentials or 14 ft. lbs. (19 Nm) for all others.

16. Thoroughly clean and dry the case cover, mating surface, bolts and bolt holes. Apply silicone sealer to the cover and install.

17. Install the drum and wheel.

18. Fill the differential with the proper lubricant.

19. Road test the vehicle and check for leaks.

Dana Model 60, 60M and 70 Differentials

1. Raise the vehicle and support safely.

2. Remove the axle flange lock bolts or nuts.

3. Remove the axle shaft.

4. Remove the locknut and remove the special adjustment nut.

5. Remove the outer bearing, brake drum and inner bearing. Remove the inner seal from the drum.

To install:

6. Lubricate and install the inner bearing to the drum and install a new seal.

7. Install the drum to the axle housing. Install the outer bearing to the drum.

8. Tighten the adjustment nut with 130 ft. lbs. (175 Nm) while rotating the wheel.

9. Loosen the adjustment nut ⅓ turn to provide about 0.005 inch of bearing endplay. Install the locknut.

10. Install the axle with a new flange gasket.

11. Install the axle flange bolts and torque to 70 ft. lbs. (95 Nm).

Front Wheel Knuckle/Spindle and Bearings

REMOVAL AND INSTALLATION

Caravan, Voyager and Town & Country

NOTE: A tie rod end puller (Chrysler tool C–3894A or equivalent) is necessary.

STEERING KNUCKLE

1. Remove the wheel cover, center hub cover, cotter pin, nut lock and spring washer from the front wheel.
2. Loosen the front hub nut and wheel lug nuts. Raise and safely support the vehicle.
3. Remove the wheel and tire assembly. Remove the center hub nut.
4. Disconnect the tie rod end from the steering knuckle arm with tool C–3894A or equivalent. Disconnect the front brake hose bracket from the strut.
5. Remove the caliper assembly and support it with a piece of wire.

Do not permit the caliper to hang from the brake hose. Remove the disc brake rotor, inner pad and caliper mounting adapter.

6. Remove the clamp bolt that secures the ball joint and steering knuckle together.
7. Insure that the splined half-shaft is loose in the hub by tapping lightly with a brass drift and hammer. Separate the ball joint and steering knuckle. Pull the knuckle assembly out and away from the half-shaft. Remove the steering knuckle from the strut assembly.

To install:

8. Service hub, bearing, seal and steering knuckle as necessary.
9. Install the steering knuckle to the strut assembly. Install the half-shaft through the hub and steering knuckle. Connect the ball joint to the knuckle and tighten the clamp bolt to 100 ft. lbs. (136 Nm).
10. Install the tie rod end and tighten the retaining nut to 35 ft. lbs. Install and bend the cotter pin.
11. Install the brake adapter, pads, rotor and caliper. Connect the brake hose bracket to the strut.
12. Install the center hub washer and retaining nut. Apply the brakes and tighten the nut to 180 ft. lbs. Install the spring washer, nut and new cotter pin. Install the wheel and tire assembly. Tighten the lug nuts to 95 ft. lbs. Lower the vehicle.

HUB AND BEARING

The bearing unit is serviced as a complete assembly. and is attached to the steering knuckle by 4 mounting bolts that are removed through a provided access hole in the hub flange.

1. Loosen the center splined retaining hub nut while the vehicle is on the ground. Loosen the wheel lug nuts slightly.
2. Raise and safely support the vehicle.
3. Remove the wheel assembly. Remove the hub nut and washer.
4. Disconnect the tie rod end from the steering arm and the clamp bolt that retains the ball joint to the knuckle.
5. Remove the disc brake caliper and suspend it with wire so there is no strain on the brake hose. Remove the rotor.
6. Separate the knuckle from the ball joint. Pull the knuckle assembly away from the halfshaft. Take care not separate the halfshaft inner CV-joint. Support the halfshaft.
7. Remove the 4 hub and bearing retaining bolts. Remove the assembly.

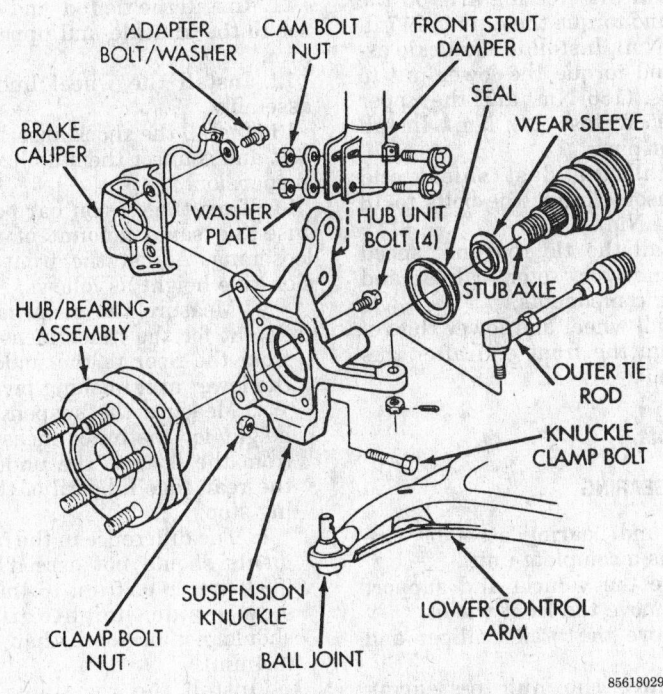

85618029

Steering knuckle assembly

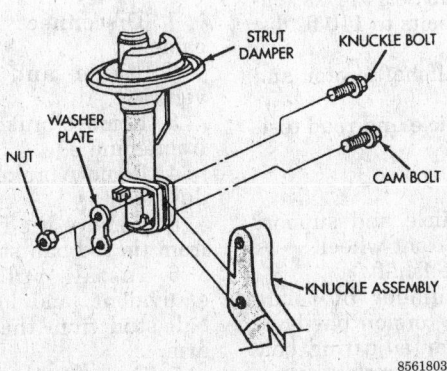

85618034

Remove/install the steering knuckle from the strut

To install:

8. Install the new bearing assembly and tighten the mounting bolts in a criss-cross manner to 45 ft. lbs. (61 Nm).

9. Install a new wear sleeve seal. Lubricate the sealing surfaces with multi-purpose grease. Install the halfshaft through the hub.

10. Install the steering knuckle onto the lower control arm. Torque the clamp bolt to 105 ft. lbs. (143 Nm).

11. Install the tie rod end and torque the nut to 35 ft. lbs. (48 Nm). Install the brake disc rotor and caliper assembly.

12. Install and tighten the hub nut reasonably tight. Install the wheel assembly, tighten the lug nuts fairly tight. Lower the vehicle and tighten the hub nut to 180 ft. lbs. (245 Nm) and the wheel lugs to 85 ft. lbs. (116 Nm).

2WD Dakota

HUB AND BEARINGS

1. Disconnect negative battery cable.

2. Raise and safely support vehicle. Remove the front wheel.

3. Remove brake caliper and rotor from spindle.

4. Remove the seal and inner bearing.

5. Remove the bearing races with a punch and hammer. Be careful not to damage the hub service.

To install:

6. Clean all components, except the hub with solvent and blow dry with shop air. The hub is porous and will absorb the solvent, causing the grease to liquefy.

7. Install the bearing races into the hub using a suitable installing tool.

8. Apply a coating of high temperature wheel bearing grease into the engine inner surface of the hub. Force grease into the bearing assemblies and install the inner bearing and seal.

9. Carefully slide the hub/rotor assembly onto the spindle.

10. Install the outer wheel bearing, washer and retaining nut.

11. Torque the nut to 30–40 ft. lbs. (41–54 Nm) while rotating the hub/rotor. Loosen the nut to release the preload. Retighten the nut finger-tight and install the nut lock and cotter pin.

12. Install the dust cap, front wheel and lower the vehicle.

KNUCKLE

1. Raise the vehicle and support safely. Place a jack under the outer end of the lower control arm.

2. Remove the wheel, brake caliper and hub/rotor. Disconnect the speed sensor connector, if equipped.

3. Disconnect the tie rod end from the knuckle.

4. Remove the dust shield and speed sensor pickup.

5. Remove the cotter pins and nuts from the upper and lower ball joints.

6. Use a ball joint remover C–3564A to free the upper and lower ball joints from the steering knuckle.

7. Remove the steering knuckle assembly.

To install:

8. Install the steering arm on the knuckle and torque the nuts to 217 ft. lbs. (294 Nm). Install the knuckle assembly and torque the lower nut to 135 ft. lbs. (183 Nm) and the upper nut to 105 ft. lbs. (142 Nm). Install new cotter pins.

9. Install the dust shield and speed sensor. Torque the bolts to 18 ft. lbs. (24 Nm).

10. Install the tie rod end, speed sensor connector, rotor, caliper and remaining components.

11. Install wheel and lower the vehicle. Align the front end after this procedure.

4WD Dakota

HUB AND BEARING

The hub and bearing assembly are serviced as a complete unit.

1. Raise the vehicle and support safely. Remove the front wheel.

2. Remove the brake caliper and rotor.

3. Remove the hub-to-steering knuckle bolts, hub and bearing assembly.

To install:

4. Install the hub/bearing assembly and torque the bolts to 110 ft. lbs. (149 Nm).

5. Install the halfshaft, rotor and caliper.

6. Lower the vehicle and road test.

KNUCKLE

1. Raise the vehicle and support safely. Remove the front wheel.

2. Remove the halfshaft.

3. Count the number of turns when loosening the torsion bar bolt. Turn the torsion bar adjusting bolt counterclockwise to completely remove tension from the torsion bar.

4. Remove the shock absorber lower bolt and disconnect the stabilizer bar from suspension.

5. Remove the wheel hub/bearing assembly.

6. Remove the tie rod and ABS sensor from the knuckle and upper control arm.

7. Remove the upper and lower ball joint cotter pins and nuts.

8. Use ball joint remover C–3564–A to remove the upper and lower ball joints from the knuckle.

9. Remove the steering knuckle from the vehicle.

To install:

10. Install the knuckle and ball joint nuts. Torque the lower nut to 115 ft. lbs. (156 Nm) and upper nut to 105 ft. lbs. (142 Nm). Install a new cotter pin in each ball joint.

11. Install the tie rod and ABS sensor to the knuckle and upper control arm.

12. Install the wheel hub/bearing assembly.

13. Install the shock absorber lower bolt and connect the stabilizer bar to suspension.

14. Turn the torsion bar bolt clockwise the same amount of turns as loosening. Adjust the front suspension ride height as follows:

   a. Measure the suspension arm height for the inner measurement from the floor to the underside of the lower arm bushing pivot bores.

   b. Measure the suspension arm height for the outer measurement from the floor to the underside of the rear edge inboard of the steering stop.

   c. The difference in the measurements should not exceed 1.50 in. (38.0mm) ± 0.25 in. (6.4mm). The side-to-side height difference should not be more than 0.25 in. (6.4mm).

15. Install the remaining components and align the front end.

Model 44–2WD Vehicles

1. Disconnect negative battery cable.

2. Raise and safely support vehicle.

3. Remove brake caliper and rotor from spindle.

4. Remove brake splash shield and dust seal.

5. Remove the cotter pin and nut from tie rod ball stud.

6. Install puller C–3894A or equivalent, and loosen tie rod end ball stud from the steering knuckle arm.

7. Remove the shock absorber from vehicle.

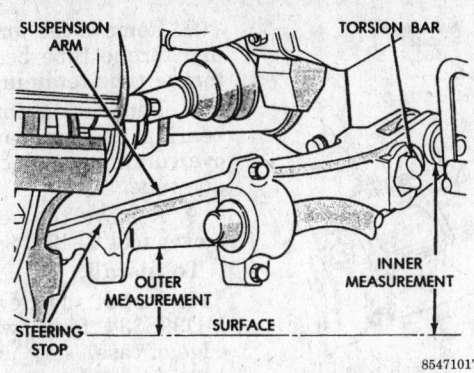

85471017

Front suspension ride height measurement — 4WD Dakota

8. Install spring compressor tool DD–1278 or equivalent, in the spring and snug nut by hand.

9. Remove cotter pins and lower and upper ball stud nuts at the steering knuckle.

10. Loosen upper and lower joint studs from the steering knuckle and remove ball studs. Slowly loosen tension on spring until spring is in a relaxed position.

11. Remove steering knuckle from vehicle. Remove the brake adapter and steering knuckle attaching bolts and separate knuckle from the steering arm.

To install:

12. Install brake adapter on steering knuckle and tighten to 100 ft. lbs. (136 Nm).

13. Install steering knuckle arm to steering knuckle bolts and torque to 215 ft. lbs. (291 Nm).

14. Mount the knuckle to the suspension arms and torque upper nut to 105 ft. lbs. (142 Nm). Torque lower nut as follows:

a. If $^{11}/_{16}$–16 bolt to 135 ft. lbs. (183 Nm). Install cotter pin.

b. If $^{3}/_{4}$–16 bolt to 175 ft. lbs. (237 Nm). Install cotter pin.

15. Connect the tie rod end. Install nut and tighten to 45 ft. lbs. (61 Nm). Install cotter pin.

16. Install new dust seal on steering knuckle. Install splash shield.

17. Install shock absorber. Install rotor and brake caliper.

18. Install wheel and tire assembly and reconnect negative battery cable.

19. Road test vehicle for proper operation.

Model 44 and 60–4WD Vehicles

1. Raise and safely support vehicle.

2. Remove the wheel tire assembly.

3. Remove the cotter pin and retaining nut from the drag link.

4. Install puller C–4150 or equivalent, on the drag link ball stud and separate from knuckle arm.

5. Remove 3 steering knuckle arm to steering knuckle nuts and washers. Remove the steering knuckle arm from the vehicle.

To install:

6. Position steering knuckle arm to steering knuckle. Install nuts and tighten to 90 ft. lbs. (122 Nm).

7. Connect drag link to steering knuckle arm and tighten nut to 60 ft. lbs. (81 Nm). Install new cotter pin. Lower vehicle.

Manual Locking Hubs

REMOVAL AND INSTALLATION

1. Raise the vehicle and support safely.

2. Remove the wheel and remove the brake caliper and pads from the rotor. Do not allow the caliper to hang by the hose.

3. Turn the shift knob to the **ENGAGE** position.

4. Apply pressure to the face of the shift knob and remove the 3 retaining screws located nearest to the flange. Pull outward and remove the shift knob from the base.

5. Remove the snapring from the axle shaft.

6. Remove the capscrews and lockwashers from the base flange.

7. Remove the locking hub from the rotor/hub. Remove and discard the gasket.

To install:

8. Install a new gasket on the hub. Install the drive flange and torque the nuts to 35 ft. lbs. (48 Nm). Install the snapring.

9. Position the locking hub shift knob on its base. Align the splines by pushing inward on the shift knob and rotating it clockwise to lock it in place.

10. Install and tighten the 3 screws.

11. Install the brake components and wheel.

12. Road test the vehicle and check for leaks.

Vacuum Disconnect Motor

REMOVAL AND INSTALLATION

Dana Model 44/60 Front Differential

1. Disconnect the vacuum and electrical connectors.

2. Remove the indicator switch.

3. Remove the shift motor housing cover, gasket and shield from the differential housing.

4. Remove the E-clips from the shift motor housing and shaft. Remove the shift motor and fork from the housing.

5. Remove the O-ring seal from the motor shaft.

To install:

6. Clean and inspect all components.

7. Install the new O-ring, shift motor shaft and shift fork. The shift fork offset should be toward the differential.

8. Install the E-clips and assembly to the differential. Torque the housing bolts to 96 inch lbs. (11 Nm).

9. Add 5 oz. (148ml) of GL5 gear lubricant to the motor housing, through the indicator switch hole.

10. Install the indicator switch, electrical and vacuum connectors.

11. Drive vehicle and check operation.

Pinion Seal

REMOVAL AND INSTALLATION

Caravan, Voyager and Town & Country AWD

FRONT OVERRUNNING CLUTCH SEAL

1. Remove the rear drive line module from the vehicle. The front overrunning clutch seal is located in the overrunning clutch case.

2. Remove the viscous coupling unit.

3. Remove the overrunning clutch cover assembly and drain the fluid.

4. Remove the clutch case from the rear carrier case.

5. Remove the inner race snapring and slide the clutch inner race off the shaft.

6. Remove the shaft snapring and slide the dog clutch off the shaft, noting the snapring positioning.

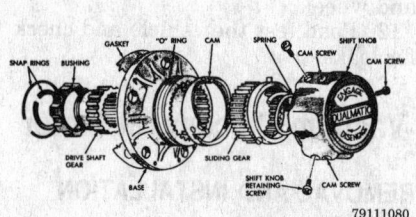

Dualmatic locking hub

79111080

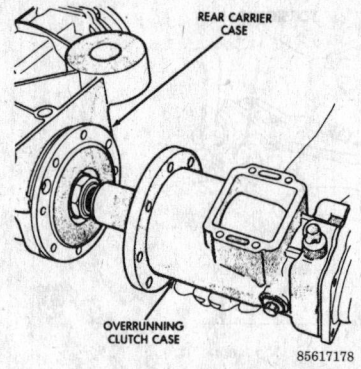

Separating the housings

85617178

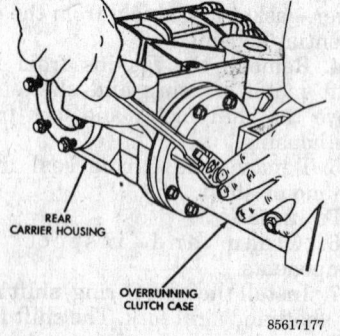

Overrunning clutch case to rear carrier bolts

85617177

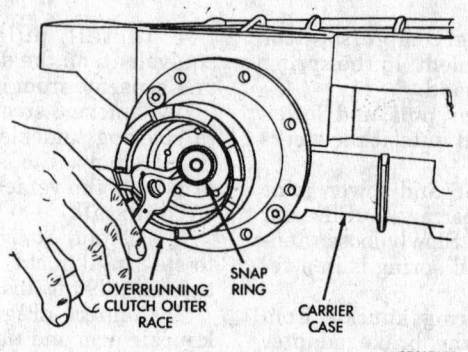

Overruning clutch snapring removal

85617179

7. Remove the torque shaft snapring, torque tube bearing shield and torque tube retaining bolts.

8. Remove the inner torque shaft bearing snapring and separate the overrunning clutch case from the torque tube.

9. Remove the seal with seal remover tool C–4967.

To install:

10. Install the new seal with tool MD998334 flush with the outside edge of case.

11. Install the rear torque shaft bearing and snapring.

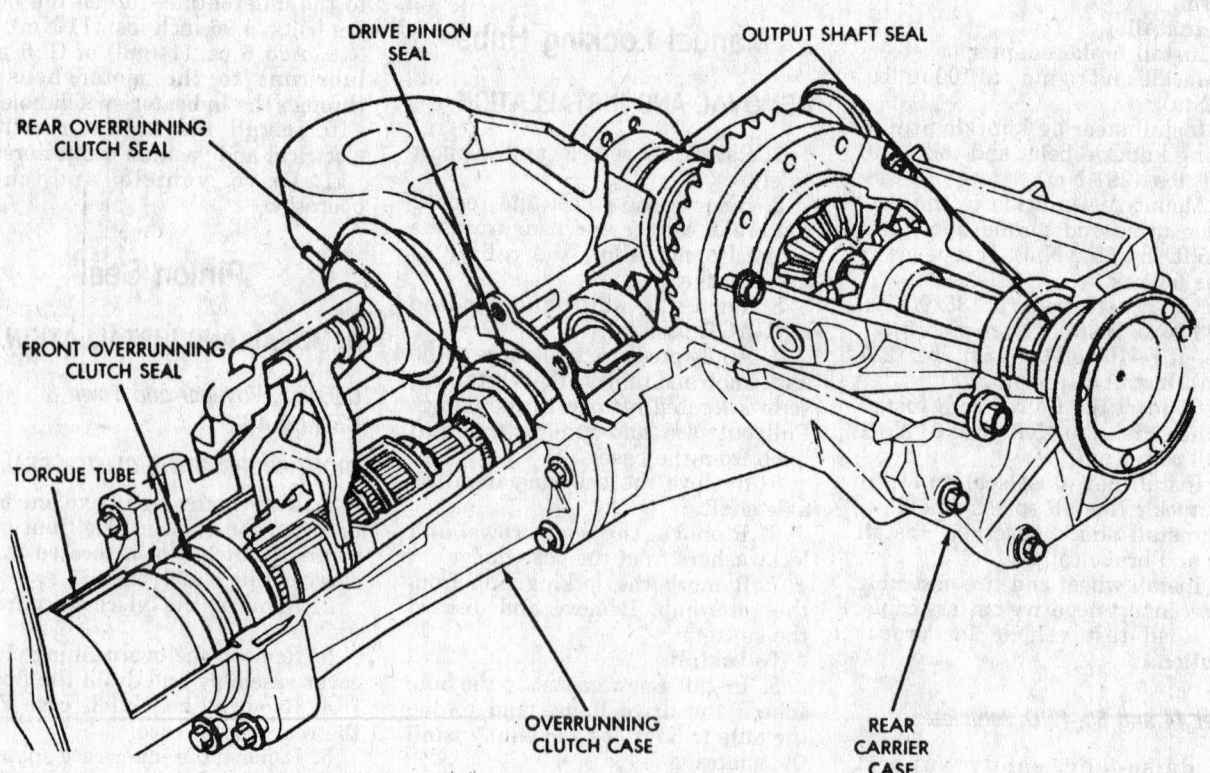

Rear driveline module seal locations — AWD Caravan, Voyager and Town & Country

85617176

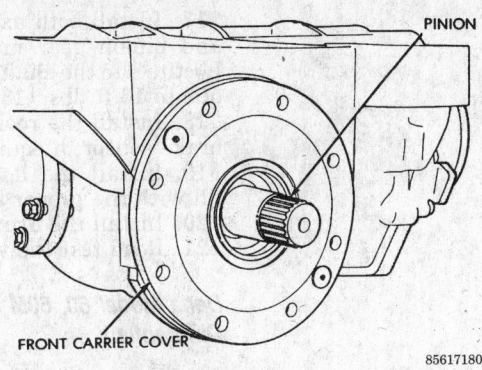

Reinstalling the front carrier cover

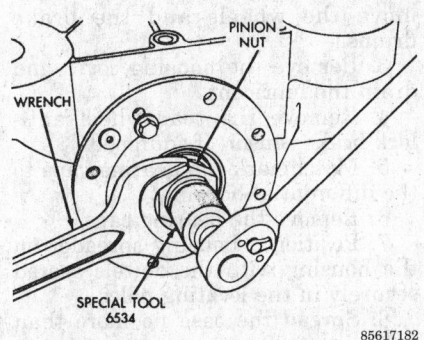

Removing the pinion nut

12. Install the overrunning clutch case onto the torque tube and torque bolts to 250 inch lbs. (28 Nm).

13. Install the torque shaft inner snapring and slide the dog clutch onto the shaft. Install the snapring.

14. Slide the overrunning clutch inner race onto shaft and install retaining snapring with the tapered end of inner race facing outward.

15. Clean the gasket surfaces and apply Mopar® Gasket Maker or equivalent. Install the overrunning clutch case to the carrier case. Torque the bolts to 250 inch lbs. (28 Nm).

16. Apply Gasket Maker or equivalent and install the overrun-ning clutch cover. Make sure the clutch fork engages the clutch dog.

17. Install the rear drive line module into the vehicle and check fluid levels.

DRIVE PINION SEAL AND/OR REAR OVERRUNNING CLUTCH SEAL

1. Remove the rear drive line module from the vehicle. The drive pinion seal is located in the front carrier cover, behind the overrunning clutch rear seal. The overrunning clutch seal must be removed to gain access to the drive pinion seal. Do not reuse the overrunning clutch seal.

2. Remove the overrunning clutch case-to-rear carrier bolts. Separate the overrunning clutch case from the differential carrier case.

3. Remove the clutch snapring and outer race off the shaft.

4. Use spline socket tool 6534 and a wrench to remove the pinion nut.

5. Remove the front carrier cover. Place a block of wood under the end of the pinion shaft. Tap the end of the pinion against the wood to drive the spacer from the pinion shaft.

NOTE: A shim should be installed with the front carrier cover. This will eliminate the potential of cutting the O-ring with the shim.

6. Install the front carrier cover and bolts into the carrier case. Torque the bolts to 105 inch lbs. (12 Nm).

7. Use seal puller tool 7794–A to remove the overrunning clutch seal and drive pinion seal. The overrunning clutch seal must be removed first to gain access to the drive pinion seal. Do not reuse old seals.

To install:

8. Coat the drive pinion seal with oil and install using installer tool 6507. Install with the spring side towards the rear carrier case.

9. Coat the drive pinion spacer with oil and install with the tapered side facing outward.

10. Coat the overrunning clutch seal with oil and install using installer tool 6508. Install with the spring side away from the rear carrier case.

11. Clean pinion and nut with brake cleaner. Apply Loctite® to the threads and install the nut. Torque the nut to 280 ft. lbs. (380 Nm).

12. Install the overrunning clutch outer race and snapring.

13. Apply Loctite® sealer to the overrunning clutch case and install to the rear carrier case. Install the rear drive line module and check fluid level.

Except Caravan, Voyager and Town & Country

1. Raise the vehicle and support safely.

2. Matchmark and remove the driveshaft.

3. Remove the rear wheel and brake drums to prevent any drag.

4. Using an inch lb. torque wrench, measure the pinion bearing preload. Read the torque while the handle of the wrench is moving through several complete revolutions.

5. Using the proper tools, hold the companion flange and remove the drive pinion nut and washer.

6. Remove the companion flange using tool C–452 or equivalent. Lower the rear of the vehicle to prevent fluid loss.

7. Using a seal remover tool, remove the seal from the carrier and clean the seal seat.

To install:

8. The outside diameter of the seal is precoated with a special sealer so no sealing compound is required for installation. The seal is properly installed when the flange contacts the housing flange face.

9. Install the companion flange and the washer with the convex side out.

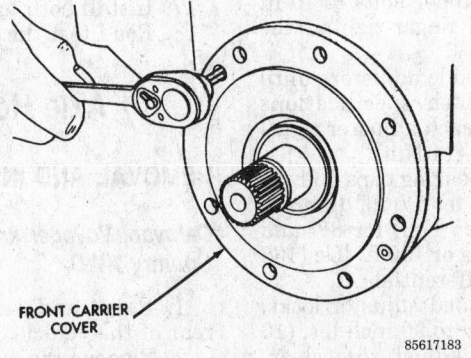

Removing the front carrier cover retaining bolts

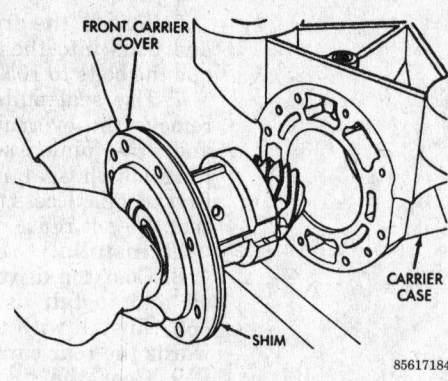

Removing the front carrier cover and pinion

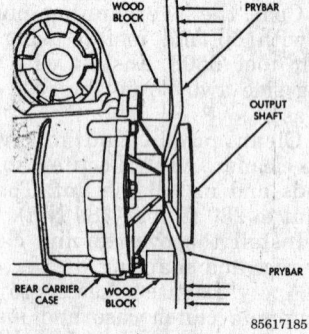

Removing the output flange using 2 pry bars

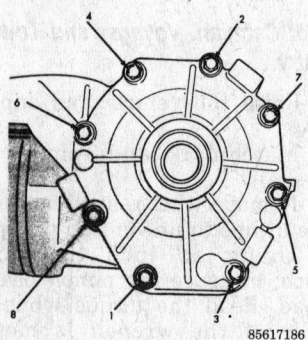

Differential side gear bolt torque sequence

10. For Chrysler differentials, tighten the pinion nut to 210 ft. lbs. (285 Nm) and check the pinion bearing preload. If the preload is less than the original preload measured, continue tightening the nut in very small increments until the proper preload is reached.

11. For Dana 60, 60M and 70 differentials, torque the pinion nut to 260 ft. lbs. (350 Nm).

12. Install the driveshaft, drums and rear wheels.

13. Refill the differential with the proper lubricant.

14. Road test the vehicle.

Differential Case

REMOVAL AND INSTALLATION

Chrysler 7¼ in., 8¼ in., 8⅜ in. and 9¼ in. Differentials

1. Raise the vehicle and support safely.

2. Remove the wheels and the brake drums.

3. Remove the rear housing cover and drain the lubricant.

4. Remove the rear wheel anti-lock brake sensor, if equipped.

5. Remove both pinion gear mate shaft, C-clips and axle shafts.

6. Matchmark the bearing caps to the differential housing.

7. Remove the differential bearing threaded adjuster lock from each cap.

8. Loosen but do not remove the bearing caps.

9. Loosen the side adjusters using tool C–4164.

10. Remove the bearing caps, the threaded adjusters and the differential case.

To install:

11. Position the assembled differential case in the housing.

12. Install the bearing caps in their original positions according to the matchmarks made during the disassembly.

13. Torque the upper bolts to 10 ft. lbs. (14 Nm) and finger-tighten the bottom bolts.

14. Tighten the side adjusters until the proper backlash specifications are reached with each adjuster tightened to 10 ft. lbs. (14 Nm).

15. Torque the bearing caps bolts to 45 ft. lbs. (61 Nm) for 7¼ in. differentials, 70 ft. lbs. (95 Nm) for 8¼ and 8⅜ in. differentials or 100 ft. lbs. (136 Nm) for 9¼ in. differentials.

16. Install threaded adjuster locks. Tighten lock screw to 90 inch lbs. (10 Nm). Check and adjust side clearance, if necessary.

17. Install both axle shafts, C-clips and pinion gear mate shaft. Apply Loctite® to the shaft lock pin and torque to 10 ft. lbs. (13 Nm).

18. Install the rear wheel anti-lock brake sensor, if equipped.

19. Install the housing cover and fill with the proper lubricant.

20. Install the drums and wheels.

21. Road test the vehicle.

Dana Model 60, 60M and 70 Differentials

1. Raise the vehicle and support safely.

2. Remove both axle shafts. Remove the wheels and the brake drums.

3. Remove the housing cover and drain the lubricant.

4. Remove the rear wheel anti-lock brake sensor, if equipped.

5. Matchmark the bearing caps to the differential housing.

6. Remove the bearing caps.

7. Position a housing spreader on the housing with the dowels seated securely in the locating holes.

8. Spread the case no more than 0.015 in. (0.38mm).

9. Remove the differential case from the housing using a small prying tool, if necessary.

To install:

10. Spread the housing and install the assembled case.

11. Install the bearing caps in their original positions according to the matchmarks made during the disassembly.

12. Torque the cap bolts to 85 ft. lbs. (115 Nm).

13. Check and adjust all measurements to specifications.

14. Install the rear wheel anti-lock brake sensor, if equipped.

15. Install the housing cover and fill with the proper lubricant. Include hypoid gear lubricant if the differential is a Trac–Lok.

16. Install the brake drums and wheels.

17. Install both axle shafts.

18. Road test the vehicle.

Axle Housing

REMOVAL AND INSTALLATION

Caravan, Voyager and Town & Country AWD

1. Raise and safely support the rear of the vehicle.

2. Remove the right and left inner halfshaft joint mounting bolts.

3. Support the inner side of the halfshaft, by hanging it from the frame using a piece of wire. Do not allow the shafts to hang freely or the joints will be damaged.

4. Remove the mounting bolts from the rear side of the propeller shaft at, the rear carrier.

5. Support the propeller shaft.

6. Remove the viscous coupling retaining nut and slide the viscous coupling off the rear driveline assembly.

7. Disconnect the vacuum line at the driveline module. Also disconnect the electrical lead from the assembly.

8. Support the rear of the driveline module with a jack.

9. Remove the rear driveline module front mounting bolts. Partially lower the unit from the vehicle.

10. Remove the rear driveline module from the vehicle.

To install:

11. Position the driveline module in the vehicle. Install the front mounting bolts and tighten to 40 ft. lbs. (54 Nm).

12. Reconnect the vacuum line and electrical lead. Install the viscous coupling and nut. Tighten the nut to 120 ft. lbs. (162 Nm).

13. Connect the propeller shaft to the driveline module, tighten to 250 inch lbs. (28 Nm).

14. Connect the rear halfshafts to the rear driveline module. Tighten the bolt to 45 ft. lbs. (61 Nm).

15. Lower the vehicle. Check the operation of the drive train.

Except Caravan, Voyager and Town & Country AWD

1. Disconnect the negative battery cable. Raise vehicle and support safely.

2. Remove the rear wheel anti-lock brake sensor, if equipped.

3. Remove the rear wheels.

4. Disconnect the brake hose at the T-fitting.

5. Disconnect the parking brake cables.

6. Matchmark and remove the driveshaft.

7. Support the weight of the assembly with the proper equipment. Disconnect the shock absorbers and remove the leaf spring nuts and U-bolts.

8. Remove the assembly from vehicle.

To install:

9. Position rear axle spring pads over spring center bolts and install U-bolts and nuts.

10. Connect the parking brake cables and rear shocks.

11. Reconnect the brake hoses. Align the reference marks and install driveshaft. Tighten the clamp bolts to 185 inch lbs. (22 Nm).

12. Install rear wheels and lower vehicle. Fill brake system, bleed and adjust brakes.

STEERING

Steering Wheel

REMOVAL AND INSTALLATION

— WARNING —
Replace air bag system components with Chrysler Mopar specified replacement parts. Substitute parts may visually appear interchangeable, but internal differences may result in inferior occupant protection. The fasteners, screws, and bolts, originally used for the air bag components, have special coatings and are specifically designed for the air bag system. They must never be replaced with any substitutes. Anytime a new fastener is needed, replace with the correct fasteners provided in the service package or fasteners listed in the Chrysler parts books.

Disconnect and isolate the battery negative cable before beginning any airbag system component removal or installation procedure. This will disable the airbag system. Failure to disconnect the battery could result in accidental airbag deployment and possible personal injury. Allow system capacitor to discharge for 2 minutes before removing any airbag components.

Caravan, Voyager and Town & Country

WITHOUT AIRBAG

NOTE: A steering wheel puller (Chrysler tool C3428B or the equivalent) is required.

1. Disconnect the negative battery cable at the battery.

2. Remove the center horn pad assembly. On standard steering wheels the horn pad is retained by 2 screws which are removed from underneath the wheel. Premium steering wheels require that the horn pad be pried from internal retainers. Pry the horn

pad up from the bottom edges of the steering wheel.

3. Disconnect the horn wires from the center pad, if necessary. Remove the pad.

4. Mark the column shaft and wheel for reinstallation reference and remove the steering wheel retaining nut.

5. Remove the steering wheel using a steering wheel puller (Chrysler tool C3428B or the equivalent).

To install:

6. Align the reference marks on the steering wheel and column shaft. Push wheel on to the shaft and draw into position with the mounting nut. Tighten the nut to 45 ft. lbs. (61 Nm). Install the center horn pad after connecting the horn connectors. Connect the negative battery cable.

WITH AIRBAG

— CAUTION —
Disconnect and isolate the negative (ground) battery cable. This will disable the air bag system. Failure to disconnect the battery could result in accidental deployment and possible personal injury. Allow system capacitor to discharge for 2 minutes then begin air bag system component removal.

1. Make sure the front wheels are straight and the steering column is locked in place.

2. Disconnect the negative battery cable at the battery and isolate.

3. Wait 2 minutes for the reserve capacitor to discharge before removing non deployed module.

4. Remove the 4 nuts attaching the air bag module from the back side of the steering wheel.

5. Lift the module and disconnect the connector from the rear of the module.

6. Remove the vehicle speed control switch and connector, if equipped or cover.

7. Mark the column shaft and wheel for reinstallation reference and remove the steering wheel retaining nut.

8. Remove the steering wheel using a steering wheel puller (Chrysler tool C3428B or the equivalent).

To install:

9. With the front wheels in a straight ahead position, position the steering wheel on the steering column, making sure to fit the flats on the hub of the steering wheel with the formations on the inside of the clockspring.

10. Pull the air bag and speed control wires through the lower, larger hole in the steering wheel and horn wire through the smaller hole at the top. Be sure not to pinch the wires.

11. Install and tighten the nut to 45 ft. lbs. (61 Nm).

12. Install the horn wire connector.

13. Connect the 4-way connector to the vehicle speed control switch and attach the switch to the steering wheel.

14. Connect the air bag lead wire to the air bag module and secure the module to the steering wheel. Tighten to 80–100 inch lbs. (9–11 Nm).

15. Do NOT connect the negative battery until an Air Bag System Check is performed as follows:

a. Remove forward console or cover as necessary.

b. Connect DRB to ACM data link 6-way connector, located at right of steering column.

c. Turn the ignition key to ON position. Exit vehicle with DRB. Use the latest version of the proper cartridge.

d. After checking that no one is inside the vehicle, connect the battery negative cable.

e. Using the DRB, read and record active diagnostic data.

f. Read and record any stored diagnostic codes.

g. Correct any problems found in steps (e) and (f).

h. Erase stored diagnostic codes if there are no active diagnostic codes. If problems remain, diagnostic codes will not erase.

i. Turn the ignition key to OFF then ON and observe the message center airbag lamp. It should go ON for 6–8 seconds, then go out; indicating system is functioning normally.

j. If airbag warning lamp either fails to light, blinks ON and OFF or goes ON and stays on, there is a system malfunction.

Except Caravan, Voyager and Town & Country

WITHOUT AIRBAG

1. Disconnect the negative battery cable.

2. Remove the horn pad.

3. Remove the steering wheel hold-down nut. Matchmark the steering wheel to the shaft.

4. Using a steering wheel puller, pull the steering wheel off the shaft.

To install:

5. Install steering wheel onto shaft and torque to 45 ft. lbs. (61 Nm).

6. Install horn pad and connect negative battery cable.

WITH AIRBAG

1. Disconnect and isolate the negative battery cable. Wait at least 2 minutes for the system capacitor to discharge before proceeding.

2. Place the steering wheel in the straight-ahead position.

3. If equipped, remove the speed control switch mounting screws from the underside of the steering wheel. Disconnect the switch connector.

4. Using a small prybar, remove the right rear steering wheel cover.

5. Remove the 4 nuts attaching the airbag module to the steering wheel. Remove the module and disconnect the electrical connector.

6. Remove the steering wheel hold-down nut. Matchmark the steering wheel to the shaft.

7. Using a steering wheel puller, pull the steering wheel off the shaft.

To install:

8. Pull the speed control and airbag wires through the lower hole in the steering wheel. Pull the horn wire through the smaller hole at the top. Make sure the wires are not pinched.

9. Install steering wheel onto shaft and torque to 45 ft. lbs. (61 Nm).

10. Connect the horn, speed control and airbag connectors. Connect the clockspring wiring connector to the module by pressing straight in on the connector. The connector should latch securely beneath the module locking clip to assure positive connection.

11. Install the 4 nuts and torque to 80–100 inch lbs. (9–11 Nm).

12. Do NOT connect the negative battery until an Air Bag System Check is performed as follows:

a. Remove forward console or cover as necessary.

b. Connect DRB to ACM data link 6-way connector, located at right of steering column.

c. Turn the ignition key to ON position. Exit vehicle with DRB. Use the latest version of the proper cartridge.

d. After checking that no one is inside the vehicle, connect the battery negative cable.

e. Using the DRB, read and record active diagnostic data.

f. Read and record any stored diagnostic codes.

g. Correct any problems found in steps (e) and (f).

h. Erase stored diagnostic codes if there are no active diagnostic codes. If problems remain, diagnostic codes will not erase.

i. Turn the ignition key to OFF then ON and observe the message center airbag lamp. It should go ON for 6–8 seconds, then go out; indicating system is functioning normally.

j. If airbag warning lamp either fails to light, blinks ON and OFF or goes ON and stays on, there is a system malfunction.

Steering Column

REMOVAL AND INSTALLATION

Caravan, Voyager and Town & Country

1992–96 MODELS

--- CAUTION ---

Disconnect and isolate the negative (ground) battery cable. This will disable the air bag system. Failure to disconnect the battery could result in accidental deployment and possible personal injury. Allow system capacitor to discharge for 2 minutes then begin air bag system component removal.

1. Make sure the front wheels are straight and the steering column is locked in place.

2. Disconnect the negative battery cable at the battery and isolate the cable from the battery terminal.

3. Remove the parking brake release rod, from the parking brake pedal assembly.

4. Remove the 5 screws attaching the steering column assembly cover.

5. Lower the steering column enough to disconnect the lift gate release switch connector.

6. Remove the fuse access/silencer panel assembly from the lower instrument panel.

7. Remove the nut from the stud, attaching the lower steering column bracket to the lower instrument panel reinforcement.

8. Remove the DRB diagnostic connector from its mounting bracket, on the lower instrument panel reinforcement.

9. Remove the 4 attaching bolts and lower instrument panel reinforcement from the lower instrument panel.

10. Position the steering wheel in the locked position and remove the key from the lock cylinder. Remove

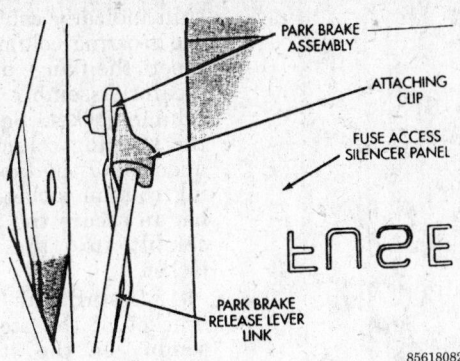

Parking brake pedal release rod — 1992–96 models

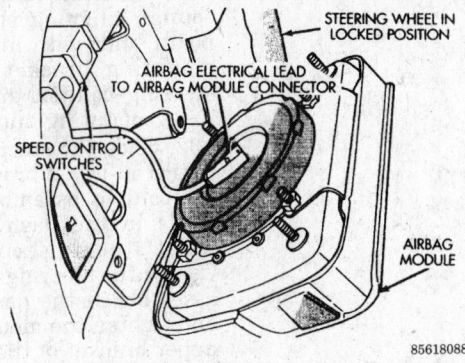

Air bag module removed from steering wheel

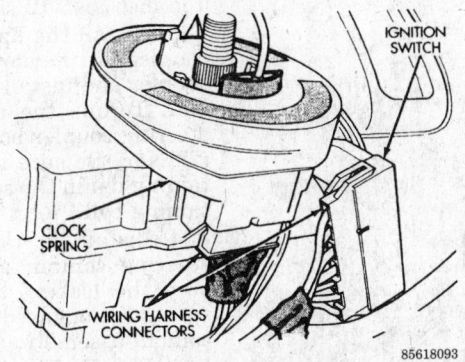

Clock spring and ignition switch wiring

17. Remove the 7 mm hex head bolt from the rear of the multi-function switch connector and disconnect the connector from the switch.

18. Remove the clock spring from the steering column assembly.

19. If the clock spring will not lift off the steering column do the following:

    a. Insert a suitable tool in the area of the clock spring's lower locking tab.

    b. Place the suitable tool against the locking tab of the clock spring assembly and push the locking tab back, and disengage the locking tab from the steering column.

    c. Remove the clock spring from the column.

20. Remove the steering column assembly wiring harness from the column.

NOTE: The nut is part of the upper steering shift coupler and will remain on the coupler when removing the bolt. Do not attempt to remove the nut from the coupler.

21. Remove the 3 nuts, attaching the lower mounting bracket of the steering column assembly to the dash panel reinforcement/steering column lower mounting bracket, then remove the 2 nuts attaching the upper mounting bracket of the steering column assembly to the dash board liner.

WARNING
During the following Step, do not allow the weight of the steering column assembly to be supported by the gear shift indicator cable.

22. Lower the steering column assembly from the dash board of the vehicle enough to access the gear shift indicator cable assembly, on the jacket of the steering column.

23. Position the gear shift lever on the steering column in the park position and remove the gear shift indicator assembly from the steering column jacket. Remove the indicator assembly, by first releasing the lock bar on the column insert and squeezing the legs of the column insert together and then lift the assembly from the column.

24. Lower the steering column to the floor of the vehicle, then remove the clip attaching the gear shift cable to the lower bracket of the steering column assembly.

25. Remove the gear shift cable from the shift lever of the steering column

the 4 nuts attaching the air bag module from the steering wheel, then remove the air bag module from the steering wheel and disconnect the electrical lead at the air bag module.

11. Disconnect the steering wheel horn switch wiring connector from the steering wheel wiring harness.

12. Remove the steering column wiring harness connector from the speed control switch assembly.

13. Remove the steering wheel retaining nut and remove the steering wheel using a puller.

14. Remove the 3 screws attaching the upper steering column shrouds to the steering column, then remove the upper and lower halves of the upper steering column shroud, from the steering column.

15. Remove the 3 screws attaching the lower steering column shrouds to the steering column, then remove the upper and lower steering column shroud, from the steering column.

16. Remove the wiring harness connectors from the clock spring and ignition switch, then remove the halo light and key in buzzer wiring harness connector from the ignition switch assembly.

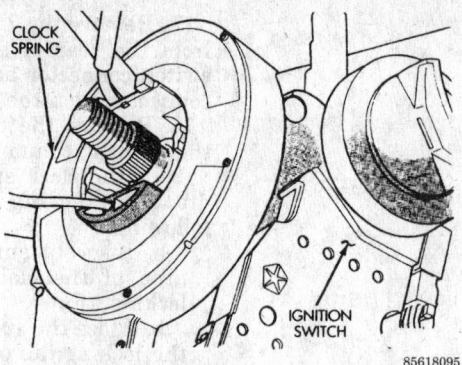

Clock spring assembly — 1992–96 models

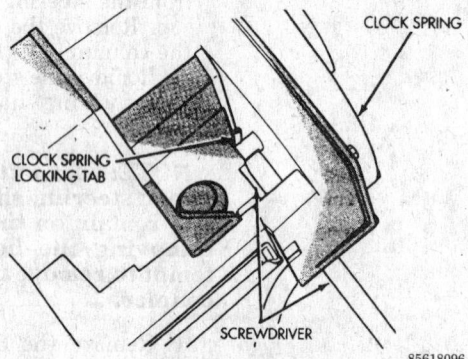

Clock spring locking tab disengagement — 1992–96 models

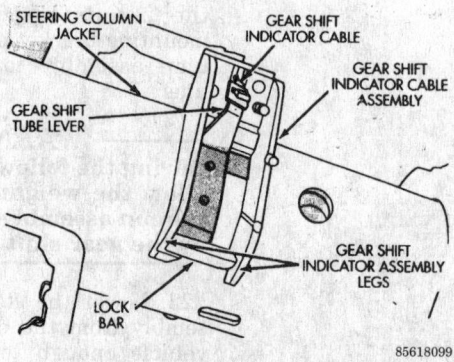

Gear shift indicator cable assembly — 1992–96 models

26. Carefully remove the steering column assembly from the vehicle.

To install:

27. Install a new gear shift cable attaching grommet into the steering column shift lever.

28. Prior to installing the steering column in the vehicle, install a ground clip on the left side capsule slot. The plastic capsules should be pre-assembled in the bracket slots. Remove the shipping lock pin, located on the lower column jacket when installing a new jacket. Place the steering column on the floor of the vehicle.

29. Install the gear shift cable on the lower mounting bracket of the steering column assembly. Install the gear shift cable into the new grommet on the steering column gear shift lever, then install the clip, attaching the shift cable to the steering column bracket.

30. Route the gear shift indicator assembly and its cable under the left upper mounting bracket of the steering column. Hook the eye of the gear shift indicator cable onto the lever of the steering column gear shift tube. Insert the flange of the gear shift indicator assembly into the steering column jacket. Squeeze the legs of the steering column insert together and install the tabs under the steering column jacket. Engage the lock bar to secure the shift indicator assembly into the steering column jacket.

31. Install the lower mounting bracket of the steering column assembly on the studs of the dash panel/reinforcement steering column mounting bracket then loosely install the 3 mounting nuts. Lift the steering column aligning studs in the dash board liner with insert in the upper mounting bracket of the steering steering column and loosely install the 2 mounting nuts.

32. Slide the steering column down until the lower bracket of the steering column assembly is against the studs in the dash panel reinforcement/steering column bracket. Center the steering column assembly assembly in the dash panel opening and tighten the mounting nuts at the upper bracket of the steering column assembly, then torque all 5 steering column assembly mounting nuts to 105 inch lbs. (12 Nm).

33. Install the upper steering shaft coupler on the lower steering shaft coupler and install the upper coupler bolt. Torque the nut on the upper steering coupler bolt to 250 inch lbs. (28 Nm). Be sure to reinstall the retaining pin in the steering coupler retaining bolt.

34. Install the clock spring on the steering column assembly, making sure the locking tabs on the clock spring are engaged with the steering column assembly.

35. Install the wiring harness connector onto the multi-function switch. Torque the multi-function switch wiring harness connector retaining bolt to 17 inch lbs. (2 (Nm).

36. Install the wiring harness connectors onto the clock spring and ignition switch assembly.

37. Move the shift lever to the neutral position and check the pointer location in the PRNDL window on the instrument cluster. If the pointer does not indicate neutral, adjust the actuator assembly to center the pointer on **N** (neutral), and then check the pointer in other gear positions.

38. Install the clips attaching the steering column assembly wiring harness to the steering column assembly.

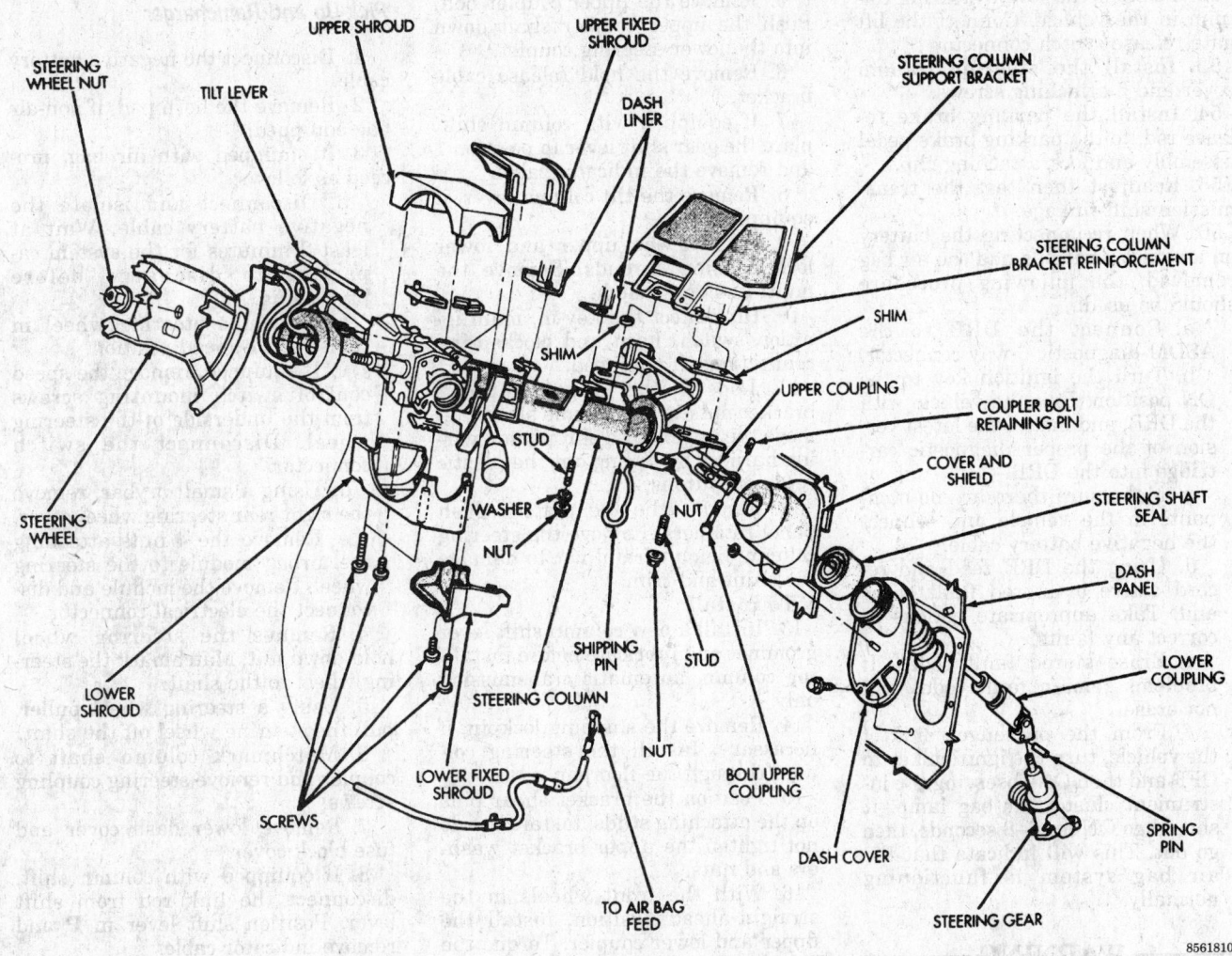

Exploded view of the Acustar steering column assembly — 1992–96 models

85618103

39. Install the upper and lower halves of the lower steering column shroud assembly on the steering column. Then install and securely tighten the 3 lower steering column shroud attaching screws.

40. Install the upper and lower halves of the upper steering column shroud assembly on the steering column. Then install and securely tighten the 3 upper steering column shroud attaching screws.

41. Install the tilt lever on the column.

42. Feed the speed control switch and air bag module wiring leads through the rectangular hole in the steering wheel, then feed the horn switch wiring lead through the round hole in the steering wheel.

43. Install the steering wheel.

44. Connect the horn switch wiring lead from the clock spring, onto the steering wheel horn switch wiring.

45. If equipped with speed control, connect the speed control wiring from the clock spring onto the speed control switch.

46. Install the wiring lead from the clock spring onto the air bag module. Make the wiring connection onto the air bag module, by pressing straight in on the connector. Make sure it is fully seated.

47. Install the air bag module into the steering wheel and then install the 4 air bag module attaching nuts. Torque all 4 air bag module attaching nuts to 100 inch lbs. (11 Nm).

48. Install the lower instrument panel reinforcement onto the instrument panel and tighten the 4 retaining bolts to 50 inch lbs. (6 Nm).

49. Install the nut on the stud attaching the lower steering column bracket to the lower instrument panel reinforcement and torque the nut to 100 inch lbs. (6 Nm).

50. Install the DRB diagnostic connector onto the instrument panel bracket on the lower instrument panel reinforcement.

51. Install the fuse access/silencer panel assembly on the lower instrument panel.

52. Position the lower steering column in the vehicle. Connect the lift gate release switch connector.

53. Install the steering column cover and 5 attaching screws.

54. Install the parking brake release rod, to the parking brake pedal assembly and lock attaching clip.

55. Readjust then test the transmission shift linkage.

56. When reconnecting the battery on a vehicle that has had the air bag removed, the following procedure should be used:

a. Connect the DRB to the ASDM diagnostic 6-way connector.

b. Turn the ignition key to the ON position. Exit the vehicle with the DRB, and install the latest version of the proper diagnostic cartridge into the DRB.

c. Make sure there are no occupants in the vehicle and connect the negative battery cable.

d. Using the DRB read and record active or stored fault codes and. Take appropriate actions to correct any faults.

e. Erase stored fault codes. If problems remain fault codes will not erase.

f. From the passenger side of the vehicle, turn the ignition key to OFF and then ON observing the instrument cluster air bag lamp. It should go ON for 6–8 seconds, then go out. This will indicate that the air bag system is functioning normally.

—— WARNING ——

If the air bag warning lamp fails to light, blinks ON and OFF or goes on and stays ON, there is an air bag system malfunction.

g. Test the operation of any steering column functions such as the horn, lights or speed control system.

Dakota

1. Make sure the front wheels are straight and the steering column is locked in place.

2. Disconnect the negative battery cable at the battery and isolate the cable from the battery terminal.

3. Remove the horn pad for non-air bag vehicles. Remove the speed control switch, right steering wheel cover and air bag module for air bag vehicles.

4. Disconnect the automatic transmission link rod by prying it out of the grommet in the shift lever.

5. Remove the upper coupler bolt. Push the upper coupler shaft down into the lower steering coupler.

6. Remove the hold release cable bracket.

7. If equipped with column shift, place the gear shift lever in position 1 and remove the indicator cable.

8. Remove the tilt column lever, if equipped.

9. Remove the upper and lower lock housing shrouds. Remove the multi-function switch.

10. Disconnect the key-in, main ignition switch, horn and clockspring connections, if equipped.

11. Loosen the upper support bracket nuts to allow some slack. Remove the upper fixed shroud and wiring harness by prying out the plastic retainer buttons.

12. Remove the toe plate-to-dash panel retainers. Remove the steering column, being careful not to damage the paint and trim.

To install:

13. Install a new column shift lever grommet and lubricate before installing column, automatic transmission only.

14. Remove the shipping lockpin, if necessary. Install the steering column through the floorpan.

15. Position the bracket shear pins on the attaching studs. Install, but do not tighten the upper bracket washers and nuts.

16. With the front wheels in the straight-ahead position, install the upper and lower coupler. Torque the bolts to 36 ft. lbs. (48 Nm).

17. Install the wiring harness and connect the column switches and install the upper shroud.

18. Make sure both spacers are fully seated in the column support bracket by pulling the column upwards. Torque the upper bracket nuts to 105 inch lbs. (12 Nm) and the toe plate bolts to 200 ft. lbs. (23 Nm).

19. Connect the wiring harness and install the lower shroud.

20. Install the lock housing shrouds and tilt lever.

21. Install the gear shift indicator cable, column shift vehicles.

22. Install the lower dash cover and steering wheel..

23. Connect the shift link rod to the transmission shift lever, column shift vehicles. Check the operation of the column shift. Slowly move the gear shift selector lever from 1 to L to P. The indicator pointer must align with each indicator position.

24. Connect the negative battery cable and check operation.

Pick-Up and Ramcharger

1. Disconnect the negative battery cable.

2. Remove the horn pad, if non-air bag equipped.

3. If equipped with air bag, proceed as follows:

a. Disconnect and isolate the negative battery cable. Wait at least 2 minutes for the system capacitor to discharge before proceeding.

b. Place the steering wheel in the straight-ahead position.

c. If equipped, remove the speed control switch mounting screws from the underside of the steering wheel. Disconnect the switch connector.

d. Using a small prybar, remove the right rear steering wheel cover.

e. Remove the 4 nuts attaching the airbag module to the steering wheel. Remove the module and disconnect the electrical connector.

4. Remove the steering wheel hold-down nut. Matchmark the steering wheel to the shaft.

5. Using a steering wheel puller, pull the steering wheel off the shaft.

6. Matchmark column shaft to coupler and remove steering coupling screws.

7. Remove lower dash cover and fuse block cover.

8. If equipped with column shift, disconnect the link rod from shift lever. Position shift lever in **P** and remove indicator cable.

9. Remove tilt lever, if equipped.

10. Remove upper and lower shrouds. Remove the turn signal multi-function switch with 7 mm socket.

11. Remove wiring harness from column by removing retainer clips. Disconnect connectors at base of column.

12. Remove the lower dash panel and support bracket. Remove nuts from upper bracket and remove column.

To install:

13. Install column in vehicle and install mount brackets and fasteners loosely in place.

14. Align master splines on steering gear shaft and coupler. Engage the coupler with the shaft and install the roll pin. Tighten mounting nuts.

15. Fasten the wiring harness and multi-function switch to the steering column and connect wires to connectors at base of column.

16. Install the gear indicator cable and lower fixed shroud.

17. Install the lock housing shrouds and tilt lever, if equipped.

18. Install steering wheel to shaft and tighten to 45 ft. lbs. (61 Nm).

19. Install horn pad and connect negative battery cable.

20. Check operation of multi-function switch and any other related switches.

Van/Wagon

1. Disconnect the negative battery cable.

2. Remove the horn pad, if non-air bag equipped.

3. If equipped with air bag, proceed as follows:

   a. Disconnect and isolate the negative battery cable. Wait at least 2 minutes for the system capacitor to discharge before proceeding.

   b. Place the steering wheel in the straight-ahead position.

   c. If equipped, remove the speed control switch mounting screws from the underside of the steering wheel. Disconnect the switch connector.

   d. Using a small prybar, remove the right rear steering wheel cover.

   e. Remove the 4 nuts attaching the airbag module to the steering wheel. Remove the module and disconnect the electrical connector.

4. Remove the steering wheel hold-down nut. Matchmark the steering wheel to the shaft.

5. Using a steering wheel puller, pull the steering wheel off the shaft.

6. Remove the lower steering column shrouds and disconnect the multi-function switch connector(s). Use a 7mm socket to remove the connector from the switch.

7. Remove the clock spring from the steering column and wiring harness from the column.

8. Remove the bolt from the upper shaft coupler and slide shaft down.

9. Remove the 4 upper and lower bracket nuts. Remove the lower shrouds to access the gear shift indicator cable. Remove the gear shift cable from the shift lever.

10. Lower the steering column to the floor and remove. Be careful to avoid damage to the paint and trim.

To install:

11. Remove the shipping lockpin located on the lower jacket when installing a new column.

12. Place the column on the floor and install the gear shift cable into the lower mounting bracket and ball stud on the gear shift lever.

13. Route the shift indicator assembly and its cable under the right upper mount bracket of column. Hook the eye of the shift indicator cable onto the steering column gear shift tube.

14. Lift the column into place and install the 4 mounting nuts and washers, loosely.

15. Firmly slide the column upward until all the brackets are against the studs in the support brackets. Make sure the plastic capsules are fully seated in the mounting brackets. Center the assembly and torque the nuts to 105 ft. lbs. (12 Nm). Do NOT overtighten.

16. Install the shaft coupler and torque the bolt to 36 ft. lbs. (48 Nm).

17. Install the clock spring with the locking tabs engaged with the column assembly.

18. Install the wiring harnesses and torque the retainers to 17 inch lbs. (2.0 Nm).

19. Move the shift lever to the **N** position and check for pointer location in the cluster window. If not, adjust the actuator.

20. Install the steering column shrouds and tilt lever.

21. Install steering wheel, horn pad or air bag module. Torque the shaft nut to 45 ft. lbs. (61 Nm).

22. Connect the negative battery cable.

23. Check operation of multi-function switch and any other related switches.

Manual Steering Gear

REMOVAL AND INSTALLATION

1. Disconnect the negative battery cable.

2. Remove the 2 bolts from the wormshaft to steering shaft coupler.

3. Raise the vehicle and support safely.

4. Matchmark and remove the pitman arm from the pitman shaft using tool C–4150 or equivalent.

5. Remove the steering gear mounting bolts and remove the gear from the vehicle.

6. The installation is the reversal of the removal procedure. Torque the pitman arm nut to 175 ft. lbs. (237 Nm).

ADJUSTMENT

Wormshaft Preload Torque

1. Raise the vehicle and support safely.

2. Remove the pitman arm from the pitman shaft.

3. Remove the horn pad.

4. Loosen the sector shaft adjusting screw locknut and back off the adjusting screw about 1½ turns.

5. Turn the steering wheel to the right stop and then back ½ turn. Measure the torque required to turn the steering while back to the straight-ahead position. The specification is 4–6 inch lbs. (0.45–0.67 Nm).

6. If not within specifications, loosen the large adjustment cap locknut and turn the adjustment cap until the proper preload is reached. Turning the adjuster clockwise increases the preload torque.

7. Tighten the locknut and recheck the preload.

8. Tighten the sector shaft adjuster screw locknut.

Sector Shaft

1. Perform the wormshaft preload procedure.

2. Center the steering wheel.

3. Loosen the sector shaft adjuster screw locknut and screw the adjuster screw all the way down. Tighten the locknut.

4. Rotate the steering wheel ¼ turn away from the overcenter position. Measure the torque required to rotate the wheel past the overcenter position. The specification is 14 inch lbs. (1.6 Nm).

5. If not within specifications, adjust the screw accordingly and tighten the locknut.

6. Install the horn pad.

7. Install the pitman arm.

Manual Rack and Pinion

REMOVAL AND INSTALLATION

Dakota 2WD

1. Raise the vehicle and support safely.

2. Remove the tie rod ends with puller tool C–3894–A.

3. Disconnect the steering shaft coupler from the pinion gear shaft.

4. Remove the bolts and steering gear from the vehicle.

To install:

5. Install the gear to the front crossmember and align the master serration of the stub shaft with column shaft.

6. Torque the gear bolts to 150 ft. lbs. (203 Nm) and steering coupler bolt to 36 ft. lbs. (49 Nm).

7. Install the tie rod ends and torque the nuts to 40 ft. lbs. (54 Nm). Install a new cotter pin.

8. Adjust the wheel alignment and road test.

ADJUSTMENT

The rack and pinion steering gear cannot be adjusted or internally serviced. If a malfunction or a fluid leak occurs, the complete unit must be replaced.

Power Steering Gear

ADJUSTMENT

Worm Thrust Bearing Preload

1. Perform this procedure before the over-center preload adjustment.

2. Remove the steering gear assembly from the vehicle.

3. Loosen the stub shaft locknut. Turn the adjuster in with spanner wrench C–4381. Tighten the plug and thrust washer in the housing until firmly bottomed in the housing.

4. Place an index mark on the housing even with one of the holes in the adjuster plug.

5. Measure back (counterclockwise) 0.050 in. (13.0mm) and mark housing. Rotate the adjustment cap back with spanner wrench until the hole is aligned with the second mark.

6. Torque the locknut to 80 ft. lbs. (109 Nm) and make sure the adjustment cap does not turn. Install the steering gear.

Over-center Adjustment

1. Remove the steering gear from the vehicle.

2. Rotate the stub shaft from stop-to-stop and count the number of turns.

3. Starting at either stop, turn the stub shaft back ½ the total number of turns. This is the center of travel.

4. Turn the pitman shaft adjuster screw back (counterclockwise) until extended, then turn clockwise 1 full turn.

5. Place an inch lbs. torque wrench in the vertical position on the stub shaft. Rotate the wrench 45 degrees each side of the center and record the highest rotational torque on center.

6. Turn the adjuster in until the torque to turn the stub shaft is 6–10 inch lbs. (0.6–1.2 Nm) more than reading in Step 5.

7. Prevent the adjusting screw from turning while tightening the locknut to 36 ft. lbs. (49 Nm).

8. Road test the vehicle. If the steering wheel does not return easily after a turn, back the screw off until the wheel returns easily.

REMOVAL AND INSTALLATION

1. Place the wheels in the straight ahead position.

2. Remove the windshield washer solvent reservoir and the coolant overflow tank, if necessary.

3. Position a drain pan under the steering gear.

4. Disconnect the fluid hoses from the gear and plug them.

5. Disconnect the steering column shaft from the stub shaft.

6. Raise the vehicle and support safely. Matchmark and remove the pitman arm from the center link on 2WD vehicles. On 4WD vehicles, disconnect the drag link from the pitman arm. Remove the pitman arm from the pitman shaft.

7. Remove the retaining bolts and remove the steering gear from the vehicle.

To install:

8. For 2WD vehicles, position steering gear at frame rail and install bolts loosely. Align steering shaft and stub shaft and install bolts to 33 ft. lbs. (45 Nm) torque. Realign gear at frame and torque bolts to 100 ft. lbs. (136 Nm).

9. On 4WD vehicles, install steering gear to reinforcement and tighten screws to 100 ft. lbs. (136 Nm). Position steering gear at frame rail and install bolts loosely. Align steering shaft and stub shaft and install bolts to 33 ft. lbs. (45 Nm) torque. Realign gear at frame and torque bolts to 100 ft. lbs. (136 Nm).

10. Install pitman arm to steering shaft and torque nut to 175 ft. lbs. (237 Nm). Connect steering linkage to arm. Install replacement cotter pins.

Power Rack and Pinion

REMOVAL AND INSTALLATION

Caravan, Voyager and Town & Country

FRONT WHEEL DRIVE

1. Loosen the wheel lugs slightly. Raise and support the front of the vehicle at the frame point below the front doors, not on the front cross-

member. Use jackstands for supporting.

2. Remove the front wheels and tire assemblies.

3. Remove the tie rod ends from the steering knuckles.

4. Lower and disconnect the steering column from the steering gear pinion shaft.

5. If equipped, remove the anti-rotation link from the crossmember and the air diverter valve from the left side of the crossmember.

6. Place a transmission jack, or floor jack with a wide lifting flange, under the front suspension K-crossmember. Support the crossmember and remove the 4 crossmember to frame attaching bolts. Slowly lower the crossmember until enough room is gained to remove the steering gear assembly. Place stands under the crossmember, if available.

7. Remove the splash and boot shields. If equipped with power steering, disconnect the power steering hoses.

8. Remove the bolts that attach the steering gear assembly to the crossmember. Remove the assembly from the left side of the vehicle.

To install:

9. Align the gear pinion with the column. Installation is in the reverse order of removal. The right rear crossmember bolt is the alignment pilot for reinstallation. Install first and tighten.

10. Attach the gear to the K-frame and secure the K-frame. Secure the anti-rotation link. Secure the K-frame. Torque all crossmember attaching bolts to 90 ft. lbs. (122 Nm). Steering gear mounting bolts are tightened to 50 ft. lbs. (68 Nm).

11. Connect the tie rod ends, torque nuts to 38 ft. lbs. (52 Nm) and install new cotter pins.

12. Fill power steering reservoir, start engine, turn the steering wheel from lock to lock and check for fluid leaks.

13. Check toe adjustment.

ALL WHEEL DRIVE (AWD)

Before removing the steering gear on AWD models, the steering column must be removed to provide clearance for steering rack removal.

1. Raise and support the vehicle. Remove the wheel and tire assemblies.

2. Remove the steering column assembly from the vehicle.

3. Remove the tie rod ends from the steering knuckle using a suitable puller.

4. Remove the 2 bolts and the 2 nuts that attach the bridge assembly

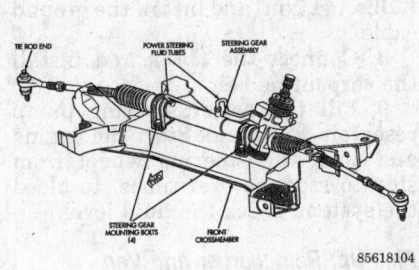

Steering gear and crossmember

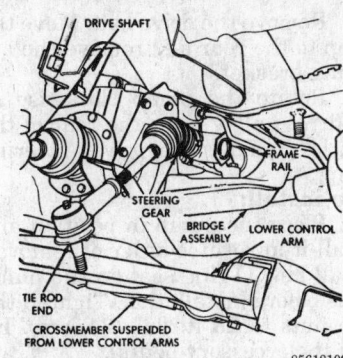

Crossmember lowered for gear removal

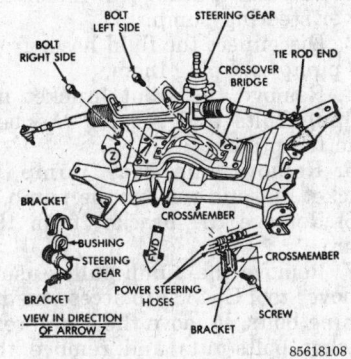

Steering gear removal and installation

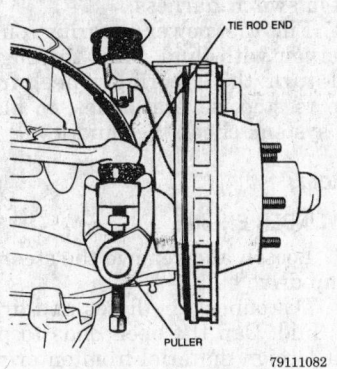

Removing the tie rod end

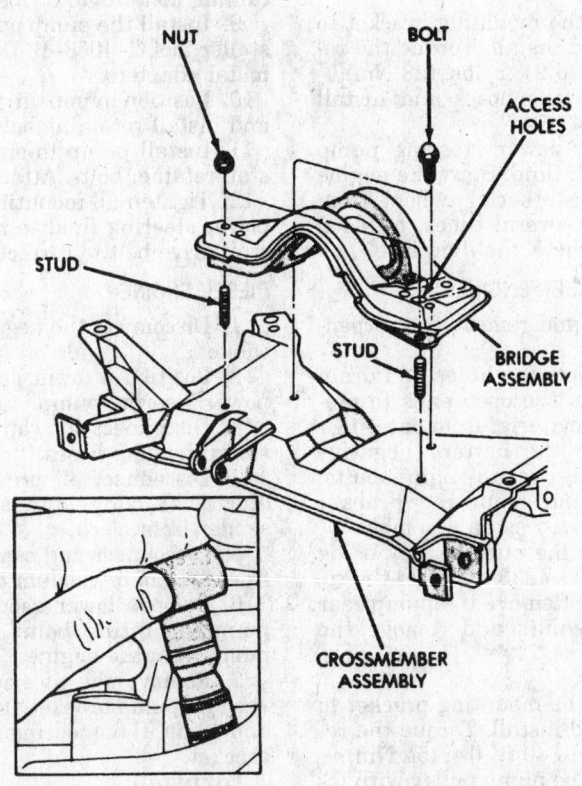

Bridge assembly removal — AWD vehicles

to the crossmember. The bolts and nuts can be reached through the access holes in the top of the bridge assembly.

5. Remove the crossmember to frame rail attaching bolts. Use a jack to lower the crossmember so it is suspended from the lower control arms. It is necessary to remove the crossmember completely from the vehicle.

6. Disconnect and plug the power steering lines from the steering gear. Remove the hose retaining bracket from the crossmember.

7. Remove the 4 bolts that retain the steering gear to the bridge assembly.

NOTE: Note the position of each bolt as it is removed, there are different bolts for the left and right sides.

8. Remove the lower steering column coupler from the steering gear. Drive the roll pin from the coupler using a punch. If this is not done, there will not be enough clearance for rack removal.

9. Remove the steering gear from the vehicle by pulling it out through the drivers side wheel well. Rotate the gear to clear the frame rail.

To install:

10. Install the steering gear into the vehicle. Work it in through the left wheel opening, rotating it as needed.

11. Install the steering column coupler, make sure to fully seat the roll pin.

12. Install the steering gear mounting bolts. Do not torque them at this time, be sure to install them in the proper locations.

13. Install the steering hose bracket in position, tighten to 70 inch lbs. (8 Nm). Install the hoses on the steering rack and tighten them to 275 inch lbs. (31 Nm).

14. Raise the crossmember into position and install the bolts to the following torques:

　a. Crossmember-to-frame rail screw and washer — 90 ft. lbs. (122 Nm)

　b. Crossmember-to-frame rail stud nut — 90 ft. lbs. (122 Nm)

15. Install the bridge assembly onto the crossmember and tighten the mounting nuts to 50 ft. lbs. (68 Nm).

16. Install the outer tie rod ends on the steering knuckle and tighten the nuts, tighten to 38 ft. lbs. (52 Nm). Be sure to install a new cotter pin.

17. Install the wheel and tire assemblies. Lower the vehicle.

18. Connect the negative battery cable. Start the vehicle and check the

power steering lines for leaks. Check the fluid level.

Dakota 2WD

1. Raise the vehicle and support safely.
2. Remove the tie rod ends with puller tool C–3894–A.
3. Drain the power steering fluid and disconnect the hoses.
4. Disconnect the steering shaft coupler from the pinion gear shaft.
5. Remove the bolts and steering gear from the vehicle.

To install:

6. Install the gear to the front crossmember and align the master serration of the stub shaft with column shaft.
7. Torque the gear bolts to 150 ft. lbs. (203 Nm) and steering coupler bolt to 36 ft. lbs. (49 Nm).
8. Install the tie rod ends and torque the nuts to 40 ft. lbs. (54 Nm). Install a new cotter pin.
9. Fill power steering reservoir, start engine, turn the steering wheel from lock to lock and check for fluid leaks.
10. Adjust the wheel alignment and road test.

ADJUSTMENT

The rack and pinion steering gear cannot be adjusted or internally serviced. If a malfunction or a fluid leak occurs, the complete unit must be replaced.

Power Steering Pump

REMOVAL AND INSTALLATION

Caravan, Voyager and Town & Country

1. Disconnect the negative battery cable from the battery. Disconnect the A/C compressor clutch wire harness connector at the compressor.
2. Remove the power steering pump adjustment bolt. Remove the power steering hose bracket from mounting.
3. Raise and safely support the vehicle.
4. Disconnect the return hose from the steering gear and drain the fluid into a container.
5. Remove the right side splash shield if it interferes with pump removal. After the fluid has drained from the pump, disconnect and plug the hoses from the pump.
6. Remove the lower pivot bolt and nut from the pump mounting.

7. Remove the drive belt. Move the pump to the rear and remove the adjusting bracket.
8. Rotate the pump clockwise so the drive pulley faces the rear of the vehicle. Remove the power steering pump.

To install:

9. Place the pump in position and install it in reverse order of removal. Install new O-ring seal on the pump hoses before installation. Tighten the tube nuts to 25 ft. lbs. (34 Nm). Install the accessory belt(s).
10. Lower the vehicle and connect the vapor hose and A/C compressor clutch switch harness..
11. Fill the power steering pump reservoir with fluid. Start the engine and turn the steering wheel from stop to stop, several times, to bleed the system. check the fluid level.

Dakota

4 CYLINDER ENGINE

1. Loosen and remove the steering pump drive belt.
2. Disconnect the hoses and drain the fluid. Cap the open ends to prevent foreign material from entering.
3. Remove the front bracket bolts where applicable. Remove the pump rear bracket bolts/nuts and remove the pump.

To install:

4. Install the mounting bracket to the pump and install. Torque the retaining bolts to 21 ft. lbs. (28 Nm).
5. Connect the hoses and install the drive belt.
6. Fill the power steering pump reservoir with fluid. Start the engine and turn the steering wheel from stop to stop, several times, to bleed the system. check the fluid level.

6 AND 8 CYLINDER ENGINES

1. Loosen and remove the serpentine belt.
2. Disconnect the hoses and drain the fluid. Cap the open ends to prevent foreign material from entering.
3. Remove the battery negative cable and bracket-to-engine bolts. The pump and mounting bracket must be removed as an assembly.
4. Remove the pump pulley using remover tool C–4333 to access the retaining bolts. Remove the pump rear bracket bolts/nuts and remove the pump.

To install:

5. Install the mounting bracket to the pump and install. Torque the retaining bolts to 40 ft. lbs. (54 Nm).
6. Install the pump pulley with installer tool C–4063–B. Do not use the metal adapters.

7. Torque the retaining bolts to 30 ft. lbs. (41 Nm) and install the ground cable.
8. Connect the hoses and install the serpentine belt.
9. Fill the power steering pump reservoir with fluid. Start the engine and turn the steering wheel from stop to stop, several times, to bleed the system. check the fluid level.

Pick-Up, Ramcharger and Van

GASOLINE ENGINE

1. Disconnect the negative battery cable.
2. Position a drain pan under the power steering pump.
3. Disconnect the fluid hoses from the pump and plug them.
4. Remove the front bracket attaching bolts and remove the belt from the pulley.
5. Remove the rear pump to bracket nut and remove the pump.
6. Remove the bracket from the pump.
7. Remove the pump pulley using remover tool C–4333 to access the retaining bolts. Remove the pump rear bracket bolts/nuts and remove the pump.

To install:

8. Install the mounting bracket to the pump and install. Torque the retaining bolts to 40 ft. lbs. (54 Nm).
9. Install the pump pulley with installer tool C–4063–B. Do not use the metal adapters.
10. Position pump in rear bracket and install retaining bolts.
11. Install pump to engine and install retainer bolts. Attach fluid lines.
12. Tighten all mounting bolts. Add power steering fluid to reservoir. Install drive belt to correct tension.

DIESEL ENGINE

1. Disconnect the negative battery cable.
2. Position a drain pan under the power steering pump.
3. Disconnect and cap vacuum and steering pump hoses.
4. Disconnect oil pressure sender electrical connector and remove sender from block.
5. Disconnect and cap the oil feed from bottom of vacuum pump.
6. Remove lower vacuum/steering pump mounting bolts, gasket and pump from the engine.
7. Remove the steering pump to vacuum pump bracket attaching nuts and slide the steering pump from bracket.

To install:

8. Install body spacers to pump and install pump into bracket. The

steering pump and spacer must mate completely with vacuum pump bracket.

9. Install new gasket to pump assembly using sealer to retain the gasket. Install pump assembly to engine.

10. Install oil pressure sending unit and electrical connector.

11. Install oil feed line and vacuum hoses to vacuum pump. Install fluid hoses to power steering pump.

12. Fill reservoir with power steering fluid. Connect negative battery cable, start engine and check for leaks.

BELT ADJUSTMENT

Except 2.5L Engine

The belt tension is automatically adjusted by the tensioner on the all engines except 2.5L engine. Periodic adjustment is not necessary.

2.5L Engine

1. Loosen the bracket mounting bolts.

2. Using a ½ in. drive breaker bar in the square hole provided in the bracket, move the pump away from the engine. Do not pry against the fluid reservoir.

3. With the pump moved enough so the belt deflects about ¼–½ in. under a 10 lb. load, tighten the bolts.

SYSTEM BLEEDING

1. Fill the reservoir with power steering fluid.

2. Turn the wheels to the full left turn position and add fluid until the reservoir is full.

3. Start the engine and add fluid to bring the level to the correct level.

4. To purge the system of air, turn the steering wheel from side to side without contacting the stops.

5. Return the wheel to the straight-ahead position and operate the engine for 2 minutes before road testing. This should bleed the system completely.

Tie Rod Ends

REMOVAL AND INSTALLATION

With Recirculating Ball-Type Steering Gear

1. Raise the vehicle and support safely.

2. Remove the cotter pin and nut from the tie rod end.

3. Using a puller tool C–3894–A or equivalent, remove the tie rod from the steering knuckle or center link.

4. Loosen the sleeve clamp nut and bolt and unscrew the tie rod end from the sleeve.

5. The installation is the reversal of the removal procedure. Torque the stud nuts to 45 ft. lbs. (61 Nm) and install a new cotter pin.

6. Perform a front end alignment as required to adjust toe-in.

With Rack and Pinion Steering Gear

1. Raise and safely support the vehicle.

2. Loosen the jam nut which connects the tie rod end to the rack.

3. Mark the tie rod position on the threads.

4. Remove the tie rod cotter pin and nut.

5. Using a puller tool C–3894–A or equivalent, remove the tie rod from the steering knuckle.

NOTE: Count the number of turns when removing tie rod end. Install the new end the same amount of turns.

6. Unscrew the tie rod end from the rack.

To install:

7. Install a new tie rod end, screw in the same number of turns as removal. Tighten the jam nut to 40 ft. lbs. (54 Nm) and install a new cotter pin.

8. Check the wheel alignment.

BRAKES

Master Cylinder

REMOVAL AND INSTALLATION

1. Disconnect the negative battery cable.

2. Remove the ABS brake valve and bracket, if equipped.

3. Disconnect and plug the brake lines from the master cylinder.

4. Remove the nuts attaching the master cylinder to the power booster.

5. Remove the master cylinder from the mounting studs.

To install:

6. Bench bleed the master cylinder.

7. Install to the studs and install the nuts.

8. Install the brake lines to the master cylinder loosely.

9. Install the ABS brake valve and bracket, if equipped.

10. Slowly push brake pedal to the floor and hold in this position while tightening brake lines at master cylinder. Refill master cylinder and check for leaks and proper pedal resistance.

11. Bleed the brake system and check operation.

Proportioning/Combination Valve

REMOVAL AND INSTALLATION

1. Disconnect the negative battery cable.

2. Raise the vehicle and support safely.

3. Tag and disconnect the brake lines from the valve.

4. Disconnect the wires to the pressure switch.

5. Remove the combination valve from the frame bracket.

6. The installation is the reversal of the removal procedure.

7. Bleed the brakes in the following order:
   a. Master cylinder
   b. Rear Wheel Anti-Lock valve, if equipped
   c. Front Wheel Anti-Lock valve, if equipped
   d. Left rear wheel cylinder
   e. Right rear wheel cylinder
   f. Right front caliper
   g. Left front caliper

Power Brake Booster

REMOVAL AND INSTALLATION

Dakota

1. Disconnect the negative battery cable.

2. Disconnect and plug the master cylinder brake lines. Remove the ground wire from the combination valve.

3. Remove the master cylinder nuts and slide the combination valve bracket off the master cylinder mounting studs. If necessary, loosen or disconnect the brake lines from the combination valve and move out of the way.

4. Remove the master cylinder and disconnect the booster vacuum line. Remove the pedal retaining clip from the pivot.

5. Remove the booster mounting nuts, booster and gasket.

To install:

6. Install the gasket, guide booster into dash panel and torque the nuts to 250 inch lbs. (28 Nm).

7. Install the pedal retaining clip to the pivot.

8. Install the master cylinder and combination valve. Torque the mounting nuts to 250 inch lbs. (28 Nm).

9. Connect the brake lines and torque to 170 inch lbs. (19 Nm) with a flarenut wrench.

10. Install the remaining components, bleed the brake system and connect the battery cable.

Caravan, Voyager and Town & Country

1. Remove the nuts that attach the master cylinder to the power brake booster. Slowly and carefully slide the master cylinder away from the booster, off the mounting studs. Allow the cylinder to rest against the fender shield.

2. Disconnect the vacuum hose from the brake booster.

NOTE: Do not remove the check valve.

3. From the inside of the vehicle under the instrument panel, locate the point where the booster linkage connects to the brake pedal. Use a small tool and position between the center tang of the booster linkage to brake pedal retaining clip. Rotate the tool and pull the retainer from the pin. disconnect the brake pedal.

4. Remove the brake booster mounting nuts and unfasten the brackets mounting the steel water line at the firewall and left frame rail. If equipped with a manual transmission, unfasten the clutch cable bracket at the shock tower and move it to the side.

5. The booster mounting bracket holes are slotted, slide the booster up and to the left. Tilt the booster inboard and up to remove from the engine compartment.

6. Position the power booster over the firewall mounting studs. Install the mounting nuts and tighten to 200–300 inch lbs.

7. install the steel heater line bracket and clutch cable bracket, if equipped.

8. Carefully install the master cylinder and tighten the mounting bolts to 200–300 inch lbs.

9. Connect the vacuum line to the power brake booster.

10. Connect the pedal linkage to the booster pushrod after lubricating

the pivot point with white grease. Install a new retainer clip. Check brake and stoplight operation.

Pick-Up, Ramcharger and Van

1. Disconnect the negative battery cable. Disconnect the vacuum hose(s) from the booster.

2. Remove the nuts attaching the master cylinder to the booster and move the master cylinder aside.

3. From inside of the vehicle, remove the clip that secures the booster pushrod to the brake pedal.

4. Remove the nuts that attach the booster to the dash panel and remove it from the vehicle.

5. Transfer the check valve to the new booster.

To install:

6. Position booster on dash panel and install retainer nuts.

7. Install booster pushrod on brake pedal and install new retainer clip.

8. Install brake master cylinder to booster and secure. Install vacuum hose to booster check valve.

Height Sensing Fuel Proportioning Valve

TESTING

NOTE: Two pressure gauges and adapter fittings (tool set C4007A or equivalent) are required of the following test.

If premature rear wheel lock-up and skid is experienced frequently, it could be an indication that the fluid pressure to the rear brakes is excessive and that a malfunction has occurred in the proportioning valve or an adjustment is necessary.

1. If a pressure gauge and adapter fittings are on hand, proceed with the following test.

2. Disconnect the external spring at the valve lever.

3. Install 1 pressure gauge and T-fitting in line from either master cylinder port to the brake valve assembly.

4. Install the second gauge to either rear brake outlet port between the valve assembly and the rear brake line. Bleed the rear brakes.

5. Have a helper apply and hold pedal pressure to get a reading on the valve inlet gauge and outlet gauge. The inlet pressure should be 500 psi and the outlet pressure should be 100–200 psi. If the required pressures are not present, replace the

valve. If the test pressures are all right, adjust the external spring and arm.

REMOVAL, INSTALLATION AND ADJUSTMENT

1. Raise and safely support the rear of the vehicle. Position jackstands at the rear contact pads so the rear axle will hang free with the tires off the ground.

2. Loosen the rear axle mounted adjustable lever assembly and remove the actuating spring. Remove the brake lines from the proportioning valve and remove the valve.

3. Install the brake lines loosely in the proportioning valve and mount valve in position.

4. Tighten the brake lines, fill the master cylinder to the correct fluid level and bleed the brakes.

5. Confirm that the axle is hanging free and at full rebound position with the wheels and tires mounted.

6. Confirm that the actuating spring is connected between the proportioning valve and axle adjusting lever. The axle adjusting lever mounting bolts should be loose so the bracket can be moved.

7. Push the control lever on the proportioning valve towards the valve until it is against the body and hold it in that position.

8. Move the axle lever up and away to apply tension to the spring. When all free play is taken out of the spring, but the spring is not stretched, tighten the mounting bolt that goes through the slotted side of the adjustment bracket. Tighten the anchor bolt. Both mounting bolts should be tightened to 150 inch lbs. (17 Nm).

Brake Caliper

REMOVAL AND INSTALLATION

1. Raise the vehicle and support safely. Remove the tire and wheel assembly.

2. Remove the caliper retaining clips and anti-rattle springs.

3. Lift the caliper off the rotor. Remove the outer pad from the caliper.

4. Remove the brake hose retaining bolt from the caliper.

To install:

5. Install the brake hose to the caliper using new copper washers.

6. Adjust the ears of the outer pad to provide a tight fit in the caliper recesses.

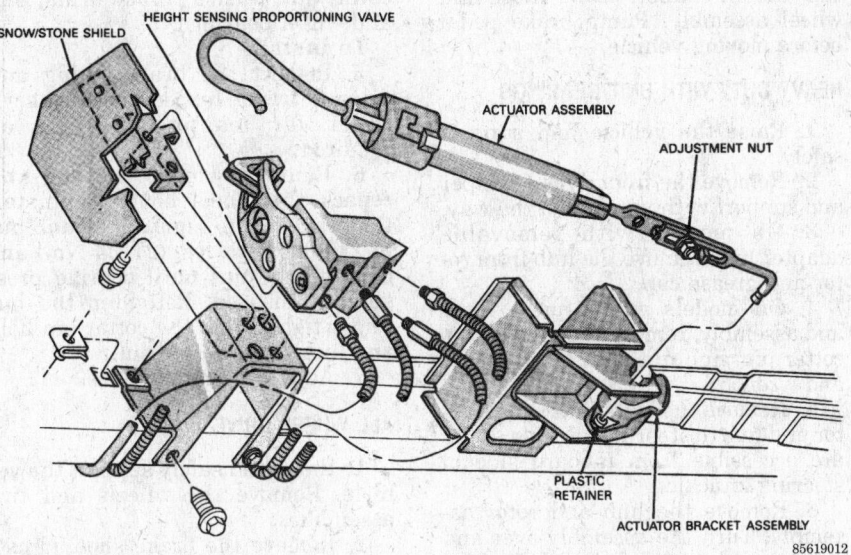

Height sensing dual proportioning valve assembly — non-ABS equipped vehicles

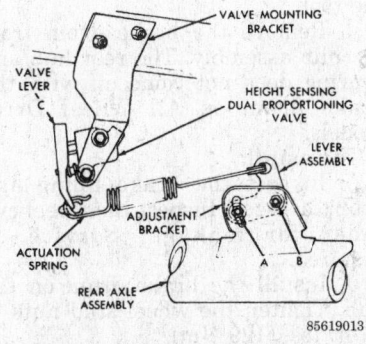

Height sensing dual proportioning valve and adjustment points

7. Position the caliper over the rotor so the caliper engages the adaptor correctly.

8. Install the anti-rattle springs and retaining clips or pins. Torque the slide pins to 22 ft. lbs. (30 Nm).

9. Fill the master cylinder and bleed the brake system.

Disc Brake Pads

REMOVAL AND INSTALLATION

1. Remove some of the fluid from the master cylinder. Raise the vehicle and support safely. Remove the tire and wheel assemblies.

2. Remove the caliper and remove the outer pad from the caliper.

3. Remove the inner pad from the adaptor.

To install:

4. Use a large C–clamp to compress the piston back into the caliper bore.

5. Adjust the ears of the outer pad to provide a tight fit in the caliper recesses.

6. Install the inner pad to the adaptor.

7. Position the caliper over the rotor so the caliper engages the adaptor correctly.

8. Install the anti-rattle springs and retaining bolt(s). Torque the retaining bolts (pins) to 22 ft. lbs. (30 Nm).

9. Install tire and wheel assembly. Refill the master cylinder. Pump brake pedal before moving the vehi-

cle. Recheck the fluid level and road test.

Brake Rotor

REMOVAL AND INSTALLATION

Caravan, Voyager and Town & Country

1. Loosen the wheel lugs slightly. Raise and safely support the vehicle.

2. Remove the front wheel and tire assembly. Relieve the brake system pressure if equipped with ABS.

3. Remove the disc brake caliper and outer brake pad.

4. Remove the disc brake rotor retaining clip and rotor.

5. Service as necessary. Place the rotor in position and install the retaining clip and caliper assembly.

6. Install the remaining components, pump the brake several times and road test.

Dakota

1. Raise the vehicle and support safely.

2. Remove the front wheel, caliper and hang caliper to suspension component.

3. On 2WD models; remove the grease cap, cotter pin, nut lock, nut, thrust washer and outer bearing. Remove the rotor and hub assembly. Remove the inner bearing and seal if the rotor is going to be serviced.

NOTE: On 2WD models with ABS, the tone wheel for the front wheel sensor is located on the rotor hub. Use caution when handling the rotor during service. The entire rotor/hub assembly will have to be replaced if the tone wheel becomes damaged.

4. On 4WD models; remove the stamped rotor retaining nuts or clips and rotor.

To install:

5. On 4WD models; install the rotor and retaining clips.

6. On 2WD models; repack and install the wheel bearing into the hub with new grease seal.

7. Install the rotor on spindle, thrust washer and nut.

8. Install the brake pads and caliper.

9. Adjust the wheel bearings to a endplay of zero to 0.003 in. (0.076mm) maximum.

10. Install the remaining components, apply brakes several times and road test.

Pick-Up, Ramcharger and Van

CHRYSLER DISC BRAKE — LIGHT DUTY

1. Raise the vehicle and support safely.
2. Remove the wheel.
3. Remove the caliper and disc brake pads. It is not necessary to remove the brake line from the caliper
4. On models with removable adapter hub, remove the hub from the rotor.
5. On models with 1-piece rotor and hub assembly; remove the dust cap, cotter pin, locknut, wheel bearing nut and washer from the spindle. Remove the outer wheel bearing. Remove the rotor with the inner wheel bearing from the spindle. Remove the grease seal.

To install:
6. Lubricate and install the inner wheel bearing. Install a new grease seal.
7. Install the rotor to the spindle.
8. Lubricate and install the outer wheel bearing, washer and nut. When the bearing preload is properly set, install the nut lock and a new cotter pin.
9. Install the grease cap.
10. Install the brake pads and caliper.
11. Install the wheel. Pump brake pedal before moving vehicle.

BENDIX DISC BRAKE

1. Raise and safely support vehicle.
2. Remove wheel and tire assembly.
3. Remove support key retaining screw and support key. Remove caliper from adapter.
4. Remove hub cap. Remove drive flange snapring, flange nuts and lockwashers. Remove drive flange and gasket.
5. Straighten tang on lockring. Remove locknut, lockring, inner adjusting nut and bearing.
6. Remove hub and rotor from spindle.

To install:
7. Repack wheel bearings and install in hub. Install hub and rotor on spindle.
8. Install outer bearing and adjuster nut and tighten to 50 ft. lbs. (68 Nm). Back off adjusting nut and retorque to 40 ft. lbs. (54 Nm) while rotating wheel. Back off adjuster nut 3/8 turn. Install lockring and nut. Bearing endplay should be 0.001–0.010 in.
9. Bend 1 tang of lock-ring over locknut and 1 tang over adjusting nut.

10. Install hub with new gasket, drive flange, lockwashers and nuts. Tighten nuts to 35 ft. lbs.
11. Install flange snapring and hub cap. Install caliper, brake shoes and wheel assembly. Pump brake pedal before moving vehicle.

HEAVY DUTY WITH UNIT BEARINGS

1. Raise the vehicle and support safely.
2. Remove the front wheel, caliper and support with wire out of the way.
3. On models with removable adapter hub, remove the hub from rotor and grease cap.
4. On models with 1-piece rotor and assembly, remove the grease cap, cotter pin, hub nut with 3/4 in. socket and wrench.
5. Remove the bolts that secure rotor and hub to steering knuckle. Bolts are accessible from inboard side of steering knuckle.
6. Remove the hub and rotor assembly. Turn the assembly over and check unit bearing and seal. Replace if necessary.

To install:
7. Apply anti-seize compound to the splines of the front driveshaft.
8. Replace the grease seal in wheel hub if old one is damaged. Install new wheel bearing assembly if necessary.
9. Install the bolts through the back of the steering knuckle. Install the hub spacer so the flat is toward the rear of the vehicle.
10. Apply Loctite® to the retaining bolts and align hub with driveshaft. Align bolt holes and hub assembly. Torque all bolts securely.
11. Install the washer, hub nut and new cotter pin.
12. Install the remaining components, pump brake pedal several times and road test.

Brake Drums

REMOVAL AND INSTALLATION

Caravan, Voyager and Town & Country

FRONT WHEEL DRIVE

1. Raise and safely support the vehicle. Remove the wheels and tire assemblies.
2. Remove the brake shoe adjusting slot cover from the rear of backing plate.
3. Insert a thin tool through the adjusting slot and hold the adjusting lever away from the star wheel. Insert an adjusting tool and back off the star wheel by prying downward with the tool.
4. Remove the center hub dust cover, nut, washer, brake drum, hub and wheel bearings.

To install:
5. Inspect the brake lining and drum for wear. Inspect the wheel cylinder for leakage. Service as required.
6. Remove, clean, inspect and repack the wheel bearings. Install the brake drum. Tighten the hub nut to 240-300 inch lbs. (27–34 Nm) and back off the nut until bearing pressure is released. Retighten the nut finger tight, align the cotter pin hole and install the cotter pin.
7. Adjust the rear brakes.

ALL WHEEL DRIVE

1. Raise and safely support the vehicle. Remove the wheels and tire assemblies.
2. Remove the brake shoe adjusting slot cover from the front the of the brake drum.
3. Insert a thin tool through the adjusting slot and hold the adjusting lever away from the star wheel. Insert an adjusting tool and back off the star wheel by prying downward with the tool.
4. Remove the brake drum from the hub assembly. The rear hub and bearing does not come off with the brake drum on All Wheel Drive models.

To install:
5. Inspect the brake lining and drum for wear. Inspect the wheel cylinder for leakage. Service as required.
6. Install the brake drum on the hub. Tighten the wheel stud nuts to 95 ft. lbs. (129 Nm).
7. Adjust the rear brakes.

Except Caravan, Voyager and Town & Country

CHRYSLER AND DANA AXLES WITH REMOVABLE DRUMS

1. Raise the vehicle and support safely.
2. Remove the wheel.
3. Remove the factory clips from the wheel studs, if equipped.
4. Remove the drum. If the drum is difficult to remove, remove the plug from the rear of the backing plate and push the self adjuster lever away from the star wheel. Rotate the star wheel to retract the shoes.
5. The installation is the reverse of the removal procedure.

DANA AXLE WITH INTEGRAL HUB/ROTOR

1. Raise the vehicle and support safely.

2. Remove the axle shafts.

3. Remove the bearing adjuster nut and the outer bearing.

4. Remove the drum. If the drum is difficult to remove, remove the plug from the rear of the backing plate and push the self adjuster lever away from the star wheel. Rotate the star wheel to retract the shoes.

5. The installation is the reversal of the removal procedure.

Brake Shoes

REMOVAL AND INSTALLATION

Caravan, Voyager, Town & Country and Dakota

1. Raise and safely support the vehicle. Remove the rear wheels and brake drums.

NOTE: Remove and install the brake shoes on one side at a time. Use the assembled side for reference.

2. Use a pair of brake spring pliers or appropriate tool and remove the shoe return springs from the top anchor. Take note that the secondary shoe spring is on top of the primary shoe spring. Install in the same position at installation time.

3. Slide the closed eye of the adjuster cable off the anchor stud. Unhook the spring end and remove the cable, overload spring, cable guide and anchor plate.

4. Remove the adjusting lever from the spring by sliding forward to clear the pivot. Work the lever out from under the spring. Remove the spring from the pivot.

5. Unhook the bottom shoe-to-shoe spring from the secondary (back) shoe and disengage from the primary (front) shoe.

6. Spread the bottom of the brake shoes apart and remove the star wheel adjuster. Remove the parking brake strut and spring assembly.

7. Locate the shoe retainer nail head at the rear of the brake backing plate. Support the nail head with a finger, press in and twist the spring retainer washer with the special retainer tool or a pair of pliers. If you are using pliers, take care not to slip and pinch your fingers.

8. Remove the retainer, spring, inner washer and nail from both shoes. Remove the parking brake lever from the secondary brake shoe. Remove

the shoes from the backing plate. Disconnect the parking brake lever from the brake cable.

To install:

9. Clean the backing plate with a safe solvent. Inspect the raised show support pads for rough or rusted contact areas. Clean and smooth as necessary. Clean and inspect the adjuster star wheels, apply a thin film of lubricant to the threads, socket and washer. Replace the star wheel if rust or threads show damage.

10. Inspect the hold-down springs, return springs and adjuster spring. If the springs have been subjected to overheating or if their strength is questionable, replace the spring.

11. Inspect the wheel cylinder. If signs of leakage are present (a small amount of fluid inside the end boot is normal) rebuild or replace the cylinder.

12. Lubricate the shoe contact area pads on the backing plate with high temperature resistant white lube.

13. Engage the parking brake lever with the cable and install the lever on the secondary brake shoe. Engage the end of the brake shoe with the wheel cylinder piston and the top anchor. Install the retainer nail, washer, spring and retainer.

14. Position the primary shoe in like manner and install hold-down pin assembly. Install the top anchor plate.

15. Install the parking brake strut and spring in position, press the lower part of the brake.

16. Straighten the adjuster cable and install the eye end over the top anchor. Be sure the lower spring end hook is facing inward.

17. Install the primary (front) shoe return spring. Place the cable guide in position on the secondary (rear) shoe (keep cable out of the way) and install the return spring. Check the cable guide and ensure proper mounting position. Squeeze the anchor ends of the return springs with pliers until they are parallel.

18. Carefully install the star wheel between the brake shoes. The wheel end goes closest the secondary (back) shoe. Wind out the star wheel until snug contact between the brake shoes will hold it in position.

19. Install the adjusting lever spring over the pivot pin on the lower shoe web of the secondary shoe. Install the adjuster lever under the spring and over the pivot pin. Slide the lever rearward until it locks in position.

20. Thread the adjuster cable over the guide and hook the end of the

overload spring on the adjuster lever. Make sure the cable is float on the guide and the eye end is against the anchor.

21. Check the operation of the adjuster by pulling the cable rearward. The star wheel should rotate upward as the adjuster lever engages the teeth.

22. Back off the star wheel, if necessary, and install the hub and drum. Adjust the brakes.

23. Repeat the procedures on the other rear wheel.

Pick-Up, Ramcharger and Van

11 INCH BRAKE DRUM

1. Raise the vehicle and support safely. Remove the wheels and drums. Remove the primary and secondary shoe return springs from the anchor pin.

2. Lift the adjuster lever and disconnect the actuator cable.

3. Remove the shoe retainers and springs.

4. Remove the shoes (held together by the lower spring) while separating the parking brake actuating lever from the shoe with a twisting motion.

To install:

5. Thoroughly clean and dry the backing plate. To prepare the backing plate, lubricate the bosses, anchor pin and parking brake actuating lever pivot surface lightly with lithium based grease.

6. Remove, clean and dry all parts still on the old shoes. Lubricate the star wheel shaft threads with antiseize lubricant and transfer all parts to their proper locations on the new shoes.

7. Spread the shoes apart, engage the parking brake lever and position them on the backing plate so the wheel cylinder pins engage and the anchor pins hold the shoes.

8. Install the parking brake strut and hold-down spring assemblies.

9. Install the anchor plate. Lubricate the sliding surface of the actuator cable plate lightly and install the cable.

10. Install the shoe return spring opposite the cable, then install the remaining spring.

11. Adjust the star wheel.

12. Remove any grease from the linings and install the drum.

13. Complete the brake adjustment with the wheels installed.

12 AND 13 INCH BRAKE DRUMS

1. Raise the vehicle and support safely. Remove the axles for integral hub/drum assemblies. Remove the

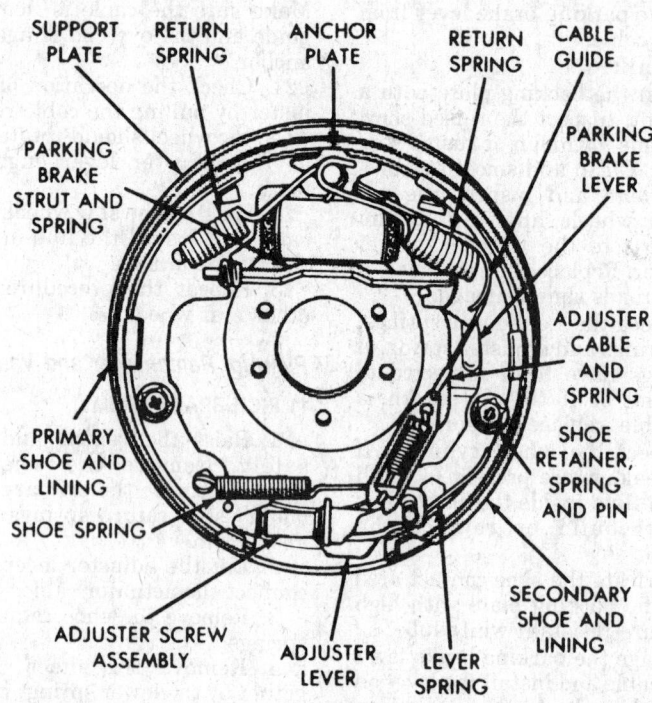

SUPPORT PLATE — RETURN SPRING — ANCHOR PLATE — RETURN SPRING — CABLE GUIDE — PARKING BRAKE STRUT AND SPRING — PARKING BRAKE LEVER — ADJUSTER CABLE AND SPRING — SHOE RETAINER, SPRING AND PIN — SECONDARY SHOE AND LINING — LEVER SPRING — ADJUSTER LEVER — ADJUSTER SCREW ASSEMBLY — SHOE SPRING — PRIMARY SHOE AND LINING

79111083

11 inch drum brakes

brake drums for removable brake drums assemblies.

2. Unhook the adjuster lever return spring from the lever.

3. Remove the lever and return spring from the lever pin.

4. Unhook the adjuster cable from the lever.

5. Remove the shoe to shoe upper spring.

6. Remove the shoe hold-down springs.

7. Disconnect the parking brake cable from the parking brake lever.

8. Remove both brake shoes, the lower spring and star wheel assembly.

To install:

9. Thoroughly clean and dry the backing plate. To prepare the backing plate, lubricate the bosses, anchor pin and parking brake actuating lever pivot surface lightly with lithium based grease.

10. Remove, clean and dry all parts still on the old shoes. Lubricate the star wheel shaft threads with anti-seize lubricant and transfer all parts to their proper locations on the new shoes. Install the assemblies to the backing plate.

11. Install the shoe hold-down springs and pins.

12. Connect the parking brake cable to the lever.

13. Install the upper spring.

14. Position the adjuster lever return spring on the pin. Install the adjuster lever and attach the cable.

15. Adjust the star wheel.

16. Remove any grease from the linings and install the drum.

17. Complete the brake adjustment with the wheels (but not the axles) installed.

18. Install the axles.

Wheel Cylinder

REMOVAL AND INSTALLATION

1. Raise the vehicle and support safely.

2. Remove the wheel, drum and brake shoes.

3. If equipped with a 12 or 13 in. drum, remove the anchor bolt and nut, washer, spring, parking brake lever, adjuster cable, cam plate and anchor spring bushing.

4. Remove the brake line from the wheel cylinder.

5. Remove the wheel cylinder bolts and remove the cylinder from the backing plate.

To install:

6. Install cylinder to backing plate and install bolts. Install brake line to cylinder.

7. If equipped with a 12 or 13 in. drum, install the anchor bolt and nut, washer, spring, parking brake lever, adjuster cable, cam plate and anchor spring bushing.

8. Install brake shoes, drum and wheel.

9. Bleed wheel cylinder and correct brake fluid level.

Parking Brake Cable

ADJUSTMENT

Caravan, Voyager and Town & Country

1. Raise and safely support the vehicle. Apply and release the parking brake several times.

2. Clean the parking park adjustment bolts with a wire brush and lubricate the threads. Back off the adjusting nut until there is slack in the cable.

3. Check the rear brake adjustment, adjust as necessary.

4. Tighten the parking brake cable adjuster until the slight drag is felt when turning the rear wheel.

5. Loosen the cable until no drag is felt on either rear wheel. Back off adjusting nut 2 full turns more.

6. Apply and release the parking brake several times to ensure there is not rear wheel drag. Lower the vehicle.

Dakota

1. Raise the vehicle and support safely.

2. Back off cable tensioner adjusting nut at equalizer to create slack in cables.

3. Remove the rear wheels and drums.

4. Check rear brake shoe adjustment with standard brake gauge. An out-of-adjustment will cause faulty parking brake operation. Check all automatic brake adjuster components before adjusting parking brake.

5. Verify that parking brake cables operate freely and are not binding.

6. Adjust the rear brake shoes to drums. Install brake drums and wheels.

7. Fully apply parking brake and leave applied until adjustment is complete.

8. Mark tensioner rod 1/4 in. (6.5mm) from edge of tensioner bracket. Tighten the nut at equalizer until mark on tensioner rod moves into alignment with bracket.

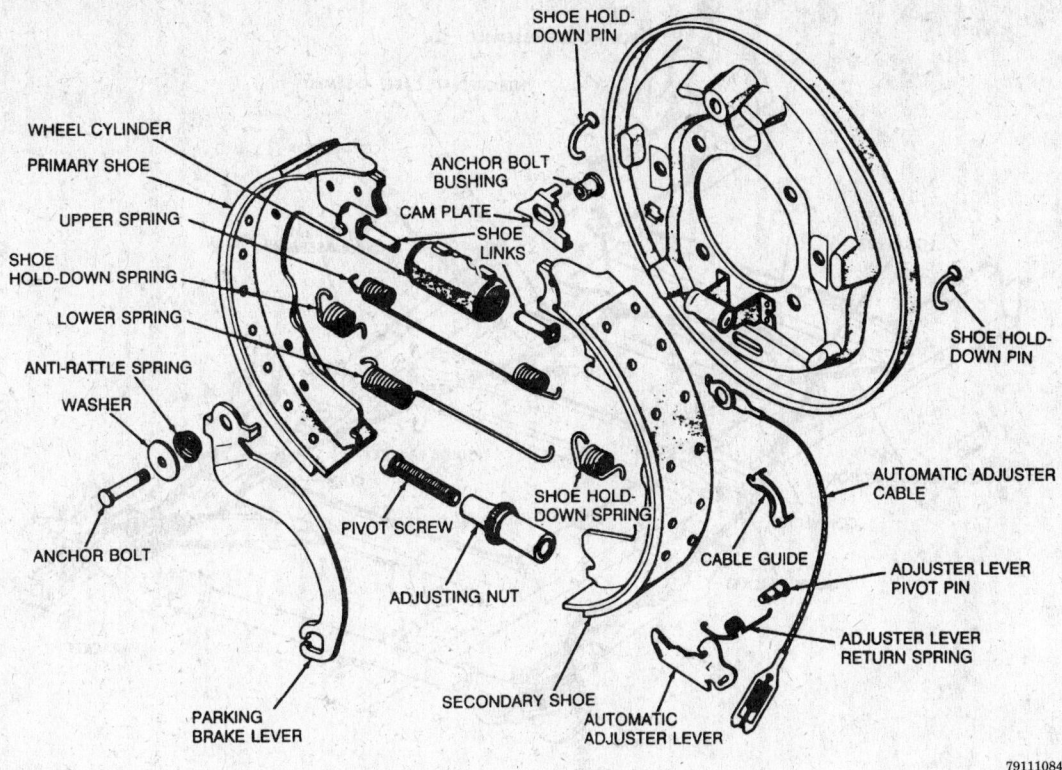

WHEEL CYLINDER

PRIMARY SHOE

UPPER SPRING

SHOE HOLD-DOWN SPRING

LOWER SPRING

ANTI-RATTLE SPRING

WASHER

ANCHOR BOLT

PARKING BRAKE LEVER

PIVOT SCREW

ADJUSTING NUT

SECONDARY SHOE

SHOE HOLD-DOWN PIN

ANCHOR BOLT BUSHING

CAM PLATE

SHOE LINKS

SHOE HOLD-DOWN SPRING

SHOE HOLD-DOWN PIN

AUTOMATIC ADJUSTER CABLE

CABLE GUIDE

ADJUSTER LEVER PIVOT PIN

ADJUSTER LEVER RETURN SPRING

AUTOMATIC ADJUSTER LEVER

79111084

12 inch drum brakes, 13 inch similar

9. Lower the vehicle until the rear wheels are 6–8 in. (15–20cm) of the floor. Release the parking brake and verify that the rear wheels rotate freely without drag.

Pick-Up, Ramcharger and Van

1. Release the parking brakes fully.
2. Raise the vehicle and support safely.
3. Adjust the rear brakes.
4. Loosen the nut on the front cable until there is slack in all the cables.
5. Rotate the rear wheels and tighten the cable adjusting nut until there is a slight drag at the wheels.
6. Continue to rotate the rear wheels and loosen the nut until all drag is eliminated.
7. Back off the nut an additional 2 turns.
8. Apply and release the parking brake several times. Upon the last release, verify that there is no drag at the rear wheels.
9. To check the operation, make sure the parking brake holds on an incline.

REMOVAL AND INSTALLATION

Caravan, Voyager and Town & Country

FRONT CABLE

1. Raise and safely support the vehicle.
2. Back off the adjuster nut until the cable can be released from the connectors.
3. Lift the floor mat for access to the floor pan. Force the seal surrounding the cable from the floor.
4. Pull the cable forward and disconnect from lever clevis. Remove the front cable from support bracket and vehicle.
5. Feed the new cable through the floor pan hole. Attach the front end of the cable to the parking brake lever clevis and support.
6. Engage intermediate cable and adjust.

INTERMEDIATE CABLE

1. Back off the parking brake adjuster. Disengage the front cable and rear cables from the intermediate cable connector.
2. Remove the intermediate cable. Install the new cable and adjust.

REAR CABLES

1. Raise and safely support the vehicle.
2. Back off the cable adjustment and disconnect the rear cable (that is to be replaced) from the intermediate cable. Remove the rear cable from the mounting clips.
3. Remove the rear wheel and the brake shoes from the side requiring replacement.
4. Disconnect the cable from the rear brake apply lever. Compress the cable lock with a mini-hose clamp and pull the cable from the backing plate.
5. Install the new cable through the brake backing plate. Engage the locks. Attach the cable to the apply lever. Install the brake shoes, drum and wheel assembly.
6. Adjust the service brakes and parking brake.

Dakota

FRONT CABLE

1. Raise the vehicle and support safely.
2. Loosen cable adjusting nut and disengage cable from intermediate cable connector.
3. Remove the clip attaching front cable to frame rail with a pry tool. Press cable out of frame rail. Remove

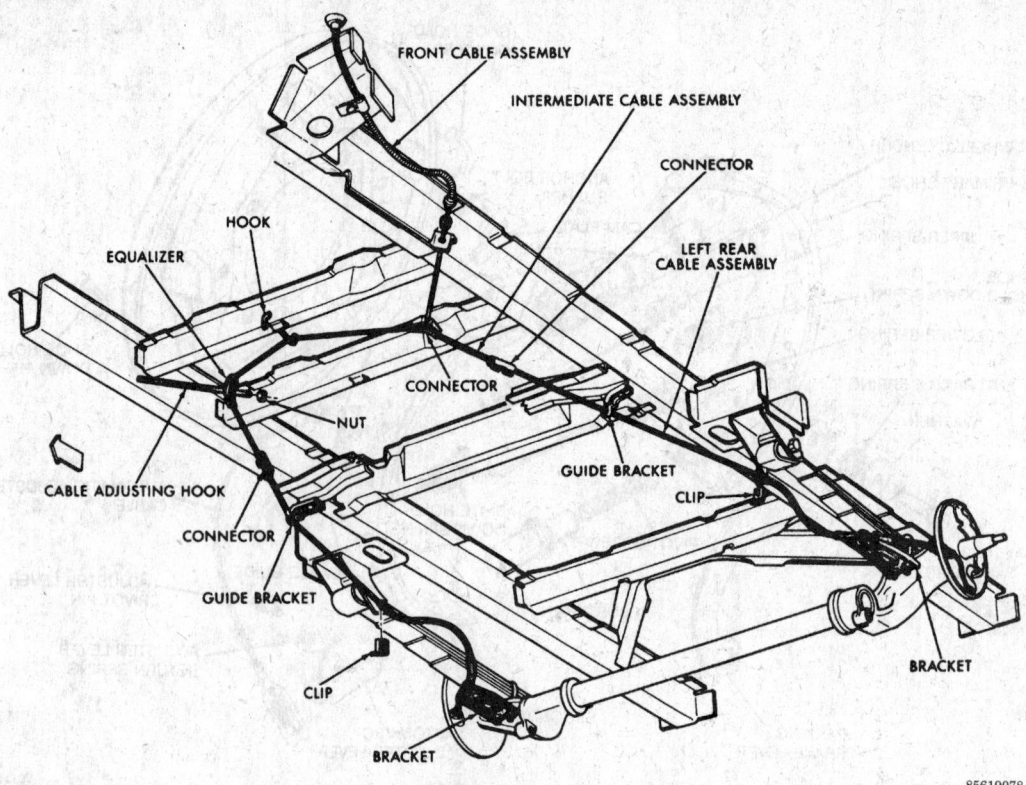

FRONT CABLE ASSEMBLY

INTERMEDIATE CABLE ASSEMBLY

CONNECTOR

HOOK

EQUALIZER

LEFT REAR CABLE ASSEMBLY

CONNECTOR

NUT

GUIDE BRACKET

CABLE ADJUSTING HOOK

CLIP

CONNECTOR

GUIDE BRACKET

BRACKET

CLIP

BRACKET

85619078

Parking brake cable routing

the guide clip from frame rail for 4WD vehicles.

4. Lower the vehicle and fold left front edge of floor covering rearward and remove the cable boot from floor pan.

5. Engage parking brake pedal and work front cable up and out of clevis linkage in pedal assembly.

6. Pry upper end of cable housing and clip downward and out of pedal bracket. Work cable and housing up through floor pan and remove from vehicle.

To install:

7. Insert cable through floor pan and insert cable retainer into hole at bottom of pedal assembly bracket. Connect cable end fitting to linkage clevis.

8. Push cable retainer inward until firmly seated against pedal bracket. Install cable boot to floor pan.

9. Route cable through frame and seat in frame rail. Raise the vehicle and support safely.

10. Attach cable to intermediate cable and guide clip to frame rail, if equipped.

11. Adjust parking brakes and lower vehicle.

INTERMEDIATE CABLE

1. Raise vehicle and support safely.

2. Loosen parking brake cable adjuster nut to create slack.

3. Disengage adjuster hook from frame rail. Disconnect the intermediate cable from rear cable connectors and cable guides.

To install:

4. Locate cable guides in frame rail slots as follows:

   a. On 2WD models, locate guides in slots that are 13.6 in. (34.54mm) rearward of weld seam in frame rail.

   b. On 4WD models, locate guides in slots that are 13.8 in. (35.07mm) rearward of weld seam in frame rail.

5. Guide cables through cables guides and attach intermediate cable ends to rear cable connectors.

6. Attach adjuster hook and equalizer to intermediate cable and connect hook to frame.

7. Adjust the parking brake cables.

REAR CABLES

1. Raise the vehicle and support safely.

2. Loosen the adjuster nut at equalizer until rear cable has 2–4 inches of slack.

3. Remove clips that secure rear cable to bracket at rear of frame rail. Remove the brake drums and brake shoes.

4. Disconnect the rear cable from lever on secondary brake shoe.

5. Compress tab on each cable retainer with hose clamp or pliers. Push cable through backing plate and remove cable. If cable tabs cannot be compressed, pry and break tabs from retainer and remove cable.

To install:

6. Install cable through frame brackets, but do not clips at this time.

7. Install cable through brake backing plates and engage retaining tabs. Connect cable to brake shoe.

8. Install brake shoes on support plate. Make sure parking brake lever strut and springs are properly positioned before installing return springs.

9. Install remaining components and adjust parking brake.

Pick-Up, Ramcharger and Van

FRONT CABLE

1. Raise the vehicle and support safely.

2. Remove the front cable adjusting nut.

3. Remove the clip securing the cable to the anchor bracket and slide the cable out of the bracket.

4. Remove the retainer attaching the cable to the pedal assembly frame. Disengage the cable from the pedal clevis.

5. Remove the cable grommet from the floor pan and remove the cable.

6. The installation is the reversal of the removal procedure.

REAR CABLES

1. Release the parking brake fully.
2. Raise the vehicle and support safely.
3. Remove the adjusting nut from the front cable.
4. Remove the brake drums. Remove the shoes, if necessary. Disconnect the cable from the lever and compress the cable retainer tabs and remove the cable from the backing plate.
5. Remove the cable from the equalizer and ratio lever.
6. The installation is the reversal of the removal procedure.

Brake System Bleeding

BENCH BLEEDING

Always bench bleed the master cylinder before installing it on the vehicle.

1. Place the master cylinder in a vise.
2. Connect 2 lines to the fluid outlet orifices, bend the lines upwards and insert the opened ends into the reservoir.
3. Fill the reservoir with brake fluid.
4. Using a wooden dowel, depress the pushrod slowly, allowing the pistons to return. do this several times until the air bubbles are all expelled.
5. Remove the bleeding tubes from the master cylinder, plug the outlets and install the caps.

NOTE: It is not necessary to bleed the entire system after replacing the master cylinder, provided that master cylinder has been bled and filled upon installation. However, if a soft pedal is experienced, bleed the entire system.

SYSTEM BLEEDING

─────── **WARNING** ───────
Do not allow brake fluid to spill on the vehicle's finish; it will remove the paint. In case of a spill, flush the area with water.

1. The sequence for bleeding is as follows:
    a. Master cylinder
    b. Rear Wheel Anti-Lock valve, if equipped
    c. Front Wheel Anti-Lock valve, if equipped
    d. Left rear wheel cylinder
    e. Right rear wheel cylinder
    f. Right front caliper
    g. Left front caliper

2. Clean all the bleeder screws. You may want to give each one a shot of penetrating solvent to help loosen the fitting. Seizure is a common problem with bleeder screws, which then brake off, sometimes requiring replacement of the part to which they are attached.

3. Check the fluid level in the master cylinder and fill with DOT 3 brake fluid, if necessary.

NOTE: Brake fluid absorbs moisture from the air. Don't leave the master cylinder or the fluid container uncovered any longer than necessary. Be careful handling the brake fluid,it is a great paint remover. If any brake fluid spills on the vehicle's finish, flush off with water immediately. Check the level of the fluid often when bleeding, and refill the reservoirs as necessary. Don't let them run dry, or you will have to repeat the process.

4. Attach a length of clear vinyl tubing to the bleeder screw at the wheel cylinder or caliper. Insert the other end of the tube into a clear, clean jar ½ filled with brake fluid. Start at a rear cylinder first, then bleed the opposite side front cylinder.

5. Have your assistant slowly depress the brake pedal. As this is done, open the bleeder screw ⅓–½ of a turn on wheel cylinders and at least 1 turn on calipers, and allow the fluid to run through the tube. Then close the bleeder screw before the pedal reaches the end of its travel. Have an assistant slowly release the pedal after the bleeder screw is closed. Repeat this process until no air bubbles appear in the expelled fluid.

6. Repeat the procedure on the other calipers and cylinders, checking the level of fluid in the master cylinder reservoir often. After finished, there should be no spongyness in the brake pedal feel. If there is, either there is still air in the line, in which case the process should be repeated, or there is a leak somewhere, which of course must be corrected before moving the vehicle.

Anti-Lock Brake System Service

PRECAUTIONS

Failure to observe the following precautions may result in system damage.

• Before performing electric arc welding on the vehicle, disconnect the Electronic Brake Control Module (EBCM) and the hydraulic modulator connectors.

• When performing painting work on the vehicle, do not expose the Electronic Brake Control Module (EBCM) to temperatures in excess of 185°F (85°C) for longer than 2 hrs. The system may be exposed to temperatures up to 200°F (95°C) for less than 15 min.

• Never disconnect or connect the Electronic Brake Control Module (EBCM) or hydraulic modulator connectors with the ignition switch ON.

• Never disassemble any component of the Anti-Lock Brake System (ABS) which is designated non-serviceable; the component must be replaced as an assembly.

• When filling the master cylinder, always use brake fluid which meets DOT-3 specifications; petroleum-based fluid will destroy the rubber parts.

ABS Electronic Control Module

NOTE: Bendix 10 ABS system can be found on 1992–93 Caravan/Voyager/Town & Country and Bendix 4 ABS system is used on 1994–96 Caravan/Voyager/Town & Country.

REMOVAL AND REPLACEMENT

Caravan, Voyager and Town & Country

The Controller Anti-lock Brake (CAB) is located in the engine compartment under the battery tray. This computer — operating separately from other on-board controllers — monitors wheel speed signals as well as several internal functions. The CAB controls the wheel circuit valves once a locking tendency is detected. This pressure modulation continues until the locking tendency is no longer detected.

1. Turn the ignition switch **OFF** and disconnect the battery cables from the battery.

2. Remove the CAB-to-battery tray support bracket bolts and pull CAB and battery tray outward.

3. Loosen bolt retaining the wiring harness 60-way connector and disconnect.

4. Remove the CAB and mounting bracket as an assembly.

Dakota

1. The ABS control module is located on the control valve assembly, left inner fender.

2. Disconnect the upper harness connector from control module. Lift connector locking handle and disconnect main harness connector from module.

3. Remove module retaining screws and module.

4. Installation is the reverse of removal. Make sure the connectors are properly seated and locked.

Pick-Up, Ramcharger and Van

The RWAL (Rear Wheel Anti-Lock) control module is located behind the instrument panel for Pick-Up and Ramcharger or under the battery tray for Van. The All Wheel ABS control unit is attached to the ABS valve assembly, left inner fender.

PICK-UP AND RAMCHARGER WITH RWAL

1. Disconnect negative battery cable.

2. The module is located by the blower motor resistor board and defroster duct. Remove the mounting screws, disconnect the harness connector and remove the module.

3. Installation is the reverse of the removal procedure.

PICK-UP AND RAMCHARGER WITH ALL WHEEL ABS AND VAN

1. The ABS control module is located on the control valve assembly, left inner fender.

2. Disconnect the upper harness connector from control module. Lift connector locking handle and disconnect main harness connector from module.

3. Remove module retaining screws and module.

4. Installation is the reverse of removal. Make sure the connectors are properly seated and locked.

Wheel Speed Sensor

REMOVAL AND REPLACEMENT

Caravan, Voyager and Town & Country

FRONT

1. Raise the vehicle and support safely. Remove the front wheel.

2. Remove grommet retainer clip that holds the grommet into fender shield.

3. Disconnect the sensor connector.

4. Remove the sensor screw and carefully slide the sensor from the steering knuckle. If the sensor is seized, use a hammer and punch to tap the sensor ear back and forth until free. Do not use pliers on the sensor.

5. Installation is the reverse of removal. Coat the sensor with high temperature grease and torque screws to 60 inch lbs. (7.0 Nm). Make sure all retainer grommets are positioned properly. If not, damage to the sensor wire could result.

REAR

1. Raise the vehicle and support safely.

2. Disconnect the sensor and remove wiring from retainer grommets. Make routing note for installation purposes.

3. Remove the sensor screw and carefully slide the sensor from the backing plate. If the sensor is seized, use a hammer and punch to tap the sensor ear back and forth until free. Do not use pliers on the sensor.

4. Installation is the reverse of removal. Coat the sensor with high temperature grease and torque screws to 60 inch lbs. (7.0 Nm). Make sure all retainer grommets are positioned properly. If not, damage to the sensor wire could result.

Pick-Up, Ramcharger, Van and Dakota

FRONT

1. Raise the vehicle and safely support. Remove the front wheel.

2. For all except 4WD Dakota: remove the caliper, hub/rotor and speed sensor-to-backing plate retaining screws.

3. For 4WD Dakota: remove the sensor-to-steering knuckle retaining screws.

4. Disconnect the harness connector and remove all grommet retainers.

5. Carefully slide the sensor from the backing plate. If the sensor is seized, use a hammer and punch to tap the sensor ear back and forth until free. Do not use pliers on the sensor.

6. Installation is the reverse of removal. Coat the sensor with high temperature grease and torque screws to 60 inch lbs. (7.0 Nm) for Dakota or 190–250 inch lbs. (21–25 Nm) for all others. Make sure all retainer grommets are positioned properly. If not, damage to the sensor wire could result.

REAR

1. Raise and safely support vehicle.

2. Remove sensor mounting bolt on rear axle housing.

3. Remove sensor shield and sensor from housing. Disconnect sensor wire harness.

4. Installation is the reversal of the removal process.

ABS (Modulator) Control Valve Assembly

REMOVAL AND INSTALLATION

Caravan, Voyager and Town & Country

1. With ignition switch **OFF**, disconnect the both battery cables and isolate from battery.

2. Remove the battery hold-down clamp, battery and battery tray.

3. Remove the control module from the bracket and move out of the way.

4. Loosen, but do not remove the bolt attaching battery tray support bracket-to-modulator mounting bracket.

5. Remove the battery tray support bracket from the vehicle.

6. Remove the acid shield from the ABS modulator.

7. Using flarenut wrenches, remove the 6 tube nuts attaching brake line bundle to modulator, thread savers and proportioning valves. Remove the brake lines an an assembly from the modulator. Brake lines do not need to be loosened at junction block.

8. Raise the vehicle and support safely. Disconnect the 10-way connector from the modulator and remove the speed control servo assembly bracket and move out of the way.

9. Loosen but do not remove the lower modulator mounting bolts. Lower the vehicle and remove the modulator and bracket assembly.

To install:

10. Inspect the bracket insulator for damage. Install the modulator onto mounting brackets and install 3 bolts. Torque bolts to 21 ft. lbs. (28 Nm).

11. Install the assembly and torque bolts to small retainers to 12 inch lbs. (1.4 Nm) and large to 250 inch lbs. (28 Nm).

12. Lower the vehicle and attach the brake line assembly. Thread all lines by hand until snug. Hold the proportioning valve with a wrench and torque the brake lines to 160 inch lbs. (18 Nm).

13. Use jumper cables to bleed the brake system.

14. Remove jumper cables and install the acid shield, battery tray, support bracket, control module, battery and cables.

15. Apply parking brake and start the vehicle. Test brakes before driving the vehicle.

Pick-Up, Ramcharger, Van and Dakota

FRONT ABS VALVE

The assembly is located on top of the left inner fender.

1. Disconnect the negative battery cable and isolate from battery.

2. Remove the battery and tray, if necessary.

3. Disconnect the brake lines at front of ABS valve using flarenut and backup wrenches.

4. Disconnect and label all electrical connectors.

5. Remove the retaining screws and lift valve/bracket assembly from vehicle.

6. Installation is the reverse of removal. Torque retaining nuts to 112 inch lbs. (13 Nm), screws to 220 inch lbs. (25 Nm) and brake lines to 140–200 inch lbs. (16–23 Nm).

7. Connect battery cable and bleed brake system.

REAR ABS VALVE

The assembly is located under the brake master cylinder.

1. Disconnect the negative battery cable and isolate from battery. Remove the battery.

2. Using a flarenut wrench, disconnect the rear brake line at ABS valve and front brake line at combination valve.

3. Disconnect the electrical connectors from both valves.

4. Remove combination-to-booster nuts and disconnect lines connecting ABS valve to master cylinder.

5. Slide combination valve bracket off booster studs and remove ABS valve, combination valve and bracket with brake lines attached. Remove the ABS valve from assembly.

6. Installation is the reverse of removal. Torque the booster nuts to 250 ft. lbs. (28 Nm) and brake line fittings to 140–200 inch lbs. (16–23 Nm).

7. Connect battery cable and bleed brake system.

Exciter Ring or Tone Wheel

The only exciter ring that is serviceable is for the rear standard differential. All others are serviced with the component they are attached to.

REMOVAL AND INSTALLATION

1. Raise and safely support vehicle.

2. Remove rear axle cover, drain fluid and remove ring gear.

3. Remove old exciter ring with a hammer and drift, wearing proper eye protection.

To install:

4. Heat replacement exciter ring with heat light or by immersing in a hot liquid not to exceed a temperature of 300°F. Do not use a torch.

5. After heating, quickly position ring on differential case adjacent to the flange.

6. Install ring gear, cover and fluid to rear axle.

FRONT SUSPENSION

Shock Absorbers

REMOVAL AND INSTALLATION

1. Raise the vehicle and support safely.

2. On 2WD vehicles, remove the upper shock nut, washer and bushing. Remove the lower mounting bolts and remove the shock from the vehicle.

3. On 4WD vehicles, remove the upper mounting nut, lower mounting stud and retainers. Remove the shock from the vehicle.

4. The installation is the reversal of the removal procedure.

MacPherson Struts

REMOVAL AND INSTALLATION

Caravan, Voyager and Town & Country

1. Loosen the front wheel lug nuts slightly. Raise and safely support the vehicle.

2. Remove the wheel and tire assemblies.

NOTE: If the original strut assemblies are to be installed, mark the camber eccentric bolt and strut for installment in same position.

3. Remove the lower camber bolt and nut (at the steering knuckle), and the knuckle bolt and nut. Remove the brake hose to strut bracket mounting bolt.

4. Remove the upper mounting nuts and washers on the fender shield in the engine compartment. Remove the strut assembly from the vehicle.

To install:

5. Inspect the strut assembly for signs of leakage. A slight amount of seepage is normal, fluid streaking down the side of the strut is not. Replace the strut if leakage is evident. Service the strut and spring assembly as required.

6. Position the strut assembly under the fender well and loosely install the upper washers and nuts. Position the lower mount over the steering knuckle and loosely install the mounting and camber bolts and nuts. Attach the brake hose retaining bracket and tighten the mounting bolts to 10 ft. lbs. (14 Nm).

7. Tighten the upper mount nuts to 20 ft. lbs. (28 Nm). Index the camber bolt to reference mark and snug the nut. Install the nut on the mounting bolt and tighten slightly.

8. Mount a 4 in. (102mm) C–clamp over the inner edge of the strut and outer edge of the steering knuckle. Tighten the clamp just enough to eliminate any looseness between the knuckle and the strut. Check the alignment of the camber bolt and strut reference marks. Tighten the mounting and camber nuts to 75 ft. lbs. (102 Nm), plug ¼ turn more. Remove the C–clamp.

9. Install the wheel and tire assembly and lower the vehicle.

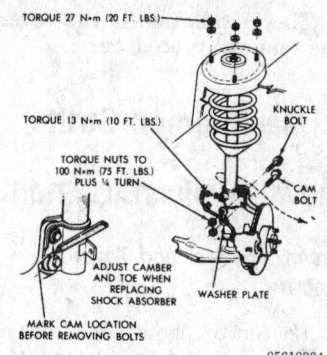

TORQUE 27 N•m (20 FT. LBS.)

TORQUE 13 N•m (10 FT. LBS.)

KNUCKLE BOLT

TORQUE NUTS TO 100 N•m (75 FT. LBS.) PLUS ¼ TURN

CAM BOLT

ADJUST CAMBER AND TOE WHEN REPLACING SHOCK ABSORBER

WASHER PLATE

MARK CAM LOCATION BEFORE REMOVING BOLTS

85618004

Strut removal

Strut Damper and Spring

REMOVAL AND INSTALLATION

Caravan, Voyager and Town & Country

NOTE: A coil spring compressor Chrysler tool C–4838 or equivalent is required.

1. Remove the strut and spring assembly from the vehicle.
2. Compress the coil spring with Chrysler tool C–4838 or equivalent.

— CAUTION —

Make sure the compressor is mounted correctly and tighten jaws evenly. If the spring slips from the compressor, bodily injury could occur.

3. Hold the strut center rod from turning and remove the assembly nut.

NOTE: The coil springs on each are rated differently. Be sure to mark the spring for side identification.

4. Remove the mount assembly and the coil spring. Inspect the assembly for rubber isolator deterioration, distortion, cracks and bonding

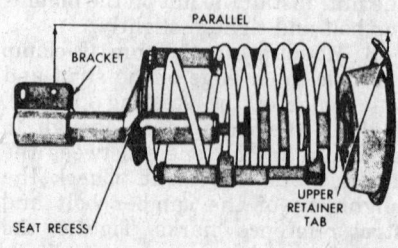

PARALLEL

BRACKET

UPPER RETAINER TAB

SEAT RECESS

85618014

A coil spring compressor Chrysler tool C–4838 in the installed position

failure. Replace as necessary. Check the mount bearings for binding and the retainers for bends and cracks. Replace as necessary.

To install:

5. Install the spring on the strut in compressed mode. Install the upper mount assembly. The spring seat tab and the end of the coil spring must be aligned. Install assembly nut and tighten while holding the center strut rod in position. Tighten the nut to 60 ft. lbs. (82 Nm).
6. Release the coil spring compressor.
7. Install the strut assembly on the vehicle.
8. Misalignment of the upper coil spring seat can cause interference between the coil spring and the inside of the mounting tower. A scraping noise on turns will be an indication if the problem. To correct, raise and support the vehicle to take the weight off the front wheels. Use 2 wrenches, one on the top of the center strut rod and one on the assembly nut. Turn both the strut rod and nut in the same direction. The spring will wind up and snap into position. Check the torque on the assembly nut 60 ft. lbs. (82 Nm).

Coil Springs

REMOVAL AND INSTALLATION

2WD Dakota, Pick-Up and Van

1. Raise the vehicle and support safely.
2. Remove the shock absorber.
3. Remove the strut bar and disconnect the sway bar from the lower control arm, if equipped.
4. Install spring compressor tool DD–1278 or equivalent, to the coil spring and tighten the nut finger-tight, then back off nut ½ turn.
5. Remove the cotter pin and lower ball joint nut.
6. Release the lower ball joint taper using ball stud loosening tool C–3564–A or equivalent.
7. Remove the tool and remove the ball stud from the control arm. Release the compressor tool from the coil spring.
8. Pull the arm down and remove the spring with the rubber isolation pad from the vehicle.

To install:

9. Install the spring with the rubber isolators. Install the compressor tool and compress it enough so the lower ball joint can be inserted through the knuckle.

10. Torque $^{11}/_{16}$-16 lower ball joint nuts to 135 ft. lbs. (183 Nm). Torque $^{3}/_{4}$-16 nuts to 175 ft. lbs. (237 Nm). Install a new cotter pin. Remove the spring compressor.
11. Install the strut bar and connect the sway bar from the lower control arm, if equipped.
12. Install the shock absorber.

1994–96 4WD Pick-Up

1. Raise the vehicle and support safely. Position a floor jack under the drive axle to support it.
2. Matchmark the lower suspension arm cam adjusters and axle bracket for installation reference.
3. Remove the upper suspension arm and loosen lower suspension arm bolts.
4. Mark and disconnect the front driveshaft.
5. Disconnect the track bar from the frame rail brackets.
6. Disconnect the drag link from the pitman arm.
7. Disconnect the stabilizer bar link and shock absorber from the axle.
8. Lower the axle until the spring is free from the upper mount and remove.

To install:

9. Position the coil spring on the axle pad and raise the axle into position.

NOTE: Do not tighten any suspension pivot bolts until the vehicle weight is resting on the suspension. Damage to the rubber bushing will occur.

10. Connect the stabilizer bar, shock absorber and track bar.
11. Install the upper suspension arm and front driveshaft.
12. Install the drag link to pitman arm and torque nut to 65 ft. lbs. (88 Nm).
13. Remove the supports, lower the vehicle and torque the suspension components to the following:
   a. Stabilizer bar nut to 87 ft. lbs. (118 Nm)
   b. Shock bolt to 89 ft. lbs. (121 Nm)
   c. Track bar bolt to 130 ft. lbs. (176 Nm)
   d. Suspension arm-to-axle to 89 ft. lbs. (121 Nm)
   e. Suspension arm-to-frame bracket to 62 ft. lbs. (84 Nm)
   f. Lower suspension arm adjusting cam to 110 ft. lbs. (149 Nm)
14. Install the remaining components and align the front end.

Leaf Springs

REMOVAL AND INSTALLATION

1992–93 Pick-Up and Ramcharger

1. Raise the vehicle and support safely.
2. Using the proper equipment, support the weight of the front axle.
3. Remove the nuts, washers and U-bolts attaching the springs to the axle housing. Remove the spring pad.
4. Remove the spring shackle bolts, shackle and spring front bolt.
5. Remove the spring from the vehicle.
6. The installation is the reverse of the removal procedure. Torque the U-bolt nuts to 110 ft. lbs. (149 Nm).

Torsion Bars

REMOVAL AND INSTALLATION

4WD Dakota

NOTE: The right and left torsion bars are not interchangeable. The bars are identified by a R or L. They do not have a front or rear end and can be installed in either direction.

1. Remove the suspension arm jounce bumpers before raising vehicle. Raise the vehicle and support safely.
2. Mark torsion bar-to-lower arm positioning.
3. Turn the adjustment bolt counterclockwise to release spring load and remove bolt.
4. Remove torsion bar and anchor from vehicle.
5. Remove all foreign material from torsion bar mounting in anchor and suspension arm.
   To install:
6. Insert torsion bar ends into anchor and lower arm. Position anchor and bushing in frame crossmember.
7. Install the adjusting bolt through bushing and anchor and into swivel.
8. Turn adjustment bolt clockwise to apply a spring load.
9. Lower the vehicle and adjust the front suspension height.

Upper Ball Joint

INSPECTION

To inspect the ball joints, unload the suspension. Upper ball joints should be replaced if any lateral play exists at all.

REMOVAL AND INSTALLATION

Except 4WD and 1994–96 2WD Pick-Up

1. Raise the vehicle and support safely.
2. Position a support at the outer end of the lower control arm and lower the vehicle so the support compresses the coil spring.
3. Remove the tire and wheel assembly.
4. With the vehicle weight on the coil spring, disconnect the ball joint from the knuckle with separator tool MB990625 or equivalent.
5. Release the upper ball joint taper using ball stud loosening tool C–3564–A or equivalent.
6. Unthread the ball joint from the control arm with tool C–3561 or equivalent.
7. The installation is the reversal of the removal procedure. Torque the ball joint itself to 125 ft. lbs. (169 Nm).
8. Torque the upper ball stud nut to 135 ft. lbs. (183 Nm).

1994–96 2WD Pick-Up

1. Remove the upper control arm from the vehicle and place in vise.
2. Position removal tools C–4212–F and 6756 onto ball joint. Press the ball joint from the upper arm.
3. Using the same tools, press the ball joint into the upper arm and install the upper arm into the vehicle.

4WD Pick-Up and Ramcharger

1. Raise the vehicle and support safely.
2. Remove the front axle shaft.
3. Disconnect the tie rod end from the steering knuckle. On the left side, disconnect the drag link ball stud from the steering knuckle.
4. On the left side, remove the nuts and washers from the steering knuckle arm and remove the arm and spring, if equipped, from the knuckle.
5. If equipped with a Model 44 front axle, remove the ball joint nuts and discard the lower nut. Use a brass drift and hammer to separate

the steering knuckle from the axle tube yoke. Use tool C–4169 to remove the sleeve from the upper yoke arm.
6. Remove the snapring from the ball joint. Install the knuckle in a vise and use tools D–150–1, D–150–3 and C–4212–L or equivalent, to remove the ball joint from the knuckle.
7. If equipped with a Dana 60 front axle, remove the bolts from the knuckle lower cap. Dislodge the cap from the steering knuckle and axle tube yoke. Remove the steering knuckle. Use tool D–192 or equivalent, to remove the upper socket pin from the axle tube upper arm bore. Remove the seal.
   To install:
8. If equipped with a Model 44, use tools C–4212–L and C–4288 or equivalent, to force the upper ball joint into the steering knuckle. Install the snapring and install a new rubber boot. Thread the replacement sleeve into the upper yoke bore so 2 threads are exposed at the top of the yoke. Position the knuckle on the axle tube yoke and install a new lower ball stud nut. Torque to 80 ft. lbs. (108 Nm). Using the special socket, torque the sleeve to 40 ft. lbs. (54 Nm). Install the upper ball stud nut and torque to 100 ft. lbs. (136 Nm) and install a new cotter pin.
9. If equipped with a Dana 60 front axle, use tool D–192 or equivalent, to install the upper socket pin to the axle tube upper arm bore. Install a new seal. Torque to 500–600 ft. lbs. (668–813 Nm). Position the knuckle over the socket pin. Fill the lower socket cavity with grease. Install the lower cap and torque the bolts to 80 ft. lbs. (110 Nm).
10. On the left side, install the spring, if equipped, and the steering knuckle arm to the steering knuckle.
11. Connect the tie rod to the end of the steering knuckle. On the left side, connect the drag link ball stud to the steering knuckle.
12. Install the front axle shaft and all related components.

Lower Ball Joint

INSPECTION

To inspect the ball joints, unload the suspension. Lower ball joints on 2WD Pick-Up and Dakota should be replaced if the have more than 0.020 in. (0.51mm) play. Any ball joint on Caravan/Voyager/Town & Country and 4WD vehicles should be replaced if any play exists.

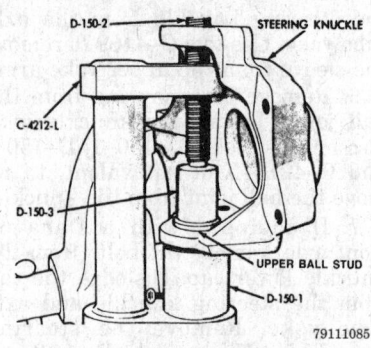

Removing the upper ball joint from the knuckle

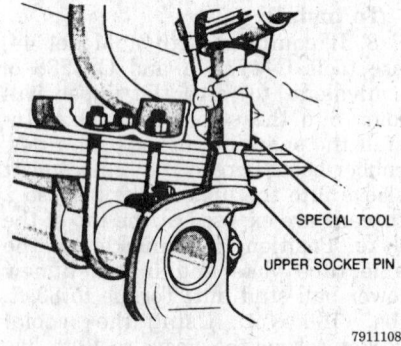

Removing or installing the upper socket pin

REMOVAL AND INSTALLATION

Caravan, Voyager and Town & Country

NOTE: Special Chrysler tools C–4699–1 and C–4699–2 or equivalents are required to remove and install the ball joint form the lower control arm.

1. Remove the lower control arm. Pry off the seal from the ball joint.
2. Position a receiving cup, special tool C–4699–2 or its equivalent to support the lower control arm.

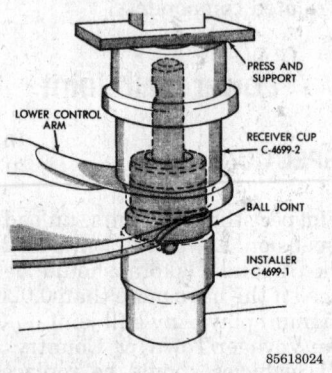

Lower ball joint installation

3. Install a 1⅛ in. deep socket over the stud and against the joint upper housing.
4. Press the joint assembly from the arm.
    To install:
5. To install, position the ball joint housing into the control arm cavity.
6. Position the assembly in a press with special tool C–4699–1 or its equivalent, supporting the control arm.
7. Align the ball joint assembly, then press it until the housing ledge stops against the control arm cavity down flange.
8. To install a new seal, support the ball joint housing with tool C–4699–2 and place a new seal over the stud, against the housing.
9. With a 1½ in. socket, press the seal onto the joint housing with the seat against the control arm. Install control arm.

2WD Pick-Up, Van and Dakota

1. Raise the vehicle and support safely.
2. Remove the shock absorber.
3. Remove the strut bar and disconnect the sway bar from the lower control arm, if equipped.
4. Install spring compressor tool DD–1278 or equivalent, to the coil spring and tighten the nut finger-tight, then back off ½ turn.
5. Remove the cotter pin and lower ball joint nut.
6. Release the lower ball joint taper using ball stud loosening tool C–3564–A or equivalent.
7. Remove the tool and remove the ball stud from the control arm. Release the compressor tool from the coil spring.
8. Pull the arm down and remove the spring with the rubber isolation pad from the vehicle. Remove the ball joint boot. Use tool C–4212 or a ball joint press, to remove the ball joint from the arm.
    To install:
9. Use the remover tool to press the ball joint into the arm. Install a new rubber boot. Install the spring with the rubber isolators. Install the compressor tool and compress it enough so the lower ball joint can be inserted through the knuckle.
10. Torque ¹¹⁄₁₆-16 lower ball joint nuts to 135 ft. lbs. (183 Nm). Torque ¾-16 nuts to 175 ft. lbs. (237 Nm). Install a new cotter pin. Remove the spring compressor.
11. Install the strut bar and connect the sway bar from the lower control arm, if equipped.
12. Install the shock absorber.

4WD Dakota

1. Raise the vehicle and support safely.
2. Remove the lower control arm assembly.
3. Pry the peened ball joint retainer sections upward from the control arm. Press the ball joint from the control arm with a hydraulic press.
    To install:
4. Press the new ball joint into the control arm and peen the housing retainer to the ball joint.
5. Install the lower control arm, adjust the alignment and lower the vehicle.

4WD Pick-Up and Ramcharger

1. Raise the vehicle and support safely.
2. Remove the front axle shaft.
3. Disconnect the tie rod end from the steering knuckle. On the left side, disconnect the drag link ball stud from the steering knuckle.
4. On the left side, remove the nuts and washers from the steering knuckle arm and remove the arm and spring, if equipped, from the knuckle.
5. If equipped with a Model 44 front axle, remove the ball joint nuts and discard the lower nut. Use a brass drift and hammer to separate the steering knuckle from the axle tube yoke.
6. Remove the snapring from the ball joint. Install the knuckle in a vise and use tools D–150–1, D–150–3 and C–4212–L to remove the ball joint from the knuckle.
7. If equipped with a Dana 60 front axle, use tools C–4212–L, C–4366–1 and C–4366–2 to remove the lower ball joint.
    To install:
8. If equipped with a Model 44, use tools C–4212–L and C–4288 or equivalent, to force the lower ball joint into the steering knuckle. Install the snapring and install a new rubber boot. Position the knuckle on the axle tube yoke and install a new lower ball stud nut. Torque to 80 ft. lbs. (108 Nm). Install the upper ball stud nut and torque to 100 ft. lbs. (136 Nm) and install a new cotter pin.
9. If equipped with a Dana 60 front axle, use tools C–4212–L, C–4366–3 and C–4366–4 to install the seal and lower bearing cup into the axle tube yoke lower bore. Reposition the tools and install the lower bearing and seal into the bore. Position the knuckle over the socket pin. Fill the lower socket cavity with

grease. Install the lower cap and torque the bolts to 80 ft. lbs. (110 Nm).

10. On the left side, install the spring, if equipped, and the steering knuckle arm to the steering knuckle.

11. Connect the tie rod to the end of the steering knuckle. On the left side, connect the drag link ball stud to the steering knuckle.

12. Install the front axle shaft and all related components.

Upper Control Arm

REMOVAL AND INSTALLATION

2WD Pick-Up, Ramcharger, Van and Dakota

1. Raise the vehicle and support safely.

2. Remove the shock absorber.

3. Remove the strut bar and disconnect the sway bar from the lower control arm, if equipped.

4. Install spring compressor tool DD–1278 or equivalent, to the coil spring and tighten the nut finger-tight, then back off nut ½ turn.

5. Remove the cotter pin and upper ball joint nut. Suspend the rotor assembly with a wire so there is not excessive pull on the brake hose.

6. Release the upper ball joint taper using ball stud loosening tool C–3564–A or equivalent.

7. Remove the tool and remove the ball stud from the control arm.

8. Remove the pivot bar retaining bolts on Van, Dakota and 1994–96 Pick-Up or the cam bolt assemblies on 1992–93 Pick-Up and Ramcharger and remove the arm from the vehicle.

To install:

9. Install the arm to the frame rail bracket and install the retaining bolts.

10. Torque the ball joint nut to 135 ft. lbs. (183 Nm). Install a new cotter pin. Remove the spring compressor.

11. Install the strut bar and connect the sway bar to the lower control arm, if equipped.

12. Install the shock absorber.

13. Align the front end. When all settings are at specifications, torque the pivot bar retaining bolts on Vans to 195 ft. lbs. (264 Nm), 150 ft. lbs. (203 Nm) on 1994–96 Pick-Up, 100 ft. lbs. (135 Nm) on 2WD Dakota or cam bolts to 70 ft. lbs. (95 Nm) on 1992–93 Pick-Up and Ramcharger.

4WD Dakota

1. Raise the vehicle and support safely. Remove the front wheel.

2. Remove the halfshaft.

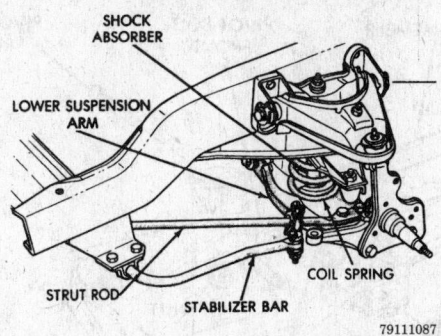

Upper control arm and related components — 2WD Pick-Up and Ramcharger, Dakota similar

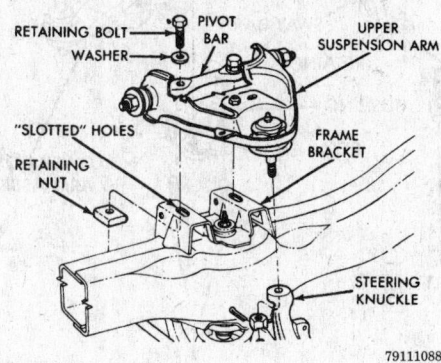

Upper control arm — Van

3. Turn the torsion bar adjusting bolt counterclockwise to remove tension from the torsion bar. Count the number of turns for installation reference.

4. Remove the brake hose brackets and shock absorber lower bolt.

5. Remove the cotter pin and nut from the upper ball joint. Position ball joint remover tool C–3564–A or equivalent, between the upper and lower ball studs.

6. Strike the knuckle sharply with a hammer to loosen the ball joint from knuckle. Do not force the stud out of the knuckle with the tool. The tool is only used to apply force.

7. Remove the upper arm pivot bar bolts and remove.

To install:

8. Install the control arm and tighten nuts temporarily to 100 ft. lbs. (136 Nm).

9. Install the ball joint-to-knuckle and torque the nut to 105 ft. lbs. (142 Nm). Install new cotter pin.

10. Install shock absorber lower bolt and brake hose brackets.

11. Turn the torsion bar adjusting bolt clockwise to apply tension to the torsion bar. Align the front end and torque the upper pivot bolts to 155 ft. lbs. (210 Nm).

Lower Control Arm

REMOVAL AND INSTALLATION

Caravan, Voyager and Town & Country

1. Raise and safely support the vehicle.

2. Remove the front inner pivot through bolt, the rear stub strut nut, retainer and bushing, and the ball joint-to-steering knuckle clamp bolts.

3. Separate the ball joint stud from the steering knuckle by prying between the ball stud retainer on the knuckle and the lower control arm.

— **WARNING** —

Pulling the steering knuckle out from the vehicle after releasing it from the ball joint can separate the inner CV-joint.

4. Remove the sway bar-to-control arm nut and reinforcement and rotate the control arm over the sway bar. Remove the rear stub strut bushing, sleeve and retainer. Remove the control arm.

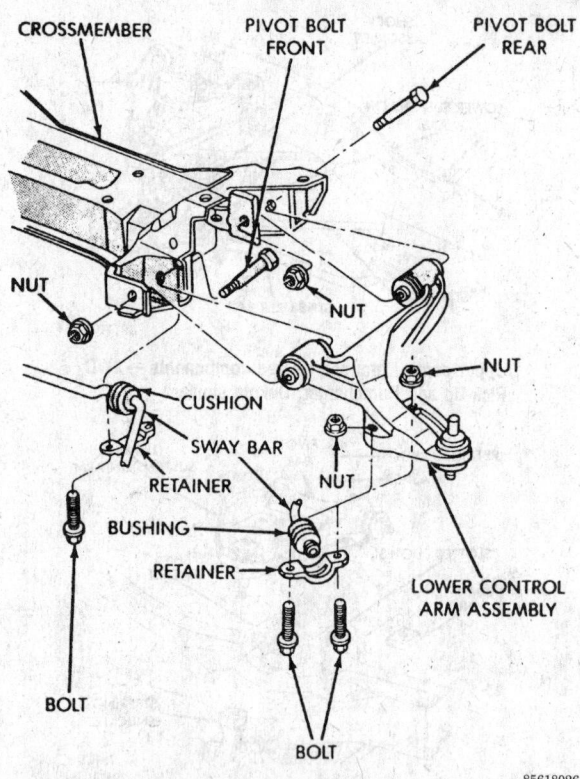

Lower ball control arm installation

85618026

To install:

NOTE: The substitution of fasteners other than those of the grade originally used is not recommended.

5. Install the retainer, bushing and sleeve on the stub strut.

6. Position the control arm over the sway bar and install the rear stub strut and front pivot into the crossmember.

7. Install the front pivot bolt and loosely install the nut.

8. Install the stub strut bushing and retainer and loosely assembly the nut.

9. Position the sway bar bracket and stud through the control arm and install the retainer nut. Tighten the nuts to 50 ft. lbs. (68 Nm).

10. Install the ball joint stud into the steering knuckle and install the clamp bolt. Torque the clamp bolt to 105 ft. lbs. (143 Nm).

11. Lower the vehicle, weight on wheels, and tighten the front pivot bolt to 125 ft. lbs. (170 Nm). Tighten the rear stub strut nut to 70 ft. lbs. (95 Nm).

4WD Dakota

1. Raise the vehicle and support safely. Remove the front wheel.

2. Remove the halfshaft.

3. Turn the torsion bar adjusting bolt counterclockwise to remove tension from the torsion bar. Count the number of turns for installation reference. Remove the torsion bar from the vehicle.

4. Remove the stabilizer bar from control arm and shock absorber bolt.

5. Remove the cotter pin and nut from the lower ball joint. Position ball joint remover tool C–3564–A or equivalent, between the upper and lower ball studs.

6. Strike the knuckle sharply with a hammer to loosen the ball joint from knuckle. Do not force the stud out of the knuckle with the tool. The tool is only used to apply force.

7. Remove the lower arm pivot bolts and remove.

To install:

8. Install the control arm, bolts and finger-tighten.

9. Install the ball joint-to-knuckle and torque the nut to 115 ft. lbs. (142 Nm). Install new cotter pin.

10. Install shock absorber lower bolt and stabilizer bar.

11. Turn the torsion bar adjusting bolt clockwise to apply tension to the torsion bar.

12. Lower the vehicle and load the front suspension. Torque the lower control arm-to-frame bolts to 130 ft. lbs. (176 Nm).

13. Align the front end.

Except 4WD Dakota

1. Raise the vehicle and support safely.

2. Remove the shock absorber.

3. Remove the strut bar and disconnect the sway bar from the lower control arm, if equipped.

4. Install spring compressor tool DD–1278 or equivalent, to the coil spring and tighten the nut finger-tight, then back off ½ turn.

5. Remove the cotter pin and lower ball joint nut.

6. Release the lower ball joint taper using ball stud loosening tool C–3564–A or equivalent.

7. Remove the tool and remove the ball stud from the control arm. Release the compressor tool from the coil spring.

8. Pull the arm down and remove the spring with the rubber isolation pad from the vehicle. Remove the lower control arm pivot bolt from the crossmember and remove the arm from the vehicle.

To install:

9. Install the arm to the crossmember finger-tight. Install the spring with the rubber isolators. Install the compressor tool and compress it enough so the lower ball joint can be inserted through the knuckle.

10. Torque $^{11}/_{16}$-16 lower ball joint nuts to 135 ft. lbs. (183 Nm). Torque $^{3}/_{4}$-16 nuts to 175 ft. lbs. (237 Nm). Install a new cotter pin. Remove the spring compressor.

11. Install the strut bar and connect the sway bar from the lower control arm, if equipped.

12. Install the shock absorber.

13. Lower the vehicle completely. When the weight of the vehicle is off the lifting apparatus, torque the lower arm pivot bolts to 175 ft. lbs. (237 Nm) on Vans or 225 ft. lbs. (305 Nm) on Pick-Up and Ramcharger.

14. Align the front end as required.

Suspension Arms

REMOVAL AND INSTALLATION

4WD 1994–96 Pick-Up

1. Raise the vehicle and support safely. Remove the front wheel. Place a hydraulic jack under the drive axle to support the assembly.

2. Matchmark the alignment marks on the cam adjuster for the lower suspension arm.

3. Remove the arm-to-axle and arm-to-frame bolts and remove suspension arm.

4. Installation is the reverse of removal. Torque the cam adjuster nut to 110 ft. lbs. (149 Nm), lower arm rear bolt to 88 ft. lbs. (118 Nm), upper arm frame bolt to 62 ft. lbs. (84 Nm) and upper arm axle bolt to 89 ft. lbs. (121 Nm).

Sway Bar

REMOVAL AND INSTALLATION

Caravan, Voyager and Town & Country

1. Raise and safely support the vehicle.

2. Remove the nuts, bolts and retainer connecting the sway bar to the control arms.

3. Remove the bolt that mount the sway bar to the crossmember. Remove the sway bar and crossmember mounting clamps from the vehicle.

4. Inspect the bushings for wear. Replace as necessary. End bushings are replaced by cutting or driving them from the retainer. Center bushings are split and are removed by opening the split and sliding from the sway bar.

5. Force the new end bushings into the retainers, allow about ½ in. (13mm) to protrude. Install the sway bar. Tighten the center bracket bolts to 50 ft. lbs. (68 Nm). Place a jack under the control arm and raise the arm to normal design height. Tighten the outer bracket bolts to 50 ft. lbs. (68 Nm). Lower the vehicle.

4WD Dakota

1. Raise and safely support the vehicle. Remove the front wheels.

2. Remove the sway bar-to-frame member bolts.

3. Remove the lower control arm-to-sway bar bolts.

4. Remove the sway bar from the vehicle. If necessary, remove the rear support brackets and bushings from the sway bar.

To install:

5. Install the sway bar hardware and assembly into the vehicle.

6. Install the retainers and torque the sway bar bolts to 20 ft. lbs. (27 Nm).

Except Caravan/Voyager/Town & Country and 4WD Dakota

1. Raise the vehicle and support safely.

2. Remove the front sway bar brackets and retainers.

3. Remove the sway bar connecting links to the control arm or front axle. Remove the sway bar from the vehicle.

4. The installation is the reversal of the removal procedure. Tighten the nuts just enough so the bushings compress to the same outer diameter as the washer adjacent to it.

Front Wheel Bearings

REMOVAL AND INSTALLATION

Caravan, Voyager and Town & Country

1. Loosen the center splined retaining hub nut while the vehicle is on the ground. Loosen the wheel lug nuts slightly.

2. Raise and safely support the vehicle.

3. Remove the wheel assembly. Remove the hub nut and washer.

4. Disconnect the tie rod end from the steering arm and the clamp bolt that retains the ball joint to the knuckle.

5. Remove the disc brake caliper and suspend it with wire so there is no strain on the brake hose. Remove the rotor.

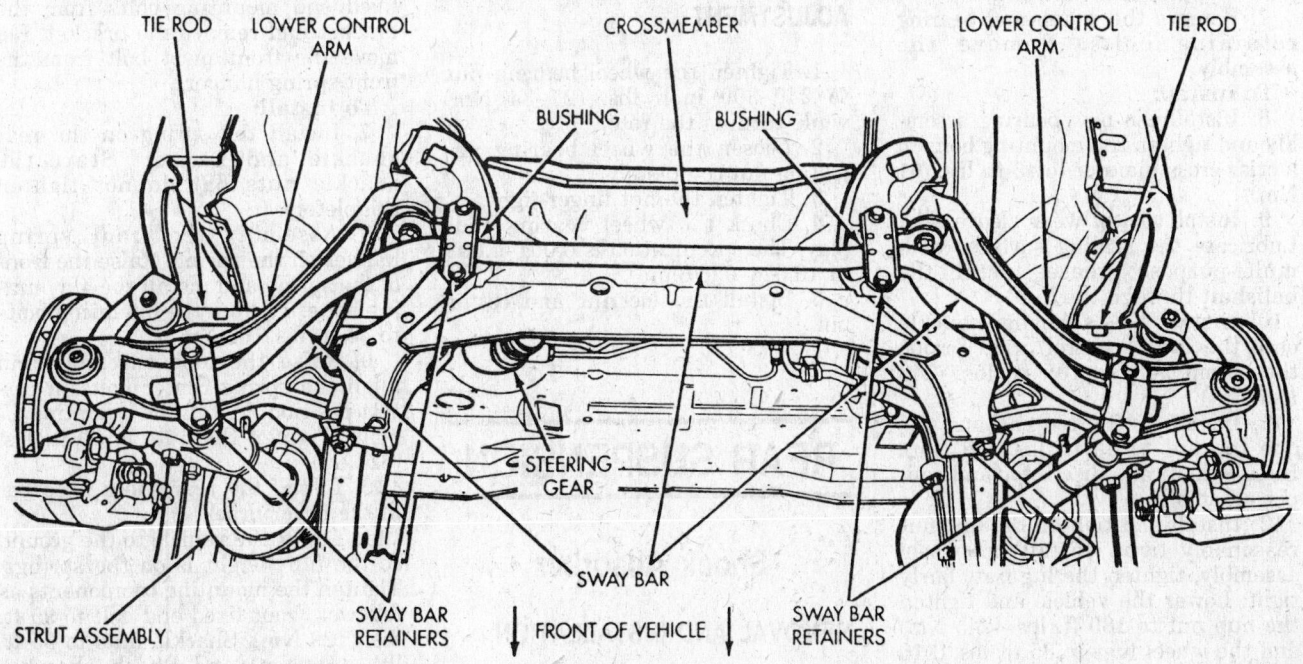

Front sway bar installation

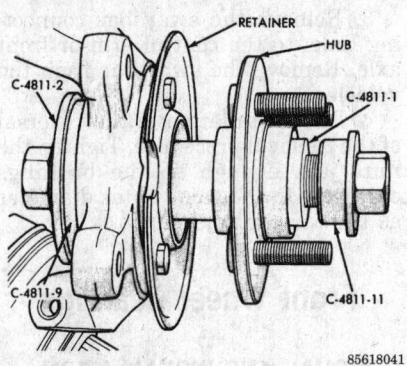

Installing the hub assembly

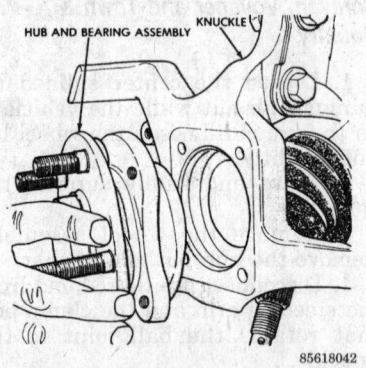

Separating the ball stud from the knuckle

6. Separate the knuckle from the ball joint. Pull the knuckle assembly away from the halfshaft. Take care not separate the halfshaft inner CV-joint. Support the halfshaft.

7. Remove the 4 hub and bearing retaining bolts. Remove the assembly.

To install:

8. Install the new bearing assembly and tighten the mounting bolts in a criss-cross manner to 45 ft. lbs. (61 Nm).

9. Install a new wear sleeve seal. Lubricate the sealing surfaces with multi-purpose grease. Install the halfshaft through the hub.

10. Install the steering knuckle onto the lower control arm. Torque the clamp bolt to 105 ft. lbs. (143 Nm).

11. Install the tie rod end and torque the nut to 35 ft. lbs. (48 Nm). Install the brake disc rotor and caliper assembly.

12. Install and tighten the hub nut reasonably tight. Install the wheel assembly, tighten the lug nuts fairly tight. Lower the vehicle and tighten the hub nut to 180 ft. lbs. (245 Nm) and the wheel lugs to 85 ft. lbs. (116 Nm).

Except Caravan, Voyager and Town & Country

1. Raise the vehicle and support safely.

2. Remove the tire and wheel assembly.

3. Remove the caliper and disc brake pads.

4. Remove the dust cap.

5. Remove the cotter pin, castelated locknut, wheel bearing nut and washer from the spindle.

6. Remove the outer wheel bearing.

7. Remove the rotor with the inner wheel bearing from the spindle. Remove the grease seal and inner wheel bearing.

8. If bearing replacement is required, remove bearing races with brass drift or puller. Install races with an appropriate installation tool.

To install:

9. Lubricate and install the inner wheel bearing. Install a new grease seal.

10. Install the rotor to the spindle.

11. Lubricate and install the outer wheel bearing, washer and nut. When the bearing preload is properly set, install the locknut and a new cotter pin.

12. Install the grease cap.

13. Install the brake pads and caliper.

14. Install the wheel.

ADJUSTMENT

1. Tighten the wheel bearing nut to 240–300 inch lbs. (27–34 Nm) while turning the rotor.

2. Loosen the wheel bearing adjusting nut completely.

3. Tighten the nut finger-tight.

4. Check the wheel bearing endplay. The specification is 0.001–0.003 in. (0.024–0.076mm).

5. Install the locknut and cotter pin.

REAR SUSPENSION

Shock Absorber

REMOVAL AND INSTALLATION

1. Raise the vehicle and support safely.

2. Remove the bolts that attach the shock to the frame or bracket.

3. Remove the shock from the vehicle.

4. The installation is the reversal of the removal procedure.

Leaf Springs

REMOVAL AND INSTALLATION

Caravan, Voyager and Town & Country

FWD MODELS

1. Raise and safely support the vehicle. Locate the jackstands under the frame contact points just ahead of the rear spring fixed ends.

2. Raise the rear axle just enough to relieve the weight on the springs and support on jackstands.

3. Disconnect the rear brake proportioning valve spring. Disconnect the lower ends of the shock absorbers at the rear axle bracket.

4. Loosen and remove the nuts from the U-bolts. Remove the washer and U-bolts.

5. Lower the rear axle assembly to permit the rear springs to hang free. Support the spring and remove the 4 bolts that mount the fixed end spring bracket. Remove the rear spring shackle nuts and plate. Remove the shackle from the spring.

6. Remove the spring. Remove the fixed end mounting bolts from the bracket and remove the bracket. Remove the front pivot bolt from the front spring hanger.

To install:

7. Install the spring on the rear shackle and hanger. Start the shackle nuts but do not tighten completely.

8. Assembly the front spring hanger on the spring. Raise the front of the spring and install the 4 mounting bolts. Tighten the mounting bolts to 45 ft. lbs. (61 Nm).

9. Raise the axle assembly and align the spring center bolts in correct position. Install the mounting U-bolts. Tighten the nuts to 60 ft. lbs. (82 Nm).

10. Install the rear shock absorber to the lower brackets.

11. Lower the vehicle to the ground so the full weight is on the springs. Tighten the mounting components as follows: Front fixed end bolt to 95 ft. lbs. (129 Nm), Shackle nuts to 35 ft. lbs. (48 Nm) and Shock absorber bolts to 50 ft. lbs. (68 Nm).

12. Raise and support the vehicle. Connect the brake valve spring and adjust the valve.

AWD MODELS

1. Raise and safely support the rear of the vehicle on jackstands. Locate the jackstands under the chassis, ahead of the springs.

2. Raise the rear axle just enough to relieve the weight on the springs and support on jackstands.

3. Disconnect the rear brake proportioning valve spring. Disconnect the lower ends of the shock absorbers at the rear axle bracket.

4. Loosen and remove the nuts from the U-bolts. Remove the washer and U-bolts.

5. Lower the rear axle assembly to permit the rear springs to hang free. Support the spring and remove the 4 bolts that mount the fixed end spring bracket. Remove the rear spring shackle nuts and plate. Remove the shackle from the spring.

6. Remove the spring. Remove the fixed end mounting bolts from the bracket and remove the bracket. Remove the front pivot bolt from the front spring hanger.

7. Separate the rear shackle plate from the shackle and pin assembly. Remove the shackle and pin assembly from the spring.

To install:

8. Assemble the shackle and pin assembly, bushing and shackle plate on rear of spring and spring hanger. Start the shackle and pin assembly through bolts, do not tighten.

9. Assemble the front spring hanger to the front of the spring eye and install pivot bolt and nut. Do not tighten.

NOTE: Pivot bolt must inboard to prevent structural damage during spring installation.

10. Raise the front of the spring into position and install the 4 hanger bolts, tighten them to 45 ft. lbs. (61 Nm). Connect the actuator assembly for the proportioning valve.

11. Raise the axle assembly into position, centered under the spring center bolt.

12. Install the U-bolts, nuts and washers. Tighten the U-bolt nuts to 65 ft. lbs. (88 Nm).

13. Install the shock absorbers and start the bolts.

14. Lower the vehicle to the ground, with the full weight of the vehicle on the wheels. Tighten all of the fasteners in the following sequence and to the listed torques:

　　a. Front pivot bolts — 105 ft. lbs. (142 Nm)

　　b. Shackle and pin assembly through bolt nuts — 35 ft. lbs. (47 Nm)

　　c. Shackle and pin assembly retaining bolts — 35 ft. lbs. (47 Nm)

　　d. Shock absorber upper bolts — 85 ft. lbs. (115 Nm)

　　e. Shock absorber lower bolts — 80 ft. lbs. (108 Nm)

15. Raise the vehicle and connect the proportioning valve.

Except Caravan, Voyager and Town & Country

1. Raise the vehicle and support safely.

2. Using the proper equipment, support the weight of the axle.

3. Remove the nuts, washers and U-bolts attaching the springs to the axle housing. Remove the spacer.

4. Remove the spring shackle bolts, shackle and spring front bolt.

5. Remove the springs and auxiliary spring, if equipped, from the vehicle.

To install:

6. Install spring on the axle tube so the spring center bolt is inserted into the locating hole in the axle tube spring pad.

7. Align front and rear spring eye and pivot bolts/nuts. Do not tighten at this time.

8. Install U-bolts with new lockwashers and retaining nuts. Align auxiliary spring with primary spring, if equipped.

9. Torque the spring eye and U-bolt nuts as follows:

　　a. U-bolt nut below 10,500 GVWR — 110 ft. lbs. (149 Nm)

　　b. U-bolt nut above 11,000 GVWR — 120 ft. lbs. (163 Nm)

　　c. Spring eye bolts below 7500 GVWR — 100 ft. lbs. (136 Nm)

　　d. Spring eye bolts above 8000 GVWR — 140 ft. lbs. (190 Nm)

10. Lower vehicle.

Rear Wheel Bearings

REMOVAL AND INSTALLATION

Caravan, Voyager and Town & Country

FRONT WHEEL DRIVE MODELS

NOTE: Sodium-based grease is not compatible with lithium-based grease. Read the package labels and be careful not to mix the 2 types. If there is any doubt as to the type of grease used, completely clean the old grease from the bearing and hub before replacing.

1. Raise and support the vehicle with the rear wheels off the floor.

2. Remove the wheel grease cap, cotter pin, nut-lock and bearing adjusting nut.

3. Remove the thrust washer and bearing.

4. Remove the drum from the spindle.

5. Thoroughly clean the old lubricant from the bearings and hub cavity. Inspect the bearing rollers for pitting or other signs of wear. Light discoloration is normal.

To install:

6. Repack the bearings with high temperature multi-purpose EP grease and add a small amount of new grease to the hub cavity. Be sure to force the lubricant between all rollers in the bearing.

7. Install the drum on the spindle after coating the polished spindle surfaces with wheel bearing lubricant.

8. Install the outer bearing cone, thrust washer and adjusting nut.

9. Tighten the adjusting nut to 20–25 ft. lbs. (27–34 Nm) while rotating the wheel.

10. Back off the adjusting nut to completely release the preload from the bearing.

11. Tighten the adjusting nut finger-tight.

12. Position the nut-lock with 1 pair of slots in line with the cotter pin hole. Install the cotter pin.

13. Clean and install the grease cap and wheel.

14. Lower the vehicle.

ALL WHEEL DRIVE MODELS

The rear wheel bearings used on these models is a bolt in type unit, this is the same unit that is used on the front knuckle assembly.

1. Raise and support the vehicle.

2. Remove the wheel and tire assembly.

3. Remove the halfshaft flange retaining bolts and remove the halfshaft assembly.

4. Remove the wheel bearing mounting bolts and remove the wheel bearing and hub assembly.

To install:

5. Install the hub and bearing assembly, tighten the bolts to 96 ft. lbs. (130 Nm) in a criss-cross pattern.

NOTE: Thoroughly clean the seal and wear sleeve, lubricate both before installation.

6. Install the halfshaft.

7. Install the washer and hub nut, with the brakes applied tighten the nut to 180 ft. lbs. (244 Nm).

8. Install the spring washer, nut lock and new cotter pin.

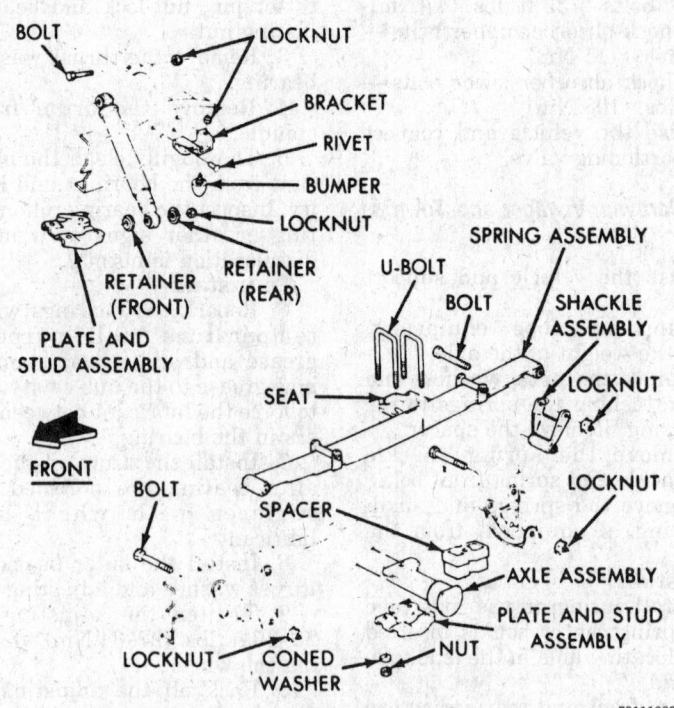

Rear suspension components — 150 models

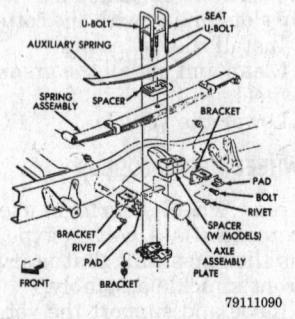

Rear suspension with auxiliary springs — D and W250 and 350 models

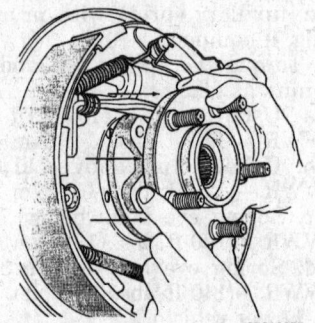

Pull the wheel bearing assembly from the housing — AWD models

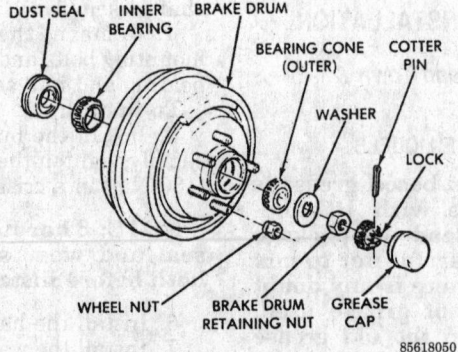

Rear brake drum and bearings — FWD models

9. Install the wheel and tire assembly.

Rear Axle

ALIGNMENT

Caravan, Voyager and Town & Country

Camber and Toe adjustment are possible through the use of shims. Shims are added or subtracted between the spindle mounting surface and the axle mounting plate. Each shim equals a wheel angle change of 0.3 degrees.

Ford Motor Company 2

FORD—Aerostar • Bronco • Bronco II • F Series • E
Series • Explorer • Lightening • Ranger • Splash **MERCURY**—Villager

2-1

FIRING ORDERS

NOTE: To avoid confusion, always replace spark plug wires one at a time.

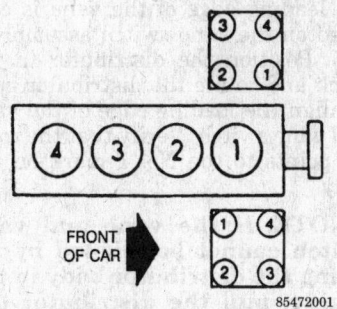

2.3L Engine
Engine Firing Order: 1–3–4–2
Distributorless Ignition System

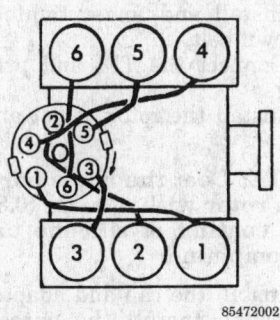

2.9L and 3.0L (VIN U) Engines
Engine Firing Order:
1–4–2–5–3–6
Distributor Rotation: Clockwise

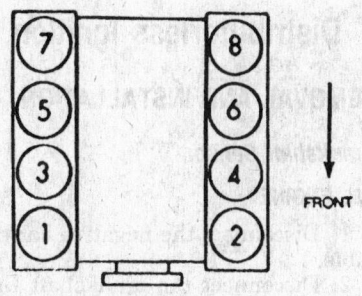

7.3L Diesel Engine
Engine Firing Order: 1–2–7–3–4–5–6–8

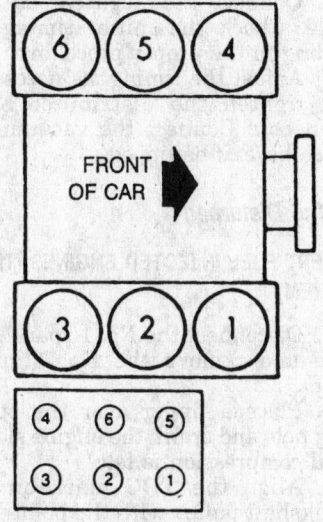

4.0L Engine
Engine Firing Order: 1–4–2–5–3–6
Distributor Rotation: Clockwise

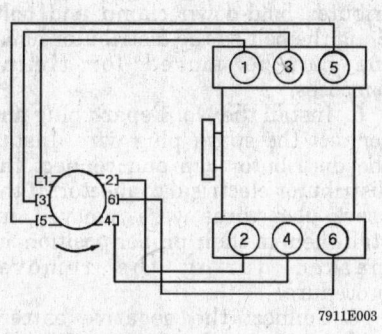

3.0L (VIN W) Engine
Engine Firing Order: 1–2–3–4–5–6
Distributor Rotation: Counterclockwise

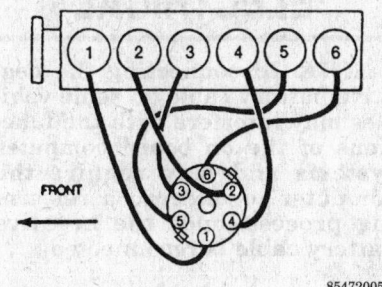

4.9L Engine
Engine Firing Order: 1–5–3–6–2–4
Distributor Rotation: Clockwise

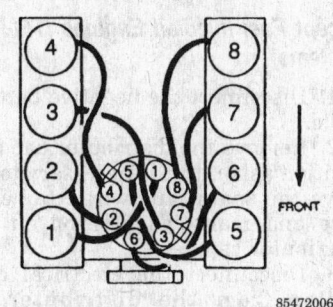

5.0L and 7.5L Engines
Engine Firing Order: 1–5–4–2–6–3–7–8
Distributor Rotation: Counterclockwise

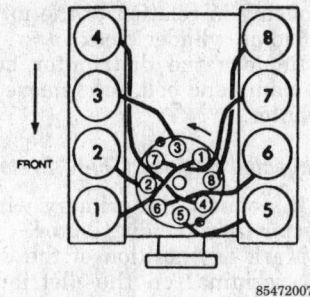

5.8L Engine
Engine Firing Order:
1–3–7–2–6–5–4–8
Distributor Rotation:
Counterclockwise

ENGINE ELECTRICAL

NOTE: Disconnecting the negative battery cable on some vehicles may interfere with the functions of the on board computer systems and may require the computer to undergo a relearning process, once the negative battery cable is reconnected.

Distributor

REMOVAL

Except Fuel Injected Engines (TFI-IV Systems)

1. Disconnect the negative battery cable.
2. Remove the distributor cap and position aside. If it is necessary to remove the spark plug wires, tag each wire and mark it's position on the distributor cap.
3. Disconnect the electrical connector from the distributor. If equipped, disconnect and plug the vacuum advance hose.
4. Mark the position of the rotor in relation to the distributor housing and mark the position of the distributor housing in relation to the intake manifold or cylinder block.
5. Remove the distributor hold-down clamp and bolt and remove the distributor.

Fuel Injected Engines (TFI-IV Systems)

1. Disconnect the primary wiring connector from the distributor.
2. Mark the position of the cap's No. 1 terminal on the distributor base.
3. Unclip and remove the cap. Remove the adapter.
4. Remove the rotor.
5. Remove the TFI connector.
6. Matchmark the distributor base and engine for installation reference.
7. Remove the hold-down bolt and lift out the distributor.

INSTALLATION

Timing Not Disturbed

1. Install the distributor assembly, aligning the marks that were made during the removal procedure.
2. Install the distributor hold-down clamp and bolt and leave it snug.

3. Connect the electrical connector to the distributor.
4. Install the distributor cap. If the spark plug wires were removed, install them in their proper position, as marked during the removal procedure.
5. Connect the negative battery cable. Check the initial timing according to the proper procedure.
6. Adjust the timing, as necessary and tighten the distributor hold-down bolt. Connect the vacuum advance hose, if equipped.

Timing Disturbed

EXCEPT FUEL INJECTED ENGINES (TFI-IV SYSTEM)

1. Disconnect the No. 1 spark plug wire and remove the No. 1 spark plug.
2. Place a finger over the spark plug hole and crank the engine slowly until compression is felt.
3. Align the TDC mark on the crankshaft pulley with the pointer on the timing cover. This places the No. 1 cylinder at TDC on the compression stroke.
4. Turn the distributor shaft until the rotor points to the No. 1 spark plug tower on the cap.
5. Install the distributor into the engine, aligning the marks made on the block or intake manifold and the distributor housing. Install the distributor hold-down clamp and bolt. Snug the bolt so the distributor housing can be moved for timing purposes.
6. Install the No. 1 spark plug and connect the spark plug wire. Install the distributor cap and connect the distributor electrical connector. If the spark plug wires were removed, install them in their proper position, as marked during the removal procedure.
7. Connect the negative battery cable and set the ignition timing. Tighten the distributor hold-down clamp bolt and recheck the ignition timing after tightening the bolt.
8. If equipped, connect the vacuum advance hose.

FUEL INJECTED ENGINES (TFI-IV SYSTEM)

1. Rotate the engine so the No. 1 piston is at TDC of the compression stroke.
2. Align the timing marks so the engine is set at the initial timing shown on the underhood sticker.
3. Install the rotor on the shaft and rotate the shaft so the rotor tip

points to the No. 1 mark made on the distributor base.
4. Continue rotating the shaft so the leading edge of the vane is centered on the vane switch assembly.
5. Position the distributor in the block and rotate the distributor body to align the leading edge of the vane and vane switch. Verify that the rotor tip points to the No. 1 mark on the body.

NOTE: If the vane and vane switch cannot be aligned by rotating the distributor body in the engine, pull the distributor out just far enough to disengage the gears and rotate the shaft to engage a different gear tooth. Repeat Steps 3, 4 and 5.

6. Install and finger tighten the holddown bolt.
7. Connect the TFI and primary wiring.
8. Install the rotor, if not already done.

NOTE: Coat the brass portions of the rotor with a 1/32 in. (0.8mm) thick coating of silicone dielectric compound.

9. Install the cap and adapter (as necessary). Install the wires and start the engine.
10. Check and set the initial timing.
11. Tighten the holddown bolt to 25 ft. lbs.

Distributorless Ignition

REMOVAL AND INSTALLATION

Crankshaft Sensor

2.3L ENGINE

1. Disconnect the negative battery cable.
2. Disconnect the crankshaft timing sensor assembly electrical connectors from the engine harness.
3. Remove the large electrical connector from the crankshaft timing sensor assembly by prying out the red retaining clip and removing the 4 wires.
4. Remove the crankshaft pulley assembly by removing the accessory drive belts and then the 4 bolts that retain it to the crankshaft pulley hub assembly.
5. Remove the timing belt outer cover.
6. Rotate the crankshaft so the keyway is at the 10 o'clock position. This will place the vane window of both inner and outer vane cups over

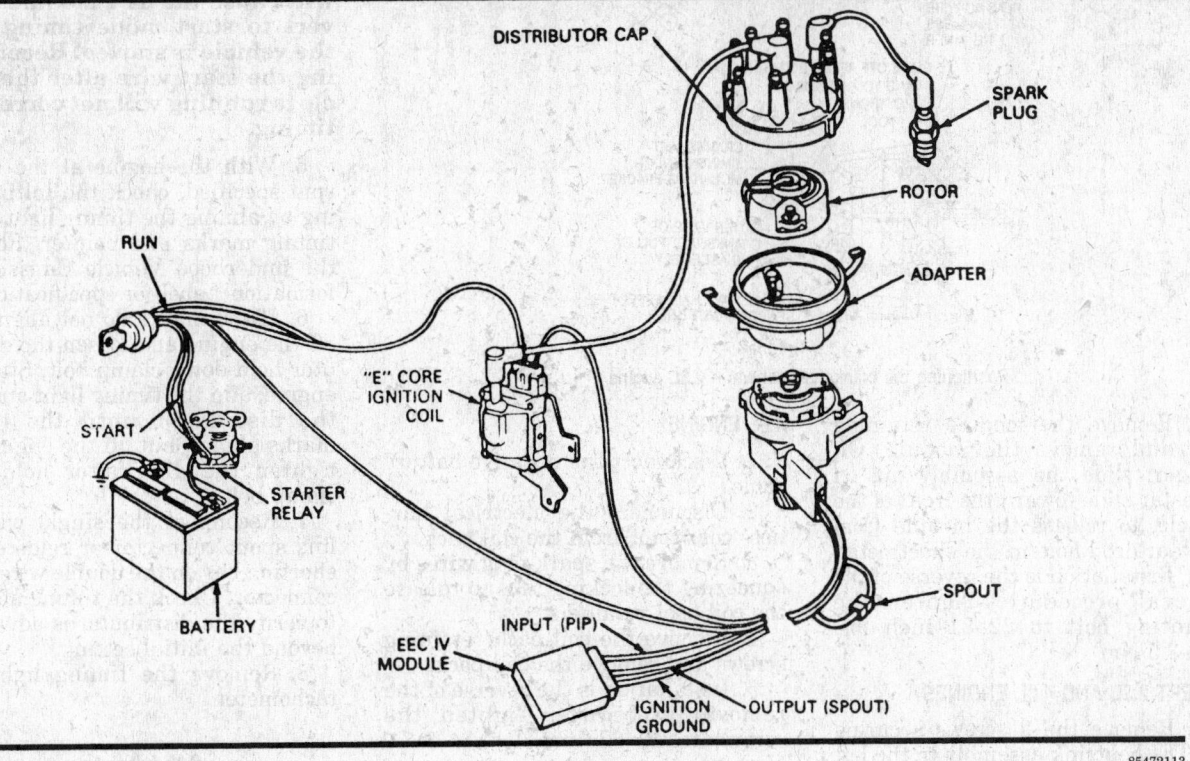

Thick Film integrated (TFI) ignition system with universal distributor — 4.9L, 5.0L, 5.8L and 7.5L engines

the crankshaft timing sensor assembly.

NOTE: The vane cups are attached to the crankshaft pulley hub assembly.

7. Remove the 2 crankshaft timing sensor assembly retaining bolts and the plastic wire harness retainer which secures the crankshaft timing sensor harness to it's mounting bracket. Then remove the crankshaft timing sensor assembly, sliding the electrical wires out from behind the inner timing belt cover.

To install:

8. Remove the large electrical connector from the new crankshaft timing sensor assembly.

9. Position the crankshaft timing sensor assembly. First slide the electrical wires behind the inner timing belt cover. Then, hold the sensor assembly loosely in place with the retaining bolts, but do not tighten at this time.

10. Install the large electrical connector onto the crankshaft timing sensor assembly.

NOTE: Make sure the 4 wires to the large electrical connector are installed in the proper locations. The sensor will not function properly if the wires are installed in the wrong locations.

11. Reconnect both of the crankshaft timing sensor electrical connectors to the engine harness.

12. Rotate the crankshaft so the outer vane on the crankshaft pulley hub assembly engages both sides of the crankshaft Hall effect sensor positioner tool T89P-6316-A or equivalent, and tighten the sensor assembly retaining bolts.

13. Rotate the crankshaft so the vane on the crankshaft pulley hub assembly is no longer engaged in the positioning tool. Remove the tool.

14. Install the new plastic wire harness retainer to secure the crankshaft timing sensor harness to it's mounting bracket. Trim off the excess.

15. Install the timing belt outer cover.

16. Install the crankshaft pulley assembly and tighten the 4 attaching bolts to 15–22 ft. lbs. (20–30 Nm). Install the accessory drive belts.

4.0L ENGINE

1. Disconnect the negative battery cable.

2. Disconnect the sensor electrical connector from the wiring harness.

3. Remove the crankshaft sensor mounting screws and remove the sensor.

4. Installation is the reverse of the removal procedure. Tighten the screws to 75–106 inch lbs. (8.5–12 Nm).

Ignition Module

2.3L ENGINE

1. Disconnect the negative battery cable.

2. Disconnect the electrical connectors at the module.

3. Remove the module retaining screws and remove the module from the lower intake manifold.

To install:

4. Apply an even coating of silicone dielectric compound WA-10, D7AZ-19A331-A or equivalent, to the mounting surface of the module.

5. Install the module and the retaining screws. Tighten the screws to 22–31 inch lbs. (2.5–3.5 Nm).

6. Connect the electrical connectors to the module and connect the negative battery cable.

4.0L ENGINE

1. On Aerostar, disconnect the negative battery cable.

2. On Explorer and Ranger, disconnect the battery cables and remove the battery.

3. Disconnect the electrical connector at the module.

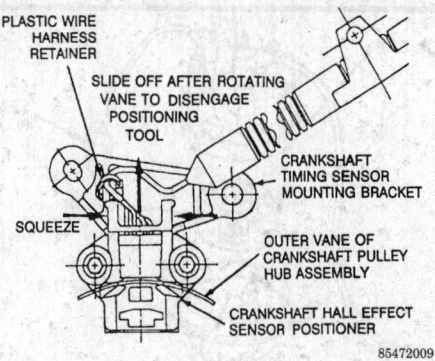

Positioning the crankshaft sensor — 2.3L engine

4. Remove the module retaining bolt and remove the module. On Ranger, slide the assembly up; on Aerostar slide toward the front of the vehicle, to release the module from the tear-drop hole in the sheetmetal.

5. Installation is the reverse of the removal procedure. Tighten the mounting bolt to 22–31 inch lbs. (2.5–3.5 Nm).

EXCEPT 2.3L AND 4.0L ENGINES

1. Remove the 2 screws securing the TFI heatsink assembly to the left fender apron.

2. Disconnect the harness from the module.

3. Remove the 2 screws securing the TFI module to the heatsink.

4. Coat the baseplate of the module with a uniform covering of silicone dielectric grease, about 1/32 in. thick.

5. Position the module on the heatsink and tighten the screws to 15-35 inch lbs.

6. Install the heatsink and connect the wiring.

Ignition Coil Pack

2.3L ENGINE

1. Disconnect the negative battery cable.

2. Squeeze the locking tabs of the coil wire retainer by hand and remove the spark plug wires with a twisting and pulling motion. Do not pull on the wire.

3. Disconnect the engine harness electrical connector from the ignition coil assembly.

4. Remove the ignition coil assembly by removing the 4 retaining screws.

NOTE: If equipped with power steering, it may be necessary to remove the intake coil and bracket as an assembly.

5. Installation is the reverse of the removal procedure.

4.0L ENGINE

1. Disconnect the negative battery cable.

2. Disconnect the electrical harness connector from the coil pack.

3. Remove the spark plug wires by squeezing the locking tabs to release the coil boot retainers.

4. Remove the coil pack retaining screws and remove the coil pack.

5. Installation is the reverse of the removal procedure. Tighten the screws to 40–62 inch lbs. (4.5–7.0 Nm).

Ignition Timing

ADJUSTMENT

NOTE: Always refer to the Vehicle Emission Information Label to verify the timing adjustment procedure.

Distributorless Ignition System

Base timing for distributorless engines is set from the factory at 10 degrees BTDC and is not adjustable.

Distributor Ignition System

1. Place automatic transmission in **P** or manual transmission in neutral. The air conditioning and heater controls should be in the **OFF** position.

2. Connect a suitable inductive timing light and a tachometer according to the manufacturer's instructions.

3. Disconnect the single wire in-line spout connector or remove the shorting bar from the double wire spout connector.

4. Start the engine and bring to normal operating temperature.

NOTE: To set timing correctly, a remote starter should not be used. Use the ignition key only to start the vehicle. Disconnecting the start wire at the starter relay will cause the TFI module to revert to start mode timing after the vehicle is started. Reconnecting the start wire after the vehicle is running will not correct the timing.

5. With the engine at the timing rpm specified, check the initial timing by aiming the timing light at the timing marks and pointer. Refer to the underhood Vehicle Emission Information Label for specifications.

6. If the marks do not align, shut off the engine and loosen the distributor hold-down clamp bolt. Start the engine, aim the timing light and turn the distributor until the timing marks align. Shut off the engine and tighten the distributor hold-down clamp bolt.

7. Reconnect the single wire in-line spout connector or reinstall the shorting bar on the double wire spout connector. Check the timing advance to verify the distributor is advancing beyond the initial setting.

8. Remove the timing light and tachometer.

Alternator

PRECAUTIONS

Several precautions must be observed with alternator equipped vehicles to avoid damage to the unit.

If the battery is removed for any reason, make sure it is reconnected with the correct polarity. Reversing the battery connections may result in damage to the one-way rectifiers.

When utilizing a booster battery as a starting aid, always connect the positive to positive terminals and the negative terminal from the booster battery to a good engine ground on the vehicle being started.

Never use a fast charger as a booster to start vehicles.

Disconnect the battery cables when charging the battery with a fast charger.

Never attempt to polarize the alternator.

Do not use test lights of more than 12V when checking diode continuity.

Do not short across or ground any of the alternator terminals.

The polarity of the battery, alternator and regulator must be matched and considered before making any electrical connections within the system.

Never separate the alternator on an open circuit. Make sure all connections within the circuit are clean and tight.

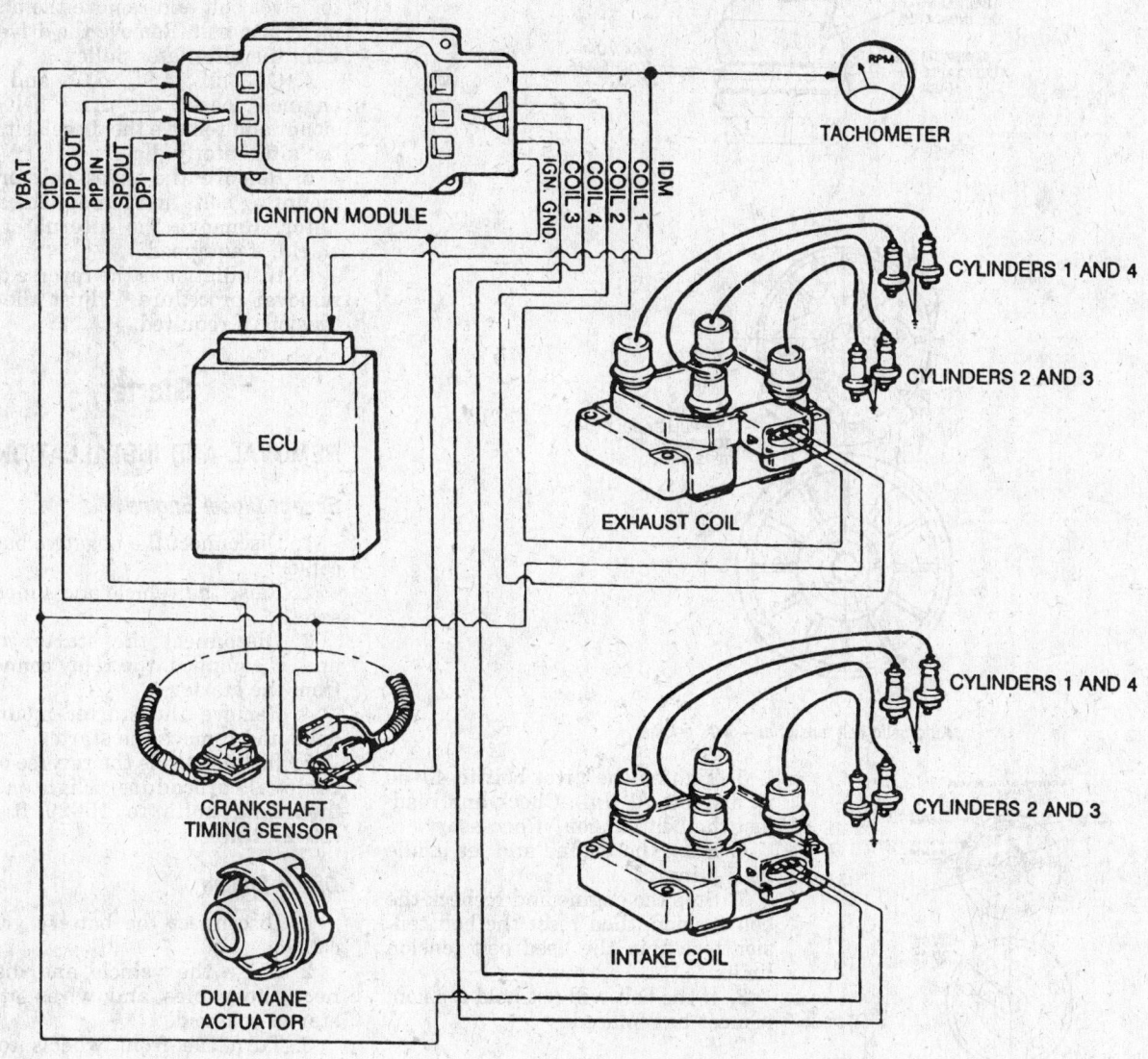

Distributorless ignition system — 2.3L engine

85472010

Disconnect the battery ground terminal when performing any service on electrical components.

Disconnect the battery if arc welding is to be done on the vehicle.

BELT TENSION ADJUSTMENT

Except 7.3L Diesel and 7.5L Engines

NOTE: On 4.0L, 4.9L, 5.0L and 5.8L engines, belt tension is maintained by an automatic tensioner. No adjustment is necessary.

1. Disconnect the negative battery cable. Loosen the alternator adjustment and pivot bolts.

2. Position a suitable belt tension gauge on an accessible belt span midway between the 2 pulleys.

3. Position the alternator housing using a suitable tool to attain correct belt tension. Be careful not to damage the alternator housing.

4. The correct belt tension for a new belt should be 150–190 lbs. on all except 2.9L engine. New belt tension on 2.9L engine should be 120–160 lbs. The correct belt tension for a used belt should be 140–160 lbs., on all except 2.9L engine. Used belt tension on 2.9L engine should be 110–130 lbs.

NOTE: A used belt has more than 10 minutes of operation.

5. Tighten the adjustment bolt and release the pressure. Tighten the pivot bolt.

6. Check the belt tension and reset, if necessary.

7.3L Diesel and 7.5L Engines

1. Position a suitable belt tension gauge midway on the longest accessible belt span.

2. Loosen the alternator adjustment and pivot bolts just enough to move the alternator.

3. Place a "C" clamp over the end of the adjusting arm and the adjusting bolt boss and tighten the belt to

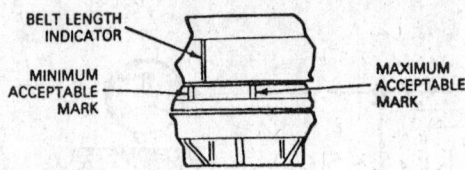

INDICATOR SHOULD BE BETWEEN MARKS

BELT LENGTH INDICATOR

MINIMUM ACCEPTABLE MARK

MAXIMUM ACCEPTABLE MARK

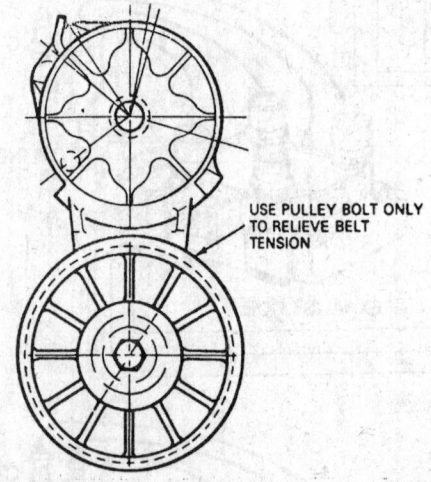

USE PULLEY BOLT ONLY TO RELIEVE BELT TENSION

85472114

Automatic belt tensioner — 4.9L engine

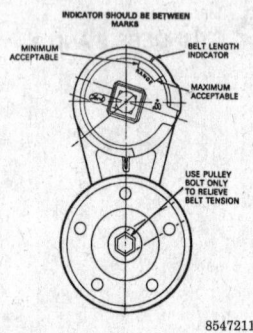

INDICATOR SHOULD BE BETWEEN MARKS

MINIMUM ACCEPTABLE

BELT LENGTH INDICATOR

MAXIMUM ACCEPTABLE

USE PULLEY BOLT ONLY TO RELIEVE BELT TENSION

85472115

Automatic belt tensioner — 5.0L and 5.8L engines

the correct tension. The correct tension is:

7.3L diesel engine

140–180 lbs. — new belt

95–115 lbs. — used belt; a used belt is one with over 5 minutes operation.

7.5L engine

160–200 lbs. — new belt

110–130 lbs. — used belt; a used belt is one with over 5 minutes operation.

4. Tighten the adjustment bolt to 30–40 ft. lbs. (40–55 Nm) and remove the "C" clamp.

5. Tighten the pivot bolt to 40–50 ft. lbs. (55–70 Nm). Check and readjust the belt tension, if necessary.

6. Start the engine and let it idle for 5 minutes.

7. Stop the engine and recheck the belt tension, then reset the belt tension to within the used belt tension limits.

8. If the belt will not hold tension, it must be replaced.

REMOVAL AND INSTALLATION

1. Disconnect the negative battery cable.

2. Disconnect the electrical connectors from the alternator.

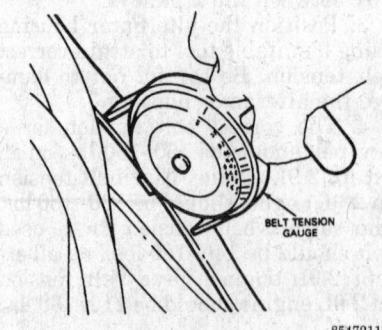

BELT TENSION GAUGE

85472116

Checking alternator belt tension — 7.3L diesel and 7.5L engines

3. On all except 4.0L, 4.9L, 5.0L and 5.8L engines, loosen the alternator pivot bolt and remove the adjustment arm bolt. Remove the drive belt from the alternator pulley.

4. On 4.0L, 4.9L, 5.0L and 5.8L engines, loosen the drive belt tensioner and remove the drive belt from the alternator pulley.

5. Remove the pivot bolt or the mounting bolts and remove the alternator. Remove the alternator fan shield, if equipped.

6. Installation is the reverse of the removal procedure. Adjust the belt tension, if required.

Starter

REMOVAL AND INSTALLATION

Except Diesel Engine

1. Disconnect the negative battery cable.

2. Raise the vehicle and support it safely.

3. Disconnect the starter cable and, if equipped, the relay connector from the starter.

4. Remove the starter mounting bolts and remove the starter.

5. Installation is the reverse of the removal procedure. Tighten the mounting bolts to 15–20 ft. lbs. (20–27 Nm).

Diesel Engine

1. Disconnect the battery ground cable.

2. Raise the vehicle and disconnect the cables and wires at the starter solenoid.

3. Turn the front wheels to the right and remove the two bolts attaching the steering idler arm to the frame.

4. Remove the starter mounting bolts and remove the starter.

5. Installation is the reverse of removal. Torque the mounting bolts to 20 ft. lbs.

Diesel Glow Plugs

REMOVAL AND INSTALLATION

1. Disconnect the negative battery cable. Disconnect the glow plug electrical leads.

2. Remove the glow plugs by unscrewing them from the cylinder head.

3. Inspect the tips of the plugs for any evidence of distortion or missing tip ends and replace, as necessary.

4. Installation is the reverse of the removal procedure.

TESTING

1. Turn the ignition switch **OFF** and disconnect the electrical connectors from the glow plugs.

2. Using a test light, check for continuity between the glow plug terminal and a power source with the glow plugs installed in the engine.

3. If there is no continuity, the glow plug must be replaced.

CHASSIS ELECTRICAL

Heater Blower Motor

REMOVAL AND INSTALLATION

Without Air Conditioning

EXCEPT BRONCO, F SERIES (PICK-UP) AND E SERIES (VAN)

1. Disconnect the negative battery cable.

2. Remove the air cleaner or air inlet duct, as necessary.

3. On Aerostar, remove the 2 screws attaching the vacuum reservoir to the blower assembly and remove the reservoir.

4. Disconnect the wire harness connector from the blower motor by pushing down on the connector tabs and pulling the connector off of the motor.

5. Disconnect the blower motor cooling tube at the blower motor.

6. Remove the 3 screws attaching the blower motor and wheel to the heater blower assembly.

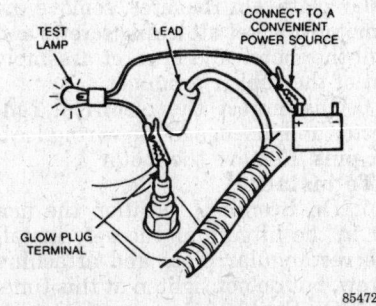

TEST LAMP   LEAD   CONNECT TO A CONVENIENT POWER SOURCE

GLOW PLUG TERMINAL

85472117

Diesel glow plug testing — 7.3L engine

7. Holding the cooling tube aside, pull the blower motor and wheel from the heater blower assembly and remove it from the vehicle.

8. Remove the blower wheel push-nut or clamp from the motor shaft and pull the blower wheel from the motor shaft.

To install:

9. tall the blower wheel on the blower motor shaft.

10. Install the hub clamp or push-nut.

11. Holding the cooling tube aside, position the blower motor and wheel on the heater blower assembly and install the 3 attaching screws.

12. Connect the blower motor cooling tube and the wire harness connector.

13. On Aerostar, install the vacuum reservoir on the hoses with the 2 screws.

14. Install the air cleaner or air inlet duct, as necessary.

15. Connect the negative battery cable and check the system for proper operation.

BRONCO, F SERIES (PICK-UP) AND E SERIES (VAN)

1. Disconnect the battery ground.

2. On vehicles built for sale in California, remove the emission module located in front of the blower.

3. Disconnect the wiring harness at the blower.

4. Disconnect the blower motor cooling tube at the blower.

5. Remove the 3 blower motor mounting screws.

6. Hold the cooling tube to one side and pull the blower motor from the housing.

7. Installation is the reverse of removal.

With Air Conditioning

EXCEPT BRONCO, F SERIES (PICK-UP) AND E SERIES (VAN)

1. Disconnect the negative battery cable.

2. In the engine compartment, disconnect the wire harness from the motor by pushing down on the tab while pulling the connection off at the motor.

3. Remove the air cleaner or air inlet duct, as necessary.

4. On Bronco II, Explorer and Ranger, remove the solenoid box cover retaining bolts and the solenoid box cover, if equipped.

5. Disconnect the blower motor cooling tube from the blower motor.

6. Remove the 3 blower motor mounting plate attaching screws and

remove the motor and wheel assembly from the evaporator assembly blower motor housing.

7. Remove the blower motor hub clamp from the motor shaft and pull the blower wheel from the shaft.

To install:

8. Install the blower motor wheel on the blower motor shaft and install a new hub clamp.

9. Install a new motor mounting seal on the blower housing before installing the blower motor.

10. Position the blower motor and wheel assembly in the blower housing and install the 3 attaching screws.

11. Connect the blower motor cooling tube.

12. Connect the electrical wire harness hardshell connector to the blower motor by pushing into place.

13. On Bronco II, Explorer and Ranger, position the solenoid box cover, if equipped, into place and install the 3 retaining screws.

14. Install the air cleaner or air inlet duct, as necessary.

15. Connect the negative battery cable and check the blower motor in all speeds for proper operation.

EXCEPT BRONCO, F SERIES (PICK-UP) AND E SERIES (VAN)

1. Disconnect the blower motor wiring at the blower.

2. Disconnect the cooling tube at the blower.

3. Remove the 4 mounting screws and pull the motor from the housing.

4. Installation is the reverse of removal. Cement the cooling tube on the nipple at the housing using Liquid Butyl Sealer D9AZ–19554–A, or equivalent.

Window Wiper Motor

REMOVAL AND INSTALLATION

Front

AEROSTAR

1. Turn the wiper switch **ON**. Turn the ignition switch to **RUN** until the wiper blades are in midpattern, then turn the ignition switch to **OFF** to keep the blades in this position.

2. Disconnect the negative battery cable, then disconnect the electrical connector from the wiper motor.

3. Remove both wiper arms and remove the cowl grille.

4. Remove the linkage retaining clip and disconnect the linkage from the motor crank arm.

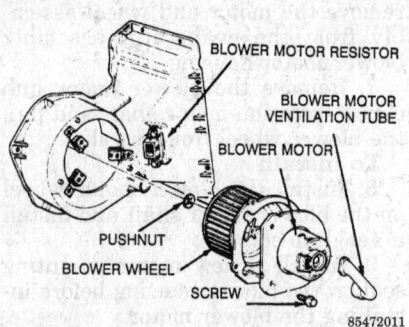

Blower motor installation — Bronco II, Explorer and Ranger

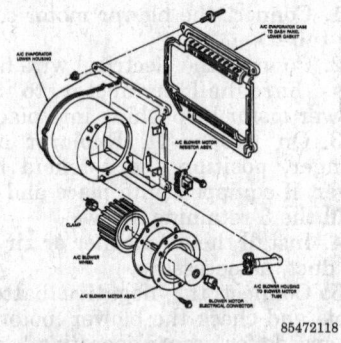

Blower motor and wheel installation — E Series

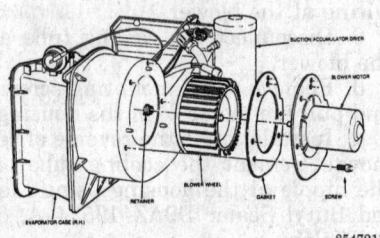

Blower motor and wheel installation — Bronco and F Series

5. Remove the motor retaining nuts while holding the motor to keep it from falling.

6. Installation is the reverse of the removal procedure.

BRONCO II, EXPLORER AND RANGER

1. Turn the wiper switch **ON**. Turn the ignition switch **ON** until the blades are straight up, then turn the ignition **OFF** to keep them there.

2. Disconnect the negative battery cable, then disconnect the electrical connector from the wiper motor.

3. Remove the right wiper arm and blade assembly. Remove the

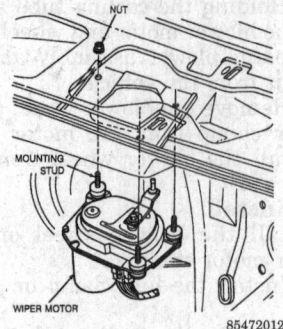

Front wiper motor installation — Aerostar

right pivot nut and allow the linkage to drop into the cowl.

4. Remove the linkage access cover, located on the right side of the dash panel, near the wiper motor.

5. Reach through the access cover opening and unsnap the wiper motor clip. Push the clip away from the linkage until it clears the nib on the crank pin, then push the clip off the linkage. Remove the linkage from the crank pin.

6. Remove the 3 attaching screws and remove the wiper motor.

To install:

7. Install the motor with the attaching screws. Tighten to 60–85 inch lbs. (6.8–9.6 Nm). Connect the motor electrical connector.

8. Install the clip completely onto the right linkage, making sure it is fully seated. Do not put the linkage on the motor crank pin and then try to install the clip.

9. Install the left and right linkage onto the wiper motor crank pin. Pull the linkage onto the crank pin until it snaps into place. The clip is properly installed if the nib is protruding through the center of the clip.

10. Install the right wiper pivot shaft and nut. Tighten the nut to 84–110 inch lbs. (9.5–12.5 Nm).

11. Connect the negative battery cable and turn the ignition **ON**. Turn the wiper switch **OFF** so the wiper motor will park, then turn the ignition **OFF**. Install the right linkage access cover.

12. Install the right wiper blade and arm assembly and test the system.

Rear

AEROSTAR

1. Disconnect the negative battery cable.

2. Remove the wiper arm.

3. Remove the motor shaft attaching nut and wedge block. Remove the liftgate trim panel.

4. Disconnect the electrical connector and remove the motor wiring pins from the inner panel. Remove the motor.

To install:

5. Position the motor so the motor shaft protrudes through the hole in the outer panel. Attach the motor to the liftgate panel with the bracket attaching screws but do not tighten at this time.

6. Install the rubber seal and wedge block over the shaft and install the pivot attaching nut. Tighten to 5.0–5.8 ft. lbs. (6.8–7.9 Nm). Tighten the motor bracket attaching screw to 5.5–6.3 ft. lbs. (7.5–8.5 Nm).

7. Attach the motor wiring to the liftgate inner panel by installing the wiring pushpins in the holes.

8. Install the articulating arm onto the drive pivot shaft.

9. Connect the negative battery cable and turn the ignition switch **ON**. Operate the wiper switch to cycle and park the wiper system in order to ensure the system linkage is in the **PARK** position before the wiper arm is installed.

10. Locate the blade in the proper position and install the arm onto the shaft with the slide latch in the unlocked position.

11. While applying a downward pressure on the arm head to ensure full seating, raise the other end of the arm sufficiently to allow the latch to slide under the pivot to the locked position. Use finger pressure only to slide the latch, then release the arm and blade against the rear window.

BRONCO II AND EXPLORER

1. Disconnect the negative battery cable.

2. Remove the wiper arm and blade assembly.

3. On Bronco II, remove the pivot shaft attaching nut washer and gasket.

4. Remove the liftgate inner trim panel.

5. On Bronco II, remove the motor bracket attaching screw and rectangular plate. On Explorer, remove the 3 motor bracket attaching screws and pull the motor and bracket assembly out of the rubber grommet.

6. Disconnect the electrical connector and disengage the wiring locator pins. Remove the motor.

To install:

7. On Bronco II, position the motor in the liftgate and loosely install the rectangular plate and attaching screw, but do not tighten at this time.

8. On Explorer, position the motor in the liftgate rubber grommet and install the attaching screws.

9. On Bronco II, install the gasket, washer and nut. Tighten the nut to 60–69 inch lbs. (6.8–7.9 Nm). Tighten the motor bracket attaching screw to 5–6 ft. lbs. (7.5–8.5 Nm).

10. Connect the electrical connector and install the wiring locator pins in the holes provided.

11. Install the wiper arm and blade assembly. Connect the negative battery cable and check wiper operation.

12. Install the liftgate inner trim panel.

Window Wiper Switch

REMOVAL AND INSTALLATION

Front

AEROSTAR

NOTE: The switch handle is an integral part of the switch and cannot be removed separately.

1. Disconnect the negative battery cable.

2. Remove the cluster finish panel retaining screws.

3. Remove the 3 left control pod retaining screws.

4. Remove the wiring connector from the switch.

5. Remove the 2 switch-to-control pod retaining screws and remove the switch.

6. Installation is the reverse of the removal procedure.

RANGER

NOTE: The switch handle is an integral part of the switch and cannot be removed separately.

1. Disconnect the negative battery cable.

2. Remove the trim shrouds.

3. Disconnect the electrical connector.

4. Peel back the foam sight shield. Remove the 2 cross-recessed screws holding the switch and remove the switch.

5. Installation is the reverse of the removal procedure.

BRONCO AND F SERIES

1. Disconnect the negative battery cable.

2. Remove the wiper switch knob, bezel nut and bezel.

3. Pull out the switch from under the instrument panel.

4. Disconnect the electrical connector from the switch and remove the switch.

5. Installation is the reverse of the removal procedures.

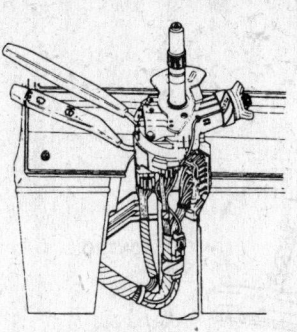

85472013

Front wiper switch location — Ranger

E SERIES

1. Disconnect the negative battery cable.

2. Remove the windshield wiper switch knob.

3. Remove the ignition switch bezel.

4. Remove the headlight switch knob and shaft by pulling the switch to the **ON** position. Then, depress the button on the top of the switch and pull the knob and shaft out.

5. Remove the 2 screws at the bottom of the finish panel, then pry the 2 upper retainers away from the instrument panel.

6. Disconnect the connector from the switch.

7. Remove the attaching screws and remove the switch.

8. Installation is the reverse of the removal procedures.

Rear

AEROSTAR

NOTE: The switch handle is an integral part of the switch and cannot be removed separately.

1. Disconnect the negative battery cable.

2. Remove the trim shrouds and the left switch pod.

3. Disconnect the electrical connector.

4. Remove the 2 cross-recessed screws holding the switch and remove the switch.

5. Installation is the reverse of the removal procedure.

EXPLORER

1. Disconnect the negative battery cable.

2. Remove the 2 ashtray retaining screws and remove the ashtray.

3. Remove the cluster trim panel, which is held on by clips.

4. Remove the snap-in switch mounting bezel containing the

switches and disconnect the electrical connector.

5. Remove the switch from the mounting bezel by pushing on the switch from the connector side until the snap-in mounting clips release.

6. Installation is the reverse of the removal procedure.

Instrument Cluster

REMOVAL AND INSTALLATION

Aerostar

CONVENTIONAL CLUSTER

1. Disconnect the negative battery cable.

2. Remove the 7 cluster housing-to-panel retaining screws and remove the cluster housing.

3. Remove the 4 instrument cluster-to-panel retaining screws.

4. Disconnect the 2 wiring harness connectors from the backplate.

5. Disconnect the speedometer cable and remove the cluster assembly.

6. Installation is the reverse of the removal procedure. Apply an approximately 3/16 in. diameter ball of silicone dielectric compound in the drive hole of the speedometer head prior to installation.

ELECTRONIC CLUSTER

1. Disconnect the negative battery cable.

2. Remove the cluster binnacle.

3. Remove the 4 cluster mounting screws.

4. Pull the top of the cluster toward the steering wheel, then reach behind the cluster and unplug the 3 connectors.

5. Swing the bottom of the cluster out and remove.

6. Installation is the reverse of the removal procedure.

Bronco II, Explorer and Ranger

1. Disconnect the negative battery cable.

2. Open the ashtray and remove the 2 screws attaching the ashtray and instrument cluster trim panel. Remove the ashtray.

3. Unsnap the cluster trim panel by pulling rearward around the edge of the panel. Depress the hazard warning switch on the steering column and remove the cluster trim panel.

4. Remove the 4 screws securing the instrument cluster to the instrument panel.

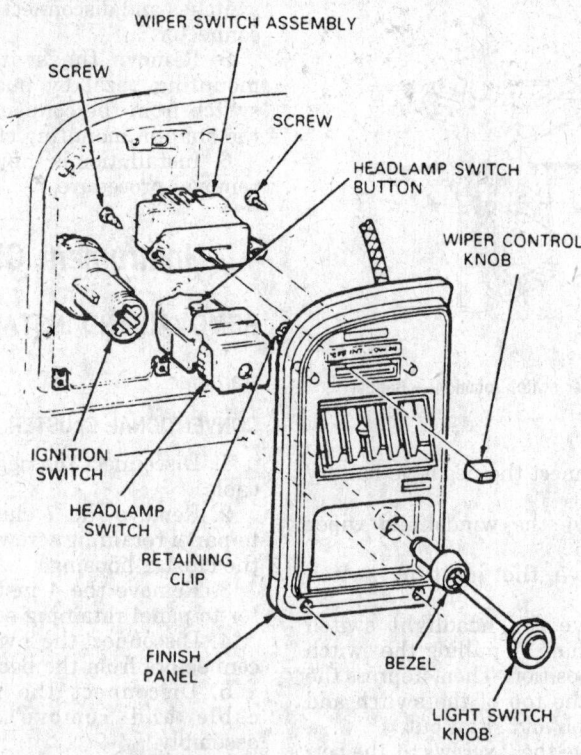

Windshield wiper switch installation — E Series

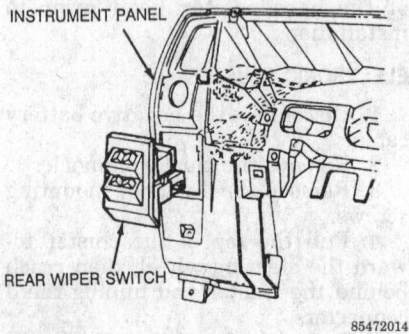

Rear wiper switch installation — Explorer

5. If equipped with automatic transmission, remove the 2 screws attaching the shift position indicator to the cluster and slide the indicator down and out of the cluster. Leave the indicator connections undisturbed.

6. Pull the cluster assembly rearward to gain access to the speedometer cable. Disconnect the cable and the 2 wiring harness connectors and remove the cluster.

NOTE: If there is not enough room to disengage the cable from the speedometer, it may be necessary to disconnect the cable at

the transmission and pull the cable through the cowl, to allow room to reach the speedometer quick disconnect.

7. Installation is the reverse of the removal procedure. Apply an approximately 3/16 in. diameter ball of silicone dielectric compound in the drive hole of the speedometer head prior to installation.

Bronco, F Series (Pick-Up) and E Series

1. Disconnect the battery ground cable.

2. Remove the wiper-washer knob. Use a hook tool to release each knob lock tab.

3. Remove the knob from the head lamp switch. Remove the fog lamp switch knob, if equipped.

4. Remove the steering column shroud. Care must be taken not to damage the transmission control selector indicator (PRNDL) cable on vehicles equipped with an automatic transmission.

5. If equipped with an automatic transmission, remove the loop on the indicator cable assembly from the retainer pin. Remove the bracket screw from the cable bracket and slide the bracket out of the slot in the tube.

6. Remove the cluster trim cover. Remove the four cluster attaching screws, disconnect the speedometer cable, wire connector from the printed circuit, 4x4 indicator light and remove the cluster.

7. Position cluster at the opening and connect the multiple connector, the speedometer cable and 4x4 indicator light. Install the four cluster retaining screws.

8. If equipped, place the loop on the transmission indicator cable assembly over the retainer on the column.

9. Position the tab on the steering column bracket into the slot on the column. Align and attach the screw.

10. Place the transmission selector lever on the steering column into **D** position.

11. Adjust the slotted bracket so the pin is within the letter band.

12. Install the trim cover.

13. Install the head lamp switch knob. If equipped, install the fog lamp switch.

14. Install the wiper washer control knobs.

15. Connect the battery cable, and check the operation of all gauges, lights and signals.

Speedometer

REMOVAL AND INSTALLATION

1. Disconnect the negative battery cable. Remove the instrument cluster.

2. Remove the lens and mask from the cluster.

3. Remove the 2 speedometer attaching screws and remove the speedometer.

4. Installation is the reverse of the removal procedure.

Headlight Switch

REMOVAL AND INSTALLATION

Aerostar

1. Disconnect the negative battery cable.

2. Remove the 5 cluster finish panel assembly retaining screws and remove the cluster finish panel.

3. Remove the 3 left control pod assembly retaining screws.

4. Disconnect the electrical connector from the switch.

5. Remove the 2 switch-to-control pod retaining screws and remove the switch.

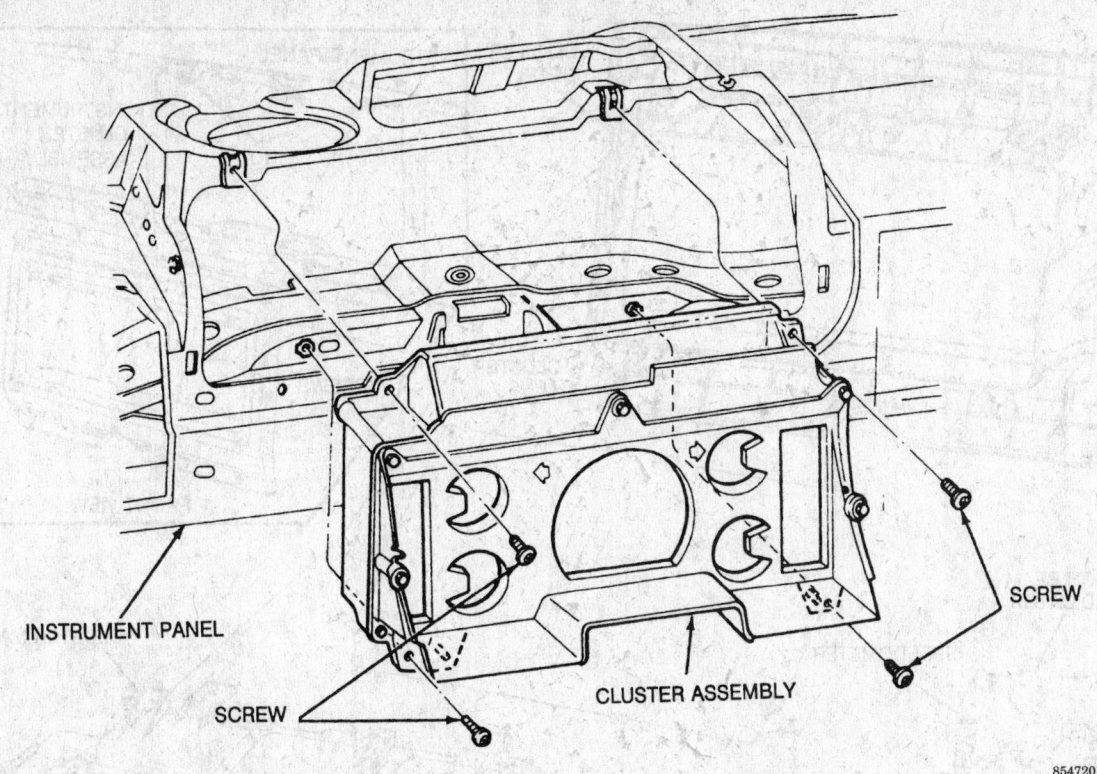

INSTRUMENT PANEL

SCREW

SCREW

CLUSTER ASSEMBLY

85472016

Instrument cluster installation — Aerostar with conventional cluster

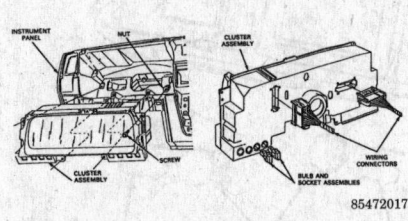

85472017

Instrument cluster installation — Bronco II, Explorer and Ranger

6. Installation is the reverse of the removal procedure.

Bronco II, Explorer and Ranger

1. Disconnect the negative battery cable.
2. Remove the ashtray and the 2 finish panel retaining screws.
3. Remove the finish panel, which snaps off.
4. Remove the rear wiper switch and rear defrost switch on Bronco II and Explorer, or the storage bin on Ranger.
5. Pull the headlight switch knob to the full **ON** position. Reach through the opening below the headlight switch, depress the shaft release button on the switch and remove the knob and shaft assembly.
6. Remove the headlight switch retaining bezel nut. Pull the switch downward and through the opening to disconnect the connector.
7. Installation is the reverse of the removal procedure.

Bronco, F Series (Pick-Up) and E Series (Van)

1. Disconnect the battery ground cable.
2. Depending on the year and model remove the wiper-washer and fog lamp switch knob if they will interfere with the headlight switch knob removal. Check the switch body (behind dash, see Step 3) for a release button. Press in on the button and remove the knob and shaft assembly. If not equipped with a release button, a hook tool may be necessary for knob removal.
3. Remove the steering column shrouds and cluster panel finish panel if they interfere with the required clearance for working behind the dash.
4. Unscrew the switch mounting nut from the front of the dash. Remove the switch from the back of the dash and disconnect the wiring harness.
5. Install in reverse order.

Combination Switch

The combination switch incorporates the turn signal and dimmer switch functions on Aerostar and Ranger. On Explorer and Ranger, the combination switch incorporates the turn signal, dimmer and windshield wiper/washer switch functions.

REMOVAL AND INSTALLATION

Aerostar

1. Disconnect the negative battery cable.
2. Remove the steering wheel.
3. If equipped with tilt column, remove the upper extension shroud by squeezing it at the 6 and 12 o'clock positions and popping it free of the retaining plate at the 3 o'clock position.
4. Open the trim shroud by removing the 4 attaching screws. Swing the trim shroud down and remove the 2 screws attaching the shroud to the steering column assembly.
5. Remove the lock cylinder.

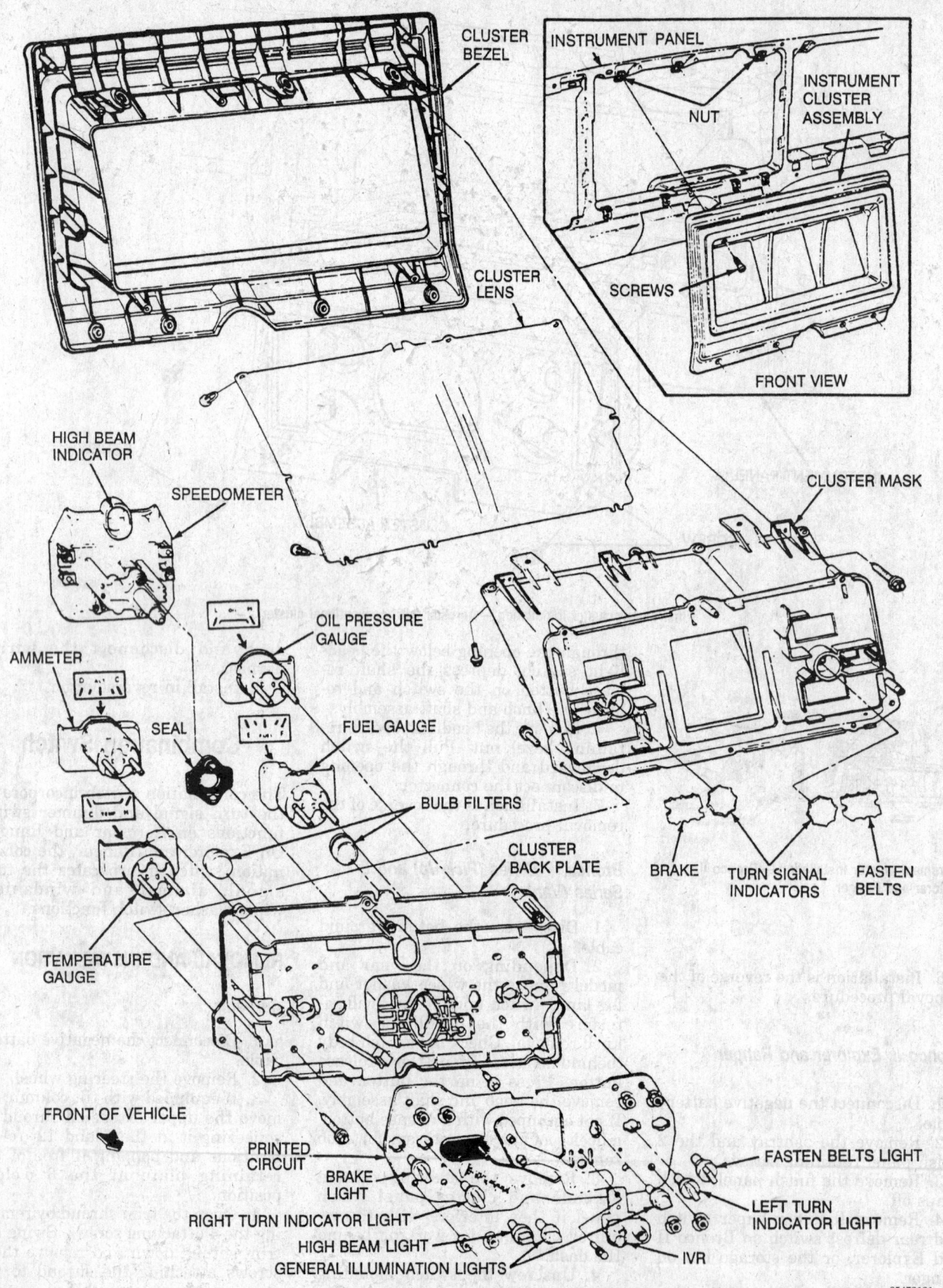

CLUSTER BEZEL

INSTRUMENT PANEL

INSTRUMENT CLUSTER ASSEMBLY

NUT

SCREWS

FRONT VIEW

CLUSTER LENS

HIGH BEAM INDICATOR

SPEEDOMETER

CLUSTER MASK

AMMETER

OIL PRESSURE GAUGE

SEAL

FUEL GAUGE

BULB FILTERS

CLUSTER BACK PLATE

BRAKE

TURN SIGNAL INDICATORS

FASTEN BELTS

TEMPERATURE GAUGE

FRONT OF VEHICLE

PRINTED CIRCUIT

BRAKE LIGHT

RIGHT TURN INDICATOR LIGHT

HIGH BEAM LIGHT

GENERAL ILLUMINATION LIGHTS

FASTEN BELTS LIGHT

LEFT TURN INDICATOR LIGHT

IVR

85472121

Instrument cluster exploded view — E Series

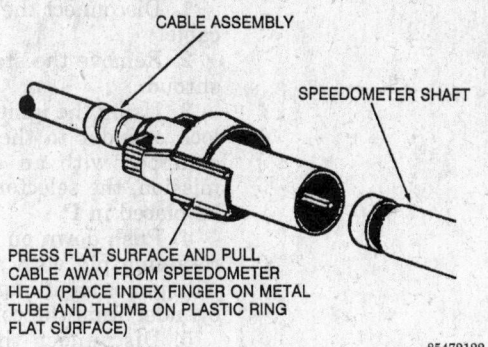

Speedometer cable quick disconnect

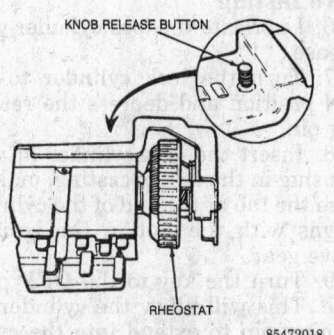

Headlight switch — Bronco II, Explorer, E Series and Ranger

6. Remove the combination switch lever by grasping the lever and using a pulling and twisting motion, pull the lever straight out from the switch. Remove the shroud.

7. Peel back the foam sight shield from the switch. Remove the 2 self-tapping screws attaching the switch to the lock cylinder housing. Disengage the switch from the housing and disconnect the switch electrical connectors.

To install:

8. Connect the switch electrical connectors.

9. Install the switch with the self-tapping screws and tighten to 18–26 inch lbs. (2.0–2.9 Nm).

10. Stick the foam sight shield to the switch and install the trim shroud.

11. Install the lock cylinder. Install the tilt collar shroud, if equipped.

12. Install the lever into the switch by aligning the key on the lever with the keyway in the switch and pushing the lever into the switch to full engagement.

13. Install the steering wheel and connect the negative battery cable.

Bronco II, Explorer and Ranger

1. Disconnect the negative battery cable.

2. Remove the steering column shroud.

3. Remove the 2 self-tapping screws that attach the combination switch to the steering column casting. Disengage the switch from the casting.

4. Disconnect the 3 electrical connectors, being careful not to damage the locking tabs. Do not damage the shift position indicator cable.

To install:

5. Connect the 3 switch electrical connectors. The wiring for the switch

is to be routed under the shift position indicator cable.

6. Install the switch with the self-tapping screws. Tighten the screws to 18–27 inch lbs. (2–3 Nm).

7. If equipped with automatic transmission, make sure the shift position indicator adjustment is correct.

8. Install the shroud and connect the negative battery cable. Check the steering column for proper operation.

Ignition Lock

REMOVAL AND INSTALLATION

Aerostar and Ranger

FUNCTIONAL LOCK

NOTE: The following procedure should be used on vehicles with functional lock cylinders. Ignition keys are available for these vehicles or the ignition key numbers are known and the proper key can be made.

1. Disconnect the negative battery cable.

2. Remove the trim shroud and disconnect the electrical connector from the key warning switch.

3. Turn the lock cylinder to the **RUN** position.

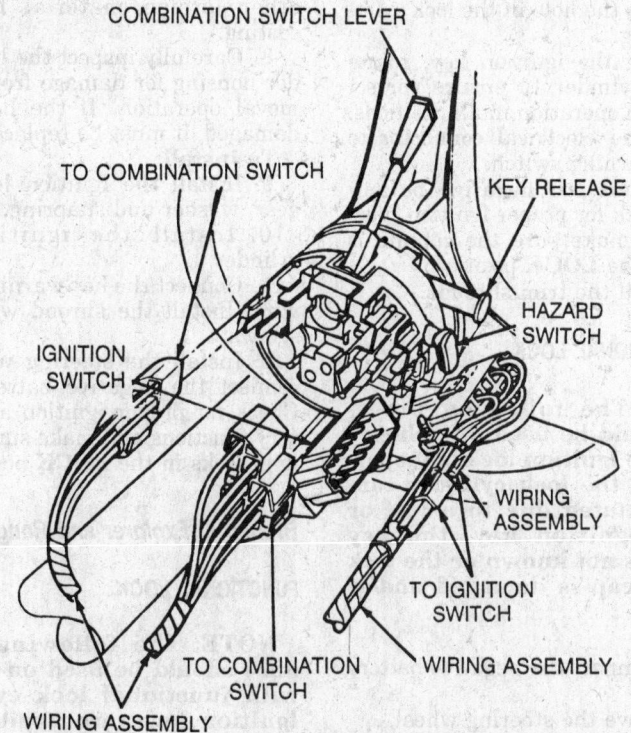

Combination switch assembly — Aerostar

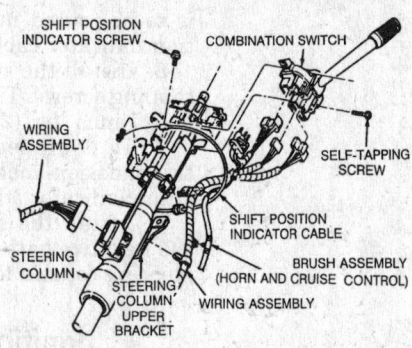

SHIFT POSITION INDICATOR SCREW — COMBINATION SWITCH

WIRING ASSEMBLY

SELF-TAPPING SCREW

SHIFT POSITION INDICATOR CABLE

STEERING COLUMN

STEERING COLUMN UPPER BRACKET

BRUSH ASSEMBLY (HORN AND CRUISE CONTROL)

WIRING ASSEMBLY

85472020

Combination switch installation — Bronco II, Explorer and Ranger

4. Place a ⅛ in. diameter pin or small drift punch in the hole located at 4 o'clock and 1¼ in. from the outer edge of the lock cylinder housing. Depress the retaining pin and pull out the lock cylinder.

To install:

5. Before installing the lock cylinder, lubricate the cylinder cavity, including the drive gear, with a suitable lock lubricant.

6. Turn the lock cylinder to the **RUN** position, depress the retaining pin and insert it into the lock cylinder housing. Make sure the cylinder is fully seated and aligned into the inter-locking washer before turning the key to the **OFF** position. This will permit the cylinder retaining pin to extend into the hole in the lock cylinder housing.

7. Using the ignition key, rotate the lock cylinder to ensure correct mechanical operation in all positions. Connect the electrical connector to the key warning switch.

8. Connect the negative battery cable. Check for proper ignition functions and make sure the column is locked in the **LOCK** position.

9. Install the trim shrouds.

NON-FUNCTIONAL LOCK

NOTE: The following procedure should be used on vehicles where the ignition lock is inoperative and the lock cylinder cannot be rotated due to a lost or broken ignition key, the key number is not known or the lock cylinder cap is damaged and/or broken.

1. Disconnect the negative battery cable.

2. Remove the steering wheel.

3. Remove the trim shrouds and disconnect the electrical connector from the key warning switch.

4. Using a ⅛ in. diameter drill bit, drill out the retaining pin, being careful not to drill deeper than ½ in.

5. Position a chisel at the base of the ignition lock cylinder cap and using a hammer, strike the chisel with sharp blows to break the cap away from the lock cylinder.

6. Using a ⅜ in. diameter drill bit, drill down the middle of the ignition lock key slot approximately 1¾ in. until the lock cylinder breaks loose from the breakaway base of the lock cylinder. Remove the lock cylinder and drill shavings from the lock cylinder housing.

7. Remove the snapring, washer and ignition lock drive gear. Thoroughly clean all drill shavings and other foreign material from the casting.

8. Carefully inspect the lock cylinder housing for damage from the removal operation. If the housing is damaged, it must be replaced.

To install:

9. Install the ignition lock drive gear, washer and snapring.

10. Install the ignition lock cylinder.

11. Connect the key warning switch wire. Install the shroud with the 2 screws.

12. Install the steering wheel and connect the negative battery cable. Check for proper ignition and accessory functions and make sure the column locks in the **LOCK** position.

Bronco II, Explorer and Ranger

FUNCTIONAL LOCK

NOTE: The following procedure should be used on vehicles with functional lock cylinders. Ignition keys are available for these vehicles or the ignition key numbers are known and the proper key can be made.

1. Disconnect the negative battery cable.

2. Remove the steering wheel and shroud.

3. Using the ignition key, turn the lock cylinder to the **ON** position. If equipped with an automatic transmission, the selector lever must first be placed in **P**.

4. Push down on the lock cylinder retaining pin with a ⅛ in. diameter wire pin or small punch. Pull the lock cylinder from the column housing.

5. Disconnect the lock cylinder wiring plug from the horn brush wiring connector.

To install:

6. Lubricate the lock cylinder with grease.

7. Turn the lock cylinder to the **ON** position and depress the retaining pin.

8. Insert the lock cylinder into its housing in the flange casting, making sure the tab at the end of the cylinder aligns with the slot in the ignition drive gear.

9. Turn the key to the **OFF** position. This will allow the cylinder retaining pin to extend into the cylinder casting housing hole.

10. Using the ignition key, rotate the lock cylinder to ensure correct mechanical operation in all positions.

11. Connect the key warning wire plug and install the steering column lower shroud.

12. Install the steering column opening trim panel and connect the negative battery cable.

13. Check for proper start in **P** or **N**. Make sure the vehicle cannot be started in **D** and **R**.

NON-FUNCTIONAL LOCK

NOTE: The following procedure should be used on vehicles where the ignition lock is inoperative and the lock cylinder cannot be rotated due to a lost or broken ignition key, the key number is not known or the lock cylinder cap is damaged and/or broken.

1. Disconnect the negative battery cable. If equipped with tilt wheel, tilt to the full up position.

2. Remove the steering wheel, tilt lever and steering column trim shrouds.

3. Punch the lock cylinder retaining pin with a prick punch, ⅛ in. maximum outside diameter. Using a ⅛ in. diameter drill, drill out the retaining pin going no deeper than ½ in. Be careful not to damage the cast housing.

4. Place a chisel at the base of the lock cylinder cap and, using a hammer, strike the chisel with sharp blows to break the cap away from the lock cylinder.

5. Using a ⅜ in. diameter drill bit, drill down the middle of the ignition lock key slot approximately 1¾ in. until the lock cylinder breaks loose from the steering column cover casting. Remove the lock cylinder and drill shavings from the base of the cover cast housing.

6. Remove the drive gear, bearing retainer and actuator from the casting. Thoroughly clean and inspect all components. If any components or the casting are damaged, they must be replaced.

To install:

7. Lubricate the drive gear, bearing and retainer with grease and install. Lubricate the lock cylinder with grease.

8. Turn the lock cylinder to the **ON** position and depress the retaining pin. Insert the cylinder into its housing in the flange casting, making sure the tab at the end of the cylinder aligns with the slot in the ignition lock drive gear.

9. Turn the key to the **OFF** position. This will allow the cylinder retaining pin to extend into the cylinder casting housing hole.

10. Using the ignition key, rotate the lock cylinder to ensure correct mechanical operation in all positions.

11. Connect the key warning wire plug and install the steering column shrouds.

12. Install the steering wheel and connect the negative battery cable. Check for proper start in **P** or **N**. Make sure the vehicle cannot be started in **D** and **R**.

Bronco, F Series and E Series

FIXED COLUMNS

1. Disconnect the battery ground.
2. Remove the steering wheel.
3. Remove the turn signal lever.
4. Remove the column trim shrouds.
5. Unbolt the steering column and lower it carefully.
6. Remove the ignition switch and warning buzzer and pin the switch in the **LOCK** position.
7. Remove the turn signal switch.
8. Remove the snapring and T-bolt nuts that retain the flange casting to the column outer tube.
9. Remove the flange casting, upper shaft bearing, lock cylinder, ignition switch actuator and the actuator

rod by pulling the entire assembly over the end of the steering column shaft.

10. Remove the lock actuator insert, the T-bolts and the automatic transmission indicator insert, or, with manual transmissions, the key release lever.

11. Upon reassembly, the following parts must be replaced with new parts:
- Flange
- Lock cylinder assembly
- Steering column lock gear
- Steering column lock bearing
- Steering column upper bearing retainer
- Lock actuator assembly

12. Assembly is a reversal of the disassembly procedure. It is best to install a new upper bearing. Check that the vehicle starts only in **P** and **NEUTRAL**.

TILT COLUMNS

1. Disconnect the battery ground.
2. Remove the steering column shrouds.
3. Using masking tape, tape the gap between the steering wheel hub and the cover casting. Cover the entire circumference of the casting. Cover the seat and floor area with a drop-cloth.
4. Pull out the hazard switch and tape it in a downward position.
5. The lock cylinder retaining pin is located on the outside of the steering column cover casting adjacent to the hazard flasher button.
6. Tilt the steering column to the full up position and pre-punch the lock cylinder retaining pin with a sharp punch.
7. Using a ⅛ in. (3mm) drill bit, mounted in a right angle drive drill adapter, drill out the retaining pin, going no deeper than ½ in. (13mm).
8. Tilt the column to the full down position. Place a chisel at the base of the ignition lock cylinder cap and using a hammer break away the cap from the lock cylinder.
9. Using a ⅜ in. (10mm) drill bit, drill down the center of the ignition lock cylinder key slot about 1¾ in. (44mm), until the lock cylinder breaks loose from the steering column cover casting.
10. Remove the lock cylinder and the drill shavings.
11. Remove the steering wheel.
12. Remove the turn signal lever.
13. Remove the turn signal switch attaching screws.
14. Remove the key buzzer attaching screw.

15. Remove the turn signal switch up and over the end of the column, but don't disconnect the wiring.

16. Remove the 4 attaching screws from the cover casting and lift the casting over the end of the steering shaft, allowing the turn signal switch to pass through the casting. The removal of the casting cover will expose the upper actuator. Remove the upper actuator.

17. Remove the drive gear, snapring and washer from the cover casting along with the upper actuator.

18. Clean all components and replace any that appear damaged or worn.

19. Installation is the reverse of removal.

Ignition Switch

REMOVAL AND INSTALLATION

Except Bronco, F Series and E Series

1. Rotate the lock cylinder to the **LOCK** position. Disconnect the negative battery cable.
2. Remove the steering wheel.
3. If equipped with tilt wheel, remove the upper extension housing shroud by squeezing it at the 6 and 12 o'clock positions and popping it free of the retaining plate at the 3 o'clock position.
4. On all except Aerostar, remove the trim shroud halves.
5. On Aerostar, proceed as follows:
    a. Remove the panel to the right of the steering column.
    b. Remove the trim shroud by removing the 4 screws at the bottom of the shroud. Swing the bottom panel of the shroud open and remove the 2 screws attaching the shroud to the retaining plate.
    c. Remove the lock cylinder.
    d. Remove the shroud by first raising the left side so the window for the combination switch lever is up past the lever receptacle, then pull up on the right side of the shroud until the lock cylinder embossment clears the lock cylinder housing.
    e. Work the shroud past the instrument panel.
6. Disconnect the switch electrical connector.
7. If equipped, remove the retaining nuts and disengage the ignition switch from the actuator pin.
8. If equipped with break-off head bolts, remove them using an ⅛ in. drill bit, then remove the bolts using an "easy-out" tool or equivalent. Dis-

engage the ignition switch from the actuator pin.

NOTE: An alternate method of removing the break-off head bolts is to use a hammer and chisel to turn the bolts 1 revolution counterclockwise. Then, using a pair of adjustable pliers, grab the bolt head and continue to rotate the bolt until removed.

To install:

9. Rotate the ignition key to the **RUN** position and align the holes in the switch casting base with the holes in the lock cylinder housing.

10. Install the nuts or if equipped, new break-off head bolts. Tighten the break-off head bolts until the heads break off.

11. Connect the electrical connector to the ignition switch and install the steering column trim shrouds.

12. On Aerostar, install the lock cylinder.

13. Install the steering wheel. Connect the negative battery cable and check the ignition switch for proper operation.

Bronco, F Series and E Series

1. Disconnect the battery ground cable.

2. Remove the steering column shroud and lower the steering column.

3. Disconnect the switch wiring at the multiple plug.

4. Remove the two nuts that retain the switch to the steering column.

5. Lift the switch vertically upward to disengage the actuator rod from the switch and remove the switch.

6. When installing the ignition switch, both the locking mechanism at the top of the column and the switch itself must be in the **LOCK** position for correct adjustment. To hold the mechanical parts of the column in the **LOCK** position, move the shift lever into **P** (with automatic transmissions) or **REVERSE** (with manual transmissions), turn the key to the **LOCK** position, and remove the key. New replacement switches, when received, are already pinned in the LOCK position by a metal shipping pin inserted in a locking hole on the side of the switch.

7. Engage the actuator rod in the switch.

8. Position the switch on the column and install the retaining nuts, but do not tighten them.

9. Move the switch up and down along the column to locate the mid-position of rod lash, and then tighten the retaining nuts.

10. Remove the locking pin, connect the battery cable, and check for proper start in **P** or **NEUTRAL**. Also check to make certain that the start circuit cannot be actuated in the **D** and **R** position.

11. Raise the steering column into position at instrument panel. Install steering column shroud.

Stoplight Switch

REMOVAL AND INSTALLATION

Bronco, F Series (Pick-Up) and E Series

1. Disconnect the negative battery cable. Disconnect the electrical connector from the switch. The locking tab must be lifted before the connector can be removed.

2. Remove the hairpin clip and slide the switch, booster pushrod, nylon washer and bushing away from the pedal. Remove the washer, then the switch by sliding the switch up or down.

To install:

3. Position the switch so the U-shaped side is nearest the pedal and directly over/under the pin. Then slide the switch up/down installing the booster pushrod and bushing between the switch side plates.

4. Push the switch and pushrod assembly firmly toward the brake pedal arm. Install the outside plastic washer to the pin and install the hairpin clip. Do not substitute for this clip. Use only factory supplied hairpin clips.

5. Connect the electrical connector to the switch and connect the negative battery cable. Make sure the switch wire harness has sufficient length to travel with the switch during the full stroke of the brake pedal. Check the switch for proper operation.

Bronco, F Series (Pick-Up) and E Series (Van)

1. Remove the hairpin retainer, slide the stop light switch, pushrod and nylon washer off of the pedal. Remove the washer, then the switch by sliding it up or down.

NOTE: If equipped with speed control, the spacer washer is replaced by the dump valve adapter washer.

2. To install the switch, position it so the U-shaped side is nearest the pedal and directly over/under the pin.

3. Slide the switch up or down, trapping the master cylinder pushrod and bushing between the switch side plates.

4. Push the switch and pushrod assembly firmly towards the brake pedal arm. Assemble the outside white plastic washer to the pin and install the hairpin retainer.

———— **CAUTION** ————
Don't substitute any other type of retainer. Use only the Ford specified hairpin retainer.

5. Assemble the connector on the switch.

6. Check stop light operation.

———— **CAUTION** ————
Make sure the stop light switch wiring has sufficient travel during a full pedal stroke!

Clutch Switch

REMOVAL AND INSTALLATION

1. Disconnect the negative battery cable. Disconnect the wiring harness from the switch.

2. Pull the orientation clip away from the switch to separate it from the pin on the switch.

3. Rotate the switch to expose the plastic retainer.

4. Push the tabs together to allow the retainer to slide rearward and separate from the switch.

5. Remove the switch from the pushrod.

6. Installation is the reverse of the removal procedure.

Neutral Safety Switch

REMOVAL AND INSTALLATION

Except Bronco, F Series (Pick-Up) and E Series (Van)

1. Disconnect the negative battery cable.

2. Disconnect the electrical harness from the switch.

3. Remove the switch and O-ring using socket tool T74P-77247-A or equivalent.

NOTE: The use of other tools could crush or puncture the walls of the switch.

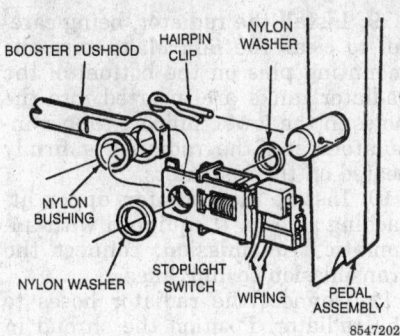

Stoplight switch assembly — Bronco, F Series (Pick-Up) and E Series (Van)

85472021

4. Installation is the reverse of the removal procedure. Tighten the switch to 7–10 ft. lbs. (9.5–13.6 Nm).

5. Check the operation of the switch with the parking brake applied. The engine should start only with the transmission selector lever in **N** or **P**. The back-up lights should illuminate only with the selector lever in **R**.

Bronco, F Series (Pick-Up) and E Series (Van)

C6 TRANSMISSION

1. Remove the downshift linkage rod return spring at the low-reverse servo cover.
2. Coat the outer lever attaching nut with penetrating oil. Remove the nut and lever.
3. Remove the 2 switch attaching bolts, disconnect the wiring at the connectors and remove the switch.
4. Installation is the reverse of removal. Adjust the switch and torque the bolts to 55–75 inch lbs.

AOD TRANSMISSION

1. Disconnect the wiring from the switch.
2. Using a deep socket, unscrew the switch.
3. Installation is the reverse of removal. Torque the switch to 10 ft. lbs.

ADJUSTMENT

C6 AND AOD TRANSMISSIONS

1. Hold the steering column transmission selector lever against the Neutral stop.
2. Move the sliding block assembly on the neutral switch to the neutral position and insert a 0.091 in. (2.3mm) gauge pin in the alignment hole on the terminal side of the switch.

3. Move the switch assembly housing so the sliding block contacts the actuating pin lever. Secure the switch to the outer tube of the steering column and remove the gauge pin.

4. Check the operation of the switch. The engine should only start in Neutral and Park.

Fuses

LOCATION

Fuse Panel — located under the instrument panel, to the left of the steering column on all vehicles.

Power Distribution Box — located in the engine compartment, on the right inner fender on Bronco II, Explorer and Ranger. Contains only high current fuses.

Circuit Breakers

LOCATION

Aerostar

Front Wiper/Washer Circuit — 6 amp circuit breaker located on the fuse panel.

Power Window Circuit — 20 amp circuit breaker located on the fuse panel.

Bronco II, Explorer and Ranger

Combination Switch Circuit — 20 amp circuit breaker located on the fuse panel.

Cigar Lighter Circuit — 20 amp circuit breaker located on the fuse panel.

Flash-to-Pass Circuit — 20 amp circuit breaker located on the fuse panel.

Front Wiper/Washer Circuit — 6 amp circuit breaker located on the fuse panel.

Headlight Circuit — 22 amp circuit breaker, integral with the headlight switch.

Power Lumbar Support Circuit — 20 amp circuit breaker located on the fuse panel.

Power Window Circuit — 30 amp circuit breaker located on the fuse panel.

Rear Wiper/Washer Circuit — 4.5 amp circuit breaker located behind the instrument panel under the glove box on Bronco II and Explorer.

Relays

LOCATION

Aerostar

Auxiliary Air Conditioner-Heater Power Relay — located at the multi-relay bracket on the left fender apron.

Courtesy Lamp Relay — located in front of the left "D" pillar, above the grommet.

Day/Night Illumination Relay — located behind the left side of the instrument panel.

Door Ajar Relay — located at the bottom of the right "B" pillar.

Door Locks Control Relay — located at the right cowl panel.

EEC Power Relay — located on the multi-relay bracket on the left fender apron.

Fuel Pump Relay — located on the multi-relay bracket on the left fender apron.

Horn Relay — located behind the left side of the instrument panel.

Low Oil Level Relay — located behind the left side of the instrument panel.

Starter Relay — located on the left fender apron, next to the battery.

Trailer Tow Relay Module — located behind the left wheelhouse.

Wide Open Throttle Cut-Out Relay — located at the multi-relay bracket on the left fender apron.

Bronco II, Explorer and Ranger

Air Conditioning Relay — located on the right fender apron.

Choke Relay — located near the test connector take off.

EEC Power Relay — located on the right fender apron.

Fuel Metering Relay — located at the cigar lighter takeoff.

Fuel Pump Relay — located on the right fender apron.

Horn Relay — located behind the instrument panel, to the right of the steering column.

Lock/Unlock Relays — located on the left fender apron.

Low Oil Level Relay — located behind the lower right side of the instrument panel.

Starter Relay — located on the right fender apron.

Stop/Turn Signal Relay — located on left rear quarter panel on Explorer.

Tail Light Relay — located on left rear quarter panel on Explorer.

Trailer Lamps Relay—located on top of the left radiator support.

Wide Open Throttle Cut-Out Relay—located at the right fender apron.

Computers

LOCATION

The engine Electronic Control Assembly (ECA) is located in the engine compartment, on the left side of the firewall on Aerostar or under the dash, at the right kick panel, on Bronco II, Explorer and Ranger.

Flashers

LOCATION

Both the turn signal and hazard flashers are attached to the fuse panel.

Cruise Control

ADJUSTMENT

Actuator Cable

1. Remove the cable retaining clip.
2. Disengage the throttle positioner.
3. Set the engine at hot idle.
4. Pull on the actuator cable to take up any slack. Maintain a light tension on the cable.
5. While holding the cable, insert the cable retaining clip and snap securely.

Vacuum Dump Valve

1. Firmly hold the brake pedal in the up, released, position.
2. Push in the dump valve until the valve bottoms against the pad on the brake pedal.
3. The dump valve housing must clear the plastic pad on the brake pedal by 0.050–0.10 in. (1.27–2.54mm) with the brake pedal pulled to the rearmost position.

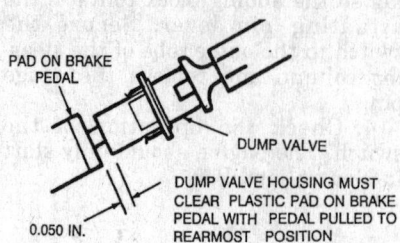

PAD ON BRAKE PEDAL

DUMP VALVE

DUMP VALVE HOUSING MUST CLEAR PLASTIC PAD ON BRAKE PEDAL WITH PEDAL PULLED TO REARMOST POSITION

0.050 IN.

85472022

View showing correctly adjusted dump valve

ENGINE COOLING

Radiator

REMOVAL AND INSTALLATION

1. Disconnect the negative battery cable and remove the radiator cap.

CAUTION

Never remove the radiator cap while the engine is running or personal injury from scalding hot coolant or steam may result. If possible, wait until the engine has cooled to remove the radiator cap. If this is not possible, wrap a thick cloth around the radiator cap and turn it slowly to the first stop, to release the pressure in the cooling system. Step back while the pressure is released. After all pressure is released, remove the radiator cap completely.

2. Position a drain pan under the radiator and open the draincock to drain the radiator.
3. Disconnect the overflow hose from the radiator and the fan shroud, if necessary.
4. Remove the shroud or finger guard upper attaching screws. Lift the shroud out of the lower retaining clips and drape it on the fan.
5. Disconnect the radiator hoses from the radiator.
6. Disconnect and plug the automatic transmission oil cooling lines, if equipped.
7. Remove the radiator upper attaching screws, tilt the radiator back and lift directly upward, clear of the radiator support and cooling fan.
To install:
8. Make sure the radiator lower support rubber insulators are in place on the lower support.

9. Install the radiator, being careful to clear the fan. Make sure the mounting pins on the bottom of the radiator tanks are inserted into the holes in the lower support rubber insulators and the radiator is firmly seated on the insulators.
10. Install the radiator upper attaching screws. If equipped with automatic transmission, connect the transmission cooling lines.
11. Connect the radiator hoses to the radiator. Position the shroud in the retainer clips and install the attaching screws.
12. Connect the overflow hose and close the draincock. Connect the negative battery cable. Fill and bleed the cooling system.

Heater Core

REMOVAL AND INSTALLATION

Except Bronco, F Series (Pick-Up) and E Series (Van)

1. Disconnect the negative battery cable.
2. Drain the cooling system into a suitable container.
3. Disconnect the heater hoses from the heater core tubes. Use the snap-lock fitting disconnect procedure, if necessary.
4. In the passenger compartment, remove the screws attaching the heater core access cover to the plenum assembly. Remove the access cover.
5. Pull the heater core rearward and down, removing it from the plenum assembly.
To install:
6. Position the heater core and seal in the plenum assembly.
7. Install the heater core access cover to the plenum assembly and secure it with the screws.
8. Connect the heater hoses to the heater core tubes. Use the snap-lock fitting connection procedure.
9. Fill the cooling system to the proper level.
10. Connect the negative battery cable and check the system for proper operation and coolant leaks.

Bronco, F Series (Pick-Up) and E Series (Van)

WITHOUT AIR CONDITIONING

1. Drain the cooling system to a level below the heater core.
2. Disconnect the coolant hoses at the heater core tubes.
3. From inside the passenger compartment, remove the 7 screws that

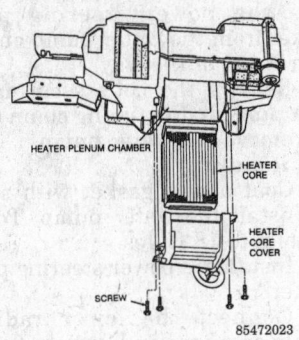

HEATER PLENUM CHAMBER
HEATER CORE
HEATER CORE COVER
SCREW
85472023

**Heater core installation —
Explorer and Ranger**

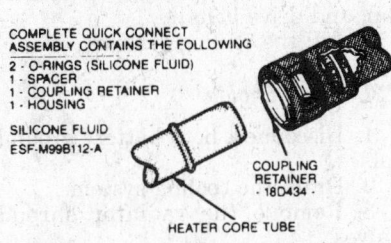

COMPLETE QUICK CONNECT
ASSEMBLY CONTAINS THE FOLLOWING
2 - O-RINGS (SILICONE FLUID)
1 - SPACER
1 - COUPLING RETAINER
1 - HOUSING

SILICONE FLUID
ESF-M99B112-A

COUPLING RETAINER - 18D434

HEATER CORE TUBE

QUICK CONNECT COUPLING - DISCONNECTED
85472025

Snap-lock fitting procedures

secure the heater core access cover to the plenum chamber. Remove the cover. On some models, it might be easier to first remove the glove compartment.

4. Remove the heater core.

5. Installation is the reverse of removal. Replace any damaged sealer.

WITH AIR CONDITIONING

1. Drain the cooling system to a level below the heater core.

2. Disconnect the coolant hoses at the heater core tubes.

3. Remove the glove compartment.

4. Disconnect the temperature and function cables.

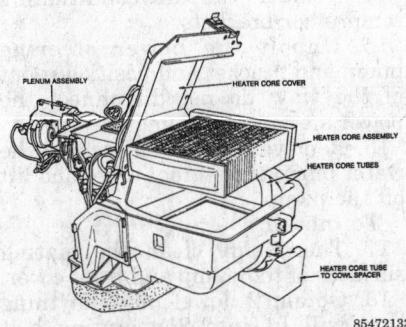

PLENUM ASSEMBLY
HEATER CORE COVER
HEATER CORE ASSEMBLY
HEATER CORE TUBES
HEATER CORE TUBE TO COWL SPACER
85472133

Heater core removal — Bronco and F Series

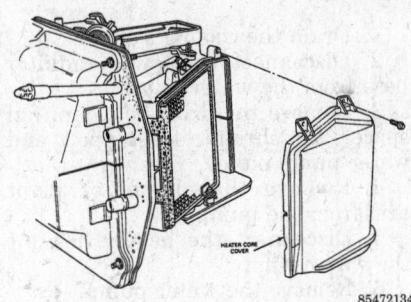

HEATER CORE COVER
85472134

Heater core removal — E Series

5. From inside the passenger compartment, remove the 7 screws that secure the heater core access cover to the plenum chamber. Remove the cover.

6. Remove the heater core.

7. Installation is the reverse of removal. Replace any damaged sealer.

Water Pump

REMOVAL AND INSTALLATION

2.3L Engine

1. Disconnect the negative battery cable and drain the cooling system.

2. Remove the bolts that retain the fan shroud and position the shroud back over the fan.

3. Remove the 4 bolts that retain the cooling fan, then remove the fan and shroud.

4. Remove the accessory drive belts.

5. Remove the water pump pulley and the vent hose to the canister.

6. Remove the heater hose at the water pump.

7. Remove the timing belt cover. Remove the lower radiator hose from the water pump.

8. Remove the water pump mounting bolts and the water pump. Clean all gasket mating surfaces.

9. Installation is the reverse of the removal procedure. Coat the threads of the mounting bolts with sealer before installation and tighten to 14–21 ft. lbs. (20–30 Nm). Fill and bleed the cooling system.

2.9L and 4.0L Engines

1. Disconnect the negative battery cable and drain the cooling system.

2. Remove the lower radiator hose and the heater return hose from the pump.

3. Remove the fan and clutch assembly using fan clutch pulley holder

T83T-6312-A and fan clutch nut wrench T83T-6312-B or equivalents. The fan clutch nut has left hand thread; remove by turning clockwise.

4. Loosen the alternator mounting bolts and remove the belt. If equipped with air conditioning, remove the alternator and bracket.

5. Remove the water pump pulley.

6. Remove the water pump attaching bolts and remove the water pump. Note the length of the bolts when removing, so they can be reinstalled in the same positions.

7. Clean all gasket mating surfaces and install in the reverse order of removal. Tighten the water pump retaining bolts to 7–9 ft. lbs. (9–12 Nm) and the fan clutch nut to 30–100 ft. lbs. (40–135 Nm). Fill and bleed the cooling system.

3.0L (VIN U) Engine

1. Disconnect the negative battery cable and drain the cooling system.

2. Loosen the nut that attaches the fan clutch to the water pump shaft using a 22mm wrench. The nut has left-hand thread and must be turned clockwise to remove. Remove the fan and clutch assembly.

3. Loosen the 4 water pump pulley bolts, then remove the accessory drive belts. Remove the water pump pulley.

4. Remove the alternator adjusting arm and brace. Disconnect the heater hose and lower radiator hose from the pump.

5. Rotate the belt adjuster out of the way.

6. Remove the water pump attaching bolts, noting their positions for reinstallation and remove the water pump. Clean all gasket mating surfaces.

7. Installation is the reverse of the removal procedure. Apply sealer to the 8mm mounting bolt at the extreme passenger side, prior to installation. Tighten the 6mm mounting bolts to 7 ft. lbs. (10 Nm) and the 8mm mounting bolts to 19 ft. lbs. (25 Nm). Tighten the fan clutch nut to 30–100 ft. lbs. (40–135 Nm). Fill and bleed the cooling system.

3.0L (VIN W) Engine

1. The timing belt cover must be removed. Disconnect the negative battery cable and drain the cooling system. Don't forget the block drain.

2. Remove the radiator hoses and, on automatic transmission, disconnect and plug the fluid cooling lines.

3. Remove the lower section of the fan shroud and remove the screws to lift the shroud from the engine. Re-

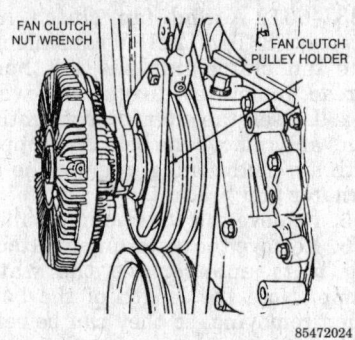

Fan and clutch assembly removal — 2.9L, 4.0L and 7.3L Diesel engines

move the bracket bolts and lift the radiator out of the vehicle.

4. Remove all the accessory drive belts.

5. Hold the pulley and remove the nuts to remove the fan and pulley from the water pump.

6. Remove the timing belt covers.

7. Remove the bolts to remove the water pump from the engine.

To install:

8. Make sure all gasket surfaces are clean and use a new gasket or silicone sealer when installing the pump to the engine. Torque the bolts to 15 ft. lbs. (21 Nm).

9. Install the timing belt covers. On 4WD models, make sure the sealing surfaces are clean and carefully install the rubber seal when installing the cover. The timing belt must be properly protected from dirt and oil.

10. Install the pulley, fan clutch and the fan.

11. Install the accessory drive belts and adjust the tension.

12. Install the radiator and fan shroud and connect the cooling system hoses.

13. Fill the system and check for leaks.

4.9L Engine

1. Drain the cooling system.
2. Disconnect the lower radiator hose from the water pump.
3. Remove the drive belt, fan, fan spacer, fan shroud, if equipped, and water pump pulley.
4. Remove the alternator pivot arm from the pump.
5. Disconnect the heater hose at the water pump.
6. Remove the water pump.

To install:

7. Before installing the old water pump, clean the gasket mounting surfaces on the pump and on the cylinder block. If a new water pump is being installed, remove the heater hose fitting from the old pump and install it on the new one.

8. Coat the new gaskets with sealer on both sides and install the water pump. Torque the mounting bolts to 18 ft. lbs.

9. Connect the heater hose at the water pump.

10. Install the alternator pivot arm on the pump.

11. Install the water pump pulley fan shroud, fan spacer, fan, and drive belt.

12. Connect the lower radiator hose at the water pump.

13. Fill the cooling system.

5.0L, 5.8L and 7.5L Engines

1. Drain the cooling system.
2. Remove the bolts securing the fan shroud to the radiator, if equipped, and position the shroud over the fan.
3. Disconnect the lower radiator hose, heater hose and by-pass hose at the water pump. Remove the drive belts, fan, fan spacer and pulley. Remove the fan shroud, if equipped.
4. Loosen the alternator pivot bolt and the bolt attaching the alternator adjusting arm to the water pump. Re-

move the power steering pump bracket from the water pump and position it out of the way.

5. Remove the bolts securing the water pump to the timing chain cover and remove the water pump.

To install:

6. Coat a new gasket with sealer and install the water pump. Torque the bolts to 18 ft. lbs.

7. Install the power steering pump bracket.

8. Connect the lower radiator hose, heater hose and by-pass hose at the water pump.

9. Install the fan shroud, if equipped.

10. Install the pulley, fan spacer, fan, and drive belts.

11. Fill the cooling system.

7.3L Diesel Engine

1. Disconnect both battery ground cables.
2. Drain the cooling system.
3. Remove the radiator shroud halves.
4. Remove the fan clutch and fan.

NOTE: The fan clutch bolts are left hand thread. Remove them by turning them clockwise.

5. Remove the power steering pump belt.
6. Remove the air conditioning compressor belt.
7. Remove the vacuum pump drive belt.
8. Remove the alternator drive belt.
9. Remove the water pump pulley.
10. Disconnect the heater hose at the water pump.
11. If installing a new pump, remove the heater hose fitting from the old pump.
12. Remove the alternator adjusting arm and bracket.
13. Unbolt the air conditioning compressor and position it out of the way; do not disconnect the refrigerant lines!
14. Remove the air conditioning compressor brackets.
15. Unbolt the power steering pump and bracket and position it out of the way; do not disconnect the power steering fluid lines.
16. Remove the bolts attaching the water pump to the front cover and lift off the pump.

To install:

17. Thoroughly clean the mating surfaces of the pump and front cover.

18. Obtain 2 dowel pins, anything that will fit into 2 mounting bolt holes in the front cover, when installing the water pump.

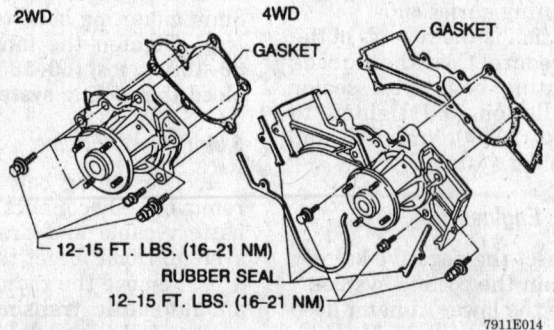

2WD   4WD

GASKET   GASKET

12–15 FT. LBS. (16–21 NM)
RUBBER SEAL
12–15 FT. LBS. (16–21 NM)

The timing belt cover must be removed to remove the water pump on 3.0L (VIN W) engine — on 4WD, the pump is part of the rear belt cover

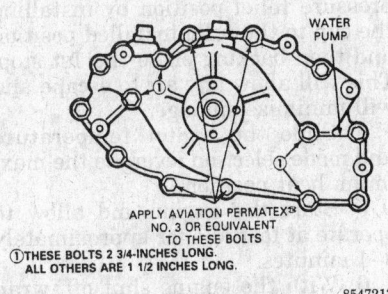

APPLY AVIATION PERMATEX®
NO. 3 OR EQUIVALENT
TO THESE BOLTS
① THESE BOLTS 2 3/4-INCHES LONG.
ALL OTHERS ARE 1 1/2 INCHES LONG.

85472136

Water pump — 7.3L diesel engine

19. Using a new gasket, position the water pump over the dowel pins and into place on the front cover.

20. Install the attaching bolts. The 2 top center and 2 bottom center bolts must be coated with RTV silicone sealant prior to installation. Also, the 4 bolts marked No. 1 are a different length than the other bolts. Torque the bolts to 14 ft. lbs.

21. Install the water pump pulley.

22. Wrap the heater hose fitting threads with Teflon® tape and screw it into the water pump. Torque it to 18 ft. lbs.

23. Connect the heater hose to the pump.

24. Install the power steering pump and bracket. Install the belt.

25. Install the air conditioning compressor bracket.

26. Install the air conditioning compressor. Install the belt.

27. Install the alternator adjusting arm and install the belt.

28. Install the vacuum pump drive belt.

29. Adjust all the drive belts.

30. Install the fan and clutch. Remember that the bolts are left hand thread. Turn them counterclockwise to tighten them. Torque them to 45 ft. lbs.

31. Install the fan shroud halves.

32. Fill and bleed the cooling system.

33. Connect the battery ground cables.

34. Start the engine and check for leaks.

Thermostat

NOTE: It is a good practice to check the operation of a new thermostat before it is installed in an engine. Place the thermostat in a pan of boiling water. If it does not open more than ¼ in. (6mm), do not install it in the engine.

REMOVAL AND INSTALLATION

2.3L, 2.9L, 3.0L (VIN U) and 4.0L Engines

1. Disconnect the negative battery cable and drain the cooling system.

2. Disconnect the upper radiator hose and, if equipped, the heater hose from the water outlet.

3. Remove the water outlet retaining bolts and remove the water outlet. Remove the thermostat from the water outlet.

To install:

4. Clean all gasket mating surfaces.

5. Apply gasket sealer to a new water outlet gasket and install on the cylinder head or intake manifold.

6. Install the thermostat in the water outlet with the bridge section toward the radiator hose. Turn the thermostat clockwise to lock it in position on the flats cast into the water outlet.

NOTE: If the water outlet is equipped with a heater outlet tube opening, check that the full width of the opening is visible within the thermostat port in the assembly. The correct port alignment is required to provide maximum coolant flow to the heater.

7. Install the water outlet with the mounting bolts. Tighten the bolts to 14–21 ft. lbs. (20–30 Nm) on 2.3L engine, 7–10 ft. lbs. (9–13 Nm) on 2.9L and 4.0L engines or 18 ft. lbs. (25 Nm) on the 3.0L (VIN U) engine.

8. Connect the radiator hose and, if equipped, the heater hose to the water outlet.

9. Connect the negative battery cable. Fill and bleed the cooling system.

3.0L (VIN W) Engine

The factory-installed thermostat opening temperature is 180°F (USA) or 190°F (Canada). The thermostat is located above the water pump.

1. Disconnect the negative battery cable.

2. Drain the engine coolant to a level below the thermostat housing.

3. Disconnect the coolant hose from the thermostat water outlet.

4. Remove the water outlet-to-thermostat housing bolts, gasket and thermostat.

NOTE: The thermostat spring must face the inside of the engine.

5. Clean the gasket mounting surfaces.

NOTE: If the thermostat is equipped with an air bleed or jiggle valve, be sure to position it in the upward direction.

6. To install, use a new gasket or sealant and reverse the removal procedures. Torque the thermostat housing bolts to 15 ft. lbs. (21 Nm).

4.9L Engine

1. Drain the cooling system below the level of the coolant outlet housing. Use the petcock valve at the bottom of the radiator to drain the system. It is not necessary to remove any of the hoses.

2. Remove the coolant outlet housing retaining bolts and slide the housing with the hose attached to one side.

3. Remove the thermostat and gasket from the cylinder head and clean both mating surfaces.

4. To install the thermostat, coat a new gasket with water resistant sealer and position it on the outlet of the engine. The gasket must be in place before the thermostat is installed.

5. Install the thermostat with the bridge (opposite end of the spring) inside the elbow connection.

6. Position the elbow connection onto the mounting surface of the outlet, so the thermostat flange is resting on the gasket and install the retaining bolts. Torque the bolts to 15 ft. lbs.

7. Fill the radiator and operate the engine until it reaches operating temperature. Check the coolant level and adjust if necessary.

5.0L, 5.8L and 7.5L Engines

1. Drain the cooling system below the level of the coolant outlet housing. Use the petcock valve at the bottom of the radiator to drain the system. It is not necessary to remove any of the hoses.

2. Disconnect the bypass hoses at the water pump and intake manifold.

3. Remove the bypass tube.

4. Remove the coolant outlet housing retaining bolts, bend the hose and lift the housing with the hose attached to one side.

5. Remove the thermostat and gasket from the intake manifold and clean both mating surfaces.

To install:

6. To install the thermostat, coat a new gasket with water resistant sealer and position it on the outlet of the engine. The gasket must be in

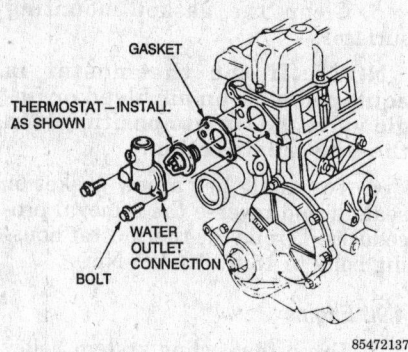

Thermostat installation — 4.9L engine

85472137

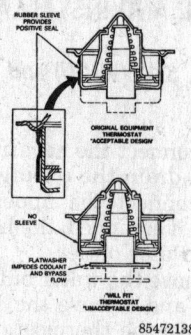

Thermostat — 7.3L
diesel engine

85472138

place before the thermostat is installed.

7. Install the thermostat with the bridge (opposite end of the spring) inside the elbow connection and the thermostat flange positioned in the recess in the manifold.

8. Position the elbow connection onto the mounting surface of the outlet. Torque the bolts to 18 ft. lbs. on the 5.0L and 5.8L engines or 28 ft. lbs. on the 7.5L engine.

9. Install the bypass tube and hoses.

10. Fill the radiator and operate the engine until it reaches operating temperature. Check the coolant level and adjust if necessary.

7.3L Diesel Engine

WARNING

The factory specified thermostat does not contain an internal bypass. On these engines, an internal bypass is located in the block. The use of any replacement thermostat other than that meeting the manufacturer's specifications will result in engine overheating! Use only thermostats meeting the specifications of Ford part number E5TZ–8575–C or Navistar International part number 1807945–C1.

1. Disconnect both battery ground cables.

2. Drain the coolant to a point below the thermostat housing.

3. Remove the alternator and vacuum pump belts

4. Remove the alternator.

5. Remove the vacuum pump and bracket.

6. Remove all but the lowest vacuum pump/alternator mounting casting bolt.

7. Loosen that lowest bolt and pivot the casting outboard of the engine.

8. Remove the thermostat housing attaching bolts, bend the hose and lift the housing up and to one side.

9. Remove the thermostat and gasket.

To install:

10. Clean the thermostat housing and block surfaces thoroughly.

11. Coat a new gasket with waterproof sealer and position the gasket on the manifold outlet opening.

12. Install the thermostat in the manifold opening with the spring element end downward and the flange positioned in the recess in the manifold.

13. Place the outlet housing into position and install the bolts. Torque the bolts to 20 ft. lbs.

14. Reposition the casting.

15. Install the vacuum pump and bracket.

16. Install the alternator.

17. Adjust the drive belts.

18. Fill and bleed the cooling system.

19. Connect both battery cables.

20. Run the engine and check for leaks.

Cooling System Bleeding

Except 3.0L (VIN W) Engine

When the entire cooling system is drained, the following procedure should be used to remove air from the cooling system and ensure a complete fill.

1. Close the radiator draincock and install the cylinder block drain plug, if removed.

2. Fill the cooling system with a 50/50 mixture of anti-freeze and water. Allow several minutes for trapped air to escape. When filling a cross flow radiator, allow time for the coolant to flow through the radiator tubes to the other end of the tank to ensure the radiator is full.

3. Install the radiator cap to the pressure relief position by installing the cap to the fully installed position and then backing off to the 1st stop. This will allow any air to escape and will minimize spillage.

4. Slide the heater temperature and mode selection levers to the maximum heat position.

5. Start the engine and allow to operate at fast idle for approximately 3–4 minutes.

6. With the engine shut off, wrap the radiator cap with a thick cloth, carefully remove the cap and add coolant to bring the coolant level up to the filler neck seat.

7. Install the cap to the fully installed position. Then, back off to the 1st stop and operate the engine at fast idle until the thermostat opens and the upper radiator hose is warm. To check the coolant level, shut the engine off, wrap the cap with a thick cloth and cautiously remove the cap. Add additional coolant, if necessary. Install the cap to the fully installed position.

CAUTION

To avoid personal injury from scalding hot coolant or steam blowing out of the radiator, use extreme care when removing the cap from a hot radiator.

8. Fill the coolant recovery reservoir to the proper level with a 50/50 mix of anti-freeze and water.

3.0L (VIN W) Engine

1. Set the heater temperature control to **HOT** and open the air relief plug. Pour coolant into the radiator until it comes out the relief plug, then close the plug.

2. Fill the reservoir and run the engine to warm it to operating temperature.

3. When the engine is cool again, check the coolant level in the reservoir.

GASOLINE FUEL SYSTEM

Fuel System Service Precautions

Safety is the most important factor when performing not only fuel sys-

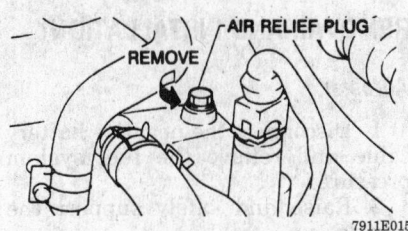

Air relief plug — 3.0L (VIN W) engine

tem maintenance but any type of maintenance. Failure to conduct maintenance and repairs in a safe manner may result in serious personal injury or death. Maintenance and testing of the vehicle's fuel system components can be accomplished safely and effectively by adhering to the following rules and guidelines.

• To avoid the possibility of fire and personal injury, always disconnect the negative battery cable unless the repair or test procedure requires that battery voltage be applied.

• Always relieve the fuel system pressure prior to disconnecting any fuel system component (injector, fuel rail, pressure regulator, etc.), fitting or fuel line connection. Exercise extreme caution whenever relieving fuel system pressure to avoid exposing skin, face and eyes to fuel spray. Please be advised that fuel under pressure may penetrate the skin or any part of the body that it contacts.

• Always place a shop towel or cloth around the fitting or connection prior to loosening to absorb any excess fuel due to spillage. Ensure that all fuel spillage (should it occur) is quickly removed from engine surfaces. Ensure that all fuel soaked cloths or towels are deposited into a suitable waste container.

• Always keep a dry chemical (Class B) fire extinguisher near the work area.

• Do not allow fuel spray or fuel vapors to come into contact with a spark or open flame.

• Always use a backup wrench when loosening and tightening fuel line connection fittings. This will prevent unnecessary stress and torsion to fuel line piping. Always follow the proper torque specifications.

• Always replace worn fuel fitting O-rings with new. Do not substitute fuel hose or equivalent where fuel pipe is installed.

RELIEVING FUEL SYSTEM PRESSURE

1. Disconnect the negative battery cable and remove the fuel filler cap.
2. Remove the cap from the pressure relief valve on the fuel supply manifold. Install pressure gauge T80L-9974-B or equivalent, to the pressure relief valve.
3. Direct the gauge drain hose into a suitable container and depress the pressure relief button.
4. Remove the gauge and replace the cap on the pressure relief valve.

NOTE: As an alternate method, disconnect the inertia switch and crank the engine for 15–20 seconds until the pressure is relieved.

Fuel Line Couplings

REMOVAL AND INSTALLATION

There are 3 methods in use to connect the fuel lines and fuel system components, the hairpin clip push connect fitting, the duck bill clip push connect fitting and the spring lock coupling. Each requires a different procedure to disconnect and connect.

Hairpin Clip Push Connect Fitting

1. Inspect the visible internal portion of the fitting for dirt accumulation. If more than a light coating of dust is present, clean the fitting before disassembly.
2. Some adhesion between the seals in the fitting and the tubing will occur with time. To separate, twist the fitting on the tube, then push and pull the fitting until it moves freely on the tube.
3. Remove the hairpin clip from the fitting by first bending and breaking the shipping tab. Next, spread the 2 clip legs by hand about

⅛ in. each to disengage the body and push the legs into the fitting. Lightly pull the triangular end of the clip and work it clear of the tube and fitting.

NOTE: Do not use hand tools to complete this operation.

4. Grasp the fitting and pull in an axial direction to remove the fitting from the tube. Be careful on 90 degree elbow connectors, as excessive side loading could break the connector body.
5. After disassembly, inspect and clean the tube end sealing surfaces. The tube end should be free of scratches and corrosion that could provide leak paths. Inspect the inside of the fitting for any internal parts such as O-rings and spacers that may have been dislodged from the fitting. Replace any damaged connector.

To install:
6. Install a new connector if damage was found. Insert a new clip into any 2 adjacent openings with the triangular portion pointing away from the fitting opening. Install the clip until the legs of the clip are locked on the outside of the body. Piloting with an index finger is necessary.
7. Before installing the fitting on the tube, wipe the tube end with a clean cloth. Inspect the inside of the fitting to make sure it is free of dirt and/or obstructions.
8. Apply a light coating of engine oil to the tube end. Align the fitting and tube axially and push the fitting onto the tube end. When the fitting is engaged, a definite click will be heard. Pull on the fitting to make sure it is fully engaged.

Duck Bill Clip Push Connect Fitting

1. Inspect the visible internal portion of the fitting for dirt accumulation. If more than a light coating of dust is present, clean the fitting before disassembly.

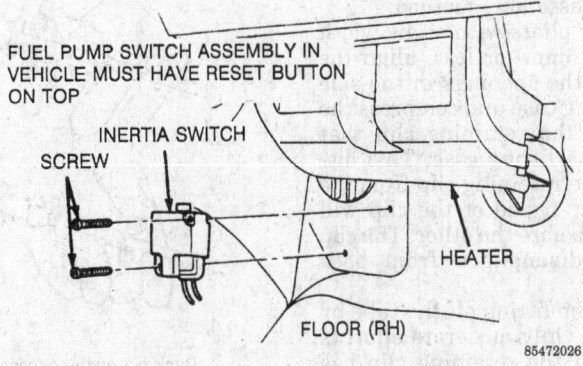

Typical inertia switch location

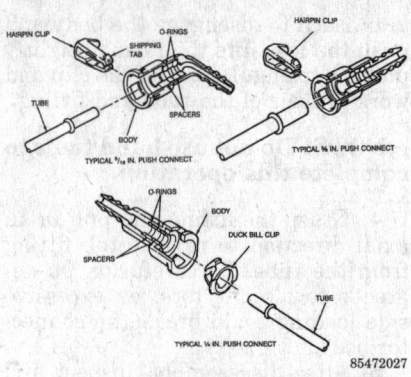

85472027

Typical push connect fittings

2. Some adhesion between the seals in the fitting and the tubing will occur with time. To separate, twist the fitting on the tube, then push and pull the fitting until it moves freely on the tube.

3. Align the slot on push connect disassembly tool T82L-9500-AH or equivalent, with either tab on the clip, 90 degrees from the slots on the side of the fitting and insert the tool. This disengages the duck bill retainer from the tube.

4. Holding the tool and the tube with 1 hand, pull the fitting away from the tube.

NOTE: Use hands only. Only moderate effort is required, if the tube has been properly disengaged.

5. After disassembly, inspect and clean the tube end sealing surfaces. The tube end should be free of scratches and corrosion that could provide leak paths. Inspect the inside of the fitting for any internal parts such as O-rings and spacers that may have been dislodged from the fitting. Replace any damaged connector.

6. Some fuel tubes have a secondary bead which aligns with the outer surface of the clip. These beads can make tool insertion difficult. If there is extreme difficulty, use the following disassembly method:

a. Using pliers with a jaw width of 0.2 in. (5mm) or less, align the jaws with the openings in the side of the fitting case and compress the portion of the retaining clip that engages the fitting case. This disengages the retaining clip from the case. Often 1 side of the clip will disengage before the other. The clip must be disengaged from both openings.

b. Pull the fitting off the tube by hand only. Only moderate effort is required, if the retaining clip has been properly disengaged.

c. After disassembly, inspect and clean the tube end sealing surfaces. The tube end should be free of scratches and corrosion that could provide leak paths. Inspect the inside of the fitting for any internal parts such as O-rings and spacers that may have been dislodged from the fitting. Replace any damaged connector.

d. The retaining clip will remain on the tube. Disengage the clip from the tube bead and remove.

To install:

7. Install a new connector if damage was found. Install the new replacement clip into the body by inserting 1 of the retaining clip serrated edges on the duck bill portion into 1 side of the window openings. Push on the other side until the clip snaps into place.

8. Before installing the fitting on the tube, wipe the tube end with a clean cloth. Inspect the inside of the fitting to make sure it is free of dirt and/or obstructions.

9. Apply a light coating of engine oil to the tube end. Align the fitting and tube axially and push the fitting onto the tube end. When the fitting is engaged, a definite click will be heard. Pull on the fitting to make sure it is fully engaged.

Spring Lock Coupling

The spring lock coupling is a fuel line coupling held together by a garter spring inside a circular cage. When the coupling is connected together, the flared end of the female fitting slips behind the garter spring inside the cage of the male fitting. The garter spring and cage then prevent the flared end of the female fitting from pulling out of the cage. As an additional locking feature, most vehicles have a horseshoe shaped retaining clip that improves the retaining reliability of the spring lock coupling.

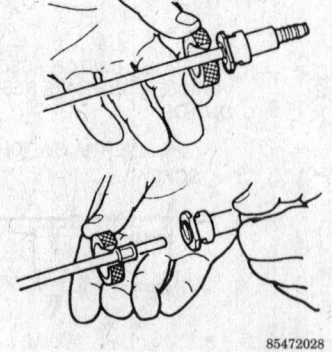

85472028

Duck bill push connect fitting removal

Fuel Tank

REMOVAL AND INSTALLATION

Aerostar

1. Disconnect the negative battery cable and relieve the fuel system pressure.
2. Raise and safely support the vehicle.
3. Drain the fuel from the fuel tank.
4. Loosen the fuel fill pipe clamp and remove the heat shield.
5. Support the tank with a jack and remove the fuel tank straps.
6. Disconnect the fuel lines, vapor hose and electrical connector from the fuel tank.
7. Lower the tank from the vehicle.

To install:

8. Raise the tank into position and install the fuel tank straps.
9. Connect the fuel lines, vapor hose and electrical connector.
10. Install the heat shield and connect the fuel filler pipe.
11. Tighten the fuel tank strap retaining bolts to 35–45 ft. lbs. (47–61 Nm).
12. Remove the jack and lower the vehicle.
13. Fill the fuel tank and check for leaks. Connect the negative battery cable.

Bronco II

1. Disconnect the negative battery cable and relieve the fuel system pressure.
2. Raise and safely support the vehicle.
3. Drain the fuel from the fuel tank. Remove the skid plate, if equipped.
4. Support the fuel tank with a jack and remove the fuel tank straps.
5. Disconnect the fill pipe and lower the tank enough to disconnect the fuel lines, vapor hoses and electrical connector.
6. Lower the tank from the vehicle.

To install:

7. Raise the fuel tank and connect the electrical connector vapor hoses and fuel lines.
8. Connect the fuel filler pipe and install the fuel tank straps. Install the skid plate, if equipped.
9. Remove the jack and lower the vehicle.
10. Fill the fuel tank and check for leaks. Connect the negative battery cable.

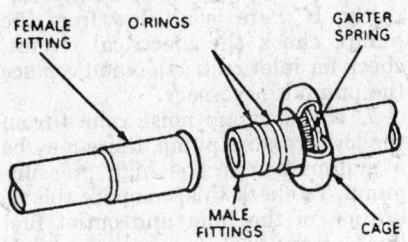

SPRING LOCK COUPLING DISCONNECTED

85472029

Spring lock coupling chart

Explorer

1. Disconnect the negative battery cable and relieve the fuel system pressure.

2. Raise and safely support the vehicle.

3. Drain the fuel from the fuel tank.

4. Remove the shield, skid plate and fuel tank front strap.

5. Support the tank with a jack and remove the bolt from the fuel tank rear strap.

6. Disconnect the filler pipe and vent pipe and lower the tank. Disconnect the vapor hose, fuel lines and electrical connector.

7. Lower the tank from the vehicle.

To install:

8. Raise the fuel tank and connect the electrical connector, fuel lines and vapor hose.

9. Connect the filler pipe and vent pipe. Attach the rear fuel tank strap.

10. Install the shield, skid plate and front strap.

11. Remove the jack and lower the vehicle.

12. Fill the fuel tank and check for leaks. Connect the negative battery cable.

Ranger

1. Disconnect the negative battery cable and relieve the fuel system pressure.

2. Raise and safely support the vehicle.

3. Drain the fuel from the fuel tank.

4. Loosen the filler pipe clamp.

5. Remove the bolts securing the skid plate and shield assembly brackets to the frame, if equipped. Remove the skid plate and shield and the brackets as an assembly.

6. Remove the heat shield. Support the tank with a jack and remove the fuel tank straps.

7. Disconnect the fuel lines, vapor hose and electrical connector. Lower the fuel tank from the vehicle.

To install:

8. Raise the tank into position and attach the fuel tank straps.

9. Connect the electrical connector, vapor hose and fuel lines.

10. Connect the fuel filler pipe. Remove the jack.

11. Install the skid plate and heat shield and bracket assembly, if equipped. Install the heat shield and lower the vehicle.

12. Fill the fuel tank and check for leaks. Connect the negative battery cable.

Bronco

1. Raise and support the rear end on jackstands.

2. Disconnect the negative battery cable.

3. Disconnect the fuel gauge sending unit wire at the fuel tank.

4. Remove the fuel drain plug or siphon the fuel from the tank into a suitable container.

5. Loosen the fuel line hose clamps, slide the clamps forward and disconnect the fuel 1 at the fuel gauge sending unit.

6. Loosen the clamps on the fuel filler pipe and vent hose as necessary and disconnect the filler pipe hose and vent hose from the tank.

7. Support the tank and remove the lower attaching bolts or skid plate bolts supporting the tank to the frame. Carefully lower the tank or tank/skid plate assembly and disconnect the vent tube from the vapor emission control valve in the top of the tank. Finish removing the filler pipe and filler pipe vent hose if not possible previously. Remove the tank from under the vehicle.

8. If the sending unit is being removed, turn the unit's retaining ring counterclockwise and remove the sending unit, retaining ring and gasket. Discard the gasket.

9. Install the tank in the reverse order of removal. Use thread locking compound on the bolt threads and torque the bolts to 27–37 ft. lbs.

F Series and E Series

STEEL MID-SHIPS FUEL TANK(S)

1. If equipped with a single fuel tank, disconnect the battery ground cable, then, drain the fuel from the tank into a suitable container by either removing the drain plug, if equipped, or siphoning through the filler cap opening.

2. If equipped with dual tanks, drain the fuel tanks by disconnecting the connector hoses, then disconnect the battery ground cable.

3. Disconnect the fuel gauge sending unit wire and fuel outlet line.

4. Disconnect the air relief tube from the filler neck and fuel tank.

5. Loosen the filler neck hose clamp at the fuel tank and pull the filler neck away from the tank.

6. Remove the retaining strap mounting nuts and/or bolts and lower the tank(s) to the floor.

7. If a new tank is being installed, change over the fuel gauge sending unit to the new tank.

8. Install the fuel tank(s) in the reverse order of removal. Torque the strap nuts to 30 ft. lbs.

PLASTIC MID-SHIPS FUEL TANK

1. Drain the fuel from the tank into a suitable container by either removing the drain plug, if equipped, or siphoning through the filler cap opening.

2. Disconnect the battery ground cable(s).

3. Remove the skid plate and heat shields.

4. Disconnect the fuel gauge sending unit wire at the tank.

5. Loosen the filler neck hose clamp at the fuel tank and pull the filler neck away from the tank.

6. Disconnect the fuel line push-connect fittings at the fuel gauge sending unit.

7. Support the tank. Remove the retaining strap mounting bolts and lower the tank to the floor.

8. If a new tank is being installed, change over the fuel gauge sending unit to the new tank.

9. Install the fuel tank(s) in the reverse order of removal. Torque the strap bolts to 12–18 ft. lbs.

PLASTIC OR STEEL BEHIND-THE-AXLE FUEL TANK

1. Raise the rear of the vehicle.

2. Disconnect the negative battery cable.

3. If equipped with a single tank, disconnect the fuel gauge sending unit wire at the fuel tank. Remove the fuel drain plug or siphon the fuel from the tank into a suitable container.

4. If equipped with dual tanks, drain the fuel tanks by disconnecting the connector hoses.

5. Disconnect the fuel line push-connect fittings at the fuel gauge sending unit.

6. Loosen the clamps on the fuel filler pipe and vent hose as necessary

and disconnect the filler pipe hose and vent hose from the tank.

7. If the tank is the metal type, support the tank and remove the bolts attaching the tank support or skid plate to the frame. Carefully lower the tank or tank/skid plate assembly and disconnect the vent tube from the vapor emission control valve in the top of the tank. Finish removing the filler pipe and filler pipe vent hose if not possible previously. Remove the tank from under the vehicle.

8. If the tank is the plastic type, support the tank and remove the bolts attaching the combination skid plate and tank support to the frame. Carefully lower the tank and disconnect the vent tube from the vapor emission control valve in the top of the tank. Finish removing the filler pipe and filler pipe vent hose if it was not possible previously. Remove the skid plate and tank from under the vehicle. Remove the skid plate from the tank.

9. If the sending unit is to be removed, turn the unit retaining ring counterclockwise and remove the sending unit, retaining ring and gasket. Discard the gasket.

10. Install the tank in the reverse order of removal. With metal tanks, use thread adhesive such as Loctite® on the bolt threads, and torque these bolts to 27–37 ft. lbs. With plastic tanks, DO NOT use thread adhesive. Torque the bolts to 25–35 ft. lbs.

Fuel Filter

REMOVAL AND INSTALLATION

1. Disconnect the negative battery cable and relieve the fuel system pressure.
2. Raise and support the vehicle safely.
3. Disconnect the fuel lines from the fuel filter.
4. Remove the fuel filter from the bracket and the retainer, if equipped. Note the direction of the flow arrow so the replacement filter can be installed correctly.
5. Installation is the reverse of the removal procedure. Start the engine and check for leaks.

Electric Fuel Pump

Aerostar, Bronco II, Explorer and Ranger are equipped with a single high-pressure pump located in the fuel tank.

PRESSURE TESTING

High Pressure Pump

1. Make sure there is an adequate fuel supply.
2. Relieve the fuel system pressure.
3. Turn the ignition key **OFF**.
4. Connect a suitable fuel pressure gauge to the schrader valve on the fuel rail.
5. Install a test lead to the **FP** terminal on the VIP test connector.
6. Turn the ignition key to the **RUN** position, then ground the test lead to run the fuel pump.
7. Observe the fuel pressure reading on the pressure gauge. The fuel pressure should be 35–45 psi.
8. Relieve the fuel system pressure and turn the ignition key **OFF**. Remove the fuel pressure gauge and the test lead.

Low Pressure Pump

1. Relieve the fuel system pressure. Open the fuel line at the high pressure pump inlet.
2. Connect a hose to the line from the fuel tank. Position the other end of the hose in a calibrated container of at least 1 quart capacity.
3. Disconnect the high pressure fuel pump electrical connector from the wiring harness.
4. Install a test lead to the **FP** terminal on the VIP test connector.
5. Turn the ignition switch to the **RUN** position and ground the test lead to energize the pump for 10 seconds, then disconnect the test lead.

NOTE: It may be necessary to momentarily block the fuel hose to prime the low pressure pump. With the outlet open and under no back pressure on the outlet, this is normal.

6. If the fuel pump produces a minimum flow of 16 oz. of fuel in 10

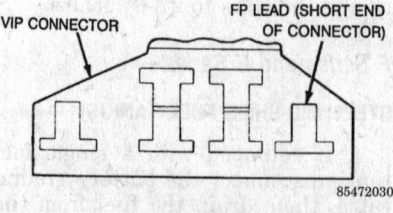

VIP test connector

seconds, the pump is operating correctly. If there is no flow from the pump, check the electrical circuit, check for inlet restriction and replace the pump if necessary.

7. If fuel pump noise comes from the low pressure pump, there may be a malfunction in the high pressure pump. To check this, compare the vibration of the inlet and outlet fuel lines at the high pressure pump. If there is a large difference between the lines in vibration level, replace the high pressure pump and recheck for noise.

REMOVAL AND INSTALLATION

Tank Mounted Pump

AEROSTAR, BRONCO II, EXPLORER AND RANGER

NOTE: On Ranger, the fuel pump may be accessed by removing the pickup box from the chassis, instead of removing the fuel tank.

1. Disconnect the negative battery cable and relieve the fuel system pressure.
2. Raise and safely support the vehicle.
3. Remove the fuel tank.
4. Remove any dirt that has accumulated around the fuel pump attaching flange so it will not enter the fuel tank during removal and installation.
5. Turn the fuel pump locking ring counterclockwise using a suitable tool. Remove the locking ring.
6. Remove the fuel pump and discard the seal ring. Separate the fuel pump from the sending unit, if required.
   To install:
7. Clean the fuel pump mounting flange and tank mounting surface and seal ring groove.
8. Apply a light coating of grease on a new seal ring and install it in the groove.
9. Install the fuel pump to the sending unit, if removed. Install the fuel pump assembly in the tank, making sure the locating keys are in the keyways and the seal ring is in place.
10. Hold the fuel pump assembly and the seal ring in place and install the locking ring. Rotate the ring clockwise using a suitable tool. Find the fuel tank part number on the front bottom of the tank and proceed as follows:
    a. If equipped with part number E59A-9002-CAE tank, tighten the

ring to 60–85 ft. lbs. (81–115 Nm), wait 5 minutes and retighten to the same specification. Use only the ring that was removed from the tank, do not replace with a ring from another tank.

b. If equipped with plastic retaining ring E99A-9A307-D, tighten to 40–55 ft. lbs. (54–74 Nm). Use the same ring that was removed from the tank. If a new tank is installed, use a new ring.

c. If equipped with part number E69A-9002-PA tank, tighten the locking ring once to 80–113 ft. lbs. (109–153 Nm).

d. On Ranger and Aerostar, tighten the polyethylene locking ring to 40–45 ft. lbs. (54–61 Nm).

11. Install the fuel tank in the vehicle.

12. Lower the vehicle and fill the fuel tank with at least 10 gallons of fuel. Connect the negative battery cable. Turn the ignition key to **RUN** for 3 seconds repeatedly, 5–10 times, to pressurize the system. Check for leaks.

13. Start the engine and check for leaks.

BRONCO, F SERIES (PICK-UP) AND E SERIES (VAN)

1. Release the fuel system pressure. Disconnect the negative battery cable.

2. Remove the fuel tank as described below.

3. On steel tanks:

a. Disconnect the wiring at the connector.

b. Remove all dirt from the area of the sender.

c. Disconnect the fuel lines.

d. Turn the locking ring counterclockwise to remove it.

4. Lift out the fuel pump and sending unit. Discard the gasket.

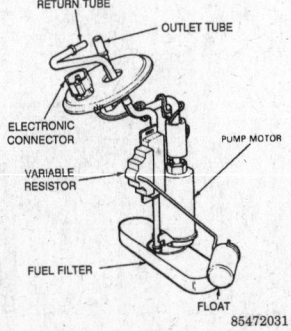

Tank mounted electric fuel pump assembly — Aerostar, Bronco II, Explorer and Ranger

5. On plastic tanks:

a. Disconnect the wiring at the connector.

b. Remove all dirt from the area of the sender.

c. Disconnect the fuel lines.

d. Turn the locking ring counterclockwise to remove it. Lift out the fuel pump and sending unit. Discard the gasket.

To install:

6. Place a new gasket in position in the groove in the tank.

7. Place the sending unit/fuel pump assembly in the tank, indexing the tabs with the slots in the tank. Make sure the gasket stays in place.

8. Hold the assembly in place and position the locking ring.

On steel tanks, turn the locking ring clockwise until the stop is against the retainer ring tab.

On plastic tanks, turn the retaining ring clockwise until hand-tight. Torque the ring to 40–55 ft. lbs.

9. Make sure the gasket is still in place.

10. Connect the fuel lines and wiring.

11. Install the tank.

Frame Mounted Pump

1. Disconnect the negative battery cable and relieve the fuel system pressure.

2. Raise and support the vehicle safely.

3. Disconnect the fuel lines and electrical connector from the pump.

4. Remove the pump from the mounting bracket.

5. Installation is the reverse of the removal procedure. Start the engine and check for leaks.

Fuel Injection

IDLE SPEED ADJUSTMENT

1992

Idle speed adjustment on Bronco, F Series (Pick-Up) and E Series (Van) requires the use of Super Star tester 007-00028 or equivalent.

IDLE MIXTURE ADJUSTMENT

The idle mixture is controlled by the electronic control unit and cannot be adjusted.

Fuel Injector

REMOVAL AND INSTALLATION

2.3L Engine

1. Disconnect the negative battery cable and relieve the fuel system pressure.

2. Disconnect the electrical connectors at the TPS, air bypass valve, injector wiring harness at the main engine harness and at the water temperature indicator sensor, ACT and ECT sensors and the ignition control assembly. Tag all lines prior to removal to aid reinstallation.

3. Remove the throttle linkage shield and disconnect the throttle linkage and cruise control. Unbolt the accelerator cable from the bracket and position out of the way.

4. Disconnect the vacuum lines at the upper intake manifold vacuum tree, EGR valve, fuel pressure regulator and canister purge line. Tag all lines prior to removal to aid reinstallation.

5. Disconnect the air intake hose and crankcase vent hose.

6. Disconnect the hose for the PCV system from the fitting on the underside of the upper intake manifold.

7. Disconnect the EGR tube from the EGR valve by removing the flange nut.

8. Remove the upper intake manifold retaining bolts and remove the upper intake manifold and throttle body assembly.

9. Disconnect the injector electrical connectors.

10. Disconnect the fuel lines from the fuel supply manifold.

11. Remove the 2 fuel supply manifold retaining bolts.

12. Carefully disengage the manifold and fuel injectors from the engine and remove the manifold and injectors.

13. Remove the injectors from the manifold by grasping the injector body and pulling while gently rocking the injector from side-to-side. Remove and discard the injector O-rings.

To install:

14. Lubricate new O-rings with clean light grade oil and install 2 on each injector.

NOTE: Never use silicone grease at it will clog the injectors.

15. Install the injectors, using a light, twisting, pushing motion.

16. Install the fuel supply manifold, pushing it down to make sure all the

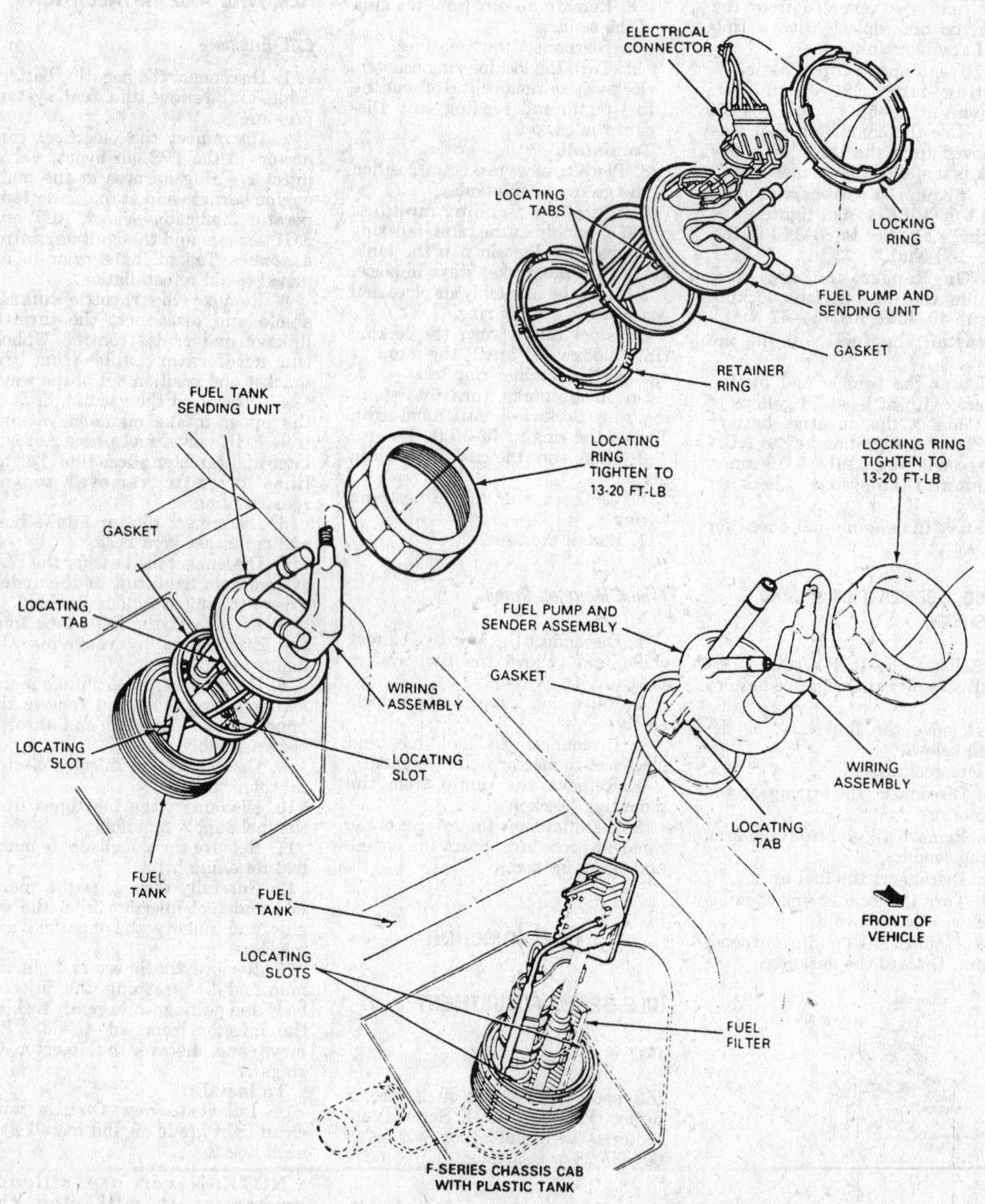

ELECTRICAL CONNECTOR

LOCATING TABS

LOCKING RING

FUEL PUMP AND SENDING UNIT

GASKET

RETAINER RING

FUEL TANK SENDING UNIT

LOCATING RING TIGHTEN TO 13-20 FT-LB

LOCKING RING TIGHTEN TO 13-20 FT-LB

GASKET

LOCATING TAB

LOCATING SLOT

WIRING ASSEMBLY

LOCATING SLOT

FUEL TANK

FUEL TANK

FUEL PUMP AND SENDER ASSEMBLY

GASKET

LOCATING TAB

WIRING ASSEMBLY

FRONT OF VEHICLE

LOCATING SLOTS

FUEL FILTER

F-SERIES CHASSIS CAB WITH PLASTIC TANK

85472139

Tank mounted Fuel pump installation — Bronco, F Series (Pick-Up) and E Series (Van)

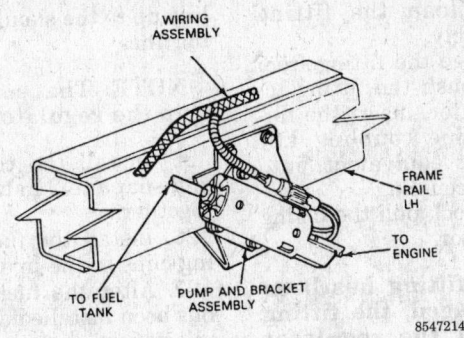

Frame mounted electric fuel pump assembly — Bronco, F Series (Pick-Up) and E Series (Van)

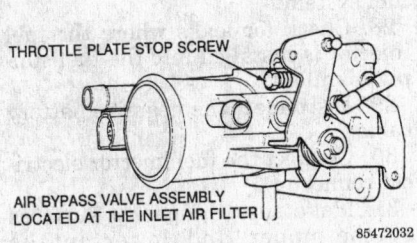

Throttle plate stop screw location — 2.3L engine

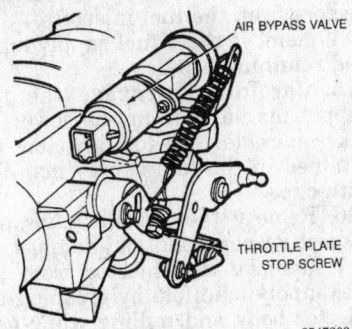

Throttle plate stop screw location — 3.0L engine

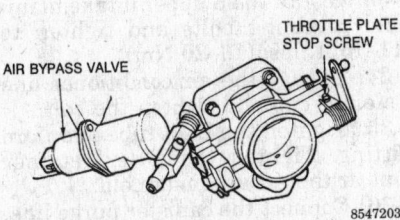

Throttle plate stop screw location — 2.9L engine

O-rings are seated in the fuel rail cups and intake manifold.

17. Install the manifold retaining bolts and tighten to 15–22 ft. lbs. (20–30 Nm) while holding the fuel manifold down.

18. Connect the fuel lines to the supply manifold.

19. After the fuel supply manifold has been installed and before the fuel injector wire connectors have been connected, connect the negative battery cable and turn the ignition **ON**. This will cause the fuel pump to run

for 2–3 seconds and pressurize the fuel system.

20. Check for leaks where the fuel injector is installed into the fuel supply manifold.

21. Disconnect the negative battery cable.

22. Connect the fuel injector electrical connectors.

23. Make sure the gasket surfaces of the upper and lower intake manifolds are clean.

24. Place a new gasket on the lower intake manifold assembly and place the upper intake manifold and throttle body assembly in position.

25. Install the retaining bolts and tighten in sequence to 15–22 ft. lbs. (20–30 Nm).

NOTE: The 3 bolts with stud heads go in hole positions 2, 3 and 4.

26. Connect the EGR tube to the EGR valve and tighten to 18–28 ft. lbs. (25–30 Nm).

27. Connect the PCV system hose to the fitting on the underside of the upper intake manifold.

28. Connect all vacuum lines and electrical connectors according to the locations that were marked during the removal procedure.

29. Hold the accelerator cable bracket in position on the upper manifold and install the retaining bolts. Tighten to 10–15 ft. lbs. (13.5–20.5 Nm).

30. Install the accelerator cable to the bracket and connect the accelerator cable and cruise control. Install the throttle linkage shield.

31. Connect the air intake hose and crankcase vent hose.

32. Connect the negative battery cable. Start the engine and let it idle for 2 minutes.

33. Turn the engine **OFF** and check for fuel leaks.

2.9L Engine

1. Disconnect the negative battery cable and relieve the fuel system pressure.

2. Disconnect the electrical connectors at the air bypass valve, TPS, EGR sensor and ACT.

3. Remove the air inlet tube from the air cleaner to throttle body.

4. Remove the snow/ice shield to expose the throttle linkage. Disconnect the throttle cable from the ball stud.

5. Disconnect the upper intake manifold vacuum connectors; both the front and rear fittings including

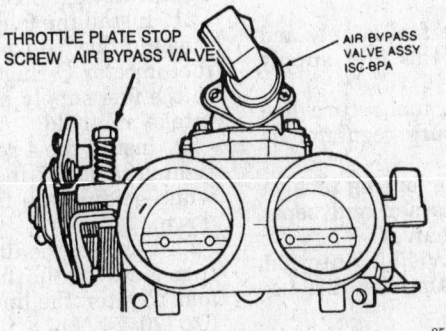

Throttle plate stop screw location — 4.9L, 5.0L and 5.8L engines

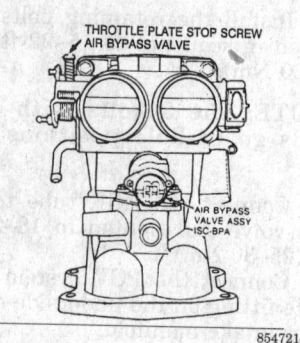

Throttle plate stop screw location — 7.5L engine

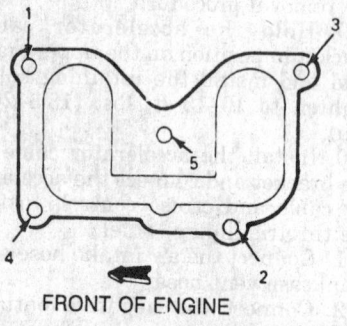

FRONT OF ENGINE

Upper intake manifold bolt torque sequence — 2.3L engine

the EGR valve and the vacuum line to the fuel pressure regulator.

6. Disconnect the PCV closure tube from under the throttle body and disconnect the PCV vacuum tube from under the manifold.

7. Remove the canister purge line from the fitting near the power steering pump.

8. Disconnect the EGR tube from the EGR valve by removing the flange nut.

9. Loosen the bolt that retains the air conditioning line at the upper rear of the upper manifold and disengage the retainer.

10. Remove the 6 upper intake manifold retaining bolts and remove the upper intake manifold and throttle body assembly.

11. Disconnect the fuel supply and return lines from the fuel supply manifold.

12. Disconnect the fuel return line from the fuel pressure regulator as follows:

a. Disengage the locking tabs on the connector retainer and separate the retainer halves.

b. Inspect the visible internal portion of the fitting for dirt ac-

cumulation. Clean the fitting before disassembly.

c. To disengage the fitting from the regulator, push the fitting toward the regulator, insert the fingers on fuel line coupling key T90P-9550-A or equivalent, into the slots in the coupling.

d. Using the tool, pull the fitting from the regulator.

NOTE: If the fitting has been properly disengaged, the fitting should slide off the regulator with minimum effort.

13. Disconnect the electrical connectors from the fuel injectors.

14. Remove the 4 fuel supply manifold retaining bolts.

15. Carefully disengage the fuel supply manifold from the lower intake manifold. The fuel injectors are retained in the fuel supply manifold with clips.

16. Remove the retainer clips and inspect for corrosion and damage.

17. Remove the injector from the fuel supply manifold by grasping the injector body and pulling while gently rocking from side-to-side. Remove and discard the injector O-rings.

18. Inspect the injector plastic pintle protection cap and washer for signs of deterioration. Replace the complete injector as required. If the plastic pintle protection cap is missing, look for it in the intake manifold.

NOTE: The plastic pintle protection cap is not available as a separate part.

To install:

19. Lubricate new O-rings with clean light grade oil and install 2 on each injector.

NOTE: Never use silicone grease at it will clog the injectors.

20. Install the injectors, using a light, twisting, pushing motion.

21. Install the fuel supply manifold, pushing down to make sure all the fuel injector O-rings are fully seated in the fuel supply manifold cups and intake manifold.

22. Install the 4 retaining bolts and tighten to 71–97 inch lbs. (8–11 Nm) while holding the fuel rail assembly down.

23. Connect the fuel supply and return lines to the fuel supply manifold. Tighten the line nut to 15–18 ft. lbs. (20–24 Nm).

24. Install the fuel return line to the fuel pressure regulator by pushing it onto the fuel pressure regulator

line up to the shoulder on the regulator line.

NOTE: The connector should grip the regulator line securely.

25. Install the connector retainer and snap the 2 halves of the retainer together.

26. Install the fuel injector retaining clips to the injectors.

27. After the fuel supply manifold has been installed and before the fuel injector wire connectors have been connected, connect the negative battery cable and turn the ignition **ON**. This will cause the fuel pump to run for 2–3 seconds and pressurize the fuel system.

28. Check for leaks where the fuel injector is installed into the fuel supply manifold.

29. Disconnect the negative battery cable.

30. Connect the fuel injector electrical connectors.

31. Make sure the gasket surfaces of the upper and lower intake manifolds are clean.

32. Place a new gasket on the lower intake manifold assembly and place the upper intake manifold and throttle body assembly in position. The use of alignment studs may be helpful. Align the EGR tube in the valve.

33. Install the 6 upper intake manifold retaining bolts and tighten to 11–15 ft. lbs. (16–20 Nm).

34. Engage the air conditioner line retainer cup and tighten the bolt.

35. Tighten the EGR tube and flare fitting. Tighten the lower retainer nut at the exhaust manifold.

36. Connect the canister purge line, PCV vacuum hose and the PCV closure hose.

37. Connect the vacuum lines to the vacuum tree, EGR valve and fuel pressure regulator.

38. Connect the throttle cable to the throttle body and install the snow/ice shield.

39. Connect the electrical connectors at the air bypass valve, TPS and ACT sensor.

40. Install the air inlet tube from the throttle body to the air cleaner.

41. Connect the negative battery cable, start the engine and let it idle for 2 minutes.

42. Turn the engine **OFF** and check for fuel leaks.

3.0L (VIN U) Engine

1. Disconnect the negative battery cable and relieve the fuel system pressure.

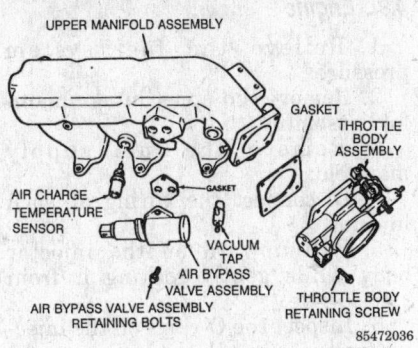

UPPER MANIFOLD ASSEMBLY

GASKET

THROTTLE BODY ASSEMBLY

AIR CHARGE TEMPERATURE SENSOR

GASKET

VACUUM TAP

AIR BYPASS VALVE ASSEMBLY

AIR BYPASS VALVE ASSEMBLY RETAINING BOLTS

THROTTLE BODY RETAINING SCREW

85472036

Upper intake manifold assembly — 2.9L engine

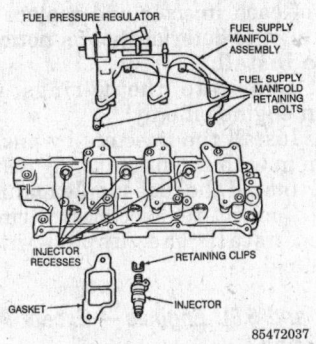

FUEL PRESSURE REGULATOR

FUEL SUPPLY MANIFOLD ASSEMBLY

FUEL SUPPLY MANIFOLD RETAINING BOLTS

INJECTOR RECESSES

RETAINING CLIPS

GASKET

INJECTOR

85472037

Fuel supply manifold assembly — 2.9L engine

2. Remove the air intake throttle body assembly as follows:

a. Remove the engine air cleaner outlet tube between the air cleaner and throttle body.

b. Remove the snow shield from the power steering pump bracket and accelerator cable bracket.

c. Tag and disconnect the vacuum lines at the vacuum fittings on the intake manifold and PCV hose.

d. Disconnect and remove the accelerator and cruise control cables from the accelerator mounting bracket and throttle lever.

e. Remove the alternator support brace.

f. Remove the throttle body-to-lower intake manifold retaining bolts and stud bolts. Remove the throttle body assembly.

3. Disconnect the fuel lines from the fuel supply manifold.

4. Disconnect the wiring harness from the injectors.

5. Disconnect the vacuum line from the fuel pressure regulator.

6. Remove the 4 fuel supply manifold retaining bolts.

7. Carefully disengage the fuel supply manifold from the fuel injec-

tors by lifting and gently rocking the manifold.

8. Remove the injectors by lifting while gently rocking from side-to-side. Remove and discard the O-rings.

To install:

9. Lubricate new O-rings with clean light grade oil and install 2 on each injector.

NOTE: Never use silicone grease at it will clog the injectors.

10. Install the injectors in the fuel supply manifold, using a light, twisting, pushing motion.

11. Carefully install the fuel supply manifold and injectors into the lower intake manifold, 1 side at a time. Push the fuel supply manifold down to ensure that all injector O-rings are fully seated in the fuel supply manifold cups and intake manifold.

12. While holding the fuel supply manifold in place, install the 2 retaining bolts hand-tight and then tighten to 6–8 ft. lbs. (8–12 Nm).

13. Repeat Steps 11 and 12 for the other side of the fuel supply manifold.

14. Connect the fuel supply and return lines.

15. After the fuel supply manifold has been installed and before the fuel injector wire connectors have been connected, connect the negative battery cable and turn the ignition **ON**. This will cause the fuel pump to run for 2–3 seconds and pressurize the fuel system.

16. Check for leaks where the fuel injector is installed into the fuel supply manifold.

17. Disconnect the negative battery cable.

18. Connect the fuel injector electrical connectors.

19. Install the air intake throttle body in the reverse order of removal. Tighten the bolts, in sequence, to 19 ft. lbs. (25 Nm).

20. Connect the vacuum line to the fuel pressure regulator.

21. Connect the negative battery cable, start the engine and let it idle for 2 minutes.

22. Turn the engine **OFF** and check for fuel leaks.

3.0L (VIN W) Engine

The engine is equipped with 6 fuel injectors, with one located at each cylinder.

1. Relieve the fuel pressure.

2. Remove the air cleaner from the throttle body.

3. Label and disconnect the vacuum hoses, electrical connectors and

throttle cable from the throttle body/upper intake manifold assembly.

4. Remove the upper intake manifold.

5. Disconnect the electrical connectors from the fuel injectors.

6. Disconnect the supply and return hoses from the fuel rail.

7. The injectors can be removed separately or as an assembly with the rail. Do not use the old O-rings or insulators when installing the injectors.

To install:

8. Replace the fuel injector O-rings.

9. Lubricate the fuel injector O-rings with automatic transmission fluid and press them into the fuel rail assembly.

10. Connect the electrical connectors to the fuel injectors.

11. Using a new gasket, install the upper intake manifold and torque the bolts to 16 ft. lbs. (22 Nm).

12. Connect the electrical connectors, the vacuum lines and the accelerator cable.

13. Install the air cleaner to the throttle body.

14. Turn the ignition switch **ON** and check for fuel leaks at the fuel rail.

4.0L Engine

1. Disconnect the negative battery cable and relieve the fuel system pressure.

2. Disconnect the electrical connectors at the air bypass valve, TPS and ACT sensor.

3. Remove the snow/ice shield to expose the throttle linkage. Remove the throttle cable bracket and disconnect the cable from the ball stud on the throttle body.

4. Remove the air inlet tube from the air cleaner to the throttle body.

5. Disconnect the PCV valve from the valve cover.

6. Disconnect the spark plug wires from the comb at the rear of the manifold.

7. Remove the canister purge line from the fitting in the throttle housing.

8. On Aerostar, remove the bolt retaining the engine oil dipstick tube.

9. Remove the bolt that retains the air conditioner line at the upper rear of the upper manifold.

10. Remove the 6 upper intake manifold retaining nuts and remove the upper intake and throttle body assembly.

11. Disconnect the fuel supply line fitting at the fuel manifold.

12. Disconnect the fuel return line from the fuel pressure regulator as follows:

   a. Disengage the locking tabs on the connector retainer and separate the retainer halves.

   b. Inspect the visible internal portion of the fitting for dirt accumulation. Clean the fitting before disassembly.

   c. To disengage the fitting from the regulator, push the fitting toward the regulator, insert the fingers on fuel line coupling key T90P-9550-A or equivalent, into the slots in the coupling.

   d. Using the tool, pull the fitting from the regulator.

NOTE: If the fitting has been properly disengaged, the fitting should slide off the regulator with minimum effort.

13. Disconnect the electrical connectors from the fuel injectors.

14. Remove the 6 bolts retaining the fuel supply manifold and remove the manifold.

15. Remove the injector retaining clips and remove the injectors from the manifold by grasping the injector body and pulling up while rocking the injector from side-to-side.

16. Remove and discard the injector O-rings.

17. Inspect the injector plastic pintle protection cap and washer for signs of deterioration. Replace the complete injector as required. If the plastic pintle protection cap is missing, look for it in the intake manifold.

NOTE: The plastic pintle protection cap is not available as a separate part.

To install:
18. Lubricate new O-rings with clean light grade oil and install 2 on each injector.

NOTE: Never use silicone grease at it will clog the injectors.

19. Install the injectors, using a light, twisting, pushing motion.

20. Install the fuel supply manifold, pushing down to make sure all the fuel injector O-rings are fully seated in the fuel supply manifold cups and intake manifold.

21. Install the 6 retaining bolts and tighten to 7–10 ft. lbs. (10–14 Nm). Install the retainer clips.

22. Install the fuel supply line and tighten the fitting to 15–18 ft. lbs. (20–24 Nm).

23. Install the fuel return line to the fuel pressure regulator by push-ing it onto the fuel pressure regulator line up to the shoulder on the regulator line.

NOTE: The connector should grip the regulator line securely.

24. Install the connector retainer and snap the 2 halves of the retainer together.

25. Clean and inspect the mounting faces of the fuel manifold and upper intake manifold.

26. Position a new gasket on the mounting studs and install the upper intake manifold on the studs.

27. Install the 6 upper intake manifold retaining nuts and tighten to 15–18 ft. lbs. (20–25 Nm).

28. Connect the spark plug wires to the retainer comb at the rear of the intake manifold.

29. Attach the air conditioner line retainer and automatic transmission vacuum line retainer at the upper intake manifold.

30. Install the canister purge line on the throttle body fitting.

31. Connect the vacuum lines to the vacuum tree. Connect the electrical connectors at the air bypass valve, TPS and ACT sensor.

32. Install the PCV valve in the grommet at the rear of the right valve cover.

33. On Aerostar, attach the engine oil dipstick tube to the upper intake manifold.

34. Attach the throttle cable bracket to the upper intake manifold, then connect the throttle cable to the ball stud and install the snow/ice shield.

35. After the upper intake manifold has been installed and before the fuel injector wire connectors have been connected, connect the negative battery cable and turn the ignition switch **ON**. This will cause the fuel pump to run for 2–3 seconds and pressurize the system.

36. Check for fuel leaks where the fuel injector is installed into the fuel supply manifold.

37. Turn the ignition switch **OFF** and disconnect the negative battery cable.

38. Connect the injector wire connectors and the vacuum line to the regulator.

39. Install the air inlet tube from the throttle body to the air cleaner.

40. Connect the negative battery cable, start the engine and let it idle for 2 minutes.

41. Turn the engine **OFF** and check for fuel leaks.

4.9L Engine

1. Relieve the fuel system pressure.

2. Remove the upper intake manifold assembly.

3. Remove the fuel supply manifold.

4. Disconnect the wiring at each injector.

5. Pull upward on the injector body while gently rocking it from side-to-side.

6. Inspect the O-rings on the injector for any sign of leakage or damage. Replace any suspected O-rings.

7. Inspect the plastic cap at the top of each injector and replace it if any sign of deterioration is noticed.

To install:
8. Lubricate the O-rings with clean engine oil only!

9. Install the injectors by pushing them in with a gentle rocking motion.

10. Install the fuel supply manifold.

11. Connect the electrical wiring.

12. Install the upper intake manifold.

5.0L and 5.8L Engines — Except Lightning

1. Relieve the fuel system pressure.

2. Disconnect the battery ground.

3. Remove the upper intake manifold.

4. Disconnect the wiring at the injectors.

5. Pull upward on the injector body while gently rocking it from side-to-side.

6. Inspect the O-rings on the injector for any sign of leakage or damage. Replace any suspected O-rings.

7. Inspect the plastic cap at the top of each injector and replace it if any sign of deterioration is noticed.

To install:
8. Lubricate the O-rings with clean engine oil !

9. Install the injectors by pushing them in with a gentle rocking motion.

10. Install the fuel supply manifold.

11. Connect the electrical wiring.

12. Install the upper intake manifold.

5.8L Engine Lightning

1. Relieve the fuel system pressure.

2. Disconnect the battery ground.

3. Remove the upper intake manifold.

4. Disconnect the wiring at the injectors.

5. Pull upward on the injector body while gently rocking it from side-to-side.

6. Inspect the O-rings on the injector for any sign of leakage or damage. Replace any suspected O-rings.

7. Inspect the plastic cap at the top of each injector and replace it if any sign of deterioration is noticed.

8. Lubricate the O-rings with clean engine oil only!

9. Install the injectors by pushing them in with a gentle rocking motion.

10. Install the fuel supply manifold.

11. Connect the electrical wiring.

12. Install the upper intake manifold.

7.5L Engine

1. Relieve the fuel system pressure.

2. Disconnect the battery ground.

3. Remove the fuel supply manifold.

4. Disconnect the wiring at the injectors.

5. Pull upward on the injector body while gently rocking it from side-to-side.

6. Inspect the O-rings (2 per injector) on the injector for any sign of leakage or damage. Replace any suspected O-rings.

7. Inspect the plastic cap at the top of each injector and replace it if any sign of deterioration is noticed.

To install:

8. Lubricate the O-rings with clean engine oil only!

9. Install the injectors by pushing them in with a gentle rocking motion.

10. Install the fuel supply manifold.

11. Connect the electrical wiring.

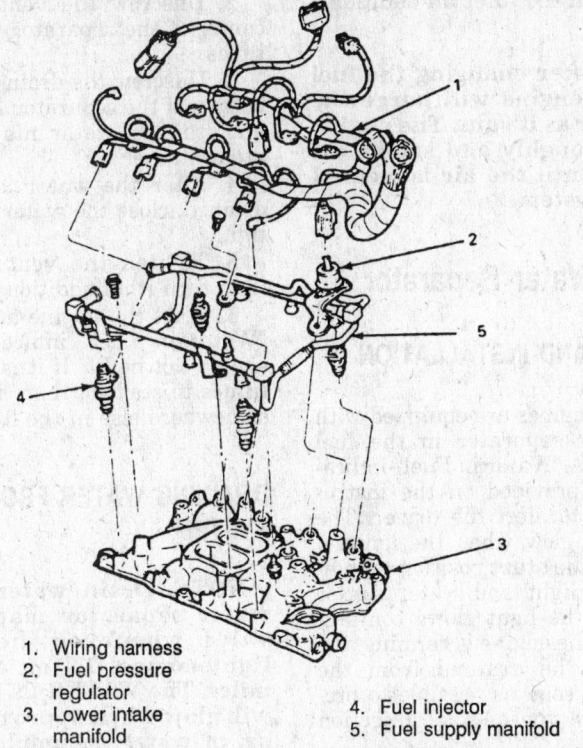

1. Wiring harness
2. Fuel pressure regulator
3. Lower intake manifold
4. Fuel injector
5. Fuel supply manifold

85472143

Fuel injector removal — 7.5L engine

DIESEL FUEL SYSTEM

Fuel System Service Precautions

Safety is the most important factor when performing not only fuel system maintenance but any type of maintenance. Failure to conduct maintenance and repairs in a safe manner may result in serious personal injury or death. Maintenance and testing of the vehicle's fuel system components can be accomplished safely and effectively by adhering to the following rules and guidelines.

• To avoid the possibility of fire and personal injury, always disconnect the negative battery cable unless the repair or test procedure requires that battery voltage be applied.

• Always relieve the fuel system pressure prior to disconnecting any fuel system component (injector, fuel rail, pressure regulator, etc.), fitting or fuel line connection. Exercise extreme caution whenever relieving fuel system pressure to avoid exposing skin, face and eyes to fuel spray. Please be advised that fuel under pressure may penetrate the skin or any part of the body that it contacts.

• Always place a shop towel or cloth around the fitting or connection prior to loosening to absorb any excess fuel due to spillage. Ensure that all fuel spillage (should it occur) is quickly removed from engine surfaces. Ensure that all fuel soaked cloths or towels are deposited into a suitable waste container.

• Always keep a dry chemical (Class B) fire extinguisher near the work area.

• Do not allow fuel spray or fuel vapors to come into contact with a spark or open flame.

• Always use a backup wrench when loosening and tightening fuel line connection fittings. This will prevent unnecessary stress and torsion to fuel line piping. Always follow the proper torque specifications.

• Always replace worn fuel fitting O-rings with new. Do not substitute fuel hose or equivalent where fuel pipe is installed.

Fuel Filter

REMOVAL AND INSTALLATION

The desel engine uses a one-piece spin-on fuel filter. Do not add fuel to the new fuel filter. Allow the engine to draw fuel through the filter.

1. Remove the spin-on filter by unscrewing it counterclockwise.

2. Clean the filter mounting surface.

3. Coat the gasket or the replacement filter with clean diesel fuel. This helps ensure a good seal.

4. Tighten the filter by hand until the gasket touches the filter mounting surface.

5. Tighten the filter an additional ½ turn.

NOTE: After changing the fuel filter, the engine will purge the trapped air as it runs. The engine may run roughly and smoke excessively until the air is cleared from the system.

Fuel/Water Separator

REMOVAL AND INSTALLATION

The diesel engines are equipped with a fuel/water separator in the fuel supply line. A "Water in Fuel" indicator light is provided on the instrument panel to alert the driver. The light should glow when the ignition switch is in the **start** position to indicate proper light and water sensor function. If the light glows continuously while the engine is running, the water must be drained from the separator as soon as possible to prevent damage to the fuel injection system.

1. Shut off the engine. Failure to shut the engine **OFF** before draining the separator will cause air to enter the system.

2. Unscrew the vent on the top center of the separator unit 2½ to 3 turns.

3. Unscrew the drain screw on the bottom of the separator 1½ to 2 turns and drain the water into an appropriate container.

4. After the water is completely drained, close the water drain finger tight.

5. Tighten the vent until snug, then turn it an additional ¼ turn.

6. Start the engine and check the "Water in Fuel" indicator light; it should not be lit. If it is lit and continues to stay so, there is a problem somewhere else in the fuel system.

DRAINING WATER FROM THE SYSTEM

NOTE: Drain water from the water separator manual drain valve whenever the warning light comes ON or every 5000 miles. The WATER IN FUEL light will glow when approximately 3.5 oz. of water accumulates in the separator.

1. Stop the vehicle and shut **OFF** the engine.

FUEL PRIMING VALVE AND CAP
CONTINUOUS VENT WITH CHECK VALVE
FILTER ASSEMBLY HEADER (F-SERIES)
VACUUM SWITCH (FUEL FILTER ELEMENT REPLACEMENT INDICATOR)
CONTINUOUS VENT WITH CHECK VALVE
FUEL PRIMING VALVE AND CAP
FUEL HEATER O-RING
FUEL HEATER
FILTER ASSEMBLY HEADER (E-SERIES)
THREADED INSERT
FUEL FILTER ELEMENT
DRAIN BOWL O-RING
DRAIN VALVE STEM CAP
DRAIN VALVE SEAL
WATER SEPARATOR DRAIN BOWL
WATER SENSOR PROBE
VENT/VALVE ASSEMBLY
MANUAL DRAIN VALVE (TURN TO DRAIN)
WATER SENSOR O-RING

85472144

Fuel filter/water separator assembly — 7.3L diesel engine

2. Place a container under the fuel filter/water separator drain tube to collect drain fluid.

3. Open the drain valve at the base of the water separator drain bowl. Allow the drain valve to remain open approximately 15 seconds or until clear, water-free diesel fuel flows from the drain tube.

4. Close the drain valve. Start the engine and make sure the WATER IN FUEL light is not on.

Diesel Fuel Pump

REMOVAL AND INSTALLATION

1. Loosen the threaded connections with the proper size wrench (a flare nut wrench is preferred) and re-tighten snugly. Do not remove the lines at this time.

2. Loosen the mounting bolts, 1–2 turns. Apply force by hand to loosen the fuel pump if the gasket is stuck. Rotate the engine by nudging the starter, until the fuel pump cam lobe is at the low position. At this position, spring tension against the fuel pump bolts will be greatly reduced.

3. Disconnect the fuel supply pump inlet, outlet and fuel return line.

4. Remove the fuel pump attaching bolts and remove the pump and gasket. Discard the old gasket.

5. Remove the remaining fuel pump gasket material from the engine and from the fuel pump if reinstalling the old pump. Make sure both mounting surfaces are clean.

To install:

6. Install the attaching bolts into the fuel supply pump and install a new gasket on the bolts. Position the fuel pump onto the mounting pad. Turn the attaching bolts alternately and evenly and tighten the bolts to the specifications according to the size bolts used on the pump. See the accompanying standard torque chart for reference.

NOTE: The cam must be at its low position before attempting to install the fuel supply pump. If it is difficult to start the mounting bolts, remove the pump and reinstall with a lever on the bottom side of the cam.

7. Install the fuel outlet line. Start the fitting by hand to avoid crossthreading.

8. Install the inlet line and the fuel return line.

9. Start the engine and observe all connections for fuel leaks for 2 minutes.

10. Stop the engine and check all fuel supply pump fuel line connections. Check for oil leaks at the pump mounting pad.

Diesel Fuel Injectors

REMOVAL AND INSTALLATION

NOTE: Before removing the nozzle assemblies, clean the exterior of each nozzle assembly and the surrounding area with clean fuel oil or solvent to prevent entry of dirt into the engine when nozzle assemblies are removed. Also, clean the fuel inlet and fuel leak-off piping connections. Blow dry with compressed air.

1. Remove the fuel line retaining clamp(s) from the nozzle lines that are to be removed.

2. Disconnect the nozzle fuel inlet (high pressure) and fuel leak-off tees from each nozzle assembly and position out of the way. Cover the open ends of the fuel inlet and outlet or nozzles with protective caps, to prevent dirt from entering.

3. Remove the injection nozzles by turning them counterclockwise. Pull the nozzle assembly with the copper washer attached from the engine. Cover the nozzle fuel opening and spray tip, with plastic caps, to prevent the entry of dirt.

NOTE: Remove the copper injector nozzle gasket from the nozzle bore with special tool, T71P–19703–C, or equivalent, whenever the gasket does not come out with the nozzle.

4. Place the nozzle assemblies in a fabricated holder as they are removed from the heads. The holder should be marked with numbers corresponding to the cylinder numbering of the engine. This will allow for reinstallation of the nozzle in the same ports from which they were removed.

To install:

5. Thoroughly clean the nozzle bore in cylinder head before reinserting the nozzle assembly with nozzle seat cleaner, special tool T83T–9527–A or equivalent. Make certain that no small particles of metal or carbon remain on the seating surface. Blow out the particles with compressed air.

6. Remove the protective cap and install a new copper gasket on the nozzle assembly, with a small dab of grease.

NOTE: Anti-seize compound or equivalent should be used on nozzle threads to aid in installation and future removal.

7. Install the nozzle assembly into the cylinder head nozzle bore.

8. Tighten the nozzle assembly to 33 ft. lbs.

9. Remove the protective caps from nozzle assemblies and fuel lines.

10. Install the leak-off tees to the nozzle assemblies.

NOTE: Install 2 new O-ring seals for each fuel return tee.

11. Connect the high pressure fuel line and tighten, using a flare nut wrench.

12. Install the fuel line retainer clamps.

13. Start the engine and check for leaks.

Diesel Injection Pump

REMOVAL AND INSTALLATION

— **WARNING** —

Before removing the fuel lines, clean the exterior with clean fuel oil or solvent to prevent entry of dirt into the engine when the fuel lines are removed. Do not wash or steam clean engine while engine is running. Serious damage to injection pump could occur.

1. Disconnect battery ground cables from both batteries.

2. Remove the engine oil filler neck.

3. Remove the bolts attaching injection pump to drive gear.

4. Disconnect the electrical connectors to injection pump.

5. Disconnect the accelerator cable and speed control cable from throttle lever, if equipped.

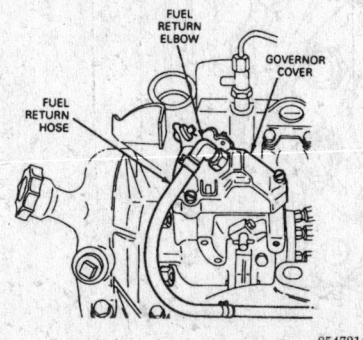

Fuel return line location — 7.3L diesel engine

6. Remove the air cleaner and install clean rags to prevent dirt from entering the intake manifold.

7. Remove the accelerator cable bracket, with cables attached, from the intake manifold and position out of the way.

NOTE: All fuel lines and fittings must be capped using Fuel System Protective Cap Set T83T–9395–A or equivalent, to prevent fuel contamination.

8. Remove the fuel filter-to-injection pump fuel line and cap fittings.

9. Remove and cap the injection pump inlet elbow and the injection pump fitting adapter.

10. Remove the fuel return line on injection pump, rotate out of the way, And cap all fittings.

NOTE: It is not necessary to remove injection lines from injection pump. If lines are to be removed, loosen injection line fittings at injection pump before removing it from engine.

11. Remove the fuel injection lines from the nozzles and cap lines and nozzles.

12. Remove the 3 nuts attaching the Injection pump to injection pump adapter using Tool T83T–9000–B.

13. If the injection pump is to be replaced, loosen the injection line retaining clips and the injection nozzle fuel lines with Tool T83T–9396–A and cap all fittings at this time with protective cap set T83T–9395–A or equivalent. Do not install the injection nozzle fuel lines until the new pump is installed in the engine.

14. Lift the Injection pump, with the nozzle lines attached, up and out of the engine compartment.

— **WARNING** —

Do not carry injection pump by injection nozzle fuel lines as this could cause lines to bend or crimp.

To install:

15. Install a new O-ring on the drive gear end of the injection pump.

16. Move the injection pump down and into position.

17. Position the alignment dowel on injection pump into the alignment hole on drive gear.

18. Install the bolts attaching the injection pump to drive gear and tighten.

19. Install the nuts attaching injection pump to adapter. Align scribe lines on the injection pump flange and the injection pump adapter and tighten to 14 ft. lbs.

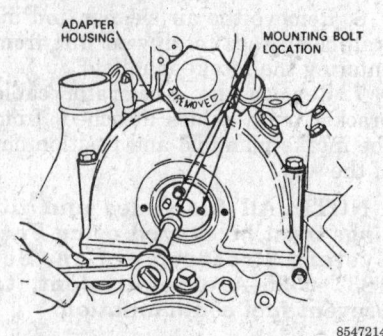

Injection pump drive gear attaching bolt removal — 7.3L diesel engine

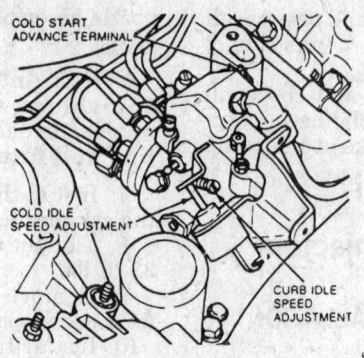

Idle speed adjusting screw location — 7.3L diesel engine

20. If the injection nozzle fuel lines were removed from the injection pump install at this time.

21. Remove the caps from nozzles and the fuel lines and install the fuel line nuts on the nozzles and tighten to 22 ft. lbs.

22. Connect the fuel return line to injection pump and tighten the nuts.

23. Install the injection pump fitting adapter with a new O-ring.

24. Clean the old sealant from the injection pump elbow threads, using clean solvent, and dry thoroughly.

Apply a light coating of pipe sealant to the elbow threads.

25. Install the elbow in the injection pump adapter and tighten to to a minimum of 6 ft. lbs. Then tighten further, if necessary, to align the elbow with the injection pump fuel inlet line, but do not exceed 360 degrees of rotation or 10 ft. lbs.

26. Remove the caps and connect the fuel filter-to-injection pump fuel line.

27. Install the accelerator cable bracket to the intake manifold.

28. Remove the rags from the intake manifold and install the air cleaner.

29. Connect the accelerator and speed control cable, if equipped, to throttle lever.

30. Install the electrical connectors on injection pump.

31. Clean the injection pump adapter and oil filler neck sealing surfaces.

32. Apply a 1/8 in. (3mm) bead of RTV sealant on the adapter housing.

33. Install the oil filler neck and tighten the bolts.

34. Connect the battery ground cables to both batteries.

35. Run the engine and check for fuel leaks.

36. If necessary, purge high pressure fuel lines of air by loosening connector 1/2–1 turn and cranking engine until solid fuel, free from bubbles flows from connection.

CAUTION

Keep eyes and hands away from nozzle spray. Fuel spraying from the nozzle under high pressure can penetrate the skin.

---

37. Check and adjust injection pump timing.

Fuel Lines

REMOVAL AND INSTALLATION

NOTE: Before removing any fuel lines, clean the exterior with clean fuel oil, or solvent to prevent entry of dirt into fuel system when the fuel lines are removed. Blow dry with compressed air.

1. Disconnect the battery ground cables from both batteries.

2. Remove the air cleaner and cap intake manifold opening with clean rags.

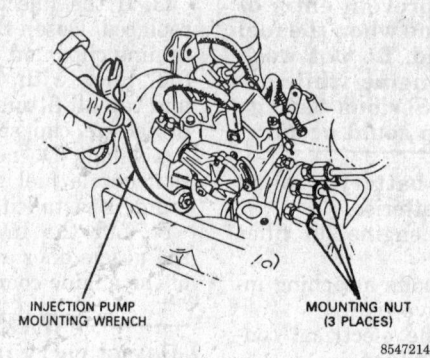

Injection pump removal and installation — 7.3L diesel engine

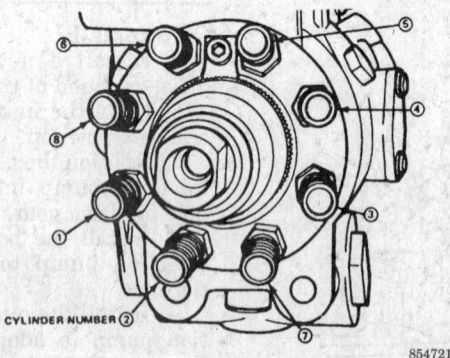

Injection pump cylinder numbering sequence — 7.3L diesel engine

3. Disconnect the accelerator cable and speed control cable, if equipped, from the injection pump.

4. remove the accelerator cable bracket from the intake manifold and position out of the way with cable(s) attached.

---------- **WARNING** ----------
To prevent fuel system contamination, cap all fuel lines and fittings.

---

5. Disconnect the fuel line from the fuel filter to injection pump and cap all fittings.

6. Disconnect and cap the nozzle fuel lines at nozzles.

7. Remove the fuel line clamps from the fuel lines to be removed.

8. Remove and cap the injection pump inlet elbow.

9. Remove and cap the inlet fitting adapter.

10. Remove the injection nozzle lines, 1 at a time, from injection pump using Tool T83T–9396–A.

NOTE: Fuel lines must be removed following this sequence: 5–6–4–8–3–1–7–2. Install caps on the end of each fuel line and pump fitting as the line is disconnected and identify each fuel line accordingly.

To install:

11. Install fuel lines on injection pump, 1 at a time, and tighten to 22 ft.lbs.

NOTE: Fuel lines must be installed in the sequence: 2–7–1–3–8–4–6–5.

12. Clean the old sealant from the injection pump elbow, using clean solvent, and dry thoroughly.

13. Apply a light coating of pipe sealant on the elbow threads.

Diesel Injection Timing

ADJUSTMENT

Static Timing

1. Break the torque of the injection pump mounting nuts (keeping the nuts snug).

2. Rotate the injection pump using Tool T83–9000–C or equivalent to bring the mark on the pump into alignment with the mark on pump mounting adapter.

3. Visually recheck the alignment of the timing marks and tighten injection pump mounting nuts.

Dynamic Timing

1. Bring the engine up to normal operating temperature.

2. Stop the engine and install a dynamic timing meter, Rotunda 78–0100 or equivalent, by placing the magnetic probe pick-up into the probe hole.

3. Remove the no. 1 glow plug wire and remove the glow plug, install the luminosity probe and tighten to 12 ft.lbs. Install the photocell over the probe.

4. Connect the dynamic timing meter to the battery and adjust the offset of the meter.

5. Set the transmission in neutral and raise the rear wheels off the ground. Using Rotunda 14–0302, throttle control, set the engine speed to 1,400 rpm with no accessory load. Observe the injection timing on the dynamic timing meter.

NOTE: Obtain the fuel sample from the vehicle and check the cetane value using the tester supplied with the Ford special tools 78–0100 or equivalent.

6. If the dynamic timing is not within ± 2 degrees of specification, then the injection pump timing will require adjustment.

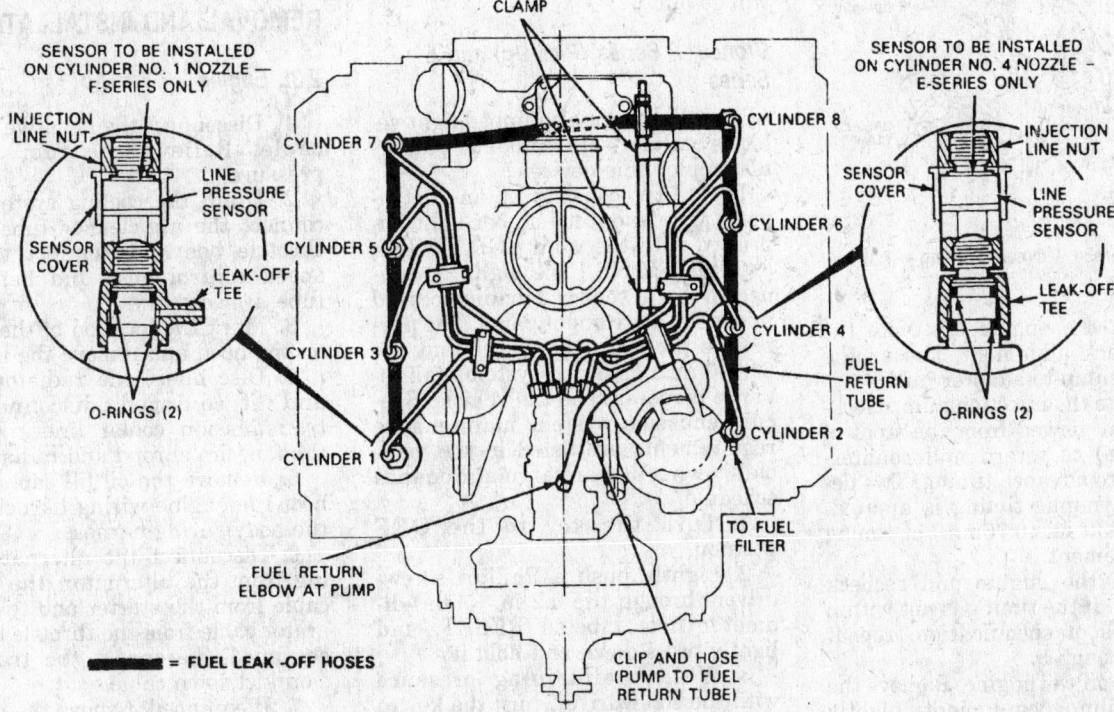

Diesel fuel routing and installation — 7.3L diesel engine

85472153

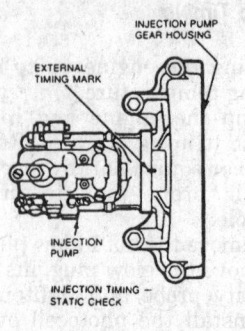

Injection pump timing marks — 7.3L diesel engine

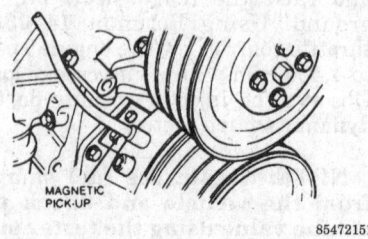

Magnetic pickup — dynamic timing — 7.3L diesel engine

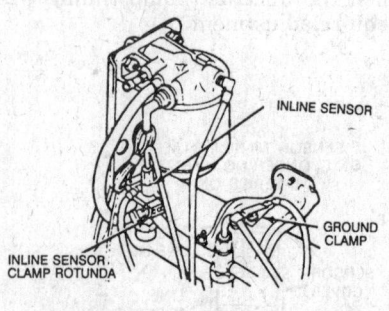

Luminosity probe — dynamic timing — 7.3L diesel engine

7. Turn the engine off. Note the timing mark alignment. Loosen the injection pump-to-adapter nuts.

8. Rotate the injection pump clockwise (when viewed from the front of the engine) to retard and counterclockwise to advance timing. Two degrees of dynamic timing is approximately 0.030 in. (0.76mm) of timing mark movement.

9. Start the engine and recheck the timing. If the timing is not within ± 1 degree of specification, repeat steps 7 through 9.

10. Turn off the engine. Remove the dynamic timing equipment. Lightly

coat the glow plug thread with anti-seize compound, install the glow plugs and tighten to 12 ft. lbs. Connect the glow plug wires.

EMISSION CONTROLS

Emission Warning Lamps

RESETTING

Except 2.3L Engine, Bronco, F Series (Pick-Up) and E Series

All vehicles are equipped with a "CHECK ENGINE" or "SERVICE ENGINE SOON" warning lamp located on the instrument cluster. This lamp should come on briefly when the ignition key is turned **ON**, but should turn off when the engine starts. If the lamp does not come ON when the ignition key is turned **ON** or if it comes ON and stays ON when the engine is running, there is a malfunction in the electronic engine control system. After the malfunction has been remedied, using the proper procedures, the "CHECK ENGINE" or "SERVICE ENGINE SOON" lamp will go out.

Bronco, F Series (Pick-Up) and E Series

All gasoline engine equipped light vehicles built for sale outside of California employ this device.

The EMW consists of an instrument panel mounted amber light imprinted with the word EGR, EMISS, or EMISSIONS. The light is connected to a sensor module located under the instrument panel. The purpose is the warn the driver that the 60,000 mile emission system maintenance is required on the vehicle. Specific emission system maintenance requirements are listed in the vehicle's owner's manual maintenance schedule.

1. Turn the key to the **OFF** position.

2. Lightly push a Phillips screwdriver through the 0.2 in. (5mm) diameter hole labeled RESET, and lightly press down and hold it.

3. While maintaining pressure with the screwdriver, turn the key to the **RUN** position. The EMW lamp will light and stay lit as long as pressure is kept on the screwdriver. Hold

the screwdriver down for about 5 seconds.

4. Remove the screwdriver. The lamp should go out within 2–5 seconds. If not, repeat Steps 1–3.

5. Turn the key **OFF**.

6. Turn the key to the **RUN** position. The lamp will light for 2–5 seconds and then go out. If not, repeat the rest procedure.

NOTE: If the light comes ON between 15,000 and 45,000 miles or between 75,000 and 105,000 miles, replace the 1,000 hour pre-timed module.

ENGINE MECHANICAL

NOTE: Disconnecting the negative battery cable on some vehicles may interfere with the functions of the on board computer systems and may require the computer to undergo a relearning process, once the negative battery cable is reconnected.

Engine Assembly

REMOVAL AND INSTALLATION

2.3L Engine

1. Disconnect the negative battery cable. Relieve the fuel system pressure.

2. Drain the cooling system. Disconnect the air cleaner tube at the throttle body. Disconnect the idle speed control hose and heat riser tube, if necessary.

3. Mark the location of the hinges on the hood and remove the hood.

4. Disconnect the radiator hoses and, if equipped, disconnect the transmission cooler lines. Remove the fan, fan shroud and radiator.

5. Remove the oil fill cap. Disconnect the engine wiring harness from the body wiring harness.

6. Disconnect the alternator wiring from the alternator, the starter cable from the starter and the accelerator cable from the throttle body. If equipped, disconnect the transmission kickdown cable.

7. If equipped, remove the air conditioner compressor from the mounting bracket and position aside, leaving the refrigerant lines attached.

8. Disconnect the power brake vacuum hose. Disconnect the fuel lines from the fuel supply manifold.

9. Disconnect the heater hoses from the engine.

10. Remove the engine mount nuts. Raise and safely support the vehicle.

11. Drain the engine oil from the crankcase and remove the starter.

12. Disconnect the exhaust pipe at the exhaust manifold. If equipped with manual transmission, remove the dust cover. If equipped with automatic transmission, remove the converter inspection plate, then remove the converter-to-flywheel bolts.

13. Remove the lower flywheel housing or converter housing attaching bolts and lower the vehicle.

14. Support the transmission and flywheel housing or converter housing with a jack.

15. Remove the flywheel housing or converter housing upper attaching bolts.

16. Attach suitable engine lifting equipment. Carefully lift the engine out of the vehicle and install on a workstand.

To install:

17. Remove the engine from the workstand and carefully lower it into the engine compartment. If equipped with automatic transmission, start the converter pilot into the crankshaft.

18. If equipped with manual transmission, start the transmission input shaft into the clutch disc. It may be necessary to adjust the position of the transmission in relation to the engine if the input shaft will not enter the clutch disc. If the engine hangs up after the shaft enters, turn the crankshaft in the clockwise direction slowly, transmission in gear, until the shaft splines mesh with the clutch disc splines.

19. Install the flywheel or converter housing attaching bolts and remove the engine lifting equipment.

20. Remove the jack from under the vehicle and raise and safely support the vehicle.

21. If equipped with automatic transmission, install the converter-to-flywheel attaching bolts. Install the lower flywheel housing or converter housing attaching bolts and install the dust plate or converter inspection cover.

22. Connect the exhaust pipe to the exhaust manifold. Install the starter and connect the starter cable.

23. Lower the vehicle and install the engine mount nuts. Tighten to 65–85 ft. lbs. (88–115 Nm).

24. Connect the heater hoses to the engine and the fuel lines to the fuel supply manifold or fuel pump. Connect the power brake vacuum hose.

25. Connect the wiring to the alternator and the accelerator cable to the throttle body. If equipped, connect the transmission kickdown rod.

26. If equipped, install the air conditioning compressor in its mounting brackets.

27. Connect the engine wiring harness to the body wiring harness.

28. Install the fan, fan shroud and radiator. Connect the radiator hoses and, if equipped, the transmission cooler lines.

29. Install the hood, aligning the hinges with the marks that were made during removal.

30. Connect the air cleaner outlet tube at the throttle body. Connect the idle speed control hose and heat riser tube, if necessary.

31. Fill the crankcase with the proper type and quantity of engine oil. Install the oil cap.

32. Connect the negative battery cable. Fill and bleed the cooling system. Run the engine and check for leaks.

2.9L Engine

1. Disconnect the negative battery cable and relieve the fuel system pressure. Drain the cooling system.

2. Mark the position of the hood on the hinges and remove the hood. Remove the air cleaner intake hose.

3. Disconnect the radiator hoses and, if equipped with automatic transmission, disconnect the transmission cooler lines. Remove the fan shroud and radiator.

4. Remove the alternator and bracket and position the alternator aside. Disconnect the alternator ground wire from the engine block.

5. If equipped, remove the air conditioning compressor and power steering pump and position aside.

6. Disconnect the heater hoses at the intake manifold and water pump. Remove the ground wires from the cylinder block.

7. Disconnect the fuel lines from the fuel supply manifold. Disconnect the throttle cable shield and linkage at the throttle body and intake manifold.

8. Tag and disconnect all necessary vacuum lines and electrical connectors.

9. Raise and safely support the vehicle.

10. Disconnect the exhaust pipes from the exhaust manifolds. Discon-

nect the starter cable and remove the starter.

11. If equipped with manual transmission, remove the flywheel housing attaching bolts and remove the hydraulic clutch hose.

12. Remove the engine front mount-to-crossmember attaching nuts or through bolts.

13. If equipped with automatic transmission, remove the converter inspection cover and disconnect the converter from the flywheel.

14. Remove the cable. Remove the converter housing-to-engine bolts and the adapter plate-to-converter housing bolt.

15. Lower the vehicle and position a jack under the transmission. Install suitable engine lifting equipment.

16. Raise the engine slightly and carefully pull it from the transmission. Carefully lift the engine out of the engine compartment so the rear cover plate is not bent or components damaged. Install the engine on a workstand.

To install:

17. Remove the engine from the workstand and lower it carefully into the engine compartment. Make sure the exhaust manifolds are properly aligned with the exhaust pipe.

18. If equipped with manual transmission, start the transmission input shaft into the clutch disc. It may be necessary to adjust the position of the transmission in relation to the engine if the input shaft will not enter the clutch disc. If the engine hangs up after the shaft enters, turn the crankshaft in the clockwise direction slowly, transmission in gear, until the shaft splines mesh with the clutch disc splines.

19. Install the flywheel housing or converter housing upper bolts, making sure the dowels in the engine block engage the flywheel housing or converter housing. Tighten the bolts to 33–45 ft. lbs. (45–61 Nm).

20. Install the clutch hose and remove the jack from under the transmission. Remove the engine lifting equipment.

21. If equipped with automatic transmission, position the kickdown rod on the transmission and engine. Raise and safely support the vehicle.

22. If equipped with automatic transmission, position the transmission linkage bracket and install the remaining converter housing bolts. Install the adapter plate-to-converter housing bolt. Install the converter-to-flywheel nuts and the inspection cover. Connect the kickdown rod on the transmission.

23. If equipped with manual transmission, install the flywheel housing attaching bolts.

24. Install the starter and connect the cable. Connect the exhaust pipes at the exhaust manifolds.

25. Install the engine front mount-to-crossmember attaching nuts or through bolts. Lower the vehicle.

26. Connect all vacuum hoses and electrical connectors to the locations marked during removal.

27. Install the throttle linkage and connect the fuel lines. Connect the heater hoses at the water pump and engine block.

28. Install the alternator and bracket and connect the ground wire to the engine block. Install the drive belt and adjust the tension.

29. Install the air conditioning compressor and power steering pump, if equipped.

30. Install the radiator and fan shroud. Connect the radiator hoses and, if equipped, transmission cooler lines.

31. Connect the negative battery cable. Fill and bleed the cooling system. Run the engine and check for leaks.

32. If equipped, evacuate and charge the air conditioning system.

33. Install the intake hose. Install the hood, aligning the hinges with the marks that were made during removal.

3.0L Engine

AEROSTAR

1. Disconnect the negative battery cable and relieve the fuel system pressure. Drain the cooling system.

2. Disconnect the upper and lower radiator hoses.

3. Remove the air cleaner hose assembly. Removal should take place at the clamp retaining the hose to the air cleaner housing assembly.

4. Remove the engine fan retaining nut or bolts and remove the fan. Remove the fan shroud retaining screws and remove the shroud.

5. Disconnect the Barometric Manifold Absolute Pressure (BMAP) sensor electrical connector and vacuum line located on the dash panel.

6. Remove the shroud covering the throttle linkage and disconnect the linkage at the throttle body.

7. Loosen the idler arm and alternator jack screw retaining bolts and remove the accessory drive belts.

8. Disconnect the injector harness connector from the main harness. Disconnect the engine coolant temperature sensor, located near the thermostat housing and the engine coolant temperature sender.

9. Disconnect the canister purge solenoid hoses from both sides of the solenoid. If equipped with power steering, disconnect the pump pressure switch.

10. Mark the inlet and outlet heater hoses with chalk prior to removing them from the engine side of the ballast tube.

11. Remove the breather tubes from the air cleaner and rocker arm cover.

12. If equipped with automatic transmission, disconnect the transmission cooler lines from the radiator. Remove the radiator.

13. If equipped with air conditioning, remove the compressor retaining bolts and retain it to a sidemember with mechanics wire.

14. Disconnect the oil fill tube from the alternator bracket. If equipped with automatic transmission, disconnect the transmission fill tube from the manifold and gently pull out from the top of the vehicle.

15. Disconnect the electrical connectors from the alternator and the brake booster vacuum line from the booster. Remove the bolt retaining the steering gear at the top of the shaft.

16. From inside the vehicle, remove the engine cover. Tag and disconnect the electrical connectors for the radio frequency interference suppressor, distributor TFI module and oil pressure sender.

17. Disconnect the fuel lines from the fuel supply manifold.

18. If equipped with manual transmission, place the shift lever in **N** and remove the screws retaining the shift lever boot to the floor. Slide the boot up the shift lever. Remove the bolt retaining the shift lever assembly to the transmission and remove the lever assembly.

19. Raise and safely support the vehicle. Disconnect the oil level sensor connector from the oil pan.

20. Mark the driveshaft to flange position. From the rear of the vehicle, remove the 4 bolts retaining the driveshaft. Slide the driveshaft forward, pull down, then pull out to release. Set the driveshaft aside.

21. Remove the bolt retaining the speedometer cable bracket to the transmission. Pull the speedometer out of the rear of the transmission.

22. Remove the starter ground strap and remove the battery connection to the starter. Remove the starter bolts and remove the starter.

23. If equipped with manual transmission, disconnect the coupling at the transmission with tool T88T-70522-A or equivalent, by sliding the white plastic sleeve toward the slave cylinder while applying a slight tug on the tube.

24. If equipped with manual transmission, disconnect the backup lamp switch and neutral sensing switch wires from the transmission.

25. If equipped with automatic transmission, proceed as follows:

   a. Disconnect the electrical connectors for the neutral safety switch and 3–4 shift solenoid connectors. Disconnect the selector and kickdown cable from the transmission lever.

   b. Disconnect the vacuum hose from the transmission vacuum modulator.

   c. Remove the converter access cover and adapter plate bolts from the lower end of the converter housing.

   d. Remove the flywheel-to-converter attaching nuts. Place a 22mm socket and breaker bar on the crankshaft pulley bolt in order to turn the crankshaft and gain access to the flywheel-to-converter nuts.

   e. Disconnect the transmission cooler lines from the transmission.

26. Disconnect the oxygen sensor.

27. Position a jack under the transmission and a safety chain around the transmission. Slightly raise the transmission.

28. Remove the mount-to-crossmember attaching nuts. Remove the nuts and bolts attaching the crossmember to the 2 mounting brackets and remove the crossmember. If required, remove the bolts attaching the mount to the transmission and remove the mount.

29. Remove the converter housing-to-engine fasteners. Move the transmission to the rear so it disengages from the dowel pins and the converter disengages from the flywheel. Lower the transmission from the vehicle.

30. Disconnect and remove the exhaust pipe and catalytic converter. Remove both front wheel and tire assemblies.

31. Remove the engine block ground straps, 1 on the cylinder head just behind the power steering pump and the other just above where the exhaust manifold and exhaust pipe connect.

32. Remove the bar nuts and disconnect the stabilizer bar from the lower control arms. Discard the bar nuts.

33. Behind the spindles, disconnect and plug the brake lines at the bracket on the frame.

34. Position a jack under the lower control arm and raise the arm until tension is applied to the coil spring. Remove the bolt and nut retaining the spindle to the upper control arm ball joint. Slowly lower the jack to disconnect the spindle from the ball joint. Install safety chains around the lower control arm and spring seat.

35. Position drive train removal lift 109-00002 or equivalent, under the crossmember and engine assembly.

36. Slowly lower the vehicle until the crossmember rests on the removal lift. Place wood blocks under the front crossmember and rear of the engine block to keep the engine and crossmember assembly level. Install safety chains around the crossmember and lift.

37. With the engine and crossmember securely supported on the lift, remove the 3 nuts from the bolts that retain the engine crossmember assembly to the frame on each side of the vehicle.

38. Slowly lower the engine assembly out of the vehicle, making sure the air conditioning compressor and wiring harnesses do not interfere. When the assembly is clear, roll the lift out from under the vehicle.

39. Separate the engine from the crossmember and position on a workstand.

To install:

40. Remove the engine from the workstand. With the front crossmember securely positioned on drive train removal lift 109-00002 or equivalent, slowly lower the engine until the motor mount studs enter the crossmember holes. Install the retaining nuts and tighten to 71–94 ft. lbs. (96–127 Nm).

NOTE: Install wood blocks under the oil pan and crossmember.

41. Roll the removal lift under the vehicle. Align the lift, engine and crossmember assembly so the 3 mounting bolts on each side of the frame are in alignment with the holes in the crossmember.

42. Slowly lower the vehicle so the bolts are piloted in the crossmember holes. Raise the lift or lower the vehicle so the crossmember is against the frame. Install the nuts retaining the crossmember to the frame and tighten to 145–195 ft. lbs. (196–264 Nm). Raise the vehicle and remove the lift.

43. If equipped with automatic transmission, position the converter

to the transmission making sure the converter hub is fully engaged in the pump gear. When the torque converter is fully installed, the distance between the converter pilot and the front of the converter housing should be 7/16–9/16 in. Make sure the converter rotates freely and is not binding.

44. If equipped with manual transmission, install the transmission on a jack and lift into position. Make sure the transmission input shaft engages the pilot bearing in the flywheel and the flywheel housing holes are aligned with the engine block dowel pins. Install the flywheel housing-to-engine block bolts and tighten to 28–38 ft. lbs. (38–51 Nm).

45. If equipped with automatic transmission, place the transmission on a jack and secure with safety chains. Rotate the converter so the drive studs are aligned with the flywheel holes. Lift the transmission into position and connect the transmission cooler lines to the case. Move the transmission forward into position, making sure the converter housing holes align with the engine block dowel pins. Install the converter housing-to-engine block bolts and tighten to 28–38 ft. lbs. (38–51 Nm).

46. Position the crossmember in the 2 mounting brackets and install the mounting nuts and bolts. Slowly lower the transmission so the mount studs are installed in the proper slots in the crossmember. Install the nuts and tighten to 71–94 ft. lbs. (97–127 Nm). Remove the safety chain and the jack.

47. Install the starter and tighten the mounting bolts to 15–20 ft. lbs. (21–27 Nm). Connect the starter cable.

48. If equipped with automatic transmission, connect the modulator vacuum hose. Position the selector cable in the case bracket and press the end of the cable on the ball stud on the lower portion of the selector lever. Install the retainer in the bracket.

49. If equipped with manual transmission, install the speedometer cable or connect the electronic speedometer wire. Connect the backup lamp and neutral sensor wires.

50. Remove the cap from the hydraulic clutch line. Insert the male coupling into the female coupling on the slave cylinder and make sure the connection is secure.

51. Install the manual transmission shift lever to the shifter. Position the rubber shift boot on the floor and install the screws.

52. If equipped with automatic transmission, install the kickdown and selector cable. Adjust the cable. Connect the neutral safety switch, converter clutch solenoid and 3–4 shift solenoid connectors. Insert the speedometer driven gear into the transmission and retain with a clamp. Tighten the retaining screw to 20–25 inch lbs. (2.25–2.82).

53. Position a 22mm socket and breaker bar on the crankshaft pulley bolt. Rotate the pulley clockwise, as viewed from the front, to gain access to each torque converter studs. Install the nuts on the studs and tighten to 20–34 ft. lbs. (27–46 Nm).

54. Position the converter access cover and adapter plate on the converter housing. Install the bolts and tighten to 12–16 ft. lbs. (16–22 Nm).

55. Remove the safety chains from around the lower control arms and spring seat. Install a jack under the lower control arms. Slowly raise the control arm until the coil spring is under tension. Continue to raise the arm until the spindle is connected to the upper arm ball joint. Install a new nut and bolt and tighten to 27–37 ft. lbs. (37–50 Nm).

56. Connect the stabilizer bar to the lower control arms. Install new bar nuts and tighten to 12–18 ft. lbs. (16–24 Nm).

57. Connect the front brake lines to the caliper hoses at the frame brackets. Install the wheel and tire assemblies.

58. Install the driveshaft, aligning the marks that were made during removal.

59. Install new gaskets on the exhaust manifold and catalytic converter. Install the exhaust pipe and catalytic converter. Tighten the converter-to-muffler nuts and bolts to 18–26 ft. lbs. (25–35 Nm). Tighten the exhaust pipe-to-exhaust manifold nuts to 25–34 ft. lbs. (34–46 Nm).

60. Connect the oxygen sensor connector and install the engine ground straps. Connect the fuel lines and the low-oil level sensor.

61. If equipped with automatic transmission, connect the transmission oil cooler lines. Install the transmission oil fill tube and lower the vehicle.

62. From inside the vehicle, connect the radio frequency interference suppressor, TFI module connector and oil pressure sender. Install the engine cover.

63. Connect the alternator electrical connectors and the brake booster vacuum hose. Connect the breather tube to the oil filler tube and attach

the bolt retaining the steering gear to the top of the shaft.

64. If equipped, connect the power steering pressure switch. Connect the heater hoses to the ballast tube by matching the chalk lines to the specific inlet and outlet hoses.

65. Install the radiator. If equipped, connect the transmission oil cooler lines.

66. Connect the canister purge solenoid hoses from both sides of the solenoid. Connect the engine coolant temperature sensor, located near the thermostat housing and connect the engine coolant temperature sender.

67. If equipped with air conditioning, untie the compressor from the sidemember and position on the mounting bracket. Install the attaching bolts.

68. Install the alternator belt and tighten the idler arm. Place the injector harness behind the belt tension idler arm and tighten the idler arm.

69. Connect the throttle linkage to the ball stud located on the throttle body. Connect the shroud covering the throttle body.

70. Connect the BMAP sensor electrical connector and vacuum line located on the dash panel.

71. Install the fan and fan shroud. Connect the radiator hoses.

72. Connect the negative battery cable and install the air cleaner and duct assembly.

73. Bleed the brakes and the hydraulic clutch. Fill and bleed the cooling system. Check all fluid levels.

74. Run the engine and check for leaks and proper operation. Check the front end alignment.

RANGER

1. Disconnect the negative battery cable and relieve the fuel system pressure. Drain the cooling system.

2. Mark the position of the hood on the hinges and remove the hood. Remove the air cleaner intake hose.

3. Disconnect the radiator hoses at the radiator. Remove the fan shroud attaching bolts and position the shroud over the fan. Remove the radiator, then remove the shroud.

4. Remove the alternator and bracket and position the alternator aside. Disconnect the alternator ground wire from the cylinder block.

5. Remove the air conditioner compressor and power steering pump and position aside, if equipped.

6. Disconnect the heater hoses at the intake manifold and water pump. Remove the ground wires from the cylinder block.

7. Disconnect the fuel lines at the chassis to engine connections. Dis-

connect the throttle cable shield and linkage at the throttle body and intake manifold.

8. Tag and disconnect the vacuum connections at the rear fitting in the upper intake manifold.

9. Tag and disconnect the wires at the ignition coil. Disconnect the 3 body wiring connectors on top of the right rocker arm cover. Disconnect the oil pressure and engine coolant temperature sender connectors.

10. Disconnect the injector harness, air charge temperature sensor and throttle position sensor. Disconnect the oxygen sensor connector at the rear of the engine and disconnect the brake booster vacuum hose.

11. Remove the engine front mount-to-crossmember attaching nuts.

12. Raise and safely support the vehicle.

13. Remove 2 lower air conditioner compressor bracket-to-engine bolts. Disconnect the wiring from the low oil level sensor and oil pressure sending unit.

14. Remove the retaining bracket holding the transmission cooling lines to the right side of the engine block.

15. Disconnect the exhaust pipes at the manifolds. Disconnect the starter cable and remove the starter.

16. If equipped with manual transmission, disconnect the hydraulic clutch line and remove the flywheel housing-to-engine block bolts.

17. If equipped with automatic transmission, remove the converter inspection cover and disconnect the converter from the flywheel.

18. Disconnect the kickdown and shift cables at the transmission. Remove the converter housing-to-engine block bolts and adapter plate-to-converter housing bolt.

19. Lower the vehicle. Remove the 2 bolts from the air conditioner compressor and position aside.

20. Attach suitable engine lifting equipment and position a jack under the transmission.

21. Raise the engine slightly and carefully pull it from the transmission. Carefully lift the engine out of the engine compartment so the rear cover plate is not bent or components damaged. Install the engine on a workstand.

To install:

22. Remove the engine from the workstand and carefully lower it into the engine compartment. Make sure the exhaust manifolds are aligned with the exhaust pipes.

23. If equipped with manual transmission, start the transmission input

shaft into the clutch disc. It may be necessary to adjust the position of the transmission in relation to the engine, if the input shaft will not enter the clutch disc. If the engine hangs up after the shaft enters, turn the crankshaft in the clockwise direction slowly, transmission in gear, until the shaft splines mesh with the clutch disc splines.

24. If equipped with automatic transmission, start the converter pilot into the crankshaft. Make sure the converter rotates freely and is not binding. When the converter is fully installed in the transmission, the distance between the converter pilot and the edge of the converter housing should be $7/16$–$9/16$.

25. Install the flywheel housing or converter housing upper bolts, making sure the engine block dowels engage the housing. If equipped, install the clutch hydraulic line.

26. Remove the jack from under the transmission and remove the engine lifting equipment. If equipped with automatic transmission, position the kickdown cable on the transmission and engine.

27. Raise and safely support the vehicle. If equipped with automatic transmission, position the transmission linkage bracket and install the remaining converter housing bolts.

28. Install the adapter plate-to-converter housing bolt. Install the converter-to-flywheel nuts and install the inspection cover. Connect the kickdown cable at the transmission.

29. If equipped with manual transmission, install the flywheel housing attaching bolts.

30. Install the starter and connect the cables. Connect the exhaust pipes at the manifolds.

31. Install the engine front mount nuts and washers or through bolts. Lower the vehicle.

32. Install the ground wires to the engine block. Connect the coil wires, the 3 body wiring connectors and the oxygen wiring connector. Connect the coolant temperature sending unit and oil pressure sending unit. Connect the brake booster vacuum hose.

33. Install the throttle linkage and connect the fuel lines. Connect the heater hoses at the water pump and cylinder block.

34. Install the alternator and bracket. Connect the alternator ground wire to the engine block. Install the drive belt and adjust the tension.

35. Install the air conditioning compressor and power steering pump, if equipped.

36. Position the fan shroud over the fan. Install the radiator and connect the radiator hoses. Install the fan shroud.

37. Connect the negative battery cable. Fill and bleed the cooling system.

38. Bleed the hydraulic clutch, if necessary. Evacuate and charge the air conditioning system, if necessary.

39. Run the engine and check for leaks and proper operation. Install the intake hose. Install the hood, aligning the marks that were made during removal.

4.0L Engine

AEROSTAR

1. Disconnect the negative battery cable and relieve the fuel system pressure.

2. Remove the front grille. Remove the air cleaner tube and the air cleaner assembly.

3. Discharge the refrigerant from the air conditioning system, if equipped. Disconnect and remove the air conditioner compressor.

4. Drain the engine oil. Drain disconnect and remove the power steering oil cooler.

5. Remove the front bumper cover. Drain, disconnect and remove the transmission oil cooler.

6. Drain the radiator and disconnect the radiator hoses. Disconnect the transmission oil cooler lines from the radiator.

7. Disconnect the fan shroud and position it over the fan. Remove the radiator and the shroud.

8. Remove the accessory drive belt and the right front air diverter flap. Remove the center hood latch support and remove the alternator.

9. If equipped, discharge the air conditioning system and remove the compressor.

10. Remove the engine oil fill tube. From inside the vehicle, remove the engine cover.

11. Remove the ice/snow shield. Remove the power steering hoses and remove the power steering pump and bracket.

12. Remove the transmission oil and engine oil dipsticks and tubes. Disconnect the exhaust system from the exhaust manifolds.

13. Disconnect and remove the starter. Working through the starter opening in the converter housing, remove the converter to flexplate bolts.

14. Remove the transmission oil cooler line bracket retaining bolt and remove the engine mount to frame bolts.

15. Remove the converter housing-to-engine bolts, except the upper bolts.

16. Remove the left motor mount from the engine, then remove the upper converter housing bolts.

17. Disconnect the transmission and transfer case electrical connectors. Disconnect the fuel lines at the fuel supply manifold.

18. Disconnect the throttle linkage and bracket and position aside. Disconnect the heater hoses.

19. Tag and disconnect the vacuum lines from the vapor canister, lower intake manifold and upper intake manifold vacuum tee.

20. Remove the spark plug wires from the coil assembly. Disconnect and remove the coil assembly with mounting bracket.

21. Disconnect the throttle position sensor electrical connector. Remove the throttle body from the upper intake manifold.

22. Tag and disconnect the engine wiring harness main connectors. Install suitable engine lifting equipment and remove the engine from the vehicle. Position the engine on a workstand.

To install:

23. Remove the engine from the workstand and position it in the vehicle. Remove the engine lifting equipment.

24. Connect the engine wiring harness main connectors. Install the throttle body on the upper intake manifold.

25. Install the ignition coil assembly and connect the spark plug wires and coil assembly wiring connector. Connect the electrical connector for the throttle position sensor.

26. Connect the heater hoses. Connect the vacuum lines to the vapor canister, lower intake manifold and upper intake manifold vacuum tee.

27. Connect the throttle linkage and bracket. Connect the fuel lines to the fuel supply manifold.

28. Install the left motor mount. Install the converter housing-to-engine bolts and connect the transmission and transfer case electrical connectors.

29. Install the engine mount-to-frame bolts and the transmission oil cooler line bracket retaining bolt.

30. Working through the starter opening in the converter housing, install the converter to flexplate bolts.

31. Install the starter and connect the starter wires. Connect the exhaust system to the exhaust manifolds.

32. Install the transmission oil and engine oil dipstick tubes and dipsticks.

33. Install the power steering pump and mounting bracket. Connect the power steering hoses.

34. Install the ice/snow shield and the engine oil fill tube. Install the engine cover.

35. Install and connect the air conditioner compressor, if equipped. Install and connect the alternator.

36. Install the center hood latch support and the right front air diverter flap. Install the accessory drive belt.

37. Install the radiator and fan shroud. Connect the transmission oil cooler lines and the radiator hoses.

38. Install the transmission oil cooler and the front bumper cover. Install and connect the power steering oil cooler.

39. Fill the engine with the proper type and quantity of engine oil.

40. Install and connect the air conditioner condenser, if equipped. Install the air cleaner assembly and air tube.

41. Install the front grille and connect the negative battery cable. Fill and bleed the cooling system.

42. If equipped, evacuate and charge the air conditioning system. Check all fluid levels.

43. Run the engine and check for leaks and for proper operation.

EXPLORER AND RANGER

1. Disconnect the negative battery cable and relieve the fuel system pressure. Drain the cooling system.

2. Mark the position of the hood on the hinges and remove the hood. Remove the air cleaner intake hose.

3. Disconnect the radiator hoses at the radiator. Disconnect the fan shroud and position it over the fan. Remove the radiator, then the shroud.

4. Remove the alternator and bracket and position the alternator aside. Disconnect the alternator ground wire from the cylinder block.

5. Remove the air conditioning compressor and power steering pump and position aside, if equipped.

6. Disconnect the heater hoses at the intake manifold and water pump. Remove the ground wires from the cylinder block.

7. Disconnect the fuel lines from the fuel supply manifold. Disconnect the throttle cable shield and linkage at the throttle body and intake manifold.

8. Tag and disconnect the vacuum connections at the rear vacuum fitting in the upper intake manifold.

9. Disconnect the wiring from the ignition coil and oil pressure and engine coolant temperature senders. Disconnect the injector harness, air charge temperature sensor and throttle position sensor. Disconnect the brake booster vacuum hose.

10. Raise and safely support the vehicle. Disconnect the exhaust pipes at the manifolds. Disconnect the starter cable and remove the starter.

11. Remove the engine front mount-to-crossmember attaching nuts or through bolts.

12. Remove the converter inspection cover and disconnect the converter from the flywheel. Remove the cable.

13. Remove the converter housing-to-engine block bolts and the adapter plate-to-converter housing bolt. Lower the vehicle.

14. Position a jack under the transmission and install suitable engine lifting equipment.

15. Raise the engine slightly and carefully pull it from the transmission. Carefully lift the engine out of the engine compartment so the rear cover plate is not bent or components damaged. Install the engine on a workstand.

To install:

16. Remove the engine from the workstand and carefully lower it into the engine compartment. Make sure the exhaust manifolds are aligned with the exhaust pipe.

17. At the transmission, start the converter pilot into the crankshaft. Install the converter housing upper bolts, making sure the dowels in the cylinder block engage the flywheel housing. Tighten the bolts to 33–45 ft. lbs. (45–61 Nm).

18. Remove the jack from under the transmission and the engine lifting equipment.

19. Position the kickdown rod on the transmission and engine. Raise and safely support the vehicle.

20. Position the transmission linkage bracket and install the remaining converter housing bolts. Install the adapter plate-to-converter housing bolt. Install the converter-to-flywheel nuts and install the inspection cover. Connect the kickdown rod on the transmission.

21. Install the starter and connect the cable. Connect the exhaust pipes at the manifolds.

22. Install the engine front mount nuts and washers or through bolts. Lower the vehicle.

23. Install the ground wires to the engine block. Connect the ignition coil wiring, then connect the coolant

temperature sending unit and oil pressure sending unit. Connect the brake booster vacuum hose.

24. Install the throttle linkage and connect the fuel lines at the fuel supply manifold.

25. Connect the ground cable at the engine block. Connect the heater hoses to the water pump and cylinder block.

26. Install the alternator and bracket. Connect the alternator ground wire to the engine block. Install the accessory drive belt.

27. Install the air conditioner compressor and power steering pump, if equipped.

28. Position the shroud over the fan. Install the radiator and connect the radiator upper and lower hoses. Install the fan shroud attaching bolts.

29. Connect the negative battery cable. Fill and bleed the cooling system.

30. Run the engine and check for leaks and proper operation. If equipped, evacuate and charge the air conditioning system.

31. Install the intake hose. Install the hood, aligning the marks that were made during removal.

4.9L Engine

1. Disconnect the negative battery cable(s) before beginning any work. Label all disconnected hoses, vacuum lines and wires.

2. Drain the cooling system and the crankcase.

3. Remove the hood.

4. Remove the throttle body inlet tubes.

5. Disconnect the positive battery cable.

6. Discharge the air conditioning system.

7. Disconnect the refrigerant lines at the compressor. Cap all openings at once.

8. Remove the compressor.

9. Disconnect the refrigerant lines at the condenser. Cap all openings at once.

10. Remove the condenser.

11. Disconnect the heater hose from the water pump and coolant outlet housing.

12. Disconnect the flexible fuel line from the fuel pump.

13. Remove the radiator.

14. Remove the fan, water pump pulley, and fan belt.

15. Disconnect the accelerator cable.

16. Disconnect the brake booster vacuum hose at the intake manifold.

17. If equipped with automatic transmission, disconnect the transmission kickdown rod at the bellcrank assembly.

18. Disconnect the exhaust pipe from the exhaust manifold.

19. Disconnect the Electronic Engine Control (EEC) harness from all the sensors.

20. Disconnect the body ground strap and the battery ground cable from the engine.

21. Disconnect the engine wiring harness at the ignition coil, the coolant temperature sending unit, and the oil pressure sensing unit. Position the wiring harness out of the way.

22. Remove the alternator mounting bolts and position the alternator out of the way.

23. Remove the power steering pump from the mounting brackets and move it to one side, leaving the lines attached.

24. Raise and support the vehicle on jackstands.

25. Remove the starter.

26. Remove the automatic transmission filler tube bracket, if equipped.

27. Remove the rear engine plate upper right bolt.

28. On manual transmission equipped vehicles:

   a. Remove the flywheel housing lower attaching bolts.

   b. Disconnect the clutch return spring.

29. On automatic transmission equipped vehicles:

   a. Remove the converter housing access cover assembly.

   b. Remove the flywheel-to-converter attaching nuts.

   c. Secure the converter in the housing.

   d. Remove the transmission oil cooler lines from the retaining clip at the engine.

   e. Remove the lower converter housing-to-engine attaching bolts.

30. Remove the nut from each of the 2 front engine mounts.

31. Lower the vehicle and position a jack under the transmission and support it.

32. Remove the remaining bellhousing-to-engine attaching bolts.

33. Attach an engine lifting device and raise the engine slightly and carefully pull it from the transmission. Lift the engine out of the vehicle.

To install:

34. Remove the engine mount brackets from the frame. Attach them to the engine mounts, making

the nuts just tight enough to hold the brackets securely to the mounts.

35. Place a new gasket on the muffler inlet pipe.

36. Carefully lower the engine into the vehicle. Make sure the dowels in the engine block engage the holes in the bellhousing and the mount bracket holes align with the frame holes.

37. On manual transmission equipped vehicles, start the transmission input shaft into the clutch disc. It may be necessary to adjust the position of the engine or transmission in order for the input shaft to enter the clutch disc. If necessary, turn the crankshaft until the input shaft splines mesh with the clutch disc splines.

38. On automatic transmission equipped vehicles, start the converter pilot into the crankshaft. Secure the converter in the housing.

39. Install the bolts securing the mount brackets to the frame.

40. Install the bellhousing upper attaching bolts. Torque the bolts to 50 ft. lbs.

41. Remove the jack supporting the transmission.

42. Remove the lifting device.

43. Install the engine mount nuts and tighten them to 70 ft. lbs. Tighten the bracket-to-frame bolts to 70 ft. lbs.

44. Install the automatic transmission coil cooler lines bracket, if equipped.

45. Install the remaining bellhousing attaching bolts. Torque them to 50 ft. lbs.

46. Connect the clutch return spring, if equipped.

47. Install the starter and connect the starter cable.

48. Attach the automatic transmission fluid filler tube bracket, if equipped.

49. If equipped with automatic transmissions, install the transmission oil cooler lines in the bracket at the cylinder block.

50. Connect the exhaust pipe to the exhaust manifold. Tighten the nuts to 25–35 ft. lbs.

51. Connect the engine ground strap and negative battery cable.

52. On a vehicle with an automatic transmission, connect the kickdown rod to the bellcrank assembly on the intake manifold.

53. Connect the accelerator linkage.

54. Connect the brake booster vacuum line to the intake manifold.

55. Connect the coil primary wire, oil pressure and coolant temperature sending unit wires, fuel line, heater hoses, and the battery positive cable.

56. Connect the EEC sensors.

57. Install the alternator on its mounting bracket.

58. Install the power steering pump on its bracket.

59. Install the water pump pulley, spacer, fan, and fan belt. Adjust the belt tension.

60. Install the air conditioning compressor. Connect the refrigerant lines.

61. Install the radiator.

62. Install the condenser and connect the refrigerant lines.

63. Charge the refrigerant system.

64. Connect the upper and lower radiator hoses to the radiator and engine.

65. Connect the automatic transmission oil cooler lines, if equipped.

66. Install and adjust the hood.

67. Fill the cooling system.

68. Fill the crankcase.

69. Start the engine and check for leaks.

70. Bleed the cooling system.

71. Adjust the clutch pedal freeplay or the automatic transmission control linkage.

72. Install the air cleaner.

5.0L and 5.8L Engines

1. Remove the hood.

2. Drain the cooling system and crankcase.

3. Disconnect the battery and alternator cables.

4. Remove the air intake hoses, PCV tube and carbon canister hose.

5. Disconnect the upper and lower radiator hoses.

6. Discharge the air conditioning system.

7. Disconnect the refrigerant lines at the compressor. Cap all openings immediately.

8. If equipped, disconnect the automatic transmission oil cooler lines.

9. Remove the fan shroud and lay it over the fan.

10. Remove the radiator and fan, shroud, fan, spacer, pulley and belt.

11. Remove the alternator pivot and adjusting bolts. Remove the alternator.

12. Disconnect the oil pressure sending unit lead from the sending unit.

13. Disconnect the fuel tank-to-pump fuel line at the fuel pump and plug the line.

14. If equipped, disconnect the chassis fuel line at the fuel rails.

15. Disconnect the accelerator linkage and speed control linkage at the throttle body.

16. Disconnect the automatic transmission kick-down rod and remove the return spring, if equipped.

17. Disconnect the power brake booster vacuum hose.

18. Disconnect the throttle bracket from the upper intake manifold and swing it out of the way with the cables still attached.

19. Disconnect the heater hoses from the water pump and tee.

20. Disconnect the temperature sending unit wire from the sending unit.

21. Remove the upper bellhousing-to-engine attaching bolts.

22. Remove the wiring harness from the left rocker arm cover and position the wires out of the way.

23. Disconnect the ground strap from the cylinder block.

24. Disconnect the air conditioning compressor clutch wire.

25. Raise the front of the vehicle and disconnect the starter cable from the starter.

26. Remove the starter.

27. Disconnect the exhaust pipe from the exhaust manifolds.

28. Disconnect the engine mounts from the brackets on the frame.

29. If equipped with automatic transmissions, remove the converter inspection plate and remove the torque converter-to-flywheel attaching bolts.

30. Remove the remaining bellhousing-to-engine attaching bolts.

31. Lower the vehicle and support the transmission with a jack.

32. Install an engine lifting device.

33. Raise the engine slightly and carefully pull it out of the transmission. Lift the engine out of the engine compartment.

To install:

34. Remove the engine mount brackets from the frame and attach them to the engine mounts. Tighten the mount-to-bracket nuts just enough to hold them securely.

35. Lower the engine carefully into the transmission. Make sure the dowel in the engine block engage the holes in the bellhousing through the rear cover plate. If the engine hangs up after the transmission input shaft enters the clutch disc (manual transmission only), turn the crankshaft with the transmission in gear until the input shaft splines mesh with the clutch disc splines.

36. Install the engine mount nuts and washers. Torque the nuts to 80 ft. lbs. Tighten the bracket-to-frame bolts to 70 ft. lbs.

37. Remove the engine lifting device.

38. Install the lower bellhousing-to-engine attaching bolts. Torque the bolts to 50 ft. lbs.

39. Remove the transmission support jack.

40. If equipped with automatic transmissions, install the torque converter-to-flywheel attaching bolts. Torque the bolts to 30 ft. lbs.

41. Install the converter inspection plate. Torque the bolts to 60 inch lbs.

42. Connect the exhaust pipe to the exhaust manifolds. Tighten the exhaust pipe-to-exhaust manifold nuts to 25–35 ft. lbs.

43. Install the starter. Torque the mounting bolts to 20 ft. lbs.

44. Connect the starter cable to the starter.

45. Lower the vehicle.

46. Install the upper bellhousing-to-engine attaching bolts. Torque the bolts to 50 ft. lbs.

47. Connect the wiring harness at the left rocker arm cover.

48. Connect the ground strap to the cylinder block.

49. Connect the air conditioning compressor clutch wire.

50. Connect the heater hoses at the water pump and tee.

51. Connect the temperature sending unit wire at the sending unit.

52. Connect the accelerator linkage and speed control linkage at the throttle body.

53. Connect the automatic transmission kick-down rod and install the return spring, if equipped.

54. Connect the power brake booster vacuum hose.

55. Connect the throttle bracket to the upper intake manifold.

56. Connect the fuel tank-to-pump fuel line at the fuel pump. If equipped, connect the chassis fuel line at the fuel rails.

57. Connect the oil pressure sending unit lead to the sending unit.

58. Install the alternator.

59. Connect the refrigerant lines to the compressor.

60. Install the radiator and fan, shroud, fan, spacer, pulley and belt.

61. Connect the upper and lower radiator hoses, and, if equipped, the automatic transmission oil cooler lines.

62. Install the air intake hoses, PCV tube and carbon canister hose.

63. Connect the battery and alternator cables.

64. Fill the cooling system and crankcase.

65. Charge the air conditioning system.

66. Install the hood.

If the torque for a particular fastener was not mentioned above, use the following torque values as a guide:

$\frac{1}{4}$ in.–20 — 6–9 ft. lbs.
$\frac{5}{16}$ in.–18 — 12–18 ft. lbs.
$\frac{3}{8}$ in.–16 — 22–32 ft. lbs.
$\frac{7}{16}$ in.–14 — 45–57 ft. lbs.
$\frac{1}{2}$ in.–13 — 55–80 ft. lbs.
$\frac{9}{16}$ in. — 85–120 ft. lbs.

7.5L Engine

1. Remove the hood.
2. Drain the cooling system.
3. Disconnect the negative battery cable from the block.
4. Remove the air cleaner assembly.
5. Remove the crankcase ventilation hose.
6. Remove the canister hose.
7. Disconnect the upper and lower radiator hoses.
8. Disconnect the transmission oil cooler lines from the radiator.
9. Disconnect the oil cooler lines at the oil filter adapter.

— WARNING —

Don't disconnect the lines at the quick-connect fittings behind or at the oil cooler. Disconnecting them may permanently damage them.

10. Discharge the air conditioning system.
11. Disconnect the refrigerant lines at the compressor. Cap the openings at once!
12. Disconnect the refrigerant lines at the condenser. Cap the openings at once!
13. Remove the condenser.
14. Remove the fan shroud from the radiator and position it up, over the fan.
15. Remove the radiator.
16. Remove the fan shroud.
17. Remove the fan, belts and pulley from the water pump.
18. Remove the compressor.
19. Remove the power steering pump from the engine, if equipped, and position it to one side. Do not disconnect the fluid lines.
20. Disconnect the fuel pump inlet line from the pump and plug the line.
21. Disconnect the oil pressure sending unit wire at the sending unit.
22. Remove the alternator drive belts and disconnect the alternator from the engine, positioning it aside.
23. Disconnect the ground cable from the right front corner of the engine.
24. Disconnect the heater hoses.

25. Remove the transmission fluid filler tube attaching bolt from the right side valve cover and position the tube out of the way.

26. Disconnect all vacuum lines at the rear of the intake manifold.

27. Disconnect the accelerator rod and the transmission kickdown rod and secure them out of the way.

28. Disconnect the engine wiring harness at the connector on the fire wall. Disconnect the primary wire at the coil.

29. Remove the upper flywheel housing-to-engine bolts.

30. Raise the vehicle and disconnect the exhaust pipes at the exhaust manifolds.

31. Disconnect the starter cable and remove the starter. Bring the starter forward and rotate the solenoid outward to remove the assembly.

32. Remove the access cover from the converter housing and remove the flywheel-to-converter attaching nuts.

33. Remove the lower the converter housing-to-engine attaching bolts.

34. Remove the engine mount through bolts attaching the rubber insulator to the frame brackets.

35. Lower the vehicle and place a jack under the transmission to support it.

36. Remove the converter housing-to-engine block attaching bolts (left side).

37. Remove the coil and bracket assembly from the intake manifold.

38. Attach an engine lifting device and carefully take up the weight of the engine.

39. Move the engine forward to disengage it from the transmission and slowly lift it from the vehicle.

To install:

40. Remove the engine mount brackets from the frame and attach them to the mounts. Tighten the nuts just enough to hold them securely.

41. Lower the engine slowly into the vehicle.

42. Slide the engine rearward to engage it with the transmission and slowly lower it onto the supports.

43. Tighten the engine support nuts to 74 ft. lbs. Tighten the bracket bolts to 70 ft. lbs.

44. Remove the engine lifting device.

45. Install the converter housing-to-engine block upper and left side attaching bolts. Torque the bolts to 50 ft. lbs.

46. Install the coil and bracket assembly on the intake manifold.

47. Remove the jack from under the transmission.

48. Lower the vehicle.

49. Install the upper converter housing-to-engine attaching bolts. Torque the bolts to 50 ft. lbs.

50. Install the flywheel-to-converter attaching nuts. Torque the nuts to 34 ft. lbs.

51. Install the access cover on the converter housing. Torque the bolts to 60–90 inch lbs.

52. Install the starter.

53. Connect the starter cable.

54. Raise the vehicle and connect the exhaust pipes at the exhaust manifolds.

55. Connect the engine wiring harness at the connector on the fire wall.

56. Connect the primary wire at the coil.

57. Connect the accelerator rod and the transmission kickdown rod.

58. Connect the speed control cable.

59. Connect all vacuum lines at the rear of the intake manifold.

60. Install the transmission fluid filler tube attaching bolt from the right side valve cover and position the tube out of the way.

61. Connect the heater hoses.

62. Connect the ground cable at the right front corner of the engine.

63. Install the alternator and drive belts.

64. Connect the oil pressure sending unit wire at the sending unit.

65. Connect the fuel pump inlet line at the pump and plug the line.

66. Install the power steering pump and belt.

67. Install air conditioning compressor. Connect the refrigerant lines.

68. Install the fan, belts and pulley on the water pump.

69. Position the fan shroud over the fan.

70. Install the radiator.

71. Attach the fan shroud.

72. Install the condenser.

73. Connect the refrigerant lines at the condenser.

74. Charge the air conditioning system.

75. Connect the oil cooler lines at the oil filter adapter.

76. Connect the transmission oil cooler lines at the radiator.

77. Connect the upper and lower radiator hoses.

78. Connect the canister hose.

79. Connect the crankcase ventilation hose.

80. Connect the negative battery cable from the block.

81. Fill the cooling system.

82. Install the air cleaner assembly.

83. Install the hood.

If the torque for a particular fastener was not mentioned above, use the following torque values as a guide:

$\frac{1}{4}$ in.–20 — 6–9 ft. lbs.
$\frac{5}{16}$ in.–18 — 12–18 ft. lbs.
$\frac{3}{8}$ in.–16 — 22–32 ft. lbs.
$\frac{7}{16}$ in.–14 — 45–57 ft. lbs.
$\frac{1}{2}$ in.–13 — 55–80 ft. lbs.
$\frac{9}{16}$ in. — 85–120 ft. lbs.

7.3L Diesel Engine

1. Remove the hood.

2. Drain the coolant.

3. Remove the air cleaner and intake duct assembly and cover the air intake opening with a clean rag to keep out the dirt.

4. Remove the upper grille support bracket and upper air conditioning condenser mounting bracket.

5. If equipped with air conditioning, the system MUST be discharged to remove the condenser.

6. Remove the radiator fan shroud halves.

7. Remove the fan and clutch assembly.

8. Detach the radiator hoses and the transmission cooler lines, if equipped.

9. Remove the condenser. Cap all openings at once!

10. Remove the radiator.

11. Remove the power steering pump and position it out of the way.

12. Disconnect the fuel supply line heater and alternator wires at the alternator.

13. Disconnect the oil pressure sending unit wire at the sending unit, remove the sender from the firewall and lay it on the engine.

14. Disconnect the accelerator cable and the speed control cable, if equipped, from the injection pump. Remove the cable bracket with the cables attached, from the intake manifold and position it out of the way.

15. Disconnect the transmission kickdown rod from the injection pump, if equipped.

16. Disconnect the main wiring harness connector from the right side of the engine and the ground strap from the rear of the engine.

17. Remove the fuel return hose from the left rear of the engine.

18. Remove the 2 upper transmission-to-engine attaching bolts.

19. Disconnect the heater hoses.

20. Disconnect the water temperature sender wire.

21. Disconnect the overheat light switch wire and position the wire out of the way.

22. Raise the vehicle and support on it on jackstands.

23. Disconnect the battery ground cables from the front of the engine and the starter cables from the starter.

24. Remove the fuel inlet line and plug the fuel line at the fuel pump.

25. Detach the exhaust pipe at the exhaust manifold.

26. Disconnect the engine insulators from the no. 1 crossmember.

27. Remove the flywheel inspection plate and the 4 converter-to-flywheel attaching nuts, if equipped with automatic transmission.

28. Remove the jackstands and lower the vehicle.

29. Supporting the transmission on a jack.

30. Remove the 4 lower transmission attaching bolts.

31. Attach an engine lifting sling and remove the engine from the vehicle.

To install:

32. Lower the engine into vehicle.

33. Align the converter to the flexplate and the engine dowels to the transmission.

34. Install the engine mount bolts and torque them to 80 ft. lbs.

35. Remove the engine lifting sling.

36. Install the 4 lower transmission attaching bolts. Torque the bolts to 65 ft. lbs.

37. Remove transmission jack.

38. Raise and support the front end on jackstands.

39. If equipped with automatic transmission, install the 4 converter-to-flywheel attaching nuts. Torque the nuts to 34 ft. lbs.

40. Install the flywheel inspection plate. Torque the bolts to 60–90 inch lbs.

41. Attach the exhaust pipe at the exhaust manifold.

42. Connect the fuel inlet line.

43. Connect the battery ground cables to the front of the engine.

44. Connect the starter cables at the starter.

45. Lower the vehicle.

46. Connect the overheat light switch wire.

47. Connect the water temperature sender wire.

48. Connect the heater hoses.

49. Install the 2 upper transmission-to-engine attaching bolts. Torque the bolts to 65 ft. lbs.

50. Connect the fuel return hose at the left rear of the engine.

51. Connect the main wiring harness connector at the right side of the engine and the ground strap from the rear of the engine.

52. Connect the transmission kickdown rod at the injection pump, if equipped.

53. Connect the accelerator cable and the speed control cable, if equipped, at the injection pump.

54. Install the cable bracket with the cables attached, to the intake manifold.

55. Install the oil pressure sending unit.

56. Connect the oil pressure sending unit wire at the sending unit.

57. Connect the fuel supply line heater and alternator wires at the alternator.

58. Install the power steering pump.

59. Install the radiator.

60. Install the condenser.

61. Connect the radiator hoses and the transmission cooler lines, if equipped.

62. Install the fan and clutch assembly.

63. Install the radiator fan shroud halves.

64. If equipped with air conditioning, charge the system.

65. Install the upper grille support bracket and upper air conditioning condenser mounting bracket.

66. Install the air cleaner and intake duct assembly.

67. Fill the cooling system.

68. Install the hood.

Engine Mounts

REMOVAL AND INSTALLATION

Front Mounts

1. Remove the fan shroud attaching screws.

2. Support the engine using a wood block and a jack placed under the oil pan.

3. Remove the nuts and washers attaching the mounts to the engine bracket. Lift the engine enough to disengage the mount upper stud from the crossmember engine bracket.

4. Remove the bolt attaching the fuel pump shield to the left engine bracket, if necessary.

5. Remove the mount-to-crossmember attaching nut and washer assembly. Remove the engine mount.

To install:

6. Install the engine mount to the crossmember.

7. Install the bolt attaching the fuel pump shield to the left bracket, if necessary.

8. Lower the engine until the mount stud engages in the slot/hole

of the engine bracket. Install the attaching nuts.

9. Remove the jack and wood block from the engine oil pan. Install the fan shroud attaching screws.

Rear Mount

1. Place a block of wood and a jack under the transmission.

2. Remove the 2 nuts attaching the mount to the crossmember. Raise the transmission enough to lift the mount from the crossmember.

3. Remove the bolts and nuts attaching the crossmember to the frame side rails and remove the crossmember.

4. If equipped, remove the fasteners attaching the exhaust hanger to the rear engine mount.

5. Remove the 2 bolts attaching the mount to the transmission and remove the mount and retainer assembly.

To install:

6. Position the mount and retainer assembly to the transmission and install the 2 attaching bolts.

7. If equipped, install the fasteners attaching the exhaust hanger to the mount.

8. Install the crossmember to the frame side rails with the attaching nuts and bolts.

9. Lower the transmission and install the mount crossmember attaching nuts. Remove the jack and wood block.

Cylinder Head

REMOVAL AND INSTALLATION

2.3L Engine

1. Disconnect the negative battery cable. Drain the cooling system.

2. Remove the air cleaner assembly. Remove the heater hose retaining screw(s) to the rocker arm cover.

3. If equipped, disconnect the distributor cap and spark plug wires and remove the assembly.

4. Remove the spark plugs. If equipped with distributorless ignition, remove the spark plug wire harnesses.

5. Remove the engine and alternator wiring harnesses. Disconnect the oxygen sensor at the exhaust manifold.

6. Tag and disconnect the required vacuum hoses. Remove the dipstick tube and bracket.

7. Remove the rocker arm cover attaching bolts and remove the cover.

Remove the intake manifold attaching bolts.

8. Loosen the alternator retaining bolts and remove the belt from the pulley. Remove the mounting bracket-to-head retaining bolts.

9. Remove the upper radiator hose. Remove the timing belt cover bolt(s) and remove the cover. If equipped with power steering, move the power steering pump bracket.

10. Loosen the timing belt idler retaining bolts. Position the idler in the unloaded position and tighten the retaining bolts. Remove the timing belt from the camshaft pulley and auxiliary pulley.

11. Remove the 4 nuts and/or stud bolts retaining the heat stove to the exhaust manifold. Remove the 8 exhaust manifold retaining bolts.

12. Remove the timing belt idler and 2 bracket bolts. Remove the timing belt idler spring stop from the cylinder head.

13. Remove the cylinder head retaining bolts and remove the cylinder head.

14. Clean all gasket mating surfaces. Check the cylinder head for flatness using a straight edge and a feeler gauge. The cylinder head must not be warped more than 0.003 in. in any 6 in. or more than 0.006 in. overall.

To install:

15. Position a new head gasket on the block. Properly position the camshaft in the cylinder head and install the cylinder head on the block.

16. Install the cylinder head bolts and tighten, in sequence, in 2 steps, first to 50–60 ft. lbs. (68–81 Nm) and then to 80–90 ft. lbs. (108–122 Nm).

17. Install a new intake manifold gasket and position the intake manifold to the cylinder head. Install the retaining bolts.

18. Install the timing belt idler spring stop to the cylinder head. Position the timing belt idler to the cylinder head and install the retaining bolts.

19. Install the 8 exhaust manifold retaining bolts and the 4 nuts and/or stud bolts retaining the heat stove to the exhaust manifold.

20. If equipped, align the distributor rotor with the No. 1 spark plug location in the distributor cap.

21. Align the cam gear with the pointer and the crank pulley with the pointer on the timing belt cover.

22. Position the timing belt to the pulleys. Loosen the idler retaining, rotate the engine and check the timing alignment.

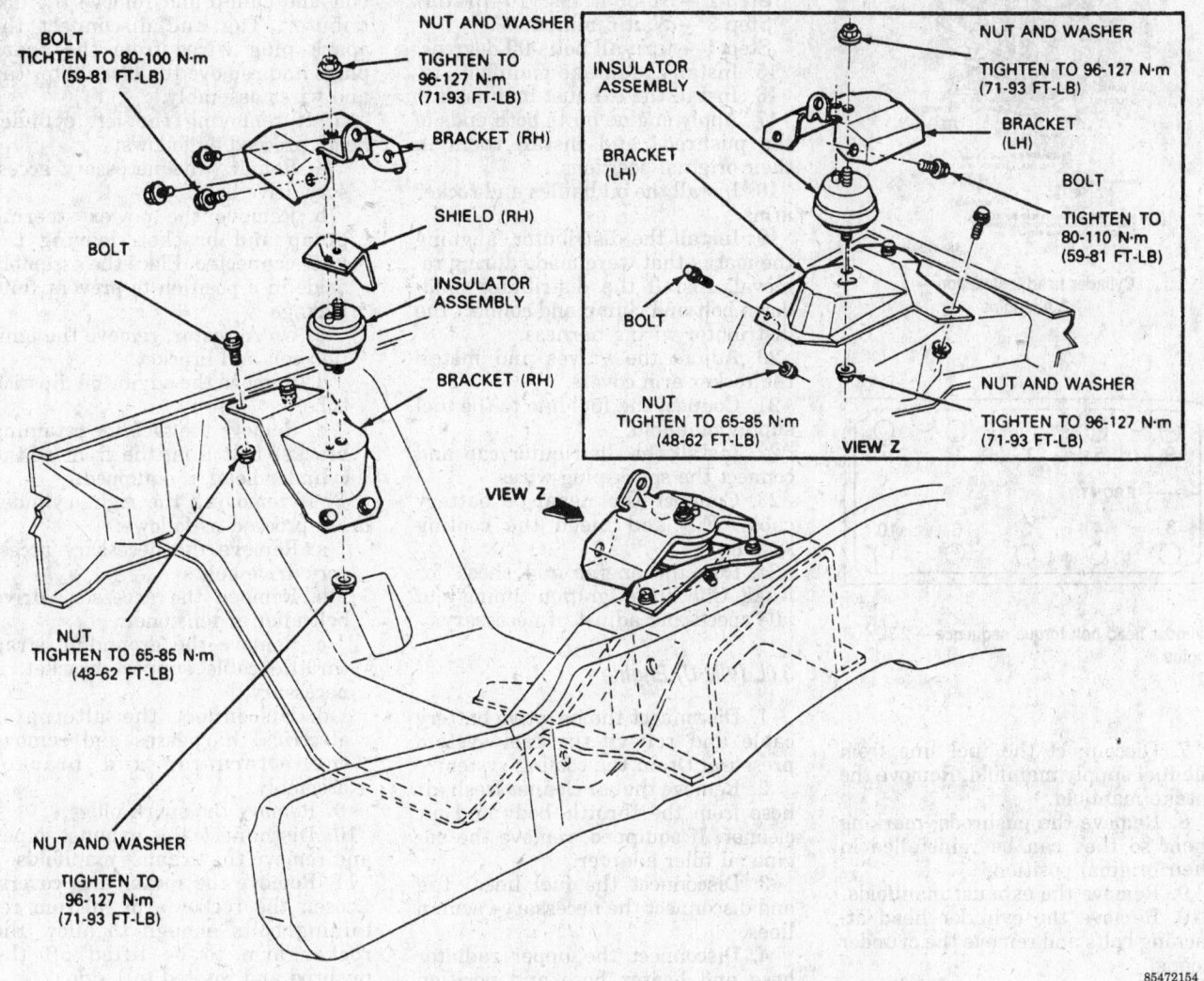

BOLT
TICHTEN TO 80-100 N·m (59-81 FT-LB)

NUT AND WASHER
TIGHTEN TO 96-127 N·m (71-93 FT-LB)

BRACKET (RH)

BOLT

SHIELD (RH)

INSULATOR ASSEMBLY

BRACKET (RH)

NUT
TIGHTEN TO 65-85 N·m (43-62 FT-LB)

NUT AND WASHER
TIGHTEN TO 96-127 N·m (71-93 FT-LB)

INSULATOR ASSEMBLY

BRACKET (LH)

BOLT

NUT
TIGHTEN TO 65-85 N·m (48-62 FT-LB)

NUT AND WASHER
TIGHTEN TO 96-127 N·m (71-93 FT-LB)

BRACKET (LH)

BOLT
TIGHTEN TO 80-110 N·m (59-81 FT-LB)

NUT AND WASHER
TIGHTEN TO 96-127 N·m (71-93 FT-LB)

VIEW Z

VIEW Z

85472154

Front engine mount installation — Bronco and F Series with 4.9L engine

23. Adjust the belt tensioner and tighten the retaining bolts. Install the timing belt cover and the retaining bolt(s).

24. Install the upper radiator hose. Position the alternator bracket to the cylinder head and install the retainers. Install the drive belt and adjust the belt tension.

25. Install a new rocker arm cover gasket on the rocker arm cover. Install the rocker arm cover on the cylinder head and install the retaining bolts.

26. Install the spark plugs. Install the spark plug wires and the distributor cap, if equipped.

27. Install the dipstick tube and bracket. Connect the vacuum hoses. Install the retaining heater hose screw(s) to the rocker arm cover.

28. Connect the negative battery cable. Fill and bleed the cooling system.

29. Start the engine and check for leaks. Install the air cleaner hose to the throttle body.

2.9L Engine

1. Disconnect the negative battery cable and relieve the fuel system pressure.

2. Drain the cooling system and remove the upper radiator hose.

3. Remove the intake tube from the throttle body and disconnect the throttle linkage and cover.

4. Tag the position of the spark plug wires and remove the distributor cap and wires as an assembly. Disconnect the distributor wiring harness.

5. Mark the position of the rotor in relation to the distributor housing and the position of the distributor housing in relation to the intake manifold. Remove the distributor hold-down bolt and clamp and remove the distributor.

6. Remove the rocker arm covers and rocker arm shafts.

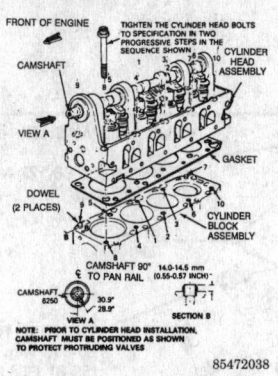

Cylinder head installation — 2.3L engine

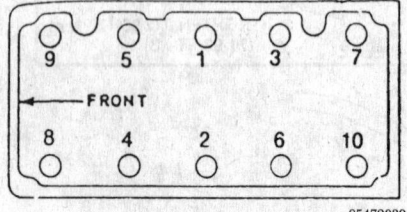

Cylinder head bolt torque sequence — 2.3L engine

7. Disconnect the fuel line from the fuel supply manifold. Remove the intake manifold.

8. Remove the pushrods, marking them so they can be reinstalled in their original positions.

9. Remove the exhaust manifolds.

10. Remove the cylinder head attaching bolts and remove the cylinder heads.

11. Clean all gasket mating surfaces. Check the cylinder head for flatness using a straight edge and a feeler gauge. The cylinder head must not be warped more than 0.003 in. in any 6 in. or more than 0.006 in. overall.

To install:

12. Position new cylinder head gaskets on the cylinder block.

NOTE: Gaskets are marked with the words "front" and "top" for correct positioning. Left and right cylinder head gaskets are not interchangeable.

13. Install fabricated alignment dowels in the cylinder block and install the cylinder heads.

14. Install new cylinder head bolts and remove the fabricated dowels.

Tighten the bolts, in sequence, as follows:

Step 1 — 22 ft. lbs. (30 Nm).
Step 2 — 51–55 ft. lbs. (70–75 Nm).
Step 3 — Wait 5 minutes.
Step 4 — turn all bolts 90 degrees.

15. Install the intake manifold.

16. Install the exhaust manifolds.

17. Apply engine oil to both ends of the pushrods and install them in their original positions.

18. Install the oil baffles and rocker arms.

19. Install the distributor, aligning the marks that were made during removal. Install the distributor hold-down bolt and clamp and connect the distributor wiring harness.

20. Adjust the valves and install the rocker arm covers.

21. Connect the fuel line to the fuel supply manifold.

22. Install the distributor cap and connect the spark plug wires.

23. Connect the negative battery cable. Fill and bleed the cooling system.

24. Run the engine and check for leaks. Check the ignition timing and idle speed and adjust, if necessary.

3.0L (VIN U) Engine

1. Disconnect the negative battery cable and relieve the fuel system pressure. Drain the cooling system.

2. Remove the air cleaner fresh air hose from the throttle body and air cleaner. If equipped, remove the engine oil filler adapter.

3. Disconnect the fuel lines. Tag and disconnect the necessary vacuum lines.

4. Disconnect the upper radiator hose and heater hose and position aside. On Ranger, disconnect the ignition coil electrical connector and remove the coil.

5. Remove the throttle body.

6. Remove the distributor cap. Mark the position of the rotor in relation to the distributor housing and

Cylinder head bolt torque sequence — 2.9L engine

the position of the distributor housing in relation to the intake manifold. Remove the distributor hold-down bolt and clamp and remove the distributor. Tag and disconnect the spark plug wires from the spark plugs and remove the distributor cap and wires assembly.

7. If removing the left cylinder head, proceed as follows:

a. Remove the necessary accessory drive belt(s).

b. Remove the power steering pump and bracket, leaving the lines connected. Place the assembly aside in a position to prevent fluid leakage.

c. On Aerostar, remove the ignition coil and bracket.

d. Remove the engine oil dipstick tube.

e. Remove the fuel line retaining bracket bolt from the front of the cylinder head, if equipped.

8. If removing the right cylinder head, proceed as follows:

a. Remove the necessary accessory drive belt(s).

b. Remove the accessory drive belt idler or tensioner.

c. Remove the grounding strap throttle cable support bracket, if necessary.

d. Disconnect the alternator electrical harnesses and remove the alternator and bracket assembly.

9. Remove the spark plugs.

10. Disconnect the exhaust pipes and remove the exhaust manifolds.

11. Remove the rocker arm covers. Loosen the rocker arm fulcrum retaining bolts enough to allow the rocker arm to be lifted off the pushrod and rotated to 1 side.

NOTE: Regardless of which head is to be removed, the No. 3 cylinder intake valve pushrod must be removed to allow removal of the intake manifold.

12. Remove the pushrods, marking them so they can be reinstalled in their original positions.

13. Remove the intake manifold.

14. Remove the cylinder head attaching bolts and remove the cylinder heads.

15. Clean all gasket mating surfaces. Check the cylinder head for flatness using a straight edge and a feeler gauge. The cylinder head must not be warped more than 0.003 in. in any 6 in. or more than 0.006 in. overall.

To install:

16. Position new head gasket(s) on the cylinder block, using the dowels for alignment.

17. Install the cylinder head(s) on the block. Oil the threads of new cylinder head bolts and hand tighten.

18. Tighten the cylinder head bolts, in sequence, to 59 ft. lbs. (80 Nm). Back off all bolts a minimum of 1 full turn. Retighten the bolts, in sequence, in 2 steps, first to 37 ft. lbs. (50 Nm) and then to 68 ft. lbs. (92 Nm).

19. Install the intake manifold.

20. Install the distributor, aligning the marks that were made during removal. Install the hold-down bolt and clamp.

21. Dip each pushrod in heavy engine oil and install them in their original positions.

22. For each valve, rotate the crankshaft until the lifter rests on the base circle of the camshaft lobe, before tightening the rocker arm fulcrum attaching bolts. Position the rocker arms over the valves and pushrods, install the fulcrums and fulcrum bolts and tighten to 24 ft. lbs. (32 Nm).

NOTE: If the original valve train components are being installed, a valve clearance check is not required. If a component has been replaced, perform a valve clearance check.

23. Install the exhaust manifolds and the spark plugs.

24. Install the rocker arm covers. Install the dipstick tube.

25. Install the fuel injector harness to the injectors and inboard rocker arm cover studs. Connect the engine harness to the main harness.

26. Install the distributor cap and connect the spark plug wires to the spark plugs.

27. Install the throttle body. Install the ignition coil and bracket, if necessary and connect the electrical connector.

28. Install the fuel line retaining bracket to the front of the cylinder head, if equipped. Tighten the retaining bolts to 26 ft. lbs. (35 Nm).

29. Install the power steering pump and bracket, if removed. Install the alternator and bracket assembly, if removed and connect the electrical harness.

30. Install the accessory drive belt(s).

31. Connect the fuel lines to the fuel supply manifold. Connect the upper radiator and heater hoses.

32. Connect the vacuum lines. Install the engine oil filler adapter on Aerostar.

33. Change the engine oil and filter.

NOTE: Engine coolant is corrosive to all engine bearing material. Replacing engine oil after removal of a coolant carrying component helps prevent engine failure later.

34. Install the air cleaner fresh air hose to the throttle body and air cleaner. Connect the negative battery cable.

35. Fill and bleed the cooling system. Run the engine and check for leaks.

36. Check the ignition timing and idle speed and adjust, if necessary.

3.0L (VIN W) Engine

1. Relieve the fuel system pressure. Disconnect the negative battery cable.

2. Remove the air cleaner. Disconnect the accelerator cable from the throttle body.

3. Drain the engine coolant, including the block drain.

4. Label and disconnect all wiring and hoses as required.

5. Remove the distributor and spark plug wires as an assembly.

6. Remove the timing belt covers and the timing belt.

7. Remove the upper intake manifold section (5 bolts).

8. Label and disconnect the wiring to the fuel injectors and disconnect the fuel supply and return hoses.

9. Remove the injectors and rail as an assembly. Place the assembly where it will stay clean.

10. Loosen the intake manifold bolts 1 turn at a time in the reverse order of the torque sequence. This is important to prevent warping the manifold.

11. Remove the bolts and lift the manifold off.

12. Mark the camshaft sprockets left and right for proper installation and remove them.

13. Remove the rear timing belt cover.

14. Without disconnecting the hydraulic or coolant hoses, remove the power steering pump and the air conditioner compressor and secure them out of the way. Remove the brackets from the cylinder heads.

15. Remove the rocker arm covers.

NOTE: It may be necessary to remove the rocker shafts and valve lifter guide to provide access to the cylinder head bolts. Before removing the valve lifter guide, secure the valve lifters with a safety wire to keep them in their original positions.

16. To prevent warping the heads, loosen the cylinder head bolts 1 turn at a time in the reverse order of the torque sequence. When they are all loose, remove the bolts and lift the heads off the engine.

To install:

17. Thoroughly clean all gasket surfaces and inspect the head and block for damage to the surfaces. Before installing, check the cylinder head for warping. The limit is 0.004 in. (0.10mm). Make sure the threads on the bolts and in the block are clean and that the bolts turn easily in the threads. Do not oil the threads.

18. Set the crankshaft to TDC on No. 1 cylinder and make sure the mark on the sprocket aligns with the mark on the oil pump body. Make sure the knock pin on the camshaft is at the top.

19. Use new gaskets and install the exhaust manifolds. Torque the nuts or bolts in the proper sequence to 16 ft. lbs. (22 Nm).

20. Apply sealant to the block cooling system drain plugs and install the plugs.

21. Make sure the new head gaskets are properly fitted and install the cylinder heads. When installing the bolts, the long bolts go into positions 4, 5, 12 and 13; the flat side of the washer goes towards the head.

22. Torque the cylinder head bolts in the proper sequence in five steps:

Step 1 — 22 ft. lbs. (30 Nm)
Step 2 — 43 ft. lbs. (58 Nm)
Step 3 — loosen all bolts
Step 4 — 22 ft. lbs. (30 Nm)
Step 5 — 40–47 ft. lbs. (54–64 Nm) or 22 ft. lbs. (30 Nm) plus 65 degrees.

23. If the lifter guide and rocker arms were removed, install them now and tighten the bolts 1 turn at a time to draw the shafts down evenly against the valve springs without bending the shafts. Torque the bolts to 16 ft. lbs. (22 Nm).

24. Install the rocker arm covers and torque the bolts to 25 inch lbs. (3 Nm).

25. Install the rear timing belt cover and the camshaft sprockets. Make sure the sprockets are on the correct side and torque the sprocket bolts to 65 ft. lbs. (88 Nm).

26. Make sure the crankshaft and camshafts are properly positioned to install the timing belt. Be careful if it is necessary to turn either shaft; this is not a free wheeling engine and the valves will contact the pistons if the crankshaft is turned without the timing belt in place.

27. Install the timing belt, set the tension and turn the crankshaft 2 full

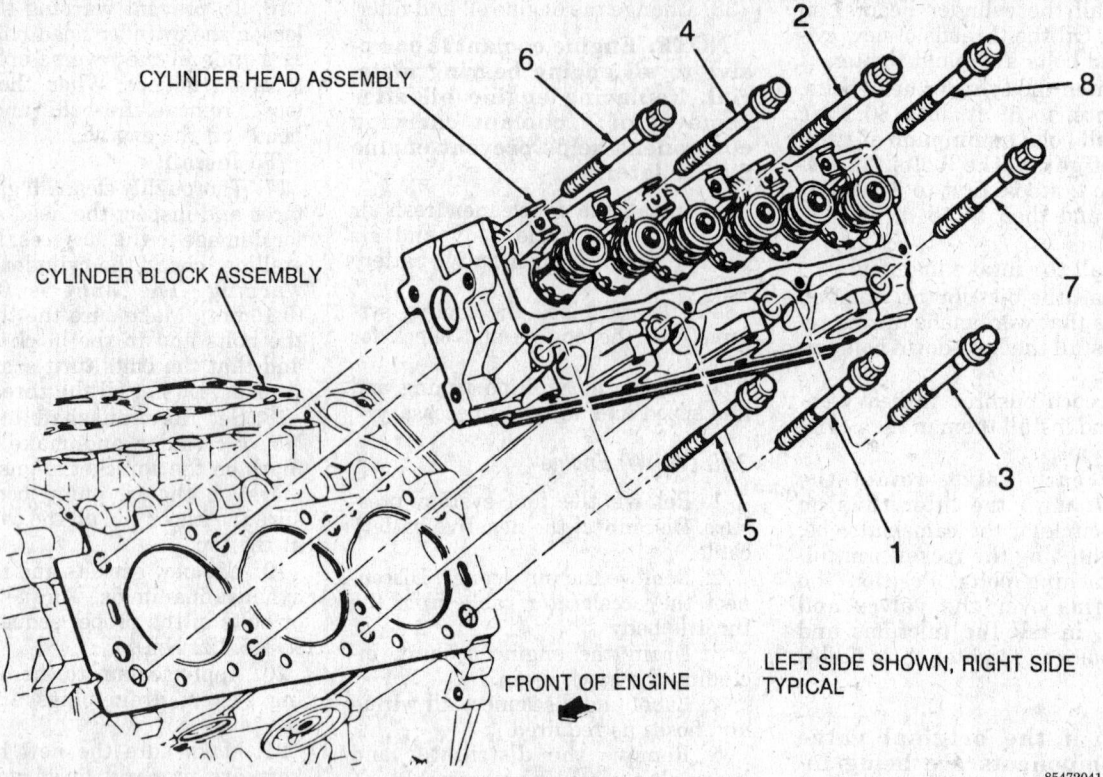

CYLINDER HEAD ASSEMBLY

CYLINDER BLOCK ASSEMBLY

FRONT OF ENGINE

LEFT SIDE SHOWN, RIGHT SIDE TYPICAL

85472041

Cylinder head bolt torque sequence — 3.0L engine

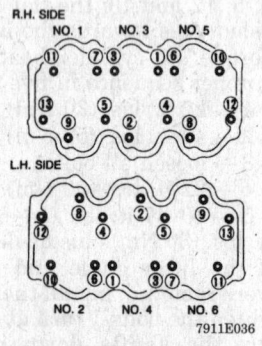

R.H. SIDE

NO. 1   NO. 3   NO. 5

L.H. SIDE

NO. 2   NO. 4   NO. 6

7911E036

Cylinder head bolt torque sequence — 3.0L (VIN W) engine

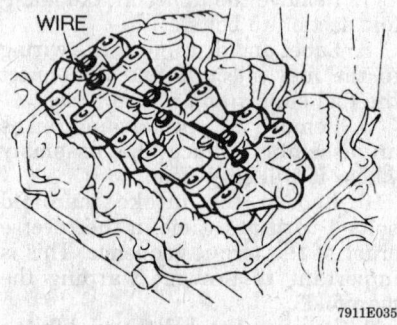

WIRE

7911E035

Secure the lifters with wire before removing the guide assembly — 3.0L (VIN W) engine

turns to make sure the timing marks still align properly.

28. Use a new gasket to install the intake manifold and torque the nuts bolts in the proper sequence in 3 steps. Torque the nuts to 20 ft. lbs. (27 Nm) and the bolts to 14 ft. lbs. (20 Nm).

29. Connect the exhaust pipes to the manifolds and torque the bolts to 20 ft. lbs. (27 Nm).

30. Install the remaining components using new gaskets, O-rings or seals as required. Adjust belt tensions and change the oil before starting the engine.

31. When the engine is first started, the hydraulic valve lifters may be noisy. Run the engine for 10–20 minutes at about 1000 rpm. If the noise has not subsided, the lifter will probably never pump up and must be replaced.

4.0L Engine

1. Disconnect the negative battery cable and relieve the fuel system pressure. Drain the cooling system.

2. Remove the upper and lower intake manifolds and rocker arm covers.

3. If the left cylinder head is being removed, proceed as follows:
   a. Remove the accessory drive belt.
   b. Discharge the refrigerant and remove the air conditioning compressor, if equipped.
   c. Remove the power steering pump and bracket and position aside.
   d. Remove the spark plugs.

4. If the right cylinder head is being removed, proceed as follows:
   a. Remove the accessory drive belt.
   b. Remove the alternator and alternator bracket.
   c. Remove the ignition coil and bracket assembly.
   d. Remove the spark plugs.

5. Disconnect the exhaust pipe and remove the exhaust manifold(s).

6. Remove the rocker arm shaft assembly. Remove the pushrods, marking them so they can be reinstalled in the same positions.

7. Remove and discard the cylinder head attaching bolts and remove the cylinder heads.

8. Clean all gasket mating surfaces. Check the cylinder head for flatness using a straight edge and a feeler gauge. The cylinder head must not be warped more than 0.003 in. in

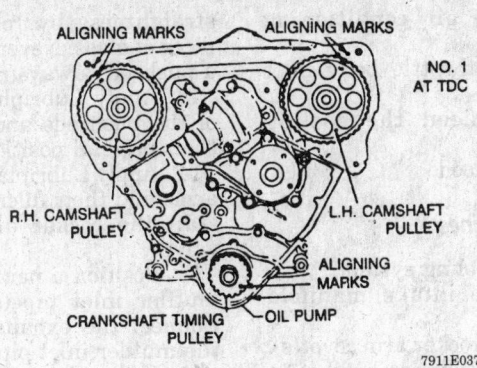

View of the camshaft sprocket timing marks — 3.0L (VIN W) engine

7911E037

any 6 in. or more than 0.006 in. overall.

To install:

9. Position new cylinder head gasket(s) on the cylinder block. Install cylinder head locating dowels.

NOTE: The cylinder head(s) and intake manifold are torqued alternately and in sequence to insure correct fit and gasket crunch.

10. Install new cylinder head bolts and tighten, in sequence, to 44 ft. lbs. (60 Nm).

11. Apply silicone sealer to the block and cylinder head mating surfaces at the 4 corners of the lifter valley opening. Install the intake manifold gasket and again apply sealer in the same locations.

12. Position the lower intake manifold on the 2 guide studs and install the nuts and bolts hand tight. Tighten the lower intake manifold bolts, in sequence, to 3–6 ft. lbs. (4–8 Nm).

13. Tighten the cylinder head bolts, in sequence, to 59 ft. lbs. (80 Nm).

14. Tighten the intake manifold, in sequence, to 6–11 ft. lbs. (8–15 Nm).

15. Turn the cylinder head bolts 80–85 degrees tighter, in sequence.

16. Tighten the intake manifold, in sequence, to 11–15 ft. lbs. (15–21 Nm) and then to 15–18 ft. lbs. (21–25 Nm), in sequence.

17. Dip both ends of each pushrod in clean engine oil and install in their original locations. Install the rocker arm and shaft assemblies and tighten the rocker arm shaft support bolts evenly to 46–52 ft. lbs. (62–70 Nm).

18. Apply silicone sealer to the 4 locations at the joint where the intake manifold and cylinder head meet. Install a new rocker arm cover gasket in each cover and install the rocker arm covers. Tighten the rocker arm

cover bolts to 3–5 ft. lbs. (4–7 Nm), wait 2 minutes and then retighten to the same specification.

19. Install the upper intake manifold and tighten the nuts to 15–18 ft. lbs. (20–25 Nm).

20. Install the exhaust manifold(s) and connect the exhaust pipe.

21. Install the spark plugs and the ignition coil and bracket assembly.

22. Install the alternator and the accessory drive belt.

23. Install the power steering pump. Install the air conditioning compressor, if equipped.

24. Connect the negative battery cable. Fill and bleed the cooling system. Run the engine and check for leaks.

4.9L Engine

1. Drain the cooling system. Remove the hood.

2. Remove the throttle body inlet tubes.

3. Remove the air conditioning compressor.

4. Remove the condenser.

5. Disconnect the battery ground cable.

6. Disconnect the heater hoses from the water pump and coolant outlet housing.

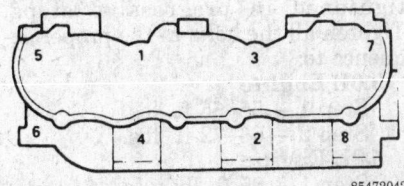

85472042

Cylinder head bolt torque sequence — 4.0L engine

7. Disconnect the fuel line at the fuel pump.

8. Remove the radiator.

9. Remove the engine fan and fan drive, the water pump pulley and the drive belt.

10. Disconnect the accelerator cable and retracting spring.

11. Disconnect the power brake hose at the manifold.

12. Disconnect the transmission kickdown rod on vehicles with automatic transmission.

13. Disconnect the muffler inlet pipe at the exhaust manifold. Pull the muffler inlet pipe down. Remove the gasket.

14. Disconnect the EEC harness from all the sensors.

15. Tag and disconnect all remaining wiring from the head and related components.

16. Remove the alternator, leaving the wires connected and position it out of the way.

17. Remove the air pump and bracket.

18. Remove the power steering pump and position it out of the way with the hoses still connected.

19. If the vehicle is equipped with an air compressor, bleed the 2 pressure lines and remove the compressor and bracket.

20. Remove the valve rocker arm cover.

21. Loosen the rocker arm bolts so they can be pivoted out of the way. Remove the pushrods in sequence so they can be identified and reinstalled in their original positions.

22. Disconnect the spark plug wires at the spark plugs.

23. Remove the cylinder head bolts and remove the cylinder head. Do not pry between the cylinder head and the block as the gasket surfaces maybe damaged.

To install:

24. Clean the head and block gasket surfaces. If the cylinder head was removed for a gasket change, check the flatness of the cylinder head and block.

25. Position the gasket on the cylinder block.

26. Install a new gasket on the flange of the muffler inlet pipe.

27. Lift the cylinder head above the cylinder block and lower it into position using 2 head bolts installed through the head as guides.

28. Coat the threads of the Nos. 1 and 6 bolts for the right side of the cylinder head with a small mount of water-resistant sealer. Oil the threads of the remaining bolts. Install, but do not tighten, 2 bolts at the

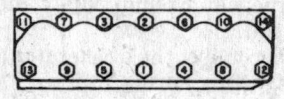

85472155

Cylinder head bolt torque sequence — 4.9L engine

opposite ends of the head to hold the head and gasket in position.

29. The cylinder head bolts are tightened in 3 progressive steps. Torque them (in the proper sequence):

Step 1 — 50–55 ft. lbs.
Step 2 — 60–65 ft. lbs.
Step 3 — 70–85 ft. lbs.

30. Apply Lubriplate® to both ends of the pushrods and install them in their original positions.

31. Apply Lubriplate® to both the fulcrum and seat and position the rocker arms on the valves and pushrods.

32. Adjust the valves, as outlined below.

33. Install the valve rocker arm cover.

34. Install the air compressor and bracket.

35. Install the power steering pump.

36. Install the air pump and bracket.

37. Install the alternator.

38. Connect all wiring at the head and related components.

39. Connect the EEC harness to all the sensors.

40. Connect the muffler inlet pipe at the exhaust manifold.

41. Connect the transmission kickdown rod on vehicles with automatic transmission.

42. Connect the power brake hose at the manifold.

43. Connect the accelerator cable and retracting spring.

44. Install the water pump pulley, the engine fan and fan drive, and the drive belt.

45. Install the radiator.

46. Connect the fuel line at the fuel pump.

47. Connect the heater hoses at the water pump and coolant outlet housing.

48. Connect the battery ground cable.

49. Install the condenser.

50. Install the air conditioning compressor.

51. Install the throttle body inlet tubes.

52. Fill and bleed the cooling system.

53. Install the hood.

5.0L and 5.8L Engines

1. Drain the cooling system.
2. Remove the intake manifold and throttle body.
3. Remove the rocker arm cover(s).
4. If the right cylinder head is to be removed, lift the tensioner and remove the drive belt. Loosen the alternator adjusting arm bolt and remove the alternator mounting bracket bolt and spacer. Swing the alternator down and out of the way. Remove the air cleaner inlet duct.

If the left cylinder head is being removed, remove the air conditioning compressor. Persons not familiar with air conditioning systems should exercise extreme caution, perhaps leaving this job to a professional. Remove the oil dipstick and tube. Remove the cruise control bracket.

5. Disconnect the exhaust manifold(s) from the muffler inlet pipe(s).
6. Loosen the rocker arm stud nuts so the rocker arms can be rotated to the side. Remove the pushrods and identify them so they can be reinstalled in their original positions.
7. Disconnect the Thermactor® air supply hoses at the check valves. Cover the check valve openings.
8. Remove the cylinder head bolts and lift the cylinder head from the block. Remove the discard the gasket.

To install:

9. Clean the cylinder head, intake manifold, the valve cover and the head gasket surfaces.
10. A specially treated composition head gasket is used. Do not apply sealer to a composition gasket. Position the new gasket over the locating dowels on the cylinder block. Then, position the cylinder head on the block and install the attaching bolts.
11. The cylinder head bolts are tightened in progressive steps. Tighten all the bolts in the proper sequence to:

5.0L Engine
Step 1 — 55–65 ft. lbs.
Step 2 — 66–72 ft. lbs.

5.8L Engine
Step 1 — 85 ft. lbs.
Step 2 — 95 ft. lbs.
Step 3 — 105–112 ft. lbs.

12. Clean the pushrods. Blow out the oil passage in the rods with compressed air. Check the pushrods for

straightness by rolling them on a piece of glass. Never try to straighten a pushrod; always replace it.

13. Apply Lubriplate® to the ends of the pushrods and install them in their original positions.

14. Apply Lubriplate® to the rocker arms and their fulcrum seats and install the rocker arms. Adjust the valves.

15. Position a new gasket(s) on the muffler inlet pipe(s) as necessary. Connect the exhaust manifold(s) at the muffler inlet pipe(s).

16. If the right cylinder head was removed, install the alternator, and air cleaner duct. Install the drive belt. If the left cylinder head was removed, install the compressor. Install the dipstick and cruise control bracket.

17. Clean the valve rocker arm cover and the cylinder head gasket surfaces. Place the new gaskets in the covers, making sure the tabs of the gasket engage the notches provided in the cover. Evacuate, charge and leak test the air conditioning system.

18. Install the intake manifold and related parts. Install the Thermactor® hoses.

19. Fill and bleed the cooling system.

7.5L Engine

1. Drain the cooling system.
2. Remove the upper and lower intake manifolds..
3. Disconnect the exhaust pipe from the exhaust manifold.
4. Loosen the air conditioning compressor drive belt, if equipped.
5. Loosen the alternator attaching bolts and remove the bolt attaching the alternator bracket to the right cylinder head.
6. Disconnect the air conditioning compressor from the engine and move it aside, out of the way. Do not discharge the air conditioning system.
7. Remove the bolts securing the power steering reservoir bracket to the left cylinder head. Position the reservoir and bracket out of the way. On motor home chassis, remove the oil filler tube.
8. Remove the valve rocker arm covers. Remove the rocker arm bolts, rocker arms, oil deflectors, fulcrums and pushrods in sequence so they can be reinstalled in their original positions.
9. Remove the cylinder head bolts and lift the head and exhaust manifold off the engine. If necessary, pry at the forward corners of the cylinder

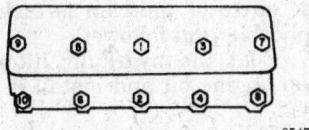

Cylinder head bolt torque sequence — 5.0L, 5.8L and 7.5L engines

85472156

head against the casting bosses provided on the cylinder block. Do not damage the gasket mating surfaces of the cylinder head and block by prying against them.

To install:

10. Remove all gasket material from the cylinder head and block. Clean all gasket material from the mating surfaces of the intake manifold. If the exhaust manifold was removed, clean the mating surfaces of the cylinder head and exhaust manifold. Apply a thin coat of graphite grease to the cylinder head exhaust port areas and install the exhaust manifold.

11. Position 2 long cylinder head bolts in the 2 rear lower bolt holes of the left cylinder head. Place a long cylinder head bolt in the rear lower bolt hole of the right cylinder head. Use rubber bands to keep the bolts in position until the cylinder heads are installed on the cylinder block.

12. Position new cylinder head gaskets on the cylinder block dowels. Do not apply sealer to the gaskets, heads, or block.

13. Place the cylinder heads on the block, guiding the exhaust manifold studs into the exhaust pipe connections. Install the remaining cylinder head bolts. The longer bolts go in the lower row of holes.

14. Tighten all the cylinder head attaching bolts in the proper sequence in 3 stages: 80–90 ft. lbs., 100–110 ft. lbs., and finally to 130–140 ft. lbs. When this procedure is used, it is not necessary to retorque the heads after extended use.

15. Make sure the oil holes in the pushrods are open and install the pushrods in their original positions. Place a dab of Lubriplate® to the ends of the pushrods before installing them.

16. Lubricate and install the valve rockers. Make sure the pushrods remain seated in their lifters.

17. Connect the exhaust pipes to the exhaust manifolds.

18. Install the upper and lower intake manifolds.

19. Install the air conditioning compressor.

20. Install the power steering reservoir.

21. Apply oil-resistant sealer to one side of the new valve cover gaskets and lay the cemented side in place in the valve cover. Install the covers.

22. Install the alternator and adjust the drive belt.

23. Adjust the air conditioning compressor drive belt tension.

24. On motor home chassis, install the oil filler tube.

25. Fill and bleed the cooling system.

26. Start the engine and check for leaks.

7.3L Diesel Engine

1. Open the hood and disconnect the negative cables from both batteries.

2. Drain the cooling system and remove the radiator fan shroud halves.

3. Remove the radiator fan and clutch assembly using special tool T83T–6312–A and B. This tool is available through the Owatonna Tool Co. whose address is listed in the front of this boot, or through Ford Dealers. It is also available through many tool rental shops.

NOTE: The fan clutch uses a left hand thread and must be removed by turning the nut clockwise.

4. Label and disconnect the wiring from the alternator.

5. Remove the adjusting bolts and pivot bolts from the alternator and the vacuum pump and remove both units.

6. Remove the fuel filter lines and cap to prevent fuel leakage.

7. Remove the alternator, vacuum pump, and fuel filter brackets with the fuel filter attached.

8. Remove the heater hose from the cylinder head.

9. Remove the fuel injection pump.

10. Remove the intake manifold and valley cover.

11. Raise the vehicle and safely support it with jackstands.

12. Disconnect the exhaust pipes from the exhaust manifolds.

13. Remove the clamp holding the oil dipstick tube in place and the bolt attaching the transmission oil dipstick to the cylinder head.

14. Lower the vehicle.

15. Remove the oil dipstick tube.

16. Remove the valve covers, rocker arms and pushrods. Keep the pushrods in order so they can be returned to their original positions.

17. Remove the nozzles and glow plugs.

18. Remove the cylinder head bolts and attach lifting eyes, using special tool T70P–6000 or equivalent, to each end of the cylinder heads.

19. Carefully lift the cylinder heads out of the engine compartment and remove the head gaskets.

NOTE: The cylinder head prechambers may fall out of the heads upon removal.

To install:

20. Position the cylinder head gasket on the engine block and carefully lower the cylinder head in place.

NOTE: Use care in installing the cylinder heads to prevent the prechambers from falling out into the cylinder bores.

21. Install the cylinder head bolt and torque in 4 steps using the sequence.

NOTE: Lubricate the threads and the mating surfaces of the bolt heads and washers with oil.

22. Dip the pushrod ends in clean oil and install the pushrods with the copper colored ends toward the rocker arms, making sure the pushrods are fully seated in the tappet pushrod seats.

23. Install the rocker arms and posts in their original positions. Apply Lubriplate® grease to the valve stem tips. Turn the engine over by hand until the timing mark is at the 11 o'clock position as viewed from the front. Install the rocker arm posts, bolts, and torque to 27 ft. lbs. Install the valve covers.

24. Install the valley pan and the intake manifold.

25. Install the fuel injection pump.

26. Connect the heater hose to the cylinder head.

27. Install the fuel filter, alternator, vacuum pump, and their drive belts.

28. Install the oil and transmission dip stick.

29. Connect the exhaust pipe to the exhaust manifolds.

30. Reconnect the alternator wiring harness and replace the air cleaner. Connect both battery ground cables.

31. Refill and bleed the cooling system.

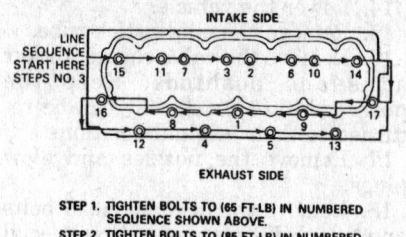

STEP 1. TIGHTEN BOLTS TO (65 FT-LB) IN NUMBERED SEQUENCE SHOWN ABOVE.
STEP 2. TIGHTEN BOLTS TO (85 FT-LB) IN NUMBERED SEQUENCE SHOWN ABOVE.
STEP 3. TIGHTEN BOLTS TO (100 FT-LB) IN LINE SEQUENCE SHOWN ABOVE.
STEP 4. REPEAT STEP NO. 3.

85472177

Cylinder head bolt torque sequence — 7.3L diesel engine

32. Run the engine and check for fuel, coolant and exhaust leaks.

NOTE: If necessary, purge the high pressure fuel lines of air by loosening the connector one half to one turn and cranking the engine until a solid stream of fuel, free from any bubbles, flows from the connections.

33. Check the injection pump timing.
34. Install the radiator fan and clutch assembly using special tools T83T-6312A and B or equivalent.

NOTE: The fan clutch uses a left hand thread. Tighten by turning the nut counterclockwise. Install the radiator fan shroud halves.

Valve Lifters

REMOVAL AND INSTALLATION

2.9L, 3.0L and 4.0L Engines

1. Disconnect the negative battery cable and relieve the fuel system pressure. Drain the cooling system.
2. Remove the intake manifold and rocker arm covers.
3. On 2.9L and 4.0L engines, loosen the rocker arm shaft support bolts 2 turns at a time until the rocker arm and shaft assembly can be removed.
4. On 3.0L engine, loosen the rocker arm fulcrum bolt enough so the rocker arm can be lifted from the pushrod and turned to 1 side.
5. Remove the pushrods, marking them so they can be reinstalled in their original positions.
6. On 2.9L engine, remove the cylinder heads.
7. Remove the lifters. Note the location of each lifter so it can be reinstalled in the same bore. If a lifter is stuck in the bore, use a suitable tool to rotate the lifter back and forth to loosen it from the gum and varnish that may have formed on the lifter.

NOTE: The 4.0L engine is equipped with roller lifters. Roller lifters have an alignment tab which fits into a locating groove in the lifter bore. Do not attempt to rotate a roller lifter in the bore.

To install:
8. Lubricate the lifters and bores with clean engine oil. Install each lifter in the same bore from which it was removed. On 4.0L engine, install the lifter with the alignment tab in the locating groove of the bore. If a new lifter is being installed, check for free fit in the bore.
9. On 2.9L engine, install the cylinder heads.
10. Check each pushrod for straightness and for damage, replace as necessary. Dip each pushrod end in clean engine oil and install in its original position.
11. On 2.9L and 4.0L engines, lubricate the rocker arm and shaft assembly and install. Draw the shaft support bolts down evenly, 2 turns at a time, until the shafts are fully down. Tighten the bolts to 43–50 ft. lbs. (59–67 Nm) on 2.9L engine or 46–52 ft. lbs. (62–70 Nm) on 4.0L engine.
12. On 3.0L engine, for each valve, rotate the crankshaft until the lifter rests on the base circle of the camshaft lobe, before tightening the rocker arm fulcrum attaching bolts. Position the rocker arms over the valves and pushrods, install the fulcrums and fulcrum bolts and tighten to 24 ft. lbs. (32 Nm).
13. Install the intake manifold and rocker arm covers.
14. Connect the negative battery cable. Fill and bleed the cooling system.
15. Run the engine and check for leaks.

2.3L Engine

1. Disconnect the negative battery cable and remove the air cleaner or air intake duct. On 2.3L engine, remove the throttle body and EGR supply tube.
2. Remove the rocker arm cover.
3. Rotate the crankshaft so the base circle of the cam is facing the applicable cam follower.
4. Using valve spring compressor lever tool T88T-6565-BH or equivalent, collapse the valve spring and slide the cam follower over the valve lifter and out.

5. Lift out the hydraulic valve lifter.

To install:
6. Rotate the crankshaft so the base circle of the cam is facing the applicable cam follower.
7. Coat the hydraulic lifter with clean engine oil and install it in the bore.
8. Collapse the valve spring using valve spring compressor lever T88T-6565-BH or equivalent. Position the cam follower over the valve lifter and the valve stem.
9. Clean the gasket surfaces of the rocker arm cover and cylinder head.
10. Coat the rocker arm cover and a new gasket with gasket adhesive and install the gasket to the cover.
11. Install the cover and tighten the retaining bolts to 5–8 ft. lbs. (7–11 Nm).
12. Install the throttle body and EGR supply tube, if necessary. Install the air cleaner or air intake duct.
13. Connect the negative battery cable.

4.9L Engine

1. Disconnect the inlet hose at the crankcase filler cap.
2. Remove the throttle body inlet tubes.
3. Disconnect the accelerator cable at the throttle body. Remove the cable retracting spring. Remove the accelerator cable bracket from the upper intake manifold and position the cable and bracket out of the way.
4. Remove the fuel line from the fuel rail. Be careful not to kink the line.
5. Remove the upper intake manifold and throttle body assembly.
6. Remove the ignition coil and wires.
7. Remove the rocker arm cover.
8. Remove the spark plug wires.
9. Remove the distributor cap.
10. Remove the pushrod cover (engine side cover).
11. Loosen the rocker arm bolts until the pushrods can be removed; keep them in order, for installation.
12. Using a magnetic lifter removal tool, remove the lifters. Wipe clean the exterior of each lifter as it's removed and mark it with an indelible marker, so it can be installed in its original bore.

To install:
13. Coat the bottom surface of each lifter with multi-purpose grease, and coat the rest of the lifter with clean oil.
14. Install each lifter in it original bore using the magnetic tool.

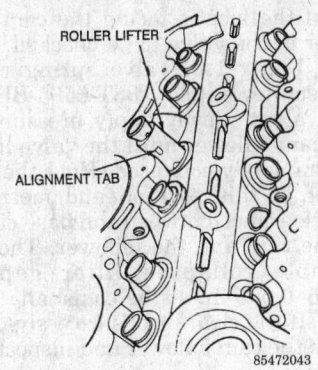

Valve lifter installation — 4.0L engine

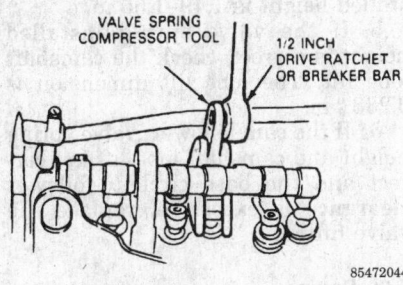

Cam follower removal — 2.3L engine

15. Coat each end of each pushrod with multi-purpose grease and install each in its original position. Make sure each pushrod is properly seated in the lifter socket.

16. Engage the rocker arms with the pushrods and tighten the rocker arm bolts enough to hold the pushrods in place.

17. Adjust the valve clearance.

18. Install the pushrod cover (engine side cover).

19. Install the distributor cap.

20. Install the spark plug wires.

21. Install the rocker arm cover.

22. Install the ignition coil and wires.

23. Install the upper intake manifold and throttle body assembly.

24. Install the fuel line at the fuel rail.

25. Install the accelerator cable bracket at the upper intake manifold. Install the cable retracting spring. Connect the accelerator cable at the throttle body.

26. Install the throttle body inlet tubes.

27. Connect the inlet hose at the crankcase filler cap.

5.0L and 5.8L Engines

NOTE: The 1993 5.0L engine uses roller lifters.

1. Remove the intake manifold.

2. Disconnect the Thermactor® air supply hose at the pump.

3. Remove the rocker arm covers.

4. Loosen the rocker arm fulcrum bolts until the rocker arms can be rotated off the pushrods.

5. Remove the pushrods and keep them in order, for installation.

6. Using a magnetic lifter removal tool, remove the lifters. Wipe clean the exterior of each lifter as it's removed and mark it with an indelible marker, so it can be installed in its original bore.

To install:

7. Coat the bottom surface of each lifter with multi-purpose grease, and coat the rest of the lifter with clean oil.

8. Install each lifter in it original bore using the magnetic tool.

9. Coat each end of each pushrod with multi-purpose grease and install each in its original position. Make sure each pushrod is properly seated in the lifter socket.

10. Engage the rocker arms with the pushrods and tighten the rocker arm fulcrum bolts to 18–25 ft. lbs. No valve adjustment should be necessary, however, if there is any question as to post-assembly collapsed lifter clearance, see the Hydraulic Lifter Clearance procedure below.

11. Install the rocker arm covers.

12. Connect the Thermactor® air supply hose at the pump.

13. Install the intake manifold.

7.5L Engine

1. Remove the intake manifold.

2. Remove the rocker arm covers.

3. Loosen the rocker arm fulcrum bolts until the rocker arms can be rotated off the pushrods.

4. Remove the pushrods and keep them in order, for installation.

5. Using a magnetic lifter removal tool, remove the lifters. Wipe clean the exterior of each lifter as it's removed and mark it with an indelible marker, so it can be installed in its original bore.

To install:

6. Coat the bottom surface of each lifter with multi-purpose grease, and coat the rest of the lifter with clean oil.

7. Install each lifter in it original bore using the magnetic tool.

8. Coat each end of each pushrod with multi-purpose grease and install each in its original position. Make sure each pushrod is properly seated in the lifter socket.

9. Rotate the crankshaft by hand until No. 1 piston is at TDC of compression. The firing order marks on the damper will be aligned at TDC with the timing pointer.

10. Engage the rocker arms with the pushrods and tighten the rocker arm fulcrum bolts to 18–25 ft. lbs. in the following sequence:

No. 1 intake and exhaust
No. 3 intake
No. 8 exhaust
No. 7 intake
No. 5 exhaust
No. 8 intake
No. 4 exhaust

11. Rotate the crankshaft 1 full turn — 360 degrees — and re-align the TDC mark and pointer. Tighten the fulcrum bolt on the following valves:

No. 2 intake and exhaust
No. 4 intake
No. 3 exhaust
No. 5 intake
No. 6 exhaust
No. 6 intake
No. 7 exhaust

12. Check the valve clearance as described under Hydraulic Valve Clearance, below.

13. Install the intake manifold.

14. Install the rocker arm covers.

7.3L Diesel Engine

1. Remove the intake manifold.

2. Remove the CDR tube and grommet from the valley pan.

3. Remove the valley pan strap from the front of the block.

4. Remove the valley pan drain plug and lift out the valley pan.

5. Remove the rocker arm covers.

6. Remove the rocker arms; keep them in order for installation.

7. Remove the pushrods; keep them in order for installation.

8. Remove the lifter guide retainer.

9. Using a magnetic lifter removal tool, remove the lifters. Wipe clean the exterior of each lifter as it's removed and mark it with an indelible marker, so it can be installed in its original bore.

To install:

10. Coat the bottom surface of each lifter with multi-purpose grease, and coat the rest of the lifter with clean oil.

11. Install each lifter in it original bore using the magnetic tool.

12. Install the lifter guide retainer.

13. Install the pushrods, copper colored end up, into their original lo-

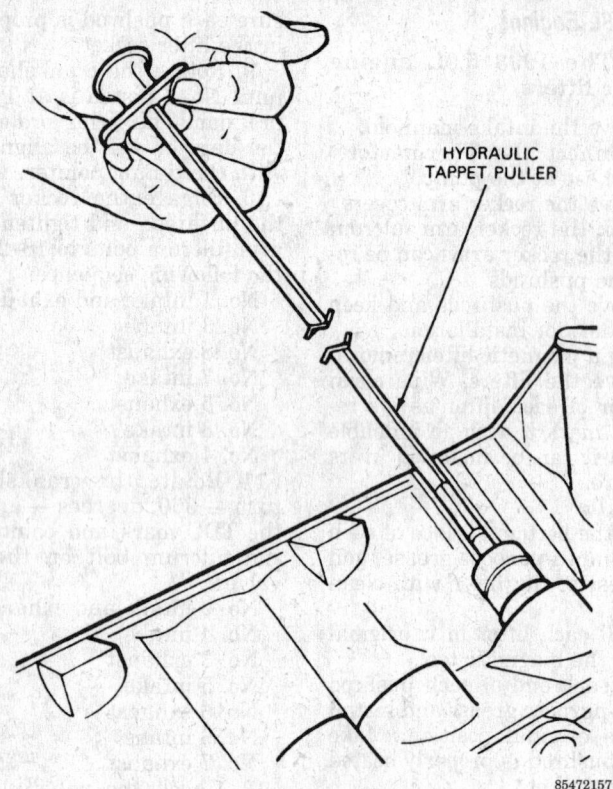

85472157

Valve lifter removal — 5.0L, 5.8L and 7.5L engines

HYDRAULIC TAPPET PULLER

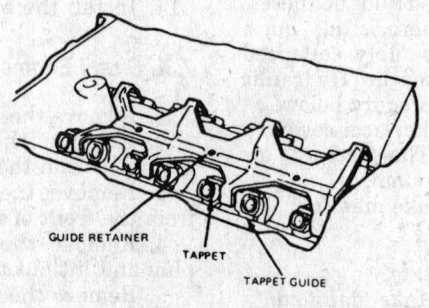

GUIDE RETAINER

TAPPET

TAPPET GUIDE

85472178

Valve lifter removal — 7.3L diesel engine

cations, making sure they are firmly seated in the lifters.

14. Coat the valve stem tips with multi-purpose grease and install the rocker arms and posts in their original positions.

15. Turn the crankshaft by hand, until the timing mark is at the 11 o'clock position — viewed from the front.

16. Install all the rocker arm post bolts and torque them to 20 ft. lbs.

17. Install the rocker arm covers.

18. Clean all old RTV gasket material from the block and run a ⅛ in. (3mm) bead of new RTV gasket mate-

rial at each end of the block. Within 15 minutes, install the valley pan. Install the pan drain plug.

19. Install the CDR tube, new grommet and new O-ring.

20. Install the intake manifold and related parts.

Valve Lash

ADJUSTMENT

2.3L Engine

1. Remove the rocker arm cover. Position the camshaft so the base cir-

cle of the lobe is facing the cam follower of the valve to be checked.

2. Using tool valve spring compressor lever tool T88T-6565-BH or equivalent, slowly apply pressure to the cam follower until the valve lifter is completely collapsed. Hold the follower in this position and measure the clearance between the base circle of the cam and the follower. The allowable collapsed lifter gap is 0.035–0.055 in. at the camshaft.

3. If the clearance is excessive, remove the cam follower and inspect for damage.

4. If the cam follower is not excessively worn, measure the valve spring installed height to make sure the valve is not sticking. The installed height is 1.49–1.55 in.

5. If the valve spring installed height is correct, check the camshaft lobe lift. The lobe lift dimension is 0.2381 in.

6. If the cam follower, valve spring height and camshaft lobe lift are correct and the base circle-to-follower clearance is excessive, replace the valve lifter.

2.9L Engine

1. Remove the rocker arm cover assembly. On the cylinder to be adjusted, position the camshaft lobe so the lifters are on the base circle.

2. Loosen the adjusting screws until a distinct lash between the rocker arm pad and the valve tip end can be noticed. The plunger of the hydraulic lifter should now be fully extended under load of the internal spring.

3. Screw in the adjustment screws until the rocker arms slightly touch the valve stem.

4. To achieve the nominal working position of the plunger, turn in the adjusting screw 1½ turns, equivalent to 0.070 in.

3.0L Engine

1. Remove the rocker arm cover.

2. Rotate the crankshaft until the lifter is on the base circle of the cam on the valve to be checked.

3. Using a suitable tool, collapse the lifter fully and measure the clearance between the valve stem tip and rocker arm. The clearance should be 0.085–0.185 in. (2.15–4.69mm).

4.9L Engine

1. Rotate the crankshaft by hand so No. 1 piston is at TDC of the compression stroke. Make a chalk mark on the damper at that point, then, make 2 more chalk marks about 120

degrees apart, dividing the damper into 3 equal parts.

2. With No. 1 at TDC, tighten the rocker arm bolts on No. 1 cylinder intake and exhaust to 17–23 ft. lbs. Then, slowly apply pressure, using Lifter Bleed-down wrench T70P-6513-A, or equivalent, to completely bottom the lifter. Take care to avoid excessive pressure that might bend the pushrod. Hold the lifter in this position and check the clearance between the rocker arm and the valve stem tip. Allowable clearance is 0.10–0.20 in. (2.5–5.0mm) with a desired clearance of 0.125–0.175 in. (3.0–4.5mm)

3. If the clearance is less than specified, install a shorter pushrod. If the clearance is greater than specified, install a longer pushrod.

4. Rotate the crankshaft clockwise — viewed from the front — until the next chalk mark is aligned with the timing pointer. Repeat the procedure for No. 5 intake and exhaust.

5. Rotate the crankshaft to the next chalk mark and repeat the procedure for No. 3 intake and exhaust.

6. Repeat the rotation/checking procedure for the remaining valves in firing order, that is: 6–2–4.

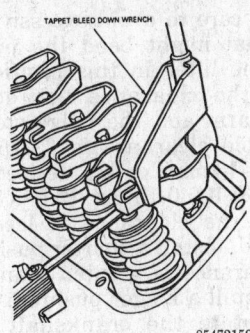

85472159

Checking valve clearance — 4.9L, 5.0L, 5.8L and 7.5L engines

5.0L Engine

1. Rotate the crankshaft by hand so No. 1 piston is at TDC of the compression stroke. Make a chalk mark on the damper at that point, then, make 2 more chalk marks about 90 degrees apart in a clockwise direction.

2. With No. 1 at TDC, slowly apply pressure, using Lifter Bleed-down wrench T70P-6513-A, or equivalent,

to completely bottom the lifter, on the following valves:

No. 1 intake and exhaust
No. 7 intake
No. 5 exhaust
No. 8 intake
No. 4 exhaust

Take care to avoid excessive pressure that might bend the pushrod. Hold the lifter in this position and check the clearance between the rocker arm and the valve stem tip. Allowable clearance is 0.071–0.193 in. (1.8–4.9mm) with a desired clearance of 0.096–0.165 in. (2.4–4.2mm).

3. If the clearance is less than specified, install a shorter pushrod. If the clearance is greater than specified, install a longer pushrod.

4. Rotate the crankshaft clockwise — viewed from the front — 180 degrees, until the next chalk mark is aligned with the timing pointer. Repeat the procedure for:

No. 5 intake
No. 2 exhaust
No. 4 intake
No. 6 exhaust

5. Rotate the crankshaft to the next chalk mark — 90 degrees — and repeat the procedure for:

No. 2 intake
No. 7 exhaust
No. 3 intake and exhaust
No. 6 intake
No. 8 exhaust

5.8L Engine

1. Rotate the crankshaft by hand so No. 1 piston is at TDC of the compression stroke. Make a chalk mark on the damper at that point, then, make 2 more chalk marks about 90 degrees apart in a clockwise direction.

2. With No. 1 at TDC, slowly apply pressure, using Lifter Bleed-down wrench T70P-6513-A, or equivalent, to completely bottom the lifter, on the following valves:

No. 1 intake and exhaust
No. 4 intake
No. 3 exhaust
No. 8 intake
No. 7 exhaust

Take care to avoid excessive pressure that might bend the pushrod. Hold the lifter in this position and check the clearance between the rocker arm and the valve stem tip. Allowable clearance is 0.098–0.198 in. (2.5–5.0mm) with a desired clearance of 0.123–0.173 in. (3.1–4.4mm).

3. If the clearance is less than specified, install a shorter pushrod. If the clearance is greater than specified, install a longer pushrod.

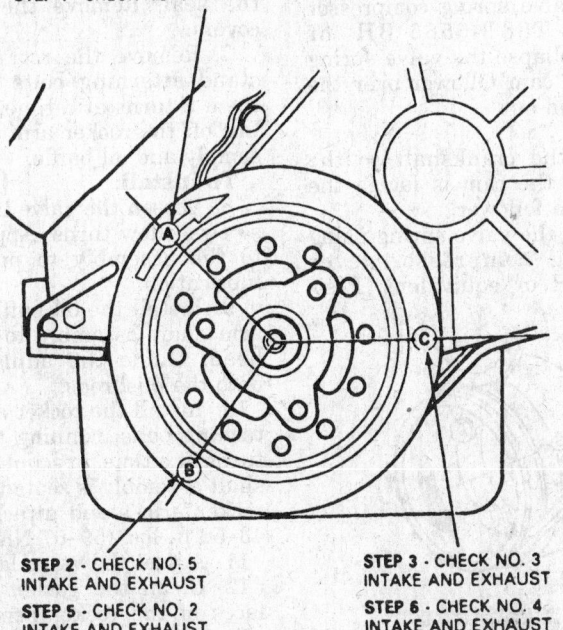

STEP 1 - SET NO. 1 PISTON ON T.D.C. AT END OF COMPRESSION STROKE ADJUST NO. 1 INTAKE AND EXHAUST

STEP 4 - CHECK NO. 6 INTAKE AND EXHAUST

STEP 2 - CHECK NO. 5 INTAKE AND EXHAUST

STEP 5 - CHECK NO. 2 INTAKE AND EXHAUST

STEP 3 - CHECK NO. 3 INTAKE AND EXHAUST

STEP 6 - CHECK NO. 4 INTAKE AND EXHAUST

85472158

Valve clearance adjustment positions — 4.9L engine

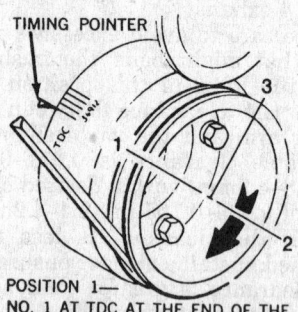

WITH NO. 1 AT TDC AT THE END OF THE COMPRESSION STROKE MAKE A CHALK MARK AT POINTS 2 AND 3 APPROXIMATELY 90 DEGREES APART.

TIMING POINTER

POSITION 1—
NO. 1 AT TDC AT THE END OF THE COMPRESSION STROKE

POSITION 2—
ROTATE THE CRANKSHAFT 180 DEGREES (ONE HALF REVOLUTION) CLOCKWISE FROM POSITION 1

POSITION 3—
ROTATE THE CRANKSHAFT 270 DEGREES (THREE QUARTER REVOLUTION CLOCKWISE FROM POSITION 2

85472160

Valve clearance adjustment positions — 5.0L and 5.8L engines

4. Rotate the crankshaft clockwise — viewed from the front — 180 degrees, until the next chalk mark is aligned with the timing pointer. Repeat the procedure for:
No. 3 intake
No. 2 exhaust
No. 7 intake
No. 6 exhaust

5. Rotate the crankshaft to the next chalk mark — 90 degrees — and repeat the procedure for:
No. 2 intake
No. 4 exhaust
No. 5 intake and exhaust
No. 6 intake
No. 8 exhaust

7.5L Engine

1. Rotate the crankshaft by hand so No. 1 piston is at TDC of the compression stroke. Make a chalk mark on the damper at that point.
2. With No. 1 at TDC, slowly apply pressure, using Lifter Bleed-down wrench T70P-6513-A, or equivalent, to completely bottom the lifter, on the following valves:
No. 1 intake and exhaust
No. 3 intake
No. 4 exhaust
No. 7 intake
No. 5 exhaust
No. 8 intake and exhaust

Take care to avoid excessive pressure that might bend the pushrod. Hold the lifter in this position and check the clearance between the rocker arm and the valve stem tip. Allowable clearance is 0.075–0.175 in. (1.9–4.4mm) with a desired clearance of 0.100-0.150 in. (2.5–3.8mm).

3. If the clearance is less than specified, install a shorter pushrod. If the clearance is greater than specified, install a longer pushrod.
4. Rotate the crankshaft clockwise — viewed from the front — 360 degrees, until the chalk mark is once again aligned with the timing pointer. Repeat the procedure for:
No. 2 intake and exhaust
No. 4 intake
No. 3 exhaust
No. 5 intake
No. 7 exhaust
No. 6 intake and exhaust

Rocker Arms/Shafts

REMOVAL AND INSTALLATION

2.3L Engine

1. Disconnect the negative battery cable and remove the air cleaner or air intake duct. On 2.3L engine, remove the throttle body and EGR supply tube.
2. Remove the rocker arm cover.
3. Rotate the crankshaft so the base circle of the cam is facing the applicable cam follower.
4. Using valve spring compressor lever tool T88T-6565-BH or equivalent, collapse the valve spring and slide the cam follower over the valve lifter and out.
To install:
5. Rotate the crankshaft so the base circle of the cam is facing the applicable cam follower.
6. Collapse the valve spring using valve spring compressor lever T88T-6565-BH or equivalent. Posi-

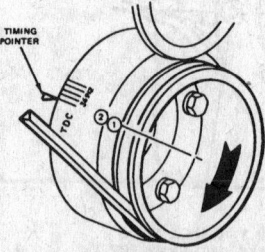

TIMING POINTER

POSITION 1—NO. 1 AT TDC AT END OF COMPRESSION STROKE.
POSITION 2—ROTATE THE CRANKSHAFT 360 DEGREES (ONE REVOLUTION) CLOCKWISE FROM POSITION 1.

85472161

Valve clearance adjustment positions — 7.5L engine

tion the cam follower over the valve lifter and the valve stem.
7. Clean the gasket surfaces of the rocker arm cover and cylinder head.
8. Coat the rocker arm cover and a new gasket with gasket adhesive and install the gasket to the cover.
9. Install the cover and tighten the retaining bolts to 5–8 ft. lbs. (7–11 Nm).
10. Install the throttle body and EGR supply tube, if necessary. Install the air cleaner or air intake duct.
11. Connect the negative battery cable.

2.9L Engine

1. Disconnect the negative battery cable and relieve the fuel system pressure.
2. Tag and disconnect the spark plug wires. If equipped, disconnect the transmission kickdown linkage.
3. Disconnect the fuel lines. If equipped with air conditioning, remove the dipstick tube and bracket and remove the left lifting eye.
4. Remove the PCV valve hose and breather. Remove the rocker arm cover attaching screws and load distribution washers. Note the position of the washers so they can be reinstalled in their original positions.
5. If equipped, remove the electrical connections from the right rocker arm cover.
6. Using a light plastic hammer, tap the rocker arm covers to break the seal. Remove the rocker arm covers.
7. Remove the rocker arm shaft stand attaching bolts by loosening them 2 turns at a time, in sequence. Lift off the rocker arm and shaft assembly and oil baffle.
To install:
8. Loosen the valve lash adjusting screws a few turns. Apply engine oil to the assembly to provide initial lubrication.
9. Install the oil baffle and rocker arm shaft assembly to the cylinder head. Guide the adjusting screws onto the pushrods.
10. Install the rocker arm stand attaching bolts, running them down 2 turns at a time, in sequence, until the shaft assembly is seated. Tighten the rocker arm stand attaching bolts to 43–50 ft. lbs. (59–67 Nm).
11. Adjust the valve lash.
12. Clean the gasket mating surfaces of the rocker arm covers and cylinder heads.
13. Install the rocker arm covers, using new gaskets. Install the attaching screws and load distribution

washers, making sure the washers are installed in their original positions. Tighten to 3–5 ft. lbs. (4–7 Nm).

14. Connect the transmission kickdown linkage, if necessary. Connect the spark plug wires.

15. Connect the fuel lines and the negative battery cable. Start the engine and check for leaks.

3.0L (VIN U) Engine

1. Disconnect the negative battery cable. Remove the air cleaner fresh air hose, if necessary.

2. Tag and disconnect the spark plug wires from the spark plugs. Remove the spark plug wire/separator assembly from the rocker arm cover attaching bolt studs and position aside.

3. If the left rocker arm cover is being removed, proceed as follows:

   a. Remove the throttle body assembly and the PCV valve.

   b. Remove the fuel injector harness stand-offs from the inboard rocker arm cover studs. Move the harness aside.

4. If the right rocker arm cover is being removed, proceed as follows:

   a. On Aerostar, remove the oil filler tube assembly and disconnect the closure hose from the oil fill adapter.

   b. On Ranger, disconnect the engine harness connectors and remove the air cleaner closure hose from the oil fill adapter.

   c. Remove the fuel injector harness stand-offs from the inboard rocker arm cover studs. Move the harness aside.

5. Remove the rocker arm cover attaching bolts and studs, noting their locations. Remove the rocker arm cover.

6. Remove the rocker arm fulcrum bolt and remove the rocker arm and fulcrum.

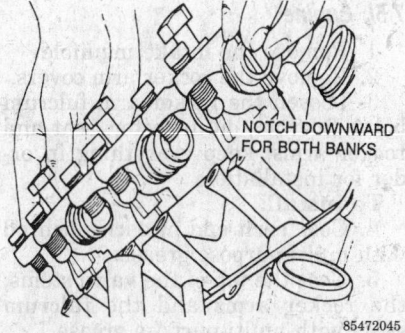

NOTCH DOWNWARD FOR BOTH BANKS

85472045

Rocker arm shaft assembly installation — 2.9L engine

To install:

7. Lubricate the valve stem tip, pushrod end, fulcrum and rocker arm fulcrum seat with clean engine oil.

8. For each valve, rotate the crankshaft until the lifter rests on the base circle of the camshaft lobe, before tightening the rocker arm fulcrum attaching bolts. Position the rocker arms over the valves and pushrods, install the fulcrums and fulcrum bolts and tighten to 24 ft. lbs. (32 Nm).

9. Clean the rocker arm cover and cylinder head gasket mating surfaces of all gasket material and/or old silicone sealer.

10. Apply a bead of silicone sealer at the cylinder head to intake manifold rail step and position the rocker arm cover on the cylinder head.

11. Install the bolts/studs in their original locations and tighten to 9 ft. lbs. (12 Nm).

12. Install the remaining components in the reverse order of their removal. Start the engine and check for leaks.

3.0L (VIN W) Engine

1. Relieve the fuel system pressure and disconnect the negative battery cable.

2. Remove the rocker arm covers.

3. Turn the crankshaft to align the timing marks at TDC on No. 1 cylinder. Remove the distributor cap and matchmark the position of the rotor to the distributor body and to the engine. Remove the distributor.

4. Loosen each rocker shaft bolt 1 turn at a time to prevent bending the shafts.

5. When all the bolts are loose, remove the rocker arm shafts with the bolts still in the shafts. This will hold the assembly together.

6. If the lifters are to be removed:

   a. Secure the valve lifters in the guide assembly with safety wire to keep them in their original positions, then remove the entire assembly.

   b. Before removing a lifter from the guide assembly, tag the lifters to make sure they are returned to their original position. Do not disassemble a lifter.

   c. Keep the lifters upright to prevent air from getting in or lay them down in a pan of new engine oil.

   d. Check the lifter for signs of wear or damage. Measure the outside diameter of the lifter and the inside diameter of the bore it came from. The clearance should

be 0.0017–0.0026 in. (0.043–0.066mm).

7. If the rocker arms are to be removed from the shafts, mark them so they can be returned into their original position. Remove the bolts from the shaft assembly and remove the rockers. Tag each shaft to tell which shaft is for the intake side and which is for the exhaust side. This is important for correct rocker arm oiling.

To install:

8. Lubricate the shafts with new engine oil and install the rockers in their original positions. Lubricate the lifters and install them into their original positions. Wire the lifters into the guide assembly.

9. Make sure the engine is at TDC on No. 1 cylinder. Install the left bank lifter guide assembly, remove the safety wire and install the rocker arm shafts. Tighten the bolts 1 turn at a time to draw the shafts down evenly. Torque the bolts to 16 ft. lbs. (22 Nm). Rotate the crankshaft to bring cylinder No. 4 to TDC. Set the right bank lifter guide assembly into place, remove the safety wire and install the rocker arm shafts. Tighten the bolts 1 turn at a time to 16 ft. lbs. (22 Nm).

11. Use new gaskets to install the rocker arm covers and torque the bolts to 24 inch lbs. (3 Nm). Install the remaining components.

12. When the engine is first started, the hydraulic valve lifters may be noisy. Run the engine for 10–20 minutes at about 1000 rpm. If the noise has not subsided, the lifter will probably never pump up and must be replaced.

4.0L Engine

1. Disconnect the negative battery cable and relieve the fuel system pressure.

2. Tag and disconnect the spark plug wires. Disconnect the fuel lines.

3. If the left rocker arm cover is being removed, upper intake manifold removal may be required.

4. If the right rocker arm cover is being removed, proceed as follows:

   a. Remove the ignition coil and bracket assembly and remove the PCV valve hose and breather.

   b. Remove the air inlet duct and the hose attached to the oil fill tube. Remove the accessory drive belt and remove the alternator.

   c. Drain the cooling system and remove the upper radiator hose. Remove the low pressure air conditioner hose bracket from the upper intake, if still installed and remove

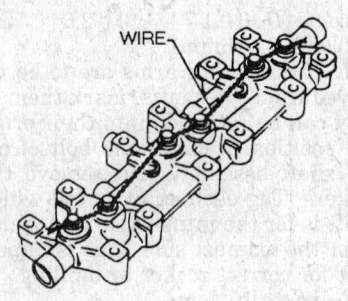

WIRE

7911E044

Hold the lifters in place with wire before removing the guide assembly — 3.0L (VIN W) engine

ROCKER SHAFT DIRECTION

EXHAUST

◄ R.H. CYLINDER HEAD FRONT   L.H. CYLINDER HEAD FRONT ►

INTAKE

7911E045

Make sure rocker arm shafts are installed in their original position — 3.0L (VIN W) engine

the vacuum hose from the air cleaner.

5. Remove the rocker arm cover attaching screws and load distribution washers. Note the position of the washers so they can be reinstalled in their original positions.

6. Using a light plastic hammer, tap the rocker arm covers to break the seal. Remove the covers.

7. Remove the rocker arm shaft stand attaching bolts by loosening the bolts 2 turns at a time, in sequence. Lift off the rocker arm and shaft assembly.

To install:

8. Apply engine oil to the valve train assembly to provide initial lubrication.

9. Install the rocker arm shaft assembly to the cylinder head, guiding the rocker arms onto the pushrods.

10. Install the rocker arm stand attaching bolts, running them down 2 turns at a time, in sequence, until the shaft assembly is seated. Tighten the rocker arm stand attaching bolts to 46–52 ft. lbs. (62–70 Nm).

11. Clean all gasket material from the rocker arm cover and cylinder head.

12. Apply silicone sealer to the parting lines where the cylinder head

and intake manifold seal. Install the rocker arm cover, using a new gasket.

13. Install the rocker arm cover attaching screws and load distribution washers, making sure the washers are in their original positions. Tighten to 3–5 ft. lbs. (4–7 Nm).

14. Install the remaining components in the reverse order of their removal. Start the engine and check for leaks.

4.9L Engine

1. Disconnect the inlet hose at the crankcase filler cap.

2. Remove the throttle body inlet tubes.

3. Disconnect the accelerator cable at the throttle body. Remove the cable retracting spring. Remove the accelerator cable bracket from the upper intake manifold and position the cable and bracket out of the way.

4. Remove the fuel line from the fuel rail. Be careful not to kink the line.

5. Remove the upper intake manifold and throttle body assembly.

6. Remove the ignition coil and wires.

7. Remove the rocker arm cover.

8. Remove the spark plug wires.

9. Remove the distributor cap.

10. Remove the pushrod cover (engine side cover).

11. Loosen the rocker arm bolts until the pushrods can be removed; keep them in order, for installation.

12. Using a magnetic lifter removal tool, remove the lifters. Wipe clean the exterior of each lifter as it's removed and mark it with an indelible marker, so it can be installed in its original bore.

To install:

13. Coat the bottom surface of each lifter with multi-purpose grease, and coat the rest of the lifter with clean oil.

14. Install each lifter in it original bore using the magnetic tool.

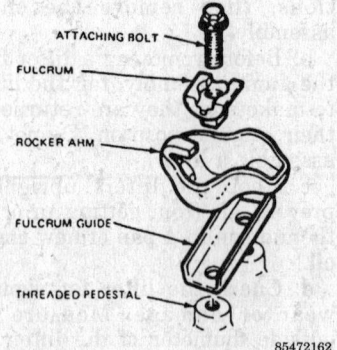

ATTACHING BOLT

FULCRUM

ROCKER AHM

FULCRUM GUIDE

THREADED PEDESTAL

85472162

Rocker arm assembly — 4.9L engine

15. Coat each end of each pushrod with multi-purpose grease and install each in its original position. Make sure each pushrod is properly seated in the lifter socket.

16. Engage the rocker arms with the pushrods and tighten the rocker arm bolts enough to hold the pushrods in place.

17. Adjust the valve clearance as described below.

18. Install the pushrod cover (engine side cover).

19. Install the distributor cap.

20. Install the spark plug wires.

21. Install the rocker arm cover.

22. Install the ignition coil and wires.

23. Install the upper intake manifold and throttle body assembly.

24. Install the fuel line at the fuel rail.

25. Install the accelerator cable bracket on the upper intake manifold. Install the cable retracting spring. Connect the accelerator cable at the throttle body.

26. Install the throttle body inlet tubes.

27. Connect the inlet hose at the crankcase filler cap.

5.0L and 5.8L Engines

1. Remove the intake manifold.

2. Disconnect the Thermactor® air supply hose at the pump.

3. Remove the rocker arm covers.

4. Loosen the rocker arm fulcrum bolts, fulcrum seats and rocker arms; keep all parts in order for installation.

To install:

5. Apply multi-purpose grease to the valve stem tips, the fulcrum seats and sockets.

6. Install the fulcrum guides, rocker arms, seats and bolts. Torque the bolts to 18–25 ft. lbs.

7. Install the rocker arm covers.

8. Connect the Thermactor® air supply hose at the pump.

9. Install the intake manifold.

7.5L Engine

1. Remove the intake manifold.

2. Remove the rocker arm covers.

3. Loosen the rocker arm fulcrum bolts, fulcrum, oil deflector, seat and rocker arms; keep everything in order for installation.

To install:

4. Coat each end of each pushrod with multi-purpose grease.

5. Coat the top of the valve stems, the rocker arms and the fulcrum seats with multi-purpose grease.

6. Rotate the crankshaft by hand until No. 1 piston is at TDC of com-

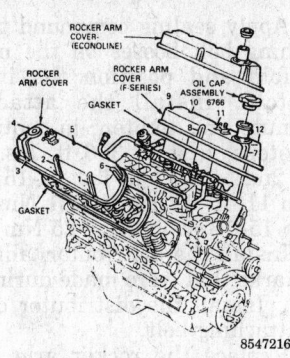

Rocker arm cover bolt torque
sequence — 5.0L and 5.8L engines

pression. The firing order marks on the damper will be aligned at TDC with the timing pointer.

7. Install the rocker arms, seats, deflectors and bolts on the following valves:

No. 1 intake and exhaust
No. 3 intake
No. 8 exhaust
No. 7 intake
No. 5 exhaust
No. 8 intake
No. 4 exhaust

Engage the rocker arms with the pushrods and tighten the rocker arm fulcrum bolts to 18–25 ft. lbs.

8. Rotate the crankshaft on full turn — 360 degrees — and re-align the TDC mark and pointer. Install the parts and tighten the bolts on the following valves:

No. 2 intake and exhaust
No. 4 intake
No. 3 exhaust
No. 5 intake
No. 6 exhaust
No. 6 intake
No. 7 exhaust

9. Install the rocker arm covers.
10. Install the intake manifold.
11. Check the valve clearance as described under Hydraulic Valve Clearance, below.

7.3L Diesel Engine

1. Disconnect the ground cables from both batteries.
2. Remove the valve cover attaching screws and remove both valve cover.
3. Remove the valve rocker arm post mounting bolts. Remove the rocker arms and posts in order and mark them with tape so they can be installed in their original positions.
4. If the cylinder heads are to be removed, then the pushrods can now be removed. Make a holder for the pushrods out of a piece of wood or cardboard, and remove the pushrods in order. It is very important that the

pushrods be re-installed in their original order. The pushrods can remain in position if no further disassembly is required.

5. If the pushrods were removed, install them in their original locations. make sure they are fully seated in the tappet seats.

NOTE: The copper colored end of the pushrod goes toward the rocker arm.

6. Apply a polyethylene grease to the valve stem tips. Install the rocker arms and posts in their original positions.
7. Turn the engine over by hand until the valve timing mark is at the 11:00 o'clock position, as viewed from the front of the engine. Install all of the rocker arm post attaching bolts and torque to 20 ft. lbs.
8. Install new valve cover gaskets and install the valve cover. Install the battery cables, start the engine and check for leaks.

Intake Manifold

REMOVAL AND INSTALLATION

2.3L Engine

1. Disconnect the negative battery cable and relieve the fuel system pressure. Drain the cooling system.
2. Tag and disconnect the electrical connectors at the throttle position sensor, air charge temperature sensor, engine coolant temperature sensor and air bypass valve, if equipped. Disconnect the knock sensor connector, if equipped.
3. Disconnect the injector wiring harness at the main engine harness and at the water temperature indicator sensor. Disconnect the ignition control assembly connector, if equipped.
4. Tag and disconnect the vacuum lines at the upper intake manifold

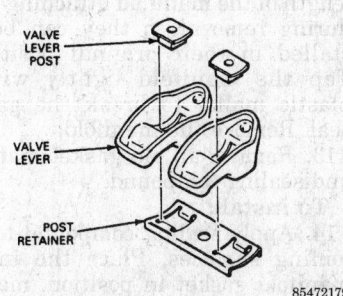

Rocker arm assembly — 7.3L diesel engine

vacuum tree, EGR valve, fuel pressure regulator and canister purge line.

5. Remove the throttle linkage shield and disconnect the throttle linkage and cruise control. Disconnect the kickdown cable, if equipped. Unbolt the accelerator cable from the bracket and position the cable aside.
6. Disconnect the air intake hose and crankcase vent hose. Disconnect the air bypass hose, if equipped.
7. Disconnect the PCV system by disconnecting the hose from the fitting on the underside of the upper intake. Disconnect the water bypass line at the lower intake manifold.
8. Disconnect the EGR tube from the EGR valve. Remove the attaching bolts and remove the upper intake manifold and throttle body assembly.
9. Remove the engine oil dipstick tube bracket attaching bolt. Disconnect the fuel lines from the fuel supply manifold.
10. Disconnect the electrical connectors from the fuel injectors and position aside. Remove the fuel supply manifold attaching bolts and remove the fuel supply manifold.
11. Remove the attaching bolts and remove the lower intake manifold.

To install:

12. Clean all gasket mating surfaces. Clean and oil the manifold bolt threads.
13. Position a new gasket and install the lower intake manifold. Install the attaching bolts and tighten, in sequence, in 2 steps, first to 5–7 ft. lbs. (7–9 Nm) and then to 15–22 ft. lbs. (20–30 Nm).
14. Install the fuel supply manifold and injectors with the 2 attaching bolts. Tighten to 15–22 ft. lbs. (20–30 Nm). Connect the electrical connectors to the injectors.
15. Position a new gasket on the lower intake manifold and install the upper intake manifold. Install the attaching bolts and tighten, in sequence, to 15–22 ft. lbs. (20–30 Nm).
16. Install the engine oil dipstick tube and retaining bolt. Connect the fuel lines to the fuel supply manifold.
17. Connect the EGR tube to the EGR valve. Tighten to 18–28 ft. lbs. (25–30 Nm).
18. Connect the water bypass line and connect the PCV hose. Connect the vacuum lines to the locations marked during removal.
19. Hold the accelerator cable bracket in position on the upper manifold and install the attaching bolts. Tighten to 10–15 ft. lbs. (13.5–20.5 Nm).

20. Install the accelerator cable to the bracket. Connect the accelerator cable and cruise control. Install the throttle linkage shield.

21. Connect the electrical connectors to the locations marked during removal.

22. Connect the air intake hose and crankcase vent hose. Connect the air bypass hose, if equipped.

23. Connect the negative battery cable. Fill and bleed the cooling system. Run the engine and check for leaks.

2.9L Engine

1. Disconnect the negative battery cable and relieve the fuel system pressure. Drain the cooling system.

2. Remove air cleaner air intake duct from the throttle body.

3. Disconnect the throttle cable and bracket assembly.

4. Disconnect the EGR tube at the EGR valve, if equipped.

5. Tag and disconnect all vacuum hoses from the fittings on the upper intake manifold.

6. Disconnect the electrical connections at the throttle body, intake manifold upper and lower, distributor and EGR pressure sensor, if equipped. Also disconnect the fuel in-

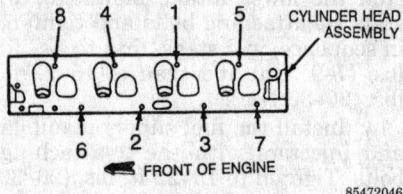

Intake manifold bolt torque sequence — 2.3L engine

85472046

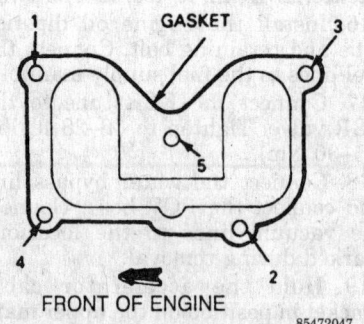

Upper intake manifold retaining bolt torque sequence — 2.3L engine

85472047

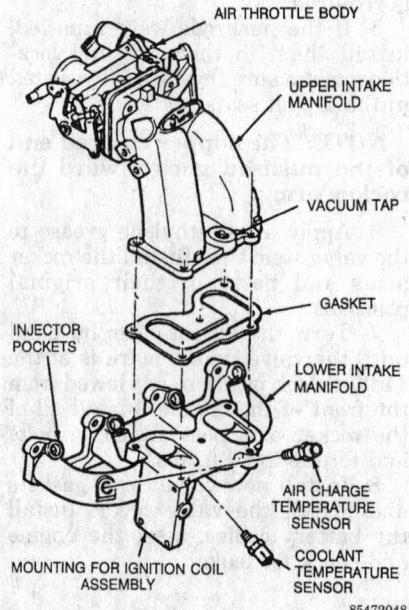

Intake manifold assembly — 2.3L engine

85472048

jector sub harness from the main EEC harness.

7. Remove the upper intake manifold assembly.

8. Disconnect and remove the hose from the water outlet to radiator and heater supply. Disconnect the fuel lines from the fuel supply manifold.

9. Tag and disconnect the spark plug wires. Remove the distributor cap and wires as an assembly.

10. Mark the position of the distributor rotor in relation to the distributor housing and the housing in relation to the engine. Remove the distributor hold-down screw and clamp and lift out the distributor.

11. Remove the rocker arm covers.

12. Remove the intake manifold attaching bolts and nuts. Note the length of the manifold attaching bolts during removal so they can be installed in their original positions. Tap the manifold lightly with a plastic mallet to break the gasket seal. Remove the manifold.

13. Remove all old gasket material and sealing compound.

To install:

14. Apply sealing compound to the joining surfaces. Place the intake manifold gasket in position, making sure the tab on the right bank cylinder head gasket fits into the cutout of the manifold gasket.

15. Apply sealing compound to the attaching bolt bosses on the intake manifold and position the intake manifold. Install the attaching bolts/nuts and tighten, in sequence, in 4 steps, first to 3–6 ft. lbs. (4–8 Nm), 2nd to 6–11 ft. lbs. (8–15 Nm), 3rd to 11–15 ft. lbs. (15–21 Nm) and 4th to 15–18 ft. lbs. (21–25 Nm).

16. Install the distributor, aligning the marks that were made during removal. Install the distributor clamp and attaching bolt.

17. Replace the rocker arm cover gaskets and install the rocker arm covers.

18. Install the distributor cap and spark plug wires. Connect the distributor wiring harness.

19. Apply sealing compound at the joining surfaces of the upper and lower intake manifold. Install new upper intake manifold gaskets.

20. Install the upper intake manifold assembly and tighten the retaining bolts in sequence, center to end, in 2 steps, first to 7 ft. lbs. (10 Nm) and then to 15–18 ft. lbs. (21–25 Nm).

21. Connect all vacuum hoses to the fittings on the upper intake manifold.

22. Connect the electrical connectors at the throttle body, intake manifolds sub harness to EEC main harness and EGR pressure sensor, if equipped.

23. Install and adjust the throttle linkage bracket assembly and cover as required.

24. Connect the hoses from the water outlet to the radiator and the bypass hose from the thermostat housing rear cover to intake manifold.

25. Connect the fuel lines.

26. Connect the negative battery cable. Fill and bleed the cooling system.

27. Check the ignition timing and reset the engine idle speed to specification. Start the engine and check for coolant and oil leaks.

3.0L (VIN U) Engine

1. Disconnect the negative battery cable and relieve the fuel system pressure. Drain the cooling system.

2. Remove the air cleaner hoses to the throttle body and rocker arm cover. Disconnect the fuel lines from the fuel supply manifold.

3. Tag and disconnect the necessary vacuum lines.

4. Tag and disconnect the electrical connectors at the air charge temperature sensor, engine coolant temperature sensor, throttle position sensor, air bypass solenoid and coolant temperature sender.

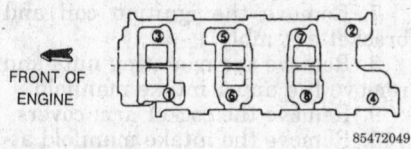

FRONT OF ENGINE

85472049

Intake manifold bolt torque sequence — 2.9L engine

5. Remove the snow shield from the power steering pump bracket and accelerator cable bracket.

6. Disconnect and remove the accelerator and cruise control cables from the accelerator mounting bracket and throttle lever.

7. Remove the alternator support brace.

8. Remove the throttle body-to-lower intake manifold retaining bolts and stud bolts and remove the throttle body assembly.

9. Disconnect the fuel injector harness stand-offs from the inboard rocker arm cover studs and each injector and remove from the engine.

10. Disconnect the upper radiator hose from the thermostat housing and disconnect the heater hoses.

11. Tag and disconnect the spark plug wires. Remove the distributor cap and wires as an assembly.

12. Mark the position of the distributor rotor in relation to the distributor housing and the housing in relation to the engine. Remove the distributor hold-down screw and clamp and lift out the distributor.

13. Remove the ignition coil from the rear of the left cylinder head, if required.

14. Remove the rocker arm covers. Loosen the No. 3 cylinder intake valve rocker arm fulcrum bolt and rotate the rocker arm away from the valve. Remove the pushrod.

15. Remove the intake manifold bolts. Break the gasket seal by wedging a large prybar between the manifold an the block using the lug on the water pump as a leverage point. Be careful to prevent damage to machines surfaces.

16. Remove the intake manifold.

To install:

17. Clean all gasket mating surface.

18. Apply silicone sealer to the intersection of the cylinder block and cylinder head at the 4 corners of the lifter valley opening.

19. Install the front and rear intake manifold seals and secure with the retaining features. Position the intake manifold gaskets on the cylinder heads and insert the locking tabs on the cylinder head gaskets.

20. Carefully lower the intake manifold into position being careful not to disturb the silicone sealer. Install the intake manifold bolts and tighten, in sequence, in 2 steps, first to 11 ft. lbs. (15 Nm) and then to 19 ft. lbs. (26 Nm).

21. Install the No. 3 cylinder intake valve pushrod. Apply oil to the pushrod and rocker arm fulcrum and position the rocker arm over the valve and pushrod. Rotate the crankshaft to place the lifter on the base circle of the cam, then tighten the fulcrum bolt to 24 ft. lbs. (32 Nm).

22. Install the rocker arm covers and the fuel injector electrical harness.

23. Install the throttle body using a new gasket. Tighten the throttle body attaching bolts, in sequence, to 19 ft. lbs. (25 Nm).

24. Install the alternator brace. Tighten the nuts to 12 ft. lbs. (16 Nm).

25. Connect the PCV valve hose. Connect the engine coolant temperature sensor, air charge temperature sensor, throttle position sensor, air bypass solenoid and coolant temperature sender connectors.

26. Install the distributor, aligning the marks that were made during removal. Install the distributor cap and connect the spark plug wires. Connect the distributor electrical connector.

27. Install the ignition coil, if removed.

28. Connect the heater hoses and the upper radiator hose. Connect the vacuum lines to the locations marked during removal.

29. Connect the fuel lines to the fuel supply manifold. Change the engine oil and filter.

NOTE: Engine coolant is corrosive to all engine bearing material. Changing the oil after removal of a coolant carrying component helps prevent engine failure.

30. Connect the negative battery cable. Fill and bleed the cooling system. Install the air cleaner hose.

31. Run the engine and check for leaks. Check the ignition timing, idle speed, throttle linkage and cruise control and adjust, if necessary.

3.0L (VIN W) Engine

1. Release the fuel system pressure and disconnect the negative battery cable.

2. Drain the cooling system to a level below the intake manifold.

3. Remove the air duct from the throttle body. Disconnect the accelerator linkage from the throttle body.

4. Remove the upper radiator hose from the water outlet housing and the exhaust tube from the EGR valve. If necessary, remove the EGR valve-to-intake manifold nuts and the EGR valve.

5. Label and disconnect the wiring and hoses as required.

6. Remove the 5 intake manifold collector-to-intake manifold bolts and the lift the collector off the engine.

7. Remove the fuel rail and the injectors as an assembly from the intake manifold.

8. To prevent warping, loosen the intake manifold nuts and bolts 1 or 2 turns at a time in the reverse of the torque sequence. Remove the manifold.

To install:

9. Clean the gasket surfaces and install new gaskets.

10. Install the intake manifold and torque the nuts and bolts in the proper sequence in the following steps:

   Step 1: all to 43 inch lbs. (5 Nm)
   Step 2:
     Bolts to 14 ft. lbs. (20 Nm)
     Nuts to 20 ft. lbs. (27 Nm)
   Step 3: repeat Step 2

11. Use new O-rings and install the fuel injectors and rail assembly. Connect the wiring.

12. Use a new gasket and install the intake manifold collector. Torque the bolts to 12 ft. lbs. (16 Nm).

13. Install the remaining components and connect the wiring and hoses. Refill the cooling system and run the engine to check ignition timing and idle speed.

4.0L Engine

1. Disconnect the negative battery cable and relieve the fuel system pressure.

2. Remove the air cleaner air intake duct from the throttle body.

3. Remove the snow/ice shield and disconnect the throttle cable and bracket assembly.

4. Tag and disconnect the vacuum hoses from the fittings on the upper intake manifold.

5. Tag and disconnect the electrical connectors at the throttle body,

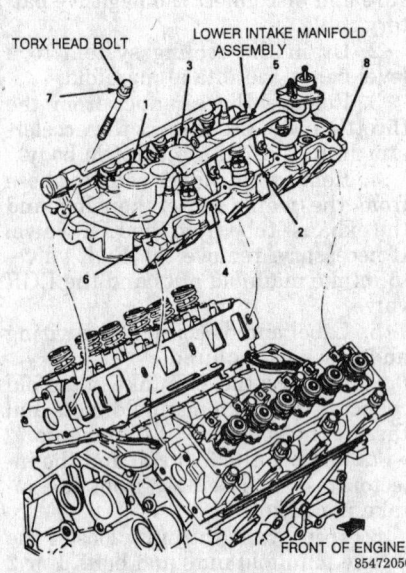

Intake manifold bolt torque sequence — 3.0L (VIN U) engine

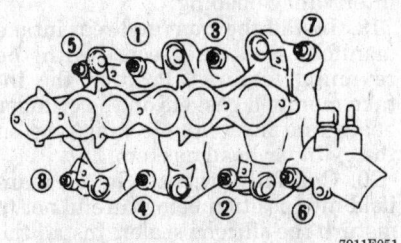

Intake manifold bolt torque sequence — 3.0L (VIN W) engine

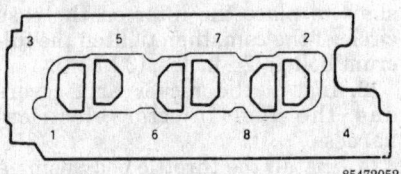

Intake manifold bolt sequence — 4.0L engine

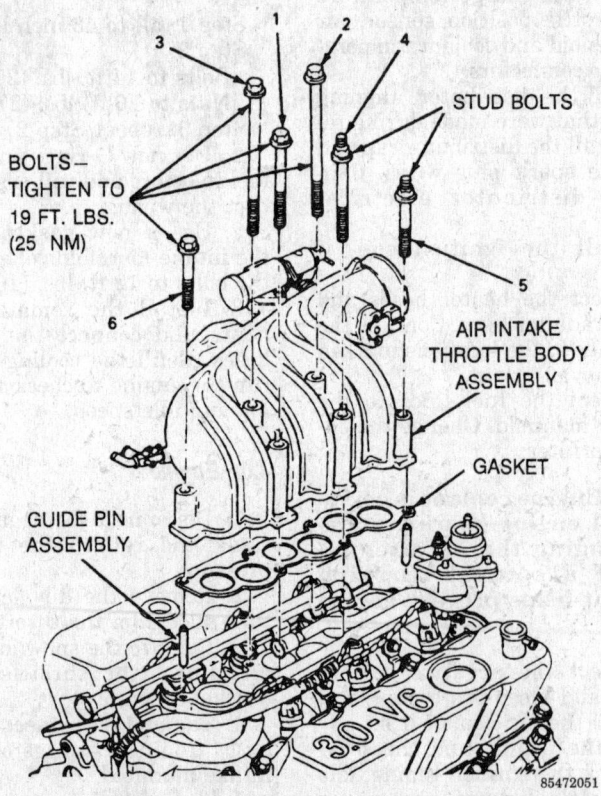

Air intake throttle body bolt torque sequence — 3.0L (VIN U) engine

upper intake manifold, lower intake manifold and injectors.

6. Disconnect the fuel lines from the fuel supply manifold.

7. Remove the ignition coil and bracket assembly.

8. Remove the mounting nuts and remove the upper intake manifold.

9. Remove the rocker arm covers.

10. Remove the intake manifold attaching bolts and nuts. Tap the manifold lightly with a plastic mallet to break the gasket seal and remove the manifold.

To install:

11. Clean all gasket mating surfaces.

12. Apply silicone sealer to the block and cylinder head mating surfaces at the 4 corners of the lifter valley opening. Install the intake manifold gaskets and again apply sealer to the same locations.

13. Position the intake manifold on the 2 guide studs and install the nuts and bolts hand tight. Tighten the bolts, in sequence, in 4 steps, first to 3–6 ft. lbs. (4–8 Nm), then to 6–11 ft. lbs. (8–15 Nm), then to 11–15 ft. lbs. (15–21 Nm) and finally to 15–18 ft. lbs. (21–25 Nm).

14. Apply silicone sealer to the 4 locations where the intake manifold and the cylinder heads meet. Install the rocker arm covers with new gaskets and tighten evenly to 3–5 ft. lbs. (4–7 Nm). Wait 2 minutes and tighten the bolts again to the same specification.

15. Install the upper intake manifold and tighten the nuts to 15–18 ft. lbs. (20–25 Nm).

16. Install the ignition coil and bracket assembly. Connect the fuel lines to the fuel supply manifold.

17. Connect the electrical connectors at the throttle body, upper intake manifold, lower intake manifold and injectors.

18. Connect the vacuum hoses to the fittings on the upper intake manifold.

19. Install the throttle cable and bracket assembly and the snow/ice shield to the throttle body.

20. Connect the air cleaner air intake duct to the throttle body.

21. Connect the negative battery cable. Fill and bleed the cooling system. Run the engine and check for leaks.

5.0L, 5.8L and 7.5L Engines, Except 5.8L Engine Lightning

NOTE: Discharge fuel system pressure before starting any work that involves disconnecting fuel system lines.

UPPER INTAKE MANIFOLD

1. Remove the air cleaner. Disconnect the electrical connectors at the air bypass valve, throttle position sensor and EGR position sensor.

2. Disconnect the throttle linkage at the throttle ball and the AOD transmission linkage from the throttle body. Remove the bolts that secure the bracket to the intake and position the bracket and cables out of the way.

3. Disconnect the upper manifold vacuum fitting connections by removing all the vacuum lines at the vacuum tree (label lines for position identification). Remove the vacuum lines to the EGR valve and fuel pressure regulator.

4. Disconnect the PCV system by disconnecting the hose from the fitting at the rear of the upper manifold.

5. Remove the 2 canister purge lines from the fittings at the throttle body.

6. Disconnect the EGR tube from the EGR valve by loosening the flange nut.

7. Remove the bolt from the upper intake support bracket to upper manifold. Remove the upper manifold retaining bolts and remove the upper intake manifold and throttle body as an assembly.

8. Clean and inspect all mounting surfaces of the upper and lower intake manifolds.

To install:

9. Position a new mounting gasket on the lower intake manifold.

10. Install the upper intake manifold and throttle body as an assembly. Install the upper manifold retaining bolts and install the bolt at the upper intake support bracket. Mounting bolts are torqued to 12–18 ft. lbs.

11. Connect the EGR tube at the EGR valve.

12. Install the 2 canister purge lines at the fittings at the throttle body.

13. Connect the PCV system hose at the fitting at the rear of the upper manifold.

14. Connect the upper manifold vacuum lines at the vacuum tree. Install the vacuum lines at the EGR valve and fuel pressure regulator.

15. Install the throttle bracket on the intake manifold. Connect the throttle linkage at the throttle ball and the AOD transmission linkage at the throttle body.

16. Connect the electrical connectors at the air bypass valve, throttle position sensor and EGR position sensor.

17. Install the air cleaner.

UPPER INTAKE MANIFOLD

1. Upper manifold and throttle body must be removed first.
2. Drain the cooling system.
3. Remove the distributor assembly, cap and wires.
4. Disconnect the electrical connectors at the engine, coolant temperature sensor and sending unit, at the air charge temperature sensor and at the knock sensor.
5. Disconnect the injector wiring harness from the main harness assembly. Remove the ground wire from the intake manifold stud. The ground wire must be installed at the same position it was removed from.
6. Disconnect the fuel supply and return lines from the fuel rails.
7. Remove the upper radiator hose from the thermostat housing. Remove the bypass hose. Remove the heater outlet hose at the intake manifold.
8. Remove the air cleaner mounting bracket. Remove the intake manifold mounting bolts and studs. Pay

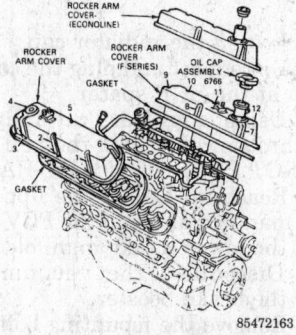

85472163

Lower intake manifold installation — 5.0L and 5.8L engines

attention to the location of the bolts and studs for reinstallation. Remove the lower intake manifold assembly.

To install:

9. Clean and inspect the mounting surfaces of the heads and manifold.

10. Apply a $1/16$ in. (1.5mm) bead of RTV sealer to the ends of the manifold seal (the junction point of the seals and gaskets). Install the end seals and intake gaskets on the cylinder heads. The gaskets must interlock with the seal tabs.

11. Install locator bolts at opposite ends of each head and carefully lower the intake manifold into position. Install and tighten the mounting bolts and studs to 23–25 ft. lbs.

12. Install the lower intake manifold assembly. Install the intake manifold mounting bolts and studs. Pay attention to the location of the bolts. Install the air cleaner mounting bracket.

13. Install the heater outlet hose at the intake manifold.

14. Install the bypass hose.

15. Install the upper radiator hose.

16. Connect the fuel supply and return lines at the fuel rails.

17. Connect the injector wiring harness from the main harness assembly. Install the ground wire from the intake manifold stud.

18. Connect the electrical connectors at the engine, coolant temperature sensor and sending unit, at the air charge temperature sensor and at the knock sensor.

19. Install the distributor assembly, cap and wires.

20. Fill the cooling system.

5.8L Engine Lightning

UPPER INTAKE MANIFOLD

1. Disconnect the battery ground.
2. Remove the air intake tube.
3. Remove the snow/ice shield from the throttle body.

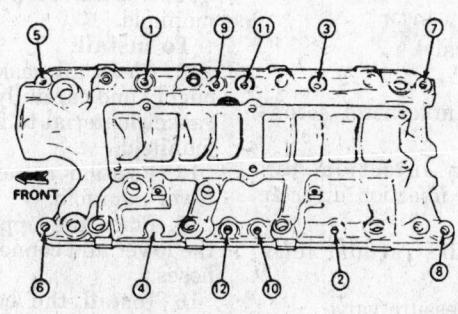

85472164

Lower intake manifold bolt sequence — 5.0L and 5.8L engines

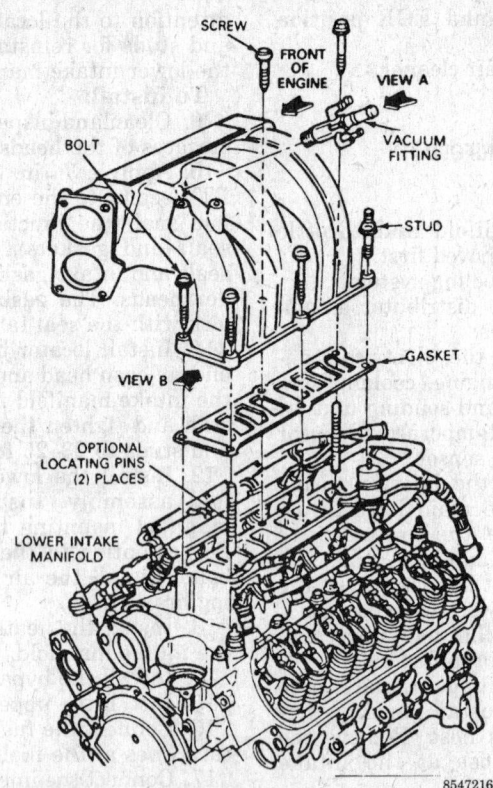

Upper intake manifold installation — 5.0L and 5.8L engines

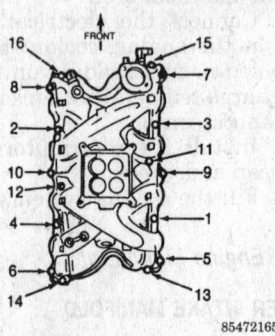

Intake manifold bolt torque sequence — 7.5L engine

4. Disconnect the electrical connectors at:

Throttle position sensor

Idle air control valve

EVP sensor

Emission vacuum control secondary regulator

Secondary air injection bypass/secondary air injection diverter solenoids

5. Disconnect the vacuum lines from:

EGR external pressure valve

EVP sensor

AIRB/AIRD solenoids

Vacuum tree

6. Disconnect the PCV fresh air tube from the throttle body and oil fill tube.

7. Loosen the radiator cap.

8. Disconnect and plug the coolant hoses at the EGR spacer.

9. Using a prybar, carefully pry the throttle cable from the ball stud. DO NOT PULL IT OFF BY HAND!

10. Reach up behind the upper intake manifold and pull the PCV valve from the lower intake manifold.

11. Disconnect the vacuum line from the brake booster.

12. Remove the mounting bolts, lift the upper manifold up and pull it forward to gain access to the vacuum hoses located below it. Disconnect the hoses and remove the upper manifold.

To install:

13. Clean all gasket surfaces thoroughly and carefully. Don't allow any gasket material to fall into the lower manifold.

14. Position a new gasket on the lower manifold.

15. Place the upper manifold onto the lower and connect all the vacuum hoses.

16. Install the bolts and tighten them, in the sequence shown, to 12-18 ft. lbs.

17. Connect the throttle cable at the ball stud.

18. Connect the coolant hoses at the EGR spacer.

19. Connect the PCV fresh air tube at the throttle body and oil fill tube.

20. Connect the vacuum lines to:

EGR external pressure valve

EVP sensor

AIRB/AIRD solenoids

Vacuum tree

21. Connect the electrical connectors at:

Throttle position sensor

Idle air control valve

EVP sensor

Emission vacuum control secondary regulator

Secondary air injection bypass/secondary air injection diverter solenoids

22. Install the snow/ice shield on the throttle body.

23. Install the air intake tube.

24. Connect the battery ground.

LOWER MANIFOLD

1. The upper manifold and throttle body must be removed first.

2. Drain the cooling system.

3. Remove the distributor assembly, cap and wires.

4. Disconnect the electrical connectors at the engine, coolant temperature sensor and sending unit, at the air charge temperature sensor and at the knock sensor.

5. Disconnect the injector wiring harness from the main harness assembly. Remove the ground wire from the intake manifold stud. The ground wire must be installed at the same position it was removed from.

6. Disconnect the fuel supply and return lines from the fuel rails.

7. Remove the upper radiator hose from the thermostat housing. Remove the bypass hose. Remove the heater outlet hose at the intake manifold.

8. Remove the air cleaner mounting bracket. Remove the intake manifold mounting bolts and studs. Pay attention to the location of the bolts and studs for reinstallation. Remove the lower intake manifold assembly.

To install:

9. Clean and inspect the mounting surfaces of the heads and manifold.

10. Apply a $1/16$ in. (1.5mm) bead of RTV sealer to the ends of the manifold seal (the junction point of the seals and gaskets). Install the end seals and intake gaskets on the cylinder heads. The gaskets must interlock with the seal tabs.

11. Install locator bolts at opposite ends of each head and carefully lower the intake manifold into position. Install and tighten the mounting bolts and studs to 23–25 ft. lbs.

12. Install the air cleaner mounting bracket.

13. Install the upper radiator hose at the thermostat housing. Install the bypass hose. Install the heater outlet hose at the intake manifold.

14. Connect the fuel supply and return lines at the fuel rails.

15. Connect the injector wiring harness at the main harness assembly. Install the ground wire at the intake manifold stud.

16. Connect the electrical connectors at the engine, coolant temperature sensor and sending unit, at the air charge temperature sensor and at the knock sensor.

17. Install the distributor assembly, cap and wires.

18. Fill the cooling system.

7.3L Diesel Engine

1. Open the hood and remove both battery ground cables.

2. Remove the air cleaner and install clean rags into the air intake of the intake manifold. It is important that no dirt or foreign objects get into the diesel intake.

3. Remove the injection pump.

4. Remove the fuel return hose from No. 7 and No. 8 rear nozzles and remove the return hose to the fuel tank.

5. Label the positions of the wires and remove the engine wiring harness from the engine.

NOTE: The engine harness ground cables must be removed from the back of the left cylinder head.

6. Remove the bolts attaching the intake manifold to the cylinder heads and remove the manifold.

7. Remove the CDR tube grommet from the valley pan.

8. Remove the bolts attaching the valley pan strap to the front of the engine block, and remove the strap.

9. Remove the valley pan drain plug and remove the valley pan.

To install:

10. Apply a ⅛ in. (3mm) bead of RTV sealer to each end of the cylinder block.

NOTE: The RTV sealer should be applied immediately prior to the valley pan installation.

11. Install the valley pan drain plug, CDR tube and new grommet into the valley pan.

12. Install a new O-ring and new back-up ring on the CDR valve.

13. Install the valley pan strap on the front of the valley pan.

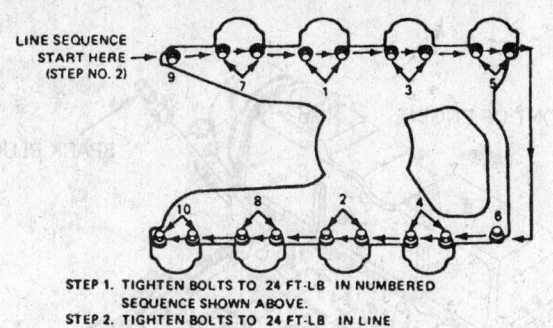

LINE SEQUENCE START HERE (STEP NO. 2)

STEP 1. TIGHTEN BOLTS TO 24 FT-LB IN NUMBERED SEQUENCE SHOWN ABOVE.
STEP 2. TIGHTEN BOLTS TO 24 FT-LB IN LINE SEQUENCE SHOWN ABOVE.

85472180

Intake manifold bolt torque sequence — 7.3L diesel engine

14. Install the intake manifold and torque the bolts to 24 ft. lbs. using the sequence.

15. Reconnect the engine wiring harness and the engine ground wire located to the rear of the left cylinder head.

16. Install the injection pump.

17. Install the No. 7 and No. 8 fuel return hoses and the fuel tank return hose.

18. Remove the rag from the intake manifold and replace the air cleaner. Reconnect the battery ground cables to both batteries.

19. Run the engine and check for oil and fuel leaks.

NOTE: If necessary, purge the nozzle high pressure lines of air by loosening the connector one half to one turn and cranking the engine until solid stream of fuel, devoid of any bubbles, flows from the connection.

CAUTION

Keep eyes and hands away from the nozzle spray. Fuel spraying from the nozzle under high pressure can penetrate the skin.

---

20. Check and adjust the injection pump timing.

Exhaust Manifold

REMOVAL AND INSTALLATION

2.3L Engine

1. Disconnect the negative battery cable. Remove the air cleaner and duct assembly.

2. Remove the EGR tube at the exhaust manifold and loosen at the EGR valve.

3. Remove the check valve at the exhaust manifold and disconnect the hose at the end of the air bypass valve, if equipped.

4. Disconnect the oxygen sensor from the exhaust manifold, if equipped. Remove the sensor, if necessary.

5. Remove the screw attaching the heater hoses to the rocker arm cover. Disconnect the exhaust pipe from the exhaust manifold.

6. Remove the exhaust manifold mounting bolts and remove the manifold.

7. Installation is the reverse of the removal procedure. Tighten the exhaust manifold mounting bolts, in sequence, in 2 steps, first to 15–17 ft. lbs. (20–23 Nm) and then to 20–30 ft. lbs. (27–41 Nm).

2.9L Engine

1. Disconnect the negative battery cable.

2. Raise and safely support the vehicle, as necessary.

3. Disconnect the exhaust pipe from the exhaust manifold.

4. Disconnect the EGR tube at the manifold, if equipped.

5. Remove the manifold attaching bolts and remove the manifold.

6. Installation is the reverse of the removal procedure. Tighten the exhaust manifold bolts to 20–30 ft. lbs. (27–40 Nm).

3.0L (VIN U) Engine

1. Disconnect the negative battery cable.

2. Raise and safely support the vehicle, as necessary.

3. If removing the left exhaust manifold, remove the engine oil dipstick tube support bracket or retaining nut, as required. Rotate the tube out of the way or remove.

4. Remove the spark plugs. Disconnect the exhaust pipe from the manifold.

5. Remove the exhaust manifold attaching nuts and remove the manifold.

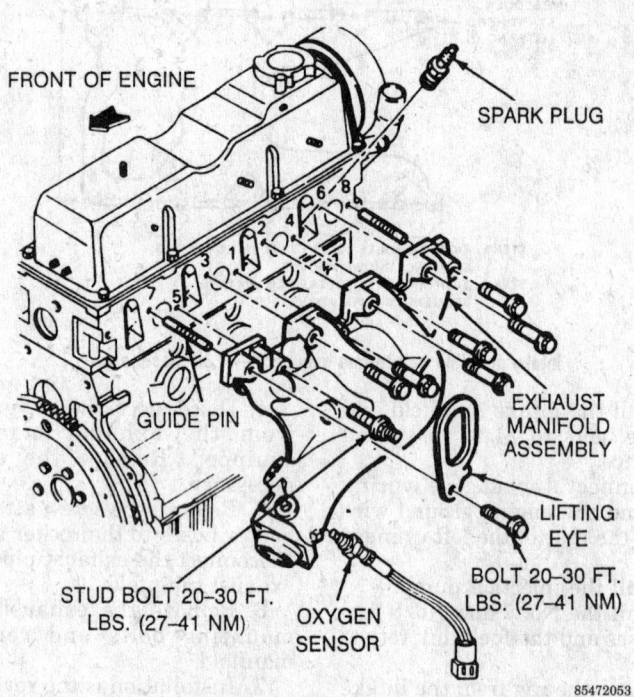

FRONT OF ENGINE

SPARK PLUG

GUIDE PIN

EXHAUST MANIFOLD ASSEMBLY

STUD BOLT 20–30 FT. LBS. (27–41 NM)

OXYGEN SENSOR

LIFTING EYE

BOLT 20–30 FT. LBS. (27–41 NM)

85472053

Exhaust manifold bolt torque sequence — 2.3L engine

6. Installation is the reverse of the removal procedure. Tighten the manifold attaching bolts to 18 ft. lbs. (25 Nm).

3.0L (VIN W) Engine

LEFT SIDE

1. Disconnect the negative battery cable.
2. Remove the hot air tube from the exhaust manifold cover. Remove the exhaust manifold cover-to-exhaust manifold bolts and cover.
3. Remove the EGR and the AIR tubes from the exhaust manifold, if equipped.

NOTE: If the alternator is in the way, remove the drive belt and the alternator.

4. Raise and safely support the vehicle.
5. Remove the exhaust pipe-to-exhaust manifold nuts and separate the exhaust pipe from the manifold.
6. Remove the exhaust manifold-to-cylinder head bolts and the manifold from the engine.
7. Clean the gasket mounting surfaces.
8. To install, use new gaskets and reverse the removal procedures. Torque the exhaust manifold-to-cylinder head nuts to 16 ft. lbs. (22 Nm) and

the exhaust pipe-to-exhaust manifold bolts to 20 ft. lbs. (27 Nm).

RIGHT SIDE

1. Disconnect the negative battery cable.
2. Remove the upper/lower exhaust manifold cover-to-exhaust manifold bolts and covers.
3. Remove the AIR tube from the exhaust manifold, if equipped.
4. Raise and safely support the vehicle.
5. Remove the exhaust pipe-to-exhaust manifold bolts and separate the exhaust pipe from the manifold.
6. Remove the exhaust manifold-to-cylinder head bolts and the manifold from the engine.
7. Clean the gasket mounting surfaces.
8. To install, use new gaskets and reverse the removal procedures. Torque the exhaust manifold-to-cylinder head nuts to 16 ft. lbs. (22 Nm) and the exhaust pipe-to-exhaust manifold bolts to 20 ft. lbs. (27 Nm).

4.0L Engine

1. Disconnect the negative battery cable.
2. Raise and safely support the vehicle, as necessary.

3. If removing the left manifold, remove the engine oil dipstick tube support bracket. Remove the power steering pump pressure and return hoses, if necessary.
4. If removing the right manifold, remove the heater hose support bracket and disconnect the heater hoses.
5. Disconnect the exhaust pipe from the manifold.
6. Remove the manifold attaching bolts and remove the manifold.
7. Installation is the reverse of the removal procedure. Tighten the mounting bolts to 19 ft. lbs. (25 Nm).

5.0L, 5.8L and 7.5L Engines

1. On the 5.0L engine, remove the dipstick bracket.
2. Disconnect the exhaust pipe or catalytic converter from the exhaust manifold. Remove and discard the doughnut gasket.
3. Remove the exhaust manifold attaching screws and remove the manifold from the cylinder head.
4. Install the exhaust manifold in the reverse order of removal. Apply a light coat of graphite grease to the mating surface of the manifold. Install and tighten the attaching bolts, starting from the center and working to both ends alternately. Tighten to the proper specifications.

7.3L Diesel Engine

1. Disconnect the ground cables from both batteries.
2. Raise the vehicle and safely support it with jackstands.
3. Disconnect the muffler inlet pipe from the exhaust manifolds.
4. Lower the vehicle to remove the right manifold. When removing the left manifold, jack the tuck up. Bend the tabs on the manifold attaching bolts, then remove the bolts and manifold.
5. Before installing, clean all mounting surfaces on the cylinder heads and the manifold. Apply an anti-seize compound on the manifold both threads and install the left manifold, using a new gasket and new locking tabs.
6. Torque the bolts to specifications and bend the tabs over the flats on the bolt heads to prevent the bolts from loosening.
7. Raise the vehicle to install the right manifold. Install the right manifold following procedures 5 and 6 above.
8. Connect the inlet pipes to the manifold and tighten. Lower the vehicle, connect the batteries and run the engine to check for exhaust leaks.

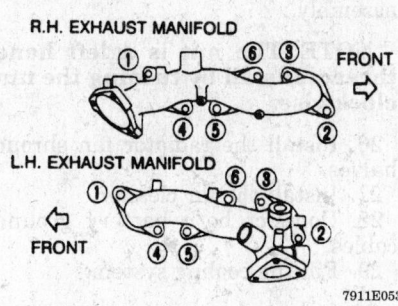

Exhaust manifolds — 3.0L (VIN W) engine

7911E053

Combination Manifold

REMOVAL AND INSTALLATION

4.9L Engine

The intake and exhaust manifolds on these engines are known as combination manifolds and are serviced as a unit.

1. Remove the air inlet hose at the crankcase filter cap.
2. Remove the throttle body inlet hoses.
3. Disconnect the accelerator cable at the throttle body.
4. Remove the cable retracting spring.
5. Remove the cable bracket from the upper intake manifold.
6. Disconnect the fuel inlet line at the fuel rail. Don't kink the line!
7. Remove the upper intake and throttle body as an assembly.
8. Tag and disconnect all vacuum lines attached to the parts in question.
9. Disconnect the inlet pipe from the exhaust manifold.
10. Disconnect the power brake vacuum line, if equipped.
11. Remove the bolts and nuts attaching the manifolds to the cylinder head. Lift the manifold assemblies

from the engine. Remove and discard the gaskets.
12. To separate the manifold, remove the nuts joining the intake and exhaust manifolds.

To install:
13. Clean the mating surfaces of the cylinder head and the manifolds.
14. If the intake and exhaust manifolds have been separated, coat the mating surfaces lightly with graphite grease and place the exhaust manifold over the studs on the intake manifold. Install the lockwashers and nuts. Tighten them finger tight.
15. Install a new intake manifold gasket.
16. Coat the mating surfaces lightly with graphite grease. Place the manifold assemblies in position against the cylinder head. Make sure the gaskets have not become dislodged. Install the attaching nuts and bolts in the proper sequence to 26 ft. lbs. If the intake and exhaust manifolds were separated, tighten the nuts joining them.
17. Position a new gasket on the muffler inlet pipe and connect the inlet pipe to the exhaust manifold.
18. Connect the crankcase vent hose to the intake manifold inlet tube and position the hose clamp.
19. Connect the power brake vacuum line, if equipped.
20. Connect the inlet pipe at the exhaust manifold.
21. Connect all vacuum lines.
22. Install the upper intake and throttle body as an assembly.
23. Connect the fuel inlet line at the fuel rail.
24. Install the accelerator cable bracket at the upper intake manifold.
25. Install the cable retracting spring.
26. Connect the accelerator cable at the throttle body.
27. Install the throttle body inlet hoses.

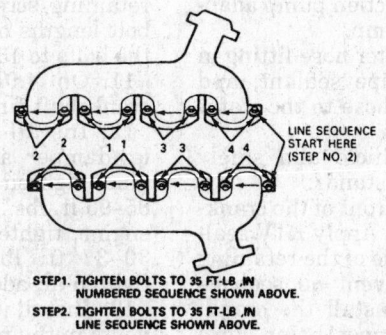

STEP1. TIGHTEN BOLTS TO 35 FT-LB IN NUMBERED SEQUENCE SHOWN ABOVE.
STEP2. TIGHTEN BOLTS TO 35 FT-LB IN LINE SEQUENCE SHOWN ABOVE.

85472181

Exhaust manifold bolt torque sequence — 7.3L diesel engine

28. Install the air inlet hose at the crankcase filter cap.

Timing Gear Front Cover

REMOVAL AND INSTALLATION

4.9L Engine

1. Drain the cooling system and disconnect the radiator upper hose at the coolant outlet elbow and remove the 2 upper radiator retaining bolts.
2. Raise the vehicle and drain the crankcase.
3. Remove the splash shield and the automatic transmission oil cooling lines, if equipped, then remove the radiator.
4. Loosen and remove the fan belt, fan and pulley.
5. Use a gear puller to remove the crankshaft pulley damper.
6. Remove the front cover retaining bolts and gently pry the cover away from the block. Remove the gasket.

To install:
7. Clean the front cover and the gasket surface of the cylinder block. Apply an oil-resistant sealer to the new front cover gasket and install the gasket onto the cover.
8. Position the front cover assembly over the end of the crankshaft and against the cylinder block. Start, but do not tighten, the cover and pan attaching screws. Slide a front cover alignment tool (Ford part no. T68P–6019–A or equivalent) over the crank stub and into the seal bore of the cover. Tighten all front cover and oil pan attaching screws to 12–18 ft. lbs. front cover; 10–15 ft. lbs. oil pan, tightening the oil pan screws first.

NOTE: Trim away the exposed portion of the old oil pan gasket flush with the front of the engine block. Cut and position the required portion of a new gasket to the oil pan and apply sealer to both sides.

9. Lubricate the hub of the crankshaft damper pulley with Lubriplate® to prevent damage to the seal during installation or on initial starting of the engine.
10. Install the fan belt, fan and pulley.
11. Install the radiator.
12. Install the splash shield and the automatic transmission oil cooling lines, if equipped.
13. Fill the crankcase.
14. Connect the radiator upper hose at the coolant outlet elbow and install the 2 upper radiator retaining bolts.

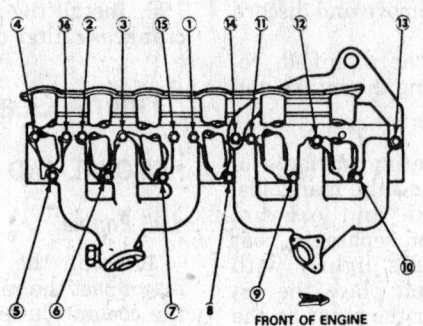

Combination manifold bolt torque sequence — 4.9L engine

15. Drain the cooling system.
16. Start the engine and check for leaks.

7.3L Diesel Engine

1. Disconnect both battery ground cables. Drain the cooling system.
2. Remove the air cleaner and cover the air intake on the manifold with clean rags. Do not allow any foreign material to enter the intake.
3. Remove the radiator fan shroud halves.
4. Remove the fan and fan clutch assembly using a puller or ford tool No. T83T–6312–A.

NOTE: The nut is a left hand thread; remove by turning the nut clockwise.

5. Remove the injection pump.
6. Remove the water pump.
7. Raise the vehicle and safely support it with jackstands.
8. Remove the crankshaft pulley and vibration damper.
9. Remove the engine ground cables at the front of the engine.
10. Remove the 5 bolts attaching the engine front cover to the engine block and oil pan.
11. Lower the vehicle.
12. Remove the front cover.

NOTE: The front cover oil seal on the diesel must be driven out with an arbor press and a 3¼ in. (82.5mm) spacer.

To install:
13. Remove all old gasket material from the front cover, engine block, oil pan sealing surfaces and water pump surfaces.
14. Coat the new front oil seal with Lubriplate® or equivalent grease.
15. The new seal must be installed using a seal installation tool, Ford part no. T83T–6700–A or an arbor press. When the seal bottoms out on the front cover surface, it is installed at the proper depth.

16. Install alignment dowels into the engine block to align the front cover and gaskets. These can be made out of round stock. Apply a gasket sealer to the engine block sealing surfaces, then install the gaskets on the block.
17. Apply a ⅛ in. (3mm) bead of RTV sealer on the front of the engine block. Apply a ¼ in. (6mm) bead of RTV sealer on the oil pan.
18. Install the front cover immediately after applying RTV sealer. The sealer will begin to cure and lose its effectiveness unless the cover is installed quickly.
19. Install the water pump gasket on the engine front cover. Apply RTV sealer to the 4 water pump bolts illustrated. Install the water pump and hand tighten all bolts.

WARNING
The 2 top water pump bolts must be no more than 1¼ in. (31.75mm) long bolts any longer will interfere with (hit) the engine drive gears.

---

20. Torque the water pump bolts to 19 ft. lbs. Torque the front cover bolts to specifications according to bolt size (see Torque Specifications chart).
21. Install the injection pump adaptor and injection pump.
22. Install the heater hose fitting in the pump using pipe sealant, and connect the heater hose to the water pump.
23. Raise the vehicle and safely support it with jackstands.
24. Lubricate the front of the crankshaft with clean oil. Apply RTV sealant to the engine side of the retaining bolt washer to prevent oil seepage past the keyway. Install the crankshaft vibration damper using Ford Special tools T83T–6316B. Torque the damper-to-crankshaft bolt to 90 ft. lbs.

25. Install the fan and fan clutch assembly.

NOTE: The nut is a left hand thread; Install by turning the nut clockwise.

26. Install the radiator fan shroud halves.
27. Install the air cleaner.
28. Connect both battery ground cables.
29. Fill the cooling system.

Timing Chain Front Cover

REMOVAL AND INSTALLATION

2.9L and 4.0L Engines

1. Disconnect the negative battery cable and drain the cooling system and crankcase.
2. Remove the oil pan and the radiator.
3. Remove the air conditioning compressor and power steering bracket, if equipped.
4. Remove the alternator and drive belt(s). Remove the fan.
5. Remove the water pump and heater and radiator hoses.
6. Remove the crankshaft pulley/damper assembly. On 4.0L engine, remove the crankshaft timing sensor.
7. Remove the front cover retaining bolts, noting their positions. If necessary, tap the cover lightly with a plastic hammer to break the gasket seal. Remove the front cover.

To install:
8. Clean all gasket mating surfaces. Apply sealer to the gasket surfaces on the cylinder block and the back side of the front cover plate. Install the guide sleeves.
9. Apply sealer to the front cover gasket surface and position a new gasket on the front cover.
10. Install the front cover with the retaining screws. Note the different bolt lengths on 4.0L engine. Tighten the bolts to 13–15 ft. lbs. (17–21 Nm).
11. On 4.0L engine, install the crankshaft timing sensor.
12. Install the crankshaft pulley/damper assembly. On 2.9L engine, tighten the attaching bolt to 85–96 ft. lbs. (115–130 Nm). On 4.0L engine, tighten the attaching bolt to 30–37 ft. lbs. (40–50 Nm), then tighten an additional 80–90 degrees.
13. Install the remaining components in the reverse order of their removal. Fill and bleed the cooling system. Run the engine and check for leaks.

3.0L Engine

AEROSTAR

1. Disconnect the negative battery cable. Remove the air cleaner fresh air hose.

2. Drain the cooling system and the crankcase. Remove the cooling fan.

3. Loosen the water pump hub bolts and remove the accessory drive belts. Remove the water pump pulley.

4. Remove the alternator adjusting arm and brace. Move the alternator aside.

5. Remove the air conditioning compressor mounting bolts, if equipped. Tie the compressor aside with mechanics wire and remove the bracket.

6. Remove the crankshaft pulley and damper. Remove the water pump, if required.

NOTE: The timing cover can be removed with the water pump installed by not removing the 6mm water pump attaching bolts.

7. Disconnect the lower radiator hose and heater hose.

8. Remove the oil pan assembly. Disconnect the oil level sensor, if equipped, before removal.

9. Remove the front cover attaching bolts and remove the front cover.

To install:

10. Clean all gasket mating surfaces. Use a seal removal tool to remove the front cover oil seal.

11. Install a new front cover oil seal, using a seal installer. Position a new front cover gasket on the engine block dowel pins.

12. Install the front cover with the attaching bolts. Apply sealer to the 3 attaching bolts on the passenger side of the cover, prior to installation. Tighten the 8mm bolts to 19 ft. lbs. (25 Nm) and the 6mm bolts to 7 ft. lbs. (10 Nm).

13. Install the oil pan. Install the water pump, if removed.

14. Install the crankshaft pulley and damper. Tighten the damper attaching bolt to 107 ft. lbs. (145 Nm).

15. Install the lower radiator hose and heater hose. Install the air conditioning bracket, compressor and brace, if equipped.

16. Install the alternator assembly, bracket, oil fill tube support and throttle body brace.

17. Install the water pump pulley and accessory drive belts. Install the cooling fan and shroud.

18. Fill the crankcase with the proper type and quantity of engine oil. Connect the negative battery cable.

19. Fill and bleed the cooling system. Run the engine and check for leaks. Install the air cleaner fresh air hose.

RANGER

1. Disconnect the negative battery cable. Drain the cooling system and crankcase.

2. Remove the cooling fan and water pump pulley bolts. Remove the accessory drive belts and the water pump pulley.

3. Remove the alternator adjusting arm and the throttle body brace. Remove the heater air intake duct.

4. Remove the motor mount upper nuts. If equipped with automatic transmission and air conditioning, remove the air conditioning compressor upper bolts, then remove the front cover front nuts.

5. Remove the distributor assembly.

NOTE: Failure to remove the distributor assembly will result in a broken distributor.

6. Raise and safely support the vehicle. Remove the lower air conditioning compressor bolts and wire the compressor aside. Remove the compressor bracket.

7. Remove the crankshaft pulley and damper. Remove the oil pan. Disconnect the oil level sensor before pan removal.

8. Lower the vehicle and remove the lower radiator hose. Remove the water pump, if required.

NOTE: The timing cover can be removed with the water pump installed by not removing the 6mm water pump attaching bolts.

9. Remove the front cover attaching bolts and remove the front cover.

To install:

10. Clean all gasket mating surfaces. Use a seal removal tool to remove the front cover oil seal.

11. Install a new front cover oil seal, using a seal installer. Position a new front cover gasket on the engine block dowel pins.

12. Install the front cover with the attaching bolts. Apply sealer to the 3 attaching bolts on the passenger side of the cover, prior to installation. Tighten the 8mm bolts to 19 ft. lbs. (25 Nm) and the 6mm bolts to 7 ft. lbs. (10 Nm).

13. Raise and safely support the vehicle. Install the oil pan and connect the oil level sensor.

14. Install the water pump, if removed.

15. Install the crankshaft pulley and damper. Tighten the damper attaching bolt to 107 ft. lbs. (145 Nm).

16. Install the air conditioning compressor bracket, if equipped, position the compressor and install the lower bolts. Lower the vehicle.

17. Install the distributor. Install the front cover front nuts and the air conditioning compressor upper bolts, if equipped.

18. Install the motor mount upper nuts and the heater air intake duct. Install the alternator adjusting arm and brace.

19. Install the water pump pulley and accessory drive belts. Install the cooling fan and coolant hoses.

20. Fill the crankcase with the proper type and quantity of engine oil. Connect the negative battery cable.

21. Fill and bleed the cooling system. Run the engine and check for leaks. Check the ignition timing and adjust, if necessary.

5.0L and 5.8L Engines

1. Drain the cooling system and the crankcase.

2. Disconnect the upper and lower radiator hoses from the water pump, transmission oil cooler lines from the radiator, and remove the radiator.

3. Disconnect the heater hose from the water pump. Slide the water pump by-pass hose clamp toward the water pump.

4. Loosen the alternator pivot bolt and the bolt which secures the alternator adjusting arm to the water pump. Position the alternator out of the way.

5. Remove the power steering pump and air conditioning compressor from their mounting brackets, if equipped.

6. Remove the bolts holding the fan shroud to the radiator, if equipped. Remove the fan, spacer, pulley and drive belts.

7. Remove the crankshaft pulley from the crankshaft damper. Remove the damper attaching bolt and washer and remove the damper with a puller.

8. Disconnect the fuel pump outlet line at the fuel pump. Disconnect the vacuum inlet and outlet lines from the fuel pump. Remove the fuel pump attaching bolts and lay the pump to one side with the fuel inlet line still attached.

9. Remove the oil level dipstick and the bolt holding the dipstick tube to the exhaust manifold on the 5.0L engine.

10. Remove the oil pan-to-cylinder front cover attaching bolts. Use a sharp, thin cutting blade to cut the oil pan gasket flush with the cylinder block. Remove the front cover and water pump as an assembly.

11. Discard the front cover gasket.

To install:

12. Place the front seal removing tool (Ford part no. T70P–6B070–A or equivalent) into the front cover plate and over the front of the seal. Tighten the 2 through bolts to force the seal puller under the seal flange, then alternately tighten the 4 puller bolts a half turn at a time to pull the oil seal from the cover.

13. Coat a new front cover oil seal with Lubriplate® or equivalent and place it onto the front oil seal alignment and installation tool (Ford part no. T70P–6B070–A or equivalent). Place the tool and the seal onto the end of the crankshaft and push it toward the engine until the seal starts into the front cover.

14. Place the installation screw, washer, and nut onto the end of the crankshaft, then thread the screw into the crankshaft. Tighten the nut against the washer and tool to force the seal into the front cover plate. Remove the tool.

15. Apply Lubriplate® or equivalent to the oil seal rubbing surface of the vibration damper inner hub to prevent damage to the seal. Coat the front of the crankshaft with oil for damper installation.

16. To install the damper, line up the damper keyway with the key on the crankshaft, then install the damper onto the crankshaft. Install the cap screw and washer, and tighten the screw to 80 ft. lbs. Install the crankshaft pulley.

17. Install the fan, spacer, pulley and drive belts.

18. Install the bolts holding the fan shroud to the radiator, if equipped.

19. Install the power steering pump and air conditioning compressor.

20. Position and tighten the alternator.

21. Connect the heater hose at the water pump.

22. Install the radiator.

23. Connect the upper and lower radiator hoses, and transmission oil cooler lines.

24. Fill the cooling system and the crankcase.

7.5L Engine

1. Drain the cooling system and crankcase.

2. Remove the radiator shroud and fan.

3. Disconnect the upper and lower radiator hoses, and the automatic transmission oil cooler lines from the radiator.

4. Remove the radiator upper support and remove the radiator.

5. Loosen the alternator attaching bolts and air conditioning compressor idler pulley and remove the drive belts with the water pump pulley. Remove the bolts attaching the compressor support to the water pump and remove the bracket (support), if equipped.

6. Remove the crankshaft pulley from the vibration damper. Remove the bolt and washer attaching the crankshaft damper and remove the damper with a puller. Remove the woodruff key from the crankshaft.

7. Loosen the by-pass hose at the water pump, and disconnect the heater return tube at the water pump.

8. Disconnect and plug the fuel inlet and outlet lines at the fuel pump, and remove the fuel pump.

9. Remove the bolts attaching the front cover to the cylinder block. Cut the oil pan seal flush with the cylinder block face with a thin knife blade prior to separating the cover from the cylinder block. Remove the cover and water pump as an assembly. Discard the front cover gasket and oil pan seal.

To install:

10. Transfer the water pump if a new cover is going to be installed. Clean all of the gasket sealing surfaces on both the front cover and the cylinder block.

11. Coat the gasket surface of the oil pan with sealer. Cut and position the required sections of a new seal on the oil pan. Apply sealer to the corners.

12. Drive out the old front cover oil seal with a pin punch. Clean out the seal recess in the cover. coat a new seal with Lubriplate® or equivalent grease. Install the seal, making sure the seal spring remains in the proper position. A front cover seal tool, Ford part no. T72J–117 or equivalent, makes installation easier.

13. Coat the gasket surfaces of the cylinder block and cover with sealer and position the new gasket on the block.

14. Position the front cover on the cylinder block. Use care not to damage the seal and gasket or misplace them.

15. Coat the front cover attaching screws with sealer and install them.

NOTE: It may be necessary to force the front cover downward to compress the oil pan seal in order to install the front cover attaching bolts. Use a prybar or drift to engage the cover screw holes through the cover and pry downward.

16. Install the fuel pump.

17. Connect the fuel inlet and outlet lines at the fuel pump.

18. Tighten the by-pass hose at the water pump.

19. Connect the heater return tube at the water pump.

20. Install the woodruff key from the crankshaft.

21. Install the damper.

22. Install the crankshaft pulley on the vibration damper.

23. Install the compressor support on the water pump and install the bracket (support), if equipped.

24. Install the drive belts with the water pump pulley.

25. Install the radiator and upper support.

26. Connect the upper and lower radiator hoses, and the automatic transmission oil cooler lines.

27. Install the radiator shroud and fan.

28. Fill the cooling system and crankcase.

Observe the following torques:

Front cover bolts — 15–20 ft. lbs.

Water pump attaching screws — 12–15 ft. lbs.

Crankshaft damper — 70–90 ft. lbs.

Crankshaft pulley — 35–50 ft. lbs.

Fuel pump — 19–27 ft. lbs.

Oil pan bolts — 9–11 ft. lbs. for the 5/16 in. screws and to 7–9 ft. lbs. for the 1/4 in. screws

Alternator pivot bolt — 45–57 ft. lbs.

Front Cover Oil Seal

REPLACEMENT

2.3L, 2.9L, 3.0L and 4.0L Engines

1. Disconnect the negative battery cable.

2. Drain the cooling system and remove the radiator, if necessary to provide access.

3. Remove the accessory drive belts and remove the crankshaft pulley and damper assembly.

4. Remove the seal from the front cover using a seal removal tool. Be

careful not to damage the seal housing or crankshaft surfaces.

To install:

5. Coat a new oil seal with clean engine oil and install in the front cover, using a seal installer.

6. Install the crankshaft pulley and damper assembly. Tighten the damper attaching bolt to 85–96 ft. lbs. (115–130 Nm) on 2.9L engine or 107 ft. lbs. (145 Nm) on 3.0L engine. On 4.0L engine, tighten the attaching bolt to 30–37 ft. lbs. (40–50 Nm), then tighten an additional 80–90 degrees.

7. Install the accessory drive belts. Install the radiator, if removed.

8. Connect the negative battery cable. Fill and bleed the cooling system, if necessary.

4.9L Engine

1. Drain the cooling system and disconnect the radiator upper hose at the coolant outlet elbow and remove the 2 upper radiator retaining bolts.

2. Raise the vehicle and drain the crankcase.

3. Remove the splash shield and the automatic transmission oil cooling lines, if equipped, then remove the radiator.

4. Loosen and remove the fan belt, fan and pulley.

5. Use a gear puller to remove the crankshaft pulley damper.

6. Remove the cylinder front cover retaining bolts and gently pry the cover away from the block. Remove the gasket.

7. Drive out the old seal with a pin punch from the rear of the cover. Clean out the recess in the cover.

To install:

8. Coat the new seal with grease and drive it into the cover until it is fully seated. Check the seal to make sure the spring around the seal is in the proper position.

9. Clean the cylinder front cover and the gasket surface of the cylinder block. Apply an oil-resistant sealer to the new front cover gasket and install the gasket onto the cover.

10. Position the front cover assembly over the end of the crankshaft and against the cylinder block. Start, but do not tighten, the cover and pan attaching screws. Slide a front cover alignment tool (Ford part no. T68P–6019–A or equivalent) over the crank stub and into the seal bore of the cover. Tighten all front cover and oil pan attaching screws to 12–18 ft. lbs. front cover; 10–15 ft. lbs. oil pan, tightening the oil pan screws first.

NOTE: Trim away the exposed portion of the old oil pan gasket flush with the front of the engine

block. Cut and position the required portion of a new gasket to the oil pan and apply sealer to both sides.

11. Lubricate the hub of the crankshaft damper pulley with Lubriplate® to prevent damage to the seal during installation or on initial starting of the engine.

12. Install the fan belt, fan and pulley.

13. Install the radiator.

14. Install the splash shield and the automatic transmission oil cooling lines, if equipped.

15. Fill the crankcase.

16. Connect the radiator upper hose at the coolant outlet elbow and install the 2 upper radiator retaining bolts.

17. Drain the cooling system.

18. Start the engine and check for leaks.

5.0L and 5.8L Engines

1. Drain the cooling system and the crankcase.

2. Disconnect the upper and lower radiator hoses from the water pump, transmission oil cooler lines from the radiator, and remove the radiator.

3. Disconnect the heater hose from the water pump. Slide the water

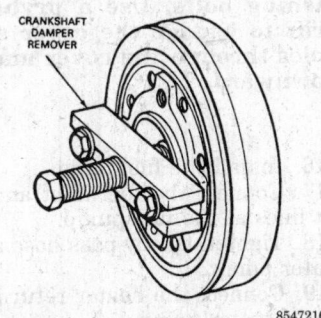

Crankshaft damper removal — 4.9L, 5.0L, 5.8L and 7.5L engines

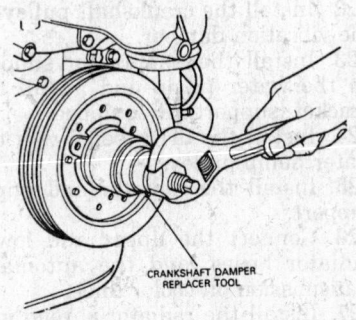

Crankshaft damper installation — 4.9L, 5.0L, 5.8L and 7.5L engines

pump by-pass hose clamp toward the water pump.

4. Loosen the alternator pivot bolt and the bolt which secures the alternator adjusting arm to the water pump. Position the alternator out of the way.

5. Remove the power steering pump and air conditioning compressor from their mounting brackets, if equipped.

6. Remove the bolts holding the fan shroud to the radiator, if equipped. Remove the fan, spacer, pulley and drive belts.

7. Remove the crankshaft pulley from the crankshaft damper. Remove the damper attaching bolt and washer and remove the damper with a puller.

8. Disconnect the fuel pump outlet line at the fuel pump. Disconnect the vacuum inlet and outlet lines from the fuel pump. Remove the fuel pump attaching bolts and lay the pump to one side with the fuel inlet line still attached.

9. Remove the oil level dipstick and the bolt holding the dipstick tube to the exhaust manifold on the 5.0L engine.

10. Remove the oil pan-to-cylinder front cover attaching bolts. Use a sharp, thin cutting blade to cut the oil pan gasket flush with the cylinder block. Remove the front cover and water pump as an assembly.

11. Discard the front cover gasket.

To install:

12. Place the front seal removing tool (Ford part no. T70P–6B070–A or equivalent) into the front cover plate and over the front of the seal. Tighten the 2 through bolts to force the seal puller under the seal flange, then alternately tighten the 4 puller bolts a half turn at a time to pull the oil seal from the cover.

13. Coat a new front cover oil seal with Lubriplate® or equivalent and place it onto the front oil seal alignment and installation tool (Ford part no. T70P–6B070–A or equivalent). Place the tool and the seal onto the end of the crankshaft and push it toward the engine until the seal starts into the front cover.

14. Place the installation screw, washer, and nut onto the end of the crankshaft, then thread the screw into the crankshaft. Tighten the nut against the washer and tool to force the seal into the front cover plate. Remove the tool.

15. Apply Lubriplate® or equivalent to the oil seal rubbing surface of the vibration damper inner hub to prevent damage to the seal.

Coat the front of the crankshaft with oil for damper installation.

16. To install the damper, line up the damper keyway with the key on the crankshaft, then install the damper onto the crankshaft. Install the cap screw and washer, and tighten the screw to 80 ft. lbs. Install the crankshaft pulley.

17. Install the fan, spacer, pulley and drive belts.

18. Install the bolts holding the fan shroud to the radiator, if equipped.

19. Install the power steering pump and air conditioning compressor.

20. Position and tighten the alternator.

21. Connect the heater hose at the water pump.

22. Install the radiator.

23. Connect the upper and lower radiator hoses, and transmission oil cooler lines.

24. Fill the cooling system and the crankcase.

7.5L Engine

1. Drain the cooling system and crankcase.

2. Remove the radiator shroud and fan.

3. Disconnect the upper and lower radiator hoses, and the automatic transmission oil cooler lines from the radiator.

4. Remove the radiator upper support and remove the radiator.

5. Loosen the alternator attaching bolts and air conditioning compressor idler pulley and remove the drive belts with the water pump pulley. Remove the bolts attaching the compressor support to the water pump and remove the bracket (support), if equipped.

6. Remove the crankshaft pulley from the vibration damper. Remove the bolt and washer attaching the crankshaft damper and remove the damper with a puller. Remove the woodruff key from the crankshaft.

7. Loosen the by-pass hose at the water pump, and disconnect the heater return tube at the water pump.

8. Disconnect and plug the fuel inlet and outlet lines at the fuel pump, and remove the fuel pump.

9. Remove the bolts attaching the front cover to the cylinder block. Cut the oil pan seal flush with the cylinder block face with a thin knife blade prior to separating the cover from the cylinder block. Remove the cover and water pump as an assembly. Discard the front cover gasket and oil pan seal.

To install:

10. Transfer the water pump if a new cover is going to be installed. Clean all of the gasket sealing surfaces on both the front cover and the cylinder block.

11. Coat the gasket surface of the oil pan with sealer. Cut and position the required sections of a new seal on the oil pan. Apply sealer to the corners.

12. Drive out the old front cover oil seal with a pin punch. Clean out the seal recess in the cover. coat a new seal with Lubriplate® or equivalent grease. Install the seal, making sure the seal spring remains in the proper position. A front cover seal tool, Ford part no. T72J–117 or equivalent, makes installation easier.

13. Coat the gasket surfaces of the cylinder block and cover with sealer and position the new gasket on the block.

14. Position the front cover on the cylinder block. Use care not to damage the seal and gasket or misplace them.

15. Coat the front cover attaching screws with sealer and install them.

NOTE: It may be necessary to force the front cover downward to compress the oil pan seal in order to install the front cover attaching bolts. Use a prybar or drift to engage the cover screw holes through the cover and pry downward.

16. Install the fuel pump.

17. Connect the fuel inlet and outlet lines at the fuel pump.

18. Tighten the by-pass hose at the water pump.

19. Connect the heater return tube at the water pump.

20. Install the woodruff key from the crankshaft.

21. Install the damper.

22. Install the crankshaft pulley on the vibration damper.

23. Install the compressor support on the water pump and install the bracket (support), if equipped.

24. Install the drive belts with the water pump pulley.

25. Install the radiator and upper support.

26. Connect the upper and lower radiator hoses, and the automatic transmission oil cooler lines.

27. Install the radiator shroud and fan.

28. Fill the cooling system and crankcase.

Observe the following torques:
Front cover bolts — 15–20 ft. lbs.
Water pump attaching screws — 12–15 ft. lbs.
Crankshaft damper — 70–90 ft. lbs.
Crankshaft pulley — 35–50 ft. lbs.
Fuel pump — 19–27 ft. lbs.
Oil pan bolts — 9–11 ft. lbs. for the $5/16$ in. screws and to 7–9 ft. lbs. for the $1/4$ in. screws
Alternator pivot bolt — 45–57 ft. lbs.

7.3L Diesel Engine

1. Disconnect both battery ground cables. Drain the cooling system.

2. Remove the air cleaner and cover the air intake on the manifold with clean rags. Do not allow any foreign material to enter the intake.

3. Remove the radiator fan shroud halves.

4. Remove the fan and fan clutch assembly using a puller or ford tool No. T83T–6312–A.

NOTE: The nut is a left hand thread; remove by turning the nut clockwise.

5. Remove the injection pump.

6. Remove the water pump.

7. Raise the vehicle and safely support it with jackstands.

8. Remove the crankshaft pulley and vibration damper.

9. Remove the engine ground cables at the front of the engine.

10. Remove the 5 bolts attaching the engine front cover to the engine block and oil pan.

11. Lower the vehicle.

12. Remove the front cover.

NOTE: The front cover oil seal on the diesel must be driven out with an arbor press and a $3\frac{1}{4}$ in. (82.5mm) spacer.

To install:

13. Remove all old gasket material from the front cover, engine block, oil pan sealing surfaces and water pump surfaces.

14. Coat the new front oil seal with Lubriplate® or equivalent grease.

15. The new seal must be installed using a seal installation tool, Ford part no. T83T–6700–A or an arbor press. When the seal bottoms out on the front cover surface, it is installed at the proper depth.

16. Install alignment dowels into the engine block to align the front cover and gaskets. These can be made out of round stock. Apply a gasket sealer to the engine block sealing surfaces, then install the gaskets on the block.

17. Apply a ⅛ in. (3mm) bead of RTV sealer on the front of the engine block. Apply a ¼ in. (6mm) bead of RTV sealer on the oil pan.

18. Install the front cover immediately after applying RTV sealer. The sealer will begin to cure and lose its effectiveness unless the cover is installed quickly.

19. Install the water pump gasket on the engine front cover. Apply RTV sealer to the 4 water pump bolts illustrated. Install the water pump and hand tighten all bolts.

WARNING

The 2 top water pump bolts must be no more than 1¼ in. (31.75mm) long bolts any longer will interfere with (hit) the engine drive gears.

---

20. Torque the water pump bolts to 19 ft. lbs. Torque the front cover bolts to specifications according to bolt size (see Torque Specifications chart).

21. Install the injection pump adaptor and injection pump.

22. Install the heater hose fitting in the pump using pipe sealant, and connect the heater hose to the water pump.

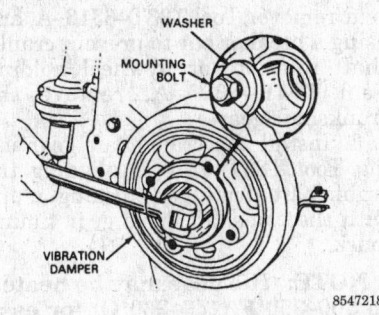

WASHER
MOUNTING BOLT
VIBRATION DAMPER
85472182

Vibration damper removal — 7.3L diesel engine

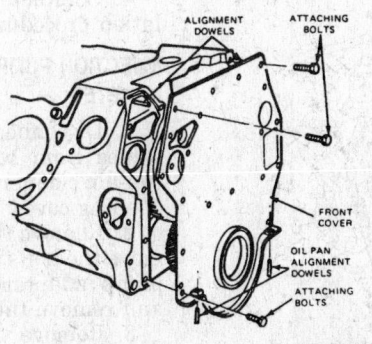

ALIGNMENT DOWELS   ATTACHING BOLTS
FRONT COVER
OIL PAN ALIGNMENT DOWELS
ATTACHING BOLTS
85472183

Cylinder block front cover installation — 7.3L engine

23. Raise the vehicle and safely support it with jackstands.

24. Lubricate the front of the crankshaft with clean oil. Apply RTV sealant to the engine side of the retaining bolt washer to prevent oil seepage past the keyway. Install the crankshaft vibration damper using Ford Special tools T83T-6316B. Torque the damper-to-crankshaft bolt to 90 ft. lbs.

25. Install the fan and fan clutch assembly.

NOTE: The nut is a left hand thread; Install by turning the nut clockwise.

26. Install the radiator fan shroud halves.

27. Install the air cleaner.

28. Connect both battery ground cables.

29. Fill the cooling system.

Timing Chain and Sprockets

REMOVAL AND INSTALLATION

2.9L and 3.0L Engines

1. Disconnect the negative battery cable and drain the cooling system.

2. Remove the timing chain front cover.

3. Rotate the crankshaft until No. 1 cylinder is at TDC and the crankshaft and camshaft sprocket timing marks are aligned.

4. Remove the camshaft sprocket retaining bolt and remove the sprocket and timing chain.

5. Remove the crankshaft sprocket.

To install:

6. Align the crankshaft sprocket with the key or dowel on the crankshaft and install the sprocket.

7. Make sure the sprocket timing marks are still in alignment.

8. Install the camshaft sprocket and timing chain. Install the camshaft sprocket retaining bolt and tighten to 19–28 ft. lbs. (26–38 Nm) on 2.9L engine or 46 ft. lbs. (63 Nm) on 3.0L engine.

NOTE: The camshaft retaining bolt on the 3.0L engine has a drilled oil passage for timing chain lubrication. If damaged, do not replace with a standard bolt. Clean the oil passage with solvent.

9. Install the timing chain front cover and the remaining components in the reverse order of their removal. Fill the crankcase with the proper type and quantity of engine oil. Fill and bleed the cooling system. Run the engine and check for leaks.

4.0L Engine

1. Disconnect the negative battery cable and drain the cooling system and crankcase.

2. Remove the oil pan and radiator. Remove the accessory drive belt and crankshaft damper.

3. Remove the water pump and timing chain front cover.

4. Remove the camshaft sprocket retaining bolt and the crankshaft sprocket key.

5. Push the timing chain tensioner into the retracted position and install the retaining clip.

6. Remove the crankshaft and camshaft sprockets with the timing chain. Remove the tensioner and guide, as required.

To install:

7. Install the timing chain guide to the cylinder block with the pin of the guide inserted into the oil hole in the block. Install the 2 retaining bolts and tighten to 7–9 ft. lbs. (10–12 Nm).

8. Position the camshaft and crankshaft so the sprocket timing marks will align.

9. Install the sprockets and timing chain together. Install the timing chain tensioner with the clip in place to lock the tensioner in the retracted position.

10. Install the crankshaft key and check the timing marks on the sprockets for correct alignment. Make sure the tensioner side of the timing chain is held inward and the guide side of the chain is straight and tight.

11. Install the camshaft sprocket retaining bolt and tighten to 44–50 ft. lbs. (60–68 Nm). Remove the clip from the tensioner assembly.

12. Install the timing chain front cover and the remaining components

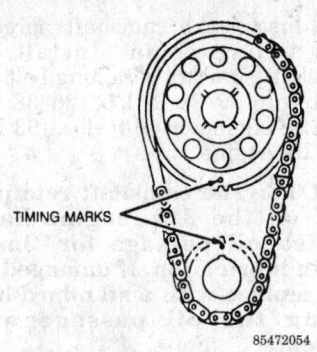

Timing chain and sprocket alignment — 3.0L engine

in the reverse order of their removal. Fill the crankcase with the proper type and quantity of engine oil. Fill and bleed the cooling system. Run the engine and check for leaks.

5.0L, 5.8L and 7.5L Engines

1. Remove the front cover.
2. Rotate the crankshaft counterclockwise to take up the slack on the left side of the chain.
3. Establish a reference point on the cylinder block and measure from this point to the chain.
4. Rotate the crankshaft in the opposite direction to take up the slack on the right side of the chain.
5. Force the left side of the chain out and measure the distance between the reference point and the chain. The timing chain deflection is the difference between the 2 measurements. If the deflection exceeds $\frac{1}{2}$ in. (13mm), replace the timing chain and sprockets.

To install:

6. Turn the crankshaft until the timing marks on the sprockets are aligned vertically.
7. Remove the camshaft sprocket retaining screw and remove the fuel pump eccentric and washers.
8. Alternately slide both of the sprockets and timing chain off the

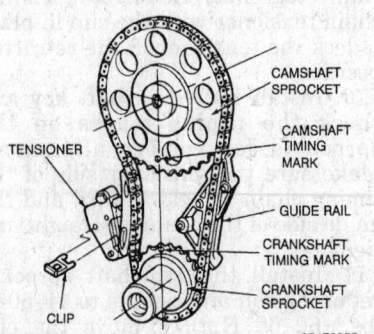

Timing chain and sprocket alignment — 4.0L engine

crankshaft and camshaft until free of the engine.

9. Position the timing chain on the sprockets so the timing marks on the sprockets are aligned vertically. Alternately slide the sprockets and chain onto the crankshaft and camshaft sprockets.
10. Install the fuel pump eccentric washers and attaching bolt on the camshaft sprocket. Tighten to 40–45 ft. lbs.
11. Install the front cover.

Timing Gears

REMOVAL AND INSTALLATION

4.9L Engine

1. Drain the cooling system and remove the front cover.
2. Crank the engine until the timing marks on the camshaft and crankshaft gears are aligned.
3. Use a gear puller to removal both of the timing gears.

To install:

4. Before installing the timing gears, be sure the key and spacer are properly installed. Align the gear keyway with the key and install the gear

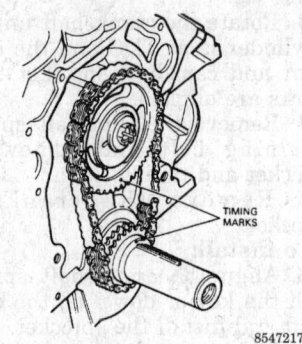

Timing chain and sprocket alignment — 5.0L and 5.8L engines

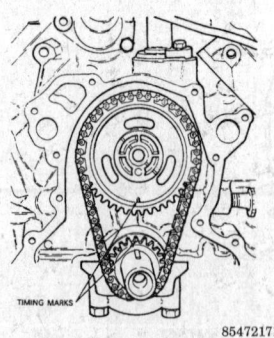

Timing chain and sprocket alignment — 7.5L engine

on the camshaft. Be sure the timing marks line up on the camshaft and the crankshaft gears and install the crankshaft gear.

5. Install the front cover, and assemble the rest of the engine in the reverse order of disassembly. Fill the cooling system.

7.3L Diesel Engine

1. Follow the procedures for timing gear cover removal and installation, and remove the front cover.
2. To remove the crankshaft gear, install gear puller (Ford part) no. T83T–6316–A or equivalent, and using a breaker bar to prevent the crankshaft from rotating, remove the crankshaft gear. To install the crankshaft gear use tool (Ford part) no. T83T–6316–B or equivalent while aligning the timing marks, and press the gear into place.
3. The camshaft gear may be removed by taking out the Allen screw and installing a gear puller, Ford part no. T83T–6316–A or equivalent and removing the gear. The gear may be replaced by using tool (Ford part) no. T83T–6316–B or equivalent. Torque the Allen screw to 12–18 ft. lbs.

CRANKSHAFT DRIVE GEAR

1. Complete the front cover removal procedures.
2. Install the crankshaft drive gear remover Tool T83T–6316–A, and using a breaker bar to prevent crankshaft rotation, or flywheel holding Tool T74R–6375–A, remove the crankshaft gear.
3. Install the crankshaft gear using Tool T83T–6316–B aligning the crankshaft drive gear timing mark with the camshaft drive gear timing mark.

NOTE: The gear may be heated to 300–350°F (149–260°C) for ease of installation. Heat it in an oven. Do not use a torch.

4. Complete the front cover installation procedures.

INJECTION PUMP DRIVE GEAR AND ADAPTER

1. Disconnect the battery ground cables from both batteries. Remove the air cleaner and install an intake opening cover.
2. Remove the injection pump. Remove the bolts attaching the injection pump adapter to the engine block, and remove the adapter.
3. Remove the engine front cover. Remove the drive gear.
4. Clean all gasket and sealant surfaces of the components removed

Timing sprocket alignment — 4.9L engine

with a suitable solvent and dry them thoroughly.

To install:

5. Install the drive gear in position, aligning all the drive gear timing marks.

NOTE: To determine that the No. 1 piston is at TDC of the compression stroke, position the injection pump drive gear dowel at the 4 o'clock position. The scribe line on the vibration damper should be at TDC. Use extreme care to avoid disturbing the injection pump drive gear, once it is in position.

6. Install the engine front cover. Apply a ⅛ in. (3mm) bead of RTV Sealant along the bottom surface of the injection pump adapter.

NOTE: RTV should be applied immediately prior to adapter installation.

7. Install the injection pump adaptor. Apply sealer to the bolt threads before assembly.

NOTE: With the injection pump adapter installed, the injection pump drive gear cannot jump timing.

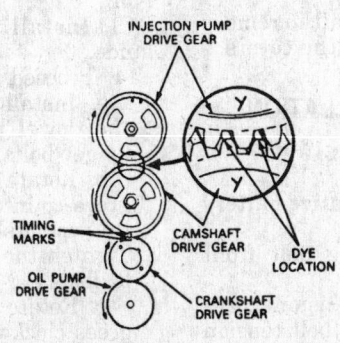

Timing sprocket alignment — 7.3L diesel engine

8. Install all removed components. Run the engine and check for leaks.

NOTE: If necessary, purge the high pressure fuel lines of air by loosening the connector one half to one turn and crank the engine until a solid flow of fuel, free of air bubbles, flows from the connection.

CAMSHAFT DRIVE GEAR, FUEL PUMP CAM, SPACER AND THRUST PLATE

1. Complete the front cover removal procedures.

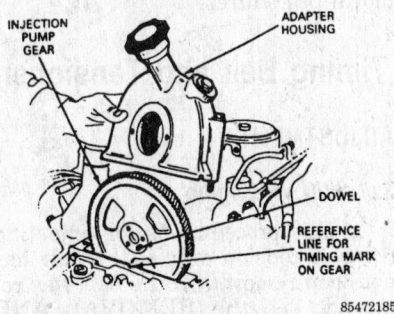

Injection pump drive sprocket cover — 7.3L diesel engine

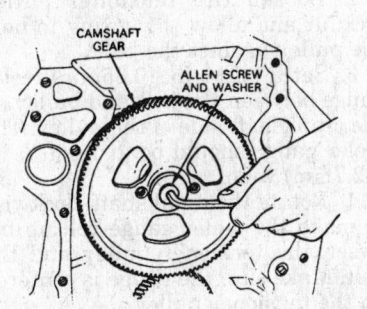

Camshaft drive sprocket removal — 7.3L diesel engine

2. Remove the camshaft allen screw.

3. Install a gear puller, Tool T83T–6316–A and remove the gear. Remove the fuel supply pump, if necessary.

4. Install a gear puller, Tool T77E–4220–B and shaft protector T83T–6316–A and remove the fuel pump cam and spacer, if necessary.

5. Remove the bolts attaching the thrust plate, and remove the thrust plate, if necessary.

6. Install a new thrust plate, if removed.

7. Install the spacer and fuel pump cam against the camshaft thrust flange, using installation sleeve and replacer Tool T83T–6316–B, if removed.

8. Install the camshaft drive gear against the fuel pump cam, aligning the timing mark with the timing mark on the crankshaft drive gear, using installation sleeve and replacer Tool T83T–6316–B.

9. Install the camshaft allen screw and tighten to 18 ft. lbs.

10. Install the fuel pump, if removed.

11. Install the front cover, following the previous procedure.

Timing Belt Front Cover

REMOVAL AND INSTALLATION

2.3L Engine

1. Disconnect the negative battery cable and drain the cooling system.

2. Loosen the thermactor pump bolts and remove the drive belt, if equipped.

3. Remove the fan blade and 4 water pump pulley bolts.

4. Loosen the alternator retaining bolts and remove the drive belt from the pulleys. Remove the upper radiator hose.

5. Remove the crankshaft pulley bolt and pulley. Remove the thermostat housing.

6. Loosen the power steering pump mounting bracket and position aside.

7. Remove the timing belt front cover retaining bolt(s). Release the cover interlocking tabs, if equipped. Remove the cover.

To install:

8. Install the front cover. If equipped, secure by snapping the interlocking tabs into place. Install the retaining bolt(s).

9. Install the power steering pump mounting bracket.

10. Install the thermostat housing and connect the upper radiator hose.

11. Install the crankshaft pulley and retaining bolt. Tighten to 103–133 ft. lbs. (140–180 Nm).

12. Position the alternator drive belt and adjust the belt tension. Install the water pump pulley and fan.

13. Position the thermactor pump drive belt, if equipped, and adjust the tension.

14. Connect the negative battery cable. Fill and bleed the cooling system. Run the engine and check for leaks.

3.0L (VIN W) Engine

1. Disconnect the negative battery cable and remove the engine under cover.

2. Drain the coolant and remove the hoses and the lower fan shroud. Remove the radiator and main shroud as an assembly.

3. Remove the accessory drive belts and remove the fan and water pump pulley.

4. Remove the spark plugs and the fresh air intake tube to the rocker arm cover.

5. Remove the idler pulley bracket and the water inlet hose.

6. Remove the crankshaft pulley bolt and use a puller to remove the crankshaft pulley. Put a spacer (a stack of washers or a large nut) on the pulley bolt and install the bolt so the crankshaft can be turned with the socket or wrench.

7. Remove the front timing belt covers. To remove the rear covers, the timing belt and camshaft sprockets must be removed.

8. Installation is the reverse of removal. Torque the crankshaft pulley bolt to 98 ft. lbs. (132 Nm).

OIL SEAL REPLACEMENT

2.3L Engine

1. Disconnect the negative battery cable.

2. Remove the timing belt front cover, timing belt and sprockets.

3. Use seal removal tool T74P-6700-B or equivalent, to remove the crankshaft, camshaft or auxiliary shaft seals. Make sure the jaws of the tool are gripping the thin edge of the seal very tightly before operating the jack-screw portion of the tool.

To install:

4. Coat the new seal with engine oil and install, using seal installation tool T74P-6150-A or equivalent.

5. Install the timing sprockets, timing belt and timing belt front cover. Connect the negative battery cable.

3.0L (VIN W) Engine

The front oil seal is a part of the oil pump.

1. Remove the oil pump.

2. Carefully pry the oil seal from the oil pump.

3. Lubricate the new seal with light grease. Using an oil seal installation tool, drive the new oil seal into the oil pump housing until it seats. Clean all oil and grease away from the seal.

4. To complete the installation, use new gaskets and reverse the removal procedures.

Timing Belt and Tensioner

ADJUSTMENT

3.0L (VIN W) Engine

1. This procedure is for adjusting the belt tension only if the belt has not been removed. If the belt was removed, see the REMOVAL AND INSTALLATION procedure. Disconnect the negative battery cable and remove the front timing belt covers.

2. Loosen the tensioner pulley locknut and allow the spring to hold the pulley against the belt.

3. Set a 0.014 in. (0.35mm) feeler gauge between the belt and pulley on the crankshaft side of the pulley. The feeler gauge should be at least ½ in. (12.7mm) wide.

4. Rotate the crankshaft clockwise to make the feeler gauge roll up between the tensioner pulley and the belt. Make sure the gauge is centered on the tensioner pulley.

5. Push in on the belt halfway between the tensioner pulley and the camshaft sprocket with a force of 22 lbs. (98 N) and torque the locknut to 43 ft. lbs. (58 Nm).

6. Rotate the crankshaft to remove the feeler gauge. Install the covers.

REMOVAL AND INSTALLATION

2.3L Engine

1. Disconnect the negative battery cable.

2. Remove the timing belt front cover.

3. Loosen the belt tensioner adjustment screw. Position belt tension adjusting tool T74P-6254-A or equivalent, on the tension spring

rollpin and retract the belt tensioner. Tighten the adjustment screw to hold the tensioner in the retracted position.

4. Remove the bolts holding the timing sensor in place and pull the sensor free of the dowel pin.

5. Remove the crankshaft pulley, hub and belt guide. Remove the timing belt.

6. If the timing belt tensioner is to be removed, remove the adjustment screw and the spring bolt and remove the tensioner.

To install:

7. If removed, install the timing belt tensioner. Install the spring bolt but do not tighten at this time. Position the tensioner in the fully retracted position and tighten the adjustment bolt.

8. Position the crankshaft sprocket to align with the TDC mark and the camshaft sprocket to align with the timing pointer.

9. Install the timing belt over the crankshaft sprocket and then counterclockwise over the auxiliary and camshaft sprockets. Align the belt fore and aft on the sprockets.

10. Loosen the tensioner adjustment bolt to allow the tensioner to move against the belt. If the spring does not have enough tension to move the roller against the belt and the belt hangs loose, it may be necessary to manually push the roller against the belt and tighten the bolt.

NOTE: The spring cannot be used to set belt tension. A wrench must be used on the tensioner assembly.

11. Remove a spark plug from each cylinder to make sure the engine does not jump time during Step 12.

12. Rotate the crankshaft 2 complete turns in the direction of normal rotation to remove the slack from the belt. Tighten the spring bolt to 28–40 ft. lbs. (38–54 Nm) and the adjustment bolt to 14–21 ft. lbs. (19–29 Nm).

13. Install the crankshaft belt guide.

14. Proceed as follows:

   a. Install the timing sensor onto the dowel pin and tighten the 2 longer bolts.

   b. Rotate the crankshaft 45 degrees counterclockwise and install the crankshaft pulley and hub. Tighten the pulley bolt to 103–133 ft. lbs. (140–180 Nm).

   c. Rotate the crankshaft 90 degrees clockwise so the vane of the crankshaft pulley engages with timing sensor positioner tool

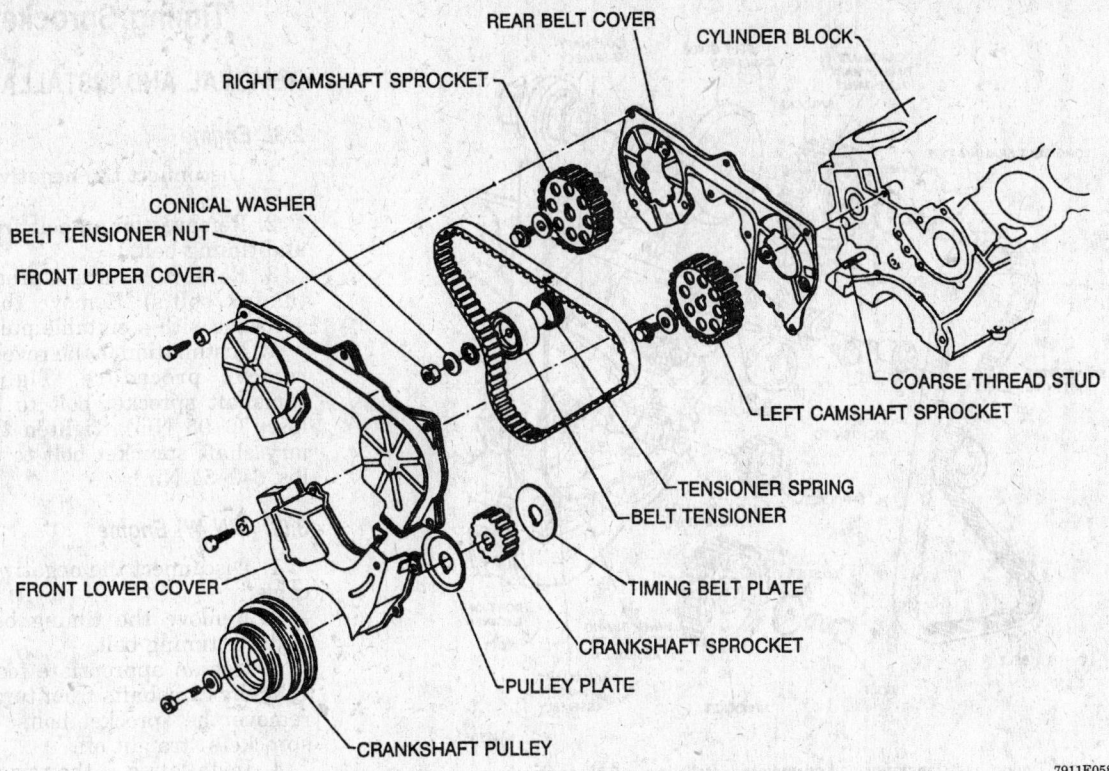

Timing belt and cover assembly — 3.0L (VIN W) engine

7911E058

T89P-6316-A or equivalent. Tighten the 2 shorter sensor bolts.

d. Rotate the crankshaft 90 degrees counterclockwise and remove the sensor positioner tool.

e. Rotate the crankshaft 90 degrees clockwise and measure the outer vane-to-sensor air gap. The air gap must be 0.018–0.039 in. (0.458–0.996mm).

15. Install the timing belt front cover and the remaining components in the reverse order of their removal.

3.0L (VIN W) Engine

1. Disconnect the negative battery cable and remove the timing belt cover.

2. Put a spacer (a stack of washers or a large nut) on the crankshaft pulley bolt and install the bolt so the crankshaft can be turned with a socket wrench.

3. Rotate the crankshaft to position the No. 1 piston on the TDC of its compression stroke. The marks on the camshaft and crankshaft sprockets will align with marks on the rear timing belt cover and the oil pump housing.

4. If the belt is to be re-used, paint an arrow on the belt pointing towards the front of the vehicle.

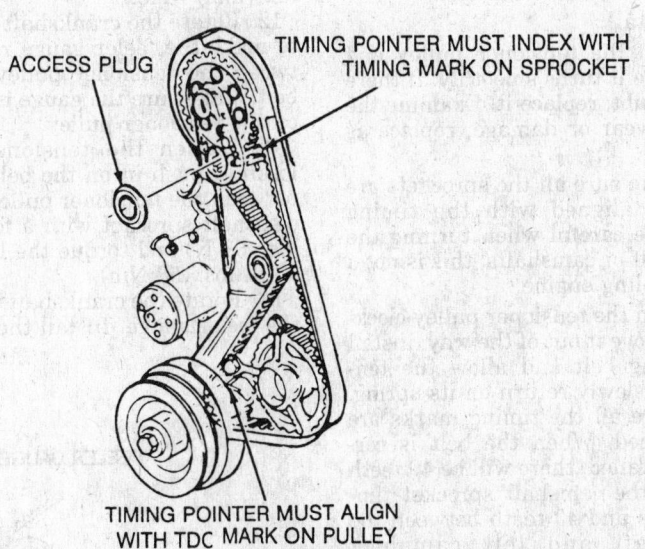

ON 1988 VEHICLES DISTRIBUTOR ROTOR MUST ALIGN WITH NO. 1 FIRING POSITION

85472056

Timing belt and sprockets alignment — 2.3L engine

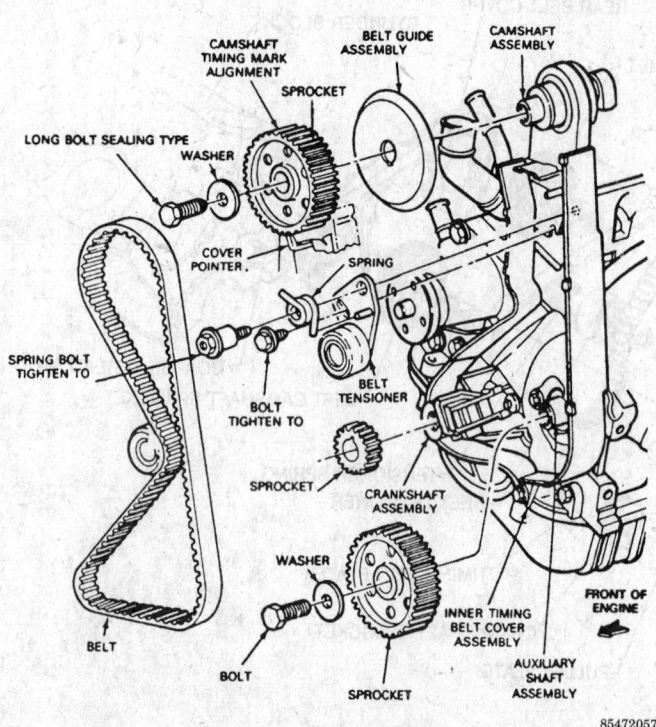

Timing belt, tensioner and sprockets installation — 2.3L engine

5. Loosen the belt tensioner pulley nut, move the pulley with an Allen wrench and remove the belt.

To install:

6. Spin the tensioner pulley and make sure it turns smoothly. If there is any doubt, replace it. Examine the belt for wear or damage, replace as necessary.

7. Make sure all the sprockets are correctly aligned with the timing marks. Be careful when turning the crankshaft or camshafts, this is not a free wheeling engine.

8. Turn the tensioner pulley clockwise to move it out of the way, install the timing belt and allow the tensioner to slowly return on its spring. Make sure all the timing marks are still aligned. When the belt is correctly installed, there will be 40 teeth between the camshaft sprocket timing marks and 43 teeth between the crankshaft and left camshaft sprocket timing marks.

9. Turn the tensioner approximately 70–80 degrees clockwise with the wrench and tighten the locknut.

10. To adjust the belt tension, turn the crankshaft clockwise several times and slowly set the No. 1 piston to TDC of the compression stroke.

11. Set a 0.014 in. (0.35mm) feeler gauge between the belt and pulley on the crankshaft side of the pulley. The feeler gauge should be at least ½ in. (12.7mm) wide.

12. Rotate the crankshaft clockwise to make the feeler gauge roll up between the tensioner pulley and the belt. Make sure the gauge is centered on the tensioner pulley.

13. Loosen the tensioner pulley locknut, push in on the belt halfway between the tensioner pulley and the camshaft sprocket with a force of 22 lbs. (98 N) and torque the locknut to 43 ft. lbs. (58 Nm).

14. Rotate the crankshaft to remove the feeler gauge. Install the covers.

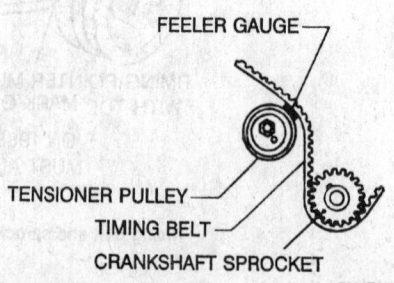

Make sure the feeler gauge is centered between the tensioner pulley and the belt — 3.0L (VIN W) engine

Timing Sprockets

REMOVAL AND INSTALLATION

2.3L Engine

1. Disconnect the negative battery cable.

2. Remove timing belt front cover and timing belt.

3. Remove timing sprockets retaining bolt(s). Remove the timing sprocket with a suitable puller.

4. Installation is the reverse of the remove procedure. Tighten the camshaft sprocket bolt to 52–70 ft. lbs. (70–95 Nm). Tighten the auxiliary shaft sprocket bolt to 30–40 ft. lbs. (40–54 Nm).

3.0L (VIN W) Engine

1. Disconnect the negative battery cable.

2. Remove the timing belt cover and the timing belt.

3. Use an appropriate tool to prevent the camshafts from turning and remove the sprocket bolts. Pull the sprockets straight off.

4. Installation is the reverse of removal. Torque the camshaft sprocket bolts to 65 ft. lbs. (88 Nm). Install the timing belt.

Camshaft

REMOVAL AND INSTALLATION

2.9L, 3.0L (VIN U) and 4.0L Engines

1. Disconnect the negative battery cable and relieve the fuel system pressure. Drain the crankcase and the cooling system.

2. Remove the rocker arm covers, rocker arms or rocker arm shaft assemblies and pushrods. Note the position of each component so it can be reinstalled in the same place.

3. Remove the intake manifold.

4. Remove the lifters. Identify each lifter so it can be reinstalled in the original position.

5. Remove the front timing chain cover and the timing chain and sprockets.

6. Remove the thrust plate bolts and remove the thrust plate. Carefully remove the camshaft, being careful not to damage the journals, lobes or bearings.

To install:

7. Coat the camshaft lobes with grease and the journals with heavy engine oil. Carefully install the camshaft, being careful not to damage the journals, lobes or bearings.

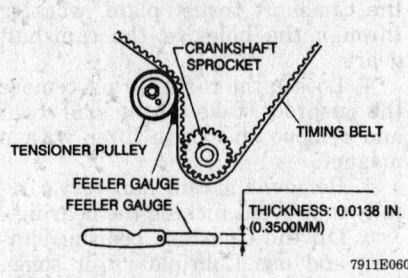

Place the feeler gauge under the tensioner pulley — 3.0L (VIN W) engine

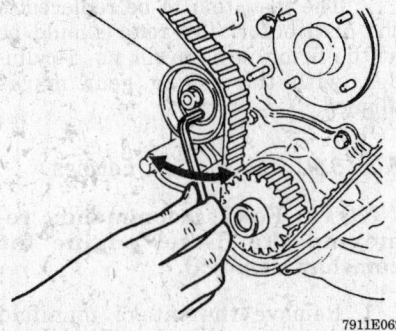

Move the tensioner pulley with an Allen wrench — 3.0L (VIN W) engine

8. Install the thrust plate and the thrust plate retaining bolts. Tighten the bolts to 13–16 ft. lbs. (17–21 Nm) on 2.9L engine, 7 ft. lbs. (10 Nm) on 3.0L engine or 7–10 ft. lbs. (10–13 Nm) on 4.0L engine.

9. Check the camshaft endplay using a dial indicator. The endplay should be 0.0008–0.004 in. on 2.9L and 4.0L engines or should not exceed 0.007 in. on 3.0L engine.

10. Install the remaining components in the reverse order of their removal. Fill the crankcase with the proper type and quantity of engine oil. Fill and bleed the cooling system. Run the engine and check for leaks.

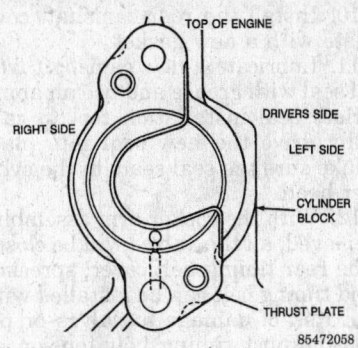

Camshaft thrust plate positioning — 2.9L engine

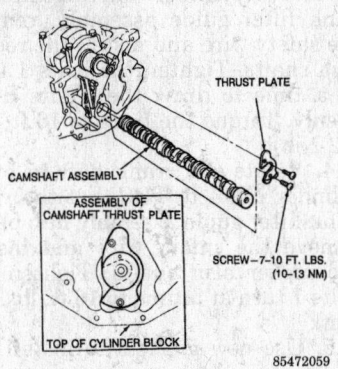

Camshaft installation — 4.0L engine

2.3L Engine

1. Disconnect the negative battery cable and drain the cooling system. Remove the air cleaner assembly.

2. Tag and disconnect the spark plug wires at the plugs and rocker arm cover and position aside. Tag and disconnect the necessary vacuum lines.

3. Remove the rocker arm cover. Remove the alternator mounting bracket-to-cylinder head mounting bolts and position aside.

4. Disconnect and remove the upper radiator hose. Remove the radiator shroud.

5. Remove the timing belt front cover. If equipped with power steering, remove the power steering pump bracket.

6. Remove the timing belt, camshaft followers and camshaft sprocket. Remove the camshaft seal using seal removal tool T74P-6700-B or equivalent.

7. Remove the 2 screws and the camshaft rear retainer.

8. Raise and support the vehicle safely. Remove the front motor mount bolts.

9. Position a jack under the engine and raise the engine carefully as far as it will go. Place blocks of wood between the engine mounts and chassis brackets and remove the jack.

10. Remove the camshaft, being careful to avoid damaging the journals, lobes and bearings.

To install:

11. Make sure the threaded plug is in the rear of the camshaft. If not, remove the threaded plug from the old camshaft and install. Tighten to 12–18 ft. lbs. (16–24 Nm).

12. Coat the camshaft lobes with grease and lubricate the journals with heavy engine oil. Carefully slide the camshaft through the bearings.

13. Install the camshaft rear retainer with the 2 screws. Tighten to 6–9 ft. lbs. (8–12 Nm).

14. Install a new camshaft seal using seal installation tool T74P-6150-A or equivalent.

15. Install the remaining components in the reverse order of their removal. Fill and bleed the cooling system. Run the engine and check for leaks.

3.0L (VIN W) Engine

The camshafts can be removed without removing the cylinder heads. When removing the timing belt covers, the radiator must be removed. This should provide the clearance for removing the camshafts.

1. Relieve the fuel system pressure and disconnect the negative battery cable.

2. Remove the rocker arm covers.

3. Turn the crankshaft to align the timing marks at TDC on No. 1 cylinder. Remove the timing belt cover and the timing belt.

4. Hold the camshafts from turning and remove the camshaft sprockets. Remove the rear timing belt cover.

5. Loosen each rocker shaft bolt 1 turn at a time to prevent bending the shafts. When all the bolts are loose, remove the rocker arm shafts with

Timing belt and sprockets — 3.0L (VIN W) engine

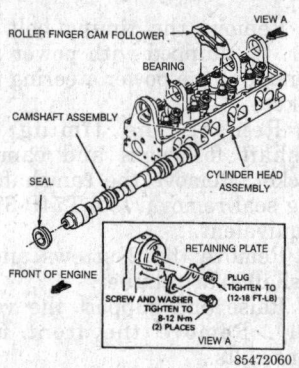

Camshaft installation — 2.3L engine

the bolts still in the shafts. This will hold the assembly together.

6. Secure the valve lifters in the guide assembly with safety wire to keep them in their original positions, then remove the entire assembly.

NOTE: Before removing a lifter from the guide assembly, tag the lifters to make sure they are returned to their original position. Keep the lifters upright to keep them from becoming air bound or lay them down in a pan of new engine oil. Do not disassemble a lifter.

7. Remove the plates from the front and rear of the cylinder heads and pry the oil seals out. Remove the bolt at the rear of the camshafts and remove the locating plates. Carefully withdraw the camshafts out towards the front.

To install:

8. Inspect the camshaft and the bearing surfaces:

a. Make sure the camshaft and the bearing surfaces are in good condition.

b. Measure the inside diameter of the bearing circle.

c. Measure the diameter of the camshaft bearings.

d. The difference between the measurements is the camshaft journal clearance; it should be no more than 0.0059 in. (0.15mm)

e. To check endplay, install the camshaft and the locating plates and torque the bolts to 65 ft. lbs. (88 Nm). The camshaft endplay should be no more than 0.0024 in. (0.06mm).

9. Lubricate the camshaft with engine oil and carefully set it in place. Install the locating plate at the rear and torque the bolt to 65 ft. lbs. (88 Nm). Turn the camshaft so the pin on the sprocket end is up.

10. Install the rear camshaft cover plate with a new gasket.

11. Lubricate a new camshaft front oil seal with grease and use an appropriate seal installation tool to carefully drive the new seal into place. Make sure the seal seats in the cylinder head.

12. With the rocker arm assemblies removed, all the valves will be closed. The rear timing belt cover, sprockets and timing belt can be installed without risk of damage to valves or pistons. Adjust timing belt tension according to correct procedure.

13. Make sure the engine is at TDC on No. 1 cylinder. Install the left bank lifter guide assembly, remove the safety wire and install the rocker arm shafts. Tighten the bolts 1 turn at a time to draw the shafts down evenly. Torque the bolts to 16 ft. lbs. (22 Nm)

14. Rotate the crankshaft to bring cylinder No. 4 to TDC. Set the right bank lifter guide assembly into place, remove the safety wire and install the rocker arm shafts. Tighten the bolts 1 turn at a time to 16 ft. lbs. (22 Nm).

15. Use new gaskets to install the rocker arm covers and torque the bolts to 24 inch lbs. (3 Nm). Install the remaining components.

16. When the engine is first started, the hydraulic valve lifters may be noisy. Run the engine for 10–20 minutes at about 1000 rpm. If the noise has not subsided, the lifter will probably never pump up and must be replaced.

4.9L Engine

1. Remove the grille, radiator, air conditioner condenser, and timing cover.

2. Remove the distributor, fuel pump, oil pan and oil pump.

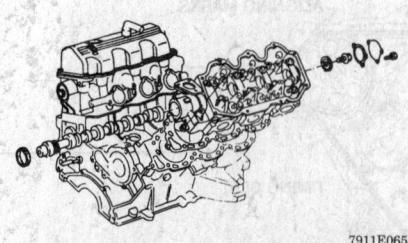

Camshaft removal on 3.0L (VIN W) engine can be done without removing the cylinder head

3. Align the timing marks. Unbolt the camshaft thrust plate, working through the holes in the camshaft gear.

4. Loosen the rocker arms, remove the pushrods, take off the side cover and remove the valve lifter with a magnet.

5. Remove the camshaft very carefully to prevent nicking the bearings.

6. Oil the camshaft bearing journals and use Lubriplate® or something similar on the lobes. Install the camshaft, gear, and thrust plate, aligning the gear marks. Tighten down the thrust plate. Make sure the camshaft end-play is not excessive.

7. The last item to be replaced is the distributor. The rotor should be at the firing position for no. 1 cylinder, with the timing gear marks aligned.

5.0L, 5.8L, 7.3L and 7.5L Engines

NOTE: Ford recommends removing the diesel engine for camshaft removal.

1. Remove the intake manifold and valley pan, if equipped.

2. Remove the rocker covers, and either remove the rocker arm shafts or loosen the rockers on their pivots and remove the pushrods. The pushrods must be reinstalled in their original positions.

3. Remove the valve lifters in sequence with a magnet. They must be replaced in their original positions.

4. Remove the timing gear cover and timing chain (timing gear on V8 diesel) and sprockets.

5. In addition to the radiator and air conditioning condenser, if equipped, it may be necessary to remove the front grille assembly and the hook lock assembly to gain the necessary clearance to code the camshaft out of the front of the engine.

NOTE: A camshaft removal tool, Ford part no. T65L–6250–A and adaptor 14–0314 are needed to remove the diesel camshaft.

6. Coat the camshaft with oil liberally before installing it. Slide the camshaft into the engine very carefully so as not to scratch the bearing bores with the camshaft lobes. Install the camshaft thrust plate and tighten the attaching screws to 9–12 ft. lbs. Measure the camshaft end-play. If the end-play is more than 0.009 in. (0.228mm), replace the thrust plate. Assemble the remaining components in the reverse order of removal.

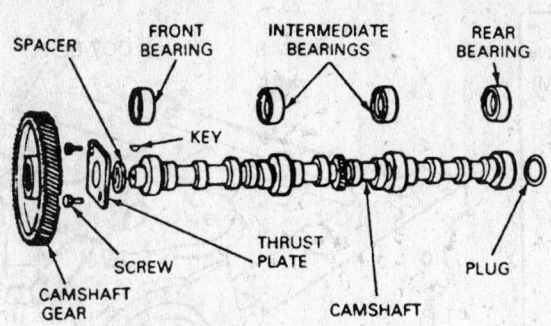

Camshaft assembly — 4.9L engine

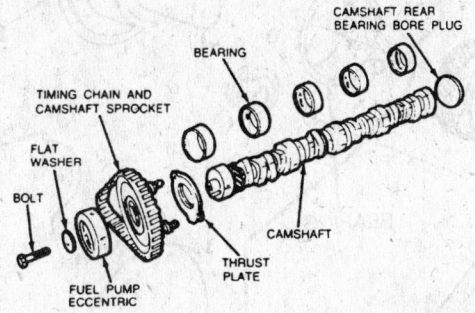

Camshaft assembly — 4.9L engine

Auxiliary Shaft

REMOVAL AND INSTALLATION

1. Disconnect the negative battery cable and drain the cooling system.
2. Remove the timing belt front cover.
3. Remove the timing belt and remove the auxiliary shaft sprocket.
4. Remove the auxiliary shaft cover bolts and the cover.
5. Remove the auxiliary shaft retaining plate screws and remove the retaining plate.
6. Remove the auxiliary shaft, being careful not to damage the journals or bearings.

To install:

7. Coat the auxiliary shaft journals with heavy engine oil. Install the auxiliary shaft, being careful not to damage the journals or bearings.
8. Install the retaining plate. Tighten the retaining plate screws to 6–9 ft. lbs. (8–12 Nm).
9. Install the auxiliary shaft cover and tighten the screws to 6–9 ft. lbs. (8–12 Nm).

10. Install the remaining components in the reverse order of their removal. Fill and bleed the cooling system. Run the engine and check for leaks.

Piston and Connecting Rod

POSITIONING

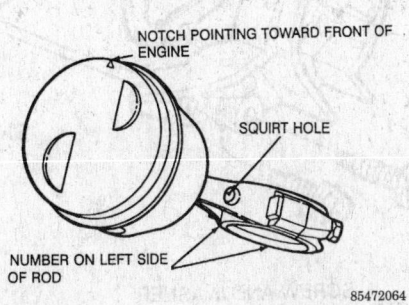

Piston and connecting rod assembly — 2.3L engine

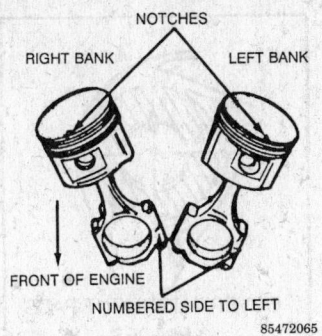

Piston and connecting rod assembly — 2.9L engine

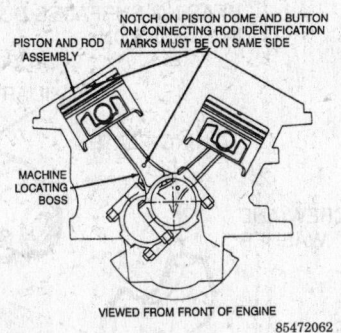

Piston and connecting rod assembly — 3.0L (VIN U) engine

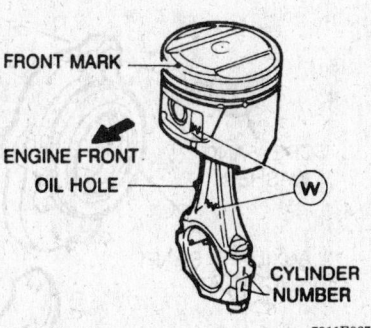

Piston and rod orientation on 3.0L (VIN W) engine

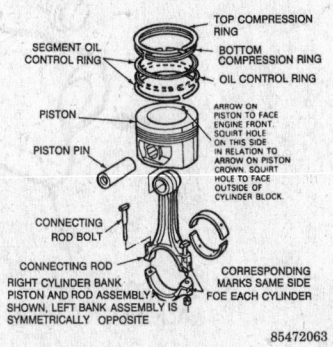

Piston and connecting rod assembly — 4.0L engine

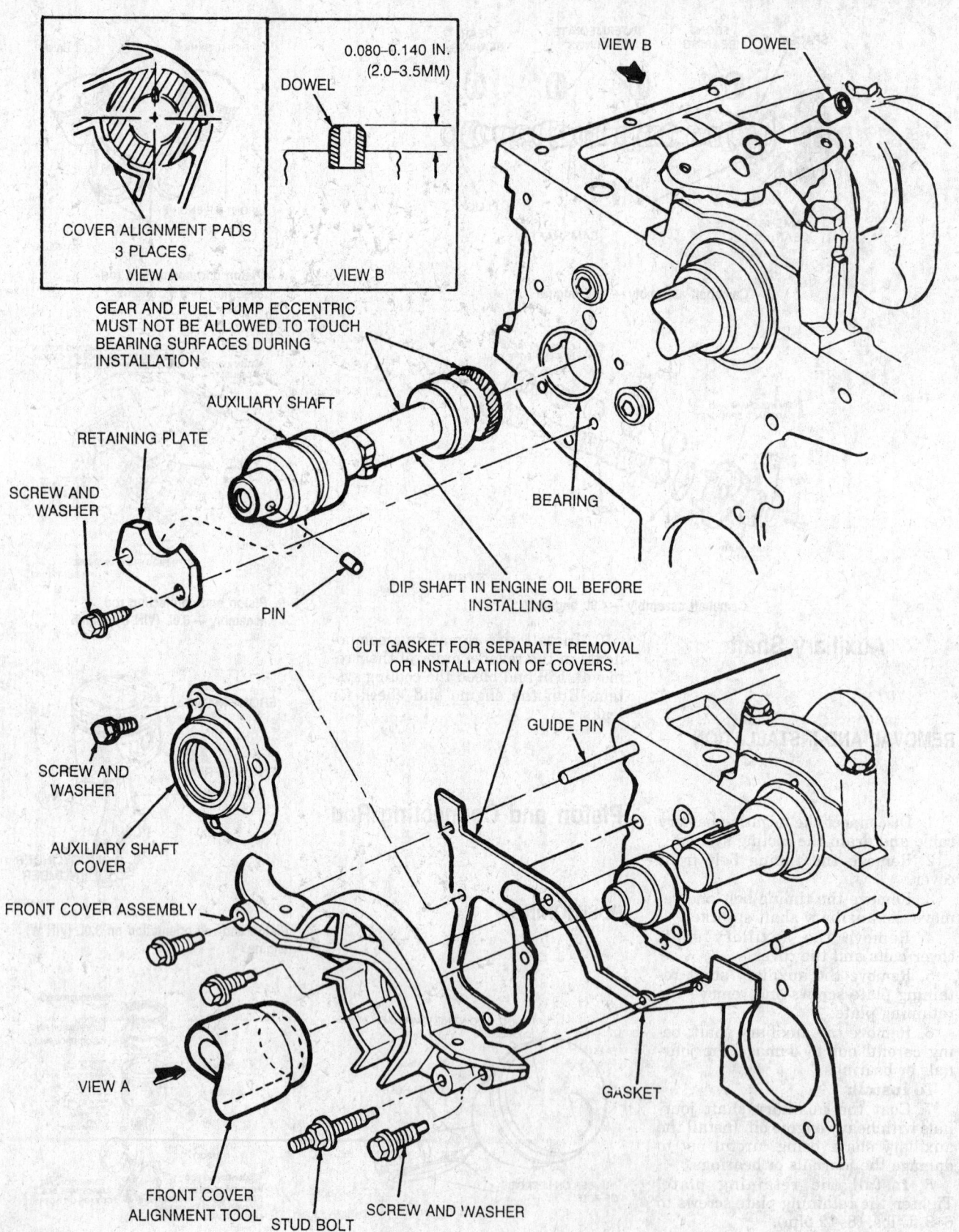

0.080–0.140 IN.
(2.0–3.5MM)

DOWEL

COVER ALIGNMENT PADS
3 PLACES

VIEW A

VIEW B

GEAR AND FUEL PUMP ECCENTRIC
MUST NOT BE ALLOWED TO TOUCH
BEARING SURFACES DURING
INSTALLATION

AUXILIARY SHAFT

RETAINING PLATE

SCREW AND
WASHER

PIN

DIP SHAFT IN ENGINE OIL BEFORE
INSTALLING

BEARING

CUT GASKET FOR SEPARATE REMOVAL
OR INSTALLATION OF COVERS.

SCREW AND
WASHER

GUIDE PIN

AUXILIARY SHAFT
COVER

FRONT COVER ASSEMBLY

VIEW A

FRONT COVER
ALIGNMENT TOOL

STUD BOLT

SCREW AND WASHER

GASKET

VIEW B   DOWEL

Auxiliary shaft installation — 2.3L engine

85472061

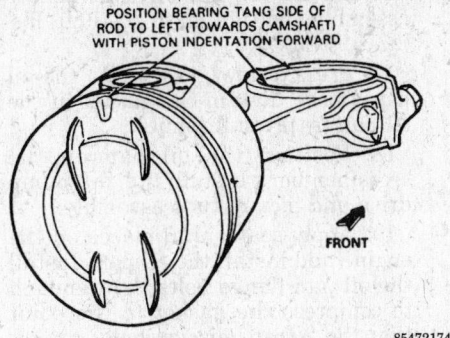

Piston and connecting rod assembly — 4.9L engine

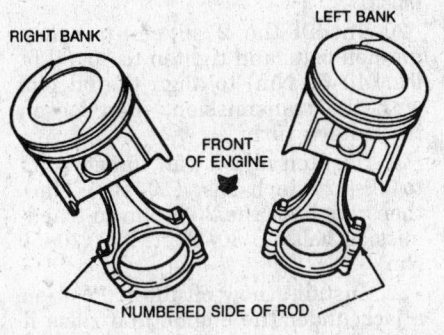

Piston and connecting rod assembly — 5.0L and 5.8L engines

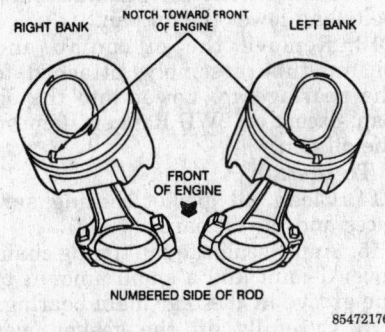

Piston and connecting rod assembly — 7.5L engine

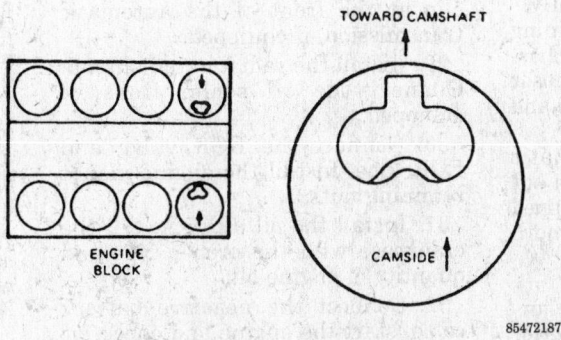

Piston orientation — 7.3L diesel engine

ENGINE LUBRICATION

Oil Pan

REMOVAL AND INSTALLATION

2.3L Engine

1. Disconnect the negative battery cable and remove the air cleaner outlet tube at the throttle body.
2. Remove the engine oil dipstick and remove the engine mount retaining nuts.
3. Disconnect the oil cooler lines at the radiator, if equipped. Remove the fan shroud.
4. If equipped with automatic transmission, remove the radiator retaining bolts and position the radiator upward and wire to the hood.
5. Raise and safely support the vehicle. Drain the engine oil.
6. Disconnect the starter cable and remove the starter. Disconnect the exhaust manifold tube to the inlet pipe bracket at the thermactor check valve.
7. Disconnect the catalytic converter at the inlet pipe.
8. Remove the insulator and retainer assembly at the transmission. Remove the transmission mount retaining nuts to the crossmember.
9. If equipped with automatic transmission, remove the oil cooler lines from the retainer at the block and remove the front crossmember.
10. If equipped with manual transmission, disconnect the right front lower shock absorber mount.
11. Position a jack under the engine. Raise the engine and position suitable wood blocks between the engine mounts and frame brackets. Remove the jack.
12. If equipped with automatic transmission, position a jack under the transmission and raise slightly.
13. Remove the oil pan retaining bolts and lower the pan to the chassis. Remove the low oil level sensor assembly and the oil pump drive and pickup tube assembly.
14. If equipped with automatic transmission, remove the oil pan out the front of the vehicle. If equipped with manual transmission, remove the oil pan out from the rear.

To install:

15. Clean all gasket mating surfaces, the oil pan, oil pump exterior and pickup tube screen.
16. Install the low oil level sensor assembly and tighten to 20–30 ft. lbs. (27–41 Nm).
17. Press a new gasket into the oil pan groove. Retain the gasket in the oil pan by press fit only.
18. Position the oil pan on the crossmember. Install the oil pump drive and pickup tube assembly.
19. Apply sealer in 6 places on the engine and install the oil pan. Install the oil pan flange bolts tight enough to compress the gasket to the point that the 2 transmission holes are aligned with the 2 tapped holes in the oil pan, but loose enough to allow movement of the pan relative to the block.
20. Install the 2 oil pan-to-transmission bolts and tighten to 30–39 ft. lbs. (40–50 Nm) to align the oil pan with the transmission, then loosen the bolts ½ turn.
21. Tighten all oil pan flange bolts to 90–120 inch lbs. (10–13.5 Nm), then retighten the 2 oil pan-to-transmission bolts to 30–39 ft. lbs. (40–50 Nm).
22. Install a new oil filter. Position a jack under the engine and raise it enough to remove the wood blocks. Shift the engine/transmission backward to its original position.
23. Install the mount/bracket assembly to the crossmember and lower the engine. Install the front crossmember, if removed.
24. Raise the transmission with the jack and install the mount. Install the stabilizer brackets to the frame, if removed.
25. Connect the automatic transmission oil cooler line retainer clip to the engine, if equipped. Install the transmission mount retaining nuts.
26. Install a new gasket and connect the rear exhaust pipe just behind the catalytic converter.
27. Connect the low oil level sensor wire. Install the starter and connect the starter cable. Lower the vehicle.
28. Connect the vacuum tube to the clip at the front of the automatic transmission, if equipped.
29. Install the radiator and shroud. Connect the oil cooler lines, if equipped.
30. Connect the EGR valve and EGR tube. Install the engine mount retaining nuts.
31. Install the oil dipstick. Fill the crankcase with the proper type and quantity of engine oil.
32. Connect the negative battery cable, start the engine and check for leaks.

2.9L Engine

1. Disconnect negative battery cable and remove the air intake tube.
2. Remove the fan shroud and position over the fan.
3. Remove the distributor cap and position forward of the dash panel. Remove the distributor and cover the bore opening.
4. Remove the nuts attaching the engine front mounts to the crossmember.
5. Raise and safely support the vehicle.
6. Drain the engine crankcase. If equipped with automatic transmission, remove the transmission fluid filler tube and plug the pan hole.
7. Remove the engine oil filter. Disconnect the muffler inlet pipe(s), except on 2WD Ranger vehicles.
8. Disconnect the oil cooler bracket and lower, if equipped. Remove the starter.
9. Position the transmission oil cooler lines aside, if equipped. Disconnect the front stabilizer bar and position forward, if equipped.
10. Position the jack under the engine. Raise the engine and install wooden blocks between the front engine mounts and No. 2 crossmember.
11. Lower the engine onto the blocks and remove the jack.
12. Remove the oil pan attaching bolts and lower the oil pan.
13. Remove the oil pump and pickup tube assembly, attached to the bearing cap. Lower into the oil pan, except on 2WD Ranger. Remove the oil pan.

To install:

14. Clean all gasket mating surfaces and the oil pan.
15. Apply sealer to the timing chain cover T-joint and a small amount to the groove in the rear main bearing.
16. Carefully lift the gasket over the 6 studs on the cylinder block, insert the ends into the grooves and align the gasket.
17. With the oil pump, oil pan baffle and pickup tube assembly positioned in the oil pan, install the oil pump and then the oil pan. Tighten the pan bolts in 2 steps. Start with bolt **A** and proceed in the direction of the arrows for the first step. Start with bolt **B** and proceed in the direction of the arrows for the second step. Final torque should be 4–6 ft. lbs. (5–8 Nm).
18. Position a jack under the engine and raise enough to remove the wooden blocks. Lower the engine and remove the jack.
19. Install the starter. Connect the muffler inlet pipes, if removed.

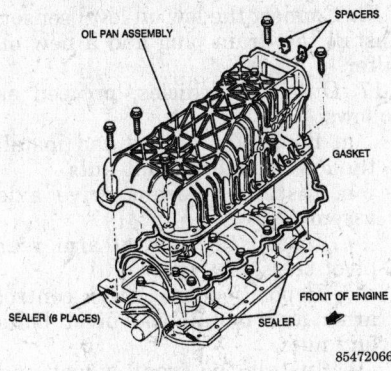

Oil pan installation — 2.3L engine

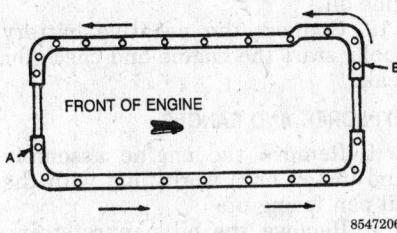

Oil pan bolt tightening procedure — 2.9L engine

20. Connect the front stabilizer bar, if equipped. Position the transmission oil cooler lines and connect the cooler bracket, if equipped.

21. Install a new oil filter. If equipped with automatic transmission, unplug the oil pan and install the filler tube.

22. Lower the vehicle. Install the nuts attaching the engine front mounts to the crossmember.

23. Install the distributor assembly and cap. Install the fan shroud.

24. Fill the engine with the proper type and quantity of engine oil. Connect the negative battery cable.

25. Run the engine and check for leaks. Check the ignition timing and adjust, if necessary.

26. Install the air intake tube. Check the transmission fluid level.

3.0L (VIN U) Engine

AEROSTAR

1. Disconnect the negative battery cable.

2. Remove the engine oil level dipstick. Raise the vehicle and support it safely.

3. If equipped with an oil level sensor, remove the retaining clip at the sensor. Disconnect the electrical connector from the sensor.

4. Drain the crankcase. Remove the starter and transmission inspection cover.

5. Remove the oil pan attaching bolts and remove the pan.

To install:

6. Clean all gasket mating surfaces and the oil pan.

7. Apply a ⅕ in. bead of silicone sealer to the junction of the rear main bearing cap and cylinder block and the junction of the front cover assembly and cylinder block.

8. Position the oil pan gasket to the oil pan and secure with sealer. Install the oil pan on the engine block with the attaching bolts and tighten to 9 ft. lbs. (12 Nm).

9. Install the starter and transmission inspection cover. Attach the low oil level sensor connector and install the retainer clip.

10. Lower the vehicle and install the engine oil level dipstick. Fill the crankcase with the proper type and quantity of engine oil.

11. Connect the negative battery cable, start the engine and check for leaks.

RANGER

1. Disconnect the negative battery cable. Remove the engine oil level dipstick.

2. Disconnect the fan shroud and drape it over the fan. Remove the motor mount nuts from the frame.

3. Mark the position of the distributor rotor in relation to the distributor housing and the position of the housing in relation to the engine. Remove the distributor.

4. Raise and safely support the vehicle. Remove the low oil level sensor retainer clip at the sensor. Disconnect the electrical connector from the sensor.

5. Drain the crankcase and remove the starter. Remove the transmission inspection cover.

6. Remove the right axle beam on 2WD vehicles.

NOTE: The brake caliper must be removed and wired out of the way.

7. Remove the oil pan bolts. Position a jack under the engine and raise it approximately 2 in. Remove the oil pan.

NOTE: The oil pan fits tightly between the transmission spacer plate and oil pump pickup tube. Use care when removing to avoid damaging the pickup tube.

To install:

8. Clean all gasket mating surfaces and the oil pan.

9. Apply a ⅕ in. bead of silicone sealer to the junction of the rear main bearing cap and cylinder block and the junction of the front cover assembly and cylinder block.

10. Position the oil pan gasket to the oil pan and secure with sealer. Install the oil pan on the engine block with the attaching bolts and tighten to 9 ft. lbs. (12 Nm).

11. Install the low oil level sensor connector and the retainer clip. Lower the engine assembly.

12. Install the right axle beam, if removed.

13. Install the transmission inspection cover and the starter. Lower the vehicle.

14. Install the fan shroud and the motor mount nuts. Install the distributor, aligning the marks that were made during removal.

15. Install the engine oil level dipstick. Fill the crankcase with the proper type and quantity of engine oil.

16. Connect the negative battery cable, start the engine and check for leaks.

3.0L (VIN W) Engine

1. Raise and safely support the vehicle.

2. Remove the undercover and drain the engine oil.

3. On 2WD models, remove the stabilizer bar bracket bolts.

4. On 4WD models, remove the front driveshaft and disconnect the halfshafts at the transfer case. Position a floor jack under the front differential carrier and remove the mounting bolts.

5. On 2WD models, remove the front crossmember.

6. Remove the idler arm and the starter motor.

7. On 4WD models, remove the transmission-to-rear engine mount bracket nuts and the engine mount nuts/bolts.

8. Remove the engine gussets.

9. On 4WD models, attach a hoist to the engine and raise the engine slightly.

10. Remove the oil pan-to-engine bolts in the correct sequence to avoid warping the pan. Insert a seal cutter tool between the cylinder block and the oil pan and tap the tool around the circumference with a hammer to remove the oil pan.

NOTE: Be careful not to drive the seal cutter into the oil pump or rear oil seal retainer for damage may occur.

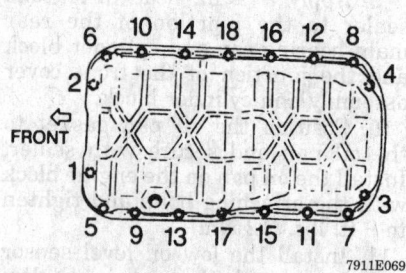

Oil pan bolt loosening sequence on 3.0L (VIN W) engine — tighten the bolts in the reverse of this sequence

11. Clean the gasket mounting surfaces.

To install:

12. Apply silicone sealant to the oil pump and oil seal retainer gasket.

13. Apply a continuous 1/8 in. bead of sealant to the oil pan mounting surface; be sure to trace sealant bead to the inside of the bolt holes where there is no groove.

14. Install the oil pan and torque the bolts in sequence to 60 inch lbs. (7 Nm).

15. To complete the installation, reverse the removal procedures.

16. Wait at least 30 minutes and refill the crankcase. Start the engine and allow it to reach normal operating temperatures and check for leaks.

4.0L Engine

AEROSTAR

1. Disconnect the negative battery cable.

2. Raise and safely support the vehicle. Remove the starter.

3. On 4WD vehicles, proceed as follows:

a. Remove the front wheel and tire assemblies.

b. Remove the pivot bolts and nuts from both lower control arms, to allow the control arms to hang.

c. Remove the control arm rear pivot crossmember.

d. Remove the lower nuts from both motor mounts.

e. Remove the front drive axle assembly.

4. Drain the crankcase and remove the oil filter. Disconnect the low oil level sensor from the engine oil pan.

5. Remove the 2 transmission-to-engine oil pan bolts. Remove the oil pan retaining bolts and nuts.

6. On 4WD vehicles, raise the engine approximately 1 in.

7. Remove the oil pan.

To install:

8. Clean all gasket mating surfaces and the oil pan.

9. Place a small amount of silicone sealer on the block at the corner where the oil pan, rear seal and block mate.

10. Install a new crankshaft rear main bearing cap wedge seal. The seal should fit snugly into the sides of the rear main bearing cap.

11. Position a new oil pan gasket into the groove in the oil pan and position the 2 oil pan spacers on the oil pan locating pads.

NOTE: If the same oil pan is being reused, the existing spacers may be used. If a new pan is being installed, the pan-to-transmission gap must be measured to find the needed spacer thickness. Failure to use the correct spacer can result in improper clearance between the oil pan and transmission, resulting in oil pan damage and/or an oil leak.

12. If a new oil pan is being installed, find the correct spacer thickness as follows:

a. Position the oil pan on the engine without the spacers and install the retaining nuts on the 4 locating studs.

b. Using a feeler gauge, measure the gap between the locating pads on the pan and the transmission converter housing.

c. If the measured gap is 0.011–0.020 in. (0.27–0.51mm), a 0.010 in. (0.254mm) spacer is required. If the measured gap is 0.021–0.029 in. (0.52–0.76mm), a 0.020 in. (0.508mm) spacer is required. If the measured gap is 0.030–0.039 in. (0.77–1.00mm), a 0.030 in. (0.762mm) spacer is required.

d. Remove the oil pan and position the correct spacers.

13. Install the oil pan with a new gasket on the engine and tighten the retaining bolts and nuts enough to compress the gasket so the transmission bolts align with the holes in the oil pan, but loose enough to allow the pan to move when the transmission bolts are installed.

14. Install the 2 transmission-to-oil pan bolts and tighten to 28–38 ft. lbs. (38–51 Nm) to align the oil pan with the transmission, then loosen the bolts 1/2 turn.

15. Tighten all the oil pan bolts and nuts evenly to 5–7 ft. lbs. (7–10 Nm), then retighten the 2 transmission-to-oil pan bolts to 28–38 ft. lbs. (38–51 Nm).

16. Connect the low oil level sensor. Install the drain plug and a new oil filter.

17. On 4WD vehicles, proceed as follows:

a. Lower the engine and install the lower motor mount nuts.

b. Install the front drive axle assembly.

c. Install the control arm rear pivot crossmember.

d. Reposition the lower control arms and install the pivot bolts and nuts.

e. Install the front wheel and tire assemblies.

18. Install the starter. Lower the vehicle and fill the crankcase with the proper type and quantity of engine oil.

19. Connect the negative battery cable, start the engine and check for leaks.

EXPLORER AND RANGER

1. Remove the engine assembly and install on a workstand with the oil pan facing up.

2. Remove the oil pan retaining bolts and remove the pan.

To install:

3. Clean all gasket mating surfaces and the oil pan.

4. Install a new crankshaft rear main bearing cap wedge seal. The seal should fit snugly into the sides of the rear main bearing cap.

5. Position a new oil pan gasket to the engine block and place the oil pan in position on the 4 locating studs. Tighten the retaining nuts and bolts evenly to 5–7 ft. lbs. (7–10 Nm).

6. Measure the gap between the surface of the rear face of the oil pan, at the spacer locations, and the rear face of the engine block as follows:

a. With the oil pan installed on the engine, position a straight edge flat on the rear of the engine block so it extends over 1 of the oil pan/transmission bolt mounting pads.

b. Using a feeler gauge, measure the gap between the mounting pad and the straight edge. Repeat the procedure for the other mounting pad.

c. If the measured gap is 0.011–0.020 in. (0.27–0.51mm), a 0.010 in. (0.254mm) spacer is required. If the measured gap is 0.021–0.029 in. (0.52–0.76mm), a 0.020 in. (0.508mm) spacer is required. If the measured gap is 0.030–0.039 in. (0.77–1.00mm), a 0.030 in. (0.762mm) spacer is required.

d. Install the selected spacers to the mounting pads on the rear of

the oil pan before bolting the engine and transmission together.

NOTE: Failure to use the correct spacer can result in improper clearance between the oil pan and transmission, resulting in oil pan damage and/or an oil leak.

7. Remove the engine from the workstand and install in the vehicle.

4.9L Engine

1. Drain the crankcase.
2. Drain the cooling system.
3. Remove the upper intake manifold and throttle body.
4. Remove the starter.
5. Remove the engine front support insulator to support bracket nuts and washers on both supports. Raise the front of the engine with a transmission jack and wood block and place 1 in. (25mm) thick wood blocks between the front support insulators and support brackets. Lower the engine and remove the transmission jack.
6. Remove the oil pan attaching bolts and lower the pan to the crossmember. Remove the 2 oil pump inlet tube and screw assembly bolts and drop the assembly in the pan. Remove the oil pan. Remove the oil pump inlet tube attaching bolts. Remove the inlet tube and screen assembly from the oil pump and leave it in the bottom of the oil pan. Remove the oil pan gaskets. Remove the inlet tube and screen from the oil pan.

To install:

7. Clean the gasket surfaces of the oil pump, oil pan and cylinder block. Remove the rear main bearing cap to oil pan seal and cylinder front cover to oil pan seal. Clean the seal grooves.
8. Apply oil-resistant sealer in the cavities between the bearing cap and cylinder block. Install a new seal in

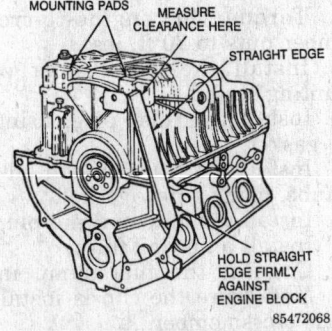

Spacer thickness measurement procedure — Explorer and Ranger with 4.0L engine

the rear main bearing cap and apply a bead of oil-resistant sealer to the tapered ends of the seal.

9. Install new side gaskets on the oil pan with oil-resistant sealer. Position a new oil pan to cylinder front cover seal on the oil pan.
10. Clean the inlet tube and screen assembly and place it in the oil pan.
11. Position the oil pan under the engine. Install the inlet tube and screen assembly on the oil pump with a new gasket. Tighten the screws to 5–7 ft. lbs. Position the oil pan against the cylinder block and install the attaching bolts. Tighten the bolts in sequence to 10–12 ft. lbs.
12. Raise the engine with a transmission jack and remove the wood blocks from the engine front supports. Lower the engine until the front support insulators are positioned on the support brackets. Install the washers and nuts on the insulator studs and tighten the nuts.
13. Install the starter and connect the starter cable.
14. Install the manifold and throttle body.
15. Fill the crankcase and cooling system.
16. Start the engine and check for coolant and oil leaks.

5.0L and 5.8L Engines

1. Drain the cooling system.
2. Remove the bolts attaching the fan shroud to the radiator and position the shroud over the fan.
3. Remove the upper intake manifold and throttle body.
4. Remove the nuts and lockwashers attaching the engine support insulators to the chassis bracket.
5. If equipped with an automatic transmission, disconnect the oil cooler line at the left side of the radiator.
6. Remove the exhaust system.
7. Raise the engine and place wood blocks under the engine supports.
8. Drain the crankcase.
9. Support the transmission with a floor jack and remove the transmission crossmember.
10. Remove the oil pan attaching bolts and lower the oil pan onto the crossmember.
11. Remove the 2 bolts attaching the oil pump pickup tube to the oil pump. Remove nut attaching oil pump pickup tube to the number 3 main bearing cap stud. Lower the pickup tube and screen into the oil pan.

12. Remove the oil pan from the vehicle.

To install:

13. Clean the oil pan, inlet tube and gasket surfaces. Inspect the gasket sealing surface for damages and distortion due to overtightening of the bolts. Repair and straighten as required.
14. Position a new oil pan gasket and seal to the cylinder block.
15. Position the oil pick-up tube and screen to the oil pump, and install the lower attaching bolt and gasket loosely. Install nut attaching to number 3 main bearing cap stud.
16. Place the oil pan on the crossmember. Install the upper pick-up tube bolt. Tighten the pick-up tube bolts.
17. Position the oil pan to the cylinder block and install the attaching bolts. Tighten to 10–12 ft. lbs.
18. Install the transmission crossmember.
19. Raise the engine and remove the blocks under the engine supports. Bolt the engine to the supports.
20. Install the exhaust system.
21. If equipped with an automatic transmission, connect the oil cooler line at the left side of the radiator.
22. Install the nuts and lockwashers attaching the engine support insulators to the chassis bracket.
23. Install the upper intake manifold and throttle body.
24. Install the fan shroud.
25. Fill the crankcase.
26. Fill and bleed the cooling system.

7.5L Engine

1. Remove the hood.
2. Disconnect the battery ground cable.
3. Drain the cooling system.
4. Remove the air intake tube and air cleaner assembly.
5. Disconnect the throttle linkage at the throttle body.
6. Disconnect the power brake vacuum line at the manifold.
7. Disconnect the fuel lines at the fuel rail.
8. Disconnect the air tubes at the throttle body.
9. Remove the radiator.
10. Remove the power steering pump and position it out of the way without disconnecting the lines.
11. Remove the oil dipstick tube. On motor home chassis, remove the oil filler tube.
12. Remove the front engine mount through-bolts.

13. Position the air conditioner refrigerant hoses so they are clear of the firewall. If necessary, discharge the system and remove the compressor.

14. Remove the upper intake manifold and throttle body.

15. Drain the crankcase. Remove the oil filter.

16. Disconnect the exhaust pipe at the manifolds.

17. Disconnect the transmission linkage at the transmission.

18. Remove the driveshaft(s).

19. Remove the transmission fill tube.

20. Raise the engine with a jack placed under the crankshaft damper and a block of wood to act as a cushion. Raise the engine until the transmission contacts the underside of the floor. Place wood blocks under the engine supports. The engine **must** remain centralized at a point at least 4 in. (102mm) above the mounts, to remove the oil pan!

21. Remove the oil pan attaching screws and lower the oil pan onto the crossmember. Remove the 2 bolts attaching the oil pump pick-up tube to the oil pump. Lower the assembly from the oil pump. Leave it on the bottom of the oil pan. Remove the oil pan and gaskets. Remove the inlet tube and screen from the oil pan.

To install:

22. Clean the gasket surfaces of the oil pan and cylinder block.

23. Apply a coating of gasket adhesive on the block mating surface and stick the 1-piece silicone gasket on the block.

24. Clean the inlet tube and screen assembly and place on the pump.

25. Position the oil pan against the cylinder block and install the retaining bolts. Torque all bolts to 10 ft. lbs.

26. Lower the engine and bolt it in place.

27. Install the transmission fill tube.

28. Install the driveshaft(s).

29. Connect the transmission linkage at the transmission.

30. Connect the exhaust pipe at the manifolds.

31. Install the oil filter.

32. Install the upper intake manifold and throttle body.

33. Install the compressor or reposition the hoses.

34. Install the oil dipstick tube. On motor home chassis, install the oil filler tube.

35. Install the power steering pump.

36. Install the radiator.

37. Connect the air tubes at the throttle body.

38. Connect the fuel lines at the fuel rail.

39. Connect the power brake vacuum line at the manifold.

40. Connect the throttle linkage at the throttle body.

41. Install the air intake tube and air cleaner assembly.

42. Fill and bleed the cooling system.

43. Fill the crankcase.

44. Connect the battery ground cable.

45. Install the hood.

7.3L Diesel Engine

1. Disconnect both battery ground cables.

2. Remove the oil dipstick.

3. Remove the transmission oil dipstick.

4. Remove the air cleaner and cover the intake opening.

5. Remove the fan and fan clutch.

NOTE: The fan uses left hand threads. Remove them by turning them clockwise.

6. Drain the cooling system.

7. Disconnect the lower radiator hose.

8. Disconnect the power steering return hose and plug the line and pump.

9. Disconnect the alternator wiring harness.

10. Disconnect the fuel line heater connector from the alternator.

11. Raise and support the front end on jackstands.

12. If equipped with automatic transmission, disconnect the transmission cooler lines at the radiator and plug them.

13. Disconnect and plug the fuel pump inlet line.

14. Drain the crankcase and remove the oil filter.

15. Remove the oil filler tube.

16. Disconnect the exhaust pipes at the manifolds.

17. Disconnect the muffler inlet pipe from the muffler and remove the pipe.

18. Remove the upper inlet mounting stud from the right exhaust manifold.

19. Unbolt the engine from the No. 1 crossmember.

20. Lower the vehicle.

21. Install lifting brackets on the front of the engine.

22. Raise the engine until the transmission contact the body.

23. Install wood blocks — 2¾ in. (70mm) on the left side; 2 in. (50mm) on the right side — between the engine insulators and crossmember.

24. Lower the engine onto the blocks.

25. Raise and support the front end on jackstands.

26. Remove the flywheel inspection plate.

27. Position fuel pump inlet line No. 1 rearward of the crossmember and position the oil cooler lines out of the way.

28. Remove the oil pan bolts.

29. Lower the oil pan.

NOTE: The oil pan is sealed to the crankcase with RTV silicone sealant in place of a gasket. It may be necessary to separate the pan from the crankcase with a utility knife.

NOTE: The crankshaft may have to be turned to allow the pan to clear the crankshaft throws.

30. Clean the pan and crankcase mating surfaces thoroughly.

To install:

31. Apply a ⅛ in. (3mm) bead of RTV silicone sealant to the pan mating surfaces, and a ¼ in. (6mm) bead on the front and rear covers and in the corners; you have 15 minutes within which to install the pan!

32. Install locating dowels into position.

33. Position the pan on the engine and install the pan bolts loosely.

34. Remove the dowels.

35. Torque the pan bolts to 7 ft. lbs. for ¼ in.-20 bolts; 14 ft. lbs. for 5/16 in.-18 bolts; 24 ft.lb for ⅜ in.-16 bolts.

36. Install the flywheel inspection cover.

37. Lower the truss.

38. Raise the engine and remove the wood blocks.

39. Lower the engine onto the crossmember and remove the lifting brackets.

40. Raise and support the front end on jackstands.

41. Torque the engine-to-crossmember nuts to 70 ft. lbs.

42. Install the upper inlet pipe mounting stud.

43. Install the inlet pipe, using a new gasket.

44. Install the transmission oil filler tube, using a new gasket.

45. Install the oil pan drain plug.

46. Install a new oil filter.

47. Connect the fuel pump inlet line. Make sure the clip is installed on the crossmember.

48. Connect the transmission cooler lines.

49. Lower the vehicle.

50. Connect all wiring.
51. Connect the power steering return line.
52. Connect the lower radiator hose.
53. Install the fan and fan clutch.

NOTE: The fan uses left hand threads. Install them by turning them counterclockwise.

54. Remove the cover and install the air cleaner.
55. Install the dipsticks.
56. Fill the crankcase.
57. Fill and bleed the cooling system.
58. Fill the power steering reservoir.
59. Connect the batteries.
60. Run the engine and check for leaks.

NOTE: The fan uses left hand threads. Install them by turning them counterclockwise.

61. Remove the cover and install the air cleaner.
62. Install the dipsticks.
63. Fill the crankcase.
64. Fill and bleed the cooling system.
65. Fill the power steering reservoir.
66. Connect the batteries.
67. Run the engine and check for leaks.

Oil Pump

REMOVAL AND INSTALLATION

2.3L, 2.9L, 3.0L (VIN U) and 4.0L Engines

1. Disconnect the negative battery cable.
2. Remove the oil pan.
3. Remove the oil pump attaching bolts and, if equipped, remove the oil pump pickup tube retaining nut from the main bearing cap.
4. Remove the oil pump and oil pump driveshaft. Remove and clean the oil pump pickup tube and screen, as necessary.
   To install:
5. Install the oil pump pickup tube and screen assembly, if removed.
6. Prime the oil pump by filling either the inlet or outlet port with clean engine oil. Rotate the pump shaft to distribute the oil within the pump body.
7. Insert the oil pump driveshaft into the opening in the block or main bearing cap. On 3.0L engine, assemble the shaft to the oil pump until the retainer clicks into place.

8. Install the oil pump, with a new gasket if equipped, and install the attaching bolts. Tighten the bolts to 14–21 ft. lbs. (19–29 Nm) on 2.3L engine, 6–10 ft. lbs. (9–13 Nm) on 2.9L engine, 35 ft. lbs. (48 Nm) on 3.0L (VIN U) engine or 13–15 ft. lbs. (17–21 Nm) on 4.0L engine.
9. On 2.3L engine, install the pickup tube retaining nut and tighten to 30–41 ft. lbs. (40–55 Nm).
10. Install the oil pan.
11. Fill the crankcase with the proper type and quantity of engine oil. Connect the negative battery cable, start the engine and check for leaks.

3.0L (VIN W) Engine

The oil pump is mounted at the front of the engine behind the crankshaft pulley.

1. Disconnect the negative battery cable.
2. Raise and safely support the vehicle. Drain the cooling system and the crankcase.
3. Remove the oil pan and the timing belt.
4. Remove the crankshaft timing sprocket using a wheel puller and the timing belt plate.
5. Remove the oil pump strainer and the pickup tube from the oil pump.
6. Remove the oil pump-to-engine bolts and the oil pump from the engine.
7. Clean the gasket mounting surfaces.

NOTE: Whenever the oil pump is removed, replace the oil seal.

8. To install, use new gaskets or silicone sealant. Pack the oil pump cavity with petroleum jelly and reverse the removal procedures. Torque as follows:
   Oil pump-to-engine:
   6mm bolts — 60 inch lbs. (7 Nm)
   8mm bolts — 12 ft. lbs. (16 Nm)
   Pickup tube-to-oil pump bolts — 15 ft. lbs. (21 Nm)

4.9L, 5.0L, 5.8L and 7.5L Engines

1. Remove the oil pan.
2. Remove the oil pump inlet tube and screen assembly.
3. Remove the oil pump attaching bolts and remove the oil pump gasket and intermediate driveshaft.
4. Before installing the oil pump, prime it by filling the inlet and outlet port with oil and rotating the shaft of the pump to distribute it.
5. Position the intermediate driveshaft into the distributor socket.

6. Position the new gasket on the pump body and insert the intermediate driveshaft into the pump body.
7. Install the pump and intermediate driveshaft as an assembly. Do not force the pump if it does not seal readily. The driveshaft may be misaligned with the distributor shaft. To align it, rotate the intermediate driveshaft into a new position.
8. Install the oil pump attaching bolts and torque them to 12–15 ft. lbs. on the inline sixes and to 20–25 ft. lbs. on the V8s.

7.3L Diesel Engine

1. Remove the oil pan.
2. Remove the oil pick-up tube from the pump.
3. Unbolt and remove the oil pump.
4. Assemble the pick-up tube and pump. Use a new gasket.
5. Install the oil pump and torque the bolts to 14 ft. lbs.

CHECKING

Except 3.0L (VIN W) Engine

1. Remove the pump and disassemble. Thoroughly clean all parts in solvent and dry with compressed air.
2. Check the inside of the pump housing and the inner and outer gears for damage or excessive wear. Check the mating surfaces of the pump cover for wear. Minor scuff marks are normal, but if the cover, gears or housing surfaces are excessively worn, scored or grooved, replace the entire pump.
3. Measure the inner to outer rotor tip clearance. With the rotor assembly removed from the pump and resting on a flat surface, the inner and outer rotor tip clearance must not exceed 0.012 in. (0.30mm) with a feeler gauge inserted ½ in. (13mm) minimum.
4. With the rotor assembly installed in the housing, place a straight edge over the rotor assembly and the housing. Measure the vertical clearance, the rotor endplay, between the straight edge and the inner rotor and outer race. Maximum clearance must not exceed 0.005 in. (0.13mm).
5. Inspect the relief valve spring for collapsed or worn condition. Check the spring tension. The tension should be 12.6–14.5 lbs. at 1.20 in. on 2.3L engine, 13.6–14.7 lbs. at 1.39 in. on 2.9L engine and 4.0L engines or 9.1–10.1 lbs. at 1.11 in. on 3.0L engine.

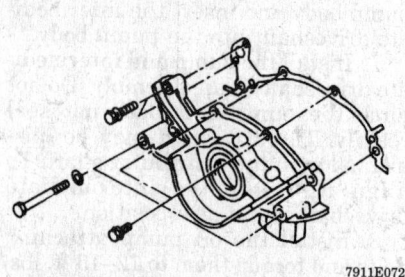

Oil pump on 3.0L (VIN W) engine is on the front of the engine block

7911E072

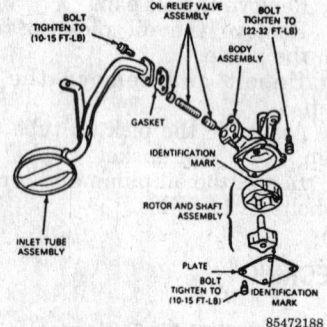

Oil pump assembly — 5.0L and 5.8L engines

85472188

6. If any part of the oil pump requires replacement, replace the complete pump assembly.

3.0L (VIN W) Engine

To check the oil pump clearances, the oil pump must be removed from the engine and disassembled. If the parts do not meet specifications, replace the oil pump as an assembly.

Using a feeler gauge, check the following clearances:

Pump body-to-outer gear — 0.0043–0.0079 in. (0.11–0.20mm)

Inner gear-to-crescent — 0.0047–0.0091 in. (0.12–0.23mm)

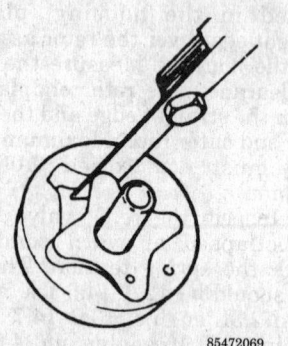

Measuring the oil pump inner-to-outer rotor tip clearance

85472069

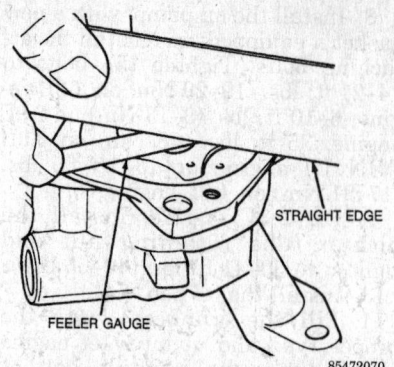

STRAIGHT EDGE

FEELER GAUGE

85472070

Measuring oil pump rotor endplay

Outer gear-to-crescent — 0.0083–0.0126 in. (0.22–0.33mm)

Housing-to-inner gear — 0.0020–0.0035 in. (0.05–0.09mm)

Housing-to-outer gear — 0.0020–0.0043 in. (0.05–0.11mm)

Rear Main Bearing Oil Seal

REMOVAL AND INSTALLATION

2.3L, 2.9L, 3.0L (VIN U) and 4.0L Engines

1. Disconnect the negative battery cable. Raise and safely support the vehicle.

2. Remove the transmission. If equipped with manual transmission, remove the clutch assembly.

3. Remove the flywheel and the engine rear cover plate.

4. Using a sharp awl or equivalent, punch a hole into the seal metal surface between the lip and block. Screw in the threaded end of plug puller T77L-9533-B or equivalent, and remove the seal. Be careful to avoid scratching or damaging the oil seal surface.

5. When the seal has been removed, clean the mounting recess.

To install:

6. Coat the new seal and the crankshaft with a light film of engine oil. Do not use grease.

7. Start the seal into the recess with the seal lip facing forward and install it with a suitable rear oil seal replacer tool. Keep the tool straight with the centerline of the crankshaft and install the seal until it is fully seated.

8. After removing the tool, inspect the seal to make sure it was not damaged during installation.

9. Install the engine rear cover plate. Position the flywheel on the crankshaft flange. Install the flywheel attaching bolts and tighten to 59 ft. lbs. (80 Nm) on all except 2.9L

engine. Tighten the bolts on 2.9L engine to 47–52 ft. lbs. (64–70 Nm).

10. If equipped with manual transmission, install the clutch assembly. Install the transmission and starter and lower the vehicle.

11. Connect the negative battery cable, start the engine and check for leaks.

3.0L (VIN W) Engine

1. Disconnect the negative battery cable.

2. Raise and safely support the vehicle. Remove the starter.

3. Remove the transmission from the vehicle.

4. If equipped with a manual transmission, remove the clutch-to-flywheel bolts and the clutch assembly from the vehicle.

5. Remove the flywheel-to-crankshaft bolts and the flywheel from the engine.

6. Remove the rear oil seal retainer-to-engine bolts, the rear oil seal retainer-to-oil pan bolts and the retainer.

7. Carefully pry the rear oil seal from the retainer; be careful not to damage the mounting surfaces. Clean the oil seal mounting surfaces.

8. Using an appropriate oil seal installation tool, lubricate the new oil seal lips with engine oil and drive the the seal into the retainer until it seats.

9. To complete the installation, reverse the removal procedures. Start the engine and check for leaks.

4.9L, 5.0L, 5.8L and 7.5L Engines

If the crankshaft rear oil seal replacement is the only operation being performed, it can be done in the vehicle as detailed in the following procedure. If the oil seal is being replaced in conjunction with a rear main bearing replacement, the engine must be removed from the vehicle and installed on a work stand.

1. Remove the starter.

2. Remove the transmission from the vehicle.

3. On manual shift transmission, remove the pressure plate and cover assembly and the clutch disc.

4. Remove the flywheel attaching bolts and remove the flywheel and engine rear cover plate.

5. Use an awl to punch 2 holes in the crankshaft rear oil seal. Punch the holes on opposite sides of the crankshaft and just above the bearing cap to cylinder block split line. Install a sheet metal screw in each hole. Use 2 small pry bars and pry against both screws at the same time

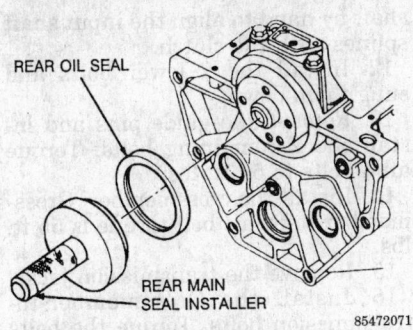

REAR OIL SEAL

REAR MAIN SEAL INSTALLER

85472071

Rear main bearing oil seal installation — 3.0L (VIN U) , 4.9L, 5.0L and 5.8L engines

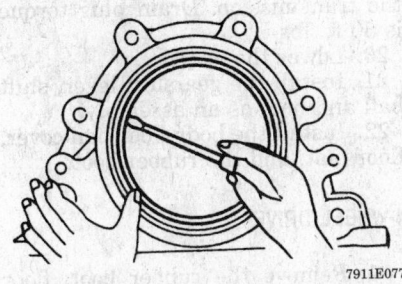

7911E077

Removing the rear oil seal from the retainer; the transmission and flywheel must be removed — 3.0L (VIN W) Engine

to remove the crankshaft rear oil seal. It may be necessary to place small blocks of wood against the cylinder block to provide a fulcrum point for the pry bars. Use caution throughout this procedure to avoid scratching or otherwise damaging the crankshaft oil seal surface.

6. Clean the oil seal recess in the cylinder block and main bearing cap.

7. Clean, inspect and polish the rear oil seal rubbing surface on the crankshaft. Coat the new oil seal and the crankshaft with a light film of oil. Start the seal in the recess with the

seal lip facing forward and install it with a seal driver. Keep the tool straight with the centerline of the crankshaft and install the seal until the tool contacts the cylinder block surface. Remove the tool and inspect the seal to be sure it was not damaged during installation.

8. Install the engine rear cover plate. Position the flywheel on the crankshaft flange. Coat the threads of the flywheel attaching bolts with oil-resistant sealer and install the bolts. Tighten the bolts in sequence.

9. On a manual shift transmission, install the clutch disc and the pressure plate assembly.

10. Install the transmission.

7.3L Diesel Engine

1. Remove the transmission, clutch and flywheel assemblies.

2. Remove the engine rear cover.

3. Using an arbor press and a $4\frac{1}{8}$ in. (104.775mm) diameter spacer, press out the rear oil seal from the cover.

To install:

4. Clean the rear cover and engine block surfaces. Remove all traces of old RTV sealant from the oil pan and rear cover sealing surface by cleaning with a suitable solvent and drying thoroughly.

5. Coat the new rear oil seal with Lubriplate® or equivalent. Using an arbor press and spacer, install the new seal into the cover.

NOTE: The seal must be installed from the engine block side of the rear cover, flush with the seal bore inner surface.

6. Install a seal pilot, ford part no. T83T–6701B or equivalent onto the crankshaft.

7. Apply gasket sealant to the engine block gasket surfaces, and install the rear cover gasket to the engine.

8. Apply a ¼ in. (6mm) bead of RTV sealant onto the oil pan sealing surface, immediately after rear cover installation.

9. Push the rear cover into position on the engine and install the cover bolts. Torque to specification.

10. Position the flywheel on the crankshaft flange. Coat the threads of the flywheel attaching bolts with sealant and install the bolts and flex-plate, if equipped. Torque the bolts to specification, alternating across from each bolt.

11. Install the clutch and transmission. Run the engine and check for oil leaks.

MANUAL TRANSMISSION

Transmission Assembly

REMOVAL AND INSTALLATION

— CAUTION —

The clutch driven disc contains asbestos, which has been determined to be a cancer causing agent. Never clean clutch surfaces with compressed air! Avoid inhaling any dust from any clutch surface! When cleaning clutch surfaces, use a commercially available brake cleaning fluid.

FM146 Transmission

1. Disconnect the negative battery cable.

2. Place the gearshift lever in the **N** position.

3. Remove the shifter boot retainer screws and slide the boot up the shift lever shaft. Remove the shift lever attaching bolt(s) and remove the shift lever. Cover the opening in the transmission to prevent dirt from entering.

4. Raise and safely support the vehicle.

5. Mark the position of the driveshaft(s) on the flange(s) and remove the driveshaft(s). Plug the transmission or transfer case opening to prevent fluid leakage.

6. Disconnect the clutch hydraulic fluid line. Plug the line to prevent fluid leakage.

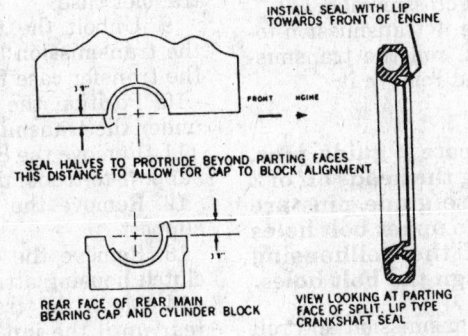

INSTALL SEAL WITH LIP TOWARDS FRONT OF ENGINE

FRONT ENGINE

SEAL HALVES TO PROTRUDE BEYOND PARTING FACES THIS DISTANCE TO ALLOW FOR CAP TO BLOCK ALIGNMENT

REAR FACE OF REAR MAIN BEARING CAP AND CYLINDER BLOCK

VIEW LOOKING AT PARTING FACE OF SPLIT, LIP TYPE CRANKSHAFT SEAL

85472189

Installilng 2 piece rear main bearing oil seal — 7.5L engine

7. Disconnect the speedometer cable from the transmission or transfer case.

8. Disconnect the starter cable, backup lamp and neutral switch wires.

9. Place a jack under the engine, with a wood block to protect the oil pan.

10. Remove the transfer case, if equipped.

11. Remove the starter. Place a transmission jack under the transmission.

12. Remove the bolts attaching the transmission and clutch housing to the engine. Remove the nuts and bolts attaching the transmission mount and damper to the crossmember.

13. Remove the nuts and/or bolts attaching the crossmember to the frame side rails and remove the crossmember.

14. Lower the engine jack. Work the clutch housing off the locating dowels and slide the clutch housing and transmission rearward until the input shaft clears the clutch disc. Remove the transmission.

15. Remove the clutch housing from the transmission, if necessary.

To install:

16. Make sure the machined mating surfaces and the locating dowels on the engine rear plate and the mating face of the clutch housing and locating dowel holes are free of burrs, dirt or paint. Install the clutch housing on the transmission, if removed.

17. Mount the transmission on a transmission jack and raise into position. Start the input shaft into the clutch disc, aligning the splines. Move the transmission forward until the clutch housing seats on the locating dowels.

18. Install the clutch housing-to-engine attaching bolts and tighten to 28–38 ft. lbs. (38–51 Nm). Remove the transmission jack.

19. Install the starter.

20. Raise the engine and install the crossmember, insulator and damper with the attaching nuts and bolts. Install the nuts and bolts attaching the transmission mount to the crossmember.

21. Install the transfer case, if equipped.

22. Remove the plug(s) and install the driveshaft(s), aligning the marks on the flange(s) that were made during the removal procedure.

23. Connect the starter cable, backup lamp switch wire, shift indi-

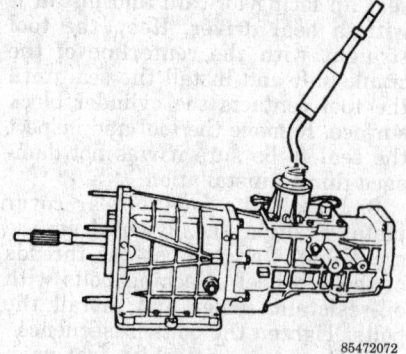

85472072

FM146 manual transmission

cator wire and neutral position switch wire, if equipped.

24. Connect the hydraulic clutch line and bleed the system.

25. Connect the speedometer cable.

26. Remove the fill plug and check the fluid level. Add if necessary.

27. Lower the vehicle and remove the cover from the transmission opening.

28. Install the gearshift lever with the attaching bolt(s). Install the shifter boot.

29. Connect the negative battery cable. Check the transmission for proper operation.

Warner T-18, T-19A, T-19C 4-Speed

2-WHEEL DRIVE

1. Remove the rubber boot, floor mat, and the body floor pan cover.

2. Remove the gearshift lever, shift ball and boot as an assembly.

3. Raise the vehicle and support it with jackstands.

4. Drain the transmission.

5. Remove the driveshaft.

6. Disconnect the speedometer cable.

7. Remove the crossmember-to-transmission bolts.

8. Secure the transmission to a transmission jack.

9. Remove the crossmember.

10. Remove the 4 transmission-to-bellhousing bolts, roll the transmission rearward and remove it.

To install:

NOTE: Fabricate 2 guide pins, made by cutting the heads off of 2 long bolts. These guide pins are inserted into the upper bolt holes in the back of the bellhousing and serve to align the bolt holes.

11. Raise the transmission and roll it forward using the guide pins to align the bolt holes. Turn the output

shaft by hand to align the input shaft splines with the clutch.

12. Install the 2 lower bolts and snug them down.

13. Remove the guide pins and install the 2 remaining bolts. Torque all 4 bolts to 50 ft. lbs.

14. Install the crossmember. Crossmember-to-frame bolt torque is 55 ft. lbs.

15. Remove the transmission jack.

16. Install the Crossmember-to-transmission bolts. Torque the bolts to 50 ft. lbs.

17. Connect the speedometer cable.

18. Install the driveshaft.

19. Install the drain plug and fill the transmission. Drain plug torque is 50 ft. lbs.

20. Lower the vehicle.

21. Install the gearshift lever, shift ball and boot as an assembly.

22. Install the body floor pan cover, floor mat, and the rubber boot.

4-WHEEL DRIVE

1. Remove the rubber boot, floor mat, and the body floor pan cover. Remove the gearshift lever. Remove the weather pad.

2. Remove the transfer case shift lever, shift ball and boot as an assembly.

3. Disconnect the back-up light switch at the rear of the gearshift housing cover.

4. Raise the vehicle and support it with jackstands. Remove the drain and fill plugs and drain the lubricant.

5. Position a transmission jack under the transfer case and disconnect the speedometer cable.

6. Matchmark the flanges and disconnect the rear driveshaft from the transfer case. Wire it up and out of the way.

7. Matchmark and disconnect the front driveshaft at the transfer case. Wire it up and out of the way.

8. Remove the shift link from the transfer case.

9. Unbolt the transfer case from the transmission (6 bolts) and lower the transfer case from the vehicle.

10. Position the transmission jack under the transmission.

11. Remove the 8 rear transmission support-to-transmission bolts.

12. Remove the rear transmission support.

13. Remove the 4 transmission-to-clutch housing attaching bolts.

14. Move the transmission to the rear until the input shaft clears the flywheel housing and lower the transmission.

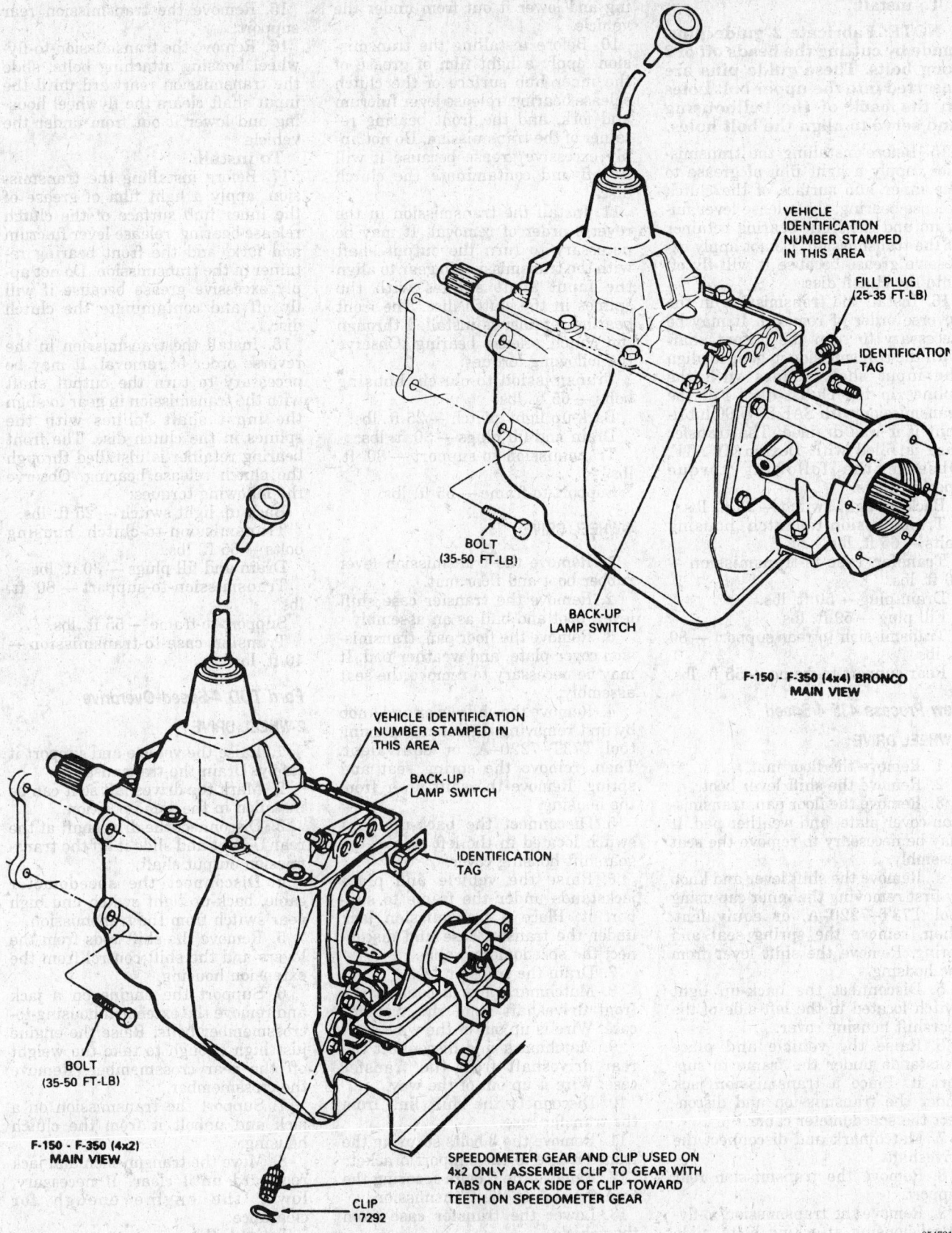

VEHICLE
IDENTIFICATION
NUMBER STAMPED
IN THIS AREA

FILL PLUG
(25-35 FT-LB)

IDENTIFICATION
TAG

BOLT
(35-50 FT-LB)

BACK-UP
LAMP SWITCH

**F-150 - F-350 (4x4) BRONCO
MAIN VIEW**

VEHICLE IDENTIFICATION
NUMBER STAMPED IN
THIS AREA

BACK-UP
LAMP SWITCH

IDENTIFICATION
TAG

BOLT
(35-50 FT-LB)

**F-150 - F-350 (4x2)
MAIN VIEW**

SPEEDOMETER GEAR AND CLIP USED ON
4x2 ONLY ASSEMBLE CLIP TO GEAR WITH
TABS ON BACK SIDE OF CLIP TOWARD
TEETH ON SPEEDOMETER GEAR

CLIP
17292

85472190

Borg-Warner T-18 manual transmission — Bronco, F Series (Pick-Up) and E Series (Van)

To install:

NOTE: Fabricate 2 guide pins, made by cutting the heads off of 2 long bolts. These guide pins are inserted into the upper bolt holes in the back of the bellhousing and serve to align the bolt holes.

15. Before installing the transmission, apply a light film of grease to the inner hub surface of the clutch release bearing, the release lever fulcrum and the front bearing retainer of the transmission. Do not apply excessive grease because it will fly off onto the clutch disc.

16. Install the transmission in the reverse order of removal. It may be necessary to turn the output shaft with the transmission in gear to align the input shaft splines with the splines in the clutch disc. Fill the transmission with SAE 80W/90 lubricant if it was drained. The transfer case is filled with Dexron®II ATF. Observe the following torque specifications:

Back-up light switch — 25 ft. lbs.
Transmission-to-clutch housing bolts — 65 ft. lbs.
Transfer case-to-transmission — 40 ft. lbs.
Drain plug — 50 ft. lbs.
Fill plug — 50 ft. lbs.
Transmission to rear support — 80 ft. lbs.
Rear support-to-frame — 55 ft. lbs.

New Process 435 4-Speed

2-WHEEL DRIVE

1. Remove the floor mat.
2. Remove the shift lever boot.
3. Remove the floor pan, transmission cover plate, and weather pad. It may be necessary to remove the seat assembly.
4. Remove the shift lever and knob by first removing the inner cap using tool T73T–7220–A, or equivalent. Then, remove the spring seat and spring. Remove the shift lever from the housing.
5. Disconnect the back-up light switch located in the left side of the gearshift housing cover.
6. Raise the vehicle and place jackstands under the frame to support it. Place a transmission jack under the transmission and disconnect the speedometer cable.
7. Matchmark and disconnect the driveshaft.
8. Remove the transmission rear support.
9. Remove the transmission-to-flywheel housing attaching bolts, slide the transmission rearward until the input shaft clears the flywheel hous-

ing and lower it out from under the vehicle.

10. Before installing the transmission, apply a light film of grease of the inner hub surface of the clutch release bearing, release lever fulcrum and fork, and the front bearing retainer of the transmission. Do not apply excessive grease because if will fly off and contaminate the clutch disc.

11. Install the transmission in the reverse order of removal. It may be necessary to turn the output shaft with the transmission in gear to align the input shaft splines with the splines in the clutch disc. The front bearing retainer is installed through the clutch release bearing. Observe the following torques:

Transmission-to-clutch housing bolts — 65 ft. lbs.
Back-up light switch — 25 ft. lbs.
Drain and fill plugs — 30 ft. lbs.
Transmission-to-support — 80 ft. lbs.
Support-to-frame — 55 ft. lbs.

4-WHEEL DRIVE

1. Remove the transmission lever rubber boot and floor mat.
2. Remove the transfer case shift lever, boot and ball as an assembly.
3. Remove the floor pan, transmission cover plate, and weather pad. It may be necessary to remove the seat assembly.
4. Remove the shift lever and knob by first removing the inner cap using tool T73T–7220–A, or equivalent. Then, remove the spring seat and spring. Remove the shift lever from the housing.
5. Disconnect the back-up light switch located in the left side of the gearshift housing cover.
6. Raise the vehicle and place jackstands under the frame to support it. Place a transmission jack under the transfer case and disconnect the speedometer cable.
7. Drain the transfer case.
8. Matchmark and disconnect the front driveshaft from the transfer case. Wire is up out of the way.
9. Matchmark and disconnect the rear driveshaft from the transfer case. Wire it up out of the way.
10. Disconnect the shift link from the transfer case.
11. Remove the 3 bolts securing the transfer case to the support bracket.
12. Remove the 6 bolts securing the transfer case to the transmission.
13. Lower the transfer case from the vehicle.
14. Place the transmission jack under the transmission.

15. Remove the transmission rear support.

16. Remove the transmission-to-flywheel housing attaching bolts, slide the transmission rearward until the input shaft clears the flywheel housing and lower it out from under the vehicle.

To install:

17. Before installing the transmission, apply a light film of grease of the inner hub surface of the clutch release bearing, release lever fulcrum and fork, and the front bearing retainer of the transmission. Do not apply excessive grease because if will fly off and contaminate the clutch disc.

18. Install the transmission in the reverse order of removal. It may be necessary to turn the output shaft with the transmission in gear to align the input shaft splines with the splines in the clutch disc. The front bearing retainer is installed through the clutch release bearing. Observe the following torques:

Back-up light switch — 25 ft. lbs.
Transmission-to-clutch housing bolts — 65 ft. lbs.
Drain and fill plugs — 30 ft. lbs.
Transmission-to-support — 80 ft. lbs.
Support-to-frame — 55 ft. lbs.
Transfer case-to-transmission — 40 ft. lbs.

Ford TOD 4-Speed Overdrive

2-WHEEL DRIVE

1. Raise the vehicle and support it safely. Drain the transmission.
2. Mark the driveshaft so it can be installed in the same position.
3. Disconnect the driveshaft at the rear U-joint and slide it off the transmission output shaft.
4. Disconnect the speedometer cable, back-up light switch and high gear switch from the transmission.
5. Remove the shift rods from the levers and the shift control from the extension housing.
6. Support the engine on a jack and remove the extension housing-to-crossmember bolts. Raise the engine just high enough to take the weight off the rear crossmember. Remove the crossmember.
7. Support the transmission on a jack and unbolt it from the clutch housing.
8. Move the transmission and jack rearward until clear. If necessary, lower the engine enough for clearance.

To install:

9. Installation is the reverse of removal. It is a good idea to install and

snug down the upper transmission-to-engine bolts first, then the lower. Adjustment linkage and check the fluid level. Observe the following torques:

Back-up light switch — 25 ft. lbs.
Transmission-to-clutch housing bolts — 65 ft. lbs.
Drain and fill plugs — 30 ft. lbs.
Transmission-to-support — 80 ft. lbs.
Support-to-frame — 55 ft. lbs.

4-WHEEL DRIVE

1. Raise the vehicle and support it safely. Drain the transmission and transfer case.
2. Mark the driveshaft so it can be installed in the same position.
3. Matchmark and disconnect the front and rear driveshafts at the transfer case.
4. Disconnect the speedometer cable and 4-wheel drive indicator switch from the transfer case; the back-up light switch and high gear switch from the transmission.
5. Remove the skid plate.
6. Disconnect the shift link from the transfer case.
7. Remove the shift lever from the transmission.
8. Support the transmission on a jack and remove the transmission housing rear support bracket.
9. Raise the transmission just high enough to take the weight off the rear crossmember.
10. Remove the 2 nuts securing the upper gusset to the frame on both sides of the frame.
11. Remove the nut and bolt connecting the gusset to the support. Remove the gusset on the left side.
12. Remove the transmission-to-support plate bolts.
13. Remove the support plate and right gusset.
14. Remove the crossmember.
15. Remove the transfer case heat shield. Be very careful if the catalytic converter is hot!
16. Support the transfer case on a jack and unbolt it from the transmission.
17. Move the transfer case and jack rearward until clear and lower it. Discard the adapter gasket.
18. Support the transmission on a jack and unbolt it from the clutch housing.
19. Move the transmission and jack rearward until clear. If necessary, lower the engine for clearance.
To install:
20. Installation is the reverse of removal. It is a good idea to install and snug down the upper transmission-

to-clutch housing bolts first, then the lower. Adjust linkage and check the fluid level. Observe the following torques:

Back-up light switch — 25 ft. lbs.
Transmission-to-clutch housing bolts — 65 ft. lbs.
Transfer case-to-transmission — 40 ft. lbs.
Rear driveshaft-to-yoke — 25 ft. lbs.
Front driveshaft-to-yoke — 15 ft. lbs.
Drain and fill plugs — 30 ft. lbs.
Transmission-to-support — 80 ft. lbs.
Support-to-frame — 55 ft. lbs.

Mazda M5OD 5-Speed

1. Raise and support the vehicle safely. Prop the clutch pedal in the full up position with a block of wood.
2. Matchmark the driveshaft-to-flange relation.
3. Disconnect the driveshaft at the rear axle and slide it off of the transmission output shaft. Lubricant will leak out of the transmission so be prepared to catch it, or plug the opening with rags or a seal installation tool.
4. Disconnect the speedometer cable at the transmission.
5. Disconnect the shift rods from the shift levers.
6. Remove the shift control from the extension housing and transmission case.
7. On 4-wheel drive models, remove the transfer case.
8. Remove the extension housing-to-rear support bolts.
9. Take up the weight of the transmission with a transmission jack. Chain the transmission to the jack.
10. Raise the transmission just enough to take the weight off of the No. 3 crossmember.
11. Unbolt the crossmember from the frame rails and remove it.
12. Place a jackstand under the rear of the engine at the bellhousing.
13. Lower the jack and allow the jackstand to take the weight of the engine. The engine should be angled slightly downward to allow the transmission to roll backward.
14. Remove the transmission-to bellhousing bolts.
15. Roll the jack rearward until the input shaft clears the bellhousing. Lower the jack and remove the transmission.

WARNING
Do not depress the clutch pedal with the transmission removed.

To install:
16. Clean all machined mating surfaces thoroughly.
17. Install a guide pin in each lower bolt hole. Position the spacer plate on the guide pins.
18. Raise the transmission and start the input shaft through the clutch release bearing.
19. Align the input shaft splines with the clutch disc splines. Roll the transmission forward so the input shaft will enter the clutch disc. If the shaft binds in the release bearing, work the release arm back and forth.
20. Once the transmission is all the way in, install the 2 upper retaining bolts and washers and remove the lower guide pins. Install the lower bolts. Torque the bolts to 50 ft. lbs.
21. Raise the transmission just enough to allow installation of the No.3 crossmember.
22. Install the crossmember on the frame rails. Torque the bolts to 80 ft. lbs.
23. Lower the transmission onto the crossmember and install the nuts. Torque the nuts to 70 ft. lbs.
24. Remove the transmission jack.
25. Install the transfer case.
26. Install the shift control on the extension housing and transmission case.
27. Connect the shift rods at the shift levers.
28. Connect the speedometer cable at the transmission.
29. Slide the driveshaft onto the output shaft and connect the driveshaft at the rear axle, aligning the matchmarks.

ZF S5-42 5-Speed

1. Place the transmission in neutral.
2. Remove the carpet or floor mat.
3. Remove the ball from the shift lever.
4. Remove the boot and bezel assembly from the floor.
5. Remove the 2 bolts and disengage the upper shift lever from the lower shift lever.
6. Raise and support the vehicle safely.
7. Disconnect the speedometer cable.
8. Disconnect the back-up switch wire.
9. Place a drain pan under the case and drain the case through the drain plug.
10. Position a transmission jack under the case and safety-chain the case to the jack.
11. Remove the driveshaft.
12. Disconnect the clutch linkage.

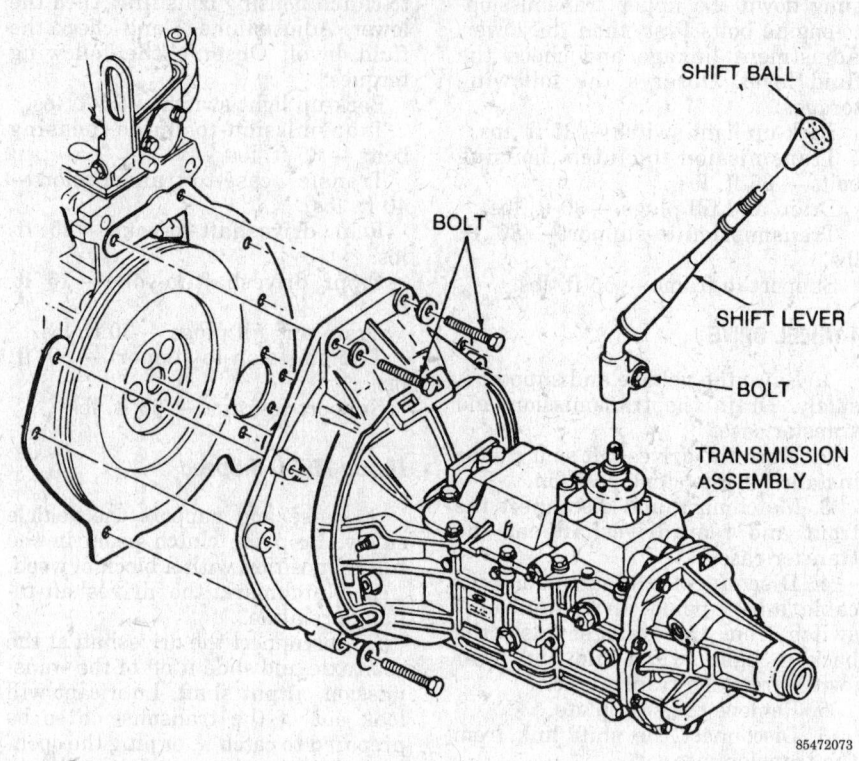

85472073

M50D manual transmission

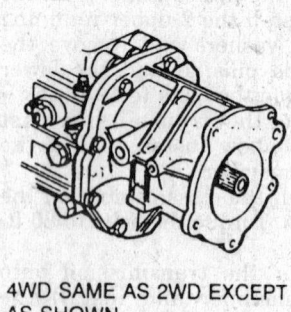

4WD SAME AS 2WD EXCEPT AS SHOWN

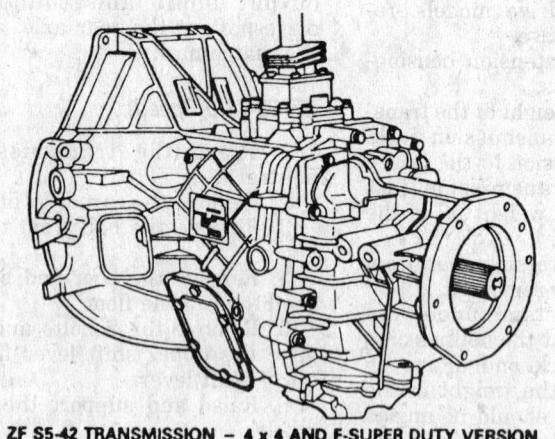

ZF S5-42 TRANSMISSION – 4 x 4 AND F-SUPER DUTY VERSION

ZFS 5-42 TRANSMISSION – 4 x 2 VERSION

85472191

S5-42 ZF manual transmission — Bronco, F Series (Pick-Up) and E Series (Van)

13. On 4-wheel drive models, remove the transfer case.

14. Remove the transmission rear insulator and lower retainer.

15. Unbolt and remove the crossmember.

16. Remove the transmission-to-engine block bolts.

17. Roll the transmission rearward until the input shaft clears, lower the jack and remove the transmission.

To install:

18. Install 2 guide studs into the lower bolt holes.

19. Raise the transmission until the input shaft splines are aligned with the clutch disc splines. The clutch release bearing and hub must be properly positioned in the release lever fork.

20. Roll the transmission forward and into position on the front case.

21. Install the bolts and torque them to 50 ft. lbs. Remove the guide studs and install and tighten the 2 remaining bolts.

22. Install the crossmember and torque the bolts to 55 ft. lbs.

23. Install the transmission rear insulator and lower retainer. Torque the bolts to 60 ft. lbs.

24. On 4-wheel drive models, install the transfer case.

25. Connect the clutch linkage.

26. Install the driveshaft.

27. Remove the transmission jack.

28. Fill the transmission.

29. Connect the back-up switch wire.

30. Connect the speedometer cable.

31. Lower the van.

32. Install the boot and bezel assembly.

33. Connect the upper shift to from the lower shift lever. Tighten the bolts to 20 ft. lbs.

34. Install the carpet or floor mat.

35. Install the ball from the shift lever.

SHIFT LINKAGE ADJUSTMENT

Ford TOD 4-Speed Overdrive

1. Attach the shift rods in the levers.

2. Rotate the output shaft to determine that the transmission is in neutral.

3. Insert a alignment pin into the shift control assembly alignment hole.

4. Attach the slotted end of the shift rods over the flats of the studs in the shift control assembly.

5. Install the lock nuts and remove the alignment pin.

CLUTCH

Clutch Assembly

REMOVAL AND INSTALLATION

Except Bronco, F Series (Pick-Up) and E Series (Van)

1. Disconnect the negative battery cable.

2. Disconnect the hydraulic clutch master cylinder from the clutch pedal.

3. Raise and safely support the vehicle. Remove the starter.

4. Use coupling disconnect tool T88T-70522-A or equivalent, to slide the white plastic sleeve toward the slave cylinder, then apply a slight tug on the tube to disconnect the hydraulic coupling. Plug the hose.

5. Remove the transmission.

6. Mark the position of the pressure plate on the flywheel so if the pressure plate is reused, it can be reinstalled in the same position.

7. Loosen the pressure plate attaching bolts evenly until the diaphragm spring is expanded. Remove the bolts, pressure plate and clutch disc.

8. Inspect the flywheel for wear, scoring and cracks. Machine or replace, as necessary. Inspect the clutch pilot bearing for wear and free movement. If replacement is necessary, remove using puller tool T58L-101-B or equivalent.

9. Inspect the clutch release bearing for wear and free movement; replace as necessary. Remove the release bearing by twisting it until resistance is felt. Turning further will allow the preload spring to push the bearing assembly off the slave cylinder.

To install:

10. If the pilot bearing was removed, a new 1 must be installed. Install using replacer tool T71P-7137-C and clutch driver tool T71P-7137-H or equivalent. Install the pilot bearing with the seal facing the transmission so the adapter is not cocked.

11. If the flywheel was removed, make sure the mating surfaces of the crank flange and flywheel are clean, and install the flywheel. Tighten the flywheel bolts to 59 ft. lbs. (80 Nm) on all except 2.9L engine. Tighten the bolts on 2.9L engine to 47–52 ft. lbs. (64–70 Nm).

12. Position the clutch disc on the flywheel so alignment tool

T74P-7137-K or equivalent, can enter the pilot bearing and align the disc.

13. Install the pressure plate. If the original pressure plate is being reused, align the marks that were made during the removal procedure. Install the attaching bolts and tighten, in sequence, to 15–24 ft. lbs. (21–32 Nm), then remove the alignment tool.

14. Install the transmission. If equipped, reuse the aluminum washers under the attaching bolts to prevent galvanic corrosion.

15. Connect the hydraulic coupling by pushing the male coupling into the slave cylinder female coupling.

16. Lower the vehicle and connect the clutch master cylinder to the brake pedal. Bleed the clutch system, if necessary.

17. Connect the negative battery cable.

Bronco, F Series (Pick-Up) and E Series (Van)

——— **CAUTION** ———

The clutch driven disc contains asbestos, which has been determined to be a cancer causing agent. Never clean clutch surfaces with compressed air! Avoid inhaling any dust from any clutch surface! When cleaning clutch surfaces, use a commercially available brake cleaning fluid.

1. Raise and support the vehicle safely.

2. If equipped with an externally mounted slave cylinder, remove the clutch slave cylinder. If equipped with an internally mounted slave cylinder, disconnect the quick-disconnect coupling with a spring coupling tool such as T88T-70522-A.

3. Remove the transmission.

4. If equipped with an internally mounted slave cylinder, remove the starter. Remove the flywheel housing attaching bolts and remove the housing. If equipped with tan externally mounted slave cylinder, remove the cover and then remove the release lever and bearing from the clutch housing. To remove the release lever:

   a. Remove the dust boot.

   b. Push the release lever forward to compress the slave cylinder.

   c. Remove the slave cylinder by prying on the steel clip to free the tangs while pulling the cylinder clear.

   d. Remove the release lever by pulling it outward.

5. Mark the pressure plate and cover assembly and the flywheel so

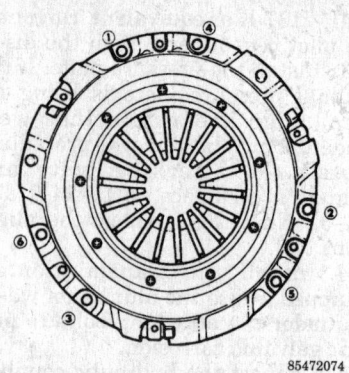

85472074

Clutch pressure plate bolt torque sequence

they can be reinstalled in the same relative position.

6. Loosen the pressure plate and cover attaching bolts evenly in a staggered sequence a turn at time until the pressure plate springs are relieved of their tension. Remove the attaching bolts.

7. Remove the pressure plate and cover assembly and the clutch disc from the flywheel.

To install:

8. Position the clutch disc on the flywheel so an aligning tool can enter the clutch pilot bearing and align the disc.

── **WARNING** ──

New pressure plate/cover bolts have been issued for use on the 7.3L diesel engine and the 7.5L gasoline engine. The bolts for the diesel are $5/16$ in. x 18 x $3/4$ in. The bolts for the 7.5L are $5/16$ in. x 18 x $59/64$ in. The $59/64$ in. bolts cannot be used with the dual mass flywheel used on the diesel, since they would interfere with the operation of the primary flywheel.

9. When reinstalling the original pressure plate and cover assembly, align the assembly and flywheel according to the marks made during removal. Position the pressure plate and cover assembly on the flywheel, align the pressure plate and disc, and install the retaining bolts. Tighten the bolts in an alternating sequence a few turns at a time until the proper torque is reached:

10 in. and 12 in. clutch — 15–20 ft. lbs.

11 in. clutch — 20–29 ft. lbs.

10. Remove the tool used to align the clutch disc.

11. With the clutch fully released, apply a light coat of grease on the sides of the driving lugs.

12. Position the clutch release bearing and the bearing hub on the re-

lease lever. On the 7.3L diesel engine and the 7.5L engine, clean and lubricate the transmission bearing retainer. Install the release lever on the fulcrum in the flywheel housing. Apply a light coating of grease to the release lever fingers and the fulcrum. Fill the groove of the release bearing hub with grease.

13. If the flywheel housing has been removed, position it against the rear engine cover plate and install the attaching bolts and tighten them to 40–50 ft. lbs.

14. Install the starter motor, if removed.

15. Install the transmission.

16. Install the salve cylinder and bleed the system.

PEDAL HEIGHT/FREE PLAY ADJUSTMENT

The hydraulic clutch system provides automatic adjustment. No adjustment of clutch linkage or pedal position is required.

Clutch Master Cylinder

REMOVAL AND INSTALLATION

1. Disconnect the negative battery cable.

2. Disconnect the clutch master cylinder pushrod from the clutch pedal by prying the retainer bushing and pushrod off the pedal pin.

3. Remove the switch from the master cylinder assembly.

4. On Bronco II, Explorer and Ranger, remove the screw retaining the fluid reservoir to the cowl access cover. On Aerostar, slide the reservoir out of the relay bracket.

5. Use coupling disconnect tool T88T-70522-A or equivalent, to slide the white plastic sleeve toward the slave cylinder, then apply a slight tug on the tube to disconnect the hydraulic coupling.

6. Remove the retaining bolts and the clutch master cylinder.

To install:

7. Install the pushrod through the hole in the engine compartment. Make sure it is located on the correct side of the clutch pedal. Install the master cylinder and tighten the bolts to 12 ft. lbs. (16 Nm).

8. Insert the coupling end into the slave cylinder and install the tube into the clips.

9. On Bronco II, Explorer and Ranger, install the fluid reservoir on the cowl access cover with the retain-

ing screw. On Aerostar, slide the reservoir into the relay bracket.

10. Replace the retainer bushing in the clutch master cylinder pushrod if worn or damaged. Install the retainer and pushrod on the clutch pedal pin. Make sure the flange of the bushing is against the pedal blade. Install the switch.

11. Connect the negative battery cable and bleed the clutch hydraulic system, if necessary.

Clutch Slave Cylinder

REMOVAL AND INSTALLATION

Except Bronco, F Series (Pick-Up) and E Series (Van)

NOTE: Before any vehicle service that requires slave cylinder removal, the clutch master cylinder pushrod must be disconnected from the clutch pedal. If not disconnected, permanent damage to the master cylinder will occur if the clutch pedal is depressed while the slave cylinder is disconnected.

1. Disconnect the negative battery cable.

2. Disconnect the coupling at the transmission using tool T88T-70522-A or equivalent, by sliding the white plastic sleeve toward the slave cylinder while applying a slight tug on the tube.

3. Raise and safely support the vehicle. Remove the transmission and clutch housing.

4. Remove the bolts retaining the slave cylinder to the transmission. Remove the slave cylinder from the transmission input shaft.

5. If necessary, remove the release bearing from the slave cylinder by twisting until resistance is felt, then turning further to allow the preload spring to push the bearing assembly off.

To install:

6. Push the release bearing into place, if removed.

7. Position the slave cylinder over the transmission input shaft with the bleed screw and coupling facing the left side of the transmission.

8. Install the slave cylinder attaching bolts and tighten to 13–19 ft. lbs. (18–26 Nm).

9. Install the transmission.

10. Insert the male coupling into the female coupling on the clutch slave cylinder and make sure the connection is secure.

11. Bleed the clutch hydraulic system, if necessary. Lower the vehicle and connect the negative battery cable.

Bronco, F Series (Pick-Up) and E Series (Van)

There are 2 types of slave cylinders used: an internally mounted (in the bellhousing) and an externally mounted type. The 5.0L, 5.8L and 7.5L gasoline engines and 7.3L diesel engines, equipped with the M50DHD transmission use the externally mounted type; 4.9L enigne uses the internally mounted type.

WARNING

Prior to any service on models with the externally mounted slave cylinder, that requires removal of the slave cylinder, such as transmission and/or clutch housing removal, the clutch master cylinder pushrod must be disconnected from the clutch pedal. Failure to do this may damage the slave cylinder if the clutch pedal is depressed while the slave cylinder is disconnected.

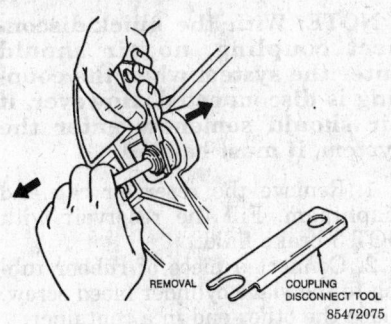

Disconnecting the hydraulic tube from the slave cylinder — Except Bronco, F Series (Pick-Up) and E Series (Van)

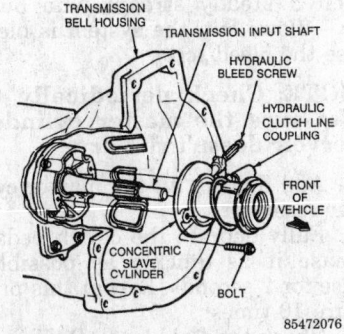

Slave cylinder installation — Except Bronco, F Series (Pick-Up) and E Series (Van)

1. From inside the cab, remove the cotter pin retaining the clutch master cylinder pushrod to the clutch pedal lever. Disconnect the pushrod and remove the bushing.
2. Remove the 2 nuts retaining the clutch reservoir and master cylinder assembly to the firewall.
3. From the engine compartment, remove the clutch reservoir and master cylinder assembly from the firewall. Note here how the clutch tubing routes to the slave cylinder.
4. Push the release lever forward to compress the slave cylinder.
5. On all models with the internally mounted slave cylinder, remove the plastic clip that retains the slave cylinder to the bracket. Remove the slave cylinder.
6. On models with the externally mounted slave cylinder, the steel retaining clip is permanently attached to the slave cylinder. Remove the slave cylinder by prying on the clip to free the tangs while pulling the cylinder clear.
7. Remove the release lever by pulling it outward.
8. Remove the clutch hydraulic system from the vehicle.
To install:
9. Position the clutch pedal reservoir and master cylinder assembly into the firewall from inside the cab, and install the 2 nuts and tighten.
10. Route the clutch tubing and slave cylinder to the bellhousing, taking care that the nylon lines are kept away from any hot exhaust system components.
11. Install the slave cylinder by pushing the slave cylinder pushrod into the cylinder. Engage the pushrod into the release lever and slide the slave cylinder into the bellhousing lugs. Seat the cylinder into the recess in the lugs.

NOTE: When installing a new hydraulic system, notice that the slave cylinder contains a shipping strap that propositions the pushrod for installation, and also provides a bearing insert. Following installation of the new slave cylinder, the first actuation of the clutch pedal will break the shipping strap and give normal clutch action.

12. Clean the master cylinder pushrod bearing and apply a light film of SAE 30 engine oil.
13. From inside the cab, install the bushing on the clutch pedal lever. Connect the clutch master cylinder pushrod to the clutch pedal lever and install the cotter pin.

14. Check the clutch reservoir and add fluid if required. Depress the clutch pedal at least 10 times to verify smooth operation and proper clutch release.

Hydraulic Clutch System Bleeding

Except Bronco, F Series (Pick-Up) and E Series (Van)

NOTE: Under normal conditions, disconnecting the clutch coupling will not let air into the system. However, if there appears to be air in the system, indicated by a spongy pedal or insufficient bearing travel, the system must be bled.

1. Clean all dirt and grease from around the reservoir cap.
2. Remove the cap and fill the reservoir with heavy duty brake fluid.
3. Raise and safely support the vehicle, as necessary. Loosen the bleed screw, located in the slave cylinder body, next to the inlet connection.
4. Fluid will now begin to flow from the master cylinder, down the tube and into the slave cylinder.

NOTE: Keep the reservoir full at all times to make sure no additional air is drawn into the system.

5. Bubbles should begin to appear at the bleed screw outlet, indicating air is being expelled. When the slave cylinder is full, a steady stream of fluid will come from the slave cylinder outlet. Tighten the bleed screw.
6. Slowly depress the clutch pedal to the floor and hold. Loosen the bleed screw to allow air and excess fluid to be expelled. Retighten the bleed screw when fluid flow stops.
7. Depress and release the clutch pedal slowly, waiting 2 seconds between each cycle. Repeat 5 times.
8. Check the fluid level in the reservoir and add, if necessary. If evidence of air still exists, repeat Steps 6 and 7.

Bronco, F Series (Pick-Up) and E Series (Van)

EXTERNALLY MOUNTED SLAVE CYLINDER

1. Clean the reservoir cap and the slave cylinder connection.
2. Remove the slave cylinder from the housing.
3. Using a $^3/_{32}$ in. punch, drive out the pin that holds the tube in place.

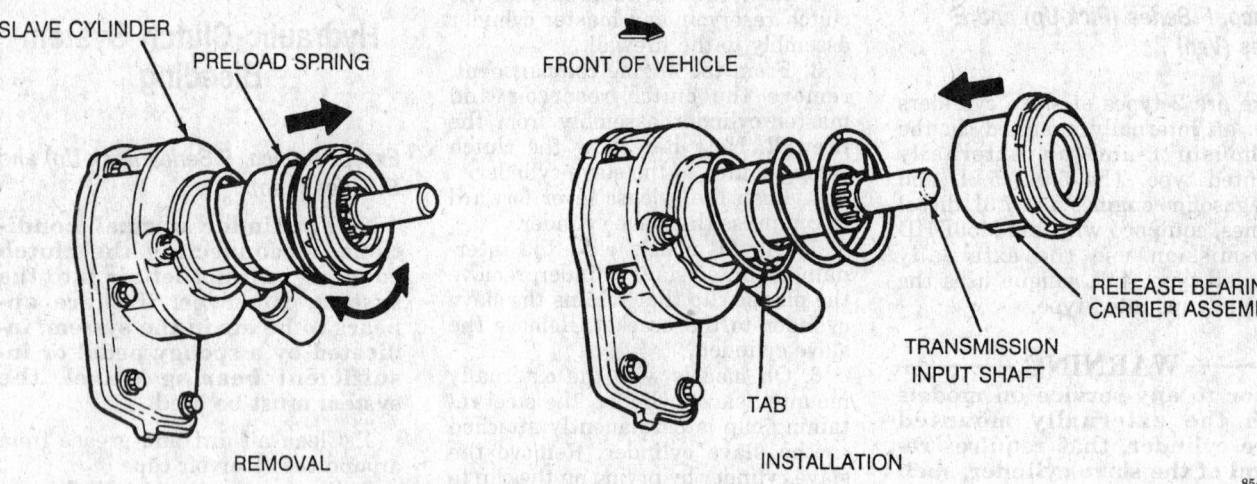

SLAVE CYLINDER
PRELOAD SPRING
FRONT OF VEHICLE

RELEASE BEARING/
CARRIER ASSEMBLY

TRANSMISSION
INPUT SHAFT

TAB

REMOVAL

INSTALLATION

85472077

Clutch release bearing removal and installation — concentric slave cylinder

4. Remove the tube from the slave cylinder and place the end of the tube in a container.

5. Hold the slave cylinder so the connector port is at the highest point, by tipping it about 30 degrees from horizontal. Fill the cylinder with DOT 3 brake fluid through the port. It may be necessary to rock the cylinder or slightly depress the pushrod to expel all the air.

WARNING
Pushing too hard on the pushrod will spurt fluid from the port!

6. When all air is expelled — no more bubble are seen — install the slave cylinder.

NOTE: Some fluid will be expelled during installation as the pushrod is depressed.

7. Remove the reservoir cap. Some fluid will run out of the tube end into the container. Pour fluid into the reservoir until a steady stream of fluid runs out of the tube and the reservoir is filled. Quickly install the diaphragm and cap. The flow should stop.

8. Connect the tube and install the pin. Check the fluid level.

9. Check the clutch operation.

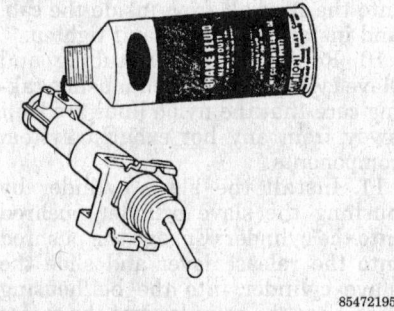

85472195

External slave cylinder bleeding — Bronco, F Series (Pick-Up) and E Series (Van)

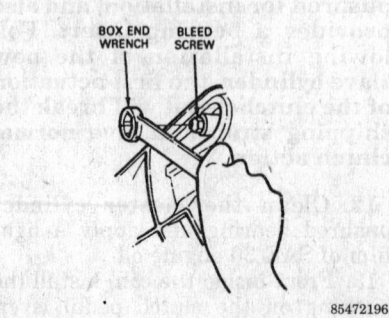

BOX END WRENCH   BLEED SCREW

85472196

Concentric slave cylinder bleeding — Bronco, F Series (Pick-Up) and E Series (Van)

INTERNALLY MOUNTED SLAVE CYLINDER

NOTE: With the quick-disconnect coupling, no air should enter the system when the coupling is disconnected. However, if air should somehow enter the system, it must be bled.

1. Remove the reservoir cap and diaphragm. Fill the reservoir with DOT 3 brake fluid.

2. Connect a piece of rubber tubing to the slave cylinder bleed screw. Place the other end in a container.

3. Loosen the bleed screw. Gravity will force fluid from the master cylinder to flow down to the slave cylinder, forcing air out of the bleed screw. When a steady stream — no bubbles — flows out, the system is bled. Close the bleed screw.

NOTE: Check periodically to make sure the master cylinder reservoir doesn't run dry.

4. Add fluid to fill the master cylinder reservoir.

5. Fully depress the clutch pedal. Release it as quickly as possible. Pause for 2 seconds. Repeat this procedure 10 times.

6. Check the fluid level. Refill it if necessary. It should be kept full.

7. Repeat Steps 5 and 6 five more times.

8. Install the diaphragm and cap.

9. Have an assistant hold the pedal to the floor while you crack the bleed screw — not too far — just far enough to expel any trapped air. Close the bleed screw, then, release the pedal.

10. Check, and if necessary, fill the reservoir.

AUTOMATIC TRANSMISSION

Transmission Assembly

REMOVAL AND INSTALLATION

Except Bronco, F Series (Pick-Up) and E-Series (Van)

1. Disconnect the negative battery cable. Raise and safely support the vehicle.

2. Position a drain pan under the transmission fluid pan. On Explorer, pry the lower clips of the transmission heat shield back slightly to allow access to the pan bolts.

3. Starting at the rear of the transmission pan and working toward the front, loosen the attaching bolts and allow the fluid to drain. Remove all the bolts except the 2 at the front to allow the fluid to further drain. After all fluid has drained, reinstall 2 bolts at the rear of the pan to temporarily hold it in place.

4. Remove the converter access cover from the converter housing. On some applications, it may only be necessary to remove 1 bolt and swing the cover open.

5. Disconnect the starter cable and remove the starter.

6. Place a 22mm socket and breaker bar on the crankshaft pulley attaching bolt. Rotate the pulley clockwise, as viewed from the front, to gain access to each converter attaching nut. Remove the nuts.

NOTE: On 2.3L engine, the converter attaching nuts are accessed through the cover on the engine oil pan. On 2.9L and 4.0L engines, the converter attaching nuts are accessed through the starter mounting hole.

7. Mark the position of the driveshaft on the axle flange and remove the driveshaft. Plug the transmission to prevent fluid leakage.

8. Disconnect the speedometer cable from the transmission.

9. Disconnect the shift rod at the transmission manual lever. Remove the kickdown cable from the ball stud lever. Depress the tab on the cable downshift retainer and remove the cable from the bracket.

10. Disconnect the neutral safety switch wires and converter clutch solenoid connector. Disconnect the vacuum line from the vacuum modulator.

11. Position a transmission jack under the transmission and raise it slightly. Remove the engine rear support-to-crossmember bolts.

12. Remove the crossmember-to-frame side support attaching bolts and remove the crossmember insulator and support and damper.

13. Lower the jack under the transmission and allow the transmission to hang. On Bronco II, Explorer and Ranger, position a jack to the front of the engine and raise it to gain access to the 2 upper converter housing-to-engine attaching bolts.

14. Disconnect the oil cooler lines at the transmission. Plug the lines and transmission to prevent the entrance of dirt.

15. Remove the lower converter housing-to-engine attaching bolts

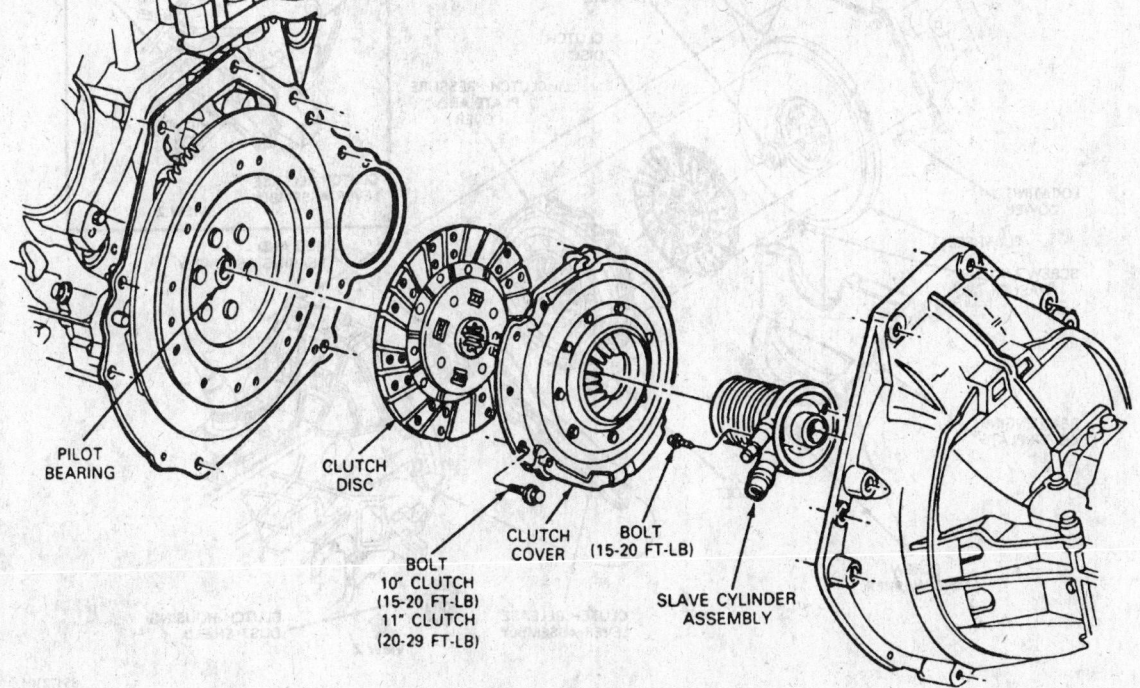

PILOT BEARING

CLUTCH DISC

BOLT
10" CLUTCH
(15-20 FT-LB)
11" CLUTCH
(20-29 FT-LB)

CLUTCH COVER

BOLT
(15-20 FT-LB)

SLAVE CYLINDER ASSEMBLY

85472192

Clutch installation — Bronco, F Series and E Series with 4.9L, 5.0L and 5.8L engines

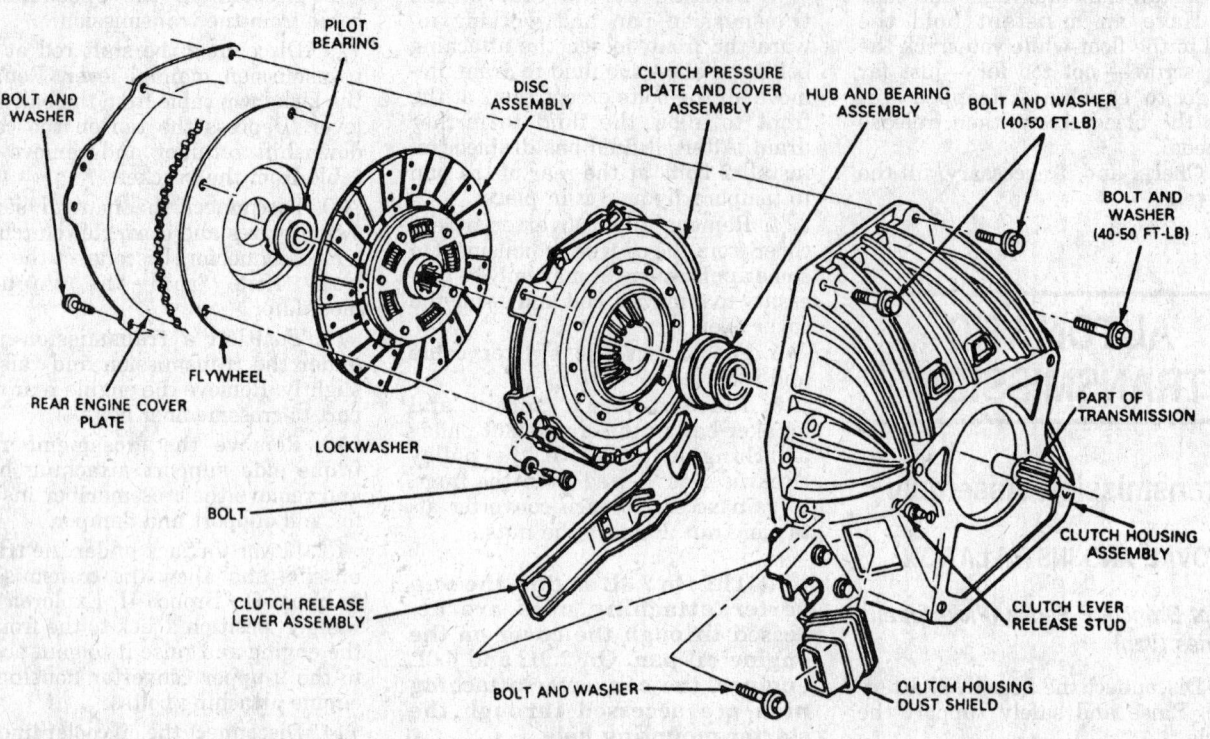

Clutch installation — Bronco and F Series with 4.9L and 5.0L engines

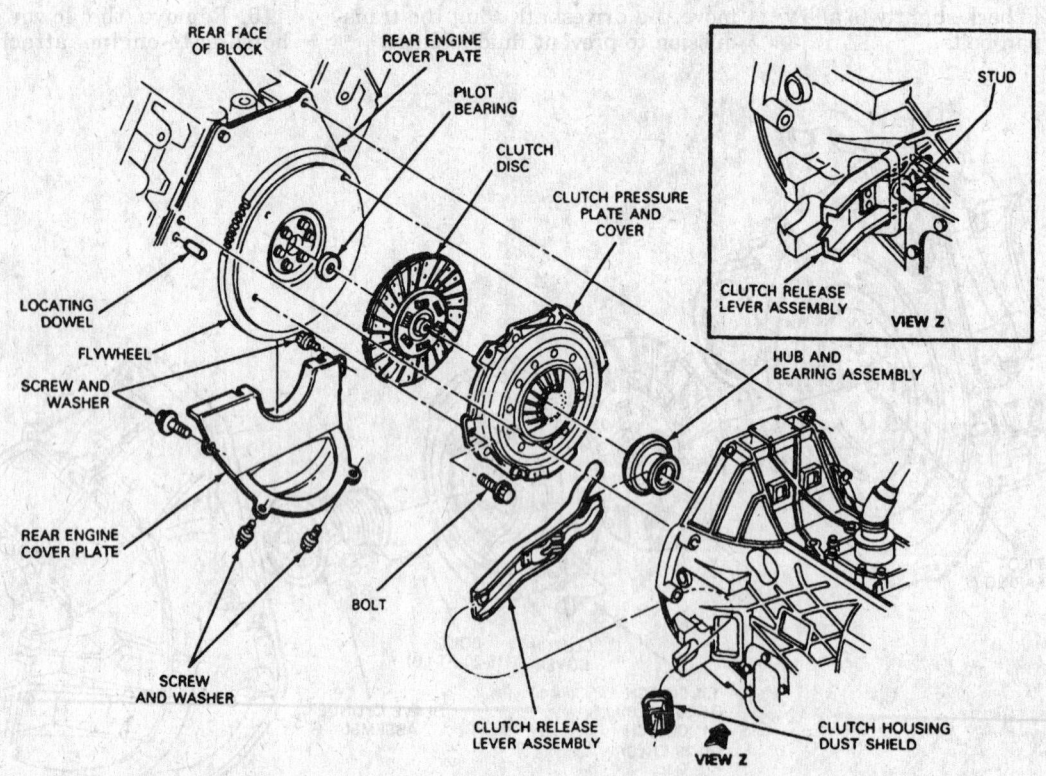

Clutch installation — F Series with 7.3L diesel and 7.5L engines

and remove the transmission filler tube.

16. Secure the transmission to the jack with a safety chain. Remove the 2 upper converter housing-to-engine attaching bolts. Move the transmission to the rear so it disengages from the dowel pins and the converter is disengaged from the flywheel. Lower the transmission from the vehicle.

NOTE: If the transmission is to be removed for an extended period, support the engine with a safety stand and wood block.

To install:

17. Position the converter to the transmission making sure the converter hub is fully engaged in the pump gear. To make sure the converter is fully engaged, push and rotate the converter until 2 "bumps" are felt. Keep pushing and rotating until the distance between the converter pilot and the edge of the converter housing is $7/16$–$9/16$ in.

18. Place the transmission on a transmission jack and secure with a safety chain. Rotate the converter so the drive studs are in alignment with the holes in the flywheel.

19. Raise the transmission and move it forward into position, being careful not to damage the flywheel and converter pilot.

NOTE: When moving the transmission, do not let the front of the transmission tilt downward. This will cause the converter to move forward and disengage from the pump gear. The converter must rest squarely against the flywheel. This indicates that the converter pilot is not binding in the engine crankshaft.

20. Install 2 converter housing-to-engine attaching bolts at the engine dowel locations and tighten to 28–38 ft. lbs. (38–51 Nm). Install the remaining attaching bolts and tighten to the same specification.

21. Remove the safety chain from the transmission.

22. Insert the filler tube in the stub tube and secure it to the cylinder block with the attaching bolt. Tighten the bolt to 28–38 ft. lbs. (38–51 Nm). If the stub tube is loosened or dislodged, it should be replaced.

23. Install the oil cooler lines in the retaining clip at the cylinder block. Connect the lines to the transmission.

24. Remove the jack supporting the front of the engine.

25. Raise the transmission and position the crossmember, insulator

and support and damper to the frame side supports. Install the attaching bolts and tighten to 20–30 ft. lbs. (27–41 Nm).

26. Lower the transmission and install the rear engine support-to-crossmember nut. Tighten the bolt to 60–80 ft. lbs. (82–108 Nm). Remove the transmission jack.

27. Install the vacuum hose on the vacuum modulator and attach the line to the clip. Connect the neutral safety switch plug and the converter clutch solenoid connector.

28. Install the flywheel-to-converter nuts and tighten to 20–34 ft. lbs. (27–46 Nm).

29. Install the converter access cover and adapter plate bolts and tighten to 12–16 ft. lbs. (16–22 Nm). On 2.3L engine, tighten the oil pan access cover bolts to 22–32 inch lbs. (2.5–3.6 Nm).

30. Install the starter and tighten the attaching bolts to 15–20 ft. lbs. (20–27 Nm). Connect the starter cable.

31. Connect the exhaust pipe to the exhaust manifold, if disconnected for removal.

32. Connect the shift rod to the manual lever and the downshift cable to the downshift lever. Connect the speedometer cable.

33. Install the driveshaft, aligning the marks on the axle flange. Adjust the manual and downshift linkage, as required.

34. Remove the bolts temporarily holding the transmission fluid pan and remove the pan. Discard the gasket and clean all old gasket material and dirt from the gasket mating surfaces.

35. Install the pan using a new gasket. Tighten the attaching bolts to 8–10 ft. lbs. (11–13.5 Nm).

36. Lower the vehicle and connect the negative battery cable. Fill the transmission with the proper type and quantity of fluid.

37. Run the vehicle and check for leaks and proper operation.

Bronco, F Series (Pick-Up) and E Series (Van)

C6 TRANSMISSION

1. From in the engine compartment, remove the 2 upper converter housing-to-engine bolts.

2. Disconnect the neutral switch wire at the inline connector.

3. Remove the bolt securing the fluid filler tube to the engine cylinder head.

4. Raise and support the vehicle safely.

5. Place the drain pan under the transmission fluid pan. Starting at the rear of the pan and working toward the front, loosen the attaching bolts and allow the fluid to drain. Finally remove all of the pan attaching bolts except 2 at the front, to allow the fluid to further drain. With fluid drained, install 2 bolts on the rear side of the pan to temporarily hold it in place.

6. Remove the converter drain plug access cover from the lower end of the converter housing.

7. Remove the converter-to-flywheel attaching nuts. Place a wrench on the crankshaft pulley attaching bolt to turn the converter to gain access to the nuts.

8. With the wrench on the crankshaft pulley attaching bolt, turn the converter to gain access to the converter drain plug. Place a drain pan under the converter to catch the fluid and remove the plug. After the fluid has been drained, reinstall the plug.

9. On 2WD models, disconnect the driveshaft from the rear axle and slide shaft rearward from the transmission. Install a seal installation tool in the extension housing to prevent fluid leakage.

10. Disconnect the speedometer cable from the extension housing.

11. Disconnect the downshift and manual linkage rods from the levers at the transmission.

12. Disconnect the oil cooler lines from the transmission.

13. Disconnect the vacuum hose from the vacuum diaphragm unit. Remove the vacuum line retaining clip.

14. Disconnect the cable from the terminal on the starter motor. Remove the 3 attaching bolts and remove the starter motor.

15. On 4WD models remove the transfer case.

16. Remove the 2 engine rear support and insulator assembly-to-attaching bolts.

17. Remove the 2 engine rear support and insulator assembly-to-extension housing attaching bolts.

18. Remove the 6 bolts securing the No. 2 crossmember to the frame side rails.

19. Raise the transmission with a transmission jack and remove both crossmembers.

20. Secure the transmission to the jack with the safety chain.

21. Remove the remaining converter housing-to-engine attaching bolts.

22. Move the transmission away from the engine. Lower the jack and

remove the converter and transmission assembly from under the vehicle.

To install:

23. Tighten the converter drain plug.

24. Position the converter on the transmission making sure the converter drive flats are fully engaged in the pump gear.

25. With the converter properly installed, place the transmission on the jack. Secure the transmission on the jack with the chain.

26. Rotate the converter until the studs and drain plug are in alignment with their holes in the flywheel.

27. Move the converter and transmission assembly forward into position, using care not to damage the flywheel and the converter pilot. The converter must rest squarely against the flywheel. This indicates that the converter pilot is not binding in the engine crankshaft.

28. Install the converter housing-to-engine attaching bolts and torque them to 65 ft. lbs. for the diesel; 50 ft. lbs. for gasoline engines.

29. Remove the transmission jack safety chain from around the transmission.

30. Position the No. 2 crossmember to the frame side rails. Install and tighten the attaching bolts.

31. Install transfer case on 4WD models.

32. Position the engine rear support and insulator assembly above the crossmember. Install the rear support and insulator assembly-to-extension housing mounting bolts and tighten the bolts to 45 ft. lbs.

33. Lower the transmission and remove the jack.

34. Secure the engine rear support and insulator assembly to the crossmember with the attaching bolts and tighten them to 80 ft. lbs.

35. Connect the vacuum line to the vacuum diaphragm making sure the line is in the retaining clip.

36. Connect the oil cooler lines to the transmission.

37. Connect the downshift and manual linkage rods to their respective levers on the transmission.

38. Connect the speedometer cable to the extension housing.

39. Secure the starter motor in place with the attaching bolts. Connect the cable to the terminal on the starter.

40. Install a new O-ring on the lower end of the transmission filler tube and insert the tube in the case.

41. Secure the converter-to-flywheel attaching nuts and tighten them to 30 ft. lbs.

42. Install the converter housing access cover and secure it with the attaching bolts.

43. Connect the driveshaft.

44. Adjust the shift linkage as required.

45. Lower the vehicle. Then install the 2 upper converter housing-to-engine bolts and tighten them.

46. Position the transmission fluid filler tube to the cylinder head and secure with the attaching bolts.

47. Make sure the drain pan is securely attached, and fill the transmission to the correct level with the Dexron®II fluid.

AOD TRANSMISSION

1. Raise the vehicle on hoist or stands.

2. Place the drain pan under the transmission fluid pan. Starting at the rear of the pan and working toward the front, loosen the attaching bolts and allow the fluid to drain. Finally remove all of the pan attaching bolts except 2 at the front, to allow the fluid to further drain. With fluid drained, install 2 bolts on the rear side of the pan to temporarily hold it in place.

3. Remove the converter drain plug access cover from the lower end of the converter.

4. Remove the converter-to-flywheel attaching nuts. Place a wrench on the crankshaft pulley attaching bolt to turn the converter to gain access to the nuts.

5. Place a drain pan under the converter to catch the fluid. With the wrench on the crankshaft pulley attaching bolt, turn the converter to gain access to the converter drain plug and remove the plug. After the fluid has been drained, reinstall the plug.

6. On 2WD models, matchmark and disconnect the driveshaft from the rear axle and slide shaft rearward from the transmission. Install a seal installation tool in the extension housing to prevent fluid leakage.

7. Disconnect the cable from the terminal on the starter motor. Remove the 3 attaching bolts and remove the starter motor. Disconnect the neutral start switch wires at the plug connector.

8. Remove the rear mount-to-crossmember attaching bolts and the 2 crossmember-to-frame attaching bolts.

9. Remove the 2 engine rear support-to-extension housing attaching bolts.

10. Disconnect the TV linkage rod from the transmission TV lever. Dis-

connect the manual rod from the transmission manual lever at the transmission.

11. Remove the 2 bolts securing the bellcrank bracket to the converter housing.

12. On 4WD models, remove the transfer case.

13. Raise the transmission with a transmission jack to provide clearance to remove the crossmember. Remove the rear mount from the crossmember and remove the crossmember from the side supports.

14. Lower the transmission to gain access to the oil cooler lines.

15. Disconnect each oil line from the fittings on the transmission.

16. Disconnect the speedometer cable from the extension housing.

17. Remove the bolt that secures the transmission fluid filler tube to the cylinder block. Lift the filler tube and the dipstick from the transmission.

18. Secure the transmission to the jack with the chain.

19. Remove the converter housing-to-cylinder block attaching bolts.

20. Carefully move the transmission and converter assembly away from the engine and, at the same time, lower the jack to clear the underside of the vehicle.

21. Remove the converter and mount the transmission in a holding fixture.

22. Tighten the converter drain plug.

To install:

23. Position the converter on the transmission, making sure the converter drive flats are fully engaged in the pump gear by rotating the converter.

24. With the converter properly installed, place the transmission on the jack. Secure the transmission to the jack with a chain.

25. Rotate the converter until the studs and drain plug are in alignment with the holes in the flywheel.

26. Move the converter and transmission assembly forward into position, using care not to damage the flywheel and the converter pilot. The converter must rest squarely against the flywheel. This indicates that the converter pilot is not binding in the engine crankshaft.

27. Install and tighten the converter housing-to-engine attaching bolts to 40–50 ft. lbs.

28. Remove the safety chain from around the transmission.

29. Install a new O-ring on the lower end of the transmission filler tube. Insert the tube in the transmis-

sion case and secure the tube to the engine with the attaching bolt.

30. Connect the speedometer cable to the extension housing.

31. Connect the oil cooler lines to the right side of transmission case.

32. Position the crossmember on the side supports. Torque the bolts to 55 ft. lbs. Position the rear mount on the crossmember and install the attaching nuts to 90 ft. lbs.

33. On 4WD models, install the transfer case.

34. Secure the rear support to the extension housing and tighten the bolts to 80 ft. lbs.

35. Lower the transmission and remove the jack.

E4OD TRANSMISSION

1. Raise and support the vehicle safely.

2. Place the drain pan under the transmission fluid pan. Starting at the rear of the pan and working toward the front, loosen the attaching bolts and allow the fluid to drain. Finally remove all of the pan attaching bolts except 2 at the front, to allow the fluid to further drain. With fluid drained, install 2 bolts on the rear side of the pan to temporarily hold it in place.

3. Remove the dipstick from the transmission.

4. On 4WD models, matchmark and remove the front driveshaft.

5. Matchmark and remove the rear driveshaft. Install a seal installation tool in the extension housing to prevent fluid leakage.

6. Disconnect the linkage from the transmission.

7. On 4WD models, disconnect the transfer case linkage.

8. Remove the heat shield and remove the manual lever position sensor connector by squeezing the tabs and pulling on the connector; never attempt to pry the connector apart!

9. Remove the solenoid body heat shield.

10. Remove the solenoid body connector by pushing on the center tab and pulling on the wiring harness; never attempt to pry apart the connector!

11. On 4WD models, remove the 4x4 switch connector from the transfer case. Be careful not to over-extend the tabs.

12. Pry the harness connector from the extension housing wire bracket.

13. On 4WD models, remove the wiring harness locators from the left side of the connector.

14. Disconnect the speedometer cable.

15. On 4WD models, remove the transfer case.

16. Remove the converter cover bolts.

17. Remove the rear engine cover plate bolts.

18. Disconnect the cable from the terminal on the starter motor. Remove the 3 attaching bolts and remove the starter motor. Disconnect the neutral start switch wires at the plug connector.

19. Remove the converter-to-flywheel attaching nuts. Place a wrench on the crankshaft pulley attaching bolt to turn the converter to gain access to the nuts.

20. Secure the transmission to a transmission jack. Use a safety chain.

21. Remove the rear mount-to-crossmember attaching nuts and the 2 crossmember-to-frame attaching bolts.

22. Disconnect each oil line from the fittings on the transmission. Cap the lines.

23. Remove the 6 converter housing-to-cylinder block attaching bolts.

24. Carefully move the transmission and converter assembly away from the engine and, at the same time, lower the jack to clear the underside of the vehicle.

25. Remove the transmission filler tube.

26. Install Torque Converter Handles T81P-7902-C, or equivalent, at the 12 o'clock and 6 o'clock positions.

To install:

27. Install the converter with the handles at the 12 o'clock and 6 o'clock positions. Push and rotate the converter until it bottoms out. Check the seating of the converter by placing a straightedge across the converter and bellhousing. There must be a gap between the converter and straightedge. Remove the handles.

28. Install the transmission filler tube.

29. Rotate the converter to align the studs with the flywheel mounting holes.

30. Carefully raise the transmission into position at the engine. The converter must rest squarely against the flywheel.

31. Install the 6 converter housing-to-cylinder block attaching bolts. Snug them alternately and evenly, then, tighten them alternately and evenly to 40-50 ft. lbs.

32. Install the converter drain plug cover.

33. Connect each oil line at the fittings on the transmission.

34. Install the rear mount-to-crossmember attaching nuts and the 2 crossmember-to-frame attaching bolts. Torque the nuts and bolts to 50 ft. lbs.

35. Remove the transmission jack.

36. Install the converter-to-flywheel attaching nuts. Place a wrench on the crankshaft pulley attaching bolt to turn the converter to gain access to the nuts. Torque the nuts to 20-30 ft. lbs.

37. Install the starter motor. Connect the cable at the terminal on the starter motor. Connect the neutral start switch wires at the plug connector.

38. Install the rear engine cover plate bolts.

39. Install the converter cover bolts.

40. On 4WD models, install the transfer case.

41. Connect the speedometer cable.

42. On 4WD models, install the wiring harness locators at the left side of the connector.

43. Connect the harness connector at the extension housing wire bracket.

44. On 4WD models, install the 4x4 switch connector at the transfer case.

45. Install the solenoid body connector. An audible click indicates connection.

46. Install the solenoid body heat shield.

47. Install the manual lever position sensor connector and the heat shield.

48. On 4WD models, connect the transfer case linkage.

49. Connect the linkage at the transmission.

50. Install the rear driveshaft.

51. On 4WD models, install the front driveshaft.

52. Install the dipstick.

53. Install the drain pan using a new gasket and sealer.

54. Lower the vehicle.

55. Refill the transmission and check for leaks.

SHIFT LINKAGE ADJUSTMENT

Aerostar

1. Raise and safely support the vehicle, as necessary. Place the console shift lever in the **OD** position.

2. From below the vehicle, loosen the shift cable adjusting screw and remove the end fitting from the transmission manual control lever ball stud.

3. Position the manual control lever in the **OD** position by moving the lever all the way rearward, then

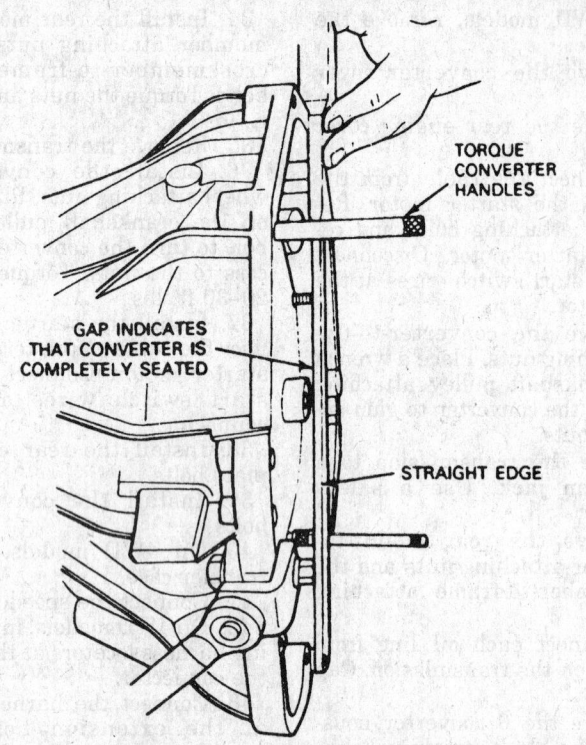

TORQUE CONVERTER HANDLES

GAP INDICATES THAT CONVERTER IS COMPLETELY SEATED

STRAIGHT EDGE

85472197

Torque converter installation — E4OD automatic transmission — Bronco, F Series (Pick-Up) and E Series (Van)

moving it 3 detents forward. Hold the console shift lever against the rear **OD** stop.

4. Connect the cable end fitting to the manual control lever.

5. Tighten the adjustment screw to 45–60 inch lbs. (5–6 Nm).

6. Check the console shift lever in all detent positions with the engine running to ensure correct adjustment.

Bronco II, Explorer and Ranger

1. Raise and safely support the vehicle, as necessary. From inside the vehicle, place the column shift selector lever in the **OD** position. Hang an 8 lb. weight on the selector lever.

2. From below the vehicle, pull down the lock tab on the shift cable and remove the fitting from the transmission manual control lever ball stud.

3. Position the transmission manual control lever in the **OD** position by moving the lever all the way rearward and then moving it 3 detents forward.

4. Connect the cable end fitting to the transmission manual control lever. Push up on the lock tab to lock the cable in the correctly adjusted position.

5. Remove the 8 lb. weight from the column shift selector.

6. After adjustment, check for **P** engagement. Check the column shift selector lever in all detent positions with the engine running to ensure correct adjustment.

Bronco, F Series (Pick-Up) and E Series (Van)

1. With the engine stopped, place the transmission selector lever at the steering column in the **D** position for the C6 or the D overdrive position for the AOD and E4OD, and hold the lever against the stop by hanging an 8 lb. weight from the lever handle.

2. Loosen the shift rod adjusting nut at the transmission lever.

3. Shift the manual lever at the transmission to the **D** position, 2 detents from the rear. On the F-150 with 4WD and Bronco, move the bellcrank lever.

4. With the selector lever and transmission manual lever in the D or D overdrive position, tighten the adjusting nut to 12–18 ft. lbs. Do not allow the rod or shift lever to move while tightening the nut. Remove the weight.

5. Check the operation of the shift linkage.

SELECTOR INDICATOR ADJUSTMENT

Bronco II, Explorer and Ranger

1. Remove the steering column shroud.

2. With the engine stopped and the parking brake applied, place the transmission selector lever at the steering column in the **OD** position.

3. Secure a 3 lb. weight to the end of the transmission selector lever.

4. Loosen the selector indicator screw on the column casting. Move the selector indicator adjustment until the orange pointer is completely within the letter "D" inside the **OD** graphic.

5. Tighten the selector indicator screw on the column to 10–15 inch lbs. (1.1–1.7 Nm).

6. Install the steering column shroud.

INTERMEDIATE BAND ADJUSTMENT

C6 Transmission

1. Raise the vehicle on a hoist or jackstands.

2. Clean all dirt away from the band adjusting screw. Remove and discard the locknut.

3. Install a new locknut and tighten the adjusting screw to 10 ft. lbs.

4. Back off the adjusting screw exactly 1½ turns.

5. Hold the adjusting screw from turning and tighten the locknut to 35–40 ft. lbs.

6. Remove the jackstands and lower the vehicle.

THROTTLE VALVE LINKAGE ADJUSTMENT

AOD Transmission with EFI Fuel System

ADJUSTMENT WITH ENGINE OFF

1. Set the parking brake and put the selector lever in **N**.

2. Remove the protective cover from the cable.

3. Make sure the throttle lever is at the idle stop. If it isn't, check for binding or interference. Never attempt to adjust the idle stop!

4. Make sure the cable is free of sharp bends or is not rubbing on anything throughout its entire length.

5. Lubricate the TV lever ball stud with chassis lube.

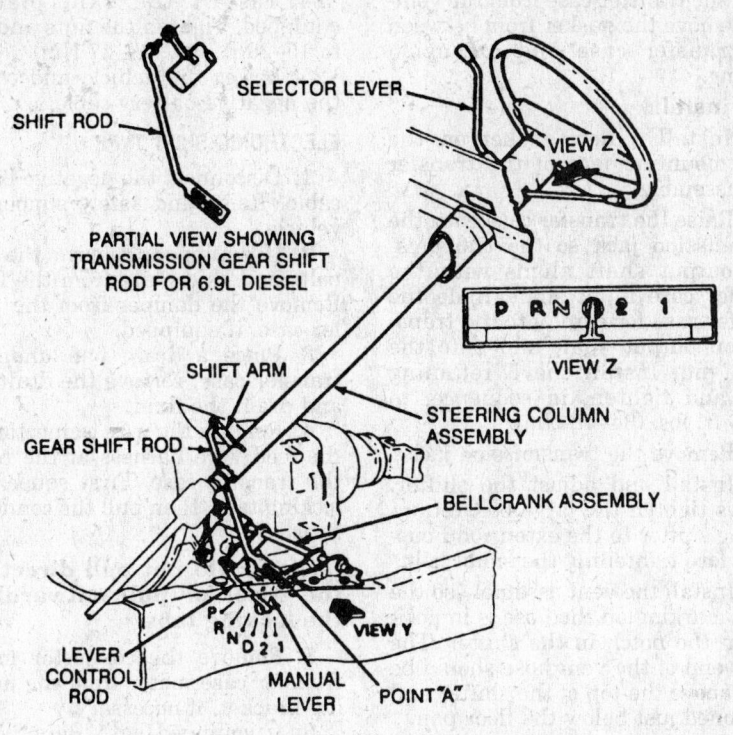

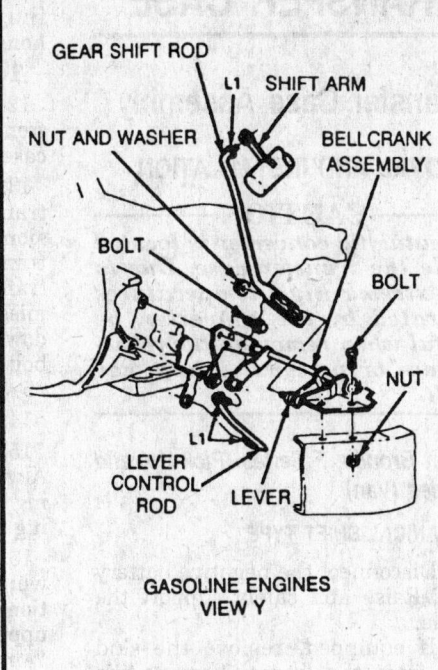

85472198

Shift linkage adjustment — C6 automatic transmission — Bronco, F Series (Pick-Up) and E Series (Van)

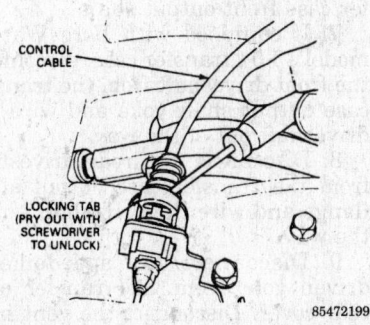

85472199

Unlocking TV cable locking tab — 5.0L engine

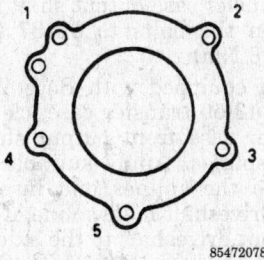

85472078

Transfer case-to-extension housing bolt torque sequence

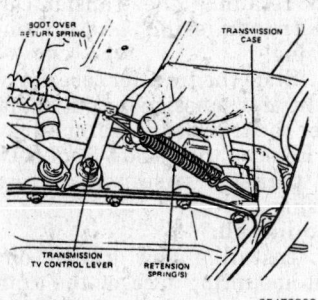

85472200

Installing retension springs — TV cable adjustment — Bronco, F Series (Pick-Up) and E Series (Van)

6. Unlock the locking tab at the throttle body by prying with a small prybar.

7. Install a spring on the TV control lever, to hold it in the rearmost travel position. The spring must exert at least 10 lbs. of force on the lever.

8. Rotate the transmission outer TV lever 10-30 degrees and slowly allow it to return.

9. Push down on the locking tab until flush.

10. Remove the retaining spring from the lever.

THROTTLE KICKDOWN LINKAGE ADJUSTMENT

1. Move the carburetor throttle linkage to the wide open position.

2. Insert a 0.060 in. thick spacer between the throttle lever and the kickdown adjusting screw.

3. Rotate the transmission kickdown lever until the lever engages the transmission internal stop. Do not use the kickdown rod to turn the transmission lever.

4. Turn the adjusting screw until it contacts the 0.060 in. spacer.

5. Remove the spacer.

TRANSFER CASE

Transfer Case Assembly

REMOVAL AND INSTALLATION

——————— CAUTION ———————

The catalytic converter is located beside the transfer case. Due to the extreme high temperatures generated by the converter, be careful when removing the transfer case or personal injury may result.

Except Bronco, F Series (Pick-Up) and E Series (Van)

MECHANICAL SHIFT TYPE

1. Disconnect the negative battery cable. Raise and safely support the vehicle.

2. If equipped, remove the skid plate from the frame. Remove the damper from the transfer case, if equipped.

3. Place a drain pan under the transfer case, remove the drain plug and drain the fluid. Disconnect the 4WD indicator switch wire connector at the transfer case.

4. If equipped with Borg Warner model 13-50 transfer case, disconnect the front driveshaft from the axle input yoke and pull the driveshaft and front boot assembly out of the transfer case front output shaft.

5. If equipped with Borg Warner model 13-54 transfer case, disconnect the front driveshaft from the transfer case output shaft yoke and wire the driveshaft out of the way.

6. Disconnect the rear driveshaft from the transfer case output shaft flange and wire the driveshaft out of the way.

7. Disconnect the speedometer driven gear from the transfer case rear cover. Disconnect the vent hose from the control lever.

8. Disconnect the nut from the shift lever and remove the shift lever, if necessary.

9. Remove the large and small bolts retaining the shifter to the extension housing. Remove the lever assembly and bushing.

10. Support the transfer case with a transmission jack. Remove the 5 bolts retaining the transfer case to the transmission and extension housing.

11. Slide the transfer case rearward off the transmission output shaft and lower the transfer case from the vehicle. Remove the gasket from between the transfer case and extension housing.

To install:

12. Install a new gasket on the front mounting face of the transfer case assembly.

13. Raise the transfer case with the transmission jack so the transmission output shaft aligns with the transfer case input shaft. Slide the transfer case forward onto the transmission output shaft and onto the dowel pin. Install the 5 retaining bolts and tighten, in sequence, to 25–35 ft. lbs. (34–48 Nm).

14. Remove the transmission jack.

15. Install and adjust the shifter. Always tighten the large bolt retaining the shifter to the extension housing before tightening the small bolt.

16. Install the vent assembly so the white marking on the hose is in position in the notch in the shifter. The upper end of the vent hose should be ¾ in. above the top of the shifter and positioned just below the floor pan.

17. Connect the speedometer driven gear to the transfer case rear cover. Tighten the screw to 20–25 inch lbs. (2.3–2.8 Nm).

18. Connect the rear driveshaft to the transfer case output shaft flange. Tighten the bolts to 61–87 ft. lbs. (83–118 Nm).

19. If equipped with Borg Warner model 13-50 transfer case, clean the transfer case front output shaft female splines. Apply suitable lubricant to the splines and insert the front driveshaft male spline. Connect the front driveshaft to the axle input yoke and tighten the bolts to 12–16 ft. lbs. (16–22 Nm). Push the driveshaft boot to engage the external groove on the transfer case front output shaft.

20. If equipped with Borg Warner model 13-54 transfer case, connect the front driveshaft to the transfer case output shaft yoke. Tighten the bolts to 12–16 ft. lbs. (16–22 Nm).

21. Connect the 4WD indicator switch wire connector at the transfer case.

22. Install the drain plug and tighten to 14–22 ft. lbs. (19–30 Nm). Remove the fill plug and fill the transfer case with the proper type of fluid to the bottom of the fill hole. Install the fill plug and tighten to 14–22 ft. lbs. (19–30 Nm).

23. Install the damper to the transfer case, if equipped. Using new damper bolts, tighten to 25–35 ft. lbs. (34–48 Nm).

24. Install the skid plate, if equipped. Tighten the nuts and bolts to 15–20 ft. lbs. (20–27 Nm).

25. Lower the vehicle and connect the negative battery cable.

ELECTRONIC SHIFT TYPE

1. Disconnect the negative battery cable. Raise and safely support the vehicle.

2. If equipped, remove the nuts, bolts and skid plate from the frame. Remove the damper from the transfer case, if equipped.

3. Place a drain pan under the transfer case, remove the drain plug and drain the fluid.

4. Remove the wire connector from the feed wire harness at the rear of the transfer case. First squeeze the locking tabs, then pull the connectors apart.

NOTE: Do not pull directly on the wires or pull outwardly on the locking tabs.

5. Remove the connector for the transfer case motor from the mounting bracket, if necessary.

6. If equipped with Borg Warner model 13-50 transfer case, disconnect the front driveshaft from the axle input yoke and pull the driveshaft and front boot assembly out of the transfer case front output shaft.

7. If equipped with Borg Warner model 13-54 transfer case, disconnect the front driveshaft from the transfer case output shaft yoke and wire the driveshaft out of the way.

8. Disconnect the rear driveshaft from the transfer case output shaft flange and wire the driveshaft out of the way.

9. Disconnect the speedometer driven gear from the transfer case rear cover. Disconnect the vent hose from the mounting bracket.

10. Support the transfer case with a transmission jack. Remove the 5 bolts retaining the transfer case to the transmission and extension housing.

11. Slide the transfer case rearward off the transmission output shaft and lower the transfer case from the vehicle. Remove the gasket from between the transfer case and extension housing.

To install:

12. Install a new gasket on the front mounting face of the transfer case assembly.

13. Raise the transfer case with the transmission jack so the transmission output shaft aligns with the transfer case input shaft. Slide the transfer case forward onto the transmission output shaft and onto the

dowel pin. Install the 5 retaining bolts and tighten, in sequence, to 25–35 ft. lbs. (34–48 Nm).

14. Remove the transmission jack.

15. Install the vent hose so the white marking on the hose aligns with the notch in the mounting bracket.

16. Connect the speedometer driven gear to the transfer case rear cover. Tighten the screw to 20–25 inch lbs. (2.3–2.8 Nm).

17. Connect the rear driveshaft to the transfer case output shaft flange. Tighten the bolts to 61–87 ft. lbs. (83–118 Nm).

18. If equipped with Borg Warner model 13-50 transfer case, clean the transfer case front output shaft female splines. Apply suitable lubricant to the splines and insert the front driveshaft male spline. Connect the front driveshaft to the axle input yoke and tighten the bolts to 12–16 ft. lbs. (16–22 Nm). Push the driveshaft boot to engage the external groove on the transfer case front output shaft.

19. If equipped with Borg Warner model 13-54 transfer case, connect the front driveshaft to the transfer case output shaft yoke. Tighten the bolts to 12–16 ft. lbs. (16–22 Nm).

20. Attach the connector for the transfer case motor to the mounting bracket, if necessary.

21. Connect the wire connectors on the rear of the transfer case, making sure the retaining tabs lock.

22. Install the drain plug and tighten to 14–22 ft. lbs. (19–30 Nm). Remove the fill plug and fill the transfer case with the proper type of fluid to the bottom of the fill hole. Install the fill plug and tighten to 14–22 ft. lbs. (19–30 Nm).

23. Install the damper to the transfer case, if equipped. Using new damper bolts, tighten to 25–35 ft. lbs. (34–48 Nm).

24. Install the skid plate, if equipped. Tighten the nuts and bolts to 15–20 ft. lbs. (20–27 Nm).

25. Lower the vehicle and connect the negative battery cable.

Bronco, F Series (Pick-Up) and E Series (Van)

BORG-WARNER MODEL 13-45

1. Raise and support the vehicle safely.

2. Drain the fluid from the transfer case.

3. Disconnect the 4WD indicator switch wire connector at the transfer case.

4. Remove the skid plate from the frame, if equipped.

5. Matchmark and disconnect the front driveshaft from the front output yoke.

6. Matchmark and disconnect the rear driveshaft from the rear output shaft yoke.

7. Disconnect the speedometer driven gear from the transfer case rear bearing retainer.

8. Remove the retaining rings and shift rod from the transfer case shift lever.

9. Disconnect the vent hose from the transfer case.

10. Remove the heat shield from the frame.

11. Support the transfer case with a transmission jack.

12. Remove the bolts retaining the transfer case to the transmission adapter.

13. Lower the transfer case from the vehicle.

To install:

14. When installing place a new gasket between the transfer case and the adapter.

15. Raise the transfer case with the transmission jack so the transmission output shaft aligns with the splined transfer case input shaft. Install the bolts retaining the transfer case to the adapter.

16. Remove the transmission jack from the transfer case.

17. Connect the rear driveshaft to the rear output shaft yoke. Torque the bolts to 15 ft. lbs.

18. Install the shift lever to the transfer case and install the retaining nut.

19. Connect the speedometer driven gear to the transfer case.

20. Connect the 4WD indicator switch wire connector at the transfer case.

21. Connect the front driveshaft to the front output yoke. Torque the bolts to 15 ft. lbs.

22. Position the heat shield to the frame crossmember and the mount-

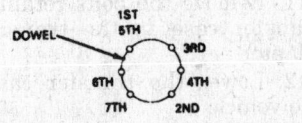

Transfer case-to-adapter bolt torque sequence — Borg Warner 13-45 transfer case — Bronco, F Series (Pick-Up) and E Series (Van)

ing lug on the transfer case. Install and tighten the retaining bolts.

23. Install the skid plate to the frame.

24. Install the drain plug. Remove the filler plug and install 6 pints of Dexron®II type transmission fluid or equivalent.

25. Lower the vehicle.

BORG-WARNER 13-56 MANUAL SHIFT

1. Raise and support the vehicle safely.

2. Drain the fluid from the transfer case.

3. Disconnect the 4WD indicator switch wire connector at the transfer case.

4. Remove the skid plate from the frame, if equipped.

5. Matchmark and disconnect the front driveshaft from the front output yoke.

6. Matchmark and disconnect the rear driveshaft from the rear output shaft yoke.

7. Disconnect the speedometer driven gear from the transfer case rear bearing retainer.

8. Remove the retaining rings and shift rod from the transfer case shift lever.

9. Disconnect the vent hose from the transfer case.

10. Remove the heat shield from the frame.

11. Support the transfer case with a transmission jack.

12. Remove the bolts retaining the transfer case to the transmission adapter.

13. Lower the transfer case from the vehicle.

To install:

14. When installing place a new gasket between the transfer case and the adapter.

15. Raise the transfer case with the transmission jack so the transmission output shaft aligns with the splined transfer case input shaft. Install the bolts retaining the transfer case to the adapter. Torque the bolts to 40 ft. lbs.

16. Remove the transmission jack from the transfer case.

17. Connect the rear driveshaft to the rear output shaft yoke. Torque the bolts to 15 ft. lbs.

18. Install the shift lever to the transfer case and install the retaining nut.

19. Connect the speedometer driven gear to the transfer case.

20. Connect the 4WD indicator switch wire connector at the transfer case.

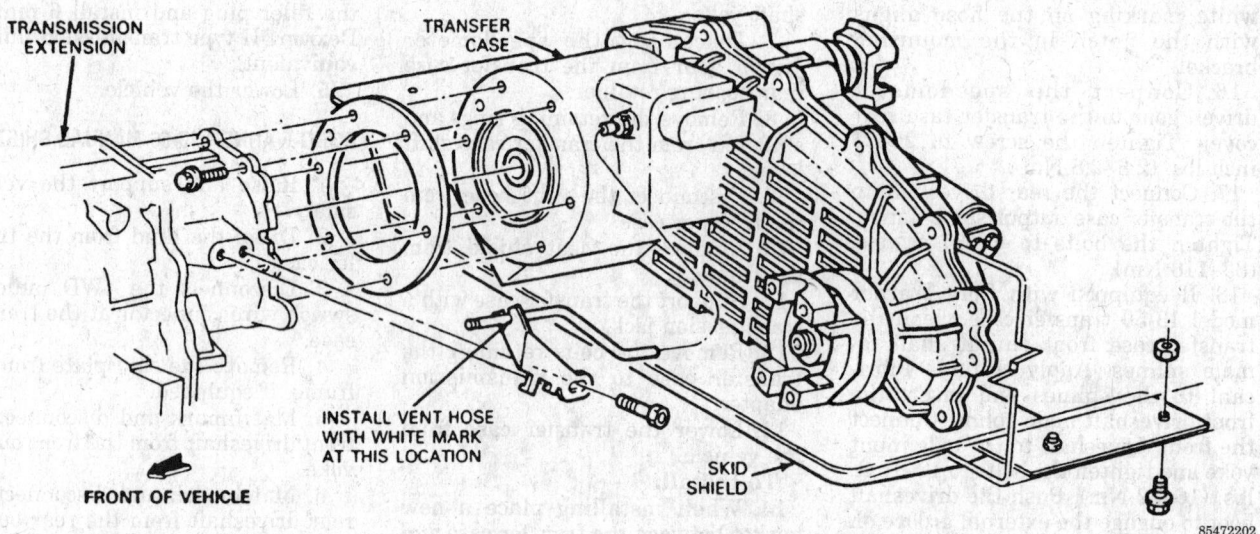

Transfer case installation — typical — Bronco, F Series (Pick-Up) and E Series (Van)

21. Connect the front driveshaft to the front output yoke. Torque the bolts to 15 ft. lbs.

22. Position the heat shield to the frame crossmember and the mounting lug on the transfer case. Install and tighten the retaining bolts.

23. Install the skid plate to the frame.

24. Install the drain plug. Remove the filler plug and install 6 pints of Dexron®II type transmission fluid or equivalent.

25. Lower the vehicle.

BORG-WARNER 13-56 ELECTRONIC SHIFT

1. Raise and support the vehicle safely.

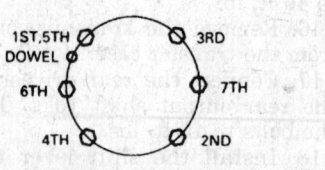

Transfer case-to-adapter bolt torque sequence — Borg Warner 13-56 electronic and manual shift transfer case — Bronco, F Series (Pick-Up) and E Series (Van)

2. Drain the fluid from the transfer case.

3. Disconnect the wire connector at the transfer case.

4. Remove the skid plate from the frame, if equipped.

5. Matchmark and disconnect the front driveshaft from the front output yoke.

6. Matchmark and disconnect the rear driveshaft from the rear output shaft yoke.

7. Disconnect the speedometer driven gear from the transfer case rear bearing retainer.

8. Disconnect the vent hose from the transfer case.

9. Remove the heat shield from the frame.

10. Support the transfer case with a transmission jack.

11. Remove the bolts retaining the transfer case to the transmission adapter.

12. Lower the transfer case from the vehicle.

13. When installing place a new gasket between the transfer case and the adapter.

To install:

14. Raise the transfer case with the transmission jack so the transmission output shaft aligns with the splined transfer case input shaft. In-

stall the bolts retaining the transfer case to the adapter. Torque the bolts to 40 ft. lbs.

15. Remove the transmission jack from the transfer case.

16. Connect the rear driveshaft to the rear output shaft yoke. Torque the bolts to 28 ft. lbs.

17. Install the shift lever to the transfer case and install the retaining nut.

18. Connect the speedometer driven gear to the transfer case. Tighten the bolt to 25 inch lbs.

19. Connect the wire connector at the transfer case.

20. Connect the front driveshaft to the front output yoke. Torque the bolts to 15 ft. lbs.

21. Position the heat shield to the frame crossmember and the mounting lug on the transfer case. Install and tighten the retaining bolts.

22. Install the skid plate to the frame.

23. Install the drain plug. Remove the filler plug and install 6 pints of Dexron®II type transmission fluid or equivalent.

24. Lower the vehicle.

LINKAGE ADJUSTMENT

Except Bronco, F Series (Pick-Up) and E Series (Van)

MECHANICAL SHIFT TYPE

1. Raise the shift boot to expose the top surface of the cam plate.
2. Loosen the bolts "A" and "B" on the control lever assembly approximately 2 turns. Move the transfer case shift lever to the **4L** position.
3. Move the cam plate rearward until the bottom chamfered corner of the neutral lug just contacts the forward right edge of the shift lever, point "C".
4. Hold the cam plate in this position and tighten bolt "A" first to 70–90 ft. lbs. (94–122 Nm), then tighten bolt "B" to 31–42 ft. lbs. (43–56 Nm).
5. Move the transfer case in-cab shift lever to all shift positions to check the positive engagement. There should be clearance, not exceeding 0.13 in. (3.30mm), between the shift lever and cam plate in **2H** front **4H** rear and **4L** shift positions.
6. Install the shift boot assembly.

DRIVE AXLE

Halfshaft

REMOVAL AND INSTALLATION

4WD Aerostar

1. Raise and safely support the vehicle.
2. Remove the wheel and tire assembly and the hub retainer nut and washer. Discard the nut.
3. Mark the differential shaft flange in relation to the halfshaft so they can be reinstalled in their original position.
4. Remove the bolts and disconnect the halfshaft inboard flanges from the differential axle shaft flanges.
5. Support the end of the shaft by suspending it from an underbody component with mechanics wire. Do not allow the shaft to hang unsupported as damage to the outboard CV-joint may result.
6. Loosen the shock absorber on the lower control arm and move it to the side. Remove the rubber jounce bumper.

7. Separate the outboard CV-joint from the hub using front hub tools T81P-1104-C with T81P-1104-A and adapters T83P-1104-BH1 and T86P-1104-A1 or equivalents, and free the hub, bearing and knuckle assembly from the halfshaft by pushing in the CV-joint outer shaft until it is loose in the assembly.

NOTE: Never use a hammer to separate the outboard CV-joint stub shaft from the hub. Damage to the CV-joint threads and internal components may result.

8. Remove the halfshaft assembly from the vehicle. Once the halfshaft(s) have been removed, the vehicle must not be driven or rolled with the vehicle weight supported by the hub bearing.

To install:

9. Carefully align the splines of the outboard CV-joint stub shaft with the splines in the hub and push the shaft into the hub as far as possible.
10. Temporarily fasten the rotor to the hub with washers and 2 lug nuts. Insert a suitable steel rod into the rotor and rotate clockwise to contact the knuckle to prevent the rotor from turning during CV-joint installation.
11. Install the hub nut washer and a new hub retainer nut. Manually thread the nut onto the halfshaft as far as possible, then tighten to 170–210 ft. lbs. (230–283 Nm).
12. Install the inboard flange of the halfshaft to the differential output flange, aligning the marks that were made during removal. Install the flange bolts and tighten to 22–29 ft. lbs. (30–40 Nm).
13. Install the wheel and tire assembly and lower the vehicle.

CV-Boot

REMOVAL AND INSTALLATION

4WD Aerostar

1. Remove the halfshaft assembly from the vehicle.
2. Clamp the halfshaft in a vise equipped with jaw caps to prevent damage to machined surfaces. Do not allow the vise jaws to contact the boot or its clamp.
3. Remove the slip yoke boot clamps and separate the outboard shaft and joint assembly from the inboard slip yoke assembly. Remove and discard the slip yoke boot.
4. Cut the large boot clamp using suitable cutters and peel away from the boot. After removing the clamp,

roll the boot back over the shaft and remove and discard the boot.
5. Clean all parts in suitable parts cleaning solvent.

NOTE: Do not submerge the slip yoke assembly U-joint in cleaning solvent.

6. Inspect the CV-joint and slip yoke assembly for excessive wear, pitting, rust and broken parts. If the CV-joint is no longer usable, the complete outer shaft assembly must be replaced.

To install:

7. Fill the CV-joint area around the balls with 2.8 oz. of suitable CV-joint grease. Then spread 1.4 oz. of grease evenly inside the large boot for a total combined fill of 4.2 oz.
8. Assemble the large outboard boot onto the outboard shaft and joint assembly, making sure the boot is seated in the boot grooves. Tighten the clamps using suitable crimping pliers, but do not overtighten, as it may damage the clamp and/or boot.
9. Assemble the small boot and clamps onto the outboard shaft and joint assembly, but do not crimp the clamps at this time.
10. Coat the spline end of the outboard shaft and joint assembly with lubricant and assemble into the inner slip yoke assembly.
11. Slip the boot into place, making sure the boot is seated in the boot grooves. Tighten the clamps using a suitable tool, but do not overtighten, as it may damage the clamp and/or boot.
12. Install the halfshaft in the vehicle.

Driveshaft and U-Joints

REMOVAL AND INSTALLATION

Single Type U-Joint

REAR ONE PIECE DRIVESHAFT

1. Matchmark the driveshaft yoke and axle pinion flange.
2. Remove the U-bolt nuts and U-bolts attaching the yoke to the axle flange.
3. Separate the yoke from the flange. It may be necessary to pry it free with a small prybar. Immediately after separation, wrap tape around the U-joint caps to keep them from falling off.
4. Slip the driveshaft off the transmission splines.
5. Installation is the reverse of removal. Align the yoke-to-flange

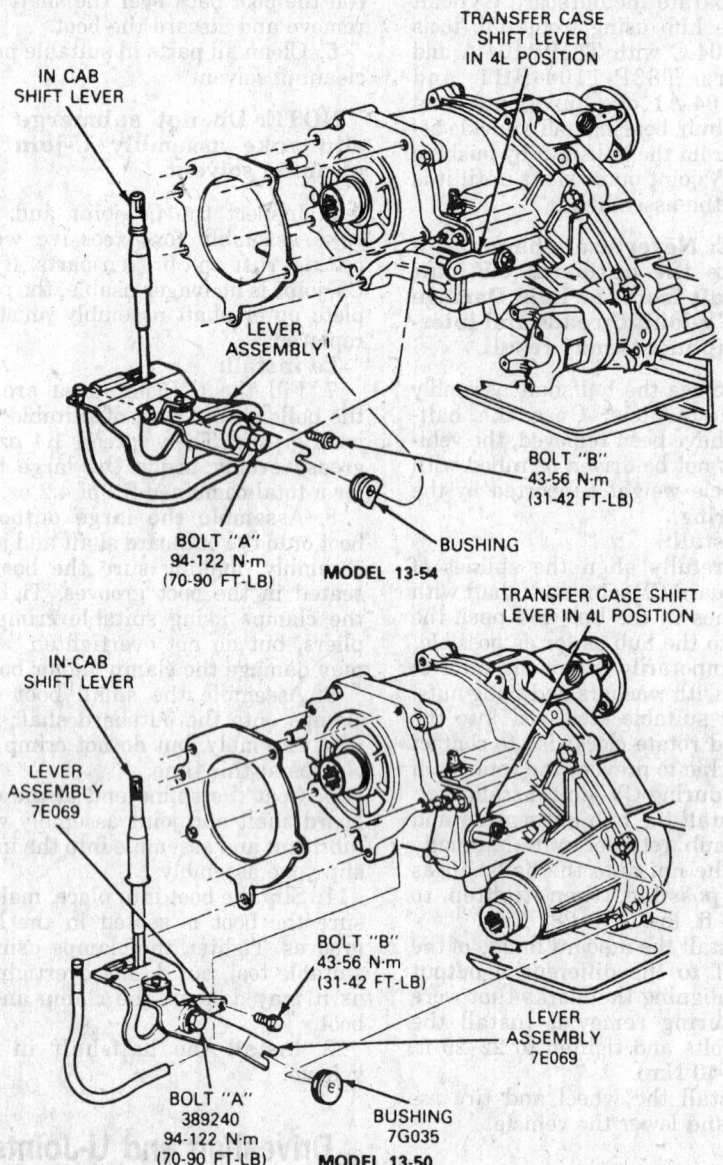

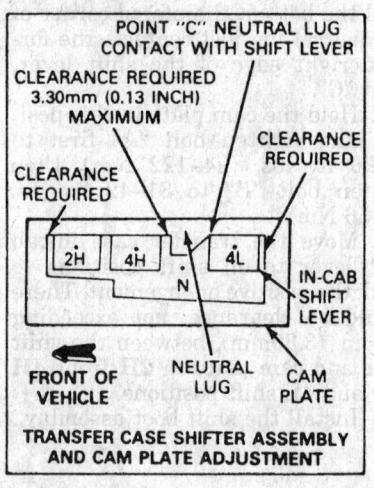

Transfer case linkage adjustment procedure — Except Bronco, F Series (Pick-Up) and E Series (Van)

matchmarks. Torque the U-bolt nuts to 15 ft. lbs.

FRONT DRIVESHAFT

1. Matchmark the driveshaft yoke and axle pinion flange.
2. Matchmark the driveshaft yoke and transfer case flange.
3. Remove the U-bolt nuts and U-bolts attaching the yoke to the axle flange.
4. Separate the yoke from the flange. It may be necessary to pry it free with a small prybar. Immediately after separation, wrap tape around the U-joint caps to keep them from falling off.

5. Remove the U-bolts and nuts (bolts for the F-350) and disconnect the driveshaft from the transfer case. It may be necessary to pry it free with a small prybar. Immediately after separation, wrap tape around the U-joint caps to keep them from falling off.

NOTE: Avoid separating the driveshaft parts at the slip joint. If the driveshaft should become separated, follow the procedure, below.

6. Installation is the reverse of removal. Align the yoke-to-flange matchmarks. Torque the U-bolt nuts

to 15 ft. lbs. Torque the F-350 bolts to 20–28 ft. lbs.

TWO PIECE DRIVESHAFT/COUPLING SHAFT

1. Matchmark the driveshaft yoke and axle pinion flange.
2. Remove the U-bolt nuts and U-bolts attaching the yoke to the axle flange.
3. Separate the yoke from the flange. It may be necessary to pry it free with a small prybar. Immediately after separation, wrap tape around the U-joint caps to keep them from falling off.
4. Slip the driveshaft off the coupling shaft splines.

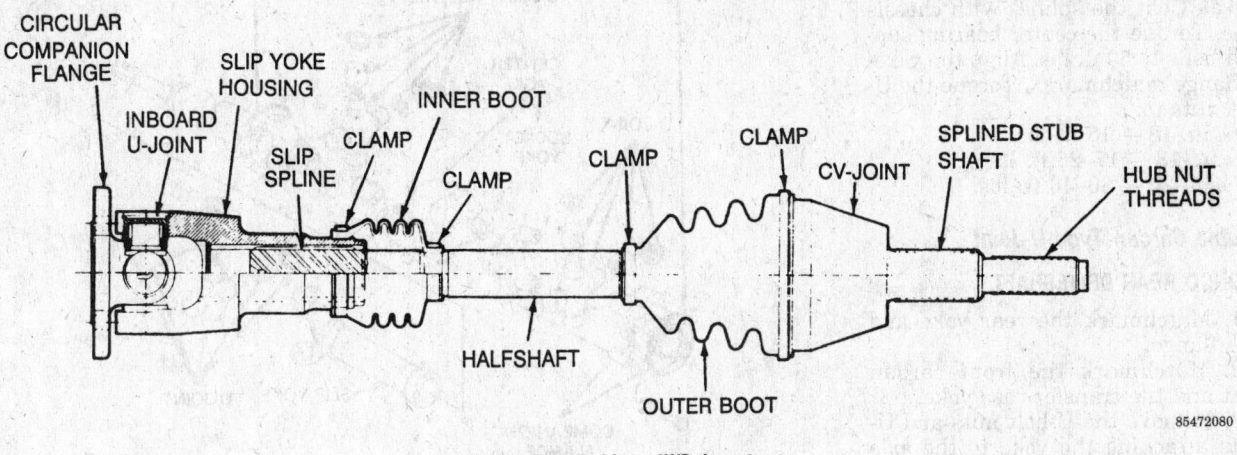

CIRCULAR COMPANION FLANGE
SLIP YOKE HOUSING
INBOARD U-JOINT
INNER BOOT
SLIP SPLINE
CLAMP
CLAMP
CLAMP
CLAMP
CV-JOINT
SPLINED STUB SHAFT
HUB NUT THREADS
HALFSHAFT
OUTER BOOT

85472080

Halfshaft assembly — 4WD Aerostar

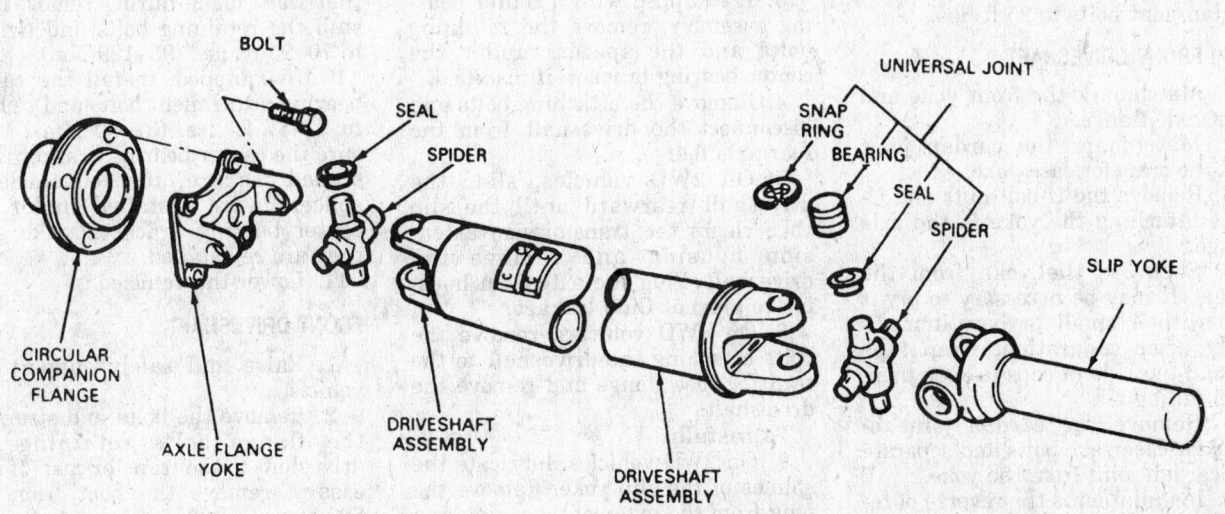

BOLT
SEAL
SPIDER
UNIVERSAL JOINT
SNAP RING
BEARING
SEAL
SPIDER
SLIP YOKE
CIRCULAR COMPANION FLANGE
AXLE FLANGE YOKE
DRIVESHAFT ASSEMBLY
DRIVESHAFT ASSEMBLY

85472204

One-piece driveshaft — Bronco, F Series (Pick-Up) and E Series (Van)

5. Remove the center bearing.

6. Slide the coupling shaft from the transmission shaft splines.

7. Clean all parts and check for damage. Do not remove the blue plastic coating from the male splines.

8. Installation is the reverse of removal. Coat the splines with chassis lube. Torque the center bearing support bolts to 50 ft. lbs. Align the yoke-to-flange matchmarks. Torque the U-bolt nuts to:

$\frac{5}{16}$ in.-18 — 15 ft. lbs.
$\frac{3}{8}$ in.-18 — 17–26 ft. lbs.
$\frac{7}{16}$ in.-20 — 30–40 ft. lbs.

Double Cardan Type U-Joint

BRONCO REAR DRIVESHAFT

1. Matchmark the rear yoke and axle flange.

2. Matchmark the front cardan joint and the transfer case yoke.

3. Remove the U-bolt nuts and U-bolts attaching the yoke to the axle flange.

4. Separate the yoke from the flange. It may be necessary to pry it free with a small prybar. Immediately after separation, wrap tape around the U-joint caps to keep them from falling off.

5. Remove the cardan joint-to-transfer case yoke bolts and separate the cardan joint from the yoke.

6. Installation is the reverse of removal. Align the matchmarks. Torque the U-bolt nuts to 15 ft. lbs.; the cardan joint bolts to 25 ft. lbs.

F-350 FRONT DRIVESHAFT

1. Matchmark the front yoke and front axle flange.

2. Matchmark the cardan joint and the transfer case yoke.

3. Remove the U-bolt nuts and U-bolts attaching the yoke to the axle flange.

4. Separate the yoke from the flange. It may be necessary to pry it free with a small prybar. Immediately after separation, wrap tape around the U-joint caps to keep them from falling off.

5. Remove the cardan joint-to-transfer case yoke bolts and separate the cardan joint from the yoke.

6. Installation is the reverse of removal. Align the matchmarks. Torque the U-bolt nuts to 15 ft. lbs.; the cardan joint bolts to 25 ft. lbs.

Except Bronco, F Series (Pick-Up) and E Series (Van)

REAR DRIVESHAFT

1. Raise and safely support the vehicle.

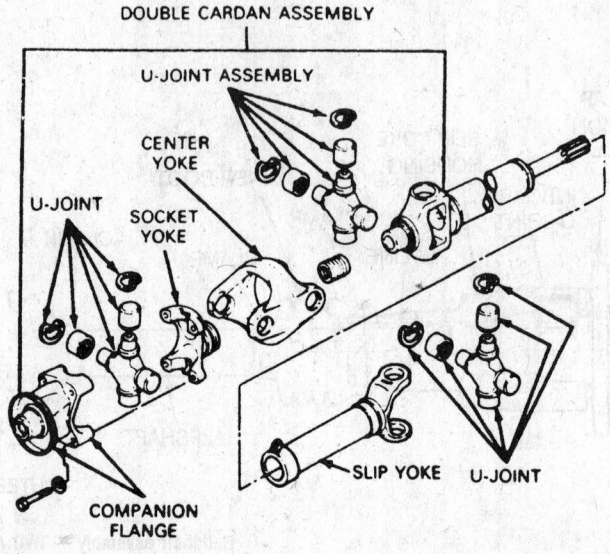

Double Cardan U-joint assembly — Bronco, F Series (Pick-Up) and E Series (Van)

2. Mark the driveshaft in relation to the rear axle flange. If necessary, mark the relation of the driveshaft to the transfer case flange.

3. If equipped with a center bearing assembly, remove the retaining bolts and the spacers under the center bearing bracket, if installed.

4. Remove the attaching bolts and disconnect the driveshaft from the rear axle flange.

5. On 2WD vehicles, slide the driveshaft rearward until the slip yoke clears the transmission extension housing and remove the driveshaft. Plug the extension housing to prevent fluid leakage.

6. On 4WD vehicles, remove the bolts attaching the driveshaft to the transfer case flange and remove the driveshaft.

To install:

7. On 2WD vehicles, lubricate the splines of the slip yoke. Remove the plug from the extension housing and install the driveshaft assembly. Do not allow the slip yoke to bottom on the output shaft with excessive force.

8. On 4WD vehicles, install the driveshaft to the transfer case flange, aligning the marks that were made during removal. Install the attaching bolts and tighten to 61–87 ft. lbs. (83–118 Nm) if equipped with constant velocity U-joints or 12–16 ft.

lbs. (17–22 Nm) if equipped with double cardan U-joints.

9. Connect the driveshaft to the rear axle flange, aligning the marks that were made during removal. Install the retaining bolts and tighten to 70–95 ft. lbs. (95–129 Nm).

10. If equipped, install the center bearing attachment bolts and tighten to 27–37 ft. lbs. (37–50 Nm). Make sure the center bearing bracket is installed "square" to the vehicle. If spacers were installed under the center bearing bracket, make sure they are reinstalled.

11. Lower the vehicle.

FRONT DRIVESHAFT

1. Raise and safely support the vehicle.

2. Remove the bolts and straps or the flange bolts retaining the driveshaft to the transfer case. If necessary, remove the boot from the transfer case to gain access to the slip yoke.

3. Remove the bolts and straps retaining the front U-joint to the front axle and remove the front driveshaft.

To install:

4. If equipped, lubricate the slip yoke splines and the edge of the inner diameter of the rubber boot. Slide the driveshaft into the transfer case, making sure the wide-tooth splines

are properly indexed. Reposition the boot and install the clamp.

5. If equipped, install the driveshaft to the transfer case flange and install the retaining bolts. Tighten to 12–16 ft. lbs. (17–22 Nm).

6. Install the driveshaft to the front axle flange with the straps and bolts. Tighten to 10–15 ft. lbs. (14–20 Nm).

7. Lower the vehicle.

Front Axle Shaft, Bearing And Seal

REMOVAL AND INSTALLATION

Except Aerostar

1. Raise and safely support the vehicle. Remove the front wheel and tire assemblies.

2. Remove the disc brake caliper and wire it to the frame. Do not let the caliper hang by the brake hose.

3. Remove the hub locks, wheel bearings and locknuts.

4. Remove the hub, rotor and outer wheel bearing.

5. Remove the grease seal from the rotor with a seal removal tool. Remove the inner wheel bearing.

6. If the wheel bearings are to be replaced, remove the inner and outer bearing races with a suitable puller or a hammer and brass drift.

7. Remove the nuts retaining the spindle to the steering knuckle. Tap the spindle with a plastic hammer to jar the spindle from the knuckle. Remove the splash shield.

8. On the left side of the vehicle, remove the shaft and joint assembly by pulling the assembly out of the carrier. On the right side of the carrier, remove and discard the clamp from the shaft and joint assembly and the stub shaft. Pull the shaft and joint assembly from the splines of the stub shaft.

9. If required, remove the oil seal and needle bearing from the spindle. If necessary, remove the slinger from the shaft by driving it off with a hammer.

To install:

10. If removed, install a new bearing and seal in the spindle and/or press on a new shaft slinger.

11. On the right side of the carrier, install the rubber boot and new keystone clamps on the stub shaft slip yoke. Slide the right shaft and joint assembly into the slip yoke making sure the splines are fully engaged. Slide the boot over the assembly and

crimp the keystone clamp using suitable pliers.

NOTE: The Dana model 28 axle has phased splines; there is only 1 way to assemble the right shaft and joint assembly into the slip yoke. The Dana model 35 axle does not have a blind spline, therefore pay special attention to make sure the yoke ears are in phase (in line) during assembly.

12. On the left side of the carrier, slide the shaft and joint assembly through the knuckle and engage the splines on the shaft in the carrier.

13. Install the splash shield and spindle onto the steering knuckle. Install and tighten the spindle nuts to 45 ft. lbs. (61 Nm).

14. If removed, drive the bearing races into the rotor using a suitable driver. Pack the inner and outer wheel bearings and the lip of a new seal with high-temperature wheel bearing grease.

15. Position the inner wheel bearing in the race and install the seal using a seal installer. Install the rotor on the spindle and install the outer wheel bearing in the race.

16. Install the wheel bearing, locknut, thrust bearing, snapring and locking hubs.

17. Install the caliper and the wheel and tire assemblies. Lower the vehicle.

Aerostar

1. Remove the axle assembly from the sub-frame and the vehicle.

2. Remove the cover plate and drain the lubricant. Mount the axle assembly in a suitable fixture.

3. Rotate the shafts so the open side of the snapring is exposed. Remove the snaprings.

4. Remove the axle shafts. Remove and discard the oil seal and needle bearings.

To install:

5. Make sure the bearing bore is free from nicks and burrs. Install a new caged needle bearing on installation tool T83T-1244-A or equivalent, with the manufacturer name and part number facing outward towards the tool. Drive the needle bearing in until it is seated in the bore. The tool controls the installation depth of the seal and bearing.

6. Coat a new seal with lubricant and install using a seal installer.

7. Install the axle shafts into the carrier so the groove in the shaft is visible in the differential case.

8. Install the snapring in the axle shaft groove. Remove the axle assembly from the holding fixture.

9. Clean all old sealer from the carrier and cover surfaces. Apply a bead of RTV sealer ⅛–¼ in. wide. The bead should be continuous and should not pass through or outside the holes.

10. Install the cover and tighten the bolts to 20–25 ft. lbs. (27–34 Nm). Fill the carrier with the proper type and quantity of fluid.

11. Install the axle assembly in the vehicle.

Rear Axle Shaft, Bearing And Seal

REMOVAL AND INSTALLATION

Ford 7.5 In. and 8.8 In. Rear Axles

1. Raise and safely support the vehicle.

2. Remove the rear wheel and tire assemblies and the brake drums.

3. Clean all dirt from the carrier cover area. Position a drain pan under the carrier, remove the cover and drain the rear axle.

NOTE: Whenever a plastic rear axle cover is removed, it must be replaced with a new cover and bolts. Steel rear axle covers may be reused.

4. For all 8.8 in. axles and all 7.5 in. axles except 3.73:1 and 4.10:1 ratio axles, proceed as follows:

a. Remove the differential pinion shaft lock bolt and pinion shaft.

b. Push the flanged end of the axle shafts toward the center of the vehicle and remove the C-lock from the button end of the axle shaft.

c. Remove the axle shaft from the housing.

d. Reinstall the pinion shaft and lock bolt to ensure the pinion gears remain in place.

5. On 7.5 in. axles equipped with 3.73:1 and 4.10:1 axle ratios, proceed as follows:

a. Remove the pinion shaft lock bolt.

b. Push out the pinion shaft until the step on the shaft contacts the ring gear.

c. Remove the C-lock from the axle shaft.

d. Remove the axle shaft from the housing.

e. Reinstall the pinion shaft and lock bolt to ensure the pinion gears remain in place.

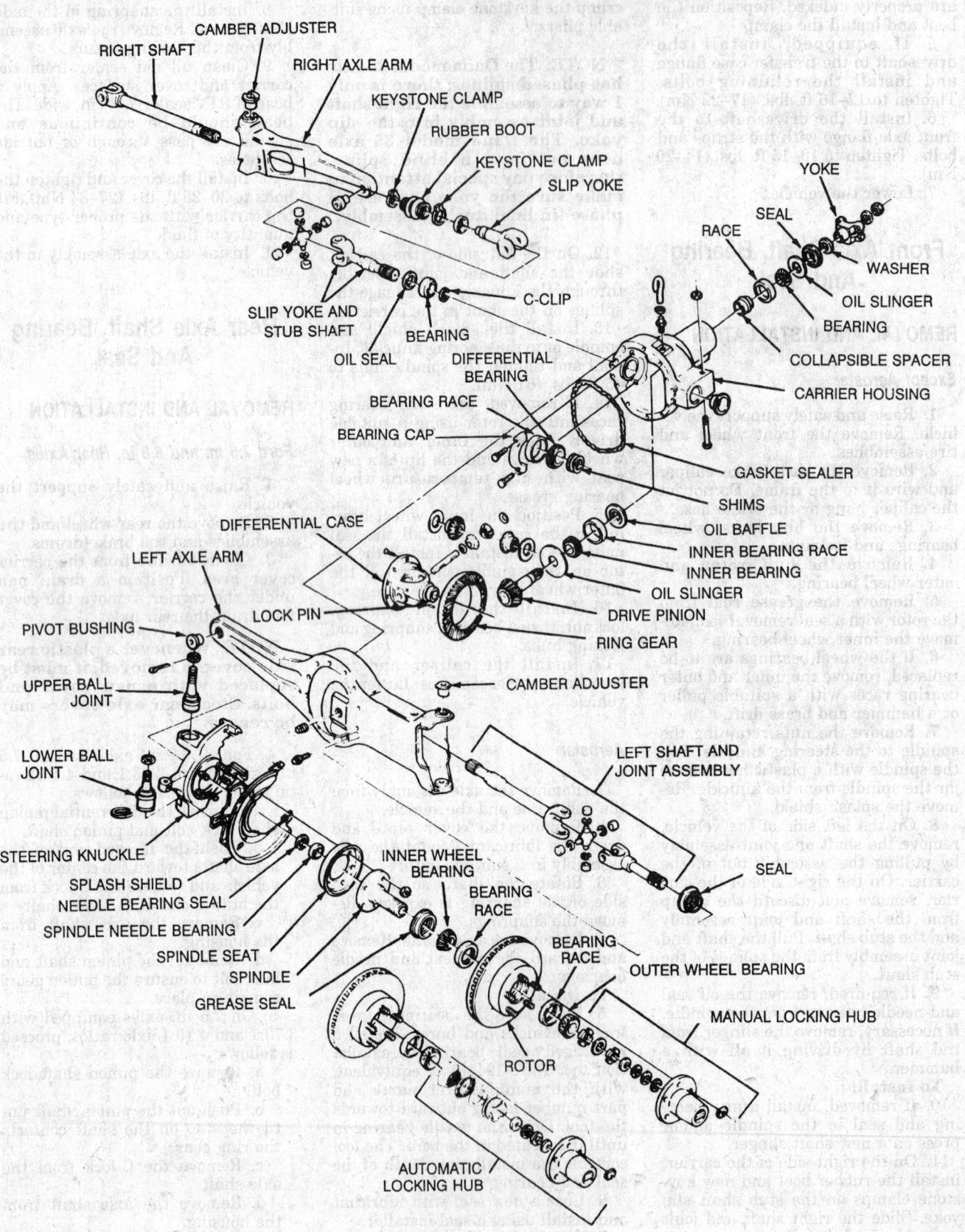

RIGHT SHAFT

CAMBER ADJUSTER

RIGHT AXLE ARM

KEYSTONE CLAMP

RUBBER BOOT

KEYSTONE CLAMP

SLIP YOKE

YOKE

SEAL

RACE

WASHER

OIL SLINGER

BEARING

COLLAPSIBLE SPACER

CARRIER HOUSING

SLIP YOKE AND STUB SHAFT

OIL SEAL

BEARING

C-CLIP

DIFFERENTIAL BEARING

BEARING RACE

BEARING CAP

GASKET SEALER

SHIMS

OIL BAFFLE

INNER BEARING RACE

INNER BEARING

OIL SLINGER

DRIVE PINION

RING GEAR

DIFFERENTIAL CASE

LEFT AXLE ARM

LOCK PIN

CAMBER ADJUSTER

PIVOT BUSHING

UPPER BALL JOINT

LOWER BALL JOINT

LEFT SHAFT AND JOINT ASSEMBLY

SEAL

STEERING KNUCKLE

SPLASH SHIELD

NEEDLE BEARING SEAL

SPINDLE NEEDLE BEARING

SPINDLE SEAT

SPINDLE

GREASE SEAL

INNER WHEEL BEARING

BEARING RACE

BEARING RACE

OUTER WHEEL BEARING

MANUAL LOCKING HUB

ROTOR

AUTOMATIC LOCKING HUB

85472081

Dana model 28 front drive axle assembly

6. Using bearing remover T85L-1225-AH or equivalent and a suitable slide hammer, remove the axle bearing and seal as a unit.

To install:

7. Lubricate a new bearing with rear axle lubricant and install in the housing bore using a suitable driver.

8. Apply grease to the lips of a new axle seal and install, using a seal installer.

9. Remove the pinion shaft lock bolt and pinion shaft. On 7.5 in. axles equipped with 3.73:1 and 4.10:1 axle ratios, push out the pinion shaft until the step contacts the ring gear.

10. Slide the axle shaft into the axle housing, being careful not to damage the seal or axle bearing. Start the splines into the side gear and push firmly until the button end of the axle shaft can be seen in the differential case.

11. Install the C-lock on the button end of the axle shaft, then pull the shaft outboard until the shaft splines engage and the C-lock seats in the counterbore of the differential side gear.

NOTE: On 8.8 in. axles, a rubber O-ring is used to hold the C-lock in position on the axle shaft. Make sure the O-ring is in the groove at the button end of the axle shaft before installing the C-lock.

12. Slide the pinion shaft through the case and pinion gears, aligning the hole in the shaft with the lock bolt hole. Install the lock bolt and tighten to 15–30 ft. lbs. (20–40 Nm).

13. Clean all old sealer from the carrier and cover surfaces. Apply a bead of RTV sealer ⅛–¼ in. wide. The bead should be continuous and should not pass through or outside the holes.

14. Install the cover and tighten the bolts to 15–20 ft. lbs. (21–27 Nm) if equipped with a plastic cover or 25–35 ft. lbs. (34–37 Nm) if equipped with a steel cover. Fill the carrier with the proper type and quantity of fluid.

15. Install the brake drums and the wheel and tire assemblies. Lower the vehicle.

Dana 30 and 35-1A Rear Axles

1. Raise and safely support the vehicle.

2. Remove the rear wheel and tire assemblies and the brake drums.

3. Working through the hole provided in the axle shaft flange, remove the nuts that secure the wheel bearing retainer plate. These are torque

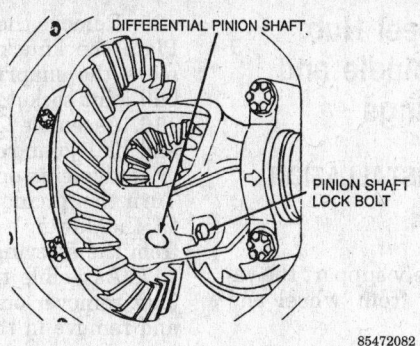

Differential pinion shaft and pinion shaft lock bolt location — Ford 7.5 in. and 8.8 in. rear axles

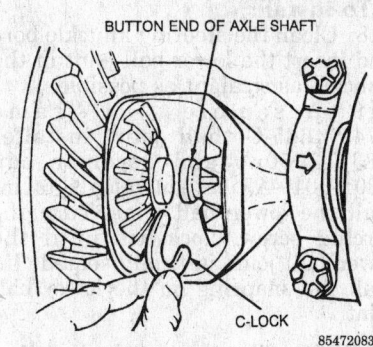

Axle shaft C-lock installation — Ford 7.5 in. and 8.8 in. rear axles

prevailing nuts and must not be reused.

4. Pull the axle shaft assembly out of the axle housing using puller adapter tool T66L-4234-A or equivalent, and a suitable slide hammer.

5. Remove the axle shaft carefully so as not to damage the outer seal. Remove the bearing race from the housing using a slide hammer type puller and bearing race puller tool T77F-1102-AA or equivalent. Remove the brake backing plate and wire it to the chassis.

6. Mount the axle shaft in a suitable fixture. Drill a ¼–½ in. hole in the outside diameter of the inner retainer ring to a depth approximately ⅜ in. the thickness of the retainer ring. Do not drill all the way through the retainer ring as this will damage the axle shaft.

7. After drilling the retainer ring, use a chisel positioned across the drilled hole and strike sharply to split the retainer ring.

8. Put the outer bearing race on the axle shaft assembly and place the axle shaft in tool T75L-1165-A, B, C or equivalent. Assemble the 2 halves of the remover collet and tighten the bolts.

9. Press the bearing and seal assembly off of the shaft. Never use heat as this would damage the axle shaft. Inspect the retainer plate for possible distortion and replace if damaged.

To install:

10. Install the outer retainer plate, if removed. Make sure it is not installed backwards.

11. Place a new lubricated seal and bearing on the axle shaft, making sure the race rib ring is facing the axle flange.

12. Press the tapered-bearing and seal assembly onto the axle shaft using tools T75L-1165-B, service plate and adapter tool T75L-1165-DA or equivalents. Apply enough pressure to seat the bearing against the axle shaft shoulder. Do not attempt to press on the bearing retainer at the same time.

13. Position a new bearing retainer on the shaft, then press it into position firmly against the bearing.

14. Apply lubricant to the outer diameter of the race and seal. Install the brake backing plate and attaching bolts.

15. Before sliding the shaft assembly into the axle housing, make sure the outer seal is fully mounted on the bearing.

16. Carefully slide the axle shaft into the housing, start the axle splines into the side gear and push the shaft in until the bearing bottoms in the housing.

17. Install the bearing retainer plate and nuts. Tighten the nuts to 25–35 ft. lbs. (34–47 Nm).

18. Install the brake drum and the wheel and tire assembly.

19. Add lubricant through the filler hole until the level reaches 3.8 ± ¼ in. below the bottom of the filler hole. The axle must be in the running position and the vehicle level.

20. Lower the vehicle.

Front Wheel Hub, Knuckle/Spindle and Bearings

REMOVAL AND INSTALLATION

Except Aerostar

1. Raise and safely support the vehicle. Remove the front wheel and tire assemblies.

2. Remove the disc brake caliper and wire it to the frame. Do not let the caliper hang by the brake hose.

3. Remove the hub locks, wheel bearings and locknuts.

4. Remove the hub, rotor and outer wheel bearing.

5. Remove the grease seal from the rotor with a seal removal tool. Remove the inner wheel bearing.

6. If the wheel bearings are to be replaced, remove the inner and outer bearing races with a suitable puller or a hammer and brass drift.

7. Remove the nuts retaining the spindle to the steering knuckle. Tap the spindle with a plastic hammer to jar the spindle from the knuckle. Remove the splash shield.

8. On the left side of the vehicle, remove the shaft and joint assembly by pulling the assembly out of the carrier. On the right side of the carrier, remove and discard the clamp from the shaft and joint assembly and the stub shaft. Pull the shaft and joint assembly from the splines of the stub shaft.

9. Place the spindle in a vise on the second step of the spindle. Wrap a shop towel around the spindle or use a brass-jawed vise to protect the spindle.

10. Remove the oil seal and needle bearing from the spindle with a slide hammer and seal remover TOOL-1175-AC or equivalent. If necessary, remove the slinger from the shaft by driving off with a hammer.

11. Remove the cotter pin from the tie rod nut and then remove the nut. Tap on the tie rod stud to free it from the steering arm.

12. Remove the upper ball joint snapring and remove the upper ball joint pinch bolt. Loosen the lower ball joint nut to the end of the stud.

13. Strike the inside of the knuckle near the upper and lower ball joints to break the knuckle loose from the ball joint studs.

14. Remove the camber adjuster sleeve. Note the position of the slot in the camber adjuster so it can be reinstalled in the same position during assembly.

15. Remove the lower ball joint nut. Place the knuckle in a vise and remove the snapring from the bottom ball joint socket, if equipped.

16. Assemble C-frame T74P-4635-C and ball joint remover T83T-3050-A or equivalents on the lower ball joint. Turn the forcing screw clockwise until the lower ball joint is removed from the steering knuckle.

17. Assemble the C-frame and ball joint remover on the upper ball joint and remove in the same manner.

NOTE: Always remove the lower ball joint first.

To install:

18. Clean the steering knuckle bore and insert the lower ball joint in the knuckle as straight as possible.

19. Assemble C-frame T74P-4635-C, ball joint installer T83T-3050-A and receiver cup T80T-3010-A3 or equivalents to install the lower ball joint. Turn the forcing screw clockwise until the lower ball joint is firmly seated. Install the snapring on the lower ball joint.

NOTE: The lower ball joint must always be installed first.

20. Assemble the C-frame, ball joint installer and receiver cup to install the upper ball joint. Turn the forcing screw clockwise until the ball joint is firmly seated.

21. Install the camber adjuster into the support arm, making sure the slot is in the original position.

NOTE: The torque sequence in Steps 22 and 23 must be followed exactly when securing the knuckle. Excessive knuckle turning effort may result in reduced steering returnability if this procedure is not followed.

22. Install a new nut on the bottom ball joint stud. Tighten the nut to 90 ft. lbs. (122 Nm) minimum, then tighten to align the next slot in the nut with the hole in the stud. Install a new cotter pin.

23. Install the snapring on the upper ball joint stud. Install the upper ball joint pinch bolt and tighten to 48–65 ft. lbs. (65–88 Nm).

NOTE: The camber adjuster will seat itself into the knuckle at a predetermined position during the tightening sequence. Do not attempt to adjust this position.

24. Clean all dirt and grease from the spindle bearing bore. The bearing bores must be free from nicks and burrs.

25. Place the bearing in the bore with the manufacturers identification facing outward. Drive the bearing into the bore using spindle bearing replacer T80T-4000-S and driver handle T80T-4000-W or equivalents.

26. Install the grease seal in the bearing bore with the lip side of the seal facing towards the tool. Drive the seal in the bore using the same tools as in Step 25. Coat the bearing seal lip with high-temperature lubricant.

27. If removed, press on a new shaft slinger.

28. On the right side of the carrier, install the rubber boot and new keystone clamps on the stub shaft slip yoke. Slide the right shaft and joint assembly into the slip yoke making sure the splines are fully engaged. Slide the boot over the assembly and crimp the keystone clamp using suitable pliers.

NOTE: The Dana model 28 axle has phased splines; there is only 1 way to assemble the right shaft and joint assembly into the slip yoke. The Dana model 35 axle does not have a blind spline, therefore pay special attention to make sure the yoke ears are in phase (in line) during assembly.

29. On the left side of the carrier, slide the shaft and joint assembly through the knuckle and engage the splines on the shaft in the carrier.

30. Install the splash shield and spindle onto the steering knuckle. Install and tighten the spindle nuts to 45 ft. lbs. (61 Nm).

31. If removed, drive the bearing races into the rotor using a suitable driver. Pack the inner and outer wheel bearings and the lip of a new seal with high-temperature wheel bearing grease.

32. Position the inner wheel bearing in the race and install the seal using a seal installer. Install the rotor on the spindle and install the outer wheel bearing in the race.

33. Install the wheel bearing, locknut, thrust bearing, snapring and locking hubs.

34. Install the caliper and the wheel and tire assemblies. Lower the vehicle.

Aerostar

1. Place the front wheels in the straight ahead position. Raise and safely support the vehicle.

2. Raise and safely support the vehicle. Remove the wheel and tire assembly.

3. Remove the caliper and support it aside with mechanics wire. Do not let the caliper hang by the brake hose. Remove the brake rotor.

4. Remove the cotter pin and nut from the tie rod end stud. Disconnect the tie rod end from the steering knuckle.

5. Support the lower control arm. Remove the cotter pin and loosen the nut retaining the knuckle to the lower control arm ball joint. Disconnect the lower ball joint using tool T64P-3590-F or equivalent. Remove the tool and ball joint retaining nut.

6. With the vehicle body securely supported, pull down on the knuckle until the lower ball joint is disengaged from the steering knuckle.

7. Install hub remover T81P-1104-A with T81P-1104-C and hub knuckle adapters T83P-1104-BH1 and T88P-1104-A1 or equivalents, and free the hub, bearing and knuckle assembly from the halfshaft by pushing in the CV-joint outer shaft until it is loose in the assembly.

8. Remove the bolt and nut retaining the spindle to the upper control arm ball joint. While supporting the halfshaft, remove the knuckle by pulling the knuckle down and out of the upper ball joint and outward away from the halfshaft. Wire the halfshaft to the body to maintain it in a level position.

9. Remove the 3 bolts retaining the hub assembly to the steering knuckle and remove the hub assembly.

NOTE: The hub and bearing assembly is not serviceable. If the bearing requires replacement, it must be replaced as an assembly.

To install:

10. Install the hub assembly into the steering knuckle and tighten the 3 bolts.

11. Position the steering knuckle on the CV-joint outer shaft and into the lower ball joint. Make sure the splines of the CV-joint shaft are in proper mesh in the hub. Install the lower ball joint nut and tighten to 80–120 ft. lbs. (108–163 Nm). If required, continue turning the nut to the next castellation and install the cotter pin.

12. Temporarily install the rotor on the hub with washers and 2 lug nuts. Insert a steel rod into the rotor diameter and rotate clockwise to contact the knuckle.

13. Install the hub nut washer and a new hub nut. Rotate the nut clockwise to seat the CV-joint, but do not final torque at this time.

14. Position the upper control arm ball joint stud to the steering knuckle. Install the nut and bolt and tighten to 27–37 ft. lbs. (37–50 Nm).

15. Connect the tie rod end to the steering knuckle. Firmly seat the tie rod end stud into the tapered hole to prevent rotation while tightening. Install the nut and tighten to 52–74 ft. lbs. (70–100 Nm). If required, continue turning the nut to the next castellation and install the cotter pin.

16. Using a steel rod inserted into the rotor as in Step 12, tighten the hub nut to 170–210 ft. lbs. (230–285 Nm). Remove the wheel nuts and washers.

17. Install the dust shield, caliper, rotor and wheel and tire assembly. Lower the vehicle.

2WD Front Wheel Bearings

ADJUSTMENT

F-150, F-250 and F-350

1. Raise and support the front end on jackstands.

2. Remove the grease cap and remove excess grease from the end of the spindle.

3. Remove the cotter pin and nut lock shown in the illustration.

4. Loosen the adjusting nut 3 full turns. Obtain a clearance between the brake rotor and brake pads by rocking the wheel in and out several times to push the pads away from the rotor. If that doesn't work, remove the caliper. The rotor must turn freely.

5. Tighten the adjusting nut to 17–25 ft. lbs. while rotating the rotor in opposite directions.

6. Back off the adjusting nut 120–180 degrees (⅓–½ turn).

7. Install the retainer and cotter pin without additional movement of the locknut.

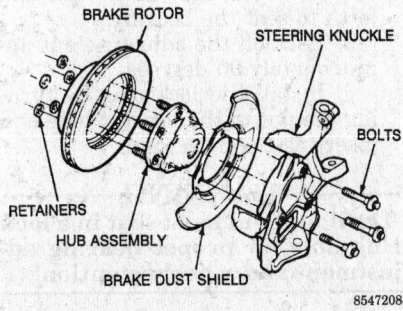

Steering knuckle and hub assembly — 4WD Aerostar

8. If a dial indicator is available, check the end-play at the hub. End-play should be 0.00024–0.0050 in. (0.006–0.127mm).

9. Install the grease cap.

10. If removed, install the caliper.

REMOVAL AND INSTALLATION

F-150, F-250 and F-350

1. Raise and support the front end on jackstands.

2. Remove the wheel cover. Remove the wheel.

3. Remove the caliper from the disc and wire it to the underbody to prevent damage to the brake hose.

4. Remove the grease cap from the hub. Then, remove the cotter pin, nut lock, adjusting nut and flat washer from the spindle. Remove the outer bearing assembly from the hub.

5. Pull the hub and disc assembly off the wheel spindle.

6. Remove and discard the old grease retainer. Remove the inner bearing cone and roller assembly from the hub.

7. Clean all grease from the inner and outer bearing cups with solvent. Inspect the cups for pits, scratches, or excessive wear. If the cups are damaged, remove them with a drift.

8. Clean the inner and outer cone and roller assemblies with solvent and shake them dry. If the cone and roller assemblies show excessive wear or damage, replace them with the bearing cups as a unit.

9. Clean the spindle and the inside of the hub with solvent to thoroughly remove all old grease.

To install:

10. Covering the spindle with a clean cloth, brush all loose dirt and dust from the brake assembly. Remove the cloth carefully so as to not get dirt on the spindle.

11. If the inner and/or outer bearing cups were removed, install the replacement cups on the hub. Be sure the cups seat properly in the hub.

12. It is imperative that all old grease be removed from the bearings and surrounding surfaces before repacking. The new lithium-based grease is not compatible with the sodium base grease used in the past.

13. Install the hub and disc on the wheel spindle. To prevent damage to the grease retainer and spindle threads, keep the hub centered on the spindle.

14. Install the outer bearing cone and roller assembly and the flat washer on the spindle. Install the adjusting nut.

15. Adjust the wheel bearings by torquing the adjusting nut to 17–25 ft. lbs. with the wheel rotating to seat the bearing. Then back off the adjusting nut ½ turn. Retighten the adjusting nut to 10–15 inch lbs. Install the locknut so the castellations are aligned with the cotter pin hole. Install the cotter pin. Bend the ends of the cotter pin around the castellations of the locknut to prevent interference with the radio static collector in the grease cap. Install the grease cap.

—— WARNING ——
New bolts must be used when servicing floating caliper units. The upper bolt must be tightened first.

16. Install the wheels.
17. Install the wheel cover.

4WD Front Wheel Bearings

REMOVAL AND INSTALLATION

Bronco, F Series (Pick-Up) and E Series (Van)

WITH MANUAL LOCKING HUBS

1. Raise the vehicle and install safety stands.
2. Refer to Manual Locking Hub Removal and Installation and remove the hub assemblies.
3. On Bronco, F-150 and F-250 LD with the Dana 44 axle: apply inward pressure on the bearing adjusting nut, using a socket made for that purpose, available at most auto parts stores, to disengage the adjusting nut locking splines, while turning it counterclockwise to remove it. On F-250 HD (Dana 50 axle) and F-350, use the hub nut tool to unscrew the outer locking nut. Then, remove the lock ring from the bearing adjusting nut. Use the locknut socket to remove the bearing adjusting nut.
4. Remove the caliper and suspend it out of the way.
5. Slide the hub and disc assembly off of the spindle. The outer wheel bearing will slide out as the hub is removed, so be prepared to catch it.
6. Lay the hub on a clean work surface. Carefully drive the inner bearing cone and grease seal out of the hub using Tool T69L–1102–A, or equivalent.
7. Inspect the bearing cups for pits or cracks. If necessary, remove them with a drift. If new cups are installed, install new bearings.

To install:
8. Lubricate the bearings with Multi-Purpose Lubricant Ford Specification, ESA–MIC7–B or equivalent. Clean all old grease from the hub. Pack the cones and rollers. If a bearing packer is not available, work as much lubricant as possible between the rollers and the cages.
9. Drive new cups into place with a driver, making sure they are fully seated.
10. Position the inner bearing cone and roller in the inner cup and install the grease retainer.
11. Carefully position the hub and disc assembly on the spindle.
12. Install the outer bearing cone and roller, and the adjusting nut.
13. On Bronco, F-150 and F-250 LD with the Dana 44 axle:
   a. Make sure the metal stamping on the adjusting nut faces inboard and the inner diameter key on the nut enters the spindle keyway.
   b. Apply inward pressure on the hub nut wrench and tighten the adjusting nut to 70 ft. lbs. while rotating the hub back and forth to seat the bearings.
   c. Apply inward pressure on the wrench and back off the nut about 90 degrees then, re-tighten the nut to 15–20 ft. lbs.
   d. Remove the wrench. End-play of the hub/rotor assembly should be 0 (zero) and the torque required to rotate the hub assembly should not exceed 20 inch lbs.
14. Install the outer bearing cone and roller, and the adjusting nut.
15. On the F-250 HD (Dana 50 axle) and F-350:

NOTE: The adjusting nut has a small dowel on one side. This dowel faces outward to engage the locking ring.

   a. Using the hub nut socket and a torque wrench, tighten the bearing adjusting nut to 50 ft. lbs., while rotating the wheel back and forth to seat the bearings.
   b. Back off the adjusting nut approximately 90 degrees.
   c. Install the lock ring by turning the nut to the nearest hole and inserting the dowel pin.

—— WARNING ——
The dowel pin must seat in a lock ring hole for proper bearing adjustment and wheel retention!

   d. Install the outer lock nut and tighten to 160–205 ft. lbs. Final end-play of the wheel on the spin-dle should be 0–0.004 in. (0–0.15mm).
16. Assemble the hub parts.
17. Install the caliper.
18. Remove the safety stands and lower the vehicle.

Bronco, F Series (Pick-Up) and E Series (Van)

WITH AUTOMATIC LOCKING HUBS

1. Raise the vehicle and install safety stands.
2. Refer to Automatic Locking Hub Removal and Installation and remove the hub assemblies.
3. Using a socket made for that purpose, available at most auto parts stores, use the hub nut tool to unscrew the outer locking nut.
4. Remove the lock ring from the bearing adjusting nut.
5. Use the locknut socket to remove the bearing adjusting nut.
6. Remove the caliper and suspend it out of the way.
7. Slide the hub and disc assembly off of the spindle. The outer wheel bearing will slide out as the hub is removed, so be prepared to catch it.
8. Lay the hub on a clean work surface. Carefully drive the inner bearing cone and grease seal out of the hub using Tool T69L–1102–A, or equivalent.
9. Inspect the bearing cups for pits or cracks. If necessary, remove them with a drift. If new cups are installed, install new bearings.

To install:
10. Lubricate the bearings with Multi-Purpose Lubricant Ford Specification, ESA–MIC7–B or equivalent. Clean all old grease from the hub. Pack the cones and rollers. If a bearing packer is not available, work as much lubricant as possible between the rollers and the cages.
11. Drive new cups into place with a driver, making sure they are fully seated.
12. Position the inner bearing cone and roller in the inner cup and install the grease retainer.
13. Carefully position the hub and disc assembly on the spindle.
14. Install the outer bearing cone and roller, and the adjusting nut.

NOTE: The adjusting nut has a small dowel on one side. This dowel faces outward to engage the locking ring.

15. Using the hub nut socket and a torque wrench, tighten the bearing adjusting nut to 50 ft. lbs., while rotating the wheel back and forth to seat the bearings.

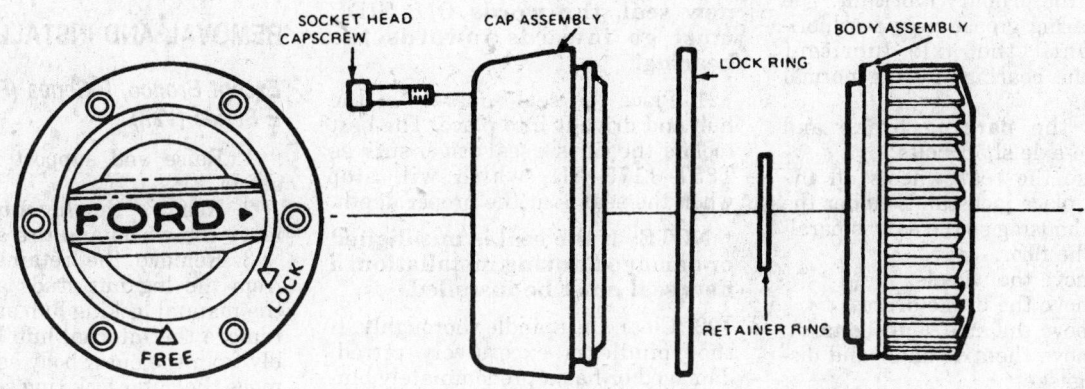

Manual locking hub assembly — Bronco, F Series (Pick-Up) and E Series (Van)

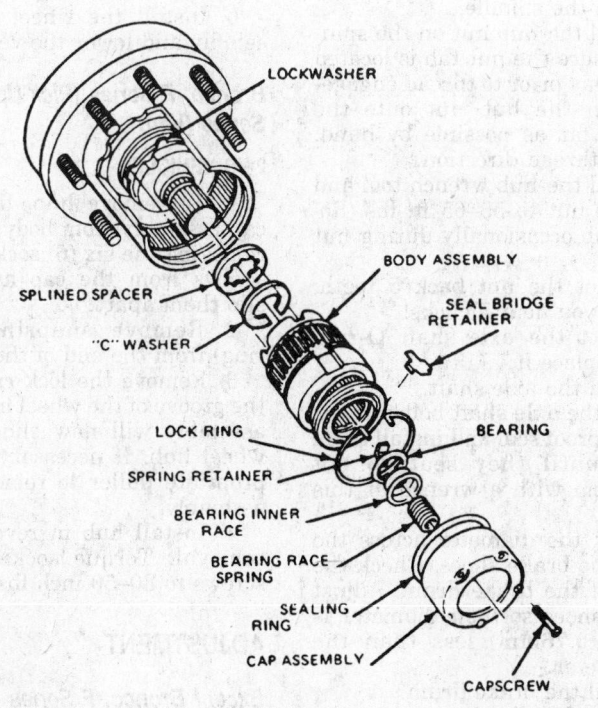

Automatic locking hub assembly — Bronco, F Series (Pick-Up) and E Series (Van)

16. Back off the adjusting nut approximately 90 degrees.

17. Install the lock ring by turning the nut to the nearest hole and inserting the dowel pin.

NOTE: The dowel pin must seat in a lock ring hole for proper bearing adjustment and wheel retention.

18. Install the outer lock nut and tighten to 160–205 ft. lbs. Final end-play of the wheel on the spindle should be 0–0.004 in. (0–0.15mm).

19. Assemble the hub parts.

20. Install the caliper.

21. Remove the safety stands and lower the vehicle.

Full Floating Rear Axle Bearings

REMOVAL AND INSTALLATION

F-250 HD and F-350

The wheel bearings on the Ford 10½ in. full floating rear axle are packed with wheel bearing grease. Axle lubricant can also flow into the wheel hubs and bearings, however, wheel bearing grease is the primary lubricant. The wheel bearing grease provides lubrication until the axle lubri-

cant reaches the bearings during normal operation.

The wheel bearings on the full floating rear axle are packed with wheel bearing grease. Axle lubricant can also flow into the wheel hubs and bearings, however, wheel bearing grease is the primary lubricant. The wheel bearing grease provides lubrication until the axle lubricant reaches the bearings during normal operation.

1. Set the parking brake and loosen the axle shaft bolts.

2. Raise the rear wheels off the floor and place jackstands under the rear axle housing so the axle is parallel with the floor.

3. Remove the wheels.

4. Remove the brake drums.

5. Remove the axle shaft bolts.

6. Remove the axle shaft and discard the gaskets.

7. With the axle shaft removed, remove the gasket from the axle shaft flange studs.

8. Install Hub Wrench T85T–4252–AH, or equivalent, so the drive tangs on the tool engage the slots in the hub nut.

NOTE: The hub nuts are right hand thread on the right hub and left hand thread on the left hub. The hub nuts should be stamped RH and LH. Never use power or impact tools on these nuts! The nuts will ratchet during removal.

9. Remove the hub nut.

10. Install step plate adapter tool D80L–630–7 or equivalent, in the hub.

11. Install puller D80L–1002–L or equivalent, and loosen the hub to the point of removal. Remove the puller and step plate.

12. Remove the hub, taking care to catch the outer bearing as the hub comes off.

13. Install the hub in a soft-jawed vise and pry out the hub seal.

14. Lift out the inner bearing.

15. Drive out the inner and outer bearing races with a drift.

16. Wash all the old grease or axle lubricant out of the wheel hub, using a suitable solvent.

17. Wash the bearing races and rollers and inspect them for pitting, galling, and uneven wear patterns. Inspect the roller for end wear. Replace any bearing and race that appears in any way damaged. Always replace the bearings and races as a set.

To install:

18. Coat the race bores with a light coat of clean, waterproof wheel bearing grease and drive the races

squarely into the bores until they are fully seated.

19. Pack each bearing cone and roller with a bearing packer.

20. Place the inner bearing cone and roller assembly in the wheel hub.

NOTE: When installing the new seal, the words OIL SIDE must go inwards towards the bearing!

21. Place the seal squarely in the hub and drive it into place. The best tool for the job is a seal driver such as T85T–1175–AH, which will stop when the seal is at the proper depth.

NOTE: If the seal is misaligned or damaged during installation, a new seal must be installed.

22. Clean the spindle thoroughly. If the spindle is excessively pitted, damaged or has a predominately bluish tint (from overheating), it must be replaced.

23. Coat the spindle with 80W/90 oil.

24. Pack the hub with clean, waterproof wheel bearing grease.

25. Pack the outer bearing with clean, waterproof wheel bearing grease.

26. Place the outer bearing in the hub and install the hub and bearing together on the spindle.

27. Install the hub nut on the spindle. Make sure the nut tab is located in the keyway prior to thread engagement. Turn the hub nut onto the threads as far as possible by hand, noting the thread direction.

28. Install the hub wrench tool and tighten the nut to 55–65 ft. lbs. Rotate the hub occasionally during nut tightening.

29. Ratchet the nut back 5 teeth; make sure you hear 5 clicks!

30. Inspect the axle shaft O-ring seal and replace it.

31. Install the axle shaft.

32. Coat the axle shaft bolt threads with waterproof seal and install them by hand until they seat;.do not tighten them with a wrench at this time!

33. Check the diameter across the center of the brake shoes. Check the diameter of the brake drum. Adjust the brake shoes so their diameter is 0.030 in. (0.76mm) less than the drum diameter.

34. Install the brake drum

35. Install the wheel.

36. Loosen the differential filler plug. If lubricant starts to run out, retighten the plug. If not, remove the plug and fill the housing with 80W/90 gear oil.

37. Lower the vehicle to the floor.

38. Tighten the wheel lugs to 140 ft. lbs.

39. Now tighten the axle shaft bolts. Torque them to 60–80 ft. lbs.

Manual Locking Hubs

REMOVAL AND INSTALLATION

Except Bronco, F Series (Pick-Up) and E Series (Van)

1. Raise and support the vehicle safely.

2. Remove the lug nuts and remove the wheel and tire assembly.

3. Remove the retainer washers from the lug nut studs and remove the manual locking hub assembly. To remove the internal hub lock assembly from the outer body assembly, remove the outer lock ring seated in the hub body groove. The internal assembly, spring and clutch gear will now slide out of the hub body. Do not remove the screw from the plastic dial.

4. Rebuild the hub assembly in the reverse order of disassembly.

5. Adjust the wheel bearing if necessary. Install the manual locking hub assembly over the spindle and place the retainer washers on the lug nut studs.

6. Install the wheel and tire assembly and lower the vehicle.

Bronco, F Series (Pick-Up) and E Series (Van)

2WD VEHICLES

1. To remove hub, first separate cap assembly from body assembly by removing the six (6) socket head capscrews from the cap assembly and slip them apart.

2. Remove snapring (retainer ring) from the end of the axle shaft.

3. Remove the lock ring seated in the groove of the wheel hub. The body assembly will now slide out of the wheel hub. If necessary, use an appropriate puller to remove the body assembly.

4. Install hub in reverse order of removal. Torque socket head capscrews to 30–50 inch lbs.

ADJUSTMENT

Except Bronco, F Series (Pick-Up) and E Series (Van)

1. Raise and safely support the vehicle. Remove the wheel and tire assembly.

2. Remove the retainer washers from the lug nut studs and remove

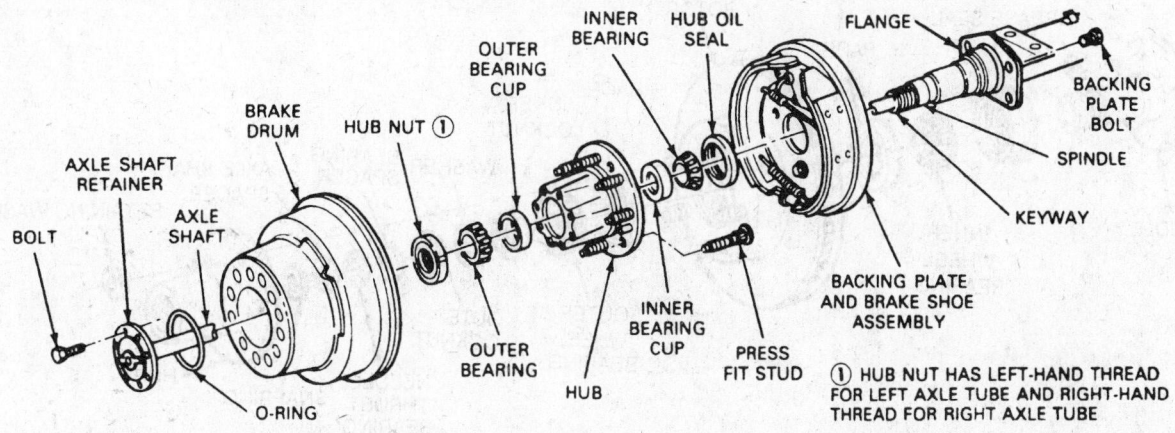

Full-floating axle shaft, bearing and hub assembly — F-250 HD and F-350

85472209

the manual locking hub assembly from the spindle.

3. Remove the snapring from the end of the spindle shaft.

4. On Dana model 28 axles, remove the axle shaft spacer, needle thrust bearing and bearing spacer. On Dana model 35 axles, remove the axle shaft spacer.

5. Remove the outer wheel bearing locknut from the spindle using locknut wrench T86T-1197-A or equivalent. Make sure the tabs on the tool engage the slots in the locknut.

6. Remove the locknut washer from the spindle.

7. Loosen the inner wheel bearing locknut using locknut wrench T86T-1197-A or equivalent. Make sure the tabs on the tool engage the slots in the locknut and the slot in the tool is centered over the locknut pin.

8. Tighten the inner locknut to 35 ft. lbs. (47 Nm) to seat the bearings.

9. Spin the rotor and back off the inner locknut ¼ turn. Retighten the inner locknut to 16 inch lbs. (1.8 Nm). Install the lockwasher on the spindle. It may be necessary to tighten the inner locknut slightly so the pin on the locknut aligns with the closest hole in the lockwasher.

10. Install the outer wheel bearing locknut using locknut wrench T86T-1197-A or equivalent. Tighten the locknut to 150 ft. lbs. (203 Nm).

11. On Dana model 28 axles, install the bearing thrust spacer, needle thrust bearing and axle shaft spacer. On Dana model 35 axles, install the axle shaft spacer.

12. Clip the snapring onto the end of the spindle. Install the manual hub assembly over the spindle and install the retainer washers.

13. Install the wheel and tire assembly. Check the endplay of the wheel and tire assembly on the spindle. Final endplay should be 0–0.003 in. (0–0.08mm). The maximum torque to rotate the hub should be 25 inch lbs. (2.8 Nm).

14. Lower the vehicle.

Automatic Locking Hubs

REMOVAL AND INSTALLATION

Except Bronco, F Series (Pick-Up) and E Series (Van)

1. Raise and support the vehicle safely. Remove the wheel lug nuts and remove the wheel and tire assembly.

2. Remove the retainer washers from the lug nut studs and remove the automatic locking hub assembly from the spindle.

3. Remove the snapring from the end of the spindle shaft.

4. On Dana model 28 axles, remove the axle shaft spacer, needle thrust bearing and the bearing spacer. On Dana model 35 axles, remove the axle shaft spacer.

5. Being careful not to damage the plastic moving cam, pull the cam assembly off the wheel bearing adjusting nut. On Dana model 28 axles, remove the thrust washer and needle thrust bearing from the adjusting nut. On Dana model 35 axles, remove the 2 plastic thrust spacers from the adjusting nut.

6. Using a magnet, remove the locking key. It may be necessary to rotate the adjusting nut slightly to relieve the pressure against the locking key, before the key can be removed.

NOTE: To prevent damage to the spindle threads, look into the spindle keyway under the adjusting nut and remove the separate locking key before removing the adjusting nut.

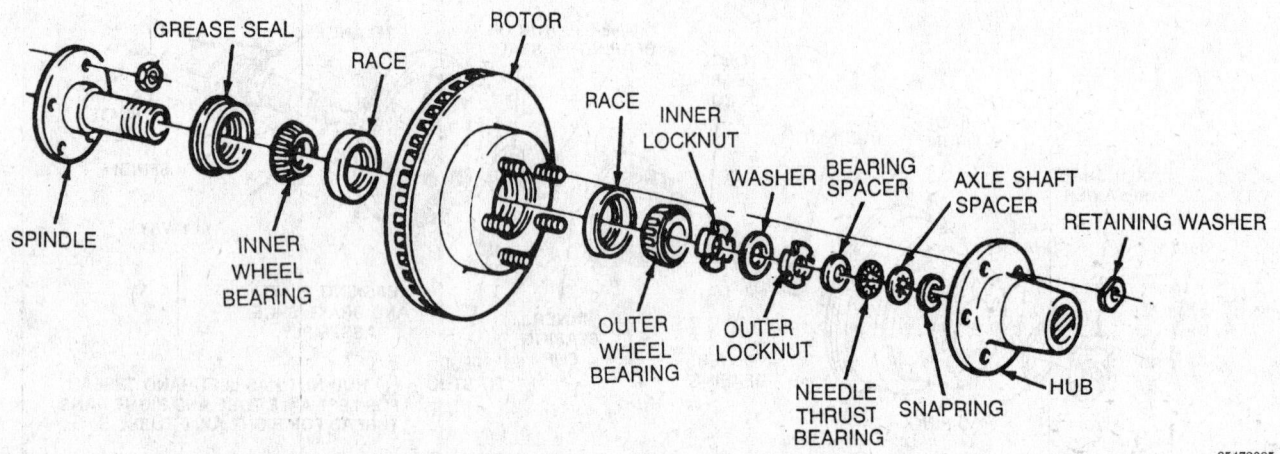

Manual locking hub assembly — Dana model 28 axle, model 35 similar

85472085

7. Loosen the wheel bearing adjusting nut from the spindle using a 2⅜ in. hex socket tool.

8. While rotating the hub and rotor assembly, tighten the wheel bearing adjusting nut to 35 ft. lbs. (47 Nm) to seat the bearings. Spin the rotor and back off the nut ¼ turn.

9. Retighten the adjusting nut to 16 inch lbs. (1.8 Nm) using a torque wrench. Align the closest hole in the wheel bearing adjusting nut with the center of the spindle keyway slot. Advance the nut to the next lug if required. Install the separate locking key in the spindle keyway under the adjusting nut.

NOTE: Extreme care must be taken when aligning the spindle nut adjustment lug with the center of the spindle keyway slot to prevent damage to the separate locking key.

10. On Dana model 28 axles, install the locknut needle bearing and thrust washer in the reverse order of removal. On Dana model 35 axles, install the 2 thrust spacers. Push or press the cam assembly onto the

locknut by lining up the key in the fixed cam with the spindle keyway.

NOTE: Extreme care must be taken when aligning the fixed cam key with the spindle keyway to prevent damage to the fixed cam.

11. On Dana model 28 axles, install the bearing thrust washer, needle thrust bearing and axle shaft spacer. On Dana model 35 axles, install the axle shaft spacer.

12. Clip the snapring onto the end of the spindle.

13. Install the automatic locking hub assembly over the spindle by lining up the 3 legs in the hub assembly with the 3 pockets in the cam assembly. Install the retainer washers.

14. Install the wheel and tire assembly. Check the endplay of the wheel and tire assembly on the spindle. Final endplay should be 0–0.003 in. (0–0.08mm). The maximum torque to rotate the hub should be 25 inch lbs. (2.8 Nm).

15. Lower the vehicle.

Bronco, F Series (Pick-Up) and E Series (Van)

2WD VEHICLES

1. Remove the 5 capscrews — Torx® bit TX25 — and remove hub cap assembly from the hub.

NOTE: Take care to avoid dropping the spring, ball bearing, bearing race or retainer!

2. Remove the rubber seal.
3. Remove the seal bridge — a small metal stamping — from the retainer ring space.
4. Remove lock ring seated in the groove of the wheel hub by compressing the ends with a needle nose pliers, while pulling the hub lock from the hub body. If body assembly does not slide out easily, use an appropriate puller.
5. If the hub and spindle are being removed:
   a. Remove the C-washer from the groove in the stub shaft.
   b. Remove the splined spacer from the shaft.
   c. Remove the outer locknut, locking washer and inner bearing locknut.
   d. Pull the hub and bearings from the spindle.

To install:

6. Position the hub and bearings on the spindle. Adjust the bearings as described below.

7. Install the splined spacer and C-washer.

8. Wipe off excess grease from the splines and start the locking hub assembly into the hub body. Make sure the large tangs are aligned with the lockwasher and the outside diameter, and the inside diameter splines are aligned with the hub and axle shaft splines.

9. Install the retaining ring while pushing the locking hub assembly into the hub body.

10. Install the seal bridge, narrow end first.

11. Install the rubber seal.

12. Install the cover, making sure the ball bearing, spring and race are in position.

13. Install the 5 Torx® screws and tighten them to 40–50 inch lbs. by tighten one, then skipping one, and so on until they are all tightened.

Steering Knuckle and Ball Joints

REMOVAL AND INSTALLATION

Independent Front Axles

1. Raise and support the vehicle safely.

2. Remove the spindles and left and right shafts and joint.

3. Remove the tie rod nut and disconnect the tie rod from the steering arm.

4. Remove the cotter pin from the top ball joint stud. Remove the nut from the top stud and loosen the nut on the lower stud inside the knuckle.

5. Hit the top stud sharply with a plastic mallet to free the knuckle from the axle arm. Remove and discard the bottom nut. New nuts should be used at assembly.

6. Note the positioning of the camber adjuster carefully for reassembly. Remove the camber adjuster. If it's hard to remove, use a puller.

7. Place the knuckle in a vise and remove the snapring from the bottom ball joint. Not all ball joints will have this snapring.

8. Remove the plug from C-frame tool T74P–4635–C and replace it with plug T80T–3010–A. Assemble C-frame tool T74P–4635–C and receiving cup D79T–3010–G (Bronco, F-150 and 250) or T80T–3010–A2 (F-250HD and F-350). on the knuckle.

9. Turn the forcing screw inward until the ball joint is separated from the knuckle.

10. Assemble the C-frame tool with receiving cup D79P–3010–BG on the upper ball joint and force it out of the knuckle.

NOTE: Always force out the bottom ball joint first.

11. Clean the ball joint bores thoroughly.

12. Insert the lower joint into its bore as straight as possible.

13. On the Bronco, F-150 and F-250, assemble the C-frame tool, receiving cup T80T–3010–A3 and installing cup D79T–3010–BF onto the lower ball joint. On the F-250HD and F-350, assemble the C-frame tool, receiving cup T80T–3010–A3 and receiving cup D79T–3010–BG on the lower ball joint.

14. Turn the screw clockwise until the ball joint is firmly seated.

NOTE: If the ball joint cannot be installed to the correct depth, realign the receiving cup on the tool.

15. On all models, assemble the C-frame, receiving cup T80T–3010–A3 and replacer T80T–3010–A1 on the upper ball joint.

16. Turn the screw clockwise until the ball joint is firmly seated.

17. Place the knuckle into position on the axle arm. Install the camber adjuster on the upper ball joint stud with the arrow point to positive or negative as noted before disassembly.

18. Install a new nut on the bottom stud, finger tight. Install a new nut on the top stud finger tight.

19. Tighten the bottom nut to 80 ft. lbs.

20. Tighten the top nut to 100 ft. lbs., then, (tighten) advance the nut until the cotter pin hole align with the castellations. Install a new cotter pin.

21. Again tighten the bottom nut, this time to 110 ft. lbs.

22. Install all other parts.

Steering Knuckle and Kingpins

REMOVAL AND INSTALLATION

Monobeam Front Axle

NOTE: For this job use a torque wrench with a capacity of at least 600 ft. lbs.

1. Raise and support the vehicle safely.

2. Remove the axle shafts.

3. Alternately and evenly remove the 4 bolts that retain the spindle cap to the knuckle. This will relieve spring tension.

4. When spring tension is relieved, remove the bolts.

5. Remove the spindle cap, compression spring and retainer. Discard the gasket.

6. Remove the 4 bolts securing the lower kingpin and retainer to the knuckle. Remove the lower kingpin and retainer.

7. Remove the tapered bushing from the top of the upper kingpin.

8. Remove the knuckle from the axle yoke.

9. Remove the upper kingpin from the axle yoke with a piece of ⁷⁄₈ in. hex-shaped case hardened metal bar stock, or, with a ⁷⁄₈ in. hex socket. Discard the upper kingpin and seal.

NOTE: The upper kingpin is tightened to 500–600 ft. lbs.

10. Using a 2-jawed puller and step plate, press out the lower kingpin grease retainer, bearing cup, bearing and seal from the axle yoke lower bore. Discard the grease seal and retainer, and the lower bearing cup.

To install:

11. Coat the mating surfaces of a new lower kingpin grease retainer with RTV silicone sealer.

12. Install the retainer in the axle yoke bore so the concave portion of the retainer faces the upper kingpin.

13. Using a bearing driver, drive a new bearing cup in the lower kingpin bore until it bottoms against the grease retainer.

14. Pack the lower kingpin bearing and the yoke bore with waterproof wheel bearing grease.

15. Using a driver, drive a new seal into the lower kingpin bore.

16. Install a new seal and upper kingpin into the yoke using tool T86T–3110–AH. Tighten the kingpin to 500–600 ft. lbs.

17. Install the knuckle on the yoke.

18. Place the tapered bushing over the upper kingpin in the knuckle bore.

19. Place the lower kingpin and retainer in the knuckle and axle yoke. Install the 4 bolts and tighten them, alternately and evenly, to 90 ft. lbs.

20. Place the retainer and compression spring on the tapered bushing.

21. Install a new gasket on the knuckle. Position the spindle cap on the gasket and knuckle. Install the 4 bolts and tighten them, alternately and evenly, to 90 ft. lbs.

22. Install the axle shafts and lubricate the upper kingpin through

Spindle and Left Shaft and Joint Installation — Typical

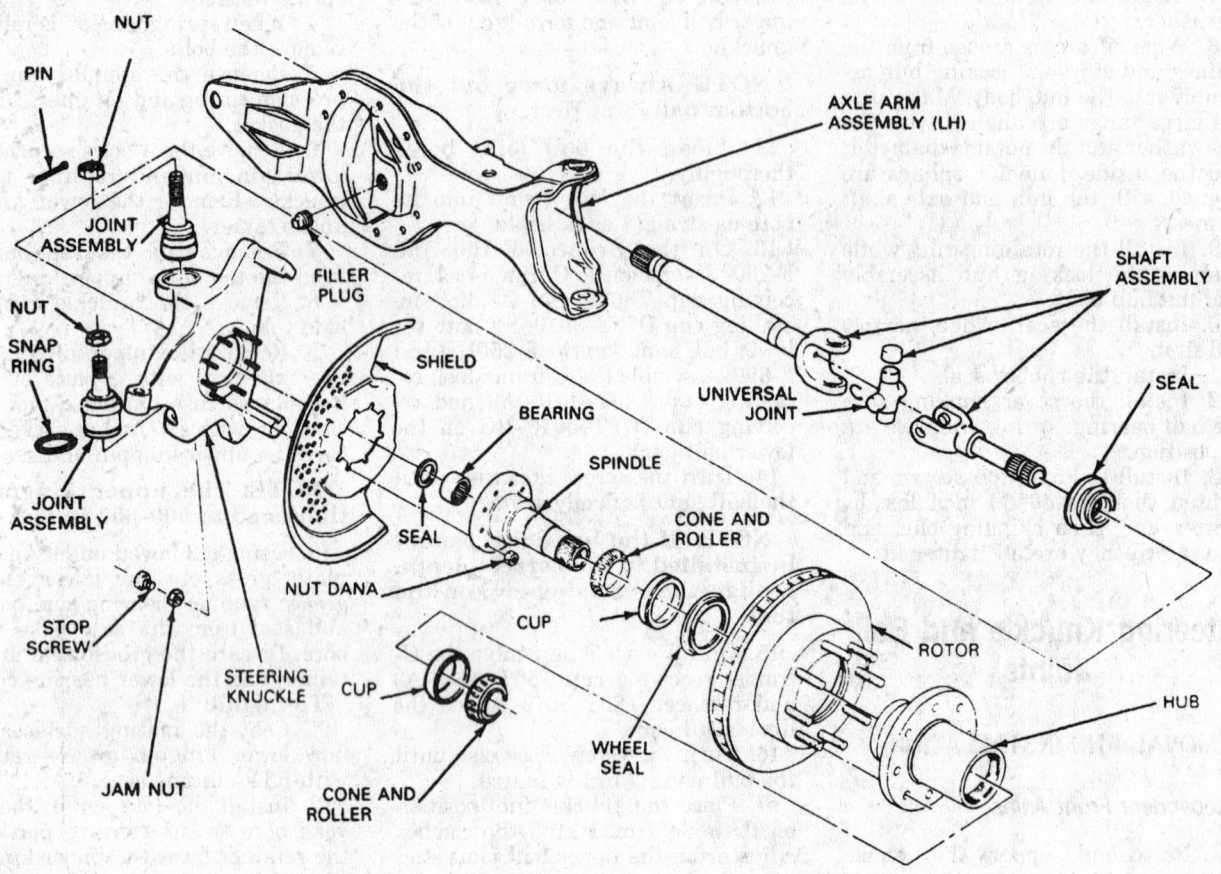

Right Hand Shaft and Joint Assembly Installation — Typical

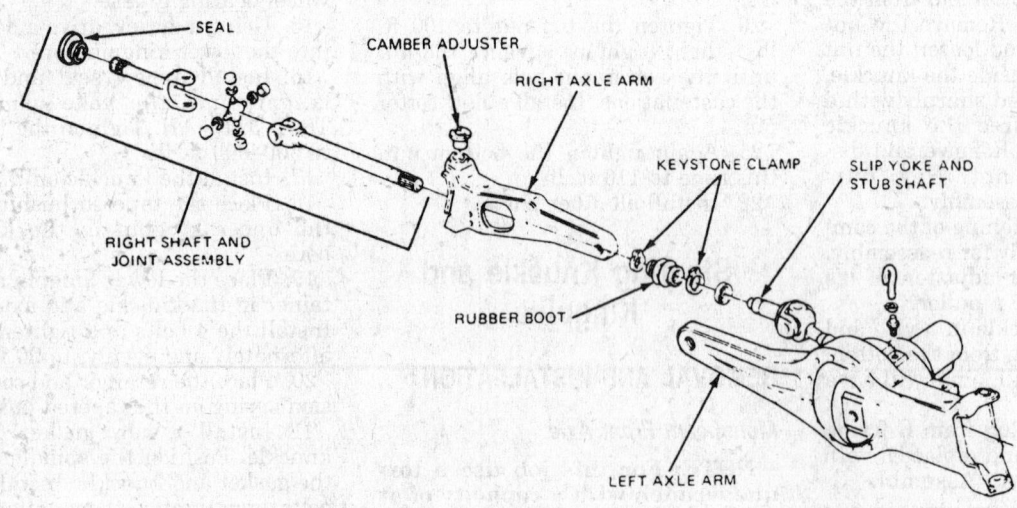

85472207

Dana models 44 and 50 axle shaft and joint assemblies — Bronco, F Series (Pick-Up) and E Series (Van)

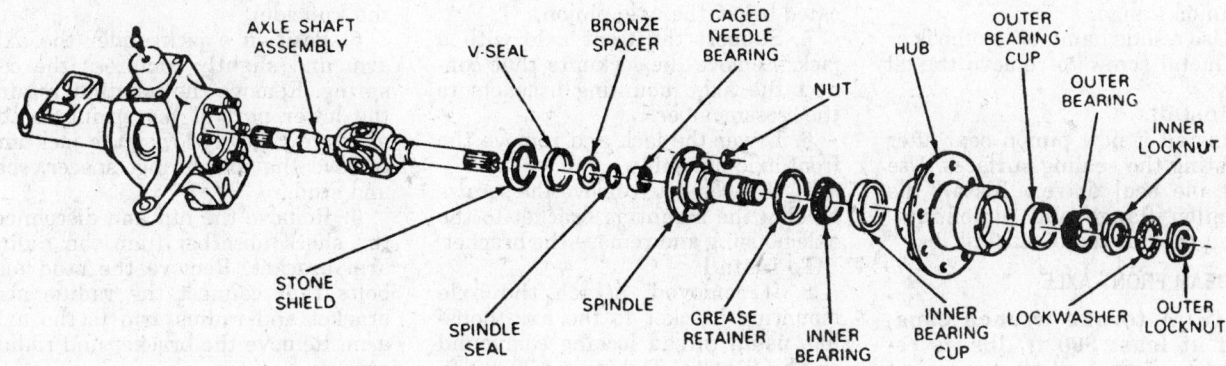

Dana model 60 Monobeam front drive axle assembly — Bronco, F Series (Pick-Up) and E Series (Van)

85472206

the zerk fitting and the lower fitting through the flush fitting. The lower fitting may be lubricated with Alemite adapter #6783, or equivalent.

Pinion Seal

REMOVAL AND INSTALLATION

Except Bronco, F Series (Pick-Up) and E Series (Van)

NOTE: This service procedure disturbs the pinion bearing preload and this preload must be carefully reset when assembling.

1. Raise the vehicle and support it safely.
2. Remove the wheels and the brake drums.
3. Mark the driveshaft and the axle companion flange so the driveshaft can be reinstalled in the same position. Remove the driveshaft.
4. Using an inch pound torque wrench on the pinion nut, record the torque required to maintain rotation of the pinion through several revolutions.
5. While holding the companion flange with a suitable tool, remove

the pinion nut. Mark the companion flange in relation to the pinion shaft so the flange can be reinstalled in the same position.
6. Using a suitable puller, remove the rear axle companion flange. Use a small prybar to remove the seal from the carrier.

To install:

7. Make sure the splines of the pinion shaft are free of burrs.
8. Apply grease to the lips of the pinion seal and install, using a seal installer.
9. Check the seal surface of the companion flange for scratches, nicks or a groove. Replace the companion flange, as necessary. Apply a small amount of lubricant to the splines. Align the mark on the flange with the mark on the pinion shaft and install the companion flange.

NOTE: The companion flange must never be hammered on or installed with power tools.

10. Install a new nut on the pinion shaft. Hold the companion flange with a suitable tool while tightening the nut.
11. Tighten the pinion nut, rotating the pinion occasionally to ensure proper bearing seating. Take frequent pinion bearing torque preload readings until the original recorded

preload reading is obtained or the following specification:
Ford 7.5 in. and 8.8 in. rear axles — 8–14 inch lbs.
Dana model 30 axle rear axles — 20–40 inch lbs.
Dana model 35-1A rear axles — 15–35 inch lbs.
Dana models 28 and Model 35 front axles — 15–25 inch lbs.
Dana model 28-2 front axles (4WD Aerostar) — 15–35 inch lbs.

NOTE: Under no circumstances should the pinion nut be backed off to reduce preload. If reduced preload is required, a new collapsible pinion spacer and pinion nut must be installed.

12. Install the driveshaft and check the fluid level in the carrier. Lower the vehicle.

Bronco, F Series (Pick-Up) and E Series (Van)

INDEPENDENT FRONT AXLE

NOTE: A torque wrench capable of at least 225 ft. lbs. is required for pinion seal installation.

1. Raise and safely support the vehicle with jackstands under the frame rails. Allow the axle to drop to

rebound position for working clearance.

2. Mark the companion flanges and U-joints for correct reinstallation position.

3. Remove the driveshaft. Use a suitable tool to hold the companion flange. Remove the pinion nut and companion flange.

4. Use a slide hammer and hook or sheet metal screw to remove the oil seal.

To install:

5. Install a new pinion seal after lubricating the sealing surfaces. Use a suitable seal driver. Install the companion flange and pinion nut. Tighten the nut to 200–220 ft. lbs.

MONOBEAM FRONT AXLE

NOTE: A torque wrench capable of at least 300 ft. lbs. is required for pinion seal installation.

1. Raise and support the vehicle safely.

2. Allow the axle to hang freely.

3. Matchmark and disconnect the driveshaft from the front axle.

4. Using a tool such as T75T–4851–B, or equivalent, hold the pinion flange while removing the pinion nut.

5. Using a puller, remove the pinion flange.

6. Use a puller to remove the seal, or punch the seal out using a pin punch.

To install:

7. Thoroughly clean the seal bore and make sure it is not damaged in any way. Coat the sealing edge of the new seal with a small amount of 80W/90 oil and drive the seal into the housing using a seal driver.

8. Coat the inside of the pinion flange with clean 80W/90 oil and install the flange onto the pinion shaft.

9. Install the nut on the pinion shaft and tighten it to 250–300 ft. lbs.

10. Connect the driveshaft.

Axle Housing

REMOVAL AND INSTALLATION

Front Axle

AEROSTAR

Raise and safely support the vehicle.

1. Mark the driveshaft and axle flanges so they can be reassembled in their original positions. Disconnect the driveshaft from the companion flange.

2. Remove the bolts that connect the inboard halfshaft flanges to the axle shafts. Wire the halfshafts to the body in a level position.

3. Remove the vent hose from the vent fitting on the axle tube and cap the fitting to prevent any fluid leakage.

4. Remove the snubber from the crossmember rear lateral support, located below the axle pinion.

5. Support the front axle with a jack. Remove the locknuts that connect the axle mounting brackets to the crossmember.

6. Lower the jack and remove the front axle assembly.

7. If necessary, remove the screws holding the mounting bracket to the axle housing and remove the bracket.

To install:

8. If removed, attach the axle mounting bracket to the axle housing, using thread locking compound on the 2 bolts. Tighten to 70–80 ft. lbs. (95–108 Nm).

9. Raise the axle into position. Insert the axle mounting bushing studs through the axle mounting bracket. Install the locknuts using thread locking compound and tighten to 65–85 ft. lbs. (88–115 Nm). Tighten in the following order: left front, right front, pinion, rear.

NOTE: When installing the axle assembly with new mounting bushings, each nut must be tightened to full torque in 1 step to avoid coring of the locking patch on the stud, before the nut is fully torqued.

10. Attach the vent hose to the vent fitting on the axle tube. Make sure the hose is not kinked.

11. Position the inboard halfshaft flanges to the axle shaft flanges, aligning the marks that were made during removal. Install the bolts and tighten to 22–29 ft. lbs. (30–40 Nm). Remove the wire that was supporting the halfshafts.

12. Position the front driveshaft flange to the front axle flange, aligning the marks that were made during removal. Install the bolts and tighten to 22–29 ft. lbs. (30–40 Nm).

13. Install the axle snubber on the crossmember just below the axle pinion. Tighten to 17–24 ft. lbs. (23–33 Nm).

14. Lower the vehicle.

BRONCO II AND RANGER

1. Raise the vehicle and support it safely under the radius arm brackets.

2. Mark the front axle yoke and the driveshaft so they can be reassembled in the same position. Disconnect the driveshaft from the front axle yoke.

3. Remove the front wheel and tire assemblies. Remove the disc brake calipers and support them on a frame rail. Do not let the calipers hang by the brake hoses.

4. Remove the cotter pin and nut retaining the steering linkage to the knuckle. Disconnect the linkage from the knuckle.

5. Position a jack under the axle arm and slightly compress the coil spring. Remove the nut that retains the lower part of the spring to the axle arm. Slowly lower the jack and remove the coil spring, spacer, seat and stud.

6. Remove the nut and disconnect the shock absorber from the radius arm bracket. Remove the stud and bolts that connect the radius arm bracket and radius arm to the axle arm. Remove the bracket and radius arm.

7. Remove the pivot bolt that secures the right axle arm assembly to the crossmember.

8. Remove the clamps securing the axle shaft boot from the axle shaft slip yoke and axle shaft. Disconnect the outer axle shaft from the slip yoke assembly. Lower the jack and remove the right axle arm assembly.

9. Position another jack under the differential housing. Remove the bolt that connects the left axle arm to the crossmember. Lower the jacks and remove the left axle arm assembly.

To install:

10. Position a jack under the left support arm and raise the arm into position in the pivot bracket. Install the nut and bolt and tighten to 120–150 ft. lbs. (163–203 Nm). Do not remove the jack from under the differential housing at this time.

11. Place new clamps for the axle shaft boot on the axle shaft assembly. Position the right support arm on a jack and raise it so the right outer axle shaft slides onto the slip yoke and the support arm is in position in the right pivot bracket. Install the nut and bolt and tighten to 120–150 ft. lbs. (163–203 Nm). Do not remove the jack from the right support arm at this time.

NOTE: When installing the outer axle shaft into the inner slip yoke on Dana model 35 axles, the yoke ears must be in alignment with each other to assure proper phasing.

12. Position the radius arm and front bracket on the support arms. Install a new stud and nut on the top of the axle and radius arm assembly and tighten to 190–230 ft. lbs. (258–311 Nm). Install the bolts in the

front of the bracket and tighten to 27–37 ft. lbs. (37–50 Nm).

13. Install the seat, spacer retainer and coil spring on the stud and nut. Raise the jack to compress the coil spring. Install the nut and tighten to 70–100 ft. lbs. (95–135 Nm).

14. Connect the shock absorber to the support arm assembly. Install the nut and tighten to 42–72 ft. lbs. (57–97 Nm).

15. Connect the tie rod ball joint to the knuckle. Install the nut and tighten to 50–75 ft. lbs. (68–101 Nm). Lower the jacks from the support arms.

16. Install the brake calipers and the wheel and tire assemblies.

17. Connect the driveshaft to the front axle yoke, aligning the marks that were made during removal. Install the U-bolts and tighten the nuts to 8–15 ft. lbs. (11–20 Nm).

18. Lower the vehicle.

EXPLORER

1. Raise and safely support the vehicle. Remove the front axle shaft and spindle assemblies.

2. Mark the front axle yoke and the driveshaft so they can be reassembled in the same position. Disconnect the driveshaft from the front axle yoke.

3. Remove the cotter pin and nut retaining the steering linkage to the knuckle. Disconnect the linkage from the knuckle.

4. Remove the left stabilizer bar link lower bolt and remove the link from the radius arm bracket.

5. Position a jack under the left axle arm and slightly compress the coil spring. Remove the shock absorber lower nut and disconnect the shock absorber from the radius arm bracket.

6. Remove the nut that retains the lower part of the spring to the axle arm. Slowly lower the jack and remove the coil spring, spacer, seat and stud.

7. Remove the stud and bolts that connect the radius arm bracket and radius arm to the axle arm. Remove the bracket and radius arm.

8. Position another jack under the differential housing. Remove the bolt that connects the left axle arm to the axle pivot bracket. Lower the jacks and remove the left axle arm assembly.

To install:

9. Position a jack under the left support arm and raise the arm into position in the pivot bracket. Install the nut and bolt and tighten to 120–150 ft. lbs. (163–203 Nm). Do not

remove the jack from under the differential housing at this time.

10. Position the radius arm and front bracket on the left axle arm. Install a new stud and nut on the top of the axle and radius arm assembly and tighten to 190–230 ft. lbs. (258–311 Nm). Install the bolts in the front of the bracket and tighten to 27–37 ft. lbs. (37–50 Nm).

11. Install the seat, spacer retainer and coil spring on the stud and nut. Raise the jack to compress the coil spring. Install the nut and tighten to 70–100 ft. lbs. (95–135 Nm).

12. Connect the shock absorber to the radius arm. Install the nut and tighten to 42–72 ft. lbs. (57–97 Nm).

13. Connect the tie rod ball joint to the knuckle. Install the nut and tighten to 50–75 ft. lbs. (68–101 Nm). Install the stabilizer bar mounting bracket and tighten to 203–240 ft. lbs. (275–325 Nm).

14. Connect the front driveshaft to the front axle yoke, aligning the marks that were made during removal. Install the U-bolts and tighten the nuts to 8–15 ft. lbs. (11–20 Nm).

15. Install the spindle and axle shaft assemblies. Lower the vehicle.

Rear Axle

AEROSTAR

1. Raise and safely support the vehicle.

2. Release the parking brake cable tension by pulling rearward on the front cable approximately 2 in. Clamp the cable behind the crossmember to release the tension on the rear parking brake cables.

3. Remove the parking brake cables from the equalizer. Compress the tabs on the retainers and pull the cables through the rear crossmember.

4. Mark the driveshaft to the rear axle so they can be reassembled in the same position. Remove the driveshaft. Remove the wheel and tire assemblies.

5. Disconnect the brake hose from the chassis brake line. Plug the line to prevent fluid loss.

6. Disconnect the shock absorbers from the lower control arm. Disconnect the axle vent tube from the clip on the frame.

7. Lower the axle until the springs are no longer under compression. Remove the spring retainers and the coil springs.

8. Raise the axle to the normal load position and disconnect the control arms at the axle.

9. Remove the bolt and nut retaining the upper control arm to the rear axle. Remove the upper control arm from the axle. Mark the position of the cam adjuster in the axle bushing.

10. Lower the axle from the vehicle.

To install:

11. Raise the axle into position.

12. Position the upper control arm over the cam adjuster and bushing. Make sure the marks scribed on the bushing and adjuster are still in alignment. Install the bolt, nut and retainer and tighten until snug. Do not final torque at this time.

13. Lower the axle to the spring unloaded position. Place the lower insulator on the control arm and the upper insulator on top of the spring. The white colored tapered coil must face upward. Install the spring in position on the control arm and axle.

14. Install the lower retainer and nut and tighten to 41–64 ft. lbs. (55–88 Nm). Install the upper retainer and bolt and tighten to 30–40 ft. lbs. (40–55 Nm).

15. Raise the axle to the normal load position and tighten the bolt and nut retaining the lower control arm to the axle to 100–129 ft. lbs. (133–176 Nm).

16. Connect the shock absorbers to the lower control arm. Install the shock bolt nut on the inside of the lower control arm bracket. Install the nut and tighten to 40–60 ft. lbs. (54–82 Nm).

17. Attach the brake hose to the frame and chassis brake line. Connect the axle vent hose, if equipped.

18. Install the wheel and tire assemblies. Install the driveshaft, aligning the marks that were made during removal.

19. Pull the parking brake cables and retainers through the clips on the vehicle underbody side rails and through the rear crossmember. Connect the brake cables to the equalizer. Unclamp the front parking brake cable to restore cable tension.

20. Bleed the brake system and lower the vehicle.

BRONCO II AND RANGER

1. Raise the vehicle and support it safely.

2. Remove the cover and drain the lubricant from the axle.

3. Remove the rear wheel and tire assemblies and remove the axle shafts.

4. Remove the 4 retaining nuts from each backing plate. Wire the backing plates to the underbody.

5. Disconnect the vent hose from the axle housing.

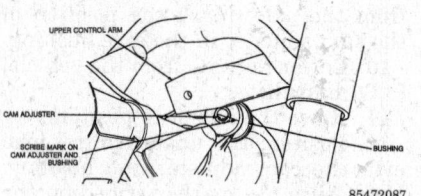

Rear axle housing removal — Aerostar

6. Remove the brake line from the clips that retain the line to the axle housing.

7. Remove the hydraulic brake T-fitting from the axle housing. Do not open the hydraulic brake system lines.

8. Mark the driveshaft and the axle companion flange so they can be reassembled in the same position. Remove the driveshaft.

9. Support the rear axle housing on a jack, then remove the spring clip U-bolt nuts. Remove the U-bolts and plates.

10. Disconnect the lower shock absorber studs or bolts from the mounting brackets on the axle housing. Lower the axle housing and remove it from under the vehicle.

To install:

11. Raise the axle housing into position so the spring clip U-bolt plates can be installed. Tighten the spring clip U-bolt nuts to 55–75 ft. lbs. (70–101 Nm).

12. Connect the lower shock absorber studs or bolts to the axle housing mounting bracket. Tighten the nut/bolt to 40–60 ft. lbs. (54–82 Nm).

13. Position the brake lines to the axle housing and secure with the retaining clips. Install the T-fitting.

14. Install the brake backing plates on the axle housing flanges. Tighten the nuts to 20–40 ft. lbs. (28–54 Nm).

15. Apply stud and bearing mount compound to the threads on the vent. Install the vent and vent tube.

16. Install the axle shafts, brake drums and wheel and tire assemblies.

17. Install the driveshaft, aligning the marks that were made during removal.

18. Clean all old sealer from the carrier and cover surfaces. Apply a bead of RTV sealer $1/8$–$1/4$ in. wide. The bead should be continuous and should not pass through or outside the holes.

19. Install the cover and tighten the bolts to 15–20 ft. lbs. (21–27 Nm) if equipped with a plastic cover or 25–35 ft. lbs. (34–37 Nm) if equipped with a steel cover.

20. Add the proper type of rear axle lubricant until the level is $1/4$–$1/9$ in. below the bottom of the filler hole with the axle in running position.

21. Lower the vehicle.

EXPLORER

1. Raise the vehicle and support it safely.

2. Remove the cover and drain the lubricant from the axle.

3. Remove the rear wheel and tire assemblies and remove the rear anti-lock brake system sensor. Remove the axle shafts.

4. Remove the 4 retaining nuts from each backing plate. Wire the backing plates to the underbody.

5. Disconnect the vent hose from the axle housing. Remove the connector from the rear anti-lock sensor.

6. Remove the brake line from the clips that retain the line to the axle housing.

7. Remove the hydraulic brake junction block from the axle housing. Do not open the hydraulic brake system lines.

8. Mark the driveshaft and the axle companion flange so they can be reassembled in the same position. Remove the driveshaft.

9. Support the rear axle housing on a jack, then remove the axle housing U-bolt nuts. Remove the U-bolts and shock absorber plates. Leave the shock absorbers attached to the plates.

10. Remove the stabilizer bar attaching bracket bolts from the axle housing and position the stabilizer bar assembly away from the axle housing.

11. Raise the axle housing off the springs with the jack and move to the right side of the vehicle. Lower the left side of the axle housing below the left spring enough to clear the spring.

12. Remove the axle housing from the vehicle by lowering the axle and moving to the left until the right axle tube clears the right spring.

To install:

13. Install the axle housing on the transmission jack. Guide the right side of the axle housing over the right spring. Lift the left side of the axle housing over the left spring and position the axle housing on the spring center bolt.

14. Install the stabilizer bar to the axle housing. Tighten the stabilizer bar bracket bolts to 30–42 ft. lbs. (40–57 Nm).

15. Install the axle housing U-bolts over the axle tube. Position the shock absorber plates under the springs and install the U-bolts through the holes. Install the nuts and tighten to 88–108 ft. lbs. (119–146 Nm).

16. Install the axle vent tube to the axle vent fitting and secure with a clamp. Connect the rear anti-lock sensor connector.

17. Install the brake backing plates on the axle housing flanges. Tighten the nuts to 20–40 ft. lbs. (28–54 Nm).

18. Position the brake lines to the axle housing and secure with the retaining clips. Position the brake junction block to the axle housing and install the retaining screw.

19. Install the axle shafts. Install the driveshaft, aligning the marks that were made during removal. Tighten the attaching bolts to 70–95 ft. lbs. (95–128 Nm).

20. Install the brake drums and the wheel and tire assemblies.

21. Clean all old sealer from the carrier surface. Apply a bead of RTV sealer $1/8$–$1/4$ in. wide. The bead should be continuous and should not pass through or outside the holes.

22. Install a new cover and tighten the bolts to 15–20 ft. lbs. (21–27 Nm) in a criss-cross pattern.

23. Add the proper type of lubricant through the filler hole until the lubricant level is $1/4$–$9/16$ in. below the bottom of the filler hole with the axle in the running position.

24. Lower the vehicle.

Bronco, F Series (Pick-Up) and E Series (Van)

INDEPENDENT FRONT AXLES

1. Raise and support the vehicle safely; place a support under the radius arms.

2. Remove the wheels.

3. Remove the calipers and wire them out of the way. Don't disconnect the brake lines.

4. Support the axle arm with a jack and remove the upper coil spring retainers.

5. Lower the jack and remove the coil springs, spring cushions and lower spring seats.

6. Disconnect the shock absorbers at the radius arms and upper mounting brackets.

7. Remove the studs and spring seats at the radius arms and axle arms.

8. Remove the bolts securing the upper attachment to the axle arm and the lower attachment to the axle arm.

9. Disconnect the vent tube at the housing. Remove the vent fitting and install a ⅛ in. pipe plug.

10. Remove the pivot bolt securing the right side axle arm to the crossmember. Remove and discard the boot clamps and remove the boot from the shaft. Remove the right drive axle assembly and pull the axle shaft from the slip shaft.

11. Support the housing with a floor jack. Remove the bolt securing the left side axle assembly to the crossmember. Remove the left side drive axle assembly.

To install:

12. Installation is, basically, a reversal of the removal procedure. Always use new boot clamps. Observe the following torques:

Left and right drive axles-to-crossmember — 120–150 ft. lbs.

Axle arm-to-radius arm — 180–240 ft. lbs.

Coil spring insulator — 30–70 ft. lbs.

Upper spring retainer — 13–18 ft. lbs.

MONOBEAM AXLE

1. Raise and support the vehicle safely; place a support under the frame.

2. Remove the wheels.

3. Remove the calipers and wire them out of the way. Don't disconnect the brake lines.

4. Disconnect the stabilizer links at the stabilizer bar.

5. Remove the U-bolts securing the stabilizer bar and mounting brackets to the axle.

6. Remove the cotter pins and nuts securing the spindle connecting rod to the steering knuckles. Separate the connecting rod to the steering knuckles. Separate the connecting rods from the knuckles with a pitman arm puller. Wire the steering linkage to the spring.

7. Matchmark and disconnect the driveshaft from the front axle.

8. Disconnect the vent tube at the axle and plug the fitting.

9. On the right side, disconnect the track bar from the right spring cap.

10. Raise the vehicle and place a support under front springs at a point about half way between the axle and spring rear hanger. Remove the support from the front of the frame and lower the vehicle onto the stands under the springs. Make sure the vehicle is securely supported.

11. Support the axle with a floor jack.

12. Remove the U-bolts securing the springs to the axle.

13. Lower the axle from the vehicle.

To install:

14. Installation is the reverse of removal. Observe the following torques:

Driveshaft-to-flange — 15–20 ft. lbs.

Track bar nut and bolt — 160–200 ft. lbs.

Stabilizer link nut — 20–30 ft. lbs.

Stabilizer bar U-bolt — 50–65 ft. lbs.

Spindle connecting rod-to-knuckle — 70–100 ft. lbs.

Front spring U-bolts — 85–100 ft. lbs.

STEERING

Steering Wheel

REMOVAL AND INSTALLATION

Except Bronco, F Series and E Series

1. Disconnect the negative battery cable.

2. Remove the screws retaining the steering wheel pad to the steering wheel spokes. Pull the pad back and disconnect the horn switch/cruise control wires. Remove the steering wheel pad.

3. Remove the steering wheel attaching bolt and damper, if equipped.

4. Using a suitable puller, remove the steering wheel from the steering column shaft.

NOTE: Do not hammer on the steering wheel or steering shaft or use a knock-off type steering wheel puller, as either will damage the steering column.

To install:

5. Install the steering wheel on the steering column shaft, aligning the mark and flat on the steering wheel with the mark and flat on the steering shaft.

6. If equipped, install the damper and align the locators with the hole in the wheel hub.

7. Install the steering wheel attaching bolt and tighten to 23–33 ft. lbs. (31–45 Nm).

8. Connect the horn switch/cruise control wires and install the steering wheel pad. Install the pad retaining screws and tighten to 8–11.5 inch lbs. (0.9–1.3 Nm).

9. Connect the negative battery and check the steering column for proper operation.

Bronco, F Series and E Series

1. Set the front wheel in the straight ahead position and make chalk marks on the column and steering wheel hub for alignment purposes during installation.

2. Disconnect the negative battery cable.

3. Remove the one screw from the underside of each steering wheel spoke, and lift the horn switch assembly (steering wheel pad) from the steering wheel. If equipped with the sport steering wheel option, pry the button cover off with a prybar.

4. Disconnect the horn switch wires at the connector and remove the switch assembly. If equipped with speed control, squeeze the J-clip ground wire terminal firmly and pull it out of the hole in the steering wheel. Don't pull the wire out without squeezing the clip.

5. Remove the horn switch assembly.

6. Remove the steering wheel retaining nut and remove the steering wheel with a puller.

—— **WARNING** ——

Never hammer on the wheel or shaft to remove it! Never use a knock-off type puller.

7. Install the steering wheel in the reverse order of removal. Tighten the shaft nut to 40 ft. lbs.

F-Super Duty Stripped Chassis Motor Home Chassis

1. Set the front wheel in the straight ahead position and make chalk marks on the column and steering wheel hub for alignment purposes during installation.

2. Disconnect the negative battery cable.

3. Remove the one screw from the underside of each steering wheel spoke, and lift the horn switch assembly (steering wheel pad) from the steering wheel.

4. Disconnect the horn switch wires at the connector and remove the switch assembly.

5. Remove the horn switch assembly.

6. Remove the steering wheel retaining nut and remove the steering wheel with a puller.

—— **WARNING** ——

Never hammer on the wheel or shaft to remove it! Never use a knock-off type puller.

7. Install the steering wheel in the reverse order of removal. Tighten the shaft nut to 30–42 ft. lbs.

Steering Column

REMOVAL AND INSTALLATION

Aerostar

1. Disconnect the negative battery cable.

2. Remove the bolt attaching the steering column shaft to the lower shaft assembly and disengage the shaft.

3. Remove the steering wheel.

4. Remove the steering column trim shrouds. If equipped with tilt column, remove the upper extension shroud by squeezing it at the 6 and 12 o'clock positions and popping it free of the retaining plate at the 3 o'clock position.

5. Remove the steering column cover directly under the column, on the instrument panel.

6. Disconnect the electrical connections to the steering column switches.

7. Loosen the 2 bolts retaining the steering column to the lower support bracket, but do not remove the bolts at this time.

8. Remove the 3 screws retaining the steering column toeplate/lower seal to the dash.

9. Remove the 2 bolts retaining the steering column to the lower support bracket.

10. Lower the steering column and pull it out from the vehicle.

To install:

11. Carefully insert the lower end of the steering column through the opening in the dash panel.

12. Align the lower support brackets and attach the bolts loosely, so the column hangs with clearance between the brackets.

13. Align the steering column toeplate 3 mounting holes to the dash weld nuts. Install the 3 bolts and tighten to 12 ft. lbs. (16 Nm).

14. Tighten the column support bolts to 17 ft. lbs. (23 Nm).

15. Connect the steering column switch electrical connectors.

16. Slide the lower steering shaft onto the steering column shaft and install the bolt and nut. On Aerostar, tighten to 30–42 ft. lbs. (41–57 Nm).

17. Attach the trim shrouds that cover the steering column upper end. If equipped with tilt column, snap the upper extension shroud in place.

18. Install the steering wheel and the steering column cover on the instrument panel.

19. Connect the negative battery cable and check the steering column for proper operation.

Ranger and Explorer

1. Disconnect the negative battery cable and apply the parking brake. Place automatic transmission in **N**.

2. Remove the bolt that holds the intermediate shaft to the steering column shaft. Using a prybar, compress the intermediate shaft until it is clear of the steering column shaft.

3. If equipped with automatic transmission, remove the nuts from the studs and remove the shift cable bracket from the steering column bracket. Disconnect the shift cable from the column lever.

4. Remove the steering wheel. If equipped with tilt column, make sure the steering wheel is in the full up position before removal.

5. If equipped with tilt column, remove the tilt lever and remove the column collar by pressing on the collar from the top and bottom while removing the collar.

6. Remove the retaining screws and remove the panel trim cover.

7. Remove the 2 screws from the bottom of the column shroud. Remove the bottom half of the shroud by pulling the shroud down and toward the rear of the vehicle. If equipped with automatic transmission, move the shift lever as required to ease shroud removal. Lift the top half of the shroud from the column.

8. If equipped with automatic transmission, disconnect the selector indicator cable by removing the screw from the column casting and the plastic plug at the end of the cable. To remove the plastic plug from the shift lever socket casting, push on the nose of the plug until the head clears the casting, then pull the plug from the casting.

9. Remove the plastic clip that holds the combination switch wiring to the steering column bracket. Remove the 2 screws from the combination switch and remove the switch from the column, leaving the wiring connectors attached to the switch. Position the switch and wiring aside.

10. Disconnect the key warning buzzer wire from the horn brush wire. Remove the screw that holds the horn brush connector to the column and remove the connector.

11. Remove the 5 screws that hold the toe plate to the dash panel and loosen the toe plate clamp bolt.

12. Support the column and remove the bolts that hold the breakaway bracket to the pedal support bracket. Pry apart the locking tabs and disconnect the ignition switch wiring harness.

13. Carefully remove the column from the vehicle.

To install:

14. Carefully position the column in the hole in the vehicle floor. Connect the ignition switch wiring harness to the column connector.

15. Install the bolts that hold the breakaway bracket to the pedal support bracket, but do not tighten at this time.

16. Tighten the bolts that hold the toe plate to the floor to 8 ft. lbs. (11 Nm), then tighten the breakaway bracket-to-pedal support bracket bolts to 19–27 ft. lbs. (25–36 Nm). Tighten the toe plate clamp to 6–13 ft. lbs. (8–18 Nm).

17. Install the horn brush connector to the column and tighten the retaining screw to 21–29 inch lbs. (2.3–3.3 Nm). Attach the key warning buzzer wire connector to the horn brush wire. Route the wiring to prevent contact with moving parts.

18. Position the combination switch on the column with the attaching screws. Tighten to 18–26 inch lbs. (2–3 Nm). Install the plastic clip that holds the switch wiring to the steering column breakaway bracket.

19. If equipped with automatic transmission, connect the selector indicator cable by pushing the plastic plug at the end of the cable into the shift lever socket casting. When installed, the nose of the plug should be facing the steering wheel and the head of the plug away from the wheel. Install the cable retaining screw in the column and adjust the cable. If the shift lever was removed, install it at this time.

20. Position the top half of the shroud on the column so the screw moldings on the shroud seat in the mounting bores in the column. Place the automatic transmission shift lever in the lowest position to aid assembly.

21. Install the bottom half of the shroud by sliding the guides in the shroud bottom half into the tabs in the shroud top half. Install the shroud retaining screws and tighten to 6–10 inch lbs. (0.7–1.1 Nm).

22. If equipped with tilt column, install the column collar by pressing on the collar from the top and bottom while installing the collar on the column, Install the tilt lever and tighten to 2.2–3.6 ft. lbs. (3–5 Nm).

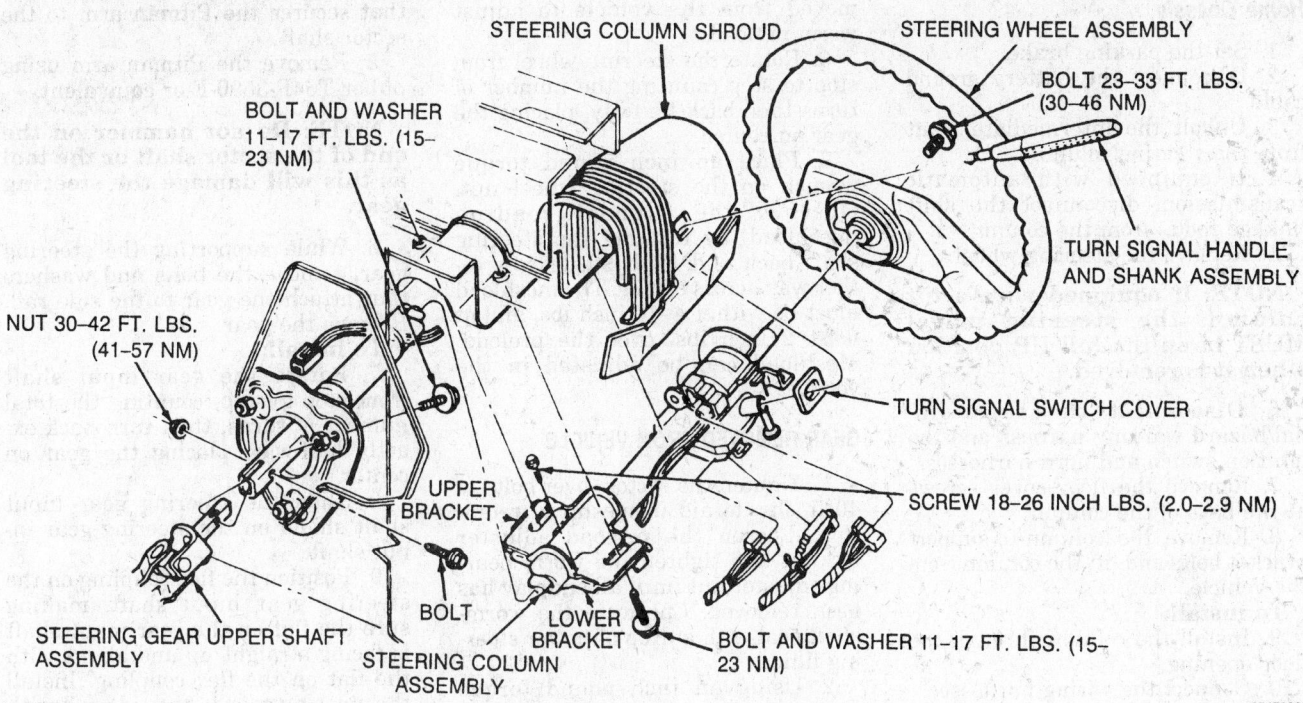

STEERING COLUMN SHROUD

STEERING WHEEL ASSEMBLY

BOLT 23–33 FT. LBS. (30–46 NM)

BOLT AND WASHER 11–17 FT. LBS. (15–23 NM)

TURN SIGNAL HANDLE AND SHANK ASSEMBLY

NUT 30–42 FT. LBS. (41–57 NM)

TURN SIGNAL SWITCH COVER

UPPER BRACKET

SCREW 18–26 INCH LBS. (2.0–2.9 NM)

STEERING GEAR UPPER SHAFT ASSEMBLY

BOLT

LOWER BRACKET

STEERING COLUMN ASSEMBLY

BOLT AND WASHER 11–17 FT. LBS. (15–23 NM)

85472088

Steering column assembly — Aerostar

23. If equipped, place the automatic transmission selector lever in **N**. Install the steering wheel and the lower trim cover panel.

24. If equipped with automatic transmission, install the nuts on the studs and install the shift cable bracket on the steering column bracket. Connect the shift cable to the column lever.

25. Connect the column shaft to the intermediate shaft U-joint and tighten the pinch bolt to 25–35 ft. lbs. (34–47 Nm). The intermediate shaft must be in collapsed state to align, both shafts have a flat side, and then pulled up the column shaft until the bolt holes align. Make sure the intermediate shaft does not contact the plastic retainer at the base of the column. If it does, pull the lower shaft of the column slightly out of the column.

26. Connect the negative battery cable and check the adjustment of the selector indicator cable. Pull the shift lever toward the steering wheel until the **OD** detent in the transmission is felt. Release the shift lever, it should be against the detent wall in the column.

27. Release the parking brake lever and test drive the vehicle.

Bronco, F Series and E Series

1. Set the parking brake.
2. Disconnect the battery ground cable.
3. Unbolt the intermediate shaft from the steering column.
4. Disconnect the shift linkage rod(s) from the column.
5. Remove the steering wheel.

NOTE: If equipped with a tilt column, the steering wheel MUST be in the full UP position when it is removed.

6. Remove the floor cover screws at the base of the column.
7. Remove the steering column shroud by place the bottom screw in the No. 1 position and pulling the shroud up and away from the column.
8. On automatics, remove the shift indicator cable.
9. Remove the instrument panel column opening cover.
10. Remove the bolts securing the column support bracket to the pedal support bracket.
11. Disconnect the turn signal/hazard warning harness and the ignition switch harness.
12. Lift the column from the vehicle.

13. Remove the column support bracket

To install:

14. Install the column support bracket making sure the wiring is outboard of the column. Torque the nuts to 35 ft. lbs.

15. Start the floor cover clamp bolt and press the plate until the clamp flats touch the stops on the column outer tube.

16. Install the column through the floor opening.

17. Connect the turn signal/hazard warning and ignition harnesses.

18. Raise the column and install the 2 support bolts.

19. Tighten the floor cover bolts to 10 ft. lbs.

20. Torque the support bracket bolts to 25 ft. lbs.

21. Torque the cover plate clamp bolt to 18 ft. lbs.

22. Install and adjust the shift indicator cable, on automatics.

23. Install the instrument panel column opening cover.

24. Install the column shroud.

25. Torque the shroud bottom screw to 15 inch lbs.

26. Connect the shifter rod(s).

27. Connect the intermediate shaft. Torque the bolt to 50 ft. lbs.

F-Super Duty Stripped Chassis Motor Home Chassis

1. Set the parking brake.
2. Disconnect the battery ground cable.
3. Unbolt the intermediate shaft from the steering column.
4. If equipped with automatic transmission, disconnect the shift linkage rod(s) from the column.
5. Remove the steering wheel.

NOTE: If equipped with a tilt column, the steering wheel MUST be in the full UP position when it is removed.

6. Disconnect the turn signal/hazard warning harness and the ignition switch and horn harnesses.
7. Remove the floor cover screws at the base of the column.
8. Remove the column-to-support bracket bolts and lift the column from the vehicle.

To install:

9. Install the column through the floor opening.
10. Connect the wiring harnesses.
11. Raise the column and install the 2 support bolts.
12. Torque the column-to-support bracket bolts to 19–27 ft. lbs.
13. Connect the intermediate shaft. Torque the bolt to 20–35 ft. lbs.
14. Tighten the floor cover bolts to 10 ft. lbs.
15. Connect the shifter rod(s).
16. Install the steering wheel.

Manual Steering Gear

ADJUSTMENT

Preload and Meshload

GEAR IN VEHICLE

Make sure the steering column is properly aligned and that the intermediate shaft flex coupling is not distorted.

1. Raise and safely support the vehicle. Disconnect the Pitman arm at the ball stud.
2. Lubricate the wormshaft seal with a drop of power steering fluid.
3. Remove the horn pad assembly from the steering wheel and turn the wheel slowly to 1 stop.
4. Using an inch pound torque wrench on the steering wheel nut, measure the torque (preload) required to rotate the steering wheel at a constant speed for approximately 1½ turns.
5. If the preload is not within 2–6 inch lbs. the preload must be ad-

justed. The steering gear must be removed from the vehicle to adjust worm preload.

6. Rotate the steering wheel from stop to stop counting the number of turns then back halfway, placing the gear on center.
7. Place an inch pound torque wrench on the steering wheel nut. Observe the highest reading (meshload) by rotating the steering shaft back and forth 90 degrees either way across center. The meshload must be within 4–10 inch lbs. and at least 2 inch lbs. over the preload. Meshload can be adjusted in the vehicle.

GEAR REMOVED FROM VEHICLE

1. Tighten the sector cover bolts to 40 ft. lbs. to aid in meshload retention. Loosen the preload adjuster locknut and tighten the worm bearing adjuster nut until all endplay has been removed. Lubricate the wormshaft seal with a drop of power steering fluid.
2. Using an inch pound torque wrench and an 11/16 in. 12-point socket, carefully turn the wormshaft all the way to the right. Measure the left turn torque (preload) required to rotate the wormshaft at a constant speed for approximately 1½ turns.
3. Tighten or loosen the adjuster nut as required until the correct preload of 5–6 inch lbs. is obtained. Tighten the adjuster locknut to 166–187 ft. lbs. (225–253 Nm).
4. Rotate the wormshaft from stop to stop, counting the total number of turns, then turn back halfway placing the gear on center.
5. Using the same torque wrench and socket, observe the highest reading (meshload) while the wormshaft is turned 90 degrees either way across center. If the reading is not within 9–11 inch lbs. and at least 4 inch lbs. over the preload, turn the sector shaft adjusting screw, as required.
6. Hold the sector shaft adjusting screw and tighten the locknut to 14–25 ft. lbs. (19–34 Nm).

REMOVAL AND INSTALLATION

1. Raise the vehicle and support it safely with the front wheels in the straight ahead position.
2. Disengage the flex coupling shield from the steering gear input shaft shield and slide it up the intermediate shaft.
3. Remove the bolt that retains the flex coupling to the steering gear.

4. Remove the nut and washer that secures the Pitman arm to the sector shaft.
5. Remove the Pitman arm using puller T64P-3590-F or equivalent.

NOTE: Do not hammer on the end of the sector shaft or the tool as this will damage the steering gear.

6. While supporting the steering gear, remove the bolts and washers that attach the gear to the side rail. Remove the gear.

To install:

7. Rotate the gear input shaft from stop-to-stop, counting the total number of turns, then turn back exactly half-way, placing the gear on center.
8. Slide the steering gear input shaft shield on the steering gear input shaft.
9. Position the flex coupling on the steering gear input shaft, making sure the flat on the gear input shaft is facing straight up and aligns with the flat on the flex coupling. Install the steering gear to the side rail with bolts and washers and tighten to 54–62 ft. lbs. (73–84 Nm).
10. Place the Pitman arm on the sector shaft and install the attaching washer and nut. Align the 2 blocked teeth on the Pitman arm with the 4 missing teeth on the steering gear sector shaft. Tighten the nut to 170–230 ft. lbs. (230–310 Nm).
11. Install the flex coupling to the steering gear input shaft with the attaching bolt and tighten to 25–35 ft. lbs. (34–47 Nm). Snap the flex coupling shield to the steering gear input shield.
12. Check the system to ensure equal turns from center to each lock position.

Power Steering Gear

ADJUSTMENT

Except Bronco, F Series and E Series

1. Raise and safely support the vehicle. Disconnect the Pitman arm from the sector shaft using puller T64P-3590-F or equivalent.
2. Disconnect the fluid return line at the reservoir and cap the reservoir return line tube. Place the end of the return line in a clean container and turn the steering wheel from stop to stop several times to empty the steering gear. Discard the fluid.
3. Turn the steering wheel to 45 degrees from the right stop.

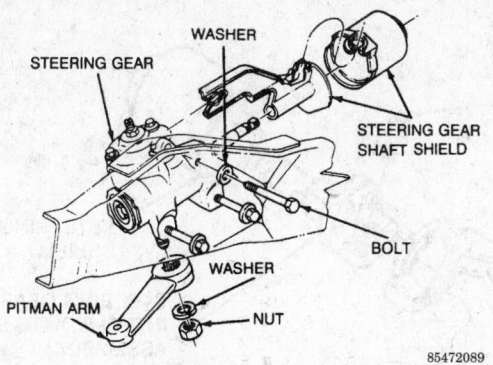

Manual steering gear installation

4. Attach an inch pound torque wrench to steering wheel nut and record the torque required to rotate the shaft slowly approximately ⅛ turn toward center from the 45 degree position.

5. Turn the steering gear back to center and record the torque required to rotate the shaft back and forth across the center position.

6. If the vehicle has less than 5000 miles, resetting is required if total meshload over center is not 12–24 inch lbs. If the vehicle has more than 5000 miles or the sector shaft has been replaced, resetting is required if meshload over center is less than 10 inch lbs. greater than the torque 45 degrees from the right stop.

7. The set torque specification is measured rocking across center to a value of 9–13 inch lbs. greater than that measured 45 degrees from the right stop.

8. If reset is required, loosen the locknut and turn the sector shaft adjusting screw until the reading is the specified value greater than the torque at 45 degrees from the stop.

9. Tighten the adjusting screw locknut and recheck. Install the Pitman arm and steering wheel cover.

10. Connect the fluid return line to the reservoir and refill the system with fluid. Bleed the system.

Bronco, F Series and E Series

FORD INTEGRAL POWER STEERING GEAR

The Ford Integral Power Steering Gear is used on all 1992 models except the F-Super Duty stripped chassis and motor home chassis

1. Raise and support the front end on jackstands.
2. Matchmark the pitman arm and gear housing.
3. Set the wheels in a straight-ahead position.
4. Disconnect the pitman arm from the sector shaft.

5. Disconnect the fluid RETURN line at the pump reservoir and cap the reservoir nipple.

6. Place the end of the return line in a clean container and turn the steering wheel lock-to-lock a few times to expel the fluid from the gear.

7. Turn the steering wheel all the way to the right stop. Place a small piece of masking tape on the steering wheel rim as a reference and rotate the steering wheel 45° from the right stop.

8. Disconnect the battery ground.

9. Remove the horn pad.

10. Using an inch-pound torque wrench on the steering wheel nut, record the amount of torque needed to turn the steering wheel ⅛ turn counterclockwise. The preload reading should be 4–9 inch lbs.

11. Center the steering wheel (½ the total lock-to-lock turns) and record the torque needed to turn the steering wheel 90° to either side of center. On a vehicle with fewer than 5000 miles, the meshload should be 15–25 inch lbs. On a vehicle with 5000 or more miles, the meshload should be 7 inch lbs. more than the preload torque. On vehicles with fewer than 5000 miles, if the meshload is not within specifications, it should be reset to a figure 14–18 inch lbs. greater than the recorded preload torque. On vehicles with 5000 or more miles, if the meshload is not within specifications, it should be reset to a figure 10–14 inch lbs. greater than the recorded preload torque.

12. If an adjustment is required, loosen the adjuster locknut and turn the sector shaft adjuster screw until the necessary torque is achieved.

13. Once adjustment is completed. hold the adjuster screw and tighten the locknut to 45 ft. lbs.

14. Recheck the adjustment readings and reset if necessary.

15. Connect the return line and refill the reservoir.

16. Install the pitman arm.
17. Install the horn pad.

FORD XR-50 POWER STEERING GEAR

The XR-50 Power Steering Gear is used on all 1993–96 models except the F-Super Duty stripped chassis and motor home chassis.

1. Raise and support the front end on jackstands.

2. Matchmark the pitman arm and gear housing.

3. Set the wheels in a straight-ahead position.

4. Disconnect the pitman arm from the sector shaft.

5. Disconnect the fluid RETURN line at the pump reservoir and cap the reservoir nipple.

6. Place the end of the return line in a clean container and turn the steering wheel lock-to-lock a few times to expel the fluid from the gear.

7. Turn the steering wheel all the way to the right stop. Place a small piece of masking tape on the steering wheel rim as a reference and rotate the steering wheel 45° from the right stop.

8. Disconnect the battery ground.

9. Remove the horn pad.

10. Using an inch-pound torque wrench on the steering wheel nut, record the amount of torque needed to turn the steering wheel ⅛ turn counterclockwise. The preload reading should be 4–9 inch lbs.

11. Center the steering wheel (½ the total lock-to-lock turns) and record the torque needed to turn the steering wheel 90° to either side of center. On a vehicle with fewer than 5000 miles, the meshload should be 15–25 inch lbs. On a vehicle with 5000 or more miles, the meshload should be 7 inch lbs. more than the preload torque. On vehicles with fewer than 5000 miles, if the meshload is not within specifications, it should be reset to a figure 14–18 inch lbs. greater than the recorded preload torque. On vehicles with 5000 or more miles, if the meshload is not within specifications, it should be reset to a figure 10–14 inch lbs. greater than the recorded preload torque

12. If an adjustment is required, loosen the adjuster locknut and turn the sector shaft adjuster screw until the necessary torque is achieved.

13. Once adjustment is completed. hold the adjuster screw and tighten the locknut to 45 ft. lbs.

14. Recheck the adjustment readings and reset if necessary

15. Connect the return line and refill the reservoir.

16. Install the pitman arm.

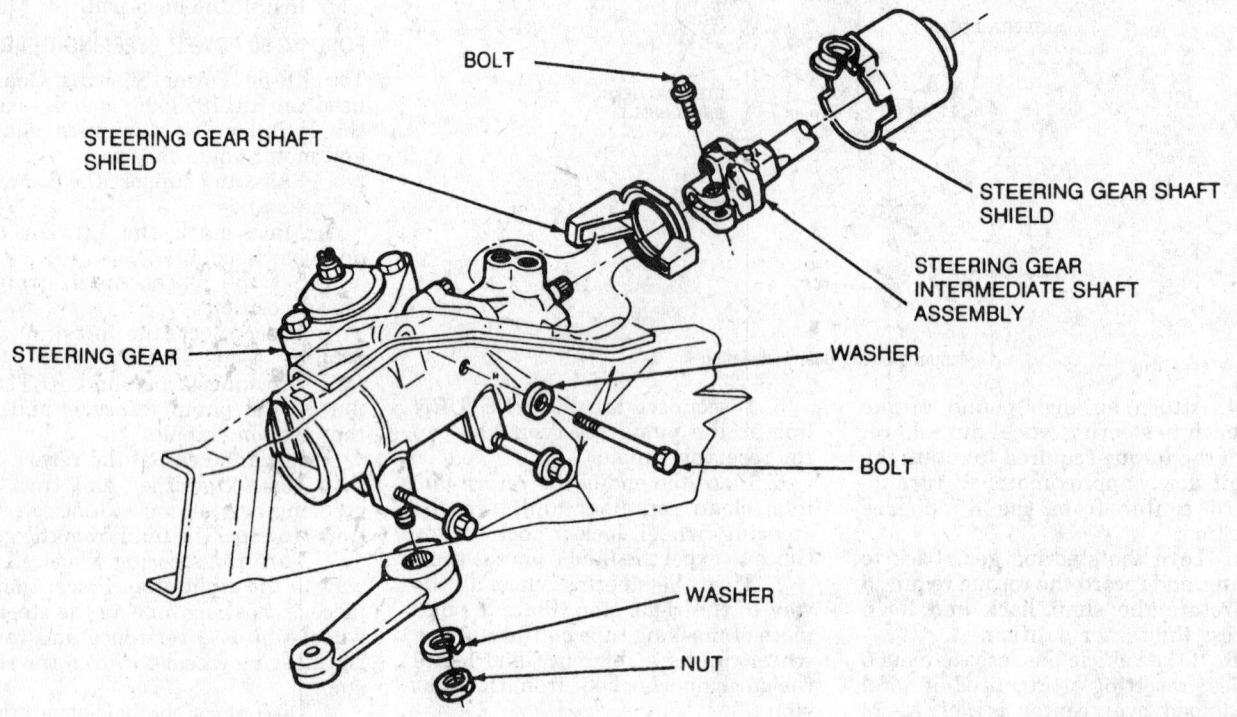

BOLT

STEERING GEAR SHAFT
SHIELD

STEERING GEAR SHAFT
SHIELD

STEERING GEAR
INTERMEDIATE SHAFT
ASSEMBLY

STEERING GEAR

WASHER

BOLT

WASHER

NUT

85472090

Power steering gear installation — Except Bronco, F Series and E Series

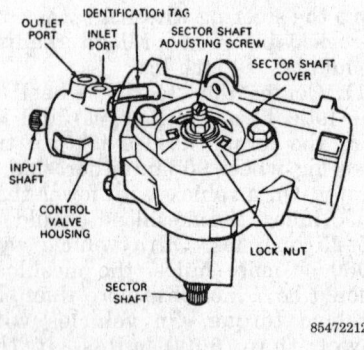

OUTLET PORT
IDENTIFICATION TAG
INLET PORT
SECTOR SHAFT ADJUSTING SCREW
SECTOR SHAFT COVER
INPUT SHAFT
CONTROL VALVE HOUSING
LOCK NUT
SECTOR SHAFT

85472212

**View of the power steering gear — Bronco,
F Series and E Series**

17. Install the horn pad.

F Series Super Duty and Motor Home Chassis

BENDIX C-300N POWER STEERING GEAR

Adjustments must be made with the steering gear removed and mounted in a vise.

NOTE: Backlash is correct when a 4–18 inch lb. increase in rotational torque is noted at the input shaft as it is rotated and the piston passes the mid-point of its total travel in the housing.

The torque increase should occur only at mid-point and should disappear after mid-point.

1. Loosen the locknut and turn the adjusting screw counterclockwise as far as it will go.

2. Using an inch-pound torque wrench, rotate the input shaft as far as it will go in one direction, then, counting the number of full turns and noting the rotational torque, rotate it to the opposite stop.

3. Turn the shaft back ½ the total number of turns to the mid-point.

4. Rotate the shaft 180° to both sides of the mid-point, noting the change in rotational torque. Turn the adjusting screw ⅛–¼ turn at a time until the proper reading of 4–18 inch lb. increase in torque is noted over the mid-point. This increase in torque must be plus the total rotational torque.

5. When the adjustment is correct, hold the adjusting screw and, using a crow's foot adapter, torque the locknut to 74–88 ft. lbs.

6. Check the adjustment to make sure it hasn't changed. Rotate the shaft through its entire travel. It must rotate smoothly.

REMOVAL AND INSTALLATION

Except Bronco, F Series and E Series

1. Disconnect the pressure and return lines from the steering gear. Plug the lines and the ports in the gear to prevent entry of dirt.

2. Remove the upper and lower steering gear shaft U-joint shield from the flex coupling. Disconnect the flex coupling at the steering gear by removing the bolt.

3. Raise the vehicle and support it safely. Remove the Pitman arm attaching nut and washer. Remove the Pitman arm from the sector shaft using tool T64P-3590-F or equivalent. Be careful not to damage the seals.

4. Support the steering gear and remove the attaching bolts. Work the steering gear free from the flex coupling and remove the gear from the vehicle.

To install:

5. Install the lower U-joint shield onto the steering gear lugs. Slide the upper U-joint shield into place on the steering shaft assembly. Turn the steering wheel so the spokes are in the horizontal position.

6. Center the steering gear input shaft with the indexing flat facing down.

7. Slide the steering gear input shaft into the flex coupling and into place on the frame side rail. Install the attaching bolts and tighten to 50–62 ft. lbs. (68–84 Nm). Tighten the flex coupling bolt to 26–34 ft. lbs. (34–47 Nm).

8. Make sure the wheels are in the straight ahead position, then install the Pitman arm on the sector shaft. Install the attaching washer and nut and tighten to 170–228 ft. lbs. (230–310 Nm).

9. Connect and tighten the pressure and return lines to the steering gear to 20–30 ft. lbs. (27–40 Nm). Snap the upper and lower steering gear shaft U-joint shields together.

10. Fill and bleed the power steering system.

Bronco, F Series and E Series

FORD INTEGRAL POWER STEERING GEAR

The Ford Integral Power Steering Gear is used on all 1992 models except the F-Super Duty stripped chassis and motor home chassis

1. Raise and support the front end on jackstands.

2. Place the wheels in the straight-ahead position.

3. Place a drain pan under the gear and disconnect the pressure and return lines. Cap the openings.

4. Remove the splash shield from the flex coupling.

5. Disconnect the flex coupling at the gear.

6. Matchmark and remove the pitman arm from the sector shaft.

7. Support the steering gear and remove the mounting bolts.

8. Remove the steering gear. It may be necessary to work it free of the flex coupling.

To install:

9. Place the splash shield on the steering gear lugs.

10. Slide the flex coupling into place on the steering shaft. Make sure the steering wheel spokes are still horizontal.

11. Center the steering gear input shaft with the indexing flat facing downward.

12. Slide the steering gear input shaft into the flex coupling and into place on the frame side rail. Install the flex coupling bolt and torque it to 30 ft. lbs.

13. Install the gear mounting bolts and torque them to 65 ft. lbs.

14. Make sure the wheels are still straight ahead and install the pitman arm. Torque the nut to 230 ft. lbs.

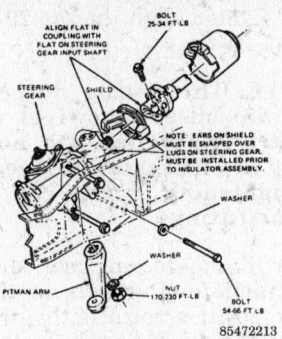

Power steering gear installation — Bronco and F Series

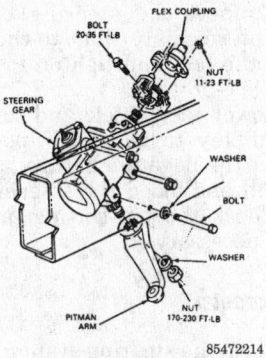

Power steering gear installation — E Series

15. Connect the pressure, then, the return lines. Torque the pressure line to 25 ft. lbs.

16. Snap the flex coupling shield into place.

17. Fill the steering reservoir.

18. Run the engine and turn the steering wheel lock-to-lock several times to expel air. Check for leaks.

FORD XR-50 POWER STEERING GEAR

The XR-50 Power Steering Gear is used on all 1993ndash;96 models except the F-Super Duty stripped chassis and motor home chassis.

1. Raise and support the front end on jackstands.

2. Place the wheels in the straight-ahead position.

3. Place a drain pan under the gear and disconnect the pressure and return lines. Cap the openings.

4. Remove the splash shield from the flex coupling.

5. Disconnect the flex coupling at the gear.

6. Matchmark and remove the pitman arm from the sector shaft.

7. Support the steering gear and remove the mounting bolts.

8. Remove the steering gear. It may be necessary to work it free of the flex coupling.

To install:

9. Place the splash shield on the steering gear lugs.

10. Slide the flex coupling into place on the steering shaft. Make sure the steering wheel spokes are still horizontal.

11. Center the steering gear input shaft with the indexing flat facing downward.

12. Slide the steering gear input shaft into the flex coupling and into place on the frame side rail. Install the flex coupling bolt and torque it to 30-42 ft. lbs.

13. Install the gear mounting bolts and torque them to 65 ft. lbs.

14. Make sure the wheels are still straight ahead and install the pitman arm. Torque the nut to 170-288 ft. lbs.

15. Connect the pressure, then, the return lines. Torque the pressure line to 25 ft. lbs.

16. Snap the flex coupling shield into place.

17. Fill the steering reservoir.

18. Run the engine and turn the steering wheel lock-to-lock several times to expel air. Check for leaks.

F Series Super Duty and Motor Home Chassis

BENDIX C-300N POWER STEERING GEAR

1. Raise and support the front end on jackstands.

2. Thoroughly clean all connections.

3. Place a drain pan under the area.

4. Disconnect the hydraulic lines at the gear. Cap all openings at once.

5. Remove the retaining bolt and nut and disconnect the pitman arm from the sector shaft.

6. Remove the bolt and nut securing the input shaft and U-joint.

7. Support the gear and remove the gear-to-frame bolts and nuts.

To install:

8. Position the gear on the frame and install the bolts and nuts. Torque the nuts to 150–200 ft. lbs.

9. Install the U-joint bolt and nut. Torque the nut to 50–70 ft. lbs.

10. Install the pitman arm.

———— **CAUTION** ————

Never hammer the pitman shaft onto the sector shaft! Hammering will damage the gear. Use a cold chisel to separate the pitman arm opening.

11. Install the bolt and nut. Torque the nut to 220–300 ft. lbs.

12. Connect the hydraulic lines, fill the reservoir, run the engine and check for leaks.

Power Rack and Pinion

ADJUSTMENT

Service adjustments are not required on the power rack and pinion gear.

REMOVAL AND INSTALLATION

Except 4WD Aerostar

1. Place the steering system in the on center position as follows:

a. Start the engine.

b. Rotate the steering wheel from lock-to-lock and record the number of steering wheel rotations.

c. Divide the number of steering wheel rotations by 2 to give the required number of turns to place the system in the on center position.

d. From the lock position, rotate the steering wheel the number of turns determined in Step c to place the gear in the on center position. Make sure the wheels are in the straight ahead position.

e. Stop the engine.

2. Disconnect the negative battery cable and turn the ignition key to the **ON** position. Raise and safely support the vehicle.

3. Disconnect the pressure and return lines from the steering gear valve housing. Plug the lines and ports in the gear valve housing to prevent the entry of dirt.

4. Remove the bolt retaining the lower intermediate steering column shaft to the steering gear. Disconnect the shaft from the gear.

5. Remove the cotter pins and nuts from the tie rod ends. Separate the tie rod ends from the spindle arms.

6. Support the steering gear and remove the 2 nuts, bolts and washers retaining the gear to the crossmember. Remove the gear from the vehicle.

To install:

7. Position the steering gear on the crossmember. Install the retaining nuts, bolts and washers and tighten to 80–105 ft. lbs. (108–142 Nm).

8. Connect the pressure and return lines to the gear valve housing

ports. Tighten the fittings to 20–25 ft. lbs. (27–34 Nm).

NOTE: The fitting design allows the hoses to swivel when properly tightened. Do not attempt to eliminate looseness by overtightening as this can damage the fittings.

9. With the steering gear, steering wheel and front wheels in the on center position, attach the tie rod ends to the spindle arms. Install the nuts and tighten to 52–73 ft. lbs. (70–100 Nm). If required, advance the nuts to the next castellation and install new cotter pins.

10. Connect the steering column lower intermediate shaft to the gear. Install the bolt and tighten to 30–42 ft. lbs. (41–56 Nm).

11. Lower the vehicle and turn the ignition key to the **OFF** position. Connect the negative battery cable.

12. Fill and bleed the steering system. Check the toe setting and adjust, if necessary.

4WD Aerostar

1. Place the steering system in the on center position as follows:

a. Start the engine.

b. Rotate the steering wheel from lock-to-lock and record the number of steering wheel rotations.

c. Divide the number of steering wheel rotations by 2 to give the required number of turns to place the system in the on center position.

d. From the lock position, rotate the steering wheel the number of turns determined in Step c to place the gear in the on center position. Make sure the wheels are in the straight ahead position.

e. Stop the engine.

2. Disconnect the negative battery cable and turn the ignition key to the **ON** position. Raise and safely sup-

port the vehicle and remove the wheel and tire assemblies.

3. Disconnect the pressure and return lines from the steering gear valve housing. Plug the lines and ports in the gear valve housing to prevent the entry of dirt.

4. Remove the bolt retaining the lower intermediate steering column shaft to the steering gear. Disconnect the shaft from the gear. Retain any dust seals which may be present.

5. Remove the cotter pins and nuts from the tie rod ends. Separate the tie rod ends from the spindle arms.

6. Remove the nut and washer with the insulator retaining the shock absorbers to the front crossmember brackets. Remove the bolts retaining the shock absorbers to the bottom of the lower control arms and remove the shock absorbers.

NOTE: Be careful during shock absorber removal as the shock absorber may extend somewhat due to gas pressure.

7. Remove the front stabilizer bar.

8. Install a suitable spring compressor through each coil spring to secure the spring and prevent extension when the control arm pivot bolts are removed.

9. Remove the lower control arm pivot bolts. Reposition and secure the lower control arms away from the brackets. Be careful not to deform the control arm pivot brackets.

10. Remove the 5 nuts from the forward edge of the crossmember lower plate assembly. Remove the nut from the left rear and the bolts from the center and right rear positions at the rear of the assembly. Remove the crossmember lower plate.

11. Support the steering gear and remove the 2 bolts, spacers and bushings retaining the steering gear. Remove the gear from the vehicle.

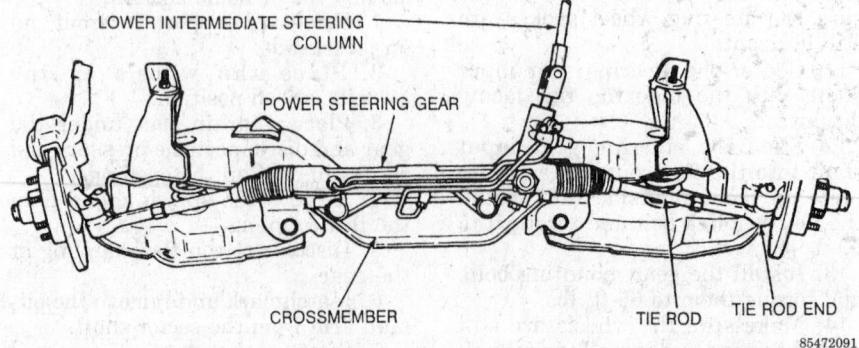

Power rack and pinion steering gear

To install:

12. Position the steering gear on the crossmember with the attaching bolts and tighten to 61–82 ft. lbs. (83–111 Nm). The large end of the spacer is installed facing the steering rack.

13. Install the crossmember lower plate with the nuts and bolt in the proper locations.

14. Position the lower control arms within the brackets and install the pivot bolts. Properly position the retaining flags.

15. Tighten all lower control arm pivot bolt nuts to 100–140 ft. lbs. (136–190 Nm).

16. Install the coil springs and remove the spring compressors.

17. Install the shock absorbers through the lower control arms and install the insulators, nuts and washers. Tighten the nuts to 2–\35 ft. lbs. (34–47 Nm). Install the lower shock absorber retaining bolts and tighten to 16–25 ft. lbs. (22–33 Nm).

18. Install the front stabilizer bar.

19. Connect the pressure and return lines to the gear valve housing ports. Tighten the fittings to 10–15 ft. lbs. (15–20 Nm).

NOTE: The fitting design allows the hoses to swivel when properly tightened. Do not attempt to eliminate looseness by overtightening as this can damage the fittings.

20. With the steering gear, steering wheel and front wheels in the on center position, attach the tie rod ends to the spindle arms. Install the nuts and tighten to 52–73 ft. lbs. (70–100 Nm). If required, advance the nuts to the next castellation and install new cotter pins.

21. Position the intermediate shaft and any dust seals over the steering rack input shaft spline and make sure no rotation from the on center

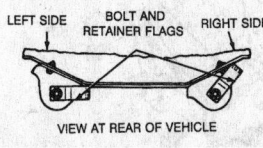

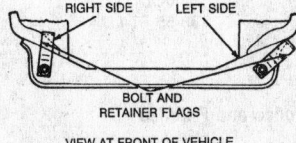

Bolt and retainer flag positioning — 4WD Aerostar

position has occurred. Install the bolt and tighten to 30–42 ft. lbs. (41–56 Nm).

22. Install the wheel and tire assemblies. Lower the vehicle and turn the ignition key to the **OFF** position. Connect the negative battery cable.

23. Fill and bleed the steering system. Check the toe setting and adjust, if necessary.

Power Steering Pump

REMOVAL AND INSTALLATION

Except Bronco, F Series and E Series

1. Remove the power steering fluid from the pump reservoir by disconnecting the fluid return hose at the reservoir and draining the fluid into a container.

2. Remove the pressure hose from the pump. If equipped, disconnect the power steering pump pressure switch.

3. If equipped with 2.3L or 3.0L engine, loosen the alternator or idler pulley assembly pivot and adjustment bolts to slacken belt tension. Remove the drive belt.

4. If equipped with 2.9L engine, loosen the adjustment nut and the slider bolts on the pump support to slacken belt tension. Remove the drive belt.

5. If equipped with 4.0L engine, slacken belt tension by lifting the tensioner pulley in a counterclockwise direction. Remove the drive belt from under the tensioner pulley and slowly lower the pulley to stop. Remove the drive belt.

6. Remove the engine oil dipstick tube, if necessary. Remove the power steering pump bracket support brace, if equipped.

7. Install steering pump pulley removal tool T69L-10300-B on the pulley. Hold the pump and rotate the tool nut counterclockwise to remove the pulley. Do not apply in and out pressure on the pump shaft as pressure will damage the internal thrust areas.

8. Remove the bolts attaching the pump to the bracket and remove the pump.

To install:

9. Install the pump on the bracket. Install and tighten the attaching bolts to 30–45 ft. lbs. (41–61 Nm). If equipped with 4.0L engine, tighten to 35–47 ft. lbs. (47–64 Nm), position the support on the bracket and in-

stall and tighten the mounting bolts to 35–47 ft. lbs. (47–64 Nm).

10. Install steering pump pulley replacement tool T65P-3A733-C and install the pulley. Remove the tool.

NOTE: Fore and aft location of the pulley on the pump shaft is critical for correct belt alignment. Make sure the pull-off groove on the pulley is facing front and flush with the end of the shaft ± 0.010 in. (0.254mm).

11. Install the drive belt.

12. If equipped with 4.0L engine, position and rotate the drive belt on the engine. While lifting the tensioner pulley in a counterclockwise direction, slide the belt under the tensioner pulley and lower the pulley to the belt.

13. If equipped with 2.3L or 3.0L engine, position the idler pulley or alternator to set the belt tension. Tighten the idler pulley or alternator pivot and adjustment bolts to 40 ft. lbs. (55 Nm) on the 2.3L engine or 35–47 ft. lbs. (47–64 Nm) on the 3.0L engine.

14. If equipped with the 2.9L engine, tighten the pump support adjustment nut to set the belt tension, then tighten the slider bolts to 35–47 ft. lbs. (47–64 Nm).

15. Install the power steering pump bracket support brace and/or engine dipstick tube, if removed.

16. Install the pressure hose to the pump fitting. Connect the return hose to the pump and tighten the clamp. If equipped, connect the power steering pump pressure switch.

17. Fill and bleed the power steering system. Check for leaks.

Bronco, F Series and E Series

FORD C-II POWER STEERING PUMP

This pump is used by all models except the F-Super Duty stripped chassis and motor home models.

1. Disconnect the return line at the pump and drain the fluid into a container.

2. Disconnect the pressure line from the pump.

3. Loosen the pump bracket nuts and remove the drive belt. On the 4.9L and 5.0L with a serpentine drive belt, remove belt tension by lifting the tensioner out of position.

4. Remove the nuts and lift out the pump/bracket assembly.

5. If a new pump or bracket is being installed, remove the pulley from the pump; use a press and adapters.

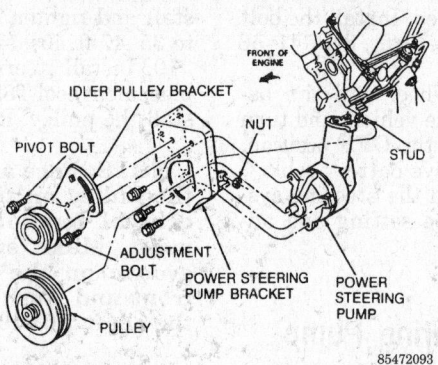

Power steering pump installation — 3.0L engine

6. Installation is the reverse of removal. Note the following torques:
- Pivot bolt (4.9L and 5.0L) — 45 ft. lbs.
- Pump-to-adjustment bracket — 45 ft. lbs.
- Support bracket-to-engine (5.8L) — 65 ft. lbs.
- Support bracket-to-water pump housing (4.9L) — 17 ft. lbs.
- Support bracket-to-water pump housing (5.0L, 5.8L) — 45 ft. lbs.
- Pressure line-to-fitting — 29 ft. lbs.
- Adjustment bracket-to-support bracket:
  - 4.9L, 5.0L, 5.8L — 45 ft. lbs.
  - 7.5L and Diesel — Long bolt — 65 ft. lbs.
  - Short bolt — 45 ft. lbs.

F Series Super Duty and Motor Home Chassis

ZF POWER STEERING PUMP

1. Disconnect the pressure line from the pump and tie up the ends of both hoses in a raised position. Cap the openings.
2. Loosen the pump pivot and adjusting bolts and remove the drive belt.
3. Remove the bolts and lift out the pump.
4. Installation is the reverse of removal. Adjust the belt tension. Tighten the bolts to 30–45 ft. lbs. Connect the hoses. Refill the reservoir. Run the engine and check for leaks.

BELT ADJUSTMENT

Except 4.0L Engine

1. Loosen the accessory adjustment and pivot bolts.
2. Position a suitable belt tension gauge mid-way between the pulleys on the longest accessible belt span.
3. On 2.3L engine, move the alternator or idler pulley to apply tension

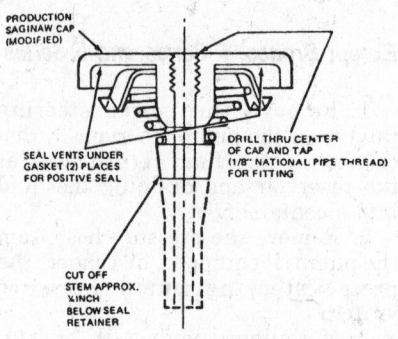

Modified pump reservoir cap — E Series

to the belt. On 2.9L and 3.0L engines, move the power steering pump to apply tension to the belt.

4. On 2.3L and 3.0L engines, the tension should be 150–190 lbs. for a new belt or 140–160 lbs. for a used belt. On 2.9L engine, the tension should be 120–160 lbs. for a new belt or 110–130 lbs. for a used belt.
5. Tighten the adjustment bolt and release pressure, then tighten the pivot bolt.
6. Recheck the belt tension and adjust, if necessary.

4.0L Engine

Belt tension is maintained by an automatic tensioner. No adjustment is necessary.

SYSTEM BLEEDING

1. Fill the power steering fluid reservoir.
2. Disconnect the coil wire.
3. Crank the engine with the starter and continue adding fluid until the level remains constant. Do not prolong cranking as the battery may be drained and the starter damaged.
4. Rotate the steering wheel approximately 30 degrees each side of center while continuing to crank the engine.

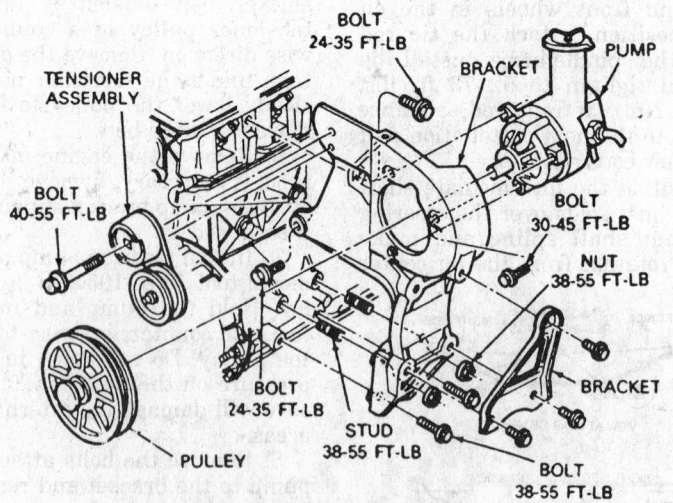

Power steering pump installation — Bronco and F Series

5. Recheck the fluid level and fill, as required.

6. Reconnect the coil wire.

7. Start the engine and allow it to run for several minutes.

8. Rotate the steering wheel from stop to stop.

9. Shut off the engine and recheck the fluid level. Add fluid, as required.

10. If air is still trapped in the system, proceed as follows:

a. Fabricate a purging tool.

b. Make sure the reservoir fluid level is correct.

c. Insert the rubber stopper end of the fabricated purging tool tightly into the filler tube.

d. Connect a suitable length of hose to the purging tool. Connect the other end of the hose to an air conditioner vacuum pump or distributor machine. Do not use engine vacuum.

e. Start the engine and let it idle for approximately 15 minutes. Turn the steering wheel 1 full cycle every 5 minutes but do not hit the stops. This will assist in removing trapped air.

f. Stop the engine and disconnect the vacuum source. Remove the purging tool.

g. Check the fluid level and install the filler tube dipstick.

Tie Rod Ends

REMOVAL AND INSTALLATION

Except Bronco, F Series and E Series

1. Place the front wheels in the straight ahead position. Raise and safely support the vehicle.

2. Remove the cotter pin and nut from the tie rod end ball stud. Discard the cotter pin.

3. Separate the tie rod end from the spindle or drag link using puller tool T64P-3590-F or equivalent.

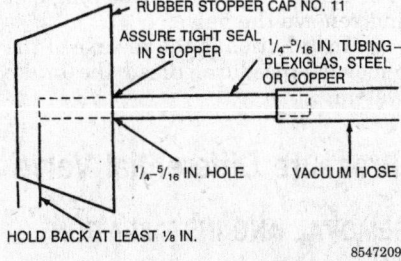

RUBBER STOPPER CAP NO. 11

ASSURE TIGHT SEAL IN STOPPER

¹/₄–⁵/₁₆ IN. TUBING – PLEXIGLAS, STEEL OR COPPER

¹/₄–⁵/₁₆ IN. HOLE

VACUUM HOSE

HOLD BACK AT LEAST ⅛ IN.

85472094

Fabricated power steering system air purging tool

4. On Aerostar, hold the tie rod with a wrench and loosen the tie rod jam nut. Mark the position of the tie rod end on the tie rod threads, grip the tie rod with suitable pliers and remove the tie rod end from the tie rod.

5. On Bronco II, Explorer and Ranger, loosen the bolts on the tie rod adjusting sleeve. Count the number of turns required to remove the tie rod from the tie rod adjusting sleeve and remove the tie rod.

To install:

6. On Aerostar, thread the replacement tie rod end onto the tie rod to the same location as the 1 that was removed. Hold the tie rod end with a wrench and tighten the jam nut to 35–50 ft. lbs. (48–68 Nm).

7. On Bronco II, Explorer and Ranger, install the tie rod into the adjusting sleeve the same number of turns required to remove it. With the adjusting sleeve clamps pointed down, tighten the adjusting sleeve nuts to 30–42 ft. lbs. (40–57 Nm).

8. Install the tie rod ball stud into the spindle or drag link. Install the nut and tighten to 50–75 ft. lbs. (70–100 Nm). Install a new cotter pin.

NOTE: If the cotter pin cannot be installed because the hole in the ball stud does not align with a castellation on the nut, continue to tighten the nut to align them. Never loosen the nut to align the hole and castellation.

9. Lower the vehicle. Check the toe-in setting and adjust, if necessary.

Bronco, F Series and E Series

1. Raise and support the front end on jackstands.

2. Place the wheels in a straight-ahead position.

3. Remove the ball stud from the pitman arm using a tie rod end remover.

4. Loosen the nuts on the adjusting sleeve clamp. Remove the ball stud from the adjuster, or the adjuster from the tie rod. Count the number of turns it takes to remove the sleeve from the tie rod or ball stud from the sleeve.

To install:

5. Install the sleeve on the tie rod, or the ball in the sleeve the same number of turns noted during removal. Make sure the adjuster clamps are in the correct position, illustrated, and torque the clamp bolts to 40 ft. lbs.

6. Keep the wheels straight ahead and install the ball studs. Torque the nuts to 75 ft. lbs. Use new cotter pins.

7. Install the drag link and connecting rod.

8. Have the front end alignment checked.

BRAKES

Master Cylinder

REMOVAL AND INSTALLATION

Except Bronco, F Series (Pick-Up) and E Series (Van)

1. Disconnect the negative battery cable. If equipped, push the brake pedal down to expel vacuum from the brake booster system.

2. Disconnect the fluid level indicator switch connector from the master cylinder.

3. If equipped with non-power brakes, disconnect the wires from the stop light switch inside the cab below the instrument panel. Remove the lock pin and spacers securing the master cylinder pushrod to the brake pedal assembly. Remove the stop light switch from the pedal.

4. Disconnect and plug the hydraulic lines at the master cylinder. Plug the master cylinder ports.

5. Remove the master cylinder-to-booster or master cylinder-to-dash panel retaining nuts and remove the master cylinder.

NOTE: On Aerostar, use care when removing the cartridge master cylinder so as not to scratch the exposed primary piston.

To install:

6. If equipped with power brakes, before installing the master cylinder on all except Aerostar, check the distance from the outer end of the vacuum booster assembly pushrod to the front face of the vacuum brake booster assembly. The distance should be 0.980–0.995 in. (24.89–25.27mm). Turn the pushrod adjusting screw in or out, as required, to obtain the proper length.

7. On Aerostar, make sure the interface seal is located in the annular groove in the cartridge master cylinder body where the cartridge master cylinder seals with the booster. Do not assemble the cartridge master

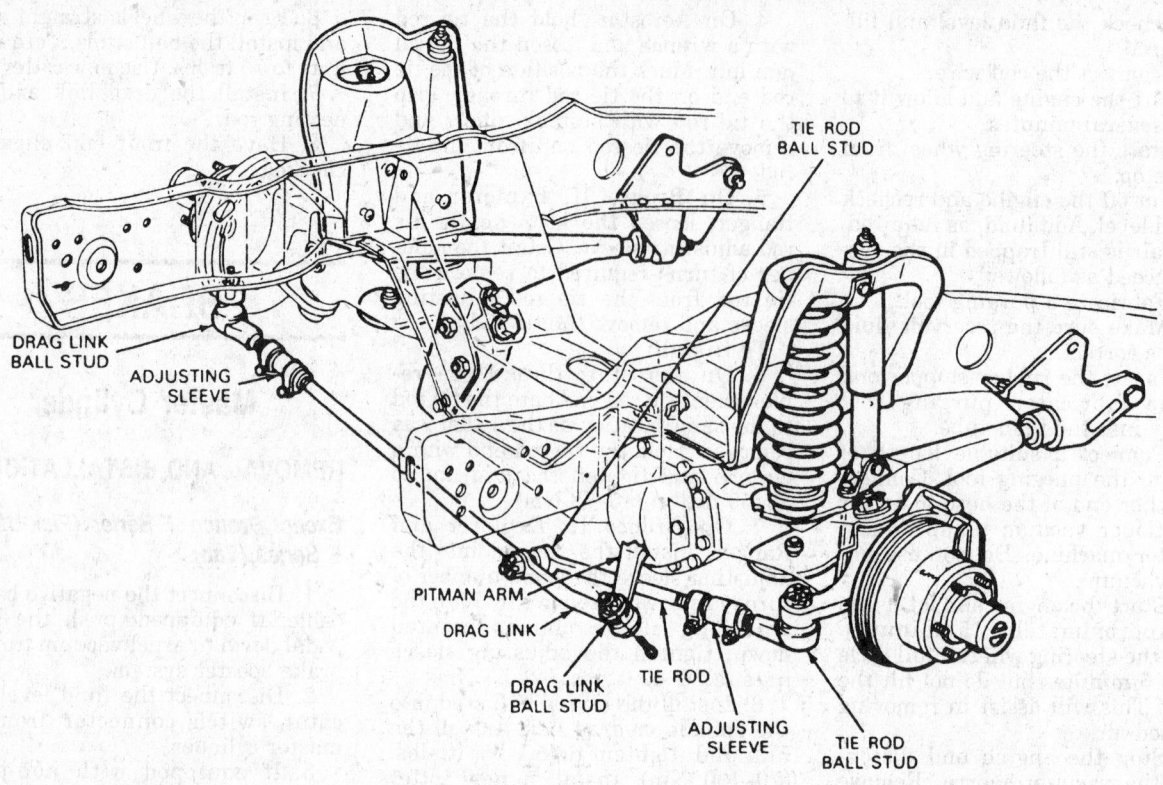

Steering linkage — 4WD Bronco and F 150

cylinder to the booster without this square section interface seal.

8. If equipped with non-power brakes and the dash spacer was removed, coat the spacer with sealer and install on the dash panel.

9. Install the master cylinder with the attaching nuts. On Aerostar, be careful not to scratch the exposed primary piston and make sure the primary piston socket engages the booster pushrod before tightening. Tighten the nuts to 20 ft. lbs. (27 Nm). Connect the fluid level indicator switch.

10. If equipped with non-power brakes, secure the pushrod to the brake pedal assembly with the pin or shoulder bolt. Make sure the bushings and spacers are installed properly. Install the lockpin and connect the wires to the stop light switch.

11. Connect the brake lines to the master cylinder and fill the master cylinder fluid reservoir. Wrap a shop cloth around the tubing below the fitting to be bled to absorb escaping brake fluid.

12. Have an assistant push the brake pedal to the floor. Crack open the brake line fitting to expel air trapped in the master cylinder. Tighten the fitting, then let the brake pedal return. Repeat this procedure until all air is expelled.

13. Repeat Step 12 on the remaining brake line fitting(s).

14. Final tighten the brake line fittings. Bleed the brake system, as required. Check the master cylinder fluid level.

Bronco, F Series (Pick-Up) and E Series (Van)

1. With the engine off, depress the brake pedal several times to expel any vacuum.

2. Disconnect the fluid level warning switch wire.

3. Disconnect the hydraulic system brake lines at the master cylinder.

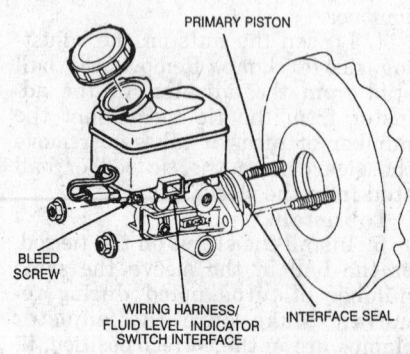

Master cylinder installation — Aerostar

4. Remove the master cylinder retaining nuts and remove the master cylinder.

To install:

5. Position the master cylinder assembly on the booster and install the retaining nuts. Torque the nuts to 18–25 ft. lbs.

6. Connect the hydraulic brake system lines to the master cylinder.

7. Connect the wiring.

8. Bleed the master cylinder.

Combination Valve

REMOVAL AND INSTALLATION

1. Disconnect and plug the brake lines at the valve.

2. Remove the valve attaching bolt and remove the valve.

3. Installation is the reverse of the removal procedure. Bleed the brake system.

Pressure Differential Valve

REMOVAL AND INSTALLATION

Except F Super Duty

1. Disconnect the electrical leads from the valve.

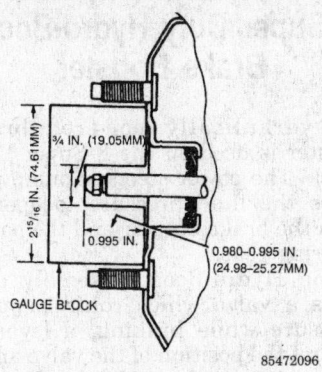

Power brake booster dimensions

2. Unscrew the valve from the master cylinder.

3. Install the valve in the reverse order of removal.

4. Bleed the master cylinder.

Height Sensing Proportioning Valve

REMOVAL AND INSTALLATION

F-Super Duty Only

NOTE: If the linkage is disconnected from the valve, the proper setting of the valve will be lost and a new valve will have to be installed. The new valve will have the shaft preset and secured internally. If the shaft of the new valve turns freely; do not use it! The valve cannot be repaired or disassembled. It is to be replaced as a unit. If the linkage is damaged or broken and requires replacement, a new sensing valve will also be required.

1. Raise and safely support the vehicle.

2. Raise the frame to obtain a clearance of 6⅝ in. (168.3mm) between the bottom edge of the rubber jounce bumper and the top of the axle tube — on BOTH sides of the axle. The is the correct indexing height for the valve.

3. Remove the nut holding the linkage arm to the valve and disconnect the arm.

4. Remove the bolt holding the flexible brake hose to the valve.

5. Disconnect the brake line from the valve.

6. Remove the 2 mounting bolts and remove the valve from its bracket.

To install:

7. Place the new valve on the bracket and tighten the mounting bolts to 12–18 ft. lbs.

8. Install the brake hose, using new copper gaskets and tighten the bolt to 28–34 ft. lbs.

9. Attach the brake line to the lower part of the valve.

10. Connect the linkage arm to the valve and tighten the nut to 8–10 ft. lbs.

11. Bleed the brakes.

NOTE: When servicing axle or suspension parts which would require disconnection of the valve, instead, remove the 2 nuts that attach the linkage arm to the axle cover plate. This will avoid disconnecting the valve and avoid having to replace the valve.

Power Brake Booster

REMOVAL AND INSTALLATION

Except Bronco, F Series (Pick-Up) and E Series (Van)

1. Disconnect the negative battery cable. Support the master cylinder from the underside with a prop.

2. Disconnect the vacuum hose from the booster check valve and remove the check valve.

3. Remove the master cylinder-to-booster retaining nuts. Pull the master cylinder off the booster and leave it supported by the prop, out of the way enough to allow booster removal.

4. Working inside the cab, remove the hairpin retainer and slide the stoplight switch, valve rod, spacers and bushing off the brake pedal arm. Remove the nuts retaining the booster and remove the booster.

To install:

5. Mount the booster assembly on the engine side of the dash panel by sliding the bracket mounting bolts and valve operating rod in through the holes in the dash panel.

6. Working inside the cab, install the booster mounting nuts and tighten to 13–25 ft. lbs. (18–33 Nm).

7. Before installing the master cylinder on all except Aerostar, check the distance from the outer end of the vacuum booster assembly pushrod to the front face of the vacuum brake booster assembly. The distance should be 0.980–0.995 in. (24.89–25.27mm). Turn the pushrod adjusting screw in or out, as required, to obtain the proper length.

8. Install the master cylinder and tighten the retaining nuts to 20 ft. lbs. (27 Nm). Remove the prop from under the master cylinder.

9. Install the booster check valve and connect the vacuum hose. Check the hose routing to make sure the hose is not crimped.

10. Working inside the cab, install the bushing and position the switch on the end of the valve rod, then install the switch and rod on the pedal arm along with the spacers and hairpin retainer.

NOTE: Use only the factory supplied hairpin retainer. Do not substitute other types of retainers.

11. Connect the negative battery cable, start the engine and check brake operation.

F-150, F-250 and Bronco

1. Disconnect the brake light switch wires.

2. Support the master cylinder from below.

3. Loosen the clamp and remove the booster check valve hose.

4. Remove the master cylinder from the booster. Keep it supported. It will not be necessary to disconnect the brake lines.

5. Working inside the vehicle below the instrument panel, disconnect the booster valve operating rod from the brake pedal assembly.

6. Remove the four bracket-to-dash panel attaching nuts.

7. Remove the booster and bracket assembly from the dash panel, sliding the valve operating rod out from the engine side of the dash panel.

To install:

8. Mount the booster and bracket assembly on the dash panel by sliding the valve operating rod in through the hole in the dash panel, and installing the attaching nuts. Torque the nuts to 18–25 ft. lbs.

9. Connect the manifold vacuum hose to the booster.

10. Install the master cylinder. Torque the nuts to 18–25 ft. lbs.

11. Connect the stop light switch wires.

12. Working inside the vehicle below the instrument panel, connect the pushrod and stoplight switch.

F-250 HD and F-350

1. Disconnect the brake light switch wires.

2. Support the master cylinder from below, with a prop of some kind.

3. Loosen the clamp and remove the booster check valve hose.

4. Remove the wraparound clip from the booster inboard stud.

5. Remove the master cylinder from the booster. Keep it supported. It will not be necessary to disconnect the brake lines.

6. Working inside the vehicle below the instrument panel, disconnect the booster valve operating rod from the brake pedal assembly.

7. Remove the four bracket-to-dash panel attaching nuts.

8. Remove the booster and bracket assembly from the dash panel, sliding the valve operating rod out from the engine side of the dash panel.

To install:

9. Mount the booster and bracket assembly on the dash panel by sliding the valve operating rod in through the hole in the dash panel, and installing the attaching nuts. Torque the nuts to 18–25 ft. lbs.

10. Connect the manifold vacuum hose to the booster.

11. Install the master cylinder. Torque the nuts to 18–25 ft. lbs.

12. Install the wraparound clip.

13. Connect the stop light switch wires.

14. Working inside the vehicle below the instrument panel, connect the pushrod and stoplight switch.

BRAKE BOOSTER PUSHROD ADJUSTMENT

Bronco, F Series (Pick-Up) and E Series (Van)

The pushrod has an adjustment screw to maintain the correct relationship between the booster control valve plunger and the master cylinder piston. If the plunger is too long it will prevent the master cylinder piston from completely releasing hydraulic pressure, causing the brakes to drag. If the plunger is too short it will cause excessive pedal travel and an undesirable clunk in the booster area. Remove the master cylinder for access to the booster pushrod.

To check the adjustment of the screw, place a gauge against the master cylinder mounting surface of the booster body. Adjust the pushrod screw by turning it until the end of the screw just touches the inner edge of the slot in the gauge. Install the master cylinder and bleed the system.

Diesel Brake Booster Vacuum Pump

The diesel is equipped with a vacuum pump, which is driven by a single belt off of the alternator. This pump is located on the top right side of the engine.

Diesel pickups are also equipped with a low vacuum indicator switch which actuates the BRAKE warning lamp when available vacuum is below a certain level. The switch senses vacuum through a fitting in the vacuum manifold that intercepts the vacuum flow from the pump. The low vacuum switch is mounted on the right side of the engine compartment, adjacent to the vacuum pump on F-250 and F-350 models.

NOTE: The vacuum pump cannot be disassembled. It is only serviced as a unit (the pulley is separate).

REMOVAL AND INSTALLATION

1. Remove the hose clamp and disconnect the pump from the hose on the manifold vacuum outlet fitting.

2. Loosen the vacuum pump adjustment bolt and the pivot bolt. Slide the pump downward and remove the drive belt from the pulley.

3. Remove the pivot and adjustment bolts and the bolts retaining the pump to the adjustment plate. Remove the vacuum pump and adjustment plate.

To install:

4. Install the pump-to-adjustment plate bolts and tighten to 11–18 ft. lbs. Position the pump and plate on the vacuum pump bracket and loosely install the pivot and adjustment bolts.

5. Connect the hose from the manifold vacuum outlet fitting to the pump and install the hose clamp.

6. Install the drive belt on the pulley. Place a ³⁄₈ in. drive breaker bar or ratchet into the slot on the vacuum pump adjustment plate. Lift up on the assembly until the proper belt tension is obtained. Tighten the pivot and adjustment bolts to 11–18 ft. lbs.

7. Start the engine and make sure the brake system functions properly.

NOTE: The BRAKE light will glow until brake vacuum builds up to the normal level.

F-Super Duty Hydro-Boost Brake Booster

A hydraulically powered brake booster is used on the F-Super Duty truck. The power steering pump provides the fluid pressure to operate both the brake booster and the power steering gear.

The Hydro-Boost assembly contains a valve which controls pump pressure while braking, a lever to control the position of the valve and a boost piston to provide the force to operate a conventional master cylinder attached to the front of the booster. The Hydro-Boost also has a reserve system, designed to store sufficient pressurized fluid to provide at least 2 brake applications in the event of insufficient fluid flow from the power steering pump. The brakes can also be applied unassisted if the reserve system is depleted.

—— **WARNING** ——

Before removing the Hydro-Boost, discharge the accumulator by making several brake applications until a hard pedal is felt.

REMOVAL AND INSTALLATION

—— **CAUTION** ——

Do not depress the brake pedal with the master cylinder removed!

1. Remove the master cylinder from the Hydro-Boost unit. Do not disconnect the brake lines from the master cylinder! Position the master cylinder out of the way.

2. Disconnect the 3 hydraulic lines from the Hydro-Boost unit.

3. Disconnect the pushrod from the brake pedal.

4. Remove the booster mounting nuts and lift the booster from the firewall.

—— **CAUTION** ——

The booster should never be carried by the accumulator. The accumulator contains high pressure nitrogen and can be dangerous if mishandled! If the accumulator is to be disposed of, do not expose it to fire or other forms of incineration! Gas pressure can be relieved by drilling a ¹⁄₁₆ in. (1.5mm) hole in the end of the accumulator can. Always wear safety goggles during the drilling!

5. Installation is the reverse of removal. Torque the booster mounting nuts to 25 ft. lbs.; the master cylinder

nuts to 25 ft. lbs.; connect the hydraulic lines, refill and bleed the booster as follows:

a. Fill the pump reservoir with Dexron®II ATF.

b. Disconnect the coil wires and crank the engine for several seconds.

c. Check the fluid level and refill, if necessary.

d. Connect the coil wires and start the engine.

e. With the engine running, turn the steering wheel lock-to-lock twice. Shut off the engine.

f. Depress the brake pedal several times to discharge the accumulator.

g. Start the engine and repeat Step e.

h. If foam appears in the reservoir, allow the foam to dissipate.

i. Repeat Step E as often as necessary to expel all air from the system.

NOTE: The system is, in effect, self-bleeding and normal vehicle operation will expel any further trapped air.

Front Brake Caliper

REMOVAL AND INSTALLATION

Except Bronco, F Series (Pick-Up) and E Series (Van)

1. Siphon part of the brake fluid out of the master cylinder to avoid overflow when the caliper piston is pressed into the caliper bore.

2. Raise the vehicle and support it safely. Remove the wheel and tire assembly.

3. Position an 8 in. C-clamp on the caliper and tighten the clamp to move the caliper piston into the bore approximately ⅛ in. Avoid clamp contact with the outer shoe spring clip. Remove the clamp.

NOTE: Do not pry the piston away from the rotor.

4. Clean excess dirt from the pin tab area.

5. Using a ¼ in. drive socket, ⅜ in. deep and a light hammer, tap the upper caliper pin towards the outboard side until the pin tabs pass the spindle face.

6. Compress the inboard pin tab, if equipped, with pliers and, with a hammer, drive the pin out until the tab slips into the spindle groove.

7. Place 1 end of a ⁷⁄₁₆ in. diameter punch against the end of the caliper pin and tap the pin out of the caliper slide groove.

8. Repeat Steps 5, 6 and 7 to remove the lower pin.

9. Disconnect and plug the brake hose at the caliper. Remove the caliper from the rotor.

To install:

10. Make sure the caliper mounting surfaces are free of dirt. Lubricate the caliper grooves with disc brake caliper grease and install the caliper.

11. From the caliper outboard side, position the pin between the caliper and spindle grooves. The pin must be positioned so the tabs will be installed against the spindle outer face.

12. Tap the pin on the outboard end with a hammer until the retention tabs on the sides of the pin contact the spindle face.

13. Repeat Steps 11 and 12 for the lower pin.

NOTE: During installation, do not allow the tabs of the caliper pin to be tapped too far into the spindle groove. If this happens, it will be necessary to tap the other end of the caliper pin until the tabs snap in place. The tabs on each end of the pin must be free to catch on the spindle face.

14. Connect the brake hose to the caliper. Bleed the brake system.

15. Install the wheel and tire assembly and lower the vehicle. Check the brake fluid level and check the brakes for proper operation.

Bronco, F Series (Pick-Up) and E Series (Van)

1. Raise and safely support the vehicle.

2. Remove the wheels.

3. Remove the caliper and the brake pads.

4. Disconnect the brake hose from the caliper.

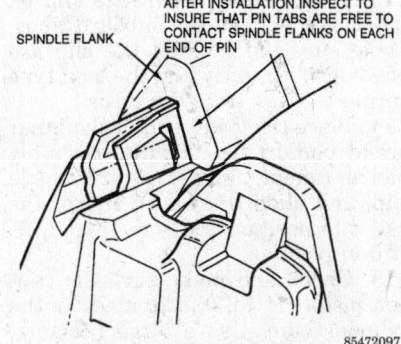

SPINDLE FLANK — AFTER INSTALLATION INSPECT TO INSURE THAT PIN TABS ARE FREE TO CONTACT SPINDLE FLANKS ON EACH END OF PIN

85472097

Correct caliper pin installation

To install:

5. Connect the brake hose to the caliper. When connecting the brake fluid hose to the caliper, it is recommended that a new copper washer be used at the connection of the brake hose and caliper.

6. Install the brake caliper and pads.

7. Install the wheels and lower the vehicle. Bleed the brake system.

Rear Brake Caliper

REMOVAL AND INSTALLATION

Bronco, F Series (Pick-Up) and E Series (Van)

1. Raise and safely support the vehicle.

2. Remove the wheels.

3. Remove the caliper and the brake pads.

4. Disconnect the brake hose from the caliper. Cap the openings at once!

5. When connecting the brake fluid hose to the caliper, it is recommended that a new copper washer be used at the connection of the brake hose and caliper.

6. Bleed the brake system and install the wheels. Lower the vehicle.

Front Disc Brake Pads

REMOVAL AND INSTALLATION

Except Bronco, F Series (Pick-Up) and E Series (Van)

1. Siphon part of the brake fluid out of the master cylinder to avoid overflow when the caliper piston is pressed into the caliper bore.

2. Raise the vehicle and support it safely. Remove the wheel and tire assembly.

3. Remove the brake caliper, but do not disconnect the brake hose. Secure the caliper aside with mechanics wire.

NOTE: Do not let the caliper hang by the brake hose.

4. Compress the anti-rattle clip and remove the inner brake pad from the caliper.

5. Press each ear of the outer brake pad away from the caliper and slide the torque buttons out of the retention notches.

To install:

6. Bottom out the caliper piston in the caliper bore using an 8 in. C-clamp and a worn out inner brake pad or block of wood to push against

the piston. Do not attempt to bottom out the piston with the outer brake pad installed.

7. Place a new anti-rattle clip on the lower end of the inner brake pad. Make sure the tabs on the clip are properly positioned and the clip is fully seated.

8. Position the inner brake pad and anti-rattle clip in the pad abutment with the ant-rattle clip tab against the pad abutment and the loop-type spring away from the rotor. Compress the anti-rattle clip and slide the upper end of the pad in position.

9. Install the outer pad, making sure the torque buttons on the pad are seated solidly in the matching holes in the caliper.

10. Install the caliper on the spindle.

11. Install the wheel and tire assembly and lower the vehicle. Apply the brakes several times before moving the vehicle to seat the pads.

12. Check the brake fluid level. Check the brakes for proper operation.

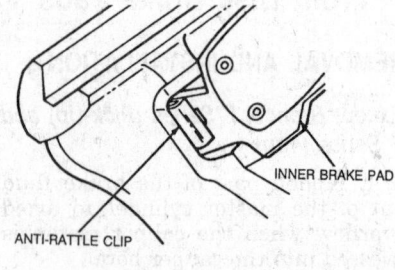

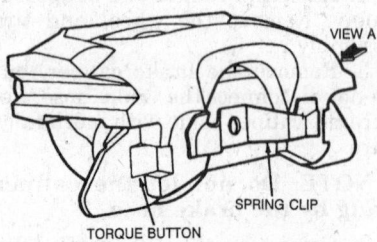

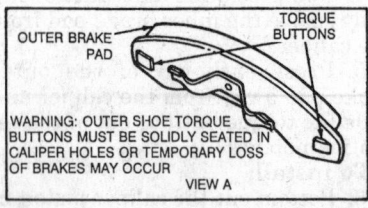

WARNING: OUTER SHOE TORQUE BUTTONS MUST BE SOLIDLY SEATED IN CALIPER HOLES OR TEMPORARY LOSS OF BRAKES MAY OCCUR

VIEW A

85472098

Correct brake pad installation — Except Bronco, F Series (Pick-Up) and E Series (Van)

Bronco, F Series (Pick-Up) and E Series (Van)

NOTE: Never replace the pads on one side only! Always replace pads on both wheels as a set!

LD SLIDING CALIPER (SINGLE PISTON)

1. To avoid overflowing of the master cylinder when the caliper pistons are pressed into the caliper cylinder bores, siphon or dip some brake fluid out of the larger reservoir.

2. Raise and safely support the vehicle and remove the wheels.

3. Place an 8 in. (203mm) C-clamp on the caliper and tighten the clamp to bottom the caliper piston in the cylinder bore. Bear the clamp on the outer pad; never press directly on the piston! Remove the C-clamp.

4. Clean the excess dirt from around the caliper pin tabs.

5. Drive the upper caliper pin inward until the tabs on the pin touch the spindle.

6. Insert a small prybar into the slot provided behind the pin tabs on the inboard side of the pin.

7. Using needlenose pliers, compress the outboard end of the pin while, at the same time, prying with the prybar until the tabs slip into the groove in the spindle.

8. Place the end of a 7/16 in. (11mm) punch against the end of the caliper pin and drive the pin out of the caliper slide groove.

9. Repeat this procedure for the lower pin.

10. Lift the caliper off of the rotor.

11. Remove the brake pads and anti-rattle spring.

NOTE: Do not allow the caliper to hand by the brake hose.

To install:

12. Thoroughly clean the areas of the caliper and spindle assembly which contact each other during the sliding action of the caliper.

13. Place a new anti-rattle clip on the lower end of the inboard shoe. Make sure the tabs on the clip are positioned correctly and the loop-type spring is away from the rotor.

14. Place the lower end of the inner brake pad in the spindle assembly pad abutment, against the anti-rattle clip, and slide the upper end of the pad into position. Be sure the clip is still in position.

15. Check and make sure the caliper piston is fully bottomed in the cylinder bore. Use a large C-clamp, bearing on a piece of wood, to bottom the piston, if necessary.

16. Position the outer brake pad on the caliper, and press the pad tabs into place with your fingers. If the pad cannot be pressed into place by hand, use a C-clamp. Be careful not to damage the lining with the clamp. Bend the tabs to prevent rattling.

17. Position the caliper on the spindle assembly. Lightly lubricate the caliper sliding grooves with caliper pin grease.

18. Position the a new upper pin with the retention tabs next to the spindle groove.

NOTE: Don't use the bolt and nut with the new pin.

19. Carefully drive the pin, at the outboard end, inward until the tabs contact the spindle face.

20. Repeat the procedure for the lower pin.

― **WARNING** ―
Don't drive the pins in too far, or it will be necessary to drive them back out until the tabs snap into place. The tabs on each end of the pin must be free to catch on the spindle sides!

21. Install the wheels.

HD SLIDING CALIPER (TWO PISTON)

1. To avoid overflowing of the master cylinder when the caliper pistons are pressed into the caliper cylinder bores, siphon or dip some brake fluid out of the larger reservoir.

2. Raise and safely support the vehicle.

3. Remove the wheels.

4. Place an 8 in. (203mm) C-clamp on the caliper and, with the clamp bearing on the outer pad, tighten the clamp to bottom the caliper pistons in the cylinder bores. Remove the C-clamp.

5. Clean the excess dirt from around the caliper pin tabs.

6. Drive the upper caliper pin inward until the tabs on the pin touch the spindle.

7. Insert a small prybar into the slot provided behind the pin tabs on the inboard side of the pin.

8. Using needlenose pliers, compress the outboard end of the pin while, at the same time, prying with the prybar until the tabs slip into the groove in the spindle.

9. Place the end of a 7/16 in. (11mm) punch against the end of the caliper pin and drive the pin out of the caliper slide groove.

10. Repeat this procedure for the lower pin.

11. Lift the caliper off of the rotor.

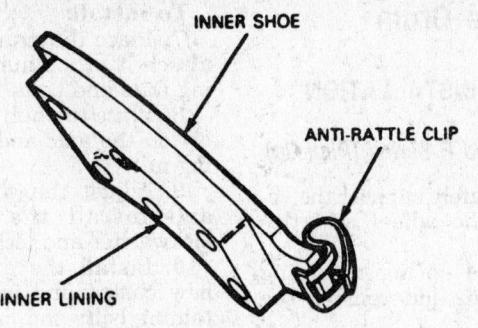

INNER SHOE

ANTI-RATTLE CLIP

INNER LINING

85472218

Installing anti-rattle clip on inner pad — single piston caliper — Bronco, F Series (Pick-Up) and E Series (Van)

12. Remove the brake pads and anti-rattle spring.

NOTE: Do not allow the caliper to hand by the brake hose.

To install:
13. Thoroughly clean the areas of the caliper and spindle assembly which contact each other during the sliding action of the caliper.
14. Place a new anti-rattle clip on the lower end of the inboard shoe. Make sure the tabs on the clip are positioned correctly and the loop-type spring is away from the rotor.
15. Place the lower end of the inner brake pad in the spindle assembly pad abutment, against the anti-rattle clip, and slide the upper end of the pad into position. Be sure the clip is still in position.
16. Check and make sure the caliper piston is fully bottomed in the cylinder bore. Use a large C-clamp to bottom the piston, if necessary.
17. Position the outer brake pad on the caliper, and press the pad tabs into place with your fingers. If the pad cannot be pressed into place by hand, use a C-clamp. Be careful not to damage the lining with the clamp. Bend the tabs to prevent rattling.
18. Position the caliper on the spindle assembly. Lightly lubricate the caliper sliding grooves with caliper pin grease.
19. Position the a new upper pin with the retention tabs next to the spindle groove.

NOTE: Don't use the bolt and nut with the new pin.

20. Carefully drive the pin, at the outboard end, inward until the tabs contact the spindle face.
21. Repeat the procedure for the lower pin.

—————— WARNING ——————
Don't drive the pins in too far, or it will be necessary to drive them back out until the tabs snap into

place. The tabs on each end of the pin MUST be free to catch on the spindle sides!

22. Install the wheels.

Rear Disc Brake Pads

REMOVAL AND INSTALLATION

Bronco, F Series (Pick-Up) and E Series (Van)

NOTE: Never replace the pads on one side only! Always replace pads on both wheels as a set!

1. To avoid overflowing of the master cylinder when the caliper pistons are pressed into the caliper cylinder bores, siphon or dip some brake fluid out of the larger reservoir.
2. Raise and safely support the vehicle.
3. Remove the wheels.
4. Place an 8 in. (203mm) C-clamp on the caliper and tighten the clamp to bottom the caliper pistons in the cylinder bores. Remove the C-clamp.
5. Clean the excess dirt from around the caliper pin tabs.
6. Drive the upper caliper pin inward until the tabs on the pin touch the caliper support.
7. Insert a small prybar into the slot provided behind the pin tabs on the inboard side of the pin.
8. Using needlenose pliers, compress the outboard end of the pin while, at the same time, prying with the prybar until the tabs slip into the groove in the caliper support.
9. Place the end of a 7/16 in. (11mm) punch against the end of the caliper pin and drive the pin out of the caliper slide groove.
10. Repeat this procedure for the lower pin.
11. Lift the caliper off of the rotor.

12. Remove the brake pads and anti-rattle spring.

NOTE: Do not allow the caliper to hand by the brake hose.

13. Thoroughly clean the areas of the caliper and caliper support assembly which contact each other during the sliding action of the caliper.
To install:
14. Place a new anti-rattle clip on the lower end of the inboard shoe. Make sure the tabs on the clip are positioned correctly and the loop-type spring is away from the rotor.
15. Place the lower end of the inner brake pad in the caliper support assembly pad abutment, against the anti-rattle clip, and slide the upper end of the pad into position. Be sure the clip is still in position.
16. Check and make sure the caliper pistons are fully bottomed in the cylinder bores. Use a large C-clamp to bottom the pistons, if necessary.
17. Position the outer brake pad on the caliper, and press the pad tabs into place with your fingers. If the pad cannot be pressed into place by hand, use a C-clamp. Be careful not to damage the lining with the clamp. Bend the tabs to prevent rattling.
18. Position the caliper on the caliper support. Lightly lubricate the caliper sliding grooves with caliper pin grease.
19. Position the a new upper pin with the retention tabs next to the support groove.

NOTE: Don't use the bolt and nut with the new pin.

20. Carefully drive the pin, at the outboard end, inward until the tabs contact the caliper support face.
21. Repeat the procedure for the lower pin.

—————— WARNING ——————
Don't drive the pins in too far, or it will be necessary to drive them back out until the tabs snap into place. The tabs on each end of the pin MUST be free to catch on the support sides!

22. Install the wheels.

Front Brake Rotor

REMOVAL AND INSTALLATION

Except Bronco, F Series (Pick-Up) and E Series (Van)

1. Raise and safely support the vehicle. Remove the wheel and tire assembly.

2. Remove the caliper and support it aside with mechanics wire. Do not let the caliper hang by the brake hose.

3. On 2WD vehicles, remove the dust cap, cotter pin, nut, washer and outer bearing and remove the rotor from the spindle.

4. On 4WD Aerostar, remove the retainers and remove the brake rotor. On all other 4WD vehicles, remove the locking hub and remove the brake rotor.

5. Inspect the rotor for scoring, wear and runout; machine or replace as necessary.

6. Install in the reverse order of removal. Adjust the wheel bearings.

Bronco, F Series (Pick-Up) and E Series (Van)

EXCEPT F-SUPER DUTY WITH 4-WHEEL DISC BRAKES

1. Raise and safely support the vehicle. Remove the front wheel.

2. Remove the caliper assembly and support it on the frame with a piece of wire without disconnecting the brake fluid hose.

3. Remove the hub and rotor assembly.

4. Install the rotor in the reverse order of removal, and adjust the wheel bearing .

F-SUPER DUTY WITH 4-WHEEL DISC BRAKES

The hub and rotor are individual pieces, allowing the rotor to be replaced independently. The front and rear rotors are the same and are attached with 10 bolts and washers. The bolts are tightened a little at a time, in a criss-cross fashion, to an ultimate torque of 74–89 ft. lbs.

Rear Brake Rotor

REMOVAL AND INSTALLATION

Bronco, F Series (Pick-Up) and E Series (Van)

1. Raise and safely support the vehicle. Remove the wheel.

2. Remove the caliper assembly and support it to the frame with a piece of wire without disconnecting the brake fluid hose.

3. Remove the axle hub and rotor assembly.

4. Install the rotor.

Brake Drum

REMOVAL AND INSTALLATION

Except Bronco and F Series (Pick-Up)

1. Raise and safely support the vehicle. Remove the wheel and tire assembly.

2. Remove the spring retaining nuts, if equipped, and remove the brake drum.

NOTE: If the brake drum will not come off, insert a narrow prybar through the brake adjusting hole in the backing plate and disengage the adjusting lever from the adjusting screw. While holding the adjusting lever away from the adjusting screw, loosen the adjusting screw with a brake adjusting tool.

3. Inspect the brake drum surface for wear, scoring and runout. Machine or replace, as necessary.

4. Installation is the reverse of the removal procedure.

Bronco, F-150 and F-250 Light Duty

1. Raise and safely support the vehicle.

2. Remove the wheel. Remove the three retaining nuts and remove the brake drum. It may be necessary to back off the brake shoe adjustment in order to remove the brake drum. This is because the drum might be grooved or worn from being in service for an extended period of time.

3. Before installing a new brake drum, be sure to remove any protective coating with carburetor degreaser.

4. Install the brake drum in the reverse order of removal and adjust the brakes.

F-250HD and F-350

1. Raise and safely support the vehicle.

2. Remove the wheel. Loosen the rear brake shoe adjustment.

3. Remove the rear axle retaining bolts and lockwashers, axle shaft, and gasket.

4. Remove the wheel bearing locknut, lockwasher, and adjusting nut.

5. Remove the hub and drum assembly from the axle.

6. Remove the brake drum-to-hub retaining screws, bolts or bolts and nut. Remove the brake drum from the hub.

To install:

7. Place the drum on the hub and attach it to the hub with the attaching nuts and bolts.

8. Place the hub and drum assembly on the axle and start the adjusting nut.

9. Adjust the wheel bearing nut and install the wheel bearing lockwasher and locknut.

10. Install the axle shaft with a new gasket and install the axle retaining bolts and lockwashers.

11. Install the wheel and adjust the brake shoes. Lower the vehicle.

ADJUSTMENTS

Drum Brakes

This procedure is used on Bronco, F Series (Pick-Up) and E Series (Van)

DRUM INSTALLED

1. Raise and safely support the vehicle.

2. Remove the rubber plug from the adjusting slot on the backing plate.

3. Insert a brake adjusting spoon into the slot and engage the lowest possible tooth on the starwheel. Move the end of the brake spoon downward to move the starwheel upward and expand the adjusting screw. Repeat this operation until the brakes lock the wheels.

4. Insert a small prybar or piece of firm wire (coat hanger wire) into the adjusting slot and push the automatic adjusting lever out and free of the starwheel on the adjusting screw and hold it there.

5. Engage the topmost tooth possible on the starwheel with the brake adjusting spoon. Move the end of the adjusting spoon upward to move the adjusting screw starwheel downward and contract the adjusting screw. Back off the adjusting screw starwheel until the wheel spins freely with a minimum of drag. Keep track of the number of turns that the starwheel is backed off, or the number of strokes taken with the brake adjusting spoon.

6. Repeat this operation for the other side. When backing off the brakes on the other side, the starwheel adjuster must be backed off the same number of turns to prevent side-to-side brake pull.

7. When the brakes are adjusted make several stops while backing the vehicle, to equalize the brakes at both of the wheels.

8. Remove the safety stands and lower the vehicle. Road test the vehicle.

DRUM REMOVED

1. Make sure the shoe-to-contact pad areas are clean and properly lubricated.

2. Using an inside caliper check the inside diameter of the drum. Measure across the diameter of the assembled brake shoes, at their widest point.

3. Turn the adjusting screw so the diameter of the shoes is 0.030 in. (0.76mm) less than the brake drum inner diameter.

4. Install the drum.

Brake Shoes

REMOVAL AND INSTALLATION

Except Bronco and F Series (Pick-Up)

1. Raise and safely support the vehicle. Remove the wheel and tire assembly and the brake drum.

2. Pull backward on the adjusting lever cable to disengage the adjusting lever from the adjusting screw. Move the outboard side of the adjusting screw upward and back off the pivot nut as far as it will go.

3. Pull the adjusting lever, cable and automatic adjuster spring down and toward the rear to unhook the pivot hook from the large hole in the secondary shoe web. Do not pry the pivot hook from the hole.

4. Remove the automatic adjuster spring and adjusting lever.

5. Remove the secondary shoe-to-anchor spring using a suitable brake spring removal/installation tool. Using the tool, remove the primary shoe-to-anchor spring and unhook the cable anchor. Remove the anchor pin plate, if equipped.

6. Remove the cable guide from the secondary shoe.

7. Remove the shoe hold-down springs, shoes, adjusting screw, pivot nut and socket. Note the color and position of each hold-down spring so they can be reassembled in the same position.

8. Remove the parking brake link and spring. Disconnect the parking brake cable from the parking brake lever.

9. Remove the secondary brake shoe. On 9 in. rear brakes, remove the parking brake lever from the shoe. On 10 in. rear brakes, remove the retainer clip and spring washer and remove the parking brake lever.

To install:

10. Clean the backing plate ledge pads and sand lightly. Apply a light coating of high temperature lithium grease to the points where the brake shoes touch the backing plate. Lubricate the adjusting cable eye and the anchor pin area.

11. Install the parking brake lever on the secondary shoe. On 10 in. brakes, secure with the spring washer and retaining clip.

12. Position the brake shoes on the backing plate and install the hold-down spring pins, springs and cups. Install the parking brake link, spring and washer. Connect the parking brake cable to the parking brake lever.

13. Install the anchor pin plate, if equipped, and place the cable anchor over the anchor pin with the crimped side toward the backing plate.

14. Install the primary shoe-to-anchor spring using the brake spring removal/installation tool.

15. Install the cable guide on the secondary shoe with the flanged hole fitted into the hole in the secondary shoe. Thread the cable around the cable guide groove.

NOTE: Make sure the cable is positioned in the groove and not between the guide and shoe web.

16. Install the secondary shoe-to-anchor (long) spring.

NOTE: Make sure the cable end is not cocked or binding on the anchor pin when installed. All parts should be flat on the anchor pin.

17. Apply high temperature lithium grease to the threads and the socket end of the adjusting screw. Turn the adjusting screw into the adjusting pivot nut to the end of the threads and then loosen, ½ turn.

18. Place the adjusting socket on the screw and install the assembly between the shoe ends with the adjusting screw nearest the secondary shoe.

NOTE: Be sure to install the adjusting screw on the same side of the vehicle from which it came. To prevent incorrect installation, the socket end of each adjusting screw is stamped with R or L, to indicate installation on the right or left side of the vehicle. The adjusting pivot nuts have lines machined around the body of the nut, 2 lines indicating the right side nut and 1 line indicating the left side nut.

19. Hook the cable hook into the hole in the adjusting lever from the outboard plate side. The adjusting levers are also stamped with an **R** or **L** to indicate right or left side installation.

20. Place the hooked end of the adjuster spring in the large hole in the primary shoe web and connect the loop end of the spring to the adjuster lever hole.

21. Pull the adjuster lever, cable and automatic adjuster spring down toward the rear to engage the pivot hook in the large hole in the secondary shoe web.

22. After installation, check the action of the adjuster by pulling the section of the cable between the cable guide and the adjusting lever toward the secondary shoe web far enough to lift the lever past a tooth on the adjusting screw wheel. The lever should snap into position behind the next tooth and releasing the cable should cause the adjuster spring to return the lever to its original position. This return action will turn the adjusting screw 1 tooth.

23. If pulling the cable does not produce the action described in Step 22 or if lever action is sluggish instead of positive and sharp, check the position of the lever on the adjusting screw toothed wheel. With the brake in a vertical position, anchor at the top, the lever should contact the adjusting wheel 1 tooth above the center line of the adjusting screw. If the contact point is below the center line, the lever will not lock on the adjusting screw wheel teeth and the screw will not turn as the lever is actuated by the cable.

24. To find the cause of the condition described in Step 23, proceed as follows:

a. Check the cable and fittings. The cable should completely fill or extend slightly beyond the crimped section of the fittings. If this does not happen, the cable assembly may be damaged and should be replaced.

b. Check the cable guide for damage. The cable groove should be parallel to the shoe web and the body of the guide should lie flat against the web. Replace the guide if it shows damage.

c. Check the pivot hook on the lever. The hook surfaces should be square with the body on the lever for proper pivoting. Repair the hook or replace the lever if the hook shows damage.

d. Be sure the adjusting screw socket is properly seated in the notch in the shoe web.

25. Adjust the brake shoes using either a brake adjustment gauge or manually with the drums installed.

26. If using a brake adjustment gauge, proceed as follows:

a. Measure the inside diameter of the brake drum with the gauge.

b. Reverse the tool and adjust the brake shoes until they touch the gauge. The gauge contact points on the shoes must be parallel to the vehicle with the center line through the center of the axle.

c. Install the drum and wheel and tire assembly. Lower the vehicle.

d. Apply the brakes sharply several times while driving the vehicle in reverse. Check brake operation by making several stops while driving forward.

27. If manually adjusting the brakes, proceed as follows:

a. a. Install the brake drum and wheel and tire assembly.

b. Remove the cover from the adjusting hole at the bottom of the backing plate and turn the adjusting screw, using a suitable brake adjusting tool, to expand the brake shoes until they drag against the brake drum.

c. When the shoes are against the drum, insert a narrow prybar through the brake adjusting hole and disengage the adjusting lever from the adjusting screw. While holding the adjusting lever away from the adjusting screw, loosen the adjusting screw with the brake adjusting tool, until the drum rotates freely without drag.

d. Install the adjusting hole cover and lower the vehicle.

e. Apply the brakes. If the pedal travels more than halfway to the floor, there is too much clearance between the brake shoes and drums. Repeat the adjustment procedure.

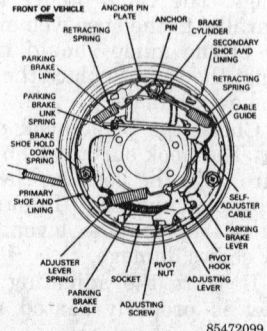

Rear brake shoe assembly — Except Bronco, F Series (Pick-Up) and E Series (Van)

Bronco, F-150 and F-250 Light Duty

1. Raise and support the vehicle and remove the wheel and brake drum from the wheel to be worked on.

2. Install a clamp over the ends of the wheel cylinder to prevent the pistons of the wheel cylinder from coming out, causing loss of fluid and much grief.

3. Contract the brake shoes by pulling the self-adjusting lever away from the starwheel adjustment screw and turn the starwheel up and back until the pivot nut is drawn onto the starwheel as far as it will come.

4. Pull the adjusting lever, cable and automatic adjuster spring down and toward the rear to unhook the pivot hook from the large hole in the secondary shoe web. Do not attempt to pry the pivot hook from the hole.

5. Remove the automatic adjuster spring and the adjusting lever.

6. Remove the secondary shoe-to-anchor spring with a brake tool. (Brake tools are very common implements and are available to auto parts stores). Remove the primary shoe-to-anchor spring and unhook the cable anchor. Remove the anchor pin plate.

7. Remove the cable guide from the secondary shoe.

8. Remove the shoe holddown springs, shoes, adjusting screw, pivot nut, and socket. Note the color of each holddown spring for assembly. To remove the holddown springs, reach behind the brake backing plate and place one finger on the end of one of the brake holddown spring mounting pins. Using a pair of pliers, grasp the washer type retainer on top of the holddown spring that corresponds to the pin. Push down on the pliers and turn them 90° to align the slot in the washer with the head on the spring mounting pin. Remove the spring and washer retainer and repeat this operation on the hold down spring on the other shoe.

9. Remove the parking brake link and spring. Disconnect the parking brake cable from the parking brake lever.

10. After removing the rear brake secondary shoe, disassemble the parking brake lever from the shoe by removing the retaining clip and spring washer.

11. Assemble the parking brake lever to the secondary shoe and secure it with the spring washer and retaining clip.

12. Apply a light coating of Lubriplate® at the points where the brake shoes contact the backing plate.

13. Position the brake shoes on the backing plate, and install the holddown spring pins, springs, and spring washer type retainers. On the rear brake, install the parking brake link, spring and washer. Connect the parking brake cable to the parking brake lever.

14. Install the anchor pin plate, and place the cable anchor over the anchor pin with the crimped side toward the backing plate.

15. Install the primary shoe-to-anchor spring with the brake tool.

16. Install the cable guide on the secondary shoe web with the flanged holes fitted into the hole in the secondary shoe web. Thread the cable around the cable guide groove.

17. Install the secondary shoe-to-anchor (long) spring. Be sure the cable end is not cocked or binding on the anchor pin when installed. All of the parts should be flat on the anchor pin. Remove the wheel cylinder piston clamp.

18. Apply Lubriplate® to the threads and the socket end of the adjusting starwheel screw. Turn the adjusting screw into the adjusting pivot nut to the limit of the threads and then back off ½ turn.

NOTE: Interchanging the brake shoe adjusting screw assemblies from one side of the vehicle to the other would cause the brake shoes to retract rather than expand each time the automatic adjusting mechanism is operated. To prevent this, the socket end of the adjusting screw is stamped with an "R" or an "L" for "RIGHT" or "LEFT". The adjusting pivot nuts can be distinguished by the number of lines machined around the body of the nut; one line indicates left hand nut and two lines indicate a right hand nut.

19. Place the adjusting socket on the screw and install this assembly between the shoe ends with the adjusting screw nearest to the secondary shoe.

20. Place the cable hook into the hole in the adjusting lever from the backing plate side. The adjusting levers are stamped with an **R** (right) or a **L** (left) to indicate their installation on the right or left hand brake assembly.

21. Position the hooked end of the adjuster spring in the primary shoe web and connect the loop end of the spring to the adjuster lever hole.

22. Pull the adjuster lever, cable and automatic adjuster spring down toward the rear to engage the pivot

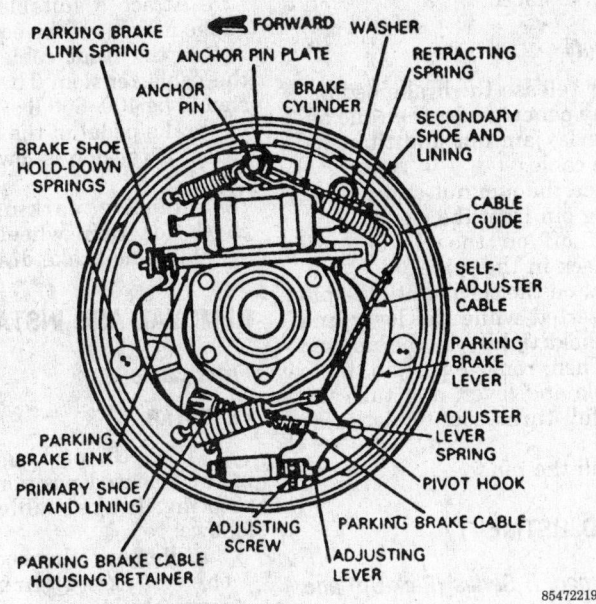

Rear brake shoe assembly — Bronco, F 150 and E 150

85472219

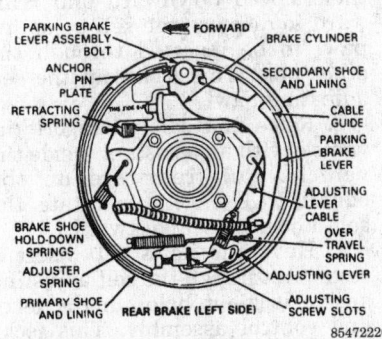

Rear brake shoe assembly — F 250, F 350, E 250 and E 350

85472220

hook in the large hole in the secondary shoe web.

23. After installation, check the action of the adjuster by pulling the section of the cable guide and the adjusting lever toward the secondary shoe web far enough to lift the lever past a tooth on the adjusting screw starwheel. The lever should snap into position behind the next tooth, and release of the cable should cause the adjuster spring to return the lever to its original position. This return action of the lever will turn the adjusting screw starwheel one tooth. The

lever should contact the adjusting screw starwheel one tooth above the centerline of the adjusting screw.

If the automatic adjusting mechanism does not perform properly, check the following:

24. Check the cable and fittings. The cable ends should fill or extend slightly beyond the crimped section of the fittings. If this is not the case, replace the cable.

25. Check the cable guide for damage. The cable groove should be parallel to the shoe web, and the body of the guide should lie flat against the web. Replace the cable guide if this is not so.

26. Check the pivot hook on the lever. The hook surfaces should be square with the body on the lever for proper pivoting. Repair or replace the hook as necessary.

27. Make sure the adjusting screw starwheel is properly seated in the notch in the shoe web.

F-250 HD and F-350

1. Raise and support the vehicle.
2. Remove the wheel and drum.
3. Remove the parking brake lever assembly retaining nut from behind the backing plate and remove the parking brake lever assembly.

4. Remove the adjusting cable assembly from the anchor pin, cable guide, and adjusting lever.
5. Remove the brake shoe retracting springs.
6. Remove the brake shoe holddown spring from each shoe.
7. Remove the brake shoes and adjusting screw assembly.
8. Disassemble the adjusting screw assembly.
9. Clean the ledge pads on the backing plate. Apply a light coat of Lubriplate® to the ledge pads (where the brake shoes rub the backing plate).

To install:

10. Apply Lubriplate® to the adjusting screw assembly and the holddown and retracting spring contacts on the brake shoes.
11. Install the upper retracting spring on the primary and secondary shoes and position the shoe assembly on the backing plate with the wheel cylinder pushrods in the shoe slots.
12. Install the brake shoe holddown springs.
13. Install the brake shoe adjustment screw assembly with the slot in the head of the adjusting screw toward the primary shoe, lower retracting spring, adjusting lever spring, adjusting lever assembly, and connect the adjusting cable to the adjusting lever. Position the cable in the cable guide and install the cable anchor fitting on the anchor pin.
14. Install the adjusting screw assemblies in the same locations from which they were removed. Interchanging the brake shoe adjusting screws from one side of the vehicle to the other will cause the brake shoes to retract rather than expand each time the automatic adjusting mechanism is operated. To prevent incorrect installation, the socket end of each adjusting screw is stamped with an **R** or an **L** to indicate their installation on the right or left side of the vehicle. The adjusting pivot nuts can be distinguished by the number of lines machined around the body of the nut. Two lines indicate a right hand nut; one line indicates a left hand nut.
15. Install the parking brake assembly in the anchor pin and secure with the retaining nut behind the backing plate.
16. Adjust the brakes before installing the brake drums and wheels. Install the brake drums and wheels.
17. Lower the vehicle and road test the brakes. New brakes may pull to one side or the other before they are

seated. Continued pulling or erratic braking should not occur.

Wheel Cylinder

REMOVAL AND INSTALLATION

1. Raise and safely support the vehicle. Remove the wheel and tire assembly, brake drum and brake shoes.
2. Remove the cylinder to shoe connecting pins.
3. Disconnect the brake line from the wheel cylinder.
4. Remove the wheel cylinder retaining bolts and remove the cylinder from the brake backing plate.
5. Installation is the reverse of the removal procedure. Adjust the brakes and bleed the system.

Parking Brake Cable

ADJUSTMENT

Aerostar

The parking brake system is self adjusting and requires no adjustment.

Bronco II, Explorer and Ranger

NOTE: Adjust the drum brakes before adjusting the parking brake. The brake drums must be cold for correct adjustment.

Bronco, F Series (Pick-Up) and E Series (Van) — Except F-Super Duty

NOTE: Adjust the drum brakes before adjusting the parking brake.

1. Raise and safely support the vehicle.
2. The brake drums should be cold.
3. Make sure the parking brake pedal is fully released.
4. While holding the tension equalizer, tighten the equalizer nut 6 full turns past its original position.
5. Fully depress the parking brake pedal. Using a cable tension gauge, check rear cable tension. Cable tension should be 350 lbs. minimum.
6. Fully release the parking brake. No drag should be noted at the wheels.
7. If drag is noted on F-250 and F-350 models, remove the drums and adjust the clearance between the parking brake lever and cam plate. Clearance should be 0.015 in. (0.38mm). Clearance is adjusted at the parking brake equalizer adjust-

ing nut. If the tension limiter on the F-150 and Bronco doesn't release the drag, the tension limiter will have to be replaced.

F-Super Duty

1. Fully release the brake pedal.
2. Spray penetrating oil on the adjusting clevis, jam nut and threaded end of the cable.
3. Loosen the jam nut and remove the locking pin from the clevis.
4. Back off on the clevis until there is slack in the cable.
5. Screw on the clevis until the pin can be inserted while the lever and cable are held tightly in the applied position, Then, remove the pin, let fo of the cable and lever, and turn the clevis 10 full turns counterclockwise (loosen).
6. Install the pin.

INITIAL ADJUSTMENT

Except Bronco, F Series (Pick-Up) and E Series (Van)

Use this procedure when a new tension limiter is install
1. Apply the parking brake pedal to the fully engaged position.
2. Raise and safely support the vehicle, as necessary. Hold the threaded rod end of the right brake cable to keep it from spinning and thread the equalizer nut 2½ in. up the rod.
3. Check to make sure the cinch strap has slipped and there are less than 1⅜ in. remaining.
4. Release the parking brake and check for proper operation.

Bronco, F Series (Pick-Up) and E Series (Van) — Except F-Super Duty

1. Raise and safely support the vehicle.
2. Depress the parking brake pedal fully.
3. Hold the tension limiter, install the equalizer nut and tighten it to a point 2½ in. ± ⅛ in. (63.5mm ± 3mm) up the rod.
4. Check to make sure the cinch strap has 1⅜ in. (35mm) remaining.

FIELD ADJUSTMENT

Use this procedure to correct a slack system if a new tension limiter is not installed.
1. Apply the parking brake pedal to the fully engaged position.
2. Raise and safely support the vehicle, as necessary. Grip the threaded rod to keep it from spinning and

tighten the equalizer nut 6 full turns past its original position on the threaded rod.
3. Attach a suitable cable tension gauge in front of the equalizer assembly on the front cable and measure the cable tension. The cable tension should be 400–600 lbs. with the parking brake pedal in the last detent position. If tension is low, repeat Steps 2 and 3.
4. Release parking brake and check for rear wheel drag. There should be no brake drag.

REMOVAL AND INSTALLATION

Front Cable

AEROSTAR

1. Place the parking brake control in the released position. Release the parking brake cable tension as follows:
   a. Remove the boot cover from the parking brake control assembly.
   b. Insert a steel pin through the pawl lockout pin hole. The pin must be inserted from the inboard side of the control (larger hole) at a slightly upward and forward angle then moved downward and rearward to displace the self adjusting pawl to be inserted through the other hole. This locks out the self adjusting pawl.
   c. Raise and safely support the vehicle with an assistant inside the vehicle. Pull rearward on the equalizer 1–2½ in. to rotate the self-adjuster reel backward.
   d. Have the assistant insert a steel pin through the self-adjusting spring lock-out holes in the lever and control assembly. This locks the ratchet wheel in the cable released position.

NOTE: Do not remove the steel lock pin until the cables are connected to the equalizer. Pin removal releases the tension in the ratchet wheel causing the spring to unwind and release tension, requiring assembly removal to reset spring tension.

2. Raise and safely support the vehicle. Disconnect the rear parking brake cables from the equalizer. Remove the equalizer from the front cable.
3. Remove the bolts retaining the cover to the underbody reinforcement bracket and remove the cover. It may be necessary to loosen fuel tank straps and partially lower the fuel tank to gain access to the cover.

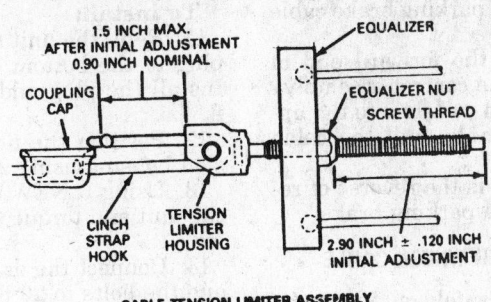

CABLE TENSION LIMITER ASSEMBLY

85472221

Parking brake cable tension limiter assembly — Bronco, F Series (Pick-Up) and E Series

4. Remove the cable anchor pin from the pivot hole in the control assembly ratchet plate. Guide the front cable from the control assembly.

5. Insert a ½ in. box end 12-point distributor lock bolt wrench over the front fitting of the front cable. Push the wrench onto the cable retainer fitting in the crossmember. Compress the retainer fingers and push the retainer rearward through the hole.

6. Insert a ½ in. box end 12-point wrench over the rear fitting of the front cable. Push the wrench onto the cable retainer fitting in the crossmember. Compress the retainer fingers and push the retainer forward through the hole.

7. Pull the cable ends through the crossmembers and remove the cable.

To install:

8. Feed the front cable through the holes in both crossmembers. Push the retainers through the holes so the fingers expand over each hole.

9. Route the front cable around the control assembly pulley and insert the cable anchor pin in the pivot hole in the ratchet plate.

10. Slide the return spring over the rear end of the front cable. Connect the equalizer to the front and rear cables.

11. Remove the lock pins from the control assembly to apply cable tension. Position the cover on the reinforcement bracket. Install and tighten the bolts after visually checking to be sure the front cable is attached to the control.

12. Position the boot over the control. Install and tighten the screws.

13. Apply and release the control several times. Make sure the parking brakes are applied, and released and not dragging. Both pins must be removed for proper adjustment.

BRONCO II, EXPLORER AND RANGER

1. Raise and safely support the vehicle.

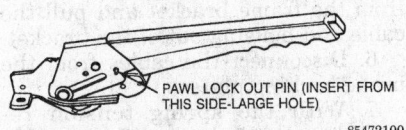

PAWL LOCK OUT PIN (INSERT FROM THIS SIDE-LARGE HOLE)

85472100

Releasing parking brake cable tension — Aerostar

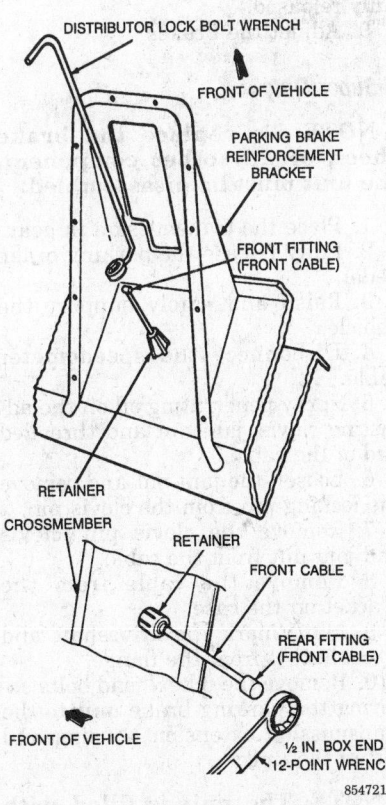

DISTRIBUTOR LOCK BOLT WRENCH

FRONT OF VEHICLE

PARKING BRAKE REINFORCEMENT BRACKET

FRONT FITTING (FRONT CABLE)

RETAINER

CROSSMEMBER

RETAINER

FRONT CABLE

REAR FITTING (FRONT CABLE)

FRONT OF VEHICLE

½ IN. BOX END 12-POINT WRENCH

85472101

Front parking brake cable removal — Aerostar

2. Back off the equalizer nut and remove slug of front cable on Bronco II and Ranger or intermediate cable on Explorer from the tension limiter.

3. On Bronco II and Ranger, remove the parking brake cable from the cable bracket. On Explorer, remove the intermediate cable from the bracket and disconnect the intermediate cable from the front cable.

4. Lower the vehicle. Remove the forward ball end of the parking brake cable from the control assembly clevis.

5. Remove the cable from the control assembly.

6. Using a cord attached to the control lever end of the cable, remove the cable from the vehicle pulling it up into the passenger compartment.

To install:

7. Transfer the cord to the new cable. Position the cable in the vehicle, routing the cable through the dash panel. Remove the cord and secure the cable to the control.

8. Connect the forward ball end of the brake cable to the clevis of the control assembly. Raise and safely support the vehicle.

9. Route the cable through the bracket. On Explorer, connect the front cable to the intermediate cable.

10. Connect the slug of the front or intermediate cable cable to the tension limiter connector. Adjust the parking brake cable at the equalizer using initial adjustment or field adjustment, as necessary.

11. Rotate both wheels to make sure the parking brakes are not dragging.

Rear Cable

1. Release parking brake control.

2. On Aerostar, to release tension on the rear cables, pull rearward on the equalizer assembly about 1–2 in. and place a clamp on the front cable behind the crossmember.

3. Raise and safely support the vehicle. Remove the wheel and tire assembly and the brake drum.

4. On Bronco II, Explorer and Ranger, remove the locknut on the threaded rod at the equalizer. Disconnect the rear parking brake cable from the equalizer.

5. Compress the prongs that retain the cable housing to the frame bracket or crossmember and pull out the cable and housing.

6. Working on the wheel side of the backing plate, compress the prongs on the cable retainer so they can pass through the hole in the brake backing plate.

7. Lift the cable out of the slot in the parking brake lever, attached to the secondary brake shoe, and remove the cable through the brake backing plate hole.

To install:

8. Route the cable through the hole in the backing plate. Insert the cable anchor behind the slot in the parking brake lever. Make sure the cable is securely engaged in the parking brake lever so the cable return spring is holding the cable in the parking brake lever.

9. Push the retainer through the hole in the backing plate so the retainer prongs engage the backing plate.

10. Properly route the cable and insert the front of the cable through the frame bracket or crossmember until the prongs expand. Connect the rear cables to the equalizer.

11. On Bronco II, Explorer and Ranger, rotate the equalizer 90 degrees and recouple the threaded rod to the equalizer.

12. On Aerostar, remove the clamping device the reapply tension.

13. Install the brake drum and wheel and tire assembly. Adjust the rear brakes.

14. On Bronco II, Explorer and Ranger, adjust the parking brake tension using the initial adjustment or the field adjustment procedure, as necessary.

15. Apply and release the parking brake control several times. Rotate both wheels to make sure the parking brakes are applied and released and not dragging.

Bronco, F Series (Pick-Up) and E Series (Van) — Except F-Super Duty

PARKING BRAKE CONTROL

1. Raise and safely support the vehicle.

2. Loosen the adjusting nut at the equalizer.

3. Working in the engine compartment, remove the nuts attaching the parking brake control to the firewall.

4. Remove the cable from the control assembly clevis by compressing the conduit end prongs.

5. Installation is the reverse of removal. Torque the attaching nuts to 15 ft. lbs.

EQUALIZER-TO-CONTROL ASSEMBLY CABLE

1. Raise and safely support the vehicle.

2. Back off the equalizer nut and disconnect the cable from the tension limiter.

3. Remove the parking brake cable from the mount.

4. Disconnect the forward end of the cable from the control assembly.

5. Using a cord attached to the upper end of the cable, pull the cable from the vehicle.

6. Installation is the reverse of removal. Adjust the parking brake.

EQUALIZER-TO-REAR WHEEL CABLE

1. Raise and safely support the vehicle.

2. Remove the wheels and brake drums.

3. Remove the tension limiter.

4. Remove the locknut from the threaded rod and disconnect the cable from the equalizer.

5. Disconnect the cable housing from the frame bracket and pull the cable and housing out of the bracket.

6. Disconnect the cables from the brake backing plates.

7. With the spring tension removed from the lever, lift the cable out of the slot in the lever and remove the cable through the backing plate hole.

8. Installation is the reverse of removal. On the F-250 and F-350, check the clearance between the parking brake operating lever and the cam plate. Clearance should be 0.015 in. (0.38mm) with the brakes fully released.

9. Adjust the brakes.

F-Super Duty

NOTE: To replace the brake shoes, or any other component, the unit must be disassembled.

1. Place the transmission in gear.

2. Fully release the parking brake pedal.

3. Raise and safely support the vehicle.

4. Disconnect the speedometer cable.

5. Spray penetrating oil on the adjusting clevis, jam nut and threaded end of the cable.

6. Loosen the jam nut and remove the locking pin from the clevis pin.

7. Remove the clevis pin, clevis and jam nut from the cable.

8. Remove the cable from the bracket on the case.

9. Matchmark the driveshaft and disconnect it from the flange.

10. Remove the 6 hex-head bolts securing the parking brake unit to the transmission extension housing and lift off the unit.

NOTE: The unit is filled with Ford Type H ATF.

To install:

11. Refill the unit through the filler plug to the bottom of the plug hole. Install the plug and tighten it to 45 ft. lbs.

12. Position the unit on the extension housing using 2 guide pins.

13. Using 6 NEW hex-bolts, attach the unit and torque the bolts to 40 ft. lbs.

14. Connect the driveshaft and torque the bolts to 20 ft. lbs.

15. Assemble the cable components. Screw on the clevis until the pin can be inserted while the lever and cable are held tightly in the applied position. Then, remove the pin, let go of the cable and lever, and turn the clevis 10 full turns counterclockwise (loosen).

16. Install the pin.

Brake System Bleeding

Except Bronco, F Series (Pick-Up) and E Series (Van)

1. Clean all dirt from the master cylinder filler cap.

2. If the master cylinder is known or suspected to have air in the bore, it must be bled before any of the wheel cylinders or calipers. Proceed as follows:

a. Loosen the brake line fitting approximately $3/4$ turn. Wrap a shop cloth around the tubing below the fitting to absorb escaping brake fluid.

b. Have an assistant depress the brake pedal slowly through it's full travel to force air trapped in the master cylinder to escape at the fitting.

c. Tighten the fitting and let the pedal return slowly to the fully released position. Do not release the pedal until the fitting is tightened or air will re-enter the master cylinder.

d. Wait 5 seconds and then repeat the operation until all air bubbles disappear.

e. Repeat Steps a–d on the remaining master cylinder brake line fitting(s).

3. On Bronco II, Explorer and Ranger equipped with Rear Anti-lock Brakes (RABS), proceed as follows:

a. Place a box wrench on the bleeder fitting On the RABS valve. Attach a rubber drain hose to the bleeder fitting, making sure the end of the hose fits snugly around the bleeder fitting.

b. Submerge the other end of the hose in a container partially filled with clean brake fluid.

c. Loosen the bleeder fitting approximately ¾ turn. Have an assistant slowly press the brake pedal all the way down. Close the bleeder fitting and let the pedal return to the fully released position.

d. Repeat this procedure until no more air bubbles come from the submerged end of the tube. Close the fitting and remove the hose.

4. On Aerostar with cartridge master cylinder, proceed as follows:

a. Place a box wrench on the bleeder fitting located on the front of the cartridge master cylinder. Attach a rubber drain hose to the bleeder fitting, making sure the end of the hose fits snugly around the bleeder fitting.

b. Submerge the other end of the hose in a container partially filled with clean brake fluid.

c. Loosen the bleeder fitting approximately ¾ turn. Have an assistant slowly press the brake pedal all the way down. Close the bleeder fitting and let the pedal return to the fully released position.

d. Repeat this procedure until no more air bubbles come from the submerged end of the tube. Close the fitting and remove the hose.

5. Continue to bleed the brake system by removing the rubber dust cap from the wheel cylinder bleeder fitting at the right-hand rear of the vehicle. Place a box wrench on the bleeder fitting and attach a rubber drain hose to the fitting. The end of the tube should fit snugly around the bleeder fitting. Submerge the other end of the tube in a container partially filled with clean brake fluid and loosen the fitting ¾ turn.

6. Have an assistant push the brake pedal down slowly through it's full travel. Close the bleeder fitting and allow the pedal to slowly return to it's full release position. Wait 5 seconds and repeat the procedure until no bubbles appear at the submerged end of the bleeder tube. Secure the bleeder fitting and remove the bleeder hose. Install the rubber dust cap on the bleeder fitting.

7. Repeat the procedure in Steps 5 and 6 and bleed the rest of the system in the following sequence: left rear, right front and left front.

8. Refill the master cylinder reservoir after each wheel cylinder or caliper has been bled and install the master cylinder cover and gasket. When brake bleeding is completed, the fluid level should be filled to the maximum level indicated on the reservoir.

9. Always make sure the disc brake pistons are returned to their normal positions by depressing the brake pedal several times until normal pedal travel is established. If the pedal feels spongy, repeat the bleeding procedure.

Bronco, F Series (Pick-Up) and E Series (Van)

When any part of the hydraulic system has been disconnected for repair or replacement, air may get into the lines and cause spongy pedal action (because air can be compressed and brake fluid cannot). To correct this condition, it is necessary to bleed the hydraulic system after it has been properly connected to be sure all air is expelled from the brake cylinders and lines.

When bleeding the brake system, bleed one brake cylinder at a time, beginning at the cylinder with the longest hydraulic line (farthest from the master cylinder) first. Keep the master cylinder reservoir filled with brake fluid during bleeding operation. Never use brake fluid that has been drained from the hydraulic system, no matter how clean it is.

It will be necessary to centralize the pressure differential valve after a brake system failure has been corrected and the hydraulic system has been bled.

The primary and secondary hydraulic brake systems are individual systems and are bled separately. During the entire bleeding operation, do not allow the reservoir to run dry. Keep the master cylinder reservoirs filled with brake fluid.

WHEEL CYLINDERS AND CALIPERS

Bronco, F Series (Pick-Up) and E Series (Van)

1. Clean all dirt from around the master cylinder fill cap, remove the cap and fill the master cylinder with brake fluid until the level is within ¼ in. (6mm) of the top of the edge of the reservoir.

2. Clean off the bleeder screws at the wheel cylinders and calipers.

3. Attach the length of rubber hose over the nozzle of the bleeder screw at the wheel to be done first. Place the other end of the hose in a glass jar, submerged in brake fluid.

4. Open the bleed screw valve ½–¾ turn.

5. Have an assistant slowly depress the brake pedal. Close the bleeder screw valve and havel your assistant slowly return the brake pedal. Continue this pumping action to force any air out of the system. When bubbles cease to appear at the end of the bleeder hose, close the bleed valve and remove the hose.

6. Check the master cylinder fluid level and add fluid accordingly. Do this after bleeding each wheel.

7. Repeat the bleeding operation at the remaining 3 wheels, ending with the one closest to the master cylinder. Fill the master cylinder reservoir.

MASTER CYLINDER

Bronco, F Series (Pick-Up) and E Series (Van)

1. Fill the master cylinder reservoirs.

2. Place absorbent rags under the fluid lines at the master cylinder.

3. Have an assistant depress and hold the brake pedal.

4. With the pedal held down, slowly crack open the hydraulic line fitting, allowing the air to escape. Close the fitting and have the pedal released.

5. Repeat Steps 3 and 4 for each fitting until all the air is released.

Anti-lock Brake System Service

PRECAUTIONS

Use caution when disassembling any hydraulic components as the system will contain residual pressure. Cover the area around the component to be removed with a shop cloth to catch any brake fluid spray. Do not allow brake fluid to come in contact with painted surfaces.

REAR ANTI-LOCK BRAKE SYSTEM (RABS)

Rear Anti-lock Brake System (RABS) Module

REMOVAL AND INSTALLATION

Aerostar

1. Disconnect the negative battery cable.
2. Disconnect the wiring harness from the RABS connector by depressing the plastic tab on the connector and pulling the connector off.
3. Remove the 2 nuts that retain the RABS module to the instrument panel anti-shake brace and remove the module.
4. Installation is the reverse of the removal procedure. Check the system for proper operation.

Bronco II, Explorer and Ranger

1. Disconnect the negative battery cable.
2. Disconnect the wiring harness from the RABS module by depressing the plastic tab on the connector and pulling the connector off.
3. Remove the 2 screws that retain the module to the dash panel and remove the module.
4. Installation is the reverse of the removal procedure. Check the system for proper operation.

RABS Valve

REMOVAL AND INSTALLATION

1. Disconnect the negative battery cable.
2. Disconnect and plug the 2 brake lines connected to the RABS valve.
3. Disconnect the wiring harness from the valve harness.
4. Remove the screw retaining the valve and remove the valve.
   To install:
5. Position the RABS valve and install the retaining screw. Tighten the retaining screw on Bronco II, Explorer and Ranger to 11–14 ft. lbs. (15–20 Nm) or on Aerostar to 30–40 inch lbs. (3.3–4.5 Nm).
6. Connect the brake valve wiring harness connector.

7. Connect the brake lines to the valve and tighten as follows:
   a. 1/2–20 threaded fittings — 10–17 ft. lbs. (14–23 Nm).
   b. 7/16–24 threaded fittings — 10–15 ft. lbs. (14–20 Nm).
   c. 3/8–24 threaded fittings — 10–15 ft. lbs. (14–20 Nm).

NOTE: Do not overtighten the fittings.

8. Bleed the brake system. It is not necessary to energize the valve electrically to bleed the rear brakes.
9. Connect the negative battery cable.

RABS Sensor

REMOVAL AND INSTALLATION

1. Disconnect the negative battery cable.
2. Pull the wiring harness connector off.
3. Remove the sensor hold-down bolt and remove the sensor from the axle housing.
   To install:
4. Clean the axle mounting surface. Use care to prevent dirt from entering the axle housing.
5. Inspect and clean the magnetized sensor pole piece to ensure that it is free from loose metal particles which could cause erratic system operation. Inspect the sensor O-ring for damage and replace, if necessary.
6. Lightly lubricate the sensor O-ring with motor oil, align the sensor bolt hole and install. Do not apply force to the plastic sensor connector. The sensor flange should slide to the mounting surface. This will insure the air gap setting is between 0.005–0.045 in. (0.127–1.14mm).
7. Install the hold down bolt and tighten to 25–30 ft. lbs. (34–40 Nm).
8. Inspect the blue sensor connector seal and replace if missing or damaged. Push the connector on the sensor.
9. Connect the negative battery cable.

RABS Exciter Ring

INSPECTION

1. Remove the RABS sensor.
2. View the exciter ring teeth through the sensor hole. Rotate the rear axle and check the exciter ring teeth for damage or breakage. Dented or broken teeth could cause

the RABS system to function when not required.

REMOVAL AND INSTALLATION

To service the exciter ring, the differential case must be removed from the axle housing and the exciter ring pressed off the case.

NOTE: Upon removal, the exciter ring is to be discarded. It is not to be reused.

4WD ANTI-LOCK BRAKE SYSTEM (ABS)

This system is used on 1993–96 Bronco.

Hydraulic Control Unit

REMOVAL AND INSTALLATION

1. Disconnect the battery ground cable.
2. Unplug the 8-pin connector from the unit, and the 4-pin connector from the pump motor.
3. Disconnect the 5 inlet and outlet tubes from the unit. Immediately plug the ports.
4. Remove the 3 unit attaching nuts and lift out the unit.
5. Installation is the reverse of removal. Torque the mounting nuts to 12–18 ft. lbs. and the tube fittings to 10–18 ft. lbs.

NOTE: After reconnecting the battery, it may take 10 miles or more of driving for the Powertrain Control Module to relearn its driveability codes.

6. Bleed the brakes.

Electronic Control Unit

REMOVAL AND INSTALLATION

1. Disconnect the battery ground cable.
2. Unplug the wiring from the ECU.
3. Remove the mounting bolts, slide the ECU off its bracket.
4. Installation is the reverse of removal. Torque the mounting screw to

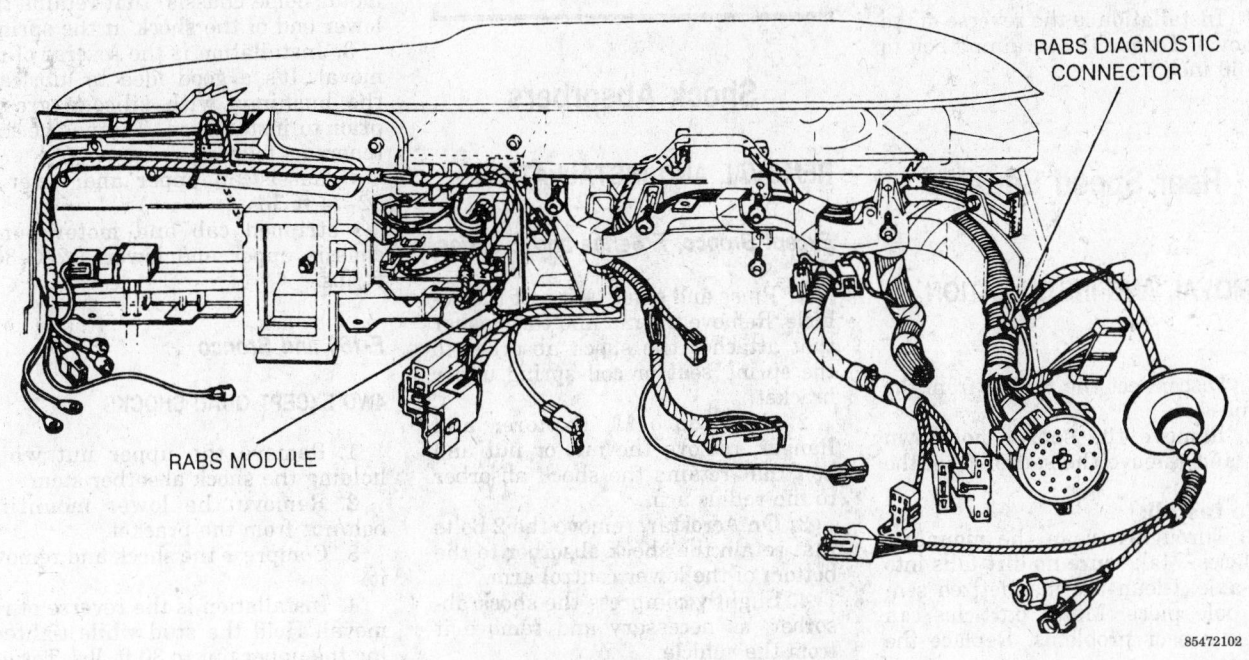

RABS module location — Bronco II, Explorer and Ranger

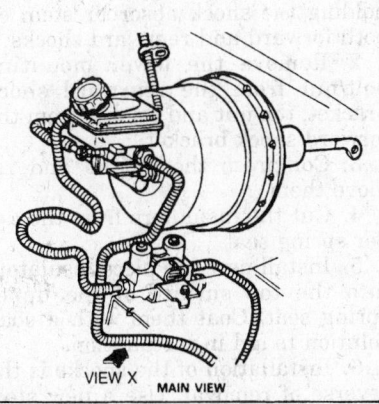

RABS valve location — Aerostar

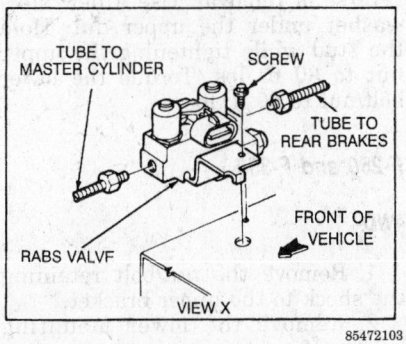

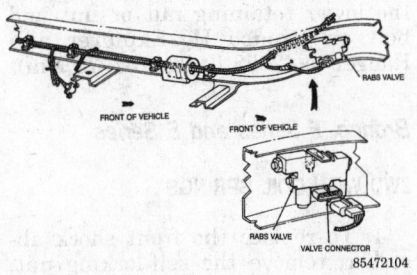

RABS valve location — Bronco II, Explorer and Ranger

5–6 ft. lbs. and the connector bolt to 4–5 ft. lbs.

NOTE: After reconnecting the battery, it may take 10 miles or more of driving for the Powertrain Control Module to relearn its driveability codes.

Front Wheel Speed Sensor

REMOVAL AND INSTALLATION

1. Inside the engine compartment, disconnect the sensor from the harness.
2. Unclip the sensor cable from the brake hose clips.

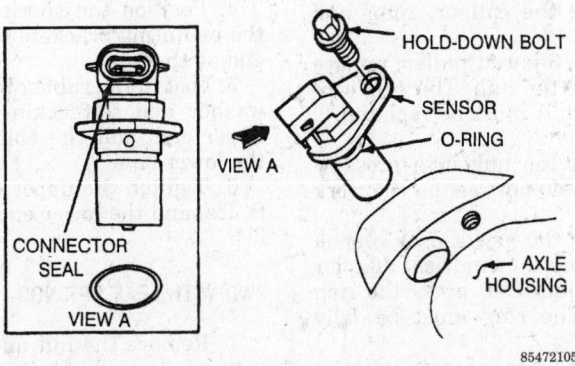

RABS sensor installation

3. Remove the retaining bolt from the spindle and slide the sensor from its hole.

4. Installation is the reverse of the removal. Torque the retaining bolt to 40–60 inch lbs.

Rear Speed Sensor

REMOVAL AND INSTALLATION

1. Disconnect the wiring from the harness.

2. Remove the sensor holddown bolt and remove the sensor from the axle.

To install:

3. Throughly clean the mounting surfaces. Make sure no dirt falls into the axle. Clean the magnetized sensor pole piece. Metal particles can cause sensor problems. Replace the O-ring.

4. Coat the new O-ring with clean engine oil.

5. Position the new sensor on the axle. It should slide into place easily. Correct installation will allow a gap of 0.005–0.045 in.

6. Torque the holddown bolt to 25–30 ft. lbs.

7. Connect the wiring.

Front Speed Sensor Ring

REMOVAL AND INSTALLATION

1. Raise and safely support the vehicle.

2. Remove the wheels.

3. Remove the caliper, rotor and hub.

4. Using a 3-jawed puller, remove the ring from the hub. The ring cannot be reused; it must be replaced.

To install:

5. Support the hub in a press so the lug studs do not rest on the work surface.

6. Position the new sensor ring on the hub. Using a cylindrical adapter 98mm x 106mm OD, press the ring into place. The ring must be fully seated!

7. The remainder of installation is the reverse of removal.

FRONT SUSPENSION

Shock Absorbers

REMOVAL AND INSTALLATION

Except Bronco, F Series and E Series

1. Raise and safely support the vehicle. Remove the nut and the washer that attaches the shock absorber to the spring seat or coil spring upper bracket.

2. On Bronco II, Explorer and Ranger, remove the nut or nut and bolt that retains the shock absorber to the radius arm.

3. On Aerostar, remove the 2 bolts that retain the shock absorber to the bottom of the lower control arm.

4. Slightly compress the shock absorber, as necessary and remove it from the vehicle.

5. Installation is the reverse of the removal procedure. Tighten the upper retaining nut to 25–35 ft. lbs. (34–38 Nm). Tighten the lower retaining bolts or nuts on Aerostar to 16–24 ft. lbs. (22–33 Nm). Tighten the lower retaining nut or nut and bolt on Bronco II, Explorer and Ranger to 42–53 ft. lbs. (57–72 Nm).

Bronco, F Series and E Series

2WD WITH COIL SPRINGS

1. To replace the front shock absorber, remove the self-locking nut, steel washer, and rubber bushings at the upper end of the shock absorber.

2. Remove the bolt and nut at the lower end and remove the shock absorber.

3. When installing a new shock absorber, use new rubber bushings.

4. Position the shock absorber on the mounting brackets with the stud end at the top.

5. Install the rubber bushing, steel washer and self-locking nut at the upper end, and the bolt and nut at the lower end.

6. Tighten the upper end to 25–35 ft. lbs. and the lower end to 40–60 ft. lbs.

2WD WITH LEAF SPRINGS

1. Remove the nut and bolt which retains the shock to the upper bracket.

2. Remove the nut (chassis/cab) or nut and bolt (stripped chassis and motor home chassis) that retains the lower end of the shock at the spring.

3. Installation is the reverse of removal. It's a good idea to lubricate the bushings with silicone grease prior to installation. Torque the fasteners as follows:

• chassis/cab upper and lower — 52–74 ft. lbs.

• stripped cab and motor home chassis upper and lower — 220–300 ft. lbs.

F-150 and Bronco

4WD EXCEPT QUAD SHOCKS

1. Remove the upper nut while holding the shock absorber stem.

2. Remove the lower mounting bolt/nut from the bracket.

3. Compress the shock and remove it.

4. Installation is the reverse of removal. Hold the stud while tightening the upper nut to 30 ft. lbs. Torque the lower bolt/nut to 60 ft. lbs.

4WD WITH QUAD SHOCKS

1. Remove the upper nut while holding the shock absorber stem on both forward and rearward shocks.

2. Remove the lower mounting bolt/nut from the rearward shock bracket; the nut and washer from the forward shock bracket.

3. Compress the shocks and remove them.

4. Cut the insulators from the upper spring seat.

5. Install new one piece insulators into the top surface of the upper spring seat. Coat them with a soap solution to aid in installation.

6. Installation of the shocks is the reverse of removal. Use a new steel washer under the upper nut. Hold the stud while tightening the upper nut to 30 ft. lbs. Torque the lower bolt/nut to 60 ft. lbs.

F-250 and F-350

4WD

1. Remove the nut/bolt retaining the shock to the upper bracket.

2. Remove the lower mounting bolt/nut from the bracket.

3. Compress the shock and remove it.

4. Installation is the reverse of removal. Tighten the upper and lower nut/bolt to 70 ft. lbs.

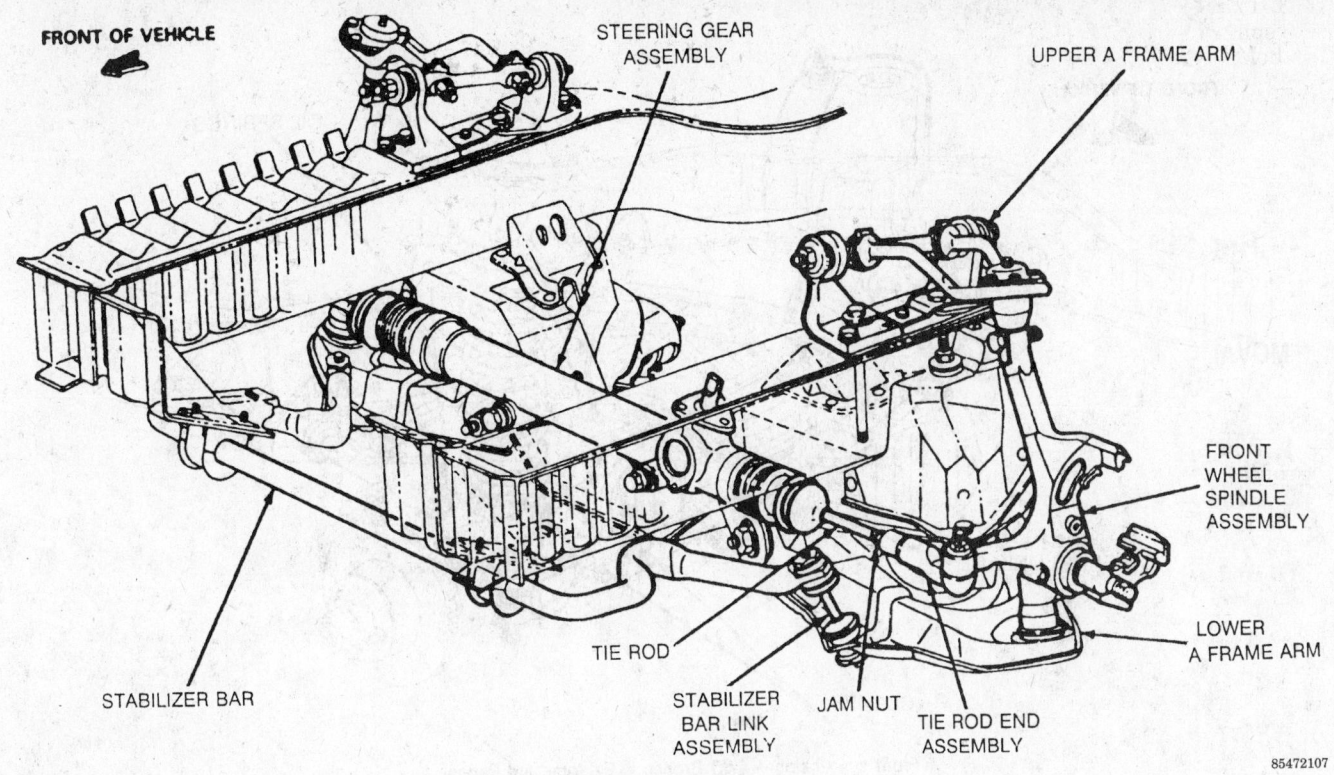

Front suspension — Aerostar

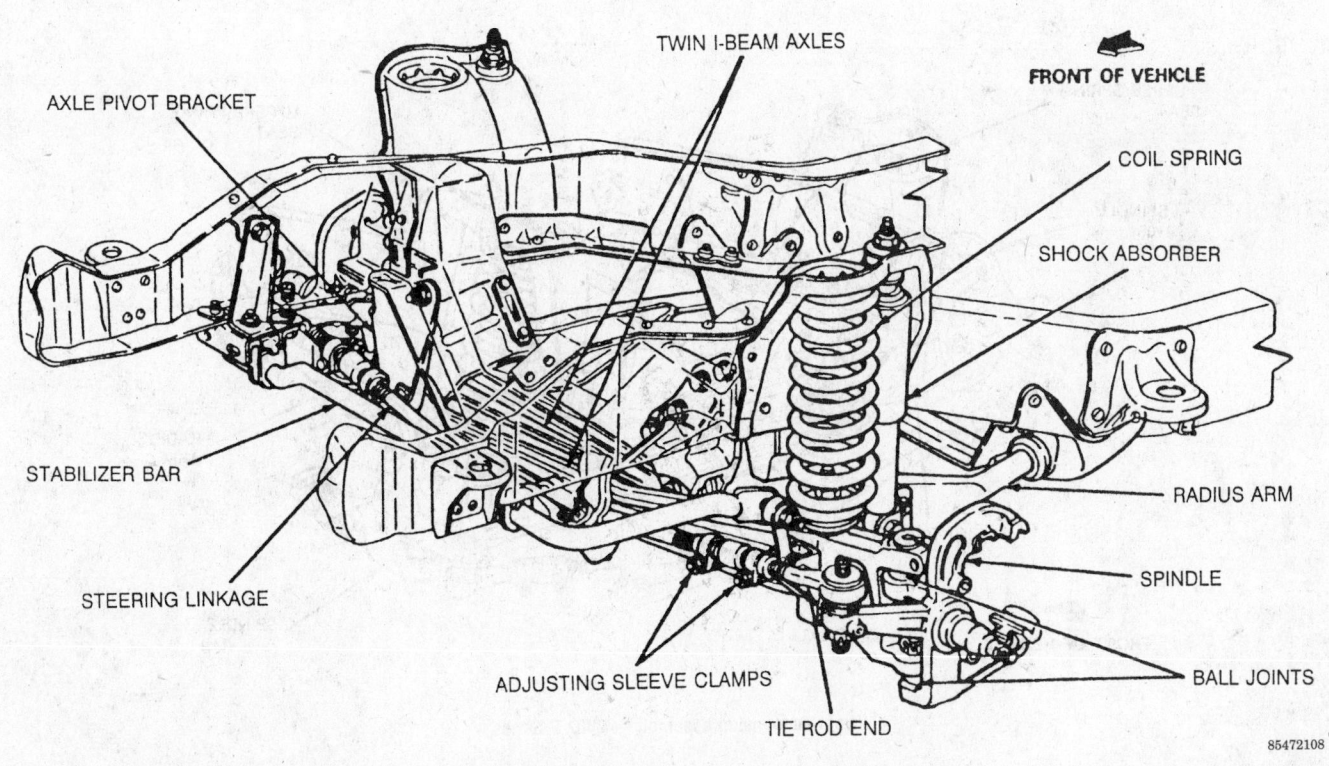

Front suspension — 2WD Bronco II, Explorer and Ranger

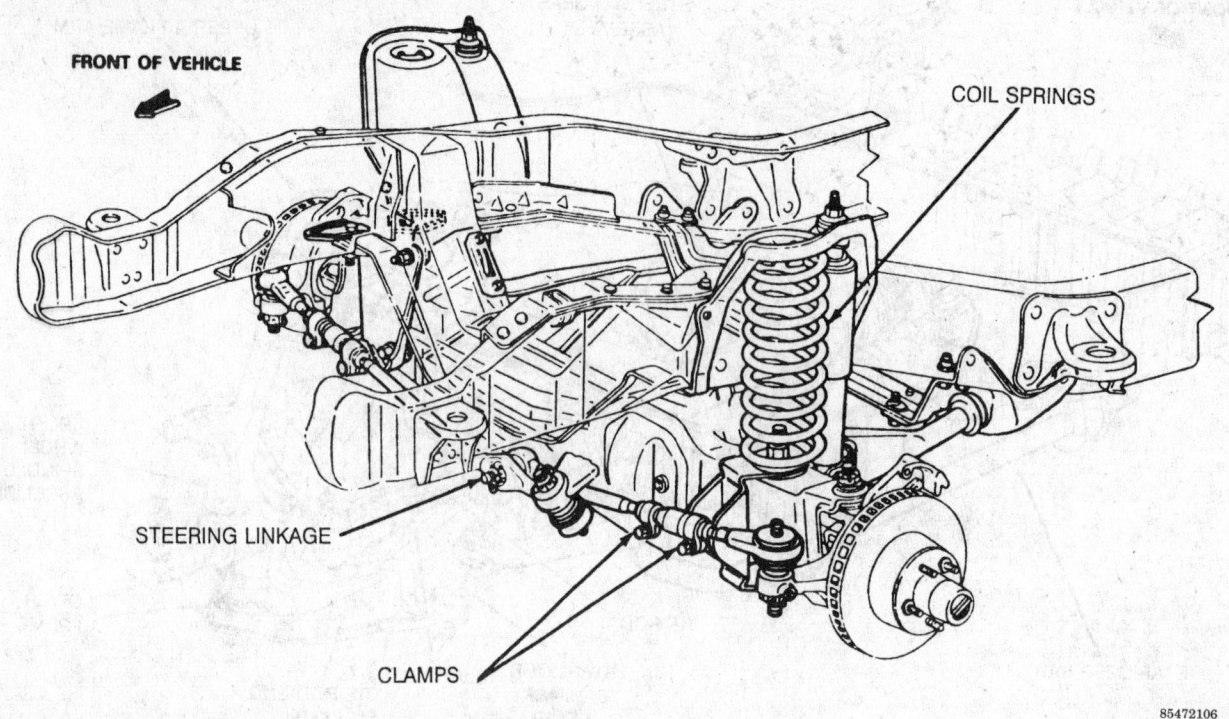

FRONT OF VEHICLE

COIL SPRINGS

STEERING LINKAGE

CLAMPS

85472106

Front suspension — 4WD Bronco II, Explorer and Ranger

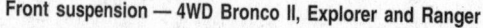

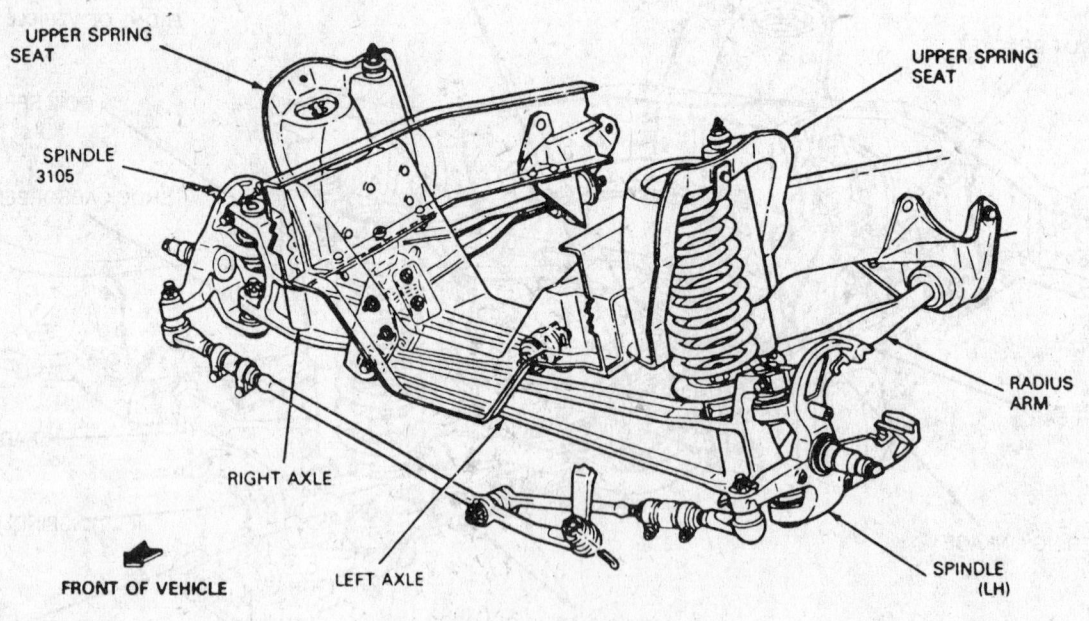

UPPER SPRING SEAT

SPINDLE 3105

UPPER SPRING SEAT

RADIUS ARM

RIGHT AXLE

LEFT AXLE

FRONT OF VEHICLE

SPINDLE (LH)

85472224

Front suspension assembly — 2WD F Series

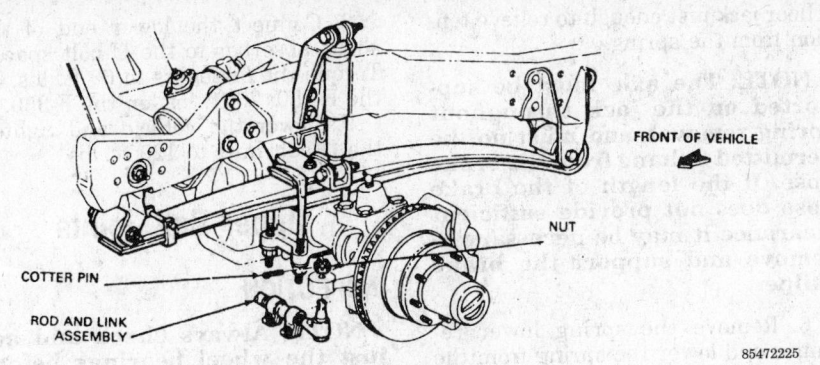

FRONT OF VEHICLE

NUT

COTTER PIN

ROD AND LINK
ASSEMBLY

85472225

Front suspension assembly — F 350

Coil Springs

REMOVAL AND INSTALLATION

Aerostar

1. Place the steering wheel and the steering system in the on center position.
2. Raise and safely support the vehicle. Remove the wheel and tire assembly.
3. Disconnect the stabilizer bar link bolt from the lower arm.
4. Remove the 2 nuts or bolts attaching the shock absorber to the lower arm. Remove the upper nut and washer and remove the shock absorber.
5. Using spring compressor tool D78P-5310-A or equivalent, install 1 plate with the pivot ball seat facing downward into the coils of the spring. Rotate the plate so it is flush with the upper surface of the lower arm.
6. Install the other plate with the pivot ball seat facing upward into the coils of the spring. Insert the upper ball nut through the coils of the spring, so the nut rests in the upper plate.
7. Insert the compression rod into the opening in the lower arm, through the upper and lower plate and upper ball nut. Insert the securing pin through the upper ball nut and the compression rod.
8. With the upper ball nut secured, turn the upper plate so it walks up the coil until it contacts the upper spring seat, then back off ½ turn.
9. Install the lower ball nut and thrust washer on the compression rod and screw on the forcing nut. Tighten the forcing nut until the spring is compressed enough so it is free in its seat.
10. Loosen the lower arm pivot bolts. Remove the cotter pin and loosen but do not remove the nut at-

taching the lower ball joint to the spindle. Using puller tool T64P-3590-F or equivalent, loosen the lower ball joint. Remove the puller tool. Support the lower control arm with a jack and remove the ball joint nut. Lower the control arm and remove the spring.
11. If a new spring is to be installed, mark the position of the plates on the spring with chalk. Compress a new spring for installation and measure the compressed length of the old spring.
12. Loosen the forcing nut to relieve spring tension and remove the tools from the spring.
   To install:
13. Assemble the spring compressor and locate in the same positions indicated in Step 11.
14. 14. Before compressing the spring, make sure the upper ball nut securing pin is inserted properly.
15. Compress the coil spring until the spring height reaches the dimension obtained in Step 11.
16. Position the coil spring in the lower control arm. To complete installation, reverse the removal procedure. Tighten the lower ball joint nut to 80–120 ft. lbs. (108–163 Nm).

Bronco II, Explorer and Ranger

1. Raise and safely support the vehicle. Place a jack under the axle.
2. Remove the nut or nut and bolt attaching the shock absorber to the radius arm.
3. Remove the nut securing the spring to the axle and remove the retainer.
4. Slowly lower the axle to relieve the spring tension. Remove the spring by rotating the upper coil out of the tabs in the upper spring seat.
   To install:
5. Install the top of the spring in the upper seat, rotating into position.
6. Raise the axle until the spring is seated in the lower spring seat. In-

stall the lower retainer and tighten the nut to 70–100 ft. lbs. (95–136 Nm).
7. Connect the shock absorber to the radius arm and lower the vehicle.

Bronco, F Series and E Series

2WD

1. Raise the front of the vehicle and place jackstands under the frame and a jack under the axle.
2. Remove the wheels.
3. Disconnect the shock absorber from the lower bracket.
4. Remove one bolt and nut and remove the rebound bracket.
5. Remove the two spring upper retainer attaching bolts from the top of the spring upper seat and remove the retainer.
6. Remove the nut attaching the spring lower retainer to the lower seat and axle and remove the retainer.
7. Place a safety chain through the spring to prevent it from suddenly coming loose. Slowly lower the axle and remove the spring.
   To install:
8. Place the spring in position and raise the front axle.
9. Position the spring lower retainer over the stud and lower seat, and install the two attaching bolts.
10. Position the upper retainer over the spring coil and against the spring upper seat, and install the two attaching bolts.
11. Tighten the upper retaining bolts to 13–18 ft. lbs.; the lower retainer attaching nuts to 70–100 ft. lbs.
12. Connect the shock absorber to the lower bracket. Torque the bolt and nut to 40–60 ft. lbs. Install the rebound bracket.
13. Remove the jack and safety stands.

Leaf Springs

REMOVAL AND INSTALLATION

Bronco, F Series and E Series

2WD

1. Raise and support the front end on jackstands with the tires still touching the ground.
2. Using jacks, take up the weight of the axle, off the U-bolts.
3. Disconnect the lower end of each shock absorber.
4. Disconnect the spring from the front bracket or shackle.

5. Disconnect the spring from the rear bracket or shackle.

6. Remove the U-bolt nuts.

7. Remove the U-bolts.

8. Disconnect the jack bracket or stabilizer bar as necessary.

9. Lower the axle slightly and remove the spring. Take note of the position of the spring spacer.

To install

10. Position the spring on its seat on the axle and raise it to align the front of the spring with the bracket or shackle.

11. Coat the bushing with silicone grease.

12. Carefully guide the attaching bolt through the bracket or shackle, and the bushing.

13. Install the nut and torque it to:
- chassis/cab spring-to-shackle — 120–150 ft. lbs.
- chassis/cab shackle-to-frame — 150–210 ft. lbs.
- stripped chassis or motor home chassis spring-to-bracket — 148–207 ft. lbs.

14. In a similar fashion, attach the rear of the spring. The torques are:
- chassis/cab spring-to-bracket — 150–210 ft. lbs.
- stripped chassis or motor home chassis spring-to-shackle or shackle-to-bracket — 74–110 ft. lbs.

15. Position the spacer on the spring.

16. Install the U-bolts. Install the jack bracket or stabilizer bar bracket on the forward U-bolt. Install the U-bolt nuts. Torque the nuts, evenly and in gradual increments, in a criss-cross fashion, to:
- chassis/cab — 150–210 ft. lbs.
- stripped chassis and motor home chassis — 220–300 ft. lbs.

17. Connect the shock absorbers. Torque them to:
- chassis/cab models, shock absorber-to-bracket nuts to 52–74 ft. lbs.
- stripped chassis or motor home chassis models, lower attaching bolt to 220–300 ft. lbs.

F-150 and Bronco

4WD

1. Raise and support the front end on jackstands.

2. Remove the shock absorber lower attaching bolt and nut.

3. Remove the spring lower retainer nuts from inside of the spring coil.

4. Remove the upper spring retainer by removing the attaching screw.

5. Position safety stands under the frame side rails and lower the axle on

a floor jack just enough to relieve tension from the spring.

NOTE: The axle must be supported on the jack throughout spring removal, and must not be permitted to hang from the brake hose. If the length of the brake hose does not provide sufficient clearance it may be necessary to remove and support the brake caliper.

6. Remove the spring lower retainer and lower the spring from the vehicle.

To install:

7. Place the spring in position and slowly raise the front axle. Make sure the springs are positioned correctly in the upper spring seats.

8. Install the lower spring retainer and torque the nut to 100 ft. lbs.

9. Position the upper retainer over the spring coil and tighten the attaching screws to 13–18 ft. lbs.

10. Position the shock absorber to the lower bracket and torque the attaching bolt and nut to 65 ft. lbs.

11. Remove the safety stands and lower the vehicle.

F-250 and F-350

4WD

1. Raise the vehicle frame until the weight is off the front spring with the wheels still touching the floor. Support the axle to prevent rotation.

2. Disconnect the lower end of the shock absorber from the U-bolt spacer. Remove the U-bolts, U-bolt cap and spacer. On F-350 models, remove the 2 bolts retaining the track bar to the spring cap and the track bar bracket.

3. Remove the nut from the hanger bolt retaining the spring at the rear and drive out the hanger bolt.

4. Remove the nut connecting the front shackle and spring eye and drive out the shackle bolt and remove the spring.

To install:

5. Position the spring on the spring seat. Install the shackle bolt through the shackle and spring. Torque the nuts to 150 ft. lbs.

6. Position the rear of the spring and install the hanger bolt. Torque the nut to 150 ft. lbs.

7. Position the U-bolt spacer and place the U-bolts in position through the holes in the spring seat cap. Install but do not tighten the U-bolt nut. On the F-350, install the track bar. Torque the track bar-to-bracket bolts to 200 ft. lbs.

8. Connect the lower end of the shock absorber to the U-bolt spacer. Torque the fasteners to 60 ft. lbs. on the F-250; 70 ft. lbs. on the F-350.

9. Lower the vehicle and tighten the U-bolt nuts to 120 ft. lbs.

Upper Ball Joints

INSPECTION

NOTE: Always check and adjust the wheel bearings before ball joint inspection.

1. Raise and safely support the vehicle.

2. On Aerostar, place a jack under the lower control arm and raise to slightly compress the spring. On Bronco II, Explorer and Ranger, place a jack under the axle beneath the coil spring.

3. Grasp the upper edge of the tire and move the wheel in and out. A $1/32$ in. or greater movement between the upper spindle arm and the upper control arm or upper part of the axle jaw indicates that the upper ball joint must be replaced.

REMOVAL AND INSTALLATION

Aerostar

If upper ball joint replacement is necessary, the entire upper control arm must be replaced.

2WD Bronco II, Explorer and Ranger

1. Raise and safely support the vehicle. Remove the wheel and tire assembly.

2. Remove the brake caliper and support it aside with mechanics wire. Do not let the caliper hang by the brake hose.

3. Remove the dust cap, cotter pin, nut retainer, washer and outer bearing and remove the brake rotor from the spindle. Remove the brake dust shield.

4. Disconnect the steering linkage from the spindle and spindle arm by removing the cotter pin and nut. Remove the tie rod end from the spindle arm.

5. Remove the cotter pin and nut from the lower ball joint stud. Remove the axle clamp bolt from the axle.

6. Remove the camber adjuster from the upper ball joint stud and axle beam.

7. Strike the inside area of the axle to pop the lower ball joint loose from the axle beam. Remove the spin-

dle and ball joint assembly from the axle.

NOTE: Do not use a pickle fork to separate the ball joint from the axle as this will damage the seal and ball joint socket.

To install:

8. Install the spindle assembly in a vise and remove the snapring from the lower ball joint. Remove the lower ball joint from the spindle using C-frame T74P-4635-C or equivalent and a suitable receiver cup to press the ball joint from the spindle.

NOTE: The lower ball joint must be removed first.

9. Repeat the procedure in Step 8 to remove the upper ball joint.

NOTE: Do not heat the ball joints or the spindle to aid in removal.

10. Assemble the C-frame and receiver cup and press in the upper ball joint.

11. Repeat the procedure in Step 10 to install the lower ball joint.

NOTE: Do not heat the ball joints or axle to aid in installation.

12. Install the snapring onto the ball joint.

13. Place the spindle and ball joints into the axle. Install the camber adjuster in the upper spindle over the ball joint stud making sure it is properly aligned.

14. Tighten the lower ball joint stud nut to 104–146 ft. lbs. (141–198 Nm). Continue tightening the castellated nut until it lines up with the hole in the stud, then install the cotter pin.

15. Install the clamp bolt into the axle boss and tighten to 48–65 ft. lbs. (65–88 Nm).

16. Install the remaining components in the reverse order of their removal.

4WD Bronco II, Explorer and Ranger

1. Raise and safely support the vehicle. Remove the front wheel and tire assemblies.

2. Remove the disc brake caliper and wire it to the frame. Do not let the caliper hang by the brake hose.

3. Remove the hub locks, wheel bearings and locknuts.

4. Remove the hub, rotor and outer wheel bearing.

5. Remove the nuts retaining the spindle to the steering knuckle. Tap the spindle with a plastic hammer to jar the spindle from the knuckle. Remove the splash shield.

6. On the left side of the vehicle, remove the shaft and joint assembly by pulling the assembly out of the carrier. On the right side of the carrier, remove and discard the clamp from the shaft and joint assembly and the stub shaft. Pull the shaft and joint assembly from the splines of the stub shaft.

7. Remove the cotter pin from the tie rod nut and then remove the nut. Tap on the tie rod stud to free it from the steering arm.

8. Remove the upper ball joint snapring and remove the upper ball joint pinch bolt. Loosen the lower ball joint nut to the end of the stud.

9. Strike the inside of the knuckle near the upper and lower ball joints to break the knuckle loose from the ball joint studs.

10. Remove the camber adjuster sleeve. Note the position of the slot in the camber adjuster so it can be reinstalled in the same position during assembly.

11. Remove the lower ball joint nut. Place the knuckle in a vise and remove the snapring from the bottom ball joint socket, if equipped.

12. Assemble C-frame T74P-4635-C and ball joint remover T83T-3050-A or equivalents on the lower ball joint. Turn the forcing screw clockwise until the lower ball joint is removed from the steering knuckle.

13. Assemble the C-frame and ball joint remover on the upper ball joint and remove in the same manner.

NOTE: Always remove the lower ball joint first.

To install:

14. Clean the steering knuckle bore and insert the lower ball joint in the knuckle as straight as possible.

15. Assemble C-frame T74P-4635-C, ball joint installer T83T-3050-A and receiver cup T80T-3010-A3 or equivalents to install the lower ball joint. Turn the forcing screw clockwise until the lower ball joint is firmly seated. Install the snapring on the lower ball joint.

NOTE: The lower ball joint must always be installed first.

16. Assemble the C-frame, ball joint installer and receiver cup to install

the upper ball joint. Turn the forcing screw clockwise until the ball joint is firmly seated.

17. Install the camber adjuster into the support arm, making sure the slot is in the original position.

NOTE: The torque sequence in Steps 18 and 19 must be followed exactly when securing the knuckle. Excessive knuckle turning effort may result in reduced steering returnability if this procedure is not followed.

18. Install a new nut on the bottom ball joint stud. Tighten the nut to 90 ft. lbs. (122 Nm) minimum, then tighten to align the next slot in the nut with the hole in the stud. Install a new cotter pin.

19. Install the snapring on the upper ball joint stud. Install the upper ball joint pinch bolt and tighten to 48–65 ft. lbs. (65–88 Nm).

NOTE: The camber adjuster will seat itself into the knuckle at a predetermined position during the tightening sequence. Do not attempt to adjust this position.

20. On the right side of the carrier, install the rubber boot and new keystone clamps on the stub shaft slip yoke. Slide the right shaft and joint assembly into the slip yoke making sure the splines are fully engaged. Slide the boot over the assembly and crimp the keystone clamp using suitable pliers.

NOTE: The Dana model 28 axle has phased splines; there is only 1 way to assemble the right shaft and joint assembly into the slip yoke. The Dana model 35 axle does not have a blind spline, therefore pay special attention to make sure the yoke ears are in phase (in line) during assembly.

21. On the left side of the carrier, slide the shaft and joint assembly through the knuckle and engage the splines on the shaft in the carrier.

22. Install the splash shield and spindle onto the steering knuckle. Install and tighten the spindle nuts to 45 ft. lbs. (61 Nm).

23. Install the rotor on the spindle and install the outer wheel bearing in the race.

24. Install the wheel bearing, locknut, thrust bearing, snapring and locking hubs.

25. Install the caliper and the wheel and tire assemblies. Lower the vehicle.

Lower Ball Joints

INSPECTION

NOTE: Always check and adjust the wheel bearings before ball joint inspection.

1. Raise and safely support the vehicle.

2. On Aerostar, place a jack under the lower control arm and raise to slightly compress the spring. On Bronco II, Explorer and Ranger, place a jack under the axle beneath the coil spring.

3. Grasp the lower edge of the tire and move the wheel in and out. A $\frac{1}{32}$ in. or greater movement between the lower control arm or lower axle and the spindle indicates that the lower ball joint must be replaced.

REMOVAL AND INSTALLATION

Aerostar

If lower ball joint replacement is necessary, the entire lower control arm must be replaced.

2WD Bronco II, Explorer and Ranger

1. Raise and safely support the vehicle. Remove the wheel and tire assembly.

2. Remove the brake caliper and support it aside with mechanics wire. Do not let the caliper hang by the brake hose.

3. Remove the dust cap, cotter pin, nut retainer, washer and outer bearing and remove the brake rotor from the spindle. Remove the brake dust shield.

4. Disconnect the steering linkage from the spindle and spindle arm by removing the cotter pin and nut. Remove the tie rod end from the spindle arm.

5. Remove the cotter pin and nut from the lower ball joint stud. Remove the axle clamp bolt from the axle.

6. Remove the camber adjuster from the upper ball joint stud and axle beam.

7. Strike the inside area of the axle to pop the lower ball joint loose from the axle beam. Remove the spindle and ball joint assembly from the axle.

NOTE: Do not use a pickle fork to separate the ball joint from the axle as this will damage the seal and ball joint socket.

To install:

8. Install the spindle assembly in a vise and remove the snapring from

the lower ball joint. Remove the lower ball joint from the spindle using C-frame T74P-4635-C or equivalent and a suitable receiver cup to press the ball joint from the spindle.

NOTE: Do not heat the ball joint or the spindle to aid in removal.

9. Assemble the C-frame and receiver cup and press in the lower ball joint.

NOTE: Do not heat the ball joint or axle to aid in installation.

10. Install the snapring onto the ball joint.

11. Place the spindle and ball joints into the axle. Install the camber adjuster in the upper spindle over the ball joint stud making sure it is properly aligned.

12. Tighten the lower ball joint stud nut to 104–146 ft. lbs. (141–198 Nm). Continue tightening the castellated nut until it lines up with the hole in the stud, then install the cotter pin.

13. Install the clamp bolt into the axle boss and tighten to 48–65 ft. lbs. (65–88 Nm).

14. Install the remaining components in the reverse order of their removal.

4WD Bronco II, Explorer and Ranger

1. Raise and safely support the vehicle. Remove the front wheel and tire assemblies.

2. Remove the disc brake caliper and wire it to the frame. Do not let the caliper hang by the brake hose.

3. Remove the hub locks, wheel bearings and locknuts.

4. Remove the hub, rotor and outer wheel bearing.

5. Remove the nuts retaining the spindle to the steering knuckle. Tap the spindle with a plastic hammer to jar the spindle from the knuckle. Remove the splash shield.

6. On the left side of the vehicle, remove the shaft and joint assembly by pulling the assembly out of the carrier. On the right side of the carrier, remove and discard the clamp from the shaft and joint assembly and the stub shaft. Pull the shaft and joint assembly from the splines of the stub shaft.

7. Remove the cotter pin from the tie rod nut and then remove the nut. Tap on the tie rod stud to free it from the steering arm.

8. Remove the upper ball joint snapring and remove the upper ball joint pinch bolt. Loosen the lower ball joint nut to the end of the stud.

9. Strike the inside of the knuckle near the upper and lower ball joints to break the knuckle loose from the ball joint studs.

10. Remove the camber adjuster sleeve. Note the position of the slot in the camber adjuster so it can be reinstalled in the same position during assembly.

11. Remove the lower ball joint nut. Place the knuckle in a vise and remove the snapring from the bottom ball joint socket, if equipped.

12. Assemble C-frame T74P-4635-C and ball joint remover T83T-3050-A or equivalents on the lower ball joint. Turn the forcing screw clockwise until the lower ball joint is removed from the steering knuckle.

To install:

13. Clean the steering knuckle bore and insert the lower ball joint in the knuckle as straight as possible.

14. Assemble C-frame T74P-4635-C, ball joint installer T83T-3050-A and receiver cup T80T-3010-A3 or equivalents to install the lower ball joint. Turn the forcing screw clockwise until the lower ball joint is firmly seated. Install the snapring on the lower ball joint.

15. Install the camber adjuster into the support arm, making sure the slot is in the original position.

NOTE: The torque sequence in Steps 16 and 17 must be followed exactly when securing the knuckle. Excessive knuckle turning effort may result in reduced steering returnability if this procedure is not followed.

16. Install a new nut on the bottom ball joint stud. Tighten the nut to 90 ft. lbs. (122 Nm) minimum, then tighten to align the next slot in the nut with the hole in the stud. Install a new cotter pin.

17. Install the snapring on the upper ball joint stud. Install the upper ball joint pinch bolt and tighten to 48–65 ft. lbs. (65–88 Nm).

NOTE: The camber adjuster will seat itself into the knuckle at a predetermined position during the tightening sequence. Do not attempt to adjust this position.

18. On the right side of the carrier, install the rubber boot and new keystone clamps on the stub shaft slip yoke. Slide the right shaft and joint assembly into the slip yoke making sure the splines are fully engaged. Slide the boot over the assembly and

crimp the keystone clamp using suitable pliers.

NOTE: The Dana model 28 axle has phased splines; there is only 1 way to assemble the right shaft and joint assembly into the slip yoke. The Dana model 35 axle does not have a blind spline, therefore pay special attention to make sure the yoke ears are in phase (in line) during assembly.

19. On the left side of the carrier, slide the shaft and joint assembly through the knuckle and engage the splines on the shaft in the carrier.
20. Install the splash shield and spindle onto the steering knuckle. Install and tighten the spindle nuts to 45 ft. lbs. (61 Nm).
21. Install the rotor on the spindle and install the outer wheel bearing in the race.
22. Install the wheel bearing, locknut, thrust bearing, snapring and locking hubs.
23. Install the caliper and the wheel and tire assemblies. Lower the vehicle.

Upper and Lower Ball Joints

INSPECTION

Bronco, F Series and E Series

1. Before an inspection of the ball joints, make sure the front wheel bearings are properly packed and adjusted.
2. Jack up the front of the vehicle and safely support it with jackstands, placing the stands under the I-beam axle beneath the spring as shown in the accompanying illustration.
3. Have a helper grab the lower edge of the tire and move the wheel assembly in and out.
4. While the wheel is being moved, observe the lower spindle arm and the lower part of the axle jaw (the end of the axle to which the spindle assembly attaches). If there is $1/32$ in. (0.8mm) or greater movement between the lower part of the axle jaw and the lower spindle arm, the lower ball must be replaced.
5. To check upper ball joints, grab the upper edge of the tire and move the wheel in and out. If there is $1/32$ in. (0.8mm) or greater movement between the upper spindle arm and the upper part of the jaw, the upper ball joint must be replaced.

REMOVAL AND INSTALLALION

Bronco, F Series and E Series

1. Remove the spindle.
2. Remove the snapring from the ball joints. Assemble the C-frame assembly T74P–4635–C and receiver cup D81T–3010–A, or equivalents, on the upper ball joint. Turn the forcing screw clockwise until the ball joint is removed from the axle.
3. Repeat Step 2 on the lower ball joint.

NOTE: The upper ball joint must always be removed first. DO NOT heat the ball joint or spindle!

To install:

NOTE: The lower ball joint must be installed first.

4. To install the lower ball joint, assemble the C-frame with ball joint receiver cup D81T–3010–A5 and installation cup D81T–3010–A1, and turn the forcing screw clockwise until the ball joint is seated. DO NOT heat the ball joint to aid in installation!
5. Install the snapring onto the ball joint.
6. Install the upper ball joint in the same manner as the lower ball joint.
7. Install the spindle assembly.

Upper Control Arms

REMOVAL AND INSTALLATION

Aerostar

1. Place the steering wheel and the steering system in the on center position.
2. Raise the vehicle and support it safely under the body rails.

NOTE: Only remove and install 1 upper control arm at a time. Never service both sides at the same time.

3. Remove the spindle or steering knuckle, as required.
4. Remove the bolt retaining the bolt retainer plate and remove the plate.
5. Mark the position of the control arm mounting brackets on the flat plate.
6. Remove the bolt and washer retaining the front mounting bracket to the flat plate.
7. From under the rail, remove the 3 nuts from the bolts retaining the 2 upper control arm mounting brackets to the body rail.

8. Remove the 3 long bolts retaining the mounting brackets to the body rail by rotating the upper control arm out of position in order to remove the bolts.
9. Remove the upper control arm, upper ball joint and mounting bracket assembly and flat plate from the vehicle. If required, remove the damper assembly from the upper control arm.

To install:

10. If removed, install the damper assembly and tighten the retaining bolts to 22–29 ft. lbs. (30–39 Nm).
11. Place the flat plate for the mounting brackets in position on the body rail. Install the bolt and tighten to 10–14 ft. lbs. (14–18 Nm).
12. Place the mounting brackets and upper control arm assembly in position on the flat plate.
13. Install the 3 long bolts and washers retaining the mounting brackets to the body rail. Rotate or rock the upper control arm and mounting bracket assembly until the bolt heads rest against the mounting bracket and the studs extend through the body rail.
14. Move the mounting brackets into the position marked on the flat plate during removal.
15. Install and tighten the nuts retaining the mounting bracket bolts to the body rail to 145–195 ft. lbs. (196–264 Nm). Make sure the mounting brackets do not move from the marked position on the flat plate.

NOTE: The torque setting for the mounting bracket-to-body rail nuts and bolts is critical. They must be tightened to the specified torque.

16. Install and tighten the bolt retaining the front mounting bracket to the flat plate to 35–47 ft. lbs. (47–64 Nm).
17. Place the bolt retaining the plate in position on the mounting bracket and flat plate assembly. Install and tighten the bolt to 10–14 ft. lbs. (14–18 Nm).
18. Install the spindle or steering knuckle, as required.
19. Lower the vehicle and check the front end alignment.

Lower Control Arms

REMOVAL AND INSTALLATION

Aerostar

1. Place the steering and the steering system in the on center position.

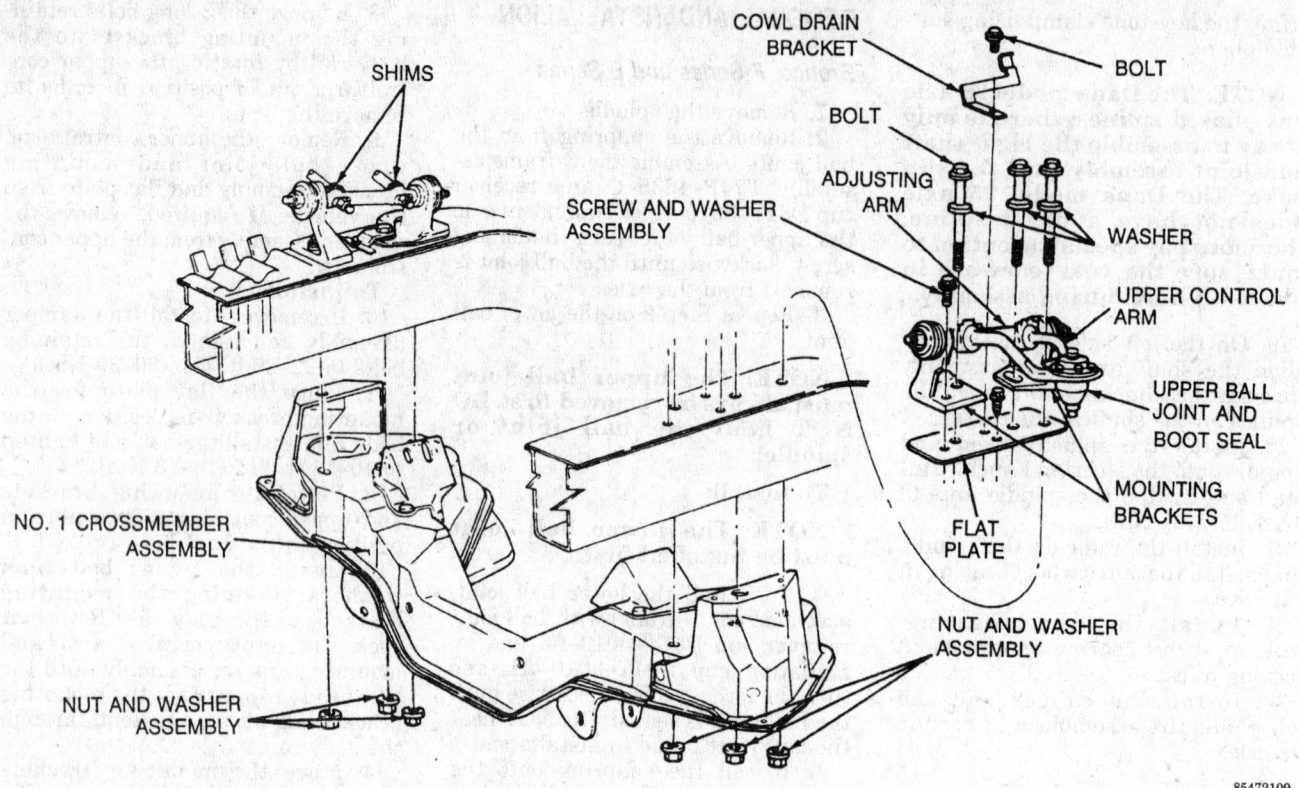

Upper control arm installation — Aerostar

85472109

2. Raise the vehicle and support it safely under the frame.

3. Remove the coil spring.

4. Remove the bolts and nuts retaining the control arm to the No. 1 crossmember. Remove the lower control arm.

To install:

5. Position the control arm in the No. 1 crossmember and install the mounting bolts. Install the nuts and tighten until snug. Do not tighten to the specified torque at this time.

6. Install the coil spring.

7. With the vehicle in the normal ride position, tighten the lower control arm retaining nuts and bolts to 100–140 ft. lbs. (136–190 Nm).

Stabilizer Bar

REMOVAL AND INSTALLATION

Aerostar

1. Raise and safely support the vehicle. Remove the nuts retaining the stabilizer bar to the lower control arm link.

2. Remove the insulators and disconnect the bar from the links. If required, remove the nuts retaining the links to the lower control arm. Re-

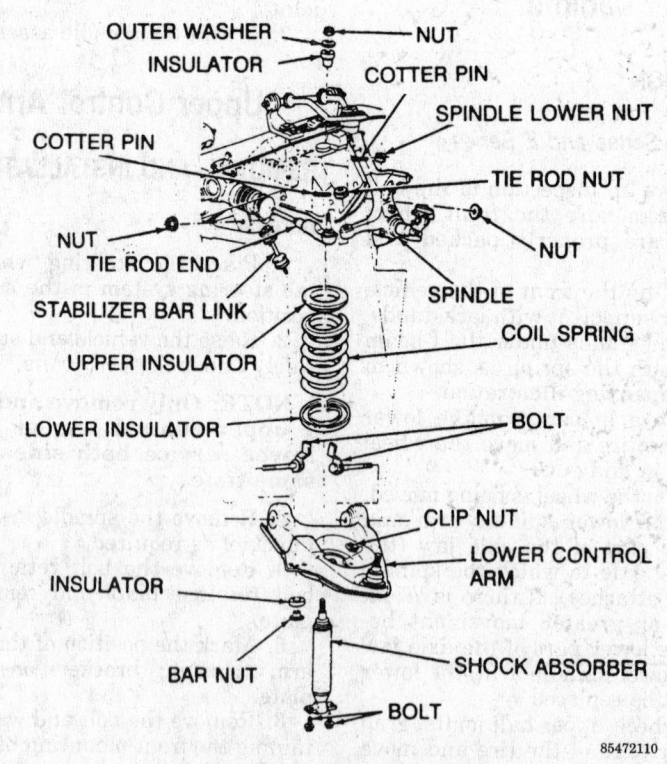

Lower control arm installation — Aerostar

85472110

move the insulators and remove the links.

3. Remove the bolts retaining the bar mounting bracket to the frame and remove the stabilizer bar. If required, remove the insulators from the stabilizer bar.

4. Installation is the reverse of the removal procedure. Tighten the mounting bracket bolts to 16–24 ft. lbs. (22–33 Nm). Tighten the link nuts to 9–12 ft. lbs. (12–16 Nm).

2WD Bronco II and explorer

1. Raise and safely support the vehicle.

2. Remove the nut and washer and disconnect the stabilizer link assembly from the front I-beam axle.

3. Remove the mounting bolts and remove the stabilizer bar retainers from the stabilizer bar assembly. Remove the stabilizer bar.

4. Installation is the reverse of the removal procedure. Tighten the retainer bolts to 35–50 ft. lbs. (47–68 Nm). Tighten the stabilizer bar link nuts to 30–44 ft. lbs. (40–60 Nm).

2WD Ranger

1. Raise and safely support the vehicle.

2. Remove the nuts and bolts retaining the stabilizer bar to the end links.

3. Remove the retainers and remove the stabilizer bar and bushings.

4. Installation is the reverse of the removal procedure. Tighten the retainer bolts to 35–50 ft. lbs. (47–68 Nm). Tighten the end link nuts to 30–44 ft. lbs. (40–60 Nm).

4WD Bronco II, Explorer and Ranger

1. Raise and safely support the vehicle.

2. Remove the bolts and retainers from the center and right end of the stabilizer bar.

3. Remove the nut, bolt and washer retaining the stabilizer bar to the stabilizer link.

4. Remove the stabilizer bar and bushings.

5. Installation is the reverse of the removal procedure. Tighten the retainer bolts to 35–50 ft. lbs. (48–68 Nm). Tighten the stabilizer bar link nut to 30–44 ft. lbs. (40–60 Nm).

Bronco, F Series and E Series

2WD

1. Raise and support the front end on jackstands.

2. Disconnect the right and left stabilizer bar ends from the link assembly.

3. Disconnect the retainer bolts and remove the stabilizer bar.

4. Disconnect the stabilizer link assemblies by loosening the right and left locknuts from their respective brackets on the I-beams.

To install:

5. Loosely install the entire assembly. The links are marked with an **R** and **L** for identification.

6. Tighten the link-to-stabilizer bar and axle bracket fasteners to 70 ft. lbs.

7. Check to make sure the insulators are properly seated and the stabilizer bar is centered.

8. On the F-150, torque the 6 stabilizer bar to crossmember attaching bolts to 35 ft. lbs. On the F-250 and F-350, torque the stabilizer bar-to-frame retainer bolts to 35 ft. lbs. Torque the frame mounting bracket nuts/bolts to 65 ft. lbs.

Chassis/Cab

2WD

1. Raise and support the front end on jackstands.

2. Disconnect each end of the bar from the links.

3. Disconnect the bar from the axle.

4. Unbolt and remove the links from the frame.

5. Installation is the reverse of removal. Replace any worn or cracked rubber parts. Install the bar loosely and make sure it is centered between the leaf springs. Make sure the insulators are seated in the retainers. When everything is in proper order, tighten the stabilizer bar-to-axle mounting bolts to 35–50 ft. lbs. Tighten the end link-to-frame bolts to 52–74 ft. lbs. Tighten the bar-to-end link nuts to 15–25 ft. lbs.

Stripped Chassis or Motor Home Chassis

2WD

1. Raise and support the front end on jackstands.

2. Disconnect the stabilizer bar ends from the links attached to the axle.

3. Remove the bar-to-frame bolts and remove the bar.

4. Remove the links from the axle brackets.

5. Installation is the reverse of removal. Replace any worn or cracked rubber parts. Assemble all parts loosely and make sure the assembly is centered on the frame. make sure the insulators are seated in the retainers. When everything is in proper order, tighten the bar-to-frame brackets bolts to 30–47 ft. lbs. Tighten the link-to-axle bracket bolts to 57–81 ft. lbs. Tighten the bar-to-link nuts to 15–25 ft. lbs.

F-150 and Bronco

4WD

1. Unbolt the stabilizer bar from the connecting links.

2. Unbolt the stabilizer bar retainers.

3. If necessary to remove the stabilizer bar mounting bracket, remove the coil springs as described above.

4. Installation is the reverse of removal. Torque the retainer nuts to 35 ft. lbs., then torque all other nuts at the links to 70 ft. lbs.

F-250 and F-350

4WD

1. Remove the bolts, washers and nuts securing the links to the spring seat caps. On models with the Monobeam axle, remove the nut, washer and bolt securing the links to the mounting brackets. Remove the nuts, washers and insulators connecting the links to the stabilizer bar. Remove the links.

2. Unbolt and remove the retainers from the mounting brackets.

3. Remove the stabilizer bar.

4. Installation is the reverse of removal. Torque the connecting links-to-spring seat caps to 70 ft. lbs. Torque the nuts securing the connecting links to the stabilizer bar to 25 ft. lbs. Torque the retainer-to-mounting bracket nuts to 35 ft. lbs.

Radius Arm

REMOVAL AND INSTALLATION

Bronco, F Series and E Series

2WD

NOTE: A torque wrench with a capacity of at least 350 ft. lbs. is necessary, along with other special tools, for this procedure.

1. Raise the front of the vehicle and place safety stands under the frame and a jack under the wheel or axle. Remove the wheels.

2. Disconnect the shock absorber from the radius arm bracket.

3. Remove the two spring upper retainer attaching bolts from the top

of the spring upper seat and remove the retainer.

4. Remove the nut which attached the spring lower retainer to the lower seat and axle and remove the retainer.

5. Lower the axle and remove the spring.

6. Remove the spring lower seat and shim from the radius arm. The, remove the bolt and nut which attach the radius arm to the axle.

7. Remove the cotter pin, nut and washer from the radius arm rear attachment.

8. Remove the bushing from the radius arm and remove the radius arm from the vehicle.

9. Remove the inner bushing from the radius arm.

10. Position the radius arm to the axle and install the bolt and nut finger-tight.

11. Install the inner bushing on the radius arm and position the arm to the frame bracket.

12. Install the bushing, washer, and attaching nut. Tighten the nut to 120 ft. lbs. and install the cotter pin.

13. Tighten the radius arm-to-axle bolt to 269–329 ft. lbs.

14. Install the spring seat and insulator on the radius arm so the hole in the seat fits over the arm-to-axle nut.

15. Install the spring.

16. Connect the shock absorber. Torque the nut and bolt to 40–60 ft. lbs.

17. Install the wheels.

F-150 and Bronco

4WD

1. Raise the vehicle and position safety stands under the frame side rails.

2. Remove the shock absorber lower attaching bolt and nut and pull the shock absorber free of the radius arm.

3. Remove the lower spring retaining bolt from the inside of the spring coil.

4. Loosen the axle pivot bolt.

5. Remove the nut attaching the radius arm to the frame bracket and remove the radius arm rear insulator. Lower the axle and allow the axle to move forward.

NOTE: The axle must be supported on a floor jack throughout this procedure, and must not be permitted to hang from the brake hose. If the length of the brake hose does not provide sufficient

clearance it may be necessary to remove and support the brake caliper.

6. Remove the spring as described above.

7. Remove the bolt and stud attaching the radius arm and bracket to the axle.

8. Move the axle forward and remove the radius arm from the axle. Then, pull the radius arm from the frame bracket.

9. Install the components in the reverse order of removal. Install new bolts and stud type bolts which attach the radius arm and bracket to the axle. Torque the bracket-to-axle bolts to 25 ft. lbs. Torque the lower radius arm-to-axle bolt to 330 ft. lbs. Tighten the upper stud-type radius arm-to-axle bolt to 250 ft. lbs. Torque the radius arm rear attaching nut to 120 ft. lbs. Torque the lower spring retainer nut to 100 ft. lbs. Torque the upper spring retainer bolts to 15 ft. lbs. Torque the axle pivot bolt to 150 ft. lbs. Torque the lower shock absorber bolt to 60 ft. lbs.

Twin I-Beam Axles

REMOVAL AND INSTALLATION

Bronco, F Series and E Series

NOTE: A torque wrench with a capacity of at least 350 ft. lbs. is necessary, along with other special tools, for this procedure.

1. Raise and support the front end on jackstands.

2. Remove the spindles.

3. Remove the springs.

4. Remove the stabilizer bar.

5. Remove the lower spring seats from the radius arms.

6. Remove the radius arm-to-axle bolts.

7. Remove the axle-to-frame pivot bolts and remove the axles.

To install:

8. Position the axle on the pivot bracket and loosely install the bolt/nut.

9. Position the other end on the radius arm and install the bolt. Torque the bolt to 269–329 ft. lbs.

10. Install the spring seats.

11. Install the springs.

12. Torque the axle pivot bolts to 120–150 ft. lbs.

13. Install the spindles.

14. Install the stabilizer bar.

I-Beam Axle

REMOVAL AND INSTALLATION

1. Raise and safely support the vehicle. Remove the front wheel spindle, the front spring and the stabilizer bar, if equipped.

2. Remove the spring lower seat from the radius arm and then remove the bolt and nut that attaches the stabilizer bar bracket, if equipped, and radius arm to the front axle.

3. Remove the axle-to-frame pivot bracket bolt and nut.

To install:

4. Position the axle to the frame pivot bracket and install the bolt and nut finger tight.

5. Position the opposite end of the of the axle to the radius arm, install the attaching bolt from underneath through the bracket, the radius arm and the axle. Install the nut and tighten to 191–220 ft. lbs. (258–298 Nm).

6. Install the spring lower seat on the radius arm so the hole in the seat indexes over the arm-to-axle bolt. Install the front spring.

7. Install the front wheel spindle and stabilizer bar, if equipped.

8. Lower the vehicle and with the weight on the suspension, tighten the axle-to-frame pivot bracket bolts to 120–150 ft. lbs. (163–203 Nm).

Track Bar

REMOVAL AND INSTALLATION

Chassis/Cab

1. Raise and support the vehicle safely.

2. Remove the wheel cover and the grease cap from the hub. Remove the cotter pin and the retainer. Discard the cotter pin.

3. Loosen the adjusting nut 3 turns.

4. Obtain running clearance between the brake rotor and disc brake pads by rocking the entire wheel and tire assembly in and out several times to push the caliper and brake pads away from the rotor.

NOTE: Do not pry on the caliper piston to obtain clearance.

5. While rotating the wheel, tighten the adjusting nut to 17–25 ft. lbs. (23–34 Nm) to seat the bearings.

6. Back off the adjusting nut ½ turn. Retighten the nut to 18–20 inch lbs. (2.0–2.3 Nm).

7. Install the retainer on the adjusting nut so the castellations line up with the hole in the spindle without moving the nut. Install a new cotter pin.

8. Check the front wheel rotation. If the wheel rotates properly, reinstall the grease cap and the wheel cover. If rotation is noisy or rough, remove, inspect and lubricate the bearings and bearing races.

9. Before driving the vehicle, pump the brake pedal several times to restore normal brake travel.

REMOVAL AND INSTALLATION

1. Raise and safely support the vehicle. Remove the wheel and tire assembly.

2. Remove the brake caliper and support it with mechanics wire. Do not let the caliper hang by the brake hose.

3. Remove the grease cap, cotter pin, retainer, adjusting nut and washer. Discard the cotter pin.

4. Remove the outer bearing and pull the hub and rotor off the spindle. Remove the grease seal using a seal removal tool. Discard the grease seal.

5. Remove the inner bearing from the hub. Remove all traces of old lubricant from the bearings, hub and spindle with solvent and dry thoroughly.

6. Inspect the bearings and bearing races for scratches, pits or cracks. If the bearings and/or races are worn or damaged, remove the races with a brass drift.

To install:

7. If the bearing races were removed, Install new races in the hub with suitable installation tools. Make sure the races are properly seated.

8. Using a bearing packer, pack the bearings with high-temperature wheel bearing grease. If a packer is not available, work as much grease as possible between the rollers and cages by hand.

9. Place a small amount of grease within the hub and grease the races. Install the inner bearing. Install a new wheel seal using a seal installer. Apply grease to the lips of the seal.

10. Install the hub and rotor assembly on the spindle. Install the outer bearing, washer and adjusting nut. Adjust the bearings.

11. Install the retainer, a new cotter pin and the grease cap.

12. Install the caliper and the wheel and tire assembly. Lower the vehicle.

13. Before driving the vehicle, pump the brake pedal several times to restore normal brake travel.

REAR SUSPENSION

Shock Absorber

REMOVAL AND INSTALLATION

Except Bronco, F Series and E Series

1. Raise and safely support the vehicle.

2. Place a jack under the rear axle and raise slightly to take the load off the shock absorbers.

3. Remove the shock absorber lower attaching nut and bolt and swing the lower end free of the mounting bracket on the axle housing.

4. Remove the upper attaching bolt or nut(s) and remove the shock absorber.

5. Installation is the reverse of the removal procedure. Tighten the lower attaching nut and bolt to 41–53 ft. lbs. (55–72 Nm). On Aerostar, tighten the upper bolt to 41–63 ft. lbs. (55–85 Nm). On Bronco II and Ranger, tighten the upper attaching nut to 41–53 ft. lbs. (55–72 Nm). On Explorer, tighten the upper mounting nuts to 15–21 ft. lbs. (21–29 Nm).

Bronco, F Series and E Series

1. Raise and support the rear end on jackstands.

2. Remove the self-locking nut, steel washer and bolt from the lower end of the shock absorber. Swing the lower end away from the bracket.

3. Remove the upper mounting nut and washer.

To install:

4. Attach the upper end first, then the lower end; don't tighten the nuts yet. If installing new gas shocks, attach the upper end loosely, aim the lower end at its bracket and cut the strap holding the shock compressed. Once extended, these shocks are very difficult to compress by hand!

5. Once the upper and lower ends are attached, tighten the nuts, for all models, as follows:

• Lower end, except Super Duty stripped chassis and motor home chassis — 52–74 ft. lbs.

• Upper end, except Super Duty stripped chassis and motor home chassis — 40–60 ft. lbs.

• Super Duty stripped chassis and motor home chassis upper and lower ends — 220–300 ft. lbs.

Coil Springs

REMOVAL AND INSTALLATION

Aerostar

1. Raise and safely support the vehicle. Place safety stands or equivalent on the frame rear lift points.

2. Remove the nut and bolt retaining the shock absorber to the axle mount on the lower control arm. Disconnect the shock absorber from the axle bracket.

3. Lower the rear axle until the coil springs are no longer under compression.

4. Remove the nut retaining the lower retainer and spring to the control arm. Remove the bolt retaining the upper retainer and spring to the frame.

5. Remove the spring and retainers. Remove the upper and lower insulators.

To install:

6. Make sure the axle is in the spring unloaded position. Place the lower insulator on the control arm and the upper insulator on top of the spring.

7. Install the coil spring. The small diameter, white colored, tapered coils must face upward with the pigtail resting against the upper insulator rubber stop.

8. With the upper pigtail resting against the rubber stop, rotate the spring with the upper insulator until the lower pigtail points in the 3 o'clock position. Install the upper retainer and bolt and tighten to 30–40 ft. lbs. (40–55 Nm).

9. Install the lower retainer and nut and tighten to 41–65 ft. lbs. (55–88 Nm).

10. Raise the axle to the normal ride position and install the shock absorber. Lower the vehicle.

Leaf Springs

REMOVAL AND INSTALLATION

Bronco II, Explorer and Ranger

1. Raise the vehicle and safely support on the frame until the weight is off the rear spring, with the tires still touching the floor.
2. Remove the nuts from the spring U-bolts and drive the U-bolts from the U-bolt plate.
3. Remove the spring-to-bracket nut and bolt at the front of the spring.
4. Remove the shackle upper and lower nuts and bolts at the rear of the spring. Remove the spring and shackle assembly from the rear shackle bracket.

To install:

5. Position the spring in the shackle and install the upper shackle-to-spring bolt and nut with the bolt head facing outboard.
6. Position the front end of the spring in the bracket and install the bolt and nut. Position the shackle in the rear bracket and install the bolt and nut.
7. On Bronco II and Ranger, position the spring on top of the axle with the spring tie bolt centered in the hole provided in the seat. On Explorer, position the spring on the bottom of the axle with the spring tie bolt centered in the hole provided in the seat.
8. Install the spring U-bolts, U-bolt plate and nuts and lower the vehicle. On Bronco II and Ranger, tighten the spring U-bolt nuts to 65–75 ft. lbs. (88–102 Nm) and the front spring bolt and the rear shackle bolts and nuts to 75–115 ft. lbs. (100–155 Nm). On Explorer, tighten the spring U-bolt nuts to 88–108 ft. lbs. (119–146 Nm), the front spring bolt and nut to 64–91 ft. lbs. (87–123 Nm) and the rear shackle bolts and nuts to 75–115 ft. lbs. (100–155 Nm).

Bronco, F Series and E Series

1. Raise the vehicle by the frame until the weight is off the rear spring with the tires still on the floor.
2. Remove the nuts from the spring U-bolts and drive the U-bolts from the U-bolt plate. Remove the auxiliary spring and spacer, if equipped.
3. Remove the spring-to-bracket nut and bolt at the front of the spring.
4. Remove the upper and lower shackle nuts and bolts at the rear of

the spring and remove the spring and shackle assembly from the rear shackle bracket.
5. Remove the bushings in the spring or shackle, if they are worn or damaged, and install new ones.

NOTE: When installing the components, snug down the fasteners. Don't apply final torque to the fasteners until the vehicle is back on the ground.

6. Position the spring in the shackle and install the upper shackle-to-spring nut and bolt with the bolt head facing outward.
7. Position the front end of the spring in the bracket and install the nut and bolt.
8. Position the shackle in the rear bracket and install the nut and bolt.
9. Position the spring on top of the axle with the spring center bolts centered in the hole provided in the seat. Install the auxiliary spring and spacer, if equipped.
10. Install the spring U-bolts, plate and nuts.
11. Lower the vehicle to the floor and tighten the attaching hardware as follows:

U-bolts nuts:
• Bronco, F-150 and F-250 under 8,500 lb. GVW — 75–115 ft. lbs.
• F-250 HD and F-350 — 150–210 ft. lbs.
• F-Super Duty chassis/cab — 200–270 ft. lbs.
• F-Super Duty stripped chassis and motor home chassis — 220–300 ft. lbs.

Spring to front spring hanger:
• F-150 2WD — 75–115 ft. lbs.
• F-250 2WD, F-350 2WD and Bronco — 150–210 ft. lbs.
• F-150, 250, 350 4WD — 150–175 ft. lbs.
• F-Super Duty — 255–345 ft. lbs.

Spring to rear spring hanger:
• All except F-250 and F-350 2WD Chassis Cab — 75–115 ft. lbs.
• F-250 and F-350 2WD Chassis Cab; F-Super Duty — 150–210 ft. lbs.

ADJUSTMENTS

Bronco, F Series and E Series

Side-to-side lean can be adjusted by about ⅜ in. (10mm) by installing a shim between the spring and axle on the low side. A vehicle that is low in the rear on both sides can be similarly raised by the insertion of 1 shim on each side.

If the side-to-side lean is greater than ½ in., try switch the springs from one side to the other.

Stabilizer Bar

REMOVAL AND INSTALLATION

Bronco, F Series and E Series

1. Remove the nuts from the lower ends of the stabilizer bar link.
2. Remove the outer washers and insulators.
3. Disconnect the bar from the links.
4. Remove the inner insulators and washers.
5. Unbolt the link from the frame.
6. Remove the U-bolts, brackets and retainers.
7. Installation is the reverse of removal. Replace all worn or cracked rubber parts. Coat all new rubber parts with silicone grease. Assemble all parts loosely and make sure the bar assembly is centered before tightening the fasteners. Observe the following torque figures:
• Stabilizer bar-to-axle nut, except Super Duty — 30–42 ft. lbs.
• Stabilizer bar-to-axle bolt, Super Duty chassis/cab — 27–37 ft. lbs.
• Stabilizer bar-to-axle bolt, Super Duty stripped chassis and motor home chassis — 30–47 ft. lbs.
• Link bracket-to-frame nut, 4WD — 30–42 ft. lbs.
• Link-to-bracket nut, 4WD — 60 ft. lbs.
• Link-to-frame nut, 2WD — 60 ft. lbs.
• Stabilizer bar-to-link — 15–25 ft. lbs.

Rear Control Arms

REMOVAL AND INSTALLATION

Aerostar

UPPER ARM

1. Raise the vehicle and support it safely. Place safety stands or equivalent on the frame rear lift points.
2. Remove the nut and bolt retaining the shock absorber to the lower axle bracket. Swing the lower end of the shock absorber free of the axle bracket.
3. Lower the rear axle assembly until the coil springs are no longer under compression.
4. Remove the bolt and nut retaining the upper control arm to the rear axle. Disconnect the upper control arm from the axle. Scribe a mark aligning the position of the cam adjuster in the axle bushing. The cam

adjuster controls the rear axle pinion angle for driveline angularity.

5. Remove the bolt and nut retaining the upper control arm to the right frame bracket. Rotate the arm to disengage from the body bracket.

6. Remove the nut and washer retaining the upper control arm to the left frame bracket. Remove the outer insulator and spacer. Remove the control arm from the bracket. Remove the inner insulator from the control arm stud.

NOTE: If the left bracket attachments are loosened prior to disengaging the arm from the right bracket, the uncompressed left bushing will force the arm against the right bracket and make removal difficult.

To install:

7. Position the inner insulator on the control arm stud. Install the control arm so the stud extends through the left frame bracket. Install the spacer and outer insulator over the stud. Install nut and washer assembly and tighten until snug. Do not torque at this time.

8. Position the upper control arm in the right frame bracket. Install the bolt and nut and tighten until snug. Do not torque at this time.

9. Align the marks on the cam adjuster and axle bushing. Install the upper control arm to the axle housing. Install the nut and bolt and tighten until snug. Do not torque at this time.

10. Raise the rear axle to the normal ride position and install the shock absorber. With the axle in the normal ride position, tighten the control arm-to-left frame bracket nut to 60–100 ft. lbs. (81–135 Nm), control arm-to-right frame bracket nut and bolt to 100–133 ft. lbs. (135–170 Nm) and control arm-to-axle housing to 155–210 ft. lbs. (210–284 Nm).

11. Remove the safety stands and lower the vehicle.

LOWER ARM

1. Raise and safely support the vehicle. Place safety stands under the frame rear lift points.

2. Remove the nut and bolt retaining the shock absorber to the lower axle bracket. Swing the lower end of the shock absorber free of the axle bracket.

3. Lower the rear axle until the coil springs are no longer under compression.

4. Remove the nut attaching the lower retainer and coil spring to the lower control arm. Remove the insulator from the arm.

5. Remove the bolt and nut retaining the lower control arm to the axle housing.

6. Remove the nut and bolt retaining the lower control arm to the frame bracket and remove the lower control arm.

To install:

7. Position the lower control arm in the bracket on the axle housing. Install the bolt so the head is inboard on the axle bracket. Install the nut but do not tighten at this time.

8. Install the insulator on the lower control arm. With the axle in the spring unloaded position, install the coil spring and lower retainer on the lower control arm.

9. Install the nut attaching the retainer and spring to the lower control arm. Tighten the nut to 41–65 ft. lbs. (55–88 Nm).

10. Raise the axle to the normal ride position. Tighten the lower control arm-to-axle housing nut and bolt and lower control arm-to-frame bracket nut and bolt to 95–130 ft. lbs. (129–177 Nm).

11. Install the shock absorber and lower the vehicle.

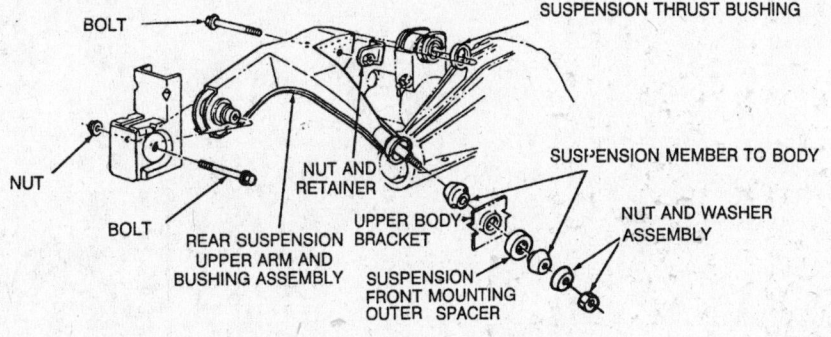

Rear upper control arm installation — Aerostar

85472111

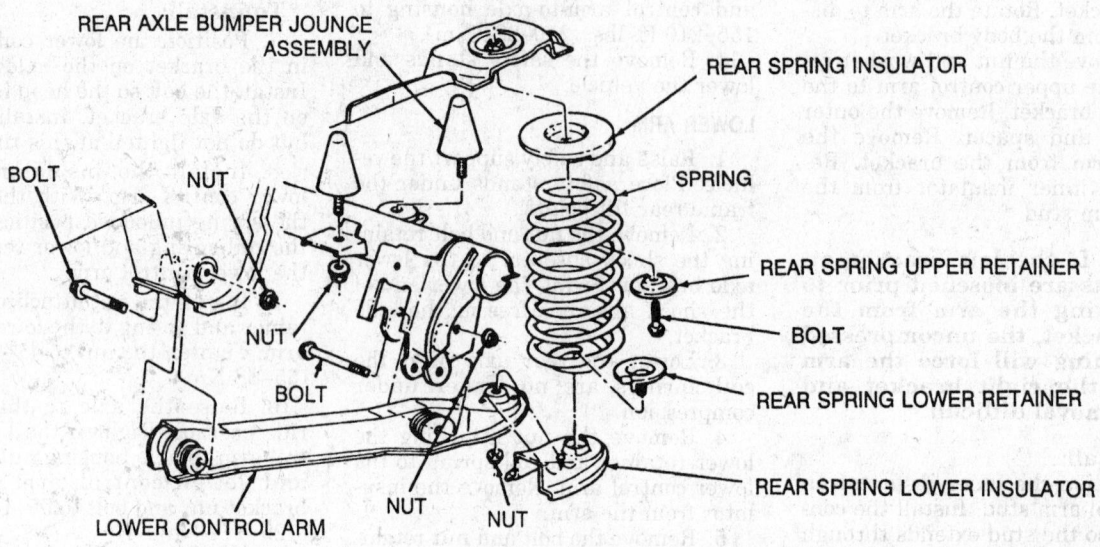

Rear lower control arm installation — Aerostar

GENERAL MOTORS

GM Mid-Size/Full-Size Vehicles

CHEVY/GMC TRUCK—Astro/Safari • S-Blazer/Jimmy • Blazer/Yukon • Bravada • Lumina APV • S10/S15 Pick-Up • C/K Pick-Up • Silhouette • Sonoma • Suburban • Syclone • Trans Sport • Typhoon • Van

FIRING ORDERS

NOTE: To avoid confusion, always replace spark plug wires one at a time.

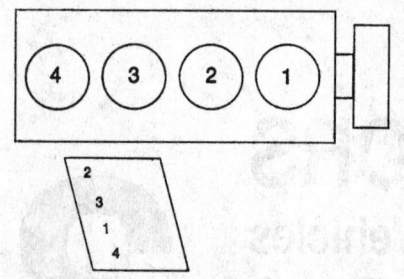

2.2L Engine
Engine Firing Order: 1–3–4–2
Distributorless Ignition System

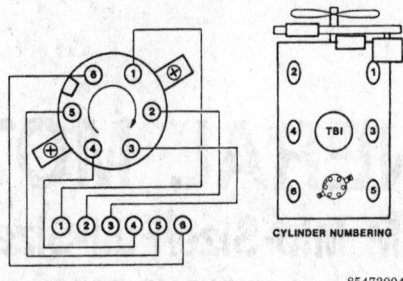

3.1L Engine
Engine Firing Order: 1–2–3–4–5–6
Distributor Rotation: Clockwise

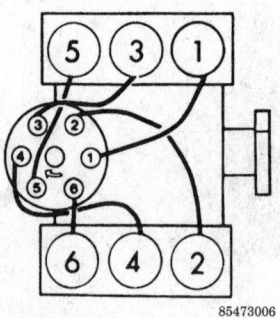

4.3L Engine
Engine Firing Order:
1–6–5–4–3–2
Distributor Rotation: Clockwise

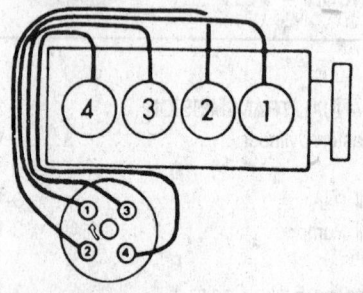

2.5L Engine
Engine Firing Order: 1–3–4–2
Distributor Rotation: Clockwise

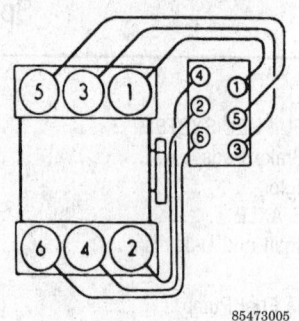

3.8L Engine
Engine Firing Order:
1–6–5–4–3–2
Distributorless Ignition System

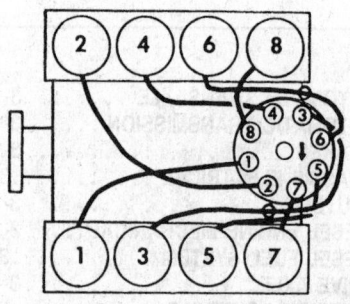

5.0L, 5.7L and 7.4L Engines
Engine Firing Order: 1–8–4–3–6–5–7–2
Distributor Rotation: Clockwise

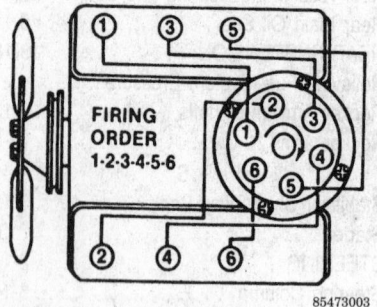

2.8L Engine
Engine Firing Order: 1–2–3–4–5–6
Distributor Rotation: Clockwise

ENGINE ELECTRICAL

NOTE: Disconnecting the negative battery cable on some vehicles may interfere with the functions of the on board computer systems and may require the computer to undergo a relearning process, once the negative battery cable is reconnected.

─────── WARNING ───────
NEVER disconnect the negative battery cable with the ignition ON. Removing power from the computer control module with the ignition ON may destroy the module.

Distributor

Most distributor equipped vehicles covered by this manual utilize a commonly recognizable distributor ignition system. However, the 1995–96 4.3L (VIN W) engine utilizes a distributor-like ignition system in which the commonly recognized distributor is replaced by a High Voltage Switch (HVS). The HVS is mounted in a fixed position so the Powertrain Control Module (PCM) may control ignition timing using input from a camshaft position sensor (usually integral to the HVS). Because of this, proper rotor alignment when removing and installing the HVS is even more critical than with the conventional distributor systems.

REMOVAL

1. Disconnect the negative battery cable.
2. Remove all necessary components in order to gain access to the distributor assembly. On most V-type engines it will be necessary to remove the air cleaner assembly for access.
3. Tag and disengage the distributor electrical connectors. If equipped, disconnect the vacuum line.
4. Remove the distributor cap. If necessary, tag and disconnect the spark plug wires.
5. Matchmark the rotor and the distributor body. Matchmark the distributor assembly and the engine block.

NOTE: Although it is only necessary to matchmark the distributor position for ease of installa-

tion, it may be advisable to first position the engine at TDC. If the distributor is being removed for further engine repair which may involve rotating the crankshaft (such as to align timing marks), setting the engine to TDC at this time will keep the distributor matchmarks valid during installation.

6. Remove the distributor holddown bolt. Carefully remove the distributor.

NOTE: As the distributor is removed from the engine, the rotor will turn counterclockwise. Observe and mark the finish position of the rotor. When reinstalling, position the rotor at the last mark and set the distributor into the engine. As the distributor drops into place, the rotor should turn to its original position, providing the engine crankshaft has not been rotated with the distributor out.

INSTALLATION

Timing Not Disturbed

NOTE: To ensure correct ignition timing if the engine has not been disturbed, the distributor must be installed with the rotor in the same position as when removed.

1. Align the rotor to the last mark made and install the distributor in the engine.

NOTE: On vehicles not equipped with the HVS system, if the distributor shaft cannot drop into the engine, remove the distributor and use a small prytool through the mounting hole to rotate the oil pump driveshaft until it can align with the distributor gear.

2. As the distributor is fully seated, the rotor should turn and end up at the first mark made. Ensure the distributor and oil pump rod are fully engaged.

NOTE: When the distributor is fully seated on the engine, make sure the rotor is properly aligned with the first timing mark. If equipped with the HVS system, if the rotor dos not align with the mark, the gear teeth of the HVS and camshaft have meshed 1 or more teeth out of time and the HVS procedure for timing disturbed should be used to assure proper installation.

3. Reconnect the distributor cap and wires. If applicable, connect the vacuum line to the distributor.
4. Tighten the distributor holddown bolt, then install the air cleaner or duct, if removed for access.

NOTE: If a check engine light is illuminated after HVS installation (Astro/Safari) and a Diagnostic Trouble Code (DTC) 1345 is found, the HVS has been installed incorrectly. Proceed to the timing disturbed installation procedure for the 1995–96 Astro/Safari Van.

5. Check and adjust the ignition timing.

Timing Disturbed

EXCEPT 1995–96 HVS IGNITION SYSTEMS

1. Set the engine to TDC: Remove the No. 1 spark plug. Place a finger over the spark plug hole and rotate the engine in the normal direction of rotation slowly, until compression is felt.
2. Align the timing mark on the crankshaft pulley to the **0** on the engine timing indicator by rotating the engine in the same direction slowly. The engine is now set on No. 1 TDC.

NOTE: An alternate method may be used to assure the engine is at TDC if the valve cover is removed. Watch the rocker arms for the No. 1 cylinder as the engine is turned. If the valves move as the crankshaft timing marker approaches the scale, the No. 1 cylinder is on its exhaust stroke. If the valves remain closed as the timing mark approaches the scale, then the No. 1 cylinder is approaching TDC of the compression stroke.

3. Install the distributor to the engine so the rotor is pointing to the No. 1 spark plug tower on the distributor cap once the distributor is fully seated in the engine.
4. Install the distributor cap, spark plug, wiring and connectors. If applicable, connect the vacuum line to the distributor.
5. If removed for access, install the air duct and/or air cleaner assembly, as applicable.
6. Check and adjust ignition timing.

1995–96 HVS IGNITION SYSTEMS

1. Set the engine to TDC: Remove the No. 1 spark plug. Place a finger over the spark plug hole and rotate the engine in the normal direction of

rotation slowly, until compression is felt.

2. Align the timing mark on the crankshaft pulley to the **0** on the engine timing indicator by rotating the engine in the same direction slowly. The engine is now set on No. 1 TDC.

NOTE: An alternate method may be used to assure the engine is at TDC if the valve cover is removed. Watch the rocker arms for the No. 1 cylinder as the engine is turned. If the valves move as the crankshaft timing marker approaches the scale, the No. 1 cylinder is on its exhaust stroke. If the valves remain closed as the timing mark approaches the scale, then the No. 1 cylinder is approaching TDC of the compression stroke.

3. Remove the HVS cap screws and cap to expose the rotor.

4. Align the pre-drilled indent hole in the HVS driven gear with the arrow cast into the upper portion of the shaft housing. The rotor should point to the cap hold-down mount nearest the flat side of the housing.

5. Using a long prytool, align the oil pump driveshaft in the engine to the mating drive tab in the HVS.

6. Guide the HVS into place, making sure the locating slot in the HVS

85473008

Proper HVS alignment — 1995–96 HVS ignition

base fits over the dowl pin in the intake manifold.

7. Once the HVS is FULLY SEATED, the rotor tip should be aligned with the pointer cast into the HVS base. this pointer will have a "6" cast into it, indicating the HVS component is designed for use in a 6-cylinder engine. If the rotor tip does not align within a few degrees of the pointer, the gear mesh between the HVS and camshaft is likely off by a tooth or more. If so, repeat the procedure again to achieve proper alignment.

8. Install the cap and mounting screws.

9. Install the HVS mounting clamp and tighten to 20 ft. lbs. (27 Nm).

10. Engage the 3-wire camshaft position sensor connector to the base of the HVS assembly.

11. Connect the spark plug and coil leads to the HVS cap. If a check engine light is illuminated and a Diagnostic Trouble Code (DTC) 1345 is found, either the HVS has been installed incorrectly or an incorrect HVS assembly has been installed.

Distributorless Ignition System

REMOVAL AND INSTALLATION

Ignition Coils

NOTE: Any 1 of the 2 coils on the 2.2L engine or 3 coils on 3.8L engine may be removed separately from the other(s).

1. Disconnect the negative battery cable.

2. Tag and disconnect the spark plug wiring from the coil(s).

3. Remove the coil retaining screws (there are usually 2 screws per coil).

4. Separate the coil from the ignition module.

To install:

5. Install the coil to the ignition module assembly.

6. Install the coil retaining screws and tighten to 40 inch lbs. (4.5 Nm).

7. Engage the spark plug wire to the coil(s) and noted during removal.

8. Connect the negative battery cable.

Ignition Module

3.8L ENGINE

1. Disconnect the negative battery cable.

2. Disconnect the wire connector from the module.

3. Remove the screws securing the module and coils to the mounting plate.

4. Separate the ignition coils from the module by pulling straight up on the coils.

NOTE: Position the coils and wiring so the assembly will not be hanging from the wires.

5. Installation is the reverse of the removal procedure.

2.2L ENGINE

1. Disconnect the negative battery cable.

2. Disengage the module electrical connectors.

3. Tag and disconnect the spark plug wiring from the coils.

4. Remove the 3 ignition module/coil assembly-to-block retaining bolts, then remove the assembly from the engine.

5. Remove the coils from the ignition module, then separate the module from the assembly plate bracket.

To install:

6. Install the module to the assembly plate bracket, then install the ignition coils.

7. Install the module/coil assembly to the engine block and tighten the retaining bolts to 15–22 ft. lbs. (20–30 Nm).

8. Engage the spark plug cables to the proper coil towers, as noted during removal.

9. Engage the module electrical connectors.

10. Connect the negative battery cable.

Crankshaft Sensor

3.8L ENGINE

1. Disconnect the negative battery cable.

2. Remove the serpentine belt from the crankshaft pulley.

3. Raise and support the vehicle safely.

4. Remove the right front tire and wheel assembly.

5. Remove the right inner fender access cover.

6. Using a 28mm socket, remove the harmonic balancer retaining bolt.

7. Using a harmonic balancer pulley removal tool such as J-38197 or equivalent, remove the balancer assembly.

8. Loosen the retaining bolts and remove the sensor shield. Do not use a prybar when removing the shield.

9. Disengage the sensor electrical connector, then remove the sensor

and sensor pedestal (1992 only) from the engine block.

10. On 1992 vehicles, remove the sensor from the pedestal.

To install:

11. On 1992 vehicles, loosely install the crankshaft sensor on the pedestal, then position the sensor with the pedestal attached onto tool J–37090. Position the sensor, pedestal and tool on the crankshaft.

12. Except for 1992 vehicles, install the sensor to the engine block.

13. Install the sensor securing bolts and torque to 14–28 ft. lbs. (20–40 Nm), except for 1993 vehicles on which the bolts should be tightened to 6–9 ft. lbs. (9–12 Nm).

14. For 1992 vehicles, torque the pedestal pinch bolt to 36–40 inch lbs. (4–4.5 Nm), then remove special tool J-37089.

15. Install the crankshaft sensor shield.

16. Engage the wire connector.

17. Except for 1994–96 vehicles, place tool J–37089 or equivalent, on the harmonic balancer and turn; if any vane of the balancer touches the tool, replace the balancer assembly.

18. Position the balancer onto the crankshaft.

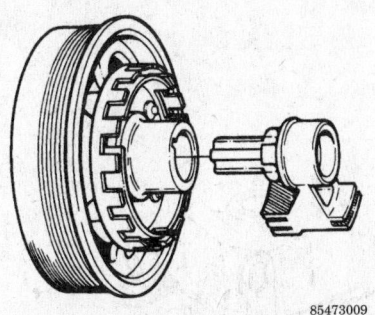

85473009

Use J-37089 or equivalent tool to check the harmonic balancer during crankshaft sensor installation on all 3.8L engines except 1994–96

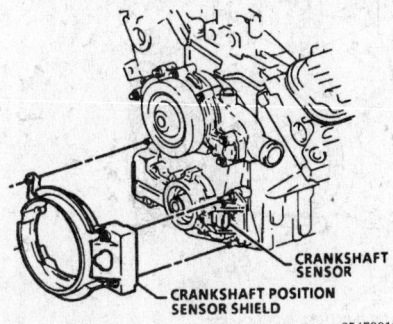

85473010

Install the shield over the crankshaft sensor — 3.8L engine

19. Apply sealer to the threads of the balancer bolt and torque the bolt to 110 ft. lbs. (150 Nm) plus turn the bolt an additional 76 degrees.

20. Install the fender shield, the install the tire and wheel assembly.

21. Lower the vehicle.

22. Install the serpentine belt, then connect the negative battery cable.

2.2L ENGINE

1. Disconnect the negative battery cable.

2. Disengage the sensor harness connector at the ignition module.

3. Remove the sensor-to-block retaining bolt.

4. Remove the sensor from the engine block.

To install:

5. Inspect the sensor O-ring for wear, cracks or leakage and replace, if necessary.

6. Lightly coat the O-ring with clean engine oil, then install the sensor to the engine block.

7. Install the sensor-to-block retaining bolt and tighten to 71 inch lbs. (8 Nm).

8. Engage the sensor wiring harness to the ignition module.

9. Connect the negative battery cable.

Ignition Timing

On gasoline engines, the timing may be adjusted only on those that are equipped with a conventional distributor ignition. If equipped with the distributorless Electronic Ignition (EI) system, the control module sets timing and makes all necessary spark changes. On these systems, the crankshaft position sensor is mounted in a fixed position, therefore not allowing for adjustment. The HVS system found on some 1995–96 vehicles is also not adjustable.

NOTE: The 1995–96 4.3L (VIN W) engine is equipped with a new distributor-like ignition component called the High Voltage Switch (HVS). On the HVS ignition system the Powertrain Control Module (PCM) utilizes a camshaft position sensor to determine spark timing, dwell and firing of the ignition coil. Because of this, positioning of the HVS (and ignition timing) is fixed and non-adjustable. Do not attempt to adjust the ignition timing by rotating the HVS or cross/mis-firing may occur.

Connect the timing light and tachometer to the engine according to

the tool manufacturers' instructions. Make sure the timing light is connected to the No. 1 spark plug wire. If equipped with a diesel engine, a special timing light and a digital tachometer must be used.

ADJUSTMENT

1. Locate and clean the timing marks on the crankshaft pulley and the front of the timing case cover.

2. Use chalk or white paint to color the mark on the scale that will indicate the correct timing, when aligned with the mark on the pulley or the pointer.

3. Attach a tachometer and a timing light to the engine.

4. On early model vehicles that are not equipped with Electronic Spark Control (EST), disconnect and plug the vacuum lines to the distributor.

5. If equipped with EST, the electronic spark timing must be disabled or bypassed to prevent the control module from advancing timing while attempting to set it. This would obviously lead to an incorrect base timing setting. There are 2 possible methods of disabling the EST system, depending on the type of engine:

• On 2.5L engines, ground the **A** and **B** terminals on the ALDL connector under the dash before adjusting the timing.

• On all other engines using the EST distributor, disengage the timing connector wire. Refer to the Vehicle Emission Control Information (VECI) label for details on the particular engine. Most vehicles are equipped with a single wire timing bypass connector. The bypass wire is normally a tan wire with a black stripe, that breaks out of the wiring harness conduit adjacent to the distributor, but on some later vehicles (1994–96) it may break out of a taped section just below the heater case in the passenger compartment.

6. Start the engine, then check and adjust the idle speed, as necessary.

7. Loosen the distributor lock bolt slightly to permit the distributor to be turned.

8. Adjust the idle to the correct specification.

9. With the timing light aimed at the pulley and the marks on the engine, turn the distributor in the direction of rotor rotation to retard the spark or in the opposite direction of rotor rotation to advance the spark. Align the marks on the pulley and

the engine with the flashes of the timing light.

10. Turn the engine **OFF**, tighten the distributor hold-down bolt and recheck the timing.

Alternator

PRECAUTIONS

Several precautions must be observed with alternator equipped vehicles in order to avoid damage to the unit.

- If the battery is removed for any reason, make sure it is reconnected with the correct polarity. Reversing the battery connections may result in damage to the 1-way rectifiers.
- When utilizing a booster battery as a starting aid, always connect the positive to positive terminals and the negative terminal from the booster battery to a good engine ground on the vehicle being started.
- Never use a fast charger as a booster to start vehicles.
- Disconnect the battery cables when charging the battery with a fast charger.
- Never attempt to polarize the alternator.
- Do not use test lamps of more than 12 volts when checking diode continuity.
- Do not short across or ground any of the alternator terminals.
- The polarity of the battery, alternator and regulator must be matched and considered before making any electrical connections within the system.
- Never separate the alternator on an open circuit. Make sure all connections within the circuit are clean and tight.
- Disconnect the battery ground terminal when performing any service on electrical components.
- Disconnect the battery if arc welding is to be done on the vehicle.

REMOVAL AND INSTALLATION

1. Disconnect the negative battery cable.
2. Remove the necessary components in order to gain access to the alternator assembly. On early models of the Astro/Safari vans, remove the upper radiator fan shroud. On most Astro/Safari vans, remove the engine cover from inside the vehicle.

3. If necessary, remove the air cleaner and/or duct work.
4. Tag and disengage the electrical connectors at the alternator.
5. Remove the alternator belt. If equipped with a serpentine belt, relieve the belt tension, the carefully remove the belt from the alternator pulley.
6. If equipped, remove the alternator brace. On 1994–96 vehicles equipped with a 2.2L engine, this may be accomplished working through the wheel well.
7. Remove the alternator retaining bolts and remove the alternator.
8. Installation is the reverse of the removal procedure. Check and adjust the belt tension, as required.

BELT TENSION ADJUSTMENT

V-Belt

1. Place a belt tension gauge at the center of the greatest span of a warm not hot drive belt and measure the tension.
2. If the belt is below the specification, loosen the component mounting bracket and adjust.

3. Run the engine at idle for 15 minutes to allow the belt to reseat itself in the pulleys.
4. Allow the drive belt to cool and re-measure the tension. Adjust as necessary to meet the following specifications:
  4.3L, 5.0L, 5.7L and 7.4L engines
  Used belt — 90 lbs. (400 N)
  New belt — 135 lbs. (600 N)
  6.2L diesel engine:
  Used belt — 67 lbs. (300 N)
  New belt — 146 lbs. (650 N)

Serpentine Belts

Serpentine belts use an automatic tensioner which is spring activated and can be turned to the left or the right to apply or release the pulley tension.

Most tensioners are equipped with a belt wear scale, make sure the belt is not stretched beyond it's serviceable life. Also, the serpentine belt grooves must match the grooves in the pulleys.

NOTE: Most tensioners are equipped to insert a $^1/_2$ in. breaker bar into the tensioner pulley in order to apply leverage and release the belt tension.

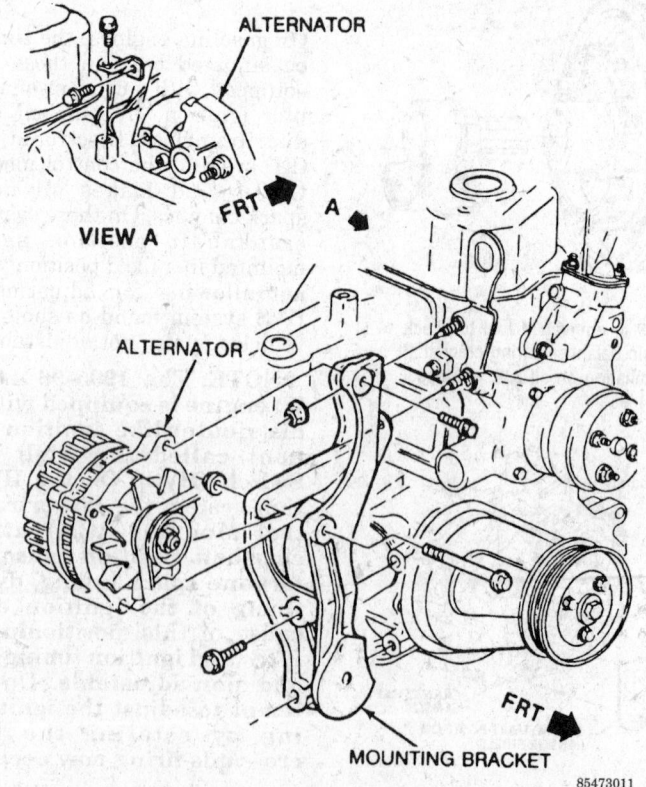

Alternator mounting — 2.5L engine

85473011

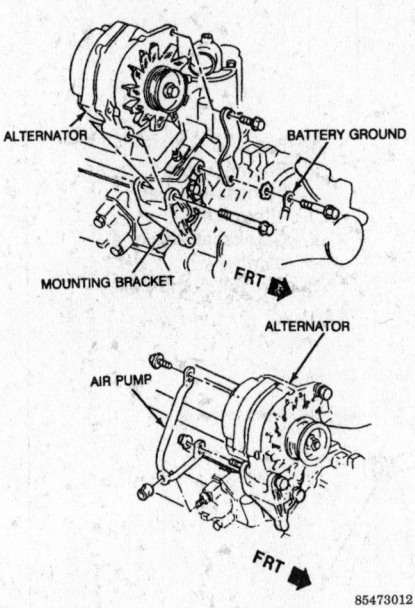

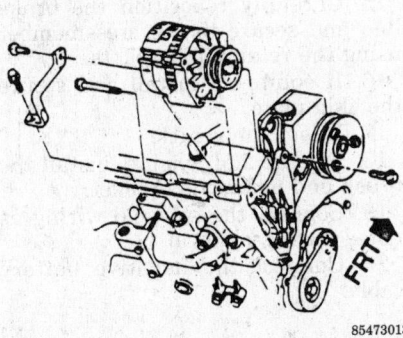

Alternator mounting — 2.8L engine

85473012

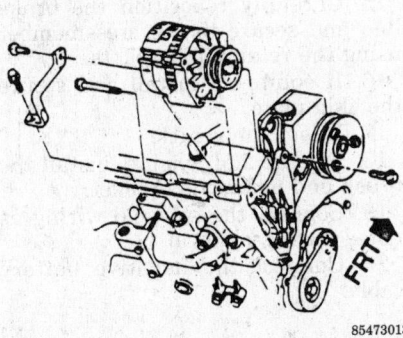

Alternator mounting — 3.1L engine

85473013

Starter

REMOVAL AND INSTALLATION

S/T-Series

1992–93 REAR WHEEL DRIVE

1. Disconnect the negative battery cable.
2. Raise and support the vehicle safely.
3. On 2.5L engines, remove the brush end mounting bracket from the starter motor.

4. Tag and disconnect the solenoid wiring.

NOTE: If the wiring is difficult to access with the starter installed, remove the bolts and partially lower the starter for access to the wiring. If this is done, be careful not to stretch or damage the wiring.

5. Remove the 2 bolts and washers (noting the location of any shims); then remove the starter and the shim.

To install:

6. Position the starter in the vehicle (along with any shims which were removed), then support while threading the starter mounting bolts.
7. Tighten the starter mounting bolts to 30–33 ft. lbs. (40–45 Nm).
8. Engage the starter solenoid wiring as noted during removal.
9. On 2.5L engines, install the brush end mounting bracket.
10. Lower the vehicle and connect the negative battery cable.

1994–96 REAR WHEEL DRIVE PICK-UP

1. Disconnect the negative battery cable.
2. Raise and support the vehicle safely.
3. Remove the cover in order to provide access to the flywheel.
4. Tag and disconnect the solenoid wiring.
5. For the 2.2L engine, remove the attaching bracket-to-engine mount bolt.
6. Remove the starter-to-engine block bolts, then carefully remove the starter noting the position of any shims (if used).
7. If necessary, remove the bracket (2.2L engine) or the shield (4.3L engine) from the starter assembly.

To install:

8. If removed, install the bracket or shield to the starter, as applicable. Tighten the bracket nuts to 97 inch lbs. (11 Nm) or the the shield nuts to 106 inch lbs. (12 Nm).
9. Carefully raise the starter and shims, if equipped, into position in the vehicle and thread 1 of the retaining bolts to hold it in position.
10. On the 2.2L engine, loosely install the bracket-to-engine mount bolt.
11. Install the remaining starter mounting bolts, then tighten all mounting fasteners to 32 ft. lbs. (43 Nm).
12. Engage the wiring to the solenoid as noted during removal.
13. Install the flywheel cover.

14. Lower the vehicle and connect the negative battery cable.

1992–93 4WD AND ALL 1994–96 UTILITY MODELS

1. Disconnect the negative battery cable.
2. Raise and support the vehicle safely.

NOTE: On some vehicles access to the wiring may be easier from above. Before raising and supporting the vehicle, check to see if the solenoid wiring is accessible. If so, tag and disconnect it at this time.

3. On 2.5L engines, remove the brush end mounting bracket from the starter motor.
4. Tag and disconnect the solenoid wiring.

NOTE: If the wiring is difficult to access with the starter installed, remove the bolts and partially lower the starter for access to the wiring. If this is done, be careful not to stretch or damage the wiring.

5. If equipped, loosen the retaining bolts and remove the skid plate.
6. Remove the retainers and the brackets holding the brake line to the crossmember located just behind the oil pan. Reposition the brake line slightly in order to clear the crossmember.
7. Remove the crossmember retaining bolts, there are usually 3 on each side, then carefully lower the crossmember and remove it from the vehicle for access.
8. As applicable and necessary, remove the bracket holding the transmission fluid cooler lines to the flywheel housing, brace rod to the flywheel housing and/or the lower flywheel housing.
9. Remove the starter-to-engine block bolts. When removing the last bolt, be sure to support the starter to keep it from falling and possibly injuring you.

NOTE: On some vehicles, even with the crossmember removed clearance for starter removal is tight. As the starter is lowered, it may be necessary to rotate it upside down in order for the end to clear the motor mount, then lower the nose behind the bellhousing and rotate it back so the solenoid is on top and the starter may be removed.

10. Carefully lower the starter and shims, if equipped.

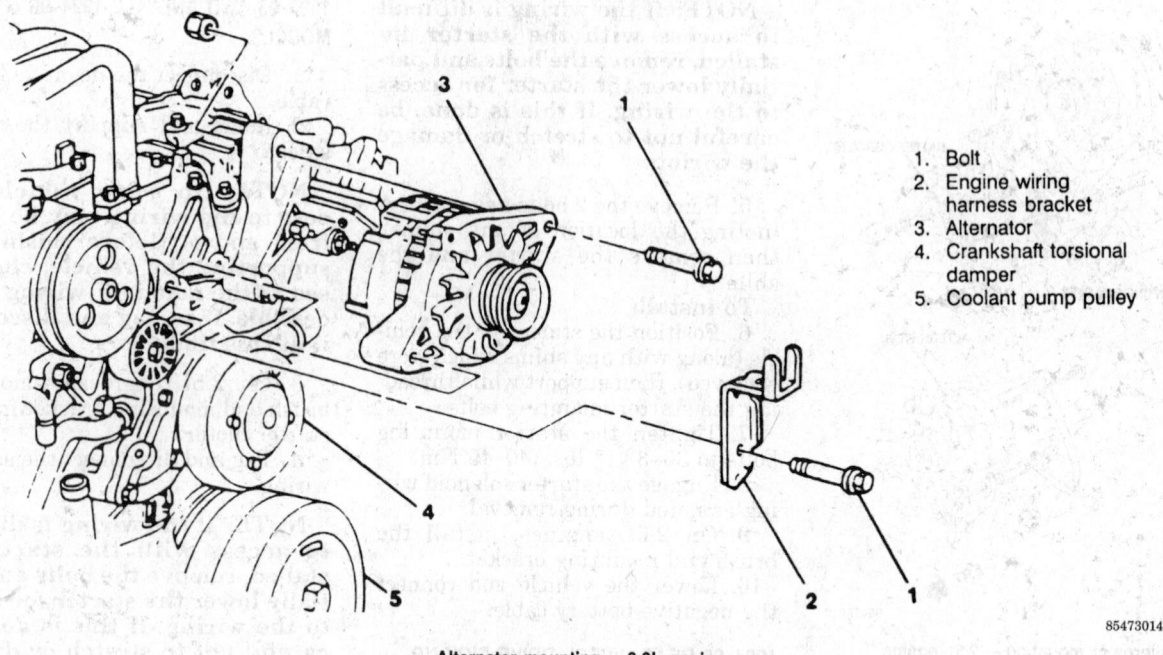

1. Bolt
2. Engine wiring harness bracket
3. Alternator
4. Crankshaft torsional damper
5. Coolant pump pulley

85473014

Alternator mounting — 3.8L engine

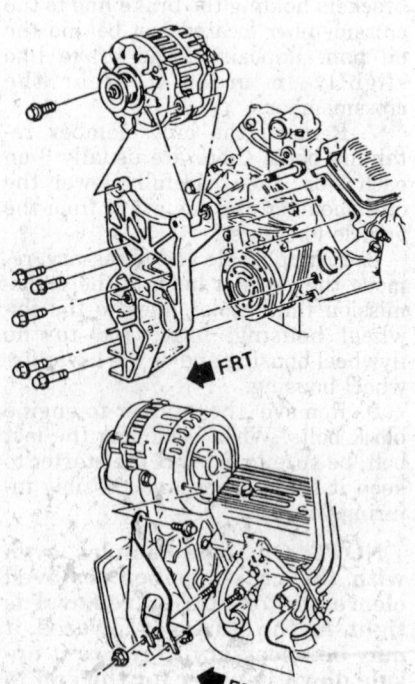

FRT

FRT

85473015

Common alternator mounting for the 4.3L engine

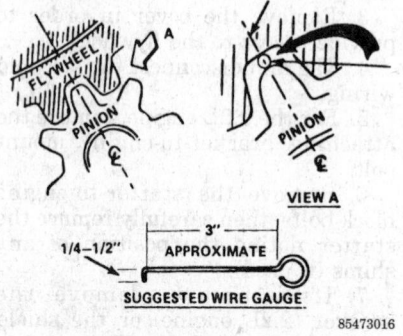

VIEW A

3"
APPROXIMATE

1/4–1/2"

SUGGESTED WIRE GAUGE

85473016

Measuring flywheel-to-starter pinion clearance during starter installation

To install:

11. Position the starter in the vehicle (along with any shims which were removed) and support while threading the starter mounting bolts. Tighten the starter mounting bolts to 30–33 ft. lbs. (40–45 Nm).

12. If removed, install the lower flywheel housing.

13. If equipped, install the transmission cooler line bracket and/or the brace rod to the housing.

14. Install the crossmember to the frame and secure using the retaining bolts.

15. Carefully reposition the brake line and secure to the crossmember using the retaining brackets.

16. If equipped, install and secure the skid plate.

17. Lower the vehicle.

18. For the 2.5L engine, install the brush end mounting bracket.

19. Connect the solenoid wiring as noted during removal.

20. Connect the negative battery cable.

1994–96 4WD PICK-UP

1. Disconnect the negative battery cable.

2. Unbolt the engine mounts, then raise and support the engine using a suitable lifting device.

3. Unbolt the transmission mount and support the transmission assembly.

4. Remove the starter-to-engine bolts and support the starter.

5. Rotate the starter as necessary for access, then tag and disconnect the solenoid wiring.

6. Carefully lower the starter and shims, if equipped. Note the location of any shims for installation purposes.

7. If necessary, remove the shield from the starter assembly.

To install:

8. Raise the starter into position in the vehicle along with any shims (making sure they are in their original positions), then tighten the mounting bolts to 32 ft. lbs. (43 Nm).

9. If removed, install the shield to the starter assembly and tighten the retaining nuts to 106 inch lbs. (12 Nm).

10. Engage the wiring to the solenoid as noted during removal.

11. Install the transmission mount and remove the supports.

12. Lower the engine and secure the engine mounts, then remove the lifting device.

13. Connect the negative battery cable.

Astro and Safari

1. Disconnect the negative battery cable.

2. Raise and support the vehicle safely.

3. If access is possible with the starter installed, tag and disconnect the solenoid wiring.

4. Remove the 2 bolts and washers (along with the shims, if equipped), then carefully the starter. If the wiring was not disconnected previously, support the starter, then tag and disconnect the wiring at this time.

5. Installation is the reverse of removal. Install the shim, if used, and torque the mounting bolts to 32 ft. lbs. (43 Nm).

Lumina APV, Silhouette and Trans Sport

3.1L ENGINE

1. Disconnect the negative battery cable.

2. Raise and support the vehicle safely.

3. If necessary, remove the air conditioning compressor brace.

4. Remove the solenoid cover, then tag and disconnect the solenoid wiring. Reposition the wiring harness, as necessary.

5. Disengage the oil pressure sensor electrical connector, then remove the sensor.

6. Either remove the 2 bolts or the 1 bolt and 1 nut retaining the starter to the engine block. Carefully remove the starter and the shim(s), noting shim position, if equipped, for installation purposes.

7. Installation is the reverse of removal. Install the shim, if used, and torque the mounting bolts to 32 ft. lbs. (43 Nm).

3.8L ENGINE

1. Disconnect the negative battery cable.

2. Raise and support the vehicle safely.

3. Remove the cover from the starter wiring, then tag and disconnect the wiring.

4. Remove the screws and harness clips retaining the wiring, then position the harness out of the way.

5. Remove the retainers and the flywheel cover.

6. Remove the starter bolts, then carefully remove the starter and any shims, if equipped, noting the shim location(s) for installation purposes.

7. Installation is the reverse of removal. Install the shim, if used, and torque the mounting bolts to 32 ft. lbs. (43 Nm).

Full Size Pick-Up, Van and Utility

1. Disconnect the negative battery cable.

2. If equipped, remove any brackets and/or shields.

3. If accessible from above, tag and disconnect the solenoid wiring at this time.

4. Raise and support the vehicle safely.

5. If not done earlier, tag and disconnect the solenoid wiring.

6. As necessary on vehicles before 1993, remove the flywheel cover, the and/or exhaust crossover pipe.

7. Remove the starter mounting bolts and/or retaining nuts, then remove the starter assembly from the vehicle noting the positioning of any shims which may be used.

8. Installation is the reverse of the removal procedure. Install any shims that were removed with the starter and torque the retaining bolts to 35 ft. lbs. (45 Nm). Where equipped, tighten the bracket bolt on diesel engines to 24 ft. lbs. (33 Nm).

9. Once installed, check the flywheel-to-starter pinion clearance with a wire gauge and adjust (using shims), if necessary.

Diesel Glow Plugs

REMOVAL AND INSTALLATION

1. Disconnect the negative battery cable.

2. Disengage the electrical connection at the glow plug.

NOTE: On some late model 6.2L engines, it will be necessary to remove the right wheel and the splash shield from the wheel well in order to access the right bank plugs. Also on the 6.2L, it may be necessary to remove the exhaust down pipe from the turbocharger for easier access to the No. 6 and No. 8 plugs.

3. Using a suitable tool, loosen and remove the glow plug. On most engines, a $^3/_8$ in. deep well socket may be used to remove the plugs.

4. Installation is the reverse of removal. Torque the glow plugs to 13 ft. lbs. (17 Nm).

TESTING

Inhibit Switch

1. Check the temperature controlled switch to make sure it is closed at low temperatures or open at temperatures above 125°F (52°C).

2. Remove the connector from the inhibit switch when the engine temperature is below 100°F (38°C).

3. Set the ohmmeter on a low range or use a self powered test light.

4. Test across the terminals. The switch should be closed (test light **ON** or a reading of less than 0.1 ohm on the meter).

5. Test terminals to ground with a test light or the ohmmeter on a high range. The light should be **OFF** or the meter show greater than 1.0 mega-ohm.

6. Replace the switch if it tests open across the terminals or if either terminal is closed to the ground.

7. Disconnect the plug from the switch terminals when the engine is above 125°F.

8. Set the ohmmeter on the highest scale or use a self powered test light and test across the terminals. Test across each terminal to ground.

9. The switch should be open (test light **OFF** or high ohm reading of greater than 1 mega-ohm on the meter).

10. Replace the switch if it is closed. Use a socket wrench when installing the switch and torque to 17 ft. lbs. (21 Nm).

Controller

The glow plug controller provides glow plug operation after starting a cold engine.

1. With the engine cold 80°F (27°C), turn the engine control switch to the **RUN** position and let the glow plugs cycle.

2. After 2 minutes of letting the glow plugs cycle, crank the engine for 1 second; it is not important that the engine starts. Return the engine control switch to **RUN**. The glow plugs

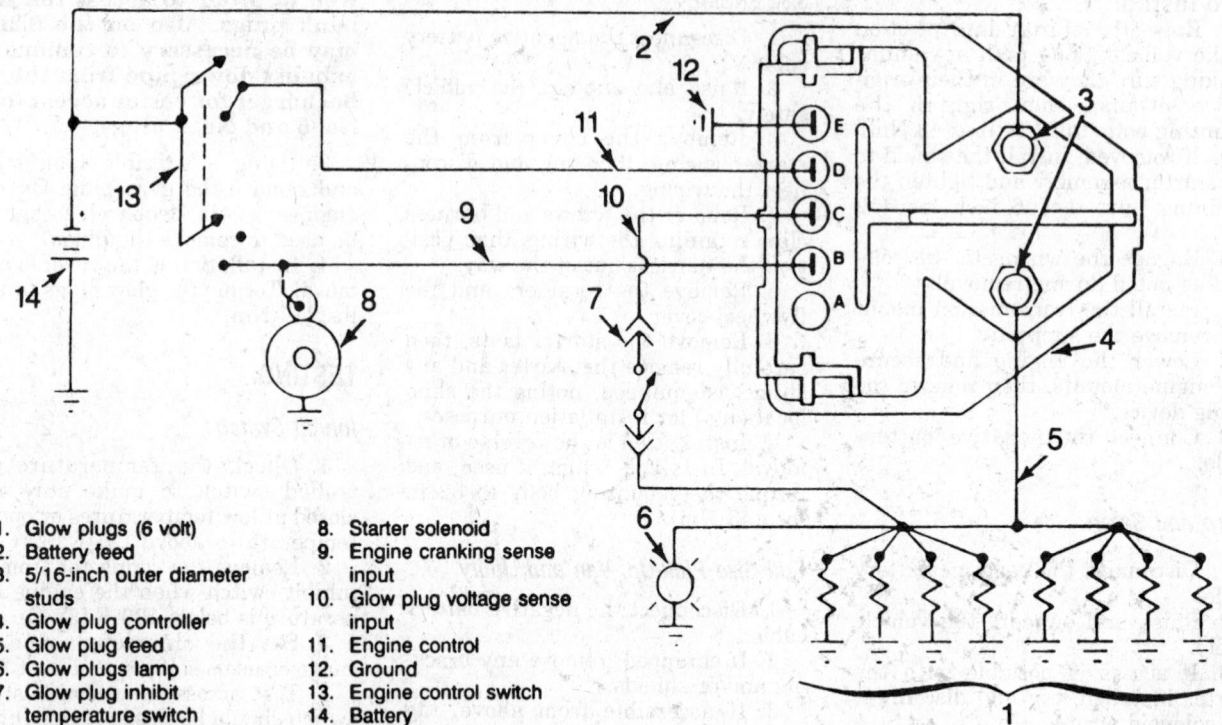

1. Glow plugs (6 volt)
2. Battery feed
3. 5/16-inch outer diameter studs
4. Glow plug controller
5. Glow plug feed
6. Glow plugs lamp
7. Glow plug inhibit temperature switch
8. Starter solenoid
9. Engine cranking sense input
10. Glow plug voltage sense input
11. Engine control
12. Ground
13. Engine control switch
14. Battery

Electronic glow plug system schematic

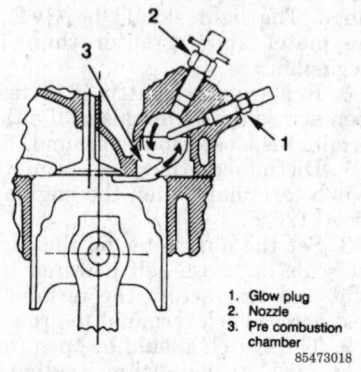

1. Glow plug
2. Nozzle
3. Pre combustion chamber

Diesel engine glow plug location

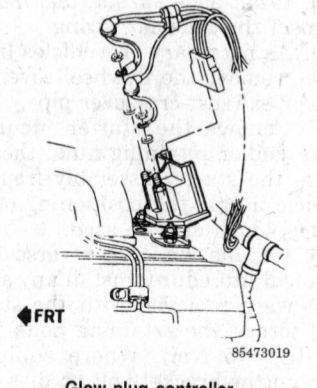

◀FRT

Glow plug controller

should cycle at least once after cranking.

3. If the plugs do not turn on, disconnect the controller connector and check terminal **B** with a grounded 12 volt test light. The light should be **OFF** with the engine control switch in **RUN**, and **ON** when the engine is cranked.

4. If the light does not operate as described, repair a short or open in the engine harness purple wire.

5. If the light works right but the afterstart glow plug feature does not, replace the controller.

CHASSIS ELECTRICAL

Air Bag

NOTE: 1994–96 Vans (Astro and Safari, Lumina, Silhouette and Trans Sport and Full Size G Van) and some 1995–96 S/T-Series vehicles are equipped with a supplemental inflatable restraint (SIR) system or driver's side air bag. Before attempting any work on or near the steering column, ALWAYS disarm the air bag to prevent a costly and possibly dangerous accidental deployment.

DISARMING

1. Turn the wheels to the straight-ahead position, then turn the ignition switch to **LOCK**.

2. On the Lumina, Silhouette and Trans Sport, remove the instrument panel lower extension for access to the fuse block.

3. Remove the "AIR BAG" or "SIR" fuse from the block, as applicable.

4. Remove the steering column filler panel or left hand sound insulator, as applicable, for access to the SIR wiring harness.

5. Remove the Connector Position Assurance (CPA) device, then disengage the yellow 2-way connector at the base of the steering column.

NOTE: With the fuse removed, the AIR BAG or SIR light will illuminate if the ignition switch is turned ON at any time. This is normal and does not indicate a problem when the system is disarmed.

To enable:

6. Make sure the ignition is in the **LOCK** position.

7. Engage the yellow SIR connector, then secure using the CPA device.

8. Install the steering column filler or sound insulator panel, as applicable.

9. Install the SIR system fuse to the fuse block.

10. Turn the ignition switch to the **ON** position and verify that the AIR BAG indicator light flashes 7 times, then extinquishes. If it does not go out, troubleshoot the SIR system fault.

11. On the Lumina, Silhouette and Trans Sport, install the instrument panel lower extension.

Heater Blower Motor

REMOVAL AND INSTALLATION

S/T-Series

1. Disconnect the negative battery cable.

2. If equipped on 1994–96 vehicles, remove the VCM from the engine compartment.

3. For 1994–96 vehicles, remove the coolant recovery reservoir.

4. Disconnect the blower motor cooling tube.

5. Disengage the electrical connector(s) from the blower motor, as necessary.

6. Remove the blower motor-to-case screws, then carefully withdraw the blower motor from the case.

To install:

7. Install the blower motor to the case and secure using the retaining screws.

8. Engage the electrical connector(s) to the motor, as necessary.

9. Connect the blower motor cooling tube.

10. For 1994–96 vehicles, install the coolant recovery reservoir, then if equipped, install the VCM.

11. Connect the negative battery cable.

Astro and Safari

1. Disconnect the negative battery cable.

2. Tag and disengage the necessary electrical connections.

3. Remove the engine coolant recovery bottle.

4. Disconnect and reposition the windshield washer bottle.

5. Disengage the cooling tube from the heater blower assembly and remove the blower motor retaining screws. If necessary, remove the blower motor relay bracket.

6. Remove the blower motor.

7. Installation is the reverse of the removal procedure. Transfer the blower motor cage, as required.

Lumina, Silhouette and Trans Sport

1. Disconnect the negative battery cable.

2. If necessary, remove the engine air cleaner assembly.

3. Remove the screws and disconnect the left windshield wiper arm linkage. Carefully move the left wiper arm linkage aside for access to the blower motor assembly.

4. Disengage the blower motor electrical harness.

5. Remove the blower motor retaining screws and remove the blower motor assembly.

6. Installation is the reverse of removal.

Full Sized Pick-Up, Van and Utility, Without Air Conditioning

EXCEPT G-SERIES 1992

1. Disconnect the negative battery cable.

2. Mark the position of the blower motor in relation to its case.

3. Remove the electrical connection at the motor.

4. Remove the blower attaching screws and remove the assembly.

5. The blower wheel can be removed from the motor shaft by removing the retaining nut.

6. Installation is the reverse of the removal procedure. Apply a bead of sealer to the mounting flange before installation.

EXCEPT G-SERIES 1993–96

1. Disconnect the negative battery cable.

2. Remove the instrument panel storage compartment for access.

3. Remove the front screw from the right door sill plate, then remove the right hinge pillar trim panel.

4. Except for 1995–96 vehicles, if necessary, disengage the ECM wiring, then remove the ECM and mounting bracket.

5. Disengage the blower motor wiring, then if equipped, remove the courtesy lamp.

6. Remove the bolt from the right lower dash support, then remove the blower motor cover and disconnect the cooling tube.

7. Loosen and remove the motor flange screws, then remove the blower motor pulling forward carefully to prevent damaging the fan. On some earlier vehicles, it may be necessary to pry very carefully on the back right side of the instrument panel.

To install:

8. Install the blower motor to the case and secure using the retaining screws.

9. Connect the cooling tube and install the cover.

10. Install the bolt to the right lower dash support, then install the courtesy lamp, if equipped.

11. Engage the blower motor wiring. If applicable, install the ECM and mounting bracket, then engage the wiring.

12. Install the right hinge pillar trim panel, then install the screw to the front door sill plate.

13. Install the instrument panel storage compartment, then connect the negative battery cable.

G-SERIES

1. Disconnect the negative battery cable.

2. If necessary on vehicles before 1993, remove the coolant overflow bottle.

3. On 1993 vehicles (and earlier vehicles, as necessary), remove the retaining screws, then remove the cover for access to the blower motor and wiring.

4. Disengage the necessary wiring.

5. For 1994–96 vehicles, remove the cooling tube.

6. Remove the attaching screws, then carefully withdraw the blower motor assembly.

7. Installation is the reverse of the removal procedure.

With Air Conditioning

R/V-SERIES

1. Disconnect the negative battery terminal.

2. Remove the insulator attaching bolts and nuts. Remove the insulating shield from the case.

3. Mark the position of the blower motor in relation to its case.

4. Disengage the electrical connection at the motor.

5. Disconnect the blower motor cooling tube.

6. Remove the blower attaching screws and remove the assembly.

7. The blower wheel can be removed from the motor shaft by removing the nut at the center.

8. Installation is the reverse of the removal procedure. Apply a bead of sealer to the mounting flange before installation.

C/K-SERIES 1992

1. Disconnect the negative battery cable.
2. Disengage the electrical connection at the motor.
3. Remove the blower attaching screws and remove the assembly.
4. The blower wheel can be removed from the motor shaft by removing the nut at the center.
5. Installation is the reverse of removal. Apply a bead of sealer to the mounting flange before installation.

C/K-SERIES 1993–96

1. Disconnect the negative battery cable.
2. Remove the instrument panel storage compartment for access.
3. Remove the front screw from the right door sill plate, then remove the right hinge pillar trim panel.
4. If necessary, disengage the ECM wiring, then remove the ECM and mounting bracket.
5. Disengage the blower motor wiring, then if equipped, remove the courtesy lamp.
6. Remove the bolt from the right lower dash support, then remove the blower motor cover and disconnect the cooling tube.
7. Loosen and remove the motor flange screws, then remove the

1. Blower motor
2. Screws
3. Gasket
4. Screw
5. Evaporator inlet line
6. Evaporator outlet line
7. Heater core tubes
8. Nut
9. Stud

85473020

Air conditioning blower motor installation — C/K-Series

blower motor pulling forward carefully to prevent damaging the fan. It may be necessary to pry very carefully on the back right side of the instrument panel.

To install:

8. Install the blower motor to the case and secure using the retaining screws.
9. Connect the cooling tube and install the cover.
10. Install the bolt to the right lower dash support, then install the courtesy lamp, if equipped.
11. Engage the blower motor wiring. If applicable, install the ECM and mounting bracket, then engage the wiring.
12. Install the right hinge pillar trim panel, then install the screw to the front door sill plate.
13. Install the instrument panel storage compartment, then connect the negative battery cable.

G-SERIES

1. Disconnect the negative battery cable.
2. Remove the coolant overflow bottle.
3. On 1993 vehicles (and earlier when applicable) remove the cooling tube.
4. Disengage the motor wiring.
5. Remove the attaching screws, then carefully withdraw the blower motor assembly.
6. Installation is the reverse of removal.

Windshield Wiper Motor

REMOVAL AND INSTALLATION

S/T-Series and 1995–96 Astro/Safari

1. Disconnect the negative battery cable.
2. Remove the wiper arms from the linkage so the cowl may be removed.
3. Remove the cowl vent grille and screen.
4. Disengage the wiring from the wiper motor.
5. Except for 1994–96 vehicles, loosen but do not remove the nuts which hold the drive link to the motor crank arm. Detach the drive link from the crank arm.
6. For 1994–96 vehicles, remove the wiper transmission from the wiper motor drive link using J-39232 or equivalent tool.
7. Remove the wiper motor-to-cowl screws. Carefully rotate the motor and guide the drive link from the hole in the cowl, then remove the motor.

To install:

8. Guide the motor drive link through the hole in the cowl, then install the motor and secure using the retainers.
9. For 1994–96 vehicles, install the drive link socket onto the crank arm ball using J-39529 or equivalent tool. The wiper transmission assembly must be installed to the crank arm PAST the 2nd detent so the seal is compressed to a maximum height of 1 in. (25.5mm)

NOTE: Before assembling the transmission drive link socket to the crank arm ball, lubricate the inside of the socket using white lithium grease.

10. Except for 1994–96 vehicles, position the drive link socket onto the crank arm ball of the wiper motor assembly. Evenly tighten the socket nuts to secure the connection.
11. Engage the wiring to the wiper motor.
12. Install the cowl vent grille and screen.
13. Install the wiper arm and blade assemblies to the transmission linkage.
14. Connect the negative battery cable and verify proper operation.

Astro and Safari 1992–94

1. Disconnect the negative battery cable.
2. Remove the wiper arms from the linkage so the cowl may be removed.
3. Remove the cowl vent grille.
4. Disengage the wiring from the wiper motor.
5. Disconnect the transmission link from the crank arm on the motor by prying it toward the rear of the vehicle.
6. Remove the motor mounting bolts and remove the motor.
7. Installation is the reverse of removal.

Lumina, Silhouette and Trans Sport

1. Disconnect the negative battery cable.
2. Disengage the wiper motor wiring harness connector.
3. Disconnect the transmission link from the crank arm on the motor by loosening the 2 crank arm screws until the ball socket release the crank arm ball. The screws are usually 8mm heads.
4. Remove the motor mounting bolts and slide the motor out of its mounting.
5. Installation is the reverse of removal.

R/V-Series

1. Make sure the wipers are in the parked position.
2. Disconnect the ground cable from the battery.
3. Disconnect the wiring harness at the wiper motor and the hoses from the washer pump.
4. Reach down through the access hole in the plenum and loosen the wiper drive rod attaching screws. Remove the drive rod from the wiper motor crank arm.
5. Remove the wiper motor attaching screws and the motor assembly and linkage.
6. To install, reverse the removal procedure.

NOTE: Lubricate the wiper motor crank arm pivot before re-installation. Failure of the washers to operate or to shut off is often caused by grease or dirt on the electromagnetic contacts. Simply unplug the wire and pull off the plastic cover for access. Likewise, failure of the wipers to park is often caused by grease or dirt on the park switch contacts. The park switch is under the cover behind the pump.

C/K-Series

1. Disconnect the negative battery cable.
2. Pivot the wiper arm away from the windshield, move the latch to the open position and lift the wiper arm off the driveshaft.
3. Remove the cowl vent grille.
4. Unplug the wiring from the motor.
5. Remove the drive link-to-crank arm retainers and slide the links from the arm. Do not remove the crank arm.
6. Remove the motor mounting bolts and lift the motor out.
7. Installation is the reverse of removal.

G-Series

1. Make sure the wipers are parked. The wiper arms should be in their normal **OFF** position.
2. Disconnect the negative battery cable.
3. Remove the wiper arms.
4. Remove the cowl vent grille.
5. Loosen the nuts holding the transmission linkage, then separate the linkage from the wiper motor crank arm.
6. Disconnect the power feed to the wiper motor at the connector next to the radio. For 1995–96 vehicles, remove the radio.
7. Separate the left defroster outlet from the flex hose.
8. Remove the screw holding the left hand heater duct to the engine shroud, then twist the heater duct down and out.
9. If necessary on vehicles before 1993, remove the windshield washer hoses from the pump.
10. Remove the screws (usually 3) holding the wiper motor to the cowl and remove the motor.

To install:

11. Position the wiper motor to the vehicle, then secure using the retaining screws.
12. If applicable, install the windshield washer hoses at the pump.
13. Position the heater duct (twisting in and up), then install the screw holding the left hand heater duct to the engine cover shroud.
14. Connect the left defroster outlet to the flex hose.
15. Engage the electrical connector to the wiper motor assembly.
16. Lubricate the inside of the crank arm socket using white lithium grease, then reach in through the access hole and connect the crank arm to the socket. Tighten the nuts hold-

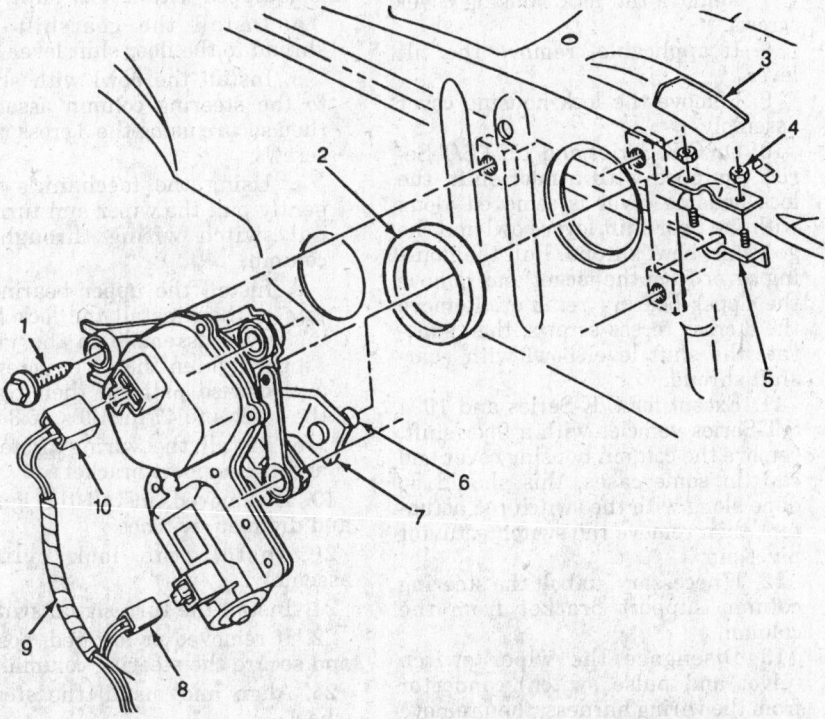

1. Screw
2. Seal
3. Access hole
4. Drive rod retaining cap nuts
5. Drive rod
6. Crank arm pivot ball
7. Crank arm
8. Motor connector
9. Wiper motor harness
10. Park switch connector

85473021

Wiper motor mounting — R/V-Series

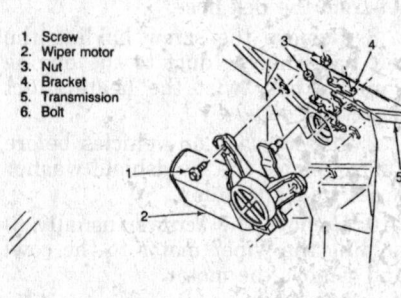

1. Screw
2. Wiper motor
3. Nut
4. Bracket
5. Transmission
6. Bolt

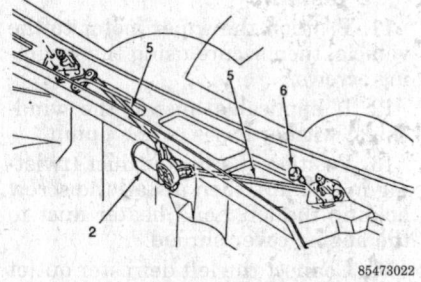

85473022

Common wiper motor mounting — C/K-Series

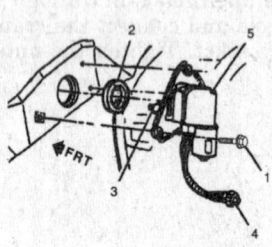

1. BOLT, 4 N·m (35 LBS. IN.)
2. SEAL
3. CRANK ARM
4. HARNESS, WIPER MOTOR
5. ASSEMBLY, WIPER MOTOR

85473023

Wiper motor mounting — 1993–96 G-Series

ing the transmission linkage to the wiper motor crank arm.

NOTE: For 1994–96 vehicles, use a pair of pliers to carefully squeeze the drive link onto the crank arm. The wiper transmission assembly must be installed to the crank arm PAST the 2nd detent so the seal is compressed to a maximum height of 1 in. (25.5mm)

17. If removed, install the radio assembly.

18. Install the cowl vent grille.
19. Install the wiper arms.
20. Connect the negative battery cable.

Windshield Wiper Switch

REMOVAL AND INSTALLATION

Steering Column Without Air Bag

1. Disconnect the negative battery cable.
2. Matchmark and remove the steering wheel.
3. On C/K-Series, 1994 S/T-Series and other vehicles as necessary, remove the steering column.

NOTE: Although in some cases the components necessary to remove the wiper switch may be removed with the steering column installed in the vehicle, it is usually necessary to at least unbolt, lower and support the column.

4. Remove the turn signal switch.
5. Remove the lock cylinder assembly.
6. On C/K-Series and 1994 S/T-Series, if not done already (and if necessary), remove the dimmer and ignition switches from the base of the column.
7. Remove the lock housing cover screws.
8. If applicable, remove the tilt lever.
9. Remove the lock housing cover assembly.
10. On C/K-Series and 1994 S/T-Series equipped with a floor shift, the lock housing cover is removed along with the floor shift lever bowl and the gearshift bowl shroud. Pull the housing cover from the jacket and remove the upper bearing retainer. Remove the 3 cross recess screws, then separate the shift level bowl with gearshift shroud.
11. Except for C/K-Series and 1994 S/T-Series vehicles with a floor shift, remove the column housing cover end cap (in some cases, this should be done along with the switch rod actuator), then remove the switch actuator pivot pin.
12. If necessary, unbolt the steering column support bracket from the column.
13. Disengage the wiper switch (pivot and pulse switch) connector from the wiring harness, then remove the wiring protector.
14. Attach a length of mechanic's wire to the switch connector, then

carefully pull the harness through the column (from the top), leaving the wire in the column for assembly.
15. Remove the switch.
To install:
16. Install the switch to the lock housing cover assembly, then install the pivot pin.
17. Except for C/K-Series and 1994 S/T-Series vehicles equipped with floor shift:
   a. Carefully pull the switch harness through the steering column using the mechanic's wire, then engage the connector to the harness.
   b. If applicable, install the column support bracket.
   c. Lubricate the dimmer switch rod actuator using lithium grease, then if removed, install the actuator to the column housing cover end cap.
   d. Install the end cap to the lock housing cover assembly. Make sure the bottom edge of the dimmer switch rod actuator is resting on the bend in the dimmer switch rod.
   e. Install the lock housing cover assembly, then secure using the retaining screws. Tighten the screw in the 12 o'clock position first, then the 8 o'clock position next and finally the screw in the 3 o'clock position.
18. On C/K-Series and 1994 S/T-Series equipped with a floor shift:
   a. Install the gearshift bowl shroud to the floor shift lever bowl.
   b. Install the bowl with shroud to the steering column assembly, then secure using the 3 cross recess screws.
   c. Using the mechanic's wire, gently pull the wiper and turn signal switch wiring through the column.
   d. Install the upper bearing retainer, then install the lock housing cover assembly to the jacket. Finger-tighten the cover screws in a clockwise pattern, then tighten the screws to 47 inch lbs. (5.3 Nm).
   e. Install the wiring protectors and the support bracket.
19. If removed, install the ignition and dimmer switches.
20. Install the lock cylinder assembly.
21. Install the turn signal switch.
22. If removed or lowered, position and secure the steering column.
23. Align and install the steering wheel.
24. Connect the negative battery cable.

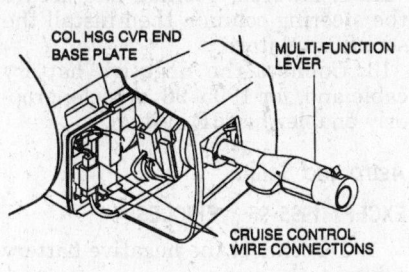

85473024

Some columns use a multi-function lever with cruise control wiring

Steering Column With Air Bag

EXCEPT 1995–96 S/T-SERIES AND C/K-SERIES

1. Properly disable the SIR (air bag) system, then disconnect the negative battery cable.
2. Matchmark and remove the steering wheel.

NOTE: Although in some cases the components necessary to remove the wiper switch may be removed with the steering column installed in the vehicle, it is usually necessary to at least unbolt, lower and support the column.

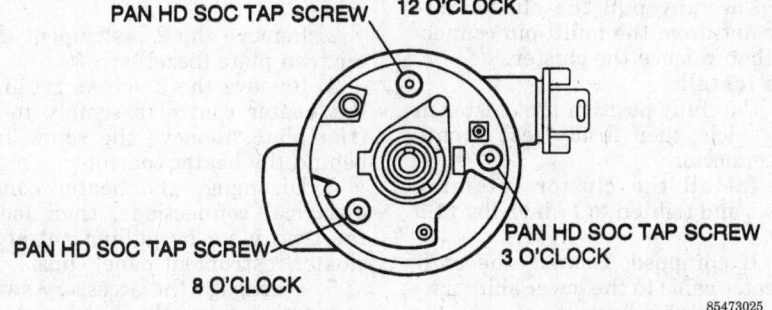

Lock housing cover assembly screw locations — except C/K-Series and 1994 S/T-Series.

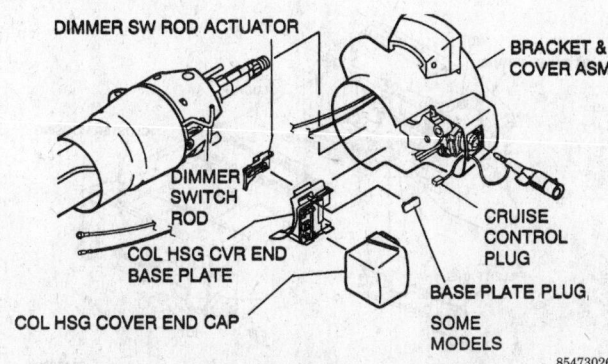

85473026

Exploded view of a common housing cover mounting

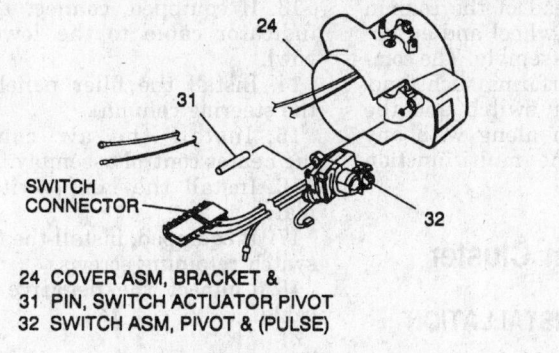

24 COVER ASM, BRACKET &
31 PIN, SWITCH ACTUATOR PIVOT
32 SWITCH ASM, PIVOT & (PULSE)

85473027

Removing the windshield wiper (pivot and pulse) switch

3. Remove the turn signal switch.
4. Remove the lock cylinder assembly.
5. Remove the lock housing cover screws.
6. If applicable, remove the tilt lever.
7. Remove the lock housing cover assembly.
8. Remove the column housing cover end cap (in some cases, this should be done along with the switch rod actuator), then remove the switch actuator pivot pin.
9. If necessary, unbolt the steering column support bracket from the column.

10. Disengage the wiper switch (pivot and pulse switch) connector from the wiring harness, then remove the wiring protector.
11. Attach a length of mechanic's wire to the switch connector, then carefully pull the harness through the column (from the top), leaving the wire in the column for assembly.
12. Remove the switch.

To install:
13. Install the switch to the lock housing cover assembly, then install the pivot pin.
14. Carefully pull the switch harness through the steering column using the mechanic's wire, then engage the connector to the harness.
15. If applicable, install the column support bracket.
16. Lubricate the dimmer switch rod actuator using lithium grease, then if removed, install the actuator to the column housing cover end cap.
17. Install the end cap to the lock housing cover assembly. Make sure the bottom edge of the dimmer switch rod actuator is resting on the bend in the dimmer switch rod.
18. Install the lock housing cover assembly, then secure using the retaining screws. Tighten the screw in the 12 o'clock position first, then the 8 o'clock position next and finally the screw in the 3 o'clock position.
19. Install the lock cylinder assembly.
20. Install the turn signal switch.
21. If removed or lowered, position and secure the steering column.
22. Align and install the steering wheel.
23. Connect the negative battery cable, then properly enable the SIR system.

1995–96 S/T-SERIES AND C/K-SERIES

Instead of the long time used steering column found on most other GM vehicles the 1995–96 S/T-Series and C/K-Series utilize a new column with a multi-function combination switch

3-15

mounted at the head of the column below the steering wheel and an upper/lower shroud assembly. The combination switch performs such functions as the wiper switch and the turn signal switch along with any other duties of the multi-function lever.

Instrument Cluster

REMOVAL AND INSTALLATION

S/T-Series

EXCEPT 1994 UTILITY AND ALL 1995–96 VEHICLES

1. Disconnect the negative battery cable.
2. If equipped (such as on the MFI-Turbo) remove the fog lamp switch retaining screws.
3. Remove the lamp switch trim plate-to-instrument panel screws and the trim plate, then disengage the electrical connector from the lamp switch.
4. Remove the air conditioning/heater control assembly-to-instrument panel screws and the assembly, the disengage the electrical connector from the lamp switch.
5. Remove the filler panel (under the steering column)-to-instrument panel screws and the filler panel.
6. If equipped, disconnect the shift indicator cable from the lower shift bowl.

NOTE: Some late model vehicles may use a single multi-pin connector to which the instrument cluster is mounted. On these vehicles, pulling the cluster outward should disengage the necessary connections. Be careful not to damage the connector during removal and installation. Do not force the cluster, but make sure it is firmly seated when installed.

7. Remove the instrument cluster housing nuts, then carefully pull the instrument cluster forward for access to the connectors.
8. Disengage the electrical connectors from the rear of the cluster.
9. Remove the instrument housing and/or cluster.
   To install:
10. Position the instrument housing and/or cluster assembly in front of the instrument panel.
11. Engage the electrical connectors to the rear of the cluster.
12. Position the cluster and secure the housing retaining nuts.

13. If equipped, connect the shift indicator cable to the lower shift bowl.
14. Install the filler panel (under the steering column).
15. Install the air conditioning/heater control assembly.
16. Install the lamp switch trim plate.
17. If equipped, install the fog lamp switch retaining screws.
18. Connect the negative battery cable.

1994 UTILITY AND ALL 1995–96 VEHICLES

1. For 1995–96 vehicles, properly disarm the SIR (air bag) system.
2. Disconnect the negative battery cable.
3. For 1995–96 vehicles, remove the sound insulators, then remove the lower steering column retainers and lower the column for access. This can be done for 1994 vehicles, if necessary.
4. Remove the instrument cluster trim bezel. Since the light switch assembly is mounted to the bezel, once the bezel is released, pull it forward in order to disengage the wiring, then the bezel may be removed.
5. If equipped on 1994 vehicles, disengage the shift indicator cable from the lower shift bowl.
6. Remove the 4 cluster-to-instrument panel retaining screws.
7. Carefully pull the cluster forward and from the multi-pin connector, then remove the cluster.
   To install:
8. Carefully position the cluster in the vehicle, then firmly seat it onto the connector.
9. Install the cluster retaining screws and tighten to 17 inch lbs. (1.9 Nm).
10. If equipped, connect the shift indicator cable to the lower shift bowl and adjust, as necessary.
11. Install the instrument cluster bezel.

12. If lowered, position and secure the steering column, then install the sound insulators.
13. Connect the negative battery cable and, for 1995–96 vehicle, properly enable the SIR system.

Astro and Safari

EXCEPT 1995–96 VEHICLES

1. Disconnect the negative battery cable.
2. Remove the instrument cluster trim plate (bezel) screws.
3. Remove the screws (usually 2) retaining the heater control assembly to the trim plate. If equipped, remove the screw from behind the heater control.
4. Disconnect the cables from the heater control, then disengage the connections from the hatch release switch.
5. Remove the screws retaining the cluster to the instrument panel.
6. Disconnect the shift indicator cable from the lower shift bowl.
7. Disconnect the instrument panel cluster harness connectors and speedometer cable, as required.
8. Remove the instrument panel cluster.
9. Installation is the reverse of the removal procedure.

1995–96 VEHICLES

1. Disconnect the negative battery cable.
2. Remove the 2 instrument cluster trim plate (bezel) screws.
3. Remove the 2 screws retaining the heater control assembly to the trim plate. Remove the screw from behind the heater control.
4. Disengage the heater control electrical connections, then loosen the trim plate by pulling out of the cluster instrument panel clips.
5. Disengage the accessory switch connection from the hatch release, rear wiper and/or defog switch, as equipped.

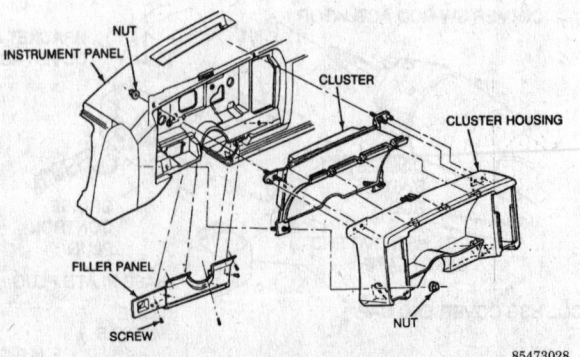

Common S/T-Series instrument cluster assembly — 1992–93

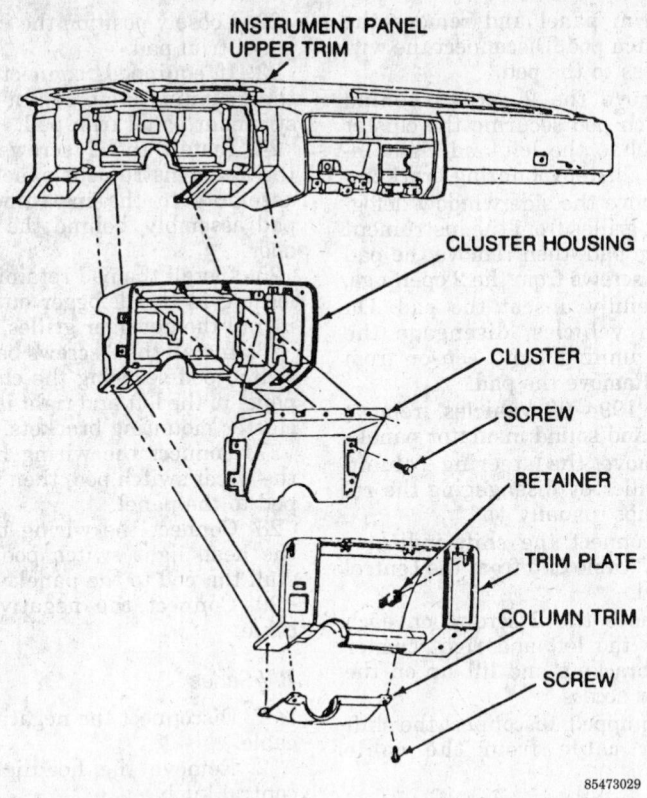

INSTRUMENT PANEL
UPPER TRIM

CLUSTER HOUSING

CLUSTER

SCREW

RETAINER

TRIM PLATE

COLUMN TRIM

SCREW

85473029

Common instrument cluster assembly — Astro and Safari

6. Disengage the head light switch electrical connector.

7. Rotate the cluster trim plate (bezel) for access.

8. Remove the engine cover and the lower instrument panel insulator.

9. Disconnect the shift indicator (PRNDL) cable.

10. Make sure all retainers are removed, then carefully pull the instrument panel cluster from the connector and remove it.

To install:

11. Position the instrument cluster to the vehicle and carefully engage it to the connector.

12. With the transmission in Neutral, pull the shift indicator (PRNDL) cable until the needle indicates Neutral. Attach the cable securely to the lower shift bowl. Make sure the cable is properly centered on Neutral, if not release the cable and adjust it again.

NOTE: Once connected, make sure the shift indicator cable rests on the shift bowl and not the column jacket.

13. Install the lower instrument panel insulator, then install the engine cover.

14. Engage the head light switch connector, then engage the accessory switch connector, if equipped.

15. Engage the heater control connections, then install the control retaining screws to the bezel.

16. Install the remaining bezel retaining screws.

17. Connect the negative battery cable.

Lumina

1992–93 VEHICLES

1. Disconnect the negative battery cable.

2. Remove the 4 screws securing the instrument panel pad to the instrument panel lower trim pad.

3. On Canadian models, if equipped, disconnect the daytime running lights sensor attached to the pad under the front left hand speaker grille.

4. Lift the instrument panel trim pad up and pull the pad rearward to disengage the pad from the 4 slots in the lower trim pad and remove the pad assembly.

5. Grip the pod and carefully pull the wiper switch out to release the 2 spring retaining clips.

6. Disengage the electrical connector and remove the switch.

7. Remove the 2 cluster housing screws attaching the trim to the instrument panel lower trim pad.

8. Feed the instrument panel harness through the switch pod openings in the housing.

9. Lift the housing up while pulling rearward to release the 2 tabs on the pad from the slots in the housing and remove the cluster housing.

10. Remove the 4 bolts securing the cluster to the right and left hand retainers.

11. Disconnect the instrument panel harness connector and remove the cluster.

To install:

12. Connect the harness to the instrument cluster.

13. Lift the housing up and push the 2 tabs on the pad into the slots in the housing.

14. Install the 2 cluster housing screws attaching the trim to the instrument panel lower trim pad.

15. Engage the electrical connector and install the switch.

16. Install the instrument panel trim pad.

17. On Canadian models, if equipped, connect the daytime running lights sensor attached to the pad under the front left hand speaker grille.

18. Install the 4 screws securing the instrument panel pad to the instrument panel lower trim pad.

19. Connect the negative battery cable.

1994–96 VEHICLES

1. Disconnect the negative battery cable.

2. Remove the rear window wiper switch from the instrument cluster housing, then disengage the electrical connector.

3. Remove the head light switch from the instrument cluster housing, then disengage the electrical connector.

4. Remove the 4 screws securing the instrument cluster housing to the instrument panel trim pad, then remove the housing from the pad.

5. Remove the left hand sound insulator panel.

6. Remove the steering column opening filler from the instrument panel lower trim pad by disengaging the 4 upper clips.

7. If necessary, disconnect the shift indicator cable from the transaxle control lever bowl.

8. Remove the screws retaining the instrument cluster to the pad.

9. Raise the instrument cluster for access to the shift indicator cable, then disconnect the cable from the cable bracket. Disengage the cluster wiring and remove the instrument cluster from the panel trim pad.

To install:

10. Position the cluster to the instrument panel trim pad, then connect the shift indicator cable to the cable bracket.

11. Engage the cluster wiring, then secure the cluster to the trim pad using the retaining screws. Tighten the screws to 27 inch lbs. (3 Nm).

12. If removed, connect the shift indicator cable to the transaxle control lever:

a. Position the transaxle control lever in the Neutral gate notch.

b. Guide the shift indicator cable around the edge of the transaxle control lever bowl and into a position that locates the cluster pointer to Neutral.

c. Push the cable onto the control lever bowl, taking care to assure the cable rests on the bowl and not the steering column jacket.

d. Check that with the control lever in Neutral, portions of the "N" are visible on either side of the pointer. Make sure each gear is indicated in the same fashion, with the pointer at the center of the indicator.

13. Install the steering column opening filler panel to the instrument panel lower trim pad by engaging the 4 clips.

14. Install the left hand sound insulator panel.

15. Install the 4 screws securing the instrument cluster housing to the instrument panel lower trim pad. Tighten the screws to 18 inch lbs. (2 Nm).

16. Engage the head light switch connector, then install the switch to the cluster housing.

17. Engage the rear wiper switch connector, then install the switch to the cluster housing.

18. Connect the negative battery cable.

Silhouette and Trans Sport

1. Disconnect the negative battery cable.

2. Open the glove box door to access the 2 screws securing the lower instrument panel trim pad assembly to the instrument panel pad assembly.

3. Remove the 2 screws securing the instrument cluster trim panel to the instrument panel pad.

4. Remove the screw retaining the head light switch pod to the cluster trim panel and remove the head light switch pod. Disconnect the wiring harness to the pod.

5. Remove the screw retaining the windshield wiper switch pod to the cluster trim panel and remove the wiper switch pod. Disconnect the wiring harness to the pod.

6. Remove the 2 screws behind each switch pod securing the cluster trim panel to the left and right instrument cluster mounting brackets.

7. Remove the side window defogger outlet grilles from the instrument panel trim pad, then remove the pad retaining screws from the 2 openings.

8. Carefully unseat the pad. On Canadian vehicles, disengage the daytime running lamp sensor from the pad. Remove the pad.

9. For 1994–96 vehicles, remove the left hand sound insulator panel.

10. Remove the steering column opening filler by disengaging the retaining clips (usually 4).

11. Disconnect the shift indicator **"PRNDL"** cable clip from the control lever bowl.

12. Remove the 2 screws on each side from the left and right cluster retainer brackets and lift up on the cluster for access.

13. If equipped, disconnect the shift indicator cable from the cable bracket.

14. Disengage the instrument panel harness connector from the the instrument cluster.

15. Remove the cluster.

To install:

16. Position the cluster, then connect the instrument panel harness connector.

17. If equipped, connect the shift indicator cable to the cable bracket.

18. Seat the cluster, then secure the cluster retainer brackets using the screws.

19. Connect the shift indicator cable to the transaxle control lever:

a. Position the transaxle control lever in the Neutral gate notch.

b. Guide the shift indicator cable around the edge of the transaxle control lever bowl and into a position that locates the cluster pointer to Neutral.

c. Push the cable onto the control lever bowl, taking care to assure the cable rests on the bowl and not the steering column jacket.

d. Check that with the control lever in Neutral, portions of the "N" are visible on either side of the pointer. Make sure each gear is indicated in the same fashion, with the pointer at the center of the indicator.

20. Install the steering column opening filler.

21. If equipped, install the left hand sound insulator panel.

22. Loosely position the instrument panel trim pad.

23. If equipped, connect the daytime running lamp sensor to the instrument panel trim pad.

24. Install the 2 screws securing the lower instrument panel trim pad assembly to the instrument panel pad assembly, behind the glove box door.

25. Install the pad retaining screws located in the defogger outlets, then install the defogger grilles.

26. Install the 2 screws behind each switch pod securing the cluster trim panel to the left and right instrument cluster mounting brackets.

27. Connect the wiring harness to the wiper switch pod, then install the pod to the panel.

28. Connect the wiring harness to the head light switch pod, then install the pod to the panel.

29. Connect the negative battery cable.

R/V-Series

1. Disconnect the negative battery cable.

2. Remove the headlight switch control knob.

3. Remove the radio control knobs, if required.

4. Remove the steering 4 column cover retaining screws.

5. Remove 8 screws and remove instrument bezel.

6. Reach under the dash, depress the speedometer cable tang, and remove the cable, if equipped.

7. Pull instrument cluster out just far enough to disconnect all lines and wires.

8. Remove the cluster.

9. Installation is the reverse of removal.

C/K-Series

1. Disconnect the negative battery cable.

2. If equipped, remove the cup holder by removing the screw under the holder and sliding it outward from the instrument panel.

3. Remove the instrument cluster trim bezel. On most vehicles, the bezel is retained by 4 clips along the underside. On some vehicles, the head light switch and dimmer switch electrical wiring must be disengaged.

4. If necessary (except for 1995–96 vehicles), remove the radio control head.

5. If necessary (except for 1995–96 vehicles), remove the heater control head.

6. On 1995–96 vehicles (and 1994 as necessary), disengage the electri-

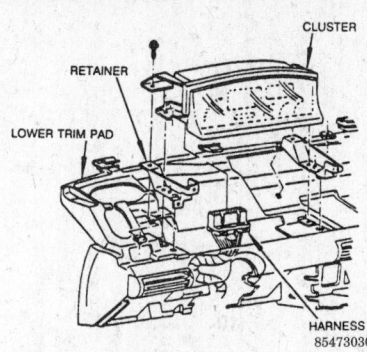

Instrument cluster assembly — Silhouette and 1994–96 Trans Sport

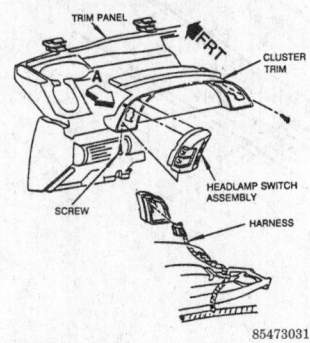

Instrument cluster assembly — Trans Sport 1992–93

cal connectors from the head light switch, dimmer control and accessory switches.

7. Remove the 4 cluster retaining screws.

8. Carefully pull the cluster towards you and unplug the electrical connector. Avoid touching the connector pins. On some late model vehicles, the connector is mounted in a fixed position, pulling the cluster away will disengage the wiring.

9. On some vehicles 1992–94 the shift indicator cable must be disconnected from the steering column lower shift bowl.

10. Installation is the reverse of removal.

G-Series

1992–93 VEHICLES

1. Disconnect the negative battery cable.

2. If equipped, reach up behind the cluster, depress the speedometer cable retaining tang and pull out the cable.

3. Remove the clock set stem knob, if equipped.

4. Remove the rear heater and fan controls knobs, if equipped.

5. Remove the interior light and headlight switch bezels.

6. Remove the instrument cluster bezel screws, then remove the bezel.

7. Remove the instrument cluster retaining screws.

8. Pull the top of the cluster away from the panel and lift out the bottom of the cluster. Pull the cluster out just far enough to unplug the wiring.

9. Installation is the reverse of removal.

1994–96 VEHICLES

1. Set the parking brake and block the drive wheels, then place the transmission in LOW gear.

2. Disconnect the negative battery cable.

3. If equipped with a tilt steering column, position it to the fully downward position.

4. If equipped, remove the rear heater and fan controls knobs.

5. Remove the instrument cluster bezel screws (3 across the top and 3 across the bottom), then remove the bezel.

6. Remove the instrument cluster retaining screws.

7. Carefully pull the cluster away from the panel to separate it from the fixed multi-pin connector.

8. Installation is the reverse of removal.

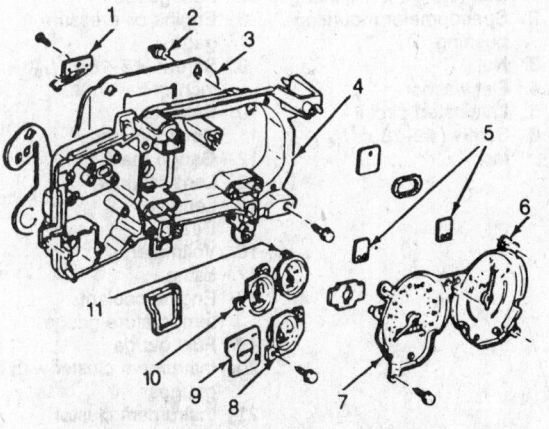

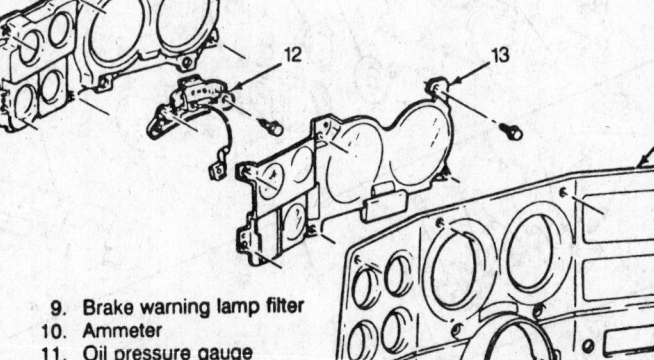

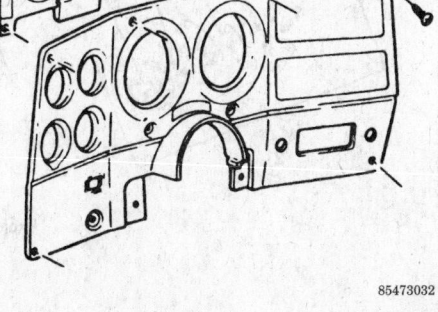

1. Speedometer cable spring clip
2. Lamp bulb socket
3. Laminated circuit
4. Cluster case
5. Indicator lamp filter (turn signal)
6. Fuel gauge
7. Speedometer
8. Temperature gauge
9. Brake warning lamp filter
10. Ammeter
11. Oil pressure gauge
12. Transmission shift indicator
13. Instrument cluster lens
14. Instrument cluster bezel
15. Retainer

Exploded view of the cluster assembly — R/V-Series

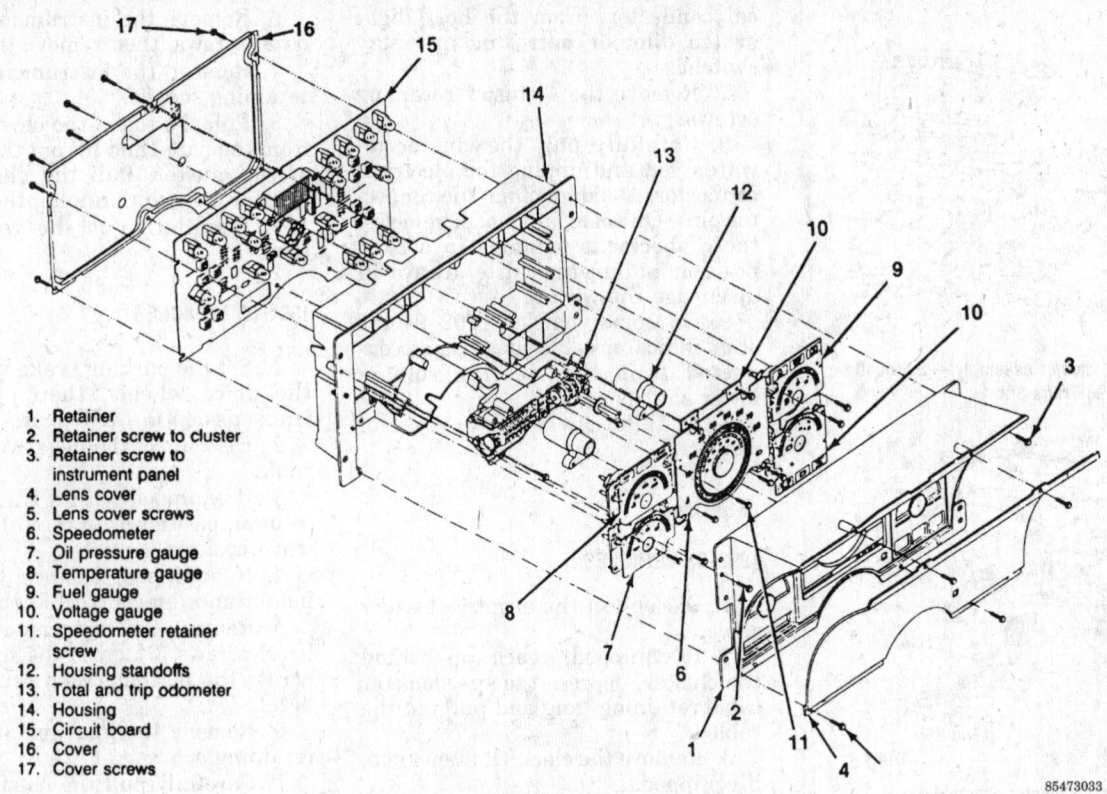

1. Retainer
2. Retainer screw to cluster
3. Retainer screw to instrument panel
4. Lens cover
5. Lens cover screws
6. Speedometer
7. Oil pressure gauge
8. Temperature gauge
9. Fuel gauge
10. Voltage gauge
11. Speedometer retainer screw
12. Housing standoffs
13. Total and trip odometer
14. Housing
15. Circuit board
16. Cover
17. Cover screws

85473033

Exploded view of the cluster assembly — C/K-Series 1992

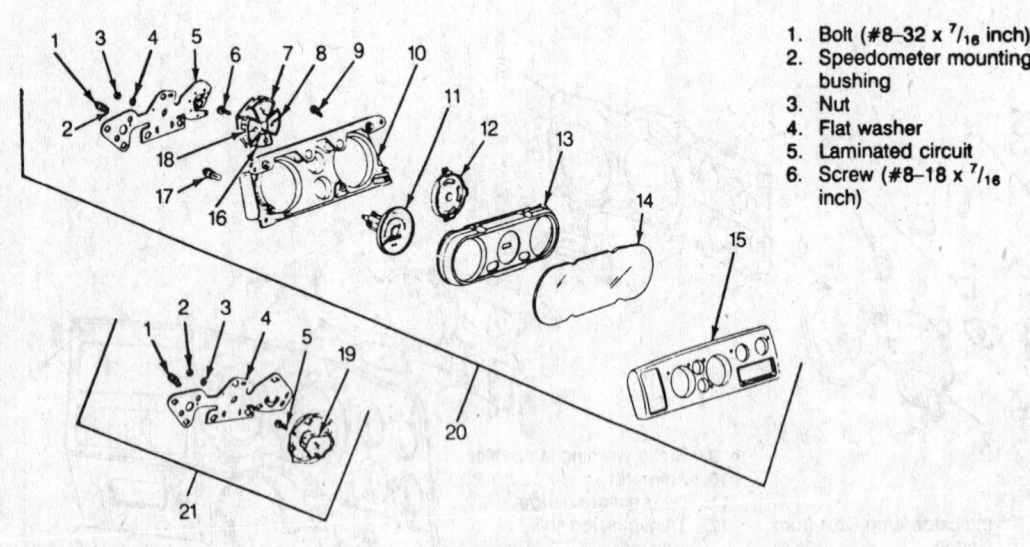

1. Bolt (#8–32 x $^{7}/_{16}$ inch)
2. Speedometer mounting bushing
3. Nut
4. Flat washer
5. Laminated circuit
6. Screw (#8–18 x $^{7}/_{16}$ inch)
7. Fuel gauge
8. Engine oil pressure gage
9. Screw (#8–16 x $^{7}/_{16}$ inch)
10. Retainer
11. Speedometer
12. Gauge mask
13. Lens retainer
14. Lens
15. Bezel
16. Voltmeter
17. Lamp
18. Engine coolant temperature gauge
19. Fuel gauge
20. Instrument cluster with gauges
21. Instrument cluster without gauges

85473034

Exploded view of the cluster assembly — G-Series 1992–94

Speedometer

On most vehicles covered by this manual, the speedometer is a non-serviceable unit. However, on some models the speedometer may be unbolted from the instrument cluster (after the cluster is removed from the vehicle and the front or rear cover, as applicable, is removed) and replaced. Before attempting to separate the cluster from the speedometer, make sure replacement components are available.

Headlight Switch

REMOVAL AND INSTALLATION

S/T-Series

1992–93 VEHICLES

1. Disconnect the negative battery cable.
2. From under the headlight switch assembly, remove the trim plate/switch assembly retaining screws.

NOTE: For some vehicles equipped with a fog lamps, the fog lamp switch may have to be removed in order to access the headlight trim plate/switch screw.

3. Pull the switch trim plate from the instrument panel. Pivot the trim plate outward at the bottom, then pull the plate downward to release it.
4. Disengage the electrical wiring connectors from the rear of the switch/trim plate assembly.
5. Remove the headlight switch from the trim plate assembly; if necessary, replace the switch.
6. To install, reverse the removal procedures.

1994–96 VEHICLES

1. Disconnect the negative battery cable.
2. Remove the instrument cluster trim bezel.
3. Disengage the electrical connector.
4. Remove the switch-to-bezel retaining screws.
5. Remove the switch from the bezel.
6. Installation is the reverse of removal. To make sure the switch is working properly, temporarily connect the negative battery cable and check switch operation BEFORE the bezel is fully installed.

Astro and Safari

1. Disconnect the negative battery cable.
2. Remove the screws (usually 5) holding the instrument panel cluster trim plate to the panel. There may also be another screw behind the heater control panel.
3. Pull the trim panel forward for access, then disengage the 2 electrical connectors from the back of the headlight switch.
4. Remove the screws (usually 4) securing the headlight switch to the back of the trim plate.
5. Remove the switch.
6. Installation is the reverse of the removal.

Lumina/Silhouette/Trans Sport

1. Separate, the head light switch from the instrument cluster housing. Most switches are snapped into position using retaining clips, though some may use a small retaining screw.
2. Disengage the wiring harness connector from the switch and remove it.
3. Installation is the reverse of the removal.

R/V-Series

1. Disconnect the negative battery cable.
2. Reaching up behind instrument cluster, depress shaft retaining button and remove switch knob and rod.
3. Remove instrument cluster bezel and trim panel screws.
4. Disengage the multiple wiring connectors at switch terminals.
5. Remove switch by rotating the switch locknut.
6. Installation is the reverse of removal.

C/K-Series

1. Disconnect the negative battery cable.
2. Remove the instrument cluster bezel.
3. Disengage the switch wiring connector.
4. If equipped, remove the headlight switch retaining screws and pull the switch away from the bezel, if not unsnap the switch from the bezel. Remove the switch.
5. Installation is the reverse of removal.

G-Series

1. Disconnect the negative battery cable.

2. Press the switch knob retaining pin and remove the knob. In most cases, the switch must be pulled out to the low beam position in order to depress the pin and remove the knob.
3. Remove the left instrument panel trim or lower trim panel, as applicable.
4. Remove the retaining nut securing the switch.
5. Disengage the electrical connector from the back of the switch.
6. Remove the switch from the instrument panel.
7. Reverse the procedure for installation.

Dimmer Switch

REMOVAL AND INSTALLATION

Except 1995–96 S/T-Series and 1995–96 C/K-Series

1. If equipped, properly disable the SIR (air bag) system.
2. Disconnect the negative battery cable.
3. If equipped, remove the lower column trim panel.
4. Remove the steering column-to-instrument panel fasteners and lower the column for access to the switch. Extreme care is necessary to prevent damage to the collapsible column.
5. On some full size vehicles it may be necessary to remove the steering wheel in order to fully lower the column. If equipped with a tilt column, position the column in the upper most position for additional lowering clearance.

NOTE: If the ignition switch shares fasteners with the dimmer switch it may be necessary to remove it first.

6. Remove the dimmer switch-to-steering column retainers, then remove the switch from the column. Disengage the switch wiring and remove it.
To install:
7. Position the switch to the column and loosely install the retainers.
8. Insert a $3/32$ in. drill bit into the adjustment hole provided in the switch in order to limit switch travel, then push the switch up against the actuator rod in order to remove lash.
9. Tighten the switch retainers, then remove the drill bit.
10. Engage the switch wiring.
11. If removed for access, install the ignition switch.
12. Raise the column into position and secure, then install any necessary trim plates.

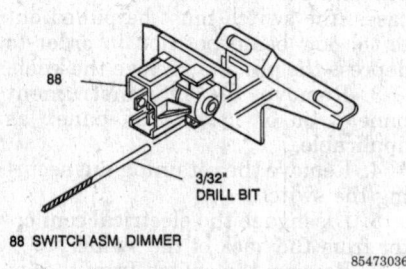

88 SWITCH ASM, DIMMER

85473036

Dimmer switch adjustment

13. If removed install the steering wheel.

14. Make sure the ignition is **OFF**, then connect the negative battery cable.

15. If equipped, properly enable the SIR system.

1995–96 S/T-Series and 1995–96 C/K-Series

Instead of the long time used steering column found on most other GM vehicles the 1995–96 S/T-Series and C/K-Series utilize a new column with a multi-function combination switch mounted at the head of the column below the steering wheel and an upper/lower shroud assembly. The combination switch performs such functions as the wiper switch and the turn signal switch along with any other duties of the multi-function lever.

Turn Signal Switch

REMOVAL AND INSTALLATION

NOTE: When servicing any components on the steering column, should any fasteners require replacement, be sure to use only nuts and bolts of the same size and grade as the original fasteners. Using screws that are too long could prevent the column from collapsing during a collision.

NOTE: The following procedures require the use of a lock plate compressor tool such as J-23653 or equivalent.

1992–96 Vehicles

EXCEPT 1995–96 S/T-SERIES AND 1995–96 C/K-SERIES

1. If equipped, make sure the wheels are locked in the straight-

ahead position, then properly disable the SIR (air bag) system.

2. Disconnect the negative battery cable.

3. Matchmark and remove the steering wheel.

4. If equipped with an SIR system, remove the SIR coil assembly retaining ring, then remove the coil assembly and allow it to hang freely from the wiring. Remove the wave washer.

5. On non-SIR equipped vehicles, remove the shaft lock cover.

6. Push downward on the shaft lock assembly until the snapring is exposed using the shaft lock compressor tool.

7. Remove the shaft lock retaining snapring, then carefully release the tool and remove the shaft lock from the column.

8. Remove the turn signal cancelling cam assembly.

9. For standard columns not equipped with SIR, remove the upper bearing spring and thrust washer.

10. For tilt columns or SIR equipped standard columns, remove the upper bearing spring, inner race seat and inner race.

11. Move the turn signal lever upward to the "Right Turn" position.

12. Remove the access cap and disengage the multi-function lever harness connector, then grasp the lever and pull it from the column.

13. Loosen and remove the hazard knob retaining screw, then remove the screw, button, spring and knob.

14. Remove the screw and the switch actuator arm.

15. Remove the turn signal switch retaining screws, then pull the switch forward and allow it to hang from the wires. If the switch is only being removed for access to other components, this may be sufficient.

16. If the switch is to be replaced, cut the wires near the top of the switch and discard the switch. Before cutting the wires, verify that the wire color codes are the same. Secure the connector of the new switch to the old wires, and pull the new harness down through the steering column while removing the old switch.

17. If the original switch is to be reused, attach a piece of wire or string around the connector and pull the harness up through the column, while pulling the string up through the column and leaving the string or wire in position to help with reinstallation later.

18. After freeing the switch wiring protector from its mounting, pull the turn signal switch straight up and re-

move the switch, switch harness, and the connector from the column.

NOTE: On some vehicles access to the connector may be difficult. If necessary, remove the column support bracket assembly and properly support the column, and/or remove the wiring protectors.

To install:

19. Install the switch and wiring harness to the vehicle. If the switch was completely removed, use the length of mechanic's wire or string to pull the switch harness through the column, then engage the connector.

NOTE: If the column support bracket or wiring protectors were removed, install them before proceeding.

20. Position the switch in the column and secure using the retaining screws.

21. Install the switch actuator arm and retaining screw.

22. Install the hazard knob assembly, then install the multi-function lever.

23. Install the thrust washer and upper bearing spring (standard columns without SIR) or the inner race, upper bearing race seat and upper bearing spring (tilt columns or standard with SIR), as applicable.

24. Lubricate the turn signal cancelling cam using a suitable synthetic grease (usually included in the service kit), then install the cam assembly.

25. Position the shaft lock and a new snapring, then use the lock compressor to hold the lock down while seating the new snapring. Make sure the ring is firmly seated in the groove, then carefully release the tool.

NOTE: The coil assembly will become uncentered if the steering column is separated from the steering gear and allowed to rotate or if the centering spring is pushed down, letting the hub rotate while the coils assembly is removed from the steering column.

26. If equipped with SIR, make sure the coil is centered, then install the wave washer, followed by the coil and the retaining ring. The coil ring must be firmly seated in the shaft groove.

27. On non SIR columns, install the shaft lock cover.

28. Align and install the steering wheel.

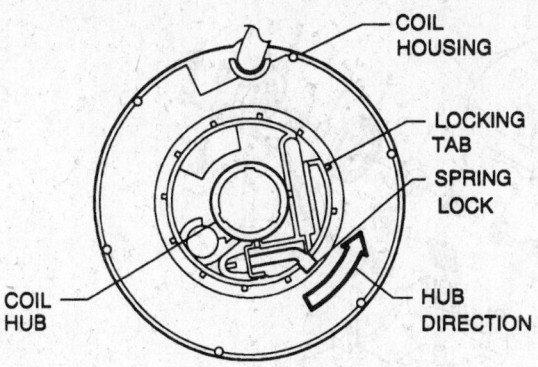

PERFORM THE FOLLOWING STEPS TO CENTER COIL ASSEMBLY

A. WHEELS STRAIGHT AHEAD.
B. REMOVE COIL ASSEMBLY.
C. HOLD COIL ASSEMBLY WITH BOTTOM UP.
D. WHILE HOLDING COIL ASSEMBLY, DEPRESS SPRING LOCK TO
   ROTATE HUB IN DIRECTION OF ARROW UNTIL IT STOPS.
E. THE COIL RIBBON SHOULD BE WOUND UP SNUG AGAINST
   CENTER HUB.
F. ROTATE COIL HUB IN OPPOSITE DIRECTION APPROXIMATELY
   TWO AND A HALF (2-1/2) TURNS. RELEASE SPRING LOCK
   BETWEEN LOCKING TABS.

85473040

Centering the SIR coil

29. Make sure the ignition is **OFF**, then connect the negative battery cable.

30. Properly enable the SIR system.

1995–96 S/T-SERIES AND 1995–96 C/K-SERIES

Instead of the long time used steering column found on most other GM vehicles the 1995–96 S/T-Series and C/K-Series utilize a new column with a multi-function combination switch mounted at the head of the column below the steering wheel and an upper/lower shroud assembly. The combination switch performs such functions as the wiper switch and the turn signal switch along with any other duties of the multi-function lever.

Combination Switch

REMOVAL AND INSTALLATION

Instead of the long time used steering column found on most other GM vehicles the 1995–96 S/T-Series and C/K-Series utilize a new column with a multi-function combination switch mounted at the head of the column below the steering wheel and an upper/lower shroud assembly. The combination switch performs such func-

tions as the wiper switch and the turn signal switch along with any other duties of the multi-function lever.

NOTE: Removal of the SIR coil is not necessary during this procedure. avoid removing the coil and make sure the steering column, if disconnected from the gear, is not allowed to rotate excessively. This is to prevent uncentering and damaging the coil. Should the coil become uncentered, it must be removed, centered and repositioned on the steering column.

1. Disconnect the negative battery cable.

2. Properly disable the SIR (air bag) system.

3. Either lower the steering column from the instrument panel for access or unbolt and remove the column. If the column is removed, prevent it from rotating so the SIR coil does not become uncentered.

4. If applicable, remove the tilt lever by pulling outward.

5. Remove the 2 pan head tapping screws from the lower column shroud, then tilt the shroud down and slide it back to disengage the locking tabs. Remove the lower shroud.

6. Remove the 2 Torx head screws from the upper shroud.

7. Lift the upper shroud for access to the lock cylinder hole. Hold the key in the **START** position and use a ¹⁄₁₆ in. Allen wrench to push on the lock cylinder retaining pin.

8. Release the key to the **RUN** position and pull the steering column lock cylinder set from the lock module assembly. Remove the upper shroud.

9. If necessary, remove the shift lever clevis, then remove the lever.

10. Remove the wiring harness straps (noting the positioning for installation purposes), then disengage the steering column bulkhead connector from the vehicle wiring harness.

11. On column shift C/K-Series, remove the axial position assurance connector from the electrical Brake Transmission Shift Interlock (BTSI) actuator. Disengage the wiring connector from the actuator.

12. Disengage the grey and black connectors for the turn signal and multi-function switch from the column bulkhead connector.

13. Remove the 2 pan head switch retaining screws, then remove the switch from the steering column.

To install:

14. Position the multi-function switch assembly, then use a suitable small bladed tool to compress the electrical contact while moving the switch into position. Make sure the electrical contact rests on the cancelling cam assembly.

15. Install the switch retaining screws and tighten to 53 inch lbs. (6.0 Nm).

16. Engage the grey and black multi-function switch connectors to the column bulkhead connector.

17. On C/K-Series with a column shift, engage the wiring connector to the BTSI actuator, then secure using the axial position assurance connector.

18. Engage the steering column bulkhead-to-vehicle connector.

19. If removed, install the shift lever and secure the clevis.

20. Install the wiring harness straps as noted during removal.

21. Position the shift lever and multi-function lever seals to ease installation of the upper and lower shrouds.

22. Install the upper shroud and lock cylinder. With the key installed to the lock cylinder and turned to the **RUN** position, make sure the sector in the lock module is also in this position.

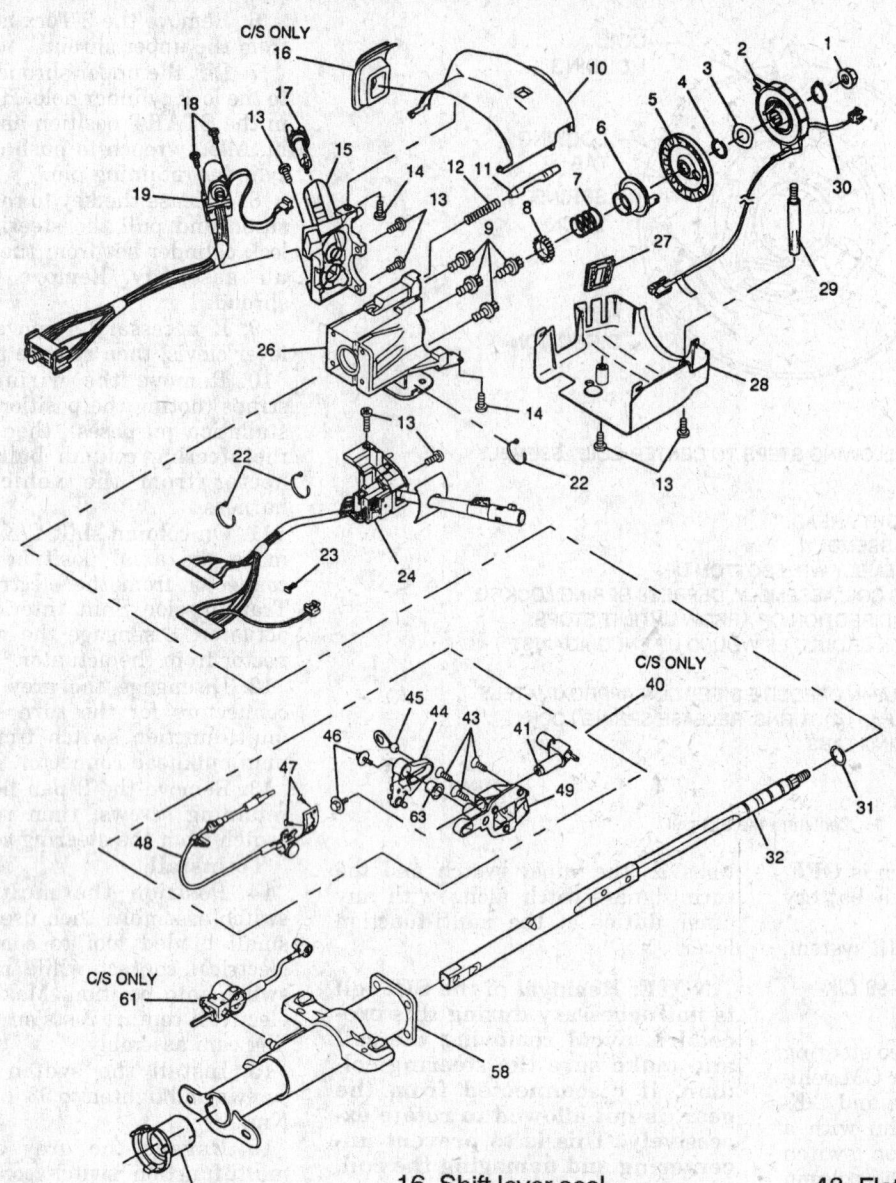

1 Hexagon locking (m14x1.5) nut	16 Shift lever seal	43 Flat hd 6-lobed soc tap
2 Sir coil asm	17 STRG column lock cyl set	44 Cable shift cam asm
3 Wave washer	18 Tapping screw	45 Ball & actuator asm
4 Retaining ring	19 Ign & key alarm switch asm	46 Hex flange head bolt
5 Shaft lock shield asm	22 Wire harness strap	47 Oval hd 6-lobed soc
6 T/SIG cancel cam asm	23 Axial posn assur connector	tap screw
7 Upper bearing spring	24 T/S & multifunc switch asm	48 Park lock cable asm
8 Thrust washer	26 Strg column housing asm	49 G/S lever asm support
9 Torx head screw	27 Shroud protector	bracket
10 Upper shroud	28 Lower shroud	58 Strg col jacket asm
11 Lock bolt asm	29 Shroud mounting stud	60 Adapter & bearing asm
12 Lock bolt spring	30 Retaining ring	61 Electrical (BTSI) actuator
13 Pan hd tapping screw	31 Retaining ring	63 Cam bushing
14 Torx head screw	32 Steering shaft asm	
15 Lock module asm	40 Linear shift asm	Service Kits
	41 Shift lever clevis	201 Grease serv kit (synthetic)

85473041

Exploded view of a standard 1995–96 C/K-Series steering column, S/T-Series column similar

23. Install the lock cylinder to the upper shroud, then align the locking tab and positioning tab with the slots in the lock module assembly. With the tabs aligned, carefully push the cylinder into position.

24. Install the upper shroud Torx head retaining screws and tighten to 12 inch lbs. (1.4 Nm).

25. Install the lower shroud, making sure the slots on the shroud engage with the upper shroud tabs. Tilt the lower shroud upward and snap the shrouds together.

26. Install the 2 lower shroud pan head retaining screws and tighten to 53 inch lbs. (6.0 Nm).

27. Move the shift and multi-function lever seals into position, then

28. If removed, install the tilt lever by aligning and pushing inward.

29. Position and secure the steering column.

30. Properly enable the SIR system, then connect the negative battery cable.

Ignition Lock Cylinder

REMOVAL AND INSTALLATION

Except 1995–96 S/T-Series and 1995–96 C/K-Series

1. If equipped, make sure the wheels are locked in the straight-ahead position, then properly disable the SIR (air bag) system.

2. Disconnect the negative battery cable.

3. Matchmark and remove the steering wheel.

4. If equipped with an SIR system, remove the SIR coil assembly retaining ring, then remove the coil assembly and allow it to hang freely from the wiring. Remove the wave washer.

NOTE: On some SIR equipped vehicles, it may be necessary to completely remove the coil and wiring from the steering column before removing the lock cylinder assembly. If so, attach a length of mechanic's wire to the coil connector at the base of the column, then carefully pull the harness and wire through the steering column towards the top. Leave the wire in position inside the column in order to pull the harness back down into position during installation.

5. Remove the turn signal switch from the column and allow it to hang from the wires (leaving them connected).

6. Remove the buzzer switch assembly. On some vehicles it may be necessary to temporarily remove the key from the lock cylinder in order to remove the buzzer. If so, the key should be reinserted before the next step.

7. Carefully remove the lock cylinder screw and the lock cylinder. If possible, use a magnetic tipped screwdriver on the screw in order to help prevent the possibility of dropping it.

— **CAUTION** —

If the screw is dropped upon removal, it could fall into the steering column, requiring complete disassembly in order to retrieve the screw and prevent damage.

To install:

8. Align and install the lock cylinder set.

9. Push the lock cylinder all the way in, then carefully install the retaining screw. Tighten the screw to 22 inch lbs. (2.5 Nm) on tilt columns or to 40 inch lbs. (4.5 Nm) on standard non-tilt columns.

10. If necessary, install the buzzer switch assembly.

11. Reposition and secure the turn signal switch assembly

NOTE: The coil assembly will become uncentered if the steering column is separated from the steering gear and allowed to rotate or if the centering spring is pushed down, letting the hub rotate while the coils assembly is removed from the steering column.

12. If equipped with SIR, make sure the coil is centered, then install the wave washer, followed by the coil and the retaining ring. The coil ring must be firmly seated in the shaft groove.

13. Align and install the steering wheel.

14. Make sure the ignition is **OFF**, then connect the negative battery cable.

15. Properly enable the SIR system.

1995–96 S/T-Series and 1995–96 C/K-Series

1. Disconnect the negative battery cable.

2. Properly disable the SIR (air bag) system.

3. Either lower the steering column from the instrument panel for access or unbolt and remove the column. If the column is removed, pre-

vent it from rotating so the SIR coil does not become uncentered.

4. If applicable, remove the tilt lever by pulling outward.

5. Remove the 2 pan head tapping screws from the lower column shroud, then tilt the shroud down and slide it back to disengage the locking tabs. Remove the lower shroud.

6. Remove the 2 Torx head screws from the upper shroud.

7. Lift the upper shroud for access to the lock cylinder hole. Hold the key in the **START** position and use a $\frac{1}{16}$ in. Allen wrench to push on the lock cylinder retaining pin.

8. Release the key to the **RUN** position and pull the steering column lock cylinder set from the lock module assembly. Remove the upper shroud.

To install:

9. Install the upper shroud and lock cylinder. With the key installed to the lock cylinder and turned to the **RUN** position, make sure the sector in the lock module is also in this position.

10. Install the lock cylinder to the upper shroud, then align the locking tab and positioning tab with the slots in the lock module assembly. With the tabs aligned, carefully push the cylinder into position.

11. Install the upper shroud Torx head retaining screws and tighten to 12 inch lbs. (1.4 Nm).

12. Install the lower shroud, making sure the slots on the shroud engage with the upper shroud tabs. Tilt the lower shroud upward and snap the shrouds together.

13. Install the 2 lower shroud pan head retaining screws and tighten to 53 inch lbs. (6.0 Nm).

14. Move the shift and multi-function lever seals into position, then

15. If removed, install the tilt lever by aligning and pushing inward.

16. Position and secure the steering column.

17. Properly enable the SIR system, then connect the negative battery cable.

Ignition Switch

REMOVAL AND INSTALLATION

Except 1995–96 S/T-Series and 1995–96 C/K-Series

1. If equipped, make sure the wheels are locked in the straight-ahead position, then properly disable the SIR (air bag) system.

2. Disconnect the negative battery cable.

3. Remove the lower column trim panel, then remove the steering column-to-instrument panel fasteners and carefully lower the column for access to the switch.

4. On some vehicles, the dimmer switch must be removed in order to remove the ignition switch. If necessary, remove the dimmer switch.

5. On 1992–96 vehicles, place the ignition switch in the **OFF-LOCK** position.

NOTE: If the lock cylinder was removed, the switch slider should be moved to the extreme right position, then 1 detent to the left.

6. Remove the ignition switch-to-steering column retainers and disengage the switch wiring, then remove the assembly.

To install:

7. Before installing the ignition switch, place it in the **OFF-LOCK** position, then make sure the lock cylinder and actuating rod are in the Locked position (1st detent from the top or 1st detent to the right of far left detent travel).

NOTE: Most replacement switches are pinned in the OFF-LOCK position for installation purposes. If so, the pins must be removed after installation or damage may occur.

8. Install the activating rod into the ignition switch and assemble the switch onto the steering column. Once the switch is properly positioned, tighten the ignition switch-to-steering column retainers to 35 inch lbs. (4.0 Nm).

NOTE: When installing the ignition switch, use only the specified screws since over length screws could impair the collapsibility of the column.

9. If removed, install the dimmer switch.

10. Raise the column into position and secure, then install any necessary trim plates.

11. Make sure the ignition is **OFF**, then connect the negative battery cable.

12. Properly enable the SIR system.

1995–96 S/T-Series and 1995–96 C/K-Series

1. Disconnect the negative battery cable.

2. Properly disable the SIR (air bag) system.

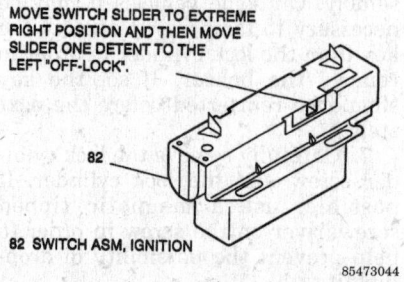

MOVE SWITCH SLIDER TO EXTREME RIGHT POSITION AND THEN MOVE SLIDER ONE DETENT TO THE LEFT "OFF-LOCK".

82

82 SWITCH ASM, IGNITION

85473044

Common ignition switch OFF-LOCK positioning for removal — 1992–96 vehicles (G Van shown)

3. Either lower the steering column from the instrument panel for access or unbolt and remove the column. If the column is removed, prevent it from rotating so the SIR coil does not become uncentered.

4. Remove the combination switch from the steering column.

5. If equipped, remove the alarm switch from the lock module assembly by gently prying the retaining clip on the alarm switch using a small blade prytool. Then, rotate the alarm switch ¼ turn and remove

6. Remove the 2 ignition switch self-tapping retaining screws.

7. Disengage the connector, then remove the wiring harness from the slot in the steering column. Remove the ignition and key alarm switch.

To install:

8. Position the switch to the column. Route the wire harness through the slot in the column housing assembly. Secure the harness using a wire strap through the hole located in the bottom of the housing assembly.

9. Install the switch retaining screws and tighten to 12 inch lbs. (1.4 Nm) in order to secure the switch.

10. If applicable, install the alarm switch to the lock module assembly by aligning the switch (with the retaining clip) parallel to the lock cylinder, then rotating the switch ¼ turn until locked in place.

11. Install the combination switch to the steering column.

12. Position and secure the steering column.

13. Properly enable the SIR system, then connect the negative battery cable.

Stoplight Switch

ADJUSTMENT

The stoplight switches used by these vehicles are either adjustable or not, depending upon the application. All vehicles 1992–93 and some later vehicles (1994–96 Lumina, Silhouette and Trans Sport) utilize an adjustable switch. On all of these vehicles except the C/K-Series and some S/T-Series vehicles, the stoplight actuator component takes the form of a ribbed tubular switch which fits into an interference clip mounted to the pedal bracket. In contrast to this, the C/K-Series vehicles 1992–93 (and some S/T-Series vehicles) utilize a flat adjusting switch. All adjusting switches should self-adjust during installation or on their first use.

On most 1994–96 models (except the Lumina, Silhouette and Trans Sport), the switch is snapped into position on the pushrod and is not adjustable.

Except C/K-Series and some S/T-Series

1. Depress the brake pedal and press the brake light switch inward until it seats firmly against the clip.

NOTE: As the switch is being pushed into the clip, audible clicks can be heard.

2. Release the brake pedal, then pull it back against the pedal stop until the audible clicks can no longer be heard. The clicks indicate that the switch is moving into position in the clip for proper adjustment.

3. Verify that the switch operates properly when the pedal is depressed and released.

C/K-Series and some S/T-Series

1. Depress the brake pedal fully and make sure the switch is properly positioned.

2. Pull the lever on the brake switch back to its stop.

3. Pull the brake pedal back to its stop position.

4. Check for proper switch operation.

REMOVAL AND INSTALLATION

Tubular Interference Switch

All 1992–93 vehicles(except C/K-Series and some S/T-Series), along with the 1994–96 Lumina, Silhouette and Trans Sport utilize this ribbed, clip mounted switch.

1. Disconnect the negative battery cable.

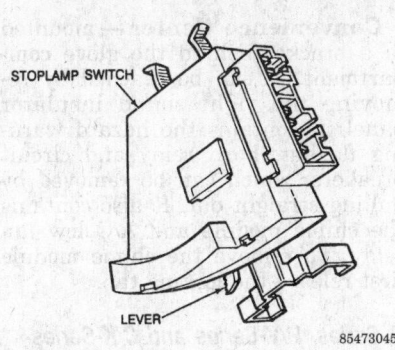

STOPLAMP SWITCH

LEVER

85473045

Stoplight switch adjustment lever — C/K-Series and some S/T-Series 1992–93

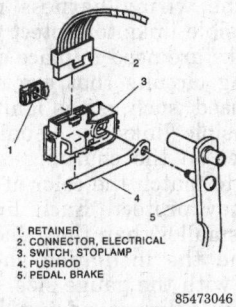

1. RETAINER
2. CONNECTOR, ELECTRICAL
3. SWITCH, STOPLAMP
4. PUSHROD
5. PEDAL, BRAKE

85473046

A non-adjustable stoplight switch is used on all 1994–96 vehicles except the Lumina, Silhouette and Trans Sport

2. Disengage the vacuum and/or electrical connector(s) from the switch.

NOTE: Some brake light switches may be combined with the cruise control release switch, therefore may contain a vacuum hose or an additional electrical connector. If so, be sure to tag all hoses/wiring before disconnecting in order to assure proper installation.

3. Grasp the switch and withdraw it from the clip. If necessary the clip can be removed from the pedal bracket as well. Some clips are designed with lock tangs and may be pivoted in order to pull them from the bracket. On these, you may twist the switch and retainer clip together and withdraw them as an assembly. Other clips are also an interference fit and must be squeezed and withdrawn.
To install:
4. If removed, install the retainer to the pedal bracket.
5. With the pedal depressed so it will not interfere, insert and fully seat the switch into the clip on the pedal bracket.

6. In order to adjust the switch, grasp the pedal and pull it fully back against the stop. While pulling the pedal backwards, a clicking sound should be heard as the switch is pushed backwards in the clip until it is in the proper position. Make sure the switch plunger is seated when the pedal is released and that the plunger fully extends as the pedal is depressed. Check the switch operation and adjust again, if necessary.
7. Engage the vacuum line and/or electrical connector(s) to the switch.
8. Connect the negative battery cable.
9. Verify proper switch operation.

Flat Adjustable Switch

The C/K-Series utilized this switch 1992–93. There are also some reports of this switch being used on some S/T-Series 1992 vehicles–93.
1. Disconnect the negative battery cable. Remove the under dash trim panel(s), as necessary for access.
2. Disengage the switch electrical connections. Remove the switch assembly from its mount.
3. Installation is the reverse of the removal procedure. Adjust the switch, as required.

Non-Adjustable Switch

All 1994–96 vehicles (except Lumina, Silhouette and Trans Sport) utilize a non-adjustable stoplight switch which is snapped to the brake pushrod.
1. Disconnect the negative battery cable.
2. Disengage the switch electrical connector.
3. Remove the retainer from the brake pedal pin, then remove the switch by unsnapping it from the pushrod.
To install:
4. Install the switch by snapping it onto the pushrod, then secure using the retainer on the pedal pin.
5. Engage the switch connector.
6. Connect the negative battery cable and verify proper switch operation.

Clutch Switch

ADJUSTMENT

On early model vehicles, the clutch switch is automatic adjusting upon installation and initial pedal depression. On all 1993–96 vehicles the switch is not adjustable.

REMOVAL AND INSTALLATION

1. Disconnect the negative battery cable.
2. Remove the lower steering column-to-instrument panel cover or under dash trim panel, as necessary for access.
3. Disengage the electrical wiring from the clutch switch.
4. If equipped, remove the switch retaining screw.
5. Remove the switch from the clutch pedal. The switch used on most later model vehicles is snapped into position.
To install:
6. On 1992 vehicles that contain an adjustable switch:
   a. Move the slider to the rear of the shaft.
   b. Push the clutch pedal to the floor.
   c. Move the slider down the shaft.
   d. Release the clutch pedal.
7. Engage the electrical wiring to the switch.
8. If removed, install the trim panel.
9. Connect the negative battery cable.

Neutral Safety Switch

ADJUSTMENT

Column Mounted Switch

Most vehicles covered by this manual utilize a column mounted, ratcheting, self-adjusting switch.
1. Move the switch all the way toward the **L** gear position.
2. Move the selector to the **P** position.
3. The main housing and housing back should ratchet, providing proper switch adjustment.

Floor Console Mounted Switch

1. Remove the center console for access to the switch.
2. Place the shift control lever in Neutral.
3. Align the carrier tang on the switch with the slot on the shifter.
4. Loosen the retaining switch nuts.
5. Rotate the switch to align the service adjustment hole with the carrier tang hold, then use a 0.09 in. (2.34mm) gauge pin to complete adjustment. Insert the pin in the service adjustment hole and rotate the switch until it drops to a depth of 0.59 in. (15mm). Hold the switch in

this position and tighten the retaining nuts to 30 inch lbs. (3.4 Nm).

REMOVAL AND INSTALLATION

Column Mounted Switch

Most vehicles covered by this manual should be equipped with ratcheting self-adjusting switches.

1. Disconnect the negative battery cable.
2. If necessary for access, remove the steering column insulator/filler panel for access to the switch.
3. Disengage the electrical harness connector from the switch.
4. Remove the switch by grasping and pulling it straight out of the steering column jacket.

To install:

5. Align the actuator on the switch with the holes in the shift tube.
6. Set the parking brake and place the gear selector in Neutral.
7. Press down on the front of the switch until the tangs snap into the rectangular holes in the steering column jacket.
8. Adjust the switch by moving the gear selector to **P**. The main housing and the housing back should ratchet, providing the proper switch adjustment.
9. Engage the harness connector to the switch.
10. Connect the negative battery cable, then verify proper switch operation. Make sure the reverse lights work and that the ignition will only work in the Neutral or **P** positions. If necessary, readjust the switch. For ratcheting type switches, move the gear selector all the way to the Low position, then repeat the adjustment.
11. If applicable, install the steering column insulator/filler panel.

Floor Console Mounted Switch

1. Disconnect the negative battery cable.
2. Remove the center console for access to the switch assembly.
3. Disengage the switch electrical connector.
4. Remove the retaining nuts, then remove the switch.
5. If necessary, remove the gauge pin from the switch.
6. If installing a new switch:
   a. Place the shift control lever in Neutral.
   b. Align the carrier tang on the back-up lamp/neutral safety switch with the slot on the shifter.

NOTE: Replacement switches are pinned in the Neutral position to ease installation. If the

switch has been rotated or the switch is broken, install the switch using the "old switch" installation and adjustment procedure.

   c. Tighten the switch retaining nuts to 30 inch lbs. (3.4 Nm), then engage the switch connector.
   d. Move the shift control lever out of Neutral in order to shear the plastic pin, then remove the accessible piece(s) of the gauge pin.
7. If installing an old switch, install and adjust the switch to assure proper operation:
   a. Place the shift control lever in Neutral.
   b. Align the carrier tang on the switch with the slot on the shifter.
   c. Loosely install the retaining switch nuts and engage the wiring connector.
   d. Rotate the switch to align the service adjustment hole with the carrier tang hold, then use a 0.09 in. (2.34mm) gauge pin to complete adjustment. Insert the pin in the service adjustment hole and rotate the switch until it drops to a depth of 0.59 in. (15mm). Hold the switch in this position and tighten the retaining nuts to 30 inch lbs. (3.4 Nm).
8. Install the center console.
9. Connect the negative battery cable.
10. Verify proper switch operation.

Fuses, Circuit Breakers and Relays

LOCATION

M/L-Series and S/T-Series

Fuse Block — located at the far left side of the instrument panel.
Convenience Center — located at the left side of the instrument panel, usually to the right of the steering column.
Hazard Warning Relay — mounted on the convenience center.
Horn Relay — mounted on the convenience center.
Alarm Module or Buzzers — mounted on the convenience center.
Circuit Breakers — mounted on the convenience center.
A/C Low Fan Relay — mounted on the convenience center.

Lumina, Silhouette and Trans Sport

Fuse Panel — located inside the glove compartment.

Convenience Center — mounted to a bracket behind the glove compartment. It can be reached by removing the right sound insulator panel. It contains the hazard warning flasher, horn relay and circuit breakers, which can be removed by pulling straight out. It also contains the chime module and A/C low fan relay. To remove the chime module first release the locking tab.

G-Series, R/V-Series and C/K-Series

FUSIBLE LINKS

In addition to circuit breakers and fuses, the wiring harness incorporates fusible links to protect the wiring. Links are used in place of a fuse in wiring circuits that are not normally fused, such as the ignition circuit. Fusible links are usually color coded red in the charging and load circuits to match the color of the circuits they protect. Each link is 4 gauges smaller than the cable it protects and the insulation should be marked with the gauge size. The engine compartment wiring harness has several fusible links. The same size wire with a special hypalon insulation must be used when replacing a fusible link. The links are normally located in the following areas:

1. A molded splice at the starter solenoid BAT terminal, a 14 gauge red wire.
2. A 16 gauge red fusible link at the junction block to protect the unfused wiring of 12 gauge or larger wire. This link stops at the bulkhead connector.
3. The alternator warning light and field circuitry is protected by a 20 gauge fusible link. The link is installed as a molded splice in the circuit at the junction block.
4. The ammeter circuit is protected by two 20 gauge fusible links installed as molded splices in the circuit at the junction block and battery to starter circuit.

CIRCUIT BREAKERS

A circuit breaker is an electrical switch which breaks the circuit in case of an overload. All models have a circuit breaker in the headlight switch to protect the headlight and parking light systems. An overload may cause the lights to flicker or flash ON and OFF or in some cases, to remain OFF. Windshield wiper motors are protected by a circuit breaker at the motor. Other circuit breakers may be found in the fuse block or convenience center depending on vehicle model and options.

FUSES

Fuses are located in the junction box below the instrument panel to the left of the steering column. Each fuse receptacle is marked as to the circuit it protects and the correct amperage of the fuse. Inline fuses are used on the underhood light and air conditioning.

FLASHERS

The turn signal flasher and the hazard/warning flasher plugs into the fuse block.

NOTE: A special heavy duty turn signal flasher is required to properly operate the turn signals when a trailer's lights are connected to the system.

Computers

LOCATION

Astro and Safari

Electronic Control Module (ECM) — located in the passenger compartment behind the right side cowl/kick panel.
Powertrain Control Module (PCM) — located in the passenger compartment behind the right side cowl/kick panel.
Electronic Spark Control (ESC) Module (4.3L engine with ECM) — located at the right side of the engine above the valve cover.
Cruise Control Module (Electronic Cluster) — located on the left of the cowl, near the brake booster.
Cruise Control Module (Standard Cluster) — located on the left side of the instrument panel on the rear of the dash.

S/T-Series

Electronic Control Module (ECM) — located in the passenger compartment either under/behind the glove box or behind the kick panel.
Powertrain Control Module (PCM) — located in the passenger compartment either under/behind the glove box or behind the kick panel.
Vehicle Control Module (VCM) — either located in the passenger compartment in the same spot as an ECM or PCM (1993) or located in the engine compartment on the right side wheel well (1994–96).
Electronic Spark Control (ESC) Module — used only on ECM vehicles and located at the center of the firewall. On PCM or VCM vehicles,

the computer control module performs this function.
Cruise Control Module — located behind the instrument panel on or near the pedal bracket.

Lumina, Silhouette and Trans Sport

Electronic Control Module (ECM) — located below the right side of instrument panel, behind the convenience center.
Powertrain Control Module (PCM) — located below the right side of instrument panel.
Electronic Spark Control (ESC) Module — located behind the instrument panel, behind the convenience center. Used on ECM equipped vehicles only, the PCM performs this function on Powertrain Control Module (PCM) equipped vehicles.
Cruise Control Module — located behind the instrument panel on the left side.

G-Series, R/V-Series and C/K-Series

Electronic Control Module (ECM): located in the passenger compartment by the right side kick panel or behind the glove box on the R/V and C/K-Series vehicles or on the drivers side under the seat on the G-Series vans.
Wiper Delay Module: R/V-Series: located on the steering column behind the lower cover. C/K-Series: located on the wiper motor. G-Series: located in the harness on the left side of the steering column.
Cruise Control Module: R/V and G-Series: located on the back of instrument panel next to the steering column. C/K-Series: located on the engine side of the cowl near the master cylinder.

Cruise Control

SERVO ADJUSTMENT

M/L-Series, 1992–94, S/T-Series 1992–93 and Lumina, Silhouette and Trans Sport

1. Disconnect the cruise control cable from the servo.
2. Ensure ignition and fast idle cam are **OFF** and throttle is fully closed before adjusting servo.
3. Except for the Lumina, Silhouette and Trans Sport, Connect the cable to the servo. The rod should have approximately 0.039–0.150 in. (1–4mm) of clearance at the stud.
4. For the Lumina, Silhouette and Trans Sport, pull the cable towards the servo WITHOUT moving the

throttle lever. If 1 of the holes in the servo tab aligns with cable pin, connect them. If not, move the cable away from the servo until the next closest hole in the tab aligns with the cable pin.
5. Install the cable retainer and check for proper operation.

G-Series 1992–94 and R/V-Series

1. Ensure ignition is **OFF** and the throttle valve fully closed before proceeding with adjustment.
2. If equipped with a gasoline engine, install the servo rod so the rod assembles over the stud per adjustment "B".
3. If equipped with a diesel engine 1992–93, position the pin on the servo rod in the hole closest to the servo that allows for adjustment "C".
4. If equipped with a 1994–96 diesel engine, connect the cable servo blade to the tightest servo chain ball which still allows the throttle lever assembly to remain at rest.
5. Make sure the servo rod is secured, then verify that the system functions properly.

C/K-Series 1992–93

1. Disconnect the engine end of the cruise control cable from the lever stud.
2. Pull lightly on the end of the cable.
3. If the cable does not pull out, the cable is adjusted properly. If the cable extends out, proceed as follows:
   a. Unlock the cable conduit lock mechanism, if equipped.
   b. If equipped with a gasoline engine, move the cable until the throttle begins to open. Then move the cable in the opposite direction enough to close the throttle.
   c. If equipped with a diesel engine, move the cable until the injection pump lever moves off the idle stop screw. Then move the cable in the opposite direction far enough to return the lever to the idle stop screw.
   d. While holding the cable securely, push down on the cable conduit lock mechanism until it snaps into place.
   e. Verify the system functions properly.

1994 S/T-Series, 1994 C/K-Series and All 1995–96 Except Lumina, Silhouette and Trans Sport

Install or connect and properly adjust the cruise control cable:
1. Attach the cable bead to the module ribbon end fitting.

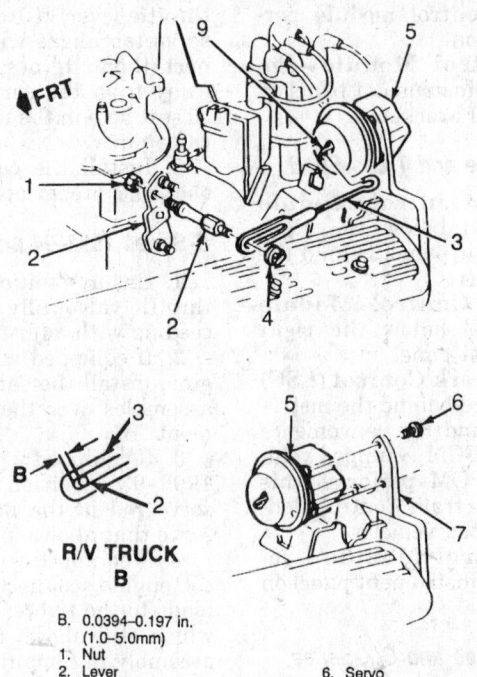

R/V TRUCK
B

B. 0.0394–0.197 in.
(1.0–5.0mm)
1. Nut
2. Lever
3. Stud
4. Rod
5. Retainer
6. Servo
7. Bolt
8. Bracket
9. Tab

85473047

Cruise control servo mounting and adjustment — G-Series 1992–94 and R/V-Series, except diesel engine

2. For the S/T-Series equipped with the 4.3L (VIN W) engine, snap the cruise cable fitting over ferrule on end of conduit until an audible "snap" is heard.

3. Pull the cruise control cable engine end fitting until the the cable is taut.

4. Turn the cruise control engine end fitting to straighten the ribbon. The ribbon must be flat and vertical.

5. Slide the cable conduit over ribbon and install tangs on the module housing.

6. Except for S/T-Series vehicles:

a. Install the cable conduit in the engine bracket, then press firmly until the tang locks into position.

b. Install the cable fitting securely over the throttle lever pin. Make sure the throttle lever is closed, this is especially important on 7.4L engines.

c. Except for M/L-Series, check the cable for approximately 0–0.197 in. (0–5mm) lash. Turn the adjuster screw as required to obtain proper clearance.

d. For the M/L-Series, route the cable through the retainers, then clip the cable mid-conduit clip to the accelerator cable. Flip the toggle lever on the adjuster to lock cable adjustment.

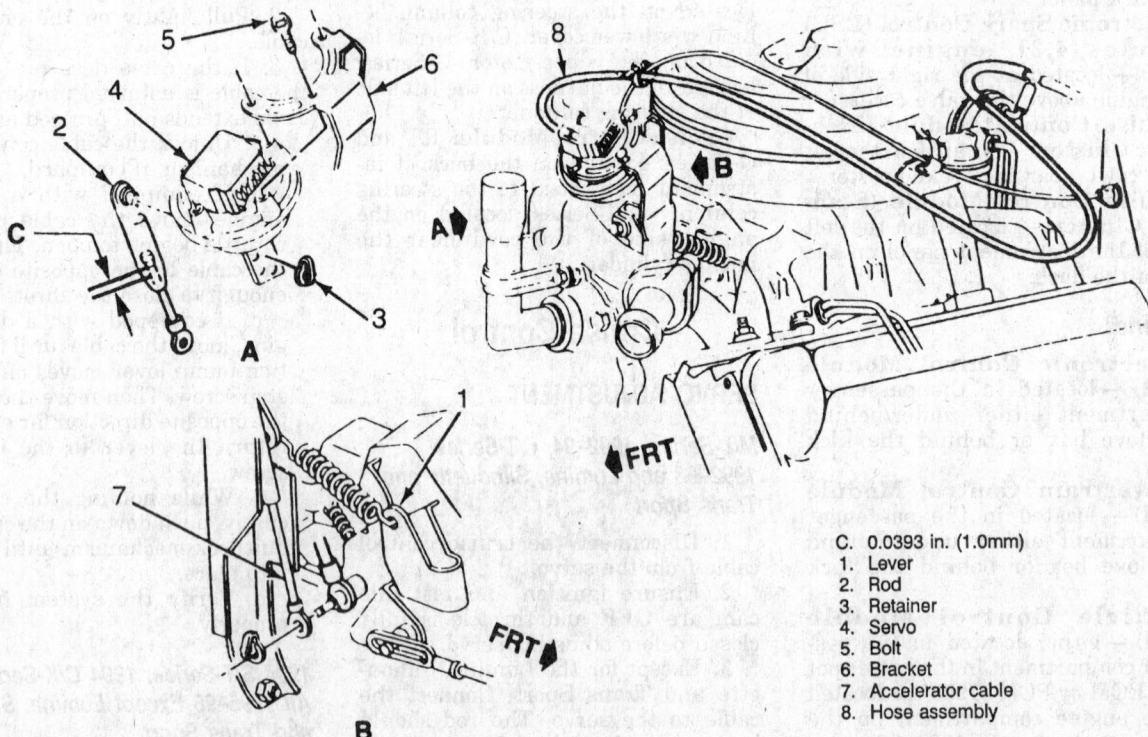

C. 0.0393 in. (1.0mm)
1. Lever
2. Rod
3. Retainer
4. Servo
5. Bolt
6. Bracket
7. Accelerator cable
8. Hose assembly

85473048

Cruise control servo mounting and adjustment — G-Series and R/V-Series with diesel engine 1992

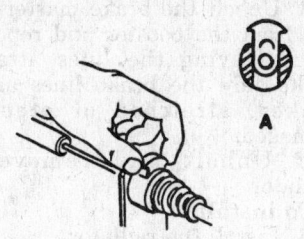

A. Unlocked Position

85473049

Unlocking cable for adjustment — C/K-Series 1992–93

7. For the 2.2L engine:

a. If equipped with A/C, route the cable over the refrigerant line.

b. Rotate the cam lever and install the cable slug into the throttle lever slot opening and the wire into the pulley groove. Do not twist or kink the cable. Make sure the cable slug is supported by sides of the throttle cam lever.

c. Slide the cable fitting into the rectangular slot in the engine bracket, while making sure the tab snaps into the locking slot. Do not install the splash shield cover until final cable adjustment is made.

d. Connect the cable locator clip to the top of the routing bracket which is mounted to the rocker cover.

e. Flip the adjuster lever down to lock final adjustment to the cable.

f. Adjustment should result in a clearance of 0–0.39 in. (0–10mm) at the throttle cam lever.

8. For the S/T-Series equipped with the 4.3L (VIN Z) engine:

a. Install the cable conduit in the engine bracket, then press firmly until the tang locks into position.

b. Rotate the cam lever rearward and snap the cable fitting securely over the throttle lever pin.

c. Push the cable adjuster tab into the locking position. Check the cable for approximately 0–0.39 in. (0–10mm) lash.

9. For the S/T-Series equipped with the 4.3L (VIN W) engine:

a. Slide the cable fitting into the rectangular slot in the engine bracket, while making sure the tab snaps into the locking slot.

b. Snap the cruise control cable fitting over the throttle lever pin.

c. Route the cable through the retainer on right rear corner of the engine. The cruise control cable must route above the accelerator cable in the retainer.

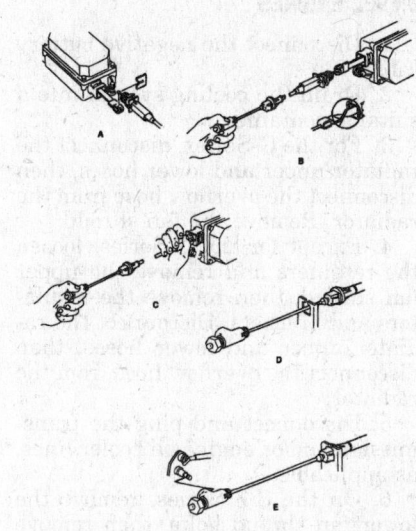

85473050

Cruise control cable installation and adjustment — C/K-Series shown (others similar)

d. Flip the adjuster toggle lever in order to lock adjustment of the cable. If properly adjusted, there should be approximately 0–0.39 in. (0–10mm) of clearance.

e. Secure the cable to the electrical junction connector using the retaining strap.

10. Check to be sure all throttle linkage operates freely, without binding.

ENGINE COOLING

Radiator

REMOVAL AND INSTALLATION

M/L-Series and S/T-Series

1. Disconnect the negative battery cable.

2. Drain the engine cooling system.

3. If equipped with the MFI-Turbo engine:

a. Remove the air cleaner and duct, then remove the turbocharger inlet elbow.

b. Disconnect the positive battery cable, then remove the battery and the battery tray.

c. Disconnect the heater hose and clamp from the radiator.

4. Disconnect the overflow hose from the radiator, then disconnect the upper and lower radiator hoses.

5. If equipped with A/C, it may be necessary to remove the A/C hose retaining clip and reposition the hose for shroud and/or radiator removal. Do not disconnect any refrigerant fittings.

NOTE: If equipped with a 1 piece shroud, the shroud may be unbolted from the radiator support and pushed back over the cooling fan instead of removing it completely.

6. Most vehicles should be equipped with a 2 piece radiator/fan shroud. Remove the upper fan shroud-to-radiator support bolts and the upper fan shroud-to-lower fan shroud retainers. Remove the upper shroud.

7. If equipped with an A/T, disconnect and plug the fluid cooler lines at the radiator. Plug all openings to prevent system contamination or excessive fluid loss.

NOTE: On some late model M/L-Series vehicles, the automatic transmission fluid cooler lines utilize a quick-connect fitting. Use J-37088-2A or equivalent quick-disconnect tool when servicing these vehicles.

8. If equipped with a factory engine oil cooler which is integral to the radiator, disconnect and plug the oil cooler lines at the radiator. Plug all openings to prevent system contamination or excessive fluid loss. Plug all openings to prevent system contamination or excessive fluid loss.

9. Lift the radiator straight upward from the supports. Be careful to lift the radiator straight upward and not to tilt it excessively as the radiator will still contain a significant amount of coolant and, if applicable, transmission fluid/engine oil.

To install:

10. Lower the radiator into position on the supports.

11. If equipped, remove the plugs, then connect the engine oil cooler lines and tighten the fittings.

12. If equipped with an A/T, remove the plugs, then connect the transmission fluid cooler lines and tighten the fittings.

13. Install the upper fan shroud and secure using the support and lower shroud retainers.

14. If applicable, reposition the A/C refrigerant hose and secure using the retaining clip.

15. Connect the overflow hose, upper and lower radiator hoses.

16. If equipped with the MFI-Turbo engine:

   a. Connect the heater hose and clamp to the radiator.

   b. Install the battery tray, then install the battery and connect the positive battery cable

   c. Install the turbocharger inlet elbow, then install the air cleaner and duct.

17. Connect the negative battery cable.

NOTE: Whenever the cooling system in a 1995–96 vehicle (except diesel engines or U-Series vehicles) is completely drained and refilled with fresh coolant, 2 sealant pellets GMSPO part 3634621 must be added to the radiator. Failure to use the correct sealant pellets may result in premature coolant pump leakage. Do not add the pellets to the coolant recovery bottle as this may prevent the system from operating properly.

18. Properly refill the engine cooling system.

Lumina APV, Silhouette and Trans Sport

1. Disconnect the negative battery cable.

2. Drain the coolant from the radiator.

3. Disconnect the engine forward strut bracket at the radiator, loosen the bolt at the other end and swing the strut rearward.

4. Disconnect the forward lamp harness from the fan frame and unplug the fan connector.

5. Remove the fan attaching bolts, then remove the fan and frame assembly.

6. Scribe the latch location then remove the hood latch from the radiator support.

7. Disconnect the coolant hoses from the radiator and the coolant recovery tank hose from the radiator neck.

8. Disconnect and plug the transaxle oil cooler lines.

9. Remove the radiator-to-support attaching bolts and clamps, then remove the radiator.

10. Installation is the reverse of removal.

G-Series, R/V-Series and C/K-Series

EXCEPT G-SERIES WITH 6.2L AND 6.5L DIESEL ENGINES

1. Disconnect the negative battery cable.

2. Drain the cooling system into a suitable container.

3. For the G-Series, disconnect the radiator upper and lower hoses, then disconnect the overflow hose from the radiator. Remove the fan shroud.

4. Except for the G-Series, loosen the retainers and remove the upper fan shroud, then remove the insulators and brackets. Disconnect the radiator upper and lower hoses, then disconnect the overflow hose from the radiator.

5. Disconnect and plug the transmission and/or engine oil cooler lines, as applicable.

6. On the C/K-Series, remove the lower fan shroud bolts, then remove the lower shroud.

7. If necessary on vehicles before 1993, remove the clutch fan.

8. Remove the radiator.

9. Installation is the reverse of the removal procedure.

NOTE: Whenever the cooling system in a 1995–96 vehicle (except diesel engines or U-Series vehicles) is completely drained and refilled with fresh coolant, 2 sealant pellets GMSPO part 3634621 must be added to the radiator. Failure to use the correct sealant pellets may result in premature coolant pump leakage. Do not add the pellets to the coolant recovery bottle as this may prevent the system from operating properly.

G-SERIES WITH 6.2L AND 6.5L DIESEL ENGINES

1. Disconnect the negative battery cables.

2. Drain the engine cooling system.

3. Remove the air intake snorkel.

4. Remove the windshield washer bottle.

5. Remove the hood release cable.

6. Remove the upper fan shroud.

7. Disconnect the upper radiator hose.

8. Disconnect and plug the transmission cooler lines.

9. Disconnect the low coolant sensor wire.

10. Disconnect the overflow hose.

11. Disconnect the engine oil cooler lines.

12. Disconnect the lower radiator hose.

13. Unbolt the brake master cylinder from the booster and reposition aside leaving the lines attached. Make sure the brake lines are not kinked, stretched or otherwise damaged.

14. Unbolt and remove the radiator.

To install:

15. Install the radiator.

16. Secure the brake master cylinder on the booster.

17. Connect the lower radiator hose.

18. Connect the engine oil cooler lines.

19. Connect the overflow hose.

20. Connect the low coolant sensor wire.

21. Connect the transmission cooler lines.

22. Connect the upper radiator hose.

23. Install the upper fan shroud.

24. Install the hood release cable.

25. Install the windshield washer bottom.

26. Install the air intake snorkle.

27. Fill the radiator with the proper type and quantity of coolant and inspect the system for leaks.

Electric Cooling Fan

REMOVAL AND INSTALLATION

The Lumina, Silhouette and Trans Sport are the only vehicles equipped with an electric cooling fan. With the exception of the auxiliary fan used on some G-Series and C/K-Series vehicles, the remainder of these vehicles utilize a belt driven fan.

1. Disconnect the negative battery cable.

2. If necessary, disconnect the engine forward strut bracket from the radiator frame and swing it rearward.

3. Disconnect the forward lamp harness from the fan frame.

4. Remove the fan attaching bolts.

5. Disconnect the fan wiring.

6. Remove the fan and frame assembly.

7. Installation is the reverse of the removal procedure.

Auxiliary Electric Cooling Fan

An electric, auxiliary fan is used on some G-Series and C/K-Series vehicles. The purpose of the fan is to provide additional cooling during extended idle and slow moving vehicle

operation. The system consists of an engine coolant temperature sensor, relay and the electric fan motor. When the engine coolant temperature reaches a predetermined point, the sensor will close the circuit to the relay, energizing it, and causing the relay to apply 12 volts to the fan motor. Once temperature falls below that point, the sensor will open the circuit, de-energizing the relay and causing it to cut power from the fan motor.

REMOVAL AND INSTALLATION

1. Disconnect the negative battery cable.
2. On the G-Series and if necessary on the C/K-Series, remove the grille for access.
3. Unplug the fan harness connector.
4. Remove the fan-to-brace bolts and lift out the fan.
5. Installation is the reverse of removal.

Heater Core

REMOVAL AND INSTALLATION

S/T-Series

ALL 1992–93 VEHICLES AND 1994 UTILITY

1. Disconnect the negative battery cable.
2. Drain the cooling system to a level below the heater core.

NOTE: Plug the heater core tubes to avoid spilling coolant in the passenger compartment during removal.

3. Disconnect the heater-to-engine coolant hoses from the core tubes.
4. From the passenger compartment (under the dash) remove the heater core rear case cover-to-cowl screws, then remove the cover.
5. Remove the straps or brackets from each end of the heater core.
6. Carefully remove the heater core from the cowl and case.
To install:
7. Insert the heater core into the case, taking care not to damage the tubes as they are inserted through the cowl.
8. Install the straps or brackets to the ends of the heater core and secure using the retaining screws.
9. Install the heater core rear case cover and secure using the retaining screws.

10. Connect the heater-to-engine coolant hoses to the core tubes.
11. Connect the negative battery cable, then properly refill the engine cooling system.
12. Run the engine at normal operating temperatures and check for leaks.

1994 UTILITY AND ALL 1995–96 VEHICLES

1. If equipped, properly disable the SIR (air bag) system.
2. Disconnect the negative battery cable and drain the engine cooling system to a level below the heater core.
3. Disconnect the heater hoses from the core tubes.

NOTE: The instrument panel carrier is designed not only to provide access to parts through removal of the carrier components, but the carrier will also tilt downward as a complete assembly to allow access from the top. If this is desired, remove the retainer screws along the top and bottom of the carrier assembly. The instrument panel will then tilt as an assembly into the cab. It is necessary to unbolt and lower the steering column from the carrier to allow for maximum movement of the instrument panel.

4. The instrument panel must be removed or repositioned for access to the heater core case. Unbolt and either tilt the instrument panel forward or disengage the instrument panel components and remove the panel. In most cases, tilting the panel forward should be sufficient for the necessary access, but if necessary remove the panel assembly.
5. Remove the heater core rear case retaining screws, then remove the rear case for access to the heater core.
6. Loosen the retainers and remove the heater core retaining straps.
7. Remove the heater core and seals.
To install:
8. Install the heater core and seals, taking care not to damage the core tubes when inserting them through the cowl.
9. Install and secure the core retaining straps.
10. Install the rear case and secure using the screws.
11. Reposition and secure the instrument panel and components.
12. Connect the heater hoses to the core tubes.

13. Connect the negative battery cable, then properly refill the engine cooling system.
14. Run the engine at normal operating temperature, then check for leaks.
15. If equipped, properly enable the SIR system.

NOTE: Whenever the cooling system in a 1995–96 vehicle (except diesel engines or the U-Series vehicles) is completely drained and refilled with fresh coolant, 2 sealant pellets GMSPO part 3634621 must be added to the radiator. Failure to use the correct sealant pellets may result in premature coolant pump leakage. Do not add the pellets to the coolant recovery bottle as this may prevent the system from operating properly.

Astro and Safari

1992 VEHICLES

1. Disconnect the negative battery cable. Drain the engine coolant.
2. Remove the engine coolant bottle. Remove the bolts from the windshield washer bottle and position it aside. Remove and plug the heater hoses at the heater core.
3. Remove the instrument panel lower right filler panel. Remove the air distributor duct. Remove the engine cover as needed.
4. Remove the air duct. Remove vacuum lines and control cables as required.
5. Remove the heater core assembly retaining screws.
6. Remove the heater core cover plate. Remove the heater core.
7. Installation is the reverse of the removal procedure.

1993–96 VEHICLES

1. Disconnect the negative battery cable.
2. Drain the engine cooling system to a level below the heater core.
3. If necessary, remove the rear seat.
4. Loosen the clamps on the auxiliary heater pipes, then disconnect the pipes from the heater core.
5. Loosen the retaining screws, then remove the heater core cover.
6. Loosen and remove the mounting strap and clamp.
7. Remove the heater core and seals. If necessary, remove the seals from the heater core.
8. Installation is the reverse of the removal.

Lumina, Silhouette and Trans Sport

1992–93 VEHICLES

1. Disconnect the negative battery cable.
2. Drain the engine cooling system.
3. Remove the right side sound insulator from under the instrument panel.
4. Disconnect the heater hoses.
5. Remove the glove box and door.
6. If necessary, remove the bolt and nut retaining the instrument panel brace, then remove the brace.
7. Disconnect the vacuum hoses and wiring from the heater core cover.

NOTE: On some vehicles it may be necessary to disconnect the vacuum harness from the vacuum electric solenoid, then remove the solenoid retaining screws and separate the solenoid from the heater core cover.

8. Remove the heater core cover and remove the heater core.
9. Installation is the reverse of the removal procedure.

1994–96 VEHICLES

1. Disconnect the negative battery cable and drain the engine cooling system.
2. Remove the 2 screws attaching the right hand windshield wiper transmission arm to the wiper frame. Move the wiper transmission for access to the heater hoses.
3. Loosen the clamps, then disconnect the outlet and inlet hoses from the heater core tubes.
4. Remove the right hand instrument panel sound insulator panel push-in retainers. Remove the screw and nut from the stud.
5. Carefully pull the sound insulator panel away from the instrument panel, then remove the courtesy lamp from the panel and remove the panel.
6. Open the instrument panel compartment (glove box) door. Remove the 3 screws from the bottom of the box insert, then remove the upper box screws with the 2 bumpers. Disengage the wiring harness connector from the box lamp and switch assembly. Remove the glove box and door from the instrument panel.
7. Remove the 2 screws retaining the instrument panel lower extension housing to the support bracket.
8. Remove the right instrument panel outer support-to-panel lower trim pad attaching bolt, then place a wedge between the outer support and the lower trim pad.
9. Disengage the heater control vacuum harness from the vacuum/electric solenoid assembly. Remove the 2 solenoid retaining screws, then remove the solenoid from the heater core cover.
10. Remove the 6 screws and 2 clips from the heater core cover, then remove the cover and seal from the heater case.
11. Remove the retaining screw and the lower heater core bracket.
12. Remove the left retaining screw from the upper heater core bracket, then loosen the right screw. Reposition the upper bracket to allow for heater core removal.
13. Carefully remove the heater core inlet/outlet tubes from the tube/case seal, then remove the heater core from the case.

To install:
14. Carefully install the heater core to the case while guiding the tubes through the seal.
15. Position the upper bracket and secure using the retaining bolts.
16. Install and secure the lower bracket.
17. Install the heater core cover and seal and secure using the screws and clips.
18. Install and secure the vacuum/electric solenoid, then connect the vacuum harness.
19. Remove the wedge, then install the outer support to the lower trim pad.
20. Install the screws retaining the instrument panel lower extension housing to the lower extension support brackets.
21. Install the glove box.
22. Install the instrument panel sound insulator.
23. Connect the heater hoses to the core tubes and secure using the retaining clamps.
24. Reposition the windshield wiper transmission and attach it to the wiper frame.
25. Connect the negative battery cable and properly refill the engine cooling system.

R/V-Series

1. Disconnect the battery ground cable.
2. Disconnect the heater hoses at the core tubes and drain the engine coolant. Plug the core tubes to prevent spillage.
3. Remove the nuts securing the assembly to the engine firewall.
4. Remove the instrument panel.
5. Disconnect the air-defrost and temperature door cables.
6. Remove the floor outlet and remove the defroster duct-to-heater case screw.
7. Remove the heater case-to-instrument panel screws. Pull the assembly rearward to gain access to the wiring harness and disconnect the wires attached to the unit.
8. Remove the heater distributor.
9. Remove the heater core retaining straps and remove the core.
10. Installation is the reverse of removal. Be sure the core-to-case and case-to-dash panel sealer is intact. Fill the cooling system and check for leaks.

NOTE: Whenever the cooling system in a 1995–96 vehicle (except diesel engines or the U-Series vehicles) is completely drained and refilled with fresh coolant, 2 sealant pellets GMSPO part 3634621 must be added to the radiator. Failure to use the correct sealant pellets may result in premature coolant pump leakage. Do not add the pellets to the coolant recovery bottle as this may prevent the system from operating properly.

C/K-Series

1992 VEHICLES

1. Disconnect the negative battery cable.
2. Drain the cooling system into a suitable container.
3. Disconnect the heater hoses at the core tubes.
4. In the passenger compartment, remove the lower heater core cover-to-case screws.
5. Remove the bracket and screws securing the heater core to the case.
6. Remove the heater core.
7. Installation is the reverse of the removal procedure.

1993–96 VEHICLES

1. If equipped, properly disable the SIR (air bag) system.
2. Disconnect the negative battery cable and drain the engine cooling system.
3. Remove the glove box.
4. Disengage the necessary electrical connectors, then remove the center floor air distribution duct.
5. On 1993–94 vehicles, remove the ECM and mounting tray.
6. Remove the hinge pillar trim panels.
7. Remove the blower motor cover, then remove the blower motor assembly.
8. Remove or lower the steering column, as necessary for access, then

remove the necessary retainers and tilt the instrument panel downward.

9. Remove the coolant recovery reservoir for access, the disconnect the heater hoses from the core tubes.

10. Remove the screw on the interior side of the cowl, near the evaporator pipe, if equipped, while holding the heater case to the cowl.

11. Remove the screws and nuts on the engine side of the cowl while still holding the heater case.

NOTE: The help of an assistant may be necessary when removing the heater case.

12. Remove the heater case.

13. Loosen the screws and remove the heater cover for access, then remove the core from the heater case.

To install:

14. Install the core to the heater case, then install the cover and secure using the retainers.

15. Install the heater case to the vehicle and secure using the screws and nut on the engine side of the cowl, then instal the screws on the interior side.

16. Connect the heater hoses, then install the coolant recovery reservoir.

17. Reposition and secure the instrument panel.

18. Reposition and secure the steering column.

19. Install the blower motor assembly, then install the cover.

20. Install the hinge pillar trim panels.

21. Make sure the ignition is in the **OFF** position, then install the ECM and mounting bracket on vehicles so equipped.

22. Install the center floor air distribution duct, then engage the wiring which was disconnected earlier.

23. Install the glove box.

24. Connect the negative battery cable and properly refill the engine cooling system.

25. If equipped, properly enable the SIR system.

NOTE: Whenever the cooling system in a 1995–96 vehicle (except diesel engines or the U-Series vehicles) is completely drained and refilled with fresh coolant, 2 sealant pellets GMSPO part 3634621 must be added to the radiator. Failure to use the correct sealant pellets may result in premature coolant pump leakage. Do not add the pellets to the coolant recovery bottle as this may prevent the system from operating properly.

G-Series

1. Disconnect the negative battery cable.

2. If necessary on 1992 vehicles, Remove the coolant recovery bottle.

3. Place a pan under the vehicle and disconnect the heater intake and outlet hoses. Quickly remove and plug the hoses, then support them in an upright position. Drain the coolant from the heater core into the pan.

NOTE: Use low pressure compressed air to blow the remaining coolant from the heater core. This will prevent the possibility of spilling it on the vehicle's interior.

4. Remove the heater distributor duct-to-case attaching screws and the duct-to-engine cover screw. Remove the duct.

5. If necessary, remove the engine housing cover.

6. Remove all the instrument panel attaching screws.

7. Carefully lower the steering column. Raise and support the right side of the instrument panel.

8. Remove the defroster duct-to-case attaching screws and the 2 screws attaching the distributor to the heater case.

9. Disconnect the temperature door cable. Carefully fold the cable back and out of the way.

10. Remove the 3 nuts from the engine compartment side of the heater case and the screw from the passenger compartment side.

11. Remove the heater case and core assembly.

12. Remove the core retaining straps and remove the core.

To install:

13. Install the core.

14. Install the core retaining straps.

15. Install the heater case and core assembly.

16. Install the 3 nuts on the engine compartment side of the distributor case and the screw on the passenger compartment side.

17. Connect the temperature door cable.

18. Install the defroster duct-to-case attaching screws and the 2 screws attaching the distributor to the heater case.

19. Install the steering column.

20. Install all the instrument panel attaching screws.

21. Install the engine cover.

22. Install the duct. Install the heater distributor duct-to-case attaching screws and the duct-to-engine cover screw.

23. Connect the heater intake and outlet hoses.

24. If removed, install the coolant recovery bottle.

25. Connect the negative battery cable.

26. Check and fill the cooling system.

Water Pump

REMOVAL AND INSTALLATION

S/T-Series

1. Disconnect the negative battery cable, then drain the engine cooling system.

2. Relieve the belt tension, then remove the accessory drive belts or the serpentine drive belt, as applicable.

3. Remove the upper fan shroud, then remove the fan or fan and clutch assembly, as applicable.

4. Remove the water pump pulley.

5. Loosen the clamp and disconnect the coolant hose(s) from the water pump.

NOTE: For the hoses on some engines, such as the heater hose on the early 2.8L, removal may be easier if the hose is left attached until the pump is free from the block. Once the pump is removed from the engine, the pump may be pulled (giving a better grip and greater leverage) from the tight hose connection.

6. Remove the retainers, then remove the water pump from the engine. Note the positions of all retainers as some engines will utilize different length fasteners in different locations and/or bolts and studs in different locations.

To install:

7. Using a gasket scraper, carefully clean the gasket mounting surfaces.

NOTE: The water pumps on some of the earlier engines covered may have been installed using sealer only, no gasket, at the factory. If a gasket is supplied with the replacement part, it should be used. Otherwise, a 1/8 in. bead of RTV sealer should be used around the sealing surface of the pump.

8. Apply 1052080 or equivalent sealant to the threads of the water pump retainers. Install the water pump to the engine using a new gasket, then thread the retainers in order to hold it in position.

9. Tighten the water pump retainers to specification:

a. For 2.2L and 2.5L gasoline engines tighten the water pump-to-engine retainers to 17 ft. lbs. (23 Nm).

b. For the 2.8L engine, tighten the retainers to 22 ft. lbs. (30 Nm) for all 1992 vehicles or to 15 ft. lbs. (21 Nm) and 89 inch lbs. (10 Nm) depending on fastener location for 1993 vehicles. The central 3 lower bolts are tightened to the inch lbs. specification.

c. For the 4.3L engine, tighten the bolts and studs to 30 ft. lbs. (41 Nm).

10. Connect the coolant hose(s) and secure using the retaining clamp(s).

11. Install the water pump pulley, then install the fan or fan and clutch assembly.

12. If equipped with a serpentine drive belt, position the belt over the pulleys, then carefully allow the tensioner back into contact with the belt.

13. If equipped with V-belts, install the accessory drive belts and adjust the tension.

14. Install the upper fan shroud, then connect the negative battery cable.

15. Properly refill the engine cooling system, then run the engine and check for leaks.

NOTE: Whenever the cooling system in a 1995–96 vehicle (except diesel engines or the U-Series vehicles) is completely drained and refilled with fresh coolant, 2 sealant pellets GMSPO part 3634621 must be added to the radiator. Failure to use the correct sealant pellets may result in premature coolant pump leakage. Do not add the pellets to the coolant recovery bottle as this may prevent the system from operating properly.

Compact Van

1. Disconnect the negative battery cable, then drain the engine cooling system.

2. On the 3.1L engine, disconnect the heater hose, then remove the serpentine drive belt shield.

3. For the 3.8L engine, loosen but do not remove the water pump pulley bolts.

4. Remove the serpentine drive belt. On the 3.1L engine, a ⅜ in. drive breaker bar may be used to pivot the belt tensioner.

5. For the M/L-Series, remove the upper fan shroud.

6. Remove the water pump pulley.

7. Loosen the clamps and disconnect any remaining hoses from the water pump, as applicable.

8. Remove the water pump retaining bolts. Remove the water pump assembly from the engine.

NOTE: On some engines, then pump retaining bolts will vary in size and thread. Be sure to note the positioning of all bolts during removal to assure proper installation.

9. Installation is the reverse of removal procedure. Use a new gasket and carefully tighten the bolts.

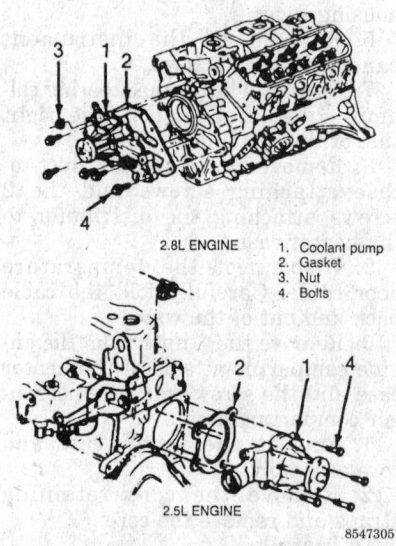

2.8L ENGINE
1. Coolant pump
2. Gasket
3. Nut
4. Bolts

2.5L ENGINE

85473051

Water pump assembly mounting — 2.5L and 2.8L engines

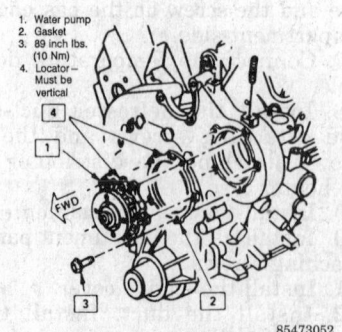

1. Water pump
2. Gasket
3. 89 inch lbs. (10 Nm)
4. Locator — Must be vertical

85473052

Water pump assembly mounting — 3.1L engine

G-Series, R/V-Series and C/K-Series

GASOLINE ENGINES

1. Disconnect the negative battery cable.

2. Except for G-Series, remove the upper fan shroud

3. On the G-Series, remove the air intake duct, then remove the upper radiator shroud.

4. Drain the engine coolant into a suitable container.

5. Remove the drive belt(s) from the water pump pulley.

6. Remove fan, clutch and pulley.

7. If necessary, remove any accessory brackets that will interfere with water pump removal.

8. Disconnect the coolant hoses from the water pump assembly.

9. Remove the bolts, pump assembly and old gasket from the engine.

To install:

10. Ensure the gasket surfaces on the pump and engine are clean.

11. Install the pump assembly with a new gasket. Tighten the bolts to 30 ft. lbs. (40 Nm).

12. Connect the hoses to the water pump assembly.

13. Install any accessory brackets which were removed for access.

14. Install the fan, clutch and pulley.

15. Install the accessory drive belt(s), as applicable.

16. Install the upper fan or radiator shroud and the air intake duct, as applicable.

17. Connect the battery, then properly refill the engine cooling system.

NOTE: Whenever the cooling system in a 1995–96 vehicle (except diesel engines or the U-Series vehicles) is completely drained and refilled with fresh coolant, 2 sealant pellets GMSPO part 3634621 must be added to the radiator. Failure to use the correct sealant pellets may result in premature coolant pump leakage. Do not add the pellets to the coolant recovery bottle as this may prevent the system from operating properly.

DIESEL ENGINES

1. Disconnect the negative battery cables.

2. Remove the fan and fan shroud.

3. Drain the engine coolant into a suitable container.

4. If necessary on 1992 vehicles, remove the air conditioning hose bracket and/or the oil filler tube, as required.

5. Remove the engine accessory drive belt(s).

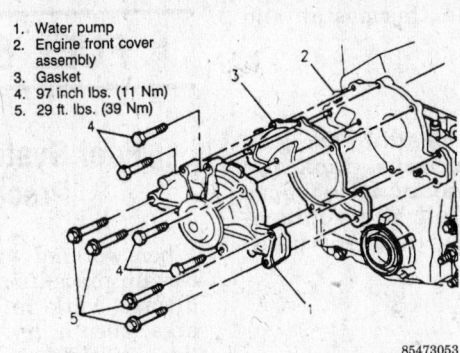

1. Water pump
2. Engine front cover assembly
3. Gasket
4. 97 inch lbs. (11 Nm)
5. 29 ft. lbs. (39 Nm)

85473053

Water pump assembly mounting — 3.8L engine

6. Raise and support the vehicle safely.

7. Remove the vacuum pump mounting bracket nuts, then remove the bolt holding the pump and alternator. Remove the vacuum pump and bracket.

8. Remove the power steering pump and bracket, then support the assembly aside.

9. Lower the vehicle, then disconnect the coolant hoses from the pump.

10. Remove the water pump plate retaining bolts, then remove the pump and plate assembly from the engine.

11. Remove the bolt on the rear of the water pump plate, then separate the pump and gasket from the plate.

To install:

12. Install the water pump and a new gasket to the plate. Tighten the retaining bolt (at the rear of the plate) to 17 ft. lbs. (23 Nm).

13. Make sure the block mating surface and the plate flanges are free of oil. Apply an anaerobic sealer GM part 1052357 or equivalent.

NOTE: The sealer must be wet to the touch when the bolts are torqued.

14. Attach the water pump and plate assembly, then install and tighten the retainers.

15. Connect the coolant hoses to the pump assembly.

16. Raise and support the vehicle safely, then reposition and secure the power steering pump and bracket.

17. Install the vacuum pump and bracket, along with the bolt holding the pump and alternator.

18. Lower the vehicle, then install the fan and pulley.

19. Install the engine accessory drive belt(s).

20. If removed on 1992 vehicles, install the oil filler tube and/or air conditioning hose bracket nuts.

21. Install the fan shroud.

22. Connect the batteries.

23. Fill the radiator with the proper type and quantity of antifreeze.

Thermostat

REMOVAL AND INSTALLATION

Except Diesel Engines

1. Disconnect the negative battery cable.

2. Drain the radiator until the level is below the thermostat (below the level of the intake manifold, cyl-

1. Water pump
2. Gasket
3. Bolt

85473054

Water pump assembly mounting — 4.3L engine

inder head or other thermostat housing, as applicable).

3. If necessary, disconnect the hose from the thermostat outlet. On most applications, the hose may be left attached to the outlet when it is removed, however on some models disconnecting the hose may make outlet removal easier.

4. Loosen and remove the thermostat outlet retainers, then remove the outlet from the housing. Note the orientation of the thermostat in the housing for installation purposes.

To install:

5. Carefully clean the all traces of the old gasket and/or sealer from the housing and outlet.

6. Install the thermostat to the housing, oriented as noted during removal, then position a new gasket (if used).

7. If sealant was used on the old component or if no gasket is provided, place a 1/8 in. bead of RTV sealant in the groove on the water outlet sealing surface, then install the outlet while the sealer is still wet.

8. Install and tighten the outlet retainers.

9. If removed, connect the hose to the outlet.

10. Connect the negative battery cable.

11. Properly refill and bleed the engine cooling system, then check for leaks.

NOTE: Whenever the cooling system in a 1995–96 vehicle (except diesel engines or the U-Series vehicles) is completely drained and refilled with fresh coolant, 2 sealant pellets GMSPO part 3634621 must be added to the radiator. Failure to use the correct sealant pellets may result in premature coolant pump leakage. Do not add the pellets to the coolant recovery bottle as this may prevent the system from operating properly.

Diesel Engines

1. Disconnect the negative battery cables.

2. Remove the upper fan shroud.

3. Drain the cooling system to a point below the thermostat.

4. Remove the engine oil dipstick tube brace and the oil fill brace.

5. If necessary, disconnect the radiator inlet hose.

6. Loosen the retainers, then remove the water outlet.

7. Remove the thermostat and gasket.

NOTE: When cleaning the gasket mating surfaces, look for traces of RTV sealant. If no traces are found, install the replacement gasket dry (without additional sealant).

8. Installation is the reverse of removal. Use a new gasket and torque the outlet retainers to 35 ft. lbs. (47 Nm).

Cooling System Bleeding

NOTE: Whenever the cooling system in a 1995–96 vehicle (except diesel engines or the U-Series vehicles) is completely drained and refilled with fresh coolant, 2 sealant pellets GMSPO part 3634621 must be added to the radiator. Failure to use the correct sealant pellets may result in premature coolant pump leakage. Do not add the pellets to the coolant recovery bottle as this may prevent the system from operating properly.

1. To bleed the system, start with the system cool, the radiator cap off and the radiator filled to about an inch below the filler neck.

2. Start the engine and run it at slightly above normal idle speed. If air bubbles appear and the coolant level drops, fill the system with a 50/50 antifreeze/water mixture to bring the level back to the proper level.

3. Run the engine until the thermostat opens and coolant flow is visible.

4. At this point, air is often expelled and the level may drop again. Keep refilling the system until the level is near the top of the radiator and remains constant.

5. Fill the radiator to the filler neck, then install the radiator filler cap.

6. Check and make sure the coolant reservoir is filled to the correct level.

FUEL SYSTEM

Fuel System Service Precaution

When working with the fuel system certain precautions should be taken; always work in a well ventilated area, keep a dry chemical (Class B) fire extinguisher near the work area. Always disconnect the negative battery cable and do not make any repairs to the fuel system until all the necessary steps for repair have been reviewed.

Relieving Fuel System Pressure

Before loosening or disconnecting any fuel fitting or system component, always relieve the fuel system pressure in order to help prevent the danger of fire or injury.

THROTTLE BODY FUEL INJECTION SYSTEMS

2.5L Engine

Unlike most GM vehicle Throttle body Fuel Injection (TBI) engines, then Throttle Body (TBI) unit used on the 2.5L engine does not contain an automatic pressure bleed down feature. Because of this, and the lack of service fittings, the pressure is relieved by disabling the fuel pump and allowing the engine to run until fuel pressure drops.

1. Place the transmission selector in **P** for automatic transmissions or Neutral for manual transmissions, then set the parking brake and block the drive wheels.

2. Loosen the fuel filler cap to relieve tank pressure.

3. Disengage the fuel pump/sending unit 3 terminal electrical connector at the fuel tank.

4. Start the engine and allow to run until it stops due to lack of fuel.

5. Engage the starter (turn key to start) for 3 seconds to dissipate pressure in the fuel lines.

6. Turn the ignition **OFF**, then reengage the connector at the fuel tank.

7. Disconnect the negative battery cable to prevent fuel spillage should the ignition key accidentally be turned **ON** with a fuel fitting disconnected.

8. When service is finished, tighten the fuel filler cap and connect the negative battery cable.

---------- CAUTION ----------

To reduce the chance of personal injury when disconnecting a fuel line, always cover the line with cloth to collect escaping fuel, then place the cloth in an approved container.

Except 2.5L Engine

Unlike most 2.5L TBI engine, the remaining GM vehicle TBI engines utilize an automatic pressure bleed down feature. But, some fuel pressure related steps should still be taken to assure safer working conditions.

1. Disconnect the negative battery cable to prevent fuel spillage should the ignition key accidentally be turned **ON** with a fuel fitting disconnected.
2. Loosen fuel filler cap to relieve fuel tank pressure.
3. The internal constant bleed feature of the Model 220 TBI unit relieves fuel pump system pressure when the engine is turned **OFF**. Therefore, no further action is required.

NOTE: Allow the engine to set for 5–10 minutes; this will allow the orifice (in the fuel system) to bleed off the pressure.

4. When fuel service is finished, tighten the fuel filler cap and connect the negative battery cable.

MULTI-PORT FUEL INJECTION SYSTEMS

The MFI, MFI-Turbo and CMFI fuel systems used on GM vehicles all operate under high fuel pressures. It is very important that the pressure be properly relieved prior to servicing the system or any of its components.

A schrader valve is provided on these fuel systems in order to conveniently test or release the system pressure. A fuel pressure gauge and adapter will be necessary to connect the gauge to the fitting. Most of the MFI and MFI-Turbo systems utilize a service valve on 1 end of the fuel rail assembly. The CMFI system covered here uses a valve located on the inlet pipe fitting, immediately before it enters the CMFI assembly (towards the rear of the engine).

1. Disconnect the negative battery cable to assure the prevention of fuel spillage if the ignition switch is accidentally turned **ON** while a fitting is still disconnected.
2. Loosen the fuel filler cap to release the fuel tank pressure.
3. Make sure the release valve on the fuel gauge is closed, then connect the fuel gauge to the pressure fitting located on the inlet fuel pipe fitting.

NOTE: When connecting the gauge to the fitting, be sure to wrap a rag around the fitting to avoid spillage. After repairs, place the rag in an approved container.

4. Install the bleed hose portion of the fuel gauge assembly into an approved container, then open the gauge release valve and bleed the fuel pressure from the system.
5. When the gauge is removed, be sure to open the bleed valve and drain all fuel from the gauge assembly.
6. When fuel service is finished, tighten the fuel filler cap and connect the negative battery cable.

Fuel Tank

REMOVAL AND INSTALLATION

Except Lumina, Silhouette and Trans Sport

EXCEPT S/T-SERIES EQUIPPED WITH SHIELD PACKAGE

1. Properly relieve the fuel system pressure, then disconnect the negative battery cable.
2. Use an approved hand operated pump to drain the fuel from the tank into a suitable container. If the pump is equipped with a static ground wire, be sure to connect it to a metal part of the tank before beginning.
3. Raise and support the vehicle safely.
4. If equipped, loosen and remove the tank plastic shield.
5. Loosen the retaining clamp and disconnect the tank filler hose from the tank neck.

NOTE: If fuel and vapor hoses or pump/sending unit wiring can be accessed at this time, they may be tagged and disconnected. If not, wait for the retaining straps to be loosened and lower the tank slightly for access.

6. Tag and disconnect and accessible wiring or hoses from the top of the fuel tank.
7. Have and assistant support the fuel tank, then remove the fuel tank-to-vehicle straps.

8. Lower the tank slightly, then remove the sending unit/pump wires, hoses and ground strap. Be sure to label all connections to ease installation.
9. Carefully lower the fuel tank from the vehicle and store in a safe place.

To install:

10. Raise the tank partially into position in the vehicle so there is access to the sending unit/pump assembly.
11. Connect the fuel/vapor hoses and wiring to the top of the fuel tank, as tagged during removal.
12. Carefully raise the fuel tank so it is fully into position and loosely secure the retaining straps. Make sure the wires and hoses are not pinched or damaged when raising the tank. Also, be sure the isolation strips (if used) are positioned between the retaining straps and the fuel tank.
13. It may be easier to connect the fuel filler hose to the tank neck at this time. If desired, connect the hose and secure the clamp.
14. Tighten the fuel tank retaining strap fasteners.
15. If not done earlier, connect the tank filler hose to the tank neck and secure using the clamp.
16. If equipped, install and secure the tank plastic shield.
17. Carefully lower the vehicle.
18. Refill the fuel tank and install the filler cap, then check for leaks.
19. Connect the negative battery cable.

S/T-SERIES EQUIPPED WITH SHIELD PACKAGE

1. Properly drain the fuel tank, then disconnect the negative battery cable.
2. Raise and support the vehicle safely.
3. Remove the shield forward support and bracket.
4. While supporting the shield and tank assembly with the help of both an assistant, remove the remaining bolts holding the assembly to the frame, then lower it sufficiently for access to the hoses and wires.
5. Tag and disengage the hoses and wires from the sending unit assembly.
6. Carefully lower the fuel tank and shield from the vehicle, then if necessary for service or replacement, separate the tank from the shield.

To install:

7. If separated, install the tank to the shield.
8. Carefully raise the tank and shield assembly partially into position with the help of an assistant.

9. Connect the wiring and hoses to the sending unit assembly, as tagged during removal.

10. Raise the tank and shield assembly fully into position, then secure to the frame using the lower retaining bolts.

11. Install the shield forward support bracket.

12. Carefully lower the vehicle.

13. Refill the fuel tank and install the filler cap, then check for leaks.

14. Connect the negative battery cable.

Lumina, Silhouette and Trans Sport

NOTE: Draining the fuel tank through the filler neck can only be performed after knocking the filler neck check ball into the tank. This will require the fuel pump/sending unit to be removed in order to retrieve and reposition the check ball.

1. Properly relieve the fuel system pressure, then disconnect the negative battery cable.

2. Using an approved pump, drain the fuel from the tank into a suitable container:

   a. Block the front wheels, then raise and support the rear of the vehicle safely so the rear bumper is 28 in. (71cm) above the ground.

   b. Loosen the fuel filler neck tube clamp at the tank, then wrap a shop towel around the neck tube and slowly disconnect the tube from the tank.

   c. Using a socket extension that is approximately 18 in. long, drive the filler neck check ball into the tank.

   d. Use a hand operated pump to drain the fuel from the tank into a suitable container.

3. Raise and support the vehicle safely and level for access to the vehicle underside.

4. For vehicles 1992–94, unbolt the rear exhaust system hangers from the converter to the tailpipe, then reposition the heat shield for access to the tank straps:

   a. Remove the tailpipe hanger attaching bolt.

   b. Remove the muffler hanger attaching bolts and the muffler hanger.

   c. Loosen the converter hanger attaching nuts.

   d. Remove the heat shield attaching screws. Note the position of the heat shield for installation purposes. .

   e. Support the exhaust and move the heat shield to gain access to the

right side fuel tank retaining strap attaching bolts.

5. Remove the in-line fuel filter body clips or attaching screws, as applicable.

6. Disengage the quick-connect fuel fittings both at the inlet side of the in-line fuel filter and at the fuel return line fitting located near the filter: Grasp both ends of a fuel line and twist ¼ turn in each direction to loosen any dirt in the quick-connect fitting. Squeeze the plastic tabs of the male ends of the connectors and pull the connections apart.

7. Disengage the fuel meter/sender assembly electrical wiring, then tag and disconnect the fuel vapor/vent hoses at the tank.

8. With the help of an assistant, properly support the fuel tank, then unbolt and remove the retaining strap.

9. Carefully lower the fuel tank. Remove the fuel sender and seal ring using J–35731 or equivalent tool, in order to recover and install the filler neck check ball.

   To install:

10. Remove the filler neck check ball from the tank and check for cracks or holes. If damaged, the filler neck extension pipe (tube) must be replaced.

11. Pop the filler neck check ball back into position in the filler neck tube.

12. Install the fuel sender and seal ring using tool J–35731 or equivalent tool.

13. With the aid of an assistant, raise the tank into position and secure using the retaining straps. Tighten the strap bolts to 18 ft. lbs. (24 Nm).

14. Connect the fuel vapor/vent hoses and electrical connections at the sender.

15. Apply a few drops of clean engine oil to the fuel feed/return line quick connect fittings, then push connectors together until a snap is heard. Pull on both lines and verify they are secure.

16. Secure the in-line fuel filter using the attaching screws or 2 new body clips, as applicable.

17. On vehicles 1992–94, reposition and secure the exhaust heat shield, the tail pipe, muffler and converter hangers. Make sure the heat shield is properly positioned as noted during removal.

18. Lower the vehicle an fill the tank.

19. Connect the negative battery cable.

20. Turn the ignition key **ON** for 2 seconds and then **OFF** for 10 seconds. Cycle the ignition as necessary to pressurize the fuel system; then check the system for leaks.

Fuel Filter

REMOVAL AND INSTALLATION

2.5L Engine

1. Properly relieve the fuel system pressure.

2. Disconnect the negative battery cable.

3. Locate the fuel filter by tracing a fuel line either from the tank forward or from the engine rearward. The filter is normally found along the frame rail or in the engine compartment.

4. Disengage the fuel line connections from the filter.

5. Remove the filter mounting clamp bolt and remove the filter.

6. Installation is the reverse of the removal procedure.

2.8L, 3.1L and 3.8L Engines

1. Disconnect the negative battery cable.

2. Remove the fuel line connections from the filter. If equipped with quick connect fittings, use tool J–37088A or equivalent to separate the lines.

NOTE: Before disengaging quick-connect fittings, always twist each side of the connection ¼ turn (in opposite directions) in order to loosen any dirt, then use compressed air (while wearing safety glasses) to blow the dirt free of the fittings.

3. Remove the filter mounting clamp bolt and remove the filter.

4. Installation is the reverse of the removal procedure. Before installing any quick-connect fittings, apply a few drops of clean engine oil to the male connector to assure proper seal and prevent a possible leak.

Except 2.5L, 2.8L, 3.1L and 3.8L Engines

The fuel filter is normally located along the frame rail of the vehicle. On some vehicles however, it may have been relocated to the engine compartment. When in doubt, trace a fuel line from the engine backwards or from the tank forward in order to locate the filter.

1. Properly relieve the fuel system pressure.

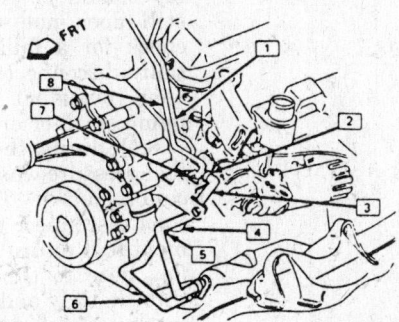

1. Fuel return pipe
2. Clamp
3. Fuel return hose
4. In-line fuel filter
5. Clamp
6. Fuel feed hose
7. O-ring
8. Tighten nut to 20 ft. lbs. (26 Nm)

85473055

Fuel filter mounting — 2.8L engine

2. Disconnect the negative battery cable.

3. Raise and support the vehicle safely.

4. Disengage the fuel line connections from the filter.

5. Remove the bolt from the filter mounting clamp, then remove the clamp and filter assembly. Separate the filter from the clamp.

6. To install, reverse the removal procedures ensuring the filter flow is in the correct direction. Start the engine and check for leaks.

NOTE: The filter has an arrow (fuel flow direction) on the side of the case, be sure to install it correctly in the system, the with arrow facing away from the fuel tank.

Electric Fuel Pump

PRESSURE TESTING

Throttle Body Injection (TBI)

1. Turn the engine **OFF** and relieve the fuel system pressure.

2. Disconnect the negative battery cable.

3. Disconnect the fuel supply line somewhere between the in-line filter and the throttle body. Install a suita-

ble fuel pressure gauge using a T fitting in the fuel line.

NOTE: On some vehicles it may be necessary to remove the air cleaner for easier access to the fuel supply line. If so, be sure to plug the THERMAC vacuum port while the cleaner is removed.

4. Connect the negative battery cable. Verify there is a sufficient quantity of fuel in the tank.

5. Run the fuel pump and check the fuel pressure. There are 3 possible methods to run the fuel pump. Start and run the engine, apply 12 volts to the fuel pressure check connector (normally a single terminal red connector located on the driver's side of the engine compartment) using a fused jumper wire or cycle the ignition without starting the engine. If cycling the ignition is chosen, each time the ignition is turned **ON**, the pump will run for 2 seconds.

6. Observe the fuel pressure with the pump running, it should be 9–13 psi. (62–90 kPa) except for 1994–96 G-Vans equipped with a 7.4L engine which should be 26–32 psi (179–220 kPa). The system pressure must be checked with the pump running because on most applications the pressure will drop immediately after the pump shuts off.

7. If the fuel pressure reading is not as specified, inspect the fuel pump for proper operation, the lines and filter for kinks or clogging.

8. On testing is complete, depressurize the fuel system, then remove the fuel pressure gauge and adapter. Reconnect the fuel line, start the engine and check for fuel leaks.

Multi-Port Fuel Injection

2.2L AND 3.8L ENGINES

1. Properly relieve the fuel system pressure.

2. Leave the gauge attached to the pressure fitting on the fuel inlet pipe.

3. If disconnected during the fuel pressure relief procedure, reconnect the negative battery terminal.

4. Verify there is a sufficient quantity of fuel in the tank.

5. Turn the ignition switch **ON**, the fuel pump should run for 2 seconds and turn **OFF**. If necessary, cycle the ignition **OFF** for 10 seconds and then **ON** again in order to build maximum system pressure. The pressure gauge reading should be approximately 41–47 psi. (284–325 kPa).

6. Turn the ignition switch **OFF** and observe the pressure gauge, the reading may vary slightly, then should hold and not leak down.

7. Start the vehicle and observe the gauge, the pressure should be 3–10 psi (21–69 kPa) lower because of vacuum applied to the regulator.

8. If not as specified, inspect the pump, regulator, filter and lines for proper operation, kinks or clogging.

4.3L (VIN Z) TURBOCHARGED ENGINE

1. Properly relieve the fuel system pressure.

2. Leave the gauge attached to the pressure fitting on the fuel inlet pipe.

3. If disconnected during the fuel pressure relief procedure, reconnect the negative battery terminal.

4. Verify there is a sufficient quantity of fuel in the tank.

5. Turn the ignition switch **ON**, the fuel pump should run for 2 seconds and turn **OFF**; the pressure gauge reading should be approximately 35–38 psi. (245–256 kPa).

6. Turn the ignition switch **OFF** and observe the pressure gauge, the reading should not leak down.

7. Start the vehicle and observe the gauge, the pressure should be 25–30 psi because of vacuum applied to the regulator.

8. If not as specified, inspect the pump, regulator, filter and lines for proper operation, kinks or clogging.

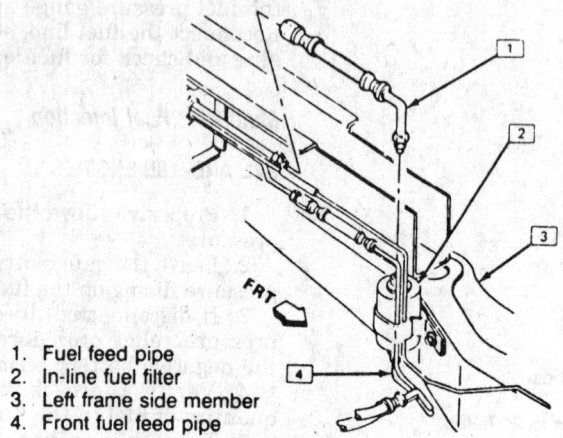

1. Fuel feed pipe
2. In-line fuel filter
3. Left frame side member
4. Front fuel feed pipe

85473056

Common fuel filter mounting for the 4.3L engine

Central Multi-Port Fuel Injection (CMFI)

1. Properly relieve the fuel system pressure.

2. Leave the gauge attached to the pressure fitting on the fuel inlet pipe.

3. If disconnected during the fuel pressure relief procedure, reconnect the negative battery terminal.

4. If the engine will run, start the engine and allow it to run at normal idle speed. The fuel pressure should be 55–61 psi (380–420 kPa). Once the engine is at normal operating temperature, open the throttle quickly while noting fuel pressure; it should quickly approach 61 psi (40 kPa) if all components are operating properly (there is no need to proceed further). If the pressure was in specification before, but does not approach 61 psi (420 kPa) on acceleration, the pressure regulator in the CMFI unit is faulty and the assembly should be replaced.

5. If the engine does not run, turn the ignition **ON**, but do not attempt to start the engine. Listen for the fuel pump to run. Within 2 seconds of turning the ignition **ON** pressure should be 55–61 psi (380–420 kPa) while the pump is running. Once the pump stops, pressure may vary by several pounds, then it should hold

steady. If the pressure does not hold steady, wait 10 seconds and repeat this step, but pinch the fuel pressure line flexible hose and watch if the pressure holds. If it still does not hold, the CMFI unit should be replaced. If the pressure holds with the pressure line pinched, check for a partially disconnected fuel dampener (pulsator) or faulty in-tank fuel pump.

6. If the fuel pump did not run or system pressure did not reach specification, locate the fuel pump test connector. The test connector is usually found on the driver's side of the engine compartment (on or near the fender), with a single wire (usually red) leading from the relay to the connector. Using a 10 amp fused jumper wire, apply battery voltage to the test connector in order to energize and run the fuel pump. The pump should run and produce fuel pressure of 55–61 psi (380–420 kPa). If the pump does not run, check the relay and fuel pump wiring.

7. If the pump pressure was lower than specification, first check for a restricted fuel line, filter or a disconnected fuel pulse dampener (pulsator) and repair/replace, as necessary. If no restrictions can be found, restrict the flexible fuel return line (by gradually pinching it) until the pres-

sure rises above 61 psi (420 kPa), but do not allow pressure to exceed 75 psi (517 kPa). If the fuel pressure rises above specification with the return line restricted, then the pressure regulator is faulty and the CMFI assembly should be replaced. If pressure still does not reach specification, check for a faulty fuel pump, partially disconnected fuel pulse dampener (pulsator), partially restricted pump strainer or an incorrect pump.

8. If during the previous steps, the fuel pressure was higher than specification, relieve the system pressure, then disconnect the engine compartment fuel return line. Attach a ⁵⁄₁₆ ID flex hose to the fuel line from the throttle body and place the other end into an approved gasoline container. Cycle the ignition in order to energize the fuel pump and watch system pressure. If pressure is still higher, check for restrictions in the line between the pressure regulator and the point where it was disconnected. Repair or replace the line if restrictions are found or replace the CMFI assembly with the faulty internal pressure regulator if no other causes of high pressure are identified. If fuel pressure is normal only with the rest of the return line out of the circuit, check that remaining line for restrictions and repair or replace, as necessary.

9. Once the test is completed, depressurize the fuel system and remove the gauge.

REMOVAL AND INSTALLATION

1. Properly relieve the fuel system pressure.

2. Disconnect the negative battery cable.

3. Drain and remove the fuel tank from the vehicle

4. Using a suitable spanner wrench, turn the fuel pump/sending unit assembly locking ring (located on top of the fuel tank) counterclockwise, then carefully lift the assembly from the tank and remove the pump from the fuel lever sending device.

5. Installation is the reverse of the removal procedure. The fuel pump/sending unit assembly O-ring should be replaced whenever the tank is removed.

Fuel Injection

IDLE SPEED ADJUSTMENT

Idle speed and mixture adjustments on these engines are controlled by the

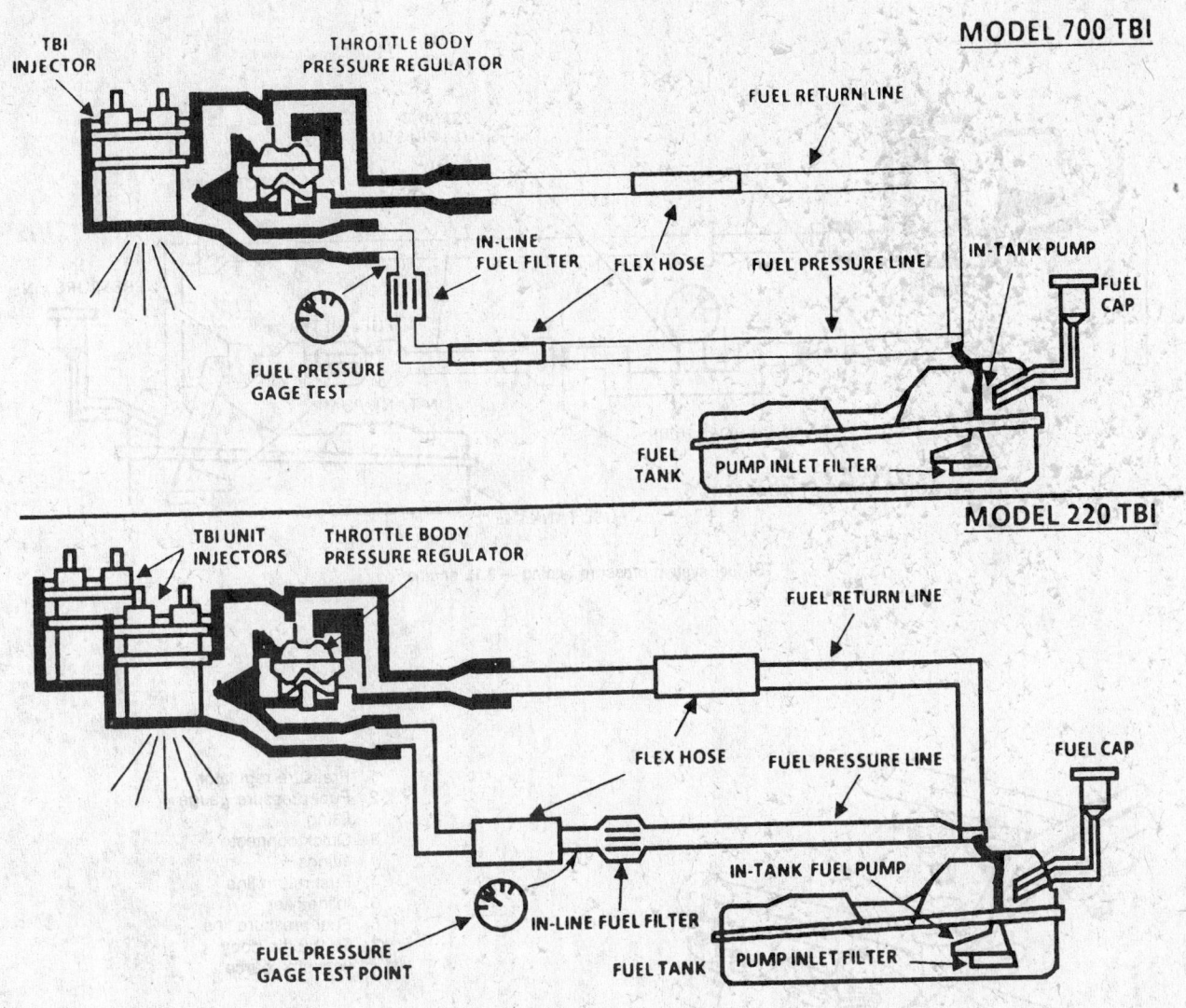

MODEL 700 TBI

TBI INJECTOR

THROTTLE BODY PRESSURE REGULATOR

FUEL RETURN LINE

IN-LINE FUEL FILTER

FLEX HOSE

FUEL PRESSURE LINE

IN-TANK PUMP

FUEL CAP

FUEL PRESSURE GAGE TEST

FUEL TANK

PUMP INLET FILTER

MODEL 220 TBI

TBI UNIT INJECTORS

THROTTLE BODY PRESSURE REGULATOR

FUEL RETURN LINE

FLEX HOSE

FUEL PRESSURE LINE

FUEL CAP

IN-TANK FUEL PUMP

IN-LINE FUEL FILTER

FUEL PRESSURE GAGE TEST POINT

FUEL TANK

PUMP INLET FILTER

85473057

Common TBI fuel system pressure testing — 2.5L, 2.8L and 4.3L (VIN Z) engines shown

computer modules, regulated through the IAC valve and fuel injector(s), respectively. No periodic check or adjustments are necessary for these systems.

However, the minimum idle speed on some systems 1992–93 and on the 7.4L engine TBI system used 1992–96 may be adjusted if the throttle body has been replaced AND an incorrect idle speed cannot be obtained. These adjustments should not be performed unless all other possible causes (vacuum leaks, bad fuel pressure, faulty wiring or components) have already been eliminated.

Compact Pick-Up, Utility and Van

2.5L ENGINE

The throttle stop screw that is used to adjust the idle speed of the vehicle is preset at the factory. The throttle stop screw is then covered with a steel plug to prevent adjustment in the field. If it is necessary to gain access to the throttle stop screw, the following procedure will allow access to the throttle stop screw without removing the TBI unit from the manifold

1. Using a small punch or equivalent, mark the center line of the throttle stop screw. Drill a 5/32 in.

diameter hole through the casting of the hardened steel plug.

2. Using a 5/16 in. diameter punch or equivalent, punch out the steel plug.

3. With the transmission in **P** for automatic transmission or neutral for manual transmission equipped vehicles, the parking brake applied and the drive wheels blocked, remove the air cleaner and plug the thermac vacuum port, as required.

4. If equipped with automatic transmission, remove the transmission detent cable from the throttle control bracket in order to gain access to the minimum air adjustment screw.

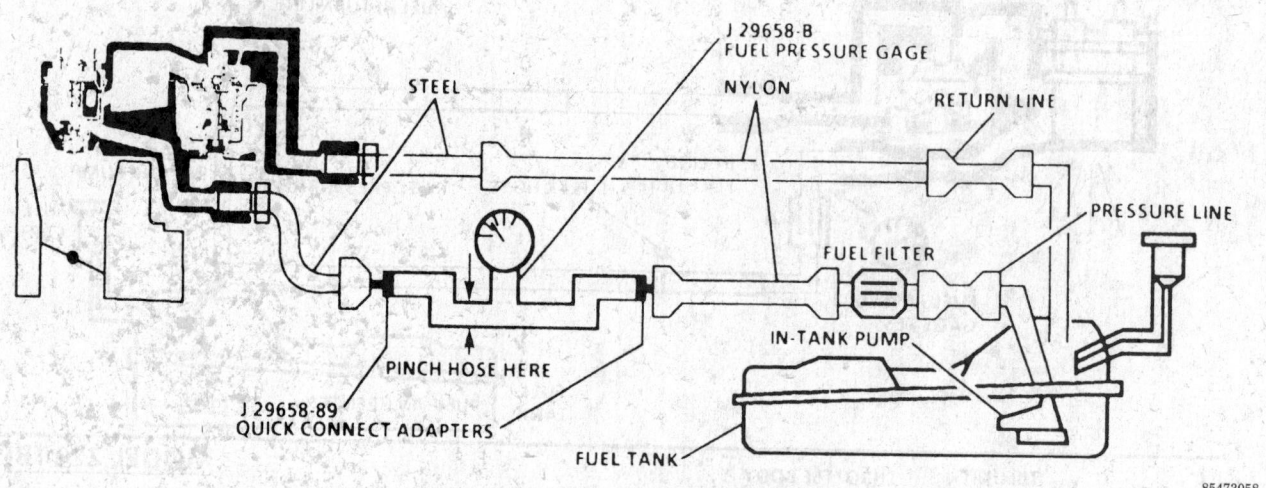

TBI fuel system pressure testing — 3.1L engine

1. Pressure regulator
2. Fuel pressure gauge fitting
3. Quick connect fittings
4. Fuel return line
5. Inline filter
6. Fuel pressure line
7. To throttle body vacuum source

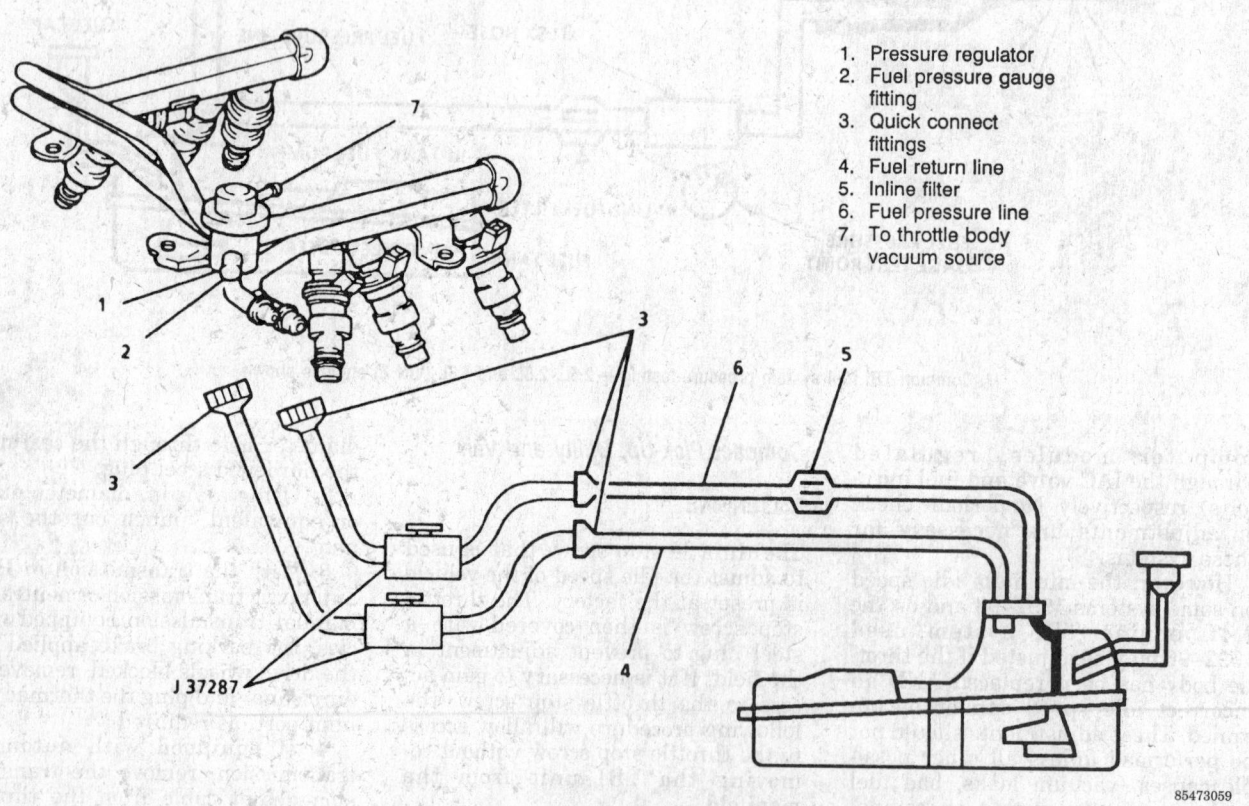

MFI system pressure testing — 3.8L engine

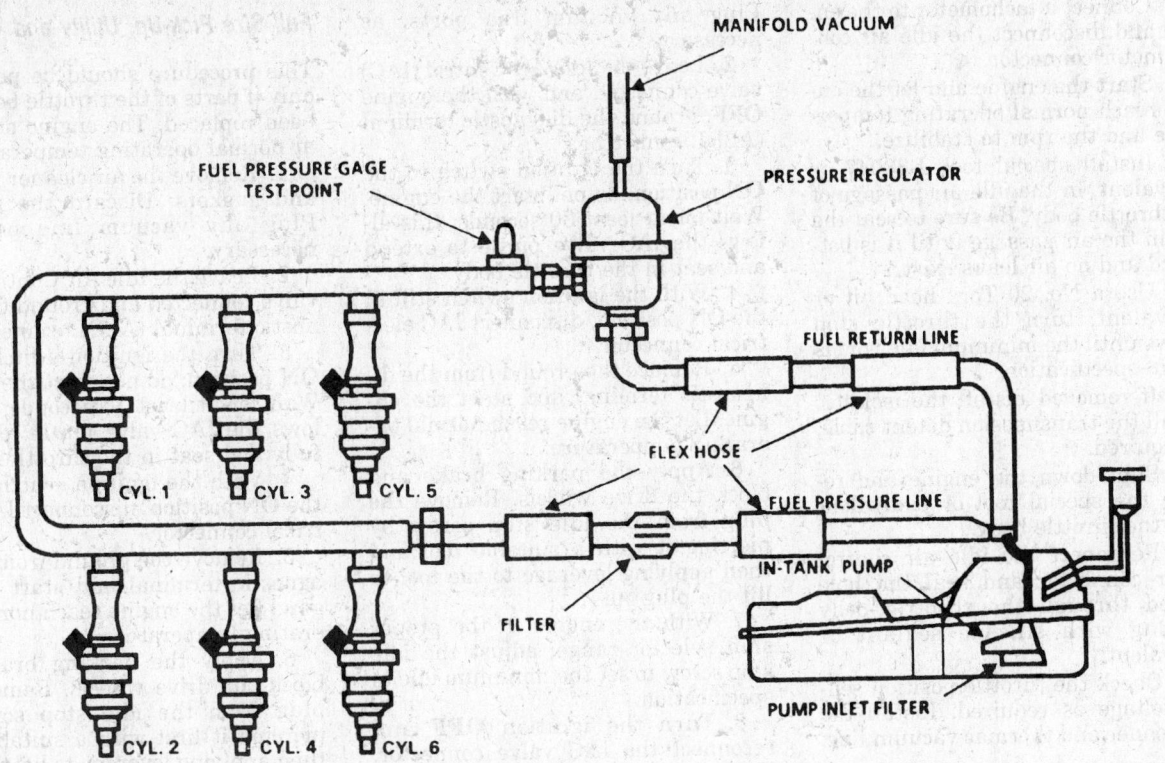

MFI system pressure testing — 4.3L (VIN Z) Turbocharged engine

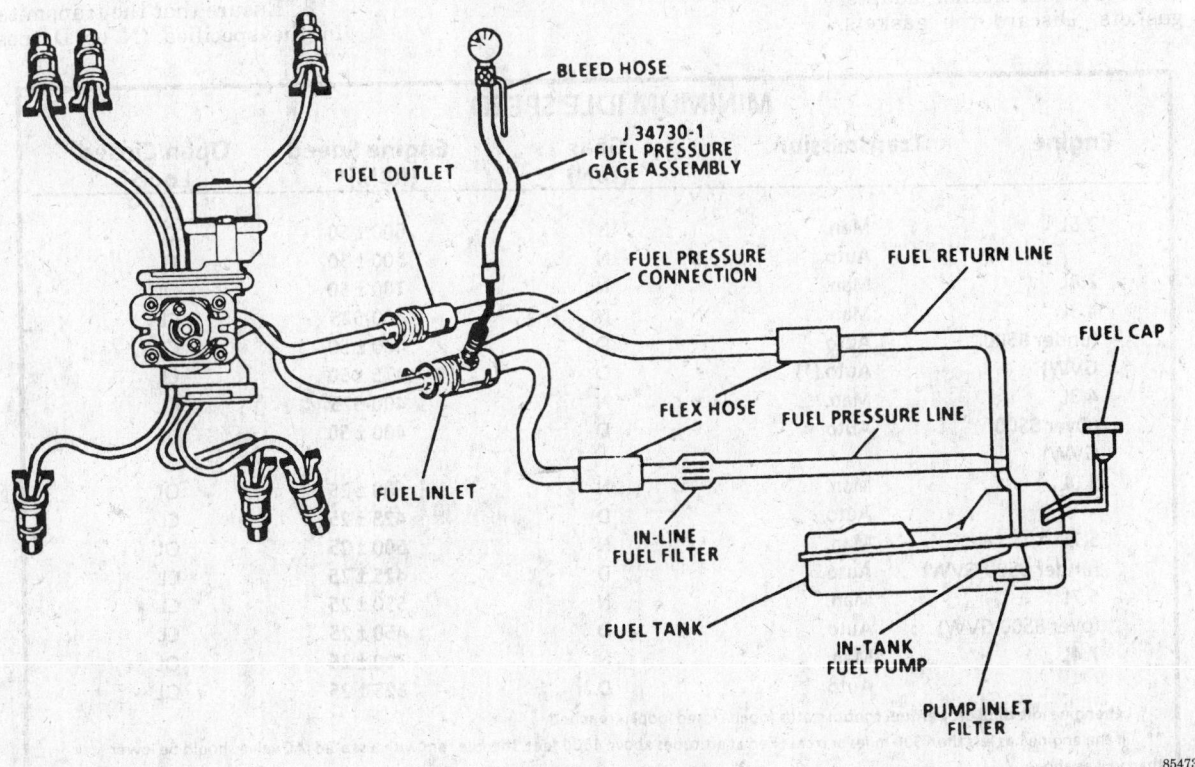

CMFI system pressure testing — 4.3L (VIN W) engine

5. Connect a tachometer to the engine and disconnect the idle air control motor connector.

6. Start the engine and let the engine reach normal operating temperature and the rpm to stabilize.

7. Install special tool J-33047 or equivalent, in the idle air passage of the throttle body. Be sure to seat the tool in the air passage until it is bottomed and no air leaks exist.

8. Use a No. 20 Torx head bit or equivalent, turn the throttle stop screws until the minimum idle rpm is within specification.

9. If removed install the isolator. Install the transmission detent cable, as required.

10. Shut down the engine and remove the special tool or equivalent from the throttle body.

11. Reconnect the idle air control motor connector and seal the hole drilled through the throttle body housing with silicone sealant or equivalent.

12. Check the throttle position sensor voltage as required. Install the air cleaner and thermac vacuum line.

2.8L, 3.1L AND 4.3L (VIN Z) TBI ENGINES

1. Remove the air cleaner, adapter and gaskets. Discard the gaskets.

Plug any vacuum line ports, as necessary.

2. Leave the Idle Air Control (IAC) valve connected and with the engine OFF, ground the diagnostic terminal (ALDL connector).

3. Turn the ignition switch to the ON position, do not start the engine. Wait for at least 30 seconds; this allows the IAC valve pintle to extend and seat in the throttle body.

4. With the ignition switch still in the ON position, disconnect IAC electrical connector.

5. Remove the ground from the diagnostic terminal and start the engine. Let the engine reach normal operating temperature.

6. Apply the parking brake and block the drive wheels. Remove the plug from the idle stop screw by piercing it with a suitable tool and then applying leverage to the tool to lift the plug out.

7. With the engine in the proper shift selector range, adjust the idle stop screw to set the minimum idle to specification.

8. Turn the ignition OFF and reconnect the IAC valve connector. Unplug any plugged vacuum line ports and install the air cleaner, adapter and new gaskets.

Full Size Pick-Up, Utility and Van

This procedure should be performed only if parts of the throttle body have been replaced. The engine should be at normal operating temperature

1. Remove the air cleaner, adapter and gaskets. Discard the gaskets. Plug any vacuum line ports, as necessary.

2. Leave the Idle Air Control (IAC) valve connected and ground the diagnostic terminal (ALDL connector).

3. Turn the ignition switch to the ON position; do not start the engine. Wait for at least 10 seconds; this allows the IAC valve pintle to extend fully and seat in the throttle body.

4. With the ignition switch still in the ON position, disconnect IAC electrical connector.

5. Remove the ground from the diagnostic terminal and start the engine. Let the engine reach normal operating temperature.

6. Apply the parking brake and block the drive wheels. Remove the plug from the idle stop screw by piercing it first with a suitable tool, then applying leverage to lift the plug out.

7. Connect a suitable tachometer to the engine.

8. Ensure that the transmission is in the specified (N or D) position,

MINIMUM IDLE SPEED				
Engine	Transmission	Gear (D/N)	Engine Speed (RPM)**	Open/Closed Loop*
2.5L	Man.	N	600 ± 50	CL
	Auto.	N	500 ± 50	CL
2.8L	Man.	N	700 ± 50	OL
4.3L	Man.	N	400-525	CL
(under 8500	Auto.	D	400 ± 50	CL
GVW)	Auto.(1)	D	475 ± 50	CL
4.3L	Man.	N	400-525	CL
(Over 8500	Auto.	D	400 ± 50	CL
GVW)				
5.0L	Man.	N	500 ± 25	OL
	Auto.	D	425 ± 25	CL
5.7L	Man.	N	500 ± 25	OL
(under 8500 GVW)	Auto.	D	425 ± 25	CL
5.7L	Man.	N	550 ± 25	CL
(over 8500 GVW)	Auto.	D	450 ± 25	CL
7.4L	Man.	N	700 ± 25	OL
	Auto.	D	625 ± 25	OL

* Let engine idle until proper fuel control status (open/closed loop) is reached.

** If the engine has less than 500 miles or is checked at altitudes above 1500 feet, the idle rpm with a seated IAC valve should be lower than valves above.

(1) 4.3L High-Output ML Van Series

Minimum idle air rate — 1992–93 vehicles

85473062

MINIMUM IDLE SPEED

Engine	Transmission	Gear (Drive/Neutral)	Engine Speed (RPM) **	Open/Closed Loop *
7.4L	MAN	NEUTRAL	625 ± 25	CL
	AUTO	DRIVE	625 ± 25	CL

*   Let engine idle until proper fuel control status ("Open/Closed Loop") is reached.

**   If the engine has less than 500 miles or is checked at altitudes above 1500 feet, the idle RPM with a seated IAC valve should be lower than valves above.

85473063

Minimum idle air rate — 1994–96 engines

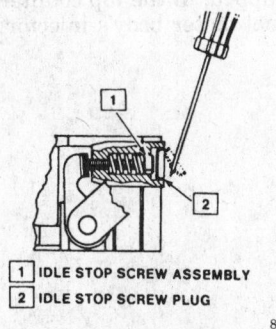

1 IDLE STOP SCREW ASSEMBLY
2 IDLE STOP SCREW PLUG

85473064

Removing idle stop screw plug for adjustment — TBI engines

with the ECM in "Open or Closed" loop as specified.

9. Adjust the idle stop screw to obtain the specified RPM reading.

10. Turn the ignition **OFF** and reconnect the IAC valve connector. Unplug any plugged vacuum line ports and install the air cleaner, adapter and new gaskets.

11. Reset the IAC valve as follows:

NOTE: If installing a new IAC valve, measure and adjust the valve accordingly. If reinstalling a used IAC valve, do not push or pull on the pintle to adjust pintle length or damage to the IAC

worm gear might occur.The valve is preset at the factory and will self-adjust when the following procedure is performed.

a. Set a new IAC valve by measuring the distance between the tip of the pintle and the valve mounting surface.

b. If greater than 1.10 in. (28mm), use light finger pressure to slowly retract the pintle. The force required to retract a new valve will not damage the valve.

c. Install the valve and connect the wire connector.

d. Reset a used IAC valve pintle position by depressing the accelerator pedal slightly, start the engine and run for 5 seconds, turn the key **OFF** for 10 seconds, then restart the vehicle and check for proper idle operation.

CONTROLLED IDLE SPEED CHECK

Idle speed adjustments are not provided for most 1994–96 vehicles (with the exception of the 7.4L engine). However, a controlled idle speed check may be made on most vehicles (except the U-Series van) to determine if the computer module is successfully regulating the idle speed. If

an improper idle speed is indicated by the check, inspect all components of the engine control systems.

1. Using a scan tool, check to be sure no codes are stored in the computer self-diagnosis memory. If codes are stored, diagnose and correct the problems before proceeding.

2. Verify that the idle air control system is working correctly, then check to make sure the ignition timing is properly set.

3. Connect the Tech 1® or equivalent scan tool to the Diagnostic Link Connector (DLC). Make sure the tool is in the OPEN mode.

4. Start and run the engine at normal operating temperature.

5. If equipped with an automatic transmission, use the scan tool to check for a proper state of the PRNDL position (R-D-L) switch.

6. Using the scan tool, compare readings of the controlled idle speed and IAC valve pintle position to the specifications for that engine.

NOTE: For purposes of the minimum idle speed and IAC valve specifications, the G-Series Van should be treated as a C/K-Series.

7. If the readings agree with specifications, the system is operating properly. If not, the system must be

3-47

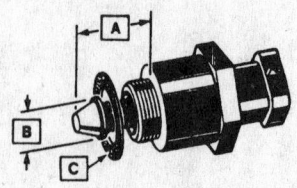

A	DISTANCE OF PINTLE EXTENSION
B	DIAMETER AND SHAPE OF PINTLE
C	IAC VALVE GASKET

85473065

A common threaded IAC valve used on GM vehicles

thoroughly checked for faulty connections or components.

Fuel Injector

REMOVAL AND INSTALLATION

TBI Engines

—————— CAUTION ——————
When removing the injector(s), be careful not to damage the electrical connector pins (on top of the injector), the injector fuel filter and the nozzle. The fuel injector is serviced as a complete assembly

ONLY, it is an electrical component and should not be immersed in any kind of cleaner.

1. Properly relieve the fuel system pressure, then disconnect the negative battery cable.

2. Remove the air cleaner assembly.

3. At the injector connector(s), squeeze the 2 tabs together and pull straight up to disengage connector from the injector.

4. Except for the 2.5L engine (which is equipped with the model 700 TBI unit), loosen the fuel meter cover retaining screws, then remove the cover from the fuel meter body, but leave the cover gasket in place.

5. For the 2.5L engine (model 700 TBI unit), loosen the injector retainer screw, then remove the screw and retainer from the top of the throttle body.

6. Using a small pry bar and a round fulcrum, carefully pry the injector until it is free, then remove the injector from the fuel meter body.

7. Remove the small O-ring from the nozzle end of the injector. If equipped and removal is necessary, carefully rotate the injector's fuel filter back and forth to remove it from the base of the injector.

8. If applicable (except for the 2.5L engine), remove and discard the fuel meter cover gasket.

9. Remove the large O-ring and back-up washer, if equipped, from the top of the counterbore of the fuel meter body injector cavity.

To install:

NOTE: Be sure the replacement injectors have an identical part number. For some applications, the 4.3L (VIN Z) uses 2 different injectors that have different flow rates. Injectors with part no. 5235134 (color coded orange and green) are located on the throttle lever side, and those with part no. 5235342 (color coded pink and brown) are located on the TPS side.

10. If removed, with the larger end of the filter facing the injector (so the filter covers the raised rib of the injector base) install the filter by twisting it into position on the injector.

11. Lubricate the new O-rings with clean automatic transmission fluid, then install the small O-ring on the nozzle end of the injector. Be sure the O-ring is pressed up against the injector or injector filter (as applicable).

12. Install the steel backup washer, if equipped, in the top counterbore of the fuel meter body's injector cavity,

CONTROLLED IDLE SPEED
NOTE: Engine at operating temperature

Engine	Transmission	Gear (Drive/Neutral)	Idle Speed (RPM)	IAC Counts *	Open/Closed Loop
4.3L (Central MFI)					
M-VAN	AUTO	DRIVE	550	5-40	CL
L-VAN	AUTO	DRIVE	625	15-50	CL

* Add 2 counts for engines with less than 500 miles. Add 2 counts for every 1000 ft. above sea level.

85473066

Controlled idle speed check specifications — M/L-Series

CONTROLLED IDLE SPEED
NOTE: Engine at operating temperature

Engine	Transmission	Gear (Drive/Neutral)	Idle Speed (RPM)	IAC Counts *	Open/Closed Loop **
2.2L S-TRK	MAN	NEUTRAL	950	5-20	CL
	AUTO	DRIVE	800	15-40	CL
4.3L (TBI) S/T-PICKUP	AUTO	DRIVE	650	5-30	CL
	MANUAL	NEUTRAL	725	3-30	
4.3L (TBI) S/T UTILITY	MANUAL	NEUTRAL	700	5-30	CL
4.3L (CMFI) S/T UTILITY	AUTO	DRIVE	600	5-40	CL
PICKUP	AUTO	DRIVE	625	15-50	CL
	MANUAL	NEUTRAL	650	15-50	CL

* On a manual transmission vehicle the Tech 1 will display RDL in neutral.

* Add 2 counts for engines with less than 500 miles. Add 2 counts for every 1000 ft. above sea level.

** Let engine idle until proper fuel control status ("Open/Closed Loop") is reached.

85473067

Controlled idle speed check specifications — S/T-Series

CONTROLLED IDLE SPEED
Note: Engine at operating temperature 92°C to 104°C (196°F to 222°F)

Engine	Transmission	Gear (Drive/Neutral)	Idle Speed (RPM)	IAC Counts *	Open/Closed Loop **
4.3L (TBI) UNDER 8500 GVW C/K-TRK	AUTO	DRIVE	590 ± 25	5-30	CL
	MANUAL	NEUTRAL	550 ± 25	5-30	
4.3L (TBI) C/K-TRK (OVER 8500 GVW)	AUTO	DRIVE	650 ± 25	5-30	CL
	MANUAL	NEUTRAL	700 ± 25	5-30	CL
5.0L C/K-TRK	MAN	NEUTRAL	650 ± 25	5-30	CL
	AUTO	DRIVE	550 ± 25	5-30	CL
5.7L C/K (under 8500 GVW)	MAN	NEUTRAL	660 ± 25	5-30	CL
	AUTO	DRIVE	525 ± 25	5-30	CL
5.7L C/K (over 8500 GVW)	MAN	NEUTRAL	590 ± 25	5-30	CL
	AUTO	DRIVE	550 ± 25	5-30	CL
7.4L C/K	MAN	NEUTRAL	750 ± 25	5-30	CL
	AUTO	DRIVE	675 ± 25	5-30	CL

* On manual transmission vehicles the Tech 1 will display RDL in neutral.

* Add 2 counts for engines with less than 500 miles. Add 2 counts for every 1000 ft. above sea level (4.3L and V8).

** Let engine idle until proper fuel control status ("Open/Closed Loop") is reached.

85473068

Controlled idle speed check specifications — G-Series and C/K-Series

then install the new large O-ring directly over the backup washer. Make sure the O-ring is properly seated in the cavity and is flush with the top of the fuel meter body casting surface.

NOTE: If the backup washer and large O-ring are not properly installed before the fuel injector, a fuel leak will likely result.

13. For the model 220 TBI unit (all engines except the 2.5L), install the fuel injector into the cavity by aligning the raised lug on the injector base with the cast notch in the fuel meter body cavity. Once the injector is aligned, carefully push down on the injector by hand until it is fully seated in the cavity. When properly aligned and installed, the injector terminals will be approximately parallel to the throttle shaft.

14. For the 2.5L engine (model 700 TBI unit), carefully align and install the injector to the cavity. Push straight down until the injector is properly seated. The injector connector should be installed parallel to the casting support rib and facing in the general direction of the cut-out in the fuel meter body provided for the wire grommet.

15. Except for the 2.5L engine, position a new fuel meter cover gasket, then install the cover to the body, making sure the gasket remains in position. Using a suitable threadlocking compound, install and tighten the cover retainers to 30 inch lbs. (4 Nm).

16. For the model 2.5L engine, install the injector retainer and coat the retainer screw threads with a suitable threadlocking compound, then install and tighten the screw to secure the injector.

17. Engage the injector electrical connector(s).

18. Connect the negative battery cable, then turn the **ON** to pressurize the fuel system and check for leaks.

19. Install the air cleaner assembly, then start the engine and check for leaks.

2.2L MFI Engine

The bottom feed fuel injectors used on the 2.2L MFI engine are installed to the lower intake manifold assembly. For access, the upper intake must first be removed.

NOTE: Take care when servicing the lower intake and fuel injectors to prevent dirt or contaminants from entering the fuel system. All openings in the fuel

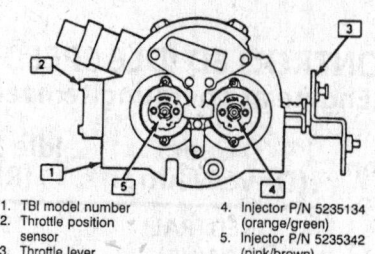

1. TBI model number
2. Throttle position sensor
3. Throttle lever
4. Injector P/N 5235134 (orange/green)
5. Injector P/N 5235342 (pink/brown)

85473069

Fuel injector location — Model 220 TBI unit (used on engines, except the 2.5L)

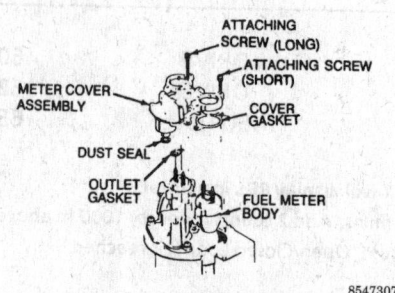

ATTACHING SCREW (LONG)
ATTACHING SCREW (SHORT)
METER COVER ASSEMBLY
COVER GASKET
DUST SEAL
OUTLET GASKET
FUEL METER BODY

85473070

Exploded view of the fuel meter cover mounting — Model 220 TBI unit

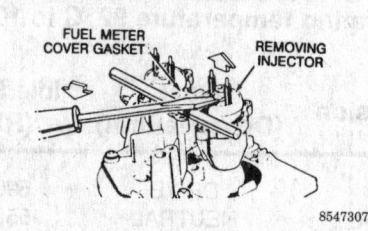

FUEL METER COVER GASKET
REMOVING INJECTOR

85473071

Removing the fuel injector — Model 220 TBI unit

lines and passages should be capped or plugged while disconnected.

1. Properly relieve the fuel system pressure, then disconnect the negative battery cable.

2. Remove the accelerator bracket retaining bolts/nuts, then remove or reposition the bracket.

3. Remove the upper intake manifold assembly.

4. Remove the fuel return line bracket nut, then remove the return

line retaining bracket and position it away from the pressure regulator.

5. Remove the fuel pressure regulator assembly.

NOTE: Do not attempt to remove the injectors from their bores while lifting upward on the retaining bracket or damage may occur. Do not attempt to remove the bracket without first removing the pressure regulator.

6. Remove the fuel injector retainer bracket attaching screws, then remove the bracket by carefully sliding it off in order to clear the injector slots and regulator.

7. Tag and disengage the injector electrical connectors.

8. Remove the fuel injectors from the lower intake manifold assembly, then remove and discard the old O-rings.

To install:

NOTE: Because each injector is calibrated for a specific flow rate, make sure to only replace fuel injectors using an identical part number to the old injectors.

9. Lubricate the new O-ring seals with clean engine oil, then position them on the injectors.

10. Carefully install the injectors assemblies into the lower manifold sockets, making sure the electrical connectors are facing inward.

11. Position the injector bracket to the retaining slots and regulator are aligned with the bracket slots.

12. Engage the injector electrical connectors as tagged during removal.

13. Install the fuel pressure regulator assembly.

14. Make sure the threads of the injector retainer bracket screws are coated with a suitable threadlocking compound such as Loctite®262 or equivalent, then install and tighten them to 31 inch lbs. (3.5 Nm).

15. Install the upper intake manifold assembly.

16. If not done already, install the accelerator cable bracket. Tighten the retaining nut to 22 ft. lbs. (30 Nm) and the retaining bolts to 18 ft. lbs. (25 Nm).

17. Connect the negative battery cable.

18. Pressurize the fuel system by cycling the ignition (without attempting to start the engine), then check for leaks.

19. If not done already, install the air inlet duct

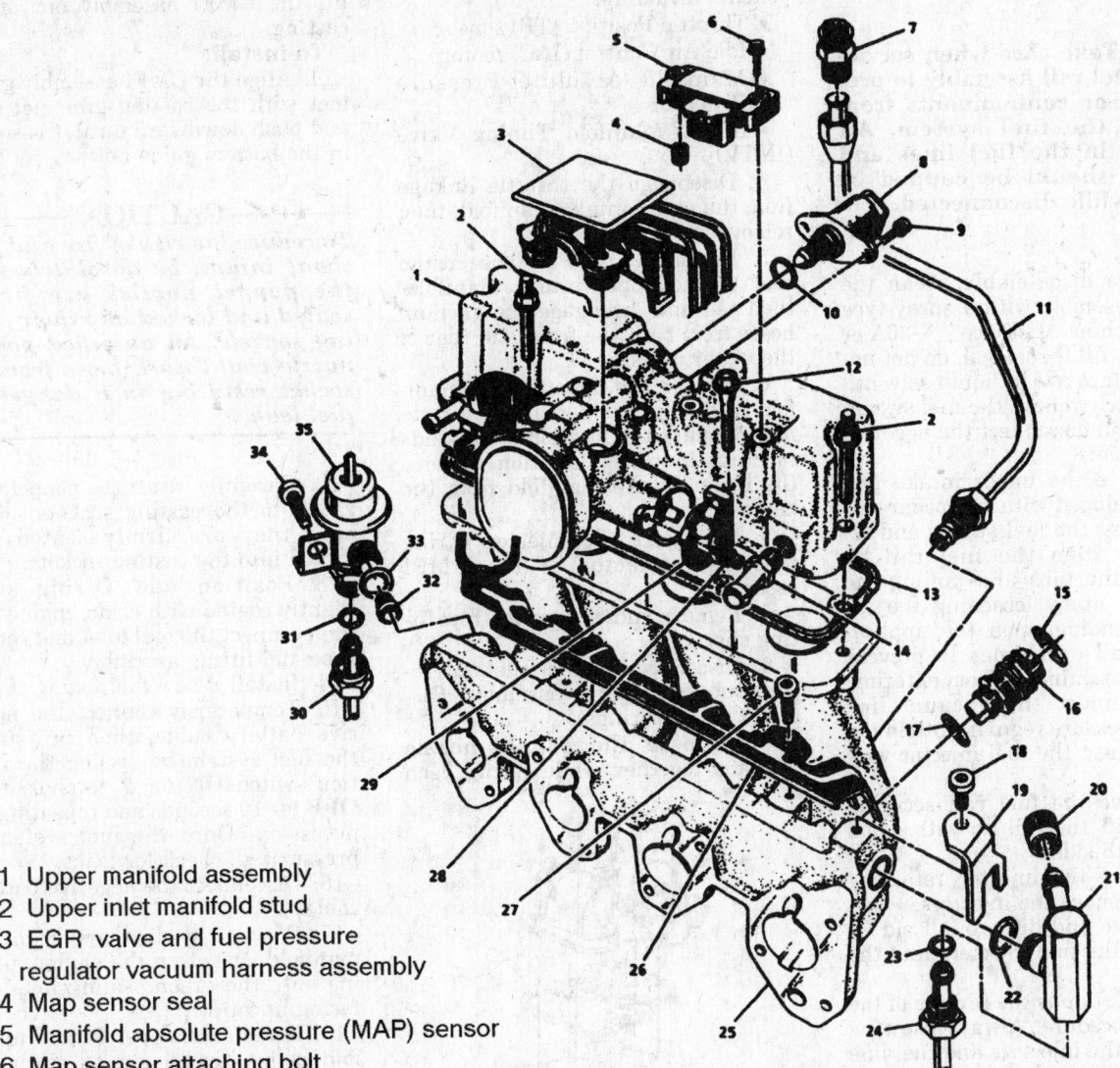

1 Upper manifold assembly
2 Upper inlet manifold stud
3 EGR valve and fuel pressure
   regulator vacuum harness assembly
4 Map sensor seal
5 Manifold absolute pressure (MAP) sensor
6 Map sensor attaching bolt
7 EGR transfer tube fitting and washer assembly
8 Idle air control (IAC) valve assembly
9 IAC valve attaching screw
10 IAC valve o-ring
11 EGR transport tube assembly
12 Upper inlet manifold bolt
13 Upper inlet manifold gasket
14 Power brake fitting
15 Fuel injector upper o-ring
16 MFI fuel injector assembly (bottom feed)
17 Fuel injector lower o-ring
18 Fuel pressure connection fitting screw
19 Fuel pressure connection fitting bracket
20 Fuel pressure connection cap
21 Fuel pressure connection fitting

22 Fuel pressure connection fitting o-ring
23 Fuel feed pipe fitting o-ring
24 Fuel feed pipe assembly
25 Lower manifold assembly
26 Injectors retainer
27 Injectors retainer attaching screw
28 TP sensor attaching screw
29 Throttle position (TP) sensor
30 Fuel return pipe assembly
31 Fuel return pipe fitting o-ring
32 Filter (if so equipped) screen
33 Fuel pressure regulator o-ring
34 Fuel pressure regulator attaching screw
35 Fuel pressure regulator assembly

85473A70

Exploded view of the upper and lower intake manifold assemblies along with related components — 2.2L MFI engine

3.8L MFI and 4.3L (VIN Z) MFI-Turbo Engines

NOTE: Take care when servicing the fuel rail assembly to prevent dirt or contaminants from entering the fuel system. All openings in the fuel lines and passages should be capped or plugged while disconnected.

1. Before disassembly, clean the fuel rail assembly with a spray type cleaner such as AC Delco® X-30A or equivalent. After removal, do not immerse the fuel rail in liquid solvent.

2. Properly relieve the fuel system pressure and disconnect the negative battery cable.

3. Remove the upper intake plenum, if equipped with turbocharger.

4. Remove the fuel supply and return lines from the fuel rail by squeezing the tabs and pulling the lines apart or by loosening the fittings, depending upon the application. Cap all open lines to prevent dirt and contaminants from entering.

5. Disconnect the vacuum line from the pressure regulator, then tag and disconnect the fuel injector wire connectors.

6. Remove the fuel rail securing bolts and lift the rail up with equal force on both sides.

7. Remove the injector retaining clips and remove the injectors.

8. Remove and discard All old O-rings from the fuel injectors and the fuel lines.

9. Installation is the reverse of the removal procedure. Always use new O-rings on the injectors and fuel line fittings.

4.3L (VIN W) CMFI Engine

The non-repairable CMFI assembly or injection unit consists of a fuel meter body, gasket seal, fuel pressure regulator, fuel injector and 6 poppet nozzles with fuel tubes. The assembly is housed in the lower intake manifold. Should a failure occur in the CMFI assembly, the entire component must be replaced as a unit.

1. Remove the plastic cover and properly relieve the fuel system pressure.

2. Disconnect the negative battery cable, then remove the air cleaner and air inlet duct.

3. Disengage the wiring harness from the necessary upper intake components including:
- Throttle Position (TP) sensor
- Idle Air Control (IAC) motor
- Manifold Absolute Pressure (MAP) sensor
- Intake Manifold Tuning Valve (IMTV)

4. Disengage the throttle linkage from the upper intake manifold, then remove the ignition coil.

5. Disconnect the PCV hose at the rear of the upper intake manifold, then tag and disengage the vacuum hoses from both the front and rear of the upper intake.

6. Remove the upper intake manifold bolts and studs, making sure to note or mark the location of all studs to assure proper installation. Remove the upper intake manifold from the engine.

7. Disengage the injector wiring harness connector at the CMFI assembly.

8. Remove and discard the fuel fitting clip.

9. Disconnect the fuel inlet and return tube and fitting assembly. Discard the old O-rings.

10. Squeeze the poppet nozzle locktabs together while lifting each

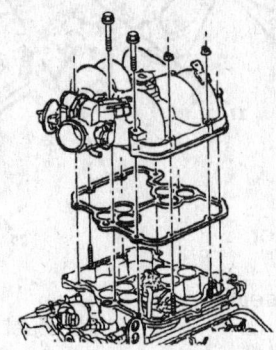

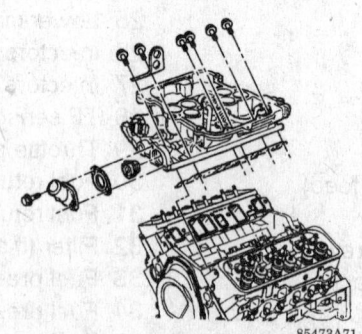

85473A71

Exploded view of the upper and lower intake manifolds along with the CMFI system components — 4.3L engine

nozzle out of the casting socket. Once all 6 nozzles are released, carefully lift the CMFI assembly out of the casting.

To install:

11. Align the CMFI assembly grommet with the casting grommet slots and push downward until it is seated in the bottom guide hole.

CAUTION

To reduce the risk of fire and personal injury, be absolutely sure the poppet nozzles are firmly seated and locked into their casting sockets. An unlocked poppet nozzle could work loose from its socket resulting in a dangerous fuel leak.

---

12. Carefully insert the poppet nozzles into the casting sockets. Make sure they are firmly seated and locked into the casting sockets.

13. Position new O-ring seals (lightly coated with clean engine oil), then connect the fuel inlet and return tube and fitting assembly.

14. Install a new fuel fitting clip.

15. Temporarily connect the negative battery cable, then pressurize the fuel system by cycling the ignition switch **ON** for 2 seconds, then **OFF** for 10 seconds and repeating, as necessary. Once the fuel system is pressurized, check for leaks.

16. Disconnect the negative battery cable.

17. Position a new upper intake manifold gasket on the engine, making sure the green sealing lines are facing upward.

18. Install the upper intake manifold being careful not to pinch the fuel injector wires between the manifolds.

19. Install the manifold retainers, making sure the studs are properly positioned, then tighten them using the proper sequence to 124 inch lbs. (14 Nm).

20. Connect the PCV hose to the rear of the upper intake manifold and the vacuum hoses to both the front and rear of the manifold assembly.

21. Connect the throttle linkage to the upper intake, then install the ignition coil.

22. Engage the necessary wiring to the upper intake components including the TP sensor, IAC motor, MAP sensor and the IMTV.

23. Install the plastic cover, the air cleaner and air inlet duct.

24. Connect the negative battery cable.

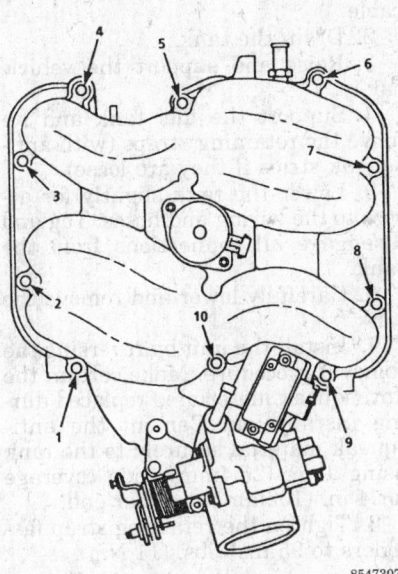

85473072

Upper intake manifold torque sequence — 4.3L engine

DIESEL FUEL SYSTEM

All 1992 vehicles utilize a mechanical diesel fuel injection pump. Starting on some 1993 vehicles and on all 1994–96 vehicles (except the non-turbocharged, heavy emission VIN Y engine), an electronically controlled diesel fuel injection pump was used. The major difference in the new electronic system is the use of the Powertrain Control Module (PCM) to control emission output by regulating the emission systems, monitoring engine operation and electronically controlling the diesel injection pump. Most system removal and installation procedures remain similar or the same as the mechanical system with subtle differences for additional or revised components.

Fuel Filter

REMOVAL AND INSTALLATION

1992–93 Vehicles

1. Turn the ignition **OFF**. Remove the fuel tank cap to release any pressure or vacuum in the tank.
2. Drain the fuel from the fuel filter by opening both the air bleed and the water drain valve allowing the fuel to drain into a suitable container.
3. Unstrap both bail wires with a suitable tool and remove the filter by pulling straight away from the filter base.
   To install:
4. Before installing the new filter, ensure that both filter mounting plate fittings are clear of dirt.
5. Position the filter, then snap into place with the bail wires.
6. Close the water drain valve and open the air bleed valve. Connect a $\frac{1}{8}$ in. (3mm) I.D. hose to the air bleed port and place the other end into a suitable container.
7. Disconnect the fuel injection pump shutdown solenoid wire.
8. Crank the engine for 10–15 seconds, then wait 1 minute for the starter motor to cool. Repeat until clear fuel is observed coming from the air bleed.

NOTE: If the engine is to be cranked or started with the air cleaner removed, care must be taken to prevent dirt from being pulled into the air inlet manifold which could result in engine damage.

9. Close the air bleed valve, reconnect the injection pump solenoid wire and replace the fuel tank cap.
10. Start the engine, allow it to idle for 5 minutes and check the fuel filter for leaks.

1994–96 Vehicles

1. Turn the ignition **OFF**. Remove the fuel tank cap to release any pressure or vacuum in the tank.

NOTE: It is not necessary to drain all the fuel from the header in order to change the element since the fuel will remain in the header's cavity.

2. Remove the element nut, turning it by hand to the left. If necessary, a strap wrench may be used to loosen the nut.
3. Remove the element by lifting straight up and out of the header assembly.

To install:
4. Make sure the mating surface between the element assembly and the header assembly is clean.
5. Install the new element by aligning the widest key slot located under the element assembly cap with the widest key in the header assembly.
6. Carefully push the element downward until the mating surfaces make contact.
7. Install the element nut and tighten securely by hand.
8. Open the air bleed valve on top of the fuel manager/filter assembly, then connect a length of hose placing the other end in a suitable container.

NOTE: Be extremely cautious when handling diesel fuel. Do not expose the fuel to sparks or open flames. Also, be cautious as the fuel coming out of the drain hose could be hot.

9. Disconnect the fuel injection pump shutdown solenoid wire.
10. Crank the engine for 10–15 seconds, then wait 1 minute for the starter motor to cool. Repeat until clear fuel is observed coming from the air bleed.
11. Close the air bleed valve, reconnect the injection pump solenoid wire and replace the fuel tank cap.
12. Start the engine, allow it to idle for 5 minutes and check the fuel manager/filter assembly for leaks.

DRAINING WATER FROM THE SYSTEM

Water is the worst enemy of the diesel fuel injection system. The injection pump and injectors, which are designed and constructed with extremely close tolerances, can be easily damaged if enough water is forced through them in the fuel. Engine performance will also be drastically affected and engine damage can occur. Diesel fuel is much more susceptible than gasoline to water contamination. Diesel engine vehicles are equipped with an indicator light system located in the instrument panel.

For 1992 vehicles, the light will be triggered if (1–2½ gallons of water is detected in the fuel tank. On 1993–96 vehicles, the water sensor is located in the fuel filter. Once the water level in the collector at the bottom of the filter assembly reaches a predetermined point (approximately 2.2 fluid ounces on 1993 vehicles) the indicator light will illuminate. The light will come ON for 2–5 seconds each time the ignition is turned ON, assur-

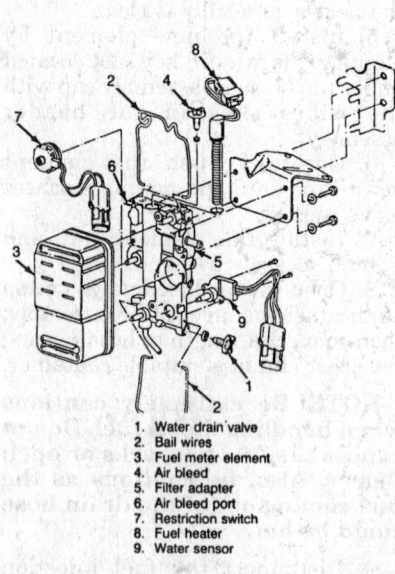

1. Water drain valve
2. Bail wires
3. Fuel meter element
4. Air bleed
5. Filter adapter
6. Air bleed port
7. Restriction switch
8. Fuel heater
9. Water sensor

85473073

Diesel engine fuel filter — vehicles 1992–93

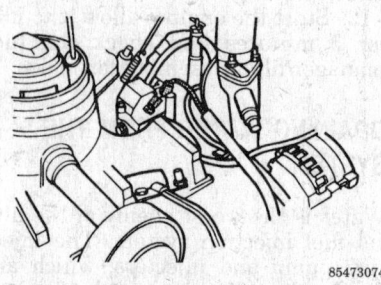

85473074

Diesel shutdown solenoid location

ing the driver the light is working. If there is water in the fuel, the light will come back ON after a 15–20 second off delay, and then remain ON.

NOTE: Water should be drained from the fuel system as soon as possible after the warning light illuminates. It is recommended that the water be drained after no longer than 2 hours of engine operation after the light comes on.

Purging The Fuel Tank

If equipped with the tank based water warning system, the fuel tank may be purged of water using the system components. The fuel tank is equipped with a filter which screens out the water and lets it lay in the bottom of the tank below the fuel pickup. When the water level reaches a point where it could be drawn into the system, a warning light flashes in the cab. A built-in siphoning system starting at the fuel tank and going to the rear spring hanger on some models, and at the midway point of the right frame rail on other models permits attaching a hose at the shut-off and siphon out the water. If it becomes necessary to drain water from the fuel tank, also check the primary fuel filter for water.

Purging The Fuel Filter

1. Make sure the engine is turned **OFF**, then firmly set the parking brake and block the drive wheels.
2. Remove the fuel filler cap to relieve any pressure or vacuum from the tank.
3. Position a suitable container under the filter drain hose, then open the drain valve 2–3 turns.
4. Start the engine and allow it to idle for 1–2 minutes or until clear fuel is observed.
5. Close the drain valve and stop the engine.
6. Install the fuel filler cap.
7. Dispose of the contaminated fuel in a proper manner.

Fuel Tank

DRAINING THE FUEL TANK

NOTE: Disconnect the negative battery cables before beginning the draining operation. Always have a dry chemical (Class B) fire extinguisher handy when working on fuel systems.

1. Remove the fuel filler cap.
2. Insert the hose from a hand operated pump into the fuel filler tube. Drain as much diesel fuel as possible from the tank using the hand pump.
3. Disconnect the main fuel line (not the return line) and use a siphon to drain the remaining fuel in the tank.

NOTE: If the vehicle is to be stored, always drain the fuel from the complete fuel system including, fuel pump supply, fuel injection pump, fuel lines and tank.

REMOVAL AND INSTALLATION

1. Disconnect the negative battery cable.
2. Drain the tank.
3. Raise and support the vehicle safely.
4. Support the fuel tank and remove the retaining straps (with anti-squeak strips if they are loose).
5. Lower the tank slightly for access to the wiring and hoses. Tag and disengage all connections from the tank.
6. Carefully lower and remove the tank.
7. Install the unit by reversing the removal procedure. Make certain the anti-squeak material is replaced during installation. Cement the anti-squeak material securely to the tank using 1 in. (25.4mm) wide coverage for 4 in. (102mm) at either end.
8. Tighten the retaining strap fasteners to 95 inch lbs. (11 Nm).

Diesel Injection Pump

Though most earlier vehicles (1992 and some 1993) utilize a mechanical injection pump, most later vehicles are equipped with an electronically controlled pump. The electronic pump is still driven by gear and rotates at the same speed as the camshaft. The major difference between the mechanical and electronic pumps is an electronic stepper motor used to control injection timing and a fuel solenoid driver used to control the fuel injection solenoid on the electronic model.

REMOVAL AND INSTALLATION

1. Disconnect both battery negative cables.
2. Remove the intake manifold.
3. Remove the fuel injection lines.
4. If necessary, disconnect the detent and/or accelerator cable at the injection pump.
5. Tag and disconnect the necessary wires and hoses at the injection pump.
6. Disconnect the fuel return line at the top of the injection pump.
7. If equipped on mechanical pump engines, remove the air conditioning hose retainer bracket.
8. If necessary, disconnect the fuel feed line at the injection pump.
9. Remove the oil fill tube (on the mechanical pump engines this should include the Crankcase Depression

Regulator (CDR) valve vent hose assembly). Remove the grommet.

NOTE: Do not engage the starter in order to rotate the engine with the injection pump removed. The pump driven gear could jam in the front housing resulting in a sheared crankshaft or camshaft gear key and possible valve train damage.

10. Scribe or paint a matchmark on the front cover and the injection pump flange.

11. Rotate the crankshaft by hand and remove the injection pump driven gear bolts, accessing the bolts through the oil filler neck hole.

12. Remove the injection pump-to-front cover attaching nuts. Remove the pump. Be sure to cap all open lines and nozzles in order to prevent system contamination and damage.

To install:

13. Position and new pump gasket.

14. Align the locating pin on the pump hub with the slot in the injection pump driven gear (the SLOT not the hole in the gear). At the same time, align the timing marks.

15. Attach the injection pump to the front cover, checking the timing marks before torquing the nuts to 30 ft. lbs. (40 Nm).

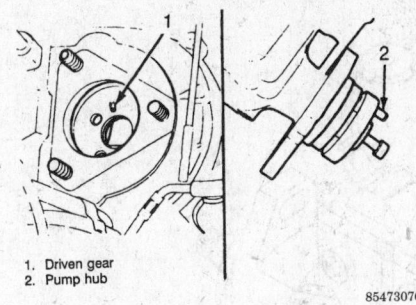

1. Driven gear
2. Pump hub

85473076

Diesel injection pump locating pin

16. Install the driven gear-to-injection pump bolts, torquing the bolts to 20 ft. lbs. (25 Nm).

17. Install the grommet and oil fill tube.

18. If applicable, install the air conditioning bracket.

19. Connect the fuel feed line and torque to 20 ft. lbs. (25 Nm).

20. If removed, connect the fuel return line to the pump.

21. If necessary, connect the detent and/or accelerator cables.

22. Connect all wires and hoses previously removed.

23. Connect the injector lines and install the intake manifold.

24. Connect the negative battery cables. Start the engine and check for leaks.

IDLE SPEED ADJUSTMENT

Idle speed is controlled by the PCM on electronically controlled injection pump engines. On mechanical pump engines, the idle speed may be adjusted:

NOTE: A special tachometer suitable for diesel engines must be used. A gasoline engine type tachometer will not work with the diesel engine.

1. Set the parking brake and block the drive wheels.

2. Run the engine up to normal operating temperature. The air cleaner must be mounted and all accessories turned **OFF**.

3. Install the diesel tachometer as per the manufacturer's instructions.

4. Adjust the low idle speed screw on the fuel injection pump to manufacturer's specification per the emission control label.

NOTE: All idle speeds are to be set within 25 rpm of the specified values.

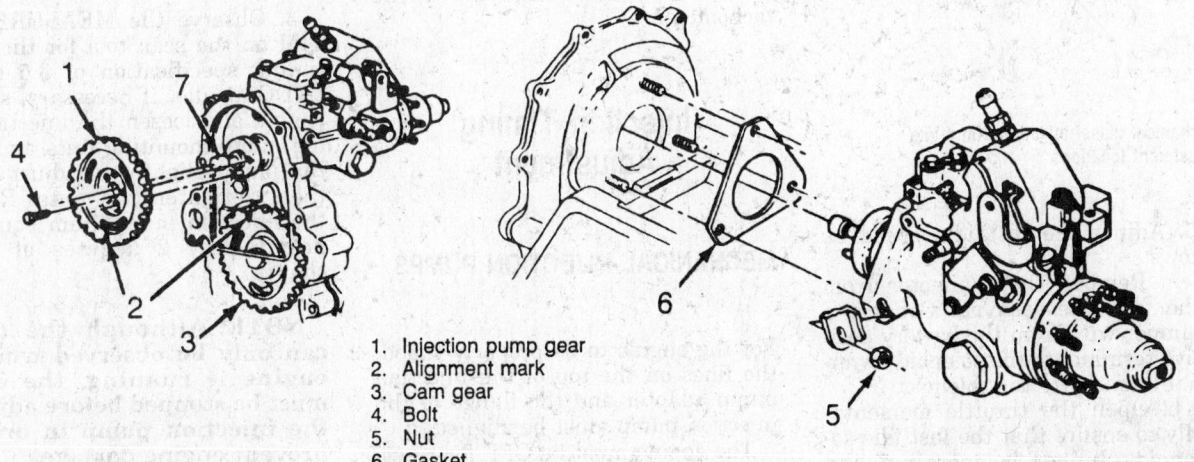

1. Injection pump gear
2. Alignment mark
3. Cam gear
4. Bolt
5. Nut
6. Gasket
7. Pump hub

85473075

Diesel injection pump installation

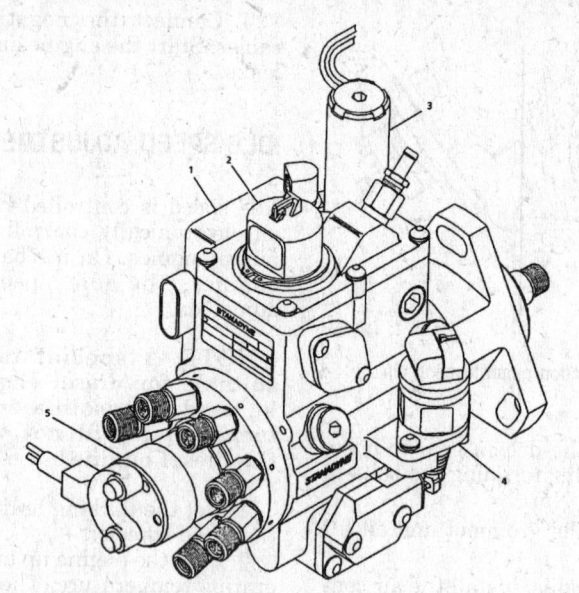

1   FUEL SOLENOID DRIVER
2   OPTICAL/FUEL TEMPERATURE SENSOR
3   ENGINE SHUT OFF SOLENOID
4   INJECTION TIMING STEPPER MOTOR
5   FUEL SOLENOID

85473077

Electronic injection pump components

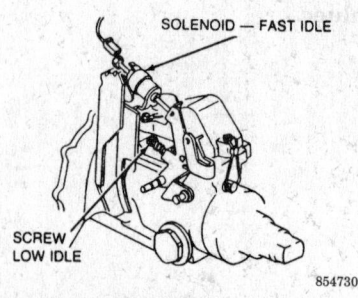

Mechanical diesel injection pump idle adjustment locations

85473078

5. Adjust the fast idle speed as follows:

a. Remove the connector from the fast idle solenoid. Connect a jumper wire from the battery positive terminal to the solenoid terminal to energize the solenoid.

b. Open the throttle momentarily to ensure that the fast idle solenoid plunger is energized and fully extended.

c. Adjust the fast idle by turning the hex-head screw to manufacturer's specification per the emission control label.

d. Remove the jumper wire and reinstall the connector to the fast idle solenoid.

6. Disconnect and remove the tachometer.

Injection Timing Adjustment

MECHANICAL INJECTION PUMPS

For the engine to be properly timed, the lines on the top of the injection pump adapter and the flange of the injection pump must be aligned.

The engine must be OFF for resetting the timing.

1. Loosen the 3 pump retaining nuts with tool J–26987, an injection pump intake manifold wrench or equivalent.

2. Align the mark on the injection pump with the marks on the front cover. Torque the nuts to 30 ft. lbs. (40 Nm). Use a ³/₄ in. open-end wrench on the boss at the front of the injection pump to aid in rotating the pump to align the marks.

ELECTRONIC INJECTION PUMPS

Checking and Adjusting Timing

The Tech 1® or equivalent scan tool must be used in order to check or adjust injection timing on these vehicles. The original factory timing is indicated with a static timing mark in the form of a line scribed across both the pump mounting flange and the front cover. This static mark may be used as a reference.

If the static mark is not present on the pump mounting flange, 1 can be scribed to further assist in determining the distance the pump needs to be rotated.

1. Start and idle the engine until warm.

2. Connect the scan tool, then activate the TDC TIME SET function (found in the OUTPUT TEST/INJ PUMP menu on the Tech 1®). If the engine stalls during the TDC TIME SET, rotate the injection pump slightly toward the driver's side of the vehicle, tighten the mounting nuts and repeat this step.

NOTE: When the TDC TIME SET is activated the DESIRED INJ TRIM value for the Tech 1® will read 0.

3. Observe the MEASURED INJ TIM on the scan tool for the proper timing specification of 3.5 degrees BTDC at idle. If necessary, stop the engine and loosen the injection timing pump mounting nuts and rotate the pump slightly to adjust timing, then re-tighten the nuts. Rotating the injection pump 1mm equals approximately 2 degrees of timing change.

NOTE: Although the timing can only be observed while the engine is running, the engine must be stopped before adjusting the injection pump in order to prevent engine damage.

4. Once the timing is adjusted, restart the engine and observe the MEASURED INJ TIM value on the scan tool. If necessary, stop the engine and readjust the timing. Keep in mind that it is normal for the value to fluctuate slightly while the PCM is in set timing mode.

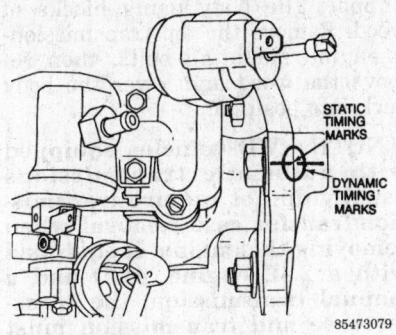

Mechanical diesel injection pump timing alignment marks

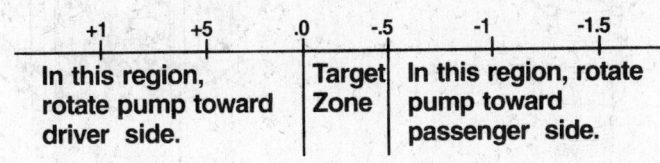

Backup timing TDC OFFSET values and pump rotation

Backup Timing Procedure

A backup timing procedure is available for use under 1 of the following conditions

- The front cover and PCM have been remove and replaced at the same time.
- The pump and the PCM have been removed and replaced at the same time.
- The front cover and/or crank sensor, pump and PCM have been removed and replaced at the same time.
- The front cover has been removed.
- A replacement engine is installed.

1. Start and idle the engine until warm.

2. Connect a Tech 1® or equivalent scan tool, then activate the TDC OFFSET LEARN function (found in the OUTPUT TEST/INJ PUMP menu on the Tech 1®). If the engine stalls during the TDC OFFSET LEARN, rotate the injection pump slightly toward the driver's side of the vehicle, tighten the mounting nuts and repeat this step.

3. If the TDC OFFSET value is between 0.00–0.50 degrees, the procedure is complete. If not, stop the engine and rotate the pump slightly, then retighten the nuts and recheck the valve.

NOTE: To achieve a negative value rotate the pump towards the driver's side. To achieve a positive value rotate the pump towards the passenger's side. 1mm of pump movement equals approximately 2 degrees of timing.

4. If loosened, tighten the pump retaining nuts to 30 ft. lbs. (40 Nm).

Fuel Injector

REMOVAL AND INSTALLATION

1. Disconnect the negative cable on both batteries.

2. Disconnect the fuel line clip, then remove the fuel return hose.

3. Remove the fuel injection line. Immediately cap the nozzle and lines to prevent system contamination and damage.

4. Using GM special tool J–29873 or equivalent, remove the injector. Always remove the injector by turning the 30mm hex portion of the injector.

5. Install the injector using a new gasket and torque to 50 ft. lbs. (70 Nm).

6. Connect the injection line and torque the nut to 20 ft. lbs. (25 Nm).

7. Install the fuel return hose, then install the fuel line clip and connect the batteries.

EMISSION CONTROLS

Emission Warning Lamps

RESETTING

These vehicles are equipped with a SERVICE ENGINE SOON Malfunction Indicator Lamp (MIL). The MIL will illuminate when the key is turned to the **ON** position as a systems check, but will extinguish shortly after the engine is started. If the computer control module (ECM, PCM or VCM, as applicable) detects a malfunction in 1 of the monitored circuits, a trouble code will be set and the lamp will be illuminated to indicate a fault.

When the computer module sets a code, the MIL will remain illuminated as long as the fault is detected. If the problem is intermittent, the light will extinguish approximately 10 seconds after the fault goes away. However the code will stay in the memory for 50 starts or until cleared.

NOTE: If a scan tool is not available, the trouble codes for most of these vehicles may be flash diagnosed. However, certain 1994–96 models equipped with a Vehicle Control Module (VCM), such as certain S/T-Series equipped with a module mounted on the fender well and not in the passenger compartment, are On-Board Diagnostic II (OBD-II) compliant. OBD-II vehicles utilize a new trouble code system in which all codes consist of 5 alpha-numeric digits. The first digit is a letter, while the remaining 4 are numbers. Nevertheless, flash diagnosis was not incorporated as it would be impractical.

Obviously, the MIL cannot be reset until the malfunction is corrected (or at least not present if intermittent) and the computer memory is cleared of the fault. Codes may be cleared using a suitable scan tool or by removing power from the computer control module. If the latter method is chosen, power must be removed from the module for a minimum of 30 seconds. The lower the ambient temperature, the longer period of time the power must be removed.

Remember, to prevent control module damage, the ignition must always be **OFF** when removing power. Power may be removed through various methods, depending on how the vehicle is equipped. The preferable method is to remove the control module fuse from the fuse box. The control module pigtail may also be un-

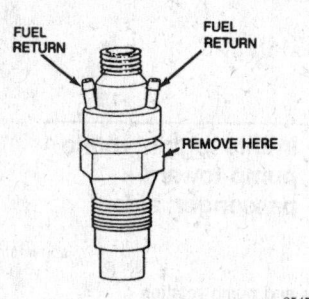

Diesel injection nozzles

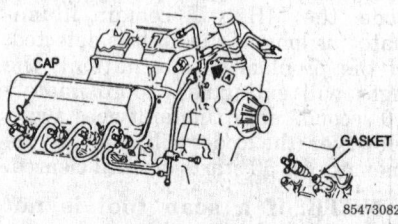

Diesel injection nozzle

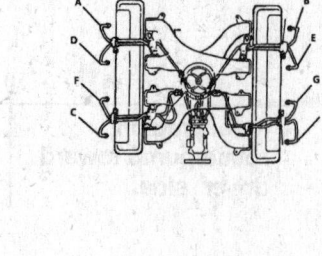

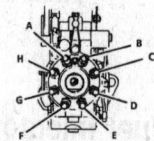

A.	CYLINDER NUMBER 8
B.	CYLINDER NUMBER 7
C.	CYLINDER NUMBER 2
D.	CYLINDER NUMBER 6
E.	CYLINDER NUMBER 5
F.	CYLINDER NUMBER 4
G.	CYLINDER NUMBER 3
H.	CYLINDER NUMBER 1

85473083

Diesel injection line routing — electronic pump shown (mechanical similar)

plugged. If necessary, the negative battery cable may be disconnected, but other on-board data such as radio presets will be lost.

ENGINE MECHANICAL

NOTE: Disconnecting the battery cable on most vehicles may interfere with the functions of the on-board computer systems and may require the computer to undergo a relearning process.

Engine Assembly

REMOVAL AND INSTALLATION

S/T-Series

2.5L AND 2.8L ENGINES

1. Properly relieve the fuel system pressure and disconnect the negative battery cable.
2. Matchmark the hood hinges for installation reference and remove the hood.

3. Drain the cooling system and remove the upper and lower radiator hoses. Disconnect the coolant overflow hose. Disconnect the heater hoses at the engine.
4. Remove the upper and lower fan shrouds. On automatic transmission equipped vehicles, disconnect and plug the transmission cooler lines.
5. Remove the air cleaner assembly and cover the carburetor/throttle body with a rag.
6. Label and disconnect all necessary hoses, vacuum lines and wires from the engine, transmission and transfer case, if equipped.
7. Disconnect the throttle cable, transmission TV cable and cruise control cable, if equipped.
8. Raise and support the vehicle safely. Disconnect the exhaust pipes at the manifold.
9. Remove the front driveshaft and skid plates on 4WD vehicles.
10. If applicable, disconnect the strut rods at the bellhousing.
11. For automatic transmission vehicles the body will have to be raised away from the engine in order for the top transmission-to-engine bolt(s) to clear the cowl. Remove the body mounting bolts, then raise the front of the body away from the frame.

Support the body using blocks of wood. Remove the top transmission-to-engine mounting bolts, then remove the wood and lower the body back into position.

NOTE: 4WD vehicles equipped with automatic transmissions usually do not require transmission/transfer case removal when removing the engine. If equipped with a 2.8L engine, 4WD and a manual transmission, the transfer case and transmission must usually be removed prior to removing the engine.

12. Remove the rear driveshaft.
13. Support the transmission and remove the transmission crossmember.
14. If equipped with automatic transmissions:
   • Remove the torque converter cover
   • Remove the torque converter-to-flexplate attaching bolts
   • If transmission removal is desired, remove the transmission shift linkage and, if equipped, the transfer case shift linkage. Remove the remaining transmission-to-engine mounting bolts, and remove the transmission and transfer case, if equipped, as an assembly
15. If equipped with manual transmissions:
   • Remove the clutch slave cylinder and set aside
   • If transmission removal is desired or necessary, remove the transmission shift linkage and shifter, and if equipped, remove the 4WD transfer case shift linkage and shifter.
   • Remove the transmission-to-bellhousing bolts, if the transmission is being removed, carefully lower the transmission and transfer case, if equipped, as an assembly.

NOTE: If the manual transmission is removed, leave the bellhousing in place to protect the clutch during engine removal. Leaving the bellhousing in place will also prevent the necessity of raising the body off the frame to access the top bellhousing-to-engine bolts which would otherwise be blocked by the cowl.

16. Remove the accessory drive belts. Remove the fan.
17. If equipped, remove the power steering pump, A/C compressor and air pump with their brackets and place aside in the engine compartment with the lines intact.

NOTE: Do not disconnect the fluid or refrigerant lines.

18. Verify that nothing else is attached to the engine and, if necessary, disconnect the remaining component(s).

19. Attach a suitable lifting device to the engine and remove. Pause several times while lifting the engine to make sure no hoses or wiring have been snagged by the powerplant.

To install:

20. Using the lifting device, carefully lower the engine into position. Loosely install the engine mount bolts at this time to hold the engine in position.

21. If equipped, reposition and secure the power steering pump and/or A/C compressor to the engine.

22. Install the engine cooling fan and the accessory drive belts.

23. If removed, install the transmission and, if equipped, transfer case.

24. Install the transmission crossmember and remove the support. Install all accessible transmission-to-engine/bellhousing bolts (as applicable) at this time.

25. Tighten the engine and transmission fasteners:

- Engine mount-to-engine: 35 ft. lbs. (47 Nm).
- Engine mount-to-frame mount: 52 ft. lbs. (70 Nm).
- Transmission mount-to-transmission: 45 ft. lbs. (61 Nm).
- Transmission mount-to-crossmember: 24 ft. lbs. (33 Nm).

26. For automatic transmission vehicles, install the torque converter-to-flexplate bolts and install the torque converter cover.

27. If the transmission/transfer case was removed, reconnect the shift linkage.

28. For manual transmission vehicles, position and install the slave cylinder assembly.

29. Install the rear driveshaft.

30. Carefully raise the front of the body away from the frame, then install the remaining transmission-to-engine bolts. Carefully lower the body back into position and secure the body mounts.

31. If applicable, connect the strut rods at the bellhousing.

32. For 4WD vehicles, install the front driveshaft and, if equipped, the skid plates.

33. Connect the throttle cable, transmission TV cable and cruise control cable, if equipped.

34. Reconnect all necessary hoses, vacuum lines and wires from the engine, transmission and transfer case, if equipped, as noted during removal.

35. Remove the cover from the throttle body/carburetor, then install the air cleaner assembly.

36. For automatic transmission equipped vehicles, remove the plugs, then reconnect the transmission cooler lines.

37. Install the upper and lower fan shrouds.

38. Connect the upper and lower radiator hoses, the coolant overflow hose and the heater hoses at the engine.

39. Align and install the hood using the matchmarks made during removal.

40. Connect the negative battery cable, then proper refill the engine cooling system.

41. Check all powertrain fluid levels and add, as necessary.

4.3L ENGINE — 1992–93 2WD

1. Disconnect the negative battery cable and properly relieve the fuel system pressure.

2. Scribe matchmarks for installation purposes, then remove the hood.

3. Properly drain the engine cooling system, then disconnect the upper radiator hose from the radiator.

4. Disconnect the overflow hose, then remove the upper fan shroud.

5. If equipped, disconnect the automatic transmission cooler lines from the radiator assembly. Plug the openings to prevent system contamination or excessive fluid loss.

6. Remove the radiator assembly.

7. Remove the engine cooling fan, then disconnect and plug the heater hoses.

8. Remove the air cleaner assembly, then tag and disconnect all necessary vacuum hoses.

9. Tag and disconnect all necessary wires at the bulkhead, ground wires and main feed wires.

10. Disconnect the throttle and cruise control cables, as equipped.

11. Remove the distributor cap.

12. Raise and support the vehicle safely.

13. Remove the catalytic converter-to-exhaust pipe bolts, then disconnect the exhaust pipes at the manifold.

14. Disconnect the strut rods at the bellhousing.

15. If equipped, remove the flywheel cover, then remove the torque converter bolts.

16. Remove the shield at the rear of the catalytic converter.

17. Disconnect the converter hanger at the exhaust pipe.

18. Remove the lower fan shroud.

19. Disconnect the fuel lines and loosen all fuel line clamps from the TBI unit and engine. Move the lines

to the rear of the engine compartment and tie them in place, but take care not to stress or damage the lines.

20. Remove the 2 outer air dam bolts.

21. Remove the left body mount bolts, then carefully raise the body from the frame and support.

22. Remove the bellhousing retaining bolts, then remove the supports and carefully lower the body back to the frame.

23. Remove the motor mount through-bolts, then lower the vehicle.

24. Remove the A/C compressor and/or power steering pump from the engine, then position them aside with the lines intact. There is no need to disconnect the lines from either of these components.

25. Support the transmission, then install a suitable lifting device and carefully lift the engine. Pause several times while lifting the engine to make sure no wires or hoses have become snagged.

To install:

26. Carefully lower the engine into the vehicle and engage it with the transmission. Remove the support from the transmission and the lifting device from the engine.

27. Raise and support the vehicle safely.

28. Install the motor mount through-bolts.

29. Raise the body from the frame for access, then install and tighten the bellhousing bolts. Lower the body back into position and install the body mount bolts.

30. If equipped, reposition and secure the power steering pump and/or A/C compressor.

31. Install and tighten the 2 outer air dam bolts.

32. Reposition the fuel lines and connect them to the TBI unit. Be sure to properly secure the lines using the clamps.

33. Install the lower fan shroud, then install the converter hanger to the exhaust pipe.

34. Install the shield at the rear of the converter

35. If applicable, install the torque converter bolts, then install the flywheel cover.

36. Connect the strut rods at the bellhousing.

37. Connect the exhaust pipes to the manifolds, then install the converter-to-exhaust pipe bolts.

38. Lower the vehicle.

39. Install the distributor cap.

40. Connect the throttle and, if equipped, cruise control cables.

41. Engage all wires at the bulkhead, ground wires and main feed wires as tagged during removal.

42. Install the vacuum hoses as noted during removal, then install the air cleaner assembly.

43. Connect the heater hoses, then install the fan.

44. Install the radiator and the upper fan shroud.

45. Connect the overflow hose, the radiator hoses and, if equipped, the transmission cooler lines.

46. Align and install the hood, then check all powertrain fluid levels.

47. Connect the negative battery cable, then properly fill the engine cooling system.

48. Start and run the engine, then check for leaks.

4.3 ENGINE — 1992–93 4WD; EXCEPT MFI-TURBO

1. Disconnect the negative battery cable and properly relieve the fuel system pressure.

2. If equipped, disconnect the underhood light.

3. Scribe matchmarks for installation purposes, then remove the hood.

4. Properly drain the engine cooling system, then raise and support the the vehicle safely.

5. Loosen the front and remove the 2 body mounts located near or under the cab.

6. Remove the outer bolts from the front air dam.

7. Raise the body away from the frame to gain the necessary clearance for transmission bolt removal. Remove the top transmission-to-engine bolts, then carefully lower the body back into position.

8. Support the transmission, then remove the remaining transmission-to-engine bolts.

9. Remove the 2nd crossmember (located 2nd back from the front of the vehicle).

10. Disconnect the exhaust pipes at the manifolds, then remove the catalytic converter hanger.

11. Remove the torque converter cover bolts and disconnect the front driveshaft from the front differential, then remove the torque converter cover.

12. Release the transmission oil cooler lines at the engine clips.

13. Remove the motor mount bolts.

14. Remove the flexplate-to-torque converter bolts.

15. Remove the front splash shield, then remove the lower fan shroud retaining bolts.

16. Carefully lower the vehicle.

17. Remove the upper fan shroud, then disconnect the hoses from the radiator.

18. Disconnect the oil filter pipe at the remote oil filter.

19. Remove the radiator assembly, then remove the engine cooling fan.

20. Remove the air cleaner assembly.

21. Remove the A/C compressor and/or power steering pump from the engine, then position them aside with the lines intact. There is no need to disconnect the lines from either of these components.

22. Disconnect the fuel lines and loosen all fuel line clamps from the TBI unit and engine. Move the lines to the rear of the engine compartment and tie them in place, but take care not to stress or damage the lines.

23. Tag and disconnect all necessary wires, vacuum lines and emission hoses.

24. Disconnect the accelerator cable and, if equipped, the cruise control cable.

25. Disconnect the engine wiring harness at the bulkhead connector.

26. Disconnect the heater hoses at the engine.

27. Make sure the transmission is supported, then install a suitable lifting device and carefully lift the engine. Pause several times while lifting the engine to make sure no wires or hoses have become snagged.

To install:

28. Carefully lower the engine into the vehicle and engage it with the transmission. Remove the support from the transmission and the lifting device from the engine.

29. Raise and support the vehicle safely.

30. Install the motor mount through-bolts.

31. Raise the body from the frame for access, then install and tighten the bellhousing bolts. Lower the body back into position and install the body mount bolts.

32. Install the flexplate-to-torque converter bolts, then install the torque converter cover.

33. Install the front driveshaft assembly, then install the catalytic converter hanger.

34. Connect the exhaust pipe to the manifolds.

35. Install the crossmember.

36. Install the lower fan shroud retaining bolts, then install the front splash shield.

37. Secure the transmission oil cooler lines at the engine clips.

38. Install the front air dam bolts, then carefully lower the vehicle.

39. Engage the engine wiring harness at the bulkhead connector.

40. Connect the accelerator cable, and if equipped, the cruise control cable.

41. Connect the heater hoses, then connect the wires, vacuum lines and emission hoses as noted during removal.

42. Reposition and connect the fuel lines making sure they are properly routed in their clamps.

43. If equipped, reposition and secure the power steering pump and/or A/C compressor.

44. Install the engine cooling fan, then install the radiator assembly.

45. Connect the oil filter pipe at the remote oil filter using new O-rings.

46. Connect the radiator hoses and install the drive belt(s).

47. Install the upper fan shroud.

48. Install the hood and check all powertrain fluid levels.

49. Connect the negative battery cable and properly refill the engine cooling system.

50. Start and run the engine, then check for leaks.

4.3L MFI-TURBO ENGINE

1. Disconnect the negative battery cable, followed by the positive cable, then properly relieve the fuel system pressure.

2. Properly drain both the engine cooling system and the turbocharger air cooler system.

3. Scribe matchmarks for installation purposes, then remove the hood.

4. Remove the air cleaner and duct assembly.

5. Remove the turbocharger air inlet elbow.

6. Remove the upper fan shroud, then remove the fan and pulley nuts.

7. Remove the serpentine drive belt, then remove the fan and pulley.

8. Remove the battery tray and vacuum tank.

9. Raise and support the vehicle safely.

10. Remove the front tire and wheel assemblies, then remove the wheel house panels

11. Disconnect the mufflers and tailpipe from the catalytic converter, then remove the catalytic converter support bolts.

12. Remove the turbocharger outlet pipe bracket and outlet pipe nuts. Move the outlet pipe and catalytic converter away from the turbocharger.

13. Disengage the electrical wiring connector from the charge air cooler

radiator temperature sensor, then disconnect the radiator hoses.

14. Remove the charge air cooler radiator.

15. Disconnect the exhaust crossover pipe. Underhood access is necessary, either install the front wheels and lower the vehicle or adjust lift for access.

16. Disconnect the transmission oil cooler lines from the radiator. Plug the openings to prevent system contamination or excessive fluid loss.

17. Remove the upper and lower radiator hoses.

18. Disconnect the engine oil cooler lines from the radiator. Plug the openings to prevent system contamination or excessive fluid loss.

19. Disconnect the heater hoses and the overflow hoses from the radiator.

20. Remove the radiator.

21. Disconnect the oil pipes at the filter adapter.

22. Remove the power steering pump hoses from the steering gear. Plug the openings to prevent system contamination or excessive fluid loss.

23. Remove the engine coolant reservoir.

24. Disconnect the A/C compress from the bracket and position aside with the lines intact.

25. Loosen the charge air cooler clamps, then disconnect the ducts and hoses.

26. Remove the charge air cooler from the supports.

27. Remove the throttle body, gasket and cable bracket from the upper intake manifold and position aside.

28. If not done already, disconnect the heater hose from the lower intake manifold.

29. Tag and disengage the electrical connectors from the upper intake manifold assembly.

30. Disconnect the fuel pipes from the fuel rail assembly.

31. Tag and disengage the remaining electrical connectors and vacuum hoses form the engine assembly.

32. If additional access is needed, further raise and support the vehicle safely.

33. Remove the rear driveshaft.

34. Position a support under the transmission, then remove the transmission crossmember and mount.

35. Remove the front driveshaft.

36. Remove the torque converter cover, then disconnect the shift linkage from the transmission.

37. Remove the torque converter bolts.

38. Disconnect the fuel pipes from the hoses near the transfer case, then

remove the fuel line bracket from the transfer case.

39. Disengage the fuel line clip and the electrical clips and connectors from the transmission and transfer case.

40. Remove the transfer case and gasket.

41. Disconnect the TV cable from the transmission.

42. Disconnect the transmission cooler lines from the transmission. Be sure to plug all openings.

43. Remove the torque converter housing bolts, then carefully lower the transmission.

44. Remove the transmission oil cooler lines from the oil pan.

45. Remove the fuel line clip, oil line and electrical harness clips from the cylinder heads.

46. Tag and disengage the starter motor electrical connections, then remove the starter from the engine.

47. Remove the engine mount through-bolts and nuts. Underhood access is necessary, either install the front wheels and lower the vehicle or adjust the lift for access.

48. Disengage the electrical connections form the oil pressure and knock sensors, then remove the ground strap.

49. Install a suitable lifting device and carefully lift the engine. Pause several times while lifting the engine to make sure no wires or hoses have become snagged.

To install:

50. Carefully lower the engine into the vehicle.

51. Engage the electrical connections to the oil pressure and knock sensors, then install the ground strap.

52. Make sure the engine is properly positioned on the engine mounts, then route the wiring harnesses into position.

53. Install the engine mount through-bolts and nuts, then tighten the bolts to 61 ft. lbs. (83 Nm) or the nuts to 52 ft. lbs. (70 Nm).

54. Install the fuel line clip, oil line and electrical harness clips to the cylinder heads.

55. Install the starter motor and engage the wiring as noted during removal.

56. Carefully raise the transmission into position in the vehicle, then install the torque converter housing bolts and tighten to 35 ft. lbs. (41 Nm).

57. Connect the transmission oil cooler lines to the transmission housing and tighten to 21 ft. lbs. (28 Nm).

58. Connect the TV cable to the transmission.

59. Install the transfer case and gasket, then tighten the retaining bolts to 39 ft. lbs. (53 Nm).

60. Install the transmission cooler lines to the oil pan clip.

61. Install the fuel line pipes to the hoses, then connect the fuel line bracket to the transfer case. Tighten the fuel line hose fittings to 19 ft. lbs. (26 Nm) and the bracket bolt to 26 ft. lbs. (35 Nm).

62. Engage the fuel line clip and the electrical wiring clips and connectors to the transmission and transfer case.

63. Install the torque converter bolts and tighten to 46 ft. lbs. (63 Nm), then connect the shift linkage to the transmission.

64. Install the torque converter cover and tighten the retaining bolts to 35 ft. lbs. (47 Nm).

65. Install the front driveshaft and tighten the retaining bolts to 52 ft. lbs. (70 Nm).

66. Install the transmission crossmember and mount, then tighten the crossmember bolts to 35 ft. lbs. (47 Nm).

67. Install the rear driveshaft and tighten the retainers to 15 ft. lbs. (20 Nm).

68. Install the turbocharger outlet pipe and nuts, then install the turbocharger outlet pipe bracket. Tighten the pipe nuts to 41 ft. lbs. (55 Nm) and the pipe support bolt to 22 ft. lbs. (30 Nm).

69. Install the catalytic converter support bolts, then install the mufflers and tailpipe to the converter. Tighten the support bolts to 25 ft. lbs. (34 Nm) and the tailpipe bolts to 24 ft. lbs. (32 Nm).

70. Connect the crossover pipe and tighten the nuts to 12 ft. lbs. (16 Nm).

71. Install the charge air cooler radiator, connect the cooler radiator hoses and engage the electrical connection.

72. Underhood access is necessary, either install the front wheels and lower the vehicle or adjust the lift for access.

73. Engage the electrical connectors and vacuum lines to the engine.

74. Connect the fuel pipes to the fuel rail assembly, then install the upper intake manifold assembly and gasket. Tighten the upper intake manifold bolts (starting at the 2 middle bolts, moving outward to each side) to 18 ft. lbs. (24 Nm).

75. Engage the electrical connectors to the upper intake manifold as-

sembly, then connect the heater hose to the lower intake manifold.

76. Install the throttle body, gasket and cable bracket to the upper intake manifold assembly. Tighten the throttle body bolts to 18 ft. lbs. (24 Nm).

77. Install the charge air cooler to the supports, then install the charge air cooler ducts and hoses (secure using the clamps).

78. Reposition the A/C compressor to the bracket and secure.

79. Install the engine coolant reservoir.

80. Install the power steering pump hoses to the steering gear and tighten the fittings to 21 ft. lbs. (28 Nm).

81. Install the oil pipes to the filter adapter and tighten the retaining bolt to 26 ft. lbs. (35 Nm).

82. Install the radiator assembly.

83. Connect the heater hoses and the overflow hose to the radiator.

84. Install the engine oil and transmission fluid cooler lines to the radiator. Tighten the engine oil line fittings to 26 ft. lbs. (35 Nm) and the transmission fluid lines to 20 ft. lbs. (27 Nm).

85. Connect the upper and lower radiator hoses.

86. Install the battery tray and vacuum tank.

87. Install the fan, pulley and nuts.

88. Install the serpentine drive belt, then tighten the pulley nuts to 18 ft. lbs. (24 Nm).

89. Install the upper radiator shroud.

90. Install the turbocharger air inlet elbow.

91. Install the air cleaner and duct.

92. Align and install the hood using the matchmarks made during removal.

93. Install the front wheel house panels.

94. Install the front tire and wheel assemblies, then carefully lower the vehicle.

95. Check all powertrain fluid levels and add, as necessary.

96. Connect the positive battery cable, followed by the negative battery cable.

97. Properly refill the charge air cooling system and bleed the air.

98. Properly refill the engine cooling system.

99. Start and run the engine, then check for leaks.

1994–96 4.3L ENGINE

1. Disconnect the negative battery cable and properly relieve the fuel system pressure.

2. Disconnect the vacuum reservoir and/or the underhood light from the hood (as equipped), then remove the outer cowl vent grilles.

3. Matchmark and remove the hood.

4. Raise and support the front of the vehicle safely. It will be most convenient if the vehicle can be supported so underhood access is still possible. Otherwise, the vehicle will have to be raised and lowered multiple times during the procedure for the necessary access.

5. Drain the engine cooling system and the engine oil into separate drain pans.

6. Disconnect the oxygen sensor and/or wiring.

7. Disconnect the exhaust at the manifolds and loosen the hanger at the catalytic converter. This is necessary to remove the rear catalytic converter cushion mounts for removal of the exhaust assembly.

8. If equipped, remove the skid plate.

9. Remove the pencil braces from the engine to the transmission.

10. If equipped, remove the slave cylinder and position aside.

11. Disconnect the line clamp at the bellhousing.

12. Tag and remove the wiring from the starter, remove the flywheel cover and remove the starter.

13. Remove the oil filter.

14. Remove the engine mount through-bolts and remove all of the bellhousing bolts, except the upper left.

15. Disconnect the battery ground (negative) cable from the engine.

16. On 4WD vehicles, remove the front drive axle bolts and roll the axle downward.

17. Remove the air cleaner assembly and duct work.

18. Remove the upper radiator shroud, then remove the fan assembly.

19. Remove the multi-ribbed serpentine drive belt, then remove the water pump pulley.

20. Disconnect the upper radiator hose, then remove the A/C compressor, if equipped, and position aside with the lines intact.

21. Disconnect the lower radiator hose, then disconnect the oil cooler and overflow lines from the radiator. Plug the cooler line openings to prevent system contamination or excessive fluid loss.

22. Remove the radiator from the vehicle, then remove the lower radiator shroud.

23. Disconnect the power steering hoses from the steering gear, then cap the openings to prevent system contamination or excessive fluid loss.

24. Disconnect the heater hoses from the intake manifold and the water pump.

25. Tag, disconnect and remove the wiring harness and vacuum lines from the engine

26. Disconnect the throttle cables, then remove the distributor cap.

27. Remove the remaining bolt from the bellhousing.

28. Disconnect the fuel lines and remove the bracket.

29. Remove the ground strap(s) from the rear of the cylinder head.

30. On 4WD vehicles, loosen the front body mount bolts.

31. Support the transmission.

32. Install a suitable lifting device and carefully lift the engine. Pause several times while lifting the engine to make sure no wires or hoses have become snagged.

To install:

33. Carefully lower the engine into the vehicle.

34. On 4WD vehicles, tighten the front body mount bolts.

35. Install the ground strap(s) to the rear of the cylinder head.

36. Connect the fuel lines and install the bracket.

37. Install the upper left bellhousing bolt.

38. Install the distributor cap and wires.

39. Connect the throttle cables.

40. Connect the vacuum lines and wiring harness connectors as noted during removal.

41. Connect the heater hoses, then uncap and connect the power steering hoses.

42. Install the lower shroud, then install the radiator.

43. Uncap and connect the oil cooler lines to the radiator, then connect the overflow hose.

44. Connect the lower radiator hose, then if equipped, reposition and secure the A/C compressor to the engine.

45. Install the upper radiator hose, then install the water pump pulley.

46. Install the serpentine drive belt, then install the fan assembly.

47. Install the upper radiator shroud, then install the air cleaner and ducts.

48. For 4WD vehicles, roll the front axle up into position, then install and tighten the retaining bolts.

49. Connect the battery ground strap to the engine block.

50. Install the remaining bellhousing bolts.

51. Install the engine mount through-bolts and tighten to 49 ft. lbs. (66 Nm).

52. Install a new oil filter, then install the starter motor.

53. Install the flywheel cover.

54. If equipped, reposition and secure the clutch slave cylinder.

55. Install the pencil brace and the skid plate, as equipped.

56. Install the catalytic converter Y-pipe assembly and hangers.

57. Carefully lower the vehicle.

58. Align the marks made during removal and install the hood.

59. Install the outer cowl vent grilles, then connect the vacuum reservoir and/or the underhood light to the hood (as equipped).

60. Check all powertrain fluid levels and add, as necessary. Be sure to properly fill the engine crankcase with clean engine oil.

61. Connect the negative battery cable and properly fill the engine cooling system.

62. Start and run the engine, then check for leaks.

2.2L (VIN 4) ENGINE

NOTE: The manufacturer recommends the discharge and recovery of the A/C system R-134a refrigerant for this procedure. Do not attempt this without the proper equipment. R-134a should not be mixed with R-12 refrigerant.

1. Disconnect the negative battery cable and properly relieve the fuel system pressure.

2. Disconnect the vacuum reservoir and/or the underhood light from the hood (as equipped).

3. Disconnect the windshield washer line from the hood, then remove the outer cowl vent grilles.

4. Matchmark and remove the hood.

5. Raise and support the vehicle safely. It will be most convenient if the vehicle can be supported so underhood access is still possible. Otherwise, the vehicle will have to be raised and lowered multiple times during the procedure for the necessary access.

6. Properly recover the R-134a refrigerant from the A/C system.

7. Drain the engine cooling system and the engine oil into separate drain pans.

8. Disconnect the oxygen sensor and/or wiring.

9. Disconnect the exhaust at the manifolds and loosen the hanger at the catalytic converter.

10. Remove the pencil braces from the engine to the transmission.

11. Remove the inspection cover.

12. Tag and remove the wiring from the starter, then remove the starter.

13. Remove the engine mount through-bolts, then remove the bellhousing bolts.

14. Remove the battery from the vehicle, then disconnect the battery ground (negative cable) from the engine.

15. Remove the air cleaner assembly and duct work.

16. Remove the upper fan shroud, then remove the engine cooling fan.

17. Remove the multi-ribbed serpentine drive belt, then remove the water pump assembly.

18. Disconnect the upper radiator hose, then remove the A/C compressor, if equipped, and position aside.

19. Disconnect the lower radiator hose, then remove the radiator and lower fan shroud.

20. Disconnect the power steering hoses from the pump, then cap the openings to prevent system contamination or excessive fluid loss.

21. Disconnect the heater hose from the intake manifold, then disconnect the ground straps at the rear of the engine.

22. Tag, disconnect and remove the wiring harness and vacuum lines from the engine.

23. Disconnect the throttle cable, then disconnect the fuel lines from the fuel rail and engine.

24. Support the transmission.

25. Install a suitable lifting device and carefully lift the engine. Pause several times while lifting the engine to make sure no wires or hoses have become snagged.

To install:

26. Carefully lower the engine into the vehicle, then remove the support and engine lifting device.

27. Connect the fuel lines and install the bracket(s).

28. Connect the throttle cable.

29. Connect the vacuum lines and wiring harness connectors as noted during removal. Engage the wiring harness clips and connect the ground straps to the rear of the engine.

30. Connect the heater hose, then uncap and connect the power steering hoses.

31. Install the lower shroud, then install the radiator.

32. Reposition and secure the A/C compressor to the engine.

33. Install the upper radiator hose, then install the water pump.

34. Install the serpentine drive belt, then install the fan assembly.

35. Install the upper radiator shroud, then install the air cleaner and ducts.

36. Connect the battery ground strap to the engine block.

37. Install the bellhousing bolts.

38. Install the engine mount through-bolts.

39. Install the starter motor.

40. Install the flywheel cover.

41. Install the pencil braces.

42. Install the catalytic converter pipe assembly and hangers.

43. Carefully lower the vehicle.

44. Align the marks made during removal and install the hood.

45. Install the outer cowl vent grilles, then connect the vacuum reservoir and/or the underhood light to the hood (as equipped).

46. Connect the windshield washer hoses.

47. Check all powertrain fluid levels and add, as necessary. Be sure to properly fill the engine crankcase with clean engine oil.

48. Connect the negative battery cable and properly fill the engine cooling system.

49. Start and run the engine, then check for leaks.

Astro and Safari

1. If equipped, properly discharge and recover the refrigerant from the A/C system.

2. Disconnect the negative battery cable.

3. Drain the cooling system.

4. Raise and safely support the vehicle. Disconnect the exhaust pipes at the manifolds.

5. If applicable, disconnect the strut rods at the flywheel housing.

6. Remove the torque converter cover, then remove the torque converter bolts.

7. Remove the starter assembly, then drain the oil and remove the and oil filter. Disconnect the wires at the transmission. Disconnect the fuel lines.

8. Tag and disengage the wires at the engine and frame. Disconnect the fuel lines at the frame.

9. Disconnect the transmission and engine oil cooler lines at the radiator.

10. Remove the lower fan shroud retainers, then remove the motor mount bolts.

11. Lower the vehicle. Remove the headlight bezels and/or grille, as necessary. On 1994–96 vehicles, remove the horns.

12. Remove the radiator close out panel and the radiator support brace.

13. Remove the hood latch mechanism. If necessary on vehicles 1992, remove the master cylinder.

14. Remove the air cleaner assembly and ducts.

15. Remove the upper fan shroud.

16. For vehicles 1992–93:

a. Remove the upper radiator core support, then if equipped, remove the A/C condenser.

b. Remove the radiator filler panels, then remove the radiator.

c. Remove the lower radiator shroud, then remove the engine cover.

d. If equipped, disconnect the A/C hose at the accumulator.

e. Remove the multi-ribbed accessory drive belt, then remove the fan.

17. For 1994–96 vehicles:

a. If equipped, remove the A/C condenser.

b. Remove the fan and clutch assembly, then remove the lower fan shroud.

c. If not done already, disconnect the remaining oil cooler-to-radiator lines.

d. Remove the radiator.

e. Remove the engine cover.

f. If equipped, remove the A/C accumulator.

g. If not done already, remove the multi-ribbed engine accessory drive belt.

18. Disconnect the power steering pump lines at the gearbox (1992–93) or from the hydro-boost, oil cooler and reservoir (1994–96).

19. If equipped, remove the A/C compressor pencil braces at the engine block.

20. Remove the power steering pump, bracket and A/C compressor as an assembly.

21. Disengage the alternator wiring, then remove the alternator and bracket assembly.

22. Disengage the wiring harness at the bulkhead. Except for 1995–96 vehicles, remove the right kick panel.

23. Disengage the wiring from the knock sensor module.

24. Disconnect the upper and lower radiator hoses, then disconnect the heater hose from the water pump.

25. Remove the oil filler tube, then remove the transmission filler tube (top bolt only).

26. Tag and disconnect the vacuum hoses at the intake manifold.

27. If equipped, remove the cruise control servo and bracket.

28. Matchmark and remove the distributor assembly or the High Voltage Switch (HVS) assembly, as applicable.

29. If equipped with the 4.3L (VIN W) engine, remove the upper intake manifold assembly, then disconnect the fuel lines and remove the lower intake manifold.

30. If equipped with the 4.3L (VIN Z) engine, disconnect the fuel lines from the TBI unit, tag and disengage all cables, wiring and hoses, then remove the TBI unit from the engine. Remove the MAP sensor bracket, then disconnect the heater hose from the engine block with bracket from the exhaust manifold.

31. Raise and support the vehicle safely, then If equipped, remove the transfer case brace.

32. For 1994–96 vehicles, remove the fuel line bracket and ground wire from the back of the left cylinder head.

33. Remove the transmission oil level indicator tube.

34. Disengage the necessary wiring from the transmission.

35. Remove the bellhousing bolts, then lower the vehicle.

36. For 1995–96 vehicles the tie bar must be cut from the vehicle in order

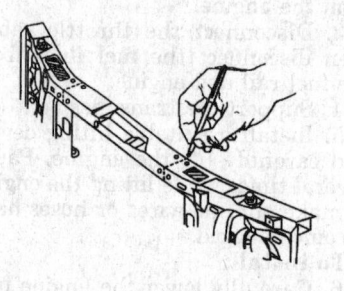

85473084

Scribing marks for cutting the tie bar — 1995–96 vehicles

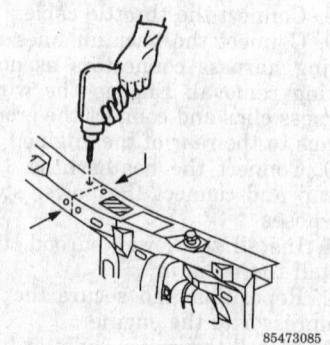

85473085

Drilling out holes for tie bar replacement brackets — 1995–96 vehicles

to create sufficient clearance for engine removal:

a. Remove the master cylinder retaining nuts, then reposition the cylinder assembly out of the way.

b. Scribe marks for cutting the tie bar assembly. The marks should be made at the centerline between the indentations on the right and left side of the bar assembly.

c. Using the replacement brackets from the service kit as a template over the indentations, center punch the holes for drilling.

d. Drill out 8mm holes for the brace bolts.

e. Carefully cut the tie bar cross section using a reciprocating power saw or hack saw.

NOTE: Extreme care must be taken when cutting out the tie bar cross section. The tie bar will be attached using brackets from the service kit. the cut out portion of the bar and the brackets must be treated with anti-corrosion materials and painted. Care taken during cutting will help save time on surface preparation and installation.

37. Attach a suitable lifting device to the engine and support the transmission, then carefully remove the engine.

To install:

38. Carefully lower the engine into position and engage it to the transmission assembly. If possible, thread the bellhousing bolts to secure the engine to the transmission.

39. Remove the engine lifting device, then raise and support the vehicle safely. Install any remaining bellhousing bolts, then tighten the bolts and remove the transmission support.

40. Engage the wiring to the transmission assembly.

41. Install the transmission oil level indicator tube.

42. On 1994–96 vehicles install the fuel line bracket and ground wire to the back of the left cylinder head.

43. If equipped, install the transfer case brace.

44. Lower the vehicle.

45. If equipped with the 4.3L (VIN Z) engine, connect the heater hose to the engine block with the exhaust manifold bracket, then install the MAP sensor bracket. Instal the TBI unit, connecting all wiring, cables and hoses. Connect the fuel lines.

46. If equipped with the 4.3L (VIN W) engine, instal the lower intake manifold assembly, then connect the

fuel lines and install the upper intake manifold assembly.

47. Align and install the distributor or the HVS assembly, as equipped.

48. If equipped, install the cruise control servo and bracket.

49. Connect the vacuum hoses to the intake manifold.

50. Install the transmission filler tube (upper bolt) and the oil filler tube.

51. If removed and applicable, install the ignition coil.

52. Except for 1996 vehicles, the air cleaner and ducts may be installed at this time.

53. Connect the heater and radiator hoses.

54. Connect the wiring harness to the knock sensor module, then for vehicles 1992–94 install the kick panel.

55. Engage the wiring harness at the bulkhead.

56. Install the alternator and bracket as an assembly, then engage the wiring.

57. Install the power steering pump, bracket and A/C compressor assembly. Connect the compressor pencil braces to the block and connect the hoses to the power steering pump, oil cooler and reservoir. Make sure all components are secure.

58. For vehicles 1992–93, install the fan.

59. Position the multi-ribbed drive belt.

60. Install the accumulator and/or connect the refrigerant hoses to the accumulator assembly, as applicable.

61. Install the lower radiator shroud, then for 1994–96 vehicles, install the fan and clutch.

62. For 1995–96 vehicles install the tie bar assembly:

a. File the rough edges of the tie bar and removed cross section.

b. Clean the assembly, cross section and brackets using a wax and grease remover.

c. Treat all bare metal surfaces with an anticorrosion primer.

d. Apply primer surfaces to the tie bar assembly, cross section and brackets.

e. Paint the components and allow to dry.

f. Install the front brackets to the tie bar cross section and to the bar assembly using the 2 bolts and nuts facing the front of the vehicle.

g. Install the U-nuts to the rear tie bar cross section and tie bar assembly.

h. Install the rear bracket and remaining nuts and bolts, then tighten to 24 ft. lbs. (31 Nm)

i. Reposition and secure the master cylinder assembly. If necessary, cut out indication hole in the air cleaner snorkel.

63. Install the radiator and connect the hoses.

64. If equipped, install the A/C condenser.

65. Instal the upper fan shroud and, if applicable, the upper radiator core support.

66. Instal the hood latch mechanism, then install the core support brace.

67. On vehicles 1992–94 install the radiator lower close out panel.

68. On 1994–96 vehicles, install the horns.

69. Install the grille and, if applicable, the headlight bezels.

70. If not done earlier, install the air cleaner and intake ducts at this time.

71. If not done earlier, connect the fuel lines at the engine.

72. Raise and support the vehicle safely, then install the motor mount fasteners.

73. If not done earlier, install the lower fan shroud retainers.

74. Connect the engine and transmission oil cooler lines./

75. Secure the fuel line bracket at the frame.

76. Engage the wiring to the engine and frame, as necessary.

77. Install the oil filter, then install the starter assembly.

78. Install the torque converter bolts, then install the cover.

79. Connect the exhaust pipes, then lower the vehicle.

80. Refill the engine crankcase with engine oil, then connect the negative battery cable.

81. Properly refill the engine cooling system.

82. If equipped, make sure all refrigerant lines are properly connected, then evacuate and charge the A/C system.

Lumina, Silhouette and Trans Sport

3.1L ENGINE

1. Disconnect the negative battery cable.

2. Drain the cooling system. Disconnect the air flow tube from the air cleaner.

3. Disconnect the electrical connector from the ECM and push it through to the engine compartment. Disconnect the harness from the clips on the body and lay it across the engine.

4. Disconnect the engine harness at the bulkhead connector. Disconnect the throttle and TV cables.

5. Disconnect the fuel lines. Disconnect the transaxle shift linkage.

6. Disconnect the cooler lines at the radiator. Disconnect the radiator and heater hoses.

NOTE: On some newer vehicles it may be necessary to disconnect the refrigerant lines from the compressor in order to prevent stressing and damaging them. If so, properly recover the refrigerant using a recovery station before loosening ANY fittings. Cap all openings to prevent system contamination or damage.

7. Remove the air conditioning compressor from the bracket and support it aside. Remove the upper engine support strut.

8. Raise and safely support the vehicle. Remove the front wheel and tire assemblies.

9. Remove the stabilizer bar. Disconnect the tie rod ends and the lower control arm ball joints.

10. Disconnect the halfshafts from the transaxle and support them aside. Disconnect the steering shaft pinch bolt.

11. Remove the starter.

12. Remove the flywheel cover, then remove the torque converter bolts.

13. Disconnect the exhaust pipe at the manifold. Support the engine and sub-frame.

14. Remove the sub-frame bolts and lower the engine/transaxle and subframe.

To install:

15. Raise the engine assembly into position, then install and tighten the subframe bolts.

16. Connect the exhaust pipe at the rear manifold. Install the starter.

17. Connect the steering shaft and install the pinch bolt. Connect the halfshafts to the transaxle.

18. Connect the lower control arm ball joints to the steering knuckles.

19. Install the stabilizer bar. Install the upper engine strut.

20. Install the wheel and tire assemblies. Lower the vehicle. Install the radiator and heater hoses.

21. Install the shift linkage. Connect the fuel lines and the throttle and TV cables.

22. Connect the harness to bulkhead connector. Connect the ECM harness to the ECM.

23. Connect the air cleaner hose and the radiator upper support.

24. Connect the negative battery cable.

25. Fill the cooling system. Install the air conditioning compressor. If lines were disconnected, properly

evacuate and recharge the A/C system.

3.8L ENGINE

1. If equipped, properly recover the refrigerant from the A/C system.
2. Properly relieve the fuel system pressure, then disconnect the negative battery cable.
3. Remove the air cleaner and duct assembly, then drain the engine cooling system.
4. Disconnect the wiring from the left side of the engine.
5. Disengage the cruise servo connector, then disengage the connector at the emergency jumper box.
6. Disengage the wiring harness retainer from the right side of the engine.
7. Disengage the electrical connector at the cooling fan.
8. Disconnect the shift cable, heat shield and bracket at the transaxle.
9. Disconnect the battery ground cable from the engine, then remove the wiring block connector from the right side of the engine.
10. Remove the screws retaining the multi-use relay bracket to the tie bar.
11. Disengage the A/C compressor and accumulator wiring.
12. Disconnect the engine fuel vapor harness from the engine.
13. Disconnect the accelerator and cruise control cables along with the bracket from the throttle body.
14. Disconnect the brake vacuum hose at the engine.
15. Remove the engine mount strut bolts and nuts from the engine.
16. Disconnect the radiator and heater inlet/outlet hoses at the engine.
17. Remove the retaining bolt and disconnect the refrigerant manifold from the A/C compressor.
18. Disconnect the fuel hoses from the rail assembly.
19. Raise and support the vehicle safely, then drain the engine oil from the crankcase.
20. Remove the left and right tire and wheel assemblies.
21. Disconnect the engine wiring harness at the front of the frame, then disengage the wiring from the starter motor assembly.
22. Remove the flywheel covers from the transaxle, then remove the starter assembly.
23. Remove the torque converter bolts.
24. Remove the steering shaft (intermediate shaft) pinch bolt.
25. Disconnect the tie rod ends from the steering knuckles, then dis-

connect the right and left lower control arm ball joints.
26. Separate the drive axles from the transaxle, then support them aside.
27. Disconnect the exhaust pipe-to-manifold bolts and springs.
28. Disconnect the transaxle oil cooler line at the transaxle.
29. Remove the engine front mount nuts from the frame.
30. Position and engine/transaxle frame support under the assembly, then lower the vehicle or raise the support so the assembly is secure.
31. Remove the bolts retaining the frame assembly, then raise the vehicle leaving the engine/transaxle frame assembly behind.
32. If necessary, remove the power steering pump from the engine and position aside. Remove the necessary components and separate the engine from the transaxle.

To install:

33. If removed install the engine to the transaxle and frame assembly. Install the engine-to-transaxle retainers and tighten to 55 ft. lbs. (75 Nm). Install the engine-to-transaxle brace and retaining bolts. Tighten the engine side bolts to 70 ft. lbs. (95 Nm) and the transaxle side bolts to 47 ft. lbs. (63 Nm). Install the necessary components, including the power steering pump.
34. Position the engine/transaxle frame assembly under the vehicle, then carefully lower the vehicle until the frame is in position.
35. Install the frame retaining bolts and tighten to 103 ft. lbs. (140 Nm).
36. Raise and support the vehicle safely for access, then connect the transaxle cooler lines.
37. Connect the exhaust pipe to the manifold and tighten the retainers to 18 ft. lbs. (25 Nm).
38. Connect the drive axles to the transaxle.
39. Install the ball joints and tie rods to the knuckles.
40. Connect the intermediate shaft pinch bolt and tighten to 33 ft. lbs. (47 Nm).
41. Install the torque converter bolts and tighten to 46 ft. lbs. (62 Nm).
42. Install the starter assembly to the engine, then install the torque converter cover. Engage the starter wiring.
43. Connect the engine wiring harness and retainers to the frame.
44. Install the front tire and wheel assemblies, then lower the vehicle.

45. Install the A/C manifold to the compressor and secure using the retaining bolt.
46. Connect the fuel lines to the rail.
47. Connect the heater/radiator pipes and hoses to the engine.
48. Install the engine mount strut bolt and nut to the engine, then tighten to 44 ft. lbs. (60 Nm).
49. Connect the vacuum hose from the engine to the brake booster.
50. Install the accelerator and cruise control bracket, heat shield and cables to the throttle body.
51. Connect the engine fuel vapor harness to the engine.
52. Engage all wiring removed earlier in the reverse order of removal.
53. Refill the engine crankcase with oil, then connect the negative battery cable.
54. Properly refill the engine cooling system.
55. If equipped, properly evacuate and recharge the A/C system.

R/V-Series and C/K-Series

1. Relieve the fuel system pressure, then disconnect the negative battery cable.
2. Remove the hood.
3. Drain the cooling system.
4. Remove the air cleaner.
5. Remove the accessory drive belt, fan and water pump pulley.
6. Remove the radiator and shroud.
7. Disconnect the heater hoses at the engine.
8. Disconnect the accelerator, cruise control and detent linkage, as applicable.
9. Disconnect the air conditioning compressor, if equipped, and lay aside.
10. Remove the power steering pump, if used, and lay aside.
11. Disconnect the engine wiring from the engine.
12. Disconnect the fuel line.
13. Disconnect the vacuum lines from the intake manifold.
14. Raise the vehicle and support it safely.
15. Drain the engine oil.
16. Disconnect the exhaust pipes from the manifolds.
17. Disconnect the strut rods at the engine mountings, if used.
18. Remove the flywheel or torque converter cover.
19. Disconnect the wiring along the oil pan rail.
20. Remove the starter.
21. If applicable, disconnect the wire for the fuel gauge.

22. If equipped with automatic transmission, remove the converter to flexplate bolts.

23. Lower the vehicle and suitably support the transmission. Attach a suitable lifting fixture to the engine.

24. Remove the bellhousing to engine bolts.

25. Remove the engine mounting to frame bolts and remove the engine.

To install:

26. Raise the vehicle and support it safely.

27. Lower the engine and install the engine mounting bolts.

28. Install the bellhousing to engine bolts and torque to 35 ft. lbs. (44 Nm).

29. Install the converter to flex bolts and torque.

30. Install the fuel gauge wiring (if applicable) and starter.

31. Install the flywheel or torque converter cover.

32. Connect the strut rods at the engine mountings, if used.

33. Install the exhaust pipes at the manifold.

34. Lower the vehicle.

35. Connect the vacuum lines to the intake manifold.

36. Install the fuel line.

37. Connect the engine wiring harness.

38. Install the power steering pump, if used.

39. Connect the air conditioning compressor, if used.

40. Connect the accelerator, cruise control and detent linkage.

41. Connect the heater hoses.

42. Install the radiator and shroud.

43. Install the accessory drive belts.

44. Install the hood.

45. Install the proper quantity and grade of coolant and engine oil.

46. Connect the negative battery cable.

G-Series

4.3L ENGINE

1. If equipped, properly recover the refrigerant from the A/C system.

2. Properly relieve the fuel system pressure, then disconnect the negative battery cable.

3. If necessary on 1992 vehicles, remove the glove box.

4. Drain the engine cooling system.

5. Remove the engine cover.

6. Remove the air cleaner assembly and air intake duct.

7. Remove the power steering reservoir.

8. Remove the upper fan shroud, then remove the fan and pulley. Remove the radiator assembly.

9. Remove the air conditioning condenser, then remove the compressor and bracket.

10. Remove the alternator.

11. If equipped, remove the cruise control servo.

12. Tag and disconnect all vacuum hoses.

13. Disconnect the accelerator linkage, cruise control and TVS cables with the mounting brackets from the throttle body, as applicable.

14. Properly relieve the fuel system pressure and remove the TBI unit.

15. Remove the distributor cap with the wires attached. If necessary, remove the coil and mounting bracket.

16. For 1993–96 vehicles (and earlier as necessary) remove the MAP sensor and mounting bracket.

17. Tag and disengage the engine wiring harness connectors from the necessary sensors and switches. Lay the harness aside.

18. Remove the upper half of the engine dipstick tube.

19. Remove the oil filler tube.

20. If necessary, remove the power steering pump and position aside.

21. Remove the headlight bezels and the grille.

22. Remove the upper radiator support.

23. If necessary on 1992 vehicles, remove the lower fan shroud and filler panel. Remove the hood latch support.

24. Raise and support the vehicle safely.

25. Drain the engine oil.

26. Disconnect the exhaust pipes at the manifolds.

27. Remove the strut rods at the torque converter underpan.

28. Remove the torque converter cover.

29. If equipped, disconnect the oil cooler lines from the engine.

30. Remove the starter.

31. Remove the flexplate-to-torque converter bolts.

32. Remove the engine mounting through bolts.

33. Remove the bellhousing-to-engine bolts.

34. Lower the vehicle and support the transmission using the proper equipment.

35. Attach an engine crane to the engine, pull the engine forward and upward and remove it.

To install:

36. Lower the engine into position and engage the transmission.

37. Install and tighten the engine mount through-bolts.

38. Install and tighten the bellhousing-to-engine bolts.

39. Raise and support the vehicle safely for access.

40. Install the flexplate-to-torque converter bolts.

41. Install the starter.

42. Install the torque converter cover.

43. Install the strut rods at the torque converter underpan.

44. If equipped, connect the oil cooler lines to the engine.

45. Connect the exhaust pipes at the manifolds, then lower the vehicle.

46. Install the radiator support.

47. Install the head light bezel and grill.

48. Install oil fill tube and the upper half of the dipstick tube.

49. If applicable, install the MAP sensor and/or ignition coil and brackets.

50. Install the distributor cap and spark plug wires.

51. Engage the engine wiring harness connectors and harness retaining clamps.

52. Install the TBI unit, then connect the accelerator cables (with cruise control and/or TVS cables as applicable) along with the brackets.

53. Connect the vacuum hoses to the engine.

54. Install the cruise control servo.

55. Install the alternator.

56. If equipped, install the air conditioning compressor and the condenser.

57. Install the radiator and lower shroud.

58. Install the cooling fan and pulley, then install the upper fan shroud.

59. Install the power steering reservoir.

60. Install the hood release cable.

61. Install the air duct and the air cleaner assembly.

62. Refill the engine crankcase.

63. Connect the negative battery cable.

64. Refill the cooling system with the proper type and quantity of antifreeze.

65. Install the engine cover.

66. If removed, install the glove box.

67. If equipped, properly evacuate and charge the air conditioning system.

5.0L AND 5.7L ENGINES

1. If equipped, properly recover the refrigerant from the A/C system.

2. Properly relieve the fuel system pressure, then disconnect the negative battery cable.

3. Drain the engine cooling system.

4. Remove the radiator coolant reservoir bottle.

5. Remove the grille and the lower grille valance.

6. Remove the upper radiator support.

7. Remove the air conditioning condenser from in front of the radiator.

8. Remove the radiator.

9. Remove the power steering pump and position it aside with the lines intact.

10. Remove the engine cover.

11. Remove the air cleaner.

12. Remove the TBI unit.

13. Disconnect the engine wiring harness from the firewall connection.

14. Tag and disengage all necessary vacuum lines and wiring harness connectors.

15. Disconnect the heater pipe or hoses at the engine, as applicable.

16. Remove the thermostat housing.

17. Remove the oil filler tube.

18. Remove the cruise control servo, bracket and transducer, as necessary.

19. Raise and support the vehicle safely.

20. Drain the engine oil.

21. Disconnect the exhaust pipes at the manifolds.

22. Remove the driveshaft from the transmission and plug the end of the transmission case to prevent fluid leakage.

23. Disconnect the transmission shift linkage and the speed sensor connector.

24. Disconnect the fuel and vapor return lines at the engine.

25. Remove the rear engine/transmission mount bolts.

——— WARNING ———

Do not jack under the oil pan, crankshaft pulley or any sheetmetal for any reason. Due to the small clearance between the oil pan and pump screen, jacking against the pan could cause it to be bent up against the pump screen resulting in a damaged oil pickup unit.

26. Support the transmission and engine.

27. Remove the engine mount bracket-to-frame bolts.

28. Remove the engine mount through bolts.

29. Raise the engine slightly and remove the engine mounts.

30. Support the engine with wood blocks.

31. Lower the vehicle.

32. Install a suitable engine lifting device.

33. Remove the engine and transmission from the vehicle as an assembly.

34. Separate the engine and transmission, as required.

To install:

35. If separated, joint the engine and transmission and support using a suitable lifting device.

36. Install the engine and transmission assembly to the vehicle, then install the engine mounts and secure.

37. Remove the engine lifting device, then raise and support the vehicle safely.

38. Connect the fuel and vapor return lines at the engine.

39. Connect the transmission shift linkage, then engage the speed sensor connector.

40. Install the driveshaft.

41. Connect the exhaust pipes at the manifolds, then lower the vehicle.

42. If equipped, install the cruise control servo, bracket and transducer.

43. Install the oil filler tube.

44. Install the thermostat housing.

45. Connect the heater hoses or pipe at the engine.

46. Connect the vacuum hoses and wiring, as tagged during removal.

47. Connect the engine wiring harness connector.

48. Install the TBI unit.

49. Install the air cleaner.

50. Reposition and secure the power steering pump.

51. Install the radiator.

52. If equipped, install the A/C condenser.

53. Install the upper radiator support, the grille and the lower grille valance.

54. Install the radiator coolant reservoir bottle.

55. Refill the engine crankcase.

56. Install the engine cover.

57. Connect the negative battery cable.

58. Refill the cooling system with the proper type and quantity of antifreeze.

59. If equipped, properly evacuate and charge the air conditioning system.

7.4L ENGINE

1. If equipped, properly recover the refrigerant from the A/C system.

2. Properly relieve the fuel system pressure, then disconnect the negative battery cable.

3. Remove the engine cover.

4. Drain the engine cooling system, then drain the crankcase of engine oil.

5. Remove the air intake duct and the air cleaner assembly.

6. Disconnect the upper radiator hoses at the engine and the upper heater hose and the rear of the engine.

7. Tag and disconnect all wiring at the TBI unit, then disconnect the accelerator linkage (including the cruise control and/or TV linkage).

8. Tag and disconnect all vacuum hoses.

9. Remove the distributor cap (lay aside) and all spark plug wiring. Matchmark and remove the distributor assembly.

10. Disconnect the fuel lines and bracket. If equipped, remove the cruise control bracket.

11. Remove the ignition coil and bracket.

12. Disconnect the ECS and MAP sensors with bracket(s).

13. Remove the transmission and engine oil dipstick tubes.

14. If applicable, remove the EGR solenoid.

15. Remove the air conditioning compressor brackets (usually 2).

16. Remove the TBI unit.

17. Disconnect the wiring at the rear of the engine.

18. Remove the headlight bezels, grille, lower grille valance or bumper filler panel and all necessary sheetmetal to ease removal and installation of the engine and transmission assembly.

19. If equipped, remove the cruise control servo.

20. Remove the hood latch and the radiator coolant reservoir bottle.

21. Remove the upper radiator brackets.

22. If not done earlier, remove the front end sheetmetal cross panel, then remove the sheetmetal vertical support with electric cooling fan.

23. Remove the air conditioning condenser from in front of the radiator. Cap all lines.

24. Remove the windshield wiper reservoir and washer pump.

25. Remove the upper cooling fan shroud.

26. Disconnect the lower radiator and heater hoses, then disconnect the engine oil and transmission cooler lines.

27. Remove the radiator, then remove the lower shroud.

28. Remove the cooling fan, then remove the multi-ribbed belt and the pump pulley.

29. Remove A/C line from the accumulator and alternator.

30. Remove the air conditioning line assembly from the back of the

compressor. Remove the right side engine accessory mounting bracket with the A/C compressor and idler pulley.

31. Remove the power steering pump and position aside.

32. Disconnect the alternator wires, then remove the left engine accessory bracket along with the alternator and belt tensioner.

33. Raise and support the vehicle safely.

34. Remove the exhaust crossover pipe heat shields, then disconnect the pipe from the manifolds.

35. Remove the starter motor heat shield, then disconnect the starter motor and, if applicable, knock sensor wires. Remove the starter motor assembly.

36. Disconnect the transmission wiring and linkage.

37. Remove the driveshaft from the transmission, then plug the end of the transmission case to prevent fluid leakage.

38. Remove the engine mount through-bolts. The bolts may be difficult to remove until the engine weight is taken off the mounts, if necessary, loosen them and wait until the engine is supported.

39. Do not position the jack under the oil pan, crankshaft pulley or any sheetmetal!.

40. Disconnect the transmission crossmember.

41. Remove the wiring from the front of the engine.

42. Lower the vehicle for access and engine/transmission assembly removal.

43. Attach a suitable lifting device to the engine.

44. Raise the engine as necessary and maneuver the engine/transmission assembly.

45. If necessary, separate the engine from the transmission, then mount the engine on a work stand.

To install:

46. If removed, connect the transmission to the engine and prepare them for installation.

47. Raise the engine/transmission and guide the assembly into position in the vehicle.

48. With the assembly still supported, carefully install the transmission crossmember and engine mount fasteners.

49. Install the driveshaft.

50. Connect the transmission shift linkage and wiring.

51. Install the starter motor assembly, then engage the starter motor and, if applicable, then knock sensor

wiring. Install the starter motor heat shield.

52. Connect the exhaust crossover pipe, then install the crossover pipe heat shields.

53. Lower the vehicle as necessary for access.

54. Install the left engine accessory bracket along with the alternator and belt tensioner. Engage the alternator wiring.

55. Reposition and secure the power steering pump.

56. Install the right accessory accessory mounting bracket with the A/C compressor and idler pulley. Connect the air conditioning line assembly to the back of the compressor.

57. Install the A/C line to the accumulator and alternator. Connect the lower radiator hose to the engine.

58. Install the water pump pulley, then install the belt and the cooling fan.

59. Install the radiator and the lower shroud.

60. Connect the lower radiator and heater hoses, along with the engine oil and transmission cooler lines.

61. Install the upper cooling fan shroud.

62. Install the windshield wiper reservoir and washer pump.

63. Install the air conditioning condenser.

64. Install the sheetmetal vertical support with electric cooling fan, then install the front end sheetmetal cross panel.

65. Install the upper radiator brackets.

66. Install the radiator coolant reservoir bottle and the hood latch.

67. If equipped, install the cruise control servo.

68. Install the remaining front end sheetmetal or trim components including the lower grille valance or bumper filler panel, grille and headlight bezels.

69. Connect the wiring at the rear of the engine.

70. Install the TBI unit.

71. Install the air conditioning compressor brackets (usually 2).

72. If applicable, install the EGR solenoid.

73. Install the transmission and engine oil dipstick tubes.

74. Connect the ECS and MAP sensors with bracket(s).

75. Install the ignition coil and bracket.

76. If equipped, install the cruise control bracket.

77. Connect the fuel lines and bracket.

78. Align and install the distributor assembly, then install the distributor cap and spark plug wiring.

79. Connect all vacuum hoses as tagged during removal.

80. Connect the accelerator linkage (including the cruise control and/or TV linkage), then connect all wiring at the TBI unit.

81. Connect the upper radiator hoses at the engine and the upper heater hose and the rear of the engine.

82. Install the air cleaner assembly and the air intake duct.

83. Refill the engine crankcase.

84. Connect the negative battery cable.

85. Refill the cooling system with the proper type and quantity of antifreeze.

86. If equipped, properly evacuate and charge the air conditioning system.

87. Install the engine cover.

Engine Mounts

NOTE: When lifting or raising the engine for any reason, do not support the assembly under the oil pan, any sheetmetal or the crankshaft pulley.

--- **CAUTION** ---

When working on the engine mounts, make sure the engine is SECURELY supported at all times. If necessary, use blocks of wood to help make sure it cannot shift suddenly.

REMOVAL AND INSTALLATION

2.2L and 2.5L Engines

1. Disconnect the negative battery cable.

2. Support the engine with a suitable lifting fixture. Do not load the engine mounts, just take the engine weight off them.

3. Remove the engine mount through-bolt and nut, then raise the engine just sufficiently to permit mount removal.

4. Remove the engine mount bolts, nuts and washers.

5. Remove the mount assembly attaching bolts, nuts and washers. Remove the mount assembly.

6. Installation is the reverse of the removal procedure.

2.8L Engine

1. Disconnect the negative battery cable.

2. Raise and support the vehicle safely. Support the engine with a suitable lifting fixture.

3. Remove the fan shroud and front wheel.

4. Remove the engine mount through-bolt and nut.

5. Raise the engine enough to permit removal of the engine mounting and block in position.

6. If necessary for access, remove the tie rod at the drag link, then remove the stabilizer link from the control arm. Remove the lower shock absorber bolts. Remove the lower control arm pivot bolts and position control arm aside.

7. Remove the mount assembly attaching bolts, nuts and washers. Remove the mount assembly.

8. Installation is the reverse of the removal procedure.

3.1L Engine

1. Disconnect the negative battery cable.

2. Raise and support the vehicle safely. Support the engine with a suitable lifting fixture just sufficiently to take the weight off the mount.

3. Remove the engine mount nuts from below the engine frame mounting bracket.

4. Raise the engine enough to permit removal of the engine mounting and block the engine in position.

5. Remove the mount assembly to engine bracket nuts and washers. Remove the mount assembly.

6. Installation is the reverse of the removal procedure. Tighten the mount retaining nuts to 35 ft. lbs. (48 Nm), then check the mounts for proper alignment. If the mount is not properly aligned, loosen the nuts and allow the mount to reposition itself before tightening again. If the mount is not properly positioned, drivetrain component failure could occur.

3.8L Engine

1. Disconnect the negative battery cable, then remove the serpentine drive belt.

2. Install an engine support fixture, then raise and support the vehicle safely. Remove the right front tire and wheel assembly, then remove the right splash shield.

3. Remove the flywheel access covers.

4. Remove the crankshaft balancer bolt and balancer using J-39096 and J-38197 or equivalents.

5. Disengage the wiring connector from the crankshaft sensor, then remove the sensor shield from the engine.

6. Disconnect the power steering lines and engine wiring at the front of the frame. Remove the power steering gear heat shield from the gear assembly, then remove the gear assembly from the frame mounts and support aside using wire.

7. Remove the engine front mount-to-frame nuts, then remove the nuts retaining the front and rear transaxle mounts to the frame.

8. Support the frame from below, then remove the frame retaining bolts. Lower the frame.

9. Remove the bolts retaining the front engine mount to the engine, then remove the mount.

10. Installation is the reverse of the removal procedure. Be sure to tighten the front engine mount-to-engine bolts to 66 ft. lbs. (90 Nm), then frame retaining bolts to 103 ft. lbs. (140 Nm) and the engine/transaxle mount-to-frame bolts to 33 ft. lbs. (44 Nm).

4.3L and V8 Engines

1. Disconnect the negative battery cable.

2. For S/T-Series or if access from underneath is preferable, raise and support the vehicle safely.

3. For the S/T-Series, remove the cab or body mounting bolts. Raise the body for clearance and block in position.

4. Support the engine with a suitable lifting fixture. Just take the weight off the mounts, do not load them.

NOTE: Do not position the jack under the oil pan, any sheetmetal or the crankshaft pulley, otherwise damage may occur.

5. Remove the engine mount through-bolt and nut.

6. Raise the engine just sufficiently to permit removal of the engine mounting and block in position. Keep a close eye on the engine-to-cowl clearance when raising it.

7. Remove the mount assembly to frame retainers. Remove the mount assembly.

8. Installation is the reverse of the removal procedure.

Cylinder Head

REMOVAL AND INSTALLATION

2.2L Engine

1. Properly relieve the fuel system pressure, then disconnect the negative battery cable.

2. Drain the engine cooling system, then disconnect the air duct from the air inlet.

3. Disconnect the upper radiator hose, then remove the upper fan shroud.

4. Remove the radiator assembly, then remove the lower fan shroud.

5. Remove the fan assembly, then remove the serpentine drive belt.

6. Remove the water pump pulley.

7. Disconnect the heater hose form the intake manifold and the thermostat housing, then remove the thermostat housing.

8. Remove the alternator support brace and disengage the alternator wiring.

9. If equipped, remove the A/C compressor with brackets, then position them aside. Do not disconnect the refrigerant lines, but be careful not to kink and damage them.

10. Disconnect and reposition the accessory bracket along with the alternator and power steering pump still attached. Be careful not to damage the steering pump lines.

11. Disconnect the throttle cable and cable support linkage, then disconnect the heater hose from the water pump.

12. Remove the oil fill tube, then disconnect the exhaust pipe and the oxygen sensor.

13. Remove the exhaust manifold bolts, then remove the manifold.

14. Tag and disconnect both the electrical wiring and the vacuum hoses from the upper intake manifold.

15. Remove the upper intake manifold, then tag and disconnect the wiring from the lower intake manifold.

16. Disconnect the fuel lines, then tag and disconnect the spark plug wires.

17. Remove the lower intake manifold from the engine.

18. Remove the rocker arm cover from the cylinder head.

19. Remove the rocker arms and pushrods.

20. Disconnect the engine lift bracket from the rear of the engine.

21. Remove the cylinder head bolts and studs, then carefully lift the cylinder head from the engine.

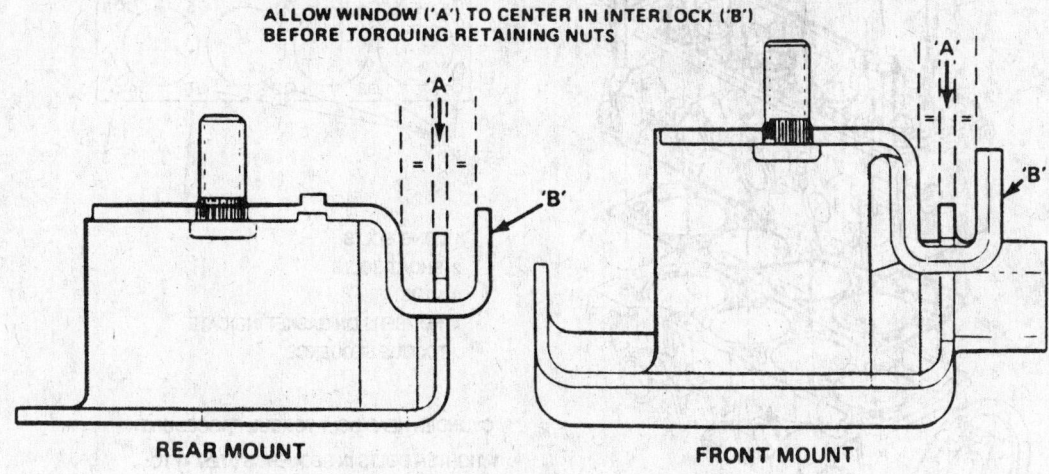

**ALLOW WINDOW ('A') TO CENTER IN INTERLOCK ('B')
BEFORE TORQUING RETAINING NUTS**

REAR MOUNT   FRONT MOUNT

85473086

Transaxle mount alignment — 3.1L engines

To install:

22. Carefully clean and inspect the gasket mounting surfaces.

NOTE: The gasket surfaces on both the head and block must be clean of any foreign matter and free of nicks or heavy scratches. The cylinder bolt threads in the block and thread on the bolts must be cleaned (dirt will affect the bolt torque).

23. Place a new gasket over the dowel pins (do not use any sealer on the gasket), then position the cylinder head over the gasket and dowels.

24. Apply a coating of 1052080 or equivalent sealer to the cylinder head bolt threads. Install the cylinder head bolts (within 15 minutes of sealer application), then tighten them in the proper sequence first to a torque of 46 ft. lbs. (63 Nm) for long bolts or to 43 ft. lbs. (58 Nm) for short bolts and then tighten all bolts an additional 90 degree turn using a torque angle meter.

25. Install the engine lift bracket.

26. Install the rocker arms and pushrods.

27. Install the rocker arm cover.

28. Install the lower intake manifold.

29. Connect the spark plug wires and the fuel lines.

30. Engage the wiring to the lower intake manifold.

31. Install the upper intake manifold.

32. Connect the vacuum hoses and electrical wiring to the upper intake, as tagged during removal.

33. Install the oil fill tube assembly.

34. Install the exhaust manifold, then connect the exhaust pipe and oxygen sensor.

35. Connect the heater hose to the water pump, then connect the throttle cable support and throttle cable.

36. Install the accessory support bracket and components.

37. If equipped, reposition and secure the A/C compressor.

38. Install the power steering support brace and the alternator support brace. Engage the alternator wiring.

39. Install the thermostat housing, then connect the heater hose to the housing.

40. Install the water pump pulley and the serpentine drive belt.

41. Install the fan assembly, then install the radiator and the lower fan shroud.

42. Install the upper fan shroud, then connect the upper radiator hose.

43. Connect the air inlet duct work, then connect the negative battery cable.

44. Properly refill the engine cooling system and check for leaks.

2.5L Engine

NOTE: Let the vehicle sit overnight before attempting to remove the cylinder head. The engine must be cold.

—————— **CAUTION** ——————

Relieve the pressure on the fuel system before disconnecting any fuel line connection.

1. Properly relieve the fuel system pressure, then disconnect the negative battery cable.

2. Drain the engine cooling system, then remove the air cleaner assembly.

3. If equipped, remove and reposition the A/C compressor with the lines intact. Make sure the lines are not kinked or otherwise damaged.

4. Remove the rocker arm cover.

5. Loosen the rocker arms and remove the pushrods.

6. Tag and disconnect the vacuum lines, fuel lines and wiring at the TBI unit. Remove the vacuum lines from the studs on the intake manifold.

7. Disconnect the accelerator, the cruise control and the TVS cables, as equipped.

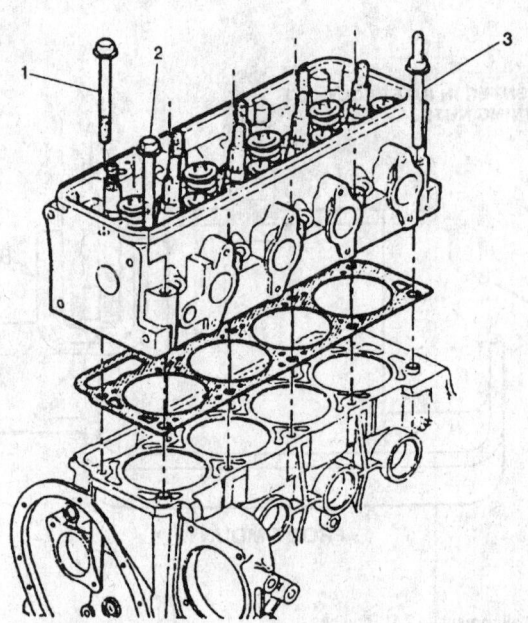

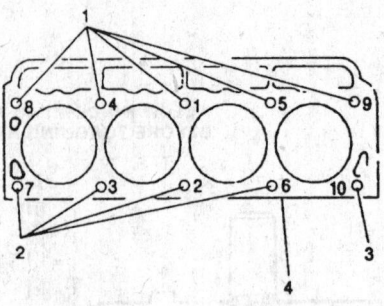

1 LONG BOLTS

2 SHORT BOLTS

3 STUD

4 NUMBERS ON GASKET INDICATE
TORQUE SEQUENCE

CYLINDER HEAD BOLT TORQUE PROCEDURE

1 TIGHTEN BOLTS IN SEQUENCE (ITEM 4) TO:
LONG BOLTS: 63 N·m (46 LBS. FT.)
SHORT BOLTS: 58 N·m (43 LBS. FT.)

2 TIGHTEN ALL BOLTS AN ADDITIONAL ANGLE
OF 90° IN SEQUENCE (ITEM 4) USING
J 36660 OR EQUIVALENT

85473087

Cylinder head bolt torque sequence — 2.2L engine

8. Remove the alternator along with the brackets and position aside.

9. Remove the water pump bypass and heater hoses from the intake manifold.

10. Disconnect the exhaust pipe from the exhaust manifold.

11. Disconnect the upper radiator hose, then remove the vacuum tube from the coolant outlet stud.

12. Remove the fuel filter and fuel line bracket at the rear of the cylinder head.

13. Remove the dipstick tube, then disconnect the wiring harness and ground strap at the rear of the cylinder head.

14. Tag and disengage the wiring connectors from the sensors and the cylinder head and the thermostat housing.

15. Remove the ignition coil wires, then tag and disconnect the spark plug wires.

16. Disengage the oxygen sensor wiring connector.

17. Remove the cylinder head-to-engine bolts, then remove the cylinder head from the engine (with the manifolds attached). If necessary, remove the intake and the exhaust manifolds from the cylinder head.

To install:

18. Carefully clean and inspect the gasket mounting surfaces.

NOTE: The gasket surfaces on both the head and block must be clean of any foreign matter and free of nicks or heavy scratches. The cylinder bolt threads in the block and thread on the bolts must be cleaned (dirt will affect the bolt torque).

19. Place a new gasket over the dowel pins, then position the cylinder head on the block over the dowel pins and gasket.

20. Apply a coating of 1052080 or equivalent sealer to the threads of the cylinder head bolts, then thread the bolts into position. Make sure the bolts are threaded within 15 minutes of the sealant application in order to allow the sealer to properly cure.

21. Tighten the cylinder head bolts to specification, using multiple passes of the proper sequence:
• Torque all bolts gradually to 18 ft. lbs. (25 Nm).
• Torque all bolts except the left front bolt (No. 9 in the sequence) to 26 ft. lbs. (35 Nm), then retorque number 9 to 18 ft. lbs. (25 Nm).
• Torque all bolts an additional ¼ turn (90°).

22. Engage the oxygen sensor connector.

23. Connect the spark plug and ignition coil wiring.

24. Engage the wiring connectors to the sensors on the cylinder head and thermostat housing.

25. Connect the wiring harness bracket and ground strap to the rear of the cylinder head.

26. Install the dipstick tube, then install the fuel filter and fuel line bracket.

27. Secure the vacuum tube at the coolant outlet stud, then connect the upper radiator hose.

28. Connect the exhaust pipe to the manifold.

29. Connect the water pump bypass and heater hoses.

30. Reposition and secure the alternator with the brackets.

31. Connect the accelerator, cruise control and TVS cables, as equipped.

32. Secure the vacuum hoses to the intake manifold studs, then engage the vacuum hoses, fuel lines and electrical wires to the TBI unit as tagged during removal.

33. Install the pushrods and secure the rocker arms.

34. Install the rocker arm cover.

35. If equipped, reposition and secure the A/C compressor along with the brackets.

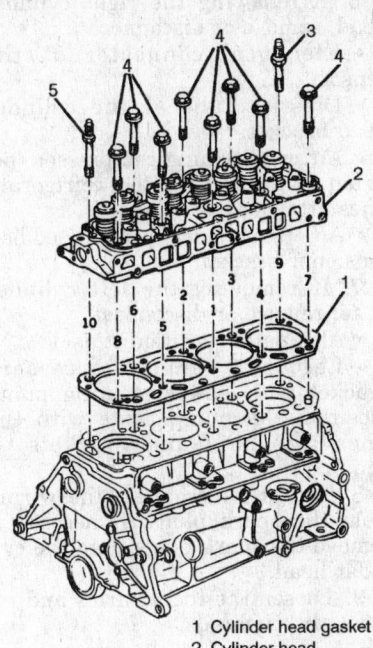

1 Cylinder head gasket
2 Cylinder head
3 Cylinder head bolt
4 Cylinder head bolt
5 Cylinder head bolt

85473088

Cylinder head bolt torque sequence — 2.5L engine

36. Install the air cleaner assembly, then connect the negative battery cable.

37. Properly refill the engine cooling system, then check for leaks.

2.8L Engine

— **CAUTION** —

Relieve the pressure on the fuel system before disconnecting any fuel line connection.

1. Properly relieve the fuel system pressure, then connect the negative battery cable.

2. Drain the engine cooling system.

3. Remove the intake manifold assembly.

4. If necessary, raise and support the vehicle safely. If it decided to disconnect the exhaust manifold and not the pipe in the next step, it may not be necessary to raise the vehicle.

5. Either disconnect the exhaust pipe from the exhaust manifold (so the manifold may be removed with the cylinder head) or, remove the exhaust manifold-to-cylinder block retainers and support the manifold out of the way.

6. If raised, lower the vehicle.

7. If removing the left side cylinder head, remove the dipstick tube, then disconnect the ground strap and the sensor connector from the cylinder head.

8. If removing the right side cylinder head, remove the drive belt, alternator, and AIR pump with mounting bracket.

NOTE: If valve train components, such as the pushrods, are to be reused, they must be tagged or arranged to insure installation in their original locations.

9. Loosen the rocker arm nuts, turn the rocker arms and remove the pushrods. Keep the pushrods in the same order as removed.

10. Loosen the cylinder head bolts using multiple passes in the reverse order of the tightening sequence.

11. Remove the cylinder head; do not pry on the head to loosen it.

To install:

12. Carefully clean and inspect the gasket mounting surfaces.

NOTE: The gasket surfaces on both the head and block must be clean of any foreign matter and free of nicks or heavy scratches. The cylinder bolt threads in the block and thread on the bolts must be cleaned (dirt will affect the bolt torque).

13. Place a new gasket over the dowel pins with the words "This Side Up" facing upwards, then position the cylinder head on the block over the dowel pins and gasket.

14. Apply a coating of 1052080 or equivalent sealer to the threads of the cylinder head bolts, then thread the bolts into position and tighten them to specification using the proper torque sequence:

• First, torque all bolts to 40 ft. lbs. (55 Nm).

• Then, torque all bolts an additional ¼ turn (90°).

15. Install the pushrods, then reposition the rocker arms and adjust the valves.

16. For the right side, install the alternator and AIR pump along with the mounting bracket, then install and tighten the drive belt.

17. For the left side, connect the ground strap and sensor connector, then install the dipstick tube.

18. If necessary, raise and support the vehicle safely.

19. Either connect the exhaust pipe to the manifold or the manifold to the cylinder head, as applicable. If raised, lower the vehicle.

20. Install the intake manifold assembly.

21. Connect the negative battery cable, then properly refill the engine cooling system.

22. Check and/or adjust the ignition timing.

3.1L Engine

1. Relieve the fuel system pressure, then disconnect the negative battery cable.

2. Drain the engine cooling system.

3. Remove the valve cover(s).

4. Remove the intake manifold.

5. Raise and support the vehicle safely, then disconnect the exhaust crossover pipe.

6. If necessary, disconnect the dipstick tube attachment and/or the the alternator bracket.

7. Lower the vehicle.

8. Loosen the rocker arms and remove the pushrods. Keep All valve train components in order for reinstallation.

9. Remove the cylinder head retaining bolts. Remove the cylinder head from the engine along with the exhaust manifold.

To install:

10. Ensure that the cylinder bolt threads in the block and threads on the bolts are cleaned, as dirt will affect bolt torque.

11. Position the new gasket over the dowel pins with THIS SIDE UP showing, then instal the cylinder head (along with the exhaust manifold).

12. Coat the threads of the cylinder head bolts with sealing compound 1052080 or equivalent.

13. Install the cylinder head retaining bolts. Torque the cylinder head bolts gradually in the proper sequence to 33 ft. lbs. (45 Nm). Then turn each bolt an additional 90 degrees.

14. Position the intake gasket, then install the pushrods in their original locations. Make sure the lower ends of the pushrods are properly positioned in the lifter seats.

15. Properly adjust the valve lash.

16. Install the intake manifold assembly.

17. Instal the valve cover(s).

18. Raise and support the vehicle safely. If removed, install the dipstick tube and/or the alternator bracket.

19. Connect the exhaust crossover pipe. Lower the vehicle.

20. Connect the negative battery cable and properly refill the engine cooling system.

85473089

Cylinder head bolt torque sequence — 2.8L and 3.1L engines

3.8L Engine

1. Relieve the fuel system pressure, then disconnect the negative battery cable.
2. Drain the engine cooling system.
3. Remove the intake manifold.
4. Remove the exhaust manifold(s).
5. Remove the valve cover(s).
6. Disconnect the electronic ignition and spark plug wires.
7. Remove the alternator bracket and 1 air conditioner bracket bolt. Remove the power steering pump.
8. As necessary, remove the belt tensioner assembly and/or the fuel pipe heat shield.
9. Remove the rocker arms, pushrods and guide plates. Keep them in order for reinstallation.
10. Remove the cylinder head retaining bolts. Remove the cylinder head from the engine.
To install:
11. Ensure that the cylinder bolt threads in the block are cleaned, as dirt will affect bolt torque.

NOTE: This engine uses special torque to yield head bolts. The procedure must be followed carefully and new bolts must be used whenever the head is removed.

12. Position the new gasket with the arrow pointing to the front of the engine.
13. Install the cylinder head onto the engine.
14. Coat the underside of the bolt heads with sealing compound 1052080 or equivalent. Coat the threads of the bolts with a suitable threadlocking compound.
15. Install the cylinder head onto the engine. Install the cylinder head retaining bolts and torque as follows:
   a. Torque the cylinder head bolts gradually in the proper sequence to 35 ft. lbs. (47 Nm).

b. Then turn each bolt an additional 130 degree turn in sequence.
   c. Finally turn the 4 center bolts an additional 30 degrees.
16. Install the rocker arms, pushrods and guide plates in the same position from which they were removed. Apply a suitable threadlocking compound to the rocker arm pedestal bolts, then install and tighten to 28 ft. lbs. (38 Nm) for vehicles 1992–93, to 19 ft. lbs. (25 Nm) plus 70 degrees for 1994 vehicles or to 11 ft. lbs. (15 Nm) plus 90 degrees for 1995–96 vehicles.
17. Install the intake manifold and the valve cover(s).
18. Raise and support the vehicle safely. Connect the exhaust manifold(s) to the exhaust pipe(s). Lower the vehicle.
19. Install the air conditioner bracket bolt. Install the alternator and bracket.
20. Install the ignition coil and spark plug wires.
21. Install the belt tensioner, then install power steering pump assembly.
22. Install the fuel pump heat shield.
23. Connect the negative battery cable, then properly refill the engine cooling system.

4.3L Engine

S/T-SERIES

———————— CAUTION ————————
Relieve the pressure on the fuel system before disconnecting any fuel line connection.

1. Properly relieve the fuel system pressure, then disconnect the negative battery cable.
2. Drain the engine cooling system.
3. Remove the rocker arm cover.
4. Remove the intake manifold.
5. Remove the exhaust manifold.

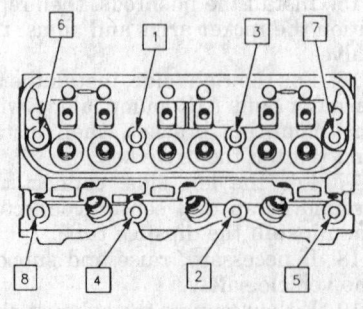

85473090

Cylinder head bolt torque sequence — 3.8L engine

6. If removing the right cylinder head, remove or disconnect:
• Electrical connector at the sensor.
• Dipstick tube at the cylinder head bracket.
• Air conditioning compressor (position it aside with the refrigerant lines attached), if equipped.
• A/C compressor, if equipped/belt tensioner bracket.
7. If removing the left cylinder head, remove or disconnect:
• Alternator (position it aside).
• Left side engine accessory bracket with power steering pump (position the pump aside with the lines attached) and brackets, if equipped.
8. Tag and disconnect the wiring from the spark plugs. If necessary, remove the spark plugs from the cylinder head.
9. Loosen the rocker arms and remove the pushrods.

NOTE: If valve train components, such as the rocker arms or pushrods, are to be reused, they must be tagged or arranged to insure installation in their original locations.

10. Remove the cylinder head bolts by loosening them in the reverse of the torque sequence, then carefully remove the cylinder head.
To install:
11. Carefully clean and inspect the gasket mounting surfaces.

NOTE: The gasket surfaces on both the head and block must be clean of any foreign matter and free of nicks or heavy scratches. The cylinder bolt threads in the block and thread on the bolts must be cleaned (dirt will affect the bolt torque).

NOTE: Do not apply sealer to composition steel-asbestos gaskets.

12. If using a steel only gasket, apply a thin and even coat of sealer to both sides of the gaskets.
13. Place a new gasket over the dowel pins with the bead or the words "This Side Up" facing upwards (as applicable), then carefully lower the cylinder head into position over the gasket and dowels.
14. Apply a coating of 1052080 or equivalent sealer to the threads of the cylinder head bolts, then thread the bolts into position until finger-

tight. Using the proper torque sequence, tighten the bolts in 3 steps:

- First, tighten the bolts to 25 ft. lbs. (34 Nm).
- Next, tighten the bolts to 45 ft. lbs. (61 Nm).
- Finally, tighten the bolts to 65 ft. lbs. (90 Nm).

15. Install the pushrods, secure the rocker arms and adjust the valves.

16. If removed, install the spark plugs. Engage the spark plug wires.

17. If the left cylinder head was removed, reposition and secure the engine accessory bracket with the power steering pump and brackets, as equipped. Install the alternator.

18. If the right cylinder head was removed, install the A/C compressor, if equipped, and A/C compressor/belt tensioner bracket, then install the dipstick tube bracket and engage the sensor electrical connector.

19. Install the exhaust manifold.

20. Install the intake manifold.

21. Install the rocker arm cover.

22. Connect the negative battery cable, then properly refill the engine cooling system.

23. Run the engine to check for leaks, then check and/or adjust the ignition timing.

EXCEPT S/T-SERIES

1. Properly relieve the fuel system pressure, then disconnect the negative battery cable.

2. On Van models, remove the engine cover for access.

3. Drain the engine cooling system.

4. Remove the intake manifold.

5. Remove the exhaust manifold.

6. Except for Van models, if equipped with AIR, remove the air pipe at the rear of the head, then remove the air pump bolt and spacer at the right cylinder head.

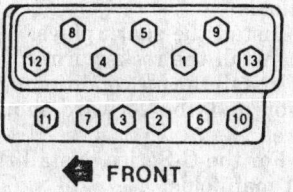

FRONT

85473091

Cylinder head bolt torque sequence — 4.3L engine

7. On the G-Series, remove the A/C compressor, if equipped, and position aside with the lines intact, then remove the alternator.

8. Remove the engine accessory bracket bolts and studs at the cylinder head. On some models, left cylinder head removal may require loosening the remaining bracket bolts in order to provide the necessary clearance.

9. Remove the spark plug wires from the brackets

10. Remove the necessary wiring harness connections from the head components and mounting clips. On most models this will include a clip and/or ground strap at the rear of the cylinder head and a connector at the coolant temperature sensor.

11. On Van models, remove the fuel pipes and bracket from the rear of the cylinder head, then remove the cruise control transducer bracket, if equipped.

12. If not done earlier, remove the rocker arm covers, then loosen the rocker arms and remove the pushrods. Tag or arrange all valve train components to assure installation in their original locations.

13. If necessary, remove the spark plugs.

14. Remove the cylinder head bolts by loosening them in the reverse of the torque sequence, then carefully remove the cylinder head.

To install:

15. Carefully clean and inspect the gasket mounting surfaces.

NOTE: The gasket surfaces on both the head and block must be clean of any foreign matter and free of nicks or heavy scratches. The cylinder bolt threads in the block and thread on the bolts must be cleaned (dirt will affect the bolt torque).

NOTE: Do not apply sealer to composition steel-asbestos gaskets.

16. If using a steel only gasket, apply a thin and even coat of sealer to both sides of the gaskets.

17. Place a new gasket over the dowel pins with the bead or the words "This Side Up" facing upwards (as applicable), then carefully lower the cylinder head into position over the gasket and dowels.

18. Apply a coating of 1052080 or equivalent sealer to the threads of the cylinder head bolts, then thread the bolts into position until finger-

tight. Using the proper torque sequence, tighten the bolts in 3 steps:

- First, tighten the bolts to 25 ft. lbs. (34 Nm).
- Next, tighten the bolts to 45 ft. lbs. (61 Nm).
- Finally, tighten the bolts to 65 ft. lbs. (90 Nm).

19. Install the pushrods, secure the rocker arms and adjust the valves. Install the rocker arm covers.

20. If removed, install the spark plugs. Engage the spark plug wires.

21. On the G-Series, install the cruise control transducer bracket to the left cylinder head, if equipped.

22. On the M/L-Series, position and secure the engine accessory bracket bolts and studs.

23. Position the wiring harness, engage the connections and secure in the clips.

24. On Van models, secure the fuel pipes and bracket to the rear of the cylinder head.

25. On the M/L-Series, secure the cruise control transducer bracket, if equipped.

26. Except the M/L-Series (on which it should be performed earlier), install the engine accessory bracket bolts and studs.

27. Except for Van models, install the AIR pump mounting bolt and spacer to the right cylinder head, then install the air pipe.

28. Install the exhaust manifold.

29. Install the intake manifold.

30. On the G-Series, reposition and secure the A/C compressor, if equipped, then install the alternator.

31. On Van models, install the engine cover.

32. Connect the negative battery cable, then properly refill the engine cooling system.

5.0L and 5.7L Engines

1. Properly relieve the fuel system pressure, then disconnect the negative battery cable.

2. For the G-Series, remove the engine cover for access.

3. Drain the engine cooling system.

4. Remove the intake manifold.

5. Remove the exhaust manifold.

6. Disconnect the ground strap from the rear of the right cylinder head.

7. If removing the right side cylinder head:

  a. Except for the G-Series, if equipped with AIR, remove the pump bolt and spacer at the cylinder head.

b. Remove the A/C compressor and position it aside with the lines attached.

c. Remove the fuel pipe, plug wire and wiring harness brackets at the rear of the cylinder head.

8. If removing the left side cylinder head:

a. For the G-Series, remove the alternator, then remove the power steering pump and position it aside with the lines attached.

b. Remove the nut and stud attaching the main accessory bracket to the cylinder head. It may be necessary to loosen the remaining bolts and studs and move the bracket forward slightly in order to gain the necessary clearance to remove the cylinder head.

9. If necessary, remove the spark plugs.

10. Remove the valve covers. Back off the rocker arm nuts and pivot the rocker arms out of the way, then remove the pushrods. Mark the pushrods so they can be installed in their original positions.

11. Remove the cylinder head bolts and remove the heads.

To install:

12. Install the cylinder heads using new gaskets. Install the gaskets with the bead up. Coat a steel gasket on both sides with sealer. If a composition gasket is used, do not use sealer.

13. Clean the cylinder head bolts, apply a coating of 1052080 or equivalent sealer to the threads. Thread the bolts into position until finger-tight. Tighten the bolts using 3 passes of the proper torque sequence:

• First, tighten the bolts to 25 ft. lbs. (34 Nm).

• Next, tighten the bolts to 45 ft. lbs. (61 Nm).

• Finally, tighten the bolts to 65 ft. lbs. (90 Nm).

14. Install the pushrods as noted or arranged during removal, then repo-

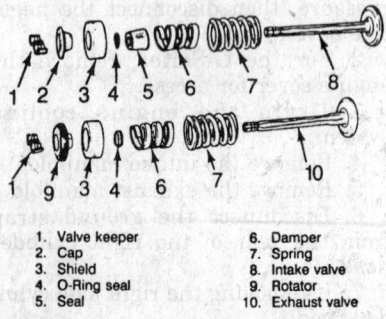

1. Valve keeper	6. Damper
2. Cap	7. Spring
3. Shield	8. Intake valve
4. O-Ring seal	9. Rotator
5. Seal	10. Exhaust valve

8547309A

Valves and components — 4.3L, 5.0L and 5.7L engines

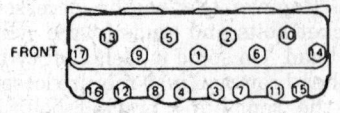

FRONT

85473092

Cylinder head bolt torque sequence — 5.0L and 5.7L engines

sition and secure the rocker arms. Properly adjust the valve lash, then install the valve covers.

15. If removed, install the spark plugs.

16. Install the intake manifold.

17. Install the exhaust manifold.

18. If the left cylinder head was removed, install the necessary components in the reverse order of their removal.

19. If the right cylinder head was removed install the necessary components in the reverse order of their remove.

20. Connect the ground strap to the rear of the right cylinder head.

21. On the G-Series, install the engine cover.

22. Connect the negative battery cable, then properly refill the engine cooling system.

7.4L Engine

1. Properly relieve the fuel system pressure, then disconnect the negative battery cable.

2. Remove the intake manifold.

3. If removing the left cylinder head, remove the alternator and power steering pump, if equipped, along with the brackets. Position the power steering pump and bracket aside with the lines attached.

4. If removing the right cylinder head, remove the A/C compressor and/or the AIR pump with brackets, as applicable, then position aside.

5. Remove the exhaust manifolds.

6. Remove the rocker arm covers.

7. If necessary, remove the spark plugs.

8. Except for the G-Series, remove the AIR pipe bolts at the rear of the cylinder head and push the pipe out of the way.

9. Disconnect the ground strap at the rear of the head.

10. Disconnect the sensor wire.

---

11. Back off the rocker arm nuts and pivot the rocker arms out of the way so the pushrods can be removed. Identify the pushrods so they can be installed in their original positions.

12. Remove the cylinder head bolts and remove the head.

To install:

13. Thoroughly clean the mating surfaces of the head and block. Clean the bolt holes thoroughly.

14. Install the cylinder heads using new gaskets. Install the gaskets with the bead up.

NOTE: Coat a steel gasket on both sides with sealer. If a composition gasket is used, do not use sealer.

15. Clean the cylinder head bolts, apply a coating of 1052080 or equivalent sealer to the threads. Thread the bolts into position until finger-tight. Tighten the bolts using 3 passes of the proper torque sequence:

• First, tighten the bolts to 30 ft. lbs. (40 Nm).

• Next, tighten the bolts to 60 ft. lbs. (80 Nm).

• Finally, tighten the bolts to 80 ft. lbs. (110 Nm).

16. Install the pushrods as noted or arranged during removal, then reposition and secure the rocker arms. Properly adjust the valve lash.

17. Connect the sensor wiring and the ground strap.

18. Except for the G-Series, connect the AIR pipe to the rear of the cylinder head.

19. For the G-Series, install the intake manifold at this time.

20. Install the rocker arm covers.

21. If removed, install the spark plugs.

22. Except for the G-Series, install the exhaust manifolds.

23. Install the power steering pump and/or alternator with brackets to the left cylinder head.

24. Install the A/C compressor and/or AIR pump with brackets to the right cylinder head.

25. Install the intake and exhaust manifolds.

26. Install the spark plugs.

27. Install the rocker arm cover.

28. Install the air conditioning compressor and the forward mounting bracket.

29. For the G-Series, install the exhaust manifolds.

30. Except for the G-Series, install the intake manifolds.

31. Connect the negative battery cable.

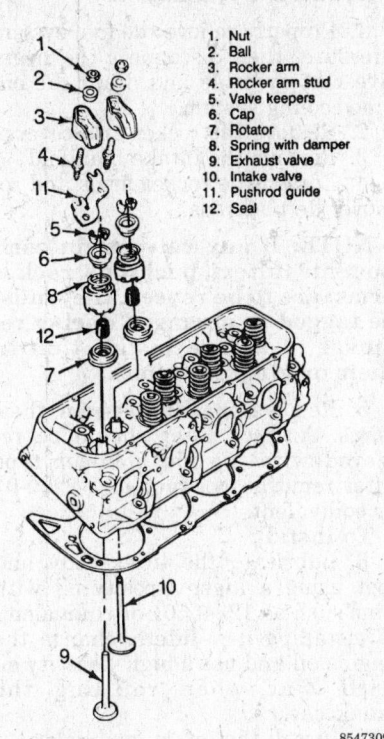

1. Nut
2. Ball
3. Rocker arm
4. Rocker arm stud
5. Valve keepers
6. Cap
7. Rotator
8. Spring with damper
9. Exhaust valve
10. Intake valve
11. Pushrod guide
12. Seal

85473093

Cylinder head and components — 7.4L engine

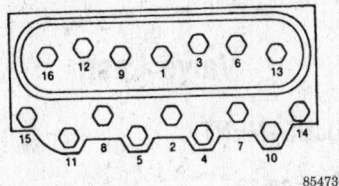

85473094

Cylinder head bolt torque sequence — 7.4L engine

Valve Lifters

REMOVAL AND INSTALLATION

When installing new lifters, a pre-lube should always be applied to the lifter body. It is also a good idea to prime hydraulic lifters by submerging them in clean engine oil a depressing the plunger using an old pushrod. This allows the internal components of the hydraulic lifter to coat with oil before initial operation in the engine. All lifters should be replaced when a new camshaft is installed.

2.2L Engine

1. Remove the rocker arm cover.
2. Remove the cylinder head assembly from the engine.
3. Remove the bolts retaining the lifter anti-rotation brackets, then remove the brackets.
4. Remove the hydraulic roller lifters from the bores.

To install:

NOTE: If installing a new lifter, coat the lifter body with a suitable camshaft pre-lube

5. Install each hydraulic lifter to its bore being careful to align the flat sides (top) of the lifters with the flat sides of the anti-rotation brackets. When properly installed the flat sides of each lifter are aligned parallel to the anti-rotation bracket. The roller at the bottom of the lifter is parallel to the camshaft lobe.

NOTE: Make sure to properly align and install each lifter as improper installation of the lifters or brackets could result in engine damage.

6. Install the anti-rotation bracket retaining bolts and tighten to 97 inch lbs. (11 Nm).
7. Install the cylinder head.
8. Install the rocker arm cover.

2.5L Engine

1. Remove the rocker arm covers.
2. Remove the pushrod cover:
   a. Remove the alternator and bracket.
   b. Disengage the ignition coil wires, then remove the spark plug wires and bracket from the intake manifold.
   c. Remove the fuel pipes and clips from the pushrod cover.
   d. Remove the oil pressure gage sender, then remove the wiring harness brackets from the pushrod cover.
   e. Unscrew the nuts from the cover attaching studs, reverse 2 of the nuts so the washers face outward and screw them back onto the 2 inner studs.
   f. Assemble the 2 remaining nuts to the same 2 inner studs with the washers facing inward, then using a small wrench on the inner nut (on each stud) jam the nuts slightly together.
   g. Again using the wrench on the inner stud, unscrew the studs until the cover breaks loose, then remove the nuts from the studs and remove the cover from the engine. Remove the studs from the cover

and reinstall them to the engine. Tighten the studs to 88 inch lbs. (10 Nm).

NOTE: Keep all components in order. If reusing components, install them into their original positions. If a new hydraulic lifter is being installed, all sealer coating inside the lifter must be removed.

3. Remove the pushrods.
4. Remove the lifter studs and retainers.
5. Remove the lifter guides and lifters.
6. Inspect the lifter and lifter bore for wear and scuffing. Examine the roller for freedom of movement and/or flat spots on the roller surface.
7. Installation is the reverse of removal, be sure to lubricate the lifter and lifter body using clean engine oil. If installing new lifters, all sealer coating inside the lifter must first be removed.
8. When installing the pushrod cover, use a thin coating of RTV sealant around the entire cover flange. Install the cover retaining nuts and tighten to 106 inch lbs. (12 Nm) starting at the front of the engine and working toward the nuts in the rear.

2.8L Engine

Some engines have both standard size and 0.25mm (0.010 in.) oversize valve lifters. The cylinder block will be marked with a white paint mark and 0.25mm O.S. stamp where the oversize lifters are used.

If lifter replacement is necessary, use new design lifters with a narrow flat along the lower ¾ of the body length. This provides additional oil to the cam lobe and lifter surfaces.

NOTE: Use of a Hydraulic Lifter Remover tool J-9290-1 (slide hammer type) or J-3049-A (pliers type) will greatly ease the removal of stuck lifters.

1. Remove the rocker arm covers.
2. Remove the intake manifold.
3. Remove the rocker arm nuts and balls.
4. Remove the rocker arms and pushrods.

NOTE: If any valve train components (lifters, pushrods, rocker arms) are to be reused, they must be tagged or arranged during removal to assure installation in their original locations.

5. Remove the lifters from the bores.

To install:

6. For proper rotation during engine operation, the lifter bottom must be convex. Check the lifter bottom for proper shape using a straight edge. If the lifter bottom is not convex, replace the lifter. Chances are if lifters are in need of replacement, so is the camshaft.

7. Lubricate and install the lifters. If installing new lifters, coat the lifter body and foot using Molykote® or equivalent prelube, then add 1051396 or equivalent engine oil supplement to the crankcase.

8. Install the pushrods, rocker arms, rocker arm nuts and balls, then properly adjust the valve lash.

9. Install the intake manifold.

10. Install the rocker arm covers.

3.1L Engine

1. Properly relieve the fuel system pressure, then disconnect the negative battery cable and drain the engine cooling system.

2. Remove the intake manifold.

3. Loosen the rocker arms, then remove the pushrod guides and remove the pushrods.

NOTE: If any valve train components (lifters, pushrods, rocker arms) are to be reused, they must be tagged or arranged during removal to assure installation in their original locations.

4. Remove the lifters.
To install:
5. Coat the foot of each lifter using a suitable prelube.

6. Install the lifters.

7. Install the pushrods and guides.

8. Coat the friction surfaces of the rocker arms with prelube, then reposition and secure the rocker arms. Properly adjust the valve lash.

9. Install the intake manifold.

10. Connect the negative battery cable and properly refill the engine cooling system.

3.8L Engine

1. Properly relieve the fuel system pressure, then disconnect the negative battery cable and drain the engine cooling system.

2. Remove the rocker arm covers.

3. Remove the intake manifold.

4. Unbolt the rocker arms and pedestals.

NOTE: If any valve train components (lifters, pushrods, rocker arms) are to be reused, they must be tagged or arranged during removal to assure installation in their original locations.

5. Remove the pushrods.

6. Remove the lifter guide retainer bolts, then remove the guides.

7. Remove the lifters.

To install:

8. Coat the foot of each lifter using a suitable prelube.

9. Install the lifters.

10. Install the lifter guides, then tighten the retainer bolts to 22 ft. lbs. (30 Nm).

11. Install the pushrods.

12. Install the rocker arms and pedestals. Apply a suitable threadlocking compound to the rocker arm pedestal bolts, then install and tighten to 28 ft. lbs. (38 Nm) for vehicles 1992–93, to 19 ft. lbs. (25 Nm) plus 70 degrees for 1994 vehicles or to 11 ft. lbs. (15 Nm) plus 90 degrees for 1995–96 vehicles.

13. Install the intake manifold.

14. Install the rocker arm covers.

15. Connect the negative battery cable and properly refill the engine cooling system.

4.3L Engine

1. Remove the rocker arm cover.

2. Remove the intake manifold assembly.

NOTE: If any valve train components (lifters, pushrods, rocker arms) are to be reused, they must be tagged or arranged during removal to assure installation in their original locations.

3. Remove the rocker arm and pushrod assemblies.

4. Remove the hydraulic lifter retainer bolts, them remove the retainers or retainers and restrictors, as equipped.

5. Remove the lifters from the engine.
To install:
6. Inspect the lifter and lifter bore for wear and scuffing. Examine the roller for freedom of movement and/or flat spots on the roller surface.

7. If new lifters are being installed, lubricate the lifters using a suitable pre-lube and add GM engine oil supplement or equivalent additive to the crankcase.

8. Install the hydraulic lifters along with the restrictors and/or retainers. Secure the retainers using the bolts and tighten to 12 ft. lbs. (16 Nm).

9. Install the pushrods and rocker arm assemblies, then adjust the valve lash.

10. Install the intake manifold assembly.

11. Install the rocker arm covers.

5.0L, 5.7L and 7.4L Engines

1. Properly relieve the fuel system pressure, then disconnect the negative battery cable and drain the engine cooling system.

2. Remove the rocker arm covers.

3. Remove the intake manifold.

4. Loosen the rocker arms and remove the pushrods.

NOTE: If any valve train components (lifters, pushrods, rocker arms) are to be reused, they must be tagged or arranged during removal to assure installation in their original locations.

5. Remove the lifters from their bores. A stuck lifter should be removed with a slide hammer type lifter removal tool such as J-9290-01 or equivalent.
To install:
6. Lubricate the lifter body and foot using a high viscosity oil with Zinc such as 12345501 or equivalent. If installing new lifters, change the engine oil and use a high viscosity oil with Zinc when refilling the crankcase.

7. Install the intake manifold.

8. Install the pushrods, then secure the rocker arms and properly adjust the valve lash.

9. Install the rocker arm covers.

10. Connect the negative battery cable, then properly refill the engine cooling system.

Valve Lash

ADJUSTMENT

2.2L Engine

Because the rocker arm fasteners are secured and torqued, valve lash is not adjustable on the 2.2L engine. If a valve train problem is suspected, check that the rocker arm nuts are tightened to 22 ft. lbs. (30 Nm). Be very careful not to overtighten the rocker arm nuts. ONLY torque the nuts when the hydraulic lifter is resting on the base circle of the camshaft and not when it is held upward on the lobe. When valve lash falls out of specification (valve tap is heard), replace the rocker arm, pushrod and hydraulic lifter on the offending cylinder.

2.5L Engine

Because the rocker arm fasteners are secured and torqued, valve lash is not adjustable on the 2.5L engine. If a valve train problem is suspected, check that the rocker arm bolts are

tightened to 22 ft. lbs. (30 Nm). Be sure to only tighten the rocker arm bolts when the hydraulic lifter for that rocker arm is on the base circle of the camshaft and not when it is held upward on the lobe. When valve lash falls out of specification (valve tap is heard), replace the rocker arm, pushrod and hydraulic lifter on the offending cylinder.

2.8L and 3.1L Engines

NOTE: These engines utilize hydraulic valve lifters which means that a valve adjustment is not a regular maintenance item. The valves must only be adjusted if the rockers arms have been disturbed for any reason such as cylinder head, camshaft, pushrod or lifter removal.

1. Remove the air cleaner and the rocker arm cover(s).
2. Rotate the crankshaft until the mark on the crankshaft pulley aligns with the **0** mark on the timing plate. Make sure the No. 1 cylinder is positioned on the compression stroke. The No. 1 piston is on it's compression stroke when both the intake and exhaust valves remain closed as the crankshaft damper mark approaches the timing scale.

NOTE: Another method to tell when the piston is coming up on the compression stroke is by removing the spark plug and placing a finger over the hole in order to feel air being forced out of the spark plug hole. Stop turning the crankshaft when pressure is felt and the TDC timing mark on the crankshaft pulley is directly aligned with the timing mark pointer or the 0 mark on the scale.

3. When the engine is on the No. 1 firing position, adjust the following valves:
- Intake — 1, 5 and 6
- Exhaust — 1, 2 and 3

4. To adjust the valves, back-out the adjusting nut until lash can be felt at the pushrod, then turn the nut until all of the lash is removed.

NOTE: To determine is all of the lash is removed, turn the pushrod between 2 fingers until the movement is removed.

5. When all of the lash has been removed, turn the adjusting an additional 1½ turns; this will center the lifter plunger.
6. Crank the engine 1 complete revolution until the timing tab (**0** degree mark) and the crankshaft pulley

mark are again in alignment. Now the engine is in the No. 4 firing position. Adjust the following valves:
- Intake — 2, 3 and 4
- Exhaust — 4, 5 and 6

7. Install the rocker arm cover(s).
8. Start and run the engine, then check and adjust the timing, as necessary.

3.8L Engine

Because the rocker arm fasteners are secured and torqued, valve lash is not adjustable on the 3.8L engine. If a valve train problem is suspected, check that the rocker arm pedestals bolts are tightened to specification. During initial installation the bolts are coated with a suitable threadlocking compound. If they are sufficiently loosened to cause valve train noise, they should be removed and thoroughly cleaned. Apply a suitable threadlocking compound to the rocker arm pedestal bolts, then install and tighten to 28 ft. lbs. (38 Nm) for vehicles 1992–93, to 19 ft. lbs. (25 Nm) plus 70 degrees for 1994 vehicles or to 11 ft. lbs. (15 Nm) plus 90 degrees for 1995–96 vehicles. When valve lash falls out of specification (valve tap is heard) and tightening the bolts does not solve the problem, replace the rocker arm, pushrod and hydraulic lifter on the offending cylinder.

4.3L (VIN Z) Engine

NOTE: This engine utilizes hydraulic valve lifters which means that a valve adjustment is not a regular maintenance item. The valves must only be adjusted if the rockers arms have been disturbed for any reason such as cylinder head, camshaft, pushrod or lifter removal.

For 1993–94, the 4.3L (VIN Z) engine may be equipped with either of 2 rocker arm retaining systems. If the engine utilizes screw-in type rocker arm studs with positive stop shoulders, no valve lash adjustment is necessary or possible. All 1995–96 4.3L engines utilize this system. If so equipped, please refer to the 4.3L (VIN W) valve lash information. If however, the engine utilizes the pressed-in rocker arm studs, use the following procedure to tighten the rocker arm nuts and properly center the pushrod on the hydraulic lifter:

1. To prepare the engine for valve adjustment, rotate the crankshaft until the mark on the damper pulley aligns with the **0** degree mark on the timing plate and the No. 1 cylinder is

on the compression stroke. When the No. 1 piston is on it's compression stroke both the intake and exhaust valves will remain closed as the crankshaft damper mark approaches the timing scale.

NOTE: Another method to tell when the piston is coming up on the compression stroke is by removing the spark plug and placing a finger over the hole in order to feel air being forced out of the spark plug hole. Stop turning the crankshaft air is felt and the TDC timing mark on the crankshaft pulley is directly aligned with the timing mark pointer or the 0 mark on the scale.

2. With the engine at No. 1 TDC, adjust the exhaust valves of cylinders No. 1, 5 and 6 and the intake valves of cylinders No. 1, 2 and 3 by performing the following procedures:
   a. Back out the adjusting nut until lash can be felt at the pushrod.
   b. While rotating the pushrod, turn the adjusting nut inward until all of the lash is removed.
   c. When the play has disappeared, turn the adjusting nut inward 1 additional turn for 1992–93 engines or 1¾ additional turns for 1994 engines.
3. Rotate the crankshaft 1 complete revolution and align the mark on the damper pulley with the **0** degree mark on the timing plate; the engine is now positioned on the No. 4 firing position. This time the No. 4 cylinder valves remain closed as the timing mark approaches the scale. Adjust the exhaust valves of cylinders No. 2, 3 and 4 and the intake valves of cylinders No. 4, 5 and 6, by performing the following procedures:
   a. Back out the adjusting nut until lash can be felt at the pushrod.
   b. While rotating the pushrod, turn the adjusting nut inward until all of the lash is removed.
   c. When the play has disappeared, turn the adjusting nut inward 1 additional turn for 1992–93 engines or 1¾ additional turns for 1994 engines.
4. Install the remaining components, then start the engine and check for oil leaks.

4.3L (VIN W) Engine

The 4.3L (VIN W) engine and some later 4.3L (VIN Z) engines (including all 1995–96 models) are equipped with screw-in type rocker arm studs with positive stop shoulders. Because

the shoulders allow the rocker arms to be torqued into proper position, no adjustments are necessary or possible. If a valve train problem is suspected, check that the rocker arm nuts are tightened to 20 ft. lbs. (27 Nm). When valve lash falls out of specification (valve tap is heard), replace the rocker arm, pushrod and hydraulic lifter on the offending cylinder.

5.0L and 5.7L Engines

NOTE: This engine utilizes hydraulic valve lifters which means that a valve adjustment is not a regular maintenance item. The valves must only be adjusted if the rockers arms have been disturbed for any reason such as cylinder head, camshaft, pushrod or lifter removal.

1. Remove the valve covers and gaskets.
2. Crank the engine until the mark on the damper aligns with the **TDC** or **0** mark on the timing tab and the engine is in No. 1 cylinder firing position. This can be determined by placing a finger on the No. 1 cylinder valves as the marks align. If the valves do not move, it is in the No. 1 firing position. If the valves move, it is in No. 6 firing position and the crankshaft should be rotated 1 more complete revolution to the No. 1 firing position.
3. With the engine in No. 1 firing position, adjust the following valves: Exhaust — 1, 3, 4, 8 Intake — 1, 2, 5, 7
4. To adjust the valves:
    a. Back off the adjusting nut until lash is felt at the pushrod.
    b. Turn in the adjusting nut until all lash is removed. This is determined by rotating the pushrod gently between 2 fingers, the point

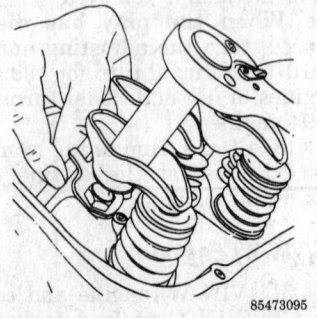

85473095

When adjusting valve lash, turn the pushrod between 2 fingers while tightening to remove lash

at which it can no longer be rotated is the point of no lash.
    c. Turn the adjusting nut in an 1 additional turn to center the lifter plunger.
5. Crank the engine 1 full revolution until the marks are again in alignment. This is the No. 6 firing position. Adjust the remaining valves in the with the engine in this position: Exhaust — 2, 5, 6, 7 Intake — 3, 4, 6, 8. Adjustment is again performed by bringing the rocker arm nut to the point of no pushrod lash, then tightening 1 additional turn.
6. Reinstall the valve covers using new gaskets.

7.4L Engine

Because the rocker arm fasteners are secured and torqued, valve lash is not adjustable on the 7.4L engine. If a valve train problem is suspected, check that the rocker arm bolts are tightened to 40 ft. lbs. (54 Nm). Be very careful not to overtighten the rocker arm bolts. In most cases it is desirable to install and tighten the bolts when the when the hydraulic lifter is resting on the base circle of the camshaft, not when it is held upward on the lobe. This will help assure proper seating of the rocker arm and valve train components. When valve lash falls out of specification (valve tap is heard), replace the rocker arm, pushrod and hydraulic lifter on the offending cylinder.

Valve Arrangement

2.2L Engine
I–E–I–E–I–E–I–E (front-to-rear)
2.5L Engine
I–E–I–E–E–I–E–I (front-to-rear)
2.8L and 3.1L Engines
E–I–E–I–I–E (right bank–front-to-rear)
E–I–I–E–I–E (left bank–front-to-rear)
3.8L and 4.3L Engines
E–I–I–E–I–E (right bank–front-to-rear)
E–I–E–I–I–E (left bank–front-to-rear)
5.0L and 5.7L Engines
E–I–I–E–E–I–I–E (right bank–front-to-rear)
E–I–I–E–E–I–I–E (left bank–front-to-rear)
7.4L Engine
I–E–I–E–I–E–I–E (right bank–front-to-rear)
E–I–E–I–E–I–E–I (left bank–front-to-rear)

Rocker Arms

REMOVAL AND INSTALLATION

2.2L Engine

1. Remove the rocker arm cover from the cylinder head.
2. Remove the rocker arm retaining nut, then remove the arm and ball. If necessary, withdraw the pushrod form the cylinder head.

NOTE: Valve train components which are to be reused must be installed in their original positions. If removed, be sure to tag or arrange all rocker arms and pushrods to assure proper installation.

To install:
3. Inspect the rocker arms, balls and pushrods for damage or wear and replace, as necessary:
    a. Check the rocker arms, balls and their mating surfaces. Make sure the surfaces are smooth and free from scoring or other damage.
    b. Check the rocker arm areas that contact the valve stems and the sockets that contact the pushrods, make sure these areas are smooth and free of both damage and wear.
    c. Make sure the pushrods are not bent; this can be determined by rolling them on a flat surface. Check the ends of the pushrods for scoring or roughness.
    d. Inspect the rocker arm bolts for thread damage. Check the rocker arm bolts in the shoulder area for contact damage with the rocker arm.
4. If removed, install the pushrods making sure they are seated within the lifters.
5. If installing new rocker arms and balls, coat the friction surfaces using Dri-Slide Molykote® or equivalent pre-lube.

NOTE: When tightening the rocker arm retainers, make sure the lifter for that valve is resting on the base circle of the camshaft not on the lobe. Do not overtighten the retainers.

6. Install the rocker arms and ball, then tighten the retaining nuts to 22 ft. lbs. (30 Nm).

NOTE: Valve lash is not adjustable on the 2.2L engine.

7. Install the rocker arm cover, then start and run the engine to check for leaks.

2.5L Engine

1. Remove the rocker arm cover from the cylinder head.

2. Remove the rocker arm bolt, the ball washer and the rocker arm.

NOTE: If only the pushrod is to be removed, back off the rocker arm bolt, swing the rocker arm aside and remove the pushrod. When removing more than 1 assembly, at the same time, be sure to keep them in order for reassembly purposes.

3. If necessary, remove the pushrods and guides.

4. Inspect the rocker arms and ball washers for scoring and/or other damage, replace them (if necessary).

NOTE: If replacing worn components with new ones, be sure to coat the new parts with Molykote® or equivalent pre-lube before installation.

To install:

5. If removed, install the pushrods and guides.

6. Install the rocker arms, ball washers and retaining bolts. Tighten the rocker arm-to-cylinder head bolt for each valve to 22 ft. lbs. (30 Nm), but only tighten the bolt with the hydraulic lifter for that valve on the base circle of the camshaft. Do not tighten the bolts while the lifter is resting on the raised portion of the lobe and do not overtighten the bolts.

NOTE: Valve lash is not adjustable on the 2.5L engine.

7. Install the rocker arm cover to the cylinder head.

NOTE: Valve train components which are to be reused must be installed in their original positions. If removed, be sure to tag or arrange all rocker arms and pushrods to assure proper installation.

2.8L and 3.1L Engines

1. Remove the rocker arm cover(s) from the cylinder head.

2. Remove the rocker arm nut, the rocker arm and the ball washer.

NOTE: If only the pushrod is to be removed, loosen the rocker arm nut, swing the rocker arm to the side and remove the pushrod.

3. Withdraw the pushrod from the cylinder head.

To install:

4. Inspect and replace components if worn or damaged.

5. Coat the bearing surfaces of the rocker arms and the rocker arm ball washers with Molykote® or equivalent pre-lube.

6. Install the pushrods making sure they seat properly in the lifter.

7. Install the rocker arms, ball washers and the nuts, then tighten the rocker arm nuts until there is little or no valve lash.

NOTE: Each valve must be adjusted when the lifter is sitting on the base circle of the camshaft, not the raised section of the lobe.

8. Properly adjust the valve lash.

9. Install the rocker arm cover.

10. Start and run the engine, then check for leaks. Check and adjust the timing, as necessary.

NOTE: Valve train components which are to be reused must be installed in their original positions. If removed, be sure to tag or arrange all rocker arms and pushrods to assure proper installation.

3.8L Engine

1. Remove the rocker arm cover from the engine.

2. Remove the rocker arm pedestal retaining bolts.

3. Remove the pedestal and rocker arm assembly.

To install:

4. Inspect and replace components if worn or damaged. Clean all old threadlocking material from the pedestal bolts.

5. Install the rocker arms and pedestals. Apply a suitable threadlocking compound to the rocker arm pedestal bolts, then install and tighten to 28 ft. lbs. (38 Nm) for vehicles 1992–93, to 19 ft. lbs. (25 Nm) plus 70 degrees for 1994 vehicles or to 11 ft. lbs. (15 Nm) plus 90 degrees for 1995–96 vehicles.

6. Install the rocker arm covers.

4.3L, 5.0L and 5.7L Engines

1. On Van models, remove the engine cover for access.

2. Remove the rocker arm cover(s) from the cylinder head.

3. Remove the rocker arm nut, the rocker arm and the ball washer.

NOTE: If only the pushrod is to be removed, loosen the rocker arm nut, swing the rocker arm to the side and remove the pushrod.

4. Withdraw the pushrod from the cylinder head.

To install:

5. Inspect and replace components if worn or damaged.

6. Coat the bearing surfaces of the rocker arms and the rocker arm ball washers with Molykote® or equivalent pre-lube.

7. Install the pushrods making sure they seat properly in the lifter.

8. Install the rocker arms, ball washers and the nuts.

9. For the 4.3L (VIN W) engine and any 1993–96 4.3L (VIN Z) engines which are equipped with screw-in type rocker arm studs with positive stop shoulders, tighten the rocker arm adjusting nuts against the stop shoulders to 20 ft. lbs. (27 Nm). No further adjustment is necessary or possible.

10. For all 1992 and some later 4.3L (VIN Z) engines, the 5.0L engine and the 5.7L engine (which are not equipped with screw-in type rocker arm studs and positive stop shoulders), properly adjust the valve lash.

11. Install the rocker arm cover(s) to the cylinder head.

12. On Van models, install the engine cover.

13. Start and run the engine, then check for leaks and for proper ignition timing adjustment.

7.4L Engine

1. Remove the rocker arm cover from the cylinder head.

2. Remove the rocker arm bolt.

NOTE: If only the pushrod is to be removed, back off the rocker arm bolt, swing the rocker arm aside and remove the pushrod. When removing more than 1 assembly, at the same time, be sure to keep them in order for reassembly purposes.

3. Remove the rocker arm and ball.

To install:

4. Inspect and replace components if worn or damaged.

5. If new rocker arms are being installed, coat the friction surfaces using a high viscosity oil with Zinc such as 12345501 or equivalent. If installing old rocker arms, it is still a good idea to coat the surfaces using clean engine oil.

6. Install the rocker arm with ball, then install the retaining bolt and tighten to 40 ft. lbs. (54 Nm).

7. Install the rocker arm cover(s).

8. Start the engine and check for leaks.

Intake Manifold

REMOVAL AND INSTALLATION

2.2L Gasoline Engine

The 2.2L (VIN 4) engine was introduced in 1994 and utilizes a Multi-Port Fuel Injection (MFI) system. The intake manifold is an assembly of separate components, an upper and a lower manifold.

1. Properly release the fuel system pressure (if the lower manifold assembly is being removed) and disconnect the negative battery cable.
2. Remove the air cleaner duct work.
3. Disconnect the throttle cable support and cable from the manifold.
4. Remove the MAP sensor and the EGR solenoid valve from the upper intake manifold and engine (if the upper manifold is not being replaced, simply disengage the wiring and hoses).
5. Tag and disengage all wiring and vacuum hoses from the upper intake manifold.
6. Loosen the retainers, then remove the upper intake manifold from the engine and lower manifold assembly.
7. Disconnect the fuel lines.

8. Tag and disconnect the spark plug wires from the Electronic Ignition (EI) coil pack.
9. Remove the lower intake manifold retaining nuts, then remove the lower intake manifold and gasket.

To install:

10. Carefully remove all traces of gasket material from the mating surfaces. Check the EGR passage to be sure it is free of excessive carbon deposits and clean, as necessary.
11. Install the lower intake manifold using a new gasket, then tighten the retaining nuts to 24 ft. lbs. (33 Nm) using the proper sequence.
12. Connect the spark plug wires to the EI coil pack and noted during removal.
13. Connect the fuel lines.
14. Install the upper intake manifold using a new gasket, then tighten the retainers to 22 ft. lbs. (30 Nm) using the proper sequence..
15. Engage the wiring connectors and vacuum hoses to the upper intake manifold assembly.
16. Install the MAP sensor and EGR solenoid valve.
17. Install and secure the throttle cable support and cable. Tighten the cable bracket bolts to 18 ft. lbs. (25 Nm).
18. Install the air cleaner duct work.

19. Connect the negative battery cable, then start and run the engine to check for leaks.

2.5L Engine

1. Properly relieve the fuel system pressure, then disconnect the negative battery cable.
2. Drain the engine cooling system and remove the air cleaner assembly.
3. Label and disconnect the wiring harnesses and connectors at the intake manifold.
4. Disconnect the accelerator, TVS, and cruise control cables (as equipped) with brackets.
5. Disconnect the EGR vacuum line.
6. Remove the emission sensor bracket at the manifold.
7. Tag and disconnect the fuel lines, vacuum lines and wiring from the TBI unit.
8. Disconnect the water pump bypass hose from the intake manifold.
9. Remove the alternator rear bracket.
10. Tag and disconnect the vacuum hoses and pipes from the intake manifold and the vacuum hold-down at the thermostat and manifold.
11. If applicable, disconnect the heater hose at the intake.
12. Disconnect the coil wires.

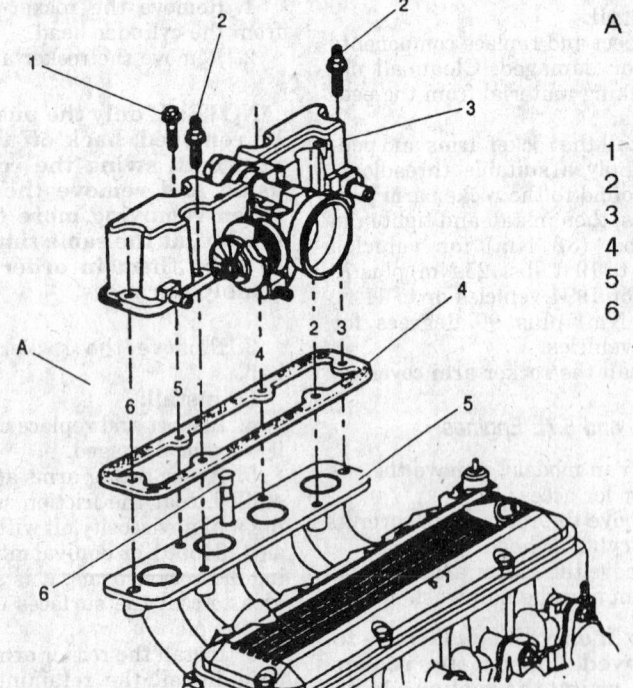

A Upper intake manifold assembly tightening sequence

1 Bolt
2 Stud
3 Upper intake manifold assembly
4 Gasket
5 Lower intake manifold
6 EGR valve injector

85473096

Upper intake manifold mounting and torque sequence — 2.2L gasoline engine

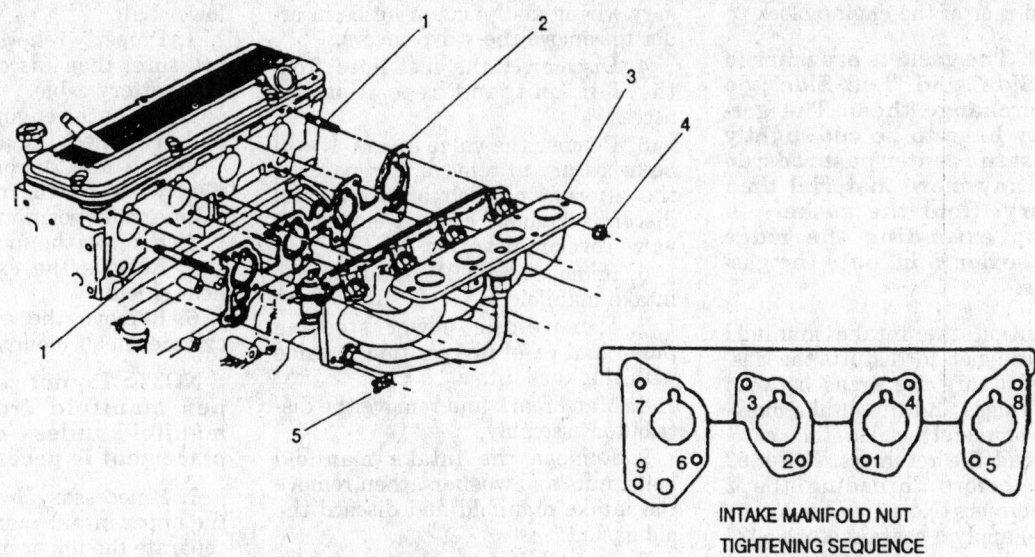

1 STUD
2 GASKET
3 INTAKE MANIFOLD
4 NUT
5 CLIP

INTAKE MANIFOLD NUT
TIGHTENING SEQUENCE

85473097

Lower intake manifold mounting and installation torque sequence — 2.2L gasoline engine

13. Remove the intake manifold bolts, then remove the manifold from the engine.

To install:

14. Using a gasket scraper, clean the gasket mounting surfaces.

15. Install the intake manifold to the engine using a new gasket and carefully thread the retainers.

16. Slowly and evenly tighten all of the retainers to 25 ft. lbs. (34 Nm).

17. Engage the coil wires.

18. If applicable, connect the heater hose at the intake.

19. Connect the vacuum hoses and pipes to the manifold and the vacuum hold-down at the thermostat as noted during removal.

20. Install the alternator rear bracket, then connect the coolant by-pass hose.

21. Connect the fuel lines, vacuum lines and the wiring to the TBI unit.

22. Install the emissions sensor bracket, then connect the EGR valve hose.

23. Connect the accelerator, TVS and cruise control cables (as equipped) with brackets.

24. Engage and secure the wiring harness connectors at the intake, as noted during removal.

25. Install the air cleaner assembly, then connect the negative battery cable.

26. Properly refill the engine cooling system, then check for leaks.

2.8L Engine

1. Properly relieve the fuel system pressure, then disconnect the negative battery cable.

2. Drain the engine cooling system and remove the air cleaner.

3. Tag and disengage the electrical connectors, vacuum hoses, fuel lines and accelerator cable(s) from the TBI unit.

4. If equipped with an AIR management system, remove the hose and the mounting bracket.

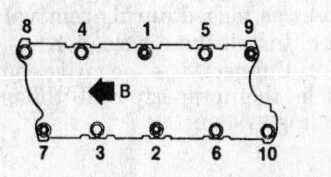

85473098

Intake manifold torque sequence — 2.8L engine

5. Label and disconnect the spark plug wires from the spark plugs and the electrical connectors from the ignition coil. Disengage the coolant switch electrical connectors on the intake manifold.

6. Remove the distributor cap (with the wires connected). Match-mark and remove the distributor from the intake manifold and engine.

7. Disconnect the EGR vacuum line and the evaporative emission hoses. Remove the pipe brackets from the rocker arm covers.

8. Remove the heater and upper radiator hoses from the intake manifold.

9. If equipped, remove the power brake vacuum hoses from the intake manifold.

10. Remove the rocker arm covers.

11. Remove the intake manifold-to-engine nuts and bolts, then the intake manifold from the engine.

To install:

12. Using a gasket scraper, clean the mating surfaces of remaining gasket and sealer. Since the manifold is made from aluminum, be sure to inspect it for warpage and/or cracks; if necessary, replace it.

13. Position new intake manifold gaskets to the engine and apply a 3/16

in. (5mm) bead of RTV sealant to the front and rear of the engine block.

NOTE: The gaskets are marked "Right Side" and "Left Side"; do not interchange them. The gaskets may have to be cut slightly to fit past the center pushrods; do not cut any more material than necessary. Hold the gaskets in place by extending the ridge bead of sealer 1/4 in. onto the gasket ends.

14. Position the intake manifold taking care not to disturb the gaskets. Make sure the areas between the case ridges and the intake manifold are completely sealed, then carefully thread the retainers. For 1993 engines, before threading the 2 center retainers (No.s 1 in the torque sequence) apply a coating of 9985427 or equivalent sealer to the threads.

15. Tighten the intake manifold-to-cylinder head fasteners to 23 ft. lbs. (31 Nm) using the proper torque sequence.

16. Install the rocker arm covers.

17. If equipped, connect the power brake vacuum hoses at the intake manifold.

18. Connect the heater and upper radiator hoses from the intake manifold.

19. Install the pipe brackets to the rocker arm covers, then connect the EGR vacuum line and the evaporative emission hoses.

20. Align the marks made during removal and install the distributor assembly, then install the distributor cap and spark plug wires.

21. Engage the electrical connectors to the ignition coil and to the coolant switch on the intake manifold.

22. If equipped with an AIR management system, install the hose and the mounting bracket.

23. Engage the electrical connectors, vacuum hoses, fuel lines and the accelerator cable(s) to the TBI unit.

24. Install the air cleaner assembly, then connect the negative battery cable.

25. Properly refill the engine cooling system, then check for leaks.

26. Adjust the ignition timing and check the coolant level after the engine has warmed up.

3.1L Engine

1. Properly relieve the fuel system pressure, then disconnect the negative battery cable.

2. Drain the engine cooling system and remove the air cleaner.

3. Tag and disconnect the necessary wiring and vacuum hoses in order to remove the valve covers.

4. Disconnect the fuel lines from the TBI unit and reposition for access.

5. Remove the valve covers. It will be necessary to remove or reposition the alternator (with brackets) and disconnect some coolant hoses for valve cover removal.

6. Remove the TBI unit from the intake manifold.

7. Remove the power steering pump and carefully position it aside with the lines intact.

8. Matchmark and remove the distributor assembly.

9. Remove the intake manifold bolts, nuts and washers, then remove the intake manifold and discard the old gasket.

To install:

10. Clean the sealing surface of the engine block and apply a 3/16 in. bead of RTV sealer to each ridge.

11. Install the new gaskets onto the heads. Hold the gaskets in place by extending the ridge bead of sealer 1/4 in. onto the gasket ends. (When the intake manifold is installed, the area between the ridges and the manifold should be completely sealed.)

12. Install the intake manifold onto the engine.

13. Coat the threads of the intake manifold studs using a sealer such as 1052080 or equivalent.

14. Install the intake manifold retainers and tighten to 13 ft. lbs. (18 Nm) using the proper sequence, then tighten the retainers (again in sequence) to 19 ft. lbs. (26 Nm).

15. Align and install the distributor assembly.

16. Reposition and secure the power steering pump assembly.

17. Install the TBI unit.

18. Install the valve covers. Reposition and secure the alternator (with brackets) and connect the coolant hoses.

19. Connect the fuel lines to the TBI unit.

20. Connect the wiring and vacuum hoses as tagged during removal.

21. Install the air cleaner.

22. Connect the negative battery cable, then properly refill the engine cooling system.

3.8L Engine

The 3.8L engine utilizes a 2-piece intake manifold assembly. The entire assembly may be removed without

separating the upper half from the lower half.

1. Properly relieve the fuel system pressure, then disconnect the negative battery cable.

2. Drain the engine cooling system and disconnect the air intake duct.

3. Tag and disconnect the spark plug wires on the right side of the engine, then position the wires aside.

4. Remove the fuel rail.

5. Remove the exhaust crossover heat shield.

6. Remove the cable bracket-to-cylinder head mounting bolt.

NOTE: Do not separate the upper manifold from the lower manifold unless component replacement is necessary.

7. If necessary, loosen and remove the upper intake manifold bolts, then separate the upper manifold from the lower manifold.

8. Remove the power steering pump support bracket.

9. Loosen the alternator and move aside to obtain clearance.

10. Disconnect the heater pipes and bypass hose.

11. Remove the lower intake manifold bolts, then remove the manifold or manifold assembly (as applicable) from the engine.

To install:

12. Thoroughly clean all manifold mating surfaces, bolts and bolt holes. Apply sealant to the ends of the manifold seals and coat the bolt threads with Loctite® or equivalent threadlocking compound. Install the lower intake manifold, gasket and bolts. Torque the lower manifold bolts in sequence, twice, to 88 inch lbs. (10 Nm) for vehicles 1992–94 or to 11 ft. lbs. (15 Nm) for 1995–96 vehicles.

───── **WARNING** ─────
The manifold surfaces used on this engine should not be scraped or wire brushed in order to clean the gaskets. The surfaces could be easily damaged if this is ignored. Instead, use a commercially available solvent to clean the mating surfaces.

13. Connect the heater pipes and bypass hose.

14. Reposition and secure the alternator.

15. Install the power steering pump support bracket.

16. If removed, prepare the upper intake manifold mating surface for installation. Apply a 1/16 bead of Loctite Instant Gasket Eliminator GM P/N 1052942 or equivalent to the

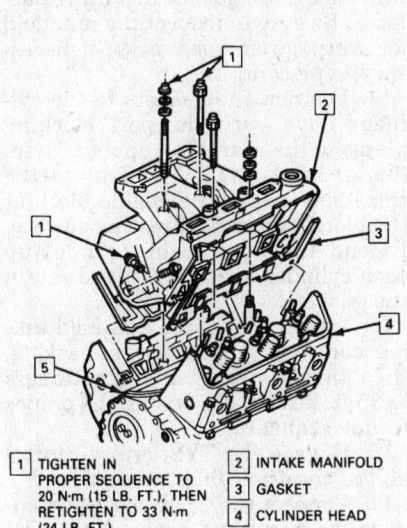

1	TIGHTEN IN PROPER SEQUENCE TO 20 N·m (15 LB. FT.), THEN RETIGHTEN TO 33 N·m (24 LB. FT.)	2	INTAKE MANIFOLD
	3	GASKET
	4	CYLINDER HEAD
⑦ ④ ③ ⑥	5	SEALER
⑧ ① ② ⑤	

85473099

Intake manifold bolt torque sequence — 3.1L engine

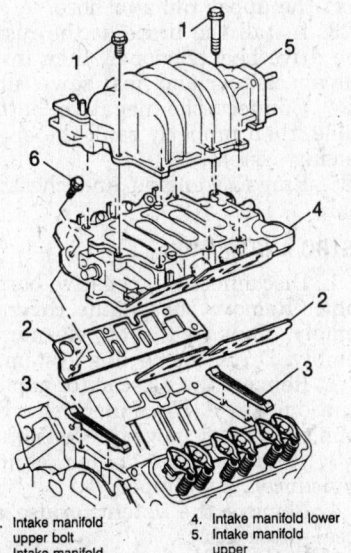

1. Intake manifold upper bolt
2. Intake manifold gasket
3. Intake manifold seal
4. Intake manifold lower
5. Intake manifold upper
6. Intake manifold lower bolt

85473100

Intake manifold assembly — 3.8L engine

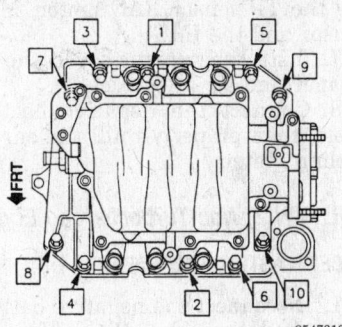

85473101

Intake manifold bolt torque sequence — 3.8L engine

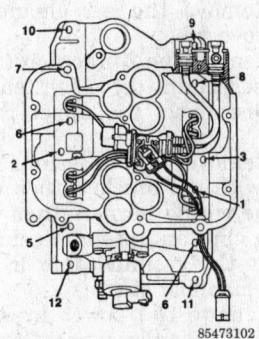

85473102

Lower intake manifold torque sequence — 4.3L VIN W engine

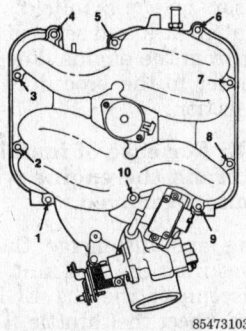

85473103

Upper intake manifold torque sequence — 4.3L VIN W engine

mating surface on the lower manifold. Be sure to circle all bolt holes. Install the upper manifold assembly, then apply threadlocking compound to the retainers. Install the upper intake manifold retainers and tighten to 22 ft. lbs. (30 Nm) for vehicles 1992–93 or to 11 ft. lbs. (15 Nm) for 1994–96 vehicles.

17. Install the cable bracket-to-cylinder head mounting bolt.
18. Install the exhaust heat shield.
19. Install the fuel rail.

20. Connect the spark plug wires on the right side of the engine.
21. Connect the air intake duct.
22. Connect the negative battery cable, then properly refill the engine cooling system.

4.3L (VIN W) Engine

NOTE: If only the upper intake manifold is being removed, the fuel system pressure does not need to be released. ALWAYS release the pressure before disconnecting any fuel lines.

1. Remove the plastic cover, then properly relieve the fuel system pressure and disconnect the negative battery cable.
2. Drain the engine cooling system, then remove the air cleaner and air inlet duct.
3. Disengage the wiring harness from the necessary upper intake components including:
 • Throttle Position (TP) sensor
 • Idle Air Control (IAC) motor
 • Manifold Absolute Pressure (MAP) sensor
 • Intake Manifold Tuning Valve (IMTV)
4. Disengage the throttle linkage from the upper intake manifold, then remove the ignition coil.
5. Disconnect the PCV hose at the rear of the upper intake manifold, then tag and disengage the vacuum hoses from both the front and rear of the upper intake.
6. Remove the upper intake manifold bolts and studs, making sure to note or mark the location of all studs to assure proper installation. Remove the upper intake manifold from the engine.
7. Disengage the distributor or HVS wiring (as equipped), then matchmark the distributor or HVS and remove the assembly from the engine.
8. Disconnect the upper radiator hose at the thermostat housing and the heater hose at the lower intake manifold.
9. Disconnect the fuel supply and return lines at the rear of the lower intake manifold.
10. Remove the pencil brace (A/C compressor bracket-to-lower intake manifold).
11. Disengage the wiring harness connectors from the necessary lower intake components including:
 • Fuel injector
 • Exhaust Gas Recirculation (EGR) valve
 • Engine Coolant Temperature (ECT) sensor

12. Remove the lower intake manifold retaining bolts, then remove the manifold from the engine.

13. Using a gasket scraper, carefully clean the gasket mounting surfaces. Be sure to inspect the manifold for warpage and/or cracks; if necessary, replace it.

14. Position the gaskets to the cylinder head with the port blocking plates to the rear and the "this side up" stamps facing upward, then apply a 3/16 in. (5mm) bead of RTV sealant to the front and rear of the engine block at the block-to-manifold mating surface. Extend the bead 1/2 in. (13mm) up each cylinder head to seal and retain the gaskets.

15. Install the lower intake manifold taking care not to disturb the gaskets, then tighten the manifold retainers to 35 ft. lbs. (48 Nm) using the proper torque sequence.

16. Engage the wiring harness to the lower manifold components, including the injector, EGR valve and ECT sensor.

17. Install the pencil brace to the A/C compressor bracket and the lower intake manifold.

18. Connect the fuel supply and return lines to the rear of the lower intake. Temporarily reconnect the negative battery cable, then pressurize the fuel system (by cycling the ignition without starting the engine) and check for leaks. Disconnect the negative battery cable and continue installation.

19. Connect the heater hose to the lower intake and the upper radiator hose to the thermostat housing.

20. Align the matchmarks and install the distributor assembly, then engage the wiring.

21. Position a new upper intake manifold gasket on the engine, making sure the green sealing lines are facing upward.

22. Install the upper intake manifold being careful not to pinch the fuel injector wires between the manifolds.

23. Install the manifold retainers, making sure the studs are properly positioned, then tighten them using the proper sequence to 124 inch lbs. (14 Nm).

24. Connect the PCV hose to the rear of the upper intake manifold and the vacuum hoses to both the front and rear of the manifold assembly.

25. Connect the throttle linkage to the upper intake, then install the ignition coil.

26. Engage the necessary wiring to the upper intake components including the TP sensor, IAC motor, MAP sensor and the IMTV.

27. Install the plastic cover, the air cleaner and air inlet duct.

28. Connect the negative battery cable, then properly refill the engine cooling system.

4.3L (VIN Z) Non-Turbocharged Engine

EXCEPT ASTRO AND SAFARI

1. Disconnect the negative battery cable and properly relieve the fuel system pressure.

2. Drain the engine cooling system.

3. Remove the air cleaner and heat stove tube.

4. Remove the 2 braces at the rear of the serpentine drive belt tensioner.

5. Disconnect the upper radiator hose.

6. Remove the emissions relays along with the bracket, then disconnect the wiring harness from the retaining clips and position aside. Disconnect the ground cable from the intake manifold stud.

7. Remove the power brake vacuum pipe, then disconnect the heater hose pipe at the manifold and fuel lines at the TBI unit.

8. Remove the ignition coil, then disengage the electrical connectors at the sensors on the manifold.

9. Matchmark and remove the distributor from the engine. For details, please refer to the procedure earlier in this section.

NOTE: For ease of installation, do not crank the engine with the distributor removed.

10. Tag and disengage the wires and hoses from the TBI unit.

11. Disconnect the the EGR hose, then disconnect the throttle, TVS and cruise control cables (as equipped).

12. Remove the intake manifold retaining studs and/or bolts, then remove the manifold and gaskets.

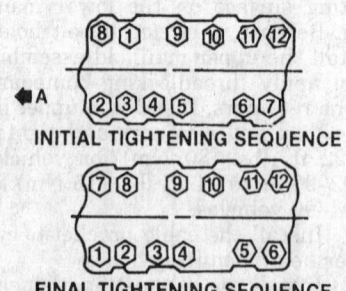

INITIAL TIGHTENING SEQUENCE

FINAL TIGHTENING SEQUENCE

A. Front Of Engine

85473104

Intake manifold torque sequence — Non-Turbo 4.3L (VIN Z) engine 1992–94

To install:

13. Using a gasket scraper, carefully clean the gasket mounting surfaces. Be sure to inspect the manifold for warpage and/or cracks; if necessary, replace it.

14. Position the gaskets to the cylinder head with the port blocking plates to the rear, then apply a 3/16 in. (5mm) bead of RTV sealant to the front and rear of the engine block at the block-to-manifold mating surface. Extend the bead 1/2 in. (13mm) up each cylinder head to seal and retain the gaskets.

15. Install the intake manifold taking care not to disturb the gaskets, then tighten the manifold retainers to 35 ft. lbs. (48 Nm) using the proper torque sequence.

16. Engage the TVS, cruise control and/or throttle cables, as equipped.

17. Connect the EGR hose then engage the wires and hoses at the TBI unit as noted during removal

18. Align and install the distributor assembly.

19. Install the ignition coil, then connect the fuel pipes.

20. Connect the heater hose pipe and the power brake vacuum pipe.

21. Connect the ground cable to the intake manifold stud, then position and secure the wiring harness using the clips.

22. Install the emissions relays along with their bracket, then connect the upper radiator hose.

23. Install the brace at the rear of the drive belt tensioner, then install the air cleaner and heat stove tube.

24. Connect the negative battery cable, then properly refill the engine cooling system.

25. Run the engine and check for leaks.

ASTRO AND SAFARI

1. Disconnect the negative battery cable. Remove the engine cover assembly. Remove the air cleaner assembly. Drain the cooling system.

2. Remove the distributor cap and ignition wires. Disconnect the ESC connector and remove the distributor.

3. Remove the cruise control transducer, if equipped.

4. Remove the detent, cruise and accelerator cables.

5. Remove the transmission and engine oil filler tubes at the alternator brace.

6. If equipped, remove the air conditioning compressor and idler pulley at the alternator brace. Remove the alternator brace.

7. Disconnect the fuel lines. Remove the necessary vacuum hoses and electrical wires.

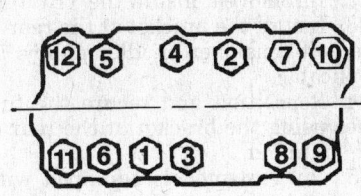

85473105

Intake manifold torque sequence — 1995–96 Non-Turbo 4.3L (VIN Z) engine

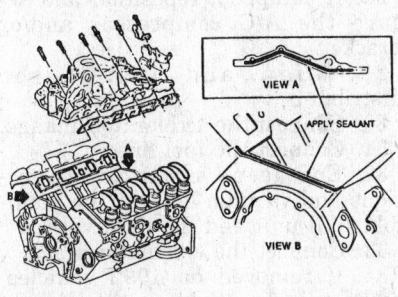

85473106

Intake manifold mounting — Non-turbo 4.3L (VIN Z) engine; note the bolt/stud usage may vary

8. Remove the AIR hoses and brackets, if equipped. Remove the upper radiator hose. Remove the heater hose at the manifold. As required, remove the TBI unit.

9. Remove the intake manifold retaining bolts. Remove the intake manifold from the engine.

To install:

10. The gaskets are marked for right and left side installation. Do not interchange them. Clean the sealing surface of the engine block and apply a 5/16 in. bead of silicone sealer to each ridge.

11. Install the new gaskets onto the heads. The gaskets will have to be cut slightly to fit past the center pushrods. Do not cut any more material than necessary. Hold the gaskets in place by extending the ridge bead of sealer 1/4 in. onto the gasket ends. (When the intake manifold is installed the area between the ridges and the manifold should be completely sealed.)

12. Install the intake manifold and torque the bolts in sequence to 35 ft. lbs. (47 Nm) except position No. 9 which is torqued to 41 ft. lbs. (56 Nm).

13. Install the AIR hoses and brackets, if equipped. Install the up-

per radiator hose. Install the heater hose at the manifold. Install the TBI unit.

14. Connect the fuel lines. Install the necessary vacuum hoses and electrical wires.

15. If equipped, install the air conditioning compressor and idler pulley at the alternator brace. Install the alternator brace.

16. Install the transmission and engine oil filler tubes at the alternator brace.

17. Install the detent, cruise and accelerator cables.

18. Install the cruise control transducer, if equipped.

19. Install the distributor, cap and ignition wires. Connect the ESC connector to the distributor.

20. Install the air cleaner assembly. Fill the cooling system with the proper type and quantity of antifreeze.

21. Connect the negative battery cable. Install the engine cover assembly.

4.3L (VIN Z) MFI-Turbocharged Engine

1. Properly relieve the fuel system pressure and disconnect the negative battery cable.

2. Drain the engine cooling system and the charge air cooling system.

3. Loosen the wing nut at the air cleaner, then position the air cleaner and duct aside.

4. Loosen the charge air cooler clamps, then remove the ducts and hoses.

5. Remove the charge air cooler from the supports, then remove the air cooler lateral (center) support.

6. Disengage the electrical connectors and hoses from the EVRV solenoid, the ignition coil and the MAP sensor located on the multi-use bracket.

7. Remove the multi-use bracket from the lower intake manifold assembly.

8. Tag and disengage the hoses and electrical connectors from the upper intake manifold assembly.

9. Loosen the throttle body retaining bolts, then remove the throttle body, gasket and cable bracket from the upper intake manifold.

10. Remove the upper intake manifold retaining bolts, then remove the manifold and gasket.

11. Disconnect the heater hose from the lower intake manifold.

12. Remove the charge air cooler coolant inlet pipe from the lower intake manifold, then disconnect it from the radiator by loosening the clamp and disengaging the hose.

13. Tag and disengage the wiring connectors from the fuel injectors, then disconnect the fuel pipes from the fuel rail assembly.

14. Loosen and remove the retaining bolts, then remove the fuel rail assembly (rail and injectors) from the lower manifold.

15. If equipped, remove the rear A/C brace,.

16. Disconnect the turbocharger coolant return line, then remove the upper radiator hose from the lower intake manifold.

17. Remove the ground strap from the lower intake manifold, then disengage the coolant sensor connector.

18. Tag and disconnect the spark plug wires from the distributor, remove the distributor cap and remove the distributor from the engine. Be sure to matchmark the distributor and rotor with the engine before removal.

19. Remove the lower intake manifold bolts and studs, then remove the manifold from the engine.

To install:

20. Using a gasket scraper, carefully clean the gasket mounting surfaces. Be sure to inspect the manifold for warpage and/or cracks; if necessary, replace it.

21. Position the gaskets to the cylinder head with the port blocking plates to the rear, then apply a 3/16 in. (5mm) bead of RTV sealant to the front and rear of the engine block at the block-to-manifold mating surface. Extend the bead 1/2 in. (13mm) up each cylinder head to seal and retain the gaskets.

22. Install the lower intake manifold taking care not to disturb the gaskets, then tighten the manifold retainers to 35 ft. lbs. (48 Nm).

23. Align the marks made during removal and install the distributor to the engine. Install the distributor cap and engage the spark plug wires.

24. Engage the coolant sensor electrical connector, then connect the ground strap.

25. Connect the upper radiator hose and the turbocharger coolant return line, then install the A/C compressor rear brace, if equipped.

26. Install the fuel rail and injectors, then connect the fuel pipes to the rail and engage the wiring connectors to the injectors. Tighten the fuel rail bolts to 58 inch lbs. (6.5 Nm) and the pipe fittings to 16 ft. lbs. (22 Nm).

27. Place the charge air cooler coolant inlet pipe into position on the lower intake manifold, then connect

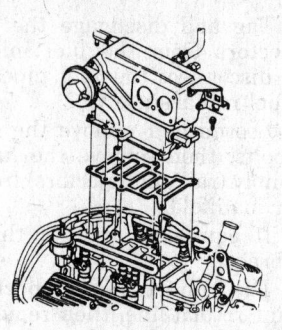

Upper intake manifold mounting — 4.3L MFI-turbo engine

the hose and clamp from the radiator to the charge air cooler inlet pipe.

28. Connect the heater hose to the lower intake manifold.

29. Install the upper intake manifold using a new gasket, then tighten the retaining bolts (starting from the 2 middle bolts working outward to each side) to 18 ft. lbs. (24 Nm).

30. Install the throttle body and cable bracket using a new throttle body gasket, then tighten the retaining bolts to 18 ft. lbs. (24 Nm).

31. Engage the upper intake manifold connectors and hoses, then install the multi-use bracket. Engage the hoses and wiring to the MAP sensor, ignition coil and EVRV solenoid.

32. Install the charge air cooler lateral support and finger-tighten the retaining nut.

33. Install and secure the charge air cooler supports, then tighten the lateral support nut.

34. Install the charge air cooler hoses and ducts, then secure using the clamps.

35. Connect the negative battery cable.

36. Properly refill the charge air cooling system and the engine cooling system.

5.0L and 5.7L Engines

1. Disconnect the negative battery cable and properly relieve the fuel system pressure.

2. On Van models, remove the engine cover.

3. Drain the engine cooling system.

4. Remove the air cleaner assembly.

5. Disconnect the heater pipe and upper radiator hose at the intake manifold.

6. If necessary on 1992 vehicles, disconnect the heater hose at the rear of the manifold.

7. Disconnect the alternator rear brace at the manifold.

8. Tag and disconnect the vacuum hoses at the manifold, TBI unit and the EGR valve.

9. Tag and disengage all electrical connections from the manifold and TBI unit.

10. Disconnect the fuel lines from the TBI unit, then disengage the accelerator and cruise control linkage (as equipped).

11. Matchmark and remove the distributor.

12. If equipped, remove the A/C compressor rear bracket (except vans) or the compressor and bracket (van models), then position aside.

13. Remove the power brake vacuum line from the vacuum booster to the manifold.

14. Disconnect the coil or spark plug wiring, as necessary, then remove the emission control sensors and bracket on the right side.

15. On Van models equipped with cruise control, remove the transducer and bracket.

16. Remove the fuel line bracket at the rear of the intake manifold and reposition the lines. Remove the bracket at the rear of the belt tensioner or idler pulley, as applicable.

17. If necessary, remove the TBI unit.

18. Remove the intake manifold bolts, studs and engine lift hooks, if necessary. Remove the intake manifold, then remove and discard the old gaskets.

To install:

NOTE: Before installing the intake manifold, ensure the gasket surfaces are thoroughly clean.

19. Apply ³⁄₁₆ in. (5mm) bead of sealant to the front and rear sealing surfaces of the engine block manifold. Extend the bead ½ in. (13mm) up each cylinder head to seal and retain the new gaskets.

20. Carefully install the manifold.

21. Install the intake manifold retainers and tighten to 35 ft. lbs. (48

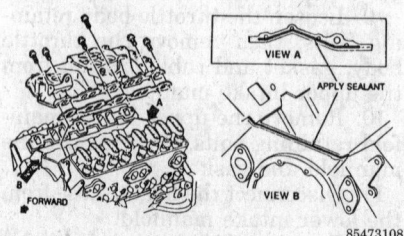

Intake manifold installation — 5.0L and 5.7L engines

Nm) using multiple passes of the proper sequence.

22. If removed, install the TBI unit.

23. Install the bracket at the rear of the belt tensioner or idler pulley, as applicable.

24. Reposition and secure the fuel lines using the bracket at the rear of the manifold.

25. On Van models equipped with cruise control, install the transducer and bracket.

26. Install the emission control sensors and bracket, then engage the coil or spark plug wiring, as necessary.

27. Install the vacuum line between the vacuum booster and manifold.

28. If equipped, reposition and secure the A/C compressor and/or bracket.

29. Align and install the distributor.

30. Connect the accelerator linkage.

31. Connect the fuel lines.

32. Engage all electrical connections and vacuum lines at the manifold, TBI unit and the EGR valve.

33. Connect the alternator brace.

34. If removed on 1992 vehicles, connect the heater hose at the rear of the manifold.

35. Connect the heater pipe and the upper radiator hose.

36. Install the air cleaner assembly.

37. On Van models, install the engine cover.

38. Connect the negative battery cable, then properly refill the engine cooling system.

7.4L Engine

1. Properly relieve the fuel system pressure, then disconnect the negative battery cable.

2. On Van models, remove the engine cover.

3. Drain the engine cooling system.

4. Remove the air cleaner assembly.

5. Remove the upper radiator hose and the water pump bypass hose.

6. Disconnect the heater hose and pipe at the TBI unit.

7. Disengage the sensor wire at the front of the manifold.

8. Tag and disengage all electrical connections, along with all vacuum lines from the manifold and TBI unit.

9. Disconnect the accelerator, cruise control and TVS linkage, as equipped.

10. Remove the wiring harness from the retaining clips or bracket and position aside.

11. Either remove the coil with bracket and/or disconnect the coil wiring.

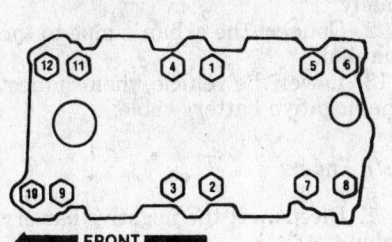

Intake manifold torque sequence — 5.0L and 5.7L engines

85473109

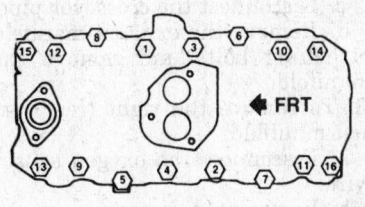

Intake manifold torque sequence — 7.4L engine

85473110

12. Disconnect the fuel lines at the TBI unit and on Van models, at the rear support.

13. If necessary, remove the TBI unit.

14. Remove the crankcase ventilation hoses.

15. Matchmark and remove the distributor assembly.

16. Remove the sensors and bracket on the right side of the engine (except vans) or remove the sensor and bracket from the front of the intake (van models).

17. On Van models, disconnect the automatic transmission dipstick tube from the manifold and move aside for clearance, then remove the MAP sensor and bracket.

18. If applicable, remove the cruise control transducer.

19. Remove the air conditioning compressor rear bracket, if equipped, then remove the alternator and rear bracket (van models) or just the rear bracket (except vans).

20. Remove the intake manifold retaining bolts.

21. Remove the intake manifold, then remove and discard both the old gaskets and seals.

To install:

22. Install the intake manifold using new gaskets and seals.

NOTE: If RTV sealer was used on the old manifold seals, apply a ³/₁₆ in. (5mm) bead of RTV sealer to the front and rear block where the seals join the cylinder heads.

23. Install the intake manifold bolts, then tighten to 30 ft. lbs. (40 Nm). using the proper torque sequence. After all bolts are torqued, retighten them in sequence to assure proper torquing.

24. Install the alternator and/or rear bracket, as applicable. If equipped, install the the air conditioning compressor rear bracket.

25. If applicable, install the cruise control transducer.

26. On Van models, install the MAP sensor and bracket.

27. Except for Van models, install the sensors and bracket on the right side of the engine.

28. If removed, install the ignition coil and bracket. Connect the coil wiring.

29. Align and install the distributor assembly.

30. If removed, install the TBI unit.

31. Connect the vacuum hoses as tagged during removal, then install the crankcase ventilation hoses.

32. Connect the fuel lines at the TBI unit and on Van models, at the rear support.

33. On Van models, install the sensor and bracket on the front of the intake.

34. Reposition and secure the wiring harness to the retaining clips or bracket.

35. Connect the accelerator, cruise control and TVS linkage, as equipped.

36. Engage all electrical connections as tagged during removal, along with the sensor wire at the front of the manifold.

37. Connect the heater hose and pipe at the TBI unit.

38. Install the upper radiator hose and the water pump bypass hose.

39. On Van models, connect the automatic transmission dipstick tube to the manifold.

40. Install the air cleaner assembly.

41. Install the engine cover.

42. Connect the negative battery cable and properly refill the engine cooling system.

Exhaust Manifold

REMOVAL AND INSTALLATION

2.2L Engine

1. Disconnect the negative battery cable, then remove the air cleaner and duct work.

2. Either disengage the wiring or remove the oxygen sensor from the manifold. If the manifold or sensor is to be replaced, remove the sensor.

3. Remove the oil fill tube assembly.

4. Loosen and remove the exhaust manifold retaining nuts, first disconnect the pipe from the manifold, then remove the manifold from the engine.

To install:

5. Carefully clean the threads of the exhaust manifold retainers, then remove all remaining traces of gasket from the mating surfaces.

6. Install the manifold to the engine using a new gasket, then tighten the manifold nuts to 115 inch lbs. (13 Nm). Connect the pipe to the manifold and tighten the retainers.

7. Install the oil fill tube assembly.

8. Either install the oxygen sensor or engage the wiring, as applicable. If the sensor or manifold was replaced, tighten the oxygen sensor to 30 ft. lbs. (41 Nm).

9. Install the air cleaner and duct work.

10. Connect the negative battery cable.

2.5L Engine

1. Disconnect the negative battery cable.

2. Remove the air cleaner and heat stove pipe.

3. Remove the A/C compressor, if equipped, drive belt, and the rear adjusting bracket (if used). Lay the compressor aside in the engine compartment.

4. Remove the dipstick tube and bracket.

5. Disconnect the exhaust pipe from the exhaust manifold.

6. Disengage the electrical connector from the oxygen sensor.

7. Remove the exhaust manifold-to-engine bolts/washers and the manifold from the engine.

To install:

8. Using a gasket scraper, clean the gasket mounting surfaces.

9. Install the manifold to the engine using a new gasket, then tighten the center retainers 36 ft. lbs. (49 Nm) and the outer retainers to 32 ft. lbs. (43 Nm) using the proper torque sequence.

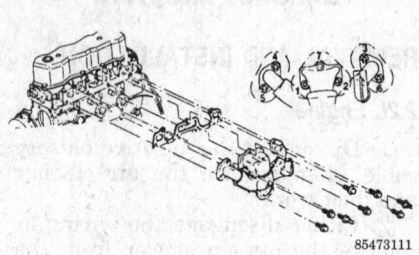

Exhaust manifold installation and torque sequence — 2.5L engine

10. Engage the oxygen sensor electrical connector, then connect and secure the exhaust pipe to the manifold.

11. Install the dipstick tube and bracket, then reposition and install the A/C compressor, if equipped, rear adjusting bracket (if used) and the drive belt.

12. Install the air cleaner and the heat stove pipe.

13. Connect the negative battery cable.

2.8L Engine

LEFT SIDE

1. Disconnect the negative battery cable, then raise and support the vehicle safely.

2. Disconnect the exhaust pipe from the exhaust manifold.

3. Remove the rear exhaust manifold-to-cylinder head bolts, then lower the vehicle for underhood access.

4. If necessary, disconnect the air management hoses and wiring.

5. If applicable, disconnect the heat stove tube.

6. If equipped, remove the P/S pump and bracket; do not disconnect the power steering hoses, instead reposition the pump with the hoses attached.

7. Remove the remaining exhaust manifold-to-cylinder head bolts, then remove the manifold from the engine.

To install:

8. Using a gasket scraper, clean the gasket mounting surfaces. Inspect the exhaust manifold for distortion, cracks or damage; replace if necessary.

9. Install the exhaust manifold to the cylinder using a new gasket, then tighten the exhaust manifold-to-cylinder head bolts to 25 ft. lbs. (34 Nm) using a circular pattern, working from the center towards the outer ends.

10. If equipped, reposition and secure the P/S pump and bracket

11. If applicable, connect the heat stove tube.

12. If necessary, reconnect the air management hoses and wiring.

13. Raise and support the vehicle safely.

14. Connect the exhaust pipe to the manifold.

15. Carefully lower the vehicle, then connect the negative battery cable.

RIGHT SIDE

1. Disconnect the negative battery cable, then raise and support the vehicle safely.

2. Disconnect the exhaust pipe from the exhaust manifold.

3. Remove the rear exhaust manifold-to-cylinder head bolts, then lower the vehicle for underhood access.

4. Remove the AIR system diverter valve and heat shield, then remove the AIR system pump and alternator brackets.

5. If necessary, disconnect the air management hoses and wiring.

6. Remove the remaining exhaust manifold-to-cylinder head bolts, then remove the manifold from the engine.

To install:

7. Using a gasket scraper, clean the gasket mounting surfaces. Inspect the exhaust manifold for distortion, cracks or damage; replace if necessary.

8. Install the exhaust manifold to the cylinder using a new gasket, then tighten the exhaust manifold-to-cylinder head bolts to 25 ft. lbs. (34 Nm) using a circular pattern, working from the center to the outer ends.

9. If necessary, reconnect the air management hoses and wiring.

10. Install the AIR system pump and alternator brackets, then install the AIR system diverter valve and heat shield.

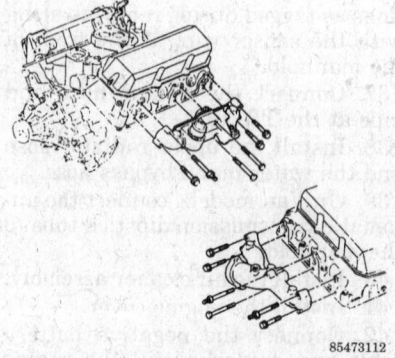

Exhaust manifold installation — 2.8L engine

11. Raise and support the vehicle safely.

12. Connect the exhaust pipe to the manifold.

13. Lower the vehicle, then connect the negative battery cable.

3.1L Engine

1. Disconnect the negative battery cable.

2. To remove the left (front) exhaust manifold:

a. Remove the serpentine belt and the air conditioning compressor. Position the compressor aside with the lines intact.

b. Remove the engine strut and bracket.

c. Disconnect the crossover pipe.

d. Remove the exhaust manifold attaching bolts and remove the manifold.

3. To remove the right (rear) exhaust manifold:

a. Disconnect the oxygen sensor wire.

b. Remove the crossover pipe.

c. Raise and support the vehicle safely.

d. Disconnect the exhaust pipe.

e. Support the rear center of the frame.

f. Remove the rear frame mount bolts.

g. Lower the frame 8–10 in. for access.

h. Remove the exhaust manifold bolts and remove the assembly.

4. Installation is the reverse of the removal procedure.

3.8L Engine

1. Disconnect the negative battery cable.

2. To remove the left (front) exhaust manifold:

a. Remove the crossover pipe.

b. Tag and disconnect the spark plug wires from the plugs.

c. Remove the exhaust manifold bolts/studs and the oil dipstick tube.

d. Remove the exhaust manifold assembly.

3. To remove the right (rear) exhaust manifolds:

a. Tag and disconnect the spark plug wires.

b. Remove the throttle cable bracket.

c. Remove the crossover pipe heat shield.

d. Remove the transaxle dipstick and tube assembly.

e. Disconnect the oxygen sensor wire.

Exhaust manifold mounting — 3.1L engine

f. Remove the fasteners connecting the crossover pipe to the manifold.

g. Remove the plastic vacuum tank mounted on the cowl.

h. Raise and support the vehicle safely.

i. Remove the catalytic converter heat shield and hanger.

j. Remove the front exhaust pipe-to-the manifold attaching nuts.

k. Remove the front exhaust pipe from the manifold. Lower the vehicle.

l. Remove the engine lift bracket and remove the manifold attaching nuts.

m. Remove the exhaust manifold assembly.

4. Installation is the reverse of the removal procedure.

4.3L Non-Turbocharged Engines

1. Disconnect the negative battery cable.

2. On Van models, remove the engine cover.

3. Raise and support the vehicle safely.

4. Disconnect the exhaust pipe from the exhaust manifold.

5. Lower the vehicle for underhood access.

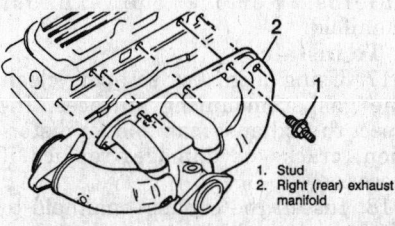

1. Stud
2. Right (rear) exhaust manifold

Exhaust manifold mounting — 3.8L engine

6. Tag and disconnect the spark plug wires from the plugs and from the retaining clips.

7. If removing the left side manifold:

a. Remove the air cleaner with heat stove pipe and cold air intake pipe.

b. Remove the power steering/alternator rear bracket.

c. Check for sufficient clearance between the manifold and the intermediate steering shaft. On some models it will be necessary to disconnect the intermediate shaft from the steering gear in order to reposition the shaft for clearance.

8. If necessary when removing the right side manifold, unbolt the A/C compressor and bracket, then position the assembly aside. Do not disconnect the lines or allow them to become kinked or otherwise damaged.

9. If necessary for the right side manifold, remove the spark plugs, dipstick tube and wiring.

10. Unbend the locktangs then remove the exhaust manifold retaining bolts, washers and tab washers. Remove the exhaust manifold, then remove and discard the old gaskets.

To install:

11. Using a gasket scraper, clean the gasket mounting surfaces. Inspect the exhaust manifold for distortion, cracks or damage; replace if necessary.

12. Install the exhaust manifold to the cylinder using a new gasket, then tighten the exhaust manifold-to-cylinder head bolts to 26 ft. lbs. (36 Nm) on the center exhaust tube and to 20 ft. lbs. (28 Nm) on the front and rear exhaust tubes. Once the bolts are tightened, bend the tabs on the washers back over the heads of all bolts in order to lock them in position.

13. If removed on the right side, install the spark plugs, dipstick tube and wiring.

14. If unbolted, reposition and secure the A/C compressor and bracket assembly.

15. If the left manifold was removed:

a. If unbolted, reconnect the intermediate shaft to the steering gear.

b. Install the power steering/alternator rear bracket.

c. Install the air cleaner along with the heat stove pipe and cold air intake pipe.

16. Connect the spark plug wires to the retainer clips and to the plugs as noted during removal.

17. Raise and support the vehicle safely.

18. Connect the exhaust pipe to the manifold.

19. Lower the vehicle.

20. On Van models, instal the engine cover.

21. Connect the negative battery cable.

4.3L Turbocharged Engine

LEFT SIDE

1. Disconnect the negative battery cable, then remove the air cleaner and duct.

2. Remove the turbocharger air inlet elbow, then remove the upper fan shroud.

3. Loosen the fan nuts, then remove the serpentine drive belt. Remove the fan and pulley assembly.

4. Using a suitable pulley remover (such as J-25034-B or equivalent) pull the power steering pump pulley from the pump.

5. Remove the rear brace from the alternator.

6. Raise and support the vehicle safely.

7. Remove the left tire and wheel, then remove the left wheel house panel.

8. Disconnect the power steering inlet and outlet hoses from the pump. Immediately plug all openings in order to prevent system contamination or excessive fluid loss.

9. Disconnect the oil filter line bracket from the power steering pump.

10. Disconnect the intermediate shaft.

11. Unbolt the exhaust crossover pipe from the manifold.

12. Remove the power steering pump and rear brace as an assembly from the front bracket.

13. Tag and disconnect the wires from the spark plugs, then remove the plugs from the left cylinder head.

14. Bend back the locktabs, then remove the exhaust manifold bolts, studs, locktabs, washers and heat shields. Remove the exhaust manifold.

To install:

15. Using a gasket scraper, clean the gasket mounting surfaces. Inspect the exhaust manifold for distortion, cracks or damage; replace if necessary.

16. Install the exhaust manifold to the cylinder using a new gasket, then tighten retainers to 33 ft. lbs. (45 Nm). Once the retainers are tightened, bend the tabs on the washers back over the hex-heads of all bolts/studs in order to lock them in position.

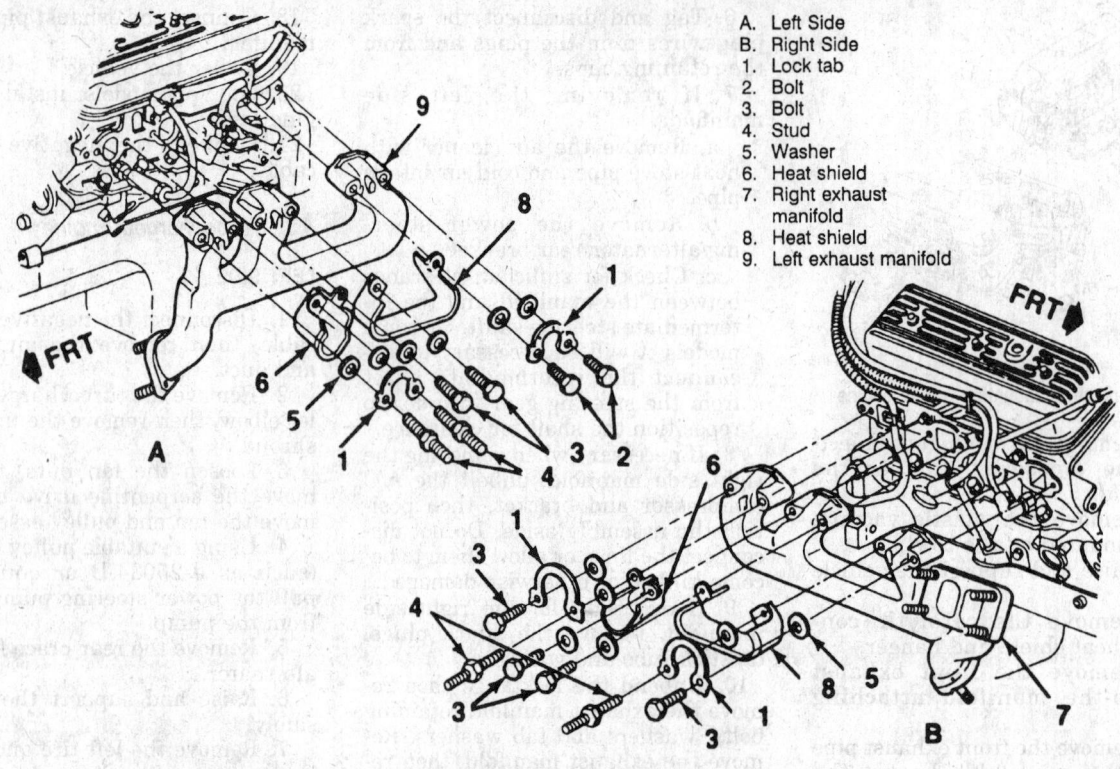

A. Left Side
B. Right Side
1. Lock tab
2. Bolt
3. Bolt
4. Stud
5. Washer
6. Heat shield
7. Right exhaust manifold
8. Heat shield
9. Left exhaust manifold

85473115

Exhaust manifold mounting — 4.3L engine

17. Install and tighten the spark plugs, then connect the spark plug wires.

18. Install the power steering pump and rear brace to the front bracket. Tighten the bracket bolts to 37 ft. lbs. (50 Nm) and the rear brace nut to 33 ft. lbs. (45 Nm).

19. Connect the crossover pipe and tighten the retaining nuts to 12 ft. lbs. (16 Nm).

20. Connect the intermediate shaft, then secure the oil filter line bracket to the power steering pump.

21. Remove the plugs, then connect the power steering outlet and inlet hoses to the pump. Tighten the hose fittings to 20 ft. lbs. (27 Nm).

22. Install the left wheel housing panel, then install the left front tire and wheel assembly.

23. Carefully lower the vehicle.

24. Install the rear brace to the alternator and tighten the retaining bolt to 18 ft. lbs. (25 Nm).

25. Install the power steering pump pulley using a suitable installer tool.

26. Install the fan and pulley to the water pump, then install the serpentine drive belt. With the belt installed, tighten the fan and pulley nuts to 18 ft. lbs. (24 Nm).

27. Install the upper fan shroud, then install the turbocharger air inlet elbow.

28. Install the air cleaner and duct.

29. Connect the negative battery cable.

30. Refill the power steering pump and bleed air from the system.

RIGHT SIDE

1. Disconnect the negative battery cable, followed by the positive cable from the battery. Loosen the battery hold-down clamp and remove the battery.

2. Drain the engine cooling system, then remove the battery tray and vacuum tank.

3. Disconnect the turbocharger oil feed hose and the coolant return pipe.

4. Disengage the oxygen sensor connector, then raise and support the vehicle safely.

5. Remove the right front tire and wheel, then remove the right wheel housing panel.

6. Disconnect the mufflers and tailpipe from the catalytic converter.

7. Remove the catalytic converter support bolts, then carefully lower the vehicle for underhood access.

8. Disengage the turbocharger solenoid electrical connector and loosen the turbocharger coolant feed line.

9. Raise and support the vehicle safely, then remove the turbocharger outlet pipe nuts.

10. Remove the turbocharger outlet pipe support bolt. Move the outlet pipe and catalytic converter away from the turbocharger.

11. Remove the turbocharger oil return pipe from the turbocharger, then remove the turbocharger mounting nuts.

12. Disconnect the coolant feed line from the turbocharger, then remove the turbocharger assembly.

13. Disconnect the exhaust crossover pipe from the manifold.

14. Tag and disconnect the wires from the spark plugs, then remove the plugs from the left cylinder head.

15. Remove the charger air cooler lower supports.

16. Bend back the locktabs, then remove the exhaust manifold bolts, studs, locktabs, washers and heat shields. Remove the exhaust manifold.

To install:

17. Using a gasket scraper, clean the gasket mounting surfaces. Inspect the exhaust manifold for distortion, cracks or damage; replace if necessary.

18. Install the exhaust manifold to the cylinder using a new gasket, then tighten retainers to 33 ft. lbs. (45 Nm). Once the retainers are tightened, bend the tabs on the washers back over the hex-heads of all

bolts/studs in order to lock them in position.

19. Install and tighten the spark plugs, then connect the spark plug wires.

20. Install the charge air cooler lower supports.

21. Connect the exhaust crossover pipe to the manifold, then tighten the retaining nuts to 12 ft. lbs. (16 Nm).

22. Position the turbocharger, then connect the coolant feed pipe and loosely install the bolt.

23. Loosely install the turbocharger mounting nuts followed by the return pipe and bolts. Tighten the coolant feed pipe bolt to 26 ft. lbs. (35 Nm), then mounting nuts to 33 ft. lbs. (45 Nm) and the oil return pipe bolts to 35 inch lbs. (4 Nm).

24. Install the turbocharger outlet pipe and nuts along with the outlet pipe support bolt. Tighten the pipe nuts to 41 ft. lbs. (55 Nm) followed by the support bolt to 22 ft. lbs. (30 Nm).

25. Engage the turbocharger solenoid electrical connector.

26. Loosely install the catalytic converter support bolts, then engage the mufflers and tailpipe to the catalytic converter. Tighten the support bolts to 25 ft. lbs. (34 Nm), then tighten the tailpipe bolts to 24 ft. lbs. (32 Nm).

27. Install the wheel housing panel.

28. Install the tire and wheel assembly, then carefully lower the vehicle.

29. Engage the oxygen sensor electrical connector.

30. Connect the turbocharger oil feed hose and the coolant return pipe. Tighten the oil hose fitting to 13 ft. lbs. (17 Nm) and the coolant pipe fittings to 16 ft. lbs. (22 Nm).

31. Install the battery tray and vacuum tank.

32. Install the battery and secure using the hold-down clamp.

33. Connect the positive cable, then the negative cable to the battery.

34. Properly refill the engine cooling system.

5.0L and 5.7L Engines

1. Disconnect the negative battery cable.

2. For Van models, remove the engine cover.

3. Remove the air cleaner.

4. Raise and support the vehicle safely.

5. Disconnect the exhaust pipe at the manifold, then lower the vehicle for underhood access.

6. If removing a manifold with the oxygen sensor mounted to it, disengage the sensor wiring.

7. If necessary, disconnect the AIR hose at the check valve.

8. Disconnect the heat stove pipe and remove the dipstick tube bracket, if working on the right side of the engine.

9. If removing the left side manifold, remove the power steering pump rear bracket at the manifold.

10. If necessary on 1992 vehicles, loosen the alternator and remove the lower bracket. Then if necessary, remove the air conditioner compressor rear bracket and the diverter valve and bracket.

NOTE: On models 1992 with air conditioning, it may be necessary to remove the compressor, and tie it out of the way. Do not disconnect the compressor lines.

11. Remove the manifold bolts and remove the manifold(s). Some models have lock tabs on the front and rear manifold bolts which must be removed before removing the bolts.

12. Installation is the reverse of removal. Tighten the 2 center retaining bolts to 26 ft. lbs. (36 Nm) and the outer manifold retaining bolts to 20 ft. lbs. (28 Nm).

7.4L Engine

1. Disconnect the negative battery cable.

2. On Van models, remove the engine cover.

3. If removing the right side manifold, remove the heat stove pipe and the dipstick tube.

4. If removing a manifold with the oxygen sensor mounted to it, disengage the sensor wiring.

5. If applicable, disconnect the AIR hose at the check valve.

6. Remove the spark plugs and wires.

7. On Van models, remove the exhaust manifold bolts and the spark plug heat shields. Leave the front bolt (left manifold) or rear bolt (right manifold) in place for support.

8. Raise and support the vehicle safely for access.

9. On Van models, if equipped, remove the heat shield bolts from the engine mount and bellhousing, then remove the shield.

10. Disconnect the exhaust pipe at the manifold.

11. Remove the manifold bolts (or bolt in the case of Van models). Except for Van models (on which it was

done earlier) remove the spark plug heat shields.

NOTE: It may be necessary to raise the engine slightly to gain sufficient clearance for removal of the manifold on some G-Series vehicles.

12. Remove the exhaust manifold.

13. Clean the mating surfaces and the retainer threads.

14. Install the manifold, spark plug heat shields and bolts. Tighten the bolts to 40 ft. lbs. (54 Nm). starting from the center bolts and working towards the outside.

15. Complete the remainder of the installation by reversing the removal procedures.

Turbocharger

The Turbocharger and multi-port fuel injection are special to the Syclone and Typhoon. They require some service procedures which are unique to the rest of the S/T-Series.

PRECAUTIONS

Proper maintenance practices must be followed in order to prolong the performance and life of the turbocharger. Failures in the turbocharger system are often caused by oil lag, restriction or lack of oil flow, dirty oil or foreign objects entering the turbocharger.

When working on or around the turbocharger system always follow these precautions:

• Do not allow dust, sand or other foreign material to enter the turbocharger. Dust or sand will erode the compressor wheel blades, while uneven blade wear can produce shaft motion causing bearing failure. Large or heavy objects will completely destroy the turbocharger and could cause severe damage to the engine.

• The air cleaner system must be properly maintained. A plugged or restricted air cleaner will reduce air pressure and volume at the compressor air inlet. The pressure drop will lower turbocharger performance and may cause oil pullover during idle. Oil pullover is a compressor end oil seal leak without seal part failure.

• The oil lube system must be properly maintained. If dirt or foreign material is introduced into the turbocharger bearing system by lube oil, the center housing bearing bore surfaces will wear. Contaminants act as an abrasive cutting tool and will eventually wear through bearing sur-

faces causing turbocharger noise and poor performance. Excessive noise and/or oil smoke may be noticed. Remember that oil will completely bypass the filter if the element becomes clogged. Adhere closely to oil and filter change intervals on turbocharged vehicles.

• Do not allow sludge to build up in the turbocharger. Sludge may occur if oil oxidation or breakdown occurs. Possible causes would include, engine overheating, excessive combustion products from piston blow-by, noncompatible oils, engine coolant leakage into the oil, incorrect grade/quality of oil or improper oil change intervals. If turbine end oil leakage is noted, check the turbocharger oil drain tube and the crankcase breathers. Remove any restrictions and check again for leaks.

• The charge air cooler system must be properly maintained. Only use the proper type and quantity of coolant in the system. If coolant becomes dirty or contaminated, the system must be flushed and refilled with fresh coolant.

REMOVAL AND INSTALLATION

1. Drain the engine cooling system, then remove the air intake duct and the turbocharger air intake duct.
2. Disconnect the negative battery cable, followed by the positive cable from the battery. Loosen the battery hold-down clamp and remove the battery.
3. Remove the battery tray and vacuum tank.
4. Remove the nut and disconnect the turbocharger oil feed line, then disengage the electrical connector from the solenoid.
5. Loosen the turbocharger coolant return line clamp nut, then disconnect the coolant return line assembly.
6. Raise and support the vehicle safely.
7. Remove the right tire and wheel, then remove the wheel house panel retaining screws and remove the panel for access.
8. If necessary, disengage the oxygen sensor electrical connector, then remove the nut from the turbocharger and the bolt from the outlet pipe support bracket. Remove the clamp from the catalytic converter and bolts from the converter support, then remove the turbocharger outlet pipe.
9. Remove the retaining bolts from the turbocharger oil return pipe, then

remove the return pipe and gasket from the turbocharger assembly.
10. Remove the turbocharger mounting nuts.
11. Disconnect the coolant feed line from the turbocharger, then remove the turbocharger assembly.

To install:
12. Inspect and clean the turbocharger and manifold mounting surfaces.
13. Position the turbocharger, then connect the coolant feed pipe with gaskets and loosely install the bolt.
14. Loosely install the turbocharger mounting nuts followed by the oil feed pipe line fitting. Tighten the coolant feed pipe bolt to 26 ft. lbs. (35 Nm), then the turbocharger mounting nuts to 33 ft. lbs. (45 Nm) and the oil feed line fitting to 13 ft. lbs. (16 Nm).
15. Connect the turbocharger oil return pipe and gaskets, then tighten the line bolt to 35 inch lbs. (4 Nm).
16. Connect the turbocharger coolant return line assembly and tighten the line nut to 16 ft. lbs. (22 Nm). Secure the coolant return line clamp and tighten to 16 inch lbs. (1.8 Nm).
17. Install the turbocharger outlet pipe to the catalytic converter and turbocharger. Install the nuts to the turbocharger, then clamp to the converter, the bolts to the converter support and the bolt to the outlet pipe bracket. Tighten the turbocharger nuts to 41 ft. lbs. (55 Nm), the converter clamp nuts to 42 ft. lbs. (57 Nm), the support bracket bolt to 22 ft. lbs. (30 Nm) and the converter support bolts to 25 ft. lbs. (34 Nm).
18. If disengaged, connect the oxygen sensor wiring to the harness.
19. Install the wheel housing panel, then install the tire and wheel assembly. Carefully lower the vehicle.
20. Engage the turbocharger solenoid electrical connector.
21. Install the battery tray and vacuum tank.
22. Install the battery and secure using the hold-down clamp.
23. Install the air intake duct and the turbocharger air intake duct.
24. Connect the positive cable, then the negative cable to the battery.
25. Properly refill the engine cooling system.

Timing Gear Front Cover

REMOVAL AND INSTALLATION

2.5L Engine

1. Disconnect the negative battery cable.

2. Remove the power steering reservoir from the fan shroud, then remove the fan shroud.
3. Remove the serpentine drive belt.
4. Remove the alternator and brackets from the engine (lay them aside).
5. Remove the crankshaft pulley and hub.

NOTE: The outer ring (weight) of the torsional damper is bonded to the hub with rubber. The damper must be removed with a puller which acts on the inner hub only. Pulling on the outer portion of the damper will break the rubber bond or destroy the tuning of the unit.

6. Drain the engine cooling system, then disconnect the lower radiator hose at the water pump.
7. Remove the timing cover bolts and cover. Check for bolts threaded from the front of the oil pan to the bottom of the cover. If present, these must be removed before attempting to loosen the cover.
8. If the front seal is to be replaced, it can be pried out of the cover with a small prytool.

To install:
9. If removed, use the GM seal installer/centering tool J-34995 or equivalent to install the replacement cover seal. Be sure to support the seal area of the cover when installing the new seal.
10. Clean all sealing surfaces and apply a ⅜ in. bead of RTV sealant to the oil pan and timing gear cover sealing surfaces.
11. Use the GM Seal Installer/Centering Tool J-34995 or equivalent align the front cover. Install the cover while the RTV sealant is still wet.
12. Install the cover (and pan) retaining bolts, then tighten the bolts to 90 inch lbs. (10 Nm). Remove the centering tool from the timing cover.
13. Connect the lower radiator hose to the water pump.
14. Install the crankshaft hub and pulley.
15. Reposition and secure the alternator and brackets.
16. Install the serpentine drive belt or install and adjust the accessory drive belts, as applicable.
17. Install the upper fan shroud, then reposition and secure the power steering reservoir.
18. Connect the negative battery cable and properly refill the engine cooling system.

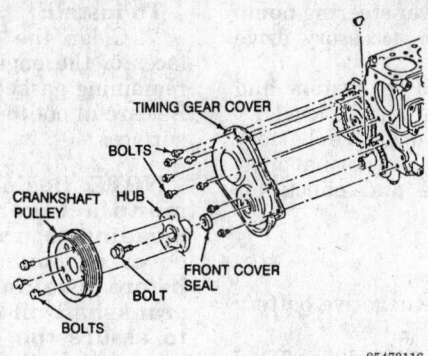

85473116

Front cover assembly — 2.5L engine

19. Run the engine until normal operating temperature is reached, then check for leaks.

Timing Chain Front Cover

It is recommended by the manufacturer that the front cover oil seal be replaced whenever the cover is removed.

REMOVAL AND INSTALLATION

2.2L Gasoline Engine

1. Disconnect the negative battery cable.
2. Remove the power steering fluid reservoir from the radiator shroud, then remove the upper fan shroud.
3. Carefully release the belt tension, then remove the serpentine drive belt.
4. Remove the alternator and brackets from the engine, then position them aside.
5. Remove the crankshaft pulley and hub.
6. As necessary, disconnect the lower radiator hose clamp at the water pump, then loosen and/or remove the oil pan.

NOTE: There may be bolts attaching the front of the oil pan to the timing cover. If so, make sure they are removed before attempting to remove the cover.

7. Remove the crankcase (timing) front cover bolts, then remove cover from the engine. Make sure all bolts are removed and be careful not to force and damage the cover.
8. If necessary, carefully remove the old crankshaft seal from the cover using a suitable prytool.

To install:

9. Carefully remove all traces of gasket or sealant from the mating surfaces.
10. If removed, lubricate the lips of a new seal with clean engine oil, then use a seal centering tool (such as J-35468 or equivalent) to install the seal to the front cover. Leave the tool in position in the seal until the cover is installed.
11. Apply a $\frac{3}{8}$ in. (10mm) wide by $\frac{5}{16}$ (5mm) thick bead of RTV sealer to the oil pan at the front crankcase cover sealing surface. Then apply a $\frac{1}{4}$ in. (6mm) by $\frac{1}{8}$ in. (3mm) thick bead of RTV to the crankcase front cover at the block sealing surface.
12. Install the crankcase front cover to the engine using the seal tool to assure it is properly centered and prevent damage to the hub. Tighten the cover retaining bolts to 97 inch lbs. (11 Nm), then remove the seal centering tool.
13. Install the lower radiator hose clamp at the water pump, then install and secure the oil pan, as applicable.
14. Install the crankshaft pulley and hub.
15. Reposition and secure the alternator with brackets.
16. Install the serpentine drive belt, then install the upper fan shroud.
17. Reposition and secure the power steering reservoir.
18. Connect the negative battery cable.

2.8L Engine

1. Disconnect the negative battery cable, then drain the engine cooling system.
2. Remove the serpentine drive belt.
3. Remove the water pump from the engine.

4. Remove the power steering pump bracket.
5. Remove the crankshaft pulley bolt, crankshaft pulley and hub (torsional damper).

NOTE: The outer ring (weight) of the torsional damper is bonded to the hub with rubber. The damper must be removed with a puller which acts on the inner hub only. Pulling on the outer portion of the damper will break the rubber bond or destroy the tuning of the unit.

6. Disconnect the lower radiator hose at the front cover.
7. Remove the timing cover bolts and cover. Check for bolts threaded from the front of the oil pan to the bottom of the cover. If present, these must be removed before attempting to loosen the cover.
8. If the front seal is to be replaced, it can be pried out of the cover with a small prytool.

To install:

9. Clean the gasket mating surfaces of the engine and cover of all remaining gasket or sealer material. Be careful not to score or damage the surfaces.
10. If removed, install a new seal to the cover using a suitable installation driver such as J-23042 (early model), J-35468 (late model) or equivalent. Be sure to support the back of the seal cover area during installation. Lightly coat the lips of the new seal with clean engine oil.
11. Lightly coat both sides of a new gasket using an anaerobic sealant, then position the gasket and cover to the engine. Install and tighten the retainers. If equipped with an oil pan sealing lip on the cover, apply a bead of sealant to the front cover at the oil pan mating surface.

NOTE: If equipped, do not forget the oil pan-to-front-cover bolts.

12. Install the water pump assembly to the engine.
13. Connect the lower radiator hose to the front cover.
14. Install the crankshaft hub and pulley.
15. Install the power steering pump bracket.
16. Install the serpentine drive belt.
17. Connect the negative battery cable, then properly refill the engine cooling system.
18. Run the engine until normal operating temperature has been reached, then check for leaks.

3.1L Engine

1. Disconnect the negative battery cable.
2. Drain the cooling system.
3. Remove the accessory drive belt and tensioner.
4. Remove the power steering pump.
5. Raise and safely support the vehicle. Remove the inner splash shield.
6. Drain the engine oil. Remove the crankshaft pulley and damper. Remove the starter and support it aside.
7. Place a support under the engine-to-transaxle mount.
8. Remove the engine mount bolts and the engine mount. Raise the engine slightly.
9. Remove the lower front cover bolts and lower the oil pan. Remove the radiator hose at the water pump.
10. Remove the heater hose at the cooling system fill pipe. Remove the bypass and overflow hoses.
11. Remove the remaining front cover bolts and remove the front cover.

To install:

12. Clean all gasket mating surfaces. Install a new gasket in position on the engine block.
13. Apply sealer to the lower edges of the front cover. Install the front cover in position on the engine block. Install and tighten the upper retainers.
14. Install the oil pan in position, then secure and tighten the lower front cover bolts.
15. Install the engine mount to the engine and lower the engine into position.
16. Install the crankshaft damper and pulley. Install the flywheel cover and inner splash shield.
17. Install the starter. Connect the heater bypass hose an the slower radiator hose to the water pump. Lower the vehicle.

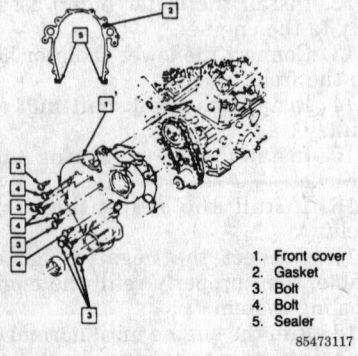

1. Front cover
2. Gasket
3. Bolt
4. Bolt
5. Sealer

85473117

Front cover assembly — 3.1L engine

18. Install the power steering pump bracket. Install the accessory drive belt and tensioner.
19. Refill the cooling system and the crankcase to the correct levels.
20. Connect the negative battery cable. Run the engine to normal operating temperature and check for leaks.

3.8L Engine

1. Disconnect the negative battery cable.
2. Remove the accessory drive belt.
3. Remove crankshaft damper using GM tool J–38197 or equivalent. The flywheel must be held from turning using J–37096 or equivalent tool.
4. Remove the crankshaft sensor shield and sensor.
5. Remove the water pump pulley.
6. Remove the oil pan-to-front cover bolts and the remaining front cover attaching bolts.
7. Remove the front cover assembly.

To install:

8. Installation is the reverse of the removal procedure.
9. Coat the threads of the cover retaining bolts with 1052080 or equivalent sealant, then install the bolts and tighten to 22 ft. lbs. (30 Nm).
10. Tighten the oil pan retaining bolts to 125 inch lbs. (14 Nm).
11. Tighten the crankshaft damper bolt to 111 ft. lbs. (150 Nm), plus an additional 76 degree turn using a torque angle meter.

4.3L Engines

1. Disconnect the negative battery cable and drain the engine cooling system.
2. Remove the crankshaft pulley and damper.

NOTE: The outer ring (weight) of the torsional damper is bonded to the hub with rubber. The damper must be removed with a puller which acts on the inner hub only. Pulling on the outer portion of the damper will break the rubber bond or destroy the tuning of the unit.

3. Remove the water pump assembly.
4. Loosen the oil pan.
5. Remove the front cover bolts and, if equipped, the reinforcements, then remove the front cover from the engine.
6. If the front cover seal is to be replaced, it may be pried front the front cover using a suitable prytool.

To install:

7. Clean the gasket mating surfaces of the engine and cover of all remaining gasket or sealer material. Be careful not to score or damage the surfaces.

NOTE: Beginning in 1992, the manufacturer began recommending to wait until the front cover is mounted to the engine before installing the replacement crankshaft oil seal. This may be to assure the cover is properly supported. On earlier vehicles, the manufacturer allowed for installation with the cover removed or installed, but waiting would be acceptable for all years of the 4.3L engine.

8. If desired on early model engines, install a new seal to the cover using a suitable installation driver, such as J-35468 or equivalent. Be sure to support the back of the seal cover area during installation. Lightly coat the lips of the new seal with clean engine oil.
9. Position a new front cover gasket to the engine or cover using gasket cement to hold it in position. For 1992–96 vehicles, lubricate the front of the oil pan seal with engine oil to aid in reassembly.
10. Install the front cover to the engine. For 1992–96 vehicles, take care while engaging the front of the oil pan seal with the bottom of the cover.
11. Install front cover retaining bolts and tighten to 124 inch lbs. (14 Nm).
12. If removed and not installed earlier, use the seal installation driver to install the new crankshaft seal at this time.
13. Secure the oil pan.
14. Install the water pump.
15. Install the crankshaft damper and pulley.
16. Connect the negative battery cable, then properly refill the engine cooling system.
17. Run the engine until normal operating temperature has been reached, then check for leaks.

5.0L, 5.7L and 7.4L Engines

1. Disconnect the negative battery cable.
2. Drain the cooling system. Remove the fan shroud assembly.
3. Remove the belts, pulleys and water pump assembly.
4. Remove the crankshaft pulley and damper.
5. Remove the oil pan-to-front cover bolts.

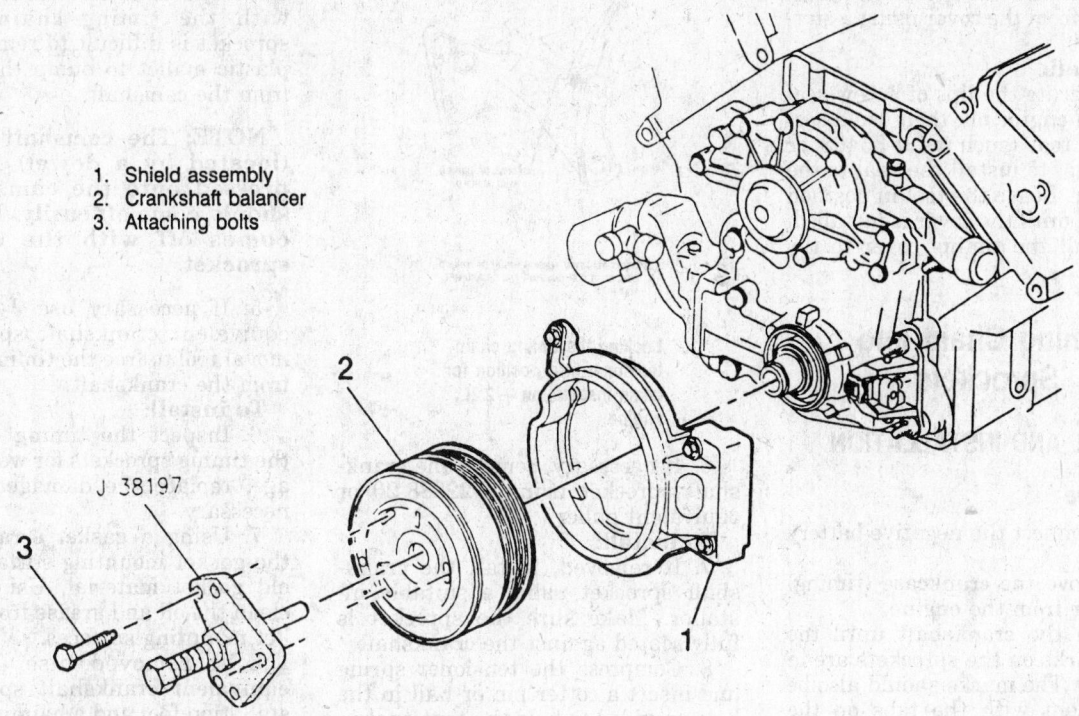

1. Shield assembly
2. Crankshaft balancer
3. Attaching bolts

J 38197

85473118

Removing crankshaft pulley hub assembly — 3.8L engine

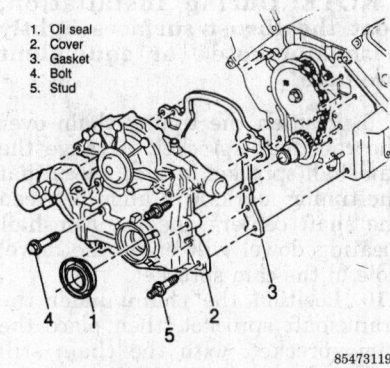

1. Oil seal
2. Cover
3. Gasket
4. Bolt
5. Stud

85473119

Front cover assembly — 3.8L engine

6. Remove the screws holding the timing chain cover to the block, pull the cover forward enough to cut the front oil pan seal. Cut the seal flush with the block on both sides.

NOTE: On some models it will be necessary to completely remove the oil pan in order to properly remove and install the front cover, assuring against oil leaks.

7. Pull off the cover and gaskets.
8. Use a suitable tool to pry the old seal out of the front face of the cover.
To install:
9. Using seal driver J–22102 or equivalent, install the new seal so the open end is toward the inside of the cover.

NOTE: Coat the lip of the new seal with oil prior to installation.

10. Install a new front pan seal, cutting the tabs off.
11. Coat a new cover gasket with adhesive sealer and position it on the block.
12. Apply a 1/8 in. bead of RTV gasket material to the front cover. Install the cover carefully onto the locating dowels.
13. Tighten the attaching screws.
14. If removed, install the oil pan.
15. Tighten the cover-to-pan bolts.
16. Install the torsional damper.
17. Install the water pump assembly.
18. Connect the negative battery cable.
19. Fill the cooling system with the proper type and quantity of antifreeze.

Front Cover Oil Seal

REPLACEMENT

On most gasoline engines it is possible to replace the timing cover front oil seal without removing the cover.

For the 2.2L gasoline engine, the manufacturer does not recommend this procedure and suggests that the front cover be removed if seal replacement is necessary.

Except 2.2L Engine

1. Disconnect the negative battery cable.
2. Remove the accessory drive belt.
3. Remove the crankshaft damper and pulley.
4. Pry the seal out of the front cover using a small prytool. Be very careful not to distort the front cover or to score the end of the crankshaft.
To install:
5. Lightly coat the lips of the replacement crankshaft seal with clean engine oil, then position the seal with the open end facing inward the engine. Use a suitable seal installation driver to position the seal in the front cover.
6. Install the crankshaft damper and pulley.
7. Install the accessory drive belt.
8. Connect the negative battery cable.

2.2L Engine

1. Remove the crankcase (timing) front cover from the engine.

2. Carefully remove the old crankshaft seal from the cover using a suitable prytool.

To install:

3. Lubricate the lips of a new seal with clean engine oil, then use a seal centering tool (such as J-35468 or equivalents) to install the seal to the front cover. Leave the tool in position in the seal until the cover is installed.

4. Install the timing cover to the engine.

Timing Chain and Sprockets

REMOVAL AND INSTALLATION

2.2L Engine

1. Disconnect the negative battery cable.

2. Remove the crankcase (timing) front cover from the engine.

3. Turn the crankshaft until the timing marks on the sprockets are in alignment. The marks should also be in alignment with the tabs on the tensioner.

4. Remove the tensioner retaining bolts.

5. Remove the camshaft sprocket retaining bolts, then remove the sprocket and timing chain.

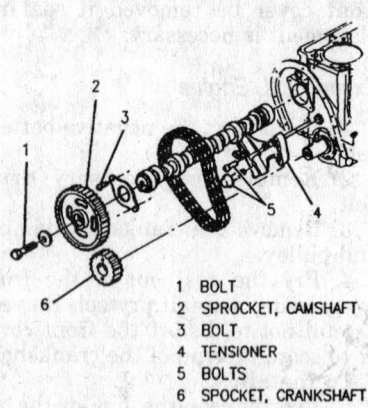

1 BOLT
2 SPROCKET, CAMSHAFT
3 BOLT
4 TENSIONER
5 BOLTS
6 SPROCKET, CRANKSHAFT

A ALIGN TABS ON TENSIONER WITH MARKS ON CAMSHAFT & CRANKSHAFT SPROCKETS.

85473120

Timing chain, sprocket and camshaft mounting — 2.2L engine

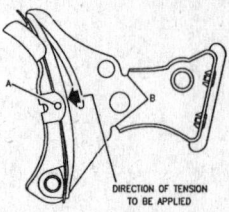

DIRECTION OF TENSION TO BE APPLIED

A INSERT PIN AFTER TENSION HAS BEEN APPLIED
B TABS, USED FOR CAMSHAFT AND CRANKSHAFT ALIGNMENT

85473121

Locking the timing chain tensioner into position for chain installation — 2.2L engine

6. If necessary, remove the crankshaft sprocket using J-22888-20 or equivalent puller.

To install:

7. If removed, install the crankshaft sprocket using a suitable installer. Make sure the sprocket is fully seated against the crankshaft.

8. Compress the tensioner spring and insert a cotter pin or nail in the hole provided to hold the tensioner in position.

9. Loosely install the tensioner retaining bolts.

10. Position the camshaft sprocket in the timing chain, position the chain under the crankshaft sprocket and the camshaft sprocket to the camshaft.

11. Verify that the timing marks are all properly aligned, then loosely install the camshaft sprocket bolt.

12. Tighten the tensioner bolts to 17 ft. lbs. (23 Nm), then tighten the camshaft sprocket bolt to 77 ft. lbs. (105 Nm).

13. Remove the cotter pin or nail holding the tensioner in position off the chain.

14. Install the timing cover to the engine.

15. Connect the negative battery cable.

2.8L Engine

1. Disconnect the negative battery cable.

2. Remove the timing cover from the engine.

3. Rotate the crankshaft until the No. 4 cylinder is on the TDC of it's compression stroke and the camshaft sprocket mark aligns with the mark on the crankshaft sprocket (facing each other at a point closest together in their travel) and in line with the shaft centers.

4. Remove the camshaft sprocket-to-camshaft nut and/or bolts, then re-

move the camshaft sprocket (along with the timing chain). If the sprocket is difficult to remove, use a plastic mallet to bump the sprocket from the camshaft.

NOTE: The camshaft sprocket (located by a dowel) is lightly pressed onto the camshaft and should come off easily. The chain comes off with the camshaft sprocket.

5. If necessary use J-5825-A or equivalent crankshaft sprocket removal tool to free the timing sprocket from the crankshaft.

To install:

6. Inspect the timing chain and the timing sprockets for wear or damage, replace the damaged parts as necessary.

7. Using a gasket scraper, clean the gasket mounting surfaces of any old gasket material. Using solvent, clean the oil and grease from the gasket mounting surfaces.

8. If removed, use J-5590 or equivalent crankshaft sprocket installation tool and a hammer to drive the crankshaft sprocket onto the crankshaft, without disturbing the position of the engine.

NOTE: During installation, coat the thrust surfaces lightly with Molykote® or equivalent pre-lube.

9. Position the timing chain over the camshaft sprocket. Arrange the camshaft sprocket in such a way that the timing marks will align between the shaft centers and the camshaft locating dowel will enter the dowel hole in the cam sprocket.

10. Position the chain under the crankshaft sprocket, then place the cam sprocket, with the chain still mounted over it, in position on the front of the camshaft. Install and tighten the camshaft sprocket-to-camshaft retainers to 17 ft. lbs. (23 Nm).

11. With the timing chain installed, turn the crankshaft 2 complete revolutions, then check to make certain that the timing marks are in correct alignment between the shaft centers.

12. Install the timing cover.

13. Connect the negative battery cable.

3.1L Engine

1. Disconnect the negative battery cable. Drain the engine cooling system.

2. Remove the right front tire and wheel assembly.

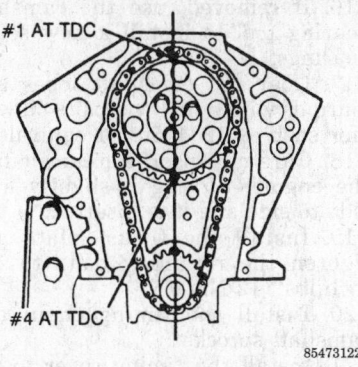

Timing mark alignment — 2.8L engine

3. Remove the front cover assembly. Ensure the marks on the crankshaft and camshaft gears are aligned using the marks on the damper stamping or cast alignment marks on cylinder and case.

4. Remove the bolts that hold the camshaft sprocket to the camshaft. This sprocket is a light press fit on the camshaft.

5. Remove the timing chain. Using a suitable puller, remove the crankshaft sprocket, as required.

To install:

6. Install the crankshaft sprocket.

7. Lubricate the camshaft thrust plate surface with Molykote® or equivalent. Install the chain onto camshaft sprocket.

8. Holding the sprocket vertically with the chain hanging down, align the marks on the camshaft and crankshaft sprockets and install the assembly onto the camshaft.

9. Install the camshaft to gear attaching bolts and torque to 18 ft. lbs. (24 Nm). After the sprockets are in place, turn the engine 2 full revolutions to make certain the timing marks are in correct alignment between the shaft centers.

10. Lubricate the chain with engine oil and install the front cover.

11. Connect the negative battery cable, then properly refill the engine cooling system.

3.8L Engine

1. Disconnect the negative battery cable, then drain the engine cooling system.

2. Align the marks on the crankshaft damper and timing cover with the engine in the No. 1 firing position. Remove the front cover assembly.

3. Ensure the marks on the crankshaft and camshaft gears are aligned.

4. Remove the timing chain damper and camshaft sprocket.

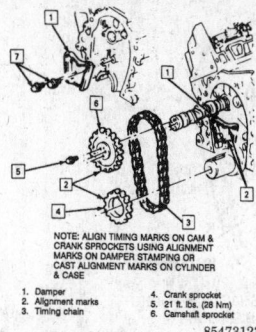

Exploded view of timing chain assembly — 3.8L engine

5. Remove the timing chain. Using a suitable puller, remove the crankshaft sprocket, as required.

To install:

6. Install the crankshaft sprocket.

7. Install the chain onto camshaft sprocket.

8. Holding the sprocket vertically with the chain hanging down, align the marks on the camshaft and crankshaft sprockets and install the assembly onto the camshaft.

9. Install the camshaft to gear attaching bolt and torque to 74 ft. lbs. (100 Nm) and then an additional 105 degree turn. Install the damper and torque to 16 ft. lbs. (22 Nm).

10. After the sprockets are in place, turn the engine 2 full revolutions to make certain the timing marks are in correct alignment between the shaft centers.

11. Lubricate the chain with engine oil and install the front cover.

12. Connect the negative battery cable, then properly refill the engine cooling system.

4.3L, 5.0L, 5.7L and 7.4L Engines

1. Disconnect the negative battery cable.

2. Remove the timing cover from the engine.

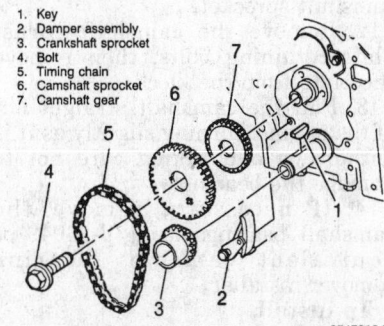

Exploded view of timing chain assembly — 3.8L engine

3. Rotate the crankshaft until the timing marks on the camshaft and crankshaft sprockets are in proper alignment.

4. Remove the camshaft sprocket-to-camshaft nut and/or bolts, then remove the camshaft sprocket (along with the timing chain). If the sprocket is difficult to remove, use a plastic mallet to bump the sprocket from the camshaft.

NOTE: The camshaft sprocket (located by a dowel) is lightly pressed onto the camshaft and should come off easily. The chain comes off with the camshaft sprocket.

5. If necessary use J-5825-A or equivalent crankshaft sprocket removal tool to free the timing sprocket from the crankshaft.

To install:

6. Inspect the timing chain and the timing sprockets for wear or damage, replace the damaged parts as necessary.

7. Using a gasket scraper, clean the gasket mounting surfaces of all remaining traces of old gasket. Using solvent, clean the oil and grease from the gasket mounting surfaces.

8. If removed, use J-5590 or equivalent crankshaft sprocket installation tool and a hammer to drive the crankshaft sprocket onto the crankshaft, without disturbing the position of the engine.

NOTE: During installation, coat the thrust surfaces lightly with Molykote® or equivalent pre-lube.

9. Position the timing chain over the camshaft sprocket. Arrange the camshaft sprocket in such a way that the timing marks will align between the shaft centers and the camshaft locating dowel will enter the dowel hole in the cam sprocket.

10. Position the chain under the crankshaft sprocket, then place the cam sprocket, with the chain still mounted over it, in position on the front of the camshaft. Install and tighten the camshaft sprocket-to-camshaft retainers.

11. With the timing chain installed, turn the crankshaft 2 complete revolutions, then check to make certain that the timing marks are in correct alignment between the shaft centers.

12. Install the timing cover.

Timing Gear Assembly

Unlike the rest of the gasoline engines utilized by these vehicles, the

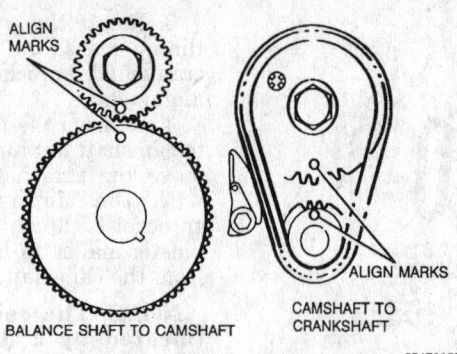

ALIGN MARKS

ALIGN MARKS

BALANCE SHAFT TO CAMSHAFT

CAMSHAFT TO CRANKSHAFT

85473125

Timing mark alignment — 3.8L engine

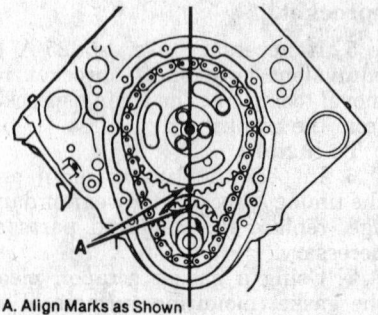

A. Align Marks as Shown

85473126

Timing mark alignment — 4.3L, 5.0L, 5.7L and 7.4L engines

2.5L engine does not use a timing chain assembly. Instead the camshaft timing gear is directly driven by the crankshaft timing gear. The timing gear (camshaft sprocket) is pressed onto the camshaft and requires the use of an arbor press to remove.

REMOVAL AND INSTALLATION

1. Remove the camshaft.
2. Using an arbor press, a press plate and the GM Gear Removal tool J-971 or equivalent, press the timing gear from the camshaft.

NOTE: When pressing the timing gear from the camshaft, be certain that the position of the press plate does not contact the woodruff key.

3. To assemble, position the press plate to support the camshaft at the back of the front journal. Place the gear spacer ring and the thrust plate over the end of the camshaft, then install the woodruff key. Press the timing gear onto the camshaft, until it bottoms against the gear spacer ring.

NOTE: The end clearance of the thrust plate should be 0.0015–0.005 in. (0.038–0.127mm).

If less than 0.0015 in. (0.038mm), replace the spacer ring; if more than 0.005 in. (0.127mm), replace the thrust plate.

4. To complete the installation, align the marks on the timing gears and install the camshaft.

Camshaft

REMOVAL AND INSTALLATION

2.2L Engine

1. Properly relieve the fuel system pressure, then disconnect the negative battery cable.
2. Drain the engine cooling system and the engine oil.
3. Remove the radiator.
4. Remove the rocker arm cover.
5. Remove the cylinder head.
6. Remove the anti-rotation bracket bolts and brackets, then remove the valve lifters.
7. Remove the oil pump drive retaining bolt, then remove the drive by lifting and twisting.
8. Remove the crankshaft pulley and hub.
9. Remove the serpentine drive belt idler pulley.
10. Remove the timing cover from the engine.
11. Remove the timing chain and camshaft sprocket.
12. Remove the camshaft thrust plate retaining bolts, then remove the plate from the block.
13. Pull the camshaft straight out of the engine, turning slightly as it is withdrawn and taking care not to damage the bearings.
14. If necessary, remove the camshaft bearings using J-33049 or equivalent camshaft bearing remover/installer.

To install:

15. Inspect the camshaft, journals and lobes for wear and replace, if necessary.

16. If removed, use the camshaft bearing tool to install a new set of bearings.
17. Coat the camshaft lobes and journals with a high viscosity oil with zinc such as 12345501 or equivalent.
18. Carefully insert the camshaft in the engine, turning it slightly from side to side and it is inserted.
19. Install the thrust plate and tighten the retaining bolts to 106 inch lbs. (12 Nm).
20. Install the timing chain and camshaft sprocket.
21. Install the timing cover to the engine.
22. Install the serpentine drive belt idler pulley.
23. Install the crankshaft pulley and hub.
24. Install the oil pump drive by inserting while twisting, then install the retaining bolt and tighten to 18 ft. lbs. (25 Nm).
25. Install the valve lifters and the anti-rotation brackets.
26. Install the cylinder head.
27. Install the rocker arm cover.
28. Install the radiator.
29. Connect the negative battery cable and properly refill the engine cooling system.

2.5L Engine

1. Disconnect the negative battery cable and drain the engine cooling system.
2. Remove the radiator.
3. If equipped with A/C, disconnect the condenser baffles and the condenser, then raise the condenser and set it aside without disconnecting the refrigerant lines.
4. Remove the grille and filler panel from the front of the vehicle.
5. Remove the timing cover from the engine.
6. Matchmark and remove the distributor.
7. Remove the oil pump drive shaft.
8. Remove the pushrod cover:
   a. Remove the alternator and bracket.
   b. Disengage the ignition coil wires, then remove the spark plug wires and bracket from the intake manifold.
   c. Remove the fuel pipes and clips from the pushrod cover.
   d. Remove the oil pressure gage sender, then remove the wiring harness brackets from the pushrod cover.
   e. Unscrew the nuts from the cover attaching studs, reverse 2 of the nuts so the washers face out-

ward and screw them back onto the 2 inner studs.

f. Assemble the 2 remaining nuts to the same 2 inner studs with the washers facing inward, then using a small wrench on the inner nut (on each stud) jam the nuts slightly together.

g. Again using the wrench on the inner stud, unscrew the studs until the cover breaks loose, then remove the nuts from the studs and remove the cover from the engine. Remove the studs from the cover and reinstall them to the engine. Tighten the studs to 88 inch lbs. (10 Nm).

9. Remove the rocker arm cover, pushrods and valve lifters from the engine.

NOTE: When removing the pushrods and the valve lifters, be sure to keep them in order for reassembly purposes.

10. Position the camshaft gear so access to the thrust plate retainers is possible. Remove the camshaft thrust plate-to-engine bolts.

11. If not done already, align the timing marks, then while supporting the camshaft (to prevent damaging the bearing or lobe surfaces), carefully remove it from the front of the engine.

To install:

12. Inspect the camshaft for scratches, pitting and/or wear on the bearing and lobe surfaces. Check the timing gear teeth for damage.

13. If necessary, replace the camshaft bearings as follows:

a. Install a camshaft bearing removal/installation tool with the shoulder toward the bearing. Ensure that enough threads are engaged.

b. Using 2 wrenches, hold the puller screw while turning the nut. When the bearing has been released from the bore, remove the tool.

c. Assemble the tool on the driver to remove the front and rear bearings.

d. Install the bearings at the correct clocking to ensure the oil holes in the block and bearings align.

e. Install a fresh camshaft bearing rear cover using sealant.

14. Lubricate the camshaft using a high viscosity oil with zinc (such as 12345501 or equivalent), then carefully insert the camshaft into the engine while aligning the timing marks.

15. Turn the camshaft as necessary, then install the camshaft thrust plate-to-engine bolts to and tighten to 90 inch lbs. (10 Nm).

16. Install the valve lifters, then install the pushrods and rocker arms to the engine.

17. Using a thin bead of RTV sealant, install the pushrod cover to the engine, then tighten the stud nuts to 106 inch lbs. (12 Nm) starting at the front nut and working toward the rear of the engine. Reposition and secure the remaining components which were removed to access the pushrod cover.

18. Install the oil pump drive shaft.

19. Align and install the distributor.

20. Install the timing cover to the engine.

21. Install the the grille and filler panel to the front of the vehicle.

22. If equipped with A/C, reposition and secure the condenser and condenser baffles.

23. Install the radiator.

24. Connect the negative battery cable, then properly refill the engine cooling system.

2.8L and 4.3L Engines

1. Properly relieve the fuel system pressure, then disconnect the negative battery cable.

2. Drain the engine cooling system.

3. Remove the radiator.

4. Remove the rocker arm covers from the engine.

5. Remove the intake manifold assembly.

6. Remove the rocker arms, pushrods and lifters.

7. Remove the crankshaft pulley and hub.

8. Remove the engine front (timing) cover.

9. Align the timing marks on the crankshaft and camshaft sprockets.

10. Remove the camshaft sprocket and timing chain.

11. If equipped, remove the balance shaft drive gear.

12. Remove the camshaft thrust plate.

13. Install the sprocket bolts or longer bolts of the same thread into the end of the camshaft as a handle, then remove the camshaft front the front of the engine while turning slightly from side to side, as necessary. Take care not to damage the camshaft bearings when removing the camshaft.

To install:

14. Lubricate the camshaft journals with clean engine oil or a suitable pre-lube, then install the camshaft into the block being extremely careful not to contact the bearings with the cam lobes.

15. Install the camshaft thrust plate.

16. If equipped, install the balance shaft drive gear.

17. Install the timing chain and camshaft sprocket.

18. Install the engine front (timing) cover.

19. Install the crankshaft pulley and hub.

20. Install the valve lifters, then install the pushrods and rocker arms. Properly adjust the valve clearance.

21. Install the intake manifold assembly.

22. Install the rocker arm covers to the engine.

23. Install the radiator to the vehicle.

24. Connect the negative battery cable and properly refill the engine cooling system.

3.1L and 3.8L Engines

1. Disconnect the negative battery cable.

2. Drain the cooling system.

3. Remove the engine from the vehicle and support it in a suitable holding fixture.

4. Remove the intake manifold. Remove the valve cover and the valve train components.

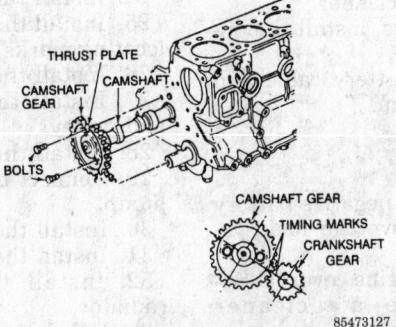

85473127

Timing gear/camshaft assembly installation and timing mark alignment — 2.5L engine

5. Remove the front cover assembly.

6. Remove the timing chain and sprocket. Remove the thrust plate, if equipped.

7. Remove the camshaft from the block. Insert 3 bolts approximately 3 in. long into the camshaft gear bolt holes to supply leverage while removing the camshaft. Use care not to damage the bearings.

To install:

8. Lubricate the camshaft with Molykote or equivalent, before installation.

9. Install the camshaft into the cylinder block, use care not to damage the bearings.

10. Install the thrust plate, if equipped. Install the timing chain and sprocket. Make sure the timing marks align correctly.

11. Install the front cover assembly.

12. Install the intake manifold assembly. Install the valve train components and the valve cover.

13. Install the engine into the vehicle.

14. Fill the cooling system to the correct level and connect the negative battery cable.

5.0L and 5.7L Engines

1. Disconnect the negative battery cable, Drain the cooling system and properly relieve the fuel system pressure.

2. On the G-Series, remove the engine cover.

3. Remove the air cleaner.

4. On the G-Series, remove the grille and center support.

5. Remove the air conditioning condenser and swing the condenser forward from its mounting, if equipped.

6. Remove the fan, the shroud and the radiator.

7. Remove the valve covers.

8. Remove the water pump assembly.

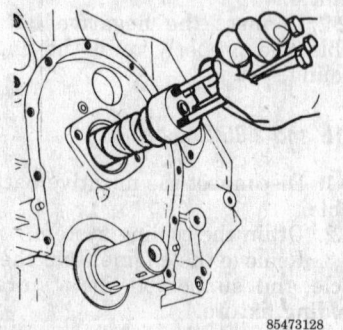

85473128

Camshaft removal and installation — 4.3L, 5.0L, 5.7L and 7.4L engines

9. Align the timing marks and remove the torsional damper.

10. Remove the timing chain cover.

11. Disconnect the electrical and vacuum connections at the intake manifold.

12. Mark the distributor rotor-to-housing location. Remove the distributor assembly.

13. Remove the intake manifold, pushrods and hydraulic lifters.

14. Remove the camshaft sprocket bolts, camshaft sprocket and timing chain. Tap the sprocket on its lower edge to loosen it.

15. Remove the crankshaft sprocket, as required.

16. As required, remove the front engine mount through bolts and raise the engine to gain sufficient clearance for camshaft removal.

17. Install two or three $5/16$–18 bolts 4–5 in. long into the camshaft threaded holes; carefully pull the camshaft from the block.

18. Inspect the shaft for signs of excessive wear or damage.

To install:

19. Liberally coat camshaft and bearing with heavy engine oil or engine assembly lubricant and insert the cam into the engine.

20. Lower the engine and install the engine mount through bolts.

21. Align the timing marks on the camshaft and crankshaft gears.

22. Install the camshaft sprocket and chain and tighten the bolts to specification.

23. Install the hydraulic lifters and pushrods and adjust the valves.

24. Install the distributor assembly.

25. Install the timing chain cover.

26. Install the torsional damper.

27. Install the water pump.

28. Install the valve covers.

29. Install the fan, the shroud and radiator.

30. Install the air conditioning condenser, if equipped.

31. On the G-Series, install the grille and center support.

32. Install the air cleaner.

33. On the G-Series, install the engine cover.

34. Connect the battery cable and fill the cooling system.

7.4L Engine

1. Disconnect the negative battery cable. Properly relieve the fuel system pressure.

2. Remove the engine cover, G-Series. Remove the air cleaner assembly.

3. Remove the grille and center support section, as required.

4. Properly discharge the air conditioning system. Remove the air conditioning compressor, condenser and auxiliary fan, if equipped.

5. Drain the cooling system.

6. Remove the fan, the shroud and radiator.

7. Remove the alternator belt, remove the alternator assembly, as required.

8. Remove the valve covers.

9. Disconnect the hoses from the water pump.

10. Remove the water pump.

11. Align the timing marks at TDC. Remove the harmonic balancer and pulley.

12. Remove the engine front cover.

13. Mark the distributor rotor-to-housing location. Remove the distributor assembly.

14. Remove the intake manifold assembly.

15. Remove the lifters, pushrods, and rocker arms.

16. Rotate the camshaft so the timing marks align.

17. Remove the camshaft sprocket bolts. Remove the camshaft sprocket and timing.

18. Remove the engine mount through bolts. Raise and support the engine to aid in camshaft removal, as required.

19. Install two or three $5/16$–18 bolts in the holes in the front of the camshaft and carefully pull the camshaft from the block.

To install:

20. Liberally coat camshaft and bearing with heavy engine oil or engine assembly lubricant and insert the cam into the engine.

21. Align the timing marks on the camshaft sprocket and crankshaft gears.

22. Install the camshaft sprocket and chain and tighten the bolts to specification. Lower the engine and install the engine mount bolts.

23. Install the lifters and pushrods and adjust the valves.

24. Install the intake manifold.

25. Install the distributor using the locating marks made during removal.

26. Install the engine front cover.

27. Install the harmonic balancer and pulley.

28. Install the water pump.

29. Connect the hoses at the water pump.

30. Install the valve covers.

31. Install the alternator.

32. Install the fan shroud and radiator.

33. Fill the cooling system with the proper type and quantity of antifreeze.

34. Install the air conditioning condenser and compressor.
35. Install the grille and center support.
36. Install the air cleaner assembly.
37. Connect the battery.

Balance Shaft

REMOVAL AND INSTALLATION

3.8L Engine

1. Disconnect the negative battery cable.
2. Remove the engine.
3. Remove the flywheel and intake manifold.
4. Remove the lifter guide retainer.
5. Remove the timing chain cover.
6. Remove the balance shaft drive gear bolt, the camshaft sprocket and timing chain.
7. Remove the balance shaft retainer bolts, retainer and gear.
8. Using tool J–6125–B, remove the balance shaft.
9. Remove the balance shaft rear plug. Using tool J–36995–5, remove the balance shaft rear bearing.

NOTE: The balance shaft and bearings are only to be serviced or replaced as a complete assembly.

To install:

10. Dip the bearings in clean engine oil before installation.
11. Using tool J–36995–5, install the balance shaft rear bearing with the rolled edge facing into the engine and the manufacturer's markings facing the flywheel side.
12. Dip the front balance shaft bearing into engine oil. Using tool J–36996, install the balance shaft into the block.
13. Temporarily install the balance shaft retainer and bolts. Install the balance shaft drive gear. Apply Loctite® to the bolt and torque to 14 ft. lbs. (20 Nm) plus turn the bolt an additional 35 degrees.
14. Install the balance shaft rear plug.
15. Measure the balance shaft endplay. Endplay should be 0–0.008 in. (0–0.203mm).
16. Measure the balance shaft radial play at both the front and rear. The front radial play should be 0–0.0011 in. (0–0.028mm). The rear radial play should be 0.0005–0.0047 in. (0.0127–0.119mm).
17. Temporarily install the camshaft gear and align the timing

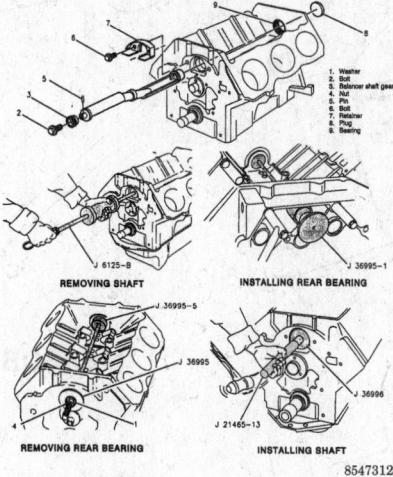

Balance shaft service — 3.8L engine

marks pointed straight down. Remove the camshaft gear and align the balance shaft marks point straight down. Install the camshaft gear and align the marks by turning the balance shaft.
18. Ensure the No. 1 piston is at TDC and install the camshaft sprocket and timing chain.
19. Measure the gear lash at 4 places, every ¼ turn. The lash should be 0.002–0.005 in. (0.050–0.127mm).
20. Tighten the balance shaft front bearing retainer to 22 ft. lbs. (30 Nm).
21. Install the timing chain cover.
22. Install the lifter guide retainer.
23. Install the flywheel and intake manifold.
24. Install the engine into the vehicle.
25. Connect the negative battery cable.

4.3L (VIN W) Engine

1. Disconnect the negative battery cable. Drain the cooling system into a suitable container. Properly relieve the fuel system pressure and discharge the air conditioning system.
2. Remove the air cleaner and air intake duct.
3. Remove the upper radiator shroud.

4. Remove the oil and transmission cooler lines at the radiator.
5. Remove the hoses from the radiator and remove the radiator.
6. Remove the air conditioner condenser and fan assembly.
7. Remove the serpentine belt.
8. Remove the brace at the coolant pump and remove the pump.
9. Remove the torsional damper.
10. Raise and support the vehicle safely.
11. Remove the flywheel cover. Drain the engine oil and loosen the oil pan bolts; remove the 2 nuts and bolts at the front of the oil pan.
12. Remove the front timing cover bolts and cover.

NOTE: Use care when removing the front cover, as not to damage the oil pan gasket.

13. Remove the crankshaft front cover oil seal.
14. Remove the camshaft sprocket, timing chain and balance shaft drive gear.
15. Remove the balance shaft retainer.
16. Remove the intake manifold assembly.
17. Remove the hydraulic lifter retainer.
18. Remove the balance shaft from the bearing using a soft faced mallet.
19. Remove the rear bearing using tool J–38834 and J–26941.

NOTE: The balance shaft and bearings are only to be serviced or replaced as a complete assembly.

To install:

20. Dip the bearings in clean engine oil before installation.
21. Using tool J–38834, install the balance shaft rear bearing with the flat edge and the manufacturer's markings facing the front of engine.
22. Dip the front balance shaft bearing into engine oil. Using tool J–36996 and J–8092, install the balance shaft into the block.
23. Install the balance shaft retainer and torque the bolts to 120 inch lbs. (14 Nm).
24. Install the balance shaft drive gear. Apply Loctite® to the bolt and torque to 15 ft. lbs. (20 Nm) plus turn the bolt an additional 35 degrees.
25. Install the lifter retainer and turn the balance shaft to ensure proper clearance.
26. Install the balance shaft rear plug.
27. Turn the camshaft so the balance shaft drive gear timing marks are aligned.

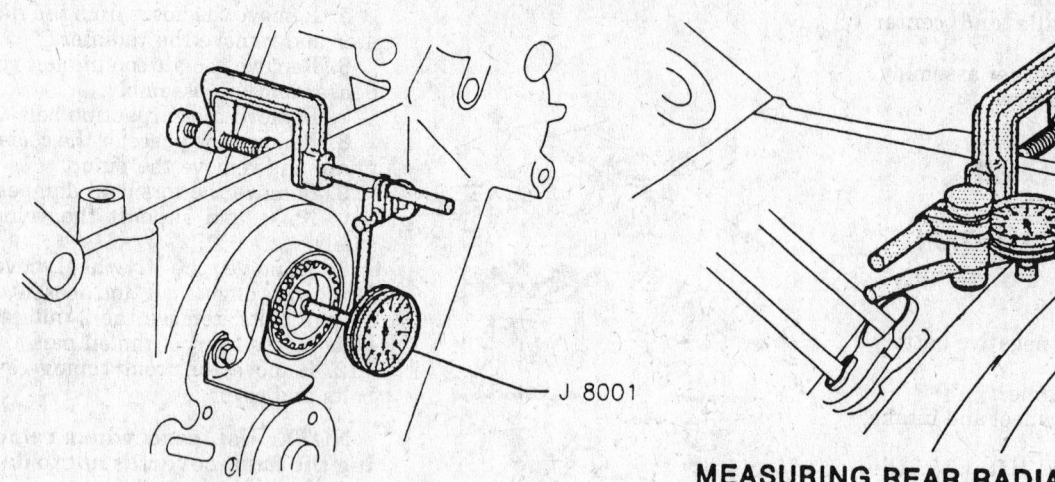

MEASURING END PLAY

MEASURING REAR RADIAL PLAY

MEASURING FRONT RADIAL PLAY

MEASURING GEAR LASH

85473130

Balance shaft clearance measurement — 3.8L engine

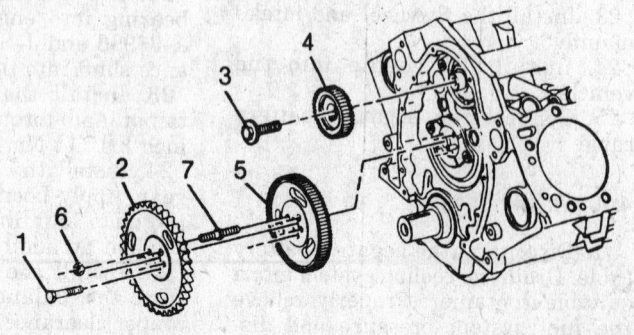

1. Camshaft sprocket bolt
2. Camshaft sprocket
3. Balance shaft driven gear bolt
4. Balance shaft driven gear
5. Balance shaft drive gear
6. Nut
7. Stud

85473131

Balance shaft drive gears — 4.3L (VIN W) engine

28. Install the balance shaft drive gear retaining stud and torque to 12 ft. lbs. (16 Nm).

29. Install the intake manifold assembly.

30. Install the timing chain and gears with the timing marks dot-to-dot; this is the No. 4 cylinder firing position, so set the distributor rotor to the No. cylinder firing position when installing. Torque the camshaft bolts and nut to 21 ft. lbs. (28 Nm).

31. Install the distributor assembly.

32. Install the timing cover oil seal and install the cover.

33. Raise and support the vehicle safely.

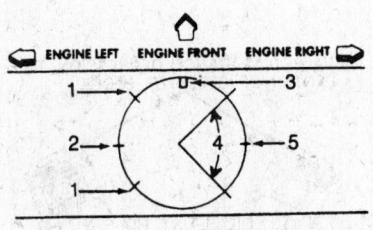

1. Balance shaft retainer
2. Balance shaft
3. Screw
4. Bearing
5. Plug

85473132

Balance shaft assembly — 4.3L (VIN W) engine

42. Install the upper radiator shroud.

43. Install the air cleaner and air intake duct.

44. Connect the negative battery cable. Fill the cooling system with proper type and quantity of antifreeze. Properly recharge the air conditioning system. Fill the engine with the correct quantity and grade of engine oil.

Piston and Connecting Rod

POSITIONING

During disassembly, note the location of the connecting rod bearing tang slots, on some engines, the slots must be on the side opposite of the camshaft. This does not apply to the 3.8L engine.

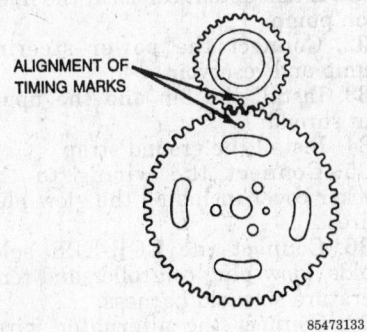

ALIGNMENT OF TIMING MARKS

85473133

Balance shaft alignment marks — 4.3L (VIN W) engine

34. Install the flywheel cover.

35. Tighten the oil pan bolts; install the 2 nuts and bolts at the front of the oil pan.

36. Install the torsional damper.

37. Install the brace at the coolant pump and install the pump.

38. Install the serpentine belt.

39. Install the air conditioner condenser and fan assembly.

40. Install the radiator and hoses.

41. Install the oil and transmission cooler lines at the radiator.

ENGINE LEFT ENGINE FRONT ENGINE RIGHT

1. Oil ring rail gaps
2. 2nd Compression ring gap
3. Notch in piston
4. Oil ring spacer gap (tang in hole or slot with arc)
5. Top compression ring gap

85473134

Piston and ring gap positioning — except 7.4L engine

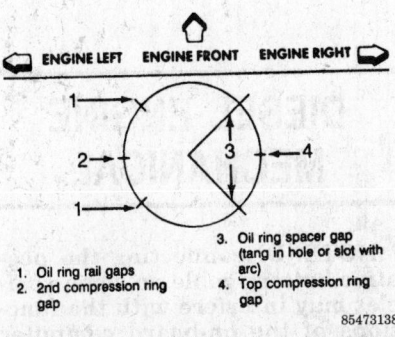

ENGINE LEFT ENGINE FRONT ENGINE RIGHT

1. Oil ring rail gaps
2. 2nd compression ring gap
3. Oil ring spacer gap (tang in hole or slot with arc)
4. Top compression ring gap

85473138

Piston ring gap locations — 7.4L engine

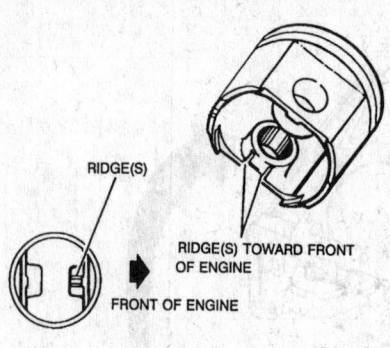

Piston installed position — 3.8L engine

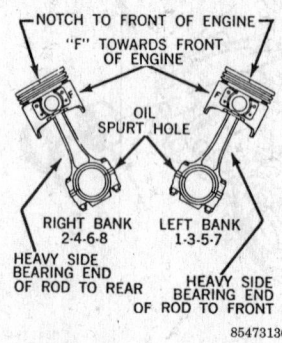

Correct relationship of the piston and rod — 5.0L and 5.7L engines

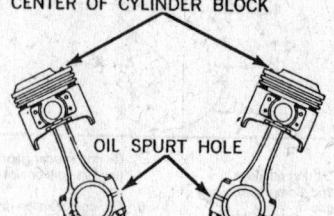

Correct relationship of the piston and rod — 7.4L engine

DIESEL ENGINE MECHANICAL

NOTE: Disconnecting the negative battery cable on some vehicles may interfere with the functions of the on-board computer systems and may require the computer to undergo a relearning process.

Engine

REMOVAL AND INSTALLATION

6.2L Engine

EXCEPT G-SERIES

1. Remove the hood. Disconnect and remove the batteries.
2. Raise the vehicle and support it safely. Drain the engine oil.
3. Remove the flywheel cover. Disconnect the torque converter from the flexplate. Disconnect the exhaust pipes from the manifolds.
4. Remove the starter bolts and remove the starter. Remove the transmission bellhousing to engine bolts, leaving 1 or more bolts loose to prevent separation.
5. Remove the engine mount through bolts. Disconnect the block heater, the wiring harness, transmission oil cooler lines and the front battery cable clamp at the oil pan.
6. Lower the vehicle. Properly relieve the fuel pump pressure. Disconnect and plug the fuel lines and the oil cooler lines at the engine block. Remove the lower fan shroud bolts.
7. Drain the engine coolant. Remove the air cleaner assembly. Disconnect the ground cable from the alternator bracket. Disconnect the alternator wires and clips.
8. Disconnect the TPS, EGR–EPR and the fuel cut-off at the injection pump. Remove the harness from the clips at the rocker covers and disconnect the glow plugs.
9. Disconnect the EGR–EPR solenoids, glow plugs, controller, temperature sender and move the harness aside. Disconnect the ground strap on the left or right side.
10. Remove the fan assembly. Remove the upper radiator hoses at the engine. Remove the fan shroud.
11. Remove the power steering pump and belt. Remove the reservoir and lay the pump and reservoir aside. If equipped with air conditioning, remove the compressor and position aside.
12. Disconnect the vacuum lines at the cruise servo and accelerator cable at the injection pump. Disconnect the heater hoses at the engine.
13. Disconnect the lower radiator hose, the oil cooler lines, the heater hose and the overflow hose at the radiator.
14. Remove the radiator assembly. Remove the detent cable.
15. Install an engine lifting device, remove the loose bolts in the bellhousing. Properly support the transmission. Carefully remove the engine.

To install:

16. Lower the engine and install the engine mounting bolts. Torque the bolts and nuts to specification
17. Install the bellhousing to engine bolts and torque to 30 ft. lbs. (40 Nm).
18. Remove the engine lifting fixture and transmission jack.
19. Raise the vehicle and support it safely.
20. Install the converter to flex bolts and torque to specification.
21. Install the starter assembly.
22. Install the flywheel or torque converter cover.
23. Install the starter.
24. Install the exhaust pipes at the manifold.
25. Connect the wiring harness, transmission cooler lines and a battery cable clamp at the oil pan.
26. Connect the fuel return lines at the engine.
27. Connect the oil cooler lines at the engine.
28. Lower the vehicle.
29. Install the radiator.
30. Install the heater hose to the engine.
31. Connect the accelerator, cruise control and detent cables at the injection pump.
32. Connect the power steering pump and reservoir.
33. Install the fan and the upper fan shroud.
34. Install the ground strap.
35. Connect the wiring to the rocker cover including the glow plug wires.
36. Connect the EGR-EPR solenoids, glow plug controller and temperature solenoid harness.
37. Connect the alternator wires and clips.
38. Connect the wiring at the injector pump.
39. Install the air cleaner and air conditioning compressor.
40. Install the hood.
41. Connect the negative battery cable.
42. Install the proper quantity and type of coolant and engine oil.

G-SERIES

1. Disconnect the negative battery cables. Properly relieve the fuel system pressure.
2. Remove the upper radiator support.
3. Remove the grille.
4. Remove the bumper.
5. Remove the lower grille valance.

6. Remove the hood latch and the upper tie bar.

7. Drain the cooling system.

8. Remove the radiator coolant reservoir bottle.

9. Remove the radiator support bracket, if equipped.

10. Remove the radiator and the fan shroud.

11. Remove the engine cover.

12. Remove the air cleaner, resonator and bracket.

13. Properly discharge the air conditioning system.

14. Remove the air conditioning condenser and cap all openings.

15. Disconnect the air cleaner bracket at the valve cover.

16. Remove the crankcase ventilator bracket and move aside.

17. Remove the intake manifold assembly. Remove the injector pump.

18. Raise and support the vehicle safely.

19. Remove the power steering pump and position aside.

20. Disconnect the exhaust pipes at the manifolds.

21. Remove the flywheel cover and remove the torque converter-to-flywheel attaching bolts.

22. Remove the engine mount through bolts.

23. Disconnect the blocker heater wires.

24. Remove the starter assembly.

25. Disconnect the fuel line at the fuel pump (lift pump).

26. Lower the vehicle.

27. Remove the bellhousing-to-engine bolts.

28. Remove the cruise control transducer, if equipped.

29. Remove the air conditioning compressor.

30. Remove the oil fill tube upper bracket.

31. Remove the wiring harness and connections from engine.

32. Unbolt the transmission dipstick tube and position aside.

33. Remove the heater hose at the engine.

34. Remove the alternator upper bracket.

35. Disconnect the glow plug temperature inhibit switch connector at the coolant crossover.

36. Remove the coolant crossover/thermostat assembly.

37. Connect a suitable engine lifting device to the center intake manifold bolt holes.

38. Support the transmission and remove the engine.

To install:

39. Install the engine into the vehicle. Raise and safely support the vehicle.

40. Install the engine mount through bolts and transmission bellhousing bolts.

41. Install the flywheel-to-converter attaching bolts.

42. Install the starter and converter housing underpan.

43. Connect the block heater wires.

44. Connect the exhaust pipes to the manifold assembly.

45. Install the power steering pump. Lower the vehicle.

46. Install the coolant crossover/thermostat assembly.

47. Install the alternator upper bracket.

48. Install the heater hoses, transmission dipstick, air cleaner resonator and bracket assembly.

49. Install the wiring harness and connectors to the engine assembly.

50. Install the oil fill tube upper bracket.

51. Install the air conditioning compressor.

52. Install the injection pump and intake manifold.

53. Install the radiator, fan and lower shroud.

54. Install the air conditioning condenser.

55. Install the upper tie bar.

56. Install the fan lower shroud, coolant recovery bottle and battery cables.

57. Install the hood latch, lower valance, bumper, grille, and headlight bezels.

58. Fill the cooling system with the proper type and quantity of antifreeze. Check all fluid levels.

59. Evacuate and recharge the air conditioning system.

60. Install the engine cover. Inspect engine for leaks.

Engine Mounts

REMOVAL AND INSTALLATION

6.2L and 6.5L Engine

1. Disconnect the negative battery cable.

2. Raise and safely support the vehicle.

3. Properly support the engine.

NOTE: Do not position the jack under the oil pan, any sheetmetal or the crankshaft pulley, otherwise damage may occur.

4. Remove the engine mount through-bolt.

5. Raise the engine to gain sufficient clearance for the mount to be removed.

6. Remove the engine mount attaching bolts, nuts and washers.

7. Remove the mount assembly.

8. Installation is the reverse of the removal procedure.

Cylinder Head

REMOVAL AND INSTALLATION

6.2L and 6.5L Engine

RIGHT SIDE

1. Disconnect the negative battery cable, relieve the fuel system pressure and drain the coolant system. Properly discharge the air conditioning system, if equipped.

2. Remove the intake manifold. Remove the fan upper shroud. Remove the compressor assembly, if equipped.

3. Raise and support the vehicle safely.

4. Remove the exhaust manifold. Lower the vehicle.

5. Remove the valve cover, rocker arm assemblies and pushrods. Mark all components so they may be returned to their original location.

6. Remove the air cleaner resonator and bracket.

7. Remove the transmission and oil dipstick tube; remove the oil fill tube from the coolant crossover pipe.

8. Remove the heater, radiator and bypass hoses.

9. Remove the alternator upper bracket and alternator.

10. Remove the fuel bleeder valve at the coolant crossover pipe.

11. Remove the fuel return crossover line clamp bolts from both cylinder heads.

12. Disconnect the wire connector from the sensor in the coolant crossover pipe.

13. Remove the coolant crossover pipe/thermostat assembly.

14. Remove the head bolts and the cylinder head.

To install:

15. Clean the mating surfaces of the head and block thoroughly.

16. Install a new head gasket on the engine block. Do not coat the gaskets with any sealer on either engine. The gaskets have a special coating that eliminates the need for sealer. Install the cylinder head onto the block.

17. Clean the head bolts thoroughly. Coat the threads of the head bolts with sealing compound GM part

1052080 or equivalent, before installation. Tighten the head bolts to 20 ft. lbs. (25 Nm), in the proper sequence, next tighten all bolts to 50 ft. lbs. (65 Nm) in the proper sequence, and finally tighten all bolts an additional 90 degree (¼ turn).

18. Install the coolant crossover pipe and thermostat.

19. Install the fuel valve and alternator assembly.

20. Connect the bypass hose.

21. Connect the upper radiator hose.

22. Connect the heater hoses at the head.

23. Install the transmission and oil dipstick tube.

24. Install the air cleaner resonator and bracket.

25. Install the pushrods, hardened ends facing up.

26. Install the rocker arm assemblies.

27. Adjust the valves.

28. Install the valve cover. Install the alternator assembly.

29. Raise and support the vehicle safely.

30. Install the exhaust manifold. Lower the vehicle.

31. Install the upper fan shroud.

32. Install the intake manifold. Connect the negative battery cables.

33. Fill the cooling system with the proper type and quantity of antifreeze. Evacuate and recharge the air conditioning system.

LEFT SIDE

1. Disconnect the negative battery cables. Drain the cooling system into a suitable container. Properly discharge the air conditioning system.

2. Remove the intake manifold.

3. Remove the air conditioning compressor belt.

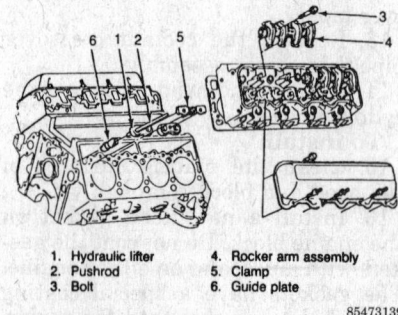

1. Hydraulic lifter
2. Pushrod
3. Bolt
4. Rocker arm assembly
5. Clamp
6. Guide plate

85473139

Cylinder head and components — 6.2L and 6.5L diesel engines

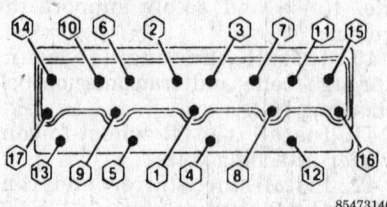

85473140

Cylinder head bolt torque sequence — 6.2L and 6.5L diesel engines

4. Remove the air conditioning compressor.

5. Remove the valve cover.

6. Remove the rocker arm assemblies. Mark the parts to ensure installation in their original location.

7. Remove the pushrods. Keep them in order.

8. Raise and support the vehicle safely.

9. Remove the exhaust manifold.

10. Remove the power steering pump and rear bracket, position the assembly aside. Lower the vehicle.

11. Remove the oil dipstick tube.

12. Disconnect the transmission detent cable.

13. Remove the glow plug controller and bracket.

14. Disconnect the wire connector from the sensor at the coolant crossover pipe.

15. Disconnect the oil fill tube, fuel bleeder valve and hoses from the coolant crossover pipe.

16. Disconnect the fuel crossover line from both cylinder heads.

17. Remove the air cleaner resonator and bracket.

18. Remove the alternator upper bracket.

19. Remove the coolant crossover pipe and thermostat.

20. Remove the head bolts.

21. Remove the cylinder head.

To install:

22. Clean the mating surfaces of the head and block thoroughly.

23. Install a new head gasket on the engine block. Do not coat the gaskets with any sealer on either engine. The gaskets have a special coating that eliminates the need for sealer. Install the cylinder head onto the block.

24. Clean the head bolts thoroughly. Coat the threads of the head

bolts with sealing compound GM part 1052080 or equivalent, before installation. Install the rear cylinder head bolt first. Tighten the head bolts to 20 ft. lbs. (25 Nm). in the proper sequence, next tighten all bolts to 50 ft. lbs. (65 Nm) in the proper sequence, and finally tighten all bolts an additional 90 degree (¼ turn).

25. Install the coolant crossover pipe and thermostat.

26. Install the fuel valve and alternator assembly.

27. Connect the bypass hose.

28. Connect the upper radiator hose.

29. Connect the heater hoses at the head.

30. Install the transmission and oil dipstick tube.

31. Install the air cleaner resonator and bracket.

32. Install the pushrods, hardened ends facing up.

33. Install the rocker arm assemblies.

34. Adjust the valves.

35. Install the valve cover. Install the air conditioner compressor and bracket assembly.

36. Raise and support the vehicle safely.

37. Install the exhaust manifold. Lower the vehicle.

38. Install the upper fan shroud.

39. Install the intake manifold. Connect the negative battery cables.

40. Fill the cooling system with the proper type and quantity of antifreeze. Evacuate and recharge the air conditioning system.

Valve Lifters

REMOVAL AND INSTALLATION

6.2L and 6.5L Engine

1. Disconnect the negative battery cables.

2. Remove the valve covers, rocker arm shafts and pushrods. Position all components in the exact order which they were removed, so they may be reinstalled in their original bore.

3. Remove the cylinder head, as required.

4. Remove the valve lifter clamps and guide plates.

5. Remove the hydraulic lifters. Position the lifters in the exact order which they were removed, so they may be reinstalled in their original bore.

To install:

6. Coat the roller tips with GM part 1052365 or equivalent.

NOTE: All new lifters must be primed by working the plunger while submerged in kerosene or diesel fuel. Some engines will have 2 sizes of lifters being used, standard and oversized. The oversized lifter will be etched "10" on the side and the block will be stamped O.S. on the cast pad adjacent to the lifter bore.

7. Install the lifters in their original bores.

8. Install the guide plates and clamps. Torque the clamps bolts to 18 ft. lbs. (26 Nm).

9. Turn the engine 2 full turns and verify the lifters move freely in the guide plates. If the engine does not turn freely, 1 or more lifters are binding in the guide plate.

10. Install the cylinder head assembly.

11. Install the rocker arm shafts and pushrods assembly. Position all components in the exact order they were removed.

12. Install the valve covers.

13. Connect the negative battery cables.

Valve Lash

ADJUSTMENT

All engines use hydraulic lifters, which require no periodic adjustment.

Rocker Arm and Shafts

REMOVAL AND INSTALLATION

1. Disconnect the negative battery cables. On the G-Series, remove the engine cover.

2. Remove all the necessary components in order to gain access to the engine valve covers. As required, properly relieve the fuel system pressure before disconnecting any fuel lines.

3. Remove the valve cover retaining bolts. Remove the valve cover from the engine.

4. Remove the rocker arm assemblies. Keep them in order for reinstallation.

5. Installation is the reverse of the removal procedure. Be sure to use new gaskets or RTV sealant, as necessary.

Intake Manifold

REMOVAL AND INSTALLATION

6.2L and 6.5L Engine

1. Disconnect both negative battery cables.

2. Drain the cooling system and properly relieve the fuel system pressure.

3. Remove the engine cover, G-Series.

4. Remove the air cleaner assembly.

5. Remove the EPR/EGR valve bracket from the intake manifold.

6. Remove the CDR valve.

7. Remove the crankcase ventilator hose and EGR.

8. Remove the air conditioning rear bracket, if equipped.

9. Remove the fuel line bracket and ground strap.

10. Remove the fuel filter bracket at the intake manifold.

11. Remove the intake manifold bolts. The injection line clips are retained by these bolts.

12. Remove the intake manifold.

NOTE: If the engine is to be further serviced with the manifold removed, install protective covers over the intake ports.

To install:

13. Clean the manifold gasket surfaces on the cylinder heads and install new gaskets before installing the manifold.

NOTE: The gaskets have an opening for the EGR valve on light duty installations. An insert covers this opening on heavy duty installations.

14. Install the intake manifold.

15. Install the intake manifold bolts and fuel injection line clips.

16. Install the fuel filter bracket at the intake manifold.

17. Install the fuel line bracket and ground strap.

18. Install the air conditioning rear bracket, if equipped.

19. Install the crankcase ventilator hose and EGR.

20. Install the CDR valve.

21. Install the EPR/EGR valve bracket from the intake manifold.

22. Install the air cleaner assembly.

23. Install the engine cover, G-Series.

24. Fill the cooling system with the proper type and quantity of antifreeze.

25. Connect both negative battery cables. Inspect for leaks.

Exhaust Manifold

REMOVAL AND INSTALLATION

6.2L and 6.5L Engines

1. Disconnect the batteries.

2. Raise and support the vehicle safely.

3. Disconnect the exhaust pipe from the manifold flange and lower the vehicle.

4. Remove the engine cover and disconnect the glow plug wires.

5. Remove the air cleaner duct bracket.

6. Remove the glow plugs. Remove the turbocharger assembly, as required.

7. Remove the air conditioner compressor rear bracket, as required.

8. Remove the manifold bolts and remove the manifold.

9. Installation is the reverse of the removal procedure. Torque the manifold bolts to 26 ft. lbs. (35 Nm).

Timing Chain Front Cover

REMOVAL AND INSTALLATION

6.2L and 6.5L Engines

1. Disconnect both negative battery cables. Drain the cooling system.

2. Remove the water pump and pulleys.

3. Rotate the crankshaft to align the marks on the torsional damper with the **0** mark on the timing tab.

4. Scribe a mark aligning the injection pump flange and the front cover, if not already marked.

5. Remove the crankshaft pulley and torsional damper.

6. Remove the front cover-to-oil pan bolts (4).

7. Remove the 2 fuel return line clips.

8. Remove the injection pump gear.

9. Remove the injection pump retaining nuts from the front cover.

10. Remove the baffle. Remove the remaining cover bolts and remove the front cover.

To install:

11. If the front cover oil seal is to be replaced, it can now be pried out of the cover with a suitable prying tool. Press the new seal into the cover evenly.

12. Clean both sealing surfaces until all traces of old sealer are gone. Apply a 3/32 in. (2mm) bead of GM sealant 1052357 or equivalent to the sealing surface. Apply a 3/16 in. (5mm)

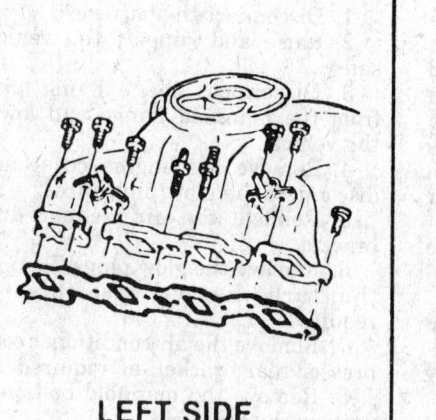

LEFT SIDE

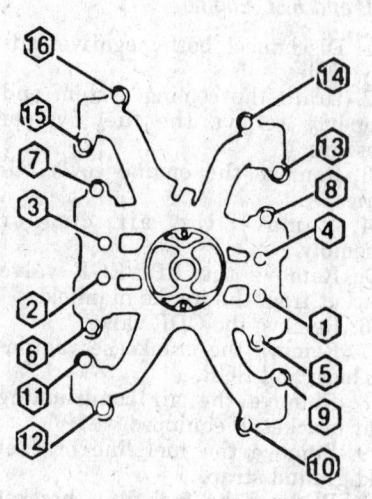

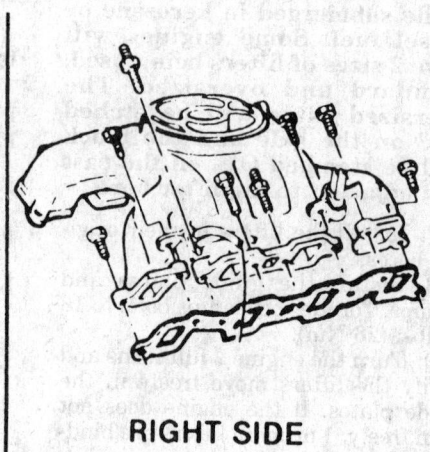

RIGHT SIDE

85473141

Intake manifold installation and torque sequence — 6.2L and 6.5L diesel engines

bead of RTV type sealer to the bottom portion of the front cover which attaches to the oil pan. Install the front cover.

13. Install the baffle.

14. Install the injection pump, making sure the scribe marks on the pump and front cover are aligned. Tighten the nuts to 31 ft. lbs. (42 Nm).

15. Install the injection pump driven gear, making sure the marks on the cam gear and pump are aligned. Torque the injection pump gear bolts to 17 ft. lbs. (23 Nm).

NOTE: Verify that there is a minimum clearance of 0.040 in. (1.0mm) between the injection pump gear and baffle or noise may be result.

16. Install the fuel line clips, the front cover-to-oil bolts, and the torsional damper and crankshaft pulley. Torque the pan and the damper bolt to specification.

17. Install the water pump and pulley assembly.

18. Fill the cooling system with the proper type and quantity of antifreeze.

19. Connect the negative battery cables. Inspect engine for leaks.

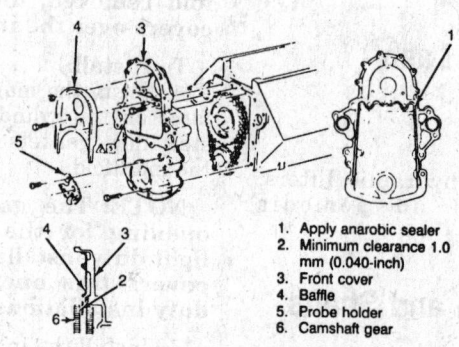

1. Apply anarobic sealer
2. Minimum clearance 1.0 mm (0.040-inch)
3. Front cover
4. Baffle
5. Probe holder
6. Camshaft gear

85473142

Front cover and components — 6.2L and 6.5L diesel engines

Front Cover Oil Seal

REMOVAL AND INSTALLATION

NOTE: The oil seal can also be replaced with the front cover installed.

1. Disconnect both negative battery cables.

2. Remove the accessory drive belt.

3. Remove the crankshaft pulley and the torsional damper assembly.

4. Pry the old seal out of the cover using a suitable tool. Use care not to damage the surface of the crankshaft. Install the new seal evenly into the cover.

5. The remaining installation is the reverse of the removal procedure.

Timing Chain

REMOVAL AND INSTALLATION

6.2L and 6.5L Engines

1. Disconnect the negative battery cables. Remove the front cover assembly.

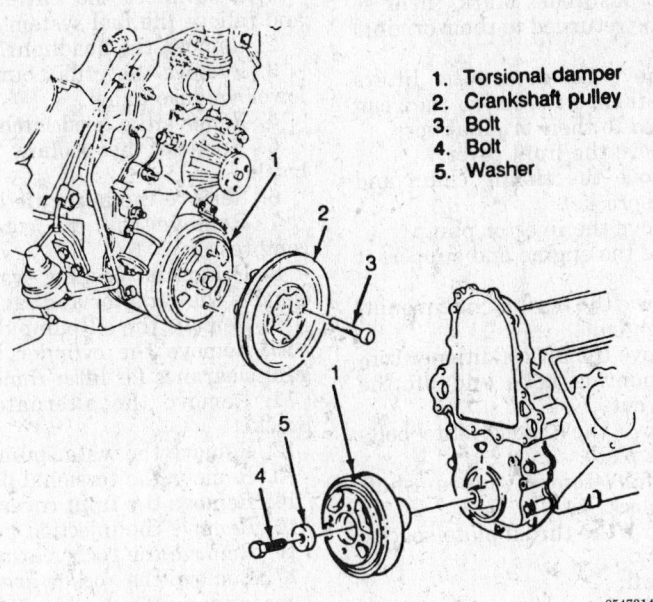

1. Torsional damper
2. Crankshaft pulley
3. Bolt
4. Bolt
5. Washer

85473143

Torsional damper and crankcase pulley installation — 6.2L and 6.5L diesel engines

2. Remove the injection pump gear.

3. Align the camshaft timing gear marks and remove the bolt and washer attaching the camshaft gear.

4. Remove the camshaft sprocket with the timing chain. Remove the crankshaft sprocket.

To install:

5. Install the cam sprocket, timing chain and crankshaft sprocket as a unit, aligning the timing marks on the sprockets.

6. Rotate the crankshaft to align the injection pump and camshaft gears. Install the injection pump gear.

7. Install the front cover. Connect the negative battery cables.

NOTE: The injection pump timing must be adjusted if a new chain, gears or sprockets were installed.

Camshaft

REMOVAL AND INSTALLATION

6.2L and 6.5L Engines

R/V-SERIES

1. Disconnect the battery cables.
2. Drain the cooling system.

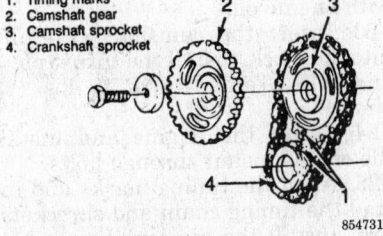

1. Timing marks
2. Camshaft gear
3. Camshaft sprocket
4. Crankshaft sprocket

85473145

Camshaft and sprockets — 6.2L and 6.5L diesel engines

3. Remove the radiator shrouds and fan.
4. Remove the vacuum pump.

NOTE: Do not run the engine while the vacuum pump is removed. The oil pump is powered by the vacuum pump drive gear and thus the engine will not have any oil pressure.

5. Remove the power steering pump.
6. Remove the alternator.
7. Remove the air conditioning compressor leaving the refrigerant lines connected and position the compressor aside.
8. Remove the rocker arm covers.
9. Remove the rocker arm assemblies and pushrods. Mark the components so they can be reinstalled in their original position.
10. Remove the hydraulic lifters keeping them in order so they can be returned to their original bore.
11. Remove the front cover.
12. Remove the injection pump.
13. Disconnect the air conditioning condenser mounting bolts and lift the condenser out of the way.
14. Remove the timing chain and camshaft sprocket.
15. Remove the engine mounting through bolts.
16. Raise the engine and support it safely.
17. Remove the camshaft thrust plate bolts and the thrust plate.
18. Carefully remove the camshaft from the block.
19. Remove the thrust plate spacer, if necessary.

To install:

20. Install the spacer with the ID chamfer toward the camshaft.

NOTE: It is recommended that the engine oil, oil filter and hydraulic lifters be replaced when installing a new camshaft.

21. Coat the camshaft lobes with Molykote® or equivalent.

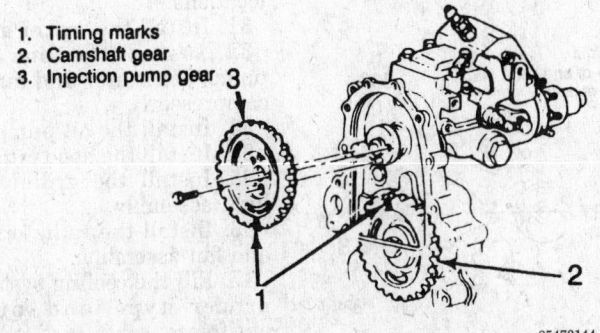

1. Timing marks
2. Camshaft gear
3. Injection pump gear

85473144

Injection pump gear and timing marks — 6.2L and 6.5L diesel engines

22. Lubricate the camshaft journals with engine oil.

23. Insert the camshaft carefully into the block, install the thrust plate and bolts and torque to 17 ft. lbs. (23 Nm).

24. Lower the engine and install the engine mount through bolts.

25. Align the timing marks and install the timing chain and sprockets.

26. Install the air conditioner condenser, if equipped.

27. Install the injection pump.

28. Install the air conditioning condenser and front timing cover.

29. Install the hydraulic lifters in the same bore as they were removed.

30. Install the rocker arm assemblies and pushrods in their original locations.

31. Install the rocker arm covers.

32. Install the air conditioner compressor.

33. Install the alternator.

34. Install the power steering pump.

35. Install the vacuum pump and align the pump so the inlet tube faces the front of the engine at a 20 degree angle.

36. Install the fan, radiator and shrouds.

37. Connect the negative battery cables.

38. Fill the cooling system with the proper type and quantity of antifreeze.

C/K-SERIES

1. Disconnect the battery cables and relieve the fuel system pressure.

2. Drain the cooling system.

3. Remove the radiator, the shroud and fan assembly.

4. Remove the grille and parking light assembly.

5. Remove the hood latch and brace assembly.

6. Remove the oil pump drive.

7. Remove the power steering pump, alternator and air conditioner compressor and position aside.

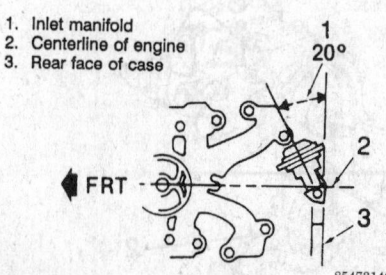

1. Inlet manifold
2. Centerline of engine
3. Rear face of case

◀ FRT

85473146

Diesel engine vacuum pump positioning

8. Remove the rocker arm covers.

9. Remove the rocker arm assemblies and pushrods. Mark them so they can be returned to their original position.

10. Remove the hydraulic lifters and keep them in order so they can be returned to their original bore.

11. Remove the front cover.

12. Remove the timing chain and camshaft sprocket.

13. Remove the injector pump.

14. Raise the engine and support it safely.

15. Remove the front engine mounting through bolts.

16. Remove the air conditioner condenser mounting bolts and lift the condenser out.

17. Remove the thrust plate bolts and thrust plate.

18. Carefully remove the camshaft from the block.

19. Remove the thrust plate spacer, if necessary.

To install:

20. Install the spacer with the ID chamfer toward the camshaft.

NOTE: It is recommended that the engine oil, oil filter and hydraulic lifters be replaced when installing a new camshaft.

21. Coat the camshaft lobes with Molykote® or equivalent.

22. Lubricate the camshaft journals with engine oil.

23. Insert the camshaft carefully into the block, install the thrust plate and bolts. Torque to 17 ft. lbs. (23 Nm).

24. Lower the engine and install the engine mount through bolts.

25. Align the timing marks and install the timing chain and sprockets.

26. Install the air conditioner condenser, if equipped.

27. Install the injector pump.

28. Install the front cover.

29. Install the hydraulic lifters in the same bore as they were removed.

30. Install the rocker arm assemblies and pushrods in their original locations.

31. Install the rocker arm covers.

32. Install the power steering pump, alternator and air conditioner compressor.

33. Install the oil pump drive.

34. Install the hood latch and brace.

35. Install the grille and parking light assembly.

36. Install the radiator, the shroud and fan assembly.

37. Fill the cooling system with the proper type and quantity of antifreeze.

38. Connect the negative battery cables.

G-SERIES

1. Disconnect the battery cables and relieve the fuel system pressure.

2. Remove the headlight bezels.

3. Remove the grille, bumper and lower valance panel.

4. Remove the hood latch.

5. Remove the coolant recovery bottle.

6. Remove the upper tie bar.

7. Remove the air conditioner compressor.

8. Drain the cooling system and remove the radiator and fan.

9. Remove the oil pump drive.

10. Remove the cylinder heads to gain clearance for lifter removal.

11. Remove the alternator lower bracket.

12. Remove the water pump.

13. Remove the torsional damper.

14. Remove the front cover.

15. Remove the injection pump.

16. Remove the rocker arm covers.

17. Remove the rocker arm assemblies and pushrods. Mark them so they can be returned to their original position.

18. Remove the hydraulic lifters and keep them in order so they can be returned to their original bore.

19. Remove the timing chain and camshaft sprocket.

20. Remove the thrust plate bolts and thrust plate.

21. Carefully remove the camshaft from the block.

22. Remove the thrust plate spacer, if necessary.

To install:

23. Install the spacer with the ID chamfer toward the camshaft.

NOTE: It is recommended that the engine oil, oil filter and hydraulic lifters be replaced when installing a new camshaft.

24. Coat the camshaft lobes with Molykote or equivalent.

25. Lubricate the camshaft journals with engine oil.

26. Insert the camshaft carefully into the block, install the thrust plate and bolts and torque to 17 ft. lbs.

27. Align the timing marks and install the timing chain and sprockets.

28. Install the hydraulic lifters in the same bore as they were removed.

29. Install the rocker arm assemblies and pushrods in their original locations.

30. Install the rocker arm covers.

31. Install the fuel pump.

32. Install the front cover.

33. Install the torsional damper and water pump.

34. Install the alternator lower bracket.

35. Install the cylinder heads.
36. Install the oil pump drive.
37. Install the radiator and fan.
38. Install the air conditioner compressor.
39. Install the upper tie bar.
40. Install the coolant recovery bottle.
41. Install the hood latch.
42. Install the grille, bumper and lower valance panel.
43. Install the headlight bezels.
44. Install the battery cables.
45. Fill the cooling system.
46. Evacuate and charge the air conditioner system.

Piston and Connecting Rod

POSITIONING

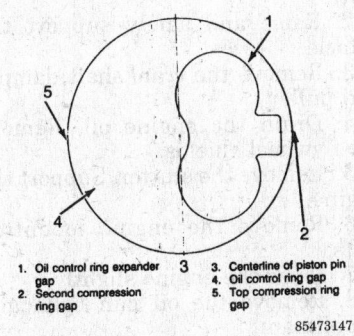

1. Oil control ring expander gap
2. Second compression ring gap
3. Centerline of piston pin
4. Oil control ring gap
5. Top compression ring gap

85473147

Piston ring gap locations — 6.2L and 6.5L diesel engines

ENGINE LUBRICATION

Oil Pan

REMOVAL AND INSTALLATION

2.2L Engine

1. Remove the engine assembly.
2. If equipped, remove the clutch pressure plate and disc from the engine.
3. Remove the flywheel.
4. Remove the oil pan nuts and bolts, then remove the pan from the bottom of the block.
   To install:
5. Carefully clean the gasket mating surfaces of any remaining old gasket or sealer material.
6. Position a new gasket and seal onto the oil pan. Use a thin bead of sealant at either side of the sealer.
7. Install the oil pan and tighten the retaining bolts to 89 inch. lbs. (10 Nm).
8. Install the flywheel.
9. If equipped, install the pressure plate and disc.
10. Install the engine to the vehicle.

2.5L Engine

2WD

1. Disconnect the negative battery cable.
2. Remove the power steering reservoir at the fan shroud.
3. Remove the radiator fan shroud.
4. Raise and support the vehicle safely.
5. Drain the engine oil.
6. Remove the strut rods.
7. Disconnect the exhaust pipes at the manifolds.
8. Remove the catalytic converter and exhaust pipe.
9. Remove the flywheel cover.
10. Remove the starter and brace.
11. Remove the brake line at the crossmember. Remove the engine mount through-bolts.
12. Carefully raise the engine, as necessary for clearance, then remove the oil pan bolts and pan.
    To install:
13. Using a gasket scraper, clean the gasket mounting surfaces. Make sure all sealing surfaces are clean and free of oil.
14. Apply RTV sealant to the oil pan flange and block.
15. Using care to avoid disturbing the RTV beads, install the oil pan onto the cylinder block. The sealant must be wet during oil pan bolt torquing.
16. Tighten oil pan bolts to 90 inch lbs. (10 Nm).
17. Carefully lower the engine into position, then install and tighten the mount through-bolts.
18. Install the brake line to the crossmember.
19. Install the starter and brace.
20. Install the flywheel cover.
21. Install the converter and exhaust pipe, then connect the exhaust pipe to the manifolds.
22. Install the strut rods, then lower the vehicle.
23. Install the radiator/fan shroud, then install the power steering reservoir.
24. Refill the engine crankcase, then connect the negative battery cable.

25. Start the engine, establish normal operating temperatures and check for leaks.

4WD

1. Disconnect the negative battery cable.
2. Remove the power steering reservoir at the fan shroud.
3. Remove the radiator fan shroud.
4. Remove the engine oil dipstick.
5. Raise and support the vehicle safely.
6. Drain the engine oil.
7. Remove the brake line at the crossmember, then remove the crossmember.
8. If equipped, remove the transmission cooler lines.
9. Disconnect the exhaust pipes at the manifolds.
10. Remove the catalytic converter hanger.
11. Remove the flywheel cover.
12. Remove the driveshaft splash shield.
13. Matchmark and remove the idler arm assembly.
14. Remove the steering gear bolts. Pull the steering gear and linkage forward.
15. Remove the differential housing mounting bolts at the bracket on the right side and at the frame on the left side.
16. Remove the starter and brace.
17. Remove the engine mount through-bolts.
18. Remove the oil pan bolts and pan.
    To install:
19. Apply RTV sealant to the oil pan flange and block.
20. Using care to avoid disturbing the RTV beads, install the oil pan onto the cylinder block. The sealant must be wet during oil pan bolt torquing.
21. Tighten oil pan bolts to 90 inch lbs. (10 Nm).
22. Install the engine mount through-bolts.
23. Install the starter and brace.
24. Install the differential housing mounting bolts at the bracket on the right side and at the frame on the left side.
25. Reposition the steering gear and linkage, then install the steering gear bolts.
26. Align and secure the idler arm assembly.
27. Install the driveshaft splash shield.
28. Install the flywheel cover.
29. Install the catalytic converter hanger.

30. Connect the exhaust pipes at the manifolds.

31. If equipped, connect the transmission cooler lines.

32. Install the crossmember, then secure the brake line at the crossmember.

33. Carefully lower the vehicle.

34. Install the engine oil dipstick.

35. Install the radiator fan shroud.

36. Install the power steering reservoir at the fan shroud.

37. Refill the engine crankcase, then connect the negative battery cable.

38. Start the engine, establish normal operating temperatures and check for leaks.

2.8L and 4.3L Engines — S/T-Series Only

2WD

1. Remove the engine.

2. Remove the oil pan retainers (nuts, studs and/or bolts) and rail reinforcements, if equipped. Remove the oil pan from the block.

To install:

3. Using a gasket scraper, clean the gasket mounting surfaces. Make sure all sealing surfaces are clean and free of oil.

4. Apply 1052080 (4.3L), 1052914 (2.8L) or equivalent sealant to the oil pan rail where it contacts the timing cover-to-block joint (front) and the crankshaft rear seal retainer-to-block joint (rear). Continue the bead of sealant about 1 in. (25mm) in both directions from each of the 4 corners.

NOTE: For the 2.8L engine, be sure all RTV is removed from the blind attaching holes to ensure proper fastener tightening can take place.

5. Using a new gasket, install the oil pan, reinforcements, if equipped, and retainers. Tighten the retainers to specification:

2.8L engines:
  1992
  Two rear bolts: 18 ft. lbs. (25 Nm)
  All other bolts, studs and nuts: 7 ft. lbs. (10 Nm)
  1993 bolts: 18 ft. lbs. (25 Nm)
4.3L engine:
  Bolts: 100 inch lbs. (11 Nm)
  Nuts at corners: 17 ft. lbs. (23 Nm)

6. Install the engine into the vehicle. Refill the crankcase with fresh oil. Start the engine, establish normal operating temperatures and check for leaks.

4WD VEHICLES

1. Disconnect the negative battery cable.

2. Remove the dipstick.

3. Raise and support the vehicle safely.

4. Remove the drive belt splash shield, the front axle shield, and the transfer case shield.

5. Remove the front skid plate and drain the engine crankcase oil, then remove the flywheel cover.

6. Remove the left and right motor mount through-bolts.

7. Raise the engine using a suitable lifting device and block in position. This may be accomplished using large wooden blocks between the motor mounts and brackets.

NOTE: Use extreme caution when blocking the engine in position. Get out from under the vehicle and rock the engine slightly once the blocks are in place to be sure the engine is properly supported.

8. Disconnect the oil cooler line, then remove the oil filter adapter.

9. Remove the pitman arm bolt, then disconnect the pitman arm.

10. Remove the idler arm bolts, then disconnect the idler arm.

11. Remove the front differential through-bolts, then disconnect or remove the front driveshaft, if necessary.

12. Roll the differential assembly forward for clearance.

13. Remove the starter motor retaining bolts, then lower the starter and either remove it from the vehicle or suspend it out of the way using mechanic's wire.

14. Remove the oil pan bolts, nuts and reinforcements, then lower the oil pan and gasket.

To install:

15. Using a gasket scraper, clean the gasket mounting surfaces. Make sure all sealing surfaces are clean and free of oil.

16. Apply 1052080 or equivalent sealant to the oil pan rail where it contacts the timing cover-to-block joint (front) and the crankshaft rear seal retainer-to-block joint (rear). Continue the bead of sealant about 1 in. (25mm) in both directions from each of the 4 corners.

17. Using a new gasket, install the oil pan, reinforcements and retainers. Tighten the bolts to 100 inch lbs. (11 Nm) and the nuts at the corners to 17 ft. lbs. (23 Nm).

18. Install the starter motor and secure using the mounting bolts.

19. Roll the differential back into position, then install/connect the front driveshaft. Install the front differential through-bolts.

20. Connect the idler arm and secure using the retaining bolts, then connect the pitman arm and secure using the bolts.

21. Install the transfer case shield.

22. Install the flywheel cover, then install the front skid plate.

23. Install the front axle shield, then install the drive belt splash shield.

24. Carefully lower the vehicle.

25. Install the dipstick, then properly refill the engine crankcase.

26. Connect the negative battery cable.

27. Start the engine, establish normal operating temperatures and check for leaks.

3.1L Engine

1. Disconnect the negative battery cable. Remove the accessory drive belt.

2. Raise and safely support the vehicle.

3. Remove the crankshaft damper and pulley.

4. Drain the engine oil. Remove the flywheel shields.

5. Remove the starter. Support the engine.

6. Remove the engine mounting bolts.

7. Raise the engine slightly.

8. Remove the oil pan bolts and the oil pan.

To install:

9. Install a new oil pan gasket and install the oil pan. Tighten M8 oil pan bolts to 19 ft. lbs. (25 Nm) and the M6 oil pan bolts to 7 ft. lbs. (10 Nm).

10. Lower the engine and install the engine mounting bolts.

11. Install the starter and flywheel shields.

12. Install the crankshaft damper and pulley.

13. Lower the vehicle and install the accessory drive belt.

14. Refill the crankcase and connect the negative battery cable.

3.8L Engine

1. Disconnect the negative battery cable. Remove the accessory drive belt.

2. Raise and safely support the vehicle.

3. Remove the crankshaft damper and pulley.

4. Drain the engine oil. Remove the flywheel shields.

5. Remove the starter. Support the engine.

6. Remove the engine mounting bolts.

7. Raise the engine slightly.

8. Remove the oil pan bolts and the oil pan.

To install:

9. Install a new oil pan gasket and install the oil pan. Tighten the oil pan bolts to 124 inch lbs. (14 Nm).

10. Lower the engine and install the engine mounting bolts.

11. Install the starter and flywheel shields.

12. Install the crankshaft damper and pulley.

13. Lower the vehicle and install the accessory drive belt.

14. Refill the crankcase and connect the negative battery cable.

4.3L Engine — M/L-Series

1. Disconnect the negative battery cable.

2. Raise and support the vehicle safely.

3. Drain the engine oil.

4. Disconnect the exhaust pipe at the manifolds.

5. Remove the torque converter cover.

6. Remove the starter assembly.

7. Remove the oil pan bolts, nuts and reinforcements.

8. Remove the oil pan and gaskets.

To install:

9. Using a gasket scraper, clean the gasket mounting surfaces. Make sure all sealing surfaces are clean and free of oil.

10. Apply 12346141 or equivalent sealant at the front cover-to-block joint and the crankshaft rear seal retainer-to-block joint (rear). Continue the bead of sealant about 1 in. (25mm) in both directions from each of the 4 corners.

11. Using a new gasket, install the oil pan, reinforcements and retainers. Tighten the retainers to specification:
Bolts: 100 inch lbs. (11 Nm)
Nuts at corners: 17 ft. lbs. (23 Nm)

12. Install the starter assembly.

13. Install the torque converter cover.

14. Connect the exhaust pipe to the manifolds.

15. Carefully lower the vehicle.

16. Properly refill the engine crankcase.

17. Connect the negative battery cable.

18. Start the engine, establish normal operating temperatures and check for leaks.

4.3L Engine — Except M/L-Series and S/T-Series

1. Disconnect the negative battery cable. Raise and support the vehicle

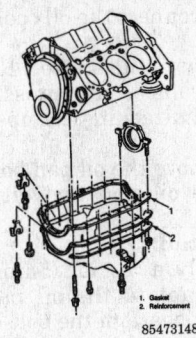

85473148

Oil pan mounting — 4.3L engine

safely. Drain the engine oil into a suitable container.

2. Remove the exhaust crossover pipe.

3. Remove the torque converter cover, if equipped with automatic transmission.

4. Remove the strut rods at the flywheel cover, if equipped.

5. Remove the strut rod at the front engine mounts, if equipped.

6. Remove the starter assembly.

7. Remove the oil pan bolts, nuts and reinforcements.

8. Remove the oil pan and gaskets.

To install:

9. Thoroughly clean all gasket surfaces and install a new gasket, using only a small amount of sealer at the front and rear corners of the oil pan.

10. Install the oil pan and new gaskets.

11. Install the oil pan bolts, nuts and reinforcements. Torque the pan bolts to specification.

12. Install the starter assembly.

13. Install the strut rod brackets at the front engine mounts.

14. Install the strut rods at the flywheel cover.

15. Install the torque converter cover, if equipped with automatic transmission.

16. Install the exhaust crossover pipe. Lower the vehicle.

17. Connect the negative battery cable.

18. Fill the engine with the proper quantity and type of oil.

5.0L and 5.7L Engines

1. Disconnect the negative battery cable. Raise the vehicle, support it safely, and drain the engine oil.

2. Remove the exhaust crossover pipe.

3. Remove the flywheel or torque converter cover.

4. Remove the strut rods at the front engine mountings, if used.

5. Remove the oil pan bolts, nuts and reinforcements.

6. Remove the oil pan and gaskets.

To install:

7. Thoroughly clean all gasket surfaces and install a new gasket, using a small amount of sealer at the front and rear corners of the oil pan.

8. Install the oil pan and new gaskets.

9. Install the oil pan bolts, nuts and reinforcements. Torque the pan bolts to specification.

10. Install the strut rods at the front engine mountings.

11. Install the torque converter or flywheel cover.

12. Install the exhaust crossover pipe.

13. Connect the negative battery cable.

14. Fill the crankcase with the proper type and quantity of oil.

6.2L and 6.5L Engines

R/V-SERIES

1. Disconnect the battery cables.

2. Raise and support the vehicle safely.

3. Drain the engine oil and remove the filter.

4. Remove the flywheel cover and oil pan dipstick.

5. Remove the left engine mount through bolts. Remove the exhaust pipes at the manifold, as required. Raise the engine.

6. Remove the strut rods, as required. Remove the battery cables, cooler lines and clamps from the oil pan.

7. Remove the oil pan bolts and remove the oil pan. Remove the oil pan gaskets and seals.

To install:

8. Clean the old RTV sealant from the oil pan and block.

9. Apply a 3/16 in. (5mm) bead of RTV sealant to the oil pan sealing surface, inboard of the bolt holes. The sealant must be wet to the touch when the oil pan is to be installed.

10. Install the oil pan rear seal.

11. Install the oil pan to the engine and install the retaining bolts. Torque the bolts to specification.

12. Lower the engine and install the oil pan dipstick.

13. Install the engine mount through bolt and nut.

14. Install the flywheel cover, strut rods.

15. Connect the battery cables, cooler lines and clamps to the oil pan and then lower the vehicle.

16. Refill with the proper grade and quantity of oil. Install the oil filter. Connect the negative battery cables.

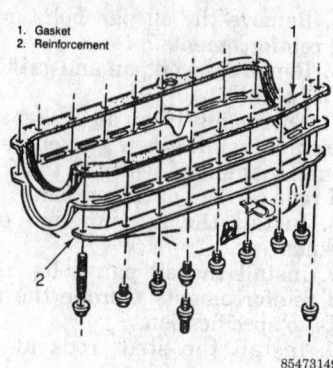

1. Gasket
2. Reinforcement

85473149

Oil pan mounting — 5.0L and 5.7L engines

C/K-SERIES

1. Disconnect the battery cables.
2. Raise the vehicle and support it safely.
3. Drain the engine oil. Remove the oil dipstick.
4. Remove the flywheel cover.
5. Disconnect the exhaust pipes from the manifolds.
6. Remove the front engine mount through bolts and raise the engine.
7. Remove the oil pan bolts and remove the oil pan.
8. Remove the oil pan rear seal.

To install:

9. Clean the old RTV sealant from the oil pan and block.
10. Apply a ³/₁₆ in. (5mm) bead of RTV sealant to the oil pan sealing surface, inboard of the bolt holes. The sealant must be wet to the touch when the oil pan is to be installed.
11. Install the oil pan rear seal.
12. Install the oil pan to the engine and install the retaining bolts. Torque all except the rear 2 bolts to 84 inch lbs. Torque the rear 2 bolts to 17 ft. lbs.
13. Lower the engine.
14. Install the engine mounting through bolt and nut.
15. Install the oil dipstick. Install the exhaust pipes to the manifolds.
16. Install the flywheel cover and lower the vehicle.
17. Refill with the proper grade and quantity of oil.
18. Install the battery cables.

G-SERIES

1. Disconnect the battery cables.
2. Remove the engine cover.
3. Remove the engine oil dipstick.
4. Remove the engine oil dipstick tube at the rocker cover.
5. Raise the vehicle and support it safely.
6. Remove the transmission flywheel cover.
7. Drain the engine oil.

8. Disconnect the oil cooler lines at the block.
9. Remove the starter. Remove the battery cables, transmission cooler lines and attaching clamps from the oil pan.
10. Remove the oil pan bolts and remove the oil pan and oil pan rear seal.

To install:

11. Apply a ³/₁₆ in. (5mm) bead of RTV sealant to the oil pan sealing surface, inboard of the bolt holes. The sealant must be wet to the touch when the oil pan is to be installed.
12. Install the oil pan rear seal.
13. Install the oil pan to the engine and install the retaining bolts. Torque all bolts to specifications.
14. Install the starter. Install the transmission, battery cables and attaching clamps to the oil pan.
15. Install the engine oil cooler lines.
16. Install the transmission flywheel cover.
17. Lower the vehicle.
18. Install the engine oil dipstick tube at the rocker cover.
19. Install the engine oil dipstick.
20. Install the engine cover.
21. Refill with the proper grade and quantity of oil.
22. Install the battery cables.

7.4L Engine

NOTE: Removal of the transmission may be necessary on the G-Series vehicles.

1. Disconnect the negative battery cable.
2. Remove the fan shroud.
3. Remove the air cleaner.
4. Remove the distributor cap.
5. Raise and support the vehicle safely.
6. Drain the engine oil. Remove the starter assembly, if equipped with manual transmission.
7. Remove the torque converter or clutch housing cover.
8. Remove the oil filter.
9. Remove the oil pressure line from the side of the block.
10. Support the engine.
11. Remove the engine mount through bolts.
12. Raise the engine just enough to remove the pan.
13. Remove the oil pan bolts, the oil pan and discard the gaskets.

To install:

14. Clean all mating surfaces thoroughly.
15. Apply RTV gasket material to the front and rear corners of the gaskets.

16. Coat the gaskets with adhesive sealer and position them on the block.
17. Install the rear pan seal in the pan with the seal ends mating with the gaskets.
18. Install the front seal on the bottom of the front cover, pressing the locating tabs into the holes in the cover.
19. Install the oil pan.
20. Install the pan bolts, clips and reinforcements. Torque the pan bolts to specification.
21. Lower the engine onto the mounts.
22. Install the engine mount through-bolts.
23. Install the oil pressure line.
24. Install the oil filter. Install the starter assembly, if removed.
25. Install the torque converter or clutch housing cover.
26. Install the distributor cap.
27. Install the air cleaner.
28. Install the fan shroud.
29. Connect the battery.
30. Fill the crankcase with the proper type and quantity of oil.

Oil Pump

REMOVAL AND INSTALLATION

Except 3.8L Engine

1. Remove the oil pan.
2. Remove the oil pump attaching bolt and, if equipped, the pickup tube nut/bolt, then remove the pump along with the pickup tube and shaft, as necessary.
3. If necessary for the 2.2L engine, remove the extension shaft and retainer (being careful not the crack the retainer) from the pump.

To install:

4. For the 2.2L engine, if the extension shaft was removed, heat the extension shaft retainer in hot water, then install the shaft and retainer to the oil pump. Make sure the retainer does not crack during installation.
5. Ensure that the pump pickup tube is tight in the pump body. If the tube should come loose, oil pressure will be lost and oil starvation will occur. If the pickup tube is loose it should be replaced.
6. If the pump has been disassembled and is being replaced or for any reason oil has been removed, it must be primed. It can either be filled with oil before installing the cover plate and oil kept within the pump during

handling or the entire pump cavity can be filled with petroleum jelly.

NOTE: If the pump is not primed, the engine could be damaged before it receives adequate lubrication when the engine is started.

7. Install the pump aligning the pump shaft with the distributor drive gear as necessary. Tighten oil pump/pickup tube retainer(s) to specification:

2.2L Engine: 32 ft. lbs. (44 Nm)

2.5L Engine:
  Pump bolts 18 ft. lbs. (25 Nm)
  Pickup tube nut to 31 ft. lbs. (42 Nm)

2.8L Engine: 30 ft. lbs. (41 Nm)

3.1L Engine: 40 ft. lbs. (54 Nm)

4.3L and all V8 Engines: 65 ft. lbs. (90 Nm)

8. Install the oil pan and refill the engine crankcase. Disable the ignition system; crank engine for approximately 10 seconds to aid in priming the oil pump and reducing the risk of engine damage.

NOTE: If the oil pump does not build up oil pressure almost immediately, remove the pan and check for a loose oil pump-to-pickup tube attachment. If necessary dismantle the pump and pack the pump cavity with petroleum jelly. Running the engine without measurable oil pressure will cause extensive damage.

3.8L Engine

1. Disconnect the negative battery cable.
2. Remove the front timing cover assembly.
3. Remove the oil pump cover attaching screws and remove the pump gears.
4. Remove the oil filter drip shield.
5. Remove the oil filter.
6. Remove the 4 bolts securing the adapter to the front cover.

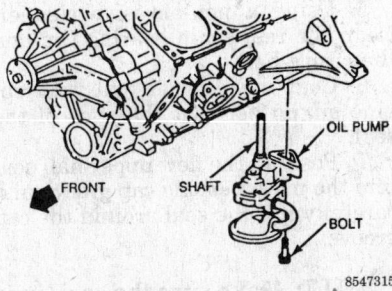

Common oil pump mounting — except 3.8L engines

7. Remove the adapter, gasket, the oil pressure valve and spring.

To install:

8. Clean all part in solvent and remove the old gaskets.
9. Check all parts for scoring, cracks or excessive wear. Check pressure regulator spring for loss of tension and replace as necessary.
10. Install the oil filter adapter, a new gasket, the oil pressure valve and spring.
11. Install the 4 adapter to front cover screws and torque to 22 ft. lbs. (30 Nm).
12. Install the oil filter.
13. Install the oil filter drip shield.
14. Install the pump gears into the cover assembly and pack with petroleum jelly. Install the oil pump cover attaching screws and torque to 97 inch lbs. (11 Nm).
15. Install the front timing cover assembly.
16. Connect the negative battery cable.

NOTE: If the oil pump pickup screen is thought to be possibly clogged or dirty the oil pan should be removed and the screen removed and cleaned with solvent.

CHECKING

1. Disconnect the negative battery cable.
2. Remove the oil pressure sending unit.
3. Connect a suitable oil pressure gauge in place of the sending unit.
4. Reconnect the negative battery cable.
5. Ensure oil level is within specification.
6. Start the engine and set to specified test RPM.
7. Verify oil pressure reading meets specifications.
8. Remove the gauge and reinstall the sending unit.

Rear Main Oil Seal

REMOVAL AND INSTALLATION

1-Piece Seal

Most of these engines will utilize a 1-piece rear main seal assembly. The seal is mounted to a housing on the rear of the block which is normally equipped with removal notches or slots to help free the old seal. A new seal is carefully driven into position using a threaded seal installation tool.

Some versions of the diesel engines and of the 7.4L gasoline engines utilize a 2-piece seal, requiring a more involved replacement procedure.

1. Remove the transmission assembly.
2. If equipped, remove the clutch assembly.
3. Remove the flywheel and verify the rear main seal is leaking.

NOTE: Most seal retainer housings are notched in order to provide a safer prying point for seal removal.

4. Remove the seal by inserting a small prybar into the notch (if provided) or through the dust lip at an angle and prying the seal out. Be careful not to score the crankshaft sealing surface.

To install:

5. Check the crankshaft and seal bore for nicks or damage. Repair as necessary.
6. Lightly coat the inner and outer diameters of the seal with clean engine oil, then position the seal on the installation tool.
7. Position the tool to the crankshaft and thread the tool's screws into the tapped holes. Tighten the screws securely using a screwdriver to attach the tool and assure proper seal installation.
8. Turn the handle of the tool until it bottoms and the seal has been completely seated.
9. Turn the handle of the tool out until it stops, then remove the tool and verify that the is seated squarely in the bore.
10. Install the flywheel to the engine.
11. If equipped, install the clutch assembly.
12. Install the transmission assembly.

2-Piece Seal

6.2L AND 6.5L ENGINES

1. Engines which are originally equipped with a 2-piece rope seal, should have their seals replaced with the 2-piece lip seal which is available as a service replacement.
2. Raise and support the vehicle safely. Drain the crankcase oil and remove the oil pan, pump and rear main bearing cap.
3. Using a suitable tool, remove the upper and lower rope seals.

To install:

4. Apply a light coat of oil to the seal lips where they contact the crankshaft. Roll 1 seal half into the block groove until a ½ in. (13mm) of 1 end is extending out of the block. In-

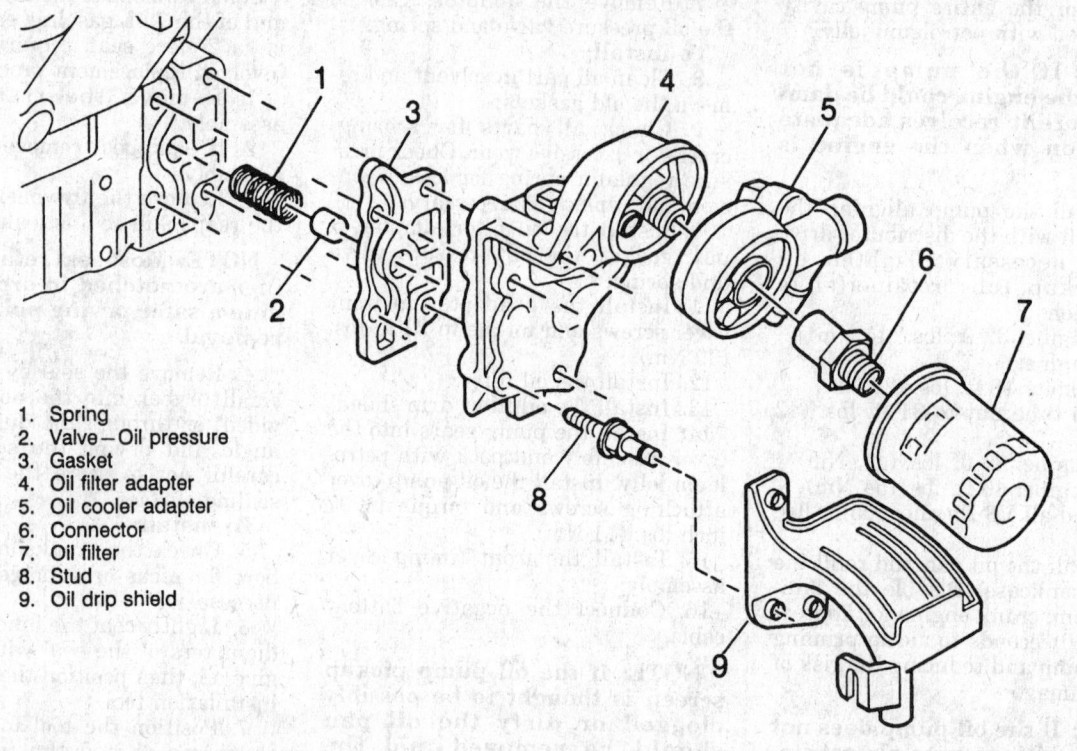

1. Spring
2. Valve—Oil pressure
3. Gasket
4. Oil filter adapter
5. Oil cooler adapter
6. Connector
7. Oil filter
8. Stud
9. Oil drip shield

Oil filter adapter and oil pressure valve — 3.8L engine

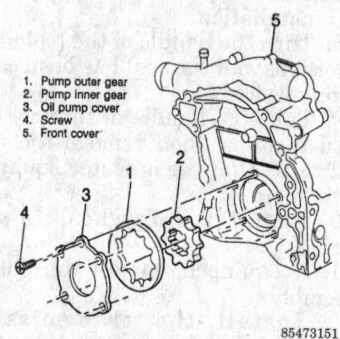

1. Pump outer gear
2. Pump inner gear
3. Oil pump cover
4. Screw
5. Front cover

Oil pump gears and housing assembly — 3.8L engine

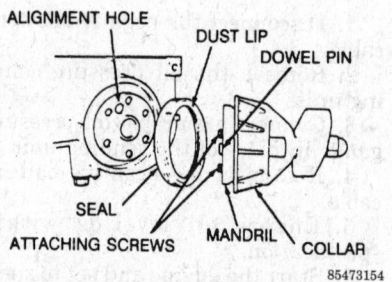

ALIGNMENT HOLE

DUST LIP

DOWEL PIN

SEAL

ATTACHING SCREWS

MANDRIL

COLLAR

Common 1-pieces rear main seal installation

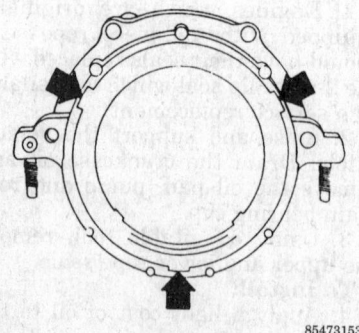

Most 1-piece rear main seal retainers are equipped with removal notches

sert the other seal half into the opposite side of the seal groove in the block.

5. The ends of the seal halves should now be positioned at the 8 and 2 o'clock or 4 and 10 o'clock positions.

6. Lightly coat the seal groove in the main bearing with adhesive Loctite 414® or equivalent.

7. Apply a thin film of anaerobic sealant or equivalent, to the main bearing cap. Do not put sealant in the oil relief slot.

8. Tap the bearing cap into place using a brass or leather mallet.

9. Install the bearing cap bolts and torque to specification.

10. Install the oil pump and oil pan.

7.4L ENGINE

The rear main bearing oil seal, both halves, can be removed without removal of the crankshaft. Always replace the upper and lower halves together.

1. Raise and support the vehicle safely, drain the oil and remove the oil pan.

2. Remove the oil pump and the rear main bearing cap.

3. Using a suitable tool, pry the oil seal from the rear main bearing cap.

4. Using a small hammer and a brass pin punch, drive the top half of the oil seal from the rear main bearing.

5. Using a non-abrasive cleaner, clean the rear main bearing cap and the crankshaft.

6. Coat the new oil seal with engine oil; do not coat the ends of the seal.

7. Position the new upper half seal into the main bearing cap groove and carefully roll the seal around the cap groove.

NOTE: Make sure the seal lip is positioned toward the front of the engine.

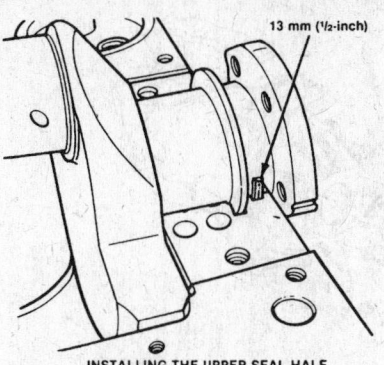

INSTALLING THE UPPER SEAL HALF

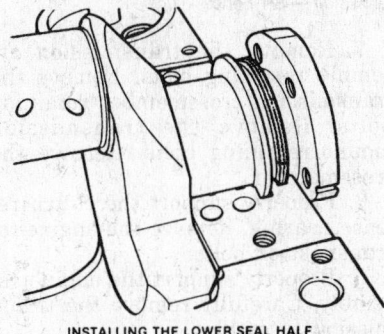

INSTALLING THE LOWER SEAL HALF

85473155

Rear main seal installation — 6.2L and 6.5L diesel engines

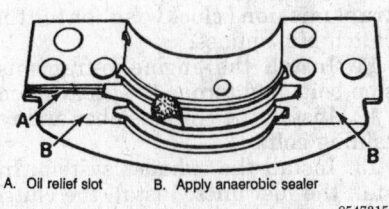

A. Oil relief slot   B. Apply anaerobic sealer

85473156

Applying sealer to the rear main bearing cap — 6.2L and 6.5L diesel engines

8. Install the lower half onto the lower half of the rear main bearing cap.

9. Apply sealant to the cap-to-case mating surfaces and install the lower rear main bearing half to the engine; keep the sealant off the seal's mating line.

10. Install the rear main bearing cap bolts and torque to 10 ft. lbs. (14 Nm). Using a lead hammer, tap the crankshaft forward and rearward, to align the thrust surfaces. Torque the main bearing bolts to 110 ft. lbs. (150 Nm).

11. Install the oil pan and pump assembly. Refill the crankcase with the proper type and quantity of engine oil.

MANUAL TRANSMISSION

Transmission Assembly

REMOVAL AND INSTALLATION

Compact Pick-Up, Van and Utility

S/T-SERIES

1. Disconnect the negative battery cable.
2. Remove the shift lever.
3. Raise and support the vehicle safely.
4. Disconnect the parking brake cable for clearance. Before disconnecting the cable, measure the adjustment or scribe marks to ease adjustment after installation.
5. Matchmark and remove the driveshaft.
6. If equipped, remove the skid plate.
7. On 4WD vehicles, remove the transfer case and shift lever.
8. Tag and disengage the necessary wiring connectors, including the reverse (backup) light switch and Vehicle Speed Sensor (VSS) connectors.
9. For 1992–96 4.3L engine, properly relieve the fuel system pressure, then disconnect the fuel lines at the engine.
10. For 2.2L engines, disconnect the fuel lines from the top cover.
11. Disconnect the exhaust pipes.

NOTE: On some vehicles 1992–93, access to and removal of the upper bellhousing bolts may be difficult. If necessary, remove the body/cab mounting bolts and

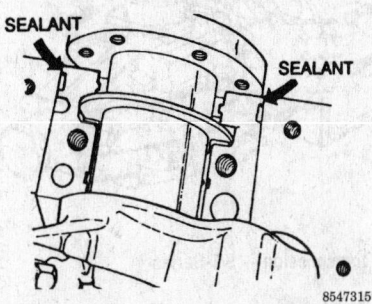

SEALANT   SEALANT

85473157

Applying sealer to the block — 7.4L engine

carefully raise the front left of the vehicle away from the frame for access.

12. Remove the slave cylinder from the transmission. If the cylinder can be repositioned with the hydraulics intact, simply support it out of the way, but make sure the line is not stretched, kinked or otherwise damaged. If necessary, disconnect the line and remove the cylinder completely.

13. Support the transmission carefully. If possible, secure the transmission to the jack to keep it from shifting suddenly and falling.

14. Remove the transmission mount retainers.

15. If necessary, remove the catalytic converter support hanger.

16. Disconnect or remove the necessary support braces.

17. If necessary, unbolt and remove the transmission crossmember.

18. Make sure the transmission is properly supported, then remove the transmission-to-bellhousing or transmission-to-engine bolts, as necessary.

19. Carefully pull the transmission assembly, straight back to disengage the input shaft splines, Do not allow the transmission to hang on the clutch. For 4.3L engine, it may be necessary to rotate the transmission counterclockwise, then pull back and disengage it from the engine. Once the transmission is disengaged, slowly lower the jack and transmission to remove it.

To install:

20. Place a THIN coat of high-temperature grease on the main drive gear (input shaft) splines, then shift the transmission into height gear.

NOTE: For 4.3L engines, it may be necessary to rotate the transmission clockwise while inserting it to the clutch hub.

21. Secure the transmission, then carefully raise it into position, directly behind the engine. Slowly insert the input shaft through the clutch. Rotate the output shaft slowly to engage the splines of the input shaft into the clutch while pushing the transmission forward into place. Do not force the transmission into position, the transmission will easily fall into place when everything is properly aligned.

22. Once the transmission is properly positioned, install the retaining bolts and tighten to 55 ft. lbs. (75 Nm).

23. If removed, install the crossmember to the vehicle.

24. Install or connect the necessary support braces.

25. If removed, install the catalytic converter support hanger.

26. Install the transmission mount bolts and tighten to 37 ft. lbs. (50 Nm).

27. Install the slave cylinder to the transmission. If the hydraulic line was disconnected, the system will have to be bled of air.

28. Connect the exhaust pipes.

29. For 2.2L engines, secure the fuel lines to the top cover.

30. For 1992–96 4.3L engines, connect the fuel lines at the engine.

31. Engage the necessary wiring harness connectors, including the reverse light switch and the VSS.

32. For 4WD vehicles, install the transfer case.

33. If equipped, install the skid plate.

34. Align and install the driveshaft.

35. Connect and adjust the parking brake cable.

36. Carefully lower the vehicle.

37. Install the shift lever.

38. Connect the negative battery cable.

EXCEPT S/T-SERIES

1. Disconnect the negative battery cable.

2. Shift the transmission into neutral and remove the shift lever boot.

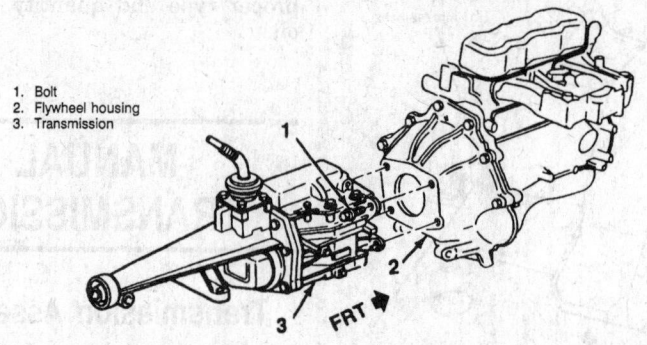

1. Bolt
2. Flywheel housing
3. Transmission

Borg-Warner T-5 manual transmission — S/T-Series

Raise and support the vehicle safely. Drain the fluid.

3. Remove the shift lever assembly. Remove the parking brake cables for clearance.

4. Remove the driveshaft and skid plate. If equipped, drain and remove the transfer case.

5. Disconnect the speedometer cable at the transmission. Disconnect all electrical wires, as required.

6. Disconnect and remove exhaust components, as required. Remove the fuel lines, as required. Properly support the transmission assembly. Remove the clutch slave cylinder from its mounting.

7. Remove the transmission assembly retaining bolts. Remove the transmission crossmember retaining bolts. Remove the transmission mount retaining bolts. Remove the crossmember.

8. Properly support the clutch release bearing. Remove the engine-to-transmission bolts.

9. Properly support the engine assembly. Carefully remove the transmission assembly.

To install:

10. Put a thin layer of high temperature grease on the transmission main shaft. Shift the transmission into high gear (5th) before installing. Carefully install the transmission assembly onto the engine. Rotate the transmission clockwise onto the clutch hub splines.

11. Install the engine-to-transmission bolts and torque to specification.

12. Install the crossmember and retaining bolts.

13. Install the exhaust system. Install the fuel lines. Install the clutch slave cylinder.

14. Connect the speedometer cable at the transmission. Connect all electrical wires, as required.

15. Install the driveshaft and skid plate. Install the transfer case and fill with the proper type and quantity of oil. Fill the transmission with the proper type and quantity of oil.

16. Install the parking brake cables.

17. Lower the vehicle.

18. Install the shift lever assembly. Connect the negative battery cable. Check for proper clutch operation.

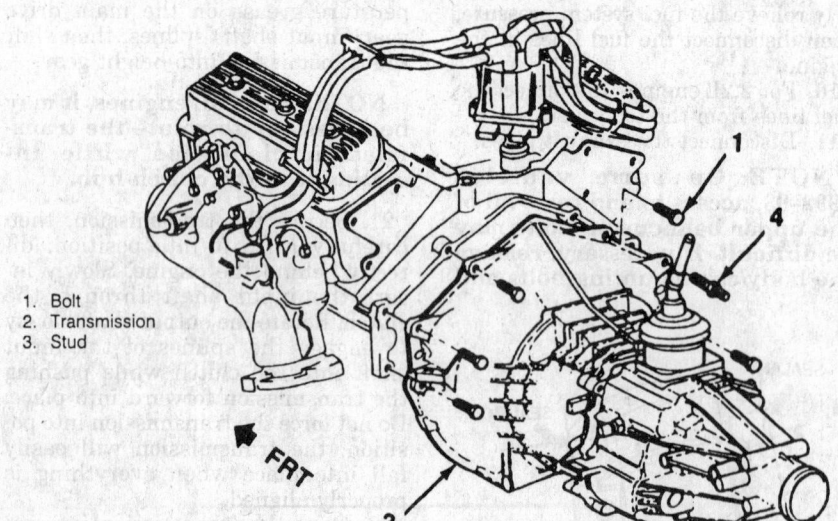

1. Bolt
2. Transmission
3. Stud

New Venture Gear 5LM60 manual transmission — S/T-Series

R/V-SERIES

1. Raise and support the vehicle safely.

2. Drain the transmission.

3. Disconnect the speedometer cable/sensor and back-up light wire at transmission.

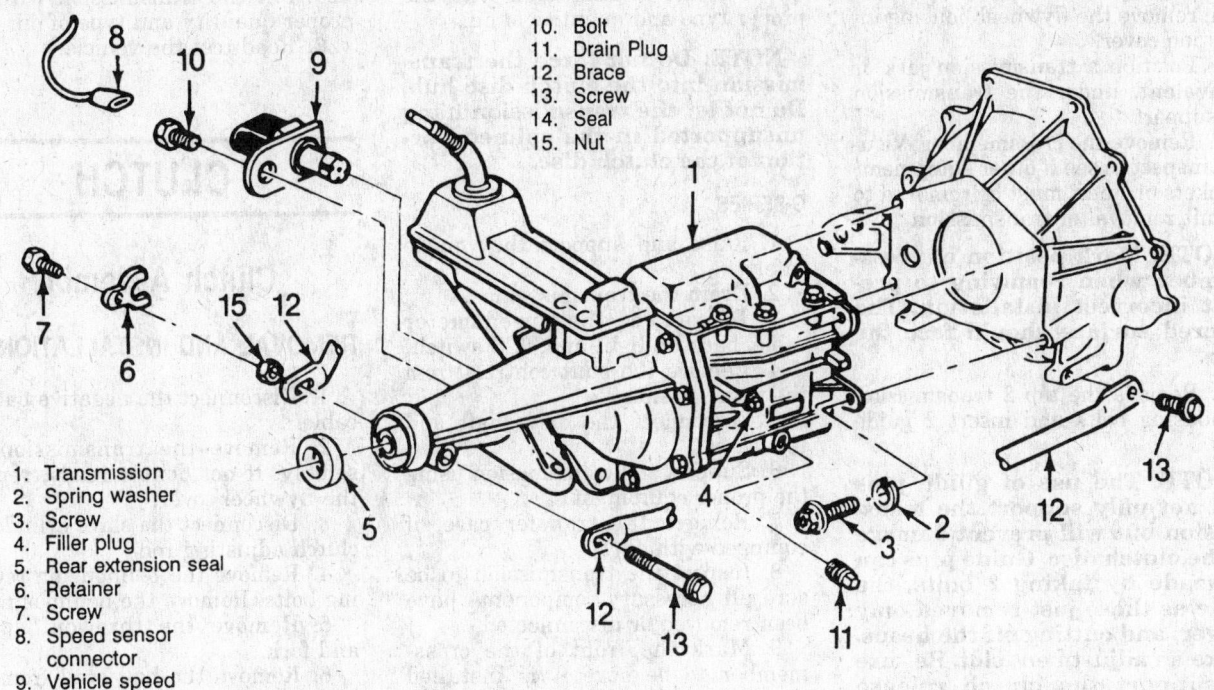

10. Bolt
11. Drain Plug
12. Brace
13. Screw
14. Seal
15. Nut

1. Transmission
2. Spring washer
3. Screw
4. Filler plug
5. Rear extension seal
6. Retainer
7. Screw
8. Speed sensor connector
9. Vehicle speed sensor

85473160

Manual transmission assembly — M/L-Series

4. Remove the shifter boot. Remove the gearshift lever by pressing down firmly on the slotted collar plate with a pair of channel lock pliers and rotating counterclockwise. Plug the opening to keep out dirt.

5. Remove the transfer case, if equipped with 4WD.

6. Remove driveshaft after marking the position of the shaft to the flange.

7. Remove the exhaust and parking brake cables, as required. Position a transmission jack under the transmission to support it.

8. Remove the crossmember. Visually inspect to see if other equipment, brackets or lines, must be removed to permit removal of transmission.

NOTE: Mark position of crossmember when removing to prevent incorrect installation. The tapered surface should face the rear.

9. Remove the flywheel housing underpan.

10. Remove the top 2 transmission to housing bolts and insert 2 guide pins.

NOTE: The use of guide pins will not only support the transmission but will prevent damage to the clutch disc. Guide pins can be made by taking 2 bolts, the

same as those just removed only longer, and cutting off the heads. Make a slot in the cut end of the bolt and use a suitable tool to install the special bolts. Be sure to support the clutch release bearing and support assembly during removal of the transmission. This will prevent the release from falling out of the flywheel housing.

11. Remove the 2 remaining bolts and slide transmission straight back from engine. Use care to keep the transmission drive gear straight in line with clutch disc hub.

12. Remove the transmission.

To install:

13. Place the transmission in high gear.

14. Coat the input shaft splines with high temperature grease.

15. Raise the transmission into position.

16. Install the guide pins in the top 2 bolt holes.

17. Roll the transmission forward and engage the clutch splines. Keep pushing the transmission forward until it mates with the engine.

18. Install the bolts, removing the guide pins. Torque the bolts to 75 ft. lbs.

19. Install the flywheel housing underpan.

20. Install the crossmember. Torque the crossmember-to-frame bolts to 55 ft. lbs.; the crossmember-to-transmission bolts to 40 ft. lbs.

21. Remove the transmission jack.

22. Install the driveshaft.

23. Install the gearshift lever.

24. Connect the speedometer cable/sensor and back-up light wire at transmission.

25. Fill the transmission with the proper quantity and type of oil.

NOTE: Do not force the transmission into the clutch disc hub. Do not let the transmission hang unsupported in the splined portion of the clutch disc.

C/K-SERIES

1. Disconnect the negative battery cable. Remove the shifter boot and lever.

2. Raise and support the vehicle safely. Drain the transmission.

3. Remove driveshaft after marking the position of the shaft to the axle flange.

4. Remove the exhaust pipes and parking brake cables.

5. Disconnect the wiring harness at the transmission.

6. Remove the transfer case, if equipped with 4WD.

7. Remove the clutch slave cylinder and support it out of the way.

8. On the 85mm (MG5) transmission, remove the flywheel housing inspection cover.

9. Position a transmission jack or equivalent, under the transmission for support.

10. Remove the crossmember. Visually inspect to see if other equipment, brackets or lines, must be removed to permit removal of transmission.

NOTE: Mark position of crossmember when removing to prevent incorrect installation. The tapered surface should face the rear.

11. Remove the top 2 transmission to housing bolts and insert 2 guide pins.

NOTE: The use of guide pins will not only support the transmission but will prevent damage to the clutch disc. Guide pins can be made by taking 2 bolts, the same as those just removed only longer, and cutting off the heads. Make an adjustment slot. Be sure to support the clutch release bearing and support assembly during removal of the transmission. This will prevent the release from falling out of the flywheel housing.

12. Remove the remaining bolts and slide transmission straight back from engine. Use care to keep the transmission drive gear straight in line with clutch disc hub.

13. Remove the transmission.

To install:

14. Place the transmission in high gear. Coat the input shaft splines with high temperature grease.

15. Raise the transmission into position.

16. Install the guide pins in the top 2 bolt holes.

17. Roll the transmission forward and engage the clutch splines. Keep pushing the transmission forward until it mates with the engine.

18. Install the bolts, removing the guide pins. Torque the bolts to specification.

19. Install the transfer case, if equipped.

20. Install the crossmember. Torque the crossmember bolts to specification. Remove the transmission jack.

21. Install the slave cylinder.

22. Install the driveshaft.

23. Install the exhaust system.

24. Install the inspection cover on the 85mm transmission.

25. Install the gearshift lever.

26. Connect the wiring harness at the transmission.

27. Fill the transmission with the proper type and quantity of oil.

NOTE: Do not force the transmission into the clutch disc hub. Do not let the transmission hang unsupported in the splined portion of the clutch disc.

G-SERIES

1. Raise and support the vehicle safely.

2. Drain the transmission.

3. Disconnect the speedometer cable, back-up light and TCS switch.

4. Remove the shift controls from the transmission.

5. Disconnect the driveshaft and remove it.

6. Support the transmission using the proper equipment.

7. Remove the transfer case, if equipped with 4WD.

8. Inspect the transmission to be sure all necessary components have been removed or disconnected.

9. Mark the front of the crossmember to be sure it is installed correctly.

10. Remove the flywheel housing under pan and transmission mounting bolts.

11. Move the transmission slowly away from the engine, keeping the mainshaft in alignment with the clutch disc hub. Support the clutch release bearing to prevent it from falling out of the flywheel housing when the transmission is removed.

12. Remove the transmission.

To install:

13. Lightly coat the mainshaft with high temperature grease. Do not use much grease, since, under normal operation, the grease will be thrown onto the clutch, causing it to fail.

14. Raise the transmission into position under the vehicle.

15. Roll the unit forward, engaging the spline of the mainshaft with the splines in the clutch hub. Continue pushing forward until the transmission mates with the bellhousing.

16. Install and tighten the transmission-to-bellhousing bolts. Install the transfer case, if equipped.

17. Install the flywheel housing under pan.

18. Install the crossmember. Torque the bolts to 50 ft. lbs.

19. Inspect the transmission to be sure all necessary components have been installed or connector.

20. Connect the driveshaft.

21. Install the shift controls.

22. Connect the speedometer cable.

23. Connect the back-up light switch.

24. Connect the TCS switch.

25. Fill the transmission with the proper quantity and type of oil.

26. Road test the vehicle.

CLUTCH

Clutch Assembly

REMOVAL AND INSTALLATION

1. Disconnect the negative battery cable.

2. Remove the transmission assembly. If not done already, remove the flywheel cover.

3. Disconnect the slave cylinder or clutch adjusting rod.

4. Remove the bellhousing retaining bolts. Remove the bellhousing.

5. Remove the throwout spring and fork.

6. Remove the ball stud from the bellhousing.

7. Install the clutch removal tool and support the clutch assembly.

NOTE: Before removing the clutch from the flywheel, matchmark the flywheel, clutch cover and 1 pressure plate lug, so these parts may be assembled in their same relative positions and retain the factory balance.

8. Loosen the clutch plate retaining bolts slowly and evenly 1 at a time until all pressure is released from the pressure plate assembly.

9. Remove the clutch, pressure plate and removal tool. Check the flywheel for damage, repair or replace, as required.

10. Check the clutch assembly, flywheel and pilot bearing for signs of wear, scoring, overheating, etc. If the clutch plate, flywheel or pressure plate is oil-soaked, inspect the engine rear main seal and the transmission input shaft seal and correct leakage as required. Replace any damaged parts.

To install:

11. Assemble the pressure plate and disc assembly, as required.

NOTE: The manufacturer recommends that new pressure plate bolts and washers be used.

12. Turn the flywheel until the previously applied mark is at the bottom.

13. Install the clutch disc, pressure plate and cover, using a suitable clutch aligning tool.

1. Lubrication fitting (R/V and C/K models only)
2. Clutch fork
3. Spring washer
4. Screw
5. Flywheel housing
6. Screw
7. Ball stud
8. Boot
9. Retainer
10. Release bearing
11. Cover assembly
12. Driveplate
13. Cover
14. Screw
15. Pilot bearing
16. Screw
17. Strap
18. Pressure plate

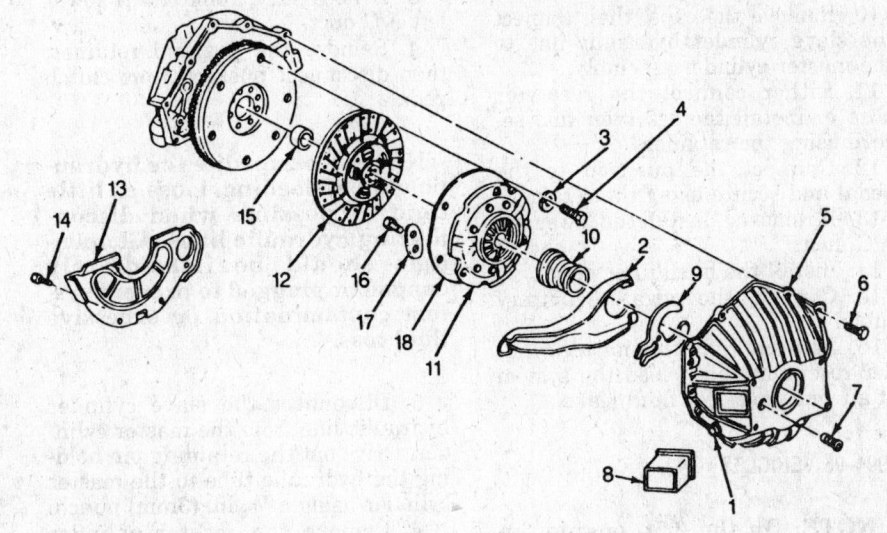

85473161

Exploded view of typical clutch assembly

14. Turn the clutch until the matchmark on the clutch cover aligns with the mark on the flywheel.

15. Install the attaching bolts and tighten them a little at a time in a crossing pattern until the spring pressure is taken up.

16. Remove the aligning tool.

17. Coat the rounded end of the ball stud with high temperature wheel bearing grease.

18. Install the ball stud in the bellhousing. Pack the ball stud from the lubrication fitting.

19. Pack the inside recess and the outside groove of the release bearing with high temperature wheel bearing grease and install the release bearing and fork. The fork must be installed so the fingers and tabs fit into the groove of the release bearing.

20. Install the release bearing seat and spring.

21. Install the bellhousing and retaining bolts, as required.

22. Install the slave cylinder or clutch rod.

23. Install the transmission and the flywheel cover.

24. Connect the negative battery cable.

25. Bleed the hydraulic system or adjust the clutch as required.

FREE PEDAL TRAVEL ADJUSTMENT

Mechanical Clutch

1. This adjustment is for the amount of clutch pedal free travel before the throwout bearing contacts the clutch release fingers. It is required periodically to compensate for clutch lining wear. Incorrect adjustment will cause gear grinding and clutch slippage or wear.

2. Raise and support the vehicle safely. Disconnect the clutch fork return spring at the fork on the clutch housing.

3. Loosen the outer locknut on the adjusting rod.

4. Move the clutch fork back until clutch spring pressure is felt.

5. Hold the clutch pedal against its bumper and turn the inner adjusting nut until it is 0.28 in. (7.1mm) from the cross lever.

6. Tighten the locknut against the cross lever.

7. Install the return spring.

8. Check the free travel at the pedal and readjust as necessary. It should be 1⅜ in. (34mm).

Clutch Master Cylinder

REMOVAL AND INSTALLATION

S/T-Series

EXCEPT 1994–96 VEHICLES

1. Disconnect the negative battery cable.

2. Remove hush panel or lower filler panel from under the dash.

3. If necessary, remove the lower left A/C duct.

4. Remove the pushrod retainer, then disconnect pushrod from clutch pedal.

5. Either disconnect the reservoir hose (if the reservoir is not being removed or if there is no clearance for reservoir removal with the hose installed) or remove the reservoir retainers.

6. Disconnect slave cylinder hydraulic line from the clutch master cylinder. Immediately plug all openings to prevent system contamination or excessive fluid loss.

7. Remove the master cylinder-to-cowl brace nuts. Remove master cylinder and overhaul (if necessary).

To install:

8. Using a gasket scraper, carefully clean all old gasket material

from the master cylinder and cowl mounting surfaces.

9. Install the master cylinder to the cowl using a new gasket. Tighten the retainers to 13 ft. lbs. (18 Nm).

10. Remove the caps, then connect the slave cylinder hydraulic line to the master cylinder assembly.

11. Either connect the reservoir hose or install the reservoir and secure using the retainers.

12. Connect the pushrod to the pedal and secure using the retainer.

13. If removed, install the lower left A/C duct.

14. Install the hush/filler panel.

15. Connect the negative battery cable.

16. Properly refill the master cylinder reservoir, then bleed the system of air and check for fluid leaks.

1994–96 VEHICLES

NOTE: On the 2.2L engine, individual components of the clutch actuating system (master cylinder/slave cylinder) may not be available for service. If so it is recommended that a complete, pre-filled and pre-bled unit should be installed and NO attempts should be made to disconnect the hydraulic lines.

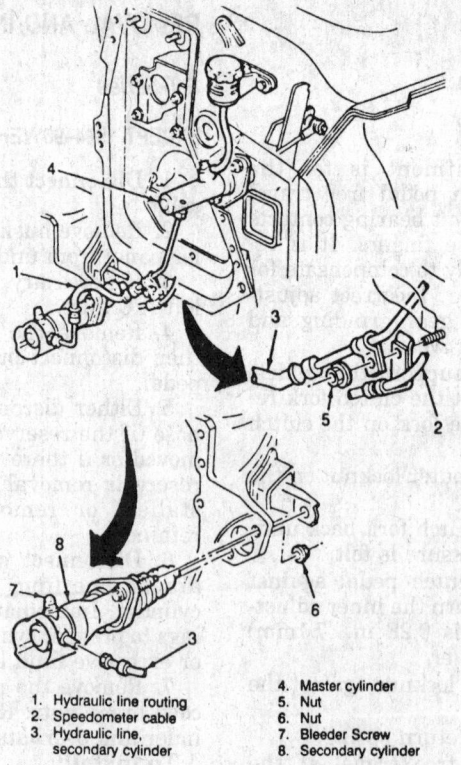

1. Hydraulic line routing
2. Speedometer cable
3. Hydraulic line, secondary cylinder
4. Master cylinder
5. Nut
6. Nut
7. Bleeder Screw
8. Secondary cylinder

85473162

Common slave cylinder mounting

1. Disconnect the negative battery cable.

2. Remove lower filler panel from under the dash.

3. If necessary, remove the lower left A/C duct.

4. Remove the pushrod retainer, then disconnect pushrod from clutch pedal.

NOTE: To expedite the hydraulic clutch bleeding, loose as little fluid as possible when disconnecting hydraulic lines. All openings should be immediately capped or plugged to prevent system contamination or excessive fluid loss.

5. Disconnect the slave cylinder hydraulic line from the master cylinder. Drive out the retaining pin holding the hydraulic tube to the master cylinder using a 7/64 in. (3mm) punch.

6. Remove the master cylinder from the cowl panel by grasping the cylinder body and rotating it about 45 degrees clockwise, then withdrawing it from the opening.

To install:

7. Hold the master cylinder assembly at a 45 degree angle (as during removal), then install the master cylinder to the cowl by inserting and twisting counterclockwise 45 degrees. Be sure not to over rotate the cylinder assembly or damage will occur.

NOTE: Use a new retaining pin and quad seal during hydraulic line installation.

8. Remove the caps, then connect the slave cylinder hydraulic line to the master cylinder assembly.

9. Connect the pushrod to the pedal and secure using the retainer.

10. If removed, install the lower left A/C duct.

11. Install the lower filler panel.

12. Connect the negative battery cable.

13. Properly refill the master cylinder reservoir, then bleed the system of air and check for fluid leaks.

Except S/T-Series

1. Disconnect the negative battery cable.

2. Remove the lower steering column cover(s) for access.

3. If necessary, remove the lower left side air conditioning duct.

4. Disconnect the pushrod from the clutch pedal.

5. If equipped, disconnect the remote reservoir hose.

6. Disconnect and plug the secondary cylinder hydraulic line to the master cylinder.

7. Remove the master cylinder retaining nuts and remove the master cylinder.

8. To install, use a new gasket, reverse the removal procedure and bleed the clutch system.

Clutch Slave Cylinder

REMOVAL AND INSTALLATION

S/T-Series

EXCEPT 1994–96 VEHICLES

1. Disconnect the negative battery cable.

2. Raise and support the front of the vehicle safely.

3. Disconnect the hydraulic line from clutch master cylinder. Immediately plug or cap all openings to prevent system contamination or excessive fluid loss. If equipped, remove the hydraulic line-to-chassis screw and the clip from the chassis.

4. Remove the slave cylinder-to-bellhousing nuts.

5. Remove the pushrod and the slave cylinder assembly from the vehicle, then overhaul it (if necessary).

To install:

6. Remove the plugs or caps, then install and secure the hydraulic line to the slave cylinder.

NOTE: If used, be sure to properly install the clip and hydraulic line-to-chassis screw.

7. Properly bleed the hydraulic system.

8. Install the slave cylinder to the bellhousing, then secure using the retaining nuts and tighten to 13 ft. lbs. (18 Nm).

9. Carefully lower the vehicle.

10. Connect the negative battery cable.

1994–96 VEHICLES

NOTE: On the 2.2L engine, individual components of the clutch actuating system (master cylinder/slave cylinder) may not be available for service. If so it is recommended that a complete, pre-filled and pre-bled unit should be installed and NO attempts should be made to disconnect the hydraulic lines.

1. Disconnect the master cylinder pushrod from the clutch pedal assembly.

NOTE: The master cylinder pushrod should be disconnected to protect the slave cylinder while it is removed from the bellhousing. If not, any attempt to depress the clutch pedal while the slave cylinder is withdrawn from the bellhousing will cause permanent damage to the slave cylinder assembly.

2. Using a 7/64 in. (3mm) punch to drive out the roll pin, disconnect the hydraulic line from the slave cylinder assembly. Immediately cap or plug all openings to prevent system contamination or excessive fluid loss.

NOTE: To expedite the hydraulic clutch bleeding process, loose as little fluid as possible.

3. Remove the slave cylinder-to-bellhousing retaining nuts.

4. Remove the slave cylinder from the bellhousing.

To install:

5. Install the slave cylinder to the bellhousing, then tighten the retaining nuts to 18 ft. lbs. (24 Nm).

6. Uncover the hydraulic line openings, then connect the hydraulic line to the slave cylinder using a new O-ring (lightly lubricated with fluid) and a new roll pin.

7. Connect the master cylinder pushrod to the clutch pedal assembly.

8. Properly bleed the hydraulic system, then check for leaks.

Except S/T-Series

1. Disconnect the negative battery cable.

2. Raise the vehicle and support it safely.

3. Disconnect and plug the hydraulic line at the slave cylinder.

4. Remove the slave cylinder retaining bolts. Remove the slave cylinder.

5. Installation is the reverse of the removal procedure. Bleed the system, as required.

Hydraulic Clutch System Bleeding

Bleeding air from the hydraulic clutch system is necessary whenever any part of the system has been disconnected or the fluid level (in the reservoir) has been allowed to fall so low, that air has been drawn into the master cylinder.

Except 1994–96 S/T-Series

1. Fill master cylinder reservoir with new brake fluid conforming to Dot 3 specifications.

— **CAUTION** —

Never, under any circumstances, use fluid which has been bled from a system to fill the reservoir as it may be aerated, have too much moisture content and possibly be contaminated.

2. Raise and support vehicle safely.

3. Remove the slave cylinder retainers.

4. Hold slave cylinder at approximately 45 degrees with the bleeder screw located at the highest point. Have an assistant fully depress and hold the clutch pedal, then open the bleeder screw.

5. Close the bleeder screw and have your assistant release the clutch pedal.

6. Repeat the procedure until all of the air is evacuated from the system. Check and refill master cylinder reservoir as required to prevent air from being drawn through the master cylinder.

NOTE: Never release a depressed clutch pedal with the bleeder screw open or air will be drawn into the system.

7. Test the clutch for proper operation.

1994–96 S/T-Series

1. Fill master cylinder reservoir with new brake fluid conforming to Dot 3 specifications.

— **CAUTION** —

Never, under any circumstances, use fluid which has been bled from a system to fill the reservoir as it may be aerated, have too much moisture content and possibly be contaminated.

2. Have an assistant fully depress and hold the clutch pedal, then open the bleeder screw.

3. Close the bleeder screw and have your assistant release the clutch pedal.

4. Repeat the procedure until all of the air is evacuated from the system. Check and refill master cylinder reservoir as required to prevent air from being drawn through the master cylinder.

NOTE: Never release a depressed clutch pedal with the bleeder screw open or air will be drawn into the system.

5. If the previous steps do not result in satisfactory pedal feel, remove the reservoir cap and pump the clutch pedal very fast for 30 seconds. Stop to let the air escape, then repeat the procedure as necessary to purge all remaining air.

6. Test the clutch for proper operation.

AUTOMATIC TRANSMISSION

Transmission Assembly

REMOVAL AND INSTALLATION

S/T-Series

1992–93 VEHICLES

1. Properly relieve the fuel system pressure, then disconnect the negative battery cable.

2. Remove the air cleaner assembly. If equipped (4L60 model), disconnect the TV cable from the TBI unit.

3. Raise and support the vehicle safely.

4. Drain the transmission fluid.

5. Disconnect the shift linkage from the transmission.

6. Disconnect and remove the fuel lines.

7. Matchmark and remove the front (if used) and rear driveshafts.

8. Remove the support bracket at the catalytic converter. Remove any components necessary for clearance.

9. Support the transmission assembly.

10. Remove the transmission crossmember. Take care not to stretch or damage any cables or wiring when attempting to remove the crossmember.

11. Lower the transmission slightly for access, then remove the dipstick tube and seal. Cover or plug the opening in the transmission housing to prevent system contamination.

12. Disengage the speedometer harness connector and the vacuum modulator line, if used.

13. Disengage the necessary electrical wiring connectors from the transmission assembly.

14. Disconnect the transmission fluid cooler lines. Plug or cap all openings to prevent system contamination or excessive fluid spillage.

15. On 4WD vehicles, disengage the transfer case shifter and position it aside.

16. Remove the transmission support braces. Be sure to tag or note the location of all support braces as they must be installed in their original positions.

17. Remove the torque converter housing cover.

18. Matchmark the flywheel-to-torque converter relationship, then remove the retaining bolts.

19. Support the engine.

20. Remove the transmission-to-engine retaining bolts. Note the positions of any brackets or clips and move them aside.

21. Slide the transmission straight back off the locating pins. Be careful not to drop the torque converter, then as soon as access is possible, install a torque converter retaining strap.

22. Carefully lower the transmission.

To install:

23. Make sure the torque converter is properly seated and a retaining strap is installed.

24. Carefully raise the transmission into position in the vehicle, then remove the converter retaining strap. Slide the transmission straight onto the locating pins while aligning the marks on the flywheel and torque converter.

NOTE: The converter must be flush on the flywheel and rotate freely by hand.

25. Install the transmission-to-engine retainers, taking care to properly reposition all brackets, clips and harness, as noted during removal. The retainers should not be torqued yet. Do not install the dipstick tube or transmission support brace screws at this time.

26. Install and finger-tighten the converter bolts, then tighten them to 50 ft. lbs. (68 Nm).

27. Remove the support from the engine.

28. Install the converter housing cover.

29. Install the transmission support braces as noted during removal.

30. On 4WD vehicles, connect the transfer case shifter assembly.

31. Uncap the openings, then connect the transmission cooler lines. Be careful not to twist or bend the lines.

32. If used, connect the vacuum modulator line.

33. Engage the speedometer harness connector and the remaining electrical wiring to the transmission housing.

34. Uncover the opening in the transmission housing and position a new seal, then install the dipstick tube.

35. Tighten the transmission-to-engine retainers and the dipstick tube retainer, then tighten the bolts to 23 ft. lbs. (32 Nm).

36. Raise the rear of the transmission (taking care not to pinch or damage any cables, wires or components), then install the crossmember. Secure the transmission mount and any components which were removed for access.

37. Remove the support from the transmission, then install the catalytic converter bracket.

38. Align and install the front, if equipped, and rear driveshafts.

39. Connect the fuel lines.

40. Connect the shift linkage and adjust, as necessary.

41. Refill the transmission using fresh fluid.

42. Carefully lower the vehicle.

43. If equipped, engage the TV cable, then check and adjust, as necessary.

44. Connect the negative battery cable, then check for proper operation.

1994–96 VEHICLES

1. Properly relieve the fuel system pressure, then disconnect the negative battery cable.

2. Raise and support the vehicle safely.

3. Drain the transmission fluid.

4. Disconnect the shift linkage from the transmission.

5. Matchmark and remove the rear driveshaft.

6. For 4WD vehicles, remove the transfer case assembly.

7. Disconnect the fuel lines.

8. Remove the transmission crossmember-to-frame retaining bolts and member-to-transmission retainer(s), then remove the crossmember. Take care not to stretch or damage any cables or wiring when attempting to remove the crossmember.

9. Disconnect the exhaust pipe(s) from the manifold(s).

10. Remove the flywheel inspection cover and matchmark the flywheel-to-torque converter relationship, then remove the flywheel-to-torque converter bolts.

11. Remove the fuel lines and wiring harness from the transmission.

12. Make sure the transmission is properly supported, then remove the transmission-to-engine bolts. Note the positioning of any brackets, clips or harnesses as they are removed.

13. Remove the dipstick tube and seal, then plug or cover the opening in the transmission housing in order to prevent system contamination.

14. Disconnect the cooler lines. Plug or cover all openings in order to prevent system contamination or excessive fluid spillage.

15. Support the engine.

16. Support the transmission, pull it straight back and disengage it from the engine. Carefully lower the transmission and remove it. If possible, install a torque converter retaining strap before attempting to lower the transmission. This will prevent the converter from possibly falling and causing damage and/or personal injury.

To install:

17. Make sure the torque converter is properly seated and a retaining strap is installed.

18. Carefully raise the transmission into position in the vehicle, then remove the converter retaining strap. Slide the transmission straight onto the locating pins while aligning the marks on the flywheel and torque converter.

NOTE: The converter must be flush on the flywheel and rotate freely by hand.

19. Install the transmission-to-engine retainers, taking care to properly reposition all brackets, clips and harness, as noted during removal. Do not install the dipstick tube or transmission support brace screws at this time.

20. Tighten the transmission-to-engine retainers to 23 ft. lbs. (32 Nm).

21. Connect the transmission cooler lines.

22. Remove the plug from the opening, then position a new seal to the transmission and install the dipstick tube.

23. If equipped, install the transfer case support rods to the transmission housing.

24. Install the wiring harness and fuel lines to the transmission housing.

25. Make sure the matchmarks are aligned, then install and finger-tighten the flywheel-to-converter bolts. Once the converter is properly seated by finger-tightening the bolts, torque them to 46 ft. lbs. (63 Nm).

26. Hook the edge of the flywheel inspection cover under the lip of the engine oil pan, then install and secure the cover.

27. Connect the exhaust pipe(s) to the manifold(s).

28. Install the transmission crossmember to the vehicle. Tighten the member-to-frame bolts to 56 ft. lbs. (77 Nm).

29. On 4WD vehicles, install the transfer case assembly.

30. Align and install the rear driveshaft.

31. Connect the shift linkage then check and adjust, as necessary.

32. Refill the transmission using fresh fluid.

33. Carefully lower the vehicle.

34. Connect the negative battery cable, then check for proper operation.

M/L-Series

1. Disconnect the negative battery cable. Remove the air cleaner assembly. Disconnect the throttle valve cable and the throttle linkage.

2. Raise and support the vehicle safely.

3. Drain the transmission fluid. Disconnect the shift linkage. Properly relieve the fuel system pressure and remove the fuel lines.

4. Remove the driveshaft. If equipped with a transfer case, also remove the front driveshaft.

5. Disconnect and remove all required exhaust system components. Support the transmission using the proper equipment.

6. Remove the crossmember retaining bolts. Remove the transmission mount retaining bolts. Remove the crossmember from the vehicle and lower the transmission enough to gain access to other components.

7. Remove the transmission dipstick and tube. Disconnect the speedometer cable. If equipped, disconnect the vacuum modulator line.

8. Disconnect all electrical connections from the transmission assembly. Disconnect and plug the fluid cooler lines.

9. Remove the damper and support, as required. Remove the flywheel housing cover and torque converter to flywheel bolts. If equipped, remove the transfer case assembly.

10. Properly support the engine assembly. Remove the transmission to engine retaining bolts. Carefully remove the automatic transmission.

To install:

11. Install the transmission into position, making sure the converter is properly seated.

12. Install the engine-to-transmission and torque converter-to-flywheel bolts. Torque the bolts to specification.

13. Install the converter housing cover. Install the damper and support.

14. Connect all electrical leads to the transmission and connect the speedometer cable.

15. Install the dipstick tube. Install the crossmember and install the transmission mount retaining bolts. Reconnect the fuel lines.

16. Connect all exhaust system components. Install the front driveshaft on 4WD vehicles.

17. Connect the shift linkage and install the skid plate, if equipped. Lower the vehicle.

18. Connect the TV cable and throttle linkage.

19. Install the air cleaner assembly. Connect the negative battery cable.

20. Check the fluid level and operation of the transmission.

Full Size Pick-Up, Van and Utility

NOTE: It may be necessary to disconnect and remove the exhaust crossover pipe on 8-cylinder engines, and to disconnect the catalytic converter and remove its support bracket, if equipped.

2WD

1. Disconnect the battery ground cable. Remove the air cleaner and disconnect the detent cable.

2. Raise and support the vehicle safely. Drain the transmission.

3. Matchmark the axle-to-driveshaft flanges and remove the driveshaft.

4. Disconnect the speedometer cable, downshift cable, vacuum modulator line, shift linkage, throttle linkage, fuel lines and fluid cooler lines at the transmission, as required. Remove the filler tube.

5. Support the transmission. Unbolt and remove the crossmember.

6. Remove the torque converter underpan, Matchmark the flywheel and converter, and remove the converter bolts.

7. Support the engine and lower the transmission slightly for access to the upper transmission to engine bolts.

8. Remove the transmission to engine bolts and pull the transmission back and out of the vehicle.

NOTE: Keep the front of the transmission up so the converter doesn't fall out.

9. Installation is the reverse of the removal procedure.

NOTE: Lubricate the internal yoke splines at the transmission end of the driveshaft with lithium base grease.

4WD

1. Disconnect the battery ground cable and remove the transmission dipstick. Detach the downshift cable. Remove the transfer case shift lever knob and boot.

2. Raise and support the vehicle safely.

3. Remove the skid plate, if any. Remove the flywheel cover.

4. Matchmark the flywheel and torque converter, remove the bolts and secure the converter so it doesn't fall out of the transmission.

5. Detach the shift linkage, speedometer cable, vacuum modulator line, downshift cable, throttle linkage and cooler times at the transmission. Remove the filler tube.

6. Remove the exhaust crossover pipe to manifold bolts.

7. Unbolt the transfer case adapter from the crossmember. Support the transmission and transfer case. Remove the crossmember.

8. Move the exhaust system aside. Detach the driveshafts after matchmarking their flanges. Disconnect the parking brake cable.

9. Unbolt the transfer case from the frame bracket. Support the engine. Unbolt the transmission from

the engine, pull the assembly back, and remove.

10. Reverse the procedure for installation.

SHIFT LINKAGE ADJUSTMENT

The shift linkage should be adjusted so transmission is in the proper gear when the selector is in the shift gate. The shift indicator position should not be relied on, instead, make sure the shifter properly engages each gate position when the transmission is shifted to each gear. After adjustment, check the back-up light/neutral safety switch to be sure the engine will only start when the transmission is in the **P** or Neutral positions.

1. Raise and support the vehicle safely.

2. At the side of the transmission, loosen the shift rod swivel-to-equalizer lever nut or retaining bolt, as equipped.

3. Inside the vehicle, place the gear selector lever into the Neutral position.

4. Rotate the transmission shift lever to the 1st detent **P** position, then turn it to the 3rd detent (Neutral) position.

5. Tightly, hold the shifting rod (swivel) in position, then tighten torque the adjusting nut or bolt, as applicable.

6. Place the gear selector lever in the **P** position and check the adjustment. Move the gear selector lever into the various positions; the engine must start in the **P** and the Neutral positions.

NOTE: If the engine will not start in the Neutral and/or P positions (or will start in gear), properly adjust the back-up light/neutral safety switch.

7. Align the gear selector lever indicator, if necessary.

8. Remove the supports and carefully lower the vehicle.

NEUTRAL START SWITCH ADJUSTMENT

The back-up lamp/neutral safety switch assembly is mounted either on the steering column or on the floor shifter assembly, under the console, depending on the vehicle and application. Most models utilize a steering column mounted shifter for the automatic transmission, therefore the switch will be found on the steering column for most vehicles. Although the switch is also responsible for activating the reverse lights on most ve-

hicles, its primary purpose is to prevent the engine from starting unless the shifter is in Neutral or **P**.

Column Mounted Switch

Two type of switches are generally found on these vehicles. Some early models will be equipped with adjustable switches which are bolted into position. Most vehicles covered by this manual should be equipped with ratcheting self-adjusting switches.

1. Disconnect the negative battery cable.

2. If necessary for access, remove the steering column insulator/filler panel for access to the switch.

3. Disengage the electrical harness connector from the switch.

4. Certain early model vehicles utilize a switch which is bolted in position. If equipped, remove the retaining bolts.

5. Remove the switch by grasping and pulling it straight out of the steering column jacket.

To install:

6. If equipped with an early model switch which is bolted into position, the switch should be equipped with a gauge hole for adjustment. If equipped, loosely install the switch to the column and adjust.

7. Most vehicles utilize a self-adjusting (ratcheting) switch. To install:

a. Align the actuator on the switch with the holes in the shift tube.

b. Set the parking brake and place the gear selector in Neutral.

c. Press down on the front of the switch until the tangs snap into the rectangular holes in the steering column jacket.

d. Adjust the switch by moving the gear selector to **P**. The main housing and the housing back should ratchet, providing the proper switch adjustment.

8. Engage the harness connector to the switch.

9. Connect the negative battery cable, then verify proper switch operation. Make sure the reverse lights work and that the ignition will only work in the Neutral or **P** positions. If necessary, readjust the switch. For ratcheting type switches, move the gear selector all the way to the **L** position, then repeat the adjustment.

10. If applicable, install the steering column insulator/filler panel.

Floor Console Mounted Switch

1. Disconnect the negative battery cable.

2. Remove the center console for access to the switch assembly.

3. Disengage the switch electrical connector.

4. Remove the retaining nuts, then remove the switch.

5. If necessary, remove the gauge pin from the switch.

6. If installing a new switch:

a. Place the shift control lever in Neutral.

b. Align the carrier tang on the back-up lamp/neutral safety switch with the slot on the shifter.

NOTE: Replacement switches are pinned in the Neutral position to ease installation. If the switch has been rotated or the switch is broken, install the switch using the "old switch" installation and adjustment procedure.

c. Tighten the switch retaining nuts, then engage the switch connector.

d. Move the shift control lever out of Neutral in order to shear the plastic pin, then remove the accessible piece(s) of the gauge pin.

7. If installing an old switch, install and adjust the switch to assure proper operation:

a. Place the shift control lever in Neutral.

b. Align the carrier tang on the switch with the slot on the shifter.

c. Loosely install the retaining switch nuts and engage the wiring connector.

d. Rotate the switch to align the service adjustment hole with the carrier tang hold, then use a 0.09 in. (2.34mm) gauge pin to complete adjustment. Insert the pin in the service adjustment hole and rotate the switch until it drops to a depth of 0.59 in. (15mm). Hold the switch in this position and tighten the retaining nuts.

8. Install the center console.

9. Connect the negative battery cable.

10. Verify proper switch operation.

THROTTLE VALVE (TV) CABLE ADJUSTMENT

1. If necessary for access, remove the air cleaner assembly.

2. If the cable has been removed and installed, pull on the upper end of the cable. It should travel a short distance with light resistance caused by the small return spring on the TV lever. When released, check to see that the cable slider returns to the 0

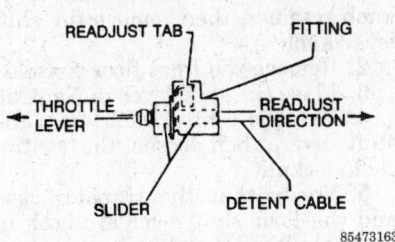

Throttle Valve (TV) Cable adjustment

or the fully adjusted position; if not, adjust the cable and slider:

a. Depress and hold the readjust tab on the end of the TV cable.

b. Move the slider back on the cable (away from the throttle lever) until it stops against the fitting.

c. Release the readjust tab.

3. Rotate the throttle lever by hand (do not use the accelerator pedal) to the full throttle stop (wide open throttle) position. The slider must move (ratchet) toward the lever in order to adjust the cable when the lever is rotated.

4. Release the throttle lever and check for proper operation.

NOTE: The throttle valve cable adjustment should be rechecked with the engine at normal operating temperature. A cable may adjustment may appear to function properly while the engine is cold, but no work properly when warmed.

AUTOMATIC TRANSAXLE

Transaxle Assembly

The automatic transaxle equipped in the Lumina, Silhouette and Trans Sport can only be removed as an assembly with the engine and transaxle/sub-frame.

REMOVAL AND INSTALLATION

1. Disconnect the negative battery cable.

2. Drain the cooling system. Disconnect the air flow tube from the air cleaner.

3. Disconnect the electrical connector from the ECM and push it through to the engine compartment. Disconnect the harness from the clips on the body and lay it across the engine.

4. Disconnect the engine harness at the bulkhead connector. Disconnect the throttle and TV cables.

5. Disconnect the fuel lines. Disconnect the transaxle shift linkage.

6. Disconnect the cooler lines at the radiator. Disconnect the radiator and heater hoses.

7. Remove the air conditioning compressor from the bracket and support it aside. Remove the upper engine support strut.

8. Raise and safely support the vehicle. Remove the front wheel and tire assemblies.

9. Remove the stabilizer bar. Disconnect the tie rod ends and the lower control arm ball joints.

10. Disconnect the halfhsafts and support them aside. Disconnect the steering shaft pinch bolt.

11. Remove the starter. Remove the torque converter bolts.

12. Disconnect the exhaust pipe at the manifold. Support the engine and sub-frame.

13. Remove the sub-frame bolts and lower the engine/transaxle and sub-frame. Remove the engine-to-transmission bolts.

To install:

14. Position the engine and transmission together in the subframe assembly and torque the engine-to-transmission bolts to 55 ft. lbs. (75 Nm). Raise the engine assembly into position and install the subframe bolts. Tighten to 38 ft. lbs. (52 Nm).

15. Connect the exhaust pipe at the rear manifold. Install the starter.

16. Connect the steering shaft and install the pinch bolt. Connect the halfshafts to the transaxle. Install the torque converter-to-flywheel bolts and torque to 35 ft. lbs. (47 Nm).

17. Connect the lower control arm ball joints to the steering knuckles.

18. Install the stabilizer bar. Install the upper engine strut.

19. Install the wheel and tire assemblies. Lower the vehicle. Install the radiator and heater hoses.

20. Install the shift linkage. Connect the fuel lines and the throttle and TV cables.

21. Connect the harness to bulkhead connector. Connect the ECM harness to the ECM.

22. Connect the air cleaner hose and the radiator upper support.

23. Fill the cooling system. Install the air conditioning compressor.

24. Connect the negative battery cable.

TV CABLE ADJUSTMENT

1. As required, remove the air cleaner assembly.

2. Depress and hold down the metal readjust tab at the engine end of the throttle valve cable.

3. Move the slider until it stops against the fitting. Release the readjustment tab.

4. Rotate the throttle lever to its full travel position. The slider must move toward the lever when the lever is rotated to its full travel position.

5. Check for proper operation. When the engine is cold, the cable may appear to be functioning properly, check the cable when the engine is hot.

6. Road test the vehicle.

NEUTRAL SAFETY SWITCH ADJUSTMENT

1. Place the transaxle in the **N** position.

2. Loosen the switch attaching screws.

3. Insert a $1/8$ in. gauge pin into the service adjustment hole.

4. Rotate the switch on the shifter assembly to align the service hole in the switch with the hole in the carrier. When the gauge pin drops into the service adjustment hole, tighten the bolts and nut.

5. Remove the gauge pin and check the operation of the switch.

6. The vehicle should only start in the **N** or **P** position.

TRANSFER CASE

Transfer Case Assembly

REMOVAL AND INSTALLATION

T-Series

1. Disconnect the negative battery cable.

2. Shift the transfer case into the **4HI** range.

3. Raise and support the vehicle safely.

4. If equipped, remove the skid plate bolts, then remove the skid plate from under the transmission/transfer case assembly.

5. Remove the plug and drain the transfer case fluid.

6. Matchmark and remove the front and rear driveshafts from the transfer case.

7. Tag and disconnect the vacuum lines and/or the electrical connectors, as equipped.

8. If applicable, disconnect the transfer case shift rod from the case.

9. If applicable, remove the support brace-to-transfer case bolts.

10. Support the transfer case, then remove the transfer case-to-transmission retaining bolts

11. Slide the transfer case rearward and off the transmission output shaft, then carefully lower it.

12. Remove all traces of old gasket material from the mating surfaces.

To install:

13. Carefully raise the transfer case into position behind the transmission. Position a new gasket, using sealer to hold it in position, then slide the transfer case onto the transmission output shaft.

14. Install the transfer case-to-transmission retaining bolts, then tighten to 24 ft. lbs. (33 Nm).

15. If equipped, install the support brace bolts and tighten to 35 ft. lbs. (47 Nm).

16. Remove the support from the transfer case.

17. If equipped, connect the shift rod to the case.

18. Engage the vacuum lines and/or electrical connections, as necessary.

19. Align and install the front and rear driveshafts.

20. Make sure the vehicle is level, then properly refill the transfer case through the filler plug.

21. If equipped, install the skid plate.

22. Carefully lower the vehicle.

23. Connect the negative battery cable.

Except T-Series

1. Disconnect the negative battery cable. If necessary, shift the transfer case into the **4HI** position to ease linkage removal.

2. Raise and support the vehicle safely.

3. If, equipped, remove the skid plate. Drain the fluid from the transfer case.

4. Drain the fluid from the transfer case.

5. Matchmark the transfer case front output shaft yoke and driveshaft for reassembly. Disconnect the driveshaft from the transfer case.

6. Matchmark the rear axle yoke and the driveshaft for reassembly. Remove the driveshaft.

7. If equipped, disconnect the speedometer cable.

8. Disconnect any vacuum or electrical connections at the transfer case.

9. If necessary, remove the parking cables.

10. If applicable, remove the catalytic converter hanger bolts at the converter assembly.

11. Support the transmission and transfer case assembly. If necessary, remove the transmission mount retaining bolts and lower the transmission and transfer case assembly to gain additional clearance.

12. Remove the transfer case retaining bolts.

13. As required, remove the shift lever bracket mounting bolts from the transfer case adapter in order to remove the upper left transfer case retaining bolt.

14. Separate the transfer case from its mounting and remove it.

15. Installation is the reverse of removal.

LINKAGE ADJUSTMENT

T-Series

1992

1. Remove the center console for access to the shift lever retainers.

2. Raise the floor shift lever boot upward on the lever.

3. Loosen the detent switch bracket retaining bolt and the floor shift lever pivot bolt (also threaded through the detent switch bracket).

4. Manually place the transfer case lever in the **4HI** position.

5. Install a suitable lock bolt to hold the transfer case lever in position.

6. Insert a 5/16 in. (8mm) drill bit (gauge pin) through the hole in the shift lever and into the upper corner of the switch bracket. This will assure that the switch is aligned with **4HI** position.

7. Tighten the floor shift lever pivot bolt to 75 ft. lbs. (102 Nm) and the detent switch bracket retaining bolt to 30 ft. lbs. (40 Nm).

8. Remove the lock bolt and the gauge pin/drill bit.

9. Verify proper shifting action.

10. Reposition the floor shift lever boot and install the center console.

1994–96 VEHICLES

1. Remove the floor shift lever knob retainer, then remove the shift lever knob

2. Remove the front floor console.

3. Place the shift lever in Neutral.

4. Pull the control cable from the shift lever, then loosen the control cable locknut.

5. Verify that the transfer case and the floor shift lever are both in Neutral. Turn the shift lever end of the cable in or out, as necessary, until it is aligned with the shifter.

6. Install the control cable to the shift lever.

7. Tighten the control cable locknut to 17 inch lbs. (1.9 Nm).

8. Verify proper shift operation.

9. Install the front floor console.

10. Install the shift lever knob and retainer.

L-Series

1. Remove the console assembly. Raise the shifter boot aside.

2. Loosen the selector lever retaining bolt. Loosen the shifter pivot bolt. Shift the transfer case into the **4HI** position.

3. Install a 5/16 in. (8mm) gauge pin through the shifter and into the bracket. Install a service bolt at the transfer case shift lever. This will lock the transfer case in the **4HI** position.

4. Tighten the selector lever retaining bolt 25–35 ft. lbs. Tighten the shifter pivot bolt 88–103 ft. lbs.

5. Remove the service bolt. Remove the gauge pin. Install the console and shifter boot.

6. Check for proper operation.

Full Size Pick-Up and Utility

MODEL NP241

1. Position the transfer case lever in the **4HI** detent. Push the lower shift lever forward to the **4HI** stop.

2. Install the rod swivel in the shift lever hole. Hang a 0.200 in. (5.19mm) gauge rod behind the swivel.

3. Install the rear rod nut against the gauge with the shifter against the **4HI** stop.

4. Remove the gauge tool. Push the rear of the swivel rearward against the nut.

5. Tighten the front rod nut against the swivel. Check for proper operation.

MODEL 205

1. Raise and support the vehicle safely. Remove the swivel from the transfer case shift lever.

2. Turn the swivel inward or outward to determine the correct shift detent.

3. Reinstall the swivel to the shift lever.

MODEL 1370

1. Position the transfer case lever in the **4HI** position.

2. Raise and support the vehicle safely.

3. Disconnect the linkage rod from the console shift lever.

4. Shift the transfer case into the **4HI** position (transfer shift lever in the forward detent).

5. Adjust the swivel to align with the hole in the console shift lever.

6. Lower the vehicle.

DRIVE AXLE

Halfshaft

REMOVAL AND INSTALLATION

L-Series and T-Series

1. Raise and support the vehicle safely. Remove the tire and wheel assemblies.

2. Remove the cotter pin, retainer, nut and washer. Remove the brake line support bracket.

3. Matchmark the axle tube-to-flange location. Loosen but do not remove the axle tube-to-flange bolts. Using the proper tools, remove the tie rods at the steering knuckles.

4. Remove the lower shock absorber retaining bolts and move the shock absorbers aside.

5. Separate the upper ball joint from the steering knuckle. Suspend the steering knuckle from the frame using a piece of wire.

6. As required, remove the skid plate. Remove the halfshaft to axle tube bolts.

7. Move the inner part of the halfshaft forward. Support it away from the frame. Using a suitable tool, remove the shaft from the hub and bearing assembly.

8. Remove the halfshaft.

To install:

9. Install the halfshaft into position. Push it into the hub.

10. Install the shaft retaining nut and washer. Tighten the halfshaft retaining nut to 160–200 ft. lbs. (220–270 Nm).

11. Install the cotter pin in the nut. Install the halfshaft-to-axle tube bolts and tighten to 60 ft. lbs. (80 Nm).

12. Install the lower shock absorber bolts. Connect the tie rods to the steering knuckle.

13. Install the skid plate, if equipped.

14. Install the wheel and tire assemblies. Lower the vehicle

Lumina APV, Silhouette and Trans Sport

1. Raise and safely support the vehicle.

2. Remove the tire and wheel assemblies.

3. Remove the halfshaft retaining nut and washer.

4. Remove the brake caliper from the rotor and support it aside.

5. Remove the brake rotor from the hub.

6. Disconnect the stabilizer shaft from the control arm and disconnect the ball joint from the steering knuckle.

7. Using a suitable axle seal protector to guard against possible boot damage. Remove the halfshaft from the transaxle using a suitable tool.

8. Remove the halfshaft from the hub and bearing assembly.

To install:

9. Install the halfshaft into the hub and bearing assembly.

10. Connect the lower ball joint to the steering knuckle.

11. Connect the stabilizer shaft to the control arm. Install the rotor.

12. Install the brake caliper. Install a new halfshaft nut and tighten the nut to 185 ft. lbs. (250 Nm).

13. Seat the halfshaft into the transaxle, by pushing it in firmly. Check that the shaft is seated by pulling on it.

14. Install the wheel and tire assemblies.

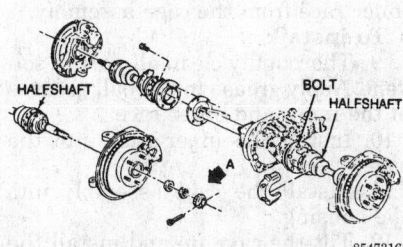

Front drive axle assembly

85473165

15. Lower the vehicle.

K-Series

1. Raise and support the vehicle safely.

2. Remove the wheel and tire assembly.

3. Remove the skid plate, as required.

4. Remove the drive axle hub nut and washer.

5. Remove the brake line support bracket from the upper control arm to allow extra travel of the control arm.

6. Remove the left outer tie rod attaching nut and cotter pin. Separate the tie rod from the steering knuckle using a suitable tie rod end splitter.

7. Position the tie rod aside and push steering linkage to the opposite side of the vehicle.

8. Remove the lower shock attaching nut and bolt; position the shock aside.

9. Remove the left stabilizer bar bracket and bushing at the frame. Remove the stabilizer bar bolt, spacer and bushings at the lower control arm.

10. Lower the vehicle, taking pressure off the upper control arm by placing a support below the lower control arm between the spring seat and the ball joint.

11. Remove the upper ball joint cotter pin and loosen (do not remove) the upper ball joint attaching nut. Using a suitable ball joint splitter, separate the ball joint stud from the steering knuckle. Remove the attaching nut.

NOTE: Cover the shock mounting bracket and lower ball joint stud with a towel to prevent the axle boot from tearing during Removal and Installation.

12. Separate the axle shaft from the hub and rotor using tool J–28733 or equivalent.

13. Remove the axle shaft inner flange bolts. Remove the shaft.

To install:

14. Lubricate the axle and hub splines with an approved high temperature wheel bearing grease. Position the shaft in the hub and install the inboard CV-joint-to-flange bolts.

15. Install the upper ball joint to steering knuckle and torque the stud nut to 61 ft. lbs. (83 Nm). Install a cotter pin through the upper ball joint stud and nut. Lubricate the ball joint as required.

16. Install the left stabilizer bar bracket and bushing at the frame. Install the stabilizer bar bolt, spacer and bushings at the lower control arm.

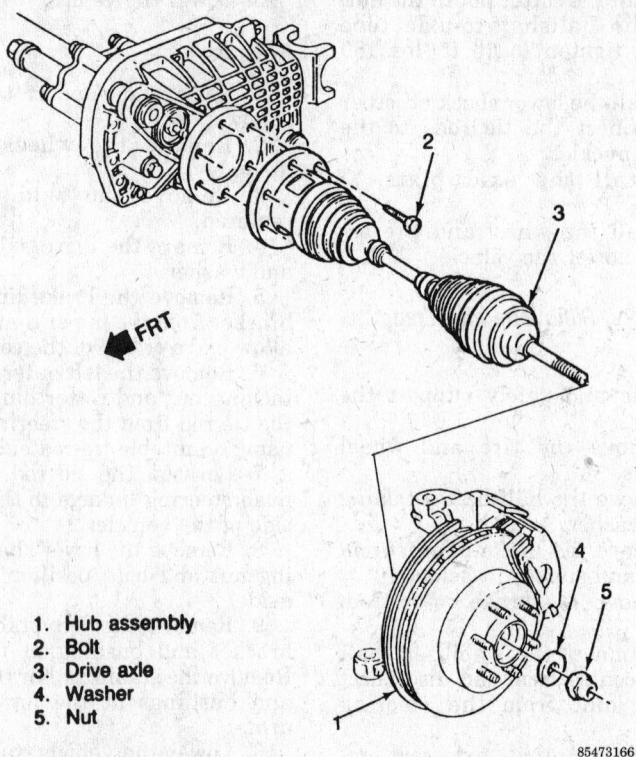

1. Hub assembly
2. Bolt
3. Drive axle
4. Washer
5. Nut

85473166

Front drive axle removal and installation — K-Series

17. Position the lower shock in the mount bracket and install the attaching nut and bolt.

18. Connect the left tie rod end at the steering knuckle. Torque the nut to 35 ft. lbs. (47 Nm). Install a cotter pin through the tie rod stud and nut.

19. Connect the brake line bracket to the control arm, ensuring the line and/or hose is not twisted or kinked.

20. Install the skid plate, as required.

21. Install the axle hub washer and nut. Insert a drift through the rotor vanes to keep the axle from turning and torque the hub nut to 180 ft. lbs. (245 Nm) and the inboard CV-joint flange bolts to 60 ft. lbs. (80 Nm).

22. Remove the drift, install the wheel and tire assembly. Remove stands and lower the vehicle.

CV-Boot and Joint

REMOVAL AND INSTALLATION

Outer

COMPACT PICK-UP, VAN AND UTILITY

1. Raise and safely support the vehicle.

2. Remove the tire and wheel assemblies.

3. Remove the halfshaft from the vehicle and place the assembly in a vise with soft jaws.

4. Cut the seal clamps and remove the boot. Slide the boot down away from the joint.

5. Clean the grease around the joint. Spread the snapring and remove the joint.

6. Discard the boot, if damaged.

7. Using a brass drift punch and hammer, tap on the joint cage until it moves enough to remove a ball, then remove the other balls in the same fashion.

8. Remove the cage and inner race by turning the assembly straight up 90 degrees to the center line of the outer housing. Maneuver the cage and inner race out of the outer race housing assembly. Then remove the inner race from the cage assembly.

To install:

9. Thoroughly clean all part in solvent. Apply grease to the ball grooves of the inner and outer race.

10. Install the inner race into the cage.

11. Install the cage assembly into the housing.

12. Tilt the cage up and install the ball into the assembly. Pack the assembly with grease.

13. Install the small boot clamp onto the axle shaft.

14. Install the axle boot onto the shaft and secure the small boot clamp using a suitable tool.

15. Install the joint assembly onto the axle shaft, the snapring will snap into place automatically. Pack the boot and outer joint with a sufficient quantity of grease.

16. Position the boot over the joint housing. Secure with the large clamp, using a suitable tool.

17. Reinstall the axle shaft assembly into the vehicle.

18. Install the tire and wheel assembly.

19. Lower the vehicle.

K-SERIES

1. Raise and support the vehicle safely.

2. Remove the wheel and tire assembly.

3. Remove the skid plate, as required.

4. Remove the drive axle and place the assembly in a suitable holding fixture.

5. Remove the large (swage) ring using a chisel, being careful not to damage the housing surface.

6. Cut and remove the small clamp on the CV-boot.

7. Slide the boot back off the joint housing. Clean excess grease from the joint area.

8. Spread the ears of the joint retaining clip and slide the joint off the axle shaft.

9. Remove the boot from the axle shaft.

To install:

10. Place the small clamp on the small neck of the CV-boot. Do not crimp the clamp.

11. Slide the boot onto the axle shaft and into the groove on the axle shaft.

12. Crimp the small clamp using tool J–35910 or equivalent.

13. Disassemble the joint and thoroughly clean out old grease. Place a sufficient quantity of approved CV-joint grease inside the boot and in the joint.

14. Pinch the large CV-boot securing ring in an oval shape and slide the ring onto the boot large end.

15. Push the CV-joint onto the axle shaft until the retaining ring is seated in the groove on the axle shaft.

16. Slide the large diameter of the CV-boot with the ring in place over the outside of the CV-joint housing and locate the seal lip in the housing groove. Release any air trapped inside the boot using a thin flat blunt tool between the boot and housing.

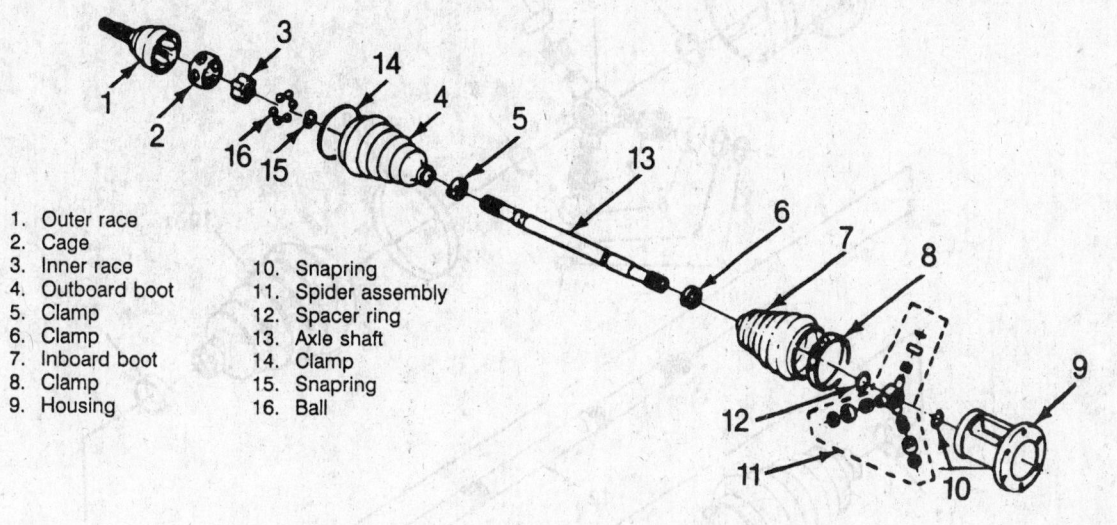

1. Outer race
2. Cage
3. Inner race
4. Outboard boot
5. Clamp
6. Clamp
7. Inboard boot
8. Clamp
9. Housing
10. Snapring
11. Spider assembly
12. Spacer ring
13. Axle shaft
14. Clamp
15. Snapring
16. Ball

85473167

Exploded view of the halfshaft assembly — compact FWD and 4WD vehicles

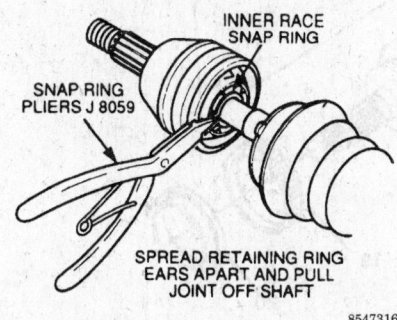

INNER RACE
SNAP RING

SNAP RING
PLIERS J 8059

SPREAD RETAINING RING
EARS APART AND PULL
JOINT OFF SHAFT

85473168

Separating the outer joint from the axle shaft — compact FWD and 4WD vehicles

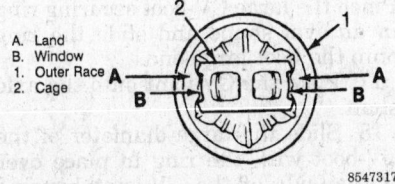

A. Land
B. Window
1. Outer Race
2. Cage

85473171

Positioning the outer joint cage and race for removal/installation — compact FWD and 4WD vehicles

17. Using a suitable ring installer tool, press the ring onto the housing until fully seated.

18. Install the halfshaft assembly, skid plate and the wheel and tire.

19. Lower the vehicle and road test.

Inner

COMPACT PICK-UP, VAN AND UTILITY

1. Raise and safely support the vehicle.

2. Remove the tire and wheel assemblies.

3. Remove the halfshaft from the vehicle and place the assembly in a vise with soft jaws.

4. Cut the seal clamps and remove the boot. Slide the joint housing off the joint and shaft assembly.

5. Clean the grease around the joint. Spread the snapring and remove the joint.

6. Discard the boot, if damaged.

To install:

7. Thoroughly clean all part in solvent.

8. Install the small boot clamp onto the axle shaft.

9. Install the axle boot onto the shaft and secure the small boot clamp using a suitable tool.

10. Install the joint assembly with the snapring counterbore facing (out)

the axle shaft housing, the snapring will snap into place automatically.

11. Install the spacer ring onto the axle shaft, ensuring the ring is fully seated in the groove.

12. Position the axle housing onto the joint and shaft assembly. Pack the boot and joint with a sufficient quantity of grease.

13. Position the boot over the joint housing. Secure with the large clamp, using a suitable tool.

14. Reinstall the axle shaft assembly into the vehicle.

15. Install the tire and wheel assembly.

16. Lower the vehicle.

K-SERIES

1. Raise and support the vehicle safely.

2. Remove the wheel and tire assembly.

3. Remove the skid plate, as required.

4. Remove the drive axle and place the assembly in a suitable holding fixture.

5. Remove the large (swage) ring using a chisel, being careful not to damage the housing surface.

6. Cut and remove the small clamp on the CV-boot.

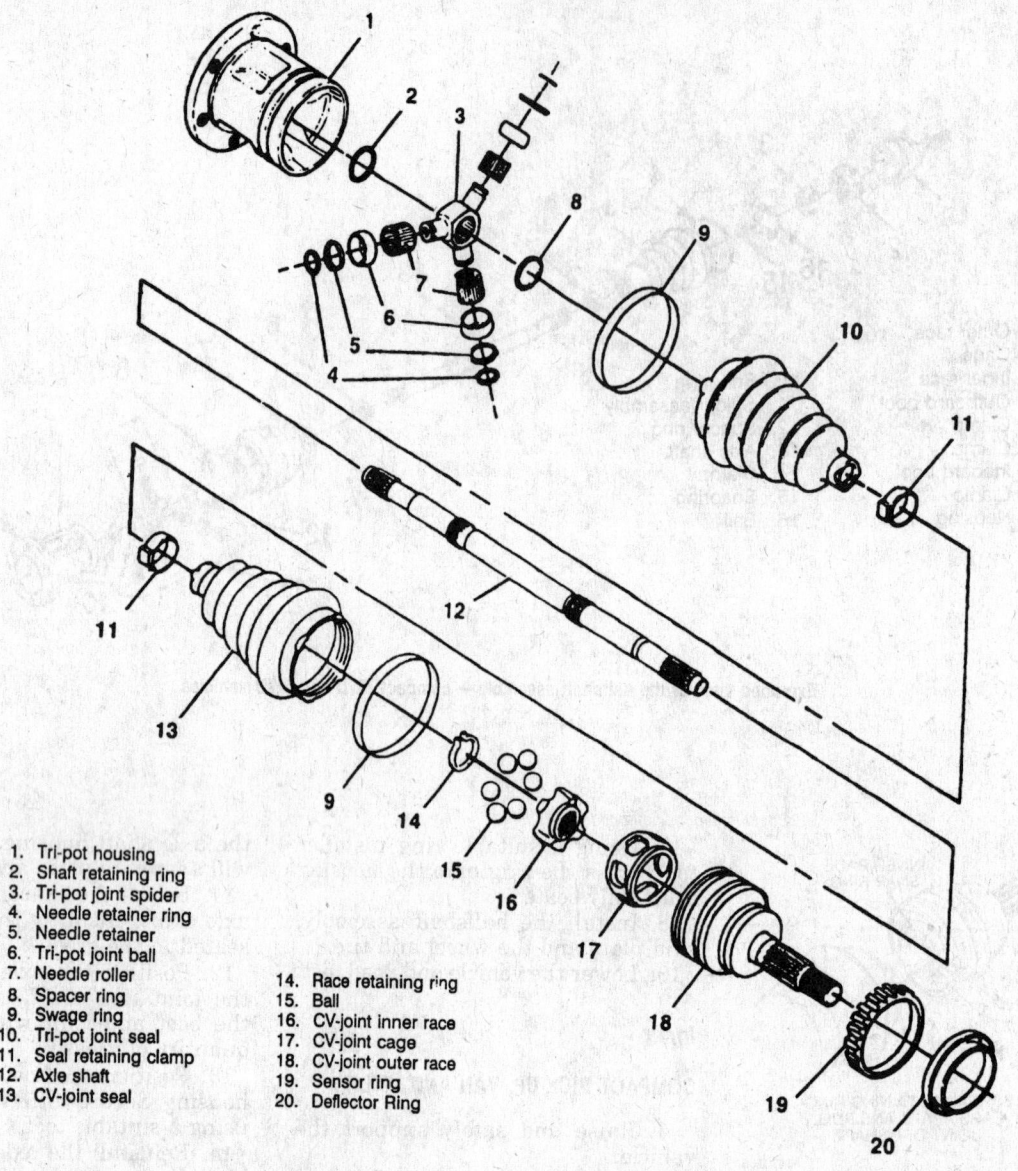

1. Tri-pot housing
2. Shaft retaining ring
3. Tri-pot joint spider
4. Needle retainer ring
5. Needle retainer
6. Tri-pot joint ball
7. Needle roller
8. Spacer ring
9. Swage ring
10. Tri-pot joint seal
11. Seal retaining clamp
12. Axle shaft
13. CV-joint seal
14. Race retaining ring
15. Ball
16. CV-joint inner race
17. CV-joint cage
18. CV-joint outer race
19. Sensor ring
20. Deflector Ring

85473169

Exploded view of the halfshaft assembly — K-Series

7. Slide the boot back off the joint housing. Remove the joint and axle shaft from the joint housing.

8. Spread the ears of the joint retaining clip and slide the joint back on the axle shaft. Remove the forward retaining ring and slide the joint off the shaft. Handle the joint with care to avoid disassembly.

9. Remove the rear retaining ring and remove the boot from the axle shaft.

To install:

10. Place the small clamp on the small neck of the CV-boot. Do not crimp the clamp.

11. Slide the boot onto the axle shaft and into the groove on the axle shaft.

12. Crimp the small clamp using tool J–35910 or equivalent. Install the forward joint retaining ring onto the axleshaft.

13. Thoroughly clean the old grease from the joint, boot and housing assembly. Place a sufficient quantity of approved CV-joint grease inside the boot.

14. Slide the joint assembly with the counterbore facing the axleshaft onto the shaft against the retaining ring.

15. Install the forward retaining ring in the groove on the axleshaft.

Slide the joint towards the end of the shaft and move the inside retaining ring into the groove.

16. Pack the joint sufficient quantity of approved CV-joint grease. Pinch the large CV-boot securing ring in an oval shape and slide the ring onto the boot large end.

17. Push the CV-joint onto the axle shaft.

18. Slide the large diameter of the CV-boot with the ring in place over the outside of the CV-joint housing and locate the seal lip in the housing groove. Release any air trapped inside the boot using a thin flat blunt tool between the boot and housing.

SWAGE CLAMP SIZE CHART

TOOL NO.	DESCRIPTION	APPLICATION
J 36652-1	Split Plate Swage Clamp	K 10/20
J 36652-2	Split Plate Swage Clamp	K 30 (Outboard)
J 36652-3	Split Plate Swage Clamp	K 30 (Inboard)

J 36652

AXLE ASSEMBLY

VISE

9. Swage Ring

MAKE SURE SWAGE RING AND SWAGE RING CLAMP ARE IN PROPER ALIGNMENT

9

HOUSING

SEAL

SWAGE RING CLAMP

9

SWAGE RING CLAMP

85473170

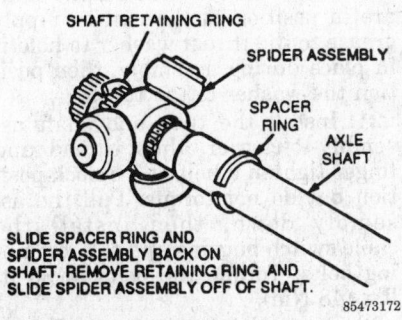

SHAFT RETAINING RING

SPIDER ASSEMBLY

SPACER RING

AXLE SHAFT

SLIDE SPACER RING AND SPIDER ASSEMBLY BACK ON SHAFT. REMOVE RETAINING RING AND SLIDE SPIDER ASSEMBLY OFF OF SHAFT.

85473172

Inner joint and snapring removal — compact FWD and 4WD vehicles

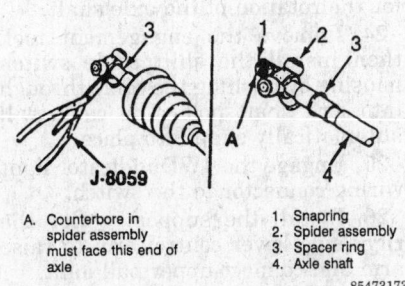

J-8059

A. Counterbore in spider assembly must face this end of axle

1. Snapring
2. Spider assembly
3. Spacer ring
4. Axle shaft

85473173

Inner joint installation — compact FWD and 4WD vehicles

Pressing the axle boot in place — K-Series

19. Using a suitable ring installer tool, press the ring onto the housing until fully seated.

20. Install the halfshaft assembly, skid plate and the wheel and tire.

21. Lower the vehicle and road test.

Driveshaft and U-Joints

REMOVAL AND INSTALLATION

Compact Pick-Up, Van and Utility

FRONT 1 PIECE — EXCEPT ASTRO AND SAFARI

1. Raise and support the vehicle safely.
2. If equipped, remove the skid plate.
3. Matchmark the rear yoke of the driveshaft to the transfer case. Matchmark the front of the driveshaft to the differential housing.
4. Remove the bolts and retainers from the rear of the driveshaft. Remove the driveshaft.
5. Installation is the reverse of the removal procedure. Tighten the bolts to 15 ft. lbs. (20 Nm).

FRONT 1 PIECE — ASTRO AND SAFARI

1. Raise and support the vehicle safely.

2. Matchmark the rear of the driveshaft to the transfer case. Matchmark the front of the driveshaft to the differential housing.

3. Remove the bolts from the rear flange of the driveshaft. Remove the bolts from the front flange of the driveshaft. Lower the driveshaft and remove it.

4. Installation is the reverse of the removal procedure. Tighten the front flange bolts to 53 ft. lbs. (72 Nm) and the rear flange bolts to 92 ft. lbs. (125 Nm).

REAR 1 PIECE

1. Raise and support the vehicle safely.

2. If equipped, remove the skid plate.

3. Matchmark the front yoke of the driveshaft to the transmission. Matchmark the rear of the driveshaft to the differential housing.

4. Remove the bolts and retainers from the rear of the driveshaft. Remove the driveshaft.

5. Installation is the reverse of the removal procedure. Tighten the bolts to 15 ft. lbs. (20 Nm).

REAR 2 PIECE

1. Raise and support the vehicle safely.

2. As required, remove the skid plate.

3. Matchmark the front yoke of the driveshaft to the transmission. Matchmark the rear of the driveshaft to the differential housing.

4. Remove the center bearing bolts and washers. Remove the center bearing.

5. Remove the front driveshaft. Remove the rear driveshaft bolts and retainers. Remove the rear driveshaft.

6. Installation is the reverse of the removal procedure. When installing the center bearing, be sure to align it 90 degrees to the driveshaft center lines. Tighten the center bearing bolts to 25 ft. lbs. (34 Nm), and the driveshaft bolts to 15 ft. lbs. (20 Nm).

Full Size Pick-Up, Van and Utility

1. Raise and support the vehicle safely.

2. Mark the relationship of the driveshaft to the front axle and transfer case flange.

3. Remove the skid plate, if equipped.

4. Remove the bolts, nuts, washers and U-bolts/retainers from the front axle flange-to-driveshaft.

5. Remove the slip yoke from the front axle.

NOTE: Do not let the U-joint caps fall off the yoke, tape the bearing caps in place to avoid loss of the bearing rollers.

6. Remove the bolts at the transfer case flange, slide the driveshaft forward and disengage the assembly from the transfer case.

7. Place the driveshaft into a holding fixture.

8. Remove the retaining rings.

9. Using 2 sockets, 1 with a diameter just smaller than the bearing cap; the other with an opening large enough to accept a bearing cap, press out the bearing caps in a vise.

10. Remove the trunnion from the slip yoke.

To install:

11. Place the trunnion in between the yoke ears of the driveshaft and begin installing both bearing caps by hand, finish the installation using a vise

12. Use a socket with a smaller diameter than the bearing cap and press the bearing cap in past the retainer ring groove. Install the retaining ring.

13. Turn the driveshaft over and repeat the procedure.

14. Install the slip yoke over the trunnion and repeat the procedure for the remaining bearing caps.

15. Install the driveshaft, U-bolt/retainers, nuts and bolts, aligning the shaft with the previous made marks on the transfer case and front axle.

16. Lower the vehicle and road test.

Front Axle Tube and Output Shaft Assembly

REMOVAL AND INSTALLATION

T-Series

EXCEPT MFI-TURBO

1. Disconnect the negative battery cable.

2. Disconnect the shift cable from the vacuum actuator by disengaging the locking spring. Then push the actuator diaphragm in to release the cable.

3. Unlock the steering wheel at steering column so the linkage is free to move.

4. Raise and support the vehicle safely.

5. Remove the front wheel assemblies and, except for 1994–96 vehicles, remove the engine drive belt shield.

6. If equipped, remove the front axle skid plate.

7. If necessary on 1994–96 vehicles, remove the right side caliper and support using safety wire.

8. Place a support under right-side lower control arm and disconnect right-side upper ball joint, then remove the support so the control arm will hang free.

NOTE: To keep the axle from turning, insert a drift through the opening in the top of the brake caliper, into the corresponding vane of the brake rotor.

9. Matchmark the right-side drive axle to the output shaft. Remove the right-side drive axle shaft-to-tube assembly bolts and separate the drive axle from the tube assembly, then remove the drift from the brake caliper and rotor.

10. Disengage the 4WD indicator lamp electrical connector from the switch.

11. Remove the 3 bolts securing the cable and switch housing-to-carrier and pull the housing away to gain access to the cable locking spring. Do not unscrew the cable coupling nut unless the cable is being replaced.

12. Disconnect the cable from the shift fork shaft by lifting spring over slot in shift fork.

13. Remove the 2 bolts securing the tube bracket to the frame.

14. Remove the remaining 2 upper bolts securing the tube assembly to the carrier. The other 3 were removed with the shift cable housing.

15. Remove the tube assembly by working around the drive axle. Be careful not to allow the sleeve, thrust washers, connector and output shaft to fall out of carrier or be damaged when removing the tube.

16. If necessary, remove the pilot bearing from the tube using J-34011 or equivalent pilot bearing remover tool.

To install:

17. If removed, lubricate the new seal lips and the new bearing using fresh axle lubricant. Install the new bearing using a pilot bearing installer tool such as J-33842 or equivalent.

18. If removed, install the new seal using J-33893 or equivalent seal installer.

19. Apply a bead of sealant on the tube-to-carrier mating surface.

20. Make sure the sleeve, thrust washers, connector and output shaft are in position in the carrier. Apply grease to the thrust washer to hold it in place during assembly, then position the washer to the tube.

21. Install the tube and shaft assembly-to-carrier, then thread and finger-tighten a bolt at 1 o'clock position but do not torque. Pull the assembly down, then install the cable/switch housing and the remaining bolts. Torque the bolts to 36 ft. lbs. (48 Nm).

22. Install the tube-to-frame nuts/bolts and torque to 55 ft. lbs. (75 Nm).

23. Using the hub engagement tool J-33798 or equivalent, check the operation of the 4WD mechanism. Insert tool into the shift fork and check for the rotation of the axle shaft.

24. Remove the engagement tool, then install the shift cable switch housing by pushing the cable through into fork shaft hole. The cable will automatically snap into place.

25. Engage the 4WD indicator light wiring connector to the switch.

26. Install the support under the right-side lower control arm to raise arm and connect upper ball joint.

27. Align and install right-side drive axle to the axle tube output shaft by installing 1 bolt first, then, rotate the axle to install and finger-

tighten the remaining bolts. Torque the bolts to 60 ft. lbs. (80 Nm).

NOTE: To hold the axle from turning, insert a drift through the opening in the top of the brake caliper into the corresponding vane of the brake rotor. If the caliper was removed, either temporarily install it or use a prybar across 2 installed lug nuts.

28. If removed on 1994–96 vehicles, reposition and secure the right side caliper.
29. If equipped, install the front axle skid plate.
30. Install the drive belt shield (except for 1994–96 vehicles), then install the front wheel assemblies.
31. Carefully lower the vehicle.
32. Connect the shift cable-to-vacuum actuator by pushing the cable end into the vacuum actuator shaft hole. The cable will snap into place, automatically.
33. Make sure the ignition is **OFF**, then connect the negative battery cable.

MFI-TURBO

1. Remove the right drive axle (halfshaft).
2. Remove the support bracket-to-frame nuts and washers.
3. Remove the tube-to-carrier retaining bolts.

NOTE: Before removing the shaft and tube assembly, position a drain pan to catch any escaping fluid.

4. Attach a slide hammer to the output shaft and pull the shaft free, then remove the shaft and tube assembly.
5. If necessary, remove the shaft along with the deflector and retaining ring. Strike the inside of the shaft flange with a brass hammer to dislodge it.
6. If necessary, remove the shaft seal and bearing using a slide hammer and axle tube bearing remover such as J-29369-2.
   To install:
7. If removed, lubricate the seal lips, bearings and bearing surfaces using axle lubricant. Install the bearing using J-33844 or equivalent bearing installer.
8. If removed, install the seal using J-33893 or equivalent seal installer. Install the shaft to the tube taking care not to cut the seal with the splines.
9. Thoroughly clean the mating surfaces of the carrier and tube.

10. Apply a bead of sealer such as Loctite®514 or equivalent to the carrier sealing surface.
11. Install the shaft and tube assembly to the carrier.
12. Install the tube-to-carrier bolts, then tighten to 35 ft. lbs. (58 Nm).
13. Install the support bracket nuts and washers, then tighten to 55 ft. lbs. (75 Nm).
14. Install the right drive axle to the output shaft.

Front Axle Shaft, Bearing and Seal

REMOVAL AND INSTALLATION

V-Series

1. Raise and support the vehicle safely.
2. Remove the wheel and tire assembly.
3. Remove the brake caliper and position the assembly aside.
4. Remove the locking hub assembly. Remove the hub and bearing assembly as follows:
   a. Using either wheel bearing nut wrench (J-6893-D on ½ or ¾ ton vehicles or J-26878-A on 1 ton vehicles), remove the locknut, ring and adjusting nut.
   b. Remove the hub and rotor assembly, bearing careful not to let the bearing fall out of the hub.
5. Remove the splash shield and brake bracket.
6. Remove the spindle from the steering knuckle.
7. Remove the axle shaft.
   To install:
8. Lube the spindle and spindle bearing with the recommended lubricant.
9. Install the spindle seal and spacer onto the axle shaft with the spacer's chamfer points facing toward the oil deflector.
10. Install the axle shaft into the housing.
11. Install the steering knuckle, brake caliper bracket and splash shield and secure with nuts and washers. Torque nuts to 65 ft. lbs. (88 Nm). Ensure the seal and oil deflector are in place on the steering knuckle.
12. Install the hub and rotor assembly as follows:
   a. If replacing the bearing, drive the races out of the hub assembly.
   b. Using a brass drift and hammer, drive the inner bearing and seal out of the hub.

   c. Remove all grease from the bearings, hub and spindle assembly using a suitable solvent.
   d. Inspect the bearings, races and spindle for heat stress, cracking or scores, repair or replace as necessary.
   e. Using a bearing race installer, drive the new races into the hub assembly until fully seated.
   f. Using an approved high-temperature wheel bearing grease pack the bearings, working the grease in between the rollers and apply a small quantity to the spindle and hub assembly.
   g. Install the inner wheel bearing and a new seal into the hub.
   h. Install the rotor/hub assembly onto the spindle.
   i. Install the outer wheel bearing and push onto the spindle until fully seated against the race. Install the adjusting nut torque to 50 ft. lbs. (60 Nm) while spinning the rotor assembly.
   j. Back off the adjusting nut and retorque the nut to 35 ft. lbs. (47 Nm) for automatic hubs or 50 ft. lbs. (60 Nm) for manual hubs.
   k. Back off the adjusting nut a maximum of ⅜ of a turn for automatic hubs or just enough to free the bearing for manual hubs.
   l. Install the ring and locknut, ensuring the tang on the inside diameter of the ring passes is aligned in the slot on the spindle.
   m. The hole in the ring must align with the pin on the locknut. Move the adjusting nut to align the pin.
   n. Torque the locknut to 160 ft. lbs. (217 Nm).
13. Install the locking hub assembly.
14. Install the brake caliper assembly.
15. Install the wheel and tire assembly.
16. Lower the vehicle, check and add gear oil to the front axle as required. Road test the vehicle.

K-Series

1. Raise and support the vehicle safely.
2. Remove the right wheel.
3. Position a drain pan under the axle.
4. Remove the stabilizer bar.
5. Remove the skid plate.
6. Disconnect the right inner tie rod end at the relay rod.
7. Remove the left halfshaft-to-axle flange bolts, turn the wheel to loosen the axle from the axle tube, push the axle towards the front of the

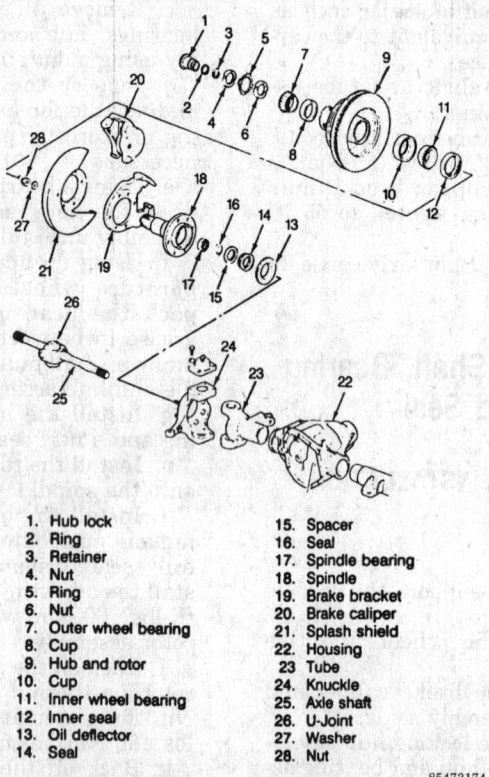

1. Hub lock	15. Spacer
2. Ring	16. Seal
3. Retainer	17. Spindle bearing
4. Nut	18. Spindle
5. Ring	19. Brake bracket
6. Nut	20. Brake caliper
7. Outer wheel bearing	21. Splash shield
8. Cup	22. Housing
9. Hub and rotor	23. Tube
10. Cup	24. Knuckle
11. Inner wheel bearing	25. Axle shaft
12. Inner seal	26. U-Joint
13. Oil deflector	27. Washer
14. Seal	28. Nut

85473174

Front driving axle components — except K-Series

vehicle and tie the axle out of the way.

8. Unplug the indicator switch and actuator electrical connectors.

9. Remove the drain plug and drain the fluid from the case.

10. Remove the right axle tube-to-frame bolts.

11. Remove the axle tube-to-carrier bolts.

12. Remove the axle tube/shaft assembly. Keep the open end up.

13. Disassemble the axle tube assembly as follows:

a. Position the axle tube, open end up, in a vise by clamping on the mounting flange.

b. Remove the snapring, sleeve, gear and thrust washer from the shaft end.

c. Tap out the axle shaft with a soft mallet.

d. Turn the axle tube over and pry out the deflector and seal.

e. Using a slide hammer and bearing remover, remove the bearing.

f. Clean all parts in a non-flammable solvent and inspect them for wear or damage. Clean off all old gasket material.

To install:

14. To install, perform the following procedures:

a. Using a bearing driver, install the new outer bearing in the tube.

b. Coat the lips of a new seal with wheel bearing grease and tap it into place in the tube.

c. Install the deflector.

d. Insert the axle shaft into the tube.

e. Coat the thrust washer with grease to hold it in place and position it on the tube end. Make sure the tabs index the slots.

f. Install the gear, sleeve, and snapring.

15. Position a new gasket, coated with sealer, on the carrier. Raise the tube assembly into position and install the tube-to-carrier bolts. Torque the bolts to 30 ft. lbs. (40 Nm).

16. Install the left halfshaft-to-flange bolts and torque to specification.

17. Install the axle tube-to-frame bolts. Torque the ½ and ¾ ton vehicle to 75 ft. lbs. (100 Nm) or the 1 ton vehicles to 106 ft. lbs. (145 Nm).

18. Connect the tie rod end to the relay rod.

19. Install the stabilizer bar.

20. Connect the actuator and indicator switch.

21. Install the drain plug. Tighten it to 24 ft. lbs. (33 Nm).

22. Fill the axle with the correct quantity and type of gear oil. Tighten the filler plug to 24 ft. lbs. (33 Nm).

23. Install the skid plate. Tighten the bolts to 25 ft. lbs.

Rear Axle Shaft, Bearing and Seal

REMOVAL AND INSTALLATION

Compact Pick-Up, Van and Utility

1. Raise and support the vehicle safely. Remove the tire, wheel and drum assemblies. Drain the lubricant.

2. Remove the carrier cover retaining bolts. Remove the carrier cover.

3. Remove the rear axle pinion shaft lock screw and the rear axle pinion shaft. Discard the lock screw.

4. Push the flanged end of the axle shaft toward the center of the vehicle. Remove the C-lock clip from the button end of the shaft.

5. Mark the axles left or right and remove the axle shaft from the housing. Be careful not to damage the oil seal.

6. Remove the rear wheel speed sensor, if equipped.

7. Remove the rear axle seal, using a suitable tool.

8. Remove the axle bearing from the housing using a suitable puller and slide hammer.

To install:

9. Install the axle bearing into the housing until the bearing bottoms against the housing shoulder, using a suitable tool.

10. Using a suitable tool, install the seal until flush with the axle housing.

11. Lubricate the seal with gear oil. Install the rear wheel speed sensor, if equipped.

12. Slide the axle into position and install the C-lock clip, use care not to damage the oil seal. Pull the axle out to secure the C-lock in place.

13. Install the pinion shaft through the case and pinion.

14. Install a new pinion shaft lock bolt, tighten it to 25 ft. lbs. (34 Nm).

15. Install the carrier cover, using a new gasket. Tighten the cover bolts to 20 ft. lbs. (27 Nm).

16. Fill the differential to within ⅜ in. of the filler opening.

17. Install the brake drum. Install the wheel and tire assembly.

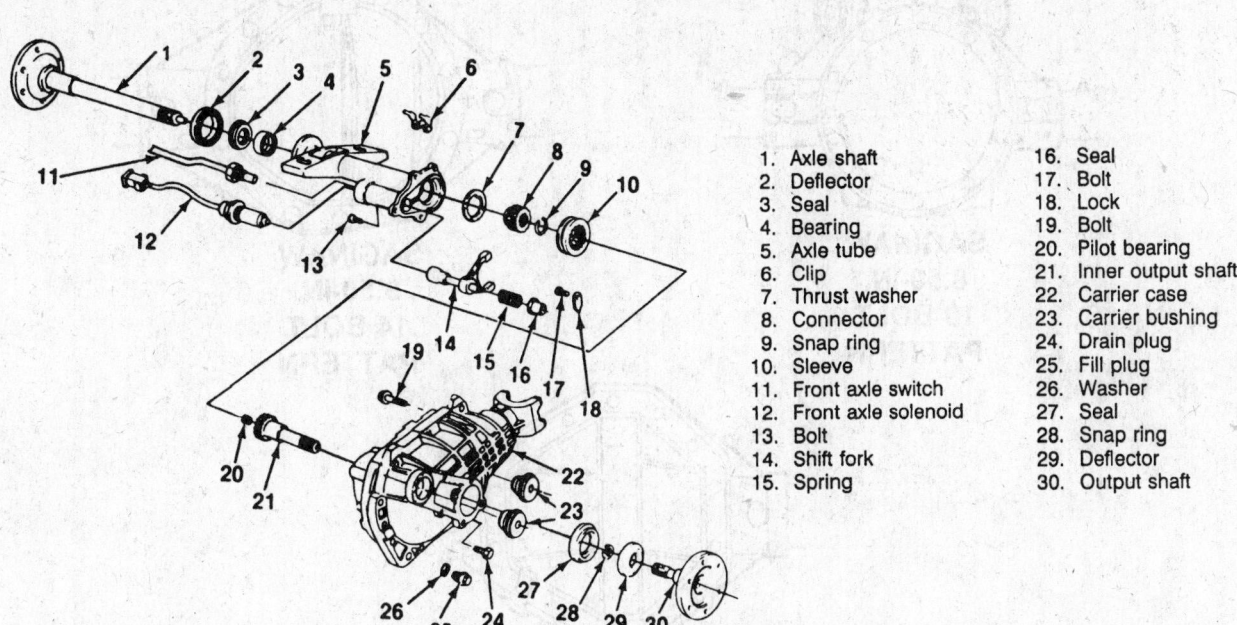

1. Axle shaft
2. Deflector
3. Seal
4. Bearing
5. Axle tube
6. Clip
7. Thrust washer
8. Connector
9. Snap ring
10. Sleeve
11. Front axle switch
12. Front axle solenoid
13. Bolt
14. Shift fork
15. Spring
16. Seal
17. Bolt
18. Lock
19. Bolt
20. Pilot bearing
21. Inner output shaft
22. Carrier case
23. Carrier bushing
24. Drain plug
25. Fill plug
26. Washer
27. Seal
28. Snap ring
29. Deflector
30. Output shaft

85473175

Front axle components — K-Series

Full Size Pick-Up, Van and Utility

SEMI-FLOATING DIFFERENTIAL (8½ AND 9½ INCH)

1. Raise and support the vehicle safely. Remove the tire and wheel assembly. Remove the brake drums.

2. Remove the carrier cover retaining bolts. Remove the carrier cover.

3. If not equipped with a locking differential, remove the rear axle pinion shaft lock screw and the rear axle pinion shaft.

4. If equipped with a locking differential, remove the shaft lock screw and pull the pinion shaft partially out. Rotate the differential until the pinion shaft touches the top of the housing. Using a suitable tool, rotate the C-lock until aligned with the thrust block.

5. Push the flanged end of the axle shaft toward the center of the vehicle. Remove the C-lock clip from the button end of the shaft.

6. Remove the axle shaft from the housing. Be careful not to damage the oil seal.

7. When removing the axle shaft on vehicles equipped with the 9½ in. ring gear, be sure the thrust washer in the differential case does not slide out.

8. Using a seal and bearing removal tool J–2619–01 and J–23689 for 8½ in. ring gear axle, insert the tool into the bore so the tool grasps behind the bearing. Slide the washer against the outside of the seal. Turn the nut finger-tight. Using a slide hammer remove the bearing and seal.

9. If equipped with the 9½ in. ring gear, use tool J–29712. Insert the tool into the axle tube so it grasps behind the bearing. Center the receiver on the axle tube and tighten the nut. Back off the nut and remove the bearing and seal from the tool.

To install:

10. Lubricate the space between where the bearing and the seal will seat with wheel bearing lubricant.

11. Using tool J–23690 for the 8½ in. ring gear or J–29709 for the 9½ in. ring gear axle, install the bearing into the housing until the tool bottoms against the tube.

12. Using tool J–21128 for the 8½ in. ring gear or J–29713 for the 9½ in. ring gear axle, install the seal until it is flush with the end of the axle tube.

13. Being careful not to damage the seal, insert the axle shaft into the housing allowing the splines to engage with the differential.

14. If not equipped with a locking differential, place the C-lock on the inside end of the axle shaft; then pull the axle shaft outward to seat the C-lock in the differential side gear. Install the pinion shaft and lock screw.

15. If equipped with a locking differential, install the pinion shaft partially into the differential; then rotate the differential until the shaft touches the top of the housing. Position the C-lock in the assembly as specified. Pull the axle shaft outward to seat the C-lock in the differential gear. Install the pinion shaft and lock screw.

16. Torque the lock screw to 25 ft. lbs. (34 Nm).

17. Install the carrier cover and gasket. Torque the bolts to 30 ft. lbs. (41 Nm).

18. Fill the axle assembly with the correct type of gear oil to the filler hole level.

19. Install the brake drum, wheel and tire assembly. Inspect the axle for leaks.

20. Lower the vehicle and road test.

FULL FLOATING DIFFERENTIAL (9¾ AND 10½ INCH)

1. Raise and support the vehicle safely. Remove the tire and wheel assembly.

2. Remove the bolts that retain the axle shaft flange to the wheel hub.

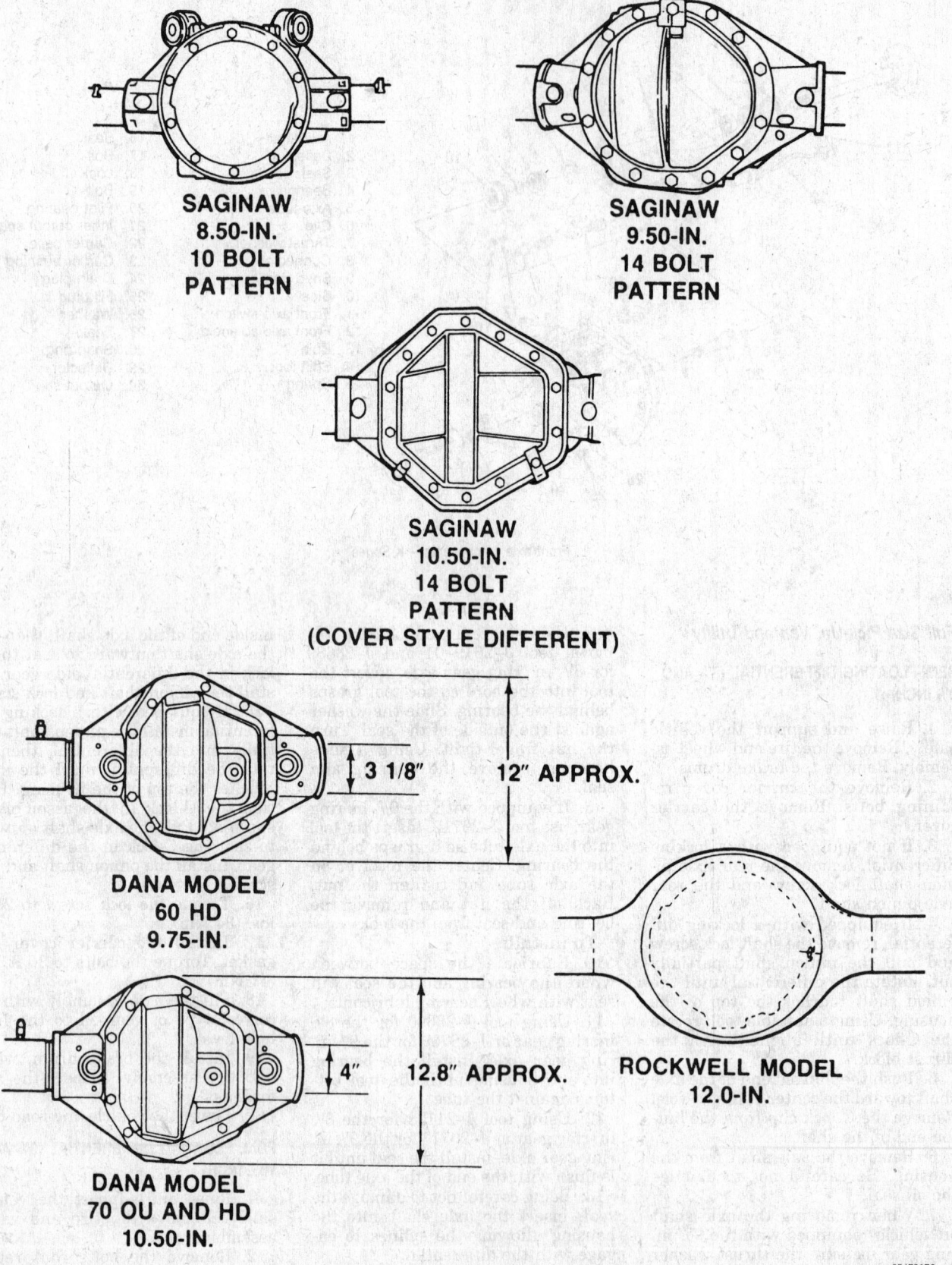

SAGINAW
8.50-IN.
10 BOLT
PATTERN

SAGINAW
9.50-IN.
14 BOLT
PATTERN

SAGINAW
10.50-IN.
14 BOLT
PATTERN
(COVER STYLE DIFFERENT)

DANA MODEL
60 HD
9.75-IN.

3 1/8″   12″ APPROX.

DANA MODEL
70 OU AND HD
10.50-IN.

4″   12.8″ APPROX.

ROCKWELL MODEL
12.0-IN.

85473176

Rear axle identification — Full Size Pick-Up, Van and Utility

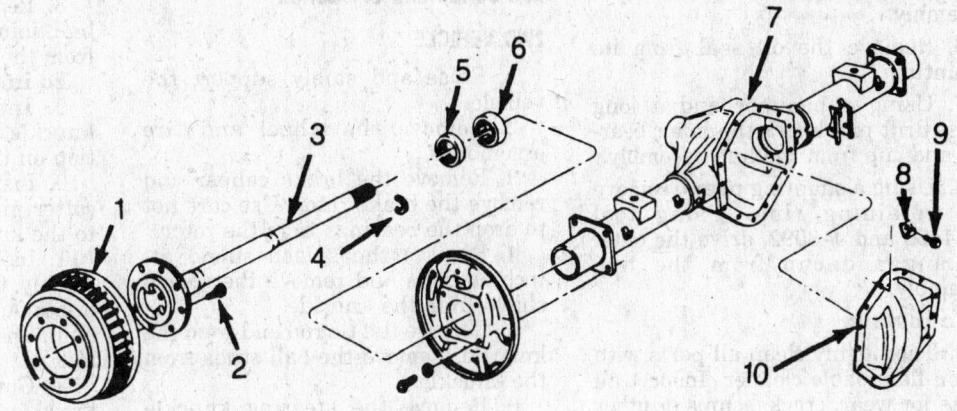

1. Drum
2. Bolt
3. Shaft
4. Lock
5. Seal
6. Bearing
7. Housing
8. Clip
9. Bolt
10. Carrier cover

Semi-floating rear axle assembly — full size vehicles

85473177

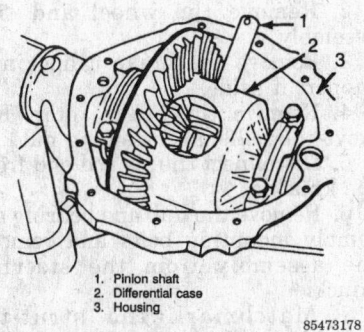

1. Pinion shaft
2. Differential case
3. Housing

85473178

Pinion shaft pin removal and installation — semi-floating rear axle

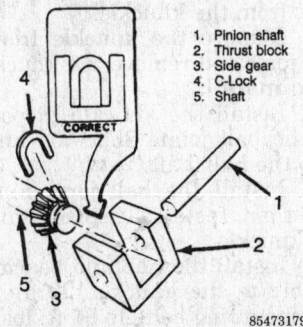

1. Pinion shaft
2. Thrust block
3. Side gear
4. C-Lock
5. Shaft

85473179

C-lock alignment for removal and installation — semi-floating rear axle

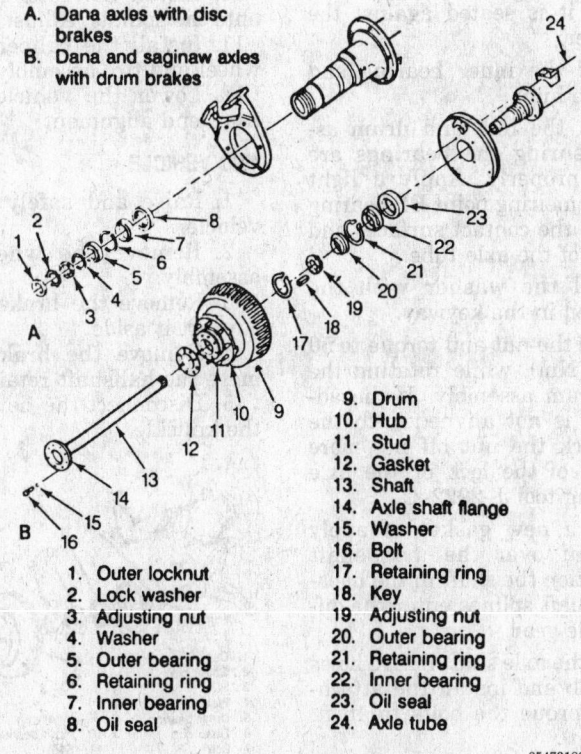

A. Dana axles with disc brakes
B. Dana and saginaw axles with drum brakes

1. Outer locknut
2. Lock washer
3. Adjusting nut
4. Washer
5. Outer bearing
6. Retaining ring
7. Inner bearing
8. Oil seal
9. Drum
10. Hub
11. Stud
12. Gasket
13. Shaft
14. Axle shaft flange
15. Washer
16. Bolt
17. Retaining ring
18. Key
19. Adjusting nut
20. Outer bearing
21. Retaining ring
22. Inner bearing
23. Oil seal
24. Axle tube

85473180

Full floating axle and components

3. Tap the flange with a soft mallet and loosen the axle shaft.

4. Twist the shaft assembly and remove it from the axle tube.

5. Remove the hub assembly retaining ring, key, adjusting nut, and washer. Remove the hub and drum assembly.

6. Remove the oil seal from its mounting.

7. Using a hammer and a long brass drift pin, knock the inner bearing and cup from the hub assembly.

8. Using a snapring pliers, remove the retaining ring. Using tool J–24426 and J–8092, drive the outer bearing and cup from the hub assembly.

To install:

9. Thoroughly clean all parts with a non-flammable cleaner. Inspect all parts for wear, cracks, chips or other damage, replace as necessary.

10. Place the outer bearing cup into the hub, drive the cup in using tool J–8608 upside down on tool J–8092 beyond the retaining ring.

11. Place the retaining ring into the groove and drive the cup back onto the retaining ring using tool J–24426.

12. Install the inner bearing cup using tool J–24426 and J–8092 into place until it is seated against the hub shoulder.

13. Install the inner bearing and seal into the hub.

14. Install the hub and drum assembly, ensuring the bearings are positioned properly. Apply a light coat of high melting point EP bearing lubricant to the contact surfaces and the outside of the axle tube.

15. Install the washer with the tang inserted in the keyway.

16. Install the nut and torque to 50 ft. lbs. (68 Nm), while rotating the hub and drum assembly. If the adjusting nut is not aligned with the keyway, back the nut off not more than 1 slot of the lock or the axle spindle using tool J–2222–C.

17. Place a new gasket or apply RTV sealant over the axle shaft flange. Position the shaft in the housing so the shaft splines enter the differential side gear.

18. Align the axle shaft flange holes with the hub and install the attaching bolts. Torque the bolts to 15 ft. lbs. (156 Nm).

19. Install the wheel assembly. Check the differential fluid level and add as required. Lower the vehicle and road test.

Front Wheel Hub, Knuckle and Bearing

REMOVAL AND INSTALLATION

M/L-Series and S/T-Series

2WD VEHICLE

1. Raise and safely support the vehicle.

2. Remove the wheel and tire assemblies.

3. Remove the brake caliper and remove the brake rotor. Use care not to drop the bearings from the rotor.

4. Remove the splash shield attaching bolts and remove the splash shield from the knuckle.

5. Remove the tie rod end from the knuckle. Remove the ball studs from the knuckle.

6. Remove the steering knuckle from the lower ball stud and the knuckle.

To install:

7. Install the upper and lower ball joint to the knuckle.

8. Attach the splash shield to the knuckle and tighten the bolts to 10 ft. lbs. (14 Nm).

9. Connect the tie rod end to the knuckle.

10. Install the rotor and bearings onto the spindle. Adjust the bearings.

11. Install the caliper. Install the wheel and tire assembly.

12. Lower the vehicle. Check the front end alignment.

4WD VEHICLE

1. Raise and safely support the vehicle.

2. Remove the wheel and tire assembly.

3. Remove the brake caliper and support it aside.

4. Remove the brake rotor. Remove the halfshaft retaining nut.

5. Disconnect the tie rod end from the knuckle.

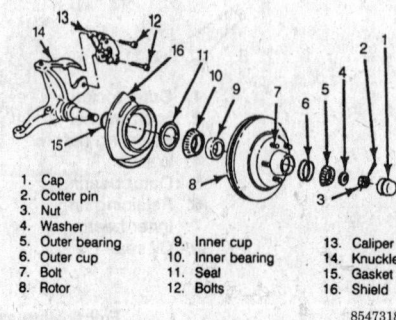

1. Cap
2. Cotter pin
3. Nut
4. Washer
5. Outer bearing
6. Outer cup
7. Bolt
8. Rotor
9. Inner cup
10. Inner bearing
11. Seal
12. Bolts
13. Caliper
14. Knuckle
15. Gasket
16. Shield

85473181

Front rotor, knuckle and bearing assembly — RWD vehicles

6. Remove the hub and bearing assembly mounting bolts and remove the assembly from the steering knuckle.

7. Remove the splash shield from the knuckle. Remove the ball joints from the knuckle.

8. Remove the knuckle from the ball joints and remove the spacer from the knuckle.

To install:

9. Install the spacer on the knuckle. Install the knuckle in position on the ball joints.

10. Install the ball joint nuts and cotter pins. Install the splash shield to the knuckle.

11. Install the hub and bearing assembly to the knuckle. Tighten the hub mounting bolts to 86 ft. lbs. (116 Nm). Install the halfshaft retaining nut.

12. Connect the tie rod to the knuckle. Install the brake rotor and the brake caliper.

13. Install the wheel and tire assembly. Lower the vehicle.

14. Check the front end alignment.

Lumina APV, Silhouette and Trans Sport

1. Raise and safely support the vehicle.

2. Remove the wheel and tire assembly.

3. Remove the brake caliper and support it aside.

4. Remove the brake rotor. Remove the halfshaft retaining nut.

5. Disconnect the tie rod end from the knuckle.

6. Remove the hub and bearing assembly mounting bolts and remove the assembly from the steering knuckle.

7. Matchmark the strut-to-knuckle positioning. Remove the strut mounting bolts from the knuckle. Remove the splash shield from the knuckle. Remove the ball joint from the knuckle.

8. Remove the knuckle from the ball joint and remove the knuckle.

To install:

9. Install the knuckle in position on the ball joint. Slide the knuckle onto the halfshaft.

10. Install the ball joint nut and cotter pin. Install the splash shield to the knuckle.

11. Install the hub and bearing assembly to the knuckle. Tighten the hub mounting bolts to 86 ft. lbs. (116 Nm). Install the halfshaft retaining nut.

12. Connect the tie rod to the knuckle. Install the brake rotor and the brake caliper.

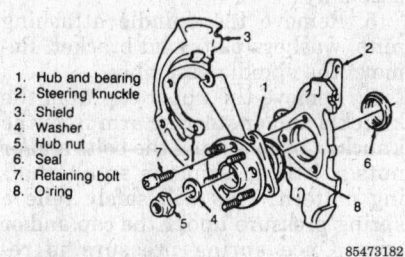

1. Hub and bearing
2. Steering knuckle
3. Shield
4. Washer
5. Hub nut
6. Seal
7. Retaining bolt
8. O-ring

85473182

Front hub and bearing assembly — Lumina, Silhouette and Trans Sport

13. Install the wheel and tire assembly. Lower the vehicle.
14. Check the front end alignment.

R and G-Series

1. Raise and support the vehicle safely.
2. Remove the wheels.
3. Dismount the caliper and suspend it out of the way without disconnecting the brake lines.
4. Remove the hub/rotor assembly as follows:
   a. Remove the dust cap, cotter pin, nut and washer.
   b. Pull the hub and rotor off the spindle and remove the outer bearing.
   c. Place the rotor upside down on a workbench and remove the inner bearing and seal.
5. Unbolt the splash shield and discard the old gasket.
6. Using a tie rod separator, disconnect the tie rod end from the knuckle.
7. Position a support under the lower control arm, near the spring seat. Raise the support to take the weight off the suspension, compressing the spring. Safety-chain the coil spring to the lower arm.
8. Remove the upper and lower ball joint nuts.
9. Using tool J-23742 or equivalent, break loose the upper ball joint from the knuckle.
10. Raise the upper control arm to disconnect the upper ball joint.
11. Using the same procedure, break loose the lower ball joint.
12. Lift the knuckle off the lower ball joint.
13. Inspect and clean the ball stud bores in the knuckle. Make sure there are no cracks or burrs. If the knuckle is damaged in any way, replace the assembly.

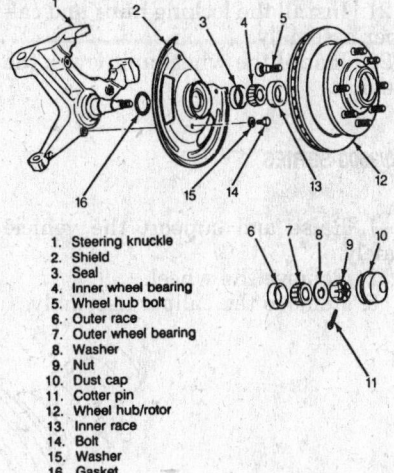

1. Steering knuckle
2. Shield
3. Seal
4. Inner wheel bearing
5. Wheel hub bolt
6. Outer race
7. Outer wheel bearing
8. Washer
9. Nut
10. Dust cap
11. Cotter pin
12. Wheel hub/rotor
13. Inner race
14. Bolt
15. Washer
16. Gasket

85473183

Hub and bearing assembly — R-Series

14. Check the spindle for wear, heat discoloration or damage. If at all damaged, replace the assembly.
   To install:
15. Maneuver the knuckle onto both ball joints.
16. Install both nuts. On ½ ton Series, torque the upper nut to 50 ft. lbs. (68 Nm) and the lower nut to 90 ft. lbs. (122 Nm). On ¾ and 1 ton Series, torque both nuts to 90 ft. lbs. (122 Nm).
17. Install the cotter pins. Advance the nut to align the cotter pin hole.

NOTE: On the upper nut which was originally torque to 50 ft. lbs. (68 Nm), do not exceed 90 ft. lbs. (122 Nm) when aligning the hole. On nuts torqued originally to 90 ft. lbs. (122 Nm), do not exceed 130 ft. lbs. (175 Nm) to align the cotter pin hole.

18. Remove the support.
19. Install a new gasket and the splash shield. Torque the bolts to 10 ft. lbs. (13.5 Nm).
20. Connect the tie rod end.
21. Install the hub/rotor assembly as follows:
   a. If replacing the bearings, drive the races out using a brass drift and hammer; place the drift behind the race in the notches in the hub.
   b. Clean all the bearings and hubs with a non-flammable solvent. Do not spin the bearings with compressed air to dry, otherwise damage may result.
   c. If reinstalling the original bearings, inspect both the race and bearing for cracks, heat stress or pitting; if either the bearing or race are damaged, replace both components.
   d. Using a suitable race installer, drive the inner and outer races into the hub until fully seated.
   e. Using an approved high temperature grease and bearing packer, fill the inner and outer wheel bearing with lubricant. Place a small amount inside the hub, in the dust cap and on the spindle.
   f. Place the inner bearing into the hub and flat block to install the seal so it is flush with the hub flange.
   g. Install the hub and rotor assembly onto the spindle, install the outer wheel bearing, washer and nut.
   h. Torque the nut to 12 ft. lbs. (16 Nm) while rotating the rotor assembly. Back off the nut until the "just loose" position. finger-tighten the nut until the cotter pin hole in the spindle aligns with the hole in the nut or cage. Do not back off the nut more than ½ of a flat.
   i. Install a new cotter pin.
   j. Rotor endplay should measure between 0.0012–0.0050 in. (0.03–0.13mm) when properly adjusted.
22. Install the caliper.
23. Install the wheels and check the front end alignment.

V-Series

EXCEPT 30/3500-SERIES

1. Raise and support the vehicle safely.
2. Remove the wheels.
3. Remove the caliper, hub and rotor assemblies.
4. Remove the spindle attaching nuts and plate. Remove the spindle assembly.
5. Disconnect the tie rod end from the knuckle.
6. Remove the knuckle-to-steering arm nuts and adapters.
7. Remove the steering arm from the knuckle.

8. Remove the cotter pins and nuts from the upper and lower ball joints.

NOTE: Do not remove the adjusting ring from the knuckle. If it is necessary to loosen the ring to remove the knuckle, do not loosen it more than 2 threads. The non-hardened threads in the yoke can be easily damaged by the hardened threads in the adjusting ring if caution is not used during knuckle removal.

9. Insert a ball joint separator between the lower ball joint and the yoke. Drive the prybar in to break the knuckle free.
10. Repeat the procedure at the upper ball joint.
11. Lift off the knuckle.
To install:
12. Position the knuckle on the yoke.
13. Start the ball joints into their sockets. Place the nuts onto the ball studs. The nut with the cotter pin slot is the upper nut. Tighten the lower nut to 30 ft. lbs. (40 Nm).
14. Using tool J–23447, tighten the adjusting ring to 50 ft. lbs. (70 Nm).
15. Tighten the upper ball joint nut to 100 ft. lbs. (135 Nm). Install a new cotter pin. Never loosen the nut to align the cotter pin hole, always tighten the nut.
16. Finish tightening the lower nut to 70 ft. lbs. (95 Nm).
17. Attach the steering arm to the knuckle using adapters and new nuts. Torque the nuts to 90 ft. lbs. (120 Nm).
18. Connect the tie rod end to the knuckle.
19. Install the spindle as follows:
   a. Mount the spindle in a holding fixture and remove the bearing seal and shaft bearing.
   b. Remove the spacer, seal and oil deflector from the shaft.
   c. Inspect all components for wear, heat stress and scoring. Replace as necessary.
   d. Lubricate the shaft bearing and spindle with a high melting point wheel bearing grease.
   e. Using tool J–8092 and J–23445–A, install the bearing and seal into the spindle.
   f. Install the oil seal onto the oil deflector with the deflector lip toward the spindle. Install the oil deflector and seal onto the axle shaft.
   g. Install the spacer onto the axle shaft with the chamfer pointing toward the oil deflector.
   h. Install the spindle onto the steering knuckle.

   i. Install the spindle plate. Install new nuts and washers. Torque the nuts to 65 ft. lbs. (88 Nm).
20. Install the hub/rotor assembly and wheel bearings. Adjust the bearings.
21. Install the locking hubs and caliper assembly.
22. Install the wheel and lower the vehicle.

30/3500-SERIES

1. Raise and support the vehicle safely.
2. Remove the wheel.
3. Remove the caliper assembly.

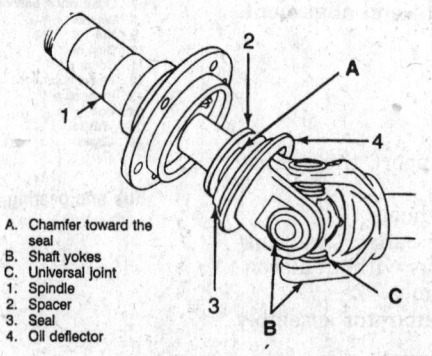

A. Chamfer toward the seal
B. Shaft yokes
C. Universal joint
1. Spindle
2. Spacer
3. Seal
4. Oil deflector

85473184

Front spindle assembly — V-Series

4. Remove the hub and rotor assembly.
5. Remove the spindle attaching nuts, washers plate and bracket. Remove the spindle assembly.
6. Remove the upper cap from the knuckle and/or steering arm from the knuckle, by loosening the bolts and/or nuts a little at a time in an alternating pattern. This will safely relieve spring pressure under the cap and/or arm. Once spring pressure is relieved, remove the bolts and/or nuts, washers and cap and/or steering arm.
7. Remove the gasket and compression spring.

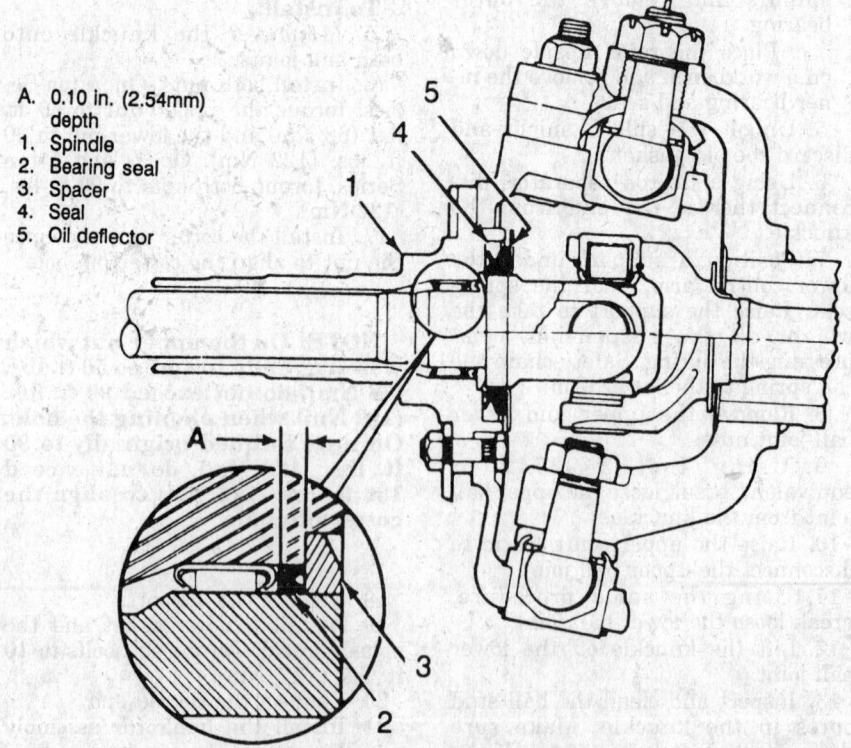

A. 0.10 in. (2.54mm) depth
1. Spindle
2. Bearing seal
3. Spacer
4. Seal
5. Oil deflector

85473185

Front spindle assembly — V-Series

8. Remove the bolts and washers and remove the lower bearing cap and the lower kingpin.

9. Remove the upper kingpin bushing by pulling it out through the knuckle.

10. Remove the knuckle from the axle yoke.

11. Remove the retainer from the knuckle.

12. Using a large breaker bar and adapter J–26871, remove the upper kingpin from the axle yoke by applying 500–600 ft. lbs. (677–813 Nm) of torque to the kingpin to break it free.

13. Using a hammer and blunt drift, drive out the retainer, race bearing and seal from the axle yoke all at once.

To install:

14. Using tool J–7817, install a new retainer and race in the axle yoke.

15. Fill the recessed area in the retainer and race with an approved high temperature wheel bearing lubricant.

16. Completely pack the upper yoke roller bearing with wheel bearing grease. A cone-type bearing packer is preferable but the bearing may be packed by hand.

17. Install the bearing and a new seal in the upper axle yoke, using a bearing driver such as J–22301. Don't distort the seal. It should protrude slightly above the yoke when fully seated.

18. Using adapter tool J–28871, install the upper kingpin. The kingpin must be torque to 550 ft. lbs. (745 Nm).

19. Position the knuckle in the yoke. Working through the knuckle, install a new felt seal over the kingpin and position the knuckle on the kingpin.

20. Install the bushing over the kingpin.

21. Install the compression spring, gasket, bearing cap and/or steering arm and bolts and/or nut and washer. Torque the bolts and/or nuts, in an alternating pattern, to 80 ft. lbs. (108 Nm).

22. Install the lower bearing cap and kingpin. Torque the bolts to 80 ft. lbs. (108 Nm) in an alternating pattern.

23. Thoroughly lube both kingpins through the grease fittings. Install the spindle as follows:

    a. Mount the spindle in a holding fixture and remove the bearing seal and shaft bearing.

    b. Remove the spacer, seal and oil deflector from the shaft.

    c. Inspect all components for wear, heat stress and scoring. Replace as necessary.

    d. Lubricate the shaft bearing and spindle with a high melting point wheel bearing grease.

    e. Using tool J–8092 and J–21465–17, install the bearing and seal into the spindle.

    f. Install the oil seal onto the oil deflector with the deflector lip toward the spindle. Install the oil deflector and seal onto the axle shaft.

    g. Install the spacer onto the axle shaft with the chamfer pointing toward the oil deflector.

    h. Install the spindle onto the steering knuckle.

    i. Install the spindle bracket and plate. Install new nuts and washers. Torque the nuts to 65 ft. lbs. (88 Nm).

24. Install the hub and rotor assembly. Adjust the bearings.

25. Install the locking hubs and caliper assembly.

26. Install the wheel and tire assembly.

27. Lower the vehicle and check the front end alignment.

C-Series

1. Raise and support the vehicle safely. Let the control arms hang freely.

2. Remove the wheels.

3. Disconnect the tie rod end from the knuckle.

4. Dismount the caliper and suspend it out of the way without disconnecting the brake lines.

5. Remove the hub/rotor assembly as follows:

    a. Remove the dust cap, cotter pin, nut and washer.

    b. Pull the hub and rotor off the spindle and remove the outer bearing.

    c. Place the rotor upside down on a workbench and remove the inner bearing and seal.

6. Unbolt the splash shield from the knuckle and discard the old gasket.

7. If a new knuckle is being installed, remove the knuckle seal carefully, without damaging it.

8. Position a support under the lower control arm, near the spring seat. Raise the support to take the weight off the suspension, compressing the spring. Safety chain the coil spring to the lower arm.

9. Remove the upper and lower ball joint nuts.

10. Using tool J–23742 or equivalent, break loose the upper ball joint from the knuckle.

11. Raise the upper control arm just enough to disconnect the ball joint.

12. Using tool J–23742 or equivalent, break loose the lower ball joint.

13. Lift the knuckle off the lower ball joint.

14. Inspect and clean the ball stud bores in the knuckle. Make sure there are no cracks or burrs. If the knuckle is damaged in any way, replace it.

15. Check the spindle for wear, heat discoloration or damage. If at all damaged, replace it.

To install:

16. Maneuver the knuckle onto both ball join

17. Install both nuts. Torque the nuts to 84 ft. lbs. (115 Nm).

18. Install new cotter pins. Always advance the nut to align the cotter pin hole.

19. Install the knuckle seal.

20. Remove the support.

21. Install a new gasket and the splash shield. Torque the bolts to 19 ft. lbs. (26 Nm).

22. Connect the tie rod end.

23. Install the hub/rotor assembly as follows:

    a. If replacing the bearings, drive the races out using a brass drift and hammer; place the drift behind the race in the notches in the hub.

    b. Clean all the bearings and hubs with a non-flammable solvent. Do not spin the bearings with compressed air to dry, otherwise damage may result.

    c. If reinstalling the original bearings, inspect both the race and bearing for cracks, heat stress or pitting; if either the bearing or race are damaged, replace both components.

    d. Using a suitable race installer, drive the inner and outer races into the hub until fully seated.

    e. Using an approved high temperature grease and bearing packer, fill the inner and outer wheel bearing with lubricant. Place a small amount inside the hub, in the dust cap and on the spindle.

    f. Place the inner bearing into the hub and flat block to install the seal so it is flush with the hub flange.

    g. Install the hub and rotor assembly onto the spindle, install the outer wheel bearing, washer and nut.

    h. Torque the nut to 12 ft. lbs. (16 Nm) while rotating the rotor

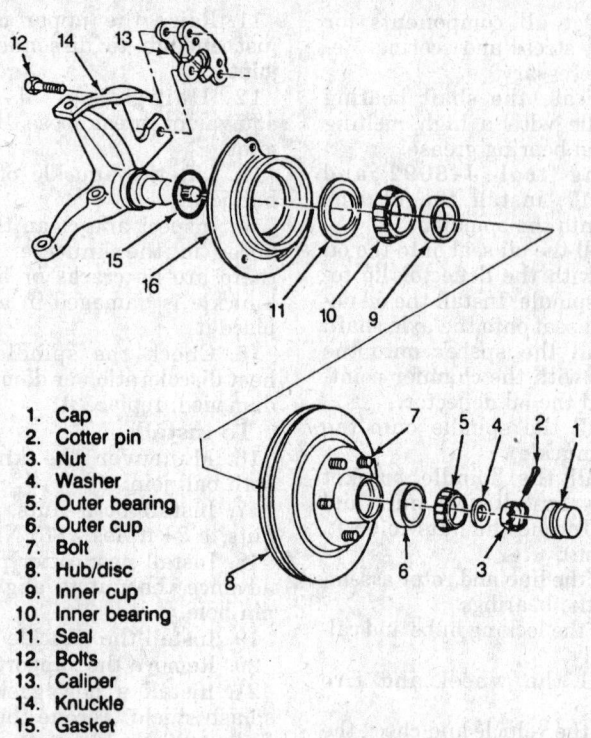

1. Cap
2. Cotter pin
3. Nut
4. Washer
5. Outer bearing
6. Outer cup
7. Bolt
8. Hub/disc
9. Inner cup
10. Inner bearing
11. Seal
12. Bolts
13. Caliper
14. Knuckle
15. Gasket
16. Shield

85473186

Hub and bearing assembly — C-Series

assembly. Back off the nut until the "just loose" position. Finger-tighten the nut until the cotter pin hole in the spindle aligns with the hole in the nut or cage. Do not back off the nut more than ½ of a flat.

i. Install a new cotter pin.

j. Rotor endplay should measure between 0.0012–0.0050 in. (0.03–0.13mm) when properly adjusted.

24. Install the caliper assembly.
25. Install the wheels.
26. Lower the vehicle and check the front end alignment.

K-Series

1. Disconnect the negative battery cable. Remove ⅔ of the brake fluid from the reservoir.
2. Raise and support the vehicle safely. Remove the wheel, caliper and brake disc. Remove the drive axle nut and washer.
3. Remove the tie rod nut and remove the tie rod end from the end of the washer.
4. Remove the hub and bearing assembly, using a puller.
5. Remove the drive axle. Remove the splash shield bolts. Remove the splash shield. Support the lower control.

6. Remove the upper and lower ball joint nut and disconnect the upper and lower ball joint from the knuckle.
7. Remove the knuckle and the knuckle seal, as required.

To install:

8. Install the seal into the knuckle, using tool J–36605 or equivalent.
9. Install the knuckle to the upper and lower ball joints and tighten the nuts to 84 ft. lbs. (115 Nm). Tighten the nuts to align the new cotter pin, but do not tighten more than ⅙ turn. Bend the pin ends against the nut flats.
10. Install the splash shield and tighten the bolts to 19 ft. lbs. (26 Nm). Install the drive axle.
11. Install the hub and bearing assembly. Align the threaded holes and tighten the bolts to 133 ft. lbs. (180 Nm).
12. Install the tie rod end to the knuckle, and tighten the tie rod nut to 35 ft. lbs. (48 Nm).
13. Install the washer and axle nut and torque to 173 ft. lbs. (245 Nm).
14. Install the brake disc and caliper. Install the axle joint cover.
15. Install the wheel and tire assembly. Lower the vehicle and check the front end alignment.

Pinion Seal

REMOVAL AND INSTALLATION

Compact Pick-Up, Van and Utility

1. Raise and support the vehicle safely. Remove the tire, wheel and drum assembly. Matchmark the driveshaft and the pinion flange.
2. Disconnect the driveshaft from the rear differential. Support the driveshaft aside.
3. Mark the position of the pinion flange, pinion shaft and nut. Using an inch lb. torque wrench, turn the pinion flange nut and record the amount of torque required to turn the pinion flange. Remove the pinion flange nut and washer.
4. Remove the pinion flange. Position a drain pan under the assembly to catch any excess lubricant.
5. Using the proper tool, remove the seal from its mounting.
6. Installation is the reverse of the removal procedure. Refill the differential to the correct level. Tighten the pinion flange nut until the torque required to turn the flange is 3–5 inch lbs. higher than the pre-disassembly reading.

Full Size Pick-Up, Van and Utility

1. Raise and support the vehicle safely. It would help to have the front end slightly higher than the rear to avoid fluid loss.
2. Mark and remove the driveshaft.
3. Release the parking brake.
4. Remove the rear wheels. Rotate the rear wheels by hand to make sure there is absolutely no brake drag. If there is brake drag, remove the drums.
5. Using an inch lb. torque wrench on the pinion nut, record the force needed to rotate the pinion.
6. Mark the pinion shaft, nut and flange. Count the number of exposed threads on the pinion shaft.
7. Install a holding tool on the pinion. A very large adjustable wrench will do or if 1 is not available, put the drums back on and set the parking brake as tightly as possible.
8. Remove the pinion nut.
9. Slide the flange off the pinion. A puller may be necessary.
10. Center punch the oil seal to distort it and pry the seal out, being careful to avoid scratching the bore.

To install:

11. Pack the cavity between the lips of the seal with a lithium-based chassis lube.

Hub, knuckle and ball joints — C/K-Series

85473187

12. Use a seal installer, as necessary, and position the seal in the bore and carefully drive it into place, leaving a space between the flange and oil seal of approximately ⅛ in.

13. Place the flange on the pinion and push it on as far as it will go.

14. Install the pinion washer and nut on the shaft and force the pinion into place by turning the nut.

NOTE: Never hammer the flange into place.

15. Tighten the nut, rotating the pinion occasionally until the exact number of threads previously noted appear and the scribed marks are aligned.

16. Measure the rotating torque of the pinion under the same circumstances as before. Compare both readings. As necessary, tighten the pinion nut in very small increments until the torque necessary to rotate the pinion is 3 inch lbs. higher than the originally recorded torque.

17. Install the driveshaft and check rear fluid level.

18. Lower the vehicle and road test.

Front Axle Housing

REMOVAL AND INSTALLATION

L-Series and T-Series

1. Unlock the steering column so the linkage is free to move. Disconnect the negative battery cable.

2. Raise and support the vehicle safely. Remove both front wheel and tire assemblies.

3. Insert a drift through the opening in the top of the brake caliper into the vanes of the brake rotor to keep the axle from turning. Remove the front driveshaft.

4. Remove the axle vent hose from the carrier fitting.

5. Disconnect the right and left halfshafts from the carrier by removing the retaining bolts.

6. Properly support the carrier assembly. Remove the carrier and axle tube to frame retaining bolts.

7. Remove the differential carrier assembly.

8. Installation is the reverse of the removal procedure.

V-Series

1. Raise and support the vehicle safely.

2. Matchmark and remove the driveshaft.

3. Disconnect the connecting rod from the steering arm.

4. Disconnect the brake caliper and position it out of the way, without disconnecting the brake line.

5. Disconnect the shock absorbers from the axle brackets.

6. Remove the front stabilizer bar.

7. Disconnect the axle vent tube clip at the differential housing.

8. Take the weight off the axle assembly.

9. Remove the nuts, washers, U-bolts and plates from the axle and separate the axle from the springs. Remove the axle assembly.

To install:

10. Position the axle under the vehicles.

11. Install the plates, U-bolts, washers and nuts. Tighten the nuts.

12. Remove the support.

13. Connect the axle vent tube clip at the differential housing.

14. Install the front stabilizer bar.

15. Connect the shock absorbers at the axle brackets. Torque the bolts.

16. Install the brake caliper assembly.

17. Connect the connecting rod at the steering arm.

18. Install the driveshaft and lower the vehicle.

3-147

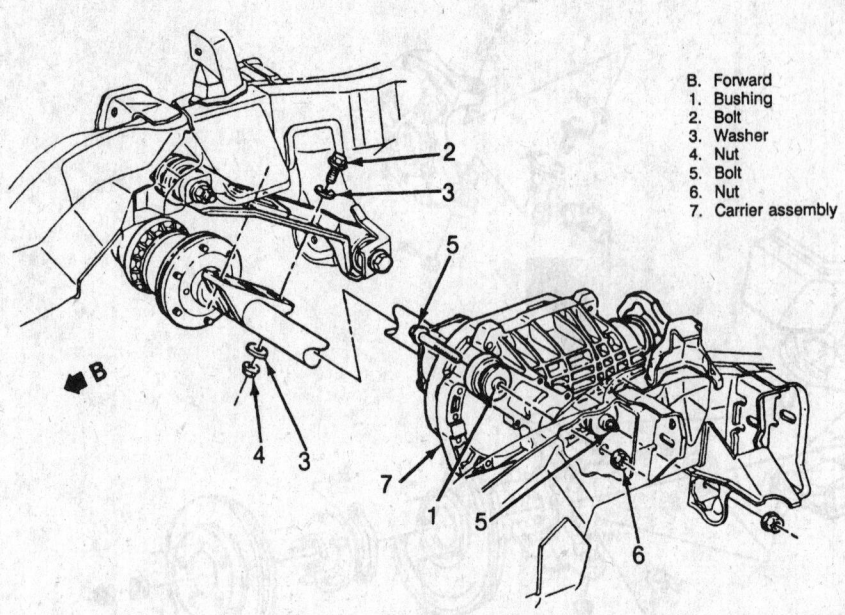

B. Forward
1. Bushing
2. Bolt
3. Washer
4. Nut
5. Bolt
6. Nut
7. Carrier assembly

85473188

Common front axle housing — L-Series and T-Series

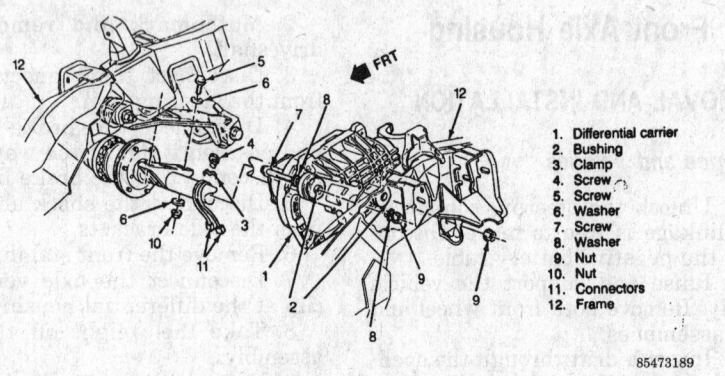

1. Differential carrier
2. Bushing
3. Clamp
4. Screw
5. Screw
6. Washer
7. Screw
8. Washer
9. Nut
10. Nut
11. Connectors
12. Frame

85473189

Front axle housing — K-Series

K-Series

1. Raise and support the vehicle safely.
2. Remove the wheels.
3. Remove the skid plate.
4. Drain the carrier.
5. Matchmark and remove the front driveshaft.
6. Disconnect the right axle shaft at the tube flange.
7. Disconnect the left axle shaft at the carrier flange.
8. Wire both axle shafts out of the way.
9. Unplug the connectors at the indicator switch and actuator.

10. Disconnect the carrier vent hose.
11. Remove the axle tube-to-frame bolts, washers and nuts.
12. Remove the lower carrier mounting bolt.
13. Disconnect the right side inner tie rod end at the relay rod.
14. Depending on model, it may be necessary to remove the engine oil filter.
15. Support the carrier. Remove the upper carrier mounting bolt.
16. Lower the carrier assembly.
    To install:
17. Raise the carrier into position.

18. Install the upper carrier mounting bolt, washers and nut. Then, install the lower carrier mounting bolt, washers and nut. Torque the bolts to 80 ft. lbs.
19. Remove the support. Install the oil filter.
20. Connect the tie rod end. Torque the nut to specification.
21. Install the axle tube-to-frame bolts, washers and nuts. Torque the nuts.
22. Connect the vent hose. Connect the wiring.
23. Connect the axle shafts at the flanges. Torque the bolts.
24. Connect the driveshaft. Torque the bolts.
25. Fill the carrier with SAE 85W-90 gear oil.
26. Install the wheels. Lower the vehicle.
27. Add any engine oil lost when the filter was removed.

Rear Axle Housing

REMOVAL AND INSTALLATION

S/T-Series

1. Raise and support the vehicle safely by the frame. Position a floor or transmission jack to support the rear axle housing. Take care when removing the U-bolts to keep the axle from suddenly dislodging.
2. Remove the rear wheels and drums for clearance and to remove some weight from the axle housing.
3. Matchmark and remove the rear driveshaft from the pinion flange. Either remove the shaft completely from the vehicle or support it aside from the undercarriage using safety wire, but do not allow the shaft to hang from the slip joint.
4. Remove the shock absorber-to-axle housing retainers, then swing the shock absorbers away from the axle housing.
5. Disconnect the brake lines from the axle housing clips and the backing plates (wheel cylinders).

NOTE: When disconnecting the brake lines from the wheel cylinders, immediately plug or cap the lines to prevent system contamination or excessive fluid loss.

6. If applicable on late model vehicles, disengage the speed sensor connectors at the junction block.
7. For 1994–96 vehicles or as necessary, disconnect the parking brake cable(s).

8. Disconnect the axle housing-to-spring U-bolt nuts, washers. U-bolts and the anchor plates.

9. Remove the vent hose from the top of the axle housing.

10. Remove the axle with the help of an assistant by moving it to clear the leaf spring or if desired, the leaf springs can be disconnected from the frame at the rear end to lower the axle down and back.

To install:

11. With the help of an assistant, carefully position the rear axle into the vehicle.

12. Connect the vent hose to the axle housing.

13. Be sure the housing is properly positioned on the leaf spring, then loosely install the U-bolts, anchor plates, washers and nuts.

14. Tighten the U-bolt nuts in a cross pattern to 18 ft. lbs. (25 Nm) to made sure everything is evenly seated. Then torque the nuts in steps to to 41 ft. lbs. (55 Nm), then to 85 ft. lbs. (115 Nm).

15. Remove the caps from the brakes lines then connect the lines and secure them to the axle housing.

16. If removed, connect the parking brake cable(s).

17. If applicable, engage the speed sensor connectors to the junction block.

18. Align and install the driveshaft assembly.

19. Install the shock absorbers to the lower mounts, then tighten the mount nuts.

20. Install the brake drums and the tire/wheel assemblies.

21. Properly refill the brake master cylinder and bleed the hydraulic brake system.

22. Check the fluid level in the rear axle assembly and add, as necessary. Make sure the vehicle is level when checking and adding fluid.

23. Remove the supports and carefully lower the vehicle.

M/L-Series

1. Raise and support the vehicle safely. Remove the tire, wheel and drums assemblies. Properly support the rear axle assembly.

2. Disconnect the shock absorbers from the anchor plate. Matchmark the driveshaft and the pinion flange. Remove the driveshaft and position aside.

3. Disconnect the brake lines from the axle housing and backing plates. Disconnect the rear wheel anti-lock speed sensor connectors, if equipped.

4. Remove the stabilizer bar, if equipped. Remove the U-bolts and anchor plates.

5. Lower the axle assembly and remove the lower spring shackle bolts.

6. Disconnect the vent hose from the axle housing. Remove the axle housing.

7. Installation is the reverse of the removal procedure. Fill and bleed the brake system.

Full Size Pick-Up, Van and Utility

1. Raise and support the vehicle safely.

2. For the 9¾ in. ring gear and the 10½ in. ring gear axles, place supports under the frame side rails for support.

3. Drain the lubricant from the axle housing and remove the driveshaft.

4. Remove the wheel, the brake drum or hub and the drum assembly.

5. Disconnect the parking brake cable from the lever and at the brake flange plate.

6. Disconnect the hydraulic brake lines from the connectors.

7. Disconnect the shock absorbers from the axle brackets.

8. Remove the vent hose from the axle vent fitting, if equipped.

9. Disconnect the height sensing and brake proportional valve linkage, if equipped.

10. Support the stabilizer shaft assembly with a hydraulic jack and remove, if equipped.

11. Remove the nuts and washers from the U-bolts.

12. Remove the U-bolts, spring plates and spacers from the axle assembly.

13. Lower and remove the axle assembly.

To install:

14. Raise the axle assembly into position.

15. Install the U-bolts, spring plates and spacers.

16. Install the nuts and washers on the U-bolts. Torque the nuts to specification.

17. Install the stabilizer shaft.

18. Connect the height sensing and brake proportional valve linkage.

19. Install the vent hose at the axle vent fitting.

20. Connect the shock absorbers at the axle brackets. Torque the nuts to 80 ft. lbs.

21. Connect the hydraulic brake lines.

22. Connect the parking brake cable.

23. Install the wheels.

24. Install the driveshaft.

25. Fill the axle housing.

STEERING

Steering Wheel

REMOVAL AND INSTALLATION

1. If equipped, properly disable the SIR (air bag) system.

2. Disconnect the negative battery cable.

3. Remove the horn pad or horn pad/air bag retaining screws. Pull the air bag and/or horn pad outward, then disconnect the electrical lead(s) and remove.

4. Matchmark the steering wheel and the shaft.

5. Remove the steering wheel retaining clip and nut.

6. Remove the steering wheel, using a suitable puller.

7. Installation is the reverse of removal. Align the matchmarks made during removal and tighten the steering wheel retaining nut to 30 ft. lbs. (40 Nm).

Steering Column

REMOVAL AND INSTALLATION

Except Lumina, Silhouette and Trans Sport

1. If equipped, properly disable the SIR (air bag) system.

2. Disconnect the negative battery cable.

3. Remove the steering wheel. Disconnect the wire harness connector under the dash.

4. Remove the transmission shift linkage from the column.

5. Remove the column upper clamp bolt; mark the relationship of the joint to the steering shaft.

6. Remove the steering column support bracket under the dash.

7. Remove the column to floor seal.

8. Rotate the column so the shift levers clear the floor opening and remove the assembly.

9. Installation is the reverse of the removal procedure.

Lumina, Silhouette and Trans Sport

1. If equipped, properly disable the SIR (air bag) system.

2. Disconnect the negative battery cable.

3. Remove the left instrument panel sound insulator and trim pad. Remove the steering column trim collar.

4. Remove the steering wheel, if column is to be disassembled.

5. Remove the column upper clamp bolt; mark the relationship of the joint to the steering shaft.

6. Remove the steering column support bracket under the dash. Remove the shift indicator cable.

7. Disconnect the wire harness connector under the dash.

8. Remove the shift cable at the actuator and housing holder.

9. Remove the column assembly.

10. Installation is the reverse of the removal procedure.

Manual Steering Gear

REMOVAL AND INSTALLATION

Compact Pick-Up, Van and Utility

1. Disconnect the negative battery cable. Raise and support the vehicle safely. Position the wheels in the straight-ahead position.

2. If equipped, remove the steering gear coupling shield. Remove the steering gear lower coupling bolt. On some vehicles it may be necessary to separate the coupling at the upper and lower flange bolts.

3. Matchmark the pitman arm to the steering gear. Remove the pitman arm retaining nut and washer. Using the proper tool, separate the pitman arm from the steering gear assembly.

4. Remove the steering gear retaining bolts. Separate the steering gear from the intermediate shaft and remove the assembly.

To install:

5. Position the steering gear into in the vehicle.

6. Install the mounting bolts. Tighten the mounting bolts to 55 ft. lbs. (75 Nm).

7. Connect the steering gear and intermediate shaft, install the coupling flange bolts.

8. Connect the pitman arm to the steering gear in the previously marked position. Tighten the pitman arm retaining bolt to 185 ft. lbs. (250 Nm).

9. Install the coupling shield. Lower the vehicle.

10. Connect the negative battery cable.

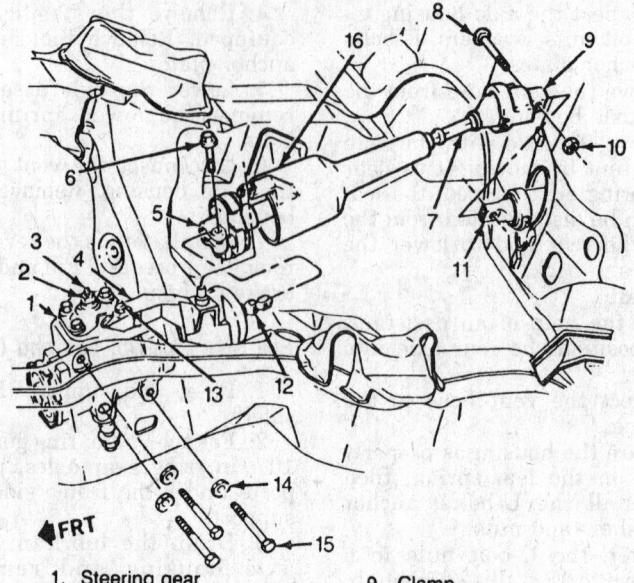

1. Steering gear
2. Jam nut
3. Adjuster screw
4. Adapter
5. Lower clamp
6. Lower clamp bolt
7. Intermediate shaft
8. Upper clamp bolt
9. Clamp
10. Retaining nut
11. Mainshaft
12. Wormshaft
13. Adapter nut and washer
14. Washer
15. Mounting bolt
16. Shield

85473190

Common steering gear mounting — compact vehicle

Full Size Pick-Up, Van and Utility

1. Set the front wheels in straight-ahead position by driving vehicle a short distance on a flat surface.

2. Raise and support the vehicle safely, as required.

3. Remove the steering shaft shield. Matchmark the relationship of the universal yoke to the wormshaft.

4. Remove the universal yoke pinch bolt.

5. Mark the relationship of the pitman arm to the pitman shaft.

6. Remove the pitman shaft nut and then remove the pitman arm from the pitman shaft, using puller J–6632 or J–29107.

7. Remove the steering gear to frame bolts and remove the gear assembly.

To install:

8. Ensure the steering gear is the centered position. Install the steering gear, guiding the steering gear shaft into the universal yoke.

9. Install the steering gear to frame bolts and torque to 100 ft. lbs. (135 Nm).

10. Install the yoke pinch bolt. Torque the pinch bolt to 22 ft. lbs. (30 Nm). Install the steering shaft shield.

11. Install the pitman arm onto the pitman shaft, lining up the marks made at removal. Install the pitman shaft nut torque to 185 ft. lbs. (250 Nm).

ADJUSTMENT

Compact Pick-Up, Van and Utility

1. Raise and safely support the vehicle.

2. Remove the coupling shield. Remove the pitman arm nut and washer.

3. Matchmark the pitman arm to the pitman shaft.

4. Remove the pitman arm, using a suitable puller.

5. Loosen the adjuster nut on the steering gear, then back out the adjuster a 1/4 turn.

6. Lower the vehicle, keeping it just above the ground.

7. Remove the horn pad. Center the steering wheel by turning the wheel all the way in 1 direction until stopped by the gear, then turn the wheel back 1½ turns to the center position.

8. Install an inch lb. torque wrench on the steering wheel nut. Use a torque wrench with no more than a 50 inch lbs. reading capability.

Check the thrust bearing preload as follows:

a. Turn the torque wrench and steering wheel through a 90 degree arc.

b. Tighten the adjuster plug until the proper preload is achieved, 5–8 inch lbs. (0.6–1.0 Nm).

c. Tighten the adjuster nut to 85 ft. lbs.

d. Turn the steering wheel to check the adjustment. The gear should turn smooth and not lumpy, from lock to lock.

9. To check the overcenter preload:

a. Turn the steering wheel from lock to lock counting the total number of turns.

b. Turn the wheel back, to exactly the ½ way point.

c. Turn the over center adjuster screw clockwise, to take out all of the lash between the ball nut and the pitman shaft sector teeth.

d. Tighten the jam nut to 22 ft. lbs. (30 Nm).

e. Check the torque at the steering wheel, taking the highest reading as the wheel is turned.

f. If necessary, loosen the adjuster nut and tighten the adjuster plug to obtain 4–10 inch lbs. (0.5–1.2 Nm).

To install:

10. Install the pitman arm onto the pitman shaft, aligning the matchmarks made during disassembly.

11. Install the pitman arm washer and nut. Install the coupling shield.

12. Lower the vehicle completely and install the horn pad.

13. Connect the negative battery cable.

Full Size Pick-Up, Van and Utility

Before any steering gear adjustments are made, it is recommended that the front end of the vehicle be raised and supported safely and a thorough inspection be made for stiffness or lost motion in the steering gear, steering linkage and front suspension. Worn or damaged parts should be replaced, since a satisfactory adjustment of the steering gear cannot be obtained, if bent or badly worn parts exist. It is also very important that the steering gear be properly aligned in the vehicle. Misalignment of the gear places a stress on the steering worm shaft, therefore a proper adjustment is impossible.

To align the steering gear, loosen the steering gear-to-frame mounting

bolts to permit the gear to align itself. Check the steering gear to frame mounting seat. If there is a gap at any of the mounting bolts, proper alignment may be obtained by placing shims where excessive gap appears. Tighten the steering gear-to-frame bolts. Alignment of the gear in the G-Series is very important and should be done carefully so a satisfactory, trouble-free gear adjustment may be obtained.

The steering gear is of the recirculating ball nut type. The ball nut, mounted on the worm gear, is driven by means of steel balls which circulate in helical grooves in both the worm and nut. Ball return guides attached to the nut serve to recirculate the 2 sets of balls in the grooves. As the steering wheel is turned to the right, the ball nut moves upward. When the wheel is turned to the left, the ball nut moves downward.

Before doing the adjustment procedures, ensure that the steering problem is not caused by faulty suspension components, bad front end alignment, etc. Then, proceed with the following adjustments.

BEARING DRAG

1. Mark the pitman arm-to-shaft relationship. Remove the pitman arm from the shaft.

2. Disconnect the battery ground cable.

3. Loosen the wormshaft nut and back the adjuster off a ¼ turn. Remove the horn cap.

4. Turn the steering wheel gently to the left stop, then back ½ turn.

5. Position an inch-pound torque wrench on the steering wheel nut and rotate it through a 90 degree arc. Note the torque required to turn the shaft. Proper torque is 5–8 inch lbs. (0.6–1 Nm).

NOTE: Do not use a torque wrench with a maximum torque reading of over 50 inch lbs. (6 Nm).

6. If the torque is incorrect, tighten the adjuster plug until the proper torque reading is achieved.

7. Hold the plug and tighten the adjuster locknut to 85 ft. lbs. (115 Nm).

NOTE: If the gear feels lumpy after adjustment this is probably due to a previous out of adjustment condition and damage has been done to the bearings. The gear will need to be replaced or rebuilt to correct the condition.

OVERCENTER PRELOAD

1. Turn the steering wheel lock-to-lock counting the total number of turns. Turn the wheel back ½ the total number of turns to the centered position.

2. Turn the lash (sector shaft) adjuster screw clockwise to remove all lash between the ball nut and sector teeth. Tighten the locknut to 22 ft. lbs. (30 Nm).

3. Using a torque wrench on the steering wheel nut, observe the highest reading while the gear is turned through the center position. It should be 16 inch lbs. (1.8 Nm) maximum torque.

4. If necessary repeat the adjustment procedure. Tighten the locknut to 22 ft. lbs. (30 Nm).

Power Steering Gear

REMOVAL AND INSTALLATION

Compact Pick-Up, Van and Utility

1. Disconnect the negative battery cable. Position the wheels in the straight-ahead position.

2. Disconnect and cap the fluid lines.

3. If equipped, remove the steering gear coupling shield. Matchmark and remove the steering gear to lower coupling and bolt. On some vehicles, it may be necessary to separate the coupling at the upper and lower flange bolts.

4. Raise and support the vehicle safely. Matchmark the pitman arm to the steering gear. Remove the pitman arm retaining nut and washer. Using the proper tool, separate the pitman arm from the steering gear assembly.

5. Remove the steering gear retaining bolts. Remove the steering gear.

To install:

6. Install the steering gear in position in the vehicle.

7. Install the mounting bolts. Tighten the mounting bolts to 55 ft. lbs. (75 Nm).

8. Connect the steering gear coupling at the flange bolts.

9. Connect the pitman arm to the steering gear. Tighten the pitman arm retaining bolt to 185 ft. lbs. (250 Nm).

10. Connect the fluid lines. Install the coupling shield. Lower the vehicle.

11. Connect the negative battery cable. Fill and bleed the power steering system.

Full Size Pick-Up, Van and Utility

R/V-SERIES

1. Set the front wheels in straight-ahead position by driving vehicle a short distance on a flat surface. Raise and support the vehicle safely as required.

2. Place a drain pan below the steering gear.

3. Disconnect the negative battery cable.

4. Disconnect the fluid lines. Cap the openings.

5. Mark the relationship of the pitman arm to the pitman shaft.

6. Remove the pitman shaft nut and then remove the pitman arm from the pitman shaft, using puller J-6632.

7. Remove the steering gear to frame bolts and remove the gear assembly.

To install:

8. Align the flat of the flexible coupling with the flat on the shaft. Push the coupling onto the shaft until the wormshaft bottoms against the end of the shaft.

9. Install the pinch bolt. Make sure the bolt passes through the shaft undercut. Tighten the pinch bolt to 75 ft. lbs. (102 Nm).

10. Place the steering gear into position, guiding the coupling bolts into the proper holes in the shaft flange.

11. Install the steering gear to frame bolts and torque to 66 ft. lbs. (90 Nm).

12. Install the coupling flange nuts and washers. Make sure the coupling alignment pins are centered in the flange slots. Tighten the nuts to 20 ft. lbs. (27 Nm). Maintain a coupling to flange dimension of 0.250–0.375 inches (6.4–9.5mm).

13. Install the pitman arm.

14. Install the hoses.

G-SERIES

1. Set the front wheels in straight-ahead position by driving vehicle a short distance on a flat surface. Raise

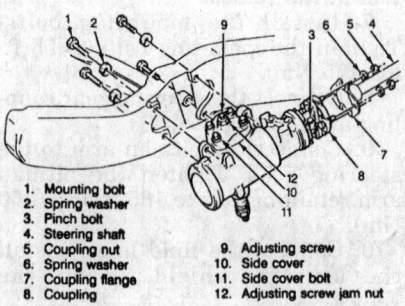

1. Mounting bolt
2. Spring washer
3. Pinch bolt
4. Steering shaft
5. Coupling nut
6. Spring washer
7. Coupling flange
8. Coupling
9. Adjusting screw
10. Side cover
11. Side cover bolt
12. Adjusting screw jam nut

85473191

Power steering gear installation — R-Series

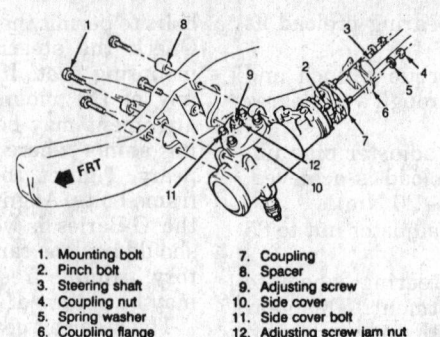

1. Mounting bolt
2. Pinch bolt
3. Steering shaft
4. Coupling nut
5. Spring washer
6. Coupling flange
7. Coupling
8. Spacer
9. Adjusting screw
10. Side cover
11. Side cover bolt
12. Adjusting screw jam nut

85473192

Power steering gear installation — V-Series

short distance on a flat surface. Raise and support the vehicle safely, as required.

2. Place a drain pan below the steering gear.

3. Disconnect the negative battery cable.

4. Disconnect the fluid lines. Cap the openings.

5. Matchmark the relationship of the universal yoke to the stubshaft.

6. Remove the universal yoke pinch bolt.

7. Mark the relationship of the pitman arm to the pitman shaft.

8. Remove the pitman shaft nut and then remove the pitman arm from the pitman shaft, using puller J-6632.

9. Remove the steering gear to frame bolts and remove the gear assembly.

To install:

10. Ensure the gear is in the centered position. Install the steering gear, guiding the steering gear shaft into the universal yoke.

11. Install the steering gear to frame bolts and torque to 66 ft. lbs. (90 Nm).

12. Install the yoke pinch bolt. Torque the pinch bolt to 46 ft. lbs. (62 Nm).

13. Install the pitman arm onto the pitman shaft, lining up the marks made at removal.

14. Connect the fluid lines and refill the reservoir. Bleed the system.

ADJUSTMENTS

Compact Pick-Up, Van and Utility

For proper adjustment, remove the gear from the vehicle and drain all the fluid from the gear and place the gear in a holding fixture. It is important that the adjustments be made in the order given.

WORM BEARING PRELOAD

1. Loosen the adjuster plug locknut.

2. Turn the adjuster plug in clockwise until firmly bottomed. Then, tighten it to 20 ft. lbs. (27 Nm).

3. Place an index mark on the gear housing in line with 1 of the holes in the adjuster plug.

4. Measure counterclockwise from the mark about ½ inch and place another mark on the housing.

5. Rotate the adjuster plug counterclockwise until the hole is aligned with the 2nd mark.

6. Install the locknut. Hold the plug and tighten the locknut to 81 ft. lbs. (110 Nm).

7. Place an inch lb. torque wrench and 12-point deep socket on the steering gear stub shaft and measure the stub shaft rotating torque, starting with the torque wrench handle in a vertical position to a point ¼ turn to either side. Note your reading. The proper torque should be 4–10 inch lbs. (0.45–1.13 Nm). If the reading is incorrect, either the adjustment was done incorrectly or there is gear damage.

OVERCENTER PRELOAD

1. Loosen the locknut and turn the pitman shaft adjuster screw counterclockwise until it is all the way out. Then, turn it in 1 turn.

2. Rotate the stub shaft from stop to stop, counting the total number of turns, then turn the shaft back ⅔ that number to center the gear. The stub shaft flat spot should face up.

3. Place the torque wrench in a vertical position on the stub shaft and measure the torque necessary to rotate the shaft to a point 45 degrees to either side of center. Record the highest reading.

4. Turn the adjuster in until the reading is 6–10 inch lbs. higher then the previous reading.

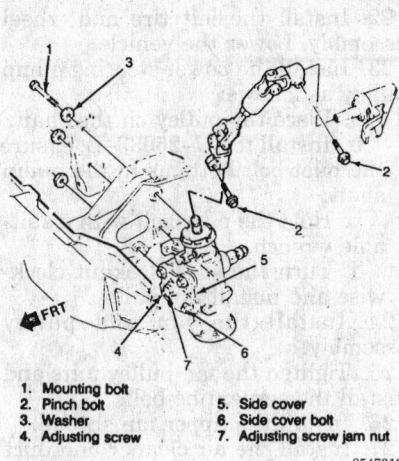

1. Mounting bolt
2. Pinch bolt
3. Washer
4. Adjusting screw
5. Side cover
6. Side cover bolt
7. Adjusting screw jam nut

85473193

Power steering gear installation — G-Series

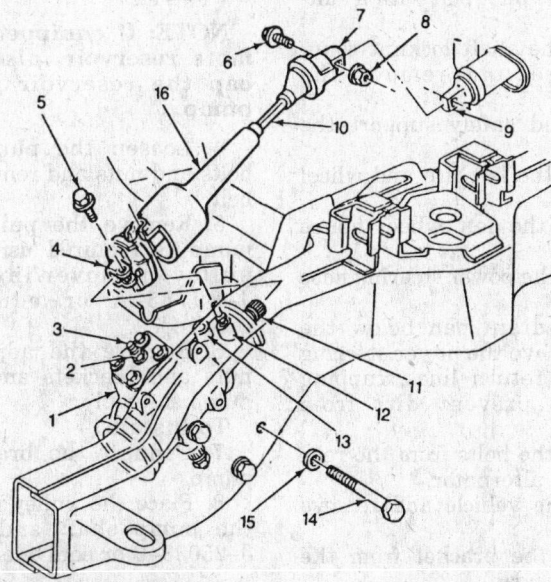

1. Steering gear
2. Jam nut
3. Adjuster screw
4. Lower intershaft clamp
5. Lower clamp bolt
6. Upper clamp bolt
7. Upper clamp
8. Retaining nut
9. Main shaft
10. Intershaft
11. Steering shaft
12. Feed
13. Return
14. Mounting bolt
15. Washer
16. Shield

85473194

Power steering gear installation — C/K-Series

5. If necessary, adjust the torque reading by turning the adjuster screw.

6. When the adjustment is made, hold the screw and tighten the locknut to 20 ft. lbs. (27 Nm).

7. Install the gear and bleed the system.

Full Size Pick-Up, Van and Utility

For proper adjustment, remove the gear from the vehicle, drain all the fluid from the gear and place the gear in a holding fixture. It is important that the adjustments be made in the order given.

WORM BEARING PRELOAD

1. Loosen the adjuster plug locknut.

2. Turn the adjuster plug in clockwise until firmly bottomed. Then, tighten it to 20 ft. lbs. (27 Nm).

3. Place an index mark on the gear housing in line with 1 of the holes in the adjuster plug.

4. Measure counterclockwise from the mark about ¼ inch and make another mark on the housing.

5. Rotate the adjuster plug counterclockwise until the hole is aligned with the 2nd mark.

6. Install the locknut. Hold the plug and tighten the locknut to 81 ft. lbs. (110 Nm).

7. Place an inch pound torque wrench and 12-point deep socket on the stub shaft and measure the stub shaft rotating torque, starting with the torque wrench handle in a vertical position to a point ¼ turn to either side. Note your reading. The proper torque should be 4–10 inch lbs. (0.45–1.13 Nm). If the reading is incorrect, either your adjustment was done incorrectly or there is gear damage.

OVERCENTER PRELOAD

1. Loosen the locknut and turn the pitman shaft adjuster screw counterclockwise until it is all the way out. Then, turn it in ½ turn.

2. Rotate the stub shaft from stop to stop, counting the total number of turns, then turn the shaft ½ that number to center the gear.

3. Place the torque wrench in a vertical position on the stub shaft and measure the torque necessary to rotate the shaft to a point 45 degrees to either side of center. Record the highest reading. On gears with less than 400 miles, the reading should be 6–10 inch lbs. higher than the worm bearing preload torque previously recorded, but not to exceed 18 inch lbs. (2 Nm). On gears with more than 400 miles, the reading should be 4–5 inch lbs. higher, but not to exceed 14 inch lbs. (1.5 Nm).

4. If necessary, adjust the torque reading by turning the adjuster screw.

5. When the adjustment is made, hold the screw and tighten the locknut to 35 ft. lbs. (47 Nm).

6. Install the gear and bleed the system.

Power Steering Rack and Pinion

REMOVAL AND INSTALLATION

1. Disconnect the negative battery cable.

2. Remove the air cleaner assembly.

3. Remove the dust boot from the steering gear.

4. Remove the intermediate shaft lower pinch bolt and disconnect the intermediate shaft from the lower stub shaft.

5. Remove the fluid line retaining clips at the pump and disconnect the lines.

6. Raise and safely support the vehicle.

7. Remove the wheel and tire assemblies. Disconnect the tie rod ends at the steering knuckle.

8. Remove the remaining brackets and clips at the crossmember. Support the body safely with the appropriate equipment, to allow lowering of the subframe.

9. Remove the rear subframe mounting bolts and carefully lower the rear of the subframe approximately 5 in. (128mm).

10. Remove the rack and pinion mounting bolts and remove the rack through the left wheel opening.

To install:

11. Install the rack and pinion through the left wheel opening.

12. Install the rack and pinion mounting nuts, tighten to 70 ft. lbs. (95 Nm).

13. Raise the subframe assembly and install the rear mounting bolts.

14. Remove any supports and install the brackets and clips to the crossmember.

15. Install the wheel and tire assemblies. Lower the vehicle.

16. Connect the fluid lines at the pump and tighten to 18 ft. lbs. (25 Nm).

17. Install the line retaining clips. Connect the intermediate shaft to the stub shaft.

18. Install the dust boot over the steering gear.

19. Install the air cleaner assembly and connect the negative battery cable.

20. Fill and bleed the steering system.

RACK BEARING PRELOAD ADJUSTMENT

1. Raise and support the vehicle safely. Ensure the steering wheel is centered.

2. Loosen the adjuster plug locknut and turn the adjuster plug clockwise until it bottoms in the housing; then back off 50–70 degrees.

3. Check the returnability of the steering wheel after the adjustment.

4. Tighten the locknut to 50 ft. lbs. (70 Nm), while holding the adjuster plug stationary.

5. Lower the vehicle.

Power Steering Pump

REMOVAL AND INSTALLATION

Compact Pick-Up, Van and Utility

EXCEPT TURBOCHARGED ENGINE

1. Disconnect the negative battery cable. Disconnect and cap the power steering pump hoses. Remove the accessory drive belt.

2. As required, remove the power steering pump pulley using a suitable puller tool or equivalent.

3. Remove the pump mounting bolts. Remove the pump.

4. Installation is the reverse of the removal procedure. Bleed the power steering system.

TURBOCHARGED ENGINE

1. Disconnect the negative battery cable.

2. Remove the air cleaner and duct assembly.

3. Remove the upper fan shroud.

4. Loosen the fan nuts and remove the serpentine belt.

5. Remove the fan and pulley assembly.

6. Remove the power steering pump pulley as follows:

a. Install tool J–25034–B, ensure the pilot bolt bottoms in the pump shaft.

b. Hold the pilot bolt with a suitable wrench.

c. Turn the shaft locknut counterclockwise and remove the pulley.

7. Raise and safely support the vehicle.

8. Remove the left tire and wheel assembly.

9. Remove the left wheel house panel.

10. Remove the power steering hose bracket.

11. Place a drain pan below the pump and remove the power steering pressure and return lines, capping the lines to prevent dirt from entering.

12. Remove the bolts from the rear bracket at the alternator.

13. Lower the vehicle and remove the assembly.

14. Remove the bracket from the pump as necessary.

To install:

15. Install the bracket to the pump, if removed.

16. Install the pump assembly and torque the bolts to 37 ft. lbs. (50 Nm).

17. Install the bolts to the rear bracket at the alternator.

18. Install the power steering pressure and return lines.

19. Install the power steering hose bracket.

20. Raise and safely support the vehicle.

21. Install the left wheel house panel.

22. Install the left tire and wheel assembly. Lower the vehicle.

23. Install the power steering pump pulley as follows:

a. Place the pulley on the shaft.

b. Install tool J–25033–B, ensure the pilot bolt bottoms in the pump shaft.

c. Hold the pilot bolt with a suitable wrench.

d. Turn the shaft locknut clockwise and install the pulley.

24. Install the fan and pulley assembly.

25. Tighten the fan pulley nuts and install the serpentine belt.

26. Install the upper fan shroud.

27. Install the air cleaner and duct assembly.

28. Connect the negative battery cable. Fill and bleed the power steering system. Check system for leaks.

Full Size Pick-Up, Van and Utility

1. Place a drain pan under the pump.

2. Disconnect the negative battery cable.

3. Disconnect and cap the hoses at the pump.

NOTE: If equipped with a remote reservoir, disconnect and cap the reservoir hose at the pump.

4. Loosen the pump adjusting bolts and nuts and remove the pump belt.

5. Remove the pulley from the pump as required using a suitable pulley remover/installer tool J–29785–A or equivalent, as required.

6. Remove the adjusting bolts, nuts and brackets and remove the pump assembly.

To install:

7. Connect the brackets to the pump.

8. Place the pulley on the end of the pump shaft and install tool J–25033–B or equivalent.

NOTE: On models with a remote reservoir fill the pump housing with as much fluid as possible before mounting.

9. Install the pump assembly and attaching parts loosely to the engine.

10. Install the hoses to the pump and fill the reservoir. Bleed the pump by turning the pulley backwards

(counterclockwise as viewed from the front) until the air bubbles cease to appear.

11. Tighten all retaining bolts and nuts.

12. Install the pump belt over the pulley and adjust.

13. Fill and bleed the system.

SYSTEM BLEEDING

1. Fill the reservoir to the proper level and let the fluid remain undisturbed for at least 2 minutes.

2. Start the engine and run it for only about 2 seconds.

3. Add fluid as necessary.

4. Repeat Steps 1–3 until the level remains constant.

5. Raise the front of the vehicle so the front wheels are off the ground. Set the parking brake and block both rear wheels front and rear. Manual transmissions should be in neutral; automatic transmissions should be in **P**.

6. Start the engine and run it at approximately 1500 rpm.

7. Turn the wheels (off the ground) to the right and left, lightly contacting the stops.

8. Add fluid as necessary.

9. Lower the vehicle and turn the wheels right and left on the ground.

10. Check the level and refill as necessary.

11. If the fluid is extremely foamy, let the vehicle stand for a few minutes with the engine off and repeat the procedure. Check the belt tension and check for a bent or loose pulley. The pulley should not wobble with the engine running.

12. Check that no hoses are contacting any parts of the vehicle, particularly sheetmetal.

13. Check the fluid level and refill as necessary.

14. Check for air in the fluid. Aerated fluid appears milky. If air is present, repeat the above operation. If it is obvious that the pump will not respond to bleeding after several attempts, a pressure test may be required.

Tie Rod Ends

REMOVAL AND INSTALLATION

M/L-Series and S/T-Series

1. Raise and support the vehicle safely. Remove the tire and wheel assemblies.

2. Remove the cotter pins and nuts. Using the proper removal tool, separate the outer tie rod from the steering knuckle.

3. Disconnect the inner tie rod from the relay rod using the proper tool. Remove the tie rod ends from the adjuster tubes.

4. Installation is the reverse of the removal procedure. Tighten the inner tie rod ball stud nut to 35 ft. lbs. (47 Nm). Tighten the outer tie rod ball stud to the steering knuckle to 35 ft. lbs. (47 Nm). The number of threads on both the inner and outer tie rod ends must be equal within 3 threads.

5. Adjust the front end alignment, as required.

Lumina, Silhouette and Trans Sport

OUTER

1. Raise and support the vehicle safely. Remove the tire and wheel assemblies.

2. Remove the cotter pins and nuts. Using the proper removal tool, separate the outer tie rod from the steering knuckle.

3. Disconnect the inner tie rod from the relay rod using the proper tool. Remove the tie rod ends from the adjuster tubes.

4. Installation is the reverse of the removal procedure. Tighten the inner tie rod ball stud nut to 35 ft. lbs. (47 Nm). Tighten the outer tie rod ball stud to the steering knuckle to 35 ft. lbs. (47 Nm). The number of threads on both the inner and outer tie rod ends must be equal within 3 threads.

5. Adjust the front end alignment, as required.

INNER

1. Disconnect the negative battery cable.

2. Raise and support the vehicle safely.

3. Remove the rack and pinion assembly.

4. Place the assembly in a holding fixture.

5. Remove the outer tie rod assembly. Remove the inner tie rod jam nut.

6. Remove the tie rod end boot clamps. Remove the boot.

7. Remove the shock dampener from the inner tie rod assembly.

8. Remove the tie rod from the rack. Place a wrench on the flat of the rack assembly and another wrench on the flats of the inner tie rod housing.

9. Installation is the reverse of the removal procedure.

C/K, R and G-Series

NOTE: Before servicing, note the position of the tie rod adjuster tube and the direction from which the bolts are installed. Do not attempt to disengage the tie rod ball stud using a wedge type tool, because seal damage could result.

1. Raise and support the vehicle safely. As required, remove the tire and wheel assembly.

2. Remove the cotter pins and nuts. Using the proper removal tool J–6627A separate the outer tie rod from the steering knuckle.

3. Disconnect the inner tie rod from the relay rod using tool J–6627A. Remove the tie rod ends from the adjuster tubes, counting the number of turns to aid in installation.

To install:

4. Grease the threads and turn the new tie rod end in as many turns as were needed to remove it. This will give approximately correct toe-in. Tighten the clamp bolts to 14 ft. lbs.

5. Secure the tie rod ends to the relay rod and steering knuckle with a new nut. Tighten the nuts to 40 ft. lbs. (54 Nm) and install new cotter pins. Tighten the nut to align the cotter pin, do not loosen it.

6. Install the tire and wheel assembly.

7. Lower the vehicle and check the front end alignment.

V-Series

1. Raise and support the vehicle safely. As required, remove the tire and wheel assembly.

2. Remove the cotter pins and nuts from the rod assembly. Disconnect the shock absorber from the tie rod assembly.

3. Using the proper removal tool, J–6627A, separate the outer tie rods from the steering knuckle.

NOTE: Do not attempt to disengage the ball joint from the steering knuckle using a wedge type tool, because seal damage could result.

4. Disconnect the tie rod end bodies. Count the number of turns needed to remove the end bodies. Remove the tie rod ends from the adjuster tube.

5. Note the position of the adjuster tube and the direction from which the bolts are installed.

To install:

6. Install the tie rod ends the same number of turns as counted previously. Tighten the locknuts.

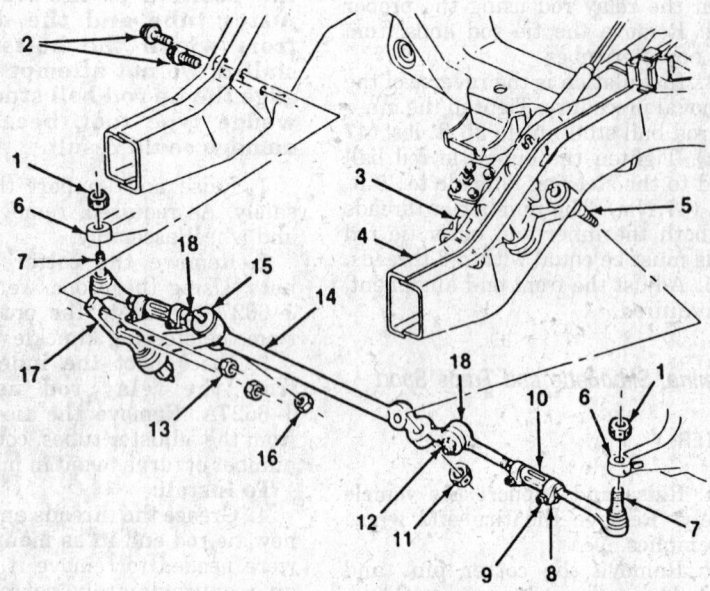

1. Tie rod outer ball joint nut
2. Idler arm frame bolts
3. Steering gear
4. Frame
5. Pitman arm ball stud
6. Knuckle
7. Tie rod ball stud
8. Clamp
9. Clamp nut
10. Adjuster tube
11. Pitman arm nut
12. Tie rod inner ball joint nut
13. Idler arm frame nut
14. Relay rod
15. Idler arm ball joint
16. Idler arm ball joint nut
17. Idler arm mounting bracket
18. Tie rod inner ball joint

85473195

Steering linkage — C-Series

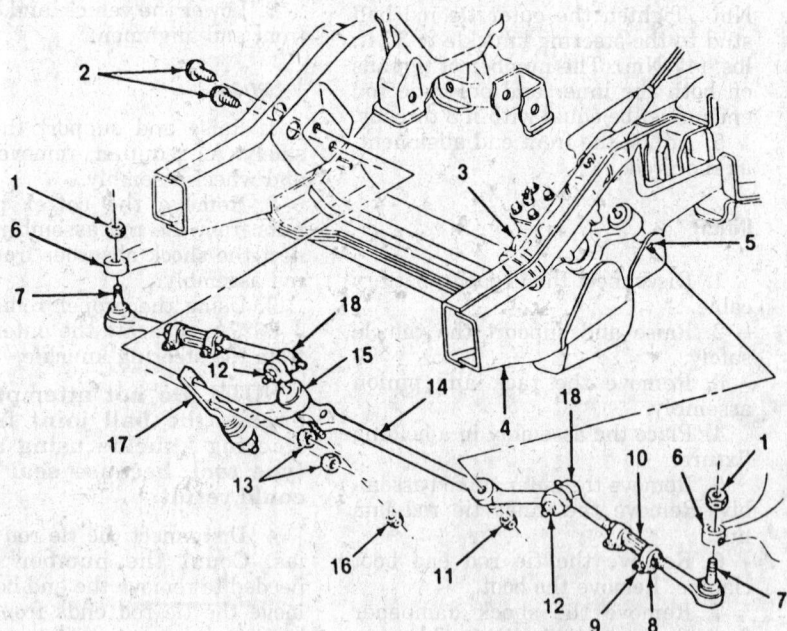

1. Tie rod outer ball joint nut
2. Idler arm frame bolts
3. Steering gear
4. Frame
5. Pitman arm ball stud
6. Knuckle
7. Tie rod ball stud
8. Clamp
9. Clamp nut
10. Adjuster tube
11. Pitman arm nut
12. Tie rod inner ball joint nut
13. Idler arm frame nut
14. Relay rod
15. Idler arm ball joint
16. Idler arm ball joint nut
17. Idler arm mounting bracket
18. Tie rod inner ball joint

85473196

Steering linkage — K-Series

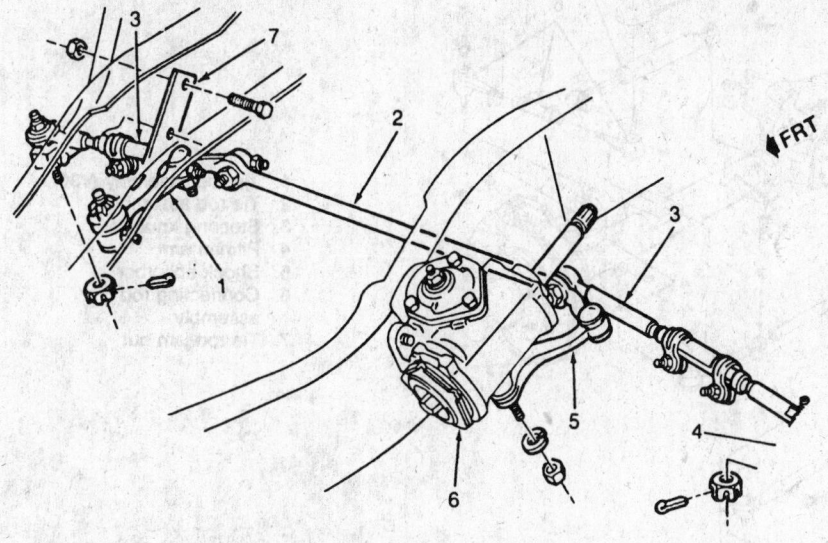

◄FRT

1. Idler arm
2. Relay rod
3. Tie rod assembly
4. Steering knuckle
5. Pitman arm
6. Steering gear
7. Idler arm frame support

85473197

Steering linkage — R-Series

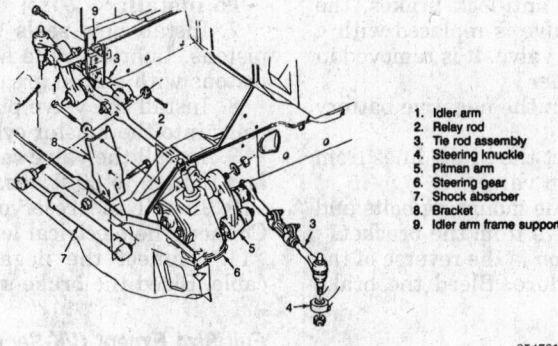

1. Idler arm
2. Relay rod
3. Tie rod assembly
4. Steering knuckle
5. Pitman arm
6. Steering gear
7. Shock absorber
8. Bracket
9. Idler arm frame support

85473198

Steering linkage — G-Series

7. Install the tie rod assembly in the knuckles and tighten the castellated nuts to 40 ft. lbs. (55 Nm). Always advance the nut to align the cotter pin hole. Never back it off.

8. Tighten the tie rod end jam nuts to 175 ft. lbs. (237 Nm).

9. Install the tire and wheel assembly. Lower the vehicle and adjust the front alignment, as required.

BRAKES

Master Cylinder

REMOVAL AND INSTALLATION

Compact Pick-Up, Van and Utility

1. Disconnect the negative battery cable.

2. Disconnect the electrical connections from the master cylinder, as required. Disconnect and plug the fluid lines.

NOTE: On Lumina APV, Silhouette and Trans Sport, the master cylinder reservoir can be removed to ease master cylinder removal.

3. Remove the master cylinder to power booster retaining bolts. Remove the RWAL control module assembly, if equipped with anti-lock brakes.

4. Remove the master cylinder. Remove the vacuum booster pushrod.
To install:

5. Install the master cylinder in position on the booster. Connect the booster pushrod.

6. Install the master cylinder retaining bolts and tighten to 20 ft. lbs. (27 Nm).

7. Connect the fluid lines to the master cylinder. Connect the RWAL control unit, if equipped with anti-lock brakes, to the bracket.

8. Connect the negative battery cable. Refill the master cylinder and bleed the brake system.

Full Size Pick-Up, Van and Utility

1. Disconnect the negative battery cable. Disconnect any electrical connections from the master cylinder, as

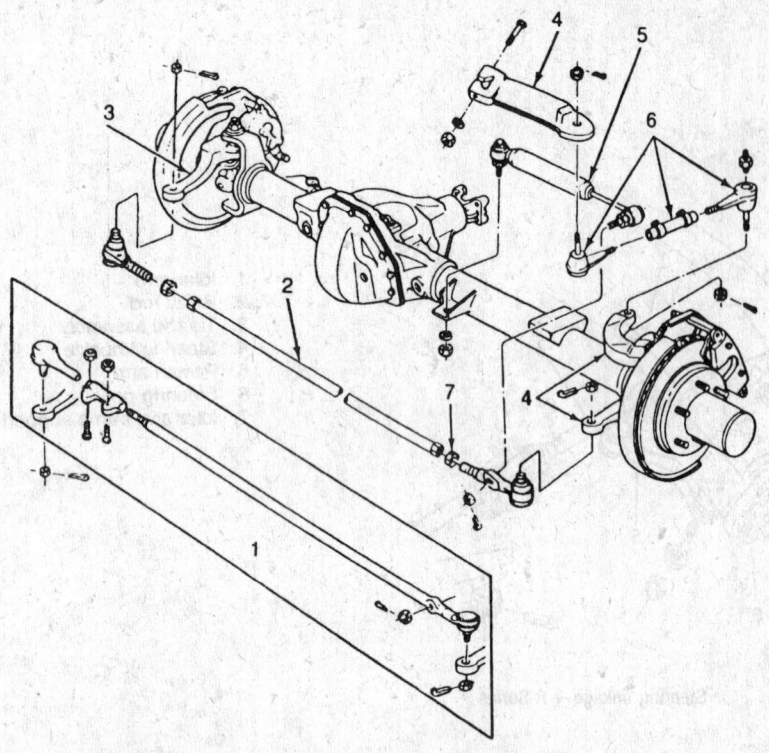

1. Tie rod assembly (V30)
2. Tie rod assembly
3. Steering knuckle
4. Pitman arm
5. Shock absorber
6. Connecting rod assembly
7. Tie rod jam nut

85473199

Steering linkage — V-Series

required. Disconnect and plug the fluid lines.

2. If equipped with power brakes, remove the master cylinder to power booster retaining bolts. Remove the Rear Wheel Anti-Lock (RWAL) control module assembly, if equipped. Do not allow fluid to leak onto the module.

3. If equipped with manual brakes, remove the master cylinder pushrod from the brake pedal and remove the RWAL control module assembly.

4. Remove the master cylinder. If equipped with power brakes remove the vacuum booster pushrod.

5. Installation is the reverse of the removal procedure. Bench bleed the master cylinder prior to installation. If equipped with power brakes be sure to install the vacuum booster pushrod. Bleed the system, as required.

Combination Valve

REMOVAL AND INSTALLATION

M/L-Series and S/T-Series

The combination valve is mounted on the master cylinder bracket. If

equipped with anti-lock brakes, the combination valve is replaced with a dump/isolation valve. It is removed in the same manner.

1. Disconnect the negative battery cable.

2. Disconnect the brake lines from the combination valve.

3. Remove the mounting bolts and remove the valve from the bracket.

4. Installation is the reverse of the removal procedure. Bleed the brake system.

Proportioning Valve

REMOVAL AND INSTALLATION

Lumina, Silhouette and Trans Sport

1. Disconnect the negative battery cable.

2. Remove the electrical connector from the master cylinder.

3. Drain and remove the master cylinder reservoir.

4. Remove the proportioning valve caps from the master cylinder.

5. Remove the O-rings, springs and the valve pistons. Use care not to scratch the valves in any way.

6. Remove the valve seals from the valve pistons.

To install:

7. Install new seals on the valve pistons. Lubricate the seals and the pistons with silicon grease.

8. Install the valve pistons and O-rings into the master cylinder.

9. Install the valve cap assemblies and tighten to 20 ft. lbs. (27 Nm).

10. Install the reservoir assembly. Connect the electrical leads.

11. Connect the negative battery cable. Bleed the brake system.

Full Size Except C/K-Series

1. Disconnect the negative battery cable. Disconnect the hydraulic lines and plug to prevent dirt from entering the system.

2. Disconnect the warning switch harness.

3. Remove the retaining bolts and remove the valve.

4. Installation is the reverse of removal procedure. Bleed the brake system.

C/K-Series

1. Disconnect the negative battery cable. Disconnect the hydraulic lines and plug to prevent dirt from entering the system.

2. Disconnect the warning switch harness.

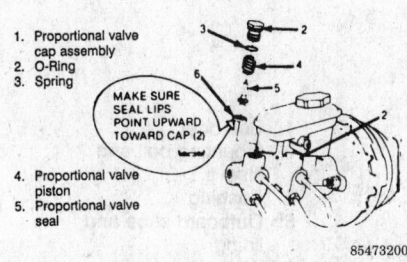

1. Proportional valve cap assembly
2. O-Ring
3. Spring

MAKE SURE SEAL LIPS POINT UPWARD TOWARD CAP (2)

4. Proportional valve piston
5. Proportional valve seal

85473200

Proportioning valve replacement — Lumina, Silhouette and Trans Sport

3. Remove the RWAL control module assembly from the bracket.

4. Remove the bolts holding the Isolation/Dump Valve to the bracket.

5. Remove the nuts that hold the master cylinder and bracket to the brake booster.

6. Remove the bracket and combination valve assembly.

7. Installation is the reverse of removal. Tighten the nuts that hold the master cylinder and bracket to the brake booster to 20 ft. lbs. (27 Nm) and the bolts holding the Isolation/Dump Valve to the bracket to 17 ft. lbs. (24 Nm).

8. Bleed the brake system.

Power Brake Booster

REMOVAL AND INSTALLATION

Vacuum Booster

COMPACT PICK-UP, VAN AND UTILITY

1. Disconnect the negative battery cable. Do not disconnect the master cylinder fluid lines, unless there is a clearance problem. Remove the master cylinder and position aside.

2. Remove the vacuum booster pushrod. Disconnect the vacuum hose from the booster assembly.

3. From inside the vehicle, remove the mounting studs which secure the vacuum booster to the fire wall.

4. Pull the booster away from the cowl and remove it.

5. Installation is the reverse of the removal procedure. Be sure to properly install the vacuum booster pushrod. Bleed the system.

FULL SIZE PICK-UP, VAN AND UTILITY

1. Disconnect the negative battery cable. Apply the parking brakes.

2. Support the master cylinder and remove the master cylinder mounting nuts.

3. Disconnect the vacuum hose from the check valve.

4. Disconnect the booster pushrod.

5. Remove the booster mounting nuts from inside the vehicle and remove the booster.

6. Installation is the reverse of removal.

Hydraulic Booster (Hydra-Boost)

1. Disconnect the negative battery cable. Apply the parking brakes.

2. Disconnect the hydraulic lines from the booster.

3. Support the master cylinder and remove the master cylinder mounting nuts.

4. Disconnect the booster pushrod.

5. Remove the booster mounting nuts from inside the vehicle and remove the booster.

6. Installation is the reverse of removal. Bleed the brake system, as follows:

   a. To bleed the hydro-boost system, fill the power steering pump to the proper level. Allow the fluid to remain undisturbed for a few minutes.

   b. Start the engine and add fluid until the level is constant with the engine running.

   c. Raise and support the vehicle safely. Start the engine and turn the wheels from stop to stop, add fluid as required. Turn the engine **OFF** and lower the vehicle.

   d. Start the engine and depress the brake pedal several times while rotating the steering wheel from stop to stop. Turn the engine off and pump the brake pedal 4–5 times.

   e. If the power steering fluid is extremely foamy, allow the vehicle to sit for a short time and then perform the procedure again.

Brake Caliper

REMOVAL AND INSTALLATION

Compact Pick-Up, Van and Utility

1. Remove $^2/_3$ of the brake fluid from the master cylinder reservoir.

2. Raise and support the vehicle safely. Remove the tire and wheel assembly.

3. Disconnect and plug the caliper fluid line. Remove the bolts retaining the caliper to the rotor. Remove the caliper from the rotor.

NOTE: If the caliper is being removed for brake pad replacement, the fluid line do not need to be disconnected.

4. Remove the disc brake pads from the caliper. Remove the disc brake pad retaining clips from inside the caliper.

To install:

5. Clean and lubricate the sleeves and bushings with silicon grease. Install the pads in the caliper.

6. Install the caliper in position over the rotor and install the mounting bolts. Tighten the mounting bolts to 38 ft. lbs. (51 Nm).

7. Connect the fluid lines to the caliper, if disconnected, and tighten to 33 ft. lbs. (45 Nm).

8. Install the wheel and tire assembly.

9. Lower the vehicle and refill the master cylinder to the correct level. Bleed the brake system if the fluid lines were disconnected from the caliper.

Full Size Pick-Up, Van and Utility

NOTE: There are 2 caliper designs and they can be identified by the method used to secure the assembly to the spindle bracket. The Delco 3000/3100 caliper is secured by a bolt and sleeve combination. The Bendix caliper assembly is secured by a slider, spring and bolt.

1. Remove the cover on the master cylinder and siphon enough fluid out of the reservoirs to bring the level to $^1/_3$ full. This step prevents spilling fluid when the piston is pushed back.

2. Raise and support the vehicle safely. Remove the front wheels and tires.

3. Position a C-clamp around the outside pad and caliper; tighten the C-clamp until the caliper piston bottoms in its bore.

4. Remove the brake hose from the caliper by removing the inlet fitting.

5. Remove the bolt and sleeve or bolt and slider assemblies which hold the caliper and then lift the caliper off the rotor.

6. Remove the inboard and outboard shoe.

To install:

7. Install the pads onto the caliper.

8. Position the caliper onto the knuckle/rotor assembly and secure the assembly with the mounting bolts or sliders.

9. Reconnect the brake line to the caliper.

10. Pump the brake pedal and verify there is minimal brake pedal travel.

11. Check the brake fluid level. Install the tire and wheel assembly.

12. Lower the vehicle.

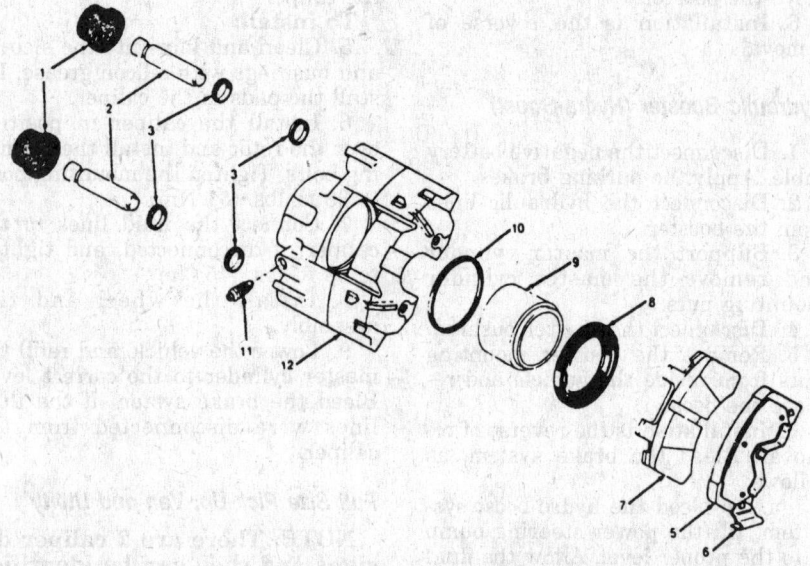

1. Bolt boot
2. Mounting bolt and sleeve
3. Bushing
5. Outboard shoe and lining
6. Wear sensor
7. Inboard shoe and lining
8. Boot
9. Piston
10. Piston seal
11. Bleeder valve
12. Caliper housing

85473201

Exploded view of a common caliper assembly — compact vehicle

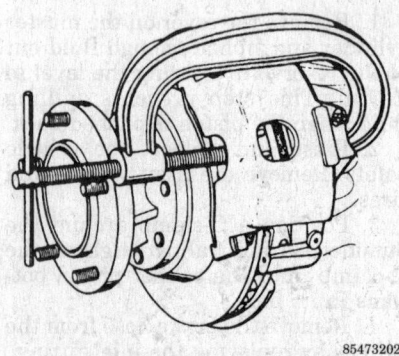

85473202

Compressing the caliper piston

Disc Brake Pads

REMOVAL AND INSTALLATION

Compact Pick-Up, Van and Utility

1. Remove ⅔ of the brake fluid from the master cylinder.
2. Raise and safely support the vehicle.
3. Place a C-clamp around the outer pad and caliper; tighten the C-clamp until the piston is fully compressed in the caliper. Remove the brake caliper.

4. Remove the inboard pad and retaining spring from the caliper.
5. Remove the outboard pad from the caliper.
6. Remove the sleeves and bushings.
   To install:
7. Clean and lubricate the sleeves and bushing with silicon lubricant and install them in the caliper.
8. Clip the retaining spring onto the inboard pad and install the pad in the caliper.
9. Install the outboard pad into the caliper.
10. Install the caliper in position over the rotor and install the mounting bolts. Bend the tabs, on the outboard brake pad, over the caliper.
11. Install the wheel and tire assemblies.
12. Lower the vehicle, refill the master cylinder and pump pedal to attain full brake pedal before road testing the vehicle.

Full Size Pick-Up, Van and Utility

DELCO TYPE

1. Remove the cover on the master cylinder and siphon out ⅔ of the fluid. This step prevents spilling fluid when the piston is pushed back into the caliper bore.

2. Raise and support the vehicle safely.
3. Remove the wheels.
4. Compress the brake piston back into its bore using a C-clamp.
5. Remove the 2 bolts which hold the caliper and then lift the caliper off the disc.

NOTE: Do not let the caliper assembly hang by the brake hose.

6. Remove the inboard and outboard shoe.
7. Remove the pad support spring from the piston, if equipped.
   To install:
8. Thoroughly inspect, clean and lubricate all caliper slide points, bolts and hardware.
9. Position the retainer spring on the inner pad and insert the assembly into the center cavity of the piston.
10. Push down on the inner pad until it lays flat against the caliper. It is important to push the piston all the way into the caliper if new linings are installed or the caliper will not fit over the rotor.
11. Position the outboard pad with the ears of the pad over the caliper ears and the tab at the bottom engaged in the caliper cutout.
12. With the 2 pads in position, place the caliper over the brake disc

and align the holes in the caliper with those of the mounting bracket.

NOTE: Make certain the brake hose is not twisted or kinked.

13. Install the mounting bracket bolts through the sleeves in the inboard caliper ears and through the mounting bracket, making sure the ends of the bolts pass under the retaining ears on the inboard pad.

14. Tighten the mounting bolts to 35 ft. lbs. (48 Nm). After both calipers are mounted pump the brake pedal to seat the pad against the rotor. Use a pair of channel lock pliers to bend over the upper ears of the outer pad so it isn't loose.

15. Install the wheels and lower the vehicle.

16. Add fluid to the master cylinder reservoirs so they are ¼ in. (6.35mm) from the top.

17. Test the brake pedal by pumping it to obtain a hard pedal. Check the fluid level again and add fluid as necessary. Do not move the vehicle until a pedal is obtained.

BENDIX TYPE

1. Remove approximately ⅓ of the brake fluid from the master cylinder. Discard the used brake fluid.

2. Raise and support the vehicle safely and remove the wheel.

3. Push the piston back into its bore. This can be done by using a C-clamp.

4. Remove the bolt at the caliper slider. Use a brass drift pin to remove the slider and spring.

5. Rotate the caliper up and forward from the bottom and lift it off the caliper support.

6. Tie the caliper out of the way with a piece of wire. Be careful not to damage the brake line.

7. Remove the inner shoe from the caliper support. Discard the inner shoe clip.

8. Remove the outer shoe from the caliper.

To install:

9. Thoroughly clean, inspect and lubricate the caliper, slider and spring with silicone.

10. Install a new inboard shoe clip on the shoe.

11. Install the lower end of the inboard shoe into the groove provided in the support. Slide the upper end of the shoe into position. Be sure the clip remains in position.

12. Position the outboard shoe in the caliper with the ears at the top of the shoe over the caliper ears and the tab at the bottom of the shoe engaged in the caliper cutout. If assembly is

difficult, a C-clamp may be used. Be careful not to damage the lining.

13. Position the caliper over the brake disc, top edge first. Rotate the caliper downward onto the support.

14. Place the spring over the caliper support key, install the assembly between the support and lower caliper groove. Tap into place until the key retaining screw can be installed.

15. Install the screw and torque to 15 ft. lbs. (20 Nm). The boss must fit fully into the circular cutout in the key.

16. Install the wheel and add brake fluid as necessary.

Brake Drums

REMOVAL AND INSTALLATION

Compact Pick-Up, Van and Utility

1. Raise and safely support the vehicle.

2. Remove the wheel and tire assembly.

3. Remove the brake drum. If the drum will not pull of the axle, use a rubber mallet and tap it around the edge.

4. Install the drum on the axle and install the wheel and tire assembly.

5. Lower the vehicle.

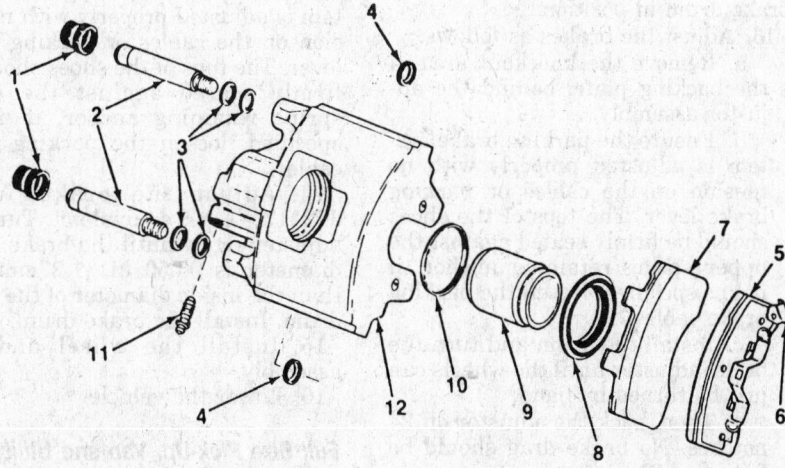

1. Bolt boot
2. Mounting bolt assembly
3. Bushing
4. Mounting bolt seal
5. Outboard shoe and lining
6. Wear sensor
7. Inboard shoe and lining
8. Boot
9. Piston
10. Piston seal
11. Bleeder valve
12. Caliper housing

85473203

Replacing the disc brake pads — Delco type

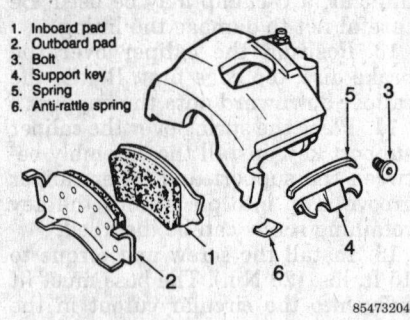

1. Inboard pad
2. Outboard pad
3. Bolt
4. Support key
5. Spring
6. Anti-rattle spring

85473204

Replacing the disc brake pads — Bendix type

Full Size Pick-Up, Van and Utility

SEMI-FLOATING AXLES

1. Raise and support the vehicle safely.

2. Mark the relationship of the wheel to the hub and remove the wheel.

3. Mark the relationship of the drum to the hub and pull the drum from the brake assembly. If the brake drums have been scored from worn linings, the brake adjuster must be backed off so the brake shoes will retract from the drum. The adjuster can be backed off by inserting a brake adjusting tool through the access hole provided. In some cases the access hole is provided in the brake drum. A metal cover plate is over the hole. This may be removed by using a hammer and chisel.

4. To install, reverse the removal procedure.

FULL FLOATING AXLES

To remove the drums from full floating rear axles, the axle shaft will have to be removed. Full floating rear axles can readily be identified by the bearing housing protruding through the center of the wheel.

1. Raise and support the vehicle safely.

2. Remove the wheel.

3. Remove the axle shaft.

4. Remove the retaining ring, key and adjusting nut.

5. Remove the hub and drum.

To install:

6. Install the hub and drum to the tube.

7. Install the adjusting nut and torque to specification.

8. Install the key and retaining ring.

9. Install the axle shaft and wheel.

Brake Shoes

REMOVAL AND INSTALLATION

M/L-Series and S/T-Series

1. Raise and safely support the vehicle.

2. Remove the wheel and tire assembly.

3. Remove the brake drum.

4. Remove the return springs from the brake shoes. Remove the shoe guide.

5. Remove the hold-down springs and pins. Remove the actuator lever and pivot.

6. Remove the lever return spring. Remove the actuator link.

7. Remove the parking brake strut and spring. Remove the parking brake lever.

8. Remove the brake shoes and the adjuster assembly.

To install:

9. Lubricate the contact points on the backing plate and the adjuster with lithium grease.

10. Install the parking brake lever, adjusting screw and spring assembly.

11. Install the shoe assembly onto the backing plate.

12. Install the parking brake lever, strut and strut spring.

13. Install the actuator lever and lever pivot. Install the actuator link.

14. Install the lever spring, the hold-down pins and springs.

15. Install the shoe guide. Install the return springs and install the brake drum in position.

16. Adjust the brakes as follows:

   a. Remove the knockout area in the backing plate, behind the adjuster assembly.

   b. Ensure the parking brake system is adjusted properly with no tension on the cables or parking brake lever. The tops of the shoes should be firmly seated against the upper spring retaining anchor, if not as specified, loosen the parking brake cables.

   c. Install the drum and turn the brake adjuster until the wheels can just be turned by hand.

   d. Then, back the adjuster off 24 notches. No brake drag should be felt after 12 notches.

   e. Install an adjusting hole plug in the backing plate to prevent dirt and moisture from entering.

   f. Readjust the parking brake cable as necessary.

17. Install the wheel and tire assemblies.

Lumina, Silhouette and Trans Sport

1. Raise and safely support the vehicle.

2. Remove the wheel and tire assembly.

3. Remove the brake drum.

4. Remove the actuator spring from the brake shoes. Remove the retractor spring from the shoe web, being careful not to over stretch the spring.

5. Remove the adjuster shoe, adjuster actuator and adjusting screw assembly.

6. Do not remove the parking brake cable from the parking brake lever, unless the lever is being replaced. Remove the parking brake shoe.

7. Remove the retractor spring, as required.

To install:

8. Lubricate the contact points on the backing plate with lithium grease. Clean and lubricate the adjuster with lithium grease.

9. Install the retractor spring, if removed.

10. Install the parking brake shoe against the backing plate and snap the retractor spring into the slot on the brake shoe. Install the parking brake lever onto the parking brake shoe.

11. Install the adjuster shoe and adjusting screw assembly. Install the retractor spring into the slot on the adjuster shoe web.

12. Lubricate and install the adjuster actuator onto the adjuster shoe. Install the actuator spring.

13. Ensure the parking brake system is adjusted properly with no tension on the cables or parking brake lever. The tops of the shoes should be firmly seated against the upper spring retaining anchor, if not as specified, loosen the parking brake cables.

14. Adjust the brakes using J–21177–A or equivalent. Turn the adjuster screw until the brake lining diameter is 0.050 in. (1.27mm) less than the inside diameter of the brake drum. Install the brake drum.

15. Install the wheel and tire assembly.

16. Lower the vehicle.

Full Size Pick-Up, Van and Utility

LEADING/TRAILING BRAKES

NOTE: This brake system is used on the lower GVW rated vehicles.

1. Raise the vehicle and support it safely.

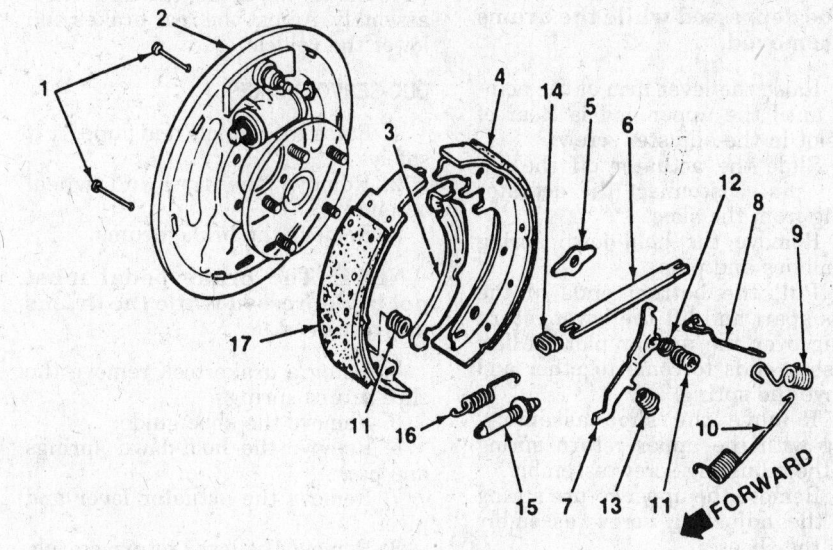

1. Hold-down pins
2. Backing plate
3. Parking brake lever
4. Secondary shoe
5. Shoe guide
6. Parking brake strut
7. Actuator lever
8. Actuator link
9. Return spring
10. Return spring
11. Hold-down springs
12. Lever pivot
13. Lever return spring
14. Strut spring
15. Adjusting screw assembly
16. Adjusting screw spring
17. Primary shoe

85473205

Exploded view of the drum brake components — M/L-Series and S/T-Series

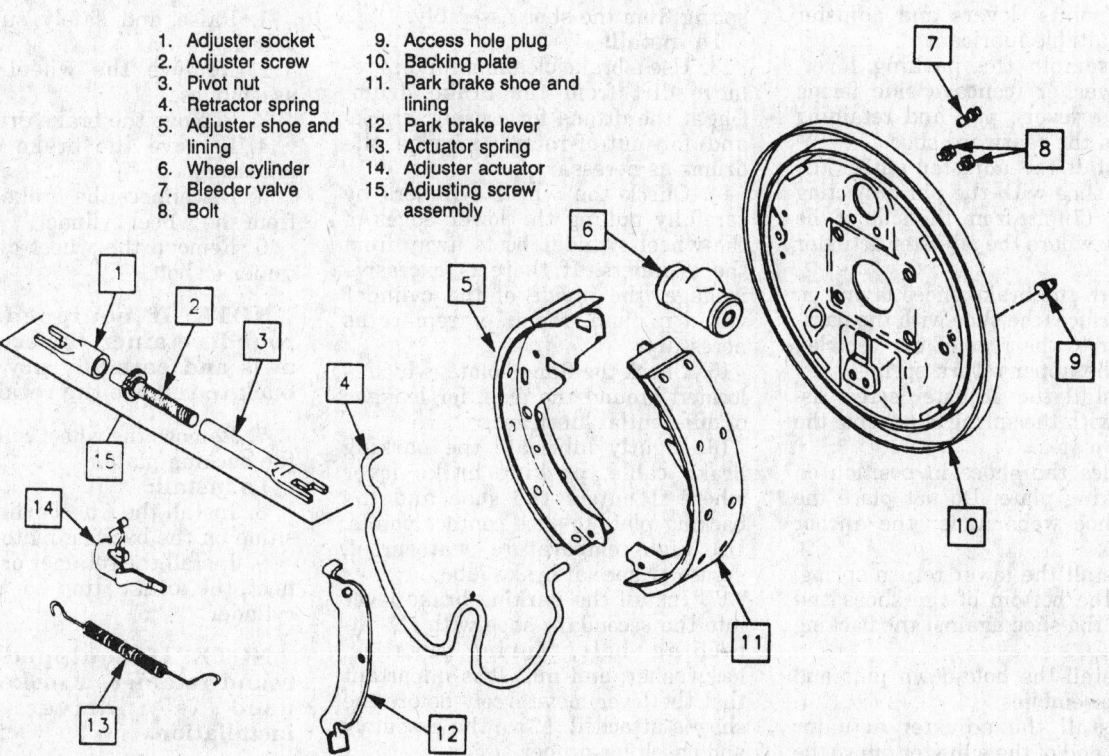

1. Adjuster socket
2. Adjuster screw
3. Pivot nut
4. Retractor spring
5. Adjuster shoe and lining
6. Wheel cylinder
7. Bleeder valve
8. Bolt
9. Access hole plug
10. Backing plate
11. Park brake shoe and lining
12. Park brake lever
13. Actuator spring
14. Adjuster actuator
15. Adjusting screw assembly

85473206

Exploded view of the drum brake components — Lumina, Silhouette and Trans Sport

2. Remove the tire and wheel assembly.

3. Remove the brake drums.

NOTE: The brake pedal must not be depressed while the drums are removed.

4. Raise the lever arm of the actuator until the upper end is clear of the slot in the adjuster screw.

5. Slide the actuator off the adjuster pin. Disconnect the actuator spring from the shoe.

6. Remove the hold-down spring assemblies and pins.

7. Pull the bottom ends of the shoes apart and lift the lower return spring over the anchor plate. Allow the shoe ends to come together and remove the spring.

8. Remove the shoe assembly, along with the upper return spring and the adjusting screw assembly.

9. Remove the upper return spring and the adjusting screw assembly from the shoes.

10. Remove the retaining ring, pin, spring washer, and parking brake lever.

To install:

11. Clean adjuster wheel and the backing plates with a suitable cleaner. Lubricate the backing plate contact points, levers and adjuster with a suitable lubricant.

12. Assemble the parking lever, spring washer (concave side facing the brake lever), pin, and retaining ring onto the rearward shoe.

13. Install the adjuster pin in the forward shoe with the pin projecting 0.276 in. (7mm) from the side of the shoe web where the adjuster actuator is installed.

14. With the brake shoes laying on a flat surface (the shoe with the parking lever to the rear of the vehicle), install the upper return spring.

15. Install the adjuster screw assembly with the spring clip facing the backing plate.

16. Place the shoes in position on the backing plate. Do not place the lower shoe webs under the anchor plate.

17. Install the lower return spring, spread the bottom of the shoes and position the shoe against the backing plate.

18. Install the hold-down pins and spring assemblies.

19. Install the adjuster actuator over the end of the adjuster pin so the top leg engages the notch in the adjuster screw.

20. Install the actuator spring, being careful not to over-stretch it more than 3.27 in. (83mm).

21. Install the parking brake cable to the lever.

22. Adjust the parking brake if the shoes will not totally retract.

23. Install the drum, tire and wheel assembly. Adjust the rear brakes and lower the vehicle.

DUO-SERVO BRAKES

1. Raise the vehicle and support it safely.

2. Remove the tire and wheel assembly.

3. Remove the brake drums.

NOTE: The brake pedal must not be depressed while the drums are removed.

4. Using a brake tool, remove the shoe return springs.

5. Remove the shoe guide.

6. Remove the hold-down springs and pins.

7. Remove the actuator lever and pivot.

8. Remove the lever return spring.

9. Remove the actuator link, parking brake strut, spring retaining ring.

10. Remove the parking brake lever and washer.

11. Remove the shoe assemblies.

12. Remove the adjuster screw and spring from the shoe assembly.

To install:

13. Use a brake cleaning fluid to remove dirt from the brake drum. Check the drums for scoring, cracks and for out-of-round; service the drums as necessary.

14. Check the wheel cylinders by carefully pulling the lower edges of the wheel cylinder boots away from the cylinders. If there is excessive leakage, the inside of the cylinder will drip fluid; repair or replace as necessary.

15. Check the flange plate, which is located around the axle, for leakage of differential lubricant.

16. Lightly lubricate the parking brake cable, parking brake lever where it enters the shoe and the backing plate-to-shoe contact points. Use high temperature, waterproof, grease or special brake lube.

17. Install the parking brake lever into the secondary shoe with the attaching bolt, spring washer, lockwasher, and nut. It is important that the lever move freely before the shoe is attached. Move the assembly and check for proper action.

18. Lubricate the adjusting screw and make sure it works freely.

19. Connect the adjuster screw and spring to the bottom portion of both shoes. Ensure the spring does not interfere with the adjuster rotation when installed. The primary (smaller shoe pad area) to the front and secondary shoe (larger shoe pad area) to the rear of the vehicle.

20. Install the shoe assembly. Ensuring the shoe webs are positioned correctly against the wheel cylinder.

21. Install the parking brake cable.

22. Secure the primary shoes with the hold-down pin and spring.

23. Install the parking brake strut and the strut spring.

24. Install the actuator lever and pivot, securing the assembly with the hold-down pin and spring. Install the actuator link and spring.

25. Install the return springs.

26. Check the operation of the self-adjusting mechanism by moving the actuating lever by hand.

27. Adjust the brakes and install the drum.

28. Adjust the parking brake.

29. Install the tire and wheel assembly.

30. Lower the vehicle.

Wheel Cylinder

REMOVAL AND INSTALLATION

1. Raise and safely support the vehicle.

2. Remove the wheel and tire assemblies.

3. Remove the brake drum.

4. Remove the brake shoes, as necessary.

5. Disconnect the brake fluid line from the wheel cylinder.

6. Remove the wheel cylinder retainer or bolt.

NOTE: If equipped with a round retainer, insert 2 small awls and carefully pry the tabs back to release the retainer.

7. Remove the wheel cylinder from the backing plate.

To install:

8. Install the wheel cylinder in position on the backing plate.

9. Install the retainer or bolt. Connect the brake line to the wheel cylinder.

NOTE: If equipped with a round retainer, a socket may be used as a driver to ease installation.

10. Install the brake linings and the brake drum.

11. Install the wheel and tire assembly. Lower the vehicle.

12. Bleed the brake system.

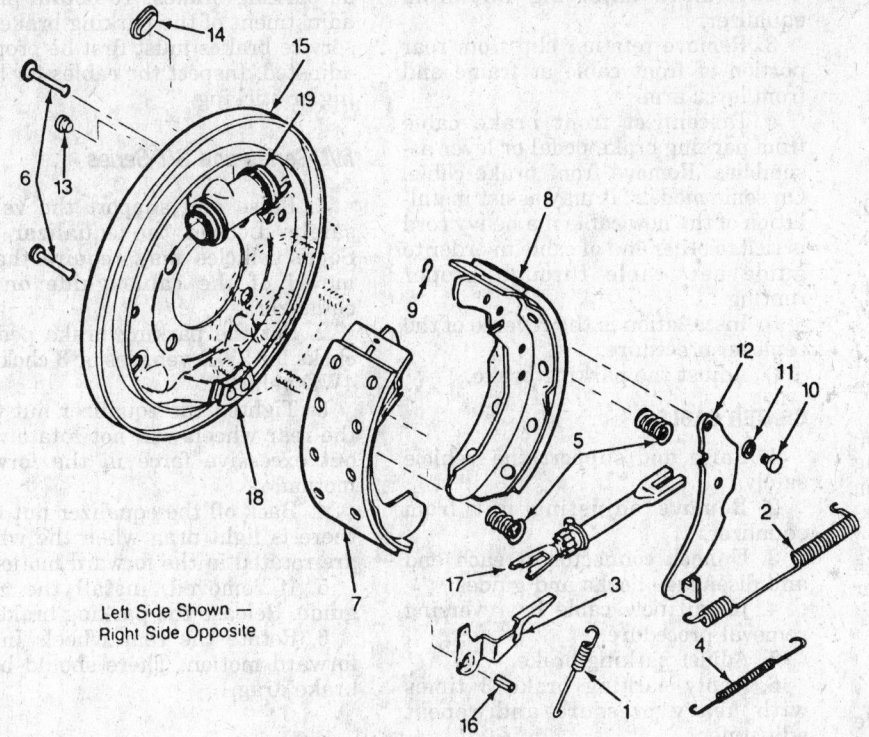

1. Actuator spring
2. Upper return spring
3. Adjuster actuator
4. Lower return spring
5. Hold-down spring assembly
6. Hold-down pin
7. Adjuster shoe and lining
8. Shoe and lining
9. Retaining ring
10. Pin
11. Spring washer
12. Park brake lever
13. Access hole plug
14. Inspection cover
15. Backing plate assembly
16. Adjuster pin
17. Adjusting screw assembly
18. Anchor plate
19. Wheel cylinder assembly

85473207

Left Side Shown —
Right Side Opposite

Exploded view of the rear drum brake assembly — Leading/Trailing type

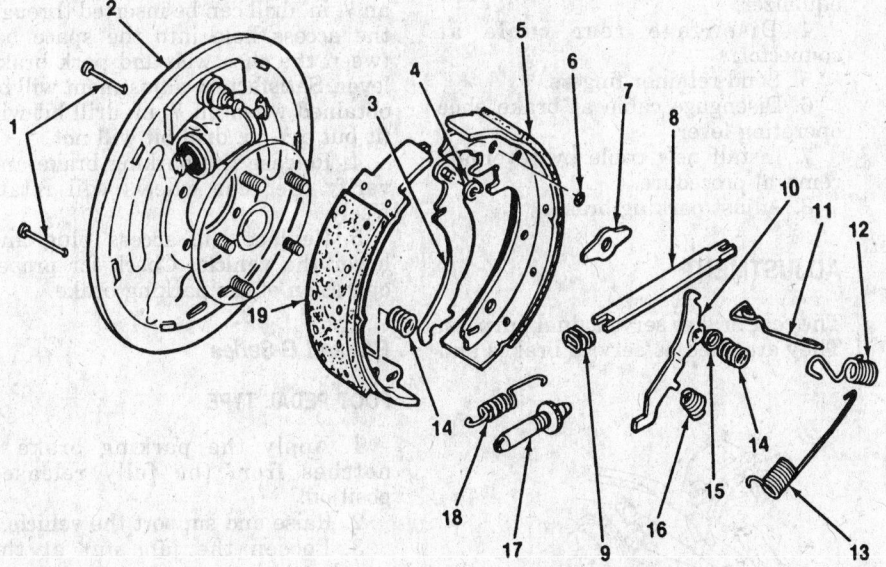

1. Hold-down pins
2. Backing plate
3. Parking brake lever
4. Washer
5. Secondary shoe
6. Retaining ring
7. Shoe guide
8. Parking brake strut
9. Strut spring
10. Actuator lever
11. Actuator link
12. Return spring
13. Return spring
14. Hold down spring
15. Lever pivot
16. Lever return spring
17. Adjusting screw assembly
18. Adjusting screw spring
19. Primary shoe

85473208

Exploded view of the rear drum brake assembly — Duo-Servo type

Parking Brake Cable

REMOVAL AND INSTALLATION

Compact Pick-Up, Van and Utility

REAR

1. Raise and support the vehicle safely. Remove the tire and wheel assembly. Remove the brake drum.
2. Loosen the equalizer and disconnect the cable at the center retainer.
3. Compress the plastic retainer fingers and remove the retainer from the frame bracket.
4. Remove the rear brake shoe assembly. Disconnect the parking brake cable. Remove the cable from the frame and from the brake backing plate.
5. Installation is the reverse of the removal procedure. Adjust the rear brakes, as required. Adjust the parking brake.

FRONT

1. Raise and support the vehicle safely. Loosen the adjuster nut and disconnect the front cable from the connector.
2. Compress the retainer fingers and loosen the assembly at the frame. Remove the supports.
3. Lower the vehicle. As required, remove dash trim panels to gain access to the parking brake pedal assembly.
4. Disconnect the cable from the parking brake pedal, compress the retainer fingers. Remove the cable.
5. Installation is the reverse of the removal procedure. Adjust the parking brake.

Full Size Pick-Up, Van and Utility

FRONT CABLE

1. Raise and support the vehicle safely.

2. Remove adjusting nut from equalizer.
3. Remove retainer clip from rear portion of front cable at frame and from lever arm.
4. Disconnect front brake cable from parking brake pedal or lever assemblies. Remove front brake cable. On some models, it may assist installation of the new cable if a heavy cord is tied to other end of cable in order to guide new cable through proper routing.
5. Installation is the reverse of the removal procedure.
6. Adjust the parking brake.

CENTER CABLE

1. Raise and support the vehicle safely.
2. Remove adjusting nut from equalizer.
3. Unhook connector at each end and disengage hooks and guides.
4. Install new cable by reversing removal procedure.
5. Adjust parking brake.
6. Apply parking brake 3 times with heavy pressure and repeat adjustment.

REAR CABLE

1. Raise and support the vehicle safely.
2. Remove rear wheel and brake drum.
3. Loosen adjusting nut at equalizer.
4. Disengage rear cable at connector.
5. Bend retainer fingers.
6. Disengage cable at brake shoe operating lever.
7. Install new cable by reversing removal procedure.
8. Adjust parking brake.

ADJUSTMENT

The rear brakes serve a dual purpose. They are used as service brakes and

as parking brakes. To obtain proper adjustment of the parking brake, the service brakes must first be properly adjusted. Inspect the cables for binding or sticking.

M/L-Series and S/T-Series

1. Raise and support the vehicle safely. Loosen the equalizer nut. Some vehicles may require the removal of the cable guide on the equalizer.
2. Set the parking brake pedal 2 clicks for 2WD vehicles or 3 clicks for 4WD vehicles.
3. Tighten the equalizer nut until the rear wheels will not rotate without excessive force in the forward motion.
4. Back off the equalizer nut until there is light drag when the wheels are rotated in the forward motion.
5. If removed, install the cable guide. Release the parking brake.
6. Rotate the rear wheels in the forward motion. There should be no brake drag.

Lumina, Silhouette and Trans Sport

1. Set the parking brake pedal 4 clicks.
2. Raise and support the vehicle safely. Remove the access plug in the backing plate.
3. Adjust the parking brake until an 1/8 in. drill can be inserted through the access hole into the space between the shoe web and park brake lever. Satisfactory adjustment will be obtained when an 1/8 in. drill bit will fit but a 1/4 in. drill bit will not.
4. Release the parking brake and verify the rear wheels will rotate freely.
5. Replace the access plug and lower the vehicle. Check for proper operation of the parking brake.

R/V and G-Series

FOOT PEDAL TYPE

1. Apply the parking brake 4 notches from the fully released position.
2. Raise and support the vehicle.
3. Loosen the jam nut at the equalizer.
4. Tighten or loosen the adjusting nut until a light drag is felt when the rear wheels are rotated forward.
5. Tighten the check nut.
6. Release the parking brake and rotate the rear wheels. No drag should be felt. If even a light drag is felt, readjust the parking brake.

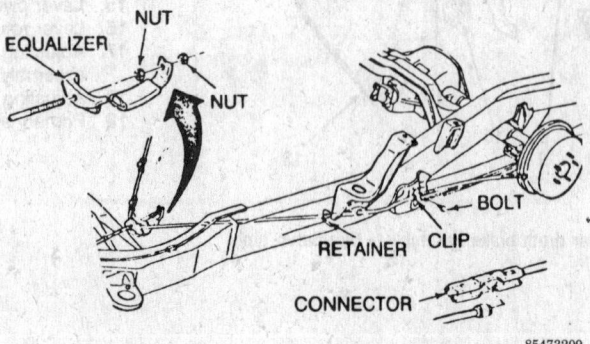

85473209

Common parking brake cable routing — M/L-Series and S/T-Series

7. Lower the vehicle.

NOTE: If a new parking brake cable is being installed, pre-stretch it by applying the parking brake hard about 3 times before making adjustments.

LEVER TYPE

1. Raise and support the vehicle safely. Turn the adjusting knob on the parking brake lever counterclockwise until it stops.

2. Apply the parking brake. Loosen the equalizer nut.

3. Tighten the equalizer nut until light drag is felt while rotating the rear wheels in the forward motion.

4. Adjust the knob on the parking brake lever until a definite snap over center is felt.

5. Release the parking brake. Rotate the rear wheels in the forward motion. There should be no brake drag.

DRIVESHAFT TYPE

1. Raise and support the vehicle safely. Remove the clevis pin connecting the pull rod and the relay lever.

2. Rotate the brake drum to align the access hole with the adjusting screw. If equipped with manual transmission the access hole is located at the bottom of the backing plate. If equipped with automatic transmission the access hole is located at the top of the shoe.

3. For first time adjustment it will be necessary to remove the driveshaft and the drum in order to remove the lanced area from the drum and clean out the metal shavings.

4. Adjust the screw until the drum cannot be rotated by hand. Back off the adjusting screw 10 notches, the drum should rotate freely.

5. Position the parking brake lever in the fully released position. Take up the slack in the cable to overcome spring tension.

6. Adjust the clevis of the pull rod to align with the hole in the relay lever. Install the clevis pin. Install a new cover in the drum access hole.

C/K-Series

1. Raise and support the vehicle safely. Matchmark the wheel to the axle flange. Remove the tire and wheel assembly.

2. Matchmark the drum to the axle flange. Remove the brake drum.

3. Using tool J–21177A or equivalent, measure and record the brake drum inside diameter.

4. Turn the adjuster nut and adjust the shoe and lining to a diameter 0.010–0.020 in. less than the measured inside diameter of the brake drum.

5. Be sure the stops on the parking brake levers are against the edge of the brake shoe web. If not, loosen the parking brake cable adjustment.

6. Tighten the parking brake cable at the adjuster nut until the lever stops begin to move off the shoe webs. Loosen the adjustment nut until the lever stops move back, barely touching the shoe webs. The final clearance between the stops and either web should be 0.5mm.

7. Install the drums and wheels. Align the assemblies with the matchmarks made during removal.

8. Apply and release the service brake pedal 30–35 times using normal pedal force. Pause about 1 second between each pedal application.

9. Depress the parking brake 6 clicks. Check the rear wheels they should not rotate.

10. Release the parking brake lever. Check for free wheel rotation.

Bleeding the Hydraulic Brake System

The hydraulic brake system must be bled any time 1 of the lines is disconnected or any time air enters the system. If a point in the system, such as a wheel cylinder or caliper brake line is the only point which was opened, the bleeder screws down stream in the hydraulic system are the only ones which must be bled. If however, the master cylinder fittings are opened or if the reservoir level drops sufficiently that air is drawn into the system, air must be bled from the entire hydraulic system. If the brake pedal feels spongy upon application, and goes almost to the floor but regains height when pumped, air has entered the system. It must be bled out. If no fittings were recently opened for service, check for leaks that would have allowed the entry of air and repair them before attempting to bleed the system.

As a general rule, once the master cylinder (and the brake pressure modulator valve or combination valve on ABS systems) is bled, the remainder of the hydraulic system should be bled starting at the furthest wheel from the master cylinder and working towards the nearest wheel. Therefore, the correct bleeding sequence is: master cylinder, modulator or combination valve (ABS only), right rear wheel cylinder, left rear, right front caliper and left front. Most master cylinder assemblies on these vehicles are not equipped with bleeder valves, therefore air must be bled from the cylinders using the front brake pipe connections.

MANUAL BLEEDING

1. Clean the top of the master cylinder, remove the cover and fill the reservoirs with clean fluid. To prevent squirting fluid, and possibly damaging painted surfaces, install the cover during the procedure, but be sure to frequently check and top off the reservoirs with fresh fluid.

—— **CAUTION** ——
Never reuse brake fluid which has been bled from the system.

2. The master cylinder must be bled first if it is suspected to contain air. If the master cylinder was removed and bench bled before installation it must still be bled, but it should take less time and effort. Bleed the master cylinder as follows:

a. Position a container under the master cylinder to catch the brake fluid.

—— **WARNING** ——
Do not allow brake fluid to spill on or come in contact with the vehicle's finish as it will remove the paint. In case of a spill, immediately flush the area with water.

b. Loosen the front brake line at the master cylinder and allow the fluid to flow from the front port.

c. Have an assistant depress the brake pedal slowly and hold (air and/or fluid should be expelled from the loose fitting). Tighten the line, then release the brake pedal and wait 15 seconds. Loosen the fitting and repeat until all air is removed from the master cylinder bore.

d. When finished, tighten the line fitting.

e. Repeat the sequence at the master cylinder rear pipe fitting.

NOTE: During the bleeding procedure, make sure your assistant does not release the brake pedal while a fitting is loosened or while a bleeder screw is opening. Air will be drawn back into the system.

3. Check and refill the master cylinder reservoir.

NOTE: Remember, if the reservoir is allowed to empty of fluid during the procedure, air will be drawn into the system and bleeding procedure must be restarted at the master cylinder assembly.

4. On late model ABS equipped vehicles, perform the special ABS procedures. On 4 wheel ABS systems the Brake Pressure Modulator Valve (BPMV) must be bled (if it has been replaced or if it is suspected to contain air) and on most Rear Wheel Anti-Lock (RWAL) systems the combination valve must be held open. In both cases, special combination valve depressor tools should be used during bleeding and a scan tool must be used for ABS function tests.

5. If a single line or fitting was the only hydraulic line disconnected, then only the caliper(s) or wheel cylinder(s) affected by that line must be bled. If the master cylinder required bleeding, then all calipers and wheel cylinders must be bled in the proper sequence:
   a. Right rear
   b. Left rear
   c. Right front
   d. Left front
6. Bleed the individual calipers or wheel cylinders as follows:
   a. Place a suitable wrench over the bleeder screw and attach a clear plastic hose over the screw end. Be sure the hose is seated snugly on the screw or you may be squirted with brake fluid.

NOTE: Be very careful when bleeding wheel cylinders and brake calipers. The bleeder screws often rust in position and may easily break off if forced. Installing a new bleeder screw will often require removal of the component and may include overhaul or replacement of the wheel cylinder/caliper. To help prevent the possibility of breaking a bleeder screw, spray it with some penetrating oil before attempting to loosen it.

   b. Submerge the other end of the tube in a transparent container of clean brake fluid.
   c. Loosen the bleed screw, then have a friend apply the brake pedal slowly and hold. Tighten the bleed screw, release the brake pedal and wait 15 seconds. Repeat the sequence (including the 15 second pause) until all air is expelled from the caliper or cylinder.

   d. Tighten the bleed screw when finished.
7. Check the pedal for a hard feeling with the engine not running. If the pedal is soft, repeat the bleeding procedure until a firm pedal is obtained.
8. If the brake warning light is on, depress the brake pedal firmly. If there is no air in the system, the light will go out.
9. After bleeding, make sure a firm pedal is achieved before attempting to move the vehicle.

PRESSURE BLEEDING

A proper pressure bleeder tool will utilize a rubber diaphragm between the air source and brake fluid in order to prevent air, moisture oil and other contaminants from entering the hydraulic system.

1. Prepare a pressure bleeder tool such as J-29567 or equivalent by making sure the pressure tank is at least 2/3 full of fresh, clean brake fluid. In most cases, the bleeder must be bled each time fluid is added. Charge the bleeder tool to 20–25 psi (140–170 kPa).
2. Install a suitable combination valve depressor tool such as J-39177 or equivalent, to the combination valve in order to hold the valve open during the bleeding operation.
3. Install the pressure bleeder tool to the master cylinder reservoir.
4. On 4 wheel ABS systems, bleed the Brake Pressure Modulator Valve (BPMV) of air.
5. Bleed each wheel cylinder or caliper in the proper sequence:
   a. Right rear
   b. Left rear
   c. Right front
   d. Left front
6. Connect a hose from the bleeder tank to the adapter at the master cylinder, then open the tank valve.
7. Attach a clear vinyl hose to the brake bleeder screw, then immerse the opposite end into a container partially filled with clean brake fluid.
8. Open the bleeder screw 3/4 turn and allow the fluid to flow until no air bubbles are seen in the fluid, then close the bleeder screw and tighten.
9. Repeat the bleeding process at each wheel.
10. Inspect the brake pedal for sponginess and if necessary, repeat the entire bleeding procedure.
11. Remove the depressor tool from the combination valve and the bleeder adapter from the master cylinder.

12. Refill the master cylinder to the proper level with brake fluid.
13. Do not attempt to move the vehicle unless a firm brake pedal is obtained.

Bleeding the RWAL Brake System

On RWAL systems 1992 the brake system may be bled in the usual manner with no special procedures. On 1993–96 vehicles a few steps (listed below) should be added to the bleeding sequence in order to ease the procedure and assure all air is removed from the system. These extra steps may be used on all RWAL vehicles to assure proper bleeding.

The use of a power bleeder is recommended, but the system may also be bled manually. If a power bleeder is used, it must be of the diaphragm type and provide isolation of the fluid from air and moisture.

Do not pump the pedal rapidly when bleeding; this can make the circuits very difficult to bleed. Instead, press the brake pedal slowly 1 time and hold it down while bleeding takes place. Tighten the bleeder screw, release the pedal and wait 15 seconds before repeating the sequence. Because of the length of the brake lines and other factors, it may take 10 or more repetitions of the sequence to bleed each line properly. When necessary to bleed all 4 wheels, the correct order is right rear, left rear, right front and left front.

CAUTION

Do not move the vehicle until a firm brake pedal is achieved. Failure to properly bleed the system may cause impaired braking and the possibility of injury and/or property damage

---

1. Make sure the ignition is in the **OFF** position to prevent setting false trouble codes.
2. After properly bleeding the master cylinder, install J-39177 or equivalent combination valve depressor tool to the combination valve. This tool is used to hold the internal valve open allowing the entire system to be completely bled.
3. Recheck the master cylinder fluid level and add, as necessary.
4. Bleed the wheel cylinders as described earlier in this section.
5. Attach the Tech-1 or equivalent scan tool, then perform 3 RWAL function tests.

6. Re-bleed the rear wheel cylinders.

7. Check for a firm brake pedal, if necessary repeat the entire bleeding procedure.

Bleeding the 4WAL Brake System

The EHCU/BPMV module is the 1 component which adds to the complexity of bleeding the 4WAL brake systems. For the most part the system is bled in the same manner as the non-ABS vehicles. But because of the EHCU/BPMV's complex internal valving additional steps are necessary if the unit has been replaced or if it is suspected to contain air. These bleeding steps are not necessary if the only connection/fitting(s) opened were downstream of the unit. These steps may or may not be necessary after master cylinder replacement. If in doubt (or without the necessary special tools) thoroughly bleed the system and see if a firm brake pedal can be obtained, if not, the EHCU/BPMV must be bled as well.

As with the RWAL brake system, the use of a power bleeder is recommended, but the system may also be bled manually. If a power bleeder is used, it must be of the diaphragm type and provide isolation of the fluid from air and moisture.

Do not pump the pedal rapidly when bleeding; this can make the circuits very difficult to bleed. Instead, press the brake pedal slowly 1 time and hold it down while bleeding takes place. Tighten the bleeder screw, release the pedal and wait 15 seconds before repeating the sequence. Because of the length of the brake lines and other factors, it may take 10 or more repetitions of the sequence to bleed each line properly. When necessary to bleed all 4 wheels, the correct order is right rear, left rear, right front and left front.

─────── CAUTION ───────

Do not move the vehicle until a firm brake pedal is achieved. Failure to properly bleed the system may cause impaired braking and the possibility of injury and/or property damage

If the EHCU/BPMV requires bleeding, the following procedures may be used to free all trapped air from the component. The procedures differ because the component used on the MFI-Turbo is equipped with external bleeders in additional to the internal bleeders found on the 1994 and later units. In either case, 3 combination valve depressor tools and a scan tool are required. The combination valve depressor tools are used to hold the internal passages (combination valve and EHCU/BPMV bleed accumulator bleed stems open allowing the entire system to be completely bled.

Finally, remember to always bleed the 4WAL brake system with the ignition **OFF** to prevent setting false trouble codes.

MFI-Turbo

The EHCU used on the MFI-Turbo is equipped with the internal bleeders AND a pair of external bleeder screws. These external bleeders look like normal brake bleeders and are found on top of the unit. Like any bleeder screw, they MUST remain closed when the unit is not pressurized.

The Internal Bleed Valves on either side of the unit must be opened ¼–½ turn before bleeding begins. These valves open internal passages within the unit. The valve located on the left side (nearest the fender) is used for the rear brake section, while the valve on the right (nearest the engine) is used for the front brakes. Actual bleeding is performed at the 2 bleeders on the top of the EHCU module. The bleeders must not be opened when the system is not pressurized. The ignition switch must be **OFF** or false trouble codes may be set.

1. Make sure the ignition is in the **OFF** position to prevent setting false trouble codes.

2. Open the internal bleed valves ¼–½ turn each.

3. Install J–35856 or equivalent combination valve depressor tool on the left accumulator bleed stem of the EHCU. Install 1 tool on the right bleed stem and install the 3rd tool on the combination valve (rear).

4. Inspect the fluid level in the master cylinder, filling if needed.

5. Have an assistant slowly depress the brake pedal and hold it down.

6. Open the left bleeder on top of the unit. Allow fluid to flow until no air is seen or until the brake pedal bottoms.

7. Close the left bleeder, then have your assistant release the pedal slowly and wait 15 seconds.

8. Repeat these steps starting with depressing the brake pedal (including the 15 second pause), until no air is seen in the fluid.

9. Tighten the left internal bleed valve to 60 inch lbs. (7 Nm).

10. Bleed air from the right bleeder screw on top of the EHCU in the same manner as the left screw.

11. When bleeding of the right port is complete, tighten the right internal bleed valve to 60 inch lbs. (7 Nm).

12. Remove the 3 special combination valve tools.

13. Check the master cylinder fluid level, refilling as necessary.

14. Bleed the individual brake circuits at each wheel.

15. Switch the ignition **ON** and use the hand scanner tool to perform 3 function tests on the system.

16. Evaluate the brake pedal feel and repeat the bleeding procedure if it is not firm.

17. Carefully test drive the vehicle at moderate speeds; check for proper pedal feel and brake operation. If any problem is noted in feel or function, repeat the entire bleeding procedure.

Except MFI-Turbo

Unlike the The EHCU/BPMV used on the MFI-Turbo, the component used on other 4WAL systems is usually not equipped with external bleeder screws. Therefore, the unit can only be bled through the downstream bleeder screws (wheel cylinders/calipers). To accomplish this the internal bleeder and the accumulator stems/combination valves must be opened to allow air/fluid to pass through the unit. The Internal Bleed Valves on either side of the unit must be opened ¼–½ turn before bleeding begins. As with most ABS systems found on these vehicles, the ignition switch must be **OFF** or false trouble codes may be set.

1. Make sure the ignition is in the **OFF** position to prevent setting false trouble codes.

2. If necessary, properly bleed the master cylinder assembly. Check and add additional fluid, as necessary.

3. Open the internal bleed valves ¼–½ turn each.

4. Install one J–39177 or equivalent combination valve depressor tool on the left accumulator bleed stem of the EHCU. Install 1 tool on the right accumulator bleed stem and install the 3rd tool on the combination valve.

5. Properly bleed the wheel cylinders and calipers.

6. Remove the 3 special tools.

7. Check the master cylinder fluid level, refilling as necessary.

8. Switch the ignition **ON** (engine not running) and use a hand scanner

to perform 6 function tests on the system.

9. Repeat the wheel cylinder and caliper bleeding procedure to remove all air that was purged from the BPMV during the function tests.

10. Check for a firm brake pedal. If necessary, repeat the entire procedure until a firm pedal is obtained.

11. Carefully test drive the vehicle at moderate speeds; check for proper pedal feel and brake operation. If any problem is noted in feel or function, repeat the entire bleeding procedure.

Anti-Lock Brake System Service

There are various systems used on these vehicles, the Four Wheel Anti-Lock (4WAL) which is available on most vehicles, the Rear Wheel Anti-Lock (RWAL) and the Zero Pressure Rear Wheel Anti-Lock (ZPRWAL) which is used only on the 3500 HD-Series vehicle.

PRECAUTION

Failure to observe the following precautions may result in system damage.

• Before performing electric arc welding on the vehicle, disconnect the Electronic Brake Control Unit.

• When performing painting work on the vehicle, do not expose the Electronic Brake Control Unit to temperatures in excess of 185°F (85°C) for longer than 2 hours. The system may be exposed to temperatures up to 200°F (95°C) for less than 15 minutes.

• Never disconnect or connect the Electronic Brake Control Unit connector with the ignition switch ON.

• Never disassemble any component of the Anti-Lock Brake System which is designated non-serviceable; the component must be replaced as an assembly.

• When filling the master cylinder, always use Delco Supreme 11 brake fluid or equivalent, which meets DOT-3 specifications; petroleum base fluid will destroy the rubber parts. Do not allow fluid to be spilled on the Electronic Brake Control Unit.

Control Module

NOTE: Some late model vehicles are equipped with Vehicle Control Modules (VCMs). On these vehicles 1 computer controls both engine/emission operation and the anti-lock brake system (no separate brake control module is used).

REMOVAL AND INSTALLATION

RWAL System

1. Disconnect the negative battery cable.
2. Disconnect the electrical connectors from the module.
3. Remove the module from the master cylinder/proportioning valve bracket.
4. Installation is the reverse of the removal procedure.

4WAL System

1. Disconnect the negative battery cable.
2. Disconnect the electrical connectors from the module.
3. Disconnect and plug the brake lines at the module.
4. Remove the bolts attaching the module to the fenderwell.
5. Remove the module and bracket assembly.
6. Remove the bracket from the module.
7. Installation is the reverse of the removal procedure.

Isolation/Dump Valve

REMOVAL AND INSTALLATION

RWAL and 4WAL System

1. Disconnect the negative battery cable.
2. Disconnect and plug the brake line fittings at the isolation/dump valve located under the master cylinder.
3. Remove the master cylinder bracket bolts.
4. Disconnect the Electronic Control Unit connector.
5. Remove the isolation/dump valve.
6. Installation is the reverse of the removal procedure.

Front Wheel Speed Sensor

REMOVAL AND INSTALLATION

4WAL System

2WD

1. Disconnect the negative battery cable.
2. Raise and support the vehicle safely.
3. Remove the wheel and tire assembly.
4. Remove the brake caliper, hub and rotor assembly.
5. Remove the sensor wire from the clips on the upper control arm and disconnect the connector.
6. Remove the sensor and backing plate attaching bolts and remove the assembly.
7. Installation is the reverse of the removal procedure.

4WD

1. Disconnect the negative battery cable.
2. Raise and support the vehicle safely.
3. Remove the wheel and tire assembly.
4. Remove the hub and rotor assembly.
5. Disconnect the sensor wire connector.
6. Remove the bolts securing the sensor and sensor wire.
7. Remove the sensor from the spindle.
8. Installation is the reverse of the removal procedure.

Rear Wheel Speed Sensor

REMOVAL AND INSTALLATION

4WAL System

1. Disconnect the negative battery cable.
2. Raise and support the vehicle safely.
3. Remove the wheel, tire and drum assembly.
4. Remove the primary (forward) brake shoe.
5. Disconnect the sensor wire connector and remove the sensor wire from the rear axle clips.
6. Remove the bolts securing the sensor and sensor wire.
7. Remove the sensor from the backing plate.
8. Installation is the reverse of the removal procedure.

FRONT SUSPENSION

Shock Absorbers

REMOVAL AND INSTALLATION

Compact Pick-Up, Van and Utility

1. Remove the top shock mounting nut and grommet.
2. Raise and safely support the vehicle.
3. Remove the wheel and tire assembly.
4. Remove the lower shock mounting bolts and remove the shock absorber.
5. Installation is the reverse of the removal procedure.

R-Series and G-Series

1. Raise and support the vehicle safely. Properly support the lower control arm assembly, as required. Remove the tire and wheel assembly.
2. Remove the upper shock absorber retaining bolt. Remove the lower shock absorber retaining bolt. Vehicles equipped with quad shocks have a spacer between them.
3. Remove the shock absorber.
4. Installation is the reverse of the removal procedure. On the R-Series vehicle, torque the bolts to specification.

V-Series

1. Raise and support the vehicle safely.
2. Remove the nuts and eye bolts securing the upper and lower shock absorber eyes. Quad shocks have a spacer between the lower end bushings.
3. Remove the shock absorber(s) and inspect the rubber eye bushings for wear or the shock for leaks, replace the shock absorber assembly as necessary.
4. Installation is the reverse of removal. Make sure the spacer is installed at the bottom end on quad shocks. Torque the upper end nut to 65 ft. lbs. (88 Nm). On dual shocks, torque the lower end to 65 ft. lbs. (88 Nm). On quad shocks, torque the lower end to 89 ft. lbs. (120 Nm).

C-Series

1. Remove the upper shock absorber retaining bolt. Raise and support the vehicle safely.

2. Properly support the lower control arm, as required. Remove the lower shock absorber retaining bolt.
3. Remove the shock absorber.
4. Installation is the reverse of removal. Tighten the upper nut to 100 inch lbs. (11 Nm); tighten the lower mounting bolts to 20 ft. lbs. (27 Nm).

K-Series

1. Raise and support the vehicle safely.
2. Remove the upper end bolt, nut and washer.
3. Remove the lower end bolt, nut and washer.
4. Remove the shock absorber and inspect the rubber bushings for wear and the shock for leaks, replace the shock absorber assembly necessary.
5. Installation is the reverse of removal. Torque the both nuts to 66 ft. lbs. (90 Nm). Make sure the bolts are inserted in the proper direction. The bolt head on the upper end should be forward; the bottom end bolt head is rearward.

MacPherson Strut Assembly

All front wheel drive vehicles are equipped with a MacPherson strut front suspension.

REMOVAL AND INSTALLATION

NOTE: Do not remove the top center nut from the strut assembly. This nut should only be removed when the strut assembly is out of the vehicle, mounted in a holding fixture and the coil spring is in a compressed position using the proper strut coil spring compressor.

1. Remove the 3 nuts that retain the top of the strut assembly.
2. Raise and safely support the vehicle.
3. Remove the wheel and tire assembly. Remove the brake line bracket from the strut mount.
4. Remove the lower strut mounting bolts.
5. Remove the strut assembly from the vehicle and place the strut in a suitable holding fixture.
6. Disassemble the strut as follows:
   a. With the strut coil spring in a compressed position approximately ½ its normal length, remove the nut from the top of the strut.
   b. Place tool J–34013–27 or equivalent guide rod on top of the

damper shaft. Use the rod to guide the damper shaft straight down through the bearing cap while decompressing the spring.
   c. Remove the coil spring and other components.
7. Installation is the reverse of the removal procedure. Ensure the spring seat flat should face 10 degrees forward of the centerline of the strut assembly spindle.
8. Tighten the strut lower bolts to 140 ft. lbs. (190 Nm) and the upper mounting nuts to 18 ft. lbs. (25 Nm).

Coil Springs

REMOVAL AND INSTALLATION

M/L-Series and S/T-Series

2WD VEHICLE

1. Raise and support the vehicle safely. Remove the wheel and tire assembly. Remove the shock absorber lower retaining bolts.
2. Push the shock absorber through the control arm and into the spring.
3. With the vehicle supported so the control arms hang free, install tool J–23028 or equivalent, onto a support and into the lower control arm bushings. Remove the stabilizer bar from the control arm.
4. Remove the stabilizer to lower control arm attachment. Raise and remove the tension on the lower control arm bolts.
5. Install a safety chain around the spring and through the lower control arm. Remove the lower control arm rear pivot bolt, than remove the other pivot bolt.
6. Lower and allow the lower control arm to hang free. Remove the spring assembly.
7. Installation is the reverse of the removal procedure. When positioning the spring in the lower control arm, be sure the spring insulator is in the proper position before lifting the control arm in place.

R-Series and G-Series

1. Raise and support the vehicle safely under the frame rails. The control arms should hang freely.
2. Remove the wheel.
3. Disconnect the shock absorber at the lower end and move it aside.
4. Disconnect the stabilizer bar from the lower control arm.
5. Support the lower control arm and install a spring compressor on

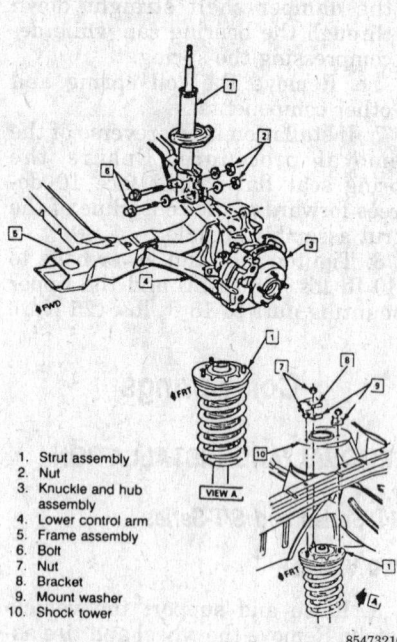

1. Strut assembly
2. Nut
3. Knuckle and hub assembly
4. Lower control arm
5. Frame assembly
6. Bolt
7. Nut
8. Bracket
9. Mount washer
10. Shock tower

85473210

Strut assembly mounting — Lumina, Silhouette and Trans Sport

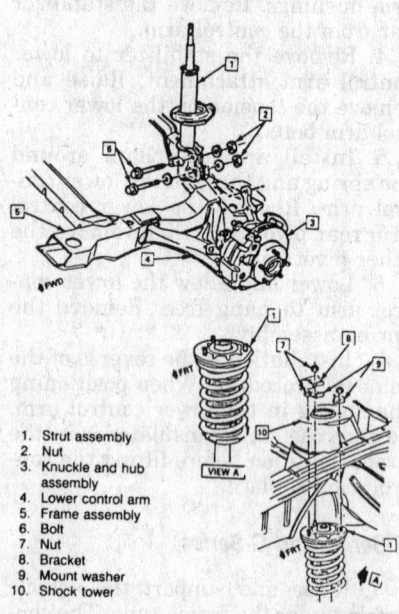

1. Strut assembly
2. Nut
3. Knuckle and hub assembly
4. Lower control arm
5. Frame assembly
6. Bolt
7. Nut
8. Bracket
9. Mount washer
10. Shock tower

85473210

MacPherson strut assembly/disassembly

the spring or chain the spring to the control arm as a safety precaution.

NOTE: If equipped with an air cylinder inside the spring, remove the valve core from the cylinder and expel the air by compressing the cylinder with a prybar. With the cylinder compressed, replace the valve core so the cylinder will stay in the compressed position. Push the cylinder as far as possible towards the top of the spring.

6. Raise to remove the tension from the lower control arm cross-shaft and remove the 2 U-bolts securing the cross-shaft to the crossmember.

NOTE: The cross-shaft and lower control arm keeps the coil spring compressed. Use care when lowering the assembly.

7. Slowly lower the control arm until the spring can be removed. Be sure all compression is relieved from the spring.
8. If the coil spring was chained, remove the chain and spring. If a compressor was used, remove the spring and slowly release the compressor.
9. Remove the air cylinder, if equipped.
To install:
10. Install the air cylinder so the protector plate is towards the upper control arm. The schrader valve should protrude through the hole in the lower control arm.
11. Install the chain and spring or compress the spring and install the assembly.
12. Slowly lower control arm. Align the indexing hole in the shaft with the crossmember attaching studs.
13. Install the 2 U-bolts securing the cross-shaft to the crossmember. Torque the nuts to 85 ft. lbs. (115 Nm).
14. Remove the support.
15. Connect the stabilizer bar to the lower control arm. Torque the nuts to 24 ft. lbs.
16. Connect the shock absorber at the lower end. Torque the bolt to specification.
17. If equipped with air cylinders, inflate the cylinder to 60 psi.
18. Install the wheel.
19. Lower the vehicle. Once the weight of the vehicle is on the wheels, reduce the air cylinder pressure to 50 psi.
20. Check the front end alignment.

C-Series

1. Raise and support the vehicle safely. Allow the control arms to hang free. Remove the tire and wheel assembly. Remove the shock absorber assembly, as required.
2. Install tool J–23028 under the lower control arm and a jack. Install a safety chain around the spring and through the lower control arm.
3. Remove the stabilizer shaft from the lower control arm. Raise and remove the tension on the lower control arm bolts.
4. Remove the lower control arm rear bolt, than remove the other retaining bolt.
5. Lower allow the lower control arm to hang free. Remove the spring assembly.
To install:
6. Install the chain and spring. If you used spring compressors, install the spring and compressors.
   a. Make sure the insulator is in place.
   b. Make sure the tape is at the lower end. New springs will have an identifying tape.
   c. Make sure the gripper notch on the top coil is in the frame bracket.
   d. Make sure 1 drain hole in the lower arm is covered by the bottom coil and the other is open.
7. Slowly raise the lower control arm. Guide the control arm into place with a prybar.
8. Install the pivot shaft bolts, front 1 first. The bolts must be installed with the heads towards the front of the vehicle. Remove the safety chain or spring compressors.

NOTE: Do not torque the bolts yet. The bolts must be torqued with the vehicle at its proper ride height.

9. Remove the jack.
10. Connect the stabilizer bar to the lower control arm. Torque the nuts to specification.
11. Install the shock absorber.
12. Install the wheel.
13. Lower the vehicle. Once the weight of the vehicle is on the wheels check the "Z" height as follows:
   a. Lift the front bumper about 1½ in. (38mm) and let it drop.
   b. Repeat this procedure 2–3 more times.
   c. Draw a line on the side of the lower control arm from the centerline of the control arm pivot shaft, dead level to the outer end of the control arm.
   d. Measure the distance between the lowest corner of the steering

knuckle and the line on the control arm. Record the figure.

e. Push down about 38mm on the front bumper and let it return. Repeat the procedure 2–3 more times.

f. Re-measure the distance at the control arm.

g. Determine the average of the 2 measurements.

h. If the figure is correct, tighten the control arm pivot nuts to 121 ft. lbs. (165 Nm). Align the front end. If the figure is incorrect, replace the coil spring.

Leaf Spring

REMOVAL AND INSTALLATION

V-Series

1. Raise and support the vehicle and front axle safely so all tension is taken off the front leaf springs.

2. Remove the shackle retaining bolts, nuts and spacers.

3. Remove the front spring-to-frame bracket bolt, washer and nut.

4. On the 10/1500 and 20/2500 both sides and the 30/3500 left side: remove the U-bolt nuts, washers, U-bolts, plate and spacers.

5. On the 30/3500 right side: remove the inboard spring plate bolts, U-bolt nuts, washers, U-bolt, plate and spacers.

6. To replace the bushing, place the spring in a press or vise and press out the bushing. Press in the new bushing. The new bushing should protrude evenly on both sides of the spring.

7. Installation is the reverse of removal. Coat all bushings with silicone grease prior to installation. Install all bolts and nuts finger-tight. When all fasteners are installed, torque the bolts. Torque the U-bolt nuts, including the inboard right side 30/3500-Series bolts, in the criss-

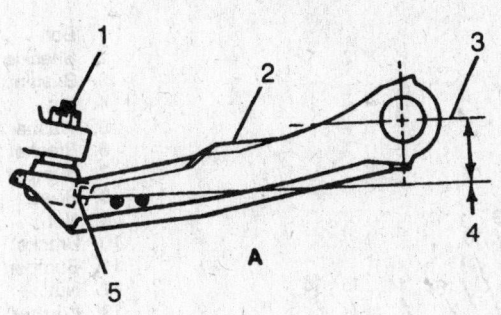

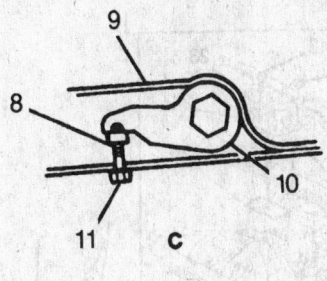

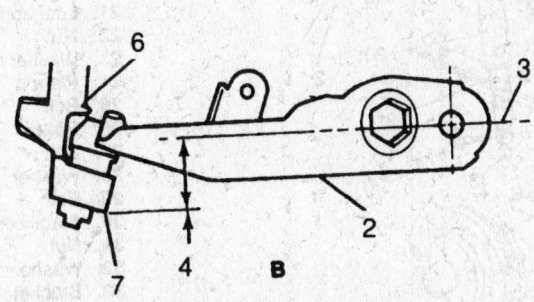

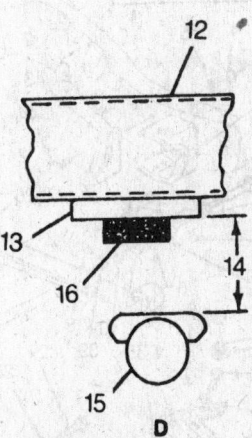

A. C-Series
B. K-Series
C. K-Series torsion bar
D. C/K-Series rear suspension
1. Lower ball joint
2. Lower control arm
3. Pivot bolt center line
4. "Z" Height
   C1, 2, 3—89–101mm
   K1, 2—151–163mm
   K3—139–151mm
5. Lower ball joint extrusion
6. Steering knuckle
7. Steering knuckle lower corner
8. Nut
9. Torsion bar support assembly
10. Torsion bar adjustment arm
11. Bolt—1 turn equals 6mm height change
12. Frame
13. Bottom surface of jounce bracket
14. "D" Height
15. Rear axle
16. Jounce bumper

85473212

Trim height adjustment — C/K-Series

cross pattern, to 150 ft. lbs. (213 Nm). Torque the shackle nuts to 50 ft. lbs. (68 Nm). Torque the front eye bolt nut to 90 ft. lbs. (122 Nm).

Torsion Bars and Support

REMOVAL AND INSTALLATION

M/L-Series and S/T-Series

1. Raise and safely support the vehicle. Remove the wheel and tire assemblies.
2. Remove the torsion bar adjusting bolt using tool J–36202 or equivalent. Count the number of tool turns required to remove the bolt.
3. Remove the torsion bar support retainer plate and insulator.
4. Remove the torsion bar by sliding it forward into the control arm and lowering it.
5. Remove the torsion bar support. Remove the adjusting arm and the adjusting arm bolt.

To install:

6. Install the adjusting arm to the support and loosely install the adjusting bolt.
7. Install the support to the frame and the insulator to the frame end.
8. Install the retainer to the support. Install the retainer mounting bolts and tighten to 26 ft. lbs. (35 Nm).
9. Tighten the center retainer bolt to 25 ft. lbs. (34 Nm).
10. Install the torsion bar to the lower control arm and raise and slide the torsion bar into the adjusting arm. The torsion bar should have 6mm clearance at the support.
11. Attach tool J–36202 to the support and tighten it against the adjusting arm the recorded number of turns.
12. Install the adjusting bolt and turn it in until it contacts the adjusting arm. Remove the tool.
13. Install the wheel and tire assemblies. Lower the vehicle.

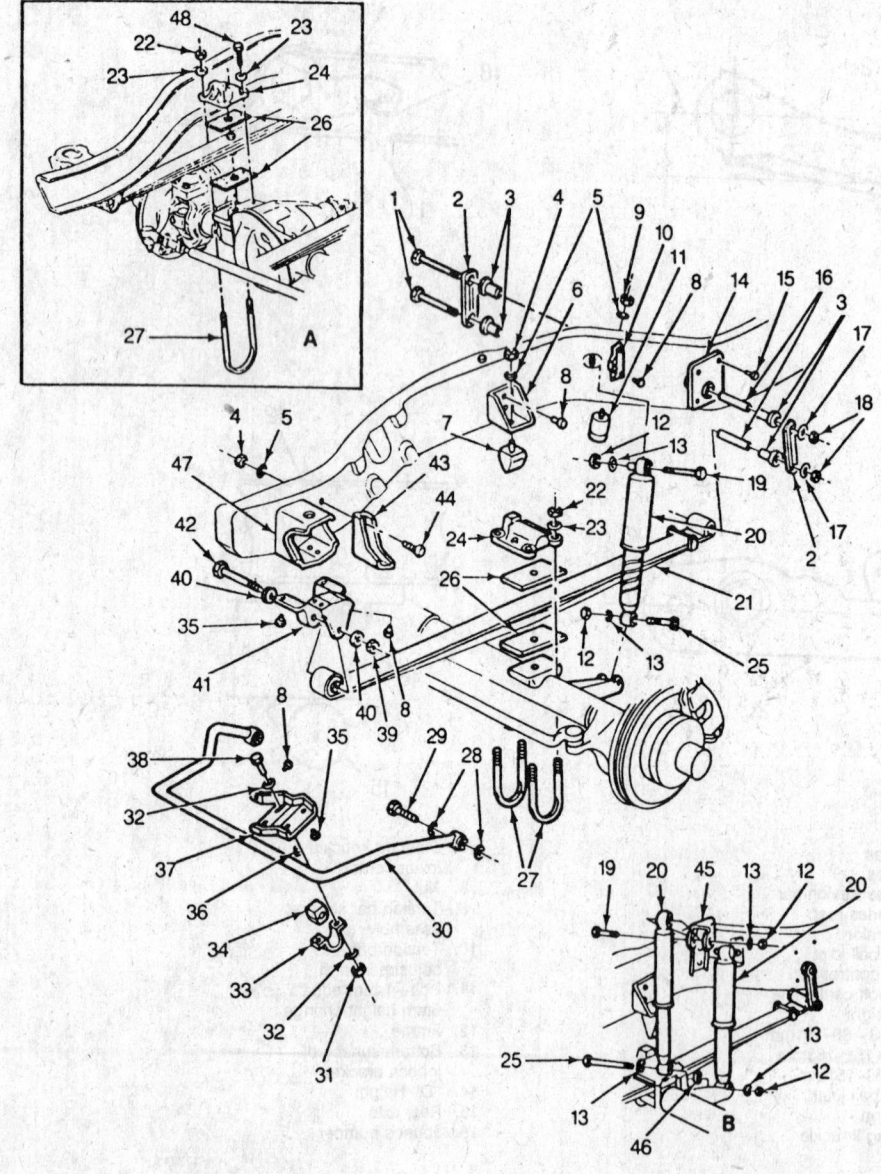

1. Bolt
2. Shackle
3. Bushing
4. nut
5. Washer
6. Bracket
7. Bumper
8. Rivet
9. Nut
10. Bracket
11. Bumper
12. Nut
13. Washer
14. hanger
15. Rivet
16. Spacer
17. Washer
18. Nut
19. Bolt
20. Shock absorber
21. Leaf spring
22. Nut
23. Washer
24. Plate
25. Bolt
26. Spacer
27. Bolt
28. Washer
29. Bolt
30. Stabilizer shaft
31. Nut
32. Washer
33. Bracket
34. Bushing
35. Rivet
36. Rivet
37. Bracket
38. Bolt
39. Nut
40. Washer
41. Hanger
42. Bolt
43. Reinforcement
44. Bracket
46. Spacer
47. Bracket
48. Bolt
A. K3500 Series – right side
B. Quad shock

Front suspension assembly — V-Series

85473213

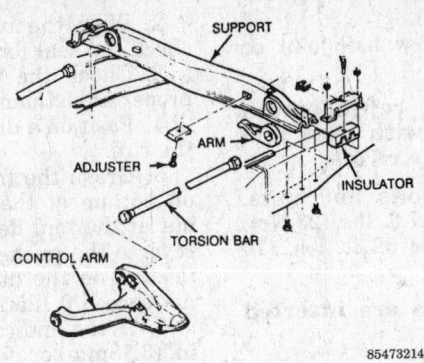

85473214

Torsion bar spring mounting — M/L-Series and S/T-Series

K-Series

1. Raise and support the vehicle safely.
2. Remove the wheels.
3. Support the lower control arm.
4. Matchmark the both torsion bar adjustment bolt positions.
5. Using tool J-36202, increase the tension on the adjusting arm.
6. Remove the adjustment bolt and retaining plate.
7. Move the tool aside.
8. Slide the torsion bars forward.
9. Remove the adjusting arms.
10. Remove the nuts and bolts from the torsion bar support crossmember and slide the support crossmember rearward.
11. Matchmark the position of the torsion bars and note the markings on the front end of each bar. They are not interchangeable. Remove the torsion bars.
12. Remove the support crossmember.
13. Remove the retainer, spacer and bushing from the support crossmember.
   To install:
14. Assemble the retainer, spacer and bushing on the support.
15. Position the support assembly on the frame, out of the way.
16. Align the matchmarks and install the torsion bars, sliding them forward until they are supported.
17. Install the adjuster arms on the torsion bars.
18. Bolt the support crossmember into position. Torque the center nut to 18 ft. lbs. (24 Nm); the edge nuts to 46 ft. lbs. (62 Nm).
19. Install the adjuster retaining plate and bolt on each torsion bar.
20. Using tool J-36202, increase tension on both torsion bars.
21. Install the adjustment retainer plate and bolt on both torsion bars.
22. Set the adjustment bolt to the marked position.

23. Release the tension on the torsion bar until the load is take up by the adjustment bolt.
24. Remove the tool.
25. Install the wheels.
26. Check the front end alignment and "Z" height.

Upper Ball Joint

INSPECTION

1. Raise the vehicle and position floor stands under the left and right lower control arm as near as possible to each lower ball joint. There should be space between the upper control arm bumper and frame after the lower control arm has been supported.
2. Wipe the ball joint clean and check the seal for cuts or tears.
3. Check the wheel bearings for proper adjustment.
4. Position a dial indicator against the tire.
5. Grasp the front wheel; push in on bottom of the tire while pulling out at the top. Read the gauge, then reverse the push-pull procedure. Deflection on the dial indicator should not exceed 0.125 in. (3.18mm).
6. If the indicator exceeds 0.125 in. (3.18mm) or if the ball stud, when disconnected from the knuckle assembly, can be twisted in its socket by hand, replace the ball joint.

REMOVAL AND INSTALLATION

Compact Pick-Up, Van and Utility

1. Raise and support the vehicle safely. Properly support the lower control arm.

   NOTE: The control arm must be supported so the spring and the control arm remain intact.

2. Remove the tire and wheel assembly. As required, remove the brake caliper and position it aside.
3. Remove the cotter pin and the upper ball joint retaining bolt. Using the proper tool separate the upper joint from its mounting. Support the knuckle assembly so its weight will not damage the brake hose.
4. Remove the rivets from the ball joint assembly, using a drill with an $\frac{1}{8}$ in. and then $\frac{1}{2}$ in. bit. Remove the ball joint from the upper control arm.
5. Installation is the reverse of the removal procedure. Tighten the replacement bolts to 17 ft. lbs. (23 Nm). Check and adjust the front end alignment, as required.

R-Series and G-Series

1. Raise and support the vehicle safely. Properly support the lower control arm.
2. Remove the wheel assembly. Remove the brake caliper and position it to the side.
3. Remove the cotter pin and the upper ball joint retaining bolt. Using the proper tool separate the upper joint from its mounting. Support the knuckle assembly so its weight will not damage the brake hose.
4. Remove the rivets from the ball joint assembly, using the proper tools. Remove the ball joint from the upper control arm.
   To install:
5. Install the new ball joint into the control arm. Position the bleed vent in the rubber boot facing inward.
6. Secure the ball joint to the control arm using the new nuts and bolts.
7. Lower the upper arm ball joint stud into the steering knuckle.
8. Install the ball stud nut and torque to specification. Tighten the nut to align the cotter pin hole.
9. Install the brake caliper, if removed.
10. Install a new lube fitting and lubricate the new joint.
11. Install the tire and wheel.
12. Lower the vehicle.

V-Series

1. Raise and support the vehicle safely. Remove the tire and wheel assembly.
2. Remove the hub and rotor assembly. Remove the spindle.
3. Remove the steering knuckle assembly. If removing the left axle yoke ball joints, remove the steering arm. Position the steering knuckle assembly in a suitable vise.

4. The lower ball joint must be removed before service can be performed on the upper ball joint. first. Remove the snapring from the lower ball joint and press the ball joint from the knuckle assembly, using the proper tools.

5. Press the upper ball joint from the knuckle assembly, using the proper tools.

6. Installation is the reverse of the removal procedure. Check and adjust front alignment, as required.

C-Series

1. Raise and support the vehicle safely. Properly support the lower control arm, using the necessary equipment.

2. Remove the tire and wheel assembly. Remove the brake caliper and position it to the side.

3. Remove the cotter pin and the upper ball joint retaining bolt. Using the proper tool separate the upper joint from its mounting. Support the knuckle assembly so its weight will not damage the brake hose.

4. Remove the rivets from the ball joint assembly, using the proper tools. Remove the ball joint from the upper control arm.

To install:

5. Install the replacement ball joint in the control arm, using the bolts and nuts supplied. Torque the nuts to 18 ft. lbs. (24 Nm).

6. Position the ball stud in the knuckle. Make sure it is squarely seated. Torque the ball stud nut to 84 ft. lbs. (115 Nm).

7. Install a new cotter pin.

8. Install a new lube fitting and lubricate the new joint.

9. If removed, install the brake caliper.

10. Install the wheel and lower the vehicle. Check and align the front end.

K-Series

1. Raise and support the vehicle safely.

2. Remove the wheel.

3. Unbolt the brake hose bracket from the control arm.

4. Using a 1/8 in. drill bit, drill a pilot hole through each ball joint rivet.

5. Drill out the rivets with a 1/2 in. drill bit. Punch out any remaining rivet material.

6. Remove the cotter pin and nut from the ball stud.

7. Support the lower control arm.

8. Using a ball joint separator, separate the stud from the knuckle.

To install:

9. Position the new ball joint on the control arm.

NOTE: Service replacement ball joints come with nuts and bolts to replace the rivets.

10. Install the bolts and nuts. Tighten the nuts to 17 ft. lbs. (23 Nm) for 15 and 25-Series; 52 ft. lbs. (70 Nm) for 35-Series.

NOTE: The bolts are inserted from the bottom.

11. Start the ball stud into the knuckle. Make sure it is squarely seated. Install the ball stud nut and pull the ball stud into the knuckle with the nut. Torque the nut after the vehicle wheel are on the ground and the suspension is loaded.

12. Install the wheel.

13. Lower the vehicle. Once the weight of the vehicle is on the wheels tighten the nut to 84 ft. lbs. (115 Nm).

Lower Ball Joint

INSPECTION

M/L-Series and S/T-Series

1. Raise and safely support the vehicle.

2. The ball joint wear is indicated by the position of the grease fitting on the bottom of the joint.

3. The round portion of the grease nipple must protrude from the bottom of the joint. If the nipple is flush with or inside of the joint, it must be replaced.

Lumina, Silhouette and Trans Sport

1. Raise and safely support the lower control arm.

2. Wipe the ball joint clean and check the seal for cuts or tears.

3. Check the wheel bearings for proper adjustment.

4. Position a dial indicator against the lowest outside point of the tire. Rock the wheel in and out.

5. Check the reading on the dial indicator. The reading should be no more than 0.125 inch (3.18mm).

Full Size Pick-Up, Van and Utility

1. Raise the vehicle and position floor stands under the left and right lower control arm as near as possible to each lower ball joint. There should be space between the upper control arm bumper and frame after the lower control arm has been supported.

2. Wipe the ball joint clean and check the seal for cuts or tears.

3. Check the wheel bearings for proper adjustment.

4. Position a dial indicator against the tire.

5. Grasp the front wheel; push in on bottom of the tire while pulling out at the top. Read the gauge, then reverse the push-pull procedure. Deflection on the dial indicator should not exceed 0.125 in. (3.18mm).

6. If the indicator exceeds 0.125 in. (3.18mm) or if the ball stud, when disconnected from the knuckle assembly, can be twisted in its socket by hand, replace the ball joint.

REMOVAL AND INSTALLATION

M/L-Series and S/T-Series

1. Raise and support the vehicle safely. Properly support the lower control arm.

NOTE: The control arm must be supported so the spring and the control arm remain intact.

2. Remove the tire and wheel assembly. As required, remove the brake caliper and position it aside.

3. Remove the cotter pin and the lower ball joint retaining bolt. Using the proper tool separate the ball joint from its mounting. Support the knuckle assembly so its weight will not damage the brake hose.

4. Remove the rivets from the ball joint assembly, using a drill with a 1/8 in. bit. Remove the ball joint from the control arm.

5. Installation is the reverse of the removal procedure. Be sure to use the nuts and bolts that are supplied with the replacement ball joint assembly. Tighten the replacement bolts to 17 ft. lbs. (23 Nm). Check and adjust the front end alignment, as required.

Lumina, Silhouette and Trans Sport

1. Raise and support the vehicle safely. Properly support the lower control arm.

NOTE: The control arm must be supported so the spring and the control arm remain intact.

2. Remove the tire and wheel assembly. As required, remove the brake caliper and position it aside.

3. Remove the pinch bolt from the lower ball joint. Using the proper tool separate the upper joint from the steering knuckle. Support the knuckle assembly so its weight will not damage the brake hose.

4. Remove the rivets from the ball joint assembly, using a drill with an ⅛ in. and then ½ in. bit.

5. Remove the stabilizer shaft bushing assembly nut.

6. Remove the ball joint from the lower control arm.

7. Installation is the reverse of the removal procedure. Tighten the ball joint pinch bolt to 33 ft. lbs. (45 Nm). Check and adjust the front end alignment, as required.

R-Series and G-Series

1. Raise and support the vehicle safely. Properly support the lower control arm, using the necessary equipment.

2. Remove the tire and wheel assembly. As required, remove the brake caliper and position it to the side.

3. Remove the cotter pin and the lower ball joint retaining bolt. Using the proper tool separate the ball joint from its mounting. Support the knuckle assembly so its weight will not damage the brake hose.

4. Press the ball joint out of the lower control arm, using the proper tool.

To install:

5. Start the new ball joint into the control arm. Position the bleed vent in the rubber boot facing inward.

6. Press the ball joint into the control arm until fully seated.

7. Lower the upper arm and insert the lower ball joint stud into the steering knuckle.

8. Install the brake caliper, if removed.

9. Install the ball stud nut and torque to 90 ft. lbs. (122 Nm) plus the additional torque necessary to align the cotter pin hole. Do not exceed 130 ft. lbs. (175 Nm) or back the nut off to align the holes with the pin.

10. Install a new lube fitting and lubricate the new joint.

11. Install the tire and wheel.

12. Lower the vehicle.

C-Series

1. Raise and support the vehicle safely. Properly support the lower control arm, using the necessary equipment.

2. Remove the tire and wheel assembly. As required, remove the brake caliper and position it to the side.

3. Remove the cotter pin and the lower ball joint retaining nut. Using the proper tool separate the ball joint from its mounting. Support the knuckle assembly so its weight will not damage the brake hose.

4. Remove the rivets from the ball joint assembly, using the proper tools. Remove the ball joint from the control arm.

To install:

5. Secure the new ball joint to the control arm.

6. Position the ball joint into the knuckle. Install the nut and tighten it to 84 ft. lbs. (115 Nm).

7. Advance the nut to align the cotter pin hole and insert the new cotter pin.

8. Install the brake caliper, if removed.

9. Install a new lube fitting and lubricate the new joint.

10. Install the wheel.

11. Lower the vehicle.

12. Check the front end alignment.

K-Series

1. Raise and support the vehicle safely.

2. Remove the wheel.

3. Remove the splash shield from the knuckle.

4. Disconnect the inner tie rod end from the relay rod using a ball joint separator.

5. Remove the hub nut and washer. Insert a long drift or dowel through the vanes in the brake rotor to hold the rotor in place.

6. Remove the axle shaft inner flange bolts.

7. Using a puller, force the outer end of the axle shaft out of the hub. Remove the shaft.

8. Using a ⅛ in. drill bit, drill a pilot hole through each ball joint rivet.

9. Drill out the rivets with a ½ in. drill bit. Punch out any remaining rivet material.

10. Remove the cotter pin and nut from the ball stud.

11. Support the lower control arm.

12. Matchmark the both torsion bar adjustment bolt positions.

13. Using tool J-36202, increase the tension on the adjusting arm.

14. Remove the adjustment bolt and retaining plate.

15. Move the tool aside.

16. Slide the torsion bars forward.

17. Using a screw-type forcing tool, separate the ball joint from the knuckle.

To install:

18. Position the new ball joint on the control arm.

NOTE: Service replacement ball joints come with nuts and bolts to replace the rivets.

19. Install the bolts and nuts. Tighten the nuts to 45 ft. lbs.

NOTE: The bolts are inserted from the bottom.

20. Start the ball stud into the knuckle. Make sure it is squarely seated. Install the ball stud nut and pull the ball stud into the knuckle with the nut. Do not final-torque the nut yet.

21. Using tool J-36202, increase tension on both torsion bars.

22. Install the adjustment retainer plate and bolt on both torsion bars.

23. Set the adjustment bolt to the marked position.

24. Release the tension on the torsion bar until the load is take up by the adjustment bolt.

25. Remove the tool.

26. Position the shaft in the hub and install the washer and hub nut. Leave the drift in the rotor vanes and tighten the hub nut to 175 ft. lbs.

27. Install the flange bolts. Tighten them to 59 ft. lbs. Remove the drift.

28. Connect the inner tie rod end at the steering relay rod. Torque the nut to 35 ft. lbs.

29. Install the splash shield.

30. Install the wheel.

31. Lower the vehicle. Once the weight of the vehicle is on the wheels:

   a. Lift the front bumper about 1½ in. (38mm) and let it drop.

   b. Repeat this procedure 2–3 more times.

   c. Draw a line on the side of the lower control arm from the centerline of the control arm pivot shaft, dead level to the outer end of the control arm.

   d. Measure the distance between the lowest corner of the steering knuckle and the line on the control arm. Record the figure.

   e. Push down about 1½ in. (38mm) on the front bumper and let it return. Repeat the procedure 2–3 more times.

   f. Re-measure the distance at the control arm.

   g. Determine the average of the 2 measurements. The average distance should be as specified.

   h. If the figure is correct, tighten the control arm pivot nuts to 94 ft. lbs. (128 Nm).

   i. If the figure is not correct, tighten the pivot bolts to 94 ft. lbs. (128 Nm) and have the front end alignment corrected.

V-Series

1. Raise and support the vehicle safely.

2. Remove the wheels.

3. Remove the locking hubs.

4. Remove the spindle.

5. Disconnect the tie rod end from the knuckle.

6. Remove the knuckle-to-steering arm nuts and adapters.

7. Remove the steering arm from the knuckle.

8. Remove the cotter pins and nuts from the upper and lower ball joints.

NOTE: Do not remove the adjusting ring from the knuckle. If it is necessary to loosen the ring to remove the knuckle, do not loosen it more than 2 threads. The non-hardened threads in the yoke can be easily damaged by the hardened threads in the adjusting ring if caution is not used during knuckle removal

9. Insert the wedge-shaped end of the heavy prybar or wedge-type ball joint tool, between the lower ball joint and the yoke. Drive the prybar in to break the knuckle free.

10. Repeat the procedure at the upper ball joint.

11. Lift off the knuckle.

12. Secure the knuckle in a vise.

13. Remove the snapring from the lower ball joint. Using tools J-9619-30, J-23454-1 and J-23454-4 or equivalent screw-type forcing tool, force the lower ball joint from the knuckle.

14. Using tools J-9619-30, J-23454-3 and J-23454-4 or equivalent screw-type forcing tool, force the upper ball joint from the knuckle.

To install:

15. Position the lower ball joint (the 1 without the cotter pin hole) squarely in the knuckle. Using tools J-9619-30, J-23454-2 and J-23454-3 or equivalent screw-type forcing tool, force the lower ball joint into the knuckle until it is fully seated.

16. Install the snapring.

17. Position the upper ball joint (the 1 with the cotter pin hole) squarely in the knuckle. Using tools J-9619-30, J-23454-2 and J-23454-3 or equivalent screw-type forcing tool, force the upper ball joint into the knuckle until it is fully seated.

18. Position the knuckle on the yoke.

19. Start the ball joints into their sockets. Place the nuts onto the ball studs. The nut with the cotter pin slot is the upper nut. Tighten the lower nut to 30 ft. lbs. (40 Nm), for now.

20. Using tool J-23447, tighten the adjusting ring to 50 ft. lbs. (68 Nm).

21. Tighten the upper nut to specification. Install a new cotter pin. Never loosen the nut to align the cotter pin hole; always tighten it.

22. Tighten the lower nut to specification.

23. Attach the steering arm to the knuckle using adapters and new nuts.

24. Connect the tie rod end to the knuckle.

25. Install the spindle.

26. Install the hub/rotor assembly and wheel bearings. Adjust the bearings.

27. Install the locking hubs.

28. Install the wheel.

29. Check the front end alignment.

Upper Control Arms

REMOVAL AND INSTALLATION

Compact Pick-Up, Van and Utility

1. Note and record the amount of shims used at the control arm retaining bolts. These shims must be installed in the same location as removed. Remove the nuts and the shims.

2. Raise and support the vehicle safely. Properly support the lower control arm. The control arm must be supported so the spring and the control arm remain intact.

3. Remove the wheel and tire assembly. Separate the upper ball joint from the steering knuckle, using the proper tool. Support the hub assembly.

4. Remove the upper control arm retaining bolts. Remove the upper control arm.

5. Installation is the reverse of the removal procedure. Tighten the upper control arm nuts to 65 ft. lbs. (88 Nm). Check and adjust the front end alignment, as required.

R-Series and G-Series

1. Note and record the amount of shims. These shims must be installed in the same location as removed. Remove the nuts and the shims.

2. Raise and support the vehicle safely. Properly support the lower control arm, using the necessary equipment. The control arm must be supported so the spring and the control arm remain intact.

3. Remove the tire and wheel assembly. Remove the brake caliper assembly and position it to the side. Loosen the upper ball joint from the

steering knuckle, using the proper tool. Support the hub assembly.

4. Remove the upper control arm retaining bolts. Remove the upper control arm.

To install:

5. Place the control arm in position and install the nuts. Before tightening the nuts, insert the caster and camber shims in the same order as when installed.

6. Install the nuts securing the control arm shaft studs to the cross-member bracket. Tighten the nuts to 70 ft. lbs. (95 Nm) for 10/1500-Series; 105 ft. lbs. (142 Nm) for all other Series.

7. Install the ball stud nut. Torque the nut to 50 ft. lbs. (68 Nm) for 10/1500-Series; 90 ft. lbs. (122 Nm) for all other Series.

8. Install the cotter pin. Never back off the nut to install the cotter pin. Always advance it.

9. Install the brake caliper. Remove the spring compressor.

10. Install the wheel.

11. Check the front end alignment.

C/K-Series

1. Raise and support the vehicle safely.

2. Support the lower control arm.

3. Remove the wheel.

4. Unbolt the brake hose bracket from the control arm.

5. Remove the air cleaner extension.

6. Remove the cotter pin from the upper control arm ball stud and loosen the stud nut until the bottom surface of the nut is slightly below the end of the stud.

7. Install a spring compressor on the coil spring for safety.

8. Using a screw-type forcing tool, break loose the ball joint from the knuckle.

9. Remove the nuts and bolts securing the control arm to the frame brackets.

10. The 35-Series bushings are replaceable. The 15/25-Series bushings are welded in place.

To install:

11. Place the control arm in position and install the shims, bolts and new nuts. Both bolt heads must be inboard of the control arm brackets. Tighten the nuts finger-tight for now.

NOTE: Do not torque the bolts yet. The bolts must be torque with the vehicle at its proper ride height.

12. Install the ball stud nut. Torque the nut to 84 ft. lbs. (115 Nm). Install

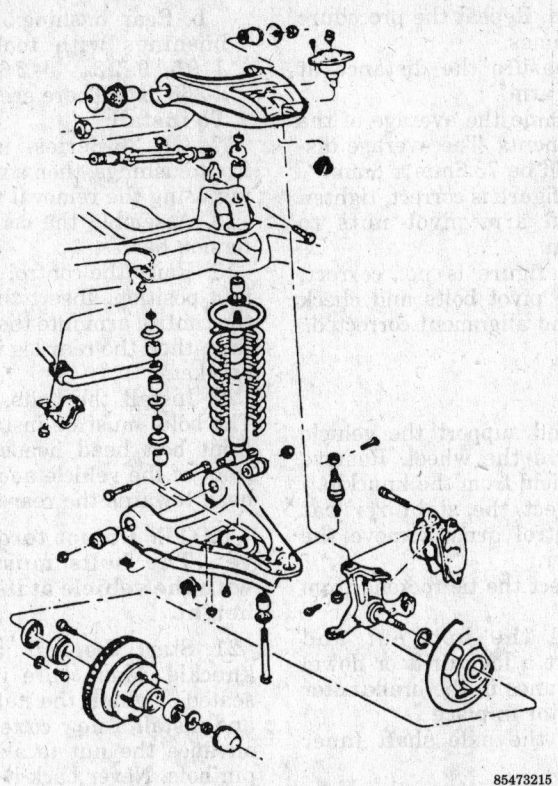

85473215

Front suspension components — M-Series and S-Series

the cotter pin. Never back off the nut to install the cotter pin.

13. Install the brake caliper.

14. Remove the spring compressor or safety chain.

15. Install the wheel.

16. Install the brake hose.

17. Install the air cleaner extension.

18. Install the battery ground cable.

19. Lower the vehicle. Once the weight of the vehicle is on the wheels:

a. Lift the front bumper about 38mm and let it drop.

b. Repeat this procedure 2–3 more times.

c. Draw a line on the side of the lower control arm from the centerline of the control arm pivot shaft, dead level to the outer end of the control arm.

d. Measure the distance between the lowest corner of the steering knuckle and the line on the control arm. Record the figure.

e. Push down about 38mm on the front bumper and let it return. Repeat the procedure 2–3 more times.

f. Re-measure the distance at the control arm.

g. Determine the average of the 2 measurements. The average distance should be as specified.

h. If the figure is correct, tighten the control arm pivot nuts to 139 ft. lbs. (190 Nm).

i. If the figure is not correct, adjust or repair the ride height.

Lower Control Arms

REMOVAL AND INSTALLATION

M/L-Series and S/T-Series

1. Raise and support the vehicle safely.

2. Remove the wheel and tire assemblies. Properly support the lower control arm assembly.

3. Remove the coil spring.

4. Remove the lower ball joint cotter pin and retaining nut.

5. Using the proper tool, separate the lower ball joint from the steering knuckle.

6. Remove the lower control arm.

7. Installation is the reverse of the removal procedure. Check and adjust front alignment, as required.

Lumina APV, Silhouette and Trans Sport

1. Raise and safely support the vehicle so the suspension hangs freely.

2. Remove the wheel and tire assemblies.

3. Remove the stabilizer shaft-to-control arm mounting bolt. Remove the lower ball joint pinch bolt.

4. Separate the steering knuckle from the lower ball joint.

5. Remove the lower control arm mounting bolts and remove the control arm.

To install:

6. Install the control arm in position on the vehicle frame. Do not tighten the control arm bolts at this time.

7. Install the stabilizer shaft to the control arm, do not tighten the bolts at this time.

8. Connect the steering knuckle to the control arm using a new pinch bolt. Tighten to 33 ft. lbs. (45 Nm). Lower the vehicle so the weight is supported by the control arms.

9. Tighten the control arm bolts to 61 ft. lbs. (83 Nm). Tighten the stabilizer shaft bolts to 32 ft. lbs. (43 Nm).

10. Install the wheel and tire assemblies. Lower the vehicle completely.

R-Series and G-Series

1. Raise and support the vehicle safely. Properly support the lower control arm assembly. Remove the tire and wheel assembly. Remove the brake caliper and position it to the side.

2. Remove the control arm u-bolts and remove the coil spring. Remove the lower ball joint cotter pin and retaining nut. Using the proper tool, separate the lower ball joint from the steering knuckle.

3. Remove the lower control arm.

To install:

4. Install the lower control arm and spring assembly. Torque the U-bolts to 85 ft. lbs. (115 Nm).

5. Install the ball stud nut. Torque the nut to 90 ft. lbs. (122 Nm). Install the cotter pin. Never back off the nut to install the cotter pin.

6. Install the brake caliper.

C-Series

1. Raise and support the vehicle safely. Remove the tire and wheel assembly. Properly support the lower control arm assembly. Remove the lower control arm bolts and coil spring.

2. Remove the lower ball joint cotter pin and retaining nut. Using the proper tool, separate the lower ball joint from the steering knuckle.

3. Remove the lower control arm.

To install:

4. Slowly raise the lower control arm with the coil spring. Guide the control arm into place with a prybar.

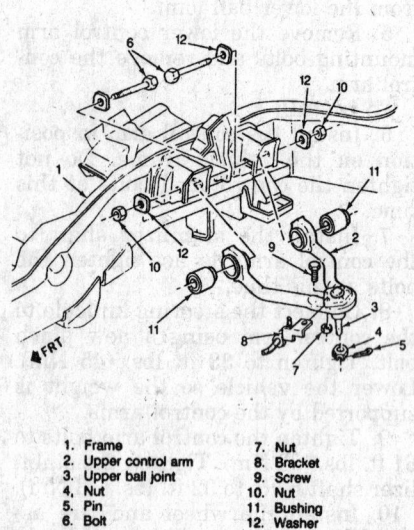

1. Frame
2. Upper control arm
3. Upper ball joint
4. Nut
5. Pin
6. Bolt
7. Nut
8. Bracket
9. Screw
10. Nut
11. Bushing
12. Washer

85473216

Upper control arm installation — K-Series

5. Install the pivot shaft bolts, front 1 first. The bolts must be installed with the heads towards the front of the vehicle. Remove the safety chain or spring compressors.

NOTE: Do not torque the bolts yet. The bolts must be torque with the vehicle at its proper ride height.

6. Remove the jack.
7. Connect the stabilizer bar to the lower control arm. Torque the nuts to specification.
8. Install the shock absorber.
9. Install the wheel.
10. Lower the vehicle. Once the weight of the vehicle is on the wheels proceed as follows:
   a. Lift the front bumper about 1½ in. (38mm) and let it drop.
   b. Repeat this procedure 2–3 more times.
   c. Draw a line on the side of the lower control arm from the center-line of the control arm pivot shaft, dead level to the outer end of the control arm.
   d. Measure the distance between the lowest corner of the steering knuckle and the line on the control arm. Record the figure.
   e. Push down about 1½ in. (38mm) on the front bumper and

let it return. Repeat the procedure 2–3 more times.
   f. Re-measure the distance at the control arm.
   g. Determine the average of the 2 measurements. The average distance should be 73.6mm ± 6mm.
   h. If the figure is correct, tighten the control arm pivot nuts to specification.
   i. If the figure is not correct, tighten the pivot bolts and check the front end alignment corrected.

K-Series

1. Raise and support the vehicle safely. Remove the wheel. Remove the splash shield from the knuckle.
2. Disconnect the stabilizer bar from the control arm. Remove the shock absorber.
3. Disconnect the tie rod end from the relay rod.
4. Remove the hub nut and washer. Insert a long drift or dowel through the vanes in the brake rotor to hold the rotor in place.
5. Remove the axle shaft inner flange bolts.
6. Using a puller, force the outer end of the axle shaft out of the hub. Remove the shaft.
7. Support the lower control arm. Matchmark the both torsion bar adjustment bolt positions.
8. Using tool J-36202, increase the tension on the adjusting arm.
9. Remove the adjustment bolt and retaining plate.
10. Move the tool aside. Slide the torsion bars forward. Remove the adjusting arm.
11. Remove the cotter pin from the lower ball stud and loosen the nut.
12. Loosen the lower ball stud in the steering knuckle using a ball joint stud removal tool. When the stud is loose, remove the nut from the stud. It may be necessary to remove the brake caliper and wire it to the frame to gain clearance.
13. Remove the control arm-to-frame bracket bolts, nuts and washers.
14. Remove the lower control arm and torsion bar as a unit.
15. Separate the control arm and torsion bar.
16. On 15 and 25-Series, the bushings are not replaceable. If they are damaged, the control arm will have to be replaced. On 35-Series, proceed as follows:
   a. Front bushing: Unbend the crimps with a punch. Force out the bushings with tools J-36618-2, J-9519-23, J-36618-4 and 36618-1.

   b. Rear bushing: Force out the bushings with tools J-36618-5, J-9519-23, J-36618-3 and J-36618-2. There are no crimps.
To install:
17. On 35-Series, install a new front bushings, then a new rear bushing using the removal tools.
18. Assemble the control arm and torsion bar.
19. Raise the control arm assembly into position. Insert the front leg of the control arm into the crossmember first, then the rear leg into the frame bracket.
20. Install the bolts, front 1 first. The bolts must be installed with the front bolt head heads towards the front of the vehicle and the rear bolt head towards the rear of the vehicle!

NOTE: Do not torque the bolts yet. The bolts must be torque with the vehicle at its proper ride height.

21. Start the ball joint into the knuckle. Make sure it is squarely seated. Tighten the nut to 96 ft. lbs. and install a new cotter pin. Always advance the nut to align the cotter pin hole. Never back it off.
22. Install the adjuster arm.
23. Using tool J-36202, increase tension on both torsion bars.
24. Install the adjustment retainer plate and bolt on both torsion bars.
25. Set the adjustment bolt to the marked position.
26. Release the tension on the torsion bar until the load is take up by the adjustment bolt.
27. Remove the tool.
28. Position the shaft in the hub and install the washer and hub nut. Leave the drift in the rotor vanes and tighten the hub nut to specification.
29. Install the flange bolts. Tighten to specification. Remove the drift.
30. Connect the inner tie rod end at the steering relay rod. Torque the nut to specification.
31. Install the splash shield.
32. Connect the stabilizer bar to the lower control arm. Torque the nuts to specification.
33. Install the shock absorber.
34. Install the wheel.
35. Lower the vehicle. Once the weight of the vehicle is on the wheels proceed as follows:
   a. Lift the front bumper about 1½ in. (38mm) and let it drop.
   b. Repeat this procedure 2–3 more times.
   c. Draw a line on the side of the lower control arm from the center-line of the control arm pivot shaft, dead level to the outer end of the control arm.

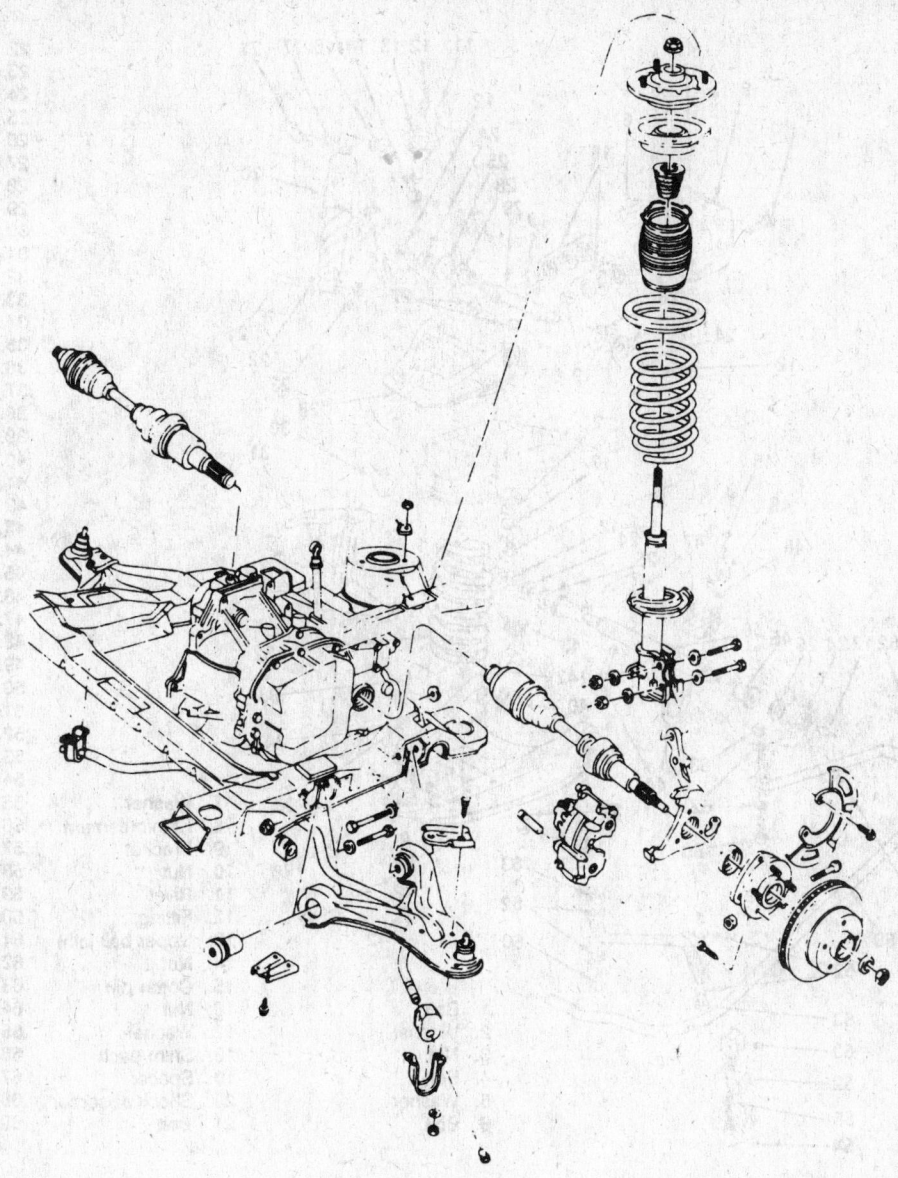

85473217

Front suspension components — Lumina, Silhouette and Trans Sport

d. Measure the distance between the lowest corner of the steering knuckle and the line on the control arm. Record the figure.

e. Push down about 1½ in. (38mm) on the front bumper and let it return. Repeat the procedure 2–3 more times.

f. Re-measure the distance at the control arm.

g. Determine the average of the 2 measurements. The average distance should be 73.6mm ± 6mm.

h. If the figure is correct, tighten the control arm nuts to specification.

i. If the figure is not correct, tighten the pivot bolts to specifica-

tion and have the front end alignment corrected.

Stabilizer Shaft/Sway Bar

REMOVAL AND INSTALLATION

Compact Pick-Up, Van and Utility

1. Raise and safely support the vehicle.

2. Remove the wheel and tire assembly.

3. Remove the left and right side stabilizer mounting bolts. Keep the sides separate for installation.

4. Remove the center stabilizer insulators and lower the stabilizer.

To install:

5. Install the stabilizer in position in the vehicle. Tighten the left and right mounting bolts to 24 ft. lbs. and the center bushing supports to 35 ft. lbs.

6. Install the wheel and tire assemblies and lower the vehicle.

R-Series and G-Series

1. Raise and support the vehicle safely. As required, remove the tire and wheel assemblies.

2. Properly support the stabilizer bar assembly. Remove the stabilizer shaft bushing retaining bolts. Re-

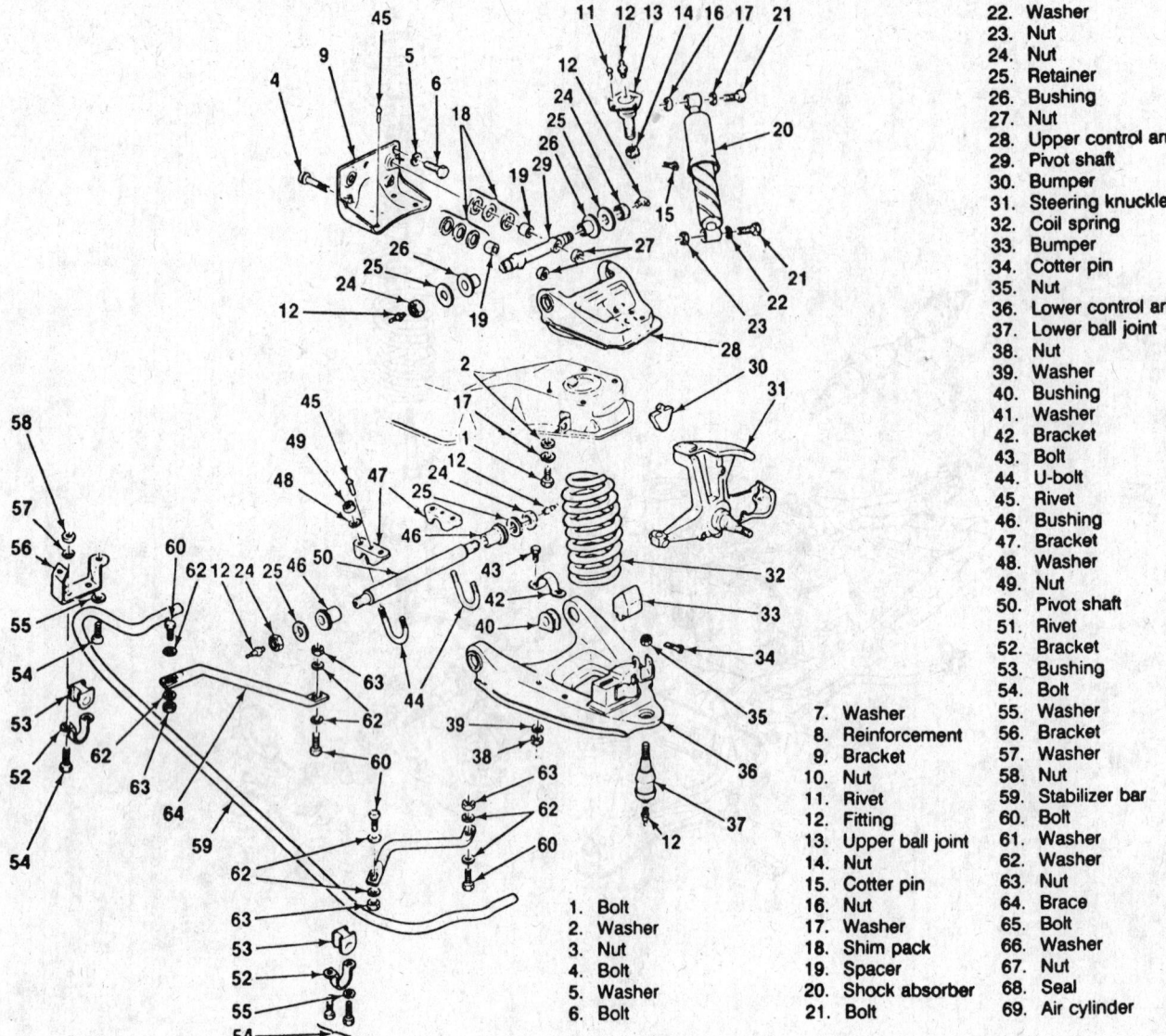

22. Washer
23. Nut
24. Nut
25. Retainer
26. Bushing
27. Nut
28. Upper control arm
29. Pivot shaft
30. Bumper
31. Steering knuckle
32. Coil spring
33. Bumper
34. Cotter pin
35. Nut
36. Lower control arm
37. Lower ball joint
38. Nut
39. Washer
40. Bushing
41. Washer
42. Bracket
43. Bolt
44. U-bolt
45. Rivet
46. Bushing
47. Bracket
48. Washer
49. Nut
50. Pivot shaft
51. Rivet
52. Bracket
53. Bushing
54. Bolt
55. Washer
56. Bracket
57. Washer
58. Nut
59. Stabilizer bar
60. Bolt
61. Washer
62. Washer
63. Nut
64. Brace
65. Bolt
66. Washer
67. Nut
68. Seal
69. Air cylinder

7. Washer
8. Reinforcement
9. Bracket
10. Nut
11. Rivet
12. Fitting
13. Upper ball joint
14. Nut
15. Cotter pin
16. Nut
17. Washer
18. Shim pack
19. Spacer
20. Shock absorber
21. Bolt

1. Bolt
2. Washer
3. Nut
4. Bolt
5. Washer
6. Bolt

85473218

Front suspension assembly — R and G-Series

move the stabilizer link bushing nuts and bolts.

3. Remove the stabilizer bar.

4. Installation is the reverse of removal. Note, the split in the bushing faces forward. Coat the bushings with silicone grease prior to installation. Install all fasteners and torque to 24 ft. lbs. (33 Nm).

V-Series

1. Raise and support the vehicle safely.

2. Remove the wheels.

3. Remove the stabilizer bar-to-frame clamps.

4. Remove the stabilizer bar-to-spring plate bolts.

5. Remove the stabilizer bar and bushings.

6. Check the bushings for wear or splitting. Replace any damaged bushings.

7. Installation is the reverse of removal. The split in the bushing faces forward. Coat the bushings with silicone grease prior to installation. Torque the stabilizer bar-to-frame nuts to 52 ft. lbs. (70 Nm). Torque the stabilizer bar-to-spring plate bolts to 133 ft. lbs. (180 Nm).

C-Series

NOTE: The end link bushings, bolts and spacers are not interchangeable from left to right.

1. Raise and support the vehicle safely.

2. Remove the nuts from the end link bolts.

3. Remove the bolts, bushings and spacers.

4. Remove the bracket bolts and remove the stabilizer bar.

5. Inspect the bushings for wear or damage. Replace them as necessary.

6. Installation is the reverse of removal. Coat the bushings with silicone grease prior to assembly. The slit in the bushings faces the front of the vehicle. Torque the frame bracket bolts to 24 ft. lbs. (33 Nm); the end link nuts to 13 ft. lbs. (18 Nm).

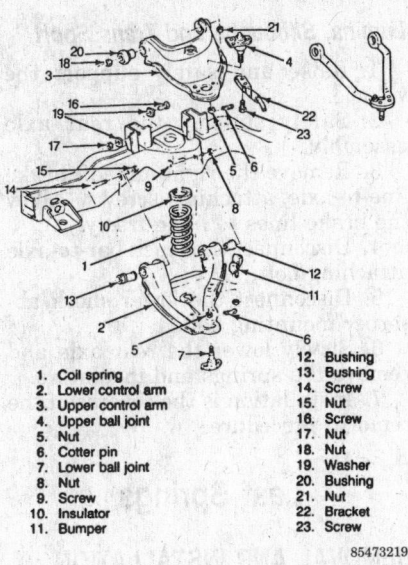

1. Coil spring
2. Lower control arm
3. Upper control arm
4. Upper ball joint
5. Nut
6. Cotter pin
7. Lower ball joint
8. Nut
9. Screw
10. Insulator
11. Bumper
12. Bushing
13. Bushing
14. Screw
15. Nut
16. Screw
17. Nut
18. Nut
19. Washer
20. Bushing
21. Nut
22. Bracket
23. Screw

85473219

Front suspension assembly — C-Series

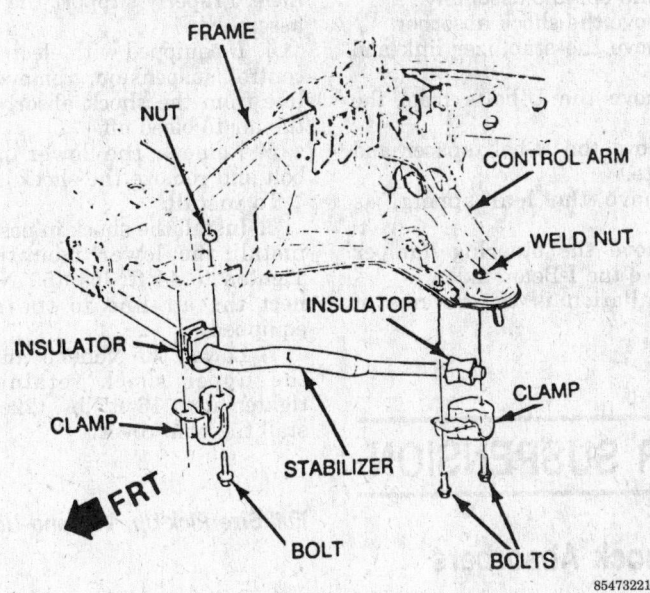

Stabilizer bar mounting — M/L-Series and S/T-Series

85473221

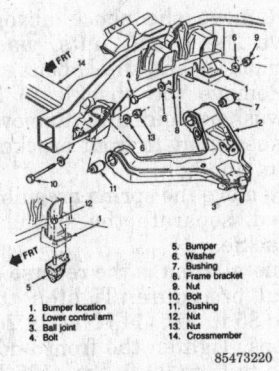

5. Bumper
6. Washer
7. Bushing
8. Frame bracket
9. Nut
10. Bolt
11. Bushing
12. Nut
13. Nut
14. Crossmember

1. Bumper location
2. Lower control arm
3. Ball joint
4. Bolt

85473220

**Lower control arm
installation — K-Series**

K-Series

NOTE: The end link bushings, bolts and spacers are not interchangeable from left to right.

1. Raise and support the vehicle safely.
2. Remove the nuts, bolts, spacer and clamp from the stabilizer bar.
3. Remove the stabilizer bar and remove the insulator.
4. Inspect all parts for wear or damage and replace them as necessary.
5. Installation is the reverse of removal.

6. Unload the torsion bar tension using tool J–36202.
7. Coat the bushings with silicone grease prior to assembly. Torque the frame bracket bolts to 13 ft. lbs. (18 Nm); the end link nuts to 12 ft. lbs. (17 Nm).

Kingpins

REMOVAL AND INSTALLATION

1. Raise and support the vehicle safely.
2. Remove the tire and wheel assembly.
3. Remove the caliper, hub and rotor assembly.
4. Remove the backing plate and steering arm.
5. Remove the upper kingpin cap, gasket and brake hose bracket.
6. Remove the lower cap and gasket. Discard the gasket.
7. Remove the locking pin and nut from the axle.
8. Drive the kingpin out using a suitable drift punch. The spacer and bushings will also come out with the kingpin.
9. Remove the steering knuckle from the drive axle.
10. Remove the dust seal, shim and thrust bearing.

To install:
11. Install new bushings into the steering knuckle and ream the new bushings to 1.1804–1.1820 in. (29.982–30.022mm). Install the steering knuckle onto the axle.
12. Prelube the thrust bearing and install the bearing, shim, and dust seal.
13. Prelube the kingpin; install the kingpin and lock pin, inserting the spacers in the correct order. Torque the lock pin to 29 ft. lbs. (40 Nm).
14. Install the upper and lower gasket and kingpin caps. Install the upper brake hose bracket.
15. Install the steering arm and backing plate. Torque the bolts to 12 ft. lbs. (16 Nm) and the nuts to 230 ft. lbs. (312 Nm).
16. Install the hub, rotor and caliper assembly.
17. Install the tire and wheel assembly.
18. Lower the vehicle and check the front end alignment.

I-Beam Axle

REMOVAL AND INSTALLATION

1. Raise and support the vehicle safely. Properly support the front axle beam.

2. Remove the tire and wheel assembly.

3. Remove the steering arm, knuckle and spindle assembly.

4. Remove the shock absorber.

5. Remove the stabilizer link and bushings.

6. Remove the U-bolts from the axle.

7. Remove the U-bolt spacer and shock plate.

8. Remove the leaf spring, as required.

9. Remove the steering damper and remove the I-Beam axle.

10. Installation is the reverse of removal.

REAR SUSPENSION

Shock Absorbers

REMOVAL AND INSTALLATION

M/L-Series and S/T-Series

1. Raise and support the vehicle safely.

2. Properly support the rear axle assembly.

3. Remove the upper shock absorber retaining bolt.

4. Remove the lower shock absorber bolt.

5. Remove the shock absorber.

To install:

6. Install the shock in position and install the mounting bolts.

7. Tighten the top mounting bolts to 17 ft. lbs. (23 Nm) and the lower mounting bolts to 47 ft. lbs. (64 Nm).

8. Lower the vehicle.

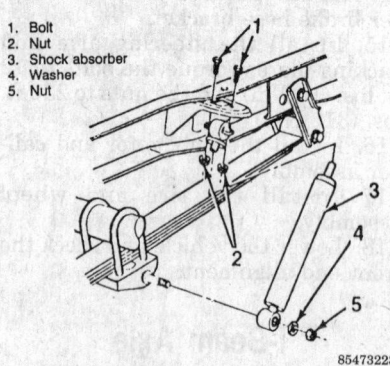

1. Bolt
2. Nut
3. Shock absorber
4. Washer
5. Nut

85473223

Common rear shock absorber mounting

Lumina, Silhouette and Trans Sport

1. Open the lift gate and open the trim cover.

2. Remove the upper shock mounting nut and grommet.

3. Raise and safely support the vehicle. Properly support the rear axle assembly.

4. If equipped with electronic level control suspension, remove the air line from the shock absorber. Allow the air to bleed off.

5. Remove the lower mounting bolt and remove the shock.

To install:

6. Install the shock in position and install the lower mounting bolt. Tighten to 44 ft. lbs. (59 Nm). Connect the air line to the shock, if equipped.

7. Lower the vehicle and install the upper shock retaining nut, tighten it to 16 ft. lbs. (22 Nm). Install the trim cover.

Full Size Pick-Up, Van and Utility

1. Raise and support the vehicle safely. Properly support the rear axle assembly. Remove the upper and lower shock absorber bolts.

2. Remove the shock absorber.

3. Installation is the reverse of the removal procedure.

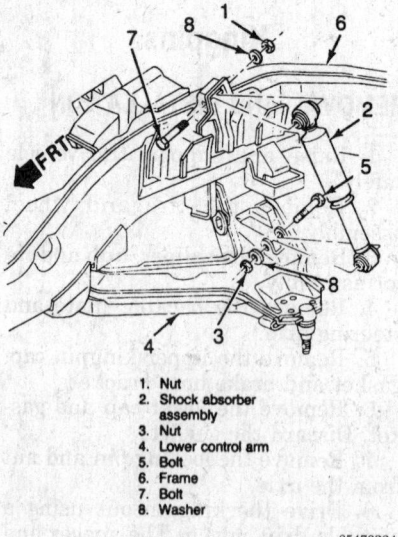

1. Nut
2. Shock absorber assembly
3. Nut
4. Lower control arm
5. Bolt
6. Frame
7. Bolt
8. Washer

85473224

Rear shock absorber mounting — K-Series

Coil Springs

REMOVAL AND INSTALLATION

Lumina, Silhouette and Trans Sport

1. Raise and safely support the vehicle.

2. Safely support the rear axle assembly.

3. Remove the right and left brake line-to-axle attaching screws. Allow the brake lines to hang freely.

4. Disconnect the track bar-to-axle attaching bolt.

5. Disconnect the lower shock absorber mounting bolts.

6. Slowly lower the rear axle and remove the springs and insulators.

7. Installation is the reverse of the removal procedure.

Leaf Springs

REMOVAL AND INSTALLATION

M/L-Series and S/T-Series

1. Raise and support the vehicle safely. Properly support the rear axle assembly to relieve tension on the springs.

2. Remove the shock absorbers. Remove the U-bolt nuts, washers, anchor plates and the U-bolts.

3. Remove the shackle to frame bolt, washers and nut. Remove the spring assembly to front bracket nut, washers and bolt.

4. Remove the spring assembly. As required, separate the spring from the shackle.

5. Installation is the reverse of the removal procedure. Tighten the U-bolts to 85 ft. lbs. (115 Nm) in 2 gradual steps. Tighten the front and rear shackle nuts to 92 ft. lbs. (125 Nm).

R/V-Series and G-Series

1. Raise and support the vehicle safely. Properly support the rear axle assembly to relieve tension on the springs.

2. If equipped, remove the stabilizer bar. Loosen, but do not remove the spring to shackle nut and bolt.

3. Remove the nut and bolt securing the shackle to the rear hanger. Remove the nut and bolt securing the leaf spring to the front hanger.

4. Remove the leaf spring from the front hanger. Remove the nut and bolt securing the shackle to the leaf spring. Remove the shackle.

5. Remove the nuts and washers holding the spring to the frame. If equipped, remove the rear stabilizer

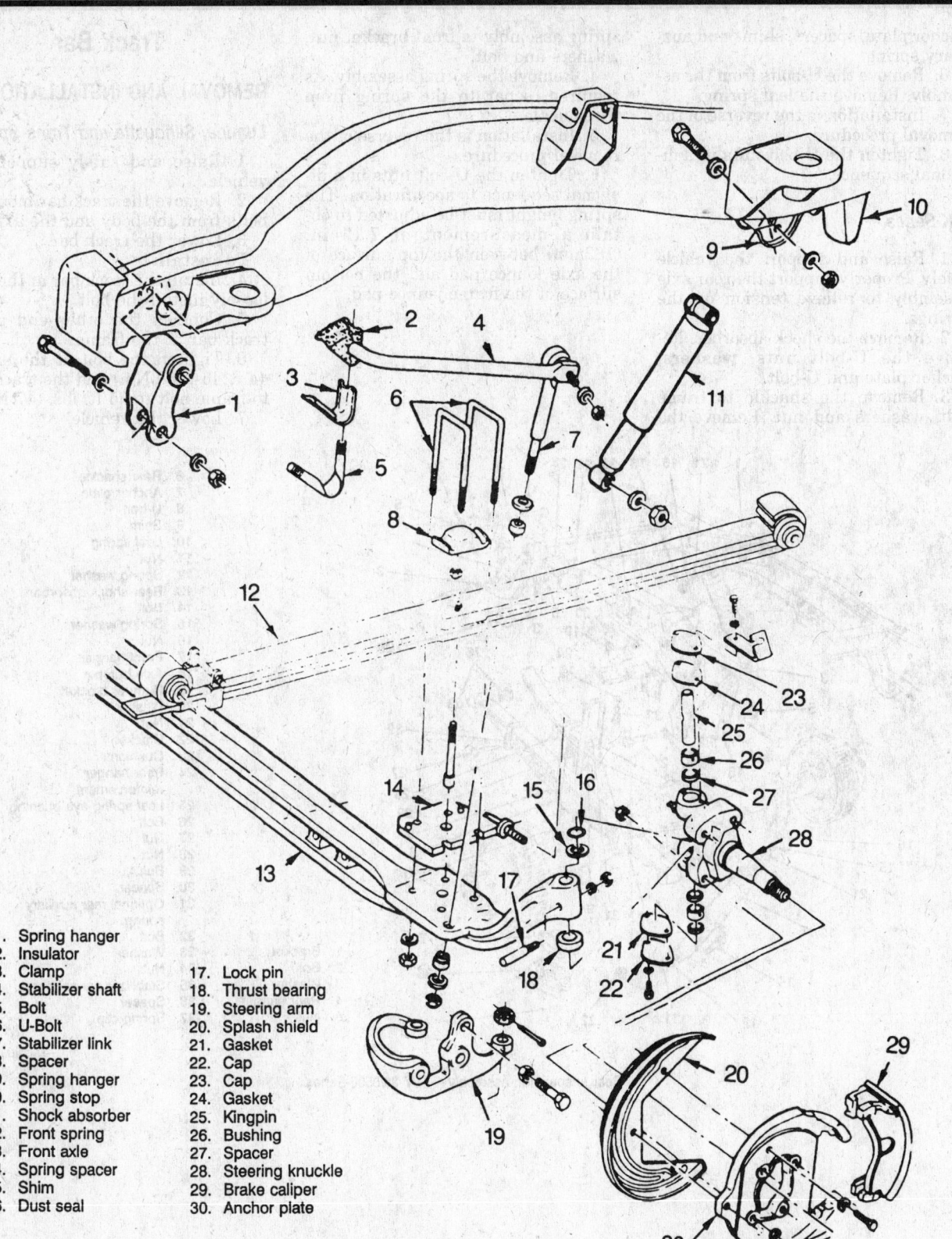

1. Spring hanger
2. Insulator
3. Clamp
4. Stabilizer shaft
5. Bolt
6. U-Bolt
7. Stabilizer link
8. Spacer
9. Spring hanger
10. Spring stop
11. Shock absorber
12. Front spring
13. Front axle
14. Spring spacer
15. Shim
16. Dust seal
17. Lock pin
18. Thrust bearing
19. Steering arm
20. Splash shield
21. Gasket
22. Cap
23. Cap
24. Gasket
25. Kingpin
26. Bushing
27. Spacer
28. Steering knuckle
29. Brake caliper
30. Anchor plate

85473222

Front I-Beam suspension — C3HD-Series

anchor plate, spacers, shims and auxiliary spring.

6. Remove the U-bolts from the assembly. Remove the leaf spring.

7. Installation is the reverse of the removal procedure.

8. Tighten the U-bolt nuts in a diagonal sequence.

C/K-Series

1. Raise and support the vehicle safely. Properly support the rear axle assembly to relieve tension on the springs.

2. Remove the shock absorber. Remove the U-bolt nuts, washers, anchor plate and U-bolt.

3. Remove the shackle to frame bolt, washers and nut. Remove the

spring assembly to front bracket nut, washers and bolt.

4. Remove the spring assembly. As required, separate the spring from the shackle.

5. Installation is the reverse of the removal procedure.

6. Tighten the U-bolt nuts in a diagonal sequence to specification. The spring height must be adjusted to obtain a measurement of 7.17 in. (182mm) between the top surface of the axle jounce pad and the bottom surface of the frame jounce pad.

Track Bar

REMOVAL AND INSTALLATION

Lumina, Silhouette and Trans Sport

1. Raise and safely support the vehicle.

2. Remove the track bar mounting bolts from the body and the axle.

3. Lower the track bar.

To install:

4. Install the track bar at the axle, loosely install the bolt.

5. Connect the other end of the track bar at the frame.

6. Tighten the bolt at the axle to 44 ft. lbs. (60 Nm) and the track bar-to-frame bolt to 35 ft. lbs. (47 Nm).

7. Lower the vehicle.

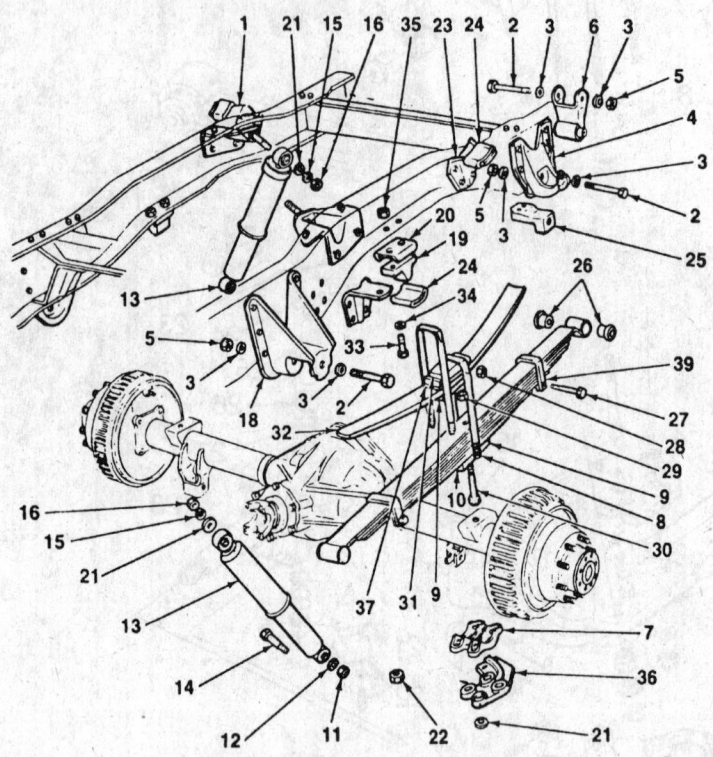

1. Bracket
2. Bolt
3. Washer
4. Rear hanger
5. Nut

6. Rear shackle
7. Anchor plate
8. U-bolt
9. Shim
10. Leaf spring
11. Nut
12. Spring washer
13. Rear shock absorber
14. Bolt
15. Spring washer
16. Nut
17. Front hanger
18. Axle bumper
19. Bumper bracket
20. Washer
21. Nut
22. Bracket
23. Cushion
24. Rear hanger reinforcement
25. Leaf spring eye bushing
26. Bolt
27. Nut
28. Nut
29. Bolt
30. Spacer
31. Optional rear auxiliary spring
32. Bolt
33. Washer
34. Nut
35. Stabilizer bar anchor
36. Spacer
37. Spring clip

85473225

Rear suspension assembly — R/V 30/3500-Series

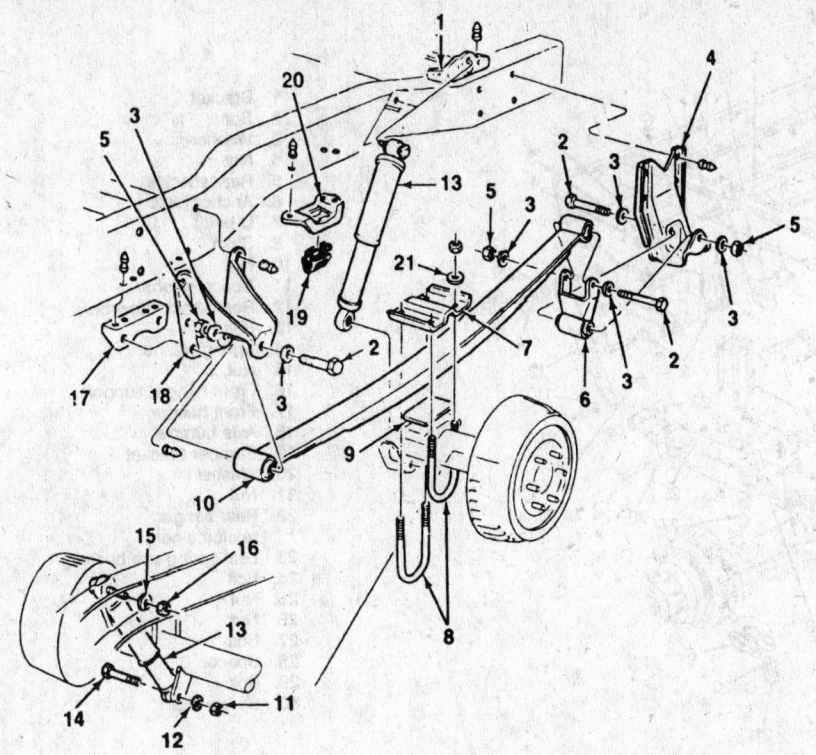

1. Bracket
2. Bolt
3. Washer
4. Rear hanger
5. Nut
6. Rear shackle
7. Anchor plate
8. U-bolt
9. Shim
10. Leaf spring
11. Nut
12. Spring washer
13. Rear shock absorber
14. Bolt
15. Spring washer
16. Nut
17. Front hanger support
18. Front hanger
19. Axle bumper
20. Bumper bracket
21. Washer
22. Nut

85473226

Rear suspension assembly — R/V 10/1500, 20/2500-Series

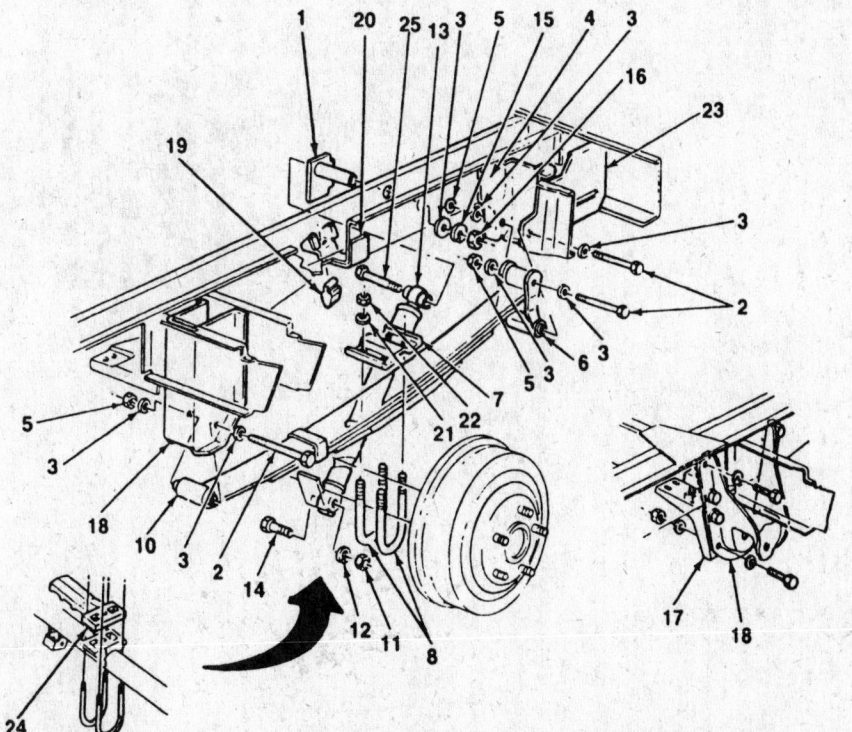

1. Bracket
2. Bolt
3. Washer
4. Rear hanger
5. Nut
6. Rear shackle
7. Anchor plate
8. U-bolt
9. Shim
10. Leaf spring
11. Nut
12. Spring washer
13. Rear shock absorber
14. Bolt
15. Spring washer
16. Nut
17. Front hanger support
18. Front hanger
19. Axle bumper
20. Bumper bracket
21. Washer
22. Nut
23. Rear hanger reinforcement
24. Spacer
25. Bolt

85473227

Rear suspension assembly — G10/1500 — G30/3500-Series

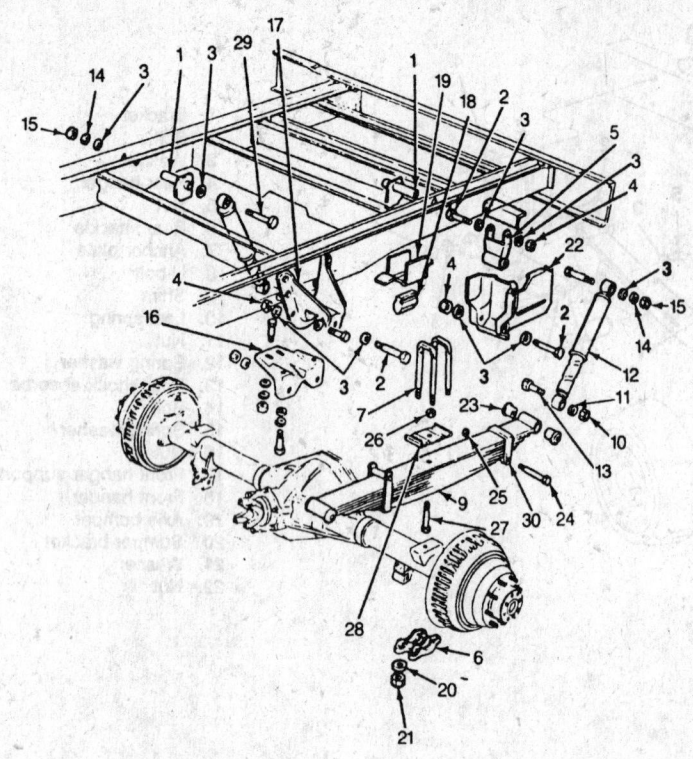

1. Bracket
2. Bolt
3. Washer
4. Nut
5. Rear shackle
6. Anchor plate
7. U-bolt
8. Shim
9. Nut
10. Nut
11. Spring washer
12. Rear shock absorber
13. Bolt
14. Spring washer
15. Nut
16. Front hanger support
17. Front hanger
18. Axle bumper
19. Bumper bracket
20. Washer
21. Nut
22. Rear hanger reinforcement
23. Leaf spring eye bushing
24. Bolt
25. Nut
26. Nut
27. Bolt
28. Spacer
29. Bolt
30. Spring clip

85473228

Rear suspension assembly — G30/3500-Series

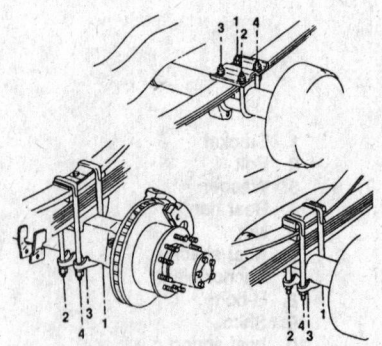

85473229

U-bolt tightening sequence — R/V and G-Series

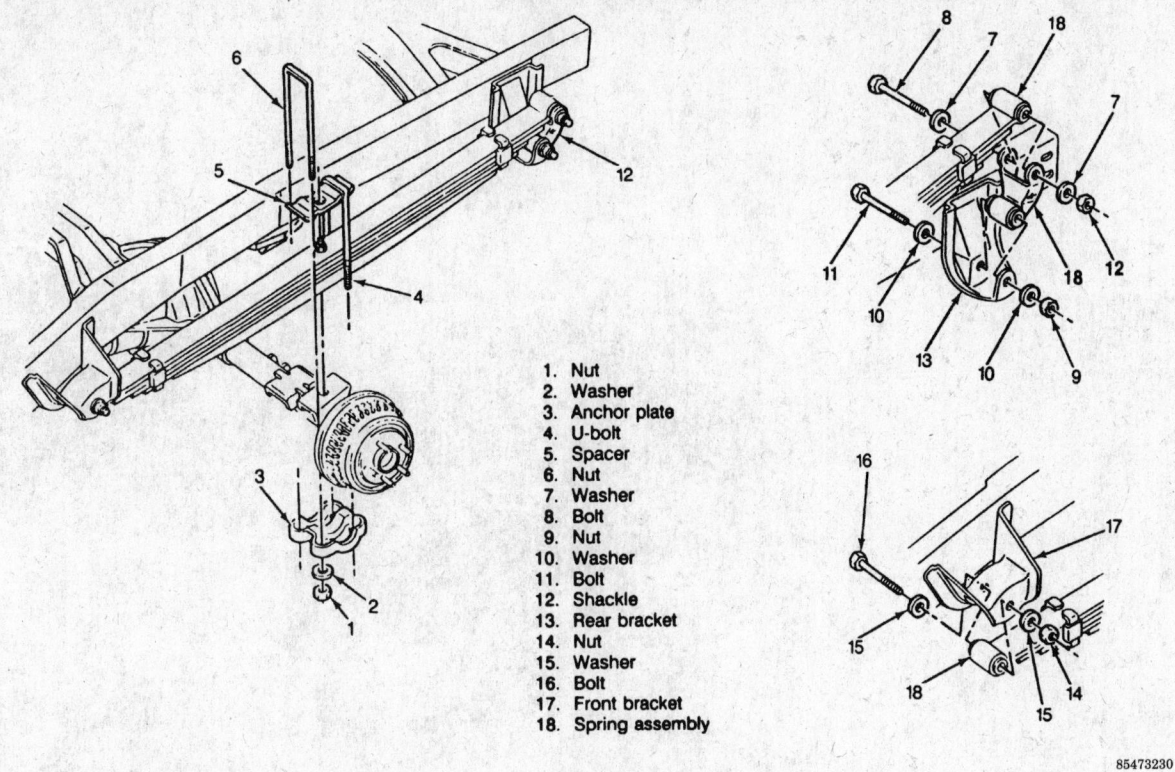

1. Nut
2. Washer
3. Anchor plate
4. U-bolt
5. Spacer
6. Nut
7. Washer
8. Bolt
9. Nut
10. Washer
11. Bolt
12. Shackle
13. Rear bracket
14. Nut
15. Washer
16. Bolt
17. Front bracket
18. Spring assembly

85473230

Rear leaf spring and components — C/K-Series

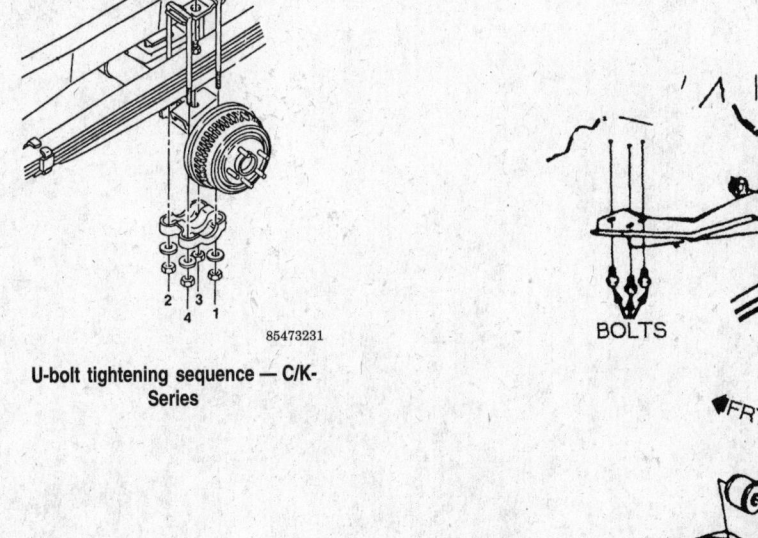

85473231

U-bolt tightening sequence — C/K-Series

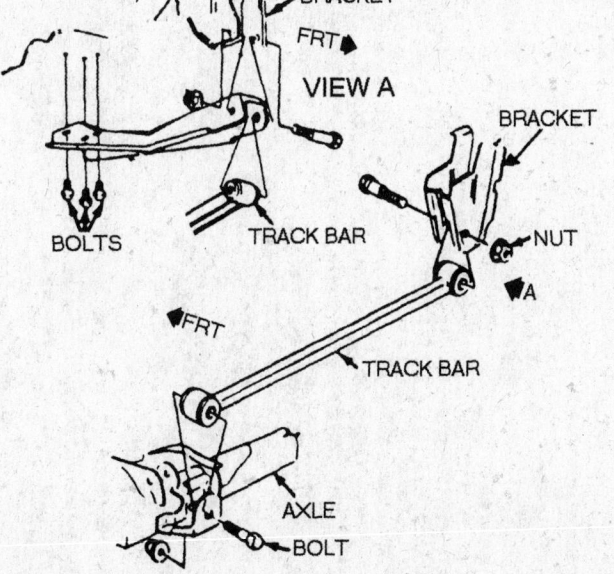

VIEW A

BRACKET
FRT
BOLTS
TRACK BAR
BRACKET
NUT
A
FRT
TRACK BAR
AXLE
BOLT

85473232

Rear track bar mounting — Lumina, Silhouette and Trans Sport

Jeep 4

Cherokee • Comanche • Grand Cherokee • Grand Wagoneer • Wrangler

FIRING ORDERS

NOTE: To avoid confusion, always replace spark plug wires one at a time.

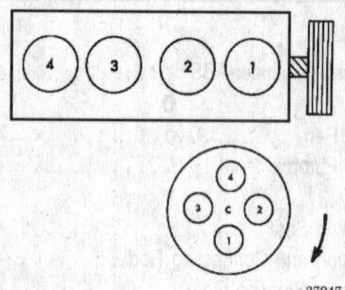

2.5L Engine
Engine Firing Order: 1–3–4–2
Distributor Rotation: Clockwise

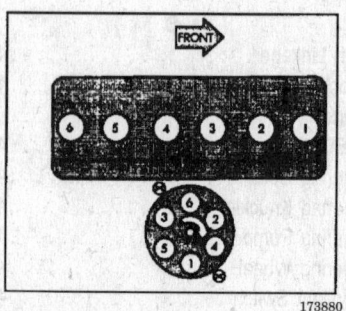

4.0L and 4.2L Engines
Engine Firing Order: 1–5–3–6–2–4
Distributor Rotation: Clockwise

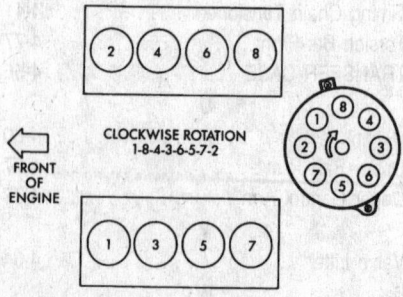

5.2L Engines
Engine Firing Order: 1–8–4–3–6–5–7–2
Distributor Rotation: Clockwise

ENGINE ELECTRICAL

Distributor

REMOVAL

Wrangler, Cherokee and Comanche

1. Disconnect the negative battery cable.
2. Unfasten the distributor cap retaining screws. Remove the distributor cap with the coil and spark plug wires attached and position them aside.
3. Disconnect the distributor primary wiring connector.
4. Scribe a mark on the distributor housing in line with the tip of the rotor.
5. Note the position of the rotor and distributor housing in relation to the surrounding engine components as reference points for installing the distributor.
6. Remove the distributor hold-down bolt and clamp.
7. Lift the distributor straight up and out of the engine.

1993–96 Grand Cherokee

The distributor contains an internal oil seal that prevents oil from entering the distributor housing. The seal is not serviceable.

1. Disconnect the negative battery cable.
2. If equipped with A/C, removing the cooling fan and shroud to gain access to the vibration damper bolt.
3. Label and remove the high tension wires from the distributor cap.
4. Remove the primary lead from the terminal post at the side of the distributor.
5. Turn the engine clockwise, using a socket on the end of the crankshaft damper bolt, until the rotor is pointing to the No. 1 spark plug wire post and the timing mark on the damper aligns with the 0 on the timing scale; No. 1 cylinder is at TDC on the compression stroke.

NOTE: The timing mark is on the edge of the vibration damper, closest to the front engine cover.

6. Remove the distributor cap. Note the position of the rotor and distributor. Scribe a mark on the base of the distributor and the engine as an installation reference.

7. Remove the bolt for the distributor hold-down clamp.
8. Remove the distributor from the engine.

1993 Grand Wagoneer

Base ignition timing is not adjustable. Base ignition timing and advance are controlled by the Powertrain Control Module (PCM).

1. Disconnect the negative battery cable.
2. Loosen the 2 screws and remove the distributor cap and position it aside.
3. Matchmark the distributor housing in relation to the engine.
4. Attach a socket to the vibration damper and rotate the crankshaft clockwise until the indicating mark on the vibration damper aligns with the **0** degree mark (TDC) on the timing chain cover.
5. The distributor rotor should now be aligned to the **cyl. No. 1** alignment mark stamped into the camshaft position sensor. If not, rotate the crankshaft through another complete 360 degree turn. Note the position of the number 1 cylinder spark plug cable (on the cap) in relation to the rotor. The rotor should now be aligned to this position.
6. Disconnect the camshaft position sensor wiring harness from the main engine wiring harness.
7. Remove the rotor.
8. Remove the distributor hold-down bolt and clamp.
9. Remove the distributor.

INSTALLATION

Engine Not Disturbed

WRANGLER, CHEROKEE AND COMANCHE

1. Clean the distributor mounting area of the cylinder block.
2. Install a new distributor mounting gasket.

NOTE: There is a fork on the distributor housing where the housing seats against the engine block. The slot in the fork aligns with the distributor hold-down bolt hole in the engine block. The distributor is correctly installed when the rotor is correctly positioned. This is the slot in the fork aligned with the hold-down bolt hole in the cylinder block. Because of the fork in the distributor housing initial ignition timing is not adjustable (the distributor cannot be rotated).

3. Position the distributor shaft in the cylinder block.

4. Align the rotor tip with the scribe mark on the distributor housing during removal.

5. Turn the rotor approximately 1/8 turn counterclockwise past the scribe mark.

——— WARNING ———
Ensure the distributor shaft fully engages into the oil pump drive gear shaft. It may be necessary to slightly rotate (bump) the engine. This is done while applying downward force on the distributor body. It should fully engage the distributor shaft with the oil pump drive gear shaft.

6. Slide the distributor shaft down into the engine.

NOTE: It may be necessary to move the rotor and shaft (slightly) to engage the distributor shaft with the slot in the oil pump shaft. the same may have to be done to engage the distributor gear with the camshaft gear. However, the rotor should align with the scribe mark when the distributor shaft is down in place.

1993–96 GRAND CHEROKEE

1. Using a flat bladed tool, turn the oil pump gear shaft, located in the distributor mounting hole, until the slot is slightly past the 11 o'clock position.

2. Install the rotor.

3. Without engaging the distributor gear into the cam gear, position the distributor into the hole in the engine block.

4. Visually align the hold-down ear of the distributor housing with the hold-down clamp hole.

5. Turn the rotor to the 4 o'clock position.

6. Slide the distributor into the block until it seats keeping the hold-down ear aligned with the hole in the block.

NOTE: The rotor should be in the 5 o'clock position with the trailing edge of the rotor blade lined up with the No. 1 spark plug post position.

7. Install the hold-down clamp and torque the bolt to 17 ft. lbs. (23 Nm).

8. Install the distributor cap.

9. Connect the distributor electrical connector.

10. If removed, install the cooling fan and shroud.

11. Connect the battery cable.

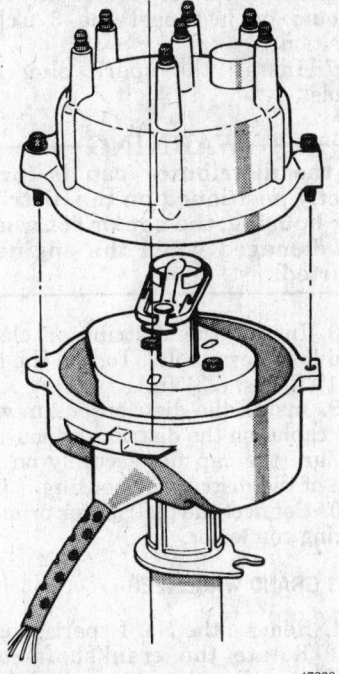

47238

Distributor cap removal — Grand Cherokee 1993–96

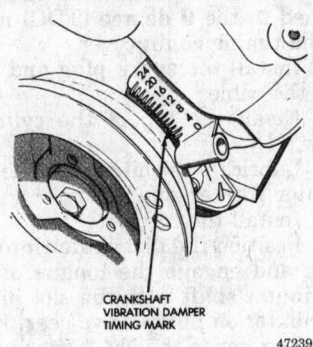

CRANKSHAFT
VIBRATION DAMPER
TIMING MARK

47239

Aligning the timing marks — Grand Cherokee 1993–96

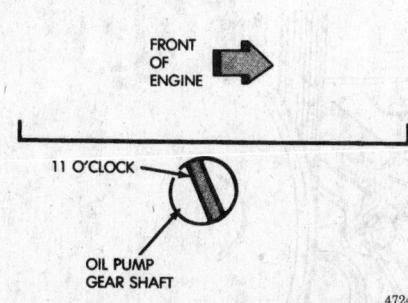

FRONT OF ENGINE

11 O'CLOCK

OIL PUMP
GEAR SHAFT

47241

Oil pump gear shaft alignment — Grand Cherokee 1993–96

1993 GRAND WAGONEER

1. Clean the top of the cylinder block.

2. Lubricate the oil seal on the distributor with engine oil.

3. Install the rotor.

4. Position the distributor into the block and engage the tongue of the distributor shaft with the slot in the distributor oil pump drive gear. Position the rotor to the No. 1 spark plug terminal position.

5. Install the hold-down clamp and loosely install the bolt.

6. Rotate the distributor housing until the rotor is aligned to the **cyl. No. 1** alignment mark on the camshaft position sensor.

7. Torque the hold-down clamp bolt to 200 inch lbs. (22 Nm).

8. Connect the camshaft position sensor wiring harness to the main engine harness.

9. Install the distributor cap and tighten the screws.

10. Ensure the spark plug wires are firmly connected to their terminals.

11. Connect the negative battery cable. Start the engine and check for proper operation.

Engine Disturbed

WRANGLER, CHEROKEE AND COMANCHE

1. Clean the distributor mounting area of the cylinder block.

2. Install a new distributor mounting gasket.

NOTE: There is a fork on the distributor housing where the housing seats against the engine block. The slot in the fork aligns with the distributor hold-down bolt hole in the engine block. The distributor is correctly installed when the rotor is correctly positioned. This is the slot in the fork aligned with the hold-down bolt hole in the cylinder block. Because of the fork in the distributor housing initial ignition timing is not adjustable (the distributor cannot be rotated).

3. Remove the No. 1 spark plug.

4. Hold a finger over the spark plug hole and rotate the engine until compression pressure is felt. Slowly continue to rotate the engine until the timing index on the vibration damper pulley aligns the Top Dead

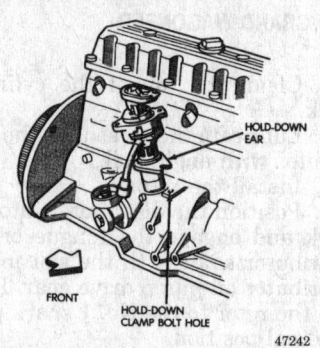

Distributor installation — Grand Cherokee 1993–96

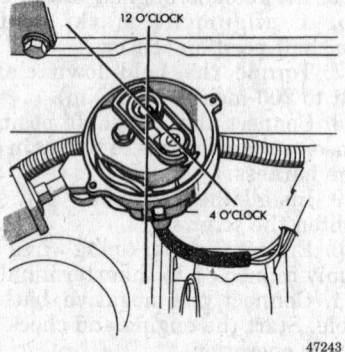

Rotor alignment — Grand Cherokee 1993–96

Center (TDC) mark (0 degree) on the timing degree scale.

NOTE: Always rotate the engine in the direction of normal rotation. Do not turn the engine backward to align the timing marks.

5. Using a flat blade prybar, rotate the oil pump gear to position the slot in the oil pump shaft slightly before the 11 O'clock position.

NOTE: With the distributor cap removed, install the distributor with the rotor located just past the 2 o'clock position.

6. With the distributor fully engaged in its correct position, the rotor should be just past the 3 o'clock position.

7. Install the spark plug and cable.

—— WARNING ——

If the distributor cap is incorrectly positioned on the distributor housing, the cap or rotor may be damaged when the engine is started.

8. Install the distributor clamp and hold-down bolts. Torque the bolt to 17 ft. lbs. (23 Nm).

9. Install the distributor cap with the cables on the distributor housing. Ensure the cap fits securely on the rim of the distributor housing.

10. Connect the distributor primary wiring connector.

1993 GRAND WAGONEER

1. Remove the No. 1 spark plug.

2. Rotate the crankshaft in a clockwise direction, as viewed from the front, until the No. 1 cylinder piston is at the top of its compression stroke. Continue to slowly rotate the engine until the indicating mark is aligned to the 0 degree (TDC) mark on the timing chain cover.

3. Install the spark plug and connect the cable.

4. Clean the top of the cylinder block.

5. Lubricate the oil seal on the distributor with engine oil.

6. Install the rotor.

7. Position the distributor into the block and engage the tongue of the distributor shaft with the slot in the distributor oil pump drive gear. Position the rotor to the No. 1 spark plug terminal position.

8. Install the hold-down clamp and loosely install the bolt.

9. Rotate the distributor housing until the rotor is aligned to the cyl.

No. 1 alignment mark on the camshaft position sensor.

10. Torque the hold-down clamp bolt to 200 inch lbs. (22 Nm).

11. Connect the camshaft position sensor wiring harness to the main engine harness.

12. Install the distributor cap and tighten the screws.

13. Ensure the spark plug wires are firmly connected to their terminals.

14. Connect the negative battery cable. Start the engine and check for proper operation.

Ignition Timing

ADJUSTMENT

Wrangler, Cherokee, Comanche, 1993–96 Grand Cherokee and 1993 Grand Wagoneer

Base ignition timing is not adjustable. The distributor does not have a built-in centrifugal or vacuum assisted advance. Base ignition timing and timing advance are controlled by the Engine Control Module (ECM) which monitors inputs from various sensors to determine and adjust correct ignition timing.

Ignition Coil

REMOVAL AND INSTALLATION

Wrangler, Cherokee, Comanche and 1993–96 Grand Cherokee

The coil is an epoxy filled type. If the coil is replaced, it must be replaced with the same type.

1. Disconnect the negative battery cable.

2. Disconnect the ignition coil secondary cable from the coil.

3. Disconnect the engine harness connector from the coil.

4. Remove the mounting bolts and coil.

To install:

5. Install the ignition coil to the bracket on the cylinder block and tighten the mounting bolts.

6. Connect the engine harness and high tension lead to the coil.

7. Connect the negative battery cable.

1993 Grand Wagoneer

The ignition coil is mounted to a bracket near the front of the right cylinder head.

1. Disconnect the negative battery cable.

Timing mark alignment — Grand Wagoneer 1993

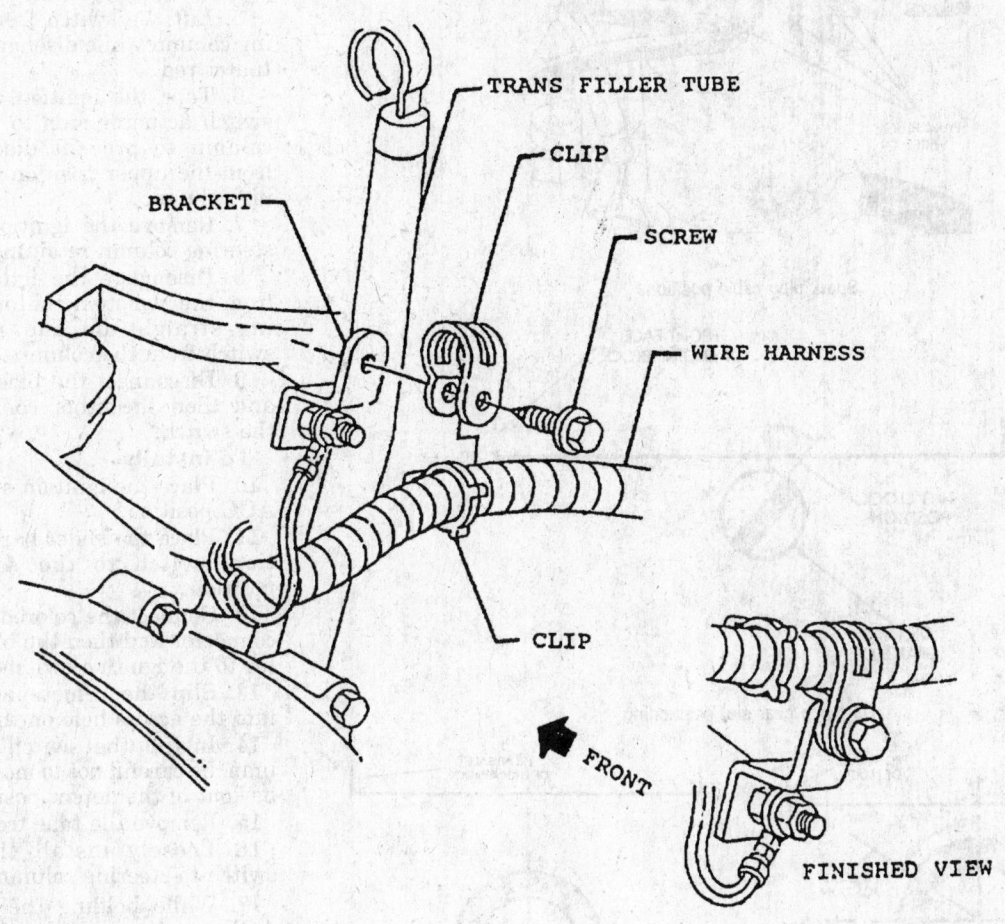

Rotor alignment mark — Grand Wagoneer 1993

47296

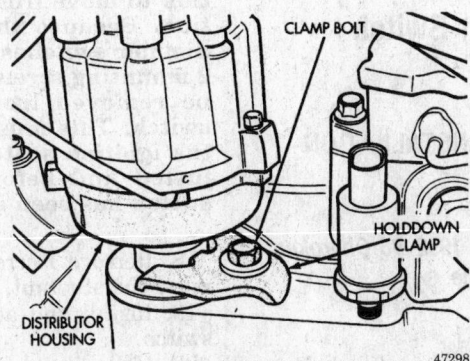

Distributor hold-down and clamp — Grand Wagoneer
1993

47298

2. Disconnect the high tension lead from the coil.

3. Disconnect the electrical connectors from the coil.

— **CAUTION** —
Do not remove the coil mounting bracket-to-cylinder head mounting bolts. The coil mounting bracket is under accessory drive belt tension. If this bracket is removed all accessory belt tension will be relieved.

4. Remove the 2 bolts securing the coil to the bracket and remove the coil.

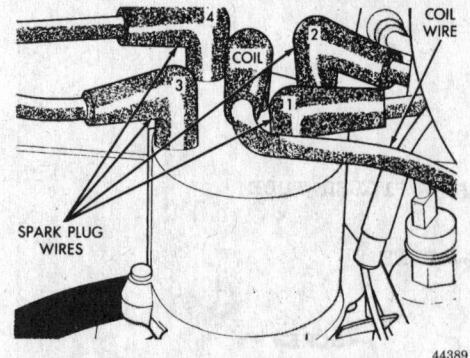

44389

Spark plug cable positions

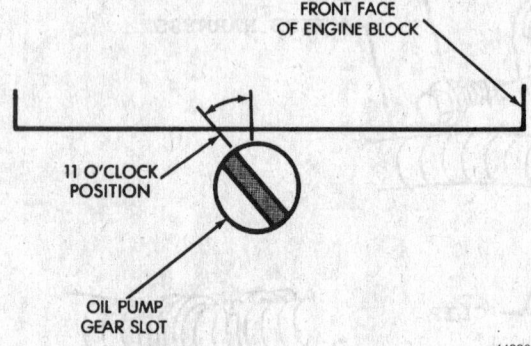

44390

Oil pump gear slot positioning

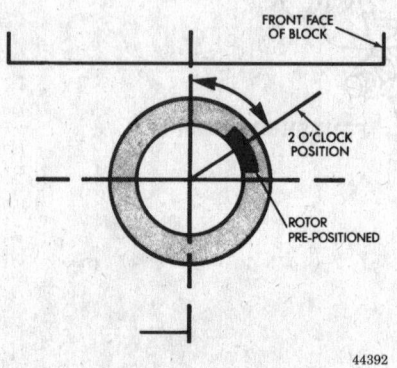

44392

Distributor installation

44398

Distributor rotor position

To install:

5. Install the coil and torque the mounting bolts to 100 inch lbs. (11 Nm).

6. Connect the high tension lead and electrical connectors tp the coil.

7. Connect the negative battery cable.

Ignition Switch

REMOVAL AND INSTALLATION

1992–96 Wrangler, 1992–96 Cherokee and 1992 Comanche

1. Disconnect the negative battery cable.

2. If equipped, remove the windshield wiper intermittent control module and its bracket.

3. Turn the ignition to the **ACC** position.

4. Remove the headlamp dimmer switch attaching nuts.

5. Lift the switch from the steering column while disengaging the actuator rod.

6. Tape the ignition and dimmer switch actuator rods to the steering column to prevent disengagement from the upper position of the steering column.

7. Remove the ignition switch-to-steering column retaining screws.

8. Disengage the ignition switch from the remote actuator rod by lifting straight up and remove the switch from the column.

9. Disconnect the black connector and then the other connector from the switch.

To install:

10. Place the ignition switch in the **ACC** position.

11. Place the slider bar in the ignition switch to the **ACC** detent position.

12. Connect the colored (non-black) connector and then the black connector to the ignition switch.

13. Slip the remote actuator rod into the access hole on the switch.

14. Install the switch to the column, be careful not to move the slider bar out of the detent position.

15. Remove the tape from the rods.

16. Loosely install the ignition switch-to-steering column screws.

17. While holding the key in the **ACC** position, slide the ignition switch up towards the steering wheel (non-tilt steering wheel) or down away from the steering wheel (tilt steering wheel) to remove slack from the switch. Tighten the attaching screws.

NOTE: Do not allow the ignition to move from the ACC position. Because the ignition and dimmer switches share the same 2 mounting screws, 1 screw must be removed from the ignition switch. This must be done after the ignition switch has been adjusted and before the dimmer switch has been installed.

18. Remove 1 screw, but do not remove the stud/nut.

19. Install and adjust the dimmer switch.

20. If equipped, install the intermittent wiper control module and bracket.

21. Connect the negative battery cable.

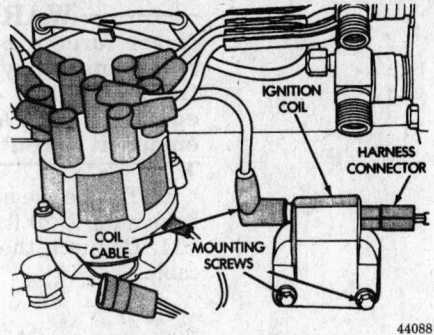

Ignition coil — 6 cylinder shown (4 cylinder similar) — Grand Cherokee 1993–96

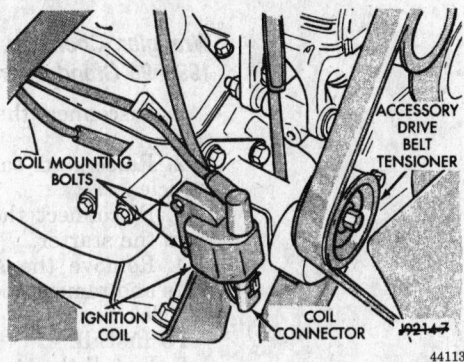

Ignition coil — Grand Wagoneer 1993

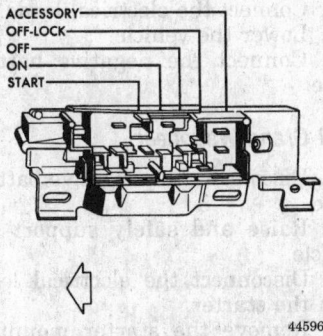

Ignition switch — non-tilt steering — Wrangler 1992–96

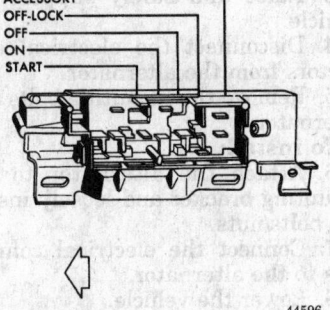

Ignition switch — tilt steering — Wrangler 1992–96

1993–96 Grand Cherokee and 1993 Grand Wagoneer

1. Disconnect the negative battery cable.

2. If equipped, remove the tilt lever.

3. Remove the upper and lower steering column covers with a suitable Torx® driver.

4. Using Snap-On tamper-proof bit TTXR20BO or equivalent, remove the ignition switch screws.

5. Pull the ignition switch away from the column.

6. Release the 2 connector locks on the 7-terminal wiring connector and remove the connector from the ignition switch.

7. Release the connector lock on the key-in-switch and halo light 4-terminal connector and remove the connector from the ignition switch.

8. Insert the key into the ignition lock and ensure it is in the **LOCK** position.

9. Using a small screwdriver, depress the key cylinder retaining pin so it is flush with the key cylinder surface.

10. Turn the ignition key to the **OFF** position and the lock will release from its seated position.

NOTE: Do not remove the cylinder at this time.

11. Turn the key to the **LOCK** position and remove the key.

12. Remove the ignition lock.

To install:

13. Install the electrical connectors to the switch. Ensure the switch locking tabs are fully seated in the wiring connectors.

14. Mount the ignition switch to the column. The dowel pin on the ignition switch assembly must engage with the column park-lock slider linkage. Ensure the ignition switch is in the lock position (flag is parallel with the ignition switch terminals).

15. Apply a dab of grease to the flag and pin. Position the park-lock link and slider to mid-travel. Position the ignition lock against the lock housing face. Ensure the pin is inserted into the park-lock link contour slot and tighten the retaining screw.

16. With the ignition lock and switch in the **LOCK** position, insert the lock into the switch assembly until it bottoms.

17. Assemble the column covers.

18. If equipped, install the tilt wheel lever.

19. Connect the negative battery cable.

Alternator

REMOVAL AND INSTALLATION

Wrangler and 1993 Grand Wagoneer

1. Disconnect the negative battery cable.

2. Loosen and remove the drive belt.

3. Disconnect the electrical connectors from the alternator.

4. Remove the mounting bolts and alternator.

To install:

5. Attach the alternator to the mounting bracket and loosely install the bolts/nuts.

6. Connect the electrical connectors to the alternator.

7. Install and tension the drive belt.

─────── **WARNING** ───────
Never force a belt over a pulley rim using a prybar, as synthetic fiber damage could result. If equipped with a serpentine belt, ensure it is routed correctly.

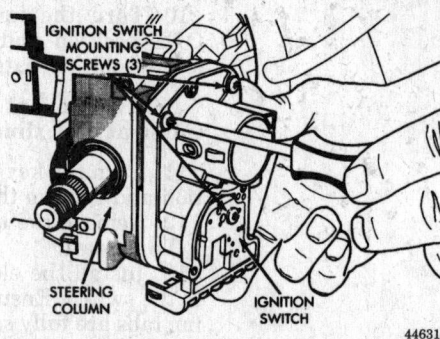

Ignition switch removal — Grand Cherokee 1993–96 and Grand Wagoneer 1993

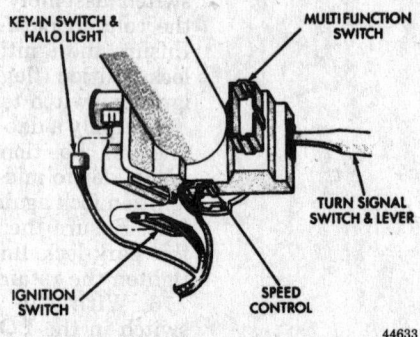

Key-in switch and halo lamp connector — Grand Cherokee 1993–96 and Grand Wagoneer 1993

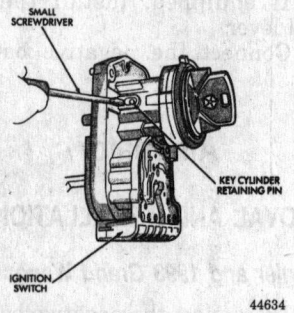

Key cylinder retaining ring — Grand Cherokee 1993–96 and Grand Wagoneer 1993

8. Torque the alternator mounting bolts/nuts to 20 ft. lbs. (27 Nm), except for 1993 Grand Wagoneer or to 30 ft. lbs. (41 Nm) for 1993 Grand Wagoneer.

9. Connect the negative battery cable.

Cherokee, Comanche and 1993–96 Grand Cherokee

1. Disconnect the negative battery cable.
2. Loosen and remove the drive belt.

3. Raise and safely support the vehicle.
4. Disconnect the electrical connectors from the alternator.
5. Remove the mounting bolts and alternator.

To install:

6. Attach the alternator to the mounting bracket and loosely install the bolts/nuts.
7. Connect the electrical connectors to the alternator.
8. Lower the vehicle.
9. Install and tension the drive belt.

WARNING

Never force a belt over a pulley rim using a prybar, as synthetic fiber damage could result. If equipped with a serpentine belt, ensure it is routed correctly.

---

10. Torque the alternator mounting bolts/nuts to 20 ft. lbs. (27 Nm).
11. Connect the negative battery cable.

Starter

REMOVAL AND INSTALLATION

Wrangler, Cherokee, Comanche, 1993–96 Grand Cherokee

1. Disconnect the negative battery cable.
2. Raise and safely support the vehicle.
3. Disconnect the electrical leads from the starter.
4. Remove the starter mounting bolts and remove the starter from the vehicle.

To install:

5. Install the starter in position.
6. Tighten the mounting bolts to 33 ft. lbs. (45 Nm).
7. Connect the electrical leads.
8. Lower the vehicle.
9. Connect the negative battery cable.

1993 Grand Wagoneer

1. Disconnect the negative battery cable.
2. Raise and safely support the vehicle.
3. Disconnect the electrical leads from the starter.
4. Remove the starter mounting bolts and remove the starter from the vehicle.

To install:

5. Install the starter.

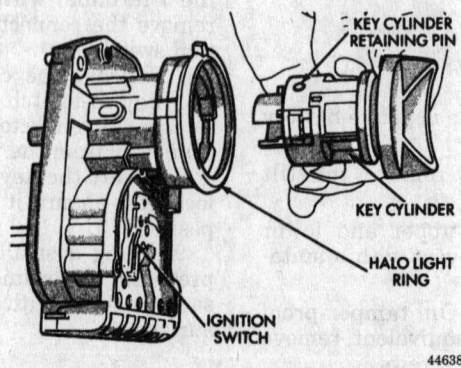

Key cylinder removal — Grand Cherokee 1993–96 and Grand Wagoneer 1993

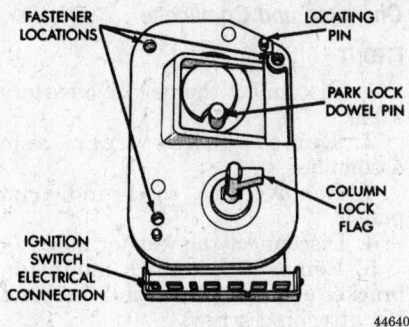

Ignition switch view from the column — Grand Cherokee 1993–96 and Grand Wagoneer 1993

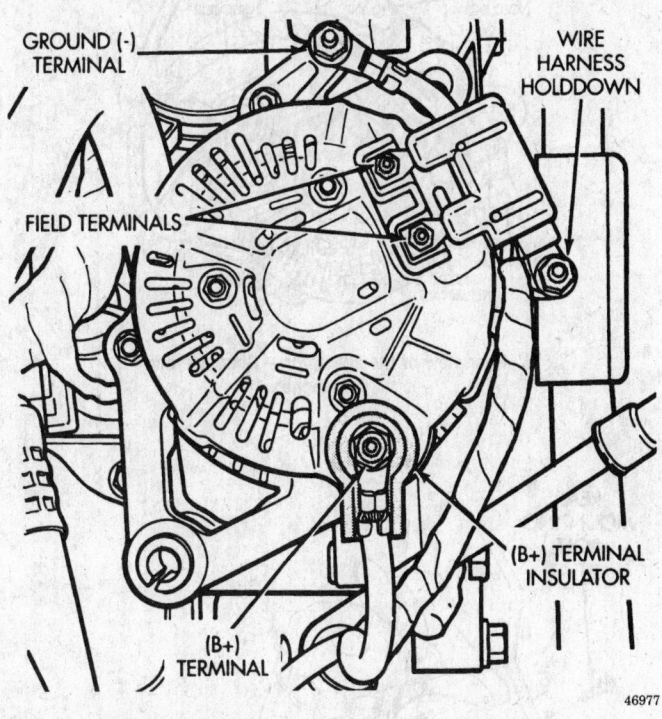

Alternator electrical connectors — Grand Wagoneer 1993

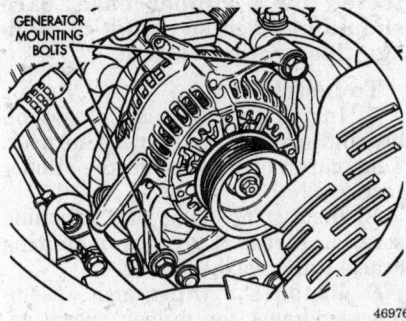

Alternator mounting bolts — Grand Wagoneer 1993

6. Tighten the mounting bolts to 50 ft. lbs. (68 Nm).

7. Connect the eletrical connectors.

8. Connect the electrical leads and lower the vehicle.

CHASSIS ELECTRICAL

Wiper Motor

REMOVAL AND INSTALLATION

Wrangler

FRONT

1. Disconnect the negative battery cable.

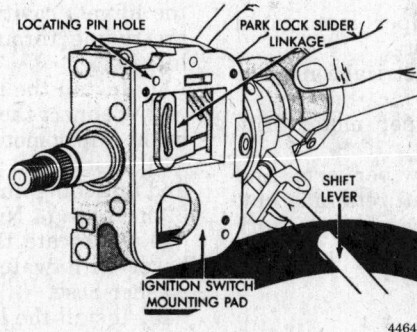

Ignition switch mounting pad — Grand Cherokee 1993–96 and Grand Wagoneer 1993

2. Remove the necessary hard or soft top components from the windshield frame.

3. Remove the left and right windshield hold-down knobs and fold the windshield forward.

4. Remove the left access hole cover.

5. Disconnect the drive link from the left wiper pivot.

6. Disconnect the wiper motor harness from the switch.

7. Grasp the motor and pull the drive arm out of the access hole. Pry the arm off the motor pivot.

NOTE: Do not remove the pivot attaching nut.

8. Remove the screws holding the intermittent wiper module bracket to the bottom of the instrument panel. Remove the motor.

To install:

9. Install and connect the wiring harness.

10. Install the screws holding the intermittent wiper module.

11. Turn the motor **ON** and check for proper operation.

12. Install the drive arm on the motor pivot. Install the motor and tighten the attaching bolts to 96 inch lbs. (11 Nm).

13. Connect the drive link at the left wiper pivot and install the har-

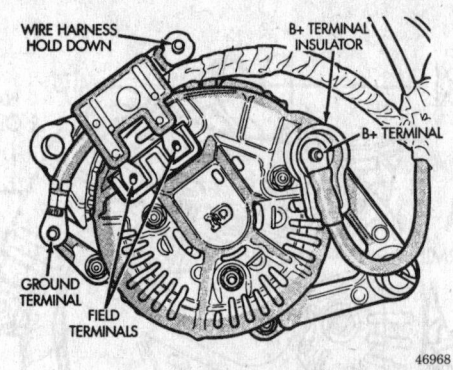

Rear view of the alternator — Cherokee and Comanche

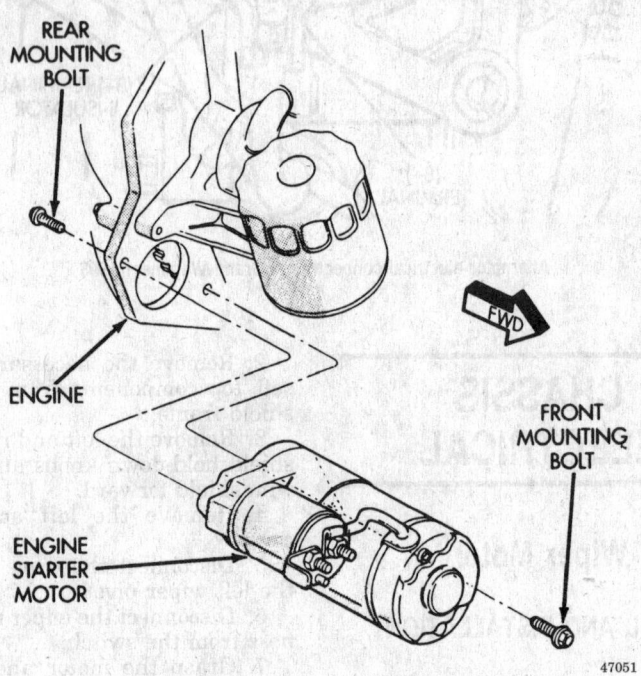

Starter removal and installation

ness clips. Install the windshield and hard or soft top assembly.

REAR

1. Disconnect the negative battery cable.
2. Remove the wiper arm from the wiper motor.
3. Remove the pivot shaft retaining nut.
4. Remove the wiper motor trim cover.
5. Disconnect the electrical connector from the wiper motor.
6. Remove the top hinge nut securing the wiper motor.

7. Remove the wiper motor.
To install:
8. Install the wiper motor and tighten the hinge nut.
9. Connect the electrical connector to the wiper motor.
10. Install the wiper motor trim cover.
11. Position the wiper arm and tighten the pivot shaft retaining nut.
12. Connect the negative battery cable.

Cherokee and Comanche
FRONT

1. Disconnect the negative battery cable.
2. Remove the wiper arm assemblies.
3. Remove the cowl and trim panel.
4. Disconnect the washer hose.
5. Remove the cowl mounting bracket attaching bolts and the pivot pin attaching screws.
6. Disconnect the wiring harness and remove the assembly.

NOTE: Some motors are protected by a rubber case, care should be used so as not to damage this protective coat.

To install:
7. Install the wiper motor assembly and connect the wiring harness. Take care not to damage the rubber case.
8. Install the pivot pin attaching screws. Install the cowl mounting bracket and washer hose.
9. Install the wiper arm assemblies and test for proper operation. Tighten the wiper motor attaching screws to 35–50 inch lbs. (47–67 Nm).

REAR

1. Remove the wiper arm from the pivot pin by depressing the tab and pulling straight out.
2. Slide the clip along the hose until the clip is off the mounting.
3. Disconnect the washer hose.
4. Remove the pivot pin retaining nut.
5. Remove the external bezel and seal.
6. Remove the liftgate interior trim panel.
7. Disconnect the electrical connector from the wiper motor.
8. Remove the wiper motor mounting screws.
9. Remove the wiper motor.
To install:
10. Position the wiper motor into the liftgate cavity with the pivot pin protruding through the hole in the liftgate.
11. Install the mounting screws.
12. Connect the electrical connector to the wiper motor.
13. Install the pivot pin, seal bezel and attaching nut. Torque the nut to 32 inch lbs. (4 Nm).
14. Lubricate the male end of the bezel with water and connect the washer hose.
15. Install the liftgate panel trim.
16. Install the wiper arm assembly and connect the extenal washer hose to the bezel.

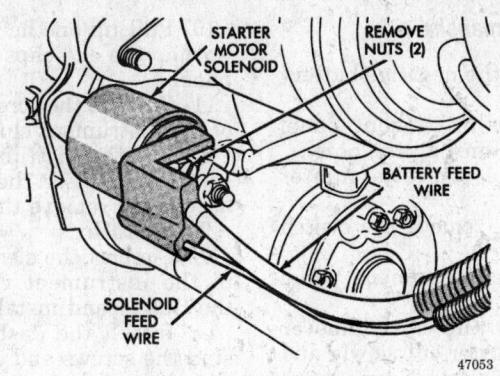

Solenoid harness removal

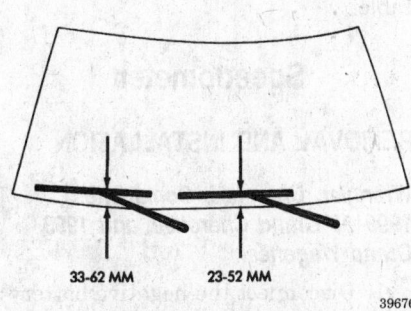

33-62 MM   23-52 MM

Front wiper arm installation

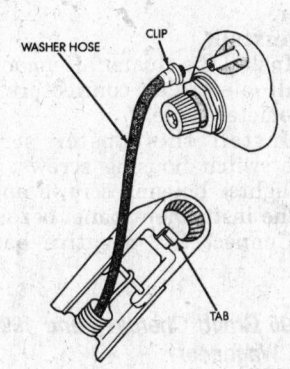

Rear wiper arm removal

17. Slide the clip along the hose until it is over the hose mount.

18. Position the arm so the blade is parallel to the window and comes no closer than 5mm to the window seal when operating on a wet surface.

19. Connect the negative battery cable.

1993–96 Grand Cherokee and 1993 Grand Wagoneer

FRONT

1. Disconnect the negative battery cable.

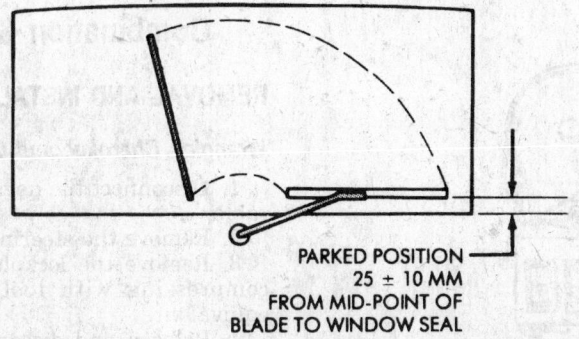

PARKED POSITION
25 ± 10 MM
FROM MID-POINT OF
BLADE TO WINDOW SEAL

Rear wiper arm positioning

2. Lift the wiper arms upward, slide the tab up and remove the wiper arms.

3. Remove the cowl grille screws, disconnect the washer hose and remove the grille.

4. Remove the bolts securing the wiper linkage.

5. Turn the linkage over and remove the nut securing the crank arm to the motor.

6. Remove the screws holding the linkage to the wiper motor and remove the motor.

To install:

7. Install the wiper motor and tighten the screws and nut.

8. Install the wiper linkage.

9. Connect the washer hose to the cowl grille and install the grille.

10. Install the wiper arm assemblies.

11. Connect the negative battery cable.

REAR

1. Disconnect the negative battery cable.

2. Lift the wiper arm and insert a ⅛ inch pin into the arm hole.

3. Remove the wiper arm assembly from the pivot pin by depressing the tab and pulling the blade straight out of the arm.

4. Remove the wiper motor retaining nut.

5. Remove the external panel.

6. Remove the 5 screws holding the liftgate interior panel.

7. Remove the panel with a wide flat bladed tool.

8. Disconnect the wiper motor electrical connector.

9. Remove the 2 wiper motor mounting bolts.

10. Remove the wiper motor.

To install:

11. Position the wiper motor in the liftgate cavity with the knurled driver protruding through the hole in the liftgate and gasket.

12. Install the mounting bolts and torque them to 10–15 inch lbs. (1–1.7 Nm).

13. Connect the electrical connector to the wiper motor.

14. Install the bezel and wiper motor retaining nut. Torque the nut to 35–50 inch lbs. (4–5.6 Nm).

15. Install the liftgate trim panel.

16. Install and position the wiper arm.

17. Connect the negative battery cable.

Instrument Cluster

REMOVAL AND INSTALLATION

Wrangler

1. Disconnect the negative battery cable.

2. Remove the 6 shroud screws.

3. Slide the shroud toward the steering wheel.

4. Remove the 3 screws holding the right side switch panel.

5. Remove the 3 screws holding the left side switch panel.

6. Remove the 2 screws holding the instrument cluster in place.

7. Lift up the top of the cluster. Roll the cluster out between the between the steering column and in-

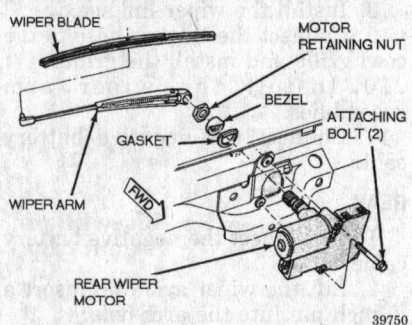

Rear wiper motor removal and installation — Grand Cherokee and Grand Wagoneer

strument panel far enough to disconnect the connector located behind the tachometer.

8. Disconnect the cluster connectors and speedometer cable. Remove the cluster.

To install:

9. Install the cluster after connecting all electrical connectors and speedometer cable.

10. Install the instrument cluster retaining screws.

11. Install the left and right switch panels.

12. Install the shroud.

13. Connect the negative battery cable.

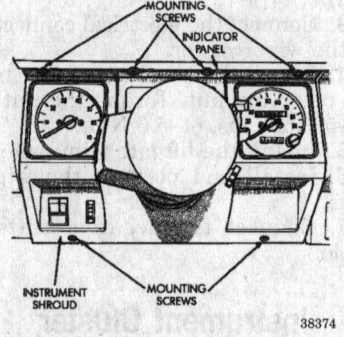

Instrument shroud screw location — Wrangler

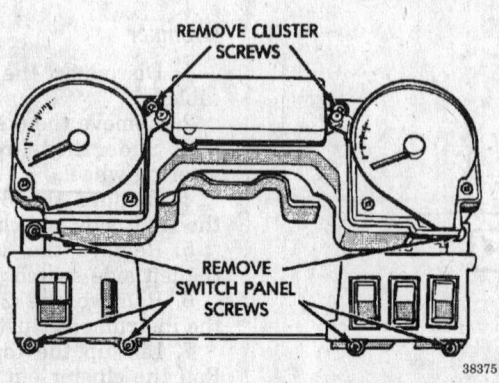

Instrument cluster removal — Wrangler

Cherokee and Comanche

1. Disconnect the negative battery cable.

2. Remove the instrument panel bezel screws and unsnap the bezel.

3. Remove the cigarette lighter housing screws.

4. If equipped, remove the switch housing screws.

5. Remove the instrument panel cluster screws.

6. Disconnect the speedometer cable, pull the cluster out slowly and disconnect the electrical connectors at the cluster back. Remove the cluster.

To install:

7. Install the cluster after connecting all electrical connectors and speedometer cable.

8. Install the cluster screws, rocker switch housing screws, cigarette lighter housing screws and install the instrument panel bezel.

9. Connect the negative battery cable.

1993–96 Grand Cherokee and 1993 Grand Wagoneer

1. Disconnect the negative battery cable.

2. Remove the ashtray.

3. Remove the screws holding the center cluster bezel and remove the bezel.

4. Remove the 2 screws holding the dash panel.

5. Gently pry the defroster grille out of the dash panel.

6. Unplug the auto headlamp and sun sensors, if equipped and remove the defroster grille.

7. Remove the screws, through the defroster duct opening, securing the dash panel.

8. Remove the 3 screws above the instrument panel cluster securing the dash panel.

9. Open the glove box and remove the 2 screws holding the dash panel.

10. Pull up on the dash panel and unsnap the end clips and remove the panel.

11. Remove the screws from the top of the instrument cluster.

12. Lift the instrument cluster upward, disconnect the electrical connector and remove the cluster.

To install:

13. Connect the electrical connector to the instrument cluster, position the cluster and install the screws.

14. Install the dash panel and install the screws and defroster grille.

15. Install the center cluster bezel.

16. Install the ashtray.

17. Connect the negative battery cable.

Speedometer

REMOVAL AND INSTALLATION

Wrangler, Cherokee, Comanche, 1993–96 Grand Cherokee, and 1993 Grand Wagoneer

1. Disconnect the negative battery cable.

2. Remove the instrument cluster.

3. Remove the lens attaching screws.

─────── **WARNING** ───────

Do not touch the face of a gauge or the back of the lens. It may leave a permanent mark.

4. Remove the screw(s) from the speedometer and pull it from the cluster.

5. Pull the speedometer out of the circuit board carefully.

To install:

6. Install the speedometer and screws.

7. Install the instrument cluster lens.

8. Install the instrument cluster.

9. Connect the negative battery cable.

Combination Switch

REMOVAL AND INSTALLATION

Wrangler, Cherokee and Comanche

1. Disconnect the negative battery cable.

2. Remove the steering wheel.

3. Remove the lockplate cover by compressing with tool C–4156 or equivalent.

4. Release and discard the steering shaft retaining snapring.

5. Remove the compressor tool.

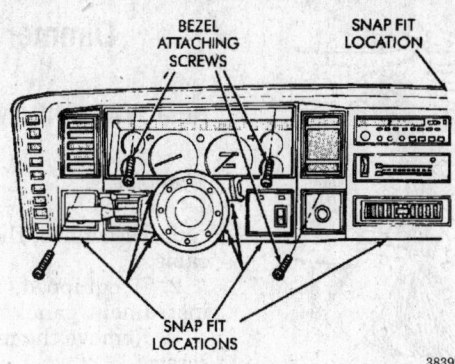

Instrument cluster bezel removal and installation —
Cherokee

38392

6. Remove the lockplate, canceling cam, upper bearing preload spring and thrust washer from the steering column.

7. Remove the horn button components from the canceling cam.

8. Remove the hazard warning switch knob.

9. Remove the dimmer switch actuator arm attaching screw.

10. Remove the turn signal switch attaching screws.

11. Remove the lower instrument panel cover trim panel.

12. Remove the lower steering column cover.

13. If equipped with automatic transmission column shift selector, remove the **PRNDL** cable clip.

14. Remove the nuts securing the steering column bracket to the brake sled.

15. Remove the bolts holding the steering column bracket to the column.

16. Loosen the column brace mounting nut at the drivers side kick panel and allow the column to drop.

17. Push the turn signal connector up and out of the steering column connector.

18. Pry up the locking tabs of the steering column connector and remove the connector from the column bracket.

19. Tape the connector flat against the wire harness to prevent it from hanging up during removal.

20. Remove the plastic harness cover by pulling it up and over the weld nuts, then open and slide the cover off the harness.

21. Remove the combination lever by pulling it out straight from the column.

   To install:

22. Position the combination switch into position on the column while guiding the harness. Ensure the wires are laying flat on the bottom of the inside column.

23. Remove the tape and connect the electrical connector.

24. Connect the turn signal connector.

25. Position the steering column and tighten the mounting nuts and bolts.

26. If equipped with a column shift selector, install the **PRNDL** cable clip with the transmission in **N**. Move the selector through all ranges and ensure the indicator is aligned.

27. Install the lower steering column cover.

28. Install the lower instrument panel cover trim panel.

29. Install the turn signal switch attaching screws.

30. Loosely install the dimmer switch actuating screws and adjust the switch as follows:

   a. Compress the switch and insert a $3/32$ inch diameter drill bit into the adjustment hole.

NOTE: The drill bit will prevent horizontal movement of the switch.

   b. Move the switch toward the steering wheel to eliminate rod lash.

   c. Tight the screw.

   d. Connect the negative battery cable.

   e. Remove the drill bit and test operation, readjust if necessary.

31. Install the hazard switch knob.

32. Assemble the canceling cam and steering column and secure the assembly with a new snapring.

33. Install the steering wheel.

34. Connect the negative battery cable.

1993–96 Grand Cherokee and 1993 Grand Wagoneer

1. Disconnect the negative battery cable.

2. If equipped, remove the tilt lever.

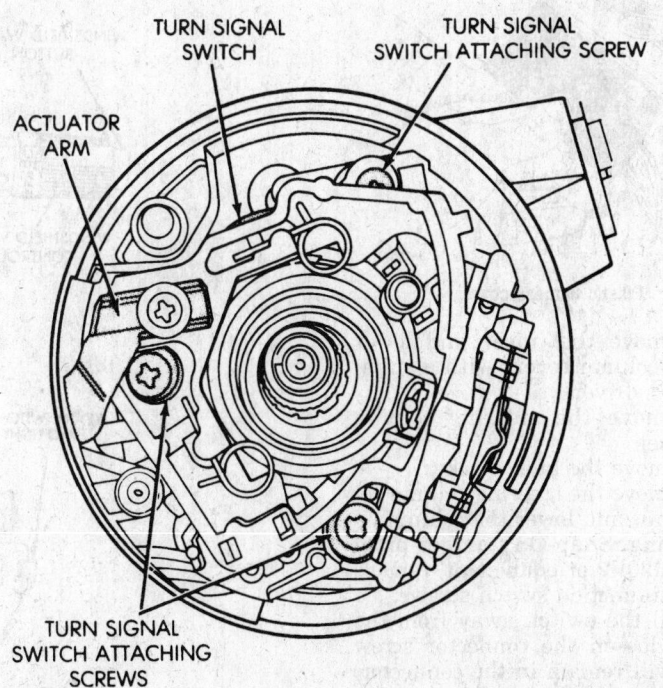

Combination switch actuating lever screws

38743

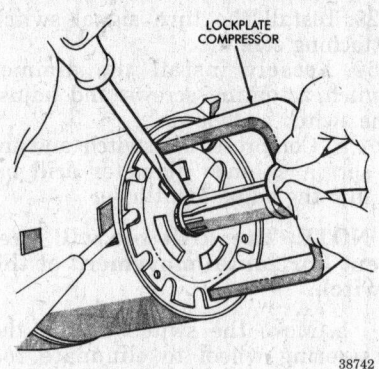

Lockplate removal

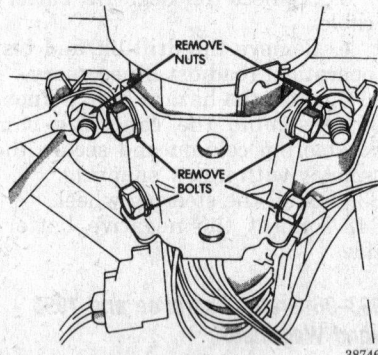

Lower steering column

Plastic harness cover

3. Remove the upper and lower steering column covers with a suitable Torx® driver.

4. Remove the steering column trim panel.

5. Remove the knee blocker.

6. Remove the steering column retaining nut and lower the column.

7. Using Snap-On tamper-proof bit TTXR20B2 or equivalent, remove the multi-function switch screws.

8. Pull the switch away from the column, loosen the connector screw (which will remain in the connector) and unplug the electrical connector.

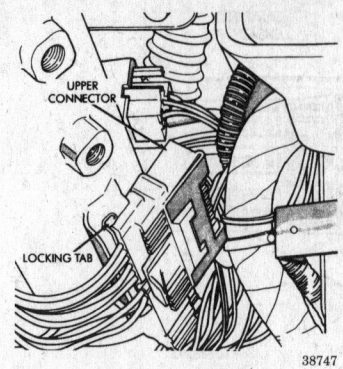

Turn signal connector

To install:

9. Connect the electrical connector to the multi-function switch and tighten the retaining screw.

10. Mount the multi-function switch to the steering column and tighten the screws.

11. Position the steering column and tighten the retaining nuts.

12. Install the knee blocker, lower trim panel and steering column covers.

13. If equipped, install the tilt steering lever.

14. Connect the negative battery cable.

Dimmer Switch

REMOVAL AND INSTALLATION

Wrangler

1. Disconnect the negative battery cable.

2. If equipped, remove the lower instrument panel cover.

3. Remove the instrument housing screws.

4. Slide the housing towards the steering wheel and apply upward pressure to the housing and downward pressure to the indicator to release the holding tabs.

5. Remove the instrument housing.

6. If equipped with A/C, perform the following:

   a. Support the A/C evaporator housing.

   b. Remove the A/C evaporator housing-to-instrument panel attaching screws.

   c. Remove the A/C evaporator housing support bracket.

   d. Lower the evaporator.

7. Disconnect the dimmer switch electrical connector.

8. Tape the actuator rod to the steering column.

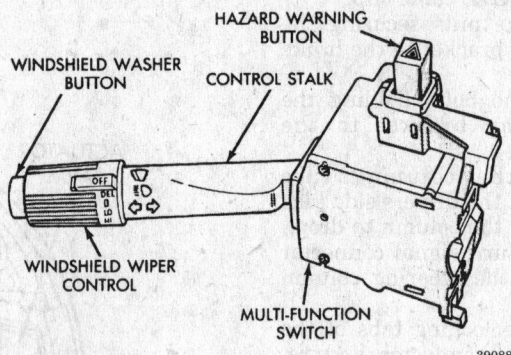

Combination switch

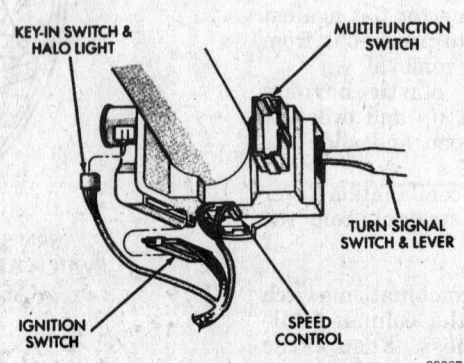

Steering column electrical connectors

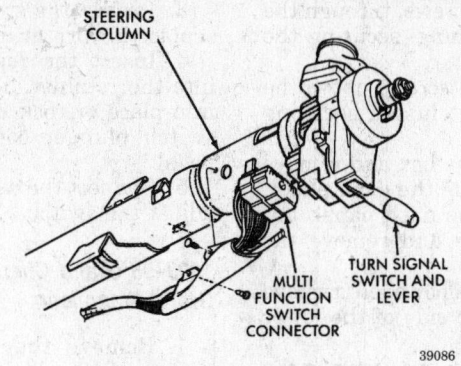

Combination switch connector

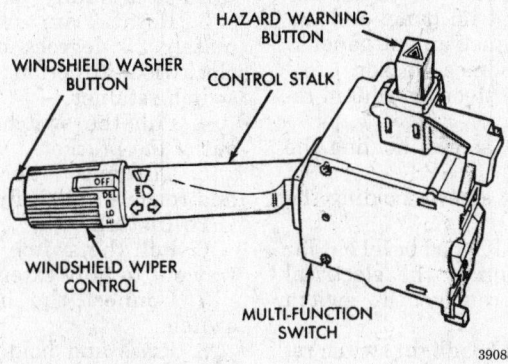

Combination switch — Grand Cherokee 1993–96 and Grand Wagoneer 1993

9. Remove the dimmer switch.

To install:

10. Force the dimmer switch onto the actuator rod and loosely install the screws.

11. Compress the switch and insert a $^3/_{32}$ inch diameter drill bit into the adjustment hole.

NOTE: The drill bit will prevent horizontal movement of the switch.

12. Move the switch toward the steering wheel to eliminate rod lash, then tighten the screw.

13. Connect the negative battery cable.

14. Remove the drill bit and test operation, readjust if necessary.

15. If equipped, install the lower instrument panel.

16. If equipped with A/C, perform the following:

    a. Raise and support the A/C evaporator housing.

    b. Install the A/C evaporator housing-to-instrument panel and support bracket screws.

17. Position the instrument panel shroud under the steering column and slide the holding tabs into the shroud notches.

18. Place the instrument panel shroud into position and install the screws.

19. Connect the negative battery cable.

Cherokee and Comanche

1. Disconnect the negative battery cable.

2. If equipped, remove the lower instrument panel cover.

3. Disconnect the dimmer switch electrical connector.

4. Tape the actuator rod to the steering column.

5. Remove the dimmer switch.

To install:

6. Force the dimmer switch onto the actuator rod and loosely install the screws.

7. Compress the switch and insert a $^3/_{32}$ inch diameter drill bit into the adjustment hole.

NOTE: The drill bit will prevent horizontal movement of the switch.

8. Move the switch toward the steering wheel to eliminate rod lash, then tight the screw.

9. Connect the negative battery cable.

10. Remove the drill bit and test operation, readjust if necessary.

11. If equipped, install the lower instrument panel.

Headlight Switch

REMOVAL AND INSTALLATION

Wrangler

1. Disconnect the negative battery cable.

2. Remove the instrument panel shroud retaining screws.

3. Pull the instrument panel shroud outward and upward while applying downward force to the indicator panel and remove the shroud.

4. Remove the screws retaining the switch, pull the switch from the instrument panel cavity and disconnect the electrical connector.

To install:

5. Connect the electrical connectors to the headlight switch and install the retaining screws.

6. Position the instrument panel shroud under the steering column and slide the holding tabs into the shroud notches.

7. Place the instrument panel shroud into position and install the screws.

8. Connect the negative battery cable.

Cherokee and Comanche

1. Disconnect the negative battery cable.

2. Pull the light switch control knob out as far as it will go.

3. If equipped, remove the instrument panel trim plate.

4. From under the dash depress the headlight switch shaft retainer button and pull the shaft along with the knob from the headlight switch assembly.

5. Remove the headlight switch retaining nut.

6. Disconnect the electrical connector from the switch.

7. Remove the headlight switch from the vehicle.

To install:

8. Connect the electrical connector, install the headlamp switch and tighten the nut.

9. Insert the shaft and knob into the switch.

10. Connect the negative battery cable.

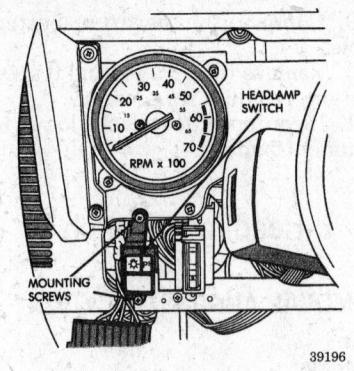

Headlight switch

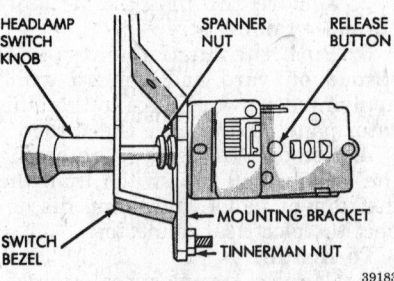

Headlight switch

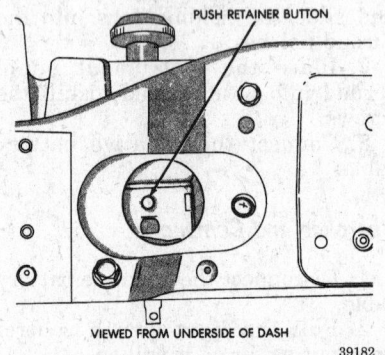

Headlight switch shaft removal

1993–96 Grand Cherokee and 1993 Grand Wagoneer

1. Disconnect the negative battery cable.
2. Remove the ashtray.
3. Remove the screws holding the center cluster bezel and remove the bezel.
4. Remove the 2 screws holding the dash panel.
5. Gently pry the defroster grille out of the dash panel.
6. Unplug the auto headlamp and sun sensors, if equipped and remove the defroster grille.

7. Remove the screws, through the defroster duct opening, securing the dash panel.
8. Remove the 3 screws above the instrument panel cluster securing the dash panel.
9. Open the glove box and remove the 2 screws holding the dash panel.
10. Pull up on the dash panel, unsnap the end clips and remove the panel.
11. With the left door open, remove the screw from the side of the lower trim panel.
12. Remove the screws securing the steering column covers.
13. Remove the screw from the bottom of the lower trim panel and unsnap it from the instrument panel.
14. Remove the knee blocker.
15. Remove the steering column retaining nuts.
16. Remove the screws holding the bezels.
17. Remove the screws holding the switch pod bezel.
18. Pull the switch pod bezel out far enough to disconnect the electrical connectors and remove the switch pod assemblies.
19. Remove the headlight switch retaining screws and switch.

To install:
20. Install the switch to the left pod assembly.
21. Connect the electrical connectors and install the switch pod assemblies.
22. Position the steering column and install the retaining nuts.
23. Install the knee blocker.
24. Install the lower trim panel.
25. Install the steering column cover screws.
26. Install the screw securing the left side of the lower trim panel.
27. Position the dash panel and install the screws and defroster grille.
28. Install the center cluster bezel.
29. Install the ashtray.
30. Connect the negative battery cable.

Stoplight Switch

REMOVAL AND INSTALLATION

Wrangler, Cherokee and Comanche

1. Remove the steering column cover and lower trim panel for access, if necessary. Disconnect the switch wiring harness.
2. Thread the switch out of the retainer or rock the switch up/down and pull it rearward.

3. Inspect the switch retainer and replace if worn or damaged.
4. Insert the replacement switch into the retainer. Thread the switch into place or rock up/down until the switch plunger contacts the brake pedal.
5. Connect the wiring harness and adjust the switch.

1993–96 Grand Cherokee and 1993 Grand Wagoneer

1. Remove the steering column cover and lower trim panel.
2. Press the brake pedal downward so it is fully applied.
3. Rotate the switch approximately 30 degrees in the counterclockwise direction to unlock the switch retainer.
4. Pull the switch rearward and out of the bracket.
5. Disconnect the switch harness and remove switch from vehicle.
To install:
6. Pull the switch plunger all the way out to fully extended position.
7. Connect the harness to the switch.
8. Press and hold brake pedal in the applied position.
9. Align the tab on the switch with the notch in the switch bracket. Insert the switch and turn it clockwise 30 degrees to lock it in place.

ADJUSTMENT

Wrangler, Cherokee and Comanche

1. Check the adjustment of the switch. Move the brake pedal forward by hand and note the operation of the plunger. The plunger should be fully extended when the pedal free-play is taken up and the brake application begins. A clearance of 1/8 inch should exist between the plunger and the pedal.
2. If adjustment is necessary, grasp the brake pedal and pull it rearward as far as possible. The switch plunger barrel will ratchet rearward in the retaining clip to the correct position.
3. Verify brakelight switch operation and proper clearance between the plunger and brake pedal.

NOTE: Ensure that the brake pedal returns to a fully released position after adjustment. The Switch can interfere with full pedal return if too far forward. The result will be brake drag caused by partial brake application.

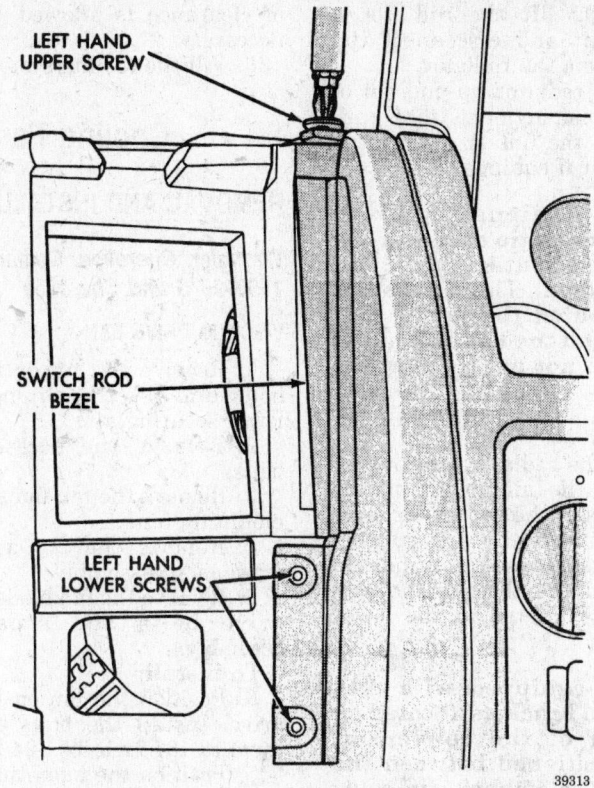

Left switch pod bezel screws

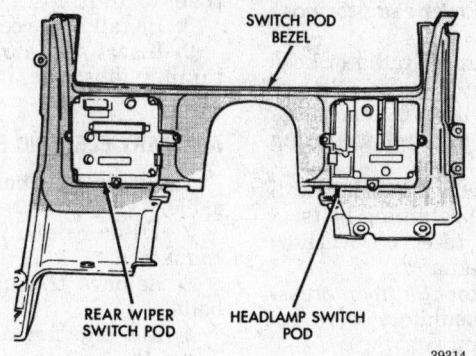

Rear view of the switch pod bezel

1993–96 Grand Cherokee and 1993 Grand Wagoneer

1. Depress and then release the brake pedal.
2. Pull the brake pedal fully rearward.
3. The brake pedal will rachet the plunger to the correct position as it is pushed into the switch body.

ENGINE COOLING

Radiator

REMOVAL AND INSTALLATION

Wrangler

1. Disconnect the negative battery cable.
2. Drain the cooling system.
3. Remove the radiator upper and lower hoses.

4. Disconnect the overflow tube from the radiator.
5. If equipped, remove the transmission cooler lines.
6. Remove the fan shroud mounting bolts and pull the fan shroud back to the engine.
7. Remove all attaching bolts and screws that secure the radiator to the radiator support.
8. Remove the condenser to radiator mounting bolts.
9. Pull the radiator out of the vehicle taking care not to damage the radiator fins.

To install:
10. Slide the radiator into position behind the condenser, if equipped and torque the mounting screws 6 ft. lbs. (8 Nm).
11. Close the radiator drain.
12. Install the fan shroud.
13. Connect the transmission cooler lines, if equipped.
14. Connect the hoses to the radiator.
15. Connect the negative battery cable.
16. Fill the cooling system.
17. Connect the reserve bottle hose and install the radiator cap.

Cherokee and Comanche

1. Disconnect the negative battery cable.
2. Remove the front grille mounting screws and grille, as necessary.
3. Drain the cooling system.
4. Remove the radiator upper and lower hoses.
5. If equipped, remove the transmission cooler lines.
6. Remove the fan shroud mounting bolts and pull the fan shroud back to the engine.
7. Remove the alignment dowel E-clip from the lower radiator mounting bracket.
8. Disconnect the overflow tube from the radiator.
9. Remove all attaching bolts and screws that secure the radiator to the radiator support.
10. Remove the condenser to radiator mounting bolts and pull the radiator out of the vehicle.

NOTE: Take care not to damage the radiator fins.

11. Empty the remaining coolant in the radiator.
To install:
12. Slide the radiator into position behind the condenser, if equipped.
13. Align the dowel pin with the bottom mounting bracket and install the E-clip.

14. Tighten the condenser-to-radiator bolts to 55 inch lbs. (6.2 Nm).

15. Install and tighten the radiator mounting bolts.

16. Install the grille.

17. Connect the transmission cooler lines, if equipped.

18. Install the fan shroud.

19. Connect the radiator hoses.

20. Connect the negative battery cable.

21. Fill the cooling system to the correct level.

1993–96 Grand Cherokee and 1993 Grand Wagoneer

1. Disconnect the negative battery cable.

2. Open the radiator valve and drain the cooling system.

3. Remove the fan and shroud assembly.

4. If equipped, disconnect the automatic transmission cooling line quick-fit connections.

5. Matchmark the upper radiator crossmember and adjust the crossmember to the left or right.

6. Eight clips are used to retain a rubber seal to the body. Gently pry up the outboard clips (2 per side) until the rubber seal can be removed. Do not remove the seals entirely. Fold back the seal on both sides to access the grille opening reinforcement mounting bolts and remove the bolts.

7. Remove the grille.

8. Remove the upper brace bolt from each of the 2 radiator braces.

9. Remove the crossmember-to-radiator mounting nuts.

10. Working through the grille opening, remove the lower bracket bolt securing the lower part of the hood latch or hood latch cable from the crossmember.

11. Lift the crossmember straight up and position it aside.

12. If equipped with A/C, remove the 2 A/C condenser-to-radiator mounting bolts which also retain the side mounted rubber air seals.

13. If not equipped with A/C, remove the bolts retaining the side mounted rubber air seals compressed between the radiator and crossmember.

NOTE: Note the location of the air seals. To prevent overheating, they must be installed in their original position.

14. Disconnect the coolant reservoir/overflow tank hose from the radiator.

15. Disconnect the upper hose from the radiator.

16. Carefully lift the radiator a slight amount and disconnect the lower hose from the radiator.

17. Lift the radiator up and out of the engine compartment, take care not to scrape the fins or disturb the A/C condenser if equipped.

NOTE: If equipped with an auxiliary automatic transmission oil cooler, use caution during radiator removal. The oil cooler lines are routed through a rubber air seal on the left side of the radiator. Do not cut or tear this seal.

To install:

18. Lower the radiator into the vehicle. Guide the alignment dowels into the hoses in the rubber air seals and then through the A/C support brackets, if equipped. Continue to guide the radiator through the rubber grommets located in the lower crossmember.

NOTE: If equipped with A/C, the L-shaped brackets, located on the bottom of the condenser, must be positioned between the bottom of the rubber air seals and top of rubber grommets.

19. Connect the lower radiator hose to the radiator.

20. Connect the upper radiator hose to the radiator.

21. If equipped with A/C, install the bolts condenser-to-radiator mounting bolts.

22. If not equipped with A/C, install the rubber air seal retaining bolts.

23. Connect the reservoir/overflow tank hose to the radiator.

24. If the radiator-to-upper crossmember rubber insulators were removed, install them.

25. Install the hood latch support bracket-to-lower frame crossmember bolt.

26. Install the bolts securing the upper radiator crossmember to the body.

27. Install the radiator-to-upper crossmember nuts.

28. Install a bolt to each upper radiator brace.

29. Install the grille.

30. Position the rubber seal and push down on the clips until seated.

31. If equipped, connect the transmission cooling lines.

32. Install the fan shroud with the fan.

33. Install the fan and shroud.

34. Rotate the fan blades and ensure they do not interfere with the shroud and at least 1.0 inch (25mm)

of clearance is allowed. Correct as necessary.

35. Fill the cooling system.

Cooling Fan

REMOVAL AND INSTALLATION

Wrangler, Cherokee, Comanche and 1993–96 Grand Cherokee

VISCOUS DRIVE FAN

1. Remove the upper fan shroud bolts and lift the shroud from its lower securing tabs.

2. Remove the accessory drive belts.

3. Remove the fan flange-to-pulley mounting nuts.

4. Remove the fan and viscous drive as an assembly.

5. Remove the fan blade-to-viscous drive bolts and separate the assembly.

To install:

6. Position the fan on the viscous drive. Install the bolts and torque them to 187 inch lbs. (24 Nm).

7. Position the mounting flange of the viscous drive assembly onto the pulley. Install the nuts and torque them to 18 ft. lbs. (24 Nm).

8. Install the accessory drive belts.

9. Insert the shroud into its retaining tabs and install the upper bolts.

AUXILIARY ELECTRIC FAN

1. Disconnect the negative battery cable.

2. Disconnect the electrical connector.

3. Remove the upper fan shroud bolts.

4. Lift the fan assembly up and out of the engine compartment.

To install:

5. Insert the shroud into its retaining tabs and install the upper bolts.

6. Connect the electrical connector.

7. Connect the negative battery cable.

1993 Grand Wagoneer

1. Disconnect the negative battery cable.

2. The viscous fan drive and blade assembly is threaded into the water pump hub shaft. Remove the fan drive and blade assembly from the water pump by turning the mounting nut counterclockwise as viewed from the front while securing the water pump pulley. Do not remove or un-

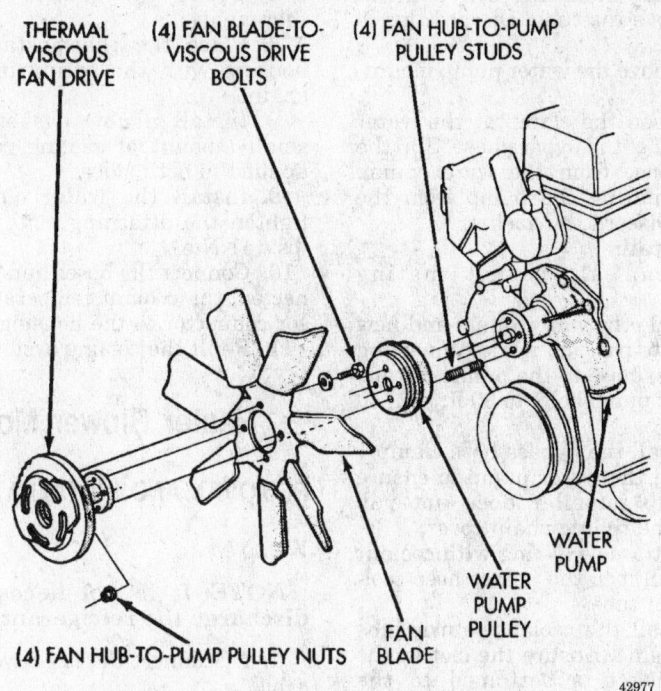

THERMAL VISCOUS FAN DRIVE

(4) FAN BLADE-TO-VISCOUS DRIVE BOLTS

(4) FAN HUB-TO-PUMP PULLEY STUDS

WATER PUMP

WATER PUMP PULLEY

FAN BLADE

(4) FAN HUB-TO-PUMP PULLEY NUTS

42977

Viscous fan removal and installation — Grand Cherokee

7. Position the fan shroud, viscous fan and blade into the engine compartment as an assembly.

8. Position the fan shroud to the radiator. Insert the lower slots of the shroud into the crossmember. Install the upper attaching nuts.

NOTE: Ensure the upper and lower portions of the fan shroud are firmly connected. All air must flow through the radiator.

9. Install the fan drive and blade assembly to the water pump shaft and tighten the nut.

NOTE: Ensure there is at least 1 inch (25mm) between the tips of the fan blades and shroud.

10. Connect the negative battery cable.

bolt the fan drive and blade at this time.

NOTE: The threads on the viscous fan drive are right hand threaded.

3. Remove the 2 fan shroud-to-upper crossmember nuts.

4. Remove the fan drive, blade and shroud as an assembly.

——— WARNING ———
Do not place the viscous fan drive in a horizontal position. If stored horizontally, silicone fluid in the viscous fan drive could drain into its bearing assembly and the assembly would have to be replaced.

——— CAUTION ———
Do not remove the water pump pulley-to-water pump bolts. The pulley is under spring tension.

5. Remove the 4 bolts securing the fan blade assembly to the viscous fan drive.
To install:
6. Install the fan blade on the viscous drive. Install the bolts and torque them to 17 ft. lbs. (23 Nm).

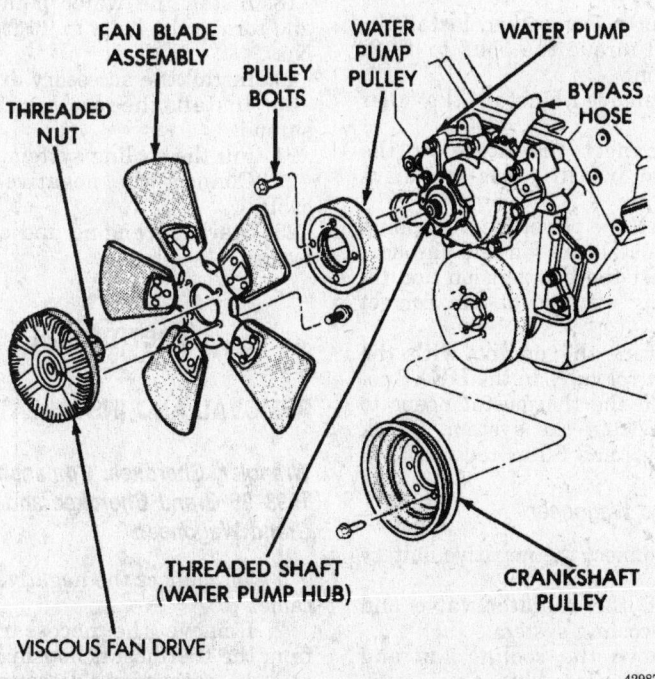

FAN BLADE ASSEMBLY

THREADED NUT

PULLEY BOLTS

WATER PUMP PULLEY

WATER PUMP

BYPASS HOSE

THREADED SHAFT (WATER PUMP HUB)

VISCOUS FAN DRIVE

CRANKSHAFT PULLEY

42987

Exploded view of the fan drive and blade — Grand Wagoneer

Water Pump

REMOVAL AND INSTALLATION

Wrangler, Cherokee, Comanche and 1993–96 Grand Cherokee

NOTE: Some vehicles use a serpentine drive belt and have a reverse rotating water pump coupled with a viscous fan drive assembly. The components are identified by the words REVERSE stamped on the cover of the viscous drive and on the inner side of the fan. The word REV is also cast into the body of the water pump.

1. Disconnect the negative battery cable.
2. Drain the cooling system.
3. Disconnect the hoses at the pump.
4. Remove the drive belts.
5. Remove the power steering pump bracket.
6. Remove the fan and shroud.
7. If equipped, remove the idler pulley to gain clearance for pump removal.
8. Unbolt and remove the pump.
To install:
9. Clean the mating surfaces thoroughly.
10. Using a new gasket, install the pump and torque the bolts to 13 ft. lbs. (18 Nm).
11. If removed, install the idler pulley.
12. Reconnect the hoses at the pump and install accessory drive belt.
13. Install the power steering pump bracket. Install the fan and shroud.
14. Adjust the belt tension and fill the cooling system to the correct level.
15. Operate the engine with the heater control valve in the **HEAT** position until the thermostat opens to purge air from the system. Check coolant level and fill as required.

1993 Grand Wagoneer

1. Disconnect the negative battery cable.
2. Open the radiator valve and drain the cooling system.
3. Remove the cooling fan and shroud as an assembly.
4. Remove the accessory drive belt.
5. Remove the water pump pulley from the hub.
6. Disconnect the hoses from the water pump.

7. Loosen the heater hose coolant return tube mounting bolt and nut and remove the tube. Discard the O-ring.
8. Remove the water pump mounting bolts.
9. Loosen the clamp at the water pump end of the bypass hose. Slip the bypass hose from the water pump while removing the pump from the engine. Discard the gasket.
To install:
10. Clean all gasket mating surfaces.
11. Guide the water pump and new gasket into position while connecting the bypass hose to the pump. Torque the water pump bolts to 30 ft. lbs. (40 Nm).
12. Install the bypass hose clamp.
13. Spin the water pump to ensure the pump impeller does not rub against the timing chain cover.
14. Coat a new O-ring with coolant and install it to the heater hose coolant return tube.
15. Install the coolant return tube to the engine. Ensure the slot in the tube bracket is bottomed to the mounting bolt. This will properly position the return tube.
16. Connect the radiator hose to the water pump.
17. Connect the heater hose and clamp to the return tube.
18. Install the water pump pulley and torque the bolts to 20 ft. lbs. (27 Nm).
19. Install the accessory drive belt.
20. Install the cooling fan and shroud.
21. Fill the cooling system.
22. Connect the negative battery cable.
23. Start the engine and check for leaks.

Thermostat

REMOVAL AND INSTALLATION

Wrangler, Cherokee, Comanche, 1993–96 Grand Cherokee and 1993 Grand Wagoneer

1. Disconnect the negative battery cable.
2. Remove the necessary hoses from the thermostat housing.
3. If necessary, disconnect the coolant temperature sensor electrical connector.
4. Remove the 2 attaching screws and lift the housing from the engine.
5. Remove the thermostat and gasket.

To install:
6. Clean all gasket surfaces thoroughly.
7. Place the thermostat in the housing with the spring inside the engine.
8. Install a new gasket with a small amount of sealing compound applied to both sides.
9. Install the water outlet and tighten the attaching bolts to 30 ft. lbs. (41 Nm).
10. Connect the hoses and if disconnected, the coolant temperature sensor connector to the housing.
11. Refill the cooling system.

Heater Blower Motor

REMOVAL AND INSTALLATION

Wrangler

NOTE: It is not necessary to discharge the refrigerant system.

1. Disconnect the negative battery cable.
2. Remove the hose clamps and dash grommet retaining screws.
3. Remove the evaporator housing-to-instrument panel screws and the housing mounting bracket screw.
4. Lower the evaporator housing to gain access to the blower motor attaching screws.
5. Remove the blower motor attaching screws and remove the blower motor. Disconnect the blower motor wiring and remove the blower motor from the vehicle.
To install:
6. Install the blower motor and connect the wiring. Install the blower motor attaching screws.
7. Position the evaporator housing and install the housing-to-instrument panel screws and housing mounting bracket screw.
8. Install the dash grommet retaining screws and hose clamps.
9. Connect the negative battery cable.

Cherokee and Comanche

NOTE: The blower motor is removed from the engine compartment.

1. Disconnect the negative battery cable.
2. If equipped with 4.0L engine, proceed as follows:
   a. Remove the coolant bottle retaining strap and move the bottle aside. Remove the coolant bottle bracket.

b. If equipped with anti-lock brakes, remove the anti-lock brake pump and bracket and position it aside.

3. Unplug the blower motor wiring connector.

4. Remove the blower motor mounting screws and lift out the motor.

To install:

5. Install the blower motor into position and connect the electrical leads.

6. If equipped with 4.0L engine, proceed as follows:

a. Install the anti-lock brake pump and bracket assembly, if equipped.

b. Install the coolant bottle bracket and coolant bottle.

7. Connect the negative battery cable.

1993–96 Grand Cherokee and 1993 Grand Wagoneer

1. Disconnect the negative battery cable.

2. Disconnect the blower motor cooling tube.

3. Unplug the blower motor wiring connector.

4. Remove the blower motor mounting screws and lift out the motor.

To install:

5. Make sure the seal is installed on the blower motor housing.

6. Install the blower motor into position and install the mounting screws.

7. Connect the wiring connector.

8. Connect the blower motor cooling tube.

9. Connect the negative battery cable.

Heater Core

REMOVAL AND INSTALLATION

Wrangler

1. Disconnect the negative battery cable.

2. Drain the coolant.

3. Disconnect the heater hoses at the core tubes.

4. Disconnect the vent door cables and the blower motor electrical connectors.

5. Disconnect the defroster duct.

6. Remove the nuts attaching the heater housing studs to the engine compartment side of the dash.

7. Remove the heater housing assembly by tilting it downward, to disengage it from the defroster duct, and

pulling it rearward and out from under the instrument panel.

8. Remove the heater housing cover and remove the heater core.

To install:

9. Install the heater core in the housing and install the cover.

10. Position the heater housing on the dash panel and install the seals on the heater core outlet and inlet tubes, and over the blower housing.

11. Install the attaching nuts and tighten alternately until 2 threads are visible beyond each nut.

NOTE: Overtightening the housing nuts can cause the housing to distort, resulting in air leaks.

12. Connect the defroster duct to the housing and the blower motor electrical connection.

13. Connect the vent door control cables and heater hoses.

14. Fill and bleed the cooling system.

15. Connect the negative battery cable and check the system for proper operation.

Cherokee and Comanche

1. Disconnect the negative battery cable.

2. Drain the coolant.

3. Disconnect the heater hoses at the core tubes.

4. If equipped with air conditioning, properly discharge the refrigerant.

5. Disconnect the air conditioning hose from the expansion valve and cap all openings. Always use a backup wrench on the fitting.

6. Disconnect the blower motor wires and vent tube.

7. Remove the center console, if equipped.

8. Remove the lower instrument panel.

9. Disconnect the wiring at the air conditioner relay, blower motor resistors and air conditioner thermostat. Disconnect the vacuum hoses at the vacuum motor.

10. Cut the plastic retaining strap that retains the evaporator housing to the heater core housing.

11. Disconnect and remove the heater control cable.

12. Remove the 3 clips at the rear blower housing flange and remove the retaining screws.

13. Remove the housing attaching nuts from the studs on the engine compartment side of the firewall.

14. Remove the evaporator drain tube.

15. Remove the right kick panel and the instrument panel support bolt.

16. Gently pull out on the right side of the dash and rotate the housing down and toward the rear to disengage the mounting studs from the firewall. Remove the housing.

17. Unbolt and remove the core from the housing.

To install:

18. Install the core in the housing.

19. Position the housing on the mounting studs on the firewall.

20. Install the right kick panel and the instrument panel support bolt.

21. Install the evaporator drain tube.

22. Install the housing attaching nuts from the studs on the engine compartment side of the firewall.

23. Install the 3 clips at the rear blower housing flange and install the retaining screws.

24. Connect the heater control cable.

25. Install a new plastic retaining strap that retains the evaporator housing to the heater core housing.

26. Connect the wiring at the air conditioner relay, blower motor resistors and air conditioner thermostat.

27. Connect the vacuum hoses at the vacuum motor.

28. Install the lower half of the instrument panel.

29. Install the center console, if equipped.

30. Connect the blower motor wires and vent tube.

31. Connect the air conditioning hose at the expansion valve. Always use a backup wrench.

32. Connect the heater hoses at the core tubes.

33. Fill the cooling system.

34. Evacuate, charge and leak test the refrigerant system.

1993–96 Grand Cherokee and 1993 Grand Wagoneer

1. Disconnect the negative battery cable.

2. Properly discharge the A/C system.

3. Disconnect the A/C hoses from the evaporator lines. Cap the openings to prevent the entrance of dirt or moisture.

4. Drain the cooling system.

5. Disconnect the heater hoses from the heater core tubes.

6. Remove the coolant reservoir/overflow tank.

7. Separate the Powertrain Control Module (PCM) from its mounting bracket and position it aside. Do not disconnect the wire harness.

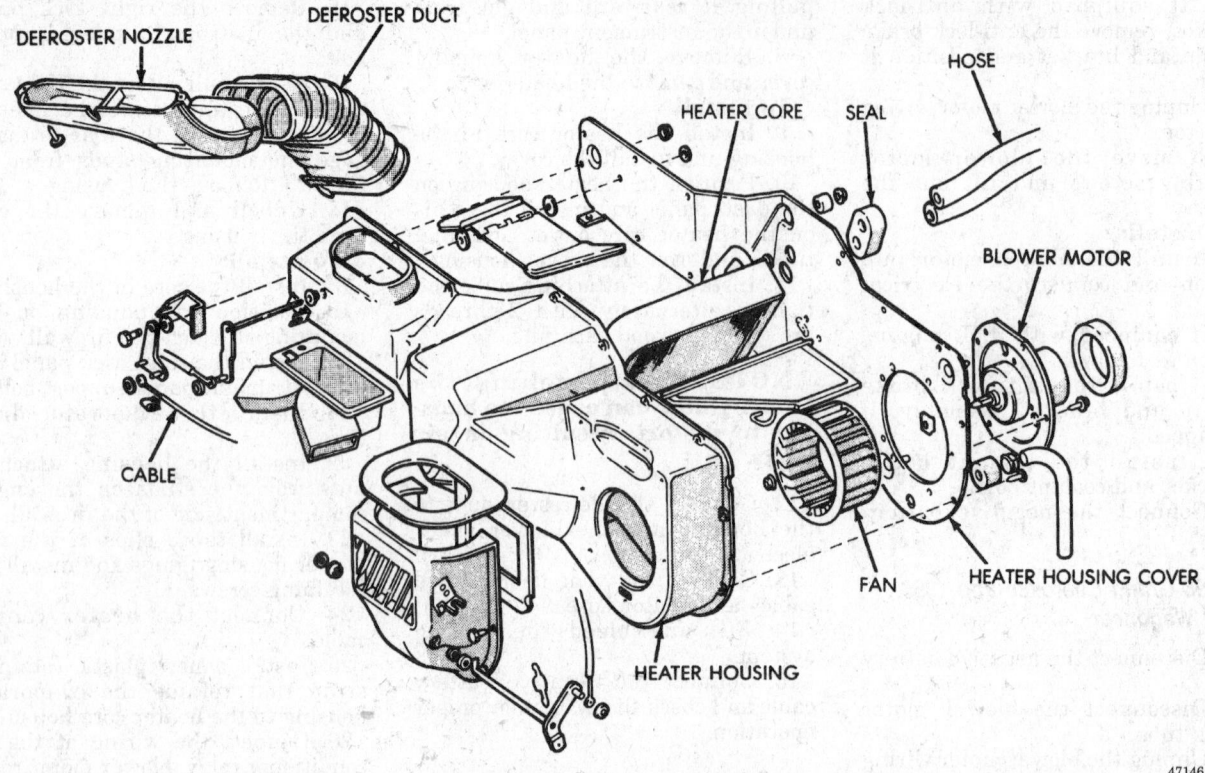

DEFROSTER NOZZLE
DEFROSTER DUCT
HEATER CORE
SEAL
HOSE
BLOWER MOTOR
CABLE
FAN
HEATER HOUSING COVER
HEATER HOUSING

47146

Heating system components — Wrangler

8. Remove the heater-A/C unit attaching nuts from the studs on the engine compartment side of the dash panel.

9. Working inside the vehicle, remove the defroster duct bezel from the instrument panel.

10. Remove the speaker grilles.

11. Remove the upper instrument panel retaining nuts.

12. Remove the screws retaining the lower left side panel at the instrument panel. Remove the mounting bolt for the instrument panel at the left side cowl through the access hole provided.

13. Remove the ashtray.

14. Remove the instrument panel mounting screw located behind the ashtray.

15. Remove the instrument panel mounting bolt located on the right side cowl.

16. Fold down the carpet at the left side of the console and remove the 2 mounting screws.

17. Remove the lower column cover.

18. Remove the knee bolster.

19. Remove the tilt lever and both steering column covers.

20. Disconnect the steering column wiring.

21. Remove the nuts at the steering column mount and lower the column.

22. Remove the instrument panel mounting bolt above the steering column.

23. Disconnect the bulkhead connect at the left side of the dash panel.

24. Disconnect the wiring cluster at the lower left side of the dash panel.

25. Remove the right side kick panel access door and disconnect the wiring at the kick panel.

26. Pull back and lower the instrument panel. Disconnect the A/C vacuum line and antenna.

27. Remove the instrument panel.

28. Remove the defroster duct.

29. Disconnect the rear floor heat duct from the center adapter heat duct.

30. Disconnect the electrical connectors.

31. Remove the attaching nuts from the studs in the passenger compartment side of the dash panel.

32. Remove the heater-A/C unit from the vehicle.

33. Remove the heater core retaining screws.

34. Pull the heater core straight out from the housing.

To install:

35. Install the heater core into the housing.

36. Position the clips over the heater core tubes. Install and tighten the screws.

37. Position the heater A/C unit into the dash panel. Be sure to position the drain tube into its hole.

38. Install the passenger compartment attaching nuts.

39. Install the attaching nuts on the engine compartment side of the dash panel.

40. Connect the heater hose to the heater core tubes.

41. Connect the A/C hoses to the evaporator lines.

42. Install the reservoir/overflow tank.

43. Install the PCM.

44. Install the defroster duct.

45. Connect the rear floor heat duct to the adaptor. Ensure the carpet is not interfering with heat duct outlets.

46. Connect the electrical connectors.

47. Connect the A/C vacuum lines and antenna to the instrument panel.

48. Position the instrument panel into place.

49. Connect the right side kick panel wiring harness.

50. Connect the wiring cluster at the lower left side of the instrument panel.

51. Connect the bulk head connector at the left side of the dash.

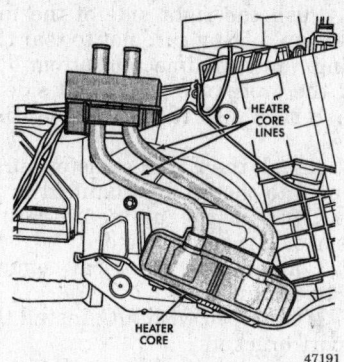

Heater core

47191

52. Install the instrument panel mounting screw above the steering column.

53. Position the steering column into place and install the mounting nuts.

54. Install the steering column covers and tilt wheel lever.

55. Install the knee bolster.

56. Install the lower column cover.

57. Install the screws located under the left side console carpet.

58. Install the instrument panel bolt located near the right side cowl.

59. Install the instrument panel bolt located behind the ashtray and install the ashtray.

60. Install the instrument panel bolt through the left side cowl.

61. Install the lower left side instrument panel mounting screws.

62. Install the upper instrument panel mounting bolts.

63. Install the speaker and defroster grilles.

64. Fill the cooling system.

65. Evacuate and recharge the A/C system.

66. Connect the negative battery cable.

67. Start the engine and check heater-A/C operations.

FUEL SYSTEM

Fuel System Service Precaution

Safety is the most important factor when performing not only fuel system maintenance but any type of maintenance. Failure to conduct maintenance and repairs in a safe manner may result in serious personal injury or death. Maintenance

and testing of the vehicle's fuel system components can be accomplished safely and effectively by adhering to the following rules and guidelines.

• To avoid the possibility of fire and personal injury, always disconnect the negative battery cable unless the repair or test procedure requires that battery voltage be applied.

• Always relieve the fuel system pressure prior to disconnecting any fuel system component (injector, fuel rail, pressure regulator, etc.), fitting or fuel line connection. Exercise extreme caution whenever relieving fuel system pressure to avoid exposing skin, face and eyes to fuel spray. Please be advised that fuel under pressure may penetrate the skin or any part of the body that it contacts.

• Always place a shop towel or cloth around the fitting or connection prior to loosening to absorb any excess fuel due to spillage. Ensure that all fuel spillage (should it occur) is quickly removed from engine surfaces. Ensure that all fuel soaked cloths or towels are deposited into a suitable waste container.

• Always keep a dry chemical (Class B) fire extinguisher near the work area.

• Do not allow fuel spray or fuel vapors to come into contact with a spark or open flame.

• Always use a backup wrench when loosening and tightening fuel line connection fittings. This will prevent unnecessary stress and torsion to fuel line piping. Always follow the proper torque specifications.

• Always replace worn fuel fitting O-rings with new. Do not substitute fuel hose or equivalent where fuel pipe is installed.

RELIEVING FUEL SYSTEM PRESSURE

Wrangler, Cherokee, Comanche, 1993–96 Grand Cherokee and 1993 Grand Wagoneer

── CAUTION ──
The fuel system is under constant pressure, even with the engine off. Fuel pressure must be released before servicing any fuel supply or fuel return system component.

1. Disconnect the negative battery cable.

2. Remove the fuel tank filler cap.

3. Remove the cap from the pressure test port on the fuel rail in the engine compartment.

── CAUTION ──
Do not allow fuel to spill onto the engine intake or exhaust manifolds. Place shop towels under and around the pressure port to absorb the fuel when the pressure is released from the fuel rail.

4. Place one end of the hose from a suitable fuel pressure gauge into an approved gasoline container.

5. Screw the other end of the hose onto the fuel pressure test port to relieve the fuel system pressure.

6. After the fuel pressure has been released, remove the hose from the test port and reinstall the test port cap.

Fuel Filter

REMOVAL AND INSTALLATION

Wrangler, Cherokee, Comanche, 1993–96 Grand Cherokee and 1993 Grand Wagoner

1. Disconnect the battery ground cable.

2. Relieve the fuel system pressure.

3. Raise and support the rear of the vehicle safely.

4. Disconnect the fuel lines from the filter.

5. Remove the filter strap bolt and remove the filter.

To install:

NOTE: The filter is marked for installation. IN goes towards the fuel tank; OUT towards the engine.

6. Place the new filter on the frame rail and tighten the strap bolt.

7. Connect the fuel lines to the filter.

8. Connect the negative battery cable.

Fuel Injector

REMOVAL AND INSTALLATION

Wrangler, Cherokee and Comanche

1. Disconnect the negative battery cable.

2. Relieve fuel system pressure.

3. Disconnect the fuel lines at the ends of the fuel rail assembly.

4. Mark and disconnect the injector wire harness connectors.

5. Remove the fuel rail retaining bolts.

6. Disconnect the vacuum line from the fuel pressure regulator.

7. Remove the fuel rail assembly from the engine.

NOTE: On models with automatic transmission, it may be necessary to remove the automatic transmission throttle pressure cable and bracket to remove the fuel rail assembly.

8. Remove the clips that retain the injectors to the fuel rail and remove the injectors.

To install:

9. Install the injectors and clips.

10. Install the fuel rail and tighten the fuel rail mounting bolts to 20 ft. lbs. (27 Nm).

11. Connect the vacuum line to the fuel pressure regulator.

12. Connect the fuel injector electrical connectors.

13. Connect the fuel lines to the injectors.

14. Connect the negative battery cable.

1993–96 Grand Cherokee and 1993 Grand Wagoneer

1. Disconnect the negative battery cable.

2. Relieve the fuel system pressure.

3. Remove the air duct from the throttle body.

4. Disconnect the Manifold Absolute Pressure (MAP) sensor, Idle Air Control (IAC) motor and Throttle Position Sensor (TPS) electrical connectors from the throttle body.

5. Disconnect the vacuum line from the throttle body.

6. Disconnect (unsnap) the control cables from the throttle body (lever) arm.

7. Remove the throttle body from the intake manifold. Discard the gasket.

8. If equipped with A/C, disconnect the compressor-to-intake manifold support bracket.

9. Disconnect the electrical connectors from the fuel injectors.

NOTE: The fuel injector wiring harness is numerically tagged (INJ. 1, INJ. 2, etc.) for injector position identification.

10. Remove the EVAP canister purge solenoid/bracket assembly from the intake manifold.

NOTE: Do not attempt to disconnect the fuel line/tubes at the rear of the fuel rail. Fuel rail connections are made under the vehicle at the frame rail.

11. Raise and support the vehicle safely.

12. Disconnect the fuel rail quick-connect fittings at the fuel lines leading to the rear of the vehicle.

13. Lower the vehicle.

14. Remove the remaining fuel rail mounting bolts.

NOTE: Do not attempt to separate the fuel rail halves at the connecting hoses and do not attempt to install clamps to the hoses. When removing the fuel rail do not bend or kink these hoses.

15. Carefully rock the left fuel rail until the fuel injectors start to clear the intake manifold. Repeat the procedure on the right side.

16. Remove the fuel rail, with the fuel injectors attached, from the engine.

17. Remove the clips retaining the injector to the fuel rail and remove the injectors.

To install:

18. Coat each injector O-ring with engine oil.

19. Install the injectors and clips to the fuel rail.

20. Position each injector to the intake manifold.

21. Push the right side of the fuel rail down, taking care not to tear the O-ring, until the injector bottom. Repeat the procedure on the left side.

22. Install the fuel rail mounting bolts.

23. Install the EVAP canister purge solenoid to the intake manifold.

24. Connect the air temperature sensor electrical connector.

25. Connect the electrical connectors to the injectors.

26. If equipped with A/C, install the support bracket.

27. Clean the mating surfaces on the throttle body.

28. Install the throttle body with a new gasket and torque the bolts to 200 inch lbs. (23 Nm).

29. Connect the control cables. If equipped with automatic transmission, the throttle cable must be adjusted.

30. Connect the vacuum line and electrical connectors to the throttle body.

31. Install the air duct to the throttle body.

32. Connect the vacuum line to the fuel pressure regulator.

33. Raise and support the vehicle safely.

34. Connect the fuel rail lines.

35. Lower the vehicle.

36. Connect the negative battery cable.

37. Start the engine and check for leaks.

Fuel Pump

REMOVAL AND INSTALLATION

Wrangler, Cherokee and Comanche

1. Disconnect the negative battery cable.

2. Remove the fuel tank filler cap.

3. Drain the fuel from the fuel tank.

4. Raise and safely support the rear of the vehicle.

5. Remove the fuel inlet and outlet hoses from the sending unit.

6. Remove the sending unit wires.

7. Using a brass punch and hammer, remove the sending unit retaining lock ring by tapping it counterclockwise.

8. Remove the sending unit, which incorporates the electric fuel pump, along with the O-ring seal from the fuel tank. Discard the O-ring.

9. Remove and discard the pump inlet filter.

10. Disconnect the fuel pump terminal wires.

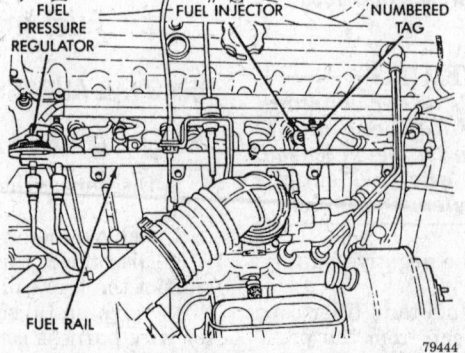

FUEL PRESSURE REGULATOR   FUEL INJECTOR   NUMBERED TAG

FUEL RAIL

79444

Fuel rail

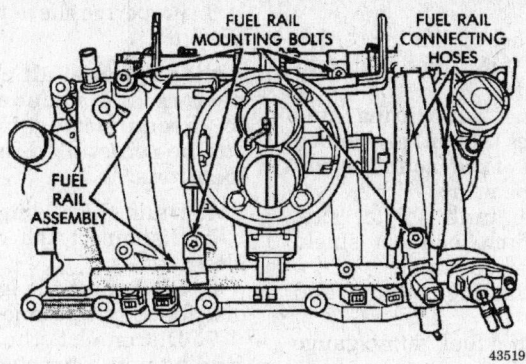

Fuel rail mounting bolts

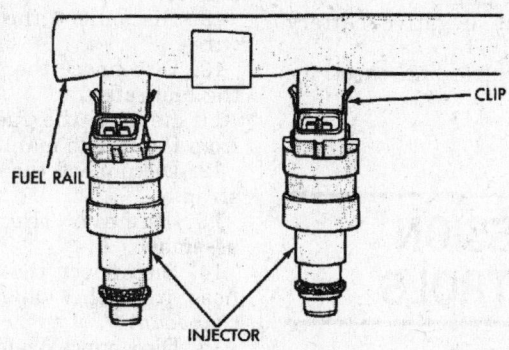

Fuel injector and rail assembly

11. Remove the pump outlet hose and clamp.

12. Remove the pump top mounting bracket nut and remove the pump.

To install:

13. Install a new inlet filter on the pump.

14. Assemble the pump and bracket.

15. Connect the hose and wiring.

16. Install the unit and new O-ring in the tank. The rubber stopper on the end of the fuel return tube must be inserted into the cup in the fuel tank reservoir.

17. Install the lock ring. Carefully tap it into place until it seats against the stop on the tank.

18. Connect the hoses.

19. Connect the wiring.

20. Lower the vehicle.

21. Refill the fuel tank.

22. Run the engine and check for leaks.

1993–96 Grand Cherokee and 1993 Grand Wagoneer

1. Disconnect the negative battery cable.

2. Remove the fuel tank filler cap.

3. Drain the fuel from the fuel tank.

4. Raise and safely support the rear of the vehicle.

5. Remove the fuel inlet and outlet hoses from the sending unit.

6. Remove the sending unit wires.

7. Using a brass punch and hammer, remove the sending unit retaining lock ring by tapping it counterclockwise.

8. Remove the sending unit, which incorporates the electric fuel pump, along with the O-ring seal from the fuel tank. Discard the O-ring.

NOTE: The fuel pump cannot be replaced separately. The sending unit and pump must be replaced as an assembly.

To install:

9. Install the unit and new O-ring in the tank. The rubber stopper on the end of the fuel return tube must be inserted into the cup in the fuel tank reservoir.

10. Install the lock ring. Carefully tap it into place until it seats against the stop on the tank.

11. Connect the hoses.

12. Connect the wiring.

13. Lower the vehicle.

14. Refill the fuel tank.

15. Run the engine and check for leaks.

Fuel Tank

REMOVAL AND INSTALLATION

Wrangler

1. Disconnect the negative battery cable.

2. Relieve the fuel system pressure.

3. Remove the fuel filler cap and drain the fuel tank.

4. Raise and support the vehicle safely.

5. Disconnect the fuel fill hose and vent hose from the filler neck.

6. Disconnect the fuel gauge electrical connectors.

7. Label and disconnect all other fuel and vent hoses attached to the fuel tank.

NOTE: The fuel tank and skid plate are removed as a unit. Do not loosen the fuel tank strap nuts. Remove the assembly by loosening the skid plate/fuel tank assembly mounting nuts.

8. Place a floorjack under the fuel tank.

9. Remove the strap nuts and pull the straps away from the tank.

10. Lower the tank from the vehicle.

To install:

11. Raise the fuel tank into position and connect all fuel filler and vent hoses.

12. Wrap the straps around the fuel tank and tighten the skid plate/fuel tank assembly mounting nuts to 65 inch lbs. (7 Nm).

13. Connect the fuel supply and vent hoses.

14. Connect the fuel gauge electrical connectors.

15. Lower the vehicle.

16. Fill the fuel tank.

17. Connect the negative battery cable.

18. Run the vehicle and check for leaks.

Cherokee and Comanche

1. Disconnect the negative battery cable.

2. Relieve the fuel system pressure.

3. Remove the fuel filler cap and drain the fuel tank.

4. Raise and support the vehicle safely.

5. Disconnect the fuel fill hose and vent hose from the filler neck.

6. Disconnect the fuel pump/gauge electrical connectors.

7. Label and disconnect all other fuel and vent hoses attached to the fuel tank.

8. Remove the skid plate.

9. Place a floorjack under the fuel tank.

10. Remove the strap nuts and pull the straps away from the tank.

11. Lower the tank from the vehicle.

To install:

12. Raise the fuel tank into position and connect all fuel filler and vent hoses.

13. Wrap the straps around the fuel tank. For Cherokee, tighten the nuts to 100 inch lbs. (11 Nm). On Comanche, tighten the nuts to 65 inch lbs. (7 Nm) for the 2 outer straps and 43 inch lbs. (5 Nm) for the center strap.

14. Install the fuel tank skid plate.

15. Connect the fuel supply and vent hoses.

16. Connect the fuel pump/gauge electrical connectors.

17. Lower the vehicle.

18. Fill the fuel tank.

19. Connect the negative battery cable.

20. Run the vehicle and check for leaks.

1993–96 Grand Cherokee and 1993 Grand Wagoneer

1. Disconnect the negative battery cable.

2. Relieve the fuel system pressure.

3. Remove the fuel filler cap and drain the fuel tank.

4. Raise and support the vehicle safely.

5. Remove the 2 tow hooks.

6. Disconnect the fuel fill hose and vent hose from the filler neck.

7. Disconnect the fuel pump/gauge electrical connectors.

8. Label and disconnect all other fuel and vent hoses attached to the fuel tank.

9. If equipped, remove the skid plate.

10. Remove the trailer hitch, if equipped and exhaust tail pipe heat shield.

11. Remove the fuel tank shield.

12. Place a floorjack under the fuel tank.

13. Remove the strap nuts and pull the straps away from the tank.

14. Lower the tank from the vehicle.

NOTE: The right side of the fuel tank must be lowered first to gain access to the 2 fuel filler hose clamps located on the left side of the tank.

To install:

15. Raise the fuel tank into position and connect all fuel filler and vent hoses.

16. Tighten the 2 mounting nuts until 3.149 inches (80mm) is attained between the end of the mounting bolt and bottom of the strap.

17. Install the tank shield, skid plate, trailer hitch, exhaust shield and tow hooks, as required.

18. Connect the fuel supply and vent hoses.

19. Connect the fuel pump/gauge electrical connectors.

20. Lower the vehicle.

21. Fill the fuel tank.

22. Connect the negative battery cable.

23. Run the vehicle and check for leaks.

EMISSION CONTROLS

Emission Warning Lamp

RESETTING

Comanche, Cherokee and 1992–93 Wrangler

1. Connect DRB-II or equivalent, to the diagnostic connector, located next to the electronic control unit in the engine compartment.

2. Follow the DRB-II Function Flow Diagram to reset the EMR light.

ENGINE MECHANICAL

Engine Assembly

REMOVAL AND INSTALLATION

Wrangler

1. Place a protective cloth on the windshield frame. Raise the hood and rest it on the frame.

2. Disconnect the battery cables and remove the battery.

3. Properly relieve the fuel system pressure.

NOTE: Label all electrical connectors and vacuum lines prior to disconnecting them, so they can be reinstalled in their proper locations.

4. Drain the cooling system.

5. Disconnect the wires from the alternator.

6. Disconnect the ignition coil and distributor wire connections.

7. Disconnect the oil pressure sending unit connector.

8. Disconnect the wires from the starter.

9. Disconnect the fuel injection wires.

10. Disconnect the fuel lines from the fuel rails.

11. Remove the fuel line bracket from the intake manifold.

12. Disconnect the engine ground strap.

13. Remove the air cleaner assembly.

14. Disconnect the canister purge hose from the vapor canister "T" connector.

15. Disconnect the idle speed actuator wire connector.

16. Disconnect the throttle cable and remove it from the bracket.

17. Disconnect the throttle rod from the bellcrank.

18. If equipped, disconnect the cruise control cable.

19. Disconnect the oxygen sensor electrical connector.

20. Disconnect the upper and lower hoses from the radiator.

21. Disconnect the coolant hoses from the rear of the intake manifold and thermostat housing.

22. Disconnect the heater hoses.

23. Remove the fan shroud screws.

24. Remove the radiator and fan shroud.

25. Remove the engine cooling fan.

26. Remove the engine cooling fan and install a $5/16$ x $1/2$ inch capscrew through the fan pulley into the water pump flange. This will maintain the pulley and water pump in alignment when the crankshaft is rotated.

27. If equipped, disconnect the check valve from the power brake booster.

28. If equipped with power steering, perform the following:

   a. Disconnect the steering hoses from the fittings at the steering gear.

   b. Drain the pump reservoir.

   c. Cap all fittings once removed.

29. Raise and support the vehicle safely.

30. Remove the oil filter.

31. Remove the starter.

32. Remove the flywheel access cover.

33. Remove the engine support cushion-to-bracket through bolts.

34. Disconnect the exhaust pipe from the manifold.

35. Remove the upper flywheel housing bolts and loosen the bottom bolts.

36. Remove the engine shock damper bracket from the sill.

37. Lower the vehicle.

38. Attach a lifting device to the engine.

39. Place a support under the bellhousing.

40. Remove the remaining flywheel bolts.

41. Lift the engine from the vehicle.

42. Install the oil filter to keep foreign material out of the engine.

To install:

43. Remove the oil filter.

44. Lower the engine into the vehicle. To ease installation, remove the engine support cushions to aid in engine-to-transmission alignment.

45. Insert the transmission shaft into the clutch spline.

46. Align the flywheel housing with the engine.

47. Install and tighten the flywheel housing bolts finger-tight.

48. If removed, install the engine support cushions.

49. Lower the engine into place and remove the lifting device.

50. Raise and support the vehicle safely.

51. Attach the engine shock damper bracket to the sill.

52. Attach the exhaust pipe to the manifold and torque the nuts to 23 ft. lbs. (31 Nm).

53. Install the flywheel access cover.

54. Install the remaining flywheel bolts and torque them to 28 ft. lbs. (38 Nm).

55. Install the starter.

56. Install the oil filter.

57. Lower the vehicle.

58. Connect the coolant lines and tighten the clamps.

59. If equipped with power steering.

a. Connect the hoses to the steering gear and torque the nut to 38 ft. lbs. (52 Nm).

b. Fill the pump reservoir with fluid.

60. Remove the alignment capscrew and install the fan assembly.

61. Install the accessory drive belt.

62. Install the radiator and shroud.

63. Connect the radiator hoses.

64. Connect the oxygen sensor electrical connector.

65. Connect the throttle valve rod and retainer. Connect the throttle cable and install the rod and spring.

66. If equipped, connect the speed control cable.

67. Install the vacuum hose and check valve to the brake booster.

68. Connect the electrical connections disconnected during removal.

69. Connect the fuel lines to the fuel rail.

70. Install the fuel line bracket to the intake manifold.

71. Install the air cleaner.

72. Install the battery and connect the cables.

73. Fill the engine to the proper level with oil.

74. Fill the cooling system.

75. Start the engine and check for leaks.

76. Fill the fluid levels to the proper level.

Comanche and Cherokee

NOTE: Disconnecting the battery cable on some vehicles may interfere with the functions of the on board computer systems and may require the computer to undergo a relearning process, once the negative battery cable is disconnected.

1. Disconnect the negative battery cable.

2. Properly relieve the fuel system pressure.

3. If equipped with A/C, properly discharge the system.

4. Matchmark the hood and hinges and remove the hood.

5. Drain the cooling system.

NOTE: Label all electrical connectors and vacuum lines prior to disconnecting them, so they can be reinstalled in their proper locations.

6. Remove the upper, lower and coolant recovery hoses.

7. Remove the fan shroud.

8. If equipped with an automatic transmission, disconnect the fluid cooler lines.

9. Remove the radiator and if equipped, A/C condenser.

10. Remove the engine cooling fan and install a $5/16$ x $1/2$ inch capscrew through the fan pulley into the water pump flange. This will maintain the pulley and water pump in alignment when the crankshaft is rotated.

11. Disconnect the heater hoses.

12. Disconnect the throttle linkages, speed control cable, if equipped and throttle valve rod.

13. Disconnect the oxygen sensor electrical connector.

14. Disconnect the fuel injection harness connectors.

15. Disconnect the quick-connection fuel lines at the fuel rail and return line.

16. Remove the fuel line bracket from the intake manifold.

17. Remove the air cleaner assembly.

18. If equipped with A/C, remove the service valves and cap the compressor ports.

19. Remove the power brake vacuum check valve from the booster, if equipped.

20. If equipped with power steering, perform the following:

a. Disconnect the steering hoses from the fittings at the steering gear.

b. Drain the pump reservoir.

c. Cap all fittings once removed.

21. Disconnect the coolant hoses from the rear of the intake manifold.

22. Identify, tag and disconnect all necessary wires and vacuum lines.

23. Raise and support the vehicle safely.

24. Remove the oil filter.

25. Remove the starter.

26. Disconnect the exhaust pipe from the manifold.

27. Remove the flywheel/converter housing access cover.

28. If equipped with an automatic transmission, matchmark the converter to the driveplate and remove the bolts.

29. Remove the upper flywheel/converter housing bolts and loosen the bottoms bolts.

30. Remove the engine mount-to-engine compartment bracket bolts.

31. Remove the engine shock damper bracket from the sill.

32. Lower the vehicle.

33. Attach a lifting device to the engine.

34. Raise the engine slightly off the front supports.

35. Place a support stand under the transmission housing.

36. Remove the remaining flywheel bolts.

37. Lift the engine out of the vehicle.

38. Install the oil filter to keep foreign material out of the engine.

To install:

39. Remove the oil filter.

40. Lower the engine into the vehicle. To ease installation, remove the engine mounts to aid in engine-to-transmission alignment.

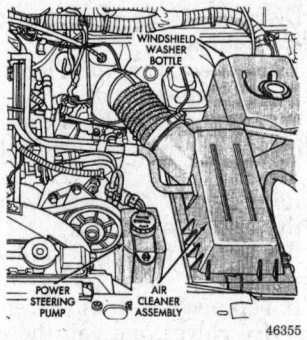

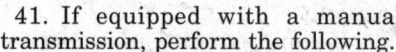

Power steering pump — Cherokee and Comanche

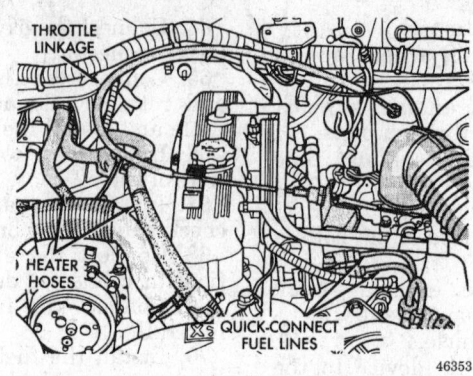

Heater hoses, throttle linkage and fuel lines

41. If equipped with a manual transmission, perform the following.

a. Insert the transmission shaft into the clutch spline.

b. Align the flywheel housing with the engine.

c. Install and tighten the flywheel housing bolts finger-tight.

42. If equipped with an automatic transmission, perform the following.

a. Align the torque converter housing with the engine.

b. Loosely install the converter housing lower bolts and install the next higher nut and bolt on each side.

c. Tighten all 4 bolts finger-tight.

43. If removed, install the engine mounts.

44. Lower the engine into place and remove the lifting device.

45. Raise and support the vehicle safely.

46. If equipped with an automatic transmission, perform the following.

a. Align the torque converter to the driveplate.

b. Install the bolts and torque them to 40 ft. lbs. (54 Nm).

c. Install the access cover.

d. Install the exhaust pipe support.

47. Install the remaining converter/flywheel bolts finger-tight.

48. Install the starter.

49. Tighten the engine support cushion bolts/nuts.

50. Torque the loose converter/flywheel bolts to 28 ft. lbs. (38 Nm).

51. Install the oil filter.

52. Connect the exhaust pipe to the manifold.

53. Lower the vehicle.

54. Connect the coolant hoses and tighten the clamps.

55. If equipped with power steering, perform the following:

a. Unplug the lines and connect them to the steering gear. Torque the fittings to 38 ft. lbs. (52 Nm).

b. Fill the pump reservoir with fluid.

56. Remove the alignment cap screw and install the fan.

57. Install the radiator, condenser, if equipped and fan shroud.

58. Connect the radiator hoses.

59. If equipped with an automatic transmission, connect the cooling lines.

60. Connect the oxygen sensor electrical connector.

61. Connect the throttle valve rod and retainer. Connect the throttle cable and install the rod and spring.

62. If equipped, connect the cruise control cable.

63. Connect the fuel lines to the throttle body.

64. Connect all vacuum lines and electrical connectors disconnected during removal.

65. If equipped with A/C, connect the service valves to the compressor ports.

66. Install the air cleaner.

67. Install the hood.

68. Connect the battery cables.

69. Fill the cooling system.

70. Start the engine and check for leaks.

71. If equipped, recharge the A/C system.

72. Check and top off fluid levels.

1993–96 Grand Cherokee

1. Matchmark the hood to the hinges and remove the hood.

2. Remove the battery.

3. Properly relieve the fuel system pressure.

4. Drain the cooling system.

5. Remove the air cleaner and tube.

6. Remove the radiator.

7. Remove the heater hoses.

8. Label and disconnect the necessary vacuum lines.

9. Remove the distributor cap and wiring.

10. Disconnect the accelerator linkage.

11. Remove the air duct from the throttle body.

12. Label and disconnect the Manifold Absolute Pressure (MAP) sensor, Idle Air Control (IAC) motor and Throttle Position Sensor (TPS) electrical connectors from the throttle body.

13. Disconnect the vacuum line from the throttle body.

14. Disconnect (unsnap) the control cables from the throttle body (lever) arm.

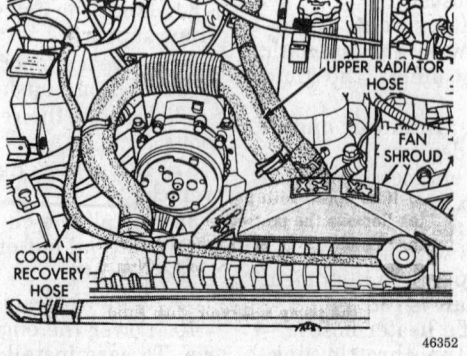

Upper radiator hose, coolant recovery hose and fan shroud

15. Remove the throttle body from the intake manifold. Discard the gasket.

16. Disconnect the oil pressure electrical connector.

17. If equipped, properly discharge the A/C system.

18. Disconnect the A/C lines from the compressor.

19. If equipped with power steering, disconnect the lines from the pump.

20. Remove the starter.

21. Remove the alternator.

22. Raise and support the vehicle safely.

23. Disconnect the fuel line connections coming from the fuel rail.

24. Disconnect the exhaust pipe from the manifold.

25. Support the transmission with a stand.

26. Remove the bell housing bolts and inspection plate.

27. Attach a C-clamp to the bottom of the torque converter housing to prevent the torque converter from coming out.

28. Matchmark the torque converter to the driveplate and remove the bolts.

29. Disconnect the engine from the torque converter driveplate.

30. Install a suitable lifting device to the engine.

——— WARNING ———
Do not lift the engine by the intake manifold.

31. Remove the front engine mount thru-bolts.

32. Lower the vehicle.

33. Remove the engine from the vehicle and mount on a suitable workstand.

To install:

34. Remove the engine from the workstand and position it in the engine compartment.

35. Raise and support the vehicle.

36. Position the torque converter and driveplate. Torque the bolts to 271 inch lbs. (31 Nm).

37. Install the front engine mount thru-bolts.

38. Install the bell housing bolts and torque them to 30 ft. lbs. (41 Nm).

39. Remove the C-clamp and install the inspection plate. Remove the stand from the transmission.

40. Connect the exhaust pipe to the manifold.

41. Connect the fuel rail lines.

42. Lower the vehicle.

43. Install the starter.

44. Install the alternator.

45. If equipped, install the power steering hoses.

46. If equipped, connect the A/C hoses.

47. Connect the accelerator linkage.

48. Connect the starter wires.

49. Connect the oil pressure electrical connector.

50. Install the distributor cap and wires.

51. Connect the vacuum lines.

52. Install the radiator, radiator hoses and heater hoses.

53. Install the fan shroud into position.

54. Install the air cleaner.

55. Install the battery.

56. Fill the cooling system.

57. Start the engine and check for leaks.

58. If equipped, recharge the A/C system.

59. Install the hood.

60. Road test the vehicle.

1993 Grand Wagoneer

1. Matchmark the hood to the hinges and remove the hood.

2. Remove the battery.

3. Properly relieve the fuel system pressure.

4. Drain the cooling system.

5. Remove the air cleaner and tube.

6. Remove the radiator.

7. Remove the heater hoses.

8. Label and disconnect the necessary vacuum lines.

9. Remove the distributor cap and wiring.

10. Disconnect the accelerator linkage.

11. Remove the air duct from the throttle body.

12. Label and disconnect the Manifold Absolute Pressure (MAP) sensor, Idle Air Control (IAC) motor and Throttle Position Sensor (TPS) electrical connectors from the throttle body.

13. Disconnect the vacuum line from the throttle body.

14. Disconnect (unsnap) the control cables from the throttle body (lever) arm.

15. Remove the throttle body from the intake manifold. Discard the gasket.

16. Disconnect the oil pressure electrical connector.

17. If equipped, properly discharge the A/C system.

18. Disconnect the A/C lines from the compressor.

19. If equipped with power steering, disconnect the lines from the pump.

20. Remove the starter.

21. Remove the alternator.

22. Raise and support the vehicle safely.

23. Disconnect the fuel line connections coming from the fuel rail.

24. Disconnect the exhaust pipe from the manifold.

25. Support the transmission with a stand.

26. Remove the bell housing bolts and inspection plate.

27. Attach a C-clamp to the bottom of the torque converter housing to prevent the torque converter from coming out.

28. Matchmark the torque converter to the driveplate and remove the bolts.

29. Disconnect the engine from the torque converter driveplate.

30. Install a suitable lifting device to the engine.

——— WARNING ———
Do not lift the engine by the intake manifold.

31. Remove the front engine mount thru-bolts.

32. Lower the vehicle.

33. Remove the engine from the vehicle and mount on a suitable workstand.

To install:

34. Remove the engine from the workstand and position it in the engine compartment.

35. Raise and support the vehicle.

36. Position the torque converter and driveplate. Torque the bolts to 271 inch lbs. (31 Nm).

37. Install the front engine mount thru-bolts.

38. Install the bell housing bolts and torque them to 30 ft. lbs. (41 Nm).

39. Remove the C-clamp and install the inspection plate. Remove the stand from the transmission.

40. Connect the exhaust pipe to the manifold.

41. Connect the fuel rail lines.

42. Lower the vehicle.

43. Install the starter.

44. Install the alternator.

45. If equipped, install the power steering hoses.

46. If equipped, connect the A/C hoses.

47. Connect the accelerator linkage.

48. Connect the starter wires.

49. Connect the oil pressure electrical connector.

50. Install the distributor cap and wires.

51. Connect the vacuum lines.

52. Install the radiator, radiator hoses and heater hoses.

53. Install the fan shroud into position.
54. Install the air cleaner.
55. Install the battery.
56. Fill the cooling system.
57. Start the engine and check for leaks.
58. If equipped, recharge the A/C system.
59. Install the hood.
60. Road test the vehicle.

Engine Mount

REMOVAL AND INSTALLATION

Comanche, 1992–93 Wrangler and 1992–93 Cherokee

1. Disconnect the negative battery cable.
2. Raise and safely support the vehicle.
3. Position a floor jack under the oil pan with a block of wood between the pan and the jack. Support the engine.
4. Remove the nut from the mount through bolt, but do not remove the through bolt.
5. Remove the engine mount-to-frame bracket retaining bolt and nut.
6. Remove the through bolt and the engine mount.

To install:

7. If the engine support bracket was removed, position the support bracket and install the attaching bolts. Tighten to 45 ft. lbs. (61 Nm).
8. Install the engine mount into position and install the through bolt and nut.
9. Install the mount-to-frame bracket bolt and nut. On Cherokee and Comanche, tighten to 30 ft. lbs. (41 Nm). On Wrangler, tighten to 48 ft. lbs. (65 Nm).
10. Tighten the through bolt to 48 ft. lbs. (65 Nm).
11. Remove the engine support and lower the vehicle.
12. Connect the negative battery cable.

1994–96 Wrangler

1. Disconnect the negative battery cable.
2. Raise and safely support the vehicle.
3. Position a floor jack under the oil pan with a block of wood between the pan and the jack. Support the engine.
4. Remove the nut from the mount through bolt, but do not remove the through bolt.

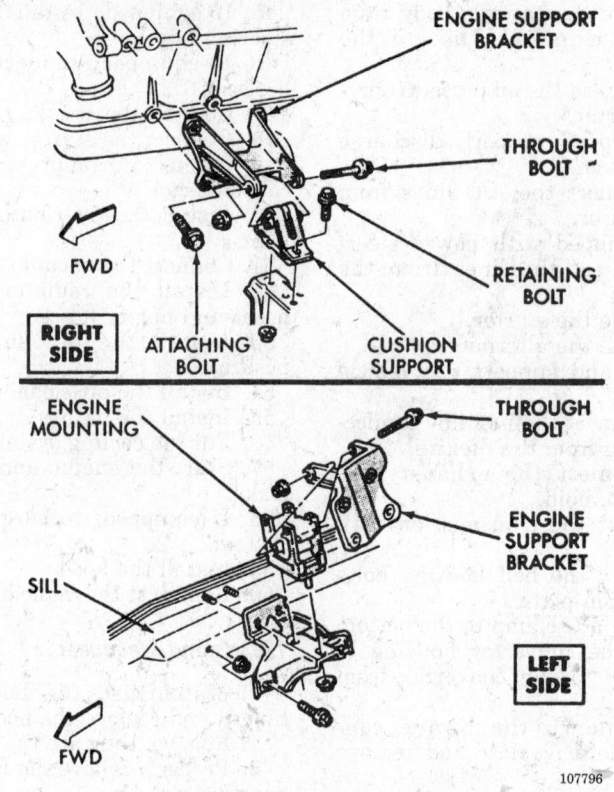

Front engine mounts — Wrangler

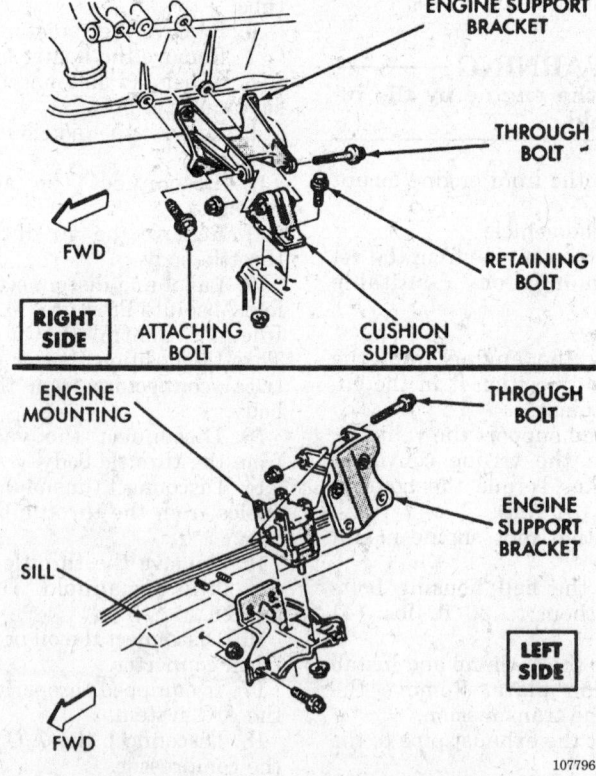

Front engine mounts — Cherokee and Comanche

5. Remove the engine mount-to-frame bracket retaining bolt and nut.

6. Remove the through bolt and the engine mount.

To install:

7. If the engine support bracket was removed, position the support bracket and install the attaching bolts. Tighten to 46 ft. lbs. (62 Nm).

8. Install the engine mount into position.

9. Install the mount-to-frame bracket bolt and nut. Tighten to 38 ft. lbs. (52 Nm).

10. Install the through bolt and nut and tighten to 51 ft. lbs. (69 Nm).

11. Remove the engine support and lower the vehicle.

12. Connect the negative battery cable.

1994–96 Cherokee

1. Disconnect the negative battery cable.

2. Raise and safely support the vehicle.

3. Position a floor jack under the oil pan with a block of wood between the pan and the jack. Support the engine.

4. Remove the nut from the mount through bolt, but do not remove the through bolt.

5. Remove the engine mount-to-frame bracket retaining bolt and nut.

6. Remove the through bolt and the engine mount.

To install:

7. If the engine support bracket was removed, position the left bracket and the right bracket with generator brace onto the cylinder block. Install the bolts and stud nuts.

8. On the right side, tighten the bolts to 45 ft. lbs. (61 Nm) and the stud nuts to 34 ft. lbs. (46 Nm). On the left side, tighten the bolts to 45 ft. lbs. (61 Nm).

9. If the frame support bracket was removed, position the brackets onto the lower front sill and install the bolts and stud nuts. Tighten the bolts to 40 ft. lbs. (54 Nm) and the stud nuts to 30 ft. lbs. (41 Nm).

10. Install the engine mount into position. Tighten the right mount nuts to 48 ft. lbs. (65 Nm) and the left mount bolt/nut to 30 ft. lbs. (41 Nm).

11. Install the through bolt and nut and tighten to 48 ft. lbs. (65 Nm).

12. Remove the engine support and lower the vehicle.

13. Connect the negative battery cable.

1993–96 Grand Cherokee

1. Disconnect the negative battery cable.

2. Raise and support the vehicle safely.

3. Support the engine using a floor jack and a block of wood under the oil pan.

4. Remove the nut from the through-bolt but do not remove the through-bolt.

5. Remove the retaining bolts and nuts from the engine support cushions.

6. Remove the engine support cushions.

To install:

7. If the engine support bracket was removed, position the bracket and install the attaching bolts. Tighten the bolts to 45–48 ft. lbs. (61–65 Nm).

8. Install the engine support cushion and the through-bolt. Install the engine support cushion attaching bolts and tighten to 30–48 ft. lbs. (41–48 Nm). Tighten the through-bolt to 89 ft. lbs. (121 Nm).

9. Remove the engine support and lower the vehicle.

10. Connect the negative battery cable.

1993 Grand Wagoneer

1. Disconnect the negative battery cable.

2. Position the fan to assure clearance for the radiator top tank and hose.

3. Raise and support the vehicle safely.

4. Support the engine using a floor jack and a block of wood under the oil pan.

5. Remove the engine support insulator through-bolts and nuts.

6. Raise the engine slightly.

7. Remove the engine support insulator bolts and remove the insulator.

To install:

8. If removed, install the sill bracket assembly.

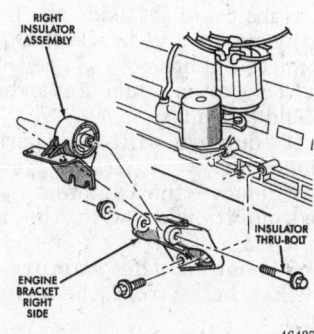

Right side engine mount — Grand Cherokee

9. Install the right side bracket onto the sill. Torque the bolts to 48 ft. lbs. (65 Nm).

10. Install the left side bracket onto the sill. Torque the top bolts to 48 ft. lbs. (65 Nm), side bolts to 70 ft. lbs. (96 Nm) and bottom bolts to 89 ft. lbs. (121 Nm).

11. With the engine raised slightly, position the support insulator assembly onto the engine block. Torque the bolts to 65 ft. lbs. (88 Nm).

12. Lower the engine while aligning the engine support insulator into the sill bracket.

13. Install the through-bolt and nut. Torque the right side nut to 48 ft. lbs. (65 Nm) and left side to 89 ft. lbs. (121 Nm).

14. Remove the engine support and lower the vehicle.

15. Connect the negative battery cable.

Cylinder Head

REMOVAL AND INSTALLATION

Wrangler, Cherokee and Comanche

1. Disconnect the negative battery cable.

2. Properly relieve the fuel system pressure.

3. Drain the cooling system.

4. Disconnect the hoses at the thermostat housing.

5. Remove the air cleaner.

6. Remove the rocker arm cover.

NOTE: The rocker arm cover has a cured gasket attached to it. This gasket should not be removed. If sections of the gasket are missing or are compressed, replace the cover. However, minor damage such as small cracks, cuts or chips can be repaired with liquid gasket material.

7. Remove the rocker arms and the pushrods. Keep them in their original order for installation.

8. Remove the power steering pump bracket. Suspend the pump aside.

9. Remove the intake and exhaust manifolds.

10. If equipped with A/C, perform the following:

   a. Remove the compressor and position it aside with the lines attached.

   b. Remove the compressor bracket bolts from the cylinder head.

   c. Loosen the through bolt at the bottom of the bracket.

11. Disconnect the fuel lines and vacuum advance hose.

12. Remove the intake and exhaust manifolds.

13. Remove the spark plugs and wires.

14. Remove the ignition coil and bracket assembly.

15. Disconnect the temperature sending unit wire.

16. Remove the cylinder head bolts in the reverse order of the installation torque sequence.

17. Lift the head off the engine and remove the head gasket.

18. Thoroughly clean the gasket mating surfaces. Remove all traces of old gasket material. Remove all carbon deposits from the combustion chambers. Lay a straight-edge across the head and check for flatness. Total deviation should not exceed 0.008 in.

To install:

19. Install the head gasket.

NOTE: Do not apply sealer as the cylinder head gaskets are of a composition type.

20. Fabricate 2 cylinder head alignment dowels from used head bolts. Using the longest bolts, trim the hex head off and cut slots into the top.

NOTE: Cylinder head bolts should be reused only once. Replace the head bolts which were previously used or are marked with paint. If head bolts are to be reused, mark each head bolt with paint for future reference. Head bolts should be installed using sealer.

21. Install the cylinder head and tighten the head bolts in the proper sequence to the following torque specifications:

a. Torque all bolts to 22 ft. lbs. (30 Nm).

b. Torque all bolts to 45 ft. lbs. 61 Nm).

c. Torque all bolts, except bolt 7, to 110 ft. lbs. (150 Nm)

d. Torque bolt 7 to 100 ft. lbs. (136 Nm).

22. Connect the temperature sending unit wire.

23. Install the ignition coil, spark plugs and wires.

24. Install the intake and exhaust manifolds.

25. Install the fuel lines and vacuum advance hose.

26. If equipped, install the power steering pump and bracket.

27. Install the pushrods and rocker arms in their original positions.

28. Install the rocker arm cover.

29. Install the A/C compressor.

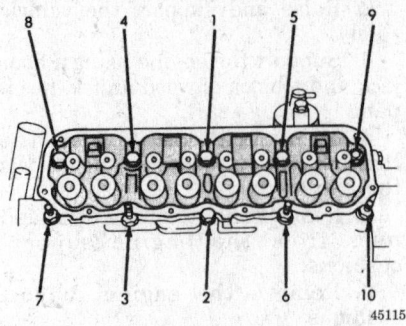

Cylinder head torque sequence — Wrangler, Cherokee and Comanche

30. Install the accessory drive belt.

31. Install the air cleaner.

32. Connect the hoses at the thermostat housing.

33. Fill the cooling system.

34. Connect the negative battery cable.

35. Run the engine to normal operating temperature and check for leaks.

1993–96 Grand Cherokee

1. Disconnect the negative battery cable.

2. Drain the cooling system.

3. Disconnect the hoses at the thermostat housing.

4. Properly relieve the fuel system pressure.

5. Remove the cylinder head cover.

6. Remove the pushrods, bridges, pivots and rocker arms.

NOTE: The valve train components must be replaced in their original positions.

7. Remove the intake and exhaust manifold from the cylinder head.

8. Disconnect the spark plug wires and remove the spark plugs.

9. Disconnect the temperature sending unit wire, ignition coil and bracket assembly from the engine.

10. Remove the accessory drive belt(s).

11. Unbolt and set aside the power steering pump and bracket. Do not disconnect the hoses.

12. Remove the intake and exhaust manifold assembly.

13. If equipped with A/C, perform the following:

a. Remove the compressor and position it aside with the lines attached.

b. Remove the compressor bracket bolts from the cylinder head.

c. Loosen the through bolt at the bottom of the bracket.

14. Remove the alternator.

15. Remove the cylinder head bolts, the cylinder head and gasket from the block.

NOTE: Bolt No. 14 cannot be removed until the head is moved forward. Pull the bolt out as far as it will go and suspend in place by wrapping with tape.

16. Discard the gasket. Thoroughly clean the head and block mating surfaces. Check them for warpage with a straight-edge. Deviation should not exceed 0.002 in. in a 6 in. span.

To install:

17. Coat a new head gasket with suitable sealing compound and place it on the block. Most replacement gaskets will have the word **TOP** stamped on them.

NOTE: Apply sealing compound only to the cylinder head gasket. Do not allow sealing compound to enter the cylinder bore.

18. Install the cylinder head and bolts. The threads of bolt No. 11 must be coated with Loctite® 592 sealant before installation. Torque the bolts in 3 steps, using the correct sequence:

a. Torque all bolts to 22 ft. lbs. (30 Nm).

b. Torque all bolts to 45 ft. lbs. (61 Nm).

c. Retorque all bolts to 45 ft. lbs. (61 Nm).

d. Torque all bolts, except bolt 11, in sequence to 110 ft. lbs. (150 Nm).

e. Torque bolt 11 to 100 ft. lbs. (136 Nm)

NOTE: Cylinder head bolts should be reused only once. Replace the head bolts which were previously used or are marked with paint. If head bolts are to be reused, mark each head bolt with paint for future reference. Head bolts should be installed using sealer.

19. Install the ignition coil.

20. Install the air conditioning compressor.

21. Install the alternator.

22. Install the intake and exhaust manifold assembly.

23. Install the power steering pump and bracket.

24. Install the accessory drive belt(s).

25. Connect the temperature sending unit wire, ignition coil and bracket.

26. Install the spark plugs and wires.

27. Install the pushrods, rocker arm assembly, gasket and cylinder head cover.

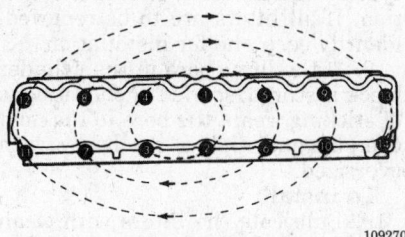

Cylinder head torque sequence — Grand Cherokee

109270

To install:

22. Apply Perfect Sealer No. 5 or equivalent, to the inner corners of the new head gaskets.

23. Position the head gaskets onto the block.

24. Position the cylinder heads onto the cylinder block.

25. Install the cylinder head bolts as follows:

    a. Torque all bolts, in sequence, to 50 ft. lbs. (68 Nm).

    b. Torque all bolts, in sequence, to 105 ft. lbs. (143 Nm).

    c. Repeat Step b to ensure the torque is correct.

26. Install the pushrods and rocker arms to their original positions.

27. Install the intake and exhaust manifolds.

28. Install the spark plugs.

29. Install the coil wires.

30. Connect the heat indicating sending unit wire.

31. Connect the heater and bypass hoses.

32. Install the distributor cap and wires.

28. Connect the hoses at the thermostat housing.

29. Fill the cooling system.

30. Connect the negative battery cable.

31. Run the engine to normal operating temperature and check for leaks.

1993 Grand Wagoneer

1. Disconnect the negative battery cable.

2. Properly relieve the fuel system pressure.

3. Drain the cooling system.

4. Remove the alternator.

5. Disconnect the PCV valve.

6. Disconnect the EVAP fuel lines.

7. Remove the air cleaner and disconnect the fuel lines.

8. Disconnect the accelerator linkage, speed control cable, if equipped, and transmission kickdown cables.

9. Remove the return spring.

10. Remove the distributor cap and wires.

11. Disconnect the coil wires.

12. Disconnect the heat indicator sending unit wire.

13. Disconnect the heater and bypass hoses.

14. Remove the cylinder head covers, discard the gaskets.

15. Remove the intake manifold and throttle body.

16. Remove the exhaust manifolds.

17. Remove the rocker arm assemblies and pushrods.

NOTE: Identify the rocker arms and pushrods for installation purposes.

18. Remove the spark plugs.

19. Remove the cylinder head bolts.

20. Remove the heads and discard the gaskets.

21. Thoroughly clean the gasket mating surfaces.

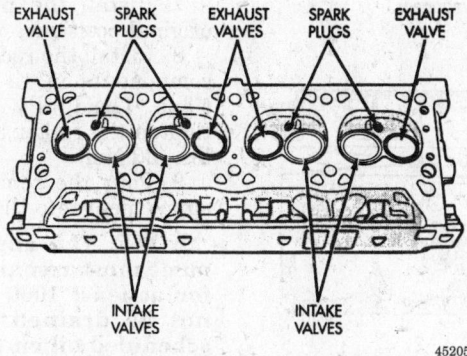

Cylinder head assembly — Grand Wagoneer

45205

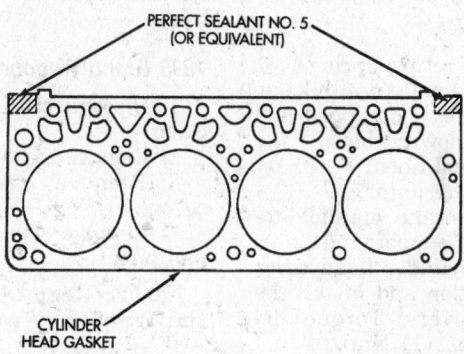

Cylinder head gasket sealant locations — Grand Wagoneer

45206

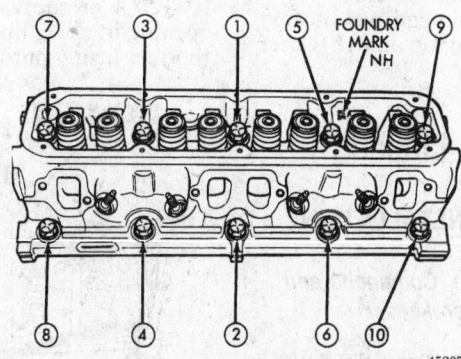

Cylinder head bolt torque sequence — Grand Wagoneer

45207

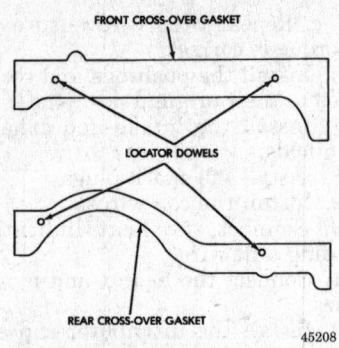

Cross-over gaskets and locator dowels — Grand Wagoneer

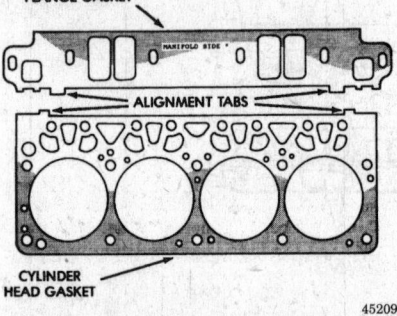

Intake manifold flange gasket alignment — Grand Wagoneer

33. Hook up the return spring.
34. Connect the accelerator linkage, speed control cable, if equipped and transmission kickdown cables.
35. Install the fuel lines.
36. Install the alternator.
37. Install the intake manifold-to-alternator bracket support rod.
38. Place new cylinder head cover gaskets into position and install the cylinder head covers. Torque the bolts to 96 inch lbs. (11 Nm).
39. Install the PCV valve.
40. Connect the EVAP lines.
41. Install the air cleaner.
42. Fill the cooling system.
43. Connect the negative battery cable. Start the engine and check for leaks.

Valve Lifter

REMOVAL AND INSTALLATION

Wrangler, Cherokee, Comanche and 1993–96 Grand Cherokee

1. Disconnect the negative battery cable.
2. Remove the rocker arm cover.
3. Remove the rocker arm assembly by alternately loosening the bolts 1 turn at a time.

4. Remove the pushrods.

NOTE: Keep all components in the order they were removed so they can be reinstalled in their original positions.

5. Remove the lifter through the pushrod opening in the cylinder head using a hydraulic lifter removal tool.
To install:
6. Dip each lifter in MOPAR engine oil supplement or equivalent, and install into the lifter bore. If reusing the old lifters, make sure they are reinstalled in their original bores.
7. Install the pushrods in their original positions.
8. Install the rocker arm assembly components in their original positions. Gradually and alternately tighten the rocker arm bolts to 19 ft. lbs. (26 Nm).
9. Pour the remaining engine oil supplement into the engine.

NOTE: The engine oil supplement must remain in the engine for at least 1000 miles but need not be drained until the next scheduled oil change.

10. Install the rocker arm cover.
11. Connect the negative battery cable.

1993 Grand Wagoneer

1. Disconnect the negative battery cable.
2. Remove the air cleaner.
3. Remove the cylinder head covers.
4. Remove the rocker assembly and pushrods.

NOTE: Keep all components in the order they were removed.

5. Remove the intake manifold.
6. Remove the yoke retainer and aligning yokes.
7. Install valve lifter tool C-4129-A or equivalent, through the opening in the cylinder head and seat the tool firmly onto the valve lifter.

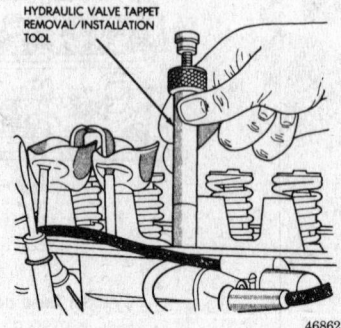

Removing the valve lifter through the pushrod bore

8. Pull the valve lifter out of the cylinder block using a twisting motion. If all lifters are to be removed, identify each one for installation.
9. If the lifter bore in the cylinder block is scored, scuffed or shows signs of sticking, ream the bore to the next oversize and replace the lifters with oversized.
To install:
10. Lubricate the lifters with clean engine oil or suitable assembly lube.
11. Install the valve lifters and pushrods into their original positions. Ensure the oil feed hole in the side of the valve lifter body faces up away from the crankshaft.
12. Install the aligning yokes with the arrow pointing toward the crankshaft.
13. Install the yoke retainer. Torque the bolts to 200 inch lbs. (23 Nm).
14. Install the rocker arms.
15. Install the intake manifold.
16. Install the cylinder head covers with new gaskets.
17. Connect the negative battery cable.
18. Start the engine and allow it to idle until the valve lifters fill with oil and become quiet. Check for leaks.

—— WARNING ——
To prevent valve mechanism damage, do not run the engine above fast idle until all lifters fill with oil and become quiet.

Rocker Arm

REMOVAL AND INSTALLATION

Wrangler, Cherokee, Comanche and 1993–96 Grand Cherokee

1. Disconnect the negative battery cable.
2. Label and disconnect the necessary hoses and vacuum lines from the cylinder head cover.
3. Remove the cylinder head cover retaining bolts and remove the cylinder head cover.
4. Alternately loosen the rocker arm bolts, one turn at a time, to avoid damaging the rocker arm bridge.
5. Remove the rocker arm bolts, bridges, pivots and rocker arms. Keep all parts in order so they can be reinstalled in their original locations.
6. Remove the pushrods. Keep them in order so they can be reinstalled in their original locations.
To install:
7. Clean all parts in solvent and allow to dry. If available, blow out the

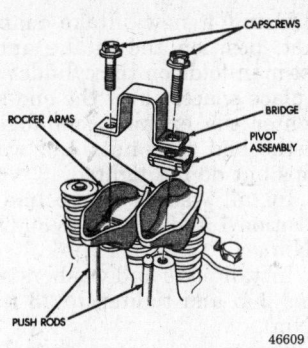

Exploded view of the rocker arm assembly

oil passages in the rocker arms and pushrods with compressed air.

8. Inspect all parts for wear or damage and replace as necessary.

9. Install the pushrods in their original locations.

10. Lubricate the pushrod tips and rocker arm bearing surfaces with clean engine oil.

11. Install the rocker arms, pivots and bridges in their original locations. Loosely install the rocker arm bolts.

12. Tighten the rocker arm bolts alternately and evenly, one turn at a time, to avoid damaging the rocker arm bridges.

13. Tighten the rocker arm bolts to 21 ft. lbs. (28 Nm).

14. Clean the cylinder head cover and cylinder head cover mating surfaces.

NOTE: Some vehicles are equipped with a cylinder head cover containing an integral gasket. This gasket should not be removed. If sections of this gasket material are missing or damaged, the cylinder head cover must be replaced. Sections of this type cover with minor damage may be repaired with liquid gasket material.

15. Install the cylinder head cover using a new gasket or sealant, as required.

16. Connect the hoses and vacuum lines.

17. Connect the negative battery cable.

1993 Grand Wagoneer

1. Disconnect the negative battery cable.

2. Label and disconnect the necessary hoses from the cylinder head cover.

3. If removing the left cylinder head cover, remove the coolant tube bracket.

4. Remove the spark plug wires from the holders and disconnect them from the spark plugs.

5. Remove the cylinder head cover and gasket. The steel backed silicon gasket can be used again if not damaged.

6. Remove the rocker arm bolts and remove the rocker arm pivots and rocker arms. Keep the rocker arm assemblies in order so they can be reinstalled in their original locations.

7. Remove the pushrods, keeping them in order so they can be reinstalled in their original locations.

To install:

8. Rotate the crankshaft until the V8 mark lines up with the TDC mark on the timing chain cover (located 17.5° ATDC from the No. 1 firing mark).

——— WARNING ———

Do not rotate or crank the engine during or immediately after rocker arm installation. Allow about 5 minutes for the hydraulic lifters to bleed down.

9. Install the pushrods in their original locations. Make sure they are seated in the lifters.

10. Lubricate the pushrod tips, rocker arm bearing surfaces and rocker arm pivots with clean engine oil.

11. Install the rocker arm and pivot assemblies in their original locations. Tighten the bolts to 21 ft. lbs. (28 Nm).

12. Install the cylinder head cover and gasket. On the left cover, install the coolant tube bracket. Tighten the cylinder head cover retaining bolts to 96 inch lbs. (11 Nm).

13. Connect the spark plug wires to the spark plugs and install the wires in the holders.

14. Connect all hoses that were disconnected during the removal procedure.

15. Connect the negative battery cable.

Intake Manifold

REMOVAL AND INSTALLATION

1993 Grand Wagoneer

The aluminum intake manifold is a single plane design with equal length runners. The manifold is sealed by flange side gaskets with front and rear cross-over gaskets. The intake manifold has an internal EGR.

1. Disconnect the negative battery cable.

2. Properly relieve the fuel system pressure.

3. Drain the cooling system.

4. Remove the air cleaner.

5. Remove the alternator.

6. Remove the fuel lines and fuel rail.

7. Disconnect the accelerator linkage and, if equipped, the cruise control and transmission kickdown cables.

8. Remove the return spring.

9. Remove the distributor cap and wires.

10. Disconnect the coil wires.

11. Disconnect the heat indicator sending unit wire.

12. Disconnect the heater and bypass hoses.

13. Disconnect the PCV and EVAP lines.

14. If equipped with A/C, remove the compressor and position it aside with the lines attached.

15. Remove the support bracket from the mounting bracket and intake manifold.

16. Remove the intake manifold and discard the gaskets.

17. Remove the throttle body and discard the gasket.

18. Turn the intake manifold upside down and support it. Remove the bolts and lift the plenum pan off the manifold. Discard the gasket.

19. Clean all gasket mating surfaces. Clean the intake manifold with solvent and blow dry with compressed air. The plenum pan rail must be clean, dry and free of all foreign material.

To install:

20. Place a new plenum pan gasket onto the seal rail of the intake manifold.

21. Position the pan over the gasket and align the holes. Hand-tighten the bolts.

22. Torque the bolts as follows:

   a. Torque all bolts, in sequence, to 24 inch lbs. (2.7 Nm).

   b. Torque all bolts, in sequence, to 48 inch lbs. (5.4 Nm).

   c. Torque all bolts, in sequence, to 84 inch lbs. (9.5 Nm).

   d. Repeat Step c to ensure proper torque.

23. Using a new gasket, install the throttle body onto the intake manifold. Tighten the bolts to 200 inch lbs. (23 Nm).

24. Place the 4 plastic locator dowels into the holes in the block.

25. Apply Mopar rubber adhesive sealant or equivalent, to the 4 corner joints.

NOTE: An excessive amount of sealant is not required to ensure a leak proof seal, however, and excessive amount of sealant may reduce the effectiveness of the flange gasket. The sealant should be slightly higher than the cross-over gaskets (approximately 0.2 inch).

26. Install the front and rear crossover gaskets onto the dowels.

27. Install the flange gaskets. Ensure the vertical port alignment tab is resting on the deck face of the block. Also, the horizontal mating alignment tabs must be in position with the mating cylinder head gasket tabs. The words MANIFOLD SIDE should be visible on the center of each flange gasket.

28. Carefully lower the intake manifold into place. Use the alignment dowels in the crossover gaskets to position the manifold. Once in place ensure the gaskets are still in position.

29. Torque the manifold bolts in sequence to the following specifications:

   a. Bolts 1–4 — 72 inch lbs. (8 Nm) in 12 inch lbs. (1.4 Nm) intervals

   b. Bolts 5–12 — 72 inch lbs. (8 Nm)

   c. Repeat Steps a and b to ensure proper torque.

   d. All bolts — 12 ft. lbs. (16 Nm)

   e. Repeat Step d to ensure proper torque.

30. Connect the PCV and EVAP lines.

31. Install the coil wires.

32. Connect the heat indicator sending unit wire.

33. Connect the heater and bypass hoses.

34. Install the distributor cap and wires.

35. Hook up the return spring.

36. Connect the accelerator linkage and, if equipped, cruise control and transmission kick down cables.

37. Install the fuel lines and fuel rail.

38. Install the support bracket.

39. Install the alternator and drive belt.

40. If equipped with A/C, install the compressor.

41. Install the air cleaner.

42. Fill the cooling system.

43. Connect the negative battery cable.

44. Start the engine and check for leaks.

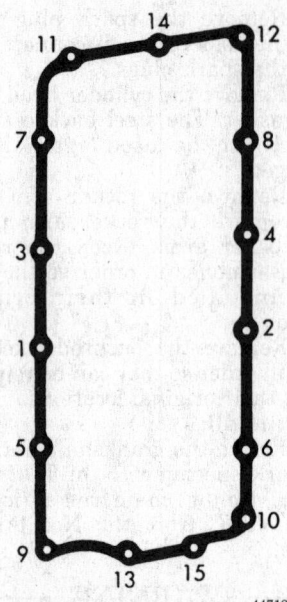

Plenum pan bolt torque sequence — Grand Wagoneer

44712

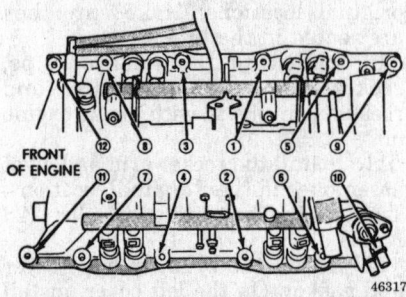

Intake manifold bolt torque sequence — Grand Wagoneer

46317

Exhaust Manifold

REMOVAL AND INSTALLATION

Wrangler, Cherokee and Comanche

1. Disconnect the negative battery cable.

2. Remove the intake manifold.

3. Disconnect the exhaust pipe at the manifold.

4. Remove the fasteners and exhaust manifold.

To install:

5. Clean the intake manifold and cylinder head mating surfaces.

6. Using a new intake manifold gasket, position the intake and exhaust manifolds on the cylinder head and place spacers over the end studs to center the exhaust manifold. Install the end stud nuts and washer clamps but do not tighten.

7. Install washer clamp and bolt at position 1 and tighten to 30 ft. lbs. (41 Nm).

8. Install bolts and washers at positions 2–5 and tighten to 23 ft. lbs. (31 Nm).

9. Tighten end stud nuts (positions 6 and 7) to 23 ft. lbs. (31 Nm).

10. Install all components removed from the intake manifold.

11. Connect the exhaust pipe and tighten the bolts to 23 ft. lbs. (31 Nm).

1993–96 Grand Cherokee and 1993 Grand Wagoneer

1. Disconnect the negative battery cable.

2. Remove the exhaust manifold heat shields.

3. Remove the spark plug wire loom and cables from the mounting stud at the rear of the valve cover and position the cables at the top of the valve cover.

4. Label and disconnect the 2 hoses from the EGR valve.

5. Disconnect the electrical connector and hoses from the EGR transducer.

6. Remove the EGR valve and discard the gasket.

7. Disconnect the oil pressure sending unit electrical connector.

8. Using oil pressure sending unit remover C-4597 or equivalent, remove the sending unit.

9. Loosen the EGR mounting nut from the intake manifold.

10. Remove the mounting bolts and EGR tube. Discard the gasket.

11. Raise and safely support the vehicle.

12. Disconnect the exhaust pipes from the manifolds.

13. Lower the vehicle.

14. Remove the fasteners and exhaust manifold.

To install:

NOTE: If the manifold mounting studs came out with the fasteners, replace the studs.

15. Position the manifold and install the conical washers on the studs.

16. Install new bolt and washer assemblies into the remaining holes. Working from the center outward, torque the fasteners to 20 ft. lbs. (27 Nm).

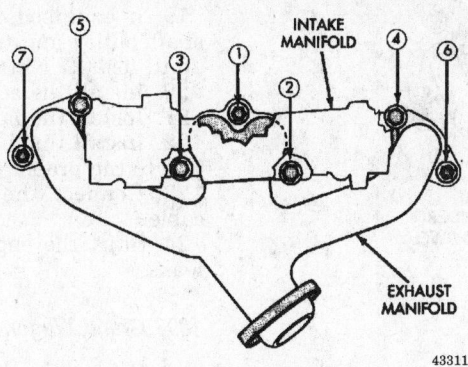

Exhaust manifold mounting bolts — Wrangler, Cherokee and Comanche

17. Raise and support the vehicle safely.

18. Connect the exhaust pipes to the manifolds and torque the fasteners to 23 ft. lbs. (31 Nm).

19. Lower the vehicle.

20. Clean the EGR and tube gasket mating surfaces.

21. Install a new gasket onto the exhaust manifold ends of the EGR tube and install the tube. Tighten the tube nut to the intake manifold and torque the tube-to-exhaust manifold bolts to 204 inch lbs. (14 Nm).

22. Coat the threads of the oil pressure sending unit with sealer taking care not to apply sealant to the opening.Install the sending unit and torque it to 130 inch lbs. (14 Nm) and connect the electrical connector.

23. Install the EGR valve and new gasket to the intake manifold and torque the bolts to 200 inch lbs. (23 Nm).

24. Position the EGR transducer and connect the vacuum lines and electrical connector.

25. Position the spark plug cables and loom into place and connect the cables.

26. Install the exhaust heat shields and torque the bolts to 20 ft. lbs. (27 Nm).

27. Connect the negative battery cable.

Combination Manifold

REMOVAL AND INSTALLATION

4.0L Engine

NOTE: The intake and exhaust manifold are mounted externally on the left side of the engine and are attached to the cylinder head. They are removed as a unit.

1. Disconnect the negative battery cable.

2. Remove the air cleaner assembly.

3. Disconnect the accelerator cable, cruise control cable, if equipped and transmission line pressure cable.

4. Disconnect all electrical connectors on the intake manifold.

5. Disconnect and remove the fuel supply and return lines from the fuel rail assembly.

6. Remove the fuel rail and injectors.

7. Loosen the accessory drive belts.

8. Remove the power steering pump.

9. Disconnect the exhaust pipe from the manifold and discard the seal.

10. Remove the intake and exhaust manifold.

To install:

11. Clean the gasket mating surfaces thoroughly. Install a new gasket over the alignment dowels and position the exhaust manifold to the cylinder head. Install bolt No. 3 finger-tight.

12. Install the intake manifold and the remaining bolts and washers.

13. Tighten bolts, in sequence, to the following torque specifications:
    a. Bolts 1–5 — 23 ft. lbs. (31 Nm)
    b. Bolts 6 and 7 — 17 ft. lbs. (23 Nm)
    c. Bolts 8–11 — 23 ft. lbs. (31 Nm)

14. Install the fuel rail and injectors.

15. Install the power steering pump and tension the accessory belt to specification.

16. Using new O-rings, install the fuel supply and return lines.

17. Connect all electrical connectors, vacuum connectors, throttle cable, cruise control cable and transmission lines pressure cable.

18. Install the air cleaner assembly.

19. Using a new seal, connect the exhaust pipe to the manifold and torque the bolts to 23 ft. lbs. (31 Nm).

20. Connect the negative battery cable.

21. Start the engine and check for leaks.

Timing Chain Front Cover

REMOVAL AND INSTALLATION

Wrangler, Cherokee, Comanche and 1993–96 Grand Cherokee

1. Disconnect the negative battery cable.

2. Remove the drive belt(s), fan and fan shroud. If equipped, remove the accessory drive belt pulley.

3. Remove the vibration damper retaining bolt and washer. Remove the vibration damper using a suitable puller.

4. Remove the accessory drive brackets attached to the timing cover.

5. Remove the A/C compressor, if equipped, and alternator bracket from the cylinder head and move to one side.

6. Remove the oil pan-to-timing case cover bolts and the cover-to-cylinder block bolts.

Right and left exhaust manifolds — Grand Cherokee

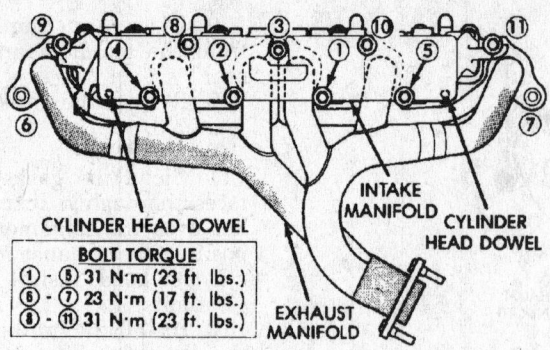

CYLINDER HEAD DOWEL

INTAKE MANIFOLD
CYLINDER HEAD DOWEL

BOLT TORQUE
① - ⑤ 31 N·m (23 ft. lbs.)
⑥ - ⑦ 23 N·m (17 ft. lbs.)
⑧ - ⑪ 31 N·m (23 ft. lbs.)

EXHAUST MANIFOLD

43359

Intake and exhaust manifold mounting bolts — 4.0L engine

7. Remove the timing case cover front seal and gasket from the engine.

NOTE: On 1993–96 Cherokee, make sure the tension spring and thrust pin do not fall out of the camshaft sprocket retaining preload bolt.

8. Cut off the oil pan side gasket end tabs and oil pan front seal tabs flush with the front face of the cylinder block. Remove the gasket tabs.

9. Clean the timing case cover, oil pan and cylinder block gasket surfaces.

10. Remove the crankshaft seal oil seal from the cover by prying it out with a suitable tool.

To install:

11. Install a new seal in the timing cover using a suitable seal installation tool.

12. Apply sealer to both sides of the replacement cover gasket and position the gasket on the cylinder block. Cut the end tabs off the replacement oil pan gasket corresponding to those cut off the original gasket. Attach the end tabs to the oil pan with sealer.

13. Coat the front cover seal end tab recesses generously with sealer and position the seal on the timing cover.

14. Apply engine oil to the seal-oil pan contact surface, then position the cover on the cylinder block.

NOTE: On 1993–96 Cherokee, make sure the tension spring and thrust pin are in place in the preload bolt, before installing the valve cover.

15. Insert timing case cover alignment tool J22248 or equivalent, in the crankshaft opening. Install the cover bolts and tighten the cover-to-cylinder block bolts to 62 inch lbs. (7 Nm); the oil pan-to-cover bolts to 11 ft. lbs. (13 Nm).

16. Remove the cover alignment tool and position a replacement oil

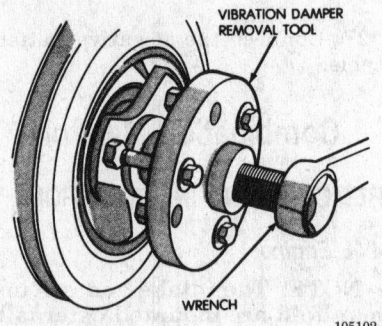

VIBRATION DAMPER REMOVAL TOOL

WRENCH

105102

Vibration damper removal — Wrangler, Cherokee and Comanche

seal on the tool with the seal lip facing outward. Apply a light coat of sealer to the seal and a light coat of oil to the crankshaft. Install the seal on the timing cover.

17. Apply a light film of oil to the vibration damper hub seal contact surface. Install the vibration damper using a suitable installation tool.

NOTE: Do not hammer the damper into place as damage may result to the damper or engine.

18. Install and tighten the crankshaft vibration damper bolt to 80 ft. lbs. (108 Nm).

19. If equipped, install the crankshaft pulley and tighten the bolts to 20 ft. lbs. (27 Nm).

20. Install the accessory brackets.

21. Install the fan and fan shroud.

22. Install the drive belt(s) and adjust to the proper tension.

23. Connect the negative battery cable.

24. Start the engine and check for leaks.

1993 Grand Wagoneer

1. Disconnect the negative battery cable.

2. Properly relieve the fuel system pressure.

3. Drain the cooling system.

4. Remove the serpentine belt.

5. Remove the cooling fan shroud and position it on the engine.

6. Remove the water pump.

7. Remove the power steering pump.

8. Remove the vibration damper using puller C-3688 or equivalent.

9. Disconnect the fuel lines.

10. Loosen the oil pan bolts and remove the front bolt at each side.

11. Remove the timing chain cover bolts. Remove the chain cover and gasket using extreme caution to avoid damaging the oil pan gasket.

To install:

12. Install a new timing chain cover gasket to the chain cover. Apply a small amount of Mopar silicone rubber adhesive sealant or equivalent, at the joint where the chain cover and oil pan gasket meet.

13. Install the timing chain cover taking care not to damage to oil pan. Torque the timing chain cover bolts to 30 ft. lbs. (41 Nm) and oil pan bolts to 215 inch lbs. (24 Nm).

14. Install the vibration damper. Torque the crankshaft bolt to 135 ft. lbs. (183 Nm) and pulley bolt to 200 inch lbs. (23 Nm).

15. Connect the fuel lines.

16. Install the water pump.

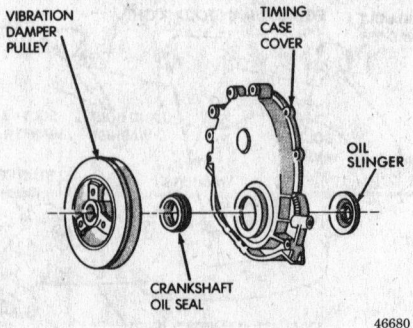

VIBRATION DAMPER PULLEY

TIMING CASE COVER

OIL SLINGER

CRANKSHAFT OIL SEAL

46680

Exploded view of the timing chain cover — Wrangler, Cherokee and Comanche

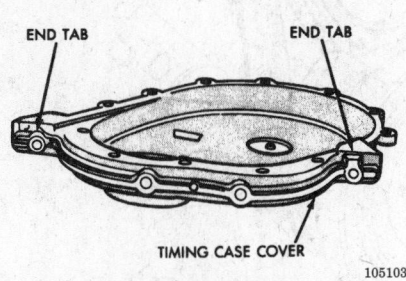

Timing case cover end tabs — Wrangler, Cherokee and Comanche

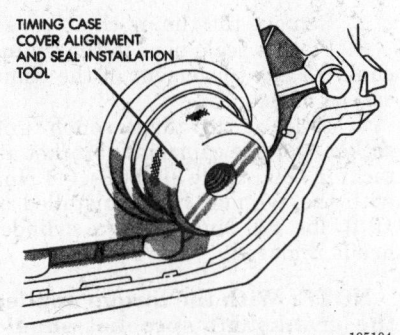

Seal installation — Wrangler, Cherokee and Comanche

17. Install the power steering pump.
18. Install the serpentine belt.
19. Install the cooling fan shroud.
20. Fill the cooling system.
21. Connect the negative battery cable.

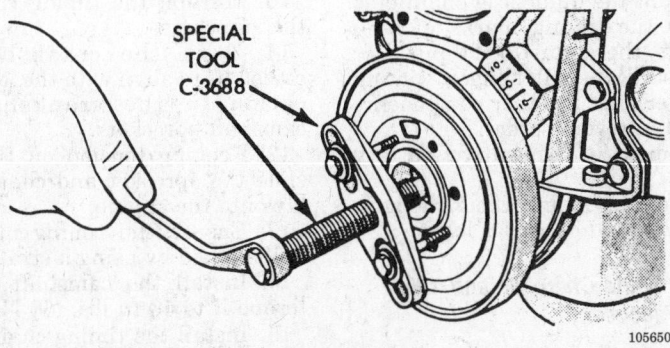

Vibration damper removal

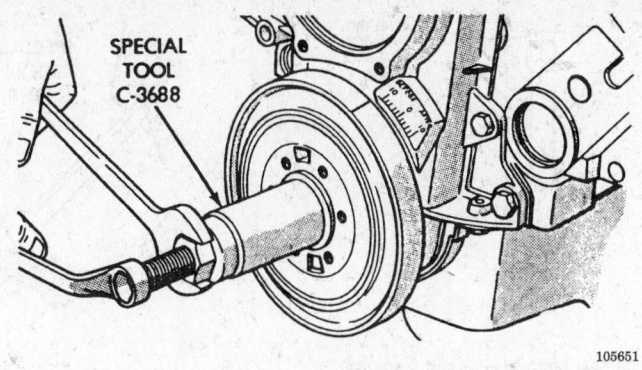

Vibration damper installation

Front Cover Seal

REMOVAL AND INSTALLATION

Wrangler, Cherokee, Comanche and 1993–96 Grand Cherokee

1. Disconnect the negative battery cable.
2. Remove the drive belts and fan shroud, if equipped.
3. If equipped, remove the crankshaft pulley. Remove the vibration damper retaining bolt.
4. Remove the vibration damper using a suitable puller.
5. Using a suitable tool, pry the oil seal from the front cover. Take care not to damage the front cover or crankshaft.
   To install:
6. Position the replacement oil seal on seal installation tool 6139 or equivalent. Install the seal in the cover.
7. Apply a light coat of oil to the seal lip and the vibration damper seal contact surface. Install the vibration damper and tighten the damper bolt to 80 ft. lbs. (108 Nm).

8. Install the crankshaft pulley and torque the bolts to 20 ft. lbs. (27 Nm).
9. Install the drive belts and fan shroud.
10. Connect the negative battery cable.
11. Start the engine and check for leaks.

1993 Grand Wagoneer

1. Disconnect the negative battery cable.
2. Remove the fan shroud retaining bolts and set the shroud back over the engine.
3. Remove the cooling fan.
4. Remove the accessory drive belt and the vibration damper pulley.
5. Remove the vibration damper bolt and washer. Remove the vibration damper using puller tool C-3688 or equivalent.
6. Using a suitable tool, pry the oil seal from the front cover. Take care not to damage the front cover.
   To install:
7. Position the replacement oil seal on seal installation tool 6635 or equivalent. Install the seal in the cover using the tool.
8. Apply a light coat of oil to the vibration damper hub seal contact surface and install the damper using a suitable installation tool. Tighten the damper bolt to 135 ft. lbs. (183 Nm).
9. Install the crankshaft pulley and torque the bolts to 200 inch lbs. (23 Nm).
10. Install the drive belt, fan and fan shroud.
11. Connect the negative battery cable.
12. Start the engine and check for leaks.

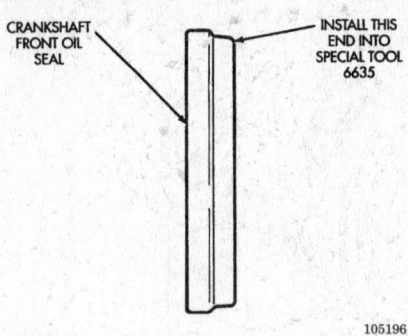

CRANKSHAFT FRONT OIL SEAL

INSTALL THIS END INTO SPECIAL TOOL 6635

105196

Front cover oil seal removal — Grand Wagoneer 1992–96

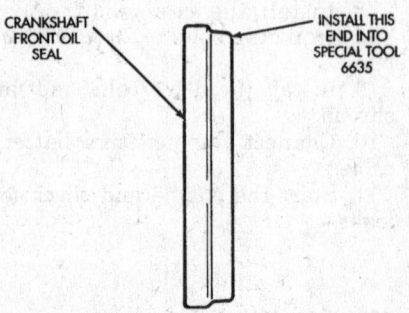

CRANKSHAFT FRONT OIL SEAL

INSTALL THIS END INTO SPECIAL TOOL 6635

105196

Position the seal on the installation tool — Grand Wagoneer 1992–96

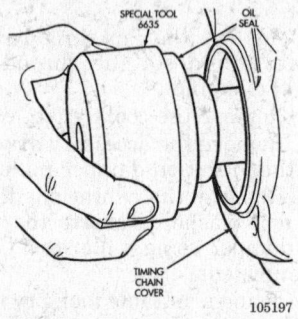

SPECIAL TOOL 6635

OIL SEAL

TIMING CHAIN COVER

105197

Install the tool and seal on the crankshaft — Grand Wagoneer 1992–96

Timing Chain and Sprockets

REMOVAL AND INSTALLATION

Wrangler, Cherokee and Comanche

1. Disconnect the negative battery cable.
2. Remove the drive belt(s), fan and fan shroud.
3. If equipped, remove the crankshaft pulley. Remove the vibration damper retaining bolt and washer.

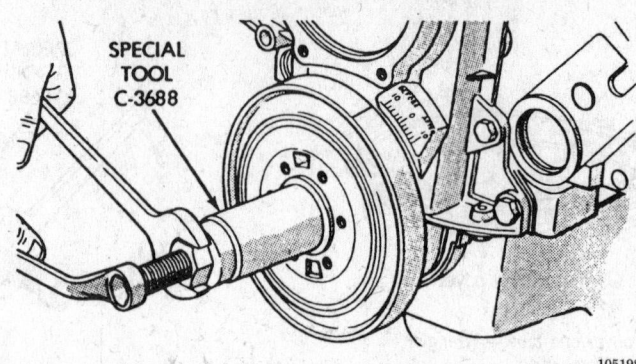

SPECIAL TOOL C-3688

105198

Vibration damper installation — Grand Wagoneer 1992–96

4. Using a puller, remove the vibration damper.
5. Remove the timing case cover.
6. Rotate the crankshaft until the **0** timing mark on the crankshaft sprocket is closest to and on a center line with the timing mark on the camshaft sprocket.
7. Remove the oil slinger from the crankshaft.
8. Remove the camshaft retaining bolt and remove the sprockets and chain as an assembly. If the timing chain tensioner is to be replaced, the oil pan must be removed.
To install:
9. Turn the timing chain tensioner lever to the unlock (down) position. Pull the tensioner block toward the tensioner lever to compress the spring. Hold the block and turn the tensioner lever to the lock (up) position.
10. Install the sprockets and timing chain. Ensure the timing marks on the sprockets are properly aligned.
11. Install the camshaft sprocket retaining bolt and washer and tighten to 80 ft. lbs. (108 Nm).
12. To verify correct alignment, turn the crankshaft to position the camshaft sprocket timing mark at the 1 o'clock position. This positions the crankshaft sprocket timing mark where the adjacent tooth meshes with the chain at the 3 o'clock position. Count the number of chain pins between the timing marks of both sprockets; there must be 20 pins.
13. Install the oil slinger, timing case cover and all other components removed in reverse order.
14. Connect the negative battery cable.
15. Start the engine, check the ignition timing and check for leaks.

1993–96 Grand Cherokee and 1993 Grand Wagoneer

1. Disconnect the negative battery cable.

2. Remove the timing chain cover.
3. Place a scale next to the timing chain so any movement of the chain can be measured.
4. Place a torque wrench and socket over the camshaft sprocket attaching bolt. Apply 30 ft. lbs. (41 Nm) with the cylinder heads installed or 15 ft. lbs. (20 Nm) with the cylinder heads removed.

NOTE: With the torque applied the crankshaft sprocket should not be permitted to move, but it may be necessary to block the crankshaft to prevent rotation.

5. Hold the scale with the dimension reading even with the edge of a chain link. Apply 30 ft. lbs. (41 Nm) with the cylinder heads installed or 15 ft. lbs. (20 Nm) with the cylinder heads removed, in the reverse direction. Note the amount of chain movement.
6. Install a new timing chain if the movement exceeds $1/8$ inch (3.175mm).
7. Remove the camshaft sprocket retaining bolt.
8. Remove the timing chain and sprockets.
To install:
9. Position the camshaft and crankshaft sprockets on a bench with the timing marks facing each other.
10. Position the timing chain onto the sprockets.
11. Turn the crankshaft and camshaft to align with the keyway location in the crankshaft and camshaft sprockets.
12. Keeping tension on the chain, slide the sprocket and chain assembly onto the engine.
13. Ensure the timing marks are still aligned by using a straight edge.
14. Install the camshaft bolt and torque it to 50 ft. lbs. (68 Nm).
15. Install the timing chain cover.
16. Connect the negative battery cable.

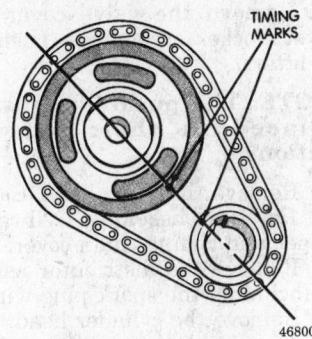

Crankshaft-to-camshaft sprocket alignment — Wrangler, Cherokee and Comanche

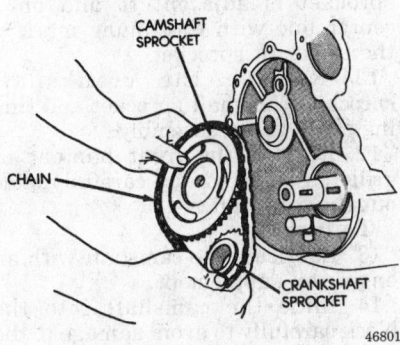

Removing the timing chain and sprockets — Wrangler, Cherokee and Comanche

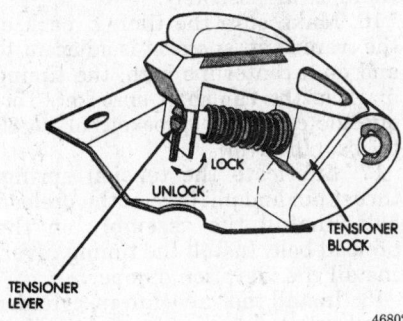

Loading the timing chain tensioner — Wrangler, Cherokee and Comanche

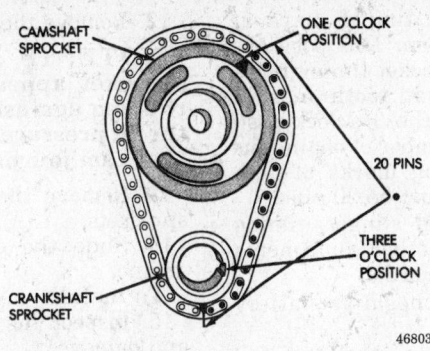

Properly installed timing chain and sprockets — Wrangler, Cherokee and Comanche

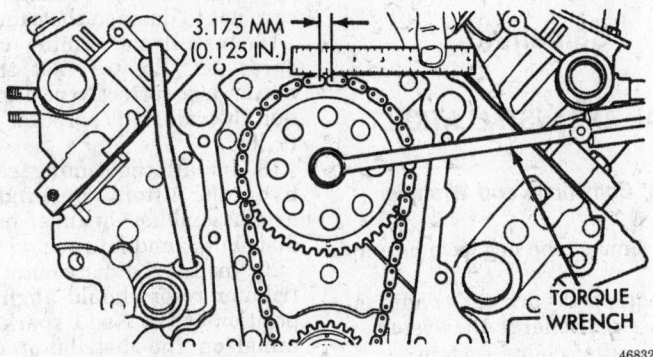

Measuring the timing chain wear — Grand Wagoneer

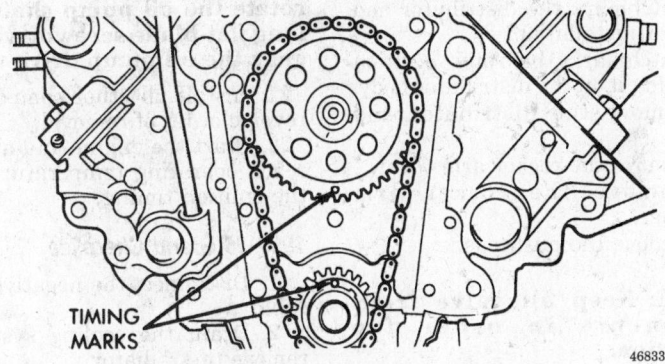

Aligning the sprocket timing marks — Grand Wagoneer

Timing Chain Tensioner

REMOVAL AND INSTALLATION

Wrangler, Cherokee and Comanche

1. Disconnect the negative battery cable.

2. Remove the drive belt(s), fan and fan shroud.

3. If equipped, remove the crankshaft pulley. Remove the vibration damper retaining bolt and washer.

4. Using a puller, remove the vibration damper.

5. Remove the timing case cover.

6. Rotate the crankshaft until the O timing mark on the crankshaft sprocket is closest to and on a center line with the timing mark on the camshaft sprocket.

7. Remove the oil slinger from the crankshaft.

8. Remove the camshaft retaining bolt and remove the sprockets and chain as an assembly. If the timing chain tensioner is to be replaced, the oil pan must be removed.

To install:

9. Turn the timing chain tensioner lever to the unlock (down) position. Pull the tensioner block toward the tensioner lever to compress the spring. Hold the block and turn the tensioner lever to the lock (up) position.

10. Install the sprockets and timing chain. Ensure the timing marks on the sprockets are properly aligned.

11. Install the camshaft sprocket retaining bolt and washer and tighten to 80 ft. lbs. (108 Nm).

12. To verify correct alignment, turn the crankshaft to position the

camshaft sprocket timing mark at the 1 o'clock position. This positions the crankshaft sprocket timing mark where the adjacent tooth meshes with the chain at the 3 o'clock position. Count the number of chain pins between the timing marks of both sprockets; there must be 20 pins.

13. Install the oil slinger, timing case cover and all other components removed in reverse order.

14. Connect the negative battery cable.

15. Start the engine, check the ignition timing and check for leaks.

Camshaft

REMOVAL AND INSTALLATION

Cherokee, Comanche and Wrangler

1. Disconnect the negative battery cable.

2. If equipped with air conditioning, properly discharge the system.

3. Drain the cooling system.

4. Remove the radiator and air conditioning condenser, if equipped.

5. Matchmark the distributor and engine for installation.

6. Matchmark the rotor position by marking it on the distributor body.

7. Remove the distributor and wires.

8. Remove the rocker arm cover.

9. Remove the rocker arm assemblies.

10. Remove the pushrods.

NOTE: Keep all valve train components in order for installation.

11. Using tool J–21884 or equivalent, remove the hydraulic lifters.

12. Remove the timing case cover.

NOTE: If the camshaft sprocket appears to have been rubbing against the cover, check the oil pressure relief holes in the rear cam journal for debris.

13. Remove the timing chain and sprockets.

14. Slide the camshaft from the engine.

To install:

15. Inspect the camshaft for wear and damage.

16. Lubricate all moving components with engine oil.

17. Install the camshaft, taking care not to damage the cam bearings.

18. Install the timing chain and sprockets. Ensure that the timing marks are correctly positioned. Torque the camshaft sprocket bolt to 50 ft. lbs.

19. Install the timing case cover, hydraulic lifters, pushrods, rocker arm assemblies, cylinder head cover, distributor and ignition wires.

20. Install the distributor. The distributor rotor should align with the position of the No. 1 spark plug terminal on the distributor cap when the distributor shaft is down in place.

NOTE: It may be necessary to rotate the oil pump shaft with a long flat-blade screwdriver to engage the oil pump drive tang.

21. Install all other components in reverse order of removal.

22. Start the engine and allow it to reach operating temperature. Check the ignition timing.

1993–96 Grand Cherokee

1. Disconnect the negative battery cable.

2. Drain the cooling system and remove the radiator.

3. Properly relieve the fuel system pressure.

4. Remove the condenser and receiver/drier as a charged unit.

5. Remove the valve cover and gasket, rocker assemblies, pushrods and lifters.

NOTE: The pushrods must be replaced in their original locations.

6. Remove the drive belts, cooling fan, fan hub assembly, vibration damper and timing chain cover.

7. Remove the distributor assembly, including the spark plug wires.

8. Remove the cylinder head.

9. Remove the valve lifters. Keep them in order for installation.

10. Rotate the crankshaft until the timing mark of the crankshaft sprocket is adjacent to and on a center line with the timing mark of the camshaft sprocket.

11. Remove the crankshaft sprocket, camshaft sprocket and timing chain as an assembly.

12. Remove the front bumper or grille as required and carefully slide out the camshaft.

To install:

13. Lubricate the camshaft with an engine oil supplement.

14. Slide the camshaft into the block carefully to avoid damage to the bearings.

15. Install the crankshaft sprocket, camshaft sprocket and the timing chain as an assembly.

16. Make sure the timing mark of the crankshaft sprocket is adjacent to and on a centerline with, the timing mark of the camshaft sprocket. Torque the camshaft sprocket bolt to 80 ft. lbs. (109 Nm).

17. Lubricate the tension spring, thrust pin and pin bore in the preload bolt. Install the assembly on the preload bolt. Install the timing cover. Install the vibration damper.

18. Install the valve lifters, cylinder head, pushrods, rocker assemblies, valve cover and gasket.

19. Install the distributor assembly. The rotor should be aligned with the No. 1 cylinder spark plug termi-

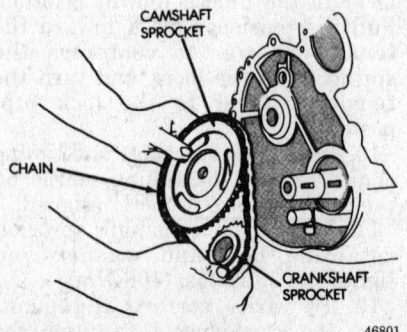

Removing the timing chain and sprockets — Wrangler, Cherokee and Comanche

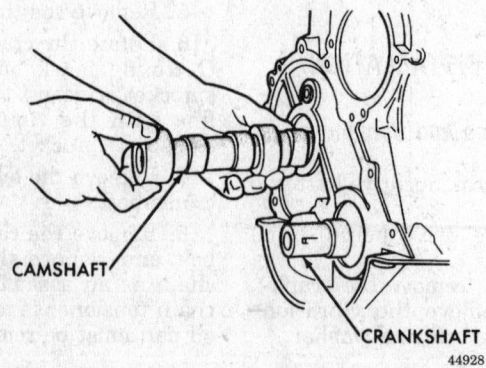

Camshaft removal — Wrangler, Cherokee and Comanche

nal on the cap when the distributor is fully seated on the cylinder block.

20. Install the condenser and receiver/drier as a charged unit.

21. Install the radiator and fill the cooling system.

22. Connect the negative battery cable.

23. Start the engine and allow it to reach operating temperature.

24. Check the ignition timing.

1993 Grand Wagoneer

1. Disconnect the negative battery cable.

2. Remove the engine from the vehicle and mount on a suitable workstand.

3. Remove the intake manifold.

4. Remove the valve covers.

5. Remove the timing case cover and timing chain.

6. Remove the rocker arms.

7. Remove the pushrods and valve lifters.

8. Remove the distributor and lift out the oil pump and distributor driveshaft.

9. Remove the camshaft thrust plate and note the location of the oil tab.

10. Install a long bolt into the camshaft to facilitate the removal of the camshaft.

11. Remove the camshaft, being careful not to damage the cam bearings with the cam lobes.

To install:

12. Lubricate the camshaft lobes and bearings with engine oil and insert the camshaft to within 2 inches (51mm) of its final position in the cylinder block.

13. Install camshaft gear installer tool C-3509 or equivalent, with the tool secured in the distributor drive gear position. Hold the tool in position with a distributor lockplate bolt.

NOTE: The tool will restrict the camshaft from being pushed in too far and prevent knocking out the plug in the rear of the cylinder block. The tool should remain installed until the camshaft and crankshaft sprockets with the chain are installed.

14. Install the camshaft thrust plate and chain oil tab. Ensure the tang enter the lower right hole in the thrust plate and torque the bolts to 210 inch lbs. (24 Nm). The top edge of the tab should be flat against the thrust plate in order to catch oil for chain lubrication.

15. Install the timing chain and sprockets.

16. Remove installer tool C-3509.

17. Ensure the camshaft end-play is 0.002–0.010 inch (0.051–0.76mm); if not, install a new thrust plate.

18. Install the driveshaft and distributor.

19. Install the lifters and pushrods.

20. Install the rocker arms.

21. Install the valve covers with new gaskets.

22. Install the intake manifold.

23. Install the engine.

24. Connect the negative battery cable.

Piston and Connecting Rod

POSITIONING

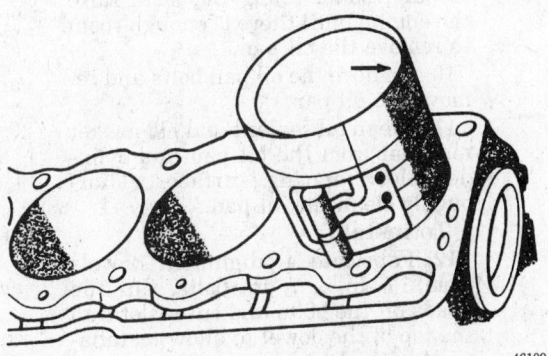

46109

Connecting rod and piston installation

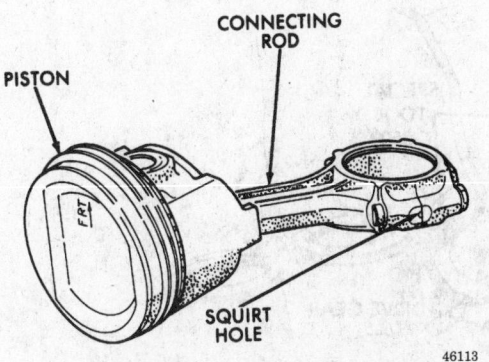

CONNECTING ROD

PISTON

F.RT

SQUIRT HOLE

46113

Correct piston and rod alignment

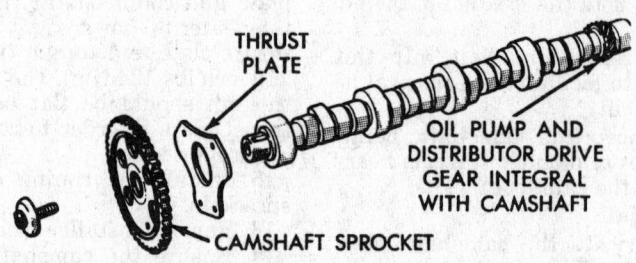

Exploded view of the camshaft and sprocket — Grand Wagoneer

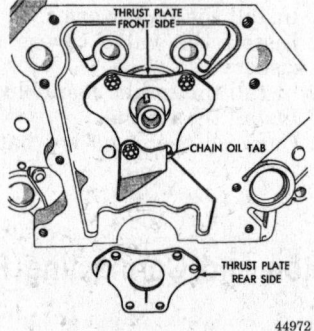

Timing chain oil tab installation — Grand Wagoneer

ENGINE LUBRICATION

Oil Pan

REMOVAL AND INSTALLATION

Comanche, 1992–96 Wrangler and Cherokee

1. Disconnect the negative battery cable.

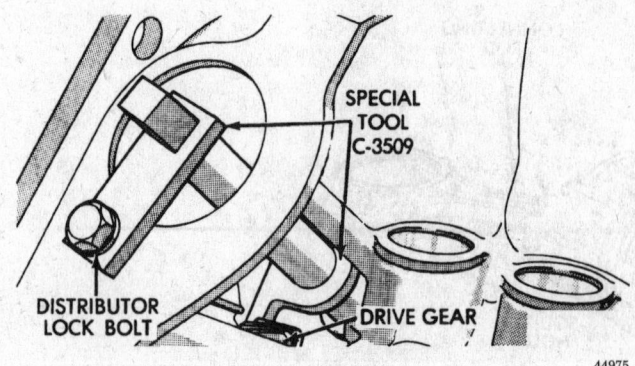

Camshaft holding tool

2. Raise and support the vehicle safely.

3. Drain the engine oil.

4. Disconnect the exhaust pipe at the manifold.

5. Disconnect the exhaust hanger at the catalytic converter and lower the pipe.

6. Remove the starter.

7. Remove the bellhousing access cover.

8. Position a jackstand directly under the vibration damper. Place a piece of wood between the jack and the vibration damper.

9. Remove the engine mount through bolts. Using the jack, raise the engine until there is enough room to remove the oil pan.

10. Remove the oil pan bolts and remove the oil pan.

11. Clean all sealant and old gasket material from the oil pan and cylinder block mating surfaces. Thoroughly clean the oil pan.

To install:

12. Fabricate 4 alignment dowels from 1½ in. x ¼ in. bolts. Cut the heads off the bolts and cut a slot into the top of the dowel to allow installation/removal with a screwdriver.

13. Install 2 dowels in the timing case cover and the other 2 in the cylinder block. Slide the one-piece gas-ket over the dowels and onto the block and timing case cover.

14. Position the oil pan over the dowels and onto the gasket. Install the ¼ in. pan bolts and tighten to 120 inch lbs. (14 Nm). Install the 5/16 in. pan bolts and tighten to 156 inch lbs. (18 Nm).

15. Remove the dowels and install the remaining ¼ in. pan bolts. Tighten to 120 inch lbs. (14 Nm).

16. Lower the engine and install the engine mount through bolts and nuts. Lower the jack and remove the piece of wood.

17. Install the bellhousing access cover.

18. Install the starter.

19. Connect the exhaust pipe to the hanger and the exhaust manifold.

20. Install the oil pan drain plug and tighten to 25 ft. lbs. (34 Nm).

21. Lower the vehicle.

22. Fill the crankcase to the proper level with the recommended oil.

23. Connect the negative battery cable. Start the engine and check for leaks.

1993–96 Grand Cherokee and 1993 Grand Wagoneer

1. Disconnect the negative battery cable.

2. Raise and safely support the vehicle.

3. Remove the oil pan drain plug and drain the engine oil.

4. Remove the oil filter.

5. Remove the starter.

6. If equipped, disconnect the oil level sensor.

7. Position the oil cooler lines out of the way.

8. Disconnect the oxygen sensor and remove the exhaust pipe.

9. Remove the oil pan bolts and carefully slide the oil pan to the rear. If equipped, be careful not to damage the oil level sensor.

10. Clean all sealant and old gasket material from the oil pan and cylinder block mating surfaces. Thoroughly clean the oil pan.

To install:

11. Fabricate 4 alignment dowels from 1½ x 5/16 in. bolts. Cut the heads off the bolts and cut a slot in the dowel to allow installation/removal with a screwdriver.

12. Install the dowels in the cylinder block. Apply a small amount of silicone sealant in the corner of the cap and cylinder block.

13. Slide the one-piece gasket over the dowels and onto the block. Position the oil pan over the dowels and onto the gasket. If equipped, be careful not to damage the oil level sensor.

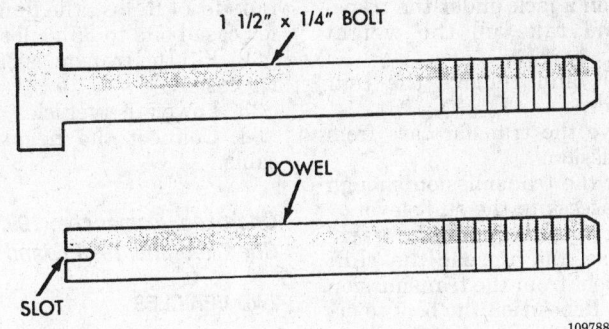

Fabricate alignment dowels from 1/4 in. bolts — Wrangler, Cherokee and Comanche

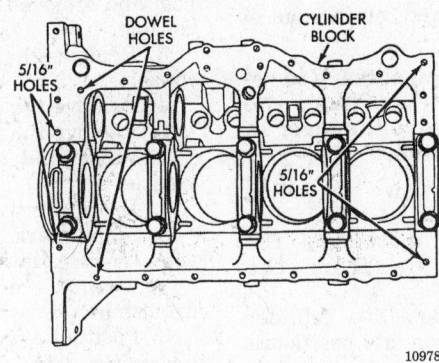

Position of dowels in cylinder block — Wrangler, Cherokee and Comanche

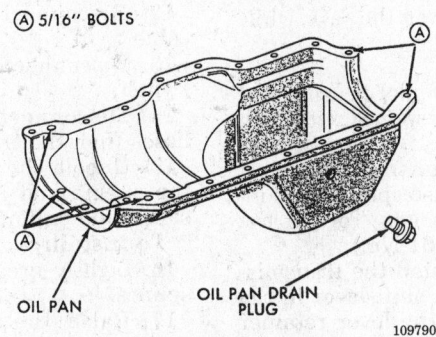

Install 5/16 in. oil pan bolts at position "A" — Wrangler, Cherokee and Comanche

14. Install the oil pan bolts and tighten to 215 inch lbs. (24 Nm). Remove the dowels and install the remaining bolts. Tighten to 215 inch lbs. (24 Nm).

15. Install the drain plug and tighten to 25 ft. lbs. (34 Nm).

16. Install the exhaust pipe and connect the oxygen sensor.

17. Install the oil filter. If equipped, connect the oil level sensor.

18. Install the starter. Move the oil cooler lines back into position.

19. Lower the vehicle and connect the negative battery cable.

20. Fill the engine with the proper type and quantity of oil. Start the engine and check for leaks.

Oil Pump

REMOVAL AND INSTALLATION

Wrangler, Cherokee, Comanche and 1993–96 Grand Cherokee

1. Disconnect the negative battery cable. Raise and safely support the vehicle.

2. Drain the engine oil and remove the oil pan.

3. Unbolt and remove the pump assembly from the block. Discard the gasket.

—— WARNING ——
If the oil pump is not to be serviced, do not disturb the position of the oil inlet tube and strainer assembly in the pump body. If the tube is moved within the pump body, a replacement tube and strainer assembly must be installed to assure an airtight seal.

To install:

4. If a new pump is being installed, prime the pump by submerging the strainer in clean engine oil and turning the pump gears until oil emerges from the pump feed hole.

5. Using a new gasket, install the pump on the cylinder block. Torque the short bolt to 10 ft. lbs. and the long bolt to 17 ft. lbs.

6. Install the oil pan and lower the vehicle.

7. Fill the engine with the proper type and quantity of oil.

8. Connect the negative battery cable. Start the engine and check for proper oil pressure.

1993 Grand Wagoneer

1. Disconnect the negative battery cable.

2. Raise and safely support the vehicle.

3. Drain the engine oil and remove the oil pan.

4. Unbolt and remove the pump assembly from the rear main bearing cap.

To install:

5. If a new pump is being installed, prime the pump by submerging the pickup in clean engine oil and turning the pump gears until oil emerges from the pump feed hole.

6. Install the oil pump. During installation, slowly rotate the pump body to ensure driveshaft-to-pump rotor shaft engagement.

7. Hold the oil pump base flush against the mating surface of the rear main bearing cap and finger tighten the pump mounting bolts. Tighten the mounting bolts to 30 ft. lbs. (41 Nm).

8. Install the oil pan and lower the vehicle. Fill the engine with the proper type and quantity of oil.

9. Connect the negative battery cable. Start the engine and check for proper oil pressure.

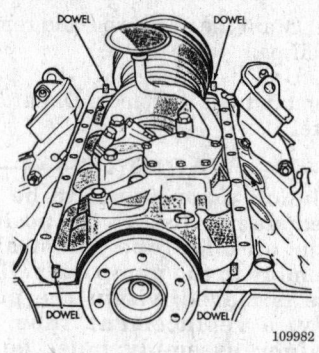

Position of dowels in cylinder block — Grand Cherokee

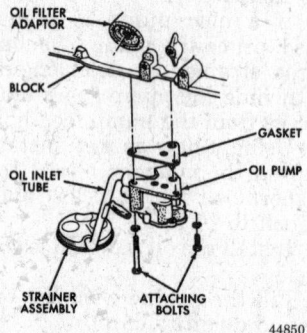

Oil pump installation — Grand Cherokee

MANUAL TRANSMISSION

Transmission Assembly

REMOVAL AND INSTALLATION

Wrangler

1. Disconnect the negative battery cable.
2. Raise and safely support the vehicle.
3. Remove the skid plate.
4. Drain the transmission and transfer case.
5. Matchmark the front and rear driveshaft and yoke for installation alignment.
6. Unbolt and remove the driveshafts.
7. Disconnect the transfer case shift linkage from the shift lever or range lever.
8. Disconnect the electrical connectors and vent hose from the transmission and differential.

9. Position a jack under the transmission and take up the weight slightly.
10. Unbolt and remove the rear crossmember.
11. Remove the transfer case from the transmission.
12. Lower the transmission enough to provide access to the shift lever.
13. Reach up and around the transmission case and unseat the shift lever dust boot from the transmission shift tower. Reposition the boot to access the lever retainer.
14. Press the shift lever retainer downward and turn it clockwise to release it.
15. Lift the lever and retainer out of the shift tower.

NOTE: It is not necessary to remove the shift lever from the floor pan boot. Leave the lever in place for installation.

16. If equipped, remove the engine timing sensor.
17. If equipped, disconnect the speedometer cable from the transmission.
18. Disconnect the slave cylinder from the transmission and position it aside.
19. Secure the transmission to the jack.
20. Unbolt the transmission from the engine and lower the jack while pulling back.

To install:
21. Lubricate the pilot bearing and transmission input splines with high temperature grease.
22. Align the transmission input shaft and clutch disc splines and install the transmission. Torque the bolts to 45 ft. lbs. (61 Nm).
23. Reach up around the transmission and insert the shift lever in the shift tower. Press the lever retainer downward and turn it clockwise to lock it in place. Install the dust lever on the dust boot.
24. Install the transfer case and torque the bolts to 26 ft. lbs. (35 Nm).
25. Install the crossmember. Torque the bolts to 26–33 ft. lbs. (37–45 Nm).
26. Install the slave cylinder to the transmission housing.
27. If equipped, install the engine timing sensor.
28. If equipped, connect the speedometer cable.
29. Connect the electrical connectors and vent hose to the transmission and transfer case.
30. Connect the transfer case shift rod to the lever.
31. Install the driveshafts using new strap bolts. Torque the strap bolt

nuts to 14 ft. lbs.; the flange-to-transfer case bolts to 35 ft. lbs.
32. Fill the transmission and transfer case.
33. Lower the vehicle.
34. Connect the negative battery cable.

Cherokee, Comanche, 1993–96 Grand Cherokee and 1993 Grand Wagoneer

2WD VEHICLES

1. Disconnect the negative battery cable.
2. Raise the outer gearshift lever boot and remove the upper part of the console.
3. Remove the lower part of the console.
4. Remove the inner boot.
5. Remove the gearshift lever.
6. Raise and safely support the vehicle.
7. Drain the transmission oil.
8. Matchmark the driveshaft and yoke for installation alignment.
9. Unbolt and remove the driveshaft.
10. Position a jack under the transmission and take the weight off the transmission slightly.
11. Unbolt and remove the rear crossmember.
12. Disconnect the speedometer cable.
13. Disconnect the backup light switch.
14. Disconnect all linkage and hoses from the transmission.
15. Unbolt the transmission from the engine and lower the transmission while pulling it back.

To install:
16. Lightly grease the input shaft splines.
17. Raise the transmission into position.
18. Roll the transmission forward and engage the input shaft and clutch disc spline. Wiggle the output shaft yoke to get the splines to mesh. Once the splines mesh, push the transmission forward all the way and align the bell housing-to-engine bolt holes. Install the attaching bolts and torque them to 28 ft. lbs. (38 Nm).
19. Connect all linkage and hoses at the transmission.
20. Connect the backup light switch.
21. Connect the speedometer cable.
22. Install the rear crossmember. Torque the crossmember attaching bolt to 30 ft. lbs. (41 Nm); the transmission to crossmember bolts to 33 ft. lbs. (45 Nm)
23. Remove the transmission jack.

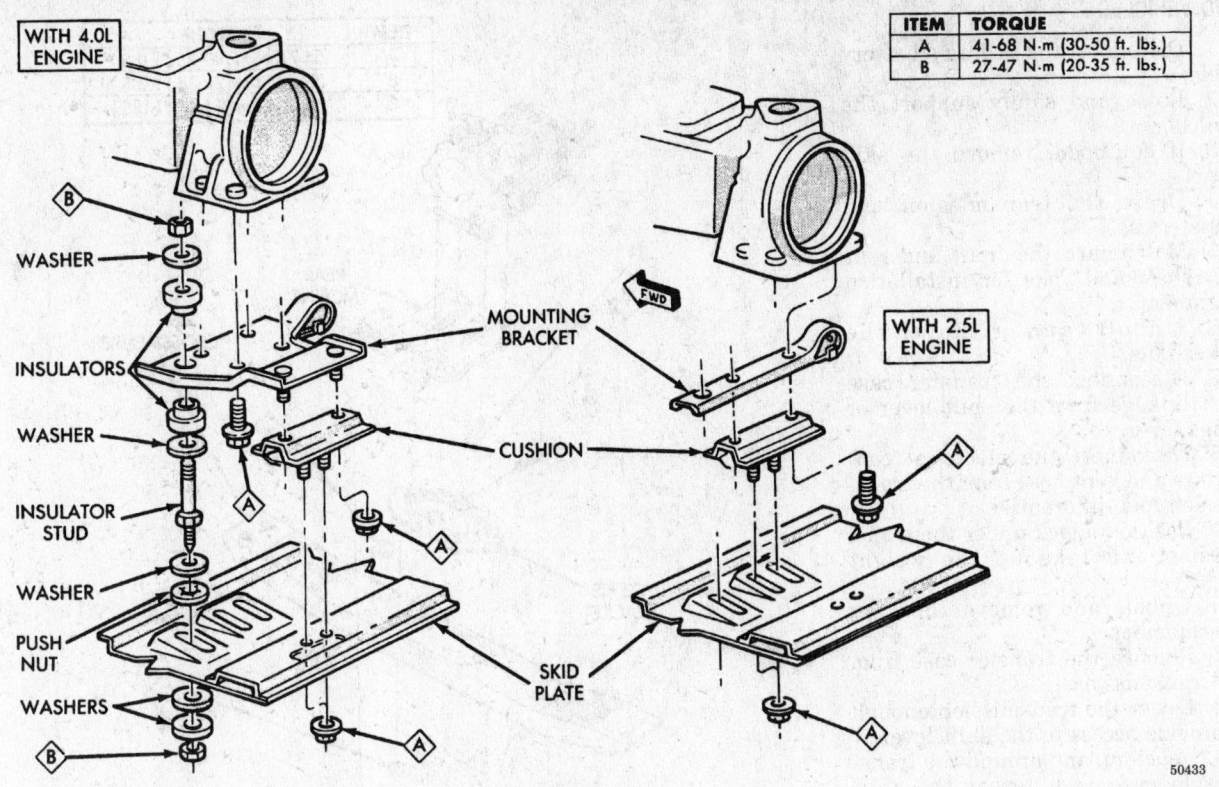

ITEM	TORQUE
A	41-68 N·m (30-50 ft. lbs.)
B	27-47 N·m (20-35 ft. lbs.)

WITH 4.0L ENGINE

WASHER

INSULATORS

WASHER

INSULATOR STUD

WASHER

PUSH NUT

WASHERS

MOUNTING BRACKET

WITH 2.5L ENGINE

CUSHION

SKID PLATE

FWD

50433

Rear transmission mounting — Wrangler

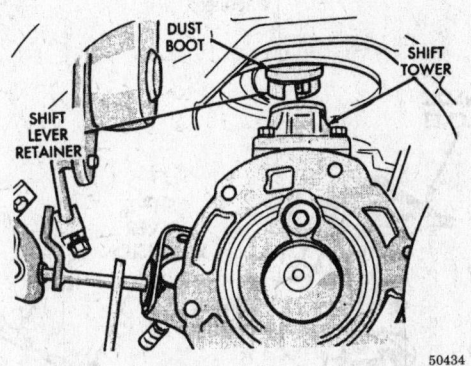

DUST BOOT

SHIFT TOWER

SHIFT LEVER RETAINER

50434

Removing and installing the shift lever — Wrangler

24. Install the driveshaft. New strap bolts should be used whenever the driveshaft is disconnected. Torque the nuts to 14 ft. lbs. (19 Nm).

25. Fill the transmission to the correct level with transmission oil.

26. Lower the vehicle.

27. Install the gearshift lever and install the inner boot.

28. Install the lower part of the console.

29. Install the upper part of the console.

30. Connect the negative battery cable.

MARK BOTH YOKES FOR ALIGNMENT AT INSTALLATION

50435

Matchmarking the propeller shafts — Wrangler

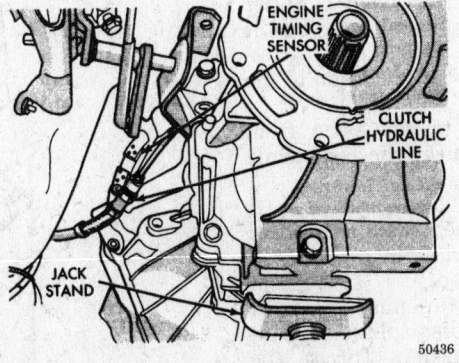

ENGINE TIMING SENSOR

CLUTCH HYDRAULIC LINE

JACK STAND

50436

Hydraulic line and timing sensor location — Wrangler

4WD VEHICLES

1. Disconnect the negative battery cable.
2. Raise and safely support the vehicle.
3. If equipped, remove the skid plate.
4. Drain the transmission and transfer case.
5. Matchmark the front and rear driveshaft and yoke for installation alignment.
6. Unbolt and remove the driveshafts.
7. Disconnect the transfer case shift linkage from the shift lever or range lever.
8. Disconnect the electrical connectors and vent hose from the transmission and differential.
9. Position a jack under the transmission and take up the weight slightly.
10. Unbolt and remove the rear crossmember.
11. Remove the transfer case from the transmission.
12. Lower the transmission enough to provide access to the shift lever.
13. Reach up and around the transmission case and unseat the shift lever dust boot from the transmission shift tower. Reposition the boot to access the lever retainer.
14. Press the shift lever retainer downward and turn it clockwise to release it.
15. Lift the lever and retainer out of the shift tower.

NOTE: It is not necessary to remove the shift lever from the floor pan boot. Leave the lever in place for installation.

16. If equipped, remove the engine timing sensor.
17. If equipped, disconnect the speedometer cable fro the transmission.
18. Disconnect the slave cylinder from the transmission and position it aside.
19. Support the transmission to the jack.
20. Unbolt the transmission from the engine and lower the jack while pulling back.

To install:

21. Lubricate the pilot bearing and transmission input splines with high temperature grease.
22. Align the transmission input shaft and clutch disc splines and install the transmission. Torque the bolts to 45 ft. lbs. (61 Nm).
23. Reach up around the transmission and insert the shift lever in the shift tower. Press the lever retainer

ITEM	TORQUE
A	54-75 N·m (40-55 FT.LBS.)
B	33-49 N·m (24-36 FT.LBS.)
C	33-60 N·m (24-44 FT.LBS.)

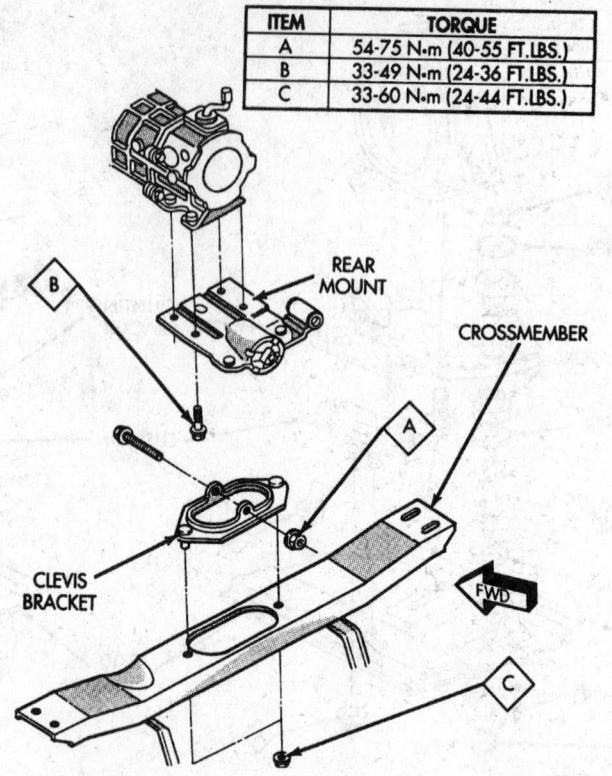

Rear transmission mounting — Grand Cherokee and Grand Wagoneer

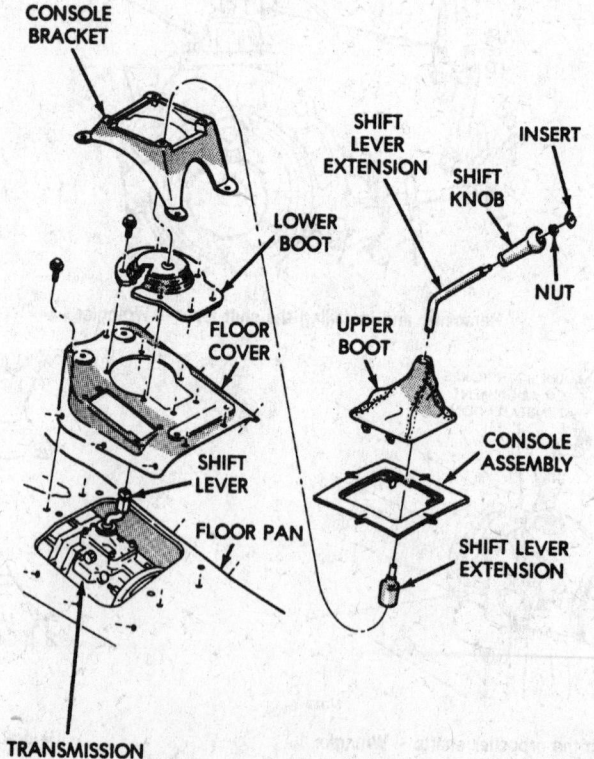

Shift lever attachment — Grand Cherokee and Grand Wagoneer

downward and turn it clockwise to lock it in place. Install the dust lever on the dust boot.

24. Install the transfer case and torque the bolts to 26 ft. lbs. (35 Nm).

25. Install the crossmember. Torque the bolts to 26–33 ft. lbs. (37–45 Nm).

26. Install the slave cylinder to the transmission housing.

27. If equipped, install the engine timing sensor.

28. If equipped, connect the speedometer cable.

29. Connect the electrical connectors and vent hose to the transmission and transfer case.

30. Connect the transfer case shift rod to the lever.

31. Install the driveshafts using new strap bolts. Torque the strap bolt nuts to 14 ft. lbs.; the flange-to-transfer case bolts to 35 ft. lbs.

32. Fill the transmission and transfer case.

33. Lower the vehicle.

34. Connect the negative battery cable.

CLUTCH

Clutch Disc and Pressure Plate

REMOVAL AND INSTALLATION

Wrangler, Cherokee, Comanche, 1993–96 Grand Cherokee and 1993 Grand Wagoneer

1. Raise and safely support the vehicle.

2. Remove the transmission or transmission/transfer case assembly.

3. Matchmark the pressure plate and flywheel. Loosen the pressure plate bolts, a little at a time, in rotation, to avoid warpage.

4. Remove the pressure plate and clutch disc.

5. Inspect the flywheel for scoring, cracks, warpage or other wear; resurface or replace as necessary.

6. Inspect the pilot bearing for excessive wear or damage and replace as necessary.

To install:

7. If removed, install the pilot bearing after lubricating with grease. Seat the bearing in the crankshaft with a clutch alignment tool.

8. Check the clutch disc runout by installing the disc on the transmission input shaft. Runout should not exceed 0.020 in. (0.5mm) when measured ¼ inch from the outer edge of the facing.

9. Install the clutch alignment tool in the pilot bearing.

10. Install the clutch disc on the tool.

11. Install the pressure plate and tighten the bolts finger-tight. The pressure plate bolts must be tightened a little at a time, in rotation, to avoid warpage. Torque the pressure plate bolts as follows:

- 2.5L engine — 23 ft. lbs. (31 Nm)
- 4.0L engine — 40 ft. lbs. (54 Nm)
- 5.2L engine — 5/16 inch bolts: 17 ft. lbs. (23 Nm) and 3/8 inch bolts 30 ft. lbs. (41 Nm)

12. Install the transmission or transmission/transfer case assembly and lower the vehicle.

Clutch Cable

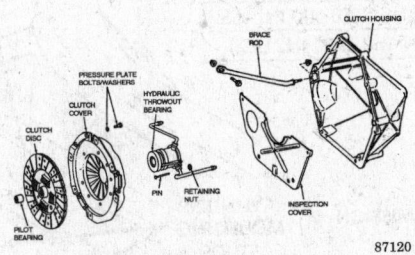

Clutch components — 2.5L engine

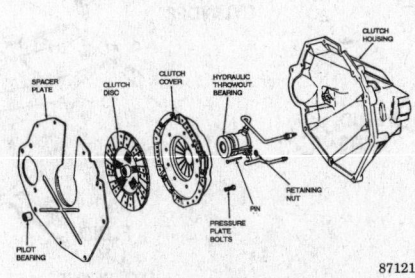

Clutch components — 4.0L engine

Clutch Master Cylinder

REMOVAL AND INSTALLATION

1994–96 Wrangler and Cherokee, 1993–96 Grand Cherokee and 1993 Grand Wagoneer

The clutch master cylinder, reservoir, slave cylinder and connecting lines are sealed units and are serviced as an assembly only.

1. Raise and safely support the vehicle.

2. Remove the slave cylinder and clip from the clutch housing.

3. Disconnect the hydraulic fluid line from the body clips.

4. Lower the vehicle.

5. Remove the retaining ring, flat washer and wave washer attaching the clutch master cylinder pushrod to the clutch pedal.

6. Slide the master cylinder pushrod off the clutch pedal pin.

7. Inspect the clutch pedal bushing, replace as necessary.

8. Remove the clutch master cylinder reservoir from the dash panel.

9. Remove the clutch master cylinder stud nuts.

10. Remove the assembly from the vehicle.

To install:

11. Position the assembly into the vehicle.

12. Torque the clutch master cylinder stud nuts to 200–300 inch lbs. (24–34 Nm).

13. Position the reservoir and tighten the screws.

14. Install the clutch master cylinder pushrod on the clutch pedal pin. Secure the rod with the wave washer, flat washer and retaining ring.

15. Raise and safely support the vehicle.

16. Insert the slave cylinder through the clutch housing into the release lever. Ensure the cap on the end of the rod is securely engaged in the lever. Torque the bolts to 200–300 inch lbs. (24–34 Nm).

17. Insert the fluid line in the body clips.

Comanche, 1992–93 Wrangler and Cherokee

1. Raise and support the vehicle safely.

2. Disconnect the quick-disconnect fitting by pushing the round disc inward to unsnap and separate the fittings.

3. Lower the vehicle.

4. Remove the lower instrument panel trim cover.

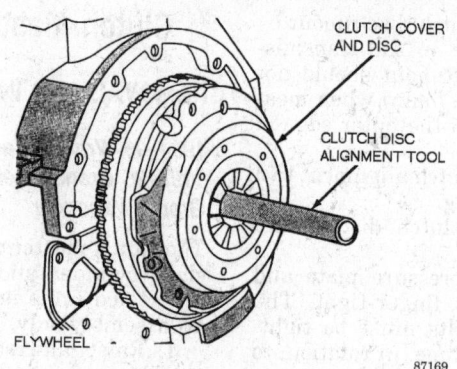

CLUTCH COVER AND DISC

CLUTCH DISC ALIGNMENT TOOL

FLYWHEEL

87169

Clutch disc alignment

5. Remove the cotter pin and washer securing the master cylinder pushrod to the pivot arm and slide the rod off the arm.

6. Unbolt the master cylinder from the firewall.

NOTE: The top bolt is installed from the engine compartment. The bottom bolt in installed from the passenger compartment.

To install:

7. Position the master cylinder and install the top bolt. Install the bottom bolt. Install the nuts and torque them to 19 ft. lbs. (26 Nm).

8. Connect the brake line. Ensure the fittings snap together securely.

9. Connect the pushrod to the pivot arm and install the washer and a new cotter pin.

10. Fill the master cylinder reservoir to the level indicated with DOT 3 brake fluid.

11. Bleed the system.

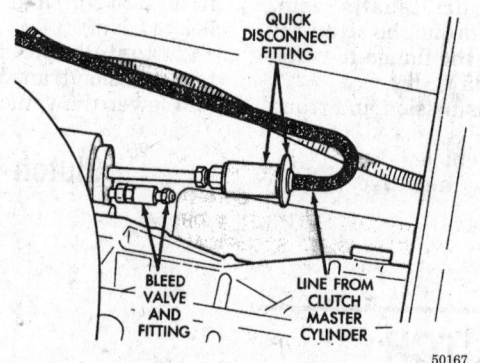

QUICK DISCONNECT FITTING

BLEED VALVE AND FITTING

LINE FROM CLUTCH MASTER CYLINDER

50167

Hydraulic fluid line fitting

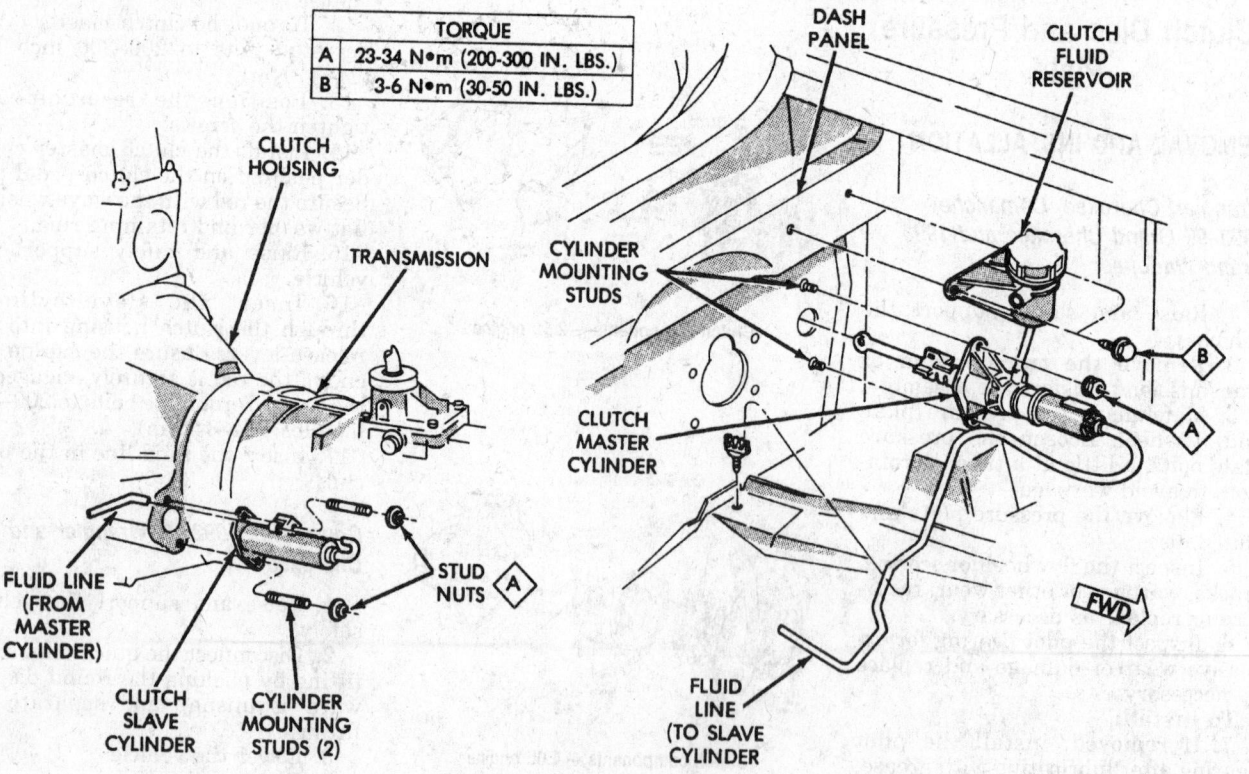

TORQUE	
A	23-34 N•m (200-300 IN. LBS.)
B	3-6 N•m (30-50 IN. LBS.)

CLUTCH HOUSING

TRANSMISSION

CYLINDER MOUNTING STUDS

DASH PANEL

CLUTCH FLUID RESERVOIR

CLUTCH MASTER CYLINDER

FLUID LINE (FROM MASTER CYLINDER)

STUD NUTS Ⓐ

CLUTCH SLAVE CYLINDER

CYLINDER MOUNTING STUDS (2)

FLUID LINE (TO SLAVE CYLINDER)

FWD

50196

Hydraulic clutch components

Clutch Slave Cylinder

REMOVAL AND INSTALLATION

Comanche, 1992–93 Wrangler and Cherokee

The hydraulic concentric bearing is serviced as an assembly only. The release bearing portion of the assembly is permanently attached to the piston. The hydraulic lines are also permanently attached.

1. Disconnect the negative battery cable.
2. Raise and support the vehicle safely.
3. Remove the transmission.
4. Disconnect the clutch master cylinder fluid line.
5. Remove the insulator plate bolts and slide the plate off the bleed line.
6. Remove the concentric bearing retaining nut.
7. Remove the concentric bearing from the transmission input shaft. If the bearing will be reused, secure the bearing and piston with rubber bands.

To install:

8. Inspect the bearing mounting pin and replace the front cover if the

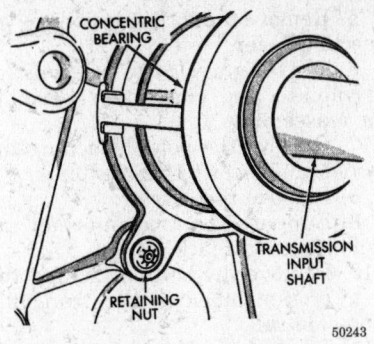

Retaining nut removal and installation — Wrangler, Cherokee and Comanche

pin is damaged. Install the concentric bearing on the transmission input shaft.

9. Guide the bearing fluid and bleed lines through the openings in the clutch housing.
10. Position the bearing boss on the mounting pin and seat the bearing against the transmission. Install a new retaining nut and unhook the T-handle straps retaining the bearing.
11. Install the insulator and plate.
12. Install the transmission and transfer case and connect the clutch master cylinder fluid line.
13. Fill and bleed the clutch hydraulic system.

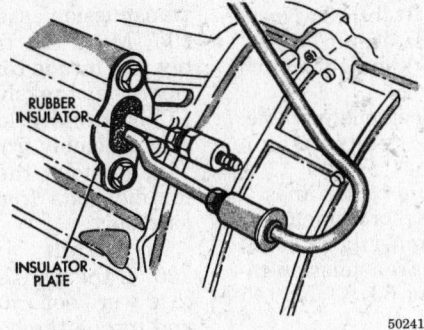

Insulator plate and bleed screw — 6 cylinder engine — Wrangler, Cherokee and Comanche

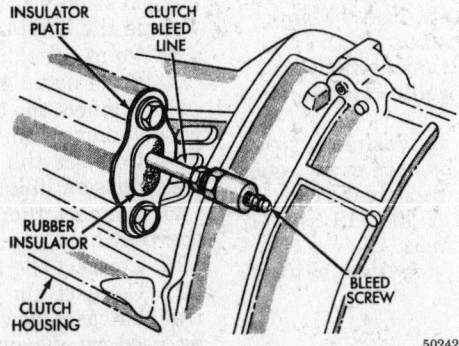

Insulator plate and bleed screw — 4 cylinder engine

AUTOMATIC TRANSMISSION

Transmission Assembly

REMOVAL AND INSTALLATION

1992–96 Wrangler

1. Disconnect the negative battery cable.
2. Raise and support the vehicle safely.
3. Matchmark the rear driveshaft and yoke for reassembly. Disconnect and remove the rear driveshaft.
4. Remove the torque converter inspection cover.
5. Matchmark the converter driveplate and converter assembly for reassembly.
6. Remove the bolts attaching the torque converter to the flexplate.
7. Support the transmission assembly with a jack.
8. Remove the bolts attaching the rear crossmember to the transmission side rail.
9. Disconnect the exhaust pipe at the catalytic converter.
10. Lower the transmission slightly in order to disconnect the fluid cooler lines.
11. Matchmark the front driveshaft assembly for installation.
12. Disconnect the driveshaft at the transfer case and secure the assembly aside.
13. Disconnect the backup light switch wire and speedometer cable.
14. Disconnect the transfer case and transmission linkage.
15. Disconnect the vacuum lines and vent hose.
16. Remove the bolts attaching the transmission assembly to the engine.
17. Move the transmission assembly and torque converter rearward to clear the crankshaft.
18. Carefully lower the transmission assembly from the vehicle.
19. Remove the transfer case retaining bolts from the transmission assembly.

To install:

20. If the transmission and transfer case were separated, re-attach them and torque the bolts to 26 ft. lbs.
21. Carefully raise the transmission into position.

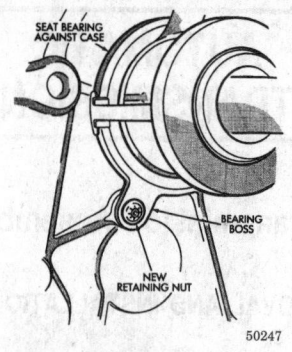

Concentric bearing
installation — Wrangler,
Cherokee and Comanche

22. Install the bolts attaching the transmission assembly to the engine. Torque the bolts as follows:
- 10mm bolts: 25 ft. lbs. (34 Nm)
- 12mm bolts: 42 ft. lbs. (57 Nm)

23. Connect the backup light switch wire and speedometer cable.

24. Connect the transfer case and transmission linkage.

25. Connect the vacuum lines and the vent hose.

26. Connect the fluid cooler lines.

27. Connect the driveshaft at the transfer case. New strap bolts should be used whenever the driveshaft is disconnected. Torque the strap bolt nuts to 14 ft. lbs (19 Nm); the flange-to-case bolts to 35 ft. lbs. (48 Nm).

28. Install the rear crossmember. Torque the crossmember attaching bolts to 30 ft. lbs. (41 Nm); the transmission-to-crossmember bolts to 33 ft. lbs. (45 Nm).

29. Connect the exhaust pipe at the catalytic converter.

30. Install the bolts attaching the torque converter to the flexplate. Torque the bolts to 40 ft. lbs. (61 Nm).

31. Remove the floor jack.

32. Install the torque converter inspection cover.

33. Install the rear driveshaft. Use new strap bolts. Torque the strap bolt nuts to 14 ft. lbs. (19 Nm); the flange bolts to 35 ft. lbs. 48 Nm).

34. Lower the vehicle.

35. Connect the negative battery cable.

Cherokee and Comanche

2WD

1. Disconnect the negative battery cable.

2. Raise and support the vehicle safely.

3. Matchmark the rear driveshaft and yoke for reassembly.

4. Disconnect and remove the rear driveshaft.

5. Remove the torque converter inspection cover.

6. Matchmark the converter driveplate and converter assembly for reassembly.

7. Remove the bolts attaching the torque converter to the flexplate.

8. Remove the starter.

9. Support the transmission assembly using a jack.

10. Remove the bolts attaching the rear crossmember to the transmission side rail.

11. Disconnect the exhaust pipe at the catalytic converter.

12. Lower the transmission slightly in order to disconnect the fluid cooler lines.

13. Disconnect the backup light switch wire and speedometer cable.

14. Disconnect the transmission linkage.

15. Remove the bolts attaching the transmission assembly to the engine.

16. Move the transmission assembly and the torque converter rearward to clear the crankshaft.

17. Carefully lower the transmission assembly from the vehicle.

To install:

18. Carefully raise the transmission into position.

19. Install the bolts attaching the transmission assembly to the engine. Torque the bolts to:
- 10mm bolts: 25 ft. lbs. (34 Nm)
- 12mm bolts: 42 ft. lbs. (57 Nm)

20. Connect the backup light switch wire.

21. Connect the speedometer cable.

22. Connect the transmission linkage.

23. Connect the fluid cooler lines.

24. Install the rear crossmember. Torque the crossmember bolts to 30 ft. lbs. (41 Nm); the transmission-to-crossmember bolts to 33 ft. lbs. (45 Nm).

25. Connect the exhaust pipe at the catalytic converter.

26. Install the bolts attaching the torque converter to the flexplate. Torque the bolts to 40 ft. lbs. (54 Nm).

27. Install the starter.

28. Remove the transmission jack.

29. Install the torque converter inspection cover.

30. Install the driveshaft. New strap bolts should be used every time the driveshaft is disconnected. Torque the nuts to 14 ft. lbs. (19 Nm).

31. Lower the vehicle.

32. Connect the negative battery cable.

4WD

1. Disconnect the negative battery cable.

2. Raise and support the vehicle safely.

3. Matchmark the rear driveshaft and yoke for reassembly. Disconnect and remove the rear driveshaft.

4. Remove the torque converter inspection cover.

5. Matchmark the converter driveplate and converter assembly for reassembly.

6. Remove the bolts attaching the torque converter to the flexplate.

7. Support the transmission assembly with a jack.

8. Remove the bolts attaching the rear crossmember to the transmission side rail.

9. Disconnect the exhaust pipe at the catalytic converter.

10. Lower the transmission slightly in order to disconnect the fluid cooler lines.

11. Matchmark the front driveshaft assembly for installation.

12. Disconnect the driveshaft at the transfer case and secure the assembly aside.

13. Disconnect the backup light switch wire and speedometer cable.

14. Disconnect the transfer case and transmission linkage.

15. Disconnect the vacuum lines and vent hose.

16. Remove the bolts attaching the transmission assembly to the engine.

17. Move the transmission assembly and torque converter rearward to clear the crankshaft.

18. Carefully lower the transmission assembly from the vehicle.

19. Remove the transfer case retaining bolts from the transmission assembly.

To install:

20. If the transmission and transfer case were separated, re-attach them and torque the bolts to 26 ft. lbs.

21. Carefully raise the transmission into position.

22. Install the bolts attaching the transmission assembly to the engine. Torque the bolts to:
- 10mm bolts: 25 ft. lbs. (34 Nm)
- 12mm bolts: 42 ft. lbs. (57 Nm)

23. Connect the backup light switch wire and speedometer cable.

24. Connect the transfer case and transmission linkage.

25. Connect the vacuum lines and the vent hose.

26. Connect the fluid cooler lines.

27. Connect the driveshaft at the transfer case. New strap bolts should be used whenever the driveshaft is disconnected. Torque the strap bolt nuts to 14 ft. lbs (19 Nm); the flange-to-case bolts to 35 ft. lbs. (48 Nm).

28. Install the rear crossmember. Torque the crossmember attaching bolts to 30 ft. lbs. (41 Nm); the transmission-to-crossmember bolts to 33 ft. lbs. (45 Nm).

29. Connect the exhaust pipe at the catalytic converter.

30. Install the bolts attaching the torque converter to the flexplate. Torque the bolts to 40 ft. lbs. (61 Nm).

31. Remove the floor jack.

32. Install the torque converter inspection cover.

33. Install the rear driveshaft. Use new strap bolts. Torque the strap bolt nuts to 14 ft. lbs. (19 Nm); the flange bolts to 35 ft. lbs. 48 Nm).

34. Lower the vehicle.

35. Connect the negative battery cable.

1993–96 Grand Cherokee and 1993 Grand Wagoneer

2WD

1. Disconnect the negative battery cable.

2. Raise and support the vehicle safely.

3. If equipped, remove the skid plate.

4. If the transmission is being removed for repair, drain the fluid and reinstall the pan.

5. Matchmark the driveshaft yoke and remove the driveshaft.

6. Disconnect the vehicle speed wires, transmission solenoid wires and park-neutral position switch wires.

7. Disconnect the wires from the transmission speed sensor at the rear of the overdrive unit.

8. Remove the exhaust Y-pipe.

9. Unclip the wire harness from the transmission clips.

10. Disconnect the throttle valve and gearshift cables from the levers on the valve body manual shaft. Position the cables aside and secure them to the underbody.

11. Remove the dust cover from the transmission converter housing.

12. Remove the starter.

13. Remove the bolts attaching the converter to the driveplate.

14. Disconnect the cooler fluid lines from the transmission.

15. Support the transmission with a jack.

16. Remove the nuts and bolts securing the rear crossmember to the insulator and remove the crossmember.

17. Lower the jack to gain access to the upper portion of the transmission.

18. Remove the crankshaft position sensor.

19. Remove the transmission fill tube and discard the O-ring.

20. Remove the bolts attaching the transmission to the engine.

21. Slide the transmission back and secure a C-clamp to the converter.

22. Remove the transmission.

To install:

23. Ensure the torque converter hub and hub drive are free from sharp edges, scratches or nicks. Polish with 400 grit sandpaper if necessary.

24. Lubricate the converter hub and pump seal with high temperature grease.

25. Secure the C-clamp to the converter.

26. Ensure the dowel pins are seated in the engine block and protrude far enough to align the transmission.

27. Align the transmission with the engine dowels and converter with the driveplate. Install 2 transmission bolts to keep it in place.

28. Remove the C-clamp and install the torque converter bolts. Torque the bolts to:

- 3 lug converter — 40 ft. lbs. (54 Nm)
- 4 lug converter — 270 inch lbs. (31 Nm)

29. Install and tighten the remaining transmission-to-engine bolts.

30. Install the crankshaft position sensor.

31. Install the dust cover on the converter housing.

32. Install the starter.

33. Connect the transmission shift and throttle valve cables to the transmission.

34. Fasten the wire harness to the transmission.

35. Connect the harness connectors disconnected during removal.

36. Install the transmission filler tube with a new O-ring.

37. Install the rear crossmember.

38. Connect the fluid cooler lines to the transmission.

39. Align and install the driveshaft.

40. Install the exhaust system components.

41. Lower the vehicle.

42. Connect the negative battery cable.

43. Check the transmission control cables; adjust if necessary.

44. If the transmission fluid was drained, fill the transmission with fluid to the proper level.

4WD

1. Disconnect the negative battery cable.

2. Raise and support the vehicle safely.

3. If equipped, remove the skid plate.

4. If the transmission is being removed for repair, drain the fluid and reinstall the pan.

5. Matchmark the driveshaft yokes and remove both driveshafts.

6. Disconnect the vehicle speed wires, transmission solenoid wires and park-neutral position switch wires.

7. Unclip the wire harness from the transmission clips.

8. Disconnect the transfer case shift linkage from the lever. Remove the linkage and bracket from the transfer case. Position the linkage aside.

9. Remove the nuts attaching the transfer case to the overdrive unit gear case.

10. Place a jack under the transfer case and remove the case.

11. Support the transmission with the jack.

12. Remove the rear transmission crossmember.

13. Remove the exhaust Y-pipe.

14. Remove the crankshaft position sensor.

15. Disconnect the gearshift linkage from the lever on the transmission.

16. Remove the transmission shift linkage torque shaft assembly from the transmission and frame rail. Position it aside.

17. Remove the transmission-to-engine brackets.

18. Remove the dust cover from the transmission converter housing.

19. Remove the starter.

20. Remove the bolts attaching the converter to the driveplate.

21. Disconnect the cooler fluid lines from the transmission.

22. Disconnect the solenoid and park/neutral position wire switch wires.

23. Remove the transmission fill tube and discard the O-ring.

24. Lower the jack to gain access to the upper portion of the transmission.

25. Remove the bolts attaching the transmission to the engine.

26. Slide the transmission back and secure a C-clamp to the converter.

27. Move the transmission rearward until it clears the engine block dowels.

NOTE: On some models, part of the flange joining the vehicle cab and dash panel may interfere with transmission removal. If necessary peen this part of the flange over with a mallet.

28. Remove the transmission.

To install:

29. Ensure the torque converter hub and hub drive are free from sharp edges, scratches or nicks. Polish with 400 grit sandpaper if necessary.

30. Lubricate the converter hub and pump seal with high temperature grease.

31. Secure the C-clamp to the converter.

32. Ensure the dowel pins are seated in the engine block and protrude far enough to align the transmission.

33. Align the transmission with the engine dowels and converter with the driveplate. Install 2 transmission bolts to keep it in place.

34. Remove the C-clamp and install the torque converter bolts. Torque the bolts as follows:

- 3 lug converter — 40 ft. lbs. (54 Nm)
- 4 lug, except 10.75 inch converter — 55 ft. lbs. (74 Nm)
- 4 lug, 10.75 inch converter — 270 inch lbs. (31 Nm)

35. Install the starter.

36. Install the strut brackets securing the transmission to the engine and front axle.

37. Install and tighten the remaining transmission–to–engine bolts.

38. Install the crankshaft position sensor.

39. Install the transmission filler tube with a new O-ring.

40. Install the exhaust system components.

41. Install the shift linkage torque bracket.

42. Connect the shift linkage to the transmission.

43. Connect the harness connectors disconnected during removal.

44. Install the rear crossmember.

45. Install the transfer case. Torque the nuts as follows:

- ³⁄₈ stud nuts — 35 ft. lbs. (47 Nm)
- ⁵⁄₁₆ stud nuts — 26 ft. lbs. (35 Nm)

46. Install the damper on the transfer case rear retainer if removed. Torque the nuts to 40 ft. lbs. (54 Nm).

47. Connect the transfer case shift linkage.

48. Connect the fluid cooler lines to the transmission.

49. Align and install the driveshafts. Torque the U-joint clamp bolts to 170 inch lbs. (19 Nm).

50. Fill the transfer case to the proper level with fluid.

51. Lower the vehicle.

52. Connect the negative battery cable.

53. Fill the transmission to the proper level with Mopar ATF Plus or equivalent.

54. Check the transmission control cables, adjust if necessary.

55. Check and adjust the transmission and transfer case shift linkage.

Shift Linkage

REMOVAL AND INSTALLATION

Wrangler

1. Shift the transmission into **P** and lock the steering column.

2. Raise and support the vehicle safely.

3. Check the condition of the shift rods, bell crank, bell crank brackets, and linkage bushings. Repair as necessary.

4. Loosen the shift rod trunnion jamnuts.

5. Remove the lockpin that retains the shift rod trunnion to the bell crank. Disengage the trunnion and shift rod at the bell crank.

6. Move the transmission lever rearward into the **P** detent. Be sure the lever is as far rearward as it will go.

7. Check the engagement of the park detent by trying to rotate the driveshaft with the rear wheels off of the ground. The shaft will not rotate if the park detent is engaged.

8. Adjust the trunnion until it will fit in the bell crank arm freely. Prevent the shift rod from turning while tightening the the bolt or nut. Tighten the jamnuts.

9. Install the lock pin.

NOTE: Gearshift linkage lash must be eliminated to obtain proper adjustment. Eliminate lash by pulling down on the shift rod and pressing up on the bell crank.

10. Check engine starting in **P** and **N**; be sure it will not start in any other gear.

Cherokee, Comanche and 1993 Grand Cherokee

1. Place the gear shift lever in the **P** position.

2. Raise and safely support the vehicle.

3. Release the cable adjuster clamp to unlock the cable.

4. Unsnap the cable from the bracket.

5. Move the transmission lever rearward into the **P** detent. Be sure the lever is as far rearward as it will go.

6. Check the engagement of the park detent by trying to rotate the driveshaft with the rear wheels off of the ground. The shaft will not rotate if the park detent is engaged.

7. Snap the cable onto the bracket.

8. Lock the cable by pressing the adjuster clamp down until it snaps into place.

9. Check engine starting in **P** and **N**; be sure it will not start in any other gear.

1994–96 Grand Cherokee

Do not attempt linkage adjustment if any components are worn or damaged. If either linkage rod must be disconnected, the plastic grommet securing the rod in the lever must be replaced. Disconnect the rod with a pry tool. Pry only where the grommet and rod attach and not on the rod itself. Then cut away the old grommet. Use pliers to snap the new grommet into the lever and to snap the rod into the grommet.

1. Shift the transmission into **P**.

2. Raise and support the vehicle safely.

3. Check the condition of the shift rods, control lever, bushings, washers and torque shaft. Repair as necessary.

4. Loosen the lock bolt in the rear shift rod adjusting swivel.

5. Slide the swivel off the torque shaft arm. Ensure the swivel turns freely on the rear shift rod.

6. Move the transmission lever rearward into the **P** detent. Be sure the lever is as far rearward as it will go.

7. Adjust the swivel position on the rear shift rod to obtain free pin fit in the torque shaft lever. Torque the swivel lock bolt to 90 inch lbs. (10 Nm).

8. Check engine starting in **P** and **N**; be sure it will not start in any other gear.

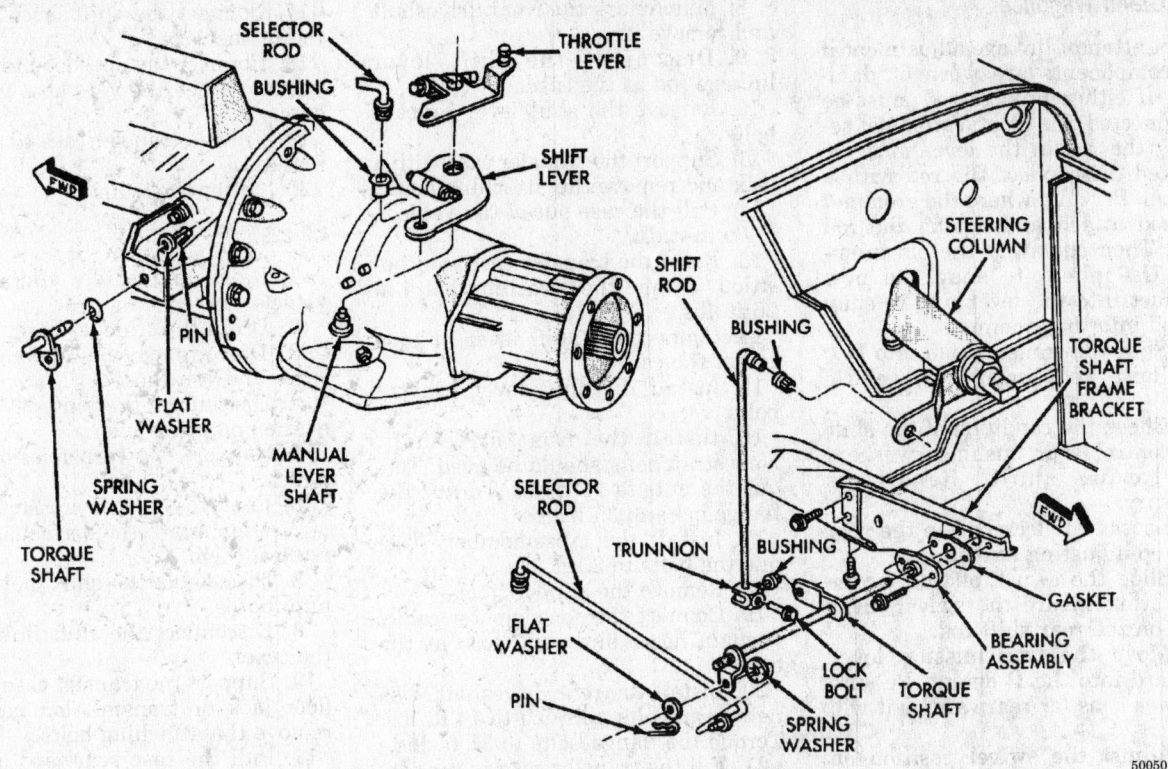

Exploded view of the shift linkage — Wrangler 1992–96

50050

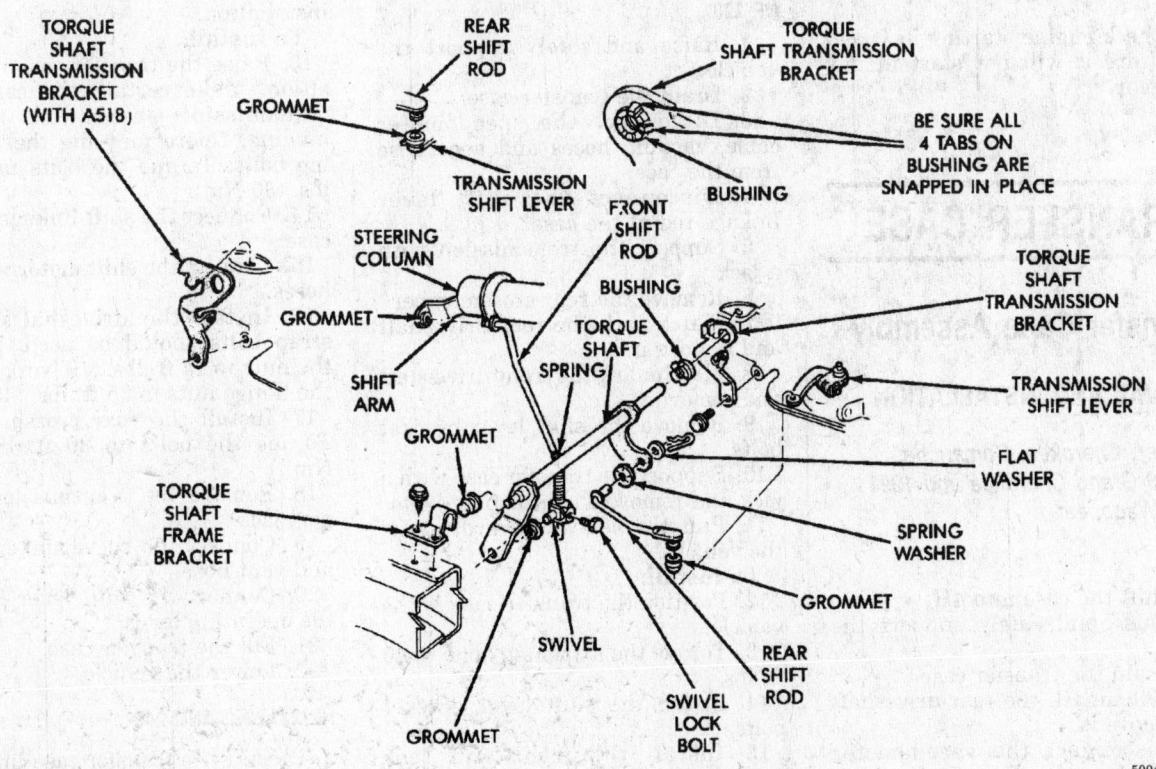

Exploded view of the shift linkage — Grand Cherokee

50046

1993 Grand Wagoneer

Do not attempt linkage adjustment if any components are worn or damaged. If either linkage rod must be disconnected, the plastic grommet securing the rod in the lever must be replaced. Disconnect the rod with a pry tool. Pry only where the grommet and rod attach and not on the rod itself. Then cut away the old grommet. Use pliers to snap the new grommet into the lever and to snap the rod into the grommet.

1. Shift the transmission into **P**.
2. Raise and support the vehicle safely.
3. Check the condition of the shift rods, control lever, bushings, washers and torque shaft. Repair as necessary.
4. Loosen the lock bolt in the rear shift rod adjusting swivel.
5. Slide the swivel off the torque shaft arm. Ensure the swivel turns freely on the rear shift rod.
6. Move the transmission lever rearward into the **P** detent. Be sure the lever is as far rearward as it will go.
7. Adjust the swivel position on the rear shift rod to obtain free pin fit in the torque shaft lever. Torque the swivel lock bolt to 90 inch lbs. (10 Nm).
8. Check engine starting in **P** and **N**; be sure it will not start in any other gear.

TRANSFER CASE

Transfer Case Assembly

REMOVAL AND INSTALLATION

Wrangler, Cherokee, Comanche, 1993–96 Grand Cherokee and 1993 Grand Wagoneer

NP 207

1. Shift the case into **4H**.
2. Raise and safely support the vehicle.
3. Drain the transfer case.
4. Matchmark the rear driveshaft and remove it.
5. Disconnect the speedometer cable, vacuum hoses and vent hose from the case.
6. Support the transmission with a transmission jack.
7. Remove the crossmember.

8. Matchmark the front driveshaft and remove it.
9. Disconnect the shift lever linkage rod at the case.
10. Remove the shift lever bracket bolts.
11. Support the transfer case with a jack and remove the attaching bolts.
12. Pull the case out of the vehicle.
   To install:
13. Raise the transfer case into position. Torque the attaching bolts to 26 ft. lbs.
14. Connect the shift lever linkage rod at the case.
15. Install the shift lever bracket bolts.
16. Install the front driveshaft. New strap bolts should be used. Torque the nuts to 14 ft. lbs. Torque the flange bolts to 35 ft. lbs.
17. Install the crossmember. Torque the bolts to 30 ft. lbs.
18. Remove the support jack.
19. Connect the speedometer cable, vacuum hoses and vent hose at the case.
20. Install the rear driveshaft. Use new strap bolts, torqued to 14 ft. lbs. Torque the flange bolts to 35 ft. lbs.
21. Fill the transfer case to the correct level.
22. Lower the vehicle.

NP 228

1. Raise and safely support the vehicle.
2. Drain the transfer case.
3. Disconnect the speedometer cable, vacuum hoses and vent hose from the case.
4. Disconnect the shift lever linkage rod at the case.
5. Support the transmission with a jack.
6. Remove the rear crossmember.
7. Matchmark the rear driveshaft and remove it.
8. Matchmark the front driveshaft and remove it.
9. Remove the shift lever bracket bolts.
10. Support the transfer case with a jack and remove the attaching bolts.
11. Pull the case rearward out of the vehicle.
   To install:
12. Position the transfer case in the vehicle.
13. Torque the attaching bolts to 40 ft. lbs.
14. Install the shift lever bracket bolts.
15. Install the front and rear driveshafts. New strap bolts should be used. Torque the strap bolt nuts to 14 ft. lbs.; the flange nuts to 35 ft. lbs.
16. Install the rear crossmember. Torque the bolts to 30 ft. lbs.

17. Connect the shift lever linkage rod at the case.
18. Connect the speedometer cable, vacuum hoses and vent hose from the case.
19. Fill the transfer case to the correct level.
20. Lower the vehicle.

NP 229

1. Raise and safely support the vehicle.
2. Drain the transfer case.
3. Disconnect the speedometer cable and vent hose.
4. Disconnect the shift lever link at the operating lever.
5. Support the transmission with a jack.
6. Remove the rear crossmember.
7. Matchmark the driveshafts and remove them.
8. Disconnect the shift motor vacuum hoses.
9. Disconnect the shift linkage at the case.
10. Support the transfer case with a floor jack or transmission jack and remove the attaching bolts.
11. Pull the case rearward and remove it.
12. Clean the gasket mating surfaces and use new gasket material for installation.
   To install:
13. Raise the transfer case into position. Make certain the case and transmission are mated without binding, before torquing the attaching bolts. Torque the bolts to 26 ft. lbs. (35 Nm).
14. Connect the shift linkage at the case.
15. Connect the shift motor vacuum hoses.
16. Install the driveshafts. New strap bolts should be used. Torque the nuts to 14 ft. lbs. (19 Nm); torque the flange nuts to 35 ft. lbs. (48 Nm).
17. Install the rear crossmember. Torque the bolts to 30 ft. lbs. (41 Nm).
18. Remove the transmission support jack.
19. Connect the speedometer cable and vent hose.
20. Connect the shift lever link at the operating lever.
21. Fill the transfer case.
22. Lower the vehicle.

NP 231, 242 AND 249

1. Shift the transfer case into **N**.
2. Raise and support the vehicle safely.
3. Drain the lubricant.
4. Matchmark and remove the front and rear driveshafts.

5. Support the transmission with a jack.

6. Remove the rear crossmember.

7. Disconnect the speedometer cable or speed sensor connector.

8. Disconnect the linkage.

9. Disconnect the vent and vacuum hoses and the indicator wire.

10. Support the transfer case with a transmission jack.

11. Remove the transfer case-to-transmission bolts.

12. Pull the case rearward to disengage it and lower it from the truck.

To install:

13. Raise the transfer case into position. Make certain the case and transmission are mated without binding, before torquing the attaching bolts. Torque the bolts to 26 ft. lbs. (35 Nm).

14. Connect the shift linkage at the case.

15. Connect the vacuum hoses.

16. Install the driveshafts. New strap bolts should be used. Torque the nuts to 14 ft. lbs. (19 Nm); torque the flange nuts to 35 ft. lbs. (48 Nm).

17. Install the rear crossmember. Torque the bolts to 30 ft. lbs. (41 Nm).

18. Remove the transmission floor jack.

19. Connect the speedometer cable or speed sensor connector and vent hose.

20. Connect the shift lever link at the operating lever.

21. Fill the transfer case to the correct lever.

22. Lower the vehicle.

DRIVE AXLE

Halfshaft

REMOVAL AND INSTALLATION

1993–96 Grand Cherokee and 1993 Grand Wagoneer

Extreme care must be used to avoid puncturing or tearing the boots. Also avoid damage to the ABS tone ring pressed onto the CV-joint.

The most common failure of CV-joints is torn or ripped boots and subsequent loss or contamination of the lubricant. Look for lubricant around the exterior of the boot. Check for loose clamps and punctured or torn boots, replace as necessary. If the joint was operating satisfactorily and the grease does not appear contaminated, the boot may be reinstalled. When the CV driveshaft is removed from the vehicle for service, the boot should be properly cleaned.

The rubber material in the CV-joint boots is not compatible with oil, gasoline or petroleum-based cleaning solvents. Use only soap and water to clean the boots. After cleaning, the rubber boot must be thoroughly rinsed and dried.

1. Remove the front axle shaft.

2. Remove and discard the CV-joint boot retaining rings.

3. Slide the boot off the axle shaft.

To install:

4. Clean the boot and check for cracks, tears, and scuffed areas on the surface. If any of these conditions exist, replace the boot.

5. Apply CV-joint lubricant to the CV-joint, as necessary.

6. Install the boot onto the shaft with the large end of the boot facing the joint and fill the boot with axle shaft lubricant.

NOTE: Ensure the boot is not twisted.

7. Ensure the clamp sealing area is in the grooved section of the housing and install new clamps.

8. Install the axle shaft.

Driveshaft

REMOVAL AND INSTALLATION

Wrangler, Cherokee, Comanche, 1993–96 Grand Cherokee and 1993 Grand Wagoneer

FRONT

NOTE: These vehicles may come equipped with one of 2 different type front driveshafts. The first type has a conventional universal joint at the axle but a double offset joint at the transfer

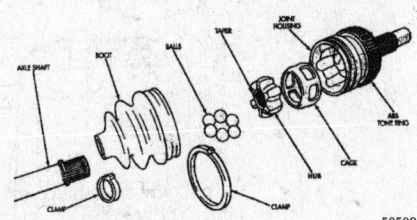

50500

Exploded view of the CV-joint — Grand Cherokee and Grand Wagoneer

case. The second type has a conventional universal joint at the axle and a double cardan joint at the transfer case.

1. Place the transmission and transfer case in **N**.

2. Raise and safely support the vehicle.

3. Matchmark the shaft ends, axle and transfer case.

4. Remove the U-joint strap bolts at the front axle yoke.

5. Remove the double offset joint flange nuts at the transfer case.

To install:

6. Position the driveshaft on the transfer case output shaft and axle yoke aligning the marks.

7. Torque the new U-joint strap-to-axle yoke bolts to 14 ft. lbs. (19 Nm).

8. Torque the new U-joint strap-to-transfer case bolts to 20 ft. lbs. (27 Nm).

9. Lower the vehicle.

REAR

NOTE: Two different driveshafts are used on these vehicles. With Command-Trac®, the driveshaft has welded yokes at each end. With Selec-Trac®, a welded yoke is used at the rear and a splined slip yoke is used at the front.

1. Place the transmission in **N**.

2. Raise and safely support the vehicle.

3. Matchmark the yokes and flanges.

4. If equipped with Command-Trac®, the driveshaft may be removed by disconnecting it at the axle and sliding it from the front yoke, leaving the front yoke attached to the transfer case. If done this way, matchmark the driveshaft and front yoke before separation.

5. If equipped with Selec-Trac®, disconnect the yokes from the axle and transfer case. Remove the driveshaft.

6. Installation is the reverse of removal. Torque the U-joint strap nuts to 19 ft. lbs. (26 Nm).

NOTE: New U-joint straps should be used.

Front Axle Shaft

REMOVAL AND INSTALLATION

1992–96 Wrangler

1. Raise and support the vehicle safely.

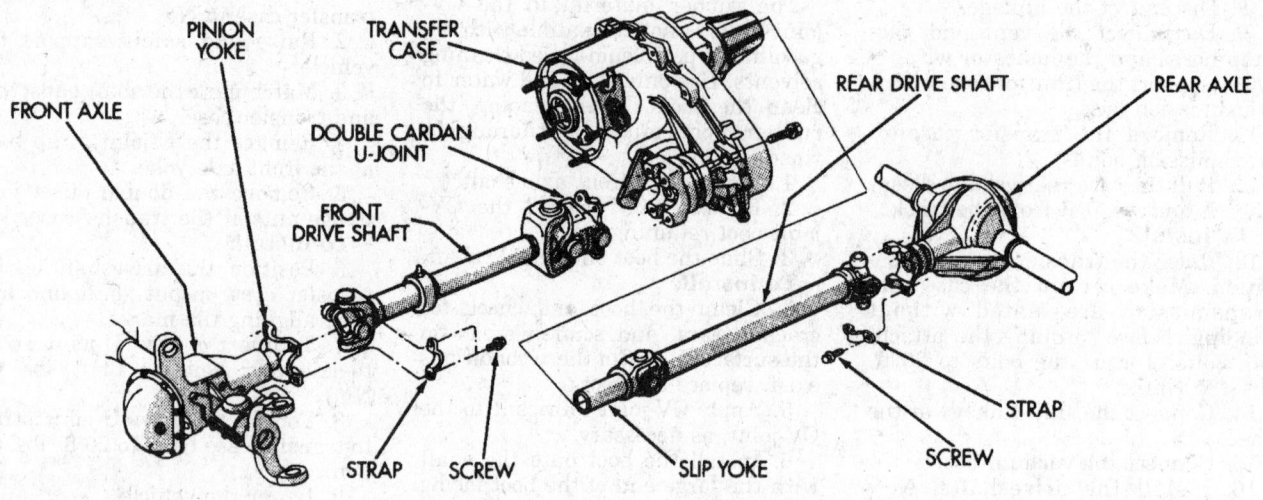

Front and rear driveshaft assemblies — 4WD Wrangler, Cherokee and Comanche

42446

2. Remove the wheel.

3. Remove the caliper and wheel.

4. Remove the hub and bearing assembly.

5. If equipped with a shift motor, perform the following:

   a. Disconnect the vacuum and wiring connector from the shift housing.

   b. Remove the indicator switch.

   c. Remove the shift motor housing cover, gasket and shield from the housing.

   d. Remove the E-clips from the shift motor housing and shaft. Remove the shift motor and fork from the housing.

   e. Remove the O-ring seal from the shift motor shaft.

6. Remove the axle from the housing, being careful to avoid damaging the axle shaft oil seals in the differential.

To install:

7. Thoroughly clean the axle shaft and apply a thin film of wheel bearing grease to the shaft splines, seal contact surface and hub bore.

8. Carefully install the axle shaft, being careful to avoid damaging the differential seals.

9. If equipped with a shift motor, perform the following:

   a. Install a new O-ring seal on the shift motor.

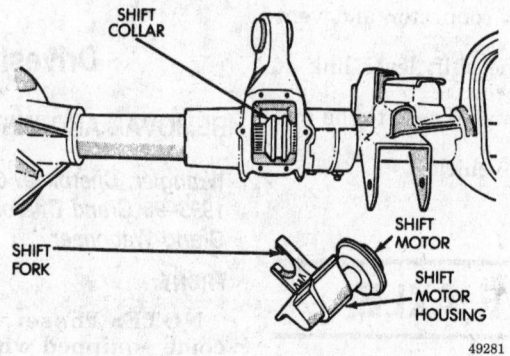

Shift motor housing and shift collar — Wrangler

49281

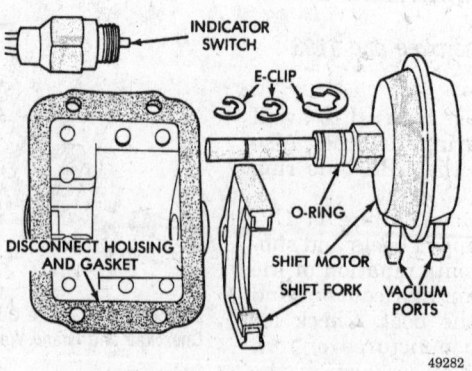

Shift motor components — Wrangler

49282

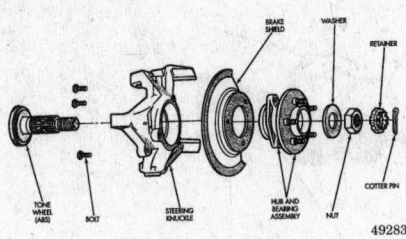

Exploded view of the hub, knuckle and shaft assembly — Wrangler

b. Insert the shift motor shaft through the hole in the housing and shift fork. The shift fork offset should be toward the differential.

c. Install the E-clips on the shift motor shaft and housing.

d. Install the shift motor housing gasket and cover. Ensure the shift fork is correctly guided into the shift collar groove.

e. Install the shift motor shield and torque the bolts to 101 inch lbs. (11 Nm).

f. Add 5 ounces of API grade 5 hydraulic gear lubricant or equivalent, into the shift motor housing through the indicator switch mounting hole.

g. Install the indicator switch.

h. Connect the electrical connector and vacuum hoses.

10. Install the wheel bearing and hub assembly.

11. Install the rotor and caliper.

12. Install the wheel.

1992–96 Cherokee, 1992 Comanche, 1993–96 Grand Cherokee and 1993 Grand Wagoneer

1. Raise and support the vehicle safely.

2. Remove the wheel.

3. Remove the caliper and disc brake rotor.

4. Remove the hub and bearing assembly.

5. Remove the disc brake rotor shield.

6. Remove the axle shaft from the housing, being careful to avoid damaging the axle shaft oil seals in the differential.

To install:

7. Thoroughly clean the axle shaft and apply a thin film of wheel bearing grease to the shaft splines, seal contact surface and hub bore.

8. Carefully install the axle shaft, being careful to avoid damaging the differential oil seals.

9. Install the brake dust shield.

10. Install the wheel bearing and hub assembly.

11. Install the rotor and caliper.

12. Install the wheel and lower the vehicle.

Front Axle Shaft Bearing and Seal

REMOVAL AND INSTALLATION

1992–96 Wrangler, 1992–96 Cherokee, 1992 Comanche, 1993–96 Grand Cherokee and 1993 Grand Wagoneer

1. Raise and support the vehicle safely.

2. Remove the wheel.

3. Remove the caliper and disc brake rotor.

4. Remove the cotter pin, nut retainer and axle hub nut.

5. Remove the hub-to-knuckle bolts and remove the hub and bearing assembly from the steering knuckle and axle shaft.

6. Remove the disc brake rotor shield from the bearing carrier.

To install:

7. Install the disc brake rotor shield on the bearing carrier.

8. Thoroughly clean the axle shaft and apply a thin film of wheel bearing grease to the shaft splines, seal contact surface and hub bore.

9. Install the hub abd bearing assembly to the knuckle. Apply Loctite® or equivalent to the threads, then install the hub-to-knuckle bolts and tighten to 75 ft. lbs. (102 Nm).

10. Install the hub washer and nut. Tighten the nut to 175 ft. lbs. (237 Nm), then install the nut retainer and a new cotter pin.

11. Install the rotor and caliper.

12. Install the wheel and lower the vehicle.

Rear Axle Shaft, Bearing and Seal

REMOVAL AND INSTALLATION

Wrangler, Cherokee, Comanche, 1993–96 Grand Cherokee and 1993 Grand Wagoneer

1. Raise and support the vehicle safely.

2. Remove the wheel and brake drum.

3. Remove the rear differential cover and drain the lubricant.

4. Rotate the differential case so the pinion gear mate shaft lock screw is accessible, then remove the lock screw and the pinion gear mate shaft.

5. Force the axle shaft toward the center of the vehicle and remove the C-clip.

6. Remove the axle shaft. Inspect the axle shaft for evidence of wear or damage; replace the axle shaft if necessary.

7. Pry the axle shaft seal from the axle tube using a small prybar. Remove the axle bearing using bearing removal tool 6310 or equivalent.

To install:

8. Wipe the axle shaft bearing bore in the axle tube clean.

9. Install a new bearing using driver handle tool C-4171 and bearing installation tool 6437 or equivalents. Insert the bearing in the axle tube, making sure it is not cocked. Tap the driver handle tool until the bearing is firmly seated.

10. Install a new axle shaft seal using driver handle tool C-4171 and seal installation tool 6437 or equivalents. The flat side of the tool must face the seal. When the installation tool contacts the axle tube face, the seal is positioned properly in the bore.

11. Lubricate the bearing bore and seal lip. Install the axle shaft, taking care not to damage the seal, and engage the axle shaft splines with the differential side gear splines.

12. Install the C-clip and force the axle shaft outward to seat the clip.

13. Insert the differential pinion gear mate shaft into the case and through the thrust washers and pinion gears. Align the hole in the shaft with the hole in the case and install the lock screw. Tighten the lock screw to 14 ft. lbs. (19 Nm).

14. Clean the differential housing and cover mating surfaces. Apply a thin bead of sealant around the bolt circle on the housing and on the cover.

15. Install the differential housing cover and tighten the attaching bolts to 35 ft. lbs. (47 Nm). Install the brake drum and wheel.

16. Fill the differential with suitable lubricant and test drive. If equipped with Trac-Lok, drive the vehicle through 10–12 slow figure 8 turns to pump the lubricant through the clutch discs.

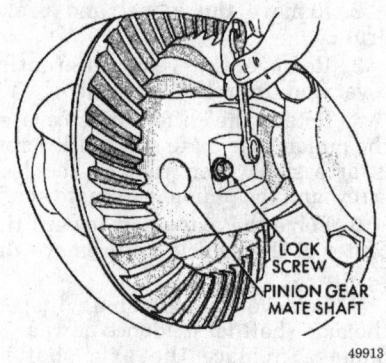

Mate shaft lock screw

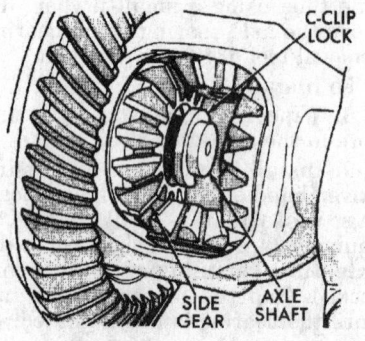

Axle shaft C-clip lock

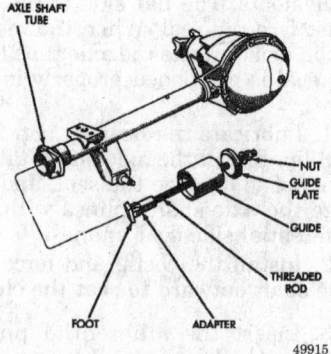

Axle shaft bearing removal tool

U-Joint

REMOVAL AND INSTALLATION

Wrangler, Cherokee, Comanche, 1993–96 Grand Cherokee and 1993 Grand Wagoneer

Most Jeep vehicles use a conventional universal joint at both ends of both driveshafts. All models have C-type retainer rings on the inside of the bearing caps. The constant velocity joint is also assembled with snaprings on the outside.

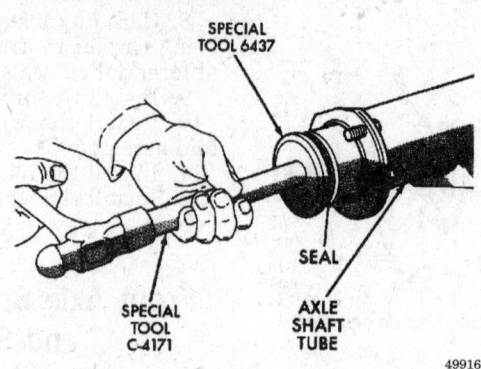

Axle shaft seal installation

The U-joints are not serviceable and if defective, must replaced as a unit. If the socket yokes, balls, springs, bearings, seals, thrust washers, spiders or bearing caps are damaged or worn, replace the complete U-joint.

SINGLE CROSS CARDAN JOINT

1. Clamp the yoke, not the tube, in a vise.
2. Remove the bearing cap C-retainers. Tap on the bearing caps to relieve pressure as necessary.
3. Support the yoke on the vise jaws.
4. Tap one bearing cap in until the opposite one comes out.
5. Turn the yoke around and tap the exposed end of the spider to drive the remaining bearing cap out.

To install:

6. Lubricate all needle bearings, bearing caps, and bearing surfaces with chassis grease.
7. Place the seals on the spider.
8. Install one cap and needle bearing assembly partway into the shaft yoke.
9. Install the spider and the opposite bearings and cap.
10. Support the yoke and seat both caps with a hammer.

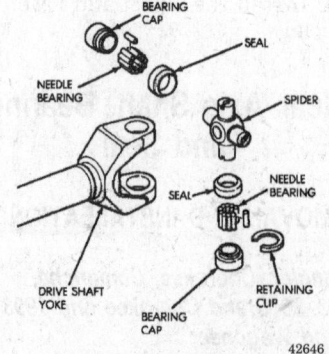

Exploded view of a single cardan U-joint

11. Install the retainer C-clips. Tap the bearing caps as necessary.
12. Install the other two cap and bearing assemblies. Hold them in place with tape until the shaft is reinstalled.

CONSTANT VELOCITY (DOUBLE CARDAN) JOINT

1. Remove the bearing cap retainer snaprings.
2. Mark all components for reassembly.
3. Use a ⅝ in. socket as a bearing cap driver and a 1¹/₁₆ in. socket as a bearing cap receiver. Squeeze the assembly in a vise to force out the bearing caps.
4. Repeat the operation of step 3 to remove the bearing caps at the other end of the joint.
5. Clean all parts in solvent and dry.

NOTE: Do not disassemble the socket yoke, centering ball, spring, needle bearings, retainer, and thrust washers. These parts are sold as an assembly only.

To install:

6. Lubricate all bearings and contact surfaces with chassis grease.
7. Install the bearing caps on the transfer case yoke ends of the rear spider. Tape them in place.
8. Assemble the socket yoke and the rear spider.
9. Place the rear spider in the link yoke and install the bearing caps. Press them into place with the ⅝ in. socket. Install the snaprings.
10. Install the front spider, bearing caps, and snaprings in the driveshaft yoke.
11. Install the thrust washer and socket spring in the ball socket bearing bore. Install the thrust washer on the ball socket bearing boss on the driveshaft yoke. Align the ball socket bearing boss with the ball socket bearing bore and insert the boss into the bore.

12. Align the front spider with the link yoke and install the bearing caps and snaprings.

Drive Axle Housing

REMOVAL AND INSTALLATION

Wrangler, Cherokee and Comanche

REAR

1. Raise and support the vehicle safely.
2. Remove the rear wheels.
3. Matchmark and remove the driveshaft.
4. Disconnect the track bar, if equipped.
5. Disconnect the vent hose, parking brake cable and shock absorbers.
6. Disconnect the brake hose at the junction.

NOTE: Do not disconnect the wheel cylinders.

7. Loosen the bolts that attach the spring front eyes to the frame.
8. Remove the spring U-bolts and support the axle with a floorjack.
9. Raise the rear just enough to relieve the axle weight from the springs.
10. Remove the bolts attaching the springs to the shackles and lower the rear.
To install:
11. Support the axle on the floorjack and raise into position.
12. Install the spring shackle bolts but do not tighten them.

NOTE: The track bar and spring eye bushing bolts must be tightened with the vehicle at ride height.

13. Align the spring center bolts with the locating holes and lower the axle onto the springs. Install the U-bolts and brackets.
14. Tighten the U-bolts to the 44–52 ft. lbs. (60–70 Nm).
15. Connect the axle vent tube, parking brake cables and brake hose.
16. Align and install the driveshaft. Tighten the bolts to 14 ft. lbs. (19 Nm).
17. Connect the track bar and torque the bolts to 74 ft. lbs. (100 Nm).
18. Install the shock absorbers.
19. Bleed the brakes.
20. Check the fluid level in the differential.
21. Install the wheels.
22. Lower the vehicle.

FRONT

1. Raise and support the vehicle safely.
2. Remove the wheels, calipers and rotors.
3. Disconnect all vacuum hoses at the axle.
4. Matchmark and remove the driveshaft.
5. Disconnect the stabilizer bar, tie rod and drag/center link, shock absorbers, steering damper, track bar and ABS brake sensors.
6. Support the front axle with a floorjack.
7. Disconnect the upper and lower control arms at the axle and lower the axle from the vehicle.
8. Disconnect the spring bushing through bolts and U-bolts from the axle tube.
9. Lower the axle.
To install:
10. Raise and support the axle assembly in position with a floor jack.
11. Install and tighten all suspension arm or spring shackle bolts. Tighten the bolts finger-tight.
12. Connect the stabilizer bar, rod and center link, shock absorbers, steering damper, track bar and ABS brake sensors. Lower the vehicle to normal ride height and tighten the suspension bolts as follows:
Upper control arm-to-axle — 55 ft. lbs. 75 Nm)
Lower control arm-to-axle — 133 ft. lbs. 181 Nm)
Track bar-to-axle — 74 ft. lbs. (101 Nm)
Steering damper-to-axle — 55 ft. lbs. (75 Nm)
Shock absorber lower bolt — 14 ft. lbs. (19 Nm)
Center link-to-knuckle — 35 ft. lbs. (48 Nm)
Stabilizer bar-to-axle — 70 ft. lbs. (96 Nm)
Stabilizer bar-to-connecting links — 55 ft. lbs. (75 Nm)
U-joint strap nuts — 14 ft. lbs. (19 Nm)
U-bolt retaining nuts — 100 ft. lbs. (136 Nm)

NOTE: Discard the U-joint straps. New replacement straps must be used whenever the straps are removed.

13. Align and install the driveshaft.
14. Connect all vacuum hoses at the axle.
15. Install the wheels, calipers and rotors.
16. Check the front wheel alignment.

1993–96 Grand Cherokee and 1993 Grand Wagoneer

REAR

1. Raise and support the vehicle safely.
2. Remove the rear wheels.
3. Matchmark and remove the driveshaft.
4. Disconnect the track bar, if equipped.
5. Disconnect the vent hose, parking brake cable and shock absorbers.
6. Disconnect the brake hose at the junction.

NOTE: Do not disconnect the wheel cylinders.

7. Loosen the bolts that attach the spring front eyes to the frame.
8. Remove the spring U-bolts and support the axle with a floorjack.
9. Raise the rear just enough to relieve the axle weight from the springs.
10. Remove the bolts attaching the springs to the shackles and lower the rear.
To install:
11. Support the axle on the floorjack and raise into position.
12. Install the spring shackle bolts but do not tighten them.

NOTE: The track bar and spring eye bushing bolts must be tightened with the vehicle at ride height.

13. Align the spring center bolts with the locating holes and lower the axle onto the springs. Install the U-bolts and brackets.
14. Tighten the U-bolts to the following specifications:
• Lower suspension arm bolts: 130 ft. lbs. (177 Nm)
• Upper suspension arm bolts: 55 ft. lbs. (75 Nm)
15. Connect the axle vent tube, parking brake cables and brake hose.
16. Align and install the driveshaft. Tighten the bolts to 14 ft. lbs. (19 Nm).
17. Connect the track bar and torque the bolts to 74 ft. lbs. (100 Nm).
18. Install the shock absorbers.
19. Bleed the brakes.
20. Check the fluid level in the differential.
21. Install the wheels.
22. Lower the vehicle.

FRONT

1. Raise and support the vehicle safely under the frame rails behind the lower suspension arm brackets.
2. Remove the front wheels.
3. Remove the brake components and if equipped, the ABS sensor.

4. Disconnect the axle vent hose and driveshaft.

5. Disconnect the stabilizer bar link at the axle bracket.

6. Disconnect the axle brackets from the axle bracket.

7. Disconnect the track bar from the axle bracket.

8. Disconnect the tie rod and drag link from the steering knuckles.

9. Disconnect the steering dampener from the axle bracket.

10. Support the axle with a hydraulic jack.

11. Disconnect the upper and lower suspension arms from the axle bracket.

12. Lower the axle with the jack.

NOTE: The coil springs will drop with the axle.

13. Remove the coil springs.
To install:

— **WARNING** —
All suspension components using rubber bushings should be tightened with the vehicle at ride height. It is important to have the springs supporting the vehicles weight when the fasteners are torqued. If the springs are not at their normal ride position, vehicle ride comfort could be affected along with premature bushing wear. The rubber bushings must never be lubricated.

14. Install the springs, retainer clip and bolts.

15. Position the axle into the vehicle and align it with the straight pads.

16. Position the upper and lower suspension arm at the axle bracket. Install the bolts finger-tight.

17. Connect the tack bar to the axle bracket and install the bolt. Do not tighten at this time.

18. Install the shock absorbers and torque the nuts to 20 ft. lbs. (27 Nm).

19. Install the stabilizer link to the axle bracket and torque the nut to 70 ft. lbs. (96 Nm).

20. Install the drag link and tie rod to the steering knuckles. Torque the nuts to 35 ft. lbs. (47 Nm).

21. Install the steering dampener to the steering axle bracket and torque the nut to 55 ft. lbs. (75 Nm).

22. Install the brake components and if equipped ABS sensor.

23. Connect the vent hose and driveshaft.

24. Check differential lubricant, add if necessary.

25. Install the wheels and tires.

26. Lower the vehicle.

27. Torque the upper suspension arm nuts to 55 ft. lbs. (75 Nm) and lower suspension arm nuts to 85 ft. lbs. (115 Nm).

28. Torque the track bar bolt at the axle bracket to 55 ft. lbs. (75 Nm).

29. Check the front wheel alignment.

Pinion Seal

REMOVAL AND INSTALLATION

Wrangler, Cherokee, Comanche, 1993–96 Grand Cherokee and 1993 Grand Wagoneer

1. Raise and support the vehicle safely.

2. Matchmark and remove the driveshaft.

3. Rotate the pinion gear 3–4 times and measure the amount of torque necessary to rotate the pinion.

4. Measure and note the amount of torque necessary to to rotate the pinion gear with a torque wrench.

NOTE: It is necessary to note the torque to properly adjust the pinion gear bearing preload torque after seal installation.

5. Remove the pinion yoke nut and washer.

6. Using a suitable puller, remove the pinion yoke.

7. Matchmark the pinion yoke and gear for installation alignment reference.

8. Carefully remove the pinion gear seal.
To install:

9. Lubricate and install the new pinion seal using a seal driver.

10. Align and install the yoke, washer and pinion nut. Tighten the pinion nut only enough to remove the shaft end-play.

— **WARNING** —
Do not over-tighten or loosen and re-tighten the nut.

11. Using a torque wrench, note the amount of torque necessary to rotate the pinion. The required pinion preload torque is equal to the measurement noted in the removal steps, plus 5 inch lbs.

12. Tighten the pinion nut in small increments and continue measuring preload torque until correct.

13. Align and install the driveshaft using new strap bolts. Torque the bolts to 14 ft. lbs. (19 Nm).

STEERING

Steering Wheel

REMOVAL AND INSTALLATION

Wrangler, Cherokee and Comanche

1. Disconnect the negative battery cable.

2. Set the front tires in a straight-ahead position.

3. Pull the horn button from the steering wheel.

4. If equipped with a standard wheel, remove the trim cover attaching screws and the trim cover. If equipped with a sport wheel, remove the horn contact and flexplate.

5. Remove the steering wheel nut and, if equipped, vibration damper.

6. Scribe a line mark on the steering wheel and steering shaft if there is not one already.

7. Remove the steering wheel using a suitable puller.
To install:

8. To install, align the scribe marks on the steering shaft with the steering wheel.

9. If equipped, install the vibration damper on the hub. Install the steering wheel retaining nut and tighten to 25 ft. lbs. (34 Nm).

10. Install the internal components, horn flexplate and the trim cover/horn button.

11. Connect the negative battery cable.

1993–96 Grand Cherokee and 1993 Grand Wagoneer

— **CAUTION** —
Before removing the steering wheel, disconnect the negative battery cable, then wait at least 2 minutes for the system capacitor to discharge, in order to disable the air bag system. Failure to do so could result in accidental air bag deployment and possible injury.

1. Disconnect the negative battery cable. Wait at least 2 minutes for the reserve capacitor to discharge.

2. Set the front tires in a straight-ahead position.

3. Remove the air bag module retaining nuts from behind the steering wheel.

4. Remove the air bag module.

5. If equipped, remove the cruise control switch.

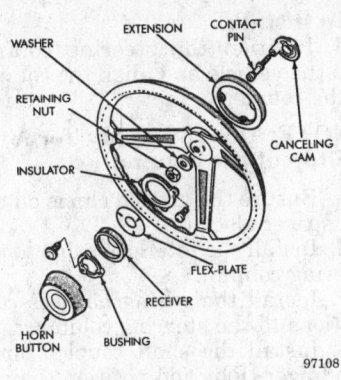

Sport wheel removal

6. Disconnect the horn wiring.
7. Remove the steering wheel retaining nut.
8. Scribe a line mark on the steering wheel and steering shaft if there is not one already.
9. Remove the steering wheel using a suitable puller.

To install:

10. To install, align the scribe marks on the steering shaft with the steering wheel.
11. Ensure the wheel compresses the 2 lock tabs on the clockspring.
12. Pull the air bag and if equipped, cruise control wires through the larger hole and horn wire through the smaller hole. Ensure they are not pinched.
13. Install the steering wheel nut and torque it to 45 ft. lbs. (61 Nm) while forcing the steering wheel don the shaft with the nut.
14. Connect the wire feed to the horn buttons.
15. Connect the feed wires and torque the air bag retaining nuts to 90 inch lbs. (10 Nm). Ensure the air bag is completely seated. the latching clip arms must be visible on top of the connector housing on the module.
16. Connect the DRB scan tool or equivalent to the ACM diagnostic 6-way connector located under the right front seat, beneath the carpet.

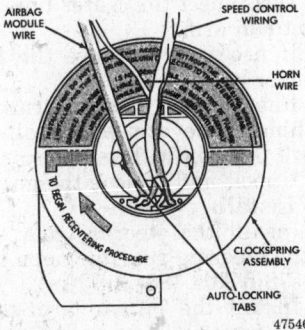

Clockspring (auto-locking) — Grand Wagoneer and Grand Cherokee

17. From the right side of the vehicle (in case of accidental deployment), turn the ignition switch to the **ON** position.
18. Insert the latest cartridge into the DRB.
19. Connect the negative battery cable.
20. Using the DRB, read and record any active or stored Diagnostic Trouble Code (DTC), repair as necessary.
21. If no DTC is found, remove the DRB.

Steering Column

REMOVAL AND INSTALLATION

1992–96 Wrangler

NOTE: Bumping, jolting and hammering on the steering column shaft and gear shift tube must be avoided during all service procedures.

1. Position the front wheels in the straight ahead position.
2. Disconnect the negative battery cable.
3. Remove the steering wheel.
4. If equipped with a column shift lever, disconnect the shift cable grommet by prying it from the shift lever.
5. Disconnect the column shaft-to-steering gear coupler upper bolt.
6. Remove the lower portion of the instrument panel.
7. Remove the nuts securing the column bracket to the brake sled.
8. Remove the bolts securing the steering column bracket to the column.
9. Disconnect the following items from the steering column connectors:
• Ignition switch
• Dimmer switch
• Turn signal switch
• Windshield wiper
• Cruise control, if equipped
• Park-lock cable, if equipped
10. Remove the bolts attaching the toe plate to the floor pan.
11. Remove the steering column from the vehicle.

To install:

12. Position the steering column into the vehicle and align the gear coupling. Torque the bolt to 25 ft. lbs. (34 Nm).
13. Connect the electrical harnesses disconnected during removal.
14. Install the support bracket on the column and torque the bolts to 180 inch lbs. (20 Nm).

15. Raise the column to the brake sled studs and connect the brace to the column. Torque the brake sled nuts or bolts to 22 ft. lbs. (30 Nm).
16. If equipped with a column shift lever, install the shift cable grommet on the shift lever.
17. Install the toe plate-to-floor pan bolts and torque them to 66 inch lbs. (8 Nm).
18. Install the lower portion of the instrument panel.
19. Install the steering wheel.
20. Connect the negative battery cable.

1992–96 Cherokee and 1992 Comanche

NOTE: Bumping, jolting and hammering on the steering column shaft and gear shift tube must be avoided during all service procedures.

1. Position the front wheels in the straight ahead position.
2. Disconnect the negative battery cable.
3. Remove the steering wheel.
4. If equipped with a column shift lever, disconnect the shift cable grommet by prying it from the shift lever.
5. Disconnect the column shaft-to-steering gear coupler upper bolt.
6. Remove the lower portion of the instrument panel.
7. If equipped with a column shift lever, disconnect the shift indicator cable from the shift housing.
8. Remove the nuts securing the column bracket to the brake sled.
9. Remove the bolts securing the steering column bracket to the column.
10. Loosen the column brace mounting nut at the drivers side kick panel and allow the column to drop.
11. Disconnect the following items from the steering column connectors:
• Ignition switch
• Dimmer switch
• Turn signal switch
• Windshield wiper
• Cruise control, if equipped
• Park-lock cable, if equipped
12. Remove the bolts attaching the toe plate to the floor pan.
13. Remove the steering column from the vehicle.

To install:

14. Position the steering column into the vehicle and align the gear coupling. Torque the bolt to 25 ft. lbs. (34 Nm).
15. Connect the electrical harnesses disconnected during removal.

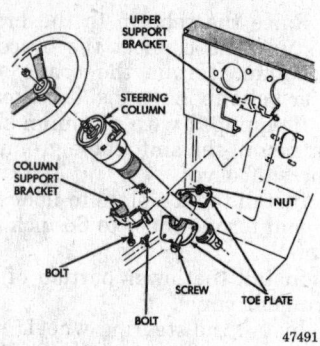

Steering column removal and installation

47491

16. Install the support bracket on the column and torque the bolts to 180 inch lbs. (20 Nm).

17. Raise the column to the brake sled studs and connect the brace to the column. Torque the brake sled nuts or bolts to 22 ft. lbs. (30 Nm).

18. If equipped with a column shift lever, install the shift cable grommet on the shift lever.

19. Install the toe plate-to-floor pan bolts and torque them to 66 inch lbs. (8 Nm).

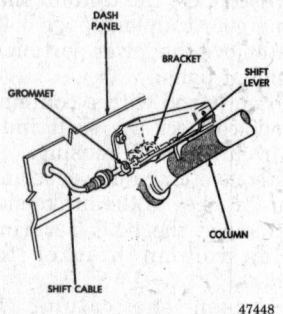

Shift cable grommet — automatic transmission — Cherokee and Comanche

47448

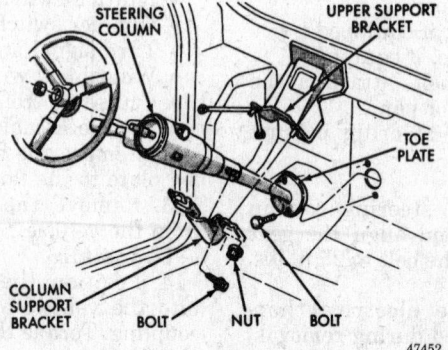

Steering column removal and installation — Cherokee and Comanche

47452

20. If equipped with a column shift lever, install the shift indicator cable on the housing.

21. Install the lower portion of the instrument panel.

22. Install the steering wheel.

23. Connect the negative battery cable.

1993–96 Grand Cherokee and 1993 Grand Wagoneer

—— CAUTION ——

Before removing the steering wheel or air bag module, disconnect the negative battery cable, then wait at least 2 minutes for the system capacitor to discharge, in order to disable the air bag system. Failure to do so could result in accidental air bag deployment and possible injury.

1. Position the front wheels in the straight ahead position.

2. Disconnect the negative battery cable.

3. Remove the steering wheel.

4. Remove the column coupler upper pinch bolt.

5. Remove the trim panel column cover and support plate.

6. If equipped, remove the tilt lever from the column.

7. Remove the upper and lower lock housing shrouds.

8. Remove the heater cross over tube from under the column.

9. Loosen the panel bracket nuts and studs and allow the column to drop.

10. Remove the wiring harness from the column.

11. Remove the interlock cable from the column.

12. Remove the toe plate-to-dash panel nuts.

13. Remove the panel bracket nuts and studs. Remove the steering column from the vehicle.

To install:

14. Position the steering column into the vehicle and align the column to the coupler.

NOTE: Do not apply force to the top of the column.

15. Ensure the ground clip is on the left spacer slot.

16. Install the interlock cable to the steering column.

17. Install the wiring harness connections to the steering column.

18. Install the shaft coupler pinch bolt finger-tight and position the column to the panel bracket.

19. Ensure both spacers are fully seated in the column support bracket and torque the nuts and studs to 105 inch lbs. (12 Nm). Ensure the nut is installed on the short threaded side of the stud.

20. Torque the toe plate attaching nuts to 105 inch lbs. (12 Nm).

21. Torque the coupler pinch bolt to 35 ft. lbs. (47 Nm).

22. Install the heater cross over tube.

23. Install the upper and lower shrouds.

24. If equipped, install the tilt lever.

25. Install the trim panel column cover and support plate.

26. Install the steering wheel.

27. If installing a new column, remove the shaft shipping lock pin.

28. Connect the negative battery cable.

Manual Steering Gear

REMOVAL AND INSTALLATION

Wrangler, Cherokee and Comanche

1. Place the front wheels in the straight ahead position.

2. Disconnect the steering shaft from the gear.

3. Raise and safely support the vehicle.

4. Disconnect the center link from the pitman arm.

5. If necessary, remove the front stabilizer bar.

6. Remove the pitman arm nut, matchmark the arm and shaft and remove the arm with a puller.

7. Unbolt and remove the gear.

To install:

8. Install the steering gear. Torque the steering gear to frame bolts to 65–78 ft. lbs. (88–106 Nm).

9. Install the pitman arm to its original position. Torque the nut to 185 ft. lbs. (252 Nm) and stake the nut securely.

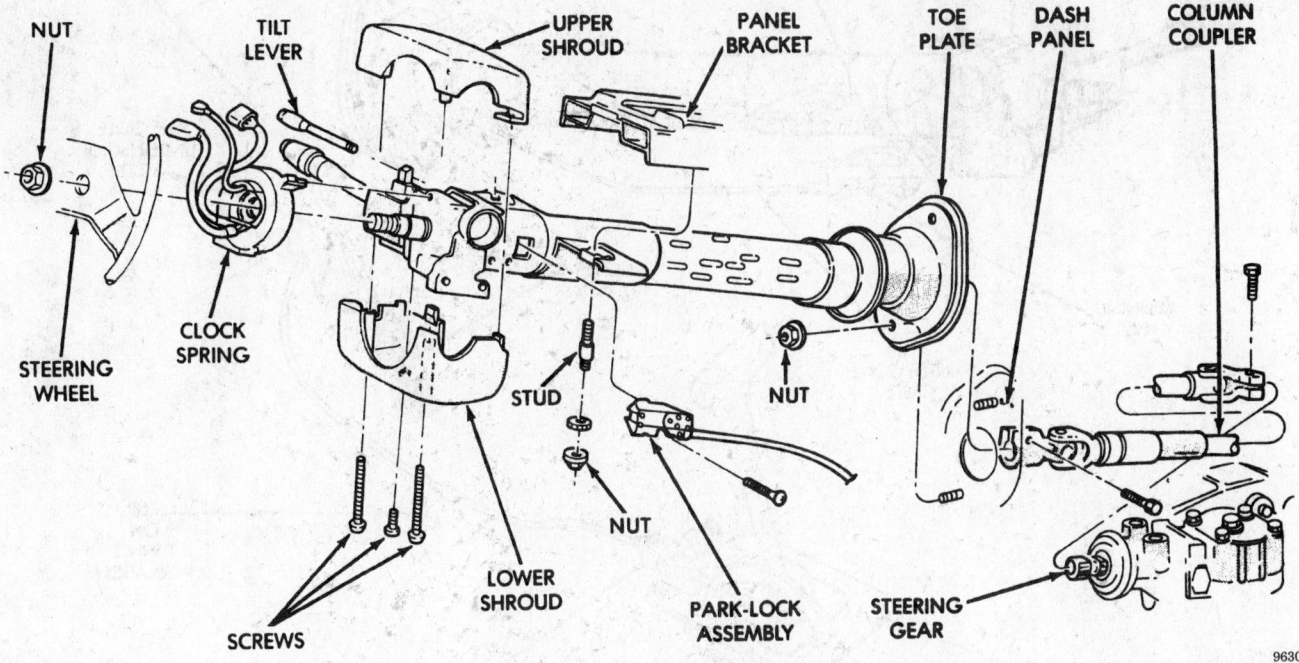

NUT   TILT LEVER   UPPER SHROUD   PANEL BRACKET   TOE PLATE   DASH PANEL   COLUMN COUPLER

CLOCK SPRING   STUD   NUT

STEERING WHEEL

NUT

SCREWS   LOWER SHROUD   PARK-LOCK ASSEMBLY   STEERING GEAR

96301

Exploded view of the steering column — Grand Cherokee and Grand Wagoneer

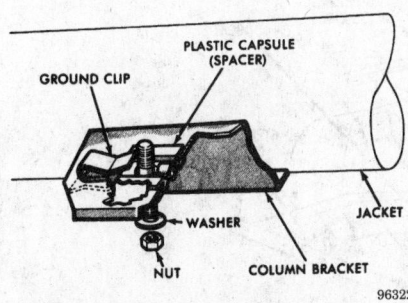

PLASTIC CAPSULE (SPACER)

GROUND CLIP

JACKET

WASHER

NUT   COLUMN BRACKET

96322

Ground clip and spacer installation — Grand Cherokee and Grand Wagoneer

10. If equipped, install the stabilizer bar and bolts as follows:
• Stabilizer bar-to-frame — 55 ft. lbs. (75 Nm)
• Stabilizer bar-to-link — 27 ft. lbs. (37 Nm)
11. Connect the center link to the pitman arm and torque the nut to 55 ft. lbs. (75 Nm).
12. Lower the vehicle.
13. Connect the steering shaft to the gear and tighten the nuts.

ADJUSTMENT

Wrangler, Cherokee and Comanche

1. Raise and safely support the vehicle.
2. Check the steering gear mounting bolt torque.
3. Matchmark the pitman arm and shaft and remove the pitman arm nut. Remove the arm with a puller.
4. Loosen the pitman adjusting screw locknut, then back off the adjusting screw 2–3 turns.
5. Remove the horn button and cover. Slowly turn the steering wheel in one direction as far as it will go, then back ½ turn.
6. Install a socket and torque wrench in the steering wheel nut. Measure the worm bearing preload by turning the wheel through a 90 degree arc (¼ turn) with the wrench. Preload should be 5–8 inch lbs.
7. If preload is not within specifications, turn the adjuster screw clockwise to increase or counterclockwise to decrease the preload.
8. When the desired preload is attained, tighten the adjuster locknut to 50 ft. lbs. and recheck the adjustment.
9. Rotate the steering wheel slowly from lock-to-lock, counting the number of turns. Turn the wheel back, ½ the number of turns to center the gear, then turn the wheel ½ turn off center.
10. Install the torque wrench and socket on the steering wheel nut. Measure the torque required to turn the gear through the center point of travel. The drag should equal the worm bearing preload torque plus 4–10 inch lbs. but not exceed a total of 18 inch lbs.
11. If adjustment is required, loosen the pitman shaft screw locknut and turn the adjusting screw to obtain the desired torque. Tighten the locknut to 25 ft. lbs. and recheck the overcenter drag.
12. Install all parts and check steering wheel alignment.

Power Steering Gear

REMOVAL AND INSTALLATION

1992–96 Wrangler, 1992–96 Cherokee, 1992 Comanche, 1993–96 Grand Cherokee and 1993 Grand Wagoneer

1. Place the wheels in the straight ahead position.
2. Disconnect and cap the power steering lines from the steering gear.

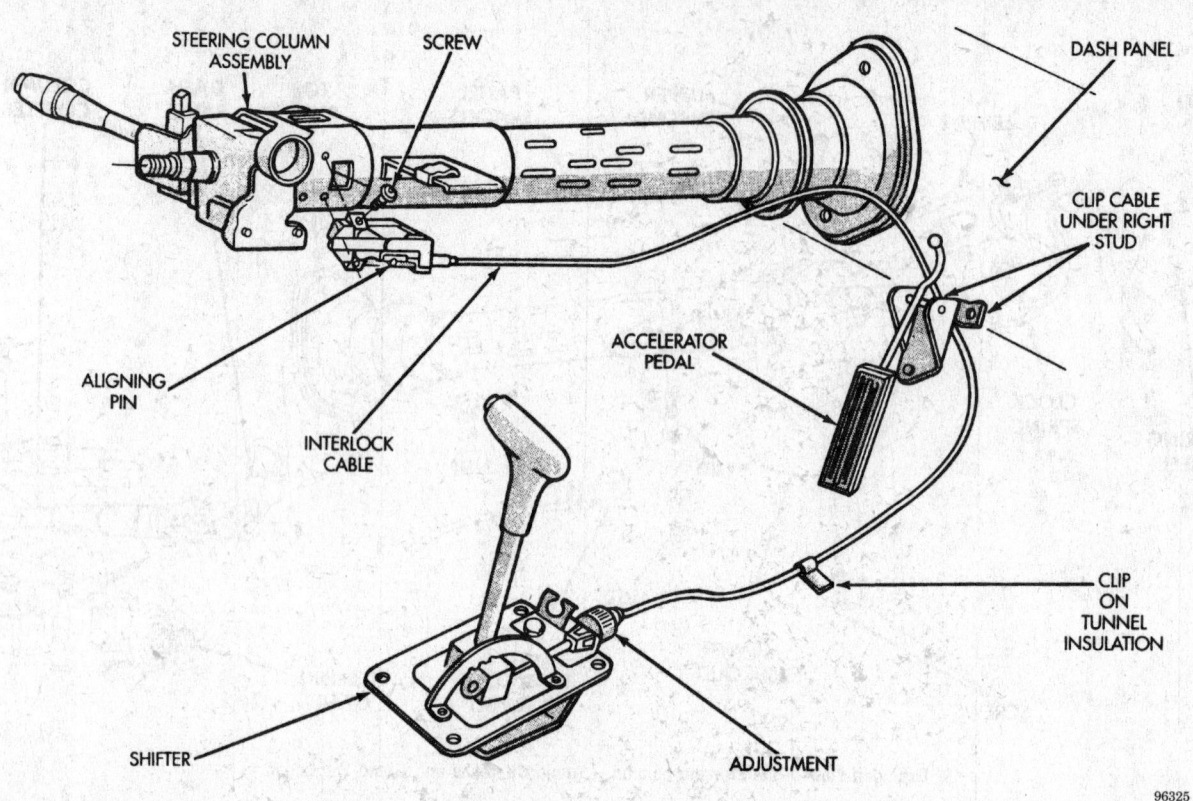

STEERING COLUMN ASSEMBLY

SCREW

DASH PANEL

CLIP CABLE UNDER RIGHT STUD

ALIGNING PIN

INTERLOCK CABLE

ACCELERATOR PEDAL

CLIP ON TUNNEL INSULATION

SHIFTER

ADJUSTMENT

96325

Ignition interlock cable routing — Grand Cherokee and Grand Wagoneer

3. Remove the column coupler shaft from the gear.

4. Matchmark the pitman arm to the gear and remove the pitman arm.

5. Remove the steering gear retaining bolts and remove the gear.

To install:

6. Align the column coupler shaft to the steering gear.

7. Position the steering gear and bracket on the frame rail and install the bolts. Torque the bolts to:

1992–96 Wrangler — 78 ft. lbs. (105 Nm)

1992–96 Cherokee and 1992 Comanche — 70 ft. lbs. (96 Nm)

1993–96 Grand Cherokee and 1993 Grand Wagoneer — 65 ft. lbs. (88 Nm)

8. Align and install the pitman arm.

9. Connect the power steering lines.

10. Fill the power steering reservoir to the proper level with fluid and bleed the system.

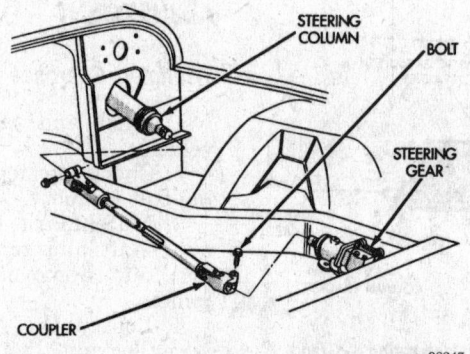

STEERING COLUMN

BOLT

STEERING GEAR

COUPLER

98247

Column shaft removal — Wrangler 1992–96

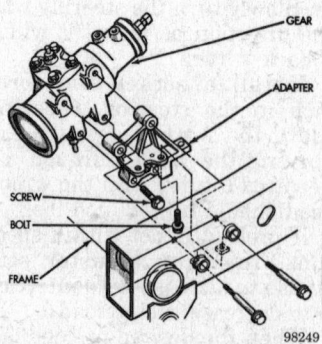

GEAR

ADAPTER

SCREW

BOLT

FRAME

98249

Steering gear installation — Wrangler 1992–96

Steering Pump

REMOVAL AND INSTALLATION

Wrangler, Cherokee and Comanche

SERPENTINE DRIVE BELT

1. Disconnect the negative battery cable.

2. Loosen and remove the serpentine drive belt.

3. Place a drain pan under the power steering pump.

4. Clamp the power steering pump pressure and return fluid lines and

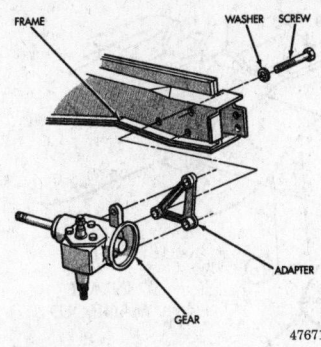

Steering gear installation — 1992–96
Cherokee and 1992 Comanche

disconnect the lines from the hose from the pump.

5. Remove the rear bracket-to-pump bolts.

6. Remove the lower nut and adjustment bracket.

7. Remove the adjuster and pivot bolts.

8. Tilt the pump forward and remove the pump and front bracket assembly from the engine bracket.

9. Remove the bracket from the pump.

To install:

10. Install the bracket to the pump and torque the bolts to 21 ft. lbs. (28 Nm).

11. Position the pump and bracket on the engine bracket.

12. Install the pivot bolt.

13. Install the adjuster bolt.

14. Install the adjuster stud nut.

15. Install the rear bracket-to-pump bolts and torque them to 21 ft. lbs. (28 Nm).

16. Install the serpentine belt.

17. Connect the power steering lines and remove the clamps.

18. Fill the pump reservoir to the proper level with fluid.

19. Connect the negative battery cable.

20. Bleed the system.

V-TYPE DRIVE BELT

1. Disconnect the negative battery cable.

2. Remove the drive belt.

3. Remove the air cleaner.

4. Disconnect the hoses at the pump and cap the hose ends.

5. Remove the front bracket-to-engine bolts.

6. Support the pump and remove the pump-to-rear bracket nuts.

7. Lift out the pump.

To install:

8. Install the pump into position and torque the pump-to-bracket nuts to 28 ft. lbs.; the bracket-to-engine bolts to 33 ft. lbs.

9. Connect the hoses.

10. Install the air cleaner.

11. Install the drive belt.

12. Connect the negative battery cable.

13. Bleed the system.

1993–96 Grand Cherokee and 1993 Grand Wagoneer

4.0L ENGINE

1. Disconnect the negative battery cable.

2. Loosen and remove the serpentine drive belt.

3. Place a drain pan under the power steering pump.

4. Clamp the power steering pump pressure and return fluid lines and disconnect the lines from the hose from the pump.

5. Remove the rear bracket-to-pump bolts.

6. Remove the lower nut and adjustment bracket.

7. Remove the adjuster and pivot bolts.

8. Tilt the pump forward and remove the pump and front bracket assembly from the engine bracket.

9. Remove the bracket from the pump.

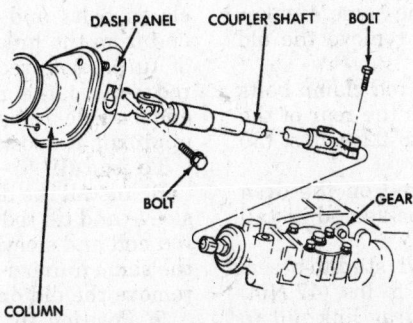

Coupling shaft removal — 1993–96 Grand
Cherokee and 1993 Grand Wagoneer

To install:

10. Install the bracket to the pump and torque the bolts to 21 ft. lbs. (28 Nm).

11. Position the pump and bracket on the engine bracket.

12. Install the pivot bolt.

13. Install the adjuster bolt.

14. Install the adjuster stud nut.

15. Install the rear bracket-to-pump bolts and torque them to 21 ft. lbs. (28 Nm).

16. Install the serpentine belt.

17. Connect the power steering lines and remove the clamps.

18. Fill the pump reservoir to the proper level with fluid.

19. Connect the negative battery cable.

20. Bleed the system.

5.2L ENGINE

1. Disconnect the negative battery cable.

2. Loosen and remove the serpentine drive belt.

3. Place a drain pan under the power steering pump.

4. Disconnect the return and pressure lines from the pump.

5. Remove the bolts attaching the pump to the bracket on the engine block.

6. If necessary, remove the bracket-to-engine block bolts.

To install:

7. Install the bracket to the engine block and torque the bolts to 30 ft. lbs. (41 Nm).

8. Mount the pump on the bracket and torque the bolts 20 ft. lbs. (27 Nm).

9. Install the serpentine belt.

10. Connect the fluid lines to the pump and remove the clamps.

11. Fill the power steering reservoir to the proper level with fluid.

12. Connect the negative battery cable.

13. Bleed the system.

Tie Rod Ends-Power Steering

REMOVAL AND INSTALLATION

Wrangler

1. Raise and safely support the vehicle.

2. Remove the cotter pins and nuts from the tie rod end ball studs, drag link end ball stud, and steering damper piston rod ball stud.

3. Use a suitable puller to loosen the ball studs, then remove the tie rod.

FASTENER TORQUE			
LETTER	N•m	IN. LBS.	FT. LBS.
A	57	—	42
B	28	250	21
C	47	—	35

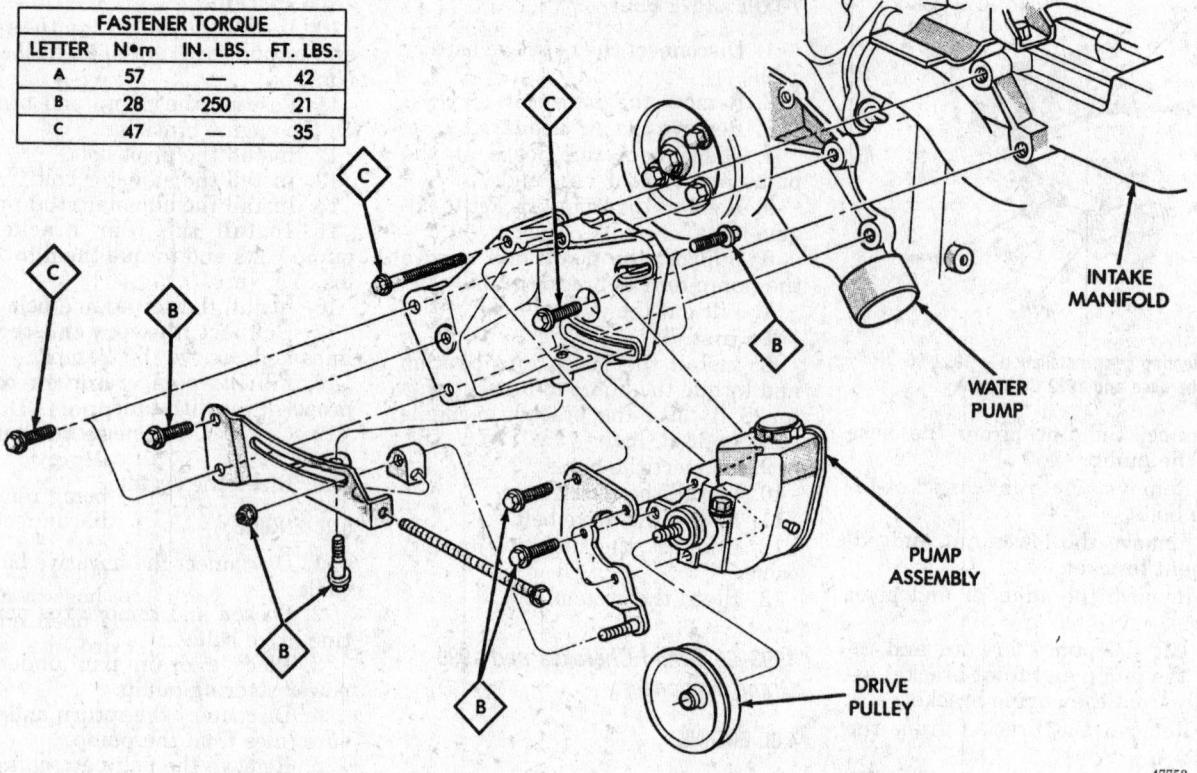

Steering pump installation — 4.0L engine

4. If necessary, loosen the adjustment sleeve clamp bolts and remove the tie rod end from the tie rod. Count the number of turns required to remove the tie rod end so the replacement can be reinstalled in approximately the same position.

To install:

5. If removed, install the tie rod end to the tie rod. Thread the tie rod end on the same number of turns that was required to remove the old one. Position the adjustment sleeve bolts so the threaded ends of the bolts face rearward and are angled upward.

6. Attach the tie rod ends to the steering knuckles and the drag link ball stud to the tie rod. Install the nuts and tighten to 35 ft. lbs. (47 Nm).

7. Install new cotter pins in the ball studs. If the ball stud hole does not align with the nut castellation, tighten the nut further until the cotter pin can be installed.

8. Attach the steering damper to the tie rod and tighten the nut to 53 ft. lbs. (71 Nm). Install a new cotter pin. If the ball stud hole does not align with the nut castellation, tighten the nut further until the cotter pin can be installed.

9. Lower the vehicle and check the toe adjustment.

1992 Cherokee and Comanche

TIE ROD

1. Raise and safely support the vehicle.

2. Remove the cotter pins at the steering knuckle and drag link.

3. Loosen the ball studs using a suitable puller.

4. If necessary, loosen the end clamp bolts and remove the tie rod ends from the tube. Count the number of turns required to remove the tie rod ends so the replacement tie rod ends can be reinstalled in the same approximate position.

To install:

5. If removed, install the tie rod ends in the tube. Thread the tie rod ends into the tube the same number of turns required to remove the old ones.

6. Position the tie rod clamp bolts so the bolt heads face the rear of the vehicle and tighten to 22 ft. lbs. (30 Nm).

7. Install the tie rod on the drag link and steering knuckle and install the retaining nuts.

8. Tighten the ball stud-to-steering knuckle nut to 35 ft. lbs. (47 Nm) and the ball stud-to-drag link nut to 55 ft. lbs. (75 Nm). Install new cotter pins. If the ball stud hole does not align with the nut castellation, fur-

ther tighten the nut in order to install the cotter pin.

9. Lower the vehicle and check the toe adjustment.

DRAG LINK

1. Raise and safely support the vehicle.

2. Remove the cotter pins and nuts at the steering knuckle, tie rod and pitman arm.

3. Remove the steering dampener ball stud from the drag link using a suitable puller tool.

4. Remove the tie rod from the drag link and remove the drag link from the steering knuckle and pitman arm using a suitable puller tool.

5. If necessary, loosen the end clamp bolts and remove the tie rod end from the link. Count the number of turns required to remove the tie rod end so the replacement tie rod end can be reinstalled in the same approximate position.

To install:

6. Install the drag link adjustment sleeve and tie rod end. Thread the tie rod end and sleeve onto the drag link the same number of turns required to remove the old ones.

7. Position the clamp bolts so the threaded ends are facing rearward and angled upward and tighten the bolts.

8. Install the drag link to the steering knuckle, tie rod and pitman arm. Install the nuts and tighten the one at the steering knuckle to 35 ft. lbs. (47 Nm) and the ones at the tie rod and pitman arm to 55 ft. lbs. (75 Nm). Install new cotter pins. If the ball stud hole does not align with the nut castellation, further tighten the nut in order to install the cotter pin.

9. Install the steering dampener onto the drag link and tighten the nut to 55 ft. lbs. (75 Nm). Install a new cotter pin. If the ball stud hole does not align with the nut castellation, further tighten the nut in order to install the cotter pin.

10. Lower the vehicle and check the toe adjustment.

1993–96 Grand Cherokee and 1993 Grand Wagoneer

TIE ROD

1. Remove the cotter pins at the steering knuckle and drag link.
2. Loosen the ball studs using a suitable puller.
3. If necessary, loosen the end clamp bolts and remove the tie rod ends from the tube. Count the number of turns required to remove the tie rod ends so the replacement tie rod ends can be reinstalled in the same approximate position.

To install:
4. If removed, install the tie rod ends in the tube. Thread the tie rod ends into the tube the same number of turns required to remove the old ones.
5. Position the tie rod clamps and tighten to 20 ft. lbs. (27 Nm).
6. Install the tie rod on the drag link and steering knuckle and install the retaining nuts.
7. Tighten the ball stud nuts to 55 ft. lbs. (75 Nm) and install new cotter pins. If the ball stud hole does not align with the nut castellation, further tighten the nut in order to install the cotter pin.
8. Check the toe adjustment.

DRAG LINK

1. Remove the cotter pins and nuts at the steering knuckle and drag link.
2. Remove the steering dampener ball stud from the drag link using a suitable puller tool.
3. Remove the tie rod from the drag link and remove the drag link from the steering knuckle and pitman arm using a suitable puller tool.
4. If necessary, loosen the end clamp bolts and remove the tie rod end from the link. Count the number of turns required to remove the tie rod end so the replacement tie rod end can be reinstalled in the same approximate position.

To install:
5. Install the drag link adjustment sleeve and tie rod end. Thread the tie rod end and sleeve onto the drag link the same number of turns required to remove the old ones.
6. Position the clamp bolts and tighten to 36 ft. lbs. (49 Nm).
7. Install the drag link to the steering knuckle, tie rod and pitman arm. Install the nuts and tighten to 55 ft. lbs. (75 Nm). Install new cotter pins. If the ball stud hole does not align with the nut castellation, further tighten the nut in order to install the cotter pin.
8. Install the steering dampener onto the drag link and tighten the nut to 55 ft. lbs. (75 Nm). Install a new cotter pin. If the ball stud hole does not align with the nut castellation, further tighten the nut in order to install the cotter pin.
9. Check the toe adjustment.

BRAKES

Brake Caliper

REMOVAL AND INSTALLATION

Wrangler, Cherokee, Comanche, 1993–96 Grand Cherokee and 1993 Grand Wagoneer

1. Drain ⅔ of the brake fluid from the front reservoir. Use the bleeder screw at the front outlet port to drain the fluid. If equipped with anti-lock brakes, relieve the system pressure.
2. Raise and safely support the vehicle.
3. Remove the wheels.
4. Place a C-clamp on the caliper so the solid end contacts the back of the caliper and screw end contacts the metal part of the outboard brake pad.
5. Tighten the clamp until the caliper moves far enough to force the piston to the bottom of the piston bore. This will back the brake pads off of the rotor surface to facilitate the removal and installation of the caliper assembly.

6. Remove the C-clamp.

NOTE: Do not push down on the brake pedal or the piston and brake pads will return to their original positions up against the rotor.

7. Remove both of the Allen head mounting bolts and lift the caliper off the rotor.

NOTE: If just the brake pads are being replaced, it is not necessary to remove the caliper assembly entirely from the vehicle. Do not remove the brake line. Rest the caliper on the front spring or other support. Do not allow the brake hose to support the weight of the caliper.

8. If the caliper is being removed, it is necessary to disconnect the brake fluid hose. Clean the brake fluid hose-to-caliper connection thoroughly. Remove the hose-to-caliper bolt. Cap or tape the open ends to keep dirt out. Discard the copper gaskets.

To install:
9. Connect the brake line to the caliper with new sealing washers and hand-tighten the fitting bolt.
10. Position the caliper into place over the rotor.
11. Coat the caliper mounting bolt with silicone grease and torque them to 7–15 ft. lbs. (10–20 Nm).
12. Position the brake line clear of all chassis components, untwisted and free of kinks. Torque the fitting bolt to 23 ft. lbs. (31 Nm).
13. Install the wheels.
14. Fill the master cylinder with fluid and bleed the brake system.
15. Before driving the vehicle, pump the brakes several times to seat the pads.

Disc Brake Pads

REMOVAL AND INSTALLATION

Wrangler, Cherokee, Comanche, 1993–96 Grand Cherokee and 1993 Grand Wagoneer

1. Raise and safely support the vehicle.
2. Drain ⅔ of the brake fluid from the front reservoir. Use the bleeder screw at the front outlet port to drain the fluid.
3. Raise and support the vehicle safely.
4. Remove the wheels.
5. Remove the brake caliper. Use a suitable tool to compress the caliper piston into the bore.

FASTENER TORQUE			
LETTER	N•m	IN. LBS.	FT. LBS.
◈	251	—	185
◈			
◈	74	—	55
◈			
◈	49	—	36
◈	27	—	20

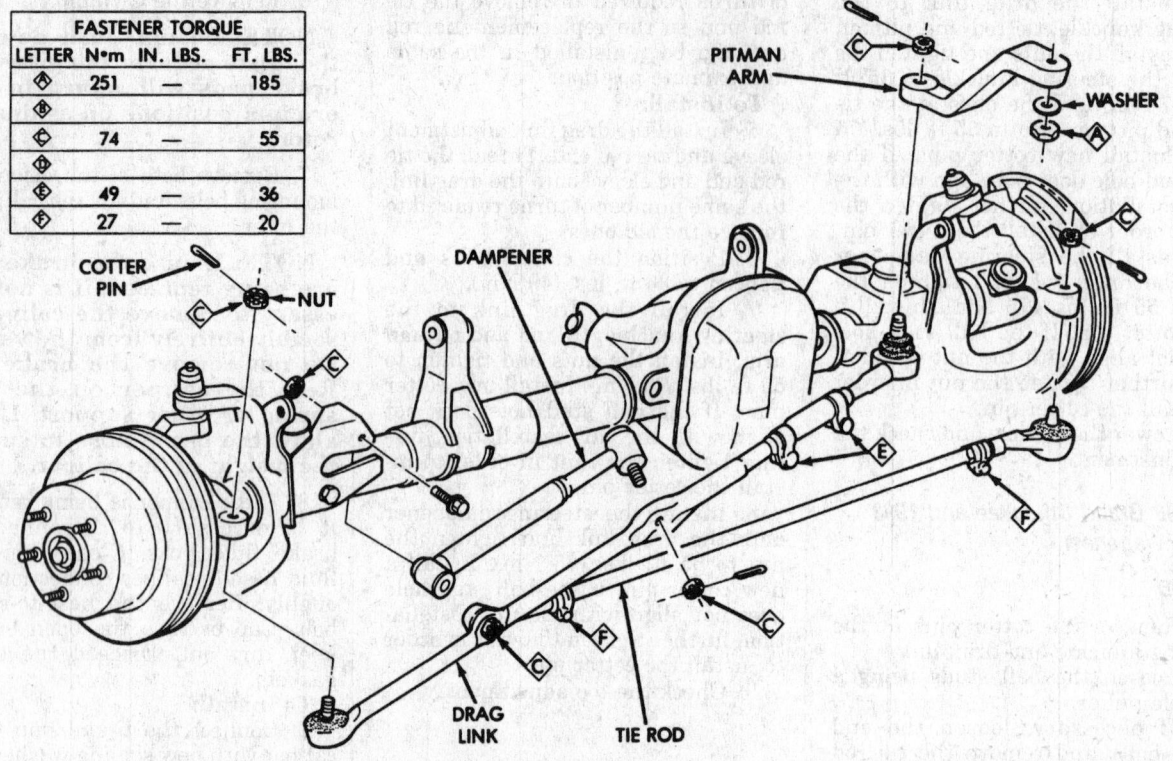

Exploded view of the steering linkage

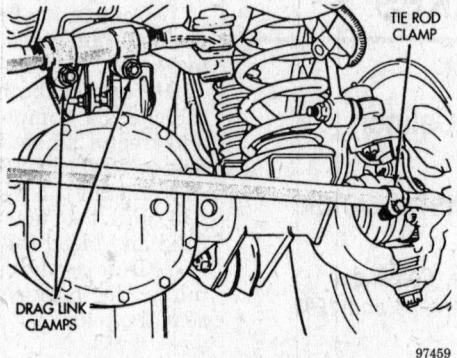

Tie rod and drag link clamp positioning

6. Hold the anti-rattle clip against the caliper anchor plate and remove the outboard brake pad.

7. Remove the inboard pad and its anti-rattle clip.

To install:

8. Clean all the mounting holes and bushing grooves in the caliper ears. Clean the mounting bolts. Replace the bolts if they are corroded or if the threads are damaged. Wipe the inside of the caliper clean, including the exterior of the dust boot. Inspect the dust boot for cuts or cracks and for proper seating in the piston bore.

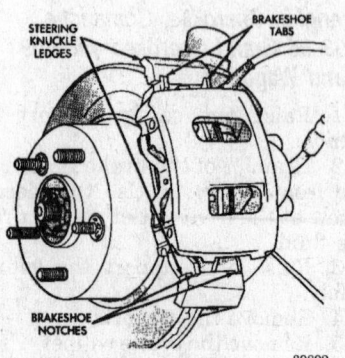

Caliper installation

If evidence of fluid leakage is noted, the caliper should be rebuilt.

NOTE: Do not use abrasives on the bolts in order not to destroy their protective plating. Do not use compressed air to clean the inside of the caliper, as it may unseat the dust boot seal.

9. Install the inboard anti-rattle clip on the trailing end of the anchor plate. The split end of the clip must face away from the rotor.

10. Install the inboard pad in the caliper. The pad must lay flat against the piston.

11. Install the outboard pad in the caliper while holding the anti-rattle clip.

12. With the pads installed, position the caliper over the rotor. Line up the mounting holes in the caliper and the support bracket and insert the mounting bolts. Make sure the bolts pass under the retaining ears on the inboard shoes. Push the bolts through until they engage the holes of the outboard pad and caliper ears. Thread the bolts into the support bracket and tighten them to 30 ft. lbs. 41 Nm).

13. Fill the master cylinder with brake fluid and pump the brake pedal to seat the pads.

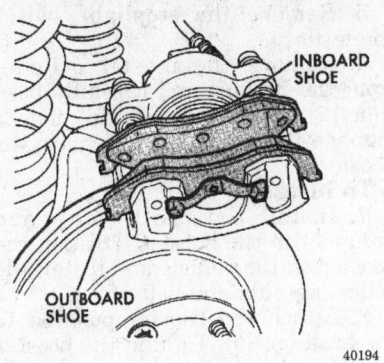

INBOARD SHOE

OUTBOARD SHOE

40194

Disc brake pads installed in the caliper

14. Install the wheel assembly and lower the vehicle. Check the level of the brake fluid in the master cylinder and fill as necessary. Test the operation of the brakes before taking the vehicle onto the road.

Brake Rotor

REMOVAL AND INSTALLATION

Wrangler, Cherokee, Comanche, 1993–96 Grand Cherokee and 1993 Grand Wagoneer

2WD

1. Raise and safely support the vehicle.
2. Remove the wheels.
3. Remove the caliper without disconnecting the brake line. Suspend the caliper aside; do not let it hang by the brake hose.
4. Remove the grease cap, cotter pin, nut cap, nut and washer from the spindle.
5. Pull slowly on the hub and catch the outer bearing as it falls.
6. Remove the hub and rotor. The inner bearing and seal can be removed by prying out and discarding the inner seal.
To install:
7. Clean and repack the hub and bearings, install the inner bearing and a new seal.
8. Position the hub and rotor on the spindle and install the outer bearing.
9. Install the washer and nut.
10. While turning the rotor, torque the nut to 25 ft. lbs. (34 Nm) to seat the bearings.
11. Back off the nut ½ turn and, while turning the rotor, torque the nut to 19 inch lbs.
12. Install the nut cap and a new cotter pin. Install the grease cap.
13. Install the caliper.

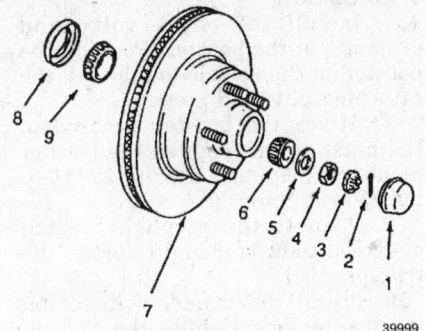

8 9   6 5 4 3 2 1

7   39999

Disc brake rotor — 2WD vehicles

14. Install the wheels and lower the vehicle. Before moving the vehicle, pump the brake pedal several times to seat the brake pads against the rotor.

4WD

1. Loosen the lug nuts on the front wheel.
2. Raise and safely support the vehicle.
3. Remove the front wheel.
4. Remove the caliper but leave the brake line connected. Suspend the caliper aside; do not let the caliper hang by the brake hose.
5. Remove the spring nuts (if equipped) and rotor.
To install:
6. Install the rotor with new spring nuts.
7. Install the caliper.
8. Install the front wheel.
9. Lower the vehicle.
10. Before moving the vehicle, pump the brake pedal several times to seat the disc brake pads against the rotor.

Brake Drum

REMOVAL AND INSTALLATION

Wrangler, Cherokee, Comanche, 1993–96 Grand Cherokee and 1993 Grand Wagoneer

1. Raise and safely support the vehicle.
2. Remove the wheel.
3. Remove the spring nuts (if installed) from the lug bolts and remove the drum from the vehicle.

NOTE: It may be necessary to back off the brake adjusters to remove the drum.

To install:
4. Ensure the contacting surfaces are clean and flat. Install the drum on the hub.
5. Adjust the brake shoes, if necessary.
6. Install the spring nuts on the lug bolts.
7. Install the wheel.

Wheel Cylinder

REMOVAL AND INSTALLATION

Wrangler, Cherokee, Comanche, 1993–96 Grand Cherokee and 1993 Grand Wagoneer

1. Raise and safely support the vehicle. If equipped with anti-lock brakes, relieve the system pressure.
2. Remove the wheel and brake drum.
3. Disconnect the brake line at the wheel cylinder.
4. Remove the brake shoes.
5. Remove the wheel cylinder attaching bolts and remove the wheel cylinder.
To install:
6. Position the wheel cylinder on the backing plate.

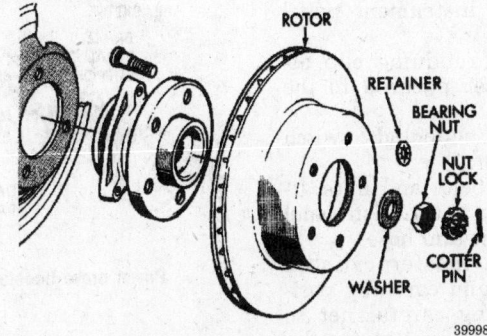

ROTOR

RETAINER

BEARING NUT

NUT LOCK

COTTER PIN

WASHER

39998

Disc brake rotor — 4WD vehicles

7. Connect the brake line to the cylinder fitting.

8. Install the wheel cylinder mounting bolts. Torque the bolts to 7 ft. lbs. (10 Nm).

9. Tighten the brake line fitting to 140 inch lbs. (16 Nm).

10. Install the brake shoes.

11. Install the brake drum and wheel.

12. Lower the vehicle.

13. Fill the brake system to the correct level and bleed the brakes.

Master Cylinder

REMOVAL AND INSTALLATION

Wrangler, Cherokee, Comanche, 1993–96 Grand Cherokee and 1993 Grand Wagoneer

1. Disconnect the negative battery cable.

2. Disconnect and plug the brake lines.

3. Disconnect the wires from the stoplight switch.

4. Remove the attaching nuts and lift the assembly from the vehicle.

To install:

5. Fill the master cylinder with brake fluid and operate the pushrod until fluid squirts from the ports.

6. Install the master cylinder. Torque the mounting nuts to 15–21 ft. lbs. (20–29 Nm).

7. Connect the stoplight switch.

8. Connect the brake lines.

9. Bleed the brake system.

Power Brake Booster

REMOVAL AND INSTALLATION

Wrangler, Cherokee and Comanche

1. Loosen but do not remove the nuts attaching the master cylinder to booster.

2. Remove the instrument panel lower trim cover.

3. Remove the retaining clip attaching the booster pushrod to the brake pedal.

4. Disconnect the stoplight switch electrical connector.

5. Remove the bolts and nuts attaching the booster to the dash panel and remove the vacuum hose.

6. Remove the master cylinder from the booster and carefully position it aside, being careful not to damage the brake lines. Remove the booster.

To install:

7. Install the check valve and grommet in the booster. Position the booster on the vehicle and install the attaching nuts and bolts.

8. Attach the booster pushrod to the brake pedal. Tighten the booster mounting bolts and nuts to 22–30 ft. lbs. (30–41 Nm).

9. Connect the stoplight switch electrical connector and reinstall the trim panels.

10. Install the master cylinder on the booster and tighten the nuts to 15–25 ft. lbs. (21–34 Nm). Top off the master cylinder, connect the vacuum hose and check for proper operation of the system.

1993–96 Grand Cherokee and 1993 Grand Wagoneer

1. Loosen but do not remove the nuts attaching the master cylinder to booster.

2. Remove the instrument panel lower trim cover.

3. Remove the air conditioner duct and lower trim panel. Remove the cotter pin, washer and bushing attaching the booster pushrod to the pedal.

4. Remove the bolts and nuts attaching the booster to the dash panel and remove the vacuum hose.

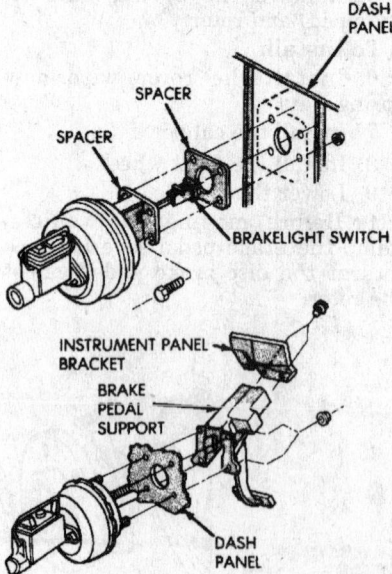

Power brake booster mounting

5. Remove the stoplight switch connector.

6. Remove the master cylinder from the booster and carefully position it aside, being careful not to damage the brake lines. Remove the booster.

To install:

7. Install the check valve and grommet in the booster. Position the booster on the vehicle and install the attaching nuts and bolts.

8. Attach the booster pushrod to the brake pedal. Tighten the booster mounting bolts and nuts to 22–30 ft. lbs. (30–41 Nm).

9. Connect the stoplight electrical connector and reinstall the trim panels and air conditioner ducts.

10. Install the master cylinder on the booster and tighten the nuts to 15–25 ft. lbs. (21–34 Nm). Top off the master cylinder, connect the vacuum hose and check for proper operation of the system.

Proportioning Valve

REMOVAL AND INSTALLATION

Comanche

1. Disconnect the linkage and spring.

2. Disconnect and cap the brake lines.

3. Unbolt and remove the valve.

To install:

4. Install the proportioning valve. Torque the valve bracket-to-frame bolts to 155 inch lbs.; the valve-to-bracket bolts to 118 inch lbs.

5. Connect the brake lines.

6. Connect the linkage and spring.

7. Bleed the brakes.

Master Cylinder-ABS

REMOVAL AND INSTALLATION

1992–96 Wrangler and Cherokee, 1992 Comanche, 1993–96 Grand Cherokee and 1993 Grand Wagoneer

NOTE: The master cylinder, modulator and accumulator are serviced as an assembly only. Do not attempt to disassemble or repair these components.

1. Disconnect the negative battery cable.

2. Remove the windshield washer reservoir.

3. Pump the brake pedal to exhaust all vacuum from the power brake booster.

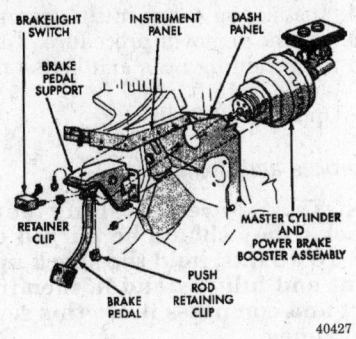

Power brake booster installation —
Grand Cherokee and Grand Wagoneer

—————— **WARNING** ——————

It is very important that all vacuum be exhausted from the booster. Failure to do so could result in damage to the master cylinder-to-booster seal when the master cylinder is removed.

4. Disconnect the anti-lock electrical harness connectors and position them aside.
5. Remove the clamps securing the reservoir hoses to the Hydraulic Control Unit (HCU) pipes.
6. Position a small drain pan under the master cylinder reservoir hoses.
7. Disconnect the reservoir hoses from the HCU pipes and allow the fluid to drain into the container. Discard the fluid.
8. Remove the combination valve.
9. Disconnect the brake lines from the master cylinder.
10. Remove the nuts attaching the master cylinder to the brake booster mounting studs.
11. Pull the master cylinder forward and out of the studs.
   To install:
12. If installing a new master cylinder, fill the reservoir with fluid and depress the pushrod until brake fluid comes out of the fluid line connections.

—————— **WARNING** ——————

The seal between the master cylinder and brake booster can be damaged if the master cylinder is improperly installed. To avoid damage, install the master cylinder only as described.

13. Have an assistant press the brake pedal until the brake booster pushrod is visible in the opening at the front of the booster. Have the assistant hold the brake pedal depressed.

14. Guide the master cylinder onto the mounting studs and onto the pushrod.

   NOTE: Ensure the pushrod is properly aligned and seated in the master cylinder.

15. Have the assistant slowly release the brake pedal while seating the master cylinder on the booster mounting studs. Keep the pushrod centered in the master cylinder while seating the cylinder.
16. Install the stud nuts and torque them to 220 inch lbs. (25 Nm).
17. Connect the brake lines and torque them to 132 inch lbs. (25 Nm).
18. Connect the reservoir hoses to the HCU pipes and tighten the clamps.
19. Ensure the master cylinder and booster are properly seated before proceeding.
20. Install the combination valve.
21. Connect the electrical connectors.
22. Fill the master cylinder reservoir and bleed the brakes.
23. Install the washer reservoir.
24. Install the air cleaner.
25. Connect the negative battery cable.

Power Brake Booster-ABS

REMOVAL AND INSTALLATION

Wrangler, Cherokee and Comanche

1. Loosen but do not remove the nuts attaching the master cylinder to booster.
2. Remove the instrument panel lower trim cover.
3. Remove the retaining clip attaching the booster pushrod to the brake pedal.
4. Disconnect the stoplight switch electrical connector.

5. Remove the bolts and nuts attaching the booster to the dash panel and remove the vacuum hose.
6. Remove the master cylinder from the booster and carefully position it aside, being careful not to damage the brake lines. Remove the booster.
   To install:
7. Install the check valve and grommet in the booster. Position the booster on the vehicle and install the attaching nuts and bolts.
8. Attach the booster pushrod to the brake pedal. Tighten the booster mounting bolts and nuts to 22–30 ft. lbs. (30–41 Nm).
9. Connect the stoplight switch electrical connector and reinstall the trim panels.
10. Install the master cylinder on the booster and tighten the nuts to 15–25 ft. lbs. (21–34 Nm). Top off the master cylinder, connect the vacuum hose and check for proper operation of the system.

1993–96 Grand Cherokee and 1993 Grand Wagoneer

1. Loosen but do not remove the nuts attaching the master cylinder to booster.
2. Remove the instrument panel lower trim cover.
3. Remove the air conditioner duct and lower trim panel. Remove the cotter pin, washer and bushing attaching the booster pushrod to the pedal.
4. Remove the bolts and nuts attaching the booster to the dash panel and remove the vacuum hose.
5. Remove the stoplight switch connector.
6. Remove the master cylinder from the booster and carefully position it aside, being careful not to damage the brake lines. Remove the booster.

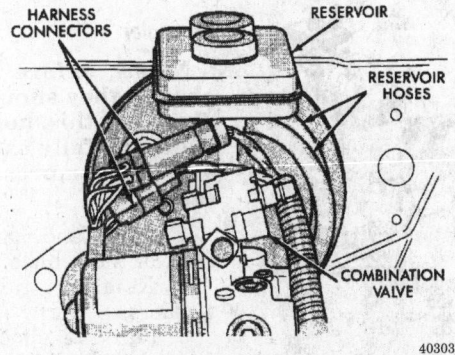

Harness, reservoir hose and valve position

To install:

7. Install the check valve and grommet in the booster. Position the booster on the vehicle and install the attaching nuts and bolts.

8. Attach the booster pushrod to the brake pedal. Tighten the booster mounting bolts and nuts to 22–30 ft. lbs. (30–41 Nm).

9. Connect the stoplight electrical connector and reinstall the trim panels and air conditioner ducts.

10. Install the master cylinder on the booster and tighten the nuts to 15–25 ft. lbs. (21–34 Nm). Top off the master cylinder, connect the vacuum hose and check for proper operation of the system.

Brake System Bleeding

BLEEDING

Wrangler, Cherokee, Comanche, 1993–96 Grand Cherokee and 1993 Grand Wagoneer

Bleeding the anti-lock braking system is basically a 3 step process consisting of a conventional manual brake bleed, a 2nd brake bleed using scan tool DRB-II or equivalent, to run the pump and a repeat of the conventional manual brake bleed. The procedure is as follows:

1. If a new master cylinder is to be installed, bench bleed the cylinder before installation.

2. Clean the master cylinder reservoir caps and reservoir exterior.

3. Fill the master cylinder with DOT 3 standard brake fluid.

4. Bleed the brake system in the following sequence:
   a. Master cylinder
   b. Hydraulic Control Unit (HCU) valve body (at fluid lines)
   c. Right rear wheel
   d. Left rear wheel
   e. Right front wheel
   f. Left front wheel

Power brake booster installation

5. Bleed the master cylinder and HCU at the brake fittings.

6. Attach a bleed hose to the bleed screw on the first wheel brake unit to be bled. Immerse the end of the bleed hose in a container partially filled with brake fluid.

7. Have an assistant apply and hold the brake pedal.

8. Open the bleed screw ½ turn and close the screw once the brake pedal reaches the floor.

NOTE: Do not pump the brake pedal at any time while bleeding. This compresses air into small bubbles which are distributed throughout the system.

9. Repeat the bleeding operation 5–7 more times at each wheel or until the fluid entering the container is free of air bubbles. Check the reservoir fluid lever frequently and add fluid if necessary.

NOTE: Do not allow the master cylinder reservoir to run dry while bleeding the system. Running the reservoir dry will allow air to reenter the system necessitating a second bleeding operation.

10. Connect the DRB-II scan tool or equivalent, to the diagnostic connector.

11. Perform the "Bleed Brake" operation as described in the scan tool manual.

12. Repeat Steps 4–9.

13. Verify proper brake operation before moving the vehicle.

FRONT SUSPENSION

Shock Absorber

REMOVAL AND INSTALLATION

Wrangler

NOTE: Before installing new shocks, they should be purged of air. To do this, hold the shock upright and fully extend it, then invert and compress it. Do this several times.

1. Raise and safely support the front of the vehicle.

2. Remove the locknuts and washers.

3. Pull the shock absorber eyes and rubber bushings from the mounting pins.

4. Install the shock in the reverse order of the removal procedure. Torque the retaining nuts and bolts to:
- Lower — 45 ft. lbs.
- Upper — 13 ft. lbs.

Cherokee and Comanche

NOTE: Before installing new shocks, they should be purged of air. To do this, hold the shock upright and fully extend it, then invert and compress it. Do this several times.

1. Raise and safely support the front of the vehicle.

2. Remove the locknuts and washers.

3. Pull the shock absorber eyes and rubber bushings from the mounting pins.

4. Install the shocks in the reverse order of the removal procedure. Torque the retaining nuts and bolts as follows:
- Lower — 14 ft. lbs.
- Upper — 8 ft. lbs.

1993–96 Grand Cherokee and 1993 Grand Wagoneer

NOTE: Before installing new shocks, they should be purged of air. To do this, hold the shock upright and fully extend it, then invert and compress it. Do this several times.

1. Remove the upper nut, retainer and grommet from the engine compartment,

2. Remove the lower bolt and nut from the mounting bracket.

3. Remove the shock absorber.

4. Install the shocks in the reverse order of the removal procedure. Torque the upper retaining nut to 14 ft. lbs. (19 Nm) and lower bolt and nut to 17 ft. lbs. (23 Nm).

Coil Spring

REMOVAL AND INSTALLATION

Cherokee and Comanche

1. Raise and safely support the vehicle, allowing the front axle to hang.

2. Support the axle with a jack.

3. Remove the wheels.

4. On 4WD vehicles, matchmark and disconnect the front driveshaft from the axle.

5. Disconnect the lower control arm at the axle.

6. Disconnect the stabilizer bar links and the shock absorbers at the axle.

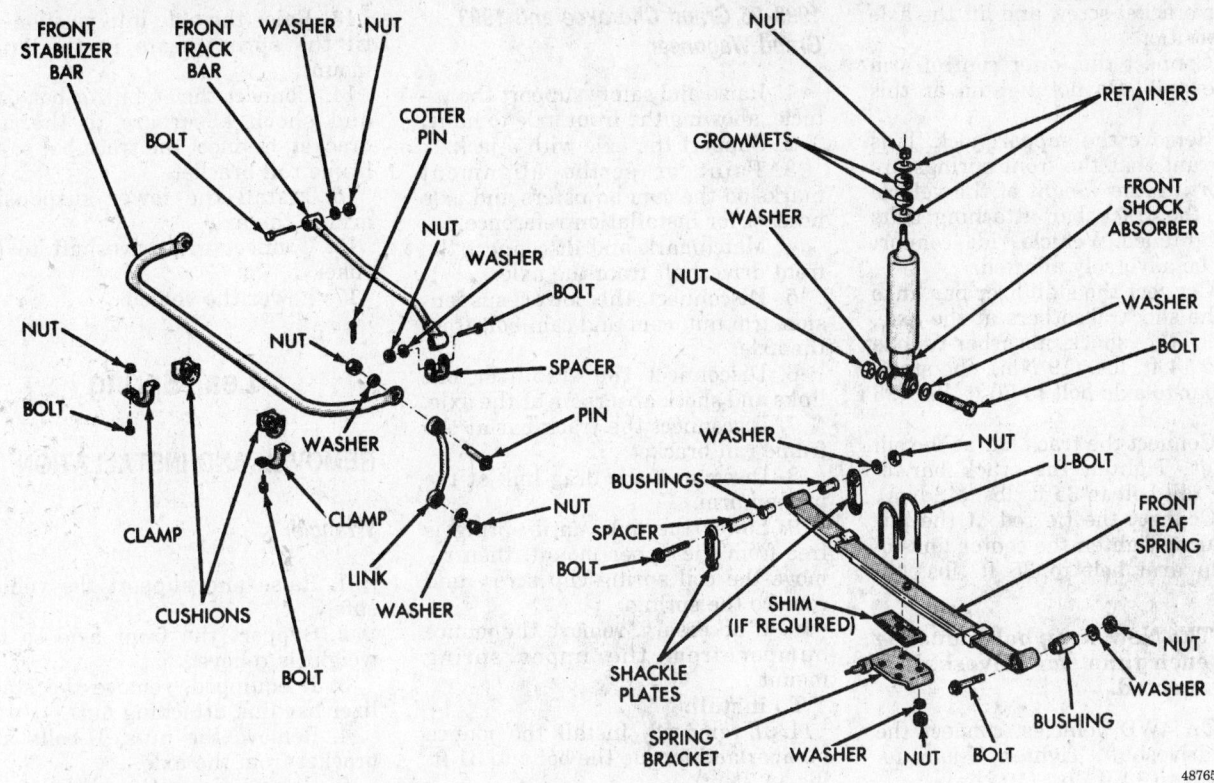

Exploded view of the front suspension — Wrangler

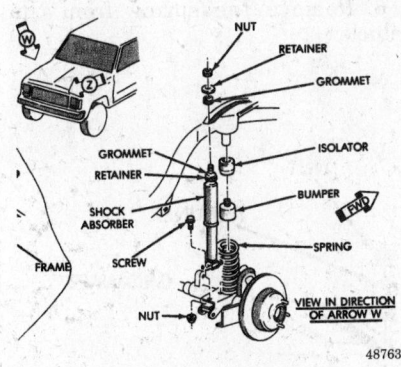

Shock absorber installation

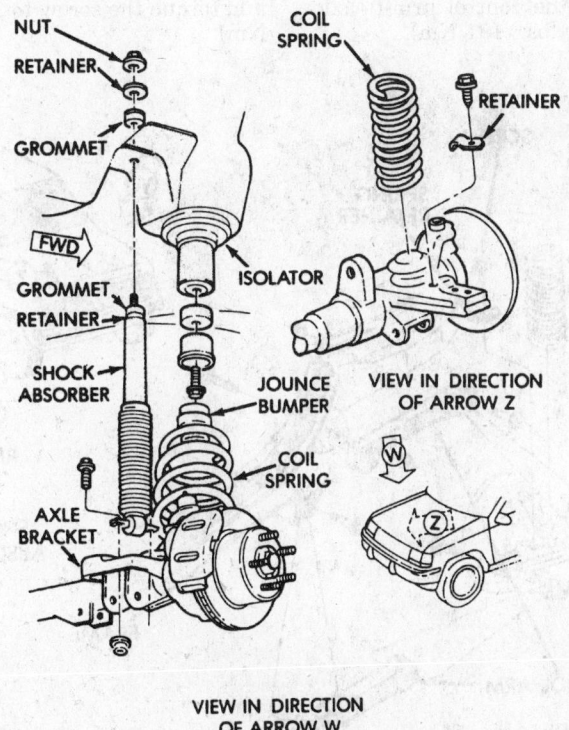

VIEW IN DIRECTION
OF ARROW W

Exploded view of the shock absorber and mounting
components — Grand Cherokee and Grand Wagoneer

7. Disconnect the track bar at the sill bracket.

8. Disconnect the tie rod at the pitman arm.

9. Lower the axle until tension is removed from the spring, then loosen the spring retainer and remove the spring.

10. If necessary, remove the jounce bumper from the upper spring mount.

To install:

11. If removed, install the jounce bumper and torque the bolts to 31 ft. lbs. (42 Nm).

12. Position the replacement spring on the retainer, tighten the spring re-

tainer bracket screw and lift the axle into position.

13. Connect the lower control arm to the axle. Do not tighten at this time.

14. Remove the support jack. It is important that the front springs are supporting the weight of the vehicle when the track bar attaching bolts are tightened. Vehicle ride comfort could be adversely affected.

15. Connect the stabilizer bar links and the shock absorbers at the axle. tighten the shock absorber-to-axle bolt to 14 ft. lbs. (19 Nm); the stabilizer bar-to-axle bolt to 70 ft. lbs. (96 Nm).

16. Connect the track bar at the sill bracket. Tighten the track bar-to-frame rail bolt to 35 ft. lbs. (48 Nm).

17. Connect the tie rod at the pitman arm. Tighten the center link-to-pitman arm bolt to 35 ft. lbs. (48 Nm).

NOTE: New strap bolts must be used each time the driveshaft is disconnected.

18. On 4WD vehicles, connect the front driveshaft. Tighten U-joint-to-axle bolt to 14 ft. lbs. (19 Nm).

19. Install the wheels and lower the vehicle.

20. Torque the control arm-to-axle bolt to 133 ft. lbs. (181 Nm).

1993–96 Grand Cherokee and 1993 Grand Wagoneer

1. Raise and safely support the vehicle, allowing the front axle to hang.

2. Support the axle with a jack.

3. Paint or scribe alignment marks on the cam adjusters and axle bracket for installation reference.

4. Matchmark and disconnect the front driveshaft from the axle.

5. Disconnect the lower suspension arm nut, cam and cam bolt from the axle.

6. Disconnect the stabilizer bar links and shock absorbers at the axle.

7. Disconnect the track bar at the frame rail bracket.

8. Disconnect the drag link at the pitman arm.

9. Lower the axle until spring is free from the upper mount, then remove the coil spring clip screw and remove the spring.

10. If necessary, remove the jounce bumper from the upper spring mount.

To install:

11. If removed, install the jounce bumper and torque the bolts to 31 ft. lbs. (42 Nm).

12. Position the replacement spring on axle pad. Install the spring clip and torque the screw to 16 ft. lbs. (21 Nm).

13. Raise the axle into position until the spring seats in the upper mount.

14. Connect the stabilizer bar links and shock absorbers to the axle bracket. Connect the track bar to the frame rail bracket.

15. Install the lower suspension arm to the axle.

16. Connect the driveshaft to the yoke.

17. Lower the vehicle.

Leaf Spring

REMOVAL AND INSTALLATION

Wrangler

1. Raise and support the vehicle safely.

2. Support the front axle so the weight is relieved.

3. If equipped, remove the stabilizer bar link attaching nut.

4. Remove the nuts, U-bolts and bracket from the axle.

5. Remove the nut and bolt attaching the spring front eye to the shackle.

6. Remove the spring from the vehicle.

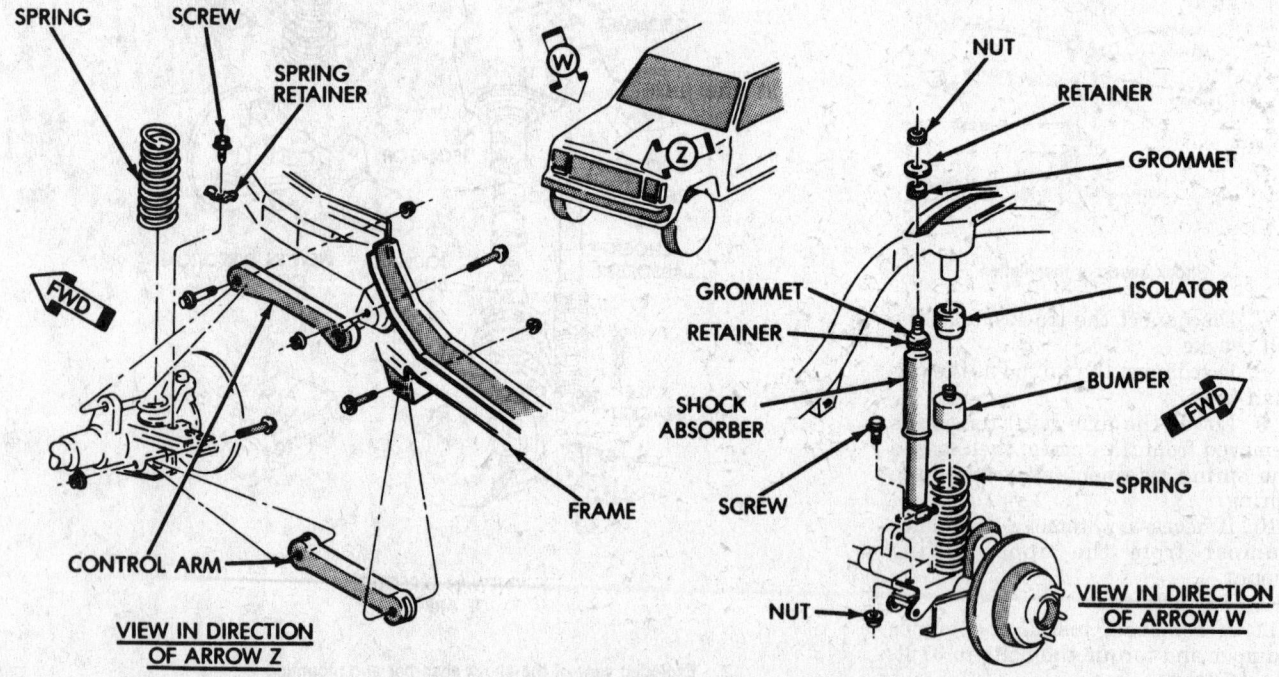

Front coil spring and shock absorber — Cherokee and Comanche

48056

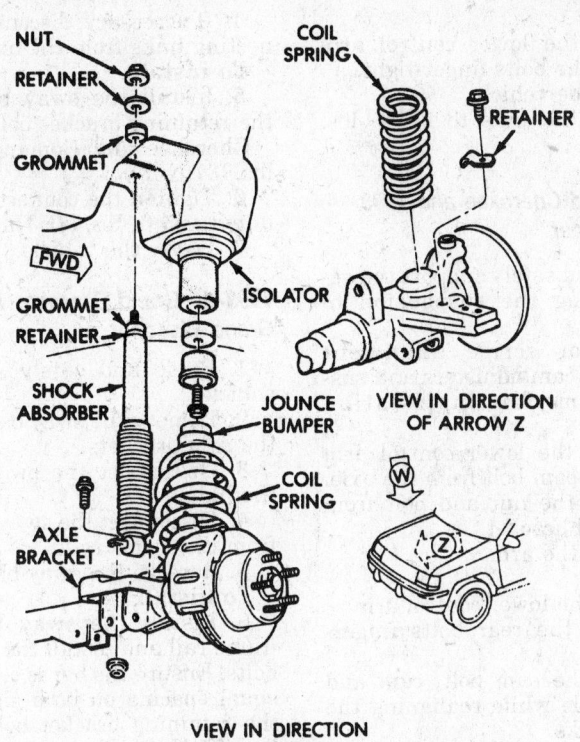

Coil spring and shock absorber — Grand Cherokee and Grand Wagoneer

To install:

7. Position the spring front eye in the shackle.

8. Position the rear eye in the hanger bracket.

9. Install the spring bracket, U-bolts and nuts. Torque the nuts to 90 ft. lbs. (122 Nm).

10. If equipped, attach the stabilizer bar links.

11. Remove the axle support.

12. Lower the vehicle.

13. Torque the front shackle plate nut to 100 ft. lbs. (135 Nm).

14. Torque the rear eye bracket nut to 105 ft. lbs. (142 Nm).

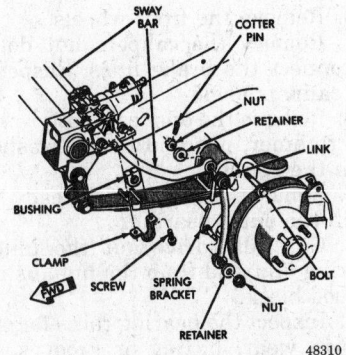

Front suspension — Wrangler

Torsion Bar-Front

Upper Ball Joint

REMOVAL AND INSTALLATION

Wrangler, Cherokee, Comanche, 1993–96 Grand Cherokee and 1993 Grand Wagoneer

1. Remove the steering knuckle.

2. Position receiver tool J34503-1 or equivalent, on top of the upper ball joint.

3. Place adapter tool J34503-3 or equivalent, in a C-clamp and position the clamp and adapter under the upper ball joint.

4. Tighten the clamp screw to remove the ball joint.

To install:

5. Place adapter tool J34503-5 on top of the replacement upper ball joint.

6. Place angled receiver tool J34503-12 or equivalent, between the C-clamp and the yoke.

7. Tighten the clamp screw and seat the ball joint.

8. Install the steering knuckle.

Lower Ball Joint

REMOVAL AND INSTALLATION

Wrangler, Cherokee, Comanche, 1993–96 Grand Cherokee and 1993 Grand Wagoneer

1. Remove the steering knuckle.

2. Position receiver tool J34503-1 or equivalent, on a C-clamp screw and adapter tool J34503-3 or equivalent between the top of the yoke and the C-clamp.

3. Tighten the clamp screw to remove the ball joint.

To install:

4. Position installer tool J34503-4 or equivalent, on the C-clamp screw and receiver tool J34503-2 or equivalent, between the top of the yoke and the C-clamp.

5. Tighten the clamp screw until the ball joint is fully seated.

6. Install the steering knuckle.

Upper Control Arm

REMOVAL AND INSTALLATION

Cherokee and Comanche

1. Raise and safely support the vehicle, allowing the suspension to hang freely.

2. Remove the wheels.

3. Remove the control arm-to-axle bolt.

4. Remove the control arm-to-frame bolt and remove the arm.

To install:

5. Install the upper control arm and tighten the bolts finger-tight.

6. Lower the vehicle and torque the control arm bolts to 55 ft. lbs. (75 Nm) at the axle; 66 ft. lbs. (90 Nm) at the frame.

1993–96 Grand Cherokee and 1993 Grand Wagoneer

1. Raise and support the vehicle safely.

2. Remove the upper control arm-to-axle bracket nut and bolt.

3. Remove the upper control arm-to-frame nut and bolt.

4. Remove the arm.

To install:

5. Install the upper control arm and tighten the bolts and nuts finger-tight.

6. Lower the vehicle.

7. Torque the upper control arm bolts to 55 ft. lbs. (75 Nm).

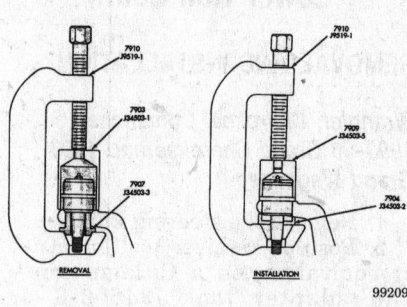

Upper ball joint removal and installation

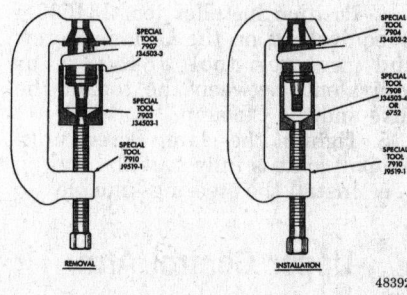

Lower ball joint removal and installation

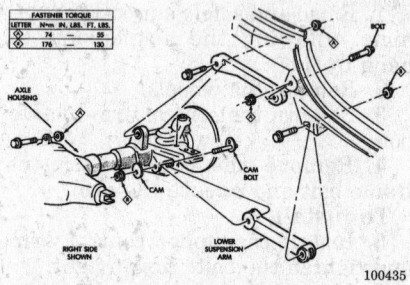

Exploded view of the suspension arms — Grand Cherokee and Grand Wagoneer

Lower Control Arm

REMOVAL AND INSTALLATION

1992–96 Cherokee and 1992 Comanche

1. Raise and safely support the vehicle, allowing the suspension to hang freely.
2. Disconnect the lower control arm at the axle and rear bracket. Remove the arm.

To install:

3. Install the lower control arm and tighten the bolts finger-tight.
4. Lower the vehicle.
5. Torque the nuts to 85 ft. lbs. (115 Nm).

1993–96 Grand Cherokee and 1993 Grand Wagoneer

1. Raise and safely support the vehicle, allowing the suspension to hang freely.
2. Paint or scribe alignment marks on the cam adjusters and suspension arm for installation reference.
3. Remove the lower control arm nut, cam and cam bolt from the axle.
4. Remove the nut and bolt from the frame rail bracket.
5. Remove the arm.

To install:

6. Install the lower control arm.
7. Tighten the rear bolts finger-tight.
8. Install the cam bolt, cam and nut in the axle while realigning the reference marks.
9. Lower the vehicle.
10. Torque the nuts to 130 ft. lbs. (176 Nm).

Sway Bar

REMOVAL AND INSTALLATION

Wrangler

1. Raise and safely support the vehicle.
2. Remove the retaining nut from the connecting link bolt.
3. Disconnect the bracket retaining nuts and brackets.
4. Remove the stabilizer bar.

To install:

5. Install the sway bar.
6. Install and torque the retaining brackets and fasteners to 30 ft. lbs. (41 Nm).
7. Install and torque the upper link bolts and nuts to 45 ft. lbs. (61 Nm).
8. Tighten the link spring bracket nuts to 45 ft. lbs. (61 Nm).
9. Lower the vehicle.

Cherokee and Comanche

1. Raise and safely support the vehicle.
2. Remove the sway bar-to-frame clamps and cushions.
3. Disconnect the sway bar at the connecting links and remove the stabilizer bar.

4. If necessary, disconnect the connecting links from the axle bracket.

To install:

5. Install the sway bar. Tighten the retaining bracket bolts to:
   Cherokee and Comanche — 27 ft. lbs. (37 Nm)
6. Tighten the connecting rod link nuts to 55 ft. lbs. (75 Nm).
7. Lower the vehicle.

1993–96 Grand Cherokee and 1993 Grand Wagoner

1. Raise and safely support the vehicle.
2. Remove the sway bar links from the axle brackets.
3. Disconnect the sway bar from the links.
4. Disconnect the sway bar clamps from the frame rails.
5. Remove the sway bar.

To install:

6. Install the sway bar on the frame rail and install the clamps and bolts. Ensure the bar is centered with equal spacing on both sides. Torque the retaining bracket bolts to 55 ft. lbs. (75 Nm).
7. Install the connecting rod link and grommets onto the stabilizer bar and brackets. Torque the nuts to 70 ft. lbs. (96 Nm).
8. Torque the sway bar-to-connecting link nut to 27 ft. lbs. (36 Nm).
9. Lower the vehicle.

Front Wheel Bearing and Hub

REMOVAL AND INSTALLATION

Comanche and 1992 Cherokee

2WD VEHICLES

1. Loosen the lug nuts on the front wheels.
2. Raise and safely support the vehicle.
3. Remove the front wheels.
4. Remove the calipers but don't disconnect the brake lines. Suspend the calipers aside.
5. Remove the dust cap, cotter pin, nut retainer, nut and thrust washer from the spindle.
6. Remove the rotor. Be ready to catch the outer bearing.
7. Carefully drive out the inner bearing and seal from the hub, using a wood block.
8. Inspect the bearing races for excessive wear, pitting or grooves. If they are cracked or grooved or if pitting and excess wear is present, drive them out with a drift or punch.

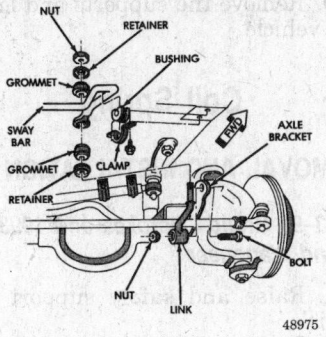

Exploded view of the sway bar and mounting components

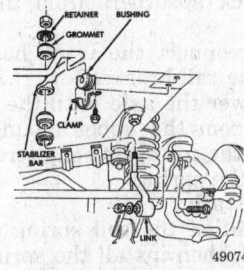

Exploded view of the sway bar and mounting components — Grand Cherokee and Grand Wagoneer

To install:

9. Check the bearing for excess wear, pitting or cracks or excess looseness.

NOTE: If it is necessary to replace either the bearing or the race, replace both. Never replace just a bearing or a race. These parts wear in a mating pattern. If just one is replaced, premature failure of the new part will result.

10. If the old parts are retained, thoroughly clean them in solvent and allow them to dry on a clean towel.

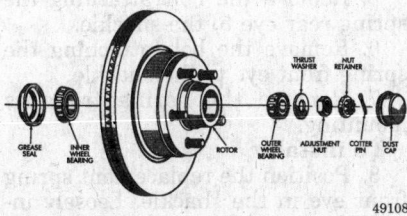

Exploded view of the hub and bearings — 2WD vehicles

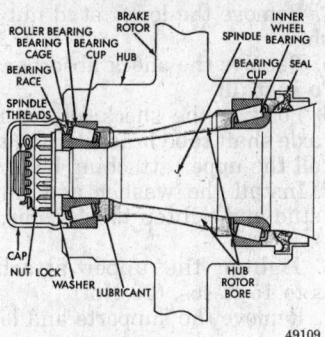

Cut-away view of the hub and bearings — 2WD vehicles

Never spin dry them with compressed air.

11. Thoroughly clean the spindle.
12. Thoroughly clean the inside of the hub.
13. Pack the inside of the hub with EP wheel bearing grease. Add grease to the hub until it is flush with the inside diameter of the bearing cup.
14. Pack the bearing with the same grease.
15. If a new race is being installed, very carefully drive it into position until it bottoms all around, using a brass drift. Be careful to avoid scratching the surface.
16. Place the inner bearing in the race and install a new grease seal.
17. Position the hub and rotor on the spindle and install the outer bearing.
18. Install the washer and nut. Adjust the wheel bearing.
19. Install the nut cap and a new cotter pin. Install the grease cap.
20. Install the caliper and wheels. Lower the vehicle.

1993–96 Cherokee, Grand Cherokee and 1993 Grand Wagoneer

1. Raise and support the vehicle safely.
2. Remove the wheel.
3. Remove the caliper and rotor.
4. Remove the cotter pin, nut retainer and axle hub nut.
5. Remove the hub-to-knuckle bolts. Remove the hub from the steering knuckle.

To install:

6. Install the hub to the steering knuckle. Torque the bolts to 75 ft. lbs. (102 Nm).
7. Install the hub washer and nut. Torque the nut to 175 ft. lbs. (237 Nm). Install the nut retainer and a new cotter pin.
8. Install the rotor and caliper.
9. Install the wheel and lower the vehicle.

Steering Knuckle

REMOVAL AND INSTALLATION

Wrangler, Cherokee, Comanche, 1993–96 Grand Cherokee and 1993 Grand Wagoneer

1. Raise and safely support the vehicle.
2. If equipped with 4WD, remove the axle shaft.
3. Remove the caliper anchor plate from the knuckle.
4. Disconnect the tie rod end or drag link from the steering knuckle.
5. If equipped, remove the ABS sensor wire and bracket.
6. Remove the knuckle-to-ball joint cotter pins and nuts.
7. Strike the knuckle with a brass hammer and remove it.

To install:

8. Position the knuckle over the ball joint studs and install the nuts.
9. Tighten the upper ball joint nut to 75 ft. lbs. (101 Nm). Tighten the lower ball joint nut to 80 ft. lbs. (109 Nm) on 1992–96 vehicles.
10. Install new cotter pins. If the ball stud hole does not align with the nut castellation, further tighten the nut until the cotter pin can be installed.
11. Connect the tie rod end or drag link.
12. If equipped, install the ABS sensor wire and bracket.
13. Install the caliper anchor plate on the knuckle. Torque the caliper anchor bolts to 77 ft. lbs. (105 Nm).
14. Install the axle shaft.

REAR SUSPENSION

Shock Absorber

REMOVAL AND INSTALLATION

Wrangler

NOTE: Before installing new shocks, they should be purged of air. To do this, hold the shock upright and fully extend it, then invert and compress it. Do this several times.

1. Raise and safely support the rear of the vehicle.
2. Using a suitable jack, relieve the axle weight from the springs.

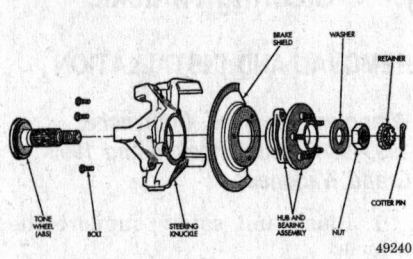

Exploded view of the hub, knuckle and axle shaft

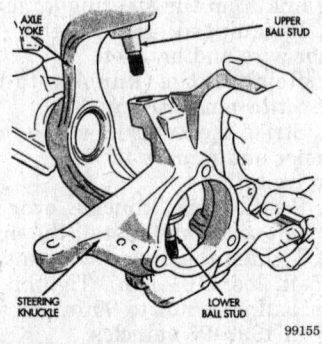

Steering knuckle removal and installation

3. Remove the upper locknut and washer from the frame bracket stud.

4. Remove the lower bolt, nut and washers from the axle shaft tube bracket.

5. Remove the shock absorber.

To install:

6. Position the shock absorber upper eye on the frame bracket stud and install the washer and nut.

7. Position the shock absorber lower eye in the axle shaft tube bracket and install the bolt, washers and nut.

8. Tighten the nuts to 44 ft. lbs. (60 Nm).

9. Remove the supports and lower the vehicle.

Cherokee

NOTE: Before installing new shocks, they should be purged of air. To do this, hold the shock upright and fully extend it, then invert and compress it. Do this several times.

1. Raise and safely support the vehicle.

2. Using a suitable jack, relieve the weight of the axle from the springs.

3. Remove the upper shock absorber-to-body bolts.

4. Remove the lower stud nut and washer.

5. Remove the shock absorber.

To install:

6. Position the shock absorber on the axle shaft tube bracket stud, then install the upper attaching bolts.

7. Install the washer and nut to the stud and tighten to 44 ft. lbs. (60 Nm).

8. Tighten the upper attaching bolts to 15 ft. lbs. (20 Nm).

9. Remove the supports and lower the vehicle.

Comanche

NOTE: Before installing new shocks, they should be purged of air. To do this, hold the shock upright and fully extend it, then invert and compress it. Do this several times.

1. Raise and safely support the rear of the vehicle.

2. Using a suitable jack, relieve the weight of the axle from the springs.

3. Remove the upper and lower stud nuts and washers.

4. Remove the shock absorber.

To install:

5. Position the shock absorber on the studs and install the washers and nuts.

6. Tighten the nuts to 44 ft. lbs. (60 Nm).

7. Remove the supports and lower the vehicle.

1993–96 Grand Cherokee and 1993 Grand Wagoneer

NOTE: Before installing new shocks, they should be purged of air. To do this, hold the shock upright and fully extend it, then invert and compress it. Do this several times.

1. Raise and safely support the rear of the vehicle.

2. Using a suitable jack, relieve the weight of the axle from the springs.

3. Remove the upper stud nut and washer from the frame rail stud.

4. Remove the lower nut and bolt from the axle bracket.

5. Remove the shock absorber.

To install:

6. Position the shock absorber on the frame rail stud and axle bracket.

7. Install the nut and retainer on the stud and tighten to 52 ft. lbs. (70 Nm).

8. Install the bolt and nut to the axle bracket and tighten to 68 ft. lbs. (92 Nm).

9. Remove the supports and lower the vehicle.

Coil Spring

REMOVAL AND INSTALLATION

1993–96 Grand Cherokee and 1993 Grand Wagoneer

1. Raise and safely support the vehicle.

2. Support the axle with a suitable jack.

3. Disconnect the sway bar links and shock absorbers from the axle bracket.

4. Disconnect the track bar from the frame rail bracket.

5. Lower the axle until the spring is free from the upper mount seat. Remove the coil spring clip screw and remove the spring.

To install:

6. Position the coil spring on the axle pad, then install the spring clip and screw. Tighten the screw to 16 ft. lbs. (22 Nm).

7. Raise the axle into position until the spring seats in the upper mount.

8. Connect the sway bar links and shock absorbers to the axle bracket. Connect the track bar to the frame rail bracket.

9. Remove the supports and lower the vehicle.

Leaf Spring

REMOVAL AND INSTALLATION

Wrangler

1. Raise the vehicle and support it safely.

2. Position a jack under the axle. Raise the axle to relieve the springs of the axle weight.

3. Remove the wheels.

4. Remove the spring U-bolts and tie plates.

5. Remove the bolt attaching the spring rear eye to the shackle.

6. Remove the bolt attaching the spring front eye to the shackle.

7. Remove the spring from its mounting.

To install:

8. Position the replacement spring front eye in the shackle. Loosely install the attaching bolt. Perform the same procedure for the rear spring eye.

9. Position and align the spring with the axle tube.

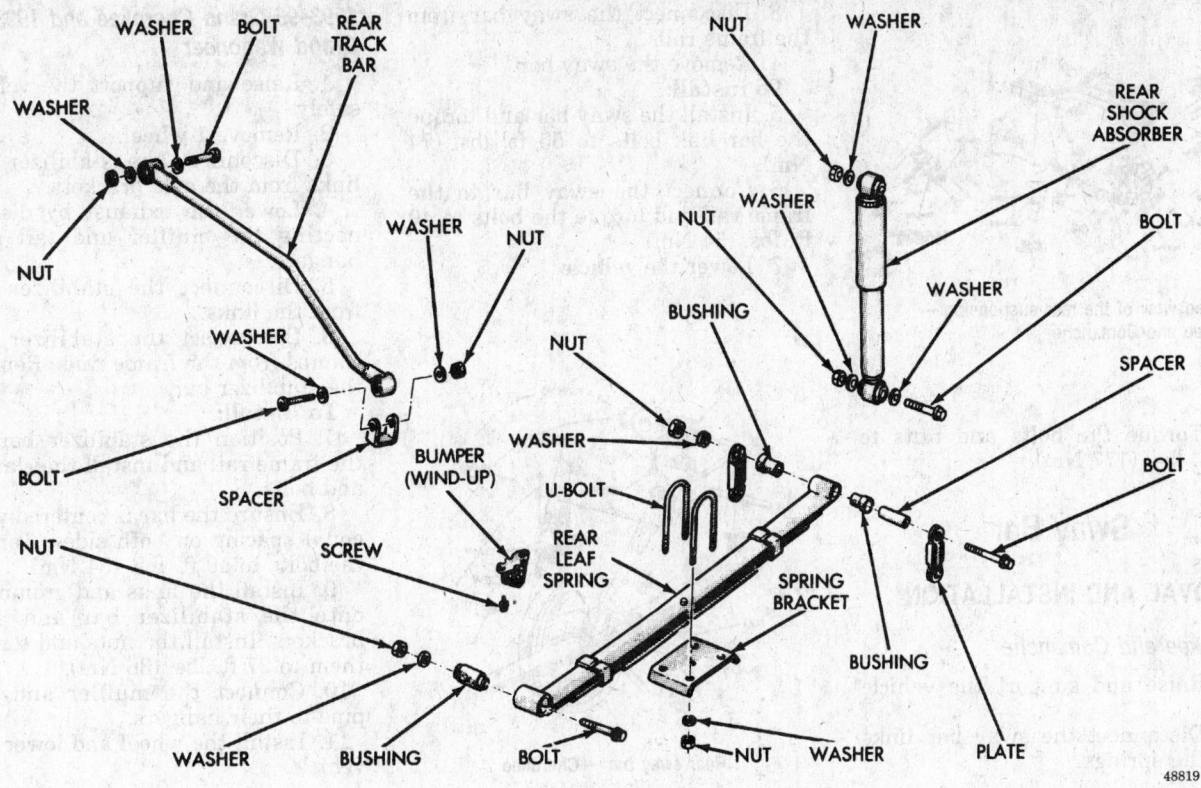

Exploded view of the rear suspension — Wrangler

48819

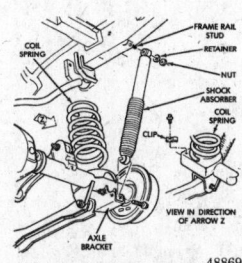

Exploded view of the shock absorber and mounting components — Grand Cherokee and Grand Wagoneer

48869

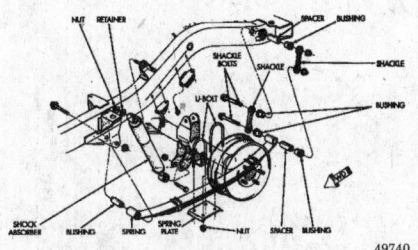

Exploded view of the rear suspension — Wrangler

49740

10. Lower the rear axle until it is completely supported by the spring.

11. Install the spring bracket, U-bolts and nuts. Torque the nuts to 90 ft. lbs. (122 Nm).

12. Install the wheels.

13. Lower the vehicle and tighten the spring eye bolts to 100 ft. lbs. (136 Nm).

Cherokee and Comanche

1. Raise the vehicle and support it safely.

2. Position a jack under the axle. Raise the axle to relieve the springs of the axle weight.

3. Remove the wheels.

4. If equipped, disconnect the sway bar links at the spring plates.

5. Remove the spring U-bolts and spring plates.

6. Remove the bolt attaching the spring rear eye to the shackle.

7. Remove the bolt attaching the spring front eye to the shackle.

8. Lower the axle and remove the spring from its mounting.

To install:

9. Position the replacement spring front eye in the shackle. Loosely install the attaching bolt. Perform the same procedure for the rear spring eye.

10. Position and align the spring with the axle tube.

11. Install the spring plates, U-bolts and nuts. Torque the nuts to 52 ft. lbs. (70 Nm) on Cherokee and Wagoneer or 65 ft. lbs. (88 Nm) on Comanche.

12. If equipped, connect the sway bar link to the spring bracket and tighten the nut to 70 ft. lbs. (96 Nm).

13. Install the wheels.

14. Lower the vehicle.

15. Torque the spring eye bolts to 65 ft. lbs..

Lower Control Arm

REMOVAL AND INSTALLATION

1993–96 Grand Cherokee and 1993 Grand Wagoneer

1. Raise and support the vehicle safely.

2. Remove the lower control arm nut and bolt at the axle bracket.

3. Remove the lower control arm nut and bolt at the frame rail.

4. Remove the lower control arm.

To install:

5. Install the lower control arm and tighten the bolts finger-tight.

6. Lower the vehicle.

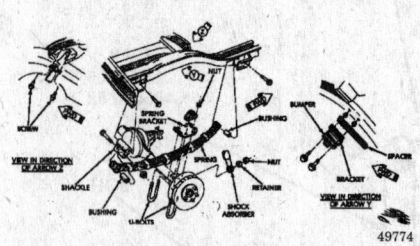

49774

Exploded view of the rear suspension — Cherokee and Comanche

7. Torque the bolts and nuts to 130 ft. lbs. (177 Nm).

Sway Bar

REMOVAL AND INSTALLATION

Cherokee and Comanche

1. Raise and support the vehicle safely.
2. Disconnect the sway bar links from the springs.

3. Disconnect the sway bar from the frame rails.
4. Remove the sway bar.

To install:
5. Install the sway bar and torque the bar link bolts to 55 ft. lbs. (74 Nm).
6. Connect the sway bar to the frame rail and torque the bolts to 40 ft. lbs. (54 Nm).
7. Lower the vehicle.

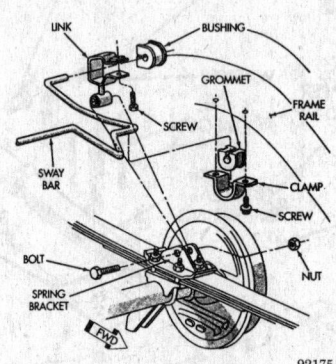

92175

Rear sway bar — Cherokee

1993–96 Grand Cherokee and 1993 Grand Wagoneer

1. Raise and support the vehicle safely.
2. Remove 1 wheel.
3. Disconnect the stabilizer bar links from the axle brackets.
4. Lower the exhaust by disconnecting the muffler and tail pipe hangers.
5. Disconnect the stabilizer bar from the links.
6. Disconnect the stabilizer bar clamps from the frame rails. Remove the stabilizer bar.

To install:
7. Position the stabilizer bar on the frame rail and install the clamps and bolts.
8. Ensure the bar is centered with equal spacing on both sides. Torque the bolts to 40 ft. lbs. (54 Nm).
9. Install the links and grommets onto the stabilizer bar and axle brackets. Install the nuts and torque them to 27 ft. lbs. (36 Nm).
10. Connect the muffler and tail pipe to their hangers.
11. Install the wheel and lower the vehicle.

Chrysler Imports 5

Ram 50

FIRING ORDERS

NOTE: To avoid confusion, always replace spark plug wires one at a time.

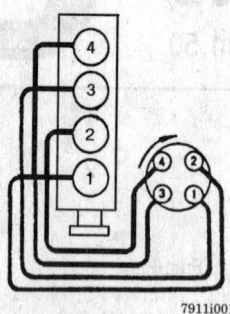

79111001

2.4L Engine
Engine Firing Order:
1–3–4–2
Distributor Rotation:
Clockwise

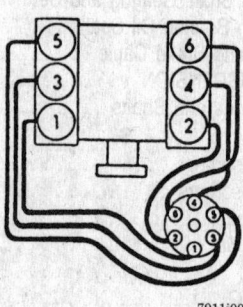

79111002

3.0L Engine
Engine Firing Order:
1–2–3–4–5–6
Distributor Rotation:
Counterclockwise

ENGINE ELECTRICAL

NOTE: Disconnecting the negative battery cable on some vehicles may interfere with the functions of the on board computer systems and may require the computer to undergo a relearning process, once the negative battery cable is reconnected.

Distributor

REMOVAL

1. Disconnect the negative battery cable.
2. Disconnect the distributor pickup lead wires and vacuum hose(s), if equipped.
3. Unfasten the distributor cap retaining clips or screws and lift off the distributor cap with all ignition wires connected. Remove the coil wire if necessary.
4. Matchmark the rotor to the distributor housing and the distributor housing to the engine.

NOTE: Do not crank the engine during this procedure. If the engine is cranked, the matchmark must be disregarded.

5. Remove the retaining nut and remove the distributor from the engine.

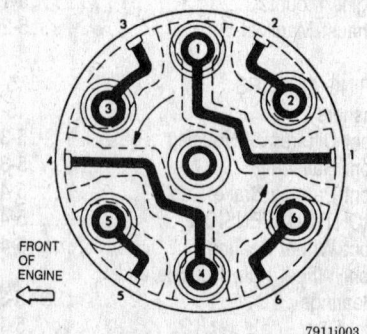

FRONT OF ENGINE

79111003

Distributor cap terminal routing viewed from the top of the cap — 3.0L engine

INSTALLATION

Timing Not Disturbed

1. Install a new distributor housing O-ring.
2. Install the distributor in the engine so the rotor is aligned with the matchmark on the housing and the housing is aligned with the matchmark on the engine. Make sure the distributor is fully seated and the distributor shaft is fully engaged.
3. Install the retaining nut finger-tight only. Connect the vacuum hose(s), if removed.
4. Connect the distributor pickup electrical harness.
5. Install the distributor cap and secure.
6. Connect the negative battery cable.

7. Check the ignition timing and adjust as required. Tighten the retaining nut.

Timing Disturbed

1. Install a new distributor housing O-ring.
2. Position the engine so No. 1 piston is on TDC of compression stroke and the timing mark on the vibration damper is aligned with **T** on the timing indicator.
3. Install the distributor so the rotor is aligned with the No. 1 ignition wire on the distributor cap. Take note that the distributor shaft is fully engaged and the housing is fully seated.

NOTE: There are distributor cap runners inside the cap on vehicles with 3.0L engine. Make sure the rotor is pointing to where the No. 1 runner originates inside the cap and not where the No. 1 ignition wire plugs into the cap.

4. Install the retaining nut finger-tight only. Connect the vacuum hose(s), if removed.
5. Connect the distributor electrical harness.
6. Install the distributor cap and secure.
7. Connect the negative battery cable.
8. Adjust the ignition timing and tighten the retaining nut.

Ignition Timing

ADJUSTMENT

1. Start the engine, set the parking brake and run the engine until normal operating temperature is reached. Keep all lights and accessories **OFF** and the transmission in neutral.
2. Without disconnecting the connector, insert a paper clip into the tachometer terminal. Connect the red lead of a tachometer to the paper clip and connect the black lead to a ground. Set the idle speed to specifications.
3. Turn the engine **OFF**. Remove the water-proof cover from the ignition timing adjusting connector. Connect a jumper wire from the ignition timing adjusting terminal to ground.
4. Connect a conventional timing light to No. 1 cylinder spark plug wire. Start the engine and allow to idle.

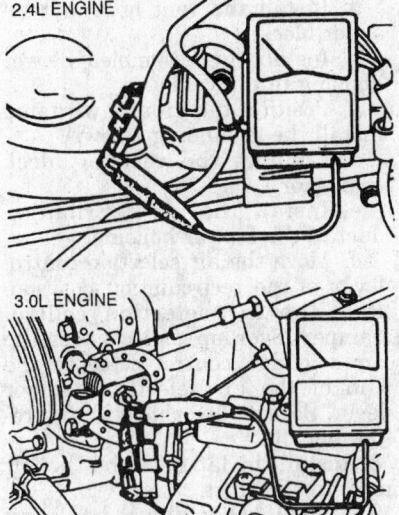

2.4L ENGINE

3.0L ENGINE

7911i006

Tachometer connector

5. Aim the timing light at the timing scale.

6. Loosen the distributor nut to allow for distributor rotation.

7. Turn the distributor in the proper direction until the specified timing is reached. Tighten the retainer nut and recheck the timing. Turn the engine **OFF**.

8. Remove the jumper wire from the ignition timing adjusting terminal and install the water-proof cover.

9. Start the engine and check the actual ignition timing. This reading should be 3 degrees more than basic timing for the 2.4L engine or 10 degrees more than basic timing for the 3.0L engine.

NOTE: The actual timing may fluctuate according to the control mode of the engine control unit; this is a normal condition.

10. Turn the engine **OFF** and remove all test equipment.

Alternator

PRECAUTIONS

Several precautions must be observed when working with the alternator to avoid damaging the unit.

• If the battery is removed for any reason, make sure it is reconnected with the correct polarity. Reversing the battery connections may result in damage to the one-way rectifiers.

• When utilizing a booster battery as a starting aid, always connect the positive to positive terminals and the negative terminal from the booster battery to a good engine ground on the vehicle being started.

• Never use a fast charger as a booster to start vehicles.

• Disconnect the battery cables when charging the battery with a fast charger.

• Never attempt to polarize the alternator.

• Do not use test lights of more than 12 volts when checking diode continuity.

• Do not short across or ground any of the alternator terminals.

• The polarity of the battery, alternator and regulator must be matched and considered before making any electrical connections within the system.

• Never separate the alternator on an open circuit. Make sure all connections within the circuit are clean and tight.

• Disconnect the battery ground terminal when performing any service on electrical components.

• Disconnect the battery if arc welding is to be done on the vehicle.

BELT TENSION ADJUSTMENT

Except 3.0L Engine

1. Loosen the pivot bolt slightly.

2. Loosen the adjuster slot bolt or adjuster bolt locknut to allow for alternator movement. Raise and safely support the vehicle if necessary.

3. Apply tension to the alternator using adjuster bolt or prybar until the belt deflects ¼–½ in. under a 10 lb. load.

4. Torque the adjuster strap bolt or locknut to 10 ft. lbs. (15 Nm). and the pivot bolt to 16 ft. lbs. (23 Nm).

3.0L Engine

1. Loosen the tensioner pulley locknut.

2. Turn the adjusting bolt to displace tensioner pulley until the belt deflects ¼–½ in. under a 10 lb. load.

3. Tighten the locknut.

REMOVAL AND INSTALLATION

1. Disconnect the negative battery cable.

2. Remove the alternator cover, if equipped.

3. Remove the alternator drive belt.

4. Remove the alternator brace bolt(s), nut(s) and applicable spacers.

5. Remove the alternator from the mounting bracket, label and disconnect all wires from the rear of the unit.

To install:

6. Connect all wiring to their proper terminals on the rear of the alternator.

7. Position the alternator in the mounting bracket.

8. Install the alternator brace bolt(s), nut(s) and applicable spacers.

9. Install the alternator belt and adjust the tension as required.

10. Install the alternator cover, if equipped.

11. Connect the negative battery cable and check the alternator for proper operation.

Starter

REMOVAL AND INSTALLATION

1. Disconnect the negative battery cable.

2. Raise the vehicle and support safely.

3. Remove the starter cover, if equipped.

4. Label and disconnect the wiring to the starter motor.

5. Remove the starter mounting bolts.

6. Remove the starter motor from the vehicle.

7. The installation is the reverse of the removal procedure. Torque the mounting bolts to 20–25 ft. lbs. (27–34 Nm).

CHASSIS ELECTRICAL

Heater Blower Motor

REMOVAL AND INSTALLATION

Without Air Conditioning

1. Disconnect the negative battery cable.
2. Remove the lap heater duct and the left side defroster duct.
3. On some vehicles, it will be necessary to remove the heater housing to extract the blower motor. Remove the housing as follows:

   a. Open the glove box lid and release the glove box stoppers. Remove the glove box from its hinge.

   b. Use a small prying device to remove the clip that holds the air selection control cable in place.

   c. Disconnect the air selection control cable from the end of the air selection damper lever.

   d. Remove the air distribution duct from the left side of the blower assembly.

   e. Disconnect the connector to the resistor block and remove the grounding screw.

   f. Remove the blower housing attaching bolts and remove the housing from the vehicle.

   g. Remove the resistor block and vent hose from the housing.
4. Remove the blower motor retaining screws and remove the motor assembly from the housing. Remove the fan from the motor.

To install:

5. Inspect the gasket on housing for cracking or breaks and repair as required.
6. Install the fan to the blower motor shaft. Install the blower motor assembly to the housing and install the retaining screws.
7. Install the heater housing as follows:

   a. Install the vent hose and resistor block.

   b. Install the assembled blower housing to the vehicle.

   c. Position the ground wire and install the grounding screw.

   d. Connect the resistor block connector.

   e. Install the air distribution duct to the blower housing.

   f. Move the air selection control lever to the recirculation position.

Pull the air selection control damper lever up and connect the air selection control cable to the end of the air selection damper lever. Secure the cable with the retaining clip.

8. Install the lap heater duct, glove box and stopper.
9. Connect the negative battery cable and check the blower motor for proper operation.

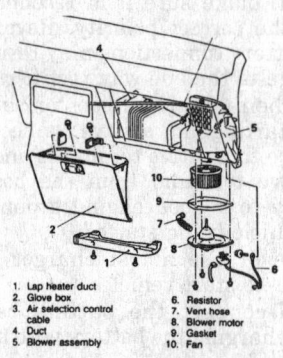

1. Lap heater duct
2. Glove box
3. Air selection control cable
4. Duct
5. Blower assembly
6. Resistor
7. Vent hose
8. Blower motor
9. Gasket
10. Fan

7911i007

Blower motor removal and installation

With Air Conditioning

1. Disconnect negative battery cable.
2. Remove the lap duct and the left side defroster duct.
3. If necessary remove the heater/air conditioner housing as follows:

   a. Open the glove box lid and release the glove box stoppers. Remove the glove box from its hinge.

   b. Use a small prying device to remove the clip that holds the air selection control cable in place.

   c. Disconnect the air selection control cable from the end of the air selection damper lever.

   d. Remove the air distribution duct from the left side of the blower assembly.

   e. Disconnect the connector to the resistor block and remove the grounding screw.

   f. Remove the blower housing attaching bolts and remove the housing from the vehicle.

   g. Remove the resistor block and vent hose from the housing.
4. Remove the blower motor retaining screws and remove the motor assembly from the housing. Remove the fan from the motor.

To install:

5. Inspect the gasket on housing for cracking or breaks and repair as required.
6. Install the fan to the blower motor shaft. Install the blower motor as-

sembly to the housing and install the retaining screws.

7. Install the heater housing as follows:

   a. Install the vent hose and resistor block.

   b. Install the assembled blower housing to the vehicle.

   c. Position the ground wire and install the grounding screw.

   d. Connect the resistor block connector.

   e. Install the air distribution duct to the blower housing.

   f. Move the air selection control lever to the recirculation position. Pull the air selection control damper lever up and connect the air selection control cable to the end of the air selection damper lever. Secure the cable with the retaining clip.

8. Install the lap duct and the left side defroster duct.
9. Install the glove box and stopper.
10. Connect the negative battery cable and check the blower motor for proper operation.

Windshield Wiper Motor

REMOVAL AND INSTALLATION

Front Wiper

1. Disconnect the negative battery cable.
2. Disconnect the wiper motor electrical connector.
3. Remove the wiper motor retaining bolts and pull the motor out far enough to gain access to the wiper linkage.
4. Matchmark position of wiper linkage to aid installation. Pry the wiper linkage from the motor output shaft.
5. Remove the wiper motor from the vehicle.
6. The installation is the reverse of the removal procedure.

Rear Wiper

1. Disconnect the negative battery cable.
2. Tilt the wiper mount nut cover up and remove the wiper arm retaining nut. Remove the wiper arm from the shaft. Remove the wiper pivot nut and washer.
3. Remove the inside door handle cover. Remove rear door inside trim panel and waterproof film.
4. Disconnect the wiper motor wire connector.

5. Remove the wiper motor retaining bolts and remove the motor from the vehicle.

To install:

6. Install the wiper motor and torque retainers to 7 ft. lbs. (10 Nm).

7. Connect the wiper motor electrical harness.

8. Install waterproof film to rear door panel. Install rear door inside trim panel and handle cover.

9. Install the wiper pivot nut and washer to motor shaft. Install the wiper arm and retainer nut to the motor shaft and torque to 7 ft. lbs. (10 Nm).

10. Reconnect the negative battery cable and check operation of the rear wiper.

Windshield Wiper Switch

The front windshield wiper switch is part of the combination switch located on the steering column. The rear wiper switch is located on the instrument panel.

REMOVAL AND INSTALLATION

Rear Wiper Switch

1. Disconnect negative battery cable.

2. Insert a trim stick between the instrument panel and the switch housing. Pry switch out from the panel.

3. Disconnect electrical connector and service the wiper/washer switch, as required.

To install:

4. Connect the electrical connector and snap switch assembly into instrument panel.

5. Connect the negative battery cable and check operation of the wiper/washer assembly.

Instrument Cluster

REMOVAL AND INSTALLATION

1. Disconnect the negative battery cable.

2. Remove the hazard flasher switch and the matching cover on the other side of the column. Remove the screws under these covers.

3. If equipped with tilt steering, operate the tilt lever to bring the steering down.

4. Remove the hood attaching screws on the underside corners of the upper hood surface, if equipped.

5. Remove the hood from the instrument meter.

6. Remove the 4 cluster attaching screws and pull out cluster. Disconnect the speedometer cable from the back of the cluster by pushing the stopper of the plug on the speedometer cable side of the connection.

7. Disconnect the electrical connectors at the cluster and remove the cluster from the vehicle.

8. To remove the speedometer or gauges, remove the cover and glass. Remove the retaining screws and remove the speedometer or gauges as required.

To install:

9. Install the speedometer or gauges into the cluster and install the retaining screws. Install the glass and the cover.

10. Connect the electrical connectors and the speedometer to the cluster and install in vehicle. Install 4 retaining screws.

11. Install the instrument cluster hood and retaining screws.

12. Install the hazard flasher switch and the matching cover on the other side of the column, if equipped.

13. Connect the negative battery cable and check operation of all gauges.

Combination Switch

REMOVAL AND INSTALLATION

NOTE: The combination switch incorporates the windshield wiper/washer, headlight, dimmer and turn signal switch functions into a single switch assembly.

1. Disconnect negative battery cable.

2. Remove the steering wheel pad. Matchmark and remove the steering wheel.

3. If equipped with tilt steering column, put the column in lowest position.

4. Remove the upper and lower column covers.

5. Remove the wiring harness band and disconnect the harness connectors.

6. Remove the combination switch mounting screws and remove the switch.

7. The installation is the reverse of the removal procedure. Torque the steering wheel nut to 30 ft. lbs. (41 Nm).

Ignition Lock/Switch

REMOVAL AND INSTALLATION

1. Disconnect the negative battery cable.

2. If equipped with tilt steering column, put the column in its lowest position.

3. Remove the upper and lower column covers.

4. Remove the wiring harness band and disconnect the ignition switch harness.

5. Remove the ignition switch to lock attaching screws, if equipped, and remove the switch from the lock.

6. Using a hacksaw blade, cut a groove into the head of the ignition switch break-off bolts and remove.

7. Remove the assembly from the steering column.

To install:

8. With the key inserted in the switch, install the switch and lock assembly to the steering column. Tighten the screws gradually making sure the key does not bind.

9. If using break-off bolts, tighten them until the heads break off.

10. Connect the switch harness and check the assembly for proper operation.

11. Install upper and lower column covers.

Stoplight Switch

ADJUSTMENT

1. Disconnect negative battery cable.

2. Loosen locknut on the brake light switch.

3. Turn the switch in the mounting bracket until the plunger does not contact the brake pedal.

4. Rotate the switch outward ½–1 revolution and secure the locknut. Reconnect the negative battery cable and check switch operation.

REMOVAL AND INSTALLATION

1. Disconnect the negative battery cable.

2. Unplug the connector to the switch.

3. Remove the locknut and remove the switch from its mount bracket.

4. The installation is the reverse of the removal procedure.

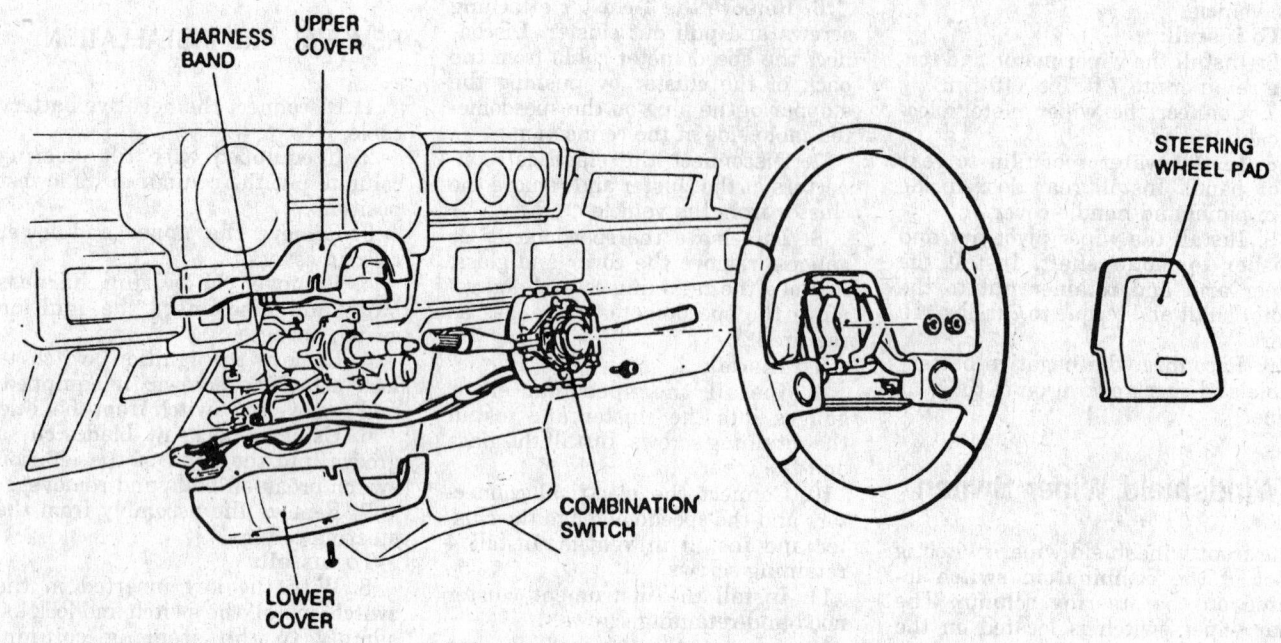

Combination switch mounting

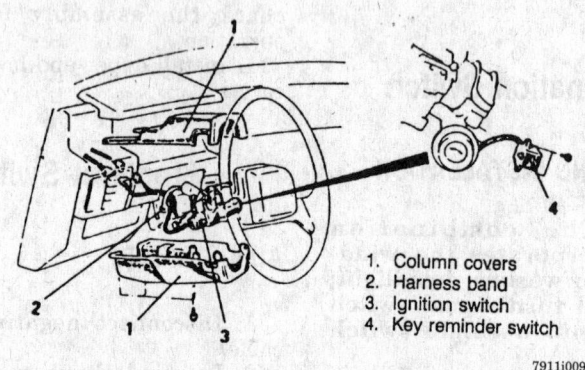

1. Column covers
2. Harness band
3. Ignition switch
4. Key reminder switch

7911i009

Ignition switch and lock assembly

Clutch Switch

ADJUSTMENT

1. Disconnect negative battery cable.
2. Loosen the locknut on the switch. Move the switch in the mounting bracket to adjust switch piston travel. Adjust the switch so distance from the bottom of the clutch pedal extension to the upper step of the switch, with the clutch depressed, measures 0–0.04 in. (0–0.5mm).

3. Reconnect the negative battery cable. Check operation of cruise control system making sure the cruise control is not operational when the pedal is depressed.

REMOVAL AND INSTALLATION

1. Disconnect negative battery cable.
2. Unplug the electrical connector from the clutch switch.
3. Remove the locknut from the top of the switch and pull the switch down from the mounting bracket.

4. The installation is the reverse of the removal procedure. Adjust switch after installed.

Neutral Safety Switch

REMOVAL AND INSTALLATION

1. Disconnect negative battery cable.
2. Raise and safely support the vehicle.
3. Remove the electrical connector from the switch. Place drain pan under the switch and remove the switch from the transmission.
4. Install switch with new seal into the transmission and tighten to 25 ft. lbs. (34 Nm).
5. Lower the vehicle and add transmission fluid to correct the level. Check operation of the switch.

Fuses, Circuit Breakers and Relays

LOCATION

Fuse Block — located to the left of the steering column, covered by a removable access panel.

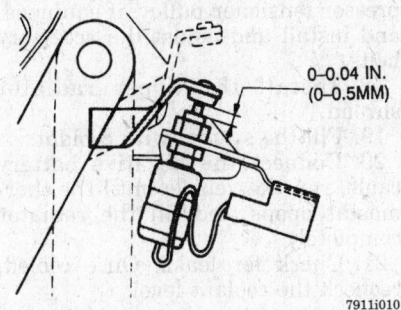

0–0.04 IN.
(0–0.5MM)

7911i010

Adjusting clutch switch — 2.4L engine

Main Fuse Link — located in the engine compartment between the battery and the fender.

Air Conditioning Relay — located behind the glove box.

Intermittent Wiper Relay — located inside of and is a function of the column combination switch.

Auto Choke Relay — located in the engine compartment on the left fender by the device box.

Over Drive Relay — located to the left of the fuse block.

Seat Belt Timer Relay — located to the left of the fuse block.

Engine Control Relay — located on the right side of the instrument panel behind a removable trim panel.

Computers

LOCATION

Engine Control Unit (ECU) — located on the right side of the dash, under a removable trim panel mounted to the kick-panel.

Automatic Free Wheeling Hub Indicator Control Unit — located on the right side of the dash mounted to the kick panel.

Auto Cruise Control Unit — located to the left of the fuse block.

Flashers

LOCATION

Turn Signal Flasher Unit — located in the central junction at the fuse block to the left of the steering column.

Hazard Warning Flasher Unit — located in the central junction at the fuse block to the left of the steering column.

Cruise Control

ADJUSTMENT

1. Run the vehicle until normal operating temperature is reached. Adjust the idle speed to match the emission sticker on the vehicle.

2. Turn the engine **OFF** and remove the actuator cover.

3. Loosen the locknuts on the accelerator cables and let the inner cables sag.

4. While keeping lever "P" and the stopper in contact with each other, turn the adjusting nut to lengthen the outer cable. Adjust until the lever "P" begins to operate. Turn the nut back ½ turn and secure the locknut. Accelerator cable "A" free-play should be 0-0.04 in. (0–1mm).

5. Install actuator cover and check operation of cruise control.

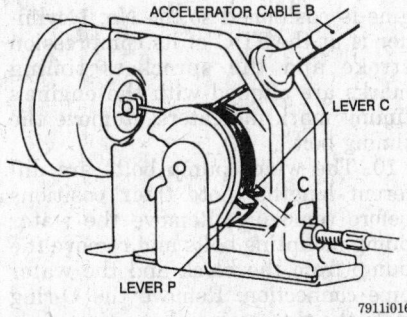

ACCELERATOR CABLE B

LEVER C

C

LEVER P

7911i016

Accelerator cable "B" adjustment — with cruise control

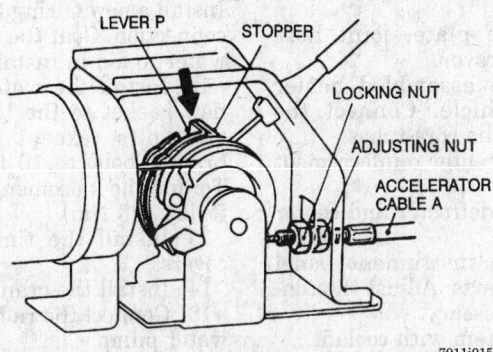

LEVER P   STOPPER

LOCKING NUT

ADJUSTING NUT

ACCELERATOR
CABLE A

7911i015

Accelerator cable "A" adjustment — with cruise control

ENGINE COOLING

Radiator

REMOVAL AND INSTALLATION

1. Disconnect the negative battery cable. Remove the air duct, as required.

2. Drain the coolant from the radiator.

3. Remove the upper hose and coolant reserve tank hose from the radiator.

4. Remove the shroud assembly from the radiator.

5. Raise the vehicle and support safely.

6. Remove the lower hose from the radiator.

7. Disconnect and plug the automatic transmission cooler hoses, if equipped. Lower the vehicle.

8. Remove the mounting screws and carefully lift the radiator out of the engine compartment.

To install:

9. Lower the radiator into position and install the mounting screws.

10. Raise the vehicle and support safely. Connect the automatic transmission cooler hoses, if removed.

11. Connect the lower radiator hose. Lower the vehicle.

12. Install the shroud assembly.

13. Connect the upper hose and coolant reserve tank hose.

14. Fill the cooling system.

15. Connect the negative battery cable and run the vehicle until the thermostat opens. Fill the radiator completely and check the automatic transmission fluid level, if equipped.

16. Check for leaks. Once vehicle has cooled, recheck coolant level.

17. Reinstall the air duct, if removed.

Heater Core

REMOVAL AND INSTALLATION

1. Disconnect the negative battery cable. Position the heater controls in the extreme right position.

2. Drain the coolant. Disconnect the heater hoses from the core tubes.

3. Remove the hazard flasher switch and the matching cover on the other side of the column. Remove the instrument cluster.

4. Remove the fuse box cover and remove the fuse box retaining screws. Position the fuse box aside.

5. Remove the glove box assembly.

6. Remove the defroster ducts.

7. Label and disconnect the air, mode and temperature control cables from the heater case.

8. Remove the front speaker grilles.

9. Remove the parcel box or clock, as equipped.

10. Remove the nut cover from the top center of the instrument panel.

11. Remove the center cover.

12. Remove the shift knob and floor console assembly, if equipped.

13. Move the tilt steering column down as far as it will go.

14. Remove the instrument panel retaining nuts and bolts and carefully remove the instrument panel from the vehicle.

15. Remove the duct from the top center of the heater case.

16. Remove the defroster duct from the the left side of the case.

17. Remove the center reinforcement braces.

18. Remove the mounting nuts and remove the heater case from the vehicle.

19. Remove the hose cover, joint hose clamp and the plate from the case.

20. Remove the heater core from the case.

To install:

21. Install the heater core to the heater case.

22. Install the plate, joint hose clamp and hose cover.

23. Install the assembled heater case to the vehicle. Connect the heater hoses to the core tubes.

24. Install the center reinforcement braces.

25. Install the defroster and center ducts to the case.

26. Install the instrument panel and all related parts. Adjust the control cables if necessary.

27. Fill the system with coolant.

28. Connect the negative battery cable, run the vehicle until the thermostat opens and fill the radiator completely.

29. Check for leaks. Once cooled, recheck the coolant level.

30. Check the entire climate control system and all gauges for proper operation.

Water Pump

REMOVAL AND INSTALLATION

2.4L Engine

1. Disconnect the negative battery cable.

2. Drain the cooling system.

3. Release the fuel pressure if equipped with fuel injection.

4. Remove the upper radiator shroud.

5. Remove all accessory belts. Remove the air conditioning compressor tensioner pulley, if equipped.

6. Remove the cooling fan assembly along with the water pump pulley.

7. Disconnect the radiator hose from the water pump.

8. Remove the crankshaft pulley(s).

9. Remove the timing belt covers. If the same timing belt will be reused, mark the direction of the timing belt's rotation, for installation in the same direction. Make sure the engine is positioned so the No. 1 cylinder is at the TDC of its compression stroke and the sprockets timing marks are aligned with the engine's timing mark indicators. Remove the timing belt.

10. The water pump bolts are different lengths, note their positions before removing. Remove the water pump mounting bolts and remove the pump from the block and the water pipe connection. Remove the O-ring from the water pipe connection.

To install:

11. Clean and dry the mating surfaces of the block and water pump. Install a new O-ring to the water pipe connection. Coat the new O-ring with water to aid in installation.

12. Install the water pump with a new gasket to the block and torque the bolts (except the alternator bracket bolt) to 10 ft. lbs. (13 Nm). Torque the aforementioned bolt to 17 ft. lbs. (23 Nm).

13. Install the timing belt(s) and covers.

14. Install the crankshaft pulley(s).

15. Connect the radiator hose to the water pump.

16. Install the water pump pulley and cooling fan assembly.

17. Install the air conditioning compressor tensioner pulley, if equipped, and install and adjust the accessory belts.

18. Install the upper radiator shroud.

19. Fill the system with coolant.

20. Connect the negative battery cable, run the vehicle until the thermostat opens and fill the radiator completely.

21. Check for leaks. Once cooled, recheck the coolant level.

3.0L Engine

1. Disconnect the negative battery cable.

2. Drain the cooling system. Remove the upper radiator hose, bypass hose and the upper radiator shroud.

3. If equipped with electric fuel pump, loosen the fuel filler cap to release fuel tank pressure and release the fuel pressure in the supply lines.

4. Remove the cooling fan assembly along with the water pump pulley. Remove all belts.

5. Remove the power steering pump from the bracket and remove the bracket.

6. Remove the tensioner pulley bracket, the air conditioning compressor and its bracket.

7. Remove the cooling fan bracket assembly. Remove the crankshaft pulley and flange.

8. Remove the timing belt covers. If the same timing belt will be reused, mark the direction of the timing belt's rotation, for installation in the same direction. Make sure the engine is positioned so the No. 1 cylinder is at the TDC of its compression stroke and the sprockets timing marks are aligned with the engine's timing mark indicators.

9. Loosen the timing belt tensioner bolt and remove the belt. Position the tensioner as far away from the center of the engine as possible and tighten the bolt. Remove the water pump mounting bolts, separate the pump from the water inlet pipe and remove the pump from the engine. Remove the water inlet fitting from the pump.

To install:

10. Clean and dry the mating surfaces of the block and water pump. Install a new O-ring to the water inlet pipe. Install the pump and water inlet fitting with new gaskets to the engine and water pipe. Torque the water pump mounting bolts to 20 ft. lbs. (27 Nm).

11. If not already done, position both camshafts so the marks line up with those on the alternator bracket

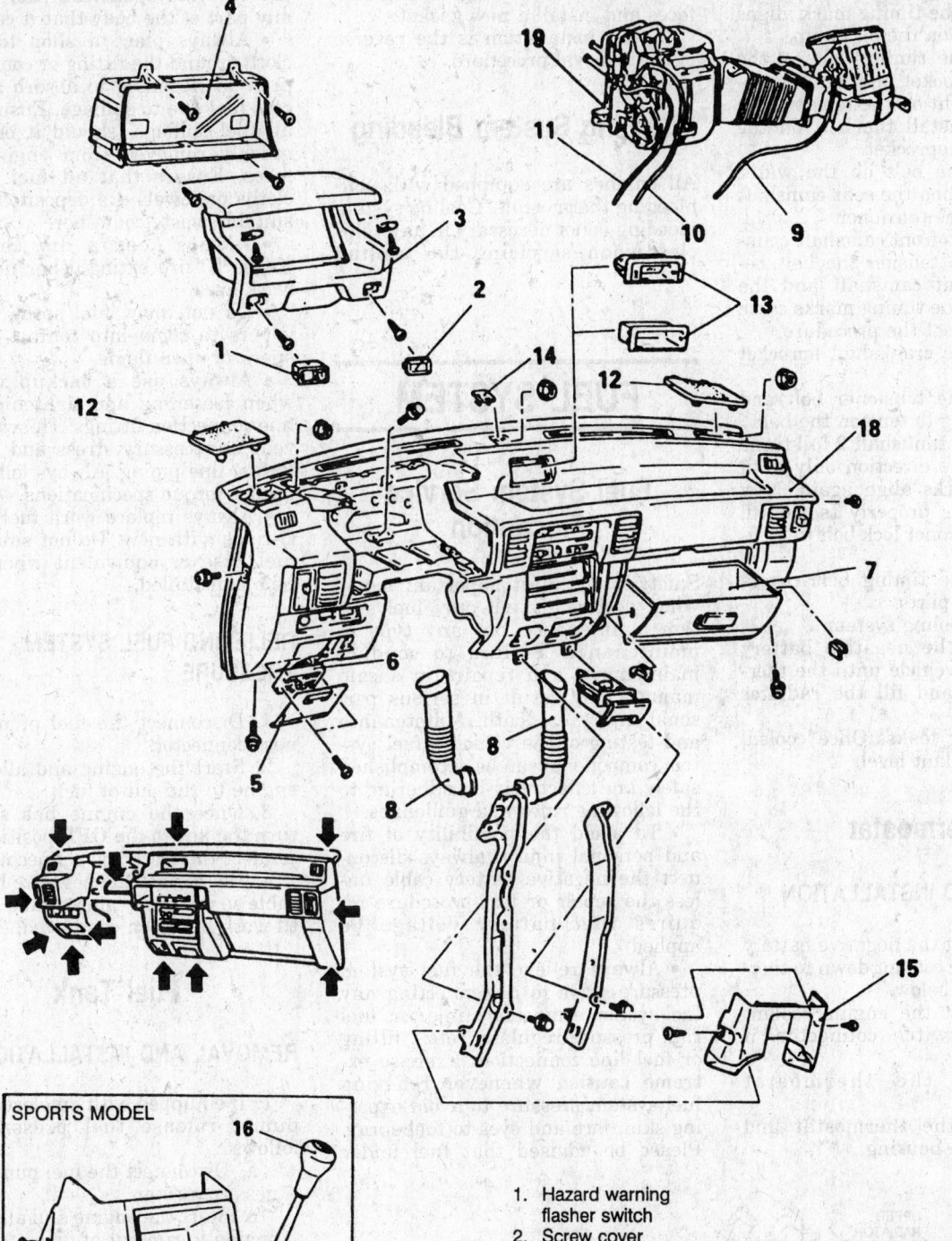

SPORTS MODEL

1. Hazard warning flasher switch
2. Screw cover
3. Instrument cluster hood
4. Instrument cluster
5. Fuse box cover
6. Fuse box
7. Glove box
8. Defroster duct
9. Air selection control cable
10. Mode selection control cable
11. Temperature control cable
12. Speaker grill
13. Parcel box or clock
14. Instrument panel attaching nut cover
15. Center cover
16. Shifter knob
17. Floor console
18. Instrument panel
19. Heater case

7911i018

Instrument panel assembly

and inner timing cover. Rotate the crankshaft so the timing mark aligns with the mark on the oil pump.

12. Install the timing belt on the crankshaft sprocket and while keeping the belt tight on the tension side (right side), install the belt on the front camshaft sprocket.

13. Install the belt on the water pump pulley, then the rear camshaft sprocket and the tensioner.

14. Rotate the front camshaft counterclockwise to tension the belt between the front camshaft and the crankshaft. If the timing marks came out of line, repeat the procedure.

15. Install the crankshaft sprocket flange.

16. Loosen the tensioner bolt and allow the spring to tension the belt.

17. Turn the crankshaft 2 full turns in the clockwise direction only until the timing marks align again. Now that the belt is properly tensioned, torque the tensioner lock bolt to 21 ft. lbs. (29 Nm).

18. Install the timing belt covers and all related parts.

19. Fill the cooling system.

20. Connect the negative battery cable, run the vehicle until the thermostat opens and fill the radiator completely.

21. Check for leaks. Once cooled, recheck the coolant level.

Thermostat

REMOVAL AND INSTALLATION

1. Disconnect the negative battery cable. Drain the coolant down to thermostat level or below.

2. Disconnect the engine coolant temperature switch connector, if equipped.

3. Remove the thermostat housing.

4. Remove the thermostat and gasket from the housing.

5. Clean the housing mating surfaces and install a new gasket.

6. The installation is the reverse of the removal procedure.

Cooling System Bleeding

All engines are equipped with self-bleeding thermostats. Cooling system bleeding is not necessary in any vehicles when servicing the cooling system.

FUEL SYSTEM

Fuel System Service Precaution

Safety is the most important factor when performing not only fuel system maintenance but any type of maintenance. Failure to conduct maintenance and repairs in a safe manner may result in serious personal injury or death. Maintenance and testing of the vehicle's fuel system components can be accomplished safely and effectively by adhering to the following rules and guidelines.

• To avoid the possibility of fire and personal injury, always disconnect the negative battery cable unless the repair or test procedure requires that battery voltage be applied.

• Always relieve the fuel system pressure prior to disconnecting any fuel system component (injector, fuel rail, pressure regulator, etc.), fitting or fuel line connection. Exercise extreme caution whenever relieving fuel system pressure to avoid exposing skin, face and eyes to fuel spray. Please be advised that fuel under

pressure may penetrate the skin or any part of the body that it contacts.

• Always place a shop towel or cloth around the fitting or connection prior to loosening to absorb any excess fuel due to spillage. Ensure that all fuel spillage (should it occur) is quickly removed from engine surfaces. Ensure that all fuel soaked cloths or towels are deposited into a suitable waste container.

• Always keep a dry chemical (Class B) fire extinguisher near the work area.

• Do not allow fuel spray or fuel vapors to come into contact with a spark or open flame.

• Always use a backup wrench when loosening and tightening fuel line connection fittings. This will prevent unnecessary stress and torsion to fuel line piping. Always follow the proper torque specifications.

• Always replace worn fuel fitting O-rings with new. Do not substitute fuel hose or equivalent where fuel pipe is installed.

RELIEVING FUEL SYSTEM PRESSURE

1. Disconnect the fuel pump harness connector.

2. Start the engine and allow the engine to run out of fuel.

3. Once the engine has stalled, turn the key to the **OFF** position and connect the electrical connector.

4. Disconnect the negative battery cable so pressure cannot build up until work has been completed.

Fuel Tank

REMOVAL AND INSTALLATION

1. If equipped with an electric fuel pump, release fuel pressure as follows:

a. Disconnect the fuel pump harness connector.

b. Start the engine and allow the engine to run out of fuel.

c. Once engine has stalled, turn the key to the **OFF** position.

d. Disconnect the negative battery cable so pressure cannot build up until work has been completed.

2. Raise the vehicle and support safely.

3. Using the proper equipment, drain the fuel tank.

4. Remove the side skirt panel, if equipped.

5. Disconnect the fuel gauge unit connector.

UPPER RADIATOR HOSE

FAN BRACKET

LOWER RADIATOR HOSE

WATER PUMP

7911i019

Water pump assembly — 3.0L engine

6. Disconnect the main hose connector.

7. Disconnect the return hose connector and the vapor hose connector.

8. Remove the filler hose connector and the breather hose connection.

9. Place a transmission jack or equivalent, under the center of the tank and apply slight pressure. Remove the tank mounting nuts.

10. Lower the tank and disconnect any lines still connected.

11. Remove the tank from the vehicle.

To install:

12. Raise the tank into position and connect all harnesses and hoses.

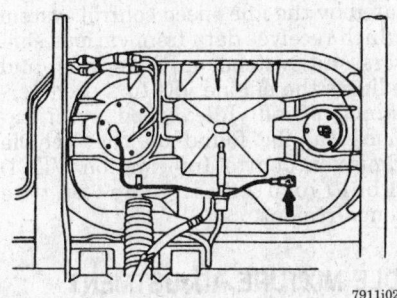

Fuel pump harness connector at the rear of the fuel tank

13. Install the fuel tank mounting nuts and torque to 18–22 ft. lbs. (25–30 Nm).

14. Reconnect the fuel gauge unit connector.

15. Install the side skirt panel, if equipped.

16. Refill the fuel tank and start the engine. Check fuel system for leaks.

Fuel Filter

REMOVAL AND INSTALLATION

——— **CAUTION** ———
Do not use conventional fuel filters, hoses or clamps when servicing this fuel system. They are not compatible with the injection system and could fail, causing personal injury or damage to the vehicle. Use only replacement parts specifically designed for fuel injection.

1. Relieve the fuel pressure.
2. Disconnect the negative battery cable.
3. Raise the vehicle and support safely.
4. Remove the fuel filter protector plate, if equipped.

5. Disconnect the main and high pressure lines. Remove any other fuel hose that are damaged or worn.

6. Remove the filter mounting bolts and remove the filter from the vehicle.

To install:

7. Install new filter onto vehicle using new gaskets. Replace any hoses that are worn or damaged.

8. Install the protector plate, if equipped.

9. Connect the negative battery cable, check for leaks and road test the vehicle.

Electric Fuel Pump

PRESSURE TESTING

1. Relieve the fuel pressure.
2. Disconnect the negative battery cable.
3. Cover the high pressure fuel hose hose with a clean shop towel to prevent fuel spray from residual pressure in the line. Disconnect the high pressure fuel hose at the delivery pipe.
4. Connect the proper fuel pressure gauge and accompanying special adaptor tools to the delivery pipe.

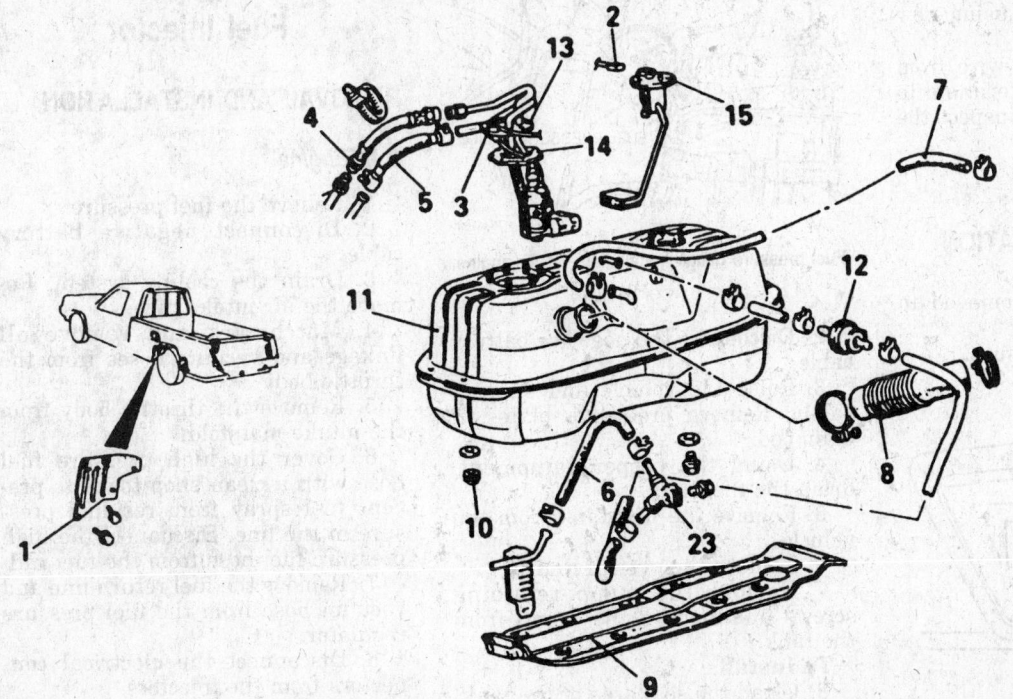

1. Side skirt stay
2. Sending unit connector
3. Fuel pump connector
4. Main hose
5. Return hose
6. Vapor hose
7. Breather hose
8. Filler hose
9. Fuel tank protector (4WD)
10. Tank mounting nut
11. Fuel tank
12. Two-way overfill limiter valve
13. Fuel pump assembly
14. Gasket
15. Sending unit

Fuel tank assembly

5. If not already done, place the key in the **OFF** position. Connect the negative battery cable.

6. Connect a jumper wire from the fuel pump activation terminal to the positive battery post. This will pressurize the system so the fuel pump installation assembly can be inspected for leaks. If a leak is found, repair it before proceeding.

7. Disconnect the jumper wire to stop the fuel pump.

8. Start the engine and allow it to idle.

9. Measure the pressure during idling. The specification for all applications is 38 psi.

10. Disconnect and plug the vacuum hose from the fuel pressure regulator.

11. With the hose disconnected, the pressure should increase to 50 psi.

12. Race the engine a few times to make sure the fuel pressure does not deviate from specifications.

13. Press on the return hose while racing the engine to make sure there is pressure in the hose. Reconnect the vacuum hose.

14. Stop the engine and allow pressure to remain in the system. There should be no decrease in pressure for at least 2 minutes.

15. Release the fuel pressure.

16. Remove the fuel pressure measuring equipment.

17. Connect the high pressure fuel hose to the delivery pipe using new O-rings where necessary.

18. Connect the jumper wire from the fuel pump activation terminal to the positive battery post, inspect the system for leaks.

19. Road test the vehicle.

REMOVAL AND INSTALLATION

The fuel tank must be removed to service the fuel pump.

1. Relieve the fuel pressure.

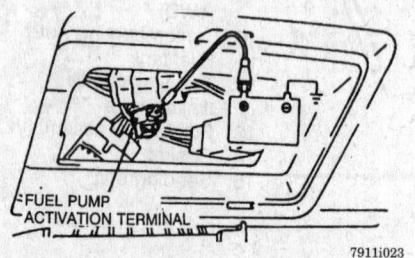

Fuel pump activation terminal located behind the fuse box

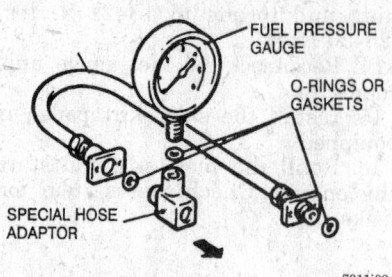

Fuel pressure testing equipment. The hose is not used with the 2.4L engine

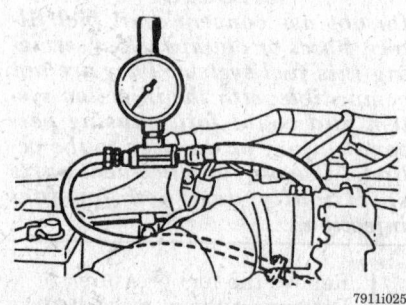

Fuel pressure gauge installation — 3.0L engine

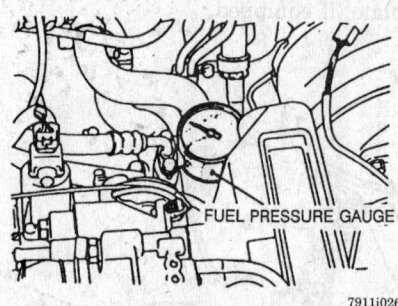

Fuel pressure gauge installation — 2.4L engine

2. Disconnect the negative battery cable.

3. Raise the vehicle and support safely. Remove protective plates, if equipped.

4. Using the proper equipment, drain the fuel tank.

5. Remove the fuel tank from the vehicle.

6. Remove the overfill limiter.

7. Remove the pump retaining screws and remove the pump from the tank.

To install:

8. Clean the seal area of the tank. Install a new gasket.

9. Install the pump in the same position as originally installed.

10. Install the retaining screws and torque them to 15 inch lbs.

11. Install the fuel tank and all related parts.

12. Connect the negative battery cable. Connect the jumper wire from the fuel pump activation terminal to the positive battery post and inspect the system for leaks.

13. Road test the vehicle.

Fuel Injection

IDLE SPEED ADJUSTMENT

The idle speed is automatically regulated by the idle speed control system which receives data from various sensors and switches in the system and adjusts the engine idle to a predetermined speed. Idle speed specifications can be found on the Vehicle Emission Control Information (VECI) label located in the engine compartment.

IDLE MIXTURE ADJUSTMENT

There is no idle mixture adjustment provided with any Mitsubishi fuel injection system.

Fuel Injector

REMOVAL AND INSTALLATION

2.4L Engine

1. Relieve the fuel pressure.

2. Disconnect negative battery cable.

3. Drain the cooling system. Remove the air intake pipe.

4. Matchmark and remove all linkage and vacuum hoses from the throttle body.

5. Remove the throttle body from the intake manifold.

6. Cover the high pressure fuel hose with a clean shop towel to prevent fuel spray from residual pressure in the line. Disconnect the high pressure fuel hose from the fuel rail.

7. Remove the fuel return line and vacuum hose from the fuel pressure regulator.

8. Disconnect the electrical connectors from the injectors.

9. Remove the fuel rail retaining bolts.

10. Lift the rail with injectors attached up and away from the engine.

11. Remove the injector from the rail by pulling straight out away from rail. Remove the lower insulator.

To install:

12. Install a new grommet and O-rings onto the injector. Coat the O-rings lightly with gasoline.

13. Install the injector to the rail, making sure injector turns freely. If it does not turn, check for a damaged or misaligned O-ring and reinstall.

14. Replace the insulators in the intake manifold. Install the fuel rail with injectors onto the manifold. Make sure the rubber bushings are correctly seated in the installation holes.

15. Tighten fuel rail retaining bolts to 18 ft. lbs. (10 Nm).

16. Install the fuel return line and vacuum hose to the fuel pressure regulator.

17. Connect the electrical harness to the injectors.

18. Replace O-ring and connect the high pressure fuel line to delivery pipe.

19. Connect the boost hose to air plenum.

20. Install the throttle body using a new base gasket.

21. Refill the cooling system. Connect the negative battery cable.

22. Connect the jumper wire from the fuel pump activation terminal to the positive battery post and inspect the system for leaks.

3.0L Engine

1. Relieve the fuel pressure.
2. Disconnect negative battery cable.
3. Remove the air intake hose from the throttle body.
4. Disconnect all wires, hoses and linkages to the throttle body.
5. Disconnect the EGR temperature sensor wire.
6. Remove the ignition coil.
7. Remove the engine oil filler neck bracket.
8. Unbolt the EGR tube from the air intake plenum.
9. Disconnect the PCV hose and vacuum hose cluster from the plenum.
10. Remove the plenum to engine brackets.
11. Unbolt the air intake plenum assembly from the intake manifold and remove.
12. Cover the high pressure fuel hose with a clean shop towel to prevent fuel spray due to residual pressure in the line. Disconnect the high pressure fuel hose from the fuel rail.

13. Remove the fuel return line and vacuum hose from the fuel pressure regulator.
14. Remove electrical connectors from the injectors.
15. Remove the fuel rail retaining bolts.
16. Lift the rail with injectors attached up and away from the engine.
17. Remove the injectors from the fuel rail pulling straight out away from the rail. Remove the lower insulator.

To install:

18. Install a new grommet and O-ring onto injector. Coat the O-ring lightly with gasoline to aid in assembly.
19. Install the injectors into the rail, making sure injector turns freely. If they do not, check for a misaligned O-ring and reinstall.
20. Replace the seats in the intake manifold. Install new rubber bushings onto mounting points of fuel rail. Install the assembled fuel rail with injectors onto the manifold.
21. Tighten the fuel rail bolts to 8 ft. lbs. (10 Nm).
22. Connect the electrical harness to the injectors.
23. Connect the fuel return hose and the vacuum hose to the pressure regulator.
24. Using a new O-ring coated lightly with gasoline, install the high pressure fuel line.
25. Install air intake plenum and all related parts.
26. Connect the negative battery cable.
27. Connect the jumper wire from the fuel pump activation terminal to the positive battery post inspect the system for leaks.

EMISSION CONTROLS

Emission Warning Lamps

RESETTING

Remove the glass from the front of the instrument cluster to access the reset switch. To reset the timer, simply flip the switch. The bulb may be removed after the 120,000 mile check is completed.

ENGINE MECHANICAL

NOTE: Disconnecting the negative battery cable on some vehicles may interfere with the functions of the on board computer systems and may require the computer to undergo a relearning process, once the negative battery cable is reconnected.

Engine Assembly

REMOVAL AND INSTALLATION

1. Relieve the fuel pressure if equipped with fuel injection. Disconnect the negative battery cable from the battery and from the engine.
2. Matchmark and remove the hood. Remove the oil dipstick.
3. Raise the vehicle and support safely. Remove the engine under cover. Drain the engine oil and coolant.
4. Remove the starter. Remove the lower radiator hose.
5. Remove the exhaust pipe from the exhaust manifold(s).
6. If equipped with 4WD, remove transfer case from vehicle.
7. If equipped with a manual transmission, remove the transmission and all related parts.
8. If equipped with an automatic transmission and 2WD, remove the inspection plate, matchmark the flexplate to the converter, remove the torque converter bolts and move the torque converter back as far as it will go. Remove the lower bell housing bolts. Lower the vehicle.
9. Remove all ductwork and air intake hoses. Disconnect all linkages and cables from the throttle body.
10. Cover the fuel line connections with a clean shop rag and disconnect and plug the fuel lines.
11. If equipped with air conditioning, unbolt the air conditioning compressor from the engine and position aside. It is not necessary to remove the lines from the compressor.
12. Remove the radiator and shroud. Remove the fan and all related parts. Disconnect the heater hoses.
13. Unbolt the power steering pump from its brackets and position it to the side. Do not remove the hoses from the pump.

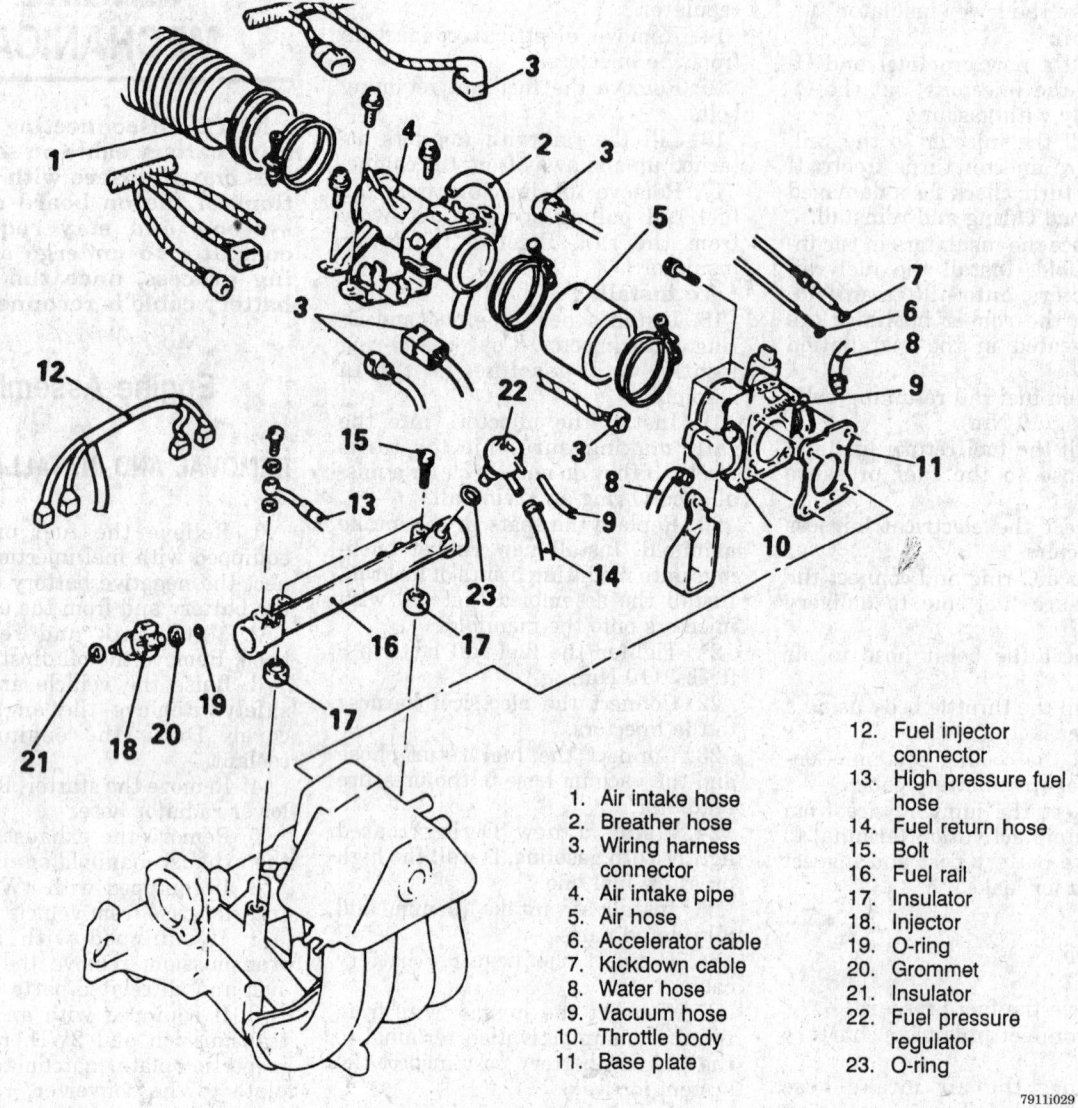

1. Air intake hose
2. Breather hose
3. Wiring harness connector
4. Air intake pipe
5. Air hose
6. Accelerator cable
7. Kickdown cable
8. Water hose
9. Vacuum hose
10. Throttle body
11. Base plate
12. Fuel injector connector
13. High pressure fuel hose
14. Fuel return hose
15. Bolt
16. Fuel rail
17. Insulator
18. Injector
19. O-ring
20. Grommet
21. Insulator
22. Fuel pressure regulator
23. O-ring

7911i029

Throttle body, fuel rail, injector and related parts — 2.4L engine

14. Remove the alternator. Remove the ignition coil and power transistor assembly, if equipped.

15. Label and disconnect all remaining electrical connectors, vacuum hoses and check for any other items preventing engine removal.

16. Attach an engine removal device to the engine support eyes on the engine.

17. If equipped with an automatic transmission, support the transmission with a floor jack or equivalent. Remove the remaining bell housing bolts.

18. Remove the engine mount nuts and remove the engine from the vehicle.

To install:

19. Lower the engine into position and install the engine mount nuts. Torque the nuts to 20 ft. lbs. (27 Nm). Install the upper bell housing bolts. Remove the engine removal device and the transmission support. Install the oil dipstick.

20. Raise the vehicle and support safely. Install the remaining bell housing bolts.

21. Install transfer case, if removed.

22. If equipped with a manual transmission, install the transmission and all related parts.

23. If equipped with an automatic transmission, align the torque converter and flexplate and install the bolts. Install the inspection plate and starter.

24. Install the exhaust pipe to the exhaust manifold(s) using new gaskets. Install the lower radiator hose. Lower the vehicle.

25. Connect the heater hoses.

26. Make sure the negative battery cable is not connected to the battery. Connect the engine side of the negative cable to the engine. Install the alternator, power steering pump and all brackets.

27. Install the air conditioning compressor.

28. Connect all linkages and cables to the throttle body.

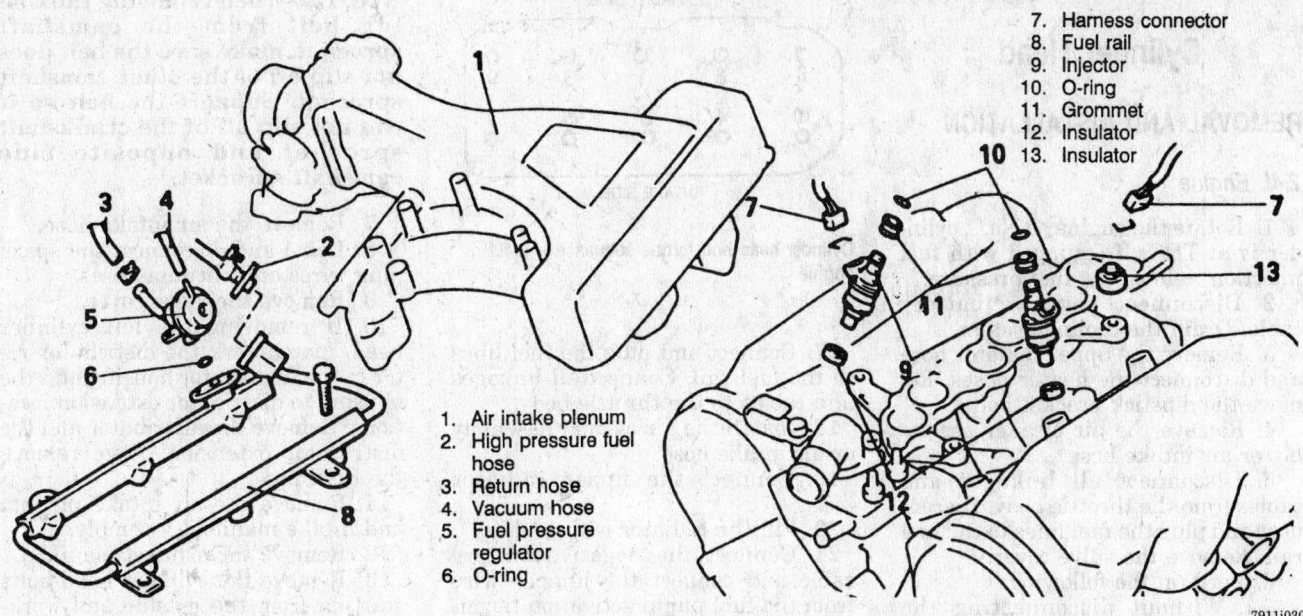

7. Harness connector
8. Fuel rail
9. Injector
10. O-ring
11. Grommet
12. Insulator
13. Insulator

1. Air intake plenum
2. High pressure fuel hose
3. Return hose
4. Vacuum hose
5. Fuel pressure regulator
6. O-ring

Fuel rail, injector and related parts — 3.0L engine

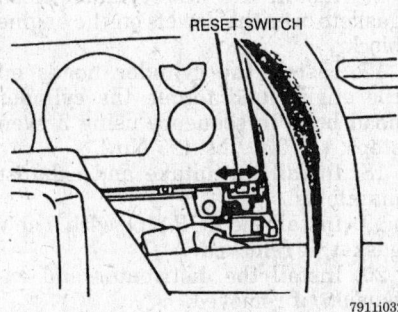

RESET SWITCH

Emissions warning light reset switch

29. Install the ignition coil and power transistor assembly, if equipped. Connect all electrical connectors and vacuum hoses that were disconnected during the engine removal procedure.

30. Install the fan and all related parts. Adjust all belt tensions, as required.

31. Install the radiator, shroud and upper hose.

32. Install the air cleaner assembly, ducts and air intake hoses.

33. Fill the engine with the specified amount of oil and fill the radiator with coolant.

34. Connect the negative battery cable and connect the jumper wire from the fuel pump activation terminal, if equipped, to the positive battery post to inspect the system for leaks.

35. Check the automatic transmission fluid level, if equipped. Set all adjustments to specifications.

36. Install and align the hood.

Engine Mounts

REMOVAL AND INSTALLATION

Front Mount

1. Disconnect negative battery cable.

2. Install engine support fixture in place. Raise and safely support the vehicle.

3. Remove the engine front support insulator.

4. Remove the front insulator stopper.

5. Remove the heat protector.

6. Unbolt the rear crossmember or mount as required.

7. Raise engine with support fixture far enough to remove mounts, remove remaining bolts and mounts. Transfer insulator and stopper to new mount.

To install:

8. Install mounts to engine block. Install stopper and heat protector to the mount.

9. Lower engine to original position and insert bolts through mounting brackets. Tighten bolts to 22–29 ft. lbs. (30-40 Nm) and mount nut to 14–22 ft. lbs. (20–30 Nm).

10. Install heat protector to insulator. Tighten heat protector nut to 6–9 ft. lbs. (8-12 Nm).

11. Lower the vehicle and remove the engine support fixture. Reconnect the negative battery cable.

Rear Mount

1. Disconnect negative battery cable.

2. Install engine support fixture in place. Raise and safely support the vehicle.

3. Install transmission jack into position and raise transmission slightly.

4. Remove rear mount attaching bolts and crossmember attaching bolts. Remove crossmember from the vehicle and transfer mounting bracket, support insulator, and plate assembly to new mount.

5. Installation is the reverse of the removal procedure. Torque crossmember retaining bolts to 29–40 ft.

lbs. (40–55 Nm). Torque the insulator to crossmember nuts to 14–18 ft. lbs. (20–25 Nm).

Cylinder Head

REMOVAL AND INSTALLATION

2.4L Engine

1. Rotate the engine so No. 1 cylinder is at TDC. If equipped with fuel injection, relieve the fuel pressure.
2. Disconnect negative battery cable. Drain the cooling system.
3. Remove the upper radiator hose and disconnect the heater hoses. Remove the dipstick bracket bolt.
4. Remove the air cleaner assembly or air intake hose.
5. Disconnect all linkages and cables from the throttle body. Disconnect and plug the fuel lines to the fuel rail. Remove the valve cover.
6. Perform the following:
   a. Without disconnecting the lines, unbolt the power steering pump from its brackets and position it to the side, if equipped.
   b. Remove the timing belt upper cover.
   c. Align the timing mark, if not already aligned. Secure the timing belt to the sprocket with wire tie.
   d. Remove the camshaft bolt.
   e. Remove the sprocket from the camshaft and allow it to rest on the lower cover. If this is not possible, tie it to a fabricated device so the belt remains taut and the timing is not lost.
7. Disconnect and label all vacuum lines, hoses and wiring connectors from the manifolds, throttle body and cylinder head.
8. Raise the vehicle and support safely.
9. Remove the exhaust pipe from the exhaust manifold. Lower the vehicle.
10. Remove head bolts, starting from the outside and working inward. Remove the cylinder head from the engine.
11. Clean the cylinder head gasket mating surfaces.
   To install:
12. Install the camshaft gear or sprocket.
13. Install the timing belt cover, if equipped.
14. Install the power steering pump, if removed.
15. Connect the heater hoses.
16. Install the dipstick bracket bolt. Install the valve cover with a new gasket.

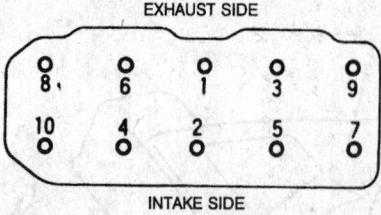

◁ TIMING BELT END

EXHAUST SIDE

8 6 1 3 9

10 4 2 5 7

INTAKE SIDE

7911i033

Cylinder head bolt torque sequence — 2.4L engine

17. Connect and plug the fuel lines to the fuel rail. Connect all linkages and cables to the throttle body.
18. Install the air cleaner assembly or air intake hose.
19. Connect the upper radiator hose.
20. Fill the radiator with coolant.
21. Connect the negative battery cable and connect the jumper wire from the fuel pump activation terminal to the positive battery post to inspect the system for leaks, if equipped.
22. Set all adjustments to specifications.
23. Install the seat underframe, if removed.

3.0L Engine

1. Relieve the fuel pressure. Disconnect the negative battery cable. Drain the cooling system. Disconnect the upper radiator hose.
2. Remove the drive belts, air conditioning compressor and power steering pump from the mounts and position them to the side.
3. Using a ½ in. drive breaker bar, insert it into the square hole of the serpentine drive belt tensioner, rotate it counterclockwise (to reduce the belt tension) and remove the belt.
4. Remove the alternator.
5. Remove the crankshaft pulley and the torsional damper.
6. To remove the timing belt, perform the following procedures:
   a. Remove the covers. Rotate the crankshaft to position No. 1 cylinder on the TDC of its compression stroke; the crankshaft sprocket timing mark should align with the oil pan timing indicator and the camshaft sprockets timing marks (triangles) should align with the rear timing belt covers timing marks.
   b. Mark the timing belt in the direction of rotation for reinstallation purposes.

c. Loosen the timing belt tensioner and remove the timing belt.

NOTE: When removing the timing belt from the camshaft sprocket, make sure the belt does not slip off of the other camshaft sprocket. Support the belt so it can not slip off of the crankshaft sprocket and opposite side camshaft sprocket.

7. Remove the air intake hose.
8. Label and disconnect the spark plug wires and vacuum hoses.
9. Remove the valve cover.
10. If removing the left cylinder head, matchmark the distributor rotor to the distributor housing and the housing to distributor extension locations. Remove the distributor and the distributor extension. Also, remove the EGR pipe.
11. Remove the air intake plenum and intake manifold assembly.
12. Remove the exhaust manifold.
13. Remove the cylinder head bolts starting from the outside and working inward.
14. Remove the cylinder head from the engine.
15. Clean the gasket mounting surfaces.
   To install:
16. Install the new cylinder head gaskets over the dowels on the engine block.
17. Install the cylinder heads on the engine and torque the cylinder head bolts in sequence using 3 even steps, to 70 ft. lbs. (95 Nm).
18. Install the intake and exhaust manifolds.
19. Install the EGR pipe with a new gasket, if removed.
20. Install the distributor and extension, if removed.
21. Install the timing belt and all related items. When installing the timing belt over the camshaft sprocket, use care not to allow the belt to slip off the opposite camshaft sprocket.
22. Make sure the timing belt is installed on the camshaft sprocket in the same position as when removed.
23. Install the alternator and power steering pump.
24. Install the air conditioning compressor and belts.
25. Connect the upper radiator hose.
26. Fill the radiator with coolant.
27. Connect the negative battery cable and connect the jumper wire from the fuel pump activation terminal to the positive battery post to inspect the system for leaks, if equipped.

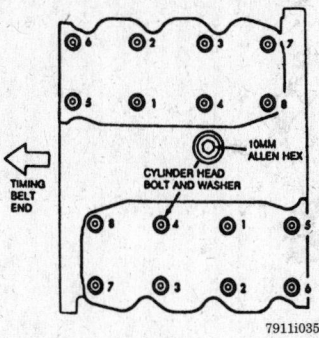

Cylinder head bolt torque sequence — 3.0L engine

28. Set all adjustments to specifications.

Valve Lifters

REMOVAL AND INSTALLATION

2.4L Engine

1. Disconnect negative battery cable.
2. Remove the valve cover.
3. Have a helper hold the rear of the camshaft down during removal. Then install the rear cap loosely to hold the camshaft in position.
4. Loosen the camshaft cap bolts but do not remove them from the caps. Remove the caps, arms, shafts and bolts all as an assembly. Install tool MD998443-01 or equivalent, on the end of all rocker arms to assure the hydraulic lifters will not fall out of the rocker arms on removal of the assembly.
5. Disassemble the unit keeping all parts in the order of removal and repair as required.

NOTE: The rocker arms have identification marks on them. Arms with 1–3 on them should only be used on cylinders 1 or 3. Arms with 2–4 on them should only be used on cylinders 2 and 4.

6. The installation is the reverse of the removal procedure. Make sure the arrows on the caps are all pointing to the front of the engine. Torque the cap bolts first to 85 inch lbs. (10 Nm), then to 175 inch lbs. (18 Nm) in the following order: No. 3 cap, No. 2 cap, No. 4 cap, Front cap and Rear cap.

3.0L Engine

1. Disconnect the negative battery cable. Remove the air cleaner assembly.
2. Remove the valve cover.

3. Using the auto lash adjuster retainer tools MD998443 or equivalent, install them on the rocker arms to keep the lash adjusters from falling out.
4. On the right side cylinder head, remove the distributor extension.
5. Have a helper hold the rear end of the camshaft down. If the rear of the camshaft cannot be held down, the belt will dislodge and the valve timing will be lost. Loosen the camshaft cap bolts but do not remove them from the caps. Remove the caps, arms, shafts and bolts all as an assembly.
6. Disassemble the unit keeping all parts in order and repair as required.
7. The installation is the reverse of the removal procedure. Apply a drop of sealant to the rear edge of the rear cap. Torque the cap bolts first to 85 inch lbs. (19 Nm), then to 180 inch lbs. (19 Nm) in the following order: No. 3 cap, No. 2 cap, No. 1 cap and No. 4 cap.

Rocker Arms and Shafts

REMOVAL AND INSTALLATION

2.4L Engine

1. Disconnect the negative battery cable.
2. Remove the valve cover.
3. Have a helper hold the rear of the camshaft down. Then install the rear cap loosely to hold the camshaft in position. If the rear of the camshaft cannot be held down, the belt will dislodge and the valve timing will be lost.
4. Loosen the camshaft cap bolts but do not remove them from the caps. Remove the caps, arms, shafts and bolts all as an assembly. Install tool MD998443-01 or equivalent, on the end of all rocker arms to assure the hydraulic lifters will not fall out of the rocker arms on removal of the assembly.
5. Disassemble the unit keeping all parts in the order of removal and repair as required.

NOTE: The rocker arms have identification marks on them. Arms with 1–3 on them should only be used on cylinders 1 or 3. Arms with 2–4 on them should only be used on cylinders 2 and 4.

6. The installation is the reverse of the removal procedure. Make sure the arrows on the caps are all pointing to the front of the engine. Torque the cap bolts first to 85 inch lbs. (10

Nm), then to 175 inch lbs. (18 Nm) in the following order: No. 3 cap, No. 2 cap, No. 4 cap, Front cap and Rear cap.

3.0L Engine

1. Disconnect the negative battery cable. Remove the air cleaner assembly.
2. Remove the valve cover.
3. Using the auto lash adjuster retainer tools MD998443 or equivalent, install them on the rocker arms to keep the lash adjusters from falling out.
4. On the right side cylinder head, remove the distributor extension.
5. Have a helper hold the rear end of the camshaft down. If the rear of the camshaft cannot be held down, the belt will dislodge and the valve timing will be lost. Loosen the camshaft cap bolts but do not remove them from the caps. Remove the caps, arms, shafts and bolts all as an assembly.
6. Disassemble the unit keeping all parts in order and repair as required.
7. The installation is the reverse of the removal procedure. Apply a drop of sealant to the rear edge of the rear cap. Torque the cap bolts first to 85 inch lbs. (19 Nm), then to 180 inch lbs. (19 Nm) in the following order: No. 3 cap, No. 2 cap, No. 1 cap and No. 4 cap.

Intake Manifold

REMOVAL AND INSTALLATION

2.4L Engine

1. Relieve the fuel pressure.
2. Disconnect the negative battery cable.
3. Drain the engine coolant. Disconnect the upper radiator hose from the thermostat housing.
4. Remove the air intake hoses, breather hose and the air intake pipe.
5. Disconnect all wires, hoses and linkages to the throttle body.
6. Remove the ignition coil.
7. Disconnect the brake booster hose and vacuum hose cluster from the air intake plenum.
8. Unbolt the air intake plenum from the intake manifold and remove the plenum from the engine.
9. Cover the fuel line with a clean shop rag and disconnect the fuel lines from the fuel rail. Keep the line covered or plugged.
10. Remove the fuel rail assembly with injectors intact.

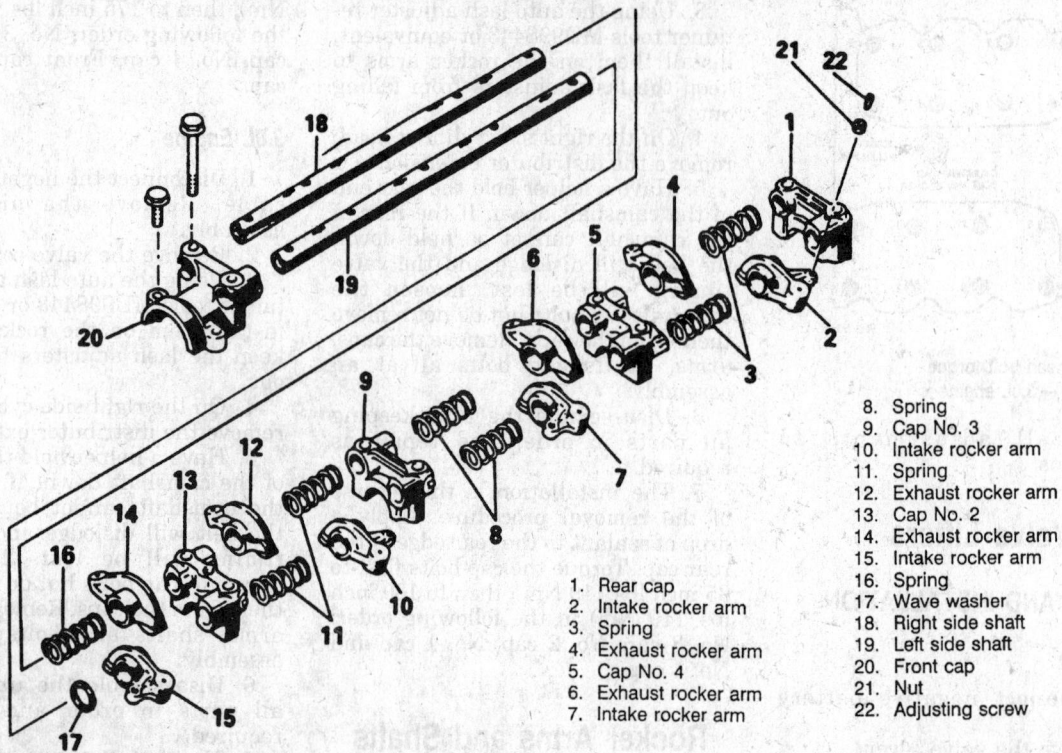

8. Spring
9. Cap No. 3
10. Intake rocker arm
11. Spring
12. Exhaust rocker arm
13. Cap No. 2
14. Exhaust rocker arm
15. Intake rocker arm
16. Spring
17. Wave washer
18. Right side shaft
19. Left side shaft
20. Front cap
21. Nut
22. Adjusting screw

1. Rear cap
2. Intake rocker arm
3. Spring
4. Exhaust rocker arm
5. Cap No. 4
6. Exhaust rocker arm
7. Intake rocker arm

7911i036

Rocker arms/shafts assembly — 2.4L engine. Note that the rocker arms are not equipped with jet valve extensions

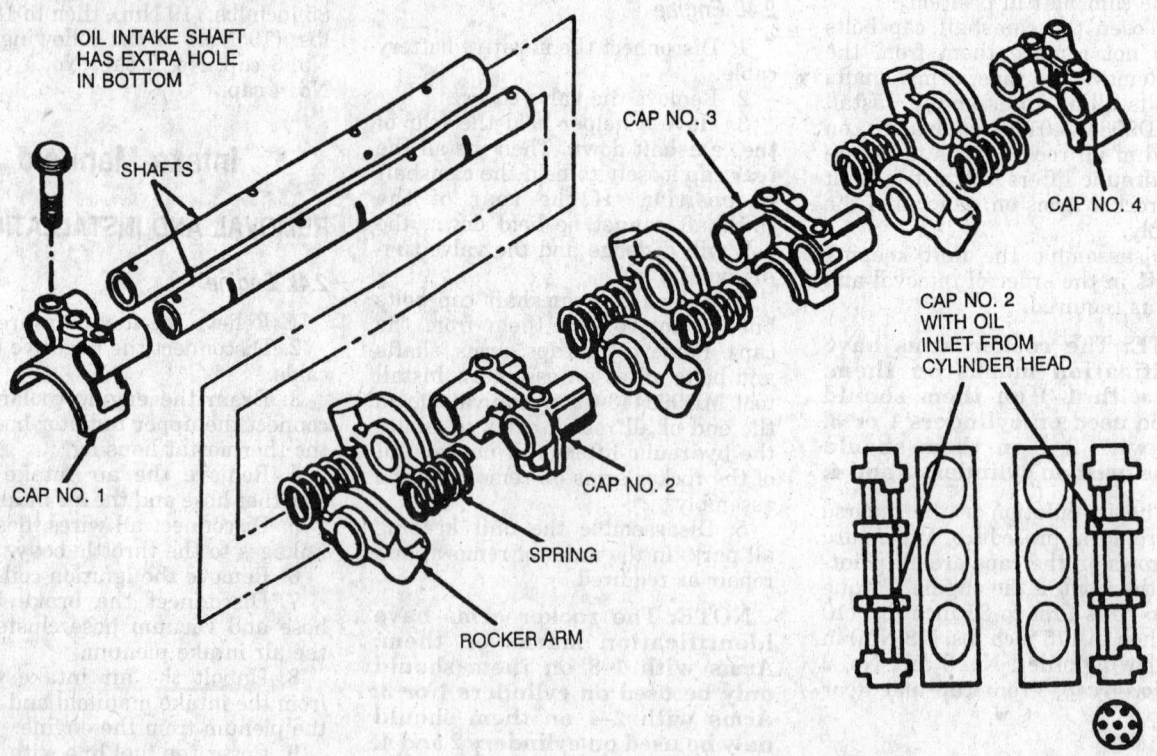

7911i038

Rocker arms/shafts assembly — 3.0L engine

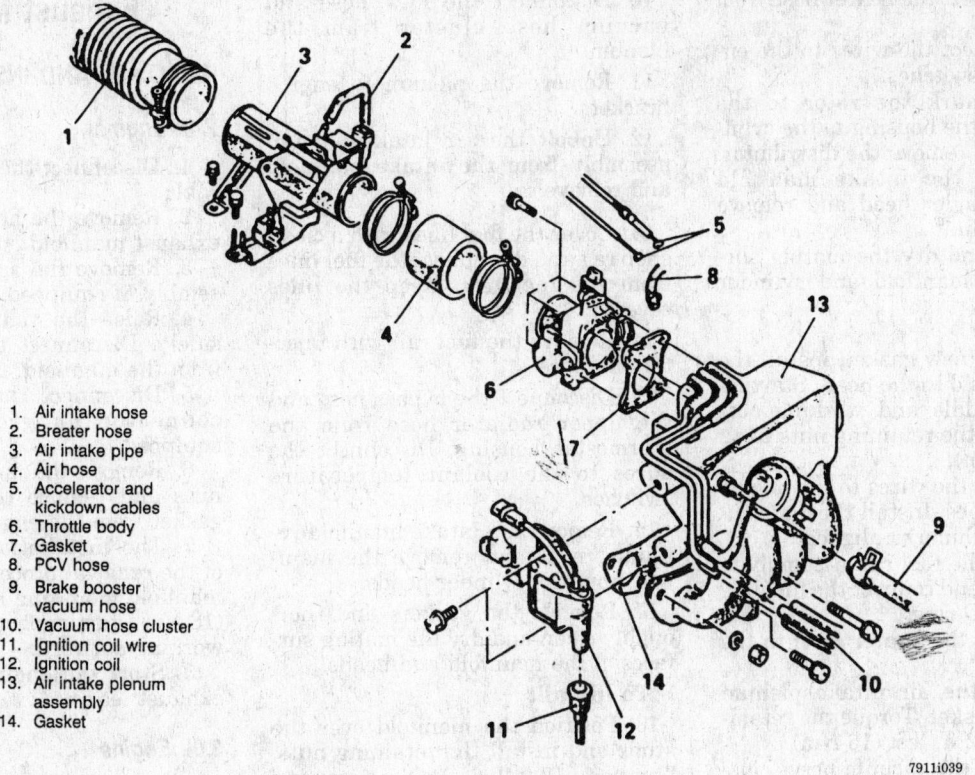

1. Air intake hose
2. Breater hose
3. Air intake pipe
4. Air hose
5. Accelerator and kickdown cables
6. Throttle body
7. Gasket
8. PCV hose
9. Brake booster vacuum hose
10. Vacuum hose cluster
11. Ignition coil wire
12. Ignition coil
13. Air intake plenum assembly
14. Gasket

7911i039

Air intake plenum assembly — 2.4L engine

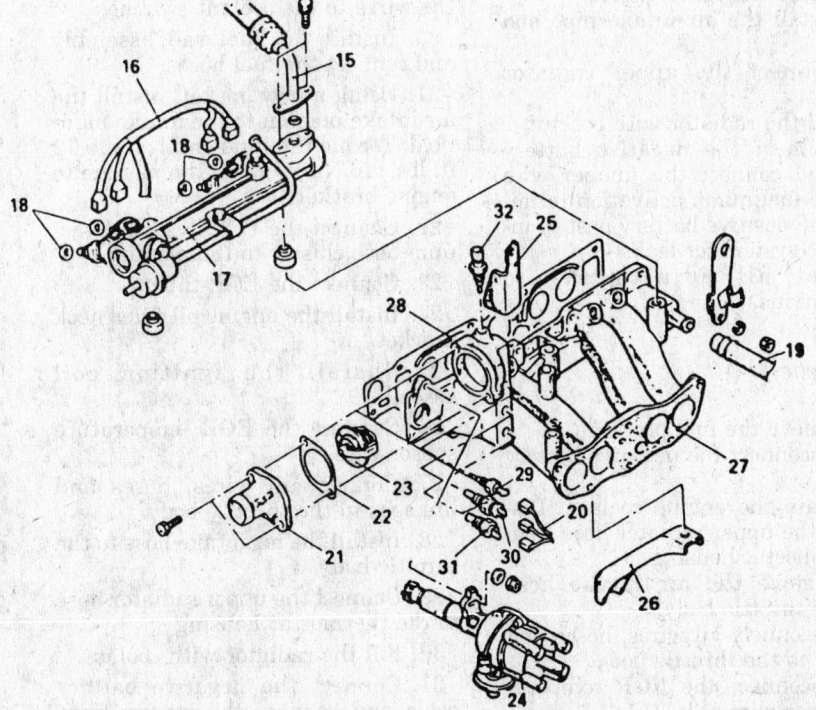

1. High pressure fuel hose
2. Injector harness connector
3. Fuel rail
4. Insulator
5. Heater hose
6. Wiring harness connector
7. Coolant outlet fitting
8. Gasket
9. Thermostat
10. Distributor
11. Plenum bracket
12. Intake manifold bracket
13. Intake manifold
14. Gasket
15. Thermo switch (automatic transmission only)
16. Coolant temperature sensor
17. Coolant temperature sending unit
18. Coolant temperature switch (automatic transmission only)

7911i040

Intake manifold assembly — 2.4L engine

11. Disconnect the heater hose from the manifold.

12. Disconnect the wires to the engine coolant switches.

13. Matchmark the rotor to the housing and the housing to the cylinder head and remove the distributor.

14. Unbolt the intake manifold from the cylinder head and remove from the engine.

15. Clean and dry the mating surfaces of the manifold and cylinder head.

To install:

16. Using a new gasket, install the intake manifold to the head. Starting from the middle and working outward, torque the retaining nuts to 12 ft. lbs. (16 Nm).

17. Connect the wires to the engine coolant switches. Install the distributor with matchmarks aligned.

18. Install the fuel rail assembly to the manifold and connect the fuel line using a new O-ring.

19. Connect the heater hose to the manifold.

20. Install the air intake plenum with a new gasket. Torque the retaining bolts to 12 ft. lbs. (16 Nm).

21. Connect the vacuum hoses cluster, brake booster hose and all wires, hoses and linkages to the throttle body.

22. Install the ignition coil.

23. Install the air intake pipe and hoses.

24. Connect the upper radiator hose.

25. Fill the radiator with coolant.

26. Connect the negative battery cable and connect the jumper wire from the fuel pump activation terminal to the positive battery post to inspect the system for leaks.

27. Set all adjustments to specifications.

3.0L Engine

1. Relieve the fuel pressure.

2. Disconnect the negative battery cable.

3. Drain the engine coolant. Disconnect the upper radiator hose from the thermostat housing.

4. Remove the air intake hose from the throttle body.

5. Disconnect all wires, hoses and linkages to the throttle body.

6. Disconnect the EGR temperature sensor wire.

7. Remove the ignition coil.

8. Remove the engine oil filler neck bracket.

9. Unbolt the EGR tube from the air intake plenum.

10. Disconnect the PCV hose and vacuum hose cluster from the plenum.

11. Remove the plenum to engine brackets.

12. Unbolt the air intake plenum assembly from the intake manifold and remove.

13. Cover the fuel lines with a clean shop rag and disconnect the fuel lines from the fuel rail. Keep the lines covered.

14. Remove the fuel rail with injectors in place.

15. Disconnect the bypass hose and the upper radiator hose from the thermostat housing. Disconnect the wires to the coolant temperature switches.

16. Remove the intake manifold retaining nuts and remove the manifold from the cylinder heads.

17. Remove the gaskets and thoroughly clean and dry the mating surfaces of the manifold and heads.

To install:

18. Position the manifold over the studs and install the retaining nuts. Torque to 12 ft. lbs. (16 Nm), starting from the center and working outward.

19. Connect the hoses and connect the wires to the coolant switches.

20. Install the fuel rail assembly and connect the fuel hoses.

21. Using a new gasket, install the air intake plenum to the intake manifold. Torque the nuts and bolts to 12 ft. lbs. (16 Nm). Install the plenum to engine brackets.

22. Connect the PCV hose and vacuum hose cluster to the plenum.

23. Connect the EGR tube.

24. Install the engine oil filler neck bracket.

25. Install the ignition coil assembly.

26. Connect the EGR temperature sensor wire.

27. Connect all wires, hoses and linkages to the throttle body.

28. Install the air intake hose to the throttle body.

29. Connect the upper radiator hose to the thermostat housing.

30. Fill the radiator with coolant.

31. Connect the negative battery cable and connect the jumper wire from the fuel pump activation terminal to the positive battery post to inspect the system for leaks.

32. Set all adjustments to specifications.

Exhaust Manifold

REMOVAL AND INSTALLATION

2.4L Engine

1. Disconnect the negative battery cable.

2. Remove the heat cowl from the exhaust manifold.

3. Remove the aspirator valve assembly, if equipped.

4. Raise the vehicle and support safely. Disconnect the exhaust pipe from the manifold. Lower the vehicle

5. Disconnect the oxygen sensor connector or ground cable, if equipped.

6. Remove the manifold mounting nuts and remove the manifold and gasket from the engine.

7. The installation is the reverse of the removal procedure. Torque the manifold mounting nuts to 13 ft. lbs. (18 Nm) starting from the middle and working outward.

8. Start the engine and check for exhaust leaks.

3.0L Engine

1. Disconnect the negative battery cable. Raise and safely support the vehicle.

2. Disconnect the exhaust pipe from the exhaust manifolds.

3. Remove the heat shield.

4. If removing the left manifold, remove EGR tube.

5. If removing the right manifold, remove alternator bracket.

6. Remove the manifold attaching nuts and remove manifold.

7. The installation is the reverse of the removal procedure. When installing, the numbers 1–3–5 on the gaskets are used with the right side cylinders and 2–4–6 are on the gasket for the left side cylinders. Torque the manifold nuts to 14 ft. lbs. (19 Nm).

8. Start the engine and check for exhaust leaks.

Timing Belt Front Cover

REMOVAL AND INSTALLATION

2.4L Engine

1. Disconnect the negative battery cable. Remove the spark plug wires from the tree on the upper cover.

2. Drain the cooling system. Remove the shroud, fan and accessory drive belts. Remove the radiator as required.

3. Remove the power steering pump, alternator, air conditioning

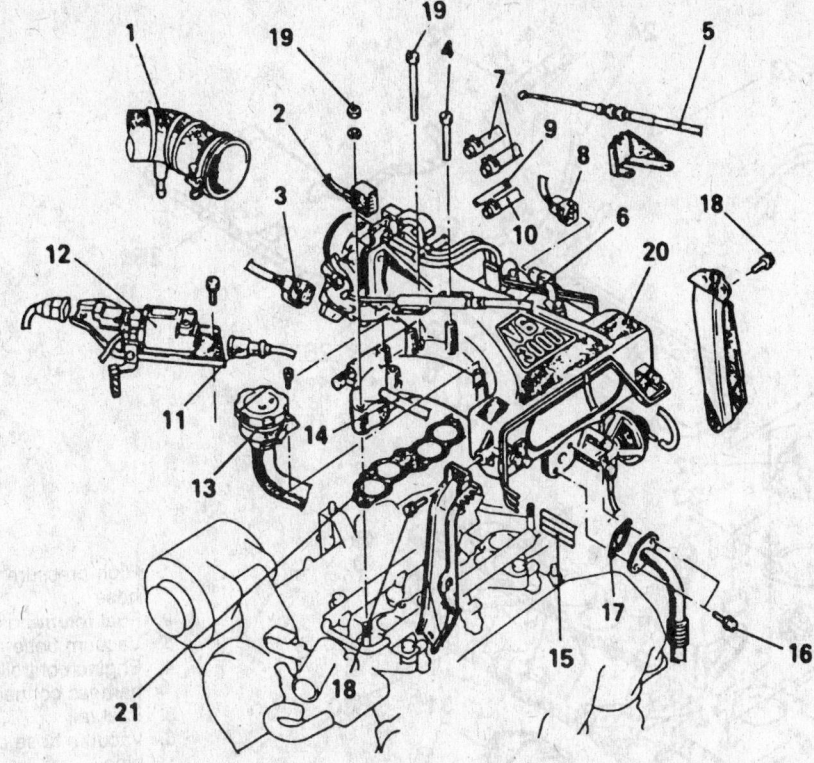

1. Air intake hose
2. Throttle position sensor connector
3. Stepper motor connector
4. Accelerator cable adjusting bolt
5. Throttle control cable (automatic transmission only)
6. Accelerator cable
7. Coolant hoses
8. EGR temperature connector
9. Vacuum hose
10. Brake booster vacuum hose
11. Ignition coil wire
12. Ignition coil
13. Oil filler neck bracket
14. PCV hose
15. Vacuum hose cluster
16. EGR pipe attaching bolt
17. Gasket
18. Bracket bolt
19. Attaching bolt and nut
20. Air intake plenum and throttle body assembly
21. Gasket

7911i041

Air intake plenum assembly — 3.0L engine

compressor, tension pulley and accompanying brackets, as required.

4. Remove the upper front timing belt cover.

5. Remove the water pump pulley and the crankshaft pulley(s).

6. Remove the lower timing belt cover to engine screws and remove the cover.

7. The installation is the reverse of the removal procedure. Make sure the packing is positioned in the inner grooves of the covers properly when installing.

3.0L Engine

1. Disconnect the negative battery cable.

2. Drain the cooling system. Remove the drive belts.

3. Remove the upper radiator shroud.

4. Remove the fan and fan pulley.

5. Without disconnecting the lines, remove the power steering pump from its bracket and position it to the side. Remove the pump brackets.

6. Remove the belt tensioner pulley bracket.

7. Without releasing the refrigerant remove the air conditioning com-

pressor from its bracket and position it to the side. Remove the bracket.

8. Remove the cooling fan bracket.

9. On some models it may be necessary to remove the pulley from the crankshaft to access the lower cover bolts.

10. Remove the timing belt cover bolts and the upper and lower covers from the engine.

To install:

11. Install the upper and lower covers to the engine and secure with the retaining screws. Make sure the packing is positioned in the inner grooves of the covers properly when installing.

12. Install the crankshaft pulley and bolts, if removed. Torque bolt to 110 ft. lbs. (150 Nm).

13. Install the air conditioning bracket and compressor to the engine. Install the belt tensioner.

14. Install the power steering pump into position. Install the fan pulley and fan.

15. Install the fan shroud to the radiator. Fill the cooling system, reconnect the negative battery cable and check for fluid leaks.

Timing Belt and Tensioner

ADJUSTMENT

2.4L Engine

1. Disconnect the negative battery cable.

2. Remove the timing belt cover.

3. Adjust the silent shaft (inner) belt first. Loosen the pulley center bolt so the pulley may be moved.

4. Move the pulley up by hand so the center span of the long side of the belt deflects ¼ inch.

5. Hold the pulley tight so the pulley itself does not rotate when the bolt is tightened. Tighten the bolt to 15 ft. lbs. (20 Nm). If the pulley has moved, the belt will be too tight.

6. Check the timing (outer) belt tension.

7. To adjust the timing (outer) belt, first loosen the tensioner pulley bolts.

8. Allow the spring to take up any slack. Check that the the deflection of the longest span (between the camshaft and oil pump sprockets) is ½ inch. Do not overtighten the belt or it will howl.

9. First tighten the lower pulley bolts to 35 ft. lbs. (47 Nm) and then the upper bolt to the same value.

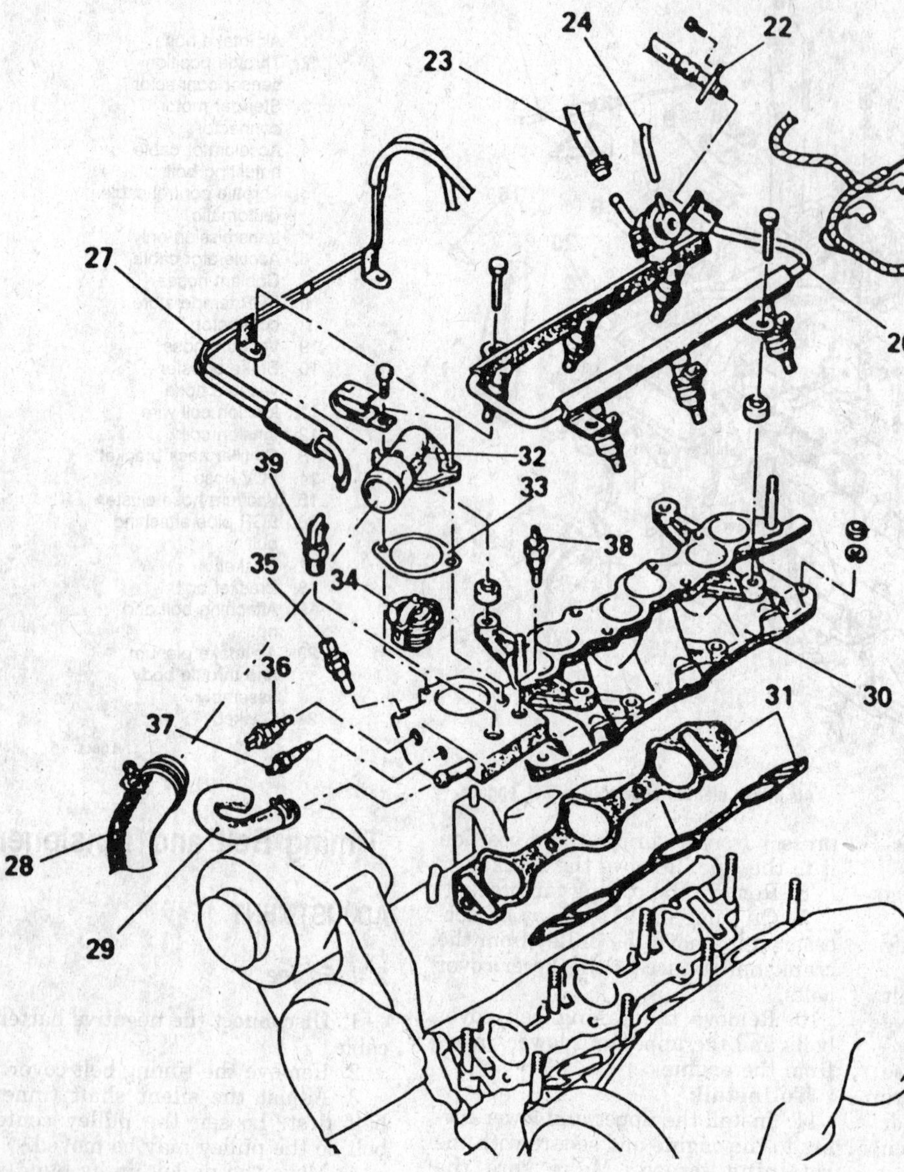

1. High pressure fuel hose
2. Fuel return hose
3. Vacuum hose
4. Engine controller harness connector
5. Fuel rail
6. Vacuum hose and pipe
7. Upper radiator hose
8. Coolant bypass hose
9. Intake manifold
10. Gasket
11. Coolant outlet fitting
12. Gasket
13. Thermostat
14. Coolant temperature switch (automatic transmission only)
15. Coolant temperature sensor
16. Thermo switch
17. Coolant temperature sending unit
18. Thermo valve

7911i042

Intake manifold assembly — 3.0L engine

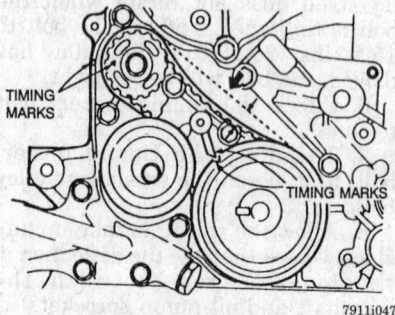

TIMING MARKS

TIMING MARKS

7911i047

Silent shaft belt installation — 2.4L engine

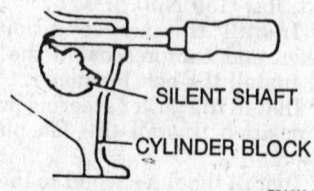

SILENT SHAFT

CYLINDER BLOCK

7911i048

Checking the left side silent shaft for positioning

10. Install the covers and all related parts.

3.0L Engine

1. Loosen the bolt that holds the timing belt tensioner in place.
2. Allow the spring to pull the tensioner in automatically.
3. Tighten the tensioner locking bolt.

REMOVAL AND INSTALLATION

2.4L Engine

1. If possible, crank the engine around so the No. 1 piston is at TDC.

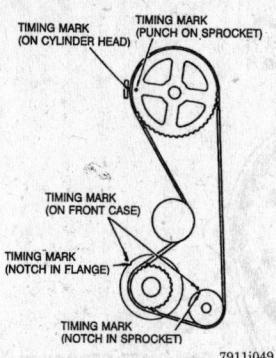

TIMING MARK
(ON CYLINDER HEAD)

TIMING MARK
(PUNCH ON SPROCKET)

TIMING MARK
(ON FRONT CASE)

TIMING MARK
(NOTCH IN FLANGE)

TIMING MARK
(NOTCH IN SPROCKET)

7911i049

Timing belt installation — 2.4L engine

2. Disconnect the negative battery cable. Remove the accessory drive belt(s).

3. Remove the timing belt covers. If the belt(s) are to be reused, mark the direction of rotation on the belt.

4. Remove the timing (outer) belt tensioner and remove the belt. Unbolt the tensioner from the block and remove.

5. Remove the outer crankshaft sprocket and flange.

6. Remove the silent shaft (inner) belt tensioner and remove the inner belt. Unbolt the tensioner from the block and remove.

To install:

7. Align the timing mark of the silent shaft belt sprockets on the crankshaft and silent shaft with the marks on the front case. Wrap the silent shaft belt around the sprockets so there is not slack in the upper span of the belt and the timing marks are still in line.

8. Install the tensioner initially so the actual center of the pulley is above and to the left of the installation bolt.

9. Move the pulley up by hand so the center span of the long side of the belt deflects about ¼ inch.

10. Hold the pulley tightly so it does not rotate when the bolt is tightened. Tighten the bolt to 15 ft. lbs. (20 Nm). If the pulley has moved, the belt will be too tight.

11. Install the timing belt tensioner fully toward the water pump and temporarily tighten the bolts. Place the upper end of the spring against the water pump body. Align the timing marks of the cam, crankshaft and oil pump sprockets with the corresponding marks on the front case or head.

NOTE: If the following step is not followed exactly, there is a chance that the silent shaft align- ment will be 180 degrees off. This will cause a noticeable vibration in the engine and the entire procedure will have to be repeated.

12. Before installing the timing belt, ensure that the left side silent shaft is in the correct position. It is possible to align the timing marks on the camshaft sprocket, crankshaft sprocket and the oil pump sprocket with the left balance shaft out of alignment. With the timing mark on the oil pump pulley aligned with the mark on the front case, check the alignment of the left balance shaft to assure correct shaft timing. To do so, remove the plug located on the left side of the block in the area of the starter. Insert a tool having a shaft diameter of 0.3 in. (8mm) into the hole. With the timing marks still aligned, the tool must be able to go in at least 2⅓ in. If it can only go in about 1 in. turn the oil pump sprocket 1 complete revolution. Recheck the position of the balance shaft with the timing marks realigned. Leave the tool in place to hold the silent shaft while continuing.

13. Install the belt to the crankshaft sprocket, oil pump sprocket and the camshaft sprocket, in that order. While doing so, make sure there is no slack between the sprockets except where the tensioner will take it up when released.

14. Recheck the timing marks' alignment. If all are aligned, loosen the tensioner mounting bolt and allow the tensioner to apply tension to the belt.

15. Remove the tool that is holding the silent shaft in place and turn the crankshaft clockwise a distance equal to 2 teeth of the camshaft sprocket. This will allow the tensioner to automatically tension the belt the proper amount.

NOTE: Do not manually apply pressure to the tensioner. This will overtighten the belt and will cause a howling noise.

16. First tighten the lower mounting bolt and then tighten the upper spacer bolt.

17. To verify that belt tension is correct, check that the deflection of the longest span (between the camshaft and oil pump sprockets) is ½ inch.

18. Install the timing belt covers and all related parts.

19. Connect the negative battery cable and road test the vehicle.

3.0L Engine

1. If possible, position engine with No. 1 cylinder at TDC. Disconnect negative battery cable. Remove the timing covers from engine.

2. If the same timing belt will be reused, mark the direction of timing belt's rotation, for installation in the same direction. Make sure engine is positioned so No. 1 cylinder is at the TDC of it's compression stroke and the sprockets timing marks are aligned with the engine's timing mark indicators.

3. Loosen the timing belt tensioner bolt and remove the belt. If not removing the tensioner, position it as far away from the center of the engine as possible and tighten the bolt.

4. If tensioner is being removed, mark outside of the spring to ensure that it is not installed backwards. Unbolt the tensioner and remove it along with the spring.

To install:

5. Install the tensioner, if removed, and hook the upper end of the spring to the water pump pin. Install the lower end of the spring to the tensioner in exactly the same position as originally installed. If not already done, position both camshafts so the timing marks line up with those on the alternator bracket (rear bank) and inner timing cover (front bank). Rotate the crankshaft so the timing mark aligns with the mark on the oil pump.

6. Install the timing belt on the crankshaft sprocket and while keeping the belt tight on the tension side (right side), install the belt on the front camshaft sprocket.

7. Install the belt on the water pump pulley, then the rear camshaft sprocket and the tensioner.

8. Rotate the front camshaft counterclockwise to tension the belt between the front camshaft and the crankshaft. If the timing marks came out of line, repeat the procedure.

9. Install the crankshaft sprocket flange.

10. Loosen the tensioner bolt and allow the spring to tension the belt.

11. Slowly turn the crankshaft 2 full turns in the clockwise direction until the timing marks align. Now that the belt is properly tensioned, torque the tensioner lock bolt to 21 ft. lbs. (29 Nm).

12. Install the timing belt covers and all related parts.

13. Connect the negative battery cable and road test the vehicle.

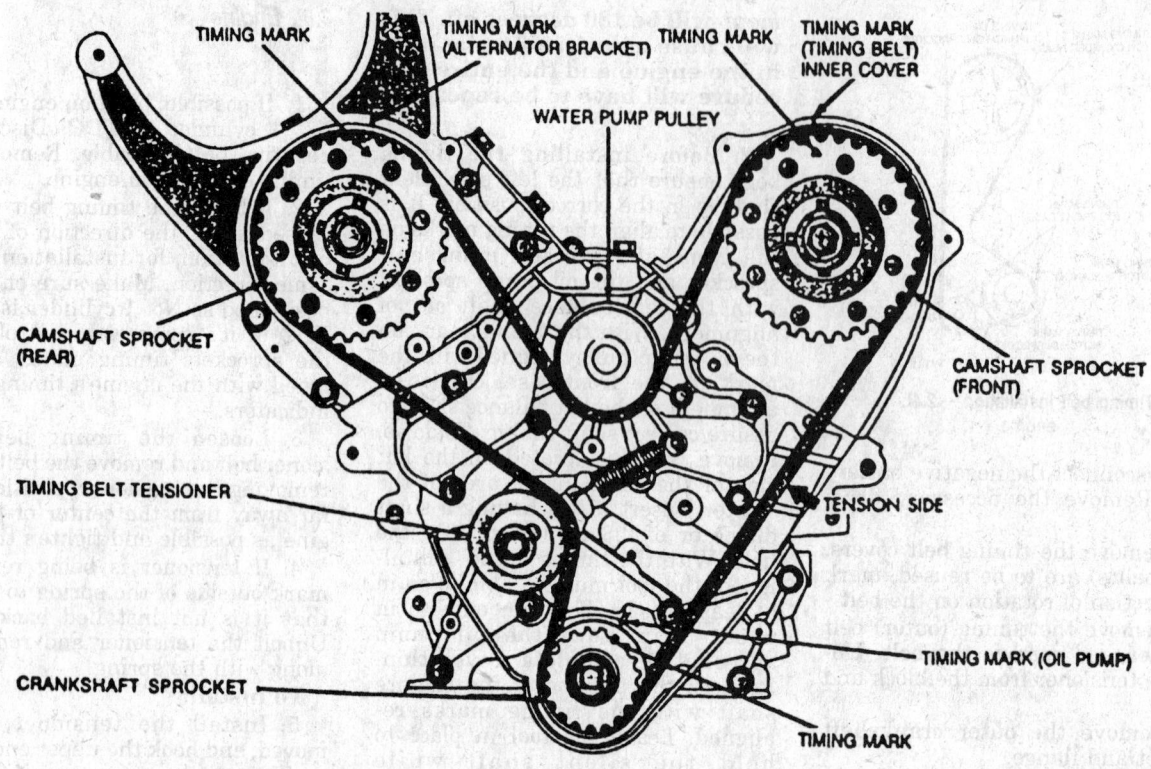

TIMING MARK

TIMING MARK (ALTERNATOR BRACKET)

TIMING MARK

TIMING MARK (TIMING BELT) INNER COVER

WATER PUMP PULLEY

CAMSHAFT SPROCKET (REAR)

CAMSHAFT SPROCKET (FRONT)

TIMING BELT TENSIONER

TENSION SIDE

CRANKSHAFT SPROCKET

TIMING MARK (OIL PUMP)

TIMING MARK

79111i050

Timing belt installation — 3.0L engine

Timing Sprockets

REMOVAL AND INSTALLATION

1. Disconnect the negative battery cable.
2. Remove the timing belt(s).
3. To remove the camshaft sprocket, hold the sprocket with a holding tool and remove the retaining bolt and washer.
4. To remove the crankshaft sprocket, remove the bolt, if equipped, and remove the sprocket from the crankshaft.
5. To remove a silent shafts sprocket, remove the retaining bolt and pry the sprocket from its mounting shaft.
6. The installation is the reverse of the removal procedure. Torque the sprocket retaining bolt to specifications.

Camshaft

REMOVAL AND INSTALLATION

2.4L Engine

1. Disconnect the negative battery cable. Remove the valve cover and the upper timing belt cover.

2. Matchmark the rotor to the distributor housing and remove the distributor.
3. Secure the belt to the sprocket and hold the sprocket up with a fabricated device to keep the belt taut. If timing is lost, it will have to be reset. Remove the camshaft sprocket from the camshaft.
4. Remove the camshaft cap bolts evenly and gradually. Install the auto lash adjuster retainers to the rocker arms.
5. Remove the caps, shafts, rocker arms and bolts together as an assembly.
6. Remove the camshaft with the front seal from the engine.

To install:

7. Install a new roll pin to the camshaft. Lubricate the camshaft and install with the front seal in place. Install the camshaft so the hole in the sprocket will line up with the roll pin.
8. Install the caps, shafts and arms assembly. Tighten the camshaft bearing cap bolts in the following order to 85 inch lbs. (10 Nm): No. 3, No. 2, No. 4, front cap, rear cap. Repeat the sequence increasing the torque to 175 inch lbs. (19 Nm).
9. Install the sprocket to the camshaft, engaging the roll pin. Tor-

que the bolt to 70 ft. lbs. (95 Nm). Install the distributor.
10. Install the valve cover and all related parts.

3.0L Engine

1. Disconnect the negative battery cable. Remove the valve cover.
2. Remove the timing belt and remove the sprocket from the camshaft.
3. Install auto lash adjuster retainers MD998443 or equivalent on the rocker arms.
4. If removing the left side camshaft, remove the distributor and the distributor extension.
5. Remove the camshaft bearing caps but do not remove the bolts from the caps. Remove the rocker arms, rocker shafts and bearing caps, as an assembly.
6. Remove the camshaft from the cylinder head.
7. Inspect the bearing journals on the camshaft, cylinder head and bearing caps.

To install:

8. Lubricate the camshaft journals and camshaft with clean engine oil and install the camshaft in the cylinder head.
9. Align the camshaft bearing caps with the arrow mark (depending on cylinder numbers) and in numerical

order. The arrow mark on the left rocker shaft bearing caps faces in same direction as the arrow marked on the left cylinder head which is away from the timing belt. The arrow on the right cylinder head and the right rocker bearing caps faces toward the timing belt.

10. Apply sealer at the ends of the bearing caps and install the assembly.

11. Torque the bearing cap bolts, in the following sequence: No. 3, No. 2, No. 1 and No. 4 to 85 inch lbs. (10 Nm).

12. Repeat the sequence increasing the torque to 175 inch lbs. (18 Nm).

13. Install the distributor, if removed.

14. Install the sprocket, timing belt and all related parts.

15. Install the valve cover.

Silent Shafts

REMOVAL AND INSTALLATION

2.4L Engine

1. Disconnect the negative battery cable. Release fuel pressure if equipped with fuel injection.

2. Raise and safely support the vehicle. Drain the engine oil.

3. Remove the oil filter and the oil pan from the engine.

4. Remove the oil pressure electrical connector and the oil pressure switch.

5. Lower the vehicle. Remove the timing belt cover(s).

6. Remove the timing belts.

7. Remove the timing belt sprockets.

8. Remove the front case from the block.

9. Remove the oil pump components.

10. Remove the shafts from the block.

To install:

11. Coat the silent shafts with clean engine oil and install into the block.

12. Install the drive and driven gears into place so the timing marks are mated with each other. Coat gears with clean engine oil.

13. Attach the special tool to the end of the crankshaft and coat the outer surface with engine oil.

14. Install the front case assembly with a new front case gasket to the block. Install retaining bolts.

15. Install the oil filter bracket together with the oil filter bracket gasket and install retaining bolts with washers. Torque bolts to 15 ft. lbs. (22 Nm).

16. Install the timing belts, covers and related parts.

17. Connect the negative battery cable, add clean oil to correct level, start engine and check for leaks.

Piston and Connecting Rod

POSITIONING

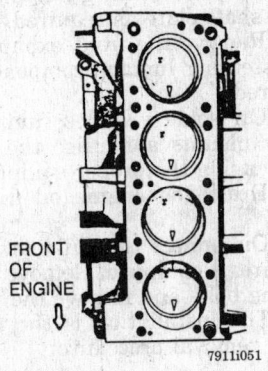

FRONT OF ENGINE

7911i051

Piston positioning — 2.4L engine

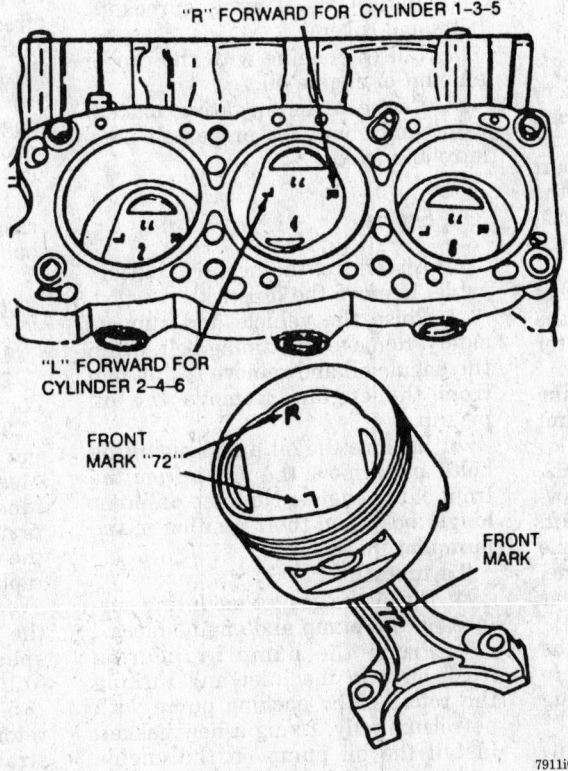

"R" FORWARD FOR CYLINDER 1–3–5

"L" FORWARD FOR CYLINDER 2–4–6

FRONT MARK "72"

FRONT MARK

7911i052

Piston positioning — 3.0L engine

ENGINE LUBRICATION

Oil Pan

REMOVAL AND INSTALLATION

1. Disconnect the negative battery cable.
2. Raise the vehicle and support safely.
3. Remove the skid plate(s), engine undercover, air guide plate and cross shaft plate as required.
4. Remove the front exhaust pipe and steering linkage components as required.
5. On some vehicles, unbolt the motor mounts and raise the engine safely using the proper equipment.
6. Drain the engine oil from the pan.
7. Disconnect the fluid level sensor wire, if equipped. Remove the attaching bolts and remove the pan.
8. The installation is the reverse of the removal procedure.

Oil Pump

REMOVAL AND INSTALLATION

2.4L Engine

1. Disconnect the negative battery cable. Remove the timing belt covers, timing belts and sprockets.
2. Raise the vehicle and support safely. Drain the oil and remove the oil filter. Remove the oil pan and gasket. Remove the oil pump pickup and gasket.
3. Remove the oil pressure relief plunger plug and gasket. Remove the spring and plunger from the oil filter bracket.
4. Remove the 4 bracket mounting bolts and remove the oil filter mount and gasket.
5. Using special tool MD998162, remove the cap and gasket that covers the oil pump driven gear shaft. This is located on the right side of the front case at the front of the engine, just above the protruding drive gear shaft.
6. Using a long socket, remove the retaining bolt from the oil pump driven gear located behind the plug removed earlier.
7. Remove the front case mounting bolts and remove the case from the block.

8. Remove the case gasket from the block.

To install:

9. Prime the pump by pouring fresh oil into the pump intake and turning the driveshaft until oil comes out the pressure port. Repeat a few times until no air bubbles are present. Replace all seals on the case assembly.
10. Install a special seal guide to the crankshaft, MD998285 or equivalent so the smaller diameter faces outward. Coat the outer diameter of the seal with clean engine oil.
11. Install a new front case gasket and install the front case by carefully positioning the crankshaft seal over the seal guide and lining up all bolt holes. Install and tighten the bolts to 17 ft. lbs. (23 Nm).
12. Remove the plug from the left side of the block. Hold the left side silent shaft by inserting a tool in the plug hole and torque the driven gear bolt to 26 ft. lbs. (35 Nm). Using a new O-ring, install the plug cover.
13. Install the oil filter mounting bracket gasket. Install the mounting bracket and bolts tightening the oil filter mounting bracket bolts to 12 ft. lbs. (16 Nm).
14. Clean or replace the oil pickup screen and install with a new gasket.
15. Install the oil pan using a new gasket.
16. Install the timing sprockets, belts and covers.
17. Fill the engine with the proper amount of engine oil.
18. Connect the negative battery cable and check for proper oil pressure and leaks.

3.0L Engine

1. Disconnect the negative battery cable. Remove the dipstick.
2. Raise the vehicle and support safely. Remove the timing belt, drain the engine oil and remove the oil pan from the engine. Remove the oil pickup.
3. Remove the oil pump mounting bolts and remove the pump from the front of the engine. Note the different length bolts and their position in the pump for installation.

To install:

4. Clean the gasket mounting surfaces of the pump and engine block.
5. Prime the pump by pouring fresh oil into the inlet and turning the rotors or by packing pump with petroleum jelly. Using a new gasket, install the oil pump on the engine and torque all bolts to 11 ft. lbs. (15 Nm).

6. Install the balancer and crankshaft sprockets.
7. Clean out the oil pickup or replace as required. Replace the oil pickup gasket ring and install the pickup to the pump.
8. Install the timing belt, oil pan and all related parts.
9. Install the dipstick. Fill the engine with the proper amount of oil.
10. Connect the negative battery cable and check the oil pressure.

CHECKING

2.4L Engine

1. Remove the oil pump cover from the front case.
2. Check the case and gear cover for stepped wear from the gears.
3. Measure the drive gear tip clearance between the teeth and the case. The specification is 0.006–0.010 in. (0.16–0.25mm).
4. Check the driven gear tip clearance in the similar manner. The specification is 0.005–0.010 in. (0.13–0.25mm).
5. Place a straight-edge across the gears resting on the opposite sides of the case. If a 0.010 in. (0.25mm) feeler gauge can be inserted under the straight-edge, replace the assembly.
6. Check the relief plunger for freedom of movement and check the spring for deformation and rust.
7. If the gears were removed from the body, install them with the mating marks aligned. If not aligned properly, the silent shaft will be out of time.
8. Install the gear cover to the case using a new gasket. Torque the bolts to 12 ft. lbs. (16 Nm).

3.0L Engine

1. Remove the rear cover.
2. Remove the pump rotors and inspect the case for excessive wear.
3. Measure the diameter of the inner rotor hub that sits in the case. Measure the inside diameter of the inner rotor hub bore. Subtract the first measurement from the second; if the result is over 0.006 in. (0.15mm), replace the oil pump assembly.
4. Measure the clearance between the outer rotor and the case. The specification is 0.004–0.007 in. (0.10–0.18mm).
5. Check the side clearance of the rotors using a feeler gauge and a straight-edge placed across the case. The specification is 0.0015–0.0035 in. (0.04–0.09mm).

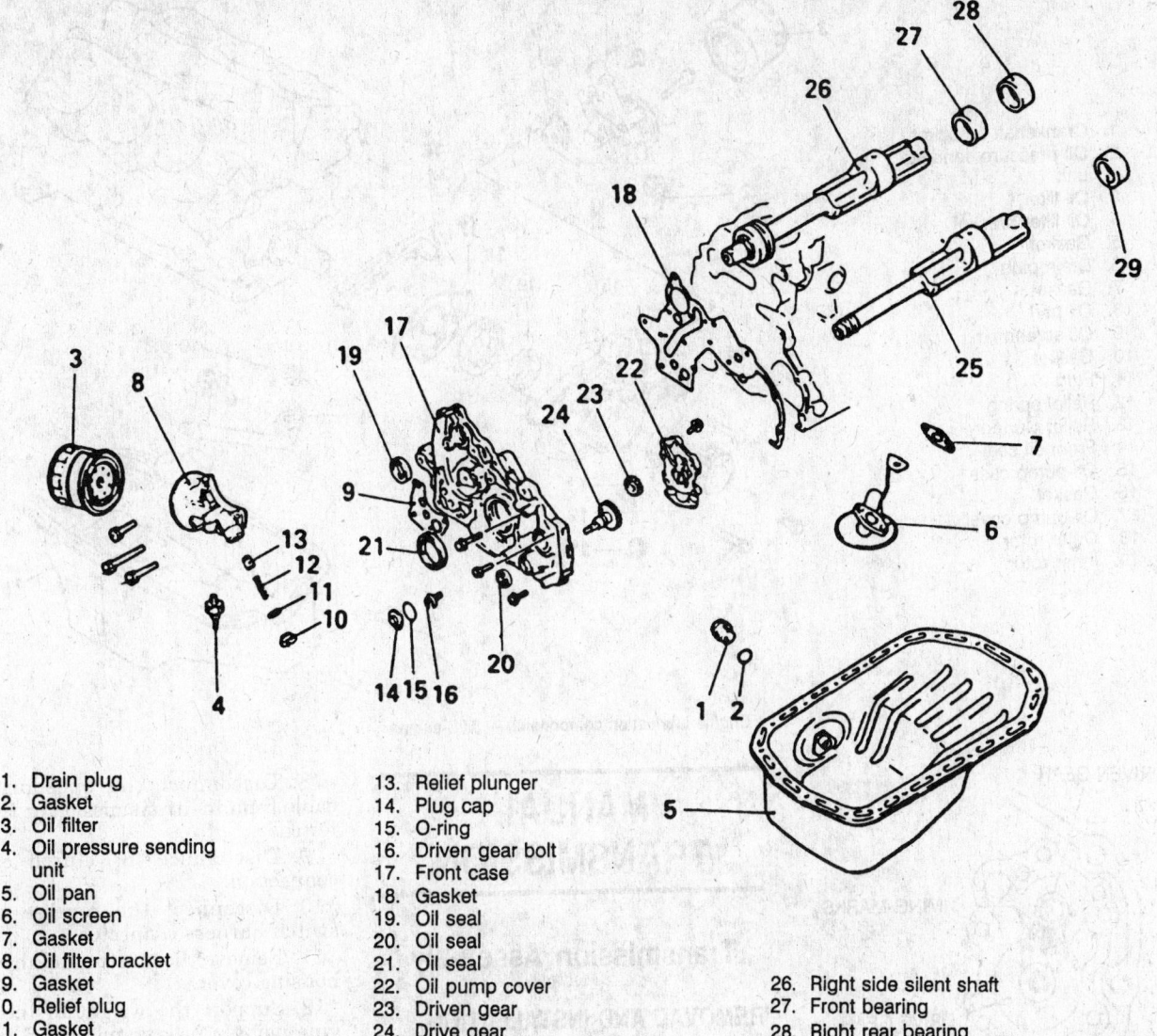

1. Drain plug
2. Gasket
3. Oil filter
4. Oil pressure sending unit
5. Oil pan
6. Oil screen
7. Gasket
8. Oil filter bracket
9. Gasket
10. Relief plug
11. Gasket
12. Relief spring
13. Relief plunger
14. Plug cap
15. O-ring
16. Driven gear bolt
17. Front case
18. Gasket
19. Oil seal
20. Oil seal
21. Oil seal
22. Oil pump cover
23. Driven gear
24. Drive gear
25. Left side silent shaft
26. Right side silent shaft
27. Front bearing
28. Right rear bearing
29. Left rear bearing

7911i053

Engine lubrication components — 2.4L engine

6. Check the relief plunger and spring for damage and replace as required.

7. Install the rear pump cover to the case.

Rear Main Bearing Oil Seal

REMOVAL AND INSTALLATION

1. Disconnect the negative battery cable.

2. Support the weight of the engine using a jack stand with a block of wood to protect the oil pan. Remove the transmission from the vehicle.

3. If equipped with manual transmission, remove the clutch cover retainer bolts in a cross fashion gradually. Remove the clutch cover and disc. Remove the retaining bolt, flywheel and ball bearing from the engine.

4. If equipped with automatic transmission, remove the adapter plate, driveplate, crankshaft adapter and bushing.

5. Remove the rear engine plate and lower bell housing cover.

6. Remove the rear oil seal case and gasket from the back of the engine.

7. Remove the oil separator if remaining on the engine block.

To install:

8. Install the new oil seal into the seal case using seal installer.

9. Press the oil separator into the seal case making sure the separator oil hole is on the very bottom of the case. In the correct position, the hole is on the adjacent to the oil pan mounting surface.

10. Clean and dry the seal case to block sealing surfaces. Install seal case to the rear of the block using a new gasket.

11. Install the rear engine plate and the lower bell housing cover.

12. If equipped with automatic transmission, install the adapter

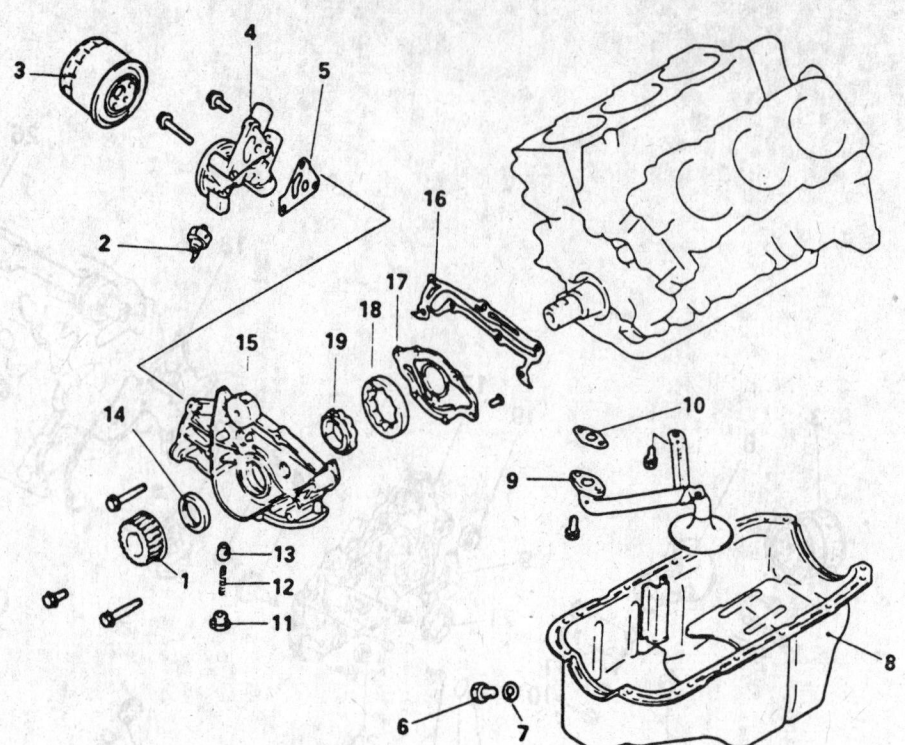

1. Crankshaft sprocket
2. Oil pressure sending unit
3. Oil filter
4. Oil filter bracket
5. Gasket
6. Drain plug
7. Gasket
8. Oil pan
9. Oil screen
10. Gasket
11. Plug
12. Relief spring
13. Relief plunger
14. Front oil seal
15. Oil pump case
16. Gasket
17. Oil pump cover
18. Outer rotor
19. Inner rotor

Engine lubrication components — 3.0L engine

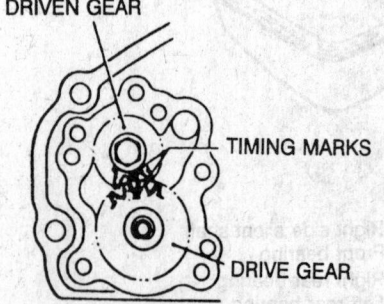

Aligning the oil pump gear timing marks — 2.4L engine

plate, driveplate, crankshaft adapter and bushing.

13. If equipped with manual transmission, install the retaining bolt, flywheel and ball bearing to the engine.

14. Install the transmission into the vehicle. Lower the vehicle and remove the engine support. Connect the negative battery cable and check the oil level, adding as required.

MANUAL TRANSMISSION

Transmission Assembly

REMOVAL AND INSTALLATION

1. Disconnect the negative battery cable.
2. Place the shifter(s) in the neutral position.
3. Unscrew the shift knob from the control lever. Remove the retainer screws from the dust cover retaining plate and slide plate and boot off of the lever.
4. Remove the retainer screws from the stopper plate and remove the lever assembly from the transmission. Cover the opening with a clean towel to prevent dirt from entering the transmission.
5. Raise the vehicle and support safely. Remove the skid plate, if equipped.
6. Drain the transmission fluid. If equipped with 4WD, drain the oil from the transfer case.
7. Matchmark and remove the driveshaft(s) from the vehicle.

8. Disconnect the speedometer cable from the transmission or transfer case.
9. Disconnect the clutch cable connection.
10. Disconnect the reverse light switch harness connector.
11. Remove the starter and the bell housing cover.
12. Support the weight of the engine using a jack stand with a block of wood to protect the oil pan.
13. Support the transmission with a transmission jack.
14. Remove the transfer case bracket, if equipped.
15. Remove the rear crossmember.
16. Remove the transmission to bell housing bolts.
17. Slide the transmission backwards until the input shaft clears the clutch disc. Remove the transmission from the vehicle.

To install:
18. Lubricate the pilot bushing and input shaft splines very lightly with high temperature lubricant.
19. Mount the transmission securely on a transmission jack and lift it in place until the input shaft is centered in the bell housing opening. Roll the transmission forward until the input shaft splines fully engage with the clutch disc.

20. Install the transmission to bell housing bolts. Torque the bolts to 35 ft. lbs. (47 Nm).

21. Lift the transmission using the transmission jack and install the rear crossmember into position. Install the transfer case bracket, if equipped. Torque the frame bolts to 50 ft. lbs. (68 Nm). Remove the transmission and engine support fixtures.

22. Install the starter and torque the mounting bolt to 20 ft. lbs. (27 Nm). Install the bell housing cover.

23. Connect the reverse light switch and clip all wiring to the transmission case.

24. Connect the speedometer cable.

25. Install the driveshaft(s) making sure to align matchmarks.

26. Connect the clutch cable, using a new cotter pin.

27. Fill the transmission and transfer case with the proper amount of SAE 80W or 75W/85W hypoid gear oil with an API classification of GL–4 or higher.

28. Install the skip plate, if equipped. Lower the vehicle.

29. Install the shift lever assembly, boot and console.

30. Connect the negative battery cable and check the transmission and transfer case for proper operation. Check operation of the reverse lights.

LINKAGE ADJUSTMENT

Since this transmission uses a direct engage shift mechanism, there are no provisions for adjustment.

CLUTCH

Clutch Assembly

REMOVAL AND INSTALLATION

1. Disconnect the negative battery cable.

2. Place the shifter(s) in the neutral position.

3. Unscrew the shift knob from the control lever. Remove the retainer screws from the dust cover retaining plate and slide plate and boot off of the lever.

4. Remove the retainer screws from the stopper plate and remove the lever assembly from the transmission. Cover the opening with a clean towel to prevent dirt from entering the transmission.

5. Raise the vehicle and support safely. Remove the skid plate, if equipped.

6. Drain the transmission fluid. If equipped with 4WD, drain the oil from the transfer case.

7. Matchmark and remove the driveshaft(s) from the vehicle.

8. Disconnect the speedometer cable from the transmission or transfer case.

9. Disconnect the clutch cable connection.

10. Disconnect the reverse light switch harness connector.

11. Remove the starter and the bell housing cover.

12. Support the weight of the engine using a jack stand with a block of wood to protect the oil pan.

13. Support the transmission with a transmission jack.

14. Remove the transfer case bracket, if equipped.

15. Remove the rear crossmember.

16. Remove the transmission to bell housing bolts.

17. Slide the transmission backwards until the input shaft clears the clutch disc. Remove the transmission from the vehicle.

18. Remove the clutch cover retainer bolts in a cross fashion gradually. Remove the clutch cover and disc.

To install:

19. Raise the clutch cover and disc into place and use a clutch aligning tool or spare input shaft to center the disc. Apply Loctite® to the threads and tighten all of the bolts finger-tight.

20. Tighten cover bolts gradually, evenly and to the proper torque to avoid distorting the cover. Torque the bolts to 15 ft. lbs. (20 Nm).

21. Lubricate the pilot bushing and input shaft splines very lightly with high temperature lubricant.

22. Mount the transmission securely on a transmission jack and raise in place until the input shaft is centered in the bell housing opening. Roll the transmission forward until the input shaft splines fully engage with the clutch disc.

23. Install the transmission to bell housing bolts. Torque the bolts to 35 ft. lbs. (47 Nm).

24. Lift the transmission using the transmission jack and install the rear crossmember into position. Install the transfer case bracket, if equipped. Torque the frame bolts to 50 ft. lbs. (68 Nm). Remove the transmission and engine support fixtures.

25. Install the starter and torque the mounting bolt to 20 ft. lbs. (27 Nm). Install the bell housing cover.

26. Connect the reverse light switch and clip all wiring to the transmission case.

27. Connect the speedometer cable.

28. Install the driveshaft(s) making sure to align matchmarks.

29. Connect the clutch cable, using a new cotter pin.

30. Fill the transmission and transfer case with the proper amount of SAE 80W or 75W/85W hypoid gear oil with an API classification of GL–4 or higher.

31. Install the skip plate, if equipped. Lower the vehicle.

32. Install the shift lever assembly and boot.

33. Connect the negative battery cable and check the transmission and transfer case for proper operation. Check operation of the reverse lights.

Pedal Height/Free-Play

ADJUSTMENT

1. Measure the distance from the face of the pedal pad to the floorboard. This distance should be about 6½–7 in.

2. If the pedal height is not correct, adjust the pedal stopper to contact the pedal at correct height.

Clutch Cable

ADJUSTMENT

1. Check the pedal's free-play. The specification is 1 inch.

2. Adjust the clutch cable by turning the star shaped adjusting wheel on the firewall. Turning the wheel counterclockwise will increase the amount of free-play in the pedal or vice-versa.

REMOVAL AND INSTALLATION

1. Disconnect the negative battery cable.

2. Turn the cable adjusting wheel counterclockwise to provide enough play to remove the cable end from the clutch lever inside the vehicle. Remove the cable from the lever.

3. Raise the vehicle and support safely.

4. Remove the cotter pin from the lever on the transmission.

5. Remove the clutch cable from the vehicle.

6. The installation is the reverse of the removal procedure. Make sure the insulator is positioning properly.

Clutch Master Cylinder

REMOVAL AND INSTALLATION

1. Disconnect the negative battery cable. Remove as much fluid as possible from the clutch master cylinder reservoir.

2. Remove the cotter pin and remove the clevis pin from the clutch pedal.

3. Disconnect and plug the fluid line from the clutch master cylinder.

4. Remove the mounting nuts and remove the cylinder from the firewall.

5. Remove the reservoir from the cylinder.

6. The installation is the reverse of the removal procedure.

7. Bleed the clutch system.

Clutch Release Cylinder

REMOVAL AND INSTALLATION

1. Disconnect the negative battery cable.

2. Raise the vehicle and support safely.

3. Remove the eye-bolt and washer from the clutch hose at the release cylinder.

4. Remove the mounting bolts and remove the slave cylinder from the transmission case.

5. Replace the eye-bolt washer.

6. The installation is the reverse of the removal procedure.

7. Bleed the system.

HYDRAULIC CLUTCH SYSTEM BLEEDING

When bleeding, keep the facial area well away from the slave cylinder and protect all painted surfaces from fluid contact. Brake fluid will damage painted surfaces and could cause physical injury.

1. Fill the clutch master cylinder with fresh DOT 3 brake fluid.

2. Have a helper sit in the vehicle. Raise the vehicle and support safely.

3. Remove the bleeder screw cap.

4. If the system is empty, the most efficient way to get fluid down to the cylinder is to loosen the bleeder about $1/2$–$3/4$ turn, place a finger firmly over the bleeder and have the helper pump the brakes slowly until fluid

pressure is felt at the bleeder. Once fluid is at the bleeder, close before the pedal is released.

NOTE: If the pedal is pump rapidly, the fluid will churn and create small air bubbles, which are difficult and time consuming to remove from the system. These air bubble will eventually congregate and will result in a spongy pedal.

5. Once fluid has been pumped to the slave cylinder, open the bleeder screw, have the helper depress the clutch pedal, lock the bleeder and have the helper release the pedal. Wait 15 seconds and repeat the procedure (including the 15 second wait) until no air bubbles flow from the bleeder. Remember to close the bleeder before the pedal is released. If the bleeder is left open when the pedal is released, air will be induced into the system.

6. If a helper is not available, connect a small hose to the bleeder, submerge the other end in a clean container of fresh brake fluid placed in a position that is visible from the driver's seat. Pump the pedal until no air comes out of the tube.

AUTOMATIC TRANSMISSION

Transmission Assembly

REMOVAL AND INSTALLATION

1. Disconnect the negative battery cable.

2. If equipped with 4WD, disconnect the 4WD indicator light switch connector and the ground cable at the transfer case. Remove the following components from the 4WD floor control console:

   a. Remove the shifter knob from the 4WD control.

   b. Remove the top trim panel around the outside of the boot, retaining screws and slide the boot(s) up and off of the shaft.

   c. Remove the center storage compartment and the rear cover plate. Remove the retaining screws the console from the vehicle.

3. Disconnect the pulse generator connector.

4. Raise and safely support the vehicle.

5. Remove the skid plate, if equipped. Drain the transmission and transfer case, as equipped.

6. Matchmark and remove the driveshaft(s).

7. Disconnect the speedometer cable from the transmission or transfer case.

8. Disconnect the shifter linkage or cable.

9. Unplug all transmission electrical connectors.

10. Remove the exhaust pipe from the vehicle. Remove the exhaust bracket from the transmission case.

11. Remove the filler neck and dipstick.

12. Remove the torque converter inspection plate. Matchmark the flexplate to the torque converter and remove the torque converter bolts.

13. Remove the starter assembly.

14. Disconnect and plug the oil cooler lines.

15. Using a transmission jack, support the transmission. Remove the retaining bolts at the crossmember.

16. Remove the rear crossmember.

17. Lower the transmission down slightly and unbolt the 4WD shifter from the transfer case, if equipped.

18. Remove the bell housing bolts and mounting brackets.

19. Pull the transmission assembly rearward to clear the aligning dowels and remove from the vehicle.

To install:

20. Install the transmission assembly to the engine using dowels as guides. Install the bell housing bolts and torque to 35 ft. lbs. (47 Nm).

21. Install the 4WD shifter, if equipped. Raise the assembly up into position and install the rear crossmember and mounting hardware. Torque the crossmember to frame bolts to 50 ft. lbs. (68 Nm).

22. Align the flexplate to torque converter. Apply Loctite® to the threads and install the torque converter bolts. Torque the bolts to 25 ft. lbs. (34 Nm). Install the inspection plate.

23. Install the filler tube with a new O-ring and the dipstick.

24. Install the exhaust and the support brackets.

25. Connect all switch connectors that were removed.

26. Connect the shifter linkage or cable and the throttle cable.

27. Align and install the driveshaft(s).

28. Install the ground wire and the 4WD indicator light switch connector to the transfer case, if equipped.

29. Fill the transfer case with hypoid gear oil with an API classification of GL–4 or higher.

30. Connect the throttle cable.

31. Install the skid plate, if equipped. Lower the vehicle.

32. Install the transfer case shifter boot and console, if equipped.

33. Fill the transmission with the proper amount of Dexron® II.

34. Connect the negative battery cable, start the engine and run through all gears. Add fluid until the transmission is properly filled.

35. Check the operation of the neutral safety switch and the reverse lights.

36. Road test the vehicle and check for leaks.

SHIFT LINKAGE ADJUSTMENT

1. Position the shifter in the **N** detent.

2. Loosen the nut or bolt on the shifter linkage or cable.

3. Make sure the lever on the transmission is in the **N** detent and the needle in the indicator is also in the **N** position. Jiggle the selector rod to settle the assembly in position. If the rod is equipped with a notch, it should be at the 6 o'clock position.

4. Tighten the adjusting bolt or nut and check for proper assembly.

5. Check the operation of the neutral safely switch.

6. Liberally lubricate all pivoting points within the system.

THROTTLE CABLE ADJUSTMENT

1. Depress the accelerator fully and make sure the throttle valve opens all the way. Adjust as required.

2. Measure the distance between the end of the rubber boot and the stopper on the cable at wide open throttle.

3. The specification is 0–0.04 in. (0–1mm).

4. Adjust the cable.

5. Road test the vehicle and check for proper shift points.

NEUTRAL SAFETY SWITCH ADJUSTMENT

NOTE: Some vehicles are not equipped with an adjustable switch.

1. Adjust the shifter linkage.

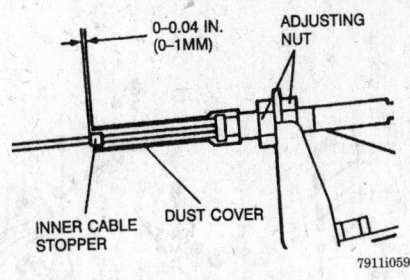

Throttle cable adjustment

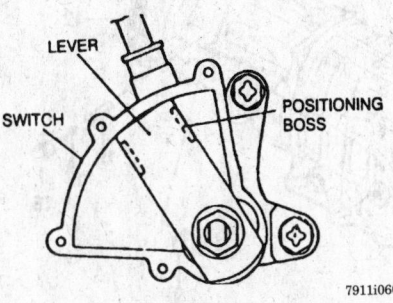

Neutral safety switch adjustment

2. Raise the vehicle and support safely. Place the shifter in the **N** detent. Loosen the mounting bolts.

3. Align the lever with the positioning boss.

4. Hold in position and tighten the bolts.

5. Check the switch and the reverse lights for proper operation.

TRANSFER CASE

Transfer Case Assembly

REMOVAL AND INSTALLATION

Automatic Transmission

1. Disconnect the negative battery cable.

2. Remove the transmission and transfer case assembly from the vehicle.

3. Remove the plug from the right side of the transfer case under the control housing.

4. Remove the select spring and plunger from the housing bore.

5. Remove the control lever housing assembly, cover and gasket.

6. Remove the transfer case to adapter attaching nuts. Pull transfer case from the adapter.

To install:

7. Install the transfer case to adapter and secure using retainer nuts. Torque nuts to 30 ft. lbs. (42 Nm).

8. Install the control lever housing assembly, cover and gasket.

9. Install the select spring and plunger into the housing and install plug in bore.

10. Install the transfer case and transmission into the vehicle, connect the negative battery cable and road test for proper operation.

Manual Transmission

1. Disconnect the negative battery cable.

2. Remove the transmission and transfer case assembly from the vehicle.

3. Remove the plug from the right side of the transfer case under the control housing.

4. Remove the select spring and plunger from the housing bore.

5. Remove the spring pin that retains the shift changer to the control shaft using a pin punch.

6. Remove the transfer case to transmission attaching nuts and remove from the transmission.

To install:

7. Install the transfer case to transmission and tighten attaching nuts to 30 ft. lbs. (42 Nm).

8. Install the shift changer to the control shaft and install new roll pin.

9. Install select spring, plunger and plug into housing bore.

10. Install the transfer case and transmission into vehicle. Connect negative battery cable and road test for proper operation.

LINKAGE ADJUSTMENT

Since this transfer case uses a directly engaging shift mechanism, there are no provisions for adjustment.

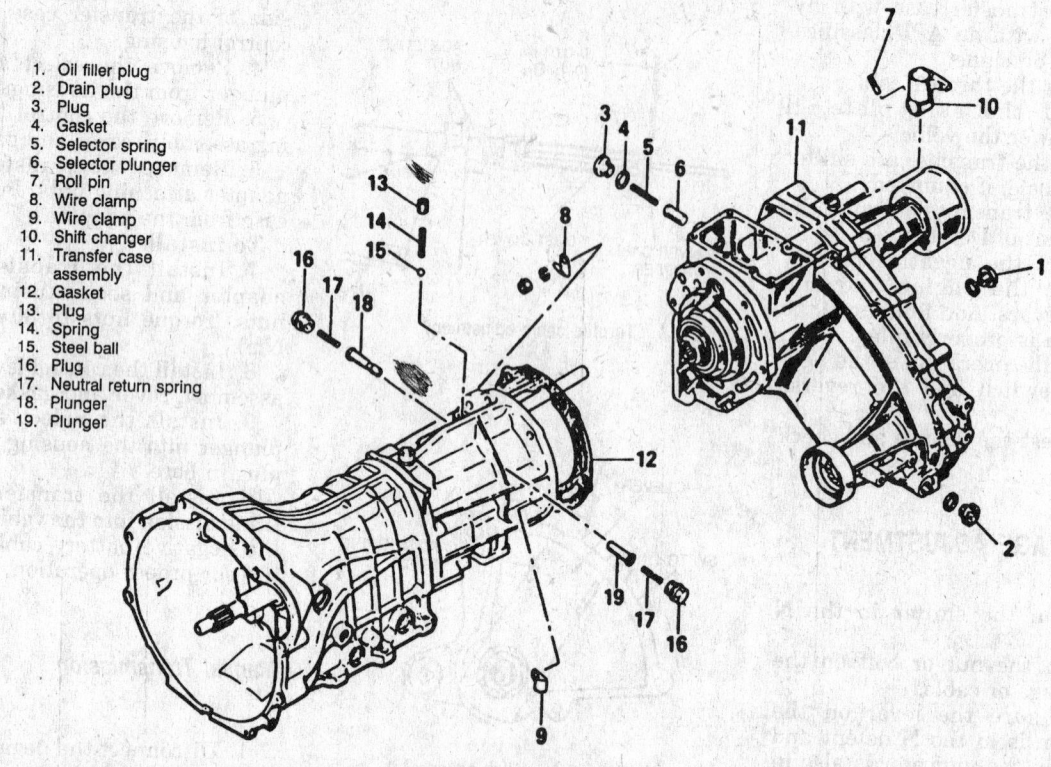

1. Oil filler plug
2. Drain plug
3. Plug
4. Gasket
5. Selector spring
6. Selector plunger
7. Roll pin
8. Wire clamp
9. Wire clamp
10. Shift changer
11. Transfer case
    assembly
12. Gasket
13. Plug
14. Spring
15. Steel ball
16. Plug
17. Neutral return spring
18. Plunger
19. Plunger

7911i061

Transfer case assembly

DRIVE AXLE

Front Halfshaft

REMOVAL AND INSTALLATION

Right Halfshaft

OUTER

1. Place the free-wheeling hub in the free condition by placing the transfer lever in the **2H** position and moving in reverse for about 6 or 7 feet.

2. Disconnect negative battery cable.

3. Raise and safely support the vehicle. Remove the skid plate, if equipped.

4. Remove the tire and wheel assembly.

5. Remove the hub cover with the use of an oil filter wrench. Install a protective cloth between the wrench and the cover to avoid damage to the cover.

6. Remove the snapring from the inside of the hub. Remove the shim.

7. Remove the front brake caliper and brake pads from the vehicle. Do

not allow the caliper to hang from the brake hose.

8. Separate the tie rod from the steering knuckle.

9. Separate the upper and lower ball joints from the steering knuckle.

10. Remove the front hub/knuckle assembly with the inner and outer bearings intact.

11. Remove the halfshaft to axle housing retaining nuts and remove the halfshaft from the vehicle.

To install:

12. Install the halfshaft and the retaining nuts and tighten to 43 ft. lbs. (60 Nm).

13. Install the front hub/knuckle and bearing assembly.

14. Install the upper ball joint to the knuckle and torque retaining nut to 130 ft. lbs. (180 Nm). Install the lower ball joint to knuckle and torque retaining nut to 65 ft. lbs. (90 Nm). Install new cotter pins.

15. Install the tie rod end to the steering knuckle and torque to 33 ft. lbs. (45 Nm). Install new cotter pin.

16. Install the shim and snapring to the axle shaft. Install the front hub cover.

17. Install front brake caliper assembly.

18. Install the tire and wheel assembly. Install skid plate, if removed.

INNER

1. Disconnect negative battery cable.

2. Raise and safely support the vehicle.

3. Remove the skid plate, if equipped.

4. Remove the right outer halfshaft.

5. Remove the lower shock absorber mounting bolts.

6. Install slide hammer to inner shaft flange and pull from housing. Press the bearing from the axle, as required.

To install:

7. Press new bearing and seal on axle, as required. Install new circlip to inner halfshaft and install into housing. Drive the axle into position.

8. Install the lower shock absorber mounting bolts.

9. Install the right outer halfshaft and related parts.

10. Install the skid plate, if equipped.

Left Halfshaft

1. Place the free-wheeling hub in the free condition by placing the transfer lever in the **2H** position and moving in reverse for about 6 or 7 feet.

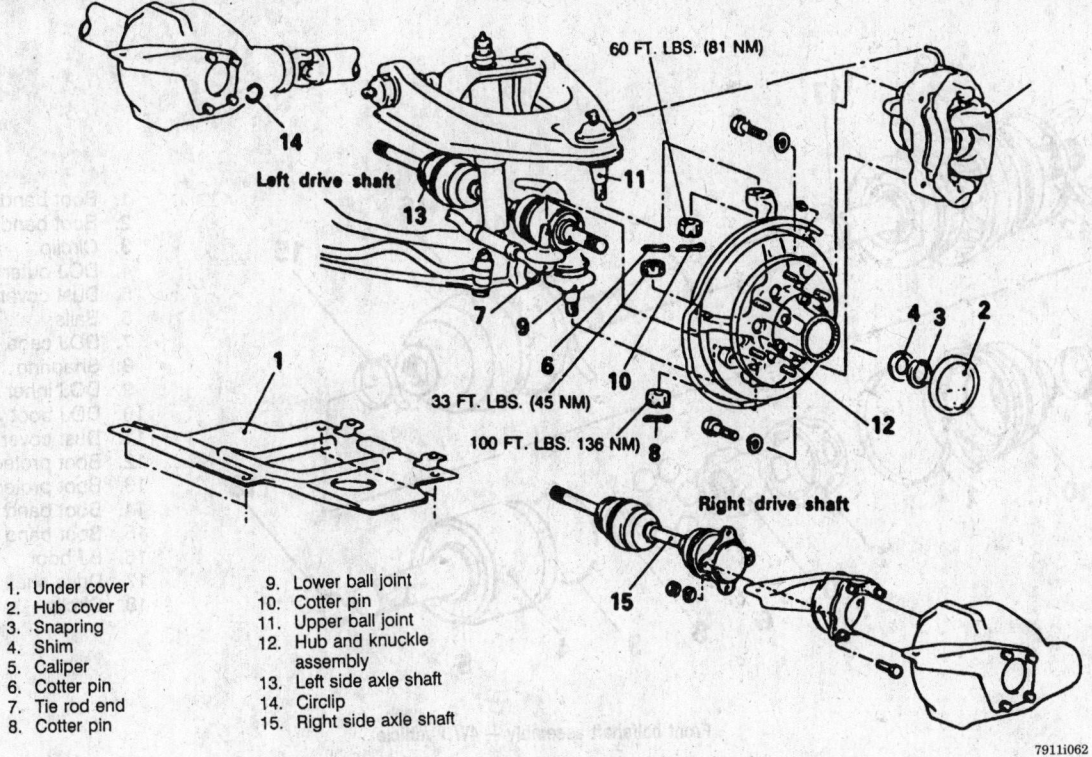

60 FT. LBS. (81 NM)

Left drive shaft

33 FT. LBS. (45 NM)

100 FT. LBS. 136 NM)

Right drive shaft

1. Under cover
2. Hub cover
3. Snapring
4. Shim
5. Caliper
6. Cotter pin
7. Tie rod end
8. Cotter pin
9. Lower ball joint
10. Cotter pin
11. Upper ball joint
12. Hub and knuckle assembly
13. Left side axle shaft
14. Circlip
15. Right side axle shaft

7911i062

Front axle shafts and related pats

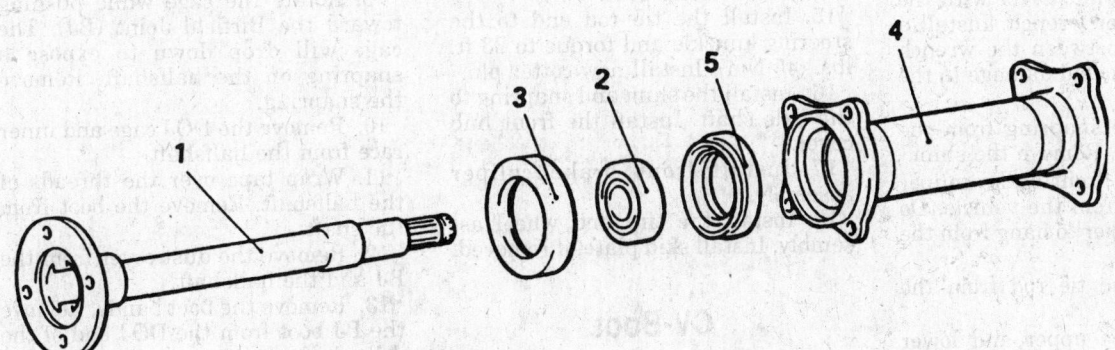

1. Inner shaft
2. Bearing
3. Dust cover
4. Housing tube
5. Dust seal

7911i063

Inner axle shaft and tube

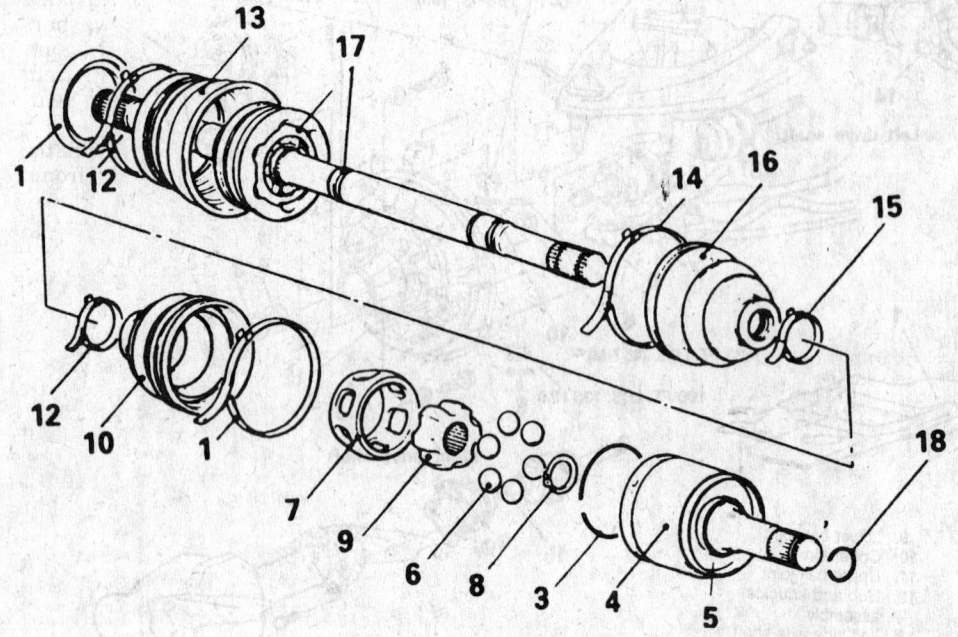

1. Boot band
2. Boot band
3. Circlip
4. DOJ outer race
5. Dust cover
6. Balls
7. DOJ cage
8. Snapring
9. DOJ inner race
10. DOJ boot
11. Dust cover
12. Boot protector band
13. Boot protector
14. Boot band
15. Boot band
16. BJ boot
17. Drive shaft and BJ
18. Circlip

Front halfshaft assembly — 4WD vehicle

2. Disconnect negative battery cable.

3. Raise and safely support the vehicle. Remove the skid plate, if equipped.

4. Remove the tire and wheel assembly.

5. Remove the hub cover with the use of an oil filter wrench. Install a protective cloth between the wrench and the cover to avoid damage to the cover.

6. Remove the snapring from the inside of the hub. Remove the shim.

7. Remove the front brake caliper and brake pads from the vehicle. Do not allow the caliper to hang from the brake hose.

8. Separate the tie rod from the steering knuckle.

9. Separate the upper and lower ball joints from the steering knuckle.

10. Remove the front hub/knuckle assembly with the inner and outer bearings intact.

11. Pull the left halfshaft out from the differential carrier. Use care not to damage the oil seal with the splines of the shaft.

To install:

12. Replace circlip on the end of the shaft. Install the halfshaft into the front differential case and drive into position using a plastic hammer.

13. Install the front hub/knuckle and bearing assembly.

14. Install the upper ball joint to the knuckle and torque retaining nut to 130 ft. lbs. (180 Nm). Install the lower ball joint to knuckle and torque retaining nut to 65 ft. lbs. (90 Nm). Install new cotter pins.

15. Install the tie rod end to the steering knuckle and torque to 33 ft. lbs. (45 Nm). Install new cotter pin.

16. Install the shim and snapring to the axle shaft. Install the front hub cover.

17. Install front brake caliper assembly.

18. Install the tire and wheel assembly. Install skid plate, if removed.

CV-Boot

REMOVAL AND INSTALLATION

1. Disconnect negative battery cable.

2. Raise and safely support the vehicle.

3. Remove the skid plate, if equipped.

4. Remove the left halfshaft.

5. Remove the boot bands on the inner Double Offset Joint (DOJ). Remove the circlip.

6. Remove the DOJ outer race from the shaft.

7. Remove the dust cover from the DOJ outer race.

8. Remove the balls from the DOJ cage prying from the inside of the cage outward.

9. Rotate the cage while pushing toward the Birfield Joint (BJ). The cage will drop down to expose a snapring on the halfshaft. Remove the snapring.

10. Remove the DOJ cage and inner race from the halfshaft.

11. Wrap tape over the threads of the halfshaft. Remove the boot from the shaft.

12. Remove the dust cover from the BJ and the halfshaft.

13. Remove the boot bands. Remove the BJ boot from the DOJ end of the driveshaft.

NOTE: Do not disassemble the Birfield Joint (BJ).

To install:

14. Install the BJ boot and bands over the DOJ end of the driveshaft. Install the DOJ boot and bands onto the halfshaft. Apply ½ of supplied grease into the BJ boot and install the bands onto the boot.

15. Install the DOJ cage onto the halfshaft with the smaller diameter

side of the cage facing the installed BJ boot. Install the snapring.

16. Apply remaining grease to the DOJ inner race, the DOJ cage and the balls. Insert the balls into the cage from the outside pushing in toward the shaft.

17. Install the outer race over the DOJ cage assembly and install the retaining circlip.

18. Install the dust cover into place and install the boot bands.

19. Install the halfshaft into the vehicle.

20. Install the skid plate, if equipped.

Driveshaft and U-Joints

REMOVAL AND INSTALLATION

1. If equipped with 4WD, place the free-wheeling hub in the free condition by placing the transfer lever in the **2H** position and moving in reverse for about 6 or 7 feet.

2. Disconnect negative battery cable.

3. Raise and safely support the vehicle.

4. Remove the skid plate, if equipped.

5. Matchmark the flange yoke and the differential companion flange. Do not damage the oil seals when marking positions.

6. Drain the transfer case. Position a drain pan under the transmission tailshaft, as required. Fluid will leak from unit on removal of the driveshaft.

7. Remove the retaining bolts and nuts from the flange(s) and remove the shaft from the vehicle.

8. Remove the U-Joint from the driveshaft as follows:

   a. Make mating marks on the yokes of the universal joint that is to be disassembled.

   b. Remove the snaprings from the yoke. When disassembling, note the position of the snaprings so they may be reinstalled in the same positions.

   c. Remove the grease fitting from the journal.

   d. Remove the journal bearings from the propeller shaft yoke using tool MB990840-01.

   e. Remove the journal and the flange yoke or sleeve yoke from the shaft.

9. Inspect the propeller shaft yokes for wear, cracks or damage. Check the sleeve yoke and the flange yoke for wear, cracks or damage. Replace as required.

To install:

10. Install the U-Joint on the driveshaft as follows:

   a. Install the sleeve yoke or flange yoke to the journal and the assembly to the driveshaft.

   b. Align the mating marks on the yokes and press the journal bearings to the yoke using tool MB990840-01.

   c. Install the snaprings in the position prior to removal. Install the grease fitting.

   d. Measure the clearance between the snaprings and the journal bearing. If the clearance is larger than 0.0024 in. (0.06mm), it will be necessary to replace the snapring.

11. With the mating marks aligned, install the driveshaft into the transfer case/transmission and the companion flange.

12. Clean the mounting nuts and bolts and install to the flange(s). Torque to 43 ft. lbs. (60 Nm).

13. Install the skid plate, if equipped.

Rear Axle Shaft, Bearing and Seal

REMOVAL AND INSTALLATION

1. Raise the vehicle and support safely.

2. Remove the rear tire and wheel assembly.

3. Remove the brake drum.

4. Disconnect the parking brake cable from the brake shoe and remove from the backing plate.

5. Disconnect and plug the brake line(s) at the wheel cylinder.

6. Remove the 4 nuts behind the backing plate.

7. Remove the backing plate, bearing case and the axle shaft as an assembly. If not possible by hand, use a slide hammer to remove the assembly.

8. Remove the O-ring and the bearing preload shims. Save the preload shims for reassembly.

9. Remove the oil seal from the axle tube with a hooked slide hammer.

10. To remove the axle shaft bearing, remove the notched locknut with tool MB990785-01 or a brass drift.

11. Remove the lock washer and flat washer.

12. Screw the locknut onto the axle shaft about 3 turns.

13. If tool MB990787-01 is not available, it will be necessary to fabricate a metal plate that fits over

the axle shaft and butts the locknut. Drill 4 holes in the plate that align with the 4 bearing case studs and fit the plate. Refit 2 nuts and washers to the bearing case studs diagonally across from each other and tighten them evenly to release the bearing case and bearing.

14. Use a hammer and drift to remove the bearing outer race from the bearing case.

15. Remove the outer oil seal from the bearing case.

To install:

16. Apply grease to the outer surface on the bearing outer race and the lip of the outer oil seal. Drive into the bearing cage.

17. Slide the bearing case and bearing over the rear axle shaft. Apply grease on the bearing rollers and install the inner race by pressing into place. Be careful not to damage the dust cover.

18. Pack the bearing with grease.

19. Install the washer, the crowned lock washer and the locknut in that order and torque the locknut to 130–159 ft. lbs. (176–220 Nm).

20. Bend the tab on the lock washer into the groove on the locknut. If the tab and the groove do not line up, tighten locknut slightly.

21. Lubricate and drive the new inner oil seal into place. Refit the assembly.

22. Install a new O-ring and the shims. Apply silicone rubber sealant to the face of the bearing case.

23. Install the entire assembly to the axle housing. Torque the retaining nuts to 40 ft. lbs. (54 Nm).

24. Check the axle shaft end-play. If not between 0.002–0.008 in. (0.05–0.20mm), proceed with the axle shaft end-play adjustment procedure.

25. Install all removed brake parts and bleed the system.

26. Install the tire and wheel assembly and road test the vehicle. Check for leaks.

END-PLAY ADJUSTMENT

1. Begin with the left side rear axle assembly and insert a 0.04 in. (1mm) shim between the bearing case and the axle shaft housing. Torque the nuts to specification.

2. Install the right side axle assembly into the right side housing without its shim and O-ring. Torque the 4 nuts to about 50 inch. lbs.

3. Using a feeler gauge, measure the gap between the bearing case and the axle housing face.

4. Remove the axle shaft and select a shim or shims that is the equal

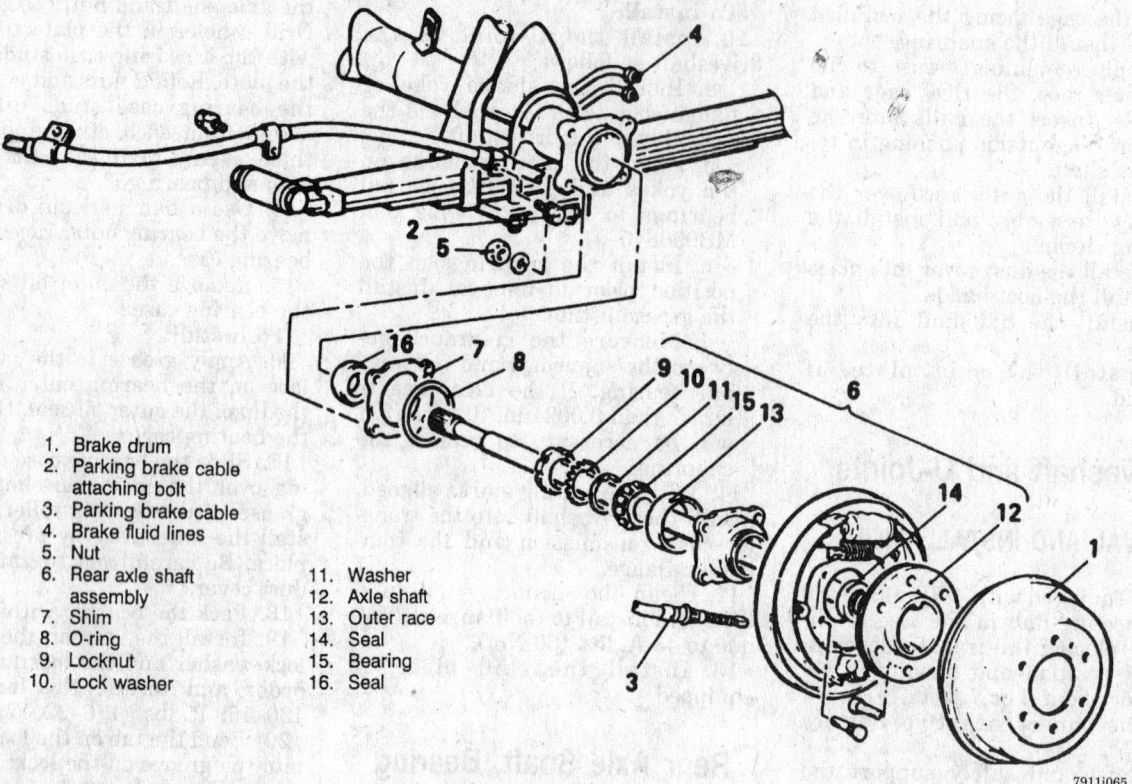

1. Brake drum
2. Parking brake cable attaching bolt
3. Parking brake cable
4. Brake fluid lines
5. Nut
6. Rear axle shaft assembly
7. Shim
8. O-ring
9. Locknut
10. Lock washer
11. Washer
12. Axle shaft
13. Outer race
14. Seal
15. Bearing
16. Seal

Rear axle shaft assembly

to the sum of the clearance measured in Step 3 plus 0.002–0.008 in. (0.05–0.20mm) and install them on the housing. Install the O-ring and apply sealant.

5. Install the axle assembly and torque the nuts to 40 ft. lbs. (54 Nm).

6. Measure the end-play and complete the installation procedure.

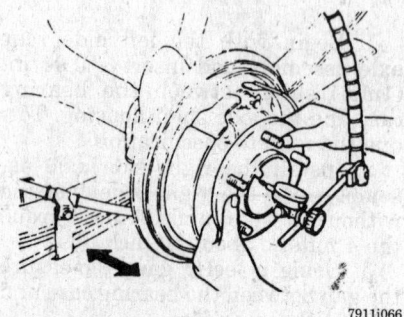

Measuring axle shaft end-play

Front Wheel Hub, Knuckle and Bearings

REMOVAL AND INSTALLATION

2WD Vehicle

1. Raise the vehicle and support safely. Remove the tire and wheel assembly.

2. Remove the brake caliper, pads and adaptor and position them out of the way.

3. Remove the grease cap.

4. Remove the cotter pin, castellated nut and washer. Remove the outer bearing.

5. Remove the front hub/rotor assembly from the steering knuckle. Remove the grease seal and inner bearing from the hub. Remove the splash shield.

6. Remove the nuts and bolts that attach the hub to the rotor and separate them. Clean out all of the old grease from the inside of the hub.

7. Remove the shock and stabilizer bar from the lower control arm, if equipped.

8. Support the lower control arm. Compress the coil spring with the special spring compressor, if equipped. Separate the ball joints and tie rod end from the knuckle.

9. Remove the steering knuckle.

To install:

10. Install the knuckle to the ball joint studs. Torque upper ball joint nuts to 65 ft. lbs. (90 Nm), and the lower joint nut to 130 ft. lbs. (180 Nm). Install new cotter pins. Remove the spring compressor, if used. Install the shock.

11. Connect the stabilizer bar to the lower control arm. Tighten the nut until the bushing is the same diameter as the washer.

12. Connect the tie rod end to the knuckle. Torque the nut to 30 ft. lbs. (41 Nm). Install a new cotter pin.

13. Assemble the rotor and front hub. Torque the nuts to 40 ft. lbs. (54 Nm).

14. Apply wheel bearing grease to the inside of the front hub.

15. Pack the inner bearing and install into hub.

16. Install a new oil seal into the hub so it is flush with the hub end face.

17. Install the assembly onto the steering knuckle, pack and install the outer bearing.

18. Install the washer and castellated nut. Spin the rotor and torque the nut to 22 ft. lbs. (30 Nm), loosen completely and retighten to 6 ft. lbs. (8 Nm) while turning the wheel.

19. Install a new cotter pin and install the grease cap.

20. Install the brake hardware and bleed the system, if opened.

21. Install the tire and wheel assembly and road test the vehicle.

Automatic Locking Hubs, Knuckle and Bearings

REMOVAL AND INSTALLATION

1. Place the free-wheeling hub in the free condition by placing the transfer lever in the **2H** position and

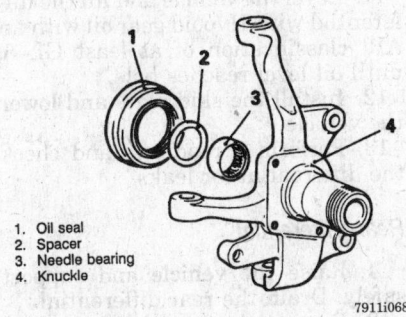

1. Oil seal
2. Spacer
3. Needle bearing
4. Knuckle

7911i068

Steering knuckle, needle bearing, spacer and seal — 4WD vehicle

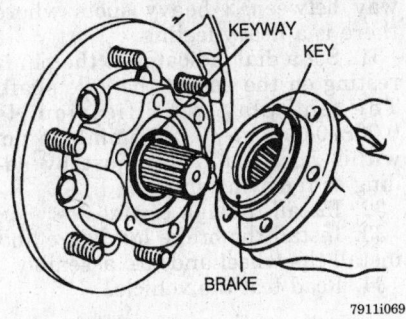

7911i069

Aligning the key in the automatic hub with the keyway in the spindle

moving in reverse for about 6 or 7 feet.

2. Disconnect negative battery cable.

3. Raise and safely support the vehicle. Remove the skid plate, if equipped.

4. Remove the tire and wheel assembly.

5. Remove the hub cover with the use of an oil filter wrench. Install a protective cloth between the wrench and the cover to avoid damage to the cover.

6. Remove the snapring from the inside of the hub. Remove the shim.

7. Remove the front brake caliper and brake pads from the vehicle. Do

not allow the caliper to hang from the brake hose.

8. Using hexagonal wrench, remove the automatic free wheeling hub assembly.

9. Remove the retaining screws from lock washer and remove lock washer.

10. Remove the outer bearing and front hub assembly from knuckle.

11. Remove the inner oil seal and inner bearing from the hub assembly.

12. To separate the hub from the brake disc, matchmark the brake disc to the front hub. Remove the retaining bolts and separate the hub from the disc.

13. Remove the dust cover from the spindle. Separate the tie rod from the steering knuckle.

14. Separate the upper and lower ball joints from the steering knuckle.

15. Remove the knuckle from the axle shaft.

16. Remove the knuckle oil seal and spacer. If damaged, drive out the needle bearing through the spindle end of the knuckle.

To install:

17. Use Chrysler tool C–4178 to press the new needle bearing into the knuckle. Lubricate the rollers and install the spacer with the chamfered side facing the center of the vehicle. Install a new seal until it is flush

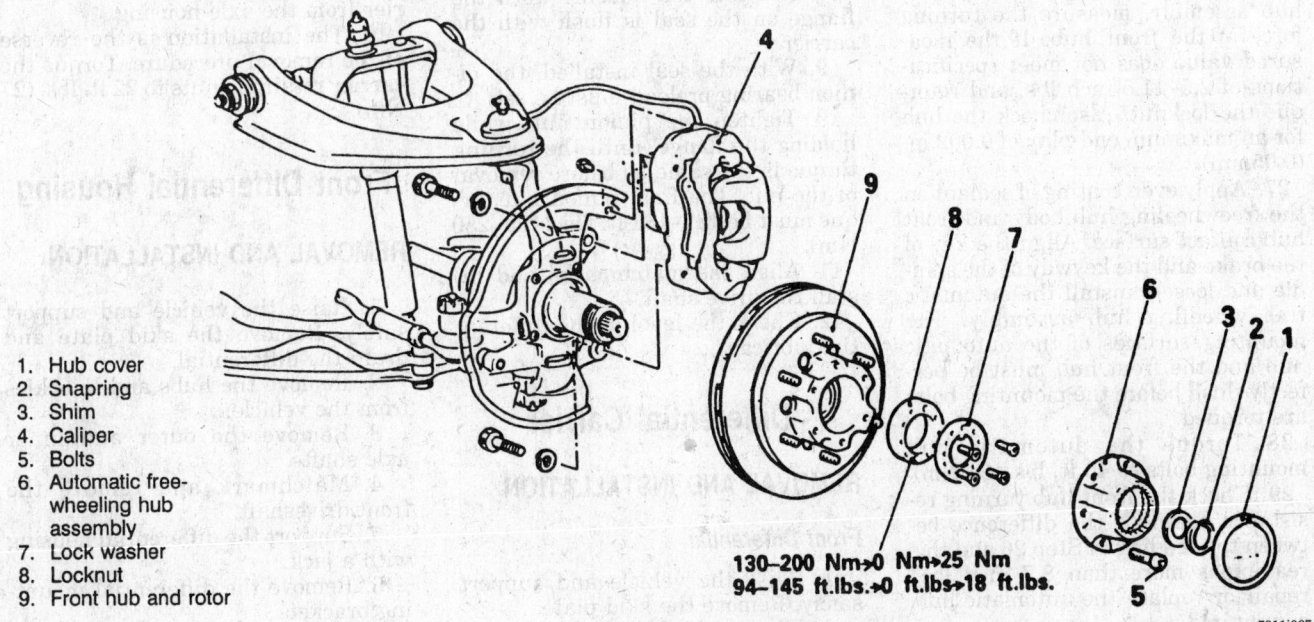

1. Hub cover
2. Snapring
3. Shim
4. Caliper
5. Bolts
6. Automatic free-wheeling hub assembly
7. Lock washer
8. Locknut
9. Front hub and rotor

130–200 Nm→0 Nm→25 Nm
94–145 ft.lbs.→0 ft.lbs.→18 ft.lbs.

7911i067

Front hub and automatic hub assembly — 4WD vehicle

with the knuckle end face and lubricate the l

18. Install the knuckle to the ball joint studs. Torque lower ball joint nut to 130 ft. lbs. (180 Nm) and the upper nut to 65 ft. lbs. (90 Nm). Install new cotter pin through castellated n

19. Connect the tie rod end to the knuckle. Torque the nut to 30 ft. lbs. (41 Nm). Install a new cotter p

20. Clean out all of the old grease from inside the front h

21. Bolt the rotor and front hub together. Torque the nuts to 40 ft. lbs. (54 Nm). Install new races and apply wheel bearing grease to the inside of the front h

22. Pack the inner bearing and install to the race.

23. Install new oil seal into the front hub until it is flush with the front hub end face.

24. Install the assembly onto the steering knuckle, pack and install the outer bearing with grease. Using special tool MB990954 or equivalent, which fits standard torque wrenches, torque the locknut to 95–145 ft. lbs. (130–200 Nm). Loosen the locknut completely, then retorque to 18 ft. lbs. (25 Nm). To complete the procedure, position the torque wrench at the 3 o'clock position and loosen the nut 30 degrees.

25. Install the lock washer. If the lock washer and locknut holes do not align, loosening the nut slight

26. Before installing the automatic hub assembly, measure the turning force of the front hub. If the measured value does not meet specifications of 2.5–11.5 inch lbs. and retorque the locknut. Also check the hub for an maximum end-play of 0.002 in. (0.05mm).

27. Apply even coating of sealant on the freewheeling hub body and front hub contact surface. Align the key of the brake and the keyway of the spindle and loosely install the automatic free wheeling hub assembly. The mounting surfaces of the automatic hub and the front hub must be perfectly flush before the mounting bolts are torqued.

28. Torque the automatic hub mounting bolts to 40 ft. lbs. (54 Nm).

29. Check the front hub turning resistance again. If the difference between the reading in Step 26 and this reading is more than 8.7 inch lbs., repair or replace the automatic hub, as required.

30. Install the shim and snapring. Rotate the axle shaft forward and backward and stop at a position midway between 2 heavy spots where there is a heavy feeling.

31. Set a dial indicator so the pin is resting on the end of the axle shaft. The end-play specification is 0.008–0.020 in. (0.2–0.5mm). If not within specifications, adjust by adding or removing shims.

32. Install the hub cover.

33. Install the brake hardware and install the wheel and tire assembly.

34. Road test the vehicle.

Pinion Seal

REMOVAL AND INSTALLATION

1. Raise the vehicle and support safely.

2. Matchmark and remove the driveshaft.

3. Check the turning torque of the pinion before proceeding. It should be 3.5–4.5 inch lbs. (0.4–0.5 Nm). This is the torque that must be reached during installation of the pinion nut.

4. Using a pinion flange holding tool, remove the pinion nut and washer.

5. Remove the companion flange from the drive pinion.

6. Pry the pinion seal out of the differential carrier.

7. Clean and inspect the sealing surface of the housing.

To install:

8. Using a seal driver, drive the new seal into the housing until the flange on the seal is flush with the carrier.

9. With the seal installed, the pinion bearing preload must be set.

10. Tighten the pinion nut, while holding the flange, until the turning torque is the same as before removal of the nut. The final pinion nut torque must be 137–181 ft. lbs. (190–250 Nm).

11. Align the matchmarks and install the drive shaft.

12. Check the level of the differential lubricant.

Differential Carrier

REMOVAL AND INSTALLATION

Front Differential

1. Raise the vehicle and support safely. Remove the skid plate.

2. Remove both side outer and right side inner axle shafts.

3. Drain the front differential and remove the cover.

4. Remove the bearing cap retaining bolts, matchmark and remove the caps.

5. Pry the differential case out of the housing.

6. Label any loose parts as removed from the assembly.

To install:

7. Install the differential case to the housing.

8. Install the caps aligning the matchmarks made previously. Torque the retaining bolts evenly and gradually to 45 ft. lbs. (61 Nm).

9. Clean the sealing surfaces of the cover and the differential housing. Reseal the cover and install to the housing.

10. Install the axle shafts.

11. Level the vehicle and fill the differential with Hypoid gear oil with an API classification of at least GL–5, until oil level reaches hole.

12. Install the skid plate and lower the vehicle.

13. Perform a road test and check the differential for leaks.

Rear Differential

1. Raise the vehicle and support safely. Drain the rear differential.

2. Remove the rear tire and wheel assemblies and brake drums.

3. Remove the axle shafts.

4. Matchmark and remove the driveshaft.

5. Remove the differential carrier retaining nuts and remove the carrier from the axle housing.

6. The installation is the reverse of the removal procedure. Torque the carrier retaining nuts to 22 ft. lbs. (27 Nm).

Front Differential Housing

REMOVAL AND INSTALLATION

1. Raise the vehicle and support safely. Remove the skid plate and drain the differential.

2. Remove the hubs and knuckles from the vehicle.

3. Remove the outer and inner axle shafts.

4. Matchmark and remove the front driveshaft.

5. Support the differential housing with a jack.

6. Remove the differential mounting brackets.

7. Remove the front suspension crossmember.

8. Lower the differential housing and remove from the vehicle.

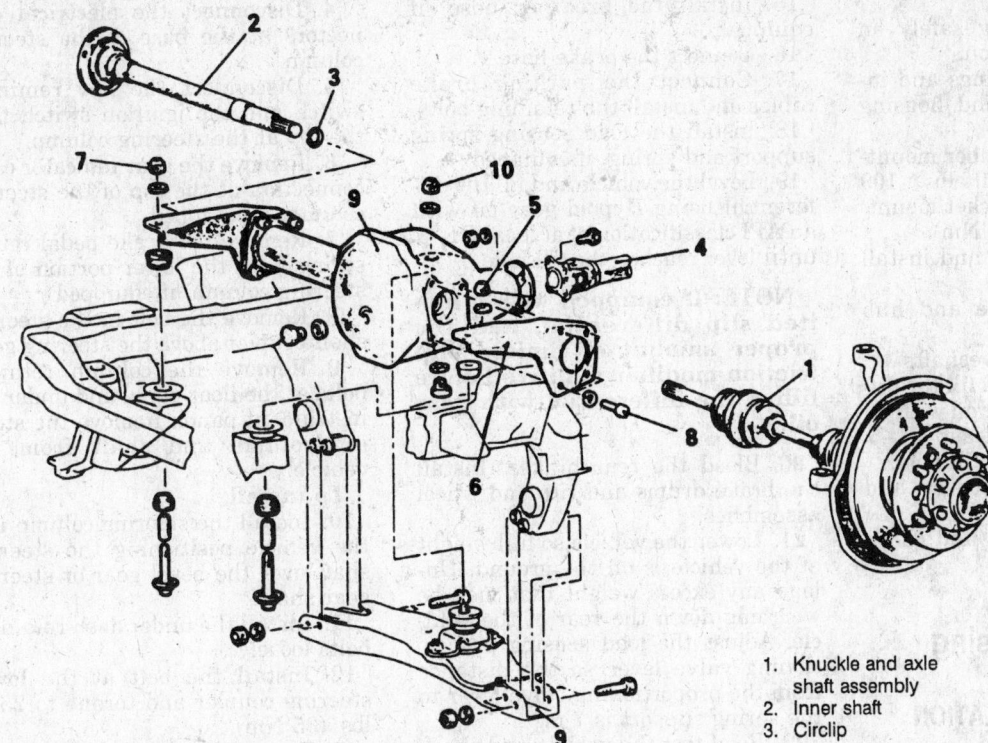

Front axle removal and installation

1. Knuckle and axle shaft assembly
2. Inner shaft
3. Circlip

4. Front driveshaft
5. Locknut
6. Left side mounting bracket
7. Locknut
8. Bolt
9. Crossmember
10. Locknut

7911i071

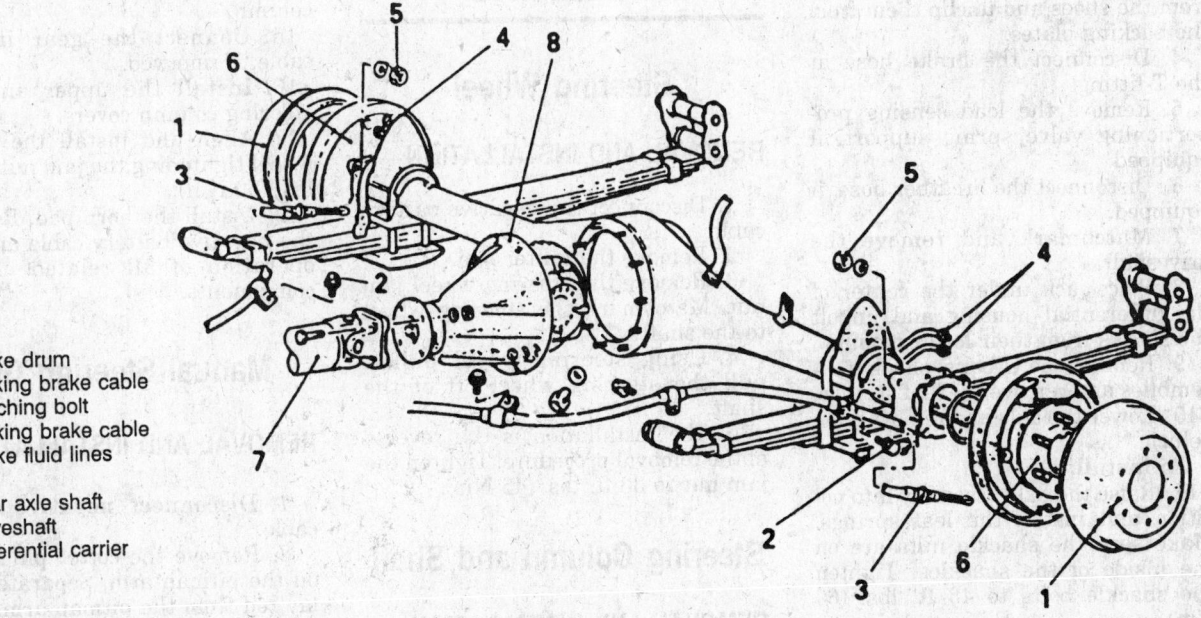

1. Brake drum
2. Parking brake cable attaching bolt
3. Parking brake cable
4. Brake fluid lines
5. Nut
6. Rear axle shaft
7. Driveshaft
8. Differential carrier

Differential carrier removal and installation

7911i070

To install:

9. Mount the housing safely on jack and raise into position.

10. Lubricate the bushings and install the crossmember and housing brackets.

11. Torque all crossmember mounting nuts and bolt to 80 ft. lbs. (109 Nm) and the housing bracket mounting bolts to 65 ft. lbs. (88 Nm).

12. Replace the circlips and install the axle shafts.

13. Install the knuckle and hub assemblies.

14. Install the front driveshaft.

15. Level the vehicle and fill the differential with Hypoid gear oil with an API classification of at least GL–5, until oil level is up to the fill hole.

16. Install the under cover and lower the vehicle.

17. Perform a road test and check the differential for leaks.

Rear Axle Housing

REMOVAL AND INSTALLATION

1. Raise the vehicle and support safely. Drain the differential

2. Remove the tire and wheel assemblies. Remove the brake drums.

3. Remove the parking brake cable attaching bolts, disconnect the cables from the shoes and unclip them from the backing plates.

4. Disconnect the brake hose at the T-fitting.

5. Remove the load sensing proportioning valve spring support, if equipped.

6. Disconnect the breather hose, if equipped.

7. Matchmark and remove the driveshaft.

8. Place jack under the center of the differential housing and unbolt the shocks from their lower mounts.

9. Remove the U-bolts, shackle assemblies and remove the leaf springs.

10. Lower the axle and remove from vehicle.

To install:

11. Raise the axle assembly into position and install the leaf springs. Make sure the shackle nuts are on the inside of the shackles. Tighten the shackle bolts to 43 ft. lbs. (60 Nm).

12. Install the U-bolt and bumper stops in position and tighten the new nuts to 87 ft. lbs. (120 Nm).

13. Install the lower shock mounting nuts tightening to 18 ft. lbs. (25 Nm).

14. Align and install the driveshaft.

15. Install the breather hose, if equipped.

16. Connect the brake hose.

17. Connect the parking brake cables and install the retaining bolts.

18. Install the load sensing spring support and spring, if equipped.

19. Level the vehicle and fill the differential using Hypoid gear oil with an API classification of at least GL–5, until level reaches the fill hole.

NOTE: If equipped with a limited slip differential, add the proper amount of limited slip friction modifier additive before filling the differential with gear oil.

20. Bleed the rear brakes. Install the brake drums and tire and wheel assemblies.

21. Lower the vehicle so full weight of the vehicle is on the ground. Unload any excess weight that may be weighing down the rear of the vehicle. Adjust the load sensing proportioning valve lever so the distance from the proportioning valve lever to the spring support is 7 in.

22. Road test the vehicle and check for leaks.

STEERING

Steering Wheel

REMOVAL AND INSTALLATION

1. Disconnect the negative battery cable.

2. Remove the center pad.

3. Remove the steering wheel jam nut. Matchmark the steering wheel to the shaft.

4. Using steering wheel puller, pull the steering wheel off of the shaft.

5. The installation is the reverse of the removal procedure. Tighten the jam nut to 33 ft. lbs. (45 Nm).

Steering Column and Shaft

REMOVAL AND INSTALLATION

1. Disconnect negative battery cable.

2. Remove the steering wheel from the vehicle.

3. Remove the upper and lower steering column covers.

4. Disconnect the electrical connectors at the base of the steering column.

5. Disconnect the key reminder switch and the ignition switch from the top at the steering column.

6. Remove the gear indicator cable connection at the top of the steering column, if equipped.

7. Remove the brake pedal return spring from the lower portion of the steering column, if equipped.

8. Remove the bolt in the steering shaft coupler above the steering gear.

9. Remove the column retainer bolts at the floor panel and under the instrument panel. Remove the steering column and shaft from the vehicle.

To install:

10. Install the steering column into the vehicle positioning the steering shaft over the bevel gear or steering gear shaft.

11. Install the under dash retaining bolts loosely.

12. Install the bolt at the lower steering coupler and torque to 25 ft. lbs. (35 Nm).

13. Tighten the bolts under the instrument panel to 14 ft. lbs. (20 Nm). Install the bolts in the column retainer at the floor panel tightening to 4 ft. lbs. (6 Nm).

14. Reconnect the electrical connectors at the base of the steering column.

15. Connect the gear indicator cable, if removed.

16. Install the upper and lower steering column covers.

17. Align and install the steering wheel tightening the jam nut to 36 ft. lbs. (50 Nm).

18. Install the horn pad. Reconnect the negative battery cable and check operation of all related electrical components.

Manual Steering Gear

REMOVAL AND INSTALLATION

1. Disconnect negative battery cable.

2. Remove the cotter pin and nut on the pitman arm. Separate the relay rod from the pitman arm.

3. Remove the bolt from the steering shaft to steering gear coupling.

4. Remove the steering gear mounting bolts and nuts, slide the gear from the steering shaft and remove the gear from the vehicle. Matchmark and remove the pitman arm, as required.

5. The installation is the reverse of the removal procedure. Torque the gear mounting nuts to 40 ft. lbs. (55 Nm). Torque the relay rod retainer nut to 33 ft. lbs. (45 Nm) and install new cotter pin.

ADJUSTMENT

1. Disconnect negative battery cable.
2. Remove the steering gear from the vehicle.
3. Turn the cross shaft 36 degrees. Position the mainshaft in the straight ahead position.
4. Using torque wrench, measure the starting torque of the mainshaft. The recommended value is 7.7–8.6 inch lbs. (0.9–1.0 Nm). If measured value is not within this value, Use tool MB990914 to screw adjusting cover to correct reading.

Power Steering Gear

REMOVAL AND INSTALLATION

1. Disconnect the negative battery cable. Raise the vehicle and support safely.
2. Fold back the dust boot which covers the steering shaft joint, if equipped. Remove the pinch bolt that holds the steering column shaft to the steering gear main shaft.
3. Remove the cotter pin, castellated nut the steering linkage from the pitman arm.
4. Disconnect and plug the fluid lines from the steering gear.
5. Remove the steering gear mounting nuts and remove the gear from the vehicle.
6. Matchmark and remove the pitman arm from the pitman shaft.
7. The installation is the reverse of the removal procedure. Torque the pitman arm nut to 100 ft. lbs. (136 Nm) and the gear mounting nuts to 28 ft. lbs. (38 Nm) on 2WD vehicles or 45 ft. lbs. (61 Nm) on 4WD vehicles.
8. Fill and bleed the system.

ADJUSTMENT

1. Attach special tool CT 1108 to the mainshaft and rotate the pinion with an inch lb. torque wrench to measure the mainshaft starting torque.
2. The specification is 4–11 inch lbs (0.45–1.25 Nm).
3. If not within specifications, loosen the adjusting cover locknut and adjust by rotating the top cover

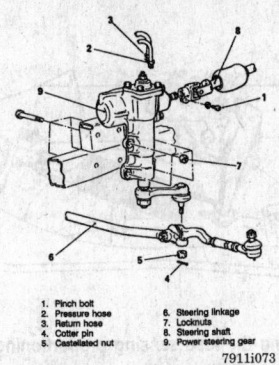

1. Pinch bolt
2. Pressure hose
3. Return hose
4. Cotter pin
5. Castellated nut
6. Steering linkage
7. Locknuts
8. Steering shaft
9. Power steering gear

7911i073

Power steering gear and related parts

until the proper starting torque is reached.
4. Tighten the valve housing locknut.

Power Steering Pump

REMOVAL AND INSTALLATION

1. Disconnect the negative battery cable.
2. Position a drain pan under the power steering pump.
3. Disconnect the fluid lines from the pump and plug them.
4. Remove the front bracket attaching bolts and remove the belt from the pulley.
5. Remove the pump from the vehicle.
6. The installation is the reverse of the removal procedure.
7. Adjust the belt tension, as required.
8. Fill and bleed the system.

BELT ADJUSTMENT

1. Loosen the pump mounting bolts. If equipped with tensioner pulley, loosen locknut on tensioner pulley only.
2. Using a prybar, move the pump away from the engine. If equipped with tensioner pulley, tighten the adjuster bolt to move the pulley.
3. Adjust the tension until the belt deflects about ¼–½ in. under a 10 lb. load, tighten the mounting bolts and adjuster bolts as required.

SYSTEM BLEEDING

1. Fill the reservoir with Dexron® II.
2. Raise the front end of the vehicle.
3. Disconnect the ignition coil wire.

4. Simultaneously crank the engine and turn the steering wheel from lock to lock. Repeat this several times.

NOTE: If the bleeding procedure is done with the engine running, high speed rotation of the pump will churn the fluid and create air bubbles filling the system with air. Bleed the system while cranking the engine only.

5. Lower the front end.
6. Connect one end of a tube to the breather plug on the steering box and place the other a container.
7. Start the engine and allow it to idle.
8. Loosen the breather plug and turn the steering wheel from lock to lock continuously until no more air bubbles appear in the fluid coming out the tube.

NOTE: Do not hold the steering wheel all the way against the stop for more than 5 seconds.

9. After the bleeding is done, tighten the breather plug and refill the reservoir.

Tie Rod Ends

REMOVAL AND INSTALLATION

1. Raise the vehicle and support safely.
2. Remove the cotter pin and nut from the tie rod end stud.
3. Using a puller, remove the tie rod from the steering knuckle or center link.
4. Loosen the sleeve clamp nut, if equipped, and unthread the tie rod end.
5. The installation is the reverse of the removal procedure. Torque the stud nuts to 33 ft. lbs. (45 Nm) and install a new cotter pin.
6. Lubricate the front end.
7. Align the front end.

BRAKES

Master Cylinder

REMOVAL AND INSTALLATION

1. Disconnect the negative battery cable. Disconnect the fluid level sensor connector.

2. Disconnect and plug the brake lines from the master cylinder.

3. Remove the nuts attaching the master cylinder to the power booster.

4. Remove the master cylinder from the mounting studs.

5. Remove the fluid reservoir from the cylinder.

To install:

6. Bench bleed the master cylinder.

7. Install master cylinder on power booster studs and install the retaining nuts.

8. Install the brake lines loosely to the master cylinder.

9. Have a helper press down on the brake pedal, holding pedal to the floor. Tighten hydraulic lines at master cylinder. Release brake pedal.

10. Connect the fluid level sensor connector and refill reservoir as required.

Load Sensing Proportioning Valve

REMOVAL AND INSTALLATION

1. Disconnect the negative battery cable.

2. Raise the vehicle and support safely.

3. Identify and disconnect the brake lines from the valve.

4. Remove the mounting bolts and remove the valve leaving the spring hanging from the lever.

To install:

5. Install the valve to the vehicle engaging the spring.

6. Connect the brake lines.

7. Bleed the brakes in the following order:

   a. Right rear
   b. Load sensing proportioning valve
   c. Left rear
   d. Right front
   e. Left front

8. Lower the vehicle so the full weight of the vehicle is on the ground. Unload any excess weight that is weighing down the rear of the vehicle. Adjust the load sensing proportioning valve lever so the distance from the proportioning valve lever to the hole in the spring support is about 7 in.

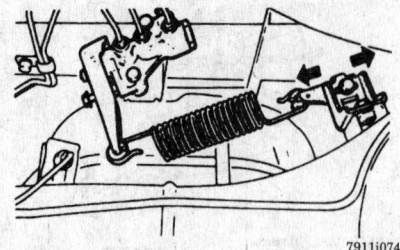

79111074

Adjusting the load sensing proportioning valve

Power Brake Booster

REMOVAL AND INSTALLATION

1. Disconnect the negative battery cable. Disconnect the vacuum hose from the booster.

2. Remove the nuts attaching the master cylinder to the booster and move the master cylinder to the side. Take care not to damage brake lines.

3. From inside of vehicle, remove the clevis pin that secures the booster pushrod to the brake pedal.

4. Remove the nuts that attach the booster to the dash panel and remove from the vehicle.

5. The installation is the reverse of the removal procedure.

Brake Caliper

REMOVAL AND INSTALLATION

1. Raise the vehicle and support safely.

2. Remove the tire and wheel assembly. Disconnect the brake line from the caliper.

3. Label and remove the 2 mounting bolts.

4. Lift the caliper off of the caliper support.

5. The installation is the reverse of the removal procedure. Make sure all anti-rattle and -squeal clips and pads are in place. Torque the guide pin bolt to 35 ft. lbs. (47 Nm) and the lock pin bolt to 30 ft. lbs. (41 Nm).

6. Bleed the brakes and road test the vehicle.

Disc Brake Pads

REMOVAL AND INSTALLATION

1. Remove ½ of the fluid from the master cylinder reservoir.

2. Raise the vehicle and support safely. Remove the tire and wheel assemblies.

3. Remove the calipers.

4. Remove the pads from the adaptor.

To install:

5. Use a large C-clamp to compress the piston into the caliper bore.

6. Install the pads to the adaptor with anti-rattle and anti-squeal clips in place.

7. Install the caliper and secure to the adapter.

8. Refill the master cylinder. Before moving the vehicle, pump brake pedal to seat brake pads against rotors.

9. Bleed the brakes if any brake lines were opened. Check the brake fluid.

Brake Rotor

REMOVAL AND INSTALLATION

1. Raise the vehicle and support safely.

2. Remove the tire and wheel assembly.

3. Remove the caliper and brake pads.

4. Remove the caliper adaptor.

5. If equipped with 4WD, remove the automatic hub, the shim, lock washer and locknut.

6. If equipped with 2WD, remove the dust cap, cotter pin, nut lock, nut, washer and outer bearing.

7. Remove the front hub and rotor assembly from the spindle.

8. To separate the hub from the rotor, remove the bolts and split the rotor from the hub.

To install:

9. Install the rotor to the hub and torque the attaching nuts and bolts to 40 ft. lbs. (54 Nm).

10. Install the hub and rotor assembly to the spindle and install the retaining nuts and bearings as removed. Adjust bearing preload.

11. Install the caliper adaptor. Torque the bolts to 70 ft. lbs. (95 Nm).

12. Install the brake pads and caliper, making sure all anti-rattle and anti-squeal clips are in place.

13. Pump the brake pedal to seat the brake pads against the rotors. Bleed the brakes if any brake lines were opened. Check the brake fluid.

14. Install the tire and wheel assembly and road test the vehicle.

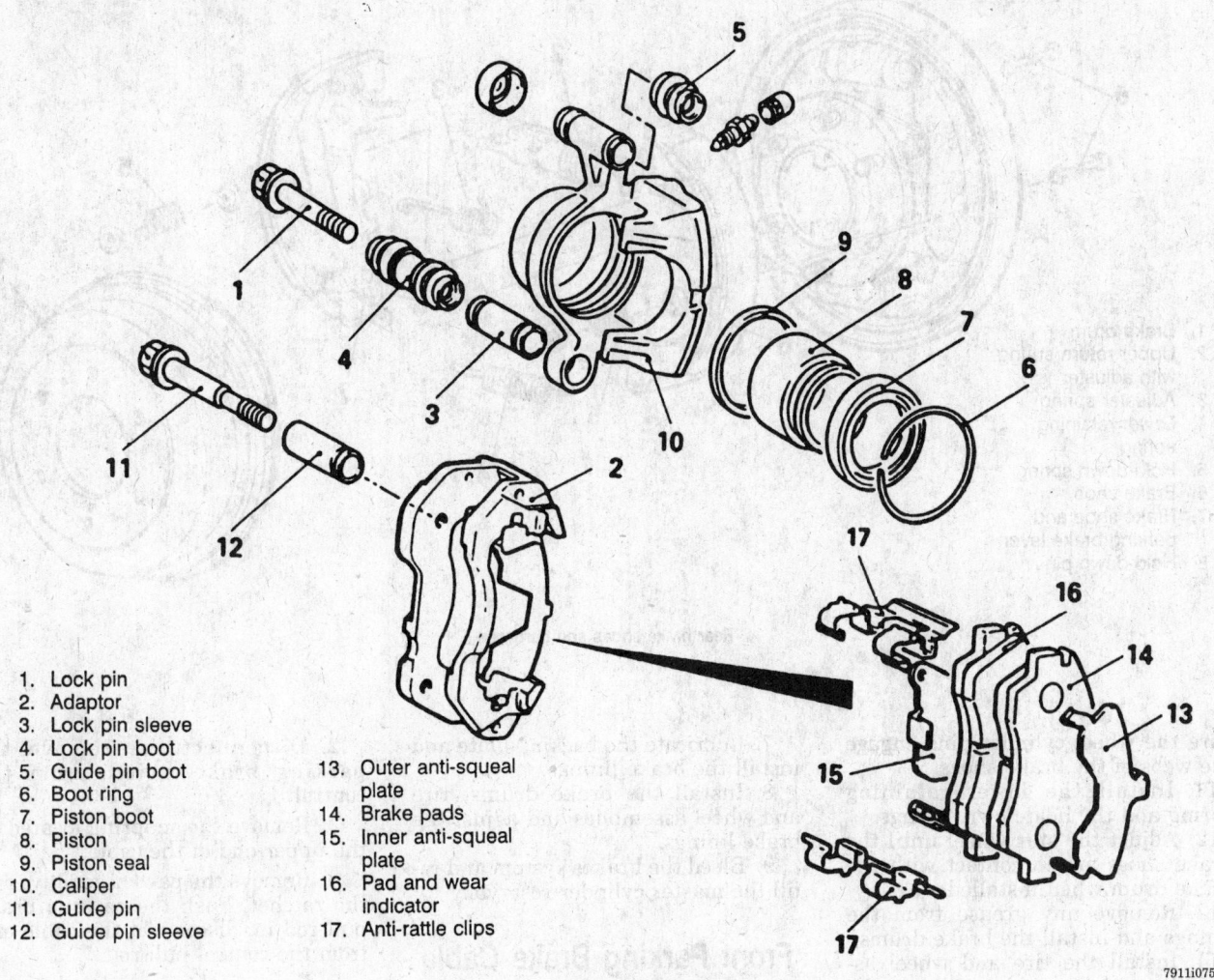

1. Lock pin
2. Adaptor
3. Lock pin sleeve
4. Lock pin boot
5. Guide pin boot
6. Boot ring
7. Piston boot
8. Piston
9. Piston seal
10. Caliper
11. Guide pin
12. Guide pin sleeve
13. Outer anti-squeal plate
14. Brake pads
15. Inner anti-squeal plate
16. Pad and wear indicator
17. Anti-rattle clips

79111i075

Front brakes

Brake Drums

REMOVAL AND INSTALLATION

1. Raise the vehicle and support safely.
2. Remove the tire and wheel assembly.
3. Remove the drum retaining screw with an impact driver if equipped.
4. Remove the drum. If difficult to remove the drum, remove the adjuster access cover in the backing plate and rotate the star wheel to loosen the adjustment on the rear brake shoes.

5. The installation is the reverse of the removal procedure.

Brake Shoes

REMOVAL AND INSTALLATION

1. Raise the vehicle and support safely.
2. Remove the tire and wheel assemblies and the brake drums.
3. Remove the upper return spring along with the adjuster.
4. Remove the adjuster spring.
5. Remove the lower retaining spring.
6. Remove the hold-down springs.

7. Remove the shoes, disengaging the parking brake lever.
   To install:
8. Clean and dry the backing plate. Lubricate the bosses, anchor contacts and wheel cylinder piston grooves where the top of the shoe fits lightly with lithium based grease.
9. Lubricate the star wheel shaft threads with anti-seize lubricant and transfer all parts to their proper locations on the new shoes. Make sure the longer end of the upper return spring is installed toward the shoe with the parking brake lever.
10. Spread the shoes apart, engage the parking brake lever and position them on the backing plate making

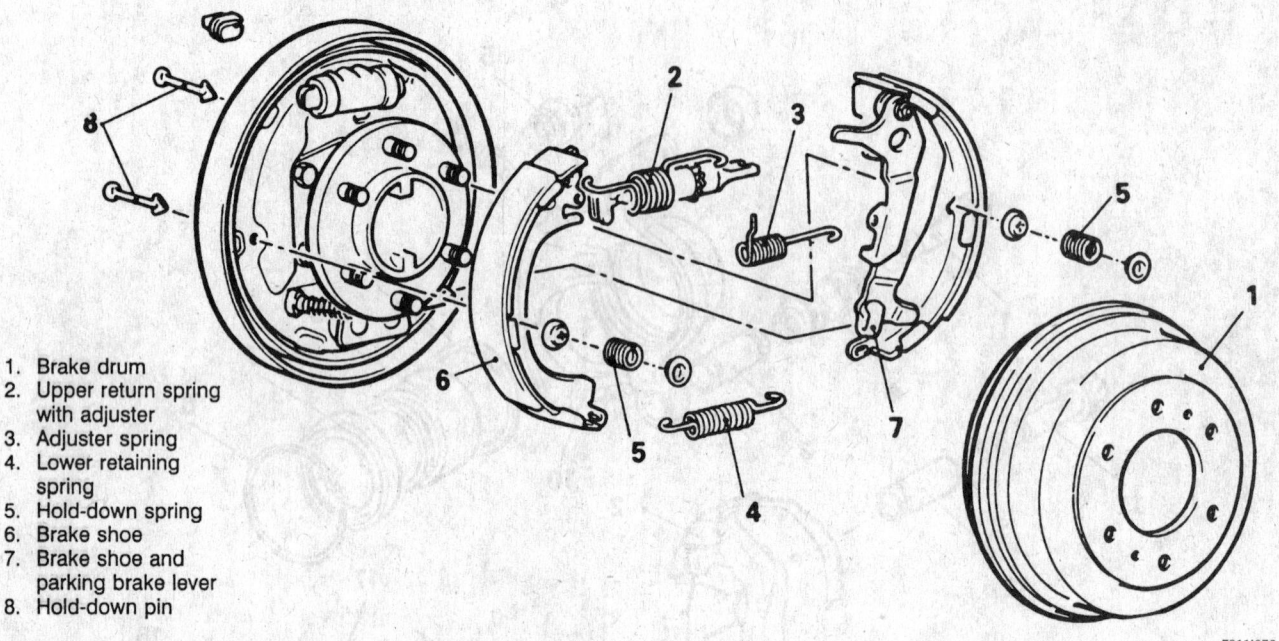

1. Brake drum
2. Upper return spring with adjuster
3. Adjuster spring
4. Lower retaining spring
5. Hold-down spring
6. Brake shoe
7. Brake shoe and parking brake lever
8. Hold-down pin

7911i076

Rear brake shoes and hardware

sure the wheel cylinder pins engage the webs of the brake shoes.

11. Install the lower retaining spring and the hold-down springs.

12. Adjust the star wheel until the brake shoes are in contact with the brake drum when installed.

13. Remove any grease from the linings and install the brake drums.

14. Install the tire and wheel assemblies and complete the brake adjustment.

Wheel Cylinder

REMOVAL AND INSTALLATION

1. Raise the vehicle and support safely.

2. Remove the wheel, drum and brake shoes.

3. Remove the hydraulic brake line from the wheel cylinder.

4. Remove the wheel cylinder mounting bolts and remove the cylinder from the backing plate.

To install:

5. Position the wheel cylinder on the backing plate and install the retaining bolts. Torque the bolts to 14 ft. lbs. (19 Nm).

6. Connect the brake line to the wheel cylinder.

7. Lubricate the backing plate and install the brake linings.

8. Install the brake drums, tire and wheel assemblies and adjust the brake linings.

9. Bleed the brakes system and refill the master cylinder reservoir.

Front Parking Brake Cable

REMOVAL AND INSTALLATION

Floor Mounted Control

1. Raise the vehicle and support safely.

2. Remove the brake lever cover.

3. Remove the pin securing the cable to the equalizer and slide the cable out of the bracket.

4. Remove the pin or retainer attaching the cable to the handle assembly. Disengage the cable from the handle.

5. Remove the cable grommet from the floor pan and remove the cable from the vehicle.

6. The installation is the reverse of the removal procedure.

Except Floor Mounted Control

1. Disconnect negative battery cable. Remove the front cable adjusting nut.

2. Disconnect the remove the parking brake switch from the control.

3. Remove the snapring located on the upper end of the cable.

4. Remove the pawl assembly from the ratchet. Push the parking brake pull rod in, disconnect the cable end from the control pull rod.

5. Remove the retainer clips and screws from the front cable.

6. Raise and safely support the vehicle.

7. Remove the pin securing the cable to the equalizer and disconnect the front cable from the rear brake cable equalizer lever. Remove the cable from the vehicle.

To install:

8. Instal the cable onto the rear brake cable actuator lever. Run cable under the vehicle and secure with retainers.

9. Lower the vehicle. Install cable into passenger compartment, install snapring to secure cable.

10. Attach the end of the cable into the parking brake control pull rod. Install paw and brake switch, adjust as required.

11. Adjust parking brake cables and connect the negative battery cable.

Rear Parking Brake Cable

REMOVAL AND INSTALLATION

1. Release the parking brakes fully.
2. Raise the vehicle and support safely.
3. Loosen the adjusting nut from the front cable.
4. Remove the brake drums. Remove the shoes, if necessary. Disconnect the cable from the lever.
5. Compress the cable retainer tabs to remove the cable from the backing plate.
6. Remove the cable from the equalizer and remove the retaining bolts from the frame.
7. The installation is the reverse of the removal procedure.

ADJUSTMENT

1. Release the parking brakes fully.
2. Raise the vehicle and support safely.
3. Adjust the rear brake linings.
4. Loosen the adjusting nut until there is slack in all the cables.
5. Rotate the rear wheels and tighten the cable adjusting nut until there is a slight drag at the wheels.
6. Continue to rotate the rear wheels and loosen the nut until all drag is eliminated.
7. Back off the nut an additional 2 turns.
8. Apply and release the parking brake several times. Upon the last release, verify that there is no drag on the wheels. The pedal should depress 4–7 notches.
9. To check operation, make sure the parking brake holds on an incline.

Brake System Bleeding

If using a pressure bleeder, follow the instructions furnished with the unit and choose the correct adaptor for the application. Do not substitute an adapter that "almost fits" as it will not work and could be dangerous.

MASTER CYLINDER

If the master cylinder is off the vehicle it can be bench bled.

1. Connect short piece(s) of brake line to the outlet fitting(s), bend them until the free end is below the fluid level in the master cylinder reservoirs.
2. Fill the reservoir with fresh brake fluid. Pump the piston slowly until no more air bubbles appear in the reservoir(s).
3. Disconnect the lines, refill the master cylinder and securely install the cylinder cap.
4. If the master cylinder is on the vehicle, it can still be bled, using a flare nut wrench.
5. Open the brake line(s) slightly with the flare nut wrench while pressure is applied to the brake pedal by a helper inside the vehicle.
6. Be sure to tighten the line before the brake pedal is released.
7. Repeat the process with both lines until no air bubbles come out.

CALIPERS AND WHEEL CYLINDERS

1. Fill the master cylinder with fresh brake fluid. Check the level often during the procedure.
2. Starting with the right rear wheel, remove the protective cap from the bleeder and place where it will not be lost. Clean the bleed screw.

— CAUTION —
When bleeding the brakes, keep face away from the brake area. Spewing fluid may cause facial and/or visual damage. Do not allow brake fluid to spill on the car's finish; it will remove the paint.

3. If the system is empty, the most efficient way to get fluid down to the wheel is to loosen the bleeder about 1/2–3/4 turn, place a finger firmly over the bleeder and have a helper pump the brakes slowly until fluid comes out the bleeder. Once fluid is at the bleeder, close it before the pedal is released inside the vehicle.

NOTE: If the pedal is pumped rapidly, the fluid will churn and create small air bubbles, which are almost impossible to remove from the system. These air bubbles will eventually congregate and a spongy pedal will result.

4. Once fluid has been pumped to the caliper or wheel cylinder, open the bleed screw again, have the helper press the brake pedal to the floor, lock the bleeder and have the helper slowly release the pedal. Wait 15 seconds and repeat the procedure (including the 15 second wait) until no more air comes out of the bleeder upon application of the brake pedal. Remember to close the bleeder before the pedal is released inside the vehicle each time the bleeder is opened. If not, air will be induced into the system.

5. If a helper is not available, connect a small hose to the bleeder, place the end in a container of brake fluid and proceed to pump the pedal from inside the vehicle until no more air comes out the bleeder. The hose will prevent air from entering the system.
6. Repeat the procedure on remaining wheel cylinders in order:
   a. Left rear
   b. Right front
   c. Left front
7. Hydraulic brake systems must be totally flushed if the fluid becomes contaminated with water, dirt or other corrosive chemicals. To flush, bleed the entire system until all fluid has been replaced with new fluid.
8. Install the bleeder cap(s) on the bleeder to keep dirt out. Always road test the vehicle after brake work of any kind is done.

FRONT SUSPENSION

Shock Absorbers

REMOVAL AND INSTALLATION

1. Raise and safely support the vehicle. Remove the upper shock nut, washer and bushing.
2. Raise the vehicle fully and support safely.
3. Remove the lower mounting bolt(s) and discard the shock.
4. The installation is the reverse of the removal procedure.

Coil Spring

REMOVAL AND INSTALLATION

1. Raise the vehicle and support safely.
2. Remove the shock absorber.
3. Disconnect the stabilizer bar from the lower control arm.
4. Install spring compressor tool MB990792 or equivalent, to the coil spring and to compress the spring.
5. Remove the cotter pin and lower ball joint nut.
6. Release the lower ball joint taper using Chrysler tool C 3564 A.
7. Remove the tool and the ball stud from the control arm. Release

the compressor tool from the coil spring.

8. Pull the arm down and remove the spring with the rubber isolation pad from the vehicle.

To install:

9. Install the spring with the rubber isolator. Install the compressor tool and compress spring so the lower ball joint can be inserted through the knuckle.

10. Torque the lower ball joint nut to 100 ft. lbs. (136 Nm). Install a new cotter pin. Remove the spring compressor.

11. Connect the sway bar to the lower control arm, if equipped.

12. Install the shock absorber. Install the wheel and tire assembly.

Torsion Bar

REMOVAL AND INSTALLATION

1. Raise the vehicle and support safely. Remove skid plate, if equipped.

2. Support the lower control arm at a point away from the torsion bar mounting point to the arm.

3. Fold the dust covers back and slide them away from the ends of the bar.

4. If the bars are to be reused, matchmark the torsion bar at both ends to the anchor and identify left from right.

5. Paint or measure the distance of the exposed threads of the rear mounting bolt down to the nut to aid in adjustment when installing. Remove the rear anchor arm mounting nut and bolt.

6. Remove the torsion bar from the front anchor arm.

To install:

7. If the bar is being reused, lubricate the ends and install the torsion bar aligning the matchmarks. If a new bar is being used, align the white stripe on the front splines with the mark on the anchor. There is a mark on the front of the torsion bar to differentiate between left and right. Do not install the bar with the mark facing the rear.

8. Install the torsion bar to the rear anchor so the length of the mounting bolt from the nut to the head of the bolt is the specified length with the rebound bumper in contact with the crossmember. The specifications are as follows: left side — 5.5–5.9 in.; right side — 5.3–5.8 in.

9. To initially set the riding height, tighten the rear anchor

mounting nut to the same point at which it was removed if the old bar is being reused. If a new bar has been installed, tighten the nut so the exposed length of the bolt threads is: left side — 3.9 in.; right side — 3.4 in.

10. Fill the dust covers with grease and fold them back into position.

11. Adjust the torsion to the correct riding height.

ADJUSTING THE TORSION BAR

1. Lower the vehicle so its full weight is on the ground. If there is

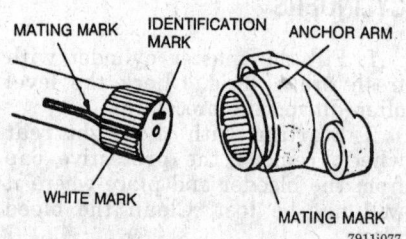

Aligning the front of the torsion bar with the front anchor

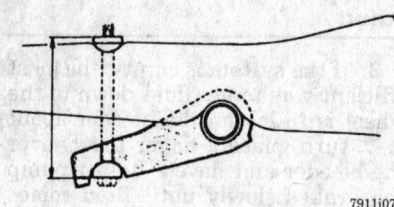

Measure this distance when installing the torsion bar to the rear anchor

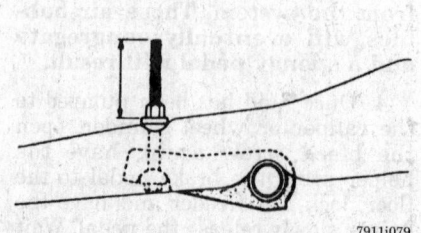

Measure this distance to initially set the riding height

any excess weight in the vehicle, unload it.

2. To set the riding height, measure the distance from the rebound bumper to its stopper bracket on the frame. Adjust the torsion bar nut until that distance is 3.1 in.

3. If, after adjusting the riding height, the exposed portion of the adjusting bolt is protruding up or down far enough to interferes with any front suspension component or is hanging down too low, the bar must be removed and repositioned.

4. Road test the vehicle and remeasure the riding height. Readjust if necessary.

Upper Ball Joint

INSPECTION

With the control arm removed, check the starting torque required to turn the ball stud. The specification for all vehicles is 7–30 inch lbs.

REMOVAL AND INSTALLATION

NOTE: The upper ball joint and upper control arm must be replaced as an assembly.

1. Raise the vehicle and support safely. Release the tension on the torsion bar and remove the upper control arm from the vehicle.

2. Remove the ring and boot from the ball joint. Remove the snapring.

3. Remove the ball joint from the control arm using special tool sets MB990800 and MB990799.

To install:

4. Align the mating mark on the upper ball joint with the mark on the arm.

5. Press the ball joint in using the same tools that were used to remove the ball joint.

6. Install the snapring. If the snapring is loose, replace with a new one.

7. Fill the boot with grease and install the boot and ring.

8. Install the upper control arm.

9. Lubricate the ball joint with a grease gun.

10. Adjust the riding height, if equipped with a torsion bar and align the front end.

Lower Ball Joint

INSPECTION

With the control arm removed, check the up and down end-play of the ball

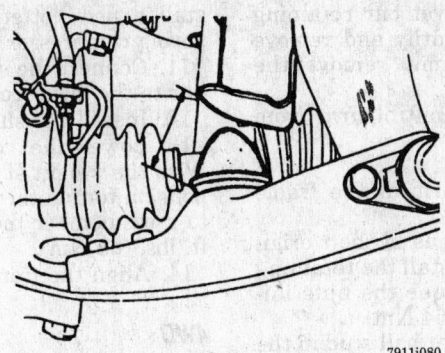

Measure this distance to set the riding height

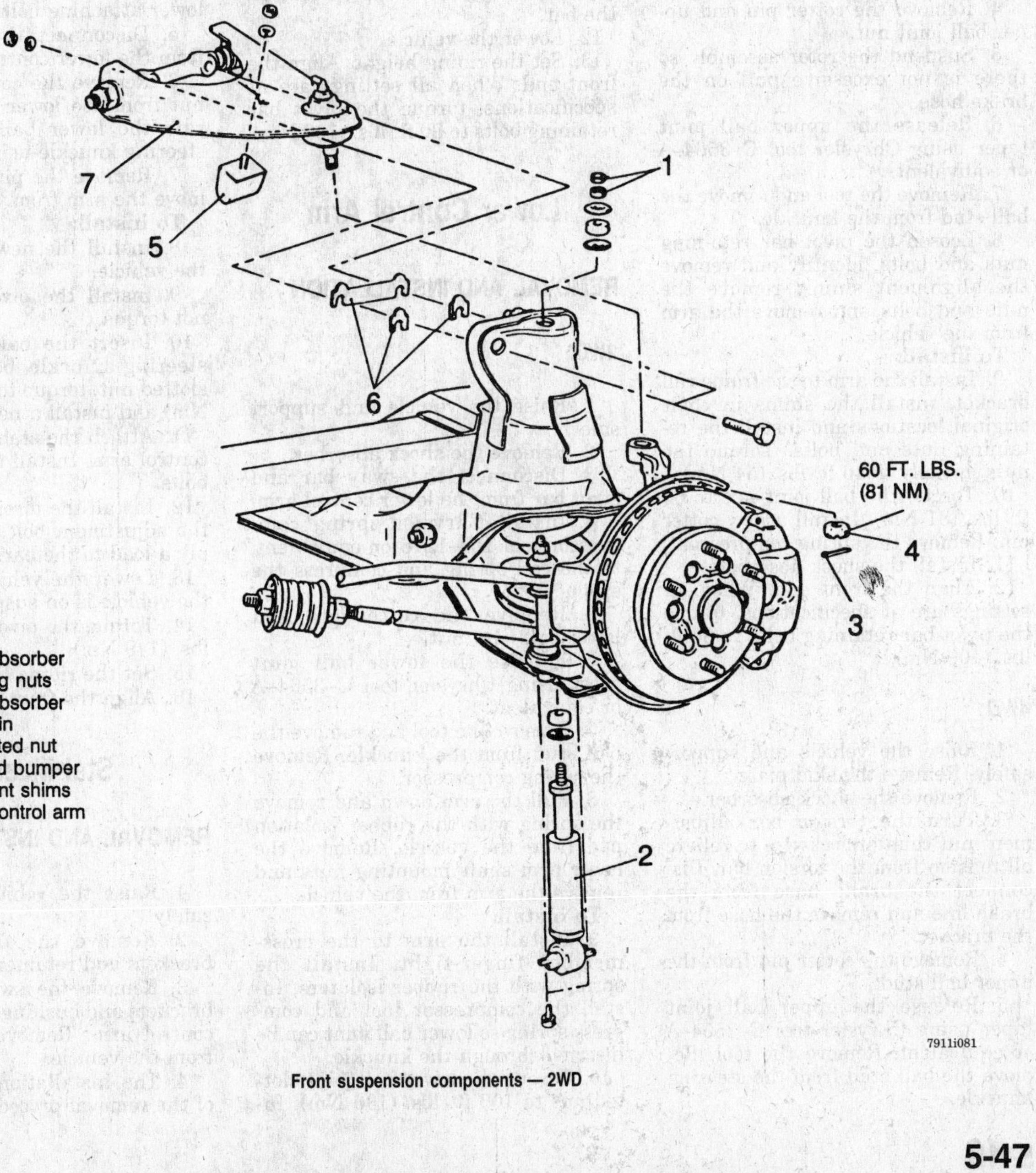

7911i080

stud. If it exceeds 0.02 in. (0.5mm), the ball joint should be replaced.

REMOVAL AND INSTALLATION

1. Raise the vehicle and support safely. Remove the lower control arm.
2. Remove the ball joint retaining nuts and bolts and remove the ball joint from the arm.
3. The installation is the reverse of the removal procedure. Torque the ball joint retaining nuts and bolts to 50 ft. lbs. (68 Nm) on 4WD vehicles or 28 ft. lbs. (38 Nm) on 2WD vehicles. Torque the ball stud nut to 100 ft. lbs. (136 Nm) and install a new cotter pin.

1. Shock absorber mounting nuts
2. Shock absorber
3. Cotter pin
4. Castellated nut
5. Rebound bumper
6. Alignment shims
7. Upper control arm

60 FT. LBS. (81 NM)

7911i081

Front suspension components — 2WD

4. Lubricate the ball joint with a grease gun.

5. Adjust the riding height, if equipped with a torsion bar.

6. Align the front suspension.

Upper Control Arm

REMOVAL AND INSTALLATION

2WD

1. Raise the vehicle and support safely. Remove the tire and wheel assembly.

2. Remove the shock absorber.

3. Install Chrysler tool DD–1278 or equivalent, to the coil spring and compress the spring.

4. Remove the cotter pin and upper ball joint nut.

5. Suspend the rotor assembly so there is not excessive pull on the brake hose.

6. Release the upper ball joint taper using Chrysler tool C–3564–A or equivalent.

7. Remove the tool and remove the ball stud from the knuckle.

8. Loosen the pivot bar retaining nuts and bolts, identify and remove the alignment shims, remove the nuts and bolts and remove the arm from the vehicle.

To install:

9. Install the arm to the frame rail bracket, install the shims in their original locations and install the retaining nuts and bolts. Torque the nuts initially to 40 ft. lbs. (54 Nm).

10. Torque the ball joint nut to 60 ft. lbs. (81 Nm). Install a new cotter pin. Remove the spring compressor.

11. Install the shock absorber.

12. Align the front end. When all settings are at specifications, torque the pivot bar retaining bolts to 80 ft. lbs. (109 Nm).

4WD

1. Raise the vehicle and support safely. Remove the skid plate.

2. Remove the shock absorber.

3. Turn the torsion bar adjustment nut counterclockwise to relieve all tension from the torsion bar. Disconnect the brake hose from the brake line and remove the hose from the bracket.

4. Remove the cotter pin from the upper ball stud.

5. Release the upper ball joint taper using Chrysler tool C–3564–A or equivalent. Remove the tool. Remove the ball stud from the steering knuckle.

6. Loosen the pivot bar retaining nuts and bolts, identify and remove the alignment shims, remove the nuts and bolts.

7. Remove the control arm from the vehicle.

To install:

8. Position the arm at the frame rail bracket.

9. Install the shims in their original locations and install the retaining nuts and bolts. Torque the nuts initially to 40 ft. lbs. (54 Nm).

10. Insert the upper ball stud in the steering knuckle arm bore and install the nut. Torque the nut to 60 ft. lbs. (81 Nm) and install a new cotter pin. Install the shock absorber and attach the brake hose.

11. Turn the torsion bar adjustment nut clockwise to apply a load on the bar.

12. Lower the vehicle.

13. Set the riding height. Align the front end. When all settings are at specifications, torque the pivot bar retaining bolts to 80 ft. lbs. (109 Nm).

Lower Control Arm

REMOVAL AND INSTALLATION

2WD

1. Raise the vehicle and support safely.

2. Remove the shock absorber.

3. Disconnect the sway bar and strut bar from the lower control arm.

4. Install Chrysler spring compressor tool DD–1278 or equivalent, to the coil spring and compress the spring.

5. Remove the cotter pin and lower ball joint nut.

6. Release the lower ball joint taper using Chrysler tool C–3564–A or equivalent.

7. Remove the tool and remove the ball stud from the knuckle. Remove the spring compressor.

8. Pull the arm down and remove the spring with the rubber isolation pad from the vehicle. Remove the lower arm shaft mounting nuts and remove the arm from the vehicle.

To install:

9. Install the arm to the crossmember finger-tight. Install the spring with the rubber isolators. Install the compressor tool and compress spring so lower ball joint can be inserted through the knuckle.

10. Torque the lower ball joint slotted nut to 100 ft. lbs. (136 Nm). In-

stall a new cotter pin. Remove the spring compressor.

11. Connect the sway bar and strut bar to the lower control arm.

12. Install the shock absorber.

13. Lower the vehicle completely. With the weight of the vehicle on suspension torque the lower control arm to crossmember mounting nut to 50 ft. lbs. (68 Nm).

14. Align the front suspension.

4WD

1. Raise the vehicle and support safely.

2. Remove the skid plate.

3. Remove the torsion bar, anchors and lower arm shaft.

4. Remove the shock absorber lower attaching bolt.

5. Disconnect the stabilizer bar from the lower control arm.

6. Remove the cotter pin and the nut from the lower ball stud. Separate the lower ball stud from the steering knuckle using a puller.

7. Remove the pivot bolts and remove the arm from the vehicle.

To install:

8. Install the new control arm to the vehicle.

9. Install the pivot bolts, but do not torque.

10. Insert the ball stud into the steering knuckle bore. Install the slotted nut, torque to 100 ft. lbs. (136 Nm) and install a new cotter pin.

11. Attach the stabilizer bar to the control arm. Install the shock mount bolts.

12. Install the torsion bar and turn the adjustment bolt clockwise to apply a load to the bar.

13. Lower the vehicle so weight of the vehicle is on suspension.

14. Torque the pivot nuts to 110 ft. lbs. (149 Nm).

15. Set the riding height.

16. Align the front suspension.

Stabilizer Bar

REMOVAL AND INSTALLATION

1. Raise the vehicle and support safely.

2. Remove the front sway bar brackets and retainers.

3. Remove the sway bar support brackets and bushings from the lower control arm. Remove the sway bar from the vehicle.

4. The installation is the reverse of the removal procedure.

1. Skid plate
2. Under cover
3. Torsion bar
4. Cotter pin
5. Lower ball joint
6. Stabilizer bar nut
7. Stabilizer bar
8. Shock absorber mounting bolts
9. Lower arm shaft
10. Front anchor arm
11. Lower control arm
12. Rebound bumper
13. Ball joint mounting nuts

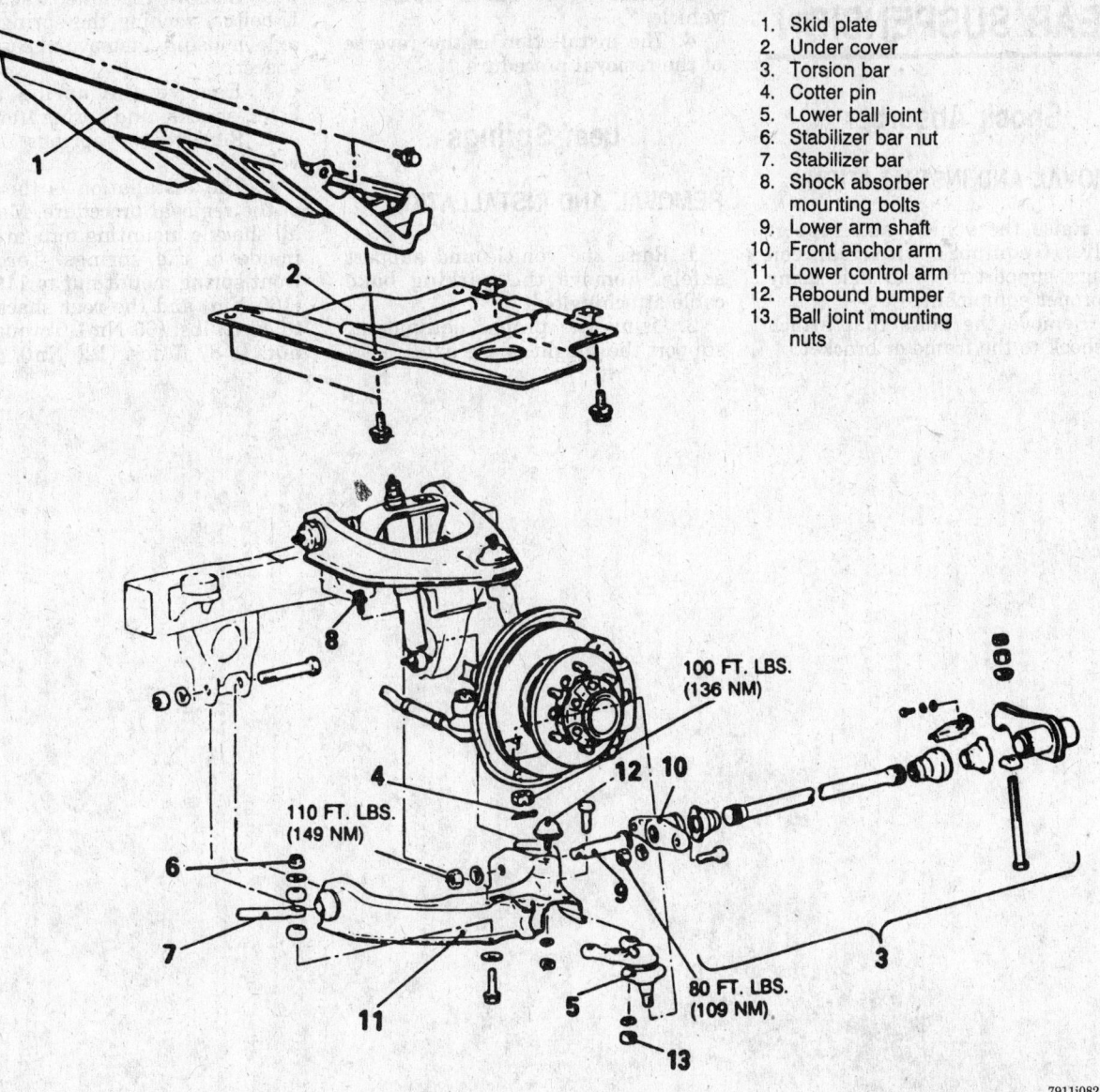

Front suspension components — 4WD

Front Wheel Bearings

ADJUSTMENT

1. Tighten the wheel bearing nut to 22 ft. lbs. (30 Nm) while turning the rotor.
2. Loosen the wheel bearing adjusting nut completely.
3. Tighten the nut to 6 ft. lbs. (8 Nm).
4. Check the wheel bearing endplay. The specification is 0.001–0.003 in.
5. Install the nut lock and cotter pin.

REMOVAL AND INSTALLATION

1. Raise the vehicle and support safely.
2. Remove the tire and wheel assembly.
3. Remove the caliper, disc brake pads and adaptor.
4. Remove the dust cap.
5. Remove the cotter pin, castellated nut lock, wheel bearing nut and washer from the spindle.
6. Remove the outer wheel bearing.
7. Remove the hub and rotor assembly with the inner intact. Remove the grease seal and inner wheel bearing.

To install:

8. Lubricate and install the inner wheel bearing. Install a new grease seal.
9. Install the hub and rotor assembly to the spindle.
10. Lubricate and install the outer wheel bearing, washer and nut. When the bearing preload is properly set, install the nut lock and a new cotter pin.
11. Install the grease cap.
12. Install the brake pads and caliper.
13. Install the tire and wheel assembly.

REAR SUSPENSION

Shock Absorber

REMOVAL AND INSTALLATION

1. Raise the vehicle and support safely. If equipped with rear coil springs, support the rear axle using the proper equipment.

2. Remove the bolts that attach the shock to the frame or bracket.

3. Remove the shock from the vehicle.

4. The installation is the reverse of the removal procedure.

Leaf Springs

REMOVAL AND INSTALLATION

1. Raise the vehicle and support safely. Remove the parking bake cable attaching bolt.

2. Using the proper equipment, support the weight of the axle.

3. Remove the nuts, washers and U-bolts attaching the springs to the axle housing. Remove the seat and spacer.

4. Remove the spring shackle bolts, shackle and spring front bolt.

5. Remove the springs from the vehicle.

6. The installation is the reverse of the removal procedure. Make sure all shackle mounting nuts are on the inside of the springs. Torque the front spring mount nut to 116 ft. lbs. (160 Nm) and the rear shackle nuts to 43 ft. lbs. (60 Nm). Torque U-bolt nuts to 87 ft. lbs. (120 Nm).

GEO 6
Tracker

FIRING ORDERS

NOTE: To avoid confusion, always replace spark plug wires one at a time.

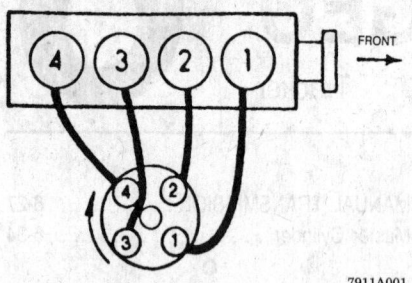

7911A001

1.6L Engine
Engine Firing Order: 1–3–4–2
Distributor Rotation: Clockwise

ENGINE ELECTRICAL

NOTE: Disconnecting the battery cable on some vehicles may interfere with the functions of the on board computer systems and may require the computer to undergo a relearning process, once the negative battery cable is disconnected.

Distributor

REMOVAL

1. Disconnect the negative battery terminal from the battery.
2. Disconnect vacuum hose and electrical connections.

NOTE: Do not bend or twist the spark plug wires to avoid internal damage. Grip the the wire boot when removing or installing the wires.

3. Remove the distributor cap.
4. Mark the rotor position on the distributor housing and the distributor housing position on the engine.
5. Remove the distributor flange bolt and remove the distributor.

NOTE: Do not crank the engine with the distributor removed.

INSTALLATION

Timing Not Disturbed

1. Install the distributor and align the marks on the distributor housing and on the engine.
2. Tighten the flange bolt to 11 ft. lbs. and install the distributor cap.
3. Connect the electrical connections and the vacuum hoses.
4. Connect the negative battery cable and set the timing to specification.

Timing Disturbed

1. Rotate the crankshaft in a clockwise position until the specified timing mark on the flywheel aligns with the timing matchmark on the engine.

NOTE: After aligning the 2 marks, remove the cylinder head cover to visually check so the rocker arms are not riding on the camshaft cams at No. 1 cylinder. If the arms are found to be riding on the cams, turn the crankshaft 360 degrees to realign the 2 marks.

2. Position the rotor to the No. 1 cylinder position and install the distributor tightening the flange bolt to 11 ft. lbs.
3. Connect the vacuum and electrical connections.
4. Connect the negative battery cable and set the timing to specification.

Ignition Timing

ADJUSTMENT

1. Start the engine and warm to normal operating temperature. Prior to any adjustment, be sure all the electrical accessories are **OFF**.
2. After warming, make sure the idle speed is 800 rpm.
3. Remove cap from monitor coupler next to battery and connect terminals **C** and **D** with a jumper wire. Connect the timing light to the No. 1 cylinder spark plug wire.
4. With the engine running at the specified idle speed, direct the timing light to the crankshaft pulley. If the specified timing mark on the timing tab is aligned with the timing notch on the crankshaft pulley the ignition is properly timed.
5. If the timing is out of adjustment, loosen the distributor flange bolt and turn the distributor housing

to advance or retard the timing. Turn the distributor counterclockwise to advance the timing and clockwise to retard the timing.
6. After the adjustment, tighten the flange bolt and recheck the timing.

Alternator

BELT TENSION ADJUSTMENT

1. Disconnect the negative battery cable.
2. Loosen the alternator bolt and pivot bolts.
3. Adjust the belt tension to 0.24–0.32 in. of deflection using a belt tension gauge.

REMOVAL AND INSTALLATION

1. Disconnect the negative battery cable.
2. Disconnect the wire coupler and white lead wire from the alternator.
3. Remove the charcoal cannister mounting bracket, if necessary.
4. Remove the alternator mounting bolt and alternator drive belt adjusting bolt.
5. Remove the alternator from the vehicle.
To install:
6. Install the alternator and tighten the mounting bolt and drive belt adjusting bolt. Adjust the drive belt tension.
7. Install the shroud under the radiator and connect the wire coupler to the alternator.
8. Connect the negative battery cable.

Starter

REMOVAL AND INSTALLATION

1. Disconnect the negative battery cable.
2. Raise and support the vehicle safely.
3. Disconnect the lead wire and battery cable from the starter motor.
4. Support the starter and remove the 2 mounting bolts.
5. Remove the starter.
To install:
6. Install the starter and tighten the 2 mounting bolts to 22 ft. lbs.
7. Connect the lead wire to the starter.
8. Lower the vehicle and connect the negative battery cable.

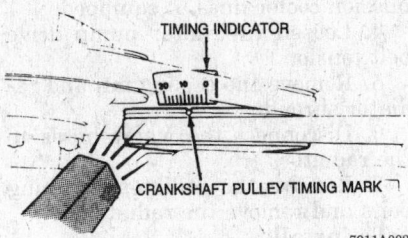

Timing mark location — Tracker

7911A002

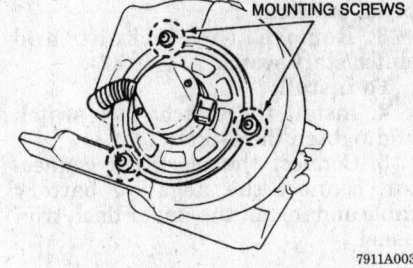

Heater blower motor mounting screws

7911A003

CHASSIS ELECTRICAL

Heater Blower Motor

REMOVAL AND INSTALLATION

1. Disconnect the negative battery cable.
2. Remove the glove box assembly.
3. Disconnect the blower motor and resistor wire connectors.
4. Disconnect the fresh air control cable from the blower motor case.
5. Loosen but do not remove the blower housing fastener bolts.
6. Remove the 3 blower motor mounting screws.
7. Remove the blower motor.
To install:
8. Install the blower motor and secure with the 3 screws.
9. Tighten the blower housing fastener bolts.
10. Connect the fresh air control cable to the blower motor case.
11. Connect the electrical connectors and install the glove box assembly.
12. Connect the negative battery cable.

Windshield Wiper Motor

REMOVAL AND INSTALLATION

1. Disconnect the negative battery cable.
2. Remove the right and left cowl grilles.
3. Remove the wiper linkage to wiper mounting nut.
4. Disconnect the wire connector from the wiper motor.

5. Remove the 4 wiper motor mounting bolts and remove the wiper motor.
To install:
6. Install the wiper motor and install the 4 mounting bolts.
7. Connect the electrical connector and connect the wiper linkage.
8. Install the cowl grilles and connect the negative battery cable.

Instrument Cluster

REMOVAL AND INSTALLATION

1. Disconnect the negative battery cable.
2. Remove the 4 screws from the front shroud.
3. Remove the front shroud.
4. Remove the 4 cluster mounting screws and slide the cluster outwards.
5. Disconnect the lead wires and speedometer cable from the speedometer.
6. Remove the instrument cluster assembly.
To install:
7. Install the lead wires and speedometer cable.
8. Install the 4 cluster screws and tighten.
9. Install the front shroud and install the 2 upper and 2 lower screws.
10. Connect the negative battery cable.

Combination Switch

The combination switch incorporates the turn signal, windshield wiper, dimmer and headlight switches into one switch.

REMOVAL AND INSTALLATION

1. Disconnect the negative battery cable.

2. Remove the horn button and the steering wheel retaining nut and remove the steering wheel.
3. Remove the upper and lower column cover screws and remove the covers.
4. Disconnect the lead wires from the combination switch at the connector.
5. Remove the combination switch assembly screws.
6. Remove the combination switch from the steering column.
To install:
7. Install the combination switch assembly and install the screws.
8. Connect the electrical connector.
9. Install the upper and lower column covers.
10. Install the steering wheel and tighten the shaft nut to 24 ft. lbs.
11. Install the horn button and connect the negative battery cable.

Ignition Switch

REMOVAL AND INSTALLATION

1. Disconnect the negative battery cable.
2. Remove the steering wheel from the vehicle.
3. Disconnect the wire connector at the ignition switch.
4. With the ignition switch in the **OFF** position, remove the mounting bolts and remove the switch.
To install:
5. Install the ignition switch and replace the mounting bolts.
6. Connect the electrical connector to the ignition switch.
7. Install the steering wheel and tighten the shaft nut to 24 ft. lbs.
8. Install the horn button and connect the negative battery cable.

Ignition Lock

REMOVAL AND INSTALLATION

1. Disconnect the negative battery cable.
2. Remove the steering wheel.
3. Disconnect the lead wires to the ignition and combination switches.
4. Disconnect the steering joint by removing the joint bolt.
5. Remove the steering column fastening bolts.
6. Remove the steering column assembly.
7. Using a center punch, loosen and remove the steering lock mounting bolts.

8. Turn the key to **ACC** or **ON** position and remove the steering lock assembly from the steering column.
To install:
9. To install the switch, position the oblong hole of the steering shaft in the center of the hole in the steering column.
10. Turn the ignition key to the **ACC** or **ON** position and install the steering lock assembly onto the column.
11. Turn the ignition key to the **LOCK** position and remove it.
12. Align the hub on the lock with oblong hole of the steering shaft.
13. Rotate the shaft to assure that the steering shaft is locked.
14. Tighten the 2 new steering lock mounting bolts.
15. Turn the ignition key to the **ACC** or **ON** position and check to be sure the steering shaft rotates smoothly. Also check the lock mechanism.
16. Install the steering column assembly by attaching the steering joint and joint bolt.
17. Install the steering column fastening bolts.
18. Reconnect the lead wires to the ignition and combination switch.
19. Replace the steering wheel and negative battery cable.

Stoplight Switch

REMOVAL AND INSTALLATION

1. Disconnect the negative battery cable. Remove the under dash trim panel, if equipped.
2. Push the brake pedal down and remove the stoplight switch locknut.
3. Disconnect the wire connector at the switch.
4. Remove the switch from the bracket.
To install:
5. Install the new switch on the bracket.
6. Adjust the switch so there is 0.02–0.04 in. clearance between the switch and the brake pedal.
7. Replace the locknut and tighten to 7.5–10.5 ft. lbs.
8. Replace the negative battery cable.

Clutch Switch

REMOVAL AND INSTALLATION

1. Disconnect the negative battery cable. Remove the under dash trim panel, if equipped.

2. Disconnect the clutch/start switch connector beside the clutch pedal bracket.
3. Remove the locknut and clutch/start switch.
To install:
4. Install the clutch/start switch and tighten the locknut.
5. Connect the electrical connector, connect the negative battery cable and install the under dash trim panel.

Fuses and Relays

LOCATION

The fuse box and turn signal relay are located under the driver side of the dashboard.

Computer

LOCATION

The Electronic Control Module (ECM) computer is located under the dash on the driver side of the vehicle.

Cruise Control

ADJUSTMENT

1. Remove the top cover from the actuator assembly.
2. Loosen the lock nuts on the cable.
3. Adjust the cable so the play range is between 0.04–0.08 in. when the actuator lever is fully closed.
4. Tighten the lock nut to 4 ft. lbs. and replace the top cover.

Flashers

LOCATION

The flashers are located under the driver side of the dashboard.

ENGINE COOLING

Radiator

REMOVAL AND INSTALLATION

1. Disconnect the negative battery cable.

2. Drain the cooling system.
3. Disconnect and plug the transmission cooler lines, if equipped.
4. Loosen the water pump drive belt tension.
5. Remove the cooling fan and radiator shroud.
6. Disconnect the water hoses to the radiator.
7. Remove the radiator retaining bolts and remove the radiator.
To install:
8. Replace the radiator mounting bolts and install the radiator.
9. Reconnect the water hoses to the radiator.
10. Install the cooling fan and radiator shroud.
11. Tighten the water pump drive belt to the proper tension.
12. Reconnect the transmission cooler lines, if necessary to the radiator.
13. Refill the cooling system.
14. Reconnect the negative battery cable.

Heater Core

REMOVAL AND INSTALLATION

1. Disconnect the negative battery cable. Drain the cooling system.
2. Disconnect the 2 heater hoses from the heater case.
3. Remove the steering wheel. Disconnect the lead wires from the ignition and combination switches.
4. Disconnect the wiring harness and remove the instrument panel.
5. Disconnect all the wiring connections and cables from the heater controls.
6. Disconnect the defroster duct and speedometer cable retaining bracket from the heater case.
7. Remove the heater assembly and remove the heater core.
To install:
8. Install the heater core and install the heater assembly.
9. Reconnect the defroster duct and speedometer cable retaining bracket to the heater case.
10. Reconnect the wiring connections and cables to the heater controls.
11. Reconnect the wiring harness and install the instrument panel.
12. Connect the lead wires to the ignition and combination switches.
13. Connect the heater hoses to the heater core.
14. Refill the cooling system with the proper coolant and replace the negative battery cable.

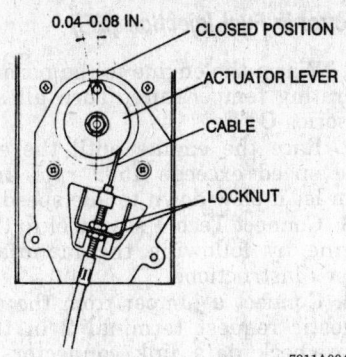

Cruise control adjustment

Water Pump

REMOVAL AND INSTALLATION

1. Disconnect the negative battery cable.

2. Drain the cooling system.

3. Loosen the drive belt tension and remove the drive belt. If equipped, loosen the air conditioning belt tension and remove the air conditioning belt.

4. Remove the radiator fan shroud mounting bolts and radiator fan mounting bolts. Remove the radiator shroud, fan and water pump pulley from the vehicle.

5. Remove the crankshaft pulley bolts and remove the crankshaft pulley.

NOTE: The crankshaft pulley bolt can be removed without removing the center crankshaft bolt.

6. Remove the timing belt cover mounting bolts and remove the cover.

7. Loosen the timing belt tensioner adjusting bolt and pivot nut. Hold the tensioner to loosen the timing belt and remove the belt from the camshaft pulley.

8. Remove the timing belt tensioner mounting bolts and remove the tensioner plate and spring.

9. Remove the water pump mounting bolts and remove the water pump assembly.

10. Remove the dipstick tube and the alternator bracket from the vehicle.

To install:

11. Clean and inspect the surface of the engine before installation.

12. Using a new gasket, install the new water pump on the engine. Torque the mounting bolts to 7.5–9.0 ft. lbs.

13. Install the dipstick tube and the alternator bracket to the vehicle.

14. Install the rubber seals between the water pump to cylinder head and water pump to oil pump.

15. Install the timing belt tensioner plate, tensioner and spring.

16. Align the marks on the timing belt and the camshaft sprocket. Install the timing belt in the same position on the camshaft sprocket as when removed.

17. Adjust the timing belt to be free of any slack. Torque the tensioner bolts to 7.5–9.0 ft. lbs.

18. Install the crankshaft and water pump pulleys. Torque the crankshaft and water pulley bolts to 7.5–9.0 ft. lbs.

19. Install the timing belt cover, cooling fan/clutch, shroud and drive belt. Adjust the belt tension.

20. As required, adjust the intake and exhaust valve lash.

21. Refill the cooling system with the proper coolant and replace the negative battery cable.

Thermostat

REMOVAL AND INSTALLATION

1. Disconnect the negative battery cable.

2. Drain the cooling system.

3. Disconnect the thermostat cap from the intake manifold and remove the thermostat.

To install:

4. Clean and inspect the surfaces of the housing and the engine.

5. Install the new thermostat with the spring facing towards the engine.

6. Install a new gasket and the thermostat cap to the intake manifold.

7. Refill the cooling system with the proper coolant and replace the negative battery cable.

COOLING SYSTEM BLEEDING

In the top portion of the thermostat, an air bleed valve is provided. This valve is for venting air, if any, that is accumulated in the system.

FUEL SYSTEM

Fuel System Service Precaution

When working with the fuel system, certain precautions should be taken; always work in a well ventilated area, keep a dry chemical (Class B) fire extinguisher near the work area. Always disconnect the negative battery cable and do not make any repairs to the fuel system until all the necessary steps for repair have been reviewed.

RELIEVING FUEL SYSTEM PRESSURE

The fuel pressure must be relieved before performing any service on the fuel system.

1. Disconnect the negative battery cable.

2. Remove the fuel filler cap from the fuel filler neck to release the fuel vapor pressure in the fuel tank. Reinstall the fuel cap.

3. Raise and support the vehicle safely.

4. Place an appropriate container under the fuel filter.

5. Cover the plug bolt on the fuel filter inlet union bolt with a rag and loosen the plug bolt slowly to release the fuel pressure gradually.

6. When the pressure has been released, tighten the plug bolt to 7.5 ft. lbs. so the fuel does not leak.

7. Lower the vehicle.

8. Reconnect the negative battery cable.

Fuel Filter

REMOVAL AND INSTALLATION

1. Disconnect the negative battery cable.

2. Remove the fuel filler cap to release the fuel vapor pressure in the fuel tank. After releasing pressure, reinstall filler cap.

3. Raise and support the vehicle safely.

4. Release the fuel pressure.

5. Disconnect the inlet and outlet hoses from the fuel filter.

6. Remove the fuel filter from the chassis frame.

To install:

7. Install the new fuel filter to the frame and connect the inlet and outlet hoses.

8. Lower the vehicle and connect the negative battery terminal.

Electric Fuel Pump

PRESSURE TESTING

1. Remove the fuel filler cap to release the fuel vapor pressure in the fuel tank. Reinstall the cap.

2. Raise and support the vehicle safely.

3. Release the fuel pressure in the fuel feed line.

4. Remove the plug bolt on the fuel filter union bolt and connect the proper fuel pressure gauge to the fuel filter inlet union bolt.

NOTE: If the pressure in the fuel tank is not released prior to system service, the fuel in the fuel tank may be forced out through the fuel hoses during disconnection.

5. Start the engine and warm to the proper operating temperature.

6. Measure the fuel pressure. At a specified idle speed or with the fuel pump operating and the engine stopped the fuel pressure should read: 34.1–39.8 psi. Within 1 minute after the fuel pump has stopped the fuel pressure should read: 21.3 psi.

7. Release the fuel pressure and remove the fuel pressure gauge.

8. Install the plug bolt to the fuel filter inlet bolt. Use a new gasket.

9. Start the engine and check for leaks.

10. Lower the vehicle.

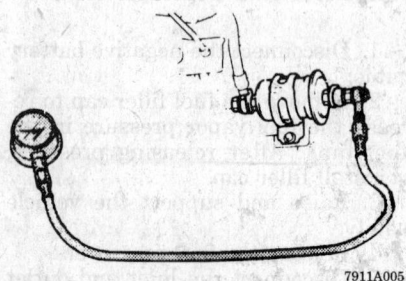

7911A005

Checking fuel pump pressure

REMOVAL AND INSTALLATION

NOTE: The fuel pump is located in the fuel tank. The fuel pump and the fuel gauge sending unit are located on the upper part of the fuel tank.

1. Disconnect the negative battery cable.

2. Remove the rear bumper assembly.

3. Disconnect the fuel gauge sending unit and fuel pump electrical connectors from the fuel tank.

4. Relieve the fuel system pressure.

5. Disconnect the fuel tank filler hose cover, filler hose and fuel tank inlet valve (breather hose).

6. Disconnect the inlet pipe from the fuel filter and remove the fuel vapor and return hoses.

7. If necessary, drain the fuel from the tank using a hand operating pump.

8. Disconnect the fuel tank protector and remove the fuel tank and cover from the vehicle.

9. Remove the fuel pump from the fuel tank.

To install:

10. Install the fuel pump to the fuel tank using a new gasket.

11. Install the fuel tank and cover to the vehicle and connect the fuel tank protector.

12. Replace the fuel vapor and return hoses and connect the inlet pipe to the fuel filter.

13. Reconnect the fuel tank inlet valve (breather hose), filler hose and fuel tank filler hose cover.

14. Connect the fuel pump and fuel gauge sending sending unit electrical connectors to the fuel tank.

15. Replace the bumper assembly and reconnect the negative battery cable.

16. If necessary, refill the fuel tank with any fuel that had been drained.

17. Start the engine and check for leaks when finished.

Fuel Injection

IDLE SPEED ADJUSTMENT

NOTE: Before starting the engine, place the gear shift lever in neutral for manual transmission or P for automatic transmission. Set the parking brake and block the drive wheels.

Electronic Fuel Injection (EFI)

1. Warm the engine to the normal operating temperature. Turn all accessories **OFF**.

2. Race the engine until the engine speed exceeds 1500 rpm and than let it slow down to idle speed.

3. Connect Tech 1 scan tool to the engine by following the manufacturer's instructions.

4. Connect a jumper from the diagnostic request terminal **2** in the duty check data link connector to ground terminal **3**.

5. Check the idle speed and Idle Air Control (IAC) duty; the IAC duty should read 50 percent with the correct idle speed.

6. If the idle speed is not 750–850 rpm, turn the idle speed/idle air control duty adjusting screw until it is correct.

7. Turn the A/C switch and the blower speed selector switch **ON**. If the idle speed is not 950–1050 rpm, check the A/C idle-up circuit or IAC valve.

8. Remove the jumper wire from the duty check Data Link Connector (DLC).

9. Disconnect the Tech 1 scan tool and install the idle speed adjusting screw cover.

Multiport Fuel Injection (MFI)

1. Warm the engine to the normal operating temperature. Turn all accessories **OFF**.

2. Race the engine until the engine speed exceeds 1500 rpm and than let it slow down to idle speed.

3. Connect Tech 1 scan tool to the engine by following the manufacturer's instructions.

4. Connect a jumper from the diagnostic request terminal **2** in the duty check data link connector to ground terminal **4**.

5. Check the idle speed and Idle Air Control (IAC) duty; the IAC duty should read 50 percent with the correct idle speed.

6. If the idle speed is not 750–850 rpm, turn the idle speed/idle air control duty adjusting screw until it is correct.

7. Remove the jumper wire from the duty check data link connector. Disconnect the Tech 1 scan tool and install the idle speed/idle air control duty adjusting screw cover.

8. Turn the A/C switch and the blower speed selector switch **ON**. If the idle speed is not 950–1050 rpm, check the A/C idle-up circuit or IAC valve circuit.

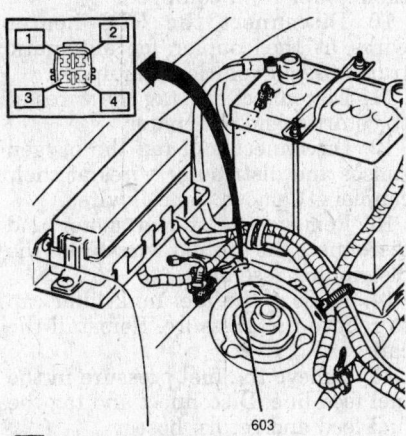

1	DUTY CHECK TERMINAL
2	DIAGNOSTIC REQUEST TERMINAL
3	GROUND TERMINAL
4	TEST SWITCH TERMINAL
603	DUTY CHECK DATA LINK CONNECTOR (DLC)

8547Z002

Duty Check Data Link Connector (DLC) — Electronic Fuel Injection (EFI) system

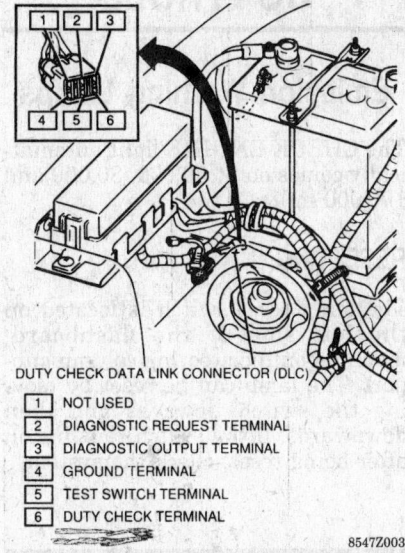

DUTY CHECK DATA LINK CONNECTOR (DLC)

1	NOT USED
2	DIAGNOSTIC REQUEST TERMINAL
3	DIAGNOSTIC OUTPUT TERMINAL
4	GROUND TERMINAL
5	TEST SWITCH TERMINAL
6	DUTY CHECK TERMINAL

8547Z003

Duty Check Data Link Connector (DLC) — Multiport Fuel Injection (MFI) system

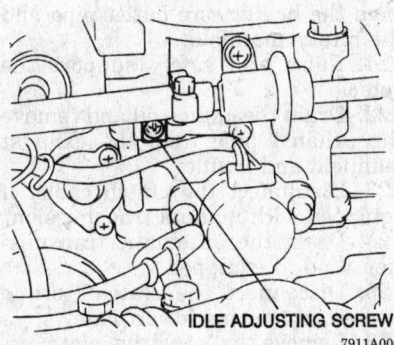

IDLE ADJUSTING SCREW

7911A006

Idle speed adjustment — Electronic Fuel Injection (EFI) system

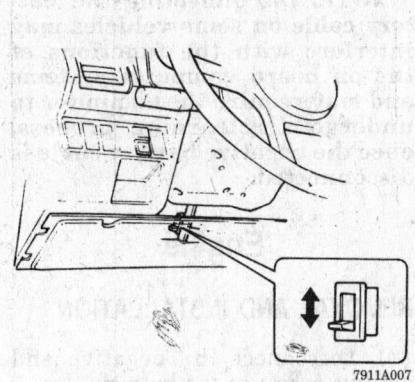

7911A007

Resetting the check engine light

THROTTLE OPENER ADJUSTMENT

NOTE: Before starting the engine, place the gear shift lever in neutral for manual transmission or P for automatic transmission. Set the parking brake and block the drive wheels.

Electronic Fuel Injection (EFI)

1. Warm the engine to the normal operating temperature. Turn all accessories **OFF**.

2. Race the engine until the engine speed exceeds 1500 rpm and than let it slow down to idle speed.

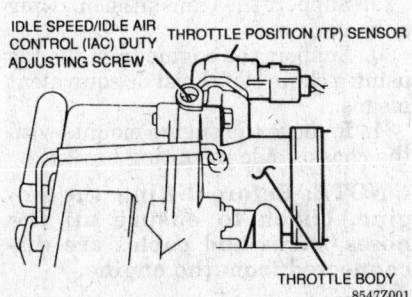

IDLE SPEED/IDLE AIR CONTROL (IAC) DUTY ADJUSTING SCREW   THROTTLE POSITION (TP) SENSOR

THROTTLE BODY

8547Z001

Idle adjustment — Multiport Fuel Injection (MFI) system

3. Connect Tech 1 scan tool to the engine by following the manufacturer's instructions.

4. Disconnect the vacuum hose from the throttle opener and plug the disconnected vacuum hose.

5. If the idle speed is not 2100–2300 rpm, turn the throttle opener adjusting screw until it is correct.

6. Reconnect the vacuum hose to the throttle opener. Disconnect the Tech 1 scan tool.

Fuel Injector

REMOVAL AND INSTALLATION

Electronic Fuel Injection (EFI)

1. Disconnect the negative battery cable.

2. Release the fuel pressure in the fuel feed line.

3. Remove the the air intake case from the throttle body.

4. Remove the fuel feed pipe clamp from the intake manifold and disconnect the fuel feed pipe from the throttle body.

5. Remove the injector cover.

6. Disconnect the injector coupler, release its wire harness from the clamp and remove its grommet from the throttle body.

7. Place a cloth over the injector and a hand on top of it. Using an air gun, blow low pressure compressed air into the fuel inlet port of the throttle body, and the injector can be removed.

NOTE: Be precise about the pressure of the compressed air. Using excessively high pressure may force the injector to jump out and may cause damage, not only to the injector itself but also to other parts.

To install:

8. Apply thin coating of gasoline to O-rings and then install the fuel injector to the throttle body.

9. Connect fuel injector wire connector and install injector cover.

10. Connect fuel feed pipe to throttle body.

11. Connect the negative battery cable and turn the ignition **ON** for 3 seconds and then **OFF** until fuel pressure is felt at the return hose.

12. Install air intake case assembly.

13. Secure all wires and check for any leaks in the system.

Multiport Fuel Injection (MFI)

1. Disconnect the negative battery cable. Release the fuel pressure in the fuel feed line.

2. Remove the the air intake case from the throttle body. Remove the throttle body.

3. Remove the Exhaust Gas Recirculation (EGR) modulator from the EGR modulator bracket.

4. Remove the 2 bolts and the EGR modulator bracket from the intake manifold.

5. Disconnect the 4 fuel injector connectors. Remove the 2 bolts and fuel pressure regulator from the fuel rail.

6. Remove the fuel pulsation damper and fuel feed pipe from the fuel rail.

7. Remove the 3 bolts and the fuel rail from the intake manifold. Remove the 4 fuel injectors from the intake manifold.

To install:

8. Install new O-rings onto the fuel injectors; be careful not to damage the O-rings. Install the grommets onto the fuel injectors.

NOTE: Inspect the insulators for breakage or scoring. If necessary, replace them.

9. Install the insulators and cushions to the intake manifold.

10. Lubricate the O-rings with fuel and install the injectors onto the fuel rail and then the whole assembly to the intake manifold.

NOTE: Make sure the fuel injectors rotate smoothly. If not, an O-ring may be installed incorrectly; replace it.

11. Install the 3 fuel rail bolts and torque to 13–20 ft. lbs. (18–28 Nm).

12. Lubricate the new gaskets with fuel. Install the fuel feed pipe, fuel pulsation damper and fuel rail. Torque the fuel pulsation damper bolts to 18.5–25 ft. lbs. (25–35 Nm).

13. Install the fuel pressure regulator and torque the bolts to 6–8.5 ft. lbs. (8–12 Nm).

14. Connect the 4 fuel injectors. Install the EGR modulator bracket and torque the bracket-to-intake manifold bolts to 17 ft. lbs. (23 Nm).

15. Install the EGR modulator to the EGR bracket. Install the throttle body.

EMISSION CONTROLS

Emission Warning Lamps

The CHECK ENGINE light automatically comes on at 50,000, 80,000 and 100,000 miles.

RESETTING

The lamp reset switch is located on the left side of the dashboard, mounted on the steering column support. The lamp can be reset by moving the switch upwards and then downwards. If the switch remains on after being reset, check the system.

ENGINE MECHANICAL

NOTE: Disconnecting the battery cable on some vehicles may interfere with the functions of the on board computer systems and may require the computer to undergo a relearning process, once the negative battery cable is disconnected.

Engine

REMOVAL AND INSTALLATION

1. Disconnect the negative and positive cables at the battery.

2. Remove the hood from the vehicle and drain the cooling system.

3. Remove the radiator reservoir tank, fan shroud, cooling fan and radiator.

4. Properly discharge the air conditioning system and remove the air conditioning condenser, if equipped.

5. Remove the air cleaner outlet hose.

6. Disconnect the accelerator and the automatic transmission kickdown cable from the throttle body, if equipped.

7. Disconnect and tag the throttle opener VSV and EGR VSV wires at the coupler.

8. Disconnect and tag the water temperature, oil pressure, air temperature and ground cable wires at the intake manifold.

9. Disconnect and tag the injector, throttle position sensor and idle speed control solenoid valve wires at their couplers, if equipped.

10. Disconnect the PTC heater wires at the coupler for automatic transmission vehicle, if equipped.

11. Disconnect and tag the wires at the starter and alternator.

12. Disconnect and tag the oxygen sensor and distributor wires at their couplers. Remove the coil wire.

13. Remove the starter motor and disconnect the ground wires from the distributor assembly.

14. Remove the fuel tank filler cap to relieve the pressure. Reinstall the cap.

15. Relieve the fuel pressure in the fuel feed line. Disconnect and tag the fuel feed and return hoses.

16. Remove the gear shift lever mounting bolts and remove the shifter.

17. Disconnect the canister purge hose and remove the pressure sensor hose from the fuel filter, if equipped.

18. Disconnect the brake booster hose from the intake manifold.

19. Remove the vacuum hose for the automatic transmission from the intake manifold, if equipped.

20. Disconnect the heater hoses from the heater core outlet pipe and the intake manifold.

21. Raise and safely support the vehicle.

22. Drain the engine oil and remove the exhaust pipe from the exhaust manifold and muffler.

23. Disconnect the clutch cable, if equipped with manual transmission.

24. Drain the automatic transmission fluid, if equipped.

25. Disconnect the clutch (torque converter) housing lower plate.

26. Remove the lock drive plate, using the special tool, if equipped with automatic transmission.

27. Lower the vehicle.

28. Remove the nuts and bolts fastening the cylinder block and transmission.

29. Support the transmission, using a stand or jack.

30. Support the engine from the top using a chain type hoist or equivalent means.

31. Remove the engine mounts with the chassis side mounting brackets.

NOTE: Before lifting the engine, check to ensure all the hoses, wires and cables are disconnected from the engine.

32. Remove the engine assembly from the chassis and transmission by sliding towards the front side and carefully hoist the engine.

To install:

33. Install the engine into the engine compartment and connect to the transmission.

34. Replace the engine mounts with the chassis side mounting brackets. Tighten to 41 ft. lbs.

35. Remove the lifting device.

36. Install the nuts and bolts fastening the cylinder block and transmission.

37. Raise and safely support the vehicle.

38. Replace the lock driveplate, if equipped.

39. Connect the clutch (torque converter) housing lower plate.

40. Connect the automatic transmission lines, if equipped.

41. Reconnect the clutch cable to the bracket, if equipped with manual transmission.

42. Replace the exhaust pipe to the exhaust manifold and muffler.

43. Lower the vehicle.

44. Reconnect the heater hoses to the heater core outlet pipe and the intake manifold.

45. Install the vacuum hose for the automatic transmission to the intake manifold, if equipped.

46. Reconnect the brake booster hose to the intake manifold.

47. Replace the pressure sensor hose to the fuel filter and connect the canister purge hose, if equipped.

48. Replace the fuel return and feed hoses.

49. Install the starter motor and connect the ground wire to the distributor.

50. Replace the coil wire and connect the oxygen sensor and distributor wires to their couplers.

51. Reconnect the wires at the alternator and starter motor.

52. Replace the PTC heater wires at the coupler, if equipped with automatic transmission.

53. Install the idle speed control solenoid valve, throttle position sensor and injector wires at their couplers, if equipped.

54. Connect the ground cable, air temperature, oil pressure and water temperature wires to the intake manifold.

55. Reconnect the throttle opener VSR and EGR VSR wires to their couplers, if equipped.

56. Connect the accelerator cable and the automatic transmission kickdown cable, if equipped, to the throttle body.

57. Replace the air cleaner outlet hose. Refill the engine oil and the transmission oil to the proper lever.

58. Replace the air conditioning condenser and properly recharge the air conditioning system, if equipped.

59. Replace the radiator, cooling fan, fan shroud and radiator reservoir tank.

60. Replace the hood and refill the cooling system with the proper coolant.

61. Reconnect the positive and negative battery cables.

62. Adjust the accelerator, clutch and the automatic transmission kickdown cable, if equipped.

63. Before starting the engine, check to see if all the parts disassembled are back in place securely.

64. Start the engine and check the timing. Check for any oil leaks.

Cylinder Head

REMOVAL AND INSTALLATION

Electronic Fuel Injection (EFI)

1. Disconnect the negative battery cable. Drain the cooling system.

2. Disconnect the air intake case.

3. Disconnect the brake booster hose from the intake manifold and the air valve water hose from the throttle body.

4. Disconnect the accelerator and the automatic transmission kickdown cable, if equipped, from the throttle body.

5. Disconnect and tag the throttle opener VSV and EGR VSV wires at the coupler.

6. Disconnect and tag the water temperature, oil pressure, air temperature sensor and ground cable wires at the intake manifold.

7. Disconnect and tag the injector, throttle position sensor and idle speed control solenoid valve wires at their couplers, if equipped.

8. Disconnect the PTC heater wires at the coupler, if equipped with automatic transmission.

9. Disconnect and tag the oxygen sensor and distributor wires at their couplers. Remove the coil wire.

10. Disconnect the ground wires from the distributor assembly.

11. Remove the fuel tank filler cap to relieve the pressure. Reinstall the cap.

12. Release the fuel pressure in the fuel feed line.

13. Disconnect the fuel feed and return hoses.

14. Disconnect the canister purge hose and remove the pressure sensor hose from the fuel filter, if equipped.

15. Remove the vacuum hose for the automatic transmission from the intake manifold, if equipped.

16. Disconnect the radiator cooling fan, fan shroud, water pump drive belt and water pump pulley.

17. Disconnect the crankshaft pulley, timing belt cover and the timing belt.

18. Raise and safely support the vehicle.

19. Disconnect the exhaust pipe from the exhaust manifold and lower the vehicle.

20. Disconnect the air conditioning compressor adjusting arm, if equipped.

21. Remove the cylinder head cover mounting bolts and remove the cylinder head cover.

22. Loosen all the valve adjusting screw locknuts, turn the adjusting screws back all the way to allow all the valves to close.

23. Remove the intake manifold from the cylinder head.

24. Remove the distributor and distributor housing from the cylinder head.

25. Remove the cylinder head mounting bolts and remove the cylinder head from the engine.

26. Remove any oil and water in the cylinder bores and on top of the pistons.

27. Clean and inspect the sealing surfaces of the cylinder head and the engine block.

To install:

28. Install the cylinder head using a new gasket.

29. Replace the cylinder head mounting bolts, using 3 steps, in sequence, and tighten to 46–54 ft. lbs.

30. Install the distributor and distributor housing to the cylinder head.

31. Replace the intake manifold on the cylinder head.

32. Tighten all the valve adjusting screw nuts.

33. Adjust the valve lash.

34. Replace the cylinder head cover and connect the air conditioning compressor adjusting arm, if equipped.

35. Raise and safely support the vehicle.

36. Connect the exhaust pipe to the exhaust manifold and safely lower the vehicle.

37. Reconnect the timing belt, timing belt cover and crankshaft pulley.

38. Replace the water pump pulley, water pump drive belt, fan shroud and the radiator cooling fan.

39. Replace the vacuum hose for the automatic transmission to the intake manifold, if equipped.

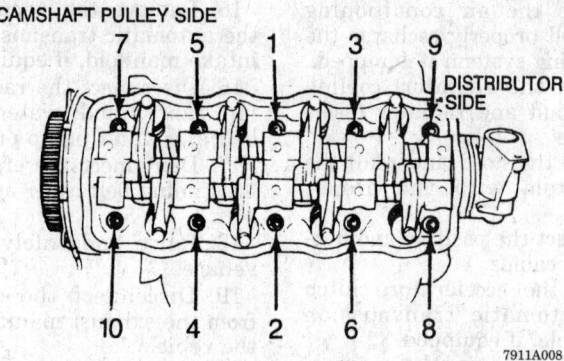

CAMSHAFT PULLEY SIDE

DISTRIBUTOR SIDE

7911A008

Cylinder head and bolt tightening sequence — Electronic Fuel Injection (EFI)

40. Replace the pressure sensor hose to the fuel filter and connect the canister purge hose, if equipped.

41. Replace the fuel return and feed hoses.

42. Connect the ground wires to the distributor assembly.

43. Replace the coil wire. Connect the oxygen sensor and distributor wires to their couplers.

44. Connect the PTC wires to the coupler.

45. Connect the idle speed control valve, throttle position sensor and injector wires to their couplers, if equipped.

46. Reconnect the ground cable, air temperature, oil pressure and water temperature sensor wires to the intake manifold.

47. Replace the throttle opener VSV and EGR VSV wires to their couplers.

48. Connect the accelerator and the automatic transmission kickdown cables, if equipped, to the throttle body.

49. Replace the air valve water hose to the throttle body and connect the brake booster hose to intake manifold.

50. Reconnect the air intake case.

51. Refill the cooling system with the proper coolant and connect the negative battery.

52. Check for any water and oil leaks when finished.

Multiport Fuel Injection (MFI)

1. Disconnect the negative battery cable. Release the fuel pressure. Remove the fuel filler cap to release the pressure in the tank, then replace the fuel filler cap.

2. Drain the cooling system. Disconnect the air intake pipe from the ACL intake hose and throttle hose.

3. Remove the throttle cover-to-intake manifold bolts and the cover.

4. If equipped with an automatic transmission, disconnect the accelerator and kickdown cables from the throttle body bellcrank.

5. Remove 1 bolt, nut, screw and accelerator cable bracket from the throttle body.

6. Disconnect the electrical connectors from the following items:
Throttle Position (TP) sensor
Idle Air Control (IAC) valve
Engine Coolant Temperature (ECT) sensor
ECT sending unit
A/C ECT switch (if equipped with A/C)
Evaporative Emissions Solenoid Purge (EVAP SP) valve
Exhaust Gas Recirculation (EGR) temperature sensor (Calif. vehicles)
EGR solenoid vacuum valve
Fuel injectors
Engine ground wire from intake surge tank

7. Disconnect the following vacuum hoses:
EVAP SP valve
Vacuum modulator supply hose (if equipped with automatic transmission)
Brake booster supply hose
EGR valve
EGR valve modulator

8. Disconnect the coolant hose from the IAC valve and the IAC hose from the IAC valve. Disconnect the coolant hoses from the fast idle air valve below the throttle body.

9. Disconnect the fuel feed hose at the fuel feed hose union and the fuel feed hose from the fuel return line. Disconnect the PCV hose from the PCV valve.

10. Loosen the upper radiator hose clamp at the thermostat housing. Disconnect the upper radiator hose from the thermostat housing. Disconnect the coolant bypass hose from the intake manifold.

11. Remove the generator adjusting arm bracket from the intake manifold. Remove the front and rear intake manifold reinforcement brackets from the intake manifold.

12. Remove the lower intake manifold support bracket from the intake manifold. Remove the intake manifold-to-cylinder head nuts/bolts, then remove the intake manifold, the intake surge tank and the throttle body from the cylinder head.

13. Remove the upper exhaust manifold heat shield from the exhaust manifold. Raise and safely support the vehicle.

14. Remove the exhaust manifold reinforcement bracket from the exhaust manifold and engine mount.

15. Remove the lower exhaust manifold heat shield from the exhaust manifold. Disconnect the Three-Way Catalytic converter (TWC) assembly from the exhaust manifold. Lower the vehicle.

16. Remove the exhaust manifold with gasket and engine hanger from the cylinder head.

17. If equipped, loosen the upper and lower A/C compressor mounting bolts. Loosen the upper and lower power steering pump mounting bolts. Remove the A/C compressor, If equipped, and/or the power steering drive belt.

18. Loosen the upper and lower generator mounting bolts. Remove the generator/water pump drive belt from the pulleys. Remove the cooling fan and the water pump pulley from the water pump.

19. Raise and safely support the vehicle. If equipped, remove the skid plate from the undercarriage. Remove the 2 lower radiator shroud bolts and lower the vehicle.

20. If equipped, remove the 2 A/C suction line bracket bolts at the right side of the radiator core support and carefully reposition the suction line for radiator shroud removal access.

21. Remove the 2 upper radiator shroud bolts and the shroud from the radiator.

NOTE: If the shroud is difficult to remove, drain the cooling system and disconnect the upper radiator hose from the radiator to gain access. If is not necessary to remove the crankshaft center bolt when removing the crankshaft pulley.

22. Remove the 5 crankshaft pulley-to-crankshaft bolts and the pulley. Remove the oil pressure sending unit wire conduit from the timing belt cover.

23. To remove the timing belt, perform the following procedure:

   a. Remove the timing belt cover from the engine.

NOTE: There are 2 sets of timing marks which must be aligned to ensure correct engine timing upon installation. A notch in the camshaft timing belt gear designated as "E" must be aligned with the notch in the cylinder head. A punch mark on the crankshaft timing belt gear should align with the arrow in the oil pump casting. Make sure to align both sets of marks prior to timing belt removal.

   b. Rotate the engine to align the timing marks on the cylinder head cover and camshaft timing belt gear; this should align the timing marks on the oil pump casting and crankshaft timing belt gear.

   c. Loosen the timing belt tensioner bolt. Remove the timing belt tensioner spring from the timing belt tensioner plate.

   d. Remove the timing belt from the camshaft and crankshaft timing belt gears.

24. Secure the camshaft sprocket, using tool J-41840 or equivalent, then remove the camshaft sprocket-to-camshaft bolt and the camshaft sprocket.

25. Remove the 2 inner timing belt cover-to-cylinder head bolts and the cover. Remove the 2 A/C compressor mounting bracket-to-cylinder head bolts and the bracket.

26. Remove the distributor from the distributor case. Remove the 6 cylinder head cover-to-cylinder head bolts and the cover. Remove the cylinder head cover gasket and O-rings from the cylinder head cover.

NOTE: A small amount of oil may drain from the distributor case upon removal from the cylinder head. Place a suitable container under the distributor case or use a shop towel to catch and absorb the oil.

27. Remove the 3 distributor case-to-cylinder head bolts and the distributor case.

28. Loosen all valve adjusting screw locknuts. Loosen all valve adjusting screws until all rocker arms move freely.

NOTE: Always loosen the camshaft carrier bolts gradually in sequence, in order to relieve tension on the camshaft; if the camshaft carrier bolts are removed at random, damage to the camshaft may occur.

29. Remove the 12 camshaft carrier cap-to-cylinder head bolts, the camshaft carrier bolts, the camshaft seal and the camshaft.

NOTE: Loosen the cylinder head bolts gradually in sequence, in order to prevent cylinder head distortion.

30. Remove the 10 cylinder head-to-block bolts, the cylinder head and gasket.

31. Clean and inspect all of the gasket mating surfaces. Inspect and/or replace any damaged parts.

   To install:

32. Install a new cylinder head gasket and the cylinder head with the distributor case onto the cylinder block. Torque the cylinder head bolts in sequence, as follows:
   Step 1: 26 ft. lbs. (35 Nm)
   Step 2: 41 ft. lbs. (55 Nm)
   Step 3: 52 ft. lbs. (70 Nm)

33. Lubricate the camshaft with clean oil. Apply RTV silicone rubber sealant to the bottom of the No. 6 camshaft carrier cap.

34. Install the camshaft and camshaft carrier caps onto the cylinder head, then, torque the camshaft carrier cap-to-cylinder head bolts to 89 inch lbs. (10 Nm).

NOTE: Always tighten the camshaft carrier cap bolts gradually in sequence; if the camshaft carrier cap bolts are tightened at random. damage to the camshaft may occur.

35. Lubricate the new camshaft seal lip with clean engine oil. Install the new camshaft seal into the cylinder head until it is flush with the camshaft carrier surface. Adjust the valve lash.

36. Adjust the valve lash.

37. Apply RTV silicone rubber sealant to the surface of the distributor case that mates with the rear of the rocker arm shaft.

38. Install the distributor case onto the cylinder head and torque the distributor case-to-cylinder head bolts to 89 inch lbs. (10 Nm).

39. Install a new cylinder head cover gasket and 4 O-rings to the cylinder head cover. Install the cylinder head cover and torque the 6 bolts to 89 inch lbs. (10 Nm).

40. Install the distributor into the distributor case. Install the A/C mounting bracket with compressor and torque the 2 mounting bracket-to-cylinder head bolts to 89 inch lbs. (10 Nm).

41. Install the inner timing belt cover and torque the 2 bolts inner timing belt cover-to-cylinder head bolts to 89 inch lbs. (10 Nm).

NOTE: During camshaft timing belt gear installation, align the camshaft dwell pin with the slot in the camshaft timing belt gear designated as "E".

42. Install the camshaft sprocket, using holding tool J-41840 or equivalent, onto the camshaft and torque the camshaft sprocket-to-camshaft bolt to 44 ft. lbs. (60 Nm).

43. Install the timing belt tensioner plate and tensioner; secure with timing belt tensioner stud and bolt only finger-tight. Push the timing belt tensioner plate up when installing the timing belt.

NOTE: When installing the timing belt, the directional arrows on the timing belt must be matched with the rotation of the crankshaft; if not, excessive wear and timing belt failure may occur.

44. Install the timing belt by performing the following procedures:

   a. Align the timing marks of the camshaft sprocket with the cylinder head cover and the oil pump housing with the crankshaft sprocket.

   b. Install the timing belt onto the camshaft and crankshaft sprockets.

   c. Rotate the crankshaft throug' 2 complete revolutions, to remove any slack from the timing belt and to properly seat the timing belt.

   d. Inspect both sets of timing marks to ensure that they are aligned. Install the belt tensioner spring to the timing belt tensioner plate.

   e. Torque the timing belt tensioner stud to 89 inch lbs. (10 Nm) and the bolt to 18 ft. lbs. (25 Nm).

45. Install the timing belt cover and torque the nut/bolts to 89 inch lbs. (10 Nm). Connect the oil pressure sending unit wire to the timing belt cover.

46. Install the crankshaft pulley to the crankshaft and torque the bolts to 12 ft. lbs. (16 Nm). Install the radiator shroud and torque both bolts to 89 inch lbs. (10 Nm).

47. If equipped, carefully, position the A/C suction line and brackets to the right side of the radiator core support and torque both bolts to 89 inch lbs. (10 Nm).

48. Raise and safely support the vehicle. Install the 2 lower radiator shroud bolts and torque to 89 inch lbs. (10 Nm). If equipped, install the front skid plate and torque the 4 bolts to 40 ft. lbs. (54 Nm). Lower the vehicle.

49. Install the water pump pulley and fan; torque the 4 nuts to 97 inch lbs. (11 Nm). Install the generator/water pump drive belt onto the pulleys. Install the A/C compressor, if equipped, and the power steering drive belt.

50. Using new gaskets, install the exhaust manifold and torque the exhaust manifold-to-cylinder head nuts to 17 ft. lbs. (23 Nm). Raise and safely support the vehicle.

51. Using new gaskets, connect the front pipe/TWC assembly to the exhaust manifold and torque the 3 bolts to 37 ft. lbs. (50 Nm). Install the lower exhaust manifold heat shield and torque both bolts to 89 inch lbs. (10 Nm). Install the exhaust manifold bracket; torque the engine mount-to-exhaust bracket bolts to 40 ft. lbs. (54 Nm) and the exhaust bracket-to-exhaust manifold nut to 37 ft. lbs. (50 Nm). Lower the vehicle.

52. Install the upper exhaust manifold heat shield and torque the nuts/bolts to 89 inch lbs. (10 Nm). Install the air intake pipe bracket and torque the bracket-to-cylinder head bolts to 89 inch (10 Nm).

53. Using a new gasket, install the intake manifold, with intake surge tank and throttle body, and torque the intake manifold-to-cylinder head bolts, in sequence, to 17 ft. lbs. (23 'm).

54. Install the lower intake manifold support bracket, the rear and the front intake manifold reinforcement bracket; torque the brackets-to-intake manifold bolts to 37 ft. lbs. (50 Nm).

55. Install the generator adjusting arm bracket and torque the bracket-to-intake manifold nut/bolt to 37 ft. lbs. (50 Nm).

56. Install the following hoses:
Coolant bypass hose to the intake manifold.
Upper radiator hose to the thermostat housing; secure with a clamp.
PCV hose to the PCV valve.
Fuel return hose to the fuel return line.
Fuel feed hose at the fuel feed hose union.

Coolant hoses to the fast idle air valve below the throttle body.
IAC air hose to the IAC valve.
Coolant hose to the IAC valve.

57. Install the following vacuum hoses:
EGR valve modulator.
EGR valve.
Brake booster supply hose.
Vacuum modulator supply hose, if equipped with an automatic transmission.
EVAP SP valve.

58. Connect the following electrical connectors:
Engine ground wire to intake surge tank.
Fuel injectors.
EGR solenoid vacuum valve.
EGR temperature sensor, California vehicles.
Evaporative Emission Solenoid Purge (EVAP SP).
A/C ECT switch, if equipped with A/C.
ECT sensor sending unit.
Engine Coolant Temperature (ECT) sensor.
Idle Air Control (IAC).
Throttle Position (TP) sensor.

59. Install the accelerator cable bracket to the throttle body and torque the nut/bolt to 17 ft. lbs. (23 Nm).

60. If equipped with an automatic transmission, connect the accelerator cable and kickdown cable to the throttle body bellcrank; adjust the cables.

61. Install the throttle cover to the intake manifold and torque the bolts to 11 ft. lbs. (15 Nm). Refill the cooling system, as necessary.

62. Install the air intake pipe to the throttle body hose and the ACL intake hose. Connect the negative battery cable.

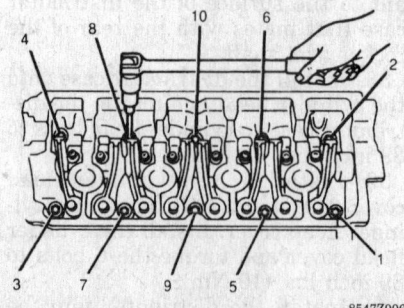

Cylinder head and bolt loosening sequence — Multiport Fuel Injection (MFI)

Valve Lash

ADJUSTMENT

Valve lash can be adjusted with the engine hot or cold. Specifications are provided for both adjustments.

1. Disconnect the negative battery cable. Remove the air intake case.
2. Remove the cylinder head cover assembly.
3. Turn the crankshaft clockwise so the **V** mark on the crankshaft pulley is aligned with the **0** mark on the timing belt cover.
4. Remove the distributor cap and confirm that the rotor is facing the No. 1 firing position. If the rotor is out of place, turn the crankshaft 360 degrees.
5. With the engine in this position, check the valve lash at valves 1, 2, 5 and 7. Clearance should be:

EFI engine
Cold
Intake 0.0051–0.0067 in. (0.13–0.17mm)
Exhaust 0.0063–0.0075 in. (0.15–0.19mm)
Hot
Intake 0.009–0.011 in. (0.23–0.27mm)
Exhaust 0.0102–0.0114 in. (0.25–0.29mm)
MFI engine
Cold
Intake 0.005–0.007 in. (0.13–0.17mm)
Exhaust 0.0053–0.007 in. (0.13–0.17mm)
Hot
Intake 0.007–0.008 in. (0.17–0.21mm)
Exhaust 0.007–0.008 in. (0.17–0.21mm)

NOTE: The valves are adjusted by loosening the locknut on the valve adjuster and turning the adjusting screw to obtain the proper clearance. Once the proper clearance is obtained, the locknut must be torqued to 11–13 ft. lbs. while holding the adjusting screw. Check the clearance after the locknut is torqued.

6. Rotate the crankshaft 360 degrees and check the valve lash at valves 3, 4, 6 and 8.
7. After adjusting and checking all the valves, install the cylinder head cover, distributor cover and intake hose. Connect the negative battery cable.

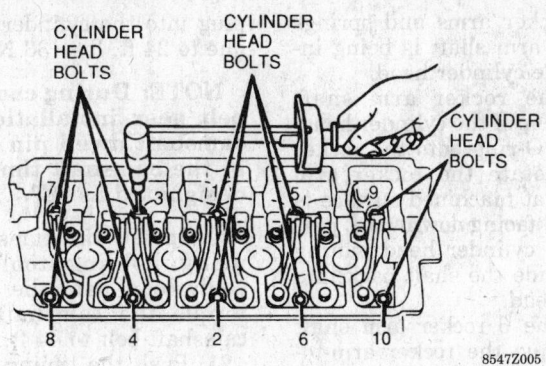

Cylinder head and bolt tightening sequence — Multiport Fuel Injection (MFI)

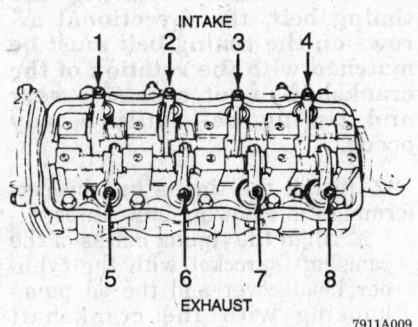

Valve lash adjustment — EFI engine

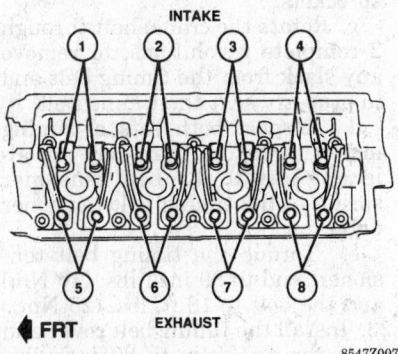

Valve lash adjustment — MFI engine

Rocker Arms/Shafts

REMOVAL AND INSTALLATION

EFI Engine

NOTE: The rocker arm shafts are not identical and must be kept in the proper order for installation. If the shafts get mixed up before installation, the intake rocker shaft has a 14mm stepped end and the exhaust rocker shaft has a 13mm stepped end. The

stepped end of the intake rocker shaft faces the front of the engine and the stepped end of the exhaust rocker shaft faces the rear of the engine.

1. Disconnect the negative battery cable. Drain the cooling system.
2. Remove the front grille.
3. Remove the radiator cooling fan and fan shroud. Properly discharge the air conditioning system and remove the air conditioning flexible suction hose, if equipped.
4. Remove the radiator.
5. Remove the water pump drive belt and the water pump pulley.
6. Remove the timing belt outside cover, timing belt and the tensioner.
7. Disconnect the air intake case and remove the cylinder head cover.
8. Remove the camshaft timing belt pulley and timing belt inside cover. Insert the proper size rod into the hole in the camshaft to lock the camshaft and loosen the pulley nut.
9. Loosen all the valve lash adjusting screw locknuts and turn the adjusting screws out all the way.
10. Remove the rocker arm shaft screws.
11. Remove the intake and exhaust rocker arm shafts, rocker arms and springs.

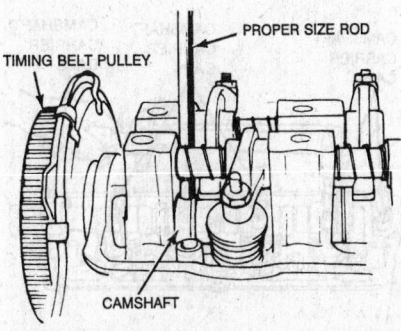

Locking the camshaft in position — EFI engine

12. Keep all the valve train parts in the order that they were removed.
   To install:
13. Apply engine oil to the rocker arms, springs and shafts. Install the shafts in the correct direction, into the cylinder head by placing the rocker arms and springs on the shafts as they are installed. With the rocker arms, springs and shafts installed, torque the rocker shaft mounting screws to 7.0–8.5 ft. lbs.
14. Install the timing belt pulley and inside cover by locking the camshaft with the proper size rod.
15. With the camshaft locked, tighten the camshaft pulley bolt to 41–46 ft. lbs.
16. The remainder of the installation is the reverse of the removal procedure.

MFI Engine

1. Disconnect the negative battery cable. Remove the front grille-to-radiator core support 3 screws and 2 clips and the grille. Remove the door latch-to-header panel bolts and the latch.
2. Disconnect the 2 electrical connectors from the horn. Remove the 12 header panel bolts and the panel from the vehicle.
3. Remove the radiator core support. Remove the timing belt from the engine.
4. Using the camshaft sprocket holding tool J-41840 or equivalent, to hold the sprocket stationary, remove the camshaft sprocket-to-camshaft bolt.
5. Remove the cylinder head cover. Remove the distributor case from the cylinder head.
6. Loosen all of the valve adjusting screw locknuts. Loosen all valve adjusting screws until the rocker arms move freely.

NOTE: Always remove the camshaft carrier bolts gradually, in sequence, in order to relieve tension on the camshaft; if the bolts are removed at random, damage may occur to the camshaft.

7. Gradually, remove the 12 camshaft carrier cap bolts, in sequence. Remove the camshaft carrier, the camshaft seal and the camshaft from the cylinder head.
8. Remove the timing belt inner cover-to-cylinder head bolts and the cover. Remove all intake rocker arms with clips from the rocker arm shaft.
9. Remove the 6 rocker arm shaft-to-cylinder head bolts. Push the rocker arm shaft through the rear of the cylinder head until the end of the

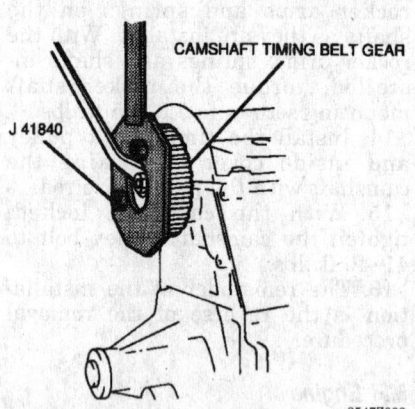

Locking the camshaft in position — MFI engine

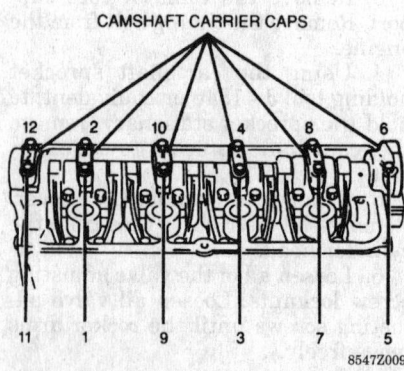

Removing camshaft carrier bolts — MFI engine

rocker arm shaft appears. Remove 1 O-ring from the rear of the rocker arm shaft.

10. Remove the exhaust rocker arms, rocker arm springs and rocker arm shaft by pulling the rocker arm shaft through the front of the cylinder head. Be sure to keep the parts in order for installation purposes.

11. Clean and inspect all of the parts for wear and/or damage; if necessary, replace the damaged parts.

To install:

12. Lubricate all of the parts with clean engine oil before installation.

13. Position the rocker arm shaft into the front of the cylinder head;

install the rocker arms and springs as the rocker arm shaft is being installed into the cylinder head.

14. Push the rocker arm shaft through the rear of the cylinder head. Install a new O-ring onto the rocker arm shaft. Rotate the rocker arm shaft so the flat machined surface is horizontal and facing downward, parallel with the cylinder head mating surface and slide the shaft back into the cylinder head.

15. Install the 6 rocker arm shaft bolts and torque the rocker arm-to-cylinder head bolts to 89 inch lbs. (10 Nm). Fill the rocker arm shaft bolt holes with clean engine oil.

16. Install the intake rocker arms with clips onto the rocker arm shaft.

NOTE: The camshaft carrier caps are embossed with numbers and arrows to ensure correct assembly. The No. 1 camshaft carrier cap must be installed at the front of the cylinder head with the remaining carrier caps following in numerical order. The directional arrows must always point toward the front of the cylinder head.

17. Lubricate the camshaft with clean engine oil. Apply RTV silicone sealant to the bottom of the No. 6 camshaft carrier cap. Install the camshaft and camshaft carrier caps onto the cylinder head and gradually, torque the 12 bolts, in sequence, to 89 inch lbs. (10 Nm); if the bolts are tightened at random, damage to the camshaft may occur.

18. Lubricate the new camshaft seal lip with clean engine oil and install it into the cylinder head until it is flush with the camshaft carrier surface.

19. Install the timing belt inner cover and torque the cover-to-cylinder head bolts to 89 inch lbs. (10 Nm). Install the rocker arm shaft

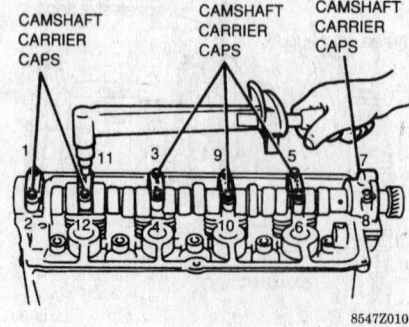

Torquing camshaft carrier bolts — MFI engine

plug into the cylinder head and torque to 24 ft. lbs. (33 Nm).

NOTE: During camshaft timing belt gear installation, align the camshaft dwell pin with the slot in the camshaft timing belt gear designated as "E".

20. Install the camshaft sprocket, using holding tool J-41840 or equivalent, onto the camshaft and torque the camshaft sprocket-to-camshaft bolt to 44 ft. lbs. (60 Nm).

21. Push the timing belt tensioner plate up when installing the timing belt.

NOTE: When installing the timing belt, the directional arrows on the timing belt must be matched with the rotation of the crankshaft; if not, excessive wear and timing belt failure may occur.

22. Install the timing belt by performing the following procedures:

a. Align the timing marks of the camshaft sprocket with the cylinder head cover and the oil pump housing with the crankshaft sprocket.

b. Install the timing belt onto the camshaft and crankshaft sprockets.

c. Rotate the crankshaft through 2 complete revolutions, to remove any slack from the timing belt and to properly seat the timing belt.

d. Inspect both sets of timing marks to ensure that they are aligned. Install the belt tensioner spring to the timing belt tensioner plate.

e. Torque the timing belt tensioner stud to 89 inch lbs. (10 Nm) and the bolt to 18 ft. lbs. (25 Nm).

23. Install the timing belt cover and torque the nut/bolts to 89 inch lbs. (10 Nm). Connect the oil pressure sending unit wire to the timing belt cover.

24. Apply RTV silicone rubber sealant to the surface of the distributor case that mates with the rear of the rocker arm shaft. Install the distributor case and torque the 3 case-to-cylinder head bolts to 89 inch lbs. (10 Nm).

25. Install the distributor into the distributor case. Adjust the valve lash.

26. Install the cylinder head cover onto the cylinder head. Install the radiator into the radiator core support.

27. Install the header panel and torque the 12 bolts to 89 inch lbs. (10 Nm). Connect the 2 electrical connectors to the horn.

28. Install the hood latch to the header panel and torque both bolts to 89 inch lbs. (10 Nm).

29. Install the front grille to the radiator core support. Connect the negative battery cable. Refill the cooling system. Start the engine, allow it to reach normal operating temperatures and check for leaks.

Intake Manifold

REMOVAL AND INSTALLATION

Electronic Fuel Injection (EFI)

1. Disconnect the negative battery cable. Drain the cooling system.

2. Remove the air intake case from the manifold.

3. Disconnect the accelerator cable and the automatic transmission kickdown cable, if equipped.

4. Disconnect the injector, throttle position sensor and idle speed control solenoid valve wires at their couplers, if equipped.

5. Disconnect the vacuum hoses from the throttle body and throttle opener. Remove the water hose from the air valve, if equipped.

6. Remove the fuel filler cap to release the fuel pressure in the fuel tank. Reinstall the cap.

7. Release the fuel pressure in the fuel line.

8. Disconnect the fuel line from the throttle body and intake manifold.

9. Remove the fuel return hose.

10. Disconnect the throttle body from the intake manifold and remove the PCV hose from the cylinder head cover.

11. Disconnect the pressure sensor hose from the fuel filter, if equipped, and remove the brake booster hose from the intake manifold.

12. Disconnect the vacuum hose for the automatic transmission from the intake manifold, if equipped.

13. Remove the VSV (for throttle opener) hose from the intake manifold.

14. Disconnect the water hose from the thermostat cap. Remove the heater inlet and water bypass hose from the intake manifold.

15. Disconnect the hoses at the EGR valve and remove the ground wire from the intake manifold.

16. Disconnect the wire couplers from the air temperature sensor, water temperature sensor, water temperature gauge and PTC heater, if equipped with automatic transmission.

17. Disconnect the wire harnesses from their clamps.

18. Remove the intake manifold mounting bolts and remove the intake manifold from the cylinder head.

19. Remove the PCV valve, EGR valve, fuel filter, thermostat from the intake manifold.

20. Clean and inspect the sealing surfaces of the intake manifold and the cylinder head.

To install:

21. Install the thermostat, fuel filter, EGR valve and PCV valve to the intake manifold.

22. Using a new gasket, install the intake manifold and tighten the mounting bolts to 13–20 ft. lbs.

23. Reconnect the wiring harnesses to their clamps and fasten the wire couplers to the air temperature sensor, water temperature sensor, water temperature gauge and PTC heater, if equipped with automatic transmission.

24. Reconnect the ground wire to the intake manifold and replace the hoses at the EGR valve.

25. Install the water heater inlet and bypass hose to the intake manifold. Replace the water hose to the thermostat cap.

26. Replace the VSV (for throttle opener) hose to the intake manifold.

27. Connect the automatic transmission vacuum hose to the intake manifold, if equipped.

28. Replace the brake booster hose to the intake manifold and connect the pressure sensor to the fuel filter, if equipped.

29. Reconnect the fuel line to the throttle body to the intake manifold.

30. Replace the water hose to the air valve. Connect the vacuum hoses to the throttle body and throttle opener, if equipped.

31. Reconnect the injector, throttle position sensor and idle speed control wires to their couplers, if equipped.

32. Connect the accelerator cable and the automatic transmission kickdown cable, if equipped, to the throttle body.

33. Install the air intake case to the manifold.

34. Refill the cooling system with the proper coolant. Connect the negative battery cable.

35. Check for vacuum, water and oil leaks when finished.

Multiport Fuel Injection (MFI)

1. Disconnect the negative battery cable. Release the fuel pressure. Remove the fuel filler cap to release the pressure in the tank, then replace the fuel filler cap.

2. Drain the cooling system. Disconnect the air intake pipe from the ACL intake hose and throttle hose.

3. Remove the throttle cover-to-intake manifold bolts and the cover.

4. If equipped with an automatic transmission, disconnect the accelerator and kickdown cables from the throttle body bellcrank.

5. Remove 1 bolt, nut, screw and accelerator cable bracket from the throttle body.

6. Disconnect the electrical connectors from the following items:
Throttle Position (TP) sensor
Idle Air Control (IAC) valve
Engine Coolant Temperature (ECT) sensor
ECT sending unit
A/C ECT switch (if equipped with A/C)
Evaporative Emissions Solenoid Purge (EVAP SP) valve
Exhaust Gas Recirculation (EGR) temperature sensor (Calif. vehicles)
EGR solenoid vacuum valve
Fuel injectors
Wiring harness from retaining clamps
Engine ground wire from intake surge tank

7. Disconnect the following vacuum hoses:
EVAP SP valve
Vacuum modulator supply hose (if equipped with automatic transmission)
Brake booster supply hose
EGR valve
EGR valve modulator

8. Disconnect the coolant hose from the IAC valve and the IAC hose from the IAC valve. Disconnect the coolant hoses from the fast idle air valve below the throttle body.

9. Disconnect the fuel feed hose at the fuel feed hose union and the fuel feed hose from the fuel return line. Disconnect the PCV hose from the PCV valve.

10. Loosen the upper radiator hose clamp at the thermostat housing. Disconnect the upper radiator hose from the thermostat housing. Disconnect the coolant bypass hose from the intake manifold.

11. Remove the generator adjusting arm bracket from the intake manifold. Remove the front and rear intake manifold reinforcement brackets from the intake manifold.

12. Remove the lower intake manifold support bracket from the intake manifold. Remove the intake manifold-to-cylinder head nuts/bolts, then remove the intake manifold, the intake surge tank and the throttle body from the cylinder head.

13. Remove the following items from the intake manifold, if necessary:

PCV valve

EGR valve

ECT sensor

ECT sensor sending unit

A/C ECT switch, if equipped with A/C

EGR temperature sensor, for California vehicles

14. Clean and inspect all of the gasket mating surfaces. Inspect and/or replace any damaged parts.

To install:

15. Install the following items onto the intake manifold, if removed:

PCV valve

EGR valve

ECT sensor

ECT sensor sending unit

A/C ECT switch, if equipped with A/C

EGR temperature sensor, for California vehicles

16. Using a new gasket, install the intake manifold, with intake surge tank and throttle body, and torque the intake manifold-to-cylinder head bolts, in sequence, to 17 ft. lbs. (23 Nm).

17. Install the lower intake manifold support bracket, the rear and the front intake manifold reinforcement bracket; torque the brackets-to-intake manifold bolts to 37 ft. lbs. (50 Nm).

18. Install the generator adjusting arm bracket and torque the bracket-to-intake manifold nut/bolt to 37 ft. lbs. (50 Nm).

19. Install the following hoses:

Coolant bypass hose to the intake manifold.

Upper radiator hose to the thermostat housing; secure with a clamp.

PCV hose to the PCV valve.

Fuel return hose to the fuel return line.

Fuel feed hose at the fuel feed hose union.

Coolant hoses to the fast idle air valve below the throttle body.

IAC air hose to the IAC valve.

Coolant hose to the IAC valve.

20. Install the following vacuum hoses:

EGR valve modulator.

EGR valve.

Brake booster supply hose.

Vacuum modulator supply hose, if equipped with an automatic transmission.

EVAP SP valve.

21. Connect the following electrical connectors:

Engine ground wire to intake surge tank.

Wiring harness to retaining clamps

Fuel injectors.

EGR solenoid vacuum valve.

EGR temperature sensor, California vehicles.

Evaporative Emission Solenoid Purge (EVAP SP).

A/C ECT switch, if equipped with A/C.

ECT sensor sending unit.

Engine Coolant Temperature (ECT) sensor.

Idle Air Control (IAC) valve.

Throttle Position (TP) sensor.

22. Install the accelerator cable bracket to the throttle body and torque the nut/bolt to 17 ft. lbs. (23 Nm).

23. If equipped with an automatic transmission, connect the accelerator cable and kickdown cable to the throttle body bellcrank; adjust the cables.

24. Install the throttle cover to the intake manifold and torque the bolts to 11 ft. lbs. (15 Nm). Refill the cooling system, as necessary.

25. Install the air intake pipe to the throttle body hose and the ACL intake hose. Connect the negative battery cable.

Exhaust Manifold

REMOVAL AND INSTALLATION

Electronic Fuel Injection (EFI)

1. Disconnect the negative cable.
2. Raise and safely support the vehicle.
3. Disconnect the exhaust pipe from the exhaust manifold and lower the vehicle.
4. Disconnect the oxygen sensor lead wire at the coupler and remove the air intake case bracket.
5. Disconnect the exhaust manifold upper and lower covers or heat shields from the exhaust manifold.
6. Remove the exhaust manifold mounting bolts and remove the exhaust manifold from the cylinder head.

To install:

7. Clean and inspect the sealing surfaces of the exhaust manifold and the cylinder head.
8. Using new gaskets, install the exhaust manifold to the cylinder head and tighten the mounting bolts to 13–20 ft. lbs.
9. The remainder of the installation is the reverse of the removal procedure.

10. Check for exhaust leaks when finished.

Multiport Fuel Injection (MFI)

1. Disconnect the negative battery cable.
2. Disconnect the air intake pipe from the ACL intake hose and throttle hose.
3. Disconnect the electrical connector from the Heated Oxygen Sensor (HO2S).
4. Remove the upper exhaust manifold heat shield from the exhaust manifold. Raise and safely support the vehicle.
5. Remove the exhaust manifold reinforcement bracket from the exhaust manifold and engine mount.
6. Remove the lower exhaust manifold heat shield from the exhaust manifold. Disconnect the Three-Way Catalytic converter (TWC) assembly from the exhaust manifold. Lower the vehicle.
7. Remove the exhaust manifold with gasket and engine hanger from the cylinder head.
8. Remove the Heated Oxygen Sensor (HO2S) from the exhaust manifold.
9. Clean and inspect all of the gasket mating surfaces. Inspect and/or replace any damaged parts.

To install:

10. Install the Heated Oxygen Sensor (HO2S) to the exhaust manifold and torque the sensor to 32 ft. lbs. (43 Nm).
11. Using new gaskets, install the exhaust manifold and torque the exhaust manifold-to-cylinder head nuts to 17 ft. lbs. (23 Nm). Raise and safely support the vehicle.
12. Using new gaskets, connect the front pipe/TWC assembly to the exhaust manifold and torque the 3 bolts to 37 ft. lbs. (50 Nm). Install the lower exhaust manifold heat shield and torque both bolts to 89 inch lbs. (10 Nm). Install the exhaust manifold bracket; torque the engine mount-to-exhaust bracket bolts to 40 ft. lbs. (54 Nm) and the exhaust bracket-to-exhaust manifold nut to 37 ft. lbs. (50 Nm). Lower the vehicle.
13. Install the upper exhaust manifold heat shield and torque the nuts/bolts to 89 inch lbs. (10 Nm). Install the air intake pipe bracket and torque the bracket-to-cylinder head bolts to 89 inch (10 Nm).
14. Connect the electrical connector to the Heated Oxygen Sensor (HO2S).
15. Install the air intake pipe to the throttle body hose and the ACL in-

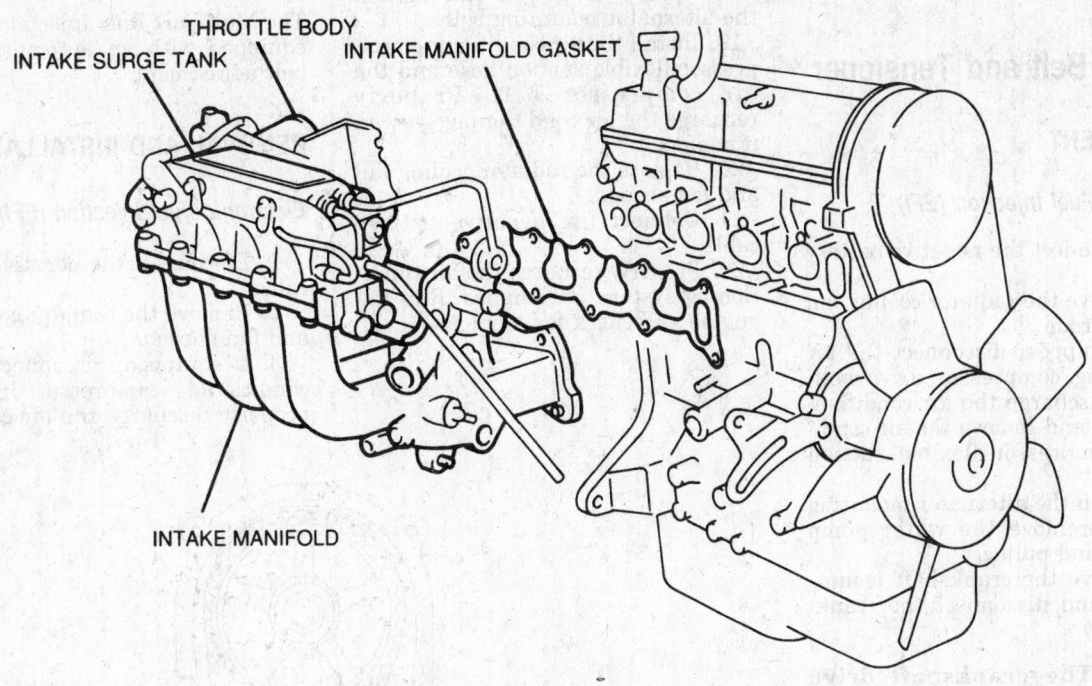

THROTTLE BODY
INTAKE SURGE TANK
INTAKE MANIFOLD GASKET
INTAKE MANIFOLD

8547Z011

Exploded view of the intake manifold — MFI engine

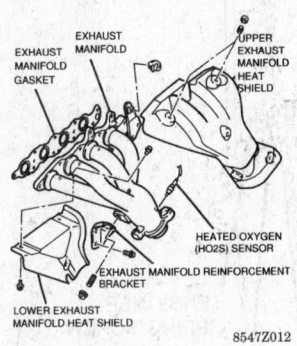

EXHAUST MANIFOLD
EXHAUST MANIFOLD HEAT SHIELD
UPPER EXHAUST MANIFOLD HEAT SHIELD
EXHAUST MANIFOLD GASKET
HEATED OXYGEN (HO2S) SENSOR
EXHAUST MANIFOLD REINFORCEMENT BRACKET
LOWER EXHAUST MANIFOLD HEAT SHIELD

8547Z012

Exploded view of the exhaust manifold — MFI engine

take hose. Connect the negative battery cable.

Timing Belt Front Cover

REMOVAL AND INSTALLATION

1. Disconnect the negative battery cable.
2. Remove the radiator cooling fan and fan shroud.
3. If equipped, disconnect the air conditioning compressor drive belt, properly discharge the air conditioning system and remove the air condi-

tioning compressor flexible suction hose.
4. Loosen the alternator mounting bolts and remove the water pump drive belt and pulley.
5. Remove the crankshaft mounting bolts and remove the crankshaft pulley.

NOTE: The crankshaft drive belt pulley can be removed without loosening the center crankshaft bolt.

6. Disconnect the timing belt cover mounting bolts and remove the timing belt cover.
   To install:
7. Clean and inspect all mounting surfaces.
8. Install the timing belt cover and tighten the bolts to 7.0–9.0 ft. lbs.
9. Install the crankshaft pulley. Replace the 5 mounting bolts and tighten to 7.0–9.0 ft. lbs.
10. Install the water pump drive belt pulley and replace the drive belt.
11. Adjust the belt tension and tighten the alternator mounting bolts.
12. Install the air conditioning flexible suction hose and replace the air conditioning compressor drive belt. Adjust the belt tension and properly

recharge the air conditioning system, if equipped.
13. Replace the radiator cooling fan and fan shroud.
14. Connect the negative battery cable.

OIL SEAL REPLACEMENT

1. Disconnect the negative battery cable.
2. Remove the the timing belt and the crankshaft sprocket.
3. Insert a suitable tool between the crankshaft and the oil seal and pull the seal outwards to remove it.

NOTE: Use care when removing or installing the oil seal, not to damage the crankshaft or the oil pump sealing surfaces.

4. Clean and inspect the surfaces of the crankshaft and the oil pump assembly.
5. Install the crankshaft sleeve, using the proper tool, onto the crankshaft.
6. Install the new seal over the crankshaft and into the oil pump, making sure the oil seal lip is not upturned.
7. Install the crankshaft sprocket and the timing belt. Check the timing.

8. Connect the negative battery cable.

Timing Belt and Tensioner

ADJUSTMENT

Electronic Fuel Injection (EFI)

1. Disconnect the negative battery cable.

2. Remove the radiator cooling fan and fan shroud.

3. If equipped, disconnect the air conditioning compressor drive belt, properly discharge the air conditioning system and remove the air conditioning compressor flexible suction hose.

4. Loosen the alternator mounting bolts and remove the water pump drive belt and pulley.

5. Remove the crankshaft mounting bolts and disconnect the crankshaft pulley.

NOTE: The crankshaft drive belt pulley can be removed without loosening the center crankshaft bolt.

6. Disconnect the timing belt cover mounting bolts and remove the timing belt cover. Loosen but do not remove the tensioner bolt.

7. Disconnect the air intake case from the intake manifold.

8. Remove the cylinder head cover and loosen all the valve adjusting screws to permit free rotation of the camshaft.

9. Turn the camshaft pulley clockwise and align the timing marks.

10. Turn the crankshaft clockwise, using a 17mm wrench to crank the timing belt pulley bolt.

11. Align the punch mark on the timing belt pulley with the arrow mark on the oil pump.

12. With the 4 marks aligned, remove any slack from the drive side of the belt. Tighten the tensioner bolt to 17.5–21.5 ft. lbs.

13. To allow the belt to be free of any slack, turn the crankshaft clockwise 2 full rotations. Confirm that the 4 marks are aligned.

14. Replace the timing cover and tighten the bolts to 7.0–8.5 ft. lbs.

15. Adjust the valve lash and install the cylinder head cover, using a new gasket.

16. Connect the air intake case to the throttle body.

17. Install the crankshaft pulley and replace the 5 mounting bolts. Tighten to 7.0–8.5 ft. lbs.

18. Replace the water pump pulley, water pump drive belt and tighten the alternator mounting bolts.

19. Install the air conditioning compressor flexible suction hose and the air compressor belt. Properly recharge the air conditioning system, if equipped.

20. Replace the radiator cooling fan and fan shroud.

21. Connect the negative battery cable.

22. Properly recharge the air conditioning system, if equipped. Run the engine and check for any leaks.

Multiport Fuel Injection (MFI)

The Multiport Fuel Injection (MFI) is equipped with an automatic timing belt adjustment.

REMOVAL AND INSTALLATION

Electronic Fuel Injection (EFI)

1. Disconnect the negative battery cable.

2. Remove the radiator cooling fan and fan shroud.

3. If equipped, disconnect the air conditioning compressor drive belt, properly discharge the air condition-

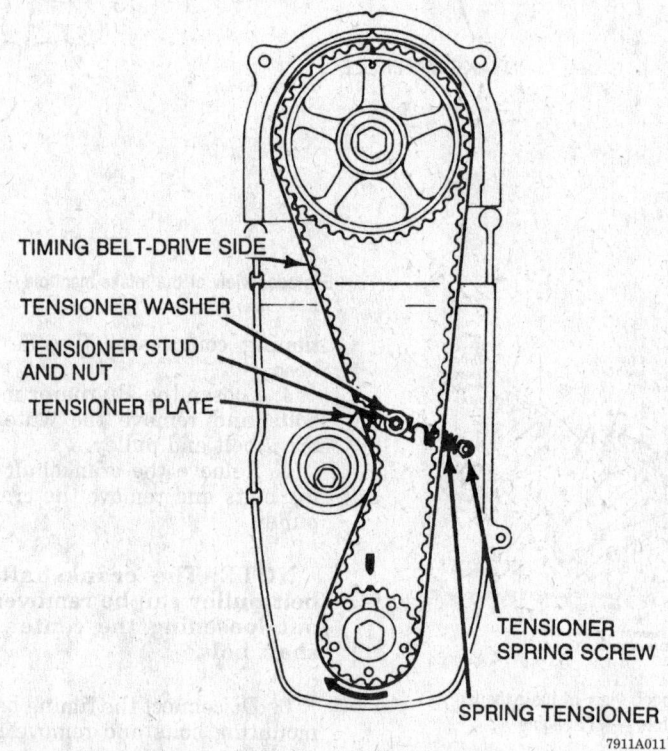

TIMING BELT-DRIVE SIDE
TENSIONER WASHER
TENSIONER STUD AND NUT
TENSIONER PLATE
TENSIONER SPRING SCREW
SPRING TENSIONER

7911A011

Exploded view of the timing belt and the tensioner assembly — EFI engine

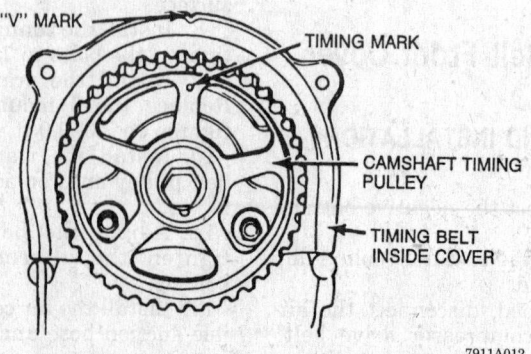

"V" MARK
TIMING MARK
CAMSHAFT TIMING PULLEY
TIMING BELT INSIDE COVER

7911A012

Timing marks on the camshaft pulley — EFI engine

ing system and remove the air conditioning compressor flexible suction hose.

4. Loosen the alternator mounting bolts and remove the water pump drive belt and pulley.

5. Remove the crankshaft mounting bolts and disconnect the crankshaft pulley.

NOTE: The crankshaft drive belt pulley can be removed without loosening the center crankshaft bolt.

6. Disconnect the timing belt cover mounting bolts and remove the timing belt cover. Loosen but do not remove the tensioner bolt.

7. Disconnect the air intake case from the intake manifold.

8. Loosen the timing belt tensioner adjusting bolt and pivot nut. Hold pressure on the tensioner to loosen the timing belt and remove the timing belt from the camshaft and crankshaft pulleys.

9. Remove the timing belt tensioner, tensioner plate and tensioner spring.

To install:

10. Install the timing belt tensioner, plate and spring. Hand tighten the tensioner bolt and stud only at this time.

11. Remove the cylinder head cover and loosen all the valve adjusting screws to permit free rotation of the camshaft.

12. Turn the camshaft pulley clockwise and align the timing marks.

13. Turn the crankshaft clockwise, using a 17mm wrench to crank the timing belt pulley bolt.

14. Align the punch mark on the timing belt pulley with the arrow mark on the oil pump

15. With the 4 marks aligned, remove any slack from the drive side of the belt. Tighten the tensioner bolt to 17.5–21.5 ft. lbs.

16. To allow the belt to be free of any slack, turn the crankshaft clockwise 2 full rotations. Confirm that the 4 marks are aligned.

17. Install the timing cover and tighten the bolts to 7.0–8.5 ft. lbs.

18. Adjust the valve lash and install the cylinder head cover, using a new gasket.

19. Connect the air intake case to the intake manifold.

20. Install the crankshaft pulley and replace the mounting bolts. Tighten to 7.0–8.5 ft. lbs.

21. Replace the water pump pulley, water pump drive belt and tighten the alternator mounting bolts.

22. If equipped, install the air conditioning compressor flexible suction

hose and replace the air conditioning compressor belt.

23. Replace the radiator cooling fan and fan shroud.

24. Connect the negative battery cable.

25. If equipped, properly recharge the air conditioning system. Run the engine and check for any leaks.

Multiport Fuel Injection (MFI)

1. Disconnect the negative battery cable.

2. Loosen the upper radiator hose clamp at the thermostat housing. Disconnect the upper radiator hose from the thermostat housing. Disconnect the coolant bypass hose from the intake manifold.

3. Remove the generator adjusting arm bracket from the intake manifold.

4. If equipped, loosen the upper and lower A/C compressor mounting bolts. Loosen the upper and lower power steering pump mounting bolts. Remove the A/C compressor, If equipped, and/or the power steering drive belt.

5. Loosen the upper and lower generator mounting bolts. Remove the generator/water pump drive belt from the pulleys. Remove the cooling fan and the water pump pulley from the water pump.

6. Raise and safely support the vehicle. If equipped, remove the skid plate from the undercarriage. Remove the 2 lower radiator shroud bolts and lower the vehicle.

7. If equipped, remove the 2 A/C suction line bracket bolts at the right side of the radiator core support and carefully reposition the suction line for radiator shroud removal access.

8. Remove the 2 upper radiator shroud bolts and the shroud from the radiator.

NOTE: If the shroud is difficult to remove, drain the cooling system and disconnect the upper radiator hose from the radiator to gain access. If is not necessary to remove the crankshaft center bolt when removing the crankshaft pulley.

9. Remove the 5 crankshaft pulley-to-crankshaft bolts and the pulley. Remove the oil pressure sending unit wire conduit from the timing belt cover.

10. Remove the timing belt cover from the engine.

NOTE: There are 2 sets of timing marks which must be aligned to ensure correct engine timing upon installation. A notch in the

camshaft timing belt gear designated as "E" must be aligned with the notch in the cylinder head. A punch mark on the crankshaft timing belt gear should align with the arrow in the oil pump casting. Make sure to align both sets of marks prior to timing belt removal.

11. Rotate the engine to align the timing marks on the cylinder head cover and camshaft timing belt gear; this should align the timing marks on the oil pump casting and crankshaft timing belt gear.

12. Loosen the timing belt tensioner bolt. Remove the timing belt tensioner spring from the timing belt tensioner plate.

13. Remove the timing belt from the camshaft and crankshaft timing belt gears.

14. Inspect and/or replace any damaged parts.

To install:

NOTE: When installing the timing belt, the directional arrows on the timing belt must be matched with the rotation of the crankshaft; if not, excessive wear and timing belt failure may occur.

15. Align the timing marks of the camshaft sprocket with the cylinder head cover and the oil pump housing with the crankshaft sprocket.

16. Install the timing belt onto the camshaft and crankshaft sprockets.

17. Rotate the crankshaft through 2 complete revolutions, to remove any slack from the timing belt and to properly seat the timing belt.

18. Inspect both sets of timing marks to ensure that they are aligned. Install the belt tensioner spring to the timing belt tensioner plate.

19. Torque the timing belt tensioner stud to 89 inch lbs. (10 Nm) and the bolt to 18 ft. lbs. (25 Nm).

20. Install the timing belt cover and torque the nut/bolts to 89 inch lbs. (10 Nm). Connect the oil pressure sending unit wire to the timing belt cover.

21. Install the crankshaft pulley to the crankshaft and torque the bolts to 12 ft. lbs. (16 Nm). Install the radiator shroud and torque both bolts to 89 inch lbs. (10 Nm).

22. If equipped, carefully, position the A/C suction line and brackets to the right side of the radiator core support and torque both bolts to 89 inch lbs. (10 Nm).

23. Raise and safely support the vehicle. Install the 2 lower radiator

shroud bolts and torque to 89 inch lbs. (10 Nm). If equipped, install the front skid plate and torque the 4 bolts to 40 ft. lbs. (54 Nm). Lower the vehicle.

24. Install the water pump pulley and fan; torque the 4 nuts to 97 inch lbs. (11 Nm). Install the generator/water pump drive belt onto the pulleys. Install the A/C compressor, if equipped, and the power steering drive belt.

25. Install the generator adjusting arm bracket and torque the bracket-to-intake manifold nut/bolt to 37 ft. lbs. (50 Nm).

26. Refill the cooling system, as necessary.

27. Connect the negative battery cable.

Timing Sprockets

REMOVAL AND INSTALLATION

Electronic Fuel Injection (EFI)

1. Disconnect the negative battery cable.

2. Remove the radiator cooling fan/clutch and fan shroud.

3. If equipped, disconnect the air conditioning compressor drive belt, properly discharge the air conditioning system and remove the air conditioning compressor flexible suction hose.

4. Loosen the alternator mounting bolts and remove the water pump drive belt and pulley.

5. Remove the crankshaft mounting bolts and disconnect the crankshaft pulley.

NOTE: The crankshaft drive belt pulley can be removed without loosening the center crankshaft bolt.

6. Disconnect the timing belt cover mounting bolts and remove the timing belt cover. Loosen but do not remove the tensioner bolt.

7. Disconnect the air intake case from the throttle body.

8. Remove the cylinder head cover and loosen all the valve adjusting screws to permit rotation of the camshaft.

9. Remove the camshaft timing belt pulley by inserting a proper size rod into the hole in the camshaft to lock the camshaft.

10. Remove the camshaft sprocket mounting bolt, sprocket and sprocket pin.

To install:

11. Install the camshaft sprocket pin in the sprocket and replace the

sprocket and the bolt on the camshaft.

12. With the camshaft locked, tighten the sprocket bolt to 41–46 ft. lbs.

13. Remove the crankshaft sprocket by using a gear stopper to hold the flywheel for manual transmission or driveplate for automatic transmission vehicles. Remove the crankshaft timing belt pulley bolt, sprocket and key.

14. With the crankshaft locked, install the crankshaft timing belt sprocket and key. Replace the crankshaft pulley bolt and tighten to 47–54 ft. lbs.

15. Align the camshaft and crankshaft timing marks, install the timing belt and tighten the timing belt tensioner.

16. Adjust the valve lash and replace the cylinder head cover.

17. Reconnect the air intake hose to the throttle body.

18. If equipped, install the air conditioning compressor flexible suction hose and replace the air conditioning compressor belt.

19. Install the water pump pulley and replace the water pump drive belt.

20. Replace the radiator cooling fan and fan shroud.

21. Install the water pump pulley and replace the water pump drive belt.

22. Connect the negative battery cable.

23. If equipped, properly recharge the air conditioning system. Run the engine and check for any leaks.

Multiport Fuel Injection (MFI)

1. Disconnect the negative battery cable.

2. Loosen the upper radiator hose clamp at the thermostat housing. Disconnect the upper radiator hose from the thermostat housing. Discon-

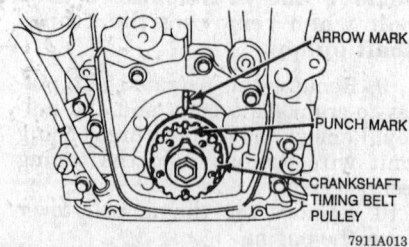

Timing marks on the crankshaft pulley — EFI engine

nect the coolant bypass hose from the intake manifold.

3. Remove the generator adjusting arm bracket from the intake manifold. Remove the front and rear intake manifold reinforcement brackets from the intake manifold.

4. Remove the lower intake manifold support bracket from the intake manifold. Remove the intake manifold-to-cylinder head nuts/bolts, then remove the intake manifold, the intake surge tank and the throttle body from the cylinder head.

5. Remove the upper exhaust manifold heat shield from the exhaust manifold. Raise and safely support the vehicle.

6. Remove the exhaust manifold reinforcement bracket from the exhaust manifold and engine mount.

7. Remove the lower exhaust manifold heat shield from the exhaust manifold. Disconnect the Three-Way Catalytic converter (TWC) assembly from the exhaust manifold. Lower the vehicle.

8. Remove the exhaust manifold with gasket and engine hanger from the cylinder head.

9. If equipped, loosen the upper and lower A/C compressor mounting bolts. Loosen the upper and lower power steering pump mounting bolts. Remove the A/C compressor, If equipped, and/or the power steering drive belt.

10. Loosen the upper and lower generator mounting bolts. Remove the generator/water pump drive belt from the pulleys. Remove the cooling fan and the water pump pulley from the water pump.

11. Raise and safely support the vehicle. If equipped, remove the skid plate from the undercarriage. Remove the 2 lower radiator shroud bolts and lower the vehicle.

12. If equipped, remove the 2 A/C suction line bracket bolts at the right side of the radiator core support and carefully reposition the suction line for radiator shroud removal access.

13. Remove the 2 upper radiator shroud bolts and the shroud from the radiator.

NOTE: If the shroud is difficult to remove, drain the cooling system and disconnect the upper radiator hose from the radiator to gain access. If is not necessary to remove the crankshaft center bolt when removing the crankshaft pulley.

14. Remove the 5 crankshaft pulley-to-crankshaft bolts and the pulley. Remove the oil pressure sending

unit wire conduit from the timing belt cover.

15. To remove the timing belt, perform the following procedure:

a. Remove the timing belt cover from the engine.

NOTE: There are 2 sets of timing marks which must be aligned to ensure correct engine timing upon installation. A notch in the camshaft timing belt gear designated as "E" must be aligned with the notch in the cylinder head. A punch mark on the crankshaft timing belt gear should align with the arrow in the oil pump casting. Make sure to align both sets of marks prior to timing belt removal.

b. Rotate the engine to align the timing marks on the cylinder head cover and camshaft timing belt gear; this should align the timing marks on the oil pump casting and crankshaft timing belt gear.

c. Loosen the timing belt tensioner bolt. Remove the timing belt tensioner spring from the timing belt tensioner plate.

d. Remove the timing belt from the camshaft and crankshaft timing belt gears.

16. Secure the camshaft sprocket, using tool J-41840 or equivalent, then remove the camshaft sprocket-to-camshaft bolt and the camshaft sprocket.

NOTE: Do not turn the crankshaft and/or camshaft independently of one another once the timing belt has been removed. If the crankshaft or camshaft is turned independently, interference between the pistons and valves may occur causing component damage.

17. Remove the crankshaft sprocket-to-crankshaft bolt and the sprocket.

18. Clean and inspect all of the gasket mating surfaces. Inspect and/or replace any damaged parts.

To install:

19. Install the crankshaft sprocket onto the crankshaft and torque the bolt to 81 ft. lbs. (110 Nm).

NOTE: During camshaft timing belt gear installation, align the camshaft dwell pin with the slot in the camshaft timing belt gear designated as "E".

20. Install the camshaft sprocket, using holding tool J-41840 or equivalent, onto the camshaft and

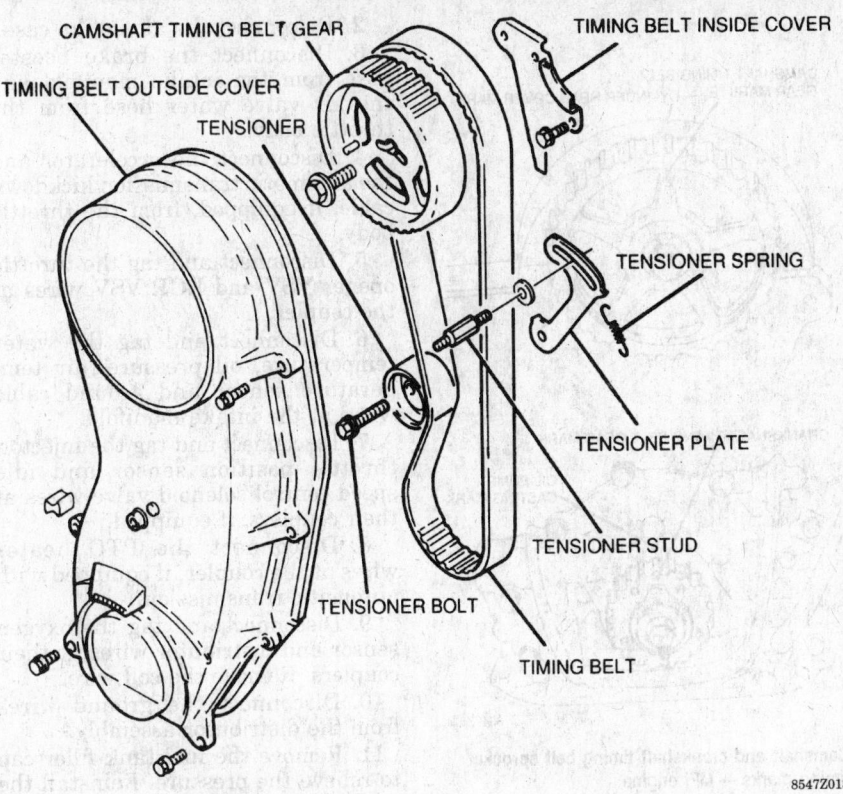

CAMSHAFT TIMING BELT GEAR
TIMING BELT INSIDE COVER
TIMING BELT OUTSIDE COVER
TENSIONER
TENSIONER SPRING
TENSIONER PLATE
TENSIONER STUD
TENSIONER BOLT
TIMING BELT

8547Z013

Timing belt, tensioner and timing belt cover — MFI engine

torque the camshaft sprocket-to-camshaft bolt to 44 ft. lbs. (60 Nm).

21. Install the timing belt tensioner plate and tensioner; secure with timing belt tensioner stud and bolt only finger-tight. Push the timing belt tensioner plate up when installing the timing belt.

NOTE: When installing the timing belt, the directional arrows on the timing belt must be matched with the rotation of the crankshaft; if not, excessive wear and timing belt failure may occur.

22. Install the timing belt by performing the following procedures:

a. Align the timing marks of the camshaft sprocket with the cylinder head cover and the oil pump housing with the crankshaft sprocket.

b. Install the timing belt onto the camshaft and crankshaft sprockets.

c. Rotate the crankshaft through 2 complete revolutions, to remove any slack from the timing belt and to properly seat the timing belt.

d. Inspect both sets of timing marks to ensure that they are aligned. Install the belt tensioner spring to the timing belt tensioner plate.

e. Torque the timing belt tensioner stud to 89 inch lbs. (10 Nm) and the bolt to 18 ft. lbs. (25 Nm).

23. Install the timing belt cover and torque the nut/bolts to 89 inch lbs. (10 Nm). Connect the oil pressure sending unit wire to the timing belt cover.

24. Install the crankshaft pulley to the crankshaft and torque the bolts to 12 ft. lbs. (16 Nm). Install the radiator shroud and torque both bolts to 89 inch lbs. (10 Nm).

25. If equipped, carefully, position the A/C suction line and brackets to the right side of the radiator core support and torque both bolts to 89 inch lbs. (10 Nm).

26. Raise and safely support the vehicle. Install the 2 lower radiator shroud bolts and torque to 89 inch lbs. (10 Nm). If equipped, install the front skid plate and torque the 4 bolts to 40 ft. lbs. (54 Nm). Lower the vehicle.

27. Install the water pump pulley and fan; torque the 4 nuts to 97 inch lbs. (11 Nm). Install the generator/water pump drive belt onto the pulleys. Install the A/C compressor, if equipped, and the power steering drive belt.

28. Install the generator adjusting arm bracket and torque the bracket-

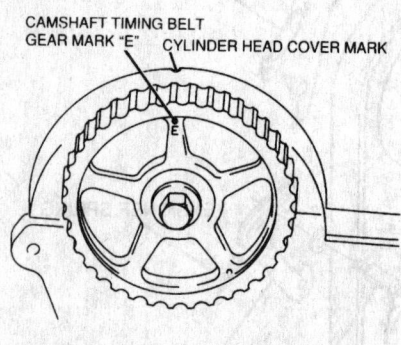

CAMSHAFT TIMING BELT GEAR MARK "E"   CYLINDER HEAD COVER MARK

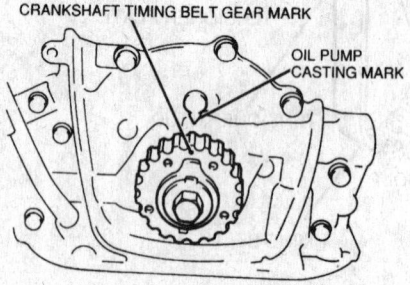

CRANKSHAFT TIMING BELT GEAR MARK

OIL PUMP CASTING MARK

8547Z014

Camshaft and crankshaft timing belt sprocket timing marks — MFI engine

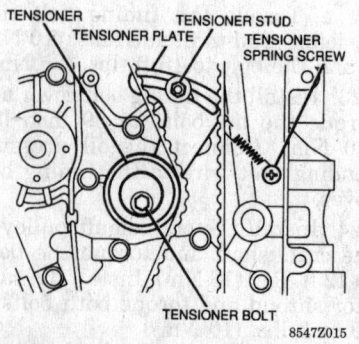

TENSIONER   TENSIONER STUD
TENSIONER PLATE   TENSIONER SPRING SCREW

TENSIONER BOLT
8547Z015

View of the timing belt tensioner assembly — MFI engine

to-intake manifold nut/bolt to 37 ft. lbs. (50 Nm).

29. Refill the cooling system, as necessary.

30. Connect the negative battery cable.

Camshaft

REMOVAL AND INSTALLATION

Electronic Fuel Injection (EFI)

1. Disconnect the negative battery cable. Drain the cooling system.

2. Disconnect the air intake case.

3. Disconnect the brake booster hose from the intake manifold and the air valve water hose from the throttle body.

4. Disconnect the accelerator and the automatic transmission kickdown cable, if equipped, from the throttle body.

5. Disconnect and tag the throttle opener VSV and EGR VSV wires at the coupler.

6. Disconnect and tag the water temperature, oil pressure, air temperature sensor and ground cable wires at the intake manifold.

7. Disconnect and tag the injector, throttle position sensor and idle speed control solenoid valve wires at their couplers, if equipped.

8. Disconnect the PTC heater wires at the coupler, if equipped with automatic transmission.

9. Disconnect and tag the oxygen sensor and distributor wires at their couplers. Remove the coil wire.

10. Disconnect the ground wires from the distributor assembly.

11. Remove the fuel tank filler cap to relieve the pressure. Reinstall the cap.

12. Release the fuel pressure in the fuel feed line.

13. Disconnect the fuel injector connections and fuel hoses.

14. Disconnect the canister purge hose and remove the pressure sensor hose from the fuel filter, if equipped.

15. Remove the vacuum hose for the automatic transmission from the intake manifold, if equipped.

16. Disconnect the radiator cooling fan, fan shroud, water pump drive belt and water pump pulley.

17. Disconnect the crankshaft pulley, timing belt cover and the timing belt.

18. Raise and safely support the vehicle.

19. Disconnect the exhaust pipe from the exhaust manifold and lower the vehicle.

20. Disconnect the air conditioner compressor adjusting arm, if equipped.

21. Remove the cylinder head cover mounting bolts and remove the cylinder head cover.

22. Loosen all the valve adjusting screw locknuts, turn the adjusting screws back all the way to allow all the valves to close.

23. Remove the intake manifold from the cylinder head.

24. Remove the distributor and distributor housing from the cylinder head.

25. Remove the cylinder head mounting bolts and remove the cylinder head from the engine.

26. Remove any oil and water in the cylinder bores and on top of the pistons.

27. Clean and inspect the sealing surfaces of the cylinder head and the engine block.

28. Disconnect the timing belt gear from the camshaft and remove the rocker arms, springs and rocker arm shafts.

29. Keep all the valve train parts in the order that they were removed.

30. Remove the camshaft from the rear of the cylinder head.

To install:

31. To install, lubricate the lobes and journals of the camshaft and the oil seal on the cylinder head with engine oil.

32. Install the camshaft to the cylinder head from the transmission side.

33. Install the cylinder head using a new gasket.

34. Install the cylinder head mounting bolts and tighten to 46–54 ft. lbs.

35. Install the distributor and distributor housing to the cylinder head.

36. Install the intake manifold to the cylinder head.

37. Tighten all the valve adjusting screw nuts.

38. Adjust the valve lash.

39. Install the cylinder head cover and connect the air conditioning compressor adjusting arm, if equipped.

40. Raise and safely support the vehicle.

41. Connect the exhaust pipe to the exhaust manifold and safely lower the vehicle.

42. Reconnect the timing belt, timing belt cover and crankshaft pulley.

43. Install the water pump pulley, water pump drive belt, fan shroud and the radiator cooling fan.

44. Install the vacuum hose for the automatic transmission to the intake manifold, if equipped.

45. Install the pressure sensor hose to the fuel filter and connect the canister purge hose, if equipped.

46. Install the fuel return and feed hoses.

47. Connect the ground wires to the distributor assembly.

48. Install the coil wire. Connect the oxygen sensor and distributor wires to their couplers.

49. Connect the PTC wires to the coupler.

50. Connect the idle speed control valve, throttle position sensor and in-

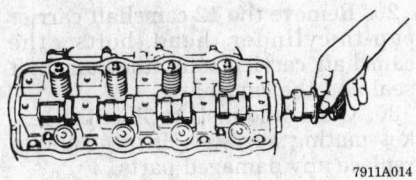

7911A014

Camshaft removal — EFI engine

jector wires to their couplers, if equipped.

51. Reconnect the ground cable, air temperature, oil pressure and water temperature sensor wires to the intake manifold.

52. Install the throttle opener VSV and EGR VSV wires to their couplers.

53. Connect the accelerator and the automatic transmission kickdown cables, if equipped, to the throttle body.

54. Install the air valve water hose to the throttle body and connect the brake booster hose to intake manifold.

55. Reconnect the air intake case.

56. Refill the cooling system with the proper coolant and connect the negative battery.

57. Check for any water and oil leaks when finished.

Multiport Fuel Injection (MFI)

1. Disconnect the negative battery cable. Release the fuel pressure. Remove the fuel filler cap to release the pressure in the tank, then replace the fuel filler cap.

2. Drain the cooling system. Disconnect the air intake pipe from the ACL intake hose and throttle body.

3. Remove the throttle cover-to-intake manifold bolts and the cover.

4. If equipped with an automatic transmission, disconnect the accelerator and kickdown cables from the throttle body bellcrank.

5. Remove 1 bolt, nut, screw and accelerator cable bracket from the throttle body.

6. Disconnect the electrical connectors from the following items:

Throttle Position (TP) sensor
Idle Air Control (IAC) valve
Engine Coolant Temperature (ECT) sensor
ECT sending unit
A/C ECT switch (if equipped with A/C)

Evaporative Emissions Solenoid Purge (EVAP SP) valve
Exhaust Gas Recirculation (EGR) temperature sensor (Calif. vehicles)
EGR solenoid vacuum valve
Fuel injectors
Engine ground wire from intake surge tank

7. Disconnect the following vacuum hoses:

EVAP SP valve
Vacuum modulator supply hose (if equipped with automatic transmission)
Brake booster supply hose
EGR valve
EGR valve modulator

8. Disconnect the coolant hose from the IAC valve and the IAC hose from the IAC valve. Disconnect the coolant hoses from the fast idle air valve below the throttle body.

9. Disconnect the fuel feed hose at the fuel feed hose union and the fuel feed hose from the fuel return line. Disconnect the PCV hose from the PCV valve.

10. Loosen the upper radiator hose clamp at the thermostat housing. Disconnect the upper radiator hose from the thermostat housing. Disconnect the coolant bypass hose from the intake manifold.

11. Remove the generator adjusting arm bracket from the intake manifold. Remove the front and rear intake manifold reinforcement brackets from the intake manifold.

12. Remove the lower intake manifold support bracket from the intake manifold. Remove the intake manifold-to-cylinder head nuts/bolts, then remove the intake manifold, the intake surge tank and the throttle body from the cylinder head.

13. Remove the upper exhaust manifold heat shield from the exhaust manifold. Raise and safely support the vehicle.

14. Remove the exhaust manifold reinforcement bracket from the exhaust manifold and engine mount.

15. Remove the lower exhaust manifold heat shield from the exhaust manifold. Disconnect the Three-Way Catalytic converter (TWC) assembly from the exhaust manifold. Lower the vehicle.

16. Remove the exhaust manifold with gasket and engine hanger from the cylinder head.

17. If equipped, loosen the upper and lower A/C compressor mounting bolts. Loosen the upper and lower power steering pump mounting bolts. Remove the A/C compressor, If equipped, and/or the power steering drive belt.

18. Loosen the upper and lower generator mounting bolts. Remove the generator/water pump drive belt from the pulleys. Remove the cooling fan and the water pump pulley from the water pump.

19. Raise and safely support the vehicle. If equipped, remove the skid plate from the undercarriage. Remove the 2 lower radiator shroud bolts and lower the vehicle.

20. If equipped, remove the 2 A/C suction line bracket bolts at the right side of the radiator core support and carefully reposition the suction line for radiator shroud removal access.

21. Remove the 2 upper radiator shroud bolts and the shroud from the radiator.

NOTE: If the shroud is difficult to remove, drain the cooling system and disconnect the upper radiator hose from the radiator to gain access. If is not necessary to remove the crankshaft center bolt when removing the crankshaft pulley.

22. Remove the 5 crankshaft pulley-to-crankshaft bolts and the pulley. Remove the oil pressure sending unit wire conduit from the timing belt cover.

23. To remove the timing belt, perform the following procedure:

a. Remove the timing belt cover from the engine.

NOTE: There are 2 sets of timing marks which must be aligned to ensure correct engine timing upon installation. A notch in the camshaft timing belt gear designated as "E" must be aligned with the notch in the cylinder head. A punch mark on the crankshaft timing belt gear should align with the arrow in the oil pump casting. Make sure to align both sets of marks prior to timing belt removal.

b. Rotate the engine to align the timing marks on the cylinder head cover and camshaft timing belt gear; this should align the timing marks on the oil pump casting and crankshaft timing belt gear.

c. Loosen the timing belt tensioner bolt. Remove the timing belt tensioner spring from the timing belt tensioner plate.

d. Remove the timing belt from the camshaft and crankshaft timing belt gears.

24. Secure the camshaft sprocket, using tool J-41840 or equivalent, then remove the camshaft sprocket-to-camshaft bolt and the camshaft sprocket.

25. Remove the 2 inner timing belt cover-to-cylinder head bolts and the cover. Remove the 2 A/C compressor mounting bracket-to-cylinder head bolts and the bracket.

26. Remove the distributor from the distributor case. Remove the 6 cylinder head cover-to-cylinder head bolts and the cover. Remove the cylinder head cover gasket and O-rings from the cylinder head cover.

NOTE: A small amount of oil may drain from the distributor case upon removal from the cylinder head. Place a suitable

container under the distributor case or use a shop towel to catch and absorb the oil.

27. Remove the 3 distributor case-to-cylinder head bolts and the distributor case.

28. Loosen all valve adjusting screw locknuts. Loosen all valve adjusting screws until all rocker arms move freely.

NOTE: Always loosen the camshaft carrier bolts gradually in sequence, in order to relieve tension on the camshaft; if the

camshaft carrier bolts are removed at random, damage to the camshaft may occur.

29. Remove the 12 camshaft carrier cap-to-cylinder head bolts, the camshaft carrier bolts, the camshaft seal and the camshaft.

30. Clean and inspect all of the gasket mating surfaces. Inspect and/or replace any damaged parts.

To install:

31. Lubricate the camshaft with clean oil. Apply RTV silicone rubber sealant to the bottom of the No. 6 camshaft carrier cap.

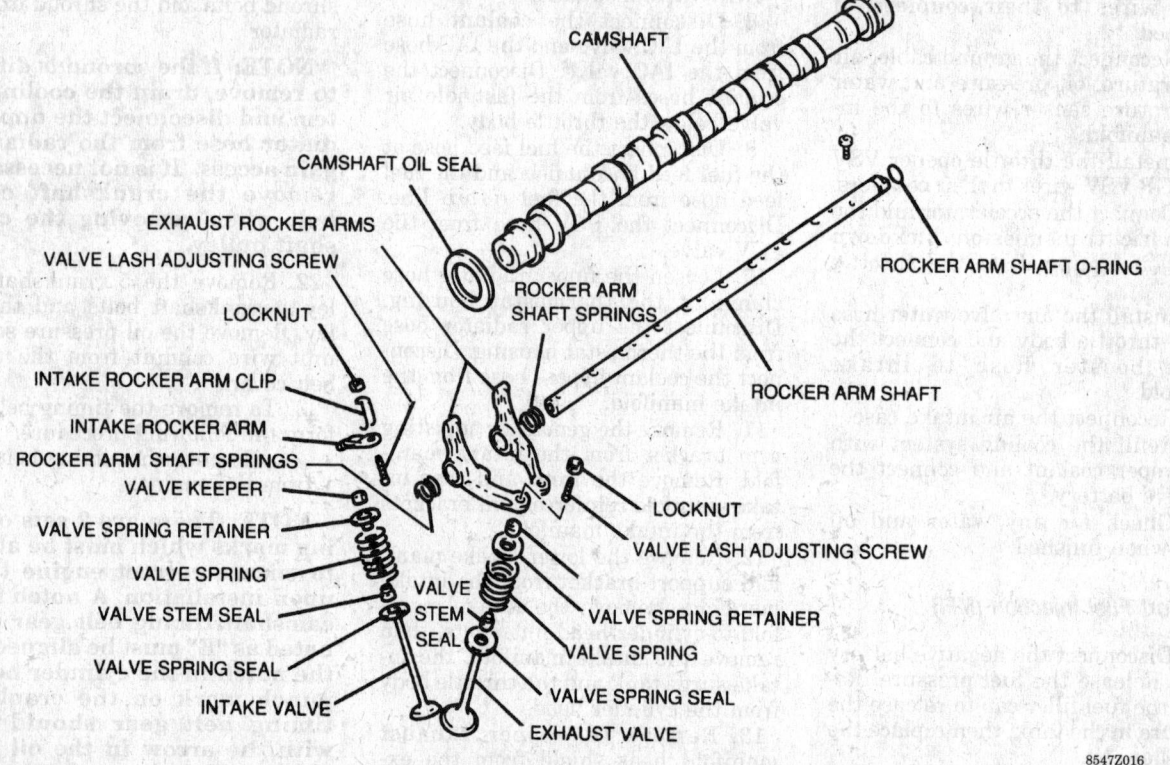

Exploded view of the camshaft, rocker arm and valve assembly — MFI engine

32. Install the camshaft and camshaft carrier caps onto the cylinder head, then, torque the camshaft carrier cap-to-cylinder head bolts to 89 inch lbs. (10 Nm).

NOTE: Always tighten the camshaft carrier cap bolts gradually in sequence; if the camshaft carrier cap bolts are tightened at random. damage to the camshaft may occur.

33. Lubricate the new camshaft seal lip with clean engine oil. Install the new camshaft seal into the cylinder head until it is flush with the camshaft carrier surface. Adjust the valve lash.

34. Adjust the valve lash.

35. Apply RTV silicone rubber sealant to the surface of the distributor case that mates with the rear of the rocker arm shaft.

36. Install the distributor case onto the cylinder head and torque the distributor case-to-cylinder head bolts to 89 inch lbs. (10 Nm).

37. Install a new cylinder head cover gasket and 4 O-rings to the cylinder head cover. Install the cylinder head cover and torque the 6 bolts to 89 inch lbs. (10 Nm).

38. Install the distributor into the distributor case. Install the A/C mounting bracket with compressor and torque the 2 mounting bracket-to-cylinder head bolts to 89 inch lbs. (10 Nm).

39. Install the inner timing belt cover and torque the 2 bolts inner timing belt cover-to-cylinder head bolts to 89 inch lbs. (10 Nm).

NOTE: During camshaft timing belt gear installation, align the camshaft dwell pin with the slot in the camshaft timing belt gear designated as "E".

40. Install the camshaft sprocket, using holding tool J-41840 or equivalent, onto the camshaft and torque the camshaft sprocket-to-camshaft bolt to 44 ft. lbs. (60 Nm).

41. Install the timing belt tensioner plate and tensioner; secure with timing belt tensioner stud and bolt only finger-tight. Push the timing belt

tensioner plate up when installing the timing belt.

NOTE: When installing the timing belt, the directional arrows on the timing belt must be matched with the rotation of the crankshaft; if not, excessive wear and timing belt failure may occur.

42. Install the timing belt by performing the following procedures:

a. Align the timing marks of the camshaft sprocket with the cylinder head cover and the oil pump housing with the crankshaft sprocket.

b. Install the timing belt onto the camshaft and crankshaft sprockets.

c. Rotate the crankshaft through 2 complete revolutions, to remove any slack from the timing belt and to properly seat the timing belt.

d. Inspect both sets of timing marks to ensure that they are aligned. Install the belt tensioner spring to the timing belt tensioner plate.

e. Torque the timing belt tensioner stud to 89 inch lbs. (10 Nm) and the bolt to 18 ft. lbs. (25 Nm).

43. Install the timing belt cover and torque the nut/bolts to 89 inch lbs. (10 Nm). Connect the oil pressure sending unit wire to the timing belt cover.

44. Install the crankshaft pulley to the crankshaft and torque the bolts to 12 ft. lbs. (16 Nm). Install the radiator shroud and torque both bolts to 89 inch lbs. (10 Nm).

45. If equipped, carefully, position the A/C suction line and brackets to the right side of the radiator core support and torque both bolts to 89 inch lbs. (10 Nm).

46. Raise and safely support the vehicle. Install the 2 lower radiator shroud bolts and torque to 89 inch lbs. (10 Nm). If equipped, install the front skid plate and torque the 4 bolts

to 40 ft. lbs. (54 Nm). Lower the vehicle.

47. Install the water pump pulley and fan; torque the 4 nuts to 97 inch lbs. (11 Nm). Install the generator/water pump drive belt onto the pulleys. Install the A/C compressor, if equipped, and the power steering drive belt.

48. Using new gaskets, install the exhaust manifold and torque the exhaust manifold-to-cylinder head nuts to 17 ft. lbs. (23 Nm). Raise and safely support the vehicle.

49. Using new gaskets, connect the front pipe/TWC assembly to the exhaust manifold and torque the 3 bolts to 37 ft. lbs. (50 Nm). Install the lower exhaust manifold heat shield and torque both bolts to 89 inch lbs. (10 Nm). Install the exhaust manifold bracket; torque the engine mount-to-exhaust bracket bolts to 40 ft. lbs. (54 Nm) and the exhaust bracket-to-exhaust manifold nut to 37 ft. lbs. (50 Nm). Lower the vehicle.

50. Install the upper exhaust manifold heat shield and torque the nuts/bolts to 89 inch lbs. (10 Nm). Install the air intake pipe bracket and torque the bracket-to-cylinder head bolts to 89 inch (10 Nm).

51. Using a new gasket, install the intake manifold, with intake surge tank and throttle body, and torque the intake manifold-to-cylinder head bolts, in sequence, to 17 ft. lbs. (23 Nm).

52. Install the lower intake manifold support bracket, the rear and the front intake manifold reinforcement bracket; torque the brackets-to-intake manifold bolts to 37 ft. lbs. (50 Nm).

53. Install the generator adjusting arm bracket and torque the bracket-to-intake manifold nut/bolt to 37 ft. lbs. (50 Nm).

54. Install the following hoses:

Coolant bypass hose to the intake manifold.

Upper radiator hose to the thermostat housing; secure with a clamp.

PCV hose to the PCV valve.

Fuel return hose to the fuel return line.

Fuel feed hose at the fuel feed hose union.

Coolant hoses to the fast idle air valve below the throttle body.

IAC air hose to the IAC valve.

Coolant hose to the IAC valve.

55. Install the following vacuum hoses:

EGR valve modulator.

EGR valve.

Brake booster supply hose.

Vacuum modulator supply hose, if equipped with an automatic transmission.

EVAP SP valve.

56. Connect the following electrical connectors:

Engine ground wire to intake surge tank.

Fuel injectors.

EGR solenoid vacuum valve.

EGR temperature sensor, California vehicles.

Evaporative Emission Solenoid Purge (EVAP SP).

A/C ECT switch, if equipped with A/C.

ECT sensor sending unit.

Engine Coolant Temperature (ECT) sensor.

Idle Air Control (IAC).

Throttle Position (TP) sensor.

57. Install the accelerator cable bracket to the throttle body and torque the nut/bolt to 17 ft. lbs. (23 Nm).

58. If equipped with an automatic transmission, connect the accelerator cable and kickdown cable to the throttle body bellcrank; adjust the cables.

59. Install the throttle cover to the intake manifold and torque the bolts to 11 ft. lbs. (15 Nm). Refill the cooling system, as necessary.

60. Install the air intake pipe to the throttle body hose and the ACL intake hose. Connect the negative battery cable.

Piston and Connecting Rod

POSITIONING

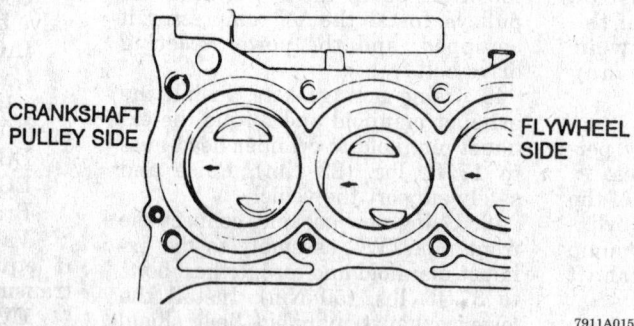

CRANKSHAFT PULLEY SIDE　　　**FLYWHEEL SIDE**

7911A015

Piston arrow marks to the cylinder head

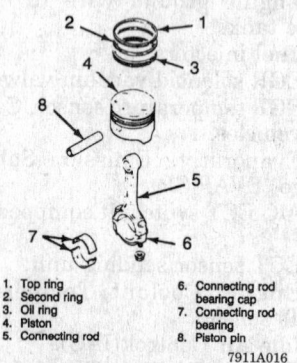

1. Top ring
2. Second ring
3. Oil ring
4. Piston
5. Connecting rod
6. Connecting rod bearing cap
7. Connecting rod bearing
8. Piston pin

7911A016

Exploded view of the piston and rod assembly

ENGINE LUBRICATION

Oil Pan

REMOVAL AND INSTALLATION

1. Raise and safely support the vehicle.
2. Drain and remove the front differential assembly from the chassis.
3. Drain the engine oil.
4. Remove the clutch housing lower plate or the torque converter housing lower plate.
5. Remove the oil pan mounting bolts and remove the pan.
   To install:
6. Clean and inspect the sealing surfaces on the oil pan and the engine block.

7. Using new gaskets, install the oil pan and tighten the oil pan bolts to 7.0–8.5 ft. lbs.

NOTE: Tightening should begin at the center moving outward on both sides.

8. Install the oil drain plug and tighten to 22.0–28.5 ft. lbs.
9. Replace the clutch housing lower plate or the torque converter.
10. Install the front differential assembly to the chassis and fill with differential oil.
11. Lower the vehicle.
12. Refill the engine with engine oil. Run the engine and check for leaks.

Oil Pump

REMOVAL AND INSTALLATION

1. Disconnect the negative battery cable.
2. Remove the radiator cooling fan, fan shroud, water pump pulley and water pump drive belt.
3. Remove the timing belt outside cover, timing belt and timing belt tensioner.
4. Disconnect the alternator and remove the bracket, if necessary.
5. If equipped, properly discharge the air conditioning system and remove the air compressor and bracket.
6. Disconnect the crankshaft timing belt pulley and the timing belt guide.

NOTE: To lock the crankshaft, engage a special tool (gear stopper) with the flywheel ring gear for manual transmission or driveplate ring gear for automatic transmission vehicles.

With the crankshaft locked, remove the crankshaft timing belt pulley bolt.

7. Raise and safely support the vehicle. Drain the engine oil.
8. Remove the clutch (torque converter) housing lower plate.
9. Remove the oil pan mounting bolts and remove the oil pan. Disconnect the oil pump strainer.
10. Remove the oil pump mounting bolts and remove the oil pump.
    To install:
11. Clean and inspect the sealing surfaces of the oil pump and the engine block.
12. Using a new gasket, install the oil pump to the engine.
13. Install the No. 1 and No. 2 mounting bolts and tighten to 7.0–8.5 ft. lbs.

NOTE: To prevent the oil seal lip from being damaged when installing the oil pump to the crankshaft, use a proper seal guide tool when installing. After installing the oil pump, check to be sure the oil lip is not upturned, then remove the special tool. The edge of the oil pump gasket might bulge out. If it does, cut off bulge with knife.

14. With the crankshaft locked, install the crankshaft timing belt guide and the timing belt pulley.
15. Replace the clutch (torque converter) housing lower plate.
16. If equipped, replace the air conditioning bracket, the air conditioning compressor and properly recharge the air conditioning system.
17. Replace the alternator and the alternator bracket, if necessary.
18. Reinstall the timing belt tensioner, timing belt and timing belt outside cover.

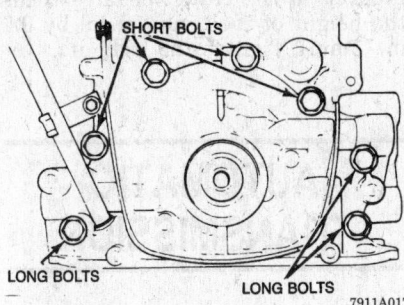

Oil pump installation — bolt location

19. Replace the water pump drive belt, water pump pulley, radiator cooling fan and fan shroud.

20. Refill the engine with engine oil and connect the negative battery cable.

21. Run the engine and check for any leaks.

CHECKING

With the oil pump removed from the engine, certain clearances must be checked on the oil pump, if it is being reused.

1. The radial clearance is the clearance between the oil pump outer rotor and the oil pump case. The maximum clearance is 0.0122 in.

2. The side clearance is measured with a straight-edge across the mounting surface of the oil pump. The measurement is taken between the oil pump gears and the straight-edge. The maximum clearance is 0.0059 in.

Rear Main Bearing Oil Seal

REMOVAL AND INSTALLATION

1. Raise and safely support the vehicle.

2. Support the engine and remove the transmission from the vehicle.

3. Disconnect the clutch and flywheel for manual transmission vehicles or the driveplate for automatic transmission vehicles.

4. Using a suitable tool, remove the seal by pulling it outwards. Use care not to damage the sealing surface of the crankshaft.

To install:

5. Clean and inspect the sealing surfaces of the crankshaft and seal housing.

6. Using a seal driver, install the new seal into the seal housing with the lip of the seal facing the engine.

7. Install the flywheel and clutch for manual transmission vehicles or the driveplate for automatic transmission vehicles.

8. Install the transmission in the vehicle.

9. Lower the vehicle and check all the fluids. Run the engine and check for any leaks.

MANUAL TRANSMISSION

Transmission Assembly

REMOVAL AND INSTALLATION

1. Disconnect the negative battery cable.

2. Remove the console cover, remove the 4 gear shift boot mounting bolts and slide the boot upwards on the gear shifter.

3. Remove the boot clamp and remove the second boot from the shift lever case.

4. Push the gear shift lever control case down with fingers, turn it counterclockwise and remove the shift control lever.

5. Remove the transfer case shift control lever the same way.

6. Disconnect the breather hose and clamp at the rear of the cylinder head.

7. Remove the clamp at the rear of the intake manifold to free up the wiring harness. Disconnect the harness coupler.

8. Raise and safely support the vehicle. Drain the oil from the transmission and the transfer case.

9. Disconnect the starter lead wires and mounting bolts and remove the starter.

10. Remove the fuel line clamp on the transmission. Disconnect the bolts fastening the engine to the transmission.

11. Disconnect the flange bolts from the front driveshaft and remove and mark the shaft.

12. Disconnect the flange bolts from the rear driveshaft and remove and mark the shaft.

13. Disconnect the clutch cable and remove the clutch housing lower plate.

14. Disconnect the center exhaust pipe and remove the nuts from the joint with the engine.

15. Disconnect the speedometer cable from the transfer case.

16. Position a transmission jack and remove the engine rear mounting member from the vehicle. Move the transmission and transfer case rearwards and lower.

17. Disconnect the wiring harness and breather hose at the transmission.

18. Separate the gear shift lever case and transfer case from the transmission. Remove the transmission from the vehicle.

To install:

19. Install the gear shift lever case and transfer case to the transmission.

20. Install the transmission wiring harness and breather hose.

21. Raise the transmission and transfer case on the transmission jack and place under the vehicle.

22. Install the engine rear mounting member and tighten the bolts.

23. Connect the speedometer cable to the transfer case and joint with the engine.

24. Remove the transmission jack and replace the center exhaust pipe.

25. Replace the clutch housing lower plate and connect the clutch cable.

26. Install the front and rear driveshaft and replace the flange bolts and tighten to 37 ft. lbs.

27. Connect the bolts attaching the engine to the transmission and tighten to 37 ft. lbs. and replace the fuel line clamp on the transmission.

28. Install the starter and replace the mounting bolts and the lead wires to the starter.

29. Lower the vehicle. Refill the transmission and transfer case with the recommended gear oil.

30. Connect the wiring coupler and replace the clamp holding the wiring harness at the rear of the intake manifold.

31. Replace the breather hose and clamp at the rear of the cylinder head.

32. Install the transfer case and the gear shift control levers. Replace the gear shift lever boots and the console cover.

33. Connect the negative battery cable. Run the engine and check for any leaks.

CLUTCH

Clutch Assembly

REMOVAL AND INSTALLATION

1. Disconnect the negative battery cable.
2. Raise and safely support the vehicle.
3. Support the engine and remove the transmission from the vehicle.
4. Support the pressure plate and remove the 6 pressure plate to flywheel mounting bolts.
5. Remove the pressure plate and the clutch disc from the flywheel.
6. Inspect the condition of the flywheel, pressure plate and clutch disc and replace as necessary.
7. Remove the flywheel mounting bolts and remove the flywheel if necessary.

To install:

8. Install the new flywheel and replace the mounting bolts, tighten to 41–47 ft. lbs.
9. Inspect the condition of the clutch release bearing and the input shaft bearing and replace if necessary.
10. Align the clutch disc to the flywheel using a clutch disc alignment tool.
11. Install the pressure plate and evenly tighten the pressure plate bolts to 13–20 ft. lbs.

NOTE: Before assembling, make sure the clutch disc and the pressure plate are clean and dry.

12. With the engine supported, install the transmission in the vehicle.
13. Lower the vehicle. Connect the negative battery cable.
14. Check and adjust the clutch pedal height. Check the clutch operation when finished.

PEDAL HEIGHT/FREE-PLAY ADJUSTMENT

The only adjustment possible is the clutch pedal free-play. The free play is adjusted by moving the joint nut on the release bearing arm. Clutch linkage free-play should be between 0.6–1.1 in.

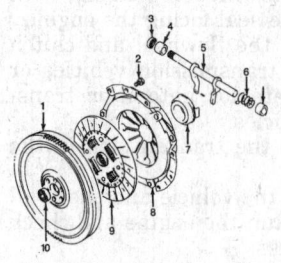

Exploded view of the clutch assembly

1. Flywheel
2. Cover bolt
3. Release shaft seal
4. Release shaft bushing
5. Clutch release shaft
6. Release return spring
7. Clutch release bearing
8. Clutch cover
9. Clutch disc
10. Input shaft bearing

7911A018

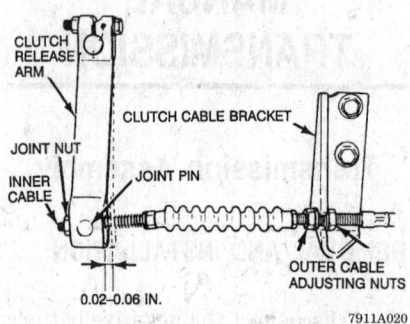

CLUTCH RELEASE ARM

CLUTCH CABLE BRACKET

JOINT NUT

INNER CABLE

JOINT PIN

OUTER CABLE ADJUSTING NUTS

0.02–0.06 IN.

7911A020

Clutch cable free travel adjustment

Clutch Cable

REMOVAL AND INSTALLATION

1. Disconnect the negative battery cable.
2. Raise and safely support the vehicle.
3. Disconnect the cable adjusting nuts on the clutch release and remove the adjusting nuts on the cable support bracket.
4. Disconnect the clutch cable from the 3 cable clamps.
5. Remove the clutch cable support bolts. Lower the vehicle.
6. Disconnect the cable hook at the clutch pedal shaft arm and remove the clutch cable.

To install:

7. Install the cable after first applying grease to the cable end hook and the joint pin.
8. Connect the cable to the 3 cable clamps and install the clutch cable support bolts.
9. Lower the vehicle and connect the negative battery cable.

ADJUSTMENT

Adjust the clutch pedal height by adjusting the bolt located on the pedal bracket so the clutch pedal exceeds the height of the brake pedal by 0.2 in. (5mm). Tighten the locknut.

AUTOMATIC TRANSMISSION

Transmission Assembly

REMOVAL AND INSTALLATION

1. Disconnect the negative battery cable.
2. Disconnect the transmission shift control lever and remove the transfer case shift control lever knob.
3. Disconnect the breather hose from the clamp at the rear of the cylinder head.
4. Disconnect the wiring harness clamp at the rear end of the intake manifold to free up the harness.
5. Disconnect the wiring harness coupler and remove the detent cable at the throttle body, if equipped.
6. Remove the vacuum modulator hose at the intake manifold.
7. Raise and safely support the vehicle.
8. Disconnect the starter lead wires and mounting bolts, remove the starter motor.
9. Drain the oil from the transmission and transfer case.
10. Disconnect the flange bolts from the front driveshaft, remove and mark the shaft.
11. Disconnect the flange bolts from the rear driveshaft, remove and mark the shaft.
12. Disconnect the select cable from the transmission and the speedometer cable from the transfer case.
13. Remove the torque converter housing lower plate and disconnect and plug the oil cooler lines.
14. Disconnect the transfer case skid plate and remove the kickdown cable from the transmission.
15. Remove the exhaust bracket at the catalytic converter and at the transmission. Disconnect the center exhaust pipe, if necessary.
16. Remove the transmission to engine retaining bolts and nuts.
17. Support the transmission using a transmission jack or equivalent. Disconnect the transmission crossmember mounting bolts and remove the crossmember.
18. Disconnect the lead wires and breather hose at the transmission

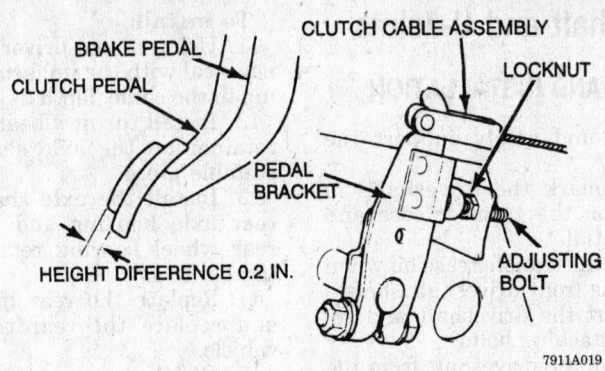

Clutch pedal height adjustment

7911A019

and lower the transmission with the transfer case from the vehicle. Remove the torque converter to flywheel bolts.

19. Disconnect the transmission-to-transfer case bolts and separate the transmission from the transfer case.

To install:

20. Connect the transfer case to the transmission and tighten the bolts to 20 ft. lbs. Replace the torque converter to flywheel bolts.

21. Raise the transmission, connect the lead wires and breather to the transmission.

22. Replace the transmission to engine retaining bolts and tighten to 62 ft. lbs.

23. Install the transmission cross member and tighten the bolts to 62 ft. lbs.

24. Connect the exhaust bracket to the catalytic converter and the transmission.

25. Reconnect the center exhaust pipe, if necessary.

26. Connect the transfer case skid plate and replace the kickdown cable to the transmission.

27. Replace the torque converter housing lower plate and connect the transmission cooler lines.

28. Reconnect the select cable to the transmission and the speedometer cable to the transfer case.

29. Replace the front and rear driveshafts and tighten the flange bolts to 37 ft. lbs.

30. Install the starter and connect the lead wires to the starter.

31. Lower the vehicle and connect the vacuum modulator hose to the intake manifold.

32. Connect the wiring coupler at the rear of the intake manifold and replace the wiring harness clamp in the proper position.

33. Connect the breather hose to the clamp at the rear of the cylinder head.

34. Install the transmission shift control lever and replace the transfer case shift control lever knob.

35. Connect the negative battery cable and refill the transmission. Run the engine and check for leaks.

SHIFT LINKAGE ADJUSTMENT

1. Adjust the shift cable assembly by moving the shift selector to the **N** position and placing a pin in the selector to hold that position.

2. Put the manual select lever in **L** position and set the cable to the cable bracket with the E-clip.

3. Adjust the manual select lever back to the **N** position and tighten the cable end locknut to 5 ft. lbs.

NOTE: When the manual selector is moved to the N position, there should be a little clearance between the lever and the adjusting nut.

THROTTLE LINKAGE ADJUSTMENT

Adjust the cable by loosening the cable locknut and adjust the cable to specifications. The cable endplay

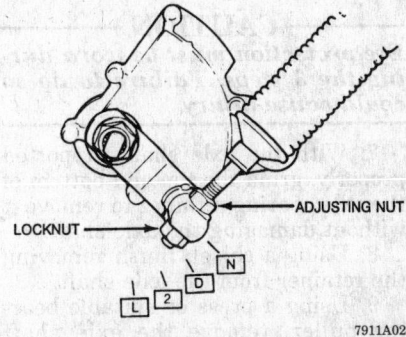

Adjusting the shift cable assembly

7911A021

should be 0.12–0.20 in. when the throttle valve is in the idle position.

DETENT CABLE ADJUSTMENT

1. Make sure accelerator play is within specifications.

2. Loosen the kickdown cable nut and adjusting nut.

3. With the accelerator pedal fully depressed and the cable pulled towards the firewall, adjust the locknut-to-bracket clearance to 0.039 in. by turning the locknut.

NOTE: When adjusting the clearance make sure the adjusting nut does not rub against the bracket.

4. Release the accelerator pedal and adjust the locknut-to-bracket clearance by tightening the adjusting nut. Tighten the locknut securely.

TRANSFER CASE

Transfer Case Assembly

REMOVAL AND INSTALLATION

1. Disconnect the negative battery cable.

2. Raise and safely support the vehicle.

3. Support the transmission and transfer case using a transmission jack.

4. Disconnect the speedometer cable from the transfer case.

5. Remove the transmission and transfer case from the vehicle.

6. Remove the 10 transmission-to-transfer case mounting bolts and separate the transfer case from the transmission.

To install:

7. Install the 10 transmission-to-transfer case mounting bolts and tighten the bolts to 20 ft. lbs.

8. Install the transmission and transfer case into the vehicle and tighten the mounting bolts to 37 ft. lbs.

9. Connect the speedometer cable to the transfer case.

10. Lower the vehicle and connect the negative battery cable.

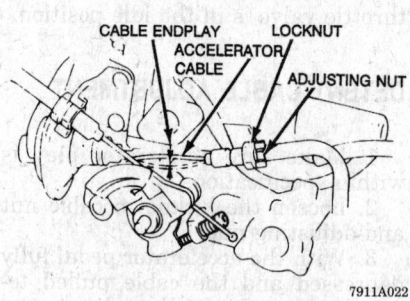

Accelerator cable adjustment

7911A022

DRIVE AXLE

Halfshaft

REMOVAL AND INSTALLATION

1. Raise and safely support the vehicle. Drain the transmission.
2. Remove the front wheels and disconnect the locking hubs.
3. Disconnect the halfshaft snaprings and remove the stabilizer bar links.
4. Disconnect the tie rod ends and remove the brake caliper and brake disc. Support the brake caliper.
5. Disconnect the wheel hub and remove the steering knuckle.
6. Disconnect the differential side joint snapring and remove the right side halfshaft by prying the joint away from the differential assembly.
7. Disconnect the left side halfshaft bolts and remove the halfshaft from the left inner axle flange.

To install:

8. Install the left side halfshaft and the halfshaft bolts and tighten to 37 ft. lbs.
9. Install the right side halfshaft and install the snapring.
10. Install the steering knuckle and wheel hub assembly.
11. Install the brake caliper and connect the tie rod end.
12. Install the left side driveshaft snapring and connect the stabilizer bar link.
13. Install the front wheels and lower the vehicle.
14. Refill the transmission with the proper fluid.

Driveshaft and U-Joints

REMOVAL AND INSTALLATION

1. Raise and safely support the vehicle.
2. Matchmark the driveshafts to the yokes on the transfer case and the differential.
3. Drain the transfer case oil when servicing the front driveshaft shaft.
4. Support the driveshaft and remove the attaching bolts.
5. Remove the driveshaft from the vehicle.

To install:

6. Install the driveshaft, by aligning the matchmarks to the vehicle.
7. Tighten the mounting bolts to 37 ft. lbs.
8. Refill the transfer case and lower the vehicle.

Rear Axle Shaft, Bearing and Seal

REMOVAL AND INSTALLATION

1. Raise and safely support the vehicle.
2. Remove the rear wheels and remove the rear brake drums from the vehicle.
3. Drain the gear oil from the rear axle housing.
4. Remove the rear wheel bearing retainer nuts from the rear axle housing.
5. Using a suitable tool, remove the axle shaft from the housing.

NOTE: Do not remove the backing plate with the axle. This may cause damage to the inner seal.

6. If the axle, axle bearing or backing plate is being replaced, support the axle in a vise with additional support under the shaft next to the bearing.

— CAUTION —
Eye protection must be worn during the 3 steps. Failure to do so could cause injury.

7. With the axle shaft supported properly, grind the top and bottom of the axle bearing retainer to remove it without damaging the axle shaft.
8. Using a chisel, finish removing the retainer from the axle shaft.
9. Using a press or suitable bearing puller, remove the axle shaft bearing from the axle shaft.
10. Using a suitable tool, remove the seal from the axle housing.

To install:

11. Using a seal driver, install the new seal with the lip facing the housing to the same depth as the old seal.
12. Install the new bearing and the retainer on the axle shaft using a suitable press.
13. Install the axle shaft into the rear axle housing and replace the rear wheel bearing retaining nuts, tighten to 17 ft. lbs.
14. Replace the rear brake drums and replace the rear tires on the vehicle.
15. Refill the rear axle housing with the proper gear oil and safely lower the vehicle.

Front Wheel Hub, Knuckle and Bearings

REMOVAL AND INSTALLATION

1. Disconnect the negative battery cable. Raise and safely support the vehicle.
2. Remove the wheels and disconnect the locking hub assembly.
3. Remove the caliper mounting bracket and position the caliper out of the way. Support the caliper.
4. Disconnect the front wheel bearing lock plate and washer and remove the wheel hub complete with bearings and seals.
5. Remove the oil seal and race from the wheel hub.
6. Clean and inspect the hub and bearing seats. Install the new bearing, race and grease seal in the same position.
7. Support the suspension with a jack and remove the dust cover.
8. Disconnect the spindle by tapping with a hammer.
9. Remove the strut bracket bolts from the steering knuckle.
10. Disconnect the tie rod end from the knuckle and the knuckle from the control arm.
11. Remove the dust seal and the spindle from the knuckle.

To install:

12. Install the new seal and the spindle to the knuckle.
13. Connect the knuckle to the ball joint and tighten the nut to 40 ft. lbs.
14. Connect the knuckle to the strut damper and tighten the bolts to 66 ft. lbs.
15. Install the tie rod end to the knuckle and tighten the nut 30 ft. lbs.
16. Install the spindle and replace the dust cover and remove the jack from under the suspension.

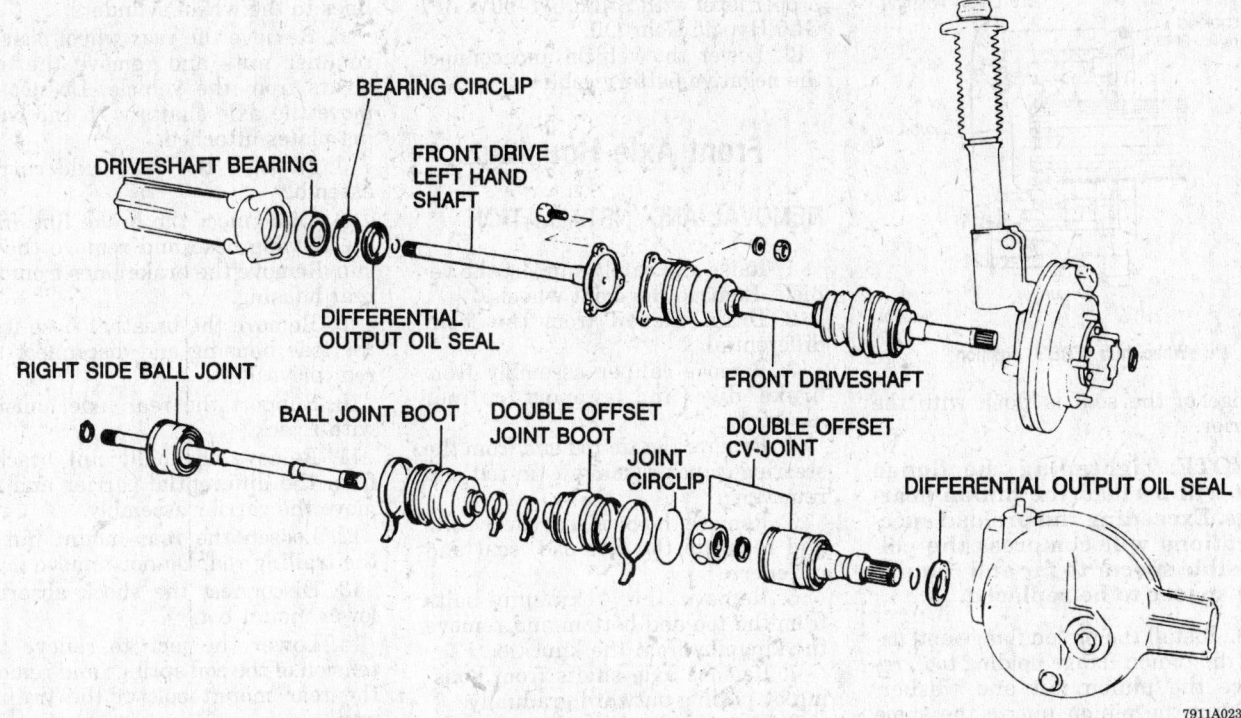

BEARING CIRCLIP

DRIVESHAFT BEARING

FRONT DRIVE
LEFT HAND
SHAFT

DIFFERENTIAL
OUTPUT OIL SEAL

RIGHT SIDE BALL JOINT

BALL JOINT BOOT

DOUBLE OFFSET
JOINT BOOT

JOINT
CIRCLIP

DOUBLE OFFSET
CV-JOINT

FRONT DRIVESHAFT

DIFFERENTIAL OUTPUT OIL SEAL

7911A023

Exploded view of the halfshaft assembly

17. Install the wheel hub assembly and connect the locking hub.

18. Install the wheels and lower the vehicle.

19. Connect the negative battery cable.

Manual Locking Hubs

REMOVAL AND INSTALLATION

1. Disconnect the negative battery cable and remove the locking hub cover.

2. Raise and support the vehicle safely.

3. Remove the locking hub body assembly.

NOTE: The manual locking hubs must not be packed with grease.

To install:

4. Install a new O-ring to the locking hub assembly.

5. Install the locking hub body assembly to the wheel hub flange and tighten the hub body bolts to 18 ft. lbs.

6. Install a new gasket in the manual locking hub cover.

7. Replace the locking hub cover and connect the negative battery cable.

8. Lower the vehicle.

NOTE: The O mark on the hub knob must be in the FREE position. Tighten the locking hub cover bolts to 106 inch lbs.

Automatic Locking Hubs

REMOVAL AND INSTALLATION

1. Disconnect the negative battery cable and remove the automatic locking hub cover.

2. Disconnect the automatic hub body assembly.

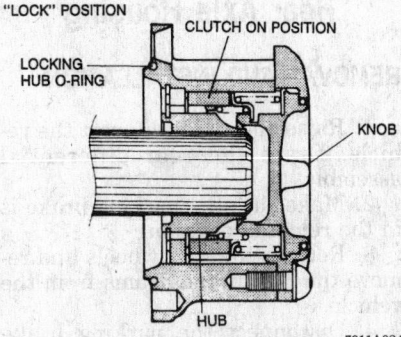

"LOCK" POSITION

CLUTCH ON POSITION

LOCKING
HUB O-RING

KNOB

HUB

7911A024

Wheel hub "LOCK" position

To install:

3. Install a new O-ring to the automatic locking hub body assembly.

4. Connect the automatic locking hub body assembly to the wheel hub flange. Tighten the hub body assembly bolts to 18 ft. lbs.

5. Install a new gasket in the automatic locking hub cover and replace the hub cover.

6. Connect the negative battery cable.

Pinion Seal

REMOVAL AND INSTALLATION

1. Raise and safely support the vehicle.

2. Matchmark and remove the driveshaft.

3. Check the turning torque of the pinion before proceeding.

4. Using a pinion flange holding tool, remove the pinion nut and the washer.

5. Remove the pinion flange from the differential carrier and pry out the pinion seal.

To install:

6. Clean and inspect the sealing surface of the carrier.

7. Using a seal driver, install the new seal into the carrier until the

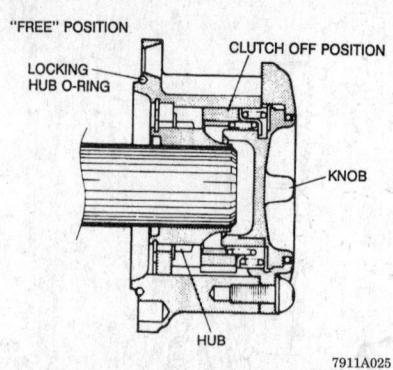

Wheel hub "FREE" position

flange of the seal is flush with the carrier.

NOTE: Tightening the flange nut will preload the pinion bearings. Exceeding the preload specifications will compress the collapsible spacer to far and require the spacer to be replaced.

8. Install the pinion flange and using the pinion flange holding tool, replace the pinion nut and washer. Tighten the pinion nut to the same torque as before.

9. Align the matchmarks and install the driveshaft.

10. Check the level of the differential fluid when finished.

Differential Carrier

REMOVAL AND INSTALLATION

1. Raise and safely support the vehicle and disconnect the negative battery cable. Drain the oil from the rear differential.

2. Remove the left and right axle shafts.

3. Disconnect the driveshaft.

4. Remove the 4 mounting bolts to the upper rear suspension arm.

5. Support the differential carrier with a proper jack.

6. Remove the differential case nuts and lower the differential assembly from the rear housing.

To install:

7. Clean and inspect the sealing surfaces of the carrier and the housing.

8. Using a liquid sealant on the carrier, install the carrier in the housing and tighten the nuts to 13–20 ft. lbs.

9. Replace the 4 mounting bolts to the upper rear suspension arm and tighten to 41 ft. lbs.

10. Connect the rear driveshaft and replace the left and rear axles.

11. Refill the rear differential to the proper level with SAE 75W–90W API GL5 Hypoid Gear Oil.

12. Lower the vehicle and connect the negative battery cable.

Front Axle Housing

REMOVAL AND INSTALLATION

1. Raise and safely support the vehicle. Remove the front wheels.

2. Drain the oil from the front differential.

3. Remove caliper assembly from brake disc and support caliper assembly.

4. Remove the tie rod end from the steering knuckle using a tie rod end remover.

5. Remove the 8 oil seal cover bolts and separate the felt pad, seal and retainer.

6. Remove the 4 kingpin bolts from the top and bottom and remove the kingpins from the knuckle.

7. Remove axle shafts from housing by pulling outward gradually.

8. Remove the bolts between the flange yoke and companion flange and disconnect the front drive shaft.

9. Remove the 8 U-joint nuts and remove the housing assembly.

To install:

10. Install the housing and torque the housing U-bolt nuts to 43 ft. lbs.

11. Connect the front drive shaft and install the bolts.

12. Install the front axle shafts and install the kingpins. Apply Loctite® to the kingpin bolts.

13. Install oil seal, felt pad and retainer and tighten the 8 cover bolts.

14. Install the tie rod end to the steering knuckle.

15. Install the front caliper to the disc and install the front wheels.

16. Refill the differential with the proper lubricant and bleed the brake system when finished.

Rear Axle Housing

REMOVAL AND INSTALLATION

1. Raise and safely support the vehicle. Drain the rear differential assembly.

2. Make sure the parking brake is in the released position.

3. Remove the rear wheels and remove the rear brake drums from the vehicle.

4. Disconnect the parking brake cables from the levers. Remove the parking brake lever stop plates.

5. Disconnect and plug the brake lines to the wheel cylinders.

6. Remove the rear wheel bearing retainer nuts and remove the axle shafts from the vehicle. Do not remove the axle shafts with the backing plates attached.

7. Remove the rear axle carrier assembly.

8. Disconnect the brake line from the flexible hose and remove the E-clip. Remove the brake lines from the rear housing.

9. Remove the breather hose from the axle housing and disconnect the rear driveshaft.

10. Support the rear axle housing with a jack.

11. Remove the ball joint bracket from the differential carrier and remove the carrier assembly.

12. Loosen the rear mount nut of the trailing rod. Do not remove it.

13. Disconnect the shock absorber lower mount bot.

14. Lower the jack to relieve the tension of the coil springs and remove the rear mount bolt of the trailing arm.

15. Remove the rear axle housing.

To install:

16. Place the rear axle housing on a jack and install the trailing rod rear mounting bolts. Mount the nuts but do not tighten.

17. Install the coil spring on the spring seat and raise the axle housing.

18. Replace the shock absorber lower mounting bolts. Do not tighten.

19. Install the differential carrier assembly and replace the rear upper ball joint bracket onto the carrier assembly and tighten to 37 ft. lbs.

20. Install the rear driveshaft and remove the jack from under the axle housing.

21. Replace the breather hose and brake lines to axle housing. Tighten them securely.

22. Connect the flexible brake hose to the bracket on the axle housing and secure with the E-clip.

23. Tighten the trailing rod nuts and the shock absorber nuts to 66 ft. lbs.

24. Install the brake line to the flexible hose and replace the axle shafts.

25. Install the brake lines to the wheel cylinders and replace the brake drums.

26. Install the wheels and refill the rear differential assembly.

27. Bleed the brake system and lower the vehicle.

STEERING

Steering Wheel

REMOVAL AND INSTALLATION

1. Disconnect the negative battery cable.
2. Disconnect the horn button and remove the steering wheel shaft nut.
3. Make matchmarks on the steering wheel and the shaft to use as a guide during reinstallation.
4. Remove the steering wheel, using a suitable steering wheel puller.
To install:
5. Install the steering wheel onto the shaft, aligning the matchmarks.
6. Install and tighten the shaft nut to 24 ft. lbs.
7. Install the horn button and connect the negative battery cable.

Manual Steering Gear

REMOVAL AND INSTALLATION

1. As required, raise and support the vehicle safely. Disconnect the steering lower shaft mounting bolts.
2. Disconnect the center link end from the pitman arm.
3. Remove the 3 steering gear box mounting bolts.
4. Disconnect the steering lower shaft joint and remove the steering gear.
To install:
5. Install the steering gear box by connecting to the lower shaft joint.

NOTE: Align the flat part of the steering gear worm shaft with the bolt hole of the lower shaft joint.

6. Replace the steering gear box mounting bolts and tighten to 50–72 ft. lbs.
7. Attach the center link to the pitman arm and tighten the nut to 22–50 ft. lbs.
8. Connect the lower shaft mounting bolts and tighten to 14–22 ft. lbs.

ADJUSTMENT

1. Check the worm shaft to make sure it is free from thrust play.
2. Place the pitman arm in a position that is nearly parallel with the worm shaft.
3. With the pitman arm in this position, the front wheels are in a straight forward position.

4. Measure the worm shaft starting torque from it's straight forward position. The torque should be 0.4–0.7 ft. lbs.
5. Adjust the worm shaft adjusting bolt to specifications.

Power Steering Gear

REMOVAL AND INSTALLATION

1. Disconnect the negative battery cable.
2. Remove the coolant reservoir tank from the radiator.
3. Disconnect the steering column lower shaft from the gear box.
4. Raise and safely support the vehicle.
5. Remove the center link nut and lock washer and disconnect the center link from the pitman arm, using a pitman arm puller.
6. Lower the vehicle. Remove the pressure hose from the power steering gear assembly and plug.
7. Disconnect the return hose and plug. Remove the 3 power steering gear mounting bolts.
8. Remove the power steering gear. Disconnect the pitman arm from the gear assembly, note the alignment marks.
To install:
9. Align the matchmarks on the pitman arm and the power steering gear sector shaft. Install the pitman arm to the gear assembly and tighten the nut to 95 ft. lbs.
10. Install the power steering gear assembly on the vehicle and tighten the mounting bolts to 72 ft. lbs.
11. Connect the power steering pressure and return hoses.
12. Raise and safely support the vehicle.
13. Install the center link to the pitman arm and tighten the nut to 40 ft. lbs. Lower the vehicle.

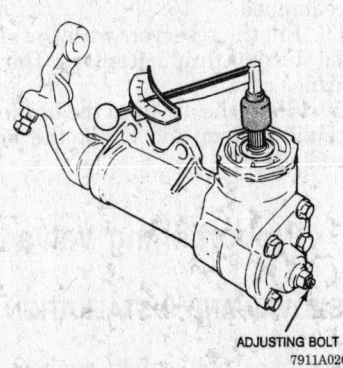

ADJUSTING BOLT
7911A026

Adjusting the steering gear assembly

14. Connect the steering column lower shaft to the gear assembly and tighten the bolts to 29 ft. lbs.
15. Install the coolant reservoir tank to the radiator. Refill the power steering pump.
16. Connect the negative battery cable. Run the engine and operate the power steering. Recheck the fluid level and for any leaks.

ADJUSTMENT

1. Check the worm shaft to make sure it is free from thrust play.
2. Place the pitman arm in a position that is nearly parallel with the worm shaft.
3. With the pitman arm in this position, the front wheels are in a straight forward state.
4. Measure the worm shaft starting torque from it's straight forward state. The torque should be 0.4–0.7 ft. lbs.
5. Adjust the worm shaft adjusting bolt to specifications.

Power steering Pump

REMOVAL AND INSTALLATION

NOTE: Before disconnecting the power steering pressure and return line at the pump assembly, make sure any dirt or grease is removed.

1. Disconnect the negative battery cable. Remove the coolant reservoir tank from the radiator.
2. Loosen the air conditioning compressor adjusting and pivot bolts, if equipped.
3. Loosen the power steering pump adjusting and mounting bolts, if not equipped with air conditioning.
4. Remove the power steering belt.
5. Disconnect the power steering pressure and return hose and plug.
6. Disconnect the power steering pressure switch lead wire at the switch terminal.
7. Remove the engine oil filter.
8. Remove the power steering pump mounting and adjusting bolts.
9. Remove the power steering pump.
To install:
10. Install the power steering pump and replace the pump mounting bolts. Do not tighten.
11. Install the power steering pump pressure switch lead wire to the switch terminal.
12. Replace the power steering pressure and return hoses.

13. Install the power steering belt and tighten the power steering pump mounting bolts to 21 ft. lbs.

14. Tighten the air conditioning mounting bolts to 21 ft. lbs., if equipped.

15. Replace the coolant reservoir tank to the radiator and connect the negative battery cable. Refill the power steering pump.

16. Replace the oil filter and fill the crankcase to the proper level.

17. Run the engine and operate the power steering. Recheck the fluid level and for any leaks.

BELT ADJUSTMENT

1. To adjust the power steering belt tension, loosen the adjusting bolt of the air conditioning compressor, if equipped, or that of the power steering pump for vehicles without air conditioning.

2. Adjust the belt tension to 0.24–0.35 in. deflection, using the proper belt tension gauge.

3. Tighten the proper adjusting and mounting bolts to the specified torque.

SYSTEM BLEEDING

1. Raise and support the vehicle safely.

2. Fill the power steering reservoir to the specified level.

3. Run the engine for 3 to 5 minutes, stop it and add fluid if necessary to reach specified level.

4. With the engine stopped, turn the steering wheel to the left and to the right as far as it turns. Repeat a few times and refill the reservoir.

5. With the engine running at idle speed, bleed air from the system by loosening the bleeder valve at the gear assembly.

6. Repeat the stop to stop turn of the steering wheel until all the foam is gone.

7. Tighten the bleed valve securely. Recheck the fluid level in the reservoir.

NOTE: When air bleeding is not complete, it is indicated by a foaming fluid on the level indicator or a humming noise from the power steering pump.

Tie Rod Ends

REMOVAL AND INSTALLATION

1. Raise and safely support the vehicle and remove the wheels.

2. Remove the tie rod end from the steering knuckle, using a suitable tie rod end remover tool.

3. Mark the tie rod end locknut position on the tie rod thread.

4. Loosen the locknut and remove the tie rod end from the tie rod.

To install:

5. Install the tie rod end locknut and the tie rod end to the tie rod. Align the locknut with the mark on the tie rod thread and tighten the locknut to 48 ft. lbs.

6. Connect the tie rod end to the steering knuckle. Tighten the castle nut until the holes of the split pin are aligned but only within the specified torque 33 ft. lbs.

BRAKES

Master Cylinder

REMOVAL AND INSTALLATION

1. Disconnect the negative battery cable. Remove the air cleaner case.

2. Disconnect the reservoir lead wire.

3. Clean the outside of the reservoir and remove the fluid from the reservoir.

4. Disconnect and plug the brake fluid lines at the master cylinder.

5. Remove the master cylinder to booster mounting bolts and remove the master cylinder.

To install:

6. Install the new master cylinder and tighten the mounting bolts to 12 ft. lbs.

7. Install the hydraulic brake lines to the master cylinder and tighten and tighten the flare nuts to 13 ft. lbs.

8. Replace the reservoir lead wire, if equipped.

9. Fill the reservoir with the specified brake fluid. Replace the air cleaner case.

10. Bleed the air from the brake hydraulic system and check the brake pedal play.

Proportioning Valve

REMOVAL AND INSTALLATION

1. Raise and safely support the vehicle.

2. Disconnect and plug the hydraulic brake lines from the proportioning valve assembly.

3. Remove the proportioning valve from the vehicle body.

NOTE: The proportioning valve should be removed with the spring attached.

To install:

4. Install the proportioning valve to the vehicle body and tighten the mounting bolts to 20 ft. lbs.

5. Connect the hydraulic brake lines to the proportioning valve and tighten the flare nuts to 13 ft. lbs.

6. Fill the brake reservoir to the proper level and bleed the brake hydraulic system. Lower the vehicle.

NOTE: Bleed the air from the proportioning valve bleeder valve.

Power Brake Booster

REMOVAL AND INSTALLATION

1. Disconnect the negative battery cable. Remove the air cleaner case.

2. Remove the fluid from the brake reservoir and remove the master cylinder.

3. Disconnect the vacuum hose from the booster. Remove the pushrod clevis pin and cotter pin from the brake pedal arm.

4. Disconnect the brake booster mounting nuts and remove the brake booster from the vehicle.

5. Disconnect the pedal attachment from the booster.

To install:

6. Connect the pedal attachment to the booster and install the booster to the vehicle. Tighten the mounting nuts to 7.5–11.5 ft. lbs.

7. Install the pushrod clevis pin and cotter pin to the brake pedal arm.

8. Connect the vacuum hose to the booster and install the master cylinder to the booster.

9. Replace the air cleaner case and connect the negative battery cable.

10. Fill the brake reservoir and bleed the brake hydraulic system.

Brake Caliper

REMOVAL AND INSTALLATION

1. Disconnect the negative battery cable. Raise and safely support the vehicle.

2. Remove the wheels. Disconnect and plug the brake line.

3. Remove the caliper mounting bolts and remove the caliper from the vehicle.

To install:

4. Install the caliper on the vehicle. Tighten the mounting bolts to 65 ft. lbs.

5. Connect the hydraulic brake line, using 2 new washers. Replace the front wheels.

6. Lower the vehicle. Connect the negative battery cable.

7. Fill the brake reservoir and bleed the hydraulic brake system.

Disc Brake Pads

REMOVAL AND INSTALLATION

1. Disconnect the negative battery cable. Raise and safely support the vehicle.

2. Remove the wheels.

3. Disconnect the brake caliper.

NOTE: Do not allow the caliper hang from the brake hose. Support it by the mounting bracket.

4. Remove the disc pads from the caliper. Disconnect the anti-rattle springs.

To install:

5. Connect the anti rattle springs and install the brake pads on to caliper assembly.

6. Connect the brake caliper and install the front wheels.

7. Lower the vehicle. Connect the negative battery cable.

Brake Rotor

REMOVAL AND INSTALLATION

1. Disconnect the negative battery cable.

2. Raise and safely support the vehicle. Remove the wheel assembly.

3. Remove the brake caliper mounting bracket, with the caliper and the brake line attached, move it out of the way and support it.

NOTE: Do not allow the caliper hang from the brake hose. Support it by the mounting bracket.

4. Install 2 bolts into the threaded holes in the brake rotor and tighten them evenly. This will remove the rotor from the hub assembly.

To install:

5. Install the new brake rotor on the hub and install the caliper assembly.

6. Install the front wheels and tighten to 65 ft. lbs.

7. Lower the vehicle and connect the negative battery cable.

Brake Drums

REMOVAL AND INSTALLATION

1. Disconnect the negative battery cable. Raise and safely support the vehicle.

2. Make sure the parking brake is released.

3. Remove the wheels and the rear drum nuts from the vehicle.

4. Remove the brake drum, using a slide hammer puller.

To install:

5. Install the brake drum, tighten the brake drum nuts to 58 ft. lbs.

6. Install the rear wheels and lower the vehicle. Connect the negative battery cable.

Brake Shoes

REMOVAL AND INSTALLATION

1. Disconnect the negative battery cable. Raise and safely support the vehicle.

2. Remove the rear wheels from the vehicle. Remove the rear brake drums.

3. Remove the brake shoe hold-down springs.

4. Disconnect the parking brake cable from the parking brake shoe lever and remove the brake shoes.

To install:

5. Install the brake shoes and install the parking brake lever and cable to the assembly.

6. Install the brake shoe hold-down springs and install the rear brake drums.

7. Install the rear wheels, lower the vehicle and connect the negative battery terminal.

Wheel Cylinder

REMOVAL AND INSTALLATION

1. Disconnect the negative battery cable. Raise and safely support the vehicle.

2. Remove the rear wheels and brake drums from the vehicle.

3. Remove the rear brake shoes and disconnect the brake line from the rear of the wheel cylinder. Plug the brake line.

4. Remove the 2 rear wheel cylinder mounting bolts. Remove the rear wheel cylinder.

To install:

5. Install the wheel cylinder and tighten the mounting bolts to 6.0–8.5 ft. lbs.

6. Connect the brake line to the wheel cylinder and install the rear brake shoes.

7. Replace the rear brake drums and the rear wheels.

8. Lower the vehicle. Connect the negative battery cable.

9. Bleed the brake system and check for any leaks when finished.

Parking Brake Cable

REMOVAL AND INSTALLATION

1. Disconnect the parking brake cable from the parking lever.

2. Raise and safely support the vehicle. Remove the rear wheels and brake drums from the vehicle.

3. Remove the rear brake shoes and disconnect the parking brake cable from the parking brake shoe lever.

4. Remove the cable from the brake backing plate by squeezing the parking brake cable stop ring.

To install:

5. Install the cable to the backing plate and to the brake shoe lever.

6. Install the brake shoes and install the rear brake drums.

7. Install the rear wheels and connect the cable to the parking brake lever.

ADJUSTMENT

1. Adjust the parking brake lever by loosening or tightening the self locking nut at the park brake lever.

2. The proper adjustment is when the parking brake lever is within 7–9 notches, when the lever is pulled up at 44 lbs.

3. Check the rear drum for dragging after adjustment.

FRONT SUSPENSION

MacPherson Strut

REMOVAL AND INSTALLATION

1. Disconnect the negative battery cable.

2. Raise and safely support the vehicle. Allow the front suspension to hang free.

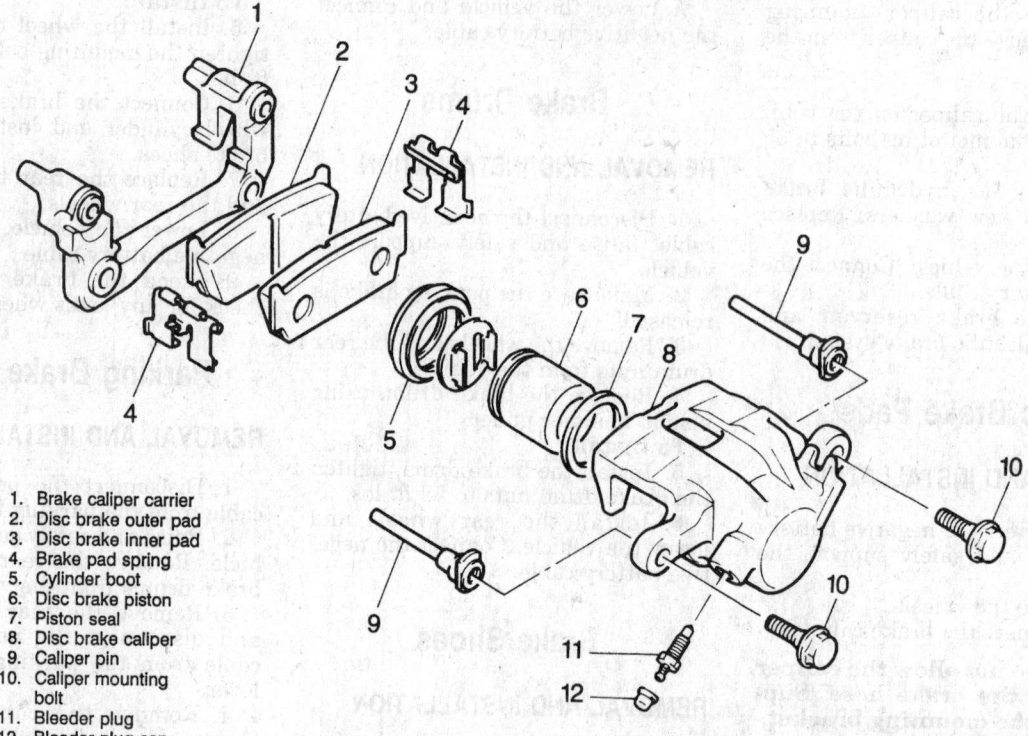

1. Brake caliper carrier
2. Disc brake outer pad
3. Disc brake inner pad
4. Brake pad spring
5. Cylinder boot
6. Disc brake piston
7. Piston seal
8. Disc brake caliper
9. Caliper pin
10. Caliper mounting bolt
11. Bleeder plug
12. Bleeder plug cap

7911A027

Exploded view of the front disc brake assembly

3. Remove the front wheel. Disconnect the E-clip mounting the brake hose and remove the brake hose from the strut bracket.

4. Remove the strut bracket to steering knuckle bolts.

5. Lower the vehicle. Remove the strut support nuts, while holding the strut by hand. Remove the strut assembly.

To install:

6. Install the strut assembly and tighten the strut support nuts to 18 ft. lbs.

7. Raise and safely support the vehicle.

8. Install the strut bracket to steering knuckle bolts and tighten to 66 ft. lbs.

9. Connect the brake hose to the strut bracket using the E-clip.

10. Replace the front wheels and lower the vehicle.

11. Connect the negative battery cable.

Coil Springs

REMOVAL AND INSTALLATION

1. Disconnect the negative battery cable.

2. Raise and safely support the vehicle. Allow the front suspension to hang free.

3. Remove the front wheel and the locking hub assembly.

4. Remove the front axle circlip and washer.

5. Remove the brake caliper mounting bracket, with the caliper and the brake line attached, move it out of the way and support it.

6. Remove the brake disc and disconnect the stabilizer link from the control arm.

7. Disconnect the tie rod end and support the lower control arm using a jack.

8. Disconnect the strut bracket and remove the ball joint castle nut.

9. Remove the steering knuckle and the wheel hub assembly while lowering the jack.

10. Remove the coil spring from the vehicle.

To install:

11. Install the coil spring to the vehicle and install the wheel hub and steering knuckle while raising the jack.

12. Connect the strut bracket and install the ball joint castle nut.

13. Connect the tie rod end and connect the stabilizer link to the control arm.

14. Install the brake disc and connect the caliper assembly.

15. Install the front axle circlip and washer and install the locking hub assembly.

16. Install the front wheels, lower the vehicle and connect the negative battery cable.

Lower Ball Joints

INSPECTION

1. Inspect for the smoothness of the rotation.

2. Check the ball stud for damage.

3. Inspect the dust shield for damage.

REMOVAL AND INSTALLATION

1. Disconnect the negative battery cable. Remove the coil spring from the vehicle.

2. Remove the control arm mounting bolts.

3. Remove the control arm.

4. Disconnect the ball joint from the control arm and remove the ball joint.

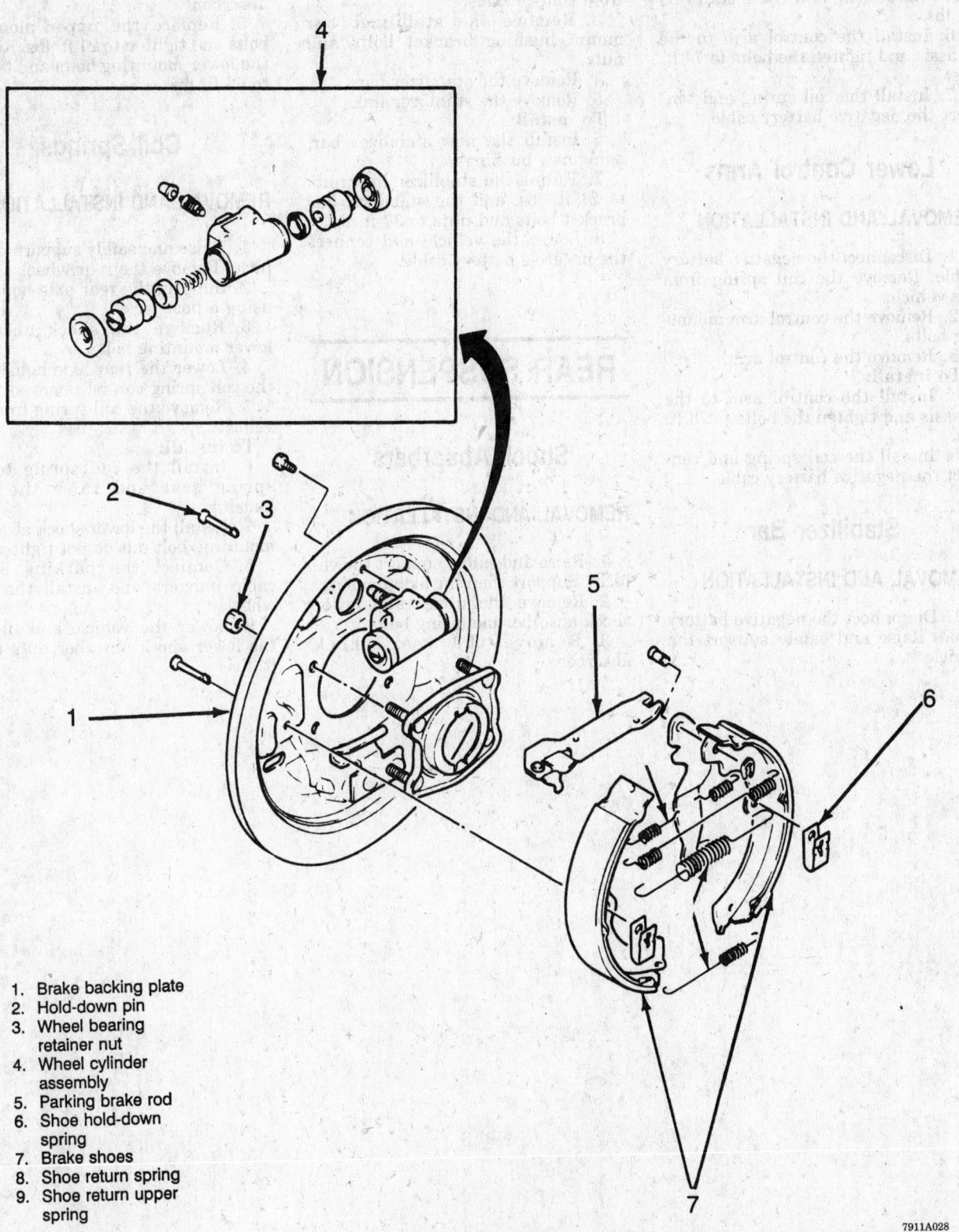

1. Brake backing plate
2. Hold-down pin
3. Wheel bearing
   retainer nut
4. Wheel cylinder
   assembly
5. Parking brake rod
6. Shoe hold-down
   spring
7. Brake shoes
8. Shoe return spring
9. Shoe return upper
   spring

Exploded view of the rear brake drum assembly

7911A028

To install:

5. Install the ball joint to the control arm and tighten the bolts to 63 ft. lbs.

6. Install the control arm to the chassis and tighten the bolts to 74 ft. lbs.

7. Install the coil spring and connect the negative battery cable.

Lower Control Arms

REMOVAL AND INSTALLATION

1. Disconnect the negative battery cable. Remove the coil spring from the vehicle.

2. Remove the control arm mounting bolts.

3. Remove the control arm.

To install:

4. Install the control arm to the chassis and tighten the bolts to 74 ft. lbs.

5. Install the coil spring and connect the negative battery cable.

Stabilizer Bar

REMOVAL AND INSTALLATION

1. Disconnect the negative battery cable. Raise and safely support the vehicle.

2. Disconnect the left and the right stabilizer ball joints from the front control arms.

3. Remove the stabilizer bar mount bushing bracket bolts and nuts.

4. Remove the stabilizer bar.

5. Remove the stabilizer links.

To install:

6. Install the new stabilizer bar, using new bushings.

7. Torque the stabilizer link nuts to 21 ft. lbs. and the stabilizer bar bracket bolts and nuts to 37 ft. lbs.

8. Lower the vehicle and connect the negative battery cable.

REAR SUSPENSION

Shock Absorbers

REMOVAL AND INSTALLATION

1. Raise and safely support the vehicle. Support the rear axle housing.

2. Remove the upper and lower shock absorber mounting bolts.

3. Remove the rear shock absorber.

To install:

4. Install the the rear shock absorber.

5. Replace the upper mounting bolts and tighten to 21 ft. lbs. Replace the lower mounting bolts and tighten to 63 ft. lbs.

Coil Springs

REMOVAL AND INSTALLATION

1. Raise and safely support the vehicle. Remove the rear wheels.

2. Support the rear axle housing, using a floor jack.

3. Remove the shock absorber lower mounting bolt.

4. Lower the rear axle housing so the coil spring can be removed.

5. Remove the coil spring from the vehicle.

To install:

6. Install the coil spring to the spring seat and raise the axle housing.

7. Install the lower shock absorber mounting bolt but do not tighten.

8. Connect the parking brake cable hangers and install the rear wheels.

9. Lower the vehicle and tighten the lower shock absorber nuts to 64 ft. lbs.

FIRING ORDERS

NOTE: To avoid confusion, always replace spark plug wires one at a time.

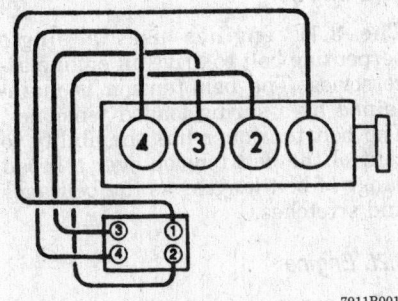

7911B001

2.3L and 2.6L Engines
Engine Firing Order: 1–3–4–2
Distributor Rotation: Counterclockwise

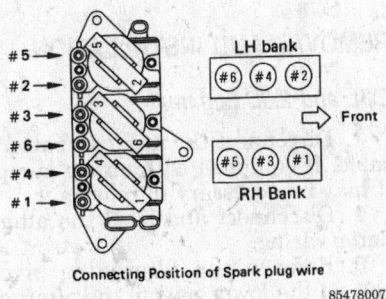

Connecting Position of Spark plug wire

85478007

3.2L Engine
Engine Firing Order: 1–2–3–4–5–6
Distributorless Ignition System

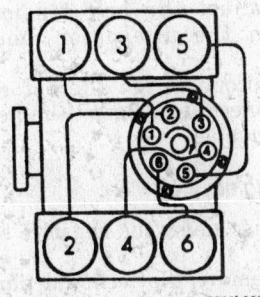

7911b002

3.1L Engines
Engine Firing Order:
1–2–3–4–5–6
Distributor Rotation: Clockwise

ENGINE ELECTRICAL

NOTE: Disconnecting the negative battery cable on some vehicles may interfere with the functions of the on board computer systems and may require the computer to undergo a relearning process, once the negative battery cable is reconnected.

Distributor

REMOVAL

2.3L and 2.6L Engines

1. Disconnect the battery ground cable and the distributor wiring connector.
2. Turn the engine to TDC of cylinder No. 4. Remove the distributor cap and mark the position of the rotor to the distributor body and the distributor body to the engine block. This allows for easier installation.
3. Remove the distributor hold-down bolt and remove the distributor.

3.1L Engines

1. Disconnect the negative battery cable.
2. Disconnect and label the spark plug wires at the distributor cap.
3. Remove the distributor cap from the distributor. Disconnect and label the distributor wiring.
4. Using a piece of chalk, match-mark the rotor to the distributor housing and the housing to the engine.
5. Remove the distributor hold-down nut, the clamp and lift the distributor from the engine.

NOTE: When removing the distributor, it may be necessary to rotate the distributor shaft slightly to disengage it from the drive gear.

INSTALLATION

Timing Not Disturbed

1. Lower the distributor into the engine and align the rotor and distributor housing to the matchmarks.

2. Check and/or adjust the ignition timing when finished.

Timing Disturbed

3.1L ENGINES

1. Remove the No. 1 spark plug.
2. Rotate the crankshaft in the normal direction of rotation until compression is felt at the spark plug hole.
3. Continue rotating the engine in the same direction while observing the timing marks at the indicator line up when No. 1 cylinder is at TDC.
4. Install the distributor and align the rotor with the No. 1 lug on the distributor cap.
5. Check and/or adjust the ignition timing when finished.

2.3L AND 2.6L ENGINES

1. Remove the valve cover. Turn the engine so cylinder No. 4 is on TDC of the compression stroke and the camshaft pulley setting mark is aligned with the setting mark on the front plate.
2. Lubricate the distributor O-ring with engine oil. Align the distributor setting mark with the distributor shaft setting mark.
3. Install the distributor on the cylinder head aligning the mark on the cylinder head with the mark on the distributor shaft.
4. Install the distributor hold-down bolt and valve cover. Install the distributor cap and the distributor wiring. Connect the negative battery terminal and time the engine. Torque the hold-down bolt to 14 ft. lbs. (19 Nm).

Distributorless Ignition

REMOVAL AND INSTALLATION

3.2L Engine

1. Disconnect negative battery cable.
2. Disconnect spark plug wires.
3. Disconnect electrical connectors on the Engine Control Module (ECM), power supply and crank angle sensor.
4. Remove the three mounting bolts from the Electronic Ignition (EI) assembly. Remove the EI assembly.

Ignition Timing

ADJUSTMENT

NOTE: The following procedures are basic outlines for timing the ignition system. As emission controls change and are updated, the timing procedures will change. Check the underhood emissions sticker for updated timing instructions and follow them exactly.

2.3L and 2.6L Engines

NOTE: Set the air gap in the distributor before timing the engine. The timing marks are located near the front crankshaft pulley and consist of a pointer with graduations attached to the engine block and a mark on the crankshaft pulley.

1. Check and correct the air gap in the distributor.
2. Locate and clean the timing marks on the crankshaft pulley and the front of the engine.
3. Using an inductive pick-up timing light, connect it to the No. 1 spark plug wire. Attach a timing light to the ignition coil.
4. If the distributor is equipped with a vacuum advance, disconnect and plug the vacuum line.
5. Make sure all wires from the timing light and tachometer are clear of the fan and belts. Start the engine.
6. Adjust the idle to the correct rpm.
7. Aim the timing light at the timing marks. Adjust the distributor until the timing marks are aligned.
8. Tighten the distributor mounting bolt and check the timing again.
9. Turn the engine OFF and remove the timing light and tachometer. Connect the distributor vacuum line.

3.1L Engine

1. Set the parking brake and block the drive wheels.
2. Operate the engine to normal operating temperatures and turn the air conditioning OFF, if equipped.
3. Verify that the Check Engine light is not turned ON.
4. Place the Electronic Spark Timing (EST) into the bypass mode by disconnect the timing connector.

NOTE: The EST is a single wire connector, located under the center console in the passenger compartment. Do not disconnect the 4-wire connector from the distributor.

5. Using an inductive pick-up timing light, connect it to the No. 1 spark plug wire.
6. Check and/or adjust the engine speed to 800 rpm.
7. Loosen the distributor hold-down bolt and turn the distributor until the timing mark, on the crankshaft pulley, is aligned with the 10 degree BTDC timing mark on the timing cover.
8. Tighten the distributor hold-down bolt.
9. Reconnect the timing connector and clear the ECM trouble code(s).

3.2L Engine

No adjustment is necessary.

Air Gap Setting

The air gap setting in the distributor should be checked and adjusted before the ignition timing is adjusted.

ADJUSTMENT

1. Remove the distributor cap, O-ring and rotor.
2. Use a feeler gauge to measure the air gap at the pick-up coil projection. The gap should be 0.008–0.016 in. for 3.1L engine or 0.012–0.020 in. for 2.3L and 2.6L engines; adjust it, if necessary.
3. Loosen the screws and move the signal generator until the gap is correct. Tighten the screws and recheck the gap.

NOTE: The electrical parts in this system are not repairable. If found to be defective, they must be replaced.

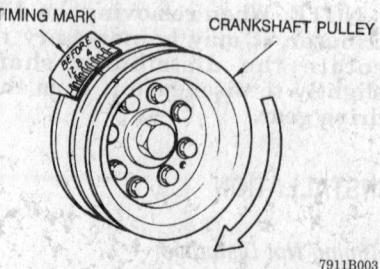

TIMING MARK   CRANKSHAFT PULLEY

7911B003

View of the ignition timing marks

Alternator

BELT TENSION ADJUSTMENT

2.3L and 2.6L Engines

1. Loosen the alternator pivot bolt.
2. Rotate the alternator to produce a belt deflection of 0.40 in. (10mm).
3. Tighten the alternator pivot bolt.

3.1L Engine

The 3.1L engines uses a single serpentine belt to drive all engine accessories. The belt tension is maintained by a spring loaded tensioner. The belt tensioner has the ability to control the belt tension over a broad range of belt lengths as the belt ages and stretches.

3.2L Engine

1. Loosen generator mounting bolt and adjuster lock bolt.
2. Adjust bolt by turning adjust bolt.
3. Install belt and tighten mounting bolt to 16 ft. lbs. (22 Nm).
4. Tighten lock bolt to 17 ft. lbs. (24 Nm).

REMOVAL AND INSTALLATION

2.3L and 2.6L Engines

1. Disconnect the negative battery cable. If equipped with an air pump, it may be necessary to remove it.
2. Disconnect and label the alternator wiring.
3. Remove the alternator pivot bolt on the lower part of the alternator. Remove the drive belt from the pulley.
4. Remove the alternator mounting bolt(s) and the alternator from the engine.
   To install:
5. Install the alternator.
6. Adjust the belt tension and tighten the alternator mounting bolts.
7. Reconnect the alternator's wiring connectors. Connect the negative battery cable.

3.1L Engine

1. Disconnect the negative battery cable.
2. Remove the terminal plug and the battery lead from the rear of the alternator.
3. Remove the drive belt.
4. Remove the bracket bolt from the rear of the alternator.

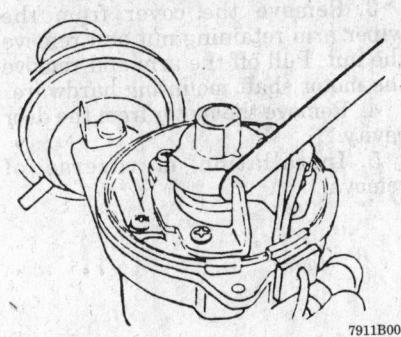

Adjusting the air gap — 2.3L engine

5. Remove the mounting bolts from the front of the alternator and the alternator from the vehicle.

To install:

6. Install the alternator and the mounting bolts.

7. Install the drive belt.

8. Torque the lower mounting bolt to 26 ft. lbs. (35 Nm), the upper mounting bolt to 18 ft. lbs. (25 Nm) and the air pump bracket bolt to 18 ft. lbs. (25 Nm).

9. Connect the terminal connector and the battery lead to the rear of the alternator. Reconnect the negative battery cable.

3.2L Engine

1. Disconnect negative battery cable.

2. Remove the front under cover.

3. Loosen the mounting bolt.

4. Loosen the lock and the adjusting bolts.

5. Remove the generator adjuster.

6. Remove the generator fixing bolt.

7. Disconnect the electrical connector from terminal "B". Remove the electrical connector from the generator.

8. Remove the generator from below.

To install:

9. Connect the electrical connector to terminal "B" and, from below, bring the generator into position to be installed.

10. Connect the electrical harness.

11. Temporarily secure the generator with mounting bolts.

12. Install the generator adjuster.

13. Loosen generator mounting bolt and adjuster lock bolt.

14. Adjust bolt by turning adjust bolt.

15. Install belt and tighten mounting bolt to 16 ft. lbs. (22 Nm).

16. Tighten lock bolt to 17 ft. lbs. (24 Nm).

17. Install the front under cover.
18. Connect negative battery cable.

Starter

REMOVAL AND INSTALLATION

Except 3.2L Engine

1. Disconnect the negative battery cable. Remove the skid plate if necessary.

2. On 4 cylinder engines, it may be necessary to disconnect and remove the EGR pipe.

3. Disconnect and label the starter wiring at the starter.

4. Remove the starter-to-engine bolts and the shims. Remove the starter from the vehicle.

To install:

5. Install the starter and shims to the engine and replace the bolts. Torque the bolts to 30 ft. lbs. (40 Nm).

6. Connect the electrical leads to the starter.

7. If the EGR pipe was removed, install it. Replace the skid plate, if removed.

8. Connect the negative battery cable.

3.2L Engine

1. Disconnect negative battery cable.

2. On vehicles equipped with automatic transmissions, disconnect Heated Oxygen Sensor connector.

3. Remove the front left exhaust pipe.

4. Remove the heat shield from the engine.

5. Disconnect the electrical connectors from terminals "B" and "S".

6. Remove the two mounting bolts starter mounting bolts.

7. Remove the starter from the bottom of the engine.

To install:

8. Install the engine from the bottom of the engine.

9. Install the two mounting bolts and tighten to 30 ft. lbs. (40 Nm).

10. Connect the electrical connector to terminals "B" and "S". Tighten the nut at terminal "B" to 73 in. lbs. (8.5 Nm).

11. Install the heat shield to the engine.

12. Install the front left exhaust pipe. Tighten the mounting nuts to 49 ft. lbs. (67 Nm).

13. Tighten the mounting bolts to 20 ft. lbs. (27 Nm).

14. On vehicles with automatic transmission, connect the Heated Oxygen Sensor connector.

15. Connect the negative battery cable.

CHASSIS ELECTRICAL

Heater Blower Motor

The heater blower motor is located under the right side of the dash.

REMOVAL AND INSTALLATION

1. Disconnect the negative battery cable.

2. Disconnect and label the blower motor electrical leads.

3. Remove the blower-to-heater unit screws and lower the blower motor assembly.

To install:

4. Install the heater blower motor, into the heater unit and install the screws.

5. Connect the electrical connectors to the heater blower motor.

6. Connect the negative battery cable.

Windshield Wiper Motor

REMOVAL AND INSTALLATION

Front

1. Disconnect the negative battery cable.

2. Disconnect the electrical connector from the wiper motor.

3. Remove the wiper motor bracket-to-chassis bolts.

4. Disconnect the wiper motor from the wiper linkage at the ball joint.

To install:

5. Connect the wiper motor to the wiper linkage at the ball joint.

6. Install the wiper motor-to-chassis bolts.

7. Connect the electrical connector to the wiper motor.

8. Connect the negative battery cable.

Rear

1. Disconnect the negative battery cable.

2. Remove the back door panel to expose the wiper motor and disconnect the motor wiring.

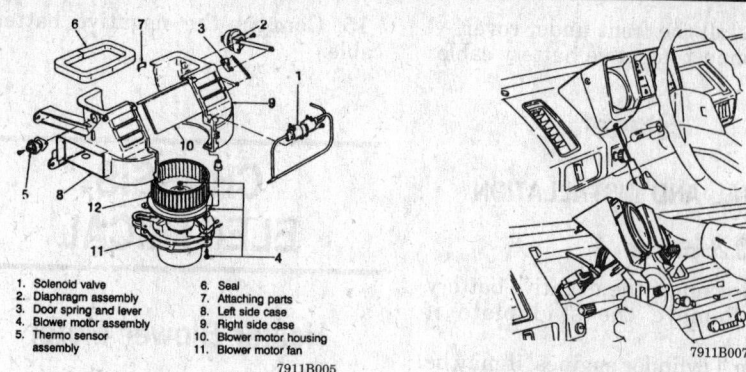

1. Solenoid valve
2. Diaphragm assembly
3. Door spring and lever
4. Blower motor assembly
5. Thermo sensor assembly
6. Seal
7. Attaching parts
8. Left side case
9. Right side case
10. Blower motor housing
11. Blower motor fan

7911B005

Exploded view of the heater blower motor

7911B007

Removing the instrument cluster — Trooper/Trooper II shown — Pick-Up similar

3. Remove the cover from the wiper arm retaining nut and remove the nut. Pull off the arm and remove the motor shaft mounting hardware.

4. Remove the motor from the door cavity.

5. Installation is reverse of removal.

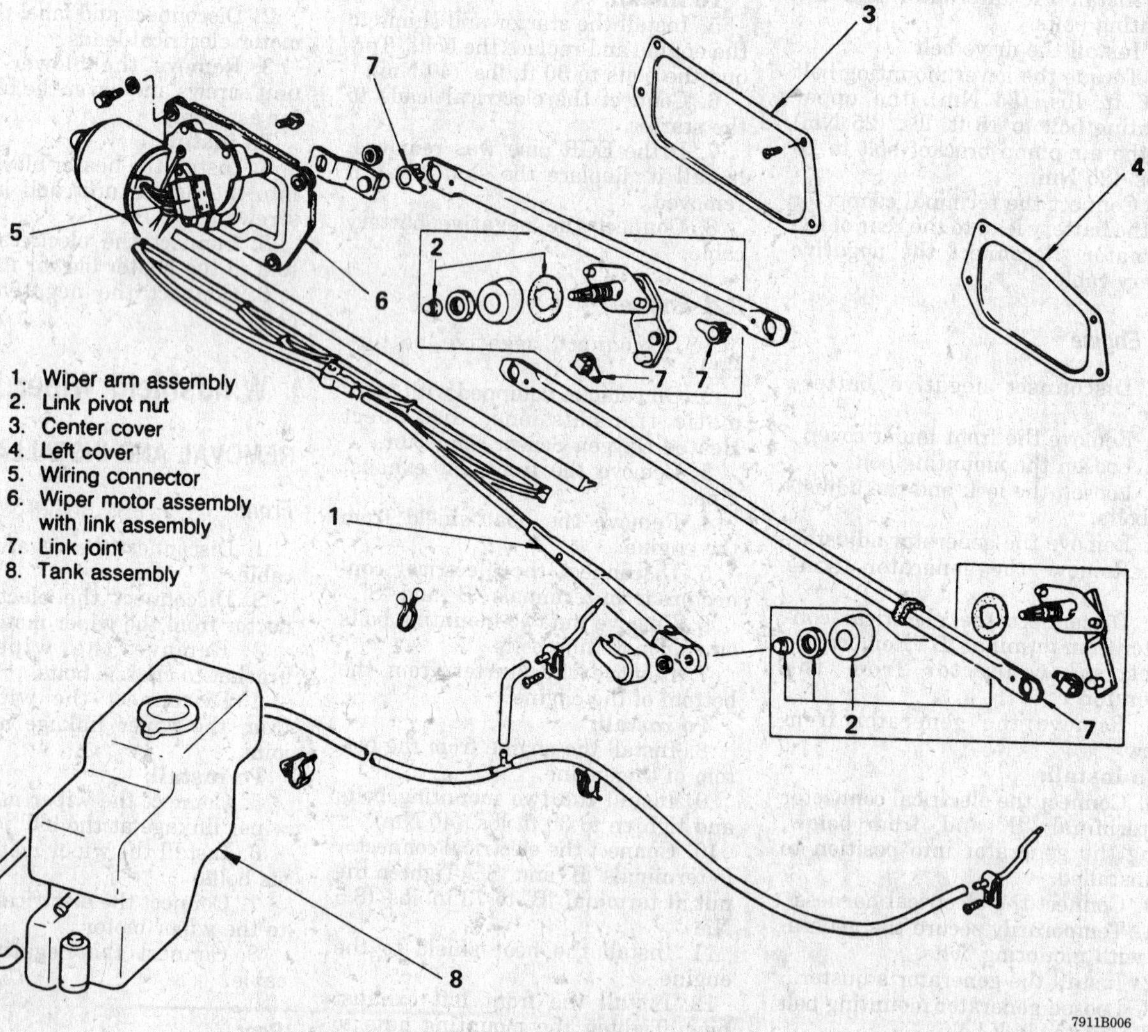

1. Wiper arm assembly
2. Link pivot nut
3. Center cover
4. Left cover
5. Wiring connector
6. Wiper motor assembly with link assembly
7. Link joint
8. Tank assembly

7911B006

Exploded view of the wiper motor and linkage assembly

Windshield Wiper Switch

REMOVAL AND INSTALLATION

Except Pick-Up and Amigo

The windshield wiper switch is a part of the combination switch located on the steering column.

Pick-Up and Amigo

The windshield wiper switch is a part of the switch cluster located on the left side of the instrument cluster.

1. Disconnect the negative battery cable.
2. Remove the instrument cluster-to-dash screws.
3. Pull the instrument cluster forward and disconnect the electrical connector from the switch cluster.
4. From the rear of the instrument cluster, loosen the switch cluster-to-instrument cluster bolts.
5. Separate the windshield wiper switch from the switch cluster.
   To install:
6. Install the windshield wiper switch to the switch cluster.
7. Tighten the switch cluster-to-instrument cluster bolts.
8. Connect the electrical connector to the switch cluster.
9. Install the instrument cluster.
10. Connect the negative battery cable.

Instrument Cluster

REMOVAL AND INSTALLATION

Trooper/Trooper II

1. Disconnect the negative battery cable.
2. Remove the steering wheel.
3. Remove the knob from the light switch.
4. Remove the cover-to-instrument panel screws and the cover.
5. Remove the instrument panel-to-dash screws and pull the panel forward.
6. Disconnect the electrical connectors and the speedometer cable from the rear of the instrument panel.
7. Remove the instrument panel from the vehicle.
   To install:
8. Connect the speedometer cable and the electrical connectors to the rear of the instrument cluster.
9. Install the instrument cluster to the dash.

10. Install the cover to the instrument cluster.
11. Install the knob to the light switch.
12. Install the steering wheel.
13. Connect the negative battery cable.

Pick-Up, Amigo and Rodeo

TILT STEERING WHEEL

1. Disconnect the negative battery cable.
2. Move the steering wheel to the fully down position.
3. Remove the instrument cluster-to-dash screws and pull the instrument cluster forward.
4. Disconnect the electrical connectors and the speedometer cable from the instrument cluster.
   To install:
5. Connect the speedometer cable and electrical connectors to the instrument cluster.
6. Install the instrument cluster to the dash.
7. Connect the negative battery cable.

EXCEPT TILT STEERING WHEEL

1. Disconnect the negative battery cable.
2. Remove the steering wheel and the steering wheel cowl.
3. Remove the instrument cluster-to-dash screws and pull the instrument cluster forward.
4. Disconnect the electrical connectors and the speedometer cable from the instrument cluster.
   To install:
5. Connect the speedometer cable and electrical connectors to the instrument cluster.
6. Install the instrument cluster to the dash.
7. Install the steering column cowl and the steering wheel.
8. Connect the negative battery cable.

Auxiliary Gauge Panel

REMOVAL AND INSTALLATION

Trooper/Trooper II

1. Disconnect the negative battery cable.
2. Remove the 2 screws holding the auxiliary gauge panel face plate and remove the face plate.
3. Remove the screws holding the gauges and pull the gauges forward.
4. Disconnect the wiring to the gauges and remove the gauge.

5. Installation is the reverse of removal.

Speedometer

REMOVAL AND INSTALLATION

Except Trooper/Trooper II

1. Disconnect the negative battery terminal.
2. Remove the instrument cluster. Remove the instrument cluster glass.
3. Pull the indicator needles off the shafts of the speedometer and tachometer.
4. Remove the speedometer fastening screws and remove the speedometer.
5. Installation is the reverse of removal. Be sure to align the instrument indicator needles when pressing them onto their shafts.

Trooper/Trooper II

1. Disconnect the negative battery cable.
2. Remove the instrument cluster.
3. Remove the speedometer holding screws from the instrument cluster and remove the speedometer.
   To install:
4. Install the speedometer to the instrument cluster.
5. Install the instrument cluster.
6. Connect the negative battery cable.

Headlight Switch

REMOVAL AND INSTALLATION

Trooper/Trooper II

The headlight switch is located on the lower left side of the dash.

1. Disconnect the negative battery cable.
2. Remove the headlight switch knob.
3. Disconnect and label the headlight switch wiring under the dashboard.
4. Remove the headlight switch locknut and the switch from the dash.
   To install:
5. Install the switch to the dash and secure with the locknut.
6. Connect the electrical connector to the headlight switch.
7. Install the headlight switch knob.
8. Connect the negative battery cable.

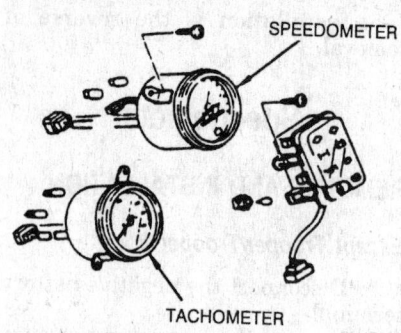

SPEEDOMETER

TACHOMETER

7911B008

Exploded view of the speedometer — Trooper/Trooper II

Pick-Up, Rodeo and Amigo

The push button headlight switch, is a part of the switch cluster located on the left side of the dash.

1. Disconnect the negative battery cable.
2. Remove the instrument cluster-to-dash screws.
3. Pull the instrument cluster forward and disconnect the electrical connector from the switch cluster.
4. From the rear of the instrument cluster, loosen the switch cluster-to-instrument cluster bolts.
5. Separate the headlight switch from the switch cluster.

To install:

6. Install the headlight switch to the switch cluster.
7. Tighten the switch cluster-to-instrument cluster bolts.
8. Connect the electrical connector to the switch cluster.
9. Install the instrument cluster.
10. Connect the negative battery cable.

Combination Switch

REMOVAL AND INSTALLATION

1. Disconnect the negative battery cable.
2. From the rear of the steering wheel, remove the horn pad screw and lift the horn pad upward to remove it.
3. Disconnect the electrical connector from the horn pad.
4. Remove the steering wheel-to-steering column nut.
5. Matchmark the steering wheel to the steering shaft for reinstallation purposes.

NOTE: Never apply a blow to the steering wheel shaft with a hammer or other impact tool, to remove the steering wheel, for the steering shaft may become damaged.

6. Using a steering wheel puller, press the steering wheel from the steering column.
7. Remove the contact ring.
8. Remove the steering column covers.
9. Disconnect the electrical connector from the combination switch.
10. Remove the combination switch-to-steering column screws and the switch.

To install:

11. Install the combination switch to the steering column and secure it with screws.
12. Connect the combination switch electrical connector.
13. Install the steering column cover.
14. Install the contact ring.
15. Align the steering wheel-to-steering column matchmarks and torque the nut to 22–29 ft. lbs. (30–40 Nm).
16. Connect the electrical connector to the horn pad.
17. Install the horn pad and the horn pad screw.
18. Connect the negative battery cable.

Ignition Lock/Switch

REMOVAL AND INSTALLATION

1. Disconnect the negative battery cable.
2. From the rear of the steering wheel, remove the horn pad screw and lift the horn pad upward to remove it.
3. Remove the steering wheel-to-steering column nut.
4. Matchmark the steering wheel to the steering shaft for ease of installation purposes.

NOTE: Never apply a blow to the steering wheel shaft with a hammer or other impact tool, to remove the steering wheel, for the steering shaft may become damaged.

5. Using the proper steering wheel puller, remove the steering wheel from the steering column.
6. Remove the horn contact ring.
7. Remove the steering column covers.
8. Disconnect the electrical connector from the combination switch.
9. Remove the combination switch-to-steering column screws and the switch.
10. On the Rodeo, Amigo and Pick-Up, remove the ignition lock/switch-to-steering column snapring and bushing.
11. Disconnect the electrical connector from the ignition lock/switch assembly.
12. On the Rodeo, Amigo and Pick-Up, remove the ignition lock/switch-to-steering column bolts and the lock/switch assembly. On the Trooper/Trooper II, remove the lock/switch pinch bolts and remove the lock/switch unit.

To install:

13. Install the ignition lock/switch-to-steering column bolts, the bushing and the snapring on the Rodeo, Amigo and Pick-Up. Install the lock/switch pinch bolts on the Trooper/Trooper II.
14. Install the combination switch to the steering column and tighten the screws.
15. Connect the combination switch electrical connector.
16. Install the steering column covers.
17. Install the contact ring.
18. Align the steering wheel-to-steering column matchmarks and torque the nut to 22–29 ft. lbs. (30–40 Nm) on the Trooper/Trooper II or 26 ft. lbs. (35 Nm) on the Rodeo, Pick-Up and Amigo.
19. Install the horn pad and the horn pad screw.
20. Connect the negative battery cable.

Stoplight Switch

ADJUSTMENT

1. Loosen the locknut on the stoplight switch.
2. Rotate the body off the switch to adjust the gap between the switch plunger and the brake pedal.
3. The gap should be 0.020–0.040 in. (0.5–1.0mm).
4. Once the gap has been set, hold the body of the stoplight switch to prevent it from rotating and tighten the locknut.

REMOVAL AND INSTALLATION

1. Disconnect the negative battery cable.
2. Locate the stoplight switch on the brake pedal support.
3. Disconnect the electrical connector from the stoplight switch.
4. Remove the locknut and the stoplight switch.

To install:

5. Install the switch on the support and adjust the switch so there is

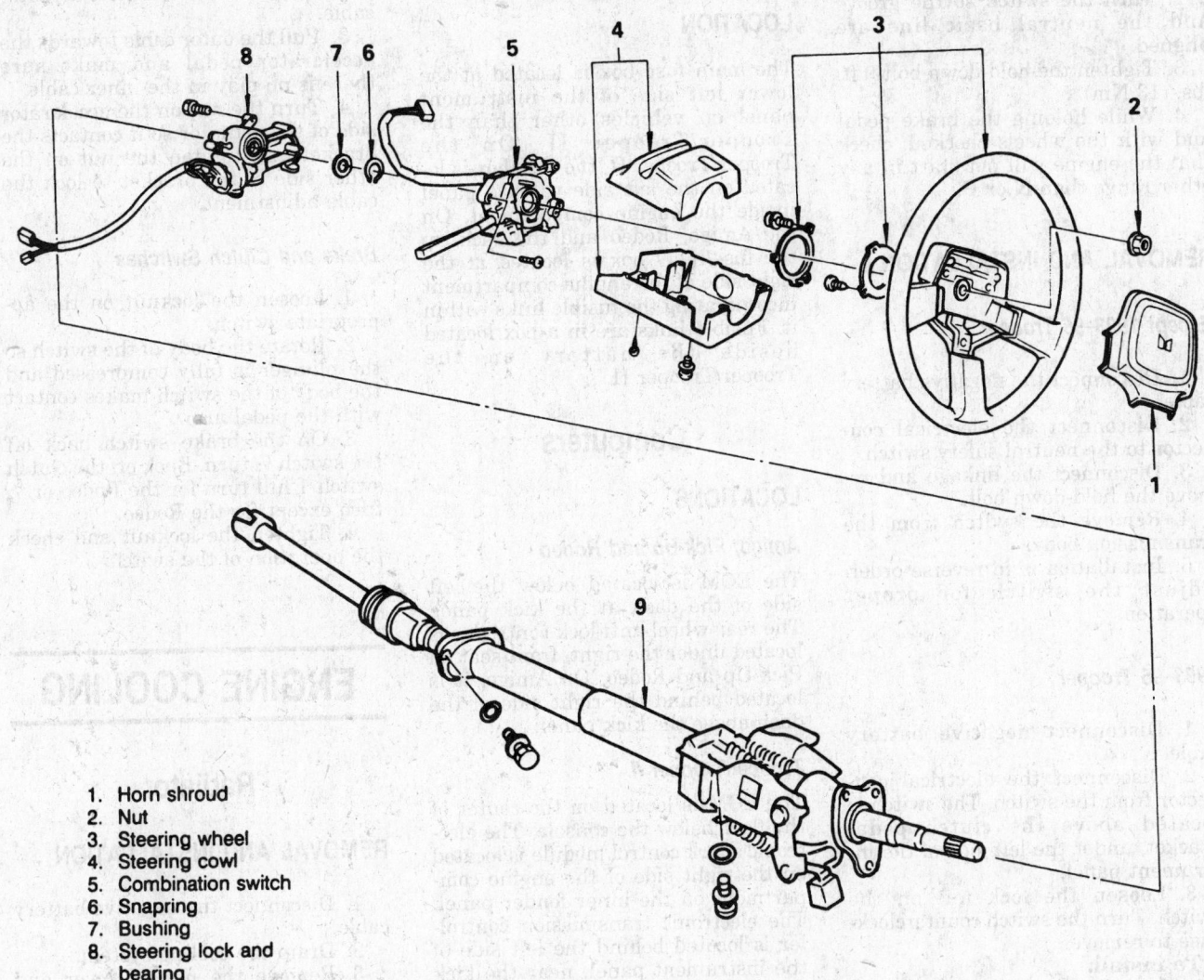

1. Horn shroud
2. Nut
3. Steering wheel
4. Steering cowl
5. Combination switch
6. Snapring
7. Bushing
8. Steering lock and bearing
9. Steering assembly

7911B009

Exploded view of the steering column — Amigo and Pick-Up — others are similar

0.020–0.040 in. (0.5–1.0mm) clearance between the switch and the brake pedal.

6. Hold the body of the stoplight switch to prevent it from turning and tighten the locknut.

7. Connect the wiring to the switch and the negative battery cable.

8. Check the operation of the switch.

Ignition Enable Clutch Switch

ADJUSTMENT

No adjustment is possible on the ignition enable clutch switch.

REMOVAL AND INSTALLATION

1. Disconnect the negative battery cable. Remove the electrical leads at the clutch switch.

2. Remove the fastening screws on the switch body and remove the switch from the linkage.

3. Install the switch and tighten the mounting screws.

4. Connect the negative battery cable and check the operation of the switch.

Neutral Safety Switch

ADJUSTMENT

Adjustment of the neutral safety switch should be done when the engine will start in any transmission range other than **N** or **P**.

1. Loosen the hold-down bolt for the neutral safety switch on the

transmission housing. Set the shifter to the **N** range.

2. Turn the switch so the groove and the neutral basic line are aligned.

3. Tighten the hold-down bolt 9 ft. lbs. (13 Nm).

4. While holding the brake pedal and with the wheels chocked, check that the engine will not start in any other range than **N** or **P**.

REMOVAL AND INSTALLATION

Except 1993–96 Trooper

1. Disconnect the negative battery cable.

2. Disconnect the electrical connector to the neutral safety switch.

3. Disconnect the linkage and remove the hold-down bolt.

4. Remove the switch from the transmission body.

5. Installation is in reverse order. Adjust the switch for proper operation.

1993–96 Trooper

1. Disconnect negative battery cable.

2. Disconnect the electrical connector from the switch. The switch is located above the clutch pedal bracket, under the left side of the instrument panel.

3. Loosen the lock nut on the switch. Turn the switch counterclockwise to remove.

To install:

4. Install the switch and turn clockwise.

5. Install the mounting bolt and tighten the lock nut.

6. Connect the electrical connector.

7. Connect the negative battery cable.

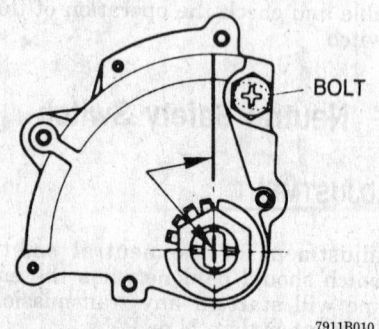

7911B010

View of the neutral start switch

Fuses and Circuit Breakers

LOCATION

The main fuse box is located at the lower left side of the instrument panel on vehicles other than the Trooper/Trooper II. On the Trooper/Trooper II, the fuse box is located on the left side valance panel inside the engine compartment. On the Amigo, Rodeo and the Pick-Up the fuse/relay box is located at the right side of the engine compartment incorporating the fusible links within it. Fusible links are in a box located beside the battery on the Trooper/Trooper II.

Computers

LOCATIONS

Amigo, Pick-Up and Rodeo

The ECM is located below the left side of the dash at the kick panel. The rear wheel anti-lock controller is located under the right, front seat on Pick-Up and Rodeo. On Amigo, it is located behind the right side of the dash above the kick panel.

Trooper/Trooper II

The ECM is located on the center of the floor below the console. The electronic spark control module is located on the right side of the engine compartment on the inner fender panel. The electronic transmission controller is located behind the left side of the instrument panel, near the kick panel.

Flashers

LOCATIONS

The flasher unit of the Amigo, Rodeo and Pick-Up is located behind the left side of the dash above the kick panel. The hazard relay on the Trooper/Trooper II is located below the left side of the instrument panel on the brake pedal support.

Cruise Control

ADJUSTMENT

Actuator Cable

1. The engine should be at normal idle speed when performing this adjustment.

2. Loosen the 2 nuts at the actuator end of the cruise control actuator cable.

3. Pull the outer cable towards the accelerator pedal and make sure there is no play in the inner cable.

4. Turn the nut on the accelerator side of the actuator so it contacts the bracket and tighten the nut on the other side of the bracket to lock the cable adjustment.

Brake and Clutch Switches

1. Loosen the locknut on the appropriate switch.

2. Rotate the body of the switch so the plunger is fully compressed and the body of the switch makes contact with the pedal arm.

3. On the brake switch back off the switch ½ turn. Back off the clutch switch 1 full turn for the Rodeo or ½ turn except for the Rodeo.

4. Tighten the locknut and check the operation of the switch.

ENGINE COOLING

Radiator

REMOVAL AND INSTALLATION

1. Disconnect the negative battery cable.

2. Drain the cooling system.

3. Remove the upper, lower and reservoir hoses from the radiator. Remove the air intake duct assembly, if necessary for Rodeo.

4. Remove the fan shroud-to-radiator bolts and the shroud. If equipped with a 2 piece shroud, unclip and remove the lower shroud section first, then unbolt and remove the main upper section.

5. Remove the automatic transmission cooling lines, if equipped.

6. Remove the radiator-to-chassis bolts and the radiator.

To install:

7. Install the radiator and the radiator-to-chassis bolts.

8. Install the automatic transmission cooling lines, if equipped.

9. Install the fan shroud and the shroud-to-radiator bolts.

10. Reconnect the radiator hoses. Replace the air intake duct.

11. Refill the cooling system.

12. Connect the negative battery cable.

Heater Core

REMOVAL AND INSTALLATION

Rodeo, Amigo and Pick-Up

1. Disconnect the negative battery cable. Drain the coolant into a clean container for reuse or dispose of the coolant in a safe and environmentally sound way. If equipped with air conditioning, discharge the system using an appropriate refrigerant recycling unit.

2. Disconnect the heater hoses at the inlet of the heater unit. Plug the hoses and inlets to prevent excess coolant from dripping into the passenger compartment.

3. Remove the instrument panel:

  a. Remove the steering wheel and its cowling.

  b. Remove the vent by inserting an appropriate prybar and carefully prying on the unit.

  c. Remove the instrument panel nuts under the vents.

  d. If equipped with an automatic transmission, remove the driving pattern indicator panel.

  e. Remove the screws holding the gauge hood and remove.

  f. Pull out the gauge cluster and remove the clips from the gauge hood.

  g. Disconnect the wiring connector blocks from the back of the cluster and remove the speedometer connection. Remove the gauge cluster.

  h. Remove the hood release handle by removing the screws on the underside of the handle.

  i. Remove the steering column lower cover, the use box, the side trim, ECM box, the front console and the lower reinforcement.

  j. Remove the screws holding the speaker grill and remove the speaker.

  k. Remove the glove box hinge pins. Remove the heater control knobs and remove the bezel.

  l. Remove the control lever assembly after disconnecting the control cables from the heater and blower units.

  m. Remove the illumination controller from the instrument panel.

  n. Remove the instrument panel nuts and bolts. Disconnect the instrument harness at the ECM location.

  o. Remove the instrument panel from the vehicle. Take appropriate measures to prevent damage to the panel.

4. Disconnect the resistor connection.

5. Remove the duct or air conditioning evaporator unit as equipped. If removing the evaporator assembly, cap the refrigerant lines to prevent moisture and foreign objects from contaminating the system.

6. Remove the instrument panel reinforcement.

7. Remove the heater unit after unclipping the harness and removing the nuts.

8. Remove the case section with the control levers.

9. Split the heater core case and remove the heater core.

To install:

10. Install the heater core in the heater core case and reassemble the heater unit.

11. Install the heater unit in the vehicle and replace the harness holding clip.

12. Install the instrument panel reinforcement and the duct or air conditioning evaporator unit as equipped. Connect the resistor wiring connection.

13. Install the instrument panel. Installation is the reverse of removal.

14. Connect the heater hoses and refill the cooling system. Recharge the air conditioning system, if equipped.

15. Connect the negative battery terminal.

Trooper/Trooper II, except 1993–96 Trooper

1. Disconnect the negative battery cable. Drain the coolant into a clean container for reuse or dispose of the coolant in a safe and environmentally sound way. If equipped with air conditioning, discharge the system using an appropriate refrigerant recycling unit.

2. Disconnect the heater hoses at the inlet of the heater unit. Plug the hoses and inlets to prevent excess coolant from dripping into the passenger compartment.

3. Remove the instrument panel:

  a. Remove the gauge cluster.

  b. Remove the screws on the underside of the gauge hood and remove the gauge assembly.

  c. Remove the glove compartment and radio.

  d. Remove the side vents by turning the vents and prying out.

  e. Remove the 10 bolts holding the instrument panel. The bolt heads are covered by a clip–on cover. Pry the covers off to expose the bolt heads.

  f. Remove the instrument panel taking care not to damage it or the interior of the vehicle.

4. Disconnect the refrigerant lines to the evaporator unit, if equipped.

5. Remove the vacuum line and the evaporator relay connection.

6. Remove the evaporator unit nuts and remove the evaporator unit, if equipped. If not air conditioner equipped, remove the duct.

7. Disconnect the air ducts from the unit.

8. Disconnect the heater unit relay connector.

9. Remove the heater unit nuts and remove the heater unit from the vehicle.

10. Remove the defroster door spring, rod and lever.

11. Remove the battery relay and air conditioning resistor.

12. Remove the plate and seal and the water valve rod.

13. Remove the core assembly.

To install:

14. Install the core assembly in the heater unit.

15. Reassemble the heater unit and install the unit in the vehicle.

16. Connect the electrical connector to the unit and install the ducts.

17. Install the evaporator unit and connect the refrigerant lines, vacuum and electric connections.

18. Install the instrument panel in reverse order of removal.

19. Connect the heater hoses and refill the cooling system. Recharge the air conditioning system, if equipped.

20. Connect the negative battery terminal.

1993–96 Trooper

1. Disconnect the negative battery cable. Drain the coolant into a clean container for reuse or dispose of the coolant in a safe and environmentally sound way. If equipped with air conditioning, discharge the system using an appropriate refrigerant recycling unit.

2. Disconnect the heater hoses at the inlet of the heater unit. Plug the hoses and inlets to prevent excess coolant from dripping into the passenger compartment.

3. Remove the instrument panel:

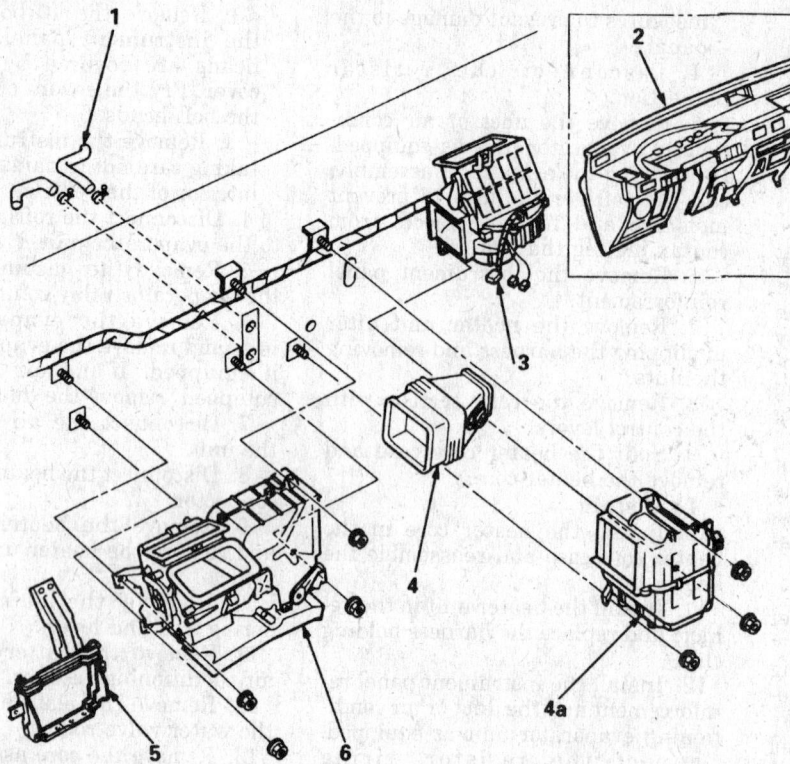

1. Heater hoses
2. Instrument panel assembly
3. Resistor connector
4. Duct (without air conditioning)
4a. Evaporator assembly (with air conditioning)
5. Instrument panel brace
6. Heater assembly

7911B011

Heater unit parts removal order — Amigo, Rodeo and Pick-Up

CAUTION

On air bag equipped vehicles, always allow at least 10 minutes between disconnecting the negative battery cable before working on or around air bag components. Failure to do so could result in personal injury or damage to the air bag system through unwanted detonation or accidental disabling of the system.

a. Remove the 5 screws from the steering cowl and remove the cowl.

b. Remove the 8 fixing screws from the instrument panel. Disconnect the windshield wiper switch, hazard warning light switch, lighting switch, illumination controller and cigar lighter electrical connectors.

c. Remove the instrument panel cluster.

d. Remove the 2 bolts securing the steering shaft.

e. Remove the 4 fixing screws from the meter assembly, disconnect the meter harness connectors and remove the meter assembly.

f. Remove the screw cover from the front of the ECM cover and remove the 3 screws. Remove the ECM cover.

g. Remove the 9 fixing screws for the instrument panel hood and remove the hood.

h. Remove the 3 screws attaching the lower steering cover and remove the cover.

i. Remove the 2 fixing screws and disconnect the engine hood opener cable.

j. Remove the hinge pins and the rivet screws from the glove box and remove the glove box.

k. Disconnect the control cables at the heater unit and blower assembly. Pull the control lever assembly out and disconnect the fan and air conditioning switch electrical connectors.

l. Remove the 2 screws retaining the audio box and remove the audio box.

m. Pry out the side defroster grille.

n. Remove the speaker grille, the side dash trim panel and the ashtray.

o. Disconnect the instrument harness connectors.

p. Remove the radio antenna cable from the fixing clips and remove the instrument panel.

4. Disconnect the resistor connector, mounted on the right heater duct. Remove the duct.

5. Remove the evaporator assembly:

a. Remove the 5 screws from the lower instrument panel reinforce and remove the reinforce.

b. Disconnect the resistor and electronic thermostat connectors on the right side of the evaporator assembly.

c. Disconnect the drain hose.

d. Disconnect and plug the refrigerant line.

e. Remove the evaporator assembly.

NOTE: Do not disconnect the ECM and the control unit connectors.

6. Remove the instrument panel stay and the front console.

7. Remove the rear heater duct and remove the heater unit.

To install:

8. Install the heater assembly and the rear heater duct.

9. Install the instrument panel stay and the front console.

10. Install the evaporator assembly:

a. Install the evaporator assembly.

b. Unplug and connect the refrigerant line.

c. Connect the drain hose.

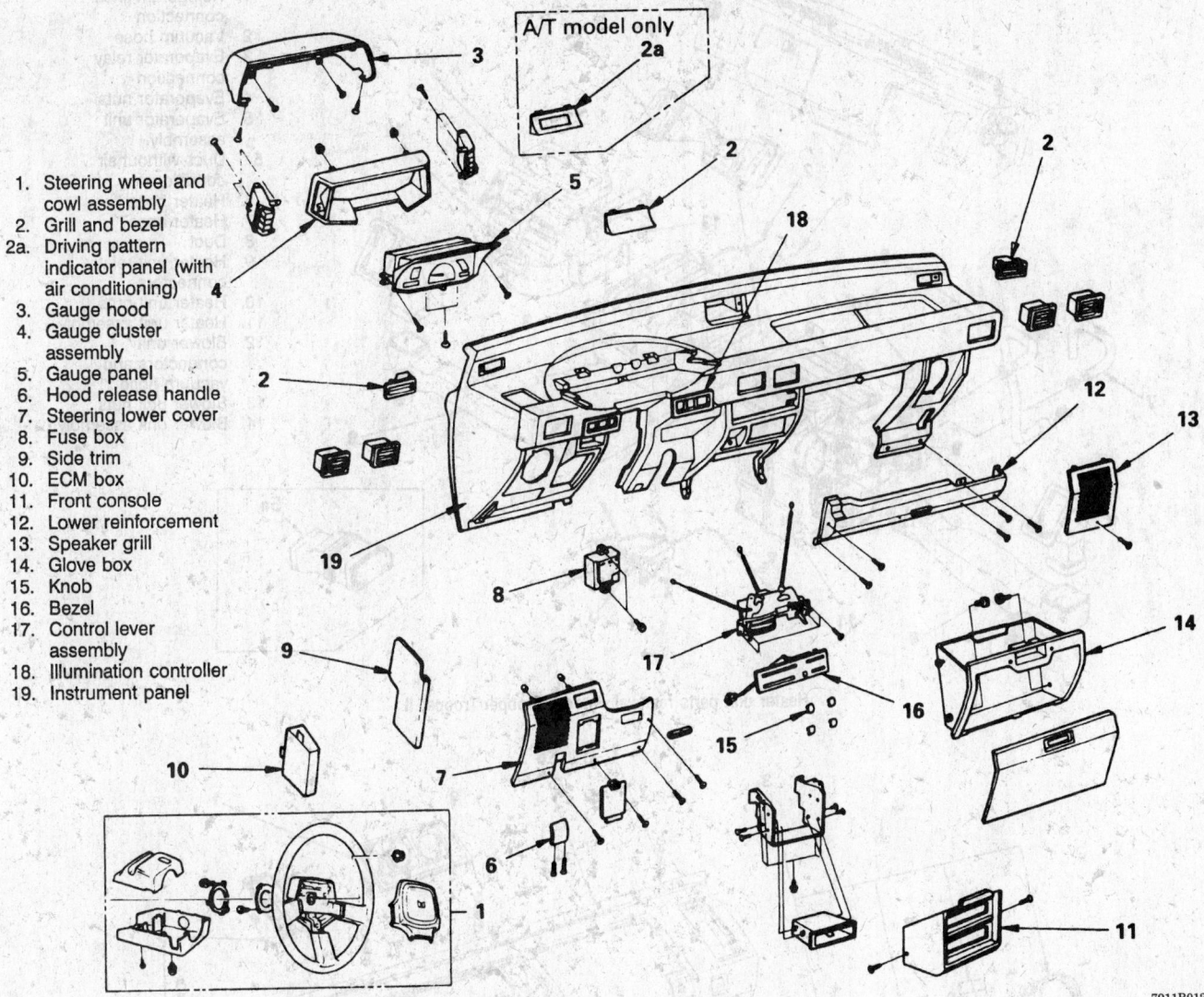

1. Steering wheel and cowl assembly
2. Grill and bezel
2a. Driving pattern indicator panel (with air conditioning)
3. Gauge hood
4. Gauge cluster assembly
5. Gauge panel
6. Hood release handle
7. Steering lower cover
8. Fuse box
9. Side trim
10. ECM box
11. Front console
12. Lower reinforcement
13. Speaker grill
14. Glove box
15. Knob
16. Bezel
17. Control lever assembly
18. Illumination controller
19. Instrument panel

A/T model only

7911B012

Instrument panel parts removal order — Amigo, Rodeo and Pick-Up

d. Connect the resistor and electronic thermostat connectors on the right side of the evaporator assembly.

e. Install the lower instrument panel reinforce and tighten the 5 screws.

11. Install the right heater duct and connect the resistor connector, on the duct.

12. Install the instrument panel:

a. Install the instrument panel. Install the radio antenna cable to the fixing clips.

b. Connect the instrument harness connectors.

c. Install the speaker grille, the side dash trim panel and the ashtray.

d. Install the side defroster grille.

e. Install the audio box and tighten the 2 screws retaining the audio box.

f. Connect the fan and air conditioning switch electrical connectors and install the switches. Connect the control cables at the heater unit and blower assembly.

g. Install the glove box. Install the hinge pins and the rivet screws to the glove box.

h. Connect the engine hood opener cable. Tighten the 2 fixing screws.

i. Install the lower steering cover and tighten the 3 screws attaching the cover.

j. Install the instrument panel hood and tighten the 9 fixing screws for the hood.

k. Install the ECM cover and tighten the 3 screws. Install the screw cover.

l. Install the meter assembly. Connect the harness to the meter and attach assembly with the 4 fixing screws.

m. Tighten the 2 bolts securing the steering shaft.

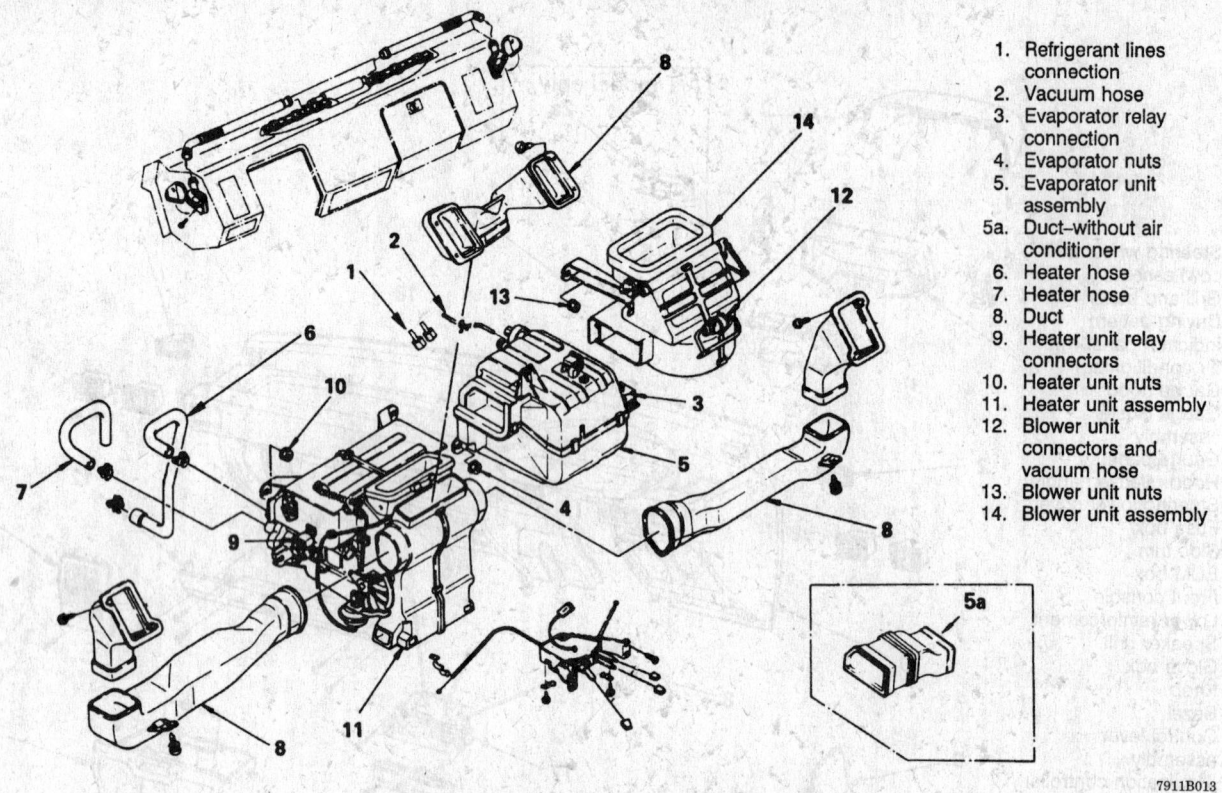

1. Refrigerant lines connection
2. Vacuum hose
3. Evaporator relay connection
4. Evaporator nuts
5. Evaporator unit assembly
5a. Duct–without air conditioner
6. Heater hose
7. Heater hose
8. Duct
9. Heater unit relay connectors
10. Heater unit nuts
11. Heater unit assembly
12. Blower unit connectors and vacuum hose
13. Blower unit nuts
14. Blower unit assembly

7911B013

Heater unit parts removal order — Trooper/Trooper II

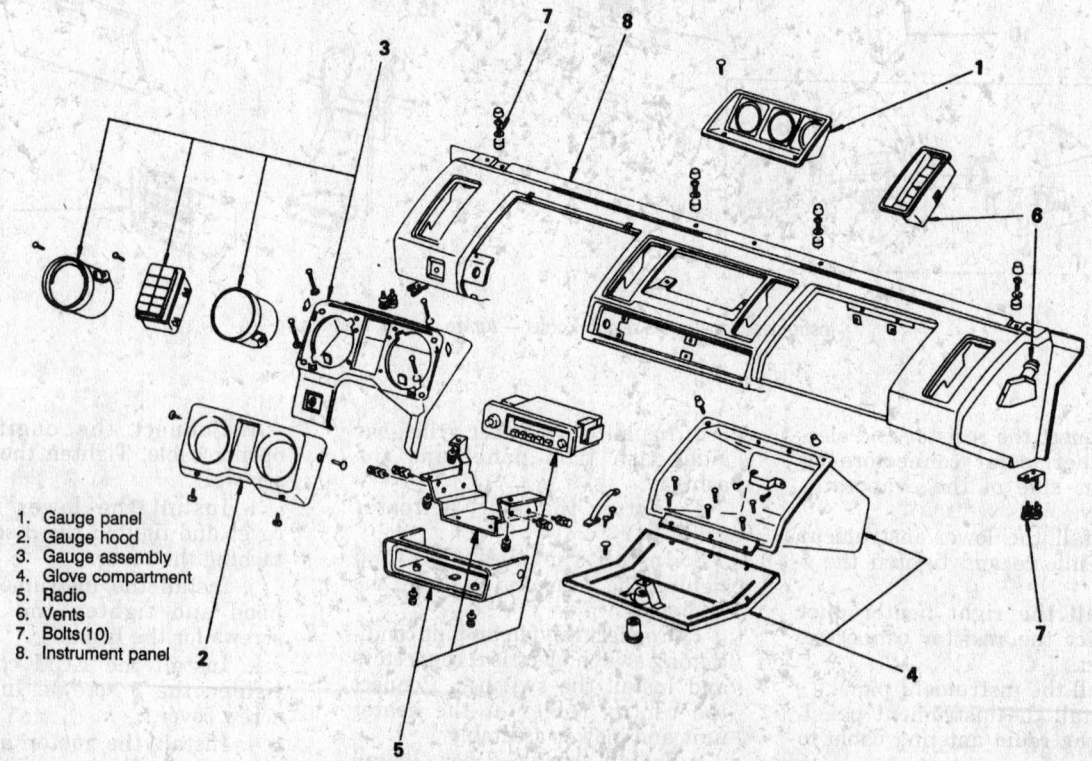

1. Gauge panel
2. Gauge hood
3. Gauge assembly
4. Glove compartment
5. Radio
6. Vents
7. Bolts (10)
8. Instrument panel

7911B014

Instrument panel parts removal order — Trooper/Trooper II

n. Install the instrument panel cluster.

o. Connect the windshield wiper switch, hazard warning light switch, lighting switch, illumination controller and cigar lighter electrical connectors. Tighten the 8 fixing screws to the instrument panel.

p. Install the steering cowl and tighten the 5 screws to the cowl.

13. Unplug and connect the heater hoses at the inlet of the heater unit.

14. Fill cooling system. If equipped with air conditioning, charge system. Connect the negative battery cable.

Water Pump

REMOVAL AND INSTALLATION

Except 2.3L and 2.6L engines

1. Disconnect the negative battery terminal.

2. Drain the coolant from the system. Collect the coolant in a clean pan for reuse or dispose of the old coolant in an environmentally safe and legally compliant way.

3. Disconnect the radiator hoses and remove the air duct assembly.

4. Unclip the lower fan shroud from the upper portion of the fan shroud and remove.

5. Remove the 4 bolts holding the upper fan shroud and remove the shroud from the engine compartment.

6. Remove the 4 nuts holding the fan, fan clutch and pulley. Remove the assembly.

7. Remove the power steering drive belt, if equipped. Loosen the bolts at the pump bracket to remove tension from the belt.

8. Loosen the air pump adjustment and remove the drive belt. Loosen the idler for the air conditioning compressor drive belt and remove the belt.

9. Remove the 2 idler pulley bolts and remove the idler.

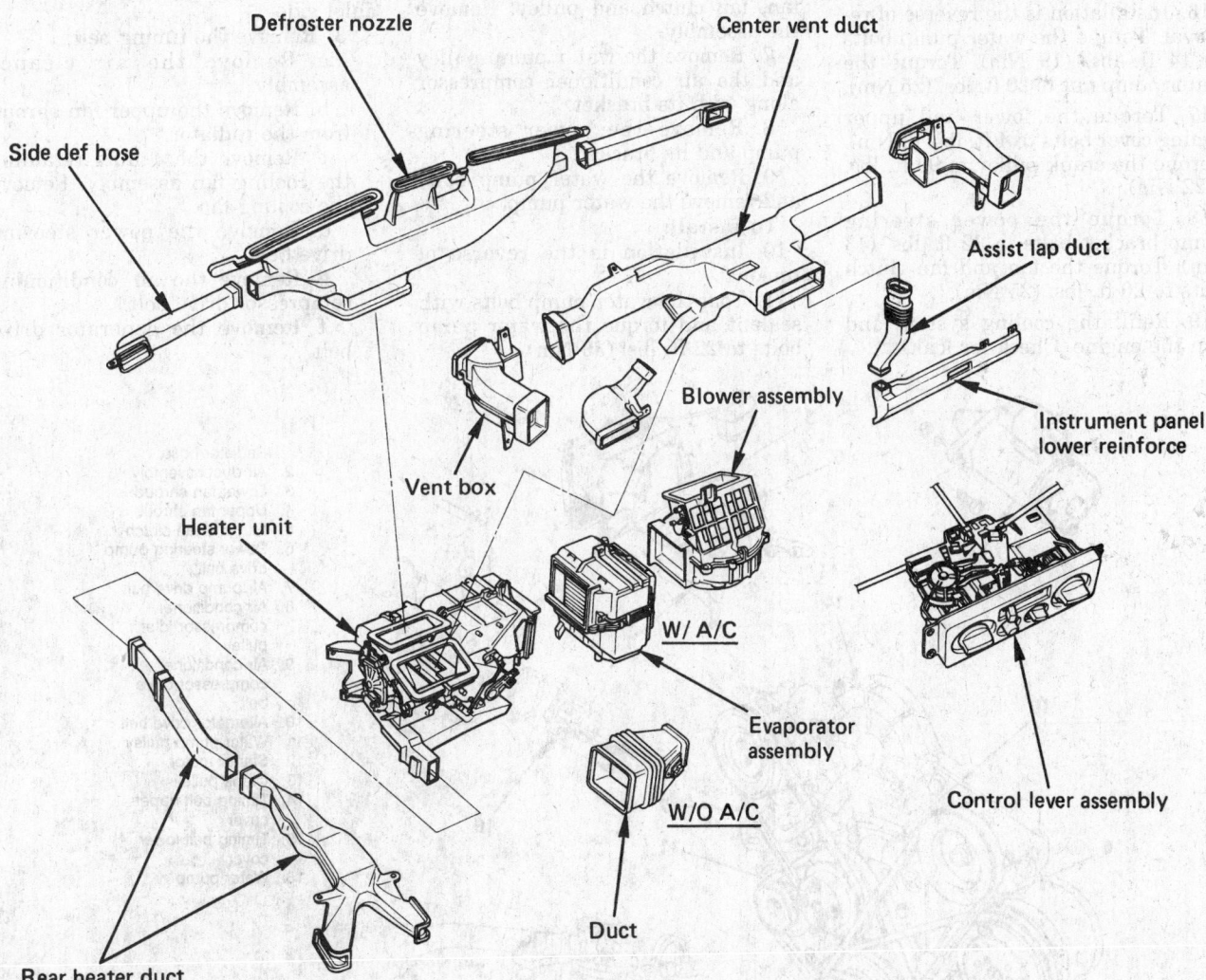

Defroster nozzle

Center vent duct

Side def hose

Assist lap duct

Instrument panel lower reinforce

Vent box

Blower assembly

W/ A/C

Heater unit

Evaporator assembly

W/O A/C

Duct

Control lever assembly

Rear heater duct

A/C - Air Conditioning

85478004

Heater and air conditioning components — 1993–96 Trooper

10. Loosen and remove the alternator drive belt.

11. Remove the 4 bolts holding the water pump pulley to the water pump hub. Remove the pulley.

12. Remove the 2 bolts holding the starter. Disconnect the starter electrical leads. Remove the starter.

13. Hold the crankshaft stationary with a flywheel lock or equivalent, and loosen the crank pulley bolt. Remove the crank pulley.

14. Remove the the upper and lower timing cover.

15. Remove the 4 bolts and 1 nut holding the water pump and remove the water pump.

To install:

16. Installation is the reverse of removal. Torque the water pump bolts to 14 ft. lbs. (19 Nm). Torque the water pump nut to 20 ft. lbs. (25 Nm).

17. Torque the lower and upper timing cover bolts to 4 ft. lbs. (6 Nm). Torque the crank pulley to 90 ft. lbs. (122 Nm).

18. Torque the power steering pump bracket bolts to 32 ft. lbs. (43 Nm). Torque the fan and fan clutch nuts to 20 ft. lbs. (25 Nm).

19. Refill the cooling system and run the engine. Check for leaks.

3.1L Engines

1. Disconnect the negative battery terminal. Drain the coolant from the system. Collect the coolant in a clean pan for reuse or dispose of the old coolant in an environmentally safe and legally compliant way.

2. Remove the serpentine drive belt.

3. Remove the upper radiator hose. Remove the air conditioner line bracket from the radiator bracket.

4. Unclip the lower fan shroud from the upper portion of the fan shroud and remove.

5. Remove the 4 bolts holding the upper fan shroud and remove the shroud from the engine compartment

6. Remove the 4 nuts holding the fan, fan clutch and pulley. Remove the assembly.

7. Remove the water pump pulley and the air conditioner compressor along with its bracket.

8. Remove the power steering pump and its bracket.

9. Remove the water pump bolts and remove the water pump.

To install:

10. Installation is the reverse of removal.

11. Coat the water pump bolts with sealant and torque the water pump bolts to 22 ft. lbs. (30 Nm).

12. Torque the power steering pump bolts to 37 ft. lbs. (50 Nm).

13. Torque the air conditioning compressor bolts to 78 ft. lbs. (58 Nm).

14. Torque the fan and fan clutch bolts to 17 ft. lbs. (23 Nm).

15. Refill the cooling system and check the system for leaks.

3.2L Engine

1. Disconnect the negative battery terminal. Drain the coolant from the system. Collect the coolant in a clean pan for reuse or dispose of the old coolant in an environmentally safe and legally compliant way.

2. Disconnect radiator hose on the inlet side.

3. Remove the timing belt:

   a. Remove the air cleaner assembly.

   b. Remove the upper fan shroud from the radiator.

   c. Remove the 4 nuts retaining the cooling fan assembly. Remove the cooling fan.

   d. Remove the power steering drive belt.

   e. Remove the air conditioning compressor drive belt.

   f. Remove the generator drive belt.

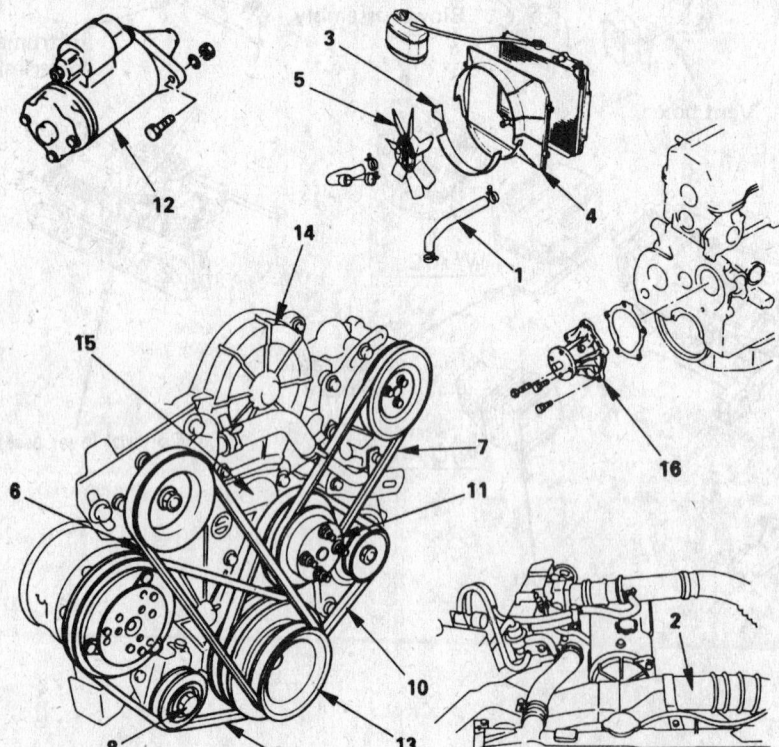

1. Radiator hose
2. Air duct assembly
3. Lower fan shroud
4. Upper fan shroud
5. Fan and fan clutch
6. Power steering pump drive belt
7. Air pump drive belt
8. Air conditioner compressor idler pulley
9. Air conditioner compressor drive belt
10. Alternator drive belt
11. Water pump pulley
12. Starter motor
13. Crank pulley
14. Timing belt upper cover
15. Timing belt lower cover
16. Water pump

7911B015

Water pump removal — 2.3L and 2.6L Engines

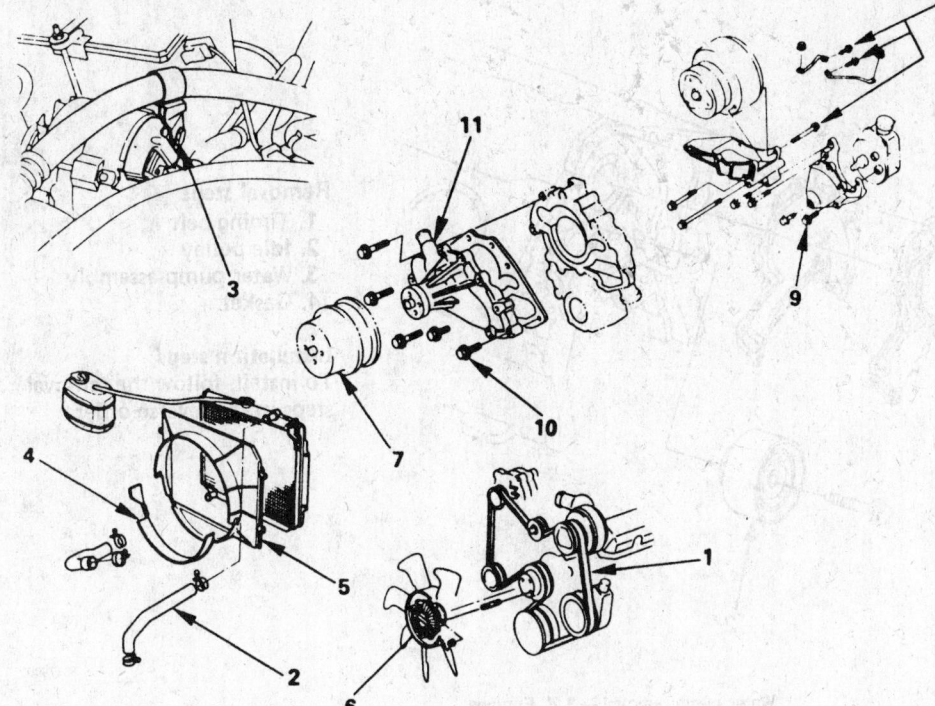

1. Serpentine drive belt
2. Radiator upper hose
3. Air conditioner line bracket
4. Lower fan shroud
5. Upper fan shroud
6. Fan and fan clutch assembly
7. Water pump pulley
8. Air conditioner compressor and bracket
9. Power steering pump with bracket
10. Water pump bolts
11. Water pump

7911B016

Water pump removal — 3.1L Engine

g. Remove the fan pulley assembly.

h. Remove the crankshaft pulley center bolt. Remove the crankshaft pulley.

i. Remove the 2 oil cooler hose bracket fixing bolts on the timing cover. Remove the oil cooler hose.

j. Remove the timing belt cover.

k. Remove the pusher. The rod must always be facing upward.

l. Mark the timing belt, cam pulley and crankshaft pulley. Remove the timing belt.

4. Remove the idle pulley.

5. Remove the 11 bolts retaining the water pump. Remove the water pump and the water pump gasket.

To install:

6. Install a new water pump gasket. Install the water pump.

7. Coat the water pump bolts with sealant and torque the water pump bolts to 13 ft. lbs. (18 Nm).

8. Install the idle pulley and tighten the bolt to 31 ft. lbs. (42 Nm).

9. Install the timing belt:

a. Align the groove on the crankshaft timing pulley with mark on the oil pump.

b. Align the marks on the camshaft timing pulleys with the dots on the front plate.

c. Install the timing belt. Align the dotted marks on the timing belt with the mark on the crankshaft gear.

d. Align the white line on the timing belt with the alignment mark on the right bank camshaft timing pulley. Secure the belt with a double clip.

e. Turn the crankshaft counterclockwise to remove the slack between the crankshaft pulley and the right camshaft timing pulley.

f. Install the belt on the water pump pulley.

g. Install the belt on the idler pulley.

h. Align the white alignment mark on the timing belt with the alignment mark on the left bank camshaft timing pulley.

i. Install the crankshaft pulley and tighten the center bolt by hand. Turn the crankshaft pulley clockwise to give slack between the crankshaft timing pulley and the right bank camshaft timing pulley.

j. Install the pusher while pushing the tension pulley to the belt.

k. Pull the pin out from the pusher.

l. Remove the double clips from the pulleys. Turn the crankshaft pulley clockwise 2 turns. Measure the rod protrusion to be sure it is between 0.16–0.24 in. (4–6 mm).

m. Tighten adjusting bolt to 31 ft. lbs. (42 Nm).

n. Tighten pusher bolt to 14 ft. lbs. (19 Nm).

o. Remove crankshaft pulley. Install the timing belt cover and tighten bolts to 12 ft. lbs. (17 Nm).

p. Install the oil cooler hose and tighten brackets to 16 ft. lbs. (22 Nm).

q. Install the crankshaft pulley and tighten bolts to 123 ft. lbs. (167 Nm).

r. Install fan pulley assembly and tighten fixing bolts to 16 ft. lbs. (22 Nm).

s. Engage and adjust generator drive belt.

t. Engage and adjust air conditioning drive belt.

u. Engage and adjust power steering pump drive belt.

v. Install cooling fan assembly and tighten bolts to 69 in. lbs. (8 Nm).

w. Install upper fan shroud to the radiator.

x. Install air cleaner assembly.

10. Connect the radiator inlet hose.

11. Refill the cooling system and check the system for leaks.

12. Connect the negative battery cable.

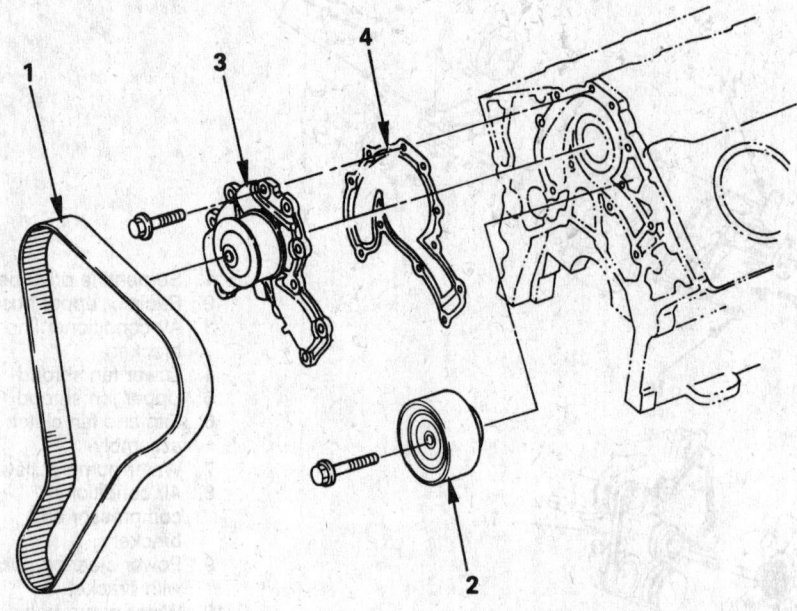

Water pump removal — 3.2L Engines

Removal steps
1. Timing belt
2. Idle pulley
3. Water pump assembly
4. Gasket

Installation steps
To install, follow the removal steps in the reverse order.

85478001

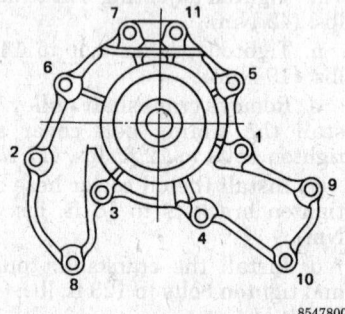

85478002

Water pump bolt tightening sequence — 3.2L Engines

Thermostat

REMOVAL AND INSTALLATION

The thermostat is located, under the thermostat housing, on top of the intake manifold at the front of the engine.

1. Disconnect the negative battery cable.

2. Drain the cooling system. Disconnect the upper radiator hose from the thermostat housing.

3. Remove the air cleaner assembly.

4. Remove the thermostat housing from the intake manifold.

5. Remove the gasket and the thermostat.

To install:

6. Install the thermostat, with the spring facing the engine.

7. Using a new gasket, install the thermostat housing.

8. Connect the radiator hose to the thermostat housing and refill the cooling system.

9. Install the air cleaner.

10. Connect the negative battery cable.

11. Operate the engine until normal operating temperatures are reached and check the thermostat operation.

Cooling System Bleeding

2.6L Engine

1. Check that the jiggle valve is located at the top of the thermostat.

2. Remove the thermal valve from the thermostat housing. Remove the radiator cap.

3. Set the heater on the highest setting. Fill the cooling system until coolant begins to flow from the thermal valve opening.

4. Apply Loctite® 262 or equivalent, to the thermal valve threads. Install the valve on the housing until the it stops. Using a wrench on the metal portion of the valve, tighten 1 full turn.

5. Continue to turn the thermal valve until the ports on the valve are parallel with the centerline of the thermostat housing mounting bolts.

6. Run the engine until it reaches operating temperature. When bubbles stop forming at the neck of the radiator, install the radiator cap.

7. Shut off engine and check the level of coolant in the reservoir tank.

FUEL SYSTEM

Fuel System Service Precautions

Disconnect the negative battery cable. Keep a Class B dry chemical fire extinguisher available. Always relieve the fuel pressure before disconnecting a fuel line. Wrap a shop cloth around the fuel line when disconnecting a fuel line. Always use

new O-rings. Do not replace the fuel pipes with fuel hoses. Always use a backup wrench when opening or closing a fuel line.

RELIEVING FUEL SYSTEM PRESSURE

Carbureted Engine

1. Release the fuel vapor pressure in the fuel tank by removing the fuel tank cap and reinstalling it.
2. Cover the fuel line with an absorbent shop cloth and loosen the connection slowly to release the fuel pressure gradually.

Fuel Injected Engines

1. Allow the engine to cool. Then, remove the fuel pump fuse from the fuse block.
2. Crank the engine, it will start and run until the fuel supply remaining in the fuel lines is exhausted. When the engine stops, engage the starter again for 3.0 seconds to assure dissipation of any remaining pressure.
3. With the ignition **OFF**, replace the fuel pump fuse.

Fuel Filter

On the Rodeo, Amigo and Pick-Up, the fuel filer is located directly in front of the fuel tank. On the Trooper/Trooper II, the fuel filter is located along the inner side of the right frame rail, near the rear of the vehicle.

REMOVAL AND INSTALLATION

1. Properly relieve the fuel system pressure.
2. Raise and safely support the vehicle.
3. Remove the fuel hose clamps and the fuel hoses from each side of the filter.
4. Cap the open fuel lines to prevent spillage and the entry of contaminants into the fuel system.
5. Remove the mounting bolt and the filter.
   To install:
6. Using a new filter, install it to the vehicle; be sure its directional arrow matches the fuel flow.
7. Install the fuel hoses and fuel hose clamps to the filter.
8. Start the engine and check for leaks at the filter.

Mechanical Fuel Pump

REMOVAL AND INSTALLATION

2.3L Engine

The fuel pump is located at the right side of the engine, directly under the intake manifold.

1. Relieve the fuel pressure.
2. Disconnect the negative battery cable.
3. Remove the air cleaner assembly.
4. Remove the intake manifold assembly.
5. Disconnect and plug the fuel lines at the fuel pump.
6. Remove the fuel pump-to-engine bolts and the pump assembly.
   To install:
7. Remove the cylinder head cover.
8. Rotate the engine to position the No. 4 cylinder at TDC.
9. Lift the fuel pump pushrod toward the camshaft and hold it in the raised position.
10. Using a new gasket, install the fuel pump on the engine; torque the bolts to 15–25 ft. lbs. (20–4 Nm).
11. Connect the fuel hoses to the fuel pump.
12. Using a new gasket, install the intake manifold.
13. Install the air cleaner assembly.
14. Connect the negative battery cable.
15. Start the engine and check for fuel leaks.

Electric Fuel Pump

PRESSURE TESTING

2.6L, 3.1L and 3.2L Engines

1. Relieve the fuel pressure.
2. Disconnect the fuel line near the engine and install fuel pressure gauge T-connector in the line.
3. Connect the fuel pressure gauge to the T-connector.
4. Start the engine and check the fuel pressure; it should be 43 psi for 2.6L and 3.1L engines, or 41–46 psi for 3.2L engine.
5. After checking, turn the engine **OFF**.
6. Relieve the fuel pressure.
7. Remove the pressure gauge from the fuel line and reconnect the fuel line.
8. Start the engine and check for leaks.

REMOVAL AND INSTALLATION

The electric fuel pump is located in the fuel tank.

2.6L and 3.1L Engines

1. Relieve the fuel pressure.
2. Disconnect the negative battery cable.
3. Raise and safely support the vehicle.
4. Drain the fuel from the fuel tank.
5. Disconnect the electrical connectors and the fuel lines from the fuel tank.
6. Remove the fuel tank-to-vehicle supports and lower the tank from the vehicle.
7. Remove the fuel sending unit cover-to-fuel tank screws and lift the assembly from the tank.
8. Remove the fuel pump from the fuel sending unit.
   To install:
9. Install the fuel pump to the fuel sending unit.
10. Using a new gasket, install the fuel sending unit to the fuel tank and tighten the screws.
11. Raise the fuel tank into the vehicle and install the tank-to-chassis connectors.
12. Connect the electrical connectors and the fuel lines to the fuel sending unit.
13. Lower the vehicle.
14. Refill the fuel tank.
15. Connect the negative battery cable.
16. Start the engine and check for fuel leaks.

Carburetor

REMOVAL AND INSTALLATION

1. Disconnect the negative battery cable.
2. Remove the air cleaner wing nut and disconnect the rubber hoses from the clips on the air cleaner cover.
3. Remove the bracket bolts, if equipped, at the air cleaner and remove the air cleaner cover and filter element.
4. Disconnect the hot air hose (to the hot air duct), the air hose to the air pump at the air cleaner and the vacuum hose at the joint nipple side of the intake manifold.
5. Loosen the bolt clamping the air cleaner to the carburetor. Separate the air cleaner body from the carburetor but do not remove it completely.

6. Disconnect the PCV hose (to the camshaft cover), the rubber hoses to the check and relief valve. Remove the air cleaner body.

7. Disconnect the vacuum hoses from the EGR valve.

8. Disconnect the choke control wire.

9. Disconnect the lead from the throttle solenoid.

10. Disconnect the throttle linkage return spring.

11. Disconnect the accelerator linkage.

12. Disconnect the fuel line at the carburetor.

13. Remove the carburetor-to-manifold nuts and the carburetor.

To install:

14. Using a new gasket, install the carburetor to the intake manifold.

15. Connect the fuel line and the accelerator linkage to the carburetor.

16. Connect the throttle linkage return spring, the throttle solenoid lead, the choke control wire and the vacuum hoses to the EGR and the PCV.

17. Install the air cleaner and any necessary hoses.

18. Start the engine and check for fuel leaks.

IDLE SPEED ADJUSTMENT

1. Firmly set the parking brake and block the drive wheels.

2. Place the transmission in **N**.

3. Operate the engine until it reaches normal operating temperatures. Be sure the choke is fully open and the air cleaner is installed. If equipped, turn the air conditioning **OFF**.

4. Disconnect and plug the distributor vacuum, the canister purge and EGR vacuum lines. Shut off the vacuum to the idle compensator by bending the rubber hose.

5. Turn the throttle adjusting screw to the required idle speed.

6. If equipped with air conditioning, turn air conditioning control to **MAX COLD** and the blower on **HIGH**.

7. Open throttle to approximately ⅓ opening and allow it to close.

NOTE: The speed-up solenoid should reach full travel.

8. Adjust the speed-up solenoid screw to 850–950 rpm.

IDLE MIXTURE ADJUSTMENT

1. Firmly set the parking brake and block the drive wheels.

2. Place the transmission in **N**.

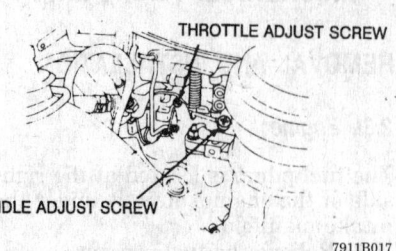

View of the idle and throttle adjusting screws — carbureted models

3. Remove the carburetor assembly.

4. Using a drill, drill a hole through the sealing plug covering the idle mixture screw and pry the plug from the carburetor.

5. Reinstall the carburetor.

6. Operate the engine until it reaches normal operating temperatures. Be sure the choke is fully open and the air cleaner is installed. If equipped, turn the air conditioning **OFF**.

7. Disconnect and plug the distributor vacuum, the canister purge and EGR vacuum lines. Shut off the vacuum to the idle compensator by bending the rubber hose.

8. Connect a dwell meter (4 cyl. scale) or duty meter to the duty monitor lead.

9. Turn the idle mixture screw all the way in and back out 1½ turns.

10. Turn the throttle adjusting screw until the engine speed is 900 rpm.

11. Adjust the idle mixture screw to achieve an average dwell of 36 degrees or duty of 40 percent.

NOTE: The dwell or duty reading specified is the average of the most constant variation.

12. Reset the throttle adjusting screw until the engine speed is 850–950 rpm.

13. Reinstall a mixture adjustment plug.

Fuel Injection

IDLE SPEED ADJUSTMENT

2.6L Engine

1. Firmly set the parking brake and block the drive wheels.

2. Place the transmission in **N**.

3. Set the engine tachometer.

4. Make sure the throttle valve is fully closed.

5. If equipped with air conditioning, turn **OFF** the air conditioning.

6. Place the manual transmission in neutral or the automatic transmission in **P**.

7. Disconnect the electrical connector from the Vacuum Switching Valve (VSV) on the pressure regulator; the idle speed should 850–950 rpm.

8. If the idle speed is not correct, turn the adjusting screw **A** on the throttle body.

3.1L and 3.2L Engines

The idle speed is controlled by the ECM and no adjustment is necessary or possible.

IDLE MIXTURE ADJUSTMENT

No idle mixture adjustment is necessary or possible.

Fuel Injector

REMOVAL AND INSTALLATION

2.6L Engine

The engine is equipped 4 fuel injectors, with 1 located at each cylinder.

1. Relieve the fuel pressure.

2. Disconnect the negative battery cable.

3. Label and disconnect the electrical connectors from the fuel injectors.

4. Disconnect the fuel rail from the fuel system.

5. Remove the fuel rail from the intake manifold; pull the fuel rail with the injectors connected from the intake manifold.

6. Separate the fuel injectors from the fuel rail.

To install:

7. Replace the fuel injector O-rings.

8. Install the fuel injectors to the fuel rail.

9. Lubricate the fuel injector O-rings with automatic transmission fluid and press them, with the fuel rail, into the intake manifold.

10. Install the fuel rail-to-intake manifold bolts.

11. Connect the fuel rail to the fuel system.

12. Connect the electrical connectors to the fuel injectors.

13. Connect the negative battery cable.

14. Turn the ignition switch **ON** and check for fuel leaks at the fuel rail.

Location of the vacuum switching valve (VSV) electrical connector — 2.6L engine

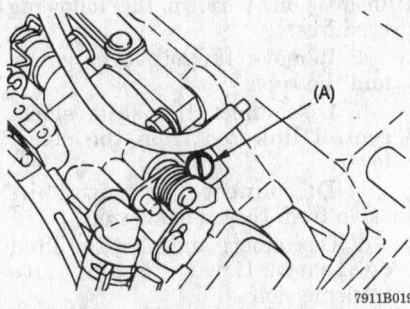

View of the throttle body adjusting screw to alter the idle speed — 2.6L engine

3.1L Engine

The engine is equipped with 2 fuel injectors, both are located in the throttle body.

1. Relieve the fuel pressure.
2. Disconnect the negative battery cable.
3. Remove the air cleaner.
4. At the injector electrical connectors, squeeze the 2 tabs together and pull them straight upward.
5. Remove the fuel meter cover and leave the cover gasket in place.
6. Using a small prybar, carefully pry the injectors upward until they are free of the throttle body.
7. Remove the small O-ring from the nozzle end of the injector. Carefully rotate the injector's fuel filter back-and-forth to remove it from the base of the injector.
8. Discard the fuel meter cover gasket.
9. Remove the large O-ring and backup washer from the top of the counterbore of the fuel meter body injector cavity.

To install:

10. Lubricate the O-rings with automatic transmission fluid and push them into the fuel injector cavities.
11. Install the new fuel meter cover gasket and cover.

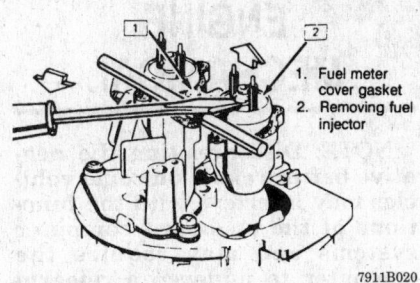

1. Fuel meter cover gasket
2. Removing fuel injector

Removing the fuel injectors from the throttle body — 3.1L Engine

12. Install the electrical connectors to the injectors.
13. Install the air cleaner and connect the negative battery cable.

3.2L Engine

The engine is equipped with 6 fuel injectors, with 1 located at each cylinder.

1. Disconnect negative battery cable and remove the engine hood.
2. Remove the air cleaner assembly.
3. Disconnect the accelerator pedal cable from the throttle body and cable brackets.
4. Disconnect the canister vacuum hose from the Vacuum Switch Valve (VSV).
5. Disconnect the vacuum booster hose from the common chamber duct.
6. Disconnect the electrical connectors from the Idle Air Control Valve, Throttle Position sensor, Manifold Absolute Pressure sensor, canister VSV, EGR VSV, Intake Air Temperature sensor and VSV.
7. Remove the high tension cable from the cylinder heads.
8. Disconnect the 3 connectors from the EI module.
9. Remove the 3 bolts from the EI bracket and remove the EI assembly.
10. Remove the 4 bolts from the throttle body and remove the throttle body.
11. Disconnect the canister VSV and the EGR VSV vacuum hose from the throttle body.
12. Disconnect the fuel pressure control valve vacuum hose from the common chamber duct.
13. Disconnect the PCV hose from the common chamber duct.
14. Disconnect the evaporative emission canister purge hose from the common chamber duct.
15. Remove the 4 bolts from the EGR valve assembly common chamber duct and remove the exhaust manifold.

16. Remove the 4 bolts, 4 nuts and 3 manifold bracket fixing bolts from the common chamber duct.
17. Remove the ground cable fixing bolt from the rear of the common chamber duct.
18. Remove the 6 bolts and 2 nuts from the common chamber duct.
19. Remove the common chamber duct bracket fixing bolts from the rear of the common chamber duct.
20. Remove the fuel feed and return hoses from the fuel pipe. Remove the 2 fixing bolts from the cylinder head.
21. Remove the fuel injector connectors from the fuel rail assembly.
22. Remove the fuel rail fixing bolts from the fuel rail assembly.
23. Remove the fuel rail assembly from the engine.

NOTE: While removing the fuel rail from the engine, if a fuel injector separates from the fuel rail and remains in the head of the engine, replace both the injector O-rings and the injector retainer clip.

24. Remove the regulator attaching screw from the fuel rail.
25. Remove the fuel pressure control valve assembly from the fuel rail.
26. Remove the fuel injector retainer clip and remove the fuel injector.

To install:

27. Install the fuel injector to the frame rail and attach with retainer clip.
28. Install the fuel pressure control valve assembly to the fuel rail.
29. Install the regulator attaching screw to the fuel rail.
30. Install the fuel rail assembly to the engine.
31. Install the fuel rail fixing bolts to the fuel rail assembly.
32. Install the fuel injector connectors to the fuel rail assembly.
33. Install the fuel feed and return hoses to the fuel pipe. Install the 2 fixing bolts to the cylinder head.
34. Install the common chamber duct bracket fixing bolts to the rear of the common chamber duct.
35. Install the 6 bolts and 2 nuts to the common chamber duct.
36. Install the ground cable fixing bolt to the rear of the common chamber duct.
37. Install the 4 bolts, 4 nuts and 3 manifold bracket fixing bolts to the common chamber duct.
38. Install the exhaust manifold and install the 4 bolts to the EGR valve assembly and common chamber duct.

39. Connect the evaporative emission canister purge hose to the common chamber duct.

40. Connect the PCV hose to the common chamber duct.

41. Connect the fuel pressure control valve vacuum hose to the common chamber duct.

42. Connect the canister VSV and the EGR VSV vacuum hose to the throttle body.

43. Install the throttle body and install the 4 bolts to the throttle body and remove the throttle body.

44. Install the EI assembly and install the 3 bolts to the EI bracket.

45. Connect the 3 connectors to the EI module.

46. Connect the high tension cable to the cylinder heads.

47. Connect the electrical connectors to the Idle Air Control Valve, Throttle Position sensor, Manifold Absolute Pressure sensor, canister VSV, EGR VSV, Intake Air Temperature sensor and VSV.

48. Connect the vacuum booster hose to the common chamber duct.

49. Connect the canister vacuum hose to the Vacuum Switch Valve (VSV).

50. Connect the accelerator pedal cable to the throttle body and cable brackets.

51. Install the air cleaner assembly.

52. Install the engine hood and connect negative battery cable.

EMISSION CONTROLS

Emission Warning Lamps

RESETTING

Once the problem in the system is corrected, the trouble codes must be cleared from the ECM memory. The Check Engine light can be reset by disconnecting the negative battery cable or the ECM fuse at the fuse box for at least 10 seconds and then reconnecting the cable.

ENGINE MECHANICAL

NOTE: Disconnecting the negative battery cable on some vehicles may interfere with the functions of the on board computer systems and may require the computer to undergo a relearning process, once the negative battery cable is reconnected.

Engine

REMOVAL AND INSTALLATION

2WD Vehicles

1. Relieve the fuel pressure. Disconnect both battery cables, the negative cable first. Remove the battery.

2. Matchmark the hood-to-hinges and remove the hood.

3. Remove the undercover, if equipped. Open the drain plugs on the radiator and the cylinder and drain the cooling system.

4. Remove the air cleaner for 2.3L and 3.1L engines or air cleaner duct and hose for 2.6L engine. Using a clean shop cloth, cover the air cleaner port to prevent dirt from entering the engine.

5. Label and disconnect the necessary hoses, electrical connectors, control cables and control rods from the engine.

6. Label and disconnect the following items:
   a. Air switch valve hose.
   b. Oxygen sensor wire.
   c. Vacuum switch valve hose.
   d. Thermal vacuum switching valve hose.
   e. Pressure regulator vacuum hose.
   f. Canister hose.
   g. ECM harness.
   h. Fuel hose(s).

7. Remove the clutch return spring, if equipped, the clutch control cable, if equipped, the backup light switch connector and the speedometer cable from the transmission.

8. Remove the radiator grille from the deflector panel.

9. Disconnect the upper and lower radiator hoses and the reservoir tank hose.

10. Remove the fan shroud, fan blade assembly and the radiator.

11. If equipped with air conditioning, remove the compressor from the engine and move it aside; do not disconnect the pressure hoses.

12. Remove the gear shift lever by performing the following procedures:
    a. Place the gear shift lever in **N**.
    b. Remove the front console from the floor panel.
    c. Pull the shift lever boot and grommet upward.
    d. Remove the shift lever cover bolts and the shift lever.

13. Raise and safely support the vehicle. Remove the front wheels.

14. Drain the oil from the engine and the transmission fluid.

15. If equipped with an automatic transmission, perform the following procedures:
    a. Remove the oil level gauge and the tube.
    b. Disconnect the shift select control link rod from the select lever.
    c. Disconnect the downshift cable from the transmission.
    d. Disconnect and plug the fluid coolant lines from the transmission.

16. If equipped with a 1-piece driveshaft, remove the driveshaft flange-to-pinion nuts, lower the driveshaft and pull it from the transmission.

17. If equipped with a 2-piece driveshaft, perform the following procedures:
    a. Remove the rear driveshaft flange-to-pinion nuts.
    b. Remove the rear driveshaft flange-to-front driveshaft flange bolts and the rear driveshaft.
    c. Remove the center bearing-to-chassis bolts, move the front driveshaft rearward and from the transmission.

18. Remove the starter-to-engine bolts and the starter.

19. Remove the exhaust pipe-to-exhaust manifold nuts, the exhaust pipe bracket-to-transmission bolts, the front exhaust pipe-to-2nd exhaust pipe bolts and the front exhaust pipe from the vehicle.

20. Attach an engine hanger to the rear of the exhaust manifold.

21. Using an engine hoist, connect it to the engine hangers and support the engine.

22. If equipped with a manual transmission, perform the following procedures:
    a. Using a transmission jack, place it under the transmission; do not support it.
    b. Remove the rear mount-to-transmission nuts.

c. Remove the rear mount-to-crossmember nuts/bolts and the mount.

NOTE: Further removal of the transmission may require an assistant.

d. Remove the clutch cover and the transmission-to-engine bolts.

e. Move the transmission rearward into the crossmember and floor pan area; the transmission may rest on the crossmember.

f. Lower the front of the transmission toward the jack.

g. Firmly, grasp the transmission the rear cover while the assistant raises the jack toward the transmission.

h. Carefully lower the transmission onto the jack and center it.

i. Lower the jack and move the transmission rearward.

23. If equipped with an automatic transmission, perform the following procedures:

NOTE: Removal of the transmission will require an assistant.

a. Remove the torque converter-to-flexplate bolts through the starter hole.

b. Using a transmission jack, place it under the transmission; do not support it.

c. Remove the rear mount-to-transmission nuts.

d. Remove the rear mount-to-crossmember nuts/bolts and the mount.

e. Remove the transmission-to-engine bolts.

f. Move the transmission rearward into the crossmember and floor pan area; the transmission may rest on the crossmember.

g. Lower the front of the transmission toward the jack.

h. Firmly, grasp the transmission the rear cover while the assistant raises the jack toward the transmission.

i. Carefully, lower the transmission onto the jack and center it.

j. Lower the jack and move the transmission rearward.

24. Remove the engine-to-mount nuts/bolts.

25. Using the hoist, slowly, lift the engine; be sure to hold the front of the engine higher than the rear.

26. Place the engine on a workstand.

To install:

27. Using the hoist, slowly, lower the engine into the vehicle; be sure to hold the front of the engine higher than the rear.

28. Install the engine-to-mount nuts/bolts.

29. If equipped with an automatic transmission, perform the following procedures:

NOTE: Installation of the transmission will require an assistant.

a. Raise the transmission into position.

b. Raise the rear of the transmission and move it into position on the crossmember.

c. Move the transmission forward and engage it with the engine.

d. Install the engine-to-transmission bolts.

e. Install the mount and the rear mount-to-crossmember nuts/bolts.

f. Install the rear mount-to-transmission nuts.

g. Install the torque converter-to-flexplate bolts through the starter hole.

30. If equipped with a manual transmission, perform the following procedures:

NOTE: Installation of the transmission may require an assistant.

a. Raise the transmission into position.

b. Raise the rear of the transmission and move it into position on the crossmember.

c. Move the transmission forward and engage it with the engine.

d. Install the engine-to-transmission bolts.

e. Install the mount and the rear mount-to-crossmember nuts/bolts.

f. Install the rear mount-to-transmission nuts.

31. Remove the engine hoist and the engine hanger from the rear of the exhaust manifold.

32. Install the front exhaust pipe, exhaust pipe-to-exhaust manifold nuts, the exhaust pipe bracket-to-transmission bolts, the front exhaust pipe-to-2nd exhaust pipe bolts.

33. Install the starter and the starter-to-engine bolts.

34. If equipped with a 2-piece driveshaft, perform the following procedures:

a. Install the front driveshaft into the transmission and the center bearing-to-chassis bolts.

b. Install the rear driveshaft and the rear driveshaft flange-to-front driveshaft flange bolts.

c. Install the rear driveshaft flange-to-pinion nuts.

35. If equipped with a 1-piece driveshaft, install the driveshaft into the transmission and the driveshaft flange-to-pinion nuts.

36. If equipped with an automatic transmission, perform the following procedures:

a. Connect the fluid coolant lines to the transmission.

b. Connect the downshift cable to the transmission.

c. Connect the shift select control link rod to the select lever.

d. Install the oil level gauge and the tube.

37. Install the front wheels and lower the vehicle.

38. Install the gear shift lever by performing the following procedures:

a. Install the shift lever and the shift lever cover bolts.

b. Push the grommet and shift lever boot downward.

c. Install the front console to the floor panel.

39. If equipped with air conditioning, install the compressor to the engine.

40. Install the radiator, the fan blade assembly and the fan shroud.

41. Connect the upper and lower radiator hoses and the reservoir tank hose.

42. Install the radiator grille to the deflector panel.

43. Install the clutch return spring, if equipped, the clutch control cable, if equipped, the backup light switch connector and the speedometer cable to the transmission.

44. Connect the following items:

a. Air switch valve hose.

b. Oxygen sensor wire.

c. Vacuum switch valve hose.

d. Thermal vacuum switching valve hose.

e. Pressure regulator vacuum hose.

f. Canister hose.

g. ECM harness.

h. Fuel hose(s).

45. Connect the necessary hoses, electrical connectors, control cables and control rods to the engine.

46. Install the air cleaner for 2.3L engine or air cleaner duct and hose for 2.6L engine.

47. Refill the engine, the transmission and the cooling system. Install the undercover, if equipped.

48. Install the hood.

49. Install the battery and connect both battery cables, the positive cable first.

50. Adjust the belt tension. Start the engine, check for leaks.

51. Check and/or adjust the idle speed and ignition timing.

4WD Vehicles

1. Relieve the fuel pressure. Disconnect both battery cables, the negative cable first. Remove the battery.

2. Matchmark the hood-to-hinges and remove the hood.

3. Remove the undercover, if equipped. Open the drain plugs on the radiator and the cylinder and drain the cooling system.

4. Remove the air cleaner for 2.3L and 3.1L engines or air cleaner duct and hose for 2.6L engine. Using a clean shop cloth, cover the air cleaner port to prevent dirt from entering the engine.

5. Label and disconnect the necessary hoses, electrical connectors, control cables and control rods from the engine.

6. Label and disconnect the following items:

   a. Air switch valve hose.

   b. Oxygen sensor wire.

   c. Vacuum switch valve hose.

   d. Thermal vacuum switching valve hose.

   e. Pressure regulator vacuum hose.

   f. Canister hose.

   g. ECM harness.

   h. Fuel hose(s).

7. Remove the clutch return spring, if equipped, the clutch control cable, if equipped, the backup light switch connector and the speedometer cable from the transmission.

8. Remove the radiator grille from the deflector panel.

9. Disconnect the upper and lower radiator hoses and the reservoir tank hose.

10. Remove the fan shroud, fan blade assembly and the radiator.

11. If equipped with air conditioning, remove the compressor from the engine and move it aside; do not disconnect the pressure hoses.

12. If equipped with a 3.1L engine, perform the following procedures:

   a. Remove the power steering pump-to-engine brackets and move the pump aside.

   b. Remove the spark plug wire from the No. 1 spark plug.

   c. Remove the distributor cap with the No. 1 spark plug wire.

   d. Remove the ignition coil.

13. Remove the gear shift lever by performing the following procedures:

   a. Place the gear shift lever in **N**.

   b. Remove the front console from the floor panel.

   c. Pull the shift lever boot and grommet upward.

   d. Remove the shift lever cover bolts and the shift lever.

14. Remove the transfer shift lever by performing the following procedures:

   a. Place the transfer shift lever in **H** for 2.3L or 2.6L engine or **2H** for 3.1L engine.

   b. Pull the shift lever boot and dust cover upward.

   c. Remove the shift lever retaining bolts.

   d. Pull the shift lever from the transfer case.

15. Raise and safely support the vehicle. Remove the front wheels. Drain the oil from the engine.

16. Drain the transmission and transfer case fluid.

17. If equipped with an automatic transmission, perform the following procedures:

   a. Remove the oil level gauge and the tube.

   b. Disconnect the shift select control link rod from the select lever.

   c. Disconnect the downshift cable from the transmission.

   d. Disconnect and plug the fluid coolant lines from the transmission.

18. If equipped with a 1-piece driveshaft, remove the driveshaft flange-to-pinion nuts, lower the driveshaft and pull it from the transmission.

19. If equipped with a 2-piece driveshaft, perform the following procedures:

   a. Remove the rear driveshaft flange-to-pinion nuts.

   b. Remove the rear driveshaft flange-to-front driveshaft flange bolts and the rear driveshaft.

   c. Remove the center bearing-to-chassis bolts, move the front driveshaft rearward and from the transmission.

20. Remove the front driveshaft's splined yoke flange-to-transfer case bolts and separate the front driveshaft from the transfer case; do not allow the splined flange to fall away from the driveshaft.

21. Remove the starter-to-engine bolts and the starter.

22. If equipped with a clutch slave cylinder, remove it from the transmission and move it aside.

23. Remove the exhaust pipe-to-exhaust manifold nuts, the exhaust pipe bracket-to-transmission bolts, the front exhaust pipe-to-2nd exhaust pipe bolts and the front exhaust pipe from the vehicle.

24. Attach an engine hanger to the rear of the exhaust manifold.

25. Using an engine hoist, connect it to the engine hangers and support the engine.

26. Remove the transmission/transfer case assembly by performing the following procedures:

   a. Using a transmission jack, place it under the transmission and support the assembly.

   b. Remove the rear mount-to-transmission nuts.

   c. Remove the rear mount-to-side mount member nuts/bolts and the mount.

   d. Remove the transmission-to-engine bolts.

   e. Move the transmission assembly rearward.

   f. Carefully lower the transmission.

27. Remove the engine-to-mount nuts/bolts.

28. Using the hoist, slowly, lift the engine; be sure to hold the front of the engine higher than the rear.

29. Place the engine on a work stand.

To install:

30. Using the hoist, slowly lower the engine into the vehicle; be sure to hold the front of the engine higher than the rear.

31. Install the engine-to-mount nuts/bolts.

32. Install the transmission/transfer assembly by performing the following procedures:

   a. Raise the transmission into position.

   b. Move the transmission forward and engage it with the engine.

   c. Install the engine-to-transmission bolts.

   d. Install the rear mount and the rear mount-to-side mount member nuts/bolts.

   e. Install the rear mount-to-transmission nuts.

   f. Remove the transmission jack.

33. If equipped with a 3.1L engine, install the catalytic converter and the parking brake cable bracket.

34. Remove the engine hoist and the engine hanger from the rear of the exhaust manifold.

35. Install the front exhaust pipe, exhaust pipe-to-exhaust manifold nuts, the exhaust pipe bracket-to-transmission bolts, the front exhaust pipe-to-2nd exhaust pipe bolts.

36. If equipped with a clutch slave cylinder, install it onto the transmission.

37. Install the starter and the starter-to-engine bolts.

38. Install the front driveshaft's splined yoke flange-to-transfer case bolts.

39. If equipped with a 2-piece driveshaft, perform the following procedures:

a. Install the front driveshaft into the transmission and the center bearing-to-chassis bolts.

b. Install the rear driveshaft and the rear driveshaft flange-to-front driveshaft flange bolts.

c. Install the rear driveshaft flange-to-pinion nuts.

40. If equipped with a 1-piece driveshaft, install the driveshaft into the transmission and the driveshaft flange-to-pinion nuts.

41. If equipped with an automatic transmission, perform the following procedures:

a. Connect the fluid coolant lines to the transmission.

b. Connect the downshift cable to the transmission.

c. Connect the shift select control link rod to the select lever.

d. Install the oil level gauge and the tube.

42. Install the front wheels and lower the vehicle.

43. Install the transfer shift lever by performing the following procedures:

a. Position the shift lever into the transfer case.

b. Install the shift lever retaining bolts.

c. Push the dust cover and the shift lever boot downward.

44. Install the gear shift lever by performing the following procedures:

a. Install the shift lever and the shift lever cover bolts.

b. Push the grommet and shift lever boot downward.

c. Install the front console to the floor panel.

45. If equipped with a 3.1L engine, perform the following procedures:

a. Install the ignition coil.

b. Install the distributor cap with the No. 1 spark plug wire.

c. Install the spark plug wire from the No. 1 spark plug and reconnect the wires to the distributor cap.

d. Install the power steering pump-to-engine brackets.

46. If equipped with air conditioning, install the compressor to the engine.

47. Install the radiator, the fan blade assembly and the fan shroud.

48. Connect the upper and lower radiator hoses and the reservoir tank hose.

49. Install the radiator grille to the deflector panel.

50. Install the clutch return spring, if equipped, the clutch control cable, if equipped, the backup light switch connector and the speedometer cable to the transmission.

51. Connect the following items:

a. Air switch valve hose.

b. Oxygen sensor wire.

c. Vacuum switch valve hose.

d. Thermal vacuum switching valve hose.

e. Pressure regulator vacuum hose.

f. Canister hose.

g. ECM harness.

h. Fuel hose(s).

52. Connect the necessary hoses, electrical connectors, control cables and control rods to the engine.

53. Install the air cleaner for 2.3L and 3.1L engines or air cleaner duct and hose for 2.6L engine.

54. Refill the engine, the transmission, the transfer case and the cooling system. Install the undercover, if equipped.

55. Install the hood.

56. Install the battery and connect both battery cables, the positive cable first.

57. Adjust the belt tension. Start the engine, check for leaks.

58. Check and/or adjust the idle speed and ignition timing.

Engine Mounts

REMOVAL AND INSTALLATION

1. Disconnect the negative battery cable. Using a hoist, lift up on the engine hoisting tabs to remove weight from the engine mounts.

2. Loosen the engine mount hardware and remove the mounts from the engine and crossmember.

3. Install the mount and replace the hardware. Torque the bolts and nuts to 38 ft. lbs. (52 Nm).

4. Lower the engine and connect the negative battery cable.

Cylinder Head

REMOVAL AND INSTALLATION

2.3L and 2.6L Engines

1. Relieve the fuel pressure. Disconnect the negative battery cable. Drain the cooling system.

2. Remove the drive belts from the power steering pump, the air pump, the air conditioning compressor, if equipped, and the cooling fan.

3. Rotate the engine to position the No. 1 cylinder on TDC.

4. Remove the distributor cap, high tension cables and the distributor.

5. Remove the exhaust manifold-to-exhaust pipe bolts.

6. Label and disconnect the electrical connectors and vacuum hoses which may be in the way.

7. On the 2.3L engine, remove the carburetor.

8. Remove the coolant hoses. It is not necessary to remove the radiator and the cooling fan assembly.

9. Remove the crankshaft pulley bolt and the pulley.

10. Remove the upper and lower timing belt covers, the tension spring and the timing belt.

11. Remove the camshaft pulley bolt, the pulley and the camshaft boss.

12. Remove the timing belt guide plate and the cylinder head front plate.

13. Remove the rocker arm cover and gasket.

14. Remove the cylinder head-to-engine bolts, the cylinder head and gasket.

15. Clean the gasket mounting surfaces.

To install:

16. Using a new gasket, install the cylinder head and torque the bolts, in sequence to 58 ft. lbs. in the 1st step, and to 65–79 ft. lbs. in the final step.

17. Install the camshaft pulley.

18. Using a new gasket, install the rocker arm cover.

19. Align the camshaft pulley mark with the mark on the front plate. Make sure the keyway on the crankshaft if facing upward, aimed at the pointer on the engine block.

20. Install the timing belt in the following order: crankshaft pulley, the oil pump pulley, the camshaft and the tensioner.

21. Install the timing belt covers, using a new gasket.

22. Install the crankshaft pulley.

23. Install the cooling fan assembly, the radiator and the coolant hoses.

24. On the 2.3L engine, install the carburetor.

25. Connect the electrical connectors and vacuum hoses.

26. Install the exhaust manifold-to-exhaust pipe bolts.

27. Install the distributor, the distributor cap and the high tension cables.

28. Install the drive belts to the power steering pump, the air pump,

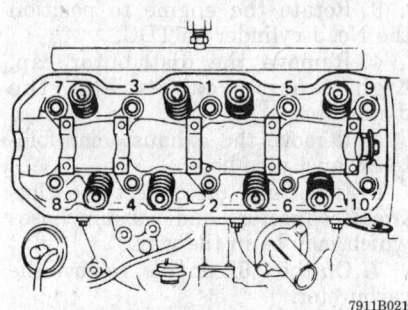

7911B021

View of the cylinder head bolt torquing sequence — 2.3L and 2.6L Engines

the air conditioning compressor, if equipped, and the cooling fan.

29. Disconnect the negative battery cable. Refill the cooling system.

30. Start the engine and check for leaks.

3.1L Engine

LEFT SIDE

1. Relieve the fuel pressure. Disconnect the negative battery cable. Drain the cooling system.

2. Remove the intake manifold.

3. Raise and safely support the vehicle.

4. Disconnect the exhaust pipe from the exhaust manifold and remove the exhaust manifold-to-cylinder head bolts.

5. Remove the dipstick tube from the engine.

6. Lower the vehicle.

7. Loosen the rocker arm nuts, turn the rocker arms and remove the pushrods; keep the pushrods in the same order as removed.

8. Remove the cylinder head bolts in stages and in the reverse order of torquing.

9. Remove the cylinder head; do not pry on the head to loosen it.

10. Clean the gasket mounting surfaces.

To install:

11. Position a new cylinder head gasket over the dowel pins with the words **This Side Up** facing upwards. Carefully, guide the cylinder head into place.

12. Install the cylinder head bolts and torque, in sequence to 41 ft. lbs. in the 1st step, and then an additional ¼ turn in the final step.

13. Install the pushrods; make sure the lower ends are in the lifter heads. Torque the rocker arm nuts to 14–20 ft. lbs. (20–27 Nm).

14. Install the intake manifold.

15. Install the dipstick tube to the engine.

16. Install the exhaust manifold-to-cylinder head bolts and the exhaust pipe-to-exhaust manifold nuts.

17. Refill the cooling system. Start the engine and check for leaks.

RIGHT SIDE

1. Relieve the fuel pressure. Disconnect the negative battery cable. Drain the cooling system.

2. Remove the intake manifold.

3. If equipped, remove the cruise control servo bracket, the air management valve and hose.

4. Raise and safely support the vehicle.

5. Disconnect the exhaust pipe from the exhaust manifold and remove the exhaust manifold-to-cylinder head bolts.

6. Remove the exhaust pipe at crossover, the crossover and the heat shield, if equipped.

7. Lower the vehicle.

8. Label and disconnect the electrical wiring and vacuum hoses that may interfere with the removal of the right cylinder head.

9. Loosen the rocker arm nuts, turn the rocker arms and remove the pushrods; keep the pushrods in the same order as removed.

10. Remove the cylinder head bolts in stages and in the reverse order of torquing.

11. Remove the cylinder head; do not pry on the head to loosen it.

12. Clean the gasket mounting surfaces.

To install:

13. Position a new cylinder head gasket over the dowel pins with the words **This Side Up** facing upwards. Carefully, guide the cylinder head into place.

14. Install the cylinder head bolts and torque, in sequence to 41 ft. lbs. in the 1st step, and then an additional ¼ turn in the final step.

15. Install the pushrods; make sure the lower ends are in the lifter heads.

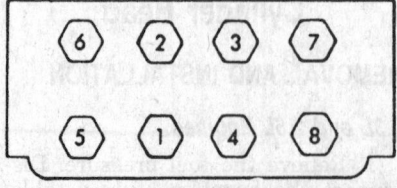

7911B022

View of the cylinder head bolt torquing sequence — 3.1L Engine

Torque the rocker arm nuts to 14–20 ft. lbs. (20–27 Nm).

16. Install the intake manifold.

17. Install the exhaust pipe at crossover, the crossover and the heat shield, if equipped.

18. Install the exhaust manifold-to-cylinder head bolts and the exhaust pipe-to-exhaust manifold nuts.

19. Connect the electrical wiring and vacuum hoses to the right cylinder head.

20. If equipped, install the cruise control servo bracket, the air management valve and hose.

21. Refill the cooling system. Start the engine and check for leaks.

3.2L SOHC Engine

1. Disconnect negative battery cable and remove the engine hood.

2. Remove the air cleaner assembly.

3. Disconnect the accelerator pedal cable from the throttle body and cable brackets.

4. Disconnect the canister vacuum hose from the Vacuum Switch Valve (VSV).

5. Disconnect the vacuum booster hose from the common chamber duct.

6. Disconnect the electrical connectors from the Idle Air Control Valve, Throttle Position sensor, Manifold Absolute Pressure sensor, canister VSV, EGR VSV, Intake Air Temperature sensor and VSV.

7. Remove the high tension cable from the cylinder heads.

8. Disconnect the 3 connectors from the EI module.

9. Remove the 3 bolts from the EI bracket and remove the EI assembly.

10. Remove the 4 bolts from the throttle body and remove the throttle body.

11. Disconnect the canister VSV and the EGR VSV vacuum hose from the throttle body.

12. Disconnect the fuel pressure control valve vacuum hose from the common chamber duct.

13. Disconnect the PCV hose from the common chamber duct.

14. Disconnect the evaporative emission canister purge hose from the common chamber duct.

15. Remove the 4 bolts from the EGR valve assembly common chamber duct and remove the exhaust manifold.

16. Remove the 4 bolts, 4 nuts and 3 manifold bracket fixing bolts from the common chamber duct.

17. Remove the ground cable fixing bolt from the rear of the common chamber duct.

18. Remove the 6 bolts and 2 nuts from the common chamber duct.

19. Remove the common chamber duct bracket fixing bolts from the rear of the common chamber duct.

20. Remove the fuel feed and return hoses from the fuel pipe. Remove the 2 fixing bolts from the cylinder head.

21. Remove the fuel injector connectors from the fuel rail assembly.

22. Remove the fuel rail fixing bolts from the fuel rail assembly.

23. Remove the fuel rail assembly from the engine.

NOTE: While removing the fuel rail from the engine, if a fuel injector separates from the fuel rail and remains in the head of the engine, replace both the injector O-rings and the injector retainer clip.

24. Remove the regulator attaching screw from the fuel rail.

25. Remove the fuel pressure control valve assembly from the fuel rail.

26. Remove the fuel injector retainer clip and remove the fuel injector.

27. Remove 11 fixing bolts and remove cylinder head cover.

28. Remove the camshaft timing pulley.

29. Remove front plate.

30. Remove camshaft:

　a. Remove thrust plate

　b. Remove camshaft bracket housing fixing bolts.

　c. Remove camshaft and camshaft bracket, together.

31. Remove the exhaust side rocker shaft assembly.

32. Remove the intake side rocker shaft assembly.

33. Remove the spark plugs.

34. Remove the cylinder head bolts and remove the cylinder head.

To install:

35. Install the cylinder head and tighten the head bolts to 47 ft. lbs. (64 Nm).

36. Install the spark plugs. Tighten to 13 ft. lbs. (18 Nm).

37. Install the intake side rocker shaft assembly.

38. Install the exhaust side rocker shaft assembly.

39. Install camshaft(s):

　a. Install camshaft and camshaft bracket, together.

　b. Install camshaft bracket housing fixing bolts. Tighten M6 bolts to 69 in. lbs. (8 Nm) and M8 bolts to 13 ft. lbs. (18 Nm).

　c. Install thrust plate. Tighten bolts to 87 in. lbs. (10 Nm).

40. Install front plate.

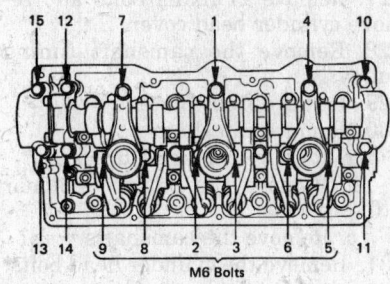

85478005

Camshaft bracket housing fixing bolts tightening sequence — 1993–96 Trooper

41. Install the camshaft timing pulley. Tighten fixing bolt to 41 ft. lbs. (55 Nm).

42. Install the cylinder head cover and tighten 11 fixing bolts to 69 in. lbs. (8 Nm).

43. Install the fuel injector to the frame rail and attach with retainer clip.

44. Install the fuel pressure control valve assembly to the fuel rail.

45. Install the regulator attaching screw to the fuel rail.

46. Install the fuel rail assembly to the engine.

47. Install the fuel rail fixing bolts to the fuel rail assembly.

48. Install the fuel injector connectors to the fuel rail assembly.

49. Install the fuel feed and return hoses to the fuel pipe. Install the 2 fixing bolts to the cylinder head.

50. Install the common chamber duct bracket fixing bolts to the rear of the common chamber duct.

51. Install the 6 bolts and 2 nuts to the common chamber duct.

52. Install the ground cable fixing bolt to the rear of the common chamber duct.

53. Install the 4 bolts, 4 nuts and 3 manifold bracket fixing bolts to the common chamber duct.

54. Install the exhaust manifold and install the 4 bolts to the EGR valve assembly and common chamber duct.

55. Connect the evaporative emission canister purge hose to the common chamber duct.

56. Connect the PCV hose to the common chamber duct.

57. Connect the fuel pressure control valve vacuum hose to the common chamber duct.

58. Connect the canister VSV and the EGR VSV vacuum hose to the throttle body.

59. Install the throttle body and install the 4 bolts to the throttle body and remove the throttle body.

60. Install the EI assembly and install the 3 bolts to the EI bracket.

61. Connect the 3 connectors to the EI module.

62. Connect the high tension cable to the cylinder heads.

63. Connect the electrical connectors to the Idle Air Control Valve, Throttle Position sensor, Manifold Absolute Pressure sensor, canister VSV, EGR VSV, Intake Air Temperature sensor and VSV.

64. Connect the vacuum booster hose to the common chamber duct.

65. Connect the canister vacuum hose to the Vacuum Switch Valve (VSV).

66. Connect the accelerator pedal cable to the throttle body and cable brackets.

67. Install the air cleaner assembly.

68. Install the engine hood and connect negative battery cable.

3.2L DOHC Engine

1. Disconnect negative battery cable and remove the engine hood.

2. Remove the air cleaner assembly.

3. Disconnect the accelerator pedal cable from the throttle body and cable brackets.

4. Disconnect the canister vacuum hose from the Vacuum Switch Valve (VSV).

5. Disconnect the vacuum booster hose from the common chamber duct.

6. Disconnect the electrical connectors from the Idle Air Control Valve, Throttle Position sensor, Manifold Absolute Pressure sensor, canister VSV, EGR VSV, Intake Air Temperature sensor and VSV.

7. Remove the high tension cable from the cylinder heads.

8. Disconnect the 3 connectors from the EI module.

9. Remove the 3 bolts from the EI bracket and remove the EI assembly.

10. Remove the 4 bolts from the throttle body and remove the throttle body.

11. Disconnect the canister VSV and the EGR VSV vacuum hose from the throttle body.

12. Disconnect the fuel pressure control valve vacuum hose from the common chamber duct.

13. Disconnect the PCV hose from the common chamber duct.

14. Disconnect the evaporative emission canister purge hose from the common chamber duct.

15. Remove the 4 bolts from the EGR valve assembly common chamber duct and remove the exhaust manifold.

16. Remove the 4 bolts, 4 nuts and 3 manifold bracket fixing bolts from the common chamber duct.

17. Remove the ground cable fixing bolt from the rear of the common chamber duct.

18. Remove the 6 bolts and 2 nuts from the common chamber duct.

19. Remove the common chamber duct bracket fixing bolts from the rear of the common chamber duct.

20. Remove the fuel feed and return hoses from the fuel pipe. Remove the 2 fixing bolts from the cylinder head.

21. Remove the fuel injector connectors from the fuel rail assembly.

22. Remove the fuel rail fixing bolts from the fuel rail assembly.

23. Remove the fuel rail assembly from the engine.

NOTE: While removing the fuel rail from the engine, if a fuel injector separates from the fuel rail and remains in the head of the engine, replace both the injector O-rings and the injector retainer clip.

24. Remove the regulator attaching screw from the fuel rail.

25. Remove the fuel pressure control valve assembly from the fuel rail.

26. Remove the fuel injector retainer clip and remove the fuel injector.

27. Remove 11 fixing bolts and remove cylinder head cover.

28. Remove the camshaft timing pulley.

29. Remove front plate.

30. Remove camshafts:

   a. Remove camshaft brackets.

   b. Remove the chain tensioner fixing bolts.

   c. Remove the camshafts.

31. Remove the cylinder head bolts. Remove the cylinder head.

To install:

32. Install the cylinder head and tighten the head bolts to 47 ft. lbs. (64 Nm).

33. Install the spark plugs. Tighten to 13 ft. lbs. (18 Nm).

34. Install camshafts:

   a. Install the camshafts.

   b. Tighten the chain tensioner fixing bolts to 14 ft. lbs. (19 Nm).

   c. Install the camshaft brackets. Tighten bolts to 87 in. lbs. (10 Nm).

35. Install front plate.

36. Install the camshaft timing pulley. Tighten fixing bolt to 41 ft. lbs. (55 Nm).

37. Install the cylinder head cover and tighten 11 fixing bolts to 69 in. lbs. (8 Nm).

38. Install the fuel injector to the frame rail and attach with retainer clip.

39. Install the fuel pressure control valve assembly to the fuel rail.

40. Install the regulator attaching screw to the fuel rail.

41. Install the fuel rail assembly to the engine.

42. Install the fuel rail fixing bolts to the fuel rail assembly.

43. Install the fuel injector connectors to the fuel rail assembly.

44. Install the fuel feed and return hoses to the fuel pipe. Install the 2 fixing bolts to the cylinder head.

45. Install the common chamber duct bracket fixing bolts to the rear of the common chamber duct.

46. Install the 6 bolts and 2 nuts to the common chamber duct.

47. Install the ground cable fixing bolt to the rear of the common chamber duct.

48. Install the 4 bolts, 4 nuts and 3 manifold bracket fixing bolts to the common chamber duct.

49. Install the exhaust manifold and install the 4 bolts to the EGR valve assembly and common chamber duct.

50. Connect the evaporative emission canister purge hose to the common chamber duct.

51. Connect the PCV hose to the common chamber duct.

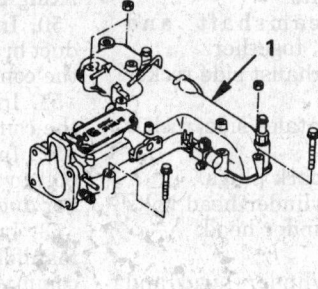

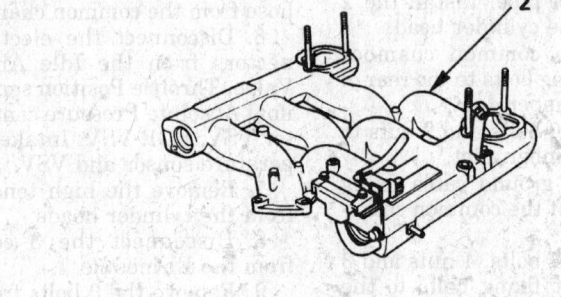

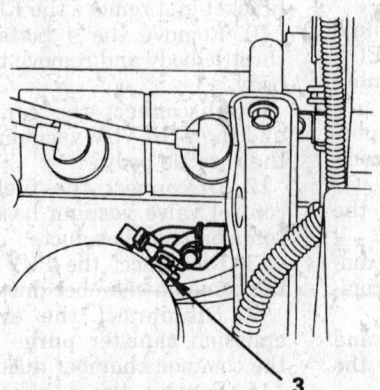

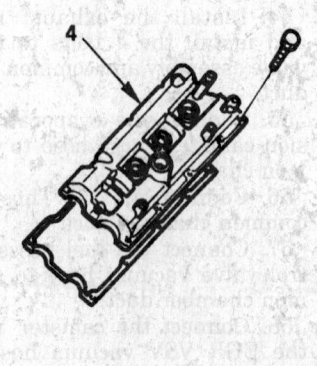

Removal steps
1. Common chamber duct
2. Common chamber
3. Fuel hose
4. Cylinder head cover

Installation steps
To install, follow the removal step in the reverse order.

85478006

Cylinder head cover removal

52. Connect the fuel pressure control valve vacuum hose to the common chamber duct.
53. Connect the canister VSV and the EGR VSV vacuum hose to the throttle body.
54. Install the throttle body and install the 4 bolts to the throttle body and remove the throttle body.
55. Install the EI assembly and install the 3 bolts to the EI bracket.
56. Connect the 3 connectors to the EI module.
57. Connect the high tension cable to the cylinder heads.
58. Connect the electrical connectors to the Idle Air Control Valve, Throttle Position sensor, Manifold Absolute Pressure sensor, canister VSV, EGR VSV, Intake Air Temperature sensor and VSV.
59. Connect the vacuum booster hose to the common chamber duct.
60. Connect the canister vacuum hose to the Vacuum Switch Valve (VSV).
61. Connect the accelerator pedal cable to the throttle body and cable brackets.
62. Install the air cleaner assembly.
63. Install the engine hood and connect negative battery cable.

Valve Lifters

REMOVAL AND INSTALLATION

3.1L Engine

1. Disconnect the negative battery cable.
2. Remove the rocker arm covers.
3. Remove the rocker arm nut, the pivot balls, the rocker arm and the pushrods. Keep all components separated so they may be reinstalled in the same location.
4. Remove the lifter from their bores using a hydraulic valve lifter J–929901 or equivalent.

NOTE: The intake and exhaust pushrods are of different lengths.

To install:
5. Lubricate the lifters with Molykote or equivalent, and install in the bores. Install the pushrods in their original location; be sure the lower ends are seated in the lifter.
6. Coat the bearing surfaces of the rocker arms and pivot balls with Molykote or equivalent.
7. Install the rocker arm nuts and torque them to 14–20 ft. lbs. (20–27 Nm).
8. Adjust the valve lash.

Valve Lash

ADJUSTMENT

2.3L and 2.6L Engines

NOTE: The valves are adjusted with the engine COLD. It is best to allow an engine to sit overnight before beginning a valve adjustment. While all valve adjustments must be made as accurately as possible, it is better to have the valve adjustment slightly loose rather than slightly tight. A burned valve may result from overly tight valve adjustments.

1. Remove the rocker arm cover and discard the gasket.
2. Make sure both the cylinder head and camshaft retaining bolts are tightened to the proper torque.
3. Rotate the crankshaft pulley until the No. 1 piston is at TDC of the compression stroke.

NOTE: To make sure the piston is on the correct stroke, remove the spark plug and place a finger over the hole. Feel for air being forced out of the spark plug hole. Both valves on No. 1 cylinder will be closed. Stop turning the crankshaft when the TDC timing mark on the crankshaft pulley is directly aligned with the timing mark pointer.

4. With the No. 1 piston at TDC of the compression stroke, adjust the clearances of the following valves: Intake 1 and 2; Exhaust 1 and 3
5. Adjust the clearance by loosening the locknut and turning the adjusting screw. Retightening the locknut when the proper thickness feeler gauge passes between the camshaft or valve stem and has a slight drag when the clearance is corrected.
6. Rotate the crankshaft 1 complete revolution (360 degrees) to position the No. 4 piston at TDC of its compression stroke and adjust the clearances of the following valves: Intake 3 and 4; Exhaust 2 and 4
7. After adjustment, use a new gasket, sealant and install the rocker arm cover.

3.1L Engine

1. Remove the valve covers.

2. Rotate the crankshaft until the No. 1 cylinder is on the TDC of its compression stroke.

NOTE: When the notch on the damper pulley is aligned with the 0 timing mark and the rocker arms of the No. 1 cylinder do not move, the engine is at the TDC of the compression stroke of the No. 1 cylinder.

3. With the engine at TDC of the No. 1 cylinder, adjust the following valves: Exhaust 1, 2 and 3; Intake: 1, 5 and 6
4. Back out the adjusting nut until lash is felt.
5. Tighten the adjusting nut until the lash is removed, then, turn the nut 1½ additional turns to center the lifter plunger.
6. Rotate the engine 1 complete revolution and reposition the notch on the damper pulley with the **0** mark on the timing tab; this is the No. 4 cylinder firing position.
7. With the engine at TDC of the No. 4 cylinder, adjust the following valves: Exhaust: 4, 5 and 6; Intake 2, 3 and 4
8. Back out the adjusting nut until lash is felt.
9. Tighten the adjusting nut until the lash is removed, plus, turn the nut 1½ additional turns to center the lifter plunger.
10. Using a new gasket and sealant, install the rocker arm covers.

Rocker Arms/Shafts

REMOVAL AND INSTALLATION

2.3L and 2.6L Engines

1. Disconnect the negative battery cable. Remove the rocker cover. Remove the accessory drive belts and the engine cooling fan and water pump pulley. Remove the starter and crankshaft pulley. Remove the timing covers and timing belt.
2. Loosen the rocker arm shaft bracket nuts a little at a time, in sequence, starting with the outer nuts.
3. Remove the nuts from the rocker arm shaft brackets. Remove shaft assembly.
4. To disassemble the rockers and shafts; remove the spring from the rocker arm shaft, the rocker brackets and arms. Keep parts in order for reassembly.
5. Before installing apply a generous amount of clean engine oil to the rocker arm shaft, rocker arms and valve stems.

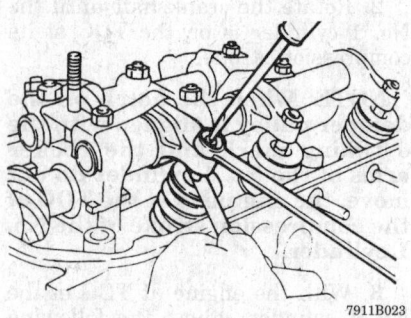

Adjusting the valves — 2.3L and 2.6L Engines

7911B023

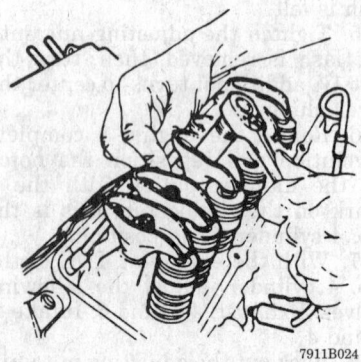

Adjusting the valves — 3.1L Engine

7911B024

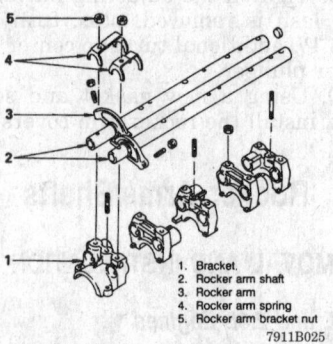

1. Bracket
2. Rocker arm shaft
3. Rocker arm
4. Rocker arm spring
5. Rocker arm bracket nut

7911B025

Exploded view of the rocker arm/shaft assembly — 2.3L and 2.6L Engines

To install:

6. Install the longer shaft on the exhaust valve side and the shorter shaft on the intake side so the aligning marks on the shafts are turned on the front side of the engine.

7. Assemble the rocker arm shaft brackets and rocker arms to the shafts so the cylinder number, on the upper face of the brackets, points toward the front of the engine.

8. Align the mark on the No. 1 rocker arm shaft bracket with the mark on the intake and exhaust valve side rocker arm shaft.

7911B026

View of the rocker arm/shaft assembly torquing sequence — 2.3L and 2.6L Engines

9. Make certain the amount of projection of the rocker arm shaft beyond the face of the No. 1 rocker arm shaft bracket, is longer on the exhaust side shaft than on the intake shaft when the rocker arm shaft stud holes are aligned with the rocker arm shaft bracket stud holes.

10. Place the rocker arm shaft springs in position between the shaft bracket and rocker arm.

11. Check that the punch mark on the rocker arm shaft is facing upward, then, install the rocker arm shaft bracket assembly onto the cylinder head studs. Align the mark on the camshaft with the mark on the No. 1 rocker arm shaft bracket.

12. Torque the rocker arm shaft brackets-to-cylinder head nuts to 16 ft. lbs. and bolts to 6 ft. lbs.

NOTE: Hold the rocker arm springs while torquing the nuts to prevent damage to the spring. Start with the center nut and work outward.

13. Adjust the valves and install the camshaft cover, with a new gasket and sealer. Install the timing covers, accessories and drive belts. Check the ignition timing.

3.1L Engine

1. Disconnect the negative battery cable.

2. Remove the rocker arm covers.

3. Remove the rocker arm nut, the pivot balls, the rocker arm and the pushrods. Keep all components separated so they may be reinstalled in the same location.

NOTE: The intake and exhaust pushrods are of different lengths.

To install:

4. Install the pushrods in their original location; be sure the lower ends are seated in the lifter.

5. Coat the bearing surfaces of the rocker arms and pivot balls with Molykote or equivalent.

6. Install the rocker arm nuts and torque them to 14–20 ft. lbs. (20–27 Nm).

7. Adjust the valve lash.

3.2L SOHC

1. Disconnect negative battery cable.

2. Remove the air cleaner assembly.

3. Disconnect the accelerator pedal cable from the throttle body and cable brackets.

4. Disconnect the canister vacuum hose from the Vacuum Switch Valve (VSV).

5. Disconnect the vacuum booster hose from the common chamber duct.

6. Disconnect the electrical connectors from the Idle Air Control Valve, Throttle Position sensor, Manifold Absolute Pressure sensor, canister VSV, EGR VSV, Intake Air Temperature sensor and VSV.

7. Remove the high tension cable from the cylinder heads.

8. Disconnect the 3 connectors from the EI module.

9. Remove the 3 bolts from the EI bracket and remove the EI assembly.

10. Remove the 4 bolts from the throttle body and remove the throttle body.

11. Disconnect the canister VSV and the EGR VSV vacuum hose from the throttle body.

12. Disconnect the fuel pressure control valve vacuum hose from the common chamber duct.

13. Disconnect the PCV hose from the common chamber duct.

14. Disconnect the evaporative emission canister purge hose from the common chamber duct.

15. Remove the 4 bolts from the EGR valve assembly common chamber duct and remove the exhaust manifold.

16. Remove the 4 bolts, 4 nuts and 3 manifold bracket fixing bolts from the common chamber duct.

17. Remove the ground cable fixing bolt from the rear of the common chamber duct.

18. Remove the 6 bolts and 2 nuts from the common chamber duct.

19. Remove the common chamber duct bracket fixing bolts from the rear of the common chamber duct.

20. Remove the timing belt:

    a. Remove the upper fan shroud from the radiator.

    b. Remove the 4 nuts retaining the cooling fan assembly. Remove the cooling fan.

    c. Remove the power steering drive belt.

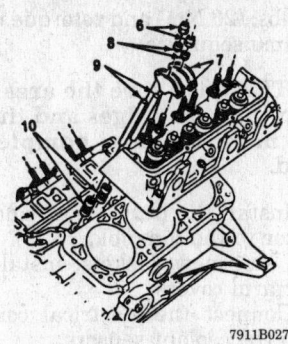

7911B027

Exploded view of the cylinder head/rocker arm assembly — 3.1L Engine

d. Remove the air conditioning compressor drive belt.

e. Remove the generator drive belt.

f. Remove the fan pulley assembly.

g. Remove the crankshaft pulley center bolt. Remove the crankshaft pulley.

h. Remove the 2 oil cooler hose bracket fixing bolts on the timing cover. Remove the oil cooler hose.

i. Remove the timing belt cover.

j. Remove the pusher. The rod must always be facing upward.

k. Mark the timing belt, cam pulley and crankshaft pulley. Remove the timing belt.

21. Remove the cylinder head cover.

22. Remove the camshaft.

23. Remove the rocker arm fixing bolts and the rocker arm.

To install:

24. Install the rocker arm and tighten the fixing bolts to 13 ft. lbs. (18 Nm).

25. Install the camshaft.

26. Install the cylinder head cover.

27. Install the timing belt:

a. Align the groove on the crankshaft timing pulley with mark on the oil pump.

b. Align the marks on the camshaft timing pulleys with the dots on the front plate.

c. Install the timing belt. Align the dotted marks on the timing belt with the mark on the crankshaft gear.

d. Align the white line on the timing belt with the alignment mark on the right bank camshaft timing pulley. Secure the belt with a double clip.

e. Turn the crankshaft counterclockwise to remove the slack between the crankshaft pulley and the right camshaft timing pulley.

f. Install the belt on the water pump pulley.

g. Install the belt on the idler pulley.

h. Align the white alignment mark on the timing belt with the alignment mark on the left bank camshaft timing pulley.

i. Install the crankshaft pulley and tighten the center bolt by hand. Turn the crankshaft pulley clockwise to give slack between the crankshaft timing pulley and the right bank camshaft timing pulley.

j. Install the pusher while pushing the tension pulley to the belt.

k. Pull the pin out from the pusher.

l. Remove the double clips from the pulleys. Turn the crankshaft pulley clockwise 2 turns. Measure the rod protrusion to be sure it is between 0.16–0.24 in. (4–6 mm).

m. Tighten adjusting bolt to 31 ft. lbs. (42 Nm).

n. Tighten pusher bolt to 14 ft. lbs. (19 Nm).

o. Remove crankshaft pulley. Install the timing belt cover and tighten bolts to 12 ft. lbs. (17 Nm).

p. Install the oil cooler hose and tighten brackets to 16 ft. lbs. (22 Nm).

q. Install the crankshaft pulley and tighten bolts to 123 ft. lbs. (167 Nm).

r. Install fan pulley assembly and tighten fixing bolts to 16 ft. lbs. (22 Nm).

s. Engage and adjust generator drive belt.

t. Engage and adjust air conditioning drive belt.

u. Engage and adjust power steering pump drive belt.

v. Install cooling fan assembly and tighten bolts to 69 in. lbs. (8 Nm).

w. Install upper fan shroud to the radiator.

28. Install the common chamber duct bracket fixing bolts to the rear of the common chamber duct.

29. Install the 6 bolts and 2 nuts to the common chamber duct.

30. Install the ground cable fixing bolt to the rear of the common chamber duct.

31. Install the 4 bolts, 4 nuts and 3 manifold bracket fixing bolts to the common chamber duct.

32. Install the exhaust manifold and install the 4 bolts to the EGR valve assembly and common chamber duct.

33. Connect the evaporative emission canister purge hose to the common chamber duct.

34. Connect the PCV hose to the common chamber duct.

35. Connect the fuel pressure control valve vacuum hose to the common chamber duct.

36. Connect the canister VSV and the EGR VSV vacuum hose to the throttle body.

37. Install the throttle body and install the 4 bolts to the throttle body and remove the throttle body.

38. Install the EI assembly and install the 3 bolts to the EI bracket.

39. Connect the 3 connectors to the EI module.

40. Connect the high tension cable to the cylinder heads.

41. Connect the electrical connectors to the Idle Air Control Valve, Throttle Position sensor, Manifold Absolute Pressure sensor, canister VSV, EGR VSV, Intake Air Temperature sensor and VSV.

42. Connect the vacuum booster hose to the common chamber duct.

43. Connect the canister vacuum hose to the Vacuum Switch Valve (VSV).

44. Connect the accelerator pedal cable to the throttle body and cable brackets.

45. Install the air cleaner assembly.

46. Install the engine hood and connect negative battery cable.

Intake Manifold

REMOVAL AND INSTALLATION

2.3L Engine

1. Relieve the fuel pressure. Disconnect the negative battery cable and remove the air cleaner assembly.

2. Remove the EGR pipe clamp bolt at the rear of the cylinder head.

3. Raise and support the vehicle safely. Remove the EGR pipe from the intake and exhaust manifolds.

4. Remove the EGR valve and bracket assembly from the intake manifold.

5. Lower the vehicle and drain the cooling system.

6. Remove the upper coolant hoses from the manifold.

7. Disconnect the accelerator linkage, vacuum lines, electrical wiring and fuel line from the intake manifold.

8. Remove the intake manifold mounting nuts and remove the manifold from the cylinder head.

9. Remove the lower heater hose while holding the manifold away from the engine. Remove the manifold from the vehicle.

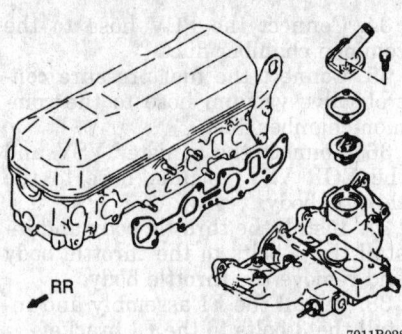

Exploded view of the intake manifold — 2.3L engine

To install:

10. Connect the lower heater hose to the manifold. Using a new gasket, install the intake manifold.

11. Connect the accelerator linkage, vacuum lines, electrical wiring and fuel line to the intake manifold.

12. Connect the upper coolant hose to the intake manifold.

13. Install the EGR valve and bracket assembly to the intake manifold.

14. Install the EGR pipe to the intake and exhaust manifolds. Lower the vehicle.

15. Install the EGR pipe clamp bolt to the rear of the cylinder head.

16. Install the air cleaner and connect the negative battery cable.

2.6L Engine

1. Relieve the fuel pressure. Disconnect the negative battery cable and remove the air duct.

2. Drain the cooling system. Remove the upper coolant hoses from the manifold.

3. Remove the air regulator rubber hose from the intake plenum.

4. Remove the EGR valve and bracket assembly from the intake manifold.

5. Disconnect the accelerator linkage, vacuum lines, electrical wiring and fuel line from the throttle body.

6. Remove the throttle body-to-plenum nuts and the throttle body.

7. Remove the plenum-to-intake manifold bolts and the plenum. Remove the fuel injector rail with the fuel injectors.

8. Remove the intake manifold-to-cylinder head nuts and the manifold from the cylinder head.

To install:

9. Using a new gasket, install the intake manifold to the cylinder head. Install the fuel injector rail with the injectors.

10. Using a new gasket, install the plenum to the intake manifold.

11. Using a new gasket, install the throttle body to the plenum.

12. Connect the accelerator linkage, vacuum lines, electrical wiring and fuel line.

13. Install the EGR valve and bracket assembly to the intake manifold.

14. Install the air regulator rubber hose to the intake plenum.

15. Install the upper coolant hoses to the manifold.

16. Install the air duct. Connect the negative battery cable. Refill the cooling system.

3.1L Engine

1. Relieve the fuel pressure. Disconnect the negative battery cable.

2. Remove the air cleaner. Drain the cooling system.

3. Label and disconnect the wires and hoses from the TBI unit and the intake manifold.

4. Disconnect and plug the fuel lines from the TBI unit.

5. Disconnect the accelerator cables from the TBI unit.

6. Disconnect the ignition wires from the spark plugs and the wires from the coil.

7. Remove the distributor cap with the wires.

8. Mark the location of the rotor to the distributor housing and the distributor housing to the intake manifold.

9. Remove the distributor holddown clamp and the distributor.

10. Label and disconnect the EGR vacuum line and the emission hoses.

11. Remove the pipe brackets from the rocker arm covers.

12. Remove the rocker arm covers.

13. Remove the upper radiator hose and the heater hose.

14. Disconnect the electrical connectors from the coolant sensors.

15. Remove the intake manifold nuts/bolts, the manifold and gaskets.

16. Clean the gasket mounting surfaces.

To install:

17. Using RTV sealant, apply an 1/8 in. bead to the front and rear of the block; make sure no water or oil is present.

18. Using new gaskets, marked right and left side, apply a 1/4 in. bead of sealant to hold them in place and install them onto the cylinder heads; the gaskets may have to be cut to be installed around the pushrods.

19. Install the intake manifold and torque the nuts/bolts, in sequence, to 19 ft. lbs. (26 Nm) and retorque using the same sequence.

NOTE: Make sure the areas between the case ridges and the intake manifold are completely sealed.

20. Install the heater hose and the radiator to the manifold.

21. Using new gaskets, install the rocker arm covers.

22. Connect the electrical connectors to the coolant sensors.

23. Install the pipe brackets.

24. Align the matchmarks and install the distributor and the distributor cap.

25. Connect the fuel lines and the accelerator cables to the TBI unit.

26. Connect all the wires and vacuum hoses.

27. Install the air cleaner. Connect the negative battery cable. Refill the cooling system.

3.2L Engine

The engine is equipped with 6 fuel injectors, with 1 located at each cylinder.

1. Disconnect negative battery cable and remove the engine hood.

2. Remove the air cleaner assembly.

3. Disconnect the accelerator pedal cable from the throttle body and cable brackets.

4. Disconnect the canister vacuum hose from the Vacuum Switch Valve (VSV).

5. Disconnect the vacuum booster hose from the common chamber duct.

6. Disconnect the electrical connectors from the Idle Air Control Valve, Throttle Position sensor, Manifold Absolute Pressure sensor, canister VSV, EGR VSV, Intake Air Temperature sensor and VSV.

7. Remove the high tension cable from the cylinder heads.

8. Disconnect the 3 connectors from the EI module.

9. Remove the 3 bolts from the EI bracket and remove the EI assembly.

10. Remove the 4 bolts from the throttle body and remove the throttle body.

11. Disconnect the canister VSV and the EGR VSV vacuum hose from the throttle body.

12. Disconnect the fuel pressure control valve vacuum hose from the common chamber duct.

13. Disconnect the PCV hose from the common chamber duct.

14. Disconnect the evaporative emission canister purge hose from the common chamber duct.

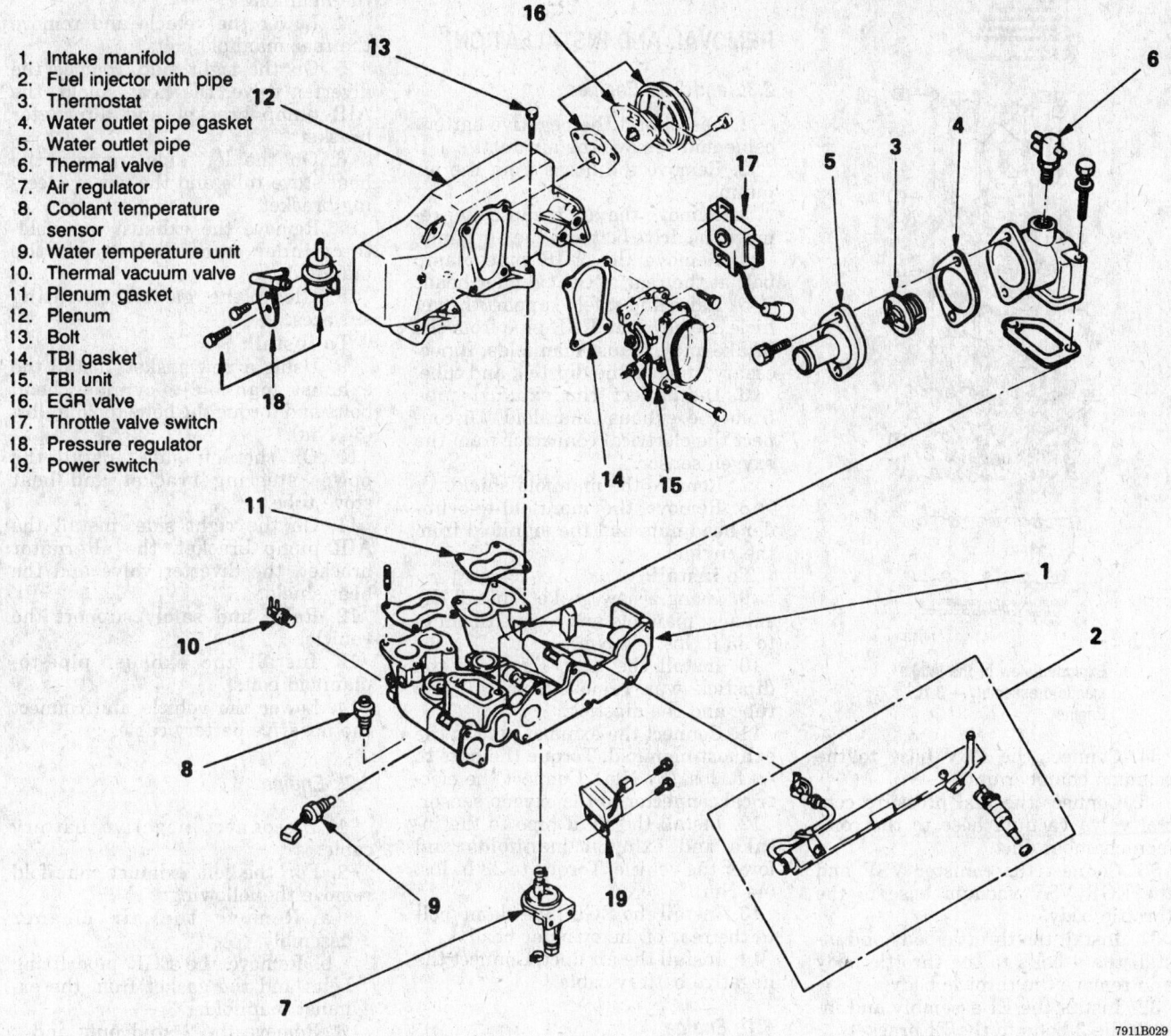

1. Intake manifold
2. Fuel injector with pipe
3. Thermostat
4. Water outlet pipe gasket
5. Water outlet pipe
6. Thermal valve
7. Air regulator
8. Coolant temperature sensor
9. Water temperature unit
10. Thermal vacuum valve
11. Plenum gasket
12. Plenum
13. Bolt
14. TBI gasket
15. TBI unit
16. EGR valve
17. Throttle valve switch
18. Pressure regulator
19. Power switch

7911B029

Exploded view of the intake manifold assembly — 2.6L engine

15. Remove the 4 bolts from the EGR valve assembly common chamber duct and remove the exhaust manifold.

16. Remove the 4 bolts, 4 nuts and 3 manifold bracket fixing bolts from the common chamber duct.

17. Remove the ground cable fixing bolt from the rear of the common chamber duct.

18. Remove the 6 bolts and 2 nuts from the common chamber duct.

19. Remove the common chamber duct bracket fixing bolts from the rear of the common chamber duct.

20. Remove the fuel feed and return hoses from the fuel pipe. Remove the 2 fixing bolts from the cylinder head.

21. Remove the fuel injector connectors from the fuel rail assembly.

22. Disconnect the thermosensor connector.

23. Remove the 2 fixing bolts and 4 nuts from the intake manifold and remove the manifold.

To install:
24. Install the intake manifold. Torque the 2 fixing bolts and 4 nuts to 17 ft. lbs. (24 Nm).

25. Connect the thermosensor connector.

26. Install the fuel injector connectors to the fuel rail assembly.

27. Install the fuel feed and return hoses to the fuel pipe. Install the 2 fixing bolts to the cylinder head.

28. Install the common chamber duct bracket fixing bolts to the rear of the common chamber duct.

29. Install the 6 bolts and 2 nuts to the common chamber duct.

30. Install the ground cable fixing bolt to the rear of the common chamber duct.

31. Install the 4 bolts, 4 nuts and 3 manifold bracket fixing bolts to the common chamber duct.

32. Install the exhaust manifold and install the 4 bolts to the EGR valve assembly and common chamber duct.

33. Connect the evaporative emission canister purge hose to the common chamber duct.

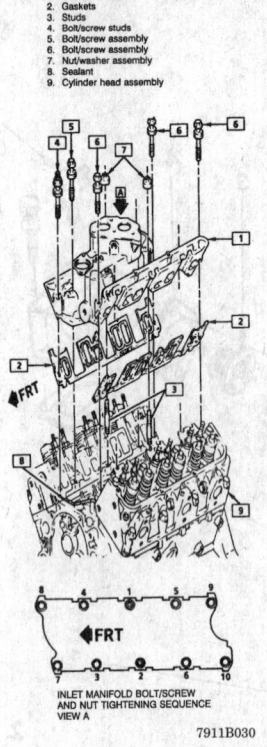

1. Intake manifold
2. Gaskets
3. Studs
4. Bolt/screw studs
5. Bolt/screw assembly
6. Bolt/screw assembly
7. Nut/washer assembly
8. Sealant
9. Cylinder head assembly

◄FRT

INLET MANIFOLD BOLT/SCREW
AND NUT TIGHTENING SEQUENCE
VIEW A

7911B030

Exploded view of the intake manifold assembly — 3.1L Engine

34. Connect the PCV hose to the common chamber duct.

35. Connect the fuel pressure control valve vacuum hose to the common chamber duct.

36. Connect the canister VSV and the EGR VSV vacuum hose to the throttle body.

37. Install the throttle body and install the 4 bolts to the throttle body and remove the throttle body.

38. Install the EI assembly and install the 3 bolts to the EI bracket.

39. Connect the 3 connectors to the EI module.

40. Connect the high tension cable to the cylinder heads.

41. Connect the electrical connectors to the Idle Air Control Valve, Throttle Position sensor, Manifold Absolute Pressure sensor, canister VSV, EGR VSV, Intake Air Temperature sensor and VSV.

42. Connect the vacuum booster hose to the common chamber duct.

43. Connect the canister vacuum hose to the Vacuum Switch Valve (VSV).

44. Connect the accelerator pedal cable to the throttle body and cable brackets.

45. Install the air cleaner assembly.

46. Install the engine hood and connect negative battery cable.

Exhaust Manifold

REMOVAL AND INSTALLATION

2.3L and 2.6L Engines

1. Disconnect the negative battery cable and remove the air duct.

2. Remove the hoses from the air pump.

3. Remove the air pump bolts, remove the drive belt and the air pump.

4. Remove the EGR pipe clamp bolt at the rear of the cylinder head.

5. Raise and safely support the vehicle. Remove the EGR pipe from the intake and exhaust manifolds. If necessary, remove the dipstick and tube.

6. Disconnect the exhaust pipe from the exhaust manifold. Disconnect the electrical connector from the oxygen sensor.

7. Remove the manifold shield.

8. Remove the manifold-to-cylinder head nuts and the manifold from the engine.

To install:

9. Using a new gasket, install the exhaust manifold and torque the nuts to 33 ft. lbs. (44 Nm).

10. Install the heat shield. If the dipstick was removed, install the tube and the dipstick.

11. Connect the exhaust pipe to the exhaust manifold. Torque the nuts to 49 ft. lbs. (67 Nm). Connect the electrical connector to the oxygen sensor.

12. Install the EGR pipe to the intake and exhaust manifolds and lower the vehicle. Torque to 33 ft. lbs. (44 Nm).

13. Install the EGR pipe clamp bolt to the rear of the cylinder head.

14. Install the air duct. Connect the negative battery cable.

3.1L Engine

1. Disconnect the negative battery cable.

2. Raise and safely support the vehicle.

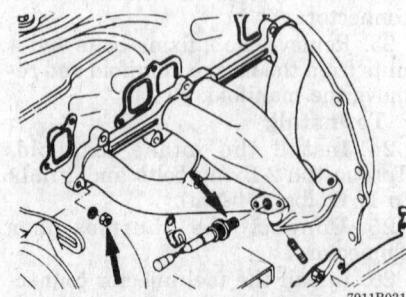

7911B031

Exploded view of the exhaust manifold — 2.6L engine

3. Remove the exhaust pipe from the manifold.

4. Lower the vehicle and remove the rear manifold bolts.

5. On the right side, remove the diverter valve, the heat shield, the AIR pump bracket and alternator bracket.

6. On the left side, remove the heat stove tube and the power steering bracket.

7. Remove the exhaust manifold-to-cylinder head bolts and the manifold.

8. Clean the gasket mounting surfaces.

To install:

9. Using a new gasket, install the exhaust manifold-to-cylinder head bolts and torque the bolts to 25 ft. lbs. (34 Nm).

10. On the left side, install the power steering bracket and heat stove tube.

11. On the right side, install the AIR pump bracket, the alternator bracket, the diverter valve and the heat shield.

12. Raise and safely support the vehicle.

13. Install the exhaust pipe-to-manifold bolts.

14. Lower the vehicle and connect the negative battery cable.

3.2L Engine

1. Disconnect negative battery cable.

2. For the left exhaust manifold remove the following:

   a. Remove the air cleaner assembly.

   b. Remove the EGR pipe fixing bolts and the gasket from the exhaust manifold.

3. Remove the 2 stud nuts and 2 bolts and nuts from the front exhaust pipe and disconnect the pipe.

4. Remove the 5 fixing bolts from the heat protector and remove the protector.

5. Remove the bolts and nuts between the exhaust manifold, cylinder head and the engine hanger.

6. Remove the 7 nuts from the exhaust manifold and remove the manifold.

To install:

7. Install the exhaust manifold and torque the nuts to 42 ft. lbs. (57 Nm).

8. Install the engine hanger.

9. Install the heat protector.

10. Install the front exhaust pipe. Torque the stud nuts to 49 ft. lbs. (67 Nm) and the bolts and nuts to 37 ft. lbs. (50 Nm).

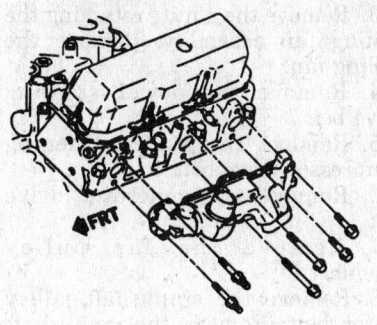

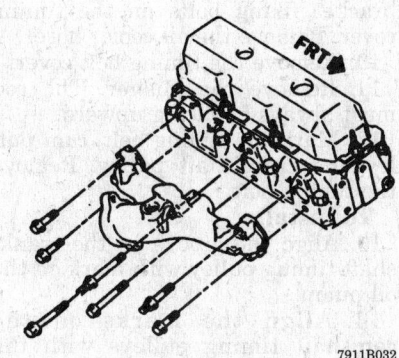

7911B032

Exploded view of the exhaust manifolds — 3.1L Engine

Timing Chain Front Cover

REMOVAL AND INSTALLATION

3.1L Engine

1. Disconnect the negative battery cable.
2. Drain the cooling system. Remove the lower radiator hose from the front cover. Raise and support the vehicle.
3. Remove the stone guard and radiator undercover from beneath the vehicle. Remove the serpentine belt and suspension crossmember.
4. Remove the starter and the flywheel cover. Loosen the oil pan nuts and bolts but do not remove them. Remove the power steering bracket, if equipped.
5. Remove the upper radiator hose and the air conditioner pipe bracket. Remove the fan shrouds. Remove the fan and clutch assembly. Remove the water pump pulley.
6. Remove the damper and pulley bolts. Remove the damper with tool J–24420B or equivalent. Remove the front cover-to-engine bolts and the cover and discard the gasket.

7. Clean the gasket mounting surfaces.

NOTE: When the front cover is removed, replace the oil seal.

To install:

8. Installation is the reverse of removal. Using a new gasket and sealant, install the front cover. torque the bolts to 20 ft. lbs. (27 Nm).
9. Install the water pump and the lower radiator hose.
10. Install the crankshaft pulley and damper. Torque the damper bolts to 70 ft. lbs. (95 Nm).
11. Install the power steering pump bracket, if equipped.
12. Install the drive belt(s).
13. Connect the negative battery cable and refill the cooling system.

Front Cover Oil Seal

REPLACEMENT

3.1L Engine

1. Disconnect the negative battery cable.
2. Remove the serpentine belt, starter, flywheel cover and damper bolt. Lock the flywheel in place and remove the crankshaft pulley and damper.
3. Using a small prybar, pry the oil seal from the front cover; be careful not to damage the sealing surface or the crankshaft.
4. Using an oil seal installation tool, lubricate the new seal with engine oil and drive it into the front cover; be careful not to cut the seal lip.
5. Install the crankshaft pulley and damper. Install the starter and flywheel cover.
6. Connect the negative battery cable.

Timing Chain and Sprockets

REMOVAL AND INSTALLATION

3.1L Engine

1. Disconnect the negative battery cable.
2. Rotate the crankshaft to position the No. 1 cylinder at the TDC of its compression stroke.
3. Remove the front cover.
4. Inspect the sprocket for chipped teeth and wear.
5. Inspect the timing chain for wear; if the chain can be pulled out

more than 0.374 in. (9.5mm) from the damper, replace the chain.
6. Remove camshaft sprocket-to-camshaft bolts, the sprocket and the timing chain; if necessary, use a mallet to tap the sprocket from the camshaft.
7. Using a puller tool, press the crankshaft sprocket from the crankshaft.

To install:

8. Using an installation tool and a hammer, drive the crankshaft sprocket onto the crankshaft; make sure the timing mark faces outward.
9. Using Molykote or equivalent, lubricate the camshaft sprocket thrust surface and install the timing chain onto the sprocket.
10. While holding the camshaft sprocket and chain vertically, align the marks on the camshaft and crankshaft sprockets.
11. Align the camshaft dowel with the camshaft sprocket hole. Install the camshaft sprocket and torque the bolts to 17 ft. lbs. (23 Nm).
12. Lubricate the timing chain with engine oil.
13. Install the front cover and crankshaft pulley.
14. Connect the negative battery cable.
15. Start the engine, then, check and/or adjust the timing.

Timing Belt Front Cover

REMOVAL AND INSTALLATION

2.3L and 2.6L Engines

1. Disconnect the negative battery cable.
2. Remove all accessory drive belts and the cooling fan assembly.
3. Remove the crankshaft pulley bolt and pulley.
4. Remove the upper timing belt cover.
5. Remove the lower timing belt cover.
6. To install, reverse the removal procedures.

OIL SEAL REPLACEMENT

2.3L and 2.6L Engines

1. Disconnect the negative battery cable. Remove the crankshaft pulley.
2. Remove the upper and lower timing belt covers.
3. Rotate the crankshaft to align the camshaft sprocket with the mark on the rear timing cover and the

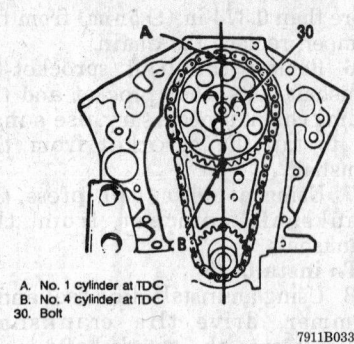

A. No. 1 cylinder at TDC
B. No. 4 cylinder at TDC
30. Bolt

7911B033

View of the timing chain alignment marks — 3.1L Engine

crankshaft sprocket keyway with the mark on the oil seal retainer cover.

NOTE: With the timing marks aligned, the engine is positioned on the TDC of the No. 4 cylinder's compression stroke.

4. Loosen the timing belt tensioner and relax the tension and remove the timing belt from the crankshaft sprocket.

5. Remove the crankshaft sprocket bolt, the sprocket, the key and deflector shield.

6. Using a small prybar, pry the oil seal from the oil seal retainer.

To install:

7. Using a new oil seal, lubricate it with engine oil and tap it into the retainer with an oil seal installation tool.

8. Install the deflector, the key, the crankshaft sprocket and bolt.

9. With the crankshaft sprocket aligned with the timing mark, install the timing belt.

10. Apply the tensioner pulley spring pressure to the timing belt.

11. Rotate the crankshaft 2 complete revolutions in the opposite direction of rotation and realign the timing marks.

12. Loosen the tensioner pulley bolt to allow the spring to adjust the correct tension. Torque the tensioner pulley bolt to 14 ft. lbs. (19 Nm).

13. Install the timing covers and the crankshaft pulley.

14. To complete the installation, reverse the removal procedures.

Timing Belt and Tensioner

ADJUSTMENT

2.3L and 2.6L Engines

1. Disconnect the negative battery cable. Remove the crankshaft pulley.

2. Remove the upper and lower timing belt covers.

3. Loosen the timing belt tensioner and relax the belt tension.

4. Apply the tensioner pulley spring pressure to the timing belt.

5. Rotate the crankshaft 2 complete revolutions in the opposite direction of rotation and realign the timing marks.

6. Loosen the tensioner pulley bolt to allow the spring to adjust the correct tension. Torque the tensioner pulley bolt to 14 ft. lbs. (19 Nm).

7. Install the timing covers and the crankshaft pulley.

8. To complete the installation, reverse the removal procedures.

REMOVAL AND INSTALLATION

2.3L and 2.6L Engines

1. Disconnect the negative battery cable. Remove the crankshaft pulley.

2. Remove the upper and lower timing belt covers.

3. Rotate the crankshaft to align the camshaft sprocket with the mark on the rear timing cover and the crankshaft sprocket keyway with the mark on the oil seal retainer cover.

NOTE: With the timing marks aligned, the engine is positioned on the TDC of the No. 4 cylinder's compression stroke.

4. Loosen the timing belt tensioner and relax the tension and remove the timing belt from the crankshaft sprocket.

To install:

5. With the crankshaft and the camshaft sprockets aligned with the timing marks, install the timing belt. Install the timing belt using the following sequence: the crankshaft sprocket, the oil pump sprocket and the camshaft sprocket.

6. Apply the tensioner pulley spring pressure to the timing belt.

7. Rotate the crankshaft 2 complete revolutions in the opposite direction of rotation and realign the timing marks.

8. Loosen the tensioner pulley bolt to allow the spring to adjust the correct tension. Torque the tensioner pulley bolt to 14 ft. lbs.

9. Install the timing covers and the crankshaft pulley.

10. To complete the installation, reverse the removal procedures.

3.2L Engine

1. Remove the air cleaner assembly.

2. Remove the upper fan shroud from the radiator.

3. Remove the 4 nuts retaining the cooling fan assembly. Remove the cooling fan.

4. Remove the power steering drive belt.

5. Remove the air conditioning compressor drive belt.

6. Remove the generator drive belt.

7. Remove the fan pulley assembly.

8. Remove the crankshaft pulley center bolt. Remove the crankshaft pulley.

9. Remove the 2 oil cooler hose bracket fixing bolts on the timing cover. Remove the oil cooler hose.

10. Remove the timing belt cover.

11. Remove the pusher. The rod must always be facing upward.

12. Mark the timing belt, cam pulley and crankshaft pulley. Remove the timing belt.

To install:

13. Align the groove on the crankshaft timing pulley with mark on the oil pump.

14. Align the marks on the camshaft timing pulleys with the dots on the front plate.

15. Install the timing belt. Align the dotted marks on the timing belt with the mark on the crankshaft gear.

16. Align the white line on the timing belt with the alignment mark on the right bank camshaft timing pulley. Secure the belt with a double clip.

17. Turn the crankshaft counterclockwise to remove the slack between the crankshaft pulley and the right camshaft timing pulley.

18. Install the belt on the water pump pulley.

19. Install the belt on the idler pulley.

20. Align the white alignment mark on the timing belt with the alignment mark on the left bank camshaft timing pulley.

21. Install the crankshaft pulley and tighten the center bolt by hand. Turn the crankshaft pulley clockwise to give slack between the crankshaft timing pulley and the right bank camshaft timing pulley.

22. Install the pusher while pushing the tension pulley to the belt.

23. Pull the pin out from the pusher.

24. Remove the double clips from the pulleys. Turn the crankshaft pulley clockwise 2 turns. Measure the rod protrusion to be sure it is between 0.16–0.24 in. (4–6 mm).

25. Tighten adjusting bolt to 31 ft. lbs. (42 Nm).

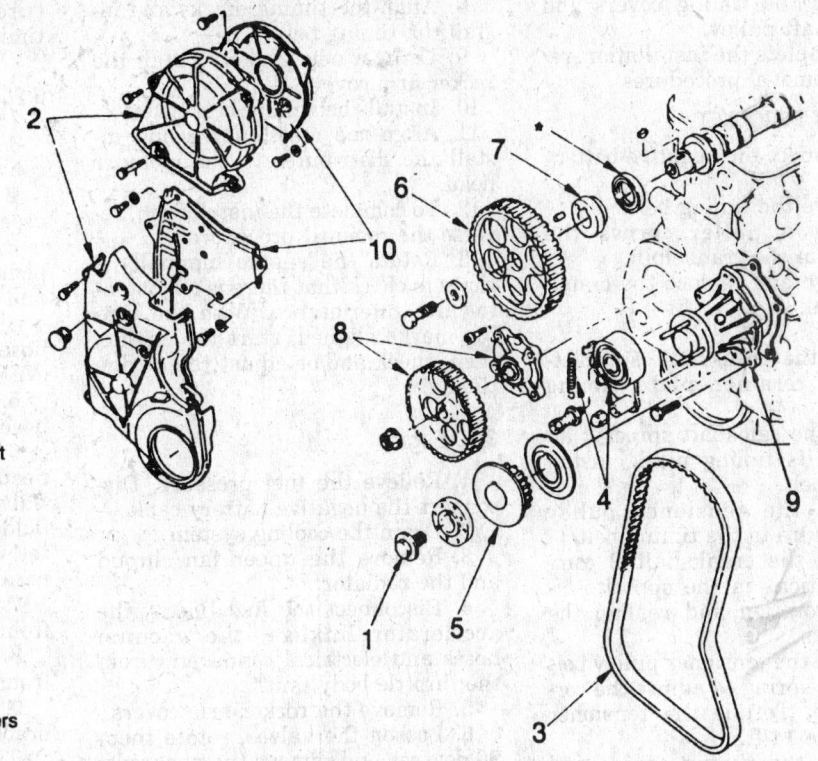

1. Crankshaft pulley bolt
2. Timing belt cover
3. Timing belt
4. Tensioner pulley and spring
5. Crankshaft timing sprocket
6. Camshaft timing sprocket
7. Camshaft boss
8. Oil pump and pulley
9. Water pump
10. Rear timing belt covers

Exploded view of the timing belt assembly — 2.3L and 2.6L Engines

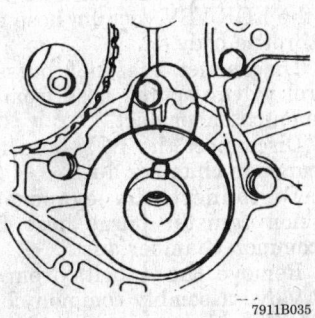

View of the crankshaft sprocket alignment mark — 2.3L and 2.6L Engines

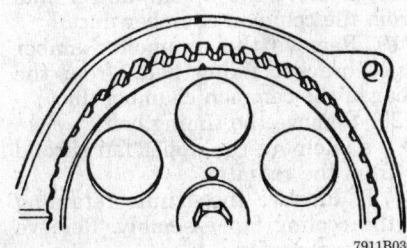

View of the camshaft sprocket alignment mark — 2.3L and 2.6L Engines

26. Tighten pusher bolt to 14 ft. lbs. (19 Nm).

27. Remove crankshaft pulley. Install the timing belt cover and tighten bolts to 12 ft. lbs. (17 Nm).

28. Install the oil cooler hose and tighten brackets to 16 ft. lbs. (22 Nm).

29. Install the crankshaft pulley and tighten bolts to 123 ft. lbs. (167 Nm).

30. Install fan pulley assembly and tighten fixing bolts to 16 ft. lbs. (22 Nm).

31. Engage and adjust generator drive belt.

32. Engage and adjust air conditioning drive belt.

33. Engage and adjust power steering pump drive belt.

34. Install cooling fan assembly and tighten bolts to 69 in. lbs. (8 Nm).

35. Install upper fan shroud to the radiator.

36. Install air cleaner assembly.

Timing Sprockets

REMOVAL AND INSTALLATION

2.3L and 2.6L Engines

CAMSHAFT SPROCKET

1. Disconnect the negative battery cable.

2. Remove the timing belt.

3. Remove the camshaft sprocket-to-camshaft bolt and the sprocket.

NOTE: It may be necessary to use a mallet to tap the sprocket from the camshaft.

4. Remove and replace the camshaft oil seal.

To install:

5. Align the camshaft sprocket-to-rear plate timing marks. With the crankshaft sprocket aligned with the timing mark, install the timing belt.

6. Apply the tensioner pulley spring pressure to the timing belt.

7. Rotate the crankshaft 2 complete revolutions in the opposite direction of rotation and realign the timing marks.

8. Loosen the tensioner pulley bolt to allow the spring to adjust the correct tension. Torque the tensioner pulley bolt to 14 ft. lbs.

9. Install the timing covers and the crankshaft pulley.

10. To complete the installation, reverse the removal procedures.

CRANKSHAFT SPROCKET

1. Disconnect the negative battery cable.

2. Remove the timing belt.

3. Using a puller, press the sprocket from the crankshaft.

4. Remove and replace the crankshaft oil seal.

To install:

5. Align the crankshaft sprocket-to-oil seal retainer plate timing marks.

6. With the camshaft sprocket aligned with its timing mark, install the timing belt.

7. Apply the tensioner pulley spring pressure to the timing belt.

8. Rotate the crankshaft 2 complete revolutions in the opposite direction of rotation and realign the timing marks.

9. Loosen the tensioner pulley bolt to allow the spring to adjust the correct tension. Torque the tensioner pulley bolt to 14 ft. lbs.

10. Install the timing covers and the crankshaft pulley.

11. To complete the installation, reverse the removal procedures.

Camshaft

REMOVAL AND INSTALLATION

2.3L and 2.6L Engines

1. Disconnect the negative battery cable.

2. Rotate the crankshaft to position the No. 4 cylinder on the TDC of its compression stroke.

3. Remove the distributor cap and move it aside. Matchmark the rotor to the distributor housing and the distributor housing to the engine. Remove the distributor.

4. Remove the rocker arm cover, the timing belt cover and the timing belt.

5. Remove the rocker arm assembly-to-cylinder head bolts, the rocker arm assembly and the camshaft. If necessary, remove the camshaft sprocket-to-camshaft bolt and the sprocket.

To install:

6. Lubricate the camshaft with engine oil and position it onto the cylinder head.

7. Install the rocker arm assembly and torque the bolts to bolts to 6 ft. lbs. (8 Nm) and the nuts to 16 ft. lbs. (22 Nm).

8. Align the timing marks and install the timing belt.

9. Using a new gasket, install the rocker arm cover.

10. Install the timing belt cover.

11. Align the matchmarks and install the distributor to the cylinder head.

12. To complete the installation, reverse the removal procedures.

13. Rotate the engine manually 2 times to check that there is no piston-to-valve interference. With the timing marks aligned, start the engine, then, check and/or adjust the engine timing.

3.1L Engine

1. Relieve the fuel pressure. Disconnect the negative battery cable.

2. Drain the cooling system.

3. Remove the upper fan shroud and the radiator.

4. Disconnect the fuel line(s), the accelerator linkage, the vacuum hoses and electrical connectors from the throttle body unit.

5. Remove the rocker arm covers.

6. Loosen the valves, rotate them 90 degrees and remove the pushrods; be sure to keep them aligned so they may be installed in their original positions.

7. Remove the intake manifold. Using a hydraulic lifter removal tool, pull the valve lifters from the engine.

8. Remove the damper, front cover, timing chain and sprocket.

9. Using 3 long bolts, thread them into the camshaft holes. Grasp the bolts and carefully, pull the camshaft from the front of the engine.

NOTE: All the camshaft bearing journals are the same diameter; exercise care in removing the camshaft so the bearings do not become damaged.

10. Lubricate the camshaft with engine oil and install it into the engine.

11. Using a hydraulic lifter installation tool, install the hydraulic lifters into the engine.

12. Using new gaskets and sealant, install the intake manifold.

13. Install the pushrods and the rocker arms.

14. Install the camshaft sprocket, the timing chain and the front cover; be sure the timing marks are aligned.

15. Adjust the valves.

16. Using new gaskets, install the rocker arm covers.

17. To complete the installation, reverse the removal procedures. Refill the cooling system.

18. Start the engine and allow it to reach normal operating temperatures. Check and/or adjust the timing.

3.2L SOHC

1. Disconnect negative battery cable.

2. Remove the air cleaner assembly.

3. Disconnect the accelerator pedal cable from the throttle body and cable brackets.

4. Disconnect the canister vacuum hose from the Vacuum Switch Valve (VSV).

5. Disconnect the vacuum booster hose from the common chamber duct.

6. Disconnect the electrical connectors from the Idle Air Control Valve, Throttle Position sensor, Manifold Absolute Pressure sensor, canister VSV, EGR VSV, Intake Air Temperature sensor and VSV.

7. Remove the high tension cable from the cylinder heads.

8. Disconnect the 3 connectors from the EI module.

9. Remove the 3 bolts from the EI bracket and remove the EI assembly.

10. Remove the 4 bolts from the throttle body and remove the throttle body.

11. Disconnect the canister VSV and the EGR VSV vacuum hose from the throttle body.

12. Disconnect the fuel pressure control valve vacuum hose from the common chamber duct.

13. Disconnect the PCV hose from the common chamber duct.

14. Disconnect the evaporative emission canister purge hose from the common chamber duct.

15. Remove the 4 bolts from the EGR valve assembly common chamber duct and remove the exhaust manifold.

16. Remove the 4 bolts, 4 nuts and 3 manifold bracket fixing bolts from the common chamber duct.

17. Remove the ground cable fixing bolt from the rear of the common chamber duct.

18. Remove the 6 bolts and 2 nuts from the common chamber duct.

19. Remove the common chamber duct bracket fixing bolts from the rear of the common chamber duct.

20. Remove the timing belt:

　a. Remove the upper fan shroud from the radiator.

　b. Remove the 4 nuts retaining the cooling fan assembly. Remove the cooling fan.

　c. Remove the power steering drive belt.

　d. Remove the air conditioning compressor drive belt.

e. Remove the generator drive belt.

f. Remove the fan pulley assembly.

g. Remove the crankshaft pulley center bolt. Remove the crankshaft pulley.

h. Remove the 2 oil cooler hose bracket fixing bolts on the timing cover. Remove the oil cooler hose.

i. Remove the timing belt cover.

j. Remove the pusher. The rod must always be facing upward.

k. Mark the timing belt, cam pulley and crankshaft pulley. Remove the timing belt.

21. Remove the cylinder head cover.
22. Remove the camshaft(s).

To install:

23. Install the camshaft(s).
24. Install the cylinder head cover.
25. Install the timing belt:

a. Align the groove on the crankshaft timing pulley with mark on the oil pump.

b. Align the marks on the camshaft timing pulleys with the dots on the front plate.

c. Install the timing belt. Align the dotted marks on the timing belt with the mark on the crankshaft gear.

d. Align the white line on the timing belt with the alignment mark on the right bank camshaft timing pulley. Secure the belt with a double clip.

e. Turn the crankshaft counterclockwise to remove the slack between the crankshaft pulley and the right camshaft timing pulley.

f. Install the belt on the water pump pulley.

g. Install the belt on the idler pulley.

h. Align the white alignment mark on the timing belt with the alignment mark on the left bank camshaft timing pulley.

i. Install the crankshaft pulley and tighten the center bolt by hand. Turn the crankshaft pulley clockwise to give slack between the crankshaft timing pulley and the right bank camshaft timing pulley.

j. Install the pusher while pushing the tension pulley to the belt.

k. Pull the pin out from the pusher.

l. Remove the double clips from the pulleys. Turn the crankshaft pulley clockwise 2 turns. Measure the rod protrusion to be sure it is between 0.16–0.24 in. (4–6 mm).

m. Tighten adjusting bolt to 31 ft. lbs. (42 Nm).

n. Tighten pusher bolt to 14 ft. lbs. (19 Nm).

o. Remove crankshaft pulley. Install the timing belt cover and tighten bolts to 12 ft. lbs. (17 Nm).

p. Install the oil cooler hose and tighten brackets to 16 ft. lbs. (22 Nm).

q. Install the crankshaft pulley and tighten bolts to 123 ft. lbs. (167 Nm).

r. Install fan pulley assembly and tighten fixing bolts to 16 ft. lbs. (22 Nm).

s. Engage and adjust generator drive belt.

t. Engage and adjust air conditioning drive belt.

u. Engage and adjust power steering pump drive belt.

v. Install cooling fan assembly and tighten bolts to 69 in. lbs. (8 Nm).

w. Install upper fan shroud to the radiator.

26. Install the common chamber duct bracket fixing bolts to the rear of the common chamber duct.
27. Install the 6 bolts and 2 nuts to the common chamber duct.
28. Install the ground cable fixing bolt to the rear of the common chamber duct.
29. Install the 4 bolts, 4 nuts and 3 manifold bracket fixing bolts to the common chamber duct.
30. Install the exhaust manifold and install the 4 bolts to the EGR valve assembly and common chamber duct.
31. Connect the evaporative emission canister purge hose to the common chamber duct.
32. Connect the PCV hose to the common chamber duct.
33. Connect the fuel pressure control valve vacuum hose to the common chamber duct.
34. Connect the canister VSV and the EGR VSV vacuum hose to the throttle body.
35. Install the throttle body and install the 4 bolts to the throttle body and remove the throttle body.
36. Install the EI assembly and install the 3 bolts to the EI bracket.
37. Connect the 3 connectors to the EI module.
38. Connect the high tension cable to the cylinder heads.
39. Connect the electrical connectors to the Idle Air Control Valve, Throttle Position sensor, Manifold Absolute Pressure sensor, canister VSV, EGR VSV, Intake Air Temperature sensor and VSV.
40. Connect the vacuum booster hose to the common chamber duct.

41. Connect the canister vacuum hose to the Vacuum Switch Valve (VSV).
42. Connect the accelerator pedal cable to the throttle body and cable brackets.
43. Install the air cleaner assembly.
44. Install the engine hood and connect negative battery cable.

Piston and Connecting Rod

POSITIONING

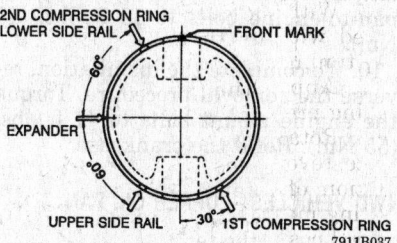

Positioning of the piston and compression rings — 2.3L and 2.6L Engines

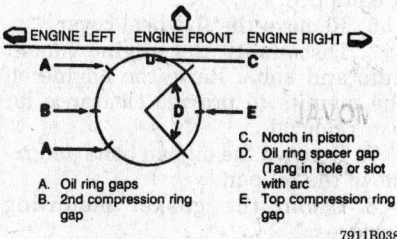

Positioning of the piston and compression rings — 3.1L Engines

ENGINE LUBRICATION

Oil Pan

REMOVAL AND INSTALLATION

2.3L and 2.6L Engines

2WD VEHICLES

1. Disconnect the negative battery cable.

2. Raise and safely support the vehicle.

3. Drain the engine oil. Remove the dipstick and the dipstick tube.

4. Remove the front splash shield, if equipped.

5. Remove the flywheel cover.

6. Disconnect the engine mount nuts and bolts. Raise the engine off the mounts to provide clearance for pan removal.

7. Remove the oil pan bolts and remove the oil pan.

8. Clean the gasket mounting surfaces.

9. Using a new gasket and sealant, install the oil pan. Torque the oil pan-to-engine bolts to 13 ft. lbs. (18 Nm).

10. To complete the installation, reverse the removal procedure. Torque the engine mount bolts to 41 ft. lbs. (55 Nm). Refill the crankcase.

4WD VEHICLES — UPPER OIL PAN

1. Disconnect the negative battery cable.

2. Raise and safely support the vehicle.

3. Drain the engine oil. Remove the dipstick and the dipstick tube.

4. Remove the front splash shield, if equipped.

5. Remove the flywheel cover.

6. Disconnect the engine mount nuts and bolts. Raise the engine off the mounts to provide clearance for pan removal.

7. Remove the oil pan bolts and remove the oil pan.

8. Clean the gasket mounting surfaces.

9. Using a new gasket and sealant, install the oil pan. Torque the oil pan-to-engine bolts to 13 ft. lbs. (18 Nm).

10. To complete the installation, reverse the removal procedure. Torque the engine mount bolts to 41 ft. lbs. (55 Nm). Refill the crankcase.

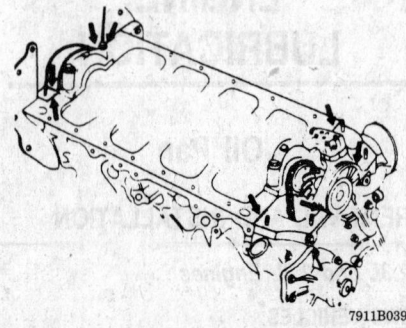

Use sealant at the indicated points when installing the pan gasket — 2.3L engine

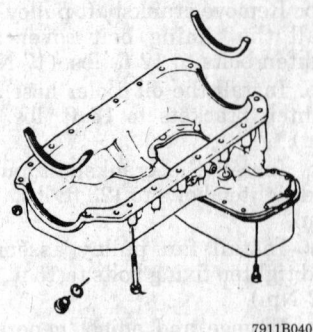

7911B040

Exploded view of the oil pan used with 4WD — 2.3L and 2.6L engines

4WD VEHICLES — LOWER OIL PAN

1. Raise and safely support the vehicle.

2. Drain the crankcase.

3. Remove the lower oil pan-to-upper oil pan bolts and the lower pan.

4. Clean the gasket mounting surfaces.

5. Using a new gasket and sealant, install the lower oil pan and torque the bolts to 47–94 inch lbs.

6. Refill the crankcase.

3.1L and 3.2L Engines

1. Disconnect the negative battery cable.

2. Remove the dipstick. Raise and safely support the vehicle. Drain the crankcase.

3. Remove the front skid plate and the crossmember.

4. Remove the exhaust pipe-to-catalytic converter bolts, the exhaust pipe-to-manifold bolts and the Y-exhaust pipe.

5. Remove the front driveshaft from the front differential.

6. Remove the braces from the flywheel cover.

7. Disconnect the electrical connectors from the starter. Remove the starter-to-engine bolts and the starter.

8. Remove the flywheel inspection cover.

9. Matchmark the pitman arm-to-pitman shaft for reassembly. Remove the pitman arm-to-pitman arm shaft nut and separate the pitman arm from the pitman shaft.

10. Remove the idler arm-to-shaft nut and separate the idler arm from the shaft.

11. Remove the rubber hose from the front axle vent and support the axle housing assembly.

12. Remove both bolts from the left axle housing isolator and the right axle housing isolator, then, lower the front axle housing assembly.

13. Remove the oil pan-to-engine bolts, the oil pan and discard the gasket.

14. Clean the gasket mounting surfaces.

To install:

15. Using a new gasket and sealant, install the oil pan. On 3.1L engines. torque both rear pan-to-engine bolts to 18 ft. lbs. (25 Nm) and the other bolts/nuts/studs to 7 ft. lbs. (10 Nm). On 3.2L engines torque oil pan fixing bolts and nuts to 87 in. lbs. (10 Nm).

16. To complete the installation, reverse the removal procedures. Torque the following fasteners: Pitman arm-to-pitman shaft nut — 159 ft. lbs. (215 Nm); Idler arm-to-shaft nut — 86 ft. lbs. (117 Nm) except on model with 3.2L engines, 33 ft. lbs. (44 Nm) on models with 3.2L engines; Front drive axle shaft bolts — 46 ft. lbs. (62 Nm).

17. Refill the crankcase. Connect the negative battery cable.

18. Start the engine and check for leaks.

Oil Pump

REMOVAL AND INSTALLATION

2.3L and 2.6L Engines

The oil pump is attached to the front, lower right side of the engine and is driven by the timing be

1. Remove the upper and lower timing belt covers.

2. Remove the timing belt from the crankshaft and oil pump sprockets.

3. Remove the oil pump sprocket-to-oil pump nut and the sprocket from the oil pump.

4. Using a 6mm Allen wrench, remove the oil pump-to-engine bolts and the oil pump.

To install:

5. Using petroleum jelly, pack the oil pump.

6. Using a new O-ring, install the oil pump and torque the bolts to 10–17 ft. lbs. (13–23 Nm).

7. Install the sprocket to the oil pump and torque the nut to 48–62 ft. lbs.

8. Align the timing marks on the camshaft and crankshaft sprockets and install the timing belt.

9. To complete the installation, reverse the removal procedures.

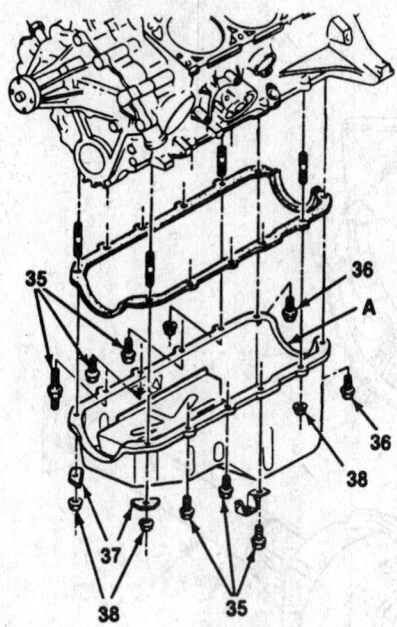

A. Apply sealant here
35. Bolts
36. Bolts
37. Reinforcements
38. Nuts

7911B041

Exploded view of the oil pan assembly — 3.1L Engines

3.1L Engine

The oil pump is attached to the cylinder block and is located in the oil pan.

1. Disconnect the negative battery cable. Raise and safely support the vehicle.
2. Drain the crankcase. Remove the oil pan.
3. Remove the oil pump-to-engine bolts and the oil pump.

To install:

4. Align the oil pump shaft with the hexagon socket and install the pump. Torque the oil pump-to-engine bolts to 30 ft. lbs. (41 Nm).
5. Install the oil pan.
6. To complete the installation, reverse the removal procedures.
7. Connect the negative battery cable. Start the engine and check for leaks.

3.2L Engines

1. Disconnect negative battery cable.
2. Remove timing belt.
3. Remove crankshaft timing pulley.
4. Remove oil pan.
5. Remove oil pipe and rubber ring.
6. Remove the oil strainer and rubber ring.

7. Remove the oil cooler assembly.
8. Remove the oil pump.
9. Remove the sealant from the mounting surfaces of the oil pump and cylinder body.

To install:

10. Apply sealant to the oil pump mounting surfaces and engine oil to the oil seal lip.
11. Install the oil pump to the cylinder body.
12. Torque bolts to 13 ft. lbs. (18 Nm).
13. Install the oil cooler assembly.
14. Install the oil pipe and rubber ring.
15. Install the oil strainer and the rubber ring.
16. Install the oil pan.
17. Install the crankshaft timing pulley.
18. Install the timing belt.

CHECKING

2.3L and 2.6L Engines

1. Visually inspect the oil pump for wear, damage or other abnormal conditions.
2. Insert the oil pump vane into the cylinder block.
3. Place a straight-edge across the oil pump opening and a feeler gauge between the straight-edge and the vane; the clearance between the vane-to-cylinder block surface should be 0.002–0.004 in. (0.04–0.09mm), if not, replace the vane.
4. Using a feeler gauge, measure the side clearance between the cylinder block and the vane; it should be 0.009–0.0014 in. (0.24–0.36mm), if not, replace the vane.
5. Position the vane onto the rotor shaft.
6. Using a feeler gauge, measure the clearance between the rotor and the vane; it should be 0.005–0.006 in. (0.13–0.15mm), if not, replace the rotor and/or vane.

3.1L Engine

1. Visually inspect the oil pump for wear, damage or other abnormal conditions.
2. Check that the regulator valve moves freely. Soak in solvent to free the piston, if stuck.
3. Lay a straight-edge across the body of the pump and the faces of the gears and measure the side lash with a feeler gauge between the straight-edge and the pump. The side lash should be 0.002–0.005 in. (0.05–0.13mm).
4. Check the gear lash between the body and the gear with a feeler

gauge. The lash should be 0.009–0.105 in. (0.23–0.38mm).

5. Check the gear lash between the gears with a feeler gauge. The lash should be 0.003–0.004 in. (0.08–0.10mm).
6. Replace the pump if any of the measurements are out of specification.

Rear Main Bearing Oil Seal

REMOVAL AND INSTALLATION

1. Disconnect the negative battery cable. Raise and safely support the vehicle.
2. If equipped with an automatic transmission, remove the transmission. If equipped with a manual transmission, remove the transmission and clutch assembly.
3. Remove the starter without disconnecting the wires and secure it aside.
4. Remove the flywheel-to-crankshaft bolts and the flywheel.
5. Using a small prybar, carefully, remove the oil seal work the tool around the diameter of the seal until the seal begins to lift out. Use care not to damage the seat and area around the seal.
6. Using a new oil seal, lubricate the seal lips with clean engine oil.
7. Using an oil seal installation tool, install the new oil seal.
8. To complete the installation, reverse the removal procedures.

MANUAL TRANSMISSION

Transmission

REMOVAL AND INSTALLATION

2WD Vehicles

1. Disconnect the negative battery cable.
2. Remove the undercover, if equipped.
3. Remove the air cleaner for 2.3L and 3.1L engines or air cleaner duct and hose for 2.6L engine. Using a clean shop cloth, cover the air cleaner port to prevent dirt from entering the engine.
4. Label and disconnect the necessary hoses and electrical connectors.

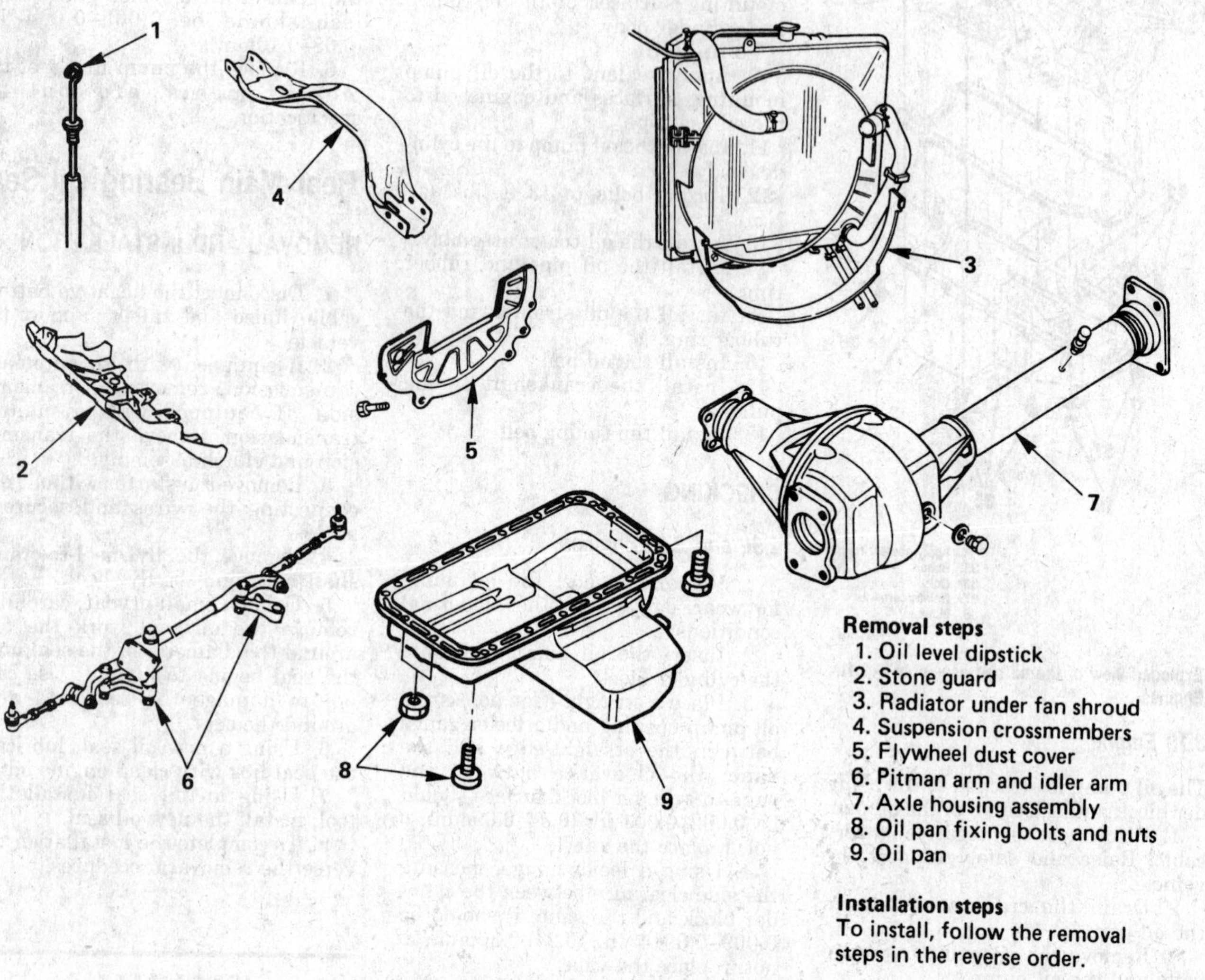

Removal steps
1. Oil level dipstick
2. Stone guard
3. Radiator under fan shroud
4. Suspension crossmembers
5. Flywheel dust cover
6. Pitman arm and idler arm
7. Axle housing assembly
8. Oil pan fixing bolts and nuts
9. Oil pan

Installation steps
To install, follow the removal steps in the reverse order.

85478003

Exploded view of the oil pan assembly — 3.2L Engines

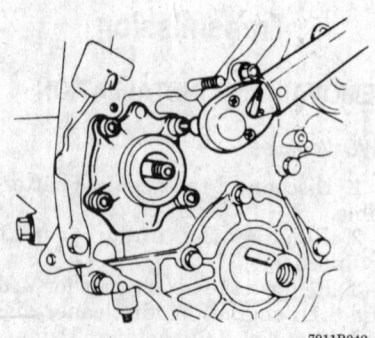

View of the oil pump — 2.3L and 2.6L Engines

7911B042

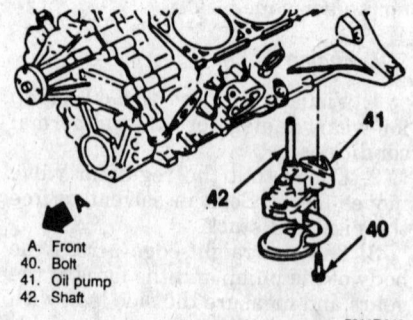

A. Front
40. Bolt
41. Oil pump
42. Shaft

Exploded view of the oil pump assembly — 3.1L Engine

7911B043

5. Remove the clutch return spring, the clutch control cable, the backup light switch connector and the speedometer cable from the transmission.

6. Remove the gear shift lever by performing the following procedures:

a. Place the gear shift lever in **N**.

b. Remove the front console from the floor panel.

c. Pull the shift lever boot and grommet upward.

d. Remove the shift lever cover bolts and the shift lever.

7. Raise and safely support the vehicle. Remove the front wheels.

8. Drain the transmission fluid.

9. If equipped with a 1-piece driveshaft, remove the driveshaft flange-to-pinion nuts, lower the driveshaft and pull it from the transmission.

10. If equipped with a 2-piece driveshaft, perform the following procedures:

   a. Remove the rear driveshaft flange-to-pinion nuts.

   b. Remove the rear driveshaft flange-to-front driveshaft flange bolts and the rear driveshaft.

   c. Remove the center bearing-to-chassis bolts, move the front driveshaft rearward and from the transmission.

11. Remove the starter-to-engine bolts and the starter.

12. Remove the exhaust pipe-to-exhaust manifold nuts, the exhaust pipe bracket-to-transmission bolts, the front exhaust pipe-to-2nd exhaust pipe bolts and the front exhaust pipe from the vehicle.

13. Attach an engine hanger to the rear of the exhaust manifold.

14. Using an engine hoist, connect it to the engine hangers and support the engine.

15. Using a transmission jack, place it under the transmission; do not support it.

16. Remove the rear mount-to-transmission nuts.

17. Remove the rear mount-to-crossmember nuts/bolts and the mount.

NOTE: Further removal of the transmission may require an assistant.

18. Remove the clutch cover and the transmission-to-engine bolts.

19. Move the transmission rearward into the crossmember and floor pan area; the transmission may rest on the crossmember.

20. Lower the front of the transmission toward the jack.

21. Firmly, grasp the transmission the rear cover while the assistant raises the jack toward the transmission.

22. Carefully, lower the transmission onto the jack and center it.

23. Lower the jack and move the transmission rearward.

To install:

NOTE: Installation of the transmission may require an assistant.

24. Raise the transmission into position.

25. Raise the rear of the transmission and move it into position on the crossmember.

26. Move the transmission forward and engage it with the engine.

27. Install the engine-to-transmission bolts.

28. Install the mount and the rear mount-to-crossmember nuts/bolts.

29. Install the rear mount-to-transmission nuts.

30. Remove the engine hoist and the engine hanger from the rear of the exhaust manifold.

31. Install the front exhaust pipe, exhaust pipe-to-exhaust manifold nuts, the exhaust pipe bracket-to-transmission bolts, the front exhaust pipe-to-2nd exhaust pipe bolts.

32. Install the starter and the starter-to-engine bolts.

33. If equipped with a 2-piece driveshaft, perform the following procedures:

   a. Install the front driveshaft into the transmission and the center bearing-to-chassis bolts.

   b. Install the rear driveshaft and the rear driveshaft flange-to-front driveshaft flange bolts.

   c. Install the rear driveshaft flange-to-pinion nuts.

34. If equipped with a 1-piece driveshaft, install the driveshaft into the transmission and the driveshaft flange-to-pinion nuts.

35. Install the front wheels and lower the vehicle.

36. Install the gear shift lever by performing the following procedures:

   a. Install the shift lever and the shift lever cover bolts.

   b. Push the grommet and shift lever boot downward.

   c. Install the front console to the floor panel.

37. Install the clutch return spring, the clutch control cable, the backup light switch connector and the speedometer cable to the transmission.

38. Connect the necessary hoses and electrical connectors.

39. Install the air cleaner for 2.3L and 3.1L engines or air cleaner duct and hose for 2.6L engine.

40. Refill the transmission. Install the undercover, if equipped.

41. Connect the negative battery cable.

4WD Vehicles

1. Disconnect the negative battery cable.

2. Remove the undercover, if equipped.

3. Remove the air cleaner for 2.3L and 3.1L engines or air cleaner duct and hose for 2.6L engine. Using a clean shop cloth, cover the air cleaner port to prevent dirt from entering the engine.

4. Label and disconnect the necessary hoses and electrical connectors.

5. Remove the clutch return spring, the clutch control cable, the backup light switch connector and the speedometer cable from the transmission.

6. Remove the gear shift lever by performing the following procedures:

   a. Place the gear shift lever in **N**.

   b. Remove the front console from the floor panel.

   c. Pull the shift lever boot and grommet upward.

   d. Remove the shift lever cover bolts and the shift lever.

7. Remove the transfer shift lever by performing the following procedures:

   a. Place the transfer shift lever in **H** for 2.3L and 2.6L engines or **2H** for 3.1L engines.

   b. Pull the shift lever boot and dust cover upward.

   c. Remove the shift lever retaining bolts.

   d. Pull the shift lever from the transfer case.

8. Raise and safely support the vehicle. Remove the front wheels.

9. Drain the transmission and transfer case fluid.

10. If equipped with a 1-piece driveshaft, remove the driveshaft flange-to-pinion nuts, lower the driveshaft and pull it from the transmission.

11. If equipped with a 2-piece driveshaft, perform the following procedures:

   a. Remove the rear driveshaft flange-to-pinion nuts.

   b. Remove the rear driveshaft flange-to-front driveshaft flange bolts and the rear driveshaft.

   c. Remove the center bearing-to-chassis bolts, move the front driveshaft rearward and from the transmission.

12. Remove the front driveshaft's splined yoke flange-to-transfer case bolts and separate the front driveshaft from the transfer case; do not allow the splined flange to fall away from the driveshaft.

13. Remove the starter-to-engine bolts and the starter.

14. If equipped with a clutch slave cylinder, remove it from the transmission and move it aside.

15. Remove the exhaust pipe-to-exhaust manifold nuts, the exhaust pipe bracket-to-transmission bolts, the front exhaust pipe-to-2nd exhaust pipe bolts and the front exhaust pipe from the vehicle.

16. Attach an engine hanger to the rear of the exhaust manifold.

17. Using an engine hoist, connect it to the engine hangers and support the engine.

18. If equipped with a 3.1L engine, remove the catalytic converter and the parking brake cable bracket.

19. Using a transmission jack, place it under the transmission and support the assembly.

20. Remove the rear mount-to-transmission nuts.

21. Remove the rear mount-to-side mount member nuts/bolts and the mount.

22. Remove the transmission-to-engine bolts.

23. Move the transmission assembly rearward.

24. Carefully lower the transmission.

To install:

25. Raise the transmission into position.

26. Move the transmission forward and engage it with the engine.

27. Install the engine-to-transmission bolts.

28. Install the rear mount and the rear mount-to-side mount member nuts/bolts.

29. Install the rear mount-to-transmission nuts.

30. Remove the transmission jack.

31. If equipped with a 3.1L engine, install the catalytic converter and the parking brake cable bracket.

32. Remove the engine hoist and the engine hanger from the rear of the exhaust manifold.

33. Install the front exhaust pipe, exhaust pipe-to-exhaust manifold nuts, the exhaust pipe bracket-to-transmission bolts, the front exhaust pipe-to-2nd exhaust pipe bolts.

34. If equipped with a clutch slave cylinder, install it onto the transmission.

35. Install the starter and the starter-to-engine bolts.

36. Install the front driveshaft's splined yoke flange-to-transfer case bolts.

37. If equipped with a 2-piece driveshaft, perform the following procedures:

a. Install the front driveshaft into the transmission and the center bearing-to-chassis bolts.

b. Install the rear driveshaft and the rear driveshaft flange-to-front driveshaft flange bolts.

c. Install the rear driveshaft flange-to-pinion nuts.

38. If equipped with a 1-piece driveshaft, install the driveshaft into the transmission and the driveshaft flange-to-pinion nuts.

39. Install the front wheels and lower the vehicle.

40. Install the transfer shift lever by performing the following procedures:

a. Position the shift lever into the transfer case.

b. Install the shift lever retaining bolts.

c. Push the dust cover and the shift lever boot downward.

41. Install the gear shift lever by performing the following procedures:

a. Install the shift lever and the shift lever cover bolts.

b. Push the grommet and shift lever boot downward.

c. Install the front console to the floor panel.

42. Install the clutch return spring, the clutch control cable, the backup light switch connector and the speedometer cable to the transmission.

43. Connect the necessary hoses and electrical connectors.

44. Install the air cleaner for 2.3L and 3.1L engines or air cleaner duct and hose for 2.6L engine.

45. Refill the transmission and the transfer case. Install the undercover, if equipped.

46. Install the negative battery cable.

LINKAGE ADJUSTMENT

No adjustments are possible on the transmission or transfer case linkage.

CLUTCH

Clutch Assembly

REMOVAL AND INSTALLATION

1. Raise and support the vehicle safely.

2. On 2WD vehicles, remove the transmission. On 4WD models, remove the transmission and transfer case as an assembly.

3. Matchmark the clutch assembly to the flywheel so the clutch assembly can be reassembled in the same position. Lock the flywheel in place to prevent it from turning.

4. Loosen the pressure plate-to-flywheel bolts, 1 turn at a time in an alternating sequence, until the spring tension is relieved to avoid distorting or bending the pressure plate.

5. Using a clutch alignment tool, support the pressure plate and cover assembly and remove the bolts and clutch assembly.

To install:

6. Apply a thin coat of grease to the pressure plate fingers, diaphragm spring, clutch cover grooves and the drive bosses on the pressure plate.

7. Apply a thin coat of lubricant to the splines in the clutch disc.

8. Using a clutch alignment tool, assemble the clutch disc and pressure plate onto the flywheel.

9. Align the matchmarks and install the pressure plate-to-flywheel bolts and torque the bolts to 12–14 ft. lbs. (16–19 Nm) using a star pattern tightening sequence. Remove the aligning tool.

10. On 2WD vehicles, install the transmission. On 4WD models, install the transmission and transfer case as an assembly.

11. To complete the installation, reverse the removal procedures. Adjust the clutch cable linkage, if equipped.

PEDAL HEIGHT ADJUSTMENT

The clutch pedal height is the distance from the center of the clutch pedal pad to the firewall.

1. Locate the clutch switch (with cruise control) or clutch pedal stop bolt (without cruise control) at the top of the clutch pedal under the dash.

2. Loosen the clutch switch or stop bolt as equipped. Loosen the clutch master cylinder pushrod yoke nut.

3. Adjust the clutch master cylinder pushrod to obtain a clutch pedal height of 6.7–7.1 in. (171–181mm) for Rodeo with 2.6L engine, 7.6–8.0 in. (192–202mm) for Rodeo with 3.1L engine or 9.15–9.55 in. (232–242mm) for Trooper/Trooper II, Pick-Up and Amigo.

4. After adjusting the pedal height, tighten the pushrod yoke nut. Screw in the clutch switch until the plunger is fully depressed and then unscrew 1 full turn and tighten the locknut. Tighten the pedal stop bolt so it just touches the pedal and tighten the locknut.

Clutch Cable

REMOVAL AND INSTALLATION

1. Loosen the clutch cable lock and adjusting nuts. Remove the clutch cable clip in the engine compartment.

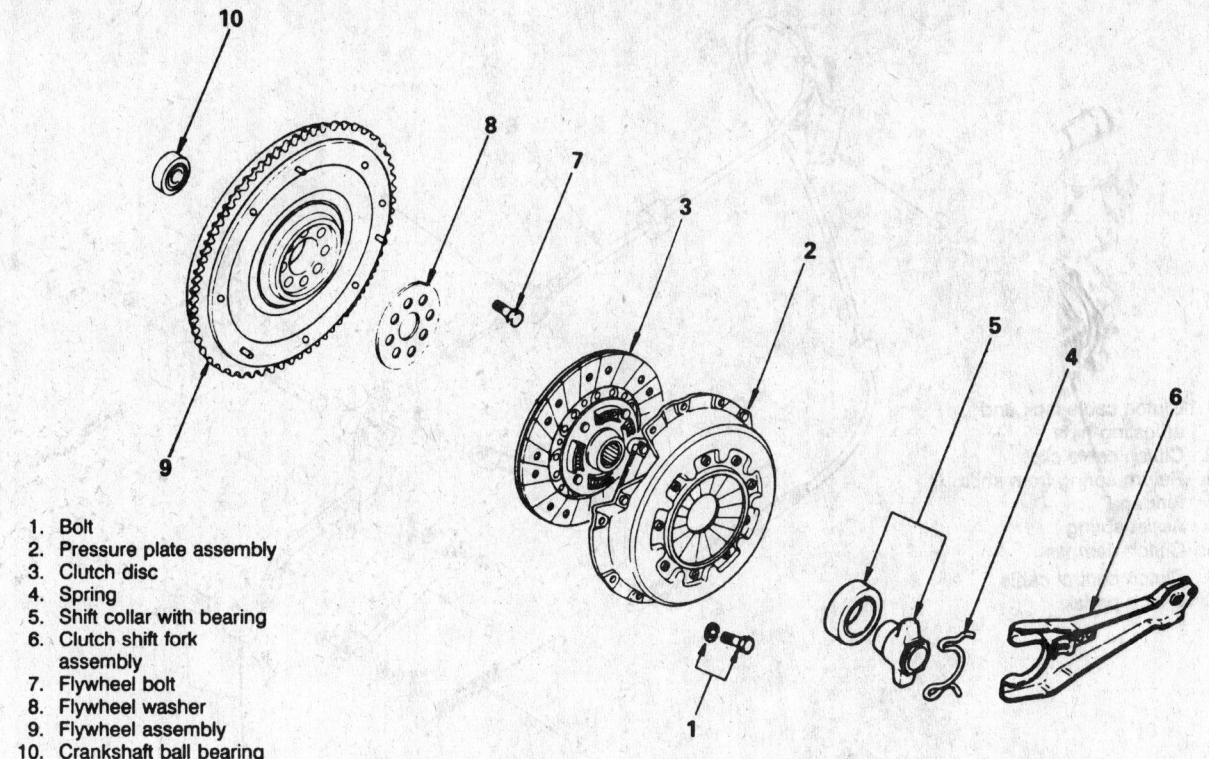

1. Bolt
2. Pressure plate assembly
3. Clutch disc
4. Spring
5. Shift collar with bearing
6. Clutch shift fork assembly
7. Flywheel bolt
8. Flywheel washer
9. Flywheel assembly
10. Crankshaft ball bearing

7911B044

Exploded view of the clutch assembly

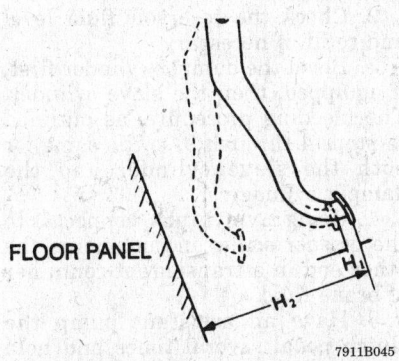

7911B045

Measuring the clutch pedal height

2. Raise and safely support the vehicle. Remove the spring from the shift fork end.

3. Disconnect the cable end from the shift fork and pull the cable assembly through the bracket.

4. Lower the vehicle enough to disengage the hooked part of the clutch pedal from the cable eye. Pull the cable assembly towards the engine compartment and remove the cable from the vehicle.

5. To install, reverse the removal procedures. Adjust the cable when finished.

ADJUSTMENT

1. Pull the outer cable, located under the hood, forward as far as possible and secure it.

2. Turn the adjusting nut inward it touches the damper rubber washer, located at the firewall.

3. Depress and release the clutch pedal 3 times.

4. Tighten the adjusting nut again.

5. Pull the outer cable forward again and fully tighten the adjusting nut.

6. Loosen the nut to provide a ⅛ in. clearance between the adjusting nut and the damper washer.

7. Release the outer cable and tighten the locknut to secure the adjusting nut.

Clutch Master Cylinder

The clutch master cylinder is located on the firewall inside the engine compartment.

REMOVAL AND INSTALLATION

1. Disconnect the negative battery cable. Remove the hydraulic line from the clutch master cylinder.

2. Disconnect the master cylinder pushrod from the clutch pedal.

3. Remove the master cylinder-to-firewall nuts and remove the master cylinder.

4. To install, reverse the removal procedures. Torque the master cylinder-to-firewall nuts to 8–15 ft. lbs. (12–20 Nm).

5. On master cylinders that use a banjo fitting, use new washers and torque the hydraulic line-to-master cylinder bolt to 22–29 ft. lbs. (30–39 Nm).

6. On master cylinders that use a flare fitting, torque the flare nut to 14.5 ft. lbs. (20 Nm).

7. Bleed the hydraulic clutch system.

Clutch Slave Cylinder

The clutch slave cylinder is attached to the bell housing.

REMOVAL AND INSTALLATION

1. Disconnect the negative battery cable. Remove the hydraulic line from the clutch slave cylinder.

2. Remove the slave cylinder-to-bell housing bolts and remove the slave cylinder.

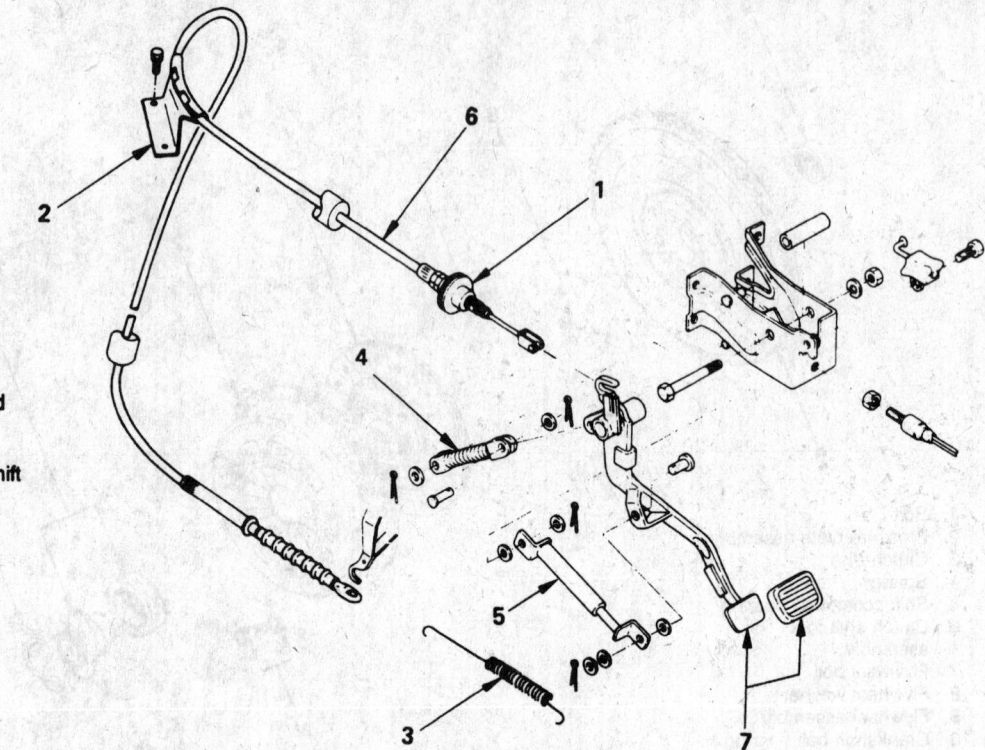

1. Clutch cable lock and adjusting nuts
2. Clutch cable clip
3. Return spring from shift fork end
4. Assist spring
5. Clutch damper
6. Clutch control cable
7. Clutch pedal

7911B046

Exploded view of the clutch cable assembly

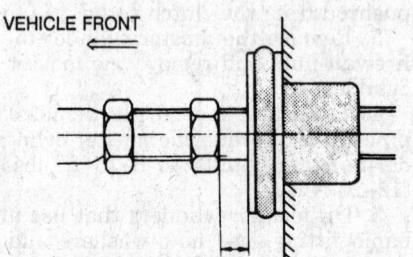

VEHICLE FRONT

0.2 IN. (5MM)

7911B047

View of the clutch cable adjustment

3. To install, reverse the removal procedures.

4. On cylinders with flare fittings, torque the hydraulic line-to-slave cylinder fitting to 11–17 ft. lbs. (16–25 Nm).

5. On cylinders with banjo fittings, use new washers and torque the hydraulic line-to-slave cylinder fitting to 25 ft. lbs. (35 Nm).

6. Bleed the hydraulic clutch system.

Clutch Damper Cylinder

REMOVAL AND INSTALLATION

6 Cylinder Vehicles

Locate the clutch hydraulic damper in the clutch hydraulic line to the slave cylinder.

1. Disconnect the hydraulic fitting from the damper body.

2. Unbolt the damper from the mounting position bracket.

3. Remove the damper and cap the hydraulic lines to prevent dirt and moisture from contaminating the system.

4. Installation is the reverse of removal. Bleed the hydraulic system.

Hydraulic Clutch System Bleeding

1. Firmly, set the parking brake.

2. Check the reservoir fluid level and refill, if necessary.

3. Bleed the damper cylinder first, if equipped, then the slave cylinder. The bleeding procedure, as outlined in steps 4 through 9, is the same for both the slave cylinder and the damper cylinder.

4. Using a vinyl tube, connect it to the bleeder screw and submerge the other end in a transparent container of brake fluid.

5. Have an assistant pump the clutch pedal several times and hold it.

6. Loosen the bleeder screw and allow the air bubble fluid to flow into the container, then, tighten the bleeder screw.

7. Release the clutch pedal.

8. Repeat this operation until the fluid is clear of air bubbles.

9. Refill the reservoir. Remove the vinyl tube and replace the rubber cap on the bleeder screw.

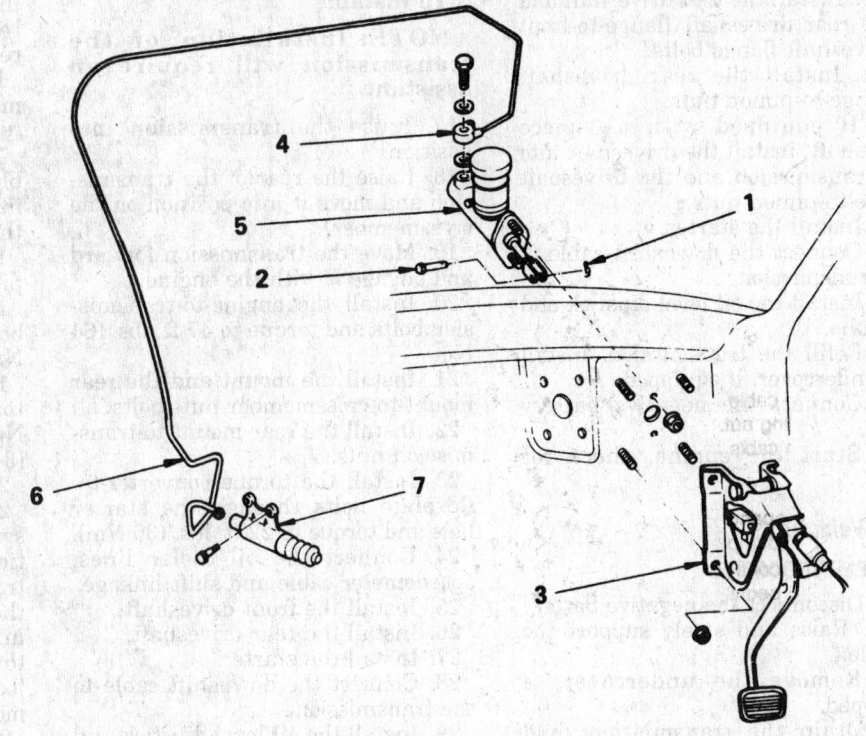

1. Pin
2. Jaw joint pin
3. Pedal assembly
4. Oil line
5. Master cylinder assembly
6. Oil line
7. Slave cylinder assembly

7911B048

Exploded view of the hydraulic system

AUTOMATIC TRANSMISSION

Transmission Assembly

REMOVAL AND INSTALLATION

2WD Vehicles

1. Disconnect the negative battery cable. Raise and safely support the vehicle.
2. Remove the undercover, if equipped.
3. Drain the transmission fluid from the oil pan.
4. Remove the throttle cable at the engine end. Remove the transmission dipstick.
5. Unbolt the starter and place it aside in a safe location. Support the starter so it does not strain the electrical connections.
6. If equipped with a 1-piece driveshaft, remove the driveshaft flange-to-pinion nuts, lower the driveshaft and pull it from the transmission.

7. If equipped with a 2-piece driveshaft, perform the following procedures:
   a. Remove the rear driveshaft flange-to-pinion nuts.
   b. Remove the rear driveshaft flange-to-front driveshaft flange bolts and the rear driveshaft.
   c. Remove the center bearing-to-chassis bolts, move the front driveshaft rearward and from the transmission.
8. Disconnect the shift lever at the shifter end.
9. Disconnect the speedometer cable
10. Disconnect the oil cooler lines and place the cooler bypass line close to the transmission case to prevent damage during transmission removal.
11. Remove the torque converter-to-flexplate bolts through the starter hole.
12. Using a transmission jack, place it under the transmission and raise it slightly.
13. Remove the rear mount-to-transmission nuts.
14. Remove the rear mount-to-crossmember nuts/bolts and the mount.
15. Remove the transmission-to-engine bolts.

16. Move the transmission back and lower the transmission out of the vehicle.
To install:

NOTE: Installation of the transmission will require an assistant.

17. Raise the transmission into position.
18. Raise the rear of the transmission and move it into position on the crossmember.
19. Move the transmission forward and engage it with the engine.
20. Install the engine-to-transmission bolts and torque to 47 ft. lbs. (64 Nm).
21. Install the mount and the rear mount-to-crossmember nuts/bolts.
22. Install the rear mount-to-transmission nuts.
23. Install the torque converter-to-flexplate bolts through the starter hole and torque to 22 ft. lbs. (30 Nm).
24. Connect the oil cooler lines, speedometer cable and shift linkage.
25. If equipped with a 2-piece driveshaft, perform the following procedures:
   a. Install the front driveshaft into the transmission and the center bearing-to-chassis bolts.

b. Install the rear driveshaft and the rear driveshaft flange-to-front driveshaft flange bolts.

c. Install the rear driveshaft flange-to-pinion nuts.

26. If equipped with a 1-piece driveshaft, install the driveshaft into the transmission and the driveshaft flange-to-pinion nuts.

27. Install the starter.

28. Connect the downshift cable to the transmission.

29. Install the oil level dipstick and the tube.

30. Refill the transmission. Install the undercover, if equipped.

31. Connect the negative battery cable.

32. Start the engine, check for leaks.

4WD Vehicles

TROOPER/TROOPER II

1. Disconnect the negative battery cable. Raise and safely support the vehicle.

2. Remove the undercover, if equipped.

3. Drain the transmission fluid from the oil pan.

4. Remove the throttle cable at the engine end. Remove the transmission dipstick.

5. Unbolt the starter and place it aside in a safe location. Support the starter so it does not strain the electrical connections.

6. Remove the front driveshaft.

7. To remove the 1-piece rear driveshaft, remove the driveshaft flange-to-pinion nuts and driveshaft-to-output flange bolts, lower the driveshaft.

8. Disconnect the shift lever at the shifter end.

9. Disconnect the speedometer cable.

10. Disconnect the oil cooler lines and place the cooler bypass line close to the transmission case to prevent damage during transmission removal.

11. Remove the torque converter-to-flexplate bolts through the starter hole.

12. Using a transmission jack, place it under the transmission and raise it slightly.

13. Remove the rear mount-to-transmission nuts.

14. Remove the rear mount-to-crossmember nuts/bolts and the mount.

15. Remove the transmission-to-engine bolts.

16. Move the transmission back and lower the transmission out of the vehicle.

To install:

NOTE: Installation of the transmission will require an assistant.

17. Raise the transmission into position.

18. Raise the rear of the transmission and move it into position on the crossmember.

19. Move the transmission forward and engage it with the engine.

20. Install the engine-to-transmission bolts and torque to 47 ft. lbs. (64 Nm).

21. Install the mount and the rear mount-to-crossmember nuts/bolts.

22. Install the rear mount-to-transmission nuts.

23. Install the torque converter-to-flexplate bolts through the starter hole and torque to 22 ft. lbs. (30 Nm).

24. Connect the oil cooler lines, speedometer cable and shift linkage.

25. Install the front driveshaft.

26. Install the rear driveshaft.

27. Install the starter.

28. Connect the downshift cable to the transmission.

29. Install the oil level dipstick and the tube.

30. Refill the transmission. Install the undercover, if equipped.

31. Connect the negative battery cable.

32. Start the engine, check for leaks.

RODEO

1. Disconnect both battery cables.

2. Remove the center console housing. Remove the transfer case control lever.

3. Disconnect the transmission shifter control linkage.

4. Remove the undercover to expose the transmission housing.

5. Remove the rear driveshaft and the front driveshaft.

6. Disconnect the parking brake cable from the relay link.

7. Disconnect the speedometer cable from the transmission housing.

8. Remove the left side exhaust pipe.

9. Remove the transmission oil cooler lines.

10. Remove the starter motor and place off to the side.

11. Remove the mode switch from the side of the transmission.

12. Remove the breather hose, dipstick, flywheel cover and the torque converter bolts.

13. Remove the rear crossmember and the exhaust Y-assembly.

14. Number the transmission mounting bolts as they are removed and note the position from which

they came. The bolts are of different lengths and this will ease reassembly.

15. Using a transmission jack, remove the transmission assembly.

To install:

16. Install the transmission assembly and replace the mounting bolts into their original locations. Torque the bolts to 55 ft. lbs. (75 Nm).

17. Install the dipstick, exhaust pipe Y-assembly and crossmember.

18. Install the torque converter bolts and torque to 40 ft. lbs. (54 Nm).

19. Install the flywheel cover and torque the M6 bolts to 6 ft. lbs. (8 Nm) and the M10 bolts to 25 ft. lbs. (34 Nm).

20. Install the breather hose.

21. Install the mode selector switch. Place the lever in the **N** position and install the switch on the transmission body. Align the slots on the support and back. Insert a 0.09 in. (2.34mm) pin into the ports and torque the mounting bolts to 104 inch lbs. (12 Nm). Remove the pin before moving the lever.

22. Install the starter motor and torque the mounting bolts to 30 ft. lbs. (40 Nm).

23. Install the oil cooler lines and torque the fittings to 33 ft. lbs. (44 Nm).

24. Install the left front exhaust pipe, the speedometer cable, the parking brake cable and the driveshafts.

25. Install the undercover, the shift linkage, the transfer control linkage and the center console.

26. Connect the battery cables and refill the transmission. Check for proper operation.

SHIFT LINKAGE ADJUSTMENT

1. Loosen the shift linkage adjusting nut.

2. Push the shift lever fully rearward.

3. Return the shift lever 2 notches to the **N** position.

4. While holding the selector lever lightly toward the **R** range side, tighten the shift linkage nut.

THROTTLE LINKAGE ADJUSTMENT

1. Depress the accelerator pedal all the way and check that the throttle valve opens fully.

NOTE: If the valve does not open fully, adjust the accelerator link.

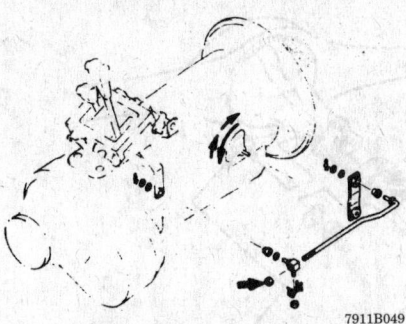

Adjusting the automatic transmission shift linkage

2. Fully depress the accelerator.

3. Loosen the adjustment nuts.

4. Adjust the cable housing so the distance between the end of the boot and stopper on the cable is the 0.03–0.06 in. (0.8–1.5mm).

5. Tighten the adjusting nuts.

6. Recheck the adjustment.

TRANSFER CASE

Transfer Case Assembly

REMOVAL AND INSTALLATION

The transfer case is an integral part of the transmission housing. Although the 2 cases can be separated, the transfer case should be removed with the transmission. The transfer case linkage is not adjustable.

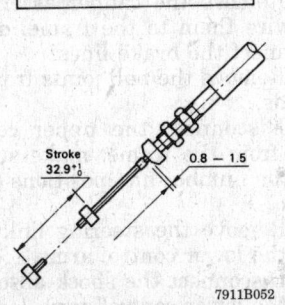

THROTTLE VALVE FULLY OPENED

Stroke 32.9⁺¹₋₀

0.8 – 1.5

7911B052

View of the throttle cable adjustment — gasoline engine

DRIVELINE

Driveshaft

REMOVAL AND INSTALLATION

2WD Driveshaft

1. Raise and support the vehicle safely.

2. Matchmark the driveshaft to the yokes.

3. Remove the driveshaft flange retaining bolts and remove the driveshaft.

4. To install, reverse the removal procedures. Torque the bolts 46 ft. lbs. (63 Nm).

4WD Driveshaft

REAR

1. Raise and safely support the vehicle.

2. Matchmark the driveshaft flange-to-differential pinion flange.

3. If equipped with a 1-piece driveshaft, remove the driveshaft flange-to-pinion nuts, lower the driveshaft and pull it from the transmission.

4. If equipped with a 2-piece driveshaft, perform the following procedures:

   a. Remove the rear driveshaft flange-to-pinion nuts.

   b. Remove the rear driveshaft flange-to-front driveshaft flange bolts and the rear driveshaft.

   c. Remove the center bearing-to-chassis bolts, move the front driveshaft rearward and from the transmission.

To install:

5. If equipped with a 2-piece driveshaft, perform the following procedures:

   a. Install the front driveshaft into the transmission and the center bearing-to-chassis bolts.

   b. Install the rear driveshaft and the rear driveshaft flange-to-front driveshaft flange bolts.

   c. Install the rear driveshaft flange-to-pinion nuts.

6. If equipped with a 1-piece driveshaft, install the driveshaft into the transmission and the driveshaft flange-to-pinion nuts.

7. To complete the installation, reverse the removal procedures. Torque

the retaining bolts to 46 ft. lbs. (63 Nm).

FRONT

1. Raise and safely support the vehicle.

2. Matchmark the driveshaft flange-to-transfer case flange and the driveshaft-to-differential pinion flange.

3. Remove the front driveshaft's splined yoke flange-to-transfer case bolts and separate the front driveshaft from the transfer case; do not allow the splined flange to fall away from the driveshaft.

4. Remove the driveshaft flange-to-differential pinion flange bolts and separate the driveshaft from the front differential.

5. To install, align the matchmarks and reverse the removal procedures. Torque the retaining bolts to 46 ft. lbs. (63 Nm).

U-Joints

REMOVAL AND INSTALLATION

1. Raise and support the vehicle safely. Remove the driveshaft.

2. If the front yoke is to be disassembled, matchmark the driveshaft and sliding splined yoke so driveline balance is preserved upon reassembly. Remove the snaprings that retain the bearing caps.

3. Select 2 press components, with one small enough to pass through the yoke holes for the bearing caps and the other large enough to receive the bearing cap.

4. Use a vise or a press and position the small and large press components on either side of the U-joint. Press in on the smaller press component so it presses the opposite bearing cap out of the yoke and into the larger press component. If the cap does not come all the way out, grasp it with a pair of pliers and work it out.

5. Reverse the position of the press components so the smaller press component presses on the cross. Press the other bearing cap out of the yoke.

6. Repeat the procedure on the other bearings.

To install:

7. To install, grease the bearing caps and needles thoroughly if they are not pregreased. Start a new bear-

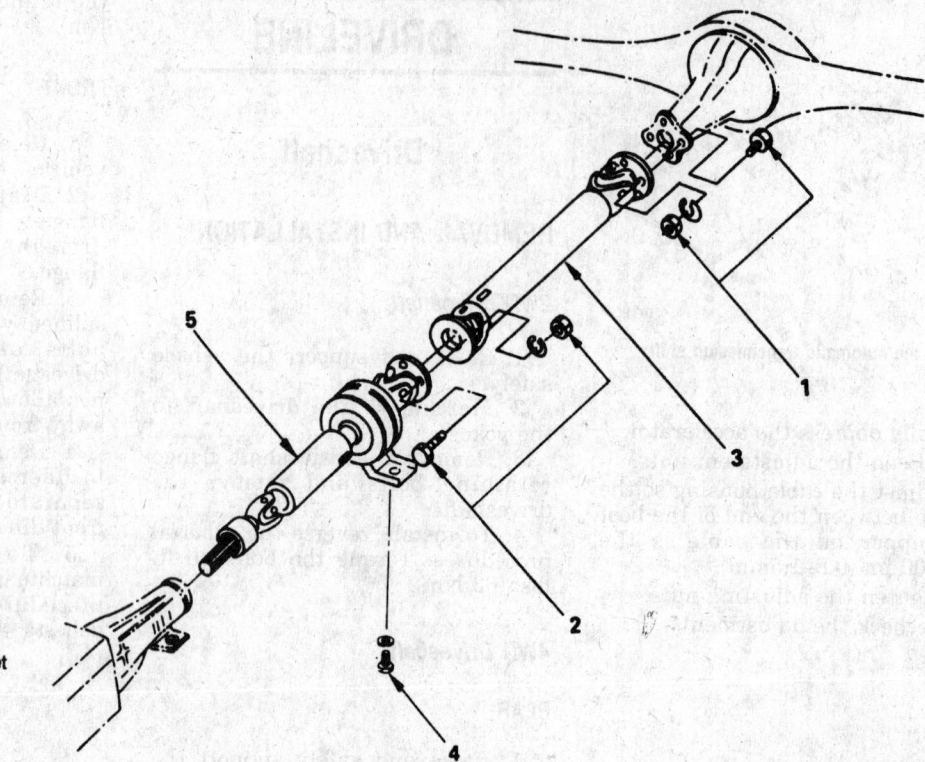

1. Differential side bolt
2. Flange bolt
3. 2nd propeller shaft assembly
4. Center bearing bracket bolt
5. 1st propeller shaft assembly

Exploded view of the rear driveshaft assembly

SPLINED YOKE FRONT PROPELLER SHAFT

TRANSFER SIDE   SETTING MARK

7911B054

View of the front driveshaft — 4WD

ing cap into a side of the yoke. Position the cross in the yoke.

NOTE: Some U-joints have a grease fitting that must be installed in the joint before assembly. When installing the fitting, make sure once the driveshaft is installed in the vehicle that the fitting is accessible to be greased at a later date.

8. Select 2 press components small enough to pass through the yoke holes. Put the press components against the cross and the cap and press the bearing cap ¼ in. below the

surface of the yoke. If there is a sudden increase in the force needed to press the cap into place or if the cross starts to bind, the bearings are cocked. They must be removed and restarted in the yoke. Failure to do so will cause premature bearing failure.

9. Install a new snapring.

10. Start the new bearing into the opposite side. Place a press component on it and press in until the opposite bearing contacts the snapring.

11. Install a new snapring.

12. Install the other bearings in the same manner.

13. Check the joint for free movement. If binding exists, smack the yoke ears with a brass or plastic faced hammer to seat the bearing needles. If binding still exists, disassemble the joint and check to see if the needles are in place. Do not strike the bearings unless the shaft is supported firmly. Do not install the driveshaft until free movement exists at all joints.

Front Axle Shaft, Bearing and Seal

REMOVAL AND INSTALLATION

Axle Shaft

1. Raise and safely support the vehicle.

2. Disconnect the front driveshaft from the differential.

3. Remove the wheels and skid plate.

4. Loosen the torsion bar completely with the height control adjusting bolts.

5. Remove the strut bars.

6. Disconnect the stabilizer bars from the lower control arms.

7. Remove the caliper assemblies and wire them to the frame; do not disconnect the brake lines.

8. Remove the ball joints from the tie rods.

9. Disconnect the upper control arms from the frame; make sure to note the number and positions of the shims.

10. Remove the steering link ends from the lower control arms.

11. Disconnect the shock absorbers from the lower control arms.

12. Disconnect the lower control arms from the frame.

13. Remove the locking hub.

14. Remove the rotors and upper links.

15. Remove the pitman arm and idler arm along with the steering linkage assembly.

16. Support the differential housing and lower it clear of the vehicle. Take care to avoid damaging the Birfield joints.

17. Drain the differential case and remove the 4 bolts attaching the axle mounting bracket to the case.

18. Pull the shaft assemblies from the case on both sides.

19. To install, reverse the removal procedures. Torque the axle mounting nuts to 112 ft. lbs. (152 Nm).

20. Check the level of the axle lubricant and bleed the brake system when finished.

Axle Shaft Seal

1. Raise and safely support the vehicle. Remove the wheel assembly.

2. Remove the axle from the housing.

3. Remove the seal from the housing.

4. Clean and inspect the sealing surfaces of the housing and axle.

5. Using a seal installer tool, drive the new seal into the housing with the lip of the seal facing the housing.

6. Lightly coat the lip of the seal with oil and install the axle in the housing.

7. To complete the installation, reverse the removal procedures.

8. Check the level of the axle lubricant when finished.

Axle Shaft Bearings

1. Raise and safely support the vehicle.

2. Remove the axle shaft from the housing.

3. Support the axle shaft and remove the bearing retainer locknut and washer.

4. Remove the retainer, bearing and seal from the axle shaft.

5. To install, reverse the removal procedures.

6. Always replace the seal and lock washer when removing the axle shaft from the housing. Torque the bearing retainer nut to 188–195 ft. lbs.

Wheel Bearings

1. Place the transfer case in **2H**. Raise and safely support the vehicle.

2. Remove the free wheeling hub cover assembly. Remove the brake caliper and hang aside.

3. Using wrench J-36827 or equivalent, remove the hub nut.

4. Remove the hub and disk assembly.

5. Remove the outer roller bearing assembly from the hub with a finger.

6. Using a brass or wood drift, drive out the inner bearing assembly along with the oil seal. Replace the seal.

7. Wash all parts in a non-flammable solvent.

8. Check all parts for cracks or wear. Thoroughly lubricate all bearing parts with a high-temperature wheel bearing grease. Remove any excess. Apply about 2 ounces of the grease to the hub.

To install:

9. Lightly coat the spindle with the same grease.

10. Place the inner bearing into the hub race and install a new seal and retaining ring.

11. Carefully install the hub on the spindle and install the outer bearing.

12. Install the spindle nut.

13. While rotating the hub, tighten the hub so the wheel can just be turned by hand.

14. Turn the hub 2–3 turns and back off the nut just enough so it can be loosened with the fingers.

15. Finger-tighten the nut so all play is taken up at the bearing.

16. Attach a pull scale to a lug nut and check the amount of pull needed to start the wheel turning. Initial pull should be 2.6–4.0 lbs. When performing this test, make sure the brake pads are not touching the rotor. If the rotating torque is not correct, tighten the spindle nut until it is.

17. Install the lockwasher so the bolt holes align. If the bolt holes do not align, reverse the position of the lock washer. The bolt head should be able to sink below the surface of the washer when tightened.

18. Clean the hub flange surface and areas surrounding the spindle and with the transfer case lever in the **2H** position, install the inner cam with the gear teeth facing out.

19. Lower the vehicle and install tools J-36835-2 and J-36836 or equivalent, on the axle shaft until it comes in contact with the lock washer.

20. Measure the gap between the tool and the snapring tool and select shims to reduce the gap to 0.00–0.10mm. Remove the tool.

21. Apply grease to the hub splines and lubrication grooves. Install the drive clutch assembly. The cut portion of the drive clutch must be aligned with the concave part of the inner cam. Match the teeth of the cam to the inner cam by turning the axle shaft.

22. Install the snapring and previously selected shims, gasket and cover. Apply Loctite® 515 or equivalent, and torque the cover bolts to 43 ft. lbs. (59 Nm).

Rear Axle Shaft, Bearing and Seal

REMOVAL AND INSTALLATION

Axle Shaft

1. Raise and safely support the vehicle.

2. Remove the rear wheel assembly and brake drum. If equipped with rear disk brakes, remove the caliper and hang aside. Remove the brake rotor.

3. Remove the 4 axle retainer bolts.

4. Using a slide hammer on the axle, pull the axle out of the housing.

5. To install, reverse the removal procedures.

6. If equipped with drum brakes, torque the axle retention bolts to 55 ft. lbs. (75 Nm). If equipped with disk brakes, torque the axle retention bolts to 75 ft. lbs. (103 Nm).

Axle Shaft Seal

1. Raise and safely support the vehicle.

2. Remove the axle shaft from the housing.

3. Support the axle shaft and remove the bearing retainer locknut.

4. Remove the retainer, bearing and seal from the axle shaft.

5. Using a seal driver tool, remove the seal and install the new seal in the retainer.

6. To install, reverse the removal procedures.

7. Torque the bearing retainer nut to 188–195 ft. lbs. (250–260 Nm).

8. Check the level of the axle lubricant when finished.

Front Wheel Hub, Knuckle and Bearings

REMOVAL AND INSTALLATION

1. Raise and safely support the vehicle. Remove the wheel assembly.

2. Remove the brake caliper and support it on a wire. Remove the rotor and dust shield.

1. Assembly of hub and disc, back plate, knuckle, knuckle arm and lower end
2. Propeller shaft
3. Nut and bolt
4. Washer
5. Front drive axle assembly
6. Washer

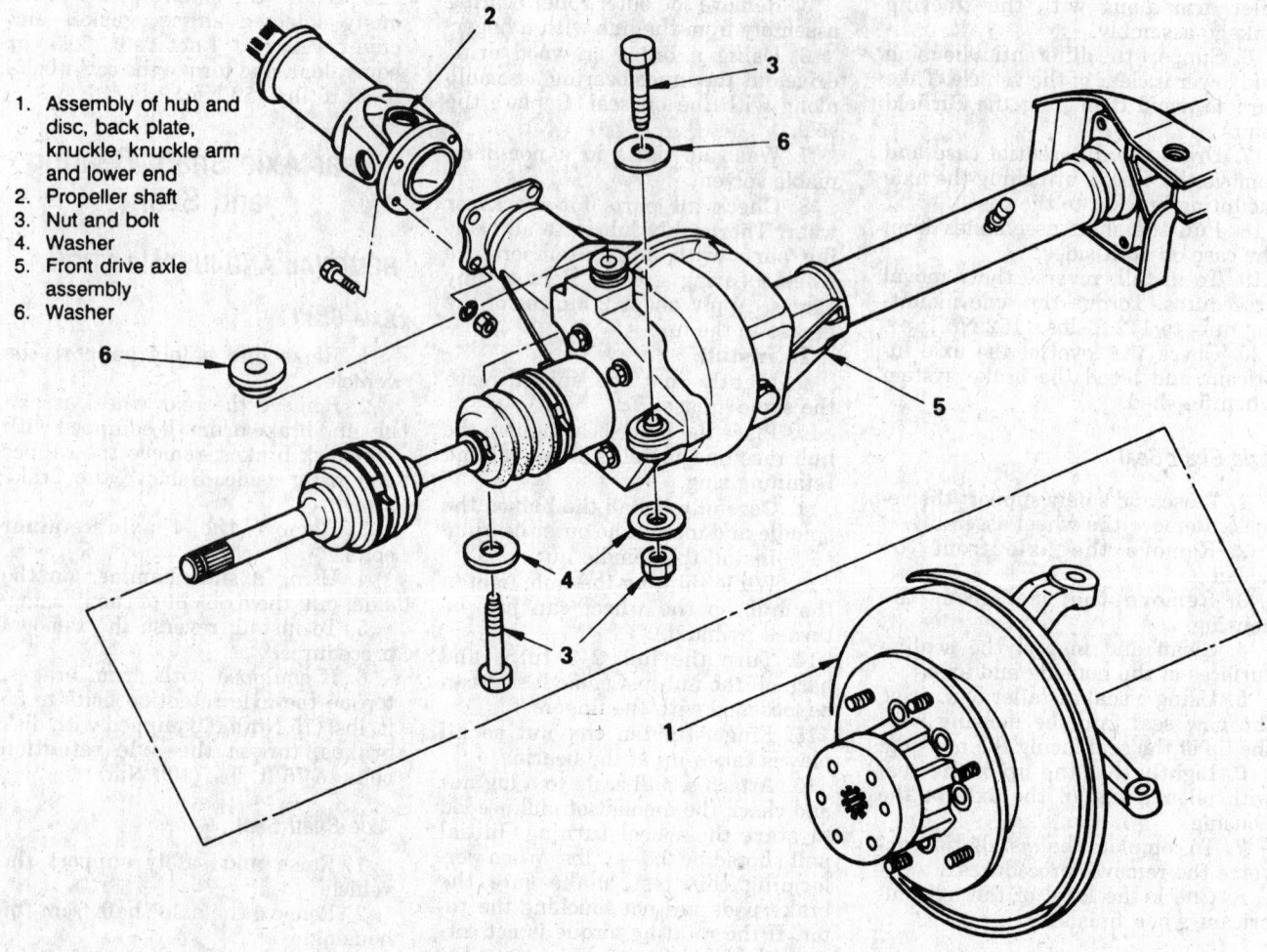

Exploded view of the front axle assembly — 4WD

7911B055

3. If equipped with 4WD, remove the axle shaft from the hub.

4. Remove the tie rod end-to-steering knuckle nut and separate the tie rod from the steering knuckle.

5. Support the lower control arm and separate the steering knuckle from the lower ball joint.

6. Separate the steering knuckle from the upper ball joint.

7. Remove the steering knuckle from the vehicle.

8. To install, reverse the removal procedures.

9. Torque the upper ball joint nut to 75 ft. lbs. (100 Nm), the lower ball joint nut to 95 ft. lbs. (127 Nm) and

the steering linkage ball nut to 75 ft. lbs. (100 Nm).

Manual Locking Hubs

REMOVAL AND INSTALLATION

1. Place the transfer case in the **2H** position. Raise and safely the vehicle.

2. Set the hubs in the **FREE** position.

3. Remove the hub cover bolts and the hub cover.

4. While pushing the follower toward the knob, turn the clutch as-

sembly clockwise and then remove the clutch assembly from the knob.

5. Remove the snapring and the knob from the cover. Do not loose the detent ball.

6. Remove the ball and spring from the knob.

7. Remove the X-ring from the knob by pressing it off.

NOTE: Do not use a sharp instrument to remove this ring because it may scratch the ring.

8. Remove the compression spring, retaining spring and the follower from the clutch assembly.

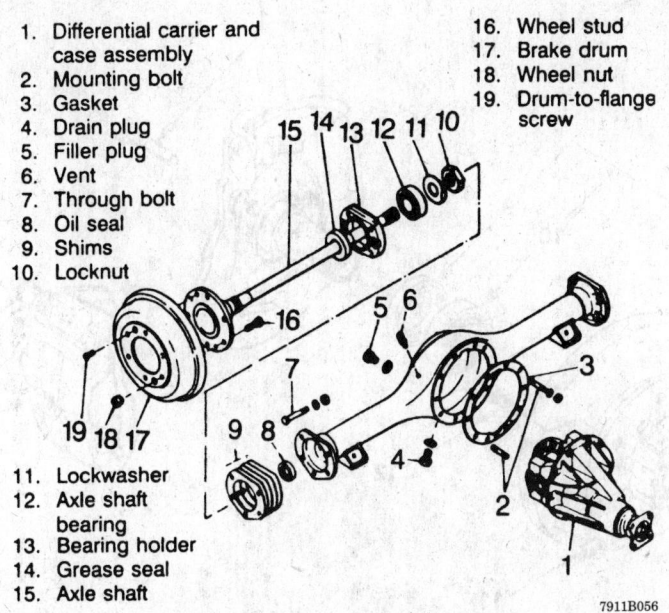

1. Differential carrier and case assembly
2. Mounting bolt
3. Gasket
4. Drain plug
5. Filler plug
6. Vent
7. Through bolt
8. Oil seal
9. Shims
10. Locknut
11. Lockwasher
12. Axle shaft bearing
13. Bearing holder
14. Grease seal
15. Axle shaft
16. Wheel stud
17. Brake drum
18. Wheel nut
19. Drum-to-flange screw

7911B056

Exploded view of the rear axle assembly

9. Remove the retaining spring from the clutch assembly by turning it counterclockwise.

10. Remove the snapring and the inner assembly from the body.

11. Separate the ring, inner and spacer by removing the snapring.

12. To install, reverse the removal procedures. Apply grease to the X-ring, the inner cover and the outside circumference of the knob.

Automatic Locking Hubs

REMOVAL AND INSTALLATION

1. Move the transfer case shift lever into **2H** and move the vehicle forward and rearward about 3 ft.

2. Remove the hub cap-to-housing bolts and the cap.

3. Loosen the wheel nuts

4. Raise and safely support the vehicle. Remove the front wheel(s).

5. Remove the brake caliper-to-steering knuckle bolts and support the caliper on a wire; do not disconnect the brake hose.

6. Using snapring pliers, remove the snapring and shims.

7. Remove the drive clutch assembly, the inner cam and lockwasher.

8. Using a hub nut wrench, loosen the hub nut.

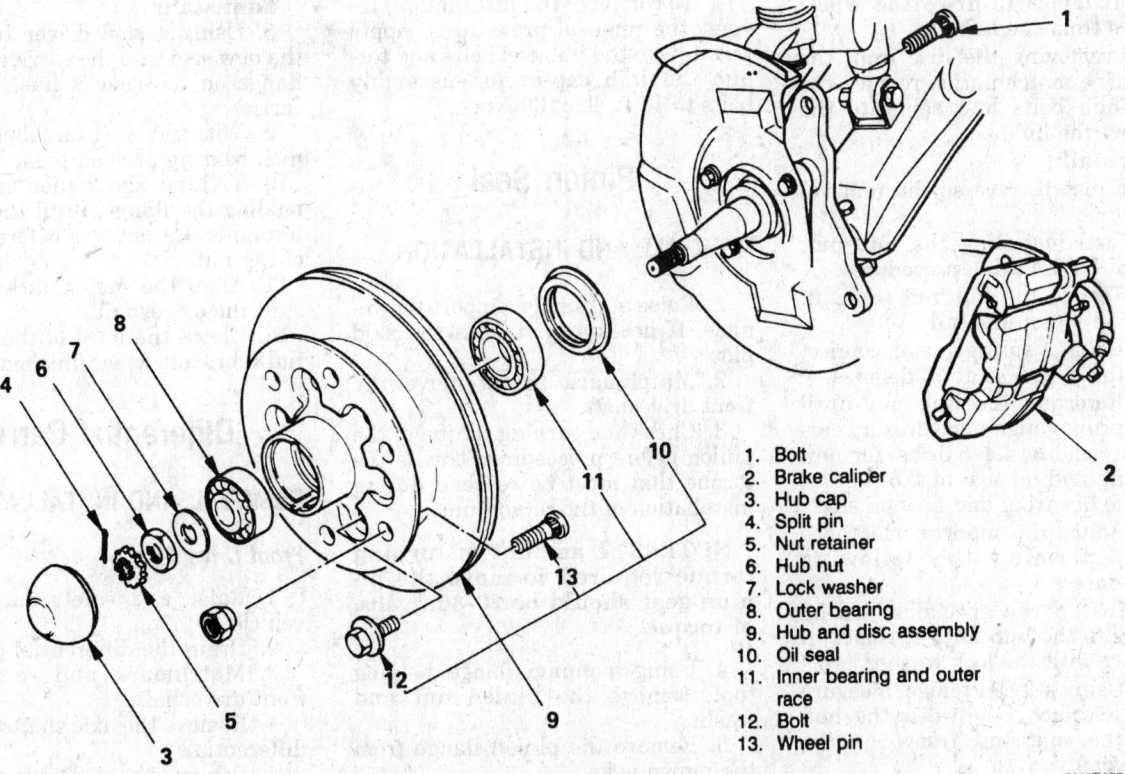

1. Bolt
2. Brake caliper
3. Hub cap
4. Split pin
5. Nut retainer
6. Hub nut
7. Lock washer
8. Outer bearing
9. Hub and disc assembly
10. Oil seal
11. Inner bearing and outer race
12. Bolt
13. Wheel pin

7911B057

Exploded view of the front wheel assembly — 2WD Pick-Up

1. Bolt
2. Brake caliper
3. Bolt
4. Cover
5. Lock washer
6. Hub nut
7. Hub and disc assembly
8. Outer bearing
9. Oil seal
10. Inner bearing
11. Bolt
12. Wheel pin

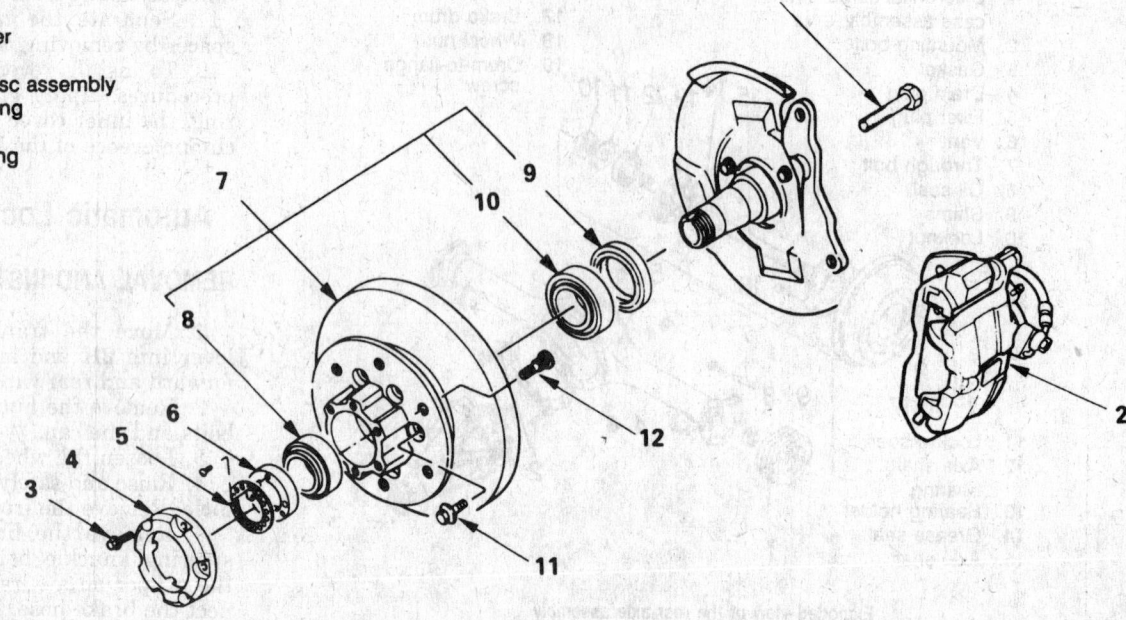

7911B058

Exploded view of the front wheel assembly — 2WD Amigo

9. Pull the hub from the spindle.

10. If necessary, use a brass drift and a hammer to drive the wheel bearings from the hub.

11. If removing the disc from the hub, scribe matchmarks, remove the disc-to-hub bolts and separate the disc from the hub.

To install:

12. To install, reverse the removal procedures.

13. When installing the hub nut, perform the following procedures:

   a. Torque the hub nut to 22 ft. lbs. and loosen the nut.

   b. Using a spring gauge, connect it to the stud bolt at 90 degrees.

   c. Retorque the hub nut until the spring gauge measures a bearing preload of 4.4–5.5 lbs. for new bearing and oil seal or 2.6–4.0 lbs. for used bearing and new oil seal.

   d. Adjust the snapring clearance by performing the following procedures:

   e. Install the special adjusting tool onto the hub until it comes in contact with the lock washer.

   f. Using a feeler gauge, measure the clearance **t** between the hub and the snapring groove on the axle shaft.

   g. If the clearance is larger than the snapring groove, install shims

on the shaft so clearance **t** is 0–0.039 in. (0–0.1mm).

14. To complete the installation, reverse the removal procedures. Apply Loctite® to the hub cap bolts and torque the hub cap-to-hub assembly bolts to 43 ft. lbs. (60 Nm).

Pinion Seal

REMOVAL AND INSTALLATION

1. Raise and safely support the vehicle. If necessary, remove the skid plate.

2. Matchmark and remove the front driveshaft.

3. Check the turning torque of the pinion before proceeding. This is the torque that must be reached during installation of the pinion nut.

NOTE: The amount of turning torque required to move the pinion gear should be 20–30 ft. lbs. of torque.

4. Using a pinion flange holding tool, remove the pinion nut and washer.

5. Remove the pinion flange from the pinion gear.

6. Pry the pinion seal out of the differential carrier.

7. Clean and inspect the sealing surface of the carrier.

To install:

8. Using a seal driver tool, drive the new seal into the carrier until the flange on the seal is flush with the carrier.

9. With the seal installed, the pinion bearing preload must be set.

10. Tighten the pinion nut while holding the flange, until the turning torque is the same as before removal of the nut.

11. Align the matchmarks and install the driveshaft.

12. Check the level of the differential lubricant when finished.

Differential Carrier

REMOVAL AND INSTALLATION

Front Drive Axle

1. Raise and safely support the vehicle.

2. Drain the differential oil.

3. Matchmark and remove the front driveshaft.

4. Remove the axle shafts from the differential.

5. Remove the differential carrier mounting bolts and remove the carrier.

1. Bolt
2. Housing assembly
3. Snapring and shims
4. Body assembly
5. Lock washer
6. Hub nut
7. Hub and disc assembly
8. Outer bearing
9. Oil seal
10. Inner bearing
11. Clutch assembly
12. Snapring
13. Knob
14. Compression spring
15. Follower
16. Retaining spring
17. Detent ball and spring
18. X-ring
19. Snapring
20. Inner assembly
21. Snapring
22. Ring
23. Spacer

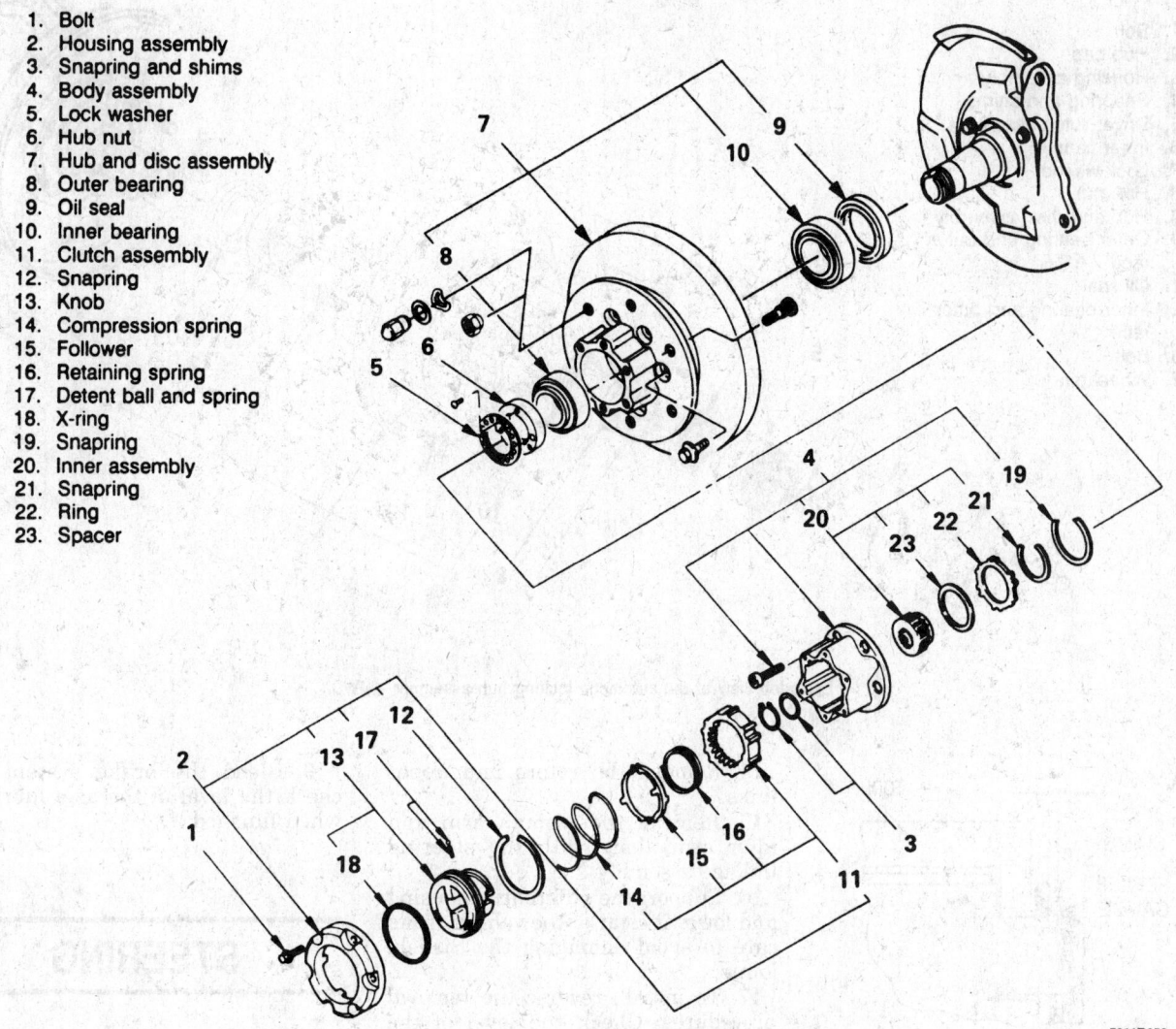

7911B059

Exploded view of the manual locking hub assembly — 4WD

To install:

6. To install, reverse the removal procedures. Use a new gasket when installing. Torque the bolts to 19 ft. lbs. (26 Nm).

7. Fill the differential to the correct level when finished.

Rear Drive Axle

1. Raise and safely support the vehicle.
2. Drain the differential oil.
3. Matchmark and remove the rear driveshaft. Remove the drum or caliper and rotor assemblies.

4. Remove the axle retainer bolts and remove the axle shafts from the axle housing.

5. Remove the differential carrier mounting bolts and the carrier.

To install:

6. To install, reverse the removal procedures. Use a new gasket when installing. Torque the differential mounting bolts to 47 ft. lbs. (64 Nm). Torque the bearing retainer bolts to 75 ft. lbs. (103 Nm) on disk brake models or 54 ft. lbs. (74 Nm) on drum brake models.

7. Fill the differential to the correct level when finished.

Axle Housing

REMOVAL AND INSTALLATION

Front Housing

1. Raise and safely support the vehicle.
2. Matchmark and disconnect the front driveshaft from the differential.
3. Remove the wheels and skid plate.
4. Loosen the torsion bar completely with the height control adjusting bolts.
5. Remove the strut bars.
6. Disconnect the stabilizer bars from the lower control arms.

1. Bolt
2. Hub cap
3. Housing assembly
4. Snapring and shims
5. Drive clutch assembly
6. Inner cam
7. Lock washer
8. Hub nut
9. Hub and disc assembly
10. Outer bearing and outer race
11. Oil seal
12. Inner bearing and outer race
13. Bolt
14. Wheel pin

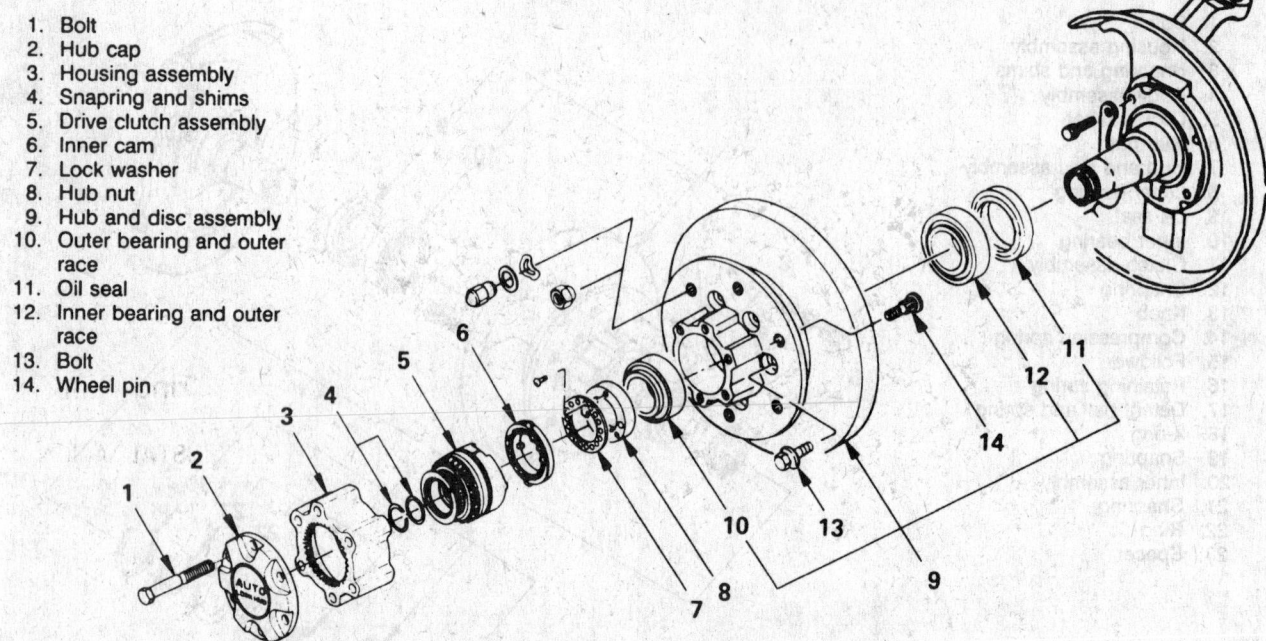

Exploded view of the automatic locking hub assembly — 4WD

7911B060

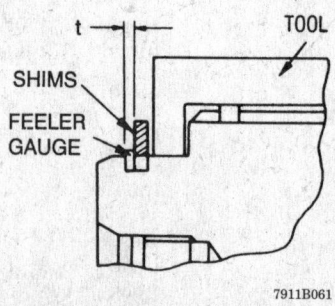

7911B061

Using a feeler gauge to measure the shim clearance on the automatic locking hub assembly — 4WD

7. Remove the caliper assemblies and suspend them on a wire; do not disconnect the brake lines.

8. Remove the tie rod ends from the steering knuckles.

9. Disconnect the upper control arms from the frame; note the number and positions of the shims.

10. Remove the steering link ends from the lower control arms.

11. Disconnect the shock absorbers from the lower control arms.

12. Disconnect the lower control arms from the frame.

13. Remove the locking hub.

14. Remove the rotors and upper links.

15. Remove the pitman arm and idler arm along with the steering linkage assembly.

16. Support the differential housing and lower it clear of the vehicle. Take care to avoid damaging the Birfield joints.

17. To install, reverse the removal procedures. Check the level of the axle lubricant when finished.

Rear Housing

1. Raise and safely support the vehicle. Remove the rear wheels.

2. Disconnect the shock absorbers from the spring plates.

3. Disconnect and plug the brake lines on the rear axle housing.

4. Disconnect the parking brake cables from the rear axle housing.

5. Support the rear axle housing and remove the housing to leaf spring U-bolts.

6. Remove the rear axle housing from the vehicle.

To install:

7. To install, reverse the removal procedures.

8. Torque the housing U-bolts to 36–43 ft. lbs. and the shock absorber bolts to 27–30 ft. lbs.

9. Bleed the brake system and check the level of the axle lubricant when finished.

STEERING

Steering Wheel

REMOVAL AND INSTALLATION

1. Disconnect the negative battery cable.

2. From the rear of the steering wheel, remove the horn pad screw. Pry the horn pad upward from the steering wheel.

3. Remove the steering wheel-to-steering column nut.

4. Matchmark the steering wheel-to-steering shaft.

5. Using a steering wheel puller, press the steering wheel from the steering shaft.

6. To install, align the matchmarks and reverse the removal procedures. Torque the steering wheel nut to 22–29 ft. lbs. (30–39 Nm).

Steering Column

REMOVAL AND INSTALLATION

1. Disconnect the negative battery cable.

2. Mark the shaft and steering wheel hub and remove the steering wheel and the column cowling. Remove the instrument cluster on the Amigo, Pick-Up and Rodeo to remove the column cowling.

3. Disconnect the electrical connections to the combination switch and the ignition switch.

4. Mark the steering shaft and universal joint and remove the bolt from the steering shaft-to-steering box universal joint. Remove the bolts from the steering column bracket at the firewall. Remove the bolts from the steering bracket under the dash panel.

5. Remove the steering column from the vehicle.

To install:

6. Install the steering column in the vehicle and match the marks on the steering shaft and the universal joint. Connect the electrical connections to the combination switch and the ignition switch.

7. Insert the bolts into the steering bracket under the dash. Torque the bolts to 11–14 ft. lbs. (1.5–2.0 Nm).

8. Insert the bolts into the firewall bracket and torque to 10–17 ft. lbs. (1.4–2.4 Nm).

9. Install the universal joint bolt and torque to 14–22 ft. lbs. (2.0–3.0 Nm).

10. Install the steering wheel, matching the marks made during removal. Torque the nut to 22–29 ft. lbs. (3.0–4.0 Nm). Install the cowling and the instrument panel. Connect the battery.

Manual Steering Gear

REMOVAL AND INSTALLATION

1. Disconnect the negative battery cable. Raise and safely support the vehicle. Remove the skid plate, if equipped.

2. Remove pitman arm nut and washer. Matchmark the pitman arm-to-pitman shaft.

3. Using a puller tool, press the pitman arm from the pitman shaft.

4. Remove the steering gear-to-steering shaft clamp bolt.

5. Remove the steering gear-to-frame bolts and the steering gear from vehicle.

To install:

6. Place the steering gear in position and install and tighten the mounting bolts.

7. Install the steering gear-to-steering shaft clamp bolt and torque to 29–40 ft. lbs. (40–49 Nm).

8. Torque the steering column mounting bolts to 13 ft. lbs.

9. Install the pitman arm-to-pitman shaft and torque the nut to 145–174 ft. lbs. (196–236 Nm).

10. Install the skid plate, if equipped.

11. Lower the vehicle.

ADJUSTMENT

1. Position the front wheel in the straight ahead position.

2. Loosen the locknut on the adjusting screw of the steering unit.

3. Turn the adjusting screw clockwise to decrease the free-play or counterclockwise to increase it.

4. With the steering wheel free-play set at 0.4–1.2 in. (10–30mm), torque the locknut to 15–22 ft. lbs. (20–29 Nm).

Power Steering Gear

REMOVAL AND INSTALLATION

1. Raise and safely support the vehicle. Remove the skip plate, if equipped.

2. Remove pitman arm nut and washer. Matchmark the pitman arm-to-pitman shaft.

3. Using a puller tool, press the the pitman arm from the pitman shaft.

4. Disconnect and plug the power steering lines at the steering gear.

5. Remove the steering gear-to-steering shaft clamp bolt.

6. Remove the steering gear-to-frame bolts and the steering gear from vehicle.

To install:

7. Place the steering gear in position and install and tighten the mounting bolts. Connect the power steering lines to the steering gear.

8. Install steering gear-to-steering shaft bolts and torque to 29–40 ft. lbs. (40–49 Nm).

9. Torque steering column mounting bolts to 13 ft. lbs.

10. Install the pitman arm to the pitman shaft. Install washer and torque nut to 145–174 ft. lbs. (196–236 Nm).

11. Install the skid plate, if equipped.

12. Lower the vehicle. Refill and bleed the power steering system.

ADJUSTMENT

1. Position the front wheel in the straight ahead position.

2. Loosen the locknut on the adjusting screw of the steering unit.

3. Turn the adjusting screw clockwise to decrease the free-play or counterclockwise to increase it.

4. With the steering wheel free-play set at 0.4 in. (10mm), torque the locknut to 26–35 ft. lbs. (37–47 Nm).

Power Steering Pump

REMOVAL AND INSTALLATION

1. Disconnect the negative battery cable.

2. Disconnect and plug the inlet and outlet fluid lines from the power steering pump.

3. Remove the drive belt from the pump.

4. Remove the pump-to-bracket bolts and the pump from the brackets.

5. To install, reverse the removal procedures.

6. Connect the negative battery cable. Refill and bleed the power steering system.

BELT ADJUSTMENT

1. Loosen the power steering pump adjusting bolts.

2. Using finger pressure, between the idler pulley and the power steering pump pulley, check the belt deflection; it should be 0.4 in. (10mm).

3. With the power steering pump adjusted to the correct belt deflection, tighten the pump bolts.

SYSTEM BLEEDING

1. Fill the power steering reservoir to the proper level when cold.

2. Start and operate the engine until it reaches normal operating temperatures.

3. Turn the engine **OFF** and check the fluid level. If necessary, fill the reservoir to the proper level.

4. Run the engine and turn the steering wheel from lock-to-lock, in both directions, 3–4 times; do not hold the steering wheel at the lock position for more than 5 seconds or temperature rise will result.

5. Return the steering wheel to center, turn the engine **OFF** and al-

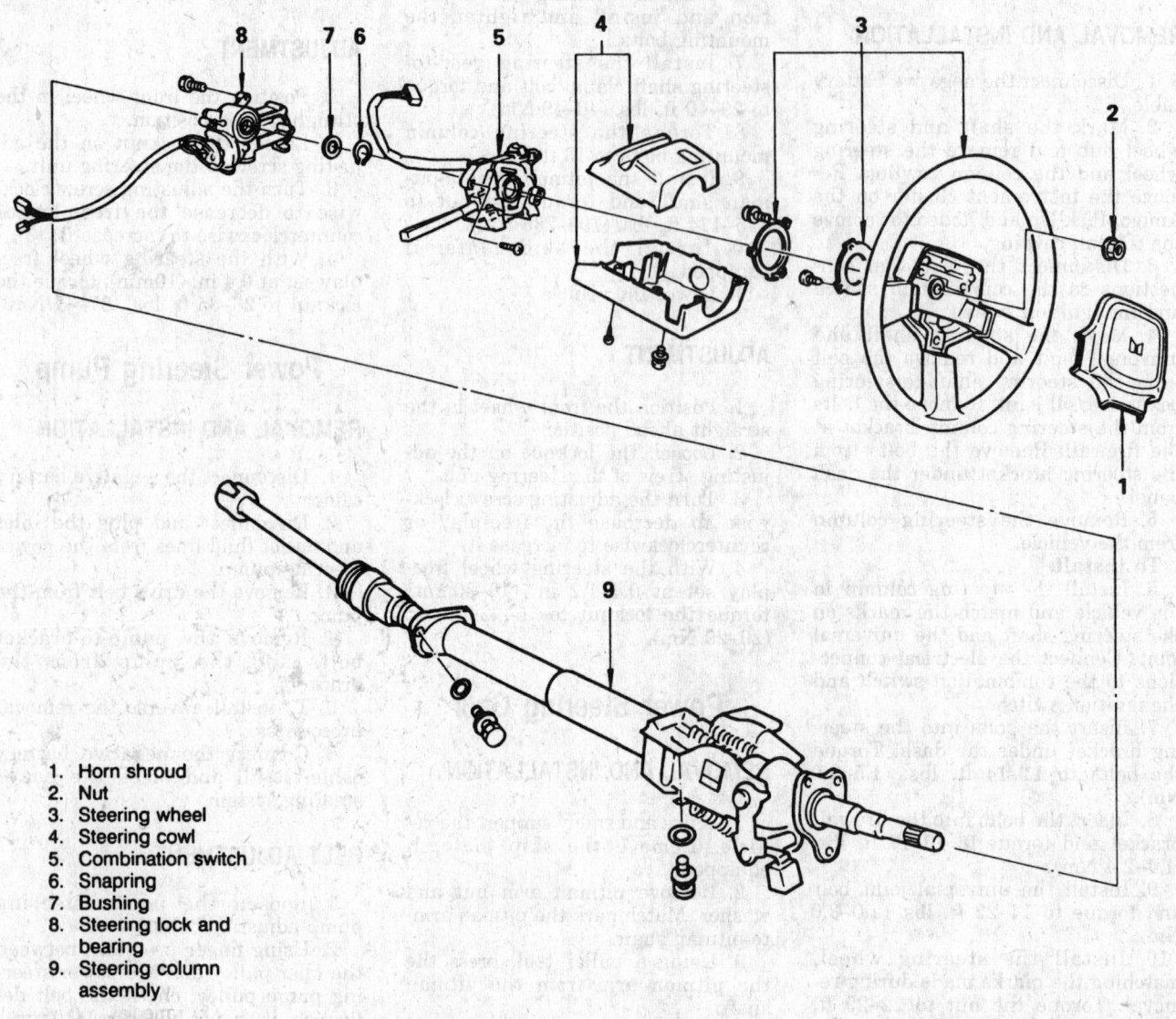

1. Horn shroud
2. Nut
3. Steering wheel
4. Steering cowl
5. Combination switch
6. Snapring
7. Bushing
8. Steering lock and bearing
9. Steering column assembly

7911B062

Exploded view of the steering column assembly

low the fluid to sit for 5 minutes before adding any more.

6. If necessary, repeat the bleeding procedure until the air bubbles are removed from the system.

7. Fill the system to the proper level when finished.

Tie Rod Ends

REMOVAL AND INSTALLATION

1. Raise and safely support the vehicle.

2. Matchmark the tie rod ends to the tie rod shaft for reinstallation purposes.

3. Remove the cotter pin and nut from the tie rod end and loosen the clamping bolts on the sleeve.

4. Using a tie rod end puller, separate the tie rod from the steering knuckle.

5. Unscrew the tie rod while counting the number of turns required to remove it.

6. Check the tie rod end for damage and replace it, if necessary.

To install:

7. Install the tie rod end in the sleeve the same number of turns as when removing it.

8. Install the tie rod end in steering knuckle. Install the nut and new cotter pin.

9. Check the toe in when finished.

Intermediate Rod and Tie Rods

REMOVAL AND INSTALLATION

1. Raise and safely support the vehicle.

2. Remove cotter pin from the ball studs connecting tie rods-to-intermediate rod and the steering damper. Remove the castellated nuts. Using a ball joint separator tool, separate the parts.

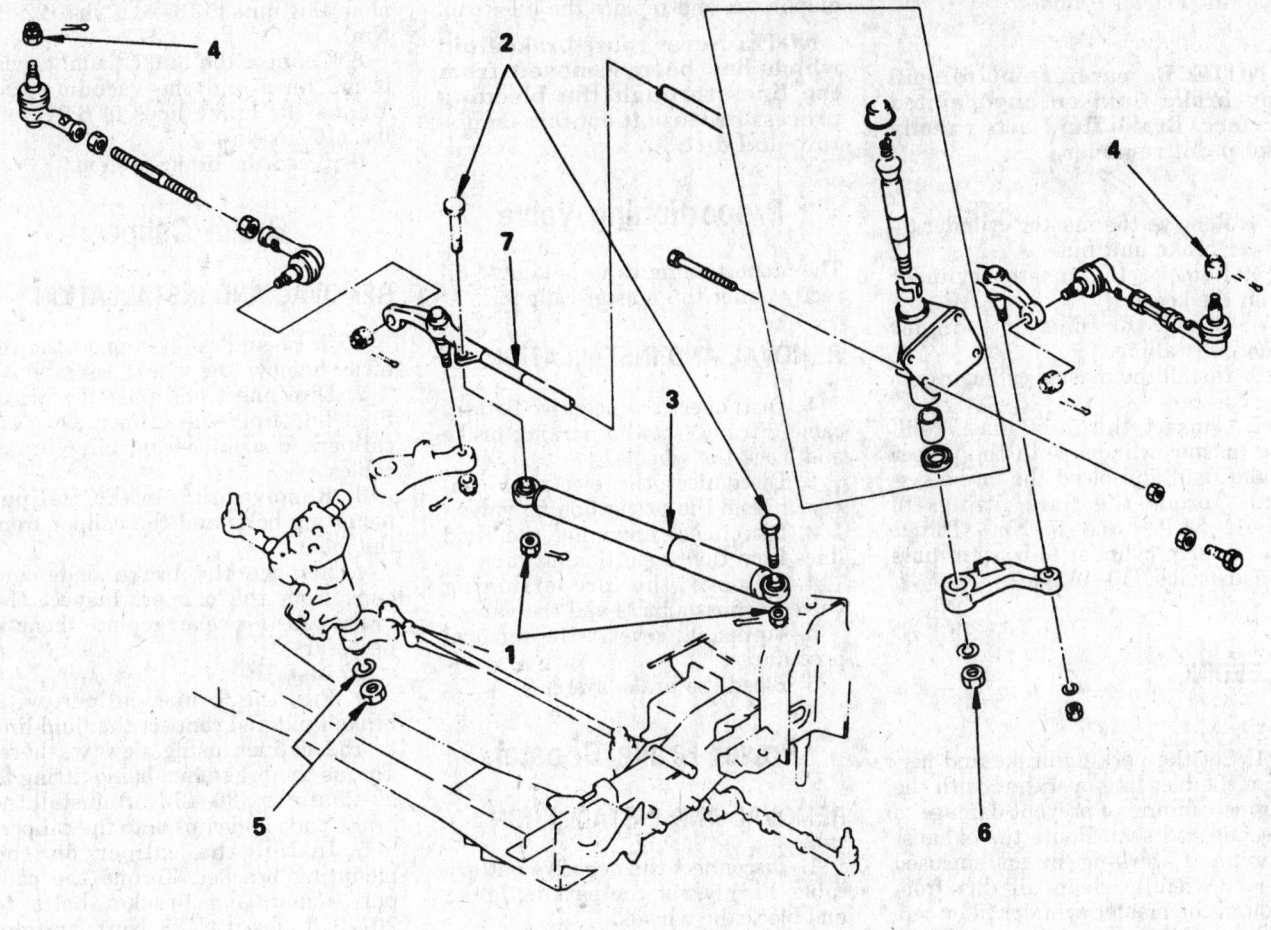

1. Nut
2. Bolt
3. Steering damper
4. Nut
5. Pitman arm nut
6. Relay lever nut
7. Intermediate rod

7911B063

Exploded view of the steering linkage assembly

3. Remove the nut and lockwasher on ball stud connecting the intermediate rod to idler arm. Using a ball joint separator tool, separate the intermediate rod from the idler arm.

4. Remove the intermediate rod with tie rods.

5. If the tie rod is replaced, disconnect the intermediate rod from tie rod.

To install:

6. Make sure the threads on the ball studs and nuts are clean and smooth.

7. Install the intermediate rod-to-idler arm and torque the nut to 50 ft. lbs. (67 Nm).

8. Raise the end of the rod and install it on the pitman arm. Torque the nut to 44 ft. lbs. (59 Nm). Tighten the nut just enough to insert cotter pin and install new cotter pin.

9. Install intermediate rod to steering damper end. Torque nut to 87 ft. lbs. (117 Nm), then, advance nut just enough to insert cotter pin and install new cotter pin.

10. Install the tie rods to adapter, torque nut to 44 ft. lbs. (59 Nm), then, advance nut just enough to insert cotter pin and install new cotter pin and lubricate tie rod ball studs.

BRAKES

Master Cylinder

REMOVAL AND INSTALLATION

1. Disconnect the negative battery cable. Firmly, set the parking brake and block the wheels.

2. Draw off the brake fluid from the reservoir with a clean syringe.

Disconnect and plug the brake lines from the master cylinder.

NOTE: Be careful not to spill any brake fluid on any painted surface. Brake fluid acts exactly like paint remover.

3. Remove the master cylinder-to-power brake unit nuts.
4. Remove the master cylinder from the booster.
5. Bleed the master cylinder before installing.
6. Install the master cylinder onto the booster.
7. Connect the fluid lines, refill the master cylinder with the proper brake fluid and bleed the brake system. Torque the flare fittings to 6.5–11 ft. lbs. (8.8–15 Nm). Torque the master cylinder-to-booster nuts to 7–1 ft. lbs. (10–16 Nm).

BLEEDING

1. Set the parking brake and perform the bleeding operation with the engine running to prevent damage to the pushrod seal. Route the exhaust outside if working in an enclosed area. Carefully clean all dirt from around the master cylinder filler cap.
2. If a bleeder tank is used, follow the manufacturer's instructions.
3. Remove the filler cap and fill the master cylinder to the lower edge of the filler neck.
4. Clean off the bleeder connections at all of the wheel cylinders or disc brake calipers. Attach the bleeder hose and fixture to the right rear wheel cylinder bleeder screw and place the end of the tube in a glass jar, submerged in brake fluid.
5. Have an assistant pump the pedal several times and hold it down. Open the bleeder valve ½–¾ of a turn. Close the valve before the pressure is completely released. Repeat this procedure until bubbles cease to appear at the end of the bleeder hose.
6. Check the level of the brake fluid in the master cylinder and add fluid, if necessary. Repeat this procedure at the left rear wheel, then right front wheel and finishing at the left front. It is a good opportunity while the bleeding equipment is available to bleed the clutch hydraulic system using the same procedure.
7. After the bleeding operation at each caliper or wheel cylinder has been completed, refill the master cyl-

inder reservoir, retract the filler cap diaphragm and replace the filler cap.

NOTE: Never reuse brake fluid which has been removed from the lines through the bleeding process because it contains moisture and dirt.

Proportioning Valve

The proportioning valve is located directly under the master cylinder.

REMOVAL AND INSTALLATION

1. Disconnect the negative battery cable. Firmly, set the parking brake and block the wheels.
2. Disconnect the electrical connector from the proportioning valve.
3. Disconnect and plug the fluid lines from the proportioning valve.
4. Remove the proportioning valve-to-chassis bolts and the valve.
5. To install, reverse the removal procedures.
6. Bleed the brake system.

Power Brake Booster

REMOVAL AND INSTALLATION

1. Disconnect the negative battery cable. Firmly, set the parking brake and block the wheels.
2. Disconnect the vacuum hose to the vacuum booster.
3. Disconnect and plug the brake fluid lines at the master cylinder. Place rags under the master cylinder to catch any leaking fluid.

NOTE: Be careful not to spill any brake fluid on any painted surface. Brake fluid will damage painted surfaces.

4. Inside the vehicle, remove the snapring from the clevis pin and separate the clevis pin from the brake pedal.
5. Remove the vacuum booster mounting nuts at the firewall and lift out the power unit and master cylinder/reservoir as an assembly.
To install:
6. Check the distance from the flange face of the vacuum booster to the end of the pushrod before installation of the master cylinder. The distance should be 0.709–0.717 in. (18.0–18.2mm). If the measurement deviates from the specified range, make an adjustment with the locknut at the end of the pushrod.
7. Apply sealer to the dashboard fitting face plate and mount the

booster assembly and torque the mounting nuts to 16–23 ft. lbs. (22–32 Nm).
8. Connect the brake pedal clevis, brake lines and the vacuum hose. Torque the brake lines to 6.5–11 ft. lbs. (10–15 Nm).
9. Bleed the brake system.

Brake Caliper

REMOVAL AND INSTALLATION

1. Raise and safely support the vehicle. Remove the wheel assembly.
2. Disconnect and plug the brake fluid line from the caliper. On rear calipers disconnect parking brake cables.
3. Remove the brake caliper mounting bolts and the caliper from the mount.
4. Remove the brake pads and clips from the caliper. Inspect the brake pads for wear; replace them, if necessary.
To install:
5. Fill the brake caliper with brake fluid and connect the fluid line to the caliper using new washers. Torque the brake line banjo fitting to 22–29 ft. lbs. (30–40 Nm). Install the brake pads and clips onto the caliper.
6. Install the caliper on the mounting bracket. Torque the caliper-to-mounting bracket bolts to 20–27 ft. lbs. (28–38 Nm) for front calipers or 12–17 ft. lbs. (16–24 Nm) for rear calipers.
7. Bleed the brake system. Install the wheel assembly and lower the vehicle.

Disc Brake Pads

REMOVAL AND INSTALLATION

Front

1. Raise and safely support the vehicle. Remove the wheel assembly.
2. Remove the brake caliper mounting bolts and remove the caliper without disconnecting the brake fluid line. Support the caliper so it does not hang on the brake line.
3. Remove the brake pads and retaining clips from the caliper.
4. Use a C-clamp and press the brake caliper piston into the caliper until it bottoms out.
To install:
5. Install the new brake pads and clips in the caliper and install the caliper in the mounting bracket.
6. Install the wheel assembly. Check the brake fluid level.

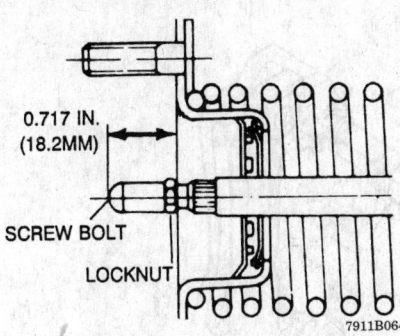

0.717 IN. (18.2MM)

SCREW BOLT

LOCKNUT

7911B064

View of the power booster pushrod adjustment

7. Pump the brake pedal until pressure is felt before moving the vehicle.

Rear

1. Raise and safely support the vehicle. Remove the wheel assembly.

2. Remove the brake caliper mounting bolts and remove the caliper without disconnecting the brake fluid line. Support the caliper so it does not hang on the brake line.

3. Remove the brake pads and retaining clips from the caliper.

4. Using tool J-37617 or equivalent, rotate the piston clockwise while retracting the piston into the bore. Align the notches of the pis-ton face so the centerline of the notches is perpendicular to the centerline of the mounting bosses.

To install:

5. Install the new brake pads and clips in the caliper and install the caliper in the mounting bracket.

6. Install the wheel assembly. Check the brake fluid level.

7. Pump the brake pedal until pressure is felt before moving the vehicle.

Brake Rotor

REMOVAL AND INSTALLATION

Front

2WD VEHICLES

1. Raise and safely support the vehicle. Remove the wheel assembly.

2. Remove the brake caliper without disconnecting the fluid line. Support the caliper aside.

3. Remove the brake caliper mounting bracket.

4. Remove the dust cover, cotter pin and locknut from the rotor.

5. Place a hand over the outer wheel bearing in the rotor and remove the rotor from the spindle.

6. Remove the rotor-to-hub bolts and pull off the rotor.

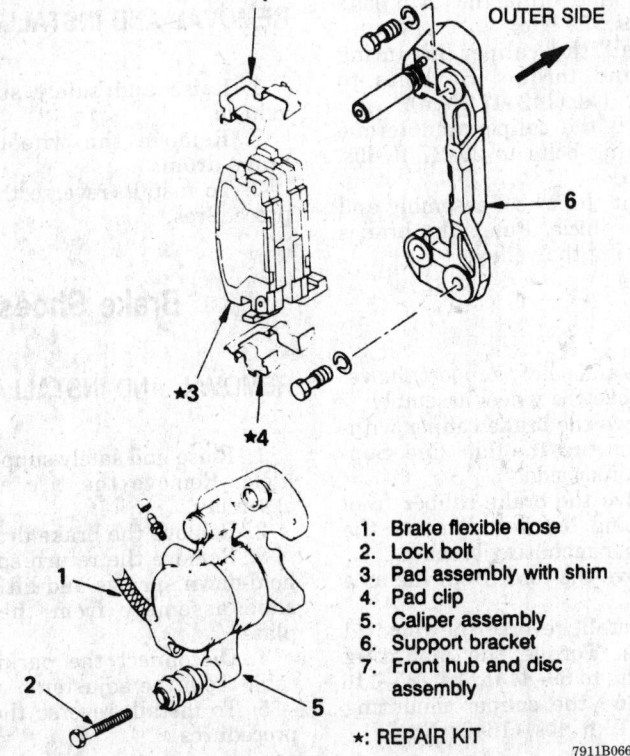

OUTER SIDE

1. Brake flexible hose
2. Lock bolt
3. Pad assembly with shim
4. Pad clip
5. Caliper assembly
6. Support bracket
7. Front hub and disc assembly

✱: REPAIR KIT

7911B066

Exploded view of the front disc brake assembly

To install:

7. Install the rotor on the hub and torque the bolts to 75 ft. lbs. (105 Nm).

8. Torque the hub nut to 22 ft. lbs. (29 Nm) and loosen the nut. Using a spring gauge, connect it to the stud bolt at 90 degrees. Retorque the hub nut until the spring gauge measures a bearing preload of 1.8–2.2 lbs.

9. Install the caliper mounting bracket and torque the bolts to 103–126 ft. lbs. (142–174 Nm).

10. Install the caliper and torque the mounting bolts to 20–27 ft. lbs. (28–38 Nm).

11. Install the wheel and lower the vehicle.

4WD VEHICLE

1. Place the transfer case in **2H**. Raise and safely support the vehicle.

2. Remove the free wheeling hub cover assembly. Remove the brake caliper and hang aside.

3. Using wrench J-36827 or equivalent, remove the hub nut.

4. Remove the hub and disk assembly. Unbolt the rotor from the hub.

5. Remove the outer roller bearing assembly from the hub with a finger.

6. Using a brass or wood drift, drive out the inner bearing assembly along with the oil seal. Replace the seal.

7. Wash all parts in a non-flammable solvent.

8. Check all parts for cracks or wear. Thoroughly lubricate all bearing parts with a high-temperature wheel bearing grease. Remove any excess. Apply about 2 ounces of the grease to the hub.

To install:

9. Bolt the rotor to the hub and torque the bolts to 75 ft. lbs. (105 Nm).

10. Lightly coat the spindle with the same grease. Place the inner bearing into the hub race and install a new seal and retaining ring.

11. Carefully install the hub on the spindle and install the outer bearing.

12. Install the spindle nut.

13. While rotating the hub, tighten the hub so the wheel can just be turned by hand.

14. Turn the hub 2–3 turns and back off the nut just enough so it can be loosened with the fingers.

15. Finger-tighten the nut so all play is taken up at the bearing.

16. Attach a pull scale to a lug nut and check the amount of pull needed to start the wheel turning. Initial pull should be 2.6–4.0 lbs. When performing this test, make sure the brake pads are not touching the ro-

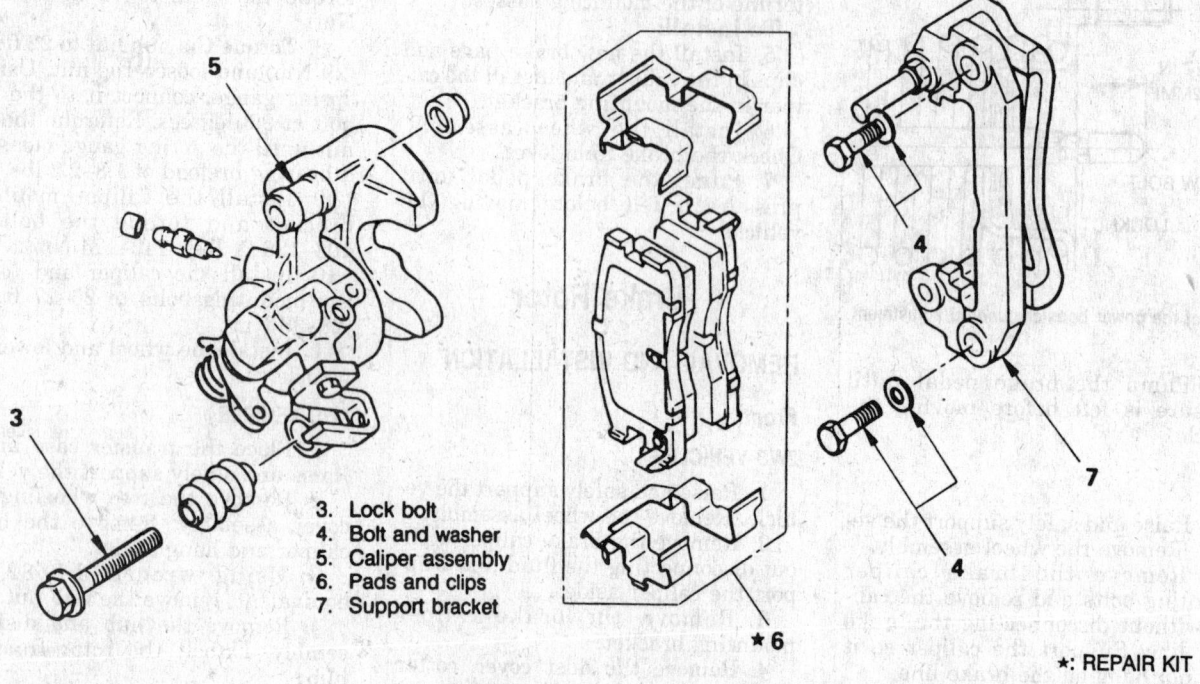

3. Lock bolt
4. Bolt and washer
5. Caliper assembly
6. Pads and clips
7. Support bracket

★: REPAIR KIT

7911B065

Exploded view of the rear disc brake assembly

tor. If the rotating torque is not correct, tighten the spindle nut until it is.

17. Install the lockwasher so the bolt holes lineup. If the bolt holes do not line up, reverse the position of the lock washer. The bolt head should be able to sink below the surface of the washer when tightened down.

18. Clean the hub flange surface and areas surrounding the spindle and with the transfer case lever in the **2H** position, install the inner cam with the gear teeth facing out.

19. Lower the vehicle and install tools J-36835-2 and J-36836 or equivalent, on the axle shaft until it comes in contact with the lock washer.

20. Measure the gap between the tool and the snapring tool and select shims to reduce the gap to 0.00–0.10mm. Remove the tool.

21. Apply grease to the hub splines and lubrication grooves. Install the drive clutch assembly. The cut portion of the drive clutch must be aligned with the concave part of the inner cam. Match the teeth of the cam to the inner cam by turning the axle shaft.

22. Install the snapring and previously selected shims, gasket and cover. Apply Loctite® 515 or equivalent, and torque the cover bolts to 43 ft. lbs. (59 Nm).

23. Install the caliper mounting bracket and torque the bolts to 103–126 ft. lbs. (142–174 Nm).

24. Install the caliper and torque the mounting bolts to 20–27 ft. lbs. (28–38 Nm).

25. Mount the wheel assembly and lower the vehicle. Pump the brakes before moving the vehicle.

Rear

1. Raise and safely support the vehicle. Remove the wheel assembly.

2. Remove the brake caliper without disconnecting the fluid line. Support the caliper aside.

3. Remove the brake caliper from the mounting bracket. Remove the brake caliper mounting bracket.

4. Remove the rotor from the axle shaft.

5. To install, reverse the removal procedures. Torque the mounting bracket bolts to 69–84 ft. lbs. (95–116 Nm). Torque the caliper mounting bolt to 12–17 ft. lbs. (16–24 Nm).

Brake Drums

REMOVAL AND INSTALLATION

1. Raise and safely support the vehicle.

2. Remove the wheel and the brake drum.

3. To install, reverse the removal procedures.

Brake Shoes

REMOVAL AND INSTALLATION

1. Raise and safely support the vehicle. Remove the tire and wheel assembly.

2. Remove the brake drum.

3. Remove the return springs, the hold-down springs and lift the brake shoe assembly from the backing plate.

4. Disconnect the parking brake cable from the adjuster.

5. To install, reverse the removal procedures.

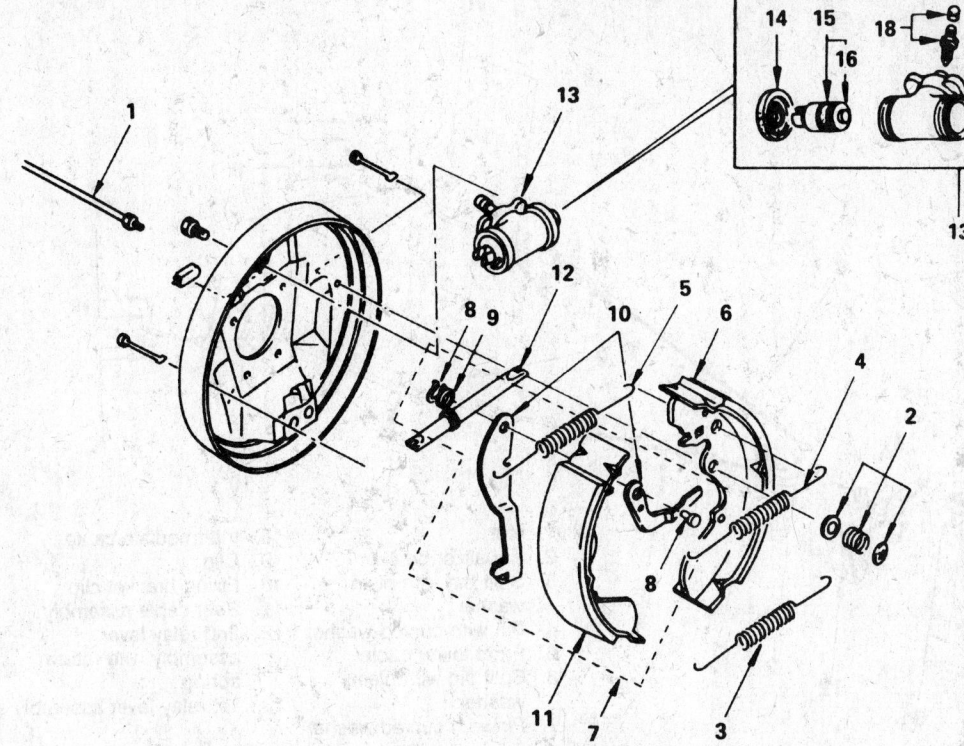

1. Brake line
2. Holding spring and cups
3. Lower return spring
4. Upper return spring (shoe-to-adjust lever)
5. Upper return spring (shoe-to-shoe)
6. Primary shoe assembly
7. Shoe assembly with lever
8. Retainer with pin
9. Wave washer
10. Automatic adjuster lever
11. Secondary shoe assembly
12. Adjuster assembly
13. Wheel cylinder assembly
14. Wheel cylinder boot
15. Piston assembly
16. Piston cup
17. Piston return spring
18. Wheel cylinder bleeder

7911B067

Exploded view of the rear brake drum/shoe assembly

Wheel Cylinder

REMOVAL AND INSTALLATION

1. Raise and safely support the vehicle. Remove the wheel assembly, brake drums and shoes.
2. Disconnect and plug the brake line at the wheel cylinder.
3. Remove the wheel cylinder-to-backing plate bolts and the cylinder.
4. Cap the openings of the brake line and the wheel cylinder.
5. To install, reverse the removal procedures. Bleed the brake system.

Parking Brake Cable

REMOVAL AND INSTALLATION

1. Raise and safely support the vehicle.
2. Loosen the cable adjusting nut and remove the lever return spring. Remove the adjusting nut.
3. Remove the cotter pin from the retaining pin on the 2nd lever assembly and remove the front cable.
4. Remove the 2 cotter pins from the retaining pins on the intermediate cable and remove the cable.

5. Remove the retaining clips from the rear fixing brackets and lower the rear brake cables.
6. Remove the rear wheel assemblies and brake drums. Remove the rear brake shoes and disconnect the rear brake cables from the lever in the rear brake shoes.
7. To install, reverse the removal procedures. Adjust the cables when finished.

ADJUSTMENT

NOTE: Adjustment of the parking brake is necessary every time the rear brake cables are disconnected or after overhauling the rear brake assembly.

1. Fully, release the parking brake lever and check the cable for free movement.
2. Firmly, grab the 2nd relay lever rod. Rotate the adjusting nut until all the slack is removed from the cable. Tighten the adjusting nut.
3. Apply the parking brake to the fully set position 3–4 times.
4. If the parking brake is properly adjusted, the traveling range should be between 12–14 notches. If the travel is incorrect, readjust to specifications.

Load Sensing Proportioning Valve

ADJUSTING

1. Connect a continuity meter between the mounting bracket and the linkage arm. The arm is insulated so be sure to cut through to the metal arm when attaching the lead.
2. Place weight into the vehicle bed to end up with a 1257 lbs. (570 kg) rear axle weight. Have an assistant sit in the drivers seat.
3. Loosen the locknut on the side of the valve body. Raise the valve body and allow to drop slowly. At the point where continuity is achieved, tighten the locknut. Torque the nut to 12 ft. lbs. (17 Nm).
4. If continuity is broken while tightening the nut, loosen the nut and lower the valve body slightly. Tighten the nut.
5. Check the adjustment by pressing down slightly on the linkage near to the valve. If continuity is broken then the adjustment is acceptable.

REMOVAL AND INSTALLATION

1. Disconnect the fluid lines to the valve body.

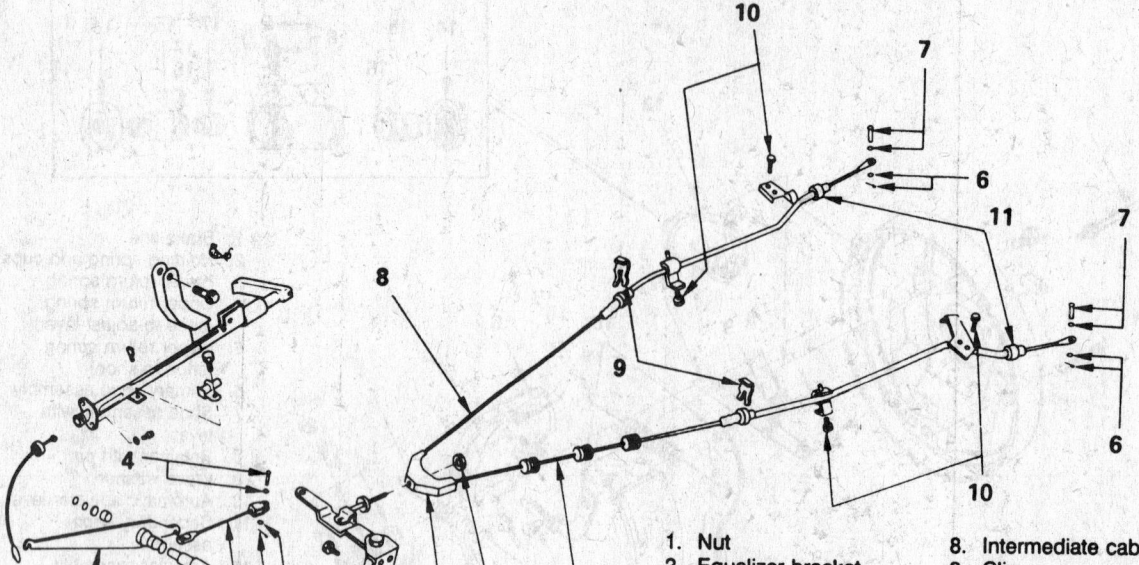

1. Nut
2. Equalizer bracket
3. Split pin with plain washer
4. Pin with curved washer
5. Front lower cable
6. Split pin with plain washer
7. Pin with curved washer
8. Intermediate cable
9. Clip
10. Fixing bracket clip
11. Rear cable assembly
12. 2nd relay lever assembly with return spring
13. 1st relay lever assembly

7911B068

Exploded view of the parking brake cable assembly

2. Disconnect the linkage at the axle housing.

3. Remove the mounting bolts at the bracket and remove the valve.

4. Mount the valve, attach the linkage and lines. Bleed the system.

Rear Wheel Anti-Lock Brake Valve

REMOVAL AND INSTALLATION

1. Disconnect the negative battery cable. Locate the valve body on the right side frame rail.

2. Disconnect the wiring harness connector from the valve body lead.

3. Disconnect the brake lines at the valve body. Cap the lines to prevent the ingress of dirt and moisture.

4. Remove the bolts holding the valve to the frame rail bracket and remove the valve.

5. Installation is the reverse of removal. Torque the brake line fittings to 11 ft. lbs. (15 Nm).

Speed Sensor

REMOVAL AND INSTALLATION

1. Disconnect the negative battery terminal. Locate the speed sensor on the top of the rear axle housing.

2. Disconnect the wiring harness lead from the sensor.

3. Remove the speed sensor bolt and remove the speed sensor.

4. Installation is the reverse of removal. Torque the bolt to 17 ft. lbs. (23 Nm).

Rear Wheel Anti-Lock Brake System ECM

REMOVAL AND INSTALLATION

1. Disconnect the negative battery terminal. Remove the 4 bolts holding the passenger seat assembly and remove the seat.

2. Disconnect the wiring harness from the ECM.

3. Unbolt the ECM from the floor and remove with the bracket.

4. Installation is the reverse of removal.

FRONT SUSPENSION

Shock Absorbers

REMOVAL AND INSTALLATION

1. Raise and support the vehicle safely.

2. Hold the upper stem of the shock absorber from turning and remove the upper stem retaining nut, retainer and rubber grommet. On some vehicles, it may be necessary to remove the bump stops to gain access to the mounting bolts.

3. Remove the bolt retaining the lower shock absorber pivot to the lower control arm and remove the shock absorber from the vehicle.

To install:

4. Install the shock absorber by first installing the lower retainer and rubber grommet over the upper stem and then, installing the shock fully extended up through the upper control arm so the upper stem passes through the mounting hole in the frame bracket.

5. Install the upper rubber grommet, retainer and attaching nut over the shock absorber upper stem.

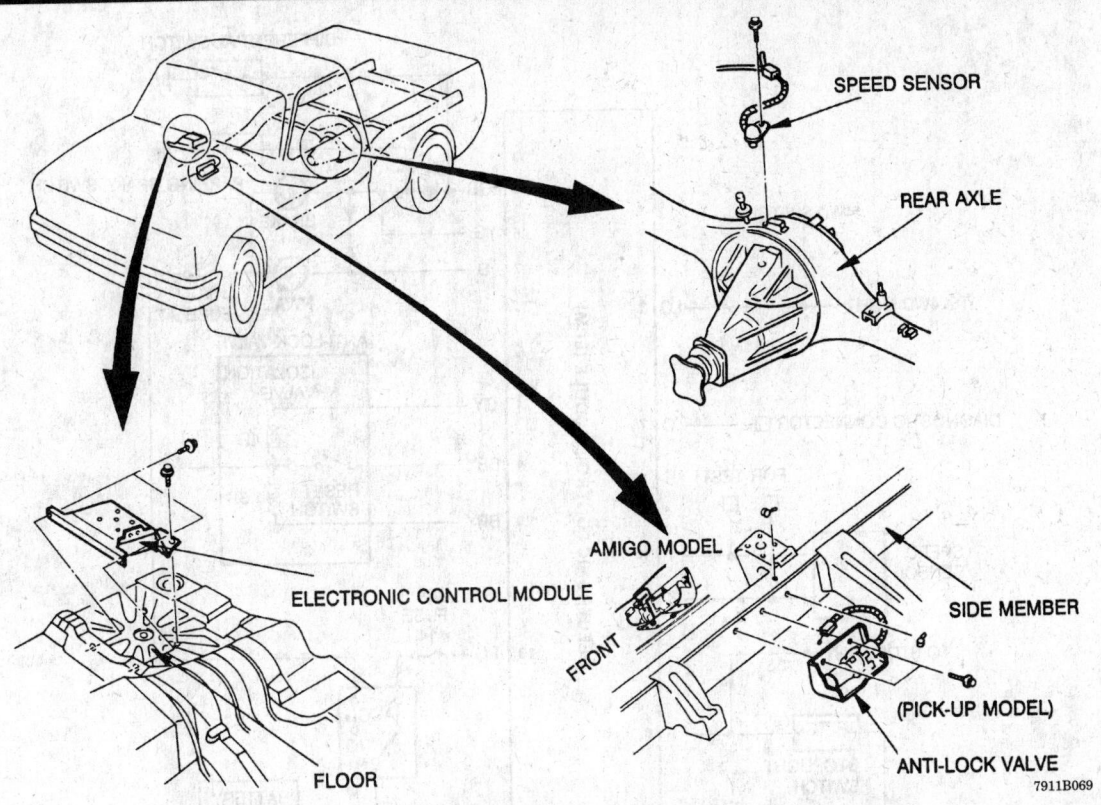

SPEED SENSOR

REAR AXLE

AMIGO MODEL

FRONT

ELECTRONIC CONTROL MODULE

SIDE MEMBER

(PICK-UP MODEL)

ANTI-LOCK VALVE

FLOOR

7911B069

Rear wheel anti-lock brake component locations — Amigo and Pick-Up — Rodeo similar

6. Hold the upper stem of the shock absorber from turning and tighten the retaining nut. Torque to 15 ft. lbs. (20 Nm).

7. Install the retainers attaching the shock absorber lower pivot to the lower control arm and tighten them. Torque the mounting bolt to 60 ft. lbs. (84 Nm).

8. Install the bump stops if removed. Lower the vehicle.

Torsion Bars

REMOVAL AND INSTALLATION

1. Raise and safely support the vehicle.

2. Mark the location of the height adjustment bolt and remove from the height control arm.

3. Mark the location and remove the height control arm from the torsion bar and the third crossmember.

4. Mark the location and withdraw the torsion bar from the lower control arm.

To install:

5. To install, apply a generous amount of grease to the serrated ends of the torsion bar.

6. Hold the rubber bumpers in contact with the lower control arm.

Raise the vehicle up under the lower control arm to accomplish this.

7. Insert the front end of the torsion bar into the control arm.

8. Install the height control arm in position so it's end is reaching the adjusting bolt. Be sure to lubricate the part of the height control arm that fits into the chassis with grease.

9. Install a new cotter pin in the control arm.

10. Turn the adjusting bolt to the location marked before removal.

11. Lower the vehicle and check the vehicle height.

Upper Ball Joints

INSPECTION

Grasp the top of the front wheel and pull it in and out several times to check for excessive movement of the ball joint; if no movement exist, the joint is in good shape.

REMOVAL AND INSTALLATION

1. Raise and safely support the vehicle. Remove the wheel and tire assembly.

2. Mark the position of the torsion bar adjuster and remove the tension from the torsion bar.

3. Remove the upper ball joint-to-steering knuckle nut.

4. Using a ball joint separator tool, separate the upper ball joint from the steering knuckle.

5. Remove the upper ball joint-to-upper control arm bolts and the ball joint.

6. To install, reverse the removal procedures. Torque the upper ball joint-to-upper control arm bolts to 21–25 ft. lbs. (29–35 Nm) and the upper ball joint-to-steering knuckle nut to 72–87 ft. lbs. (96–117 Nm) for 2WD or to 65–80 ft. lbs. (88–108 Nm) for 4WD.

7. Adjust the tension on the torsion bar to its original position and lower the vehicle.

Lower Ball Joints

INSPECTION

1. Raise and safely support the front of the vehicle.

2. Using a large prybar, place it under the front wheel and try to pry the wheel upwards.

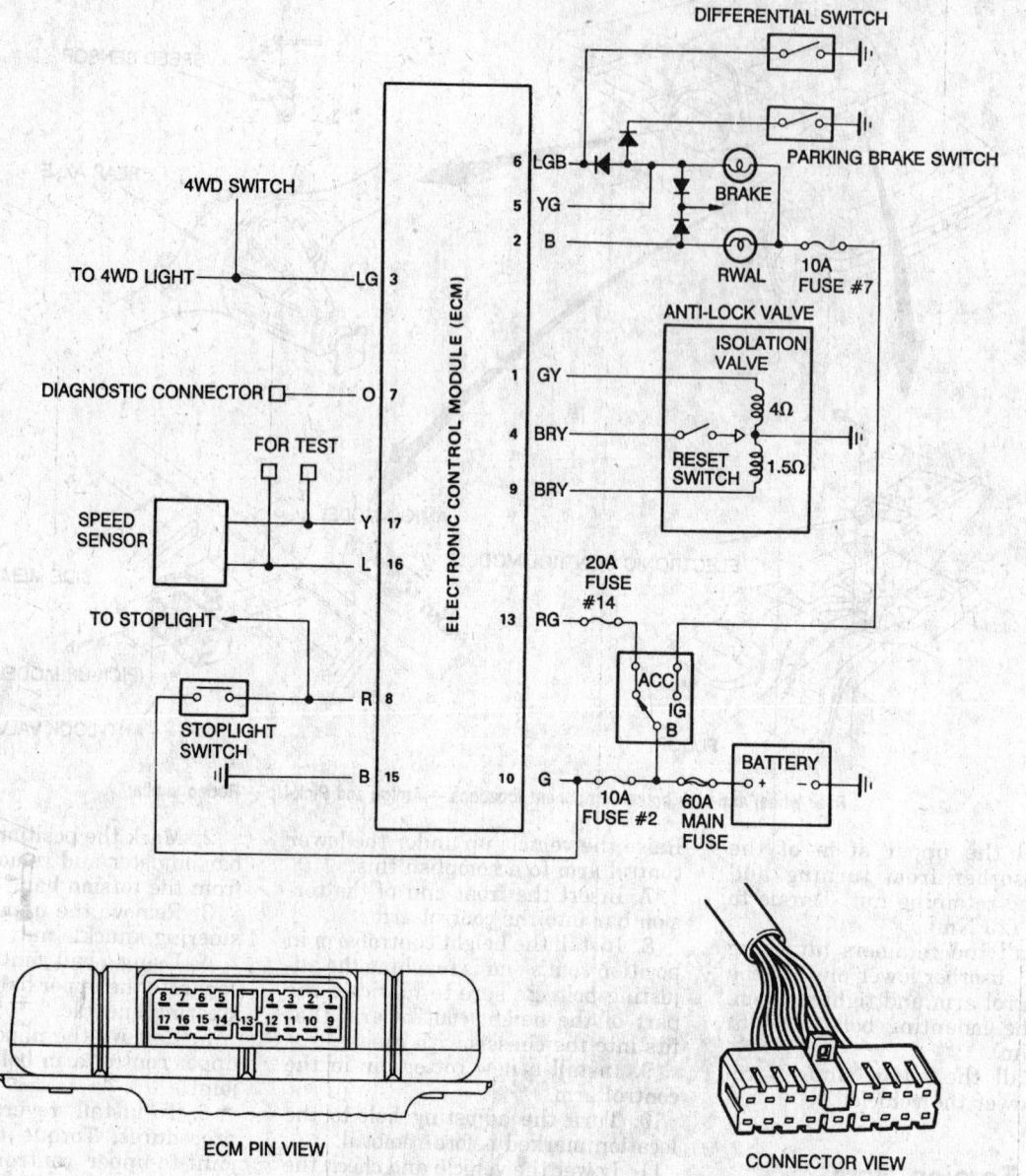

Rear wheel anti-lock brake system schematic

7911B070

3. If excessive upward movement or clunking is noticed, the ball joint is damaged and requires replacement.

REMOVAL AND INSTALLATION

1. Raise and safely support the vehicle.
2. Remove the wheel and tire assembly.
3. Mark the position of the torsion bar adjuster and release the torsion bar tension.
4. Remove the cotter pin and castellated nut which retains the ball joint to the steering knuckle.
5. Remove the lower ball joint-to-lower control arm and strut rod.

6. Remove the ball joint.
To install:
7. Install the lower ball joint by mounting the joint to the lower control arm and torque the bolts to 45–56 ft. lbs. (61–76 Nm) for 2WD or to 68–83 ft. lbs. (93–113 Nm) for 4WD.
8. Install the ball joint stud into the steering knuckle and install the castellated nut and torque it to 101–116 ft. lbs. (137–157 Nm) for 2WD or to 87–111 ft. lbs. (117–137 Nm) for 4WD and just enough additional torque to align the cotter pin hole with a castellation on the nut. Install a new cotter pin.

9. Lubricate the lower ball joint through the grease fitting.
10. Adjust the torsion bar tension to its original position.
11. Install the wheel assembly and lower the vehicle.

Upper Control Arms

REMOVAL AND INSTALLATION

NOTE: The upper control arm and ball joint are replaced as an assembly.

1. Raise and safely support the vehicle.

1. Adjust bolt, seat, lock plate and bolt
2. Height control arm
3. Torsion bar
4. Nut and washer
5. Rubber bushing and washer
6. Bolt and washer
7. Strut bar
8. Rubber bushing, washer and tube
9. Bolt
10. Bracket
11. Nut
12. Rubber bushing and washer
13. Rubber bushing and washer
14. Bracket
15. Bolt and nut
16. Rubber bushing and washer
17. Stabilizer bar
18. Nut
19. Rubber bushing and washer
20. Bolt, nut and washer
21. Shock absorber
22. Rubber bushing and washer
23. Lower link bumper
24. Upper link bumper

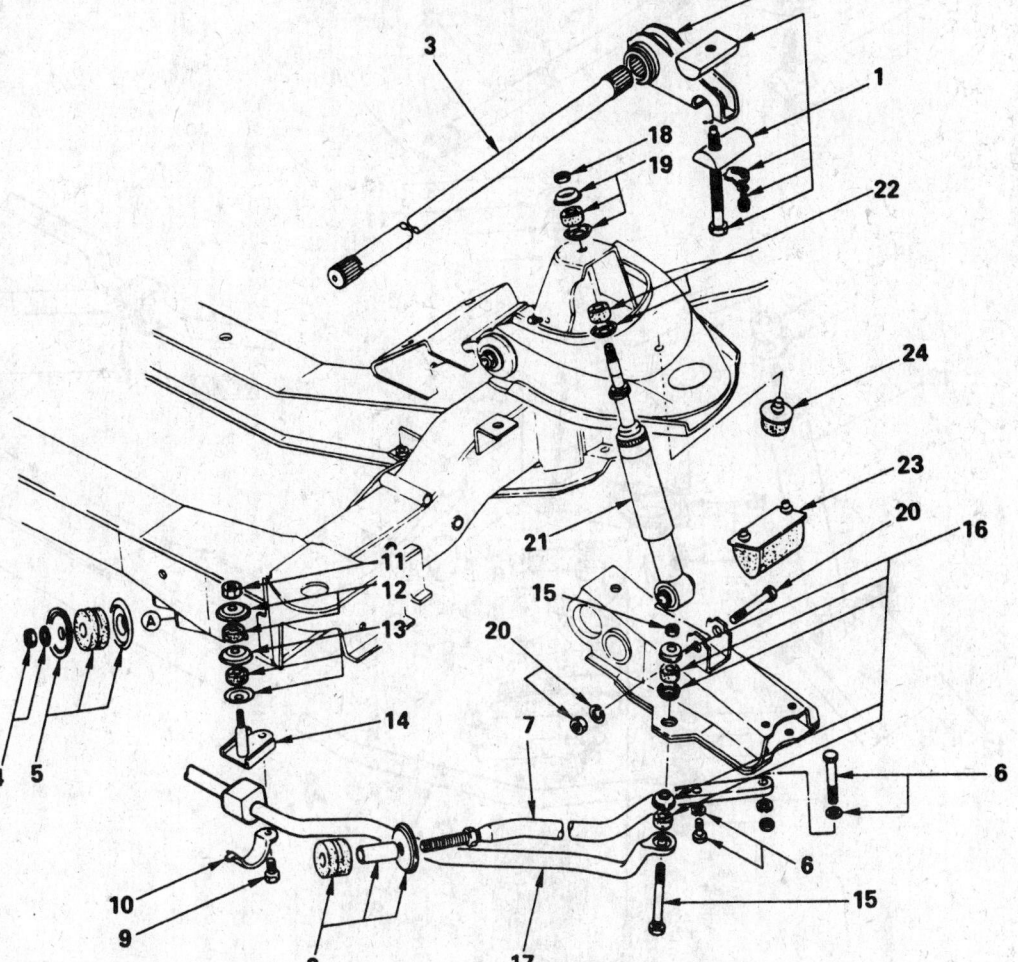

Exploded view of the front suspension — 2WD

7911B071

2. Remove the wheel and tire assembly. Mark the position of the torsion bar adjuster and release the torsion bar tension.

3. Remove the cotter pin nut fastening the upper control arm and upper ball joint assembly and disconnect the upper control arm from the steering knuckle.

NOTE: Do not allow the steering knuckle to hang by the flexible brake line. Wire the steering knuckle up to the frame temporarily.

4. Remove the bolts from the upper pivot shaft and remove the upper control arm from the bracket. Be sure to note the position and number of shims used for adjusting the camber and caster angles when removing the upper control arm. The shims must be replaced in their original position.

5. To remove the pivot shaft and bushings from the upper control arm assembly, remove the bushing nuts from the pivot shaft by loosening them alternately, then remove the pivot shaft.

To install:

6. To install the upper control arm and ball joint assembly, first install the pivot shaft boots to the pivot shaft.

7. Fill the internal part of the bushings with grease and screw the bushings into the pivot shaft. Be sure to screw the right side and the left side bushings alternately into the pivot shafts carefully avoiding getting grease on the outer face of the bushings. Tighten the nuts to 250 ft. lbs. (333 Nm).

NOTE: Be sure the control arm and bushings are centered properly and the control arm rotates with resistance but not binding on the pivot shaft when tightened to the proper torque.

8. Install the grease fittings and lubricate the parts with grease through the grease fittings.

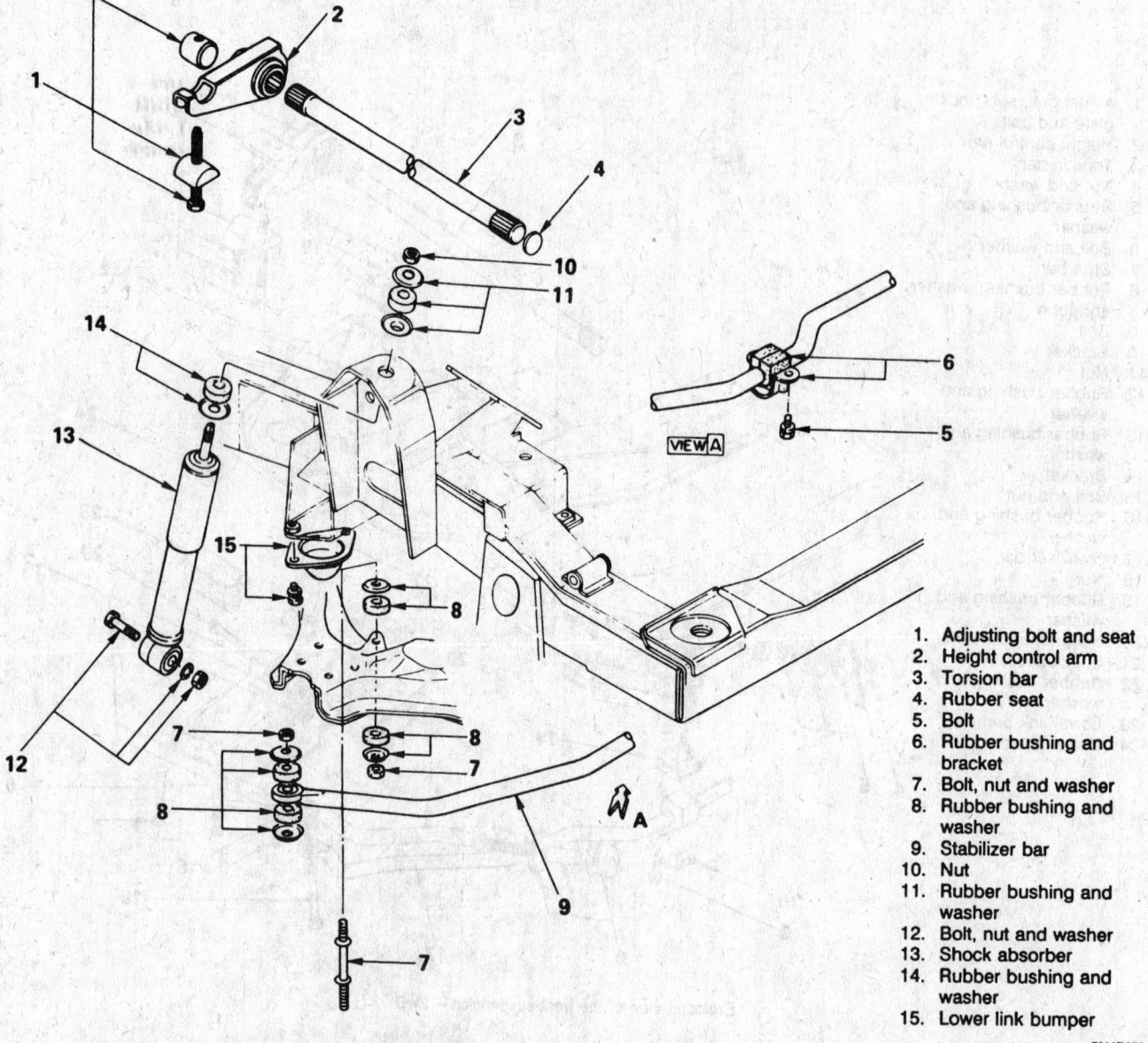

1. Adjusting bolt and seat
2. Height control arm
3. Torsion bar
4. Rubber seat
5. Bolt
6. Rubber bushing and bracket
7. Bolt, nut and washer
8. Rubber bushing and washer
9. Stabilizer bar
10. Nut
11. Rubber bushing and washer
12. Bolt, nut and washer
13. Shock absorber
14. Rubber bushing and washer
15. Lower link bumper

7911B072

Exploded view of the front suspension — 4WD

9. Install the ball joint stud through the steering knuckle. Install the castellated nut and tighten it to 75 ft. lbs. and just enough additional torque to install the cotter pin. Use a new cotter pin.

10. Mount the upper control arm to the chassis frame and install the shims in their original positions between the pivot shaft and bracket. Tighten the pivot shaft attaching nuts to 55 ft. lbs.

NOTE: Tighten the thinner shim pack's nut first for improved shaft-to-frame clamping force and torque retention.

11. Install the dust cover. Adjust the torsion bar to its original position.

12. Install the wheel assembly and lower the vehicle.

Lower Control Arms

REMOVAL AND INSTALLATION

1. Raise and safely support the vehicle.

2. Remove the wheel and tire assembly. Mark the position of the torsion bar adjuster and release the torsion bar tension.

3. Remove the strut bar by removing the frame side bracket and the double nuts, washer and the rubber bushing from the front side of the strut bar. Remove the strut bar-to-lower control arm bolts and remove the bar.

4. Disconnect the stabilizer bar from the lower control arm.

5. Remove the torsion bar.

6. Disconnect the shock absorber from the lower control arm.

7. Remove the lower ball joint from the lower control arm joint.

8. Remove the retaining nut and drive out the bolt holding the lower control arm to the chassis with a soft

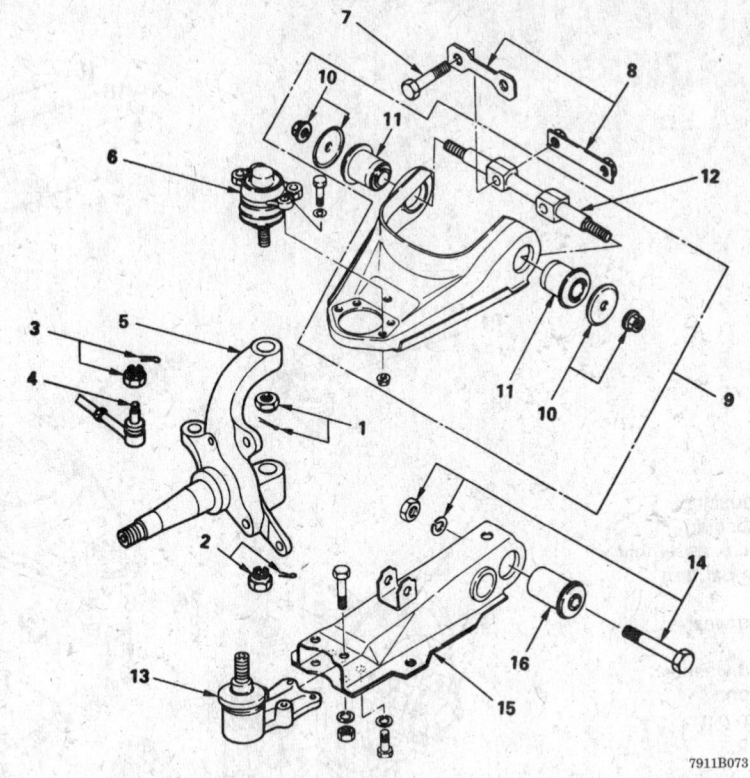

1. Nut and cotter pin
2. Nut and cotter pin
3. Nut and cotter pin
4. Steering link end
5. Knuckle
6. Upper end
7. Bolt and washer
8. Nut assembly
9. Upper link assembly
10. Nut and plate
11. Bushing
12. Fulcrum pin
13. Lower end
14. Bolt, nut and washer
15. Lower link assembly
16. Bushing

7911B073

Exploded view of the steering knuckle and control arm assembly — 2WD

metal drift. Remove the lower control arm from the vehicle.

To install:

9. To install the lower control arm, install the lower ball joint to the lower control arm. Tighten the retaining nuts to 45 ft. lbs.

10. Mount the lower control arm to the frame. Drive the bolt into position carefully. Use care not to damage the serrated portions. Tighten the nut on the end of the pivot bolt to 135 ft. lbs.

11. Install the stabilizer bar to the lower control arm.

12. Place the washers and bushings on the strut rod and install it through the frame bracket. Install the second set of washers and bushings on the strut rod together with the lockwashers and nut. Leave the nut loose temporarily.

13. Install the strut rod to the lower control arm and tighten the bolts to 45 ft. lbs.

14. Assemble the lower ball joint to the steering knuckle. Adjust the torsion bar to the original position.

15. Install the wheel assembly and lower the vehicle.

16. Tighten the 1st strut bar-to-chassis frame attaching nut to 175 ft. lbs. and the 2nd locknut to 55 ft. lbs. with the vehicle on the ground.

Stabilizer Bar

REMOVAL AND INSTALLATION

1. Raise and safely support vehicle.
2. Remove the endlink nuts and remove the endlinks
3. Unbolt the frame bushing brackets and remove the stabilizer bar.
4. Installation is the reverse of removal. Torque the bracket bolts to 20 ft. lbs. (28 Nm) and the endlink nuts to 10 ft. lbs. (14 Nm).

Front Wheel Bearings — 2WD

REMOVAL AND INSTALLATION

1. Raise and safely support the vehicle. Remove the wheel assembly. Remove the hub assembly.
2. Remove the outer roller bearing assembly from the hub. Pry out the inner bearing lip seal and remove the inner bearing assembly.
3. Wash all parts in a cleaning solvent and allow to air dry.

4. Check the bearings for pitting or scoring. Also check for smooth rotation and lack of noise.

To install:

5. Thoroughly lubricate the bearings with new wheel bearing lubricant.
6. Apply a light coat of lubricant to the spindle and inside surface of the hub.
7. Place the inner bearing in the race of the hub and install a new grease seal.
8. Install the hub assembly on the spindle.
9. Install the outer wheel bearing, washer and adjust nut.
10. Adjust the wheel bearings.
11. Install the dust cap on the hub.
12. Install the brake caliper and support assembly.
13. Install the wheel assembly.

ADJUSTMENT

1. With the wheel raised, remove the hub cap and dust cap and then remove the cotter pin and nut retainer from the end of the spindle.
2. While rotating the wheel, tighten the spindle nut to 22 ft. lbs. (29 Nm).
3. Turn the hub 2–3 turns and loosen the nut just enough so it can be turned by hand.

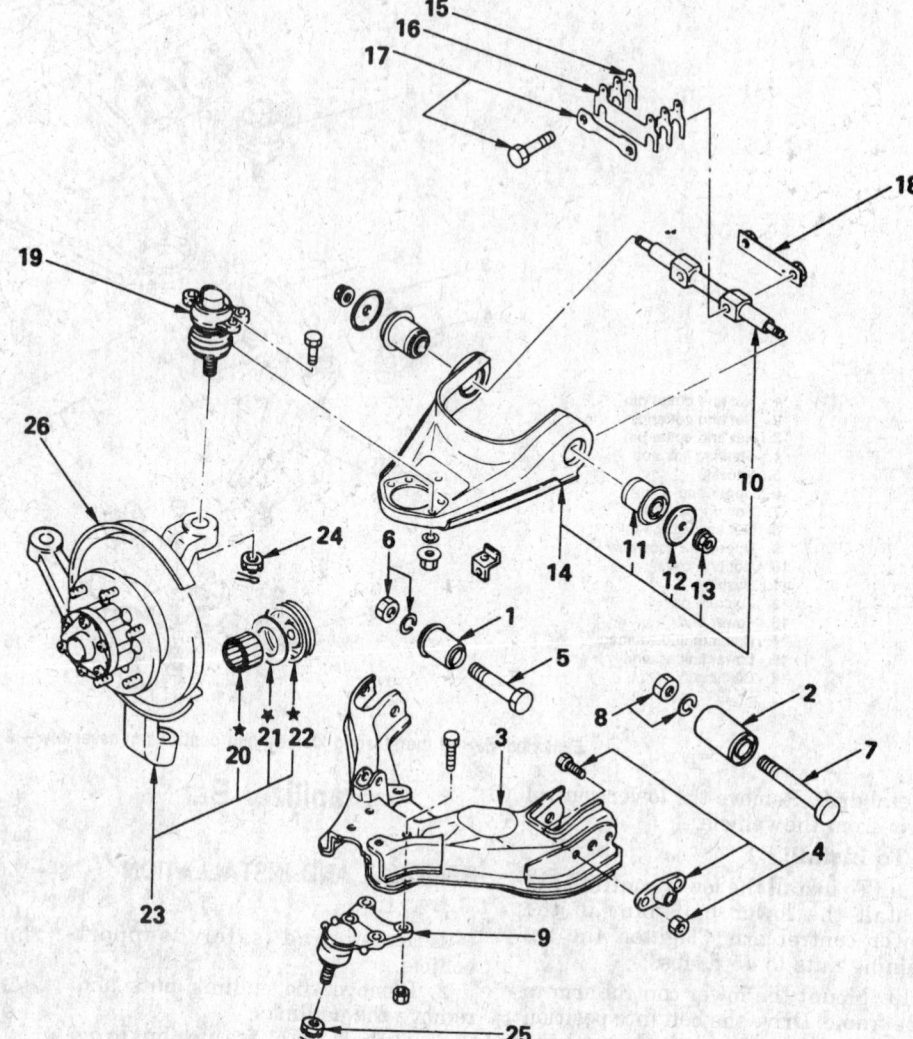

1. Front bushing
2. Rear bushing
3. Lower link assembly
4. Torsion bar arm
5. Bolt
6. Nut and washer
7. Bolt
8. Nut and washer
9. Lower end
10. Fulcrum pin
11. Bushing
12. Plate
13. Nut
14. Upper link assembly
15. Caster shims
16. Camber shims
17. Bolt and plate
18. Nut assembly
19. Upper end
20. Needle bearing
21. Washer
22. Oil seal
23. Knuckle assembly
24. Nut and cotter pin
25. Nut and cotter pin
26. Back plate

Exploded view of the steering knuckle and control arm assembly — 4WD

7911B074

4. Turn the nut all the way hand tight and check to be sure the hub has no free-play.

5. Measure the starting torque by pulling a wheel hub stud with a pull scale. Tighten the spindle nut so the pull scale reads 1.1–2.6 lbs. when the hub begins to rotate.

NOTE: Make sure the brake pads are not in contact with the drum when measuring rotating torque.

6. Install the nut retainer, new cotter pin, dust cap and hub cap.

REAR SUSPENSION

Shock Absorbers

REMOVAL AND INSTALLATION

1. Raise and safely support the vehicle.
2. Remove the shock absorber-to-lower mount nut, washers and bushings.
3. Remove the shock absorber-to-chassis nut, washers and bushings.

4. Remove the shock absorber.
5. To install, reverse the removal procedures. Torque the mounting nuts to 30 ft. lbs. (40 Nm.)

Leaf Springs

REMOVAL AND INSTALLATION

1. Raise and safely support the vehicle so the leaf springs are hanging freely. Remove the wheel assemblies.
2. Remove the rear shock absorbers.
3. Remove the parking brake cable clips.

4. Remove the nuts from the U-bolts holding the springs to the axle housing.

5. Support the rear axle housing to remove the weight of the axle housing from the springs.

6. Remove the front and rear shackle pin nuts.

7. Drive out the rear shackle pin by using a hammer and drift. Lower the rear end of the leaf spring assembly to the floor.

8. Drive out the front shackle pin and remove the leaf spring assembly rearward.

9. Remove the shackle pin from the rear spring bracket and remove the shackle.

10. Check the leaf springs for cracks, wear and broken leaves. Replace any leaves found to be cracked, broken, fatigued or seriously worn.

11. Check the shackles for bending and the pins for wear.

12. Check the U-bolts for distortion or other damage.

To install:

13. Mount the shackle to the bracket.

14. Align the front end of the leaf spring assembly with the front bracket and install the shackle pin.

15. Align the rear end of the leaf spring assembly with the shackle and install the shackle pin.

16. Loosely install the shackle pin nuts and install the U-bolts.

17. Install the shock absorbers.

18. Clip the parking brake cable to the bracket.

19. Tighten the front shackle pin nut to 112 ft. lbs. (152 Nm).

20. Tighten the rear shackle pin nuts to 72 ft. lbs. (98 Nm). Tighten the U-bolt nuts to 48 ft. lbs. (67 Nm).

21. Install the wheels. Remove the axle housing support and lower the vehicle so the weight is on the leaf springs.

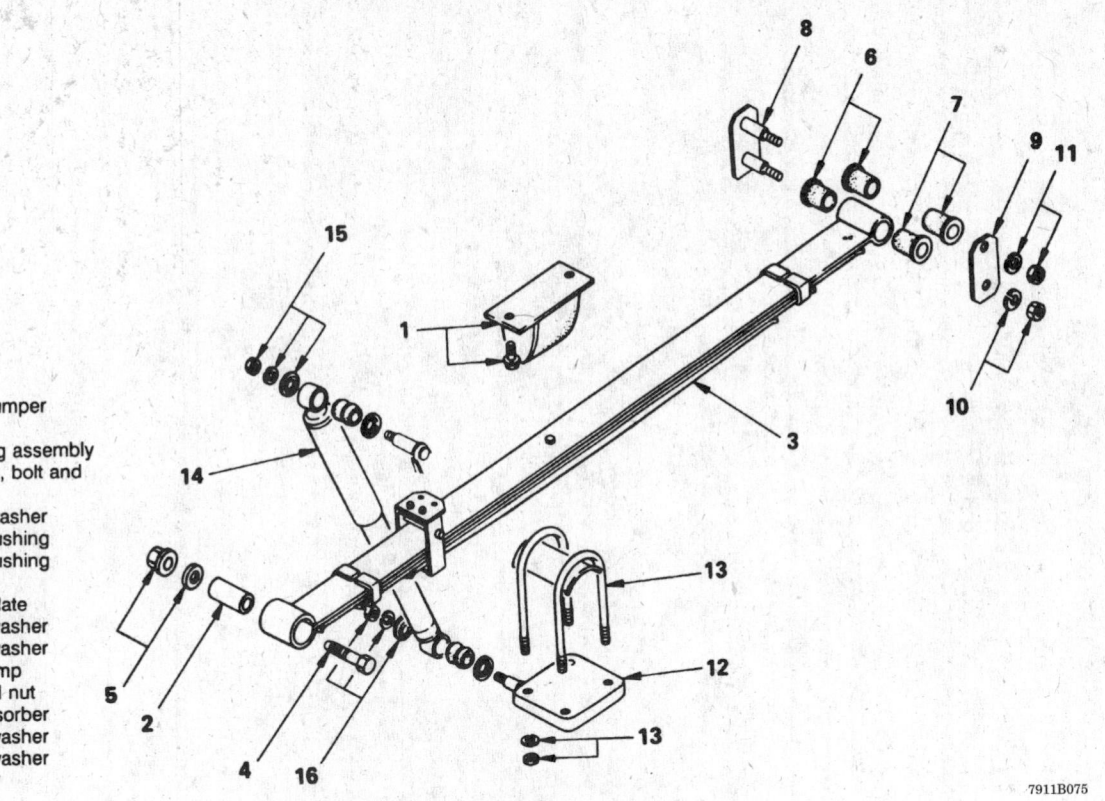

1. Rubber bumper
2. Bushing
3. Leaf spring assembly
4. Spring pin, bolt and washer
5. Nut and washer
6. Rubber bushing
7. Rubber bushing
8. Shackle
9. Shackle plate
10. Nut and washer
11. Nut and washer
12. Lower clamp
13. U-bolt and nut
14. Shock absorber
15. Nut and washer
16. Nut and washer

7911B075

Exploded view of the rear suspension assembly

FIRING ORDERS

NOTE: To avoid confusion, always replace spark plug wires one at a time.

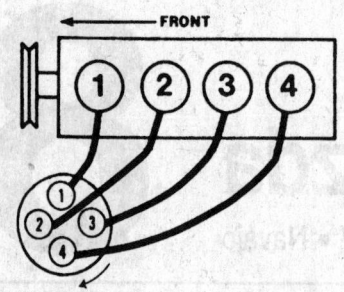

7911C001

2.2L Engine
Engine Firing Order: 1–3–4–2
Distributor Rotation: Clockwise

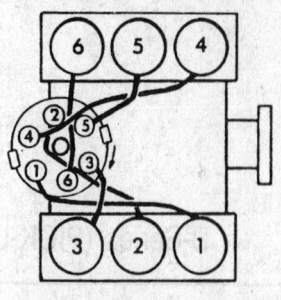

85472002

3.0L (VIN U) Engine
Engine Firing Order:
1–4–2–5–3–6
Distributor Rotation: Clockwise

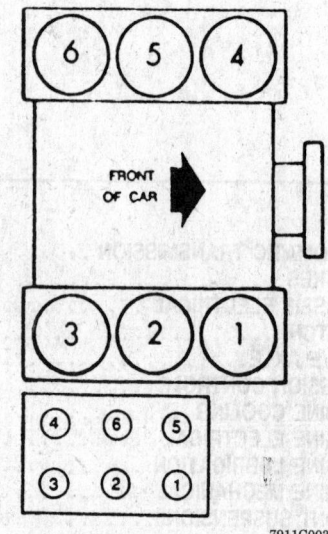

7911C003

4.0L Engine
Engine Firing Order: 1–4–2–5–3–6
Distributorless Ignition System

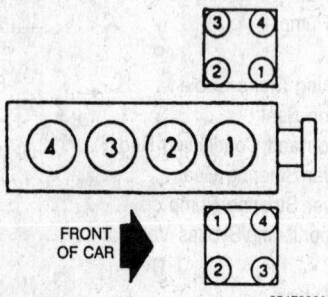

85472001

2.3L Engine
Engine Firing Order: 1–3–4–2
Distributorless Ignition System

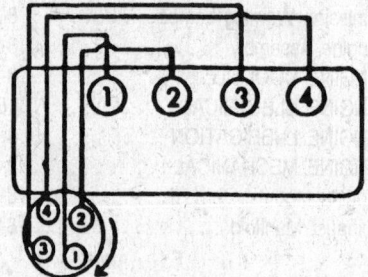

7911C002

2.6L (2606cc) Engine
Engine Firing Order: 1–3–4–2
Distributor Rotation: Clockwise

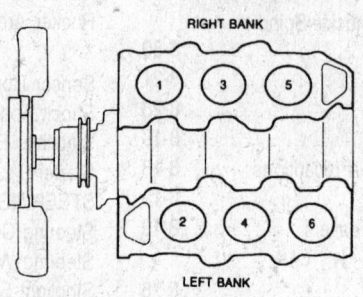

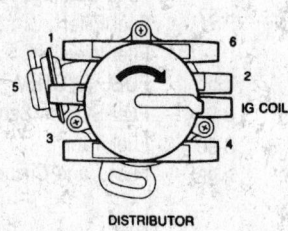

7911C004

3.0L (JE) Engine
Engine Firing Order: 1–2–3–4–5–6
Distributor Rotation: Clockwise

ENGINE ELECTRICAL

NOTE: Disconnecting the negative battery cable on some vehicles may interfere with the functions of the on board computer systems and may require the computer to undergo a relearning process, once the negative battery cable is reconnected.

Distributor

REMOVAL

1. Disconnect the negative battery cable.
2. Remove the distributor cap from the distributor, leaving the spark plug wires attached. If spark plug wire removal is necessary to remove the distributor cap, tag the wires prior to removal so they can be reinstalled in the correct position.
3. Disconnect the electrical connectors and vacuum hose(s), if equipped, from the distributor.
4. Mark the position of the rotor in relation to the distributor housing and the position of the distributor housing on the cylinder head.
5. Remove the distributor hold-down bolt(s) and remove the distributor.
6. Check the distributor O-ring for cuts or other damage and replace, if necessary.

INSTALLATION

Timing Not Disturbed

1. Lubricate the distributor O-ring with clean engine oil.
2. Install the distributor with the hold-down bolt(s), aligning the marks that were made during removal. Tighten the hold-down bolt(s) to 14–19 ft. lbs. (19–25 Nm).
3. Connect the electrical connectors and vacuum hose(s), if equipped.
4. Install the distributor cap on the distributor. Connect the spark plug wires, if removed.
5. Connect the negative battery cable. Start the engine and check the ignition timing.

Timing Disturbed

1. Disconnect the spark plug wire from the No. 1 cylinder spark plug and remove the spark plug. Place a finger over the spark plug hole.

2. Turn the crankshaft in the normal direction of rotation until compression is felt at the spark plug hole.
3. Align the mark on the crankshaft pulley with the TDC mark on the timing belt cover.
4. Lubricate the distributor O-ring with clean engine oil.
5. Turn the distributor shaft until the rotor points to the No. 1 spark plug tower on the distributor cap and install the distributor. Install the distributor hold-down bolt(s) and align the distributor housing with the mark made on the cylinder head during removal. Snug the bolt(s).
6. Connect the electrical connectors and vacuum hose(s), if equipped.
7. Install the distributor cap on the distributor. Connect the spark plug wires, if removed.
8. Install the spark plug in the No. 1 cylinder and connect the spark plug wire.
9. Connect the negative battery cable. Start the engine and adjust the ignition timing. Tighten the distributor hold-down bolt(s) to 14–19 ft. lbs. (19–25 Nm) after the timing has been set.

Distributorless Ignition

REMOVAL AND INSTALLATION

Crankshaft Sensor

1. Disconnect the negative battery cable.
2. Disconnect the sensor electrical connector from the wiring harness.
3. Remove the crankshaft sensor mounting screws and remove the sensor.
4. Installation is the reverse of the removal procedure. Tighten the screws to 75–106 inch lbs. (8.5–12 Nm).

Ignition Module

1. Disconnect the battery cables and remove the battery.
2. Disconnect the electrical connector at the module.
3. Remove the module retaining bolt and remove the module.
4. Installation is the reverse of the removal procedure. Tighten the mounting bolt to 22–31 inch lbs. (2.5–3.5 Nm).

Ignition Coil Pack

1. Disconnect the negative battery cable.
2. Disconnect the electrical harness connector from the coil pack.

3. Remove the spark plug wires by squeezing the locking tabs to release the coil boot retainers.
4. Remove the coil pack retaining screws and remove the coil pack.
5. Installation is the reverse of the removal procedure. Tighten the screws to 40–62 inch lbs. (4.5–7.0 Nm).

Ignition Timing

ADJUSTMENT

Except 2.3L, 3.0L (VIN U) and 4.0L Engines

1. Before starting the engine, clean and mark the timing marks on the timing belt cover and crankshaft pulley.
2. Connect a timing light and tachometer according to the manufacturers instructions.
3. Start the engine and bring to normal operating temperature. Turn all electric loads **OFF**.
4. On fuel injected vehicles, connect a jumper wire between the green 1-pin test connector and ground.
5. Check the idle speed and adjust, if necessary, to the specification on the underhood emission information label.
6. Aim the timing light and verify that the timing marks on the crankshaft pulley and timing belt cover are aligned. If the marks are aligned, proceed to Step 8.
7. If the marks are not aligned, loosen the distributor hold-down bolts and turn the distributor housing to adjust the timing. Tighten the hold-down bolts to 14–19 ft. lbs. (19–25 Nm) and recheck the timing.
8. Shut off the engine. Remove the jumper wire and all test equipment.

2.3L and 4.0L Engines

Timing is preset from the factory at 10 degrees BTDC and is not adjustable.

3.0L (VIN U) Engine

1. Place automatic transmission in **P** or manual transmission in neutral. The air conditioning and heater controls should be in the **OFF** position.
2. Connect a suitable inductive timing light and a tachometer according to the manufacturer's instructions.
3. Disconnect the single wire in-line spout connector or remove the shorting bar from the double wire spout connector.

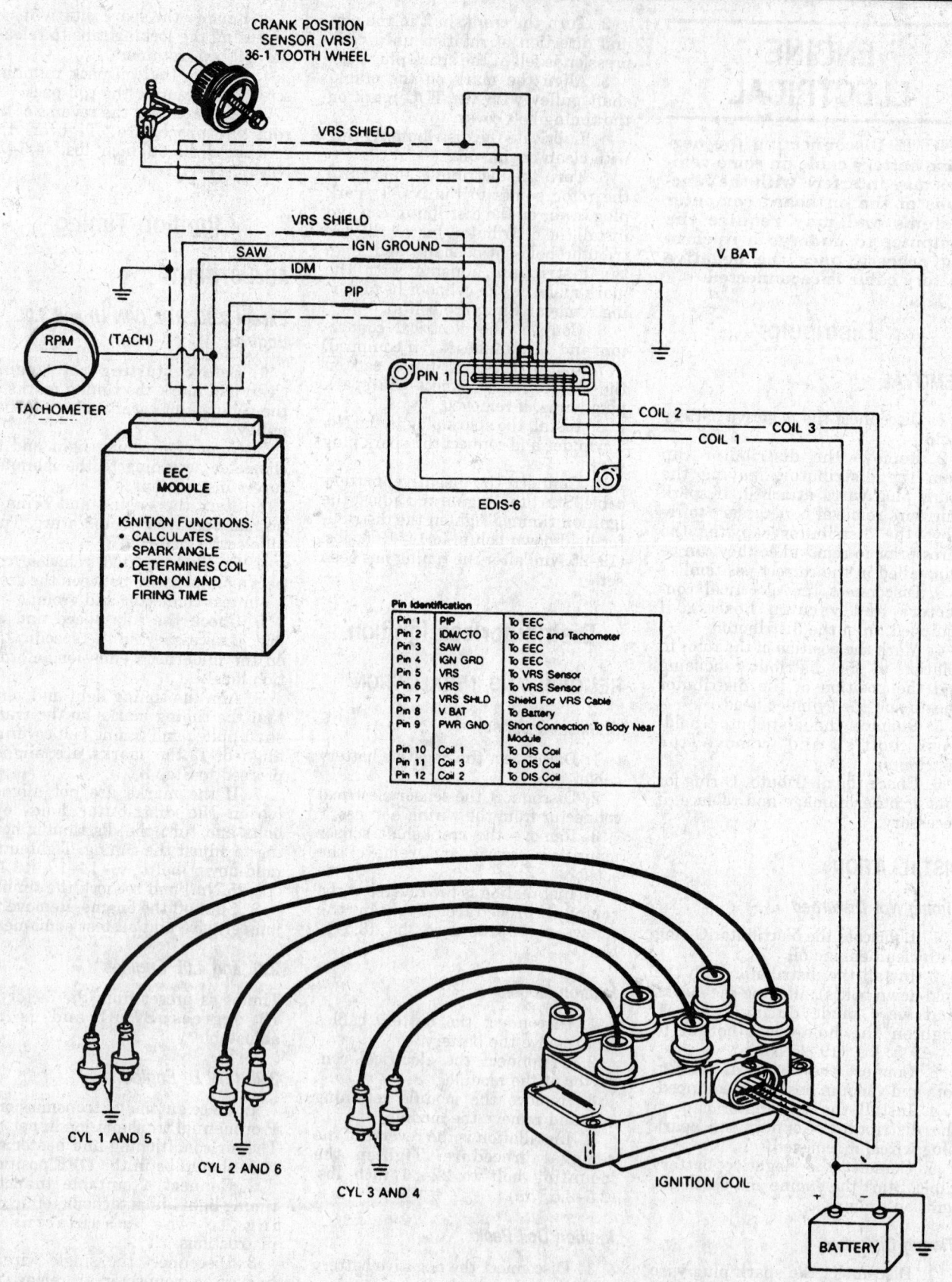

CRANK POSITION
SENSOR (VRS)
36-1 TOOTH WHEEL

VRS SHIELD

VRS SHIELD

SAW
IGN GROUND
IDM
PIP

V BAT

RPM (TACH)

TACHOMETER

PIN 1

COIL 2
COIL 3
COIL 1

EDIS-6

EEC
MODULE

IGNITION FUNCTIONS:
• CALCULATES
  SPARK ANGLE
• DETERMINES COIL
  TURN ON AND
  FIRING TIME

Pin Identification

Pin 1	PIP	To EEC
Pin 2	IDM/CTO	To EEC and Tachometer
Pin 3	SAW	To EEC
Pin 4	IGN GRD	To EEC
Pin 5	VRS	To VRS Sensor
Pin 6	VRS	To VRS Sensor
Pin 7	VRS SHLD	Shield For VRS Cable
Pin 8	V BAT	To Battery
Pin 9	PWR GND	Short Connection To Body Near Module
Pin 10	Coil 1	To DIS Coil
Pin 11	Coil 3	To DIS Coil
Pin 12	Coil 2	To DIS Coil

CYL 1 AND 5

CYL 2 AND 6

CYL 3 AND 4

IGNITION COIL

BATTERY

7911C005

Distributorless ignition system — 4.0L engine

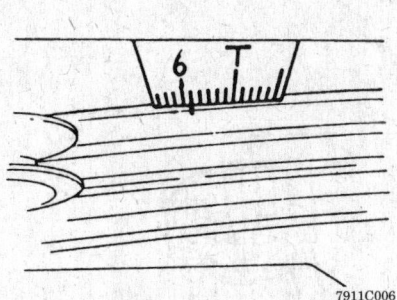

7911C006

Timing mark location — 2.2L and 2.6L engines

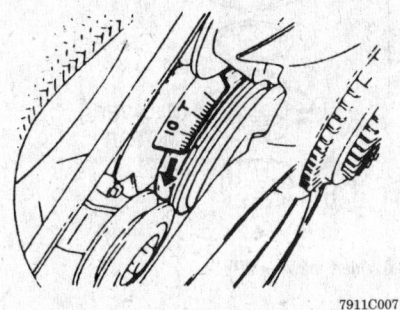

7911C007

Timing mark location — 3.0L (JE) engine

4. Start the engine and bring to normal operating temperature.

NOTE: To set timing correctly, a remote starter should not be used. Use the ignition key only to start the vehicle. Disconnecting the start wire at the starter relay will cause the TFI module to revert to start mode timing after the vehicle is started. Reconnecting the start wire after the vehicle is running will not correct the timing.

5. With the engine at the timing rpm specified, check the initial timing by aiming the timing light at the timing marks and pointer. Refer to the underhood Vehicle Emission Information Label for specifications.

6. If the marks do not align, shut off the engine and loosen the distributor hold-down clamp bolt. Start the engine, aim the timing light and turn the distributor until the timing marks align. Shut off the engine and tighten the distributor hold-down clamp bolt.

7. Reconnect the single wire in-line spout connector or reinstall the shorting bar on the double wire spout connector. Check the timing advance to verify the distributor is advancing beyond the initial setting.

8. Remove the timing light and tachometer.

Alternator

PRECAUTIONS

Several precautions must be observed with alternator equipped vehicles to avoid damage to the unit.

• If the battery is removed for any reason, make sure it is reconnected with the correct polarity. Reversing the battery connections may result in damage to the one-way rectifiers.

• When utilizing a booster battery as a starting aid, always connect the positive to positive terminals and the negative terminal from the booster battery to a good engine ground on the vehicle being started.

• Never use a fast charger as a booster to start vehicles.

• Disconnect the battery cables when charging the battery with a fast charger.

• Never attempt to polarize the alternator.

• Do not use test lights of more than 12V when checking diode continuity.

• Do not short across or ground any of the alternator terminals.

• The polarity of the battery, alternator and regulator must be matched and considered before making any electrical connections within the system.

• Never separate the alternator on an open circuit. Make sure all connections within the circuit are clean and tight.

• Disconnect the battery ground terminal when performing any service on electrical components.

• Disconnect the battery if arc welding is to be done on the vehicle.

BELT TENSION ADJUSTMENT

Except 4.0L Engine

1. Disconnect the negative battery cable.

2. Check the belt tension by applying approximately 22 lbs. pressure mid-way between the pulleys and measuring the belt deflection. Belt deflection specifications are as follows:

2.2L engines — New belt: 0.28–0.31 in., Used belt: 0.31–0.35 in.

2.6L engine — New belt: 0.39–0.47 in., Used belt: 0.43–0.51 in.

3.0L engine — New belt: 0.35–0.39 in., Used belt: 0.39–0.47 in.

3. If belt tension is incorrect, loosen the alternator pivot and adjusting bolts. Position the alternator housing using a suitable tool to attain correct belt tension. Be careful not to damage the alternator housing.

4. When correct belt tension is achieved, tighten the alternator adjusting bolt to 14–19 ft. lbs. (19–25 Nm) on all except 2.2L engine. On 2.2L engine, tighten the adjusting bolt to 23–34 ft. lbs. (31–46 Nm).

5. Tighten the alternator pivot bolt to 27–38 ft. lbs. (37–52 Nm).

6. Connect the negative battery cable.

4.0L Engine

Belt tension is maintained by an automatic tensioner; no adjustment is necessary.

REMOVAL AND INSTALLATION

1. Disconnect the negative battery cable.

2. Disconnect the electrical connectors at the alternator. Remove the wiring connector bracket on 4.0L engine.

3. On the 3.0L engine, loosen the power steering pump drive belt adjusting locknut and remove the drive belt. Remove the power steering pump pulley.

4. On all except 4.0L engine, loosen the alternator adjusting and pivot bolts and remove the drive belt. On 4.0L engine, loosen the drive belt tensioner and remove the drive belt.

5. Remove the alternator bolts and remove the alternator.

6. Installation is the reverse of the removal procedure. Tighten the alternator mounting bolts on 4.0L engine to 22–30 ft. lbs. (30–40 Nm). Adjust the belt tension on all except 4.0L engine.

7. Tighten the power steering pump pulley nut to 29–43 ft. lbs. (39–59 Nm).

Starter

REMOVAL AND INSTALLATION

Except 4WD MPV

1. Disconnect the negative battery cable. Raise and safely support the vehicle.

2. Disconnect the electrical connectors from the starter.

3. Remove the starter mounting bolts and remove the starter.

4. Installation is the reverse of the removal procedure. Tighten the starter mounting bolts to 27–38 ft. lbs. (37–52 Nm) except 4.0L engine or 15–20 ft. lbs. (21–27 Nm) on 4.0L engine.

4WD MPV

1. Disconnect the negative battery cable.
2. Remove the alternator.
3. Raise and safely support the vehicle. Remove the splash shields.
4. Remove the power steering pump mounting bolts and position the pump aside, without disconnecting the power steering hoses.
5. Remove the automatic transmission cooler line brackets.
6. Mark the position of the driveshaft on the axle flange and remove the front driveshaft.
7. Remove the wiring harness bracket and the automatic transmission cooler line bracket that is next to the starter.
8. Disconnect the electrical connectors from the starter.
9. Remove the fuel and brake line shield.
10. Remove the starter mounting bolts and remove the starter.
11. Installation is the reverse of the removal procedure. Tighten the starter mounting bolts to 27–38 ft. lbs. (37–52 Nm).

CHASSIS ELECTRICAL

Heater Blower Motor

REMOVAL AND INSTALLATION

Except 1994–96 B-Series Pick-Up and Navajo

1. Disconnect the negative battery cable.
2. On 1992–93 B-Series Pick-Up, remove the ECU. On MPV, remove the passenger side lower panel and undercover.
3. Disconnect the electrical connector from the blower motor.
4. Remove the attaching screws and remove the blower motor.
5. Installation is the reverse of removal procedure.

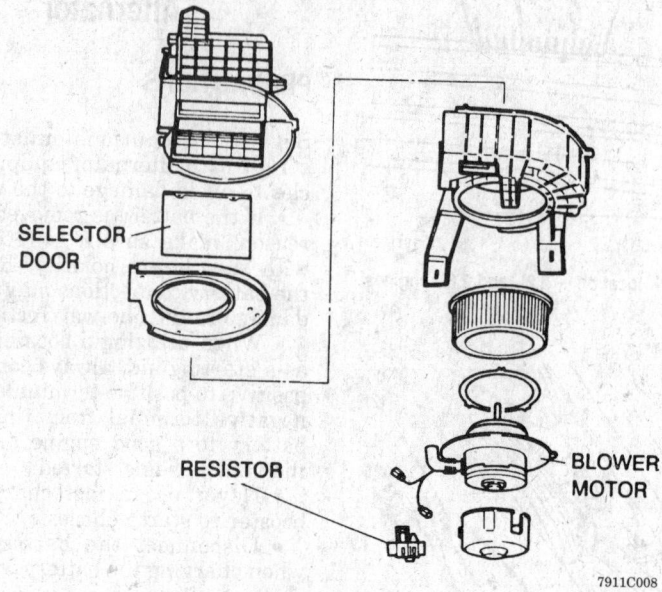

Blower motor assembly exploded view — MPV

7911C008

1994–96 B-Series Pick-Up and Navajo

1. Disconnect the negative battery cable.
2. Remove the air cleaner.
3. Disconnect the wire harness connector from the blower motor by pushing down on the tab while pulling the connector off at the motor.
4. If equipped with air conditioning, remove the 3 solenoid box cover retaining bolts and the solenoid box cover.
5. Disconnect the blower motor cooling tube at the blower motor.
6. Remove the 3 attaching screws and remove the blower motor.
7. If necessary, remove the blower wheel hub push-nut and remove the blower wheel.
8. Installation is the reverse of the removal procedure.

Window Wiper Motor

REMOVAL AND INSTALLATION

Front

1992–93 B-SERIES PICK-UP

1. Disconnect the negative battery cable. Remove the wiper arm/blade assembly.

2. Remove the rubber seal from the leading edge of the cowl grille.
3. Remove the attaching screws and remove the cowl grille.
4. Remove the access hole covers.
5. Remove the bolts attaching the wiper shaft drives.
6. Matchmark the position of the wiper linkage in relation to the face of the wiper motor. Disconnect the wiper linkage from the wiper motor.
7. Disconnect the electrical connector from the wiper motor.
8. Remove the mounting bolts and the wiper motor.
To install:
9. Position the wiper motor and install the mounting bolts. Tighten to 61–87 inch lbs. (6.9–9.8 Nm).
10. Connect the electrical connector.
11. Attach the wiper linkage to the motor, aligning the mark that was made during removal.
12. Install the bolts attaching the wiper shaft drives and tighten to 61–87 inch lbs. (6.9–9.8 Nm).
13. Install the access hole covers, cowl grille and seal.
14. Install the wiper arm/blade assemblies. Adjust the arm height to 0.8 in. (20mm) from the lower windshield moulding and tighten the arm retaining nuts to 7.2–10 ft. lbs. (9.8–14 Nm).

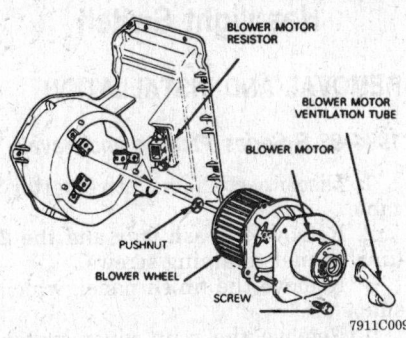

Blower motor assembly exploded view — Navajo

15. Connect the negative battery cable and check wiper operation.

MPV

1. Disconnect the negative battery cable.

2. Disconnect the electrical connector from the wiper motor.

3. Disconnect the wiper linkage from the motor crank arm. If necessary to remove the crank arm from the motor, matchmark the arm to the bracket prior to removal.

4. Remove the mounting bolts and remove the wiper motor.

To install:

5. Position the wiper motor and install the mounting bolts. Tighten to 61–87 inch lbs. (6.9–9.8 Nm).

6. If removed, install the motor crank arm, aligning the marks that were made during removal.

7. Connect the wiper linkage to the motor crank arm. Connect the electrical connector.

8. Make sure when in the park position, the wiper blades are 0.98–1.38 in. (25–35mm) from the lower windshield moulding.

1994–96 B–SERIES PICK-UP AND NAVAJO

1. Turn the wiper switch **ON**. Turn the ignition switch **ON** until the blades are straight up, then turn the ignition **OFF** to keep them there.

2. Disconnect the negative battery cable, then disconnect the electrical connector from the wiper motor.

3. Remove the right wiper arm and blade assembly. Remove the right pivot nut and allow the linkage to drop into the cowl.

4. Remove the linkage access cover, located on the right side of the dash panel, near the wiper motor.

5. Reach through the access cover opening and unsnap the wiper motor clip. Push the clip away from the linkage until it clears the nib on the crank pin, then push the clip off the linkage. Remove the linkage from the crank pin.

6. Remove the 3 attaching screws and remove the wiper motor.

To install:

7. Install the motor with the attaching screws. Tighten to 60–85 inch lbs. (6.8–9.6 Nm). Connect the motor electrical connector.

8. Install the clip completely onto the right linkage, making sure it is fully seated. Do not put the linkage on the motor crank pin and then try to install the clip.

9. Install the left and right linkage onto the wiper motor crank pin. Pull the linkage onto the crank pin until it snaps into place. The clip is properly installed if the nib is protruding through the center of the clip.

10. Install the right wiper pivot shaft and nut. Tighten the nut to 84–110 inch lbs. (9.5–12.5 Nm).

11. Connect the negative battery cable and turn the ignition **ON**. Turn the wiper switch **OFF** so the wiper motor will park, then turn the ignition **OFF**. Install the right linkage access cover.

12. Install the right wiper blade and arm assembly and test the system.

Rear

MPV

1. Disconnect the negative battery cable.

2. Remove the wiper arm cover, retaining nut and the wiper arm/blade assembly.

3. Remove the seal cap and outer bushing.

4. Remove the liftgate trim panel and screen.

5. Disconnect the electrical connector, remove the mounting bolts and remove the wiper motor.

To install:

6. Position the wiper motor and install the attaching bolts. Tighten to 61–87 inch lbs. (6.9–9.8 Nm).

7. Connect the electrical connector.

8. Install the screen and liftgate trim panel.

9. Install the seal cap and outer bushing.

10. Connect the negative battery cable. Set the motor shaft to the park position by turning the rear wiper switch from **ON** to **OFF**.

11. Install the wiper arm/blade assembly so the blade is 0.98–1.38 in. (25–35mm) from the lower window moulding.

12. Install the arm retaining nut and tighten to 52–87 inch lbs. (5.9–9.8 Nm). Install the wiper arm cover.

1994–96 B–SERIES PICK-UP AND NAVAJO

1. Disconnect the negative battery cable.

2. Remove the wiper arm and blade assembly.

3. Remove the liftgate inner trim panel.

4. Remove the 3 motor bracket attaching screws and pull the motor and bracket assembly out of the rubber grommet.

5. Disconnect the electrical connector and disengage the wiring locator pins. Remove the motor.

To install:

6. Position the motor in the liftgate rubber grommet and install the attaching screws.

7. Connect the electrical connector and install the wiring locator pins in the holes provided.

8. Install the wiper arm and blade assembly. Connect the negative battery cable and check wiper operation.

9. Install the liftgate inner trim panel.

Window Wiper Switch

REMOVAL AND INSTALLATION

Front

The function of the front wipers is controlled by the combination switch.

Rear

MPV

1. Disconnect the negative battery cable.

2. Remove the front cluster panel.

3. Remove the attaching screws from the left cluster switch, disconnect the electrical connectors and remove the rear wiper switch.

4. Installation is the reverse of the removal procedure.

1994–96 B–SERIES PICK-UP AND NAVAJO

1. Disconnect the negative battery cable.

2. Remove the 2 ash tray retaining screws and remove the ash tray.

3. Remove the cluster trim panel, which is held on by clips.

4. Remove the snap-in switch mounting bezel containing the switches and disconnect the electrical connector.

5. Remove the switch from the mounting bezel by pushing on the switch from the connector side until the snap-in mounting clips release.

6. Installation is the reverse of the removal procedure.

Instrument Cluster

REMOVAL AND INSTALLATION

1992–93 B-Series Pick-Up

1. Disconnect the negative battery cable.
2. Remove the screws and the instrument cluster hood.
3. Remove the instrument cluster attaching screws.
4. Pull the cluster rearward enough to gain access to the rear of the cluster. Disconnect the electrical connectors and speedometer cable.
5. Remove the instrument cluster.
6. Installation is the reverse of the removal procedure.

MPV

1. Disconnect the negative battery cable.
2. Remove the screws attaching the front cluster assembly. Disconnect the electrical connectors from the cluster assembly switches and remove the cluster assembly.
3. Remove the instrument cluster attaching screws.
4. Pull the cluster rearward enough to gain access to the rear of the cluster. Disconnect the electrical connectors and speedometer cable.
5. If equipped with automatic transmission, remove the lock pin from the shift position indicator wire end.
6. Remove the instrument cluster.
7. Installation is the reverse of the removal procedure. If equipped with automatic transmission, adjust the shift position indicator as follows:
   a. Using moderate force, pull the shift position indicator wire end out fully to set the indicator position. Only pull the wire until the indicator is felt to bottom. Do not use excessive force.
   b. Using a small prybar, properly align the spring hook. Pull the indicator wire until it just stops. Be careful not to move the position indicator after aligning.
   c. Install a suitable adjusting pin in the position indicator wire end.
   d. Install the instrument cluster.
   e. Make sure the transmission selector lever is in **P**.
   f. Mount the shift position indicator wire housing to the outer bracket using the clip. Hook the position indicator wire to the selector.

   g. Turn the ignition switch to **ACC**. Move the selector lever from **P** to **L** to **P**.
   h. Remove the adjusting pin and install the lock pin.

1994–96 B-Series Pick-Up and Navajo

1. Disconnect the negative battery cable.
2. Open the ash tray and remove the 2 screws attaching the ash tray and instrument cluster trim panel. Remove the ash tray.
3. Unsnap the cluster trim panel by pulling rearward around the edge of the panel. Depress the hazard warning switch on the steering column and remove the cluster trim panel.
4. Remove the 4 screws securing the instrument cluster to the instrument panel.
5. If equipped with automatic transmission, remove the 2 screws attaching the shift position indicator to the cluster and slide the indicator down and out of the cluster. Leave the indicator connections undisturbed.
6. Pull the cluster assembly rearward to gain access to the speedometer cable. Disconnect the cable and the 2 wiring harness connectors and remove the cluster.

NOTE: If there is not enough room to disengage the cable from the speedometer, it may be necessary to disconnect the cable at the transmission and pull the cable through the cowl, to allow room to reach the speedometer quick disconnect.

7. Installation is the reverse of the removal procedure. Apply an approximately ³/₁₆ in. diameter ball of silicone dielectric compound in the drive hole of the speedometer head prior to installation.

Speedometer

REMOVAL AND INSTALLATION

1. Disconnect the negative battery cable. Remove the instrument cluster.
2. Remove the trip meter and/or clock adjusting knob(s), if necessary.
3. Separate the lens and mask assembly from the cluster.
4. Remove the mounting screws and remove the speedometer.
5. Installation is the reverse of the removal procedure.

Headlight Switch

REMOVAL AND INSTALLATION

1994–96 B-Series Pick-Up and Navajo

1. Disconnect the negative battery cable.
2. Remove the ash tray and the 2 finish panel retaining screws.
3. Remove the finish panel, which snaps off.
4. Remove the rear wiper switch and rear defrost switch.
5. Pull the headlight switch knob to the full **ON** position. Reach through the opening below the headlight switch, depress the shaft release button on the switch and remove the knob and shaft assembly.
6. Remove the headlight switch retaining bezel nut. Pull the switch downward and through the opening to disconnect the connector.
7. Installation is the reverse of the removal procedure.

Combination Switch

REMOVAL AND INSTALLATION

Except 1994–96 B-Series Pick-Up and Navajo

1. Disconnect the negative battery cable.
2. Remove the steering wheel.
3. Remove the upper and lower column shroud halves.
4. Disconnect the electrical connectors to the switch.
5. Remove the attaching screw(s), release the lock, if required and remove the switch.
6. Installation is the reverse of the removal procedure.

1994–96 B-Series Pick-Up and Navajo

1. Disconnect the negative battery cable.
2. Remove the steering column shroud.
3. Remove the 2 self-tapping screws that attach the combination switch to the steering column casting. Disengage the switch from the casting.
4. Disconnect the 3 electrical connectors, being careful not to damage the locking tabs. Do not damage the shift position indicator cable.
To install:
5. Connect the 3 switch electrical connectors. The wiring for the switch is to be routed under the shift position indicator cable.

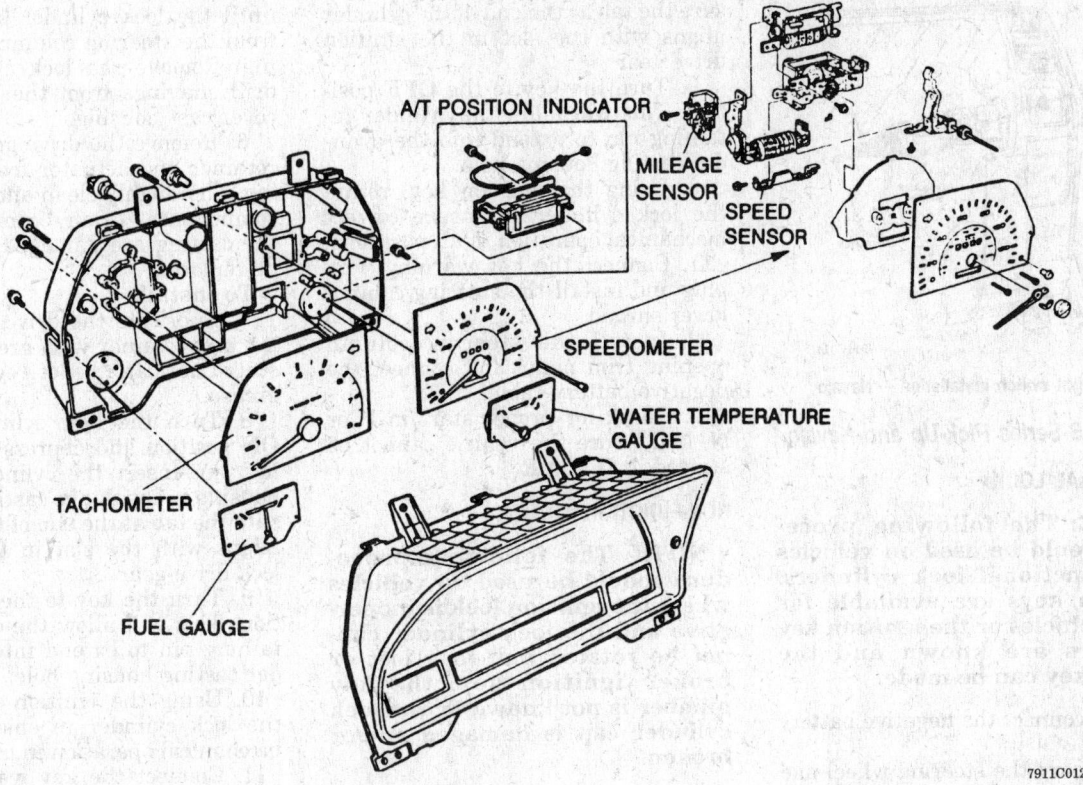

Instrument cluster exploded view — MPV

7911C012

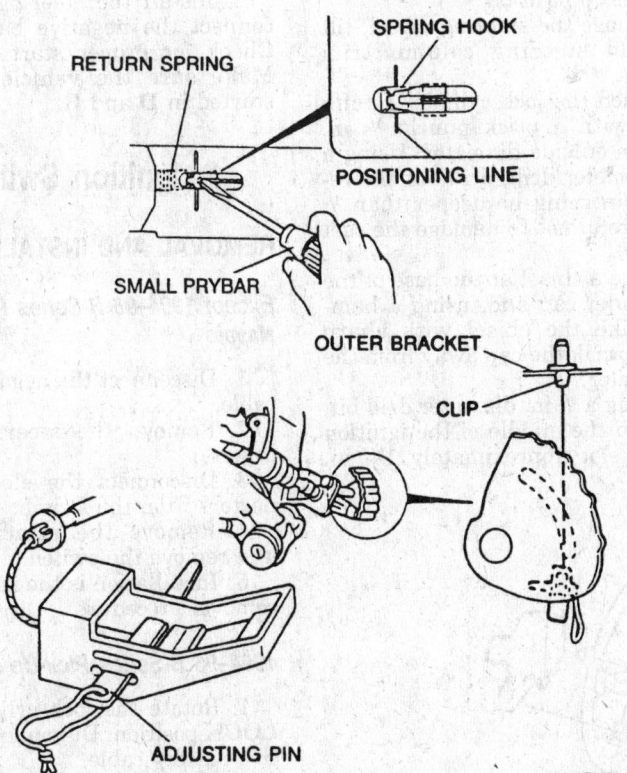

7911C010

Shift position indicator adjustment — MPV

6. Install the switch with the self-tapping screws. Tighten the screws to 18–27 inch lbs. (2–3 Nm).

7. If equipped with automatic transmission, make sure the shift position indicator adjustment is correct.

8. Install the shroud and connect the negative battery cable. Check the steering column for proper operation.

Ignition Lock

REMOVAL AND INSTALLATION

Except 1994–96 B-Series Pick-Up and Navajo

1. Disconnect the negative battery cable.

2. Remove the combination switch.

3. Use a chisel to make a groove in the head of each lock retaining bolt, then remove the bolts using a suitable tool.

4. Remove the lock assembly.

5. Installation is the reverse of the removal procedure. Install new lock retaining bolts and tighten them until the heads break off.

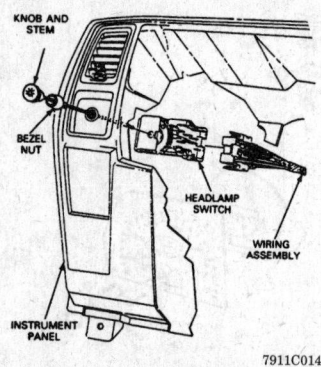

7911C014

Headlight switch installation — Navajo

1994–96 B-Series Pick-Up and Navajo

FUNCTIONAL LOCK

NOTE: The following procedure should be used on vehicles with functional lock cylinders. Ignition keys are available for these vehicles or the ignition key numbers are known and the proper key can be made.

1. Disconnect the negative battery cable.

2. Remove the steering wheel and shroud.

3. Using the ignition key, turn the lock cylinder to the **ON** position. If equipped with an automatic transmission, the selector lever must first be placed in **P**.

4. Push down on the lock cylinder retaining pin with a ⅛ in. diameter wire pin or small punch. Pull the lock cylinder from the column housing.

5. Disconnect the lock cylinder wiring plug from the horn brush wiring connector.

To install:

6. Lubricate the lock cylinder with grease.

7. Turn the lock cylinder to the **ON** position and depress the retaining pin.

8. Insert the lock cylinder into its housing in the flange casting, making

sure the tab at the end of the cylinder aligns with the slot in the ignition drive gear.

9. Turn the key to the **OFF** position. This will allow the cylinder retaining pin to extend into the cylinder casting housing hole.

10. Using the ignition key, rotate the lock cylinder to ensure correct mechanical operation in all positions.

11. Connect the key warning wire plug and install the steering column lower shroud.

12. Install the steering column opening trim panel and connect the negative battery cable.

13. Check for proper start in **P** or **N**. Make sure the vehicle cannot be started in **D** and **R**.

NON-FUNCTIONAL LOCK

NOTE: The following procedure should be used on vehicles where the ignition lock is inoperative and the lock cylinder cannot be rotated due to a lost or broken ignition key, the key number is not known or the lock cylinder cap is damaged and/or broken.

1. Disconnect the negative battery cable. If equipped with tilt wheel, tilt to the full up position.

2. Remove the steering wheel, tilt lever and steering column trim shrouds.

3. Punch the lock cylinder retaining pin with a prick punch, ⅛ in. maximum outside diameter. Using a ⅛ in. diameter drill, drill out the retaining pin going no deeper than ½ in. Be careful not to damage the cast housing.

4. Place a chisel at the base of the lock cylinder cap and, using a hammer, strike the chisel with sharp blows to break the cap away from the lock cylinder.

5. Using a ⅜ in. diameter drill bit, drill down the middle of the ignition lock key slot approximately 1¾ in.

until the lock cylinder breaks loose from the steering column cover casting. Remove the lock cylinder and drill shavings from the base of the cover cast housing.

6. Remove the drive gear, bearing retainer and actuator from the casting. Thoroughly clean and inspect all components. If any components or the casting are damaged, they must be replaced.

To install:

7. Lubricate the drive gear, bearing and retainer with grease and install. Lubricate the lock cylinder with grease.

8. Turn the lock cylinder to the **ON** position and depress the retaining pin. Insert the cylinder into its housing in the flange casting, making sure the tab at the end of the cylinder aligns with the slot in the ignition lock drive gear.

9. Turn the key to the **OFF** position. This will allow the cylinder retaining pin to extend into the cylinder casting housing hole.

10. Using the ignition key, rotate the lock cylinder to ensure correct mechanical operation in all positions.

11. Connect the key warning wire plug and install the steering column shrouds.

12. Install the steering wheel and connect the negative battery cable. Check for proper start in **P** or **N**. Make sure the vehicle cannot be started in **D** and **R**.

Ignition Switch

REMOVAL AND INSTALLATION

Except 1994–96 B-Series Pick-Up and Navajo

1. Disconnect the negative battery cable.

2. Remove the steering column covers.

3. Disconnect the electrical connectors from the switch.

4. Remove the attaching screw and remove the switch.

5. Installation is the reverse of the removal procedure.

1994–96 B-Series Pick-Up and Navajo

1. Rotate the lock cylinder to the **LOCK** position. Disconnect the negative battery cable.

2. Remove the steering wheel.

3. If equipped with tilt wheel, remove the upper extension housing shroud by squeezing it at the 6 and 12 o'clock positions and popping it

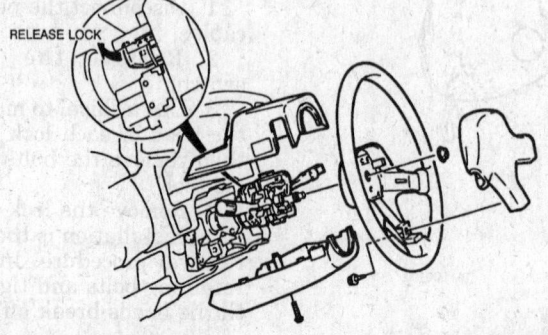

7911C015

Combination switch removal — MPV; B-Series Pick-Up similar

free of the retaining plate at the 3 o'clock position.

4. Remove the trim shroud halves.

5. Disconnect the switch electrical connector.

6. Remove the retaining nuts and disengage the ignition switch from the actuator rod.

7. Installation is the reverse of the removal procedure.

Stoplight Switch

ADJUSTMENT

Except 1994–96 B-Series Pick-Up and Navajo

1. Disconnect the negative battery cable.

2. Disconnect the electrical connector from the switch.

3. Loosen the switch locknut and turn the switch until it does not contact the pedal.

4. Loosen the booster pushrod locknut and turn the rod to adjust the pedal height to;

7.09–7.28 in. (180–185mm)—B-Series Pick-Up

7.52–7.91 in. (191–201mm)—MPV

5. Depress the brake pedal a few times to eliminate the vacuum in the system. Gently depress the pedal and check the free-play. Turn the booster pushrod to adjust the free-play to 0.16–0.28 in. (4–7mm).

6. Tighten the booster pushrod locknut.

7. Turn the stoplight switch until it contacts the pedal, then turn an additional ½ turn. Tighten the switch locknut.

8. Connect the electrical connector and the negative battery cable.

1994–96 B-Series Pick-Up and Navajo

The stoplight switch is not adjustable.

REMOVAL AND INSTALLATION

Except 1994–96 B-Series Pick-Up and Navajo

1. Disconnect the negative battery cable.

2. Disconnect the electrical connector from the switch.

3. Loosen the switch locknut and remove the switch.

4. Installation is the reverse of the removal procedure. Adjust the switch.

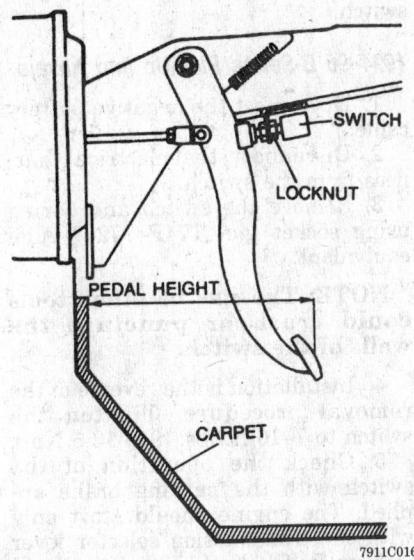

Pedal height measurement location for stoplight switch and clutch switch adjustment

1994–96 B-Series Pick-Up and Navajo

1. Disconnect the negative battery cable. Disconnect the electrical connector from the switch. The locking tab must be lifted before the connector can be removed.

2. Remove the hairpin clip and slide the switch, booster pushrod, nylon washer and bushing away from the pedal. Remove the washer, then the switch by sliding the switch up or down.

To install:

3. Position the switch so the U-shaped side is nearest the pedal and directly over/under the pin. Then slide the switch up/down installing the booster pushrod and bushing between the switch side plates.

4. Push the switch and pushrod assembly firmly toward the brake pedal arm. Install the outside plastic washer to the pin and install the hairpin clip. Do not substitute for this clip. Use only factory supplied hairpin clips.

5. Connect the electrical connector to the switch and connect the negative battery cable. Make sure the switch wire harness has sufficient length to travel with the switch during the full stroke of the brake pedal. Check the switch for proper operation.

Clutch Switch

ADJUSTMENT

Except 1994–96 B-Series Pick-Up and Navajo

1. Disconnect the negative battery cable.

2. Disconnect the electrical connector from the switch.

3. Loosen the switch locknut and turn the switch until the clutch pedal height is:

7.13–7.52 in. (181–191mm)—B2200

7.52–7.91 in. (191–201mm)—B2600

8.19–8.58 in. (208–218mm)—MPV

4. Tighten the locknut.

5. Connect the electrical connector and the negative battery cable.

1994–96 B-Series Pick-Up and Navajo

The clutch switch is not adjustable.

REMOVAL AND INSTALLATION

Except 1994–96 B-Series Pick-Up and Navajo

1. Disconnect the negative battery cable.

2. Disconnect the electrical connector from the switch.

3. Loosen the switch locknut and remove the switch.

4. Installation is the reverse of the removal procedure. Adjust the switch.

1994–96 B-Series Pick-Up and Navajo

1. Disconnect the negative battery cable. Disconnect the wiring harness from the switch.

2. Pull the orientation clip away from the switch to separate it from the pin on the switch.

3. Rotate the switch to expose the plastic retainer.

4. Push the tabs together to allow the retainer to slide rearward and separate from the switch.

5. Remove the switch from the pushrod.

6. Installation is the reverse of the removal procedure.

Neutral Safety Switch

ADJUSTMENT

Except 1994–96 B-Series Pick-Up and Navajo

HYDRAULICALLY-CONTROLLED TRANSMISSION

1. Raise and safely support the vehicle.
2. Move the manual shaft to the **N** position.
3. Loosen the switch mounting bolts.
4. Remove the screw on the switch body and move the switch so the screw hole is aligned with the small hole inside the switch. Check the alignment by inserting an approximately 0.079 in. (2mm) diameter pin through the holes.
5. Tighten the mounting bolts to 43–61 inch lbs. (4.9–6.9 Nm) and remove the alignment pin.
6. Install the screw in the switch body and check for proper operation. The starter should operate only when the transmission is in the **P** or **N** range.

ELECTRONICALLY-CONTROLLED TRANSMISSION

1. Raise and safely support the vehicle.
2. Move the manual shaft to the **N** position.
3. Loosen the switch mounting bolts.
4. Align the holes of the switch and the manual shaft lever and insert an approximately 0.157 in. (4mm) diameter pin through the holes.
5. Tighten the mounting bolts to 22–35 inch lbs. (2.5–3.9 Nm) and remove the pin.
6. Check the switch for proper operation. The starter should operate only when the transmission is in the **P** or **N** range.

1994–96 B-Series Pick-Up and Navajo

The neutral safety switch is not adjustable.

REMOVAL AND INSTALLATION

Except 1994–96 B-Series Pick-Up and Navajo

1. Disconnect the negative battery cable. Raise and safely support the vehicle.
2. Disconnect the manual shaft lever from the transmission.

3. Remove the mounting bolts and the switch.
4. Installation is the reverse of the removal procedure. Adjust the switch.

1994–96 B-Series Pick-Up and Navajo

1. Disconnect the negative battery cable.
2. Disconnect the electrical harness from the switch.
3. Remove the switch and O-ring using socket tool T74P–77247–A or equivalent.

NOTE: The use of other tools could crush or puncture the walls of the switch.

4. Installation is the reverse of the removal procedure. Tighten the switch to 7–10 ft. lbs. (9.5–13.6 Nm).
5. Check the operation of the switch with the parking brake applied. The engine should start only with the transmission selector lever in **N** or **P**. The back-up lights should illuminate only with the selector lever in **R**.

Fuses and Circuit Breakers

LOCATION

1992–93 B-Series Pick-Up

The fuse box is located under the instrument panel, to the left of the steering column. There is also a small fuse box under the hood, on the right inner fender, that contains the main vehicle fuses.

MPV

The main fuse block is located on the right side of the engine compartment. There is also a fuse box located above the left kick panel.

1994–96 B-Series Pick-Up and Navajo

The fuse panel is located under the instrument panel to the left of the steering column. There is also a power distribution box located in the engine compartment on the right inner fender, next to the starter relay, which contains mostly high-current fuses.

NOTE: All circuit breakers on Navajo are located in the fuse panel except for a 4.5 amp circuit breaker for the rear wiper/washer and a 22 amp circuit breaker for the high beams which is integral with the headlight switch.

Relays

LOCATION

1992–93 B-Series Pick-Up

Circuit Open Relay — located on the left kick panel.
Daytime Running Lights (DRL) Relay — located on the firewall in the engine compartment on Canadian vehicles.
EGI Main Relay — located at the right front of the engine compartment.
Fuel Cut Relay — located under the left side of the dash.
Horn Relay — located on the right inner fender in the engine compartment.

MPV

Air Conditioning Relay — located on the right inner fender in the engine compartment.
ALL Relay — located on the left inner fender in the engine compartment.
Blower Motor Relay — located on the left inner fender in the engine compartment.
Change Motor Relay No. 1 — located on the firewall in the engine compartment.
Change Motor Relay No. 2 — located on the firewall in the engine compartment.
Circuit Opening Relay — located in the front of the engine compartment.
Condenser Fan Relay — located on the right inner fender in the engine compartment.
Daytime Running Light (DRL) Relay — located on the left inner fender in the engine compartment.
EGI Main Relay — located on the left inner fender in the engine compartment.
Horn Relay — located on the left inner fender in the engine compartment.
Kickdown Relay — located on the left inner fender in the engine compartment.
Rear Blower Motor Relay — located on the rear blower unit.
Rear Cooler Relay No. 1 — located on the rear cooling unit.
Rear Cooler Relay No. 2 — located on the rear cooling unit.
Rear Cooler Relay No. 3 — located on the rear cooling unit.
Rear Wheel Anti-Lock Brake Relay — located on the left inner fender in the engine compartment.

1994–96 B-Series Pick-Up and Navajo

Air Conditioning Cutoff Relay — located under the power distribution box at the right fender apron.

Fuel Pump Relay — located under the power distribution box at the right fender apron.

Stop/Turn Signal Relays — located on the left rear quarter panel.

Low Oil Level Relay — located on right side of dash panel.

Starter Relay — located on the fender apron in the right front of the engine compartment.

Tail light Relay — located at the left rear quarter panel.

Computers

LOCATION

The Engine Control Unit (ECU) is located at the right kick panel on B-Series Pick-Ups and Navajo or under the center of the dash on MPV.

Flashers

LOCATION

The turn signal/hazard flasher unit is located under the left side of the dash on B-Series Pick-Up or behind the driver's side kick panel on MPV. On Navajo, both the turn signal and hazard flashers are attached to the fuse panel.

Cruise Control

ADJUSTMENT

Actuator Cable

EXCEPT 1994–96 B–SERIES PICK-UP AND NAVAJO

1. Remove the clamp.
2. Adjust the nut so the actuator cable free-play is 0.04–0.12 in. (1–3mm) when the cable is pressed lightly.
3. Reinstall the clamp.

1994–96 B–SERIES PICK-UP AND NAVAJO

1. Remove the cable retaining clip.
2. Disengage the throttle positioner.
3. Set the engine at hot idle.
4. Pull on the actuator cable to take up any slack. Maintain a light tension on the cable.
5. While holding the cable, insert the cable retaining clip and snap securely.

(B2200)

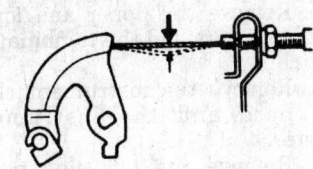

(B2600I)

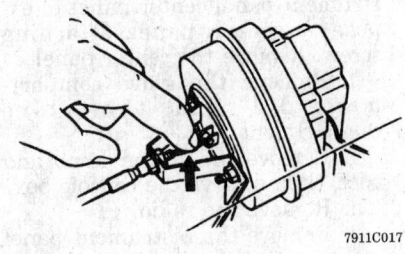

7911C017

Actuator cable free-play adjustment — B Series Pick-Up

Vacuum Dump Valve

1994–96 B–SERIES PICK-UP AND NAVAJO

1. Firmly hold the brake pedal in the up, released, position.
2. Push in the dump valve until the valve bottoms against the pad on the brake pedal.

Clutch and Stoplight Switches

EXCEPT 1994–96 B–SERIES PICK-UP AND NAVAJO

When replacing these switches, be sure to adjust the pedal height to the proper specification.

ENGINE COOLING

Radiator

REMOVAL AND INSTALLATION

Except 1994–96 B-Series Pick-Up and Navajo

1. Disconnect the negative battery cable and remove the radiator cap.

2. Position a drain pan under the radiator and open the draincock to drain the radiator.
3. On MPV, remove the fresh air duct.
4. Disconnect the upper and lower radiator hoses and the coolant reservoir hose.
5. If equipped with automatic transmission, disconnect and plug the oil cooler lines at the radiator.
6. Remove the cooling fan retaining nuts and the fan.
7. Remove the fan shroud attaching bolts and remove the shroud. Disconnect the thermoswitch electrical connector, if necessary.
8. Remove the radiator attaching bolts and remove the radiator.

To install:

9. Position the radiator and install the attaching bolts. Tighten to 16–22 ft. lbs. (22–30 Nm).
10. Install the fan shroud with the attaching bolts and tighten to 69–95 inch lbs. (7.8–11.0 Nm). Connect the thermoswitch electrical connector, if necessary.
11. Install the cooling fan with the retaining nuts and tighten to 69–95 inch lbs. (7.8–11.0 Nm).
12. If equipped with automatic transmission, unplug and connect the oil cooler lines at the radiator.
13. Connect the coolant reservoir hose and the upper and lower radiator hoses.
14. On MPV, install the fresh air duct.
15. Close the draincock and connect the negative battery cable. Fill and bleed the cooling system.
16. Run the engine and check for leaks.

1994–96 B-Series Pick-Up and Navajo

1. Disconnect the negative battery cable and remove the radiator cap.

CAUTION

Never remove the radiator cap while the engine is running or personal injury from scalding hot coolant or steam may result. If possible, wait until the engine has cooled to remove the radiator cap. If this is not possible, wrap a thick cloth around the radiator cap and turn it slowly to the first stop, to release the pressure in the cooling system. Step back while the pressure is released. After all pressure is released, remove the radiator cap completely.

2. Position a drain pan under the radiator and open the draincock to drain the radiator.

3. Disconnect the overflow hose from the radiator and the fan shroud, if necessary.

4. Remove the shroud or fan guard upper attaching screws. Lift the shroud out of the lower retaining clips and drape it on the fan.

5. Disconnect the radiator hoses from the radiator.

6. Disconnect and plug the automatic transmission oil cooling lines, if equipped.

7. Remove the radiator upper attaching screws, tilt the radiator back and lift directly upward, clear of the radiator support and cooling fan.

To install:

8. Make sure the radiator lower support rubber insulators are in place on the lower support.

9. Install the radiator, being careful to clear the fan. Make sure the mounting pins on the bottom of the radiator tanks are inserted into the holes in the lower support rubber insulators and the radiator is firmly seated on the insulators.

10. Install the radiator upper attaching screws. If equipped with automatic transmission, connect the transmission cooling lines.

11. Connect the radiator hoses to the radiator. Position the shroud in the retainer clips and install the attaching screws.

12. Connect the overflow hose and close the draincock. Connect the negative battery cable. Fill and bleed the cooling system.

Heater Core

REMOVAL AND INSTALLATION

1992–93 B-Series Pick-Up

1. Disconnect the negative battery cable. Drain the cooling system.

2. Disconnect the heater hoses from the heater unit and remove the grommet.

3. Remove the instrument panel as follows:

  a. Remove the steering wheel.

  b. Remove the upper and lower column covers and the combination switch.

  c. Remove the instrument cluster hood and the instrument cluster.

  d. Remove the left side panel from the instrument panel.

  e. Remove the hole cover from the upper right corner of the instrument panel center panel to expose a center panel attaching screw. Remove the center panel.

  f. Remove the glove compartment lid and the glove compartment.

  g. Remove the shifter knob and boot, then remove the console box.

  h. Remove the radio.

  i. Remove the instrument panel retaining bolt covers from the top and sides of the instrument panel.

  j. Remove the instrument panel retaining bolts and remove the instrument panel.

4. Disconnect the cables from the heater unit, remove the nuts and bolts and remove the heater unit.

5. Disassemble the heater unit and remove the heater core.

To install:

6. Install the heater core and assemble the heater unit.

7. Install the heater unit and tighten the retaining nuts and bolts to 69–95 inch lbs. (7.8–11.0 Nm). Connect the control cables.

8. Install the instrument panel in the reverse order of removal.

9. Install the grommet and connect the heater hoses.

10. Connect the negative battery cable. Fill and bleed the cooling system.

11. Run the engine and check heater operation. Check for leaks.

MPV

1. Disconnect the negative battery cable. Drain the cooling system.

2. Remove the instrument panel as follows:

  a. Disconnect the hood release knob from the instrument panel.

  b. Remove the steering wheel.

  c. Remove the upper and lower column covers.

  d. Disconnect the electrical connectors from the combination switch. Loosen the screw, release the lock and remove the switch.

  e. Remove the front cluster assembly and the instrument cluster.

  f. Remove the covers from the left and right side of the instrument panel.

  g. If equipped, remove the undercover from the lower right side of the instrument panel.

  h. Remove the right and left lower panels.

  i. Remove the duct from the driver's side under the steering column.

  j. Remove the ashtray and radio trim panel.

  k. Remove the radio housing and the radio.

  l. Remove the knobs and the switch panel assembly.

  m. Remove the temperature and blower controls and the airflow mode control.

  n. Remove the bolt covers, 3 bolts and the upper garnish.

  o. Remove the retaining bolts and remove the instrument panel.

3. Disconnect the heater hoses from the heater core.

4. Remove the nuts and the instrument panel stay.

5. Remove the nuts and the heater unit case. Use caution to prevent spilling coolant from the heater core.

6. Disassemble the heater unit and remove the heater core.

To install:

7. Install the heater core and assemble the heater unit.

8. Install the heater unit case with the attaching nuts.

9. Install the instrument panel stay with the attaching nuts.

10. Connect the heater hoses to the heater core.

11. Install the instrument panel in the reverse order of removal. When attaching the airflow mode control wire, proceed as follows:

  a. Set the control knob to the far left position.

  b. Set the mode control link to the extreme stop position, then install the wire loop on the link.

  c. Clamp the wire into position with the clip.

  d. Move the mode lever to be sure the wire is attached. Make sure it can move the full stroke between DEF and VENT.

12. When attaching the Rec-Fresh control wire, proceed as follows:

  a. Set the control knob to the far right position.

  b. Set the air-mix control link to the extreme stop position, then install the wire loop on the link.

  c. Clamp the wire into position with the clip.

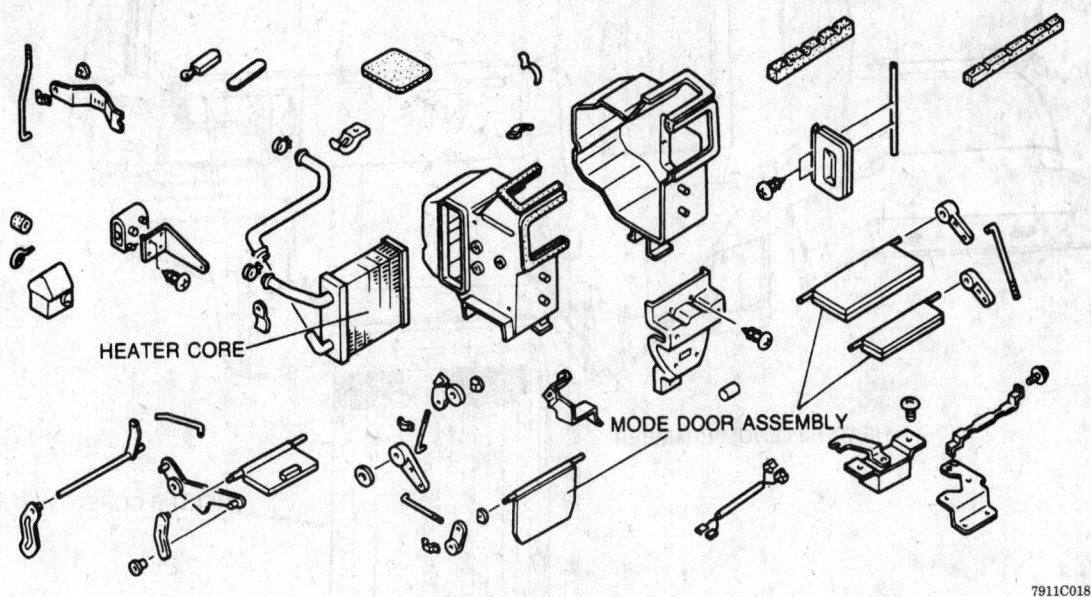

HEATER CORE

MODE DOOR ASSEMBLY

7911C018

Heater unit disassembled view — B-Series Pick-Up

d. Move the Rec-Fresh lever to be sure the wire is attached. Make sure it can move the full stroke between REC and FRESH.

13. When attaching the temperature control wire, proceed as follows:

a. Set the control knob to the full clockwise position.

b. Set the temperature control link to the extreme stop position, then install the wire loop on the link.

c. Clamp the wire into position with the clip.

d. Move the temperature control lever to be sure the wire is attached. Make sure it can move the full stroke between HOT and COLD.

14. Connect the negative battery cable. Fill and bleed the cooling system.

15. Run the engine and check heater operation. Check for leaks.

1994–96 B-Series Pick-Up and Navajo

1. Disconnect the negative battery cable.

2. Drain the cooling system into a suitable container.

3. Disconnect the heater hoses from the heater core tubes. Use the snap-lock fitting disconnect procedure, if necessary.

4. In the passenger compartment, remove the screws attaching the heater core access cover to the plenum assembly. Remove the access cover.

5. Pull the heater core rearward and down, removing it from the plenum assembly.

To install:

6. Position the heater core and seal in the plenum assembly.

7. Install the heater core access cover to the plenum assembly and secure it with the screws.

8. Connect the heater hoses to the heater core tubes. Use the snap-lock fitting connection procedure.

9. Fill the cooling system to the proper level.

10. Connect the negative battery cable and check the system for proper operation and coolant leaks.

Water Pump

REMOVAL AND INSTALLATION

2.2L Engine

1. Disconnect the negative battery cable. Drain the cooling system.

2. Remove the cooling fan and the fan shroud.

3. Remove the water pump drive belt and the water pump pulley.

4. Remove the timing belt front covers and the timing belt and tensioner. Remove the timing belt idler pulley.

5. Remove the coolant inlet pipe, if necessary.

6. Remove the mounting bolts and the water pump.

To install:

7. Clean all gasket mating surfaces.

8. Install a new water pump gasket and the water pump. Tighten the water pump mounting bolts to 14–19 ft. lbs. (19–25 Nm).

9. Install a new gasket and the coolant inlet pipe, if removed.

10. Install the timing belt idler pulley, timing belt and timing belt front cover.

11. Install the water pump pulley and drive belt. Install the cooling fan and shroud.

12. Adjust the drive belt tension. Connect the negative battery cable.

13. Fill and bleed the cooling system. Run the engine and check for leaks.

2.6L Engine

1. Disconnect the negative battery cable. Drain the cooling system.

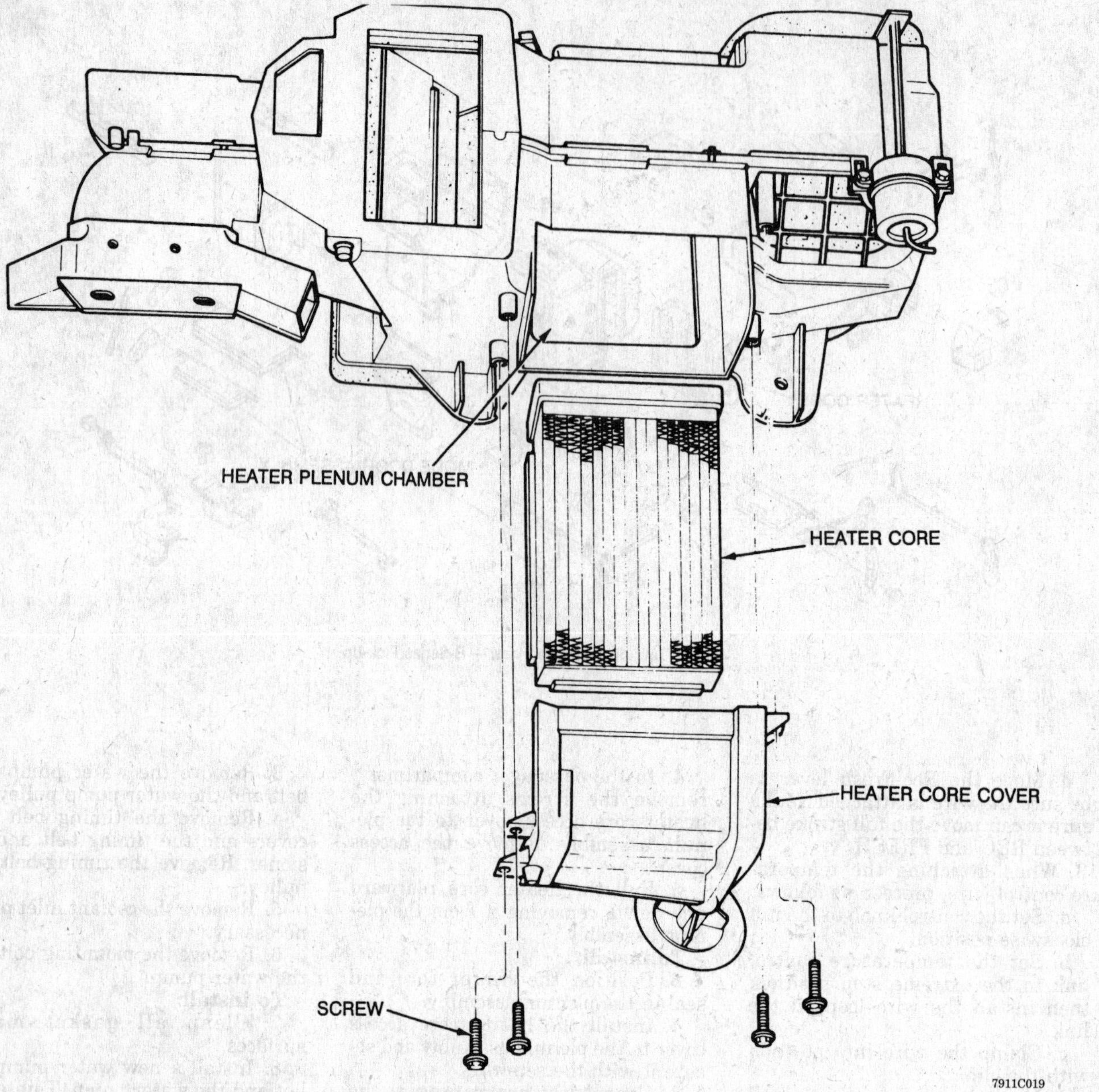

HEATER PLENUM CHAMBER

HEATER CORE

HEATER CORE COVER

SCREW

7911C019

Heater core installation — Navajo

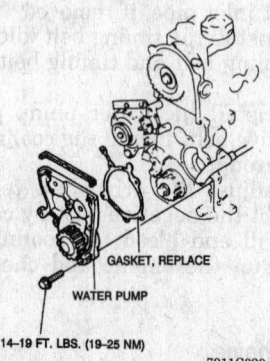

GASKET, REPLACE

WATER PUMP

14–19 FT. LBS. (19–25 NM)

7911C020

Water pump installation — 2.2L engine

2. Remove the cooling fan and the fan shroud.

3. Remove the water pump drive belt and the water pump pulley.

4. Remove the mounting bolts/nuts and the water pump.

To install:

5. Clean all gasket mating surfaces.

6. Install a new gasket and the water pump. Tighten the mounting bolts/nuts to 14–19 ft. lbs. (19–25 Nm).

7. Connect the water bypass hose, if necessary.

8. Install the water pump pulley and the drive belt. Install the cooling fan and shroud.

9. Adjust the drive belt tension. Connect the negative battery cable.

10. Fill and bleed the cooling system. Run the engine and check for leaks.

3.0L Engine

1. Disconnect the negative battery cable. Drain the cooling system.

2. Remove the fresh air duct.

3. Remove the cooling fan and the fan shroud. Loosen the drive belt and remove the water pump pulley.

4. Remove the timing belt front covers and the timing belt.

5. Remove the water pump mounting bolts/nuts and the water pump.

To install:

6. Clean all gasket mating surfaces.

7. Install a new gasket and the water pump. Tighten the mounting bolts/nuts to 14–19 ft. lbs. (19–25 Nm).

8. Install the timing belt and the timing belt front covers.

9. Install the water pump pulley and drive belt. Install the cooling fan and shroud.

10. Adjust the drive belt tension. Install the fresh air duct.

11. Connect the negative battery cable. Fill and bleed the cooling system.

12. Run the engine and check for leaks.

4.0L Engine

1. Disconnect the negative battery cable and drain the cooling system.

2. Remove the lower radiator hose and the heater return hose from the pump.

3. Remove the fan and clutch assembly using fan clutch pulley holder 49 UN01 007 and fan clutch nut wrench 49 UN01 008 or equivalents. The fan clutch nut has left hand thread; remove by turning clockwise.

4. Loosen the alternator mounting bolts and remove the belt. If equipped with air conditioning, remove the alternator and bracket.

5. Remove the water pump pulley.

6. Remove the water pump attaching bolts and remove the water pump. Note the length of the bolts when removing, so they can be reinstalled in the same positions.

7. Clean all gasket mating surfaces and install in the reverse order of removal. Tighten the water pump retaining bolts to 7–9 ft. lbs. (9–12 Nm) and the fan clutch nut to 30–100 ft. lbs. (40–135 Nm). Fill and bleed the cooling system.

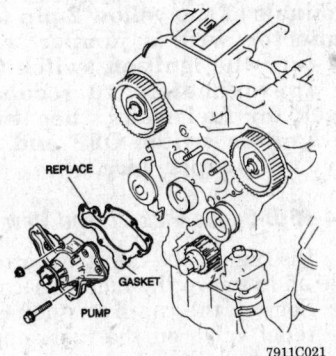

REPLACE
GASKET
PUMP
7911C021

Water pump installation — 3.0L engine

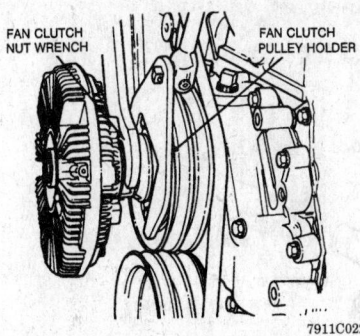

FAN CLUTCH NUT WRENCH   FAN CLUTCH PULLEY HOLDER
7911C022

Fan clutch-to-water pump installation — 4.0L engine

Thermostat

REMOVAL AND INSTALLATION

Except 4.0L Engine

1. Disconnect the negative battery cable. Drain the cooling system.

2. On 2.2L and 2.6L engines, disconnect the upper radiator hose from the water outlet. On 3.0L engine, disconnect the lower radiator hose from the water outlet.

3. Remove the water outlet and the thermostat.

To install:

4. Clean all gasket mating surfaces. On 3.0L engine, make sure the thermostat O-ring is not damaged.

5. Install the thermostat. If equipped, the jiggle pin should be on the side facing the water outlet.

6. On 2.2L and 2.6L engines, install a new gasket with the seal print facing the cylinder head.

7. Install the water outlet. On 3.0L engine, face the mark on the water outlet to the front of the engine.

8. Install the water outlet retaining bolts/nuts and tighten to 14–19 ft. lbs. (19–25 Nm).

9. Connect the radiator hose and the negative battery cable.

10. Fill and bleed the cooling system. Run the engine and check for leaks.

4.0L Engine

1. Disconnect the negative battery cable and drain the cooling system.

2. Disconnect the coolant hose from the water outlet.

3. Remove the water outlet retaining bolts and remove the water outlet. Remove the thermostat from the water outlet.

To install:

4. Clean all gasket mating surfaces.

5. Apply gasket sealer to a new water outlet gasket and install on the engine.

6. Install the thermostat in the water outlet with the bridge section toward the coolant hose. Turn the thermostat clockwise to lock it in position on the flats cast into the water outlet.

NOTE: Make sure the thermostat is aligned so the full width of the heater outlet tube opening is visible within the thermostat port in the assembly. The correct port alignment is required to provide maximum coolant flow to the heater.

7. Install the water outlet with the mounting bolts. Tighten the bolts to 7–10 ft. lbs. (9–13 Nm).

8. Connect the coolant hose.

9. Connect the negative battery cable. Fill and bleed the cooling system.

Cooling System Bleeding

Except Navajo

1. Use the following steps to remove air from the system and ensure a complete fit.

2. Close the radiator draincock and install the cylinder block drain plug, if removed.

3. Slowly pour a 50/50 mixture of water and antifreeze into the radiator up to the coolant filler port.

4. Fill the coolant reservoir with the same mixture up to the FULL level.

5. Install the radiator cap securely and start the engine.

6. Run the engine at idle speed until it reaches normal operating temperature.

NOTE: If the temperature increases beyond normal, there is excessive air in the system. Stop the engine, allow it to cool and repeat Steps 2–4.

7. Run the engine up to 2200–2800 rpm for 5 seconds and return to idle. Repeat several times.

8. Stop the engine and wait until the system has cooled down. Remove the radiator cap and check the coolant level. If the coolant level has dropped, repeat the procedure from Step 2.

1994–96 B-Series Pick-Up and Navajo

1. Use the following steps to remove air from the system and ensure a complete fit.

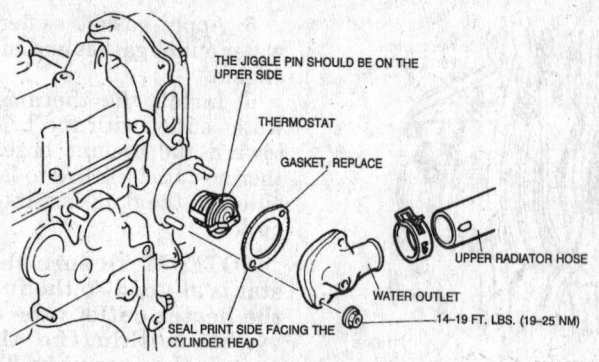

THE JIGGLE PIN SHOULD BE ON THE UPPER SIDE

THERMOSTAT

GASKET, REPLACE

UPPER RADIATOR HOSE

WATER OUTLET

SEAL PRINT SIDE FACING THE CYLINDER HEAD

14–19 FT. LBS. (19–25 NM)

7911C023

Thermostat installation — 2.2L engine

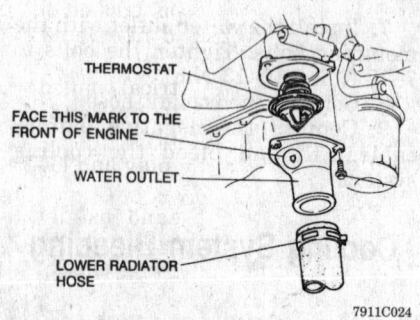

THERMOSTAT

FACE THIS MARK TO THE FRONT OF ENGINE

WATER OUTLET

LOWER RADIATOR HOSE

7911C024

Thermostat installation — 3.0L engine

2. Close the radiator draincock and install the cylinder block drain plug, if removed.

3. Fill the cooling system with a 50/50 mixture of water and antifreeze. Allow several minutes for trapped air to escape and for coolant mixture to flow through the radiator.

4. Install the radiator cap to the fully installed position, then back off to the first stop.

5. Slide the heater temperature and mode selection levers to maximum heat position.

6. Start the engine and operate at approximately 2000 rpm for 3–4 minutes.

7. Shut the engine off. Wrap the radiator cap with a thick cloth and carefully remove the cap.

8. Add coolant mixture to bring the coolant level up to the filler neck seat.

—————— **CAUTION** ——————
Use caution when adding coolant to the radiator to avoid hot coolant or steam blowing out from the radiator and possibly causing personal injury.

9. Install the radiator cap to the fully installed position, then back off to the first stop.

10. Run the engine at fast idle until the upper radiator hose is warm, indicating the thermostat is open.

11. Shut the engine off. Wrap the radiator cap with a thick cloth and carefully remove the cap. Add coolant, if necessary and reinstall the cap to the fully installed position.

12. Remove the coolant reservoir cap and add 1.1 qts. of coolant mixture to the reservoir. Install the cap.

FUEL SYSTEM

Fuel System Service Precautions

Safety is the most important factor when performing not only fuel system maintenance but any type of maintenance. Failure to conduct maintenance and repairs in a safe manner may result in serious personal injury or death. Maintenance and testing of the vehicle's fuel system components can be accomplished safely and effectively by adhering to the following rules and guidelines.

• To avoid the possibility of fire and personal injury, always disconnect the negative battery cable unless the repair or test procedure requires that battery voltage be applied.

• Always relieve the fuel system pressure prior to disconnecting any fuel system component (injector, fuel rail, pressure regulator, etc.), fitting or fuel line connection. Exercise extreme caution whenever relieving fuel system pressure to avoid exposing skin, face and eyes to fuel spray. Please be advised that fuel under pressure may penetrate the skin or any part of the body that it contacts.

• Always place a shop towel or cloth around the fitting or connection prior to loosening to absorb any excess fuel due to spillage. Ensure that all fuel spillage (should it occur) is quickly removed from engine surfaces. Ensure that all fuel soaked cloths or towels are deposited into a suitable waste container.

• Always keep a dry chemical (Class B) fire extinguisher near the work area.

• Do not allow fuel spray or fuel vapors to come into contact with a spark or open flame.

• Always use a backup wrench when loosening and tightening fuel line connection fittings. This will prevent unnecessary stress and torsion to fuel line piping. Always follow the proper torque specifications.

• Always replace worn fuel fitting O-rings with new. Do not substitute fuel hose or equivalent where fuel pipe is installed.

RELIEVING FUEL SYSTEM PRESSURE

Fuel lines on fuel injected vehicles will remain pressurized after the engine is shut off. This residual pressure must be relieved before any fuel lines or components are disconnected.

Except 1994–96 B-Series Pick-Up and Navajo

1. Start the engine.
2. Disconnect the circuit opening relay connector, airflow meter connector or fuel pump connector.
3. After the engine stalls, turn **OFF** the ignition switch.
4. Reconnect the electrical connector.

NOTE: After releasing fuel system pressure, the system must be primed before starting the engine to avoid excessive cranking. To prime the system, connect the terminals of the yellow 2-pin test connector with a jumper wire and turn the ignition switch ON for approximately 10 seconds. Check for fuel leaks, then turn the ignition switch OFF and remove the jumper wire.

1994–96 B-Series Pick-Up and Navajo

1. Disconnect the negative battery cable and remove the fuel filler cap.
2. Remove the cap from the pressure relief valve on the fuel supply manifold. Install pressure gauge 49 UN01 010 or equivalent, to the pressure relief valve.

3. Direct the gauge drain hose into a suitable container and depress the pressure relief button.

4. Remove the gauge and replace the cap on the pressure relief valve.

NOTE: As an alternate method, disconnect the inertia switch and crank the engine for 15–20 seconds until the pressure is relieved.

Fuel Line Couplings

REMOVAL AND INSTALLATION

1994–96 B-Series Pick-Up and Navajo

There are 2 methods in use to connect the fuel lines and fuel system components on Navajo, the hairpin clip push connect fitting and the spring lock coupling. Each requires a different procedure to disconnect and connect.

HAIRPIN CLIP PUSH CONNECT FITTING

1. Inspect the visible internal portion of the fitting for dirt accumulation. If more than a light coating of dust is present, clean the fitting before disassembly.

2. Some adhesion between the seals in the fitting and the tubing will occur with time. To separate, twist the fitting on the tube, then push and pull the fitting until it moves freely on the tube.

3. Remove the hairpin clip from the fitting by first bending and breaking the shipping tab. Next, spread the 2 clip legs by hand about ⅛ in. each to disengage the body and push the legs into the fitting. Lightly pull the triangular end of the clip and work it clear of the tube and fitting.

NOTE: Do not use hand tools to complete this operation.

4. Grasp the fitting and pull in an axial direction to remove the fitting from the tube. Be careful on 90 degree elbow connectors, as excessive side loading could break the connector body.

5. After disassembly, inspect and clean the tube end sealing surfaces. The tube end should be free of scratches and corrosion that could provide leak paths. Inspect the inside of the fitting for any internal parts such as O-rings and spacers that may have been dislodged from the fitting. Replace any damaged connector.

To install:

6. Install a new connector if damage was found. Insert a new clip into any 2 adjacent openings with the tri-

angular portion pointing away from the fitting opening. Install the clip until the legs of the clip are locked on the outside of the body. Piloting with an index finger is necessary.

7. Before installing the fitting on the tube, wipe the tube end with a clean cloth. Inspect the inside of the fitting to make sure it is free of dirt and/or obstructions.

8. Apply a light coating of engine oil to the tube end. Align the fitting and tube axially and push the fitting onto the tube end. When the fitting is engaged, a definite click will be heard. Pull on the fitting to make sure it is fully engaged.

SPRING LOCK COUPLING

The spring lock coupling is a fuel line coupling held together by a garter spring inside a circular cage. When the coupling is connected together, the flared end of the female fitting slips behind the garter spring inside the cage of the male fitting. The garter spring and cage then prevent the flared end of the female fitting from pulling out of the cage. As an additional locking feature, most couplings have a horseshoe shaped retaining clip that improves the retaining reliability of the spring lock coupling.

Fuel Tank

REMOVAL AND INSTALLATION

1992–93 B-Series Pick-Up

1. Relieve the fuel system pressure and disconnect the negative battery cable.

2. Remove the fuel filler cap. Raise and safely support the vehicle.

3. Position a suitable container under the fuel tank. Remove the drain plug and drain the tank.

4. Disconnect the electrical connector from the sending unit or sending unit/fuel pump assembly.

5. Disconnect the fuel filler hose, evaporative hoses, breather hose and fuel lines.

6. Position a jack under the fuel tank and remove the tank attaching nuts. Lower the tank from the vehicle.

To install:

7. Raise the tank into position and install the attaching nuts. Remove the jack.

8. Connect the fuel lines and evaporative hoses, making sure they are pushed onto the fuel tank fittings at least 1 in. (25mm). Connect the breather hose.

9. Connect the fuel filler hose, making sure the hose is pushed onto the fuel tank pipe and filler pipe at least 1.4 in. (35mm).

10. Connect the electrical connector to the sending unit or sending unit/fuel pump assembly.

11. Install the drain plug and lower the vehicle.

12. Fill the fuel tank and install the filler cap. Check for leaks.

13. Start the engine and check for leaks.

MPV

1. Relieve the fuel system pressure and disconnect the negative battery cable.

2. Remove the fuel filler cap. Raise and safely support the vehicle.

3. Position a suitable container under the fuel tank. Remove the drain plug and drain the tank.

4. Disconnect the fuel pump electrical connector.

5. Disconnect the fuel lines, evaporative hoses, breather hose and fuel filler hose.

6. Support the tank with a jack. Remove the retaining bolts and the fuel tank straps.

7. Lower the fuel tank from the vehicle.

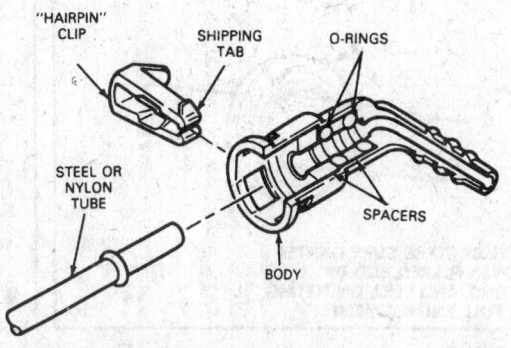

7911C026

Hairpin clip push connect fitting — Navajo

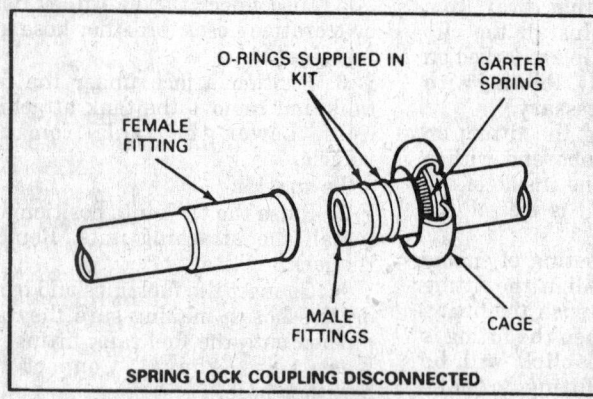

SPRING LOCK COUPLING DISCONNECTED

- FEMALE FITTING
- O-RINGS SUPPLIED IN KIT
- GARTER SPRING
- MALE FITTINGS
- CAGE

TO CONNECT COUPLING

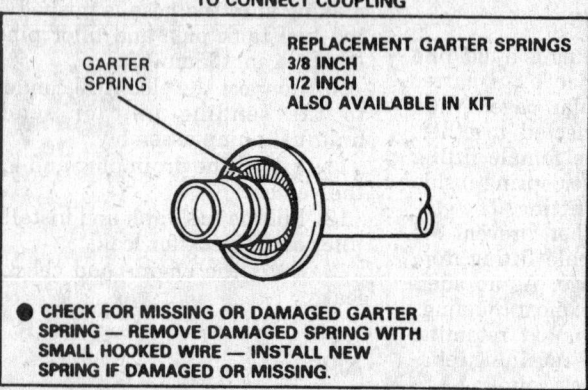

GARTER SPRING

REPLACEMENT GARTER SPRINGS
3/8 INCH
1/2 INCH
ALSO AVAILABLE IN KIT

- CHECK FOR MISSING OR DAMAGED GARTER SPRING — REMOVE DAMAGED SPRING WITH SMALL HOOKED WIRE — INSTALL NEW SPRING IF DAMAGED OR MISSING.

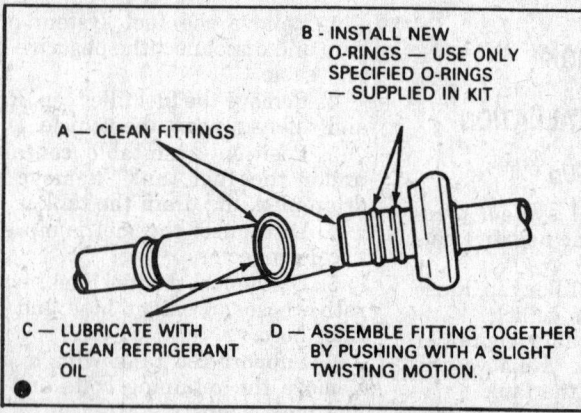

A — CLEAN FITTINGS

B - INSTALL NEW O-RINGS — USE ONLY SPECIFIED O-RINGS — SUPPLIED IN KIT

C — LUBRICATE WITH CLEAN REFRIGERANT OIL

D — ASSEMBLE FITTING TOGETHER BY PUSHING WITH A SLIGHT TWISTING MOTION.

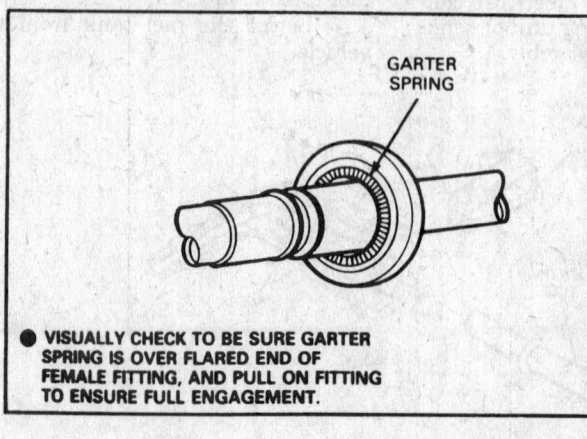

GARTER SPRING

- VISUALLY CHECK TO BE SURE GARTER SPRING IS OVER FLARED END OF FEMALE FITTING, AND PULL ON FITTING TO ENSURE FULL ENGAGEMENT.

TO DISCONNECT COUPLING
CAUTION — DISCHARGE SYSTEM BEFORE DISCONNECTING COUPLING

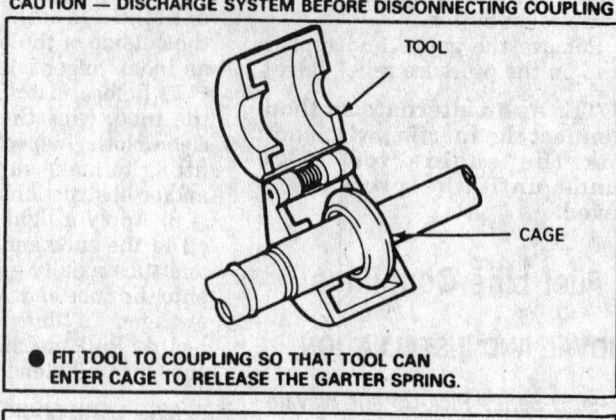

- TOOL
- CAGE

- FIT TOOL TO COUPLING SO THAT TOOL CAN ENTER CAGE TO RELEASE THE GARTER SPRING.

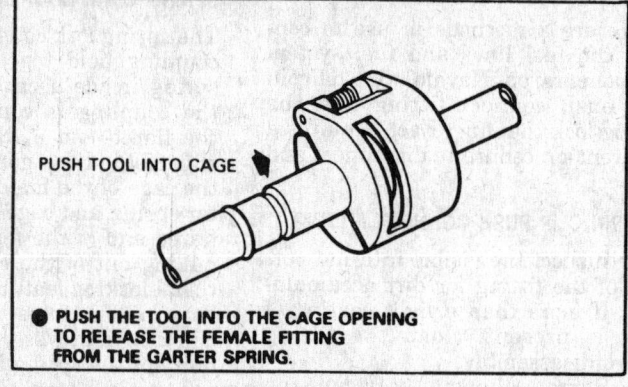

PUSH TOOL INTO CAGE

- PUSH THE TOOL INTO THE CAGE OPENING TO RELEASE THE FEMALE FITTING FROM THE GARTER SPRING.

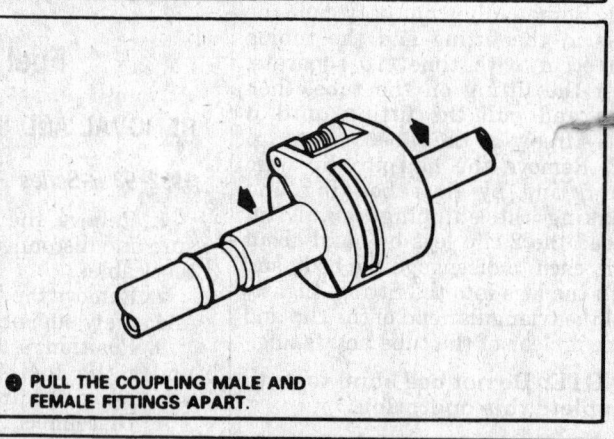

- PULL THE COUPLING MALE AND FEMALE FITTINGS APART.

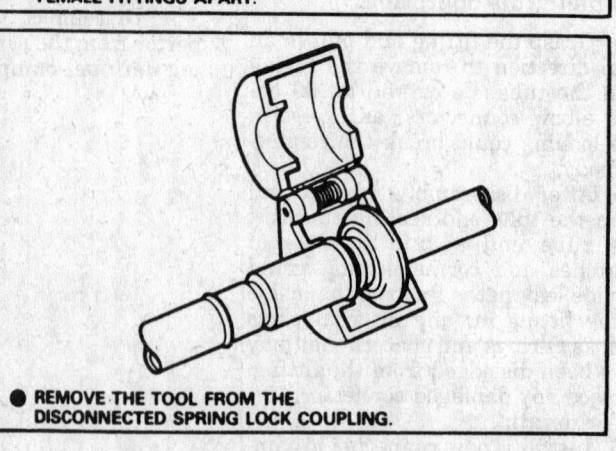

- REMOVE THE TOOL FROM THE DISCONNECTED SPRING LOCK COUPLING.

7911C025

Spring lock coupling connect and disconnect procedure

To install:

8. Raise the fuel tank into position and install the straps and retaining bolts. Tighten to 32–44 ft. lbs. (43–61 Nm). Remove the jack.

9. Connect the fuel lines and evaporative hoses, making sure they are pushed onto the fuel tank fittings at least 1 in. (25mm). Connect the breather hose.

10. Connect the fuel filler hose, making sure the hose is pushed onto the fuel tank pipe and filler pipe at least 1.4 in. (35mm).

11. Connect the fuel pump electrical connector.

12. Install the drain plug and lower the vehicle.

13. Fill the fuel tank and install the filler cap. Check for leaks.

14. Start the engine and check for leaks.

1994–96 B-Series Pick-Up and Navajo

1. Disconnect the negative battery cable and relieve the fuel system pressure.

2. Raise and safely support the vehicle.

3. Drain the fuel from the fuel tank.

4. Remove the shield, skid plate and fuel tank front strap.

5. Support the tank with a jack and remove the bolt from the fuel tank rear strap.

6. Disconnect the filler pipe and vent pipe and lower the tank. Disconnect the vapor hose, fuel lines and electrical connector.

7. Lower the tank from the vehicle.

To install:

8. Raise the fuel tank and connect the electrical connector, fuel lines and vapor hose.

9. Connect the filler pipe and vent pipe. Attach the rear fuel tank strap.

10. Install the shield, skid plate and front strap.

11. Remove the jack and lower the vehicle.

12. Fill the fuel tank and check for leaks. Connect the negative battery cable.

Fuel Filter

REMOVAL AND INSTALLATION

1992–93 B-Series Pick-Up

The fuel filter is located in the engine compartment.

1. Relieve the fuel system pressure. Disconnect the negative battery cable.

2. Raise and safely support the vehicle, if necessary.

3. Disconnect the fuel lines from the fuel filter.

4. Remove the fuel filter or, if equipped, remove the fuel filter and bracket assembly.

5. Installation is the reverse of the removal procedure. Make sure the flow arrow on the fuel filter is facing in the proper direction of fuel flow.

MPV

1. The fuel filter is located in the engine compartment, next to the pulsation damp

2. Relieve the fuel system pressure. Disconnect the negative battery cable.

3. Disconnect the fuel lines from the filter.

4. Remove the filter bracket bolts and remove the filter and bracket assembly.

5. Remove the fuel filter from the mounting bracket, if necessary.

6. Installation is the reverse of the removal procedure. Make sure the flow arrow on the fuel filter is facing in the proper direction of fuel flow.

1994–96 B-Series Pick-Up and Navajo

1. The fuel filter is located on the underside of the vehicle, attached to the frame rail.

2. Disconnect the negative battery cable and relieve the fuel system pressure.

3. Raise and support the vehicle safely.

4. Disconnect the fuel lines from the fuel filter.

5. Remove the fuel filter from the bracket. Note the direction of the flow arrow so the replacement filter can be installed correctly.

6. Installation is the reverse of the removal procedure. Start the engine and check for leaks.

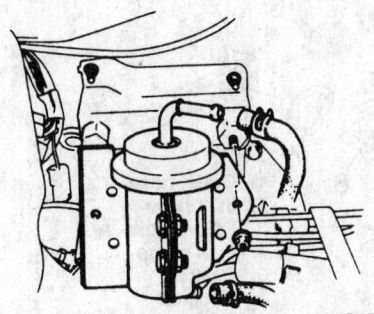

7911C027

Fuel filter location — B-Series Pick-Up with fuel injection

Mechanical Fuel Pump

PRESSURE TESTING

1. Disconnect the negative battery cable.

2. Disconnect the fuel line from the carburetor.

3. Connect a fuel pressure gauge to the fuel line.

4. Disconnect the fuel return hose from the fuel pump and plug the fuel pump return outlet.

5. Connect the negative battery cable and start the engine.

6. Check the fuel pressure while the engine is idling. The fuel pressure should be 3.7–4.7 psi.

7. Replace the pump if the pressure is not as specified.

8. Shut off the engine and disconnect the negative battery cable. Remove the fuel pressure gauge and reconnect the fuel lines.

9. Connect the negative battery cable.

REMOVAL AND INSTALLATION

1. Disconnect the negative battery cable.

2. Disconnect and plug the inlet, outlet and return hoses at the fuel pump.

3. Remove the fuel pump mounting bolts and remove the fuel pump, insulator and gaskets.

To install:

4. Clean all gasket mating surfaces.

5. Install new gaskets and the insulator and fuel pump. Install the mounting bolts and tighten to 14–19 ft. lbs. (19–25 Nm).

6. Unplug and connect the fuel lines.

7. Connect the negative battery cable, start the engine and check for leaks.

Electric Fuel Pump

PRESSURE TESTING

Carbureted Engines

1. Turn the ignition switch **OFF** and disconnect the negative battery cab

2. Disconnect the main fuel hose and connect a pressure gauge to it.

3. Connect the negative battery cable. Connect a jumper wire between the **B** and **D** terminals of the fuel pump control unit.

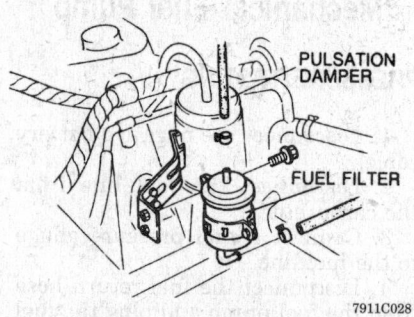

Fuel filter location — MPV

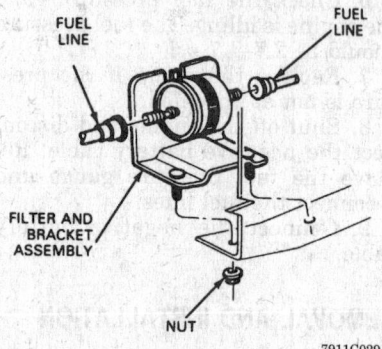

Fuel filter location — Navajo

4. Turn the ignition switch **ON** and check the fuel pressure. It should be 2.8–3.6 psi.

5. If the fuel pressure is not as specified, replace the fuel pump.

6. Turn the ignition switch **OFF** and disconnect the negative battery cable.

7. Remove the fuel pressure gauge and reconnect the main fuel hose. Remove the jumper wire from the fuel pump control unit.

8. Connect the negative battery cable.

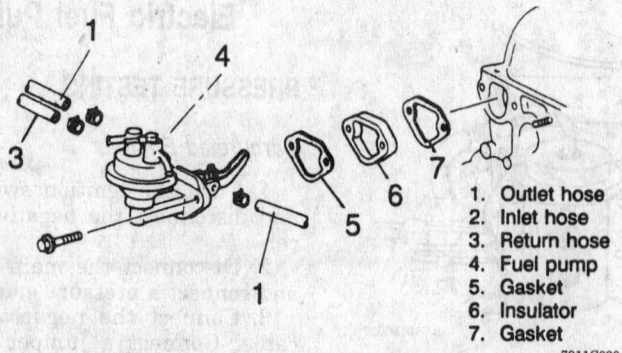

1. Outlet hose
2. Inlet hose
3. Return hose
4. Fuel pump
5. Gasket
6. Insulator
7. Gasket

Mechanical fuel pump installation

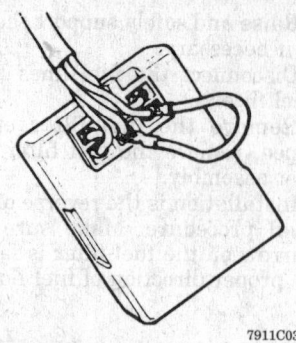

Connecting the jumper wire to the fuel pump control unit

Fuel Injected Engines

EXCEPT NAVAJO

1. Relieve the fuel system pressure and disconnect the negative battery cable.

2. Disconnect the fuel line from the fuel filter outlet. Connect a fuel pressure gauge to the fuel filter outlet.

3. Connect the negative battery cable. Connect the terminals of the yellow 2-pin test connector with a jumper wire.

4. Turn the ignition switch **ON** to operate the fuel pump and check the fuel pressure. It should be 64–85 psi.

5. If the fuel pressure is not as specified, replace the fuel pump.

6. Turn the ignition switch **OFF** and disconnect the negative battery cable. Remove the jumper wire from the test connector.

7. Remove the fuel pressure gauge and reconnect the fuel line to the fuel filter outlet.

8. Connect the negative battery cable.

1994-96 B-SERIES PICK-UP AND NAVAJO

1. Make sure there is an adequate fuel supply.

2. Relieve the fuel system pressure.

3. Turn the ignition key **OFF**.

4. Connect a suitable fuel pressure gauge to the schrader valve on the fuel rail.

5. Install a test lead to the **FP** terminal on the VIP test connector.

6. Turn the ignition key to the **RUN** position, then ground the test lead to run the fuel pump.

7. Observe the fuel pressure reading on the pressure gauge. The fuel pressure should be 35–45 psi.

8. Relieve the fuel system pressure and turn the ignition key **OFF**. Remove the fuel pressure gauge and the test lead.

REMOVAL AND INSTALLATION

NOTE: The fuel pump is located inside the fuel tank, attached to the tank sending unit assembly.

1992-93 B-Series Pick-Up

1. Relieve the fuel system pressure and disconnect the negative battery cable.

2. Remove the fuel tank.

3. Remove any dirt that has accumulated around the sending unit/fuel pump assembly so it will not enter the fuel tank during removal and installation.

4. Remove the attaching screws and remove the sending unit/fuel pump assembly.

5. If necessary, disconnect the electrical connectors and the fuel hose and remove the pump from the sending unit assembly.

6. Installation is the reverse of removal procedure. Be sure to install a new seal rubber gasket.

MPV

1. Relieve the fuel system pressure and disconnect the negative battery cable.

2. Remove the rear seat and lift up the rear floormat. Remove the fuel pump cover.

3. Disconnect the sending unit/fuel pump assembly electrical connector and the fuel lines.

4. Remove any dirt that has accumulated around the sending unit/fuel pump assembly so it will not enter the fuel tank during removal and installation.

5. Remove the attaching screws and remove the sending unit/fuel pump assembly.

6. If necessary, disconnect the electrical connectors and the fuel hose and remove the pump from the sending unit assembly.

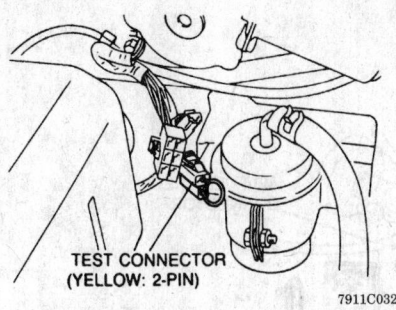

TEST CONNECTOR
(YELLOW: 2-PIN)

7911C032

Test connector location — B-Series Pick-Up

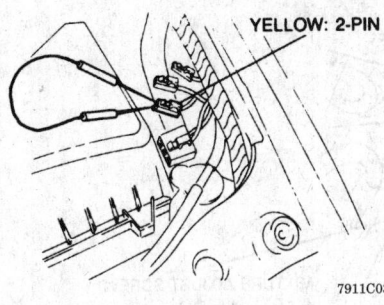

YELLOW: 2-PIN

7911C033

Test connector location — MPV

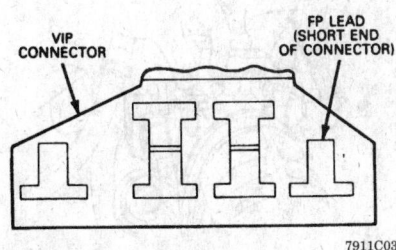

VIP
CONNECTOR

FP LEAD
(SHORT END
OF CONNECTOR)

7911C034

FP terminal location on VIP connector — Navajo

7. Installation is the reverse of the removal procedure. Be sure to install a new seal rubber gasket.

1994–96 B-Series Pick-Up and Navajo

1. Disconnect the negative battery cable and relieve the fuel system pressure.
2. Raise and safely support the vehicle.
3. Remove the fuel tank.
4. Remove any dirt that has accumulated around the fuel pump attaching flange so it will not enter the fuel tank during removal and installation.
5. Turn the fuel pump locking ring counterclockwise using a suitable tool. Remove the locking ring.
6. Remove the fuel pump and discard the seal ring. Separate the fuel pump from the sending unit, if required.

To install:
7. Clean the fuel pump mounting flange and tank mounting surface and seal ring groove.
8. Apply a light coating of Molybdenum grease on a new seal ring and install it in the groove.
9. Install the fuel pump to the sending unit, if removed. Install the fuel pump assembly in the tank, making sure the locating keys are in the keyways and the seal ring is in place.
10. Hold the fuel pump assembly and the seal ring in place and install the locking ring. Rotate the ring clockwise using a suitable tool. Tighten the locking ring to 40–45 ft. lbs. (54–61 Nm).
11. Install the fuel tank in the vehicle.
12. Lower the vehicle and fill the fuel tank with at least 10 gallons of fuel. Connect the negative battery cable. Turn the ignition key to **RUN** for 3 seconds repeatedly, 5–10 times, to pressurize the system. Check for leaks.
13. Start the engine and check for leaks.

Carburetor

REMOVAL AND INSTALLATION

1. Disconnect the negative battery cable.
2. Remove the air cleaner assembly.
3. Disconnect the accelerator cable and, if equipped, the cruise control cable.
4. Tag and disconnect the vacuum hoses and electrical connectors.
5. Disconnect the fuel lines.
6. Remove the attaching nuts and remove the carburetor.
7. Installation is the reverse of the removal procedure. Be sure to use a new gasket. Tighten the carburetor attaching nuts in a criss-cross pattern.

IDLE SPEED ADJUSTMENT

1. Make sure the ignition timing, spark plugs, and carburetor float level are all in normal operating condition. Turn off all lights and other unnecessary electrical loads.
2. Connect a tachometer to the engine.
3. Start the engine and allow it to reach normal operating temperature. Make sure the choke valve has fully opened.
4. Check the idle speed. If necessary, adjust it to specification by turning the throttle adjusting screw. The idle speed should be 800–850 rpm with manual transmission in neutral or automatic transmission in **P**.

IDLE MIXTURE ADJUSTMENT

1. Start the engine and allow it to reach normal operating temperature. Let the engine run at idle.
2. Connect a dwell meter (90 degrees, 4 cylinder) to the air/fuel check connector (Br/Y).
3. Check the idle mixture at the specified idle speed. The idle mixture should be 20–70 degrees. If the idle mixture is not as specified, adjust as follows:
   a. Remove the carburetor and knock out the spring pin. Reinstall the carburetor.
   b. Install the air cleaner and make sure the idle compensator is closed. Make sure all vacuum hoses are properly connected.
   c. Connect a tachometer to the engine.
   d. Warm the engine and run it at idle. Make sure the idle speed is correct.
   e. Reconnect the dwell meter to the air/fuel check connector.
   f. Adjust the idle mixture to 27–45 degrees by turning the mixture adjust screw.
   g. Tap in the spring pin.

Fuel Injection

IDLE SPEED ADJUSTMENT

Except 1994–96 B-Series Pick-Up and Navajo

1. Place manual transmission in neutral or automatic transmission in **P**.
2. Make sure all accessories are **OFF**.
3. Connect a tachometer and timing light to the engine.
4. Warm the engine to normal operating temperature.
5. Check the ignition timing and adjust, if necessary.

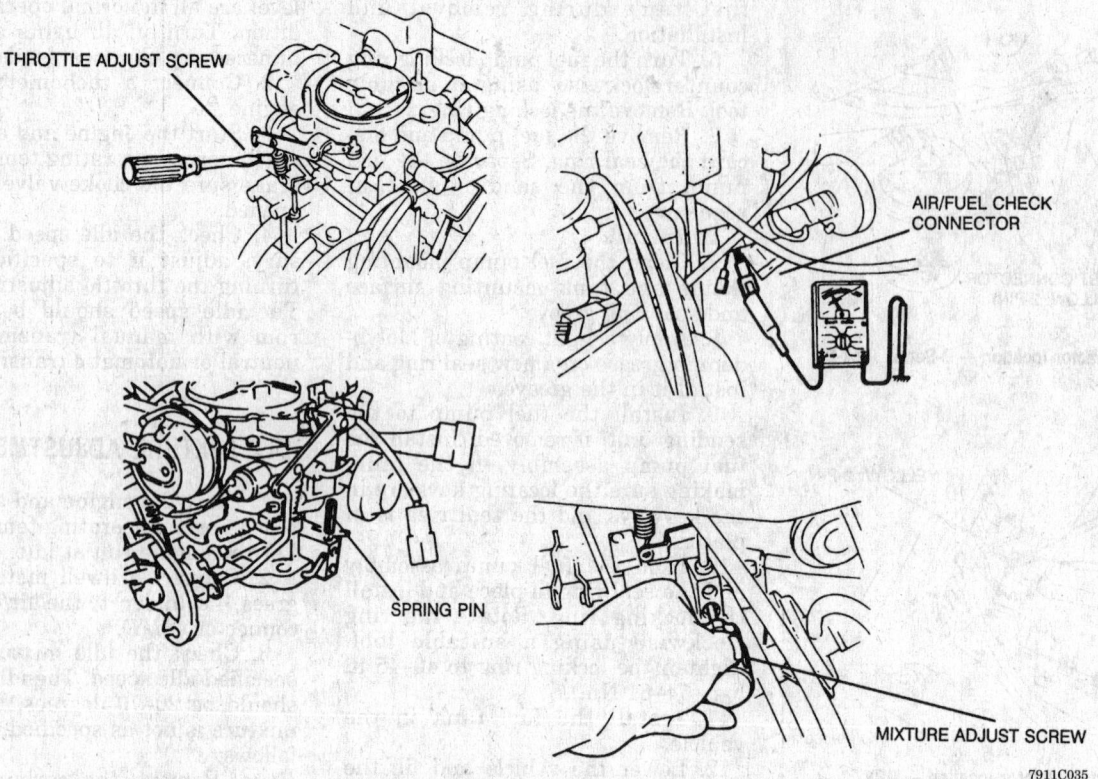

Idle speed and idle mixture adjustment — 2.2L engine

6. Ground the green 1-pin test connector to the body with a jumper wire.

7. Check the idle speed.

2.2L and 2.6L engines

Manual transmission: 730–770 rpm.

Automatic transmission: 750–790 rpm.

3.0L engine

Manual and automatic transmission: 780–820 rpm.

8. If the idle speed is not within specification, adjust by turning the air adjusting screw.

9. After adjustment, disconnect the jumper wire from the test connector. Recheck the ignition timing.

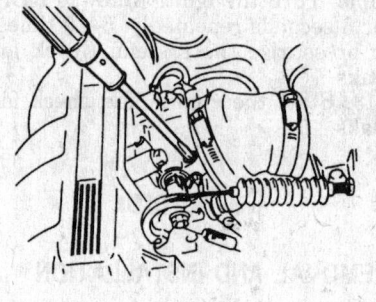

B SERIES PICK-UP

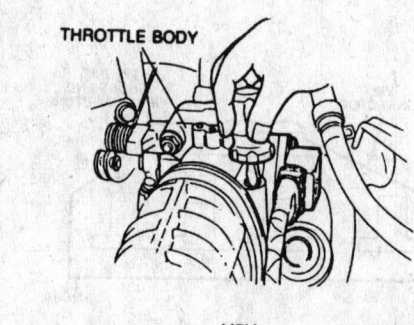

MPV

Air adjusting screw locations

1994–96 B-Series Pick-Up and Navajo

1. Place manual transmission in neutral or automatic transmission in **P**. Apply the parking brake.

2. Make sure the heater and accessories are **OFF**.

3. Start the engine and bring to normal operating temperature. Make sure the throttle lever is resting on the throttle plate stop screw.

4. Check the ignition timing and adjust, if necessary.

5. Shut off the engine and disconnect the negative battery cable for 5 minutes minimum. Reconnect the negative battery cable.

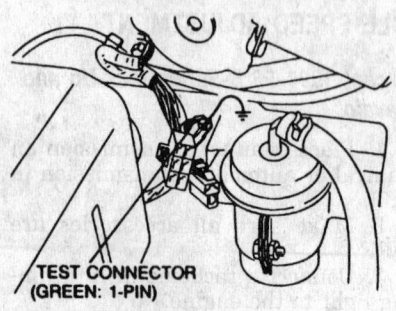

TEST CONNECTOR (GREEN: 1-PIN)

B SERIES PICK-UP

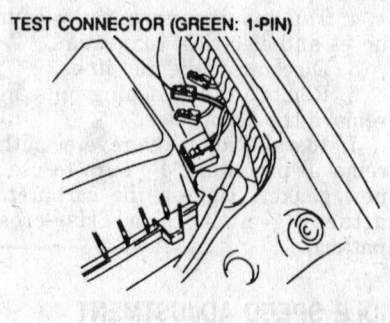

MPV

Test connector locations

6. Start the engine and let it stabilize for 2 minutes. Rev the engine and let it return to idle, lightly depress and release the accelerator and let the engine idle.

7. If the engine does not idle properly, shut off the engine and disconnect the idle speed control-air bypass solenoid.

8. Run the engine at 2500 rpm for 30 seconds, then let it idle for 2 minutes.

9. Check/adjust the idle rpm to 675 rpm by turning the throttle plate stop screw.

NOTE: If the screw must be turned in, shut the engine off and make the estimated adjustment, then start the engine and repeat Steps 8 and 9.

10. Shut the engine off and repeat Steps 8 and 9.

11. Shut the engine off and disconnect the negative battery cable for 5 minutes minimum.

12. With the engine off, reconnect the idle speed control-air bypass solenoid. Make sure the throttle is not stuck in the bore and the linkage is not preventing the throttle from closing.

13. Start the engine and let it stabilize for 2 minutes. Rev the engine and let it return to idle, lightly depress and release the accelerator and let the engine idle.

NOTE: A condition may occur where the engine rpm will oscillate. This can be caused by the throttle plates being open enough to allow purge flow. To make sure of this condition, disconnect the carbon canister purge line and plug it. If purge is present, the throttle plates must be closed until the purge flow induced idle oscillations stop.

IDLE MIXTURE ADJUSTMENT

The idle mixture is controlled by the Electronic Control Unit (ECU) and is not adjustable.

Fuel Injector

REMOVAL AND INSTALLATION

2.2L and 2.6L Engines

1. Relieve the fuel system pressure and disconnect the negative battery cable. Drain the cooling system.

2. Disconnect the intake air hose and the ventilation hose.

3. Remove the air pipe and resonance chamber on 2.6L engine.

4. Disconnect the accelerator cable from the throttle lever.

5. Disconnect the water hoses.

6. Tag and disconnect the electrical connectors from the idle speed control valve, throttle sensor and idle switch.

7. Remove the attaching nuts and the throttle body.

8. Remove the upper intake manifold brackets.

9. Tag and disconnect the vacuum hoses and PCV hose. Tag and disconnect the intake air thermosensor connector and ground wire.

10. Remove the injector harness bracket. Remove the nuts and bolts and the upper intake manifold.

11. Disconnect the vacuum hose and fuel lines from the fuel supply manifold.

12. Remove the fuel supply manifold with the pressure regulator.

13. Disconnect the electrical connector(s) from the injector(s). Remove the grommet(s), injector(s) and insulator(s).

To install:

14. Clean all gasket mating surfaces.

15. Apply a small amount of clean engine oil to new O-ring(s) and install on the injector(s). Install the injector(s) and insulator(s) and connect the electrical connector(s).

16. Install the fuel supply manifold and tighten the attaching bolts to 14–19 ft. lbs. (19–25 Nm).

17. Connect the fuel lines and vacuum hose.

18. Position a new gasket on the lower intake manifold and install the upper intake manifold. Tighten the attaching nuts and bolts to 14–19 ft. lbs. (19–25 Nm).

19. Install the injector harness bracket.

20. Connect the ground wire and the intake air thermosensor connec-

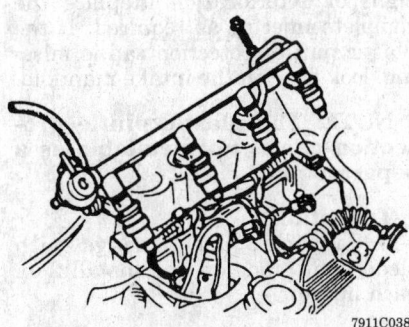

Fuel supply manifold installation — 2.2L and 2.6L engines

tor. Connect the PCV hose and the vacuum hoses.

21. Install the upper intake manifold brackets and tighten the bolts to 14–19 ft. lbs. (19–25 Nm).

22. Position a new gasket and install the throttle body. Tighten the attaching nuts to 14–19 ft. lbs. (19–25 Nm).

23. Connect the electrical connectors to the idle speed control valve, throttle sensor and idle switch.

24. Connect the water hoses. Connect the accelerator cable to the throttle lever.

25. Install the air pipe and resonance chamber, if equipped.

26. Connect the ventilation hose and intake air hose.

27. Connect the negative battery cable. Fill and bleed the cooling system.

28. Run the engine and check for leaks.

3.0L Engine

1. Relieve the fuel system pressure and disconnect the negative battery cable. Drain the cooling system.

2. Tag and disconnect all necessary vacuum, air and water hoses. Remove the airflow meter-to-throttle body intake air tube.

3. Disconnect the accelerator cable and the throttle sensor connector.

4. Remove the throttle body attaching nuts and the throttle body.

5. Remove the bypass air control valve and remove the throttle body-to-upper intake manifold intake air pipe.

6. Remove the extension manifolds. Remove the upper intake manifold along with the shutter valve actuator.

7. Disconnect the fuel lines and remove the fuel supply manifold. Disconnect the electrical connector(s) from the injector(s). Remove the injector(s) and insulator(s).

To install:

8. Clean all gasket mating surfaces.

9. Apply a small amount of clean engine oil to new O-ring(s) and install on the injector(s). Install the injector(s) and insulator(s).

10. Install the fuel supply manifold and tighten the attaching nuts to 14–19 ft. lbs. (19–25 Nm).

11. Connect the fuel lines to the fuel supply manifold. Before installing the remaining components, check for fuel leaks as follows:

a. Connect the negative battery cable.

b. Connect the terminals of the fuel pump test connector with a

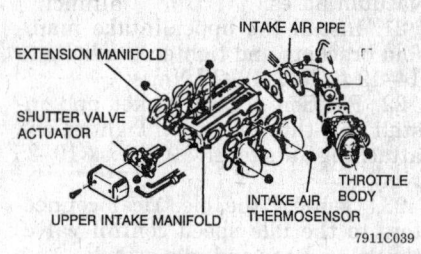

EXTENSION MANIFOLD

INTAKE AIR PIPE

SHUTTER VALVE
ACTUATOR

THROTTLE
BODY

UPPER INTAKE MANIFOLD

INTAKE AIR
THERMOSENSOR

7911C039

Upper intake manifold, throttle body and related components — 3.0L engine

jumper wire and turn the ignition switch **ON** to run the fuel pump and pressurize the system.

c. Check for fuel leaks and correct as necessary.

d. Turn the ignition switch **OFF**, remove the jumper wire and disconnect the negative battery cable.

12. Connect the electrical connectors to the fuel injectors.

13. Install a new O-ring on the lower intake manifold, then install the upper intake manifold and extension manifolds. Tighten the attaching nuts to 14–19 ft. lbs. (19–25 Nm).

14. Position a new gasket and install the intake air pipe. Tighten the attaching nuts/bolt to 14–19 ft. lbs. (19–25 Nm).

15. Position a new gasket and install the throttle body. Tighten the attaching nuts/bolt to 14–19 ft. lbs. (19–25 Nm).

16. Connect the accelerator cable and the throttle sensor connector.

17. Connect the intake air tube between the airflow meter and the throttle body. Connect all vacuum, air and water hoses.

18. Connect the negative battery cable. Fill and bleed the cooling system.

19. Run the engine and check for leaks.

4.0L Engine

1. Disconnect the negative battery cable and relieve the fuel system pressure.

2. Disconnect the electrical connectors at the air bypass valve, TPS and ACT sensor.

3. Remove the snow/ice shield to expose the throttle linkage. Remove the throttle cable bracket and disconnect the cable from the ball stud on the throttle body.

4. Remove the air inlet tube from the air cleaner to the throttle body.

5. Disconnect the PCV valve from the valve cover.

6. Disconnect the spark plug wires from the comb at the rear of the manifold.

7. Remove the canister purge line from the fitting in the throttle housing.

8. Remove the bolt that retains the air conditioner line at the upper rear of the upper manifold.

9. Remove the 6 upper intake manifold retaining nuts and remove the upper intake and throttle body assembly.

10. Disconnect the fuel supply line fitting at the fuel manifold.

11. Disconnect the fuel return line from the fuel pressure regulator as follows:

a. Disengage the locking tabs on the connector retainer and separate the retainer halves.

b. Inspect the visible internal portion of the fitting for dirt accumulation. Clean the fitting before disassembly.

c. To disengage the fitting from the regulator, push the fitting toward the regulator, insert the fingers on fuel line coupling key 49 UN01 006 or equivalent, into the slots in the coupling.

d. Using the tool, pull the fitting from the regulator.

NOTE: If the fitting has been properly disengaged, the fitting should slide off the regulator with minimum effort.

12. Disconnect the electrical connectors from the fuel injectors.

13. Remove the 6 bolts retaining the fuel supply manifold and remove the manifold.

14. Remove the injector retaining clips and remove the injectors from the manifold by grasping the injector body and pulling up while rocking the injector from side-to-side.

15. Remove and discard the injector O-rings.

16. Inspect the injector plastic pintle protection cap and washer for signs of deterioration. Replace the complete injector as required. If the plastic pintle protection cap is missing, look for it in the intake manifold.

NOTE: The plastic pintle protection cap is not available as a separate part.

To install:

17. Lubricate new O-rings with clean light grade oil and install 2 on each injector.

NOTE: Never use silicone grease at it will clog the injectors.

18. Install the injectors, using a light, twisting, pushing motion.

19. Install the fuel supply manifold, pushing down to make sure all the fuel injector O-rings are fully seated in the fuel supply manifold cups and intake manifold.

20. Install the 6 retaining bolts and tighten to 7–10 ft. lbs. (10–14 Nm). Install the retainer clips.

21. Install the fuel supply line and tighten the fitting to 15–18 ft. lbs. (20–24 Nm).

22. Install the fuel return line to the fuel pressure regulator by pushing it onto the fuel pressure regulator line up to the shoulder on the regulator line.

NOTE: The connector should grip the regulator line securely.

23. Install the connector retainer and snap the 2 halves of the retainer together.

24. Clean and inspect the mounting faces of the fuel manifold and upper intake manifold.

25. Position a new gasket on the mounting studs and install the upper intake manifold on the studs.

26. Install the 6 upper intake manifold retaining nuts and tighten to 15–18 ft. lbs. (20–25 Nm).

27. Connect the spark plug wires to the retainer comb at the rear of the intake manifold.

28. Attach the air conditioner line retainer and automatic transmission vacuum line retainer at the upper intake manifold.

29. Install the canister purge line on the throttle body fitting.

30. Connect the vacuum lines to the vacuum tree. Connect the electrical connectors at the air bypass valve, TPS and ACT sensor.

31. Install the PCV valve in the grommet at the rear of the right valve cover.

32. Attach the throttle cable bracket to the upper intake manifold, then connect the throttle cable to the ball stud and install the snow/ice shield.

33. After the upper intake manifold has been installed and before the fuel injector wire connectors have been connected, connect the negative battery cable and turn the ignition switch **ON**. This will cause the fuel pump to run for 2–3 seconds and pressurize the system.

34. Check for fuel leaks where the fuel injector is installed into the fuel supply manifold.

35. Turn the ignition switch **OFF** and disconnect the negative battery cable.

36. Connect the injector wire connectors and the vacuum line to the regulator.

37. Install the air inlet tube from the throttle body to the air cleaner.

38. Connect the negative battery cable, start the engine and let it idle for 2 minutes.

39. Turn the engine **OFF** and check for fuel leaks.

EMISSION CONTROLS

Emission Warning Lamps

RESETTING

1992–93 B-Series Pick-Up

On Federal and Canadian vehicles, the Malfunction Indicator Light (MIL) will come on at 60,000 and 80,000 mile intervals to indicate the need for scheduled maintenance of the emission control system. On California vehicles, the MIL will come on any time an engine management input device malfunctions, indicating that service is necessary. After the required service or maintenance has been performed, the MIL can be reset by changing the connector connections.

MPV

Federal and Canadian vehicles are equipped with a mileage sensor which is linked to the odometer. At every 80,000 miles, the mileage sensor will cause the Malfunction Indicator Light (MIL) to illuminate, indicating that the oxygen sensor must be

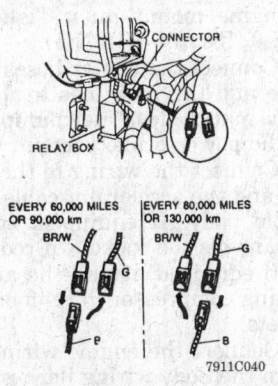

Resetting the MIL — B-Series Pick-Up

replaced. After replacing the oxygen sensor, remove the instrument cluster and reset the MIL by reversing the position of the MIL set screw.

1994–96 B-Series Pick-Up and Navajo

All vehicles are equipped with a "CHECK ENGINE" or warning light located on the instrument cluster. This light should come on briefly when the ignition key is turned **ON**, but should turn off when the engine starts. If the light does not come ON when the ignition key is turned **ON** or if it comes ON and stays ON when the engine is running, there is a mal-

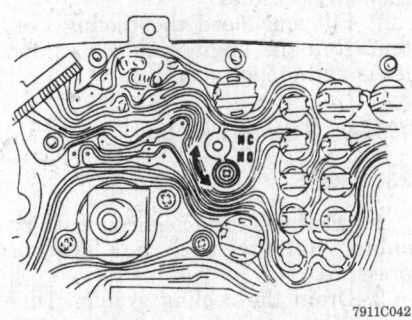

MIL reset screw location at rear of instrument cluster — MPV

function in the electronic engine control system. After the malfunction has been remedied, using the proper procedures, the "CHECK ENGINE" light will go out.

ENGINE MECHANICAL

NOTE: Disconnecting the negative battery cable on some vehicles may interfere with the functions of the on board computer systems and may require the computer to undergo a relearning process, once the negative battery cable is reconnected.

Engine Assembly

REMOVAL AND INSTALLATION

1992–93 B-Series Pick-Up

1. Relieve the fuel system pressure, disconnect the battery cables and remove the battery.

2. Raise and safely support the vehicle. Drain the engine oil and cool-

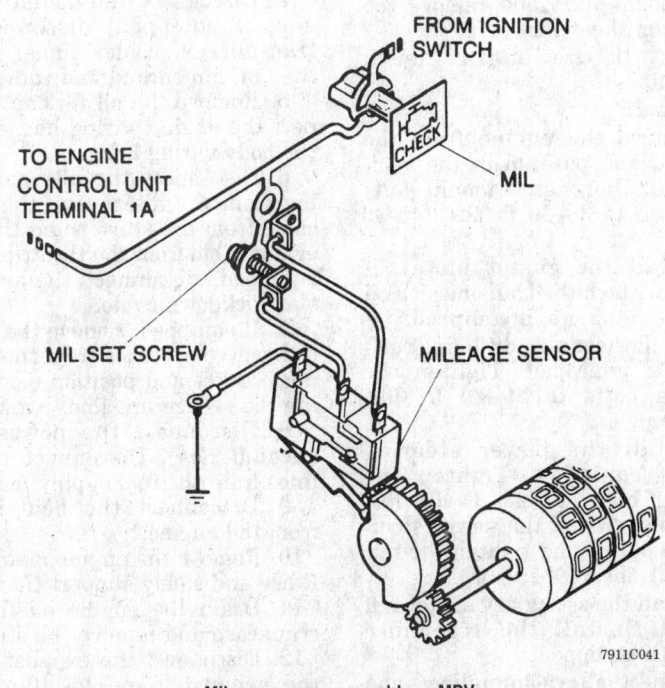

Mileage sensor assembly — MPV

ant. Remove the splash shields, as necessary.

3. Remove the starter and the transmission.

4. Disconnect the exhaust system from the exhaust manifold. Lower the vehicle.

5. Remove the air cleaner assembly, if carburetor equipped. Disconnect the accelerator cable.

6. Remove the cooling fan and the radiator shroud. Disconnect the radiator hoses and transmission oil cooler lines, if equipped and remove the radiator.

7. Disconnect the fuel lines, heater hoses and brake vacuum hose.

8. Tag and disconnect the necessary electrical connectors and vacuum hoses.

9. If carburetor equipped, disconnect the secondary air pipe assembly. On 2.6L engine, remove the resonance chamber.

10. Remove the accessory drive belt(s). If equipped, remove the power steering pump pulley and the power steering pump. Position the pump aside, leaving the hoses connected.

11. If equipped, remove the air conditioning compressor and position aside, leaving the hoses attached.

12. Remove the gusset plates, if equipped. Remove the transmission oil cooler line retainers, if equipped.

13. Attach suitable engine lifting equipment to the engine. Remove the engine mount nuts and remove the engine from the vehicle.

14. Install the engine on a workstand.

To install:

15. Remove the engine from the workstand and position in the vehicle. Install the engine mount nuts and tighten to 30–36 ft. lbs. (40–49 Nm).

16. Install the gusset plates, if equipped. Attach the transmission oil cooler line retainers, if equipped.

17. Install the air conditioning compressor, if equipped. Tighten the mounting bolts to 29–40 ft. lbs. (39–54 Nm).

18. Install the power steering pump, if equipped. Tighten the mounting bolts to 23–34 ft. lbs. (31–46 Nm). Install the power steering pump pulley and tighten the nut to 36–43 ft. lbs. (49–59 Nm).

19. Install the secondary air pipe, if equipped. Install the resonance chamber, if equipped.

20. Connect all vacuum lines and electrical connectors. Connect the brake vacuum hose, heater hoses and fuel lines.

21. Install the accessory drive belt(s) and cooling fan. Install the fan shroud, radiator and radiator hoses.

22. Adjust the accessory drive belt tension.

23. Connect the accelerator cable. Install the air cleaner assembly on carbureted engine.

24. Raise and safely support the vehicle. Connect the exhaust pipe to the exhaust manifold and tighten the attaching nuts to 30–36 ft. lbs. (40–49 Nm).

25. Install the starter and the transmission assembly. Install the splash shields and lower the vehicle.

26. Fill the crankcase with the proper type and quantity of engine oil. Install the battery and connect the battery cables.

27. Fill and bleed the cooling system. Run the engine and check for leaks and proper operation.

1994–96 B-Series Pick-Up

2.3L ENGINE

1. Disconnect the negative battery cable. Relieve the fuel system pressure.

2. Drain the cooling system. Disconnect the air cleaner tube at the throttle body. Disconnect the idle speed control hose and heat riser tube, if necessary.

3. Mark the location of the hinges on the hood and remove the hood.

4. Disconnect the radiator hoses and, if equipped, disconnect the transmission cooler lines. Remove the fan, fan shroud and radiator.

5. Remove the oil fill cap. Disconnect the engine wiring harness from the body wiring harness.

6. Disconnect the alternator wiring from the alternator, the starter cable from the starter and the accelerator cable from the throttle body. If equipped, disconnect the transmission kickdown cable.

7. If equipped, remove the air conditioner compressor from the mounting bracket and position aside, leaving the refrigerant lines attached.

8. Disconnect the power brake vacuum hose. Disconnect the fuel lines from the fuel supply manifold.

9. Disconnect the heater hoses from the engine.

10. Remove the engine mount nuts. Raise and safely support the vehicle.

11. Drain the engine oil from the crankcase and remove the starter.

12. Disconnect the exhaust pipe at the exhaust manifold. If equipped with manual transmission, remove the dust cover. If equipped with automatic transmission, remove the con-

verter inspection plate, then remove the converter-to-flywheel bolts.

13. Remove the lower flywheel housing or converter housing attaching bolts and lower the vehicle.

14. Support the transmission and flywheel housing or converter housing with a jack.

15. Remove the flywheel housing or converter housing upper attaching bolts.

16. Attach suitable engine lifting equipment. Carefully lift the engine out of the vehicle and install on a workstand.

To install:

17. Remove the engine from the workstand and carefully lower it into the engine compartment. If equipped with automatic transmission, start the converter pilot into the crankshaft.

18. If equipped with manual transmission, start the transmission input shaft into the clutch disc. It may be necessary to adjust the position of the transmission in relation to the engine if the input shaft will not enter the clutch disc. If the engine hangs up after the shaft enters, turn the crankshaft in the clockwise direction slowly, transmission in gear, until the shaft splines mesh with the clutch disc splines.

19. Install the flywheel or converter housing attaching bolts and remove the engine lifting equipment.

20. Remove the jack from under the vehicle and raise and safely support the vehicle.

21. If equipped with automatic transmission, install the converter-to-flywheel attaching bolts. Install the lower flywheel housing or converter housing attaching bolts and install the dust plate or converter inspection cover.

22. Connect the exhaust pipe to the exhaust manifold. Install the starter and connect the starter cable.

23. Lower the vehicle and install the engine mount nuts. Tighten to 65–85 ft. lbs. (88–115 Nm).

24. Connect the heater hoses to the engine and the fuel lines to the fuel supply manifold or fuel pump. Connect the power brake vacuum hose.

25. Connect the wiring to the alternator and the accelerator cable to the throttle body. If equipped, connect the transmission kickdown rod.

26. If equipped, install the air conditioning compressor in its mounting brackets.

27. Connect the engine wiring harness to the body wiring harness.

28. Install the fan, fan shroud and radiator. Connect the radiator hoses

and, if equipped, the transmission cooler lines.

29. Install the hood, aligning the hinges with the marks that were made during removal.

30. Connect the air cleaner outlet tube at the throttle body. Connect the idle speed control hose and heat riser tube, if necessary.

31. Fill the crankcase with the proper type and quantity of engine oil. Install the oil cap.

32. Connect the negative battery cable. Fill and bleed the cooling system. Run the engine and check for leaks.

3.0L (VIN U) ENGINE

1. Disconnect the negative battery cable and relieve the fuel system pressure. Drain the cooling system.

2. Mark the position of the hood on the hinges and remove the hood. Remove the air cleaner intake hose.

3. Disconnect the radiator hoses at the radiator. Remove the fan shroud attaching bolts and position the shroud over the fan. Remove the radiator, then remove the shroud.

4. Remove the alternator and bracket and position the alternator aside. Disconnect the alternator ground wire from the cylinder block.

5. Remove the air conditioner compressor and power steering pump and position aside, if equipped.

6. Disconnect the heater hoses at the intake manifold and water pump. Remove the ground wires from the cylinder block.

7. Disconnect the fuel lines at the chassis to engine connections. Disconnect the throttle cable shield and linkage at the throttle body and intake manifold.

8. Tag and disconnect the vacuum connections at the rear fitting in the upper intake manifold.

9. Tag and disconnect the wires at the ignition coil. Disconnect the 3 body wiring connectors on top of the right rocker arm cover. Disconnect the oil pressure and engine coolant temperature sender connectors.

10. Disconnect the injector harness, air charge temperature sensor and throttle position sensor. Disconnect the oxygen sensor connector at the rear of the engine and disconnect the brake booster vacuum hose.

11. Remove the engine front mount-to-crossmember attaching nuts.

12. Raise and safely support the vehicle.

13. Remove 2 lower air conditioner compressor bracket-to-engine bolts. Disconnect the wiring from the low oil level sensor and oil pressure sending unit.

14. Remove the retaining bracket holding the transmission cooling lines to the right side of the engine block.

15. Disconnect the exhaust pipes at the manifolds. Disconnect the starter cable and remove the starter.

16. If equipped with manual transmission, disconnect the hydraulic clutch line and remove the flywheel housing-to-engine block bolts.

17. If equipped with automatic transmission, remove the converter inspection cover and disconnect the converter from the flywheel.

18. Disconnect the kickdown and shift cables at the transmission. Remove the converter housing-to-engine block bolts and adapter plate-to-converter housing bolt.

19. Lower the vehicle. Remove the 2 bolts from the air conditioner compressor and position aside.

20. Attach suitable engine lifting equipment and position a jack under the transmission.

21. Raise the engine slightly and carefully pull it from the transmission. Carefully lift the engine out of the engine compartment so the rear cover plate is not bent or components damaged. Install the engine on a workstand.

To install:

22. Remove the engine from the workstand and carefully lower it into the engine compartment. Make sure the exhaust manifolds are aligned with the exhaust pipes.

23. If equipped with manual transmission, start the transmission input shaft into the clutch disc. It may be necessary to adjust the position of the transmission in relation to the engine, if the input shaft will not enter the clutch disc. If the engine hangs up after the shaft enters, turn the crankshaft in the clockwise direction slowly, transmission in gear, until the shaft splines mesh with the clutch disc splines.

24. If equipped with automatic transmission, start the converter pilot into the crankshaft. Make sure the converter rotates freely and is not binding. When the converter is fully installed in the transmission, the distance between the converter pilot and the edge of the converter housing should be 7/16–9/16

25. Install the flywheel housing or converter housing upper bolts, making sure the engine block dowels engage the housing. If equipped, install the clutch hydraulic line.

26. Remove the jack from under the transmission and remove the engine lifting equipment. If equipped with

automatic transmission, position the kickdown cable on the transmission and engine.

27. Raise and safely support the vehicle. If equipped with automatic transmission, position the transmission linkage bracket and install the remaining converter housing bolts.

28. Install the adapter plate-to-converter housing bolt. Install the converter-to-flywheel nuts and install the inspection cover. Connect the kickdown cable at the transmission.

29. If equipped with manual transmission, install the flywheel housing attaching bolts.

30. Install the starter and connect the cables. Connect the exhaust pipes at the manifolds.

31. Install the engine front mount nuts and washers or through bolts. Lower the vehicle.

32. Install the ground wires to the engine block. Connect the coil wires, the 3 body wiring connectors and the oxygen wiring connector. Connect the coolant temperature sending unit and oil pressure sending unit. Connect the brake booster vacuum hose.

33. Install the throttle linkage and connect the fuel lines. Connect the heater hoses at the water pump and cylinder block.

34. Install the alternator and bracket. Connect the alternator ground wire to the engine block. Install the drive belt and adjust the tension.

35. Install the air conditioning compressor and power steering pump, if equipped.

36. Position the fan shroud over the fan. Install the radiator and connect the radiator hoses. Install the fan shroud.

37. Connect the negative battery cable. Fill and bleed the cooling system.

38. Bleed the hydraulic clutch, if necessary. Evacuate and charge the air conditioning system, if necessary.

39. Run the engine and check for leaks and proper operation. Install the intake hose. Install the hood, aligning the marks that were made during removal.

4.0L ENGINE

1. Disconnect the negative battery cable and relieve the fuel system pressure. Drain the cooling system.

2. Mark the position of the hood on the hinges and remove the hood. Remove the air cleaner intake hose.

3. Disconnect the radiator hoses at the radiator. Disconnect the fan shroud and position it over the fan. Remove the radiator, then the shroud.

4. Remove the alternator and bracket and position the alternator aside. Disconnect the alternator ground wire from the cylinder block.

5. Remove the air conditioning compressor and power steering pump and position aside, if equipped.

6. Disconnect the heater hoses at the intake manifold and water pump. Remove the ground wires from the cylinder block.

7. Disconnect the fuel lines from the fuel supply manifold. Disconnect the throttle cable shield and linkage at the throttle body and intake manifold.

8. Tag and disconnect the vacuum connections at the rear vacuum fitting in the upper intake manifold.

9. Disconnect the wiring from the ignition coil and oil pressure and engine coolant temperature senders. Disconnect the injector harness, air charge temperature sensor and throttle position sensor. Disconnect the brake booster vacuum hose.

10. Raise and safely support the vehicle. Disconnect the exhaust pipes at the manifolds. Disconnect the starter cable and remove the starter.

11. Remove the engine front mount-to-crossmember attaching nuts or through bolts.

12. Remove the converter inspection cover and disconnect the converter from the flywheel. Remove the cable.

13. Remove the converter housing-to-engine block bolts and the adapter plate-to-converter housing bolt. Lower the vehicle.

14. Position a jack under the transmission and install suitable engine lifting equipment.

15. Raise the engine slightly and carefully pull it from the transmission. Carefully lift the engine out of the engine compartment so the rear cover plate is not bent or components damaged. Install the engine on a workstand.

To install:

16. Remove the engine from the workstand and carefully lower it into the engine compartment. Make sure the exhaust manifolds are aligned with the exhaust pipe.

17. At the transmission, start the converter pilot into the crankshaft. Install the converter housing upper bolts, making sure the dowels in the cylinder block engage the flywheel housing. Tighten the bolts to 33–45 ft. lbs. (45–61 Nm).

18. Remove the jack from under the transmission and the engine lifting equipment.

19. Position the kickdown rod on the transmission and engine. Raise and safely support the vehicle.

20. Position the transmission linkage bracket and install the remaining converter housing bolts. Install the adapter plate-to-converter housing bolt. Install the converter-to-flywheel nuts and install the inspection cover. Connect the kickdown rod on the transmission.

21. Install the starter and connect the cable. Connect the exhaust pipes at the manifolds.

22. Install the engine front mount nuts and washers or through bolts. Lower the vehicle.

23. Install the ground wires to the engine block. Connect the ignition coil wiring, then connect the coolant temperature sending unit and oil pressure sending unit. Connect the brake booster vacuum hose.

24. Install the throttle linkage and connect the fuel lines at the fuel supply manifold.

25. Connect the ground cable at the engine block. Connect the heater hoses to the water pump and cylinder block.

26. Install the alternator and bracket. Connect the alternator ground wire to the engine block. Install the accessory drive belt.

27. Install the air conditioner compressor and power steering pump, if equipped.

28. Position the shroud over the fan. Install the radiator and connect the radiator upper and lower hoses. Install the fan shroud attaching bolts.

29. Connect the negative battery cable. Fill and bleed the cooling system.

30. Run the engine and check for leaks and proper operation. If equipped, evacuate and charge the air conditioning system.

31. Install the intake hose. Install the hood, aligning the marks that were made during removal.

MPV

1. Relieve the fuel system pressure, disconnect the battery cables and remove the battery.

2. Raise and safely support the vehicle. Drain the engine oil and coolant. Remove the splash shield.

3. Remove the starter and the transmission.

4. Disconnect the exhaust pipes from the exhaust manifolds and lower the vehicle.

5. Remove the fresh air duct and the radiator hoses. Disconnect the

transmission oil cooler lines from the radiator, if equipped.

6. Remove the radiator, fan shroud and cooling fan. Remove the accessory drive belts.

7. Tag and disconnect the necessary electrical connectors and vacuum lines. Disconnect the brake vacuum hose, heater hoses and fuel lines.

8. On 2.6L engine, disconnect the accelerator cable and remove the resonance chamber and air cleaner. On 3.0L engine, disconnect the accelerator cable and remove the air cleaner and airflow meter.

9. Remove the shroud upper panel and the air conditioning pipe bracket. On 3.0L engine, remove the protector cover from the front of the engine.

10. If equipped, remove the power steering pump and position aside, leaving the hoses attached. It is necessary to remove the power steering pulley prior to removing the pump.

11. If equipped, remove the air conditioning compressor and position aside, leaving the hoses attached.

12. Remove the lower grille and radiator grille. Remove the shroud upper plate and the additional condenser fan, if equipped.

13. Attach suitable engine lifting equipment to the engine. Remove the engine mount nuts and remove the engine from the vehicle.

14. Install the engine on a workstand.

To install:

15. Remove the engine from the workstand. Lower the engine into the vehicle, being careful not to damage the piping.

NOTE: Lean the air conditioning condenser forward to ease engine installation.

16. Install the engine mount nuts and tighten to 25–36 ft. lbs. (34–49 Nm). Install the additional condenser fan, if equipped.

17. Apply a bead of sealer to each side of the front support, then install the shroud upper plate. Tighten the mounting bolts to 61–87 inch lbs. (6.9–9.8 Nm).

18. Install the radiator grille and lower grille.

19. Install the air conditioning compressor, if equipped. Tighten the mounting bolts to 13–20 ft. lbs. (18–26 Nm). Install the air conditioner pipe bracket and tighten the mounting nuts to 61–87 inch lbs. (6.9–9.8 Nm).

20. Install the power steering pump, if equipped. Tighten the mounting bolts to 23–34 ft. lbs. (31–46 Nm). Install the pump pulley

and tighten the nut to 29–43 ft. lbs. (39–59 Nm).

21. Install the shroud upper panel and tighten the bolts to 69–95 inch lbs. (7.8–11.0 Nm).

22. Connect the accelerator cable. On 2.6L engine, install the resonance chamber and air filter. On 3.0L engine, install the air cleaner and airflow meter.

23. Connect all electrical connectors and vacuum hoses.

24. Connect the brake vacuum hose, heater hoses and fuel lines.

25. Install the accessory drive belts and the cooling fan. Install the fan shroud and the radiator. Adjust the drive belt tension.

26. Install the radiator hoses and fresh air duct. If equipped, connect the transmission oil cooler lines.

27. Raise and safely support the vehicle. Connect the exhaust pipes to the exhaust manifolds. Tighten the nuts to 25–36 ft. lbs. (34–49 Nm).

28. Install the starter and transmission assembly. Install the splash shield and lower the vehicle.

29. Install the battery and connect the negative battery cables. Fill the crankcase with the proper type and quantity of engine oil.

30. Fill and bleed the cooling system. Run the engine and check for leaks and proper operation.

Navajo

1. Disconnect the negative battery cable and relieve the fuel system pressure. Drain the cooling system.

2. Mark the position of the hood on the hinges and remove the hood. Remove the air cleaner intake hose.

3. Disconnect the radiator hoses at the radiator. Disconnect the fan shroud and position it over the fan. Remove the radiator, then the shroud.

4. Remove the alternator and bracket and position the alternator aside. Disconnect the alternator ground wire from the cylinder block.

5. Remove the air conditioning compressor and power steering pump and position aside, if equipped.

6. Disconnect the heater hoses at the intake manifold and water pump. Remove the ground wires from the cylinder block.

7. Disconnect the fuel lines from the fuel supply manifold. Disconnect the throttle cable shield and linkage at the throttle body and intake manifold.

8. Tag and disconnect the vacuum connections at the rear vacuum fitting in the upper intake manifold.

9. Disconnect the wiring from the ignition coil and oil pressure and engine coolant temperature senders. Disconnect the injector harness, air charge temperature sensor and throttle position sensor. Disconnect the brake booster vacuum hose.

10. Raise and safely support the vehicle. Disconnect the exhaust pipes at the manifolds. Disconnect the starter cable and remove the starter.

11. Remove the engine front mount-to-crossmember attaching nuts or through bolts.

12. Remove the converter inspection cover and disconnect the converter from the flywheel. Remove the cable.

13. Remove the converter housing-to-engine block bolts and the adapter plate-to-converter housing bolt. Lower the vehicle.

14. Position a jack under the transmission and install suitable engine lifting equipment.

15. Raise the engine slightly and carefully pull it from the transmission. Carefully lift the engine out of the engine compartment so the rear cover plate is not bent or components damaged. Install the engine on a workstand.

To install:

16. Remove the engine from the workstand and carefully lower it into the engine compartment. Make sure the exhaust manifolds are aligned with the exhaust pip

17. At the transmission, start the converter pilot into the crankshaft. Install the converter housing upper bolts, making sure the dowels in the cylinder block engage the flywheel housing. Tighten the bolts to 33–45 ft. lbs. (45–61 Nm).

18. Remove the jack from under the transmission and the engine lifting equipment.

19. Position the kickdown rod on the transmission and engine. Raise and safely support the vehicle.

20. Position the transmission linkage bracket and install the remaining converter housing bolts. Install the adapter plate-to-converter housing bolt. Install the converter-to-flywheel nuts and install the inspection cover. Connect the kickdown rod on the transmission.

21. Install the starter and connect the cable. Connect the exhaust pipes at the manifolds.

22. Install the engine front mount nuts and washers or through bolts. Lower the vehicle.

23. Install the ground wires to the engine block. Connect the ignition

coil wiring, then connect the coolant temperature sending unit and oil pressure sending unit. Connect the brake booster vacuum hose.

24. Install the throttle linkage and connect the fuel lines at the fuel supply manifold.

25. Connect the ground cable at the engine block. Connect the heater hoses to the water pump and cylinder block.

26. Install the alternator and bracket. Connect the alternator ground wire to the engine block. Install the accessory drive belt.

27. Install the air conditioner compressor and power steering pump, if equipped.

28. Position the shroud over the fan. Install the radiator and connect the radiator upper and lower hoses. Install the fan shroud attaching bolts.

29. Connect the negative battery cable. Fill and bleed the cooling system.

30. Run the engine and check for leaks and proper operation. If equipped, evacuate and charge the air conditioning system.

31. Install the intake hose. Install the hood, aligning the marks that were made during removal.

Engine Mounts

REMOVAL AND INSTALLATION

Front Mounts

1. Remove the fan shroud attaching bolts.

2. Support the engine using a wood block and a jack under the oil pan.

3. Remove the engine mount bracket nut(s). Raise the engine with the jack just enough to remove the mount.

4. Remove the attaching nuts/bolts and remove the mount.

5. Installation is the reverse of the removal procedure.

Rear Mounts

1. Raise and safely support the vehicle.

2. Support the transmission with a jack.

3. Remove the mount-to-crossmember nuts/bolts and the mount-to-transmission bolts.

4. Raise the transmission just enough to remove the mount.

5. Installation is the reverse of the removal procedure.

Cylinder Head

REMOVAL AND INSTALLATION

2.2L Engine

1. Relieve the fuel system pressure and disconnect the negative battery cable.
2. Remove the splash shield and drain the cooling system.
3. If carburetor equipped, remove the air cleaner assembly. If fuel injected, remove the air intake hose.
4. Disconnect the accelerator cable.
5. Remove the cooling fan and fan shroud.
6. Disconnect the fuel lines. If equipped with carburetor and manual transmission, remove the fuel pump.
7. Disconnect the heater hoses and brake vacuum hose. Tag and disconnect the necessary electrical connectors and vacuum hoses.
8. Tag and disconnect the spark plug wires and remove the spark plugs. Remove the distributor.
9. If carburetor equipped, disconnect the secondary air pipe assembly.
10. Disconnect the upper radiator and water bypass hoses.
11. Remove the intake and exhaust manifolds.
12. Remove the timing belt front cover and the timing belt tensioner and timing belt.
13. Remove the rocker arm cover.
14. Loosen the cylinder head bolts in 2–3 steps in the proper sequence. Remove the bolts and remove the cylinder head.
15. Clean all gasket mating surfaces. Measure the cylinder head for distortion in 6 directions using a straight-edge. The maximum allowable distortion is 0.006 in. (0.15mm).
16. If distortion is excessive, resurface or replace the cylinder head. If resurfacing, do not remove more than 0.008 in. (0.20mm). The cylinder head height should be 3.620–3.624 in. (91.95–92.05mm).

NOTE: If resurfacing the cylinder, it will be necessary to remove the rocker arm/shaft assemblies.

To install:

17. Position a new head gasket on the cylinder block and install the cylinder head. Apply oil to the threads and seat faces of the cylinder head bolts and install.
18. Tighten the cylinder head bolts in 2–3 steps in the proper sequence. The final torque specification is 59–64 ft. lbs. (80–86 Nm).
19. Apply silicone sealer to each side of the front and rear camshaft bearing caps where the cap meets the cylinder head. Install the rocker arm cover and tighten the bolts to 26–35 inch lbs. (2.9–3.9 Nm).
20. Install the timing belt and tensioner. install the timing belt front cover.
21. Install the intake and exhaust manifolds.
22. Install the upper radiator and water bypass hoses. If carburetor equipped, install the secondary air pipe.
23. Install the distributor. Install the spark plugs and connect the spark plug wires.
24. Connect all vacuum hoses and electrical connectors. Connect the heater hoses and the brake vacuum hose.
25. If equipped, install the fuel pump. Connect the fuel lines.
26. Install the cooling fan and shroud.
27. Connect the accelerator cable. Install the air cleaner or air intake hose.
28. Install the splash shield. Connect the negative battery cable.
29. Fill and bleed the cooling system. Run the engine and check for leaks.
30. Check and adjust the ignition timing.

2.3L Engine

1. Disconnect the negative battery cable. Drain the cooling system.
2. Remove the air cleaner assembly. Remove the heater hose retaining screw(s) to the rocker arm cover.
3. If equipped, disconnect the distributor cap and spark plug wires and remove the assembly.
4. Remove the spark plugs. If equipped with distributorless ignition, remove the spark plug wire harnesses.
5. Remove the engine and alternator wiring harnesses. Disconnect the oxygen sensor at the exhaust manifold.
6. Tag and disconnect the required vacuum hoses. Remove the dipstick tube and bracket.
7. Remove the rocker arm cover attaching bolts and remove the cover. Remove the intake manifold attaching bolts.
8. Loosen the alternator retaining bolts and remove the belt from the pulley. Remove the mounting bracket-to-head retaining bolts.
9. Remove the upper radiator hose. Remove the timing belt cover bolt(s) and remove the cover. If equipped with power steering, move the power steering pump bracket.
10. Loosen the timing belt idler retaining bolts. Position the idler in the unloaded position and tighten the retaining bolts. Remove the timing belt from the camshaft pulley and auxiliary pulley.
11. Remove the 4 nuts and/or stud bolts retaining the heat stove to the exhaust manifold. Remove the 8 exhaust manifold retaining bolts.
12. Remove the timing belt idler and 2 bracket bolts. Remove the timing belt idler spring stop from the cylinder head.
13. Remove the cylinder head retaining bolts and remove the cylinder head.
14. Clean all gasket mating surfaces. Check the cylinder head for flatness using a straight edge and a feeler gauge. The cylinder head must not be warped more than 0.003 in. in any 6 in. or more than 0.006 in. overall.

To install:

15. Position a new head gasket on the block. Properly position the camshaft in the cylinder head and install the cylinder head on the block.
16. Install the cylinder head bolts and tighten, in sequence, in 2 steps,

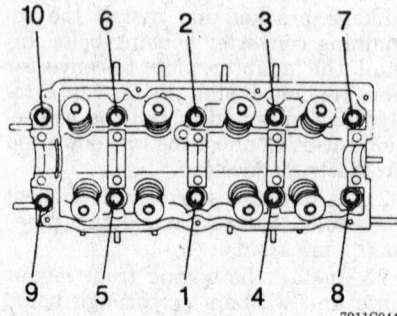

Cylinder head bolt removal sequence — 2.2L engine

7911C043

Cylinder head bolt torque sequence — 2.2L engine

7911C044

first to 50–60 ft. lbs. (68–81 Nm) and then to 80–90 ft. lbs. (108–122 Nm).

17. Install a new intake manifold gasket and position the intake manifold to the cylinder head. Install the retaining bolts.

18. Install the timing belt idler spring stop to the cylinder head. Position the timing belt idler to the cylinder head and install the retaining bolts.

19. Install the 8 exhaust manifold retaining bolts and the 4 nuts and/or stud bolts retaining the heat stove to the exhaust manifold.

20. If equipped, align the distributor rotor with the No. 1 spark plug location in the distributor cap.

21. Align the cam gear with the pointer and the crank pulley with the pointer on the timing belt cover.

22. Position the timing belt to the pulleys. Loosen the idler retaining, rotate the engine and check the timing alignment.

23. Adjust the belt tensioner and tighten the retaining bolts. Install the timing belt cover and the retaining bolt(s).

24. Install the upper radiator hose. Position the alternator bracket to the cylinder head and install the retainers. Install the drive belt and adjust the belt tension.

25. Install a new rocker arm cover gasket on the rocker arm cover. Install the rocker arm cover on the cylinder head and install the retaining bolts.

26. Install the spark plugs. Install the spark plug wires and the distributor cap, if equipped.

27. Install the dipstick tube and bracket. Connect the vacuum hoses. Install the retaining heater hose screw(s) to the rocker arm cover.

28. Connect the negative battery cable. Fill and bleed the cooling system.

29. Start the engine and check for leaks. Install the air cleaner hose to the throttle body.

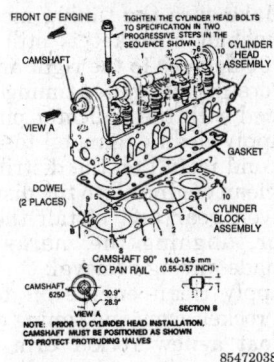

Cylinder head installation — 2.3L engine

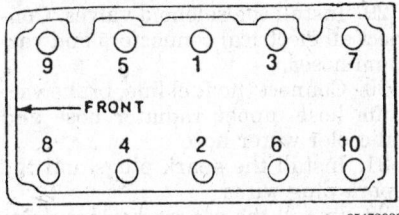

Cylinder head bolt torque sequence — 2.3L engine

2.6L Engine

1. Relieve the fuel system pressure and disconnect the negative battery cable. Drain the cooling system.

2. Disconnect the accelerator cable and remove the air intake pipe and resonance chamber.

3. Remove the air conditioning drive belt and idler.

4. Tag and disconnect the spark plug wires. Remove the spark plugs.

5. Remove the upper radiator and oil cooler water hoses. Disconnect the brake vacuum hose, canister hose and fuel line.

6. Tag and disconnect the oxygen sensor connector and emission harness connectors. Remove the solenoid valves.

7. Remove the rocker arm cover. Turn the crankshaft pulley until the timing mark on the camshaft sprocket is 90 degrees to the right. The mark should be parallel to the top of the cylinder head surface. Make sure the yellow crankshaft pulley timing mark is aligned with the indicator pin.

8. Mark the position of the distributor rotor in relation to the distributor housing and the distributor housing in relation to the cylinder head. Remove the distributor.

NOTE: Do not rotate the engine after distributor removal.

9. Hold the crankshaft pulley with a suitable tool and remove the distributor drive gear/camshaft pulley retaining bolt and the drive gear.

10. Remove the service cover on the timing chain cover. Push the chain adjuster sleeve in toward the left and insert a 0.08 in. (2mm) diameter by 1.77 in. (45mm) long pin into the lever hole to hold it. Be careful that the pin does not fall.

11. Secure the camshaft sprocket and chain with a wire to hold the chain in place on the sprocket. Do not allow the sprocket and chain to fall down into the engine and cause the chain to become disengaged from the crankshaft sprocket.

12. Loosen the cylinder head bolts in 2–3 steps in the proper sequence. Remove the bolts and remove the cylinder head.

13. If necessary, remove the intake and exhaust manifolds from the cylinder head.

14. Clean all gasket mating surfaces. Measure the cylinder head for distortion in 6 directions using a straight-edge. The maximum allowable distortion is 0.006 in. (0.15mm).

15. If distortion is excessive, resurface or replace the cylinder head. If resurfacing, do not remove more than 0.008 in. (0.20mm). The cylinder head height should be 3.541–3.545 in. (89.95–90.05mm).

NOTE: It will be necessary to remove the rocker arm/shaft assembly if resurfacing is necessary.

To install:

16. If removed, install the intake and exhaust manifolds.

17. Apply silicone sealer to the cylinder block head gasket surface at the mating junction of the cylinder block and the timing chain cover.

18. Position a new head gasket and install the cylinder head. Apply clean engine oil to the head bolt threads and seat faces and install the bolts.

19. Tighten the cylinder head bolts, in sequence, in 2–3 steps. The final torque specification is 59–64 ft. lbs. (80–86 Nm). Tighten the 2 cylinder head-to-timing chain cover bolts to 12–17 ft. lbs. (16–23 Nm).

20. Install the camshaft sprocket onto the camshaft dowel pin, then remove the wire securing the camshaft sprocket and chain.

21. Remove the retaining pin from the chain adjuster and install the ser-

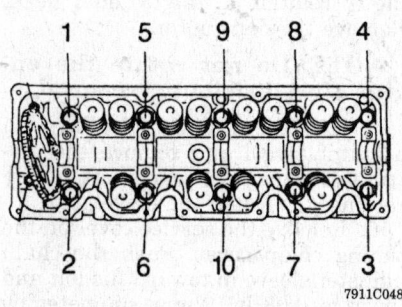

Cylinder head bolt removal sequence — 2.6L engine

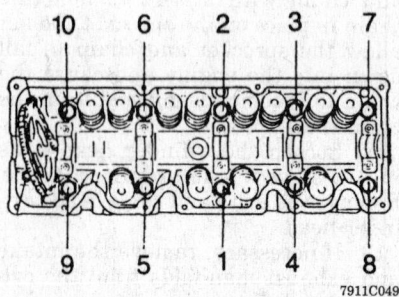

Cylinder head bolt torque sequence — 2.6L engine

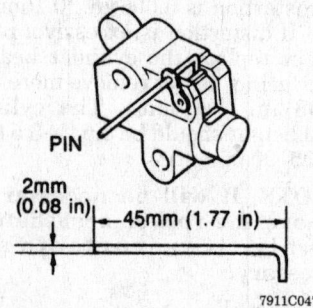

Retaining the chain adjuster — 2.6L engine

vice cover with a new gasket. Tighten the mounting bolts to 69–95 inch lbs. (7.8–11.0 Nm) and the mounting nuts to 61–87 inch lbs. (6.9–9.8 Nm).

22. Install the distributor drive gear with a new washer and lock bolt. Position a shop cloth to protect the cylinder head and place a small prybar between the cylinder head and the small tab on the camshaft between the lobes, to hold the camshaft in place. Tighten the lock bolt to 36–45 ft. lbs. (49–61 Nm).

23. Apply sealer to the cylinder head and install the half circle seals.

24. Make sure the timing mark on the camshaft sprocket is still positioned 90 degrees to the right and the yellow crankshaft pulley timing mark is aligned with the indicator pin.

25. Apply clean engine oil to a new O-ring and install on the distributor. Apply clean engine oil to the distributor driven gear and install the distributor, aligning the marks that were made during removal.

26. Apply clean engine oil to the valves, rocker arms and timing chain.

27. Coat a new rocker arm cover gasket with sealer and install on the rocker arm cover.

28. Apply silicone sealer to the front and rear half circle seals and install the rocker arm cover. Tighten the attaching bolts to 52–78 inch lbs. (5.9–8.8 Nm).

29. Install the solenoid valves. Connect all electrical connectors and vacuum hoses.

30. Connect the fuel line, brake vacuum hose, upper radiator hose and oil cooler water hose.

31. Install the spark plugs and the spark plug wires.

32. Install the air conditioner drive belt and idler, if equipped. Install the air intake pipe and resonance chamber and connect the accelerator cable.

33. Connect the negative battery cable. Fill and bleed the cooling system.

34. Run the engine and check for leaks. Check and adjust the ignition timing.

3.0L (JE) Engine

1. Relieve the fuel system pressure and disconnect the negative battery cable. Drain the cooling system.

2. Remove the air intake hose and disconnect the accelerator cable.

3. Turn the crankshaft to align the timing marks on the timing belt sprockets. Mark the direction of rotation on the belt and remove the timing belt.

4. Disconnect the brake vacuum hose and the fuel line. Tag and disconnect all necessary electrical connectors and vacuum hoses.

5. Mark the position of the distributor rotor in relation to the distributor housing and the distributor housing in relation to the cylinder head. Remove the distributor.

6. Remove the extension manifolds. Loosen the intake manifold bolts, in sequence, in 2–3 steps and remove the bolts and intake manifold.

7. Remove the rocker arm cover. Remove the center exhaust pipe insulator and center exhaust pipe.

8. Remove the exhaust manifold insulator and exhaust manifold. Remove the seal plate.

9. Loosen the cylinder head bolts, in sequence, in 2–3 steps and remove the bolts and cylinder head.

10. Clean all gasket mating surfaces. Measure the cylinder head for distortion in 6 directions using a straight-edge. The maximum allowable distortion is 0.004 in. (0.10mm).

11. If distortion is excessive, resurface or replace the cylinder head. If resurfacing, do not remove more than 0.006 in. (0.15mm). The cylinder head height should be 4.931–4.935 in. (125.25–125.35mm).

NOTE: It will be necessary to remove the rocker arm/shaft assembly if resurfacing is necessary.

To install:

12. Check the oil control plug projection from the cylinder block. It should be 0.209–0.224 in. (5.3–5.7mm).

13. Apply clean engine oil to a new O-ring and install on the oil control plug. Install a new cylinder head gasket, making sure the **L** mark, for left bank or **R** mark, for right bank, is facing upward.

14. Install the cylinder head, being careful not to damage the oil control plug O-ring.

15. Measure the length of the cylinder head bolts prior to installation and replace if not within specification. The intake side bolts should be 4.25 in. (108mm) and should not exceed 4.29 in. (109mm). The exhaust side bolts should be 5.43 in. (138mm) and should not exceed 5.47 in. (139mm).

16. Apply clean engine oil to the threads and the seat face of the cylinder head bolts and install. Tighten the bolts as follows:

Step 1: Tighten each bolt, in sequence, to 14 ft. lbs. (20 Nm)

Step 2: Tighten each bolt, in sequence, an additional 90 degree turn

Step 3: Repeat Step 2

17. Install the seal plate, exhaust manifold and exhaust manifold insulator.

18. Install the center exhaust pipe and exhaust pipe insulator.

19. Coat a new rocker arm cover gasket with silicone sealant and install onto the rocker arm cover. Install the rocker arm cover with new seal washers and tighten the bolts to 30–39 inch lbs. (3.4–4.4 Nm).

20. Connect the injector harness and position a new intake manifold gasket. Install the intake manifold and tighten the bolts, in sequence in

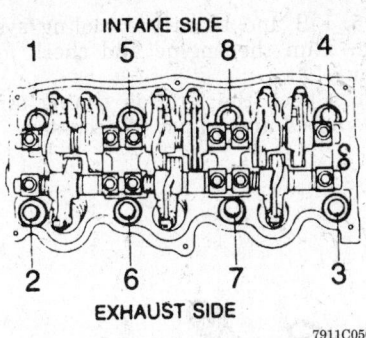

INTAKE SIDE

EXHAUST SIDE

7911C050

Cylinder head bolt removal sequence — 3.0L (JE) engine

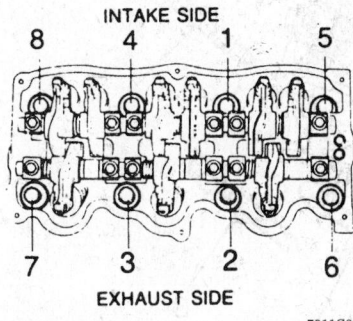

INTAKE SIDE

EXHAUST SIDE

7911C051

Cylinder head bolt torque sequence — 3.0L (JE) engine

2–3 steps. The final torque specification is 14–19 ft. lbs. (19–25 Nm).

21. Apply clean engine oil to new O-rings and install the extension manifolds with new gaskets. Tighten to 14–19 ft. lbs. (19–25 Nm).

22. Install the distributor, aligning the marks that were made during removal.

23. Connect all electrical connectors and vacuum hoses. Connect the fuel line and brake vacuum hose.

24. Install the timing belt.

25. Connect the accelerator cable and install the air intake hose.

26. Connect the negative battery cable. Fill and bleed the cooling system.

27. Run the engine and check for leaks. Check and adjust the ignition timing.

3.0L (VIN U) Engine

1. Disconnect the negative battery cable and relieve the fuel system pressure. Drain the cooling system.

2. Remove the air cleaner fresh air hose from the throttle body and air cleaner. If equipped, remove the engine oil filler adapter.

3. Disconnect the fuel lines. Tag and disconnect the necessary vacuum lines.

4. Disconnect the upper radiator hose and heater hose and position aside. Disconnect the ignition coil electrical connector and remove the coil.

5. Remove the throttle body.

6. Remove the distributor cap. Mark the position of the rotor in relation to the distributor housing and the position of the distributor housing in relation to the intake manifold. Remove the distributor hold-down bolt and clamp and remove the distributor. Tag and disconnect the spark plug wires from the spark plugs and remove the distributor cap and wires assembly.

7. If removing the left cylinder head, proceed as follows:

a. Remove the necessary accessory drive belt(s).

b. Remove the power steering pump and bracket, leaving the lines connected. Place the assembly aside in a position to prevent fluid leakage.

c. Remove the engine oil dipstick tube.

d. Remove the fuel line retaining bracket bolt from the front of the cylinder head, if equipped.

8. If removing the right cylinder head, proceed as follows:

a. Remove the necessary accessory drive belt(s).

b. Remove the accessory drive belt idler or tensioner.

c. Remove the grounding strap throttle cable support bracket, if necessary.

d. Disconnect the alternator electrical harnesses and remove the alternator and bracket assembly.

9. Remove the spark plugs.

10. Disconnect the exhaust pipes and remove the exhaust manifolds.

11. Remove the rocker arm covers. Loosen the rocker arm fulcrum retaining bolts enough to allow the rocker arm to be lifted off the pushrod and rotated to 1 side.

NOTE: Regardless of which head is to be removed, the No. 3 cylinder intake valve pushrod must be removed to allow removal of the intake manifold.

12. Remove the pushrods, marking them so they can be reinstalled in their original positions.

13. Remove the intake manifold.

14. Remove the cylinder head attaching bolts and remove the cylinder heads.

15. Clean all gasket mating surfaces. Check the cylinder head for flatness using a straight edge and a feeler gauge. The cylinder head must not be warped more than 0.003 in. in any 6 in. or more than 0.006 in. overall.

To install:

16. Position new head gasket(s) on the cylinder block, using the dowels for alignment.

17. Install the cylinder head(s) on the block. Oil the threads of new cylinder head bolts and hand tighten.

18. Tighten the cylinder head bolts, in sequence, to 59 ft. lbs. (80 Nm). Back off all bolts a minimum of 1 full turn. Retighten the bolts, in sequence, in 2 steps, first to 37 ft. lbs. (50 Nm) and then to 68 ft. lbs. (92 Nm).

19. Install the intake manifold.

20. Install the distributor, aligning the marks that were made during removal. Install the hold-down bolt and clamp.

21. Dip each pushrod in heavy engine oil and install them in their original positions.

22. For each valve, rotate the crankshaft until the lifter rests on the base circle of the camshaft lobe, before tightening the rocker arm fulcrum attaching bolts. Position the rocker arms over the valves and pushrods, install the fulcrums and fulcrum bolts and tighten to 24 ft. lbs. (32 Nm).

NOTE: If the original valve train components are being installed, a valve clearance check is not required. If a component has been replaced, perform a valve clearance check.

23. Install the exhaust manifolds and the spark plugs.

24. Install the rocker arm covers. Install the dipstick tube.

25. Install the fuel injector harness to the injectors and inboard rocker arm cover studs. Connect the engine harness to the main harness.

26. Install the distributor cap and connect the spark plug wires to the spark plugs.

27. Install the throttle body. Install the ignition coil and bracket, if necessary and connect the electrical connector.

28. Install the fuel line retaining bracket to the front of the cylinder head, if equipped. Tighten the retaining bolts to 26 ft. lbs. (35 Nm).

29. Install the power steering pump and bracket, if removed. Install the alternator and bracket assembly, if removed and connect the electrical harness.

30. Install the accessory drive belt(s).

31. Connect the fuel lines to the fuel supply manifold. Connect the upper radiator and heater hoses.

32. Connect the vacuum lines.

33. Change the engine oil and filter.

NOTE: Engine coolant is corrosive to all engine bearing material. Replacing engine oil after removal of a coolant carrying component helps prevent engine failure later.

34. Install the air cleaner fresh air hose to the throttle body and air cleaner. Connect the negative battery cable.

35. Fill and bleed the cooling system. Run the engine and check for leaks.

36. Check the ignition timing and idle speed and adjust, if necessary.

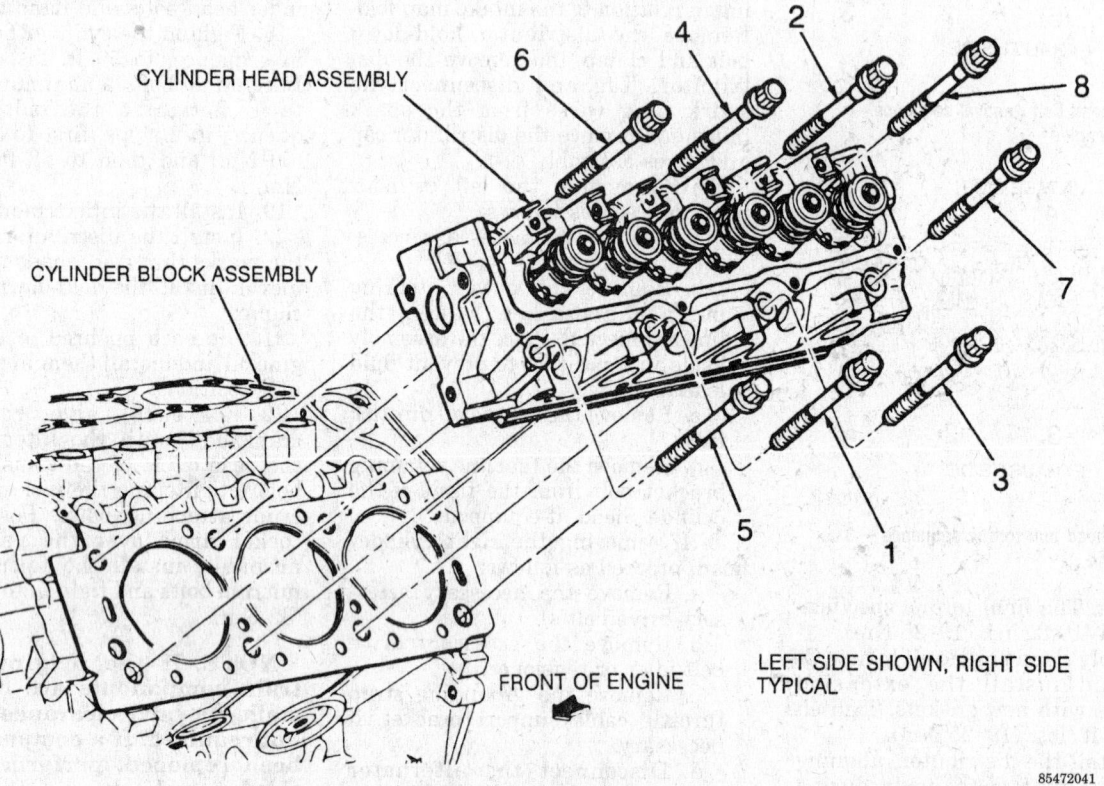

Cylinder head bolt torque sequence — 3.0L (VIN U) engine

4.0L Engine

1. Disconnect the negative battery cable and relieve the fuel system pressure. Drain the cooling system.

2. Remove the upper and lower intake manifolds and rocker arm covers.

3. If the left cylinder head is being removed, proceed as follows:

    a. Remove the accessory drive belt.

    b. Discharge the refrigerant and remove the air conditioning compressor, if equipped.

    c. Remove the power steering pump and bracket and position aside.

    d. Remove the spark plugs.

4. If the right cylinder head is being removed, proceed as follows:

    a. Remove the accessory drive belt.

    b. Remove the alternator and alternator bracket.

    c. Remove the ignition coil and bracket assembly.

    d. Remove the spark plugs.

5. Disconnect the exhaust pipe and remove the exhaust manifold(s).

6. Remove the rocker arm shaft assembly. Remove the pushrods, marking them so they can be reinstalled in the same positions.

7. Remove and discard the cylinder head attaching bolts and remove the cylinder heads.

8. Clean all gasket mating surfaces. Check the cylinder head for flatness using a straight-edge and a feeler gauge. The cylinder head must not be warped more than 0.003 in. in any 6 in. or more than 0.006 in. overall.

To install:

9. Position new cylinder head gasket(s) on the cylinder block. Install cylinder head locating dowels.

NOTE: The cylinder head(s) and intake manifold are torqued alternately and in sequence to insure correct fit and gasket crunch.

10. Install new cylinder head bolts and tighten, in sequence, to 44 ft. lbs. (60 Nm).

11. Apply silicone sealer to the block and cylinder head mating surfaces at the 4 corners of the lifter valley opening. Install the intake manifold gasket and again apply sealer in the same locations.

12. Position the lower intake manifold on the 2 guide studs and install the nuts and bolts hand tight. Tighten the lower intake manifold bolts, in sequence, to 3–6 ft. lbs. (4–8 Nm).

Valve Lifters

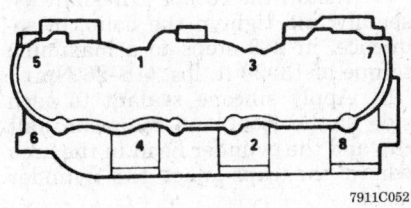

Cylinder head bolt torque sequence — 4.0L engine

7911C052

REMOVAL AND INSTALLATION

Except 2.3L, 3.0L (VIN U) and 4.0L Engines

All engines except 2.3L, 3.0L (VIN U) and 4.0L engines are equipped with hydraulic lash adjusters located in the rocker arms. The hydraulic lash adjusters can be removed by hand or with suitable pliers after the rocker arm/shaft assembly is removed.

2.3L Engine

1. Disconnect the negative battery cable and remove the air cleaner or air intake duct. On 2.3L engine, remove the throttle body and EGR supply tube.
2. Remove the rocker arm cover.
3. Rotate the crankshaft so the base circle of the cam is facing the applicable cam follower.
4. Using valve spring compressor lever tool T88T-6565-BH or equivalent, collapse the valve spring and slide the cam follower over the valve lifter and out.
5. Lift out the hydraulic valve lifter.

To install:
6. Rotate the crankshaft so the base circle of the cam is facing the applicable cam follower.
7. Coat the hydraulic lifter with clean engine oil and install it in the bore.
8. Collapse the valve spring using valve spring compressor lever T88T-6565-BH or equivalent. Position the cam follower over the valve lifter and the valve stem.
9. Clean the gasket surfaces of the rocker arm cover and cylinder head.
10. Coat the rocker arm cover and a new gasket with gasket adhesive and install the gasket to the cover.
11. Install the cover and tighten the retaining bolts to 5–8 ft. lbs. (7–11 Nm).
12. Install the throttle body and EGR supply tube, if necessary. Install the air cleaner or air intake duct.
13. Connect the negative battery cable.

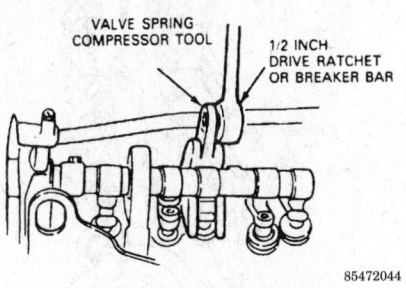

Cam follower removal — 2.3L engine

85472044

3.0L (VIN U) and 4.0L Engines

1. Disconnect the negative battery cable and relieve the fuel system pressure. Drain the cooling system.
2. Remove the intake manifold and rocker arm covers.
3. Loosen the rocker arm shaft support bolts 2 turns at a time until the rocker arm and shaft assembly can be removed.
4. Remove the pushrods, marking them so they can be reinstalled in their original positions.
5. Remove the lifters. Note the location of each lifter so it can be reinstalled in the same bore. The roller lifters have an alignment tab which fits into a locating groove in the lifter bore. Do not attempt to rotate a roller lifter in the bore in an effort to remove it.

To install:
6. Lubricate the lifters and bores with clean engine oil. Install each lifter in the same bore from which it was removed. Install the lifter with the alignment tab in the locating groove of the bore. If a new lifter is being installed, check for free fit in the bore.
7. Check each pushrod for straightness and for damage, replace as necessary. Dip each pushrod end in clean engine oil and install in its original position.
8. Lubricate the rocker arm and shaft assembly and install. Draw the shaft support bolts down evenly, 2 turns at a time, until the shafts are fully down. Tighten the bolts to 46–52 ft. lbs. (62–70 Nm).
9. Install the intake manifold and rocker arm covers.
10. Connect the negative battery cable. Fill and bleed the cooling system.
11. Run the engine and check for leaks.

13. Tighten the cylinder head bolts, in sequence, to 59 ft. lbs. (80 Nm).
14. Tighten the intake manifold, in sequence, to 6–11 ft. lbs. (8–15 Nm).
15. Turn the cylinder head bolts 80–85 degrees tighter, in sequence.
16. Tighten the intake manifold, in sequence, to 11–15 ft. lbs. (15–21 Nm) and then to 15–18 ft. lbs. (21–25 Nm), in sequence.
17. Dip both ends of each pushrod in clean engine oil and install in their original locations. Install the rocker arm and shaft assemblies and tighten the rocker arm shaft support bolts evenly to 46–52 ft. lbs. (62–70 Nm).
18. Apply silicone sealer to the 4 locations at the joint where the intake manifold and cylinder head meet. Install a new rocker arm cover gasket in each cover and install the rocker arm covers. Tighten the rocker arm cover bolts to 3–5 ft. lbs. (4–7 Nm), wait 2 minutes and then retighten to the same specification.
19. Install the upper intake manifold and tighten the nuts to 15–18 ft. lbs. (20–25 Nm).
20. Install the exhaust manifold(s) and connect the exhaust pipe.
21. Install the spark plugs and the ignition coil and bracket assembly.
22. Install the alternator and the accessory drive belt.
23. Install the power steering pump. Install the air conditioning compressor, if equipped.
24. Connect the negative battery cable. Fill and bleed the cooling system. Run the engine and check for leaks.

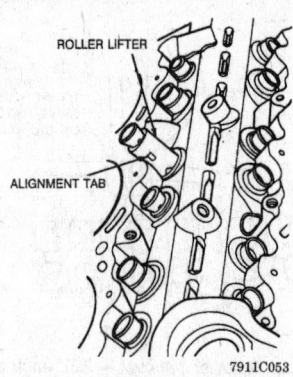

Valve lifters — 3.0L (VIN U) and 4.0L engines

Valve Lash

ADJUSTMENT

2.3L Engine

1. Remove the rocker arm cover. Position the camshaft so the base circle of the lobe is facing the cam follower of the valve to be checked.

2. Using tool valve spring compressor lever tool T88T-6565-BH or equivalent, slowly apply pressure to the cam follower until the valve lifter is completely collapsed. Hold the follower in this position and measure the clearance between the base circle of the cam and the follower. The allowable collapsed lifter gap is 0.035–0.055 in. at the camshaft.

3. If the clearance is excessive, remove the cam follower and inspect for damage.

4. If the cam follower is not excessively worn, measure the valve spring installed height to make sure the valve is not sticking. The installed height is 1.49–1.55 in.

5. If the valve spring installed height is correct, check the camshaft lobe lift. The lobe lift dimension is 0.2381 in.

6. If the cam follower, valve spring height and camshaft lobe lift are correct and the base circle-to-follower clearance is excessive, replace the valve lifter.

3.0L (VIN U) Engine

1. Remove the rocker arm cover.

2. Rotate the crankshaft until the lifter is on the base circle of the cam on the valve to be checked.

3. Using a suitable tool, collapse the lifter fully and measure the clearance between the valve stem tip and rocker arm. The clearance should be 0.085–0.185 in. (2.15–4.69mm).

Rocker Arms/Shafts

REMOVAL AND INSTALLATION

2.2L Engine

1. Disconnect the negative battery cable.

2. Remove the air cleaner assembly or air intake hose, as required.

3. Remove the rocker arm cover.

4. Loosen the rocker arm/shaft assembly mounting bolts in 2–3 steps in the proper sequence. Remove the rocker arm/shaft assembly together with the bolts.

5. If necessary, disassemble the rocker arm/shaft assembly, noting the position of each component to ease reassembly.

6. Check for wear or damage to the contact surfaces of the shafts and rocker arms; replace as necessary.

7. Measure the rocker arm inner diameter, it should be 0.6300–0.6310 in. (16.000–16.027mm). Measure the rocker arm shaft diameter, it should be 0.6286–0.6293 in. (15.966–15.984mm).

8. Subtract the shaft diameter from the rocker arm diameter to get the oil clearance. The oil clearance should be 0.0006–0.0024 in. (0.016–0.061mm) and should not exceed 0.004 in. (0.10mm). Replace parts, as necessary, if the oil clearance is not within specification.

To install:

9. Apply clean engine oil to the rocker arm shafts and rocker arms and assemble the rocker arm/shaft assembly in the reverse order of disassembly. Make sure the rocker arm shaft oil holes in the center camshaft cap face each other.

NOTE: Use the mounting bolts for alignment.

10. Apply silicone sealant to the cylinder head on the front and rear camshaft cap mounting surface. Ap-

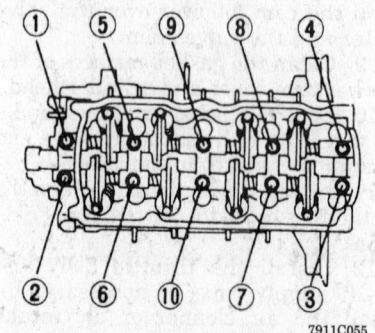

Rocker arm/shaft assembly mounting bolts removal sequence — 2.2L engine

ply clean engine oil to the camshaft journals and valve stem tips.

11. Install the rocker arm/shaft assembly and tighten the bolts, in sequence, in 2–3 steps to a maximum torque of 13–20 ft. lbs. (18–26 Nm).

12. Apply silicone sealant to each side of the front and rear camshaft cap and the cylinder head in the area where the caps meet the cylinder head.

13. Install the rocker arm cover and tighten the mounting bolts to 26–35 inch lbs. (2.9–3.9 Nm).

14. Install the air cleaner assembly or air intake tube. Connect the negative battery cable, start the engine and check for leaks and proper operation.

2.3L Engine

1. Disconnect the negative battery cable and remove the air cleaner or air intake duct. On 2.3L engine, remove the throttle body and EGR supply tube.

2. Remove the rocker arm cover.

3. Rotate the crankshaft so the base circle of the cam is facing the applicable cam follower.

4. Using valve spring compressor lever tool T88T-6565-BH or equivalent, collapse the valve spring and slide the cam follower over the valve lifter and out.

To install:

5. Rotate the crankshaft so the base circle of the cam is facing the applicable cam follower.

6. Collapse the valve spring using valve spring compressor lever T88T-6565-BH or equivalent. Position the cam follower over the valve lifter and the valve stem.

7. Clean the gasket surfaces of the rocker arm cover and cylinder head.

8. Coat the rocker arm cover and a new gasket with gasket adhesive and install the gasket to the cover.

9. Install the cover and tighten the retaining bolts to 5–8 ft. lbs. (7–11 Nm).

10. Install the throttle body and EGR supply tube, if necessary. Install the air cleaner or air intake duct.

11. Connect the negative battery cable.

2.6L Engine

1. Disconnect the negative battery cable.

2. Remove the air intake hose.

3. Remove the rocker arm cover.

4. Loosen the rocker arm/shaft assembly mounting bolts in 2–3 steps in the proper sequence. Remove the

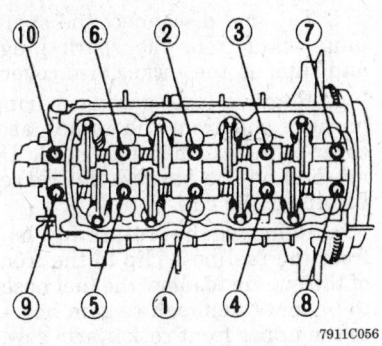

Rocker arm/shaft assembly mounting bolts torque sequence — 2.2L engine

rocker arm/shaft assembly together with the bolts.

5. If necessary, disassemble the rocker arm/shaft assembly, noting the position of each component to ease reassembly.

6. Check for wear or damage to the contact surfaces of the shafts and rocker arms; replace as necessary.

7. Measure the rocker arm inner diameter, it should be 0.8268–0.8281 in. (21.000–21.033mm). Measure the rocker arm shaft diameter, it should be 0.8252–0.8260 in. (20.959–20.980mm).

8. Subtract the shaft diameter from the rocker arm diameter to get the oil clearance. The oil clearance should be 0.0008–0.0029 in. (0.020–0.074mm) and should not exceed 0.004 in. (0.10mm). Replace parts, as necessary, if the oil clearance is not within specification.

To install:

9. Apply clean engine oil to the rocker arm shafts and rocker arms and assemble the rocker arm/shaft assembly in the reverse order of disassembly, noting the following:

a. The intake side shaft has twice as many oil holes as the exhaust side shaft.

b. The No. 4 camshaft cap has an oil hole from the cylinder head; make sure it is installed correctly.

10. Apply clean engine oil to the camshaft journals and valve stem tips.

11. Install the rocker arm/shaft assembly and tighten the mounting bolts, in sequence, in 2–3 steps to a maximum torque of 14–19 ft. lbs. (19–25 Nm).

12. Coat a new gasket with silicone sealer and install on the rocker arm cover. Apply sealer to the cylinder head in the area of the half circle seals and install the rocker arm cover. Install the mounting bolts and tighten to 52–78 inch lbs. (5.9–8.8 Nm).

13. Install the air intake hose. Connect the negative battery cable, start the engine and check for leaks and proper operation.

3.0L (JE) Engine

1. Disconnect the negative battery cable.

2. If removing the driver's side rocker arm/shaft assembly, proceed as follows:

a. Remove the air inlet tube.

b. Disconnect the necessary electrical connectors and vacuum hoses from the throttle body and intake air pipe.

c. Disconnect the throttle cable.

d. Remove the throttle body and intake air pipe.

3. Remove the rocker arm cover.

4. Loosen the rocker arm/shaft assembly mounting bolts in sequence, in 2–3 steps. Remove the assembly with the bolts.

5. If necessary, disassemble the rocker arm/shaft assembly, noting the position of each component to ease reassembly.

6. Check for wear or damage to the contact surfaces of the shafts and rocker arms; replace as necessary.

7. Measure the rocker arm inner diameter, it should be 0.7480–0.7493 in. (19.000–19.033mm). Measure the rocker arm shaft diameter, it should

be 0.7464–0.7472 in. (18.959–18.980mm).

8. Subtract the shaft diameter from the rocker arm diameter to get the oil clearance. The oil clearance should be 0.0008–0.0029 in. (0.020–0.074mm) and should not exceed 0.004 in. (0.10mm). Replace parts, as necessary, if the oil clearance is not within specification.

To install:

9. Apply clean engine oil to the rocker arm shafts and rocker arms and assemble the rocker arm/shaft assembly in the reverse order of disassembly, noting the following. The intake side shaft has twice as many oil holes as the exhaust side shaft.

10. Apply clean engine oil to the camshaft journals and valve stem tips.

11. Install the rocker arm/shaft assembly and tighten the mounting bolts, in sequence, in 2–3 steps to a maximum torque of 14–19 ft. lbs. (19–25 Nm).

NOTE: Be careful that the rocker arm shaft spring does not get caught between the shaft and mounting boss during installation.

12. Coat a new gasket with silicone sealant and install on the rocker arm cover. Install the rocker arm cover with new seal washers and tighten the bolts to 30–39 inch lbs. (3.4–4.4 Nm).

13. Install the intake air pipe, throttle body and air intake tube, if removed. Connect the throttle cable and the necessary electrical connectors and vacuum hoses.

14. Connect the negative battery cable, start the engine and check for leaks and proper operation.

3.0L (VIN U) Engine

1. Disconnect the negative battery cable. Remove the air cleaner fresh air hose, if necessary.

2. Tag and disconnect the spark plug wires from the spark plugs. Remove the spark plug wire/separator assembly from the rocker arm cover attaching bolt studs and position aside.

3. If the left rocker arm cover is being removed, proceed as follows:

a. Remove the throttle body assembly and the PCV valve.

b. Remove the fuel injector harness stand-offs from the inboard rocker arm cover studs. Move the harness aside.

Rocker arm/shaft assembly mounting bolts removal sequence — 2.6L engine

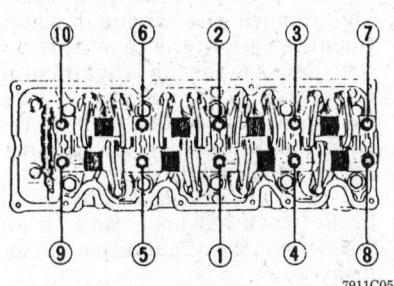

Rocker arm/shaft assembly mounting bolts torque sequence — 2.6L engine

INTAKE SIDE

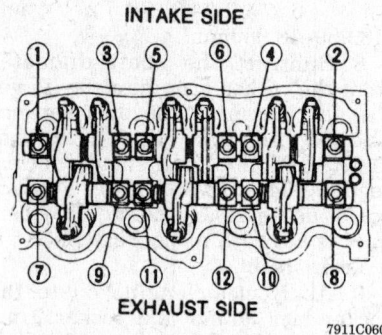

EXHAUST SIDE

7911C060

Rocker arm/shaft assembly mounting bolts removal sequence — 3.0L (JE) engine

EXHAUST SIDE

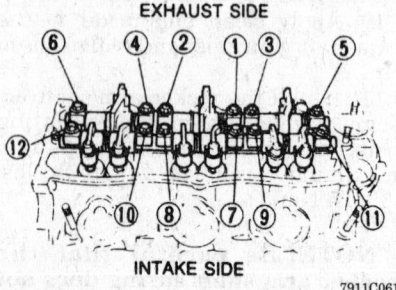

INTAKE SIDE

7911C061

Rocker arm/shaft assembly mounting bolts torque sequence — 3.0L (JE) engine

4. If the right rocker arm cover is being removed, proceed as follows:

  a. Disconnect the engine harness connectors and remove the air cleaner closure hose from the oil fill adapter.

  b. Remove the fuel injector harness stand-offs from the inboard rocker arm cover studs. Move the harness aside.

5. Remove the rocker arm cover attaching bolts and studs, noting their locations. Remove the rocker arm cover.

6. Remove the rocker arm fulcrum bolt and remove the rocker arm and fulcrum.

To install:

7. Lubricate the valve stem tip, pushrod end, fulcrum and rocker arm fulcrum seat with clean engine oil.

8. For each valve, rotate the crankshaft until the lifter rests on the base circle of the camshaft lobe, before tightening the rocker arm fulcrum attaching bolts. Position the rocker arms over the valves and pushrods, install the fulcrums and fulcrum bolts and tighten to 24 ft. lbs. (32 Nm).

9. Clean the rocker arm cover and cylinder head gasket mating surfaces

of all gasket material and/or old silicone sealer.

10. Apply a bead of silicone sealer at the cylinder head to intake manifold rail step and position the rocker arm cover on the cylinder head.

11. Install the bolts/studs in their original locations and tighten to 9 ft. lbs. (12 Nm).

12. Install the remaining components in the reverse order of their removal. Start the engine and check for leaks.

4.0L Engine

1. Disconnect the negative battery cable. Remove the intake shield and air intake tube.

2. If removing the right rocker arm/shaft assembly, proceed as follows:

  a. Remove the alternator and the coil pack.

  b. Remove the retaining bolt from the air conditioning pipe over the upper intake manifold.

  c. Remove the spark plug wires from the clips on the valve cover.

  d. Remove the 2 wiring harnesses from the right rocker arm cover.

  e. Disconnect the vacuum hose at the coupling over the rocker arm cover.

  f. Remove the engine wiring harness clip from the rocker arm cover-to-intake manifold stud. Do not pull on the harness but rather lift up on the clip.

  g. Remove the right rocker arm cover bolts, reinforcement plate and the cover.

3. If removing the right rocker arm/shaft assembly, proceed as follows:

  a. Remove the bolt from the air conditioning pipe over the upper intake manifold, if not already done.

  b. Disconnect the air conditioning compressor clutch connector and remove the wiring harness from the back of the compressor.

  c. Remove the air conditioning compressor bolts, pull up the tube that goes around the back of the engine and reposition the compressor and tube aside.

  d. Tag and disconnect the power brake vacuum hose and other hoses from the vacuum tee on the plenum.

  e. Remove the PCV hose and valve. Remove the wiring harness from the valve cover and position aside.

  f. Tag and disconnect the spark plug wires from the spark plugs and clips on the rocker arm cover.

  g. Remove the engine wiring harness clip from the rocker arm cover-to-intake manifold stud. Do not pull on the harness but rather lift up on the clip.

  h. Remove the retaining bolt from the fuel hose clip to the front of the engine to allow the fuel hoses to be moved enough to gain access to the upper front rocker arm cover bolt.

  i. Remove the bolts, reinforcement plates and left rocker arm cover.

4. Remove the rocker arm shafts by loosening the support bolts 2 turns at a time until the shaft can be removed.

5. If necessary, disassemble the rocker arm/shaft assembly by removing the spring washer and pin from each end of the shaft and sliding the rocker arms, springs and rocker arm shaft supports off the shaft. Note the position of each component to ease reassembly.

6. Inspect all components for wear and replace, as necessary.

To install:

7. Coat the rocker arms and shafts with clean engine oil and reassemble. The oil holes in the shaft must point down when the shaft is installed. This position can be recognized by a notch on the front face of the shaft.

8. Lubricate the pushrod ends and valve stem tips.

9. Install the rocker arm/shaft assembly and draw the shaft support bolts down evenly, 2 turns at a time, until the rocker arm/shaft assembly is fully down. Tighten the shaft support bolts to 46–52 ft. lbs. (62–70 Nm).

10. Clean all gasket mating surfaces.

11. Apply silicone sealant to the intake manifold-to-cylinder head parting seam and an 1/8 in. ball of sealer to the rocker arm cover bolt holes on the exhaust side.

12. Install a new gasket on the rocker arm cover and install the cover, reinforcing plates and bolts. Tighten the bolts to 53–70 inch lbs. (6–8 Nm) working in a criss-cross pattern and starting at the center bolts.

13. Install the remaining components in the reverse order of their removal. Connect the negative battery cable, start the engine and check for leaks and proper operation.

Intake Manifold

REMOVAL AND INSTALLATION

2.2L Carbureted Engine

1. Relieve the fuel system pressure and disconnect the negative battery cable. Drain the cooling system.
2. Remove the air cleaner assembly.
3. Disconnect the accelerator cable. Tag and disconnect the necessary electrical connectors and vacuum hoses.
4. Disconnect the coolant hoses and fuel line.
5. Remove the intake manifold mounting nuts and remove the intake manifold.

To install:

6. Clean all gasket mating surfaces.
7. Position a new intake manifold gasket on the cylinder head and install the intake manifold.
8. Install the intake manifold mounting nuts and tighten, in 2–3 steps, to 14–19 ft. lbs. (19–25 Nm). Tighten the nuts at the center of the manifold 1st and work towards the ends.
9. Connect the fuel line and the coolant hoses.
10. Connect the electrical connectors and vacuum hoses. Connect the accelerator cable.
11. Install the air cleaner assembly and connect the negative battery cable.
12. Fill and bleed the cooling system. Run the engine and check for leaks.

2.2L and 2.6L EFI Engines

1. Relieve the fuel system pressure and disconnect the negative battery cable. Drain the cooling system.
2. Disconnect the air intake tube and ventilation hose. Remove the air pipe and resonance chamber on 2.6L engine.
3. Disconnect the accelerator cable and coolant hoses. Tag and disconnect the electrical connectors to the solenoid valve, throttle sensor and idle switch.
4. Remove the throttle body.
5. Remove the upper intake manifold brackets.
6. Tag and disconnect the vacuum hoses and PCV hose. Tag and disconnect the intake air thermosensor connector and ground wire.
7. Remove the injector harness bracket and remove the upper intake manifold.

8. Tag and disconnect the vacuum hoses from the lower intake manifold. Disconnect the fuel lines.
9. Remove the fuel supply manifold and the injectors. Remove the injector harness and bracket.
10. Remove the pulsation damper and the intake manifold bracket. Remove the attaching nuts and remove the lower intake manifold.

To install:

11. Clean all gasket mating surfaces.
12. Position a new intake manifold-to-cylinder head gasket and install the lower intake manifold. Tighten the nuts to 14–19 ft. lbs. (19–25 Nm).
13. Install the intake manifold bracket and pulsation damper. Install the injector harness and bracket. Tighten the pulsation damper and injector harness bracket bolts to 69–95 inch lbs. (7.8–11.0 Nm).
14. Install the injectors and the fuel supply manifold. Tighten the fuel supply manifold attaching bolts and tighten to 14–19 ft. lbs. (19–25 Nm).
15. Connect the fuel lines. Connect the vacuum hoses to the lower intake manifold.
16. Position a new gasket and install the upper intake manifold. Tighten the attaching bolts/nuts to 14–19 ft. lbs. (19–25 Nm).
17. Install the injector harness bracket. Connect the ground wire and air thermosensor electrical connector. Connect the PCV hose and the vacuum hoses to the upper intake manifold.
18. Install the upper intake manifold brackets.
19. Position a new gasket and install the throttle body. Tighten the mounting nuts to 14–19 ft. lbs. (19–25 Nm).
20. Connect the electrical connectors at the idle switch, throttle sensor and solenoid valve.
21. Connect the coolant hoses and the accelerator cable. On 2.6L engine, install the air pipe and resonance chamber.
22. Connect the ventilation hose and air intake hose. Connect the negative battery cable.
23. Fill and bleed the cooling system. Run the engine and check for leaks and proper operation.

2.3L Engine

1. Disconnect the negative battery cable and relieve the fuel system pressure. Drain the cooling system.
2. Tag and disconnect the electrical connectors at the throttle position

sensor, air charge temperature sensor, engine coolant temperature sensor and air bypass valve, if equipped. Disconnect the knock sensor connector, if equipped.
3. Disconnect the injector wiring harness at the main engine harness and at the water temperature indicator sensor. Disconnect the ignition control assembly connector, if equipped.
4. Tag and disconnect the vacuum lines at the upper intake manifold vacuum tree, EGR valve, fuel pressure regulator and canister purge line.
5. Remove the throttle linkage shield and disconnect the throttle linkage and cruise control. Disconnect the kickdown cable, if equipped. Unbolt the accelerator cable from the bracket and position the cable aside.
6. Disconnect the air intake hose and crankcase vent hose. Disconnect the air bypass hose, if equipped.
7. Disconnect the PCV system by disconnecting the hose from the fitting on the underside of the upper intake. Disconnect the water bypass line at the lower intake manifold.
8. Disconnect the EGR tube from the EGR valve. Remove the attaching bolts and remove the upper intake manifold and throttle body assembly.
9. Remove the engine oil dipstick tube bracket attaching bolt. Disconnect the fuel lines from the fuel supply manifold.
10. Disconnect the electrical connectors from the fuel injectors and position aside. Remove the fuel supply manifold attaching bolts and remove the fuel supply manifold.
11. Remove the attaching bolts and remove the lower intake manifold.

To install:

12. Clean all gasket mating surfaces. Clean and oil the manifold bolt threads.
13. Position a new gasket and install the lower intake manifold. Install the attaching bolts and tighten, in sequence, in 2 steps, first to 5–7 ft. lbs. (7–9 Nm) and then to 15–22 ft. lbs. (20–30 Nm).
14. Install the fuel supply manifold and injectors with the 2 attaching bolts. Tighten to 15–22 ft. lbs. (20–30 Nm). Connect the electrical connectors to the injectors.
15. Position a new gasket on the lower intake manifold and install the upper intake manifold. Install the attaching bolts and tighten, in sequence, to 15–22 ft. lbs. (20–30 Nm).
16. Install the engine oil dipstick tube and retaining bolt. Connect the fuel lines to the fuel supply manifold.

17. Connect the EGR tube to the EGR valve. Tighten to 18–28 ft. lbs. (25–30 Nm).

18. Connect the water bypass line and connect the PCV hose. Connect the vacuum lines to the locations marked during removal.

19. Hold the accelerator cable bracket in position on the upper manifold and install the attaching bolts. Tighten to 10–15 ft. lbs. (13.5–20.5 Nm).

20. Install the accelerator cable to the bracket. Connect the accelerator cable and cruise control. Install the throttle linkage shield.

21. Connect the electrical connectors to the locations marked during removal.

22. Connect the air intake hose and crankcase vent hose. Connect the air bypass hose, if equipped.

23. Connect the negative battery cable. Fill and bleed the cooling system. Run the engine and check for leaks.

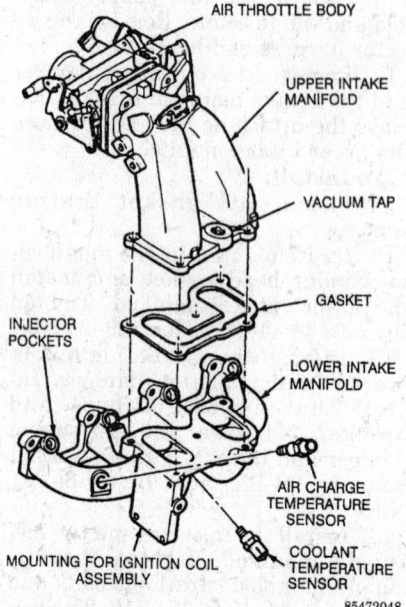

Intake manifold assembly — 2.3L engine

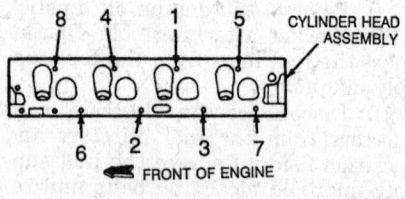

Intake manifold bolt torque sequence — 2.3L engine

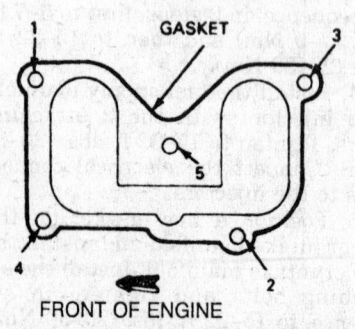

Upper intake manifold retaining bolt torque sequence — 2.3L engine

3.0L (JE) Engine

1. Relieve the fuel system pressure and disconnect the negative battery cable. Drain the cooling system.

2. Remove the air intake tube from the throttle body. Disconnect the accelerator cable.

3. Disconnect the throttle sensor connector and the coolant hoses. Remove the throttle body.

4. Tag and disconnect the vacuum hoses. Remove the bypass air control valve and the intake air pipe.

5. Remove the extension manifolds. Remove the upper intake plenum with the shutter valve actuator.

6. Remove the fuel supply manifold and the injectors. Disconnect the coolant hoses.

7. Loosen the lower intake manifold nuts, in sequence, in 2 steps and remove the lower intake manifold.

To install:

8. Clean all gasket mating surfaces.

9. Position new lower intake manifold-to-cylinder head gaskets and install the lower intake manifold.

10. Install the intake manifold washers with the white paint mark upward. Install the nuts and tighten, in sequence, in 2 steps to a maximum torque of 14–19 ft. lbs. (19–25 Nm).

11. Install the injectors and the fuel supply manifold. Tighten the attaching bolts to 14–19 ft. lbs. (19–25 Nm).

12. Connect the coolant hoses.

13. Install a new O-ring on the lower intake manifold and install the upper intake plenum. Apply clean engine oil to new O-rings and install on the extension manifolds. Position new gaskets and install the extension manifolds. Tighten the attaching nuts to 14–19 ft. lbs. (19–25 Nm).

14. Position a new gasket and install the intake air pipe. Install the bypass air control valve. Tighten the attaching bolts/nuts to 14–19 ft. lbs. (19–25 Nm).

15. Position a new gasket and install the throttle body. Tighten the attaching nuts to 14–19 ft. lbs. (19–25 Nm).

16. Connect the coolant and vacuum hoses. Connect the throttle sensor connector and accelerator cable.

17. Adjust the accelerator cable deflection to 0.039–0.118 in. (1–3mm).

18. Connect the air intake tube and the negative battery cable.

19. Fill and bleed the cooling system. Run the engine and check for leaks and proper operation.

3.0L (VIN U) Engine

1. Disconnect the negative battery cable and relieve the fuel system pressure. Drain the cooling system.

2. Remove the air cleaner hoses to the throttle body and rocker arm cover. Disconnect the fuel lines from the fuel supply manifold.

3. Tag and disconnect the necessary vacuum lines.

4. Tag and disconnect the electrical connectors at the air charge temperature sensor, engine coolant temperature sensor, throttle position sensor, air bypass solenoid and coolant temperature sender.

5. Remove the snow shield from the power steering pump bracket and accelerator cable bracket.

6. Disconnect and remove the accelerator and cruise control cables from the accelerator mounting bracket and throttle lever.

7. Remove the alternator support brace.

8. Remove the throttle body-to-lower intake manifold retaining bolts and stud bolts and remove the throttle body assembly.

9. Disconnect the fuel injector harness stand-offs from the inboard rocker arm cover studs and each injector and remove from the engine.

10. Disconnect the upper radiator hose from the thermostat housing and disconnect the heater hoses.

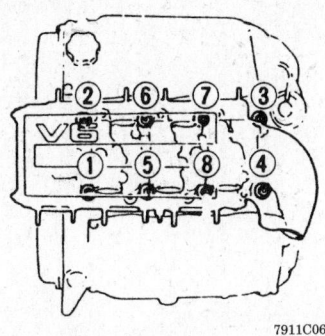

7911C062

Intake manifold mounting nuts removal sequence — 3.0L (JE) engine

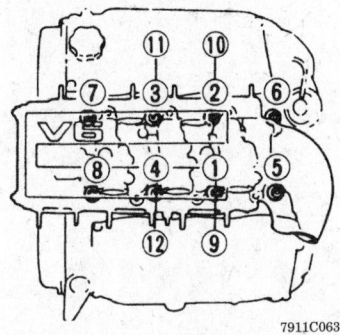

7911C063

Intake manifold mounting nuts torque sequence — 3.0L (JE) engine

11. Tag and disconnect the spark plug wires. Remove the distributor cap and wires as an assembly.

12. Mark the position of the distributor rotor in relation to the distributor housing and the housing in relation to the engine. Remove the distributor hold-down screw and clamp and lift out the distributor.

13. Remove the ignition coil from the rear of the left cylinder head, if required.

14. Remove the rocker arm covers. Loosen the No. 3 cylinder intake valve rocker arm fulcrum bolt and rotate the rocker arm away from the valve. Remove the pushrod.

15. Remove the intake manifold bolts. Break the gasket seal by wedging a large prybar between the manifold an the block using the lug on the water pump as a leverage point. Be careful to prevent damage to machines surfaces.

16. Remove the intake manifold.

To install:

17. Clean all gasket mating surface.

18. Apply silicone sealer to the intersection of the cylinder block and cylinder head at the 4 corners of the lifter valley opening.

19. Install the front and rear intake manifold seals and secure with the retaining features. Position the intake manifold gaskets on the cylinder heads and insert the locking tabs on the cylinder head gaskets.

20. Carefully lower the intake manifold into position being careful not to disturb the silicone sealer. Install the intake manifold bolts and tighten, in sequence, in 2 steps, first to 11 ft. lbs. (15 Nm) and then to 19 ft. lbs. (26 Nm).

21. Install the No. 3 cylinder intake valve pushrod. Apply oil to the pushrod and rocker arm and position the rocker arm over the valve and pushrod. Rotate the crankshaft to place the lifter on the base circle of the cam, then tighten the fulcrum bolt to 24 ft. lbs. (32 Nm).

22. Install the rocker arm covers and the fuel injector electrical harness.

23. Install the throttle body using a new gasket. Tighten the throttle body attaching bolts, in sequence, to 19 ft. lbs. (25 Nm).

24. Install the alternator brace. Tighten the nuts to 12 ft. lbs. (16 Nm).

25. Connect the PCV valve hose. Connect the engine coolant temperature sensor, air charge temperature sensor, throttle position sensor, air bypass solenoid and coolant temperature sender connectors.

26. Install the distributor, aligning the marks that were made during removal. Install the distributor cap and connect the spark plug wires. Connect the distributor electrical connector.

27. Install the ignition coil, if removed.

28. Connect the heater hoses and the upper radiator hose. Connect the vacuum lines to the locations marked during removal.

29. Connect the fuel lines to the fuel supply manifold. Change the engine oil and filter.

NOTE: Engine coolant is corrosive to all engine bearing material. Changing the oil after removal of a coolant carrying component helps prevent engine failure.

30. Connect the negative battery cable. Fill and bleed the cooling system. Install the air cleaner hose.

31. Run the engine and check for leaks. Check the ignition timing, idle speed, throttle linkage and cruise control and adjust, if necessary.

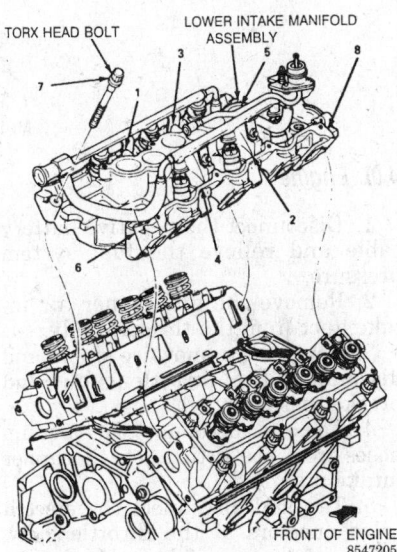

85472050

Intake manifold bolt torque sequence — 3.0L (VIN U) engine

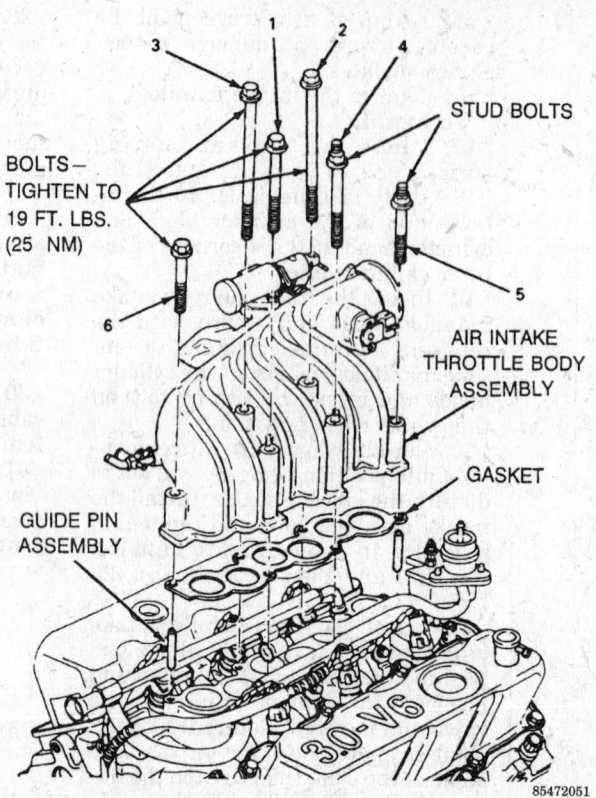

BOLTS—
TIGHTEN TO
19 FT. LBS.
(25 NM)

STUD BOLTS

AIR INTAKE
THROTTLE BODY
ASSEMBLY

GASKET

GUIDE PIN
ASSEMBLY

85472051

Air intake throttle body bolt torque sequence — 3.0L (VIN U) engine

4.0L Engine

1. Disconnect the negative battery cable and relieve the fuel system pressure.

2. Remove the air cleaner air intake duct from the throttle body.

3. Remove the snow/ice shield and disconnect the throttle cable and bracket assembly.

4. Tag and disconnect the vacuum hoses from the fittings on the upper intake manifold.

5. Tag and disconnect the electrical connectors at the throttle body, upper intake manifold, lower intake manifold and injectors.

6. Disconnect the fuel lines from the fuel supply manifold.

7. Remove the ignition coil and bracket assembly.

8. Remove the mounting nuts and remove the upper intake manifold.

9. Remove the rocker arm covers.

10. Remove the intake manifold attaching bolts and nuts. Tap the manifold lightly with a plastic mallet to break the gasket seal and remove the manifold.

   To install:

11. Clean all gasket mating surfaces.

12. Apply silicone sealer to the block and cylinder head mating surfaces at the 4 corners of the lifter val-ley opening. Install the intake manifold gaskets and again apply sealer to the same location.

13. Position the intake manifold on the 2 guide studs and install the nuts and bolts hand tight. Tighten the bolts, in sequence, in 4 steps, first to 3–6 ft. lbs. (4–8 Nm), then to 6–11 ft. lbs. (8–15 Nm), then to 11–15 ft. lbs. (15–21 Nm) and finally to 15–18 ft. lbs. (21–25 Nm).

14. Apply silicone sealer to the 4 locations where the intake manifold and the cylinder heads meet. Install the rocker arm covers with new gaskets and tighten evenly to 3–5 ft. lbs. (4–7 Nm). Wait 2 minutes and

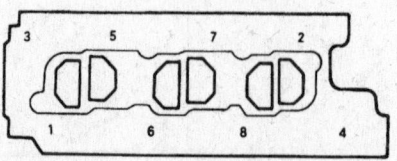

7911C064

Intake manifold bolts/nuts torque sequence — 4.0L engine

tighten the bolts again to the same specification.

15. Install the upper intake manifold and tighten the nuts to 15–18 ft. lbs. (20–25 Nm).

16. Install the ignition coil and bracket assembly. Connect the fuel lines to the fuel supply manifold.

17. Connect the electrical connectors at the throttle body, upper intake manifold, lower intake manifold and injectors.

18. Connect the vacuum hoses to the fittings on the upper intake manifold.

19. Install the throttle cable and bracket assembly and the snow/ice shield to the throttle body.

20. Connect the air cleaner air intake duct to the throttle body.

21. Connect the negative battery cable. Fill and bleed the cooling system. Run the engine and check for leaks.

Exhaust Manifold

REMOVAL AND INSTALLATION

2.3L Engine

1. Disconnect the negative battery cable. Remove the air cleaner and duct assembly.

2. Remove the EGR tube at the exhaust manifold and loosen at the EGR valve.

3. Remove the check valve at the exhaust manifold and disconnect the hose at the end of the air bypass valve, if equipped.

4. Disconnect the oxygen sensor from the exhaust manifold, if equipped. Remove the sensor, if necessary.

5. Remove the screw attaching the heater hoses to the rocker arm cover. Disconnect the exhaust pipe from the exhaust manifold.

6. Remove the exhaust manifold mounting bolts and remove the manifold.

7. Installation is the reverse of the removal procedure. Tighten the exhaust manifold mounting bolts, in sequence, in 2 steps, first to 15–17 ft. lbs. (20–23 Nm) and then to 20–30 ft. lbs. (27–41 Nm).

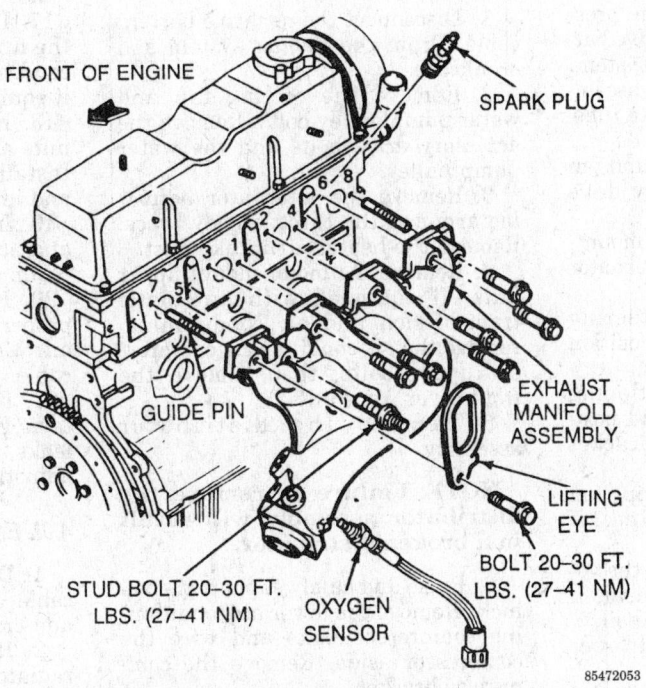

FRONT OF ENGINE

SPARK PLUG

GUIDE PIN

EXHAUST MANIFOLD ASSEMBLY

LIFTING EYE

STUD BOLT 20–30 FT. LBS. (27–41 NM)

OXYGEN SENSOR

BOLT 20–30 FT. LBS. (27–41 NM)

85472053

Exhaust manifold bolt torque sequence — 2.3L engine

2.2L, 2.6L and 3.0L (JE) Engines

1. Disconnect the negative battery cable. Raise and safely support the vehicle.

2. Disconnect the exhaust pipe from the exhaust manifold. If necessary, disconnect the electrical connector from the oxygen sensor.

3. Lower the vehicle.

4. Remove the exhaust manifold insulator, if equipped.

5. If necessary, remove the engine oil dipstick and the dipstick tube. If necessary, remove the power steering pump pressure and return hoses.

6. On 3.0L engine, disconnect or remove the exhaust manifold crossover.

7. If removing the right manifold, remove the heater hose support bracket and disconnect the heater hoses.

8. Remove the exhaust manifold attaching bolts/nuts and remove the exhaust manifold.

9. Installation is the reverse of the removal procedure. Tighten the exhaust manifold attaching bolts/nuts to 19 ft. lbs. (25 Nm).

3.0L (VIN U) Engine

1. Disconnect the negative battery cable.

2. Raise and safely support the vehicle, as necessary.

3. If removing the left exhaust manifold, remove the engine oil dipstick tube support bracket or retaining nut, as required. Rotate the tube out of the way or remove.

4. Remove the spark plugs. Disconnect the exhaust pipe from the manifold.

5. Remove the exhaust manifold attaching nuts and remove the manifold.

6. Installation is the reverse of the removal procedure. Tighten the manifold attaching bolts to 18 ft. lbs. (25 Nm).

4.0L Engine

1. Disconnect the negative battery cable.

2. Raise and safely support the vehicle, as necessary.

3. If removing the left manifold, remove the engine oil dipstick tube support bracket. Remove the power steering pump pressure and return hoses, if necessary.

4. If removing the right manifold, remove the heater hose support bracket and disconnect the heater hoses.

5. Disconnect the exhaust pipe from the manifold.

6. Remove the manifold attaching bolts and remove the manifold.

7. Installation is the reverse of the removal procedure. Tighten the mounting bolts to 19 ft. lbs. (25 Nm).

Timing Chain Front Cover

REMOVAL AND INSTALLATION

2.6L Engine

1. Relieve the fuel system pressure and disconnect the negative battery cable. Drain the cooling system.
2. Remove the air cleaner assembly or disconnect the air intake tube.
3. Remove the cylinder head.
4. Remove the cooling fan and fan shroud. Remove the accessory drive belts.
5. Remove the alternator mounting bolts and remove the alternator and bracket.
6. Remove the power steering pump mounting bolts and position the pump and bracket aside.
7. Remove the air conditioning compressor mounting bolts and position the compressor and bracket aside.
8. Remove the water pump and disconnect the bypass pipe, if equipped.
9. Raise and safely support the vehicle. Remove the splash shield, if equipped and drain the engine oil.
10. Remove the oil pan and lower the vehicle.
11. Remove the retaining bolt and the crankshaft pulley.
12. Remove the attaching bolts and remove the timing chain cover.
   To install:
13. Clean all gasket mating surfaces.
14. Coat new timing chain cover gaskets with sealer and install on the cylinder block. Install the timing chain cover and tighten the mounting bolts to 14–19 ft. lbs. (19–25 Nm).
15. Install the crankshaft pulley. Tighten the retaining bolt to 130–145 ft. lbs. (177–196 Nm).
16. Raise and safely support the vehicle. Install the oil pan and the splash shield, if equipped.
17. Lower the vehicle and install the water pump. If equipped, apply vegetable oil to a new O-ring and install the coolant bypass pipe. Tighten the attaching bolt to 27–38 ft. lbs. (37–52 Nm).
18. Install the air conditioning compressor, if equipped, power steering pump and alternator. Install the accessory drive belts.
19. Install the cooling fan and fan shroud. Adjust the drive belt tension.

20. Install the cylinder head.
21. Fill the crankcase with the proper type and quantity of engine oil.
22. Connect the negative battery cable. Fill and bleed the cooling system.
23. Run the engine and check for leaks and proper operation.

3.0L (VIN U) Engine

1. Disconnect the negative battery cable. Drain the cooling system and crankcase.
2. Remove the cooling fan and water pump pulley bolts. Remove the accessory drive belts and the water pump pulley.
3. Remove the alternator adjusting arm and the throttle body brace. Remove the heater air intake duct.
4. Remove the motor mount upper nuts. If equipped with automatic transmission and air conditioning, remove the air conditioning compressor upper bolts, then remove the front cover front nuts.
5. Remove the distributor assembly.

NOTE: Failure to remove the distributor assembly will result in a broken distributor.

6. Raise and safely support the vehicle. Remove the lower air conditioning compressor bolts and wire the compressor aside. Remove the compressor bracket.
7. Remove the crankshaft pulley and damper. Remove the oil pan. Disconnect the oil level sensor before pan removal.
8. Lower the vehicle and remove the lower radiator hose. Remove the water pump, if required.

NOTE: The timing cover can be removed with the water pump installed by not removing the 6mm water pump attaching bolts.

9. Remove the front cover attaching bolts and remove the front cover.
   To install:
10. Clean all gasket mating surfaces. Use a seal removal tool to remove the front cover oil seal.
11. Install a new front cover oil seal, using a seal installer. Position a new front cover gasket on the engine block dowel pins.
12. Install the front cover with the attaching bolts. Apply sealer to the 3 attaching bolts on the passenger side of the cover, prior to installation. Tighten the 8mm bolts to 19 ft. lbs. (25 Nm) and the 6mm bolts to 7 ft. lbs. (10 Nm).

13. Raise and safely support the vehicle. Install the oil pan and connect the oil level sensor.
14. Install the water pump, if removed.
15. Install the crankshaft pulley and damper. Tighten the damper attaching bolt to 107 ft. lbs. (145 Nm).
16. Install the air conditioning compressor bracket, if equipped, position the compressor and install the lower bolts. Lower the vehicle.
17. Install the distributor. Install the front cover front nuts and the air conditioning compressor upper bolts, if equipped.
18. Install the motor mount upper nuts and the heater air intake duct. Install the alternator adjusting arm and brace.
19. Install the water pump pulley and accessory drive belts. Install the cooling fan and coolant hoses.
20. Fill the crankcase with the proper type and quantity of engine oil. Connect the negative battery cable.
21. Fill and bleed the cooling system. Run the engine and check for leaks. Check the ignition timing and adjust, if necessary.

4.0L Engine

1. Disconnect the negative battery cable and drain the cooling system and crankcase.
2. Remove the oil pan and the radiator.
3. Remove the air conditioning compressor and power steering bracket, if equipped.
4. Remove the alternator and drive belt(s). Remove the fan.
5. Remove the water pump and heater and radiator hoses.
6. Remove the crankshaft pulley/damper assembly and the crankshaft timing sensor.
7. Remove the front cover retaining bolts, noting their positions. If necessary, tap the cover lightly with a plastic hammer to break the gasket seal. Remove the front cover.
   To install:
8. Clean all gasket mating surfaces. Apply sealer to the gasket surfaces on the cylinder block and the back side of the front cover plate. Install the guide sleeves.
9. Apply sealer to the front cover gasket surface and position a new gasket on the front cover.
10. Install the front cover with the retaining screws. Note the different bolt lengths. Tighten the bolts to 13–15 ft. lbs. (17–21 Nm).
11. Install the crankshaft timing sensor.

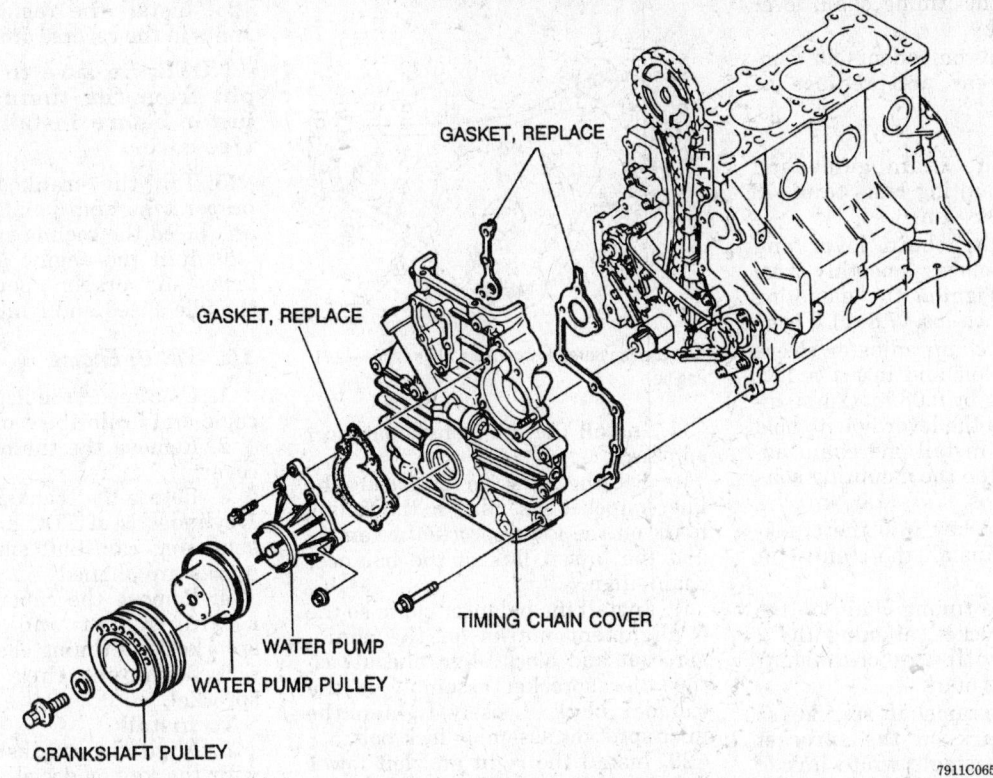

GASKET, REPLACE

GASKET, REPLACE

TIMING CHAIN COVER

WATER PUMP

WATER PUMP PULLEY

CRANKSHAFT PULLEY

7911C065

Timing chain cover installation — 2.6L engine

12. Install the crankshaft pulley/damper assembly. Tighten the attaching bolt to 30–37 ft. lbs. (40–50 Nm), then tighten an additional 80–90 degrees.

13. Install the remaining components in the reverse order of their removal. Fill and bleed the cooling system. Run the engine and check for leaks.

Front Cover Oil Seal

REPLACEMENT

1. Disconnect the negative battery cable and drain the cooling system.
2. Remove the cooling fan and fan shroud.
3. Disconnect the upper and lower radiator hoses and remove the radiator, if necessary to provide access.
4. Remove the accessory drive belt(s).
5. Remove the crankshaft pulley.
6. Pry the seal from the front cover, using a suitable prybar. Be careful not to damage the seal housing.
7. Clean the pulley and seal area. Inspect the crankshaft pulley surface for grooving or other damage. Repair or replace, as necessary.

To install:

8. Install a new seal into the cover using a seal installer. The seal must be flush with the edge of the timing chain cover.
9. Apply clean engine oil to the seal lip and the crankshaft pulley. Install the crankshaft pulley and tighten the retaining bolt to 130–145 ft. lbs. (177–196 Nm) or 30–37 ft. lbs. (40–50 Nm), then tighten an additional 80–90 degrees on 3.0L (VIN U) and 4.0L engines.
10. Install the accessory drive belt(s). Install the radiator, if removed.
11. Install the cooling fan and fan shroud. Adjust the drive belt tension.
12. Connect the negative battery cable, start the engine and check for leaks.

Timing Chain and Sprockets

REMOVAL AND INSTALLATION

2.6L Engine

1. Relieve the fuel system pressure and disconnect the negative battery cable. Drain the cooling system and engine oil.

2. Remove the cylinder head, oil pan and timing chain cover.
3. Before replacing any further components, check the following:
   a. Check the timing chain tension; if the adjuster sleeve protrudes 13 notches or more, replace the timing chain.
   b. Push the chain lever towards the driver's side of the vehicle. If there is excessive movement, there will be a chain adjuster malfunction or worn chain lever, chain guide, camshaft sprocket or crankshaft sprocket. Inspect and replace as necessary.
   c. Push the chain adjuster sleeve towards the passenger's side of the vehicle. If it moves back, the chain adjuster ratchet will be faulty and the chain adjuster must be replaced.
4. Remove the crankshaft spacer.
5. Loosen the idler sprocket lock bolt, then remove the balancer shaft chain guides.
6. Remove the idler sprocket assembly, crankshaft balancer chain sprocket and balancer chain.
7. Remove the timing chain adjuster.
8. Remove the camshaft sprocket, timing chain and crankshaft sprocket. Remove the key from the crankshaft.

9. Remove the timing chain lever and chain guide.

10. Inspect all components for damage and/or wear and replace as necessary.

To install:

11. Install the chain guide and tighten the mounting bolts to 61–78 inch lbs. (6.9–8.8 Nm).

12. Install the chain lever and check that it moves smoothly from right to left. Tighten the mounting bolt to 69–95 inch lbs. (7.8–11.0 Nm).

13. Push the chain adjuster sleeve in toward the left and insert a 1.77 in. (45mm) long by 0.08 in. (2mm) diameter pin into the lever hole to hold it in position. Install the chain adjuster and tighten the mounting bolts to 69–95 inch lbs. (7.8–11.0 Nm).

14. Install the key into the crankshaft keyway. Install the crankshaft sprocket.

15. Install the timing chain on the crankshaft sprocket, aligning the 2 white links with the crankshaft sprocket timing mark.

16. Install the camshaft sprocket so the timing mark on the sprocket aligns with the single white link of the timing chain. Secure the timing chain to the sprocket with wire and temporarily rest it between the chain lever and guide.

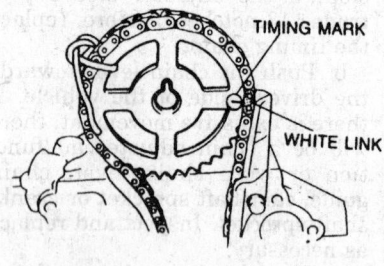

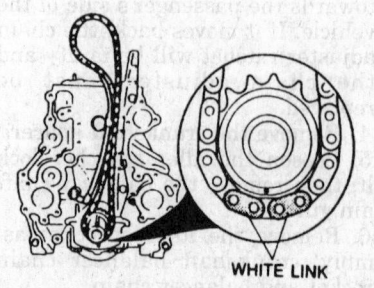

Timing chain and sprockets alignment — 2.6L engine

7911C068

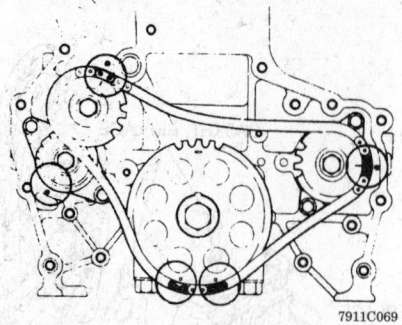

7911C069

Balancer chain and sprockets alignment — 2.6L engine

17. Install the crankshaft balancer sprocket.

18. Set the balancer chain on the idler sprocket assembly so the timing mark on the idler sprocket assembly and the brown link of the balancer chain align.

19. Install the balancer chain so the 5 alignment marks on the chain, sprocket and block align and attach the idler sprocket assembly to the cylinder block. Loosely tighten the idler sprocket assembly lock bolt.

20. Install the right and left lower balancer chain guides and tighten the mounting bolts to 69–95 inch lbs. (7.8–11.0 Nm).

21. Install the upper chain guide and loosely tighten the mounting and adjusting bolts.

22. Tighten the idler sprocket assembly lock bolt to 27–38 ft. lbs. (37–52 Nm) and install the spacer.

23. On all 1992–96 B-Series Pick-Up with automatic transmission, adjust the balancer chain tension as follows:

   a. Fabricate a piece of wood, 0.118–0.138 in. (3.0–3.5mm) thick and 0.335–0.374 in. (8.5–9.5mm) wide.

   b. Insert the piece of wood in the notch in the upper chain guide.

   c. Push on the chain guide just above the adjusting slot with a force of 2.9–3.7 lbs. and tighten the adjusting and pivot bolts to 69–95 inch lbs. (7.8–11.0 Nm).

   d. Remove the wood from between the chain and chain guide, making sure no wood shavings are left.

   e. Measure the chain slack. It should be 0.039–0.059 in. (1.0–1.5mm) at the notch in the guide.

NOTE: If the upper chain guide bottoms on the adjusting bolt during the adjustment procedure, the balancer chain must be replaced.

24. Install the remaining components in the reverse order of removal.

NOTE: Be sure to remove the pin from the timing chain adjuster before installing the service cover.

25. Fill the crankcase with the proper type and quantity of oil. Fill and bleed the cooling system.

26. Run the engine and check for leaks and proper operation. Check the idle speed and ignition timing.

3.0L (VIN U) Engine

1. Disconnect the negative battery cable and drain the cooling system.

2. Remove the timing chain front cover.

3. Rotate the crankshaft until No. 1 cylinder is at TDC and the crankshaft and camshaft sprocket timing marks are aligned.

4. Remove the camshaft sprocket retaining bolt and remove the sprocket and timing chain.

5. Remove the crankshaft sprocket.

To install:

6. Align the crankshaft sprocket with the key or dowel on the crankshaft and install the sprocket.

7. Make sure the sprocket timing marks are still in alignment.

8. Install the camshaft sprocket and timing chain. Install the camshaft sprocket retaining bolt and tighten to 46 ft. lbs. (63 Nm).

NOTE: The camshaft retaining bolt has a drilled oil passage for timing chain lubrication. If damaged, do not replace with a standard bolt. Clean the oil passage with solvent.

9. Install the timing chain front cover and the remaining components in the reverse order of their removal. Fill the crankcase with the proper type and quantity of engine oil. Fill and bleed the cooling system. Run the engine and check for leaks.

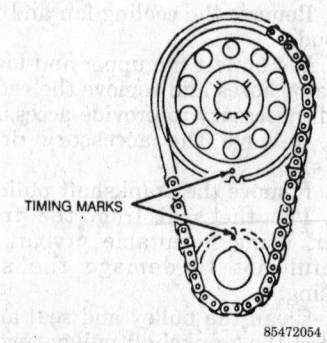

Timing chain and sprocket alignment — 3.0L (VIN U) engine

85472054

4.0L Engine

1. Disconnect the negative battery cable and drain the cooling system and crankcase.

2. Remove the oil pan and radiator. Remove the accessory drive belt and crankshaft damper.

3. Remove the water pump and timing chain front cover.

4. Remove the camshaft sprocket retaining bolt and the crankshaft sprocket key.

5. Push the timing chain tensioner into the retracted position and install the retaining clip.

6. Remove the crankshaft and camshaft sprockets with the timing chain. Remove the tensioner and guide, as required.

To install:

7. Install the timing chain guide to the cylinder block with the pin of the guide inserted into the oil hole in the block. Install the 2 retaining bolts and tighten to 7–9 ft. lbs. (10–12 Nm).

8. Position the camshaft and crankshaft so the sprocket timing marks will align.

9. Install the sprockets and timing chain together. Install the timing chain tensioner with the clip in place to lock the tensioner in the retracted position.

10. Install the crankshaft key and check the timing marks on the sprockets for correct alignment. Make sure the tensioner side of the timing chain is held inward and the guide side of the chain is straight and tight.

11. Install the camshaft sprocket retaining bolt and tighten to 44–50 ft. lbs. (60–68 Nm). Remove the clip from the tensioner assembly.

12. Install the timing chain front cover and the remaining components in the reverse order of their removal. Fill the crankcase with the proper type and quantity of engine oil. Fill and bleed the cooling system. Run the engine and check for leaks.

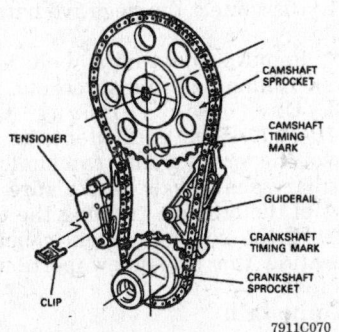

7911C070

Timing chain and sprockets alignment — 4.0L engine

Timing Belt Front Cover

REMOVAL AND INSTALLATION

2.2L Engine

1. Disconnect the negative battery cable and drain the cooling system.

2. Remove the cooling fan and fan shroud.

3. Remove the accessory drive belt(s) and the cooling fan pulley and bracket.

4. If carburetor equipped, remove the secondary air pipe assembly.

5. Remove the retaining bolts and the crankshaft pulley.

6. Remove the upper and lower timing belt covers.

7. Installation is the reverse of the removal procedure. Install the timing belt covers with new gaskets. Tighten the bolts to 61–87 inch lbs. (6.9–9.8 Nm).

8. Tighten the crankshaft pulley retaining bolts to 9–13 ft. lbs. (12–17 Nm). Fill and bleed the cooling system.

2.3L Engine

1. Disconnect the negative battery cable and drain the cooling system.

2. Loosen the thermactor pump bolts and remove the drive belt, if equipped.

3. Remove the fan blade and 4 water pump pulley bolts.

4. Loosen the alternator retaining bolts and remove the drive belt from the pulleys. Remove the upper radiator hose.

5. Remove the crankshaft pulley bolt and pulley. Remove the thermostat housing.

6. Loosen the power steering pump mounting bracket and position aside.

7. Remove the timing belt front cover retaining bolt(s). Release the cover interlocking tabs, if equipped. Remove the cover.

To install:

8. Install the front cover. If equipped, secure by snapping the interlocking tabs into place. Install the retaining bolt(s).

9. Install the power steering pump mounting bracket.

10. Install the thermostat housing and connect the upper radiator hose.

11. Install the crankshaft pulley and retaining bolt. Tighten to 103–133 ft. lbs. (140–180 Nm).

12. Position the alternator drive belt and adjust the belt tension. Install the water pump pulley and fan.

13. Position the thermactor pump drive belt, if equipped, and adjust the tension.

14. Connect the negative battery cable. Fill and bleed the cooling system. Run the engine and check for leaks.

3.0L (JE) Engine

1. Disconnect the negative battery cable and drain the cooling system.

2. Tag and disconnect the spark plug wires from the spark plugs. Remove the spark plugs.

3. Remove the fresh air duct, cooling fan and fan shroud.

4. Remove the accessory drive belt(s) and the air conditioning compressor idler pulley.

5. Remove the retaining bolt and remove the crankshaft pulley.

6. Remove the coolant bypass hose and upper radiator hose.

7. Remove the timing belt covers and gaskets.

8. Installation is the reverse of the removal procedure. Install the timing belt covers with new gaskets. Tighten the 6mm bolts to 69–95 inch lbs. (7.8–11.0 Nm) and the 10mm bolt to 27–38 ft. lbs. (37–52 Nm).

9. Tighten the crankshaft pulley bolt to 116–123 ft. lbs. (157–167 Nm).

OIL SEAL REPLACEMENT

2.2L Engine

CRANKSHAFT SEAL

1. Disconnect the negative battery cable and drain the engine oil.

2. Remove the timing belt cover and timing belt.

3. Remove the crankshaft sprocket retaining bolt and the crankshaft sprocket.

4. Remove the oil seal using a small prybar. Be careful not to damage the seal housing.

To install:

5. Apply clean engine oil to the lip of a new seal and fit the seal into the oil pump body.

6. Tap the seal in place using a seal installer until the seal is flush with the edge of the pump body.

7. Install the crankshaft sprocket and tighten the retaining bolt to 116–123 ft. lbs. (157–167 Nm).

8. Install the timing belt and timing belt cover. Connect the negative battery cable.

9. Fill the engine with the proper type and quantity of engine oil. Run the engine and check for leaks.

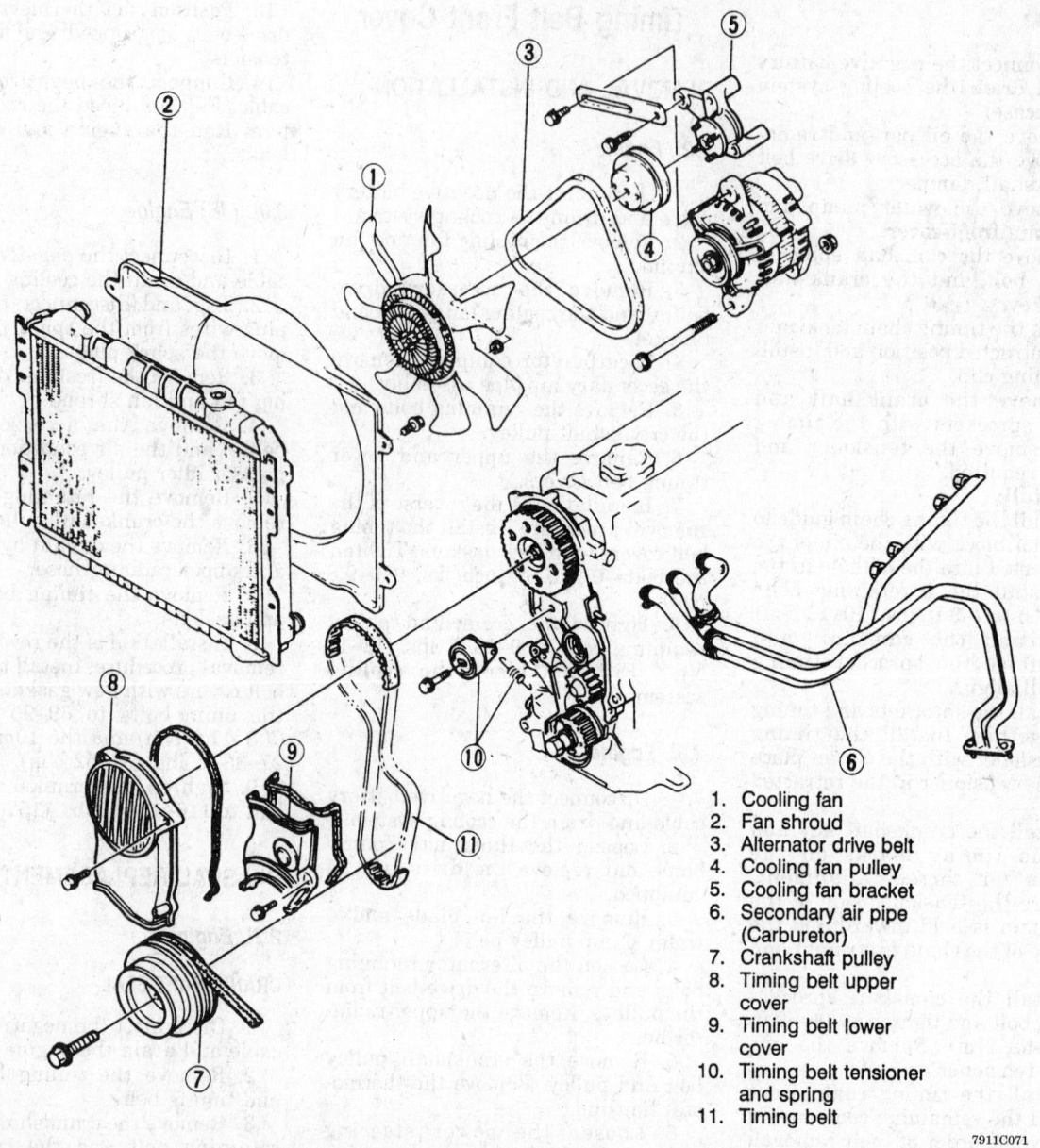

1. Cooling fan
2. Fan shroud
3. Alternator drive belt
4. Cooling fan pulley
5. Cooling fan bracket
6. Secondary air pipe (Carburetor)
7. Crankshaft pulley
8. Timing belt upper cover
9. Timing belt lower cover
10. Timing belt tensioner and spring
11. Timing belt

7911C071

Timing belt covers and timing belt installation — 2.2L engine

CAMSHAFT SEAL

1. Disconnect the negative battery cable and drain the cooling system.

2. Remove the timing belt cover and the timing belt.

3. Remove the camshaft sprocket retaining bolt and remove the sprocket.

4. Disconnect the upper radiator hose and remove the distributor.

5. Remove the front housing.

6. Pry or press the oil seal from the front housing.

To install:

7. Clean all gasket mating surfaces.

8. Apply engine oil to the front housing and a new oil seal. Press the seal into the front housing.

9. Apply engine oil to the seal lip and install the front housing with a new gasket. Tighten the mounting bolts to 14–19 ft. lbs. (19–25 Nm).

10. Connect the upper radiator hose and install the distributor.

11. Install the camshaft sprocket and tighten the retaining bolt to 35–48 ft. lbs. (47–65 Nm).

12. Install the timing belt and the timing belt cover. Connect the negative battery cable.

13. Fill and bleed the cooling system. Run the engine and check for leaks. Check the ignition timing.

2.3L Engine

1. Disconnect the negative battery cable.

2. Remove the timing belt front cover, timing belt and sprockets.

3. Use seal removal tool T74P-6700-B or equivalent, to remove the crankshaft, camshaft or auxiliary shaft seals. Make sure the jaws of the tool are gripping the thin edge of the seal very tightly before operating the jack-screw portion of the tool.

To install:

4. Coat the new seal with engine oil and install, using seal installation tool T74P-6150-A or equivalent.

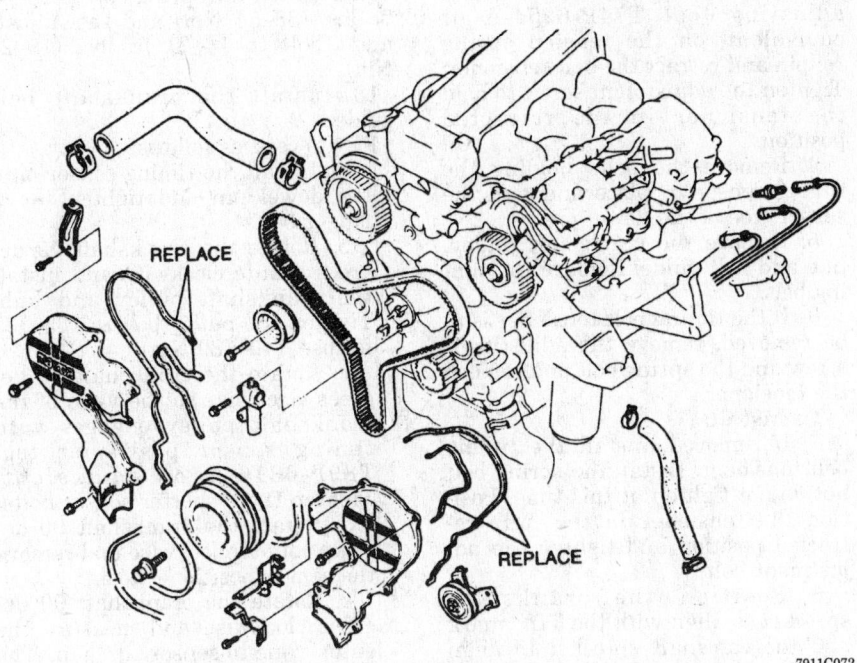

Timing belt covers and timing belt installation — 3.0L (JE) engine

7911C072

5. Install the timing sprockets, timing belt and timing belt front cover. Connect the negative battery cable.

3.0L (JE) Engine

CRANKSHAFT SEAL

1. Disconnect the negative battery cable. Drain the engine oil and the cooling system.
2. Remove the timing belt cover and timing belt. Remove the crankshaft sprocket.
3. Remove the thermostat assembly.
4. Remove the oil pan and oil pump pickup.
5. Remove the oil pump.
6. Remove the oil seal from the pump using a suitable driver. Be careful not to damage the seal housing.
To install:
7. Coat the lip of a new seal and the seal housing with clean engine oil. Install the seal using a seal installer.
8. Install the oil pump, pickup and oil pan.
9. Install the thermostat assembly.
10. Install the crankshaft sprocket, timing belt and timing belt covers.

11. Fill the crankcase with the proper type and quantity of engine oil. Connect the negative battery cable.
12. Fill and bleed the cooling system. Run the engine and check for leaks.

CAMSHAFT SEAL

1. Disconnect the negative battery cable.
2. Remove the timing belt cover and timing belt.
3. Remove the camshaft sprocket retaining bolt and remove the camshaft sprocket.
4. Remove the seal plate and the camshaft seal.
To install:
5. Lubricate the oil seal lip with clean engine oil and install in the cylinder head, using a seal installer.
6. Install the seal plate and tighten the bolts to 69–95 inch lbs. (7.8–11.0 Nm).
7. Install the camshaft sprocket and tighten the retaining bolt to 52–59 ft. lbs. (71–80 Nm).
8. Install the timing belt and timing belt cover. Connect the negative battery cable, start the engine and check for leaks.

Timing Belt and Tensioner

REMOVAL AND INSTALLATION

2.2L Engine

1. Disconnect the negative battery cable and drain the cooling system.
2. Remove the timing belt cover.
3. Turn the crankshaft to align the mark of the camshaft sprocket with the front housing matching mark.
4. Remove the tensioner and spring. Mark the timing belt direction of rotation if it is to be reused.
5. Remove the timing belt.
To install:
6. Make sure the mark on the crankshaft sprocket is aligned with the matching mark on the oil pump body.
7. Make sure the mark on the camshaft sprocket is aligned with the matching mark on the front housing.
8. Install the timing belt tensioner and spring. Temporarily secure it with the spring fully extended.
9. Install the timing belt so there is no looseness at the water pump pulley and idler pulley side. If the timing belt is being reused, it must be installed in the same direction of rotation.
10. Remove the spark plugs to make engine rotation easier.
11. Turn the crankshaft twice clockwise in the direction of rotation. Make sure the matching marks are correctly aligned; if not repeat the installation procedure.
12. Loosen the tensioner lock bolt and apply tension to the belt. Tighten the tensioner lock bolt to 27–38 ft. lbs. (37–52 Nm).
13. Turn the crankshaft twice clockwise in the direction of rotation and align the matching marks. Check the timing belt deflection. The deflection should be 0.31–0.35 in. (8–9mm) on a new belt or 0.35–0.39 in. (9–10mm) on a used belt. Do not apply tension other than that of the tensioner spring.
14. If the deflection is not correct, repeat Steps 11–13.
15. Install the remaining components in the reverse order of removal. Fill and bleed the cooling system.
16. Run the engine and check for leaks and proper operation. Check the idle speed and the ignition timing.

2.3L Engine

1. Disconnect the negative battery cable.
2. Remove the timing belt front cover.

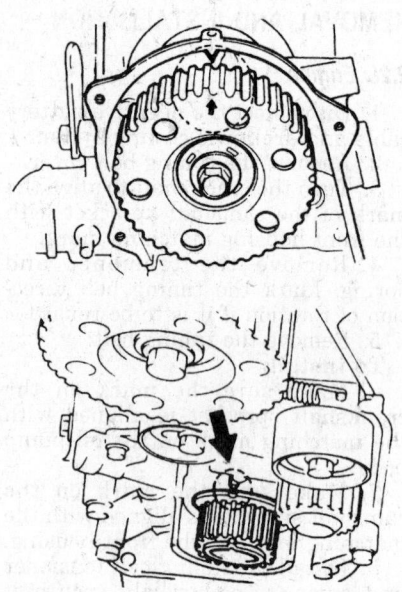

Timing belt sprocket matching marks — 2.2L engine

7911C073

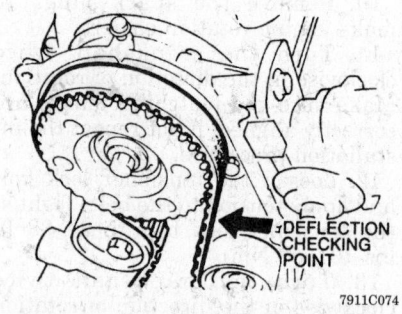

Timing belt deflection checking point — 2.2L engine

7911C074

3. Loosen the belt tensioner adjustment screw. Position belt tension adjusting tool T74P-6254-A or equivalent, on the tension spring rollpin and retract the belt tensioner. Tighten the adjustment screw to hold the tensioner in the retracted position.

4. Remove the bolts holding the timing sensor in place and pull the sensor free of the dowel pin.

5. Remove the crankshaft pulley, hub and belt guide. Remove the timing belt.

6. If the timing belt tensioner is to be removed, remove the adjustment screw and the spring bolt and remove the tensioner.

To install:

7. If removed, install the timing belt tensioner. Install the spring bolt but do not tighten at this time. Position the tensioner in the fully retracted position and tighten the adjustment bolt.

8. Position the crankshaft sprocket to align with the TDC mark and the camshaft sprocket to align with the timing pointer.

9. Install the timing belt over the crankshaft sprocket and then counterclockwise over the auxiliary and camshaft sprockets. Align the belt fore and aft on the sprockets.

10. Loosen the tensioner adjustment bolt to allow the tensioner to move against the belt. If the spring does not have enough tension to move the roller against the belt and the belt hangs loose, it may be necessary to manually push the roller against the belt and tighten the bolt.

NOTE: The spring cannot be used to set belt tension. A wrench must be used on the tensioner assembly.

11. Remove a spark plug from each cylinder to make sure the engine does not jump time during Step 12.

12. Rotate the crankshaft 2 complete turns in the direction of normal rotation to remove the slack from the belt. Tighten the spring bolt to 28–40 ft. lbs. (38–54 Nm) and the adjustment bolt to 14–21 ft. lbs. (19–29 Nm).

13. Install the crankshaft belt guide.

14. Proceed as follows:

a. Install the timing sensor onto the dowel pin and tighten the 2 longer bolts.

b. Rotate the crankshaft 45 degrees counterclockwise and install the crankshaft pulley and hub. Tighten the pulley bolt to 103–133 ft. lbs. (140–180 Nm).

c. Rotate the crankshaft 90 degrees clockwise so the vane of the crankshaft pulley engages with timing sensor positioner tool T89P-6316-A or equivalent. Tighten the 2 shorter sensor bolts.

d. Rotate the crankshaft 90 degrees counterclockwise and remove the sensor positioner tool.

e. Rotate the crankshaft 90 degrees clockwise and measure the outer vane-to-sensor air gap. The air gap must be 0.018–0.039 in. (0.458–0.996mm).

15. Install the timing belt front cover and the remaining components in the reverse order of their removal.

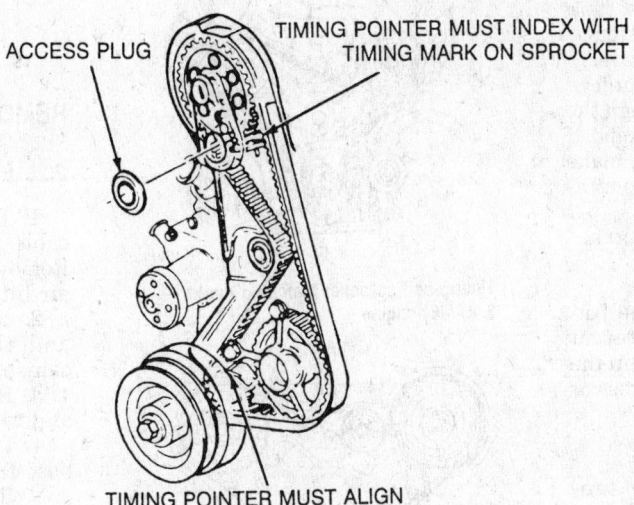

ACCESS PLUG

TIMING POINTER MUST INDEX WITH
TIMING MARK ON SPROCKET

TIMING POINTER MUST ALIGN
WITH TDC MARK ON PULLEY

ON 1988 VEHICLES DISTRIBUTOR ROTOR
MUST ALIGN WITH NO. 1 FIRING POSITION

85472056

Timing belt and sprockets alignment — 2.3L engine

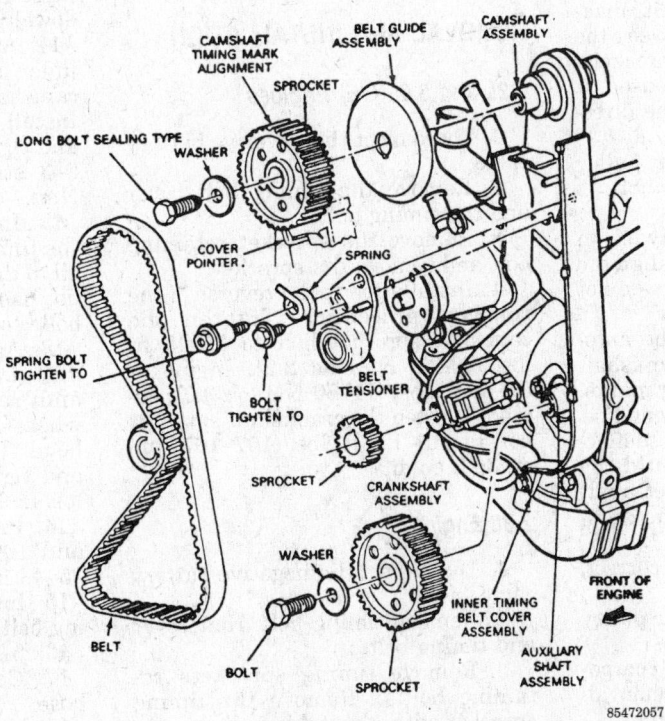

CAMSHAFT
TIMING MARK
ALIGNMENT

BELT GUIDE
ASSEMBLY

CAMSHAFT
ASSEMBLY

SPROCKET

LONG BOLT SEALING TYPE   WASHER

COVER
POINTER

SPRING

SPRING BOLT
TIGHTEN TO

BELT
TENSIONER

BOLT
TIGHTEN TO

SPROCKET

CRANKSHAFT
ASSEMBLY

BELT

WASHER

BOLT

SPROCKET

INNER TIMING
BELT COVER
ASSEMBLY

AUXILIARY
SHAFT
ASSEMBLY

FRONT OF
ENGINE

85472057

Timing belt, tensioner and sprockets installation — 2.3L engine

3.0L (JE) Engine

1. Disconnect the negative battery cable and drain the cooling system.
2. Remove the timing belt cover.
3. Remove the upper idler pulley.
4. Turn the crankshaft to align the matching marks on the sprockets. If the timing belt is to be reused, make an arrow on the belt to indicate rotation direction.
5. Remove the timing belt and automatic tensioner.

To install:

6. Set a plane washer at the bottom of the tensioner body to prevent damage to the body plug. Press in the tensioner rod slowly, using a press or a vise.

NOTE: Do not press the tensioner rod more than 2200 lbs.

7. Insert a pin to hold the tensioner rod in the body. Install the automatic tensioner and tighten the mounting bolts to 14–19 ft. lbs. (19–25 Nm).
8. Install the crankshaft pulley lock bolt and loosely tighten. Check the alignment of the matching marks on the sprockets.
9. With the upper idler pulley removed, install the timing belt, making sure there is no slack between the crankshaft and camshaft sprockets. If the timing belt is being reused, it must be installed in the same direction of rotation.
10. Install the upper idler pulley and tighten the attaching bolt to 27–38 ft. lbs. (37–52 Nm).
11. Turn the crankshaft twice in the direction of rotation and align the matching marks. If the marks do not align, repeat Steps 8–11.
12. Remove the pin from the automatic tensioner. Turn the crankshaft twice and align the matching marks. Make sure the marks are aligned.
13. Check the timing belt deflection. The deflection should be 0.20–0.28 in. (5–7mm). Do not apply tension other than that of the automatic tensioner.
14. If the deflection is not correct, repeat Steps 10–13.
15. Remove the crankshaft pulley lock bolt.
16. Install the remaining components in the reverse order of removal. Fill and bleed the cooling system.
17. Run the engine and check for leaks and proper operation. Check the idle speed and the ignition timing.

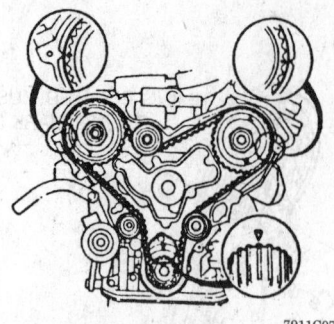

7911C075

Timing belt sprocket matching marks — 3.0L (JE) engine

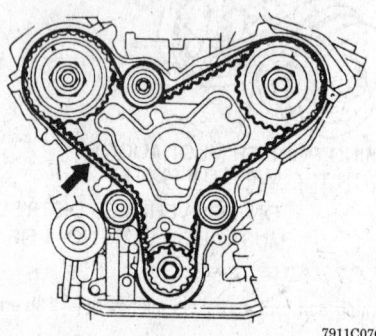

7911C076

Timing belt deflection checking point — 3.0L (JE) engine

Timing Sprockets

REMOVAL AND INSTALLATION

2.2L and 3.0L (JE) Engines

1. Disconnect the negative battery cable.
2. Remove the timing belt cover and the timing belt.
3. Remove the sprocket retaining bolt and remove the sprocket.
4. Installation is the reverse of the removal procedure. Tighten the camshaft sprocket bolt to 35–48 ft. lbs. (47–65 Nm) on 2.2L engine or 52–59 ft. lbs. (71–80 Nm) on 3.0L engine. Tighten the crankshaft sprocket bolt to 116–123 ft. lbs. (157–167 Nm) on 2.2L engine.

2.3L Engine

1. Disconnect the negative battery cable.
2. Remove timing belt front cover and timing belt.
3. Remove timing sprockets retaining bolt(s). Remove the timing sprocket with a suitable puller.
4. Installation is the reverse of the remove procedure. Tighten the camshaft sprocket bolt to 52–70 ft. lbs. (70–95 Nm). Tighten the auxiliary shaft sprocket bolt to 30–40 ft. lbs. (40–54 Nm).

Camshaft

REMOVAL AND INSTALLATION

2.2L Engine

1. Disconnect the negative battery cable and drain the cooling system. Remove the air cleaner assembly or air intake tube.
2. Remove the timing belt cover and the timing belt. Remove the camshaft sprocket.
3. Remove the rocker arm cover and rocker arm/shaft assembly.
4. Disconnect the upper radiator hose from the thermostat housing.
5. Remove the distributor.
6. Remove the front housing.
7. Remove the seal cap from the rear of the cylinder head and remove the camshaft.
8. Check the camshaft for wear and/or damage and replace, as necessary.

To install:

9. Clean all gasket mating surfaces.
10. Apply clean engine oil to the camshaft journals, lobes and bearings. Install the camshaft with the dowel pin facing straight up.
11. Apply silicone sealer to the cylinder head on the front and rear camshaft bearing cap mating surface. Install the rocker arm/shaft assembly and tighten the bolts in sequence, in 2–3 steps to 13–20 ft. lbs. (18–26 Nm).
12. Install a new camshaft seal in the front housing. Apply clean engine oil to the seal lip and install the housing using a new gasket. Tighten the bolts to 14–19 ft. lbs.
13. Apply silicone sealer to the cylinder head and both sides of the front and rear camshaft bearing caps where the caps meet the cylinder head. Install the rocker arm cover and tighten the bolts to 26–35 inch lbs. (2.9–3.9 Nm).
14. Install the camshaft sprocket and tighten the retaining bolt to 35–48 ft. lbs. (47–65 Nm).
15. Install the timing belt and timing belt cover.
16. Install the distributor.
17. Connect the upper radiator hose.
18. Install the remaining components in the reverse order of removal. Fill and bleed the cooling system.
19. Run the engine and check for leaks and proper operation. Check

the idle speed and the ignition timing.

2.3L Engine

1. Disconnect the negative battery cable and drain the cooling system. Remove the air cleaner assembly.

2. Tag and disconnect the spark plug wires at the plugs and rocker arm cover and position aside. Tag and disconnect the necessary vacuum lines.

3. Remove the rocker arm cover. Remove the alternator mounting bracket-to-cylinder head mounting bolts and position aside.

4. Disconnect and remove the upper radiator hose. Remove the radiator shroud.

5. Remove the timing belt front cover. If equipped with power steering, remove the power steering pump bracket.

6. Remove the timing belt, camshaft followers and camshaft sprocket. Remove the camshaft seal using seal removal tool T74P-6700-B or equivalent.

7. Remove the 2 screws and the camshaft rear retainer.

8. Raise and support the vehicle safely. Remove the front motor mount bolts.

9. Position a jack under the engine and raise the engine carefully as far as it will go. Place blocks of wood between the engine mounts and chassis brackets and remove the jack.

10. Remove the camshaft, being careful to avoid damaging the journals, lobes and bearings.

To install:

11. Make sure the threaded plug is in the rear of the camshaft. If not, remove the threaded plug from the old camshaft and install. Tighten to 12–18 ft. lbs. (16–24 Nm).

12. Coat the camshaft lobes with grease and lubricate the journals with heavy engine oil. Carefully slide the camshaft through the bearings.

13. Install the camshaft rear retainer with the 2 screws. Tighten to 6–9 ft. lbs. (8–12 Nm).

14. Install a new camshaft seal using seal installation tool T74P-6150-A or equivalent.

15. Install the remaining components in the reverse order of their removal. Fill and bleed the cooling system. Run the engine and check for leaks.

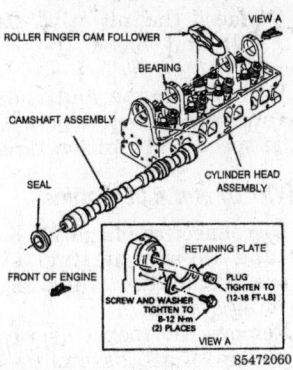

Camshaft installation — 2.3L engine

2.6L Engine

1. Disconnect the negative battery cable.

2. Remove the air cleaner assembly or air intake tube.

3. Remove the rocker arm cover.

4. Remove the distributor.

5. Remove the rocker arm/shaft assembly.

6. Remove the service cover on the timing chain cover. Push the chain adjuster sleeve toward the left and insert a 1.77 in. (45mm) long by 0.08 in. (2mm) diameter pin into the lever hole to hold it.

7. Remove the bolt and the distributor drive gear. Remove the camshaft sprocket from the camshaft and hold it in position with mechanics wire.

NOTE: Do not allow the timing chain to become disconnected from the camshaft sprocket or engine timing will be disturbed.

8. Remove the camshaft. Inspect the camshaft for wear or damage and replace, if ne. Inspect the camshaft for wear or damage and replace, if necessary.

To install:

9. Install the camshaft, aligning the dowel with the camshaft sprocket.

10. If equipped, coat the circular packing with sealant and install in the end of the cylinder head.

11. Install the rocker arm/shaft assembly and tighten the bolts, in sequence, in 2–3 steps to 14–19 ft. lbs. (19–25 Nm).

12. Install the camshaft sprocket to the camshaft. Install the distributor drive gear and lock bolt. Tighten the lock bolt to 36–43 ft. lbs. (49–58 Nm).

13. Remove the chain adjuster sleeve retaining pin and install the service cover with a new gasket. Tighten the bolts to 69–95 inch lbs. (7.8–11.0 Nm) and the nuts to 61–87 inch lbs. (6.9–9.8 Nm).

14. Apply sealant to the half circle seal(s) and install in the cylinder head. Apply sealer to the tops of the seals and to the cylinder head in the seal area.

15. Coat a new gasket with sealant and install the rocker arm cover. Tighten the bolts to 52–78 inch lbs. (5.9–8.8 Nm).

16. Install the distributor.

17. Install the air cleaner assembly or air intake tube. Connect the negative battery cable.

18. Run the engine and check for leaks and proper operation. Check the idle speed and ignition timing.

3.0L (JE) Engine

1. Disconnect the negative battery cable and drain the cooling system.

2. Remove the timing belt covers and timing belt.

3. Remove the rocker arm cover.

4. If removing the driver's side camshaft, remove the distributor and the distributor spacer.

5. Remove the bolt and the camshaft sprocket.

6. Remove the seal plate. Pry out the camshaft seal, being careful not to damage the seal housing.

7. Remove the rocker arm/shaft assembly.

8. Remove the thrust plate bolts and remove the thrust plate. Slide the camshaft out of the cylinder head. If removing the driver's side camshaft, remove the distributor drive gear.

NOTE: Components such as the radiator, radiator support and air conditioning condenser may have to be removed to allow camshaft removal. It may be necessary to remove the cylinder head to remove the camshaft.

9. Inspect the camshaft for wear and/or damage and replace if necessary.

To install:

10. If installing the driver's side camshaft, remove all old sealer from the distributor drive gear and apply sealer to the gear face, then seat the gear fully on the camshaft.

11. Apply clean engine oil to the camshaft journals, lobes and bearings. Install the camshaft and the thrust plate. Tighten the thrust plate to 69–95 inch lbs. (7.8–11.0 Nm).

12. Apply clean engine oil to a new camshaft seal lip and press the seal into the cylinder head, using a seal installer.

13. Install the rocker arm/shaft assembly and tighten the bolts, in sequence, in 2–3 steps to 14–19 ft. lbs.

(19–25 Nm). Make sure the rocker arm shaft spring does not get caught between the shaft and mounting boss during installation.

14. Install the seal plates and tighten the bolts to 69–95 inch lbs. (7.8–11.0 Nm).

15. Install the camshaft sprocket and tighten the bolt to 52–59 ft. lbs. (71–80 Nm).

16. If installing the driver's side camshaft, apply clean engine oil to a new O-ring and install on the distributor spacer. Install the spacer and tighten the nuts to 69–95 inch lbs. (7.8–11.0 Nm).

17. Coat a new gasket with silicone sealant and install on the rocker arm cover. Install the cover and tighten the bolts to 30–39 inch lbs. (3.4–4.4 Nm).

18. Install the timing belt and timing belt covers.

19. Install the distributor.

20. Connect the negative battery cable. Fill and bleed the cooling system.

21. Run the engine and check for leaks and proper operation. Check the idle speed and ignition timing.

3.0L (VIN U) and 4.0L Engines

1. Disconnect the negative battery cable and relieve the fuel system pressure. Drain the crankcase and the cooling system.

2. Remove the rocker arm covers, rocker arm shaft assemblies and pushrods. Note the position of each component so it can be reinstalled in the same place.

3. Remove the intake manifold.

4. Remove the lifters. Identify each lifter so it can be reinstalled in the original position.

5. Remove the front timing chain cover and the timing chain and sprockets.

6. Remove the thrust plate bolts and remove the thrust plate. Carefully remove the camshaft, being careful not to damage the journals, lobes or bearings.

To install:

7. Coat the camshaft lobes with grease and the journals with heavy engine oil. Carefully install the camshaft, being careful not to damage the journals, lobes or bearings.

8. Install the thrust plate and the thrust plate retaining bolts. Tighten the bolts to 7–10 ft. lbs. (10–13 Nm).

9. Check the camshaft endplay using a dial indicator. The endplay should be 0.0008–0.004 in.

10. Install the remaining components in the reverse order of their removal. Fill the crankcase with the proper type and quantity of engine oil. Fill and bleed the cooling system. Run the engine and check for leaks.

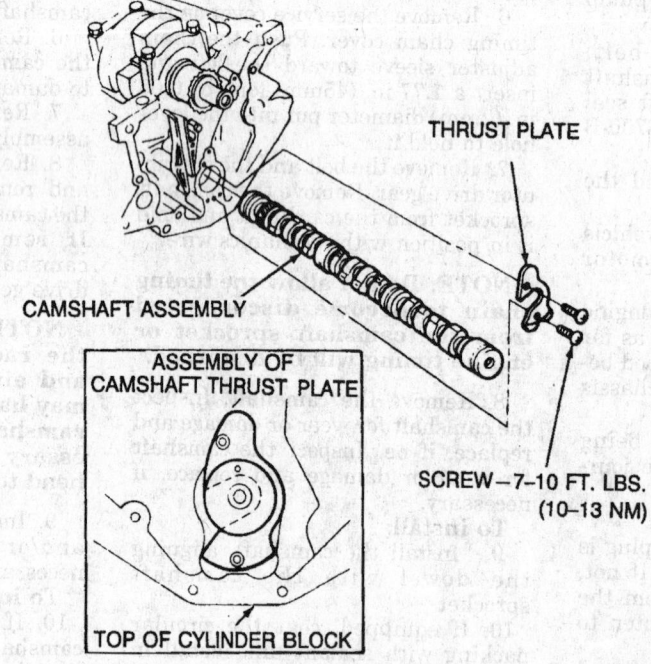

THRUST PLATE

CAMSHAFT ASSEMBLY

ASSEMBLY OF CAMSHAFT THRUST PLATE

TOP OF CYLINDER BLOCK

SCREW—7–10 FT. LBS. (10–13 NM)

85472059

Camshaft installation — 3.0L (VIN U) and 4.0L engines

Balancer Shafts

REMOVAL AND INSTALLATION

2.6L Engine

1. Relieve the fuel system pressure and disconnect the negative bat-

tery cable. Drain the engine engine oil and the cooling system.

2. Remove the cylinder head, oil pan and timing chain cover.

3. Remove the balancer shaft chain.

4. Remove the thrust plate lock bolts and remove the balancer shaft(s). Be careful not to damage the

balancer shaft journals and bushing during removal.

5. Check the balancer shaft(s) and bushings for wear and/or damage and replace as necessary.

To install:

6. Apply clean engine oil to the balancer shaft journals and install in the cylinder block, being careful not to damage the bushings and journals.

7. Loosely tighten the thrust plate lock bolts and make sure the balancer shaft(s) rotate smoothly. Tighten the lock bolts to 69–95 inch lbs. (7.8–11.0 Nm).

8. Install the crankshaft balancer sprocket.

9. Set the balancer chain on the idler sprocket assembly so the timing mark on the idler sprocket assembly and the brown link of the balancer chain align.

10. Install the balancer chain so the 5 alignment marks on the chain, sprocket and block align and attach the idler sprocket assembly to the cylinder block. Loosely tighten the idler sprocket assembly lock bolt.

11. Install the right and left lower balancer chain guides and tighten the mounting bolts to 69–95 inch lbs. (7.8–11.0 Nm).

12. Install the upper chain guide and loosely tighten the mounting and adjusting bolts.

13. Tighten the idler sprocket assembly lock bolt to 27–38 ft. lbs. (37–52 Nm) and install the spacer.

14. On all 1992–96 B-Series Pick-Up with automatic transmission, adjust the balancer chain tension as follows:

   a. Fabricate a piece of wood, 0.118–0.138 in. (3.0–3.5mm) thick and 0.335–0.374 in. (8.5–9.5mm) wide.

   b. Insert the piece of wood in the notch in the upper chain guide.

   c. Push on the chain guide just above the adjusting slot with a force of 2.9–3.7 lbs. and tighten the adjusting and pivot bolts to 69–95 inch lbs. (7.8–11.0 Nm).

   d. Remove the wood from between the chain and chain guide, making sure no wood shavings are left.

   e. Measure the chain slack. It should be 0.039–0.059 in. (1.0–1.5mm) at the notch in the guide.

NOTE: If the upper chain guide bottoms on the adjusting bolt during the adjustment procedure, the balancer chain must be replaced.

15. Install the remaining components in the reverse order of removal.

NOTE: Be sure to remove the pin from the timing chain adjuster before installing the service cover.

16. Fill the crankcase with the proper type and quantity of oil. Fill and bleed the cooling system.

17. Run the engine and check for leaks and proper operation. Check the idle speed and ignition timing.

Auxiliary Shaft

REMOVAL AND INSTALLATION

2.3L Engine

1. Disconnect the negative battery cable and drain the cooling system.

2. Remove the timing belt front cover.

3. Remove the timing belt and remove the auxiliary shaft sprocket.

4. Remove the auxiliary shaft cover bolts and the cover.

5. Remove the auxiliary shaft retaining plate screws and remove the retaining plate.

6. Remove the auxiliary shaft, being careful not to damage the journals or bearings.

To install:

7. Coat the auxiliary shaft journals with heavy engine oil. Install the auxiliary shaft, being careful not to damage the journals or bearings.

8. Install the retaining plate. Tighten the retaining plate screws to 6–9 ft. lbs. (8–12 Nm).

9. Install the auxiliary shaft cover and tighten the screws to 6–9 ft. lbs. (8–12 Nm).

10. Install the remaining components in the reverse order of their removal. Fill and bleed the cooling system. Run the engine and check for leaks.

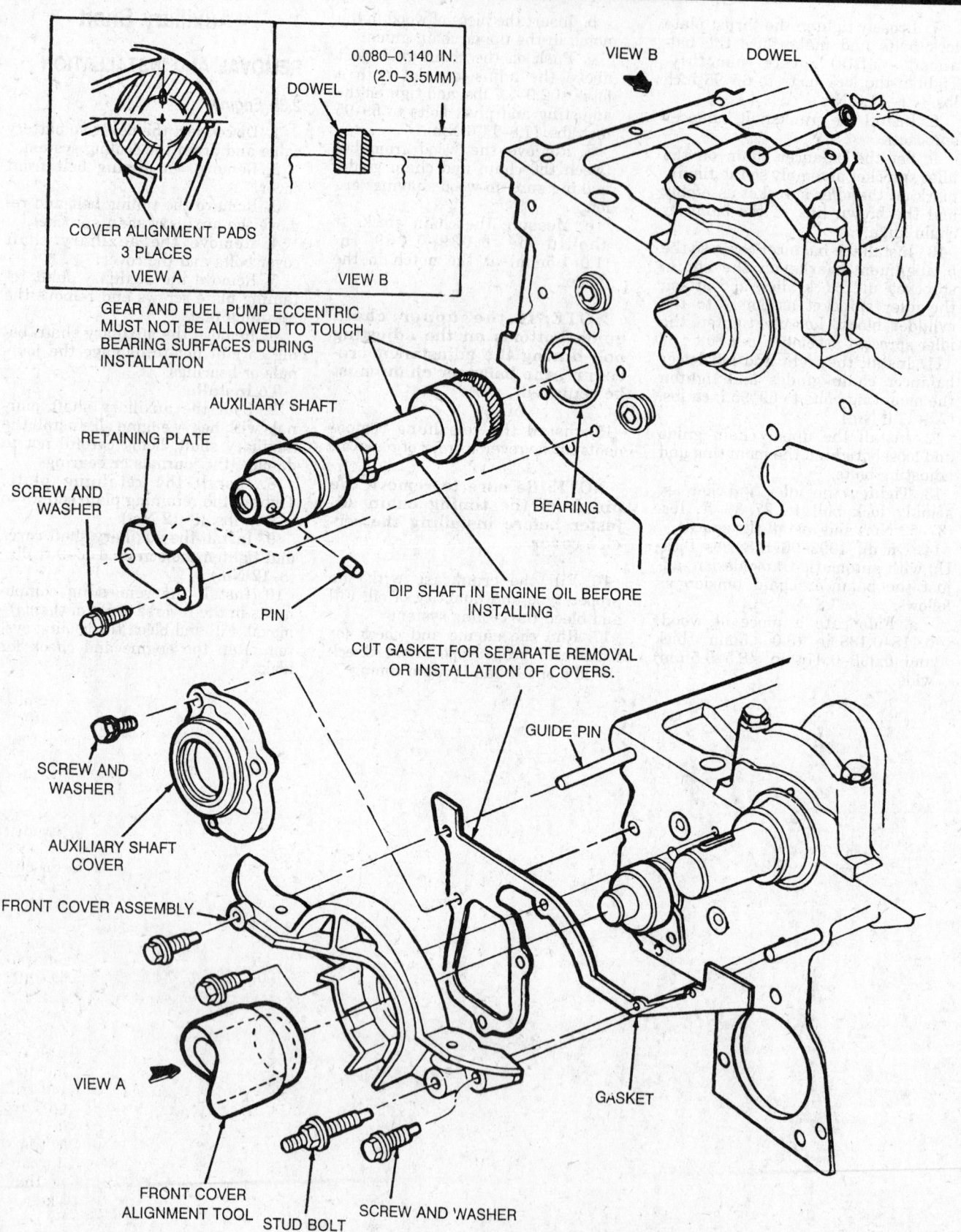

0.080–0.140 IN.
(2.0–3.5MM)

DOWEL

COVER ALIGNMENT PADS
3 PLACES
VIEW A

VIEW B

VIEW B   DOWEL

GEAR AND FUEL PUMP ECCENTRIC
MUST NOT BE ALLOWED TO TOUCH
BEARING SURFACES DURING
INSTALLATION

AUXILIARY SHAFT

RETAINING PLATE

SCREW AND
WASHER

PIN

BEARING

DIP SHAFT IN ENGINE OIL BEFORE
INSTALLING

CUT GASKET FOR SEPARATE REMOVAL
OR INSTALLATION OF COVERS.

SCREW AND
WASHER

AUXILIARY SHAFT
COVER

FRONT COVER ASSEMBLY

GUIDE PIN

VIEW A

GASKET

FRONT COVER
ALIGNMENT TOOL   STUD BOLT   SCREW AND WASHER

85472061

Auxiliary shaft installation — 2.3L engine

Piston and Connecting Rod

POSITIONING

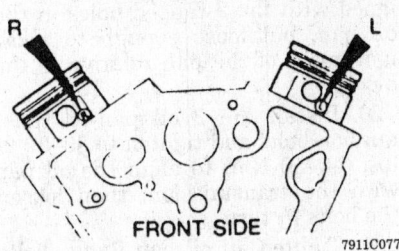

Install the piston with the L mark (left bank) and the R mark (right bank) facing the front of the engine — 3.0L (JE) engine

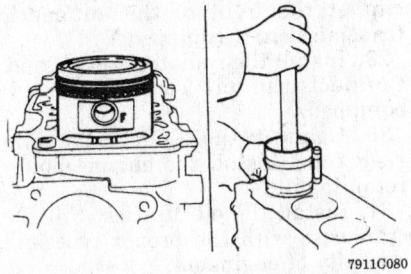

Install the piston with the F mark facing the front of the engine — 2.2L and 2.6L engine

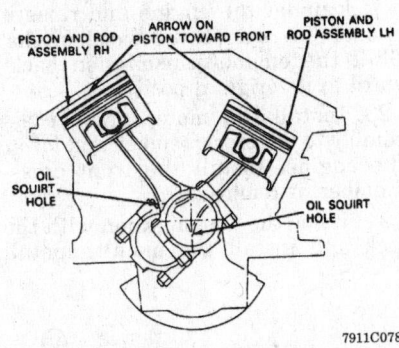

Piston and connecting rod positioning — 4.0L engine

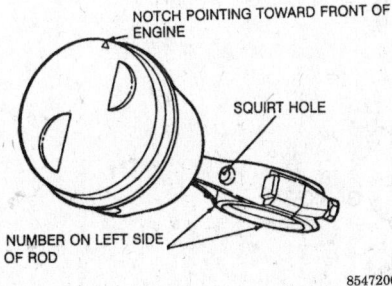

Piston and connecting rod assembly — 2.3L engine

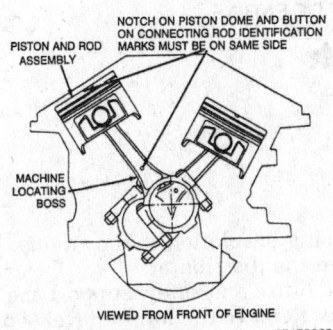

Piston and connecting rod assembly — 3.0L (VIN U) engine

ENGINE LUBRICATION

Oil Pan

REMOVAL AND INSTALLATION

2.2L and 2.6L B-Series Pick-Up Engines

1. Disconnect the negative battery cable.
2. Raise and support the vehicle safely.
3. Remove the necessary splash shields.
4. Position a drain pan under the oil pan. Remove the drain plug and drain the engine oil.
5. If equipped with 4WD, remove the front differential.
6. Remove the necessary steering linkage.
7. Remove the gusset plates and the clutch housing cover, if equipped.
8. Remove the oil pan mounting bolts and remove the oil pan. If necessary, insert a scraper or other suitable tool between the oil pan and block to separate them. Be careful not to bend the pan.

To install:

9. Clean all gasket mating surfaces and the oil p
10. Apply sealant to the cylinder block and install a new gasket.
11. Install the oil pan with the attaching bolts. Tighten the bolts to 61–104 inch lbs. (6.9–12.0 Nm) on 2.2L engine, or 69–95 inch lbs. (7.8–11.0 Nm) on 2.6L engine.

NOTE: Apply Loctite® to the bolt threads on 2.6L engine before installation.

12. Install the remaining components in the reverse order of removal. Lower the vehicle and connect the negative battery cable.
13. Fill the crankcase with the proper type and quantity of engine oil. Run the engine and check for leaks.

2.3L Engine

1. Disconnect the negative battery cable and remove the air cleaner outlet tube at the throttle body.
2. Remove the engine oil dipstick and remove the engine mount retaining nuts.
3. Disconnect the oil cooler lines at the radiator, if equipped. Remove the fan shroud.
4. If equipped with automatic transmission, remove the radiator retaining bolts and position the radiator upward and wire to the hood.
5. Raise and safely support the vehicle. Drain the engine oil.
6. Disconnect the starter cable and remove the starter. Disconnect the exhaust manifold tube to the inlet pipe bracket at the thermactor check valve.
7. Disconnect the catalytic converter at the inlet pipe.
8. Remove the insulator and retainer assembly at the transmission. Remove the transmission mount retaining nuts to the crossmember.
9. If equipped with automatic transmission, remove the oil cooler lines from the retainer at the block and remove the front crossmember.
10. If equipped with manual transmission, disconnect the right front lower shock absorber mount.
11. Position a jack under the engine. Raise the engine and position suitable wood blocks between the engine mounts and frame brackets. Remove the jack.
12. If equipped with automatic transmission, position a jack under the transmission and raise slightly.

13. Remove the oil pan retaining bolts and lower the pan to the chassis. Remove the low oil level sensor assembly and the oil pump drive and pickup tube assembly.

14. If equipped with automatic transmission, remove the oil pan out the front of the vehicle. If equipped with manual transmission, remove the oil pan out from the rear.

To install:

15. Clean all gasket mating surfaces, the oil pan, oil pump exterior and pickup tube screen.

16. Install the low oil level sensor assembly and tighten to 20–30 ft. lbs. (27–41 Nm).

17. Press a new gasket into the oil pan groove. Retain the gasket in the oil pan by press fit only.

18. Position the oil pan on the crossmember. Install the oil pump drive and pickup tube assembly.

19. Apply sealer in 6 places on the engine and install the oil pan. Install the oil pan flange bolts tight enough to compress the gasket to the point

that the 2 transmission holes are aligned with the 2 tapped holes in the oil pan, but loose enough to allow movement of the pan relative to the block.

20. Install the 2 oil pan-to-transmission bolts and tighten to 30–39 ft. lbs. (40–50 Nm) to align the oil pan with the transmission, then loosen the bolts ½ turn.

21. Tighten all oil pan flange bolts to 90–120 inch lbs. (10–13.5 Nm), then retighten the 2 oil pan-to-transmission bolts to 30–39 ft. lbs. (40–50 Nm).

22. Install a new oil filter. Position a jack under the engine and raise it enough to remove the wood blocks. Shift the engine/transmission backward to its original position.

23. Install the mount/bracket assembly to the crossmember and lower the engine. Install the front crossmember, if removed.

24. Raise the transmission with the jack and install the mount. Install

the stabilizer brackets to the frame, if removed.

25. Connect the automatic transmission oil cooler line retainer clip to the engine, if equipped. Install the transmission mount retaining nuts.

26. Install a new gasket and connect the rear exhaust pipe just behind the catalytic converter.

27. Connect the low oil level sensor wire. Install the starter and connect the starter cable. Lower the vehicle.

28. Connect the vacuum tube to the clip at the front of the automatic transmission, if equipped.

29. Install the radiator and shroud. Connect the oil cooler lines, if equipped.

30. Connect the EGR valve and EGR tube. Install the engine mount retaining nuts.

31. Install the oil dipstick. Fill the crankcase with the proper type and quantity of engine oil.

32. Connect the negative battery cable, start the engine and check for leaks.

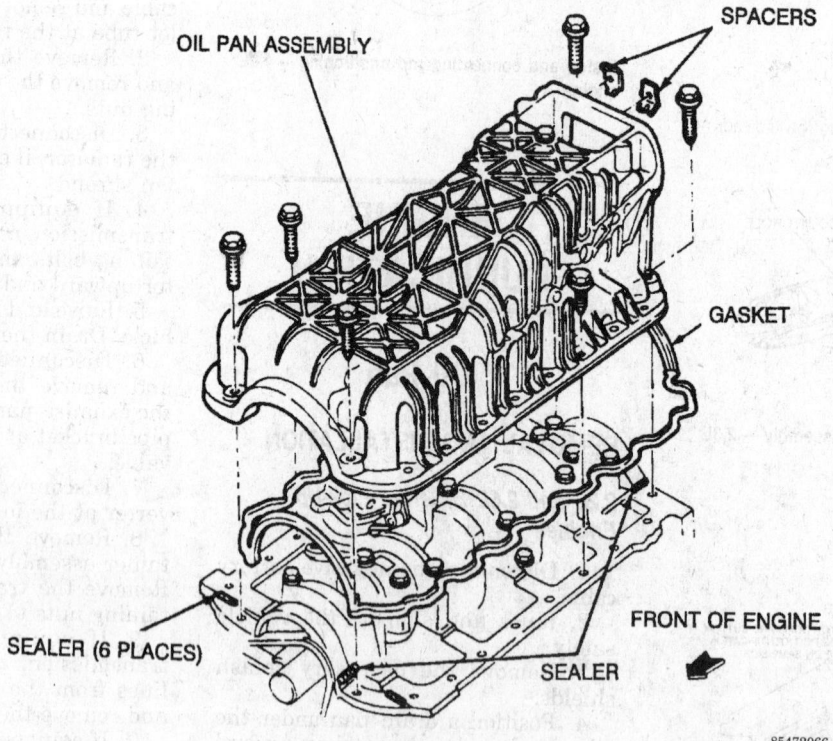

Oil pan installation — 2.3L engine

85472066

3.0L (VIN U) Engine

1. Disconnect the negative battery cable. Remove the engine oil level dipstick.

2. Disconnect the fan shroud and drape it over the fan. Remove the motor mount nuts from the frame.

3. Mark the position of the distributor rotor in relation to the distributor housing and the position of the

housing in relation to the engine. Remove the distributor.

4. Raise and safely support the vehicle. Remove the low oil level sensor retainer clip at the sensor. Disconnect the electrical connector from the sensor.

5. Drain the crankcase and remove the starter. Remove the transmission inspection cover.

6. Remove the right axle beam on 2WD vehicles.

NOTE: The brake caliper must be removed and wired out of the way.

7. Remove the oil pan bolts. Position a jack under the engine and raise it approximately 2 in. Remove the oil pan.

NOTE: The oil pan fits tightly between the transmission spacer plate and oil pump pickup tube. Use care when removing to avoid damaging the pickup tube.

To install:

8. Clean all gasket mating surfaces and the oil pan.

9. Apply a $1/5$ in. bead of silicone sealer to the junction of the rear main bearing cap and cylinder block and the junction of the front cover assembly and cylinder block.

10. Position the oil pan gasket to the oil pan and secure with sealer. Install the oil pan on the engine block with the attaching bolts and tighten to 9 ft. lbs. (12 Nm).

11. Install the low oil level sensor connector and the retainer clip. Lower the engine assembly.

12. Install the right axle beam, if removed.

13. Install the transmission inspection cover and the starter. Lower the vehicle.

14. Install the fan shroud and the motor mount nuts. Install the distributor, aligning the marks that were made during removal.

15. Install the engine oil level dipstick. Fill the crankcase with the proper type and quantity of engine oil.

16. Connect the negative battery cable, start the engine and check for leaks.

MPV

2.6L ENGINE

1. Disconnect the negative battery cable. Remove the fan shroud.

2. Install engine support tool 49 G017 5A0 or equivalent. Remove the engine mount nuts and lift the engine slightly to gain removal clearance.

3. Raise and safely support the vehicle. Support the transmission with a transmission jack and remove the transmission lower mount.

4. Remove the splash shield.

5. Position a drain pan under the oil pan. Remove the drain plug and drain the engine oil.

6. Remove the gusset plates and stabilizer bar brackets.

7. Remove the oil pan mounting bolts and remove the oil pan. If necessary, insert a scraper or other suitable tool between the oil pan and block to separate them. Be careful not to bend the pan.

To install:

8. Clean all gasket mating surfaces and the oil pan.

9. Apply sealant to the cylinder block and install a new gasket.

10. Install the oil pan with the attaching bolts. Tighten the bolts to 69–95 inch lbs. (7.8–11.0 Nm). Apply Loctite® to the bolt threads before installation.

11. Install the remaining components in the reverse order of removal. Lower the vehicle and remove the engine support tool. Install the engine mount nuts.

12. Connect the negative battery cable. Fill the crankcase with the proper type and quantity of engine oil. Run the engine and check for leaks.

3.0L (JE) ENGINE — 2WD

1. Disconnect the negative battery cable.

2. Raise and safely support the vehicle.

3. Remove the splash shield.

4. Position a drain pan under the oil pan. Remove the drain plug and drain the engine oil.

5. Remove the gusset plates.

6. Remove the oil pan mounting bolts and remove the oil pan. If necessary, insert a scraper or other suitable tool between the oil pan and block to separate them. Be careful not to bend the pan.

To install:

7. Clean all gasket mating surfaces and the oil pan.

8. Apply sealant to the cylinder block and install a new gasket.

9. Install the oil pan with the attaching bolts. Tighten to 61–87 inch lbs. (6.9–9.8 Nm).

10. Install the remaining components in the reverse order of removal. Lower the vehicle and connect the negative battery cable.

11. Fill the crankcase with the proper type and quantity of engine oil. Run the engine and check for leaks.

3.0L (JE) ENGINE — 4WD

1. Disconnect the negative battery cable. Remove the fresh air duct and fan shroud.

2. Install engine support tool 49 G017 5A0 or equivalent. Remove the

engine mount nuts and lift the engine slightly to gain removal clearance.

3. Raise and safely support the vehicle. Support the transmission with a transmission jack and remove the transmission lower mount.

4. Remove the splash shields.

5. Position a drain pan under the oil pan. Remove the drain plug and drain the engine oil.

6. If equipped with automatic transmission, disconnect and reposition the oil cooler hose and tube.

7. Remove the stabilizer bar.

8. Remove the oil pan mounting bolts and remove the oil pan. If necessary, insert a scraper or other suitable tool between the oil pan and block to separate them. Be careful not to bend the pan.

To install:

9. Clean all gasket mating surfaces and the oil pan.

10. Apply sealant to the cylinder block and install a new gasket.

11. Install the oil pan with the attaching bolts. Tighten to 61–87 inch lbs. (6.9–9.8 Nm).

12. Install the remaining components in the reverse order of removal. Lower the vehicle and remove the engine support tool. Install the engine mount nuts.

13. Connect the negative battery cable. Fill the crankcase with the proper type and quantity of engine oil. Run the engine and check for leaks.

4.0L Engine

1. Remove the engine assembly and install on a workstand with the oil pan facing up.

2. Remove the oil pan retaining bolts and remove the pan.

To install:

3. Clean all gasket mating surfaces and the oil pan.

4. Install a new crankshaft rear main bearing cap wedge seal. The seal should fit snugly into the sides of the rear main bearing cap.

5. Position a new oil pan gasket to the engine block and place the oil pan in position on the 4 locating studs. Tighten the retaining nuts and bolts evenly to 5–7 ft. lbs. (7–10 Nm).

6. Measure the gap between the surface of the rear face of the oil pan, at the spacer locations, and the rear face of the engine block as follows:

   a. With the oil pan installed on the engine, position a straight-edge flat on the rear of the engine block so it extends over one of the oil pan/transmission bolt mounting pads.

b. Using a feeler gauge, measure the gap between the mounting pad and the straight-edge. Repeat the procedure for the other mounting pad.

c. If the measured gap is 0.011–0.020 in. (0.27–0.51mm), a 0.010 in. (0.254mm) spacer is required. If the measured gap is 0.021–0.029 in. (0.52–0.76mm), a 0.020 in. (0.508mm) spacer is required. If the measured gap is 0.030–0.039 in. (0.77–1.00mm), a 0.030 in. (0.762mm) spacer is required.

d. Install the selected spacers to the mounting pads on the rear of the oil pan before bolting the engine and transmission together.

NOTE: Failure to use the correct spacer can result in improper clearance between the oil pan and transmission, resulting in oil pan damage and/or an oil leak.

7. Remove the engine from the workstand and install in the vehicle.

Measuring oil pan-to-transmission gap — Navajo

7911C081

Oil Pump

REMOVAL AND INSTALLATION

2.2L and 2.6L Engines

1. Disconnect the negative battery cable and drain the cooling system.
2. Raise and safely support the vehicle. Remove the splash shield and drain the engine oil.
3. Remove the oil pan, stiffener and oil pump pickup.
4. Lower the vehicle.
5. On 2.2L engine, remove the timing belt cover, timing belt and crankshaft sprocket. Remove the oil pump mounting bolts and remove the oil pump.
6. On 2.6L engine, remove the cylinder head and the timing chain cover. The oil pump is part of the timing chain cover.
7. If necessary, disassemble the oil pump and check for wear and/or damage. Replace parts as necessary.
8. Pry out the crankshaft oil seal, being careful not to damage the seal housing.

To install:
9. Clean all gasket material.
10. Apply clean engine oil to the lip of a new seal and press the seal into the pump, using a seal installer.

11. On 2.2L engine, proceed as follows:

a. Apply a continuous bead of silicone sealant to the contact surface of the oil pump. Do not allow sealant to get into the oil hole.

b. Lubricate a new O-ring and install into the pump body.

c. Install the oil pump and tighten the **A** bolts to 14–19 ft. lbs. (19–25 Nm) and the **B** bolts to 27–38 ft. lbs. (37–52 Nm).

d. Install the crankshaft sprocket, timing belt and timing belt cover.

12. On 2.6L engine, install the timing chain cover and cylinder head.
13. Raise and safely support the vehicle.
14. Install the stiffener. Install a new gasket and the oil pump pickup. Tighten the bolts to 69–95 inch lbs. (7.8–11.0 Nm).
15. Install the oil pan and the splash shield.
16. Lower the vehicle and connect the negative battery cable. Fill the engine with the proper type and quantity of engine oil.
17. Run the engine and check for leaks and proper operation.

2.3L and 3.0L (VIN U) Engines

1. Disconnect the negative battery cable.
2. Remove the oil pan.
3. Remove the oil pump attaching bolts and, if equipped, remove the oil pump pickup tube retaining nut from the main bearing cap.
4. Remove the oil pump and oil pump driveshaft. Remove and clean the oil pump pickup tube and screen, as necessary.

To install:
5. Install the oil pump pickup tube and screen assembly, if removed.
6. Prime the oil pump by filling either the inlet or outlet port with clean engine oil. Rotate the pump shaft to distribute the oil within the pump body.
7. Insert the oil pump driveshaft into the opening in the block or main bearing cap. On 3.0L engine, assemble the shaft to the oil pump until the retainer clicks into place.
8. Install the oil pump, with a new gasket if equipped, and install the attaching bolts. Tighten the bolts to 14–21 ft. lbs. (19–29 Nm) on 2.3L engine or 35 ft. lbs. (48 Nm) on 3.0L engine.
9. On 2.3L engine, install the pickup tube retaining nut and tighten to 30–41 ft. lbs. (40–55 Nm).
10. Install the oil pan.

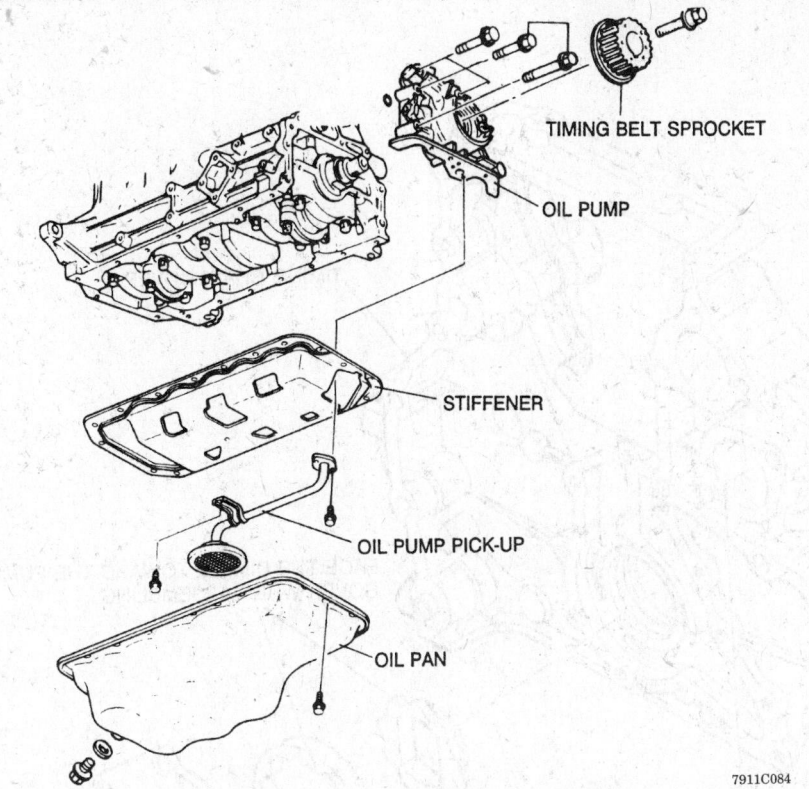

Oil pan and pump removal — 2.2L engine

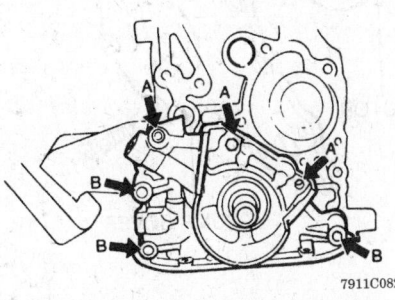

Oil pump mounting bolt identification — 2.2L engine

11. Fill the crankcase with the proper type and quantity of engine oil. Connect the negative battery cable, start the engine and check for leaks.

3.0L (JE) Engine

1. Disconnect the negative battery cable and drain the cooling system.
2. Raise and safely support the vehicle. Remove the splash shield and drain the engine oil. Remove the oil pan and oil pump pickup.
3. Lower the vehicle.
4. Remove the timing belt cover, timing belt and crankshaft sprocket.

5. Remove the thermostat assembly.
6. Remove the attaching bolts and remove the oil pump. Disassemble the pump, if necessary and inspect all components for wear and/or damage. Replace components, as necessary.
7. Pry out the crankshaft seal from the pump, being careful not to damage the seal housing.
To install:
8. Clean all gasket mating surfaces.
9. Apply clean engine oil to a new crankshaft seal and install in the pump, using a seal installer.
10. Install a new gasket and the oil pump. Tighten the mounting bolts to 14–19 ft. lbs. (19–25 Nm).
11. Install a new gasket and the thermostat housing. Tighten the mounting bolts to 14–19 ft. lbs. (19–25 Nm).
12. Install the crankshaft sprocket, timing belt and timing belt cover.
13. Raise and safely support the vehicle.
14. Lubricate and install a new O-ring and the oil pump pickup. Tighten the mounting bolts to 69–95 inch lbs. (7.8–11.0 Nm).
15. Install the oil pan and the splash shield. Lower the vehicle.
16. Fill the crankcase with the proper type and quantity of engine

oil. Connect the negative battery cable.
17. Fill and bleed the cooling system. Run the engine and check for leaks and proper operation.

4.0L Engine

1. Remove the engine assembly.
2. Remove the oil pan.
3. Remove the oil pump attaching bolts and withdraw the oil pump driveshaft.
To install:
4. Prime the oil pump by filling either the inlet or outlet port with clean engine oil. Rotate the pump shaft to distribute the oil within the pump body.
5. Insert the oil pump driveshaft into the block with the pointed end facing inward. The pointed end is closest to the pressed-on flange. Position the pump with a new gasket and install the attaching bolts. Tighten to 13–15 ft. lbs. (17–21 Nm).
6. Clean and install the oil pump pickup with a new gasket. Tighten the bolts to 7–10 ft. lbs. (9–13 Nm).
7. Install the oil pan and install the engine assembly.
8. Fill the crankcase with the proper type and quantity of engine oil. Run the engine and check for leaks.

CHECKING

2.2L, 2.6L and 3.0L (JE) Engines

1. Remove the pump and disassemble. Clean all parts in solvent and allow to dry.
2. Check for a distorted or damaged oil pump body or cover.
3. Check the relief valve plunger for wear or damage. Check for a weak or broken plunger spring. The spring free length should be 1.827 in. (46.4mm).
4. Check the rotor side clearance as follows: Lay a straightedge across the pump body and, using a feeler gauge, measure between the gear faces and the straight-edge. If the clearance exceeds 0.0039 in. (0.10mm) on 2.2L and 2.6L engines or 0.0051 in. (0.13mm) on 3.0L engine, replace the pump.
5. Check the rotor tooth tip clearance as follows: Insert a feeler gauge between the gears at the gear tip. If the clearance exceeds 0.0071 in. (0.18mm) on 2.2L and 2.6L engines or 0.0094 in. (0.24mm) on 3.0L engine, replace the gears or pump.
6. Check the outer rotor-to-pump body clearance as follows: Insert a feeler gauge between the outer gear

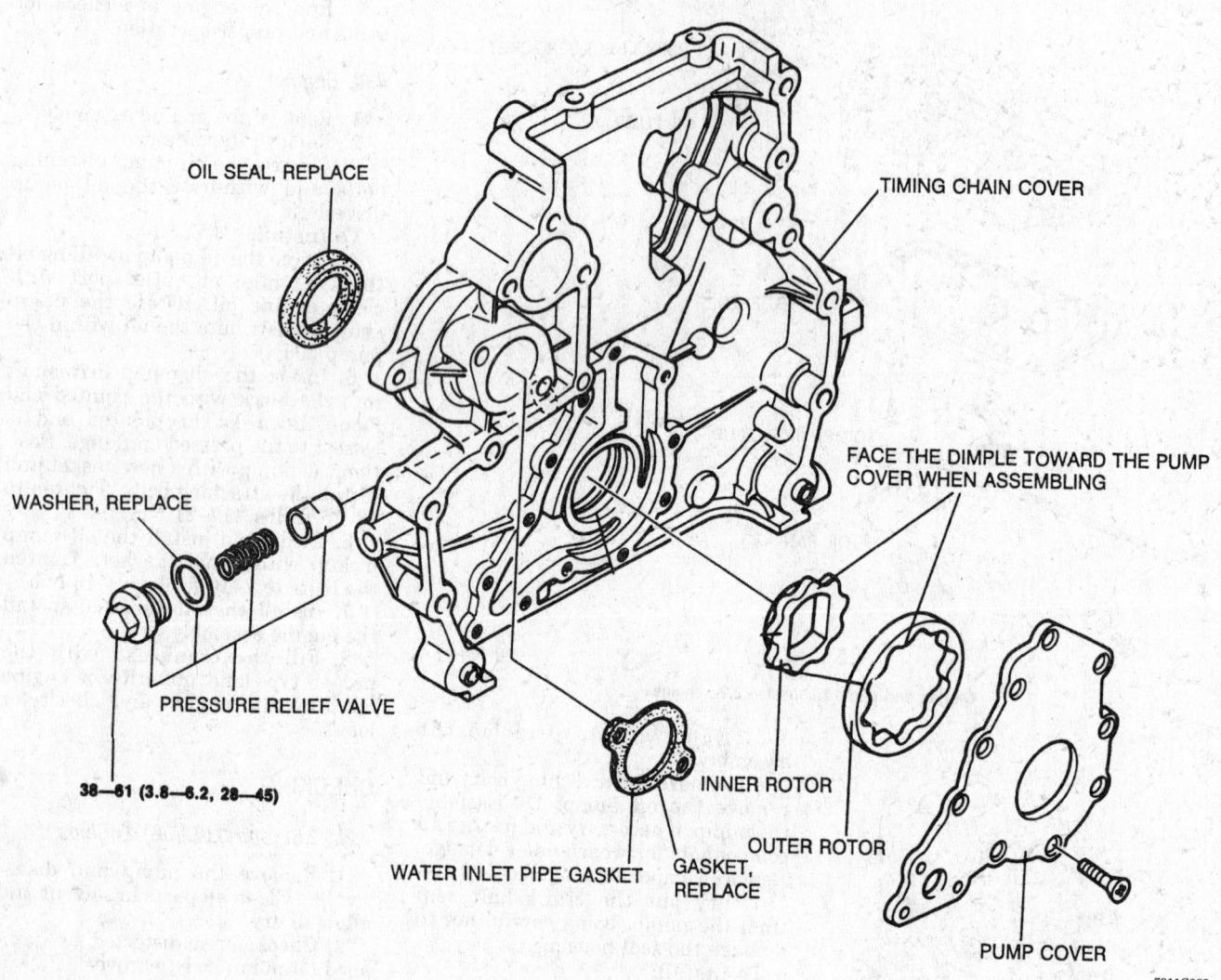

OIL SEAL, REPLACE

TIMING CHAIN COVER

FACE THE DIMPLE TOWARD THE PUMP
COVER WHEN ASSEMBLING

WASHER, REPLACE

PRESSURE RELIEF VALVE

38—61 (3.8—6.2, 28—45)

INNER ROTOR

OUTER ROTOR

WATER INLET PIPE GASKET

GASKET,
REPLACE

PUMP COVER

7911C083

Oil pump exploded view — 2.6L engine

and the pump body. If the clearance exceeds 0.0078 in. (0.20mm) on 2.2L and 2.6L engine or 0.0091 in. (0.23mm) on 3.0L engine, replace the pump.

7. Apply clean engine oil to the pump components and reassemble. Apply oil to the lip of a new seal and install in the pump, using a seal installer.

2.3L, 3.0L (VIN U) and 4.0L Engines

1. Remove the pump and disassemble. Thoroughly clean all parts in solvent and dry with compressed air.

2. Check the inside of the pump housing and the inner and outer gears for damage or excessive wear. Check the mating surfaces of the pump cover for wear. Minor scuff marks are normal, but if the cover, gears or housing surfaces are excessively worn, scored or grooved, replace the entire pump.

3. Measure the inner to outer rotor tip clearance. With the rotor assembly removed from the pump and resting on a flat surface, the inner and outer rotor tip clearance must not exceed 0.012 in. (0.30mm) with a feeler gauge inserted ½ in. (13mm) minimum.

4. With the rotor assembly installed in the housing, place a straight edge over the rotor assembly and the housing. Measure the vertical clearance, the rotor endplay, between the straight edge and the inner rotor and outer race. Maximum clearance must not exceed 0.005 in. (0.13mm).

5. Inspect the relief valve spring for collapsed or worn condition. Check the spring tension. The tension should be 12.6–14.5 lbs. at 1.20 in. on 2.3L engine, 9.1–10.1 lbs. at 1.11 in. on 3.0L engine or 13.6–14.7 lbs. at 1.39 in. on 4.0L engine.

6. If any part of the oil pump requires replacement, replace the complete pump assembly.

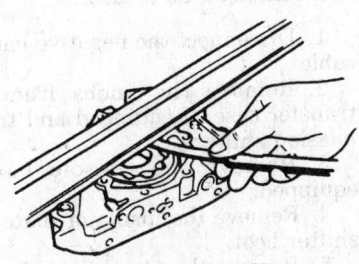

SIDE CLEARANCE

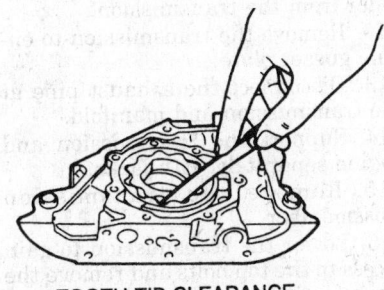

TOOTH TIP CLEARANCE

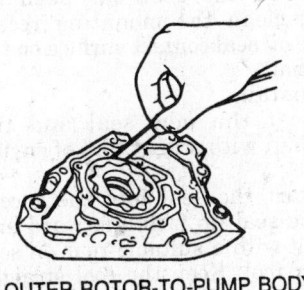

OUTER ROTOR-TO-PUMP BODY
CLEARANCE

7911C086

Oil pump checking — 2.2L engine; 2.6L and 3.0L (JE) engines similar

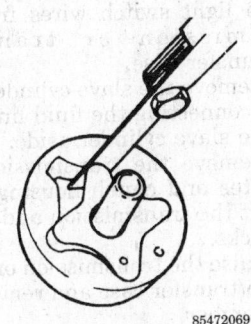

85472069

Measuring the oil pump
inner-to-outer rotor tip
clearance — 2.3L, 3.0L (VIN
U) and 4.0L Engines

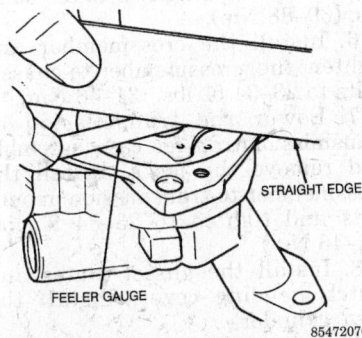

STRAIGHT EDGE

FEELER GAUGE

85472070

Measuring oil pump rotor endplay — 2.3L,
3.0L (VIN U) and 4.0L Engines

Rear Main Oil Seal

REMOVAL AND INSTALLATION

2.2L, 2.6L and 3.0L (JE) Engines

1. Disconnect the negative battery cable. Raise and safely support the vehicle.
2. Drain the engine oil.
3. Remove the transmission. If equipped with manual transmission, remove the clutch assembly.
4. Remove the flywheel.
5. Using a small prybar and a rag, remove the oil seal, being careful not to damage the crankshaft or seal housing.
6. When the seal has been removed, clean the mounting recess.

To install:

7. Coat the new seal and the crankshaft with a light film of clean engine oil.
8. Start the seal into the recess with the seal lip facing forward and install it with a suitable rear oil seal replacer tool. Install the seal until it is flush with the edge of the rear cover.

9. Position the flywheel on the crankshaft flange. Install the flywheel attaching bolts and tighten to:
   71–76 ft. lbs. (96–103 Nm) — 2.2L engine
   67–72 ft. lbs. (91–98 Nm) — 2.6L engine
   76–81 ft. lbs. (103–110 Nm) — 3.0L engine
10. If equipped with manual transmission, install the clutch assembly. Install the transmission and lower the vehicle.
11. Fill the crankcase with the proper type and quantity of engine oil. Connect the negative battery cable, start the engine and check for leaks.

2.3L, 3.0L (VIN U) and 4.0L Engines

1. Disconnect the negative battery cable. Raise and safely support the vehicle.
2. Remove the transmission. If equipped with manual transmission, remove the clutch assembly.
3. Remove the flywheel.
4. Using a sharp awl or equivalent, punch 2 holes into the seal on opposite sides of the crankshaft and just above the bearing cap-to-cylinder block split line. Install a sheet metal screw in each hole.

5. Using 2 small prybars, pry against both screws and remove the seal. It may be necessary to place small blocks of wood against the cylinder block to provide a fulcrum point for the prybars. Be careful not to damage the crankshaft oil seal surface or seal housing.

6. When the seal has been removed, clean the mounting recess and the oil seal contact surface on the crankshaft.

To install:

7. Coat the new seal and the crankshaft with a light film of engine oil.

8. Start the seal into the recess with the seal lip facing forward and install it with a suitable rear oil seal replacer tool. Keep the tool straight with the centerline of the crankshaft and install the seal until it is fully seated.

9. After removing the tool, inspect the seal to make sure it was not damaged during installation.

10. Position the flywheel on the crankshaft flange. Install the flywheel attaching bolts and tighten to 59 ft. lbs. (80 Nm).

11. If equipped with manual transmission, install the clutch assembly. Install the transmission and lower the vehicle.

12. Connect the negative battery cable, start the engine and check for leaks.

MANUAL TRANSMISSION

Transmission Assembly

REMOVAL AND INSTALLATION

B2200

1. Disconnect the negative battery cable.

2. Remove the gearshift knob and shift console attaching screws. Remove the console.

3. Remove the shift lever to extension housing attaching bolts and remove the shift lever.

4. Raise and support the vehicle safely.

5. Drain the transmission oil.

6. Matchmark and remove the driveshaft.

7. Disconnect the speedometer cable from the transmission.

8. Remove the starter motor.

9. Disconnect and the back-up light switch wiring at the transmission.

10. Disconnect the parking brake return spring and parking brake cables.

11. Disconnect the clutch slave cylinder from the transmission.

12. Remove the transmission-to-engine gusset plate.

13. Disconnect the exhaust pipe at the transmission and manifold.

14. Support the transmission and engine separately with jacks.

15. Remove the transmission crossmember.

16. Lower the transmission to gain access to the top bolts and remove the transmission-to-engine bolts.

17. Pull the transmission straight back, away from the engine and remove transmission from the vehicle.

To install:

18. Raise the transmission into position. Install the transmission-to-engine bolts and tighten to 51–65 ft. lbs. (69–88 Nm).

19. Install the transmission crossmember and tighten the crossmember-to-chassis bolts to 23–34 ft. lbs. (31–46 Nm).

20. Lower the transmission onto the crossmember and remove the jacks. Install the crossmember-to-mount bolts to 12–17 ft. lbs. (16–23 Nm).

21. Connect the exhaust pipe to the manifold and transmission bracket. Tighten the exhaust pipe-to-manifold nuts to 30–41 ft. lbs. (40–55 Nm) and the exhaust pipe-to-transmission bracket bolt to 13–20 ft. lbs. (18–26 Nm).

22. Install the gusset plate and tighten the bolts to 27–38 ft. lbs. (37–52 Nm).

23. Install the clutch slave cylinder and tighten the bolts to 12–17 ft. lbs. (16–23 Nm).

24. Install the parking brake cables and the return spring.

25. Connect the back-up light switch wiring connector and connect the speedometer cable.

26. Install the driveshaft, aligning the marks that were made during removal.

27. Install the starter. Fill the transmission with the proper type and quantity of engine oil.

28. Lower the vehicle. Install the shift lever and tighten the attaching bolts to 69–95 inch lbs. (7.8–11.0 Nm).

29. Install the console and the shift knob.

30. Connect the negative battery cable. Check the transmission for leaks and proper operation.

B2600

NOTE: On 4WD vehicles, the transmission and transfer case are removed as a unit.

1. Disconnect the negative battery cable.

2. Remove the knobs from the transfer case, if equipped and transmission shifters.

3. Remove the console box, if equipped.

4. Remove the insulator plate and shifter boot.

5. Remove the attaching bolts and the shift lever(s).

6. Raise and support the vehicle safely. Drain the transfer case, if equipped and transmission oil.

7. Remove the transmission and transfer case, if equipped, splash shields. Remove the starter.

8. Disconnect and remove the front exhaust pipe.

9. Matchmark and remove the driveshaft(s).

10. Disconnect the speedometer cable, 4WD switch, if equipped and backup light switch wires from the transmission or transmission/transfer case.

11. Remove the slave cylinder without disconnecting the fluid line. Support the slave cylinder aside.

12. Remove the transmission gusset plates and clutch housing cover. Support the transmission and engine with jacks.

13. Raise the transmission or transmission/transfer case and remove the crossmember.

14. Remove the transmission or transmission/transfer case.

To install:

15. Raise the transmission or transmission/transfer case assembly into position. Install the transmission-to-engine bolts and tighten to 51–65 ft. lbs. (69–88 Nm).

16. Install the crossmember and tighten the crossmember-to-chassis bolts to 23–34 ft. lbs. (31–46 Nm).

17. Lower the transmission or transmission/transfer case assembly and remove the jacks. Install the crossmember-to-transmission mount nuts and tighten to 23–34 ft. lbs. (31–46 Nm).

18. Install the gusset plates and clutch housing cover. Install the slave cylinder.

19. Connect the backup light and, if equipped, 4WD switch electrical connectors and the speedometer cable.

20. Install the driveshaft(s), aligning the marks that were made during removal.

21. Install the front exhaust pipe and the starter. Install the splash shields.

22. Fill the transmission and, if equipped, transfer case with the proper type and quantity of fluid. Lower the vehicle.

23. Install the shift lever(s) and tighten the mounting bolts to 25–37 ft. lbs. (34–50 Nm).

24. Install the shifter boot and insulator plate. Tighten the mounting bolts to 25–37 ft. lbs. (34–50 Nm).

25. Install the console box and the shifter knob(s).

26. Connect the negative battery cable. Check the transmission for leaks and proper operation.

MPV

NOTE: On 4WD vehicles, the transmission and transfer case are removed as a unit.

1. Disconnect the negative battery cable.

2. Remove the shift lever knob and boot.

3. Shift the transmission into **N** and unbolt and remove the shift lever.

4. Raise and safely support the vehicle.

5. Drain the transmission and, if equipped, transfer case fluid.

6. Disconnect the speedometer cable and, if equipped, the Hi-Lo shift cable.

7. Disconnect the electrical connectors at the transmission.

8. Matchmark and remove the driveshaft(s). Stuff a rag in the double offset joint to prevent damage to the boot from the driveshaft.

9. On the 2.6L engine, unbolt the support bracket from the transmission, if equipped.

10. Remove the starter.

11. Remove the clutch slave cylinder and hydraulic line bracket. It is not necessary to disconnect the hydraulic line. Remove the bellhousing inspection plate.

12. Remove the front exhaust pipe and heat shield.

13. Remove the gusset plates and support the transmission and engine with jacks.

14. Remove the transmission-to-crossmember bolts. Remove the crossmember.

15. Remove the transmission-to-engine bolts.

16. Pull the transmission straight back on the jack until the mainshaft clears the clutch. Lower the transmission and pull it out from under the vehicle.

To install:

17. Raise the transmission into position.

18. Push the transmission straight forward on the jack until the mainshaft enters the clutch and the transmission engages the locating dowels on the engine.

19. Install the transmission-to-engine bolts and tighten to 27–38 ft. lbs. (37–52 Nm) on 3.0L engine or 51–65 ft. lbs. (69–88 Nm) on 2.6L engine.

20. Install the starter. Install the crossmember and tighten the crossmember-to-chassis bolts to 32–45 ft. lbs. (43–61 Nm).

21. Lower the transmission and remove the jacks. Install the transmission-to-crossmember bolts and tighten the nuts to 23–34 ft. lbs. (31–46 Nm) or bolts/nuts to 32–45 ft. lbs. (43–61 Nm).

22. Install the front exhaust pipe and heat shield.

23. Install the transmission gusset plates. Install the clutch release cylinder and bracket.

24. Connect the speedometer cable and, if equipped, Hi-Lo shift cable. Connect the electrical wiring.

25. Install the driveshaft(s), aligning the marks that were made during removal. Install the bellhousing inspection plate.

26. Fill the transmission and, if equipped, transfer case with the proper type and quantity of fluid. Lower the vehicle.

27. Install the shift lever.

28. Install the shifter knob and boot.

29. Connect the negative battery cable. Check the transmission for leaks and proper operation.

1994–96 B-Series Pick-Up and Navajo

1. Disconnect the negative battery cable.

2. Place the gearshift lever in the **N** position.

3. Remove the shifter boot retainer screws and slide the boot up the shift lever shaft. Remove the shift lever attaching bolt(s) and remove the shift lever. Cover the opening in the transmission to prevent dirt from entering.

4. Raise and safely support the vehicle. Drain the transmission fluid.

5. Mark the position of the driveshaft(s) on the flange(s) and remove the driveshaft(s). Plug the transmission or transfer case opening to prevent fluid leakage.

6. Disconnect the clutch hydraulic fluid line. Plug the line to prevent fluid leakage.

7. Disconnect the speedometer cable from the transmission or transfer case.

8. Disconnect the starter and backup lamp switch wires.

9. Place a jack under the engine, with a wood block to protect the oil pan.

10. Remove the transfer case, if equipped.

11. Remove the starter. Place a transmission jack under the transmission.

12. Remove the bolts attaching the transmission and clutch housing to the engine. Remove the nuts and bolts attaching the transmission mount and damper to the crossmember.

13. Remove the nuts and/or bolts attaching the crossmember to the frame side rails and remove the crossmember.

14. Lower the engine jack. Work the clutch housing off the locating dowels and slide the clutch housing and transmission rearward until the input shaft clears the clutch disc. Remove the transmission.

15. Remove the clutch housing from the transmission, if necessary.

To install:

16. Make sure the machined mating surfaces and the locating dowels on the engine rear plate and the mating face of the clutch housing and locating dowel holes are free of burrs, dirt or paint. Install the clutch housing on the transmission, if removed.

17. Mount the transmission on a transmission jack and raise into position. Start the input shaft into the clutch disc, aligning the splines. Move the transmission forward until the clutch housing seats on the locating dowels.

18. Install the clutch housing-to-engine attaching bolts and tighten to 28–38 ft. lbs. (38–51 Nm). Remove the transmission jack.

19. Install the starter.

20. Raise the engine and install the crossmember, insulator and damper with the attaching nuts and bolts. Install the nuts and bolts attaching the transmission mount to the crossmember.

21. Install the transfer case, if equipped.

22. Remove the plug(s) and install the driveshaft(s), aligning the marks on the flange(s) that were made during the removal procedure.

23. Connect the starter cable and backup lamp switch wires.

24. Connect the hydraulic clutch line and bleed the system.

25. Connect the speedometer cable.

26. Fill the transmission with the proper type and quantity of flu

27. Lower the vehicle and remove the cover from the transmission opening.

28. Install the gearshift lever with the attaching bolt(s). Install the shifter bolts.

29. Connect the negative battery cable. Check the transmission for leaks and proper operation.

CLUTCH

Clutch Assembly

REMOVAL AND INSTALLATION

1. Disconnect the negative battery cable.

2. On Navajo, disconnect the hydraulic clutch master cylinder from the clutch pedal.

3. Raise and safely support the vehicle. Remove the starter.

4. On all except Navajo, remove the slave cylinder, leaving the hydraulic line connected. On Navajo, use coupling disconnect tool T88T–70522–A or equivalent, to slide the white plastic sleeve toward the slave cylinder, then apply a slight tug on the tube to disconnect the hydraulic coupling. Plug the hose.

5. Remove the transmission.

6. Mark the position of the pressure plate on the flywheel so if the pressure plate is reused, it can be reinstalled in the same position.

7. Loosen the pressure plate attaching bolts evenly until the diaphragm spring is expanded. Remove the bolts, pressure plate and clutch disc.

8. Inspect the flywheel for wear, scoring and cracks. Machine or replace, as necessary. Inspect the clutch pilot bearing for wear and free movement. If replacement is necessary, remove using puller tool T58L–101–B or equivalent.

9. Inspect the clutch release bearing for wear and free movement; replace as necessary. On Navajo, remove the release bearing by twisting it until resistance is felt, then turning further will allow the preload spring to push the bearing assembly off the slave cylinder.

To install:

10. If the pilot bearing was removed, a new one must be installed. Install using a suitable driver. On Navajo, install the pilot bearing with the seal facing the transmission so the adapter is not cock

11. If the flywheel was removed, make sure the mating surfaces of the crank flange and flywheel are clean, and install the flywheel. Tighten the flywheel bolts to:

71–76 ft. lbs. (96–103 Nm)—2.2L engine

67–72 ft. lbs. (91–98 Nm)—2.6L engine

76–81 ft. lbs. (103–110 Nm)—3.0L engine

59 ft. lbs. (80 Nm)—4.0L engine

12. Position the clutch disc on the flywheel so a suitable alignment tool can enter the pilot bearing and align the disc.

13. Install the pressure plate. If the original pressure plate is being reused, align the marks that were made during the removal procedure. Install the attaching bolts and tighten, in sequence, to 13–20 ft. lbs. (18–26 Nm) on all except 4.0L engine where the torque is 15–24 ft. lbs. (21–32 Nm), then remove the alignment tool.

14. On all except Navajo, lightly lubricate the release bearing fork pivot and release bearing contact surfaces with high temperature grease. Install the fork and the release bearing.

15. On Navajo, lubricate the release bearing bore and bearing carrier with high temperature grease and install over the transmission input shaft and onto the slave cylinder.

16. Install the transmission. If equipped, reuse the aluminum washers under the attaching bolts to prevent galvanic corrosion.

17. On all except Navajo, install the slave cylinder to the transmission. On Navajo, connect the hydraulic coupling by pushing the male coup

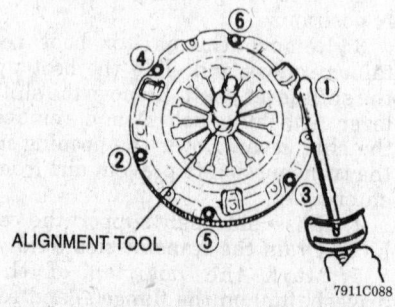

Clutch pressure plate bolt torque sequence — except 4.0L engine

ling into the slave cylinder female coupling.

18. Lower the vehicle. On Navajo, connect the clutch master cylinder to the brake pedal and bleed the clutch system, if necessary.

19. Connect the negative battery cable.

PEDAL HEIGHT/FREE-PLAY ADJUSTMENT

Except 1994–96 B-Series Pick-Up and Navajo

1. Measure the distance from the top of the clutch pedal pad to the carpet. The distance should be as follows:

B2200: 7.13–7.52 in. (181–191mm)
B2600: 7.52–7.91 in. (191–201mm)
MPV: 8.19–8.58 in. (208–218mm)

2. If the distance is not within specification, loosen the clutch switch locknut and turn the switch until the distance is correct. Tighten the lock nut.

3. Check the free-play by pressing the pedal by hand until clutch resistance is felt. The free-play should be 0.02–0.12 in. (0.6–3.0mm).

4. If the free-play is not within specification, loosen the locknut on the actuator rod and turn the actuator rod until the free-play is correct.

5. Check that the disengagement height from the upper surface of the pedal height to the carpet is correct when the pedal is fully depressed. The disengagement height should be as follows:

B2200: 2.60 in. (66mm)
B2600: 2.80 in. (71mm)
MPV: 1.38 in. (35mm)

6. Tighten the actuator rod locknut to 8.7–12.0 ft. lbs. (12–17 Nm).

7. Recheck the pedal height.

1994–96 B-Series Pick-Up and Navajo

The hydraulic clutch system provides automatic adjustment. No adjustment of clutch linkage or pedal position is required.

Clutch Master Cylinder

REMOVAL AND INSTALLATION

Except 1994–96 B-Series Pick-Up and Navajo

1. Disconnect the negative battery cable. Disconnect and plug the fluid outlet line at the fitting on the master cylinder.

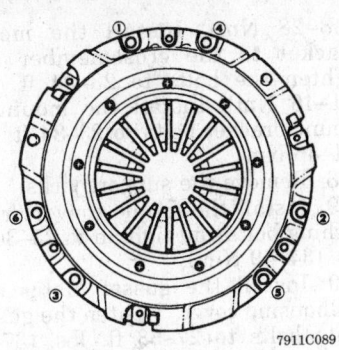

Clutch pressure plate bolt torque sequence — 1994–96 B-Series Pick-Up and 4.0L engine

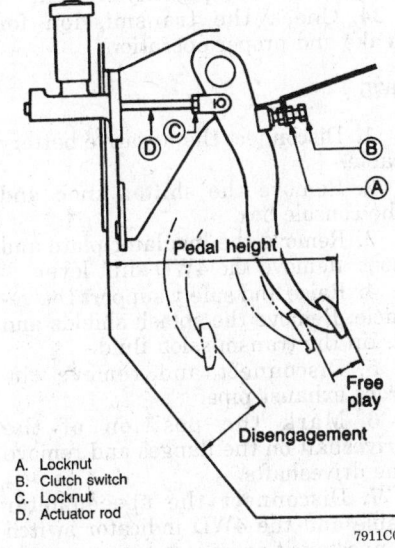

A. Locknut
B. Clutch switch
C. Locknut
D. Actuator rod

7911C090

Clutch pedal height/free-play measurement points — except Navajo

2. Working inside the vehicle, remove the nuts mounting the master cylinder to the firewall.

3. On MPV, remove the fluid reservoir mounting bolts.

4. On B-Series Pick-Up, remove the master cylinder from the firewall. On MPV, remove the master cylinder and the remote fluid reservoir as an assembly.

To install:

5. Start the pedal pushrod into the master cylinder and position the master cylinder on the firewall.

6. Working inside the vehicle, install the mounting nuts and tighten to 12–17 ft. lbs. (16–23 Nm) on B-Series Pick-Up or 14–19 ft. lbs. (19–25 Nm) on MPV.

7. On MPV, install the remote fluid reservoir mounting bolts and tighten to 69–95 inch lbs. (7.8–11.0 Nm).

8. Connect the fluid outlet line to the master cylinder fitting.

9. Bleed the hydraulic clutch system.

10. Check the clutch pedal height/free-play and adjust if necessary.

1994–96 B-Series Pick-Up and Navajo

1. Disconnect the negative battery cable.

2. Disconnect the clutch master cylinder pushrod from the clutch pedal by prying the retainer bushing and pushrod off the pedal pin.

3. Remove the switch from the master cylinder assembly.

4. Remove the screw retaining the fluid reservoir to the cowl access cover.

5. Use coupling disconnect tool T88T–70522–A or equivalent, to slide the white plastic sleeve toward the slave cylinder, then apply a slight tug on the tube to disconnect the hydraulic coupling.

6. Remove the retaining bolts and the clutch master cylinder.

To install:

7. Install the pushrod through the hole in the engine compartment. Make sure it is located on the correct side of the clutch pedal. Install the master cylinder and tighten the bolts to 12 ft. lbs. (16 Nm).

8. Insert the coupling end into the slave cylinder and install the tube into the clips.

9. Install the fluid reservoir on the cowl access cover with the retaining screw.

10. Replace the retainer bushing in the clutch master cylinder pushrod if worn or damaged. Install the retainer and pushrod on the clutch pedal pin. Make sure the flange of the bushing is against the pedal blade. Install the switch.

11. Connect the negative battery cable and bleed the clutch hydraulic system, if necessary.

Clutch Slave Cylinder

REMOVAL AND INSTALLATION

Except 1994–96 B-Series Pick-Up and Navajo

1. Disconnect the negative battery cable. Raise and support the vehicle safely.

2. Disconnect the flexible hose from the slave cylinder or hydraulic tube. Plug the hose.

3. Pull off the hose retaining clip, if equipped. Remove the tube from the slave cylinder on MPV.

4. Remove the slave cylinder attaching bolts and the slave cylinder.

5. Installation is the reverse of the removal procedure.

6. Tighten the slave cylinder mounting bolts to 12–17 ft. lbs. (16–23 Nm) on B-Series Pickup or 14–19 ft. lbs. (19–25 Nm) on MPV.

7. Bleed the clutch hydraulic system.

1994–96 B-Series Pick-Up and Navajo

NOTE: Before any vehicle service that requires slave cylinder removal, the clutch master cylinder pushrod must be disconnected from the clutch pedal. If not disconnected, permanent damage to the master cylinder will occur if the clutch pedal is depressed while the slave cylinder is disconnected.

1. Disconnect the negative battery cable.

2. Disconnect the coupling at the transmission using tool T88T–70522–A or equivalent, by sliding the white plastic sleeve toward the slave cylinder while applying a slight tug on the tube.

3. Raise and safely support the vehicle. Remove the transmission and clutch housing.

4. Remove the bolts retaining the slave cylinder to the transmission. Remove the slave cylinder from the transmission input shaft.

5. If necessary, remove the release bearing from the slave cylinder by twisting until resistance is felt, then turning further to allow the preload spring to push the bearing assembly off.

To install:

6. Push the release bearing into place, if removed.

7. Position the slave cylinder over the transmission input shaft with the bleed screw and coupling facing the left side of the transmission.

8. Install the slave cylinder attaching bolts and tighten to 13–19 ft. lbs. (18–26 Nm).

9. Install the transmission.

10. Insert the male coupling into the female coupling on the clutch slave cylinder and make sure the connection is secure.

11. Bleed the clutch hydraulic system, if necessary. Lower the vehicle and connect the negative battery cable.

Hydraulic Clutch System Bleeding

NOTE: On Navajo, under normal conditions, disconnecting the clutch coupling will not let air into the system. However, if there appears to be air in the system, indicated by a spongy pedal or insufficient bearing travel, the system must be bled.

1. Clean all dirt and grease from around the reservoir cap.

2. Remove the cap and fill the reservoir with heavy duty brake fluid.

3. Raise and safely support the vehicle, as necessary. Loosen the bleed screw, located in the slave cylinder body, next to the inlet connection.

4. Fluid should now begin to flow from the master cylinder, down the tube and into the slave cylinder.

NOTE: Keep the reservoir full at all times to make sure no additional air is drawn into the system.

5. Bubbles should begin to appear at the bleed screw outlet, indicating air is being expelled. When the slave cylinder is full, a steady stream of fluid will come from the slave cylinder outlet. Tighten the bleed screw.

6. Slowly depress the clutch pedal to the floor and hold. Loosen the bleed screw to allow air and excess

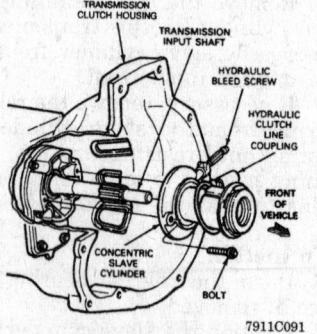

TRANSMISSION CLUTCH HOUSING
TRANSMISSION INPUT SHAFT
HYDRAULIC BLEED SCREW
HYDRAULIC CLUTCH LINE COUPLING
FRONT OF VEHICLE
CONCENTRIC SLAVE CYLINDER
BOLT

7911C091

Slave cylinder installation — 1994–96 B-Series Pick-Up and Navajo

fluid to be expelled. Retighten the bleed screw when fluid flow stops.

7. Depress and release the clutch pedal slowly, waiting 2 seconds between each cycle. Repeat 5 times.

8. Check the fluid level in the reservoir and add, if necessary. If evidence of air still exists, repeat Steps 6 and 7.

AUTOMATIC TRANSMISSION

Transmission Assembly

REMOVAL AND INSTALLATION

1992–93 B-Series Pick-Up

2WD

1. Disconnect the negative battery cable. Raise and safely support the vehicle.

2. Drain the transmission fluid.

3. Mark the position of the driveshaft on the axle flange and remove the driveshaft.

4. Disconnect the speedometer cable, vacuum hose and shift lever. Remove the vacuum line bracket from the transmission.

5. Remove the gusset plates and bellhousing cover.

6. Remove the torque converter attaching bolts from the flywheel.

7. Support the transmission and engine with jacks.

8. Remove the transmission mount and mount bracket.

9. Tag and disconnect the electrical connectors from the neutral safety switch, kickdown solenoid and overdrive cancel solenoid.

10. Remove the transmission fluid dipstick and tube.

11. Disconnect and plug the transmission fluid lines.

12. Remove the transmission.

To install:

13. Raise the transmission into position. Install the transmission-to-engine bolts and tighten to 27–38 ft. lbs. (37–52 Nm).

14. Unplug and connect the transmission fluid lines. Tighten the banjo bolts to 17–26 ft. lbs. (24–35 Nm).

15. Install the transmission fluid dipstick and tube.

16. Connect the electrical connectors.

17. Install the transmission mount and tighten the bolts to 7.2–17 ft. lbs.

(9.8–23 Nm). Install the mount bracket to the crossmember and tighten the bolts to 23–34 ft. lbs. (31–46 Nm). Install the mount-to-mount bracket bolts to 23–34 ft. lbs. (31–46 Nm).

18. Remove the support jacks.

19. Install the torque converter attaching bolts and tighten to 25–36 ft. lbs. (34–49 Nm).

20. Install the gusset plates and bellhousing cover. Tighten the gusset plate bolts to 27–38 ft. lbs. (37–52 Nm).

21. Connect the shift lever, vacuum hose and speedometer cable. Attach the vacuum line bracket.

22. Install the driveshaft and lower the vehicle.

23. Connect the negative battery cable. Fill the transmission with the proper type and quantity of fluid.

24. Check the transmission for leaks and proper operation.

4WD

1. Disconnect the negative battery cable.

2. Remove the shifter knob and the console box.

3. Remove the insulator plate and boot. Remove the 4WD shift lever.

4. Raise and safely support the vehicle. Remove the splash shields and drain the transmission fluid.

5. Disconnect and remove the front exhaust pipe.

6. Mark the position of the driveshaft on the flanges and remove the driveshafts.

7. Disconnect the speedometer cable and the 4WD indicator switch connector, if equipped.

8. Disconnect the shift cable and vacuum hose, if equipped.

9. Remove the gusset plate, if equipped.

10. Loosen the front differential mounting bolts and remove the No. 2 crossmember.

11. Remove the torque converter attaching bolts.

12. Support the transmission and engine with jacks. Remove the transmission-to-engine bolts.

13. Disconnect and plug the transmission fluid lines at the transmission. Remove the bracket from the transmission.

14. Remove the rear transmission crossmember.

15. Tag and disconnect the electrical connectors at the transmission.

16. Remove the transmission dipstick and tube.

17. Lower the transmission from the vehicle.

To install:

18. Raise the transmission into position and install the transmission-to-engine bolts. Tighten to 27–38 ft. lbs. (37–52 Nm).

19. Install the dipstick and tube.

20. Connect the electrical connectors.

21. Install the rear transmission crossmember and tighten the transmission-to-chassis bolts to 23–34 ft. lbs. (31–46 Nm).

22. Lower the transmission to the crossmember and install the mount-to-crossmember nuts. Tighten to 23–34 ft. lbs. (31–46 Nm). Remove the jacks.

23. Connect the transmission fluid lines to the transmission and tighten the banjo bolts to 17–26 ft. lbs. (24–35 Nm). Attach the fluid line bracket.

24. Install the torque converter attaching bolts and tighten to 27–40 ft. lbs. (36–54 Nm). Install the bellhousing cover.

25. Install the No. 2 crossmember.

26. Install the gusset plates, if equipped.

27. Connect the shifter cable and the bracket, if equipped. Connect the speedometer cable.

28. Install the driveshafts, aligning the marks that were made during removal.

29. Install the front exhaust pipe and the splash shields. Lower the vehicle.

30. Install the 4WD shift lever and the insulator plate and boot.

31. Install the console box and the shifter knob.

32. Connect the negative battery cable. Fill the transmission with the proper type and quantity of fluid.

33. Check the transmission for leaks and proper operation.

MPV

1. Disconnect the negative battery cable. Raise and safely support the vehicle.

2. Drain the transmission fluid.

3. Disconnect the speedometer cable. Tag and disconnect the necessary electrical connectors.

4. Disconnect and remove the front exhaust pipe and heat shield.

5. Mark the position of the driveshaft on the flanges and remove the driveshaft(s).

6. Disconnect and remove the shift linkage from the transmission.

7. Remove the dipstick and tube.

8. Remove the bellhousing cover and then remove the torque converter bolts.

9. Remove the starter and bracket, if equipped.

10. Remove the exhaust pipe bracket and the gusset plates.

11. Support the engine and transmission with jacks. Remove the transmission crossmember.

12. Disconnect and plug the transmission fluid lines at the transmission. Disconnect the vacuum line, if equipped.

13. Remove the transmission-to-engine bolts and lower the transmission from the vehicle.

To install:

14. Raise the transmission into position. Install the transmission-to-engine bolts. Tighten all bolts to 27–38 ft. lbs. (37–52 Nm) except the 4 larger diameter bolts on the hydraulically controlled transmission which are tightened to 51–65 ft. lbs. (69–88 Nm).

15. Install the transmission crossmember and tighten the crossmember-to-chassis bolts to 32–45 ft. lbs. (43–61 Nm). Tighten the mount-to-crossmember nuts to 23–34 ft. lbs. (31–46 Nm) or bolts/nuts to 32–45 ft. lbs. (43–61 Nm). Remove the jacks.

16. Connect the transmission fluid lines and tighten the banjo bolts to 17–26 ft. lbs. (24–35 Nm). Connect the vacuum line, if equipped.

17. Install the exhaust pipe bracket and gusset plates. Tighten the gusset plate bolts to 27–38 ft. lbs. (37–52 Nm).

18. Install the starter and the bracket, if equipped.

19. Install the torque converter bolts and tighten to 27–40 ft. lbs. (36–54 Nm). Install the bellhousing cover.

20. Install the dipstick and tube. Connect the shift linkage.

21. Install the driveshaft(s), aligning the marks that were made during removal.

22. Install the front exhaust pipe and heat shield.

23. Connect the electrical connectors and speedometer cable. Lower the vehicle.

24. Connect the negative battery cable. Fill the transmission with the proper type and quantity of fluid.

25. Check the transmission for leaks and proper operation.

1994–96 B-Series Pick-Up and Navajo

1. Disconnect the negative battery cable. Raise and safely support the vehicle.

2. Position a drain pan under the transmission fluid pan. Pry the lower clips of the transmission heat shield back slightly to allow access to the pan bolts.

3. Starting at the rear of the transmission pan and working toward the front, loosen the attaching bolts and allow the fluid to drain. Remove all the bolts except the 2 at the front to allow the fluid to further drain. After all fluid has drained, reinstall 2 bolts at the rear of the pan to temporarily hold it in place.

4. Disconnect the starter cable and remove the starter.

5. Place a 22mm socket and breaker bar on the crankshaft pulley attaching bolt. Rotate the pulley clockwise, as viewed from the front, to gain access to each converter attaching nut. Remove the nuts through the starter mounting hole.

6. Mark the position of the driveshaft on the axle flange and remove the driveshaft. Plug the transmission to prevent fluid leakage.

7. Disconnect the speedometer cable from the transmission.

8. Disconnect the shift cable at the transmission manual lever. Remove the kickdown cable from the ball stud lever. Depress the tab on the cable downshift retainer and remove the cable from the bracket.

9. Disconnect the neutral safety switch wires and converter clutch solenoid connector. Disconnect the vacuum line from the vacuum modulator.

10. Position a transmission jack under the transmission and raise it slightly. Remove the engine rear support-to-crossmember bolts.

11. Remove the crossmember-to-frame side support attaching bolts and remove the crossmember insulator and support and damper.

12. Lower the jack under the transmission and allow the transmission to hang. Position a jack to the front of the engine and raise it to gain access to the 2 upper converter housing-to-engine attaching bolts.

13. Disconnect the oil cooler lines at the transmission. Plug the lines and transmission to prevent the entrance of dirt.

14. Remove the lower converter housing-to-engine attaching bolts and remove the transmission filler tube.

15. Secure the transmission to the jack with a safety chain. Remove the 2 upper converter housing-to-engine attaching bolts. Move the transmission to the rear so it disengages from the dowel pins and the converter is

disengaged from the flywheel. Lower the transmission from the vehicle.

NOTE: If the transmission is to be removed for an extended period, support the engine with a safety stand and wood block.

To install:

16. Position the converter to the transmission making sure the converter hub is fully engaged in the pump gear. To make sure the converter is fully engaged, push and rotate the converter until 2 "bumps" are felt. Keep pushing and rotating until the distance between the converter pilot and the edge of the converter housing is 7/16–9/16.

17. Place the transmission on a transmission jack and secure with a safety chain. Rotate the converter so the drive studs are in alignment with the holes in the flywheel.

18. Raise the transmission and move it forward into position, being careful not to damage the flywheel and converter pilot.

NOTE: When moving the transmission, do not let the front of the transmission tilt downward. This will cause the converter to move forward and disengage from the pump gear. The converter must rest squarely against the flywheel. This indicates that the converter pilot is not binding in the engine crankshaft.

19. Install 2 converter housing-to-engine attaching bolts at the engine dowel locations and tighten to 28–38 ft. lbs. (38–51 Nm). Install the remaining attaching bolts and tighten to the same specification.

20. Remove the safety chain from the transmission.

21. Insert the filler tube in the stub tube and secure it to the cylinder block with the attaching bolt. Tighten the bolt to 28–38 ft. lbs. (38–51 Nm). If the stub tube is loosened or dislodged, it should be replaced.

22. Install the oil cooler lines in the retaining clip at the cylinder block. Connect the lines to the transmission.

23. Remove the jack supporting the front of the engine.

24. Raise the transmission and position the crossmember, insulator and support and damper to the frame side supports. Install the attaching bolts and nuts and tighten to 65–85 ft. lbs. (88–115 Nm).

25. Lower the transmission and install the rear engine support-to-crossmember nuts. Tighten the nuts to 65–85 ft. lbs. (88–115 Nm). Remove the transmission jack.

26. Install the vacuum hose on the vacuum modulator and attach the line to the clip. Connect the neutral safety switch plug and the converter clutch solenoid connector.

27. Install the flywheel-to-converter nuts and tighten to 20–34 ft. lbs. (27–46 Nm).

28. Install the starter and tighten the attaching bolts to 15–20 ft. lbs. (20–27 Nm). Connect the starter cable.

29. Connect the exhaust pipe to the exhaust manifold, if disconnected for removal.

30. Connect the shift cable to the manual lever and the downshift cable to the downshift lever. Connect the speedometer cable.

31. Install the driveshaft, aligning the marks on the axle flange. Adjust the manual and downshift linkage, as required.

32. Remove the bolts temporarily holding the transmission fluid pan and remove the pan. Discard the gasket and clean all old gasket material and dirt from the gasket mating surfaces.

33. Install the pan using a new gasket. Tighten the attaching bolts to 8–10 ft. lbs. (11–13.5 Nm).

34. Lower the vehicle and connect the negative battery cable. Fill the transmission with the proper type and quantity of fluid.

35. Run the vehicle and check for leaks and proper operation.

SHIFT LINKAGE ADJUSTMENT

1992–93 B-Series Pick-Up

HYDRAULICALLY CONTROLLED TRANSMISSION

1. Move the gearshift lever to the **P** range.

2. Loosen locknuts A and B so they are both at least 0.039 in. (1mm) away from the adjustment lever.

3. Shift the transmission to the **P** range by moving the manual shaft of the transmission.

4. With the link at 90 degrees to the lever, adjust the clearance using a feeler gauge to 0.039 in. (1mm) between the adjustment lever and locknut A.

5. Remove the feeler gauge and tighten locknut B to 69–95 inch lbs. (8–11 Nm).

6. Measure the clearance between the guide plate and the guide pin in the **P** range. There should be 0.039 in. (1mm) clearance in front of the pin and 0.020 in. (0.5mm) clearance behind the pin.

7. Move the gearshift lever to the **N** and **D** ranges and check that the clearance between the guide plate and guide pin is the same in both ranges. If not, readjust locknuts A and B.

ELECTRONICALLY CONTROLLED TRANSMISSION

1. Disconnect the negative battery cable to deactivate the shift-lock.

2. Remove the selector knob and console.

3. Loosen locknuts A and B and lock bolt C.

4. Shift the transmission manual shaft to the **P** range.

5. Push and hold the selector lever forward with a force of approximately 22 lbs., then tighten lock bolt C to 67–95 inch lbs. (8–11 Nm).

6. Turn locknut A by hand until it just touches the spacer, then tighten locknut B to 67–95 inch lbs. (8–11 Nm).

7. Check the lever so the clearance between the guide plate and the guide pin in the **P** range with the pushrod lightly depressed is as specified.

8. Move the selector lever to the **N** and **D** ranges and make sure there is the same clearance between the guide plate and guide pin. If not, readjust the lever.

9. Install the console. Clean and apply locking compound to the selector knob screw threads and tighten the screws to 13–26 inch lbs. (1.5–2.9 Nm).

10. Connect the negative battery cable.

MPV

1. Move the selector lever to the **P** range.

2. Remove the column covers.

3. Pull the selector lever rearward, toward the driver and insert a 0.197 in. (5mm) outer diameter pin into the gearshift rod assembly.

4. Remove the air intake tube.

5. Loosen the shift lever and the top lever mounting bolts.

6. Shift the transmission manual shaft to the **P** range position.

7. Adjust the clearance between the lower bracket and the shift lever bushing by sliding the shift lever assembly until there is no clearance.

8. Tighten the shift lever mounting bolts to 12–17 ft. lbs. (16–23 Nm).

9. Make sure the detent ball is positioned in the center of the **P** range detent. If not, loosen bolts A and turn the bracket to adjust the position, then retighten bolts A to 61–87 inch lbs. (6.9–9.8 Nm).

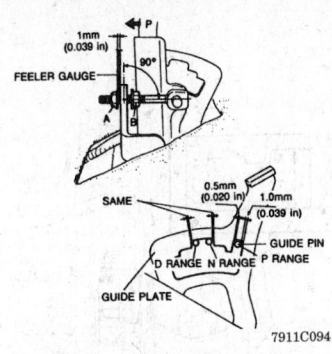

Shift linkage adjustment — B-Series Pick-Up with hydraulically controlled transmission

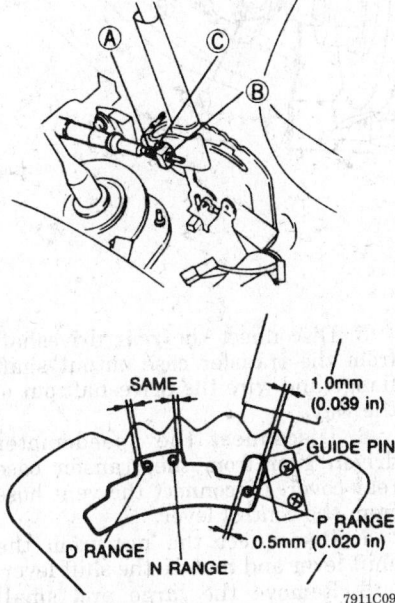

Shift linkage adjustment — B series Pick-Up with electronically controlled transmission

10. Adjust the clearance between the lower bracket and the shift lever bushing by turning the top lever until there is no clearance. Tighten the top lever mounting bolt A then retighten bolt B to 12–17 ft. lbs. (16–23 Nm).

11. Remove the pin from the gear shift rod assembly and install the column covers. Check selector lever operation.

1994–96 B-Series Pick-Up and Navajo

1. Raise and safely support the vehicle, as necessary. From inside the vehicle, place the column shift selec-

tor lever in the **OD** position. Hang an 8 lb. weight on the selector lever.

2. From below the vehicle, pull down the lock tab on the shift cable and remove the fitting from the transmission manual control lever ball stud.

3. Position the transmission manual control lever in the **OD** position by moving the lever all the way rearward and then moving it 3 detents forward.

4. Connect the cable end fitting to the transmission manual control lever. Push up on the lock tab to lock the cable in the correctly adjusted position.

5. Remove the 8 lb. weight from the column shift selector.

6. After adjustment, check for **P** engagement. Check the column shift selector lever in all detent positions with the engine running to ensure correct adjustment.

KICKDOWN SWITCH ADJUSTMENT

Except 1994–96 B-Series Pick-Up and Navajo

1. Disconnect the negative battery cable.

2. Disconnect the switch connector, located above the accelerator pedal.

3. Loosen the locknut and back the switch out fully.

4. Depress the accelerator pedal fully and hold it.

5. With the accelerator pedal fully down, turn the kickdown switch clockwise until it turns **ON** (clicking sound heard), then turn the switch ¼ turn further clockwise.

6. Tighten the locknut to 10–13 ft. lbs. (14–18 Nm) and release the accelerator pedal.

7. Reconnect the connector and the negative battery cable.

8. Depress the accelerator pedal fully and verify that the kickdown switch clicks at the fully depressed position.

SELECTOR INDICATOR ADJUSTMENT

1994–96 B-Series Pick-Up and Navajo

1. Remove the steering column shroud.

2. With the engine stopped and the parking brake applied, place the transmission selector lever at the steering column in the **OD** position.

3. Secure a 3 lb. weight to the end of the transmission selector lever.

4. Rotate the thumb wheel until the orange pointer is completely within the letter "D" inside the **OD** graphic.

5. Install the steering column shroud.

TRANSFER CASE

Transfer Case Assembly

REMOVAL AND INSTALLATION

1992–93 B-Series Pick-Up

1. Disconnect the negative battery cable. Raise and safely support the vehicle.

2. Remove the transmission assembly from the vehicle.

3. Place the transmission in a vertical position, converter housing down.

4. Remove the control cover assembly, roll pin and control lever end from the transfer case.

5. Remove the extension housing-to-transfer case attaching bolts. Lift the transfer case off vertically to prevent damaging the control rod.

To install:

6. Install the input sleeve, if removed.

7. Coat the contacting surfaces of the transfer case and extension housing with sealant.

8. Install the transfer case to the extension housing. Apply sealant to the bolt threads and tighten to 27–35 ft. lbs. (36–47 Nm).

9. Install the control lever end and secure with a new roll pin.

10. Coat the contacting surfaces of the control cover assembly and transfer case with sealant and install the control cover assembly on the transfer case.

11. Apply sealant to the bolt threads and tighten to 16–22 ft. lbs. (22–30 Nm).

12. Install the transmission assembly and lower the vehicle. Connect the negative battery cable.

13. Check the transfer case for leaks and proper operation.

MPV

1. Disconnect the negative battery cable. Raise and safely support the vehicle. Drain the transfer case.

2. Mark the position of the driveshafts on the flanges and remove the driveshafts. Push a rag into

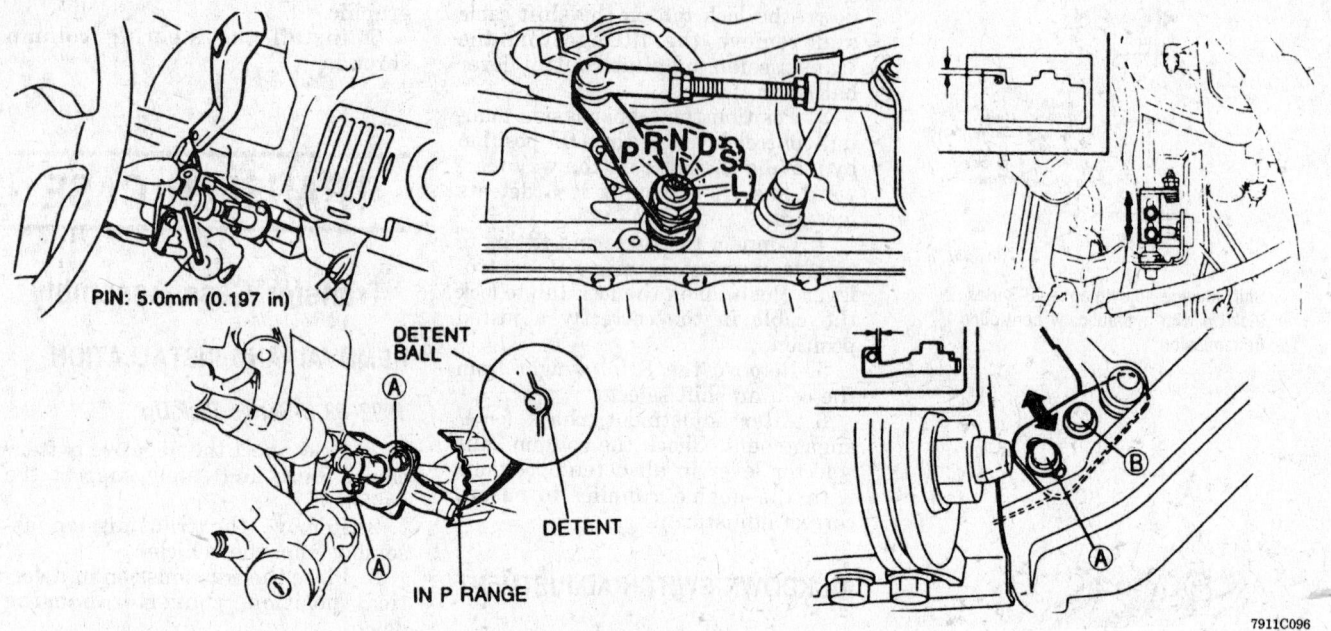

PIN: 5.0mm (0.197 in)

DETENT BALL

Ⓐ

DETENT

IN P RANGE

Ⓐ

Ⓑ

Ⓐ

7911C096

Shift linkage adjustment — MPV

the double-offset joint to hold the rear driveshaft straight to prevent damaging the boot.

3. Support the transmission with a jack and remove the transmission lower mount. Remove the upper mount.

4. Remove the front exhaust pipe and heat insulator.

5. Disconnect the speedometer and transfer case shift cable. Tag and disconnect the electrical connectors.

6. Support the transfer case with a jack and remove the transfer case attaching bolts. Remove the transfer case.

To install:

7. Apply silicone sealant to the transfer case flange.

8. Support the transfer case with a jack and install the transfer case. Apply sealant to the bolt threads and tighten to 27–40 ft. lbs. (36–54 Nm).

9. Connect the electrical connectors, transfer case shift cable and speedometer cable. Adjust the transfer case shift cable.

10. Install the exhaust pipe and heat insulator.

11. Install the upper transmission mount.

12. Install the lower transmission mount. Loosely install the center washers and nuts and tighten the outer bolts to 32–45 ft. lbs. (43–61

Nm), then tighten the center nuts to 23–34 ft. lbs. (31–46 Nm).

13. Remove the support jacks.

14. Install the driveshafts, aligning the marks that were made during removal. Remove the rag from the double-offset joint and check the boot for damage.

15. Fill the transfer case with the proper type and quantity of fluid.

16. Lower the vehicle and connect the negative battery cable. Check transfer case for leaks and proper operation.

1994–96 B-Series Pick-Up and Navajo

MECHANICAL SHIFT TYPE

1. Disconnect the negative battery cable. Raise and safely support the vehicle.

2. If equipped, remove the skid plate from the frame. Remove the damper from the transfer case, if equipped.

3. Place a drain pan under the transfer case, remove the drain plug and drain the fluid. Disconnect the 4WD indicator switch wire connector at the transfer case.

4. Disconnect the front driveshaft from the transfer case output shaft yoke and wire the driveshaft out of the way.

5. Disconnect the rear driveshaft from the transfer case output shaft flange and wire the driveshaft out of the way.

6. Disconnect the speedometer driven gear from the transfer case rear cover. Disconnect the vent hose from the control lever.

7. Disconnect the nut from the shift lever and remove the shift lever.

8. Remove the large and small bolts retaining the shifter to the extension housing. Remove the lever assembly and bushing.

9. Support the transfer case with a transmission jack. Remove the 5 bolts retaining the transfer case to the transmission and extension housing.

10. Slide the transfer case rearward off the transmission output shaft and lower the transfer case from the vehicle. Remove the gasket from between the transfer case and extension housing.

To install:

11. Install a new gasket on the front mounting face of the transfer case assembly.

12. Raise the transfer case with the transmission jack so the transmission output shaft aligns with the transfer case input shaft. Slide the transfer case forward onto the transmission output shaft and onto the

dowel pin. Install the 5 retaining bolts and tighten, in sequence, to 25–43 ft. lbs. (34–58 Nm).

13. Remove the transmission jack.

14. Install and adjust the shifter. Always tighten the large bolt retaining the shifter to the extension housing before tightening the small bolt.

15. Install the vent assembly so the white marking on the hose is in position in the notch in the shifter. The upper end of the vent hose should be ¾ in. above the top of the shifter and positioned just below the floor pan.

16. Connect the speedometer driven gear to the transfer case rear cover. Tighten the screw to 20–25 inch lbs. (2.3–2.8 Nm).

17. Connect the rear driveshaft to the transfer case output shaft flange. Tighten the bolts to 61–87 ft. lbs. (83–118 Nm).

18. Connect the front driveshaft to the transfer case output shaft yoke. Tighten the bolts to 12–16 ft. lbs. (16–22 Nm).

19. Connect the 4WD indicator switch wire connector at the transfer case.

20. Install the drain plug and tighten to 14–22 ft. lbs. (19–30 Nm). Remove the fill plug and fill the transfer case with the proper type of fluid to the bottom of the fill hole. Install the fill plug and tighten to 14–22 ft. lbs. (19–30 Nm).

21. Install the damper to the transfer case, if equipped. Using new damper bolts, tighten to 25–35 ft. lbs. (34–48 Nm).

22. Install the skid plate, if equipped. Tighten the nuts and bolts to 15–20 ft. lbs. (20–27 Nm).

23. Lower the vehicle and connect the negative battery cable.

ELECTRONIC SHIFT TYPE

1. Disconnect the negative battery cable. Raise and safely support the vehicle.

2. If equipped, remove the nuts, bolts and skid plate from the frame. Remove the damper from the transfer case, if equipped.

3. Place a drain pan under the transfer case, remove the drain plug and drain the fluid.

4. Remove the wire connector from the feed wire harness at the rear of the transfer case. First squeeze the locking tabs, then pull the connectors apart.

NOTE: Do not pull directly on the wires or pull outwardly on the locking tabs.

5. Remove the connector for the transfer case motor from the mounting bracket.

6. Disconnect the front driveshaft from the transfer case output shaft yoke and wire the driveshaft out of the way.

7. Disconnect the rear driveshaft from the transfer case output shaft flange and wire the driveshaft out of the way.

8. Disconnect the speedometer driven gear from the transfer case rear cover. Disconnect the vent hose from the mounting bracket.

9. Support the transfer case with a transmission jack. Remove the 5 bolts retaining the transfer case to the transmission and extension housing.

10. Slide the transfer case rearward off the transmission output shaft and lower the transfer case from the vehicle. Remove the gasket from between the transfer case and extension housing.

To install:

11. Install a new gasket on the front mounting face of the transfer case assembly.

12. Raise the transfer case with the transmission jack so the transmission output shaft aligns with the transfer case input shaft. Slide the transfer case forward onto the transmission output shaft and onto the dowel pin. Install the 5 retaining bolts and tighten, in sequence, to 25–43 ft. lbs. (34–58 Nm).

13. Remove the transmission jack.

14. Install the vent hose so the white marking on the hose aligns with the notch in the mounting bracket.

15. Connect the speedometer driven gear to the transfer case rear cover. Tighten the screw to 20–25 inch lbs. (2.3–2.8 Nm).

16. Connect the rear driveshaft to the transfer case output shaft flange. Tighten the bolts to 61–87 ft. lbs. (83–118 Nm).

17. Connect the front driveshaft to the transfer case output shaft yoke. Tighten the bolts to 12–16 ft. lbs. (16–22 Nm).

18. Attach the connector for the transfer case motor to the mounting bracket.

19. Connect the wire connectors on the rear of the transfer case, making sure the retaining tabs lock.

20. Install the drain plug and tighten to 14–22 ft. lbs. (19–30 Nm). Remove the fill plug and fill the transfer case with the proper type of fluid to the bottom of the fill hole. Install the fill plug and tighten to 14–22 ft. lbs. (19–30 Nm).

21. Install the damper to the transfer case, if equipped. Using new damper bolts, tighten to 25–35 ft. lbs. (34–48 Nm).

22. Install the skid plate, if equipped. Tighten the nuts and bolts to 15–20 ft. lbs. (20–27 Nm).

23. Lower the vehicle and connect the negative battery cable.

LINKAGE ADJUSTMENT

MPV

NOTE: Make sure the Hi-Low lever and transfer case are in Low mode while adjusting the Hi-Low lever.

1. Shift the Hi-Low lever to the 4LO position.

2. Remove the column covers.

3. Pull the column lever rearward, toward the driver and insert a 0.197 in. (5mm) outside diameter pin into the shift rod assembly.

4. Raise and safely support the vehicle.

5. Mark the position of the front driveshaft on the flanges and remove the front driveshaft.

6. Loosen the locknuts of the transfer case side.

7. Remove the air intake tube.

8. Loosen the shift lever mounting bolts and adjust the clearance between the lower bracket and the shift lever bushing by sliding the shift lever assembly until there is no clearance.

9. Tighten the shift lever mounting bolts to 12–17 ft. lbs. (16–23 Nm).

10. Install the air intake tube.

11. While pushing the outer cable toward the transfer case, turn locknut B until it touches Z surface. Tighten locknut A to 18–29 ft. lbs. (25–39 Nm) and locknut C to 25–37 ft. lbs. (34–50 Nm).

12. Install the front driveshaft, aligning the marks that were made during removal.

13. Remove the pin from the shift rod assembly and install the column covers. Check the Hi-Low lever operation.

1994–96 B-Series Pick-Up and Navajo

MECHANICAL SHIFT TYPE

1. Raise the shift boot to expose the top surface of the cam plate.

2. Loosen the bolts "A" and "B" on the control lever assembly approximately 1 turn. Move the transfer case shift lever to the 4L position.

3. Rotate the cam plate clockwise around bolt "A" until the bottom chamfered corner of the neutral lug just contacts the forward right edge of the shift lever, point "C".

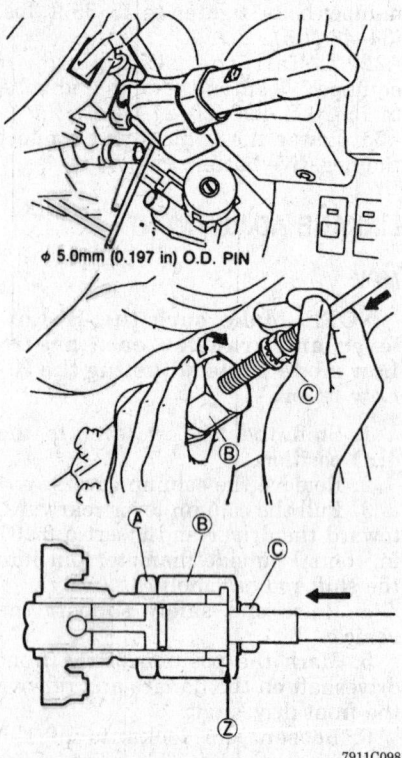

φ 5.0mm (0.197 in) O.D. PIN

7911C098

Transfer case linkage adjustment — MPV

4. Hold the cam plate in this position and tighten bolt "A" first to 70–90 ft. lbs. (94–122 Nm), then tighten bolt "B" to 31–42 ft. lbs. (43–56 Nm).

5. Move the transfer case in-cab shift lever to all shift positions to check the positive engagement. There should be clearance, not exceeding 0.13 in. (3.30mm), between the shift lever and cam plate in **2H** front **4H** rear and **4L** shift positions.

6. Install the shift boot assembly.

DRIVE AXLE

Halfshaft

REMOVAL AND INSTALLATION

1992–93 B-Series Pick-Up

1. Raise and safely support the vehicle. Remove the wheel and tire assembly.

2. Remove the drive flange hub.

3. Remove the caliper, mounting support and knuckle arm. Support the caliper aside with rope or mechanics wire; do not let the caliper hang by the brake hose.

4. Disconnect the stabilizer bar and the tie rod end.

5. Remove the lower mount of the shock absorber.

6. Remove the snapring and spacer.

7. Support the lower control arm with a jack.

8. Disconnect the upper and lower ball joints and the knuckle.

9. Lower the lower control arm and remove the knuckle assembly.

10. Remove the splash shield.

11. Using a suitable prybar, pry out the halfshaft from the differential and remove the halfshaft from the vehicle. Be careful not to damage the dust cover or oil seal.

To install:

12. Install a new clip on the halfshaft. Coat the differential seal with clean transmission fluid.

13. Install the halfshaft in the differential, being careful not to damage the seal. After installation, attempt to pull the halfshaft outward to make sure it does not come out.

14. Install the knuckle and hub to the halfshaft and ball joints. Install the spacer and a new snapring.

15. Install the lower mount of the shock absorber and loosely tighten the boot.

16. Connect the stabilizer bar and tie rod end.

17. Install the caliper assembly, knuckle arm and wheel and tire assembly. Apply sealant to the drive flange and install it.

18. Install the splash shield and lower the vehicle.

19. Tighten the lower shock absorber mount to 41–59 ft. lbs. (55–80 Nm).

20. Check the front end alignment.

MPV

1. Raise and safely support the vehicle. Remove the wheel and tire assembly.

2. Remove and discard the halfshaft locknut.

3. Disconnect the tie rod end from the knuckle.

4. Remove the caliper and brake rotor from the knuckle. Support the caliper aside with rope or mechanics wire; do not let it hang by the brake hose.

5. Remove the nut and bolts and remove the lower ball joint. Remove the bolts and nuts and remove the knuckle/hub assembly from the strut.

NOTE: If the halfshaft is stuck to the hub, install a used locknut so it is flush with the end of the shaft, then tap the nut with a soft mallet.

6. Remove the splash shield.

7. Using a suitable prybar, pry out the halfshaft from the differential and remove the halfshaft from the vehicle. Be careful not to damage the dust cover or oil seal.

To install:

8. Install a new clip on the halfshaft. Coat the differential seal with clean transmission fluid.

9. Install the halfshaft in the differential, being careful not to damage the seal. After installation, attempt to pull the halfshaft outward to make sure it does not come out.

10. Install the knuckle/hub assembly to the strut and tighten the nuts to 69–86 ft. lbs. (93–117 Nm).

11. Install the lower ball joint. Tighten the bolts to 75–101 ft. lbs. (102–137 Nm) and the nut to 115–137 ft. lbs. (157–187 Nm). Install a new cotter pin.

12. Install the brake rotor and caliper.

13. Connect the tie rod end to the knuckle.

14. Install a new locknut and tighten to 174–231 ft. lbs. (235–314 Nm). After tightening, stake the locknut using a blunt chisel.

15. Install the splash shield. Install the wheel and tire assembly and lower the vehicle.

16. Check the front end alignment.

CV-Boot

REMOVAL AND INSTALLATION

NOTE: Do not attempt to disassemble the outer CV-joint. If outer CV-boot replacement is necessary, the inner CV-joint and boot must first be removed.

Inner Boot

1. Remove the halfshaft from the vehicle and mount it in a vise with protective jaw caps.

2. Pry up the boot band locking clips with a small prybar and remove the bands with pliers.

3. Slide the boot back on the shaft to expose the inner CV-joint.

4. Mark the CV-joint housing and cage for proper reassembly and remove the retaining clip with a small prybar. Remove the housing.

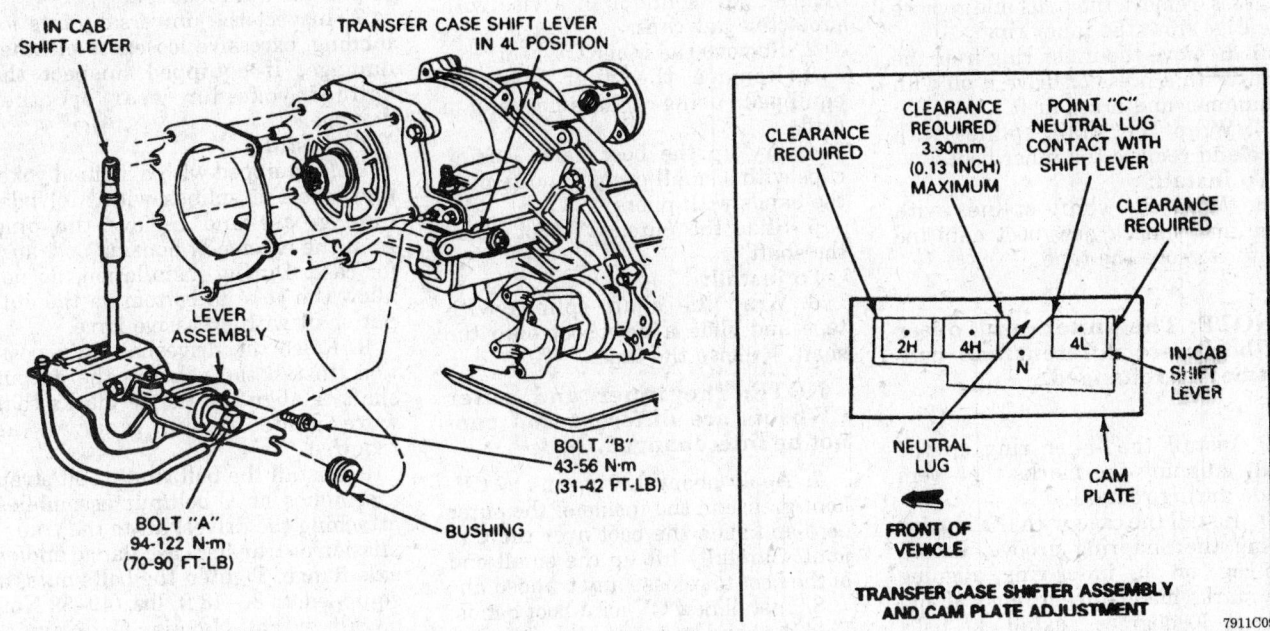

Transfer case linkage adjustment — 1994–96 B-Series Pick-Up and Navajo with mechanical shift transfer case

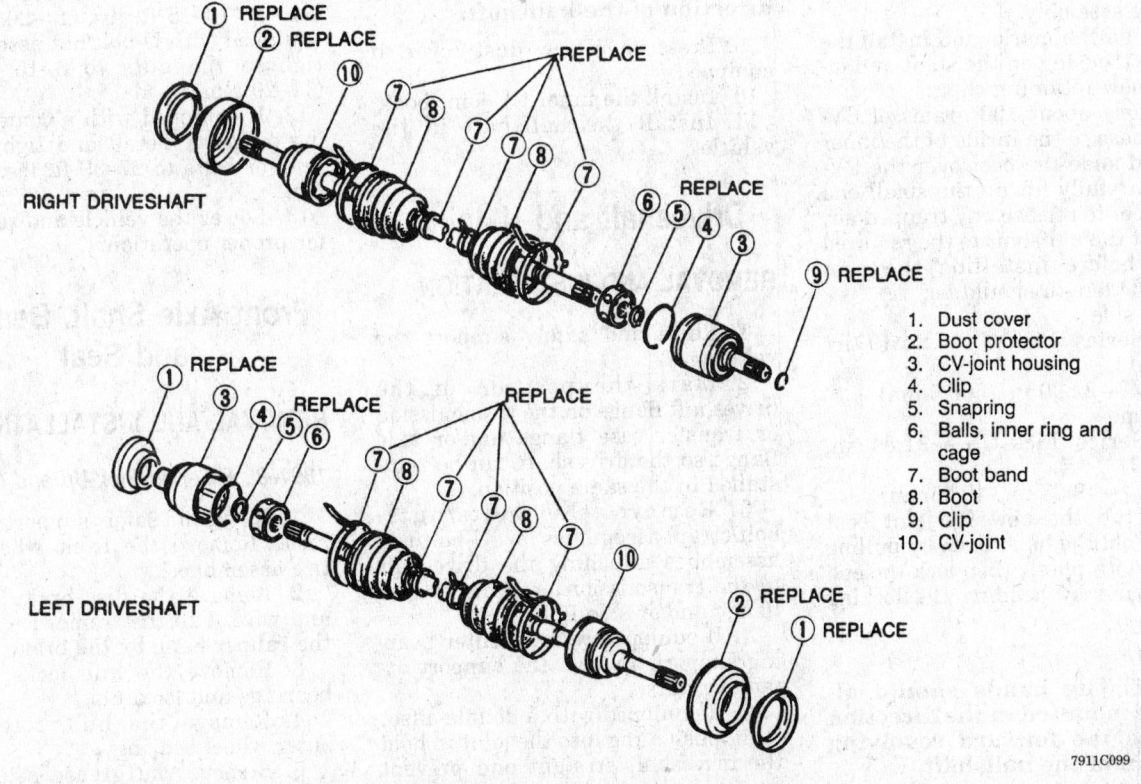

1. Dust cover
2. Boot protector
3. CV-joint housing
4. Clip
5. Snapring
6. Balls, inner ring and cage
7. Boot band
8. Boot
9. Clip
10. CV-joint

Halfshaft assembly exploded view — 1992–93 B-Series Pick-Up

5. Mark the shaft, cage, balls and inner ring for reassembly and remove the snapring. Turn the cage about 30 degrees, remove the balls and remove the cage from the inner ring.

6. Remove the inner ring from the shaft with a press or drive it off with a hammer and brass drift.

7. Wrap the shaft splines with tape and remove the inner boot.

To install:

8. Wrap the shaft splines with tape and slide a new boot onto the shaft. Remove the tape.

NOTE: The inner and outer CV-boots are different and cannot be interchanged.

9. Install the inner ring on the shaft, aligning the marks that were made during removal.

10. Install the cage with the big end facing the snapring groove. Install the cage on the inner ring, aligning the marks made during removal and turn it 30 degrees. Install the balls into their proper positions and install a new snapring in the groove.

11. Fill the CV-joint housing with the proper quantity and type of CV-joint grease and apply the grease thoroughly to the cage, inner ring and ball assembly.

12. Align the marks and install the CV-joint housing on the shaft and install a new retaining clip.

13. Apply about 120 grams of CV-joint grease to the inside of the inner boot and slide the boot over the CV-joint. Carefully lift up the small end of the boot to release any trapped air.

14. Set the halfshaft to the required length before installing the boot bands; the length should be:

Right side
B-Series Pick-Up — 24.49 in. (622mm)
MPV — 22.30 in. (566.5mm)
Left side
B-Series Pick-Up — 21.81 in. (554mm)
MPV — 19.63 in. (498.5mm)

15. Install the new CV-joint boot bands. Fold the band back by pulling the end with pliers, then lock the end of the band by bending the locking clips.

NOTE: The bands should always be mounted in the direction opposite the forward revolving direction of the halfshaft.

16. Remove the halfshaft from the vise and install it in the vehicle.

Outer Boot

1. Remove the halfshaft from the vehicle and mount it in a vise with protective jaw caps.

2. Remove the inner CV-boot.

3. Remove the dust cover, if equipped, using a hammer and a drift.

4. Pry up the boot band locking clips with a small prybar and remove the bands with pliers.

5. Slide the outer CV-boot off of the shaft.

To install:

6. Wrap the shaft splines with tape and slide a new boot onto the shaft. Remove the tape.

NOTE: The inner and outer CV-boots are different and cannot be interchanged.

7. Apply about 120 grams of CV-joint grease to the inside of the outer boot and slide the boot over the CV-joint. Carefully lift up the small end of the boot to release any trapped air.

8. Install new CV-joint boot bands. Fold the band back by pulling the end with pliers, then lock the end of the band by bending the locking clips.

NOTE: The bands should always be mounted in the direction opposite the forward revolving direction of the halfshaft.

9. Press on a new dust cover, if equipped.

10. Install the inner CV-joint boot.

11. Install the halfshaft in the vehicle.

Driveshaft and U-Joints

REMOVAL AND INSTALLATION

1. Raise and safely support the vehicle.

2. Mark the position of the driveshaft flange on the transmission or transfer case flange and/or axle flange so the driveshaft can be reinstalled in the same position.

3. Remove the bolts/nuts, bolt/strap assemblies or U-bolt/nut assemblies attaching the driveshaft to the transmission or transfer case flange and/or axle flange.

4. If equipped with a center bearing support, remove the support attaching nuts.

5. If equipped with a double-offset joint, push a rag into the joint to hold the driveshaft straight and prevent damaging the boot.

6. Remove the driveshaft assembly. If equipped with a splined yoke, pull the driveshaft out until the yoke

clears the extension housing or transfer case, then install a suitable plug to prevent fluid leakage.

7. Inspect the universal joints for binding, excessive looseness or other damage. If equipped, inspect the splined yoke for wear or other damage.

To install:

8. If equipped with a splined yoke, lubricate the splines with Molybdenum grease and remove the plug from the extension housing or transfer case. During installation, do not allow the yoke to bottom on the output shaft with excessive force.

9. Raise the driveshaft into position. Install the yoke on the output shaft or align the flange marks that were made during removal, as required.

10. Install the bolts/nuts, bolt/strap assemblies or U-bolt/nut assemblies attaching the driveshaft to the transmission or transfer case flange and/or axle flange. Tighten the bolts/nuts, if equipped, to 36–43 ft. lbs. (49–59 Nm) on all except Navajo. On Navajo, tighten the axle flange bolts to 70–95 ft. lbs. (95–129 Nm) and the transfer case bolts to 12–16 ft. lbs. (17–22 Nm).

11. On Navajo, if equipped with bolt/strap assemblies, tighten the bolts to 10–15 ft. lbs. (14–20 Nm). If equipped with U-bolt/nut assemblies, tighten the nuts to 8–15 ft. lbs. (11–20 Nm).

12. If equipped with a center bearing support, install and tighten the nuts or bolts to 27–39 ft. lbs. (36–53 Nm).

13. Lower the vehicle and road test for proper operation.

Front Axle Shaft, Bearing and Seal

REMOVAL AND INSTALLATION

1994–96 B-Series Pick-Up and Navajo

1. Raise and safely support the vehicle. Remove the front wheel and tire assemblies.

2. Remove the disc brake caliper and wire it to the frame. Do not let the caliper hang by the brake hose.

3. Remove the hub locks, wheel bearings and locknuts.

4. Remove the hub, rotor and outer wheel bearing.

5. Remove the grease seal from the rotor with a seal removal tool. Remove the inner wheel bearing.

6. If the wheel bearings are to be replaced, remove the inner and outer

bearing races with a suitable puller or a hammer and brass drift.

7. Remove the nuts retaining the spindle to the steering knuckle. Tap the spindle with a plastic hammer to jar the spindle from the knuckle. Remove the splash shield.

8. On the left side of the vehicle, remove the shaft and joint assembly by pulling the assembly out of the carrier. On the right side of the carrier, remove and discard the clamp from the shaft and joint assembly and the stub shaft. Pull the shaft and joint assembly from the splines of the stub shaft.

9. If required, remove the oil seal and needle bearing from the spindle. If necessary, remove the slinger from the shaft by driving it off with a hammer.

To install:

10. If removed, install a new bearing and seal in the spindle and/or press on a new shaft sling

11. On the right side of the carrier, install the rubber boot and new keystone clamps on the stub shaft slip yoke. Slide the right shaft and joint assembly into the slip yoke making sure the splines are fully engaged. Slide the boot over the assembly and crimp the keystone clamp using suitable pliers.

NOTE: Make sure the yoke ears are in phase (in line) during assembly.

12. On the left side of the carrier, slide the shaft and joint assembly through the knuckle and engage the splines on the shaft in the carrier.

13. Install the splash shield and spindle onto the steering knuckle. Install and tighten the spindle nuts to 45 ft. lbs. (61 Nm).

14. If removed, drive the bearing races into the rotor using a suitable driver. Pack the inner and outer wheel bearings and the lip of a new seal with high-temperature wheel bearing grease.

15. Position the inner wheel bearing in the race and install the seal using a seal installer. Install the rotor on the spindle and install the outer wheel bearing in the race.

16. Install the wheel bearing, locknut, thrust bearing, snapring and locking hubs.

17. Install the caliper and the wheel and tire assemblies. Lower the vehicle.

Rear Axle Shaft, Bearing and Seal

REMOVAL AND INSTALLATION

1992–93 B-Series Pick-Up

1. Raise and safely support the vehicle. Remove the wheel and tire assembly.

2. Remove the brake drum and the brake shoes.

3. Disconnect the parking brake cable from the brake backing plate. Disconnect and plug the brake line at the wheel cylinder.

4. Remove the axle shaft/backing plate assembly from the axle housing, then pry out the axle seal. On 4WD vehicles, remove the O-ring from the axle housing.

5. Install the axle shaft in a vise, attached at the axle flange. Remove the lockwasher and the bearing locknut.

NOTE: Left side axles have left-hand thread; remove by turning clockwise.

6. Reposition the axle shaft in the vise so the jaws grip the shaft. Use protective jaw caps on the vise to protect the axle shaft.

7. Use a suitable puller to remove the bearing and bearing housing.

8. Remove the bearing and seal from the hub, then remove the outer bearing race using a suitable drift.

9. Clean all components and inspect for wear and/or damage. Replace as necessary. If bearing replacement is necessary, the bearing races must also be replaced.

To install:

10. Press in a new seal and inner race, using suitable drivers. Liberally apply high temperature wheel bearing grease to the area of the race and seal.

11. Using a suitable seal installer, tap a new seal into the axle housing until it is flush with the end of the housing. Coat the seal lip with grease.

12. Install the spacer on the axle shaft and position the axle shaft and backing plate in a press. Using suitable press tools, press the wheel bearing onto the axle shaft.

NOTE: The standard press-fit force should be 30,379–44,121 lbs. If the force is too high or too low, replace the bearing collar or shaft.

13. Position the axle shaft in a vise, attached at the axle flange. Install

the bearing locknut and a new lockwasher. Tighten the locknut to 145–217 ft. lbs. (196–294 Nm). Align the lockwasher craws to the locknut notches and crimp the lockwasher.

14. Install a new O-ring in the axle housing, if removed. Install the axle shaft assembly, being careful not to damage the axle seal. Adjust the wheel bearing play as follows:

   a. There can only be one axle shaft installed in the housing during the adjustment procedure. If only one shaft was removed, remove the other shaft at this time. If both shafts were removed, leave the other shaft out of the axle housing for now.

   b. Attach a dial indicator to the backing plate and place the indicator foot on the end of the axle shaft.

   c. Check the axle shaft endplay; it should be 0.026–0.037 in. (0.65–0.95mm).

   d. If the bearing play is not within specification, remove the axle and install shims which are available from Mazda.

   e. If both axle shafts were removed, at this time, remove the axle shaft that has been adjusted and install and adjust the bearing play of the other shaft.

15. Install the backing plate mounting nuts and tighten to 72–87 ft. lbs. (98–118 Nm).

16. Connect the brake line and the parking brake cable.

17. Install the brake shoes and the brake drum.

18. Install the wheel and tire assembly. Bleed the brakes and lower the vehicle.

MPV

1. Raise and safely support the vehicle. Remove the wheel and tire assembly.

2. Remove the brake drum and the brake shoes.

3. Disconnect the parking brake cable from the brake backing plate. Disconnect and plug the brake line at the wheel cylinder.

4. Remove the axle shaft/backing plate assembly using a slide hammer. Remove the axle seal using a prybar.

5. Remove and discard the retaining ring from the axle shaft.

6. Using a suitable grinder, grind a section of the bearing collar until only approximately 0.0197 in. (0.5mm) remains. Be careful not to damage the axle shaft.

7. Cut the bearing collar with a chisel at the ground section and remove the bearing collar.

8. Use a suitable bearing puller to remove the bearing from the shaft. Remove the seal.

To install:

9. Apply grease to the lip of a new seal and install on the backing plate.

10. Install a new bearing over the axle shaft. Make sure there is no oil or grease on the new collar or axle shaft, then install the collar on the axle shaft.

11. Position the axle shaft/backing plate assembly in a press and press the bearing and collar onto the axle shaft.

NOTE: If the press-fit force of the collar is 5952 lbs. (2.7 tons) or less, replace the collar or the axle shaft.

12. Apply grease to the lip of a new axle seal and install the seal into the axle housing, using a suitable seal installer.

13. Install the axle shaft/backing plate assembly in the axle housing, being careful not to damage the axle seal. Install the backing plate nuts and tighten to 72–87 ft. lbs. (98–118 Nm).

14. Connect the brake line and the parking brake cable.

15. Install the brake shoes and the brake drum.

16. Install the wheel and tire assembly. Bleed the brakes and lower the vehicle.

1994–96 B-Series Pick-Up and Navajo

1. Raise and safely support the vehicle.

2. Remove the rear wheel and tire assemblies and the brake drums.

3. Clean all dirt from the carrier cover area. Position a drain pan under the carrier, remove the cover and drain the rear axle.

4. Remove the differential pinion shaft lock bolt and pinion shaft.

5. Push the flanged end of the axle shafts toward the center of the vehicle and remove the C-lock from the button end of the axle shaft. Be careful not to lose or damage the rubber O-ring which is in the axle shaft groove under the C-lock.

6. Remove the axle shaft from the housing.

7. Reinstall the pinion shaft and lock bolt to ensure the pinion gears remain in place.

8. Using bearing remover 49 UN01 033 or equivalent and a suitable slide hammer, remove the axle bearing and seal as a unit.

To install:

9. Lubricate a new bearing with rear axle lubricant and install in the housing bore using a suitable driver.

10. Apply grease to the lips of a new axle seal and install, using a seal installer.

11. Remove the pinion shaft lock bolt and pinion shaft.

12. Slide the axle shaft into the axle housing, being careful not to damage the seal or axle bearing. Start the splines into the side gear and push until the button end of the axle shaft can be seen in the differential case.

13. Install the C-lock on the button end of the axle shaft, then pull the shaft outboard until the shaft splines engage and the C-lock seats in the counterbore of the differential side gear. Make sure the O-ring is in the groove at the button end of the axle shaft before installing the C-lock.

14. Slide the pinion shaft through the case and pinion gears, aligning the hole in the shaft with the lock bolt hole. Apply stud and bearing mount compound and install the lock bolt. Tighten to 15–30 ft. lbs. (20–40 Nm).

15. Clean all old sealer from the carrier surface. Apply a bead of RTV sealer 1/8–1/4 in. wide. The bead should be continuous and should not pass through or outside the holes.

16. Install a new cover and new bolts. Tighten the bolts to 15–20 ft. lbs. (21–27 Nm). Fill the carrier with the proper type and quantity of fluid.

17. Install the brake drums and the wheel and tire assemblies. Lower the vehicle.

Front Wheel Hub, Knuckle/Spindle and Bearings

REMOVAL AND INSTALLATION

1992–93 B-Series Pick-Up

1. Raise and safely support the vehicle. Remove the wheel and tire assembly.

2. Remove the drive flange.

3. Remove the brake caliper. Support the caliper aside with rope or mechanics wire; do not let the caliper hang by the brake hose.

4. Remove the snapring and spacer. Remove the set bolts and bearing set plate.

5. Remove the bearing locknut using a suitable removal tool. Remove the hub and rotor without letting the washer and bearing fall.

6. Remove the dust cover.

7. Disconnect the tie rod end from the knuckle. Disconnect the stabilizer bar and the lower shock mount.

8. Support the lower control arm with a jack. Remove the lower ball joint nut and separate the knuckle from the lower arm using a suitable tool.

9. Remove the upper ball joint nut and separate the knuckle from the lower arm using a suitable tool.

10. Lower the lower control arm and remove the knuckle.

11. Inspect the knuckle, hub and bearings for wear and or damage. Replace components, as necessary.

12. Remove the oil seal and the bearing inner race from the knuckle. Using a suitable drift, remove the bearing outer race by tapping lightly with a hammer.

13. Using a slide hammer, remove the needle bearing from the knuckle.

14. Mark the position of the disc brake rotor on the hub, then remove the bolts and disassemble the rotor and hub.

15. Remove the oil seal and the bearing inner race from the hub. Using a suitable drift, remove the bearing outer race by tapping lightly with a hammer.

To install:

16. Press a new needle bearing into the knuckle using a suitable driver.

17. After installing the inner bearing into the knuckle, press in a new oil seal. Apply wheel bearing grease to the oil seal lip.

18. Press fit the outer side bearing outer race, then the inner side bearing outer race, into the hub using suitable drivers. Press in a new oil seal until it is flush with the hub end surface. Apply wheel bearing grease to the seal lip.

19. Align the matching marks of the hub and brake rotor and tighten the mounting bolts to 40–51 ft. lbs. (54–69 Nm).

20. Liberally apply high temperature wheel bearing grease to the inside of the hub. Install the outer bearing race and washer in the hub.

21. Insert the halfshaft into the knuckle and install the nut for the lower ball joint. Tighten the nut by hand.

22. Raise the lower control arm with the jack until the upper ball joint is connected to the knuckle. Install the nut and tighten by hand.

23. Tighten the upper ball joint nut to 22–38 ft. lbs. (29–51 Nm) and the lower ball joint nut to 87–116 ft. lbs. (118–157 Nm). Install new cotter pins.

1. Freewheel hub bolts
2. Snapring
3. Spacer
4. Bearing set plate
5. Locknut
6. Bearing
7. Hub assembly
8. Bearing
9. Oil seal
10. Rotor
11. Dust cover
12. Knuckle
13. Needle bearing
14. Halfshaft

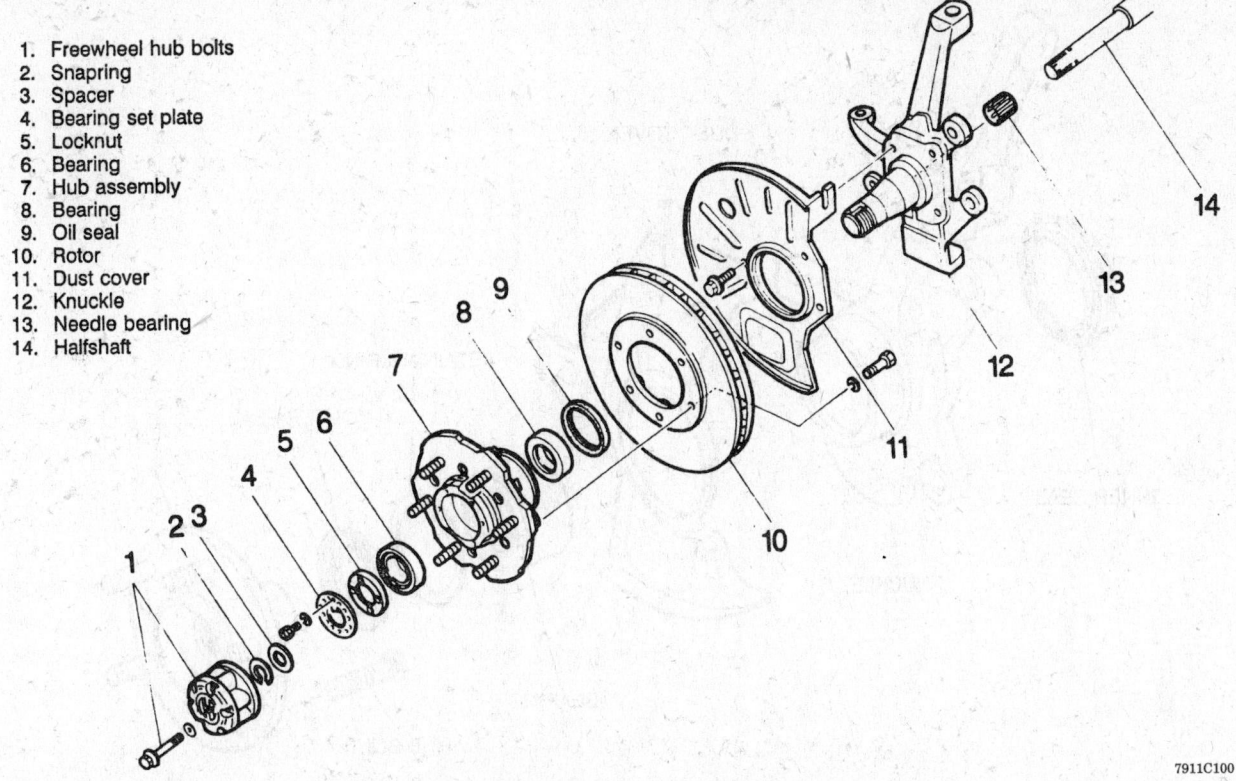

Front hub, knuckle and bearing assembly — 1992–93 4WD B-Series Pick-Up

24. Connect the tie rod end to the knuckle, tighten the nut to 23–43 ft. lbs. (44–59 Nm) and install a new cotter pin.

25. Install the dust cover to the knuckle and tighten to 14–19 ft. lbs. (19–26 Nm).

26. After loosely installing the lower shock absorber mount, install the stabilizer bar.

27. Install the hub and rotor assembly, then adjust the bearing preload as follows:

 a. Tighten the locknut, then turn the hub and rotor 2–3 times to seat the bearing.

 b. Loosen the locknut so they can be turned by hand.

 c. Attach a suitable pull scale to a wheel lug bolt and measure the frictional forces. The preload is the frictional force plus 1.3–2.6 lbs.

 d. Tighten the locknut until the preload is as specified.

 e. Install the bearing set plate using 2 bolts. Tighten the bolts to 43–61 inch lbs. (5–7 Nm).

 f. Coat the spacer with grease and install it. Install a new snapring.

28. Install the caliper, wheel and tire assembly and drive flange. Lower the vehicle.

29. Tighten the lower shock mount to 41–59 ft. lbs. (55–80 Nm) with the vehicle unloaded.

30. Check the front end alignment.

MPV

1. Raise and safely support the vehicle. Remove the wheel and tire assembly.

2. Remove and discard the locknut from the end of the halfshaft.

3. Remove the brake caliper and disc brake rotor. Support the caliper aside with rope or mechanics wire; do not let the caliper hang by the brake hose.

4. Remove the cotter pin and nut and, using a suitable tool, disconnect the tie rod end from the knuckle.

5. Remove the cotter pin and loosen the lower ball joint nut. Separate the lower arm from the knuckle using a suitable tool.

6. Remove the knuckle-to-strut bolts and nuts and remove the knuckle/hub assembly from the vehicle.

7. Pry out the inner oil seal from the knuckle.

8. Position the knuckle/hub assembly in a press and, using a suita-ble driver, press the hub from the knuckle.

NOTE: If the inner bearing race remains on the hub, position the hub in a vise, secured by the flange. Move the race away from the hub using a hammer and chisel, then position the hub in a press and press the race off of the hub.

9. Pry out the outer oil seal from the knuckle.

10. Remove the retaining ring and position the knuckle in a press. Using a suitable driver, press the wheel bearing from the knuckle.

11. If necessary, mark the position of the dust shield on the knuckle and remove the dust shield, using a hammer and chisel. Do not reuse the dust cover, if removed.

To install:

12. If the dust cover was removed, mark the new cover in the same place as the old was marked during removal. Align the cover and knuckle marks and press the cover onto the knuckle.

13. Press a new wheel bearing into the knuckle, using a suitable driver. Install the retaining ring and a new outer seal. Apply grease to the seal lip.

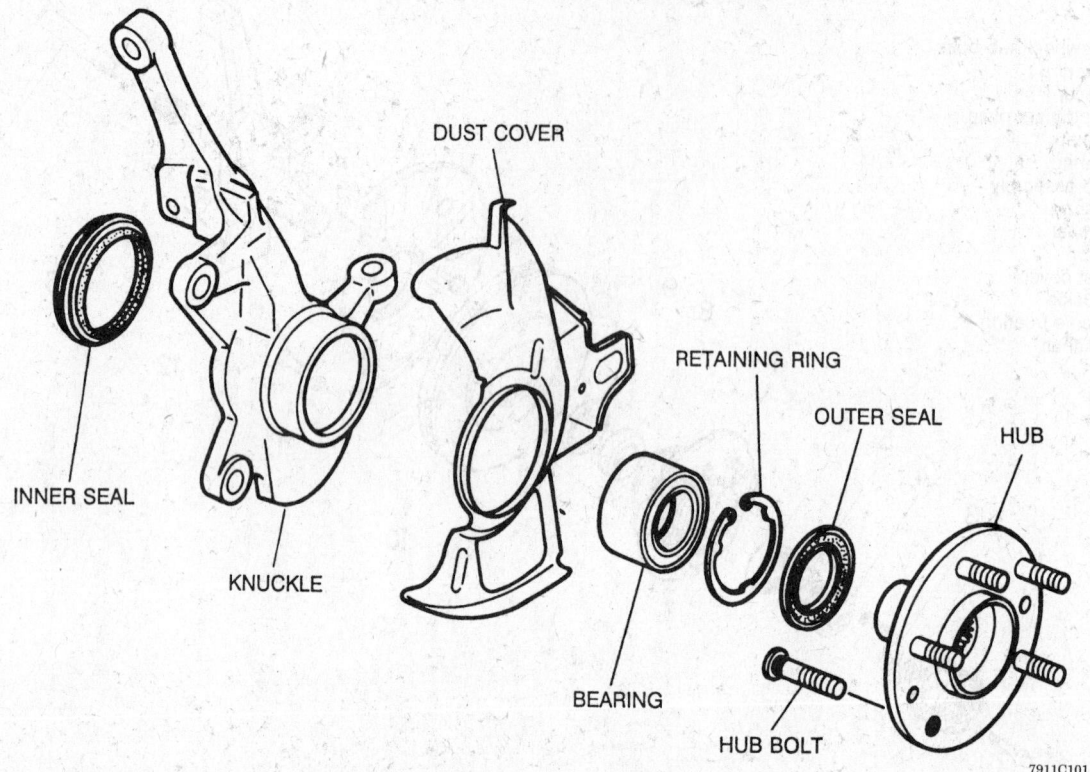

Front wheel hub, knuckle and bearing assembly — 4WD MPV

14. Press the hub into the knuckle, using a suitable driver. Install a new inner seal and lubricate the seal lip with grease.

15. Install the knuckle/hub assembly onto the strut, install the bolts and nuts and tighten to 69–86 ft. lbs. (93–117 Nm).

16. Install the lower ball joint into the knuckle and tighten the nut to 115–137 ft. lbs. (157–187 Nm). Install a new cotter pin.

17. Connect the tie rod to the knuckle and install the nut. Tighten to 43–58 ft. lbs. (59–78 Nm) and install a new cotter pin.

18. Install the brake rotor and caliper.

19. Install a new locknut on the end of the halfshaft and tighten to 174–231 ft. lbs. (235–314 Nm). After tightening, stake the nut with a blunt chisel.

20. Install the wheel and tire assembly and lower the vehicle. Check the front end alignment.

1994–96 B-Series Pick-Up and Navajo

1. Raise and safely support the vehicle. Remove the front wheel and tire assemblies.

2. Remove the disc brake caliper and wire it to the frame. Do not let the caliper hang by the brake hose.

3. Remove the hub locks, wheel bearings and locknuts.

4. Remove the hub, rotor and outer wheel bearing.

5. Remove the grease seal from the rotor with a seal removal tool. Remove the inner wheel bearing.

6. If the wheel bearings are to be replaced, remove the inner and outer bearing races with a suitable puller or a hammer and brass drift.

7. Remove the nuts retaining the spindle to the steering knuckle. Tap the spindle with a plastic hammer to jar the spindle from the knuckle. Remove the splash shield.

8. On the left side of the vehicle, remove the shaft and joint assembly by pulling the assembly out of the carrier. On the right side of the carrier, remove and discard the clamp from the shaft and joint assembly and the stub shaft. Pull the shaft and joint assembly from the splines of the stub shaft.

9. Place the spindle in a vise on the second step of the spindle. Wrap a shop towel around the spindle or use a brass-jawed vise to protect the spindle.

10. Remove the oil seal and needle bearing from the spindle with a slide hammer and seal remover TOOL–1175–AC or equivalent. If necessary, remove the slinger from the shaft by driving off with a hammer.

11. Remove the cotter pin from the tie rod nut and then remove the nut. Tap on the tie rod stud to free it from the steering arm.

12. Remove the upper ball joint snapring and remove the upper ball joint pinch bolt. Loosen the lower ball joint nut to the end of the stud.

13. Strike the inside of the knuckle near the upper and lower ball joints to break the knuckle loose from the ball joint studs.

14. Remove the camber adjuster sleeve. Note the position of the slot in the camber adjuster so it can be reinstalled in the same position during assembly.

15. Remove the lower ball joint nut. Place the knuckle in a vise and remove the snapring from the bottom ball joint socket, if equipped.

16. Assemble C-frame T74P–4635–C and ball joint remover T83T–3050–A or equivalents on the lower ball joint. Turn the forcing screw clockwise until the lower ball joint is removed from the steering knuckle.

17. Assemble the C-frame and ball joint remover on the upper ball joint and remove in the same manner.

NOTE: Always remove the lower ball joint first.

To install:

18. Clean the steering knuckle bore and insert the lower ball joint in the knuckle as straight as possible.
19. Assemble C-frame T74P-4635-C, ball joint installer T83T-3050-A and receiver cup T80T-3010-A3 or equivalents to install the lower ball joint. Turn the forcing screw clockwise until the lower ball joint is firmly seated. Install the snapring on the lower ball joint.

NOTE: The lower ball joint must always be installed first.

20. Assemble the C-frame, ball joint installer and receiver cup to install the upper ball joint. Turn the forcing screw clockwise until the ball joint is firmly seated.
21. Install the camber adjuster into the support arm, making sure the slot is in the original position.

NOTE: The torque sequence in Steps 22 and 23 must be followed exactly when securing the knuckle. Excessive knuckle turning effort may result in reduced steering returnability if this procedure is not followed.

22. Install a new nut on the bottom ball joint stud. Tighten the nut to 90 ft. lbs. (122 Nm) minimum, then tighten to align the next slot in the nut with the hole in the stud. Install a new cotter pin.
23. Install the snapring on the upper ball joint stud. Install the upper ball joint pinch bolt and tighten to 48–65 ft. lbs. (65–88 Nm).

NOTE: The camber adjuster will seat itself into the knuckle at a predetermined position during the tightening sequence. Do not attempt to adjust this position.

24. Clean all dirt and grease from the spindle bearing bore. The bearing bores must be free from nicks and burrs.
25. Place the bearing in the bore with the manufacturers identification facing outward. Drive the bearing into the bore using spindle bearing replacer T80T-4000-S and driver handle T80T-4000-W or equivalents.
26. Install the grease seal in the bearing bore with the lip side of the seal facing towards the tool. Drive the seal in the bore using the same tools as in Step 25. Coat the bearing seal lip with high-temperature lubricant.
27. If removed, press on a new shaft slinger.
28. On the right side of the carrier, install the rubber boot and new keystone clamps on the stub shaft slip yoke. Slide the right shaft and joint assembly into the slip yoke making sure the splines are fully engaged. Slide the boot over the assembly and crimp the keystone clamp using suitable pliers.

NOTE: The Dana model 35 axle does not have a blind spline, therefore pay special attention to make sure the yoke ears are in phase (in line) during assembly.

29. On the left side of the carrier, slide the shaft and joint assembly through the knuckle and engage the splines on the shaft in the carrier.
30. Install the splash shield and spindle onto the steering knuckle. Install and tighten the spindle nuts to 45 ft. lbs. (61 Nm).
31. If removed, drive the bearing races into the rotor using a suitable driver. Pack the inner and outer wheel bearings and the lip of a new seal with high-temperature wheel bearing grease.
32. Position the inner wheel bearing in the race and install the seal using a seal installer. Install the rotor on the spindle and install the outer wheel bearing in the race.
33. Install the wheel bearing, locknut, thrust bearing, snapring and locking hubs.
34. Install the caliper and the wheel and tire assemblies. Lower the vehicle.

Manual Locking Hubs

REMOVAL AND INSTALLATION

1994–96 B-Series Pick-Up and Navajo

1. Raise and support the vehicle safely.
2. Remove the lug nuts and remove the wheel and tire assembly.
3. Remove the retainer washers from the lug nut studs and remove the manual locking hub assembly. To remove the internal hub lock assembly from the outer body assembly, remove the outer lock ring seated in the hub body groove. The internal assembly, spring and clutch gear will now slide out of the hub body. Do not remove the screw from the plastic dial.
4. Rebuild the hub assembly in the reverse order of disassembly.
5. Adjust the wheel bearing if necessary. Install the manual locking hub assembly over the spindle and place the retainer washers on the lug nut studs.
6. Install the wheel and tire assembly and lower the vehicle.

ADJUSTMENT

1994–96 B-Series Pick-Up and Navajo

1. Raise and safely support the vehicle. Remove the wheel and tire assembly.
2. Remove the retainer washers from the lug nut studs and remove the manual locking hub assembly from the spindle.
3. Remove the snapring from the end of the spindle shaft.
4. Remove the axle shaft spacer.
5. Remove the outer wheel bearing locknut from the spindle using locknut wrench 49 UN01 042 or equivalent. Make sure the tabs on the tool engage the slots in the locknut.
6. Remove the locknut washer from the spindle.
7. Loosen the inner wheel bearing locknut using the locknut wrench. Make sure the tabs on the tool engage the slots in the locknut and the slot in the tool is centered over the locknut pin.
8. Tighten the inner locknut to 35 ft. lbs. (47 Nm) to seat the bearings.
9. Spin the rotor and back off the inner locknut 1/4 turn. Retighten the inner locknut to 16 inch lbs. (1.8 Nm). Install the lockwasher on the spindle. It may be necessary to tighten the inner locknut slightly so the pin on the locknut aligns with the closest hole in the lockwasher.
10. Install the outer wheel bearing locknut using the locknut wrench. Tighten the locknut to 150 ft. lbs. (203 Nm).
11. Install the axle shaft spacer.
12. Clip the snapring onto the end of the spindle. Install the manual hub assembly over the spindle and install the retainer washers.
13. Install the wheel and tire assembly. Check the endplay of the wheel and tire assembly on the spindle. Final endplay should be 0–0.003 in. (0–0.08mm). The maximum torque to rotate the hub should be 25 inch lbs. (2.8 Nm).
14. Lower the vehicle.

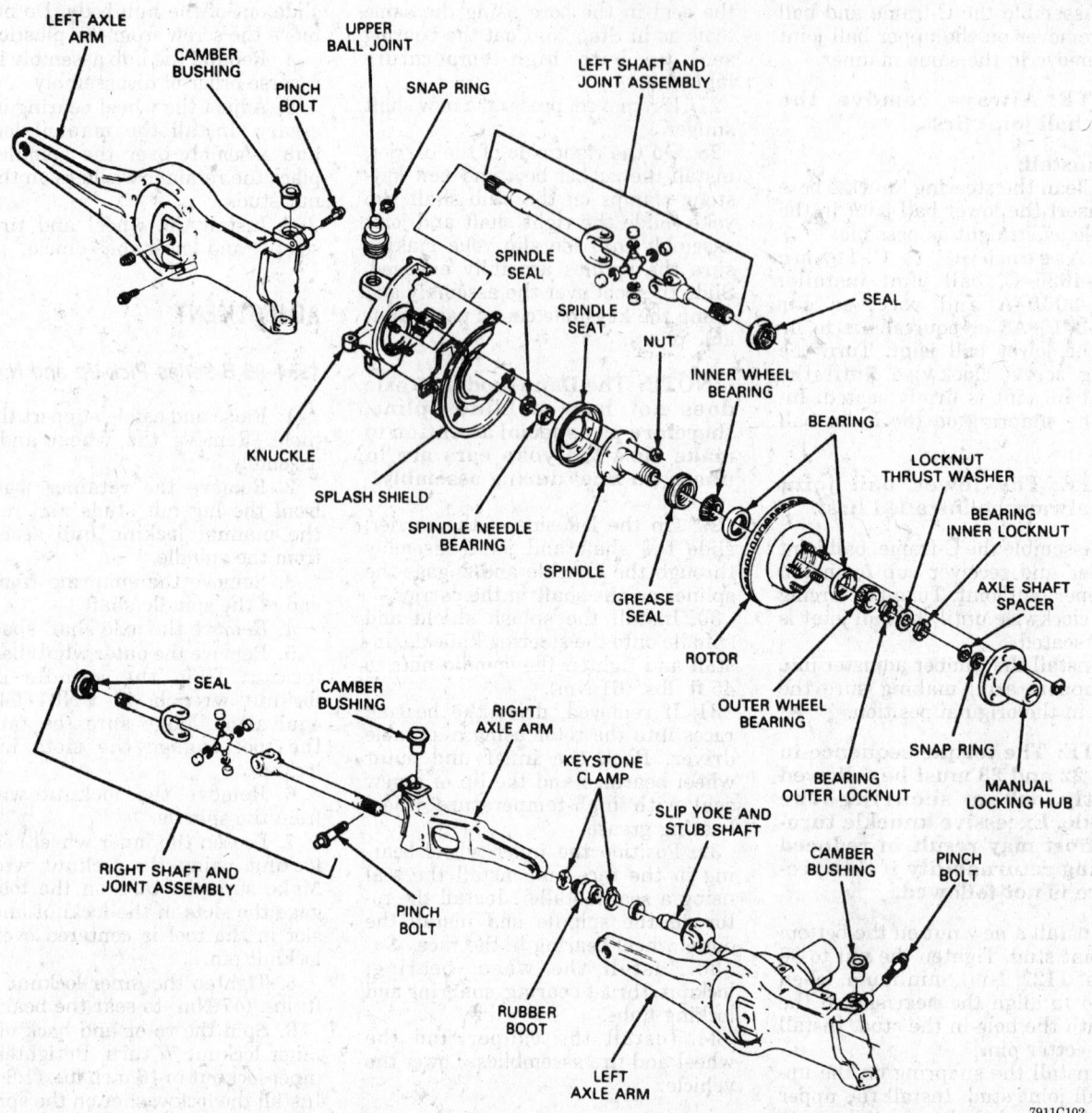

Front axle shaft, hub, knuckle and bearing assembly — 1994–96 B-Series Pick-Up and Navajo

Automatic Locking Hubs

REMOVAL AND INSTALLATION

1994–96 B-Series Pick-Up and Navajo

1. Raise and support the vehicle safely. Remove the wheel lug nuts and remove the wheel and tire assembly.

2. Remove the retainer washers from the lug nut studs and remove the automatic locking hub assembly from the spindle.

3. Remove the snapring from the end of the spindle shaft.

4. Remove the axle shaft spacer.

5. Being careful not to damage the plastic moving cam or thrust spacers, pull the cam assembly off the wheel bearing adjusting nut. Remove the 2 plastic thrust spacers from the adjusting nut.

6. Using a magnet, remove the locking key. It may be necessary to rotate the adjusting nut slightly to relieve the pressure against the locking key, before the key can be removed.

NOTE: To prevent damage to the spindle threads, look into the spindle keyway under the adjusting nut and remove the separate locking key before removing the adjusting nut.

7. Loosen the wheel bearing adjusting nut from the spindle using a 2⅜ in. hex socket tool.

8. While rotating the hub and rotor assembly, tighten the wheel bearing adjusting nut to 35 ft. lbs. (47 Nm) to seat the bearings. Spin the rotor and back off the nut ¼ turn.

9. Retighten the adjusting nut to 16 inch lbs. (1.8 Nm) using a torque wrench. Align the closest hole in the wheel bearing adjusting nut with the center of the spindle keyway slot. Advance the nut to the next lug if required. Install the separate locking

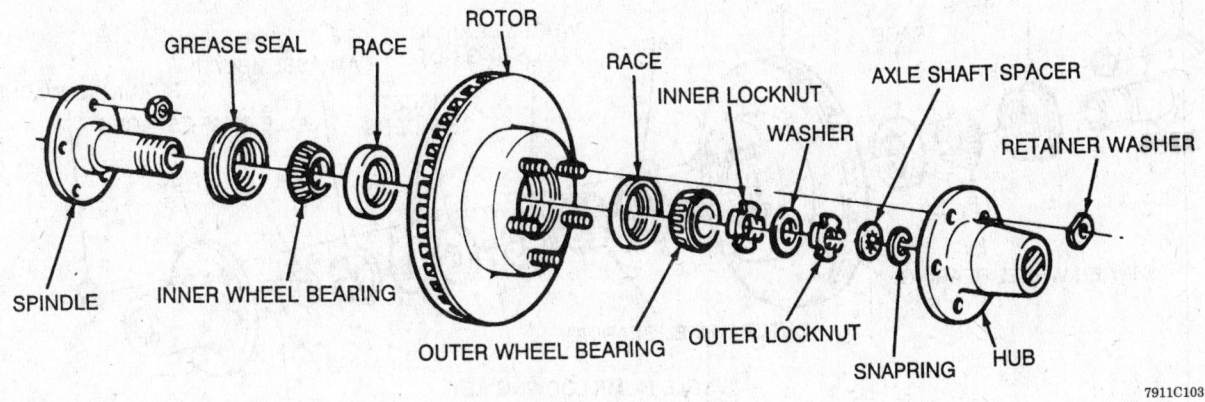

GREASE SEAL   RACE   ROTOR   RACE   INNER LOCKNUT   AXLE SHAFT SPACER   WASHER   RETAINER WASHER

SPINDLE   INNER WHEEL BEARING   OUTER WHEEL BEARING   OUTER LOCKNUT   SNAPRING   HUB

7911C103

Manual locking hub assembly — Navajo

key in the spindle keyway under the adjusting nut.

NOTE: Extreme care must be taken when aligning the spindle nut adjustment lug with the center of the spindle keyway slot to prevent damage to the separate locking key.

10. Install the 2 thrust spacers. Push or press the cam assembly onto the locknut by lining up the key in the fixed cam with the spindle keyway.

NOTE: Extreme care must be taken when aligning the fixed cam key with the spindle keyway to prevent damage to the fixed cam.

11. Install the axle shaft spacer.
12. Clip the snapring onto the end of the spindle.
13. Install the automatic locking hub assembly over the spindle by lining up the 3 legs in the hub assembly with the 3 pockets in the cam assembly. Install the retainer washers.
14. Install the wheel and tire assembly. Check the endplay of the wheel and tire assembly on the spindle. Final endplay should be 0–0.003

in. (0–0.08mm). The maximum torque to rotate the hub should be 25 inch lbs. (2.8 Nm).
15. Lower the vehicle.

Freewheel Mechanism

REMOVAL AND INSTALLATION

NOTE: The Remote Freewheel Mechanism on 4WD B-Series Pick-Up and the Automatic Freewheel Mechanism on 4WD MPV are used in place of automatic locking hubs.

1. Disconnect the negative battery cable. Raise and safely support the vehicle. Remove the left front wheel and tire assembly.
2. Drain the fluid from the front differential.
3. Remove the left side halfshaft assembly.
4. Tag and disconnect the vacuum hoses and electrical connector from the control box assembly.
5. Remove and discard the snap pin at the control box assembly.
6. Remove the attaching bolts and remove the joint shaft assembly.

7. Remove the attaching bolts and remove the control box assembly.
8. Remove the gear sleeve from the side of the differential, if necessary.
9. If necessary, remove the output shaft from the differential using a slide hammer.
To install:
10. If removed, install a new clip on the end of the output shaft and install in the differential. Install the gear sleeve, if removed.
11. Install the control box and tighten the attaching bolts to 17–20 ft. lbs. (23–26 Nm).
12. Install the joint shaft assembly and tighten the attaching bolts to 27–40 ft. lbs. (36–54 Nm). On MPV, install the attaching nut and tighten to 49–72 ft. lbs. (67–97 Nm).
13. Install a new snap pin at the control box assembly.
14. Connect the electrical connector and vacuum hoses at the control box assembly.
15. Install the left side halfshaft assembly.
16. Fill the differential with the proper type and quantity of fluid.
17. Install the wheel and tire assembly and lower the vehicle.

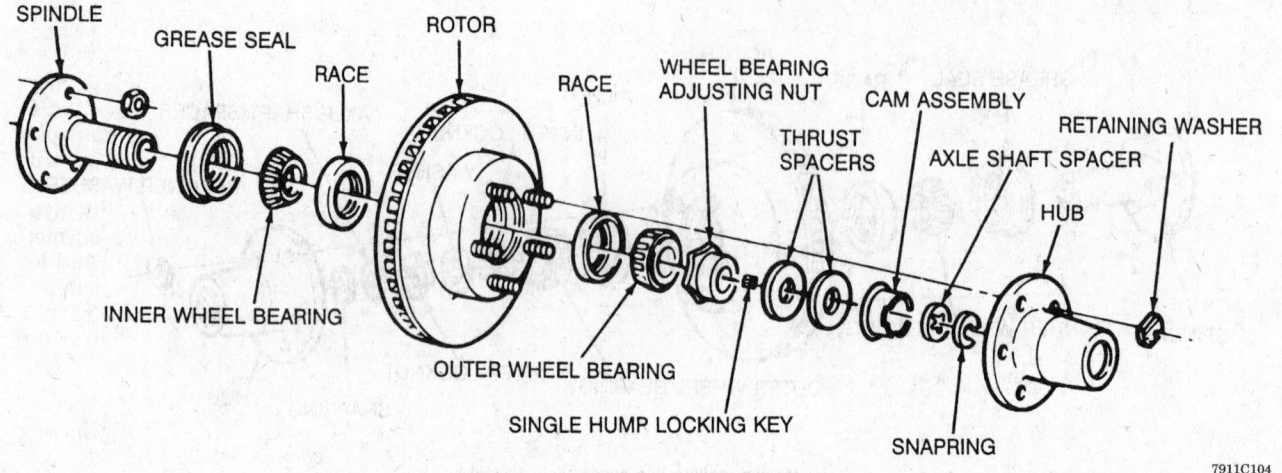

SPINDLE
GREASE SEAL
RACE
ROTOR
RACE
WHEEL BEARING ADJUSTING NUT
THRUST SPACERS
CAM ASSEMBLY
AXLE SHAFT SPACER
RETAINING WASHER
HUB
INNER WHEEL BEARING
OUTER WHEEL BEARING
SINGLE HUMP LOCKING KEY
SNAPRING

7911C104

Automatic locking hub assembly — 1994–96 B-Series Pick-Up and Navajo

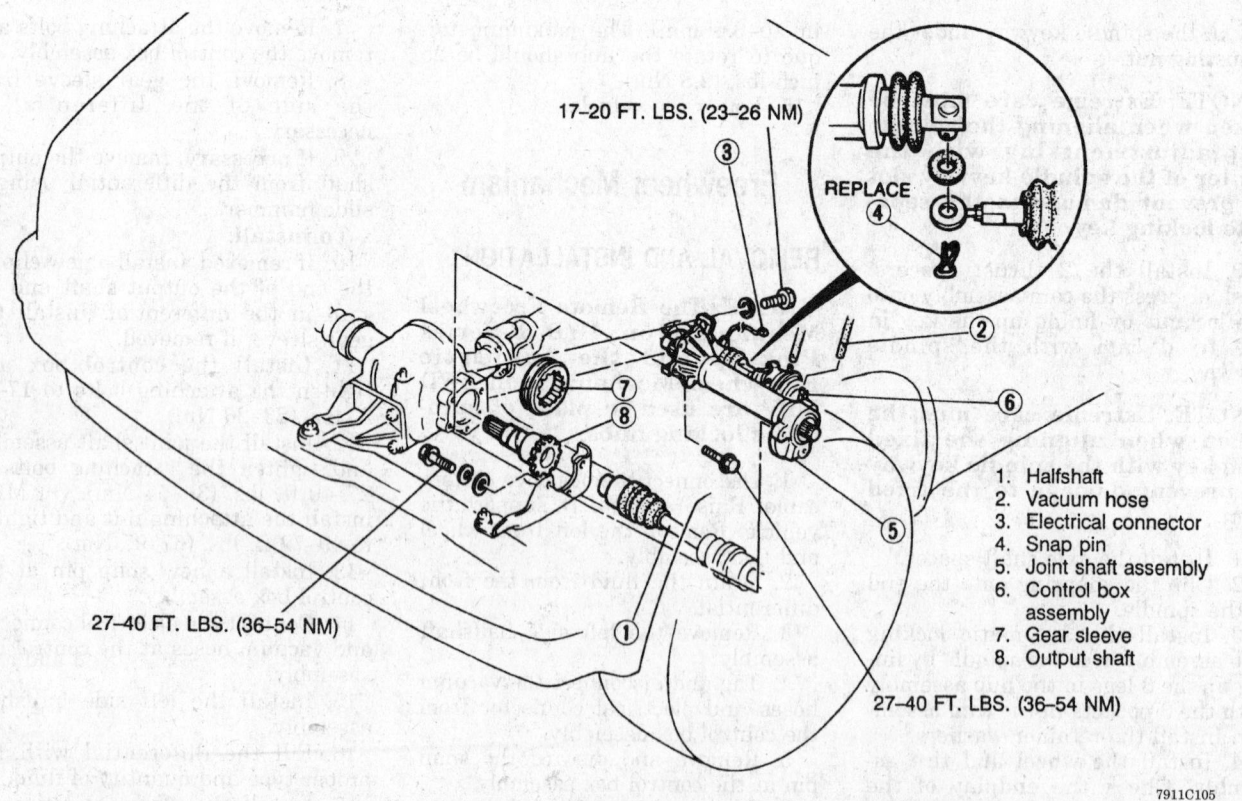

17–20 FT. LBS. (23–26 NM)

REPLACE

27–40 FT. LBS. (36–54 NM)

27–40 FT. LBS. (36–54 NM)

1. Halfshaft
2. Vacuum hose
3. Electrical connector
4. Snap pin
5. Joint shaft assembly
6. Control box assembly
7. Gear sleeve
8. Output shaft

7911C105

Remote Freewheel Mechanism installation — 4WD B-Series Pick-Up; MPV similar

Pinion Seal

REMOVAL AND INSTALLATION

NOTE: This service procedure disturbs the pinion bearing preload and this preload must be carefully reset when assembling.

1. Raise the vehicle and support it safely.
2. Remove the wheels and the brake drums.
3. Mark the driveshaft and the axle companion flange so the driveshaft can be reinstalled in the same position. Remove the driveshaft.
4. Using an inch pound torque wrench on the pinion nut, record the torque required to maintain rotation of the pinion through several revolutions.
5. While holding the companion flange with a suitable tool, remove the pinion nut. Mark the companion flange in relation to the pinion shaft so the flange can be reinstalled in the same position.
6. Using a suitable puller, remove the rear axle companion flange. Use a small prybar to remove the seal from the carrier.
To install:
7. Make sure the splines of the pinion shaft are free of burrs.
8. Apply grease to the lips of the pinion seal and install, using a seal installer.
9. Check the seal surface of the companion flange for scratches, nicks or a groove. Replace the companion flange, as necessary. Apply a small amount of lubricant to the splines. Align the mark on the flange with the mark on the pinion shaft and install the companion flange.

NOTE: The companion flange must never be hammered on or installed with power tools.

10. Install a new nut on the pinion shaft. Hold the companion flange with a suitable tool while tightening the nut.
11. Tighten the pinion nut, rotating the pinion occasionally to ensure proper bearing seating. Take frequent pinion bearing torque preload readings until the original recorded preload reading is obtained.

NOTE: Under no circumstances should the pinion nut be backed off to reduce preload. If reduced preload is required, a new collapsible pinion spacer and pinion nut must be installed.

12. Install the driveshaft and check the fluid level in the carrier. Lower the vehicle.

Differential Carrier

REMOVAL AND INSTALLATION

Front

B SERIES PICK-UP

NOTE: The differential is removed as a unit with the freewheel mechanism. After removal, the differential can then be separated from the freewheel mechanism, if necessary.

1. Raise and safely support the vehicle. Remove the wheel and tire assemblies.
2. Remove the splash shield and drain the differential fluid.
3. Remove the halfshafts.
4. Mark the position of the driveshaft on the axle flange and remove the driveshaft.
5. Tag and disconnect the vacuum hoses and electrical connector from the freewheel mechanism control box.
6. Support the differential with a jack.
7. Remove the crossmember bolts adjacent to the lower control arm. Lower the differential/crossmembers assembly from the vehicle.
8. Remove the crossmembers from the differential, if necessary. Remove the freewheel mechanism from the differential, if necessary.
To install:
9. If removed, install the freewheel mechanism.
10. If removed, install the differential to the crossmembers.
11. Raise the differential/crossmembers assembly into position. Install the crossmember mounting bolts and tighten to 69–85 ft. lbs. (93–116 Nm). Remove the jack.
12. Install the remaining components in the reverse order of their removal. Fill the differential with the proper type and quantity of fluid.

MPV

NOTE: The differential is removed as a unit with the freewheel mechanism. After removal, the differential can then be separated from the freewheel mechanism, if necessary.

1. Raise and safely support the vehicle. Remove the wheel and tire assemblies.
2. Remove the splash shield and drain the differential fluid.
3. Remove the halfshafts.
4. Mark the position of the driveshaft on the axle flange and remove the driveshaft.
5. Tag and disconnect the vacuum hoses and electrical connector from the freewheel mechanism control box.
6. Support the differential with a jack.
7. Remove the bolts/nuts attaching the differential/freewheel mechanism assembly in 3 places and lower the assembly from the vehicle.
8. If necessary, separate the freewheel mechanism from the differential.
To install:
9. If removed, install the freewheel mechanism.
10. Raise the differential/freewheel mechanism assembly into position and install the attaching bolts/nuts. Tighten to 49–72 ft. lbs. (67–97 Nm). Remove the jack.
11. Install the remaining components in the reverse order of their removal. Fill the differential with the proper type and quantity of fluid.

Rear

1. Raise and safely support the vehicle. Remove the wheel and tire assemblies.
2. Drain the fluid from the differential.
3. Remove the axle shafts.
4. Mark the position of the driveshaft on the axle flange and remove the driveshaft.
5. Disconnect the rear wheel anti-lock brake sensor, if equipped.
6. Remove the differential attaching nuts/bolts and remove the differential.
To install:
7. Clean all old sealant from the axle housing and differential mating surfaces.
8. Apply sealant to the stud threads and the differential and axle housing surfaces.
9. Install the differential to the axle housing. Tighten the attaching nuts/bolts to 17–20 ft. lbs. (23–26 Nm).
10. Install the remaining components in the reverse order of removal. Fill the differential with the proper type and quantity of fluid.

Axle Housing

REMOVAL AND INSTALLATION

Front

1994-96 B-SERIES PICK-UP AND NAVAJO

1. Raise and safely support the vehicle. Remove the front axle shaft and spindle assemblies.

2. Mark the front axle yoke and the driveshaft so they can be reassembled in the same position. Disconnect the driveshaft from the front axle yoke.

3. Remove the cotter pin and nut retaining the steering linkage to the knuckle. Disconnect the linkage from the knuckle.

4. Remove the left stabilizer bar link lower bolt and remove the link from the radius arm bracket.

5. Position a jack under the left axle arm and slightly compress the coil spring. Remove the shock absorber lower nut and disconnect the shock absorber from the radius arm bracket.

6. Remove the nut that retains the lower part of the spring to the axle arm. Slowly lower the jack and remove the coil spring, spacer, seat and stud.

7. Remove the stud and bolts that connect the radius arm bracket and radius arm to the axle arm. Remove the bracket and radius arm.

8. Position another jack under the differential housing. Remove the bolt that connects the left axle arm to the axle pivot bracket. Lower the jacks and remove the left axle arm assembly.

To install:

9. Position a jack under the left support arm and raise the arm into position in the pivot bracket. Install the nut and bolt and tighten to 120-150 ft. lbs. (163-203 Nm). Do not remove the jack from under the differential housing at this time.

10. Position the radius arm and front bracket on the left axle arm. Install a new stud and nut on the top of the axle and radius arm assembly and tighten to 190-230 ft. lbs. (258-311 Nm). Install the bolts in the front of the bracket and tighten to 27-37 ft. lbs. (37-50 Nm).

11. Install the seat, spacer retainer and coil spring on the stud and nut. Raise the jack to compress the coil spring. Install the nut and tighten to 70-100 ft. lbs. (95-135 Nm).

12. Connect the shock absorber to the radius arm. Install the nut and tighten to 42-72 ft. lbs. (57-97 Nm).

13. Connect the tie rod ball joint to the knuckle. Install the nut and tighten to 50-75 ft. lbs. (68-101 Nm). Install the stabilizer bar mounting bracket and tighten to 203-240 ft. lbs. (275-325 Nm).

14. Connect the front driveshaft to the front axle yoke, aligning the marks that were made during removal. Install the U-bolts and tighten the nuts to 8-15 ft. lbs. (11-20 Nm).

15. Install the spindle and axle shaft assemblies. Lower the vehicle.

Rear

2WD 1992-93 B-SERIES PICK-UP

1. Raise and safely support the vehicle. Remove the rear wheel and tire assemblies.

2. Remove the brake drums and brake shoes. Disconnect the parking brake cables from the backing plate.

3. Mark the position of the driveshaft on the axle flange and remove the driveshaft.

4. Disconnect and plug the flexible brake hose at the axle housing or chassis.

5. Disconnect the rear wheel anti-lock brake sensor, if equipped.

6. Support the axle housing with a jack.

7. Disconnect the shock absorbers at the spring clamp.

8. Remove the nuts from the U-bolts and remove the U-bolts and spring clamp.

9. While supporting the axle housing with the jack, move the axle housing to one side of the vehicle until the axle flange clears the leaf spring.

10. Tilt the axle housing downward and move it to the other side of the vehicle while lowering the jack. Lower the axle housing completely when the other axle flange clears the leaf spring.

To install:

11. Raise the axle housing to just below the leaf springs.

12. Move the axle housing to one side of the vehicle until the axle flange will clear the leaf spring, then tilt the axle housing upward and raise it until one side of the axle housing is over the leaf spring.

13. Move the axle housing to the opposite side of the vehicle and raise it until the other side of the housing is above the leaf spring. Move the housing into position on the leaf springs.

14. Install the spring clamps, U-bolts and nuts. Tighten the nuts to 47-58 ft. lbs. (64-78 Nm).

15. Connect the shock absorbers to the spring clamp and tighten the

nuts to 47-58 ft. lbs. (64-78 Nm). Remove the jack.

16. Install the remaining components in the reverse order of removal. Bleed the brake system.

4WD 1992-93 B-SERIES PICK-UP

1. Raise and safely support the vehicle. Remove the rear wheel and tire assemblies.

2. Remove the brake drums and brake shoes. Disconnect the parking brake cables from the backing plate.

3. Mark the position of the driveshaft on the axle flange and remove the driveshaft.

4. Disconnect and plug the flexible brake hose at the axle housing or chassis.

5. Disconnect the rear wheel anti-lock brake sensor, if equipped.

6. Support the axle housing with a jack.

7. Disconnect the shock absorbers at the axle housing.

8. Remove the nuts from the U-bolts and remove the U-bolts and spring clamp.

9. Lower the axle housing from the vehicle.

To install:

10. Raise the axle housing into position.

11. Install the U-bolts and spring clamps and tighten to 88-101 ft. lbs. (120-137 Nm).

12. Connect the shock absorbers at the axle housing and tighten the nuts and bolts to 47-58 ft. lbs. (64-78 Nm). Remove the jack.

13. Install the remaining components in the reverse order of removal. Bleed the brake system.

MPV

1. Raise and safely support the vehicle. Remove the rear wheel and tire assemblies.

2. Remove the brake drums and brake shoes. Disconnect the parking brake cables from the backing plate.

3. Mark the position of the driveshaft on the axle flange and remove the driveshaft.

4. Disconnect and plug the flexible brake hose at the axle housing or chassis.

5. Disconnect the rear wheel anti-lock brake sensor, if equipped.

6. Remove the rear stabilizer bar, if equipped.

7. Support the axle housing with a jack.

8. Disconnect the shock absorbers at the axle housing.

9. If equipped, remove the nut and disconnect the height sensor link from the axle housing.

10. Remove the lateral rod.

11. Slowly lower the axle housing until the coil spring tension is relieved. Remove the coil springs.

12. Remove the upper and lower control arms from the axle housing and lower the housing from the vehicle.

To install:

13. Raise the axle housing into position.

14. Connect the upper and lower control arms to the axle housing and snug the attaching bolts and nuts.

15. Install the coil springs. Install the lateral rod and snug the attaching bolts. Connect the height sensor link, if equipped.

16. Connect the shock absorbers to the axle housing and snug the attaching bolts and nuts. Remove the jack from the axle housing.

17. Install the stabilizer bar and snug the attaching bolts.

18. Connect the rear wheel anti-lock brake sensor, if equipped. Connect the height sensor link to the axle housing, if equipped.

19. Connect the brake hose to the brake line.

20. Install the driveshaft, aligning the marks that were made during the removal procedure.

21. Connect the parking brake cables to the backing plates. Install the brake shoes and the brake drums.

22. Install the wheel and tire assemblies and lower the vehicle.

23. With the vehicle in the normal ride height position, tighten the following to specification:

Control arm nuts and bolts: 108–127 ft. lbs. (146–167 Nm)

Lateral arm nuts: 108–127 ft. lbs. (146–167 Nm)

Shock absorber nuts and bolts: 56–76 ft. lbs. (76–103 Nm)

Stabilizer bar bushing mount bolts: 23–38 ft. lbs. (34–51 Nm)

1994–96 B-SERIES PICK-UP AND NAVAJO

1. Raise the vehicle and support it safely.

2. Remove the cover and drain the lubricant from the axle.

3. Remove the rear wheel and tire assemblies and remove the rear anti-lock brake system sensor. Remove the axle shafts.

4. Remove the 4 retaining nuts from each backing plate. Wire the backing plates to the underbody.

5. Disconnect the vent hose from the axle housing. Remove the connector from the rear anti-lock sensor.

6. Remove the brake line from the clips that retain the line to the axle housing.

7. Remove the hydraulic brake junction block from the axle housing. Do not open the hydraulic brake system lines.

8. Mark the driveshaft and the axle companion flange so they can be reassembled in the same position. Remove the driveshaft.

9. Support the rear axle housing on a jack, then remove the axle housing U-bolt nuts. Remove the U-bolts and shock absorber plates. Leave the shock absorbers attached to the plates.

10. Remove the stabilizer bar attaching bracket bolts from the axle housing and position the stabilizer bar assembly away from the axle housing.

11. Raise the axle housing off the springs with the jack and move to the right side of the vehicle. Lower the left side of the axle housing below the left spring enough to clear the spring.

12. Remove the axle housing from the vehicle by lowering the axle and moving to the left until the right axle tube clears the right spring.

To install:

13. Install the axle housing on the transmission jack. Guide the right side of the axle housing over the right spring. Lift the left side of the axle housing over the left spring and position the axle housing on the spring center bolts.

14. Install the stabilizer bar to the axle housing. Tighten the stabilizer bar bracket bolts to 30–42 ft. lbs. (40–57 Nm).

15. Install the axle housing U-bolts over the axle tube. Position the shock absorber plates under the springs and install the U-bolts through the holes. Install the nuts and tighten to 88–108 ft. lbs. (119–146 Nm).

16. Install the axle vent tube to the axle vent fitting and secure with a clamp. Connect the rear anti-lock sensor connector.

17. Install the brake backing plates on the axle housing flanges. Tighten the nuts to 20–40 ft. lbs. (28–54 Nm).

18. Position the brake lines to the axle housing and secure with the retaining clips. Position the brake junction block to the axle housing and install the retaining screw.

19. Install the axle shafts. Install the driveshaft, aligning the marks that were made during removal. Tighten the attaching bolts to 70–95 ft. lbs. (95–128 Nm).

20. Install the brake drums and the wheel and tire assemblies.

21. Clean all old sealer from the carrier surface. Apply a bead of RTV sealer ⅛–¼ in. wide. The bead should be continuous and should not pass through or outside the holes.

22. Install a new cover and tighten the bolts to 15–20 ft. lbs. (21–27 Nm) in a criss-cross pattern.

23. Add the proper type of lubricant through the filler hole until the lubricant level is ¼–⁹⁄₁₆ in. below the bottom of the filler hole with the axle in the running position.

24. Lower the vehicle.

STEERING

Steering Wheel

REMOVAL AND INSTALLATION

1. Disconnect the negative battery cable.

2. Remove the steering wheel pad from the steering wheel. Pull the pad back and disconnect the horn switch and, if equipped, cruise control wires. Remove the steering wheel pad.

3. Remove the steering wheel attaching bolt or nut. Check to see if the steering wheel and steering shaft have alignment marks or flats. If there are no steering wheel-to-steering column shaft alignment marks or flats, matchmark the steering wheel and column shaft so they can be reassembled in the same position.

4. Using a suitable puller, remove the steering wheel from the steering column shaft.

NOTE: Do not hammer on the steering wheel or steering shaft or use a knock-off type steering wheel puller, as either will damage the steering column.

To install:

5. Install the steering wheel on the steering column shaft, aligning the marks or flats on the steering wheel with the marks or flats on the steering shaft.

6. On all except Navajo, install the steering wheel attaching nut and tighten to 29–36 ft. lbs. (39–49 Nm). On Navajo, install the steering wheel attaching bolt and tighten to 23–33 ft. lbs. (31–45 Nm).

7. Connect the horn switch and, if equipped, cruise control wires and install the steering wheel pad.

8. Connect the negative battery and check the steering column for proper operation.

Steering Column

REMOVAL AND INSTALLATION

Except 1994–96 B-Series Pick-Up and Navajo

1. Disconnect the negative battery cable. Place the front wheels in the straight-ahead position.
2. Remove the steering wheel.
3. Remove the steering column covers and remove the combination switch.
4. Remove the necessary dash panels from under the steering column.
5. Disconnect the automatic transmission interlock cable, if equipped. Tag and disconnect the necessary electrical connectors.
6. Disconnect the steering column from the steering linkage by removing the bolt at the intermediate shaft universal joint. Mark the position of the intermediate shaft on the column shaft before disconnecting so they can be reassembled in the same position.
7. Remove the nuts attaching the column at the firewall.
8. Support the steering column and remove the bolts attaching the column to the underside of the dash. Remove the steering column.
9. Installation is the reverse of the removal procedure. Tighten the bolts attaching the steering column to the underside of the dash to 12–17 ft. lbs. (16–23 Nm). Tighten the nuts attaching the column at the firewall to 14–19 ft. lbs. (19–26 Nm) on B-Series Pick-Up or 12–17 ft. lbs. (16–23 Nm) on MPV.
10. Align the marks that were made on the intermediate shaft and steering column shaft during removal. Tighten the intermediate shaft universal joint bolt to 13–18 ft. lbs. (18–25 Nm).

1994–96 B-Series Pick-Up and Navajo

1. Disconnect the negative battery cable and apply the parking brake. Place automatic transmission in **N**.
2. Remove the bolt that holds the intermediate shaft to the steering column shaft. Using a prybar, compress the intermediate shaft until it is clear of the steering column shaft.
3. If equipped with automatic transmission, remove the nuts from the studs and remove the shift cable bracket from the steering column bracket. Disconnect the shift cable from the column lever.
4. Remove the steering wheel. If equipped with tilt column, make sure

the steering wheel is in the full up position before removal.
5. If equipped with tilt column, remove the tilt lever and remove the column collar by pressing on the collar from the top and bottom while removing the collar.
6. Remove the retaining screws and remove the panel trim cover.
7. Remove the 2 screws from the bottom of the column shroud. Remove the bottom half of the shroud by pulling the shroud down and toward the rear of the vehicle. If equipped with automatic transmission, move the shift lever as required to ease shroud removal. Lift the top half of the shroud from the column.
8. If equipped with automatic transmission, disconnect the selector indicator cable by removing the screw from the column casting and the plastic plug at the end of the cable. To remove the plastic plug from the shift lever socket casting, push on the nose of the plug until the head clears the casting, then pull the plug from the casting.
9. Remove the plastic clip that holds the combination switch wiring to the steering column bracket. Remove the 2 screws from the combination switch and remove the switch from the column, leaving the wiring connectors attached to the switch. Position the switch and wiring aside.
10. Disconnect the key warning buzzer wire from the horn brush wire. Remove the screw that holds the horn brush connector to the column and remove the connector.
11. Remove the 5 screws that hold the toe plate to the dash panel and loosen the toe plate clamp bolt.
12. Support the column and remove the bolts that hold the breakaway bracket to the pedal support bracket. Pry apart the locking tabs and disconnect the ignition switch wiring harness.
13. Carefully remove the column from the vehicle.
To install:
14. Carefully position the column in the hole in the vehicle floor. Connect the ignition switch wiring harness to the column connect
15. Install the bolts that hold the breakaway bracket to the pedal support bracket, but do not tighten at this ti
16. Tighten the bolts that hold the toe plate to the floor to 8 ft. lbs. (11 Nm), then tighten the breakaway bracket-to-pedal support bracket bolts to 19–27 ft. lbs. (25–36 Nm). Tighten the toe plate clamp to 6–13 ft. lbs. (8–18 Nm).

17. Install the horn brush connector to the column and tighten the retaining screw to 21–29 inch lbs. (2.3–3.3 Nm). Attach the key warning buzzer wire connector to the horn brush wire. Route the wiring to prevent contact with moving parts.
18. Position the combination switch on the column with the attaching screws. Tighten to 18–26 inch lbs. (2–3 Nm). Install the plastic clip that holds the switch wiring to the steering column breakaway bracket.
19. If equipped with automatic transmission, connect the selector indicator cable by pushing the plastic plug at the end of the cable into the shift lever socket casting. When installed, the nose of the plug should be facing the steering wheel and the head of the plug away from the wheel. Install the cable retaining screw in the column and adjust the cable. If the shift lever was removed, install it at this time.
20. Position the top half of the shroud on the column so the screw moldings on the shroud seat in the mounting bores in the column. Place the automatic transmission shift lever in the lowest position to aid assembly.
21. Install the bottom half of the shroud by sliding the guides in the shroud bottom half into the tabs in the shroud top half. Install the shroud retaining screws and tighten to 6–10 inch lbs. (0.7–1.1 Nm).
22. If equipped with tilt column, install the column collar by pressing on the collar from the top and bottom while installing the collar on the column. Install the tilt lever and tighten to 2.2–3.6 ft. lbs. (3–5 Nm).
23. If equipped, place the automatic transmission selector lever in **N**. Install the steering wheel and the lower trim cover panel.
24. If equipped with automatic transmission, install the nuts on the studs and install the shift cable bracket on the steering column bracket. Connect the shift cable to the column lever.
25. Connect the column shaft to the intermediate shaft U-joint and tighten the pinch bolt to 25–35 ft. lbs. (34–47 Nm). The intermediate shaft must be in collapsed state to align, both shafts have a flat side, and then pulled up the column shaft until the bolt holes align. Make sure the intermediate shaft does not contact the plastic retainer at the base of the column. If it does, pull the lower shaft of the column slightly out of the column.
26. Connect the negative battery cable and check the adjustment of the

selector indicator cable. Pull the shift lever toward the steering wheel until the **OD** detent in the transmission is felt. Release the shift lever, it should be against the detent wall in the column.

27. Release the parking brake lever and test drive the vehicle.

Manual Steering Gear

ADJUSTMENT

1992–93 B-Series Pick-Up

1. Remove the steering gear and mount the assembly in a vise.
2. Set the toe of a dial indicator at the end of the Pitman arm.
3. Loosen the locknut and turn the adjusting screw until there is no backlash.

NOTE: Adjust the backlash with the steering gear in the center position. Otherwise, the backlash becomes excessively small and the gears may become damaged.

4. Reinstall the steering gear in the vehicle.

REMOVAL AND INSTALLATION

1992–93 B-Series Pick-Up

1. Position the front wheels in the straight-ahead position. Raise and safely support the vehicle.
2. Remove the pinch bolt securing the worm shaft to the intermediate shaft coupling.
3. Remove the cotter pin and nut from the Pitman arm stud. Use separator tool 49 0118 850C or equivalent, to separate the Pitman arm from the center link.
4. Support the steering gear and remove the steering gear attaching bolts/nuts. Remove the steering gear from the vehicle.

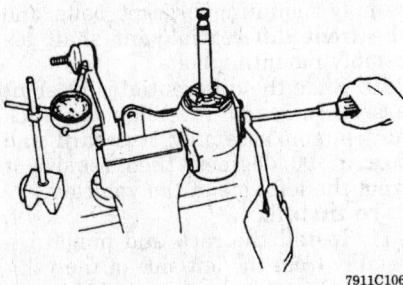

7911C106

Manual steering gear adjustment — B-Series Pick-Up

5. Installation is the reverse of the removal procedure. Tighten the steering gear-to-chassis bolts/nuts to 46–69 ft. lbs. (63–93 Nm). Tighten the Pitman arm stud nut to 33–43 ft. lbs. (44–59 Nm) and install a new cotter pin. Tighten the worm shaft-to-intermediate shaft coupling pinch bolt to 22–38 ft. lbs. (30–38 Nm).

Power Steering Gear

ADJUSTMENT

1992–93 B-Series Pick-Up

1. Remove the power steering gear from the vehicle and install in a suitable holding fixture.
2. Position the worm shaft in the center position.
3. Install tool 49 0180 510B or equivalent, on the end of the worm shaft and attach a pull scale to the end of the tool.
4. Set the sector shaft adjusting screw so the preload with the worm shaft in the center position is 1.3–2.0 lbs.

NOTE: The preload at the center position must be 0.4–0.9 lbs. higher than the preload when the worm shaft is turned 360 degrees to the left and right.

5. If the specified preload is not obtained, disassemble the steering gear and check for dirt and foreign material and that the oil seal is correctly installed. Reassemble the steering gear and adjust the preload.
6. After adjustment, tighten the sector shaft adjusting screw locknut to 25–35 ft. lbs. (34–47 Nm).
7. Reinstall the steering gear in the vehicle.

1994–96 B-Series Pick-Up and Navajo

1. Raise and safely support the vehicle. Disconnect the Pitman arm from the sector shaft using puller T64P–3590–F or equivalent.
2. Disconnect the fluid return line at the reservoir and cap the reservoir return line tube. Place the end of the return line in a clean container and turn the steering wheel from stop to stop several times to empty the steering gear. Discard the fluid.
3. Turn the steering wheel to 45 degrees from the right stop.
4. Attach an inch pound torque wrench to steering wheel nut and record the torque required to rotate the shaft slowly approximately 1/8 turn toward center from the 45 degree position.

5. Turn the steering gear back to center and record the torque required to rotate the shaft back and forth across the center position.
6. If the vehicle has less than 5000 miles, resetting is required if total mesh-load over center is not 12–24 inch lbs. If the vehicle has more than 5000 miles or the sector shaft has been replaced, resetting is required if mesh-load over center is less than 10 inch lbs. greater than the torque 45 degrees from the right stop.
7. The set torque specification is measured rocking across center to a value of 9–13 inch lbs. greater than that measured 45 degrees from the right stop.
8. If reset is required, loosen the locknut and turn the sector shaft adjusting screw until the reading is the specified value greater than the torque at 45 degrees from the stop.
9. Tighten the adjusting screw locknut and recheck. Install the Pitman arm and steering wheel cover.
10. Connect the fluid return line to the reservoir and refill the system with fluid. Bleed the system.

REMOVAL AND INSTALLATION

1992–93 B-Series Pick-Up

1. Position the front wheels in the straight-ahead position. Raise and safely support the vehicle.
2. Remove the pinch bolt securing the worm shaft to the intermediate shaft coupling.
3. Disconnect and plug the power steering fluid lines at the steering gear.
4. Remove the cotter pin and nut from the Pitman arm stud. Use separator tool 49 0118 850C or equivalent, to separate the Pitman arm from the center link.
5. Support the steering gear and remove the steering gear attaching bolts/nuts. Remove the steering gear from the vehicle.

To install:

6. Install the steering gear and tighten the steering gear-to-chassis bolts/nuts to 46–69 ft. lbs. (63–93 Nm).
7. Connect the Pitman arm and tighten the Pitman arm stud nut to 33–43 ft. lbs. (44–59 Nm). Install a new cotter pin.
8. Connect the worm shaft-to-intermediate shaft coupling and tighten the worm shaft-to-intermediate shaft coupling pinch bolt to 22–38 ft. lbs. (30–38 Nm).
9. Connect the power steering fluid lines. Tighten the pressure line nut to 17–26 ft. lbs. (24–35 Nm) and

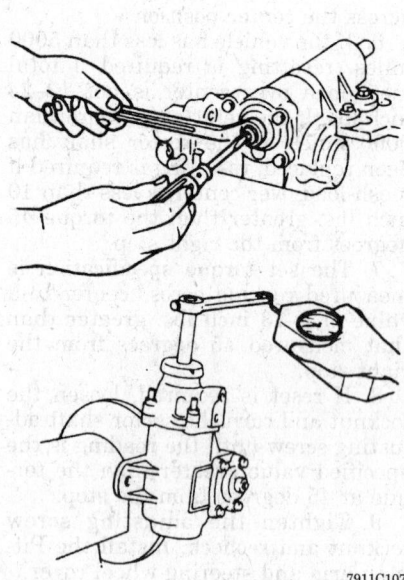

7911C107

Power steering gear adjustment — B-Series Pick-Up

the return line nut to 23–35 ft. lbs. (31–47 Nm).

10. Lower the vehicle. Fill and bleed the power steering system.

1994–96 B-Series Pick-Up and Navajo

1. Disconnect the pressure and return lines from the steering gear. Plug the lines and the ports in the gear to prevent entry of dirt.

2. Remove the upper and lower steering gear shaft U-joint shield from the flex coupling. Disconnect the flex coupling at the steering gear by removing the bolt.

3. Raise the vehicle and support it safely. Remove the Pitman arm attaching nut and washer. Remove the Pitman arm from the sector shaft using tool T64P–3590–F or equivalent. Be careful not to damage the seals.

4. Support the steering gear and remove the attaching bolts. Work the steering gear free from the flex coupling and remove the gear from the vehicle.

To install:

5. Install the lower U-joint shield onto the steering gear lugs. Slide the upper U-joint shield into place on the steering shaft assembly. Turn the steering wheel so the spokes are in the horizontal position.

6. Center the steering gear input shaft with the indexing flat facing down.

7. Slide the steering gear input shaft into the flex coupling and into place on the frame side rail. Install the attaching bolts and tighten to 50–62 ft. lbs. (68–84 Nm). Tighten the flex coupling bolt to 26–34 ft. lbs. (34–47 Nm).

8. Make sure the wheels are in the straight-ahead position, then install the Pitman arm on the sector shaft. Install the attaching washer and nut and tighten to 170–228 ft. lbs. (230–310 Nm).

9. Connect and tighten the pressure and return lines to the steering gear to 20–30 ft. lbs. (27–40 Nm). Snap the upper and lower steering gear shaft U-joint shields together.

10. Fill and bleed the power steering system.

Power Rack and Pinion

REMOVAL AND INSTALLATION

MPV

2WD

1. Place the front wheels in the straight-ahead position. Raise and safely support the vehicle.

2. Remove the wheel and tire assemblies. Remove the splash shield.

3. Remove the cotter pins and nuts from both tie rod end studs. Use separator tool 49 0727 575 or equivalent, to separate the tie rod ends from the knuckles.

4. Remove the pinch bolt from the intermediate shaft-to-pinion shaft coupling.

5. Disconnect and plug the pressure line from the rack and pinion assembly. Loosen the clamp and disconnect the return line from the rack and pinion assembly. Plug the line.

6. If equipped with automatic transmission, remove the change counter assembly to remove the protector plate mounting bolt indicated by the arrow.

7. Remove the steering bracket mounting bolts and remove the rack and pinion assembly and brackets.

8. If necessary, remove the brackets.

To install:

9. If removed, install the brackets and tighten the mounting bolts, in sequence, to 54–69 ft. lbs. (74–93 Nm).

10. Install the rack and pinion assembly and brackets in the vehicle. Tighten the bracket-to-chassis bolts to 46–69 ft. lbs. (63–93 Nm).

11. If equipped with automatic transmission, install the change counter assembly.

12. Connect the return line and tighten the clamp. Connect the pressure line and tighten the nut to 23–35 ft. lbs. (31–47 Nm).

13. Install the pinch bolt in the intermediate shaft-to-pinion shaft coupling and tighten to 13–20 ft. lbs. (18–26 Nm).

14. Position the tie rod end studs in the knuckles and install the nuts. Tighten the nuts to 43–58 ft. lbs. (59–78 Nm) and install new cotter pins.

15. Install the splash shield and the wheel and tire assemblies. Lower the vehicle and bleed the power steering system.

4WD

1. Place the front wheels in the straight-ahead position. Raise and safely support the vehicle.

2. Remove the wheel and tire assemblies. Remove the splash shield.

3. Remove the cotter pins and nuts from both tie rod end studs. Use separator tool 49 0727 575 or equivalent, to separate the tie rod ends from the knuckles.

4. Disconnect and plug the pressure and return hoses at the pressure and return lines.

5. Remove the pressure and return lines from the rack and pinion assembly.

6. Remove the pinch bolt from the intermediate shaft-to-pinion shaft coupling.

7. Working inside the vehicle, remove the lower panel and column cover from under the steering column. Remove the steering column mounting bolts and nuts and pull the column and intermediate shaft rearward to separate the intermediate shaft from the pinion shaft.

8. Mark the position of the front driveshaft on the axle flange and remove the front driveshaft.

9. Remove the rack and pinion assembly mounting bracket bolts and the front differential/joint shaft assembly mounting bolts.

10. Slide the differential/joint shaft assembly rearward. Slide the rack and pinion assembly rearward and turn it 90 degrees, then remove it from the left side of the vehicle.

To install:

11. Install the rack and pinion assembly from the left side of the vehicle, turn it 90 degrees and move it forward into position. Install the mounting bolts and tighten, in sequence, to 54–69 ft. lbs. (74–93 Nm).

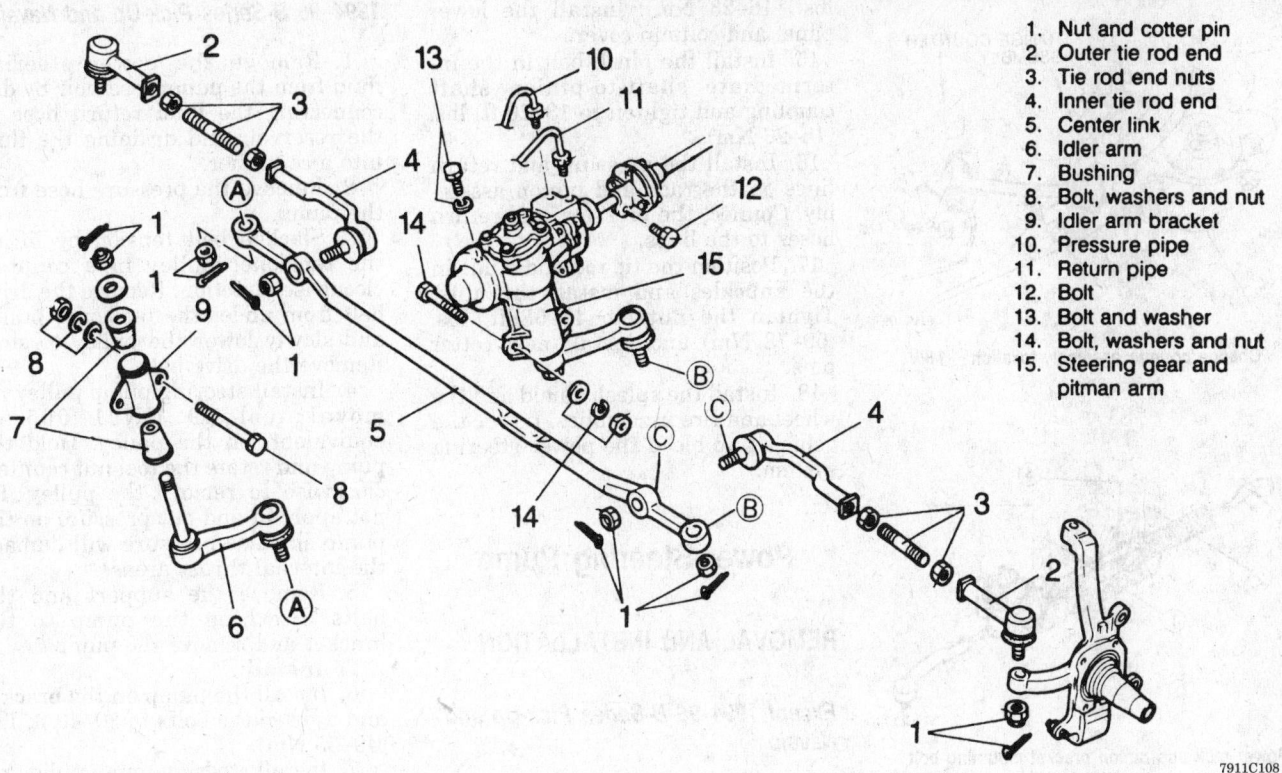

1. Nut and cotter pin
2. Outer tie rod end
3. Tie rod end nuts
4. Inner tie rod end
5. Center link
6. Idler arm
7. Bushing
8. Bolt, washers and nut
9. Idler arm bracket
10. Pressure pipe
11. Return pipe
12. Bolt
13. Bolt and washer
14. Bolt, washers and nut
15. Steering gear and pitman arm

7911C108

Power steering gear and linkage exploded view — 1992–93 B-Series Pick-Up

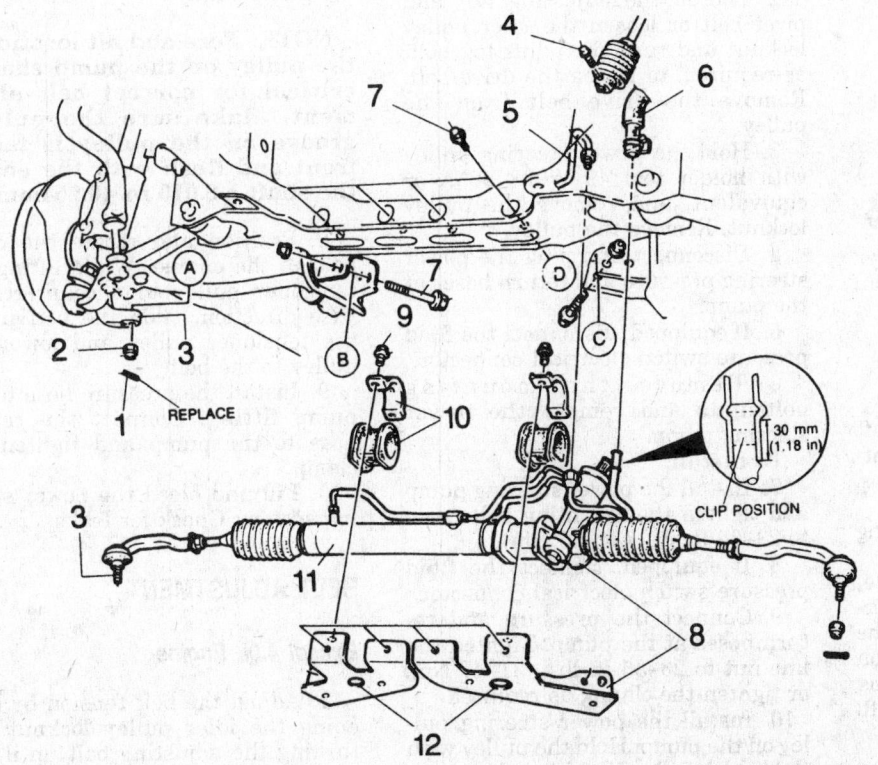

1. Cotter pin
2. Nut
3. Tie rod end and steering knuckle
4. Fixing bolt
5. Pressure pipe
6. Return hose
7. Steering bracket mounting bolts
8. Steering gear and linkage bracket assembly
9. Mounting bracket bolts
10. Mounting bracket and rubbers
11. Steering gear and linkage
12. Steering brackets

CLIP POSITION
30 mm (1.18 in)

REPLACE

7911C111

Power rack and pinion removal — 2WD MPV

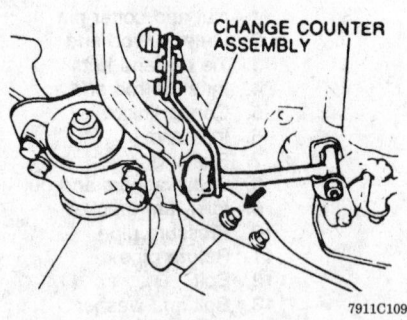

CHANGE COUNTER ASSEMBLY

7911C109

Change counter assembly location — MPV

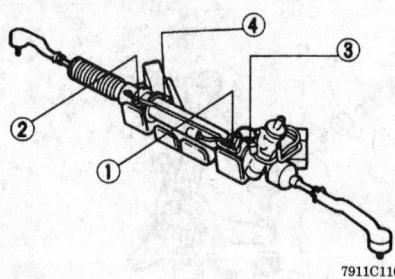

7911C110

Power rack and pinion bracket mounting bolt torque sequence — 2WD MPV

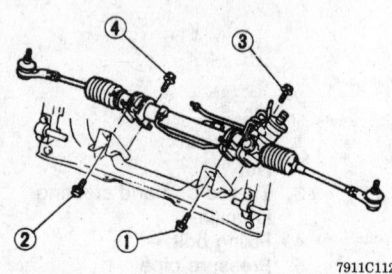

7911C112

Power rack and pinion bracket mounting bolt torque sequence — 4WD MPV

12. Move the differential/joint shaft assembly forward, install the mounting bolts and tighten to 49–72 ft. lbs. (67–97 Nm).

13. Install the driveshaft, aligning the marks made during removal.

14. Working inside the vehicle, move the steering column and intermediate shaft forward to engage the intermediate shaft with the pinion shaft. Install and tighten the steering column nuts and bolts to 12–17 ft.

lbs. (16–23 Nm). Install the lower panel and column cover.

15. Install the pinch bolt in the intermediate shaft-to-pinion shaft coupling and tighten to 13–20 ft. lbs. (18–26 Nm).

16. Install the pressure and return lines on the rack and pinion assembly. Connect the pressure and return hoses to the lines.

17. Position the tie rod end studs in the knuckles and install the nuts. Tighten the nuts to 43–58 ft. lbs. (59–78 Nm) and install new cotter pins.

18. Install the splash shield and the wheel and tire assemblies. Lower the vehicle and bleed the power steering system.

Power Steering Pump

REMOVAL AND INSTALLATION

Except 1994–96 B-Series Pick-Up and Navajo

1. Disconnect the negative battery cable.

2. Loosen the adjusting nut and pivot bolt or loosen the idler pulley locknut and turn the adjusting bolt, as required, to loosen the drive belt. Remove the drive belt from the pulley.

3. Hold the power steering pulley with holder tool 49 W023 585A or equivalent, and remove the pulley locknut. Remove the pulley.

4. Disconnect and plug the power steering pressure and return hoses at the pump.

5. If equipped, disconnect the fluid pressure switch electrical connector.

6. Remove the mounting bolts/nuts and remove the power steering pump.

To install:

7. Install the power steering pump and tighten the mounting bolts/nuts to 23–34 ft. lbs. (31–46 Nm).

8. If equipped, connect the fluid pressure switch electrical connector.

9. Connect the pressure and return hoses at the pump. Tighten the line nut to 23–35 ft. lbs. (31–47 Nm) or tighten the clamp, as required.

10. Install the power steering pulley on the pump. Hold the pulley with the holder tool and tighten the nut to 36–43 ft. lbs. (49–59 Nm).

11. Install the drive belt and adjust the tension. Fill and bleed the power steering system. Check for leaks.

1994–96 B-Series Pick-Up and Navajo

1. Remove the power steering fluid from the pump reservoir by disconnecting the fluid return hose at the reservoir and draining the fluid into a container.

2. Remove the pressure hose from the pump.

3. Slacken belt tension by lifting the tensioner pulley in a counterclockwise direction. Remove the drive belt from under the tensioner pulley and slowly lower the pulley to stop. Remove the drive belt.

4. Install steering pump pulley removal tool 49 UN01 005 or equivalent, on the pulley. Hold the pump and rotate the tool nut counterclockwise to remove the pulley. Do not apply in and out pressure on the pump shaft as pressure will damage the internal thrust areas.

5. Remove the support and the bolts attaching the pump to the bracket and remove the pump.

To install:

6. Install the pump on the bracket and tighten the bolts to 30–40 ft. lbs. (40–55 Nm).

7. Install steering pump pulley replacement tool 49 UN01 006 or equivalent and press the pulley on the pump shaft.

NOTE: Fore and aft location of the pulley on the pump shaft is critical for correct belt alignment. Make sure the pull-off groove on the pulley is facing front and flush with the end of the shaft ± 0.010 in. (0.254mm).

8. Position and rotate the drive belt on the engine. While lifting the tensioner pulley in a counterclockwise direction, slide the belt under the tensioner pulley and lower the pulley to the belt.

9. Install the pressure hose to the pump fitting. Connect the return hose to the pump and tighten the clamp.

10. Fill and bleed the power steering system. Check for leaks.

BELT ADJUSTMENT

Except 4.0L Engine

1. Adjust the belt tension by loosening the idler pulley locknut and turning the adjusting bolt until belt tension is as specified.

2. To obtain the correct belt tension, measure the belt deflection at the center of the belt span between the idler pulley and power steering

1. Oil pump belt
2. Locknut
3. Oil pump pulley
4. Pressure switch coupler
5. Pressure pipe
6. Return hose
7. Oil pump assembly

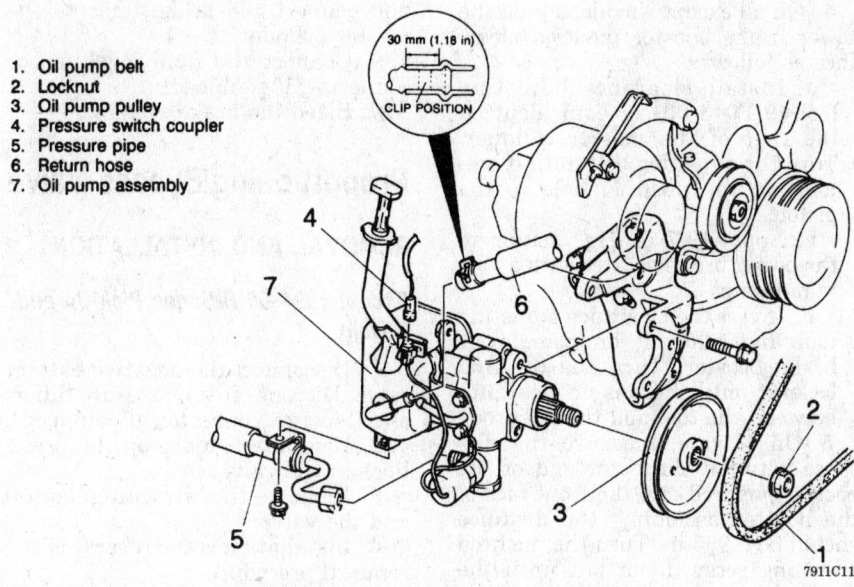

30 mm (1.18 in)

CLIP POSITION

7911C113

Power steering pump installation — 3.0L engine

pump pulley. Deflection specifications are as follows:

2.2L Engine — New belt: 0.28–0.31 in. (7–8mm); Used belt: 0.31–0.35 in. (8–9mm)

2.6L Engine — New belt: 0.26–0.28 in. (6.6–7.2mm); Used belt: 0.28–0.31 in. (7.2–8.0mm)

3.0L Engine — New belt: 0.28–0.30 in. (7.0–7.5mm); Used belt: 0.30–0.32 in. (7.5–8.2mm)

3. After correct belt tension is obtained, tighten the idler pulley locknut or the adjusting nut and pivot bolt, as required.

4.0L Engine

Belt tension is maintained by an automatic tensioner. No adjustment is necessary.

SYSTEM BLEEDING

Except 1994–96 B-Series Pick-Up and Navajo

1. Raise and safely support the vehicle.
2. Check the fluid level and add, if necessary.
3. Turn the steering wheel fully left and right several times with the engine not running.

4. Recheck the fluid level and add, if necessary.
5. Repeat Steps 3 and 4 until the fluid level stabilizes. Lower the vehicle.
6. Start the engine and let it run at idle. Turn the steering wheel fully left and right several times. If noise is heard in the oil line, air is still present.
7. Put the wheels in the straight-ahead position and turn the engine **OFF**. The fluid level in the pump should not increase; if it does, air is still present. Repeat Step 6.
8. Recheck the fluid level and check for leaks.

NOTE: If air is still present in the system, raise the fluid temperature to 122–176°F (50–80°C) by turning the steering wheel right and left, stop the engine and repeat Step 6 for 5–10 minutes. Air can be completely bled in this manner.

1994–96 B-Series Pick-Up and Navajo

1. Fill the power steering fluid reservoir.
2. Disconnect the distributorless ignition module connector.
3. Crank the engine with the starter and continue adding fluid until the level remains constant. Do not

prolong cranking as the battery may be drained and the starter damaged.

4. Rotate the steering wheel approximately 30 degrees each side of center while continuing to crank the engine.
5. Recheck the fluid level and fill, as required.
6. Reconnect the distributorless ignition module connector.
7. Start the engine and allow it to run for several minutes.
8. Rotate the steering wheel from stop to stop.
9. Shut off the engine and recheck the fluid level. Add fluid, as required.
10. If air is still trapped in the system, proceed as follows:

a. Fabricate a purging tool.

b. Make sure the reservoir fluid level is correct.

c. Insert the rubber stopper end of the fabricated purging tool tightly into the filler tube.

d. Connect a suitable length of hose to the purging tool. Connect the other end of the hose to an air conditioner vacuum pump or distributor machine. Do not use engine vacuum.

e. Start the engine and let it idle for approximately 15 minutes. Turn the steering wheel 1 full cycle every 5 minutes but do not hit the stops. This will assist in removing trapped air.

f. Stop the engine and disconnect the vacuum source. Remove the purging tool.

g. Check the fluid level and install the filler tube dipstick.

Tie Rod Ends

REMOVAL AND INSTALLATION

1. Place the front wheels in the straight-ahead position. Raise and safely support the vehicle.
2. Remove the cotter pin and nut from the tie rod end ball stud. Discard the cotter pin.
3. Separate the tie rod end from the knuckle or center link using separator tool 49 0118 850C or equivalent.
4. On all except Navajo, mark the position of the locknut and tie rod end on the tie rod threads. Grip the tie rod with suitable pliers, loosen the locknut and remove the tie rod end from the tie rod.
5. On Navajo, loosen the bolts on the tie rod adjusting sleeve. Count the number of turns required to remove the tie rod from the tie rod adjusting sleeve and remove the tie rod.

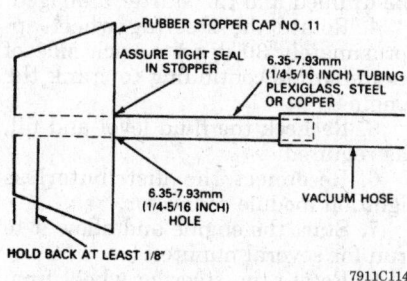

RUBBER STOPPER CAP NO. 11

ASSURE TIGHT SEAL IN STOPPER

6.35-7.93mm (1/4-5/16 INCH) TUBING PLEXIGLASS, STEEL OR COPPER

6.35-7.93mm (1/4-5/16 INCH) HOLE

VACUUM HOSE

HOLD BACK AT LEAST 1/8"

7911C114

Fabricated purging tool dimensions — Navajo

To install:

6. On all except Navajo, thread the replacement tie rod end onto the tie rod to the same location as the one that was removed. Hold the tie rod end with a wrench and tighten the locknut to 51–58 ft. lbs. (69–78 Nm).

7. On Navajo, install the tie rod into the adjusting sleeve the same number of turns required to remove it. With the adjusting sleeve clamps pointed down, tighten the adjusting sleeve nuts to 30–42 ft. lbs. (40–57 Nm).

8. Install the tie rod ball stud into the knuckle or center link. Install the nut and tighten to:

33–43 ft. lbs. (44–59 Nm)—B-Series Pick-Up

43–58 ft. lbs. (59–78 Nm)—MPV

50–75 ft. lbs. (70–100 Nm)—Navajo and Pick-Up

9. Install a new cotter pin.

NOTE: If the cotter pin cannot be installed because the hole in the ball stud does not align with a castellation on the nut, continue to tighten the nut to align them. Never loosen the nut to align the hole and castellation.

10. Lower the vehicle. Check the toe-in setting and adjust, if necessary.

BRAKES

Master Cylinder

REMOVAL AND INSTALLATION

1. Disconnect the negative battery cable. Disconnect the fluid level sensor connector, if equipped.

2. Disconnect and plug the brake lines at the master cylinder.

3. Remove the attaching nuts from the power brake booster studs and remove the master cylinder.

To install:

4. On all except Navajo, adjust the power brake booster pushrod clearance as follows:

a. Install clearance adjusting tool 49 F043 001 or equivalent on the rear of the master cylinder. Turn the adjusting bolt until it bottoms in the pushrod hole in the piston.

b. Apply 19.7 in. Hg vacuum to the power brake booster with a vacuum pump.

c. Invert the clearance adjusting tool and place it on the power brake booster. Turn the pushrod locknut until there is no clearance between the tool and the pushrod.

5. On Navajo, measure the distance between the outer end of the booster pushrod and the front face of the booster assembly; the distance should be 0.995 in. Turn the pushrod adjusting screw in or out until the distance is as specified.

6. If a new or dry master cylinder is being installed, bench bleed the master cylinder as follows:

a. Support the master cylinder in a suitable holding fixture. Fill the reservoir with the proper type of brake fluid.

b. Install plugs in the brake outlet ports.

c. Loosen an outlet port plug and depress the master cylinder piston slowly to force air out of the master cylinder. Tighten the plug while the piston is depressed or air will enter the master cylinder.

d. Repeat the procedure until there is no more air at the outlet port.

e. Repeat the procedures in Steps c and d at the other outlet ports.

7. Install the master cylinder over the booster studs. Install the attaching nuts and tighten to 7.2–12.0 ft.

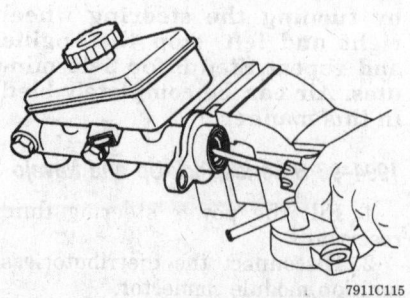

7911C115

Master cylinder bench bleeding

lbs. (9.8–16.0 Nm) on all except Navajo. On Navajo, tighten the nuts to 20 ft. lbs. (27 Nm).

8. Remove the outlet port plugs and connect the brake lines to the master cylinder.

9. Connect the fluid level sensor connector, if equipped.

10. Bleed the brake system.

Proportioning/Bypass Valve

REMOVAL AND INSTALLATION

Except 1994–96 B-Series Pick-Up and Navajo

1. Disconnect the negative battery cable. Disconnect the pressure differential switch connector, if equipped.

2. Disconnect and plug the brake lines at the valve.

3. Remove the attaching bolt(s) and the valve.

4. Installation is the reverse of the removal procedure.

5. Bleed the brake system.

Power Brake Booster

REMOVAL AND INSTALLATION

Except 1994–96 B-Series Pick-Up and Navajo

1. Disconnect the negative battery cable.

2. On MPV with 3.0L engine, remove the wiper arms, wiper motor and wiper linkage.

3. Remove the master cylinder.

4. Disconnect the vacuum hose at the booster.

5. Working inside the vehicle, remove the cotter pin and clevis pin from the booster pushrod. Remove the booster attaching nuts.

6. Remove the power brake booster and gasket.

7. Installation is the reverse of the removal procedure. Apply gasket sealant to the booster gasket and grease to the clevis pin prior to installation. Tighten the booster attaching nuts to 12–17 ft. lbs. (16–23 Nm) on B-Series Pick-Up or 14–19 ft. lbs. (19–25 Nm) on MPV.

8. Bleed the brake system.

1994–96 B-Series Pick-Up and Navajo

1. Disconnect the negative battery cable. Support the master cylinder from the underside with a prop.

2. Disconnect the vacuum hose from the booster check valve and remove the check valve.

3. Remove the master cylinder-to-booster retaining nuts. Pull the master cylinder off the booster and leave it supported by the prop, out of the way enough to allow booster removal.

4. Working inside the cab, remove the hairpin retainer and slide the stoplight switch, valve rod, spacers and bushing off the brake pedal arm. Remove the nuts retaining the booster and remove the booster.

To install:

5. Mount the booster assembly on the engine side of the dash panel by sliding the bracket mounting bolts and valve operating rod in through the holes in the dash panel.

6. Working inside the cab, install the booster mounting nuts and tighten to 13–25 ft. lbs. (18–33 Nm).

7. Before installing the master cylinder, check the distance from the outer end of the vacuum booster assembly pushrod to the front face of the vacuum brake booster assembly. The distance should be 0.995 in. Turn the pushrod adjusting screw in or out, as required, to obtain the proper length.

8. Install the master cylinder and tighten the retaining nuts to 20 ft. lbs. (27 Nm). Remove the prop from under the master cylinder.

9. Install the booster check valve and connect the vacuum hose. Check the hose routing to make sure the hose is not crimped.

10. Working inside the cab, install the bushing and position the switch on the end of the valve rod, then install the switch and rod on the pedal arm along with the spacers and hairpin retainer.

NOTE: Use only the factory supplied hairpin retainer. Do not substitute other types of retainers.

11. Connect the negative battery cable, start the engine and check brake operation.

Brake Caliper

REMOVAL AND INSTALLATION

Except 1994–96 B-Series Pick-Up and Navajo

1. Raise and safely support the vehicle. Remove the wheel and tire assembly.

2. Remove the banjo bolt and disconnect the brake hose from the cali-

per. Plug the hose to prevent fluid leakage.

3. On B-Series Pick-Up, remove the caliper mounting bolt and pivot the caliper about the mounting pin and off of the brake rotor. Remove the caliper from the pin.

4. On MPV, remove the caliper mounting bolts and remove the caliper.

5. Installation is the reverse of the removal procedure. Lubricate the caliper mounting bolts or bolt and pin prior to installation.

6. Tighten the caliper mounting bolt(s) to 23–30 ft. lbs. (31–41 Nm) on B-Series Pick-Up or 61–69 ft. lbs. (83–93 Nm) on MPV. Bleed the brake system.

1994–96 B-Series Pick-Up and Navajo

1. Siphon part of the brake fluid out of the master cylinder to avoid overflow when the caliper piston is pressed into the caliper bore.

2. Raise the vehicle and support it safely. Remove the wheel and tire assembly.

3. Position an 8 in. C-clamp on the caliper and tighten the clamp to move the caliper piston into the bore approximately 1/8 in. Avoid clamp contact with the outer shoe spring clip. Remove the clamp.

NOTE: Do not pry the piston away from the rotor.

4. Clean excess dirt from the pin tab area.

5. Using a 1/4 in. drive socket, 3/8 in. deep and a light hammer, tap the upper caliper pin towards the outboard side until the pin tabs pass the spindle face.

6. Place one end of a 7/16 in. diameter punch against the end of the caliper pin and tap the pin out of the caliper slide groove.

7. Repeat Steps 5 and 6 to remove the lower pin.

8. Disconnect and plug the brake hose at the caliper. Remove the caliper from the rotor.

To install:

9. Make sure the caliper mounting surfaces are free of dirt. Lubricate the caliper grooves with disc brake caliper grease and install the caliper.

10. From the caliper outboard side, position the pin between the caliper and spindle grooves. The pin must be positioned so the tabs will be installed against the spindle outer face.

11. Tap the pin on the outboard end with a hammer until the retention tabs on the sides of the pin contact the spindle face.

12. Repeat Steps 10 and 11 for the lower pin.

NOTE: During installation, do not allow the tabs of the caliper pin to be tapped too far into the spindle groove. If this happens, it will be necessary to tap the other end of the caliper pin until the tabs snap in place. The tabs on each end of the pin must be free to catch on the spindle face.

13. Connect the brake hose to the caliper. Bleed the brake system.

14. Install the wheel and tire assembly and lower the vehicle. Check the brake fluid level and check the brakes for proper operation.

Disc Brake Pads

REMOVAL AND INSTALLATION

Except 1994–96 B-Series Pick-Up and Navajo

1. Siphon part of the brake fluid out of the master cylinder to avoid overflow when the caliper piston is pressed into the caliper bore.

2. Raise the vehicle and support it safely. Remove the wheel and tire assembly.

3. Remove the brake caliper, but do not disconnect the brake hose. Secure the caliper aside with mechanics wire.

NOTE: Do not let the caliper hang by the brake hose.

4. Remove the disc brake pads, shims and guide plates from the mounting support, noting the position of the shims and guide plates for reassembly.

To install:

5. Using a C-clamp or similar tool, bottom out the caliper piston in the caliper bore.

6. Install the new disc pads along with the shims and guide plates in the mounting support. Make sure the shims and guide plates are installed in their original positions.

7. Install the brake caliper.

8. Install the wheel and tire assembly and lower the vehicle. Apply the brakes several times before moving the vehicle to seat the pads.

9. Check the brake fluid level. Check the brakes for proper operation.

1994–96 B-Series Pick-Up and Navajo

1. Siphon part of the brake fluid out of the master cylinder to avoid

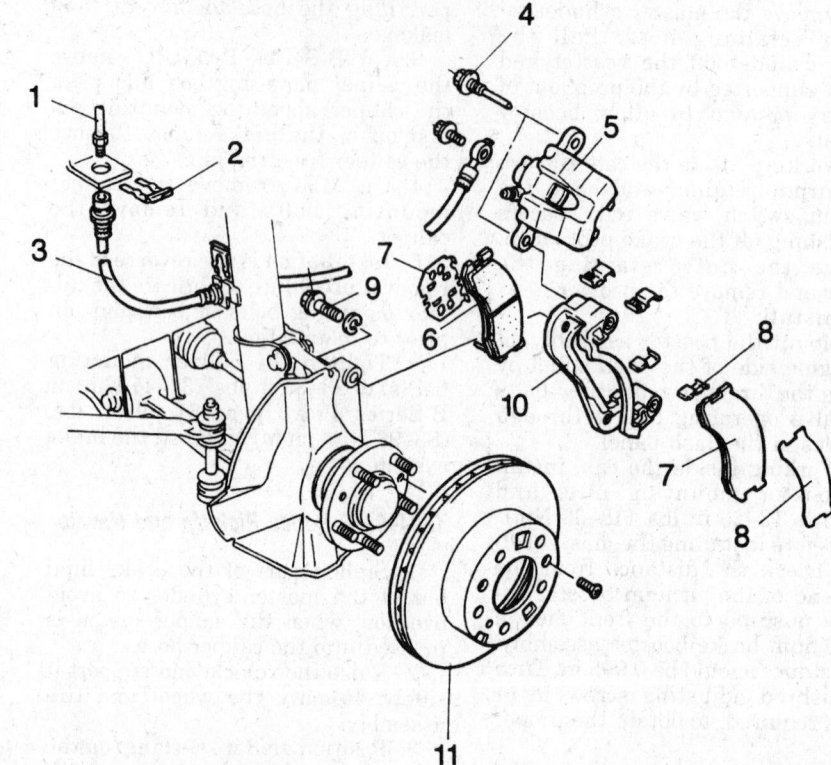

1. Brake pipe
2. Clip
3. Brake hose
4. Lockbolt
5. Brake caliper assembly
6. Disc pad
7. Shim
8. Guide plate
9. Bolt
10. Mounting support
11. Disc plate

7911C117

Disc brake assembly — MPV

overflow when the caliper piston is pressed into the caliper bore.

2. Raise the vehicle and support it safely. Remove the wheel and tire assembly.

3. Remove the brake caliper, but do not disconnect the brake hose. Secure the caliper aside with mechanics wire.

NOTE: Do not let the caliper hang by the brake hose.

4. Compress the anti-rattle clip and remove the inner brake pad from the caliper.

5. Press each ear of the outer brake pad away from the caliper and slide the torque buttons out of the retention notches.

To install:

6. Bottom out the caliper piston in the caliper bore using an 8 in. C-clamp and a worn out inner brake pad or block of wood to push against the piston. Do not attempt to bottom out the piston with the outer brake pad installed.

7. Place a new anti-rattle clip on the lower end of the inner brake pad. Make sure the tabs on the clip are properly positioned and the clip is fully seated.

8. Position the inner brake pad and anti-rattle clip in the pad abutment with the ant-rattle clip tab against the pad abutment and the loop-type spring away from the rotor. Compress the anti-rattle clip and slide the upper end of the pad in position.

9. Install the outer pad, making sure the torque buttons on the pad are seated solidly in the matching holes in the caliper.

10. Install the caliper on the spindle.

11. Install the wheel and tire assembly and lower the vehicle. Apply the brakes several times before moving the vehicle to seat the pads.

12. Check the brake fluid level. Check the brakes for proper operation.

Brake Rotor

REMOVAL AND INSTALLATION

1. Raise and safely support the vehicle. Remove the wheel and tire assembly.

2. Remove the caliper and support it aside with mechanics wire; do not let the caliper hang by the brake

hose. On all except Navajo, remove the disc brake pads and mounting support.

3. On 2WD B-Series Pick-Up and Navajo, remove the dust cap, cotter pin, nut, washer and outer bearing and remove the rotor from the spindle.

4. On 4WD B-Series Pick-Up, remove the locking hub or drive flange, snapring and spacer, set bolts and bearing set plate. Remove the bearing locknut using a suitable puller and remove the hub and rotor assembly, being careful not to let the washer and bearing fall.

5. On 4WD Navajo, remove the locking hub and remove the brake rotor.

6. On MPV, remove the attaching screw and remove the rotor.

7. Inspect the rotor for scoring, wear and runout; machine or replace as necessary.

8. If rotor replacement is necessary on B-Series Pick-Up, remove the attaching bolts and separate the rotor from the hub.

9. Install in the reverse order of removal. On B-Series Pick-Up, tighten the rotor-to-hub bolts to 40–51 ft. lbs. (54–69 Nm). Adjust the wheel bearings.

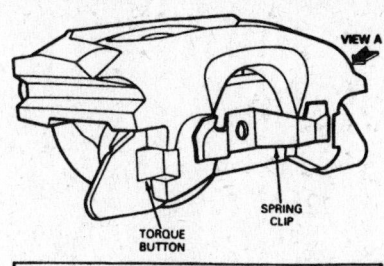

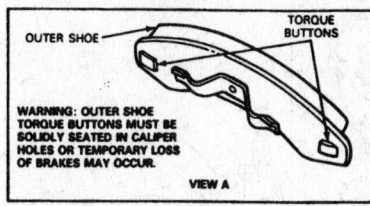

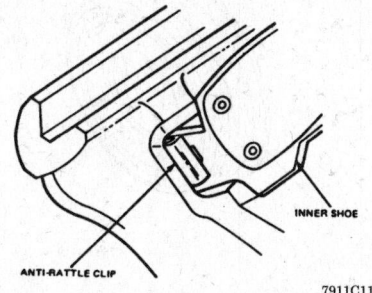

7911C118

Correct disc brake pad installation — Navajo

Brake Drums

REMOVAL AND INSTALLATION

1. Make sure the parking brake is released.

2. Raise and safely support the vehicle. Remove the wheel and tire assembly.

3. On all except Navajo, remove the retaining screw, if equipped, and remove the brake drum.

4. On Navajo, remove the spring retaining nuts, if equipped, and remove the brake drum.

NOTE: If the brake drum will not come off, insert a narrow prybar through the appropriate hole in the backing plate and disengage the adjusting lever from the adjusting screw. While holding the adjusting lever away from the adjusting screw, insert a brake adjusting tool through the backing plate hole adjacent to the star wheel of the adjusting screw and loosen the adjusting screw.

5. Inspect the brake drum surface for wear, scoring and runout. Machine or replace, as necessary.

6. Installation is the reverse of the removal procedure.

Brake Shoes

REMOVAL AND INSTALLATION

2WD 1992–93 B-Series Pick-Up

1. Raise and safely support the vehicle. Remove the wheel and tire assembly and the brake drum.

2. Remove the upper and lower return springs from the brake shoes.

3. Compress the forward brake shoe spring and remove the forward brake shoe, spring and pin.

4. Remove the adjuster screw, pawl lever return spring and pawl lever.

5. Compress the rearward brake shoe spring and remove the rearward brake shoe, spring and pin.

6. Pull back the spring on the parking brake cable and disengage the brake shoe parking brake lever from the cable.

7. Remove the clip and pin and the parking brake lever from the brake shoe, if necessary.

To install:

8. Lubricate the adjusting screw threads, backing plate shoe sliding surfaces and wheel cylinder and anchor sliding points with a small amount of grease.

9. If removed, install the parking brake lever to the rearward brake shoe with the pin and clip. Make sure the clip is secure.

10. Pull back the spring on the parking brake cable and connect the cable end to the parking brake lever.

11. Install the brake shoes to the backing plate and secure with the pins and shoe springs.

12. Turn the adjusting screw all the way in and install the adjusting screw, pawl lever return spring and pawl lever.

13. Install the upper and lower return springs.

14. Install the brake drum.

15. Adjust the brake shoes as follows:

  a. Remove the 2 adjusting hole plugs from the back of the backing plate.

  b. Place a suitable brake adjusting tool against the star wheel of the adjust screw through the hole adjacent to the star wheel and turn the star wheel toward the arrow direction marked on the backing plate until the wheel is locked.

  c. Insert a suitable drift through the other adjusting hole and push the pawl lever of the self-adjuster away from the star wheel, then back off the star wheel about 6–7 notches with the brake adjusting

tool, so the drum rotates freely without drag.

  d. Repeat the adjustment to the other wheel. The adjustment must be the same on both rear wheels.

  e. Check the parking brake adjustment and install the backing plate plugs.

16. Install the wheel and tire assembly and lower the vehicle.

MPV and 4WD 1992–93 B-Series Pick-Up

1. Raise and safely support the vehicle. Remove the wheel and tire assembly and the brake drum.

2. Remove the upper return springs from the spring anchor and the primary and secondary shoes. Remove the adjuster lever link spring.

3. Remove the primary shoe holding spring assembly and disengage the primary shoe from the lower shoe spring. Remove the primary shoe and the holding spring pin.

NOTE: The primary shoe holding spring is yellow and the secondary shoe holding spring is white. The springs cannot be interchanged.

4. Remove the parking brake lever strut, lower shoe spring and adjuster screw assembly.

5. Remove the secondary shoe holding spring assembly and remove the secondary shoe, adjust lever and parking brake lever assembly and the holding spring pin.

6. Pull back the spring on the parking brake cable and disengage the brake shoe parking brake lever from the cable.

7. Remove the clip and the parking brake lever from the brake shoe, if necessary.

To install:

8. Lubricate the adjusting screw threads, backing plate shoe sliding surfaces and spring anchor sliding points with a small amount of grease.

9. If removed, install the parking brake lever to the secondary shoe with the clip. Make sure the clip is secure.

10. Pull back the spring on the parking brake cable and connect the cable end to the parking brake lever.

11. Install the secondary shoe with the adjust lever to the backing plate and secure with the pin and holding spring assembly.

12. Install the primary shoe to the backing plate and secure with the pin and holding spring assembly.

13. Install the lower shoe spring to the primary and secondary shoes.

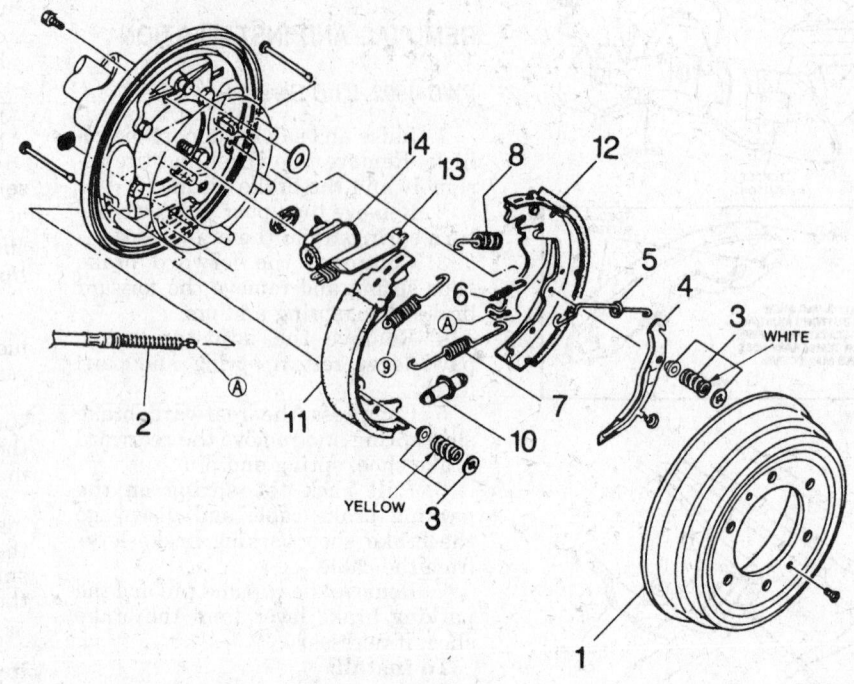

1. Brake drum
2. Parking brake cable
3. Hold spring and sleeve
4. Adjust lever
5. Link
6. Pull-off spring
7. Shoe spring
8. Return spring
9. Return spring
10. Adjuster
11. Primary brake shoe
12. Secondary brake shoe
13. Strut
14. Wheel cylinder
   assembly

Drum brake assembly — MPV and 4WD B-Series Pick-Up

14. Turn the adjuster screw assembly all the way in. Pry the shoes apart slightly and install the adjuster screw assembly between the shoes. Make sure the star wheel is toward the secondary shoe and is in contact with the adjust lever.

15. Install the parking brake lever strut.

16. Install the adjuster lever link spring between the adjust lever and the spring anchor.

17. Install the primary and secondary shoe upper return springs between the shoes and the spring anchor.

18. Install the brake drum.

19. Adjust the brake shoes as follows:

a. Remove the 2 adjusting hole plugs from the back of the backing plate.

b. Place a suitable brake adjusting tool against the star wheel of the adjust screw through the hole adjacent to the star wheel and turn the star wheel toward the arrow direction marked on the backing plate until the wheel is locked.

c. Insert a suitable drift through the other adjusting hole and push the pawl lever of the self-adjuster away from the star wheel, then back off the star wheel about 8–10 notches on B-Series Pick-Up or

13–15 notches on MPV with the brake adjusting tool, so the drum rotates freely without drag.

d. Repeat the adjustment to the other wheel. The adjustment must be the same on both rear wheels.

e. Check the parking brake adjustment and install the backing plate plugs.

20. Install the wheel and tire assembly and lower the vehicle.

1994–96 B-Series Pick-Up and Navajo

1. Raise and safely support the vehicle. Remove the wheel and tire assembly and the brake drum.

2. Pull backward on the adjusting lever cable to disengage the adjusting lever from the adjusting screw. Move the outboard side of the adjusting screw upward and back off the pivot nut as far as it will go.

3. Pull the adjusting lever, cable and automatic adjuster spring down and toward the rear to unhook the pivot hook from the large hole in the secondary shoe web. Do not pry the pivot hook from the hole.

4. Remove the automatic adjuster spring and adjusting lever.

5. Remove the secondary shoe-to-anchor spring using a suitable brake spring removal/installation tool. Using the tool, remove the primary

shoe-to-anchor spring and unhook the cable anchor. Remove the anchor pin plate, if equipped.

6. Remove the cable guide from the secondary shoe.

7. Remove the shoe hold-down springs, shoes, adjusting screw, pivot nut and socket. Note the color and position of each hold-down spring so they can be reassembled in the same position.

8. Remove the parking brake link and spring. Disconnect the parking brake cable from the parking brake lever.

9. Remove the secondary brake shoe. Remove the retainer clip and spring washer and remove the parking brake lever.

To install:

10. Clean the backing plate ledge pads and sand lightly. Apply a light coating of high temperature lithium grease to the points where the brake shoes touch the backing plate.

11. Install the parking brake lever on the secondary shoe and secure with the spring washer and retaining clip.

12. Position the brake shoes on the backing plate and install the hold-down spring pins, springs and cups. Install the parking brake link, spring and washer. Connect the parking

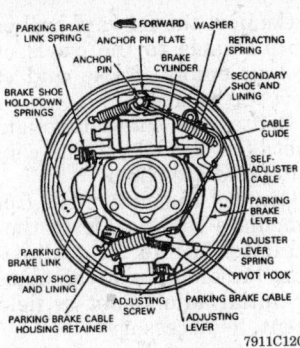

Rear brake shoe assembly — 1994–96 B-Series Pick-Up and Navajo

brake cable to the parking brake lever.

13. Install the anchor pin plate, if equipped, and place the cable anchor over the anchor pin with the crimped side toward the backing plate.

14. Install the primary shoe-to-anchor spring using the brake spring removal/installation tool.

15. Install the cable guide on the secondary shoe with the flanged hole fitted into the hole in the secondary shoe. Thread the cable around the cable guide groove.

NOTE: Make sure the cable is positioned in the groove and not between the guide and shoe web.

16. Install the secondary shoe-to-anchor (long) spring.

NOTE: Make sure the cable end is not cocked or binding on the anchor pin when installed. All parts should be flat on the anchor pin.

17. Apply high temperature lithium grease to the threads and the socket end of the adjusting screw. Turn the adjusting screw into the adjusting pivot nut to the end of the threads and then loosen, 1/2 turn.

18. Place the adjusting socket on the screw and install the assembly between the shoe ends with the adjusting screw nearest the secondary shoe.

NOTE: Be sure to install the adjusting screw on the same side of the vehicle from which it came. To prevent incorrect installation, the socket end of each adjusting screw is stamped with R or L, to indicate installation on the right or left side of the vehicle. The adjusting pivot nuts have lines machined around the body of the nut, two lines indicating the right side nut and one line indicating the left side nut.

19. Hook the cable hook into the hole in the adjusting lever from the outboard plate side. The adjusting levers are also stamped with an **R** or **L** to indicate right or left side installation.

20. Place the hooked end of the adjuster spring in the large hole in the primary shoe web and connect the loop end of the spring to the adjuster lever hole.

21. Pull the adjuster lever, cable and automatic adjuster spring down toward the rear to engage the pivot hook in the large hole in the secondary shoe web.

22. After installation, check the action of the adjuster by pulling the section of the cable between the cable guide and the adjusting lever toward the secondary shoe web far enough to lift the lever past a tooth on the adjusting screw wheel. The lever should snap into position behind the next tooth and releasing the cable should cause the adjuster spring to return the lever to its original position. This return action will turn the adjusting screw 1 tooth.

23. If pulling the cable does not produce the action described in Step 22 or if lever action is sluggish instead of positive and sharp, check the position of the lever on the adjusting screw toothed wheel. With the brake in a vertical position, anchor at the top, the lever should contact the adjusting wheel 1 tooth above the center line of the adjusting screw. If the contact point is below the center line, the lever will not lock on the adjusting screw wheel teeth and the screw will not turn as the lever is actuated by the cable.

24. To find the cause of the condition described in Step 23, proceed as follows:
  a. Check the cable and fittings. The cable should completely fill or extend slightly beyond the crimped section of the fittings. If this does not happen, the cable assembly may be damaged and should be replaced.
  b. Check the cable guide for damage. The cable groove should be parallel to the shoe web and the body of the guide should lie flat against the web. Replace the guide if it shows damage.
  c. Check the pivot hook on the lever. The hook surfaces should be square with the body on the lever for proper pivoting. Repair the hook or replace the lever if the hook shows damage.

  d. Be sure the adjusting screw socket is properly seated in the notch in the shoe web.

25. Adjust the brake shoes using either a brake adjustment gauge or manually with the drums installed.

26. If using a brake adjustment gauge, proceed as follows:
  a. Measure the inside diameter of the brake drum with the gauge.
  b. Reverse the tool and adjust the brake shoes until they touch the gauge. The gauge contact points on the shoes must be parallel to the vehicle with the center line through the center of the axle.
  c. Install the drum and wheel and tire assembly. Lower the vehicle.
  d. Apply the brakes sharply several times while driving the vehicle in reverse. Check brake operation by making several stops while driving forward.

27. If manually adjusting the brakes, proceed as follows:
  a. Install the brake drum and wheel and tire assembly.
  b. Remove the cover from the adjusting hole at the bottom of the backing plate and turn the adjusting screw, using a suitable brake adjusting tool, to expand the brake shoes until they drag against the brake drum.
  c. When the shoes are against the drum, insert a narrow prybar through the brake adjusting hole and disengage the adjusting lever from the adjusting screw. While holding the adjusting lever away from the adjusting screw, loosen the adjusting screw with the brake adjusting tool, until the drum rotates freely without drum.
  d. Install the adjusting hole cover and lower the vehicle.
  e. Apply the brakes. If the pedal travels more than halfway to the floor, there is too much clearance between the brake shoes and drums. Repeat the adjustment procedure.

Wheel Cylinder

REMOVAL AND INSTALLATION

1. Raise and safely support the vehicle. Remove the wheel and tire assembly, brake drum and brake shoes.
2. Disconnect and plug the brake line at the wheel cylinder.
3. Remove the wheel cylinder retaining bolts and remove the cylinder from the brake backing plate.

4. Installation is the reverse of the removal procedure. Adjust the brakes and bleed the system.

Parking Brake Cable

ADJUSTMENT

Except 1994–96 B-Series Pick-Up and Navajo

1. Make sure the rear brake shoes are properly adjusted.
2. Start the engine and depress the brake pedal several times while the vehicle is moving in reverse.
3. Stop the engine.
4. On MPV, remove the screw and remove the parking brake lever cover. Remove the adjusting nut clip.
5. On B-Series Pick-Up, loosen the locknut at the end of the front cable, near the parking brake lever.
6. Turn the adjusting nut until the parking brake is fully applied when the lever is pulled 7–12 notches on B-Series Pick-Up or 5–7 notches on MPV.
7. Tighten the locknut on B-Series Pick-Up.
8. Install the adjusting nut clip and the parking brake lever cover on MPV.

1994–96 B-Series Pick-Up and Navajo

NOTE: Adjust the drum brakes before adjusting the parking brake. The brake drums must be cold for correct adjustment.

INITIAL ADJUSTMENT

1. Use this procedure when a new tension limiter is install
2. Apply the parking brake pedal to the fully engaged position.
3. Raise and safely support the vehicle, as necessary. Hold the threaded rod end of the right brake cable to keep it from spinning and thread the equalizer nut 2½ in. up the rod.
4. Check to make sure the cinch strap has slipped and there are less than 1⅜ in. remaining.
5. Release the parking brake and check for proper operation.

FIELD ADJUSTMENT

1. Use this procedure to correct a slack system if a new tension limiter is not install
2. Apply the parking brake pedal to the fully engaged position.
3. Raise and safely support the vehicle, as necessary. Grip the threaded rod to keep it from spinning and tighten the equalizer nut 6 full turns

past its original position on the threaded rod.
4. Attach a suitable cable tension gauge in front of the equalizer assembly on the front cable and measure the cable tension. The cable tension should be 400–600 lbs. with the parking brake pedal in the last detent position. If tension is low, repeat Steps 2 and 3.
5. Release parking brake and check for rear wheel drag. There should be no brake drag.

REMOVAL AND INSTALLATION

Front

EXCEPT 1994–96 B-SERIES PICK-UP AND NAVAJO

1. Make sure the parking brake is fully released.
2. Remove the parking brake lever adjusting nut from the forward end of the front cable.
3. Remove the seat(s) and roll back the front floormat, as required. On MPV, remove the cable cover.
4. Raise and safely support the vehicle, as necessary.
5. Disengage the rear cables from the equalizer and remove the spring. Disconnect the front cable from the equalizer.
6. Remove the bolts from the cable retaining straps and remove the cable.
7. Installation is the reverse of the removal procedure. Adjust the parking brake.

1994–96 B-SERIES PICK-UP AND NAVAJO

1. Raise and safely support the vehicle.
2. Back off the equalizer nut and remove the cable end of the intermediate cable from the tension limiter.
3. Remove the intermediate cable from the bracket and disconnect the intermediate cable from the front cable.
4. Lower the vehicle. Remove the forward ball end of the parking brake cable from the control assembly clevis.
5. Remove the cable from the control assembly.
6. Using a cord attached to the control lever end of the cable, remove the cable from the vehicle pulling it up into the passenger compartment.
   To install:
7. Transfer the cord to the new cable. Position the cable in the vehicle, routing the cable through the dash panel. Remove the cord and secure the cable to the control.

8. Connect the forward ball end of the brake cable to the clevis of the control assembly. Raise and safely support the vehicle.
9. Route the cable through the bracket. Connect the front cable to the intermediate cable.
10. Connect the slug of the front or intermediate cable cable to the tension limiter connector. Adjust the parking brake cable at the equalizer using initial adjustment or field adjustment, as necessary.
11. Rotate both wheels to make sure the parking brakes are not dragging.

Rear

EXCEPT 1994–96 B-SERIES PICK-UP AND NAVAJO

1. Make sure the parking brake is fully released.
2. Loosen the parking brake lever adjusting nut.
3. Remove the seat(s) and roll back the front floormat, as required. On MPV, remove the cable cover.
4. Raise and safely support the vehicle.
5. Disconnect the rear cable from the equalizer.
6. Remove the rear wheel and tire assembly, brake drum and brake shoes.
7. Disconnect the cable from the backing plate.
8. Remove the bolts from the cable retaining straps and disconnect the spring from the cable. Remove the cable.
9. Installation is the reverse of the removal procedure. Adjust the parking brake.

1994–96 B-SERIES PICK-UP AND NAVAJO

1. Release the parking brake control.
2. Raise and safely support the vehicle. Remove the wheel and tire assembly, brake drum and brake shoes.
3. Remove the locknut on the threaded rod at the equalizer. Disconnect the rear parking brake cable from the equalizer.
4. Compress the prongs that retain the cable housing to the frame bracket or crossmember and pull out the cable and housing.
5. Working on the wheel side of the backing plate, compress the prongs on the cable retainer so they can pass through the hole in the brake backing plate.
6. Lift the cable out of the slot in the parking brake lever, attached to the secondary brake shoe, and re-

move the cable through the brake backing plate hole.

To install:

7. Route the cable through the hole in the backing plate. Insert the cable anchor behind the slot in the parking brake lever. Make sure the cable is securely engaged in the parking brake lever so the cable return spring is holding the cable in the parking brake lever.

8. Push the retainer through the hole in the backing plate so the retainer prongs engage the backing plate.

9. Properly route the cable and insert the front of the cable through the frame bracket or crossmember until the prongs expand. Connect the rear cables to the equalizer.

10. Rotate the equalizer 90 degrees and recouple the threaded rod to the equalizer.

11. Install the brake shoes, brake drum and wheel and tire assembly. Adjust the rear brakes.

12. Adjust the parking brake tension using the initial adjustment or the field adjustment procedure, as necessary.

13. Apply and release the parking brake control several times. Rotate both wheels to make sure the parking brakes are applied and released and not dragging.

BRAKE SYSTEM BLEEDING

1. Clean all dirt from the master cylinder filler cap.

2. If the master cylinder is known or suspected to have air in the bore, it must be bled before any of the wheel cylinders or calipers. Proceed as follows:

   a. Loosen the brake line fitting approximately 3/4 turn. Wrap a shop cloth around the tubing below the fitting to absorb escaping brake fluid.

   b. Have an assistant depress the brake pedal slowly through its full travel to force air trapped in the master cylinder to escape at the fitting.

   c. Tighten the fitting and let the pedal return slowly to the fully released position. Do not release the pedal until the fitting is tightened or air will reenter the master cylinder.

   d. Wait 5 seconds and then repeat the operation until all air bubbles disappear.

   e. Repeat Steps a–d on the remaining master cylinder brake line fitting(s).

3. Continue to bleed the brake system by removing the rubber dust cap from the wheel cylinder bleeder fitting at the right-hand rear of the vehicle. Place a box wrench on the bleeder fitting and attach a rubber drain hose to the fitting. The end of the tube should fit snugly around the bleeder fitting. Submerge the other end of the tube in a container partially filled with clean brake fluid and loosen the fitting 3/4 turn.

4. Have an assistant push the brake pedal down slowly through its full travel. Close the bleeder fitting and allow the pedal to slowly return to its full release position. Wait 5 seconds and repeat the procedure until no bubbles appear at the submerged end of the bleeder tube. Secure the bleeder fitting and remove the bleeder hose. Install the rubber dust cap on the bleeder fitting.

5. Repeat the procedure in Steps 3 and 4 and bleed the rest of the system in the following sequence: left rear, right front and left front.

NOTE: If equipped with anti-lock brakes, the electro-hydraulic valve must also be bled. It is not necessary to energize the valve to bleed it.

6. Refill the master cylinder reservoir after each wheel cylinder or caliper has been bled and install the master cylinder cover and gasket. When brake bleeding is completed, the fluid level should be filled to the maximum level indicated on the reservoir.

7. Always make sure the disc brake pistons are returned to their normal positions by depressing the brake pedal several times until normal pedal travel is established. If the pedal feels spongy, repeat the bleeding procedure.

Anti-Lock Brake System Service

PRECAUTIONS

Use caution when disassembling any hydraulic components as the system will contain residual pressure.

Cover the area around the component to be removed with a shop cloth to catch any brake fluid spray.

Do not allow brake fluid to come in contact with painted surfaces.

Electronic Control Unit

REMOVAL AND INSTALLATION

1. Disconnect the negative battery cable.

2. On B-Series Pick-Up, remove the driver's seat. On MPV, remove the inside trim panel from the left rear of the vehicle. The control unit is located under the dash on Navajo.

3. Disconnect the electrical connector from the control unit.

4. Remove the attaching screws and remove the control unit.

5. Installation is the reverse of the removal procedure. Check the system for proper operation.

Electro-Hydraulic Valve

REMOVAL AND INSTALLATION

1. Disconnect the negative battery cable.

2. Disconnect and plug the 2 brake lines connected to the valve.

3. Disconnect the wiring harness from the valve harness.

4. Remove the screw(s) retaining the valve and remove the valve.

5. Installation is the reverse of the removal procedure. Tighten the valve retaining screw(s) to 14–19 ft. lbs. (19–25 Nm) on all except Navajo where the torque is 11–14 ft. lbs. (15–20 Nm). Bleed the brake system.

Speed Sensor

REMOVAL AND INSTALLATION

Except 1994–96 B-Series Pick-Up and Navajo

1. Disconnect the negative battery cable.

2. Pull the wiring harness connector off.

3. Remove the sensor hold-down bolt and remove the sensor from the axle housing.

To install:

4. Clean the axle mounting surface. Use care to prevent dirt from entering the axle housing.

5. Inspect the sensor O-ring for damage and replace, if necessary.

6. Check the sensor-to-sensor rotor clearance as follows:

   a. Measure the distance between the sensor attaching surface and the sensor rotor teeth.

   b. Measure the distance between the sensor attaching surface and the sensor pole piece.

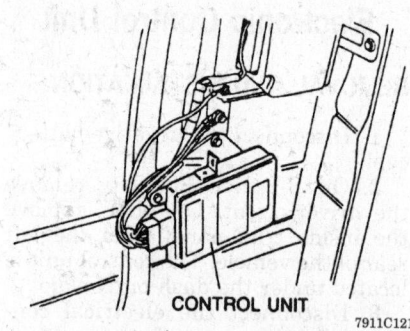

CONTROL UNIT

7911C121

Rear anti-lock brake system electronic control unit location — MPV

c. Subtract the distance recorded in Step b from the distance recorded in Step a.

d. The clearance should be 0.020–0.039 in. (0.5–1.0mm) on B2200 or 0.020–0.047 in. (0.5–1.2mm) on B2600 and MPV.

7. If the clearance is less than specified, increase it using adjusting shim P049 27 155 or equivalent, during sensor installation. If the clearance is more than specified, replace the speed sensor.

8. Lubricate the speed sensor with clean engine oil and install the speed

sensor. Tighten the attaching bolt to 12–17 ft. lbs. (16–23 Nm).

1994–96 B-Series Pick-Up and Navajo

1. Disconnect the negative battery cable.

2. Pull the wiring harness connector off.

3. Remove the sensor hold-down bolt and remove the sensor from the axle housing.

To install:

4. Clean the axle mounting surface. Use care to prevent dirt from entering the axle housing.

5. Inspect and clean the magnetized sensor pole piece to ensure that it is free from loose metal particles which could cause erratic system operation. Inspect the sensor O-ring for damage and replace, if necessary.

6. Lightly lubricate the sensor O-ring with motor oil, align the sensor bolt hole and install. Do not apply force to the plastic sensor connector. The sensor flange should slide to the mounting surface. This will insure the air gap setting is between 0.005–0.045 in. (0.127–1.14mm).

7. Install the hold-down bolt and tighten to 25–30 ft. lbs. (34–40 Nm).

8. Inspect the blue sensor connector seal and replace if missing or damaged. Push the connector on the sensor.

9. Connect the negative battery cable.

Sensor Rotor

INSPECTION

1. Remove the speed sensor.

2. View the sensor rotor teeth through the sensor hole. Rotate the rear axle and check the sensor rotor teeth for damage or breakage. Dented or broken teeth could cause the rear anti-lock brake system to function when not required.

REMOVAL AND INSTALLATION

To service the sensor rotor, the differential case must be removed from the axle housing and the sensor rotor pressed off the case.

NOTE: Upon removal, the sensor rotor is to be discarded. It is not to be reused.

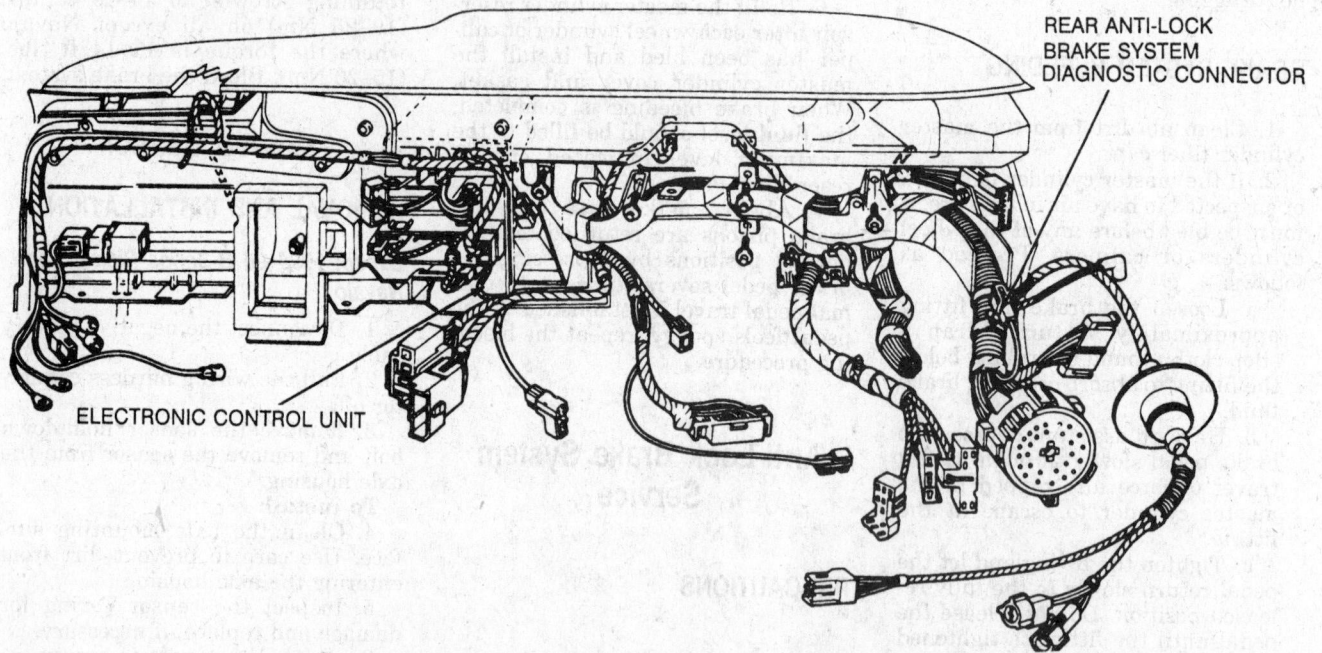

REAR ANTI-LOCK BRAKE SYSTEM DIAGNOSTIC CONNECTOR

ELECTRONIC CONTROL UNIT

7911C122

Rear anti-lock brake system electronic control unit location — 1994–96 B-Series Pick-Up and Navajo

FRONT SUSPENSION

Shock Absorbers

REMOVAL AND INSTALLATION

1992–93 B-Series Pick-Up

1. Raise and safely support the vehicle. Remove the wheel and tire assembly.
2. Remove the upper shock absorber nuts, retainer and bushing.
3. Remove the lower shock absorber-to-lower control arm mounting bolt, nut and washer.
4. Slightly compress the shock absorber and remove it from the vehicle. Remove the remaining retainers and bushing from the upper shock absorber stud.
To install:
5. Install the shock absorber and install the mounting bolts, nuts, washers and bushings. Do not tighten at this time.
6. Install the wheel and tire assembly and lower the vehicle.
7. With the vehicle unladen, tighten the upper shock absorber mounting nuts until the stud protrudes 0.28 in. (7mm) above the upper nut. Tighten the lower mounting bolt and nut to 41–59 ft. lbs. (55–80 Nm).
8. Check the front end alignment.

1994–96 B-Series Pick-Up and Navajo

1. Raise and safely support the vehicle. Remove the wheel and tire assembly.
2. Remove the shock absorber upper attaching nut, washer and bushing from the upper spring seat.
3. Remove the shock absorber lower mounting nut and washer from the radius arm stud.
4. Slide the shock absorber off the stud. Slightly compress the shock absorber and remove it from the vehicle.
5. Installation is the reverse of the removal procedure. Tighten the lower mounting nut to 39–53 ft. lbs. (53–72 Nm) and the upper mounting nut to 25–35 ft. lbs. (34–48 Nm).

MacPherson Strut

REMOVAL AND INSTALLATION

MPV

1. Raise and safely support the vehicle. Remove the wheel and tire assembly.
2. Support the lower control arm with a jack.
3. Remove the clip attaching the brake hose to the strut and disconnect the hose from the strut.
4. Remove the strut-to-knuckle attaching bolts and nuts.
5. Working in the engine compartment, remove the 4 attaching nuts from the strut tower and remove the strut assembly from the vehicle.
6. Remove the rubber cap from the upper mounting block. Loosen the upper attaching nut, but do not remove it.
7. Install a suitable spring compressor and compress the coil spring.
8. Remove the upper attaching nut and slowly relieve the tension on the coil spring, using the spring compressor. When the spring is no longer under tension, remove the spring compressor.
9. Remove the upper mounting block, upper spring seat, spring seat, coil spring, bump stopper and ring rubber from the strut.
To install:
10. Secure the strut in a vise equipped with protective jaw covers, so the strut will not be damaged.
11. Apply a suitable rubber grease to the ring rubber and install it on the bump stopper. Install the bump stopper on the strut.
12. Attach the spring compressor to the coil spring and compress the spring.
13. Install the compressed spring on the strut and install the spring seat.
14. Install the upper spring seat. The flat of the strut rod must fit correctly into the upper spring seat.
15. Install the upper mounting block. Install and loosely tighten the upper attaching nut.
16. Remove the spring compressor. Make sure the spring is properly seated in the upper and lower spring seats.
17. Secure the upper spring seat in a vise and tighten the upper attaching nut to 47–59 ft. lbs. (64–80 Nm). Install the rubber cap on the upper mounting blots.
18. Install the strut assembly in the strut tower, making sure the white mark on the upper mounting block is

in the front-inside direction. Install the attaching nuts and tighten to 22–27 ft. lbs. (29–36 Nm).
19. Install the strut to the knuckle and tighten the attaching bolts and nuts to 69–86 ft. lbs. (93–117 Nm).
20. Position the brake hose on the strut and install the clip. Remove the jack from under the lower control arm.
21. Install the wheel and tire assembly and lower the vehicle. Check the front end alignment.

Coil Springs

REMOVAL AND INSTALLATION

1994–96 B-Series Pick-Up and Navajo

1. Raise and safely support the vehicle. Place a jack under the axle.
2. Remove the nut attaching the shock absorber to the radius arm and slide the shock absorber off of the stud.
3. Remove the nut securing the spring to the axle and remove the retainer.
4. Slowly lower the axle to relieve the spring tension. Remove the spring by rotating the upper coil out of the tabs in the upper spring seat.
To install:
5. Install the top of the spring in the upper seat, rotating into position.
6. Raise the axle until the spring is seated in the lower spring seat. Install the lower retainer and tighten the nut to 70–100 ft. lbs. (95–136 Nm).
7. Connect the shock absorber to the radius arm and lower the vehicle.

Torsion Bar

REMOVAL AND INSTALLATION

1992–93 B-Series Pick-Up

1. Raise and safely support the vehicle. Remove the wheel and tire assembly.
2. Support the lower control arm with a jack.
3. Remove the cotter pin and nut from the lower ball joint stud. Separate the ball joint from the knuckle using tool 49 0727 575 or equivalent.
4. Remove the bolt, washer and nut attaching the shock absorber to the lower control arm.
5. Mark the position of the anchor bolt and swivel for reference during reassembly and remove the anchor bolt and swivel.

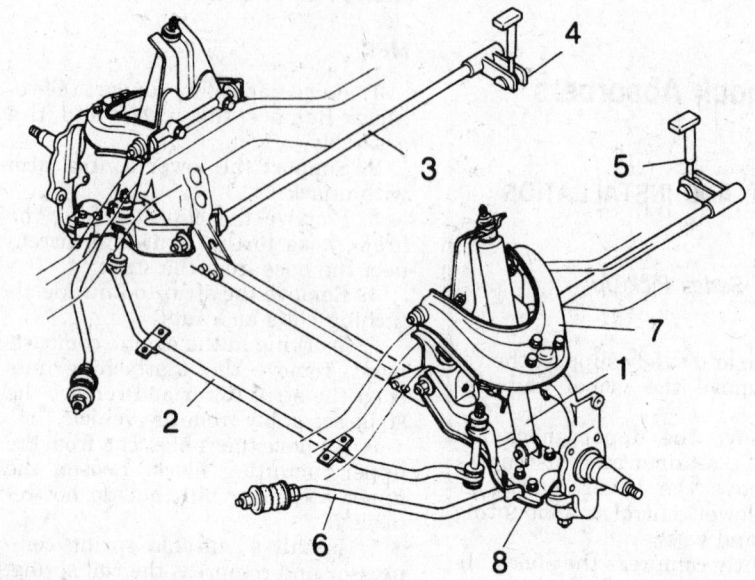

1. Shock absorber
2. Stabilizer
3. Torsion bar
4. Anchor arm
5. Anchor bolt
6. Tension rod
7. Upper arm
8. Lower arm

7911C123

Front suspension assembly — 2WD B-Series Pick-Up

1. Shock absorber
2. Stabilizer
3. Torsion bar
4. Anchor arm
5. Anchor bolt
6. Upper arm
7. Lower arm

7911C124

Front suspension assembly — 4WD B-Series Pick-Up

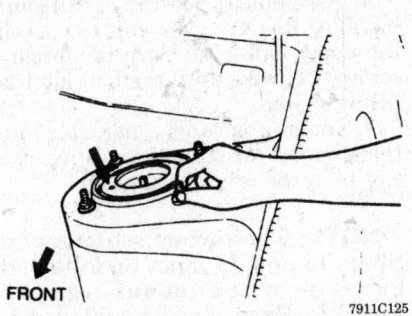

FRONT

7911C125

Strut upper mounting block positioning — MPV

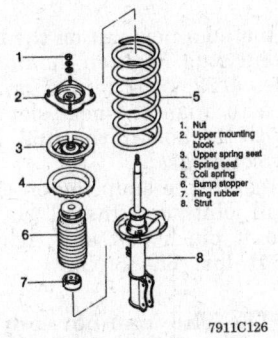

7911C126

1. Nut
2. Upper mounting block
3. Upper spring seat
4. Spring seat
5. Coil spring
6. Bump stopper
7. Ring rubber
8. Strut

MacPherson strut assembly exploded view — MPV

6. Mark the position of the torsion bar on the anchor arm and remove the anchor arm.

7. Mark the position of the torsion bar on the torque plate and remove the torsion bar. If removing the torsion bar from both sides of the vehicle, mark their positions as the torsion bars are not interchangeable.

8. Remove the attaching bolts and remove the torque plate.

9. Check the torsion bar for bending or for looseness between the serrations of the torsion bar and anchor arm and/or torque plate, replace as necessary.

To install:

10. Install the torque plate and tighten the attaching bolts to 55–69 ft. lbs. (75–93 Nm).

11. Coat the serrations of the torsion bar with grease and install in the torque plate, aligning the marks made during the removal procedure. If both torsion bars were removed, make sure the correct torsion bar is being installed.

12. Coat the serrations on the other end of the torsion bar with grease and install the anchor arm onto the torsion bar, aligning the marks made during the removal procedure.

13. Install the anchor bolt and swivel. Tighten the anchor bolt until the marks made during removal are aligned.

14. Connect the shock absorber to the lower control arm and loosely tighten the nut and bolt. Connect the lower ball joint to the knuckle; install the nut and tighten to 87–116 ft. lbs. (118–157 Nm). Install a new cotter pin.

15. Install the wheel and tire assembly and lower the vehicle. With the vehicle unladen, tighten the shock absorber-to-lower control arm bolt and nut to 41–59 ft. lbs. (55–80 Nm).

16. Check vehicle ride height as follows:

    a. Check the front and rear tire pressures and bring to specification.

    b. Measure the distance from the center of each front wheel to the fender brim. The difference must not be greater than 0.39 in. (10mm).

    c. If the difference is not as specified, turn the necessary torsion spring anchor bolt to adjust.

17. Check the front end alignment.

Upper Ball Joints

INSPECTION

1992–93 B-Series Pick-Up

1. Raise and safely support the vehicle. Remove the wheel and tire assembly.

2. Support the lower control arm with a jack.

3. Remove the clip attaching the brake hose to the upper control arm and disconnect the hose from the arm.

4. Remove the cotter pin and nut from the upper ball joint stud. Using tool 49 0727 575 or equivalent, separate the upper ball joint from the knuckle.

5. Install tool 49 0180 510B or equivalent to the ball joint stud and attach a suitable pull scale to the stud.

6. After rocking the ball joint stud back and forth 3–4 times, measure the pull scale reading while the ball joint stud is rotating. The pull scale reading should be 4.4–7.7 lbs.

7. If the pull scale reading is not as specified, replace the upper ball joint.

1994–96 B-Series Pick-Up and Navajo

NOTE: Always check and adjust the wheel bearings before ball joint inspection.

1. Raise and safely support the vehicle.

2. Place a jack under the axle beneath the coil spring.

3. Grasp the upper edge of the tire and move the wheel in and out. A $\frac{1}{32}$ in. or greater movement between the upper spindle arm and the upper control arm or upper part of the axle jaw indicates that the upper ball joint must be replaced.

REMOVAL AND INSTALLATION

1992–93 B-Series Pick-Up

1. Raise and safely support the vehicle. Remove the wheel and tire assembly.

2. Support the lower control arm with a jack.

3. Remove the clip attaching the brake hose to the upper control arm and disconnect the hose from the arm.

4. Remove the cotter pin and nut from the upper ball joint stud. Using tool 49 0727 575 or equivalent, separate the upper ball joint from the knuckle.

5. Remove the upper ball joint-to-upper control arm attaching bolts and remove the upper ball joint.

6. Installation is the reverse of the removal procedure. Tighten the upper ball joint-to-upper control arm attaching bolts to 18–25 ft. lbs. (25–33 Nm) and the upper ball joint stud nut to 22–38 ft. lbs. (29–51 Nm). Install a new cotter pin.

7. Check the front end alignment.

1994–96 B-Series Pick-Up and Navajo

2WD

1. Raise and safely support the vehicle. Remove the wheel and tire assembly.

2. Remove the brake caliper and support it aside with mechanics wire. Do not let the caliper hang by the brake hose.

3. Remove the dust cap, cotter pin, nut retainer, washer and outer bearing and remove the brake rotor from the spindle. Remove the brake dust shield.

4. Disconnect the steering linkage from the spindle and spindle arm by removing the cotter pin and nut. Remove the tie rod end from the spindle arm.

5. Remove the cotter pin and nut from the lower ball joint stud. Remove the axle clamp bolt from the axle.

6. Remove the camber adjuster from the upper ball joint stud and axle beam.

7. Strike the inside area of the axle to pop the lower ball joint loose from the axle beam. Remove the spindle and ball joint assembly from the axle.

NOTE: Do not use a pickle fork to separate the ball joint from the axle as this will damage the seal and ball joint socket.

To install:

8. Install the spindle assembly in a vise and remove the snapring from the lower ball joint. Remove the lower ball joint from the spindle using C-frame T74P-4635-C or equivalent and a suitable receiver cup to press the ball joint from the spindle.

NOTE: The lower ball joint must be removed first.

9. Repeat the procedure in Step 8 to remove the upper ball joint.

NOTE: Do not heat the ball joints or the spindle to aid in removal.

10. Assemble the C-frame and receiver cup and press in the upper ball joint.

11. Repeat the procedure in Step 10 to install the lower ball joint.

NOTE: Do not heat the ball joints or axle to aid in installation.

12. Install the snapring onto the ball joint.

13. Place the spindle and ball joints into the axle. Install the camber adjuster in the upper spindle over the ball joint stud making sure it is properly aligned.

14. Tighten the lower ball joint stud nut to 104–146 ft. lbs. (141–198 Nm). Continue tightening the castellated nut until it lines up with the hole in the stud, then install the cotter pin.

15. Install the clamp bolt into the axle boss and tighten to 48–65 ft. lbs. (65–88 Nm).

16. Install the remaining components in the reverse order of their removal.

4WD

1. Raise and safely support the vehicle. Remove the front wheel and tire assemblies.

2. Remove the disc brake caliper and wire it to the frame. Do not let the caliper hang by the brake hose.

3. Remove the hub locks, wheel bearings and locknuts.

4. Remove the hub, rotor and outer wheel bearing.

5. Remove the nuts retaining the spindle to the steering knuckle. Tap the spindle with a plastic hammer to jar the spindle from the knuckle. Remove the splash shield.

6. On the left side of the vehicle, remove the shaft and joint assembly by pulling the assembly out of the carrier. On the right side of the carrier, remove and discard the clamp from the shaft and joint assembly and the stub shaft. Pull the shaft and joint assembly from the splines of the stub shaft.

7. Remove the cotter pin from the tie rod nut and then remove the nut. Tap on the tie rod stud to free it from the steering arm.

8. Remove the upper ball joint snapring and remove the upper ball joint pinch bolt. Loosen the lower ball joint nut to the end of the stud.

9. Strike the inside of the knuckle near the upper and lower ball joints to break the knuckle loose from the ball joint studs.

10. Remove the camber adjuster sleeve. Note the position of the slot in the camber adjuster so it can be reinstalled in the same position during assembly.

11. Remove the lower ball joint nut. Place the knuckle in a vise and remove the snapring from the bottom ball joint socket, if equipped.

12. Assemble C-frame T74P-4635-C and ball joint remover T83T-3050-A or equivalents on the lower ball joint. Turn the forcing screw clockwise until the lower ball joint is removed from the steering knuckle.

13. Assemble the C-frame and ball joint remover on the upper ball joint and remove in the same manner.

NOTE: Always remove the lower ball joint first.

To install:

14. Clean the steering knuckle bore and insert the lower ball joint in the knuckle as straight as possible.

15. Assemble C-frame T74P-4635-C, ball joint installer T83T-3050-A and receiver cup T80T-3010-A3 or equivalents to install the lower ball joint. Turn the forcing screw clockwise until the lower ball joint is firmly seated. Install the snapring on the lower ball joint.

NOTE: The lower ball joint must always be installed first.

16. Assemble the C-frame, ball joint installer and receiver cup to install the upper ball joint. Turn the forcing screw clockwise until the ball joint is firmly seated.

17. Install the camber adjuster into the support arm, making sure the slot is in the original position.

NOTE: The torque sequence in Steps 18 and 19 must be followed exactly when securing the knuckle. Excessive knuckle turning effort may result in reduced steering returnability if this procedure is not followed.

18. Install a new nut on the bottom ball joint stud. Tighten the nut to 90 ft. lbs. (122 Nm) minimum, then tighten to align the next slot in the nut with the hole in the stud. Install a new cotter pin.

19. Install the snapring on the upper ball joint stud. Install the upper ball joint pinch bolt and tighten to 48–65 ft. lbs. (65–88 Nm).

NOTE: The camber adjuster will seat itself into the knuckle at a predetermined position during the tightening sequence. Do not attempt to adjust this position.

20. On the right side of the carrier, install the rubber boot and new keystone clamps on the stub shaft slip yoke. Slide the right shaft and joint assembly into the slip yoke making sure the splines are fully engaged. Slide the boot over the assembly and crimp the keystone clamp using suitable pliers.

NOTE: The Dana model 35 axle does not have a blind spline, therefore pay special attention to make sure the yoke ears are in phase (in line) during assembly.

21. On the left side of the carrier, slide the shaft and joint assembly through the knuckle and engage the splines on the shaft in the carrier.

22. Install the splash shield and spindle onto the steering knuckle. Install and tighten the spindle nuts to 45 ft. lbs. (61 Nm).

23. Install the rotor on the spindle and install the outer wheel bearing in the race.

24. Install the wheel bearing, locknut, thrust bearing, snapring and locking hubs.

25. Install the caliper and the wheel and tire assemblies. Lower the vehicle.

Lower Ball Joints

INSPECTION

1992–93 B-Series Pick-Up and 4WD MPV

1. Raise and safely support the vehicle. Remove the wheel and tire assembly.
2. On B-Series Pick-Up, support the lower control arm with a jack.
3. On 4WD MPV, disconnect the stabilizer bar from the lower control arm.
4. Remove the cotter pin and nut from the lower ball joint stud. Separate the ball joint from the knuckle using tool 49 0727 575 or equivalent.
5. Install tool 49 0180 510B or equivalent to the ball joint stud and attach a suitable pull scale to the stud.
6. After rocking the ball joint stud back and forth 3–4 times, measure the pull scale reading while the ball joint stud is rotating. The pull scale reading should be 4.4–7.7 lbs.
7. If the pull scale reading is not as specified, replace the lower ball joint.

2WD MPV

1. Raise and safely support the vehicle. Remove the wheel and tire assembly.
2. Remove the brake caliper and support it aside with mechanics wire; do not let it hang by the brake hose.
3. Remove the nuts, bolts, spacer, washers and bushings and remove the compression rod from the lower control arm and chassis and disconnect the stabilizer bar from the lower control arm.

NOTE: The left-hand compression rod nut has left-hand threads.

4. Remove the cotter pin and nut and, using tool 49 0118 850C or equivalent, separate the tie rod end from the knuckle.
5. Remove the bolts and nuts and disconnect the strut from the knuckle.
6. Remove the cotter pin and nut from the lower ball joint stud. Using tool 49 0727 575 or equivalent, separate the lower ball joint from the knuckle.
7. Install tool 49 0180 510B or equivalent to the ball joint stud and attach a suitable pull scale to the stud.
8. After rocking the ball joint stud back and forth 3–4 times, measure the pull scale reading while the ball joint stud is rotating. The pull scale reading should be 39.6 lbs. or less. The rotation torque should be 156.2 inch lbs. (18 Nm) or less.
9. If the pull scale reading or rotation torque is not as specified, replace the entire lower control arm.

1994–96 B-Series Pick-Up and Navajo

NOTE: Always check and adjust the wheel bearings before ball joint inspection.

1. Raise and safely support the vehicle.
2. Place a jack under the axle beneath the coil spring.
3. Grasp the lower edge of the tire and move the wheel in and out. A $\frac{1}{32}$ in. or greater movement between the lower control arm or lower axle and the spindle indicates that the lower ball joint must be replaced.

REMOVAL AND INSTALLATION

1992–93 B-Series Pick-Up

1. Raise and safely support the vehicle. Remove the wheel and tire assembly.
2. Support the lower control arm with a jack.
3. On 2WD vehicles, remove the bolts attaching the tension rod to the lower control arm.
4. Remove the cotter pin and nut from the lower ball joint stud. Separate the ball joint from the knuckle using tool 49 0727 575 or equivalent.
5. Remove the bolts/nuts attaching the lower ball joint to the lower control arm and remove the lower ball joint.
6. Installation is the reverse of the removal procedure. Tighten the lower ball joint-to-lower control arm bolts/nuts to 32–40 ft. lbs. (43–54 Nm) on 2WD vehicles or 41–50 ft. lbs. (55–68 Nm) on 4WD vehicles. Tighten the lower ball joint stud nut to 87–116 ft. lbs. (118–157 Nm) and install a new cotter pin.
7. Check the front end alignment.

MPV

2WD

If the lower ball joint needs replacement, the entire lower control arm must be replaced.

4WD

1. Raise and safely support the vehicle. Remove the wheel and tire assembly.

2. Disconnect the stabilizer bar from the lower control arm.
3. Remove the cotter pin and nut from the lower ball joint stud. Separate the ball joint from the knuckle using tool 49 0727 575 or equivalent.
4. Remove the lower ball joint-to-lower control arm bolts and remove the lower ball joint.
5. Installation is the reverse of the removal procedure. Tighten the lower ball joint-to-lower control arm bolts to 75–101 ft. lbs. (102–137 Nm). Tighten the lower ball joint stud nut to 115–137 ft. lbs. (157–186 Nm) and install a new cotter pin.

1994–96 B-Series Pick-Up and Navajo

2WD

1. Raise and safely support the vehicle. Remove the wheel and tire assembly.
2. Remove the brake caliper and support it aside with mechanics wire. Do not let the caliper hang by the brake hose.
3. Remove the dust cap, cotter pin, nut retainer, washer and outer bearing and remove the brake rotor from the spindle. Remove the brake dust shield.
4. Disconnect the steering linkage from the spindle and spindle arm by removing the cotter pin and nut. Remove the tie rod end from the spindle arm.
5. Remove the cotter pin and nut from the lower ball joint stud. Remove the axle clamp bolt from the axle.
6. Remove the camber adjuster from the upper ball joint stud and axle beam.
7. Strike the inside area of the axle to pop the lower ball joint loose from the axle beam. Remove the spindle and ball joint assembly from the axle.

NOTE: Do not use a pickle fork to separate the ball joint from the axle as this will damage the seal and ball joint socket.

To install:

8. Install the spindle assembly in a vise and remove the snapring from the lower ball joint. Remove the lower ball joint from the spindle using C-frame T74P-4635-C or equivalent and a suitable receiver cup to press the ball joint from the spindle.

NOTE: Do not heat the ball joint or the spindle to aid in removal.

9. Assemble the C-frame and receiver cup and press in the lower ball joint.

NOTE: Do not heat the ball joint or axle to aid in installation.

10. Install the snapring onto the ball joint.

11. Place the spindle and ball joints into the axle. Install the camber adjuster in the upper spindle over the ball joint stud making sure it is properly aligned.

12. Tighten the lower ball joint stud nut to 104–146 ft. lbs. (141–198 Nm). Continue tightening the castellated nut until it lines up with the hole in the stud, then install the cotter pin.

13. Install the clamp bolt into the axle boss and tighten to 48–65 ft. lbs. (65–88 Nm).

14. Install the remaining components in the reverse order of their removal.

4WD

1. Raise and safely support the vehicle. Remove the front wheel and tire assemblies.

2. Remove the disc brake caliper and wire it to the frame. Do not let the caliper hang by the brake hose.

3. Remove the hub locks, wheel bearings and locknuts.

4. Remove the hub, rotor and outer wheel bearing.

5. Remove the nuts retaining the spindle to the steering knuckle. Tap the spindle with a plastic hammer to jar the spindle from the knuckle. Remove the splash shield.

6. On the left side of the vehicle, remove the shaft and joint assembly by pulling the assembly out of the carrier. On the right side of the carrier, remove and discard the clamp from the shaft and joint assembly and the stub shaft. Pull the shaft and joint assembly from the splines of the stub shaft.

7. Remove the cotter pin from the tie rod nut and then remove the nut. Tap on the tie rod stud to free it from the steering arm.

8. Remove the upper ball joint snapring and remove the upper ball joint pinch bolt. Loosen the lower ball joint nut to the end of the stud.

9. Strike the inside of the knuckle near the upper and lower ball joints to break the knuckle loose from the ball joint studs.

10. Remove the camber adjuster sleeve. Note the position of the slot in the camber adjuster so it can be reinstalled in the same position during assembly.

11. Remove the lower ball joint nut. Place the knuckle in a vise and remove the snapring from the bottom ball joint socket, if equipped.

12. Assemble C-frame T74P–4635–C and ball joint remover T83T–3050–A or equivalents on the lower ball joint. Turn the forcing screw clockwise until the lower ball joint is removed from the steering knuckle.

To install:

13. Clean the steering knuckle bore and insert the lower ball joint in the knuckle as straight as possible.

14. Assemble C-frame T74P–4635–C, ball joint installer T83T–3050–A and receiver cup T80T–3010–A3 or equivalents to install the lower ball joint. Turn the forcing screw clockwise until the lower ball joint is firmly seated. Install the snapring on the lower ball joint.

15. Install the camber adjuster into the support arm, making sure the slot is in the original position.

NOTE: The torque sequence in Steps 16 and 17 must be followed exactly when securing the knuckle. Excessive knuckle turning effort may result in reduced steering returnability if this procedure is not followed.

16. Install a new nut on the bottom ball joint stud. Tighten the nut to 90 ft. lbs. (122 Nm) minimum, then tighten to align the next slot in the nut with the hole in the stud. Install a new cotter pin.

17. Install the snapring on the upper ball joint stud. Install the upper ball joint pinch bolt and tighten to 48–65 ft. lbs. (65–88 Nm).

NOTE: The camber adjuster will seat itself into the knuckle at a predetermined position during the tightening sequence. Do not attempt to adjust this position.

18. On the right side of the carrier, install the rubber boot and new keystone clamps on the stub shaft slip yoke. Slide the right shaft and joint assembly into the slip yoke making sure the splines are fully engaged. Slide the boot over the assembly and crimp the keystone clamp using suitable pliers.

NOTE: The Dana model 35 axle does not have a blind spline, therefore pay special attention to make sure the yoke ears are in phase (in line) during assembly.

19. On the left side of the carrier, slide the shaft and joint assembly through the knuckle and engage the splines on the shaft in the carrier.

20. Install the splash shield and spindle onto the steering knuckle. Install and tighten the spindle nuts to 45 ft. lbs. (61 Nm).

21. Install the rotor on the spindle and install the outer wheel bearing in the race.

22. Install the wheel bearing, locknut, thrust bearing, snapring and locking hubs.

23. Install the caliper and the wheel and tire assemblies. Lower the vehicle.

Upper Control Arms

REMOVAL AND INSTALLATION

1992–93 B-Series Pick-Up

1. Raise and safely support the vehicle. Remove the wheel and tire assembly.

2. Support the lower control arm with a jack.

3. Remove the clip attaching the brake hose to the upper control arm and disconnect the hose from the arm.

4. Remove the cotter pin and nut from the upper ball joint stud. Using tool 49 0727 575 or equivalent, separate the upper ball joint from the knuckle.

5. Remove the bolts and washers retaining the upper control arm shaft to the chassis and remove the upper control arm. Note the position of the alignment shims so they can be reassembled in their original positions.

6. Installation is the reverse of the removal procedure. Tighten the upper control arm shaft-to-chassis bolts to 54–69 ft. lbs. (74–93 Nm) on 2WD vehicles or 69–85 ft. lbs. (93–117 Nm) on 4WD vehicles. Tighten the upper ball joint stud nut to 22–38 ft. lbs. (29–51 Nm) and install a new cotter pin.

Lower Control Arms

REMOVAL AND INSTALLATION

1992–93 B-Series Pick-Up

1. Raise and safely support the vehicle. Remove the wheel and tire assembly.

2. Support the lower control arm with a jack.

3. Remove the cotter pin and nut from the lower ball joint stud. Separate the ball joint from the knuckle using tool 49 0727 575 or equivalent.

4. Remove the bolt, washer and nut attaching the shock absorber to the lower control arm.

5. Remove the torsion bar, anchor arm and torque plate assembly.

6. Remove the bolt(s) and nut(s) attaching the lower control arm to the frame.

7. On 2WD vehicles, remove the bolts attaching the tension rod to the lower control arm.

8. Remove the bolts, bushings, retainers, spacer and nuts connecting the stabilizer bar to the lower control arm.

9. Remove the lower control arm from the vehicle. Remove the lower ball joint, if necessary.

To install:

10. Position the lower control to the frame and install the attaching bolt(s) and nut(s), but do not tighten at this time.

11. Install the torsion bar, anchor arm and torque plate assembly.

12. On 2WD vehicles, install the tension rod bolt and tighten to 69–86 ft. lbs. (93–117 Nm).

13. Attach the stabilizer bar to the control arm with the bolts, bushings, retainers, spacer and nuts. Tighten the nuts so 0.73 in. (18.5mm) of thread is exposed at the end of the bolt.

14. Install the shock absorber to the lower control arm and loosely tighten the mounting bolt and nut.

15. Install the wheel and tire assembly and lower the vehicle.

16. With the vehicle unladen, tighten the lower control arm-to-frame bolt and nut on 2WD vehicles and the front side lower control arm-to-frame bolt and nut on 4WD vehicles to 87–116 ft. lbs. (118–157 Nm). Tighten the rear side lower control arm-to-frame bolt and nut on 4WD vehicles to 116–145 ft. lbs. (157–196 Nm).

17. With the vehicle unladen, tighten the shock absorber-to-lower control arm bolt and nut to 41–59 ft. lbs. (55–80 Nm).

18. Check vehicle ride height as follows:

　a. Check the front and rear tire pressures and bring to specification.

　b. Measure the distance from the center of each front wheel to the fender brim. The difference must not be greater than 0.39 in. (10mm).

　c. If the difference is not as specified, turn the necessary torsion spring anchor bolt to adjust.

19. Check the front end alignment.

MPV

2WD

1. Raise and safely support the vehicle. Remove the wheel and tire assembly.

2. Remove the brake caliper and support it aside with mechanics wire; do not let it hang by the brake hose.

3. Remove the nuts, bolts, spacer, washers and bushings and remove the compression rod from the lower control arm and chassis and disconnect the stabilizer bar from the lower control arm.

4. Remove the cotter pin and nut and, using tool 49 0118 850C or equivalent, separate the tie rod end from the knuckle.

5. Remove the bolts and nuts and disconnect the strut from the knuckle.

6. Remove the cotter pin and nut from the lower ball joint stud. Using tool 49 0727 575 or equivalent, separate the lower ball joint from the knuckle.

7. Remove the mounting bolt and nut and remove the lower control arm from the vehicle.

To install:

8. Position the lower control arm to the chassis and install the bolt and nut, but do not tighten at this time.

9. Install the knuckle to the lower control arm. Tighten the lower ball joint stud nut to 87–116 ft. lbs. (118–157 Nm) and install a new cotter pin.

10. Connect the strut to the knuckle and tighten the attaching bolts and nuts to 69–86 ft. lbs. (93–117 Nm).

11. Connect the tie rod end to the knuckle. Tighten the tie rod end stud nut to 43–58 ft. lbs. (59–78 Nm) and install a new cotter pin.

12. Install the compression rod to the lower control arm and chassis. Tighten the compression rod-to-lower control arm mounting bolts to 76–93 ft. lbs. (103–126 Nm) and the compression rod bushing-to-chassis bolts to 61–76 ft. lbs. (83–103 Nm). Install the compression rod nut but do not tighten at this time.

NOTE: The left-hand compression rod nut has left-hand threads.

13. Connect the stabilizer bar to the control arm with the bolt, washers, bushings, spacer and nuts. Tighten the nuts so 0.24 in. (6mm) of thread is exposed at the end of the bolt.

14. Install the caliper and the wheel and tire assembly. Lower the vehicle.

15. With the vehicle unladen, tighten the lower control arm-to-chassis bolt and nut to 94–108 ft. lbs. (146–172 Nm). Tighten the compression rod nut to 108–127 ft. lbs. (146–172 Nm).

16. Check the front end alignment.

4WD

1. Raise and safely support the vehicle. Remove the wheel and tire assembly.

2. Remove the bolt, retainers, bushings, spacer and nuts and disconnect the stabilizer bar from the lower control arm.

3. Remove the cotter pin and nut from the lower ball joint stud. Separate the ball joint from the knuckle using tool 49 0727 575 or equivalent.

4. Remove the lower control arm-to-chassis nuts and bolts and remove the lower control arm.

To install:

5. Position the lower control arm to the chassis and install the bolts and nuts. Do not tighten at this time.

6. Connect the lower ball joint to the knuckle and tighten the ball joint stud nut to 115–137 ft. lbs. (157–186 Nm). Install a new cotter pin.

7. Install the bolt, retainers, bushings, spacer and nuts and connect the stabilizer bar to the lower control arm. Tighten the nuts so 0.24 in. (6mm) of thread is exposed at the end of the bolt.

8. Install the wheel and tire assembly and lower the vehicle. With the vehicle unladen, tighten the lower control arm-to-chassis nuts and bolts to 101–127 ft. lbs. (137–172 Nm).

9. Check the front end alignment.

Stabilizer Bar

REMOVAL AND INSTALLATION

Except 1994–96 B-Series Pick-Up and Navajo

1. Raise and safely support the vehicle. Remove the wheel and tire assembly.

2. On MPV, remove the splash shield.

3. Remove the bolt, retainers, bushings, spacer and nuts connecting the stabilizer bar end to the lower control arm.

4. Remove the stabilizer bar bushing bracket bolts and remove the stabilizer bar.

To install:

5. Install the stabilizer bar to the vehicle and loosely tighten the bushing bracket bolts.

6. Install the bolt, retainers, bushings, spacer and nuts connecting the stabilizer bar end to the lower control arm. Tighten the nuts so 0.73 in. (18.5mm) of thread is exposed at the end of the bolt on B-Series Pick-Up or 0.24 in. (6mm) of thread is exposed at the end of the bolt on MPV.

7. Install the wheel and tire assembly and lower the vehicle.

8. With the vehicle unladen, tighten the stabilizer bar bushing bracket bolts to 16–20 ft. lbs. (22–26 Nm) on B-Series pickup, 37–45 ft. lbs. (50–61 Nm) on 2WD MPV or 14–19 ft. lbs. (19–26 Nm) on 4WD MPV.

9. Check the front end alignment.

1994–96 B-Series Pick-Up and Navajo

2WD

1. Raise and safely support the vehicle.

2. Remove the nut and washer and disconnect the stabilizer link assembly from the front I-beam axle.

3. Remove the mounting bolts and remove the stabilizer bar retainers from the stabilizer bar assembly. Remove the stabilizer bar.

4. Installation is the reverse of the removal procedure. Tighten the retainer bolts to 35–50 ft. lbs. (47–68 Nm). Tighten the stabilizer bar link nuts to 30–44 ft. lbs. (40–60 Nm).

4WD

1. Raise and safely support the vehicle.

2. Remove the bolts and retainers from the center and right end of the stabilizer bar.

3. Remove the nut, bolt and washer retaining the stabilizer bar to the stabilizer link.

4. Remove the stabilizer bar and bushings.

5. Installation is the reverse of the removal procedure. Tighten the retainer bolts to 35–50 ft. lbs. (48–68 Nm). Tighten the stabilizer bar link nut to 30–44 ft. lbs. (40–60 Nm).

I-Beam Axle

REMOVAL AND INSTALLATION

2WD Navajo

1. Raise and safely support the vehicle. Remove the front wheel spindle, the front spring and the stabilizer bar, if equipped.

2. Remove the spring lower seat from the radius arm and then remove the bolt and nut that attaches the stabilizer bar bracket, if equipped, and radius arm to the front axle.

3. Remove the axle-to-frame pivot bracket bolt and nut.

To install:

4. Position the axle to the frame pivot bracket and install the bolt and nut finger tight.

5. Position the opposite end of the of the axle to the radius arm, install the attaching bolt from underneath through the bracket, the radius arm and the axle. Install the nut and tighten to 191–220 ft. lbs. (258–298 Nm).

6. Install the spring lower seat on the radius arm so the hole in the seat indexes over the arm-to-axle bolt. Install the front spring.

7. Install the front wheel spindle and stabilizer bar, if equipped.

8. Lower the vehicle and with the weight on the suspension, tighten the axle-to-frame pivot bracket bolts to 120–150 ft. lbs. (163–203 Nm).

Front Wheel Bearings

ADJUSTMENT

2WD Vehicles

B SERIES PICK-UP

1. Raise and safely support the vehicle. Remove the wheel and tire assembly.

2. Remove the brake caliper and suspend it aside with rope or mechanics wire; do not let the caliper hang by the brake hose.

3. Remove the dust cap and cotter pin.

4. Tighten the locknut to 14–22 ft. lbs. (20–29 Nm) and turn the hub and rotor 2–3 times to seat the bearings.

5. Loosen the locknut until it can be turned by hand.

6. Attach a suitable pull scale to a wheel lug bolt and measure the frictional force.

7. Tighten the locknut until the pull scale reading, the initial turning torque, reaches the frictional force plus 1.3–2.4 lbs. Insert the retainer and secure with a new cotter pin.

8. Install the dust cap and the caliper. Install the wheel and tire assembly and lower the vehicle.

9. Before driving the vehicle, pump the brake pedal several times to restore normal brake travel.

1994–96 B-SERIES PICK-UP AND NAVAJO

1. Raise the vehicle and support it safely.

2. Remove the wheel cover and the grease cap from the hub. Remove the cotter pin and the retainer. Discard the cotter pin.

3. Loosen the adjusting nut 3 turns.

4. Obtain running clearance between the brake rotor and disc brake pads by rocking the entire wheel and tire assembly in and out several times to push the caliper and brake pads away from the rotor.

NOTE: Do not pry on the caliper piston to obtain clearance.

5. While rotating the wheel, tighten the adjusting nut to 17–25 ft. lbs. (23–34 Nm) to seat the bearings.

6. Back off the adjusting nut 1/2 turn. Retighten the nut to 18–20 inch lbs. (2.0–2.3 Nm).

7. Install the retainer on the adjusting nut so the castellations line up with the hole in the spindle without moving the nut. Install a new cotter pin.

8. Check the front wheel rotation. If the wheel rotates properly, reinstall the grease cap and the wheel cover. If rotation is noisy or rough, remove, inspect and lubricate the bearings and bearing races.

9. Before driving the vehicle, pump the brake pedal several times to restore normal brake travel.

REMOVAL AND INSTALLATION

2WD Vehicles

1. Raise and safely support the vehicle. Remove the wheel and tire assembly.

2. Remove the brake caliper and support it with mechanics wire. Do not let the caliper hang by the brake hose.

3. Remove the grease cap, cotter pin, retainer, adjusting nut and washer. Discard the cotter pin.

4. Remove the outer bearing and pull the hub and rotor off the spindle. Remove the grease seal using a seal removal tool. Discard the grease seal.

5. Remove the inner bearing from the hub. Remove all traces of old lubricant from the bearings, hub and spindle with solvent and dry thoroughly.

6. Inspect the bearings and bearing races for scratches, pits or cracks. If the bearings and/or races are worn or damaged, remove the races with a brass drift.

To install:

7. If the bearing races were removed, install new races in the hub with suitable installation tools. Make sure the races are properly seated.

8. Using a bearing packer, pack the bearings with high-temperature wheel bearing grease. If a packer is not available, work as much grease

as possible between the rollers and cages by hand.

9. Place a small amount of grease within the hub and grease the races. Install the inner bearing. Install a new wheel seal using a seal installer. Apply grease to the lips of the seal.

10. Install the hub and rotor assembly on the spindle. Install the outer bearing, washer and adjusting nut. Adjust the bearings.

11. Install the retainer, a new cotter pin and the grease cap.

12. Install the caliper and the wheel and tire assembly. Lower the vehicle.

13. Before driving the vehicle, pump the brake pedal several times to restore normal brake travel.

REAR SUSPENSION

Shock Absorber

REMOVAL AND INSTALLATION

1. Raise and safely support the vehicle.

2. Place a jack under the rear axle and raise slightly to take the load off the shock absorbers.

3. On MPV equipped with automatic load leveling, disconnect the air line from the shock absorber.

4. Remove the shock absorber lower attaching nut or nut and bolt and swing the lower end free of the mounting bracket or stud on the axle housing or spring plate.

5. Remove the upper attaching bolt and/or nut(s) and remove the shock absorber.

6. Installation is the reverse of the removal procedure. Tighten the lower attaching nut or nut and bolt to 47–58 ft. lbs. (64–78 Nm) on B-Series Pick-Up, 56–76 ft. lbs. (76–103 Nm) on MPV or 41–53 ft. lbs. (55–72 Nm) on Navajo.

7. Tighten the upper attaching bolt and/or nut(s) to 47–58 ft. lbs. (64–78 Nm) on B-Series Pick-Up, 56–76 ft. lbs. (76–103 Nm) on MPV or 15–21 ft. lbs. (21–29 Nm) on Navajo.

Coil Springs

REMOVAL AND INSTALLATION

MPV

1. Raise and safely support the vehicle. Remove the splash shield.

2. Remove the stabilizer bar.

3. Remove the nut and disconnect the height sensor from the rear axle.

4. Remove the bolt attaching the parking brake cable bracket.

5. Support the rear axle housing with a jack. Raise the jack slightly to take the load off the shock absorbers.

6. Remove the attaching bolts and nuts and disconnect the shock absorbers from the lower axle housing.

7. Slowly lower the axle housing until the spring tension is relieved. Remove the coil springs.

8. Remove the spring seats and bump stopper, if equipped.

To install:

9. Install the upper and lower spring seats and the bump stopper, if removed.

10. Install the coil springs, making sure the larger diameter coil is toward the axle housing.

11. Raise the axle housing enough to connect the shock absorbers. Install the attaching bolts and nuts and tighten to 56–76 ft. lbs. (76–103 Nm). Remove the jack.

12. Install the bolt attaching the parking brake cable bracket and the nut attaching the height sensor.

13. Install the stabilizer bar. Tighten the link bolt nut until 0.28 in. (7mm) of thread is exposed at the top of the link bolt. Do not tighten the stabilizer bar bushing bracket bolts at this time.

14. Lower the vehicle. With the vehicle unladen, tighten the stabilizer bar bushing bracket bolts to 23–38 ft. lbs. (34–51 Nm).

15. Install the splash shield.

Leaf Springs

REMOVAL AND INSTALLATION

1992–93 B-Series Pick-Up

2WD

1. Raise and safely support the vehicle. Remove the wheel and tire assembly.

2. Support the rear axle housing with a jack. Raise the jack slightly to take the load off the shock absorber.

3. Remove the nut and washers and slide the shock absorber off of the spring clamp stud. Lower the jack just enough to relieve the spring tension.

4. Remove the nuts and washers and remove the U-bolts, spring clamp and rubber stopper.

5. Support the leaf spring and remove the attaching bolts and the spring pin at the front of the leaf spring.

6. Remove the nuts and washers and remove the shackle pin and shackle plate at the rear of the leaf spring.

7. Remove the leaf spring and bushings.

8. Installation is the reverse of the removal procedure. Tighten the shackle pin nuts to 43–58 ft. lbs. (59–78 Nm). Tighten the spring pin attaching bolts to 12–17 ft. lbs. (16–23 Nm) and the spring pin nut to 58–72 ft. lbs. (78–98 Nm).

9. Tighten the U-bolt nuts to 47–58 ft. lbs. (64–78 Nm) and the lower shock absorber mounting nut to 47–58 ft. lbs. (64–78 Nm).

4WD

1. Raise and safely support the vehicle.Remove the wheel and tire assembly.

2. Support the rear axle housing with a jack. Raise the jack slightly to take the load off the shock absorber.

3. Remove the nut and bolt and disconnect the shock absorber from the axle housing. Lower the jack just enough to relieve the spring tension.

4. Remove the nuts and washers and remove the U-bolts, spring clamp and rubber stopper.

5. Remove the attaching bolts and the spring pin at the front of the leaf spring.

6. Remove the nuts and washers and remove the shackle pin and shackle plate at the rear of the leaf spring.

7. Lower the axle enough to allow clearance for the leaf spring to be removed. Remove the leaf spring and bushings.

8. Installation is the reverse of the removal procedure. Tighten the shackle pin nuts to 43–58 ft. lbs. (59–78 Nm). Tighten the spring pin attaching bolts to 12–17 ft. lbs. (16–23 Nm) and the spring pin nut to 58–72 ft. lbs. (78–98 Nm).

9. Tighten the U-bolt nuts to 88–101 ft. lbs. (120–137 Nm) and the lower shock absorber mounting bolt and nut to 47–58 ft. lbs. (64–78 Nm).

1994–96 B-Series Pick-Up and Navajo

1. Raise the vehicle and safely support on the frame until the weight

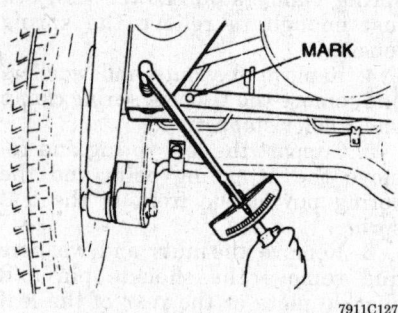

Lateral rod positioning — MPV

is off the rear spring, with the tires still touching the floor.

2. Remove the nuts from the spring U-bolts and drive the U-bolts from the U-bolt plate.

3. Remove the spring-to-bracket nut and bolt at the front of the spring.

4. Remove the shackle upper and lower nuts and bolts at the rear of the spring. Remove the spring and shackle assembly from the rear shackle bracket.

To install:

5. Position the spring in the shackle and install the upper

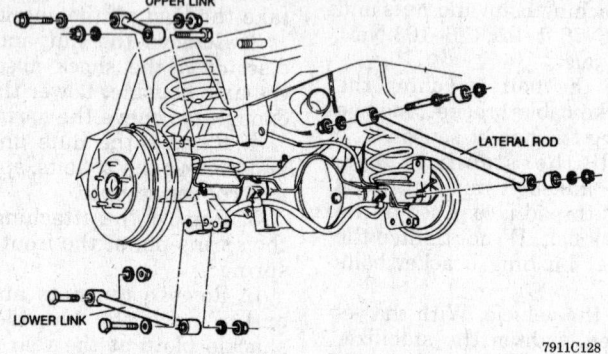

Rear control arm installation — MPV

shackle-to-spring bolt and nut with the bolt head facing outboard.

6. Position the front end of the spring in the bracket and install the bolt and nut. Position the shackle in the rear bracket and install the bolt and nut.

7. Position the spring on the bottom of the axle with the spring tie bolt centered in the hole provided in the seat.

8. Install the spring U-bolts, U-bolt plate and nuts and lower the vehicle. Tighten the spring U-bolt nuts to 88–108 ft. lbs. (119–146 Nm), the front spring bolt and nut to 64–91 ft. lbs. (87–123 Nm) and the rear shackle bolts and nuts to 75–115 ft. lbs. (100–155 Nm).

Rear Control Arms

REMOVAL AND INSTALLATION

MPV

LATERAL ROD

1. Raise and safely support the vehicle.

2. Support the axle housing with a jack.

3. Remove the lateral rod-to-chassis stud bolt and nut and the lateral rod-to-axle housing nut.

4. Remove the lateral rod.

5. Installation is the reverse of the removal procedure. Make sure the lateral rod is installed with the identification mark toward the body.

6. Tighten the lateral rod-to-axle housing nut to 108–127 ft. lbs. (146–167 Nm). Tighten the lateral rod-to-chassis stud bolt and nuts to 94–127 ft. lbs. (128–167 Nm).

UPPER CONTROL ARMS

1. Raise and safely support the vehicle.

2. Support the axle housing with a jack.

3. Remove the upper control arm-to-chassis bolt and nut and the upper control arm-to-axle housing bolt and nut.

4. Remove the upper control arm.

5. Installation is the reverse of the removal procedure. Tighten the upper control arm attaching bolts and nuts to 94–127 ft. lbs. (128–167 Nm).

LOWER CONTROL ARMS

1. Raise and safely support the vehicle.

2. Support the axle housing with a jack.

3. Remove the lower control arm-to-chassis bolt and nut and the lower control arm-to-axle housing bolt and nut.

4. Remove the lower control arm.

5. Installation is the reverse of the removal procedure. Tighten the upper control arm attaching bolts and nuts to 101–127 ft. lbs. (137–167 Nm).

FIRING ORDERS

NOTE: To avoid confusion, always replace spark plug wires one at a time.

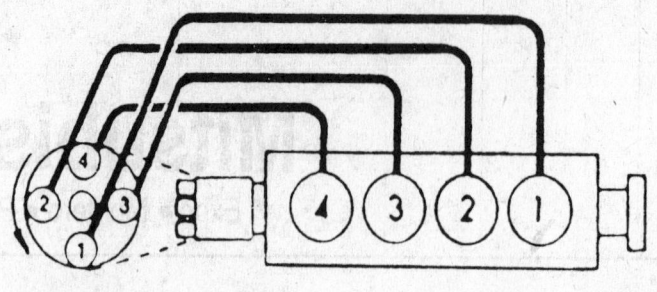

84701001

1.8L and 1993–96 2.4L Engines
Engine Firing Order: 1–3–4–2
Distributor Rotation: Counterclockwise

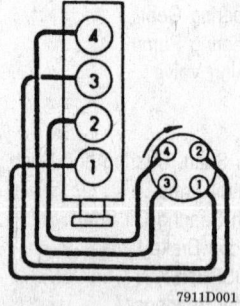

7911D001

1992 2.4L engine
Engine Firing Order:
1–3–4–2
Distributor Rotation:
Clockwise

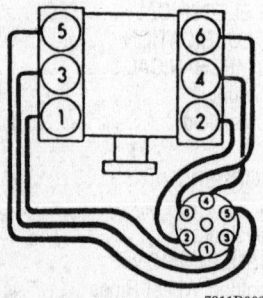

7911D002

3.0L engine
Engine Firing Order:
1–2–3–4–5–6
Distributor Rotation:
Counterclockwise

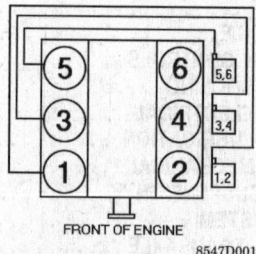

FRONT OF ENGINE

8547D001

3.5L engine
Engine Firing Order:
1–2–3–4–5–6
Distributor Rotation:
Counterclockwise

ENGINE ELECTRICAL

NOTE: Disconnecting the negative battery cable on some vehicles may interfere with the functions of the on board computer systems and may require the computer to undergo a relearning process, once the negative battery cable is reconnected.

Distributor

REMOVAL

1. Disconnect the negative battery cable.
2. Disconnect the distributor pickup lead wires and vacuum hose(s), if equipped.
3. Unfasten the distributor cap retaining clips or screws and lift off the distributor cap with all ignition wires connected. Remove the coil wire if necessary.
4. Matchmark the rotor to the distributor housing and the distributor housing to the engine.

NOTE: Do not crank the engine during this procedure. If the engine is cranked, the matchmark must be disregarded.

5. Remove the retaining nut and remove the distributor from the engine.

INSTALLATION

Timing Not Disturbed

1. Install a new distributor housing O-ring.
2. Install the distributor in the engine so the rotor is aligned with the matchmark on the housing and the housing is aligned with the matchmark on the engine. Make sure the distributor is fully seated and that the distributor shaft is fully engaged.
3. Install the retaining nut finger-tight only. Connect the vacuum hose(s), if removed.
4. Connect the distributor pickup electrical harness.
5. Install the distributor cap and secure.
6. Connect the negative battery cable.
7. Check the ignition timing and adjust as required. Tighten the retaining nut.

Timing Disturbed

1. Install a new distributor housing O-ring.
2. Position the engine so No. 1 piston is on TDC of compression stroke and the timing mark on the vibration damper is aligned with **0** on the timing indicator.
3. Install the distributor so the rotor is aligned with the No. 1 ignition wire on the distributor cap. Take note that the distributor shaft is fully engaged and the housing is fully seated.

NOTE: There are distributor cap runners inside the cap on vehicles with 3.0L engine. Make sure the rotor is pointing to where the No. 1 runner originates inside the cap and not where the No. 1 ignition wire plugs into the cap.

4. Install the retaining nut finger-tight only. Connect the vacuum hose(s), if removed.
5. Connect the distributor electrical harness.
6. Install the distributor cap and secure.
7. Connect the negative battery cable.
8. Adjust the ignition timing and tighten the retaining nut.

Distributorless Ignition System

REMOVAL AND INSTALLATION

NOTE: The 3.5L engine is equipped with distributorless ignition that consists of 3 separate coils that drive 2 cylinders each, ignition power transistor, camshaft sensor and crankshaft sensor. The coils are paired by 1-2, 3-4 and 5-6 cylinders. The ignition power transistor is located on top of the intake plenum, the crankshaft sensor is located next

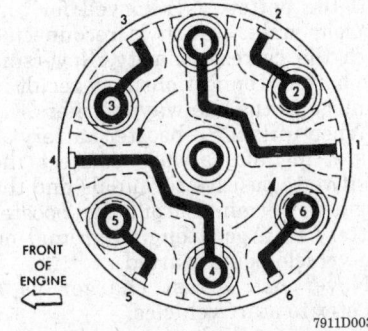

FRONT OF ENGINE

7911D003

Distributor cap terminal routing viewed from the top of the cap — 3.0L engine

to the vibration damper and the camshaft sensor is mounted to the driver side cylinder head.

Camshaft Sensor

1. Disconnect the negative battery cable.
2. Remove the upper intake manifold plenum cover and timing belt cover.
3. Disconnect the sensor connector and wiring harness. Remove the camshaft sensor from the vehicle.
4. Install the sensor and torque screw to 7 ft. lbs. (9 Nm). Install the remaining components.

Crankshaft Sensor

1. Disconnect the negative battery cable.
2. Disconnect the sensor connector and wiring harness. Remove the crankshaft sensor from the vehicle.
3. Install the sensor and torque screw to 7 ft. lbs. (9 Nm). Install the remaining components.

Ignition Power Transistor

1. Disconnect the negative battery cable.
2. Remove the upper intake manifold plenum cover.
3. Disconnect the transistor connector and wiring harness. Remove the transistor from the vehicle.
4. Install the transistor and torque screw to 7 ft. lbs. (9 Nm). Install the remaining components.

Ignition Coil

1. Disconnect the negative battery cable.
2. Remove the driver side center cover from the rocker cover.
3. Disconnect the spark plug and coil electrical connectors.
4. Remove the coil retaining screws and pull coil from the rocker cover.
5. Install the coil and torque the retaining bolts to 7 ft. lbs. (9 Nm).
6. Install the remaining components.

Ignition Timing

ADJUSTMENT

1. Start the engine, set the parking brake and run the engine until normal operating temperature is reached. Keep all lights and accessories **OFF** and the transmission in neutral.
2. Without disconnecting the connector, insert a paper clip into the

tachometer terminal. Connect the red lead of a tachometer to the paper clip and connect the black lead to a ground. Set the idle speed to specifications.

3. Turn the engine **OFF**. Remove the water-proof cover from the ignition timing adjusting connector. Connect a jumper wire from the ignition timing adjusting terminal to ground.

4. Connect a conventional timing light to No. 1 cylinder spark plug wire. Start the engine and allow to idle.

5. Aim the timing light at the timing scale.

6. Loosen the distributor nut to allow for distributor rotation.

7. Turn the distributor in the proper direction until the specified timing is reached. Tighten the retainer nut and recheck the timing. Turn the engine **OFF**.

8. Remove the jumper wire from the ignition timing adjusting terminal and install the water-proof cover.

9. Start the engine and check the actual ignition timing. This reading should be 3 degrees more than basic timing for the 2.4L engine or 10 de-

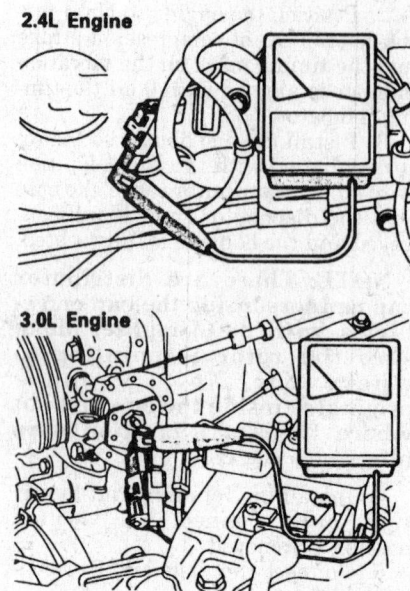

2.4L Engine

3.0L Engine

7911D006

Tachometer connector — Pick-Up

grees more than basic timing for the 3.0L engine.

NOTE: The actual timing may fluctuate according to the control mode of the engine control unit; this is a normal condition.

10. Turn the engine **OFF** and remove all test equipment.

Alternator

PRECAUTIONS

Several precautions must be observed when working with the alternator to avoid damaging the unit.

If the battery is removed for any reason, make sure it is reconnected with the correct polarity. Reversing the battery connections may result in damage to the one-way rectifiers.

When utilizing a booster battery as a starting aid, always connect the positive to positive terminals and the negative terminal from the booster battery to a good engine ground on the vehicle being started.

Never use a fast charger as a booster to start vehicles.

Disconnect the battery cables when charging the battery with a fast charger.

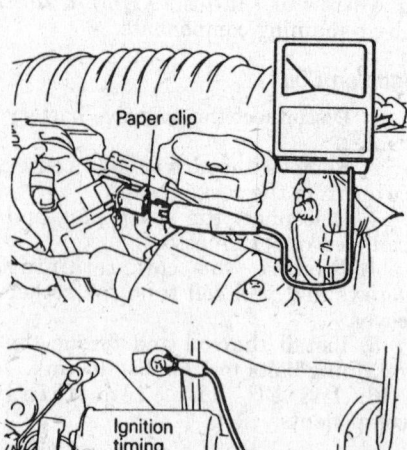

Paper clip

Ignition timing adjusting connector

7911D005

Tachometer terminal and ignition timing adjusting connector — Montero with 3.0L engine

Never attempt to polarize the alternator.

Do not use test lights of more than 12 volts when checking diode continuity.

Do not short across or ground any of the alternator terminals.

The polarity of the battery, alternator and regulator must be matched and considered before making any electrical connections within the system.

Never separate the alternator on an open circuit. Make sure all connections within the circuit are clean and tight.

Disconnect the battery ground terminal when performing any service on electrical components.

Disconnect the battery if arc welding is to be done on the vehicle.

BELT TENSION ADJUSTMENT

Except 3.0L Engine

1. Loosen the pivot bolt slightly.
2. Loosen the adjuster slot bolt so the alternator can be moved. Raise and safely support the vehicle if necessary.
3. On Montero, use a prybar and apply tension to the alternator until the belt deflects ¼–½ in. under a 10 lb. load.
4. Except Montero, loosen the brace bolt and increase the tension by tightening the adjustment bolt. The belt should deflect ¼–½ in. under a 10 lb. load.
5. Torque the adjuster strap bolt to 10 ft. lbs. (15 Nm). and the pivot bolt to 16 ft. lbs. (23 Nm).

3.0L Engine

1. Loosen the tensioner pulley locknut.
2. Turn the adjusting bolt until the belt deflects ¼–½ in. under a 10 lb. load.
3. Tighten the locknut.

REMOVAL AND INSTALLATION

1. Disconnect the negative battery cable.
2. Remove the alternator cover, if equipped.
3. Remove the alternator belt.
4. Remove the alternator brace bolt(s), nut(s) and applicable spacers.
5. Remove the alternator from the mounting bracket, label and disconnect all wires from the rear of the unit.

To install:

6. Connect all wiring to their proper terminals on the rear of the alternator.

7. Position the alternator in the mounting bracket.

8. Install the alternator brace bolt(s), nut(s) and applicable spacers.

9. Install the alternator belt and adjust the tension as required.

10. Install the alternator cover, if equipped.

11. Connect the negative battery cable and check the alternator for proper operation.

Starter

REMOVAL AND INSTALLATION

1. Disconnect the negative battery cable. This procedure is very important.

2. Raise the vehicle and support safely.

3. Remove the starter cover, if equipped.

4. Label and disconnect the wiring to the starter motor.

5. Remove the starter mounting bolts.

6. Remove the starter motor from the vehicle.

7. The installation is the reverse of the removal procedure. Torque the mounting bolts to 20–25 ft. lbs. (27–34 Nm).

CHASSIS ELECTRICAL

Air Bag

DISARMING

─── **CAUTION** ───

After disconnecting the battery cable, wait 60 seconds or more before proceeding with air bag procedures. The SRS system is designed to retain enough voltage to deploy the air bag for a short time even after the battery has been disconnected, so serious injury may result from unintended air bag deployment if work is done on the SRS system immediately after the battery cables are disconnected.

1. Position the front wheels in the straight-ahead position and place the key in the **LOCK** position. Remove the key from the ignition lock cylinder.

2. Disconnect the negative battery cable and insulate the cable end with high-quality electrical tape or similar non-conductive wrapping.

3. Wait at least 1 minute before working on the vehicle. The air bag system is designed to retain enough voltage to deploy the air bag for a short period of time even after the battery has been disconnected.

Heater Blower Motor

REMOVAL AND INSTALLATION

Expo

1. Disconnect the negative battery cable.

2. Remove the glove box assembly and pry off the speaker cover to the lower right of the glove box.

3. Remove the passenger side lower cowl side trim kick panel.

4. Remove the passenger side knee protector which is the panel surrounding in the glove box opening.

5. Remove the glove frame along top of glove box opening.

6. Remove the lap heater duct. This is a small piece on vehicles without a rear heater and much larger on vehicles with a rear heater.

7. Disconnect the electrical connector from the blower motor.

8. Remove the cooling tube from the blower assembly.

9. Remove the blower motor assembly.

10. Separate the blower assembly case and packing seal from the blower motor flange.

11. Remove the fan retaining nut and fan in order to renew the motor.

To install:

12. Check that the blower motor shaft is not bent and that the packing and blower case are in good condition.

13. Assemble the fan and motor. Install the blower assembly and connect the wiring and cooling tube.

14. Install the MPI control unit as required. Install the lap heater duct.

15. Install the glove box frame, interior trim pieces and glove box assembly.

16. Connect the negative battery cable and check the entire climate control system for proper operation.

Except Expo

WITHOUT AIR CONDITIONING

1. Disconnect the negative battery cable.

2. Remove the lap heater duct and the left side defroster duct.

3. Remove the blower motor retaining screws and remove the motor assembly from the housing. Remove the fan from the motor.

To install:

4. Inspect the gasket on housing for cracking or breaks and repair as required.

5. Install the fan to the blower motor shaft. Install the blower motor assembly to the housing and install the retaining screws.

6. Install the heater housing as follows:

   a. Install the vent hose and resistor block.

   b. Install the assembled blower housing to the vehicle.

   c. Position the ground wire and install the grounding screw.

   d. Connect the resistor block connector.

   e. Install the air distribution duct to the blower housing.

   f. Move the air selection control lever to the recirculation position. Pull the air selection control damper lever up and connect the air selection control cable to the end of the air selection damper lever. Secure the cable with the retaining clip.

7. Install the lap heater duct, glove box and stopper.

8. Connect the negative battery cable and check the blower motor for proper operation.

WITH AIR CONDITIONING

1. Disconnect negative battery cable.

2. Remove the lap duct and the left side defroster duct.

3. If necessary remove the heater/air conditioner housing as follows:

   a. Open the glove box lid and release the glove box stoppers. Remove the glove box from its hinge.

   b. Use a small prying device to remove the clip that holds the air selection control cable in place.

   c. Disconnect the air selection control cable from the end of the air selection damper lever.

   d. Remove the air distribution duct from the left side of the blower assembly.

   e. Disconnect the connector to the resistor block and remove the grounding screw.

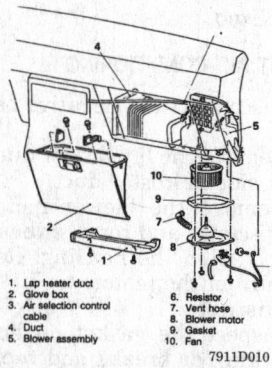

1. Lap heater duct
2. Glove box
3. Air selection control cable
4. Duct
5. Blower assembly
6. Resistor
7. Vent hose
8. Blower motor
9. Gasket
10. Fan

7911D010

Blower motor removal and installation

f. Remove the blower housing attaching bolts and remove the housing from the vehicle.

g. Remove the resistor block and vent hose from the housing.

4. Remove the blower motor retaining screws and remove the motor assembly from the housing. Remove the fan from the motor.

To install:

5. Inspect the gasket on housing for cracking or breaks and repair as required.

6. Install the fan to the blower motor shaft. Install the blower motor assembly to the housing and install the retaining screws.

7. Install the heater housing as follows:

a. Install the vent hose and resistor block.

b. Install the assembled blower housing to the vehicle.

c. Position the ground wire and install the grounding screw.

d. Connect the resistor block connector.

e. Install the air distribution duct to the blower housing.

f. Move the air selection control lever to the recirculation position. Pull the air selection control damper lever up and connect the air selection control cable to the end of the air selection damper lever. Secure the cable with the retaining clip.

8. Install the lap duct and the left side defroster duct.

9. Install the glove box and stopper.

10. Connect the negative battery cable and check the blower motor for proper operation.

Windshield Wiper Motor

REMOVAL AND INSTALLATION

Expo

FRONT

1. Disconnect the negative battery cable.

2. Remove the windshield wiper arms by unscrewing the cap nuts and lifting the arms from the linkage posts.

3. Remove the front deck garnish panel.

4. Remove both windshield holders.

5. Remove the clips that hold the deck cover. If they are the pin type, they may be removed using the following procedure:

a. Remove the clip by pressing down on the center pin with a suitable blunt pointed tool. Press down a little more than $1/16$ in. (2mm). This releases the clip. Pull the clip outward to remove it.

b. Do not push the pin inward more than necessary because it may damage the grommet or if pushed too far, the pin may fall in. Once the clips are removed, use a plastic trim stick to pry the deck cover loose.

6. Loosen the wiper motor assembly mounting bolts and remove the windshield wiper motor. Disconnect the linkage from the motor assembly. If necessary, remove the linkage from the vehicle.

NOTE: The installation angle of the crank arm and motor has been factory set, do not remove them unless it is necessary to do so. If arm must be removed, remove them only after marking their mounting positions.

To install:

7. Install the windshield wiper motor and connect the linkage. Connect the electrical harness to the motor.

8. When installing the trim and garnish pieces and reusing pin type clips, use the following procedure:

a. With the pin pulled out, insert the trim clip into the hole in the trim.

b. Push the pin inward until the pin's head is flush with the grommet.

c. Check that the trim is secure.

9. Install the wiper arms and tighten nuts to 17 ft. lbs. (24 Nm).

10. Connect the negative battery cable and check the wiper system for proper operation.

REAR

1. Disconnect the negative battery cable.

2. Remove the rear wiper arm by removing the cap nut cover, unscrewing the cap nut and lifting the arm from the linkage post.

3. Remove the large interior trim panel. Use a plastic trim stick to unhook the trim clips of the liftgate trim. There will be a row of metal liftgate clips across the top. There will be 2 rows of trim clips that retain the rest of the panel.

4. Disconnect the electrical harness at the wiper motor. Remove the rear wiper assembly. Do not loosen the grommet for the wiper post.

To install:

5. Install the motor and grommet. Mount the grommet so the arrow on the grommet is pointing downward.

6. Install the wiper arm.

7. Connect the negative battery cable and check rear wiper system for proper operation.

8. If operation is satisfactory, fit the tabs on the upper part of the liftgate trim into the liftgate clips and secure the liftgate trim.

Except Expo

FRONT

1. Disconnect the negative battery cable.

2. Disconnect the wiper motor electrical connector.

3. Remove the wiper motor retaining bolts and pull the motor out far enough to gain access to the wiper linkage.

4. Matchmark position of wiper linkage to aid installation. Pry the wiper linkage from the motor output shaft.

5. Remove the wiper motor from the vehicle.

6. The installation is the reverse of the removal procedure.

REAR

1. Disconnect the negative battery cable.

2. Tilt the wiper mount nut cover up and remove the nut. Remove the wiper arm from the shaft. Remove the wiper pivot nut and washer, if equipped.

3. Remove rear door inside trim panel and waterproof film.

4. Disconnect the wiper motor wire connector.

5. Remove the wiper motor retaining bolts and remove the motor from the vehicle.

6. The installation is the reverse of the removal procedure.

Windshield Wiper Switch

The front windshield wiper switch is part of the combination switch located on the steering column. The rear wiper switch is located on the instrument panel.

REMOVAL AND INSTALLATION

Rear Wiper Switch

1. Disconnect negative battery cable.
2. Insert a trim stick between the instrument panel and the switch housing. Pry switch out from the panel.
3. Disconnect electrical connector and service the wiper/washer switch, as required.
To install:
4. Connect the electrical connector and snap switch assembly into instrument panel.
5. Connect the negative battery cable and check operation of the wiper/washer assembly.

Instrument Cluster

REMOVAL AND INSTALLATION

Expo

1. Disconnect negative battery cable.
2. Remove the 2 retainer screws on the lower surface of the meter hood.
3. Remove the retainer screws from the under side top portion of the meter hood.
4. Carefully remove the meter hood from the face of the combination meter.
5. Remove the 4 retainer screws and the combination meter assembly with the bezel attached. Remove the front bezel and remove gauges or the speedometer as required.

NOTE: If the speedometer cable adapter requires service, disconnect the cable at the transaxle end. Pull the cable slightly toward the vehicle interior, release the lock by turning the adapter to the right or left and remove the adapter.

6. Assemble instrument cluster and attach front bezel or face trim using retaining screws.
7. Install the combination meter, secure with 4 retaining screws and attach the speedometer cable.
8. Install 2 retaining screws to meter hood.

9. Connect the negative battery cable and check all cluster-related items for proper operation.

Pick-Up and Montero

1. Disconnect the negative battery cable.
2. On Pick-Up, remove the hazard flasher switch and the matching cover on the other side of the column.
3. If equipped with tilt steering, operate the tilt lever to bring the steering down. Remove the hood attaching screws and remove the hood.
4. Remove the 4 cluster attaching screws and pull out cluster. Disconnect the speedometer cable from the back of the cluster by pushing the stopper of the plug on the speedometer cable side of the connection.
5. Disconnect the electrical connectors at the cluster and remove the cluster from the vehicle.
6. To remove the speedometer, remove the cover and glass. Remove the retaining screws and remove the speedometer or gauges as required.
To install:
7. Install the speedometer or gauges into the cluster and install the retaining screws. Install the cover and the glass.
8. Connect the electrical connectors and the speedometer to the cluster and install in vehicle. Install 4 retaining screws.
9. Install the instrument cluster hood and retaining screws.
10. Install the hazard flasher switch and the matching cover on the other side of the column.
11. Connect the negative battery cable.

Combination Switch

REMOVAL AND INSTALLATION

NOTE: The combination switch incorporates the windshield, headlight, dimmer and turn signal switches into a single switch assembly.

1. Disconnect negative battery cable.
2. Remove the steering wheel pad. Matchmark and remove the steering wheel.
3. If equipped with tilt steering column, put the column in lowest position.
4. Remove the upper and lower column covers.
5. Remove the wiring harness band and disconnect the harness connectors.

6. Remove the combination switch mounting screws and remove the switch.
7. The installation is the reverse of the removal procedure. Torque the steering wheel nut to 30 ft. lbs. (41 Nm).

Ignition Lock/Switch

REMOVAL AND INSTALLATION

1. Disconnect the negative battery cable.
2. If equipped with tilt steering column, put the column in its lowest position.
3. Remove the upper and lower column covers.
4. Remove the wiring harness band and disconnect the ignition switch harness.
5. Remove the ignition switch retaining screw, if equipped and remove the switch from the lock.
6. Using a hacksaw blade, cut a groove into the head of the ignition switch break-off bolts and remove.
7. Remove the assembly from the steering column.
To install:
8. With the key inserted in the switch, install the switch and lock assembly to the steering column. Tighten the screws gradually making sure the key does not bind.
9. If using break-off bolts, tighten them until the heads break off.
10. Connect the switch harness and check the assembly for proper operation.
11. Install upper and lower column covers.

Stoplight Switch

ADJUSTMENT

1. Disconnect negative battery cable.
2. Loosen locknut on the brake light switch.
3. Turn the switch in the mounting bracket until the plunger does not contact the brake pedal.
4. Rotate the switch outward 1/2-1 revolution and secure the locknut. Reconnect the negative battery cable and check switch operation.

REMOVAL AND INSTALLATION

1. Disconnect the negative battery cable.
2. Unplug the connector to the switch.

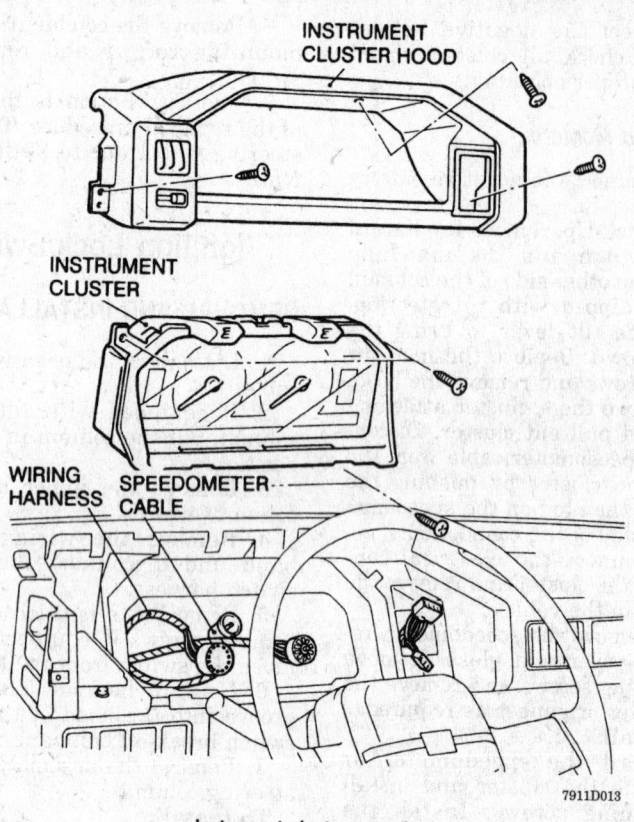

Instrument cluster mounting

3. Remove the locknut and remove the switch from its mount bracket.

4. The installation is the reverse of the removal procedure.

Clutch Switch

ADJUSTMENT

1. Disconnect negative battery cable.

2. Loosen the locknut on the switch. Adjust the switch so the distance from the floorboard to the top of the pedal pad in a released position is 7½ in. for Montero, 6½ in. for Pick-Up or 6 in. for Expo.

3. Reconnect the negative battery cable. Check operation of cruise control system making sure the cruise control is not operational when the pedal is depressed.

REMOVAL AND INSTALLATION

1. Disconnect the negative battery cable.

2. Unplug the connector to the switch.

3. Remove the locknut and the switch from its mounting bracket.

4. The installation is the reverse of the removal procedure.

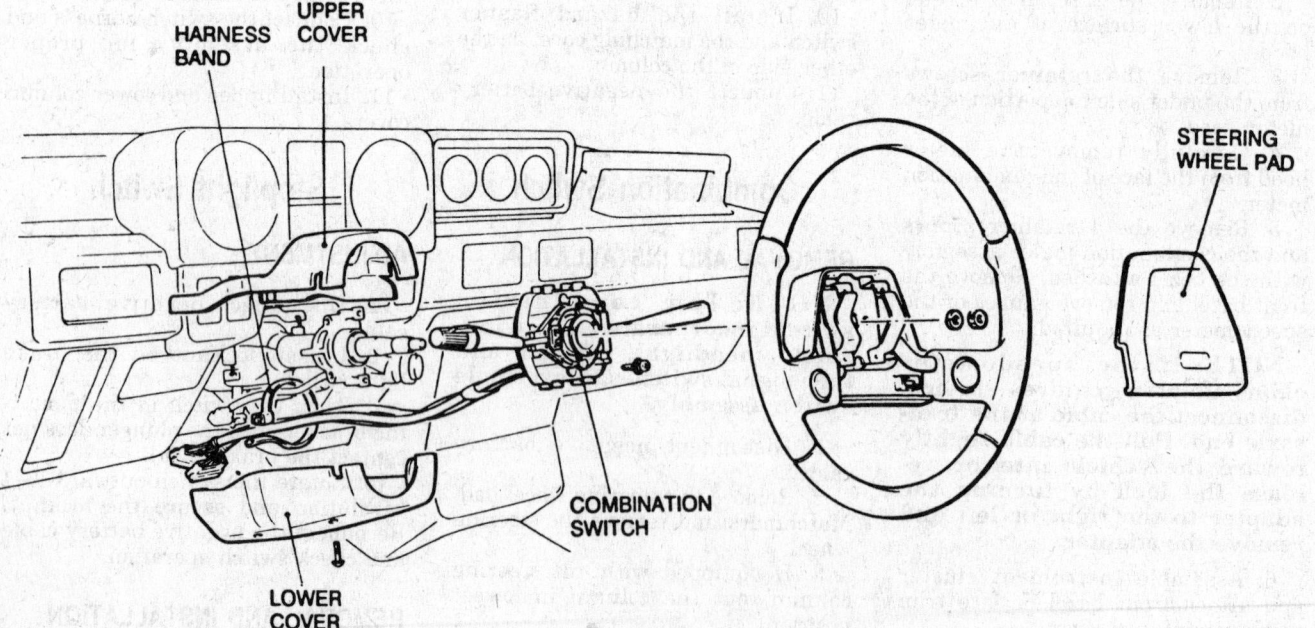

Combination switch mounting

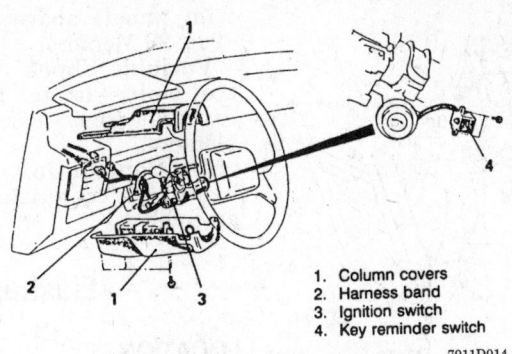

1. Column covers
2. Harness band
3. Ignition switch
4. Key reminder switch

7911D014

Ignition switch and lock assembly

Neutral Safety Switch

ADJUSTMENT

1. Disconnect the negative battery cable and locate the neutral safety switch on the top of the transaxle.

NOTE: Apply parking brake and chock wheels before placing transaxle into the N position

2. At the transmission, loosen the shift cable adjustment nut and inside the vehicle place the gearshift selector lever in **N**.
3. Place the manual shift control lever in **N**.
4. Loosen neutral safety switch mounting screws and rotate switch body so the manual control lever 0.20 in. (5mm) hole and the switch body 0.20 in. (5mm) holes are aligned.
5. Tighten switch body mounting bolts to 7–9 ft. lbs. (10–12 Nm).
6. At the shift cable adjusting nut, gently pull cable to remove any slack. Tighten locknut to 7–10 ft. lbs. 10–14 Nm).
7. Verify that the switch lever moves to positions corresponding to each position of the selector lever. Connect the negative battery terminal.
8. Make sure the engine only starts in the **P** and **N** positions. Also make sure the reverse lights operate only in the **N** selection.

REMOVAL AND INSTALLATION

1. Disconnect negative battery cable.
2. Raise and safely support the vehicle.
3. Remove the electrical connector from the switch. Place drain pan under the switch and remove the switch from the transmission.
4. Install switch with new seal into the transmission and tighten to 25 ft. lbs. (34 Nm).

5. Lower the vehicle and add transmission fluid to correct the level. Check operation of the switch.

Fuses, Circuit Breakers and Relays

LOCATION

Expo

FUSES AND FUSIBLE LINKS

Main fuse panel — passenger's side, under the hood, just behind the battery.

Main relay bank — passenger's side, under the hood, just behind the battery.

Fuse links — passenger's side, under the hood, just behind the battery.

Air conditioning control relay center — passenger's side, under the hood, up front behind the headlight.

Multi-purpose fuse block — inside the vehicle, on the left side behind the driver's knee protector.

RELAYS

Headlight relay, power window relay, radiator fan motor relay and alternator relay — passenger's side, under the hood, just behind the battery.

Air conditioner compressor relay, the condenser fan motor relay and the condenser fan motor control relay — under the hood, up front behind the headlight.

Intermittent wiper relay — incorporated into the column switch.

Seat belt warning timer relay — behind the instrument panel to the right of the center air conditioning outlets.

Multi-Point Injection control relay — inside the passenger compartment behind the right kick panel.

Starter relay — right side of the vehicle in the relay box.

Defogger relay — under the driver's left side knee protector.

Door lock relay — behind the driver's side kick panel, at the bottom.

Heater relay, the turn signal and hazard flasher unit and the defogger timer — located in the multi-purpose fuse panel located under the driver's left side knee protector.

Automatic seatbelt motor relay — located inside the trim panel on the driver's side rear quarter panel, just behind the front door post.

Montero

Main Fuse Block/Relay Box — located on the left side of the instrument panel, covered by a removable access panel. There are also several dedicated fuses located throughout the vehicle.

Air Conditioning Compressor Power Relay — located in the engine compartment on the left fender.

Engine Control Relay — located on the right side of the instrument panel, mounted under a removable trim panel.

Pick-Up

Fuse Block/Relay Box — located to the left of the steering column, covered by a removable access panel or mounted to the left kick-panel.

Air Conditioning Compressor Power Relay — located in the engine compartment on the left fender.

Engine Control Relay — located on the right side of the instrument panel behind a removable trim panel.

Computers

LOCATION

Expo

Multi-Point Injection (MPI) control unit — located under the instrument panel at the top of the passenger side kick panel next to the blower motor.

Air conditioning control unit — mounted behind the glove box.

Automatic transaxle control unit — mounted on the floor at the very front of the console.

Cruise control unit — under the instrument panel behind the driver's side knee protector.

Electric door lock control unit — fastened to the body struc-

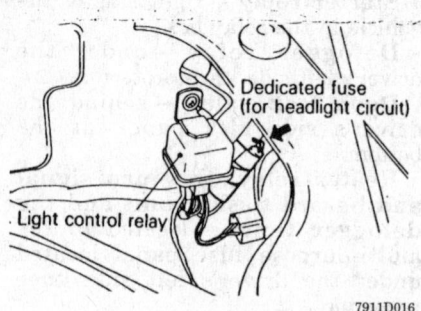

Headlight circuit fuse location — Montero

7911D016

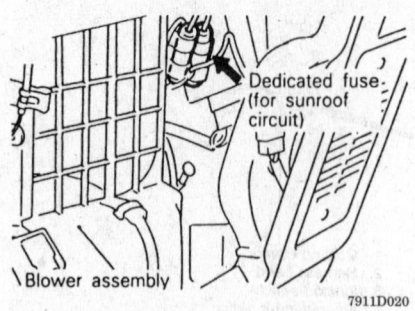

Sunroof fuse location — Montero

7911D020

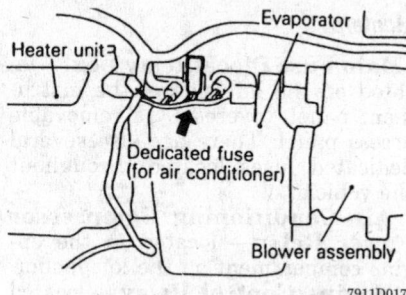

Air conditioning fuse location — Montero

7911D017

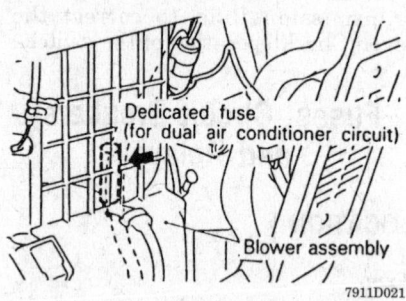

Dual air conditioning fuse location — Montero

7911D021

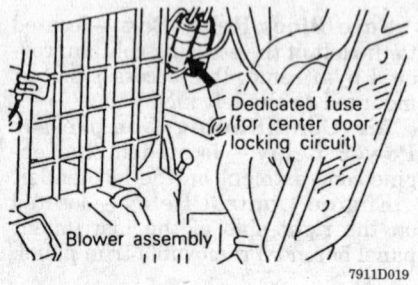

Electric door locks fuse location — Montero

7911D019

ture behind the driver's side kick panel.

Automatic seat belt control unit — under the console next to hand brake handle.

ELC 4-speed automatic transaxle control unit — under the console next to hand brake handle.

Anti-lock Braking System (ABS) control unit — under the instrument panel at center of dash.

Pick-Up and Montero

Engine Control Unit (ECU) — located on the right side of the dash,

under a removable trim panel mounted to the kick-panel.

Auto-Cruise Control Unit — located on the left side of the steering column, under the instrument panel for Pick-Up or to right of steering column for Montero.

Automatic Transmission Control Unit — located on the right side of the instrument panel, next to junction block for Montero.

SRS Diagnosis Unit — located behind center console.

4WD Indicator Control Unit — located behind center console.

Power Antenna Control Unit — located behind center console.

Door Lock Control Unit — located left instrument panel speaker.

Sunroof Control Unit — located at sunroof, under head liner.

Keyless Entry Control Unit — located behind right side rear trim panel, above wheelwell for Montero.

ABS Control Unit — located behind right side rear trim panel, above wheelwell for Montero.

Rear Differential Lock Control Unit — located under carpet, at driveshaft tunnel, near rear of vehicle for 1992–93 Montero.

Rear Differential Lock Control Unit — located behind left side rear

trim panel, above wheelwell for 1994–96 Montero.

Variable Shock Absorber Control Unit — located behind left side rear trim panel, above wheelwell for Montero.

A/C Control Unit — located above heater/air conditioning plenum assembly.

Flashers

LOCATION

Turn signal and hazard flasher unit — located in the multi-purpose fuse panel located under the driver's left side knee protector.

Cruise Control

ADJUSTMENT

Expo

Before starting adjustments, turn air conditioner and lights **OFF**. Warm engine until the idle is stable and the rpm is correct. Stop engine and set the ignition switch to **OFF**. Confirm there are no sharp bends in the accelerator, throttle and cruise control cables. Check the inner cables for correct slack. If too loose or too tight, adjust with the following procedure:

1. Remove the air cleaner. If equipped with a protective cover over the actuator, remove it.

2. First, adjust the accelerator cable on the throttle valve side. After loosening the adjustment bolts at the air intake plenum side and freeing the inner cable, use the adjusting bolts that secure the plate so the free-play of the inner cable becomes 0.040–0.080 in (1–2mm). If there is excessive play of the accelerator cable, when climbing a hill the vehicle speed will drop substantially. If there is no play, the idling speed will increase.

3. After adjusting the accelerator cable, confirm that the throttle lever touches the idle position switch.

4. Next, adjust the accelerator cable on the accelerator pedal side. Loosen the adjusting bolt or locknut. While keeping the intermediate link of the actuator in close contact with the stop, adjust the inner cable play of accelerator cable **A** to 0–0.040 in. (0–1mm) for manual transaxle vehicles or 0.080–0.120 in. (2–3mm) for automatic transaxle vehicles.

5. After making the adjustment of the cable, make sure the throttle lever at the engine side moves

0.040–0.080 in (1–2mm) when the actuator link is turned. If the throttle lever movement is incorrect, adjust by turning adjusting nut **B**.

6. Confirm that the throttle valve fully opens and closes by operating the accelerator pedal.

7. Install the air cleaner.

Pick-Up and Montero

1. Run the vehicle until normal operating temperature is reached. Adjust the idle speed to match the emission sticker on the vehicle.

2. Turn the engine **OFF** and remove the actuator cover.

3. Loosen the locknuts on the accelerator cables and let the inner cables sag.

4. While keeping lever "P" and the stopper in contact with each other, turn the adjusting nut to lengthen the outer cable. Adjust until the lever "P" begins to operate. Turn the nut back ½ turn and secure the locknut. Accelerator cable "A" free-play should be 0–0.04 in. (0–1mm).

5. To adjust accelerator cable "B", alter the adjusting nuts to meet the preferred free-play setting of 0–0.08 in. (0–2mm).

6. Install actuator cover and check operation of cruise control.

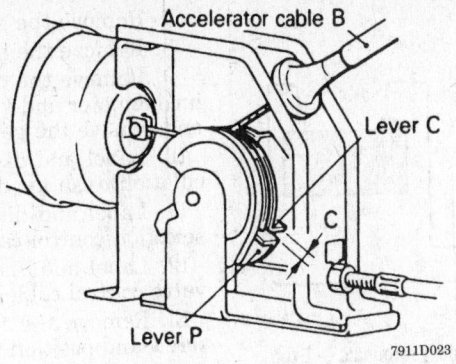

Accelerator cable "B" adjustment — with cruise control

7911D023

ENGINE COOLING

Radiator

REMOVAL AND INSTALLATION

1. Disconnect the negative battery cable.

2. Drain the coolant from the radiator.

3. Remove the upper hose and coolant reserve tank hose from the radiator.

4. Remove the shroud assembly from the radiator.

5. Raise the vehicle and support safely.

6. Remove the lower hose from the radiator.

7. Disconnect and plug the automatic transmission cooler hoses, if equipped. Lower the vehicle.

8. Remove the mounting screws and carefully lift the radiator out of the engine compartment.

To install:

9. Lower the radiator into position and install the mounting screws.

10. Raise the vehicle and support safely. Connect the automatic transmission cooler hoses, if removed.

11. Connect the lower radiator hose. Lower the vehicle.

12. Install the shroud assembly.

13. Connect the upper hose and coolant reserve tank hose.

14. Fill the cooling system.

15. Connect the negative battery cable and run the vehicle until the thermostat opens. Fill the radiator completely and check the automatic transmission fluid level, if equipped.

16. Check for leaks. Once vehicle has cooled, recheck coolant level.

Electric Cooling Fan

An electric radiator and condenser cooling fan is used on the Expo and Montero. The condenser on Pick-Up is cooled by the belt-driven fan.

TESTING

1. Disconnect negative battery cable.

— **CAUTION** —
Make sure the key is in the OFF position when checking the electric cooling fan. If not the fan could turn on at any time, causing serious personal injury.

2. Disconnect the electrical connector from the condenser fan.

3. Connect the green-with-black-tracer wire to 12 volt supply and ground the black wire.

4. Make sure the fan runs smoothly, without abnormal noise or vibration.

5. Connect the negative battery cable.

REMOVAL AND INSTALLATION

Montero

1. Disconnect negative battery cable.

2. Open the hood and remove the grille. It is fastened with 3 screws along the top and 3 nuts along the bottom.

3. Disconnect the electrical connector from the fan.

4. Remove the mounting screws and the fan through the grille opening.

5. The installation is the reverse of the removal procedure.

6. Connect the negative battery cable and check the fan for proper operation.

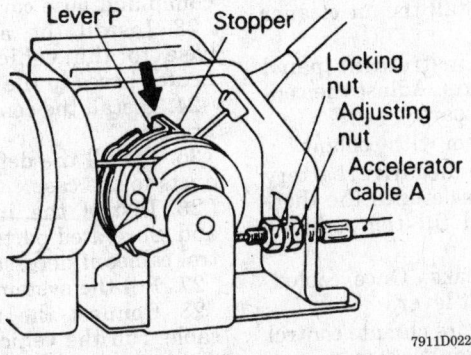

Accelerator cable "A" adjustment — with cruise control

7911D022

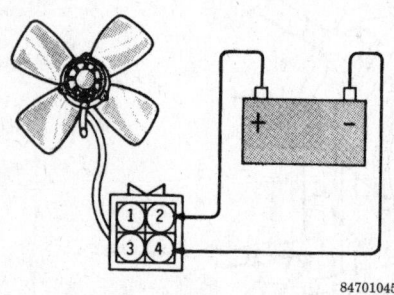

Radiator fan motor testing terminals — Expo

Expo

1. Disconnect the negative battery cable. Drain the cooling system only when radiator and engine are at safe temperatures.

2. Unplug the cooling fan and radiator sensor connector(s). Most of these connectors employ a waterproof connector. When disconnecting, make sure all parts of the connector remain intact.

3. Disconnect the upper radiator hose from the radiator and remove overflow tank.

4. Remove the fan mounting screws. The radiator and condenser cooling fans are separately removable.

5. Remove the fan assembly and disassemble as required.

6. The installation is the reverse of the removal procedure.

7. Check the coolant level and refill, as required.

8. Connect the negative battery cable and check the fan for proper operation.

Heater Core

REMOVAL AND INSTALLATION

Montero

1. Disconnect the negative battery cable.

2. Set the temperature control to the extreme right position and drain the cooling system.

3. Remove the air filter assembly. Remove the heater hose clamps and disconnect the heater hoses.

4. Remove the lap heater ducts and the hood release cable bracket.

5. Remove the side demister grills by carefully prying them from the instrument panel.

6. Remove the glove box and center console assembly. Remove the center reinforcement.

7. Remove the steering wheel.

8. Remove the instrument cluster.

9. Remove the oil pressure gauge, inclinometer and voltmeter pod cover and remove the gauge assembly.

10. Label and disconnect the recirculation/fresh air door control cable.

11. Label and disconnect the mode selection control cable.

12. Label and disconnect the water valve control cable.

13. Remove the fuse box retaining screw and position the fuse box aside.

14. Remove the instrument panel retaining nuts and bolts and carefully remove the instrument panel from the vehicle.

15. Remove the air cleaner or air intake plenum, as required.

16. Remove the duct from the top of the heater case.

17. Remove the retaining nuts and bolts and remove the heater case from the vehicle.

18. Remove the water valve cover and carefully remove the water valve from the case.

19. Remove the foot/defroster selection link from the mode selection lever.

20. Move the lever up to a position which will not interfere with the removal of the heater core.

21. Remove the heater core from the heater case. If the mode lever is in the way, remove it.

To install:

22. Install the heater core to the heater case. Install the mode lever, if removed.

23. Install the foot/defroster selection link to the mode selection lever.

24. Install the water valve assembly and its cover to the case.

25. Install the assembled heater case to the vehicle and install the retaining nuts and bolts.

26. Install the duct to the top of the case.

27. Connect the heater hoses to the core tubes and install the air cleaner or intake plenum.

28. Install the instrument panel and all related parts. Adjust the control cables if necessary.

29. Fill the system with coolant.

30. Connect the negative battery cable, run the vehicle until the thermostat opens and fill the radiator completely.

31. Check for leaks. Once cooled, recheck the coolant lever.

32. Check the entire climate control system and all gauges for proper operation.

Pick-Up

1. Disconnect the negative battery cable. Position the heater controls in the extreme right position.

2. Drain the coolant. Disconnect the heater hoses from the core tubes.

3. Remove the hazard flasher switch and the matching cover on the other side of the column. Remove the instrument cluster.

4. Remove the fuse box cover and remove the fuse box retaining screws. Position the fuse box aside.

5. Remove the glove box assembly.

6. Remove the defroster ducts.

7. Label and disconnect the air, mode and temperature control cables from the heater case.

8. Remove the front speaker grilles.

9. Remove the parcel box or clock, as equipped.

10. Remove the nut cover from the top center of the instrument panel.

11. Remove the center cover.

12. Remove the shift knob and floor console assembly, if equipped.

13. Move the tilt steering column down as far as it will go.

14. Remove the instrument panel retaining nuts and bolts and carefully remove the instrument panel from the vehicle.

15. Remove the duct from the top center of the heater case.

16. Remove the defroster duct from the the left side of the case.

17. Remove the center reinforcement braces.

18. Remove the mounting nuts and remove the heater case from the vehicle.

19. Remove the hose cover, joint hose clamp and the plate from the case.

20. Remove the heater core from the case.

To install:

21. Install the heater core to the heater case.

22. Install the plate, joint hose clamp and hose cover.

23. Install the assembled heater case to the vehicle. Connect the heater hoses to the core tubes.

24. Install the center reinforcement braces.

25. Install the defroster and center ducts to the case.

26. Install the instrument panel and all related parts. Adjust the control cables if necessary.

27. Fill the system with coolant.

28. Connect the negative battery cable, run the vehicle until the thermostat opens and fill the radiator completely.

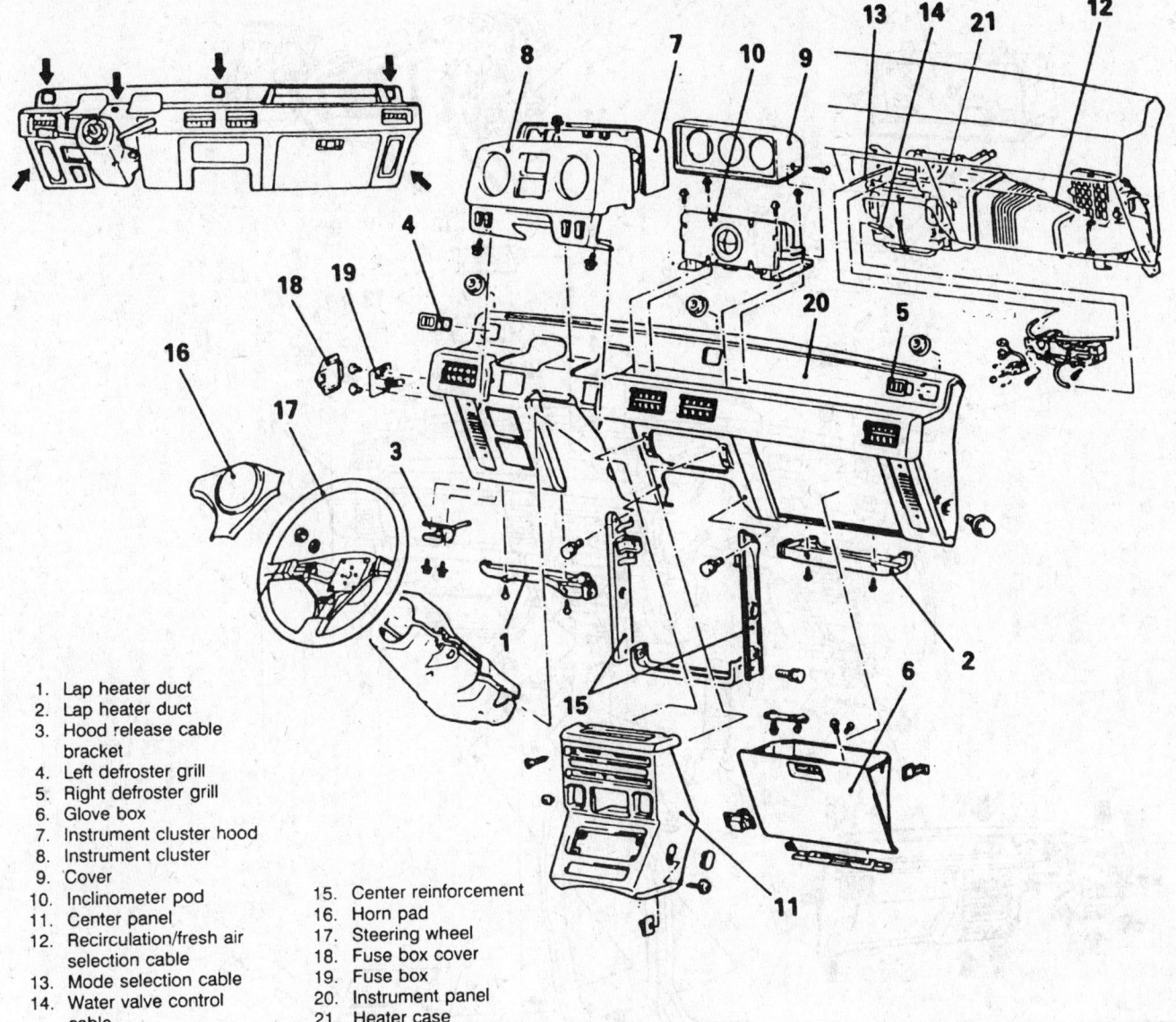

1. Lap heater duct
2. Lap heater duct
3. Hood release cable bracket
4. Left defroster grill
5. Right defroster grill
6. Glove box
7. Instrument cluster hood
8. Instrument cluster
9. Cover
10. Inclinometer pod
11. Center panel
12. Recirculation/fresh air selection cable
13. Mode selection cable
14. Water valve control cable

15. Center reinforcement
16. Horn pad
17. Steering wheel
18. Fuse box cover
19. Fuse box
20. Instrument panel
21. Heater case

7911D024

Instrument panel assembly — Montero

29. Check for leaks. Once cooled, recheck the coolant level.

30. Check the entire climate control system and all gauges for proper operation.

Expo

1. Disconnect the negative battery cable. Drain the engine coolant.

2. Remove the hood lock release handle, instrument panel undercover, lower frame, foot duct, lap duct and the lap heater duct.

3. Remove the glove box speaker harness and the glove box frame.

4. Remove the meter hood and combination meter from the instrument panel. Remove the adapter lock and pull the speedometer cable into the passenger compartment slightly. Remove the rear of the adapter from the cable. Next, turn the adapter so the notch section is aligned with the tab on the cable section and slide adapter outward to remove.

5. Remove the ashtray from the center panel. Remove the mounting screws, radio and the center panel from the vehicle.

6. Remove the center air outlet from the instrument panel by removing the clip on the lower section of the outlet. Next insert a flat tipped tool in between the fins and remove the clip on the top section while pulling the lock spring toward the inside. Remove the center air outlet assembly.

7. Disconnect the air selection, temperature and mode selection control cables from the heater box and remove the heater control assembly.

8. Remove the clock or plug from the upper instrument panel. Remove the instrument panel retaining bolt under the plug.

9. Lower the steering column by removing the bolt and nut under the column. Remove the floor console side covers. If equipped with manual transaxle, remove the shifter knob.

10. Remove the floor console switch panel, mounting bolts and the floor console from the vehicle. Remove the

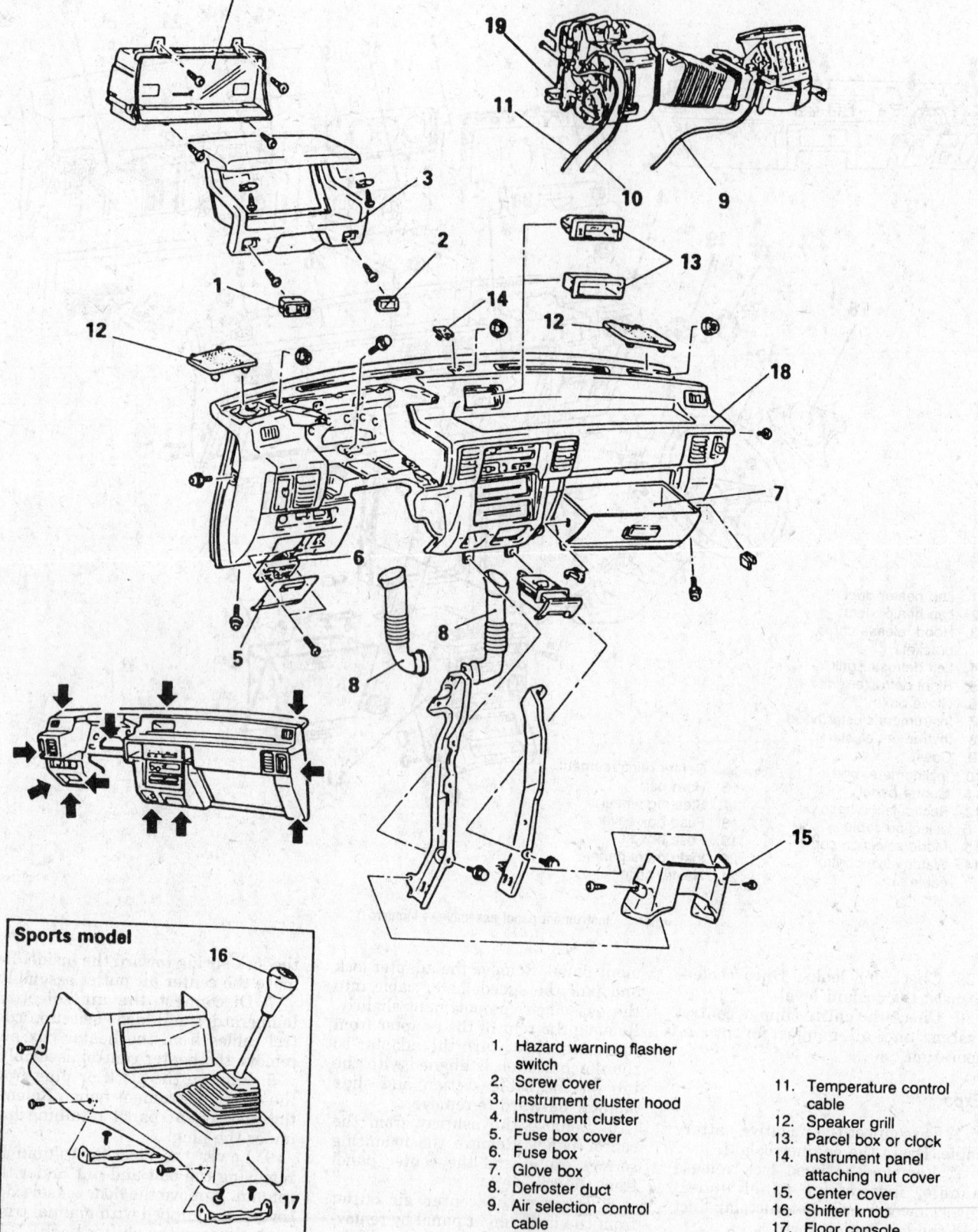

Sports model

1. Hazard warning flasher switch
2. Screw cover
3. Instrument cluster hood
4. Instrument cluster
5. Fuse box cover
6. Fuse box
7. Glove box
8. Defroster duct
9. Air selection control cable
10. Mode selection control cable
11. Temperature control cable
12. Speaker grill
13. Parcel box or clock
14. Instrument panel attaching nut cover
15. Center cover
16. Shifter knob
17. Floor console
18. Instrumnent panel
19. Heater case

7911D025

Instrument panel assembly — Pick-Up

instrument panel retainer bolts and the instrument panel. Disconnect the heater hoses at the heater box.

11. Remove the heater joint duct by first removing the pin type retainer clips on the duct using the following procedure:

a. This type of clip is removed by pressing down on the center pin with a blunt pointed tool. Press down a little more than 1/16 in. (2mm); this releases the clip. Pull the clip outward to remove it.

b. Do not push the pin inward more than necessary because it may damage the grommet or the pin may fall in if pushed in too far. Once the clips are removed, use a plastic trim stick to pry the piece loose.

12. Remove the center reinforcement. Remove the cooling unit mounting nut, if equipped with air conditioning.

13. Disconnect and remove the ABS control unit and the automatic transmission ELC control unit.

14. Remove the foot distribution duct and disconnect the rear heater duct connection. Remove both stamped steel instrument panel supports.

15. Remove the mounting bolts and the heater unit from the vehicle. Be careful not to damage the heater tubes or to spill coolant inside the vehicle.

16. Remove the cover plate around the heater tubes and the core fastener clips. Pull the heater core from the heater box, being careful not to damage the fins or tank ends.

To install:

17. Thoroughly clean and dry the inside of the case. Install the heater core to the heater box. Install the clips and cover.

18. Install the heater unit into position on the vehicle and install the evaporator and heater unit mounting nuts and clips.

19. Install the automatic transaxle ELC box and the ABS control unit.

20. Connect the air selection, temperature and mode selection control cables from the heater box and install the heater control assembly.

21. Install both stamped steel instrument panel supports. Connect the connector for the ECI control relay. Install the remaining instrument panel components reversing the removal procedure.

22. Install the center console as follows:

a. Install the front console box assembly.

b. Install the shift lever knob on manual transaxle vehicles.

c. Install the rear console box assembly.

d. Install the floor console switch panel.

e. Install the coin holder and the console box tray.

23. Refill the cooling system. Evacuate and recharge the air conditioning system. Add 2 oz. of refrigerant oil during the recharge, if the evaporator was replaced.

24. Connect the negative battery cable and check the entire climate control system for proper operation. Check the system for leaks.

Water Pump

REMOVAL AND INSTALLATION

1.8L Engine

1. Disconnect the negative battery cable.

2. Drain the cooling system.

3. Remove the engine undercover.

4. Disconnect the clamp bolt from the power steering hose.

5. Support the engine with the appropriate equipment and remove the engine mount bracket.

6. Remove the timing belt(s) from the front of the engine.

7. Disconnect the coolant hoses from the pump, if equipped.

8. Remove the alternator brace.

9. Remove the water pump, gasket and O-ring where the water inlet pipe(s) joins the pump.

To install:

10. Thoroughly clean and dry both gasket surfaces of the water pump and block.

11. Install a new O-ring into the groove on the front end of the water inlet pipe. Do not apply oils or grease to the O-ring. Wet with water only.

12. Install the gasket and pump assembly and tighten the bolts.

13. Connect the hoses to the pump.

14. Reinstall the timing belt and related parts.

15. Install the engine drive belts and adjust.

16. Fill the system with coolant.

17. Connect the negative battery cable, run the vehicle until the thermostat opens and fill the radiator completely.

18. Once the vehicle has cooled, recheck the coolant level.

2.4L Engine

1. Disconnect the negative battery cable.

2. Drain the cooling system.

3. Release the fuel pressure if equipped with fuel injection.

4. Remove the upper radiator shroud.

5. Remove all accessory belts. Remove the air conditioning compressor tensioner pulley, if equipped.

6. Remove the cooling fan assembly along with the water pump pulley.

7. Disconnect the radiator hose from the water pump.

8. Remove the crankshaft pulley(s).

9. Remove the timing belt covers. If the same timing belt will be reused, mark the direction of the timing belt's rotation, for installation in the same direction. Make sure the engine is positioned so the No. 1 cylinder is at the TDC of its compression stroke and the sprockets timing marks are aligned with the engine's timing mark indicators. Remove the timing belt.

10. The water pump bolts are different lengths, note their positions before removing. Remove the water pump mounting bolts and remove the pump from the block and the water pipe connection. Remove the O-ring from the water pipe connection.

To install:

11. Clean and dry the mating surfaces of the block and water pump. Install a new O-ring to the water pipe connection. Coat the new O-ring with water to aid in installation.

12. Install the water pump with a new gasket to the block and torque the bolts (except the alternator bracket bolt) to 10 ft. lbs. (13 Nm). Torque the aforementioned bolt to 17 ft. lbs. (23 Nm).

13. Install the timing belt(s) and covers.

14. Install the crankshaft pulley(s).

15. Connect the radiator hose to the water pump.

16. Install the water pump pulley and cooling fan assembly.

17. Install the air conditioning compressor tensioner pulley, if equipped, and install and adjust the accessory belts.

18. Install the upper radiator shroud.

19. Fill the system with coolant.

20. Connect the negative battery cable, run the vehicle until the thermostat opens and fill the radiator completely.

21. Check for leaks. Once cooled, recheck the coolant level.

22. Install the seat underframe and all related parts, if removed.

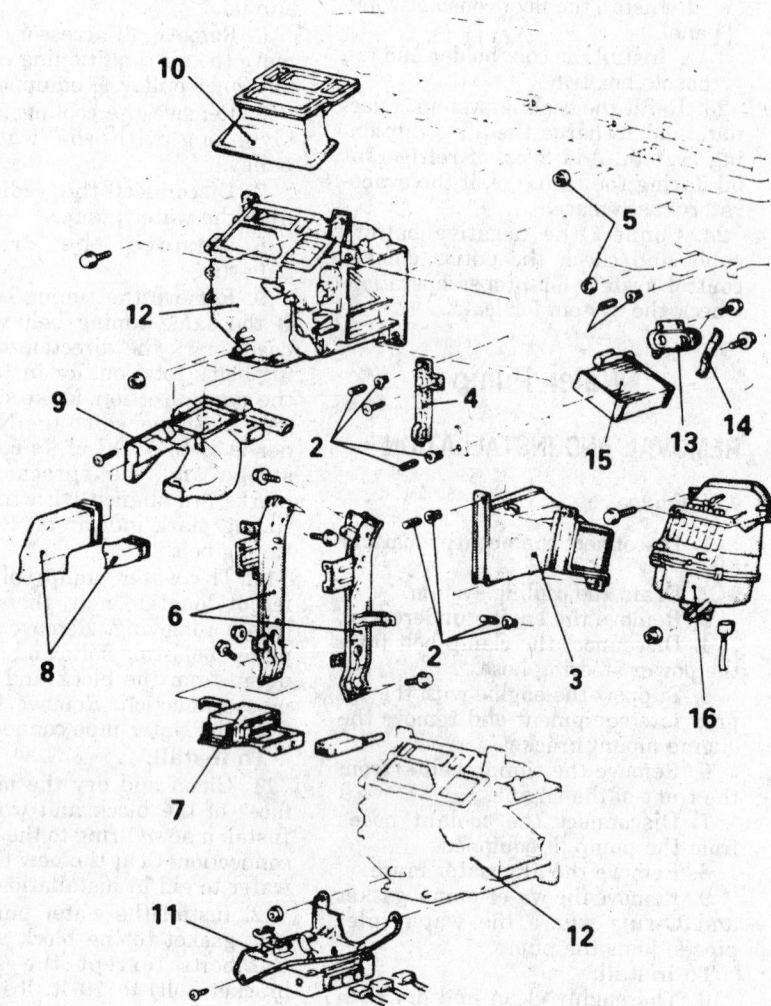

1. Heater hose connection
2. Retainer clips
3. Joint duct
4. Plate sub-assembly (vehicles with air conditioning)
5. Cooling unit installation nut (vehicles with air conditioning)
6. Center reinforcement
7. ABS Control unit assembly
8. Rear heater duct connection
9. Foot distribution duct
10. Center ventilation duct assembly
11. Automatic transaxle control unit
12. Heater unit
13. Plate
14. Clamp
15. Heater core

85691006

Heater case and related parts — Expo

3.0L Engine

1. Disconnect the negative battery cable.

2. Drain the cooling system. Remove the upper radiator hose and the upper radiator shroud.

3. If equipped with electric fuel pump, loosen the fuel filler cap to release fuel tank pressure and release the fuel pressure in the supply lines.

4. Remove the cooling fan assembly along with the water pump pulley. Remove all belts.

5. Remove the power steering pump from the bracket and remove the bracket.

6. Remove the tensioner pulley bracket, the air conditioning compressor and its bracket.

7. Remove the cooling fan bracket assembly. Remove the crankshaft pulley and flange.

8. Remove the timing belt covers. If the same timing belt will be reused, mark the direction of the timing belt's rotation, for installation in the same direction. Make sure the engine is positioned so the No. 1 cylinder is at the TDC of its compression stroke and the sprockets timing marks are aligned with the engine's timing mark indicators.

9. Loosen the timing belt tensioner bolt and remove the belt. Posi-

tion the tensioner as far away from the center of the engine as possible and tighten the bolt. Remove the water pump mounting bolts, separate the pump from the water inlet pipe and remove the pump from the engine. Remove the water inlet fitting from the pump.

To install:

10. Clean and dry the mating surfaces of the block and water pump. Install a new O-ring to the water inlet pipe. Install the pump and water inlet fitting with new gaskets to the engine and water pipe. Torque the water pump mounting bolts to 20 ft. lbs. (27 Nm).

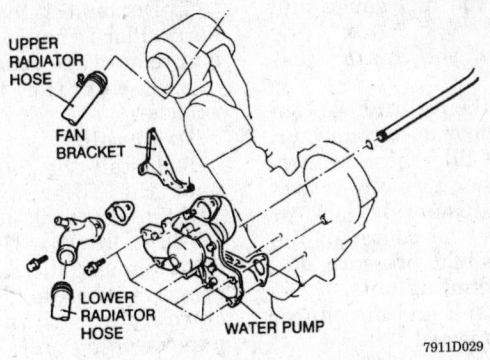

UPPER RADIATOR HOSE

FAN BRACKET

LOWER RADIATOR HOSE

WATER PUMP

7911D029

Water pump assembly — 3.0L engine

11. If not already done, position both camshafts so the marks line up with those on the alternator bracket and inner timing cover. Rotate the crankshaft so the timing mark aligns with the mark on the oil pump.

12. Install the timing belt on the crankshaft sprocket and while keeping the belt tight on the tension side (right side), install the belt on the front camshaft sprocket.

13. Install the belt on the water pump pulley, then the rear camshaft sprocket and the tensioner.

14. Rotate the front camshaft counterclockwise to tension the belt between the front camshaft and the crankshaft. If the timing marks came out of line, repeat the procedure.

15. Install the crankshaft sprocket flange.

16. Loosen the tensioner bolt and allow the spring to tension the belt.

17. Turn the crankshaft 2 full turns in the clockwise direction only until the timing marks align again. Now that the belt is properly tensioned, torque the tensioner lock bolt to 21 ft. lbs. (29 Nm).

18. Install the timing belt covers and all related parts.

19. Fill the cooling system.

20. Connect the negative battery cable, run the vehicle until the thermostat opens and fill the radiator completely.

21. Check for leaks. Once cooled, recheck the coolant level.

3.5L Engine

1. Drain the cooling system and disconnect the negative battery cable.

2. Remove the timing belt and thermostat.

3. Disconnect the radiator hose and water outlet fitting.

4. Remove the thermostat housing and related components.

5. Remove the water pump-to-thermostat housing adapter.

6. Remove the bolts, water pump and gasket.

7. Remove all O-rings and clean gasket mating surfaces.

To install:

8. Install new O-ring onto water pipe and lubricate with water only. Install the water pump and torque bolts to 17 ft. lbs. (24 Nm).

9. Install the thermostat housing and torque bolts to 14 ft. lbs. (20 Nm).

10. Install the remaining components, refill engine with coolant, start engine and check for leaks.

Thermostat

REMOVAL AND INSTALLATION

1. Disconnect the negative battery cable. Drain the coolant down to thermostat level or below.

2. Disconnect the engine coolant temperature switch connector, if equipped.

3. Remove the thermostat housing.

4. Remove the thermostat and gasket from the housing.

5. Clean the housing mating surfaces and install a new gasket.

6. The installation is the reverse of the removal procedure. Torque mounting bolts to 14 ft. lbs. (20 Nm).

Cooling System Bleeding

All engines are equipped with self-bleeding thermostats. Cooling system bleeding is not necessary in any vehicles when servicing the cooling system.

FUEL SYSTEM

Fuel System Service Precaution

Safety is the most important factor when performing not only fuel system maintenance but any type of maintenance. Failure to conduct maintenance and repairs in a safe manner may result in serious personal injury or death. Maintenance and testing of the vehicle's fuel system components can be accomplished safely and effectively by adhering to the following rules and guidelines.

To avoid the possibility of fire and personal injury, always disconnect the negative battery cable unless the repair or test procedure requires that battery voltage be applied.

Always relieve the fuel system pressure prior to disconnecting any fuel system component (injector, fuel rail, pressure regulator, etc.), fitting or fuel line connection. Exercise extreme caution whenever relieving fuel system pressure to avoid exposing skin, face and eyes to fuel spray. Please be advised that fuel under pressure may penetrate the skin or any part of the body that it contacts.

Always place a shop towel or cloth around the fitting or connection prior to loosening to absorb any excess fuel due to spillage. Ensure that all fuel spillage (should it occur) is quickly removed from engine surfaces. Ensure that all fuel soaked cloths or towels are deposited into a suitable waste container.

Always keep a dry chemical (Class B) fire extinguisher near the work area.

Do not allow fuel spray or fuel vapors to come into contact with a spark or open flame.

Always use a backup wrench when loosening and tightening fuel line connection fittings. This will prevent unnecessary stress and torsion to fuel line piping. Always follow the proper torque specifications.

Always replace worn fuel fitting O-rings with new. Do not substitute fuel hose or equivalent where fuel pipe is installed.

RELIEVING FUEL SYSTEM PRESSURE

1. Disconnect the fuel pump harness connector.

2. Start the engine and allow the engine to run out of fuel.

3. Once the engine has stalled, turn the key to the **OFF** position and connect the electrical connector.

4. Disconnect the negative battery cable pressure cannot build up until work has been completed.

Fuel Tank

REMOVAL AND INSTALLATION

Pick-Up and Montero

1. If equipped with an electric fuel pump, release fuel pressure as follows:

   a. Disconnect the fuel pump harness connector.

   b. Start the engine and allow the engine to run out of fuel.

   c. Once engine has stalled, turn the key to the **OFF** position.

   d. Disconnect the negative battery cable so pressure cannot build up until work has been completed.

2. Raise the vehicle and support safely.

3. Using the proper equipment, drain the fuel tank.

4. Remove the side skirt panel, if equipped.

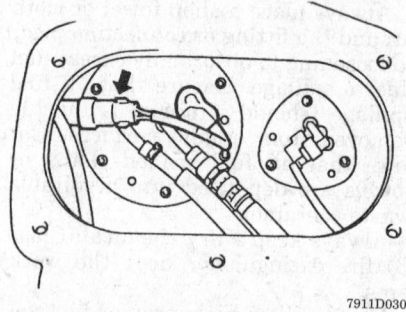

Fuel pump harness connector at the rear of the fuel tank — Montero

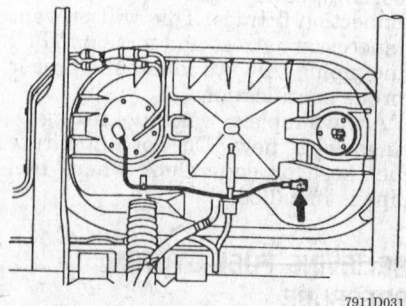

Fuel pump harness connector at the rear of the fuel tank — Pick-Up

5. Disconnect the fuel gauge unit connector.

6. Disconnect the main hose connector.

7. Disconnect the return hose connector and the vapor hose connector.

8. Remove the filler hose connector and the breather hose connection.

9. Place a transmission jack or equivalent, under the center of the tank and apply slight pressure. Remove the tank mounting nuts.

10. Lower the tank and disconnect any lines still connected.

11. Remove the tank from the vehicle.

To install:

12. Raise the tank into position and connect all harnesses and hoses.

13. Install the fuel tank mounting nuts and torque to 18–22 ft. lbs. (25–30 Nm).

14. Reconnect the fuel gauge unit connector.

15. Install the side skirt panel, if equipped.

16. Refill the fuel tank and start the engine. Check fuel system for leaks.

Expo

1. Relieve fuel system pressure.

2. Disconnect the negative battery cable.

3. Raise the vehicle and support safely.

4. Drain the fuel from the fuel tank into an approved container.

5. On Expo AWD, remove the propeller shaft as follows:

   a. Remove the center exhaust pipe bracket.

   b. Matchmark the differential companion flange to the propeller flange yoke.

   c. Remove the bolts, washers and nuts from the center support. Remove the propeller shaft assembly in a straight and level manner to avoid damage to the boot caused by pinching.

   d. Install cover into the rear end of the transfer case to prevent the entry of foreign materials.

6. Disconnect the return hose, high pressure hose and all other hoses and connectors connected to the pump/sending unit.

─────── **CAUTION** ───────
Cover all fuel hose connections with a shop towel, prior to disconnecting, to prevent splash of fuel that could be caused by residual pressure remaining in the fuel line.

7. Disconnect the filler and vent hoses. Place a support under the tank and remove the retaining nuts.

8. Lower the tank from the vehicle.

To install:

9. Install the fuel tank and connect the filler and vent hoses. Tighten the tank retaining nuts to 17–22 ft. lbs. (24–31 Nm).

10. Connect the return hose, high pressure hose and all other hoses and connectors connected to the pump/sending unit.

11. Install the propeller shaft aligning the matchmarks prior to installation. Tighten the rear yoke nuts to 22–25 ft. lbs. (30–35 Nm) and the center support self-locking nuts to 22 ft. lbs. (30 Nm). Install the exhaust pipe center bracket.

12. Lower the vehicle and return fuel to the gas tank.

13. Connect the negative battery cable and check the entire system for proper operation and leaks.

Fuel Filter

REMOVAL AND INSTALLATION

─────── **CAUTION** ───────
Do not use conventional fuel filters, hoses or clamps when servicing this fuel system. They are not compatible with the injection system and could fail, causing personal injury or damage to the vehicle. Use only replacement parts specifically designed for fuel injection.

1. Relieve the fuel pressure.

2. Disconnect the negative battery cable.

3. Raise the vehicle and support safely.

4. Remove the fuel filter protector plate, if equipped.

5. Disconnect the main and high pressure lines. Remove any other fuel hose that are damaged or worn.

6. Remove the filter mounting bolts and remove the filter from the vehicle.

To install:

7. Install new filter onto vehicle using new gaskets. Replace any hoses that are worn or damaged.

8. Install the protector plate, if equipped.

9. Connect the negative battery cable, check for leaks and road test the vehicle.

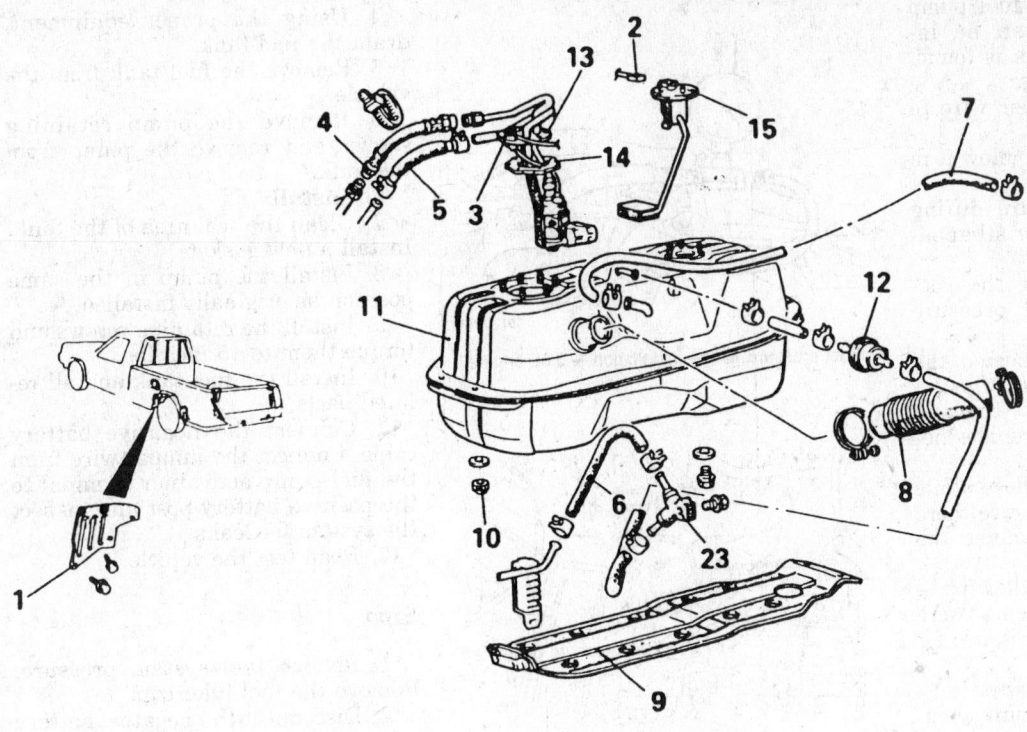

1. Side skirt stay
2. Sending unit connector
3. Fuel pump connector
4. Main hose
5. Return hose
6. Vapor hose
7. Breather hose
8. Filler hose
9. Fuel tank protector (4WD)
10. Tank mounting nut
11. Fuel tank
12. Two-way overfill limiter valve
13. Fuel pump assembly
14. Gasket
15. Sending unit

7911D038

Fuel tank assembly — Pick-Up

Mechanical Fuel Pump

REMOVAL AND INSTALLATION

1. Remove the oil filter.
2. Disconnect the fuel lines from the pump.
3. Plug the lines to prevent fuel leakage.
4. Remove the fuel pump blocker strut from front engine mount to blocker assembly.
5. Remove the fuel pump mounting bolts.
6. Clean all gasket material from engine block mounting surface and spacer block.
7. Assemble the new gaskets and spacer block to fuel pump.
8. Install the fuel pump mounting bolts in pump mounting flange.
9. Position the pump assembly on engine block and torque bolts alternately to 250 inch lbs.
10. Connect the fuel lines to the pump.
11. Position the fuel pump blocker strut on blocker assembly and front engine mount. Tighten assembly.
12. Install the oil filter. Check and adjust oil level.
13. Start the engine and check fuel fittings for leaks.

TESTING

Volume Test

The fuel pump should supply 1 qt. of fuel in 1 minute or less at idle.

Pressure Test

1. Insert a T-fitting in the fuel line at the carburetor.
2. Connect a six inch piece of hose between the T-fitting and a pressure gauge. A longer piece of hose will result in an inaccurate reading.
3. Disconnect the inlet line to the carburetor at the fuel pump and vent the pump. Failure to vent the pump will result in low pressure reading. Reconnect the fuel line.
4. Connect a tachometer to the engine. Start the engine and allow to idle. The pressure gauge should show a constant 2.8–4.2 psi reading. When the engine is turned off, the pressure should slowly drop to zero. An instant drop to zero indicates a leaky diaphragm or weak spring. If pressure is too high, the main spring is too strong or the air vent is plugged.
5. Proceed with vacuum test.

Vacuum Test

1. Remove the inlet and outlet fuel lines from the pump.

2. Plug the fuel line to the carburetor to prevent fuel leakage.
3. Connect a vacuum gauge to the fuel pump inlet fitting.
4. Using the starter motor, turn the engine over several times and observe the vacuum gauge. The fuel pump should develop a minimum of 11 inches of vacuum.
5. If the vacuum readings are below specification, replace the pump.

Electric Fuel Pump

PRESSURE TESTING

1. Relieve the fuel pressure.
2. Disconnect the negative battery cable.
3. Cover the high pressure fuel hose hose with a clean shop towel to prevent fuel spray from residual pressure in the line. Disconnect the high pressure fuel hose at the delivery pipe.
4. Connect the proper fuel pressure gauge and accompanying special adaptor tools to the delivery pipe.
5. If not already done, place the key in the **OFF** position. Connect the negative battery cable.
6. Connect a jumper wire from the fuel pump activation terminal to the positive battery post. This will pres-

surize the system so the fuel pump installation assembly can be inspected for leaks. If a leak is found, repair it before proceeding.

7. Disconnect the jumper wire to stop the fuel pump.

8. Start the engine and allow it to idle.

9. Measure the pressure during idling. The specification for all applications is 38 psi.

10. Disconnect and plug the vacuum hose from the fuel pressure regulator.

11. With the hose disconnected, the pressure should increase to 50 psi.

12. Race the engine a few times to make sure the fuel pressure does not deviate from specifications.

13. Press on the return hose while racing the engine to make sure there is pressure in the hose. Reconnect the vacuum hose.

14. Stop the engine and allow pressure to remain in the system. There should be no decrease in pressure for at least 2 minutes.

15. Release the fuel pressure.

16. Remove the fuel pressure measuring equipment.

17. Connect the high pressure fuel hose to the delivery pipe using new O-rings where necessary.

18. Connect the jumper wire from the fuel pump activation terminal to the positive battery post, inspect the system for leaks.

19. Road test the vehicle.

REMOVAL AND INSTALLATION

Montero

1. Relieve the fuel pressure.
2. Disconnect the negative battery cable.
3. Remove the pump and sending unit access panel.
4. Cover the high pressure fuel hose with a clean shop towel to prevent fuel spray from residual pres-

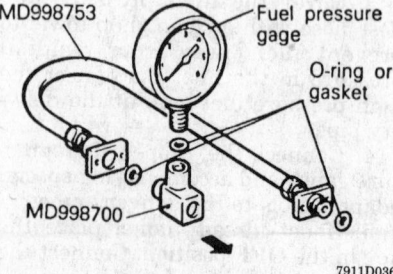

Fuel pressure testing equipment. The hose is not used on Pick-Up with 2.4L engine.

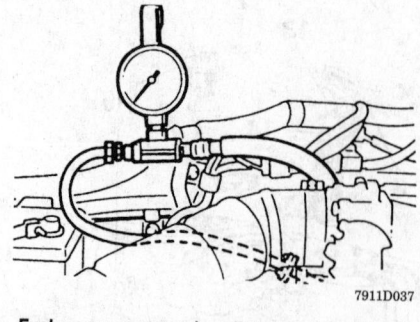

Fuel pressure gauge installation — 3.0L engine

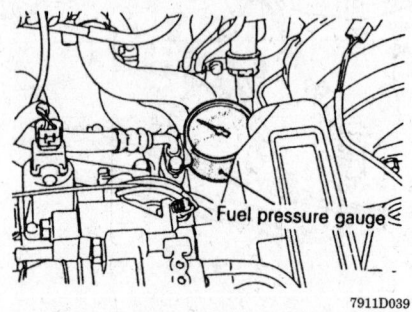

Fuel pressure gauge installation — Pick-Up with 2.4L engine

sure in the line. Disconnect the fuel hose and pipe from the pump.

5. Remove the fuel pump mounting screws and remove the pump from the tank.

6. The installation is the reverse of the removal procedure.

Pick-Up

1. Relieve the fuel pressure.
2. Disconnect the negative battery cable.
3. Raise the vehicle and support safely. Remove protective plates, if equipped.

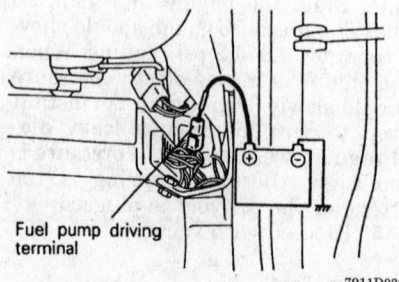

Fuel pump activation terminal — Montero

4. Using the proper equipment, drain the fuel tank.

5. Remove the fuel tank from the vehicle.

6. Remove the pump retaining screws and remove the pump from the tank.

To install:

7. Clean the seal area of the tank. Install a new gasket.

8. Install the pump in the same position as originally installed.

9. Install the retaining screws and torque them to 15 inch lbs.

10. Install the fuel tank and all related parts.

11. Connect the negative battery cable. Connect the jumper wire from the fuel pump activation terminal to the positive battery post and inspect the system for leaks.

12. Road test the vehicle.

Expo

1. Relieve fuel system pressure. Remove the fuel filler cap.

2. Disconnect the negative battery cable.

3. Raise and safely support the vehicle.

4. The fuel pump is located in the fuel tank. Drain the fuel from the fuel tank.

5. On Expo equipped with AWD, remove the rear propeller shaft from the vehicle as follows:

a. Remove the center exhaust pipe bracket.

b. Matchmark the differential companion flange to the propeller flange yoke.

c. Remove the bolts, washers and nuts from the center support. Remove the propeller shaft assembly in a straight and level manner to avoid damage to the boot caused by pinching.

d. Install cover into the rear end of the transfer case to prevent the entry of foreign materials.

6. Disconnect the return hose, high pressure hose and all other hoses and connectors connected to the pump and sending unit.

7. Disconnect the filler and vent hoses. Place a support under the tank and remove the retaining nuts. Lower the tank from vehicle.

8. Remove retaining nuts and remove the fuel pump assembly from tank.

To install:

9. Install the replacement pump using a new gasket. Be certain the pump is installed in the same location, facing the same direction as before.

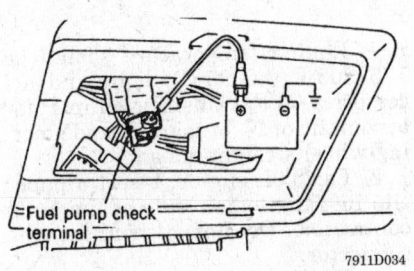

Fuel pump activation terminal located behind the fuse box — Pick-Up

10. Install the fuel tank and secure the retainer nuts. Connect all electrical harness connectors. Reconnect all vent hoses, fuel supply and fuel return hoses securing with the proper clamps.

11. On Expo equipped with AWD, install the propeller shaft aligning the matchmarks prior to installation. Tighten the rear yoke nuts to 22–25 ft. lbs. (30–35 Nm) and the center support self-locking nuts to 22 ft. lbs. (30 Nm).

12. Install the exhaust pipe center bracket. Check that electrical connectors are properly installed and all fuel hose connections are tight.

13. Connect the negative battery cable and check the entire fuel system for proper operation and leaks. If repairing of a fuel leak is required, release the fuel system pressure prior to repairing system.

Carburetor

REMOVAL AND INSTALLATION

1. Disconnect the negative battery cable.

2. Remove the air cleaner.

3. Remove the fuel tank filler cap.to relieve fuel system pressure.

4. Disconnect the carburetor protector and all carburetor electrical wiring.

5. Drain the cooling system. Label and remove the vacuum hoses and coolant hoses at carburetor.

6. Disconnect the carburetor inlet line and block off line to prevent fuel leakage.

7. Disconnect the throttle linkage.

8. Remove the carburetor mounting bolts and nuts and remove carburetor.

9. Inspect the mating surfaces of the carburetor and intake manifold for nicks, burrs, dirt or other damage.

10. Install a new gasket on intake manifold.

11. Carefully install the carburetor on the engine. Install mounting bolts and nuts. Tighten evenly and torque to 150 inch lbs. Make certain throttle plates and choke plate opens and closes properly when operated.

12. Connect the throttle linkage, fuel line and electrical connectors.

13. Install and tighten carburetor protector.

14. Fill the cooling system.

15. Connect the negative battery cable.

16. Install the air cleaner and adjust the carburetor.

ADJUSTMENTS

Idle RPM

1. Check and adjust ignition timing.

2. Set the parking brake and place transaxle in neutral. Turn off all accessories.

3. Disconnect the radiator fan.

4. Connect a tachometer to the engine.

5. Start engine and run until operating temperature is reached.

6. Disconnect cooling fan. Run engine at 2500 RPM for 10 seconds and return to idle.

7. Wait 2 minutes and record RPM. If RPM differs from VECI under hood specification label, turn idle speed adjusting screw until specification is obtained.

8. On air condition models, set the temperature lever to the coldest position and turn air conditioning switch on. With the air condition running, set the engine speed to 900 RPM using the idle-up adjustment screw.

9. Shut engine off. Connect the cooling fan and remove tachometer.

Fast Idle

1. Connect a tachometer to the engine. Check and adjust ignition timing.

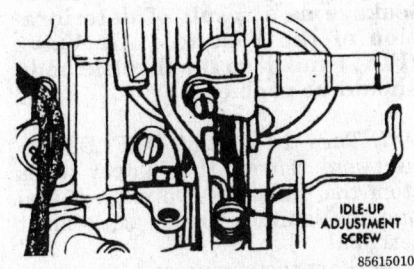

Idle up adjustment

2. Set the parking brake and place transaxle in neutral. Turn off all accessories.

3. Start engine and run until operating temperature is reached.

4. Disconnect radiator fan. Remove and plug vacuum advance hose at distributor.

5. Open the throttle slightly and install Tool C-4812 on cam follower pin.

6. Release throttle lever and adjust fast idle adjusting screw to specification shown on VECI under hood label.

7. Remove tool and shut engine off. Reconnect fan, unplug and reconnect vacuum hose, and remove tachometer.

Idle Mixture (Propane Assist)

NOTE: The following procedures require the use of a propane cylinder, vacuum hose and a special control valve to provide proper enrichment. Any adjustments made other than those in the following procedures, may violate Federal and State Laws.

1. Remove concealment plug. Check and adjust ignition timing.

2. Set the parking brake and place transaxle in neutral. Turn off all accessories.

3. Disconnect the cooling fan.

4. Connect a tachometer to the engine.

5. Start engine and run until operating temperature is reached.

6. Disconnect cooling fan. Run engine at 2500 RPM for 10 seconds and return to idle. Allow engine to idle for 2 minutes.

7. Remove the air cleaner fresh air duct. Place the propane bottle in a safe location and in an upright position. Insert the propane supply hose approximately 4 inches into the air cleaner snorkel.

8. Open the propane bottle main valve. Slowly open the metering valve until the highest engine RPM is reached. If too much propane is added, the engine RPM will decrease. Fine Tune the propane metering valve to obtain the highest engine RPM.

9. With the propane still flowing, adjust the idle speed screw to the specified RPM shown on VECI under hood label. Again Fine Tune the propane metering valve to get the highest engine RPM. If the RPM increases, readjust the idle speed screw to specification.

10. Shut off the propane main valve and allow the engine speed to stabilize. Slowly adjust the carburetor

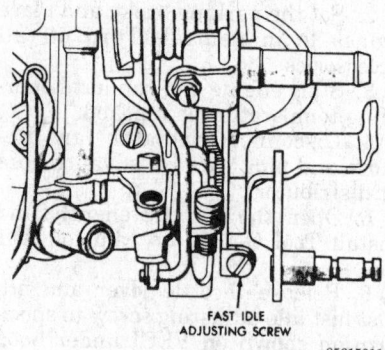

FAST IDLE
ADJUSTING SCREW

85615011

Fast idle adjustment

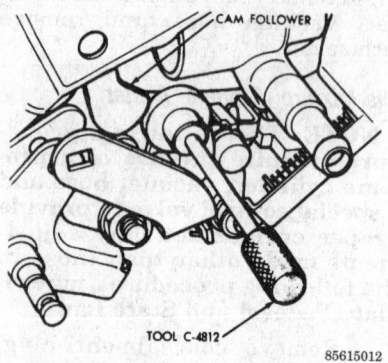

CAM FOLLOWER

TOOL C-4812

85615012

Installing tool C-4812

mixture screws to obtain the specified idle RPM. Pause between each adjustment to allow engine speed to stabilize.

11. Again turn on the propane main valve, Fine Tune the metering valve to get the highest engine RPM. If the RPM changes, repeat Step 8 through 10.

12. Shut off the propane main valve and metering valve. Remove the propane supply hose. Install the air cleaner fresh air duct. Install the concealment plug and impact plate.

Concealment Plug Removal

1. Remove the impact plate, if used.

2. Remove the vacuum connector from high altitude compensator (HAC) fitting on carburetor, if used.

3. With an eight inch long ¼" diameter drill bit, drill out concealment plug at location show.

4. Remove concealment plug.

Fuel Injection

IDLE SPEED ADJUSTMENT

The idle speed is automatically regulated by the idle speed control system

which receives data from various sensors and switches in the system and adjusts the engine idle to a predetermined speed. Idle speed specifications can be found on the Vehicle Emission Control Information (VECI) label located in the engine compartment.

NOTE: The idle speed is controlled electronically and adjustment is usually unnecessary. However, the idle speed may be checked using the following procedures.

1.8L and 2.4L Engines

1. Warm the engine to operating temperature, leave lights, electric cooling fan and accessories **OFF**. The transaxle should be in **N** or **P** for automatic transaxle. The steering wheel in a neutral position for vehicles with power steering.

2. Insert the paper clip into the single terminal rpm connector in the engine compartment, and connect the primary voltage detection type tachometer to the paper clip.

3. Ground the self-diagnostic control terminal of the diagnostic connector with a jumper wire.

4. Remove the waterproof female connector from the ignition timing adjustment connector. Ground the ignition timing adjustment terminal.

5. Start the engine and run at idle. Check the basic idle speed, the desired value is 700–800 rpm.

6. If the value is not within specifications, turn the Speed Adjusting Screw (SAS) to make the necessary adjustment.

NOTE: If the idle speed is higher than the standard value, inspect the SAS screw for evidence of movement. If there is evidence that the SAS screw has been adjusted, readjust to the proper setting. If the screw does not look as though it has been adjusted, it is possible that there is leakage as a result of deterioration of the Fast Idle Air Valve (FIAV) and, if so the throttle body should be replaced.

7. Turn the ignition **OFF**. Disconnect and remove the jumper wires from the diagnosis control terminal and the ignition timing adjustment terminal.

8. Start the engine and let run at idle speed for about 10 minutes, check to be sure the idling condition is normal.

3.0L and 3.5L Engines

1. Engine temperature should be 176–203°F (80–95°C), light and accessories OFF, transmission in **P** for automatic or **N** for manual and steering wheel straight-ahead.

2. For 3.0L engine; insert a paper clip into the female side of the 1-pin connector. Do not disconnect the connector.

3. For 3.5L engine; insert a paper clip into the 1-pin blue connector as shown.

4. Connect a tachometer to the paper clip.

5. For 1992–93 vehicles, use a jumper wire to ground the diagnostic test control terminal No. 10 of the data link connector.

6. For 1994–96 vehicles, use special tool MB991529 to connect the diagnostic test mode control terminal No. 1 of the data link connector (16-pin) located near fuse block.

7. Remove the cover from the female connector from the ignition timing adjusting connector (brown) and jumper to ground.

8. Start the engine and run at idle. Idle speed should be 650–750 rpm.

9. If not within specifications, adjust by turning the engine speed adjusting screw (SAS).

NOTE: If the idle speed is higher then specs even with the speed adjusting screw fully tightened, check to see if the fixed SAS has been moved. If the closed throttle position switch seems to have been moved, adjust it. If the switch is OK, there may be a leak caused by a deteriorated fast idle air valve. If so, replace the throttle body.

10. Turn ignition switch **OFF** and remove all testing equipment.

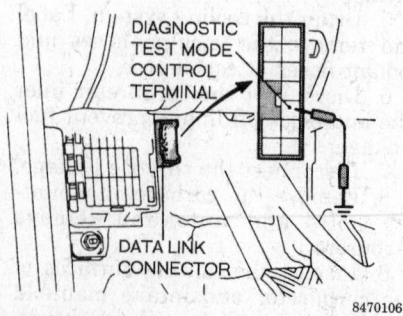

DIAGNOSTIC
TEST MODE
CONTROL
TERMINAL

DATA LINK
CONNECTOR

84701061

Grounding the diagnostic terminal — Expo

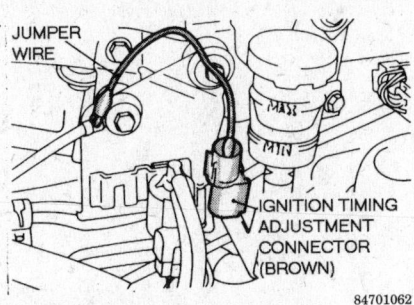

Grounding the ignition timing adjustment terminal — Expo

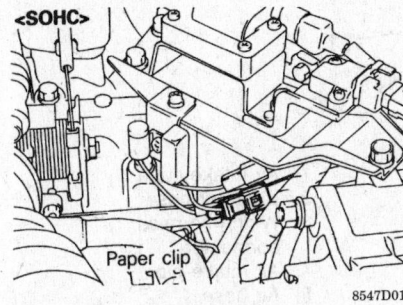

Idle speed adjustment connector location — 3.0L engine

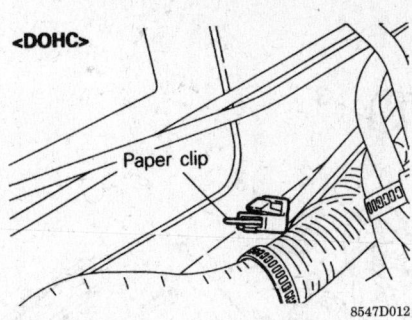

Idle speed adjustment connector location — 3.5L engine

Fuel Injector

REMOVAL AND INSTALLATION

1.8L and 2.4L Engines

1. Relieve the fuel system pressure.
2. Disconnect the negative battery cable.
3. Disconnect and remove the air intake hoses, as required.
4. Wrap the connection with a shop towel and disconnect the high pressure fuel line at the fuel rail.
5. Disconnect the fuel return hose and remove the O-ring.
6. Disconnect the accelerator cable connection from the throttle body and position aside.
7. Disconnect the vacuum connection from the fuel pressure regulator.

8. Disconnect the electrical harness connector from each fuel injector.
9. Remove the injector rail retaining bolts. Make sure the rubber mounting insulators do not get lost.
10. Lift the rail assembly up and away from engine.
11. Remove the injectors from the rail by pulling gently. Discard the lower insulator. Check the resistance through the injector. The specification is 13–16 ohms at 70°F (20°C).

To install:

12. Install a new grommet and O-ring to the injector. Coat the O-ring with light weight oil.
13. Install the injector to the fuel rail.
14. Install the fuel rail and injectors to the manifold. Make sure the rubber bushings are in place before tightening the mounting bolts.
15. Tighten the retaining bolts to 8.7 ft. lbs. (12 Nm).
16. Connect the electrical connectors to the injectors.
17. Replace the O-ring on the fuel pressure regulator, lightly lubricate and install on the delivery pipe. Connect the vacuum hose to the fuel pressure regulator.
18. Connect the fuel return hose.
19. Replace the O-ring on high pressure fuel line, lightly lubricate it and connect to delivery pipe.
20. Reconnect the accelerator cable to the throttler body and adjust to specifications.
21. Connect the negative battery cable and check the entire system for proper operation and leaks.

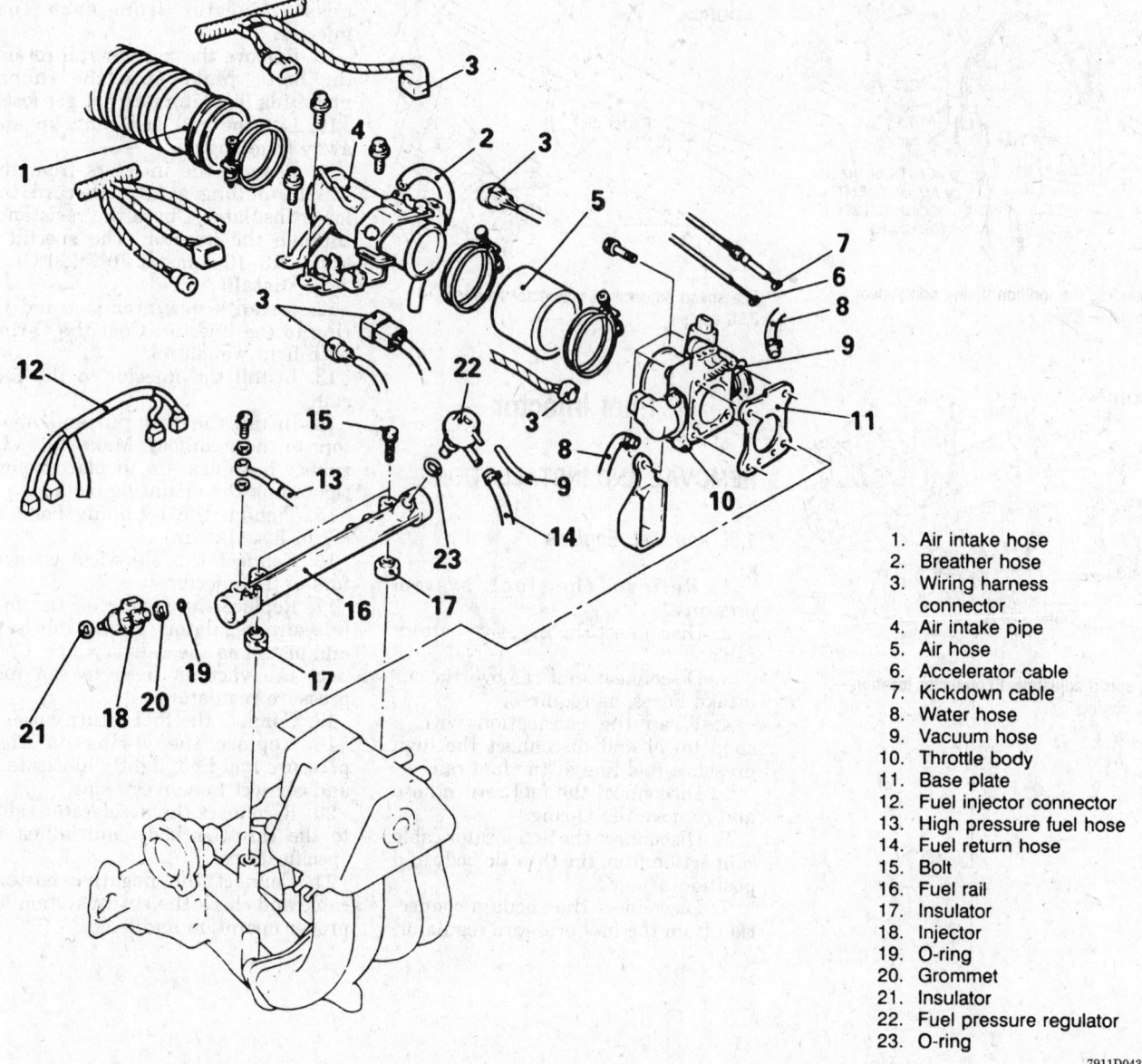

1. Air intake hose
2. Breather hose
3. Wiring harness connector
4. Air intake pipe
5. Air hose
6. Accelerator cable
7. Kickdown cable
8. Water hose
9. Vacuum hose
10. Throttle body
11. Base plate
12. Fuel injector connector
13. High pressure fuel hose
14. Fuel return hose
15. Bolt
16. Fuel rail
17. Insulator
18. Injector
19. O-ring
20. Grommet
21. Insulator
22. Fuel pressure regulator
23. O-ring

7911D043

Throttle body, fuel rail, injector and related parts — 2.4L engine

3.0L and 3.5L Engines

1. Relieve the fuel pressure.

2. Disconnect negative battery cable.

3. Remove the air intake hose from the throttle body.

4. Disconnect all wires, hoses and linkages to the throttle body.

5. Disconnect the EGR temperature sensor wire, if equipped.

6. Remove the ignition coil.

7. Remove the engine oil filler neck bracket.

8. Unbolt the EGR tube from the air intake plenum, if equipped.

9. Disconnect the PCV hose and vacuum hose cluster from the plenum.

10. Remove the plenum to engine brackets.

11. Unbolt the air intake plenum assembly from the intake manifold and remove.

12. Cover the high pressure fuel hose with a clean shop towel to prevent fuel spray due to residual pressure in the line. Disconnect the high pressure fuel hose from the fuel rail.

13. Remove the fuel return line and vacuum hose from the fuel pressure regulator.

14. Remove electrical connectors from the injectors.

15. Remove the fuel rail retaining bolts.

16. Lift the rail with injectors attached up and away from the engine.

17. Remove the injectors from the fuel rail pulling straight out away from the rail. Remove the lower insulator.

To install:

18. Install a new grommet and O-ring onto injector. Coat the O-ring lightly with gasoline to aid in assembly.

19. Install the injectors into the rail, making sure injector turns freely. If they do not, check for a misaligned O-ring and reinstall.

20. Replace the seats in the intake manifold. Install new rubber bushings onto mounting points of fuel rail.

Install the assembled fuel rail with injectors onto the manifold.

21. Tighten the fuel rail bolts to 8 ft. lbs. (10 Nm).

22. Connect the electrical harness to the injectors.

23. Connect the fuel return hose and the vacuum hose to the pressure regulator.

24. Using a new O-ring coated lightly with gasoline, install the high pressure fuel line.

25. Install air intake plenum and all related parts.

26. Connect the negative battery cable.

27. Connect the jumper wire from the fuel pump activation terminal to the positive battery post inspect the system for leaks.

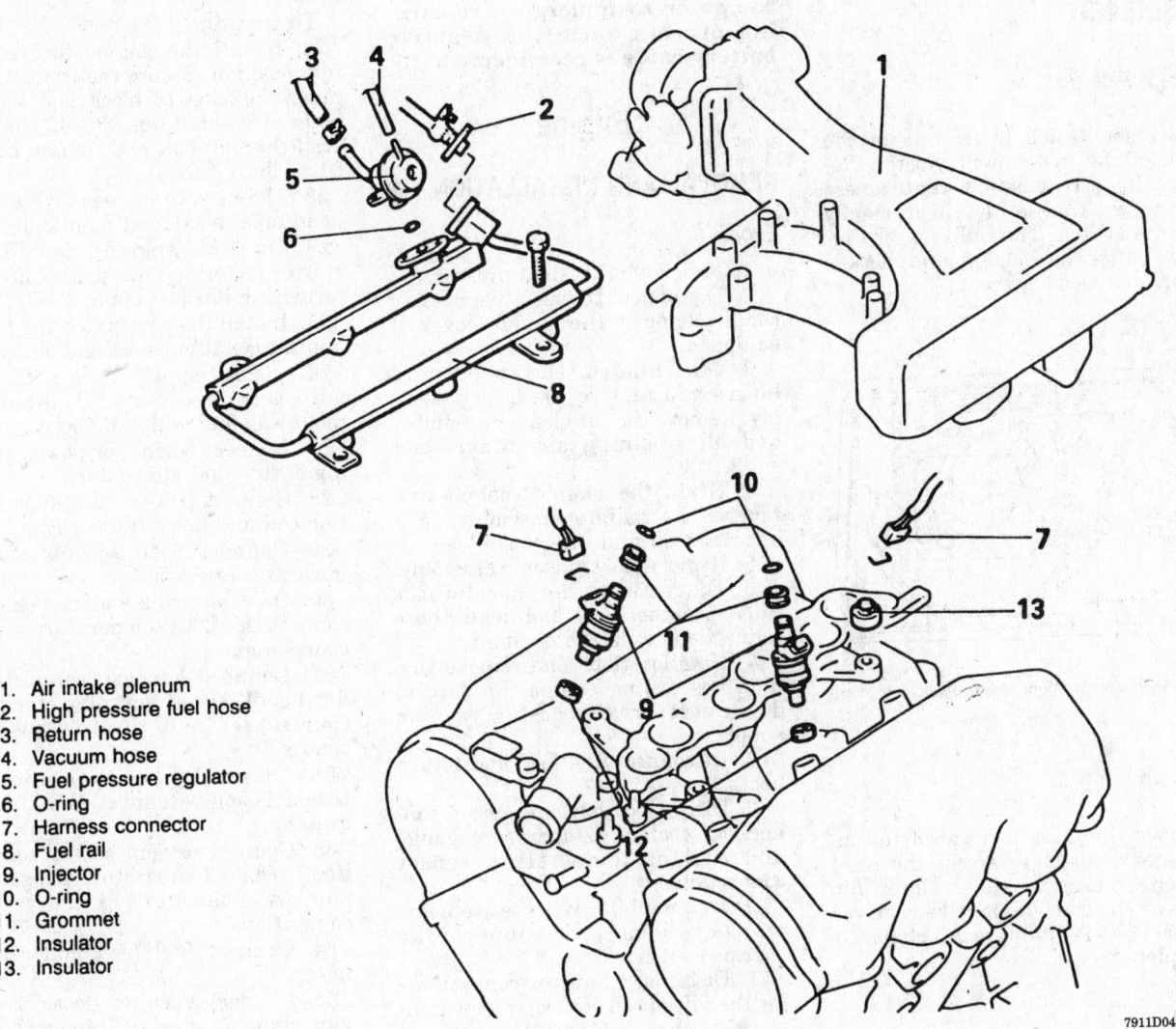

1. Air intake plenum
2. High pressure fuel hose
3. Return hose
4. Vacuum hose
5. Fuel pressure regulator
6. O-ring
7. Harness connector
8. Fuel rail
9. Injector
10. O-ring
11. Grommet
12. Insulator
13. Insulator

7911D044

Fuel rail, injector and related parts — 3.0L engine, 3.5L similar

EMISSION CONTROLS

Emission Warning Lamps

RESETTING

Except Pick-Up

The reset switch is located on the back of the instrument cluster. Remove the instrument cluster to access the switch. To reset the timer, simply flip the switch. The bulb may be removed after the 150,000 mile check is completed on Montero.

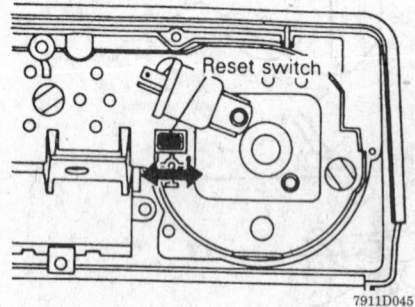

Emissions warning light reset switch — Montero

Pick-Up

Remove the glass in from of the instrument cluster to access the reset switch. To reset the timer, simply flip the switch. The bulb may be removed after the 120,000 mile check is completed.

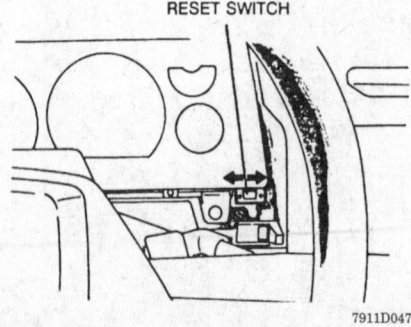

Emissions warning light reset switch — Pick-Up

ENGINE MECHANICAL

NOTE: Disconnecting the negative battery cable on some vehicles may interfere with the functions of the on board computer systems and may require the computer to undergo a relearning process, once the negative battery cable is reconnected.

Engine

REMOVAL AND INSTALLATION

Expo

1. Relieve fuel system pressure.
2. Disconnect the negative battery cable. Remove the under cover if equipped.
3. Matchmark the hood and hinges and remove the hood assembly. Remove the air cleaner assembly and all adjoining air intake duct work.
4. Drain the engine coolant and remove the radiator assembly, coolant reservoir and intercooler.
5. Remove the transaxle assembly.
6. Disconnect the accelerator cable, breather hose and heater hose connections from the engine.
7. Note locations and remove vacuum hoses from engine. Be sure to disconnect brake booster vacuum supply.
8. Disconnect fuel feed and return hoses.
9. Disconnect oxygen sensor connection, coolant temperature gauge and coolant temperature sensor connections.
10. On models with automatic transmissions , disconnect the thermo switch.
11. Disconnect harness connections for the idle speed control, motor position sensor and throttle position sensor.
12. Disconnect EGR temperature sensor (California).
13. Note locations for reassembly and disconnect injector connections.
14. Disconnect power transistor, ignition coil and noise filter connections.
15. Disconnect alternator and power steering switch wiring.
16. Remove the air conditioner drive belt and the air conditioning compressor. Leave the hoses attached and do not discharge the system. Wire the compressor aside.

17. Remove the power steering pump and wire aside.
18. Remove the starter and alternator harness clamp (1.8L engine).
19. Remove the exhaust manifold to head pipe nuts. Discard the gasket.
20. Attach a hoist to the engine and support the engine weight. Remove the engine mount brackets.
21. Remove the engine assembly from the vehicle.
    To install:
22. Install the engine and secure into position. Secure the front engine mount bracket to block and tighten bolts to 29–36 ft. lbs. (39–49 Nm). Install through bolt and tighten bolt to 51 ft. lbs. (70 Nm).
23. Using a new gasket, attach head pipe to exhaust manifold.
24. On 1.8L engines, install the starter motor and attach the alternator wiring harness clamp.
25. Install the power steering pump and air conditioner assemblies.
26. Install engine drive belts and adjust as necessary. Tighten all mounting and adjusting bolts.
27. Connect wiring for power steering switch and alternator.
28. Connect power transistor, ignition coil and noise filter wiring.
29. Connect fuel injector wiring harness connections.
30. On California model vehicles, connect the EGR temperature sensor connection.
31. Connect harness connections for the idle speed control, motor position sensor and throttle position sensor.
32. On models with automatic transmissions, connect the thermo switch.
33. Connect oxygen sensor connection, coolant temperature gauge and coolant temperature sensor connections.
34. Connect fuel feed and return hoses.
35. Connect vacuum hoses to engine and be sure to connect brake booster vacuum supply.
36. Connect the accelerator cable, breather hose and heater hose connections to the engine.
37. Install the transaxle assembly.
38. Install the radiator and overflow assembly. Refill the cooling system.
39. Install the hood assembly, air cleaner assembly and all adjoining air intake duct work.
40. Connect negative battery cable and run engine.
41. Inspect all connections and check all fluid levels.

Pick-Up and Montero with 2.4L and 3.0L Engines

1. Relieve the fuel pressure if equipped with fuel injection. Disconnect the negative battery cable from the battery and from the engine.

2. Matchmark and remove the hood. Remove the oil dipstick.

3. Raise the vehicle and support safely. Remove the engine under cover. Drain the engine oil and coolant.

4. Remove the starter. Remove the lower radiator hose.

5. Remove the exhaust pipe from the exhaust manifold(s).

6. If equipped with a manual transmission, remove the transmission and all related parts.

7. If equipped with an automatic transmission, remove the inspection plate, matchmark the flexplate to the converter, remove the torque converter bolts and push the torque converter backwards as far as it will go. Remove the lower bell housing bolts. Lower the vehicle.

8. Remove all ductwork and air intake hoses. Disconnect all linkages and cables from the throttle body.

9. Cover the fuel line connections with a clean shop rag and disconnect and plug the fuel lines.

10. If equipped with air conditioning, unbolt the air conditioning compressor from the engine and position aside. It is not necessary to remove the lines from the compressor.

11. Remove the radiator and shroud. Remove the fan and all related parts. Disconnect the heater hoses.

12. Unbolt the power steering pump from its brackets and position it to the side. Do not remove the hoses from the pump.

13. Remove the alternator. Remove the ignition coil and power transistor assembly, if equipped.

14. Label and disconnect all remaining electrical connectors, vacuum hoses and check for any other items preventing engine removed.

15. Attach an engine removal device to the engine support eyes on the engine.

16. If equipped with an automatic transmission, support the transmission with a floor jack or equivalent. Remove the remaining bell housing bolts.

17. Remove the engine mount nuts and remove the engine from the vehicle.

To install:

18. Lower the engine into position and install the engine mount nuts. Torque the nuts to 20 ft. lbs. (27 Nm).

Install the upper bell housing bolts. Remove the engine removal device. Install the oil dipstick.

19. Raise the vehicle and support safely.

20. Install the remaining bell housing bolts.

21. If equipped with a manual transmission, install the transmission and all related parts.

22. If equipped with an automatic transmission, align the torque converter and flexplate and install the bolts. Install the inspection plate and starter.

23. Install the exhaust pipe to the exhaust manifold(s) using new gaskets. Install the lower radiator hose. Lower the vehicle.

24. Connect the heater hoses.

25. Make sure the negative battery cable is not connected to the battery. Connect the engine side of the negative cable to the engine. Install the alternator, power steering pump and all brackets.

26. Install the air conditioning compressor.

27. Connect all linkages and cables to the throttle body.

28. Install the ignition coil and power transistor assembly, if equipped. Connect all electrical connectors and vacuum hoses that were disconnected during the engine removal procedure.

29. Install the fan and all related parts. Adjust all belt tensions, as required.

30. Install the radiator, shroud and upper hose.

31. Install the air cleaner assembly, ducts and air intake hoses.

32. Fill the engine with the specified amount of oil and fill the radiator with coolant.

33. Connect the negative battery cable and connect the jumper wire from the fuel pump activation terminal, if equipped, to the positive battery post to inspect the system for leaks.

34. Check the automatic transmission fluid level, if equipped. Set all adjustments to specifications.

35. Install and align the hood.

Montero with 3.5L Engine

1. Relieve the fuel pressure if equipped with fuel injection. Disconnect the negative battery cable from the battery and from the engine. Drain the engine coolant.

2. Matchmark and remove the hood with an assistant.

3. Remove the battery and tray. Disconnect the cruise control intermediate link, if equipped.

4. Disconnect the radiator hoses and automatic transmission cooler lines. Remove the radiator from the vehicle.

5. Raise the vehicle and support safely with jackstands. Remove the skid plates and undercovers.

6. Remove the front exhaust pipe and move out of the way.

7. Remove the transmission/transfer case assembly.

8. Remove the intake manifold plenum cover, accessory drive belts, cooling fan and water pump pulley.

9. Remove the A/C compressor and power steering pump. Position out of the way without disconnecting the hoses.

10. Disconnect and label all engine, ground and accessory electrical connectors.

11. Disconnect and label all cables and hoses from the engine.

12. Install an approved engine lifting device and remove engine, making sure all components are disconnected before removal.

To install:

13. Install the engine and torque mount bolts to 33 ft. lbs. (44 Nm) and nuts to 19 ft. lbs. (26 Nm).

14. Connect all cables and hoses to the engine.

15. Connect all engine, ground and accessory electrical connectors.

16. Install the A/C compressor and power steering pump.

17. Install the intake manifold plenum cover, accessory drive belts, cooling fan and water pump pulley.

18. Install the transmission/transfer case assembly.

19. Install the front exhaust pipe.

20. Install the skid plates and undercovers.

21. Install the radiator and connect the radiator hoses and automatic transmission cooler lines.

22. Install the battery and tray. Connect the cruise control intermediate link, if equipped.

23. Install the hood with an assistant.

24. Refill the engine coolant and oil, start the engine and check for leaks.

Engine Mounts

REMOVAL AND INSTALLATION

Pickup and Montero

FRONT MOUNT

1. Disconnect negative battery cable.

1. Throttle position sensor connector
2. Ignition coil connector
3. Power transistor connector
4. EGR temperature sensor connector
5. Coolant temperature sending unit connector
6. Coolant temperature sensor connector
7. Thermo switch connector (automatic transmission only)
8. Oxygen sensor connector
9. Alternator connector
10. Oil pressure sending unit connector
11. Coolant temperature switch connector (automatic transmission only)
12. Ground cable
13. Emission control vacuum hose
14. Brake booster vacuum hose
15. Ground cable
16. I.S.C. connector
17. Motor position sensor connector
18. Engine controller wiring harness
19. Heat shield
20. Engine mount bolt

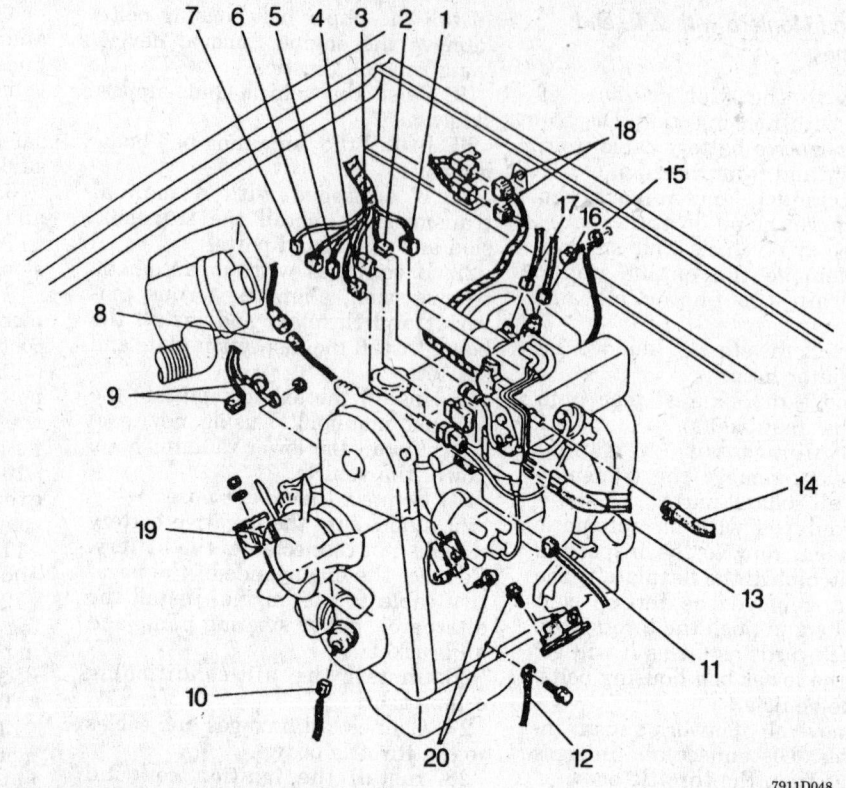

Identifying electrical connectors — Pick-Up with 2.4L engine

7911D048

2. Install engine support fixture in place. Raise and safely support the vehicle.

3. Remove the engine front support insulator.

4. Remove the front insulator stopper.

5. Remove the heat protector.

6. Unbolt the rear crossmember or mount as required.

7. Raise engine with support fixture far enough to remove mounts, remove remaining bolts and mounts. Transfer insulator and stopper to new mount.

To install:

8. Install mounts to engine block. Install stopper and heat protector to the mount.

9. Lower engine to original position and insert bolts through mounting brackets. Tighten bolts to 22–29 ft. lbs. (30–40 Nm) and mount nut to 14–22 ft. lbs. (20–30 Nm).

10. Install heat protector to insulator. Tighten heat protector nut to 6–9 ft. lbs. (8–12 Nm).

11. Lower the vehicle and remove the engine support fixture. Reconnect the negative battery cable.

REAR MOUNT

1. Disconnect negative battery cable.

2. Install engine support fixture in place. Raise and safely support the vehicle.

3. Install transmission jack into position and raise transmission slightly.

4. Remove rear mount attaching bolts and crossmember attaching bolts. Remove crossmember from the vehicle and transfer mounting bracket, support insulator plate assembly to new mount.

5. Installation is the reverse of the removal procedure. Torque crossmember retaining bolts to 29–40 ft. lbs. (40–55 Nm). Torque the insulator to crossmember nuts to 14–18 ft. lbs. (20–25 Nm).

Expo

1. Disconnect the negative battery cable. Remove the air cleaner and all necessary air duct work.

2. Raise and safely support the engine so it is not resting on the engine mount. One suggested way is a block of wood between a floor jack and the oil pan. Use care not to bend or damage any components.

3. Remove the retainer bolt from the clamp securing the power steering pressure hose and the air conditioning low pressure hose.

4. Remove the engine mount bracket and body connection through bolt. Take note of the position of the arrow on the oval shaped mounting stopper plate. This is important.

5. Remove the engine mounting bracket and stopper plate.

6. Lower mounts (roll stoppers) are removed by removing the through bolt, then the frame bolts.

To install:

7. Install the engine mounting bracket and stopper plate. Note the arrows on the stopper plates and make sure they are installed properly. On most engines the arrows will face the towards the center of the engine.

8. Install the lower front roll stopper so the part of the bracket with the hole in it is facing the front of the vehicle.

9. The front lower mount through bolt nut should not be tightened until the full weight of the engine is on the mount. Torque specifications are as follows:

1992–96 — Upper mount to engine nuts and bolts — 42 ft. lbs. (58 Nm)

1992–96 — Upper mount through bolt nut — 51 ft. lbs. (70 Nm)

1992–96 — Lower mount through bolt nut — 42 ft. lbs. (58 Nm)

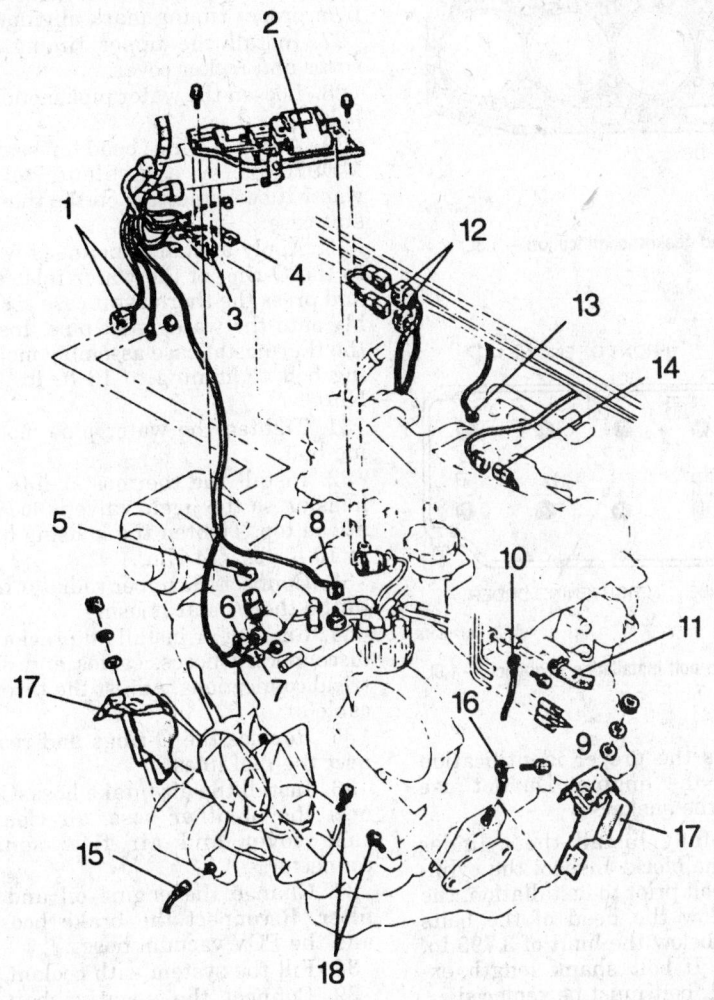

1. Alternator connector
2. Ignition coil and power transistor assembly
3. I.S.C. connector
4. Throttle position sensor connector
5. Coolant temperature switch connector (automatic transmission only)
6. Coolant temperature sensor connector
7. Thermo switch connector (automatic transmission only)
8. Coolant temperature sending unit connector
9. Emission control vacuum hose
10. Ground cable
11. Brake booster vacuum hose
12. Engine controller wiring harness
13. Ground cable
14. EGR temperature sensor connector
15. Oil pressure sending unit connector
16. Oil pressure sending unit connector
17. Ground cable
18. Heat shield

7911D049

Identifying electrical connectors — 3.0L engine

Cylinder Head

REMOVAL AND INSTALLATION

Expo

1.8L ENGINE

1. Relieve fuel system pressure. Disconnect the negative battery cable.
2. Drain the cooling system. Disconnect the brake booster vacuum hose and PVC valve connection.
3. Remove the upper radiator hose, overflow tube and the water hose from the thermostat to the throttle body.

4. Disconnect the air flow sensor connector. Remove the air cleaner case cover and the air intake hose.
5. Wrap the connection with a shop towel and disconnect the high pressure fuel line at the fuel rail.
6. Disconnect the fuel return hose and remove the O-ring.
7. Disconnect the accelerator cable connection from the throttle body and position aside.
8. Disconnect the electrical harnesses at the oil pressure switch, oxygen sensor, water temperature sensor connector and distributor.
9. Disconnect the wiring from condenser, idle speed control, throttle position sensor and knock sensor.

10. Note harness plug connections for reassembly and disconnect fuel injectors.
11. Disconnect the spark plug cables from each spark plug.
12. Unbolt the control harness assembly and position aside.
13. Remove the thermostat housing, thermostat and the thermostat case with O-ring from the engine.
14. Remove the rocker cover.
15. Remove the timing belt upper cover.
16. Rotate the crankshaft in the clockwise direction to align the camshaft timing marks. Matchmark the camshaft sprocket and the timing belt. Tie the camshaft sprocket and

the timing belt together so the sprocket will not move with respect to the timing belt.

17. While holding the camshaft sprocket in position using the appropriate wrench, remove the camshaft sprocket and with the belt attached. Wire the sprocket and belt aside making sure constant tension is maintained on the belt. Do not allow the belt to slacken or engine timing may be altered.

NOTE: When removing the camshaft sprocket, do not allow the crankshaft to rotate. If crankshaft rotation did occur, the engine timing may have been changed. Confirm proper engine timing during installation.

18. Loosen the cylinder head bolts in 2 or 3 Steps in the appropriate order and remove from the cylinder head.

19. Remove the cylinder head from the engine.

--- CAUTION ---
When removing the cylinder head, take care not to bend or damage the plug guide. The plug guide can not be replaced.

20. Remove the cylinder head gasket from the block.

To install:

21. Thoroughly clean and dry the mating surfaces of the head and block. Check the cylinder head for cracks, damage or engine coolant leakage. Remove scale, sealing compound and carbon. Clean oil passages thoroughly. Check the head for flatness. End to end, the head should be within 0.002 in. normally with 0.008 in. the maximum allowed out of true. The total thickness allowed to be removed from the head and block is 0.008 in. maximum.

22. Place a new head gasket on the cylinder block with the identification marks facing upward. Make sure the

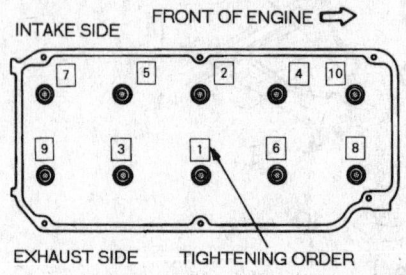

Cylinder head bolt removal sequence — 1.8L engine

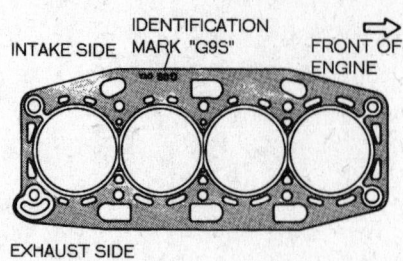

Cylinder head gasket identification — 1.8L engine

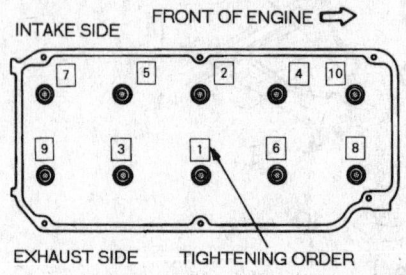

Cylinder head bolt installation sequence — 1.8L engine

gasket has the proper identification mark for the engine. Do not use sealer on the gasket.

23. Carefully install the cylinder head on the block. Inspect the cylinder head bolt prior to installation, the length below the head of the bolts should be below the limit of 3.795 in. (96.4mm). If bolt shank length exceeds limit, bolt must be replaced.

24. Apply a small amount of engine oil to the thread section and the washer of the cylinder head bolt and install so the sagging side made by tapping out the washer is facing upward. (chamfer edge faces up).

25. Tighten the cylinder head bolts in the proper order as follows:

a. In the proper tightening sequence, torque bolts to 54 ft. lbs. (75 Nm).

b. In the reverse order of the tightening sequence, fully loosen bolts.

c. In the proper tightening sequence, torque bolts to 14 ft. lbs. (20 Nm).

d. In the proper tightening sequence, tighten bolts an additional ¼turn (90 degrees).

e. In the proper tightening sequence, tighten bolts an additional ¼turn (90 degrees).

26. Install the camshaft sprocket and tighten bolt to 65 ft. lbs. (90 Nm), while holding the sprocket in place using the appropriate wrench. Confirm proper timing mark alignment.

27. Install the upper timing belt cover and rocker cover.

28. Loosen the water pipe mounting bolt.

29. Apply a thin bead of sealant MD970389 or equivalent, to the water tube connection on the thermostat case.

30. Apply a small amount of water to the O-ring of the water inlet pipe and press the thermostat case assembly onto the water inlet pipe. Install the thermostat case assembly mounting bolt tightening to 16 ft. lbs. (22 Nm).

31. Tighten the water pipe mounting bolt.

32. Install the thermostat into the housing so the jiggle valve is located at the top. Tighten the housing bolts to 10 ft. lbs. (14 Nm).

33. Connect the upper radiator hose to the thermostat housing.

34. Connect or install all previously disconnected hoses, cables and electrical connections. Adjust the throttle cable(s).

35. Replace the O-rings and reconnect the fuel lines.

36. Install the air intake hose. Connect the breather hose, air cleaner case cover and air flow sensor connector.

37. Change the engine oil and oil filter. Reconnect the brake booster and the PCV vacuum hoses.

38. Fill the system with coolant.

39. Connect the negative battery cable, run the vehicle until the thermostat opens, fill the radiator completely.

40. Check and adjust the idle speed and ignition timing.

41. Check all systems for leaks. Allow the engine to cool and recheck the coolant level.

2.4L ENGINE

1. Relieve fuel system pressure. Disconnect the negative battery cable.

2. Drain the cooling system.

3. Disconnect the accelerator cable.

4. Disconnect the air flow sensor connector and the air intake hose. Remove the air cleaner cover.

5. Disconnect the PCV hose and brake booster hose connection.

6. Disconnect the water hose connection at the throttle body to water inlet pipe.

7. Disconnect the water hose connection at the throttle body to thermostat hose.

8. Wrap the connection with a shop towel and disconnect the high pressure fuel line at the fuel rail.

9. Disconnect the fuel return hose and remove the O-ring.

10. Disconnect the accelerator cables connection at the throttle body.

11. Disconnect the spark plug cables from the spark plugs.

12. Disconnect the electrical connectors from the oxygen sensor, water temperature gauge unit, engine coolant temperature sensor and throttle position sensor.

13. Disconnect wiring for the power transistor connector, ignition coil, distributor, and air conditioner compressor.

14. Label prior to disconnecting and remove the fuel injector wiring harness connections.

15. Remove the bolt retaining the power steering hose and air conditioner hose clamp.

16. Remove the bolt holding the ground wire to the manifold.

17. Remove the upper and lower radiator hose connections at the engine.

18. Remove the exhaust pipe to manifold nuts and discard the gasket.

19. Remove the timing belt upper cover.

20. Remove the valve cover, gasket and half-round seal.

21. Rotate the crankshaft clockwise until the timing marks are aligned. Matchmark the timing sprocket to the belt.

22. Remove the sprocket bolt and remove the sprocket with the timing belt attached. Attach a flexible cord to the hood and suspend the sprocket so it cannot turn and there is no slack in the belt. Remove the timing belt rear upper cover.

23. Loosen the head bolts in the correct sequence in 2 or 3 steps. Remove the cylinder head bolts and head assembly from the block.

To install:

24. Thoroughly clean and dry the mating surfaces of the head and block. Check the cylinder head for cracks, damage or engine coolant leakage. Remove scale, sealing compound and carbon. Clean oil passages thoroughly. Check the head for flatness. End to end, the head should be within 0.002 in. normally with 0.008 in. the maximum allowed out of true. The total thickness allowed to be removed from the head and block is 0.008 in. maximum.

25. Place a new head gasket on the cylinder block with the identification marks at the top (upward) position. Make sure the gasket has the proper identification mark for the engine. Do not use sealer on the gasket. Replace the turbo gasket and ring, if equipped.

26. For 1992–96 model years torque specifications are as follows. All torque specifications apply to a cold engine.

   a. In the proper tightening sequence, torque bolts to 54 ft. lbs. (75 Nm).

   b. In the reverse order of the tightening sequence, fully loosen bolts.

   c. In the proper tightening sequence, torque bolts to 14 ft. lbs. (20 Nm).

   d. In the proper tightening sequence, tighten bolts an additional 1/4 turn (90 degrees).

   e. In the proper tightening sequence, tighten bolts an additional 1/4 turn (90 degrees).

NOTE: Install the head bolt washer so the sagging side made by tapping out the washer is facing upward.

27. Install the camshaft sprocket and tighten bolt to 65 ft. lbs. (90 Nm), while holding the sprocket in place using the appropriate wrench. Confirm proper timing mark alignment.

28. Apply sealer to the perimeter of the half-round seal and to the lower edges of the half-round portions of the belt-side of the new gasket. Install the valve cover and tighten bolts to 26.5–30 inch lbs. (3–3.5 Nm).

29. Install the power steering and air conditioning compressor hose clamp in position and secure with the retainer bolt. Tighten the bolt to 9 ft. lbs. (12 Nm).

30. Connect the exhaust pipe to the manifold using new self-locking nuts and replace gasket. Tighten nuts to 29–36 ft. lbs. (40–50 Nm).

31. Reconnect fuel injector harness connections.

32. Attach the upper and lower radiator hose connections at the engine.

33. Connect wiring for the power transistor connector, ignition coil, distributor, and air conditioner compressor.

34. Connect the electrical connectors from the oxygen sensor, water temperature gauge unit, engine coolant temperature sensor and throttle position sensor.

35. Connect the spark plug cables to the spark plugs.

36. Connect the accelerator cables connection at the throttle body.

37. Connect the fuel feed and return hoses, replace O-rings.

38. Connect the water hose connection at the throttle body to water inlet pipe.

39. Connect the water hose connection at the throttle body to thermostat hose.

40. Connect the PCV hose and brake booster hose connection.

41. Connect the air flow sensor connector and the air intake hose. Install the air cleaner cover.

42. Connect the ground wire to the manifold.

43. Fill the system with coolant. Adjust the accelerator cable.

44. Firmly set the parking brake. Start the engine and allow to idle until the thermostat opens, add coolant as required to fill system to the appropriate level.

45. Check all systems for leaks. Allow the engine to cool and recheck the coolant level.

Pick-Up 2.4L Engine

1. Rotate the engine so No. 1 cylinder is at TDC. If equipped with fuel injection, relieve the fuel pressure.

2. Disconnect negative battery cable. Drain the cooling system.

3. Remove the upper radiator hose and disconnect the heater hoses. Remove the dipstick bracket bolt.

4. Remove the air cleaner assembly or air intake hose.

5. Disconnect all linkages and cables from the throttle body. Disconnect and plug the fuel lines to the fuel rail. Remove the valve cover.

6. On the 2.4L engines, perform the following:

   a. Without disconnecting the lines, unbolt the power steering pump from its brackets and position it to the side, if equipped.

   b. Remove the timing belt upper cover.

   c. Align the timing mark, if not already aligned. Secure the timing belt to the sprocket with wire tie.

   d. Remove the camshaft bolt.

   e. Remove the sprocket from the camshaft and allow it to rest on the lower cover. If this is not possible, tie it to a fabricated device so the belt remains taut and the timing is not lost.

7. Disconnect and label all vacuum lines, hoses and wiring connectors from the manifolds, throttle body and cylinder head.

8. Raise the vehicle and support safely.

9. Remove the exhaust pipe from the exhaust manifold. Lower the vehicle.

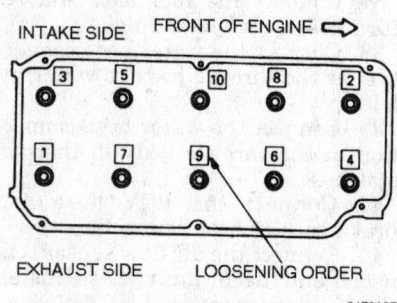

Cylinder head bolt removal sequence — Expo 2.4L engine

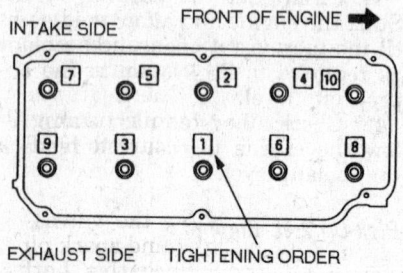

Cylinder head bolt installation sequence — Expo 2.4L engine

10. Remove the cylinder head from the engine.

11. Clean the cylinder head gasket mating surfaces.

To install:

12. Install the camshaft gear or sprocket.

13. Install the timing belt cover, if equipped.

14. Install the power steering pump, if removed.

15. Connect the heater hoses.

16. Install the dipstick bracket bolt. Install the valve cover with a new gasket.

Cylinder head bolt torque sequence — Pick-Up 2.4L engine

17. Connect and plug the fuel lines to the fuel rail. Connect all linkages and cables to the throttle body.

18. Install the air cleaner assembly or air intake hose.

19. Connect the upper radiator hose.

20. Fill the radiator with coolant.

21. Connect the negative battery cable and connect the jumper wire from the fuel pump activation terminal to the positive battery post to inspect the system for leaks, if equipped.

22. Set all adjustments to specifications.

23. Install the seat underframe, if removed.

3.0L and 3.5L Engines

1. Relieve the fuel pressure. Disconnect the negative battery cable. Drain the cooling system. Disconnect the upper radiator hose.

2. Remove the drive belts, air conditioning compressor and power steering pump from the mounts and position them to the side.

3. Using a 1/2 in. drive breaker bar, insert it into the square hole of the serpentine drive belt tensioner, rotate it counterclockwise (to reduce the belt tension) and remove the belt.

4. Remove the alternator.

5. Remove the crankshaft pulley and the torsional damper.

6. To remove the timing belt, perform the following procedures:

   a. Remove the covers. Rotate the crankshaft to position No. 1 cylinder on the TDC of its compression stroke; the crankshaft sprocket timing mark should align with the oil pan timing indicator and the camshaft sprockets timing marks (triangles) should align with the rear timing belt covers timing marks.

   b. Mark the timing belt in the direction of rotation for reinstallation purposes.

   c. Loosen the timing belt tensioner and remove the timing belt.

NOTE: When removing the timing belt from the camshaft sprocket, make sure the belt does not slip off of the other camshaft sprocket. Support the belt so it can not slip off of the crankshaft sprocket and opposite side camshaft sprocket.

7. Remove the air intake hose.

8. Label and disconnect the spark plug wires and vacuum hoses.

9. Remove the valve cover.

10. If removing the left cylinder head, matchmark the distributor ro-

tor to the distributor housing and the housing to distributor extension locations. Remove the distributor and the distributor extension. Also, remove the EGR pipe.

11. Remove the air intake plenum and intake manifold assembly.

12. Remove the exhaust manifold.

13. Remove the cylinder head bolts starting from the outside and working inward.

14. Remove the cylinder head from the engine.

15. Clean the gasket mounting surfaces.

To install:

16. Install the new cylinder head gaskets over the dowels on the engine block.

17. Install the cylinder heads on the engine and torque the cylinder head bolts in sequence using 3 even steps, to 70 ft. lbs. (95 Nm).

18. Install the intake and exhaust manifolds.

19. Install the EGR pipe with a new gasket, if removed.

20. Install the distributor and extension, if removed.

21. Install the timing belt and all related items. When installing the timing belt over the camshaft sprocket, use care not to allow the belt to slip off the opposite camshaft sprocket.

22. Make sure the timing belt is installed on the camshaft sprocket in the same position as when removed.

23. Install the alternator and power steering pump.

24. Install the air conditioning compressor and belts.

25. Connect the upper radiator hose.

26. Fill the radiator with coolant.

27. Connect the negative battery cable and connect the jumper wire from the fuel pump activation terminal to the positive battery post to inspect the system for leaks, if equipped.

28. Set all adjustments to specifications.

Valve Lifters

REMOVAL AND INSTALLATION

1.8L and 2.4L Engines

1. Disconnect the negative battery cable.

2. Remove the valve cover. Install lash adjuster retainer tools MD998443 or equivalent, to prevent the auto-lash adjuster from falling out of the rocker arm.

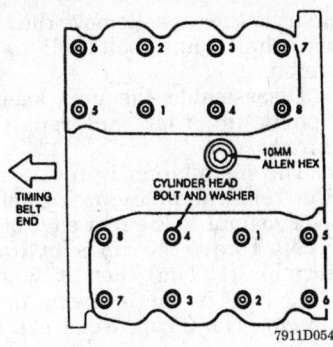

Cylinder head bolt torque sequence — 3.0L and 3.5L engines

3. Rotate the engine clockwise and position at TDC compression stroke.

4. Remove the timing belt assembly.

5. Loosen rocker arm and shaft assembly evenly in several steps. Remove the rocker arm and shaft assembly as a complete unit.

6. Remove the lifters from the rocker arms. It is recommended that all lash adjusters and rockers be replaced as a complete set.

To install:

7. Immerse the lash adjusters in clean diesel fuel. Using a small wire, move the plunger of the lash adjuster up and down 4 or 5 times while pushing down lightly on the check ball in order to bleed out the air. Install the lash adjusters in the rocker arms.

8. Lubricate the camshaft and rocker shaft with heavy engine oil and position on the cylinder head.

9. Apply a drop of sealant to the rear edges of the end caps.

10. Install the assembly into the front bearing cap making sure the notches in the rocker shafts are facing up. Insert the installation bolt but do not tighten at this point.

11. Install the remaining cap bolts and tighten evenly and gradually to 15 ft. lbs. (20 Nm). Tighten the front cap retaining bolts to 17 ft. lbs. (24 Nm). Remove the lash adjuster retainers.

12. Install the distributor extension, if removed.

13. Install the valve cover with a new gasket and tighten to 4–5 ft. lbs. (5–7 Nm).

14. Connect the negative battery cable.

3.0L Engine

1. Disconnect the negative battery cable. Remove the air cleaner assembly.

2. Remove the valve cover.

3. Using the auto lash adjuster retainer tools MD998443 or equivalent, install them on the rocker arms to keep the lash adjusters from falling out.

4. On the right side cylinder head, remove the distributor extension.

5. Have a helper hold the rear end of the camshaft down. If the rear of the camshaft cannot be held down, the belt will dislodge and the valve timing will be lost. Loosen the camshaft cap bolts but do not remove them from the caps. Remove the caps, arms, shafts and bolts all as an assembly.

6. Disassemble the unit keeping all parts in order and repair as required.

7. The installation is the reverse of the removal procedure. Apply a drop of sealant to the rear edge of the rear cap. Torque the cap bolts first to 85 inch lbs. (19 Nm), then to 180 inch lbs. (19 Nm) in the following order: No. 3 cap, No. 2 cap, No. 1 cap and No. 4 cap.

3.5L Engine

NOTE: Make sure the piston is in the down position from which the valve lifter is being removed. The cam lobe must be on the base circle to remove the rocker arm and valve lifter.

1. Remove the rocker arm cover and gasket.

2. Using special tool MD998782, press the valve down and remove the roller rocker arm.

3. Pull the valve lifter from the cylinder head.

4. Install the valve lifter and rocker arm using special spring compressor tool MD9987821.

Valve Lash

ADJUSTMENT

Expo 1.8L Engine

NOTE: Incorrect valve clearances will cause unsteady engine operation, excessive noise and reduced engine output. Check the valve clearances and adjust as required while the engine is cold.

1. Warm the engine to operating temperature, turn **OFF** and disconnect the negative battery cable.

2. Remove all spark plugs so engine can be easily turned by hand.

3. Remove the valve cover.

4. Turn the crankshaft clockwise to position the engine at Top Dead Center (TDC). The notch on the crankshaft pulley will be aligned with the **T** mark on the timing belt lower cover. This brings both No. 1 and No. 4 cylinder pistons to TDC.

5. Check the valve lash at cylinder No. 1 intake, cylinder No. 1 exhaust, cylinder No. 2 intake and cylinder No. 3 exhaust valves.

6. Rotate the crankshaft clockwise 1 complete turn. Check the valve lash at cylinder No. 2 exhaust, cylinder No. 3 intake and cylinder No. 4 intake and exhaust valves.

7. Valve lash specifications are: intake–0.004 in. (0.09mm) cold: exhaust–0.008 in. (0.20mm) cold.

8. If the valve clearances are out of specification, loosen the rocker arm locknut and adjust the clearance using a feeler gauge while turning the adjusting screw. Be sure to hold the screw to prevent it from turning when tightening the locknut.

9. After adjusting the valves, install the valve cover and spark plugs, and connect the negative battery cable.

Rocker Arms and Shafts

REMOVAL AND INSTALLATION

1.8L Engine

1. Disconnect the negative battery cable.

2. Remove the valve cover and discard the gasket.

3. Remove the rocker shaft holddown bolts gradually and evenly and remove the rocker shaft/arm assemblies.

4. If disassembly is required, keep all parts in the exact order of removal. Inspect the roller surfaces of the rockers. Replace if there are any signs of damage or if the roller does not turn smoothly. Check the inside bore of the rockers and the adjuster tip for wear.

To install:

5. Lubricate the rocker shaft with clean engine oil and install the rockers and springs in their proper places.

6. Install the rocker shaft assemblies on the engine and tighten the bolts gradually and evenly. Torque the rocker shaft bolts to 23 ft. lbs. (32 Nm).

7. Install the valve cover with a new gasket.

8. Connect the negative battery cable.

1992 2.4L Engine

1. Disconnect the negative battery cable.

2. Remove the valve cover. Install lash adjuster retainer tools MD998443 or equivalent, to prevent the auto-lash adjuster from falling out of the rocker arm.

3. Rotate the engine clockwise and position at TDC compression stroke.

4. Remove the timing belt assembly.

5. Loosen rocker arm and shaft assembly evenly in several steps. Remove the rocker arm and shaft assembly as a complete unit.

6. Remove the rear camshaft bearing cap and slide rocker arms, springs and washers from shaft. Note location and positioning of all rocker shaft components.

7. Visually inspect the rocker arm roller and replace if damage or seizure is evident. Check the roller for smooth rotation. Replace if excess play or binding is present. Also, inspect valve contact surface for possible damage or seizure. It is recommended that all rocker arms and lash adjusters be replaced together.

To install:

8. Immerse the lash adjusters in clean diesel fuel. Using a small wire, move the plunger of the lash adjuster up and down 4 or 5 times while pushing down lightly on the check ball in order to bleed out the air. Install the lash adjusters in the rocker arms.

9. Lubricate the camshaft and rocker shaft with heavy engine oil and position on the cylinder head.

10. Apply a drop of sealant to the rear edges of the end caps.

11. Install the assembly into the front bearing cap making sure the notches in the rocker shafts are facing up. Insert the installation bolt but do not tighten at this point.

12. Install the remaining cap bolts and tighten evenly and gradually to 15 ft. lbs. (20 Nm). Tighten the front cap retaining bolts to 17 ft. lbs. (24 Nm). Remove the lash adjuster retainers.

13. Install the distributor extension, if removed.

14. Install the valve cover with a new gasket and tighten to 4–5 ft. lbs. (5–7 Nm).

15. Connect the negative battery cable.

1993–96 2.4L Engine

1. Disconnect the negative battery cable.

2. Remove the valve cover. Install lash adjuster retainer tools MD998443 or equivalent, to prevent the auto-lash adjuster from falling out of the rocker arm.

3. Loosen intake rocker arm and shaft assembly evenly in several steps. Remove the intake rocker arm and shaft assembly as a complete unit.

4. Loosen exhaust rocker arm and shaft assembly evenly in several steps. Remove the exhaust rocker arm and shaft assembly as a complete unit.

NOTE: Order in reference to removal and installation of rocker arm shafts is critical to prevent damage.

5. Visually inspect the rocker arm roller and replace if damage or seizure is evident. Check the roller for smooth rotation. Replace if excess play or binding is present. Also, inspect valve contact surface for possible damage or seizure. It is recommended that all rocker arms and lash adjusters be replaced together.

— **WARNING** —
Do not disassemble the rocker arm and shaft assembly.

6. Install the exhaust rocker arm and shaft assembly as a complete unit. Tighten the exhaust rocker arm and shaft assembly evenly in several steps to 21–25 ft. lbs. (28–34 Nm).

7. Install the intake rocker arm and shaft assembly as a complete unit. Tighten the intake rocker arm and shaft assembly evenly in several steps to 21–25 ft. lbs. (28–34 Nm).

8. Remove the lash adjuster retainers and confirm that notches of rocker arm shafts are positioned toward the outside of the cylinder head.

9. Install the valve cover with a new gasket and tighten to 26–30 inch lbs. (3.0–3.5 Nm).

10. Connect the negative battery cable.

3.0L Engine

1. Disconnect the negative battery cable. Remove the air cleaner assembly.

2. Remove the valve cover.

3. Using the auto lash adjuster retainer tools MD998443 or equivalent, install them on the rocker arms to keep the lash adjusters from falling out.

4. On the right side cylinder head, remove the distributor extension.

5. Have a helper hold the rear end of the camshaft down. If the rear of the camshaft cannot be held down, the belt will dislodge and the valve timing will be lost. Loosen the camshaft cap bolts but do not remove

them from the caps. Remove the caps, arms, shafts and bolts all as an assembly.

6. Disassemble the unit keeping all parts in order and repair as required.

7. The installation is the reverse of the removal procedure. Apply a drop of sealant to the rear edge of the rear cap. Torque the cap bolts first to 85 inch lbs. (19 Nm), then to 180 inch lbs. (19 Nm) in the following order: No. 3 cap, No. 2 cap, No. 1 cap and No. 4 cap.

3.5L Engine

NOTE: Make sure the piston is in the down position from which the valve lifter is being removed. The cam lobe must be on the base circle to remove the rocker arm and valve lifter.

1. Remove the rocker arm cover and gasket.

2. Using special tool MD998782, press the valve down and remove the roller rocker arm.

3. Pull the valve lifter from the cylinder head.

4. Install the valve lifter and rocker arm using special spring compressor tool MD9987821.

Intake Manifold

REMOVAL AND INSTALLATION

1.8L Engine

1. Relieve the fuel system pressure.

2. Disconnect battery negative cable and drain the cooling system.

3. Disconnect the accelerator cable, breather hose and air intake hose.

4. Disconnect the upper radiator hose, heater hose and water bypass hose.

5. Remove all vacuum hoses and pipes as necessary, including the brake booster vacuum line.

6. Disconnect the high pressure fuel line, fuel return hose and remove throttle control cable brackets.

7. Tag and disconnect the electrical connectors from the oxygen sensor, coolant temperature sensor, thermo switch, idle speed control connection, EGR temperature sensor, spark plug wires, etc. that may interfere with the manifold removal procedure.

8. Remove the fuel rail, fuel injectors, pressure regulator and insulators.

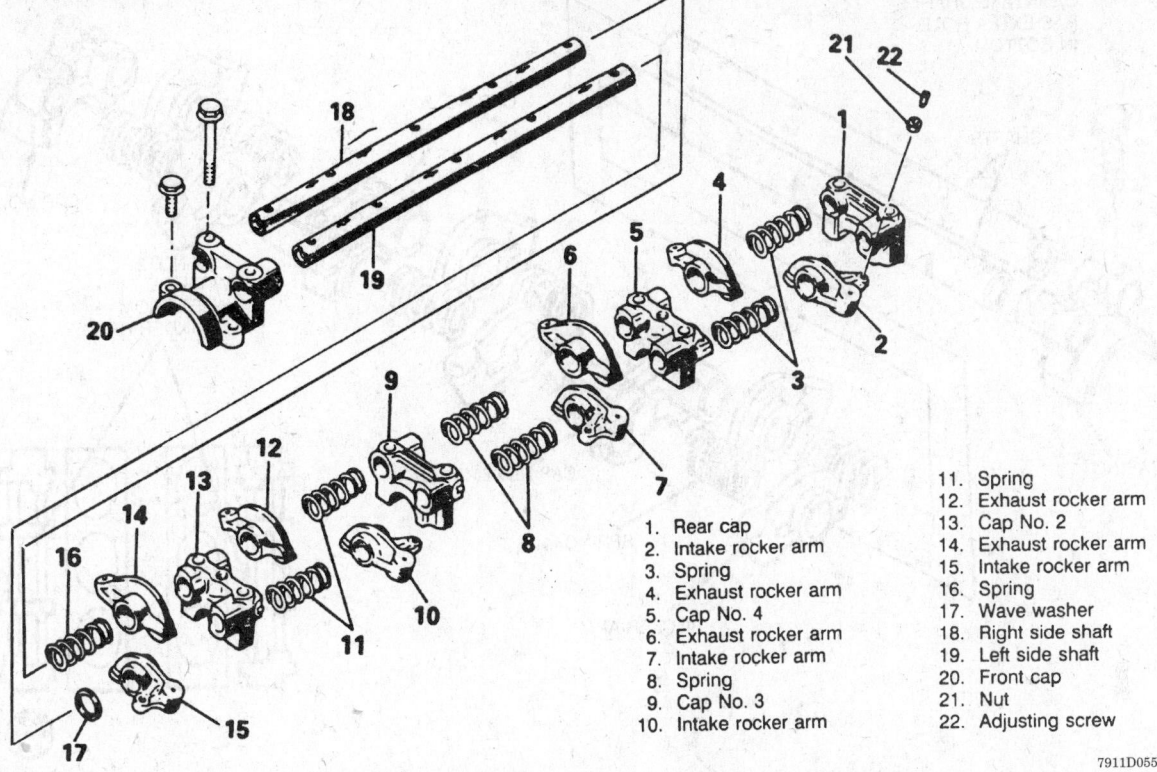

1. Rear cap
2. Intake rocker arm
3. Spring
4. Exhaust rocker arm
5. Cap No. 4
6. Exhaust rocker arm
7. Intake rocker arm
8. Spring
9. Cap No. 3
10. Intake rocker arm
11. Spring
12. Exhaust rocker arm
13. Cap No. 2
14. Exhaust rocker arm
15. Intake rocker arm
16. Spring
17. Wave washer
18. Right side shaft
19. Left side shaft
20. Front cap
21. Nut
22. Adjusting screw

7911D055

Rocker arms/shafts assembly — 2.4L engine. Note that 2.4L rocker arms are not equipped with jet valve extensions.

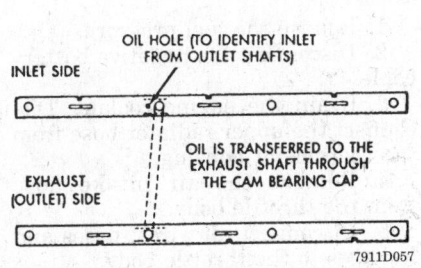

Identifying rocker shafts — 3.0L engine

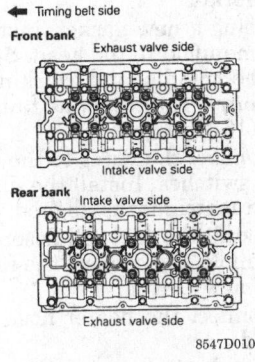

Identifying rocker arms — 3.5L engine

9. Remove the fuel delivery pipe, injectors and pressure regulator from the engine.

10. Remove the intake manifold bracket.

11. Disconnect the water hose connections at the throttle body, water inlet, and heater assembly.

12. If the thermostat housing is preventing removal of the intake manifold, remove it.

13. Disconnect the vacuum connection at the power brake booster and the PCV valve if still connected.

14. Remove the intake manifold mounting bolts and remove the in-take manifold assembly. Disassemble manifold from the intake plenum on a work bench as required.

To install:

15. Assemble the intake manifold assembly using all new gaskets. Torque air intake plenum bolts to 11–14 ft. lbs. (15–19 Nm).

16. Clean all gasket material from the cylinder head intake mounting surface and intake manifold assembly. Check both surfaces for cracks or other damage. Check the intake manifold water passages and jet air passages for clogging. Clean if necessary.

17. Install a new intake manifold gasket to the head and install the manifold. Torque the manifold in a criss-cross pattern, starting from the inside and working outwards to 11–14 ft. lbs. (15–19 Nm).

18. Install the fuel delivery pipe, injectors and pressure regulator from the engine. Torque the retaining bolts to 7–9 ft. lbs. (10–13 Nm).

19. Install the thermostat housing, intake manifold brace bracket, distributor and throttle body stay bracket.

20. Connect or install all hoses, cables and electrical connectors that were removed or disconnected during the removal procedure.

21. Fill the system with coolant.

22. Connect the negative battery cable, run the vehicle until the thermostat opens, fill the radiator completely.

23. Adjust the accelerator cable. Check and adjust the idle speed and ignition timing.

24. Once the vehicle has cooled, recheck the coolant level.

2.4L Engine

1. Relieve the fuel pressure.
2. Disconnect the negative battery cable.

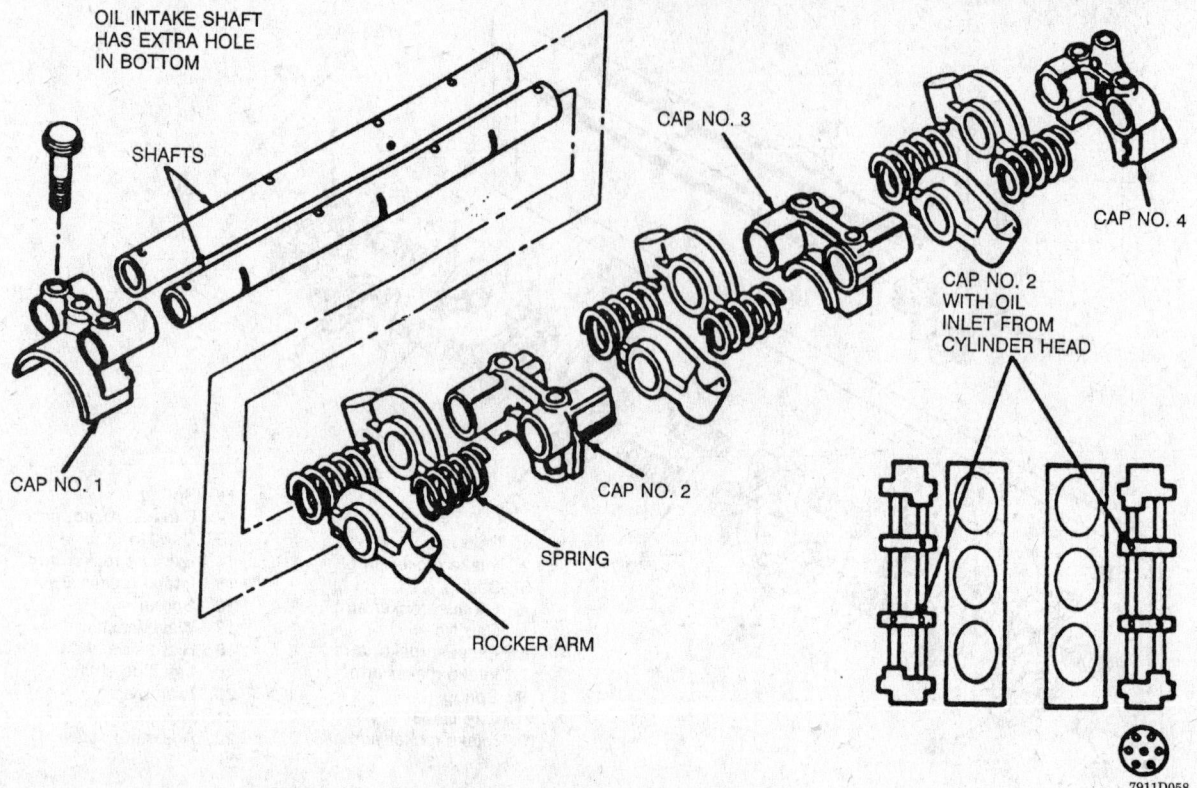

OIL INTAKE SHAFT
HAS EXTRA HOLE
IN BOTTOM

SHAFTS

CAP NO. 3

CAP NO. 4

CAP NO. 2
WITH OIL
INLET FROM
CYLINDER HEAD

CAP NO. 1

CAP NO. 2

SPRING

ROCKER ARM

7911D058

Rocker arms/shafts assembly — 3.0L engine

3. Drain the engine coolant. Disconnect the upper radiator hose from the thermostat housing.

4. Remove the air intake hoses and the air intake pipe.

5. Disconnect all wires, hoses and linkages to the throttle body.

6. Remove the ignition coil.

7. Disconnect the brake booster hose and vacuum hose cluster from the air intake plenum.

8. Unbolt the air intake plenum from the intake manifold and remove the plenum from the engine.

9. Cover the fuel line with a clean shop rag and disconnect the fuel lines from the fuel rail. Keep the line covered or plugged.

10. Remove the fuel rail assembly with injectors.

11. Disconnect the heater hose from the manifold.

12. Disconnect the wires to the engine coolant switches.

13. Matchmark the rotor to the housing and the housing to the cylinder head and remove the distributor.

14. Unbolt the intake manifold from the cylinder head and remove from the engine.

15. Clean and dry the mating surfaces of the manifold and cylinder head.

To install:

16. Using a new gasket, install the intake manifold to the head. Starting from the middle and working outward, torque the retaining nuts to 12 ft. lbs. (16 Nm).

17. Connect the wires to the engine coolant switches. Install the distributor with matchmarks aligned.

18. Install the fuel rail assembly to the manifold and connect the fuel line using a new O-ring.

19. Connect the heater hose to the manifold.

20. Install the air intake plenum with a new gasket. Torque the retaining bolts to 12 ft. lbs. (16 Nm).

21. Connect the vacuum hoses cluster, brake booster hose and all wires, hoses and linkages to the throttle body.

22. Install the ignition coil.

23. Install the air intake pipe and hoses.

24. Connect the upper radiator hose.

25. Fill the radiator with coolant.

26. Connect the negative battery cable and connect the jumper wire from the fuel pump activation terminal to the positive battery post to inspect the system for leaks.

27. Set all adjustments to specifications.

3.0L Engine

1. Relieve the fuel pressure.

2. Disconnect the negative battery cable.

3. Drain the engine coolant. Disconnect the upper radiator hose from the thermostat housing.

4. Remove the air intake hose from the throttle body.

5. Disconnect all wires, hoses and linkages to the throttle body.

6. Disconnect the EGR temperature sensor wire.

7. Remove the ignition coil.

8. Remove the engine oil filler neck bracket.

9. Unbolt the EGR tube from the air intake plenum.

10. Disconnect the PCV hose and vacuum hose cluster from the plenum.

11. Remove the plenum to engine brackets.

12. Unbolt the air intake plenum assembly from the intake manifold and remove.

13. Cover the fuel lines with a clean shop rag and disconnect the fuel lines from the fuel rail. Keep the lines covered.

14. Remove the fuel rail with injectors in place.

15. Disconnect the bypass hose and the upper radiator hose from the

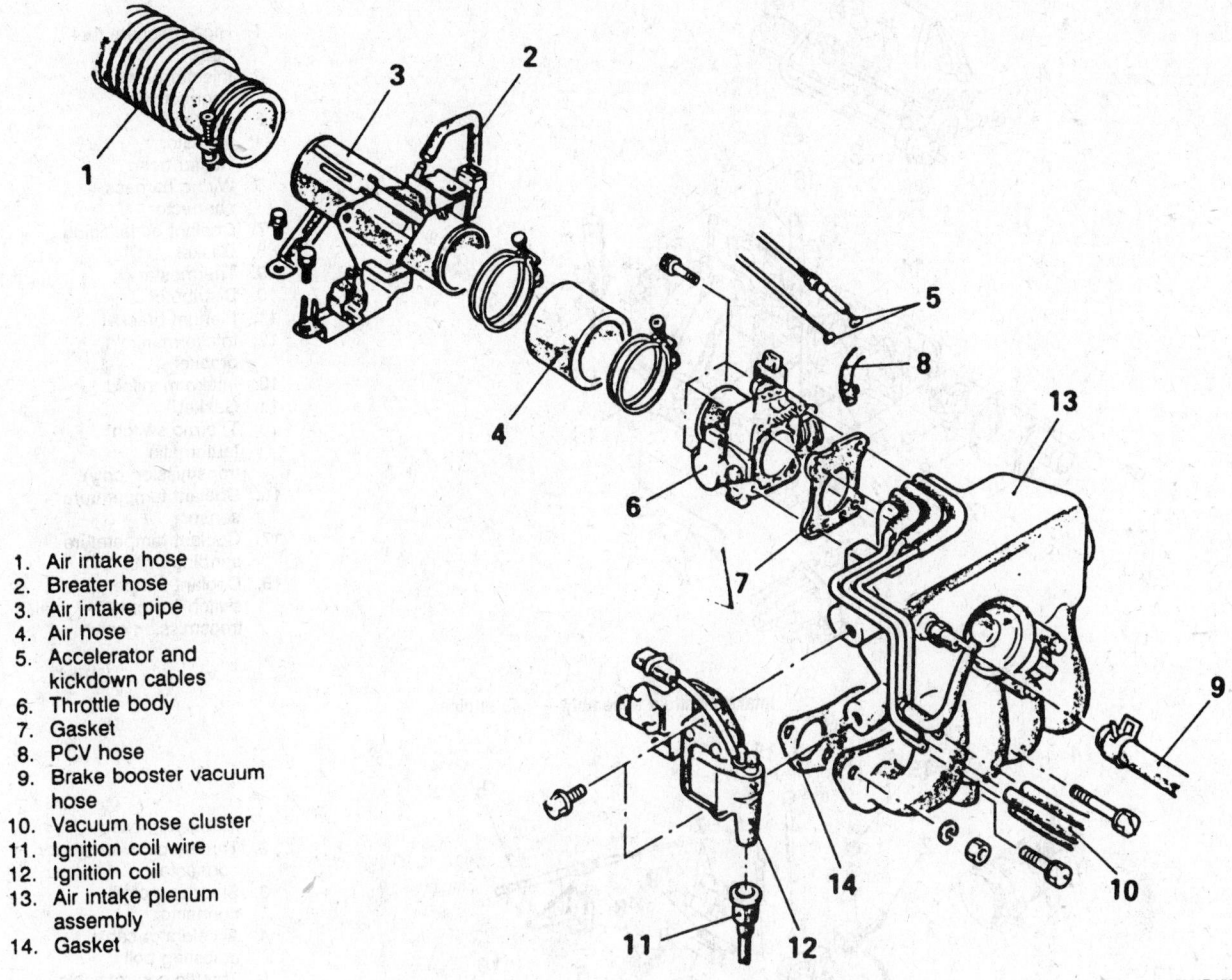

1. Air intake hose
2. Breater hose
3. Air intake pipe
4. Air hose
5. Accelerator and
   kickdown cables
6. Throttle body
7. Gasket
8. PCV hose
9. Brake booster vacuum
   hose
10. Vacuum hose cluster
11. Ignition coil wire
12. Ignition coil
13. Air intake plenum
    assembly
14. Gasket

7911D059

Air intake plenum assembly — 2.4L engine

thermostat housing. Disconnect the wires to the coolant temperature switches.

16. Remove the intake manifold retaining nuts and remove the manifold from the cylinder heads.

17. Remove the gaskets and thoroughly clean and dry the mating surfaces of the manifold and heads.

To install:

18. Position the manifold over the studs and install the retaining nuts. Torque to 12 ft. lbs. (16 Nm), starting from the center and working outward.

19. Connect the hoses and connect the wires to the coolant switches.

20. Install the fuel rail assembly and connect the fuel hoses.

21. Using a new gasket, install the air intake plenum to the intake manifold. Torque the nuts and bolts to 12 ft. lbs. (16 Nm). Install the plenum to engine brackets.

22. Connect the PCV hose and vacuum hose cluster to the plenum.

23. Connect the EGR tube.

24. Install the engine oil filler neck bracket.

25. Install the ignition coil assembly.

26. Connect the EGR temperature sensor wire.

27. Connect all wires, hoses and linkages to the throttle body.

28. Install the air intake hose to the throttle body.

29. Connect the upper radiator hose to the thermostat housing.

30. Fill the radiator with coolant.

31. Connect the negative battery cable and connect the jumper wire from the fuel pump activation terminal to the positive battery post to inspect the system for leaks.

32. Set all adjustments to specifications.

3.5L Engine

1. Relieve fuel system pressure and disconnect the negative battery cable.

2. Drain the engine coolant.

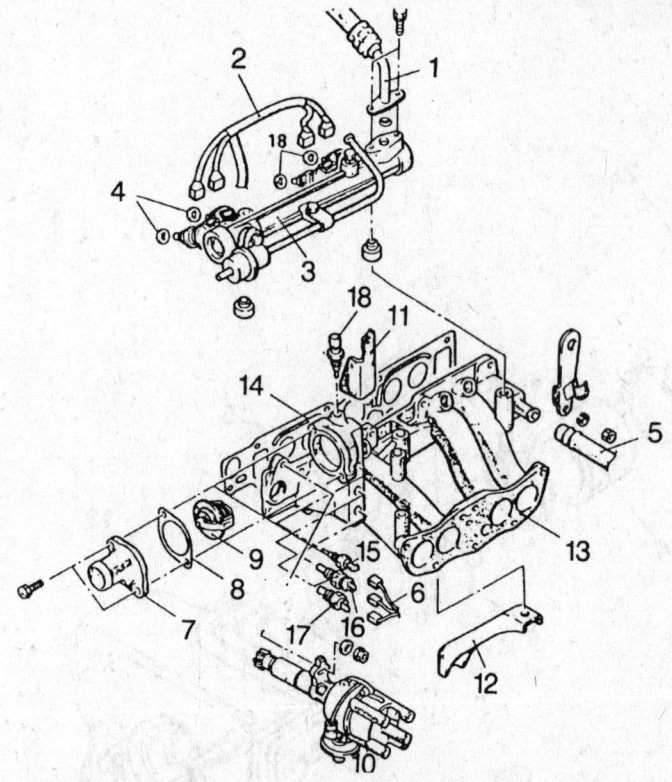

1. High pressure fuel hose
2. Injector harness connector
3. Fuel rail
4. Insulator
5. Heater hose
6. Wiring harness connector
7. Coolant outlet fitting
8. Gasket
9. Thermostat
10. Distributor
11. Plenum bracket
12. Intake manifold bracket
13. Intake manifold
14. Gasket
15. Thermo switch (automatic transmission only)
16. Coolant temperature sensor
17. Coolant temperature sending unit
18. Coolant temperature switch (automatic transmission only)

7911D060

Intake manifold assembly — 2.4L engine

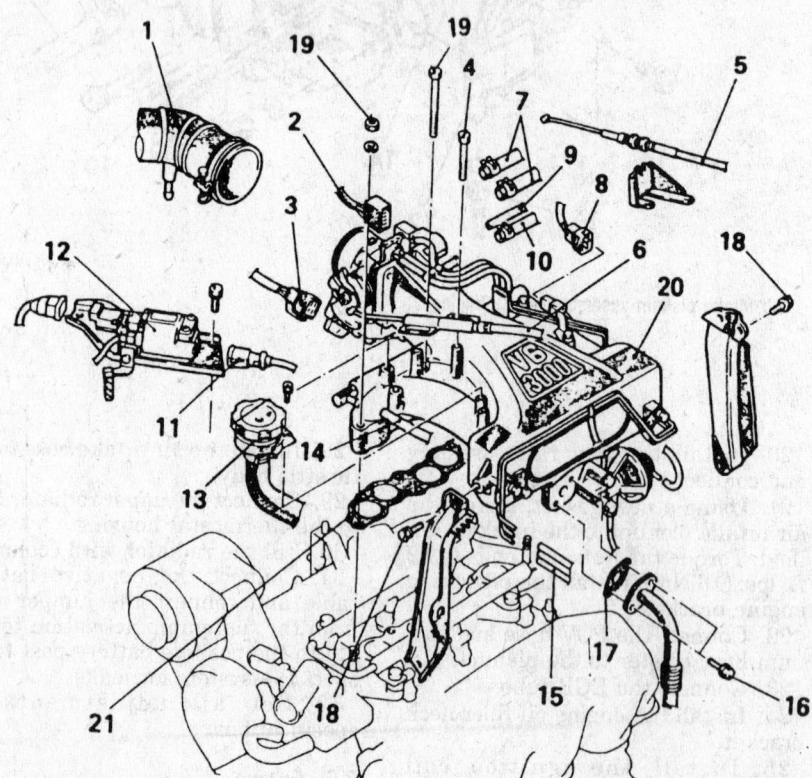

1. Air intake hose
2. Throttle position sensor connector
3. Stepper motor connector
4. Accelerator cable adjusting bolt
5. Throttle control cable (automatic transmission only)
6. Accelerator cable
7. Coolant hoses
8. EGR temperature connector
9. Vacuum hose
10. Brake booster vacuum hose
11. Ignition coil wire
12. Ignition coil
13. Oil filler neck bracket
14. PCV hose
15. Vacuum hose cluster
16. EGR pipe attaching bolt
17. Gasket
18. Bracket bolt
19. Attaching bolt and nut
20. Air intake plenum and throttle body assembly
21. Gasket

7911D061

Air intake plenum assembly — 3.0L engine

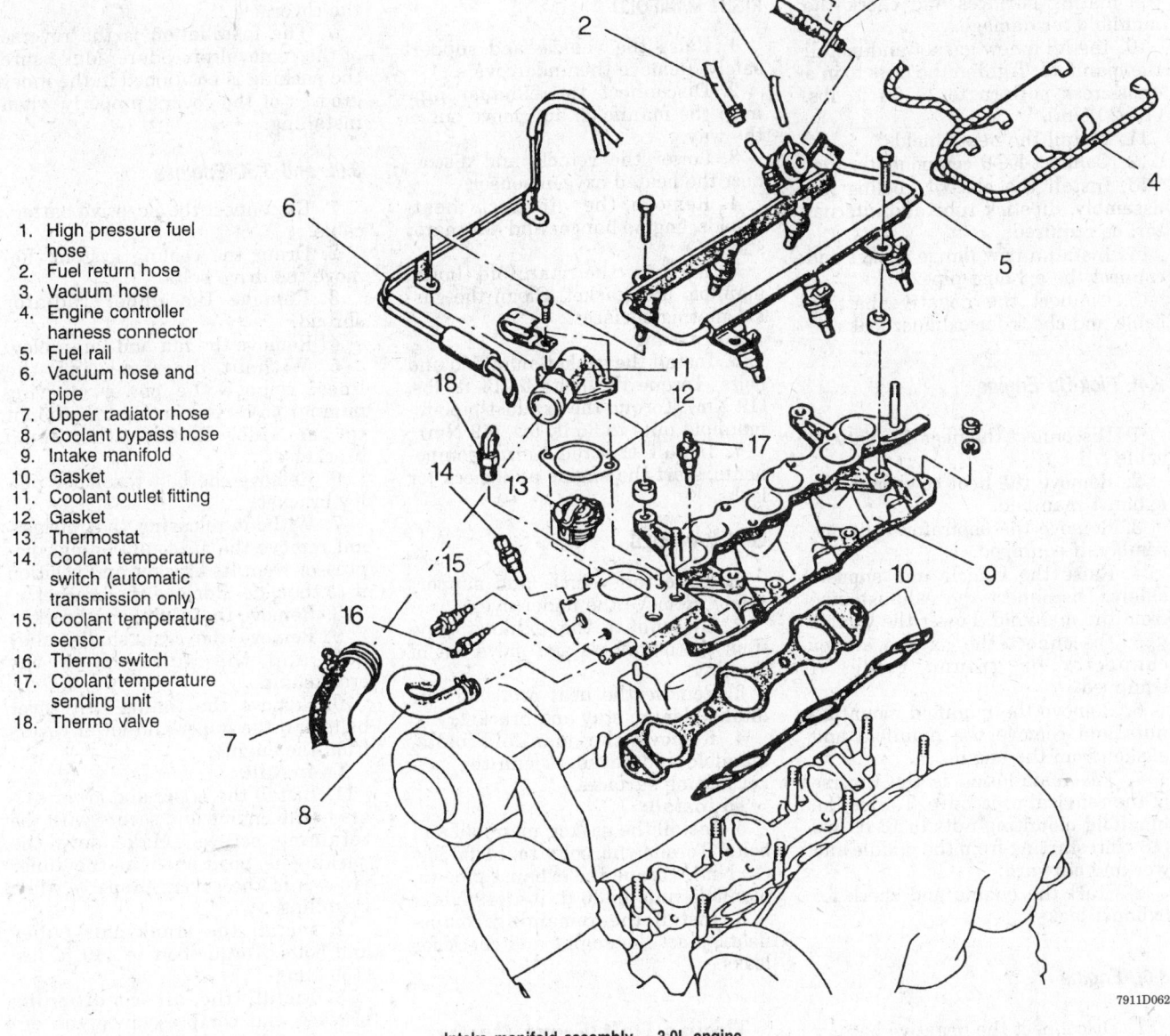

1. High pressure fuel hose
2. Fuel return hose
3. Vacuum hose
4. Engine controller harness connector
5. Fuel rail
6. Vacuum hose and pipe
7. Upper radiator hose
8. Coolant bypass hose
9. Intake manifold
10. Gasket
11. Coolant outlet fitting
12. Gasket
13. Thermostat
14. Coolant temperature switch (automatic transmission only)
15. Coolant temperature sensor
16. Thermo switch
17. Coolant temperature sending unit
18. Thermo valve

7911D062

Intake manifold assembly — 3.0L engine

3. Remove the upper intake manifold cover and plenum.

4. Disconnect the fuel injector harness, high pressure fuel line and remove O-ring.

5. Disconnect the fuel return hose and vacuum hose.

6. Remove the fuel rail assembly with the injectors installed.

7. Remove the intake manifold bolts, manifold and gasket.

To install:

8. Clean the gasket mating surface and install manifold with new gaskets. Torque the bolts on right bank to 4 ft. lbs. (5 Nm) and bolts on left bank to 11 ft. lbs. (15 Nm). Retor-que the right bank bolts to 11 ft. lbs. (15 Nm). Make sure the protrusions face the exhaust manifolds.

9. Install the remaining components and check operation.

Exhaust Manifold

REMOVAL AND INSTALLATION

1.8L and 2.4L Expo Engines

1. Disconnect battery negative cable.

2. Raise the vehicle and support safely.

3. Remove the exhaust pipe to exhaust manifold nuts and separate exhaust pipe. Discard gasket.

4. Lower vehicle.

5. Remove electric cooling fan assembly and dipstick tube, if necessary.

6. Disconnect necessary EGR components, if equipped.

7. Remove outer exhaust manifold heat shield and engine hanger. Disconnect the electrical connector and remove the oxygen sensor.

8. Remove the exhaust manifold mounting bolts, the inner heat shield and the exhaust manifold.

To install:

9. Clean all gasket material from the mating surfaces and check the manifold for damage.

10. Install a new gasket and install the manifold. Tighten the nuts to in a criss-cross pattern to 11–14 ft. lbs. (15–20 Nm).

11. Install the heat shields.

12. Connect EGR components.

13. Install the electric cooling fan assembly, dipstick tube and alternator, as required.

14. Install a new flange gasket and connect the exhaust pipe.

15. Connect the negative battery cable and check for exhaust leaks.

2.4L Pick-Up Engine

1. Disconnect the negative battery cable.

2. Remove the heat cowl from the exhaust manifold.

3. Remove the aspirator valve assembly, if equipped.

4. Raise the vehicle and support safely. Disconnect the exhaust pipe from the manifold. Lower the vehicle

5. Disconnect the oxygen sensor connector or ground cable, if equipped.

6. Remove the manifold mounting nuts and remove the manifold and gasket from the engine.

7. The installation is the reverse of the removal procedure. Torque the manifold mounting nuts to 13 ft. lbs. (18 Nm) starting from the middle and working outward.

8. Start the engine and check for exhaust leaks.

3.0L Engine

1. Disconnect the negative battery cable. Raise and safely support the vehicle.

2. Disconnect the exhaust pipe from the exhaust manifolds.

3. Remove the heat shield.

4. If removing the left manifold, remove the EGR tube.

5. If removing the right manifold, remove the alternator bracket.

6. Remove the manifold attaching nuts and remove the manifold.

7. The installation is the reverse of the removal procedure. When installing, the numbers 1–3–5 on the gaskets are used with the right side cylinders and 2–4–6 are on the gasket for the left side cylinders. Torque the manifold nuts to 14 ft. lbs. (19 Nm).

8. Start the engine and check for exhaust leaks.

3.5L Engine

RIGHT MANIFOLD

1. Raise the vehicle and support safely. Remove the undercovers.

2. Disconnect the exhaust pipe from the manifolds and move out of the way.

3. Lower the vehicle and disconnect the heated oxygen sensor.

4. Remove the air duct, heatshields, engine hanger and alternator stay.

5. Remove the manifold bolts, manifold and gasket. Clean the gasket mating surfaces.

To install:

6. Install the gasket, manifold and bolts. Torque the bolts to 14 ft. lbs. (19 Nm). Torque the exhaust pipe-to-manifold nuts to 36 ft. lbs. (49 Nm).

7. Install the remaining components, start the engine and check for leaks.

LEFT MANIFOLD

1. Raise the vehicle and support safely. Remove the undercovers.

2. Disconnect the exhaust pipe from the manifolds and move out of the way.

3. Remove the heat protector, air intake plenum stay and bracket.

4. Remove the manifold bolts, manifold and gasket. Clean the gasket mating surfaces.

To install:

5. Install the gasket, manifold and bolts. Torque the bolts to 14 ft. lbs. (19 Nm). Torque the exhaust pipe-to-manifold nuts to 36 ft. lbs. (49 Nm).

6. Install the remaining components, start the engine and check for leaks.

Timing Belt Front Cover

REMOVAL AND INSTALLATION

1.8L and 2.4L Engines

1. Disconnect the negative battery cable. Remove the spark plug wires from the tree on the upper cover.

2. Drain the cooling system. Remove the shroud, fan, belts and radiator as required.

3. Remove the power steering pump, alternator, air conditioning compressor, tension pulley and accompanying brackets, as required.

4. Remove the upper front timing belt cover.

5. Remove the water pump pulley and the crankshaft pulley(s).

6. Remove the lower timing belt cover to engine screws and remove the cover.

7. The installation is the reverse of the removal procedure. Make sure the packing is positioned in the inner grooves of the covers properly when installing.

3.0L and 3.5L Engines

1. Disconnect the negative battery cable.

2. Drain the cooling system. Remove the drive belts.

3. Remove the upper radiator shroud.

4. Remove the fan and fan pulley.

5. Without disconnecting the lines, remove the power steering pump from its bracket and position it to the side. Remove the pump brackets.

6. Remove the belt tensioner pulley bracket.

7. Without releasing the refrigerant remove the air conditioning compressor from its bracket and position it to the side. Remove the bracket.

8. Remove the cooling fan bracket.

9. Remove the crankshaft pulley bolt and the pulley from the crankshaft.

10. Remove the timing belt cover bolts and the upper and lower covers from the engine.

To install:

11. Install the upper and lower covers to the engine and secure with the retaining screws. Make sure the packing is positioned in the inner grooves of the covers properly when installing.

12. Install the crankshaft pulley and bolts. Torque bolt to 110 ft. lbs. (150 Nm).

13. Install the air conditioning bracket and compressor to the engine. Install the belt tensioner.

14. Install the power steering pump into position. Install the fan pulley and fan.

15. Install the fan shroud to the radiator. Fill the cooling system, reconnect the negative battery cable and check for fluid leaks.

Timing Belt and Tensioner

ADJUSTMENT

Expo

1.8L AND 1992 2.4L ENGINES

1. Disconnect negative battery cable.

2. Remove the timing belt covers.

3. On 2.4L engine, adjust the silent shaft (inner) belt tension first as follows:

a. Loosen the idler pulley center bolt so the pulley can be moved.

b. Move the pulley by hand so the long side of the belt deflects about ¼ in.

c. Hold the pulley tightly so the pulley cannot rotate when the bolt is tightened. Tighten the bolt to 15 ft. lbs. (20 Nm) and recheck the deflection amount.

4. To adjust the timing (outer) belt, first loosen the pivot side tensioner bolt and then the slot side bolt. Allow the spring to remove the slack.

5. Check to make sure the timing marks on each sprocket are aligned. Turn the crankshaft in clockwise direction, by 2 teeth of the crankshaft sprocket.

NOTE: The purpose of Step 5 is to apply the proper amount of tension to the tension side of the timing belt, be sure not to turn the crankshaft in the opposite direction (counterclockwise).

6. Tighten the slot side tensioner bolt and then the pivot side bolt. If the pivot side bolt is tightened first, the tensioner could turn with bolt, causing over tension.

7. Lightly clamp the center of the span between the camshaft sprocket and the water pump sprocket on the belt tension side with your thumb and forefinger. Check to be sure the clearance between the reverse surface of the belt and the inside of the undercover seal line is at the standard value.

a. 1.8L engine — 1.18 in. (30mm).

b. 2.4L engine — 0.55 in. (14mm).

8. Install the timing belt covers and all related items.

9. Connect the negative battery cable.

1993–96 2.4L ENGINE

The 1993–96 2.4L engine incorporates the use of an auto-tensioner to control tension of the timing belt. The following procedure refers to adjustment of new belts. This engine also uses a second timing belt to drive a silent shaft.

1. Disconnect the negative battery cable.

2. Remove the timing belt covers.

3. Adjust the silent shaft (inner) belt tension first. Loosen the idler pulley center bolt so the pulley can be moved.

4. Move the pulley by hand so the long side of the belt deflects 0.20–0.28 in. (5–7mm).

5. Hold the pulley tightly so the pulley cannot rotate when the bolt is tightened. Tighten the bolt to 15 ft. lbs. (20 Nm) and recheck tension.

6. To adjust the timing (outer) belt, turn the crankshaft clockwise and position No. 1 cylinder to TDC of compression stroke.

7. Loosen the center bolt of tensioner pulley and unbolt auto-tensioner assembly. The auto-tensioner assembly must be reset to correctly adjust belt tension.

8. Remove and position the auto-tensioner into a vise with soft jaws. The plug at the rear of tensioner protrudes, be sure to use a washer as a spacer, to protect the plug from contacting vise jaws.

9. Slowly push the rod into the tensioner until the set hole in rod is aligned with set hole in the auto-tensioner.

10. Insert a 0.055 in. (1.4mm) wire into the aligned set holes. Unclamp the tensioner from vise and install to vehicle. Tighten tensioner to 14–20 ft. lbs. (20–27 Nm).

11. Align all timing marks and raise tensioner against belt to remove slack, snug tensioner bolt.

12. Loosen the center bolt. Using tool No. MD998752 or equivalent and a torque wrench, apply a torque of 22.5–24 inch lbs. (2.6–2.8 Nm). If the body of the vehicle interferes with the special tool and the torque wrench, use a jack and slightly raise the engine assembly.

13. Screw tool MD998738 or exact equivalent into the engine left support bracket until its end makes contact with the tensioner arm.

14. Tighten tensioner pulley to 35 ft. lbs. (48 Nm).

15. Screw tool MD998738 or exact equivalent several more turns so the set wire in the auto-tensioner can be removed. Remove the tool assembly.

16. Rotate the crankshaft 2 complete turns clockwise and let it sit for approximately 15 minutes. Then, measure the auto tensioner protrusion (the distance between the tensioner arm and auto tensioner body) to ensure that it is within 0.15–0.18 in. (3.8–4.5mm). If out of specification, repeat adjustment until the specified value is obtained.

17. If the timing belt tension adjustment is being performed with the engine mounted in the vehicle, and clearance between the tensioner arm and the auto tensioner body cannot be measured, the following alternative method can be used:

a. Screw in special tool MD998738 or equivalent, until its end makes contact with the tensioner arm.

b. After the special tool makes contact with the arm, screw it in some more to retract the auto tensioner pushrod while counting the number of turns the tool makes until the tensioner arm is brought into contact with the auto tensioner body. Make sure the number of turns the special tool makes conforms with the standard value of 2.5–3 turns.

c. Install the rubber plug to the timing belt rear cover.

18. Install the timing belt covers and all related items.

19. Connect the negative battery cable.

2.4L Pick-Up Engine

1. Disconnect the negative battery cable.

2. Remove the timing belt cover.

3. Adjust the silent shaft (inner) belt first. Loosen the pulley center bolt so the pulley may be moved.

4. Move the pulley up by hand so the center span of the long side of the belt deflects ¼ inch.

5. Hold the pulley tight so the pulley itself does not rotate when the bolt is tightened. Tighten the bolt to 15 ft. lbs. (20 Nm). If the pulley has moved, the belt will be too tight.

6. Check the timing (outer) belt tension.

7. To adjust the timing (outer) belt, first loosen the tensioner pulley bolts.

8. Allow the spring to take up any slack. Check that the the deflection of the longest span (between the camshaft and oil pump sprockets) is ½ inch. Do not overtighten the belt or it will howl.

9. First tighten the lower pulley bolts to 35 ft. lbs. (47 Nm) and then the upper bolt to the same value.

10. Install the covers and all related parts.

3.0L Engine

1. Loosen the bolt that holds the timing belt tensioner in place.

2. Allow the spring to pull the tensioner in automatically.

3. Tighten the tensioner locking bolt.

3.5L Engine

1. Turn the crankshaft ¼ turn counterclockwise, then clockwise to align the timing marks.

2. Loosen the center bolt on the tensioner pulley. Using the special tool MD998767 and torque wrench, apply torque to the timing belt and tighten the center bolt to 7 ft. lbs. (9 Nm).

3. If installed, remove the set pin from the auto-tensioner. Rotate the crankshaft 2 turns clockwise and leave for 5 minutes. Make sure the set pin can be easily installed in the auto-tensioner. If the set pin can not be easily installed, check the protrusion. It should be 0.149–0.177 in. (3.8–4.5mm). If not, repeat the adjustment process.

REMOVAL AND INSTALLATION

1.8L Engine

1. Disconnect the negative battery cable. Remove the engine under cover.

2. Rotate crankshaft clockwise and position engine at TDC compression stroke.

3. Raise and safely support the weight of the engine using the appropriate equipment. Remove the front engine mount bracket and accessory drive belts.

4. Remove the coolant reservoir tank.

5. Remove timing belt upper and lower covers.

6. Make a mark on the back of the timing belt indicating the direction of rotation so it may be reassembled in the same direction if it is to be reused. Loosen the timing belt tensioner and remove the timing belt.

NOTE: If coolant or engine oil comes in contact with the timing belt, they will drastically shorten its life. Also, do not allow engine oil or coolant to contact the timing belt sprockets or tensioner assembly.

7. Remove the tensioner spacer, tensioner spring and tensioner assembly.

8. Inspect the timing belt for cracks on back surface, sides, bottom and check for separated canvas. Check the tensioner pulley for smooth rotation.

To install:

9. Position the tensioner, tensioner spring and tensioner spacer on engine block.

10. Align the timing marks on the camshaft sprocket and crankshaft

sprocket. This will position No. 1 piston on TDC on the compression stroke.

11. Position the timing belt on the crankshaft sprocket and keeping the tension side of the belt tight, set it on the camshaft sprocket.

12. Apply counterclockwise force to the camshaft sprocket to give tension to the belt and make sure all timing marks are aligned.

13. Loosen the pivot side tensioner bolt and the slot side bolt. Allow the spring to remove the slack.

14. Tighten the slot side tensioner bolt and then the pivot side bolt. If the pivot side bolt is tightened first, the tensioner could turn with bolt, causing over tension.

15. Turn the crankshaft clockwise. Loosen the pivot side tensioner bolt and then the slot side bolt to allow the spring to take up any remaining slack. Tighten the adjuster bolt to 18 ft. lbs. (24 Nm).

16. Install the timing belt covers and all related items.

17. Connect the negative battery cable.

1992 2.4L Engine

1. Position the engine so the No. 1 piston is at TDC of compression stroke.

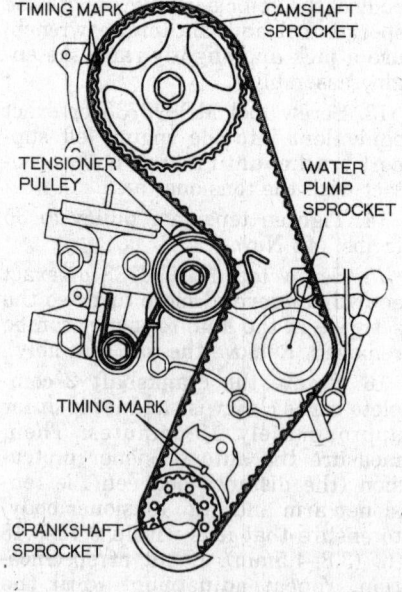

TIMING MARK — CAMSHAFT SPROCKET — TENSIONER PULLEY — WATER PUMP SPROCKET — TIMING MARK — CRANKSHAFT SPROCKET

84701088

Timing alignment marks — 1.8L engine

2. Disconnect the negative battery cable. Remove the coolant reservoir and the power steering and air conditioner hose clamp bolt.

3. Remove the timing belt covers.

4. Remove the timing belt tensioner pulley, tensioner arm, idler pulley.

5. Locate the access plug on the side of block. Remove the plug and install a Phillips screwdriver. Remove the oil pump sprocket nut, oil pump sprocket, special washer, flange and spacer.

6. Remove the outer crankshaft sprocket and flange.

7. Remove the silent shaft (inner) belt tensioner and remove the belt.

To install:

8. Align the timing marks of the silent shaft sprockets and the crankshaft sprocket with the timing marks on the front case. Wrap the timing belt around the sprockets so there is no slack in the upper span of the belt and the timing marks are still aligned.

9. Install the tensioner pulley and move the pulley by hand so the long side of the belt deflects 0.20–0.28 in. (5–7mm).

10. Hold the pulley tightly so the pulley cannot rotate when the bolt is tightened. Tighten the bolt to 15 ft. lbs. (20 Nm) and recheck the deflection amount.

11. Install the timing belt tensioner fully toward the water pump and tighten the bolts. Place the upper end of the spring against the water pump body.

12. Align the timing marks of the camshaft, crankshaft and oil pump sprockets with their corresponding marks on the front case or rear cover.

NOTE: There is a possibility to align all timing marks and have the oil pump sprocket out of time, causing an engine vibration during operation. If the following step is not followed exactly, there is a 50 percent chance that the oil pump shaft alignment will be 180 degrees off.

13. Before installing the timing belt, ensure that the oil pump sprocket is in the correct position as follows:

a. Remove the plug from the rear side of the block and insert a Phillips screwdriver with shaft diameter of 0.31 in. (8mm) into the hole.

b. With the timing marks still aligned, the shaft of the tool must be able to go in at least 2.36 in. (60mm). If the tool can only go in 0.79–0.98 in. (20–25mm), the shaft is not in the correct orientation and

will cause a vibration during engine operation. Remove the tool from the hole and turn the oil pump sprocket 1 complete revolution. Realign the timing marks and insert the tool. The shaft of the tool must go in at least 2.36 in. (60mm).

c. Recheck and realign the timing marks.

d. Leave the tool in place to hold the oil pump shaft while continuing.

14. Install the belt to the crankshaft sprocket, oil pump sprocket, then camshaft sprocket. While doing so, make sure there is no slack between the sprocket except where the tensioner is installed.

15. Tighten oil pump sprocket bolt to 26–29 ft. lbs. (34–40 Nm) and tighten crankshaft bolt to 80–94 ft. lbs. (110–130 Nm).

16. Recheck the timing mark alignment. If all are aligned, loosen the tensioner mounting bolt and allow the tensioner to apply tension to the belt.

17. Remove the tool that is holding the silent shaft and rotate the crankshaft a distance equal to 2 teeth on the camshaft sprocket. This will allow the tensioner to automatically apply the proper tension on the belt. Do not manually overtighten the belt or it will howl.

18. Tighten the lower mounting bolt first, then the upper spacer bolt.

19. To verify correct belt tension, check that the deflection at the longest span of the belt has 0.40 in. (12mm) clearance from the belt cover.

20. Install the timing belt covers and all related items.

21. Connect the negative battery cable.

1993–96 2.4L Engine

1. Disconnect the negative battery cable.

2. Remove the timing belt upper and lower covers.

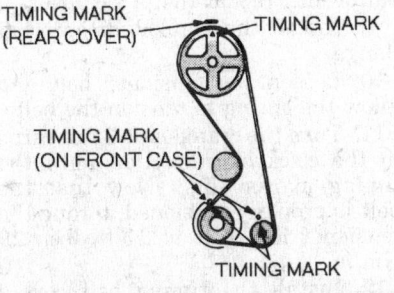

TIMING MARK (REAR COVER)

TIMING MARK

TIMING MARK (ON FRONT CASE)

TIMING MARK

84701092

Timing belt alignment marks — 1992 2.4L engine

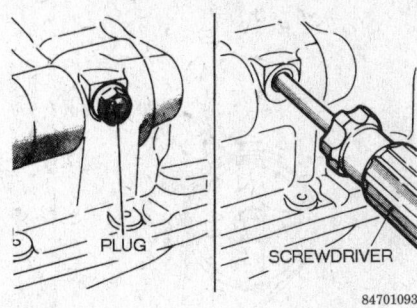

PLUG

SCREWDRIVER

84701093

Checking oil pump sprocket shaft — 1992 2.4L engine

3. Rotate the crankshaft clockwise and align the timing marks so No. 1 piston will be at TDC of the compression stroke. At this time the timing marks on the camshaft sprocket and the upper surface of the cylinder head should coincide, and the dowel pin of the camshaft sprocket should be at the upper side.

NOTE: Always rotate the crankshaft in a clockwise direction. Make a mark on the back of the timing belt indicating the direction of rotation so it may be reassembled in the same direction if it is to be reused.

4. Remove the auto tensioner and remove the outermost timing belt.

5. Remove the timing belt tensioner pulley, tensioner arm, idler pulley.

6. Locate the access plug on the side of block. Remove the plug and install a Phillips screwdriver. Remove the oil pump sprocket nut, oil pump sprocket, special washer, flange and spacer.

7. Remove the silent shaft (inner) belt tensioner and remove the belt.

To install:

8. Align the timing marks on the crankshaft sprocket and the silent shaft sprocket. Fit the inner timing belt over the crankshaft and silent shaft sprocket. Ensure that there is no slack in the belt.

9. While holding the inner timing belt tensioner with your fingers, adjust the timing belt tension by applying a force towards the center of the belt, until the tension side of the belt is taut. Tighten the tensioner bolt.

NOTE: When tightening the bolt of the tensioner, ensure that the tensioner pulley shaft does not rotate with the bolt. Allowing it to rotate with the bolt can cause excessive tension on the belt.

10. Check belt for proper tension by depressing the belt on long side with your finger and noting the belt deflection. The desired reading is 0.20–0.28 in. (5–7mm). If tension is not correct, readjust and check belt deflection.

11. Install the flange, crankshaft and washer to the crankshaft. The flange on the crankshaft sprocket must be installed towards the inner timing belt sprocket. Tighten bolt to 80–94 ft. lbs. (110–130 Nm).

NOTE: There is a possibility to align all timing marks and have the oil pump sprocket out of time, causing an engine vibration during operation. If the following step is not followed exactly, there is a 50 percent chance that the oil pump shaft alignment will be 180 degrees off.

12. Before installing the timing belt, ensure that the oil pump sprocket is in the correct position as follows:

a. Remove the plug from the rear side of the block and insert a Phillips screwdriver with shaft diameter of 0.31 in. (8mm) into the hole.

b. With the timing marks still aligned, the shaft of the tool must be able to go in at least 2.36 in. (60mm). If the tool can only go in 0.79–0.98 in. (20–25mm), the shaft is not in the correct orientation and will cause a vibration during engine operation. Remove the tool from the hole and turn the oil pump sprocket 1 complete revolution. Realign the timing marks and insert the tool. The shaft of the tool must go in at least 2.36 in. (60mm).

c. Recheck and realign the timing marks.

d. Leave the tool in place to hold the silent shaft while continuing.

13. To install the oil pump sprocket and tighten the nut to 36–43 ft. lbs. (50–60 Nm).

14. Position the auto-tensioner into a vise with soft jaws. The plug at the rear of tensioner protrudes, be sure to use a washer as a spacer to protect the plug from contacting vise jaws.

15. Slowly push the rod into the tensioner until the set hole in rod is aligned with set hole in the auto-tensioner.

16. Insert a 0.055 in. (1.4mm) wire into the aligned set holes. Unclamp the tensioner from vise and install to vehicle. Tighten tensioner to 17 ft. lbs. (24 Nm).

17. When installing timing belt, the camshaft sprocket dowel pin should be located on top. Align all timing marks.

18. Align the crankshaft sprocket, camshaft sprocket and oil pump sprocket timing marks.

19. Install the timing belt as follows:

a. Install the timing belt around the idler pulley, oil pump sprocket, crankshaft sprocket, camshaft and the tensioner pulley.

b. Lift upward on the tensioner pulley in a clockwise direction and tighten the center bolt. Make sure all timing marks are aligned.

c. Rotate the crankshaft ¼ turn counterclockwise. Then, turn in clockwise until the timing marks are aligned again.

20. Loosen the center bolt. Using tool No. MD998752 or equivalent and a torque wrench, apply a torque of 1.88–2.03 ft. lbs. (2.6–2.8 Nm). Tighten the center bolt.

21. Screw the tool No. MD998738 into the engine left support bracket until its end makes contact with the tensioner arm and tighten tensioner pulley to 35 ft. lbs. (48 Nm). At this point, screw the special tool in some more and remove the set wire attached to the auto tensioner. Then remove the special tool.

22. Rotate the crankshaft 2 complete turns clockwise and let it sit for approximately 15 minutes. Then, measure the auto tensioner protrusion (the distance between the tensioner arm and auto tensioner body) to ensure that it is within 0.15–0.18 in. (3.8–4.5mm). If out of specification, repeat belt adjustment procedure until the specified value is obtained.

23. If the timing belt tension adjustment is being performed with the engine mounted in the vehicle, and clearance between the tensioner arm and the auto tensioner body cannot be measured, the following alternative method can be used:

a. Screw in tool No. MD998738 or equivalent, until its end makes contact with the tensioner arm.

b. After the tool makes contact with the arm, screw it in some more to retract the auto tensioner pushrod while counting the number of turns the tool makes until the tensioner arm is brought into contact with the auto tensioner body. Make sure the number of turns the tool makes conforms with the standard value of 2.5–3 turns.

c. Install the rubber plug to the timing belt rear cover.

24. Install the timing belt covers and all related items.

25. Connect the negative battery cable.

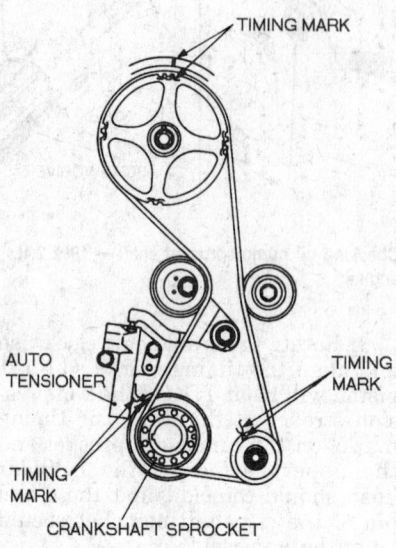

Timing belt alignment marks — 1993–96 2.4L engine

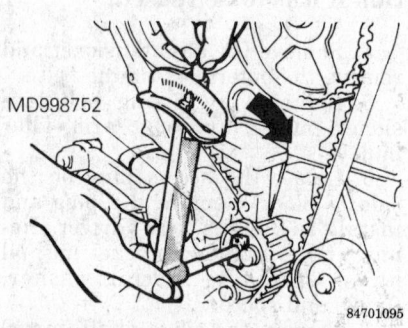

Timing belt adjusting tool No. MD998752 — 1993–96 2.4L engine

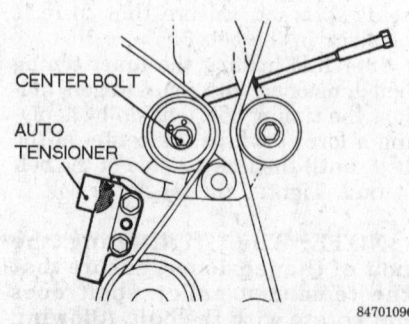

Timing belt adjusting tool No. MD998738 — 1993–96 2.4L engine

3.0L Engine

1. If possible, position engine with No. 1 cylinder at TDC. Disconnect negative battery cable. Remove the timing covers from engine.

2. If the same timing belt will be reused, mark the direction of timing belt's rotation, for installation in the same direction. Make sure engine is positioned so No. 1 cylinder is at the TDC of its compression stroke and the sprockets timing marks are aligned with the engine's timing mark indicators.

3. Loosen the timing belt tensioner bolt and remove the belt. If not removing the tensioner, position it as far away from the center of the engine as possible and tighten the bolt.

4. If tensioner is being removed, mark outside of the spring to ensure that it is not installed backwards. Unbolt the tensioner and remove it along with the spring.

To install:

5. Install the tensioner, if removed, and hook the upper end of the spring to the water pump pin. Install the lower end of the spring to the tensioner in exactly the same position as originally installed. If not already done, position both camshafts so the timing marks line up with those on the alternator bracket (rear bank) and inner timing cover (front bank). Rotate the crankshaft so the timing mark aligns with the mark on the oil pump.

6. Install the timing belt on the crankshaft sprocket and while keeping the belt tight on the tension side (right side), install the belt on the front camshaft sprocket.

7. Install the belt on the water pump pulley, then the rear camshaft sprocket and the tensioner.

8. Rotate the front camshaft counterclockwise to tension the belt between the front camshaft and the crankshaft. If the timing marks came out of line, repeat the procedure.

9. Install the crankshaft sprocket flange.

10. Loosen the tensioner bolt and allow the spring to tension the belt.

11. Turn the crankshaft 2 full turns in the clockwise direction until the timing marks align. Now that the belt is properly tensioned, torque the tensioner lock bolt to 21 ft. lbs. (29 Nm).

12. Install the timing belt covers and all related parts.

13. Connect the negative battery cable and road test the vehicle.

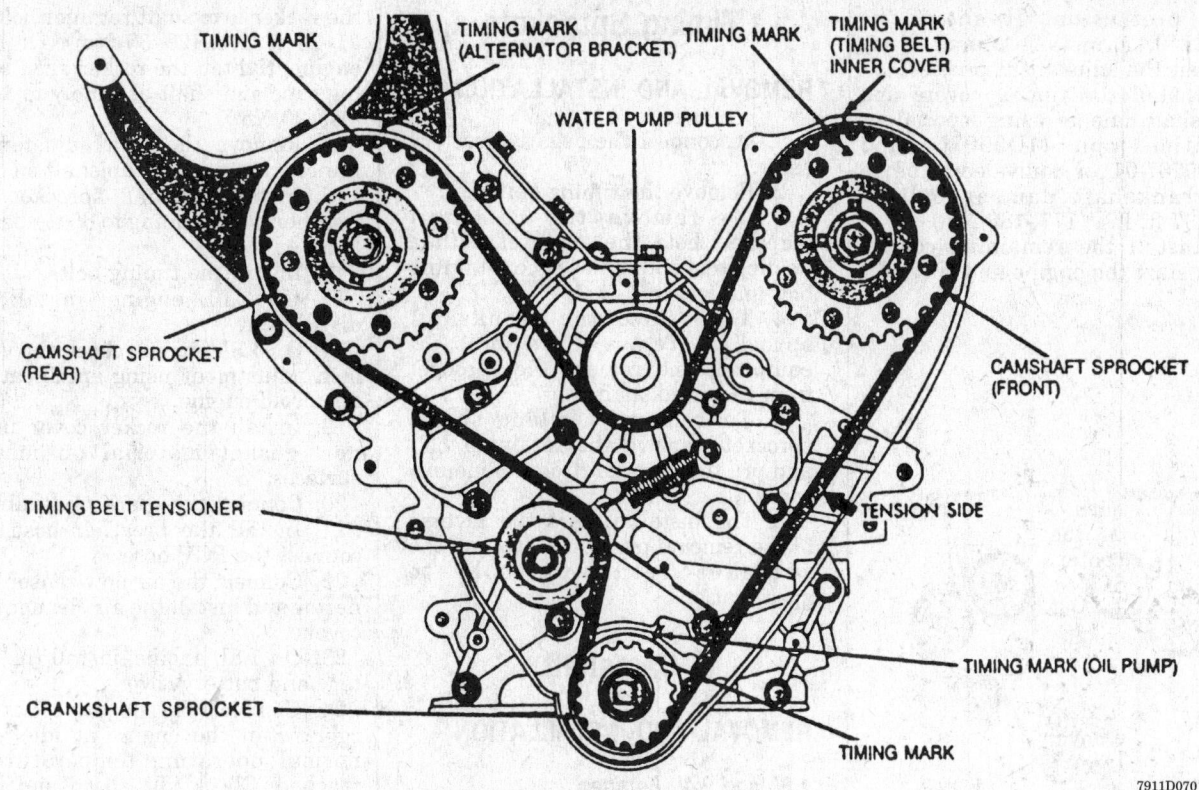

Timing belt installation — 3.0L engine

7911D070

3.5L Engine

1. Disconnect the negative battery cable and drain the engine coolant.

2. Remove the radiator, generator, battery, battery tray and undercovers.

3. Remove the cooling fan clutch, water pump pulley.

4. Remove the power steering pump and A/C compressor and leave the hoses attached. Support with wire out of the way.

5. Remove the accessory mount stay and mount assembly.

6. Remove the timing belt upper cover and crankshaft position sensor connector.

7. Remove the crankshaft pulley using removing tools MD998754 and MB990767-01, or equivalent.

8. Remove the timing belt lower cover.

9. Turn the crankshaft until all timing marks are aligned and the No. 1 cylinder is at TDC.

10. Loosen the center bolt on the auto-tensioner to remove the timing belt. If installing the old belt, make a mark on the back of the belt to indicate direction of rotation. Remove the timing belt from the sprockets.

11. Remove the auto-tensioner from the vehicle.

To install:

12. If the auto-tensioner is in the fully extended position, reset as follows:

   a. Keep the tensioner level and clamp in a soft vise.

   b. Push in the rod in very slowly with the vise until the set hole in the housing is aligned with the set hole in the cylinder.

   c. Insert a wire 0.055 in. (1.4mm) into the set holes. Remove the tensioner from the vise with the wire in the set holes.

13. Install the crankshaft pulley and turn the crankshaft sprocket timing mark forward 3 teeth to move the piston slightly past No. 1 TDC. Do NOT turn any further because the piston may hit the valves.

14. Align the timing mark on the left side camshaft sprocket.

15. Align the timing mark on the right side camshaft sprocket and support it not to turn with a closed wrench.

16. Install the timing belt to the camshaft sprockets.

17. Check that the camshaft sprocket timing mark of the right side is aligned and clamp the timing belt with double clips.

18. Set the timing belt onto the water pump pulley and idler pulley.

Make sure all camshaft marks are aligned.

19. After aligning the crankshaft sprocket timing marks, turn the crankshaft 1 notch counterclockwise.

20. Set the timing belt on the crankshaft sprocket and tensioner pulley.

21. Place the tensioner pulley pin hole so that it is towards the top. Press the tensioner pulley onto the timing belt and tighten the fixing bolt.

22. Align the crankshaft timing marks and check that each sprocket timing mark is aligned. Remove the double clips.

23. To adjust the timing belt, proceed as follows:

   a. Turn the crankshaft ¼ turn counterclockwise, then clockwise to align the timing marks.

   b. Loosen the center bolt on the tensioner pulley. Using the special tool MD998767 and torque wrench, apply torque to the timing belt and tighten the center bolt to 7 ft. lbs. (9 Nm).

   c. If installed, remove the set pin from the auto-tensioner. Rotate the crankshaft 2 turns clockwise and leave for 5 minutes. Make sure the set pin can be easily installed in the auto-tensioner. If the set pin can not be easily installed, check

the protrusion. It should be 0.149–0.177 in. (3.8–4.5mm). If not, repeat the adjustment process.

24. Install the timing covers and crankshaft damper using special installation tools MD998754 and MB990767-01, or equivalent. Torque the crankshaft damper bolt to 130–137 ft. lbs. (177–186 Nm).

25. Install the remaining components, start the engine and check for leaks.

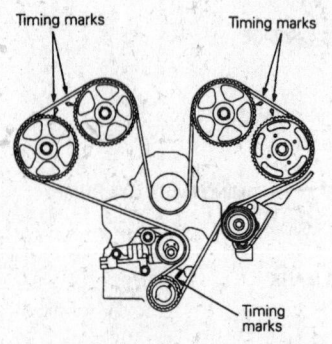

Timing belt alignment marks — 3.5L engine

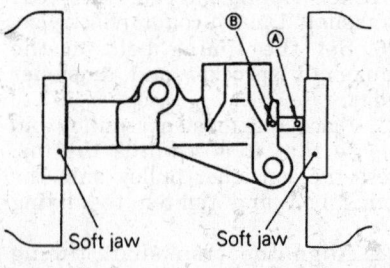

Auto-tensioner set pin hole locations — 3.5L engine

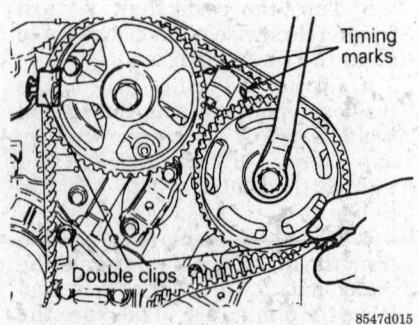

Timing belt-to-camshaft sprocket double clips — 3.5L engine

Timing Sprockets

REMOVAL AND INSTALLATION

1. Disconnect the negative battery cable.

2. Remove the timing belt(s).

3. To remove the camshaft sprocket, hold the sprocket with a holding tool and remove the retaining bolt and washer.

4. To remove the crankshaft sprocket, remove the bolt, if equipped, and remove the sprocket from the crankshaft.

5. To remove a silent shafts sprocket, remove the retaining bolt and pry the sprocket from its mounting shaft.

6. The installation is the reverse of the removal procedure. Torque the sprocket retaining bolt to specifications.

Camshaft

REMOVAL AND INSTALLATION

1.8L and 2.4L Engines

1. Disconnect the negative battery cable.

2. On 1.8L engine, remove the battery and battery cover. Disconnect the air flow sensor connector and remove the air cleaner case cover.

3. Remove the breather hose. Disconnect the PCV hose.

4. Label and disconnect the spark plug cables.

5. On 1.8L engine, remove the distributor assembly.

6. Remove the rocker cover and the timing belt assembly.

7. Remove the camshaft sprocket retainer bolt while holding shaft stationary with appropriate spanner wrench. Remove the sprocket from the shaft.

8. Remove the camshaft oil seal.

9. Install lash adjuster retainers on 2.4L engine. Remove both rocker arm shaft assemblies from the head. Do not disassembly rocker arms and rocker arm shaft assemblies.

10. Remove the camshaft from the cylinder.

11. Inspect the bearing journals on the camshaft, cylinder head, and bearing caps.

To install:

12. Lubricate the camshaft journals and camshaft with clean engine oil and install the camshaft in the cylinder head.

13. Install the rocker arm and shaft assemblies. On 1.8L engine, tighten

the rocker arm shaft retainer bolts to 21–25 ft. lbs. (29–35 Nm). On 2.4L engine, tighten the rocker arm, bearing caps and shaft assembly to 14 ft. lbs. (20 Nm).

14. Remove the lash adjuster retainers. Install new camshaft oil seal.

15. Install camshaft sprocket and retainer bolt torquing to 65 ft. lbs. (90 Nm).

16. Install the timing belt.

17. On 1.8L engine, install the distributor.

18. On 1.8L engine, check the valve lash adjustment using specifications for a cold engine.

19. Install the rocker cover using new gasket material on mating surfaces.

20. Connect the spark plug cables.

21. Install the breather hose and connect the PCV hose.

22. Connect the air flow sensor connector and install the air cleaner case cover.

23. On 1.8L engine, install the battery and battery cover.

24. Connect the negative battery cable. Run the engine at idle until normal operating temperature is reached. Check idle speed and ignition timing and adjust as required.

3.0L Engine

1. Disconnect the negative battery cable. Remove the valve cover.

2. Remove the timing belt and remove the sprocket from the camshaft.

3. Install auto lash adjuster retainers MD998443 or equivalent on the rocker arms.

4. If removing the left side camshaft, remove the distributor and the distributor extension for 3.0L engine.

5. Remove the camshaft bearing caps but do not remove the bolts from the caps. Remove the rocker arms, rocker shafts and bearing caps, as an assembly.

6. Remove the camshaft from the cylinder head.

7. Inspect the bearing journals on the camshaft, cylinder head and bearing caps.

To install:

8. Lubricate the camshaft journals and camshaft with clean engine oil and install the camshaft in the cylinder head.

9. Align the camshaft bearing caps with the arrow mark (depending on cylinder numbers) and in numerical order.

10. Apply sealer at the ends of the bearing caps and install the assembly.

11. Torque the bearing cap bolts, in the following sequence: No. 3, No. 2, No. 1 and No. 4 to 85 inch lbs. (10 Nm).

12. Repeat the sequence increasing the torque to 175 inch lbs. (18 Nm).

13. Install the distributor, if removed.

14. Install the sprocket, timing belt and all related parts.

15. Install the valve cover.

3.5L Engine

1. Disconnect the negative battery cable.

2. Remove the ignition coils or spark plug wires, valve cover and upper timing cover.

3. Use a wrench at the hexagonal part of the camshaft to prevent from turning. Loosen the camshaft sprocket bolts. Do not remove the bolt at this time.

4. Be very careful to disrupt the timing belt. Dislodge the camshaft sprocket with a rubber hammer. Remove the sprocket bolt and slide the sprocket with timing belt off the camshaft. Use a piece of wire to hang the sprocket and timing belt from the hood.

NOTE: The timing belt will have to be retimed if the belt alignment is lost during this procedure. Remove the sprocket with timing belt in its original position. Always keep tension on the belt and hang assembly by an overhead component.

5. Remove the camshaft bearing cap bolts starting in the center and working outward. Remove the bearing caps and camshaft.

6. Lubricate the bearings with engine oil and install so the sprocket timing mark is in alignment.

7. Torque the bearings to 15 ft. lbs. (20 Nm). Install the camshaft sprocket and torque the bolt to 65 ft. lbs. (88 Nm).

8. Install the remaining components, start the engine and check for leaks.

Silent Shafts

REMOVAL AND INSTALLATION

1.8L and 2.4L Engines

1. Disconnect the negative battery cable.

2. Remove the oil filter, oil pressure switch, oil gauge sending unit, oil filter mounting bracket and gasket.

3. Raise and safely support the vehicle. Drain engine oil. Remove engine oil pan, oil screen and gasket.

4. Lower the vehicle. Remove the timing belts.

5. Remove the front engine cover which is also the oil pump cover. Different length bolts are used. Take note of their locations. On 1.8L engine, if the cover sticks to the block, look for a special slot provided and pry with a flat edge tool. Discard the shaft seal and gasket.

6. Remove the oil pump driven gear flange bolt. When loosening this bolt, first insert a tool approximately ³⁄₈ in. diameter into the plug hole on the left side of the cylinder block to hold the silent shaft. Remove the oil pump gears and remove the front case assembly. Remove the threaded plug, the oil pressure relief spring and plunger.

7. Remove the silent shaft oil seals, the crankshaft oil seal and front case gasket.

8. Remove the silent shafts.

To install:

9. Carefully install the silent shafts to the block.

10. Install the oil pump components.

11. Install new seals and install the front case with a new gasket.

12. Install the timing belts and all related items. Make sure the orientation of the silent shafts is correct using alignment tool as specified in the timing belt section of this chapter.

NOTE: The timing of the oil pump sprocket and connected silent shaft can be incorrect, even with the timing mark aligned. Incorrect orientation of the silent shaft will result in engine vibration during operation. Follow the alignment procedure in the timing belt section of this chapter.

13. Install the oil pan, oil filter mounting bracket, oil switches oil filter and oil.

14. Connect the negative battery cable and check for leaks.

Piston and Connecting Rod

POSITIONING

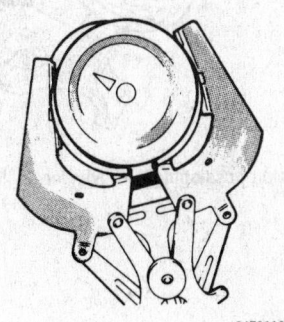

Piston identification marks — 1.8L and 2.4L engines

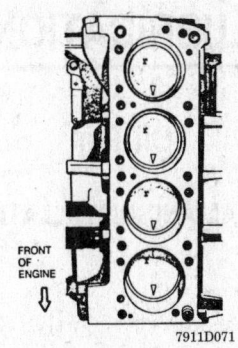

Piston positioning — 4 cylinder engine

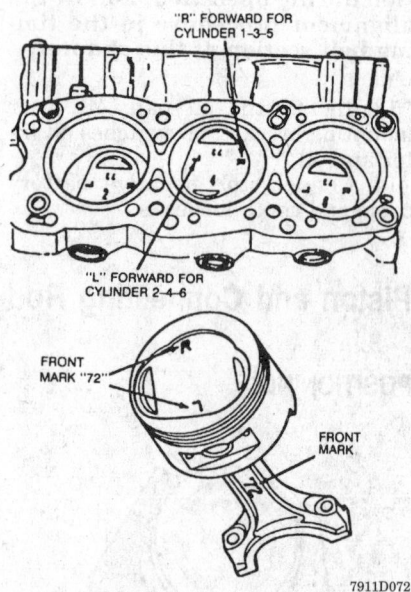

Piston positioning — 6 cylinder engine

ENGINE LUBRICATION

Oil Pan

REMOVAL AND INSTALLATION

Expo

1. Disconnect negative battery cable.
2. Raise and safely support the vehicle.
3. Remove the front exhaust pipe and gasket.
4. If equipped with AWD, remove the transfer assembly with the propeller shaft still installed.
5. Remove the bell housing cover.
6. If equipped with 2.4L engine and FWD, remove the front left driveshaft from the transaxle.
7. Remove the oil pan mounting bolts and nuts. Remove the oil pan using tool MD998727 or equivalent, and a brass bar. Take care not to deform the pan flange during removal.

To install:

8. Thoroughly clean and dry the oil pan, cylinder block bolts and bolt holes.
9. Apply a thin bead of sealer around the flange surface of the oil pan. Make sure the bead of sealer is on the area between the bolt holes and the inside of the pan, and in the shallow groove around the flange of the oil pan.
10. Assemble the oil pan to the cylinder block within 15 minutes after applying the sealant.
11. Install the oil pan mounting bolts and nuts and tighten to 5 ft. lbs. (7 Nm).
12. Install the bellhousing cover.
13. Install the front driveshaft.
14. Install the transfer assembly.
15. Install the front exhaust pipe.
16. Lower the vehicle and add clean engine oil to the correct level. Reconnect the negative battery cable and check for leaks.

Except Expo and 3.5L Engine

1. Disconnect the negative battery cable.
2. Raise the vehicle and support safely.
3. Remove the skid plate(s), engine undercover, air guide plate and cross shaft plate as required.
4. Remove the front exhaust pipe and steering linkage components as required.
5. On some vehicles, unbolt the motor mounts and raise the engine safely using the proper equipment.
6. On 4WD vehicles, the front suspension/crossmember/drive axle may have to be lowered to gain access to the oil pan.
7. Drain the engine oil from the pan.
8. Disconnect the fluid level sensor wire, if equipped. Remove the attaching bolts and remove the pan.
9. The installation is the reverse of the removal procedure. Torque the pan bolts to 7–9 ft. lbs. (10–12 Nm).

3.5L Engine

LOWER PAN

1. Drain the engine oil. Raise the vehicle and support safely.
2. Remove the skid plate and exhaust pipe.
3. Remove the lower oil pan.
4. Installation is the reverse of removal. Apply RTV sealer around the entire sealing surfaces and install the oil pan within 5 minutes. Torque the oil pan bolts to 7–9 ft. lbs. (10–12 Nm).

UPPER PAN

1. Drain the engine oil. Raise the vehicle and support safely.
2. Remove the skid plate and exhaust pipe.
3. Remove the lower oil pan.
4. Remove the differential carrier assembly, if 4WD equipped.
5. Remove the dipstick tube, upper oil pan and oil screen.

To install:

6. Clean the oil screen and torque the bolts to 13 ft. lbs. (19 Nm).
7. Clean the gasket mating surfaces and apply RTV sealer to the entire sealing surfaces. Install the oil pan within 5 minutes. Torque the oil pan bolts to 4 ft. lbs. (6 Nm).
8. Install the remaining components, refill engine oil, start the engine and check for leaks.

Oil Pump

REMOVAL AND INSTALLATION

1.8L and 2.4L Engines

1. Disconnect the negative battery cable. Remove the timing belt covers, timing belts and sprockets.
2. Raise the vehicle and support safely. Drain the oil and remove the oil filter. Remove the oil pan and gasket. Remove the oil pump pickup and gasket.
3. Remove the oil pressure relief plunger plug and gasket. Remove the spring and plunger from the oil filter bracket.
4. Remove the 4 bracket mounting bolts and remove the oil filter mount and gasket.
5. Using special tool MD998162, remove the cap and gasket that covers the oil pump driven gear shaft. This is located on the right side of the front case at the front of the engine, just above the protruding drive gear shaft.
6. Using a long socket, remove the retaining bolt from the oil pump driven gear located behind the plug removed earlier.
7. Remove the front case mounting bolts and remove the case from the block.
8. Remove the case gasket from the block.

To install:

9. Prime the pump by pouring fresh oil into the pump intake and turning the driveshaft until oil comes out the pressure port. Repeat a few times until no air bubbles are present. Replace all seals on the case assembly.

10. Install a special seal guide to the crankshaft MD998285 or equivalent so the smaller diameter faces outward. Coat the outer diameter of the seal with clean engine oil.

11. Install a new front case gasket and install the front case by carefully positioning the crankshaft seal over the seal guide and lining up all bolt holes. Install and tighten the bolts to 17 ft. lbs. (23 Nm).

12. Remove the plug from the left side of the block. Hold the left side silent shaft by inserting a tool in the plug hole and torque the driven gear bolt to 26 ft. lbs. (35 Nm). Using a new O-ring, install the plug cover.

13. Install the oil filter mounting bracket gasket. Install the mounting bracket and bolts tightening the oil filter mounting bracket bolts to 12 ft. lbs. (16 Nm).

14. Clean or replace the oil pickup screen and install with a new gasket.

15. Install the oil pan using a new gasket.

16. Install the timing sprockets, belts and covers.

17. Fill the engine with the proper amount of engine oil.

18. Connect the negative battery cable and check for proper oil pressure and leaks.

3.0L and 3.5L Engines

1. Disconnect the negative battery cable. Remove the dipstick.

2. Raise the vehicle and support safely. Remove the timing belt, drain the engine oil and remove the oil pan from the engine. Remove the oil pickup.

3. Remove the oil pump mounting bolts and remove the pump from the front of the engine. Note the different length bolts and their position in the pump for installation.

To install:

4. Clean the gasket mounting surfaces of the pump and engine block.

5. Prime the pump by pouring fresh oil into the inlet and turning the rotors or by packing pump with petroleum jelly. Using a new gasket, install the oil pump on the engine and torque all bolts to 11 ft. lbs. (15 Nm).

6. Install the balancer and crankshaft sprockets.

7. Clean out the oil pickup or replace as required. Replace the oil pickup gasket ring and install the pickup to the pump.

8. Install the timing belt, oil pan and all related parts.

9. Install the dipstick. Fill the engine with the proper amount of oil.

10. Connect the negative battery cable and check the oil pressure.

CHECKING

1.8L and 2.4L Engines

1. After disassembling the oil pump, clean all parts.

2. Assemble the oil pump gear to the front case and rotate it to ensure smooth rotation and no looseness. Make sure there is no ridge wear on the contact surface between the front case and the gear surface of the oil pump front cover.

3. The gear clearance should be checked using the following procedure:

a. On 2.4L engine, with the drive and driven gears installed in the front case, measure the tip clearance of the gears. The distance between the tips of the drive gear's teeth and the case should be 0.0063–0.0083 in. with a limit of 0.0098 in. The distance between the tips of the driven gear's teeth and the case should be 0.0051–0.0071 in. with a limit of 0.0098 in. The endplay is checked by placing a straight-edge across the machined cover surface and measuring with a feeler gauge. The endplay for the drive gear should

1. Drain plug	12. Relief spring	24. Drive gear
2. Gasket	13. Relief plunger	25. Left side silent shaft
3. Oil filter	14. Plug cap	26. Right side silent shaft
4. Oil pressure sending unit	15. O-ring	27. Front bearing
5. Oil pan	16. Driven gear bolt	28. Right rear bearing
6. Oil screen	17. Front case	29. Left rear bearing
7. Gasket	18. Gasket	
8. Oil filter bracket	19. Oil seal	
9. Gasket	20. Oil seal	
10. Relief plug	21. Oil seal	
11. Gasket	22. Oil pump cover	
	23. Driven gear	

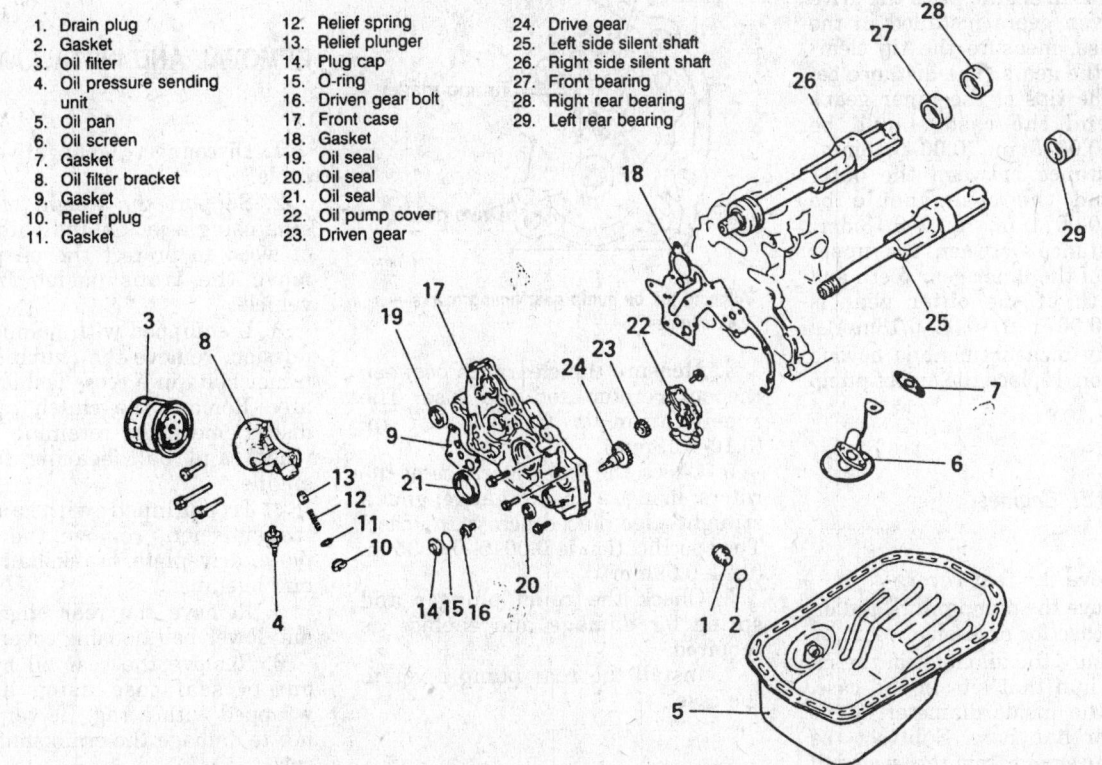

Engine lubrication components — 2.4L engine

7911D073

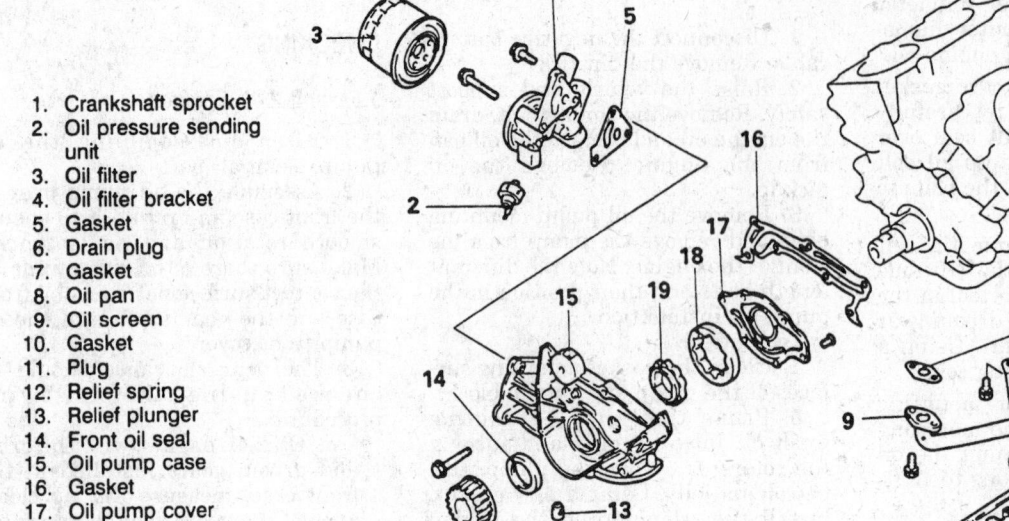

1. Crankshaft sprocket
2. Oil pressure sending unit
3. Oil filter
4. Oil filter bracket
5. Gasket
6. Drain plug
7. Gasket
8. Oil pan
9. Oil screen
10. Gasket
11. Plug
12. Relief spring
13. Relief plunger
14. Front oil seal
15. Oil pump case
16. Gasket
17. Oil pump cover
18. Outer rotor
19. Inner rotor

Engine lubrication components — 3.0L engine

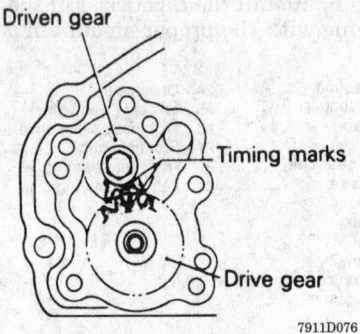

Aligning the oil pump gear timing marks — 2.4L engine

be 0.0031–0.0055 in. with a limit of 0.0098 in.

b. On 1.8L engine, with the drive and driven gears installed in the front case, measure the tip clearance of the gears. The distance between the tips of the inner gear's teeth and the case should be 0.0016–0.0039 in. (0.06–0.18mm). The distance between the outer gear and the case should be 0.0039–0.0071 in. (0.10–0.18mm). The distance between the upper portion of the inner gear teeth and the teeth of the outer gear is 0.0024–0.0071 in. (0.06–0.18mm).

4. If any measurement is beyond specification, replace the entire pump assembly.

3.0L and 3.5L Engines

1. Remove the rear cover.
2. Remove the pump rotors and inspect the case for excessive wear.
3. Measure the diameter of the inner rotor hub that sits in the case. Measure the inside diameter of the inner rotor hub bore. Subtract the first measurement from the second; if the result is over 0.006 in. (0.15mm), replace the oil pump assembly.

4. Measure the clearance between the outer rotor and the case. The specification is 0.004–0.007 in. (0.10–0.18mm).
5. Check the side clearance of the rotors using a feeler gauge and a straight-edge placed across the case. The specification is 0.0015–0.0035 in. (0.04–0.09mm).
6. Check the relief plunger and spring for damage and replace as required.
7. Install the rear pump cover to the case.

Rear Main Bearing Oil Seal

REMOVAL AND INSTALLATION

1. Disconnect the negative battery cable.
2. Support the weight of the engine using a jack stand with a block of wood to protect the oil pan. Remove the transmission from the vehicle.
3. If equipped with manual transmission, remove the clutch cover retainer bolts in a cross fashion gradually. Remove the clutch cover and disc. Remove the retaining bolt, flywheel and ball bearing from the engine.
4. If equipped with automatic transmission, remove the adapter plate, driveplate, crankshaft adapter and bushing.
5. Remove the rear engine plate and lower bell housing cover.
6. Remove the rear oil by prying out of seal case using a prybar wrapped with a rag. Be very careful not to damage the crankshaft or seal case.
7. Remove the oil separator if remaining on the engine block.

To install:

8. Lubricate the seal and install the new oil seal into the seal case using seal installer.

9. Press the oil separator into the seal case making sure the separator oil hole is on the very bottom of the case. In the correct position, the hole is on the adjacent to the oil pan mounting surface.

10. If the seal case was removed, clean and dry the seal case to block sealing surfaces. Install seal case to the rear of the block using a new gasket.

11. Install the rear engine plate and the lower bell housing cover.

12. If equipped with automatic transmission, install the adapter plate, driveplate, crankshaft adapter and bushing.

13. If equipped with manual transmission, install the retaining bolt, flywheel and ball bearing to the engine.

14. Install the transmission into the vehicle. Lower the vehicle and remove the engine support. Connect the negative battery cable and check the oil level, adding as required.

MANUAL TRANSMISSION

Transmission Assembly

REMOVAL AND INSTALLATION

1. Disconnect the negative battery cable.

2. Place the shifter(s) in the neutral position.

3. Unscrew the shift knob from the control lever. Remove the retainer screws from the dust cover retaining plate and slide plate and boot off of the lever.

4. Remove the retainer screws from the stopper plate and remove the lever assembly from the transmission. Cover the opening with a clean towel to prevent dirt from entering the transmission.

5. Raise the vehicle and support safely. Remove the skid plate, if equipped.

6. Drain the transmission fluid. If equipped with 4WD, drain the oil from the transfer case.

7. Matchmark and remove the driveshaft(s) from the vehicle.

8. Disconnect the speedometer cable from the transmission or transfer case.

9. Disconnect the clutch cable connection.

10. Disconnect the reverse light switch harness connector.

11. Remove the starter and the bell housing cover.

12. Support the weight of the engine using a jack stand with a block of wood to protect the oil pan.

13. Support the transmission with a transmission jack.

14. Remove the transfer case bracket, if equipped.

15. Remove the rear crossmember.

16. Remove the transmission to bell housing bolts.

17. Slide the transmission backwards until the input shaft clears the clutch disc. Remove the transmission from the vehicle.

To install:

18. Lubricate the pilot bushing and input shaft splines very lightly with high temperature lubricant.

19. Mount the transmission securely on a transmission jack and lift it in place until the input shaft is centered in the bell housing opening. Roll the transmission forward until the input shaft splines fully engage with the clutch disc.

20. Install the transmission to bell housing bolts. Torque the bolts to 35 ft. lbs. (47 Nm).

21. Lift the transmission using the transmission jack and install the rear crossmember into position. Install the transfer case bracket, if equipped. Torque the frame bolts to 50 ft. lbs. (68 Nm). Remove the transmission and engine support fixtures.

22. Install the starter and torque the mounting bolt to 20 ft. lbs. (27 Nm). Install the bell housing cover.

23. Connect the reverse light switch and clip all wiring to the transmission case.

24. Connect the speedometer cable.

25. Install the driveshaft(s) making sure to align matchmarks.

26. Connect the clutch cable, using a new cotter pin.

27. Fill the transmission and transfer case with the proper amount of SAE 80W or 75W/85W hypoid gear oil with an API classification of GL–4 or higher.

28. Install the skip plate, if equipped. Lower the vehicle.

29. Install the shift lever assembly, boot and console.

30. Connect the negative battery cable and check the transmission and transfer case for proper operation. Check operation of the reverse lights.

LINKAGE ADJUSTMENT

Since this transmission uses a direct engage shift mechanism, there are no provisions for adjustment.

MANUAL TRANSAXLE

Transaxle Assembly

NOTE: If the vehicle is going to be rolled while the halfshafts are out of the vehicle, obtain 2 outer CV-joints or proper equivalent tools and install to the hubs. If the vehicle is rolled without the proper torque applied to the front wheel bearings, the bearings will no longer be usable.

REMOVAL AND INSTALLATION

Expo

1. Disconnect negative battery cable. Support the weight of the engine using the appropriate fixture.

2. Remove the air cleaner assembly. Remove the transaxle upper coupling bolts.

3. Raise and safely support the vehicle.

4. Disconnect the control cable connection from the transaxle.

5. Disconnect the reverse light switch connection.

6. Disconnect the speedometer cable from the transaxle.

7. Remove the starter motor leaving the harness connected and secure aside.

8. Disconnect the tie rod end from the steering knuckle. Disconnect the stabilizer bar.

9. Remove the right side under cover. Drain the transaxle fluid.

10. Insert a prybar between the transaxle case and the driveshaft and pry the shaft from the transaxle. Turn the driveshaft and suspend with a wire so there are no sharp bends in any of the joints. Turn the right side shaft 90 degrees towards the front of the vehicle so it will not be a hindrance.

NOTE: When removing the shaft, use a prybar. Do not pull on the driveshaft; doing so will damage the inboard joint. Do not insert the prybar so deep as to damage the oil seal.

11. Remove the clutch oil line bracket bolt and remove the release cylinder. Suspend cylinder out of the way leaving the oil lines connected.

12. On AWD models, remove the front exhaust pipe and transfer assembly.

13. Remove the center support member.

14. Remove the bellhousing cover. Support the transaxle using a transmission jack.

15. Remove the transaxle mount bolt.

16. Remove the transaxle assembly lower part coupling bolts.

17. Slide the transaxle assembly away from the engine and remove from the vehicle.

To install:

18. Position the transaxle assembly against the engine. Install the transaxle assembly lower part coupling bolts.

19. Install the transaxle mount bolt and tighten nut to 51 ft. lbs. (70 Nm).

20. On 1.8L engine, install the center support member.

21. Remove the transaxle jack. Install the bellhousing cover.

22. Install the clutch oil line bracket bolt and release cylinder.

23. Install the front driveshafts so the inboard joint part of the shaft is straight in relation to the transaxle. Care must be taken to ensure that the oil seal lip part of the transaxle is not damaged by the serrated part of the driveshaft.

24. Connect the tie rod end from the steering knuckle. Disconnect the stabilizer bar.

25. Install the right side under cover. Install the starter motor.

26. Connect the tie rod ends to the steering knuckle and secure using new cotter pin.

27. Reconnect the speedometer cable, backup switch connector and the control cable connector.

28. Refill the transaxle assembly with Hypoid gear oil or equivalent, GL-4 or higher. Install the air cleaner assembly.

29. Connect the negative battery cable and check the transaxle and transfer case for proper operation. Make sure the reverse lights come ON when in reverse.

LINKAGE ADJUSTMENT

There are 2 cables, the select cable and the shift cable.

1. On the transaxle, put select lever in **N** and move the transaxle shift lever to put it in **4th** gear. Depress the clutch, if necessary, to shift.

2. Move the shift lever in the vehicle to the **4th** gear position until it contacts the stop.

3. Turn the adjuster turn buckle so the shift cable eye aligns with the eye in the gear shift lever. When installing the cable eye, make sure the flange side of the plastic bushing at the shift cable end is on the cotter pin side.

4. The cables should be adjusted so the clearance between the shift lever and the 2 stoppers are equal when the shift lever is moved to 3rd and 4th gear. Move the shift lever to each position and check that the shifting is smooth.

CLUTCH

Clutch Assembly

REMOVAL AND INSTALLATION

Expo

1. Disconnect the negative battery cable. Raise and safely support the vehicle.

2. Remove the transaxle assembly from the vehicle.

3. Remove the pressure plate attaching bolts. If the pressure plate is to be reused, loosen the bolts in succession, 1 or 2 turns at a time to prevent warping the the cover flange.

4. Remove the pressure plate release bearing assembly and the clutch disc. Do not use solvent to clean the bearing.

5. Inspect the condition of the clutch components and replace any worn parts.

To install:

6. Inspect the flywheel for heat damage or cracks. Resurface or replace the flywheel as required, using new bolts.

7. Using the proper alignment tool, install the clutch disc to the flywheel. Install the pressure plate assembly and tighten the pressure plate bolts evenly to 14–16 ft. lbs. (19–22 Nm). Remove the alignment tool.

8. Apply a very light coat of high temperature grease to the clutch fork at the ball pivot and where the fork contacts the bearing. Also a little bit of grease can be applied to end of the release cylinder's pushrod and to the pushrod hole on the fork. Apply a

light coat of grease on the transaxle input shaft splines.

9. Install a new clutch release bearing. Pack its inner surface with high temperature grease.

10. Install the transaxle assembly and check for proper clutch operation.

Except Expo

1. Disconnect the negative battery cable.

2. Place the shifter(s) in the neutral position.

3. Unscrew the shift knob from the control lever. Remove the retainer screws from the dust cover retaining plate and slide plate and boot off of the lever.

4. Remove the retainer screws from the stopper plate and remove the lever assembly from the transmission. Cover the opening with a clean towel to prevent dirt from entering the transmission.

5. Raise the vehicle and support safely. Remove the skid plate, if equipped.

6. Drain the transmission fluid. If equipped with 4WD, drain the oil from the transfer case.

7. Matchmark and remove the driveshaft(s) from the vehicle.

8. Disconnect the speedometer cable from the transmission or transfer case.

9. Disconnect the clutch cable connection.

10. Disconnect the reverse light switch harness connector.

11. Remove the starter and the bell housing cover.

12. Support the weight of the engine using a jack stand with a block of wood to protect the oil pan.

13. Support the transmission with a transmission jack.

14. Remove the transfer case bracket, if equipped.

15. Remove the rear crossmember.

16. Remove the transmission to bell housing bolts.

17. Slide the transmission backwards until the input shaft clears the clutch disc. Remove the transmission from the vehicle.

18. Remove the clutch cover retainer bolts in a cross fashion gradually. Remove the clutch cover and disc.

To install:

19. Raise the clutch cover and disc into place and use a clutch aligning tool or spare input shaft to center the disc. Apply Loctite® to the threads and tighten all of the bolts finger tight.

20. Tighten cover bolts gradually, evenly and to the proper torque to avoid distorting the cover. Torque the bolts to 15 ft. lbs. (20 Nm).

21. Lubricate the pilot bushing and input shaft splines very lightly with high temperature lubricant.

22. Mount the transmission securely on a transmission jack and raise in place until the input shaft is centered in the bell housing opening. Roll the transmission forward until the input shaft splines fully engage with the clutch disc.

23. Install the transmission to bell housing bolts. Torque the bolts to 35 ft. lbs. (47 Nm).

24. Lift the transmission using the transmission jack and install the rear crossmember into position. Install the transfer case bracket, if equipped. Torque the frame bolts to 50 ft. lbs. (68 Nm). Remove the transmission and engine support fixtures.

25. Install the starter and torque the mounting bolt to 20 ft. lbs. (27 Nm). Install the bell housing cover.

26. Connect the reverse light switch and clip all wiring to the transmission case.

27. Connect the speedometer cable.

28. Install the driveshaft(s) making sure to align matchmarks.

29. Connect the clutch cable, using a new cotter pin.

30. Fill the transmission and transfer case with the proper amount of SAE 80W or 75W/85W hypoid gear oil with an API classification of GL–4 or higher.

31. Install the skip plate, if equipped. Lower the vehicle.

32. Install the shift lever assembly and boot.

33. Connect the negative battery cable and check the transmission and transfer case for proper operation. Check operation of the reverse lights.

Pedal Height/Free-Play Adjustment

1. Measure the clutch pedal height from the face of the pedal pad to the firewall. The desired distances are as follows:
    a. Expo — 7.68–7.87 in. (195–200mm)
    b. Pick-Up — 6.50–7.00 in. (165–178mm)
    c. Montero — 7.30–7.50 in. (185–190mm)

2. Measure the clutch pedal clevis pin play at the face of the pedal pad. The standard values are is 0.04–0.12 in. (1–3mm)

3. If the clutch pedal height or clevis pin play are not within the standard values, adjust as follows:
    a. Turn and adjust the bolt so the pedal height is the standard value, then tighten the locknut.
    b. Turn the pushrod to adjust the clutch pedal clevis pin play to agree with the standard value and secure the pushrod with the locknut.

NOTE: When adjusting the clutch pedal height or the clutch pedal clevis pin play, be careful not to push the pushrod toward the master cylinder.

    c. Check that when the clutch pedal is depressed all the way, the interlock switch switches over from **ON** to **OFF**.

4. If the pedal height is not correct, adjust the pedal stopper to contact the pedal at correct height.

Clutch Cable

ADJUSTMENT

1. Check the pedal's free-play. The specification is 1 inch.

2. Adjust the clutch cable by turning the star shaped adjusting wheel on the firewall. Turning the wheel counterclockwise will increase the amount of free-play in the pedal or vice-versa.

REMOVAL AND INSTALLATION

1. Disconnect the negative battery cable.

2. Turn the cable adjusting wheel counterclockwise to provide enough play to remove the cable end from the clutch lever inside the vehicle. Remove the cable from the lever.

3. Raise the vehicle and support safely.

4. Remove the cotter pin from the lever on the transmission.

5. Remove the clutch cable from the vehicle.

6. The installation is the reverse of the removal procedure. Make sure the insulator is positioning properly.

Clutch Master Cylinder

REMOVAL AND INSTALLATION

1. Disconnect the negative battery cable. Remove as much fluid as possible from the clutch master cylinder reservoir.

2. Remove the cotter pin and remove the clevis pin from the clutch pedal.

3. Disconnect and plug the fluid line from the clutch master cylinder.

4. Remove the mounting nuts and remove the cylinder from the firewall.

5. Remove the reservoir from the cylinder.

6. The installation is the reverse of the removal procedure.

7. Bleed the system.

Clutch Slave Cylinder

REMOVAL AND INSTALLATION

1. Disconnect the negative battery cable.

2. Raise the vehicle and support safely.

3. Remove the eye-bolt and washer from the slave cylinder.

4. Remove the mounting bolts and remove the slave cylinder from the transmission case.

5. Replace the eye-bolt washer.

6. The installation is the reverse of the removal procedure.

7. Bleed the system.

Hydraulic Clutch System Bleeding

—— **CAUTION** ——
When bleeding, keep the facial area well away from the slave cylinder and protect all painted surfaces from fluid contact. Brake fluid will damage painted surfaces and could cause physical injury.

1. Fill the clutch master cylinder with fresh DOT 3 brake fluid.

2. Have a helper sit in the vehicle. Raise the vehicle and support safely.

3. Remove the bleeder screw cap.

4. If the system is empty, the most efficient way to get fluid down to the cylinder is to loosen the bleeder about 1/2–3/4 turn, place a finger firmly over the bleeder and have the helper pump the brakes slowly until fluid pressure is felt at the bleeder. Once fluid is at the bleeder, close before the pedal is released.

NOTE: If the pedal is pump rapidly, the fluid will churn and create small air bubbles, which are difficult and time consuming to remove from the system. These air bubbles will eventually congregate and will result in a spongy pedal.

5. Once fluid has been pumped to the slave cylinder, open the bleeder screw, have the helper depress the clutch pedal, lock the bleeder and have the helper release the pedal. Wait 15 seconds and repeat the procedure (including the 15 second wait) until no air bubbles flow from the bleeder. Remember to close the bleeder before the pedal is released. If the bleeder is left open when the pedal is released, air will be induced into the system.

6. If a helper is not available, connect a small hose to the bleeder, submerge the other end in a clean container of fresh brake fluid placed in a position that is visible from the driver's seat. Pump the pedal until no air comes out of the tube.

AUTOMATIC TRANSMISSION

Transmission Assembly

REMOVAL AND INSTALLATION

1. Disconnect the negative battery cable.

2. If equipped with 4WD, disconnect the 4WD indicator light switch connector and the ground cable at the transfer case.

3. Disconnect the pulse generator connector.

4. Raise and safely support the vehicle.

5. Remove the skid plate, if equipped. Drain the transmission and transfer case, as equipped.

6. Matchmark and remove the driveshaft(s).

7. Disconnect the speedometer cable from the transmission or transfer case.

8. Disconnect the shifter linkage or cable.

9. Unplug all transmission electrical connectors.

10. Remove the exhaust pipe from the vehicle. Remove the exhaust bracket from the transmission case.

11. Remove the filler neck and dipstick.

12. Remove the torque converter inspection plate. Matchmark the flexplate to the torque converter and remove the torque converter bolts.

13. Remove the starter assembly.

14. Disconnect and plug the oil cooler lines.

15. Using a transmission jack, support the transmission. Remove the retaining bolts at the crossmember.

16. Remove the crossmember.

17. Lower the transmission down slightly and unbolt the 4WD shifter from the transfer case, if equipped.

18. Remove the bell housing bolts and mounting brackets.

19. Pull the transmission assembly rearward to clear the aligning dowels and remove from the vehicle.

To install:

20. Install the transmission assembly to the engine using dowels as guides. Install the bell housing bolts and torque to 35 ft. lbs. (47 Nm).

21. Install the 4WD shifter, if equipped. Raise the assembly up into position and install the rear crossmember and mounting hardware. Torque the crossmember to frame bolts to 50 ft. lbs. (68 Nm).

22. Align the flexplate to torque converter. Apply Loctite® to the threads and install the torque converter bolts. Torque the bolts to 25 ft. lbs. (34 Nm). Install the inspection plate.

23. Install the filler tube with a new O-ring and the dipstick.

24. Install the exhaust and the support brackets.

25. Connect all switch connectors that were removed.

26. Connect the shifter linkage or cable and the throttle cable.

27. Align and install the driveshaft(s).

28. Install the ground wire and the 4WD indicator light switch connector to the transfer case, if equipped.

29. Fill the transfer case with hypoid gear oil with an API classification of GL–4 or higher.

30. Connect the throttle cable.

31. Install the skid plate, if equipped. Lower the vehicle.

32. Install the transfer shifter boot, if equipped.

33. Fill the transmission with the proper amount of Dexron® II.

34. Connect the negative battery cable, start the engine and run through all gears. Add fluid until the transmission is properly filled.

35. Check the operation of the neutral safety switch and the reverse lights.

36. Road test the vehicle and check for leaks.

SHIFT LINKAGE ADJUSTMENT

1. Position the shifter in the **N** detent.

2. Loosen the nut or bolt on the shifter linkage or cable.

3. Make sure the lever on the transmission is in the **N** detent and the needle in the indicator is also in the **N** position. Jiggle the selector rod to settle the assembly in position. If the rod is equipped with a notch, it should be at the 6 o'clock position.

4. Tighten the adjusting bolt or nut and check for proper assembly.

5. Check the operation of the neutral safely switch.

6. Liberally lubricate all pivoting points within the system.

THROTTLE CABLE ADJUSTMENT

1. Depress the accelerator fully and make sure the throttle valve opens all the way. Adjust as required.

2. Measure the distance between the end of the rubber boot and the stopper on the cable at wide open throttle.

3. The specification is 0–0.04 in. (0–1mm). Adjust the cable itself.

4. Road test the vehicle and check for proper shift points.

NEUTRAL SAFETY SWITCH ADJUSTMENT

NOTE: Some vehicles are not equipped with an adjustable switch.

1. Adjust the shifter linkage.

2. Raise the vehicle and support safely. Place the shifter in the **N** detent. Loosen the mounting bolts.

3. Align the lever with the positioning boss.

4. Hold in position and tighten the bolts.

5. Check the switch and the reverse lights for proper operation.

AUTOMATIC TRANSAXLE

Transaxle Assembly

NOTE: If the vehicle is going to be rolled while the halfshafts are out of the vehicle, obtain 2 outer CV-joints or proper equivalent tools and install to the hubs. If the vehicle is rolled without the proper torque applied to the front wheel bearings, the bearings will no longer be usable.

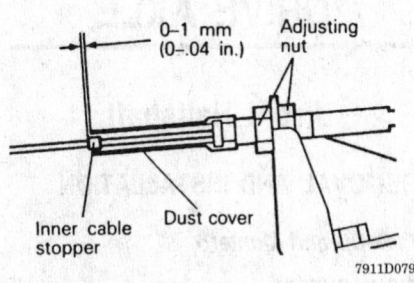

Throttle cable adjustment

7911D079

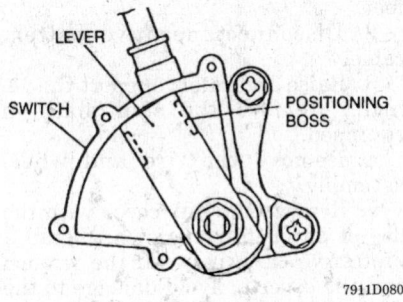

Neutral safety switch adjustment

7911D080

REMOVAL AND INSTALLATION

1. Disconnect negative battery cable.

2. Remove the air cleaner assembly.

3. Disconnect the transaxle control lever. Disconnect and plug the oil cooler lines.

4. Disconnect the pulse generator connector, oil temperature connector, kickdown servo switch connector, inhibitor switch connector and solenoid valve connection.

5. Disconnect the speedometer cable connection. Remove the oil level dipstick and tube.

6. Install holding fixture to the top of the engine to support engine weight.

7. Remove the top transaxle upper coupling bolts. Raise and safely support the vehicle.

8. Remove the starter motor leaving wire harness attached.

9. Remove the right side under cover. Drain the transaxle fluid.

10. Disconnect the tie rod ends, stabilizer bar and lower ball joints.

11. If equipped with AWD, it will be necessary to remove the right driveshaft from the vehicle.

12. Except AWD vehicles, remove the driveshafts from the transfer case, insert a prybar between the driveshaft and the transaxle case and pry the shaft from the transaxle housing. Swing the shafts out of the way keeping the joints straight and suspend using wire. Turn the right shaft 90 degrees toward the front of the vehicle so it will not be a hindrance.

NOTE: Do not pull on the shaft during removal from the transaxle; doing so will damage the inboard joint. Do not insert the prybar so deep as to damage the oil seal.

13. Remove the lower bellhousing cover. Scribe a mark on the driveplate and transaxle converter face using chalk. Remove the driveplate connecting bolts while turning the crankshaft.

14. Support the transaxle using a transmission jack. Remove the center support.

15. Remove the transaxle mount bolt and bracket.

16. If equipped with AWD, disconnect the front exhaust pipe and remove the transfer assembly.

17. Remove the lower transaxle case coupling bolts, press the torque converter towards the transfer case to prevent separation during removal and lower the transfer case from the vehicle.

To install:

18. Install the transaxle into the vehicle and secure using the lower case coupling bolts.

19. Install the transaxle mount bolt and bracket, torque through bolt nut to 51 ft. lbs. (70 Nm).

20. Align the scribe marks on the converter and the driveplate. Install the driveplate connecting bolts torquing to 33–38 ft. lbs. (46–53 Nm).

21. Install the transfer assembly and the center crossmember. Remove the transmission jack.

22. Install the center exhaust pipe.

23. Install the drive axles into the transfer case taking care not to damage the oil seal lip part of the transaxle with the serrated part of the driveshaft.

24. Connect the tie rod ends, stabilizer bar and lower ball joints.

25. Install the right side under cover.

26. Lower the vehicle. Install the upper transaxle coupling bolts.

27. Connect the speedometer cable and the electrical harness connectors disconnected during the removal procedure.

28. Install the starter motor torquing the retainer bolts to 35 ft. lbs. (49 Nm).

29. Connect the transaxle cooler hoses and the connections for the manual controls.

30. Install the air cleaner assembly and the oil level dipstick and tube.

31. Refill with Dexron® II, Mopar ATF Plus type 7176 or equivalent, automatic transaxle fluid.

32. Start the engine and allow to idle for 2 minutes. Apply parking brake and move selector through each gear position, ending in **N**. Recheck fluid level and add if necessary. Fluid level should be between the marks in the **HOT** range. Check operation of all gauges and meters.

SHIFTER CONTROL CABLE ADJUSTMENT

1. The shifter cable adjustment is done at the neutral safety switch (inhibitor switch). Locate the switch on the transaxle and note the alignment holes in the arm and the body of the switch. Place the selector lever in **N**. Place the manual lever of the transaxle in the **N** position.

2. Check alignment of the hole in the manual control lever to the hole in the inhibitor switch body. If the holes do not align, adjustment is required.

3. To adjust, loosen the nut on the cable end and pull the cable end by hand until the alignment holes match. Tighten the nut. Check that the transaxle shifts and conforms to the positions of the selector lever.

THROTTLE CONTROL CABLE ADJUSTMENT

Some vehicles do not use a throttle linkage. Instead, the throttle position sensor provides an electric signal to the transaxle, so no linkage adjustment is required.

1. Check that the throttle lever is in the curb idle position, with the engine **OFF** but at normal operating temperature.

2. At the lower cable bracket, raise the cone shaped cover to uncover a small fitting on the cable. By loosening the locknut and adjuster nut, make the distance between the fitting on the cable and the lower collar is 0.020–0.060 in.

3. With the throttle in the wide open position, check that the cable does not bind.

TRANSFER CASE

Transfer Case Assembly

REMOVAL AND INSTALLATION

Pick-Up and Montero

AUTOMATIC TRANSMISSION

1. Disconnect the negative battery cable.
2. Remove the transmission and transfer case assembly from the vehicle.
3. Remove the plug from the right side of the transfer case under the control housing.
4. Remove the select spring and plunger from the housing bore.
5. Remove the control lever housing assembly, cover and gasket.
6. Remove the transfer case to adapter attaching nuts. Pull transfer case from the adapter.
To install:
7. Install the transfer case to adapter and secure using retainer nuts. Torque nuts to 30 ft. lbs. (42 Nm).
8. Install the control lever housing assembly, cover and gasket.
9. Install the select spring and plunger into the housing and install plug in bore.
10. Install the transfer case and transmission into the vehicle, connect the negative battery cable and road test for proper operation.

MANUAL TRANSMISSION

1. Disconnect the negative battery cable.
2. Remove the transmission and transfer case assembly from the vehicle.
3. Remove the plug from the right side of the transfer case under the control housing.
4. Remove the select spring and plunger from the housing bore.
5. Remove the spring pin that retains the shift changer to the control shaft using a pin punch.
6. Remove the transfer case to transmission attaching nuts and remove from the transmission.
To install:
7. Install the transfer case to transmission and tighten attaching nuts to 30 ft. lbs. (42 Nm).
8. Install the shift changer to the control shaft and install new roll pin.
9. Install select spring, plunger and plug into housing bore.

10. Install the transfer case and transmission into vehicle. Connect negative battery cable and road test for proper operation.

Expo

1. Disconnect the battery negative cable.
2. Raise the vehicle and support safely. Drain the oil from the transfer assembly.
3. Disconnect the front exhaust pipe.
4. Make mating marks on the differential companion flange and the flange yoke. Remove the propeller shaft.

NOTE: Remove the propeller shaft in a straight and level manner so as to ensure that the boot is not damaged through pinching. Damage can be avoided if a piece of cloth or similar material is inserted into the boot. Cover the opening of the transfer assembly to prevent dirt from entering the transfer assembly.

5. Remove the transfer assembly mounting bolts and the transfer assembly from the vehicle.
To install:
6. Position the transfer assembly into the vehicle and secure using the mounting bolts, tightened to 51 ft. lbs. (70 Nm).
7. Align the mating marks and install propeller shaft.
8. Attach the front exhaust pipe using new gasket.
9. Reconnect the negative battery and lower the vehicle. Refill the transfer case and check oil levels in transaxle and transfer case.

LINKAGE ADJUSTMENT

Since this transfer case uses a directly engaging shift mechanism, there are no provisions for adjustment.

DRIVE AXLE

Front Halfshaft

REMOVAL AND INSTALLATION

Pick-Up and Montero

RIGHT OUTER

1. Place the free-wheeling hub in the free condition by placing the transfer lever in the **2H** position and moving in reverse for about 6 or 7 feet.
2. Disconnect negative battery cable.
3. Raise and safely support the vehicle. Remove the skid plate, if equipped.
4. Remove the tire and wheel assembly.
5. Remove the hub cover with the use of an oil filter wrench. Install a protective cloth between the wrench and the cover to avoid damage to the cover.
6. Remove the snapring from the inside of the hub. Remove the shim.
7. Remove the front brake caliper and brake pads from the vehicle. Do not allow the caliper to hang from the brake hose.
8. Separate the tie rod from the steering knuckle.
9. Separate the upper and lower ball joints from the steering knuckle.
10. Remove the front hub/knuckle assembly with the inner and outer bearings intact.
11. Remove the halfshaft to axle housing retaining nuts and remove the halfshaft from the axle.
To install:
12. Install the halfshaft and the retaining nuts and tighten to 43 ft. lbs. (60 Nm).
13. Install the front hub/knuckle and bearing assembly.
14. Install the upper ball joint to the knuckle and torque retaining nut to 130 ft. lbs. (180 Nm). Install the lower ball joint to knuckle and torque retaining nut to 65 ft. lbs. (90 Nm). Install new cotter pins.
15. Install the tie rod end to the steering knuckle and torque to 33 ft. lbs. (45 Nm). Install new cotter pin.
16. Install the shim and snapring to the axle shaft. Install the front hub cover.
17. Install front brake caliper assembly.
18. Install the tire and wheel assembly. Install skid plate, if removed.

1. Oil filler plug
2. Drain plug
3. Plug
4. Gasket
5. Selector spring
6. Selector plunger
7. Roll pin
8. Wire clamp
9. Wire clamp
10. Shift changer
11. Transfer case assembly
12. Gasket
13. Plug
14. Spring
15. Steel ball
16. Plug
17. Neutral return spring
18. Plunger
19. Plunger

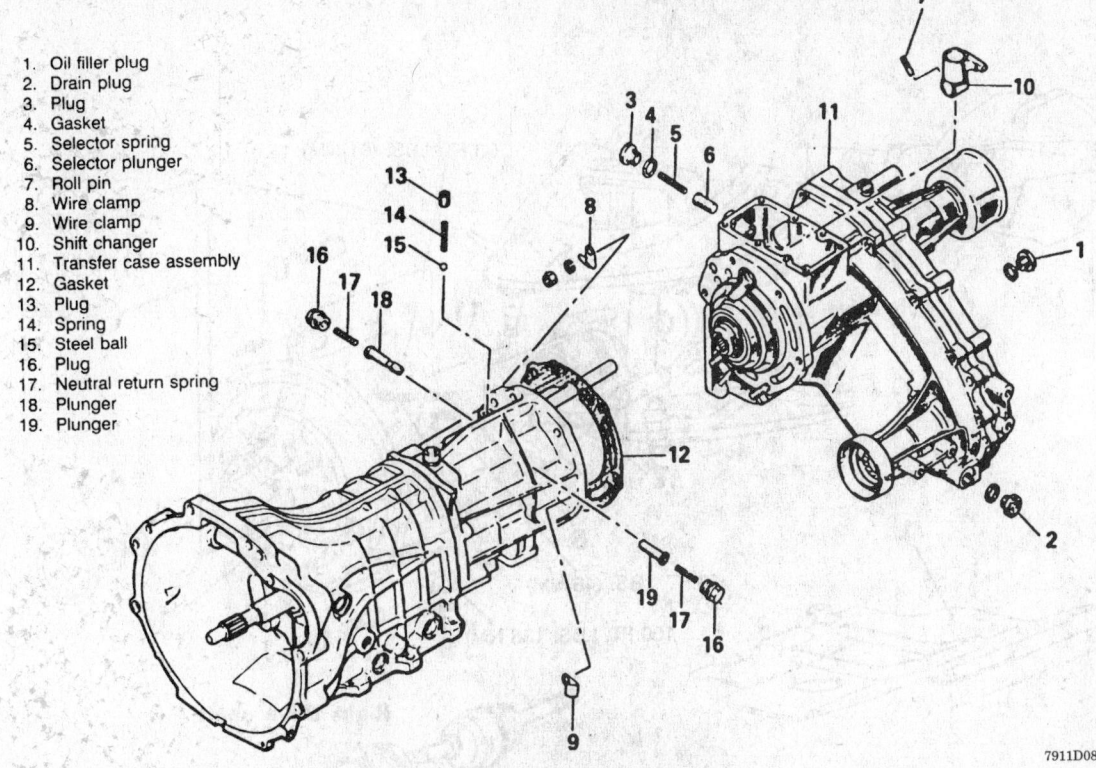

7911D081

Transfer case assembly — Pick-Up and Montero

RIGHT INNER

1. Disconnect negative battery cable.

2. Raise and safely support the vehicle.

3. Remove the skid plate, if equipped.

4. Remove the right outer halfshaft.

5. Remove the lower shock absorber mounting bolts.

6. Install slide hammer to inner shaft flange and pull from housing. Press the bearing from the axle, as required.

To install:

7. Press new bearing and seal on axle, as required. Install new circlip to inner halfshaft and install into housing. Drive the axle into position.

8. Install the lower shock absorber mounting bolts.

9. Install the right outer halfshaft.

10. Install the skid plate, if equipped.

LEFT HALFSHAFT

1. Place the free-wheeling hub in the free condition by placing the transfer lever in the **2H** position and moving in reverse for about 6 or 7 feet.

2. Disconnect negative battery cable.

3. Raise and safely support the vehicle. Remove the skid plate, if equipped.

4. Remove the tire and wheel assembly.

5. Remove the hub cover with the use of an oil filter wrench. Install a protective cloth between the wrench and the cover to avoid damage to the cover.

6. Remove the snapring from the inside of the hub. Remove the shim.

7. Remove the front brake caliper and brake pads from the vehicle. Do not allow the caliper to hang from the brake hose.

8. Separate the tie rod from the steering knuckle.

9. Separate the upper and lower ball joints from the steering knuckle.

10. Remove the front hub/knuckle assembly with the inner and outer bearings intact.

11. Pull the left halfshaft out from the differential carrier. Use care not to damage the oil seal with the splines of the shaft.

To install:

12. Replace circlip on the end of the shaft. Install the halfshaft into the front differential case and drive into position using a plastic hammer.

13. Install the front hub/knuckle and bearing assembly.

14. Install the upper ball joint to the knuckle and torque retaining nut to 130 ft. lbs. (180 Nm). Install the lower ball joint to knuckle and torque retaining nut to 65 ft. lbs. (90 Nm). Install new cotter pin.

15. Install the tie rod end to the steering knuckle and torque to 33 ft. lbs. (45 Nm). Install new cotter pin.

16. Install the shim and snapring to the axle shaft. Install the front hub cover.

17. Install front brake caliper assembly.

18. Install the tire and wheel assembly. Install skid plate, if removed.

Expo

NOTE: If the vehicle is going to be rolled while the halfshafts are out of the vehicle, obtain 2 outer CV-joints or proper equivalent tools and install to the hubs. If the vehicle is rolled without the proper torque applied to the front wheel bearings, the bearings will no longer be usable.

1. Disconnect the negative battery cable.

2. Remove the cotter pin, halfshaft nut and washer.

3. Raise the vehicle and support safely. Remove the lower ball joint

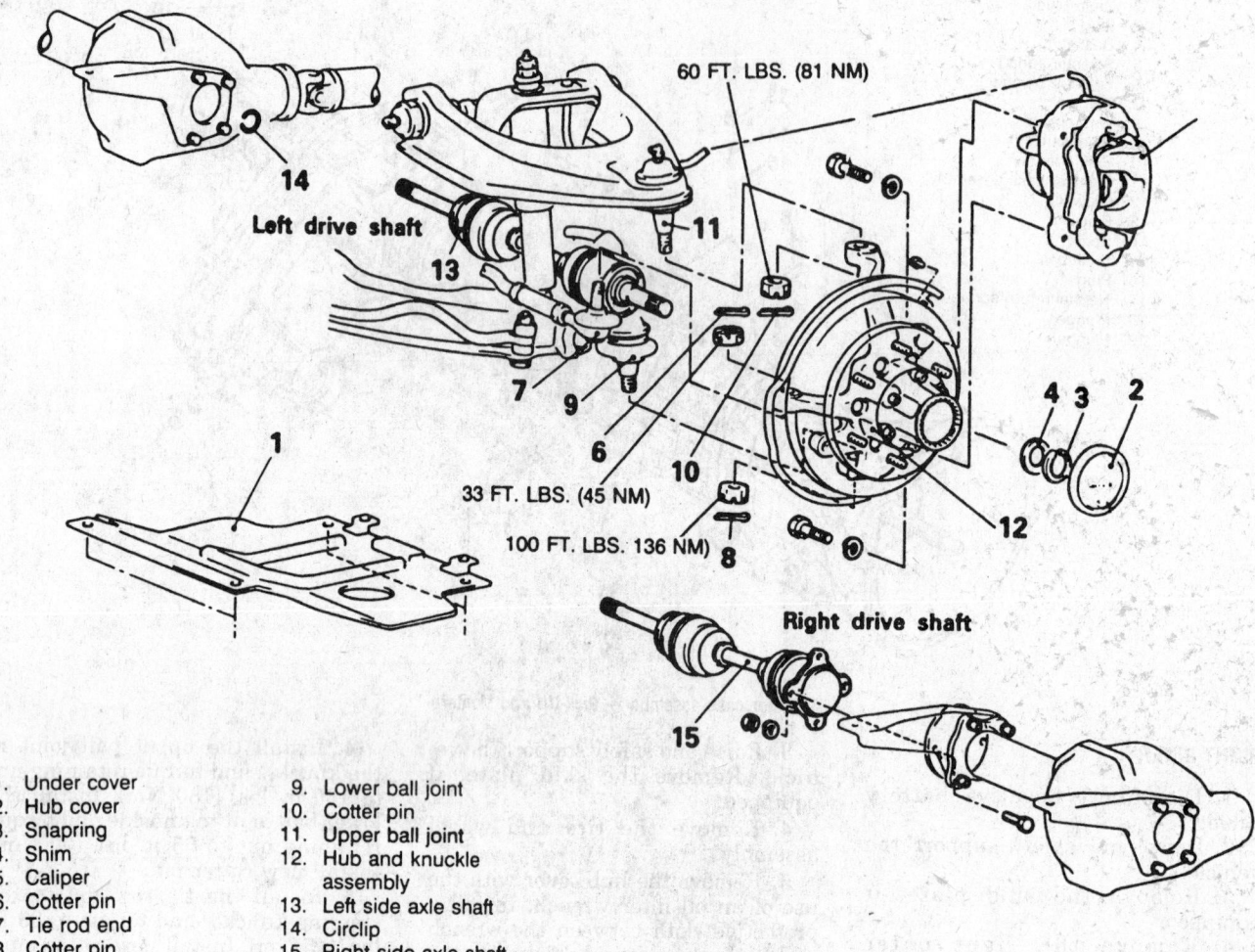

60 FT. LBS. (81 NM)

Left drive shaft

14

11

13

7   9

6

10

1

33 FT. LBS. (45 NM)

100 FT. LBS. 136 NM)   8

4 3 2

12

Right drive shaft

15

1. Under cover
2. Hub cover
3. Snapring
4. Shim
5. Caliper
6. Cotter pin
7. Tie rod end
8. Cotter pin
9. Lower ball joint
10. Cotter pin
11. Upper ball joint
12. Hub and knuckle assembly
13. Left side axle shaft
14. Circlip
15. Right side axle shaft

7911D082

Front axle shafts and related parts

and the tie rod end from the steering knuckle.

4. On vehicles with an inner shaft, remove the center support bearing bracket bolts and washers.

5. On vehicles with an inner shaft, remove the halfshaft by setting up a puller on the outside wheel hub and pushing the halfshaft from the front hub. Then tap the shaft union at the joint case with a plastic hammer to remove the halfshaft shaft and inner shaft from the transaxle.

6. On vehicles without an inner shaft, remove the halfshaft by setting up a puller on the outside wheel hub and pushing the halfshaft from the

front hub. After pressing the outer shaft, insert a prybar between the transaxle case and the halfshaft and pry the shaft from the transaxle. Do not pull on the shaft; doing so damages the inboard joint. Do not insert the prybar too far or the oil seal in the case may be damaged.

To install:

7. Inspect the halfshaft boot for damage or deterioration. Check the ball joints and splines for wear.

8. Replace the circlips on the ends of the halfshafts.

9. Insert the halfshaft into the transaxle. Make sure it is fully seated.

10. Pull the strut assembly out and install the other end to the hub.

11. Install the center bearing bracket bolts and tighten to 33 ft. lbs. (45 Nm).

12. Install the washer so the chamfered edge faces outward. Install the nut and tighten temporarily.

13. Install the tie rod end and ball joint.

14. Install the wheel and lower the vehicle to the floor. Tighten the axle nut with the brakes applied. Tighten the nut to a maximum torque of 188 ft. lbs. (260 Nm). Install the cotter pin and bend to secure.

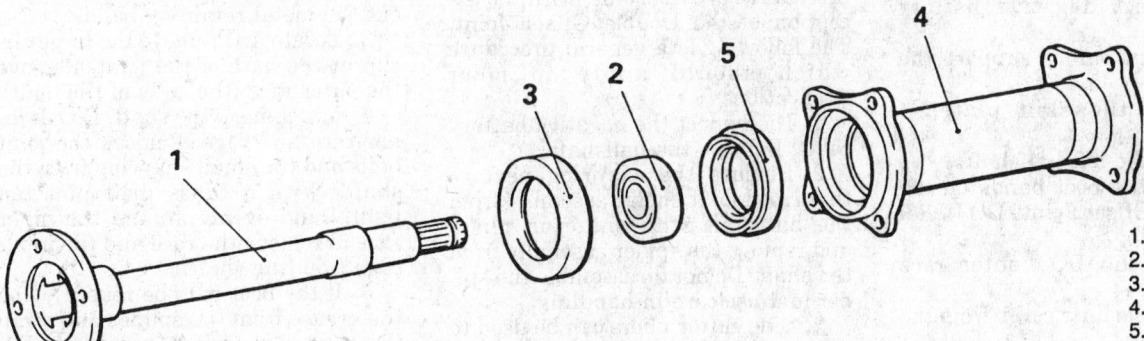

1. Inner shaft
2. Bearing
3. Dust cover
4. Housing tube
5. Dust seal

7911D083

Inner axle shaft and tube

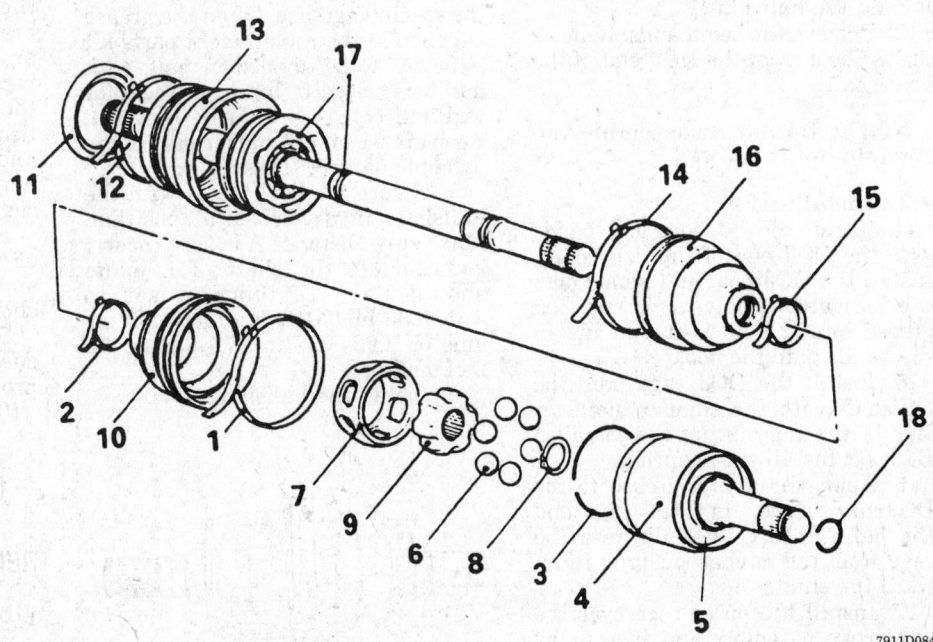

1. Boot band
2. Boot band
3. Circlip
4. DOJ outer race
5. Dust cover
6. Balls
7. DOJ cage
8. Snapring
9. DOJ inner race
10. DOJ boot
11. Dust cover
12. Boot protector band
13. Boot protector
14. Boot band
15. Boot band
16. BJ boot
17. Drive shaft and BJ
18. Circlip

7911D084

Front halfshaft assembly — 4WD Pick-Up and Montero

CV-Boot

REMOVAL AND INSTALLATION

Pick-Up and Montero

1. Disconnect negative battery cable.
2. Raise and safely support the vehicle.
3. Remove the skid plate, if equipped.
4. Remove the left halfshaft.
5. Remove the boot bands on the inner Double Offset Joint (DOJ). Remove the circlip.
6. Remove the DOJ outer race from the shaft.
7. Remove the dust cover from the DOJ outer race.
8. Remove the balls from the DOJ cage prying from the inside of the cage outward.
9. Rotate the cage while pushing toward the Birfield Joint (BJ). The cage will drop down to expose a snapring on the halfshaft. Remove the snapring.
10. Remove the DOJ cage and inner race from the halfshaft.
11. Wrap tape over the threads of the halfshaft. Remove the boot from the shaft.
12. Remove the dust cover from the BJ and the halfshaft.
13. Remove the boot bands. Remove the BJ boot from the DOJ end of the driveshaft.

NOTE: Do not disassemble the Birfield Joint (BJ).

To install:

14. Install the BJ boot and bands over the DOJ end of the driveshaft. Install the DOJ boot and bands onto the halfshaft. Apply ½ of supplied grease into the BJ boot and install the bands onto the boot.
15. Install the DOJ cage onto the halfshaft with the smaller diameter side of the cage facing the installed BJ boot. Install the snapring.
16. Apply remaining grease to the DOJ inner race, the DOJ cage and the balls. Insert the balls into the cage from the outside pushing in toward the shaft.
17. Install the outer race over the DOJ cage assembly and install the retaining circlip.
18. Install the dust cover into place and install the boot bands.
19. Install the halfshaft into the vehicle.
20. Install the skid plate, if equipped.

Expo

EXCEPT DOUBLE OFF-SET JOINT

Although joint types vary, the basic procedures are the same, with the exception of the Double Offset Joint. The following is a general procedure which should apply to most applications.

1. Disconnect the negative battery cable. Remove the halfshaft.
2. Remove the snapring next to the tripod joint spider assembly from the halfshaft with snapring pliers and remove the spider assembly from the shaft. Do not disassemble the spider and use care in handling.
3. Side cutter pliers can be used to cut the metal retaining bands.
4. If the boot is be reused, wrap vinyl tape around the spline part of the shaft so the boot will not be damaged when removed. Remove the dynamic damper, if used, and boots from the shaft.

To install:

5. Double check that the correct replacement parts are being installed. Wrap vinyl tape around the splines to protect the boot and install the boots and damper, if used, in the correct order.
6. Fill the inside of the boot with the specified grease. Often the grease supplied in the replacement parts kit is meant to be divided in half, with half being used to lubricate the joint and half being used inside the boot. Keep grease off the rubber part of the dynamic damper (if used).
7. Secure the boot bands with the halfshaft in a horizontal position. Make sure Distance A is set properly according to the chart. T.J. joints should have Distance A set to 3.11–3.35 in. (79–85mm) for 1.8L engine or 3.03–3.27 in. (77–83mm) for 2.4L engine.
8. Install the halfshaft.

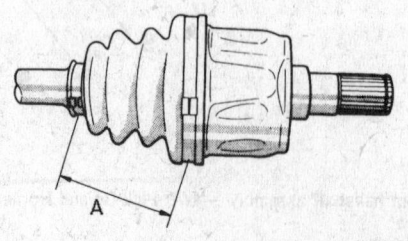

84701106

CV-joint measured distance

DOUBLE OFF-SET JOINT

1. Remove the halfshaft. The Double Off-set Joint (D.O.J.) is bigger than other joints and in these applications, is only used as an inboard joint.
2. Side cutter pliers can be used to cut the metal retaining bands.
3. Locate and remove the large circlip at the base of the joint. Remove the outer race (the body of the joint).
4. Matchmark the shaft, D.O.J. inner race and cage. Remove the joint balls and the small snapring from the shaft. With a brass drift pin, tap lightly and evenly around the inner race to remove the race and the inner cage from the shaft.
5. If the boot is to be reused, wipe the grease from the splines and wrap the splines in vinyl tape before sliding the boot from the shaft.

To install:

6. Be sure to tape the shaft splines before installing the boots. Fill the inside of the boot with the specified grease. Often the grease supplied in the replacement parts kit is meant to be divided in half, with half being used to lubricate the joint and half being used inside the boot.
7. Install the cage onto the halfshaft so the small diameter side of the cage is installed first. Align the matchmarks made at disassembly on the inner race and shaft. With a brass drift pin, tap lightly and evenly around the inner race to install the race until it comes into contact with the rib of the shaft. Apply the specified grease to the inner race and cage and fit them together aligning the matchmarks. Insert the balls into the cage.
8. Install the outer race (the body of the joint) after filling with the specified grease. The outer race should be filled with this grease.
9. Tighten the boot bands securely. Make sure Distance A is set properly according to the chart.
10. Install the halfshaft.

Driveshaft and U-Joints

REMOVAL AND INSTALLATION

Pick-Up and Montero

1. If equipped with 4WD, place the free-wheeling hub in the free condition by placing the transfer lever in the **2H** position and moving in reverse for about 6 or 7 feet.
2. Disconnect negative battery cable.

DISTANCE A—SUMMIT

TRIPOD JOINTS

1.5L, 1.6L w/A.T.,	LH Shaft—3.15 in. ±.12 in. (80mm ± 3mm)
	RH Shaft—3.35 in. ±.12 in. (85mm ± 3mm)
1.6L, w/M.T.,	—3.35 in. ±.12 in. (80mm ± 3mm)

DOUBLE OFFSET JOINTS

1.6L Non Turbo	—2.92 in. ±.12 in. (75mm ± 3mm)
1.6L Turbo	—3.15 in. ±.12 in. (80mm ± 3mm)

DISTANCE A—LASER/TALON

1.8L from 5-89	LH Shaft—2.95 in. ±.12 in. (75mm ± 3mm)
1.8L from 5-89	RH Shaft—3.35 in. ±.12 in. (85mm ± 3mm)
2.0L from 5-89	2WD-LH Shaft—3.15 in. ±.12 in. (80mm ± 3mm)
2.0L Turbo	2WD LH Shaft—3.15 in. ±.12 in. (80mm ± 3mm)
2.0L	2WD RH Shaft—3.15 in. ±.12 in. (80mm ± 3mm)
2.0L Turbo	2WD RH Shaft—3.15 in. ±.12 in. (80mm ± 3mm)
2.0L	4WD LH Shaft—3.35 in. ±.12 in. (85mm ± 3mm)
2.0L	4WD RH Shaft—3.35 in. ±.12 in. (85mm ± 3mm)

84701107

CV-joint measurements — installed length

3. Raise and safely support the vehicle.

4. Remove the skid plate, if equipped.

5. Matchmark the flange yoke and the differential companion flange. Do not damage the oil seals when marking positions.

6. Drain the transfer case. Position a drain pan under the transmission tailshaft, as required. Fluid will leak from unit on removal of the driveshaft.

7. Remove the retaining bolts and nuts from the flange(s) and remove the shaft from the vehicle.

8. Remove the U-Joint from the driveshaft as follows:

a. Make mating marks on the yokes of the universal joint that is to be disassembled.

b. Remove the snaprings from the yoke. When disassembling, note the position of the snaprings so they may be reinstalled in the same positions.

c. Remove the grease fitting from the journal.

d. Remove the journal bearings from the propeller shaft yoke using tool MB990840-01.

e. Remove the journal and the flange yoke or sleeve yoke from the shaft.

9. Inspect the propeller shaft yokes for wear, cracks or damage. Check the sleeve yoke and the flange yoke for wear, cracks or damage. Replace as required.

To install:

10. Install the U-Joint on the driveshaft as follows:

a. Install the sleeve yoke or flange yoke to the journal and the assembly to the driveshaft.

b. Align the mating marks on the yokes and press the journal bearings to the yoke using tool MB990840-01.

c. Install the snaprings in the position prior to removal. Install the grease fitting.

d. Measure the clearance between the snaprings and the journal bearing. If the clearance is larger than 0.0024 in. (0.06mm), it will be necessary to replace the snapring.

11. With the mating marks aligned, install the driveshaft into the transfer case/transmission and the companion flange.

12. Clean the mounting nuts and bolts and install to the flange(s). Torque to 43 ft. lbs. (60 Nm).

13. Install the skid plate, if equipped.

Expo AWD

1. Disconnect the battery negative cable.

2. Raise the vehicle and support safely. Drain the oil from the transfer assembly.

3. Disconnect the front exhaust pipe.

4. Make mating marks on the differential companion flange and the flange yoke. Remove the locking nut from the center support and remove the propeller shaft. Make note of washers and spacers used so they can be reinstalled in their original location.

NOTE: Remove the propeller shaft in a straight and level manner so as to ensure that the boot is not damaged through pinching. Damage can be avoided if a piece of cloth or similar material is inserted into the boot. Cover the opening of the transfer assembly to prevent dirt from entering the transfer assembly.

5. Installation is the reverse of the removal procedure. Tighten the rear flange bolts and nuts to 22–25 ft. lbs. (30–35 Nm), the locking nuts on the center support to 22 ft. lbs. (30 Nm), refill the transfer assembly and check the fluid level in the transaxle assembly.

Rear Axle Shaft, Bearing and Seal

REMOVAL AND INSTALLATION

Pick-Up and Montero

1. Raise the vehicle and support safely.

2. Remove the rear tire and wheel assembly.

3. Remove the brake drum.

4. Disconnect the parking brake cable from the brake shoe and remove from the backing plate.

5. Disconnect and plug the brake line(s) at the wheel cylinder.

6. Remove the 4 nuts behind the backing plate.

7. Remove the backing plate, bearing case and the axle shaft as an assembly. If not possible by hand, use a slide hammer to remove the assembly.

8. Remove the O-ring and the bearing preload shims. Save the preload shims for reassembly.

9. Remove the oil seal from the axle tube with a hooked slide hammer.

10. To remove the axle shaft bearing, remove the notched locknut with tool MB990785–01 or a brass drift.

11. Remove the lock washer and flat washer.

12. Screw the locknut onto the axle shaft about 3 turns.

13. If tool MB990787–01 is not available, it will be necessary to fabricate a metal plate that fits over the axle shaft and butts the locknut. Drill 4 holes in the plate that align with the 4 bearing case studs and fit the plate. Refit 2 nuts and washers to the bearing case studs diagonally across from each other and tighten them evenly to release the bearing case and bearing.

14. Use a hammer and drift to remove the bearing outer race from the bearing case.

15. Remove the outer oil seal from the bearing case.

To install:

16. Apply grease to the outer surface on the bearing outer race and the lip of the outer oil seal. Drive into the bearing case.

17. Slide the bearing case and bearing over the rear axle shaft. Apply grease on the bearing rollers and install the inner race by pressing into place. Be careful not to damage the dust cover.

18. Pack the bearing with grease.

19. Install the washer, the crowned lock washer and the locknut in that order and torque the locknut to 130–159 ft. lbs. (176–220 Nm).

20. Bend the tab on the lock washer into the groove on the locknut. If the tab and the groove do not line up, tighten locknut slightly.

21. Lubricate and drive the new inner oil seal into place. Refit the assembly.

22. Install a new O-ring and the shims. Apply silicone rubber sealant to the face of the bearing case.

23. Install the entire assembly to the axle housing. Torque the retaining nuts to 40 ft. lbs. (54 Nm).

24. Check the axle shaft endplay. If not between 0.002–0.008 in. (0.05–0.20mm), proceed with the axle shaft endplay adjustment procedure.

25. Install all removed brake parts and bleed the system.

26. Install the tire and wheel assembly and road test the vehicle. Check for leaks.

Expo AWD

1. Disconnect the negative battery cable. Raise the vehicle and support safely.

2. Remove the bolts that attach the rear halfshaft to the rear carrier.

3. Remove the cotter pin, driveshaft nut cover and nut from the rear driveshaft.

NOTE: Do not apply the vehicle weight to the wheel bearing while loosening the driveshaft nut or bearing damage may occur.

4. Separate the shaft from the hub using a puller. Remove the shaft from the flange and lift from the vehicle.

5. Installation is the reverse of the removal procedure. Torque the retainers on the rear carrier to 40–47 ft. lbs. (55–65 Nm) and the shaft end nut to 145–188 ft. lbs. (200–260 Nm).

ENDPLAY ADJUSTMENT PROCEDURE

Pick-Up and Montero

1. Begin with the left side rear axle assembly and insert a 0.04 in. (1mm) shim between the bearing case and the axle shaft housing. Torque the nuts to specification.

2. Install the right side axle assembly into the right side housing without its shim and O-ring. Torque the 4 nuts to about 50 inch. lbs. (5.6 Nm).

3. Using a feeler gauge, measure the gap between the bearing case and the axle housing face.

4. Remove the axle shaft and select a shim or shims that is the equal to the sum of the clearance measured in Step 3 plus 0.002–0.008 in. (0.05–0.20mm) and install them on the housing. Install the O-ring and apply sealant.

5. Install the axle assembly and torque the nuts to 40 ft. lbs. (54 Nm).

6. Measure the endplay and complete the installation procedure.

Expo AWD

1. Release the parking brake. Raise the vehicle and support safely.

2. Remove the wheel and brake drum or rotor.

3. Place a dial indicator to the hub and measure the endplay when the axle hub is moved in the axial direction (in and out).

4. The endplay should not exceed 0.002 in. (0.05mm). If so, replace the wheel bearing assembly.

Front Wheel Hub, Knuckle and Bearings

REMOVAL AND INSTALLATION

2WD Pick-Up

1. Raise the vehicle and support safely. Remove the tire and wheel assembly.

2. Remove the brake caliper, pads and adaptor and position them out of the way.

3. Remove the grease cap.

4. Remove the cotter pin, castellated nut and washer. Remove the outer bearing.

5. Remove the front hub/rotor assembly from the steering knuckle. Remove the grease seal and inner bearing from the hub. Remove the splash shield.

6. Remove the nuts and bolts that attach the hub to the rotor and separate them. Clean out all of the old grease from the inside of the hub.

7. Remove the shock and stabilizer bar from the lower control arm, if equipped.

8. Support the lower control arm. Compress the coil spring with the special spring compressor, if equipped. Separate the ball joints and tie rod end from the knuckle.

9. Remove the steering knuckle.

To install:

10. Install the knuckle to the ball joint studs. Torque all ball joint nuts, except the upper nut on Pick-Up to 100 ft. lbs. (136 Nm). Torque the nut on Pick-Up to 60 ft. lbs. (82 Nm). Install new cotter pins. Remove the spring compressor, if used. Install the shoes.

11. Connect the stabilizer bar to the lower control arm. Tighten the nut until the bushing is the same diameter as the washer.

12. Connect the tie rod end to the knuckle. Torque the nut to 30 ft. lbs. (41 Nm). Install a new cotter pin.

13. Assemble the rotor and front hub. Torque the nuts to 40 ft. lbs. (54 Nm).

14. Apply wheel bearing grease to the inside of the front hub.

15. Pack the inner bearing and install into hub.

16. Install a new oil seal into the hub so it is flush with the hub end face.

17. Install the assembly onto the steering knuckle, pack and install the outer bearing.

18. Install the washer and castellated nut. Spin the rotor and torque the nut to 22 ft. lbs. (30 Nm), loosen

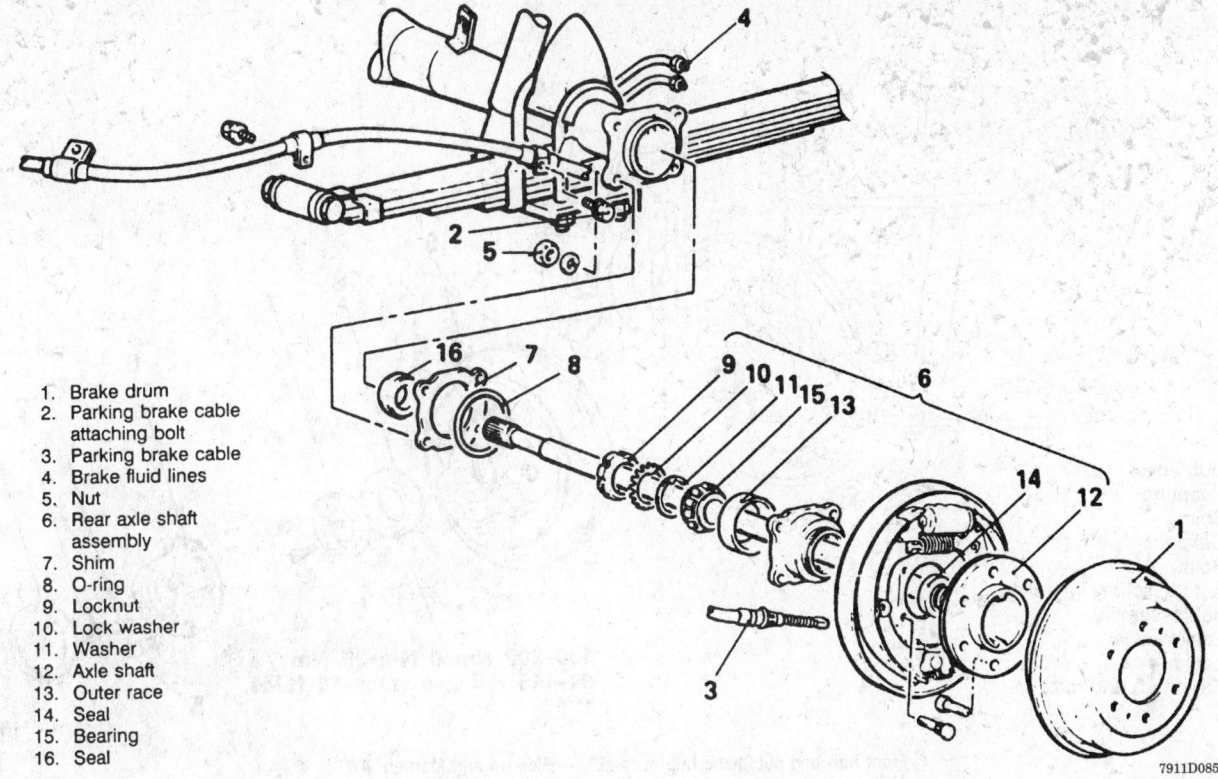

1. Brake drum
2. Parking brake cable attaching bolt
3. Parking brake cable
4. Brake fluid lines
5. Nut
6. Rear axle shaft assembly
7. Shim
8. O-ring
9. Locknut
10. Lock washer
11. Washer
12. Axle shaft
13. Outer race
14. Seal
15. Bearing
16. Seal

Rear axle shaft assembly — Pick-Up and Montero

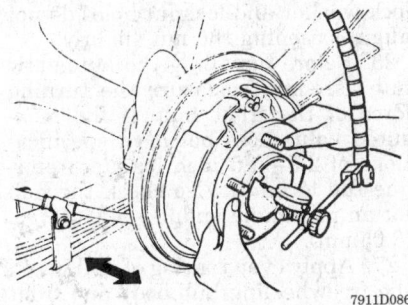

Measuring axle shaft endplay

completely and retighten to 6 ft. lbs. (8 Nm) while turning the wheel.

19. Install a new cotter pin and install the grease cap.

20. Install the brake hardware and bleed the system, if opened.

21. Install the tire and wheel assembly and road test the vehicle.

Automatic Locking Hubs, Knuckle and Bearings

REMOVAL AND INSTALLATION

Pick-Up and Montero 4WD

1. Place the free-wheeling hub in the free condition by placing the transfer lever in the **2H** position and moving in reverse for about 6 or 7 feet.

2. Disconnect negative battery cable.

3. Raise and safely support the vehicle. Remove the skid plate, if equipped.

4. Remove the tire and wheel assembly.

5. Remove the hub cover with the use of an oil filter wrench. Install a protective cloth between the wrench and the cover to avoid damage to the cover.

6. Remove the snapring from the inside of the hub. Remove the shim.

7. Remove the front brake caliper and brake pads from the vehicle. Do not allow the caliper to hang from the brake hose.

8. Using hexagonal wrench, remove the automatic free wheeling hub assembly.

9. Remove the retaining screws from lock washer and remove lock washer.

10. Remove the outer bearing and front hub assembly from the steering knuckle.

11. Remove the inner oil seal and inner bearing from the hub assembly.

12. To separate the hub from the brake disc, matchmark the brake disc to the front hub. Remove the retaining bolts and separate the hub from the disc.

13. Remove the dust cover from the spindle. Separate the tie rod from the steering knuckle.

14. Separate the upper and lower ball joints from the steering knuckle.

15. Remove the knuckle from the axle shaft.

16. Remove the knuckle oil seal and spacer. If damaged, drive out the needle bearing through the spindle end of the knuckle.

To install:

17. Use Mitsubishi tool MB990985 to press the new needle bearing into the knuckle. Lubricate the rollers and install the spacer with the chamfered side facing the center of the vehicle. Install a new seal until it is flush with the knuckle end face and lubricate the l

18. Install the knuckle to the ball joint studs. Torque all ball joint nuts

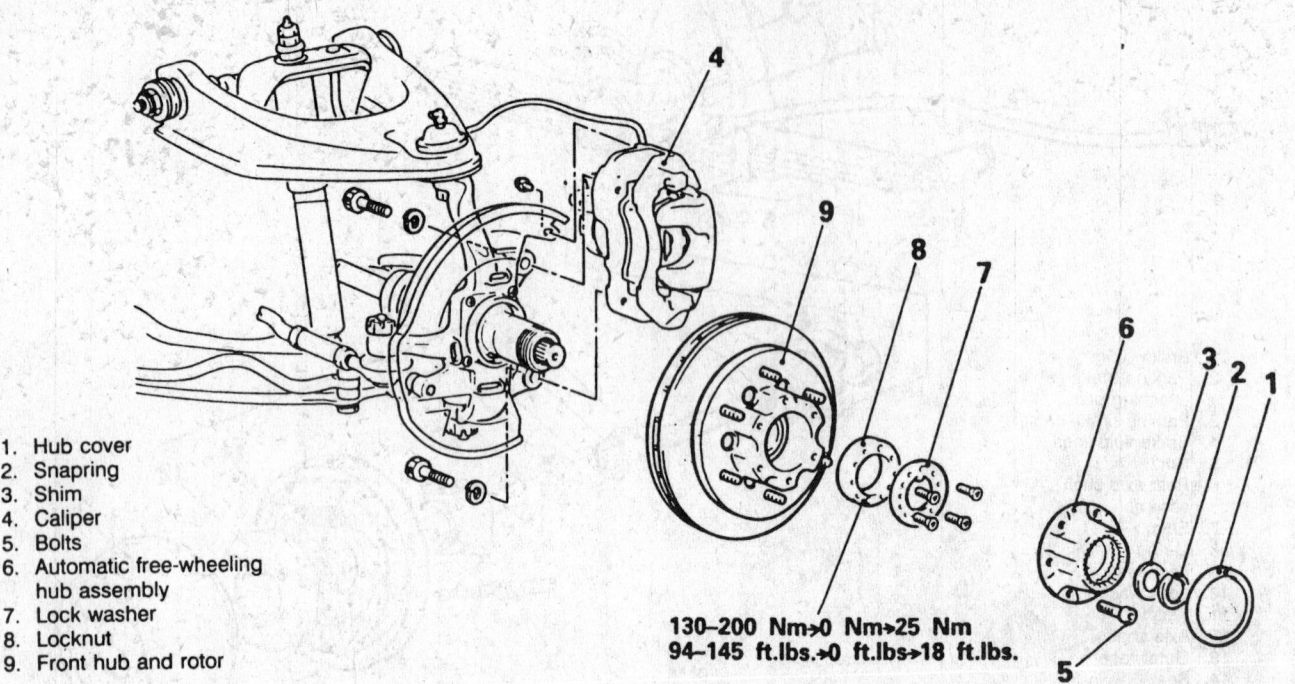

1. Hub cover
2. Snapring
3. Shim
4. Caliper
5. Bolts
6. Automatic free-wheeling hub assembly
7. Lock washer
8. Locknut
9. Front hub and rotor

130–200 Nm→0 Nm→25 Nm
94–145 ft.lbs.→0 ft.lbs→18 ft.lbs.

7911D087

Front hub and automatic hub assembly — Pick-Up and Montero 4WD

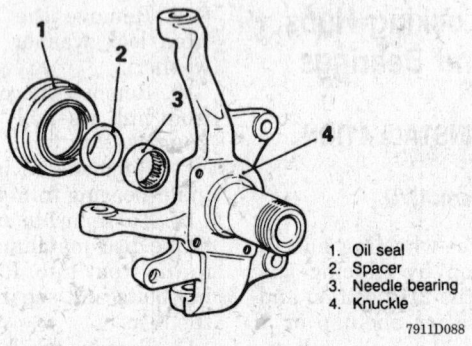

1. Oil seal
2. Spacer
3. Needle bearing
4. Knuckle

7911D088

Steering knuckle, needle bearing, spacer and seal —
Pick-Up and Montero 4WD

except the upper nut on Pick-Up to 100 ft. lbs. (136 Nm). Torque the nut on Pick-Up to 60 ft. lbs. (82 Nm). Install new cotter pins.

19. Connect the tie rod end to the knuckle. Torque the nut to 30 ft. lbs. (41 Nm). Install a new cotter pin.

20. Clean out all of the old grease from inside the front hub.

21. Bolt the rotor and front hub together. Torque the nuts to 40 ft. lbs. (54 Nm). Install new races and apply wheel bearing grease to the inside of the front hub.

22. Pack the inner bearing and install to the race.

23. Install new oil seal into the front hub until it is flush with the front hub end face.

24. Install the assembly onto the steering knuckle, pack and install the outer bearing with grease. Using special tool MB990954 or equivalent, which fits standard torque wrenches, torque the locknut to 95–145 ft. lbs. (130–200 Nm). Loosen the locknut completely, then retorque to 18 ft. lbs. (25 Nm). To complete the procedure, position the torque wrench at the 3 o'clock position and loosen the nut 30 degrees.

25. Install the lock washer. If the lock washer and locknut holes do not align, loosening the nut slightly.

26. Before installing the automatic hub assembly, measure the turning force of the front hub. If the measured value does not meet specifications of 2.5–11.5 inch lbs. and retorque the locknut. Also check the hub for an maximum endplay of 0.002 in. (0.05mm).

27. Apply even coating of sealant on the freewheeling hub body and front hub contact surface. Align the key of the brake and the keyway of the spindle and loosely install the automatic free wheeling hub assembly. The mounting surfaces of the automatic hub and the front hub must be perfectly flush before the mounting bolts are torqued.

28. Torque the automatic hub mounting bolts to 40 ft. lbs. (54 Nm).

29. Check the front hub turning resistance again. If the difference between the reading in Step 26 and this reading is more than 8.7 inch lbs., repair or replace the automatic hub, as required.

30. Install the shim and snapring. Rotate the axle shaft forward and backward and stop at a position midway between 2 heavy spots where there is a heavy feeling.

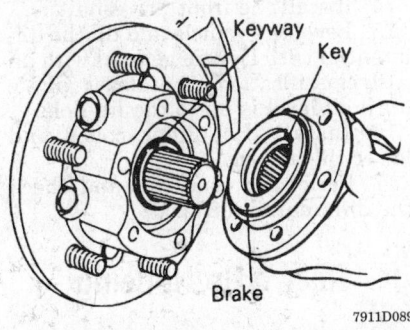

Aligning the key in the automatic hub with the keyway in the spindle

31. Set a dial indicator so the pin is resting on the end of the axle shaft. The endplay specification is 0.008–0.020 in. (0.2–0.5mm). If not within specifications, adjust by adding or removing shims.

32. Install the hub cover.

33. Install the brake hardware and install the wheel and tire assembly.

34. Road test the vehicle.

Expo

1. Disconnect the negative battery cable.

2. Remove the cotter pin, halfshaft nut and washer.

3. Raise the vehicle and support safely. If equipped with ABS, remove the front wheel speed sensor. Remove the ball joint and tie rod end from the steering knuckle.

4. Remove the caliper and brake pads and suspend with a wire.

5. On vehicles with an inner shaft, remove the center support bearing bracket bolts and washers. Remove the halfshaft by setting up a puller on the outside wheel hub and pushing the halfshaft from the front hub. Then tap the joint case with a plastic hammer to remove the halfshaft shaft and inner shaft from the transaxle.

6. On vehicles without an inner shaft, remove the halfshaft by setting up a puller on the outside wheel hub and pushing the halfshaft from the front hub. After pressing the outer shaft, insert a prybar between the transaxle case and the halfshaft and pry the shaft from the transaxle.

7. Unbolt the lower end of the strut and remove the hub and steering knuckle assembly.

8. Set up a puller with the knuckle/hub in a vise and pull the hub from the knuckle. Do not use a hammer to accomplish this or the bearing will be damaged.

9. Once the hub and outer bearing inner race are removed with a puller,

the bearing outer races can be removed by tapping out with a brass drift pin and a hammer.

To install:

10. Assemble the hub/knuckle assembly with pressing tools, using new parts as required.

11. Install the knuckle assembly to the vehicle and install the strut bolts.

12. Apply a thin coat of grease to the outside of the outer races and install into the hub with a bearing driver.

13. Apply multi-purpose grease to the bearings, inside surface of the hub and the lip of the grease seal. Place the outside bearing into the knuckle and install the seal with a driver.

14. The hub is assembled to the knuckle with a puller. Draw the parts together firmly to seat the bearings. Use a small torque wrench to check the bearing turning torque. It should be 11 lbs. or less. Check that the bearings feel smooth when rotated.

15. Apply a thin coat of grease to the lip of the halfshaft side axle seal and drive into place until it contacts the inner bearing outer race.

16. Replace the circlips on the ends of the halfshafts.

17. Insert the halfshaft into the transaxle. Make sure it is fully seated.

18. Pull the strut assembly out and install the other end to the hub.

19. Install the center bearing bracket bolts and tighten to 33 ft. lbs. (45 Nm).

20. Install the washer so the chamfered edge faces outward. Install the nut and tighten temporarily.

21. Install the tie rod end and ball joint.

22. Install the wheel and lower the vehicle to the floor. Tighten the axle nut with the brakes applied. Tighten the nut to a torque of 145–188 ft. lbs. (200–260 Nm). Install the cotter pin and bend to secure.

Pinion Seal

REMOVAL AND INSTALLATION

Pick-Up and Montero

1. Raise the vehicle and support safely.

2. Matchmark and remove the driveshaft.

3. Check the turning torque of the pinion before proceeding. It should be 3.5–4.5 inch lbs. (0.4–0.5 Nm). This is the torque that must be reached during installation of the pinion nut.

4. Using a pinion flange holding tool, remove the pinion nut and washer.

5. Remove the companion flange from the drive pinion.

6. Pry the pinion seal out of the differential carrier.

7. Clean and inspect the sealing surface of the housing.

To install:

8. Using a seal driver, drive the new seal into the housing until the flange on the seal is flush with the carrier.

9. With the seal installed, the pinion bearing preload must be set.

10. Tighten the pinion nut, while holding the flange, until the turning torque is the same as before removal of the nut. The final pinion nut torque must be 137–181 ft. lbs. (190–250 Nm).

11. Align the matchmarks and install the drive shaft.

12. Check the level of the differential lubricant.

Expo

FRONT DIFFERENTIAL

1. Disconnect the negative battery cable.

2. Remove the front halfshaft.

3. Using a prying tool, pry the seal from the case.

To install:

4. Apply a thin coat of multi-purpose grease to the seal lip and the seal contact surface.

5. Install the new seal with an appropriate driver.

6. Install the front halfshaft.

REAR DIFFERENTIAL

1. Raise the vehicle and support safely.

2. Matchmark the rear propeller shaft and companion flange and remove the shaft. Don't let it hang from the transaxle. Tie it up to the underbody.

3. Hold the companion flange stationary and remove the large self-locking nut in the center of the companion flange.

4. Using a puller, remove the flange. Pry the old seal out.

To install:

5. Apply a thin coat of multi-purpose grease to the seal lip and the companion flange seal contacting surface. Install the new seal with an appropriate driver.

6. Install the companion flange. Install a new locknut and torque to 137 ft. lbs. (190 Nm). The rotation torque of the drive pinion should be 10 inch lbs. (1.12 Nm) for new bear-

ings or 4 inch lbs. (0.448 Nm) for used bearings.

7. Install the propeller shaft.

Differential Carrier

REMOVAL AND INSTALLATION

Pick-Up and Montero

FRONT DIFFERENTIAL

1. Raise the vehicle and support safely. Remove the skid plate.
2. Remove both side outer and right side inner axle shafts.
3. Drain the front differential and remove the cover.
4. Remove the bearing cap retaining bolts, matchmark and remove the caps.
5. Pry the differential case out of the housing.
6. Label any loose parts as removed from the assembly.

To install:
7. Install the differential case to the housing.
8. Install the caps aligning the matchmarks made previously. Torque the retaining bolts evenly and gradually to 45 ft. lbs. (61 Nm).
9. Clean the sealing surfaces of the cover and the differential housing. Reseal the cover and install to the housing.
10. Install the axle shafts.
11. Level the vehicle and fill the differential with Hypoid gear oil with an API classification of at least GL-5, until oil level reaches hole.
12. Install the skid plate and lower the vehicle.
13. Perform a road test and check the differential for leaks.

REAR DIFFERENTIAL

1. Raise the vehicle and support safely. Drain the rear differential.
2. Remove the rear tire and wheel assemblies and brake drums.
3. Remove the axle shafts.
4. Matchmark and remove the driveshaft.
5. Remove the differential carrier retaining nuts and remove the carrier from the axle housing.
6. The installation is the reverse of the removal procedure. Torque the carrier retaining nuts to 22 ft. lbs. (27 Nm).

Expo AWD

1. Raise the vehicle and support safely.
2. Drain the differential gear oil and remove the center exhaust pipe.

3. Remove the rear halfshafts from the carrier and support out of the way.
4. Matchmark the differential companion flange and flange yoke for reference during installation and disconnect the propeller shaft from the carrier. Support shaft out of the way leaving attached to the transfer assembly.
5. Support the rear carrier assembly using the appropriate equipment. Remove the carrier mounting bolts and lower carrier from the vehicle.

To install:
6. Raise the rear carrier into position and torque the side retaining bolts to 72–87 ft. lbs. (100–120 Nm). Tighten the retainer bolts through the rear support member to 69 ft. lbs. (95 Nm).
7. Install the propeller shaft, with matchmarks aligned, and the rear halfshafts to the carrier. Tighten the halfshaft flange nuts to 40–47 ft. lbs. (55–65 Nm).
8. Install the center exhaust pipe using new gasket.
9. With the vehicle level, fill the rear differential.

Front Differential Housing

REMOVAL AND INSTALLATION

Pick-Up and Montero 4WD

1. Raise the vehicle and support safely. Remove the skid plate and drain the differential.
2. Remove the hubs and knuckles from the vehicle.
3. Remove the outer and inner axle shafts.
4. Matchmark and remove the front driveshaft.
5. Support the differential housing with a jack.
6. Remove the differential mounting brackets.
7. Remove the front suspension crossmember.
8. Lower the differential housing and remove from the vehicle.

To install:
9. Mount the housing safely on jack and raise into position.
10. Lubricate the bushings and install the crossmember and housing brackets.
11. Torque all crossmember mounting nuts and bolt to 80 ft. lbs. (109 Nm) and the housing bracket mounting bolts to 65 ft. lbs. (88 Nm).
12. Replace the circlips and install the axle shafts.
13. Install the knuckle and hub assemblies.

14. Install the front driveshaft.
15. Level the vehicle and fill the differential with Hypoid gear oil with an API classification of at least GL-5, until oil level is up to the fill hole.
16. Install the under cover and lower the vehicle.
17. Perform a road test and check the differential for leaks.

Rear Axle Housing

REMOVAL AND INSTALLATION

Except Expo and Montero with Coil Springs

1. Raise the vehicle and support safely. Drain the differential
2. Remove the tire and wheel assemblies. Remove the brake drums.
3. Remove the parking brake cable attaching bolts, disconnect the cables from the shoes and unclip them from the backing plates.
4. Disconnect the brake hose at the T-fitting.
5. Remove the load sensing proportioning valve spring support, if equipped.
6. Disconnect the breather hose, if equipped.
7. Matchmark and remove the driveshaft.
8. Place jack under the center of the differential housing and unbolt the shocks from their lower mounts.
9. Remove the U-bolts, shackle assemblies and remove the leaf springs.
10. Lower the axle and remove from vehicle.

To install:
11. Raise the axle assembly into position and install the leaf springs. Make sure the shackle nuts are on the inside of the shackles.
12. Install the lower shock mounting bolts.
13. Matchmark and install the driveshaft.
14. Install the breather hose, if equipped.
15. Connect the brake hose.
16. Connect the parking brake cables and install the retaining bolts.
17. Install the load sensing spring support and spring, if equipped.
18. Level the vehicle and fill the differential using Hypoid gear oil with an API classification of at least GL-5, until level reaches the fill hole.

NOTE: If equipped with a limited slip differential, add the proper amount of limited slip friction modifier additive before filling the differential with gear oil.

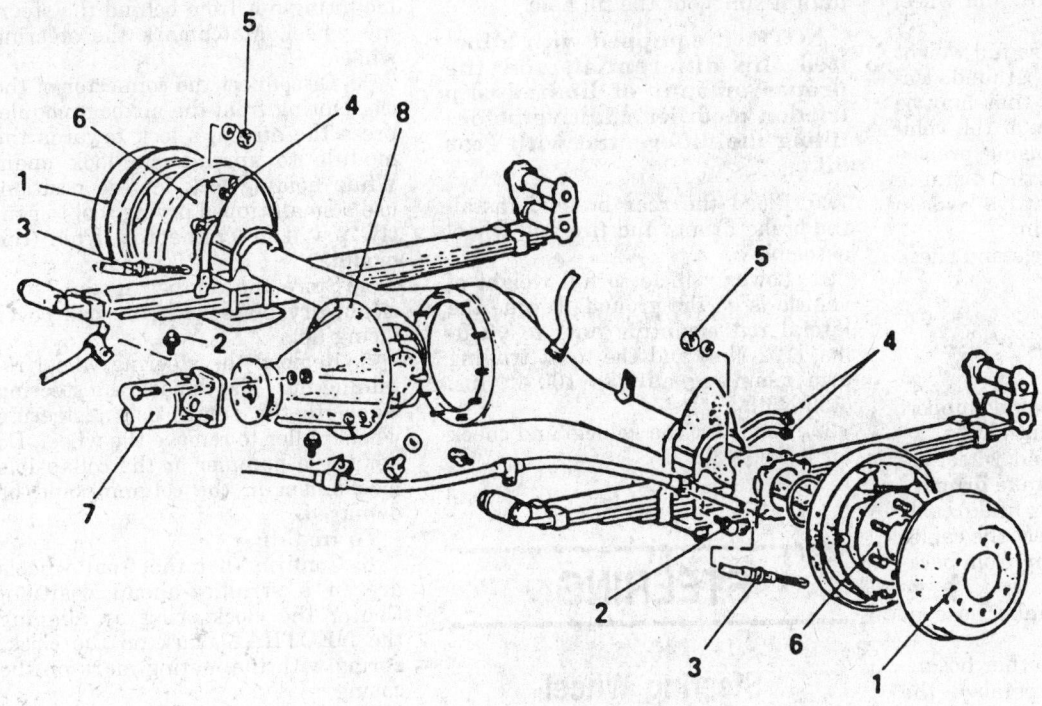

1. Brake drum
2. Parking brake cable attaching bolt
3. Parking brake cable
4. Brake fluid lines
5. Nut
6. Rear axle shaft
7. Driveshaft
8. Differential carrier

7911D090

Differential carrier removal and installation

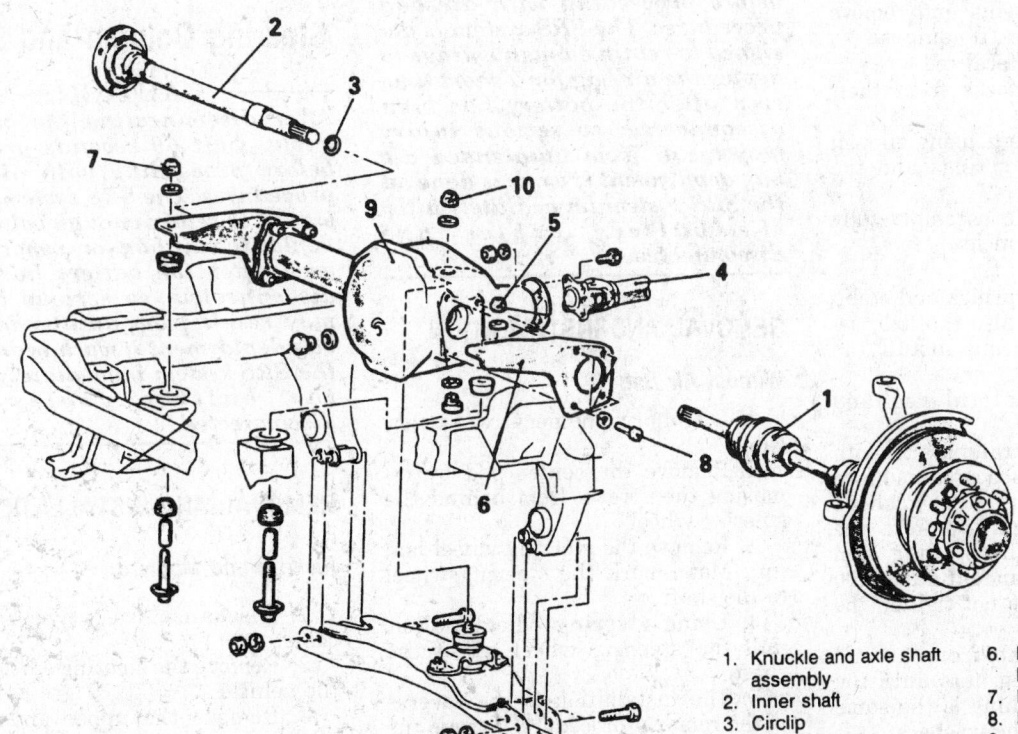

1. Knuckle and axle shaft assembly
2. Inner shaft
3. Circlip
4. Front driveshaft
5. Locknut
6. Left side mounting bracket
7. Locknut
8. Bolt
9. Crossmember
10. Locknut

7911D091

Front axle removal and installation

19. Bleed the rear brakes. Install the brake drums and tire and wheel assemblies.

20. Lower the vehicle so full weight of the vehicle is on the ground. Unload any excess weight that may be weighing down the rear of the vehicle. Adjust the load sensing proportioning valve lever so the distance from the proportioning valve lever to the spring support is 7 in.

21. Road test the vehicle and check for leaks.

Montero with Coil Springs

1. Raise the vehicle and support safely. Drain the differential.

2. Remove the tire and wheel assemblies. Remove the brake drums.

3. Remove the parking brake cable attaching bolts, disconnect the cables from the shoes and unclip from backing plates.

4. Disconnect the brake hose at the T-fitting.

5. Disconnect the breather hose.

6. Matchmark and remove the driveshaft.

7. Remove the rear stabilizer bar attaching bolts, links and bushings.

8. Place jack under the center of the differential housing and remove the rear trailing arm, if equipped.

9. Remove the lateral rod.

10. Unbolt the shocks from their lower mounts.

11. Lower the axle housing enough to remove the coil springs and the stabilizer bar.

12. Lower the axle assembly fully and remove from vehicle.

To install:

13. With the coil springs and stabilizer bar in place, raise the axle assembly into place and install the lower shock mounting bolts.

14. Install the lateral rod and tighten nuts loosely.

15. Assemble the trailing arm with its front mounting spacers, bushings and nuts. Make sure the washer's concave side faces away from the bushings. Install the trailing arm and torque the rear mount nuts to 90 ft. lbs. (122 Nm). Do not tighten the front mounting nuts yet.

16. Install the stabilizer bar and tighten the mounting nuts until the diameter of the bushing is the same as the diameter of the washers.

17. Install the driveshaft and breather hose.

18. Connect the parking brake cables and install the retaining bolts.

19. Level the vehicle and fill the differential with Hypoid gear oil with an API classification of at least GL–5, until it spills out the fill hole.

NOTE: If equipped with a limited slip differential, add the proper amount of limited slip friction modifier additive before filling the differential with gear oil.

20. Bleed the rear brakes. Install the brake drums and tire and wheel assemblies.

21. Lower vehicle so full weight of vehicle is on the ground. Torque the lateral rod mounting nuts to 90 ft. lbs. (122 Nm) and the front trailing arm mounting nuts to 100 ft. lbs. (150 Nm).

22. Road test the vehicle and check for leaks.

STEERING

Steering Wheel

——— CAUTION ———

After disconnecting the battery cable, wait 60 seconds or more before proceeding with air bag procedures. The SRS system is designed to retain enough voltage to deploy the air bag for a short time even after the battery has been disconnected, so serious injury may result from unintended air bag deployment if work is done on the SRS system immediately after the battery cables are disconnected.

REMOVAL AND INSTALLATION

Without Air Bag

1. Disconnect the negative battery cable.

2. Remove the center pad by removing the screws from behind the steering wheel.

3. Remove the steering wheel jam nut. Matchmark the steering wheel to the shaft.

4. Using steering wheel puller, pull the steering wheel off of the shaft.

5. The installation is the reverse of the removal procedure. Torque the shaft jam nut to 25–33 ft. lbs. (35–45 Nm).

With Air Bag

1. Disconnect the negative battery cable.

2. Remove the air bag module mounting nut from behind the steering wheel. Matchmark the steering wheel.

3. Disconnect the connector of the clockspring from the air bag module, press the air bag's lock towards the module to spread the lock open. While holding lock in this position, use a small tipped prying tool to gently pry the connector from the module.

4. Store the air bag module in a clean, dry place with the pad cover facing up.

5. Remove the steering wheel retaining nut. Matchmark the steering wheel to the shaft. Use a steering wheel puller to remove the wheel. Do not use a hammer or the collapsible mechanism in the column could be damaged.

To install:

6. Confirm that the front wheels are in a straight-ahead position. Center the clockspring by aligning the **NEUTRAL** mark on the clockspring with the mating mark on the casing.

7. Line up and install the steering wheel. Torque the retaining nut to 29 ft. lbs. (40 Nm).

Steering Column and Shaft

——— CAUTION ———

After disconnecting the battery cable, wait 60 seconds or more before proceeding with air bag procedures. The SRS system is designed to retain enough voltage to deploy the air bag for a short time even after the battery has been disconnected, so serious injury may result from unintended air bag deployment if work is done on the SRS system immediately after the battery cables are disconnected.

REMOVAL AND INSTALLATION

Pick-Up and Montero

1. Disconnect negative battery cable.

2. Remove the steering wheel from the vehicle.

3. Remove the upper and lower steering column covers.

4. Disconnect the electrical connectors at the base of the steering column.

5. Remove the gear indicator cable connection at the top of the steering column, if equipped.

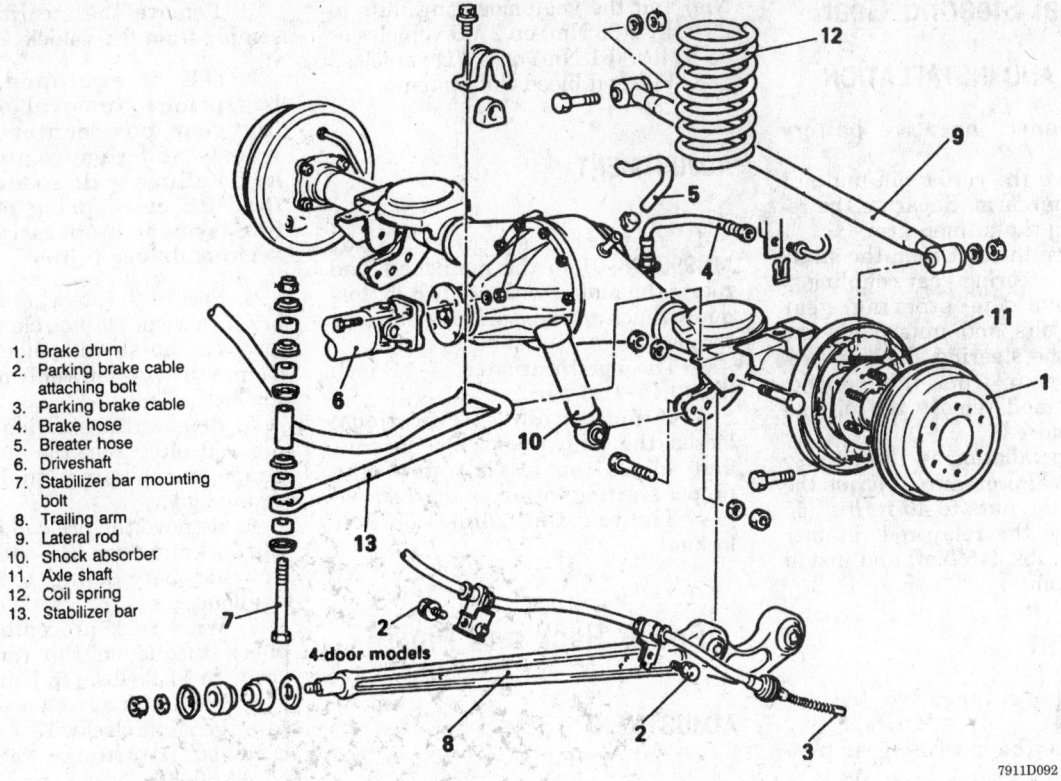

1. Brake drum
2. Parking brake cable attaching bolt
3. Parking brake cable
4. Brake hose
5. Breater hose
6. Driveshaft
7. Stabilizer bar mounting bolt
8. Trailing arm
9. Lateral rod
10. Shock absorber
11. Axle shaft
12. Coil spring
13. Stabilizer bar

4-door models

7911D092

Rear axle assembly — Montero with coil springs

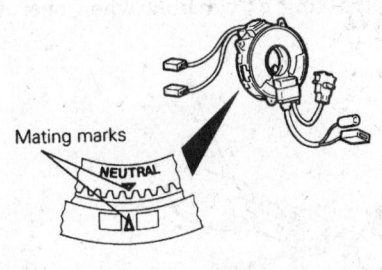

Mating marks

NEUTRAL

8547d016

Air bag clockspring "NEUTRAL" position indicator

6. Remove the brake pedal return spring from the lower portion of the steering column, if equipped.

7. Remove the bolt in the steering shaft coupler above the steering gear.

8. Remove the column retainer bolts at the floor panel and under the instrument panel. Remove the steering column and shaft from the vehicle.

To install:

9. Install the steering column into the vehicle positioning the steering shaft over the bevel gear or steering gear shaft.

10. Install the under dash retaining bolts loosely.

11. Install the bolt at the lower steering coupler and torque to 25 ft. lbs. (35 Nm).

12. Tighten the bolts under the instrument panel to 14 ft. lbs. (20 Nm). Install the bolts in the column retainer at the floor panel tightening to 4 ft. lbs. (6 Nm).

13. Reconnect the electrical connectors at the base of the steering column.

14. Connect the gear indicator cable, if removed.

15. Install the upper and lower steering column covers.

16. Align and install the steering wheel tightening the jam nut to 36 ft. lbs. (50 Nm).

17. Install the horn pad. Reconnect the negative battery cable and check operation of all related electrical components.

Expo

1. Disconnect the negative battery cable.

2. Remove the instrument panel undercover or knee protector.

3. Remove the trim clip, foot shower duct and lap shower duct.

4. Remove the steering wheel and air bag module as required. Remove the column upper and lower cover. Disconnect the key interlock cable if equipped.

5. Disconnect all connector to column-mounted items.

6. Remove the band from the steering joint cover. Remove the joint assembly and gear box connecting bolt.

7. Remove the screws that attach the rubber seal to the firewall.

8. Remove the lower and upper column mounting bolts.

9. Remove the steering column assembly.

To install:

10. Install the column so the splines are inserted around the rack input shaft. Install the pinch bolt.

11. Install the mounting bolts.

12. Install the rubber seal screws.

13. Connect the connectors and interlock cable.

14. Install the column covers.

15. Install the remaining interior pieces.

16. Connect the negative battery cable and check all column-mounted switches for proper operation.

Manual Steering Gear

REMOVAL AND INSTALLATION

1. Disconnect negative battery cable.

2. Remove the cotter pin and nut on the pitman arm. Separate the relay rod from the pitman arm.

3. Remove the bolt from the steering shaft to steering gear coupling.

4. Remove the steering gear mounting bolts and nuts, slide the gear from the steering shaft and remove the gear from the vehicle. Matchmark and remove the pitman arm, as required.

5. The installation is the reverse of the removal procedure. Torque the gear mounting nuts to 40 ft. lbs. (55 Nm). Torque the relay rod retainer nut to 33 ft. lbs. (45 Nm) and install new cotter pin.

ADJUSTMENT

1. Disconnect negative battery cable.

2. Remove the steering gear from the vehicle.

3. Turn the cross shaft 36 degrees. Position the mainshaft in the straight ahead position.

4. Using torque wrench, measure the starting torque of the mainshaft. The recommended value is 7.7–8.6 inch lbs. (0.9–1.0 Nm). If measured value is not within this value, Use tool MB990914 to screw adjusting cover to correct reading.

Power Steering Gear

REMOVAL AND INSTALLATION

1. Disconnect the negative battery cable. Raise the vehicle and support safely.

2. Fold back the dust boot which covers the steering shaft joint, if equipped. Remove the pinch bolt that holds the steering column shaft to the steering gear main shaft.

3. Remove the cotter pin, castellated nut the steering linkage from the pitman arm.

4. Disconnect and plug the fluid lines from the steering gear.

5. Remove the steering gear mounting nuts and remove the gear from the vehicle.

6. Matchmark and remove the pitman arm from the pitman shaft.

7. The installation is the reverse of the removal procedure. Torque the pitman arm nut to 100 ft. lbs. (136

Nm) and the gear mounting nuts to 28 ft. lbs. (38 Nm) on 2WD vehicles or 45 ft. lbs. (61 Nm) on 4WD vehicles.

8. Fill and bleed the system.

ADJUSTMENT

1. Attach special tool MB990228–01 to the mainshaft and rotate the pinion with an inch lb. torque wrench to measure the starting torque.

2. The specification is 4–11 inch lbs. (0.45–1.23 Nm).

3. If not within specifications, loosen the adjusting screw locknut and adjust the locknut until the proper starting torque is reached.

4. Tighten the adjusting bolt locknut.

Power Rack and Pinion

ADJUSTMENT

1. Disconnect the negative battery cable.

2. Raise the vehicle and support safely.

3. Remove the steering rack assembly from the vehicle.

NOTE: If equipped with air bag, prior to removal of the steering gear box, center the front wheels and remove the ignition key. Failure to do so may damage the SRS clockspring and render SRS system inoperative, risking serious driver injury.

4. Secure the steering rack assembly in a vise. Do not clamp the vise jaws on the steering housing tubes. Clamp the vise jaws only on the housing cast metal.

5. Remove the steering gear housing end plug from the steering gear shaft bore using tool 6103 or equivalent.

6. Remove the preload adjustment cap locknut from the steering gear housing bore using tool 6097 or equivalent.

7. With rack at center position, check torque on the rack support cover to 11 ft. lbs. (15 Nm).

8. With rack at center position, rotate the shaft clockwise 1 turn in 4–6 seconds. Return the rack support cover 30–60 degrees and adjust the total pinion torque to 5–11 inch lbs. Set the standard value at its highest value when adjusting. Assure no ratcheting or catching when operat-

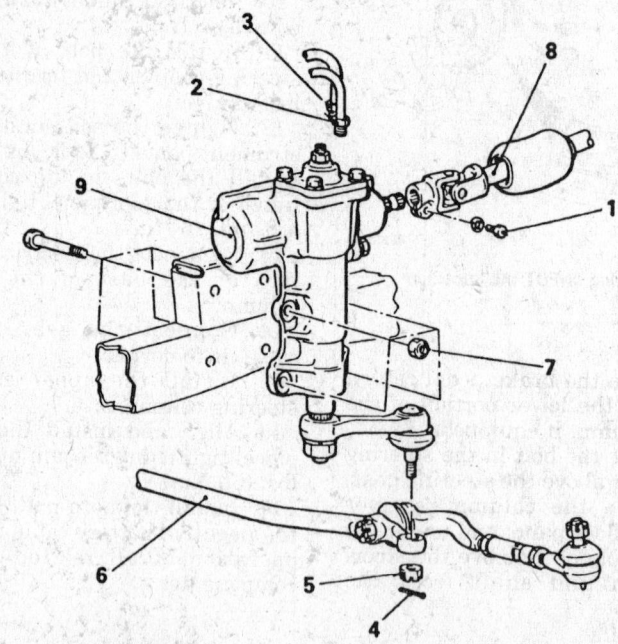

1. Pinch bolt
2. Pressure hose
3. Return hose
4. Cotter pin
5. Castellated nut
6. Steering linkage
7. Locknuts
8. Steering shaft
9. Power steering gear

7911D093

Power steering gear and related parts — Montero and Pick-Up

ing the rack towards the shaft direction.

9. Secure the preload adjustment cap with a new locknut using tool 6097 or equivalent. Do not allow the adjustment cap to rotate when tightening the locknut.

10. Install the end plug using tool 6103 or equivalent.

REMOVAL AND INSTALLATION

1. Disconnect the battery negative cable. Raise the vehicle and support safely.

2. Remove the pinch bolt holding the lower steering column joint to the rack and pinion input shaft.

3. Remove the cotter pins and disconnect the tie rod ends from the steering knuckle.

4. On Expo AWD, remove the transfer case rear bracket.

5. On 2.4L Expo with FWD, disconnect the stabilizer bar and remove as required.

6. Disconnect the power steering fluid pressure pipe and return hose from the rack fittings.

7. Remove the rack and pinion steering assembly and its rubber mounts.

To install:

8. Install the steering gear into the vehicle and secure using the retainer clamps and bolts.

9. Connect the power steering fluid lines to the rack fittings.

10. Install the stabilizer bar and rear transaxle bracket.

11. Connect the tie rod ends to the steering knuckles.

12. Connect the negative battery cable. Refill the reservoir and bleed the system.

13. Perform a front end alignment.

Power Steering Pump

REMOVAL AND INSTALLATION

Pick-Up and Montero

1. Disconnect the negative battery cable.

2. Position a drain pan under the power steering pump.

3. Disconnect the fluid lines from the pump and plug them.

4. Remove the front bracket attaching bolts and remove the belt from the pulley.

5. Remove the pump from the vehicle.

6. The installation is the reverse of the removal procedure.

7. Adjust the belt tension, as required.

8. Fill and bleed the system.

Expo

1. Disconnect the battery negative cable.

2. Remove the pressure switch connector from the side of the pump.

3. If the alternator is located under the oil pump, cover it with a shop towel to protect it from oil.

4. Disconnect the return fluid line. Remove the reservoir cap and allow the return line to drain the fluid from the reservoir. If the fluid is contaminated, disconnect the ignition high tension cable and crank the engine several times to drain the fluid from the gearbox.

5. For 2.4L engine, remove the alternator drive belt and the heat protector.

6. Disconnect the pressure line.

7. Remove the pump drive belt and unbolt the pump from its bracket.

To install:

8. Install the pump, wrap the belt around the pulley and tighten the bolts.

9. Replace the O-rings and connect the pressure line. Connect the pressure line so the notch in the fitting aligns and contacts the pump's guide bracket.

10. Connect the return line.

11. Connect the pressure switch connector.

12. Adjust the belt tension and tighten the adjusting bolts.

13. Refill the reservoir and bleed the system.

BELT ADJUSTMENT

Except 3.0L Engine

1. Loosen the pump mounting bolts.

2. Using a pry bar, move the pump away from the engine.

3. Adjust the tension until the belt deflects about ¼–½ in. under a 10 lb. load, tighten the mounting bolts.

3.0L Engine

1. Loosen the tensioner pulley locknut.

2. Tighten the adjuster bolt until the belt deflects about ¼–½ in. under a 10 lb. load

3. Tighten the tensioner lock bolt.

SYSTEM BLEEDING

1. Fill the reservoir with Dexron® II.

2. Raise the front end of the vehicle.

3. Disconnect the ignition coil wire.

4. Simultaneously crank the engine and turn the steering wheel from lock to lock. Repeat this several times.

NOTE: If the bleeding procedure is done with the engine running, high speed rotation of the pump will churn the fluid and create air bubbles filling the system with air. Bleed the system while cranking the engine only.

5. Lower the front end.

6. Connect one end of a tube to the breather plug on the steering box and place the other a container.

7. Start the engine and allow it to idle.

8. Loosen the breather plug and turn the steering wheel from lock to lock continuously until no more air bubbles appear in the fluid coming out the tube.

NOTE: Do not hold the steering wheel all the way against the stop for more than 5 seconds.

9. After the bleeding is done, tighten the breather plug and refill the reservoir.

Tie Rod Ends

REMOVAL AND INSTALLATION

1. Raise the vehicle and support safely.

2. Remove the cotter pin and nut from the tie rod end stud.

3. Using a puller, remove the tie rod from the steering knuckle or center link.

4. Loosen the sleeve clamp nut, if equipped, and unthread the tie rod end.

5. The installation is the reverse of the removal procedure. Torque the stud nuts to 33 ft. lbs. (45 Nm) and install a new cotter pin.

6. Lubricate the front end.

7. Align the front end.

BRAKES

Master Cylinder

REMOVAL AND INSTALLATION

1. Disconnect the negative battery cable. Disconnect the fluid level sensor connector.
2. Disconnect and plug the brake lines from the master cylinder.
3. Remove the nuts attaching the master cylinder to the power booster.
4. Remove the master cylinder from the mounting studs.
5. Remove the fluid reservoir from the cylinder.
To install:
6. Bench bleed the master cylinder.
7. Install master cylinder on power booster studs and install the retaining nuts.
8. Install the brake lines loosely to the master cylinder.
9. Have a helper press down on the brake pedal, holding pedal to the floor. Tighten hydraulic lines at master cylinder.
10. Connect the fluid level sensor connector and refill reservoir as required.

Proportioning Valve

REMOVAL AND INSTALLATION

Montero

1. Disconnect the negative battery cable.
2. Raise the vehicle and support safely.
3. Identify and disconnect the brake lines from the proportioning valve.
4. Disconnect the wires to the valve, if any.
5. Remove the proportioning valve from the vehicle.
6. The installation is the reverse of the removal procedure.
7. Bleed the brakes in the following order:
   a. Right rear
   b. Left rear
   c. Right front
   d. Left front

Expo

1. Disconnect the negative battery cable.

2. Locate the proportioning valve, usually below the master cylinder.
3. Tag and disconnect the brake lines from the valve.
4. Remove the proportioning valve from the engine compartment. Remove the master cylinder retainer nuts to remove the proportioning valve assembly.
5. The installation is the reverse of the removal procedure.
6. Bleed the brakes in the following order:
   a. Left rear wheel cylinder or caliper.
   b. Right front cylinder.
   c. Right rear wheel cylinder or caliper.
   d. Left front caliper.
7. Connect the negative battery cable and check the brakes for proper operation.

Load Sensing Proportioning Valve

REMOVAL AND INSTALLATION

Pick-Up

1. Disconnect the negative battery cable.
2. Raise the vehicle and support safely.
3. Identify and disconnect the brake lines from the valve.
4. Remove the mounting bolts and remove the valve leaving the spring hanging from the lever.
To install:
5. Install the valve to the vehicle engaging the spring.
6. Connect the brake lines.
7. Bleed the brakes in the following order:
   a. Right rear
   b. Load sensing proportioning valve
   c. Left rear
   d. Right front
   e. Left front
8. Lower the vehicle so the full weight of the vehicle is on the ground. Unload any excess weight that is weighing down the rear of the vehicle. Adjust the load sensing proportioning valve lever so the distance from the proportioning valve lever to the spring support is about 7 in.

Power Brake Booster

REMOVAL AND INSTALLATION

Pick-Up and Montero

1. Disconnect the negative battery cable. Disconnect the vacuum hose from the booster.
2. Remove the nuts attaching the master cylinder to the booster and move the master cylinder to the side.
3. From inside of the vehicle, remove the clevis pin that secures the booster pushrod to the brake pedal.
4. Remove the nuts that attach the booster to the dash panel and remove from the vehicle.
5. The installation is the reverse of the removal procedure.

Expo

1. Disconnect the negative battery cable. On some models, relocate the relay box and the solenoid valve located at the power brake unit.
2. Disconnect the vacuum hose from the booster. Pull it straight off. Prying off the vacuum hose could damage the check valve installed in the brake booster.
3. Disconnect the brake level sensor connector.
4. Remove the nuts attaching the master cylinder to the booster and remove the master cylinder.
5. From inside the passenger compartment, remove the cotter pin and clevis pin that secures the booster pushrod to the brake pedal.
6. Remove the nuts that attach the booster to the dash panel and remove it from the vehicle.
7. The installation is the reverse of the removal procedure.
8. Connect the negative battery cable, bleed the brakes and check for proper operation.

Brake Caliper

REMOVAL AND INSTALLATION

Front

1. Raise the vehicle and support safely.
2. Remove the tire and wheel assembly. Disconnect the brake line from the caliper.
3. Label and remove the 2 mounting bolts.
4. Lift the caliper off of the adaptor.
5. The installation is the reverse of the removal procedure. Make sure all anti-rattle and anti-squeal clips

7911D095

Adjusting the load sensing proportioning valve

and pads are in place. Torque the guide pin bolt to 35 ft. lbs. (47 Nm) and the lock pin bolt to 30 ft. lbs. (41 Nm).

6. Bleed the brakes and road test the vehicle.

Disc Brake Pads

REMOVAL AND INSTALLATION

1. Remove ½ of the fluid from the master cylinder reservoir.
2. Raise the vehicle and support safely. Remove the tire and wheel assemblies.
3. Remove the calipers.
4. Remove the pads from the adaptor.

To install:

5. Use a large C-clamp to compress the piston into the caliper bore.
6. Install the pads to the adaptor with anti-rattle and anti-squeal clips in place.
7. Install the caliper and secure to the adapter.
8. Refill the master cylinder.
9. Bleed the brakes if any brake lines were opened.

Brake Rotor

REMOVAL AND INSTALLATION

Front

PICK-UP AND MONTERO

1. Raise the vehicle and support safely.
2. Remove the tire and wheel assembly.
3. Remove the caliper and brake pads.
4. Remove the caliper adaptor.
5. If equipped with 4WD, remove the automatic hub, the shim, lock washer and locknut.

6. If equipped with 2WD, remove the dust cap, cotter pin, nut lock, nut, washer and outer bearing.
7. Remove the front hub and rotor assembly from the spindle.
8. To separate the hub from the rotor, remove the bolts and split the rotor from the hub.

To install:

9. Install the rotor to the hub and torque the attaching nuts and bolts to 40 ft. lbs. (54 Nm).
10. Install the hub and rotor assembly to the spindle and install the retaining nuts and bearings as removed. Adjust bearing preload.
11. Install the caliper adaptor. Torque the bolts to 70 ft. lbs. (95 Nm).
12. Install the brake pads and caliper, making sure all anti-rattle and anti-squeal clips are in place.
13. Bleed the brakes if any brake line was opened.
14. Install the tire and wheel assembly and road test the vehicle.

EXPO

1. Raise the vehicle and support safely. Remove appropriate wheel assembly.
2. Remove the caliper and brake pads.
3. The rotor on most models is held to the hub by 2 small threaded screws. Remove screws, if equipped, and pull off the rotor.
4. Installation is the reverse of the removal process.

Rear

1. Raise the vehicle and support safely. Remove appropriate wheel assembly.
2. Make sure the parking brake is fully released.
3. Remove the caliper, brake pads and caliper support bracket.
4. The rotor on most models is held to the hub by 2 small threaded screws. Remove screws, if equipped, and pull off the rotor.
5. Installation is the reverse of the removal process.

Brake Drums

REMOVAL AND INSTALLATION

1. Raise the vehicle and support safely.
2. Remove the tire and wheel assembly.
3. Remove the drum retaining screw with an impact driver if equipped.
4. Remove the drum. If difficult to remove the drum, remove the ad-

juster access cover in the backing plate and rotate the star wheel to loosen the adjustment on the rear brake shoes.

5. The installation is the reverse of the removal procedure.

Service Brake Shoes

REMOVAL AND INSTALLATION

1. Raise the vehicle and support safely.
2. Remove the tire and wheel assemblies and the brake drums.
3. Remove the upper return spring along with the adjuster.
4. Remove the adjuster spring.
5. Remove the lower retaining spring.
6. Remove the hold-down springs.
7. Remove the shoes, disengaging the parking brake lever.

To install:

8. Clean and dry the backing plate. Lubricate the bosses, anchor contacts and wheel cylinder piston grooves where the top of the shoe fits lightly with lithium based grease.
9. Lubricate the star wheel shaft threads with anti-seize lubricant and transfer all parts to their proper locations on the new shoes. Make sure the longer end of the upper return spring is installed toward the shoe with the parking brake lever.
10. Spread the shoes apart, engage the parking brake lever and position them on the backing plate making sure the wheel cylinder pins engage the webs of the brake shoes.
11. Install the lower retaining spring and the hold-down springs.
12. Adjust the star wheel until the brake shoes are in contact with the brake drum when installed.
13. Remove any grease from the linings and install the brake drums.
14. Install the tire and wheel assemblies and complete the brake adjustment.

Wheel Cylinder

REMOVAL AND INSTALLATION

1. Raise the vehicle and support safely.
2. Remove the wheel, drum and brake shoes.
3. Remove the hydraulic brake line from the wheel cylinder.
4. Remove the wheel cylinder mounting bolts and remove the cylinder from the backing plate.

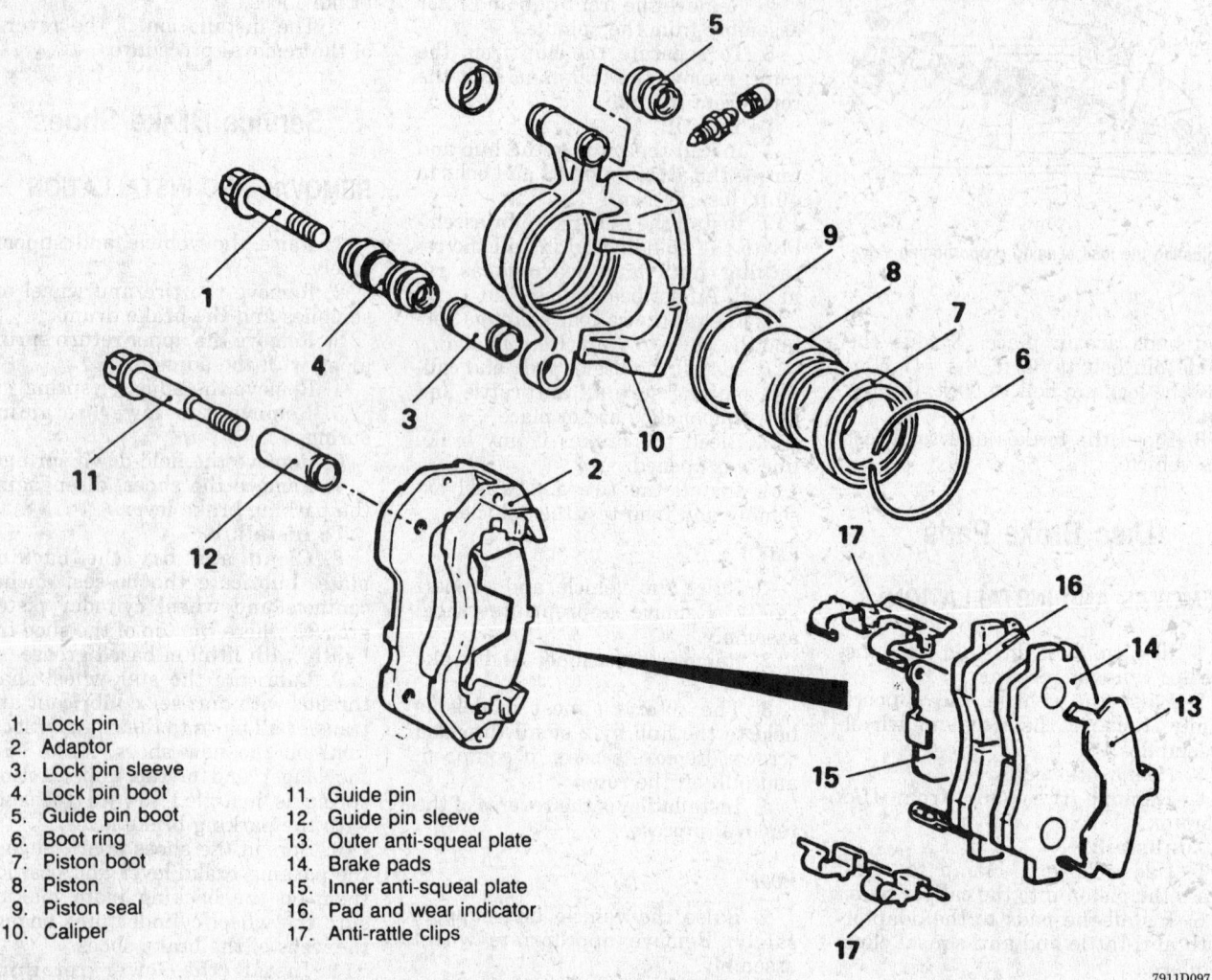

1. Lock pin
2. Adaptor
3. Lock pin sleeve
4. Lock pin boot
5. Guide pin boot
6. Boot ring
7. Piston boot
8. Piston
9. Piston seal
10. Caliper
11. Guide pin
12. Guide pin sleeve
13. Outer anti-squeal plate
14. Brake pads
15. Inner anti-squeal plate
16. Pad and wear indicator
17. Anti-rattle clips

7911D097

Front brakes — Montero and Pick-Up

To install:

5. Position the wheel cylinder on the backing plate and install the retaining bolts. Torque the bolts to 14 ft. lbs. (19 Nm).

6. Connect the brake line to the wheel cylinder.

7. Lubricate the backing plate and install the brake linings.

8. Install the brake drums, tire and wheel assemblies and adjust the brake linings.

9. Bleed the brakes system and refill the master cylinder reservoir.

Front Parking Brake Cable

REMOVAL AND INSTALLATION

1. Raise the vehicle and support safely. Remove the front cable adjusting nut.

2. Remove the brake lever cover, if floor mounted.

3. Remove the pin securing the cable to the equalizer and slide the cable out of the bracket.

4. Remove the pin or retainer attaching the cable to the handle assembly. Disengage the cable from the handle.

5. Remove the cable grommet from the floor pan and remove the cable from the vehicle.

6. The installation is the reverse of the removal procedure.

Rear Parking Brake Cable

REMOVAL AND INSTALLATION

1. Release the parking brakes fully.

2. Raise the vehicle and support safely.

3. Loosen the adjusting nut from the front cable.

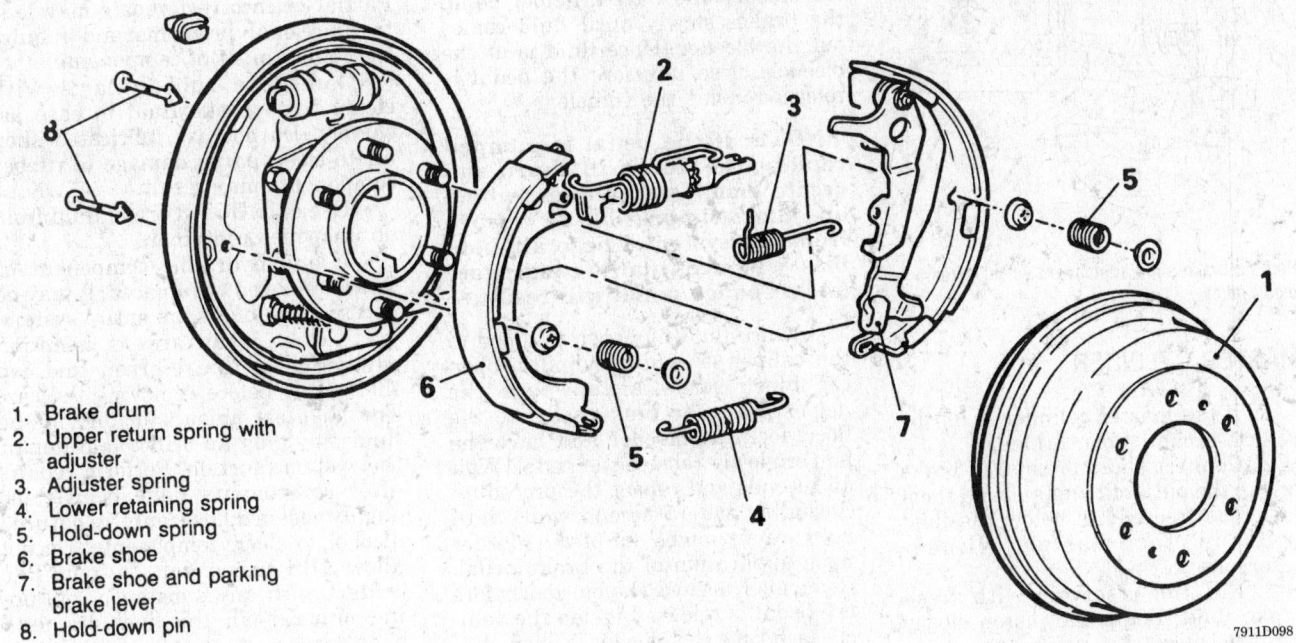

1. Brake drum
2. Upper return spring with adjuster
3. Adjuster spring
4. Lower retaining spring
5. Hold-down spring
6. Brake shoe
7. Brake shoe and parking brake lever
8. Hold-down pin

7911D098

Rear brake shoes and hardware

4. Remove the brake drums. Remove the shoes, if necessary. Disconnect the cable from the lever.

5. Compress the cable retainer tabs to remove the cable from the backing plate.

6. Remove the cable from the equalizer and remove the retaining bolts from the frame.

7. The installation is the reverse of the removal procedure.

ADJUSTMENT

Rear Drum Brakes

1. Release the parking brakes fully.

2. Raise the vehicle and support safely.

3. Adjust the rear brake linings.

4. Loosen the adjusting nut until there is slack in all the cables.

5. Rotate the rear wheels and tighten the cable adjusting nut until there is a slight drag at the wheels.

6. Continue to rotate the rear wheels and loosen the nut until all drag is eliminated.

7. Back off the nut an additional 2 turns.

8. Apply and release the parking brake several times. Upon the last release, verify that there is no drag on the wheels. The pedal should depress 4–7 notches.

9. To check operation, make sure the parking brake holds on an incline.

Rear Disc Brakes

NOTE: The parking brake shoes are located behind the brake rotor and are adjusted by means of a star wheel adjuster, similar to conventional drum brake shoes.

1. Make sure the parking brake cable is free and is not frozen or sticking. With the engine running, forcefully depress the brake pedal 5–6 times. Check the parking brake stroke. It should be 5–7 for Expo or 4–6 notches for Montero. If not, adjust using the following procedure.

2. Make sure the parking brake mechanism is not frozen or sticking.

3. For Expo, remove the floor console. For Montero, raise the vehicle and support safely to locate the adjuster under the parking brake handle. Loosen the adjuster nut to slacken the cables.

4. Remove the rear wheel and locate the parking brake shoe adjuster hole. It is located in the front face of the rotor for Expo or in the backing plate for Montero.

5. Remove the hole plug and insert a flat tipped tool. Turn the star wheel in the direction of the arrow until the disc rotor will not turn.

6. Return the adjuster 3–4 notches in the opposite direction of the arrow. After the adjustment is made, make sure to see if there is no play between the adjusting nut and pin, at the parking brake handle.

7. Check that the parking brake stroke is 5–7 notches for Expo or 4–6 notches for Montero.

8. After adjusting the lever stroke, raise the rear of the vehicle and safely support. With the parking brake lever in the released position, turn the rear wheels to confirm that the rear brakes are not dragging.

9. Check that the parking brake holds the vehicle on an incline.

Brake System Bleeding

If using a pressure bleeder, follow the instructions furnished with the unit and choose the correct adaptor for the application. Do not substitute an adapter that "almost fits" as it will not work and could be dangerous.

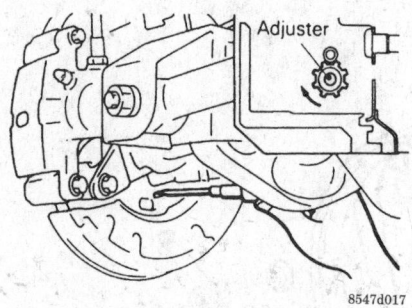

Parking brake shoe adjustment wheel — rear disc brakes

MASTER CYLINDER

1. If the master cylinder is off the vehicle it can be bench bled.

2. Connect short piece(s) of brake line to the outlet fitting(s), bend them until the free end is below the fluid level in the master cylinder reservoirs.

3. Fill the reservoir with fresh brake fluid. Pump the piston slowly until no more air bubbles appear in the reservoir(s).

4. Disconnect the lines, refill the master cylinder and securely install the cylinder cap.

5. If the master cylinder is on the vehicle, it can still be bled, using a flare nut wrench.

6. Open the brake line(s) slightly with the flare nut wrench while pressure is applied to the brake pedal by a helper inside the vehicle.

7. Be sure to tighten the line before the brake pedal is released.

8. Repeat the process with both lines until no air bubbles come out.

CALIPERS AND WHEEL CYLINDERS

1. Fill the master cylinder with fresh brake fluid. Check the level often during the procedure.

2. Starting with the right rear wheel, remove the protective cap from the bleeder and place where it will not be lost. Clean the bleed screw.

--- CAUTION ---
When bleeding the brakes, keep face away from the brake area. Spewing fluid may cause facial and/or visual damage. Do not allow brake fluid to spill on the car's finish; it will remove the paint.

3. If the system is empty, the most efficient way to get fluid down to the wheel is to loosen the bleeder about ½–¾ turn, place a finger firmly over the bleeder and have a helper pump the brakes slowly until fluid comes out the bleeder. Once fluid is at the bleeder, close it before the pedal is released inside the vehicle.

NOTE: If the pedal is pumped rapidly, the fluid will churn and create small air bubbles, which are almost impossible to remove from the system. These air bubbles will eventually congregate and a spongy pedal will result.

4. Once fluid has been pumped to the caliper or wheel cylinder, open the bleed screw again, have the helper press the brake pedal to the floor, lock the bleeder and have the helper slowly release the pedal. Wait 15 seconds and repeat the procedure (including the 15 second wait) until no more air comes out of the bleeder upon application of the brake pedal. Remember to close the bleeder before the pedal is released inside the vehicle each time the bleeder is opened. If not, air will be induced into the system.

5. If a helper is not available, connect a small hose to the bleeder, place the end in a container of brake fluid and proceed to pump the pedal from inside the vehicle until no more air comes out the bleeder. The hose will prevent air from entering the system.

6. Repeat the procedure on remaining wheel cylinders in order:
   a. Left rear
   b. Right front
   c. Left front

7. Hydraulic brake systems must be totally flushed if the fluid becomes contaminated with water, dirt or other corrosive chemicals. To flush, bleed the entire system until all fluid has been replaced with new fluid.

8. Install the bleeder cap(s) on the bleeder to keep dirt out. Always road test the vehicle after brake work of any kind is done.

Anti-lock Brake System Service

PRECAUTIONS

• Certain components within the ABS system are not intended to be serviced or repaired individually. Only those components with REMOVAL AND INSTALLATION procedures should be serviced.

• Do not use rubber hoses or other parts not specifically designed for the ABS system. When using repair kits, replace all parts included in the kit. Partial or incorrect repair may lead to functional problems and require the replacement of components.

• Lubricate rubber parts with clean, fresh brake fluid to ease assembly. Do not use lubricated shop air to clean parts; damage to rubber components may result.

• Use only DOT 3 brake fluid from an unopened container.

• If any hydraulic component or line is removed or replaced, it may be necessary to bleed the entire system.

• A clean repair area is essential. Always clean the reservoir and cap thoroughly before removing the cap. The slightest amount of dirt in the fluid may plug an orifice and impair the system function. Perform repairs after components have been thoroughly cleaned; use only denatured alcohol to clean components. Do not allow ABS components to come into contact with any substance containing mineral oil; this includes used shop rags.

• The Anti-Lock control unit is a microprocessor similar to other computer units in the vehicle. Ensure that the ignition switch is **OFF** before removing or installing controller harnesses. Avoid static electricity discharge at or near the controller.

• If any arc welding is to be done on the vehicle, the ALCU connectors should be disconnected before welding operations begin.

Hydraulic Unit

REMOVAL AND INSTALLATION

Expo

1. Disconnect the negative battery cable. Remove the splash shield from under the vehicle.

2. Use a syringe or similar device to remove as much fluid as possible from the reservoir. Some fluid will be spilled from lines during removal of the hydraulic unit; protect adjacent painted surfaces.

3. Remove the dust cover and the oil reservoir.

4. Disconnect the brake lines from the hydraulic unit. Correct reassembly is critical. Label or identify the lines before removal. Plug each line immediately after removal.

5. Disconnect the hydraulic unit electrical harness connectors.

6. Disconnect the hydraulic unit ground strap from the chassis.

7. Remove the 3 nuts holding the hydraulic unit. Remove the unit upwards.

NOTE: The hydraulic unit is heavy; use care when removing it. The unit must remain in the upright position at all times and be protected from impact and shock.

8. Set the unit upright supported by blocks on the workbench. The hydraulic unit must not be tilted or turned upside down. No component of the hydraulic unit should be loosened or disassembled.

9. The bracket assemblies and relays may be removed, if desired.

To install:

10. Install the relays and brackets, if removed.

11. Install the hydraulic unit into the vehicle, keeping it upright at all times.

12. Install the retaining nuts and tighten.

13. Connect the ground strap to the chassis bracket. Connect the hydraulic unit wiring harness.

14. Connect the hydraulic unit electrical harness connectors.

15. Install the dust cover and the oil reservoir.

16. Connect each brake line loosely to the correct port and double check the placement. Tighten each line to 10 ft. lbs. (13.5 Nm).

17. Fill the reservoir to the MAX line with brake fluid.

18. Bleed the master cylinder, then bleed the brake lines. Refill the master cylinder and check for proper operation.

Montero

1. Disconnect the negative battery cable.

2. Disconnect the brake lines from the hydraulic unit. Correct reassembly is critical. Label or identify the lines before removal. Plug each line immediately after removal.

3. Remove the cover from the relay box. Disconnect the electrical harness to the hydraulic unit.

4. Disconnect the hydraulic unit ground strap from the chassis.

5. Remove the 3 nuts holding the hydraulic unit. Remove the unit upwards.

NOTE: The hydraulic unit is heavy; use care when removing it. The unit must remain in the upright position at all times and be protected from impact and shock.

6. Set the unit upright supported by blocks on the workbench. The hydraulic unit must not be tilted or turned upside down. No component of the hydraulic unit should be loosened or disassembled.

7. The bracket assemblies and relays may be removed, if desired.

To install:

8. Install the relays and brackets, if removed

9. Install the hydraulic unit to the vehicle, keeping it upright at all times.

10. Install the retaining nuts and tighten.

11. Connect the ground strap to the chassis bracket. Connect the hydraulic unit wiring harness.

12. Install the cover on the relay box.

13. Connect each brake line loosely to the correct port and double check the placement. Tighten each line to 10 ft. lbs. (13.5 Nm).

14. Fill the reservoir to the MAX line with brake fluid.

15. Bleed the master cylinder, then bleed the brake lines.

16. Connect the negative battery cable and clean all trouble codes.

Anti-Lock Control Unit

REMOVAL AND INSTALLATION

Montero

1. Ensure that the ignition switch is **OFF** throughout the procedure.

2. Remove the interior right rear quarter trim panel. Remove the rear seat back and/or cushion, if equipped with 3rd seat.

3. Release the lock on the bottom of the connector; disconnect the multi-pin connector from the control unit.

4. Remove the retaining nuts and remove the control unit from its bracket. The bracket may be removed, if desired.

To install:

5. Place the bracket in position. Install the controller and tighten the retaining nuts.

6. Connect the ground wire to the bracket, if removed. Ensure a proper, tight connection. The ground must be connected before the multi-pin harness is connected.

7. Connect the multi-pin connector and secure the lock. Install the rear quarter trim panel and seat.

Pick-Up and Expo

1. Ensure that the ignition switch is **OFF** throughout the procedure.

2. Remove the cup holder in front of the center console.

3. Remove the console side covers.

4. Disconnect the electrical harness from the control unit.

5. Remove the fasteners and the control unit from the vehicle.

6. Installation is the reverse of the removal procedures.

G-Sensor

The G-sensor is located under the parking brake handle cover for Montero or under the center console for Pick-Up and Expo.

REMOVAL AND INSTALLATION

1. Disconnect the negative battery cable.

2. Remove the floor console. The sensor is located at the Rear ABS control unit for Pick-Up.

3. Disconnect the wiring harness connector from the sensor.

4. Remove the retaining screw and G-sensor from the mounting bracket.

5. Installation is the reverse of the removal procedure.

Wheel Speed Sensors

— **CAUTION** —
Vehicles equipped with air bag systems will have wiring and system components in the fender or wheel well area. The ABS components must be correctly identified before beginning repairs. Improper work procedures may cause impaired function of the ABS and/or SRS systems.

REMOVAL AND INSTALLATION

Except Pick-Up

1. Disconnect the negative battery cable. Raise and safely support the vehicle.

2. Remove the wheel and tire. Remove the inner fender or splash shield.

3. Beginning at the sensor end, carefully disconnect or release each clip and retainer along the sensor wire. Take careful note of the exact position of each clip; they must be reinstalled in the identical position. Rear wheel sensor harnesses will be held by plastic wire ties; these may

be cut away but must be replaced at reassembly.

4. Disconnect the sensor connector at the end of the harness.

5. For the Expo front, remove the front hub. For Expo rear, remove the rear hub and halfshaft assembly.

6. Remove the 1 or 2 bolts holding the speed sensor bracket to the knuckle or backing plate and remove the assembly from the vehicle.

NOTE: The speed sensor has a pole piece projecting from it. This exposed tip must be protected from impact or scratches. Do not allow the pole piece to contact the toothed wheel during removal or installation.

7. Remove the sensor from the bracket.

To install:

8. Assemble the sensor onto the bracket and tighten the bolt to 10 ft. lbs. (14 Nm). Note that the brackets are different for the left and right front wheels. Each bracket has identifying letters stamped on it.

9. Temporarily install the speed sensor to the knuckle; tighten the bolts only finger-tight.

10. Route the cable correctly and loosely install the clips and retainers. All clips must be in their original position and the sensor cable must not be twisted. Improper installation may cause cable damage and system failure.

NOTE: The wiring in the harness is easily damaged by twisting and flexing. Use the white stripe on the outer insulation to keep the sensor harness properly placed.

11. Use a brass of other non-magnetic feeler gauge to check the air gap between the tip of the pole piece and the toothed wheel. The gap is as follows:

a. Expo front sensor — 0.012–0.035 in. (0.3–0.9mm)

b. Expo FWD rear sensor — 0.008–0.028 in. (0.2–0.7mm)

c. Expo AWD rear sensor — 0.012–0.035 in. (0.3–0.9mm)

d. Montero front sensor — 0.008–0.039 in. (0.2–1.0mm)

e. Montero rear sensor — 0.012–0.035 in. (0.3–0.9mm)

12. Torque the sensor bracket bolts to 10 ft. lbs. (14 Nm) with the sensor located so the gap is the same at several points on the toothed wheel. If the gap is incorrect, it is likely that the toothed wheel is worn or improperly installed.

13. Tighten the screws and bolts for the cable retaining clips.

14. Install the inner fender or splash shield. Install the wheel and tire. Lower the vehicle to the ground.

Pick-Up

The Pick-Up is equipped with Rear ABS and has 1 speed sensor located in the rear differential housing. Remove the sensor retaining screw and pry from the differential housing. Inspect seal and install in the reverse of removal.

Front Toothed Wheel Rings

REMOVAL AND INSTALLATION

1. Disconnect the negative battery cable. Raise and safely support the vehicle.

2. Remove the wheel and tire.

3. Remove the wheel speed sensor and disconnect sufficient harness clips to allow the sensor and wiring to be moved out of the work area.

NOTE: The speed sensor has a pole piece projecting from it. This exposed tip must be protected from impact or scratches. Do not allow the pole piece to contact the toothed wheel during removal or installation.

4. Remove the front hub for Montero. Remove the hub/knuckle assembly for Expo. Remove the hub from the knuckle

5. Support the hub in a vise with protected jaws. Remove the retaining bolts from the toothed wheel and remove the toothed wheel.

To install:

6. Fit the new toothed wheel onto the hub and tighten the retaining bolts to 7 ft. lbs. (10 Nm).

7. Assemble the hub to the knuckle. Install the hub and knuckle assembly to the vehicle.

8. Install the wheel speed sensor. Install the wheel and tire. Lower the vehicle to the ground.

Rear Toothed Wheel Rings

REMOVAL AND INSTALLATION

Expo FWD

1. Disconnect the negative battery cable. Remove the wheel and tire.

2. Remove the wheel speed sensor and disconnect sufficient harness

clips to allow the sensor and wiring to be moved out of the work area.

NOTE: The speed sensor has a pole piece projecting from it. This exposed tip must be protected from impact or scratches. Do not allow the pole piece to contact the toothed wheel during removal or installation.

3. Remove the hub assembly.

4. Support the hub in a vise with protected jaws. Remove the retaining bolts from the toothed wheel and remove the toothed wheel.

To install:

5. Fit the new toothed wheel onto the hub and tighten the retaining bolts to 7 ft. lbs. (10 Nm).

6. Install the hub assembly to the vehicle.

7. Install the tongued washer and hub nut. Tighten to 166 ft. lbs. (230 Nm). Install the cotter pin and grease cap.

8. Install the wheel speed sensor. Install the wheel and tire. Lower the vehicle to the ground.

Expo AWD

1. Disconnect the negative battery cable. Raise and safely support the vehicle. Remove the wheel and tire assembly.

2. Remove the cotter pin cover and driveshaft nut.

3. Remove the speed sensor and its O-ring. Disconnect sufficient clamps and wire ties to allow the sensor to be moved well out of the work area.

NOTE: The speed sensor has a pole piece projecting from it. This exposed tip must be protected from impact or scratches. Do not allow the pole piece to contact the toothed wheel during removal or installation.

4. Remove the rear driveshaft from the vehicle.

5. Fit the shaft assembly in a press with the toothed wheel completely supported by a bearing plate such as special tool MB990560 or equivalent.

6. Press the toothed wheel off the axle shaft.

To install:

7. Press the new toothed wheel onto the shaft with the groove facing the axle shaft flange.

8. Install the axle on the vehicle. Tighten the inner flange retainers to 40–47 ft. lbs. (55–65 Nm).

9. Install the driveshaft nut and torque to 145–188 ft. lbs. (200–260 Nm). Secure using a new cotter pin.

10. Install the speed sensor and secure the wiring harness in its original location. Always use a new O-ring.

11. Install the wheel and tire assembly.

Montero

1. Raise the vehicle and support safely.

2. Remove the rear wheel, caliper, caliper bracket and rotor.

3. Remove the parking brake cable bolt, cable end, parking brake shoes and speed sensor.

4. Remove the axleshaft from the housing using a slide hammer and hub puller MB990241-01, or equivalent.

5. Remove 1 retainer bolt from the backing plate. Use a grinder to partially cut the bearing retainer.

6. Use a chisel to crack the retainer, being careful not to damage the axle. Using a press or appropriate pulling tool, remove the axle shaft bearings and retainers.

7. Insert an iron plate of 0.04 in. (1.0mm) thick between the ABS rotor and axle shaft. Use a press to remove the rotor assembly. Remove the bearing outer race.

8. Remove the axle seal from the axle housing using a slide hammer and jaw.

To install:

NOTE: The axle shaft lengths are different for vehicles equipped with rear differential lock. The right side is longer, so do not interchange axle shafts.

9. Drive the new oil seal into the housing using a seal driver.

10. Install the bearing outer race and ABS rotor using a press.

11. Install the oil seal, bearing inner race and retainer using a press. Install the snapring and check the clearance between the snapring and retainer. The specification is 0.0065 in. (0.166mm) or less. If excessive, install a thicker snapring.

12. Install the axle shaft and torque the retaining bolts to 145 ft. lbs. (196 Nm).

13. Installation is the reverse of removal. Refill the axle with gear lubricant.

Pick-Up

1. Remove the axle shafts, driveshaft, speed sensor and differential carrier from the vehicle.

2. Matchmark the side bearing retainers and adjusters.

3. Remove the bearing caps, adjusters and differential case.

4. Matchmark the case to the ring gear. Remove the ring gear bolts and ABS rotor.

To install:

5. Install the ring gear and ABS rotor to the original position. Torque the bolts to 65 ft. lbs. (90 Nm).

6. Install the differential case, adjusters and caps. Apply thread locking compound to the bolts and torque to 70 ft. lbs. (95 Nm).

7. Install the remaining components and check operation.

FRONT SUSPENSION

Shock Absorbers

REMOVAL AND INSTALLATION

1. Raise and safely support the vehicle. Remove the upper shock nut, washer and bushing.

2. Raise the vehicle fully and support safely.

3. Remove the lower mounting bolt(s) and discard the shock.

4. The installation is the reverse of the removal procedure.

MacPherson Strut

REMOVAL AND INSTALLATION

1. Disconnect the negative battery cable.

2. If removing the right front strut, remove the auto-cruise control actuator.

3. Disconnect and remove the daytime running lamp delay and control unit from the mounting bracket located on top of the left strut tower.

4. Raise and safely support vehicle.

5. Remove the brake hose and tube bracket. Do not pry the brake hose and tube clamp away when removing it.

6. If equipped with ABS, disconnect the front speed sensor mounting clamp from the strut.

7. Support the lower arm and remove the strut to knuckle bolts. Use a piece of wire to suspend the knuckle to keep the weight off the brake hose.

8. Before removing the top bolts, make matchmarks on the body and the strut insulator for proper reassembly. If this plate is installed improperly, the wheel alignment will be wrong. Remove the strut upper bolts and remove the strut assembly from the vehicle.

To install:

9. Install the strut to the vehicle and install the top bolts.

10. Connect the ECS connector.

11. Install to the knuckle and install the bolts.

12. Install the brake hose bracket and the ABS clamp.

13. Install the daytime running lamp delay and control unit to the mounting bracket located on top of the left strut tower.

14. Install the auto-cruise control actuator.

15. Install the wheel and tire assembly.

16. Perform a front end alignment.

Strut Cartridge

REPLACEMENT

———— **CAUTION** ————
Use extreme care when disassembling struts. Coil springs must be compressed into a loaded position for strut removal. Never remove the strut cap nut without using proper spring compression tools or equipment.

1. Hold the spring upper seat and loosen the self-locking nut.

———— **CAUTION** ————
The self-locking nut should be loosened only, not removed.

2. Position the strut assembly into spring compression tool No. MB991237/MB991238 or equivalent.

3. Compress spring only enough to free top spring cap. Secure the strut body and remove the self-locking nut.

4. Note position and location when removing the top insulator, upper spring seat with rubber insulator and bump rubber with dust shield.

5. Remove the strut cartridge body and replace only as a complete assembly.

6. Inspect all parts for wear or damage, be sure to check top spring support bearing for smooth operation. Replace any parts found to be worn or defective.

To install:

7. Install strut cartridge body into spring assembly.

8. Install dust boot, spring seat with rubber spring pad and top spring insulator.

9. Install washer and self-locking nut. Tighten nut to 14–22 ft. lbs. (20–30 Nm).

10. Release spring compression tool while seating spring against perch.

Coil Spring

REMOVAL AND INSTALLATION

2WD Pick-Up and Montero

1. Raise the vehicle and support safely.

2. Remove the shock absorber.

3. Disconnect the stabilizer bar from the lower control arm.

4. Install spring compressor tool MB990792 or equivalent, to the coil spring and to compress the spring.

5. Remove the cotter pin and lower ball joint nut.

6. Release the lower ball joint taper using Mitsubishi tool MB990809–01.

7. Remove the tool and the ball stud from the control arm. Release the compressor tool from the coil spring.

8. Pull the arm down and remove the spring with the rubber isolation pad from the vehicle.

To install:

9. Install the spring with the rubber isolator. Install the compressor tool and compress spring so the lower ball joint can be inserted through the knuckle.

10. Torque the lower ball joint nut to 100 ft. lbs. (136 Nm). Install a new cotter pin. Remove the spring compressor.

11. Connect the sway bar to the lower control arm, if equipped.

12. Install the shock absorber.

Torsion Bar

REMOVAL AND INSTALLATION

4WD Pick-Up and Montero

1. Raise the vehicle and support safely. Remove skid plate, if equipped.

2. Support the lower control arm at a point away from the torsion bar mounting point to the arm.

3. Fold the dust covers back and slide them away from the ends of the bar.

4. If the bars are to be reused, matchmark the torsion bar at both ends to the anchor and identify left from right.

5. Paint or measure the distance of the exposed threads of the rear

mounting bolt down to the nut to aid in adjustment when installing. Remove the rear anchor arm mounting nut and bolt.

6. Remove the torsion bar from the front anchor arm.

To install:

7. If the bar is being reused, lubricate the ends and install the torsion bar aligning the matchmarks. If a new bar is being used, align the white stripe on the front splines with the mark on the anchor. There is a "L or R" mark on the front of the torsion bar to differentiate between left and right. Do not install the bar with the mark facing the rear.

8. Install the torsion bar to the rear anchor so the length of the mounting bolt from the nut to the head of the bolt is the specified length with the rebound bumper in contact with the crossmember. The specifications are as follows:
- Montero left side: 5.3–5.6 in.
- Montero right side: 4.9–5.2 in.
- Pick-Up left side: 5.5–5.8 in.
- Pick-Up right side: 5.3–5.6 in.

9. To initially set the riding height, tighten the rear anchor mounting nut to the same point at which it was removed if the old bar is being reused. If a new bar has been installed, tighten the nut so the exposed length of the bolt threads is the specification:
- Montero left side: 2.4 in.
- Montero right side: 2.8 in.
- Pick-Up left side: 3.9 in.
- Pick-Up right side: 3.4 in.

10. Fill the dust covers with grease and fold them back into position.

11. Adjust the torsion to the correct riding height.

ADJUSTING THE TORSION BAR

1. Lower the vehicle so its full weight is on the ground. If there is

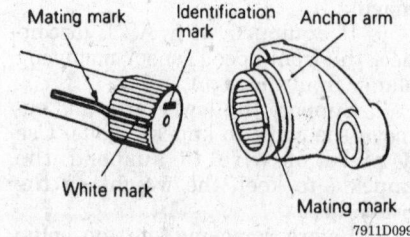

Aligning the front of the torsion bar with the front anchor

any excess weight in the vehicle, unload it.

2. To set the riding height, measure the distance from the rebound bumper to its stopper bracket on the frame. Adjust the torsion bar nut until that distance is within the specification: 1992–96 Montero and Pick-Up to 3.1 in.

3. If, after adjusting the riding height, the exposed portion of the adjusting bolt is protruding up or down far enough to interfere with any front suspension component or is hanging down too low, the bar must be removed and repositioned.

4. Road test the vehicle and remeasure the riding height. Readjust if necessary.

Upper Ball Joint

INSPECTION

With the control arm removed, check the starting torque required to turn the ball stud. The specification for all vehicles is 7–30 inch lbs. (0.8–3.5 Nm).

REMOVAL AND INSTALLATION

NOTE: The upper ball joint and upper control arm must be replaced as an assembly on Pick-Up.

1. Raise the vehicle and support safely. Release the tension on the torsion bar and remove the upper control arm from the vehicle.

2. Remove the ring and boot from the ball joint. Remove the snapring.

3. Remove the ball joint from the control arm using tool sets MB990800 and MB990799.

To install:

4. Align the mating mark on the upper ball joint with the mark on the arm.

5. Press the ball joint in using the same tools that were used to remove the ball joint.

6. Install the snapring. If the snapring is loose, install a new one.

7. Fill the boot with grease and install the boot and ring.

8. Install the upper control arm.

9. Lubricate the ball joint with a grease gun.

10. Adjust the riding height, if equipped with a torsion bar and align the front end.

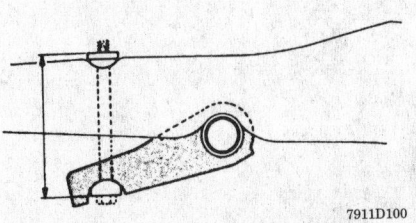

Measure this distance when installing the torsion bar to the rear anchor

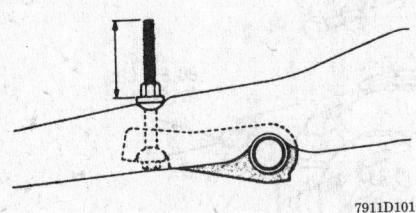

Measure this distance to initially set the riding height

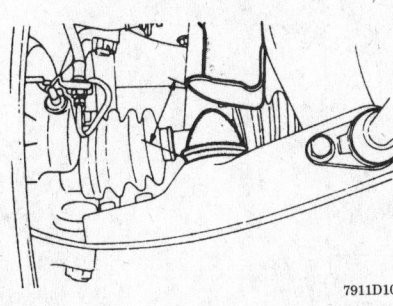

Measure this distance to set the riding height

Lower Ball Joint

INSPECTION

Pick-Up and Montero

With the control arm removed, check the up and down endplay of the ball stud. If it exceeds 0.02 in. (0.5mm), the ball joint should be replaced.

Expo

The lower ball joints on these vehicles are not serviceable. If defective, the entire lower arm must be replaced. The ball joints can be checked using the following procedure:

1. Wiggle the ball joint a few times to make sure it is free.

2. Double-nut the stud and use a torque wrench to measure how much torque is required to turn it. Starting torque should be 17–78 inch lbs. (2–9 Nm).

3. If the stud has more resistance than specified, replace the lower arm assembly. If the resistance is less, it may still be reused unless it has excessive play.

4. A new grease boot can be installed using a large socket for a driver.

REMOVAL AND INSTALLATION

Pick-Up and Montero

1. Raise the vehicle and support safely. Remove the lower control arm.

2. Remove the ball joint retaining nuts and bolts and remove the ball joint from the arm.

3. The installation is the reverse of the removal procedure. Torque the ball joint retaining nuts and bolts to 50 ft. lbs. (68 Nm) on 4WD vehicles or 28 ft. lbs. (38 Nm) on 2WD vehicles. Torque the ball stud nut to 100 ft. lbs. (136 Nm) and install a new cotter pin.

4. Lubricate the ball joint with a grease gun.

5. Adjust the riding height, if equipped with a torsion bar.

6. Align the front suspension.

Upper Control Arm

REMOVAL AND INSTALLATION

2WD Pick-Up

1. Raise the vehicle and support safely. Remove the tire and wheel assembly.

2. Remove the shock absorber.

3. Install Mitsubishi spring compressor tool MB990792 or equivalent, to the coil spring and compress the spring.

4. Remove the cotter pin and upper ball joint nut.

5. Suspend the rotor assembly so there is not excessive pull on the brake hose.

6. Release the upper ball joint taper using Mitsubishi tool MB990809–01 or equivalent.

7. Remove the tool and remove the ball stud from the knuckle.

8. Loosen the pivot bar retaining nuts and bolts, identify and remove the alignment shims, remove the nuts and bolts and remove the arm from the vehicle.

To install:

9. Install the arm to the frame rail bracket, install the shims in their original locations and install the retaining nuts and bolts. Torque the nuts initially to 40 ft. lbs. (54 Nm).

10. Torque the ball joint nut to 60 ft. lbs. (81 Nm). Install a new cotter pin. Remove the spring compressor.

11. Install the shock absorber.

12. Align the front end. When all settings are at specifications, torque the pivot bar retaining bolts to 80 ft. lbs. (109 Nm).

Montero and 4WD Pick-Up

1. Raise the vehicle and support safely. Remove the skid plate.

2. Remove the shock absorber.

3. Turn the torsion bar adjustment nut counterclockwise to relieve all tension from the torsion bar. Disconnect the brake hose from the brake line and remove the hose from the bracket.

4. Remove the cotter pin from the upper ball stud.

5. Release the upper ball joint taper using Mitsubishi tool MB990809–01 or equivalent. Remove the tool. Remove the ball stud from the steering knuckle.

6. Loosen the pivot bar retaining nuts and bolts, identify and remove the alignment shims, remove the nuts and bolts.

7. Remove the control arm from the vehicle.

To install:

8. Position the arm at the frame rail bracket.

9. Install the shims in their original locations and install the retaining nuts and bolts. Torque the nuts initially to 40 ft. lbs. (54 Nm).

10. Insert the upper ball stud in the steering knuckle arm bore and install the nut. Torque the nut to 60 ft. lbs. (81 Nm) and install a new cotter pin. Install the shock absorber and attach the brake hose.

11. Turn the torsion bar adjustment nut clockwise to apply a load on the bar.

12. Lower the vehicle.

13. Set the riding height and align the front end.

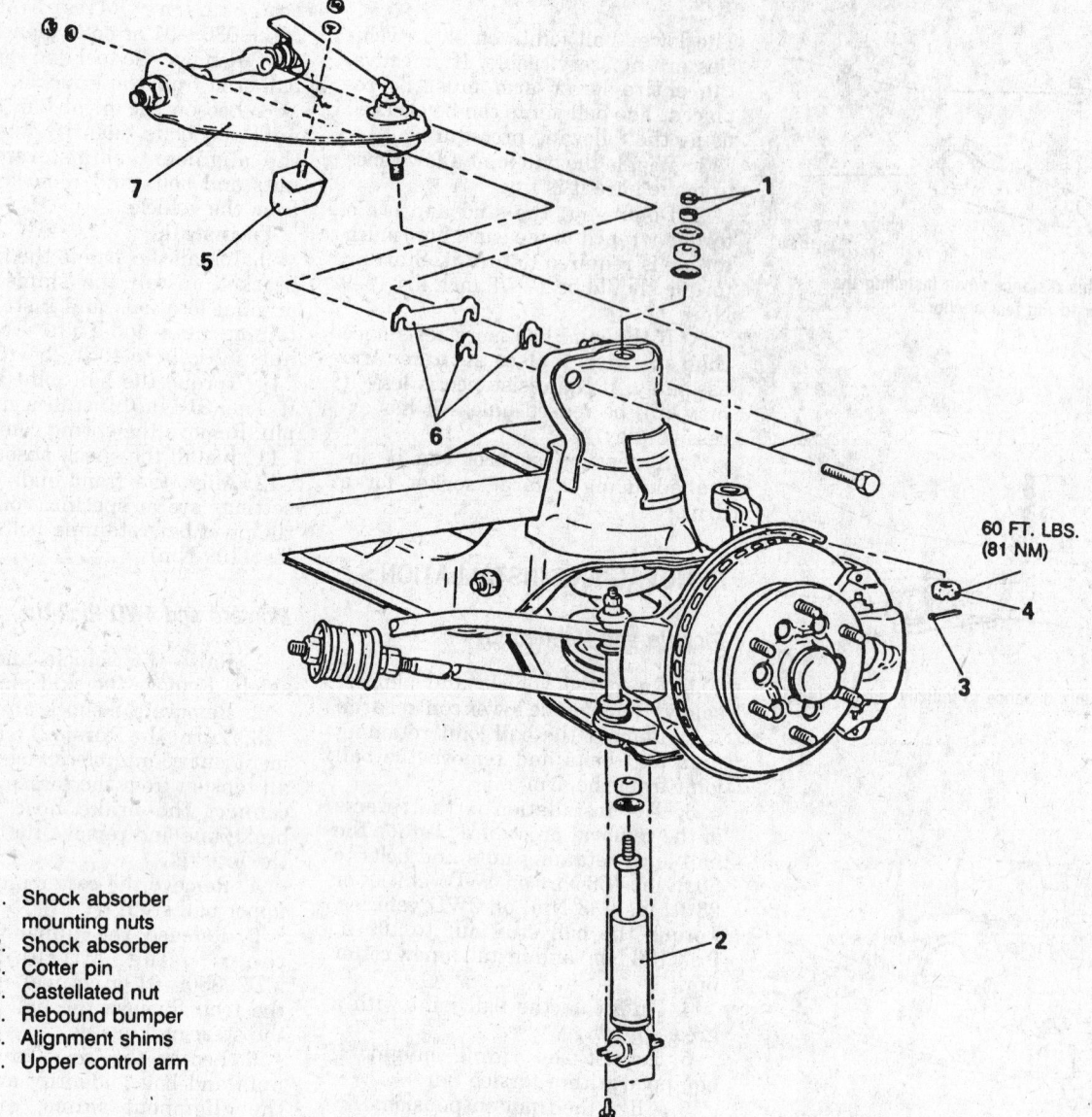

1. Shock absorber
   mounting nuts
2. Shock absorber
3. Cotter pin
4. Castellated nut
5. Rebound bumper
6. Alignment shims
7. Upper control arm

60 FT. LBS.
(81 NM)

7911D106

Front suspension components — 2WD Pick-Up

Lower Control Arm

REMOVAL AND INSTALLATION

2WD Pick-Up

1. Raise the vehicle and support safely.
2. Remove the shock absorber.
3. Disconnect the sway bar and strut bar from the lower control arm.
4. Install Mitsubishi spring compressor tool MB990792 or equivalent, to the coil spring and compress the spring.
5. Remove the cotter pin and lower ball joint nut.

6. Release the lower ball joint taper using Mitsubishi tool MB990809–01 or equivalent.
7. Remove the tool and remove the ball stud from the knuckle. Remove the spring compressor.
8. Pull the arm down and remove the spring with the rubber isolation pad from the vehicle. Remove the lower arm shaft mounting nuts and remove the arm from the vehicle.

To install:

9. Install the arm to the cross-member finger tight. Install the spring with the rubber isolators. Install the compressor tool and compress spring so lower ball joint can be inserted through the knuckle.

10. Torque the lower ball joint nut to 100 ft. lbs. (136 Nm). Install a new cotter pin. Remove the spring compressor.
11. Connect the sway bar and strut bar to the lower control arm.
12. Install the shock absorber.
13. Lower the vehicle completely. With the weight of the vehicle on suspension torque the lower control arm to crossmember mounting nut to 50 ft. lbs. (68 Nm).
14. Align the front suspension.

Montero and 4WD Pick-Up

1. Raise the vehicle and support safely.
2. Remove the skid plate.

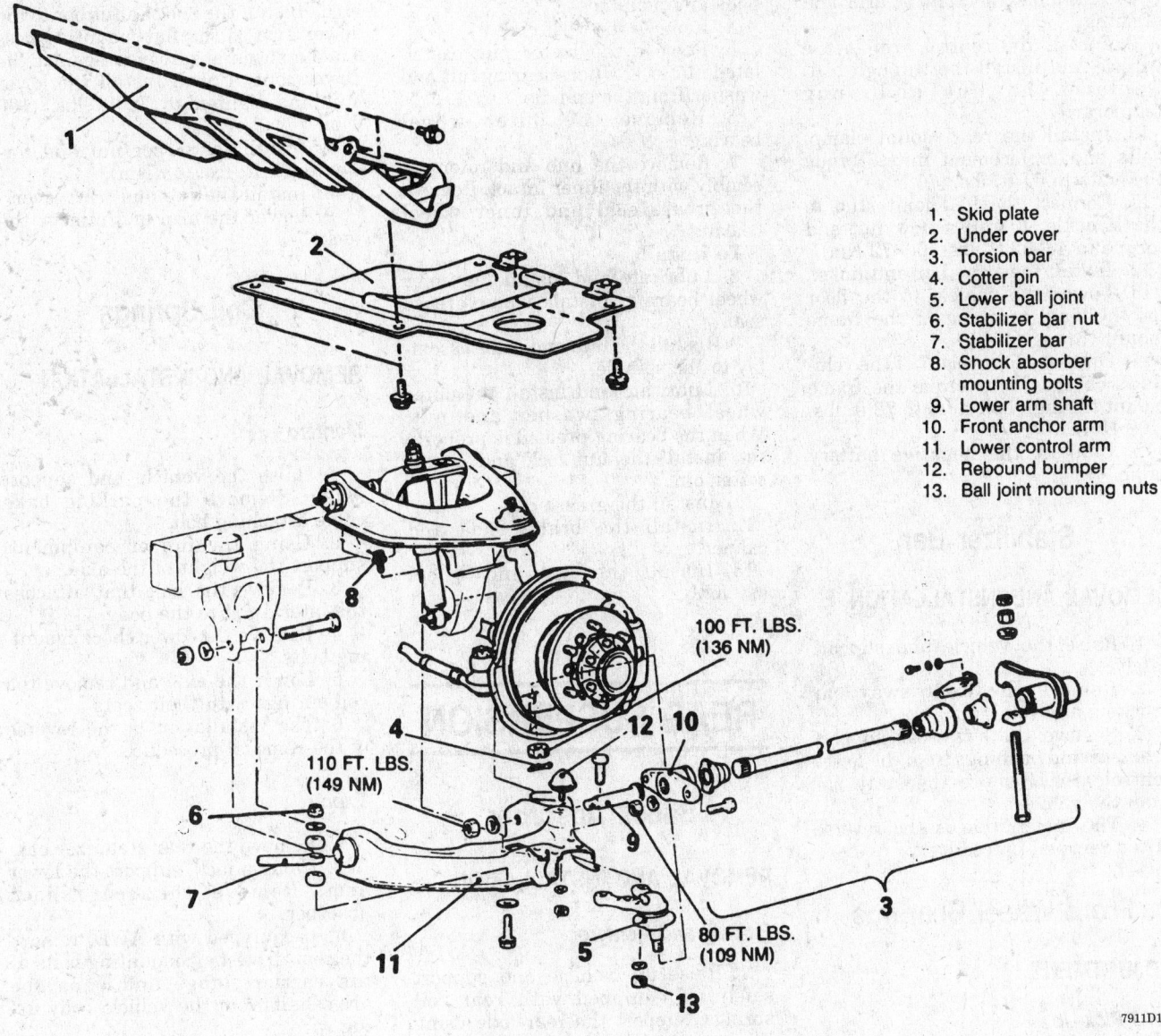

1. Skid plate
2. Under cover
3. Torsion bar
4. Cotter pin
5. Lower ball joint
6. Stabilizer bar nut
7. Stabilizer bar
8. Shock absorber mounting bolts
9. Lower arm shaft
10. Front anchor arm
11. Lower control arm
12. Rebound bumper
13. Ball joint mounting nuts

100 FT. LBS. (136 NM)

110 FT. LBS. (149 NM)

80 FT. LBS. (109 NM)

7911D107

Front suspension components — 4WD Vehicle

3. Remove the torsion bar, anchors and lower arm shaft.

4. Remove the shock absorber lower attaching bolt.

5. Disconnect the stabilizer bar from the lower control arm.

6. Remove the cotter pin and the nut from the lower ball stud. Separate the lower ball stud from the steering knuckle using a puller.

7. Remove the pivot bolts and remove the arm from the vehicle.

To install:

8. Install the new control arm to the vehicle.

9. Install the pivot bolts, but do not torque.

10. Insert the ball stud into the steering knuckle bore. Install the nut, torque to 100 ft. lbs. (136 Nm) and install a new cotter pin.

11. Attach the stabilizer bar to the control arm. Install the shock mount bolts.

12. Install the torsion bar and turn the adjustment bolt clockwise to apply a load to the bar.

13. Lower the vehicle so weight of the vehicle is on suspension.

14. Torque the pivot nuts to 110 ft. lbs. (149 Nm).

15. Set the riding height.

16. Align the front suspension.

Expo

1. Disconnect the negative battery cable.

2. Raise the vehicle and support safely allowing wheels and suspension to hang freely.

3. Remove sway bar links from lower control arm.

4. Disconnect the ball joint stud from the steering knuckle.

5. Remove the inner mounting frame-through bolt and nut.

6. Remove the rear mount bolts. Remove the clamp if equipped.

7. Remove the rear rod bushing if servicing.

To install:

8. Assemble the control arm and bushing.

9. Install the control arm to the vehicle and install the through bolt. Replace the nut and snug temporarily.

10. Install the rear mount clamp, bolts and replacement nuts. Torque the bolts to 51 ft. lbs. (70 Nm).

11. Connect the ball joint stud to the knuckle. Install a new nut and torque to 43–52 ft. lbs. (60–72 Nm).

12. Install the sway bar and links.

13. Lower the vehicle to the floor for the final torquing of the frame mount through bolt.

14. Once the full weight of the vehicle is on the floor, torque the frame mount through bolt nuts to 78 ft. lbs. (108 Nm).

15. Connect the negative battery cable.

Stabilizer Bar

REMOVAL AND INSTALLATION

1. Raise the vehicle and support safely.

2. Remove the front sway bar brackets and retainers.

3. Remove the sway bar support brackets and bushings from the lower control arm. Remove the sway bar from the vehicle.

4. The installation is the reverse of the removal procedure.

Front Wheel Bearings

ADJUSTMENT

2WD Pick-Up

1. Tighten the wheel bearing nut to 22 ft. lbs. (30 Nm) while turning the rotor.

2. Loosen the wheel bearing adjusting nut completely.

3. Tighten the nut to 6 ft. lbs. (8 Nm).

4. Check the wheel bearing endplay. The specification is 0.001–0.003 in.

5. Install the nut lock and cotter pin.

REMOVAL AND INSTALLATION

2WD Pick-Up

1. Raise the vehicle and support safely.

2. Remove the tire and wheel assembly.

3. Remove the caliper, disc brake pads and adaptor.

4. Remove the dust cap.

5. Remove the cotter pin, castellated nut lock, wheel bearing nut and washer from the spindle.

6. Remove the outer wheel bearing.

7. Remove the hub and rotor assembly with the inner intact. Remove the grease seal and inner wheel bearing.

To install:

8. Lubricate and install the inner wheel bearing. Install a new grease seal.

9. Install the hub and rotor assembly to the spindle.

10. Lubricate and install the outer wheel bearing, washer and nut. When the bearing preload is properly set, install the nut lock and a new cotter pin.

11. Install the grease cap.

12. Install the brake pads and caliper.

13. Install the tire and wheel assembly.

REAR SUSPENSION

Shock Absorber

REMOVAL AND INSTALLATION

Pick-Up and Montero

1. Raise the vehicle and support safely. If equipped with rear coil springs, support the rear axle using the proper equipment.

2. Remove the bolts that attach the shock to the frame or bracket.

3. Remove the shock from the vehicle.

4. The installation is the reverse of the removal procedure.

Expo

1. Disconnect the negative battery cable.

2. Remove the trim cover inside the hatch area for access to the top mounting nuts.

3. Support the lower arm with a jack and compress the coil spring. Remove the lower mounting nut.

4. Remove the cap from the upper end of the shock.

5. Remove the upper mounting nut and the shock from the vehicle.

To install:

6. Install the shock absorber to the lower arm so the flat mounting boss on the shock absorber is against the lower control arm. Install the lower nut and tighten to 72 ft. lbs. (100 Nm).

7. Install the upper nut and torque to 33 ft. lbs. (45 Nm).

8. Install the cap and trim cover.

9. Lower the arm and remove the jack.

Coil Springs

REMOVAL AND INSTALLATION

Montero

1. Raise the vehicle and support safely. Remove the parking bake cable attaching bolt.

2. Using the proper equipment, support the weight of the axle.

3. Remove the bolt that attaches the lateral rod to the body.

4. Remove the lower shock mounting bolts.

5. Lower the axle and remove the coil springs with their seats.

6. The installation is the reverse of the removal procedure.

Expo

1. Remove the rear stabilizer bar.

2. Using a jack, support the lower arm. Remove the rear shock absorber.

3. If equipped with AWD, remove the rear driveshaft mounting bolts at the carrier flange and hang the driveshaft from the vehicle body using wire.

4. If equipped with ABS, remove the speed sensor clamp bolt and relocate out of the way. Do not apply tension to the wire harness of the connector.

5. Scribe mating marks on the lower arm shaft assembly and the crossmember. To remove the coil spring, loosen the shaft assembly nut and slowly lower the rear end of the lower arm. It is not necessary to remove the nut, only to loosen it.

To install:

6. Install the coil spring into the seats making sure both ends of the spring are correctly aligned with the spring seat groove.

7. Slowly raise the rear the rear end of the lower arm and align the scribe marks made during disassembly. Tighten shaft assembly nut to 69 ft. lbs. (95 Nm).

8. Install the speed sensor clamp to it's original location and secure the wire harness making.

9. Install the rear driveshaft to the flange and secure tightening mounting bolts to 40–47 ft. lbs. (55–65 Nm).

10. Reconnect the lower portion of the shock and tighten the retaining bolt to 72 ft. lbs. (100 Nm).

11. Lower the arm and remove the jack.

Leaf Springs

REMOVAL AND INSTALLATION

1. Raise the vehicle and support safely. Remove the parking bake cable attaching bolt.

2. Using the proper equipment, support the weight of the axle.

3. Remove the nuts, washers and U-bolts attaching the springs to the axle housing. Remove the seat and spacer.

4. Remove the spring shackle bolts, shackle and spring front bolt.

5. Remove the springs from the vehicle.

6. The installation is the reverse of the removal procedure. Make sure all shackle mounting nuts are on the inside of the springs. Torque the front spring mount nut to 116 ft. lbs. (160 Nm) and the rear shackle nuts to 43 ft. lbs. (60 Nm). Torque U-bolt nuts to 87 ft. lbs. (120 Nm).

Rear Control Arms

REMOVAL AND INSTALLATION

Expo

1. Disconnect negative battery cable.

2. Remove the rear stabilizer bar.

3. If equipped with AWD, remove the rear axle shaft.

4. Remove the rear brake drum.

5. If equipped with ABS, remove the rear caliper assembly and brake disc.

6. Remove the rear hub assembly. If equipped with ABS, take care not

to damage the rotor teeth during hub removal.

7. Disconnect the parking brake cable from the rear brake shoe.

8. If equipped with ABS, disconnect and remove the rear wheel sensor.

NOTE: The speed sensor has a pole piece projecting from it. This exposed tip must be protected from impact or damage. Do not allow the pole piece to contact the toothed wheel during removal or installation.

9. Remove the rear shock and coil spring.

10. Remove the brake line and parking brake mounting bolts from the lower control arm.

11. Matchmark and remove the inboard lower arm pivot bolt. Remove the flange bolt and the arm from the vehicle.

To install:

12. Install the arm on the vehicle and secure with the flange bolt, temporarily tighten the nut. Install the arm pivot bolt and temporarily tighten the nut.

13. Install the rear shock and coil spring.

14. Install the brake line and parking brake mounting bolts to the lower control arm.

15. Connect the parking brake cable to the rear brake shoe.

16. Install the rear hub assembly.

17. Install the rear brake drum or, if equipped with ABS, install the rear caliper assembly and brake disc.

18. Install the rear axle shaft.

19. Install and connect the rear wheel speed sensor. Use a brass or other non-magnetic feeler gauge to check the air gap between the tip of the pole piece and the toothed wheel. Correct gap is 0.012–0.035 in. (0.3–0.9mm). Tighten the 2 sensor bracket bolts to 10 ft. lbs. (14 Nm) with the sensor located so the gap is the same at several points on the toothed wheel. If the gap is incorrect, it is likely that the toothed wheel is worn or improperly installed.

20. Lower the vehicle and tighten the lower arm flange bolt nut and the arm pivot bolt to 69 ft. lbs. (95 Nm).

21. Install the rear stabilizer bar and reconnect the negative battery cable.

22. Bleed the brake system if any lines where opened. Adjust the parking brake and perform a rear wheel alignment.

Rear Wheel Bearings

For RWD and 4WD applications, please refer to "Drive Axle" section in this repair manual.

REMOVAL AND INSTALLATION

Expo

1. Raise the vehicle and support safely. Remove the tire and wheel assembly.

2. If equipped with ABS, remove the caliper assembly, brake disc and rear wheel speed sensor from the adapter. If not equipped with ABS, remove the brake drum.

NOTE: The speed sensor has a pole piece projecting from it. This exposed tip must be protected from impact or damage. Do not allow the pole piece to contact the toothed wheel during removal or installation.

3. Remove the dust cap, nut and tongued washer. Do not use an air gun to remove the nut.

4. Remove the rear hub assembly taking care not to scrape or damage the teeth of the speed rotor, if equipped.

5. Inspect the hub unit bearing for wear or damage. If replacement of the bearing is required, the hub assembly and bearing is to be replaced as a unit. The rear hub unit bearing assembly should should not be dismantled.

6. Installation is the reverse of the removal procedure.

Rear Axle Assembly

For RWD, AWD and 4WD applications, please refer to "Drive Axle" section of this manual.

NISSAN

10

Pathfinder • Pickup • Quest

FIRING ORDERS

NOTE: To avoid confusion, always replace spark plug wires one at a time.

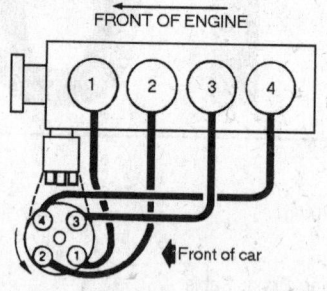

FRONT OF ENGINE

Front of car

7911E002

2.4L (KA24E) Engine
Engine Firing Order: 1-3-4-2
Distributor Rotation: Counterclockwise

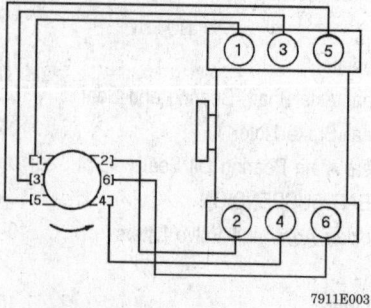

7911E003

3.0L (VG30E) Engines
Engine Firing Order: 1-2-3-4-5-6
Distributor Rotation: Counterclockwise

ENGINE ELECTRICAL

NOTE: Disconnecting the negative battery cable on some vehicles may interfere with the functions of the on board computer systems and may require the computer to undergo a relearning process when the battery cable is reconnected. This usually requires only a few minutes of driving.

Distributor

REMOVAL

1. Disconnect the negative battery cable.

2. Remove the distributor cap without disconnecting the spark plug wires. Unplug the distributor connector.

3. Rotate the crankshaft to TDC of No. 1 cylinder, if possible. Mark the position of the rotor to the distributor body and to the engine.

4. Remove the hold-down bolt and lift the distributor out of the engine.

INSTALLATION

Timing Not Disturbed

1. If necessary, install a new O-ring on the distributor body. Lightly oil the O-ring and make sure the distributor mounting boss is clean.

2. If the crankshaft was not rotated with the distributor removed, align the rotor with the mark on the distributor body and insert the distributor into place. Some distributors have alignment marks on the shaft and housing. Align the shaft mark with the protruding mark on the housing.

3. The rotor may turn as the distributor is pushed in; remove it and turn the rotor back or forward 1 tooth and try again. When installing the distributor, it is important to make sure the rotor points to the mark made on the engine.

4. Check and adjust ignition timing as required.

Timing Disturbed

1. If the crankshaft was turned or if no alignment marks were made when the distributor was removed, make sure the engine is at TDC of No. 1 cylinder.

a. Remove the spark plug from No. 1 cylinder.

b. Rotate the crankshaft while holding a thumb over the spark plug hole to determine that the piston is coming up on the compression stroke.

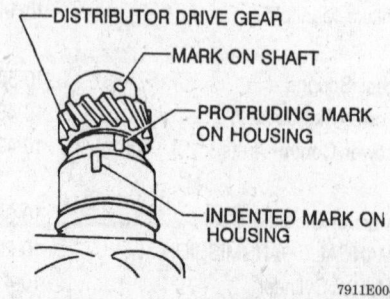

DISTRIBUTOR DRIVE GEAR

MARK ON SHAFT

PROTRUDING MARK ON HOUSING

INDENTED MARK ON HOUSING

7911E004

Some distributors have alignment marks on the shaft and body — 3.0L engine shown

c. Align the red TDC mark on the crankshaft pulley with the pointer on the cover.

2. Check the O-ring on the distributor body and replace as necessary. Lightly lubricate the O-ring and make sure the mounting boss is clean.

3. Align the marks on the distributor shaft and body and install the distributor. The rotor may turn as the distributor is pushed in; remove it and turn the rotor back or forward 1 tooth and try again. When installing the distributor, it is important to make sure the rotor points to the mark made on the engine.

4. Check and adjust ignition timing as required.

Ignition Timing

ADJUSTMENT

The ignition timing is controlled by the ECU, but a basic setting is required if the distributor has been removed. Always check and adjust ignition timing and idle speed together.

Locate the timing marks on the crankshaft pulley and the front of the engine. The timing marks are in 5 degree increments and the TDC mark is always painted red.

1. Connect a tachometer and a timing light to the engine, according to the manufacturer's instructions. Make sure the wires do not interfere with the fan.

2. Make sure all lights and accessories are switched **OFF** and run the engine to warm it to normal operating temperature.

3. With the transmission out of gear, run the engine at 2000 rpm for about 2 minutes, then check idle speed and ignition timing. If timing and idle speed are different from specification, look for another engine problem such as a vacuum leak or bad electrical connection. If no other obvious problem is found, a full diagnostic test should be run.

4. Check idle speed; on engines with throttle body fuel injection, ignition timing is not adjustable.

5. On models with automatic transmission, idle speed should be 750 rpm in **N**.

6. To adjust timing on 3.0L engines with multi-point fuel injection:

a. If timing is not correct, disconnect the wiring for the air control valve at the back of the intake manifold. Idle speed should be 700 rpm. The adjusting screw is on the

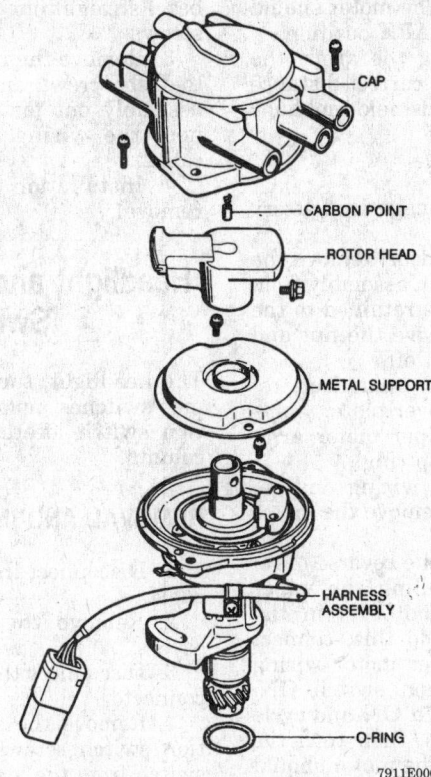

7911E006

Exploded view of the distributor — 3.0L engine

same body assembly as the air control valve.

b. Reconnect the wiring, idle speed should be about 750 rpm. Do not change it with the wiring connected.

c. Check and adjust timing as required to 15 degrees BTDC. Adjust by rotating the distributor. Idle speed should remain at about 750 rpm.

7. To adjust timing on the 2.4L engine with multi-point fuel injection:

a. Check idle speed at about 800 rpm. If not correct, disconnect the throttle sensor wiring and adjust the speed to less than 800 rpm.

b. Check and adjust ignition timing to 10 degrees.

8. Run the engine at 2000 rpm for about 2 minutes and check idle speed and timing again. If idle speed or timing are not correct, other problems exist with the engine control system and a full diagnostic test must be run.

Alternator

PRECAUTIONS

Several precautions must be observed with alternator equipped vehicles to avoid damage to the unit.

If the battery is removed for any reason, make sure it is reconnected with the correct polarity. Reversing the battery connections may result in damage to the one-way rectifiers.

When utilizing a booster battery as a starting aid, always connect the positive to positive terminals and the negative terminal from the booster battery to a good engine ground on the vehicle being started.

Never use a fast charger as a booster to start vehicles.

Disconnect the battery cables when charging the battery with a fast charger.

Never attempt to polarize the alternator.

Do not use test lights of more than 12 volts when checking diode continuity.

Do not short across or ground any of the alternator terminals.

The polarity of the battery, alternator and regulator must be matched and considered before making any electrical connections within the system.

Never separate the alternator on an open circuit. Make sure all connections within the circuit are clean and tight.

Disconnect the battery ground terminal when performing any service on electrical components.

Disconnect the battery if arc welding is to be done on the vehicle.

BELT TENSION ADJUSTMENT

Belt tension can be checked with a gauge made for the purpose. If a tension gauge is not available, belt deflection can be measured in inches. Press on the belt with 22 lbs. (10 kg) of force at a point halfway between the alternator and water pump pulleys. Deflection should be 0.200–0.310 in. (5–8mm) on the 3.0L engine or 0.310–0.470 in. (8–12mm) on the 2.4L engine.

1. Loosen the alternator's pivot bolt and the tension adjuster lock bolt.

2. Turn the adjuster bolt as required until the tension is correct.

3. Tighten the bolts and recheck the tension. If new belts have been installed, run the engine for a few minutes, then check tension again. The ideal adjustment is toward the looser end of the specification, belts adjusted too tight will cause bearing failure.

REMOVAL AND INSTALLATION

1. Disconnect the negative battery cable.

2. Label and disconnect the wiring from the alternator.

3. Loosen the drive belt tension and remove the belt from the pulley.

4. Remove the alternator-to-bracket bolts and the alternator from the vehicle.

5. To install, reverse the removal procedures. Adjust the drive belt tension. Torque the lower bracket bolt to 35 ft. lbs. (47 Nm) and the adjuster lock bolt to 10 ft. lbs. (13 Nm).

6. Connect all wiring before connecting the battery cable. Terminal **E** is always alternator ground.

Starter

REMOVAL AND INSTALLATION

1. If necessary, raise and safely support the vehicle.

2. Disconnect the negative battery cable.

3. Disconnect the electrical connectors from the starter, taking note of the positions for reinstallation purposes.

4. Remove the starter-to-engine bolts and the starter from the vehicle.

5. To install, reverse the removal procedures. Torque the starter

mounting bolts to 29–36 ft. lbs. (39–49 Nm).

CHASSIS ELECTRICAL

Heater Blower Motor

REMOVAL AND INSTALLATION

The blower motor is accessible from under the right side of the instrument pan

1. Disconnect the negative battery cable.
2. Disconnect the electrical connector from the blower motor.
3. Remove the blower motor-to-heater unit screws and the blower motor from the unit. It may be necessary to remove the glove box or package tray.
4. To install, reverse the removal procedures.

Windshield Wiper Motor

REMOVAL AND INSTALLATION

Front Wiper

1. Disconnect the negative battery cable.
2. Remove the wiper blades and arms as an assembly from the pivots. The arms are retained to the pivots by nuts; remove the nuts and pull the arms straight off.
3. Remove the cowl top grille screws (from the front edge) and pull the grille forward to disengage the rear tabs.
4. Remove the wiper motor arm-to-connecting rod stop ring.
5. From under the instrument panel, disconnect the electrical connector from the wiper motor harness.
6. Remove the wiper motor-to-cowl screws and the wiper motor from the vehicle.

To install:

7. Install the motor and secure the bolts. Install the cowl grille.
8. Before installing the wiper arms, be sure the motor is in the PARK position. To do this, connect the battery and wiper motor wiring and turn the ignition switch **ON**. Turn the wiper switch **ON** and cycle the motor 3–4 times, then turn the

wiper switch **OFF**. The motor should stop in the correct PARK position.

9. When installing the arms, the blades should be the correct distance above the lower windshield molding.

Rear Wiper

1. Disconnect the negative battery cable.
2. From the rear door, remove the wiper blade/arm as an assembly from the pivot. The arm is retained to the pivots by a nut; remove the nut and pull the arm straight off.
3. From inside the rear door, remove wiper motor cover plate.
4. Remove the wiper motor arm-to-connecting rod stop ring.
5. Disconnect the wiring and remove the screws to remove the motor from the door.
6. Installation is the reverse of removal. Before installing the wiper arm, be sure the motor is in the PARK position. To do this, connect the battery and wiper motor wiring and turn the ignition switch **ON**. Turn the wiper switch **ON** and cycle the motor 3–4 times, then turn the wiper switch **OFF**. The motor should stop in the correct PARK position.

Windshield Wiper Switch

The windshield wiper switch is a part of the combination switch located on the steering column. The switch can be removed without removing the steering wheel.

REMOVAL AND INSTALLATION

1. Disconnect the negative battery cable.
2. Remove the steering column covers.
3. Disconnect the windshield wiper switch electrical connector.
4. Remove the windshield wiper switch-to-combination switch screws and the windshield wiper switch from the steering column.
5. To install, reverse the removal procedures.

Instrument Cluster

REMOVAL AND INSTALLATION

1. Disconnect the negative battery cable.
2. Remove the instrument cluster bezel screws and the bezel. The bezel is also secured with clips; pull the

bezel straight out after removing the screws.

3. Remove the instrument cluster-to-dash screws and pull the cluster assembly out far enough to disconnect the wiring and speedometer cable.
4. Installation is the reverse of removal.

Headlight and Turn Signal Switch

The headlight, turn signal and dimmer switches make up the combination switch located on the steering column.

REMOVAL AND INSTALLATION

1. Disconnect the negative battery cable.
2. Remove the steering column covers.
3. Disconnect the switch electrical connector.
4. Remove the switch-to-combination switch screws and remove the switch from the steering column.
5. To install, reverse the removal procedures.

Combination Switch

The combination switch includes switches for headlights and dimmer, windshield washer and wiper, turn signal, horn contacts and cruise control, if equipped. The steering wheel must be removed to remove the combination switch as an assembly. The 2 switch stalks can be removed separately as described above.

REMOVAL AND INSTALLATION

1. Disconnect the negative battery cable.
2. Remove the steering column covers.
3. Remove the horn pad and the steering wheel nut. Use a puller to remove the steering wheel.
4. Disconnect the wiring harness from the clip which retains it to the lower instrument panel.
5. Disconnect the electrical connectors from the combination switch.
6. Loosen the combination switch-to-steering column screw and remove the switch assembly.
7. To install, align the hole in the steering column with the protrusion on the switch base and reverse the removal procedures.

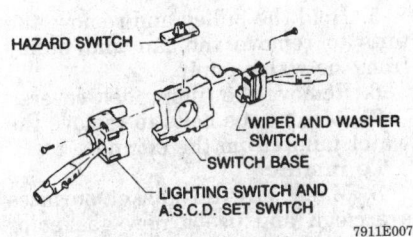

Combination switch assembly — the steering wheel must be removed to remove the base

Ignition Lock/Switch

REMOVAL AND INSTALLATION

1. Disconnect the negative battery cable.
2. From the upper steering column, remove the shell cover screws and the covers.
3. Disconnect the electrical connector from the rear of the ignition switch.
4. Drill out the 2 self shear screws from the ignition lock holder.
5. Remove the screws and the ignition switch.
6. To install, reverse the removal procedures. Torque the shear-type screws until the heads shear.

Stoplight Switch

The stoplight switch is attached to a bracket at the top of the brake pedal.

REMOVAL AND INSTALLATION

1. Disconnect the negative battery cable.
2. From under the dash, disconnect the electrical connector from the stoplight switch.
3. Loosen and remove the locknut from the stoplight switch.
4. Unscrew the stoplight switch from the brake pedal bracket.
5. To install, reverse the removal procedures. Adjust the switch, torque the stoplight switch locknut to 11 ft. lbs. (15 Nm) and adjust the pedal height and free-play.

ADJUSTMENT

1. Start the engine and press the brake pedal by hand until pushrod resistance is felt.
2. Use a feeler gauge to measure stoplight switch-to-brake pedal gap:

it should be 0.012–0.039 in. (0.3–1.0mm).
3. If necessary, disconnect the electrical connector from the stoplight switch, loosen the switch locknut and adjust the gap. Torque the lock nut to 11 ft. lbs. (15 Nm).

Clutch Cruise Control Switch

If equipped with cruise control, the clutch switch is attached to a bracket mounted to the upper portion of the clutch pedal bracket. This switch replaces the stopper bolt and is used to set pedal height.

REMOVAL AND INSTALLATION

1. Disconnect the negative battery cable.
2. Disconnect the electrical connector from the clutch switch.
3. Loosen the locknut and unscrew the switch from the bracket.
4. To install, screw the clutch switch into the bracket until the correct pedal height is established. Torque the locknut to 11 ft. lbs. (15 Nm). Pedal height should be;
   2.4L engine — 9.29–9.69 in. (236–246mm)
   3.0L engine — 8.94–9.33 in. (227–237mm)

NOTE: The pedal height is the distance from the floor board to the pedal pad with the carpet removed.

Clutch Interlock Switch

The clutch interlock switch is attached to a bracket mounted to the cowl.

REMOVAL AND INSTALLATION

1. Disconnect the negative battery cable.
2. Disconnect the electrical connector from the clutch interlock switch.
3. Loosen the locknut and unscrew the switch from the bracket.
4. To install, use a feeler gauge and screw the clutch interlock switch into the bracket.
5. Fully depress the clutch pedal and adjust the gap between the clutch pedal stopper bracket and the threaded end of the clutch interlock switch. The gap should be 0.012–0.039 in. (0.3–1.0mm).
6. Torque the locknut to 11 ft. lbs. (15 Nm), reconnect the wiring and make sure the started operates only when the clutch pedal is fully depressed.

Fuses, Circuit Breakers and Relays

LOCATION

The main fuse block is behind a panel to the right or the steering column. The turn signal flasher is to the left of the brake pedal. A series relays in mounted under the hood on the right fender. All relays are color coded according to internal circuitry and should be replaced with relays of the same color.

Computers

LOCATION

The main engine ECU is under the passenger's seat along with the automatic transmission control unit. The power window amplifier is behind the passenger's side kick panel. The door

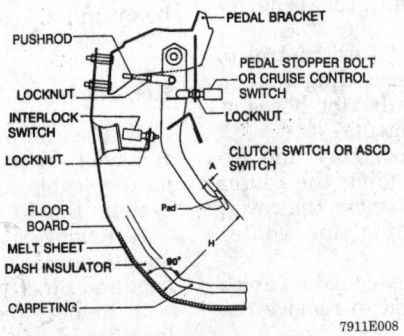

Clutch pedal switch adjustment;vehicles with cruise control use the switch to set pedal height

lock timer and cruise control ECU are under the driver's seat.

Turn Signal Flasher

LOCATION

The turn signal flasher is to the left of the brake pedal.

ENGINE COOLING

Radiator

REMOVAL AND INSTALLATION

1. Disconnect the negative battery cable.

2. Drain the engine cooling system and disconnect the radiator hoses. If equipped with an automatic transmission, disconnect and plug the transmission oil cooler lines at the radiator.

3. There is a lower section that can be removed from the fan shroud. Remove this section, unbolt the 2 upper radiator brackets and lift the radiator and shroud out together.

4. Installation is the reverse of removal. Make sure the lower radiator mounting rubbers are in place before installing radiator.

5. If equipped with an automatic transmission, check and/or refill the transmission.

Heater Core

REMOVAL AND INSTALLATION

1. The dashboard must be removed. Disconnect the negative battery cable. On vehicles with theft protected radios, obtain the security code.

2. Set the temperature control to full hot and drain the cooling system.

3. Disconnect the heater hoses at the engine compartment.

4. Remove the ash tray and remove the screws holding the center console face cover. Remove the cover, heater controls, radio and center vent.

5. Disconnect the control cables and wiring as needed to remove the dashboard.

6. Disconnect the ducts and remove the heater unit. Remove the clips or screws and split the case to remove the heater core. Note how the air flow control doors fit into the case.

7. Install the heater core and assemble the case halves. Use a new gasket and make sure the air flow doors work properly.

8. Install the heater unit and use a new gasket to seal it to the cooling unit or blower fan housing. Connect the ducts.

9. Install the instrument panel.

10. Install the heater control assembly, center vent and radio.

11. Adjust the heater controls and air flow doors as required.

12. Connect the heater hoses, fill the cooling system and start the engine to test the system.

Water Pump

REMOVAL AND INSTALLATION

2.4L Engine

1. Disconnect the negative battery cable and drain the cooling system. Don't forget the block drain.

2. Remove the upper radiator hose to provide working room and loosen the alternator to remove the drive belt from the pulleys.

3. Remove the lower section of the fan shroud and remove the screws to lift the shroud from the engine. Hold the pulley and remove the nuts to remove the fan and pulley from the water pump.

4. Remove the bolts and remove the water pump from the engine.

To install:

5. Make sure all gasket surfaces are clean and use a new gasket or silicone sealer when installing the pump to the engine. Torque the 6mm bolts to 7 ft. lbs. (10 Nm) and the 8mm bolts to 12 ft. lbs. (16 Nm).

6. Install the fan clutch, fan and pulley and torque the nuts or bolts to 7 ft. lbs. (10 Nm).

7. Install the fan shroud and drive belts and fill the cooling system to check for leaks.

3.0L Engine

1. The timing belt cover must be removed. Disconnect the negative battery cable and drain the cooling system. Don't forget the block drain.

2. Remove the radiator hoses and, on automatic transmission, disconnect and plug the fluid cooling lines.

3. Remove the lower section of the fan shroud and remove the screws to lift the shroud from the engine. Remove the bracket bolts and lift the radiator out of the vehicle.

4. Remove all the accessory drive belts.

5. Hold the pulley and remove the nuts to remove the fan and pulley from the water pump.

6. Remove the timing belt covers.

7. Remove the bolts to remove the water pump from the engine.

To install:

8. Make sure all gasket surfaces are clean and use a new gasket or silicone sealer when installing the pump to the engine. Torque the bolts to 15 ft. lbs. (21 Nm).

9. Install the timing belt covers. On 4WD models, make sure the sealing surfaces are clean and carefully install the rubber seal when installing the cover. The timing belt must be properly protected from dirt and oil.

10. Install the pulley, fan clutch and the fan.

11. Install the accessory drive belts and adjust the tension.

12. Install the radiator and fan shroud and connect the cooling system hoses.

13. Fill the system and check for leaks.

Thermostat

The factory-installed thermostat opening temperature is 180°F (USA) or 190°F (Canada). The thermostat is located above the water pump.

REMOVAL AND INSTALLATION

1. Disconnect the negative battery cable.

2. Drain the engine coolant to a level below the thermostat housing.

3. Disconnect the coolant hose from the thermostat water outlet.

4. Remove the water outlet-to-thermostat housing bolts, gasket and thermostat.

NOTE: The thermostat spring must face the inside of the engine.

5. Clean the gasket mounting surfaces.

NOTE: If the thermostat is equipped with an air bleed or jiggle valve, be sure to position it in the upward direction.

6. To install, use a new gasket or sealant and reverse the removal procedures. Torque the thermostat housing bolts to 6 ft. lbs. (8 Nm) on 2.4L engine or 15 ft. lbs. (21 Nm) on 3.0L engine.

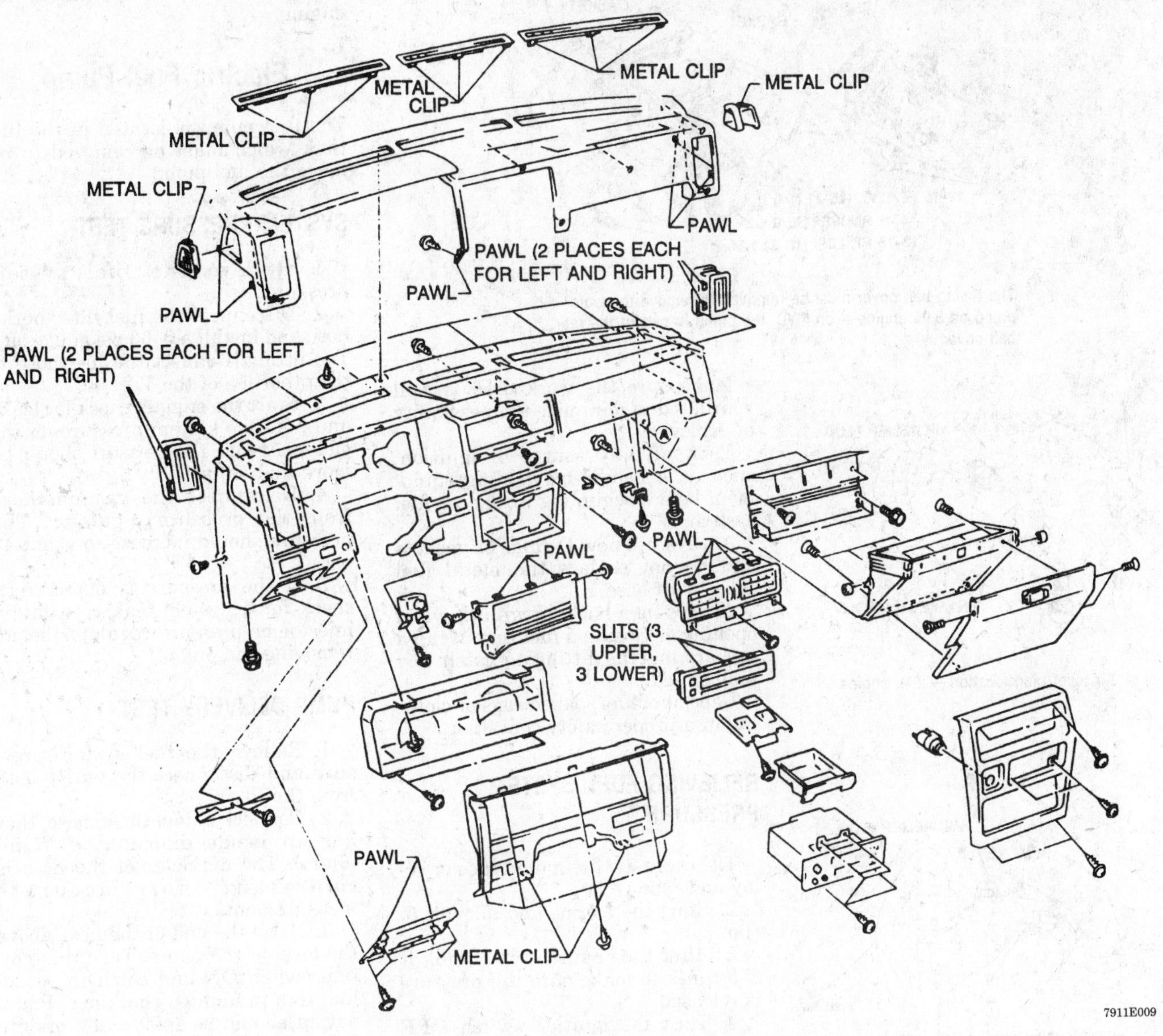

METAL CLIP

METAL CLIP

METAL CLIP

METAL CLIP

METAL CLIP

METAL CLIP

PAWL

PAWL

PAWL (2 PLACES EACH FOR LEFT AND RIGHT)

PAWL

PAWL (2 PLACES EACH FOR LEFT AND RIGHT)

PAWL

PAWL

SLITS (3 UPPER, 3 LOWER)

PAWL

METAL CLIP

7911E009

Dashboard assembly must be removed to remove the heater core

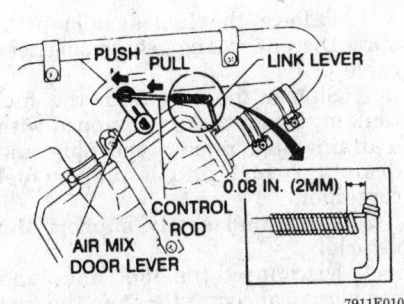

PUSH PULL LINK LEVER

0.08 IN. (2MM)

CONTROL ROD

AIR MIX DOOR LEVER

7911E010

Water valve and air mix door control rod adjustment

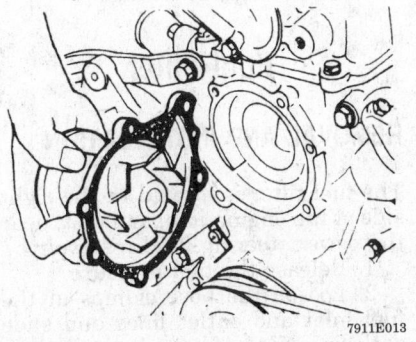

7911E013

Water pump replacement — 2.4L engine

Cooling System Bleeding

1. Set the heater temperature control to **HOT** and open the air relief plug. Pour coolant into the radiator until it comes out the relief plug, then close the plug.

2. Fill the reservoir and run the engine to warm it to operating temperature.

3. When the engine is cool again, check the coolant level in the reservoir.

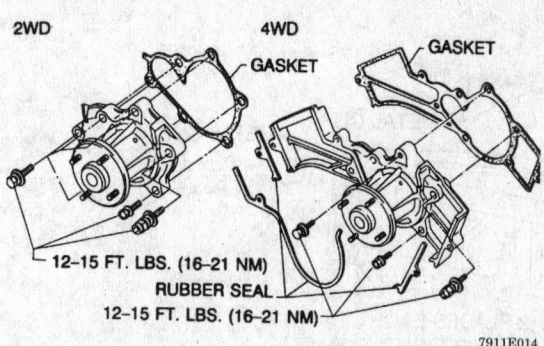

2WD — 4WD

GASKET — GASKET

12-15 FT. LBS. (16-21 NM)
RUBBER SEAL
12-15 FT. LBS. (16-21 NM)

7911E014

The timing belt cover must be removed to remove the water pump on 3.0L engine — on 4WD, the pump is part of the rear belt cover

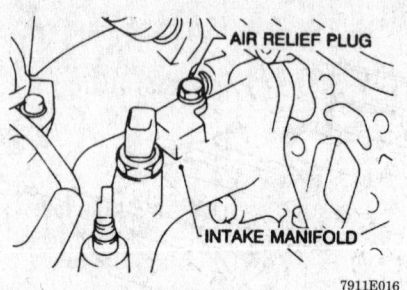

AIR RELIEF PLUG

INTAKE MANIFOLD

7911E016

Air relief plug location — 2.4L engine

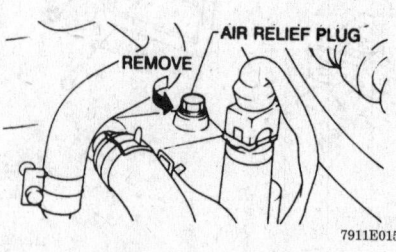

AIR RELIEF PLUG

REMOVE

7911E015

Air relief plug — 3.0L engine

FUEL SYSTEM

Fuel System Service Precautions

Keep a Class B dry chemical fire extinguisher available.

Always relieve the fuel system pressure before disconnecting any fitting.

Make sure the work area is well ventilated to minimize the possibility of explosion.

Turn off any source of ignition, such as a heater or welding equipment before beginning work on a fuel system.

Always use new O-rings or gaskets and do not replace the metal fuel pipes with hose.

Always us a back-up wrench when opening or closing a fuel line. Wrap a rag around the fitting to catch any fuel spilled.

Deposit of fuel soaked rags or clothing in a proper safety container.

RELIEVING FUEL SYSTEM PRESSURE

1. Locate the fuel pump fuse or relay and remove it.
2. Start the engine and allow it to run.
3. After the engine stalls, crank it 2–3 times to make sure the pressure is released.
4. Turn the ignition switch **OFF** and replace the fuse. There may still be some pressure in the system, make sure to take proper precautions when loosening any fittings.

Fuel Filter

REMOVAL AND INSTALLATION

The fuel filter is located in the right side of the engine compartment, near the power steering fluid reservoir.
1. Release the fuel pressure.
2. Loosen the hose clamps at the fuel inlet and outlet lines and slide each line off the filter nipples.
3. Remove the fuel filter.
4. Installation is the reverse of removal. Be sure to use a high pressure type filter and that the flow direction

arrow on the filter points to the engine.

Electric Fuel Pump

The fuel pump is located in the fuel tank which must be removed to remove the fuel pump.

SYSTEM PRESSURE TEST

1. Relieve the fuel system pressure.
2. Disconnect the fuel filter outlet hose and install a 0–60 psi gauge on a Tee fitting. Connect the fuel hose to the other leg of the Tee.
3. Start the engine, check for leaks and note the system pressure on the gauge. At idle, the pressure should be more than 33 psi.
4. Disconnect the vacuum hose from the pressure regulator. The pressure should increase to about 43 psi.
5. If the pressure is not correct, check for a system leak or a faulty injector or pressure regulator before removing the pump.

PUMP DELIVERY TEST

1. Relieve the fuel system pressure and disconnect the outlet hose from the filter.
2. Connect a length of hose that has an inside diameter of 1/4 in. (6mm). The diameter of the hose is important for accurate measurements.
3. Raise the end of the hose above the level of the pump. Turn the ignition switch **ON** and catch the gasoline in a graduated container. Pump output should be 1400cc in a minute or less.

REMOVAL AND INSTALLATION

1. Relieve the fuel system pressure. Disconnect the negative battery cable.
2. Siphon the fuel from the fuel tank or, if fuel tank is equipped with a drain plug, remove the plug and drain the fuel into a proper fuel container.
3. Raise and safely support the vehicle.
4. Disconnect the fuel lines and the electrical connector from the fuel pump assembly. For 4WD models, remove the fuel tank protector from the bottom of the fuel tank.
5. Remove the fuel tank filler tube-to-vehicle bolts or nuts and the outer plate.

6. Remove the fuel tank-to-chassis bolts and lower the tank from the vehicle.

7. Remove the fuel pump assembly-to-tank screws and lift the assembly from the tank.

8. To install, use a new fuel pump assembly-to-tank O-ring and reverse the removal procedures. Torque the fuel pump assembly-to-tank screws to 24 inch lbs. (3 Nm) and the fuel tank protectors-to-chassis bolts to 26 ft. lbs. (35 Nm).

Fuel Injection

IDLE SPEED ADJUSTMENT

NOTE: Idle speed and ignition timing must be checked together.

1. Visually inspect the air cleaner for clogging, the hoses/ducts for leaks, the EGR valve operation, the electrical connectors, the gaskets, the throttle valve and throttle sensor operation and the AIV hose.

2. Start the engine and allow it to reach normal operating temperature.

3. Operate the engine under no-load for 2 minutes at about 2000 rpm. Make sure all accessories and lights are **OFF**. Race the engine 2–3 times, then let it run at idle speed for 1 minute.

4. To adjust idle speed on the 3.0L engine with multi-point fuel injection:

a. Disconnect the wiring for the Auxiliary Air Control (AAC) valve at the back of the intake manifold. Idle speed should drop to about 700 rpm. The adjusting screw is on the same body assembly as the AAC.

b. Reconnect the wiring, idle speed should be about 750 rpm. Do not change it with the wiring connected. If idle speed is not correct, look for another problem in the engine control system.

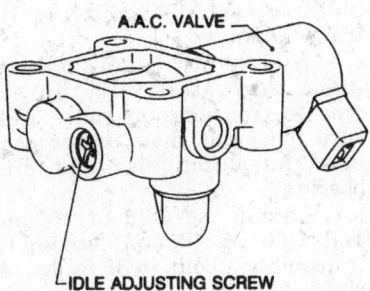

A.A.C. VALVE

IDLE ADJUSTING SCREW

7911E018

Idle speed adjustment on engines with multipoint fuel injection is on the Idle Air Adjusting unit — 3.0L engine shown

c. Check and adjust timing as required to 15 degrees BTDC by rotating the distributor. Idle speed should remain at about 750 rpm.

5. To adjust timing on the 2.4L engine with multi-point fuel injection:

a. Check idle speed at about 800 rpm. If it is not correct, disconnect the throttle sensor wiring and adjust the speed to less than 800 rpm. The adjustment is on the throttle body Idle Air Adjusting (IAA) unit that has small engine coolant hoses connected to it.

b. Check and adjust ignition timing to 15 degrees BTDC.

6. Run the engine at 2000 rpm for about 2 minutes and check idle speed and timing again. If idle speed or timing are not correct, other problems exist with the engine control system and a full diagnostic test must be run.

Fuel Injector

REMOVAL AND INSTALLATION

2.4L Engine

The engine is equipped with 4 fuel injectors, with one located at each cylinder.

1. Relieve the fuel pressure.

2. Label and disconnect the electrical connectors from the fuel injectors.

3. Disconnect the fuel hoses from the rail.

4. Remove the fuel rail with injectors attached from the intake manifold.

5. Separate the fuel injectors from the fuel rail.

To install:

6. Replace the fuel injector O-rings.

7. Install the fuel injectors to the fuel rail.

8. Lubricate the fuel injector O-rings with automatic transmission fluid and press them, with the fuel rail, into the intake manifold.

9. Install the fuel rail-to-intake manifold bolts.

10. Connect the fuel hoses to the rail.

11. Connect the electrical connectors to the fuel injectors.

12. Turn the ignition switch **ON** and check for fuel leaks at the fuel rail.

3.0L Engine

The engine is equipped with 6 fuel injectors, with one located at each cylinder.

1. Relieve the fuel pressure.

2. Remove the air cleaner from the throttle body.

3. Label and disconnect the vacuum hoses, electrical connectors and throttle cable from the throttle body/upper intake manifold assembly.

4. Remove the upper intake manifold.

5. Disconnect the electrical connectors from the fuel injectors.

6. Disconnect the supply and return hoses from the fuel rail.

7. The injectors can be removed separately or as an assembly with the rail. Do not use the old O-rings or insulators when installing the injectors.

To install:

8. Replace the fuel injector O-rings.

9. Lubricate the fuel injector O-rings with automatic transmission fluid and press them into the fuel rail assembly.

10. Connect the electrical connectors to the fuel injectors.

11. Using a new gasket, install the upper intake manifold and torque the bolts to 16 ft. lbs. (22 Nm).

12. Connect the electrical connectors, the vacuum lines and the accelerator cable.

13. Install the air cleaner to the throttle body.

14. Turn the ignition switch **ON** and check for fuel leaks at the fuel rail.

EMISSION CONTROLS

Emission Warning Lamp

The check engine light is located on the instrument panel of California vehicles only and indicates an emission performance malfunction.

RESETTING

1. Turn the ignition switch **ON**.

2. If the check engine light turns **ON**, perform the self-diagnosis procedures to determine the malfunction.

3. Turn the ignition switch **OFF**.

4. Locate and repair the malfunction.

NOTE: When the malfunction is repaired and the fault code memory cleared, the check engine light will stay OFF.

ENGINE MECHANICAL

NOTE: Disconnecting the negative battery cable on some vehicles may interfere with the functions of the on board computer systems and may require the computer to undergo a relearning process when the battery cable is reconnected. This usually requires only a few minutes of driving.

Engine

REMOVAL AND INSTALLATION

On vehicles equipped with the 3.0L engine, the transmission must be removed before removing the engine. If equipped with the 2.4L engine, the engine and transmission are removed together. On vehicles with 4WD, the front torsion bar must be removed to remove the transfer case.

1. Relieve the fuel system pressure.
2. Disconnect the battery cables and remove the battery.
3. Using a scribing tool, mark the location of the hood hinges on the body and remove the hood.
4. Drain the engine oil and the cooling system, including the block drains. Dispose of old fluids properly.
5. Remove the air cleaner. Wrap a shop rag around the fuel filter outlet and disconnect the hose.
6. Raise and safely support the vehicle. If equipped, remove the splash pan from under the engine.
7. To remove the radiator:
   a. Remove the upper and lower radiator hoses.
   b. If equipped with an automatic transmission, disconnect and plug the transmission oil cooler lines from the radiator.
   c. Remove the lower radiator shroud.
   d. Remove the bracket bolts and lift the radiator and shroud out together.

8. If equipped with air conditioning, loosen the belt tension and remove the belt. Disconnect the wiring, remove the compressor and secure it out of the way. Do not disconnect the pressure hoses.
9. If equipped with power steering, remove the drive belt and the power steering pump and secure it out of the way. Do not disconnect the pressure hoses.
10. Label and disconnect all wiring and vacuum hoses.
11. Disconnect the heater hoses from the engine and disconnect the throttle cable.
12. Remove the starter.
13. Matchmark the driveshaft flange at the rear pinion flange and remove the driveshaft. Plug the extension housing opening to prevent the oil from draining out.
14. If equipped with 4WD, matchmark both front driveshaft flanges so the shaft can be installed in the same position. Remove the driveshaft.
15. Disconnect the exhaust pipe from the manifold(s) and from the catalytic converter and remove the pipe.
16. Disconnect the speedometer cable and the wiring from the transmission.
17. If equipped an automatic transmission:
   a. Disconnect the selector lever and throttle cables from the transmission.
   b. Remove the dipstick tube and disconnect the cooler lines.
   c. Remove the torque converter housing dust cover. Matchmark the converter with the driveplate for reassembly; these are balanced together at the factory. Remove the torque converter-to-driveplate (flywheel) bolts. Use a wrench on the crankshaft pulley bolt to rotate the crankshaft to expose the hidden torque converter bolts.
18. On vehicles with a manual transmission:
   a. Remove the shifter knob and boot and remove the snapring to lift the shift lever out of the transmission. Stuff a rag in the opening to keep dirt out of the transmission.
   b. Without disconnecting the hydraulic hose, remove the clutch slave cylinder from the transmission and secure it aside.
19. If equipped with 4WD:
   a. Working under the vehicle, measure and note the length of the threads on the torsion bar adjustment. At the front of the bar, pull the boot back and matchmark the

bar to the mounting plate. The spline on the bar must be re-installed in the same position on the plate.
   b. Remove the locknut and adjustment nut from both torsion bars. Remove the 3 nuts at the mounting plate and remove the bars. Mark the bars left and right side for proper installation.
   c. Remove the transfer case shift lever assembly from the transfer case.
   d. If necessary, the transfer case can be removed at this point so the jack will be available to remove the transmission.
   e. If equipped with a 3.0L engine, remove the gusset securing the engine to the transmission.
20. Using a chain hoist, attach it to the engine and lift the engine slightly to take the weight off the mounts. Using an appropriate transmission jack, properly support the transmission and remove the transmission mount and crossmember.
21. Remove the transmission-to-engine bolts and move the transmission back away from the engine. On automatic transmissions, secure the torque converter so it does not fall out. Lower the transmission from the vehicle.

NOTE: When removing the engine mounts, do not loosen the 4 mount cover nuts. The mount is fluid filled and will not function properly if the fluid leaks out.

22. Check to make sure all wires and hoses have been disconnected. Remove the front engine mount bolts and carefully lift the engine out.
To install:
23. Carefully guide the engine into place and start the mount bolts. Tighten the bolts temporarily.
24. On manual transmission:
   a. Lightly grease the input shaft splines. On 4WD, apply a silicone sealant to the engine block or rear plate to seal the engine to the transmission.
   b. Fit the transmission into place and start all the engine-to-transmission bolts. Make sure the input shaft fits properly into the clutch disc and pilot bearing.
   c. Torque the 2.36 in. (60mm) and 2.56 in. (65mm) engine-to-transmission bolts to 36 ft. lbs. (49 Nm).
   d. Torque the remaining bolts to 18 ft. lbs. (25 Nm) on the 2.4L cylinder engine, 29 ft. lbs. (39 Nm) on the 3.0L engine.

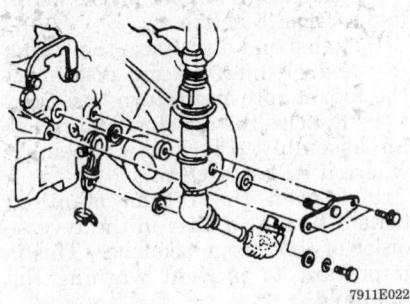

Removing the transfer case shift lever on 4WD

7911E022

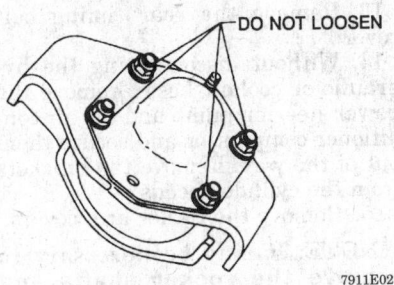

DO NOT LOOSEN

Do not remove these engine mount nuts

7911E023

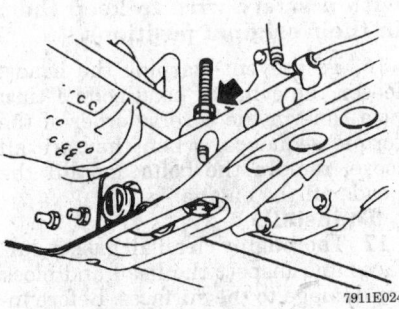

Measure thread length before removing torsion bar

7911E024

25. On automatic transmission:

a. Use a dial indicator to check the driveplate runout while turning the crankshaft. Maximum allowable runout is 0.020 in. (0.5mm); if beyond specifications, replace the driveplate.

b. Measure and adjust how far the torque converter is recessed into the transmission housing. The distance between the front mounting surface of the transmission and the torque converter-to-driveplate

bolt boss should be at least 1.024 in. (26mm).

c. Install the transmission and torque transmission-to-engine bolts to 36 ft. lbs. (49 Nm). Torque to transmission-to-engine gusset bolts to 29 ft. lbs. (39 Nm).

26. Install the crossmember and torque the crossmember-to-chassis bolts to 38 ft. lbs. (52 Nm) on 2WD or 31 ft. lbs. (42 Nm) on 4WD.

27. Install the rear transmission mount bolts, loosen the engine mount bolts, then torque all the mount bolts to 31 ft. lbs. (42 Nm), starting at the rear.

28. On automatic transmission, align the matchmarks on the driveplate and torque converter, install the bolts and torque to 36 ft. lbs. (49 Nm). Turn the crankshaft after tightening the bolts to make sure there is no binding at the driveplate.

29. If the torsion bars were removed, install them in their original location. Make sure the splines are in their original position and set the adjustment to its original position.

30. If the transfer case was removed, apply silicone sealant to seal the case to the transmission. Install the transfer case and torque the bolts to 30 ft. lbs. (41 Nm). Install the shift lever.

31. When installing the driveshafts, be sure to align the matchmarks. Torque the bolts on the front driveshaft (4WD) to 33 ft. lbs. (44 Nm). On single piece rear driveshafts, torque the bolts to 65 ft. lbs. (88 Nm). On 2 piece driveshafts, torque the bolts to 33 ft. lbs. (44 Nm). Torque the center bearing bracket bolts to 16 ft. lbs. (22 Nm).

32. When installing the exhaust system, use new gaskets and torque the flange bolts to 27 ft. lbs. (36 Nm).

33. Install the remaining components in order of removal and connect the wiring and hoses.

Cylinder Head

REMOVAL AND INSTALLATION

2.4L Engine

1. Relieve the fuel system pressure. Disconnect the negative battery cable.

2. Remove the air cleaner. Disconnect the accelerator cable from the throttle body.

3. Drain the engine coolant, including the block drain.

4. Label and disconnect all wiring and hoses as required.

5. Remove the intake and exhaust manifolds.

6. Remove the steering pump, alternator and/or air conditioner compressor as required and remove the brackets as required. When removing the steering pump or air conditioner compressor, disconnect the drive belt, remove the unit pump and move it aside; do not disconnect the pressure hoses.

7. Remove the distributor cap and rotor and disconnect the wires from the spark plugs.

8. Remove the valve cover.

9. Rotate the crankshaft until the No. 1 cylinder is on the TDC of its compression stroke. Make sure the TDC mark on the crankshaft pulley is aligned with the pointer. The silver link on the timing chain should be aligned with the mark on the camshaft sprocket and the knock pin on the camshaft will be at the top.

10. To remove the camshaft sprocket:

a. Fabricate a wooden wedge tool to hold the timing chain in place.

b. Remove the camshaft sprocket bolt and the camshaft sprocket. Hold the sprocket up to keep tension on the chain.

c. Install the wedge tool and rest the chain on the tool with the driver's side of the chain pulled snug against the crankshaft sprocket. If the chain falls off the crankshaft sprocket or if the crankshaft is turned, the front cover must be removed to properly set the valve timing.

11. Remove the cylinder head-to-timing chain cover bolts.

12. Carefully loosen the cylinder head bolts one turn at a time in the reverse order of the tightening sequence. When all bolts are loose, remove the bolts and remove the cylinder head.

To install:

13. Thoroughly clean all gasket surfaces and inspect the head and block for damage to the surfaces. Before installing, check the cylinder head for warping. The limit is 0.006 in. (0.15mm). Make sure the threads on the bolts and in the block are clean and that the bolts turn easily in the threads. Do not oil the threads.

14. Make sure the camshaft knock pin is at the top; both valves for No. 1 cylinder will be closed.

15. Install the new gasket and carefully install the cylinder head. Tor-

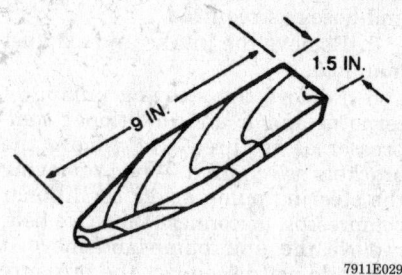

Make a wooden wedge to support the timing chain when removing 2.4L engine cylinder head

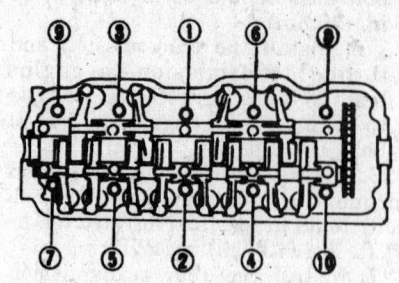

Cylinder head bolt torque sequence — 2.4L engine

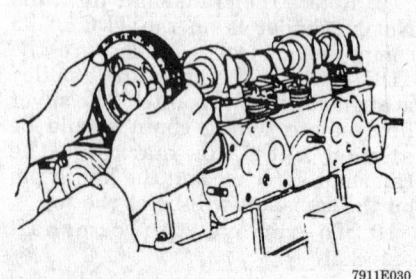

Remove the camshaft sprocket with chain attached — 2.4L engine

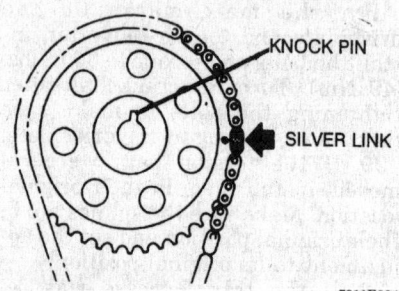

KNOCK PIN

SILVER LINK

To install the camshaft sprocket, the knock pin will be at the top and the silver link will align with the mark

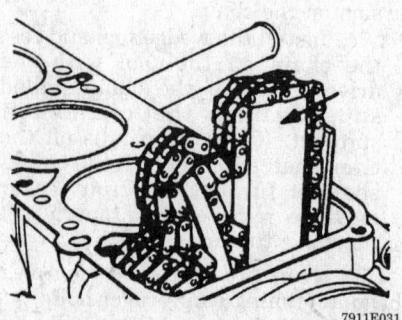

Support the chain with the wedge to keep it engaged with the crankshaft sprocket

que the cylinder head bolts in the sequence shown in 5 steps:

Step 1 — 22 ft. lbs. (29 Nm)
Step 2 — 58 ft. lbs. (78 Nm)
Step 3 — loosen all bolts
Step 4 — 22 ft. lbs. (29 Nm)
Step 5 — 54–61 ft. lbs. (74–83 Nm)

16. Correctly position the camshaft sprocket into the timing chain with the silver link aligned with the mark on the sprocket. Install the sprocket onto the camshaft, install the sprocket bolt but do not fully torque it yet.

17. Carefully turn the crankshaft 2 full turns and make sure the timing marks still line up. If not, remove the camshaft sprocket and try again. Torque the sprocket bolt to 87–116 ft. lbs. (118–157 Nm).

18. Adjust the valves.

19. Use a silicone sealer when installing the rubber covers at each end of the camshaft. Install the valve cover with a new gasket and torque the bolts in a circular pattern to 7 ft. lbs. (10 Nm). Loosen all the bolts and torque them again in the same pattern.

20. Complete the installation of the remaining components. Change the oil before running the engine.

3.0L Engine

1. Relieve the fuel system pressure. Disconnect the negative battery cable.

2. Remove the air cleaner. Disconnect the accelerator cable from the throttle body.

3. Drain the engine coolant, including the block drain.

4. Label and disconnect all wiring and hoses as required.

5. Remove the distributor and spark plug wires as an assembly.

6. Remove the timing belt covers and the timing belt.

7. Remove the upper intake manifold section (5 bolts).

8. Label and disconnect the wiring to the fuel injectors and disconnect the fuel supply and return hoses.

9. Remove the injectors and rail as an assembly. Place the assembly where it will stay clean.

10. Loosen the intake manifold bolts 1 turn at a time in the reverse order of the torque sequence. This is important to prevent warping the manifold.

11. Remove the bolts and lift the manifold off.

12. Mark the camshaft sprockets left and right for proper installation and remove them.

13. Remove the rear timing belt cover.

14. Without disconnecting the hydraulic or coolant hoses, remove the power steering pump and the air conditioner compressor and secure them out of the way. Remove the brackets from the cylinder heads.

15. Remove the rocker arm covers.

NOTE: It may be necessary to remove the rocker shafts and valve lifter guide to provide access to the cylinder head bolts. Before removing the valve lifter guide, secure the valve lifters with a safety wire to keep them in their original positions.

16. To prevent warping the heads, loosen the cylinder head bolts 1 turn at a time in the reverse order of the torque sequence. When they are all loose, remove the bolts and lift the heads off the engine.

To install:

17. Thoroughly clean all gasket surfaces and inspect the head and block for damage to the surfaces. Before installing, check the cylinder head for warping. The limit is 0.004 in. (0.10mm). Make sure the threads on the bolts and in the block are clean and that the bolts turn easily in the threads. Do not oil the threads.

18. Set the crankshaft to TDC on No. 1 cylinder and make sure the mark on the sprocket aligns with the mark on the oil pump body. Make sure the knock pin on the camshaft is at the top.

19. Use new gaskets and install the exhaust manifolds. Torque the nuts or bolts in the proper sequence to 16 ft. lbs. (22 Nm).

20. Apply sealant to the block cooling system drain plugs and install the plugs.

21. Make sure the new head gaskets are properly fitted and install the cylinder heads. When installing the bolts, the long bolts go into posi-

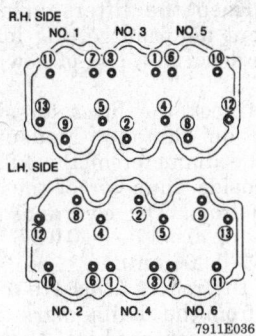

Cylinder head bolt torque sequence — 3.0L engine

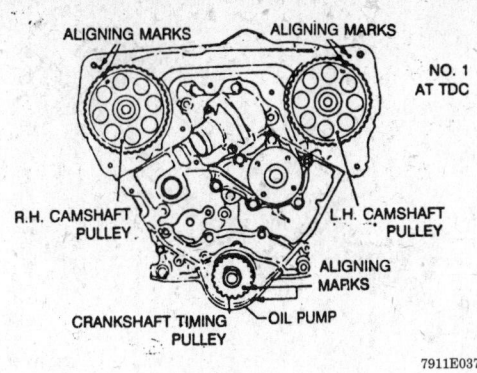

View of the camshaft sprocket timing marks — 3.0L engine

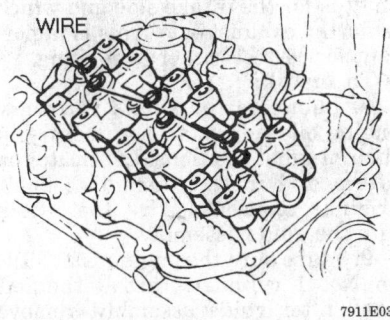

Secure the lifters with wire before removing the guide assembly — 3.0L engine

tions 4, 5, 12 and 13; the flat side of the washer goes towards the head.

22. Torque the cylinder head bolts in the proper sequence in five steps:

Step 1 — 22 ft. lbs. (30 Nm)

Step 2 — 43 ft. lbs. (58 Nm)

Step 3 — loosen all bolts

Step 4 — 22 ft. lbs. (30 Nm)

Step 5 — 40–47 ft. lbs. (54–64 Nm) or 22 ft. lbs. (30 Nm) plus 65 degrees.

23. If the lifter guide and rocker arms were removed, install them now and tighten the bolts 1 turn at a time to draw the shafts down evenly against the valve springs without bending the shafts. Torque the bolts to 16 ft. lbs. (22 Nm).

24. Install the rocker arm covers and torque the bolts to 25 inch lbs. (3 Nm).

25. Install the rear timing belt cover and the camshaft sprockets. Make sure the sprockets are on the correct side and torque the sprocket bolts to 65 ft. lbs. (88 Nm).

26. Make sure the crankshaft and camshafts are properly positioned to install the timing belt. Be careful if it is necessary to turn either shaft; this is not a free wheeling engine and the valves will contact the pistons if the crankshaft is turned without the timing belt in place.

27. Install the timing belt, set the tension and turn the crankshaft 2 full turns to make sure the timing marks still align properly.

28. Use a new gasket to install the intake manifold and torque the nuts bolts in the proper sequence in 3 steps. Torque the nuts to 20 ft. lbs. (27 Nm) and the bolts to 14 ft. lbs. (20 Nm).

29. Connect the exhaust pipes to the manifolds and torque the bolts to 20 ft. lbs. (27 Nm).

30. Install the remaining components using new gaskets, O-rings or seals as required. Adjust belt tensions and change the oil before starting the engine.

31. When the engine is first started, the hydraulic valve lifters may be noisy. Run the engine for 10–20 minutes at about 1000 rpm. If the noise has not subsided, the lifter will probably never pump up and must be replaced.

Rocker Arms and Valve Lifters

REMOVAL AND INSTALLATION

2.4L Engine

The hydraulic lifters are built into the rocker arms. Do not allow the arms to lay on their side or they will become air bound. Keep the rocker arms upright or lay them in a pan of new engine oil. On all models, the same bolts that hold the rocker arm assembly also hold the camshaft bearing caps. To avoid damage to the bearing surfaces, the camshaft sprocket must be removed.

1. Relieve the fuel system pressure and disconnect the negative battery cable.

2. Remove the rocker arm cover and turn the crankshaft to align the timing marks at TDC on No. 1 cylinder.

3. Use a wire tie or wire to secure the timing chain to the camshaft sprocket.

4. Hold the camshaft sprocket to loosen the bolt and remove the sprocket. Secure the sprocket so the chain does not fall off the crankshaft sprocket.

5. Loosen each rocker shaft bolt 1 turn at a time to prevent bending the shafts.

6. When all the bolts are loose, remove the rocker arm shafts with the bolts still in the shafts. This will hold the assembly together.

7. If the rocker arms are to be removed from the shafts, mark them so they can be returned into their original position. Remove the bolts from the shaft assembly and remove the parts. Keep the rocker arms upright or lay them in a pan of new engine oil. Note the punch marks on the front of each shaft that tell which shaft is for the intake side and which is for the exhaust side. This is important for correct rocker arm oiling.

To install:

8. Lubricate the shafts with engine oil and assemble them with the punch marks facing up. Use the bolts to hold the assembly together. Make sure the camshaft and the bearing surfaces are in good condition and lubricate with engine oil. Make sure the pin on the camshaft sprocket end is up.

9. Install the rocker arm shafts and tighten the bolts in the proper sequence 1 turn at a time to draw the shafts down evenly against the valve springs without bending the shafts. Torque the bolts to 16 ft. lbs. (22 Nm).

10. Install the camshaft sprocket and remove the tie securing the chain. Install the sprocket bolt but do not torque it yet. Rotate the crankshaft 2 full turns to make sure the

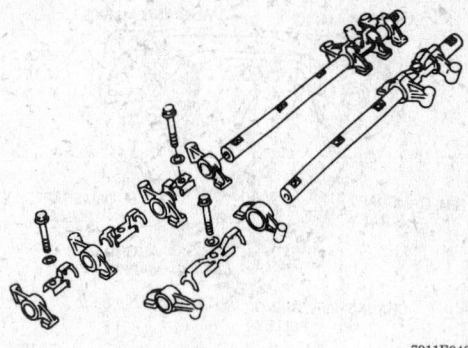

7911E040

Rocker arm assembly on 2.4L engine with hydraulic lash adjusters

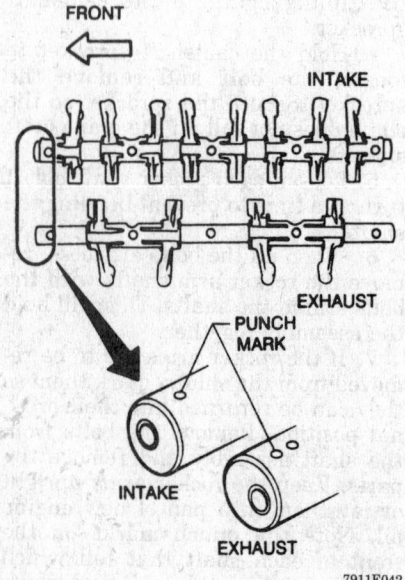

7911E042

Make sure the rocker arm shafts are returned to their correct position — 2.4L engine shown

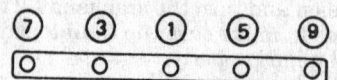

7911E043

Rocker arm shaft tightening sequence — 2.4L engine

c. Keep the lifters upright to prevent air from getting in or lay them down in a pan of new engine oil.

d. Check the lifter for signs of wear or damage. Measure the outside diameter of the lifter and the inside diameter of the bore it came from. The clearance should be 0.0017–0.0026 in. (0.043–0.066mm).

7. If the rocker arms are to be removed from the shafts, mark them so they can be returned into their original position. Remove the bolts from the shaft assembly and remove the rockers. Tag each shaft to tell which shaft is for the intake side and which is for the exhaust side. This is important for correct rocker arm oiling.

To install:

8. Lubricate the shafts with new engine oil and install the rockers in their original positions. Lubricate the lifters and install them into their original positions. Wire the lifters into the guide assembly.

9. Make sure the engine is at TDC on No. 1 cylinder. Install the left bank lifter guide assembly, remove the safety wire and install the rocker arm shafts. Tighten the bolts 1 turn at a time to draw the shafts down evenly. Torque the bolts to 16 ft. lbs. (22 Nm).

10. Rotate the crankshaft to bring cylinder No. 4 to TDC. Set the right bank lifter guide assembly into place, remove the safety wire and install the rocker arm shafts. Tighten the bolts 1 turn at a time to 16 ft. lbs. (22 Nm).

11. Use new gaskets to install the rocker arm covers and torque the bolts to 24 inch lbs. (3 Nm). Install the remaining components.

12. When the engine is first started, the hydraulic valve lifters may be noisy. Run the engine for 10–20 minutes at about 1000 rpm. If the noise has not subsided, the lifter will probably never pump up and must be replaced.

Intake Manifold

REMOVAL AND INSTALLATION

2.4L Engine

1. Release the fuel pressure. Disconnect the negative battery cab

2. Remove the air cleaner assembly together with all of the attending hoses. Remove the EGR tube.

3. Label and disconnect all wiring and hoses as required.

will probably never pump up and must be replaced.

3.0L Engine

1. Relieve the fuel system pressure and disconnect the negative battery cable.

2. Remove the rocker arm covers.

3. Turn the crankshaft to align the timing marks at TDC on No. 1 cylinder. Remove the distributor cap and matchmark the position of the rotor to the distributor body and to the engine. Remove the distributor.

4. Loosen each rocker shaft bolt 1 turn at a time to prevent bending the shafts.

5. When all the bolts are loose, remove the rocker arm shafts with the bolts still in the shafts. This will hold the assembly together.

6. If the lifters are to be removed:

a. Secure the valve lifters in the guide assembly with safety wire to keep them in their original positions, then remove the entire assembly.

b. Before removing a lifter from the guide assembly, tag the lifters to make sure they are returned to their original position. Do not disassemble a lifter.

timing marks line up. When the valve timing is correct, torque the sprocket bolt to 116 ft. lbs. (157 Nm).

11. If required, adjust the valves.

12. Use a silicone sealer on the rubber end plugs and install the rocker arm cover with a new gasket. Torque the bolts to 7 ft. lbs. (10 Nm) in a crisscross pattern starting at the middle. Install the remaining components.

13. When the engine is first started, the hydraulic valve lifters may be noisy. Run the engine for 10–20 minutes at about 1000 rpm. If the noise has not subsided, the lifter

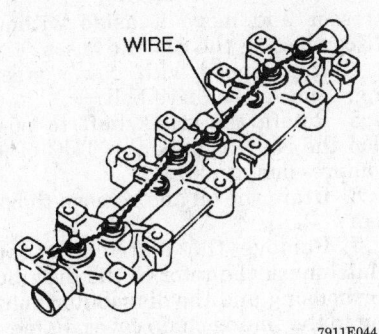

WIRE

7911E044

Hold the lifters in place with wire before removing the guide assembly — 3.0L engine

ROCKER SHAFT DIRECTION

EXHAUST

◀ R.H. CYLINDER HEAD FRONT   L.H. CYLINDER HEAD FRONT ▶

INTAKE

7911E045

Make sure rocker arm shafts are installed in their original position — 3.0L engine

4. Drain the engine coolant to a level below the thermostat housing, then, disconnect the upper coolant hose from the thermostat housing.

5. Disconnect the throttle linkage from the throttle body. The throttle body and/or fuel injectors can be removed from the manifold at this point or the entire assembly can be removed.

6. Remove the manifold bracket, if equipped, and remove the bolts and the intake manifold.

To install:

7. Clean the gasket mounting surfaces and use new gaskets. Install the manifold and tighten the bolts in 2 steps working from the center out. Torque the bolts to 15 ft. lbs. (21 Nm).

8. If it was removed, install the throttle body with a new gasket and torque the nuts to 13 ft. lbs. (18 Nm). Use new O-rings to install the injectors.

9. Install the remaining components and connect the wiring and hoses. Fill the cooling system and run the engine to check ignition timing and idle speed.

3.0L Engine

1. Release the fuel system pressure and disconnect the negative battery cable.

2. Drain the cooling system to a level below the intake manifold.

3. Remove the air duct from the throttle body. Disconnect the accelerator linkage from the throttle body.

4. Remove the upper radiator hose from the water outlet housing and the exhaust tube from the EGR valve. If necessary, remove the EGR valve-to-intake manifold nuts and the EGR valve.

5. Label and disconnect the wiring and hoses as required.

6. Remove the 5 intake manifold collector-to-intake manifold bolts and the lift the collector off the engine.

7. Remove the fuel rail and the injectors as an assembly from the intake manifold.

8. To prevent warping, loosen the intake manifold nuts and bolts 1 or 2 turns at a time in the reverse of the torque sequence. Remove the manifold.

To install:

9. Clean the gasket surfaces and install new gaskets.

10. Install the intake manifold and torque the nuts and bolts in the proper sequence in the following steps:

    Step 1: all to 43 inch lbs. (5 Nm)
    Step 2:
      Bolts to 14 ft. lbs. (20 Nm)
      Nuts to 20 ft. lbs. (27 Nm)
    Step 3: repeat Step 2

11. Use new O-rings and install the fuel injectors and rail assembly. Connect the wiring.

12. Use a new gasket and install the intake manifold collector. Torque the bolts to 12 ft. lbs. (16 Nm).

13. Install the remaining components and connect the wiring and hoses. Refill the cooling system and run the engine to check ignition timing and idle speed.

Exhaust Manifold

REMOVAL AND INSTALLATION

2.4L Engine

1. Disconnect the negative battery cable.

2. If equipped, remove the hot air duct from the exhaust manifold cover.

3. Disconnect the spark plug wires from the exhaust side of the engine; if necessary, remove the spark plugs from the exhaust side of the engine.

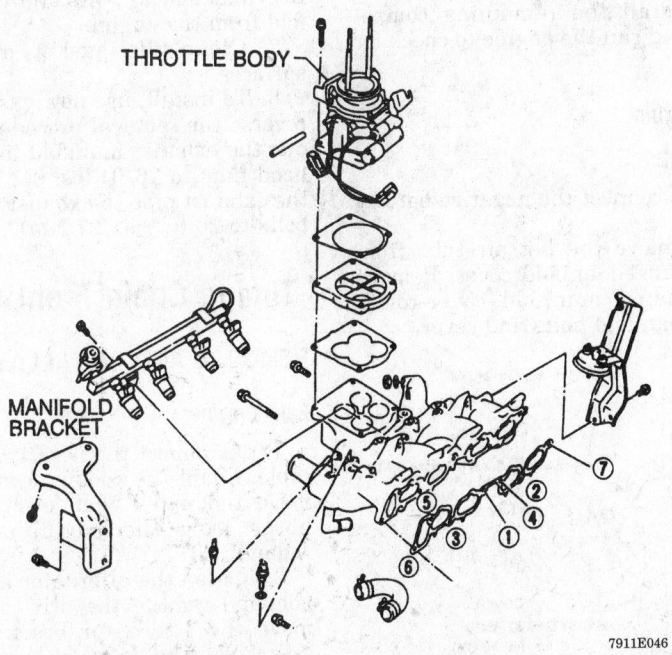

THROTTLE BODY

MANIFOLD BRACKET

7911E046

Intake manifold assembly — 2.4L engine

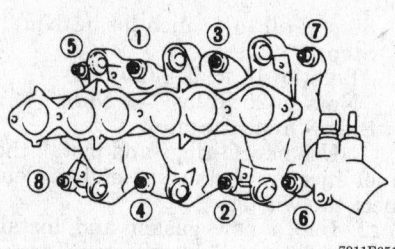

Intake manifold bolt torque sequence — 3.0L engine

7911E051

4. If necessary, raise and safely support the vehicle.

5. If equipped, remove the air induction tubes from the exhaust manifold. Remove the EGR tube from the exhaust manifold.

6. Remove the hot air cover and the exhaust pipe from the exhaust manifold.

7. Remove the exhaust manifold-to-engine nuts and the manifold from the engine.

To install:

8. Clean the gasket mounting surfaces and install new gaskets.

9. Install the manifold and torque the nuts/bolts to 15 ft. lbs. (20 Nm), working from the center to the ends, in 2 steps.

10. Use new gaskets and connect the exhaust pipe to the manifold. Torque the nuts to 27 ft. lbs. (36 Nm).

11. Install the remaining components and run the engine to check for leaks.

3.0L Engine

LEFT SIDE

1. Disconnect the negative battery cable.

2. Remove the hot air tube from the exhaust manifold cover. Remove the exhaust manifold cover-to-exhaust manifold bolts and cover.

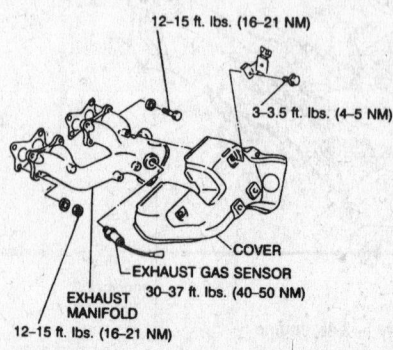

12–15 ft. lbs. (16–21 NM)

3–3.5 ft. lbs. (4–5 NM)

COVER

EXHAUST GAS SENSOR

30–37 ft. lbs. (40–50 NM)

EXHAUST MANIFOLD

12–15 ft. lbs. (16–21 NM)

7911E052

Exhaust manifold — 2.4L engine

3. Remove the EGR and the AIR tubes from the exhaust manifold, if equipped.

NOTE: If the alternator is in the way, remove the drive belt and the alternator.

4. Raise and safely support the vehicle.

5. Remove the exhaust pipe-to-exhaust manifold nuts and separate the exhaust pipe from the manifold.

6. Remove the exhaust manifold-to-cylinder head bolts and the manifold from the engine.

7. Clean the gasket mounting surfaces.

8. To install, use new gaskets and reverse the removal procedures. Torque the exhaust manifold-to-cylinder head nuts to 16 ft. lbs. (22 Nm) and the exhaust pipe-to-exhaust manifold bolts to 20 ft. lbs. (27 Nm).

RIGHT SIDE

1. Disconnect the negative battery cable.

2. Remove the upper/lower exhaust manifold cover-to-exhaust manifold bolts and covers.

3. Remove the AIR tube from the exhaust manifold, if equipped.

4. Raise and safely support the vehicle.

5. Remove the exhaust pipe-to-exhaust manifold bolts and separate the exhaust pipe from the manifold.

6. Remove the exhaust manifold-to-cylinder head bolts and the manifold from the engine.

7. Clean the gasket mounting surfaces.

8. To install, use new gaskets and reverse the removal procedures. Torque the exhaust manifold-to-cylinder head nuts to 16 ft. lbs. (22 Nm) and the exhaust pipe-to-exhaust manifold bolts to 20 ft. lbs. (27 Nm).

Timing Chain Front Cover

REMOVAL AND INSTALLATION

2.4L Engine

1. Disconnect the negative battery cable. Drain the cooling system. Remove the upper and lower coolant hoses from the engine and the radiator.

2. Loosen the alternator adjusting bolt and remove the drive belt. Remove the alternator bracket-to-engine bolts and move the alternator aside.

3. If equipped with air conditioning, remove the drive belt. If necessary, remove the air conditioner com-

pressor and move it aside without disconnecting the coolant hoses.

4. If equipped with power steering, remove the drive belt.

5. Rotate the crankshaft to position the No. 1 cylinder on TDC of its compression stroke.

6. Drain the oil and remove the oil pan.

7. Remove the distributor cap. Matchmark the rotor to the distributor housing and the distributor housing to the timing chain cover. Remove the distributor hold-down bolt and the distributor.

8. Remove the oil pump-to-timing cover bolts, the oil pump and its drive spindle.

9. On RWD vehicles, remove the cooling fan-to-water pump bolts, the fan, the fan coupling if equipped and the water pump pulley.

10. Remove the crankshaft pulley-to-crankshaft bolt and the crankshaft pulley.

11. Remove the timing chain cover-to-cylinder head bolts, the timing chain cover-to-engine bolts, and remove the cover. Clean the gasket mounting surfaces.

NOTE: Whenever the timing cover is removed, replace the oil seal.

12. Install a new oil seal and use new gaskets and silicone sealant as necessary to install the front cover.

13. Install the oil pan.

14. When installing the oil pump. place the new gasket over the shaft and make sure the drive spindle mark aligns with the hole in the pump body. This will align the shaft properly for the distributor.

15. Install the distributor and make sure the rotor aligns with the matchmark.

16. Install the crankshaft pulley and torque the bolt to 116 ft. lbs. (157 Nm).

17. Install the remaining components and refill the cooling system. Run the engine to check ignition timing and idle speed.

Front Cover Oil Seal

REPLACEMENT

2.4L Engine

1. Disconnect the negative battery cable.

2. Remove the radiator shroud as required and remove crankshaft pulley.

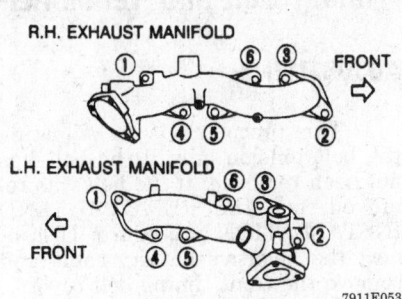

R.H. EXHAUST MANIFOLD

L.H. EXHAUST MANIFOLD

7911E053

Exhaust manifolds — 3.0L engine

3. Carefully pry the front oil seal out of the timing cover without damaging the crankshaft.

4. Lubricate the new seal with light grease. Using an oil seal installation tool, drive the new oil seal into the timing cover until it seats. Clean all oil and grease away from the seal and crankshaft area.

5. To complete the installation, reverse the removal procedures. Torque the crankshaft pulley-to-crankshaft bolt to 116 ft. lbs. (157 Nm). Start the engine, allow it reach normal operating temperatures and check for leaks.

Timing Chain and Sprockets

REMOVAL AND INSTALLATION

2.4L Engine

1. Disconnect the negative battery cable.

2. Rotate the crankshaft to align the timing marks on the crankshaft pulley at TDC of No. 1 cylinder. Remove the timing chain cover and the rocker arm cover.

3. Make sure the No. 1 piston is at TDC of its compression stroke; the No. 1 camshaft lobes will both be

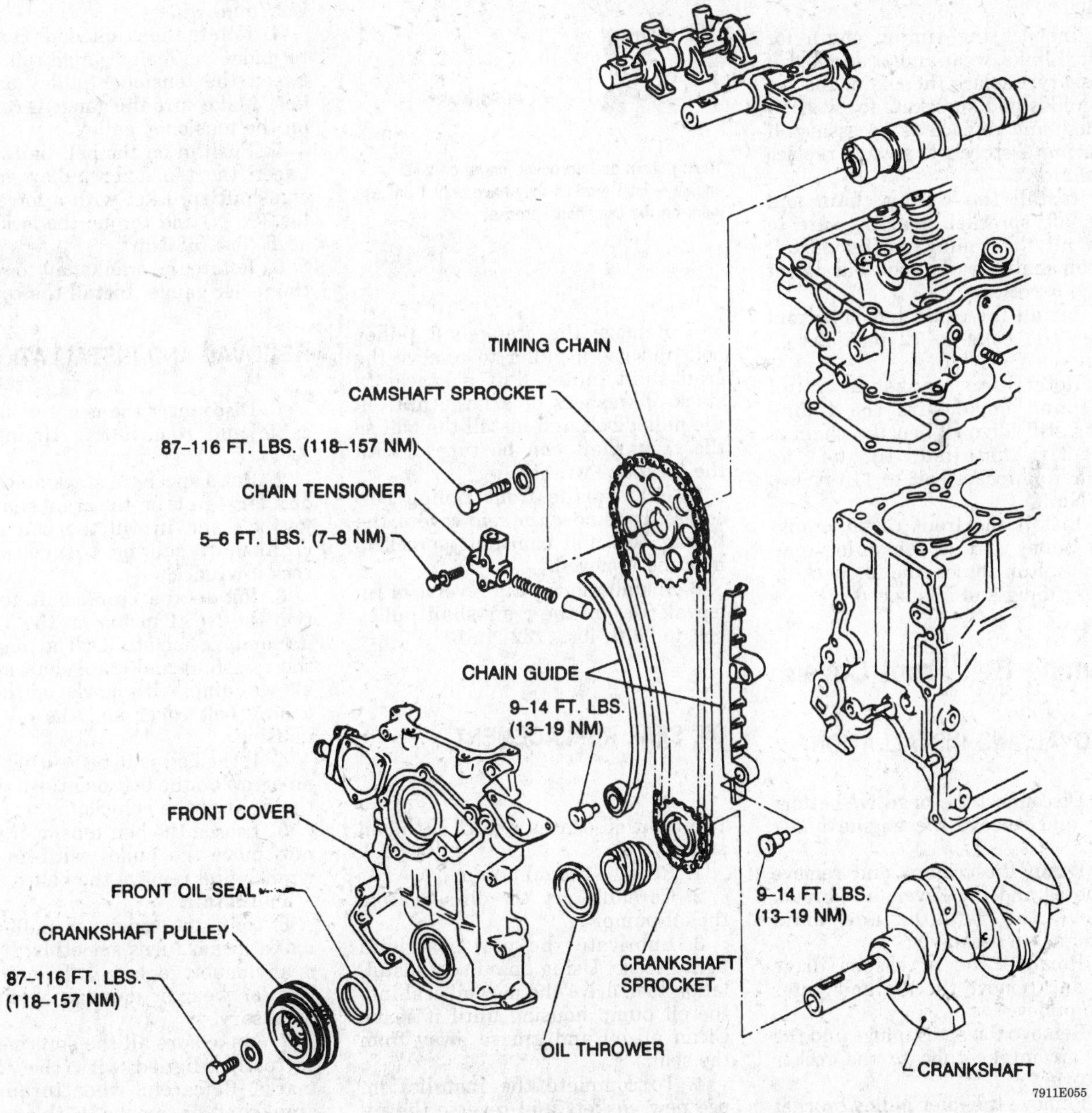

TIMING CHAIN

CAMSHAFT SPROCKET

87–116 FT. LBS. (118–157 NM)

CHAIN TENSIONER

5–6 FT. LBS. (7–8 NM)

CHAIN GUIDE

9–14 FT. LBS. (13–19 NM)

FRONT COVER

FRONT OIL SEAL

CRANKSHAFT PULLEY

87–116 FT. LBS. (118–157 NM)

CRANKSHAFT SPROCKET

9–14 FT. LBS. (13–19 NM)

OIL THROWER

CRANKSHAFT

7911E055

Timing chain assembly — 2.4L engine

down. The timing marks on the camshaft sprocket and crankshaft sprocket should align with the silver links on the timing chain. If the chain has no silver links, paint alignment marks on the chain.

4. Remove the chain tensioner.

NOTE: When the chain tensioner bolts are removed, the tensioner will come apart. Hold on to the piston and do not drop any of the parts into the oil pan. There is no need to remove the chain guide unless it is being replaced.

5. Hold the camshaft sprocket from turning, remove the bolt and remove the sprocket along with the chain.

6. Inspect the timing chain for cracked links, wear and/or damage; if necessary, replace the chain. Inspect the guides and sprockets for wear or damage and replace as necessary. If replacing a sprocket, always replace the chain.

7. Install the timing chain and camshaft sprocket, making sure to align all the timing marks. Install the camshaft sprocket bolt but do not torque it yet.

8. Install the chain tensioner and torque the bolts to 72 inch lbs. (8 Nm).

9. Rotate the crankshaft 2 full turns and make sure the timing marks still align. When the chain is correctly installed, torque the camshaft sprocket bolt to 116 ft. lbs. (157 Nm).

10. Install the front cover, crankshaft pulley and all remaining components. Run the engine to check ignition timing and idle speed.

Timing Belt Front Cover

REMOVAL AND INSTALLATION

1. Disconnect the negative battery cable and remove the engine under cover.

2. Drain the coolant and remove the hoses and the lower fan shroud. Remove the radiator and main shroud as an assembly.

3. Remove the accessory drive belts and remove the fan and water pump pulley.

4. Remove the spark plugs and the fresh air intake tube to the rocker arm cover.

5. Remove the idler pulley bracket and the water inlet hose.

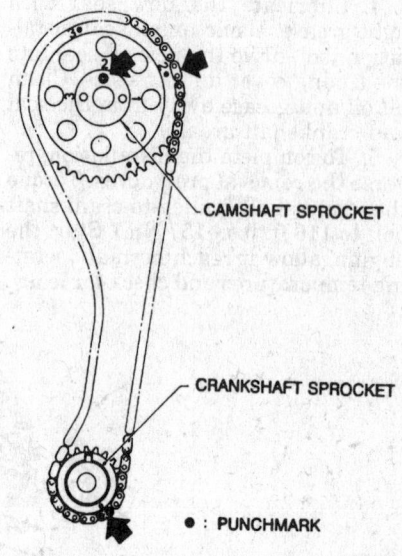

CAMSHAFT SPROCKET

CRANKSHAFT SPROCKET

● : PUNCHMARK

7911E057

Timing chain and sprocket marks on 2.4L engine — later models may have only 1 timing mark on the camshaft sprocket

6. Remove the crankshaft pulley bolt and use a puller to remove the crankshaft pulley. Put a spacer (a stack of washers or a large nut) on the pulley bolt and install the bolt so the crankshaft can be turned with the socket or wrench.

7. Remove the front timing belt covers. To remove the rear covers, the timing belt and camshaft sprockets must be removed.

8. Installation is the reverse of removal. Torque the crankshaft pulley bolt to 98 ft. lbs. (132 Nm).

OIL SEAL REPLACEMENT

The front oil seal is a part of the oil pump.

1. Remove the oil pump.

2. Carefully pry the oil seal from the oil pump.

3. Lubricate the new seal with light grease. Using an oil seal installation tool, drive the new oil seal into the oil pump housing until it seats. Clean all oil and grease away from the seal.

4. To complete the installation, use new gaskets and reverse the removal procedures.

Timing Belt and Tensioner

ADJUSTMENT

1. This procedure is for adjusting the belt tension only if the belt has not been removed. If the belt was removed, see the REMOVAL AND INSTALLATION procedure. Disconnect the negative battery cable and remove the front timing belt covers.

2. Loosen the tensioner pulley locknut and allow the spring to hold the pulley against the belt.

3. Set a 0.014 in. (0.35mm) feeler gauge between the belt and pulley on the crankshaft side of the pulley. The feeler gauge should be at least ½ in. (12.7mm) wide.

4. Rotate the crankshaft clockwise to make the feeler gauge roll up between the tensioner pulley and the belt. Make sure the gauge is centered on the tensioner pulley.

5. Push in on the belt halfway between the tensioner pulley and the camshaft sprocket with a force of 22 lbs. (98 N) and torque the locknut to 43 ft. lbs. (58 Nm).

6. Rotate the crankshaft to remove the feeler gauge. Install the covers.

REMOVAL AND INSTALLATION

1. Disconnect the negative battery cable and remove the timing belt cover.

2. Put a spacer (a stack of washers or a large nut) on the crankshaft pulley bolt and install the bolt so the crankshaft can be turned with a socket wrench.

3. Rotate the crankshaft to position the No. 1 piston on the TDC of its compression stroke. The marks on the camshaft and crankshaft sprockets will align with marks on the rear timing belt cover and the oil pump housing.

4. If the belt is to be re-used, paint an arrow on the belt pointing towards the front of the vehicle.

5. Loosen the belt tensioner pulley nut, move the pulley with an Allen wrench and remove the belt.

To install:

6. Spin the tensioner pulley and make sure it turns smoothly. If there is any doubt, replace it. Examine the belt for wear or damage, replace as necessary.

7. Make sure all the sprockets are correctly aligned with the timing marks. Be careful when turning the crankshaft or camshafts, this is not a free wheeling engine.

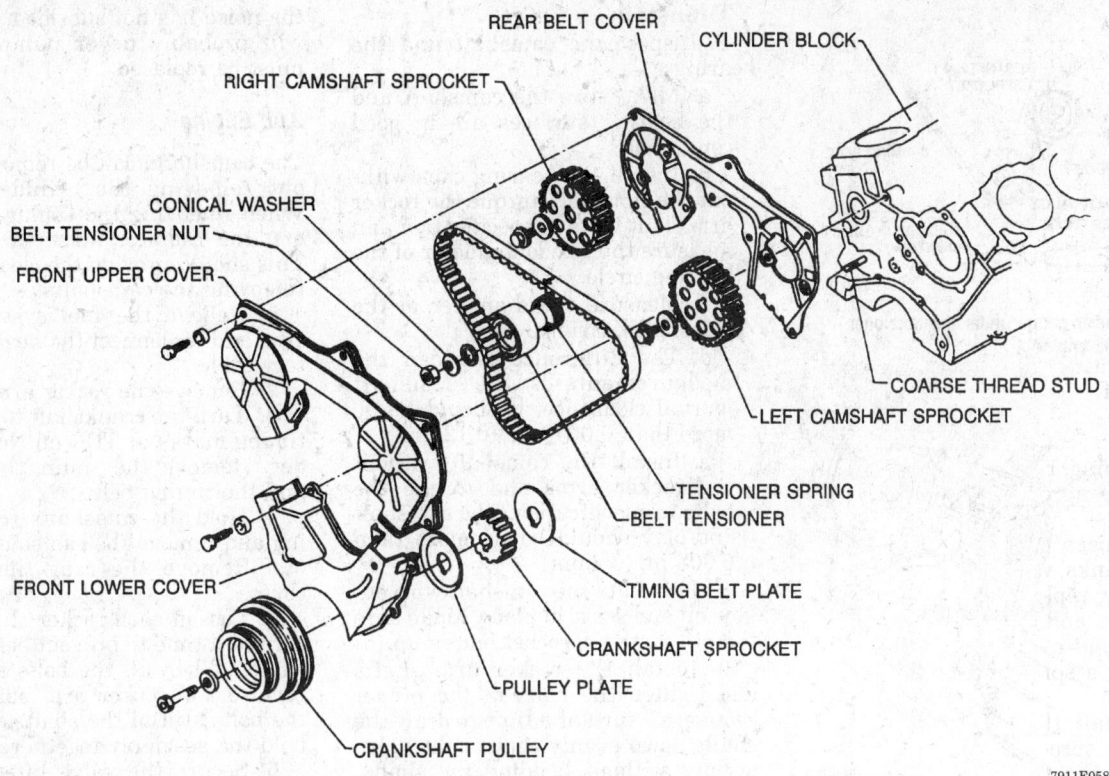

RIGHT CAMSHAFT SPROCKET

CONICAL WASHER

BELT TENSIONER NUT

FRONT UPPER COVER

REAR BELT COVER

CYLINDER BLOCK

COARSE THREAD STUD

LEFT CAMSHAFT SPROCKET

TENSIONER SPRING

BELT TENSIONER

TIMING BELT PLATE

CRANKSHAFT SPROCKET

PULLEY PLATE

FRONT LOWER COVER

CRANKSHAFT PULLEY

7911E058

Timing belt and cover assembly — 3.0L engine

8. Turn the tensioner pulley clockwise to move it out of the way, install the timing belt and allow the tensioner to slowly return on its spring. Make sure all the timing marks are still aligned. When the belt is correctly installed, there will be 40 teeth between the camshaft sprocket timing marks and 43 teeth between the crankshaft and left camshaft sprocket timing marks.

9. Turn the tensioner approximately 70–80 degrees clockwise with the wrench and tighten the locknut.

10. To adjust the belt tension, turn the crankshaft clockwise several times and slowly set the No. 1 piston to TDC of the compression stroke.

11. Set a 0.014 in. (0.35mm) feeler gauge between the belt and pulley on the crankshaft side of the pulley. The feeler gauge should be at least ½ in. (12.7mm) wide.

12. Rotate the crankshaft clockwise to make the feeler gauge roll up between the tensioner pulley and the belt. Make sure the gauge is centered on the tensioner pulley.

13. Loosen the tensioner pulley locknut, push in on the belt halfway between the tensioner pulley and the camshaft sprocket with a force of 22 lbs. (98 N) and torque the locknut to 43 ft. lbs. (58 Nm).

14. Rotate the crankshaft to remove the feeler gauge. Install the covers.

Timing Sprockets

REMOVAL AND INSTALLATION

1. Disconnect the negative battery cable.

2. Remove the timing belt cover and the timing belt.

3. Use an appropriate tool to prevent the camshafts from turning and remove the sprocket bolts. Pull the sprockets straight off.

4. Installation is the reverse of removal. Torque the camshaft sprocket

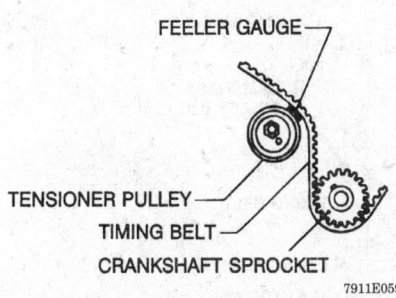

FEELER GAUGE

TENSIONER PULLEY

TIMING BELT

CRANKSHAFT SPROCKET

7911E059

Make sure the feeler gauge is centered between the tensioner pulley and the belt — 3.0L engine

bolts to 65 ft. lbs. (88 Nm). Install the timing belt.

Camshaft

REMOVAL AND INSTALLATION

2.4L Engine

The same bolts that hold the rocker arm assembly also hold the camshaft bearing caps. The hydraulic lifters are built into the rocker arms. If the rocker arm shafts are disassembled, do not allow the arms to lay on their side or they will become air bound. Keep the rocker arms upright or lay them in a pan of new engine oil.

1. Relieve the fuel system pressure and disconnect the negative battery cable.

2. Remove the rocker arm cover and turn the crankshaft to align the timing marks at TDC on No. 1 cylinder.

3. If the timing chain is not being removed, use a wire tie or wire to secure the timing chain to the camshaft sprocket.

4. Hold the camshaft sprocket to loosen the bolt and remove the sprocket. Secure the sprocket so the chain does not fall off the crankshaft sprocket.

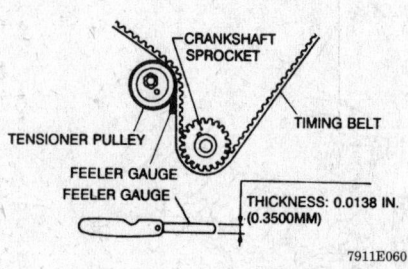

Place the feeler gauge under the tensioner pulley — 3.0L engine

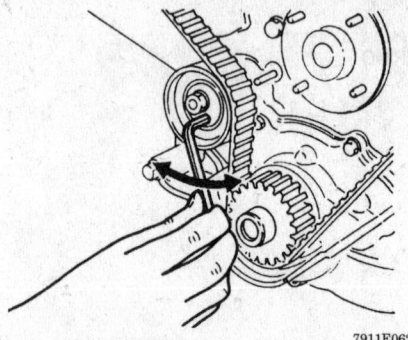

Move the tensioner pulley with an Allen wrench

5. Loosen each rocker shaft bolt 1 turn at a time to prevent bending the shafts.

6. When all the bolts are loose, remove the rocker arm shafts with the bolts still in the shafts. This will hold the assembly together.

7. If they are not already identified, mark the bearing caps so they can be installed in their original position facing the same direction. Lift the caps off and lift the camshaft out.

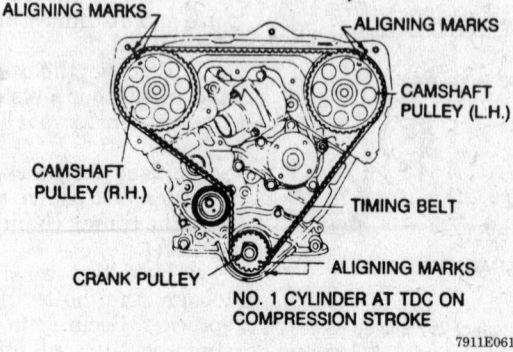

Timing belt and sprockets — 3.0L engine

To install:

8. Inspect the camshaft and the bearings:

a. Make sure the camshaft and the bearing surfaces are in good condition.

b. Install the bearing caps without the camshaft, torque the rocker arm shaft bolts to specification and measure the inside diameter of the bearing circle.

c. Measure the diameter of the camshaft bearings.

d. The difference between the measurements is the camshaft journal clearance; it should be no more than 0.0047 in. (0.12mm)

e. Install the camshaft without the rocker arms and torque the bolts to specification. The camshaft end-play should be no more than 0.008 in. (0.2mm).

9. Lubricate the camshaft with engine oil and set it in place. Make sure the pin on the sprocket end is up.

10. Install the rocker arm shafts and tighten the bolts in the proper sequence 1 turn at a time to draw the shafts down evenly against the valve springs without bending the shafts. Torque the bolts to 16 ft. lbs. (22 Nm).

11. Install the camshaft sprocket and remove the tie securing the chain. Install the sprocket bolt but don't torque it yet. Rotate the crankshaft 2 full turns to make sure the timing marks line up. When the valve timing is correct, torque the sprocket bolt to 116 ft. lbs. (157 Nm).

12. Use a silicone sealer on the rubber end plugs and install the rocker arm cover with a new gasket. Torque the bolts to 7 ft. lbs. (10 Nm) in a crisscross pattern starting at the middle. Install the remaining components.

13. When the engine is first started, the hydraulic valve lifters may be noisy. Run the engine for 10–20 minutes at about 1000 rpm. If the noise has not subsided, the lifter will probably never pump up and must be replaced.

3.0L Engine

The camshafts can be removed without removing the cylinder heads. When removing the timing belt covers, the radiator must be removed. This should provide the clearance for removing the camshafts.

1. Relieve the fuel system pressure and disconnect the negative battery cable.

2. Remove the rocker arm covers.

3. Turn the crankshaft to align the timing marks at TDC on No. 1 cylinder. Remove the timing belt cover and the timing belt.

4. Hold the camshafts from turning and remove the camshaft sprockets. Remove the rear timing belt cover.

5. Loosen each rocker shaft bolt 1 turn at a time to prevent bending the shafts. When all the bolts are loose, remove the rocker arm shafts with the bolts still in the shafts. This will hold the assembly together.

6. Secure the valve lifters in the guide assembly with safety wire to keep them in their original positions, then remove the entire assembly.

NOTE: Before removing a lifter from the guide assembly, tag the lifters to make sure they are returned to their original position. Keep the lifters upright to keep them from becoming air bound or lay them down in a pan of new engine oil. Do not disassemble a lifter.

7. Remove the plates from the front and rear of the cylinder heads and pry the oil seals out. Remove the bolt at the rear of the camshafts and remove the locating plates. Carefully withdraw the camshafts out towards the front.

To install:

8. Inspect the camshaft and the bearing surfaces:

a. Make sure the camshaft and the bearing surfaces are in good condition.

b. Measure the inside diameter of the bearing circle.

c. Measure the diameter of the camshaft bearings.

d. The difference between the measurements is the camshaft journal clearance; it should be no more than 0.0059 in. (0.15mm)

e. To check endplay, install the camshaft and the locating plates and torque the bolts to 65 ft. lbs. (88 Nm). The camshaft endplay

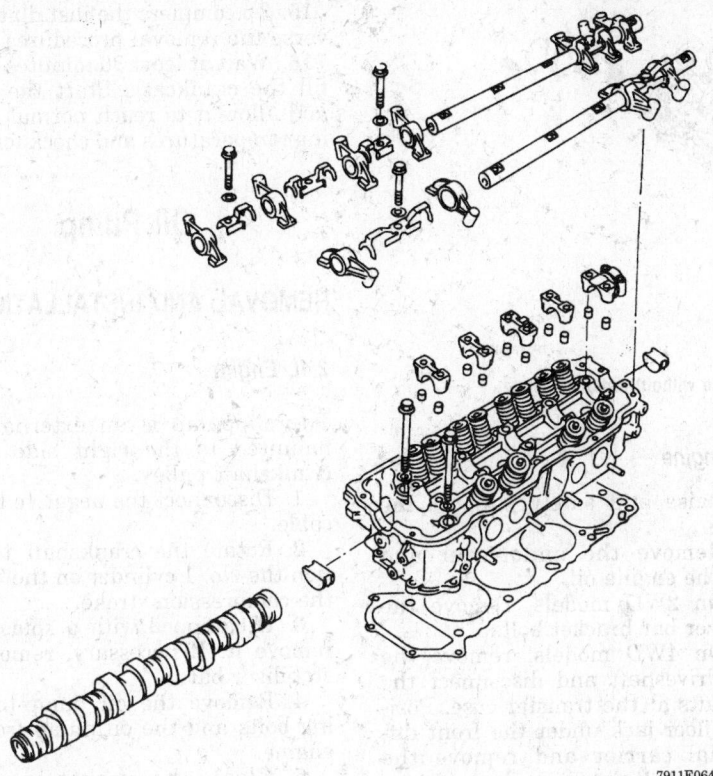

Camshaft removal — 2.4L engine

Piston and Connecting Rod

POSITIONING

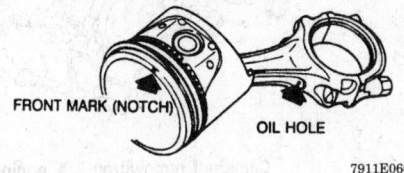

FRONT MARK (NOTCH)   OIL HOLE

7911E066

Piston and rod orientation on 2.4L engine

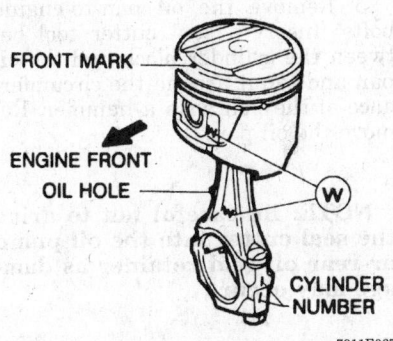

FRONT MARK

ENGINE FRONT

OIL HOLE

W

CYLINDER NUMBER

7911E067

Piston and rod orientation on 3.0L engine

should be no more than 0.0024 in. (0.06mm).

9. Lubricate the camshaft with engine oil and carefully set it in place. Install the locating plate at the rear and torque the bolt to 65 ft. lbs. (88 Nm). Turn the camshaft so the pin on the sprocket end is up.

10. Install the rear camshaft cover plate with a new gasket.

11. Lubricate a new camshaft front oil seal with grease and use an appropriate seal installation tool to carefully drive the new seal into place. Make sure the seal seats in the cylinder head.

12. With the rocker arm assemblies removed, all the valves will be closed. The rear timing belt cover, sprockets and timing belt can be installed without risk of damage to valves or pistons. Adjust timing belt tension according to correct procedure.

13. Make sure the engine is at TDC on No. 1 cylinder. Install the left bank lifter guide assembly, remove the safety wire and install the rocker arm shafts. Tighten the bolts 1 turn at a time to draw the shafts down evenly. Torque the bolts to 16 ft. lbs. (22 Nm).

14. Rotate the crankshaft to bring cylinder No. 4 to TDC. Set the right bank lifter guide assembly into place,

remove the safety wire and install the rocker arm shafts. Tighten the bolts 1 turn at a time to 16 ft. lbs. (22 Nm).

15. Use new gaskets to install the rocker arm covers and torque the bolts to 24 inch lbs. (3 Nm). Install the remaining components.

16. When the engine is first started, the hydraulic valve lifters may be noisy. Run the engine for 10–20 minutes at about 1000 rpm. If the noise has not subsided, the lifter will probably never pump up and must be replaced.

ENGINE LUBRICATION

Oil Pan

REMOVAL AND INSTALLATION

2.4L Engine

1. Raise and safely support the vehicle.

2. Remove the engine undercover and drain the engine oil.

3. On 4WD models, perform the following procedures:

   a. Remove the bolt from the front differential carrier member.

   b. Position a floor jack under the front differential carrier and remove the mounting bolts.

   c. Remove the transmission-to-rear engine mount bracket nuts.

   d. Remove the engine mount nuts and bolts.

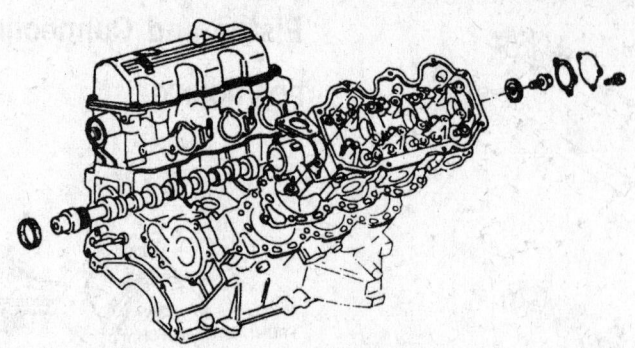

Camshaft removal on 3.0L engine can be done without removing the cylinder head

7911E065

e. Attach an engine hoist and raise the engine slightly.

4. On 2WD models, remove the front crossmember.

5. Remove the oil pan-to-engine bolts. Insert a seal cutter tool between the cylinder block and the oil pan and tap it around the circumference of the pan with a hammer. Remove the oil pan.

NOTE: Be careful not to drive the seal cutter into the oil pump or rear oil seal retainer as damage may occur.

6. Clean the gasket mounting surfaces.

7. Apply a continuous 1/8 in. bead of silicone sealant to the oil pan mounting surface; be sure to trace sealant bead to the inside of the bolt holes where there is no groove.

8. Install the oil pan and torque the bolts in sequence to 60 inch lbs. (7 Nm).

9. To complete the installation, reverse the removal procedures.

10. Wait at least 30 minutes and refill the crankcase. Start the engine and allow it to reach normal operating temperatures and check for leaks.

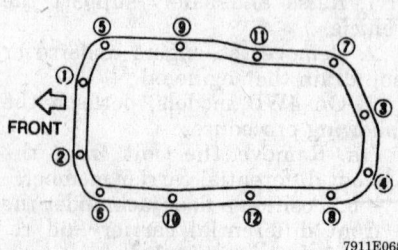

Oil pan bolt tightening sequence on 2.4L engine

7911E068

3.0L Engine

1. Raise and safely support the vehicle.

2. Remove the undercover and drain the engine oil.

3. On 2WD models, remove the stabilizer bar bracket bolts.

4. On 4WD models, remove the front driveshaft and disconnect the halfshafts at the transfer case. Position a floor jack under the front differential carrier and remove the mounting bolts.

5. On 2WD models, remove the front crossmember.

6. Remove the idler arm and the starter motor.

7. On 4WD models, remove the transmission-to-rear engine mount bracket nuts and the engine mount nuts/bolts.

8. Remove the engine gussets.

9. On 4WD models, attach a hoist to the engine and raise the engine slightly.

10. Remove the oil pan-to-engine bolts in the correct sequence to avoid warping the pan. Insert a seal cutter tool between the cylinder block and the oil pan and tap the tool around the circumference with a hammer to remove the oil pan.

NOTE: Be careful not to drive the seal cutter into the oil pump or rear oil seal retainer for damage may occur.

11. Clean the gasket mounting surfaces.

To install:

12. Apply silicone sealant to the oil pump and oil seal retainer gasket.

13. Apply a continuous 1/8 in. bead of sealant to the oil pan mounting surface; be sure to trace sealant bead to the inside of the bolt holes where there is no groove.

14. Install the oil pan and torque the bolts in sequence to 60 inch lbs. (7 Nm).

15. To complete the installation, reverse the removal procedures.

16. Wait at least 30 minutes and refill the crankcase. Start the engine and allow it to reach normal operating temperatures and check for leaks.

Oil Pump

REMOVAL AND INSTALLATION

2.4L Engine

The oil pump is an external type, mounted to the right side of the crankshaft pulley.

1. Disconnect the negative battery cable.

2. Rotate the crankshaft to position the No. 1 cylinder on the TDC of the compression stroke.

3. If equipped with a splash pan, remove it. If necessary, remove the stabilizer bar.

4. Remove the oil pump-to-housing bolts and the oil pump from the engine.

5. Clean the gasket mounting surfaces.

6. Install a new gasket onto the pump and fill the pump with oil.

7. Align the distributor drive spindle punch mark with the oil hole on the oil pump. This will properly align the drive spindle with the distributor.

8. Insert the oil pump into the housing until the drive spindle tang fits into the distributor shaft notch. Torque the oil pump-to-engine housing bolts to 11 ft. lbs. (15 Nm).

9. Start the engine to check the ignition timing and to check for leaks.

3.0L Engine

The oil pump is mounted at the front of the engine behind the crankshaft pulley.

1. Disconnect the negative battery cable.

2. Raise and safely support the vehicle. Drain the cooling system and the crankcase.

3. Remove the oil pan and the timing belt.

4. Remove the crankshaft timing sprocket using a wheel puller and the timing belt plate.

5. Remove the oil pump strainer and the pickup tube from the oil pump.

6. Remove the oil pump-to-engine bolts and the oil pump from the engine.

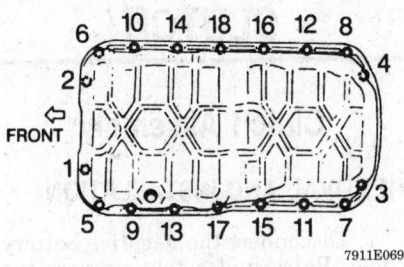

Oil pan bolt loosening sequence on 3.0L engine — tighten the bolts in the reverse of this sequence

When installing the oil pump on 2.4L engine, align the mark on the shaft with the oil hole

7. Clean the gasket mounting surfaces.

NOTE: Whenever the oil pump is removed, replace the oil seal.

8. To install, use new gaskets or silicone sealant. Pack the oil pump cavity with petroleum jelly and reverse the removal procedures. Torque as follows:

Oil pump-to-engine:
6mm bolts — 60 inch lbs. (7 Nm)
8mm bolts — 12 ft. lbs. (16 Nm)
Pickup tube-to-oil pump bolts — 15 ft. lbs. (21 Nm)

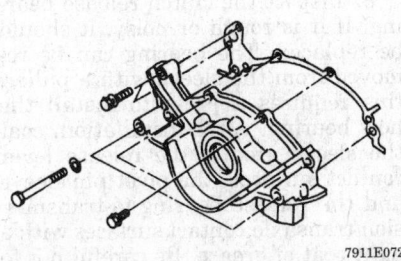

Oil pump on 3.0L engine is on the front of the engine block

CHECKING

To check the oil pump clearances, the oil pump must be removed from the engine and disassembled. If the parts do not meet specifications, replace the oil pump as an assembly.

2.4L Engine

Using a feeler gauge, check the following clearances:
Inner rotor tip-to-outer rotor — 0.0047 in. (0.12mm) max.
Outer rotor-to-housing — 0.0059–0.0083 in. (0.15–0.21mm)
Side clearance (with gasket) — 0.0016–0.0031 in. (0.04–0.07mm)

3.0L Engine

Using a feeler gauge, check the following clearances:
Pump body-to-outer gear — 0.0043–0.0079 in. (0.11–0.20mm)
Inner gear-to-crescent — 0.0047–0.0091 in. (0.12–0.23mm)
Outer gear-to-crescent — 0.0083–0.0126 in. (0.22–0.33mm)
Housing-to-inner gear — 0.0020–0.0035 in. (0.05–0.09mm)
Housing-to-outer gear — 0.0020–0.0043 in. (0.05–0.11mm)

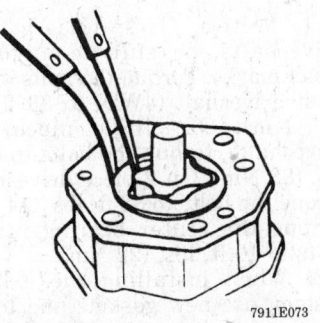

Inspecting oil pump rotor clearance — 2.4L engine

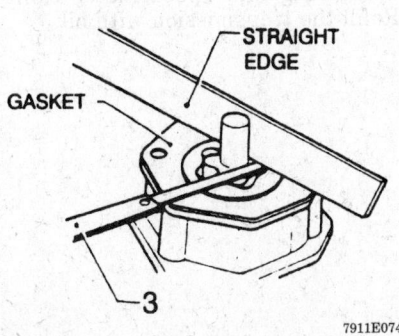

Inspecting oil pump side clearance — 2.4L engine

Rear Main Bearing Oil Seal

REMOVAL AND INSTALLATION

1. Disconnect the negative battery cable.
2. Raise and safely support the vehicle. Remove the starter.
3. Remove the transmission from the vehicle.
4. If equipped with a manual transmission, remove the clutch-to-flywheel bolts and the clutch assembly from the vehicle.
5. Remove the flywheel-to-crankshaft bolts and the flywheel from the engine.
6. Remove the rear oil seal retainer-to-engine bolts, the rear oil seal retainer-to-oil pan bolts and the retainer.
7. Carefully pry the rear oil seal from the retainer; be careful not to damage the mounting surfaces. Clean the oil seal mounting surfaces.
8. Using an appropriate oil seal installation tool, lubricate the new oil seal lips with engine oil and drive the the seal into the retainer until it seats.
9. To complete the installation, reverse the removal procedures. Start the engine and check for leaks.

MANUAL TRANSMISSION

Transmission Assembly

REMOVAL AND INSTALLATION

1. Disconnect the negative battery cable.
2. Remove the shifter knob and boot and remove the snapring to lift the shift lever out of the transmission. Stuff a rag in the opening to keep dirt out of the transmission.
3. Raise and safely support the vehicle. If equipped, remove the splash pan or skid plate.
4. Remove the starter and drain the oil from the transmission.
5. Matchmark the driveshaft flange at the rear pinion flange and remove the driveshaft. Plug the extension housing opening to prevent dirt from getting in.
6. If equipped with 4WD, matchmark both front driveshaft flanges so

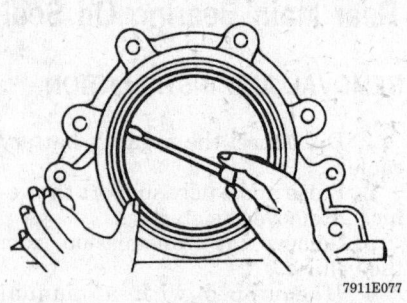

7911E077

Removing the rear oil seal from the retainer; the transmission and flywheel must be removed

the shaft can be installed in the same position. Remove the driveshaft.

7. Disconnect the exhaust pipe from the manifolds and from the catalytic converter and remove the pipe.

8. Disconnect the speedometer cable and the wiring from the transmission.

9. Without disconnecting the hydraulic hose, remove the clutch slave cylinder from the transmission and secure it aside.

10. If equipped with 4WD, the torsion bars must be removed.

   a. Working under the vehicle, measure and record the length of the threads on the torsion bar adjustment. At the front of the bar, pull the boot back and matchmark the bar to the mounting plate. The spline on the bar must be re-installed in the same position on the plate.

   b. Remove the locknut and adjustment nut from both torsion bars. Remove the 3 nuts at the mounting plate and remove the bars. Mark the bars left and right side for proper installation.

   c. Remove the transfer case shift lever assembly from the transfer case.

   d. If necessary, the transfer case can be removed at this point so the jack will be available to remove the transmission.

   e. If equipped with a 3.0L engine, remove the gusset securing the engine to the transmission.

11. Using a chain hoist, attach it to the engine and lift the engine slightly to take the weight off the mounts. Using an appropriate transmission jack, properly support the transmission and remove the transmission mount and crossmember.

12. Remove the transmission-to-engine bolts and move the transmission back away from the engine. Lower the transmission carefully from the vehicle.

To install:

13. Lightly grease the input shaft splines. On 4WD, apply a silicone sealant to the engine block or rear plate to seal the engine to the transmission.

14. Fit the transmission into place and start all the engine-to-transmission bolts. Make sure the input shaft fits properly into the clutch disc and pilot bearing.

15. Torque the 2.36 in. (60mm) and 2.56 in. (65mm) engine-to-transmission bolts to 36 ft. lbs. (49 Nm).

16. Torque the remaining bolts to 18 ft. lbs. (25 Nm) on 2.4L engine or 29 ft. lbs. (39 Nm) on 3.0L engine.

17. Install the crossmember and torque the crossmember-to-chassis bolts to 38 ft. lbs. (52 Nm) on 2WD or 31 ft. lbs. (42 Nm) on 4WD.

18. Install the rear transmission mount bolts, loosen the engine mount bolts, then torque all the mount bolts to 31 ft. lbs. (42 Nm), starting at the rear.

19. If the torsion bars were removed, install them in their original location. Make sure the splines are in their original position and set the adjustment to its original position.

20. If the transfer case was removed, apply silicone sealant to seal the case to the transmission. Install the transfer case and torque the bolts to 30 ft. lbs. (41 Nm). Install the shift lever.

21. When installing the driveshafts, be sure to align the matchmarks. Torque the bolts on the front driveshaft (4WD) to 33 ft. lbs. (44 Nm). On single piece rear driveshafts, torque the bolts to 65 ft. lbs. (88 Nm). On 2 piece driveshafts, torque the bolts to 33 ft. lbs. (44 Nm). Torque the center bearing bracket bolts to 16 ft. lbs. (22 Nm).

22. When installing the exhaust system, use new gaskets and torque the flange bolts to 27 ft. lbs. (36 Nm).

23. Install the remaining components in order of removal and connect the wiring and speedometer cable. Refill the transmission with oil.

CLUTCH

Clutch Assembly

REMOVAL AND INSTALLATION

1. Disconnect the negative battery cable. Raise and safely support the vehicle.

2. Remove the transmission or the transaxle.

3. Using a piece of chalk, paint or a center punch, mark the clutch assembly-to-flywheel relationship so it can be reassembled in the same position from which it is removed.

4. Using a clutch aligning tool, insert it into the clutch disc hub.

5. Loosen the clutch cover-to-flywheel bolts, a turn at a time in an alternating sequence, until the spring tension is relieved to avoid distorting or bending the clutch cover. Remove the clutch assembly.

6. Inspect the flywheel for scoring, roughness or signs of overheating. Light scoring may be cleaned up with emery cloth, but any deep grooves or overheating (blue marks) warrant replacement or refacing of the flywheel. If the clutch facings or flywheel are oily, inspect the transmission/transaxle front cover oil seal, the pilot bushing and engine rear seals, etc. for leakage; replace any leaking seals before replacing the clutch.

7. If the crankshaft pilot bushing is worn, replace it. Install it using a soft hammer. The factory supplied part does not have to be oiled, but check the procedure if using an aftermarket part. Inspect the clutch cover for wear or scoring and replace it, if necessary.

NOTE: The pressure plate and spring cannot be disassembled; replace the clutch cover as an assembly.

To install:

8. Inspect the clutch release bearing. If it is rough or noisy, it should be replaced. The bearing can be removed from the sleeve with a puller; this requires a press to install the new bearing. After installation, coat the sleeve groove, the release lever contact surfaces, the pivot pin/sleeve and the release bearing-to-transmission/transaxle contact surfaces with a light coat of grease. Be careful not to use too much grease, which will run at high temperatures and get onto the clutch facings. Reinstall the release bearing on the lever.

9. Apply a thin coat of grease to the pressure plate wire ring, diaphragm spring, clutch cover grooves and the pressure plate drive bosses.

10. Apply a thin coat of Lubriplate® to the splines in the driven plate. Slide the clutch disc onto the splines and move it back and forth several times. Remove the disc and wipe off the excess lubricant. Be very careful not to get any grease on the clutch facings.

11. Assemble the clutch cover and the clutch plate on the clutch alignment arbor.

12. To complete the installation, align the clutch assembly-to-flywheel alignment marks and install the bolts. Tighten the bolts 1 or 2 turns at a time in a crisscross pattern to avoid distorting the cover. Torque the bolts to 22 ft. lbs. (30 Nm).

13. Install the transmission/transaxle and adjust the pedal height as necessary.

PEDAL HEIGHT/FREE-PLAY ADJUSTMENT

The pedal height is the distance from the top of the clutch pedal to the floor board without the carpet. The pedal free-play is the distance the clutch pedal pad moves from the released position to the point where resistance is felt.

1. To adjust the pedal height:

   a. From under the dash, loosen the pedal stopper locknut.

   b. Turn the pedal stopper until the specified pedal height is obtained: 9.29–9.69 in. (236–246mm) with the 2.4L engine or 8.94–9.33 in. (227–236mm) with the 3.0L engine.

   c. After adjustment, torque the pedal stopper locknut to 16 ft. lbs. (22 Nm).

2. To adjust the pedal free-play, perform the following procedures:

   a. Loosen the clutch pedal, pushrod locknut.

   b. Using a ruler, measure the clutch pedal free-play.

   c. Turn the clutch pedal pushrod to set the free-play at 0.040–0.120 in. (1–3mm).

   d. After adjustment, torque the locknut to 9 ft. lbs. (12 Nm).

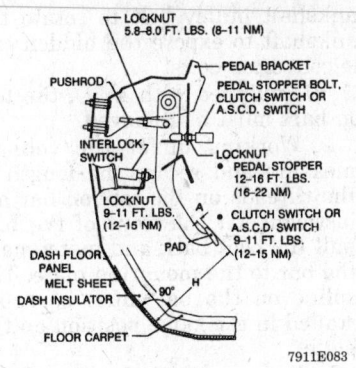

Clutch pedal

Clutch Master Cylinder

REMOVAL AND INSTALLATION

The master cylinder is attached to a bracket located under the dash.

1. Disconnect the negative battery cable.

2. From under the dash, remove the clevis pin snap pin and pull the clevis pin from the clutch pedal.

3. Disconnect the clutch pedal arm from the pushrod clevis. Remove the dust cover (boot) from the master cylinder body and pushrod. It will not go through the cowl without tearing.

4. Disconnect and plug the hydraulic line from the clutch master cylinder.

NOTE: Take precautions to keep brake fluid from coming in contact with any painted surfaces.

5. Remove the clutch master cylinder.

6. Installation is the reverse of removal. Torque the clutch master cylinder-to-cowl bolts/nuts to 9 ft. lbs. 12 Nm) on all others.

7. Bleed the clutch hydraulic system.

Clutch Slave Cylinder

REMOVAL AND INSTALLATION

1. If necessary, raise and safely support the vehicle.

2. Remove the slave cylinder-to-clutch housing bolts and the pushrod from the shift fork.

3. Disconnect and plug the hydraulic hose from the slave cylinder, then, remove the cylinder from the vehicle.

4. To install, reverse the removal procedures. Torque the slave cylinder-to-clutch housing bolts to 30 ft. lbs. (40 Nm).

5. Bleed the clutch hydraulic system.

Hydraulic Clutch System Bleeding

1. Check and refill the clutch fluid reservoir to the full mark. During the bleeding process, continue to check and replenish the reservoir to prevent the fluid level from getting lower than ½ full.

2. Connect a clear vinyl hose to the bleeder screw on the slave cylinder. Immerse the other end of the hose in a clear jar ½ filled with brake fluid.

3. Have an assistant pump the clutch pedal several times and hold it down. Loosen the bleeder screw slowly.

4. Tighten the bleeder screw and release the clutch pedal gradually. Repeat this operation until the air bubbles disappear from the brake fluid being expelled out through the bleeder screw.

5. When the air is completely removed, securely tighten the bleeder screw and replace the dust cap.

6. Check and refill the master cylinder reservoir as necessary.

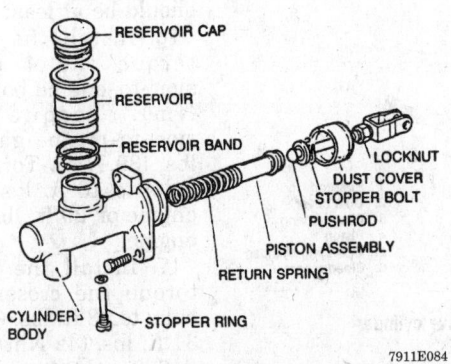

Clutch master cylinder assembly

7. Depress the clutch pedal several times to check the operation of the clutch and check for leaks.

AUTOMATIC TRANSMISSION

Transmission Assembly

REMOVAL AND INSTALLATION

1. Disconnect the negative battery cable.
2. Raise and safely support the vehicle. If equipped, remove the splash pan or skid plate.
3. Remove the starter.
4. Matchmark the driveshaft flange at the rear pinion flange and remove the driveshaft. Plug the extension housing opening to prevent fluid from leaking out.
5. If equipped with 4WD, matchmark both front driveshaft flanges so the shaft can be installed in the same position. Remove the driveshaft.
6. Disconnect the exhaust pipe from the manifolds and from the catalytic converter and remove the pipe.
7. Disconnect the speedometer cable and the wiring from the transmission.
8. Disconnect the selector lever and throttle cables from the transmission.
9. Remove the dipstick tube and disconnect the cooling lines from the transmission.
10. Remove the torque converter housing dust cover. Matchmark the torque converter with the driveplate for reassembly; these are balanced together at the factory. Remove the torque converter-to-driveplate (flywheel) bolts. Use a wrench on the

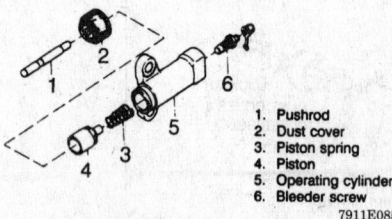

1. Pushrod
2. Dust cover
3. Piston spring
4. Piston
5. Operating cylinder
6. Bleeder screw

7911E085

Clutch slave cylinder

crankshaft pulley bolt to rotate the crankshaft to expose the hidden torque converter bolts.

11. If equipped with 4WD, the torsion bars must be removed.

a. Working under the vehicle, measure and record the length of the threads on the torsion bar adjustment. At the front of the bar, pull the boot back and matchmark the bar to the mounting plate. The spline on the bar must be re-installed in the same position on the plate.

b. Remove the locknut and adjustment nut from both torsion bars. Remove the 3 nuts at the mounting plate and remove the bars. Mark the bars left and right side for proper installation.

c. Remove the transfer case shift lever assembly from the transfer case.

d. If necessary, the transfer case can be removed at this point.

e. If equipped with a 3.0L engine, remove the gusset securing the engine to the transmission.

12. Using a chain hoist, attach it to the engine and lift the engine slightly to take the weight off the mounts. Using an appropriate transmission jack, properly support the transmission and remove the transmission mount and crossmember.

13. Remove the transmission-to-engine bolts and move the transmission back away from the engine. Lower the transmission carefully from the vehicle.

To install:

14. Use a dial indicator to check the driveplate runout while turning the crankshaft. Maximum allowable runout is 0.020 in. (0.5mm); if beyond specification, replace the driveplate.

15. Measure and adjust how far the torque converter is recessed into the transmission housing. The distance between the front mounting surface of the transmission and the torque converter-to-driveplate bolt boss should be at least 1.024 in. (26mm).

16. Install the transmission and torque the 4 upper transmission-to-engine bolts to 36 ft. lbs. (49 Nm). Torque to transmission-to-engine gusset bolts to 29 ft. lbs. (39 Nm). Torque the remaining bolts to 18 ft. lbs. (25 Nm) on 2.4L engine or 29 ft. lbs. (39 Nm) on 3.0L engine.

17. Install the crossmember and torque the crossmember-to-chassis bolts to 38 ft. lbs. (52 Nm) on 2WD or 31 ft. lbs. (42 Nm) on 4WD.

18. Install the rear transmission mount bolts, loosen the engine mount

bolts, then torque all the mount bolts to 31 ft. lbs. (42 Nm), starting at the rear.

19. Align the matchmarks on the driveplate and torque converter, install the bolts and torque to 36 ft. lbs. (49 Nm). Turn the crankshaft after tightening the bolts to make sure there is no binding at the driveplate.

20. If the torsion bars were removed, install them in their original location. Make sure the splines are in their original position and set the adjustment to its original position.

21. If the transfer case was removed, apply silicone sealant to seal the case to the transmission. Install the transfer case and torque the bolts to 30 ft. lbs. (41 Nm). Install the shift lever.

22. When installing the driveshafts, be sure to align the matchmarks. Torque the bolts on the front driveshaft (4WD) to 33 ft. lbs. (44 Nm). On single piece rear driveshafts, torque the bolts to 65 ft. lbs. (88 Nm). On 2 piece driveshafts, torque the bolts to 33 ft. lbs. (44 Nm). Torque the center bearing bracket bolts to 16 ft. lbs. (22 Nm).

23. When installing the exhaust system, use new gaskets and torque the flange bolts to 27 ft. lbs. (36 Nm).

24. Install the remaining components in order of removal and connect the wiring, cooling lines and speedometer cable. Refill the transmission with fluid and adjust as required.

SHIFT LINKAGE ADJUSTMENT

2WD Floor Shift Models

1. Place the shift selector in the **P** position.
2. Raise and safely support the vehicle.
3. From under the vehicle, loosen the shift lever locknuts.
4. Tighten the rear locknut **X** until it touches the trunnion.
5. Pull the selector lever toward the **R** position without pushing the button. Back off the rear locknut **X** a complete revolution, adjust the front locknut **Y** and torque the locknuts to 8.0 ft. lbs. (11 Nm).
6. After adjustment, move the selector lever through the gears to make sure it moves smoothly.

2WD Column Shift Models

1. Place the shift selector in the **P** position.
2. Raise and safely support the vehicle.
3. From under the vehicle, loosen the shift lever locknuts.

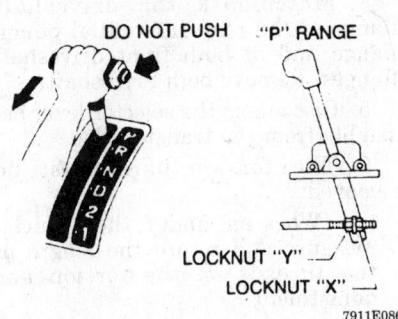

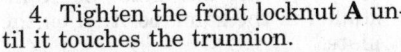

Automatic with 2WD and floor shift

4. Tighten the front locknut **A** until it touches the trunnion.

5. Pull the selector lever toward the **R** position without pushing the button. Back off the front locknut **A** 2 complete revolutions, adjust the rear locknut **B** and torque the locknuts to 8.0 ft. lbs. (11 Nm).

6. After adjustment, move the selector lever through the gears to make sure it moves smoothly.

4WD Floor Shift Models

1. Place the shift selector in the **P** position.

2. Raise and safely support the vehicle.

3. Remove the console cover.

4. Loosen the turn buckle locknuts.

5. Tighten the turn buckle until it aligns with the inner cable.

6. Pull the selector lever toward the **R** position without pushing the button. Back off the turn buckle a complete revolution, torque the locknuts to 48 inch lbs. (5 Nm).

7. After adjustment, move the selector lever through the gears to make sure it moves smoothly.

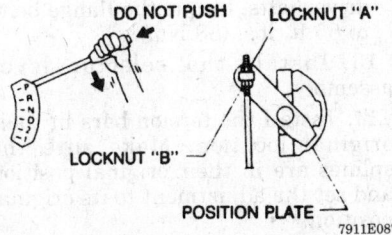

Automatic with 2WD and column shift

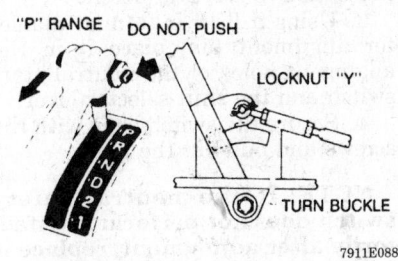

Automatic with 4WD and floor shift

KICKDOWN SWITCH ADJUSTMENT

With 71B Transmission

A kickdown switch is located inside the vehicle at the upper post of the accelerator pedal. Its purpose is to provide transmission downshifting when the accelerator pedal is fully depressed; a click can be heard just before the pedal bottoms out.

With the ignition switch in the **ON** position and the engine **OFF**, when the accelerator pedal is depressed fully, the kick-down switch contacts should be closed and the downshift solenoid activated, emitting a clicking sound. If the components fail to operate in this manner, check for continuity at the switch and then at the solenoid. Replace either of the components as necessary.

VACUUM MODULATOR ADJUSTMENT

With 71B Transmission

1. Raise and safely support the vehicle.

2. Remove the vacuum modulator from the transmission.

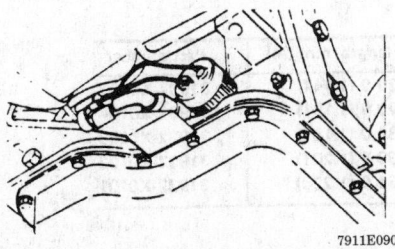

Downshift solenoid on with 71B transmission

3. Using a depth gauge, measure the **L** depth; be sure the vacuum throttle valve is pushed into the valve body as far as possible.

4. Select the correct length rod and install it into the vacuum modulator.

5. Using a new O-ring, install the modulator into the transmission.

THROTTLE LINKAGE ADJUSTMENT

With RL4R01A Transmission

1. Press the lock plate and move the adjusting tube in the direction **T**.

2. Release the lock plate.

3. Quickly move the throttle drum from P-to-P.

4. Ensure the throttle wire stroke **L** is within specified range between full throttle and idle; the throttle wire stroke **L** should be 1.50–1.65 in. (38–42mm).

NOTE: Adjust the throttle wire stroke when the throttle wire/accelerator wire is installed. Place marks on the throttle wire to facilitate measuring the wire stroke.

5. If the throttle wire stroke is not adjusted, the following problems may arise:

    a. When full-open position **P** of the throttle drum is closer to the direction **T**, the kickdown range will greatly increase.

    b. When the full-open position **P** of the throttle drum is closer to the direction **U**, the kickdown range will not occur.

NEUTRAL SAFETY SWITCH ADJUSTMENT

The neutral safety switch is located on the transmission shift selector lever. The switch operates the back-up lights and controls the operation of the starter. The starter should only operate when the transmission is in **P** or **N**.

With 71B Transmission

1. Unscrew the securing nut of the shift selector lever and the switch-to-transmission screws.

2. Position the shift selector to the **N** position (in vertical detent position). Move the switch slightly aside so the screw hole will be aligned with the pin hole of the shift selector lever.

3. Using a 0.080 in. (2mm) diameter alignment pin, place it in the

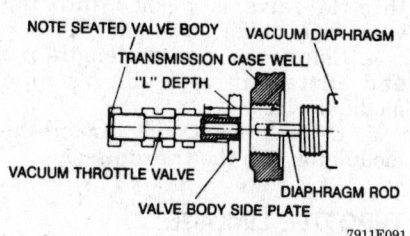

NOTE SEATED VALVE BODY | VACUUM DIAPHRAGM
TRANSMISSION CASE WELL
"L" DEPTH
VACUUM THROTTLE VALVE
DIAPHRAGM ROD
VALVE BODY SIDE PLATE
7911E091

Vacuum diaphragm with 71B transmission

alignment holes of the neutral start switch and the shift selector lever.

NOTE: A No. 47 drill bit will substitute for the pin gauge.

4. Secure the switch body with the screws and pull out the pin.

NOTE: If the neutral safety switch does not perform satisfactorily after adjustment, replace it with a new one.

With "R" Series Transmission

1. Unscrew the securing nut of the shift selector lever and the switch-to-transmission screws.

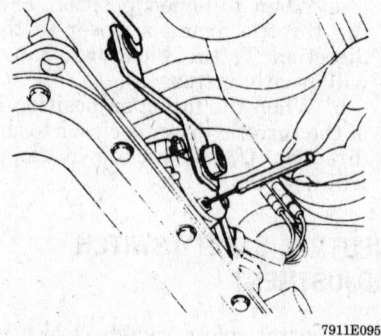

7911E095

Neutral safety switch alignment with 71B transmission

2. Position the shift selector to the **N** position (in vertical detent).

3. Using a 0.16 in. (4mm) diameter alignment pin, place it in the alignment holes of the neutral start switch and the shift selector lever.

4. Secure the switch body with the screws and pull out the pin.

NOTE: If the neutral safety switch does not perform satisfactorily after adjustment, replace it with a new one.

TRANSFER CASE

Transfer Case

REMOVAL AND INSTALLATION

1. Disconnect the negative battery cable.

2. Raise and safely support the vehicle. If equipped, remove the splash pan or skid plate.

3. Remove the starter. Drain the oil from both the transmission and the transfer case.

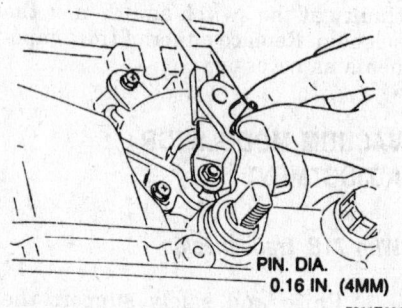

PIN. DIA.
0.16 IN. (4MM)
7911E096

Neutral safety switch alignment with "R" series transmission

4. Matchmark the driveshaft flange at the rear differential pinion flange and at both front driveshaft flanges. Remove both driveshafts.

5. Disconnect the selector lever assembly from the transfer case.

6. The torsion bars must be removed:

   a. Working under the vehicle, measure and record the length of the threads on the torsion bar adjustment.

   b. At the front of the bar, pull the boot back and matchmark the bar to the mounting plate. The spline on the bar must be re-installed in the same position on the plate.

   c. Remove the locknut and adjustment nut and remove the 3 nuts at the mounting plate to remove each bar. Mark the bars left and right side for proper installation.

7. Using an appropriate transmission jack, properly support the transmission and remove the transmission mount and crossmember.

8. Remove the transfer case–to–transmission bolts and move the unit back away from the transmission.

To install:

9. Clean the mating surfaces and apply a bead of silicone sealant to the transfer case mounting flange.

10. Carefully fit the case into place and start all the mounting bolts. Torque the bolts to 30 ft. lbs. (41 Nm).

11. Install the crossmember and torque the bolts to 58 ft. lbs. (78 Nm). Install the mount bolts and torque to 38 ft. lbs. (52 Nm).

12. Install the driveshafts and make sure to align the matchmarks:

   a. On the front driveshaft, torque the bolts to 33 ft. lbs. (44 Nm).

   b. On 2 piece rear driveshafts, torque the flange bolts to 33 ft. lbs. (44 Nm) and the center bearing bracket bolts to 16 ft. lbs. (22 Nm).

   c. On single piece rear driveshafts, torque the flange bolts to 65 ft. lbs. (88 Nm).

13. Install the selector lever assembly.

14. Install the torsion bars in their original location. Make sure the splines are in their original position and set the adjustment to its original position.

15. Install the remaining components and fill the transfer case and transmission with oil. Check and adjust front suspension height.

Measured depth "L" mm (in)	Rod length mm (in)	Part number
Under 25.55 (1.0059)	29.0 (1.142)	31932-X0103
25.65 - 26.05 (1.0098 - 1.0256)	29.5 (1.161)	31932-X0104
26.15 - 26.55 (1.0295 - 1.0453)	30.0 (1.181)	31932-X0100
26.65 - 27.05 (1.0492 - 1.0650)	30.5 (1.201)	31932-X0102
Over 27.15 (1.0689)	31.0 (1.220)	31932-X0101

7911E092

Vacuum diaphragm rod selection chart — 71B transmission

DRIVE AXLE

Halfshaft

REMOVAL AND INSTALLATION

4WD

The front steering knuckle must be removed to remove the halfshaft.

1. Raise and safely support the vehicle.
2. Have an assistant depress the brake pedal and remove the halfshaft-to-differential flange bolts.
3. Remove the locking hub and front drive clutch assemblies.
4. Remove the steering knuckle with the halfshaft and clamp the knuckle in a vise.
5. Using a hammer and a block of wood, tap the halfshaft from the steering knuckle.
6. Installation is the reverse of removal. Torque the inner halfshaft drive flange bolts to 33 ft. lbs. (44 Nm).
7. Measure halfshaft end-play with a dial indicator against the end of the shaft; it should be 0.004–0.012 in. (0.1–0.3mm). Endplay can be adjusted with different thickness snaprings available at the dealer.

Driveshaft and U-Joints

REMOVAL AND INSTALLATION

One Piece Rear Driveshaft

1. Raise and safely support the vehicle.
2. Matchmark the driveshaft flange to the pinion flange on the differential.
3. Remove the flange bolts, lower the driveshaft and pull it from the transmission.
4. Using a clean rag, plug the rear of the transmission to keep the oil from leaking out.
5. To install, insert the sleeve yoke into the transmission, align the matchmarks and fit the driveshaft into place. Torque the driveshaft flange nuts/bolts to 65 ft. lbs. (88 Nm).

Two Piece Rear Driveshaft

1. Raise and safely support the vehicle.
2. Matchmark the driveshaft flange to the pinion flange on the dif-

ferential and to the transmission drive flange.
3. Remove the bolts from both flanges, then remove the bolts from the center bearing flange-to-chassis bracket and lower the driveshaft out of the vehicle.
4. Using a clean rag, plug the rear of the transmission to keep the oil from leaking out.
5. If necessary, separate the front section of the driveshaft from the rear section.
6. To install, align the matchmarks and reverse the removal procedures. Torque as follows:
Center bearing-to-chassis bolts to 16 ft. lbs. (22 Nm)
Driveshaft-to-differential flange nuts/bolts
   Model 3S63 — 33 ft. lbs. (44 Nm)
   Model 3S80 — 65 ft. lbs. (88 Nm)
7. If the center bearing was separated from the front driveshaft, torque as follows:
Companion flange-to-front driveshaft nut — 174–203 ft. lbs. (235–275 Nm)
Rear driveshaft-to-center bearing flange nuts/bolts
   Model 3S63 — 17–24 ft. lbs. (24–32 Nm)
   Model 3S71H — 29–33 ft. lbs. (39–44 Nm)
   Model 3S80 — 58–65 ft. lbs. (78–88 Nm)

4WD Front Driveshaft

1. Raise and safely support the vehicle.
2. Matchmark the driveshaft flange to the pinion flange on the differential and to the transfer case drive flange.
3. Remove the nuts and bolts and remove the front driveshaft.
4. To install, align the matchmarks and reverse the removal procedures. Torque the all the flange nuts and bolts to 33 ft. lbs. (44 Nm).

Rear Axle Shaft, Bearing and Seal

REMOVAL AND INSTALLATION

Single Rear Wheels

1. Raise and safely support the vehicle and remove the rear wheels.
2. Using a floor jack, support the differential.
3. If equipped with rear drum brakes:
   a. Remove the brake drum.
   b. Disconnect the parking brake cable from the brake shoes.

c. Disconnect and plug the hydraulic line from wheel cylinder.
   d. Remove the brake shoe assembly.
4. If equipped with rear disc brakes:
   a. Disconnect the parking brake cable from the caliper.
   b. Remove the caliper-to-knuckle bolts and hang the caliper from the body on a piece of wire. Do not disconnect the hydraulic line.
   c. Remove the rotor disc.
5. Remove the backing plate nuts.
6. Attach a slide hammer to the wheel lugs and pull the axle shaft/backing plate assembly from the axle housing. Whenever the axle shaft is removed, the oil seal should be replaced.
7. To replace the wheel bearing, leave the slide hammer attached to the lugs and secure it in a vise with the axle pointing up.
   a. At the rear of the backing plate, unbend and discard the lockwasher.
   b. Using a brass drift and a hammer, loosen and remove the locknut.
   c. Using a shop press, press the axle shaft out of the bearing.
   d. Press the bearing out of the bearing housing.
8. To install the wheel bearing:
   a. Press the new bearing into the housing. Be sure to press only on the outer race of the bearing.
   b. Grease the inside of the bearing housing.
   c. To install a new oil seal, lubricate the seal lips and carefully press it into the bearing housing.
   d. Position the back plate on the bearing housing, support the inner bearing race and press the axle into the bearing.
   e. Grease the flat washer and lockwasher, lay them into place and install the locknut. Torque the locknut to 217 ft. lbs. (294 Nm).
   f. Bend the lockwasher tabs into place.
9. Lubricate the bearing housing and recess in the axle housing with wheel bearing grease. Coat the axle splines with gear oil. Coat the seal surface of the shaft with grease.
10. Install a new axle housing seal behind the shim pack and install the axle into the housing. Torque the nuts to 46 ft. lbs. (63 Nm) and check the endplay of the axle with a dial indicator.
11. The axle endplay should be 0.0008–0.0059 in. (0.02–0.15mm) when servicing only one axle. When servicing both sides, endplay should

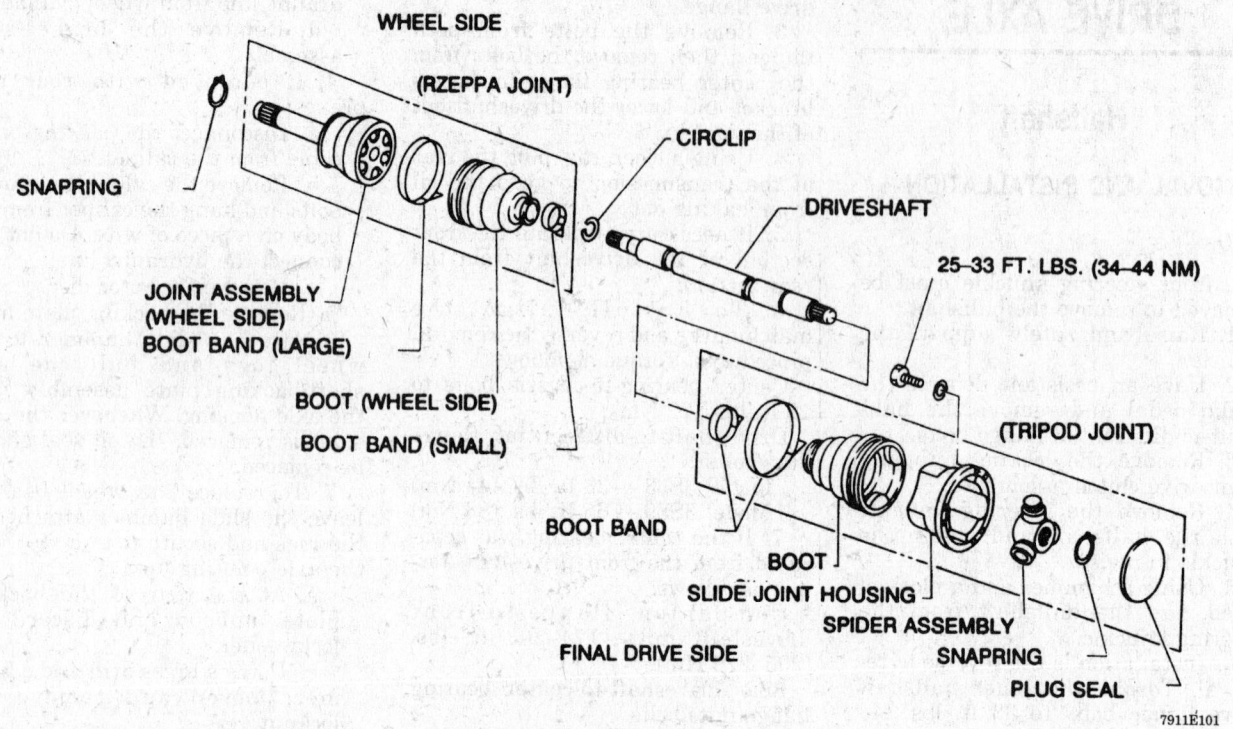

WHEEL SIDE

(RZEPPA JOINT)

SNAPRING

CIRCLIP

DRIVESHAFT

JOINT ASSEMBLY
(WHEEL SIDE)

BOOT BAND (LARGE)

BOOT (WHEEL SIDE)

BOOT BAND (SMALL)

25-33 FT. LBS. (34-44 NM)

(TRIPOD JOINT)

BOOT BAND

BOOT

SLIDE JOINT HOUSING

SPIDER ASSEMBLY

FINAL DRIVE SIDE

SNAPRING

PLUG SEAL

7911E101

Front halfshaft — 4WD with 2.4L engine

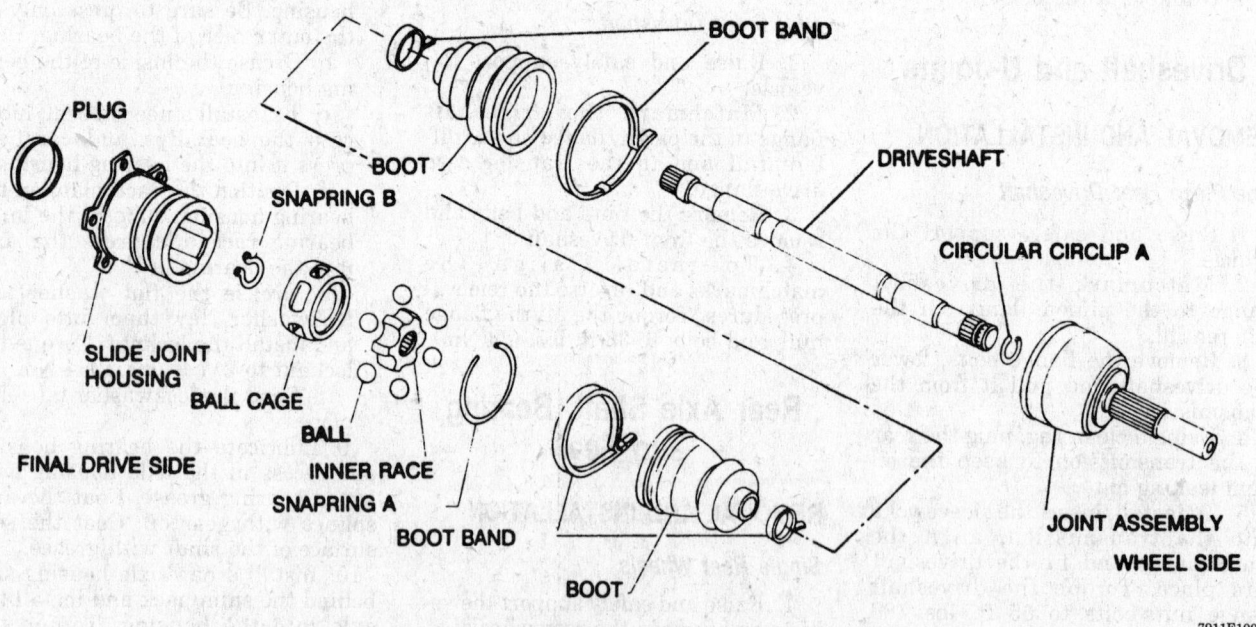

BOOT BAND

PLUG

BOOT

DRIVESHAFT

SNAPRING B

CIRCULAR CIRCLIP A

SLIDE JOINT
HOUSING

BALL CAGE

BALL

INNER RACE

SNAPRING A

FINAL DRIVE SIDE

BOOT BAND

JOINT ASSEMBLY

WHEEL SIDE

BOOT

7911E100

Front halfshaft — 4WD with 3.0L engine

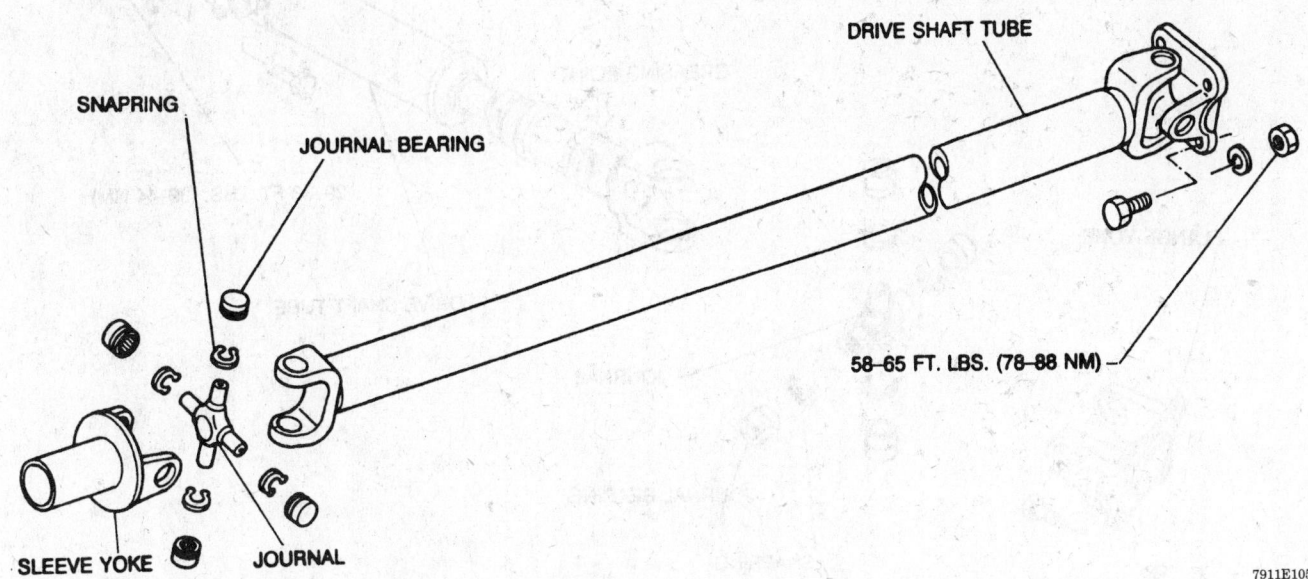

SNAPRING

JOURNAL BEARING

DRIVE SHAFT TUBE

58–65 FT. LBS. (78–88 NM)

SLEEVE YOKE

JOURNAL

7911E105

Single piece driveshaft

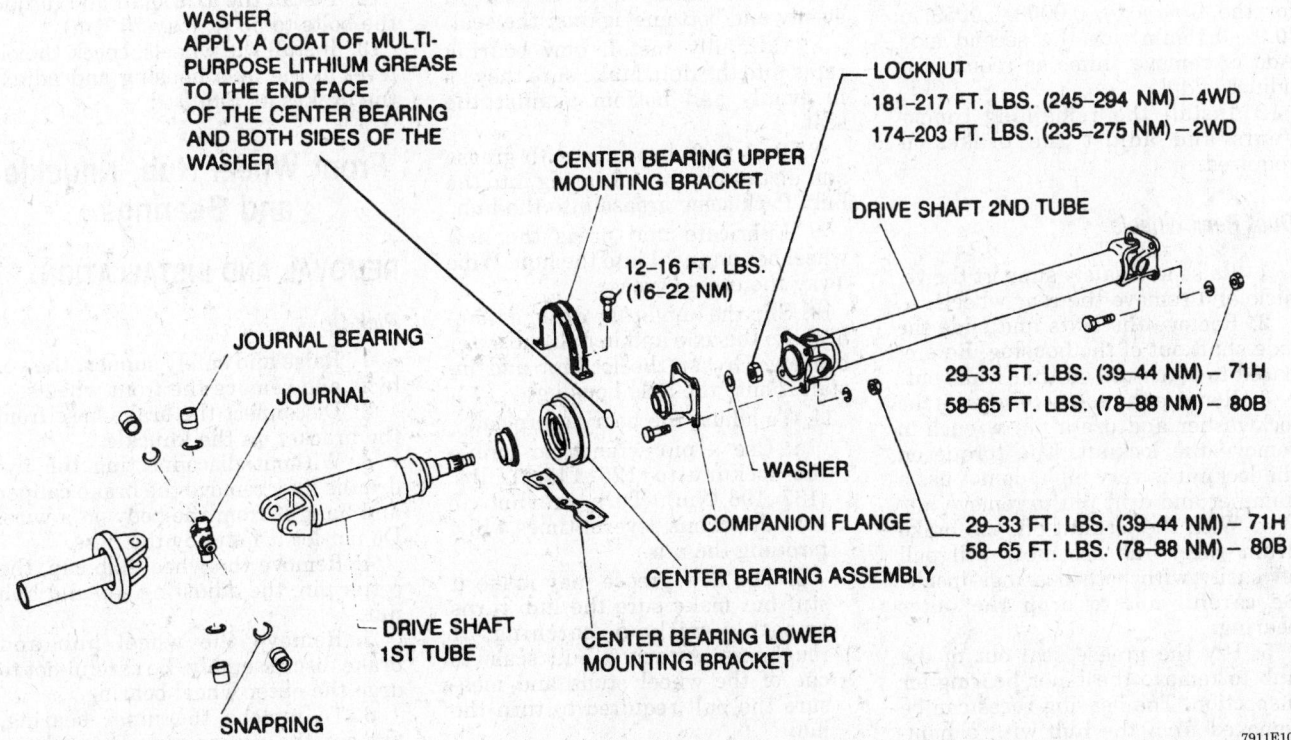

WASHER
APPLY A COAT OF MULTI-
PURPOSE LITHIUM GREASE
TO THE END FACE
OF THE CENTER BEARING
AND BOTH SIDES OF THE
WASHER

CENTER BEARING UPPER
MOUNTING BRACKET

LOCKNUT
181–217 FT. LBS. (245–294 NM) – 4WD
174–203 FT. LBS. (235–275 NM) – 2WD

DRIVE SHAFT 2ND TUBE

12–16 FT. LBS.
(16–22 NM)

JOURNAL BEARING

JOURNAL

29–33 FT. LBS. (39–44 NM) – 71H
58–65 FT. LBS. (78–88 NM) – 80B

WASHER

COMPANION FLANGE

29–33 FT. LBS. (39–44 NM) – 71H
58–65 FT. LBS. (78–88 NM) – 80B

CENTER BEARING ASSEMBLY

DRIVE SHAFT
1ST TUBE

CENTER BEARING LOWER
MOUNTING BRACKET

SNAPRING

7911E106

Two piece driveshaft

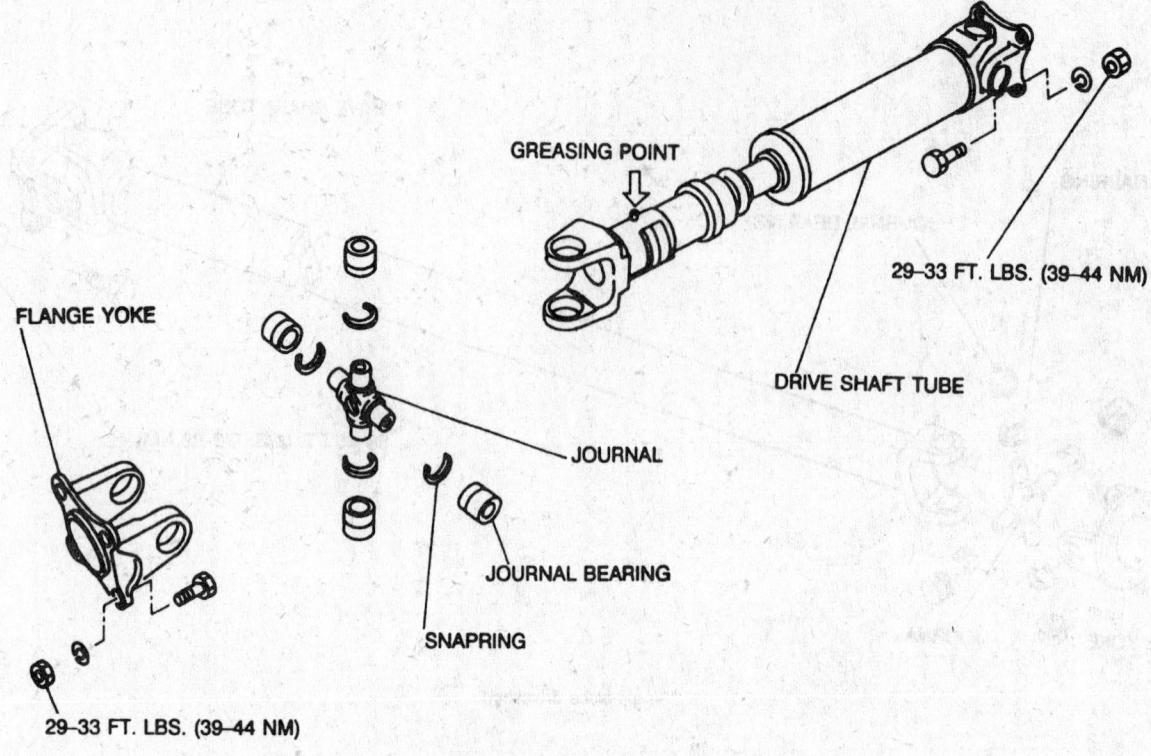

FLANGE YOKE

GREASING POINT

29-33 FT. LBS. (39-44 NM)

DRIVE SHAFT TUBE

JOURNAL

JOURNAL BEARING

SNAPRING

29-33 FT. LBS. (39-44 NM)

7911E107

Front driveshaft used on 4WD

be 0.0118–0.0354 in. (0.30–0.90mm) for the first axle, 0.0008–0.0059 in. (0.02–0.15mm) for the second axle. Add or remove shims as required to adjust endplay.

12. Install the remaining components and adjust the brakes as required.

Dual Rear Wheels

1. Raise and safely support the vehicle and remove the rear wheels.

2. Remove the bolts and slide the axle shaft out of the housing. Be prepared to catch the oil that leaks out.

3. Remove the screw to remove the lockwasher and use a pin wrench to remove the locknut. The torque on the locknut is very high, do not use a hammer and drift pin to remove it.

4. With the locknut off, the brake drum/wheel hub assembly will pull off easily with both bearings inside. Be careful not to drop the outer bearing.

5. Pry the grease seal out of the hub to remove the inner bearing for inspection. The bearing races can be removed from the hub with a hammer and a soft drift pin.

6. To replace the oil seal, pry the old seal out of the axle housing. Lubricate and carefully install the new seal with an appropriate seal instal-

lation tool. Make sure it goes in evenly and bottoms against the seat.

7. Carefully install new bearing races into the hub. Make sure they go in evenly and bottom against the seat.

8. Pack both bearings with grease and install the inner bearing into the hub. Pack some grease into the hub.

9. Lubricate and press the new wheel bearing seal into the hub. Wipe away the excess grease.

10. Slip the hub/brake drum assembly onto the axle and install the outer bearing. Grease the locknut and install it onto the axle housing.

11. To adjust the bearing preload:

a. Use a pin wrench to torque the locknut to 125–145 ft. lbs. (167–196 Nm). Turn the hub in both directions several times while torquing the nut.

b. The new grease may make it stiff but make sure the hub turns smoothly without catching or roughness. Attach a pull scale to one of the wheel studs and measure the pull required to turn the hub.

c. If it is not smooth or if more than 4.7 lbs. of pull is required to turn the hub, remove the hub and look for improperly installed bearing races or dirt in the bearings.

12. Install the axle shaft and torque the bolts to 55 ft. lbs. (75 Nm).

13. Install the wheels, check the oil level in the axle housing and adjust the brakes as required.

Front Wheel Hub, Knuckle and Bearings

REMOVAL AND INSTALLATION

Pick-Up

1. Raise and safely support the vehicle and remove the front wheels.

2. Disconnect the brake hose from the bracket on the knuckle.

3. Without disconnecting the hydraulic line, remove the brake caliper and hang it from the body on a wire. Do not let it hang by the hose.

4. Remove the wheel hub cup, the cotter pin, the adjusting cap and hub nut.

5. Remove the wheel hub and brake disc assembly. Be careful not to drop the outer wheel bearing.

6. To remove the inner bearing, pry out the grease seal. Discard the seal.

7. To remove the knuckle, remove the cotter pins from the upper and lower ball joint nuts and the tie rod nut. Remove the tie rod nut and

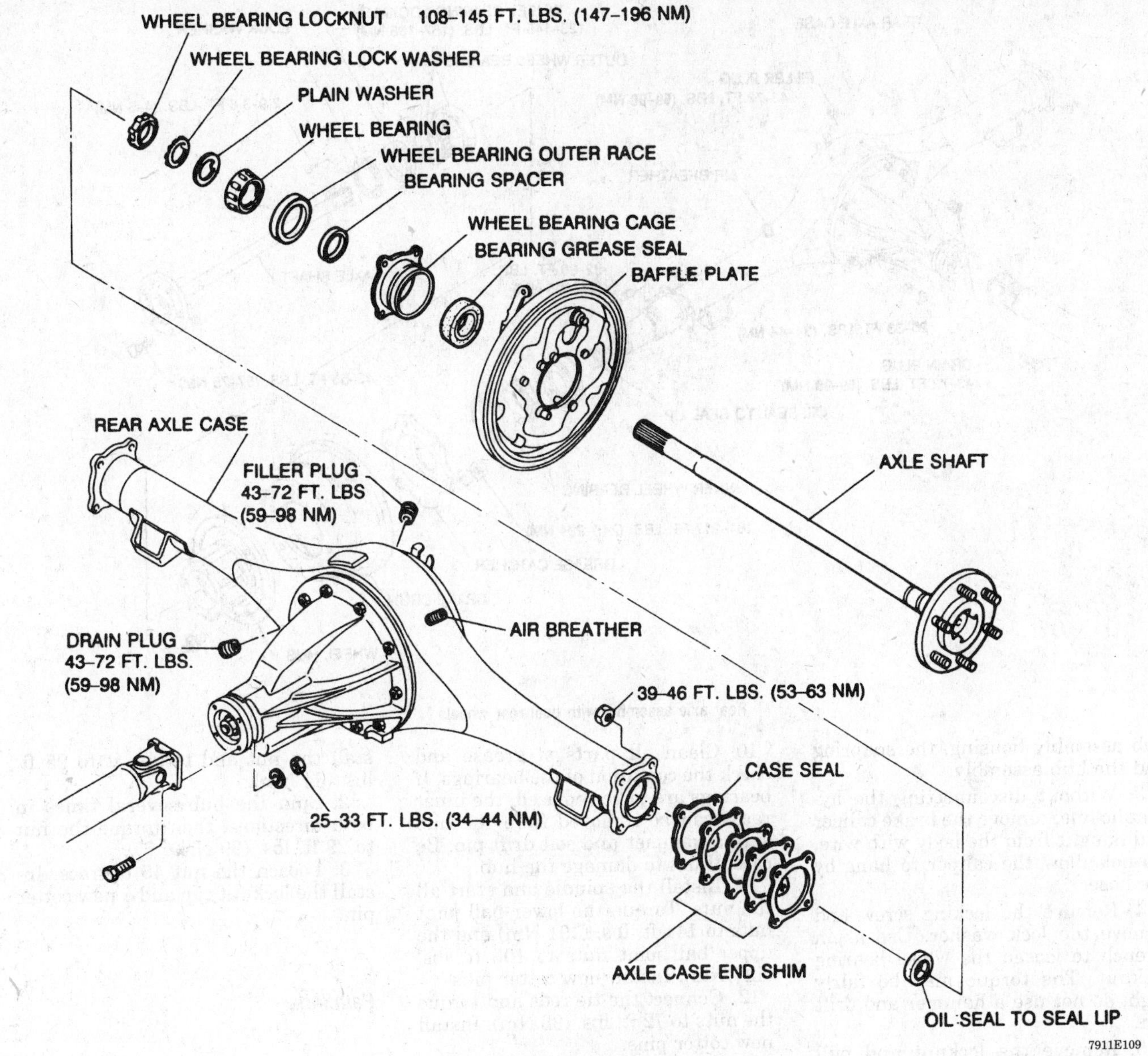

WHEEL BEARING LOCKNUT   108–145 FT. LBS. (147–196 NM)

WHEEL BEARING LOCK WASHER

PLAIN WASHER

WHEEL BEARING

WHEEL BEARING OUTER RACE

BEARING SPACER

WHEEL BEARING CAGE

BEARING GREASE SEAL

BAFFLE PLATE

REAR AXLE CASE

FILLER PLUG
43–72 FT. LBS
(59–98 NM)

AXLE SHAFT

DRAIN PLUG
43–72 FT. LBS.
(59–98 NM)

AIR BREATHER

39–46 FT. LBS. (53–63 NM)

CASE SEAL

25–33 FT. LBS. (34–44 NM)

AXLE CASE END SHIM

OIL SEAL TO SEAL LIP

7911E109

Rear axle assembly with single rear wheels

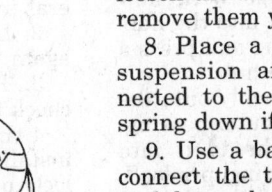

7911E110

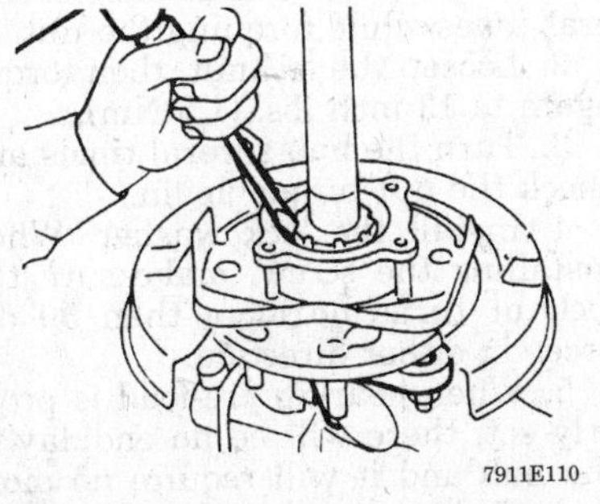

Unbend the lockwasher and remove the
locknut, then press the bearing off, with
single rear wheels

loosen the ball joint nuts but do not
remove them yet.

8. Place a jack under the lower
suspension arm. The arm is connected to the torsion bar and will
spring down if not supported.

9. Use a ball joint press and disconnect the tie rod end and upper
and lower ball joints. Remove the
front spindle.

10. Install the spindle and start all
the nuts. Torque the lower ball joint
nuts to 141 ft. lbs. (191 Nm) and the
upper ball joint nuts to 108 ft. lbs.
(147 Nm). Install new cotter pins.

11. Make sure the bearings are
clean and in good condition. Pack the
bearings and the hub with new

grease and install the bearings into
the hub. Install a new grease seal.

12. Make sure the spindle is clean.
Install the spacer with the chamfer
facing in on the spindle.

13. Lightly grease the lips on the
seal and slide the hub and bearings
onto the spindle. Install the washer
and nut and adjust the pre-load on
the bearing. Check and adjust front
wheel alignment.

Pathfinder

1. Raise and safely support the vehicle and remove the front wheels.

2. Have an assistant hold the
brake pedal and loosen the locking
front hub housing bolts. Remove the

10-33

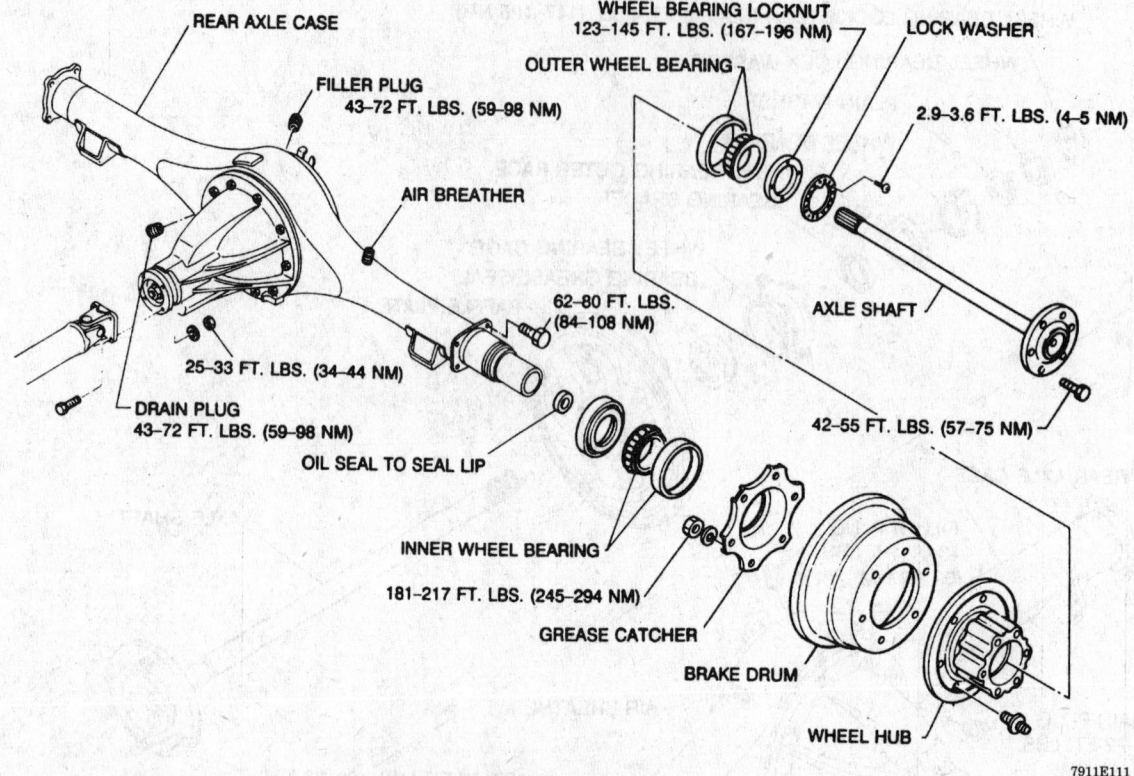

REAR AXLE CASE

FILLER PLUG
43–72 FT. LBS. (59–98 NM)

AIR BREATHER

25–33 FT. LBS. (34–44 NM)

DRAIN PLUG
43–72 FT. LBS. (59–98 NM)

OIL SEAL TO SEAL LIP

62–80 FT. LBS.
(84–108 NM)

INNER WHEEL BEARING

181–217 FT. LBS. (245–294 NM)

GREASE CATCHER

BRAKE DRUM

WHEEL HUB

WHEEL BEARING LOCKNUT
123–145 FT. LBS. (167–196 NM)

OUTER WHEEL BEARING

LOCK WASHER

2.9–3.6 FT. LBS. (4–5 NM)

AXLE SHAFT

42–55 FT. LBS. (57–75 NM)

7911E111

Rear axle assembly with dual rear wheels

hub assembly housing, the snapring and the hub assembly.

3. Without disconnecting the hydraulic line, remove the brake caliper and hang it from the body with wire. Do not allow the caliper to hang by the hose.

4. Remove the locking screw and remove the lock washer. Use a pin wrench to loosen the wheel bearing locknut. The torque may be fairly high, do not use a hammer and drift pin.

5. Remove the locknut and pull the hub off with the bearings. Pry the inner grease seal out to remove the inner bearing. Discard the seal.

6. Use a block of wood and hammer to tap on the end of the halfshaft to break it loose from the hub spline.

7. To remove the knuckle, remove the cotter pins from the upper and lower ball joint nuts and the tie rod nut. Remove the tie rod nut and loosen the ball joint nuts but do not remove them yet.

8. Place a jack under the lower suspension arm. The arm is connected to the torsion bar and will spring down if not supported.

9. Use a ball joint press and disconnect the tie rod end and upper and lower ball joints. Remove the front spindle.

10. Clean all parts of grease and check the condition of the bearings. If bearings are to be replaced, the inner races can be removed from the hub with a hammer and soft drift pin. Be careful not to damage the hub.

11. Install the spindle and start all the nuts. Torque the lower ball joint nuts to 141 ft. lbs. (191 Nm) and the upper ball joint nuts to 108 ft. lbs. (147 Nm). Install new cotter pins.

12. Connect the tie rods and torque the nuts to 72 ft. lbs. (98 Nm). Install new cotter pins.

13. Carefully install the new inner races with the drift pin, making sure they seat in the hub.

14. Pack the bearings with new grease and pack grease into the hub. Install the inner bearing and press a new inner seal into the hub.

15. Slip the hub assembly onto the spindle and install the outer bearing. Grease the locknut, thread it into place and set the bearing pre-load. Check and adjust front wheel alignment.

BEARING PRE-LOAD ADJUSTMENT

Pick-Up

1. With the bearings and hub properly cleaned and lubricated, install the nut and torque it to 25 ft. lbs. (34 Nm).

2. Spin the hub several times in both directions, then torque the nut to 29 ft. lbs. (39 Nm).

3. Loosen the nut 45 degrees. Install the locknut cap and a new cotter pin.

Pathfinder

1. Use a pin wrench to torque the locknut to 58–72 ft. lbs. (78–98 Nm). Turn the hub in both directions several times while torquing the nut.

2. Loosen the locknut, then torque again to 13 inch lbs. (1.5 Nm).

3. Turn the hub several times and check the nut torque again.

4. Install the lock washer. When installing the screw, make sure the locknut turns no more than 30 degrees in either direction.

5. When bearing pre-load is properly set, there will be no endplay in the hub and it will require no more than 4.7 lbs. of pull at the wheel stud to turn the hub.

6. Install the locking hub and the brake caliper. Torque the caliper carrier bolts to 72 ft. lbs. (98 Nm) and the hub bolts to 25 ft. lbs. (34 Nm).

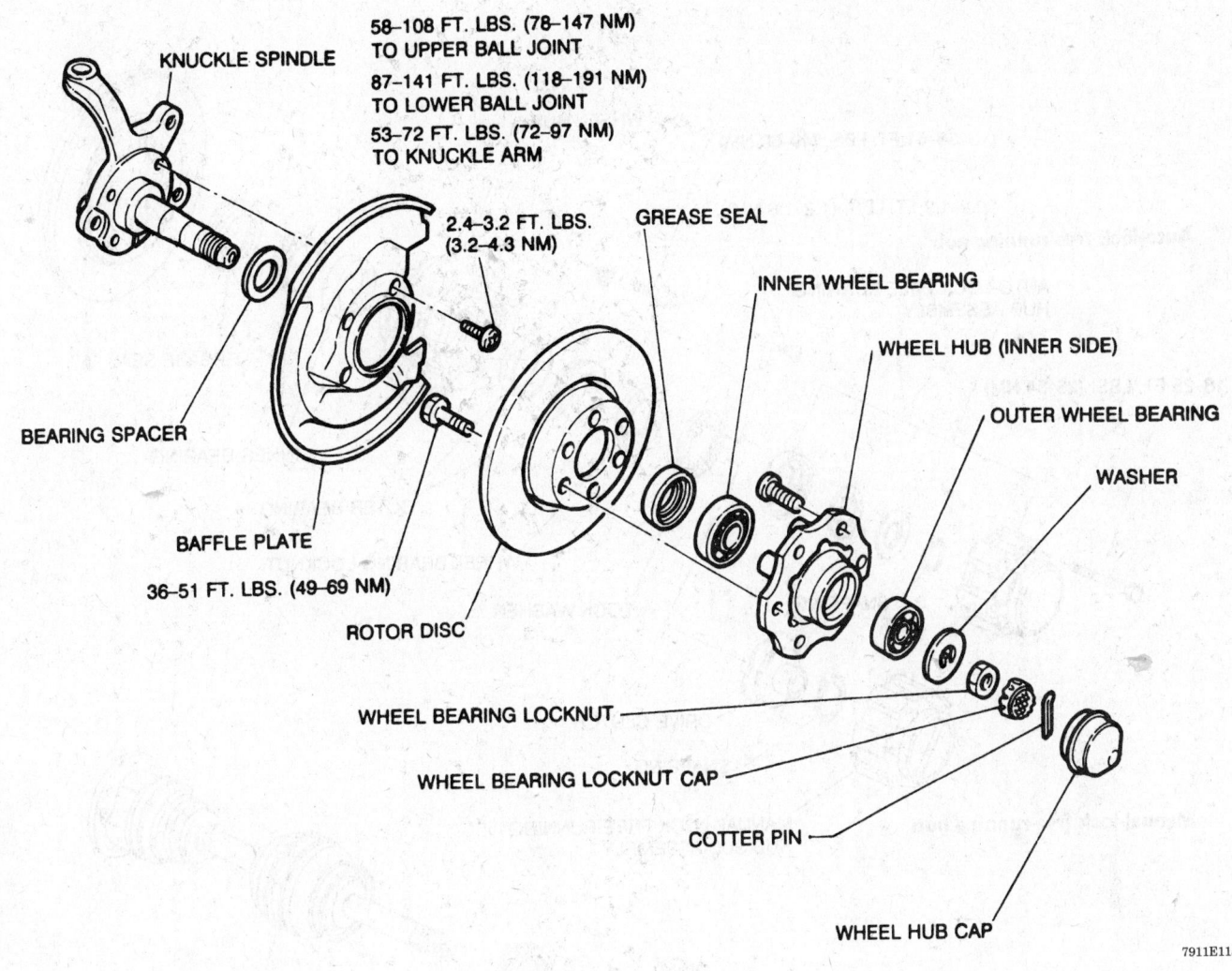

KNUCKLE SPINDLE

58–108 FT. LBS. (78–147 NM)
TO UPPER BALL JOINT

87–141 FT. LBS. (118–191 NM)
TO LOWER BALL JOINT

53–72 FT. LBS. (72–97 NM)
TO KNUCKLE ARM

2.4–3.2 FT. LBS.
(3.2–4.3 NM)

GREASE SEAL

INNER WHEEL BEARING

WHEEL HUB (INNER SIDE)

OUTER WHEEL BEARING

WASHER

BEARING SPACER

BAFFLE PLATE

36–51 FT. LBS. (49–69 NM)

ROTOR DISC

WHEEL BEARING LOCKNUT

WHEEL BEARING LOCKNUT CAP

COTTER PIN

WHEEL HUB CAP

7911E115

Front wheel bearing — 2WD

Manual Locking Hubs

REMOVAL AND INSTALLATION

1. Raise and safely support the vehicle and remove the wheels.
2. Set the knob of the manual lock to the **FREE** position.
3. Have an assistant hold the brake pedal and use a Torx® wrench to remove the locking hub housing bolts.
4. Remove the snapring to disassemble the drive clutch.
5. Installation is the reverse of removal. Make sure the parts are clean and lubricated with new grease. With the hub in the **FREE** position, torque the bolts to 25 ft. lbs. (34 Nm).

Automatic Locking Hubs

REMOVAL AND INSTALLATION

1. Raise and safely support the vehicle and remove the wheels.
2. Set the knob of the manual lock to the **FREE** position.
3. Have an assistant hold the brake pedal and use a Torx® wrench to remove the locking hub housing bolts.
4. Remove the snapring to disassemble the drive clutch.
5. Installation is the reverse of removal. Make sure the parts are clean and lubricated with new grease. With the hub in the **FREE** position, torque the bolts to 25 ft. lbs. (34 Nm).

Pinion Seal

REMOVAL AND INSTALLATION

The pinion oil seal on Models H190A, H233B and C200 differentials can not be replaced without disassembling the differential. A collapsible

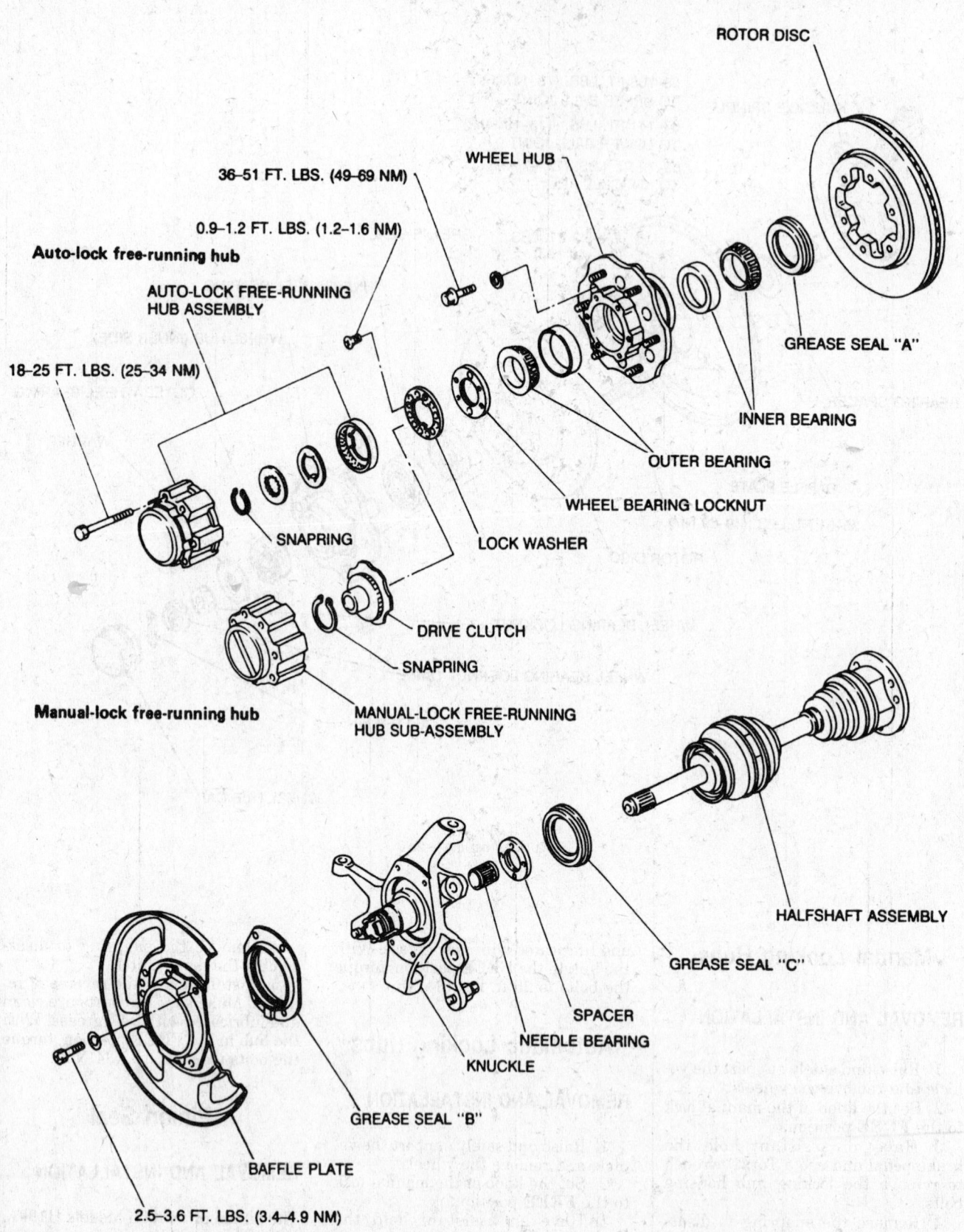

ROTOR DISC

WHEEL HUB

36–51 FT. LBS. (49–69 NM)

0.9–1.2 FT. LBS. (1.2–1.6 NM)

Auto-lock free-running hub

AUTO-LOCK FREE-RUNNING
HUB ASSEMBLY

GREASE SEAL "A"

18–25 FT. LBS. (25–34 NM)

INNER BEARING

OUTER BEARING

WHEEL BEARING LOCKNUT

SNAPRING

LOCK WASHER

DRIVE CLUTCH

SNAPRING

Manual-lock free-running hub

MANUAL-LOCK FREE-RUNNING
HUB SUB-ASSEMBLY

HALFSHAFT ASSEMBLY

GREASE SEAL "C"

SPACER

NEEDLE BEARING

KNUCKLE

GREASE SEAL "B"

BAFFLE PLATE

2.5–3.6 FT. LBS. (3.4–4.9 NM)

7911E116

Front wheel bearing and hub assembly — Pathfinder with 2WD and Pick-Up and Pathfinder with 4WD

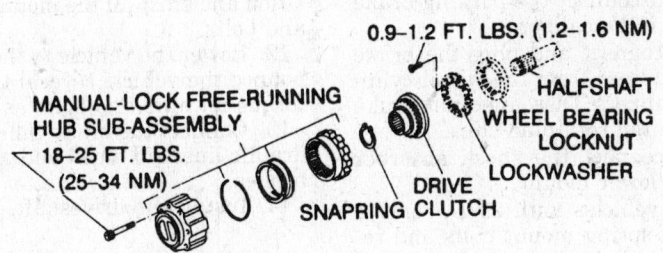

0.9-1.2 FT. LBS. (1.2-1.6 NM)

MANUAL-LOCK FREE-RUNNING HUB SUB-ASSEMBLY

18–25 FT. LBS. (25–34 NM)

HALFSHAFT

WHEEL BEARING LOCKNUT

LOCKWASHER

DRIVE CLUTCH

SNAPRING

7911E121

Manual locking hubs — 4WD

spacer is used to set pinion bearing pre-lo

1. Raise and safely support the vehicle.

2. Remove the driveshaft.

3. Using a socket wrench and the differential flange holding tool, hold the differential flange and the remove the differential pinion nut.

4. Using a wheel puller tool, pull the pinion flange from the differential.

5. Using a small prybar, pry the oil seal from the differential.

6. Using the oil seal driver tool (Model R180A and H190A differentials), lubricate the new oil seal lips

with multi-purpose grease and drive the new seal into the differential housing until it is flush with the end of the housing.

7. Using a soft hammer, tap the pinion flange onto the pinion shaft.

8. Using a socket wrench and the differential flange holding tool (Model H233B), hold the differential flange and torque the pinion flange nut as follows:

Model R180 — 123–145 ft. lbs. (166–196 Nm)

Model R190A — 94–217 ft. lbs. (127–294 Nm)

Model H233B — 145–181 ft. lbs. (196–245 Nm)

9. Check the oil level in the differential and install the driveshaft and wheels.

Differential Carrier

REMOVAL AND INSTALLATION

4WD

FRONT

1. Raise and safely support the vehicle. Drain the differential.

2. Matchmark and disconnect the front halfshafts from the front differential.

3. Matchmark the front driveshaft to the flanges and remove the driveshaft.

4. Attach a chain hoist to the engine, remove the front engine mount bolts and raise the engine slightly.

5. Remove the differential crossmember-to-chassis bolts and lower the differential with the crossmember as an assembly.

6. Fit the differential without the crossmember into place and start all the bolts. Torque all nuts and bolts to 64 ft. lbs. (87 Nm) in the following sequence to avoid excess vibration:

   a. First tighten the differential mounts to the frame.

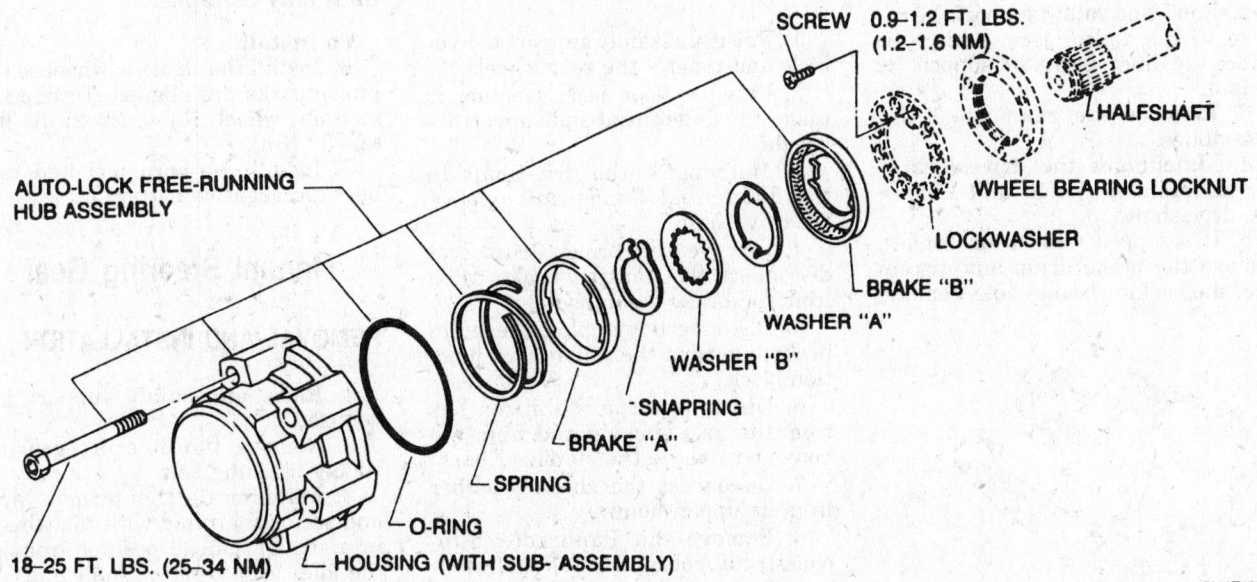

SCREW 0.9-1.2 FT. LBS. (1.2-1.6 NM)

HALFSHAFT

WHEEL BEARING LOCKNUT

LOCKWASHER

BRAKE "B"

WASHER "A"

WASHER "B"

SNAPRING

BRAKE "A"

SPRING

AUTO-LOCK FREE-RUNNING HUB ASSEMBLY

O-RING

18–25 FT. LBS. (25–34 NM)

HOUSING (WITH SUB-ASSEMBLY)

7911E122

Automatic locking hubs used on 4WD

b. Tighten the 2 long differential mount bolts.

c. Install the crossmember and tighten the differential mount bolts.

d. Tighten the crossmember mount bolts.

7. Install the front driveshaft and halfshafts, making sure to align the matchmarks.

REAR

1. Raise and safely support the vehicle.
2. Matchmark the driveshaft to the differential flange and remove the driveshaft.
3. Drain all fluid from the differential carrier and remove the axle shafts.
4. Remove the differential carrier-to-axle housing bolts and remove the carrier.
5. Installation is the reverse of removal. Be sure the gasket is correctly installed and torque the bolts to 18 ft. lbs. (25 Nm).
6. Install the remaining components and fill the differential with oil.

Axle Housing

REMOVAL AND INSTALLATION

Pick-Up

1. Block the front wheels.
2. Raise and safely support the vehicle. Using a floor jack, position it under the differential and support its weight.
3. Remove the rear wheel/tire assemblies.
4. Matchmark the driveshaft to the differential flange and remove the driveshaft.
5. If equipped with drum brakes, remove the brake drum and disconnect the parking brake cable from the

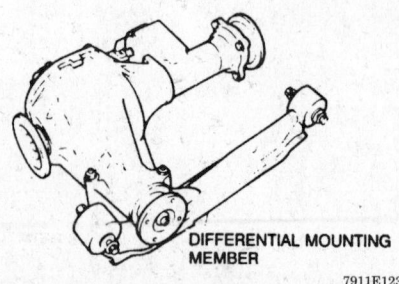

DIFFERENTIAL MOUNTING MEMBER

7911E123

When removing the front differential from, remove the crossmember

brake assembly. If equipped with disc brakes, disconnect the parking brake cable from the caliper.

6. Disconnect and plug the brake hydraulic lines from the wheel cylinders or calipers. Disconnect the brake line from the retaining clips.
7. Disconnect the shock absorber from the lower mount.
8. On vehicles with 2WD, remove all 4 leaf spring mount bolts and remove the axle housing and leaf springs together. Remove the U-bolts to remove the springs from the axle housing.
9. On vehicles with 4WD, remove the nuts from the U-bolts and lower the axle housing away from the leaf springs.
10. Raise the axle housing into position and start all the mounting bolts and nuts.
11. On 2WD vehicles, torque the rear leaf spring mount nuts to 50 ft. lbs. (68 Nm), then the front mount nuts to 72 ft. lbs. (98 Nm).
12. On 4WD vehicles, torque the U-bolt nuts to 72 ft. lbs. (98 Nm).
13. Connect the shock absorbers to the lower mounts and torque the nut to 30 ft. lbs. (40 Nm).
14. Connect the brake parking cable and hydraulic line and bleed and adjust the brakes.
15. Install the driveshaft with the matchmarks aligned.

Pathfinder

1. Raise and safely support the vehicle and remove the rear wheels.
2. Using a floor jack, position it under the differential and support its weight.
3. Matchmark the driveshaft to the differential flange and remove the driveshaft.
4. Remove the brake drum and disconnect the parking brake cable from the brake assembly.
5. Disconnect and plug the main brake line from the differential junction block.
6. Disconnect the stabilizer bar from the axle housing and from the body and remove the stabilizer bar.
7. Disconnect the shock absorber from its upper mount.
8. Remove the Panhard rod-to-chassis nut/bolt and lower the rod.
9. Remove the upper and lower links-to-chassis nuts/bolts, then separate the links from the chassis supports.
10. Lower the axle housing and remove the coil springs.

11. Raise the axle housing into position and start all the mounting nuts and bolts.
12. Lower the vehicle to the ground, bounce the vehicle several times and torque all nuts and bolts as shown.
13. Connect the brake cable and hydraulic line and bleed and adjust the brakes.
14. Install the driveshaft.

STEERING

Steering Wheel

REMOVAL AND INSTALLATION

1. Position the steering wheel in the straight-ahead position.
2. Disconnect the negative battery cable.
3. Remove the horn pad by removing the screws from the rear of the steering wheel crossbar.
4. Matchmark the top of the steering column shaft and the steering wheel flange.
5. Remove the attaching nut and remove the steering wheel with a puller.

NOTE: Do not strike the shaft with a hammer, the steering column may collapse.

To install:

6. Install the steering wheel so the punchmarks are aligned. Torque the steering wheel nut to 22–29 ft. lbs. (29–39 Nm).
7. Install the horn pad and connect the negative battery cable.

Manual Steering Gear

REMOVAL AND INSTALLATION

1. Raise and safely support the vehicle.
2. Remove the steering gear-to-rubber coupling bolt.
3. Matchmark the pitman arm and sector shaft and with the wheels in a straight-ahead position, remove the idler arm-to-sector shaft nut.
4. Using the steering gear arm puller tool, press the arm from the steering gear.
5. Remove the steering gear-to-chassis bolts and the steering gear from the vehicle.

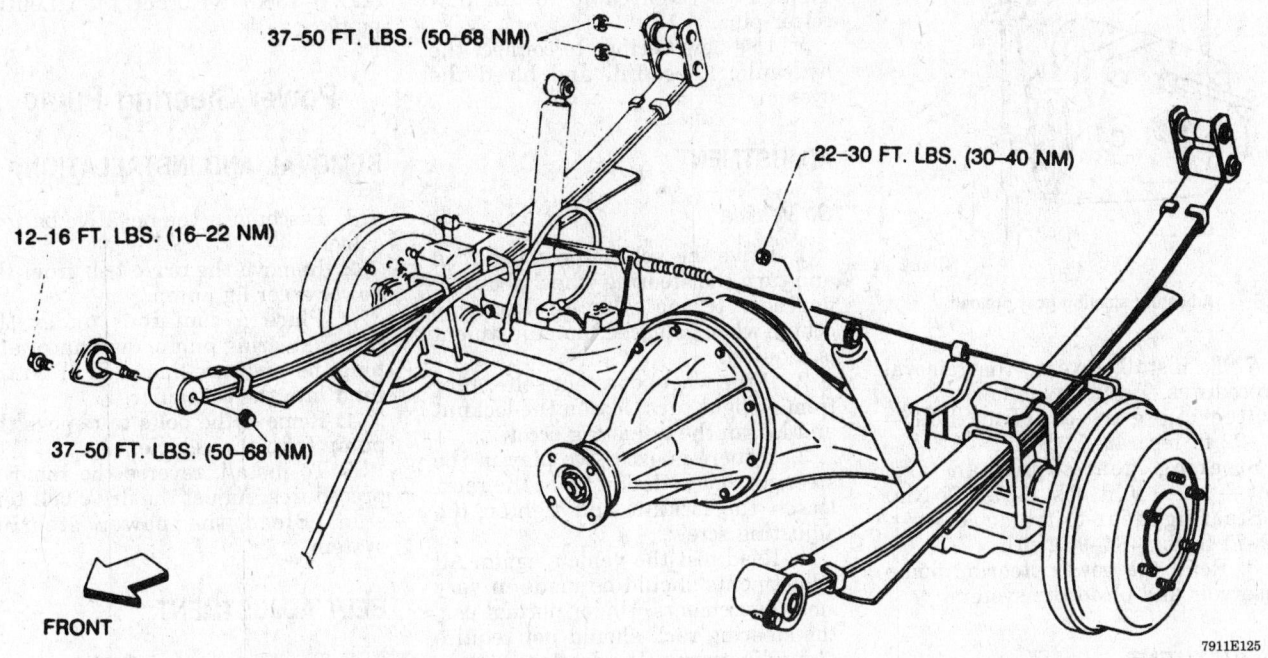

37–50 FT. LBS. (50–68 NM)

22–30 FT. LBS. (30–40 NM)

12–16 FT. LBS. (16–22 NM)

37–50 FT. LBS. (50–68 NM)

FRONT

7911E125

Rear axle housing — Pick-Up with 4WD — on 2WD, the leaf springs must be removed to remove the axle housing

6. To install, reverse the removal procedures. Torque as follows:
Steering gear-to-coupling bolt — 17–22 ft. lbs. (24–29 Nm)
Steering gear-to-pitman arm nut — 94–108 ft. lbs. (127–147 Nm)
Steering gear-to-frame bolts — 62–71 ft. lbs. (84–96 Nm)

ADJUSTMENT

Worm Gear Preload

For this procedure, the steering gear must be removed from the vehicle and placed in a vise.
1. Using the locknut wrench tool, loosen the locknut.
2. Rotate the worm shaft a few times, in both directions, to settle the worm bearing and check the preload.
3. Using the adjusting plug wrench, the torque wrench and an adapter socket, check the worm bearing preload; it should be 1.7–5.2 inch lbs. (0.20–0.59 Nm).
4. To adjust the worm gear preload, turn the adjusting plug with the special pin wrench and recheck the preload.

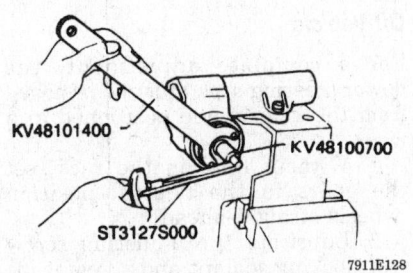

KV48101400

KV48100700

ST3127S000

7911E128

Use the special wrench to adjust worm gear preload

5. With the worm gear preload set, hold the adjusting plug and tighten the locknut. Check preload again.

Steering Gear Preload

1. Loosen the adjusting screw locknut.
2. Rotate the worm shaft a few times in both directions to settle the worm bearing and check the preload.
3. Set the worm gear in the straight ahead position.
4. Using the torque wrench tool and an adapter socket, check the worm gear preload; it should be 7.4–10.9 inch lbs. (0.83–1.23 Nm) for new parts or 5.2–8.7 inch lbs. (0.59–0.98 Nm) for used parts.
5. If necessary, loosen the locknut and turn the adjusting screw to obtain the correct preload.
6. With the preload set, tighten the locknut.

Power Steering Gear

REMOVAL AND INSTALLATION

1. Raise and safely support the vehicle.
2. Remove the wormshaft-to-rubber coupling bolt.
3. Matchmark the idler arm and sector shaft and with the wheels in a straight-ahead position, remove the idler arm-to-sector shaft nut.
4. Disconnect the fluid lines from the gear and cap the lines and openings in the gear.
5. Using the steering gear arm puller, press the gear arm from the steering knuckle.
6. Remove the steering gear-to-chassis bolts and the steering gear from the vehicle.

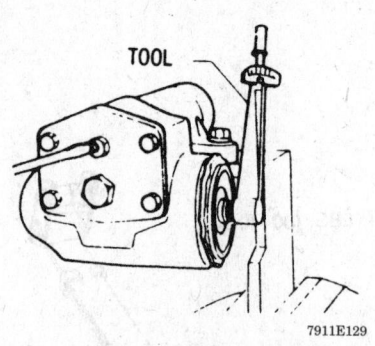

TOOL

7911E129

Adjusting steering gear preload

7. To install, reverse the removal procedures. Torque as follows:

Steering gear coupling bolt — 17–22 ft. lbs. (49–51 Nm)

Steering gear-to-pitman arm nut — 101–130 ft. lbs. (137–177 Nm)

Steering gear-to-frame bolts — 62–71 ft. lbs. (84–96 Nm).

8. Refill the power steering pump reservoir and bleed the system.

ADJUSTMENT

1. Remove the power steering gear and position it in a vise.

2. Loosen the adjusting screw locknut.

3. Set the worm gear in the straight-ahead position.

4. Using the torque wrench and an adapter socket, check the turning torque; it should be 0.9–3.5 inch lbs. (0.1–0.4 Nm).

5. If necessary, use a screwdriver, then, turn the adjusting screw to obtain the correct preload.

6. With the preload set, tighten the adjusting screw nut.

Power Steering Rack

REMOVAL AND INSTALLATION

1. Raise and safely support the vehicle and remove the front wheels.

2. Remove the cotter pins and nuts and use a ball joint press to separate the tie rod ends from the steering knuckles.

3. Remove the rubber coupling pinch bolt.

4. Disconnect and plug the hydraulic lines coming from the pump.

5. Remove the bracket bolts and remove the rack from the chassis.

6. Installation is the reverse of removal. Torque the bracket bolts to 72 ft. lbs. (98 Nm). Torque the coupling pinch bolt to 22 ft. lbs. (29 Nm).

7. Connect the tie rod ends and torque the nuts to 29 ft. lbs. (39 Nm). Tighten as required to install new cotter pins.

8. Use new O-rings to connect the hydraulic lines. Fill and bleed the system.

ADJUSTMENT

On Vehicle

1. Drive the vehicle on a flat road and turn the steering wheel about 20 degrees. If the wheel returns to center when released, no adjustment is required.

2. If the wheel does not self-center from a slight turn, loosen the locknut and loosen the adjusting screw.

3. If there is excessive play in the steering that is definitely in the rack, loosen the locknut and tighten the adjusting screw.

4. Road test the vehicle again. All adjustments should be made in very small increments. Under normal use, the steering rack should not require any adjustment. If adjustment does not cure the symptom, look for other problems in the steering system such as contaminated fluid, pump or suspension failure or incorrect wheel alignment.

Off Vehicle

For a complete adjustment, the power steering rack must be removed from the vehicle and positioned in a vise.

1. Without fluid in the rack, set the gears in the neutral position (wheels straight-ahead).

2. Lubricate the adjusting screw with locking sealant and screw it in.

3. Lightly, tighten the locknut.

4. Torque the adjusting screw to 43–52 inch lbs. (4.9–5.9 Nm).

5. Loosen the adjusting screw and retorque it to 0.43–1.74 inch lbs. (0.05–0.20 Nm).

6. Move the rack over its entire stroke several times.

7. Using an inch lb. torque wrench, measure the pinion rotating torque within the range of 180 degrees from the neutral position.

8. Loosen the adjusting screw and retorque it to 43–52 inch lbs. (4.9–5.9 Nm).

9. Loosen the adjusting screw 40–60 degrees.

10. While securing the adjusting screw in position, torque the locknut to 29–43 ft. lbs. (39–59 Nm).

11. Using a spring gauge, connect it to the tie rod end, pull the tie rod to check the frictional sliding force; it

should be 27.6–37.5 lbs. (122.6–166.7 N) at neutral point or 27.6–41.9 lbs. (122.6–186.3 N) other than neutral point.

Power Steering Pump

REMOVAL AND INSTALLATION

1. Disconnect the negative battery cable.

2. Remove the drive belt from the power steering pump.

3. Place a container under the power steering pump, disconnect and plug the pressure lines and drain the fluid into the container.

4. Remove the bolts to remove the pump from the vehicle.

5. To install, reverse the removal procedures. Adjust the drive belt tension. Bleed the power steering system.

BELT ADJUSTMENT

1. To check belt deflection, press on the belt at a point mid-way between the pulleys with a force of 22 lbs. (98 N) and measure how far the belt moves.

2. Loosen the adjuster locking bolt and turn the adjuster bolt as required. Be careful not to make the belts too tight or bearings will fail. Check belt deflection specifications.

3. Torque the adjuster locking bolt to:

2.4L Engine: Used belt — 0.35–0.43 in. (9–11mm)

3.0L Engine:

Used belt — 0.43–0.51 in. (11–13mm)

New belt — 0.35–0.43 in. (9–11mm)

SYSTEM BLEEDING

1. Raise and support the vehicle safely.

2. Check and add fluid to the reservoir, if necessary.

3. Start the engine. Turn the steering wheel quickly (all the way), right and left, just touching the stops; turn the steering wheel at least 10 times.

NOTE: When bleeding the system, make sure the temperature of the fluid reaches 140–176°F (60–80°C).

4. Stop the engine, check the fluid level, add as required.

5. Start and run the engine for 3–5 seconds.

6. Stop the engine, check the fluid level, add as required.

7. Start the engine. Turn the steering wheel (all the way) right and left, just touching the stops; turn the steering wheel at least 10 times.

8. Stop the engine, check the fluid level, add as required.

9. Repeat the steps until all of the air is bled from the system.

10. If the air cannot be bleed from the system, turn and hold the steering wheel at each stop for at least 5 seconds but never more than 15 seconds.

Tie Rod Ends

REMOVAL AND INSTALLATION

1. Raise and safely support the vehicle. Remove the wheel/tire assembly.

2. If removing the tie rod as an assembly:

a. Remove the tie rod-to-cross rod cotter pin and nut.

b. Remove the tie rods-to-steering knuckle cotter pin and nut.

c. Using the ball joint remover tool, press the tie rod from the steering knuckle and the tie rod from the cross rod.

3. If removing a defective tie rod end:

a. Remove the cotter pin and nut from the end being removed.

b. Loosen the tie rod clamp or locknut.

c. Using the ball joint remover tool, press the tie rod from the cross rod or steering knuckle and unscrew the tie rod end from the tie rod.

d. Measure the tie rod end-to-tie rod clamp distance.

e. Unscrew the tie rod end from the tie rod.

f. Using a new tie rod end, screw the new tie rod end into the tie rod clamp until the measured distance is the same, then, torque the tie rod clamp bolt to 10–14 ft. lbs. (14–20 Nm) or nut to 58–72 ft. lbs. (78–98 Nm).

4. Inspect the tie rod ball joint for wear; if necessary, replace it.

5. To install, use new cotter pins and reverse the removal procedures. Torque the tie rod-to-steering knuckle nut to 40–72 ft. lbs. (54–98 Nm) and the tie rod-to-cross rod nut to 40–72 ft. lbs. (54–98 Nm). Check and/or adjust the front-end alignment.

BRAKES

Master Cylinder

NOTE: Be careful not to spill brake fluid on the painted surfaces of the vehicle; it will damage the paint.

REMOVAL AND INSTALLATION

1. Using a syringe, remove the brake fluid from the master cylinder.

2. Disconnect and plug the hydraulic lines at the master cylinder.

3. If equipped, disconnect the fluid level warning switch connector from the master cylinder.

4. Remove the clevis pin connecting the master cylinder to the pedal.

5. Remove the nuts or bolts securing the master cylinder to the firewall or power brake booster unit and pull the master cylinder out.

6. To install, reverse the removal procedures. Torque the master cylinder nuts to 8 ft. lbs. (11 Nm) and the brake lines-to-master cylinder to 13 ft. lbs. (18 Nm). Refill the master cylinder with new brake fluid and bleed the brake system.

NOTE: Before tightening the master cylinder mounting nuts or bolts, screw the hydraulic line fitting into the cylinder body a few turns.

Load Sensing Proportioning Valve

The purpose of this valve is to control the fluid pressure applied to the brakes to prevent rear wheel lock-up during weight transfer at high speed stops.

REMOVAL AND INSTALLATION

1. Raise and safely support the vehicle.

2. Disconnect and plug the lines going to the valve.

3. Remove the valve-to-chassis bolts and the valve.

4. To install, reverse the removal procedures.

5. Bleed the brake system.

ADJUSTMENT

1. Ensure the fuel tank, the cooling system and the engine crankcase are filled. Make sure the spare tire,

the jack, the hand tools and the mats are installed.

2. Position a person in the driver's seat and one on the rear end, then have the person on the rear end slowly get off.

3. Attach a lever to the stopper bolt and adjust the length **L** to approx. 7.44 in. (189mm).

4. Install pressure gauges at the front and rear brakes.

5. Depress the brake pedal until the front brake pressure is approximately 1422 psi (9805 KPa). Check that the rear brake pressure is 327–441 psi (2255–3041 KPa).

6. Slowly, set a 220 lbs. (100 kg) weight on the rear axle.

7. Depress the brake pedal until the front brake pressure is approximately 1422 psi. Check that the rear brake pressure is 711–995 psi (4902–6861 KPa) for all except heavy duty, or 640–924 psi (4413–6371 KPa) for heavy duty.

8. If the rear brake pressure is above specification, adjust the bracket away from the valve.

9. If the rear brake pressure is below specification, adjust the bracket towards the valve.

Power Brake Booster

REMOVAL AND INSTALLATION

1. Remove the master cylinder from the power brake booster.

2. Remove the vacuum hose form the power brake booster.

3. Working under the instrument panel, remove the brake pedal-to-brake booster rod clevis pin. Remove the power brake booster mounting bolts and the booster from the vehicle.

4. To install, reverse the removal procedures. Torque the power brake booster-to-cowl nuts to 5.8–8 ft. lbs. (8–11 Nm). Check and/or adjust the brake pedal height.

NOTE: When installing the power brake booster, make sure there is 0.40–0.41 in. (10–10.5mm) clearance between the pushrod end and the master cylinder piston.

Brake Caliper

REMOVAL AND INSTALLATION

1. Raise and safely support the vehicle. Remove the wheel assembly.

2. Remove the lower sliding pin bolt and swing the caliper up to re-

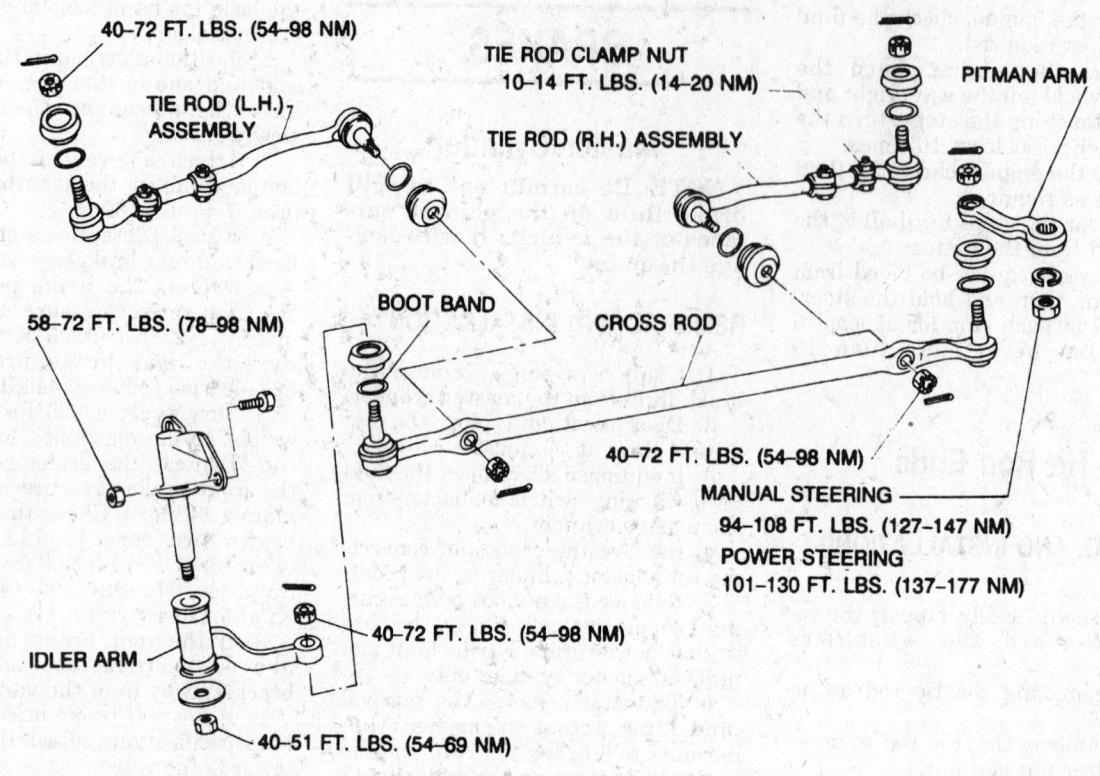

40–72 FT. LBS. (54–98 NM)

TIE ROD CLAMP NUT
10–14 FT. LBS. (14–20 NM)

PITMAN ARM

TIE ROD (L.H.)
ASSEMBLY

TIE ROD (R.H.) ASSEMBLY

58–72 FT. LBS. (78–98 NM)

BOOT BAND

CROSS ROD

40–72 FT. LBS. (54–98 NM)

MANUAL STEERING
94–108 FT. LBS. (127–147 NM)

POWER STEERING
101–130 FT. LBS. (137–177 NM)

40–72 FT. LBS. (54–98 NM)

IDLER ARM

40–51 FT. LBS. (54–69 NM)

7911E131

Steering linkage — 2WD

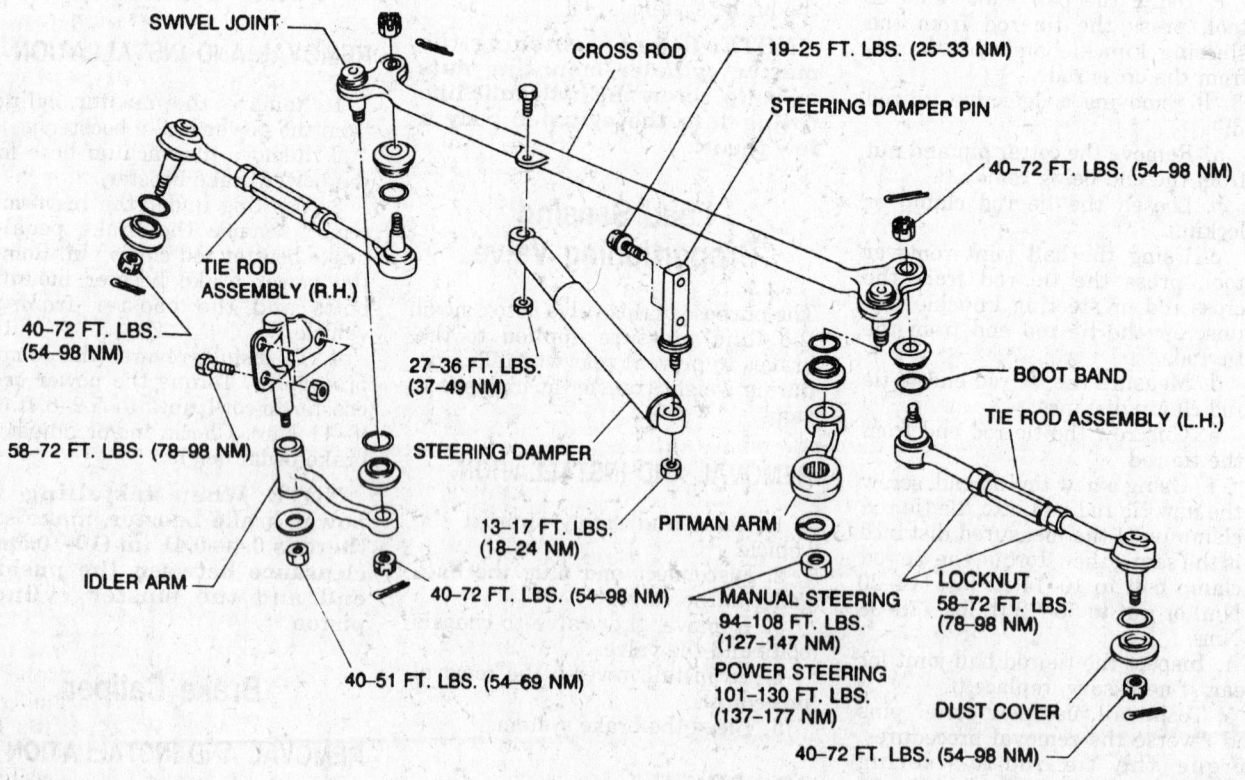

SWIVEL JOINT

CROSS ROD

19–25 FT. LBS. (25–33 NM)

STEERING DAMPER PIN

40–72 FT. LBS. (54–98 NM)

TIE ROD
ASSEMBLY (R.H.)

40–72 FT. LBS.
(54–98 NM)

27–36 FT. LBS.
(37–49 NM)

58–72 FT. LBS. (78–98 NM)

STEERING DAMPER

BOOT BAND

TIE ROD ASSEMBLY (L.H.)

13–17 FT. LBS.
(18–24 NM)

PITMAN ARM

IDLER ARM

40–72 FT. LBS. (54–98 NM)

MANUAL STEERING
94–108 FT. LBS.
(127–147 NM)

POWER STEERING
101–130 FT. LBS.
(137–177 NM)

LOCKNUT
58–72 FT. LBS.
(78–98 NM)

40–51 FT. LBS. (54–69 NM)

DUST COVER

40–72 FT. LBS. (54–98 NM)

7911E132

Steering linkage — 4WD

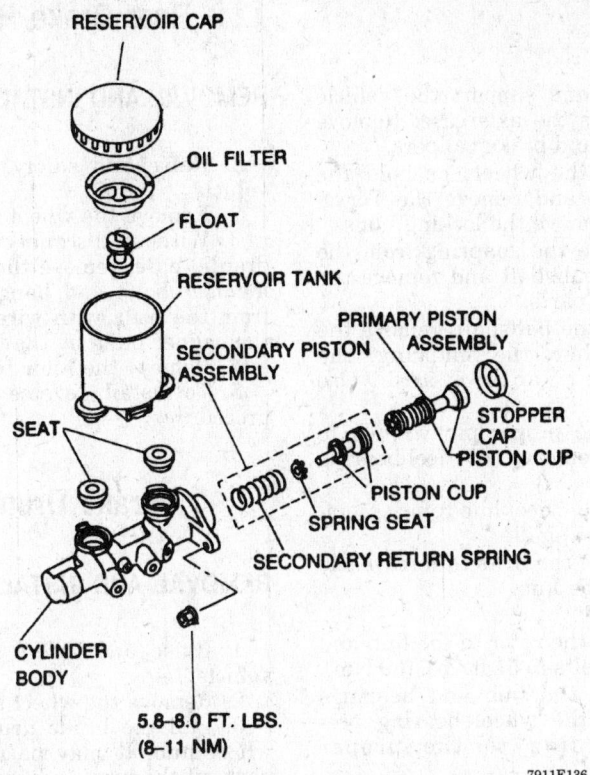

RESERVOIR CAP

OIL FILTER

FLOAT

RESERVOIR TANK

PRIMARY PISTON ASSEMBLY

SECONDARY PISTON ASSEMBLY

SEAT

STOPPER CAP

PISTON CUP

PISTON CUP

SPRING SEAT

SECONDARY RETURN SPRING

CYLINDER BODY

5.8–8.0 FT. LBS.
(8–11 NM)

7911E136

Master cylinder assembly

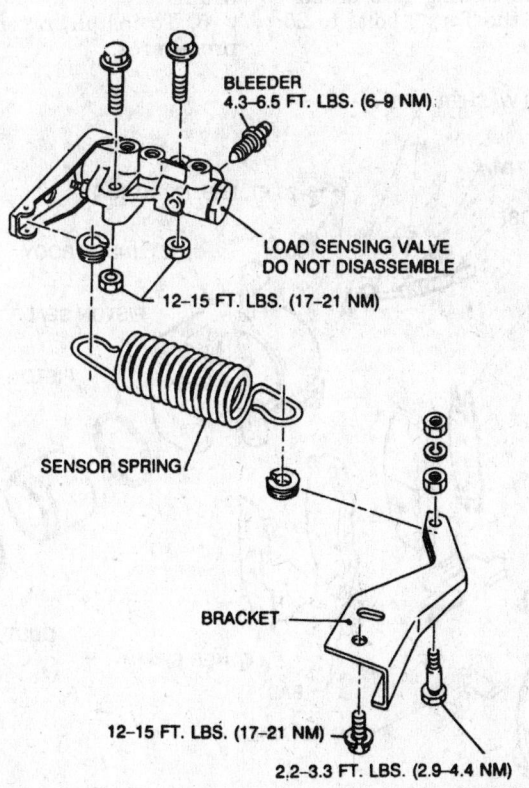

BLEEDER
4.3–6.5 FT. LBS. (6–9 NM)

LOAD SENSING VALVE
DO NOT DISASSEMBLE

12–15 FT. LBS. (17–21 NM)

SENSOR SPRING

BRACKET

12–15 FT. LBS. (17–21 NM)

2.2–3.3 FT. LBS. (2.9–4.4 NM)

7911E137

Load sensing brake valve

move disc brake pads from the caliper.

3. Disconnect and plug the brake hose from the brake caliper.

4. Remove the caliper torque member bolts and the caliper from the vehicle.

5. Make sure the caliper moves freely on the sliding pins. Clean, repair or replace as necessary. Use a small amount of light grease to lubricate the pins.

6. To install, reverse the removal procedures. Torque the sliding pin bolts to 31 ft. lbs. (42 Nm). If the torque member was removed, torque the bolts to 72 ft. lbs. (97 Nm) on front calipers, 38 ft. lbs. (52 Nm) on rear calipers.

7. Bleed the brake system.

Disc Brake Pads

REMOVAL AND INSTALLATION

1. Raise and safely support the vehicle. Remove the wheels and the brake fluid reservoir cap.

2. Remove the bottom sliding pin bolt and swing the caliper upward.

3. Remove the pad retainers, the inner/outer retainers and the brake pads.

4. Using a medium C-clamp and a block of wood, place the wood against the caliper piston(s) and use the C-clamp press the piston into the caliper. Some brake fluid may be expelled from the reservoir.

5. Inspect the caliper for signs of fluid leakage; if necessary, replace or rebuild the caliper.

6. Make sure the caliper moves freely on the sliding pins. Clean, repair or replace as necessary. Use a small amount of light grease to lubricate the pins.

7. To install, use new brake pads and reverse the removal procedures. Torque the sliding pin bolts to 31 ft. lbs. (42 Nm).

Front Brake Rotor

REMOVAL AND INSTALLATION

2WD

1. Raise and safely support the vehicle. Remove the wheel assembly.

2. Without disconnecting the hydraulic hose, remove the and torque member bolts and hang the caliper from the body with wire. Do not let the caliper hang by the hose.

3. Remove the wheel bearing grease cup, cotter pin, adjusting nut

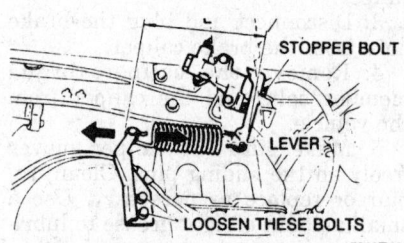

Adjust load sensing valve spring length

cap, hub nut, thrust washer and wheel bearing.

4. Pull the wheel hub/brake rotor assembly from the wheel spindle.

5. From the rear of the brake rotor, remove the rotor-to-wheel hub bolts and the rotor.

6. Inspect the rotor for cracks, wear and/or other damage; if necessary, replace it.

To install:

7. Install the rotor to the hub and torque the bolts to 51 ft. lbs. (69 Nm).

8. Install the hub and wheel bearings and adjust the bearing pre-load according to the proper procedure.

9. Install the caliper and pump the brake pedal to adjust the brakes.

4WD

1. Raise and support the vehicle safely under the axle case. Remove the wheels and brake calipers.

2. Block the wheels or hold the brake pedal and remove the Torx® screws to remove the locking hubs.

3. Remove the snapring from the end of the halfshaft and remove the locking hub parts.

4. From the halfshaft, remove the thrust washer, the snapring, the lockwasher screw and the lockwasher.

5. Use the proper pin wrench to loosen and remove the wheel bearing locknut.

6. Pull the wheel hub/rotor assembly from the spindle.

7. Remove the bolts to remove the rotor from the hub.

To install:

8. Install the rotor to the hub and torque the bolts to 51 ft. lbs. (69 Nm).

9. Install the hub and bearings and adjust the wheel bearing pre-load according to the proper procedure.

10. Install the brake caliper.

11. Install the locking hub assembly and torque the Torx® bolts to 25 ft. lbs. (34 Nm).

Rear Brake Rotor

REMOVAL AND INSTALLATION

1. Raise and safely support the vehicle.

2. Remove the wheel assembly.

3. Without disconnecting the hydraulic hose, remove the and torque member bolts and hang the caliper from the body with wire. Do not let the caliper hang by the hose.

4. Remove the rotor from the hub.

5. To install, reverse the removal procedures.

Brake Drums

REMOVAL AND INSTALLATION

1. Raise and safely support the vehicle.

2. Remove the wheel assembly.

3. Pull the brake drum from the wheel hub. It may be necessary to back off the brake adjustment.

4. Inspect and/or replace the brake drum.

5. To install, reverse the removal procedures.

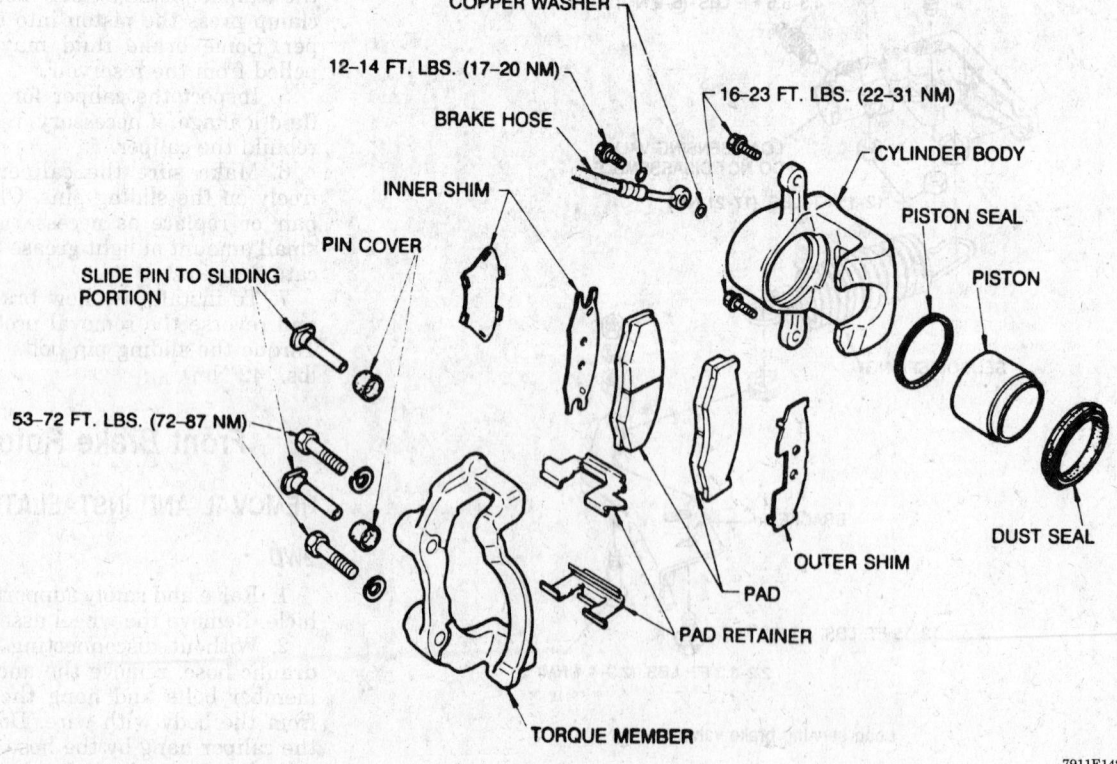

Single piston front caliper

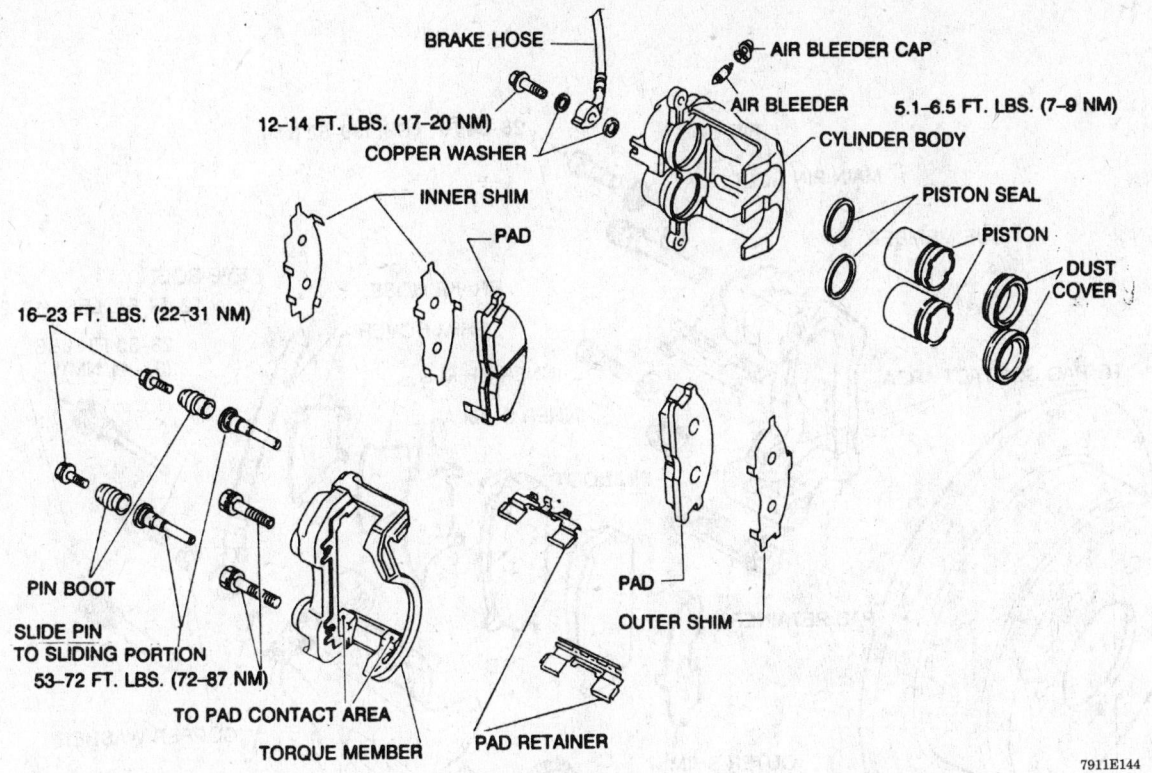

BRAKE HOSE
AIR BLEEDER CAP
12–14 FT. LBS. (17–20 NM)
COPPER WASHER
AIR BLEEDER
5.1–6.5 FT. LBS. (7–9 NM)
CYLINDER BODY
INNER SHIM
PAD
PISTON SEAL
PISTON
DUST COVER
16–23 FT. LBS. (22–31 NM)
PIN BOOT
SLIDE PIN
TO SLIDING PORTION
53–72 FT. LBS. (72–87 NM)
TO PAD CONTACT AREA
TORQUE MEMBER
PAD RETAINER
PAD
OUTER SHIM
7911E144

Dual piston front caliper

Brake Shoes

REMOVAL AND INSTALLATION

1. Fully release the parking brake.
2. Raise and safely support the vehicle. Remove the wheel assembly.
3. If equipped with rear disc brakes and drum type parking brakes, remove the brake caliper. Without disconnecting the hydraulic hose, remove the torque member bolts and hang the caliper from the body with wire. Do not let the caliper hang by the hose.
4. Remove the brake drum. If the drum is difficult to remove, insert 2 — 8mm x 1.25 screws in the disc/drum holes, tighten the screws to press the drum from the hub.
5. When removing the brake shoes and springs, be sure to remove only one side at a time so the other side is available as a reference. Remove the brake shoe retainers and the springs.
6. Separate the parking brake cable from the from the parking brake lever.
7. Using brake grease, lubricate the shoe adjuster and the backing plate contact points.
8. Turn the shoe adjuster all the way inward.

9. To install, reverse the removal procedures. Adjust the parking brakes by turning the adjuster wheel.

ADJUSTMENT

1. Raise and safely support the vehicle. Make sure the parking brake lever is fully released.
2. From the rear of the backing plate, remove the adjuster hole plug.
3. Using a small prybar, rotate the adjuster wheel until the wheel will not turn.
4. Back off the adjuster wheel 7–8 notches. Make sure the wheel turns freely.
5. Install the adjuster hole plug.

Wheel Cylinder

REMOVAL AND INSTALLATION

1. Raise and safely support the vehicle.
2. Remove the wheel, brake drum and brake shoes.
3. Disconnect the hydraulic line from the rear of the wheel cylinder.
4. Remove the wheel cylinder-to-backing plate bolts and the wheel cylinder from the backing plate.

5. To install, reverse the removal procedures. Torque the wheel cylinder-to-backing plate nuts to bolt to 65 inch lbs. (7 Nm). Bleed the brake hydraulic system.

Parking Brake Cable

REMOVAL AND INSTALLATION

Rear Cable

1. Fully release the parking brake handle.
2. Raise and safely support the vehicle.
3. Loosen the adjusting nut at the adjuster cable lever.
4. Disconnect the cable from the balance lever or adjuster.
5. Disconnect the rear parking brake cable(s) from the parking brake toggle levers of the rear service brake assemblies.
6. Remove the rear parking brake cable brackets-to-chassis bracket screws.
7. Remove parking brake cable(s) from the vehicle.
8. To install, reverse the removal procedures. Apply a light coat of grease to the cables to make sure they slide properly. Adjust the parking brake cables.

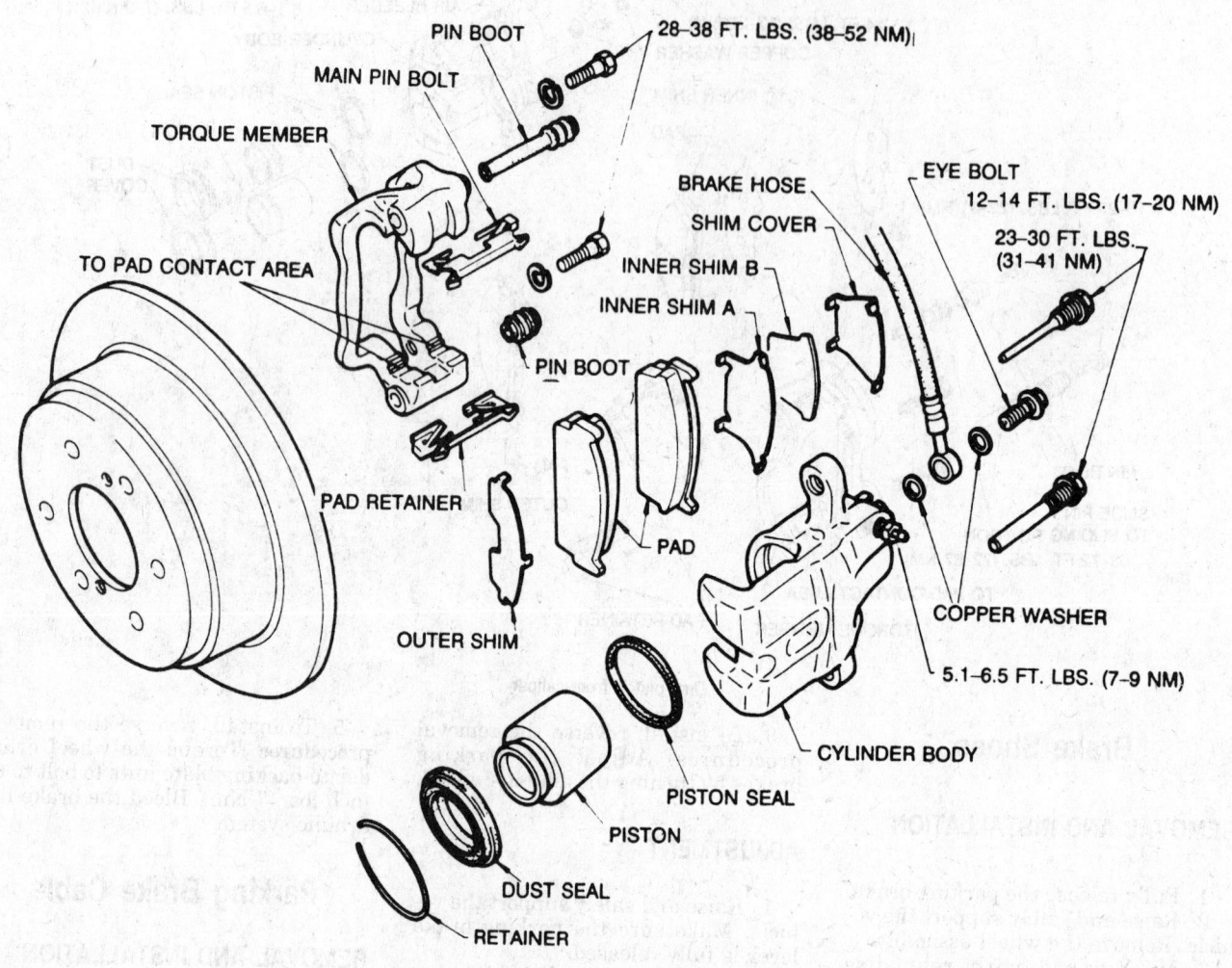

PIN BOOT

MAIN PIN BOLT

TORQUE MEMBER

28–38 FT. LBS. (38–52 NM)

BRAKE HOSE

SHIM COVER

EYE BOLT

12–14 FT. LBS. (17–20 NM)

23–30 FT. LBS. (31–41 NM)

TO PAD CONTACT AREA

INNER SHIM B

INNER SHIM A

PIN BOOT

PAD RETAINER

COPPER WASHER

PAD

5.1–6.5 FT. LBS. (7–9 NM)

OUTER SHIM

CYLINDER BODY

PISTON SEAL

PISTON

DUST SEAL

RETAINER

7911E145

Single piston rear caliper

Front Cable

1. Fully release the parking brake control lever.
2. Raise and safely support the vehicle.
3. Loosen the adjusting nut at the adjuster cable lever.
4. Disconnect the cable from the balance lever or adjuster.
5. Remove the front cable bracket-to-chassis bolt(s) and the cable from the vehicle.
6. To install, reverse the removal procedures. Apply a light coat of grease to the cable to make sure it slides properly. Adjust the parking brake cables.

ADJUSTMENT

1. Raise and safely support the vehicle.
2. Adjust the rear brakes.
3. From under the vehicle, adjust the parking brake cable locknut(s). Turn the adjusting nut until the parking brake control lever operating stroke is (using 44 lbs. force):
Console lever — 10–12 clicks
Stick lever
   2WD — 9–11 clicks
   4WD — 7–9 clicks
4. Release the parking brake and make sure the rear wheels turn freely with no drag.

Brake System Bleeding

1. Raise and safely support the vehicle.
2. Make sure the brake fluid reservoir is full. Keep checking the level during the procedure, do not allow the level to fall too low.
3. Have an assistant pump the brake pedal, then hold pressure on the pedal.
4. Connect a tube to the bleeder at the right rear wheel and put the other end in a container. Open the bleeder until the pressure is released, then close it before releasing pressure on the pedal.

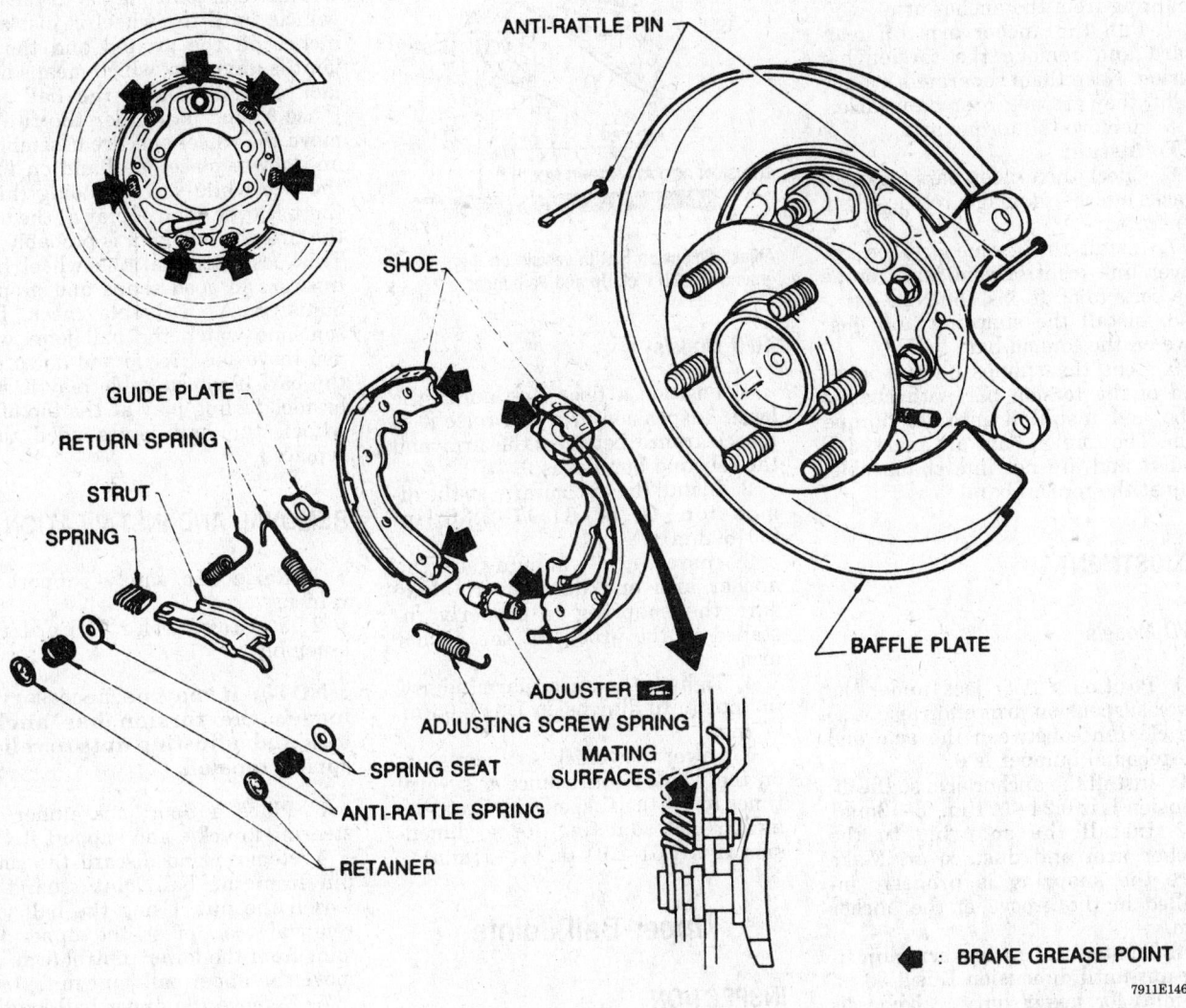

ANTI-RATTLE PIN

SHOE

GUIDE PLATE

RETURN SPRING

STRUT

SPRING

ADJUSTER

ADJUSTING SCREW SPRING

MATING SURFACES

SPRING SEAT

ANTI-RATTLE SPRING

RETAINER

BAFFLE PLATE

◀ : BRAKE GREASE POINT

7911E146

Rear brake shoe assembly on vehicles with rear disc brakes and drum parking brakes; lightly lubricate the backing plate in the areas indicated with arrows

5. Repeat the procedure until fluid flows from the bleeder with no air bubbles. If the bubbles do not stop, a problem is indicated in the master cylinder.

6. Repeat the procedure on the left rear, right front, then left front brakes in order.

7. Fill the fluid reservoir.

FRONT SUSPENSION

Shock Absorbers

REMOVAL AND INSTALLATION

1. Raise and safely support the vehicle. Remove the wheel assembly.

2. While holding the upper stem of the shock absorber, remove the shock absorber-to-chassis nut and/or bolt, washer and rubber bushing.

3. Remove the lower shock absorber-to-lower control arm nut and/or bolt and remove the shock absorber from the vehicle.

4. To install, use new rubber bushings and reverse the removal procedures. Torque the shock absorber-to-lower control arm nut/bolt to 58 ft. lbs. (78 Nm) and the shock absorber-to-chassis nut to 16 ft. lbs. (22 Nm).

Torsion Bars

REMOVAL AND INSTALLATION

1. Raise and safely support the vehicle with supports placed under the frame. Remove the wheel assemblies.

2. Remove the torsion bar spring adjusting nut.

3. Remove the dust cover and the snapring from the anchor arm.

4. Pull the anchor arm off rearward and remove the torsion bar spring. Keep them separated left and right, they are not interchangeable.

5. Remove the torque arm.

To install:

6. Check the torsion bars for wear, cracks or other damage; replace them if necessary.

7. Install the torque arm on the lower link (control arm) and torque the bolts to 50 ft. lbs. (68 Nm).

8. Install the snapring and dust cove on the torsion bar.

9. Coat the splines on the inner end of the torsion bar with chassis lube and install it into the torque arm. The torsion bars are marked **L** and **R** and are not interchangeable. Adjust the torsion bars.

ADJUSTMENT

2WD Models

1. Position a floor jack under the lower suspension arm and raise it so the clearance between the arm and the rebound bumper is 0.

2. Install the anchor arm so the dimension **L** is 0.24–0.71 in. (6–18mm).

3. Install the snapring to the anchor arm and dust cover. Make sure the snapring is properly installed in the groove of the anchor arm.

4. Tighten the anchor arm adjusting nut until dimension **L** is 1.38 in. (35mm) for heavy duty, cab/chassis and std models or 1.93 in. (49mm) for all other models.

5. Lower the vehicle so it is resting on the wheels and bounce it several times to set the suspension. Turn the anchor bolt adjusting nut so dimension **H** is 4.25–4.65 in. (108–118mm).

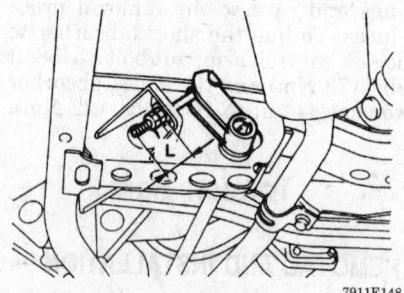

Adjusting torsion bar anchor arm bolt length L — 2WD Pick-Up and Pathfinder

7911E148

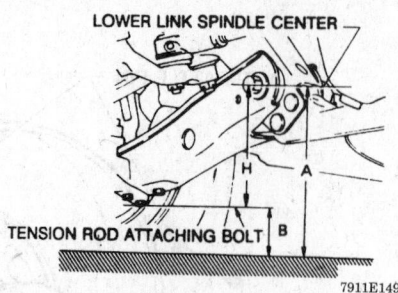

7911E149

Adjust dimension H with vehicle on the ground — 2WD Pick-Up and Pathfinder

4WD Models

1. Position a floor jack under the lower suspension arm and raise it so the clearance between the arm and the rebound bumper is 0.

2. Install the anchor arm so the dimension **G** is 01.97–2.36 in. (50–60mm).

3. Install the snapring to the anchor arm and dust cover. Make sure the snapring is properly installed in the groove of the anchor arm.

4. Tighten the anchor arm adjusting nut until dimension **L** is 3.03 in. (77mm).

5. Lower the vehicle so it is resting on the wheels and bounce it several times to set the suspension. Turn the anchor bolt adjusting nut so dimension **H** is 1.61–2.01 in. (41–51mm).

Upper Ball Joints

INSPECTION

The ball joint(s) should be replaced when play becomes excessive. The manufacturer does not publish specifications on just what constitutes excessive play, relying instead on a method of determining the force (in

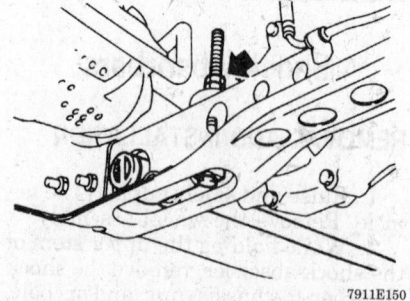

Adjusting torsion bar — 4WD Pick-Up and Pathfinder

7911E150

inch lbs.) required to keep the ball joint turning. An effective way to determine ball joint play is to raise the vehicle until the wheel is just a few inches off the ground and the ball joint is unloaded, which means not to jack directly under the ball joint. Place a long bar under the tire and move the wheel and tire assembly up and down; place one hand on top of the tire while you are doing this. If there is over ¼ in. of play at the top of the tire, the ball joint is probably bad. This assumes that the wheel bearings are in good shape and properly adjusted. As a double check, have someone watch the ball joint while you move the tire up and down with the bar. If considerable play is seen, besides feeling play at the top of the wheel, the ball joints need to be replaced.

REMOVAL AND INSTALLATION

1. Raise and safely support the vehicle.

2. Remove the wheel/tire assembly.

NOTE: It may be necessary to loosen the torsion bar anchor lock and adjusting nuts to relieve spring tension.

3. Place a floor jack under the steering knuckle and support it.

4. Remove and discard the cotter pin from the ball joint stud, then loosen the nut. Using the ball joint removal tool, press the upper ball joint from the lower control arm. Remove the upper ball joint nut.

5. Remove the upper ball joint-to-upper control arm bolts and the ball joint from the vehicle.

6. To install, use a new ball joint, a new cotter pin and reverse the removal procedures. Torque as follows:

Upper ball joint-to-upper control arm bolts — 16 ft. lbs. (22 Nm)

Upper ball-to-steering knuckle nut — 108 ft. lbs. (146 Nm)

7. Check and/or adjust the ride height and the front end alignment.

Lower Ball Joints

REMOVAL AND INSTALLATION

The lower control arm ball joint on the 2WD models is not removable; if the ball joint is defective, replace the lower control arm.

1. Raise and safely support the vehicle.

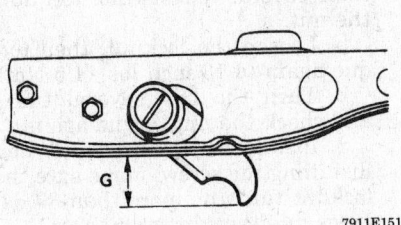

Anchor arm length G — 4WD Pick-Up and Pathfinder

7911E151

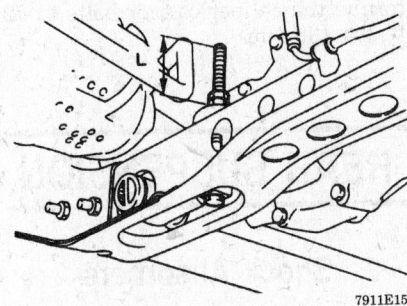

Torsion bar adjusting bolt length L — 4WD Pick-Up and Pathfinder

7911E152

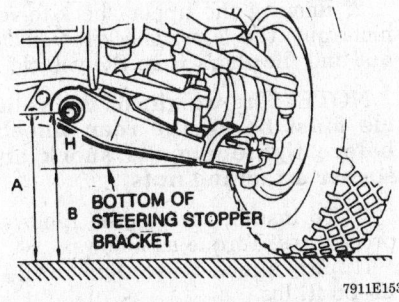

Adjust dimension H with vehicle on the ground — 4WD Pick-Up and Pathfinder

7911E153

2. Remove the wheel/tire assembly.

NOTE: Loosen the torsion bar spring anchor lock and adjusting nuts and remove the anchor arm bolt from the anchor arm. Remove the snapring, then move the anchor arm and torsion bar fully rearward. This procedure is to relieve the spring pressure on the lower control arm.

3. If equipped, it may be necessary to disconnect the sway bar from the lower arm.

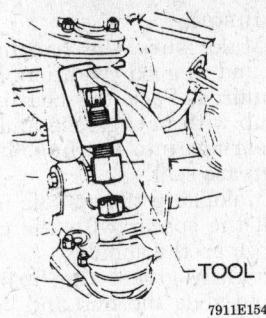

—TOOL

7911E154

Use a ball joint press to disconnect the ball joints and tie rod ends

4. Disconnect the tension rod from the lower arm.

5. Remove the cotter pin from the ball joint stud and loosen the nut.

6. Using the ball joint separator tool, press the ball joint from the steering knuckle.

7. Remove the lower ball joint-to-lower control arm bolts and the ball joint.

8. To install, use a new cotter pin and reverse the removal procedures. Torque as follows:

Ball joint-to-control arm bolts — 4WD — 45 ft. lbs. (61 Nm)

Ball joint-to-steering knuckle nut — 141 ft. lbs. (190 Nm)

9. Check and/or adjust the torsion bar ride height assembly and the front end alignment.

Upper Control Arms

REMOVAL AND INSTALLATION

1. Raise and safely support the vehicle.

2. Remove the wheels.

3. Remove the upper shock absorber-to-chassis nut and compress the shock absorber.

NOTE: If may be necessary to loosen the torsion bar anchor lock and adjusting nuts to relieve the torsion bar tension.

4. Remove the upper ball joint-to-upper control arm bolts.

5. Using a floor jack, raise the lower control arm.

6. Remove the upper control arm-to-chassis bolts and the upper control arm from the vehicle.

NOTE: If shims are used, be sure to keep them in order for re-installation purposes.

7. Inspect the ball joint, replace as required.

8. To install, replace the shims, if used, in their original locations and

reverse the removal procedures. Torque the:

Upper control arm-to-chassis bolts to 108 ft. lbs. (146 Nm)

Ball joint-to-upper control arm bolts to 15 ft. lbs. (20 Nm)

Upper shock absorber-to-chassis nut to 16 ft. lbs. (21 Nm)

9. Lower the vehicle and adjust the ride height. Check and/or adjust the front end alignment.

Lower Control Arms

REMOVAL AND INSTALLATION

2WD Pick-Up

1. Raise and safely support the vehicle and remove the front wheels.

2. Remove the shock absorber.

3. Remove the torsion bar.

4. Disconnect the stabilizer bar linkage from the lower control arm.

5. Disconnect the tension rod-to-lower control arm bolts.

6. Remove the cotter pin from the ball joint and use a ball joint press to separate the ball joints from the control arm.

7. Remove the lower control arm-to-chassis nut/bolt, tap the pivot shaft from the bushing. Push down on the tension rod and remove the lower control arm.

To install:

8. Install the control arm and the pivot bolt and torque the bolt to 108 ft. lbs. (147 Nm).

9. Connect the lower ball joint and sway bar. Torque the ball joint nut to 141 ft. lbs. (191 Nm) and tighten as required to install a new cotter pin.

10. Connect the tension rod and torque the bolts to 47 ft. lbs. (64 Nm). Install the stabilizer bar linkage and torque to 16 ft. lbs. (22 Nm).

11. Install the torsion bar and shock absorber. Adjust the torsion bar height and front wheel alignment.

4WD Pick-Up and Pathfinder

1. Raise and safely support the vehicle and remove the front wheels.

2. Remove the torsion bar.

3. Remove the shock absorber.

4. Disconnect the stabilizer bar linkage.

5. Remove the cotter pin and lower ball joint nut and use a ball joint press to separate the ball joint from the lower control arm.

6. Remove the lower arm spindle bolt and the bushing nut and remove the lower control arm.

To install:

7. Fit the arm into place and start the bushing nut. Torque this nut when the vehicle is on the wheels. Torque the spindle bolt to 108 ft. lbs. (147 Nm).

8. Connect the lower ball joint and torque the nut to 141 ft. lbs. (191 Nm) and tighten as required to install a new cotter pin.

9. Connect the stabilizer bar linkage and install the shock absorber. Torque the stabilizer bar linkage when the vehicle is on the wheels to 16 ft. lbs. (22 Nm).

10. Install the torsion bar and adjust the bar and front wheel alignment.

Stabilizer Bar

REMOVAL AND INSTALLATION

1. Raise and safely support the vehicle.

2. From both sides of the vehicle, remove the stabilizer bar-to-lower control arm connecting rod nut, bushings and tube.

3. Remove the bracket bolts and brackets and remove the stabilizer bar.

4. Installation is the reverse of removal. Make sure the brackets are to the outside of the white painted marks on the stabilizer bar. Torque the bracket bolts to 16 ft. lbs. (22 Nm) and the connecting rod nut to 22 ft. lbs. (30 Nm).

Front Wheel Bearings

For the 4WD models, please refer to the Drive Axle section.

REMOVAL AND INSTALLATION

2WD Pick-Up

1. Raise and safely support the vehicle and remove the front wheels.

2. Disconnect the brake hose from the bracket on the knuckle.

3. Without disconnecting the hydraulic line, remove the brake caliper and hang it from the body on a wire. Do not let it hang by the hose.

4. Remove the wheel hub cup, the cotter pin, the adjusting cap and hub nut.

5. Remove the wheel hub and brake disc assembly. Be careful not to drop the outer wheel bearing.

6. To remove the inner bearing, pry out the grease seal. Discard the seal.

To install:

7. Make sure the bearings are clean and in good condition. Replace as required. Pack the bearings and the hub with new grease and install the bearings into the hub. Install a new grease seal.

8. Make sure the spindle is clean. Install the spacer with the chamfer facing in on the spindle.

9. Lightly grease the lips on the seal and slide the hub and bearings onto the spindle. Install the washer and nut.

10. To adjust the pre-load on the bearing:

a. Torque the wheel bearing nut to 25 ft. lbs. (34 Nm).

b. Spin the hub several times in both directions, then torque the nut to 29 ft. lbs. (39 Nm).

c. Loosen the nut 45 degrees. Install the locknut cap and a new cotter pin.

11. Install the brake caliper and torque the caliper carrier bolts to 72 ft. lbs. (98 Nm).

2WD Pathfinder

1. Raise and safely support the vehicle and remove the front wheels.

2. Without disconnecting the hydraulic line, remove the brake caliper and hang it from the body with wire. Do not allow the caliper to hang by the hose.

3. Remove the hub cap and locking screw and remove the lock washer. Use a pin wrench to loosen the wheel bearing locknut. The torque may be fairly high, do not use a hammer and drift pin.

4. Remove the locknut and pull the hub off with the bearings. Pry the inner grease seal out to remove the inner bearing. Discard the seal.

To install:

5. Clean all parts of grease and check the condition of the bearings. If bearings are to be replaced, the inner races can be removed from the hub with a hammer and soft drift pin. Be careful not to damage the hub.

6. Carefully install the new inner races with the drift pin, making sure they seat in the hub.

7. Pack the bearings with new grease and pack grease into the hub. Install the inner bearing and press a new inner seal into the hub.

8. Slip the hub assembly onto the spindle and install the outer bearing. Grease the locknut and thread it into place.

9. To adjust bearing pre-load:

a. Use a pin wrench to torque the locknut to 58–72 ft. lbs. (78–98

Nm). Turn the hub in both directions several times while torquing the nut.

b. Loosen the locknut, then torque again to 13 inch lbs. (1.5 Nm).

c. Turn the hub several times and check the nut torque again.

d. Install the lock washer. When installing the screw, make sure the locknut turns no more than 30 degrees in either direction.

e. When bearing pre-load is properly set, there will be no end-play in the hub and it will require no more than 4.7 lbs. of pull at the wheel stud to turn the hub.

10. Install the brake caliper and torque the caliper carrier bolts to 72 ft. lbs. (98 Nm).

REAR SUSPENSION

Shock Absorbers

REMOVAL AND INSTALLATION

1. Raise and safely support the vehicle.

2. Remove the upper shock-to-vehicle nut, the lower shock-to-vehicle nut and the shock from the vehicle.

NOTE: The weight of the vehicle must be on the rear wheels before tightening the shock absorber attaching nuts.

3. To install, reverse the removal procedures. Torque as follows:

Upper shock-to-vehicle nut — 22–30 ft. lbs.

Lower shock absorber-to-axle nut
2WD — 12–16 ft. lbs.
4WD — 22–30 ft. lbs.

Leaf Springs

REMOVAL AND INSTALLATION

————— CAUTION —————
The leaf springs are under a considerable amount of tension. Be very careful when removing or installing them; they can exert enough force to cause serious injuries.

1. Raise and safely support the vehicle. Using a floor jack, support the axle housing.

2. Disconnect the shock absorbers at their lower end.

3. Remove the axle housing-to-spring pad U-bolt nuts and the spring pad.

4. Raise the axle housing to remove the weight off the springs.

5. Remove the spring shackle nuts, drive out the shackle pins and remove the spring from the vehicle.

NOTE: The weight of the vehicle must be on the rear wheels before torquing the front pin, shackle and shock absorber nuts.

6. To install, reverse the removal procedures. Torque as follows:

Front pin and shackle nuts — 94 ft. lbs. (127 Nm)

U-bolt nuts — 72 ft. lbs. (98 Nm)

Shock absorber lower end nut
2WD — 16 ft. lbs. (22 Nm)
4WD — 30 ft. lbs. (41 Nm)

FIRING ORDERS

NOTE: To avoid confusion, always replace spark plug wires one at a time.

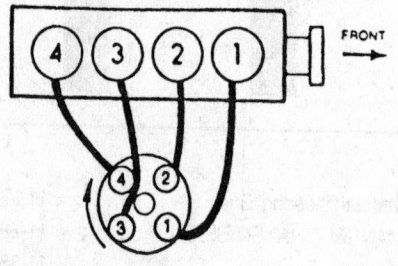

FRONT →

7911F001

1.3L and 1.6L Engines
Engine Firing Order: 1–3–4–2
Distributor Rotation: Clockwise

ENGINE ELECTRICAL

NOTE: Disconnecting the battery cable on some vehicles may interfere with the functions of the on board computer systems and may require the computer to undergo a relearning process, once the negative battery cable is disconnected.

Distributor

REMOVAL

1. Disconnect the negative battery terminal at the battery.
2. Disconnect the electrical connections and the vacuum hoses.

NOTE: Do not bend or twist the spark plug wires to avoid internal damage. Grip the the wire boot when removing or installing the wires.

3. Remove the distributor cap.
4. Mark the rotor position on the distributor housing and the distributor housing position on the engine.
5. Remove the distributor flange bolt and remove the distributor.

NOTE: Do not crank the engine with the distributor removed.

INSTALLATION

Timing Not Disturbed

1. Install the distributor and align the marks on the distributor housing and on the engine.
2. Tighten the flange bolt and install the distributor cap.
3. Connect the electrical connections and the vacuum hoses.
4. Connect the negative battery cable and set the timing to specification.

Timing Disturbed

1. Rotate the crankshaft in a clockwise position until the specified timing mark on the flywheel aligns with the timing matchmark on the engine.

NOTE: After aligning the 2 marks, remove the cylinder head cover to visually check that the rocker arms are not riding on the camshaft cams at No. 1 cylinder. If the arms are found to be riding on the cams, turn the crankshaft 360 degrees to realign the 2 marks.

2. Position the rotor to the No. 1 cylinder position and install the distributor.
3. Connect the vacuum and electrical connections.
4. Connect the negative battery cable and set the timing to specification.

Ignition Timing

ADJUSTMENT

1. Start the engine and warm up to normal operating temperature. Prior to any adjustment, be sure all the electrical accessories are **OFF**.
2. After warming up, make sure the idle speed is within the proper specification.
3. Remove cap from monitor coupler next to battery and connect terminals **C** and **D** with a jumper wire. Connect the timing light to the No. 1 cylinder spark plug wire.
4. With the engine running at the specified idle speed, direct the timing light to the crankshaft pulley. If the specified timing mark on the timing tab is aligned with the timing notch on the crankshaft pulley the ignition is properly timed.
5. If the timing is out of adjustment, loosen the distributor flange bolt and turn the distributor housing

to advance or retard the timing. Turn the distributor counterclockwise to advance the timing and clockwise to retard the timing.
6. After the adjustment, tighten the flange bolt and recheck the timing.

Alternator

BELT TENSION ADJUSTMENT

1. Disconnect the negative battery cable.
2. Loosen the alternator bolt and pivot bolts.
3. Adjust the belt tension to 0.24–0.32 in. of deflection using a belt tension gauge and measuring at the midpoint between the 2 pulleys.

REMOVAL AND INSTALLATION

1. Disconnect the negative battery cable.
2. Disconnect the wire coupler and white lead wire from the alternator.
3. Remove the radiator shroud from under the radiator.
4. Remove the alternator mounting bolt and alternator drive belt adjusting bolt.
5. Remove the alternator from the vehicle.
To install:
6. Install the alternator and tighten the mounting bolt and drive belt adjusting bolt. Adjust the drive belt tension.
7. Install the shroud under the radiator and connect the wire coupler to the alternator.
8. Connect the negative battery cable.

Starter

REMOVAL AND INSTALLATION

1. Disconnect the negative battery cable.
2. Raise and support the vehicle safely.
3. Disconnect the lead wire and battery cable from the starter motor.
4. Support the starter and remove the 2 mounting bolts.
5. Remove the starter.
To install:
6. Install the starter and tighten the 2 mounting bolts to 22 ft. lbs..
7. Connect the lead wire and battery cable to the starter.
8. Lower the vehicle and connect the negative battery cable.

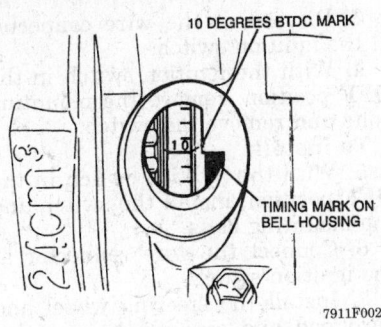

Timing mark alignment — Samurai
The timing marks are visible by removing
the rubber plug in the bell housing

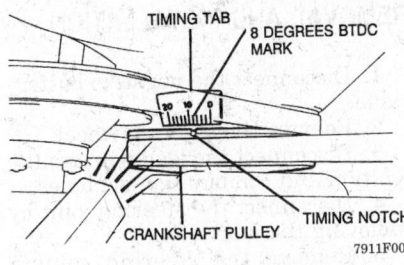

Timing marks — Sidekick

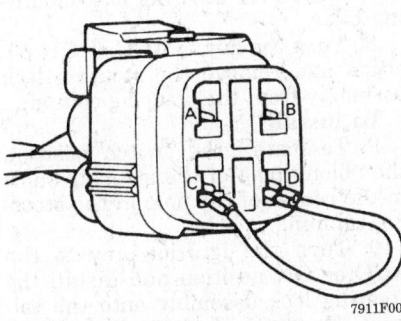

Installed jumper wire at monitor coupler

CHASSIS ELECTRICAL

Heater Blower Motor

REMOVAL AND INSTALLATION

Samurai

1. Disconnect the negative battery cable. Drain the cooling system.

2. Disconnect the inlet and outlet heater hoses from the heater core.

3. Remove the horn pad and the steering wheel retaining nut and remove the steering wheel by using the proper puller.

4. Disconnect and tag the radio and cigar lighter wires. Remove the radio from the vehicle.

5. Remove the ash tray and mounting plate.

6. Disconnect the hood release cable from the release lever.

7. Disconnect and tag the heater control cables and wires at the controls.

8. Remove the heater control lever knobs and facing plate. Loosen the lever case screws.

9. Remove the defroster and side ventilator hoses.

10. Disconnect the lead wires and speedometer cable from the speedometer and remove the lead wires from the heater controls.

11. Disconnect the wiring harness clamps from the instrument panel.

12. Loosen the instrument panel mounting screws and remove the instrument panel.

NOTE: When removing the heater lever case which is fitted in the steering column holder, be very careful not to damage it.

13. Loosen the front door opening stop screws and remove the steering column bracket.

14. Disconnect and tag the blower motor and resistor connections at the coupler.

15. Loosen the heater case securing nut on the engine side.

16. Remove the heater assembly from the vehicle.

17. Remove the blower motor from the case.

To install:

18. Install the blower motor in the heater case and install the assembly in the vehicle.

19. Tighten the heater case securing nut on the engine side.

20. Install the blower motor and resistor connections at the coupler.

21. Tighten the front door opening stop screws and install the steering column holder.

22. Tighten the instrument panel mounting screws and replace the instrument panel.

23. Reconnect the wiring harness clamps to the instrument panel.

24. Reconnect the lead wires and speedometer cable to the speedometer.

25. Install the defroster and side ventilator hoses.

26. Install the heater control knobs and plate, and tighten the lever case screws.

27. Reconnect the heater control cables at the controls.

28. Reconnect the hood release cable to the release lever.

29. Install the ash tray and mounting plate.

30. Reconnect the radio and cigar lighter wires. Install the radio in the vehicle.

31. Install the horn pad and steering wheel retaining nut and install the steering wheel.

32. Reconnect the inlet and outlet heater hoses to heater core.

33. Refill the cooling system with the proper coolant. Install the negative battery cable.

Sidekick

1. Disconnect the negative battery cable.

2. Remove the glove box assembly.

3. Disconnect the blower motor and resistor wire connectors.

4. Disconnect the fresh air control cable from the blower motor case.

5. Loosen but do not remove the blower housing fastener bolts.

6. Remove the 3 blower motor mounting screws.

7. Remove the blower motor.

To install:

8. Install the blower motor and install the 3 mounting screws.

9. Tighten the blower housing fastener bolts.

10. Connect the fresh air control cable to the blower motor case.

11. Connect the blower motor and resistor wire connectors.

12. Install the glove box assembly and connect the negative battery cable.

Windshield Wiper Motor

REMOVAL AND INSTALLATION

Samurai

SOFT TOP

1. Disconnect the negative battery cable.

2. Remove the wiper linkage to wiper mounting nut.

3. Disconnect the wire connector from the wiper motor.

4. Remove the 3 wiper mounting bolts and remove the wiper motor.

To install:

5. Install the wiper motor and install the 3 mounting bolts.

6. Connect the wire connector and linkage to the wiper motor and tighten the linkage mounting nut.

7. Connect the negative battery cable.

HARD TOP

NOTE: On some models, the windshield frame may have to be removed.

1. Disconnect the negative battery cable.

2. Remove the wiper linkage to wiper mounting nut.

3. Disconnect the wire connector from the wiper motor.

4. Remove the 3 wiper mounting bolts and remove the wiper motor.

To install:

5. Install the 3 wiper motor mounting bolts and install the motor.

6. Install the linkage and mounting nut and connect the negative battery cable.

Sidekick

1. Disconnect the negative battery cable.

2. Remove the right and left cowl grilles.

3. Remove the wiper linkage to wiper mounting nut.

4. Disconnect the wire connector from the wiper motor.

5. Remove the 4 wiper mounting bolts and remove the wiper motor.

To install:

6. Install the 4 wiper mounting bolts and the wiper motor.

7. Connect the wiper motor wire connector and wiper linkage.

8. Install the right and left cowl grilles and connect the negative battery cable.

Instrument Cluster

REMOVAL AND INSTALLATION

1. Disconnect the negative battery cable.

2. Remove the lower instrument panel cover.

3. Loosen, but do not remove the 2 upper and 4 lower steering column mounting bolts. Lower and support the steering column, if necessary.

4. Remove the outer instrument cluster cover.

5. Remove the 4 cluster mounting screws and slide the cluster outwards.

6. Disconnect the lead wires and speedometer cable from the speedometer.

7. Remove the speedometer.

8. Disconnect and tag the wire connector from the rear of the instrument cluster.

9. Remove the instrument cluster.

To install:

10. Install the instrument cluster and connect the wire connector to the rear.

11. Install the speedometer and connect the speedometer cable and lead wires.

12. Install the 4 cluster mounting screws.

13. Install the outer instrument cluster cover.

14. Secure the steering column and the column mounting bolts.

15. Install the lower instrument cover panel and connect the negative battery cable.

Combination Switch

The combination switch incorporates the turn signal, windshield wiper, dimmer and headlight switches into 1 switch.

REMOVAL AND INSTALLATION

1. Disconnect the negative battery cable.

2. Remove the horn button and remove the steering wheel retaining nut and remove the steering wheel.

3. Remove the upper and lower column cover screws and remove the covers.

4. Disconnect the lead wires from the combination switch at the connector.

5. Remove the combination switch assembly screws.

6. Remove the combination switch from the steering column.

To install:

7. Install the combination switch to the steering column and install the assembly screws.

8. Connect the lead wires at the connector to the combination switch.

9. Install the lower and upper column covers and reinstall the steering wheel.

10. Install the horn button and connect the negative battery cable.

Ignition Switch

REMOVAL AND INSTALLATION

1. Disconnect the negative battery cable.

2. Remove the steering wheel from the vehicle.

3. Disconnect the wire connector at the ignition switch.

4. With the ignition switch in the **OFF** position, remove the mounting bolts and remove the switch.

To install:

5. With the ignition switch in the **OFF** position, install the switch and the mounting bolts.

6. Connect the wire connector at the ignition switch.

7. Install the steering wheel and horn pad and connect the negative battery cable.

Ignition Lock

REMOVAL AND INSTALLATION

1. Disconnect the negative battery cable.

2. Remove the steering wheel.

3. Disconnect the lead wires to the ignition and combination switches.

4. Disconnect the steering joint by removing the joint bolt.

5. Remove the steering column fastening bolts.

6. Remove the steering column assembly.

7. Using a center punch, loosen and remove the steering lock mounting bolts.

8. Turn the key to **ACC** or **ON** position and remove the steering lock assembly from the steering column.

To install:

9. To install the switch position the oblong hole of the steering shaft in the center of the hole in the steering column.

10. Turn the ignition key to the **ACC** or **ON** position and install the steering lock assembly onto the column. Turn the ignition key to the **LOCK** position and remove it. Align the hub on the lock with oblong hole of the steering shaft.

11. Rotate the shaft to assure that the steering shaft is locked.

12. Tighten the 2 new steering lock mounting bolts.

13. Turn the ignition key to the **ACC** or **ON** position and check to be sure the steering shaft rotates smoothly and check the lock mechanism operation.

14. Install the steering column assembly by attaching the joint and joint bolt.

15. Install the steering column attaching bolts.

16. Connect the wires to the ignition and combination switches.

17. Install the steering wheel and connect the negative battery cable.

Stoplight Switch

REMOVAL AND INSTALLATION

1. Disconnect the negative battery cable. Remove the under dash trim panel, if equipped.
2. Push the brake pedal down and remove the stoplight locknut.
3. Disconnect the wire connector at the switch:
4. Remove the switch from the bracket.
To install:
5. Install the new switch on the bracket.
6. Adjust the switch so there is 0.02–0.04 in. clearance between the switch and the brake pedal.
7. Install the locknut and tighten to 7.5–10.5 ft. lbs.
8. Install the negative battery cable.

Clutch Switch

REMOVAL AND INSTALLATION

Sidekick

1. Disconnect the negative battery cable. Remove the under dash trim panel, if equipped.
2. Disconnect the start switch connector beside the clutch pedal bracket.
3. Remove the locknut and start switch.
To install:
4. Installation is the reverse of the removal procedure.

Fuses and Relays

LOCATION

The fuse box and turn signal relay are located under the driver side of the dashboard.

Computers

LOCATION

Sidekick

The Electronic Control Module computer is located under the dash on the driver side of the vehicle.

Cruise Control

ADJUSTMENT

Sidekick

1. Remove the top cover from the actuator assembly.
2. Loosen the lock nuts on the cable.
3. Adjust the cable so the play range is between 0.04–0.08 in. when the actuator lever is fully closed.
4. Tighten the locknut to 4 ft. lbs. and replace the top cover.

ENGINE COOLING

Radiator

REMOVAL AND INSTALLATION

1. Disconnect the negative battery cable.
2. Drain the cooling system.
3. Disconnect and plug the transmission cooler lines, if equipped.
4. Loosen the water pump drive belt tension.
5. Remove the cooling fan and radiator shroud.
6. Disconnect the water hoses to the radiator.
7. Remove the radiator retaining bolts and remove the radiator.
To install:
8. Install the radiator mounting bolts and install the radiator.
9. Reconnect the water hoses to the radiator.
10. Install the cooling fan and radiator shroud.
11. Tighten the water pump drive belt to the proper tension.

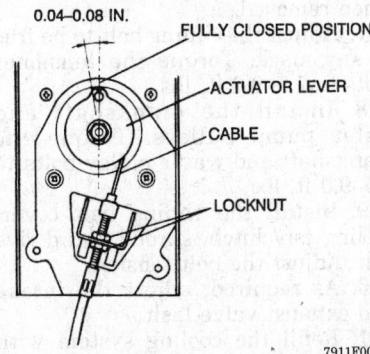

0.04–0.08 IN.
FULLY CLOSED POSITION
ACTUATOR LEVER
CABLE
LOCKNUT

7911F005

View of the cruise control adjustment

12. Reconnect the transmission cooler lines, if necessary, to the radiator.
13. Refill the cooling system.
14. Reconnect the negative battery cable.

Heater Core

REMOVAL AND INSTALLATION

Samurai

1. Disconnect the negative battery cable. Drain the cooling system.
2. Disconnect the heater hoses from the heater core.
3. Disconnect the radio and cigar lighter lead wires, and remove the radio from the vehicle.
4. Remove the ash tray and mounting plate.
5. Disconnect the hood release cable from the release lever.
6. Disconnect and tag the heater control cables and wires at the controls.
7. Remove the heater control lever knobs and facing plate, and loosen the lever case screws.
8. Remove the defroster and side ventilator hoses.
9. Disconnect the lead wires and speedometer cables from the speedometer.
10. Disconnect the wiring harness from the instrument panel.
11. Loosen the instrument panel mounting screws and remove the instrument panel.
12. Loosen the front door opening stop screws and remove the steering column holder.
13. Disconnect and tag the blower motor and resistor connections at the coupler.
14. Loosen the heater securing nut on the engine side.
15. Remove the heater assembly from the vehicle.
16. Remove the clips holding the heater case together, separate the case and remove the heater core.
To install:
17. Install the heater core into the heater case and install the clips holding the case together.
18. Install the heater assembly in the vehicle and tighten the securing nut on the engine side.
19. Reconnect the blower motor and resistor connections at the coupler.
20. Install the steering column holder and tighten the front door opening stop screws.
21. Install the instrument panel and tighten panel mounting screws.

22. Reconnect the wiring harness to the instrument panel.

23. Install the defroster and side ventilator hoses.

24. Tighten the heater control case screws and install the control knobs and facing plate.

25. Reconnect the heater control cable and wires to the heater control.

26. Reconnect the hood release cable the release lever.

27. Install the ash tray and mounting plate.

28. Install radio and connect the cigar lighter and radio wires.

29. Reconnect the heater hoses to the heater core.

30. Refill the cooling system to the proper with the proper coolant. Install the negative cable.

Sidekick

1. Disconnect the negative battery cable. Drain the cooling system.

2. Disconnect the 2 water hoses from the heater assembly.

3. Remove the steering wheel. Disconnect the lead wires from the ignition and combination switches.

4. Disconnect the wiring harness and remove the instrument panel and related parts.

5. Disconnect all the wiring connections and cables from the heater controls.

6. Disconnect the defroster duct and speedometer cable retaining bracket from the heater case.

7. Remove the heater assembly and remove the heater core.

To install:

8. Install the heater core and install the heater assembly.

9. Reconnect the defroster duct and speedometer cable retaining bracket to the heater case.

10. Reconnect the wiring connections and cables to the heater controls.

11. Reconnect the wiring harness and install the instrument panel.

12. Connect the lead wires to the ignition and combination switches and install the steering wheel.

13. Connect the water hoses to the heater assembly.

14. Refill the cooling system with the proper coolant and replace the negative battery cable.

Water Pump

REMOVAL AND INSTALLATION

1. Disconnect the negative battery cable.

2. Drain the cooling system.

3. Loosen the drive belt tension and remove the drive belt. If equipped, loosen the air conditioning belt tension and remove the air conditioning belt.

4. Remove the radiator fan shroud mounting bolts and radiator fan mounting bolts. Remove the radiator shroud, fan and water pump pulley from the vehicle.

5. Remove the crankshaft pulley bolts and remove the crankshaft pulley.

NOTE: The crankshaft pulley bolt can be removed without removing the center crankshaft bolt.

6. Remove the timing belt cover mounting bolts and remove the cover.

7. Loosen the timing belt tensioner adjusting bolt and pivot nut. Hold the tensioner to loosen the timing belt and remove the belt from the camshaft pulley.

8. Remove the timing belt tensioner mounting bolts and remove the tensioner plate and spring.

9. Remove the water pump mounting bolts and remove the water pump assembly.

10. On Sidekick, it is necessary to remove the dipstick tube and the alternator bracket from the vehicle.

To install:

11. Clean and inspect the surface of the engine before installation.

12. Using a new gasket, install the new water pump on the engine. Torque the mounting bolts to 8 ft. lbs.

13. On Sidekick, install the dipstick tube and the alternator bracket to the vehicle.

14. Install the rubber seals between the water pump to cylinder head and water pump to oil pump.

15. Install the timing belt tensioner plate, tensioner and spring.

16. Align the marks on the timing belt and the camshaft sprocket. Install the timing belt in the same position on the camshaft sprocket as when removed.

17. Adjust the timing belt to be free of any slack. Torque the tensioner bolts to 7.5–9.0 ft. lbs.

18. Install the crankshaft and water pump pulleys. Torque the crankshaft and water pulley bolts to 7.5–9.0 ft. lbs.

19. Install the timing belt cover, cooling fan/clutch, shroud and drive belt. Adjust the belt tension.

20. As required, adjust the intake and exhaust valve lash.

21. Refill the cooling system with the proper coolant and replace the negative battery cable.

Thermostat

REMOVAL AND INSTALLATION

1. Disconnect the negative battery cable.

2. Drain the cooling system.

3. Disconnect the thermostat cap from the intake manifold and remove the thermostat.

To install:

4. Clean and inspect the surfaces of the housing and the engine.

5. Install the new thermostat with the spring facing towards the engine.

6. Install a new gasket and the thermostat cap to the intake manifold.

7. Refill the cooling system with the proper coolant and replace the negative battery cable.

FUEL SYSTEM

Fuel System Service Precaution

When working with the fuel system, certain precautions should be taken; always work in a well ventilated area, keep a dry chemical (Class B) fire extinguisher near the work area. Always disconnect the negative battery cable and do not make any repairs to the fuel system until all the necessary steps for repair have been reviewed.

RELIEVING FUEL SYSTEM PRESSURE

The fuel pressure must be relieved before performing any service on the fuel system.

1. Disconnect the negative battery cable.

2. Remove the fuel filler cap from the fuel filler neck to release the fuel vapor pressure in the fuel tank. Reinstall the fuel cap.

3. Raise and support the vehicle safely.

4. Place an appropriate container under the fuel filter.

5. Cover the plug bolt on the fuel filter inlet union bolt with a rag and loosen the plug bolt slowly to release the fuel pressure gradually.

6. When the pressure has been released, tighten the plug bolt to 7.5 ft. lbs. so the fuel does not leak.

7. Lower the vehicle.

8. Reconnect the negative battery cable.

Fuel Filter

REMOVAL AND INSTALLATION

1. Disconnect the negative battery cable.

2. Remove the fuel filler cap to release the fuel vapor pressure in the fuel tank. After releasing pressure, reinstall filler cap.

3. Raise and support the vehicle safely.

4. Release the fuel pressure.

5. Disconnect the inlet and outlet hoses from the fuel filter.

6. Remove the fuel filter from the chassis frame.

To install:

7. Install the new fuel filter to the frame and connect the inlet and outlet hoses.

8. Lower the vehicle and connect the negative battery cable.

Electric Fuel Pump

PRESSURE TESTING

1. Remove the fuel filler cap to release the fuel vapor pressure in the fuel tank. Reinstall the cap.

2. Raise and support the vehicle safely.

3. Release the fuel pressure in the fuel feed line.

4. Remove the plug bolt on the fuel filter union bolt and connect the proper fuel pressure gauge to the fuel filter inlet union bolt.

NOTE: If the pressure in the fuel tank is not released prior to system service, the fuel in the fuel tank may be forced out through the fuel hoses during disconnection.

5. Start the engine and warm up to the proper operating temperature.

6. Measure the fuel pressure under each of the following conditions.

    a. At a specified idle speed or with the fuel pump operating and the engine stopped the fuel pressure should read: 34.1–39.8 psi.

    b. Within 1 minute after the fuel pump has stopped the fuel pressure should read: 21.3 psi.

7. Release the fuel pressure and remove the fuel pressure gauge.

8. Install the plug bolt to the fuel filter inlet bolt. Use a new gasket.

9. Start the engine and check for leaks.

10. Lower the vehicle.

REMOVAL AND INSTALLATION

The fuel pump is located in the fuel tank. The fuel pump and the fuel gauge sending unit are located on the upper part of the fuel tank.

1. Disconnect the negative battery cable.

2. Remove the rear bumper assembly.

3. Disconnect the fuel gauge sending unit and fuel pump electrical connectors from the fuel tank.

4. Relieve the fuel system pressure.

5. Disconnect the fuel tank filler hose cover, filler hose, and fuel tank inlet valve (breather hose).

6. Disconnect the inlet pipe from the fuel filter and remove the fuel vapor and return hoses.

7. If necessary, drain the fuel from the tank using a hand operated pump.

8. Disconnect the fuel tank protector and remove the fuel tank and cover from the vehicle.

9. Remove the fuel pump from the fuel tank.

To install:

10. Install the fuel pump to the fuel tank using a new gasket.

11. Install the fuel tank and cover to the vehicle and connect the fuel tank protector.

12. Install the fuel vapor and return hoses and connect the inlet pipe to the fuel filter.

13. Reconnect the fuel tank inlet valve (breather hose), filler hose, and fuel tank filler hose cover.

14. Connect the fuel pump and fuel gauge sending sending unit electrical connectors to the fuel tank.

15. Install the bumper assembly and reconnect the negative battery cable.

16. If necessary, refill the fuel tank with any fuel that had been drained.

17. Start the engine and check for leaks when finished.

Fuel Injection

IDLE SPEED ADJUSTMENT

1.3L Engine

1. Place the transmission lever in Neutral.

2. Set the parking brake and block the drive wheels.

3. Operate the engine to normal operating temperatures.

4. Connect a spare fuse to the diagnostic swtich terminal in the fuse box and make sure the CHECK ENGINE light indicates the diagnostic Code No. 12.

5. Stop the engine and connect a duty meter between the duty check terminal and ground terminal of the monitor coupler.

NOTE: The monitor coupler is located beside the battery.

6. Set the tachometer.

7. Turn the ignition switch **ON** and wait for 5 seconds. Start the engine and operate it at 2000 rpm for 5 minutes; then allow it to slow to idle.

8. Check the Idle Speed Control duty; it should be 50 percent.

9. Check the idle speed; it should be 750–850 rpm. If adjustment is necessary, turn the idle speed adjusting screw.

10. If equipped with air conditioning, turn it **ON**, set the heater blower swtich to the **LOW** speed and check the idle speed; it should be 950–1050 rpm. If the idle speed and the ISC duty are not correct, turn the A/C VSV adjusting screw until specificatons are correct.

11. Remove the fuse from the diagnostic switch terminal and install the cap to the monitor coupler.

1.6L Engine

ELECTRONIC FUEL INJECTION (EFI)

1. Place the transmission lever in Neutral for manual transmission or **P** for an automatic transmission.

2. Set the parking brake and block the drive wheels.

3. Operate the engine to normal operating temperatures.

4. Using a jumper wire, ground the diagnostic swtich terminal in the monitor coupler and make sure the malfunction indicator (CHECK

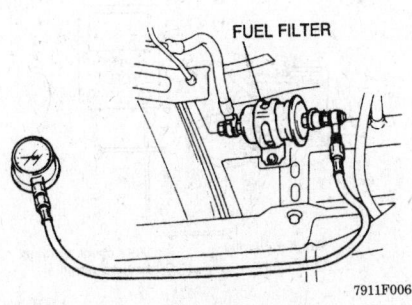

7911F006

Checking fuel pump pressure

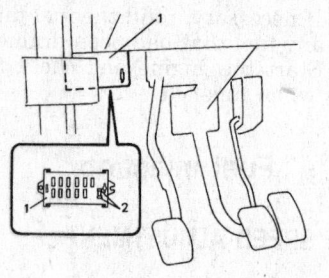

1. Fuse box
2. Diagnosis switch terminal

8547F012

View of the grounding disgnostic switch terminal — 1.3L engine

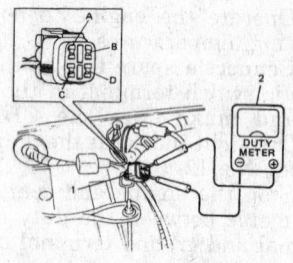

1. Monitor coupler
2. Duty meter
A: Duty check terminal
C: Ground terminal

8547F009

View of the duty meter connected to the monitor coupler — 1.3L engine

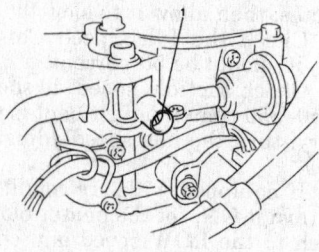

1. Idle speed adjusting screw

8547F010

View of the idle speed adjusting screw — 1.3L engine

ENGINE) light indicates the diagnostic trouble Code No. 12.

NOTE: The monitor coupler is located beside the battery.

5. Stop the engine and connect a duty meter between the duty check terminal and ground terminal of the monitor coupler.

6. Disconnect the noise suppressor coupler and connect an Adapter wire tool No. 09931-96010 or equivalent. Set the tachometer.

7. Turn the ignition switch **ON** and wait for 5 seconds. Start the en-

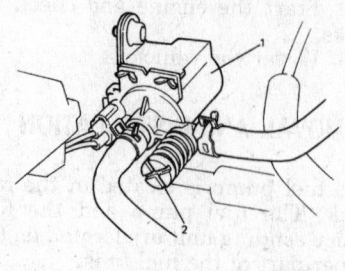

1. A/C VSV
2. Adjusting screw

8547F011

View of the A/C VSV adjusting screw — 1.3L engine

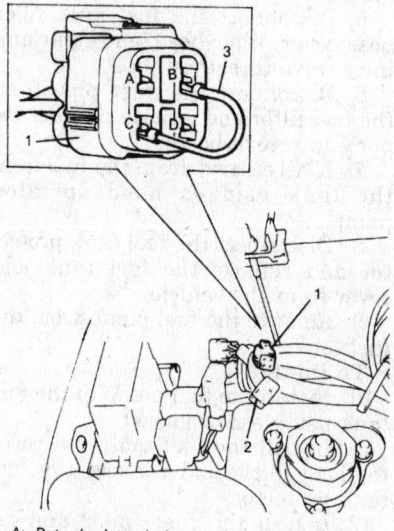

A: Duty check terminal
B: Diagnosis switch terminal
C: Ground terminal
D: Test switch terminal

1. Monitor coupler
2. Cap
3. Service wire

8547F001

View of the monitor coupler — 1.6L EFI engine

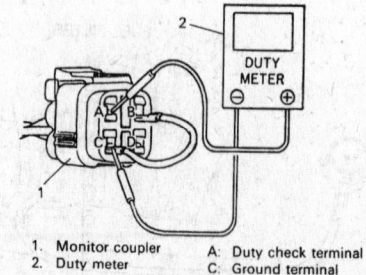

1. Monitor coupler
2. Duty meter
A: Duty check terminal
C: Ground terminal

8547F002

View of the duty meter connected to the monitor coupler — 1.6L EFI engine

gine and operate it at 2000 rpm for 5 minutes; then allow it to slow to idle.

8. Check the Idle Air Control duty; it should be 50 percent.

9. Check the idle speed; it should be 750–850 rpm. If adjustment is necessary, turn the idle speed adjusting screw.

10. If equipped with air conditioning, turn it **ON** and check the idle speed; it should be 950–1050 rpm. If the idle speed is not correct, check the A/C ON signal circuit and the Idle Air Control (IAC) valve.

11. Remove the equipment and install the adjustment caps.

MULTIPORT FUEL INJECTION (MFI)

1. Place the transmission lever in Neutral for manual transmission or **P** for an automatic transmission.

2. Set the parking brake and block the drive wheels.

3. Operate the engine to normal operating temperatures.

4. Using a jumper wire, ground the diagnostic swtich terminal in the monitor coupler and make sure the malfunction indicator (CHECK ENGINE) light indicates the diagnostic trouble Code No. 12.

NOTE: The monitor coupler is located beside the battery.

5. Stop the engine and connect a duty meter between the duty check terminal and ground terminal of the monitor coupler.

6. Turn the ignition switch **ON** and wait for 5 seconds. Start the engine and operate it at 2000 rpm for 5 minutes; then allow it to slow to idle.

7. Check the Idle Air Control duty; it should be 50 percent.

8. Check the idle speed; it should be 750–850 rpm. If adjustment is necessary, turn the idle speed adjusting screw.

9. If equipped with air conditioning, turn it **ON** and check the idle speed; it should be 950–1050 rpm. If the idle speed is not correct, check the A/C ON signal circuit and the Idle Air Control (IAC) valve.

10. Remove the equipment and install the adjustment caps.

THROTTLE OPENER ADJUSTMENT

1.3L EFI Engine

1. Place the transmission lever in Neutral for manual transmission or **P** for an automatic transmission.

2. Set the parking brake and block the drive wheels.

3. Turn the ignition switch **ON** and allow it to stand for 5 seconds.

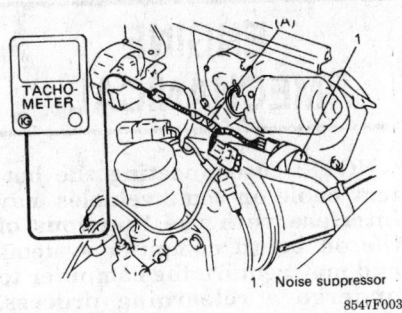

1. Noise suppressor

8547F003

View of the noise suppressor, adapter wire and tachometer — 1.6L EFI engine

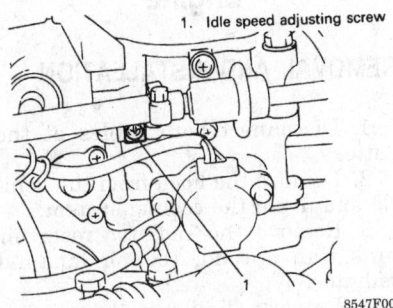

1. Idle speed adjusting screw

8547F004

View of the idle speed adjusting screw — 1.6L EFI engine

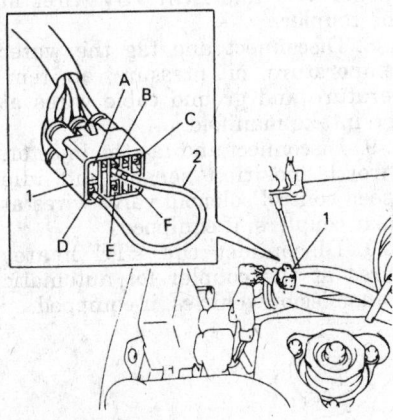

1. Monitor coupler
2. Service wire

A: Blank
B: Diagnosis switch terminal
C: Diagnosis output terminal
D: Ground terminal
E: Test switch terminal
F: Duty output terminal

8547F005

View of the monitor coupler — 1.6L MFI engine

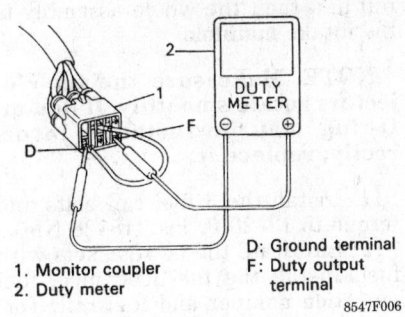

1. Monitor coupler
2. Duty meter

D: Ground terminal
F: Duty output terminal

8547F006

View of the duty meter connected to the monitor coupler — 1.6L MFI engine

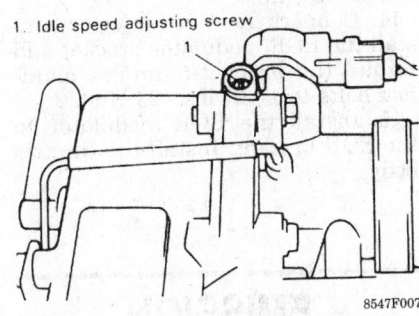

1. Idle speed adjusting screw

8547F007

View of the idle speed adjusting screw — 1.6L MFI engine

4. Operate the engine at 2000 rpm for 5 minutes and allow it to slow to idle speed.

5. Check and make sure no electrical load is applied to the engine.

6. Disconnect and plug the vacuum hose from the throttle opener. Check the idle speed; it should be 2150–2250 rpm.

7. If the idle speed is not correct, turn the throttle opener adjusting screw.

8. When the idle speed is correct, connect the vacuum hose to the throttle opener.

1.6L EFI Engine

1. Place the transmission lever in Neutral for manual transmission or **P** for an automatic transmission.

2. Set the parking brake and block the drive wheels.

3. Turn the ignition switch **ON** and allow it to stand for 5 seconds.

4. Operate the engine at 2000 rpm for 5 minutes and allow it to slow to idle speed.

5. Check and make sure no electrical load is applied to the engine.

6. Disconnect and plug the vacuum hose from the throttle opener. Check the idle speed; it should be 2100–2300 rpm.

7. If the idle speed is not correct, turn the throttle opener adjusting screw.

8. When the idle speed is correct, connect the vacuum hose to the throttle opener.

Fuel Injector

REMOVAL AND INSTALLATION

1.6L Engine

ELECTRONIC FUEL INJECTION (EFI)

1. Disconnect the negative battery cable.

2. Release the fuel pressure.

3. Remove the the air intake case from the throttle body.

4. Remove the fuel feed pipe clamp from the intake manifold and disconnect the fuel feed pipe from the throttle body.

5. Remove the injector cover.

6. Disconnect the injector coupler, release its wire harness from the clamp and remove its grommet from the throttle body.

7. Place a cloth over the injector and a hand on top of it. Using an air gun, blow low pressure compressed air into the fuel inlet port of the throttle body and the injector can be removed.

NOTE: Be precise about the pressure of the compressed air. Using excessively high pressure may force the injector to jump out and may cause damage, not only to the injector itself but also to other parts.

To install:

8. Apply thin coating of gasoline to O-rings and then install the fuel injector to the throttle body.

9. Connect fuel injector wire connector and install injector cover.

10. Connect fuel feed pipe to throttle body.

11. Connect the negative battery cable and turn the ignition **ON** for 3 seconds and then **OFF** until fuel pressure is felt at the return hose.

12. Install air intake case assembly.

13. Secure all wires and check for any leaks in the system.

MULTIPORT FUEL INJECTION (MFI)

1. Disconnect the negative battery cable. Release the fuel pressure in the fuel feed line.

2. Remove the the air intake case from the throttle body. Remove the throttle body.

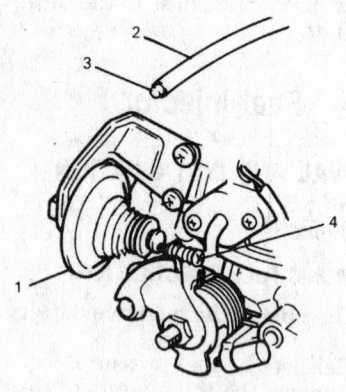

1. Throttle opener
2. Vacuum hose
3. Blind plug
4. Opener adjusting screw

8547F008

View of the throttle opener adjustment screw — 1.3L and 1.6L EFI engines

3. Remove the Exhaust Gas Recirculation (EGR) modulator from the EGR modulator bracket.

4. Remove the 2 bolts and the EGR modulator bracket from the intake manifold.

5. Disconnect the 4 fuel injector connectors. Remove the 2 bolts and fuel pressure regulator from the fuel rail.

6. Remove the fuel pulsation damper and fuel feed pipe from the fuel rail.

7. Remove the 3 bolts and the fuel rail from the intake manifold. Remove the 4 fuel injectors from the intake manifold.

To install:

8. Install new O-rings onto the fuel injectors; be careful not to damage the O-rings. Install the grommets onto the fuel injectors.

NOTE: Inspect the insulators for breakage or scoring. If necessary, replace them.

9. Install the insulators and cushions to the intake manifold.

10. Lubricate the O-rings with fuel and install the injectors onto the fuel

rail and then the whole assembly to the intake manifold.

NOTE: Make sure the fuel injectors rotate smoothly. If not, an O-ring may be installed incorrectly; replace it.

11. Install the 3 fuel rail bolts and torque to 13–20 ft. lbs. (18–28 Nm).

12. Lubricate the new gaskets with fuel. Install the fuel feed pipe, fuel pulsation damper and fuel rail. Torque the fuel pulsation damper bolts to 18.5–25 ft. lbs. (25–35 Nm).

13. Install the fuel pressure regulator and torque the bolts to 6–8.5 ft. lbs. (8–12 Nm).

14. Connect the 4 fuel injectors. Install the EGR modulator bracket and torque the bracket-to-intake manifold bolts to 17 ft. lbs. (23 Nm).

15. Install the EGR modulator to the EGR bracket. Install the throttle body.

EMISSION CONTROLS

Emission Warning Lamps

The CHECK ENGINE light automatically comes on at 50,000, 80,000 and 100,000 miles.

RESETTING

The lamp reset switch is located on the left side of the dashboard, mounted on the steering column support. The lamp can be reset by moving the switch upwards and then downwards. If the switch remains on after being reset, check the system.

ENGINE MECHANICAL

NOTE: Disconnecting the battery cable on some vehicles may interfere with the functions of the on board computer systems and may require the computer to undergo a relearning process, once the negative battery cable is disconnected.

Engine

REMOVAL AND INSTALLATION

1. Disconnect both cables at the battery.

2. Remove the hood from the vehicle and drain the cooling system.

3. Remove the radiator reservoir tank, fan shroud, cooling fan and radiator.

4. Properly discharge the air conditioning system and remove the air conditioning condenser, if equipped.

5. Remove the air cleaner outlet hose.

6. Disconnect the accelerator and the automatic transmission kickdown cable from the throttle body, if equipped.

7. Disconnect and tag the throttle opener VSV and EGR VSV wires at the coupler.

8. Disconnect and tag the water temperature, oil pressure, air temperature and ground cable wires at the intake manifold.

9. Disconnect and tag the injector, throttle position sensor and idle speed control solenoid valve wires at their couplers, if equipped.

10. Disconnect the PTC heater wires at the coupler for automatic transmission vehicles, if equipped.

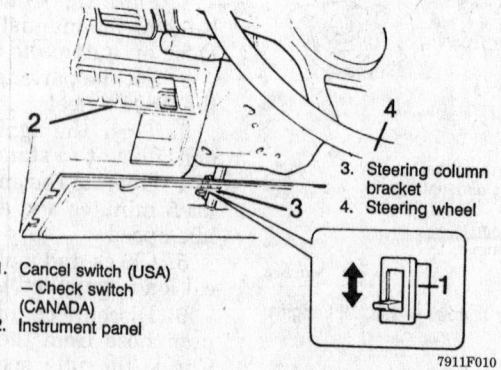

1. Cancel switch (USA) —Check switch (CANADA)
2. Instrument panel
3. Steering column bracket
4. Steering wheel

7911F010

Resetting the check engine light

11. Disconnect and tag the wires at the starter and alternator.

12. Disconnect and tag the oxygen sensor and distributor wires at their couplers. Remove the coil wire.

13. Remove the starter motor and disconnect the ground wires from the distributor.

14. Remove the fuel tank filler cap to relieve the pressure. Reinstall the cap.

15. Relieve the fuel pressure in the fuel feed line. Disconnect and tag the fuel feed and return hoses.

16. Remove the gear shift lever mounting bolts and remove the shifter.

17. Disconnect the canister purge hose and remove the pressure sensor hose from the fuel filter, if equipped.

18. Disconnect the brake booster hose from the intake manifold.

19. Remove the vacuum hose from the intake manifold, if equipped with automatic transmission.

20. Disconnect the heater hoses from the intake manifold and from the heater core outlet.

21. Raise and safely support the vehicle.

22. Drain the engine oil and disconnect the exhaust pipe from the exhaust manifold and muffler.

23. Disconnect the clutch cable, if equipped with manual transmission.

24. Drain the automatic transmission fluid, if equipped.

25. Disconnect the clutch (torque converter) housing lower plate.

26. Remove the lock driveplate, using the special tool, if equipped with automatic transmission.

27. Lower the vehicle.

28. Remove the nuts and bolts between the cylinder block and transmission.

29. Support the transmission, using an appropriate stand or jack.

30. Support the engine from the top using a chain type hoist.

31. Remove the engine mount assemblies.

NOTE: Before lifting the engine, check to ensure all the hoses, wires and cables are disconnected from the engine.

32. Remove the engine assembly from the chassis and transmission by sliding towards the front and carefully hoist the engine.

To install:

33. Install the engine into the engine compartment and connect to the transmission.

34. Install the engine mounts with the chassis side mounting brackets. Tighten to 41 ft. lbs.

35. Remove the lifting device.

36. Install the nuts and bolts fastening the cylinder block and transmission.

37. Raise and safely support the vehicle.

38. Install the lock driveplate, if equipped.

39. Connect the clutch (torque converter) housing lower plate.

40. Connect the automatic transmission lines, if equipped.

41. Reconnect the clutch cable to the bracket, if equipped with manual transmission.

42. Connect the exhaust pipe to the exhaust manifold and muffler.

43. Lower the vehicle.

44. Reconnect the heater hoses to the outlet pipe and the intake manifold.

45. Install the vacuum hose for the automatic transmission to the intake manifold, if equipped.

46. Reconnect the brake booster hose to the intake manifold.

47. Install the pressure sensor hose to the fuel filter and connect the canister purge hose, if equipped.

48. Install the fuel return and feed hoses.

49. Install the starter motor and connect the ground wire to the distributor.

50. Install the coil wire and connect the oxygen sensor and distributor wires to their couplers.

51. Reconnect the wires at the alternator and starter motor.

52. Install the PTC heater wires at the coupler, if equipped with automatic transmission.

53. Install the idle speed control solenoid valve, throttle position sensor and injector wires at their couplers, if equipped.

54. Connect the ground cable, air temperature, oil pressure and water temperature wires to the intake manifold.

55. Reconnect the throttle opener VSR and EGR VSR wires to their couplers, if equipped.

56. Connect the accelerator cable and the automatic transmission kickdown cable, if equipped, to the throttle body.

57. Install the air cleaner outlet hose. Refill the engine oil and the transmission oil to the proper level.

58. Install the air conditioning condenser and properly recharge the air conditioning system, if equipped.

59. Install the radiator, cooling fan, fan shroud and radiator reservoir tank.

60. Install the hood and refill the cooling system with the proper coolant.

61. Reconnect the positive and negative battery cables.

62. Adjust the accelerator, clutch and the automatic transmission kickdown cable, if equipped.

63. Before starting the engine, check to see if all the parts disassembled are back in place securely.

64. Start the engine and check the timing. Check for any oil leaks.

Cylinder Head

REMOVAL AND INSTALLATION

Electronic Fuel Injection (EFI)

NOTE: When removing the cylinder head, remove the pools from the top of the cylinder head before loosening the head bolts to avoid possible contamination.

1. Disconnect the negative battery cable. Drain the cooling system.

2. Disconnect the air intake case.

3. Disconnect the brake booster hose from the intake manifold and the air valve water hose from the throttle body.

4. Disconnect the accelerator and the automatic transmission kickdown cable, if equipped, from the throttle body.

5. Disconnect and tag the throttle opener VSV and EGR VSV wires at the coupler.

6. Disconnect and tag the water temperature, oil pressure, air temperature sensor and ground cable wires at the intake manifold.

7. Disconnect and tag the injector, throttle position sensor and idle speed control solenoid valve wires at their couplers, if equipped.

8. Disconnect the PTC heater wires at the coupler, if equipped with automatic transmission.

9. Disconnect and tag the oxygen sensor and distributor wires at their couplers. Remove the coil wire.

10. Disconnect the ground wires from the distributor assembly.

11. Remove the fuel tank filler cap to relieve the pressure. Reinstall the cap.

12. Release the fuel pressure in the fuel feed line.

13. Disconnect the fuel feed and return hoses.

14. Disconnect the canister purge hose and remove the pressure sensor hose from the fuel filter, if equipped.

15. Remove the vacuum hose for the automatic transmission from the intake manifold, if equipped.

16. Disconnect the radiator cooling fan, fan shroud, water pump drive belt and water pump pulley.

17. Disconnect the crankshaft pulley, timing belt cover and the timing belt.

18. Raise and safely support the vehicle.

19. Disconnect the exhaust pipe from the exhaust manifold and lower the vehicle.

20. Disconnect the air conditioner compressor adjusting arm, if equipped.

21. Remove the cylinder head cover mounting bolts and remove the cylinder head cover.

22. Loosen all the valve adjusting screw locknuts, turn the adjusting screws back all the way to allow all the valves to close.

23. Remove the intake manifold from the cylinder head.

24. Remove the distributor and distributor housing from the cylinder head.

25. Remove the cylinder head mounting bolts and remove the cylinder head from the engine.

26. Remove any oil and water in the cylinder bores and on top of the pistons.

27. Clean and inspect the sealing surfaces of the cylinder head and the engine block.

To install:

28. Install the cylinder head using a new gasket.

29. Install the cylinder head mounting bolts and tighten in the proper sequence to 46–54 ft. lbs.

30. Install the distributor and distributor housing to the cylinder head.

31. Install the intake manifold to the cylinder head.

32. Tighten all the valve adjusting screw nuts.

33. Adjust the valve lash.

34. Install the cylinder head cover and connect the air conditioning compressor adjusting arm, if equipped.

35. Raise and safely support the vehicle.

36. Connect the exhaust pipe to the exhaust manifold and safely lower the vehicle.

37. Reconnect the timing belt, timing belt cover and crankshaft pulley.

38. Install the water pump pulley, water pump drive belt, fan shroud and the radiator cooling fan.

39. Install the vacuum hose for the automatic transmission to the intake manifold, if equipped.

40. Install the pressure sensor hose to the fuel filter and connect the canister purge hose, if equipped.

41. Install the fuel return and feed hoses.

42. Connect the ground wires to the distributor assembly.

43. Install the coil wire. Connect the oxygen sensor and distributor wires to their couplers.

44. Connect the PTC wires to the coupler.

45. Connect the idle speed control valve, throttle position sensor and injector wires to their couplers, if equipped.

46. Reconnect the ground cable, air temperature, oil pressure and water temperature sensor wires to the intake manifold.

47. Install the throttle opener VSV and EGR VSV wires to their couplers.

48. Connect the accelerator and the automatic transmission kickdown cables, if equipped, to the throttle body.

49. Install the air valve water hose to the throttle body and connect the brake booster hose to intake manifold.

50. Reconnect the air intake case.

51. Refill the cooling system with the proper coolant and connect the negative battery.

52. Check for any water and oil leaks when finished.

Multiport Fuel Injection (MFI)

1. Disconnect the negative battery cable. Release the fuel pressure. Remove the fuel filler cap to release the pressure in the tank, then replace the fuel filler cap.

2. Drain the cooling system. Disconnect the air intake pipe from the ACL intake hose and throttle hose.

3. Remove the throttle cover-to-intake manifold bolts and the cover.

4. If equipped with an automatic transmission, disconnect the accelerator and kickdown cables from the throttle body bellcrank.

5. Remove 1 bolt, nut, screw and accelerator cable bracket from the throttle body.

6. Disconnect the electrical connectors from the following items:
Throttle Position (TP) sensor
Idle Air Control (IAC) valve
Engine Coolant Temperature (ECT) sensor
ECT sending unit
A/C ECT switch (if equipped with A/C)
Evaporative Emissions Solenoid Purge (EVAP SP) valve
Exhaust Gas Recirculation (EGR) temperature sensor (Calif. vehicles)
EGR solenoid vacuum valve
Fuel injectors
Engine ground wire from intake surge tank

7. Disconnect the following vacuum hoses:
EVAP SP valve
Vacuum modulator supply hose (if equipped with automatic transmission)
Brake booster supply hose
EGR valve
EGR valve modulator

8. Disconnect the coolant hose from the IAC valve and the IAC hose from the IAC valve. Disconnect the coolant hoses from the fast idle air valve below the throttle body.

9. Disconnect the fuel feed hose at the fuel feed hose union and the fuel feed hose from the fuel return line. Disconnect the PCV hose from the PCV valve.

10. Loosen the upper radiator hose clamp at the thermostat housing. Disconnect the upper radiator hose from the thermostat housing. Disconnect the coolant bypass hose from the intake manifold.

11. Remove the generator adjusting arm bracket from the intake manifold. Remove the front and rear intake manifold reinforcement brackets from the intake manifold.

12. Remove the lower intake manifold support bracket from the intake manifold. Remove the intake mani-

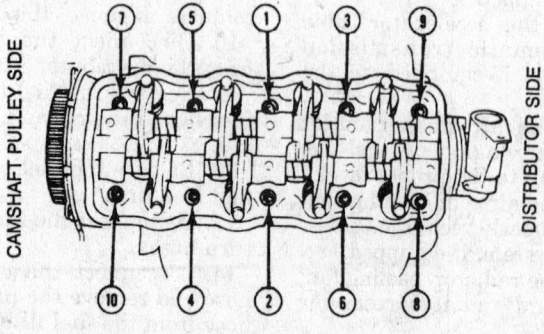

7911F011

Cylinder head bolt tightening sequence — Electronic Fuel Injection (EFI)

fold-to-cylinder head nuts/bolts, then remove the intake manifold, the intake surge tank and the throttle body from the cylinder head.

13. Remove the upper exhaust manifold heat shield from the exhaust manifold. Raise and safely support the vehicle.

14. Remove the exhaust manifold reinforcement bracket from the exhaust manifold and engine mount.

15. Remove the lower exhaust manifold heat shield from the exhaust manifold. Disconnect the Three-Way Catalytic converter (TWC) assembly from the exhaust manifold. Lower the vehicle.

16. Remove the exhaust manifold with gasket and engine hanger from the cylinder head.

17. If equipped, loosen the upper and lower A/C compressor mounting bolts. Loosen the upper and lower power steering pump mounting bolts. Remove the A/C compressor, If equipped, and/or the power steering drive belt.

18. Loosen the upper and lower generator mounting bolts. Remove the generator/water pump drive belt from the pulleys. Remove the cooling fan and the water pump pulley from the water pump.

19. Raise and safely support the vehicle. If equipped, remove the skid plate from the undercarriage. Remove the 2 lower radiator shroud bolts and lower the vehicle.

20. If equipped, remove the 2 A/C suction line bracket bolts at the right side of the radiator core support and carefully reposition the suction line for radiator shroud removal access.

21. Remove the 2 upper radiator shroud bolts and the shroud from the radiator.

NOTE: If the shroud is difficult to remove, drain the cooling system and disconnect the upper radiator hose from the radiator to gain access. If is not necessary to remove the crankshaft center bolt when removing the crankshaft pulley.

22. Remove the 5 crankshaft pulley-to-crankshaft bolts and the pulley. Remove the oil pressure sending unit wire conduit from the timing belt cover.

23. To remove the timing belt, perform the following procedure:

    a. Remove the timing belt cover from the engine.

NOTE: There are 2 sets of timing marks which must be aligned to ensure correct engine timing

upon installation. A notch in the camshaft timing belt gear designated as "E" must be aligned with the notch in the cylinder head. A punch mark on the crankshaft timing belt gear should align with the arrow in the oil pump casting. Make sure to align both sets of marks prior to timing belt removal.

    b. Rotate the engine to align the timing marks on the cylinder head cover and camshaft timing belt gear; this should align the timing marks on the oil pump casting and crankshaft timing belt gear.

    c. Loosen the timing belt tensioner bolt. Remove the timing belt tensioner spring from the timing belt tensioner plate.

    d. Remove the timing belt from the camshaft and crankshaft timing belt gears.

24. Secure the camshaft sprocket, using tool J-41840 or equivalent, then remove the camshaft sprocket-to-camshaft bolt and the camshaft sprocket.

25. Remove the 2 inner timing belt cover-to-cylinder head bolts and the cover. Remove the 2 A/C compressor mounting bracket-to-cylinder head bolts and the bracket.

26. Remove the distributor from the distributor case. Remove the 6 cylinder head cover-to-cylinder head bolts and the cover. Remove the cylinder head cover gasket and O-rings from the cylinder head cover.

NOTE: A small amount of oil may drain from the distributor case upon removal from the cylinder head. Place a suitable container under the distributor case or use a shop towel to catch and absorb the oil.

27. Remove the 3 distributor case-to-cylinder head bolts and the distributor case.

28. Loosen all valve adjusting screw locknuts. Loosen all valve adjusting screws until all rocker arms move freely.

NOTE: Always loosen the camshaft carrier bolts gradually in sequence, in order to relieve tension on the camshaft; if the camshaft carrier bolts are removed at random, damage to the camshaft may occur.

29. Remove the 12 camshaft carrier cap-to-cylinder head bolts, the

camshaft carrier bolts, the camshaft seal and the camshaft.

NOTE: Loosen the cylinder head bolts gradually in sequence, in order to prevent cylinder head distortion.

30. Remove the 10 cylinder head-to-block bolts, the cylinder head and gasket.

31. Clean and inspect all of the gasket mating surfaces. Inspect and/or replace any damaged parts.

To install:

32. Install a new cylinder head gasket and the cylinder head with the distributor case onto the cylinder block. Torque the cylinder head bolts in sequence, as follows:

    Step 1: 26 ft. lbs. (35 Nm)
    Step 2: 41 ft. lbs. (55 Nm)
    Step 3: 52 ft. lbs. (70 Nm)

33. Lubricate the camshaft with clean oil. Apply RTV silicone rubber sealant to the bottom of the No. 6 camshaft carrier cap.

34. Install the camshaft and camshaft carrier caps onto the cylinder head, then, torque the camshaft carrier cap-to-cylinder head bolts to 89 inch lbs. (10 Nm).

NOTE: Always tighten the camshaft carrier cap bolts gradually in sequence; if the camshaft carrier cap bolts are tightened at random. damage to the camshaft may occur.

35. Lubricate the new camshaft seal lip with clean engine oil. Install the new camshaft seal into the cylinder head until it is flush with the camshaft carrier surface. Adjust the valve lash.

36. Adjust the valve lash.

37. Apply RTV silicone rubber sealant to the surface of the distributor case that mates with the rear of the rocker arm shaft.

38. Install the distributor case onto the cylinder head and torque the distributor case-to-cylinder head bolts to 89 inch lbs. (10 Nm).

39. Install a new cylinder head cover gasket and 4 O-rings to the cylinder head cover. Install the cylinder head cover and torque the 6 bolts to 89 inch lbs. (10 Nm).

40. Install the distributor into the distributor case. Install the A/C mounting bracket with compressor and torque the 2 mounting bracket-to-cylinder head bolts to 89 inch lbs. (10 Nm).

41. Install the inner timing belt cover and torque the 2 bolts inner

timing belt cover-to-cylinder head bolts to 89 inch lbs. (10 Nm).

NOTE: During camshaft timing belt gear installation, align the camshaft dwell pin with the slot in the camshaft timing belt gear designated as "E".

42. Install the camshaft sprocket, using holding tool J-41840 or equivalent, onto the camshaft and torque the camshaft sprocket-to-camshaft bolt to 44 ft. lbs. (60 Nm).

43. Install the timing belt tensioner plate and tensioner; secure with timing belt tensioner stud and bolt only finger-tight. Push the timing belt tensioner plate up when installing the timing belt.

NOTE: When installing the timing belt, the directional arrows on the timing belt must be matched with the rotation of the crankshaft; if not, excessive wear and timing belt failure may occur.

44. Install the timing belt by performing the following procedures:
   a. Align the timing marks of the camshaft sprocket with the cylinder head cover and the oil pump housing with the crankshaft sprocket.
   b. Install the timing belt onto the camshaft and crankshaft sprockets.
   c. Rotate the crankshaft through 2 complete revolutions, to remove any slack from the timing belt and to properly seat the timing belt.
   d. Inspect both sets of timing marks to ensure that they are aligned. Install the belt tensioner spring to the timing belt tensioner plate.
   e. Torque the timing belt tensioner stud to 89 inch lbs. (10 Nm) and the bolt to 18 ft. lbs. (25 Nm).

45. Install the timing belt cover and torque the nut/bolts to 89 inch lbs. (10 Nm). Connect the oil pressure sending unit wire to the timing belt cover.

46. Install the crankshaft pulley to the crankshaft and torque the bolts to 12 ft. lbs. (16 Nm). Install the radiator shroud and torque both bolts to 89 inch lbs. (10 Nm).

47. If equipped, carefully, position the A/C suction line and brackets to the right side of the radiator core support and torque both bolts to 89 inch lbs. (10 Nm).

48. Raise and safely support the vehicle. Install the 2 lower radiator

shroud bolts and torque to 89 inch lbs. (10 Nm). If equipped, install the front skid plate and torque the 4 bolts to 40 ft. lbs. (54 Nm). Lower the vehicle.

49. Install the water pump pulley and fan; torque the 4 nuts to 97 inch lbs. (11 Nm). Install the generator/water pump drive belt onto the pulleys. Install the A/C compressor, if equipped, and the power steering drive belt.

50. Using new gaskets, install the exhaust manifold and torque the exhaust manifold-to-cylinder head nuts to 17 ft. lbs. (23 Nm). Raise and safely support the vehicle.

51. Using new gaskets, connect the front pipe/TWC assembly to the exhaust manifold and torque the 3 bolts to 37 ft. lbs. (50 Nm). Install the lower exhaust manifold heat shield and torque both bolts to 89 inch lbs. (10 Nm). Install the exhaust manifold bracket; torque the engine mount-to-exhaust bracket bolts to 40 ft. lbs. (54 Nm) and the exhaust bracket-to-exhaust manifold nut to 37 ft. lbs. (50 Nm). Lower the vehicle.

52. Install the upper exhaust manifold heat shield and torque the nuts/bolts to 89 inch lbs. (10 Nm). Install the air intake pipe bracket and torque the bracket-to-cylinder head bolts to 89 inch (10 Nm).

53. Using a new gasket, install the intake manifold, with intake surge tank and throttle body, and torque the intake manifold-to-cylinder head bolts, in sequence, to 17 ft. lbs. (23 Nm).

54. Install the lower intake manifold support bracket, the rear and the front intake manifold reinforcement bracket; torque the brackets-to-intake manifold bolts to 37 ft. lbs. (50 Nm).

55. Install the generator adjusting arm bracket and torque the bracket-to-intake manifold nut/bolt to 37 ft. lbs. (50 Nm).

56. Install the following hoses:
   Coolant bypass hose to the intake manifold.
   Upper radiator hose to the thermostat housing; secure with a clamp.
   PCV hose to the PCV valve.
   Fuel return hose to the fuel return line.
   Fuel feed hose at the fuel feed hose union.
   Coolant hoses to the fast idle air valve below the throttle body.
   IAC air hose to the IAC valve.
   Coolant hose to the IAC valve.

57. Install the following vacuum hoses:
   EGR valve modulator.
   EGR valve.
   Brake booster supply hose.
   Vacuum modulator supply hose, if equipped with an automatic transmission.
   EVAP SP valve.

58. Connect the following electrical connectors:
   Engine ground wire to intake surge tank.
   Fuel injectors.
   EGR solenoid vacuum valve.
   EGR temperature sensor, California vehicles.
   Evaporative Emission Solenoid Purge (EVAP SP).
   A/C ECT switch, if equipped with A/C.
   ECT sensor sending unit.
   Engine Coolant Temperature (ECT) sensor.
   Idle Air Control (IAC).
   Throttle Position (TP) sensor.

59. Install the accelerator cable bracket to the throttle body and torque the nut/bolt to 17 ft. lbs. (23 Nm).

60. If equipped with an automatic transmission, connect the accelerator cable and kickdown cable to the throttle body bellcrank; adjust the cables.

61. Install the throttle cover to the intake manifold and torque the bolts to 11 ft. lbs. (15 Nm). Refill the cooling system, as necessary.

62. Install the air intake pipe to the throttle body hose and the ACL intake hose. Connect the negative battery cable.

Valve Lash

ADJUSTMENT

Valve lash can be adjusted with the engine hot or cold. Specifications are provided for both adjustments.

1. Disconnect the negative battery cable. Remove the air intake case.

2. Remove the cylinder head cover assembly.

3. Turn the crankshaft clockwise so the **V** mark on the crankshaft pulley is aligned with the **0** mark on the timing belt cover.

4. Remove the distributor cap and confirm that the rotor is facing the No. 1 firing position. If the rotor is out of place, turn the crankshaft 360 degrees.

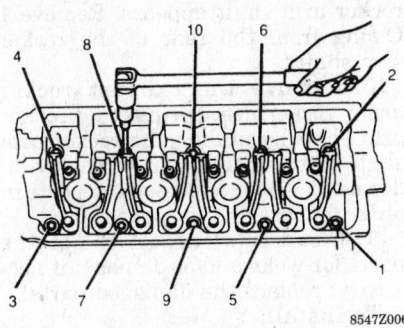

Cylinder head and bolt loosening sequence — Multiport Fuel Injection (MFI)

5. With the engine in this position, check the valve lash at valves 1, 2, 5 and 7. Clearance should be:

EFI engine
Cold
      Intake 0.0051–0.0067 in. (0.13–0.17mm)
      Exhaust 0.0063–0.0075 in. (0.15–0.19mm)
Hot
      Intake 0.009–0.011 in. (0.23–0.27mm)
      Exhaust 0.0102–0.0114 in. (0.25–0.29mm)
MFI engine
Cold
      Intake 0.005–0.007 in. (0.13–0.17mm)
      Exhaust 0.0053–0.007 in. (0.13–0.17mm)
Hot
      Intake 0.007–0.008 in. (0.17–0.21mm)
      Exhaust 0.007–0.008 in. (0.17–0.21mm)

NOTE: **The valves are adjusted by loosening the locknut on the valve adjuster and turning the adjusting screw to obtain the proper clearance. Once the proper clearance is obtained, the locknut must be torqued to 11–13**

ft. lbs. while holding the adjusting screw. Check the clearance after the locknut is torqued.

6. Rotate the crankshaft 360 degrees and check the valve lash at valves 3, 4, 6 and 8.

7. After adjusting and checking all the valves, install the cylinder head cover, distributor cover and intake hose. Connect the negative battery cable.

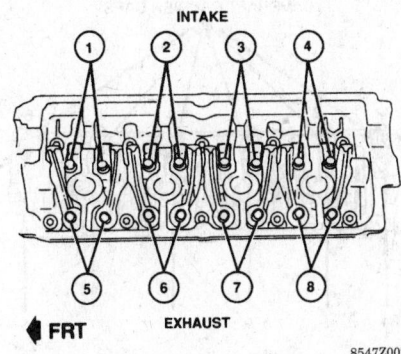

Valve lash adjustment — MFI engine

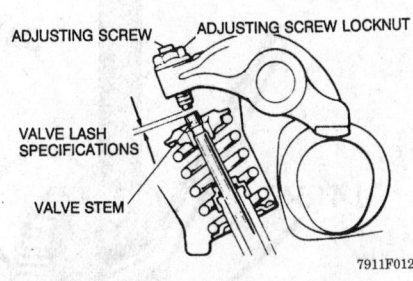

Valve lash adjustment screw and locknut — Electronic Fuel Injection (EFI)

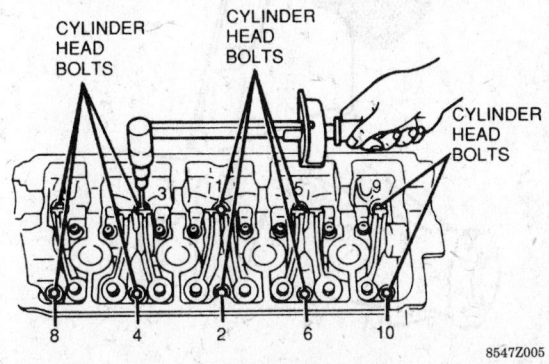

Cylinder head and bolt tightening sequence — Multiport Fuel Injection (MFI)

Rocker Arms/Shafts

REMOVAL AND INSTALLATION

EFI Engine

NOTE: **The rocker arm shafts are not identical and must be kept in the proper order for installation. If the shafts get mixed up before installation, the intake rocker shaft has a 14mm stepped end and the exhaust rocker shaft has a 13mm stepped end. The stepped end of the intake rocker shaft faces the front of the engine and the stepped end of the exhaust rocker shaft faces the rear of the engine.**

1. Disconnect the negative battery cable. Drain the cooling system.
2. Remove the front grille for Sidekick.
3. Remove the radiator cooling fan and fan shroud. Properly discharge the air conditioning system and remove the air conditioning flexible suction hose, if equipped.
4. Remove the radiator for Sidekick.
5. Remove the water pump drive belt and the water pump pulley.
6. Remove the timing belt outside cover, timing belt and the tensioner.
7. Disconnect the air intake case and remove the cylinder head cover.
8. Remove the camshaft timing belt pulley and timing belt inside cover. Insert the proper size rod into the hole in the camshaft to lock the camshaft and loosen the pulley nut.
9. Loosen all the valve lash adjusting screw locknuts and turn the adjusting screws out all the way.
10. Remove the rocker arm shaft screws.
11. Remove the intake and exhaust rocker arm shafts, rocker arms and springs.
12. Keep all the valve train parts in the order that they were removed.
To install:
13. Apply engine oil to the rocker arms, springs and shafts. Install the shafts in the correct direction, into the cylinder head by placing the rocker arms and springs on the shafts as they are installed. With the rocker arms, springs and shafts installed, torque the rocker shaft mounting screws to 7.0–8.5 ft. lbs.
14. Install the timing belt pulley and inside cover by locking the camshaft with the proper size rod.
15. With the camshaft locked, tighten the camshaft pulley bolt to 41–46 ft. lbs.

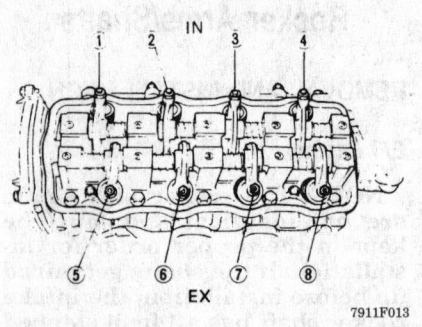

Valve adjustment sequence — Electronic Fuel Injection (EFI)

16. The remainder of the installation is the reverse of the removal procedure.

MFI Engine

1. Disconnect the negative battery cable. Remove the front grille-to-radiator core support 3 screws and 2 clips and the grille. Remove the door latch-to-header panel bolts and the latch.

2. Disconnect the 2 electrical connectors from the horn. Remove the 12 header panel bolts and the panel from the vehicle.

3. Remove the radiator core support. Remove the timing belt from the engine.

4. Using the camshaft sprocket holding tool J-41840 or equivalent, to hold the sprocket stationary, remove the camshaft sprocket-to-camshaft bolt.

5. Remove the cylinder head cover. Remove the distributor case from the cylinder head.

6. Loosen all of the valve adjusting screw locknuts. Loosen all valve adjusting screws until the rocker arms move freely.

NOTE: Always remove the camshaft carrier bolts gradually, in sequence, in order to relieve tension on the camshaft; if the

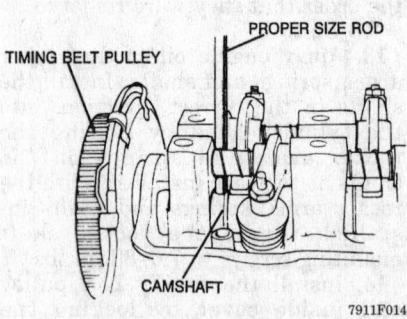

Locking the camshaft in position — EFI Engine

bolts are removed at random, damage may occur to the camshaft.

7. Gradually, remove the 12 camshaft carrier cap bolts, in sequence. Remove the camshaft carrier, the camshaft seal and the camshaft from the cylinder head.

8. Remove the timing belt inner cover-to-cylinder head bolts and the cover. Remove all intake rocker arms with clips from the rocker arm shaft.

9. Remove the 6 rocker arm shaft-to-cylinder head bolts. Push the rocker arm shaft through the rear of the cylinder head until the end of the

CAMSHAFT CARRIER CAPS

12 2 10 4 8 6

11 1 9 3 7 5

8547Z009

Removing camshaft carrier bolts — MFI engine

rocker arm shaft appears. Remove 1 O-ring from the rear of the rocker arm shaft.

10. Remove the exhaust rocker arms, rocker arm springs and rocker arm shaft by pulling the rocker arm shaft through the front of the cylinder head. Be sure to keep the parts in order for installation purposes.

11. Clean and inspect all of the parts for wear and/or damage; if necessary, replace the damaged parts.

To install:

12. Lubricate all of the parts with clean engine oil before installation.

13. Position the rocker arm shaft into the front of the cylinder head; install the rocker arms and springs as the rocker arm shaft is being installed into the cylinder head.

14. Push the rocker arm shaft through the rear of the cylinder head. Install a new O-ring onto the rocker arm shaft. Rotate the rocker arm shaft so the flat machined surface is horizontal and facing downward, parallel with the cylinder head mating surface and slide the shaft back into the cylinder head.

15. Install the 6 rocker arm shaft bolts and torque the rocker arm-to-cylinder head bolts to 89 inch lbs. (10 Nm). Fill the rocker arm shaft bolt holes with clean engine oil.

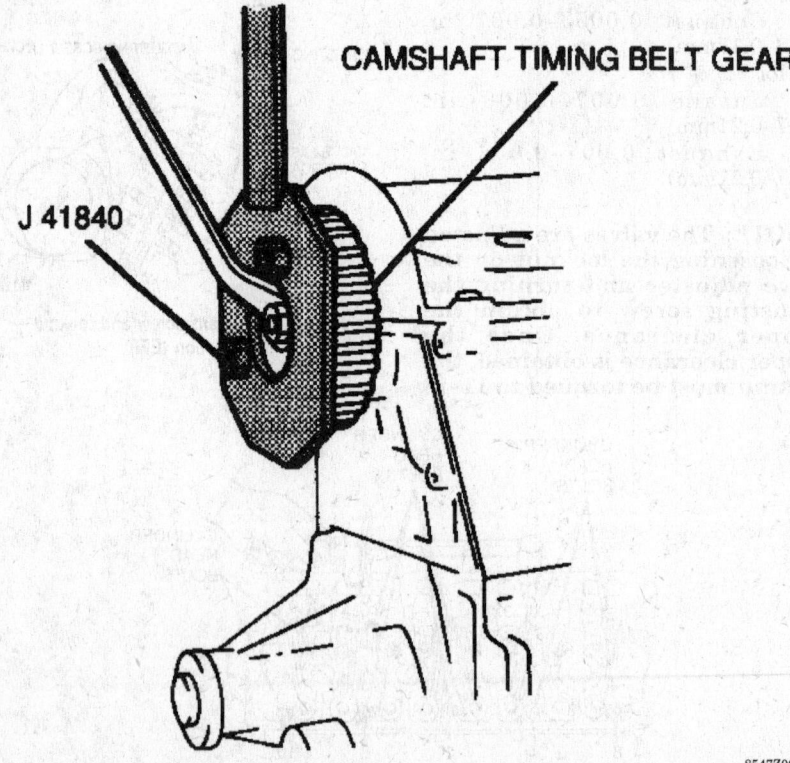

Locking the camshaft in position — MFI engine

16. Install the intake rocker arms with clips onto the rocker arm shaft.

NOTE: The camshaft carrier caps are embossed with numbers and arrows to ensure correct assembly. The No. 1 camshaft carrier cap must be installed at the front of the cylinder head with the remaining carrier caps following in numerical order. The directional arrows must always point toward the front of the cylinder head.

17. Lubricate the camshaft with clean engine oil. Apply RTV silicone sealant to the bottom of the No. 6 camshaft carrier cap. Install the camshaft and camshaft carrier caps onto the cylinder head and gradually, torque the 12 bolts, in sequence, to 89 inch lbs. (10 Nm); if the bolts are tightened at random, damage to the camshaft may occur.

18. Lubricate the new camshaft seal lip with clean engine oil and install it into the cylinder head until it is flush with the camshaft carrier surface.

19. Install the timing belt inner cover and torque the cover-to-cylinder head bolts to 89 inch lbs. (10 Nm). Install the rocker arm shaft plug into the cylinder head and torque to 24 ft. lbs. (33 Nm).

NOTE: During camshaft timing belt gear installation, align the camshaft dwell pin with the slot in the camshaft timing belt gear designated as "E".

20. Install the camshaft sprocket, using holding tool J-41840 or equivalent, onto the camshaft and torque the camshaft sprocket-to-camshaft bolt to 44 ft. lbs. (60 Nm).

21. Push the timing belt tensioner plate up when installing the timing belt.

NOTE: When installing the timing belt, the directional arrows on the timing belt must be

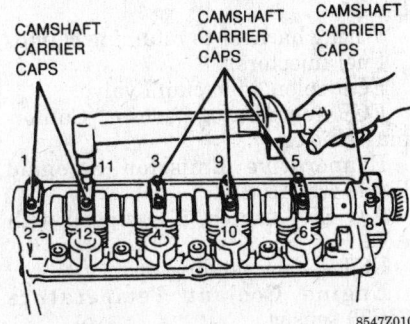

CAMSHAFT CARRIER CAPS   CAMSHAFT CARRIER CAPS   CAMSHAFT CARRIER CAPS

8547Z010

Torquing camshaft carrier bolts — MFI engine

matched with the rotation of the crankshaft; if not, excessive wear and timing belt failure may occur.

22. Install the timing belt by performing the following procedures:

   a. Align the timing marks of the camshaft sprocket with the cylinder head cover and the oil pump housing with the crankshaft sprocket.

   b. Install the timing belt onto the camshaft and crankshaft sprockets.

   c. Rotate the crankshaft through 2 complete revolutions, to remove any slack from the timing belt and to properly seat the timing belt.

   d. Inspect both sets of timing marks to ensure that they are aligned. Install the belt tensioner spring to the timing belt tensioner plate.

   e. Torque the timing belt tensioner stud to 89 inch lbs. (10 Nm) and the bolt to 18 ft. lbs. (25 Nm).

23. Install the timing belt cover and torque the nut/bolts to 89 inch lbs. (10 Nm). Connect the oil pressure sending unit wire to the timing belt cover.

24. Apply RTV silicone rubber sealant to the surface of the distributor case that mates with the rear of the rocker arm shaft. Install the distributor case and torque the 3 case-to-cylinder head bolts to 89 inch lbs. (10 Nm).

25. Install the distributor into the distributor case. Adjust the valve lash.

26. Install the cylinder head cover onto the cylinder head. Install the radiator into the radiator core support.

27. Install the header panel and torque the 12 bolts to 89 inch lbs. (10 Nm). Connect the 2 electrical connectors to the horn.

28. Install the hood latch to the header panel and torque both bolts to 89 inch lbs. (10 Nm).

29. Install the front grille to the radiator core support. Connect the negative battery cable. Refill the cooling system. Start the engine, allow it to reach normal operating temperatures and check for leaks.

Intake Manifold

REMOVAL AND INSTALLATION

Electronic Fuel Injection (EFI)

   1. Disconnect the negative battery cable. Drain the cooling system.

   2. Remove the air intake case from the manifold.

   3. Disconnect the accelerator cable and the automatic transmission kickdown cable, if equipped.

   4. Disconnect the injector, throttle position sensor and idle speed control solenoid valve wires at their couplers, if equipped.

   5. Disconnect the vacuum hoses from the throttle body and throttle opener. Remove the water hose from the air valve, if equipped.

   6. Remove the fuel filler cap to release the fuel pressure in the fuel tank. Reinstall the cap.

   7. Release the fuel pressure in the fuel line.

   8. Disconnect the fuel line from the throttle body and intake manifold.

   9. Remove the fuel return hose.

10. Disconnect the throttle body from the intake manifold and remove the PCV hose from the cylinder head cover.

11. Disconnect the pressure sensor hose from the fuel filter, if equipped, and remove the brake booster hose from the intake manifold.

12. Disconnect the vacuum hose for the automatic transmission from the intake manifold, if equipped.

13. Remove the VSV (for throttle opener) hose from the intake manifold.

14. Disconnect the water hose from the thermostat cap. Remove the heater inlet and water bypass hose from the intake manifold.

15. Disconnect the hoses at the EGR valve and remove the ground wire from the intake manifold.

16. Disconnect the wire couplers from the air temperature sensor, water temperature sensor, water temperature gauge and PTC heater, if equipped with automatic transmission.

17. Disconnect the wire harnesses from their clamps.

18. Remove the intake manifold mounting bolts and remove the intake manifold from the cylinder head.

19. Remove the PCV valve, EGR valve, fuel filter, thermostat from the intake manifold.

20. Clean and inspect the sealing surfaces of the intake manifold and the cylinder head.

   To install:

21. Install the thermostat, fuel filter, EGR valve and PCV valve to the intake manifold.

22. Using a new gasket, install the intake manifold and tighten the mounting bolts to 13–20 ft. lbs.

23. Reconnect the wiring harnesses to their clamps and fasten the wire couplers to the air temperature sensor, water temperature sensor, water temperature gauge and PTC heater, if equipped with automatic transmission.

24. Reconnect the ground wire to the intake manifold and replace the hoses at the EGR valve.

25. Install the water heater inlet and bypass hose to the intake manifold. Install the water hose to the thermostat cap.

26. Install the VSV (for throttle opener) hose to the intake manifold.

27. Connect the automatic transmission vacuum hose to the intake manifold, if equipped.

28. Install the brake booster hose to the intake manifold and connect the pressure sensor to the fuel filter, if equipped.

29. Reconnect the fuel line to the throttle body.

30. Install the water hose to the air valve. Connect the vacuum hoses to the throttle body and throttle opener, if equipped.

31. Reconnect the injector, throttle position sensor and idle speed control wires to their couplers, if equipped.

32. Connect the accelerator cable and the automatic transmission kickdown cable, if equipped, to the throttle body.

33. Install the air intake case to the manifold.

34. Refill the cooling system with the proper coolant. Connect the negative battery cable.

35. Check for vacuum, water and oil leaks when finished.

Multiport Fuel Injection (MFI)

1. Disconnect the negative battery cable. Release the fuel pressure. Remove the fuel filler cap to release the pressure in the tank, then replace the fuel filler cap.

2. Drain the cooling system. Disconnect the air intake pipe from the ACL intake hose and throttle hose.

3. Remove the throttle cover-to-intake manifold bolts and the cover.

4. If equipped with an automatic transmission, disconnect the accelerator and kickdown cables from the throttle body bellcrank.

5. Remove 1 bolt, nut, screw and accelerator cable bracket from the throttle body.

6. Disconnect the electrical connectors from the following items:

Throttle Position (TP) sensor
Idle Air Control (IAC) valve
Engine Coolant Temperature (ECT) sensor

ECT sending unit
A/C ECT switch (if equipped with A/C)
Evaporative Emissions Solenoid Purge (EVAP SP) valve
Exhaust Gas Recirculation (EGR) temperature sensor (Calif. vehicles)
EGR solenoid vacuum valve
Fuel injectors
Wiring harness from retaining clamps
Engine ground wire from intake surge tank

7. Disconnect the following vacuum hoses:

EVAP SP valve
Vacuum modulator supply hose (if equipped with automatic transmission)
Brake booster supply hose
EGR valve
EGR valve modulator

8. Disconnect the coolant hose from the IAC valve and the IAC hose from the IAC valve. Disconnect the coolant hoses from the fast idle air valve below the throttle body.

9. Disconnect the fuel feed hose at the fuel feed hose union and the fuel feed hose from the fuel return line. Disconnect the PCV hose from the PCV valve.

10. Loosen the upper radiator hose clamp at the thermostat housing. Disconnect the upper radiator hose from the thermostat housing. Disconnect the coolant bypass hose from the intake manifold.

11. Remove the generator adjusting arm bracket from the intake manifold. Remove the front and rear intake manifold reinforcement brackets from the intake manifold.

12. Remove the lower intake manifold support bracket from the intake manifold. Remove the intake manifold-to-cylinder head nuts/bolts, then remove the intake manifold, the intake surge tank and the throttle body from the cylinder head.

13. Remove the following items from the intake manifold, if necessary:

PCV valve
EGR valve
ECT sensor
ECT sensor sending unit
A/C ECT switch, if equipped with A/C
EGR temperature sensor, for California vehicles

14. Clean and inspect all of the gasket mating surfaces. Inspect and/or replace any damaged parts.

To install:

15. Install the following items onto the intake manifold, if removed:

PCV valve
EGR valve
ECT sensor
ECT sensor sending unit
A/C ECT switch, if equipped with A/C
EGR temperature sensor, for California vehicles

16. Using a new gasket, install the intake manifold, with intake surge tank and throttle body, and torque the intake manifold-to-cylinder head bolts, in sequence, to 17 ft. lbs. (23 Nm).

17. Install the lower intake manifold support bracket, the rear and the front intake manifold reinforcement bracket; torque the brackets-to-intake manifold bolts to 37 ft. lbs. (50 Nm).

18. Install the generator adjusting arm bracket and torque the bracket-to-intake manifold nut/bolt to 37 ft. lbs. (50 Nm).

19. Install the following hoses:

Coolant bypass hose to the intake manifold.
Upper radiator hose to the thermostat housing; secure with a clamp.
PCV hose to the PCV valve.
Fuel return hose to the fuel return line.
Fuel feed hose at the fuel feed hose union.
Coolant hoses to the fast idle air valve below the throttle body.
IAC air hose to the IAC valve.
Coolant hose to the IAC valve.

20. Install the following vacuum hoses:

EGR valve modulator.
EGR valve.
Brake booster supply hose.
Vacuum modulator supply hose, if equipped with an automatic transmission.
EVAP SP valve.

21. Connect the following electrical connectors:

Engine ground wire to intake surge tank.
Wiring harness to retaining clamps
Fuel injectors
EGR solenoid vacuum valve.
EGR temperature sensor, California vehicles.
Evaporative Emission Solenoid Purge (EVAP SP).
A/C ECT switch, if equipped with A/C.
ECT sensor sending unit.
Engine Coolant Temperature (ECT) sensor.
Idle Air Control (IAC) valve.
Throttle Position (TP) sensor.

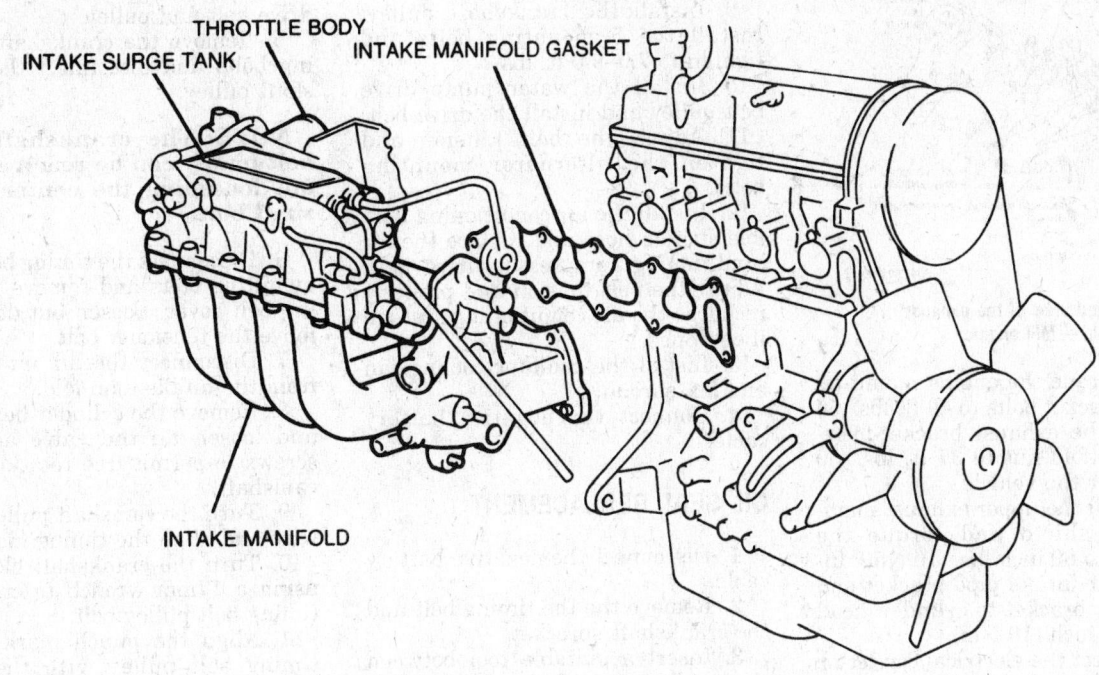

THROTTLE BODY

INTAKE SURGE TANK

INTAKE MANIFOLD GASKET

INTAKE MANIFOLD

8547Z011

Exploded view of the intake manifold — MFI engine

22. Install the accelerator cable bracket to the throttle body and torque the nut/bolt to 17 ft. lbs. (23 Nm).

23. If equipped with an automatic transmission, connect the accelerator cable and kickdown cable to the throttle body bellcrank; adjust the cables.

24. Install the throttle cover to the intake manifold and torque the bolts to 11 ft. lbs. (15 Nm). Refill the cooling system, as necessary.

25. Install the air intake pipe to the throttle body hose and the ACL intake hose. Connect the negative battery cable.

Exhaust Manifold

REMOVAL AND INSTALLATION

Electronic Fuel Injection (EFI)

1. Disconnect the negative cable.
2. Raise and safely support the vehicle.
3. Disconnect the exhaust pipe from the exhaust manifold and lower the vehicle.
4. Disconnect the oxygen sensor lead wire at the coupler and remove the air intake case bracket for 1.6L engine.

5. Disconnect the exhaust manifold upper and lower covers or heat shields from the exhaust manifold.
6. Remove the exhaust manifold mounting bolts and remove the exhaust manifold from the cylinder head.

To install:

7. Clean and inspect the sealing surfaces of the exhaust manifold and the cylinder head.
8. Using new gaskets, install the exhaust manifold to the cylinder head and tighten the mounting bolts to 13–20 ft. lbs.
9. The remainder of the installation is the reverse of the removal procedure.
10. Check for exhaust leaks when finished.

Multiport Fuel Injection (MFI)

1. Disconnect the negative battery cable.
2. Disconnect the air intake pipe from the ACL intake hose and throttle hose.
3. Disconnect the electrical connector from the Heated Oxygen Sensor (HO2S).
4. Remove the upper exhaust manifold heat shield from the exhaust manifold. Raise and safely support the vehicle.

5. Remove the exhaust manifold reinforcement bracket from the exhaust manifold and engine mount.
6. Remove the lower exhaust manifold heat shield from the exhaust manifold. Disconnect the Three-Way Catalytic converter (TWC) assembly from the exhaust manifold. Lower the vehicle.
7. Remove the exhaust manifold with gasket and engine hanger from the cylinder head.
8. Remove the Heated Oxygen Sensor (HO2S) from the exhaust manifold.
9. Clean and inspect all of the gasket mating surfaces. Inspect and/or replace any damaged parts.

To install:

10. Install the Heated Oxygen Sensor (HO2S) to the exhaust manifold and torque the sensor to 32 ft. lbs. (43 Nm).
11. Using new gaskets, install the exhaust manifold and torque the exhaust manifold-to-cylinder head nuts to 17 ft. lbs. (23 Nm). Raise and safely support the vehicle.
12. Using new gaskets, connect the front pipe/TWC assembly to the exhaust manifold and torque the 3 bolts to 37 ft. lbs. (50 Nm). Install the lower exhaust manifold heat shield and torque both bolts to 89 inch lbs. (10 Nm). Install the exhaust manifold

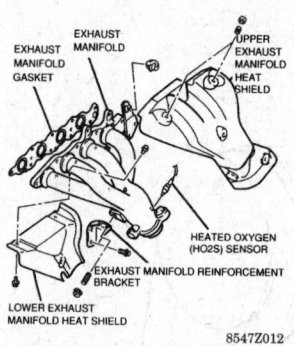

EXHAUST MANIFOLD
EXHAUST MANIFOLD GASKET
UPPER EXHAUST MANIFOLD HEAT SHIELD
HEATED OXYGEN (HO2S) SENSOR
EXHAUST MANIFOLD REINFORCEMENT BRACKET
LOWER EXHAUST MANIFOLD HEAT SHIELD

8547Z012

Exploded view of the exhaust manifold — MFI engine

bracket; torque the engine mount-to-exhaust bracket bolts to 40 ft. lbs. (54 Nm) and the exhaust bracket-to-exhaust manifold nut to 37 ft. lbs. (50 Nm). Lower the vehicle.

13. Install the upper exhaust manifold heat shield and torque the nuts/bolts to 89 inch lbs. (10 Nm). Install the air intake pipe bracket and torque the bracket-to-cylinder head bolts to 89 inch (10 Nm).

14. Connect the electrical connector to the Heated Oxygen Sensor (HO2S).

15. Install the air intake pipe to the throttle body hose and the ACL intake hose. Connect the negative battery cable.

Timing Belt Front Cover

REMOVAL AND INSTALLATION

1. Disconnect the negative battery cable.
2. Remove the radiator cooling fan and fan shroud.
3. If equipped, disconnect the air conditioning compressor drive belt, properly discharge the air conditioning system and remove the air conditioning compressor flexible suction hose.
4. Loosen the alternator mounting bolts and remove the water pump drive belt and pulley.
5. Remove the crankshaft mounting bolts and remove the crankshaft pulley.

NOTE: The crankshaft drive belt pulley can be removed without loosening the center crankshaft bolt.

6. Disconnect the timing belt cover mounting bolts and remove the timing belt cover.
To install:
7. Clean and inspect all mounting surfaces.

8. Install the timing belt cover and tighten the bolts to 7.0–9.0 ft. lbs.
9. Install the crankshaft pulley. Install the 5 mounting bolts and tighten to 7.0–9.0 ft. lbs.
10. Install the water pump drive belt pulley and install the drive belt.
11. Adjust the belt tension and tighten the alternator mounting bolts.
12. Install the air conditioning flexible suction hose and replace the air conditioning compressor drive belt. Adjust the belt tension and properly recharge the air conditioning system, if equipped.
13. Install the radiator cooling fan and fan shroud.
14. Connect the negative battery cable.

OIL SEAL REPLACEMENT

1. Disconnect the negative battery cable.
2. Remove the the timing belt and the crankshaft sprocket.
3. Insert a suitable tool between the crankshaft and the oil seal and pull the seal outwards to remove it.

NOTE: Use care when removing or installing the oil seal, not to damage the crankshaft or the oil pump sealing surfaces.

4. Clean and inspect the surfaces of the crankshaft and the oil pump assembly.
5. Install the crankshaft sleeve, using the proper tool, onto the crankshaft.
6. Install the new seal over the crankshaft and into the oil pump, making sure the oil seal lip is not upturned.
7. Install the crankshaft sprocket and the timing belt. Check the timing.
8. Connect the negative battery cable.

Timing Belt and Tensioner

ADJUSTMENT

Electronic Fuel Injection (EFI)

1. Disconnect the negative battery cable.
2. Remove the radiator cooling fan and fan shroud.
3. If equipped, disconnect the air conditioning compressor drive belt, properly discharge the air conditioning system and remove the air conditioning compressor flexible suction hose.

4. Loosen the alternator mounting bolts and remove the water pump drive belt and pulley.
5. Remove the crankshaft mounting bolts and disconnect the crankshaft pulley.

NOTE: The crankshaft drive belt pulley can be removed without loosening the center crankshaft bolt.

6. Disconnect the timing belt cover mounting bolts and remove the timing belt cover. Loosen but do not remove the tensioner bolt.
7. Disconnect the air intake case from the intake manifold.
8. Remove the cylinder head cover and loosen all the valve adjusting screws to permit free rotation of the camshaft.
9. Turn the camshaft pulley clockwise and align the timing marks.
10. Turn the crankshaft clockwise, using a 17mm wrench to crank the timing belt pulley bolt.
11. Align the punch mark on the timing belt pulley with the arrow mark on the oil pump.
12. With the 4 marks aligned, remove any slack from the drive side of the belt. Tighten the tensioner bolt to 17.5–21.5 ft. lbs.
13. To allow the belt to be free of any slack, turn the crankshaft clockwise 2 full rotations. Confirm that the 4 marks are aligned.
14. Install the timing cover and tighten the bolts to 7.0–8.5 ft. lbs.
15. Adjust the valve lash and install the cylinder head cover, using a new gasket.
16. Connect the air intake case to the throttle body.
17. Install the crankshaft pulley and install the 5 mounting bolts. Tighten to 7.0–8.5 ft. lbs.
18. Install the water pump pulley, water pump drive belt and tighten the alternator mounting bolts.
19. Install the air conditioning compressor flexible suction hose and the air compressor belt. Properly recharge the air conditioning system, if equipped.
20. Install the radiator cooling fan and fan shroud.
21. Connect the negative battery cable.
22. Properly recharge the air conditioning system, if equipped. Run the engine and check for any leaks.

Multiport Fuel Injection (MFI)

The Multiport Fuel Injection (MFI) is equipped with an automatic timing belt adjustment.

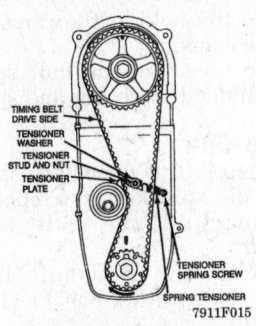

Exploded view of the timing belt and the tensioner assembly — Electronic Fuel Injection (EFI)

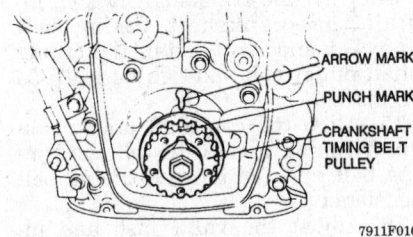

Timing marks on the crankshaft pulley — Electronic Fuel Injection (EFI)

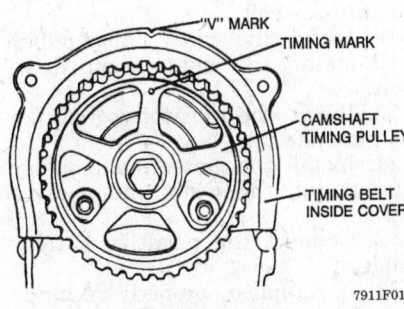

Timing marks on the camshaft pulley — Electronic Fuel Injection (EFI)

REMOVAL AND INSTALLATION

Electronic Fuel Injection (EFI)

1. Disconnect the negative battery cable.

2. Remove the radiator cooling fan and fan shroud.

3. If equipped, disconnect the air conditioning compressor drive belt, properly discharge the air conditioning system and remove the air condi-

tioning compressor flexible suction hose.

4. Loosen the alternator mounting bolts and remove the water pump drive belt and pulley.

5. Remove the crankshaft mounting bolts and disconnect the crankshaft pulley.

NOTE: The crankshaft drive belt pulley can be removed without loosening the center crankshaft bolt.

6. Disconnect the timing belt cover mounting bolts and remove the timing belt cover. Loosen but do not remove the tensioner bolt.

7. Disconnect the air intake case from the intake manifold.

8. Loosen the timing belt tensioner adjusting bolt and pivot nut. Hold pressure on the tensioner to loosen the timing belt and remove the timing belt from the camshaft and crankshaft pulleys.

9. Remove the timing belt tensioner, tensioner plate and tensioner spring.

To install:

10. Install the timing belt tensioner, plate and spring. Hand tighten the tensioner bolt and stud only at this time.

11. Remove the cylinder head cover and loosen all the valve adjusting screws to permit free rotation of the camshaft.

12. Turn the camshaft pulley clockwise and align the timing marks.

13. Turn the crankshaft clockwise, using a 17mm wrench to crank the timing belt pulley bolt.

14. Align the punch mark on the timing belt pulley with the arrow mark on the oil pump.

15. With the 4 marks aligned, remove any slack from the drive side of the belt. Tighten the tensioner bolt to 17.5–21.5 ft. lbs.

16. To allow the belt to be free of any slack, turn the crankshaft clockwise 2 full rotations. Confirm that the 4 marks are aligned.

17. Install the timing cover and tighten the bolts to 7.0–8.5 ft. lbs.

18. Adjust the valve lash and install the cylinder head cover, using a new gasket.

19. Connect the air intake case to the intake manifold.

20. Install the crankshaft pulley and install the mounting bolts. Tighten to 7.0–8.5 ft. lbs.

21. Install the water pump pulley, water pump drive belt and tighten the alternator mounting bolts.

22. If equipped, install the air conditioning compressor flexible suction hose and install the air conditioning compressor belt.

23. Install the radiator cooling fan and fan shroud.

24. Connect the negative battery cable.

25. If equipped, properly recharge the air conditioning system. Run the engine and check for any leaks.

Multiport Fuel Injection (MFI)

1. Disconnect the negative battery cable.

2. Loosen the upper radiator hose clamp at the thermostat housing. Disconnect the upper radiator hose from the thermostat housing. Disconnect the coolant bypass hose from the intake manifold.

3. Remove the generator adjusting arm bracket from the intake manifold.

4. If equipped, loosen the upper and lower A/C compressor mounting bolts. Loosen the upper and lower power steering pump mounting bolts. Remove the A/C compressor, If equipped, and/or the power steering drive belt.

5. Loosen the upper and lower generator mounting bolts. Remove the generator/water pump drive belt from the pulleys. Remove the cooling fan and the water pump pulley from the water pump.

6. Raise and safely support the vehicle. If equipped, remove the skid plate from the undercarriage. Remove the 2 lower radiator shroud bolts and lower the vehicle.

7. If equipped, remove the 2 A/C suction line bracket bolts at the right side of the radiator core support and carefully reposition the suction line for radiator shroud removal access.

8. Remove the 2 upper radiator shroud bolts and the shroud from the radiator.

NOTE: If the shroud is difficult to remove, drain the cooling system and disconnect the upper radiator hose from the radiator to gain access. If is not necessary to remove the crankshaft center bolt when removing the crankshaft pulley.

9. Remove the 5 crankshaft pulley-to-crankshaft bolts and the pulley. Remove the oil pressure sending unit wire conduit from the timing belt cover.

10. Remove the timing belt cover from the engine.

NOTE: There are 2 sets of timing marks which must be aligned to ensure correct engine timing upon installation. A notch in the camshaft timing belt gear designated as "E" must be aligned with the notch in the cylinder head. A punch mark on the crankshaft timing belt gear should align with the arrow in the oil pump casting. Make sure to align both sets of marks prior to timing belt removal.

11. Rotate the engine to align the timing marks on the cylinder head cover and camshaft timing belt gear; this should align the timing marks on the oil pump casting and crankshaft timing belt gear.

12. Loosen the timing belt tensioner bolt. Remove the timing belt tensioner spring from the timing belt tensioner plate.

13. Remove the timing belt from the camshaft and crankshaft timing belt gears.

14. Inspect and/or replace any damaged parts.

To install:

NOTE: When installing the timing belt, the directional arrows on the timing belt must be matched with the rotation of the crankshaft; if not, excessive wear and timing belt failure may occur.

15. Align the timing marks of the camshaft sprocket with the cylinder head cover and the oil pump housing with the crankshaft sprocket.

16. Install the timing belt onto the camshaft and crankshaft sprockets.

17. Rotate the crankshaft through 2 complete revolutions, to remove any slack from the timing belt and to properly seat the timing belt.

18. Inspect both sets of timing marks to ensure that they are aligned. Install the belt tensioner spring to the timing belt tensioner plate.

19. Torque the timing belt tensioner stud to 89 inch lbs. (10 Nm) and the bolt to 18 ft. lbs. (25 Nm).

20. Install the timing belt cover and torque the nut/bolts to 89 inch lbs. (10 Nm). Connect the oil pressure sending unit wire to the timing belt cover.

21. Install the crankshaft pulley to the crankshaft and torque the bolts to 12 ft. lbs. (16 Nm). Install the radiator shroud and torque both bolts to 89 inch lbs. (10 Nm).

22. If equipped, carefully, position the A/C suction line and brackets to the right side of the radiator core support and torque both bolts to 89 inch lbs. (10 Nm).

23. Raise and safely support the vehicle. Install the 2 lower radiator shroud bolts and torque to 89 inch lbs. (10 Nm). If equipped, install the front skid plate and torque the 4 bolts to 40 ft. lbs. (54 Nm). Lower the vehicle.

24. Install the water pump pulley and fan; torque the 4 nuts to 97 inch lbs. (11 Nm). Install the generator/water pump drive belt onto the pulleys. Install the A/C compressor, if equipped, and the power steering drive belt.

25. Install the generator adjusting arm bracket and torque the bracket-to-intake manifold nut/bolt to 37 ft. lbs. (50 Nm).

26. Refill the cooling system, as necessary.

27. Connect the negative battery cable.

Timing Sprockets

REMOVAL AND INSTALLATION

Electronic Fuel Injection (EFI)

1. Disconnect the negative battery cable.

2. Remove the radiator cooling fan/clutch and fan shroud.

3. If equipped, disconnect the air conditioning compressor drive belt, properly discharge the air conditioning system and remove the air conditioning compressor flexible suction hose.

4. Loosen the alternator mounting bolts and remove the water pump drive belt and pulley.

5. Remove the crankshaft mounting bolts and disconnect the crankshaft pulley.

NOTE: The crankshaft drive belt pulley can be removed without loosening the center crankshaft bolt.

6. Disconnect the timing belt cover mounting bolts and remove the timing belt cover. Loosen, but do not remove the tensioner bolt.

7. Disconnect the air intake case from the throttle body.

8. Remove the cylinder head cover and loosen all the valve adjusting screws to permit rotation of the camshaft.

9. Remove the camshaft timing belt pulley by inserting a proper size

rod into the hole in the camshaft to lock the camshaft.

10. Remove the camshaft sprocket mounting bolt, sprocket and sprocket pin.

To install:

11. Install the camshaft sprocket pin in the sprocket and replace the sprocket and the bolt on the camshaft.

12. With the camshaft locked, tighten the sprocket bolt to 41–46 ft. lbs.

13. Remove the crankshaft sprocket by using a gear stopper to hold the flywheel (driveplate for automatic transmission vehicles). Remove the crankshaft timing belt pulley bolt, sprocket and key.

14. With the crankshaft locked, install the crankshaft timing belt sprocket and key. Install the crankshaft pulley bolt and tighten to 47–54 ft. lbs.

15. Align the camshaft and crankshaft timing marks, install the timing belt and tighten the timing belt tensioner.

16. Adjust the valve lash and install the cylinder head cover.

17. Reconnect the air intake hose to the throttle body.

18. If equipped, install the air conditioning compressor flexible suction hose and install the air conditioning compressor belt.

19. Install the water pump pulley and install the water pump drive belt.

20. Install the radiator cooling fan and fan shroud.

21. Install the water pump pulley and install the water pump drive belt.

22. Connect the negative battery cable.

23. If equipped, properly recharge the air conditioning system. Run the engine and check for any leaks.

Multiport Fuel Injection (MFI)

1. Disconnect the negative battery cable.

2. Loosen the upper radiator hose clamp at the thermostat housing. Disconnect the upper radiator hose from the thermostat housing. Disconnect the coolant bypass hose from the intake manifold.

3. Remove the generator adjusting arm bracket from the intake manifold. Remove the front and rear intake manifold reinforcement brackets from the intake manifold.

4. Remove the lower intake manifold support bracket from the intake manifold. Remove the intake manifold-to-cylinder head nuts/bolts, then

remove the intake manifold, the intake surge tank and the throttle body from the cylinder head.

5. Remove the upper exhaust manifold heat shield from the exhaust manifold. Raise and safely support the vehicle.

6. Remove the exhaust manifold reinforcement bracket from the exhaust manifold and engine mount.

7. Remove the lower exhaust manifold heat shield from the exhaust manifold. Disconnect the Three-Way Catalytic converter (TWC) assembly from the exhaust manifold. Lower the vehicle.

8. Remove the exhaust manifold with gasket and engine hanger from the cylinder head.

9. If equipped, loosen the upper and lower A/C compressor mounting bolts. Loosen the upper and lower power steering pump mounting bolts. Remove the A/C compressor, If equipped, and/or the power steering drive belt.

10. Loosen the upper and lower generator mounting bolts. Remove the generator/water pump drive belt from the pulleys. Remove the cooling fan and the water pump pulley from the water pump.

11. Raise and safely support the vehicle. If equipped, remove the skid plate from the undercarriage. Remove the 2 lower radiator shroud bolts and lower the vehicle.

12. If equipped, remove the 2 A/C suction line bracket bolts at the right side of the radiator core support and carefully reposition the suction line for radiator shroud removal access.

13. Remove the 2 upper radiator shroud bolts and the shroud from the radiator.

NOTE: If the shroud is difficult to remove, drain the cooling system and disconnect the upper radiator hose from the radiator to gain access. If is not necessary to remove the crankshaft center bolt when removing the crankshaft pulley.

14. Remove the 5 crankshaft pulley-to-crankshaft bolts and the pulley. Remove the oil pressure sending unit wire conduit from the timing belt cover.

15. To remove the timing belt, perform the following procedure:

a. Remove the timing belt cover from the engine.

NOTE: There are 2 sets of timing marks which must be aligned to ensure correct engine timing upon installation. A notch in the

camshaft timing belt gear designated as "E" must be aligned with the notch in the cylinder head. A punch mark on the crankshaft timing belt gear should align with the arrow in the oil pump casting. Make sure to align both sets of marks prior to timing belt removal.

b. Rotate the engine to align the timing marks on the cylinder head cover and camshaft timing belt gear; this should align the timing marks on the oil pump casting and crankshaft timing belt gear.

c. Loosen the timing belt tensioner bolt. Remove the timing belt tensioner spring from the timing belt tensioner plate.

d. Remove the timing belt from the camshaft and crankshaft timing belt gears.

16. Secure the camshaft sprocket, using tool J-41840 or equivalent, then remove the camshaft sprocket-to-camshaft bolt and the camshaft sprocket.

NOTE: Do not turn the crankshaft and/or camshaft independently of one another once the timing belt has been removed. If the crankshaft or camshaft is turned independently, interference between the pistons and valves may occur causing component damage.

17. Remove the crankshaft sprocket-to-crankshaft bolt and the sprocket.

18. Clean and inspect all of the gasket mating surfaces. Inspect and/or replace any damaged parts.

To install:

19. Install the crankshaft sprocket onto the crankshaft and torque the bolt to 81 ft. lbs. (110 Nm).

NOTE: During camshaft timing belt gear installation, align the camshaft dwell pin with the slot in the camshaft timing belt gear designated as "E".

20. Install the camshaft sprocket, using holding tool J-41840 or equivalent, onto the camshaft and torque the camshaft sprocket-to-camshaft bolt to 44 ft. lbs. (60 Nm).

21. Install the timing belt tensioner plate and tensioner; secure with timing belt tensioner stud and bolt only finger-tight. Push the timing belt tensioner plate up when installing the timing belt.

NOTE: When installing the timing belt, the directional arrows on the timing belt must be

matched with the rotation of the crankshaft; if not, excessive wear and timing belt failure may occur.

22. Install the timing belt by performing the following procedures:

a. Align the timing marks of the camshaft sprocket with the cylinder head cover and the oil pump housing with the crankshaft sprocket.

b. Install the timing belt onto the camshaft and crankshaft sprockets.

c. Rotate the crankshaft through 2 complete revolutions, to remove any slack from the timing belt and to properly seat the timing belt.

d. Inspect both sets of timing marks to ensure that they are aligned. Install the belt tensioner spring to the timing belt tensioner plate.

e. Torque the timing belt tensioner stud to 89 inch lbs. (10 Nm) and the bolt to 18 ft. lbs. (25 Nm).

23. Install the timing belt cover and torque the nut/bolts to 89 inch lbs. (10 Nm). Connect the oil pressure sending unit wire to the timing belt cover.

24. Install the crankshaft pulley to the crankshaft and torque the bolts to 12 ft. lbs. (16 Nm). Install the radiator shroud and torque both bolts to 89 inch lbs. (10 Nm).

25. If equipped, carefully, position the A/C suction line and brackets to the right side of the radiator core support and torque both bolts to 89 inch lbs. (10 Nm).

26. Raise and safely support the vehicle. Install the 2 lower radiator shroud bolts and torque to 89 inch lbs. (10 Nm). If equipped, install the front skid plate and torque the 4 bolts to 40 ft. lbs. (54 Nm). Lower the vehicle.

27. Install the water pump pulley and fan; torque the 4 nuts to 97 inch lbs. (11 Nm). Install the generator/water pump drive belt onto the pulleys. Install the A/C compressor, if equipped, and the power steering drive belt.

28. Install the generator adjusting arm bracket and torque the bracket-to-intake manifold nut/bolt to 37 ft. lbs. (50 Nm).

29. Refill the cooling system, as necessary.

30. Connect the negative battery cable.

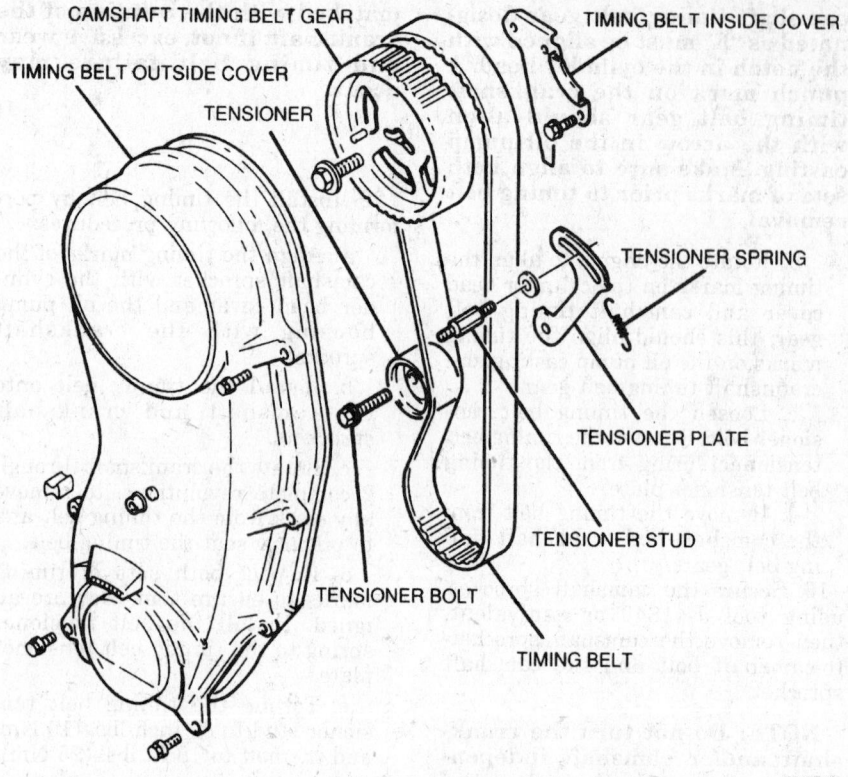

Timing belt, tensioner and timing belt cover — MFI engine

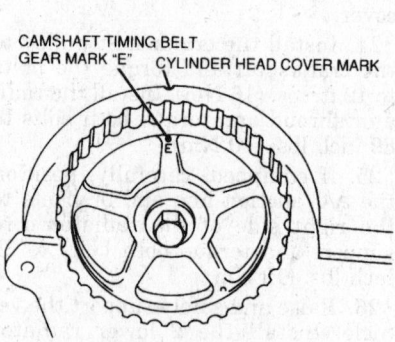

Camshaft and crankshaft timing belt sprocket timing marks — MFI engine

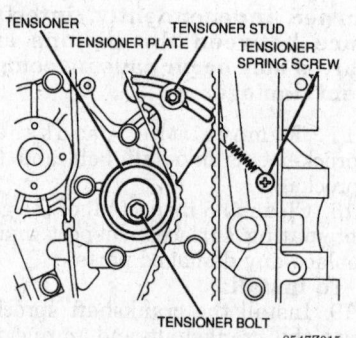

View of the timing belt tensioner assembly — MFI engine

Camshaft

REMOVAL AND INSTALLATION

Electronic Fuel Injection (EFI)

1. Disconnect the negative battery cable. Drain the cooling system.
2. Disconnect the air intake case.
3. Disconnect the brake booster hose from the intake manifold and the air valve water hose from the throttle body.
4. Disconnect the accelerator and the automatic transmission kickdown cable, if equipped, from the throttle body.

5. Disconnect and tag the throttle opener VSV and EGR VSV wires at the coupler.
6. Disconnect and tag the water temperature, oil pressure, air temperature sensor and ground cable wires at the intake manifold.
7. Disconnect and tag the injector, throttle position sensor and idle speed control solenoid valve wires at their couplers, if equipped.
8. Disconnect the PTC heater wires at the coupler, if equipped with automatic transmission.
9. Disconnect and tag the oxygen sensor and distributor wires at their couplers. Remove the coil wire.
10. Disconnect the ground wires from the distributor assembly.
11. Remove the fuel tank filler cap to relieve the pressure. Reinstall the cap.
12. Release the fuel pressure in the fuel feed line.
13. Disconnect the fuel feed and return hoses.
14. Disconnect the canister purge hose and remove the pressure sensor hose from the fuel filter, if equipped.
15. Remove the vacuum hose for the automatic transmission from the intake manifold, if equipped.
16. Disconnect the radiator cooling fan, fan shroud, water pump drive belt and water pump pulley.
17. Disconnect the crankshaft pulley, timing belt cover and the timing belt.
18. Raise and safely support the vehicle.
19. Disconnect the exhaust pipe from the exhaust manifold and lower the vehicle.
20. Disconnect the air conditioner compressor adjusting arm, if equipped.
21. Remove the cylinder head cover mounting bolts and remove the cylinder head cover.
22. Loosen all the valve adjusting screw locknuts, turn the adjusting screws back all the way to allow all the valves to close.
23. Remove the intake manifold from the cylinder head.
24. Remove the distributor and distributor housing from the cylinder head.
25. Remove the cylinder head mounting bolts and remove the cylinder head from the engine.
26. Remove any oil and water in the cylinder bores and on top of the pistons.
27. Clean and inspect the sealing surfaces of the cylinder head and the engine block.

28. Disconnect the timing belt gear from the camshaft and remove the rocker arms, springs and rocker arm shafts.

29. Keep all the valve train parts in the order that they were removed.

30. Remove the camshaft from the rear of the cylinder head.

To install:

31. To install, lubricate the lobes and journals of the camshaft and the oil seal on the cylinder head with engine oil.

32. Install the camshaft to the cylinder head from the transmission side.

33. Install the cylinder head using a new gasket.

34. Install the cylinder head mounting bolts and tighten to 46–54 ft. lbs.

35. Install the distributor and distributor housing to the cylinder head.

36. Install the intake manifold to the cylinder head.

37. Tighten all the valve adjusting screw nuts.

38. Adjust the valve lash.

39. Install the cylinder head cover and connect the air conditioning compressor adjusting arm, if equipped.

40. Raise and safely support the vehicle.

41. Connect the exhaust pipe to the exhaust manifold and safely lower the vehicle.

42. Reconnect the timing belt, timing belt cover and crankshaft pulley.

43. Install the water pump pulley, water pump drive belt, fan shroud and the radiator cooling fan.

44. Install the vacuum hose for the automatic transmission to the intake manifold, if equipped.

45. Install the pressure sensor hose to the fuel filter and connect the canister purge hose, if equipped.

46. Install the fuel return and feed hoses.

47. Connect the ground wires to the distributor assembly.

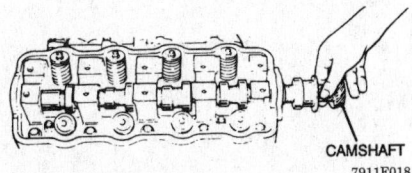

Camshaft removal — Electronic Fuel Injection (EFI)

CAMSHAFT
7911F018

48. Install the coil wire. Connect the oxygen sensor and distributor wires to their couplers.

49. Connect the PTC wires to the coupler.

50. Connect the idle speed control valve, throttle position sensor and injector wires to their couplers, if equipped.

51. Reconnect the ground cable, air temperature, oil pressure and water temperature sensor wires to the intake manifold.

52. Install the throttle opener VSV and EGR VSV wires to their couplers.

53. Connect the accelerator and the automatic transmission kickdown cables, if equipped, to the throttle body.

54. Install the air valve water hose to the throttle body and connect the brake booster hose to intake manifold.

55. Reconnect the air intake case.

56. Refill the cooling system with the proper coolant and connect the negative battery.

57. Check for any water and oil leaks when finished.

Multiport Fuel Injection (MFI)

1. Disconnect the negative battery cable. Release the fuel pressure. Remove the fuel filler cap to release the pressure in the tank, then replace the fuel filler cap.

2. Drain the cooling system. Disconnect the air intake pipe from the ACL intake hose and throttle hose.

3. Remove the throttle cover-to-intake manifold bolts and the cover.

4. If equipped with an automatic transmission, disconnect the accelerator and kickdown cables from the throttle body bellcrank.

5. Remove 1 bolt, nut, screw and accelerator cable bracket from the throttle body.

6. Disconnect the electrical connectors from the following items:

Throttle Position (TP) sensor
Idle Air Control (IAC) valve
Engine Coolant Temperature (ECT) sensor
ECT sending unit
A/C ECT switch (if equipped with A/C)
Evaporative Emissions Solenoid Purge (EVAP SP) valve
Exhaust Gas Recirculation (EGR) temperature sensor (Calif. vehicles)
EGR solenoid vacuum valve
Fuel injectors
Engine ground wire from intake surge tank

7. Disconnect the following vacuum hoses:

EVAP SP valve
Vacuum modulator supply hose (if equipped with automatic transmission)
Brake booster supply hose
EGR valve
EGR valve modulator

8. Disconnect the coolant hose from the IAC valve and the IAC hose from the IAC valve. Disconnect the coolant hoses from the fast idle air valve below the throttle body.

9. Disconnect the fuel feed hose at the fuel feed hose union and the fuel feed hose from the fuel return line. Disconnect the PCV hose from the PCV valve.

10. Loosen the upper radiator hose clamp at the thermostat housing. Disconnect the upper radiator hose from the thermostat housing. Disconnect the coolant bypass hose from the intake manifold.

11. Remove the generator adjusting arm bracket from the intake manifold. Remove the front and rear intake manifold reinforcement brackets from the intake manifold.

12. Remove the lower intake manifold support bracket from the intake manifold. Remove the intake manifold-to-cylinder head nuts/bolts, then remove the intake manifold, the intake surge tank and the throttle body from the cylinder head.

13. Remove the upper exhaust manifold heat shield from the exhaust manifold. Raise and safely support the vehicle.

14. Remove the exhaust manifold reinforcement bracket from the exhaust manifold and engine mount.

15. Remove the lower exhaust manifold heat shield from the exhaust manifold. Disconnect the Three-Way Catalytic converter (TWC) assembly from the exhaust manifold. Lower the vehicle.

16. Remove the exhaust manifold with gasket and engine hanger from the cylinder head.

17. If equipped, loosen the upper and lower A/C compressor mounting bolts. Loosen the upper and lower power steering pump mounting bolts. Remove the A/C compressor, If equipped, and/or the power steering drive belt.

18. Loosen the upper and lower generator mounting bolts. Remove the generator/water pump drive belt from the pulleys. Remove the cooling fan and the water pump pulley from the water pump.

19. Raise and safely support the vehicle. If equipped, remove the skid

plate from the undercarriage. Remove the 2 lower radiator shroud bolts and lower the vehicle.

20. If equipped, remove the 2 A/C suction line bracket bolts at the right side of the radiator core support and carefully reposition the suction line for radiator shroud removal access.

21. Remove the 2 upper radiator shroud bolts and the shroud from the radiator.

NOTE: If the shroud is difficult to remove, drain the cooling system and disconnect the upper radiator hose from the radiator to gain access. If is not necessary to remove the crankshaft center bolt when removing the crankshaft pulley.

22. Remove the 5 crankshaft pulley-to-crankshaft bolts and the pulley. Remove the oil pressure sending unit wire conduit from the timing belt cover.

23. To remove the timing belt, perform the following procedure:

a. Remove the timing belt cover from the engine.

NOTE: There are 2 sets of timing marks which must be aligned to ensure correct engine timing upon installation. A notch in the camshaft timing belt gear designated as "E" must be aligned with the notch in the cylinder head. A punch mark on the crankshaft timing belt gear should align with the arrow in the oil pump casting. Make sure to align both sets of marks prior to timing belt removal.

b. Rotate the engine to align the timing marks on the cylinder head cover and camshaft timing belt gear; this should align the timing marks on the oil pump casting and crankshaft timing belt gear.

c. Loosen the timing belt tensioner bolt. Remove the timing belt tensioner spring from the timing belt tensioner plate.

d. Remove the timing belt from the camshaft and crankshaft timing belt gears.

24. Secure the camshaft sprocket, using tool J-41840 or equivalent, then remove the camshaft sprocket-to-camshaft bolt and the camshaft sprocket.

25. Remove the 2 inner timing belt cover-to-cylinder head bolts and the cover. Remove the 2 A/C compressor mounting bracket-to-cylinder head bolts and the bracket.

26. Remove the distributor from the distributor case. Remove the 6 cylinder head cover-to-cylinder head bolts and the cover. Remove the cylinder head cover gasket and O-rings from the cylinder head cover.

NOTE: A small amount of oil may drain from the distributor case upon removal from the cylinder head. Place a suitable container under the distributor case or use a shop towel to catch and absorb the oil.

27. Remove the 3 distributor case-to-cylinder head bolts and the distributor case.

28. Loosen all valve adjusting screw locknuts. Loosen all valve adjusting screws until all rocker arms move freely.

NOTE: Always loosen the camshaft carrier bolts gradually in sequence, in order to relieve tension on the camshaft; if the camshaft carrier bolts are removed at random, damage to the camshaft may occur.

29. Remove the 12 camshaft carrier cap-to-cylinder head bolts, the camshaft carrier bolts, the camshaft seal and the camshaft.

30. Clean and inspect all of the gasket mating surfaces. Inspect and/or replace any damaged parts.

To install:

31. Lubricate the camshaft with clean oil. Apply RTV silicone rubber sealant to the bottom of the No. 6 camshaft carrier cap.

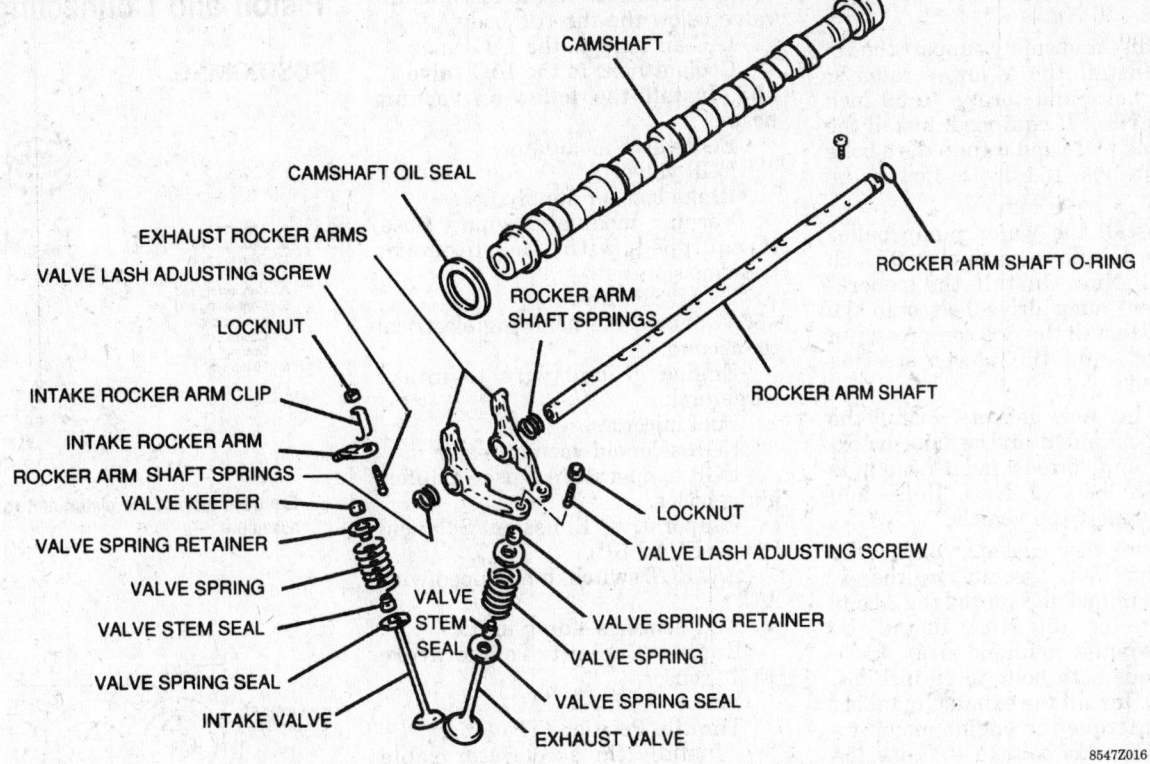

CAMSHAFT

CAMSHAFT OIL SEAL

EXHAUST ROCKER ARMS

VALVE LASH ADJUSTING SCREW

LOCKNUT

INTAKE ROCKER ARM CLIP

INTAKE ROCKER ARM

ROCKER ARM SHAFT SPRINGS

VALVE KEEPER

VALVE SPRING RETAINER

VALVE SPRING

VALVE STEM SEAL

VALVE SPRING SEAL

INTAKE VALVE

ROCKER ARM SHAFT O-RING

ROCKER ARM SHAFT SPRINGS

ROCKER ARM SHAFT

LOCKNUT

VALVE LASH ADJUSTING SCREW

VALVE STEM SEAL

VALVE SPRING RETAINER

VALVE SPRING

VALVE SPRING SEAL

EXHAUST VALVE

8547Z016

Exploded view of the camshaft, rocker arm and valve assembly — MFI engine

32. Install the camshaft and camshaft carrier caps onto the cylinder head, then, torque the camshaft carrier cap-to-cylinder head bolts to 89 inch lbs. (10 Nm).

NOTE: Always tighten the camshaft carrier cap bolts gradually in sequence; if the camshaft carrier cap bolts are tightened at random. damage to the camshaft may occur.

33. Lubricate the new camshaft seal lip with clean engine oil. Install the new camshaft seal into the cylinder head until it is flush with the camshaft carrier surface. Adjust the valve lash.

34. Adjust the valve lash.

35. Apply RTV silicone rubber sealant to the surface of the distributor case that mates with the rear of the rocker arm shaft.

36. Install the distributor case onto the cylinder head and torque the distributor case-to-cylinder head bolts to 89 inch lbs. (10 Nm).

37. Install a new cylinder head cover gasket and 4 O-rings to the cylinder head cover. Install the cylinder head cover and torque the 6 bolts to 89 inch lbs. (10 Nm).

38. Install the distributor into the distributor case. Install the A/C mounting bracket with compressor

and torque the 2 mounting bracket-to-cylinder head bolts to 89 inch lbs. (10 Nm).

39. Install the inner timing belt cover and torque the 2 bolts inner timing belt cover-to-cylinder head bolts to 89 inch lbs. (10 Nm).

NOTE: During camshaft timing belt gear installation, align the camshaft dwell pin with the slot in the camshaft timing belt gear designated as "E".

40. Install the camshaft sprocket, using holding tool J-41840 or equivalent, onto the camshaft and torque the camshaft sprocket-to-camshaft bolt to 44 ft. lbs. (60 Nm).

41. Install the timing belt tensioner plate and tensioner; secure with timing belt tensioner stud and bolt only finger-tight. Push the timing belt tensioner plate up when installing the timing belt.

NOTE: When installing the timing belt, the directional arrows on the timing belt must be matched with the rotation of the crankshaft; if not, excessive wear and timing belt failure may occur.

42. Install the timing belt by performing the following procedures:

a. Align the timing marks of the camshaft sprocket with the cylinder head cover and the oil pump housing with the crankshaft sprocket.

b. Install the timing belt onto the camshaft and crankshaft sprockets.

c. Rotate the crankshaft through 2 complete revolutions, to remove any slack from the timing belt and to properly seat the timing belt.

d. Inspect both sets of timing marks to ensure that they are aligned. Install the belt tensioner spring to the timing belt tensioner plate.

e. Torque the timing belt tensioner stud to 89 inch lbs. (10 Nm) and the bolt to 18 ft. lbs. (25 Nm).

43. Install the timing belt cover and torque the nut/bolts to 89 inch lbs. (10 Nm). Connect the oil pressure sending unit wire to the timing belt cover.

44. Install the crankshaft pulley to the crankshaft and torque the bolts to 12 ft. lbs. (16 Nm). Install the radiator shroud and torque both bolts to 89 inch lbs. (10 Nm).

45. If equipped, carefully, position the A/C suction line and brackets to the right side of the radiator core

support and torque both bolts to 89 inch lbs. (10 Nm).

46. Raise and safely support the vehicle. Install the 2 lower radiator shroud bolts and torque to 89 inch lbs. (10 Nm). If equipped, install the front skid plate and torque the 4 bolts to 40 ft. lbs. (54 Nm). Lower the vehicle.

47. Install the water pump pulley and fan; torque the 4 nuts to 97 inch lbs. (11 Nm). Install the generator/water pump drive belt onto the pulleys. Install the A/C compressor, if equipped, and the power steering drive belt.

48. Using new gaskets, install the exhaust manifold and torque the exhaust manifold-to-cylinder head nuts to 17 ft. lbs. (23 Nm). Raise and safely support the vehicle.

49. Using new gaskets, connect the front pipe/TWC assembly to the exhaust manifold and torque the 3 bolts to 37 ft. lbs. (50 Nm). Install the lower exhaust manifold heat shield and torque both bolts to 89 inch lbs. (10 Nm). Install the exhaust manifold bracket; torque the engine mount-to-exhaust bracket bolts to 40 ft. lbs. (54 Nm) and the exhaust bracket-to-exhaust manifold nut to 37 ft. lbs. (50 Nm). Lower the vehicle.

50. Install the upper exhaust manifold heat shield and torque the nuts/bolts to 89 inch lbs. (10 Nm). Install the air intake pipe bracket and torque the bracket-to-cylinder head bolts to 89 inch (10 Nm).

51. Using a new gasket, install the intake manifold, with intake surge tank and throttle body, and torque the intake manifold-to-cylinder head bolts, in sequence, to 17 ft. lbs. (23 Nm).

52. Install the lower intake manifold support bracket, the rear and the front intake manifold reinforcement bracket; torque the brackets-to-intake manifold bolts to 37 ft. lbs. (50 Nm).

53. Install the generator adjusting arm bracket and torque the bracket-to-intake manifold nut/bolt to 37 ft. lbs. (50 Nm).

54. Install the following hoses:
Coolant bypass hose to the intake manifold.
Upper radiator hose to the thermostat housing; secure with a clamp.
PCV hose to the PCV valve.
Fuel return hose to the fuel return line.
Fuel feed hose at the fuel feed hose union.

Coolant hoses to the fast idle air valve below the throttle body.
IAC air hose to the IAC valve.
Coolant hose to the IAC valve.

55. Install the following vacuum hoses:
EGR valve modulator.
EGR valve.
Brake booster supply hose.
Vacuum modulator supply hose, if equipped with an automatic transmission.
EVAP SP valve.

56. Connect the following electrical connectors:
Engine ground wire to intake surge tank.
Fuel injectors.
EGR solenoid vacuum valve.
EGR temperature sensor, California vehicles.
Evaporative Emission Solenoid Purge (EVAP SP).
A/C ECT switch, if equipped with A/C.
ECT sensor sending unit.
Engine Coolant Temperature (ECT) sensor.
Idle Air Control (IAC).
Throttle Position (TP) sensor.

57. Install the accelerator cable bracket to the throttle body and torque the nut/bolt to 17 ft. lbs. (23 Nm).

58. If equipped with an automatic transmission, connect the accelerator cable and kickdown cable to the throttle body bellcrank; adjust the cables.

59. Install the throttle cover to the intake manifold and torque the bolts to 11 ft. lbs. (15 Nm). Refill the cooling system, as necessary.

60. Install the air intake pipe to the throttle body hose and the ACL intake hose. Connect the negative battery cable.

Piston and Connecting Rod

POSITIONING

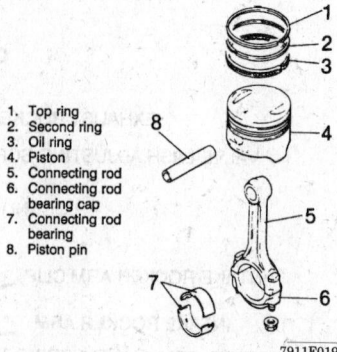

1. Top ring
2. Second ring
3. Oil ring
4. Piston
5. Connecting rod
6. Connecting rod bearing cap
7. Connecting rod bearing
8. Piston pin

7911F019

Exploded view of the piston and rod assembly

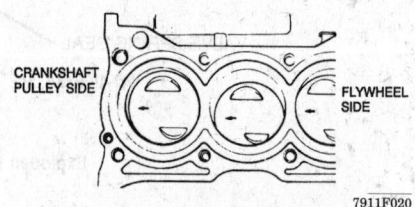

CRANKSHAFT PULLEY SIDE

FLYWHEEL SIDE

7911F020

Piston arrow marks to the cylinder head

ENGINE LUBRICATION

Oil Pan

REMOVAL AND INSTALLATION

1. Raise and safely support the vehicle.
2. On Sidekick, drain and remove the front differential assembly from the chassis.
3. Drain the engine oil.
4. Remove the clutch housing lower plate or the torque converter housing lower plate on the Sidekick.
5. Remove the oil pan mounting bolts and remove the pan.

To install:

6. Clean and inspect the sealing surfaces on the oil pan and the engine block.

7. Using new gaskets, install the oil pan and tighten the oil pan bolts to 7.0–8.5 ft. lbs.

NOTE: Tightening should begin at the center moving outward on both sides.

8. Install the oil drain plug and tighten to 22.0–28.5 ft. lbs.
9. Install the clutch housing lower plate or the torque converter on the Sidekick.
10. Install the front differential assembly to the chassis and fill with differential oil on the Sidekick.
11. Lower the vehicle.
12. Refill the engine with engine oil. Run the engine and check for leaks.

Oil Pump

REMOVAL AND INSTALLATION

1. Disconnect the negative battery cable.
2. Remove the radiator cooling fan, fan shroud, water pump pulley and water pump drive belt.
3. Remove the timing belt outside cover, timing belt and timing belt tensioner.
4. Disconnect the alternator and remove the bracket, if necessary.
5. If equipped, properly discharge the air conditioning system and remove the air compressor and bracket.
6. Disconnect the crankshaft timing belt pulley and the timing belt guide.

NOTE: To lock the crankshaft, engage a special tool (gear stopper) with the flywheel ring gear (driveplate ring gear for automatic transmission vehicles). With the crankshaft locked, remove the crankshaft timing belt pulley bolt.

7. Raise and safely support the vehicle. Drain the engine oil.
8. Remove the clutch (torque converter) housing lower plate.
9. Remove the oil pan mounting bolts and remove the oil pan. Disconnect the oil pump strainer.
10. Remove the oil pump mounting bolts and remove the oil pump.
   To install:
11. Clean and inspect the sealing surfaces of the oil pump and the engine block.
12. Using a new gasket, install the oil pump to the engine.

13. Install the No. 1 and No. 2 mounting bolts and tighten to 7.0–8.5 ft. lbs.

NOTE: To prevent the oil seal lip from being damaged when installing the oil pump to the crankshaft, use a proper seal guide tool when installing. After installing the oil pump, check to be sure the oil lip is not upturned, then remove the special tool. The edge of the oil pump gasket might bulge out. If it does, cut off bulge with knife.

14. With the crankshaft locked, install the crankshaft timing belt guide and the timing belt pulley.
15. Install the clutch (torque converter) housing lower plate.
16. If equipped, install the air conditioning bracket, the air conditioning compressor and properly recharge the air conditioning system.
17. Install the alternator and the alternator bracket, if necessary.
18. Reinstall the timing belt tensioner, timing belt and timing belt outside cover.
19. Install the water pump drive belt, water pump pulley, radiator cooling fan and fan shroud.
20. Refill the engine with engine oil and connect the negative battery cable.
21. Run the engine and check for any leaks.

CHECKING

With the oil pump removed from the engine, certain clearances must be checked on the oil pump, if it is being reused.

1. The radial clearance is the clearance between the oil pump outer rotor and the oil pump case. The maximum clearance is 0.0122 in.
2. The side clearance is measured with a straightedge across the mounting surface of the oil pump.

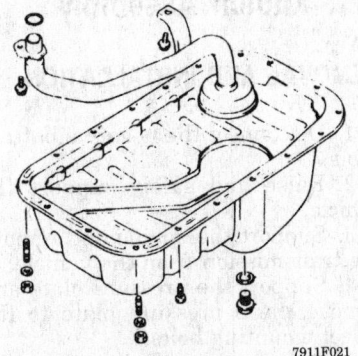

7911F021

Oil pump installation — bolt location

The measurement is taken between the oil pump gears and the straight-edge. The maximum clearance is 0.0059 in.

Rear Main Bearing Oil Seal

REMOVAL AND INSTALLATION

1. Raise and safely support the vehicle.
2. Support the engine and remove the transmission from the vehicle.
3. Disconnect the clutch and flywheel, for manual transmission vehicles or the driveplate, for automatic transmission vehicles.
4. Using a suitable tool, remove the seal by pulling it outwards. Use care not to damage the sealing surface of the crankshaft.
   To install:
5. Clean and inspect the sealing surfaces of the crankshaft and seal housing.
6. Using a seal driver, install the new seal into the seal housing with the lip of the seal facing the engine.
7. Install the flywheel and clutch, for manual transmission vehicles or the driveplate, for automatic transmission vehicles.
8. Install the transmission in the vehicle.
9. Lower the vehicle and check all the fluids. Run the engine and check for any leaks.

MANUAL TRANSMISSION

Transmission Assembly

REMOVAL AND INSTALLATION

1. Disconnect the negative battery cable.
2. Remove the console cover, remove the 4 gear shift boot mounting bolts and slide the boot upwards on the gear shifter.
3. On Samurai, loosen the 3 gear shift lever mounting bolts and remove the gear shift lever.
4. On the Sidekick remove the boot clamp and remove the second boot from the shift lever case.
5. Push the gear shift lever control case down with fingers, turn it counterclockwise and remove the shift control lever.

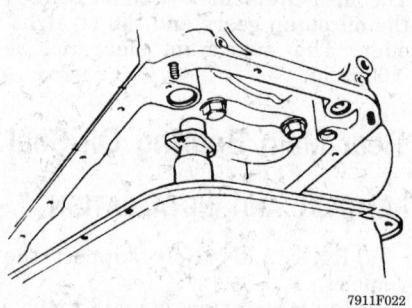

7911F022

Oil pump installation

6. Remove the transfer case shift control lever the same way.

7. Disconnect the breather hose and clamp at the rear of the cylinder head.

8. Remove the clamp at the rear of the intake manifold to free up the wiring harness. Disconnect the harness coupler.

9. Raise and safely support the vehicle. Drain the oil from the transmission and the transfer case.

10. Disconnect the starter lead wires and mounting bolts and remove the starter.

11. Remove the fuel line clamp on the transmission. Disconnect the bolts fastening the engine to the transmission.

12. Disconnect the flange bolts from the front driveshaft and remove and mark the shaft.

13. Disconnect the flange bolts from the rear driveshaft and remove and mark the shaft.

14. Disconnect the clutch cable and remove the clutch housing lower plate.

15. Disconnect the center exhaust pipe and remove the nuts from the joint with the engine.

16. Disconnect the speedometer cable from the transfer case.

17. Position a transmission jack and remove the engine rear mounting member from the vehicle. Move the transmission and transfer case rearwards and lower.

18. Disconnect the wiring harness and breather hose at the transmission.

19. Separate the gearshift lever case and transfer case from the transmission. Remove the transmission from the vehicle.

To install:

20. Install the gear shift lever case and transfer case to the transmission.

21. Install the transmission wiring harness and breather hose.

22. Raise the transmission and transfer case on the transmission jack and place under the vehicle.

23. Install the engine rear mounting member and tighten the bolts. Tighten the Samurai mounting bolts to 19 ft. lbs. or the Sidekick mounting bolts to 37 ft. lbs.

24. Connect the speedometer cable to the transfer case and joint with the engine.

25. Remove the transmission jack and install the center exhaust pipe.

26. Install the clutch housing lower plate and connect the clutch cable.

27. Install the front and rear driveshaft and install the flange bolts. Tighten the Samurai flange bolts to 20 ft. lbs. or the Sidekick flange bolts to 37 ft. lbs.

28. Connect the bolts attaching the engine to the transmission and install the fuel line clamp on the transmission.

29. Install the starter and install the mounting bolts and the lead wires to the starter.

30. Lower the vehicle. Refill the transmission and transfer case with the recommended gear oil.

31. Connect the wiring coupler and install the clamp holding the wiring harness at the rear of the intake manifold.

32. Install the breather hose and clamp at the rear of the cylinder head.

33. Install the transfer case and the gear shift control levers. Install the gear shift lever boots and the console cover.

34. Connect the negative battery cable. Run the engine and check for any leaks.

CLUTCH

Clutch Assembly

REMOVAL AND INSTALLATION

1. Disconnect the negative battery cable.

2. Raise and safely support the vehicle.

3. Support the engine and remove the transmission from the vehicle.

4. Support the pressure plate and remove the 6 pressure plate to flywheel mounting bolts.

5. Remove the pressure plate and the clutch disc from the flywheel.

6. Inspect the condition of the flywheel, pressure plate and clutch disc and install as necessary.

7. Remove the flywheel mounting bolts and remove the flywheel.

To install:

8. Install the new flywheel and install the mounting bolts, tighten to 41–47 ft. lbs.

9. Inspect the condition of the clutch release bearing and the input shaft bearing and install if necessary.

10. Align the clutch disc to the flywheel using a clutch disc alignment tool.

11. Install the pressure plate and evenly tighten the pressure plate bolts to 13–20 ft. lbs.

NOTE: Before assembling, make sure the clutch disc and the pressure plate are clean and dry.

12. With the engine supported, install the transmission in the vehicle.

13. Lower the vehicle. Connect the negative battery cable.

14. Check and adjust the clutch pedal height. Check the clutch operation when finished.

PEDAL HEIGHT/FREE-PLAY ADJUSTMENT

The only adjustment possible is the clutch pedal free-play. The free-play is adjusted by moving the joint nut on the release bearing arm. Clutch linkage free-play should be between 0.8–1.1 in. for the Samurai or 0.6–1.1 in. for the Sidekick.

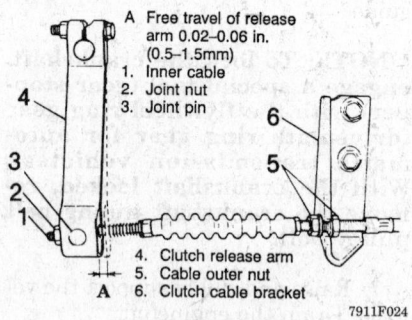

A Free travel of release arm 0.02–0.06 in. (0.5–1.5mm)
1. Inner cable
2. Joint nut
3. Joint pin
4. Clutch release arm
5. Cable outer nut
6. Clutch cable bracket

7911F024

Clutch cable free travel adjustment

Clutch Cable

REMOVAL AND INSTALLATION

1. Disconnect the negative battery cable.

2. Raise and safely support the vehicle.

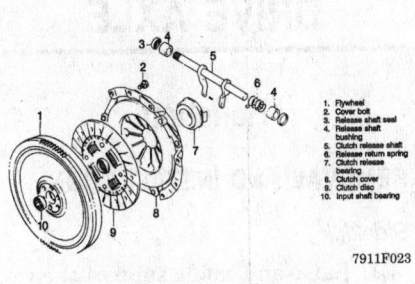

1. Flywheel
2. Cover bolt
3. Release shaft seal
4. Release shaft bushing
5. Clutch release shaft
6. Release return spring
7. Clutch release bearing
8. Clutch cover
9. Clutch disc
10. Input shaft bearing

79111F023

Exploded view of the clutch assembly

3. Disconnect the cable adjusting nuts on the clutch release and remove the adjusting nuts on the cable support bracket.

4. Disconnect the clutch cable from the 3 cable clamps.

5. Remove the clutch cable support bolts. Lower the vehicle.

6. Disconnect the cable hook at the clutch pedal shaft arm and remove the clutch cable.

To install:

7. Install the cable after first applying grease to the cable end hook and the joint pin.

8. Install the clutch cable support bolts and connect the cable to the 3 clamps.

9. Connect the clutch cable adjusting nuts and adjust to proper setting.

10. Lower the vehicle and connect the negative battery terminal.

ADJUSTMENT

Adjust the clutch pedal height by adjusting the bolt located on the pedal bracket so the clutch pedal exceeds the height of the brake pedal by 0.2 in. (5mm). Tighten the locknut.

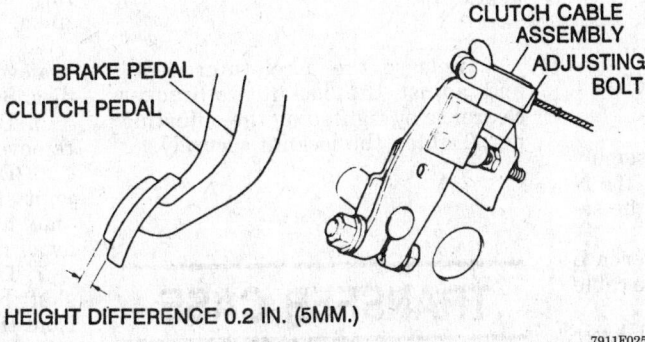

HEIGHT DIFFERENCE 0.2 IN. (5MM.)

BRAKE PEDAL
CLUTCH PEDAL

CLUTCH CABLE ASSEMBLY
ADJUSTING BOLT

79111F025

Clutch pedal height adjustment

AUTOMATIC TRANSMISSION

Transmission Assembly

REMOVAL AND INSTALLATION

1. Disconnect the negative battery cable.

2. Disconnect the transmission shift control lever and remove the transfer case shift control lever knob.

3. Disconnect the breather hose from the clamp at the rear of the cylinder head.

4. Disconnect the wiring harness clamp at the rear end of the intake manifold to free up the harness.

5. Disconnect the wiring harness coupler and remove the detent cable at the throttle body, if equipped.

6. Remove the vacuum modulator hose at the intake manifold.

7. Raise and safely support the vehicle.

8. Disconnect the starter lead wires and mounting bolts, remove the starter motor.

9. Drain the oil from the transmission and transfer case.

10. Disconnect the flange bolts from the front driveshaft, remove and mark the shaft.

11. Disconnect the flange bolts from the rear driveshaft, remove and mark the shaft.

12. Disconnect the select cable from the transmission and the speedometer cable from the transfer cases.

13. Remove the torque converter housing lower plate and disconnect and plug the oil cooler lines.

14. Disconnect the transfer case skid plate and remove the kickdown cable from the transmission.

15. Remove the exhaust bracket at the catalytic converter and at the transmission. Disconnect the center exhaust pipe, if necessary.

16. Remove the transmission to engine retaining bolts and nuts.

17. Support the transmission using a transmission jack or equivalent. Disconnect the transmission crossmember mounting bolts and remove the crossmember.

18. Disconnect the lead wires and breather hose at the transmission and lower the transmission with the transfer case from the vehicle. Remove the torque converter-to-flywheel bolts.

19. Disconnect the transmission-to-transfer case bolts and separate the transmission from the transfer case.

To install:

20. Connect the transfer case to the transmission and tighten the bolts to 20 ft. lbs. Install the torque converter to flywheel bolts.

21. Raise the transmission, connect the lead wires and breather to the transmission.

22. Install the transmission to engine retaining bolts and tighten to 62 ft. lbs.

23. Install the transmission cross member and tighten the bolts to 62 ft. lbs.

24. Connect the exhaust bracket to the catalytic converter and the transmission.

25. Reconnect the center exhaust pipe, if necessary.

26. Connect the transfer case skid plate and install the kickdown cable to the transmission.

27. Install the torque converter housing lower plate and connect the transmission cooler lines.

28. Reconnect the select cable to the transmission and the speedometer cable to the transfer case.

29. Install the front and rear driveshafts and tighten the flange bolts to 37 ft. lbs.

30. Install the starter and connect the lead wires to the starter.

31. Lower the vehicle and connect the vacuum modulator hose to the intake manifold.

32. Connect the wiring coupler at the rear of the intake manifold and install the wiring harness clamp in the proper position.

33. Connect the breather hose to the clamp at the rear of the cylinder head.

34. Install the transmission shift control lever and install the transfer case shift control lever knob.

35. Connect the negative battery cable and refill the transmission. Run the engine and check for leaks.

SHIFT LINKAGE ADJUSTMENT

1. Adjust the shift cable assembly by moving the shift selector to the **N** position and placing a pin in the selector to hold that position.

2. Put the manual select lever in **L** position and set the cable to the cable bracket with the E-clip.

3. Adjust the manual select lever back to the **N** position and tighten the cable end locknut to 5 ft. lbs.

NOTE: When the manual selector is moved to the N position, there should be a little clearance between the lever and the adjusting nut.

THROTTLE LINKAGE ADJUSTMENT

Adjust the cable by loosening the cable locknut and adjust the cable to specifications. The cable endplay should be 0.12–0.20 in. when the throttle valve is in the idle position.

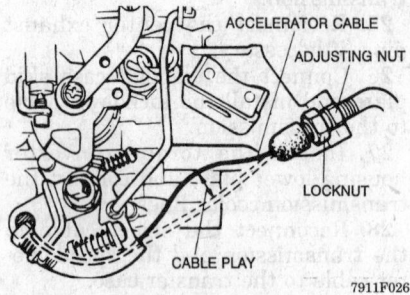

Accelerator cable adjustment

DETENT CABLE ADJUSTMENT

1. Make sure accelerator play is within specifications.

2. Loosen the kickdown cable nut and adjusting nut.

3. With the accelerator pedal fully depressed and the cable pulled towards the firewall, adjust the locknut-to-bracket clearance to 0.039 in. by turning the locknut.

NOTE: When adjusting the clearance make sure the adjusting nut does not rub against the bracket.

4. Release the accelerator pedal and adjust the locknut-to-bracket clearance by tightening the adjusting nut. Tighten the locknut securely.

TRANSFER CASE

Transfer Case Assembly

REMOVAL AND INSTALLATION

1. Disconnect the negative battery cable.

2. Raise and safely support the vehicle.

3. Support the transmission and transfer case using a suitable transmission jack.

4. Disconnect the speedometer cable from the transfer case.

5. Remove the transmission and transfer case from the vehicle.

6. Remove the 10 transmission-to-transfer case mounting bolts and separate the transfer case from the transmission.

To install:

7. Install the 10 transmission-to-transfer case mounting bolts and tighten the bolts to 20 ft. lbs.

8. Install the transmission and transfer case into the vehicle and tighten the mounting bolts to 20 ft. lbs. on the Samurai or 37 ft. lbs. on the Sidekick.

9. Connect the speedometer cable to the transfer case.

10. Lower the vehicle and connect the negative battery cable.

DRIVE AXLE

Halfshaft

REMOVAL AND INSTALLATION

Sidekick

1. Raise and safely support the vehicle. Drain the transmission.

2. Remove the front wheels and disconnect the locking hubs.

3. Disconnect the halfshaft snaprings and remove the stabilizer bar links.

4. Disconnect the tie rod ends and remove the brake caliper and brake disc. Support the brake caliper.

5. Disconnect the wheel hub and remove the steering knuckle.

6. Disconnect the differential side joint snapring and remove the right side halfshaft by prying the joint away from the differential assembly.

7. Disconnect the left side halfshaft bolts and remove the halfshaft from the left inner axle flange.

To install:

8. Install the left side halfshaft and the halfshaft bolts and tighten to 37 ft. lbs.

9. Install the right side halfshaft and install the snapring.

10. Install the steering knuckle and wheel hub assembly.

11. Install the brake caliper and connect the tie rod ends.

12. Install the left side driveshaft snapring and connect the stabilizer bar links.

13. Install the front wheels and lower the vehicle.

14. Refill the transmission with the proper fluid.

Driveshaft and U-Joints

REMOVAL AND INSTALLATION

1. Raise and safely support the vehicle.

2. Matchmark the driveshafts to the yokes on the transfer case and the differential.

3. Drain the transfer case oil, when servicing the front driveshaft shaft.

4. Support the driveshaft and remove the attaching bolts.

5. Remove the driveshaft from the vehicle.

To install:

6. Install the driveshaft, by aligning the matchmarks to the vehicle.

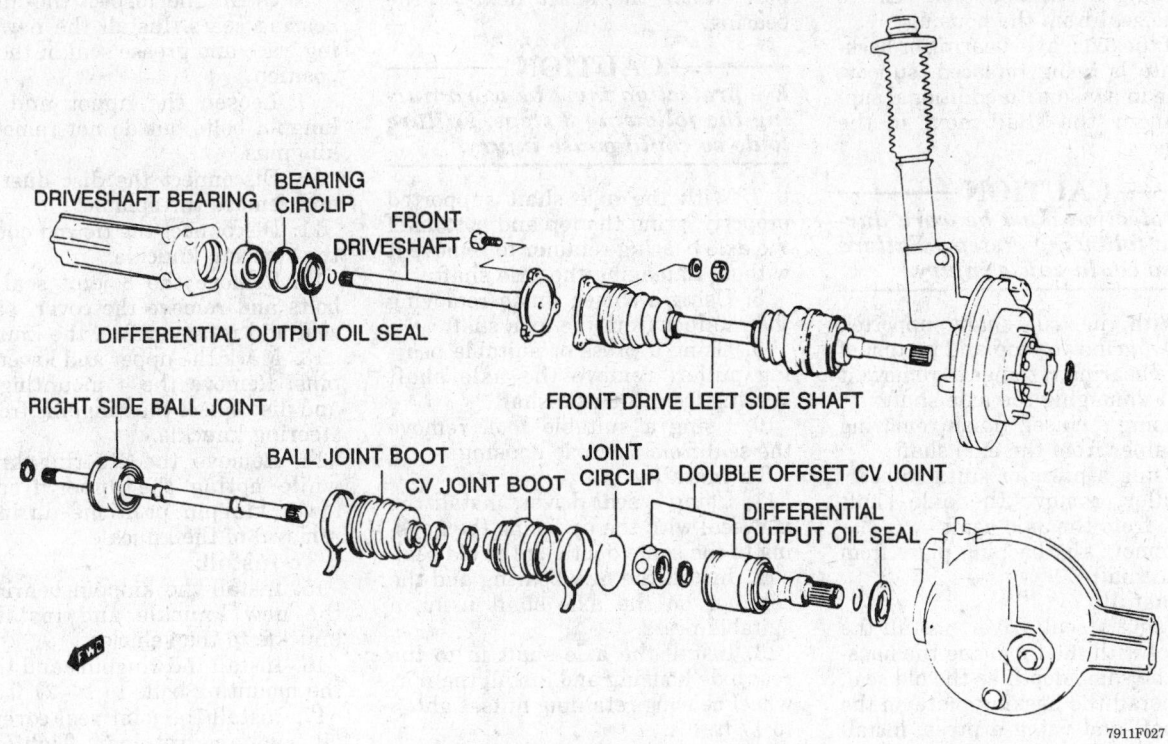

Exploded view of the halfshaft assembly

7. Tighten the mounting bolts to 17–21 ft. lbs. on Samurai or 37 ft. lbs. on the Sidekick.

8. Refill the transfer case and lower the vehicle.

Front Axle Shaft

REMOVAL AND INSTALLATION

Samurai

1. Raise and safely support the vehicle.

2. Drain the oil in the front differential.

3. Remove the front wheels and disconnect the brake caliper. Support the brake caliper.

4. Disconnect the tie rod end from the steering knuckle. The tie rod end removal may require the use of a puller.

5. Remove the 8 oil seal cover mounting bolts and disconnect the felt pad, oil seal and the retainer from the steering knuckle.

6. Mark the upper and lower kingpins. Remove the 4 mounting bolts and disconnect the kingpins from the steering knuckle.

7. Remove the axle shaft from the housing with the steering knuckle attached.

To install:

8. Transfer the steering knuckle to the new axle.

9. Align the marks on the upper and lower kingpins and install the kingpins and tighten to 14–21 ft. lbs.

10. Install the steering knuckle oil seal and install the 8 mounting bolts and tighten to 6–8 ft. lbs.

11. Connect the tie rod end to the steering knuckle and tighten the bolts to 22–39 ft. lbs. Install the front brake caliper assembly.

12. Install the front wheels and refill the differential with the proper fluid.

13. Lower the vehicle.

Front Axle Shaft, Bearing and Seal

REMOVAL AND INSTALLATION

Samurai

1. Raise and safely support the vehicle. Drain the front differential assembly.

2. Disconnect the front wheel hub and remove the bearing.

3. Support the hub and drive out the seal in the hub.

4. Using a seal driver, install the new seal in the hub until it is flush with the hub face. Apply a thin film of oil to the lip of the seal before installation to the vehicle.

5. Install the hub and the bearing to the vehicle.

6. Refill the front differential assembly and safely lower the vehicle.

Rear Axle Shaft, Bearing and Seal

REMOVAL AND INSTALLATION

Samurai

1. Raise and safely support the vehicle. Drain the rear differential assembly.

2. Make sure the rear brake is released.

3. Remove the rear wheels and remove the rear brake drums from the vehicle.

4. Disconnect the parking brake cables from the levers. Remove the parking brake lever stop plates.

5. Disconnect and plug the brake lines to the wheel cylinders.

6. Remove the backing plate mounting bolts.

7. Remove the rear axles with the backing plates attached using a slide hammer type puller.

8. Using a suitable tool, remove the axle seal from the housing.

9. If the axle, axle bearing or backing plate is being replaced, support the axle in a vise with additional support under the shaft next to the bearing.

——— CAUTION ———

Eye protection must be worn during the following 3 steps. Failure to do so could cause injury.

10. With the axle shaft supported properly, grind the top and bottom of the axle bearing retainer to remove it without damaging the axle shaft.

11. Using a chisel, finish removing the retainer from the axle shaft.

12. Using a press or suitable bearing puller, remove the axle shaft bearing from the axle shaft.

13. Remove the backing plate from the axle shaft.

To install:

14. Using a seal driver, install the new seal with the lip facing the housing to the same depth as the old seal.

15. Install the backing plate on the axle shaft and using a press, install the bearing and the retainer on the axle shaft.

16. Install the axle shaft in the housing.

17. Install the backing plate mounting bolts and connect the brake lines to the wheel cylinders.

18. Install the parking brake lever plates and connect the brake cables to the parking brake lever.

19. Install the rear brake drums and install the rear wheels.

20. Adjust the brakes and bleed the brake system.

21. Refill the rear differential and safely lower the vehicle.

Sidekick

1. Raise and safely support the vehicle.

2. Remove the rear wheels and remove the rear brake drums from the vehicle.

3. Drain the gear oil from the rear axle housing.

4. Remove the rear wheel bearing retainer nuts from the rear axle housing.

5. Using a suitable tool, remove the axle shaft from the housing.

NOTE: Do not remove the backing plate with the axle. This may cause damage to the inner seal.

6. If the axle, axle bearing or backing plate is being replaced, support the axle in a vise with additional sup-

port under the shaft next to the bearing.

——— CAUTION ———

Eye protection must be worn during the following 3 steps. Failure to do so could cause injury.

7. With the axle shaft supported properly, grind the top and bottom of the axle bearing retainer to remove it without damaging the axle shaft.

8. Using a chisel, finish removing the retainer from the axle shaft.

9. Using a press or suitable bearing puller, remove the axle shaft bearing from the axle shaft.

10. Using a suitable tool, remove the seal from the axle housing.

To install:

11. Using a seal driver, install the new seal with the lip facing the housing to the same depth as the old seal.

12. Install the new bearing and the retainer on the axle shaft using a suitable press.

13. Install the axle shaft in to the rear axle housing and install the rear wheel bearing retaining nuts, tighten to 17 ft. lbs.

14. Install the rear brake drums and install the rear tires on the vehicle.

15. Refill the rear axle housing with the proper gear oil and safely lower the vehicle.

Front Wheel Hub, Knuckle and Bearings

REMOVAL AND INSTALLATION

Samurai

1. Raise and safely support the vehicle. Remove the front wheels.

2. Disconnect the locking hub. Remove the caliper mounting bolts and move the caliper out of position with the brake line attached.

NOTE: Do not allow the caliper to hang on the brake hose. Support it by the mounting bracket.

3. Install 2 (8mm) bolts into the threaded holes and tighten evenly. This will remove the rotor from the hub assembly.

4. Remove the front axle shaft cap and the circlip. Remove the drive flange from the steering knuckle.

5. Straighten the bent lock washer and remove the hub nut and washer.

6. Remove the front wheel hub and bearing from the spindle.

7. Remove the oil seal and race from the wheel hub.

8. Clean and inspect the hub and bearing seats. Install the new bearing, race and grease seal in the same position.

9. Loosen the upper and lower kingpin bolts but do not remove the kingpins.

10. Disconnect the disc dust cover and remove the spindle.

11. Disconnect the tie rod end from the steering knuckle.

12. Remove the 8 joint seal cover bolts and remove the cover, pad, oil seal and retainer from the knuckle.

13. Mark the upper and lower kingpins. Remove the 4 mounting bolts and disconnect the kingpins from the steering knuckle.

14. Remove the steering knuckle while noting the upper from the lower kingpin positions during the removal of the knuckle.

To install:

15. Install the kingpin bearings in the new knuckle and install the knuckle to the vehicle.

16. Install the kingpins and tighten the mounting bolts to 14–21 ft. lbs.

17. Install the joint seal cover, pad oil seal and retainer. Tighten the joint seal cover bolts to 6.0–8.5 ft. lbs.

18. Connect the tie rod end to the steering knuckle.

19. Install the spindle and connect disc dust cover.

20. Install the front wheel hub and bearing to the spindle.

21. Install the front hub nut and lock washer and install the drive flange to the steering knuckle.

22. Install the front axle cap and circlip. Connect the rotor to the hub assembly.

23. Place the brake caliper into position and install the caliper mounting bolts.

24. Reconnect the locking hub assembly and install the front wheels.

25. Lower the vehicle.

Sidekick

1. Disconnect the negative battery cable. Raise and safely support the vehicle.

2. Remove the wheels and disconnect the locking hub assembly.

3. Remove the caliper mounting bracket and position the caliper out of the way. Support the caliper.

4. Disconnect the front wheel bearing lock plate and washer and remove the wheel hub complete with bearings and seals.

5. Remove the oil seal and race from the wheel hub.

6. Clean and inspect the hub and bearing seats. Install the new bear-

ing, race and grease seal in the same position.

7. Support the suspension with a jack and remove the dust cover.

8. Disconnect the spindle by tapping with a hammer.

9. Remove the strut bracket bolts from the steering knuckle.

10. Disconnect the tie rod end from the knuckle and the knuckle from the control arm.

11. Remove the dust seal and the spindle from the knuckle.

To install:

12. Install the new seal and the spindle to the knuckle.

13. Connect the knuckle to the ball joint and tighten the nut to 40 ft. lbs.

14. Connect the knuckle to the strut damper and tighten the bolts to 66 ft. lbs.

15. Install the tie rod end to the knuckle and tighten the nut 30 ft. lbs.

16. Install the spindle and install the dust cover and remove the jack from under the suspension.

17. Install the wheel hub assembly and connect the locking hub.

18. Install the wheels and lower the vehicle.

19. Connect the negative battery cable.

Manual Locking Hubs

REMOVAL AND INSTALLATION

1. Disconnect the negative battery cable and remove the locking hub cover.

2. Raise and support the vehicle safely.

3. Remove the locking hub body assembly.

NOTE: The manual locking hubs must not be packed with grease.

To install:

4. Install a new O-ring to the locking hub assembly.

5. Install the locking hub body assembly to the wheel hub flange and tighten the hub body bolts to 18 ft. lbs.

6. Install a new gasket in the manual locking hub cover.

7. Install the locking hub cover and tighten the bolts to 106 inch lbs.

8. Connect the negative battery cable and lower the vehicle.

NOTE: The O mark on the hub knob must be in the FREE position.

Automatic Locking Hubs

REMOVAL AND INSTALLATION

1. Disconnect the negative battery cable and remove the automatic locking hub cover.

2. Disconnect the automatic hub body assembly.

To install:

3. Install a new O-ring to the automatic locking hub body assembly.

4. Connect the automatic locking hub body assembly to the wheel hub flange. Tighten the hub body assembly bolts to 18 ft. lbs.

5. Install a new gasket in the automatic locking hub cover and install the hub cover.

6. Connect the negative battery cable.

Pinion Seal

REMOVAL AND INSTALLATION

1. Raise and safely support the vehicle.

2. Matchmark and remove the driveshaft.

3. Check the turning torque of the pinion before proceeding.

4. Using a pinion flange holding tool, remove the pinion nut and the washer.

5. Remove the pinion flange from the differential carrier and pry out the pinion seal.

To install:

6. Clean and inspect the sealing surface of the carrier.

7. Using a seal driver, install the new seal into the carrier until the flange of the seal is flush with the carrier.

NOTE: Tightening the flange nut will preload the pinion bearings. Exceeding the preload specifications will compress the collapsible spacer too far and require the spacer to be replaced.

8. Install the pinion flange and using the pinion flange holding tool, install the pinion nut and washer. Tighten the pinion nut to the same torque as before.

9. Align the matchmarks and install the driveshaft.

10. Check the level of the differential fluid when finished.

Differential Carrier

REMOVAL AND INSTALLATION

1. Raise and safely support the vehicle. Drain the oil from the rear differential.

2. Remove the left and right axle shafts.

3. Disconnect the driveshaft.

4. Remove the 4 mounting bolts to the upper rear suspension arm.

5. Support the differential carrier with a proper jack.

6. Remove the differential case nuts and lower the differential assembly from the rear housing.

7. Clean and inspect the sealing surfaces of the carrier and the housing.

To install:

8. Using a liquid sealant on the carrier, install the carrier in the housing and tighten the nuts to 16 ft. lbs.

9. Install the 4 mounting bolts to the upper rear suspension arm and tighten to 41 ft. lbs.

10. Connect the rear driveshaft and install the left and rear axles.

11. Refill the rear differential to the proper level with SAE 75W-90W API GL5 Hypoid Gear Oil.

12. Lower the vehicle.

Front Axle Housing

REMOVAL AND INSTALLATION

Samurai and Sidekick

1. Raise and safely support the vehicle. Remove the front wheels.

2. Drain the oil from the front differential.

3. Remove caliper assembly from brake disc and support caliper assembly.

4. Remove the tie rod end from the steering knuckle using a tie rod end remover.

5. Remove the 8 oil seal cover bolts and separate the felt pad, seal and retainer.

6. Remove the 4 kingpin bolts from the top and bottom and remove the kingpins from the knuckle.

7. Remove axle shafts from housing by pulling outward gradually.

8. Remove the bolts between the flange yoke and companion flange and disconnect the front drive shaft.

9. Remove the 8 U-joint nuts and remove the housing assembly.

To install:

10. Install the housing and torque the housing U-bolt nuts to 43 ft. lbs.

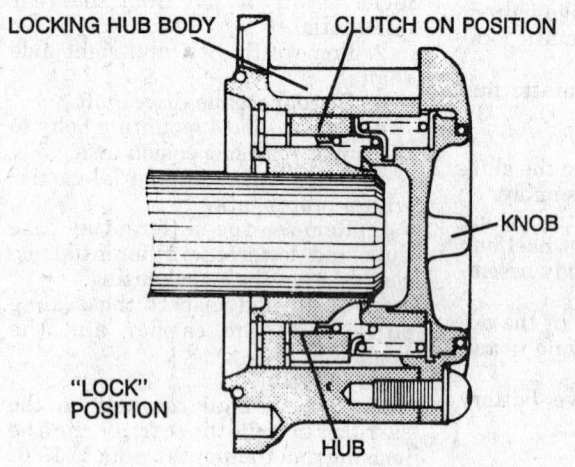

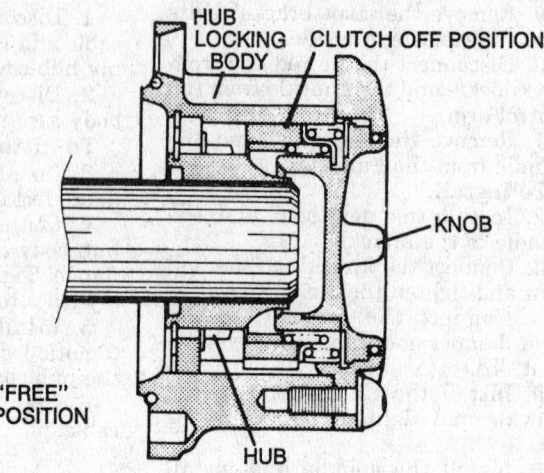

Wheel hub "LOCK" and "FREE" positions

7911F028

11. Connect the front drive shaft and install the bolts.

12. Install the front axle shafts and install the kingpins. Apply Loctite° to the kingpin bolts.

13. Install oil seal, felt pad and retainer and tighten the 8 cover bolts.

14. Install the tie rod end to the steering knuckle.

15. Install the front caliper to the disc and install the front wheels.

16. Refill the differential with the proper lubricant and bleed the brake system when finished.

Rear Axle Housing

REMOVAL AND INSTALLATION

Samurai

1. Raise and safely support the vehicle. Drain the rear differential assembly.

2. Make sure the parking brake is in the released position.

3. Remove the rear wheels and remove the rear brake drums from the vehicle.

4. Disconnect the parking brake cables from the levers. Remove the parking brake lever stop plates.

5. Disconnect and plug the brake lines to the wheel cylinders.

6. Remove the backing plate mounting bolts and remove the axle shafts with the backing plates attached.

7. Disconnect the driveshaft and remove from the transmission.

8. Remove the brake line from the flexible hose and remove the E-clip.

9. Disconnect the brake clamps and remove the brake lines from the rear housing.

10. Disconnect the mounting bolts to the rear suspension arm and remove the housing to leaf spring U-bolts and nuts.

11. Remove shock absorber lower mount bolt.

12. Slide the housing to one side while tilting the opposite side under the leaf spring and remove the housing from the vehicle.

To install:

13. Install the housing and connect the shock absorber lower bolt.

14. Connect the U-bolts to the leaf spring and tighten the bolts to 50 ft. lbs.

15. Connect brake lines to the rear housing and install the driveshaft.

16. Install the axle shafts with backing plates attached and tighten the backing plate bolts to 19 ft. lbs.

17. Connect the brake lines to the rear wheel cylinders.

18. Install the parking brake lever stop plates and connect the parking brake cables.

19. Install the rear brake drums and install the rear wheels.

20. Lower the vehicle and refill the rear differential with the proper fluid.

Sidekick

1. Raise and safely support the vehicle. Drain the rear differential assembly.

2. Make sure the parking brake is in the released position.

3. Remove the rear wheels and remove the rear brake drums from the vehicle.

4. Disconnect the parking brake cables from the levers. Remove the parking brake lever stop plates.

5. Disconnect and plug the brake lines to the wheel cylinders.

6. Remove the rear wheel bearing retainer nuts and remove the axle shafts from the vehicle. Do not remove the axle shafts with the backing plates attached.

7. Remove the rear axle carrier assembly.

8. Disconnect the brake line from the flexible hose and remove the E-clip. Remove the brake lines from the rear housing.

9. Remove the breather hose from the axle housing and disconnect the rear driveshaft.

10. Support the rear axle housing with a jack.

11. Remove the ball joint bracket from the differential carrier and remove the carrier assembly.

12. Loosen the rear mount nut of the trailing rod. Do not remove it.

13. Disconnect the shock absorber lower mount bolt.

14. Lower the jack to relieve the tension of the coil springs and remove the rear mount bolt of the trailing rod.

15. Remove the rear axle housing.

To install:

16. Place the rear axle housing on a jack and install the trailing rod rear mounting bolts. Mount the nuts but do not tighten.

17. Install the coil spring on the spring seat and raise the axle housing.

18. Install the shock absorber lower mounting bolts. Do not tighten.

19. Install the differential carrier assembly and install the rear upper ball joint bracket onto the carrier assembly and tighten to 37 ft. lbs.

20. Install the rear driveshaft and remove the jack from under the axle housing.

21. Install the breather hose and brake lines to axle housing. Tighten them securely.

22. Connect the flexible brake hose to the bracket on the axle housing and secure with the E-clip.

23. Tighten the trailing rod nuts and the shock absorber nuts to 66 ft. lbs.

24. Install the brake line to the flexible hose and install the axle shafts.

25. Install the brake line to the wheel cylinders and install the brake drums.

26. Install the wheels and refill the rear differential assembly.

27. Bleed the brake system and lower the vehicle.

STEERING

Steering Wheel

REMOVAL AND INSTALLATION

1. Disconnect the negative battery cable.

2. Disconnect the horn button and remove the steering wheel shaft nut.

3. Make matchmarks on the steering wheel and the shaft to use as a guide during reinstallation.

4. Remove the steering wheel, using a suitable steering wheel puller.

To install:

5. Install the steering wheel onto the shaft, aligning the matchmarks.

6. Install and tighten the shaft nut to 24 ft. lbs.

7. Install the horn button and connect the negative battery cable.

Manual Steering Gear

REMOVAL AND INSTALLATION

Samurai

1. Remove the steering shaft coupler bolt and disconnect the coupler from the steering box. As required, raise and support the vehicle safely.

2. Remove the radiator under cover and disconnect the ball stud of the drag rod. Remove the steering damper from the pitman arm.

3. Support the steering gear and remove the mounting bolts.

4. Remove the steering gear from the vehicle.

To install:

5. Install the steering gear in the vehicle and tighten the nuts to 55 ft. lbs.

6. Install the steering damper to the pitman arm tighten the nut to 30 ft. lbs.

7. Install the radiator under cover and connect the drag rod.

8. Connect the steering coupler to the steering box and tighten the bolt to 18 ft. lbs. Lower the vehicle.

Sidekick

1. As required, raise and support the vehicle safely. Disconnect the steering lower shaft mounting bolts.

2. Disconnect the center link end from the pitman arm.

3. Remove the 3 steering gear box mounting bolts.

4. Disconnect the steering lower shaft joint and remove the steering gear.

To install:

5. Install the steering gear box by connecting to the lower shaft joint.

NOTE: Align the flat part of the steering gear worm shaft with the bolt hole of the lower shaft joint.

6. Install the steering gear box mounting bolts and tighten to 60 ft. lbs.

7. Attach the center link to the pitman arm and tighten the nut to 35 ft. lbs.

8. Connect the lower shaft mounting bolts and tighten to 18 ft. lbs.

ADJUSTMENT

1. Check the worm shaft to make sure it is free from thrust play.

2. Place the pitman arm in a position that is nearly parallel with the worm shaft.

3. With the pitman arm in this position, the front wheels should be in a straight forward position.

4. Measure the worm shaft starting torque from its straight forward position. The torque should be 0.4–0.7 ft. lbs.

5. Adjust the worm shaft adjusting bolt to specifications.

Power Steering Gear

REMOVAL AND INSTALLATION

1. Disconnect the negative battery cable.

2. Remove the coolant reservoir tank from the radiator.

3. Disconnect the steering column lower shaft from the gear box.

4. Raise and safely support the vehicle.

5. Remove the center link nut and lock washer and disconnect the center link from the pitman arm, using a pitman arm puller.

6. Lower the vehicle. Remove the pressure hose from the power steering gear assembly and plug.

7. Disconnect the return hose and plug. Remove the 3 power steering gear mounting bolts.

8. Remove the power steering gear. Disconnect the pitman arm from the gear assembly, note the alignment marks.

To install:

9. Align the matchmarks on the pitman arm and the power steering gear sector shaft. Install the pitman arm to the gear assembly and tighten the nut to 95 ft. lbs.

10. Install the power steering gear assembly on the vehicle and tighten the mounting bolts to 72 ft. lbs.

11. Connect the power steering pressure and return hoses.

12. Raise and safely support the vehicle.

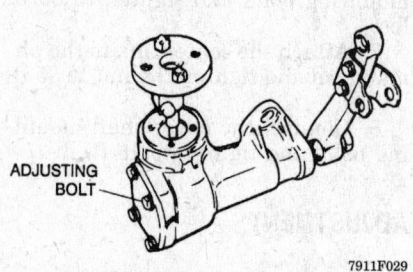

ADJUSTING
BOLT

7911F029

Adjusting the steering gear assembly

13. Install the center link to the pitman arm and tighten the nut to 40 ft. lbs. Lower the vehicle.

14. Connect the steering column lower shaft to the gear assembly and tighten the bolts to 29 ft. lbs.

15. Install the coolant reservoir tank to the radiator. Refill the power steering pump.

16. Connect the negative battery cable. Run the engine and operate the power steering. Recheck the fluid level and for any leaks.

ADJUSTMENT

1. Check the worm shaft to make sure it is free from thrust play.

2. Place the pitman arm in a position that is nearly parallel with the worm shaft.

3. With the pitman arm in this position, the front wheels are in a straight-forward state.

4. Measure the worm shaft starting torque from its straight-forward state. The torque should be 0.5 ft. lbs.

5. Adjust the worm shaft adjusting bolt to specifications.

Power steering Pump

REMOVAL AND INSTALLATION

NOTE: Before disconnecting the power steering pressure and return line at the pump assembly, make sure any dirt or grease is removed.

1. Disconnect the negative battery cable. Remove the coolant reservoir tank from the radiator.

2. Loosen the air conditioning compressor adjusting and pivot bolts, if equipped.

3. Loosen the power steering pump adjusting and mounting bolts, if not equipped with air conditioning.

4. Remove the power steering belt.

5. Disconnect the power steering pressure and return hose and plug.

6. Disconnect the power steering pressure switch lead wire at the switch terminal.

7. Remove the engine oil filter.

8. Remove the power steering pump mounting and adjusting bolts.

9. Remove the power steering pump.

To install:

10. Install the power steering pump and install the pump mounting bolts. Do not tighten.

11. Install the power steering pump pressure switch lead wire to the switch terminal.

12. Install the power steering pressure and return hoses.

13. Install the power steering belt and tighten the power steering pump mounting bolts to 21 ft. lbs.

14. Tighten the air conditioning mounting bolts to 21 ft. lbs., if equipped.

15. Install the coolant reservoir tank to the radiator and connect the negative battery cable. Refill the power steering pump.

16. Install the oil filter and fill the crankcase to the proper level.

17. Run the engine and operate the power steering. Recheck the fluid level and for any leaks.

BELT ADJUSTMENT

1. To adjust the power steering belt tension, loosen the adjusting bolt of the air conditioning compressor, if equipped, or that of the power steering pump for vehicles without air conditioning.

2. Adjust the belt tension to 0.30 in. deflection, using the proper belt tension gauge and measuring at the midpoint between the 2 pulleys.

3. Tighten the proper adjusting and mounting bolts to the specified torque.

SYSTEM BLEEDING

1. Raise and support the vehicle safely.

2. Fill the power steering reservoir to the specified level.

3. Run the engine for 3–5 minutes, stop the engine and add fluid if necessary to reach specified level.

4. With the engine stopped, turn the steering wheel to the left and to the right as far as it turns. Repeat a few times and refill the reservoir.

5. With the engine running at idle speed, bleed air from the system by loosening the bleeder valve at the gear assembly.

6. Repeat the stop to stop turn of the steering wheel until all the foam is gone.

7. Tighten the bleed valve securely. Recheck the fluid level in the reservoir.

NOTE: When air bleeding is not complete, it is indicated by a foaming fluid on the level indicator or a humming noise from the power steering pump.

Tie Rod Ends

REMOVAL AND INSTALLATION

1. Raise and safely support the vehicle and remove the wheels.

2. Remove the tie rod end from the steering knuckle, using a suitable tie rod end remover tool.

3. Mark the tie rod end locknut position on the tie rod thread.

4. Loosen the locknut and remove the tie rod end from the tie rod.

To install:

5. Install the tie rod end locknut and the tie rod end to the tie rod. Align the locknut with the mark on the tie rod thread and tighten the locknut to 48 ft. lbs.

6. Connect the tie rod end to the steering knuckle. Tighten the castle nut until the holes of the split pin are aligned but only within the specified torque 33 ft. lbs.

BRAKES

Master Cylinder

REMOVAL AND INSTALLATION

1. Disconnect the negative battery cable. Remove the air cleaner case.

2. Disconnect the reservoir lead wire.

3. Clean the outside of the reservoir and drain the fluid from the reservoir.

4. Disconnect and plug the brake fluid lines at the master cylinder.

5. Remove the master cylinder to booster mounting bolts and remove the master cylinder.

To install:

6. Install the new master cylinder and tighten the mounting bolts to 12 ft. lbs.

7. Install the hydraulic brake lines to the master cylinder and tighten

and tighten the flare nuts to 13 ft. lbs.

8. Install the reservoir lead wire, if equipped.

9. Fill the reservoir with the specified brake fluid. Install the air cleaner case.

10. Bleed the air from the brake hydraulic system and check the brake pedal play.

Proportioning Valve

REMOVAL AND INSTALLATION

1. Raise and safely support the vehicle.

2. Disconnect and plug the hydraulic brake lines from the proportioning valve assembly.

3. Remove the proportioning valve from the vehicle body.

NOTE: The proportioning valve should be removed with the spring attached.

To install:

4. Install the proportioning valve to the vehicle body and tighten the mounting bolts to 20 ft. lbs.

5. Connect the hydraulic brake lines to the proportioning valve and tighten the flare nuts to 13 ft. lbs.

6. Fill the brake reservoir to the proper level and bleed the brake hydraulic system. Lower the vehicle.

NOTE: Bleed the air from the proportioning valve bleeder valve.

Power Brake Booster

REMOVAL AND INSTALLATION

1. Disconnect the negative battery cable. Remove the air cleaner case.

2. Drain the fluid from the brake reservoir and remove the master cylinder.

3. Disconnect the vacuum hose from the booster. Remove the pushrod clevis pin and cotter pin from the brake pedal arm.

4. Disconnect the brake booster mounting nuts and remove the brake booster from the vehicle.

5. Disconnect the pedal attachment from the booster.

To install:

6. Connect the pedal attachment to the booster and install the booster to the vehicle. Tighten the mounting nuts to 7.5–11.5 ft. lbs.

7. Install the pushrod clevis pin and cotter pin to the brake pedal arm.

8. Connect the vacuum hose to the booster and install the master cylinder to the booster.

9. Install the air cleaner case and connect the negative battery cable.

10. Fill the brake reservoir and bleed the brake hydraulic system.

Brake Caliper

REMOVAL AND INSTALLATION

1. Disconnect the negative battery cable. Raise and safely support the vehicle.

2. Remove the wheels. Disconnect and plug the brake line.

3. Remove the caliper mounting bolts and remove the caliper from the vehicle.

To install:

4. Install the caliper on the vehicle. Tighten the mounting bolts to 65 ft. lbs.

5. Connect the hydraulic brake line, using 2 new washers. Replace the front wheels.

6. Lower the vehicle. Connect the negative battery cable.

7. Fill the brake reservoir and bleed the hydraulic brake system.

Disc Brake Pads

REMOVAL AND INSTALLATION

1. Disconnect the negative battery cable. Raise and safely support the vehicle.

2. Remove the wheels.

3. Disconnect the brake caliper.

NOTE: Do not allow the caliper to hang from the brake hose. Support it by the mounting bracket.

4. Remove the disc pads from the caliper. Disconnect the anti-rattle springs.

To install:

5. Connect the anti-rattle springs and install the brake pads on to caliper assembly.

6. Connect the brake caliper and install the front wheels.

7. Lower the vehicle. Connect the negative battery cable.

Brake Rotor

REMOVAL AND INSTALLATION

1. Disconnect the negative battery cable.

2. Raise and safely support the vehicle. Remove the front wheels.

3. Remove the brake caliper mounting bracket, with the caliper and the brake line attached, move it out of the way and support it.

NOTE: Do not allow the caliper to hang from the brake hose. Support it by the mounting bracket.

4. Install 2 bolts into the threaded holes in the brake rotor and tighten them evenly. This will remove the rotor from the hub assembly.

To install:

5. Install the new brake rotor on the hub and install the caliper assembly.

6. Install the front wheels and tighten to 65 ft. lbs.

7. Lower the vehicle and connect the negative battery terminal.

Brake Drums

REMOVAL AND INSTALLATION

1. Disconnect the negative battery cable. Raise and safely support the vehicle.

2. Make sure the parking brake is released.

3. Remove the wheels and the rear drum nuts from the vehicle.

4. Remove the brake drum, using a slide hammer.

To install:

5. Install the brake drum, tighten the brake drum nuts to 58 ft. lbs.

6. Install the rear wheels and lower the vehicle. Connect the negative battery cable.

Brake Shoes

REMOVAL AND INSTALLATION

1. Disconnect the negative battery cable. Raise and safely support the vehicle.

2. Remove the rear wheels from the vehicle. Remove the rear brake drums.

3. Remove the brake shoe hold-down springs.

4. Disconnect the parking brake cable from the parking brake shoe lever and remove the brake shoes.

To install:

5. Install the brake shoes and install the parking brake lever and cable to the assembly.

6. Install the brake shoe hold-down springs and install the rear brake drums.

7. Install the rear wheels, lower the vehicle and connect the negative battery terminal.

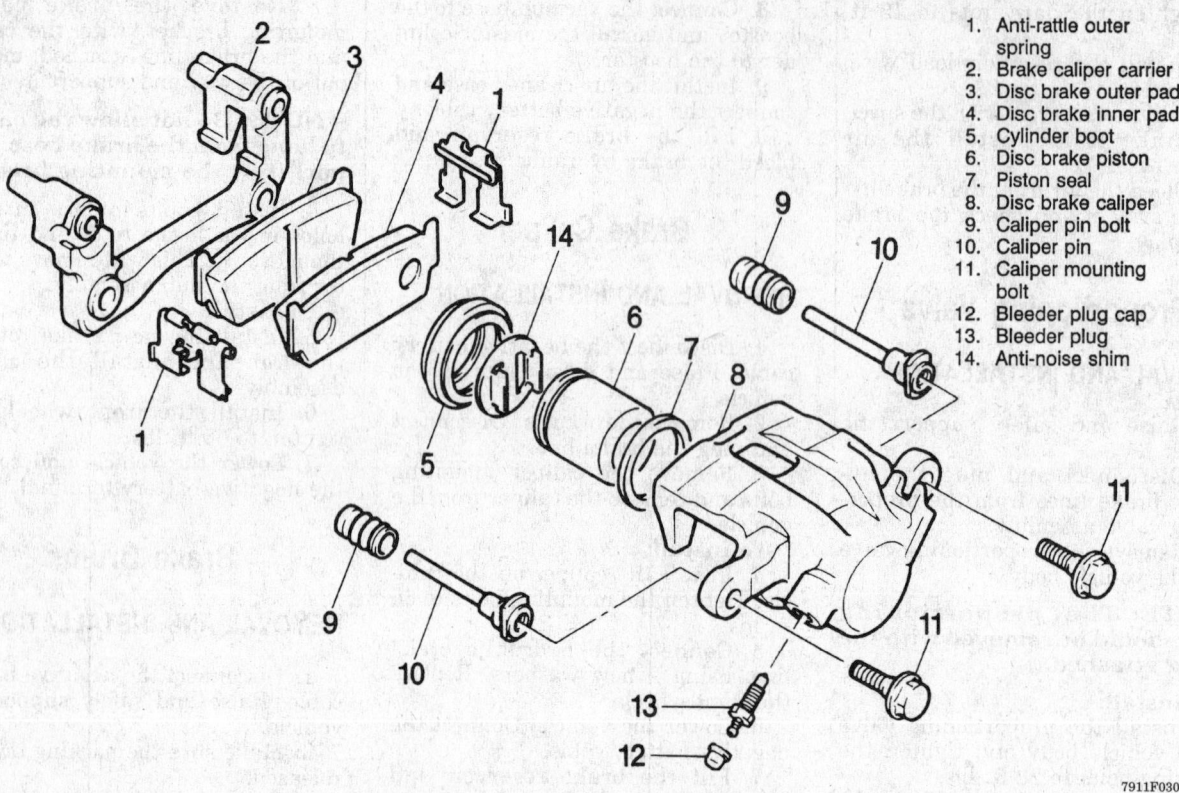

1. Anti-rattle outer spring
2. Brake caliper carrier
3. Disc brake outer pad
4. Disc brake inner pad
5. Cylinder boot
6. Disc brake piston
7. Piston seal
8. Disc brake caliper
9. Caliper pin bolt
10. Caliper pin
11. Caliper mounting bolt
12. Bleeder plug cap
13. Bleeder plug
14. Anti-noise shim

7911F030

Exploded view of the front disc brake assembly

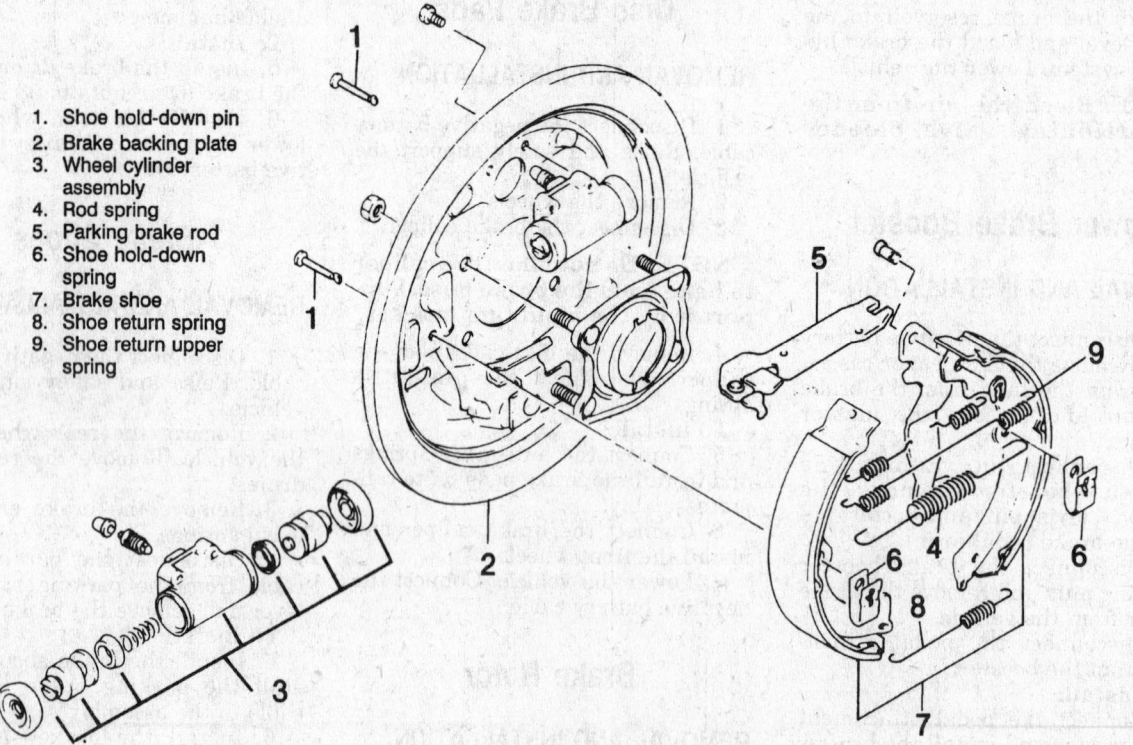

1. Shoe hold-down pin
2. Brake backing plate
3. Wheel cylinder assembly
4. Rod spring
5. Parking brake rod
6. Shoe hold-down spring
7. Brake shoe
8. Shoe return spring
9. Shoe return upper spring

7911F031

Exploded view of the rear brake drum assembly

Wheel Cylinder

REMOVAL AND INSTALLATION

1. Disconnect the negative battery cable. Raise and safely support the vehicle.

2. Remove the rear wheels and brake drums from the vehicle.

3. Remove the rear brake shoes and disconnect the brake line from the rear of the wheel cylinder. Plug the brake lines.

4. Remove the 2 rear wheel cylinder mounting bolts. Remove the rear wheel cylinder.

To install:

5. Install the wheel cylinder and tighten the mounting bolts to 7 ft. lbs.

6. Connect the brake line to the wheel cylinder and install the rear brake shoes.

7. Install the rear brake drums and the rear wheels.

8. Lower the vehicle. Connect the negative battery cable.

9. Bleed the brake system and check for any leaks when finished.

Parking Brake Cable

REMOVAL AND INSTALLATION

1. Disconnect the parking brake cable from the parking lever.

2. Raise and safely support the vehicle. Remove the rear wheels and brake drums from the vehicle.

3. Remove the rear brake shoes and disconnect the park brake cable from the park brake shoe lever.

4. Remove the cable from the brake backing plate by squeezing the park brake cable stop ring.

To install:

5. Install the cable to the backing plate and to the brake shoe lever.

6. Install the brake shoes and install the rear brake drums.

7. Install the rear wheels and lower the vehicle. Connect the cable to the parking brake lever.

ADJUSTMENT

1. Adjust the parking brake lever by loosening or tightening the self locking nut at the park brake lever.

2. The proper adjustment is when the park brake lever is within 7–9 notches, when the lever is pulled up at 44 lbs.

3. Check the rear drum for dragging after adjustment.

FRONT SUSPENSION

Shock Absorbers

REMOVAL AND INSTALLATION

1. Raise and safely support the vehicle.

2. Support the axle assembly and remove the upper shock absorber mounting nut.

3. Remove the lower shock absorber mounting nut and remove the shock absorber.

To install:

4. Install the shock absorber and install the lower mounting nut to the bolt.

5. Torque the upper mounting nut to 20 ft. lbs. and the lower nut to 33 ft. lbs. and lower the vehicle.

MacPherson Strut

REMOVAL AND INSTALLATION

1. Disconnect the negative battery cable.

2. Raise and safely support the vehicle. Allow the front suspension to hang free.

3. Remove the front wheel. Disconnect the E-clip mounting the brake hose and remove the brake hose from the strut bracket.

4. Remove the strut bracket to steering knuckle bolts.

5. Lower the vehicle. Remove the strut support nuts, while holding the strut by hand. Remove the strut assembly.

To install:

6. Install the strut assembly and tighten the strut support nuts to 18 ft. lbs.

7. Raise and safely support the vehicle.

8. Install the strut bracket to steering knuckle bolts and tighten to 66 ft. lbs.

9. Connect the brake hose to the strut bracket using the E-clip.

10. Install the front wheels and lower the vehicle.

11. Connect the negative battery cable.

Coil Springs

REMOVAL AND INSTALLATION

Sidekick

1. Disconnect the negative battery cable.

2. Raise and safely support the vehicle. Allow the front suspension to hang free.

3. Remove the front wheel and the locking hub assembly.

4. Remove the front axle circlip and washer.

5. Remove the brake caliper mounting bracket, with the caliper and the brake line attached, move it out of the way and support it.

6. Remove the brake disc and disconnect the stabilizer link from the control arm.

7. Disconnect the tie rod end and support the lower control arm using a jack.

8. Disconnect the strut bracket and remove the ball joint castle nut.

9. Remove the steering knuckle and the wheel hub assembly while lowering the jack.

10. Remove the coil spring from the vehicle.

To install:

11. Install the coil spring in the vehicle and install the wheel hub and steering knuckle while raising the jack.

12. Connect the strut bracket and install the ball joint castle nut.

13. Connect the tie rod end and connect the stabilizer link to the control arm.

14. Install the brake disc and connect the caliper assembly.

15. Install the front axle circlip and washer and install the locking hub assembly.

16. Install the front wheels, lower the vehicle and connect the negative battery cable.

Leaf Springs

REMOVAL AND INSTALLATION

Samurai

1. Disconnect the negative battery cable.

2. Raise and safely support the vehicle. Allow the front suspension to hang free.

3. Remove the stabilizer bar pivot bolt.

4. Support the front axle assembly with an adjustable stand.

5. Remove the leaf spring to spring plate mounting U-bolts.

6. Remove the shackle pin and the nut from the front of the leaf spring.

7. Disconnect the leaf spring bolt and remove the leaf spring.

NOTE: Removal of the leaf spring causes the axle housing to hang. Support it with a safety stand to prevent it from damaging the U-joint of the driveshaft.

To install:

8. Install the leaf spring and leaf spring bolts and tighten to 57 ft. lbs.

9. Install the shackle pin and nut to the front of the leaf spring and install the spring plate and U-bolts.

10. Install the stabilizer bar pivot bolt.

11. Lower the vehicle and connect the negative battery terminal.

Lower Ball Joints

INSPECTION

Sidekick

1. Inspect for the smoothness of the rotation.
2. Check the ball stud for damage.
3. Inspect the dust shield for damage.

REMOVAL AND INSTALLATION

Sidekick

1. Disconnect the negative battery cable. Remove the coil spring from the vehicle.
2. Remove the control arm mounting bolts.
3. Remove the control arm.
4. Disconnect the ball joint from the control arm and remove the ball joint.

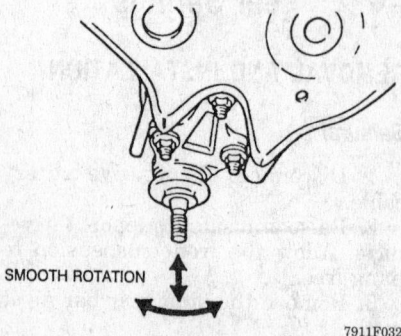

SMOOTH ROTATION

7911F032

Checking ball joint play

To install:

5. Install the ball joint to the control arm and tighten the bolts to 63 ft. lbs.

6. Install the control arm to the chassis and tighten the bolts to 74 ft. lbs.

7. Install the coil spring and connect the negative battery cable.

Lower Control Arms

REMOVAL AND INSTALLATION

Sidekick

1. Disconnect the negative battery cable. Remove the coil spring from the vehicle.
2. Remove the control arm mounting bolts.
3. Remove the control arm.

To install:

4. Install the control arm to the chassis and tighten the bolts to 74 ft. lbs.

5. Install the coil spring and connect the negative battery cable.

Stabilizer Bar

REMOVAL AND INSTALLATION

1. Disconnect the negative battery cable. Raise and safely support the vehicle.
2. Disconnect the left and the right stabilizer ball joints from the front control arms on the Sidekick.
3. Disconnect the stabilizer bar pivot bolts on the Samurai.
4. Remove the stabilizer bar mount bushing bracket bolts and nuts.
5. Remove the stabilizer bar.
6. Remove the stabilizer links on the Sidekick.

To install:

7. Install the new stabilizer bar, using new bushings.

8. Torque the stabilizer bar pivot bolts to 51–65 ft. lbs. and the mounting bracket nuts to 13–20 ft. lbs. for the Samurai. Torque the stabilizer link nuts to 21 ft. lbs. and the stabilizer bar bracket bolts and nuts to 37 ft. lbs. for the Sidekick.

9. Lower the vehicle and connect the negative battery cable.

Kingpin and Bushings

REMOVAL AND INSTALLATION

Samurai

1. Raise and safely support the vehicle.
2. Remove the steering knuckle from the vehicle.

NOTE: When the steering knuckle is pulled, the lower kingpin bearing sometimes falls off.

3. Remove the upper and the lower kingpins, mark them. Check the number of shims on each side.

To install:

4. Install the new kingpin bearings in the steering knuckle holding them in with grease.

5. Install the steering knuckle on the axle assembly.

6. Install the new kingpins in the steering knuckle, shim them correctly and torque the bolts to 17 ft. lbs.

NOTE: The correct procedure for installing the kingpins is to check the turning torque of the spindle while pulling it outwards from the tie rod end hole. A spring type gauge is required for this procedure. The correct force should be 2.20–3.96 lbs. of force required to turn the spindle without the oil seal being installed. Use additional shims, if necessary, to correct the turning torque.

7. With the turning torque of the spindle correct and the oil seal installed, install the front wheels and lower the vehicle.

REAR SUSPENSION

Shock Absorbers

REMOVAL AND INSTALLATION

1. Raise and safely support the vehicle. Support the rear axle housing.
2. Remove the upper and lower shock absorber mounting bolts.
3. Remove the rear shock absorber.

To install:

4. Install the the rear shock absorber.

5. On the Sidekick, install the upper mounting bolts and tighten to 21

ft. lbs. Install the lower mounting bolts and tighten to 63 ft. lbs.

6. On Samurai, tighten the upper and the lower mounting bolts to 25 ft. lbs.

Coil Springs

REMOVAL AND INSTALLATION

Sidekick

1. Raise and safely support the vehicle. Remove the rear wheels.
2. Support the rear axle housing, using a floor jack.
3. Remove the shock absorber lower mounting bolt and disconnect the parking brake cable hangers.
4. Lower the rear axle housing so the coil spring can be removed.
5. Remove the coil spring from the vehicle.
   To install:
6. Install the coil spring to the spring seat and raise the axle housing.

7. Install the lower shock absorber mounting bolt but do not tighten.
8. Connect the parking brake cable hangers and install the rear wheels.
9. Lower the vehicle and tighten the lower shock absorber nut to 64 ft. lbs.

Leaf Springs

REMOVAL AND INSTALLATION

Samurai

1. Raise and safely support the vehicle. Remove the rear wheels.
2. Safely support the axle housing separately and disconnect the shocks.
3. Disconnect the stabilizer bar from the shackle plate under the leaf spring.

NOTE: Do not let the axle housing hang on the brake hoses or lines.

4. Remove the rear axle housing U-bolt nuts and remove the bolts.
5. Raise the rear axle housing to release spring tension and remove the shackle plate.
6. Support the leaf spring and disconnect the rear leaf spring mounting bolts.
7. Remove the leaf spring assembly.
   To install:
8. Install the leaf spring and shackle assembly and tighten the mounting bolts to 56 ft. lbs.
9. Install the U-bolt nuts and tighten to 50 ft. lbs.
10. Connect the stabilizer bar under the shackle plate. Install the shocks and tighten to 30 ft. lbs.
11. Install the rear wheels and lower the vehicle.

TOYOTA 12

Land Cruiser • Pick-Up • Previa • 4Runner

FIRING ORDERS

NOTE: To avoid confusion, always replace spark plug wires one at a time.

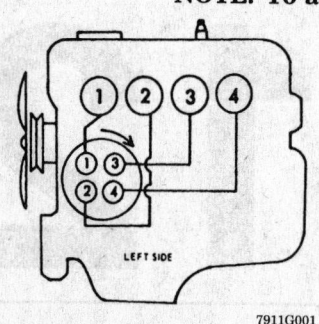

7911G001

22R-E and 2TZ-FE Engines
Engine Firing Order: 1–3–4–2
Distributor Rotation: Clockwise

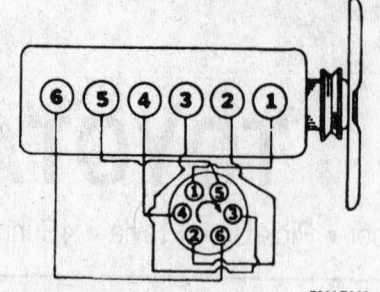

7911G002

3F-E Engine
Engine Firing Order: 1–5–3–6–2–4
Distributor Rotation: Clockwise

7911G003

3VZ-E Engine
Engine Firing Order: 1–2–3–4–5–6
Distributor Rotation: Counterclockwise

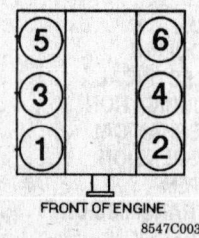

FRONT OF ENGINE

8547C003

1FZ-FE Engine
Engine Firing Order:
1–5–3–6–2–4
Distributor Rotation:
Counterclockwise

ENGINE ELECTRICAL

NOTE: Disconnecting the battery cable on some vehicles may interfere with the functions of the on board computer systems and may require the computer to undergo a relearning process, once the negative battery cable is disconnected.

Distributor

REMOVAL

3F-E, 22R-E, 3VZ-E and 1FZ-FE Engines

1. Disconnect the negative battery cable. Label and disconnect the high tension cables from the spark plugs. Remove the high tension cable from the coil.
2. Remove the primary wire or the electrical connector and the vacuum line, if equipped, from the distributor. Remove the distributor cap spring clips or screws, then the cap.
3. Using a piece of chalk, match-mark the rotor-to-distributor housing and the distributor-to-engine block. This will aid in correct positioning of the distributor during installation.
4. Remove the distributor hold-down clamp bolt and the distributor from the engine.

NOTE: It is easier to install the distributor if the engine timing is not disturbed while it is removed.

2TZ-FE Engine

1. Disconnect the negative battery cable.
2. Label and disconnect the spark plug wires.
3. Disconnect the distributor connector and ventilation hoses.
4. Remove the cap and packing.
5. Set the No. 1 cylinder to TDC of the compression stroke. Install the service bolt and nut into the equipment driveshaft to turn the crankshaft pulley. Turn the crankshaft 1 turn if the rotor is not facing No. 1 spark plug wire.
6. Remove the distributor hold-down and pull the distributor from the engine.

INSTALLATION

Timing Not Disturbed

ALL ENGINES

1. Insert the distributor into the engine block by aligning the matchmarks made during removal.
2. Engage the distributor drive with the oil pump driveshaft.
3. Install the distributor hold-down clamp, the cap, the high tension wire, the primary wire or the electrical connector and the vacuum line(s).
4. Install the spark plugs cables.
5. Connect the negative battery cable.

Timing Disturbed

3F-E, 22R-E, 3VZ-E AND 1FZ-FE ENGINES

If the engine has been cranked, dismantled or the timing otherwise lost, proceed as follows:
1. Determine the Top Dead Center (TDC) of the No. 1 cylinder's compression stroke by removing the spark plug from the No. 1 cylinder and placing a finger or a compression gauge over the spark plug hole.

NOTE: Using a wrench, turn the crankshaft until the compression pressure starts to build up. Continue cranking the engine until the timing marks indicate TDC (0 degrees).

2. Turn the crankshaft to align the timing marks on the 22R-E engines to 5 degrees BTDC or on the 3VZ-E engines to 0 degree TDC.
3. Temporarily install the rotor on the distributor shaft so the rotor is pointing toward the No. 1 terminal of the distributor cap.
4. Using a small prybar, align the slot on the distributor drive (oil pump driveshaft) with the key on the bottom of the distributor shaft.
5. Install the distributor in the block by rotating it slightly (no more than a gear tooth in either direction) until the driven gear meshes with the drive.

NOTE: Oil the distributor drive gear and the oil pump driveshaft end before installation.

6. Temporarily tighten the lock bolt.
7. Remove the rotor, then install the dust cover, the rotor and the distributor cap.

8. Install the primary wire or the electrical connector and the vacuum line(s).
9. Install the No. 1 cylinder spark plug. Connect the cables to the spark plugs in the proper order. Install the high tension wire on the coil.
10. Start the engine and adjust the ignition timing.

2TZ-FE ENGINE

1. Remove the No. 1 spark plug, place a finger over the opening and rotate the equipment driveshaft, using a turning tool, in the clockwise direction, until pressure is felt, then replace the spark plug.

NOTE: Make sure the slit in the exhaust camshaft is in the proper position.

2. Remove the service bolt and nut.
3. Align the cut-out portion of the coupling with the groove on the housing.
4. Install the distributor and align the center of the flange with the bolt hole on the cylinder head.
5. Install the hold-down bolt loosely.
6. Install the seal packing, distributor cap and connect the wiring.
7. Adjust the timing to specifications and torque the hold-down bolt to 14 ft. lbs. (19 Nm).

Ignition Timing

ADJUSTMENT

Except 2TZ-FE and 1FZ-FE Engines

NOTE: The timing mark locations differ between the engines used in the Pick-Up and 4Runner for 22R-E and 3VZ-E engines, and Land Cruiser for 3F-E engine. On the 22R-E, and 3VZ-E engines, the timing marks are located on the crankshaft pulley (painted notch) and the timing cover (plate). On the 3F-E engine, the timing marks are located on the flywheel (ball) and the bell housing (pointer).

1. Set the parking brake and block the wheels.
2. Clean off the timing marks and mark them with chalk or paint. The crankshaft may have to rotated to find the marks.
3. Warm the engine to operating temperatures. Connect a tachometer

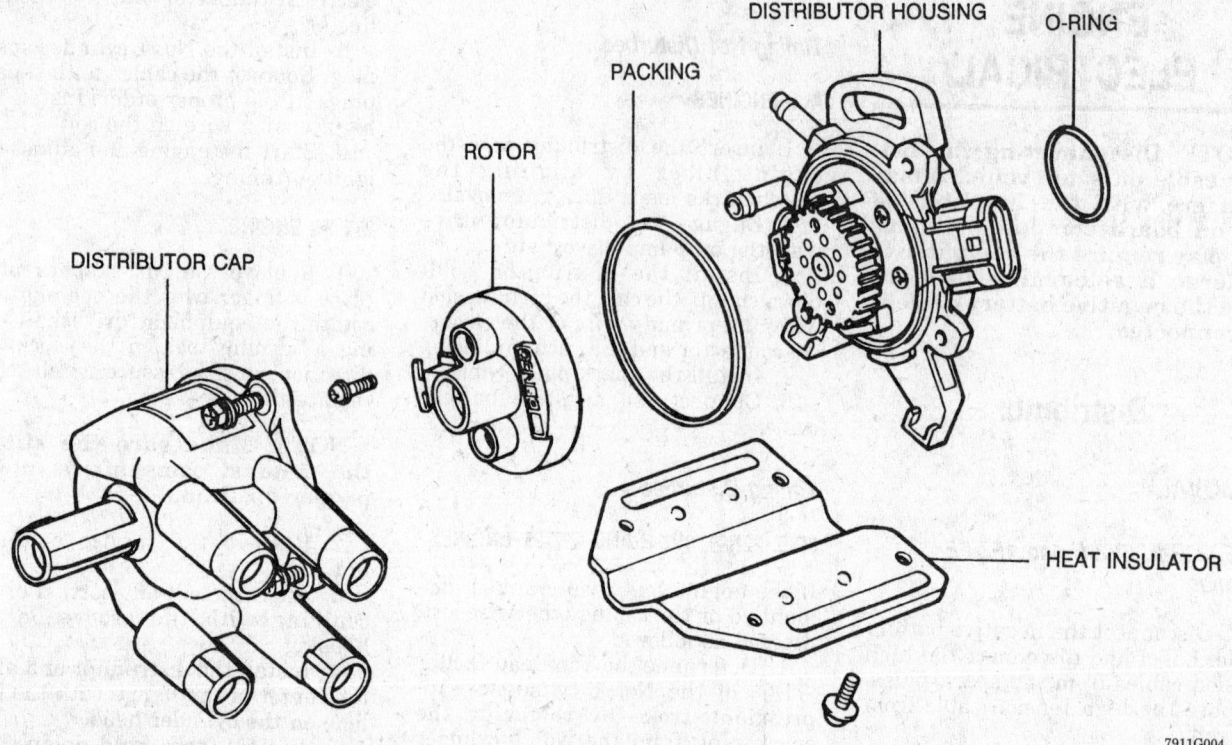

DISTRIBUTOR HOUSING

O-RING

PACKING

ROTOR

DISTRIBUTOR CAP

HEAT INSULATOR

7911G004

Distributor assembly — 2TZ-FE engine

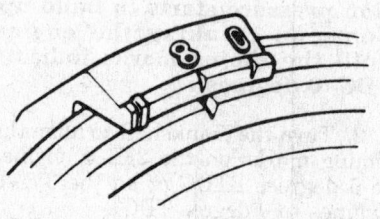

7911G007

Timing mark location — 22R-E engine

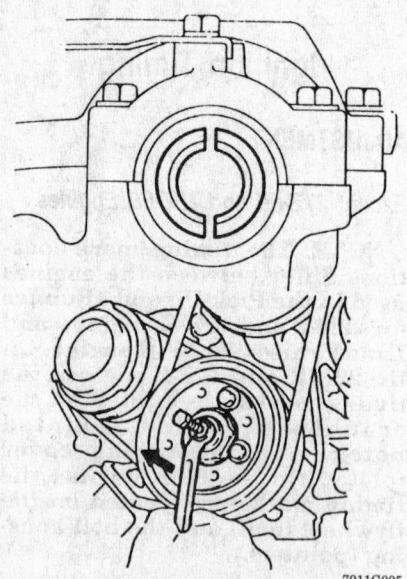

7911G005

Exhaust camshaft positioning — 2TZ-FE engine

to the engine, then, check and/or adjust the engine idle speed.

NOTE: On the 22R-E, and 3VZ-E engines, connect the positive (+) tachometer terminal either to the negative (-) ignition coil terminal or to the yellow service connector. On the 3VZ-E engines, use a service wire to short the engine check connector.

4. Turn **OFF** the engine and connect a timing light according to the manufacturer's directions.

5. On the 22R-E engines, disconnect and short the **T** and the **E$_1$** connector of the engine check harness (near the front of the vehicle). On all other engines, disconnect and plug the vacuum hose(s) from the distributor vacuum unit.

NOTE: If equipped with a High Altitude Compensation (HAC) system there are 2 vacuum hoses which connect to the distributor. Both must be disconnected and plugged. These systems require an extra step in the timing procedure.

6. Be sure the timing light wires are clear of the fan and pulleys, then start the engine.

7. Allow the engine to run at the specified idle speed with the shift selector in neutral for manual transmission or **D** for automatic transmission.

8. Point the timing light at the marks. With the engine at the specified idle, the marks should align.

9. If the timing is incorrect, loosen the bolt at the base of the distributor just enough so the distributor can be turned. Hold the distributor by its base and turn it slightly to advance or retard the timing as required. Once the marks are seen to align properly, tighten the bolt.

10. After tightening the distributor bolt or adjusting the octane selector, recheck the timing. Turn **OFF** the

engine, then, disconnect the timing light and connect the vacuum line(s) at the distributor or the electrical **T** and **E₁** connector, except on engines with HAC.

11. On engines with HAC after setting the initial timing, reconnect the vacuum hoses at the distributor. Recheck the timing.

12. If the advance is still low, pinch the hose between the HAC valve and the 3 way connector; it should now be to specifications. If not, the HAC valve should be checked for proper operation.

2TZ-FE Engine

NOTE: On the 2TZ-FE engine the timing mark is on the equipment driveshaft U-joint and front cover.

Ground terminals **TE1** and **E1** of the check connector using tool SST 09843-18020 or equivalent. The check connector is next to the emergency brake lever.

1. Connect a timing light terminal to terminal **30** of the starter and test probe to the No. 1 spark plug wire (light blue).

2. Start the engine and warm up. Slowly turn the distributor until the timing mark on the crankshaft pulley is aligned with the **5** mark. Tighten the distributor bolt and recheck timing.

3. Remove the grounding tool from the check connector and timing light.

1FZ-FE Engine

NOTE: On the 1FZ-FE engine, the timing marks are on the crankshaft pulley and the engine block.

1. Connect a tachometer and a timing light. Connect the test probe from the tachometer to the negative terminal, large upper right terminal, of the DLC1 connector.

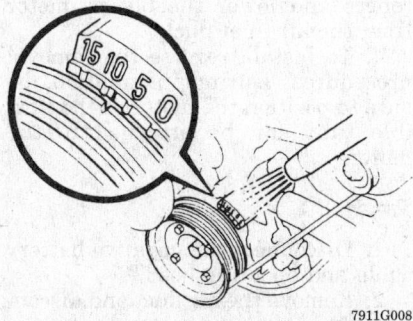

7911G008

Timing mark location — 3VZ-E engine

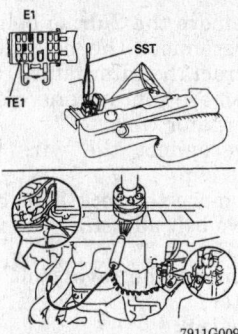

7911G009

Grounding the check connector and timing location — 2TZ-FE engine

2. Connect SST 09843-18020 or equivalent, to terminals **E1**, 3rd from the left at the top, and **TE1**, 2nd from the left on the 2nd row, of the DLC1 connector.

3. Point the timing light at the flywheel and check for correct timing of 3 degrees BTDC, with the vehicle in neutral and the air conditioner turned **OFF**.

4. If the timing is incorrect, loosen the hold-down bolt and adjust the distributor.

5. Torque the hold-down bolt to 13 ft. lbs. (18 Nm) and recheck the timing.

6. Remove the SST09843-18020 or equivalent, from the DLC1 connector.

7. Check that the timing is 2–13 degrees BTDC.

8. Disconnect the tachometer and the timing light from the engine.

Alternator

PRECAUTIONS

Several precautions must be observed with alternator equipped vehicles to avoid damage to the unit.

• If the battery is removed for any reason, make sure it is reconnected with the correct polarity. Reversing the battery connections may result in damage to the one-way rectifiers.

• When utilizing a booster battery as a starting aid, always connect the positive to positive terminals and the negative terminal from the booster battery to a good engine ground on the vehicle being started.

• Never use a fast charger as a booster to start vehicles.

• Disconnect the battery cables when charging the battery with a fast charger.

• Never attempt to polarize the alternator.

• Do not use test lights of more than 12 volts when checking diode continuity.

• Do not short across or ground any of the alternator terminals.

• The polarity of the battery, alternator and regulator must be matched and considered before making any electrical connections within the system.

• Never separate the alternator on an open circuit. Make sure all connections within the circuit are clean and tight.

• Disconnect the battery ground terminal when performing any service on electrical components.

• Disconnect the battery if arc welding is to be done on the vehicle.

BELT TENSION ADJUSTMENT

Inspection and adjustment to the alternator drive belt should be performed every 30,000 miles or if the alternator has been removed.

1. Inspect the drive belt to see that it is not cracked or worn. Be sure its surfaces are free of grease or oil.

2. If not using a belt tension gauge, push down on the belt halfway between the fan and the alternator pulleys, (or crankshaft pulley) with thumb pressure; belt deflection should be ⅜–½ in.

3. If using the an appropriate belt tension gauge, position it in the middle of the drive belt and check the belt tension; a new belt should be 100–150 lbs. (135–202 N) for Pick-Up, 4Runner and 1993–96 Land Cruiser, a used belt should be 60–100 lbs. (81–136 N) for Pick-Up, 4Runner and 1993–96 Land Cruiser.

4. If the belt tension requires adjustment, loosen the adjusting link bolt and move the alternator until the proper belt tension is obtained.

5. Tighten the adjusting link bolt.

REMOVAL AND INSTALLATION

NOTE: On some engines the alternator is mounted very low. On these engines it may be necessary to remove the gravel shield and work from under the vehicle in order to gain access to the alternator.

Except 2TZ-FE and 1FZ-FE Engines

1. Disconnect the negative battery cable.

2. Remove the air cleaner, if necessary, to gain access to the alternator.

3. On the 22R-E engines, drain the engine coolant. If necessary, remove the under engine cover.

4. If equipped with power steering, remove the water inlet pipe bolts and the water inlet hose from the engine.

NOTE: If equipped with air conditioning, it may be necessary to remove the No. 2 fan shroud.

5. Remove the nut or the wiring connector and the wire(s) from the alternator.

6. Remove the adjusting lock, the pivot and the adjusting bolt(s), then the drive belt from the alternator.

7. Remove the alternator attaching bolt and then withdraw the alternator from its bracket.

8. To install, reverse the removal procedures. Rotate the drive belt 8 revolutions for new belt or 5 revolutions for used belt. Adjust the drive belt tension.

9. Refill the cooling system, if it was drained.

10. Connect the negative battery cable.

2TZ-FE Engine

NOTE: To service many engine components, the engine service hole covers may have to be removed. Remove the front seats, scuff plate and seat legs to access the service hole covers.

1. Disconnect the negative battery cable.

2. Raise the vehicle and safely support it.

3. Disconnect the alternator connectors.

4. Loosen the lock bolt, adjusting bolt and pivot bolt. Remove the drive belt.

5. Remove the pivot and lock bolts. Remove the alternator.

To install:

6. Install the alternator and bolts.

7. Install the belt and adjust. Do not pry against the housing.

8. Connect the alternator wiring and battery cable.

9. Lower the vehicle and check operation.

1FZ-FE Engine

1. Disconnect the negative battery cable.

2. Remove the 3 bolts retaining the power steering reservoir tank and disconnect the reservoir tank.

3. Loosen the lock bolt, pivot bolt and adjusting bolt from the alternator.

4. Remove the 2 drive belts.

5. Disconnect the electrical connector from the alternator.

6. Remove the nut and disconnect the alternator wire.

7. Disconnect the wire harness from the clip.

8. Remove the lock bolt, bolt, nut and drive belt adjusting bar from the alternator.

9. Remove the pivot bolt and the alternator.

To install:

10. Install the alternator on the alternator bracket with the pivot bolt.

11. Install the drive belt adjusting bar and torque the bolt and nut to 15 ft. lbs. (21 Nm).

12. Temporarily install the lock bolt.

13. Connect the alternator electrical connector. Connect the alternator wire with the nut. Connect the wire harness to the clip.

14. Install the 2 drive belts.

15. Measure the belt tension. Belt tension should be 100–150 lbs. for a new belt and 60–100 for a used belt.

16. Torque the pivot bolt to 43 ft. lbs. (59 Nm) and the adjusting lock bolt to 15 ft. lbs. (21 Nm).

17. Connect the power steering reservoir tank and tighten the 3 bolts.

18. Connect the negative battery cable.

Starter

REMOVAL AND INSTALLATION

Except 2TZ-FE Engine

1. If necessary, raise and support the vehicle safely.

2. Disconnect the negative battery terminal from the battery.

NOTE: On some 22R-E engines equipped with an automatic transmission, it may be necessary to remove the transmission oil filler tube.

3. Disconnect the wiring connectors and the wiring from the starter.

4. Remove the starter-to-engine bolts and the starter from the engine.

5. To install, reverse the removal procedures.

2TZ-FE Engine

1. Disconnect the negative battery cable.

2. Raise the vehicle and safely support it.

3. Disconnect the starter connectors.

4. Remove the front driveshaft for 4WD only.

5. Remove the clutch release cylinder (manual transmission only).

6. Remove the 3 bolts and starter for 2WD. Remove the 4 bolts, 2 nuts, center support bracket and starter for 4WD.

To install:

7. Install the starter and torque the long bolts to 41 ft. lbs. (54 Nm) and short bolts to 30 ft. lbs. (41 Nm).

8. Connect the starter connectors.

9. Install the front driveshaft and clutch release cylinder, if removed.

10. Connect the battery cable and lower the vehicle.

CHASSIS ELECTRICAL

Heater Blower Motor

REMOVAL AND INSTALLATION

Pick-Up and 4Runner

1. Disconnect the negative battery cable.

2. Disconnect the electrical connector from motor.

3. Remove the blower motor-to-case screws and lift the motor from the case.

4. To install, reverse the removal procedures. Make sure the seal around the motor flange is in good condition.

Land Cruiser

1. Disconnect the negative battery cable. Disconnect the electrical connector from the blower motor.

2. Disconnect the flexible tube from the side of the blower motor.

3. Remove the blower motor fasteners and lower the blower motor from the air inlet duct.

4. To install, reverse the removal procedures. During installation, be sure to position the motor so the flexible tube can be attached to the motor.

Previa

1. Disconnect the negative battery cable and open the hood.

2. Remove the air duct and disconnect the motor connectors.

3. Remove the blower motor from the housing.

4. Installation is the reverse of removal.

Windshield Wiper Motor

REMOVAL AND INSTALLATION

Pick-Up and 4Runner

FRONT

1. Disconnect the negative battery cable. Disconnect the wiring from the wiper motor. Remove the motor from the fire wall.
2. Remove the nut, then, pry the wiper link from the crank arm.
3. Remove the motor.
4. To install, reverse the removal procedures and inspect he operation.

REAR

1. Disconnect the negative battery cable. At the rear of the vehicle, remove the wiper motor cover panel.
2. Remove the wiper arm from the wiper motor.
3. Disconnect the electrical connector from the wiper motor.
4. Remove the wiper motor-to-door bolts and the motor from the vehicle.
5. To install, reverse the removal procedures and inspect the operation.

Land Cruiser and Previa

NOTE: The wiper motor is removed with the linkage assembly.

1. Disconnect the negative battery cable. Remove the wiper arm retaining nuts, then, the wiper arm/blade assemblies.
2. Remove both wiper arm pivot covers and the pivot-to-cowl attaching screws.
3. Remove the service hole covers from the cowl area of the engine compartment.
4. Disconnect the wiring from the wiper motor.

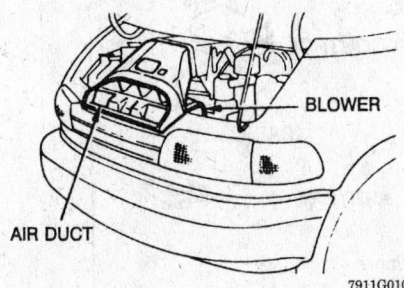

7911G010

Blower motor location — Previa

5. From the engine compartment, remove the wiper motor plate-to-cowl screws. Withdraw the wiper motor and the linkage from the cowl panel as an assembly.
6. Pry the linkage from of the wiper motor.
7. To install, reverse the removal procedures.

Windshield Wiper Linkage

REMOVAL AND INSTALLATION

Pick-Up, 4Runner and Previa

1. Disconnect the negative battery cable. Remove the wiper motor.
2. Remove the wiper arms by removing their retaining nuts and working them off their shafts.
3. Remove the wiper shafts nuts/spacers and push the shafts down into the body cavity. Pull the linkage from the cavity through the wiper motor hole.
4. To install, reverse the removal procedures.

Land Cruiser

1. Disconnect the negative battery cable. Remove the wiper arm assemblies.
2. Remove the endplate from the pivot housing.
3. Remove the wiper motor with the linkage cable.
4. Separate the wiper motor and the transmission.
5. Remove the linkage cable.
6. To install, reverse the removal procedures.

Windshield Wiper Switch

REMOVAL AND INSTALLATION

Front

1. Disconnect negative battery terminal from the battery.
2. Remove the upper and the lower steering column shrouds.
3. Disconnect the combination switch electrical connector.
4. Remove the terminal from the horn contact.
5. To remove the windshield/wiper switch wires from the electrical connector, place a small prybar into the end of the connector, pry up on the retaining tab and pull the wire(s) from the connector.
6. Remove the windshield/wiper switch-to-combination switch screw and the switch.

7. Installation is the reverse of the removal procedure. To install, place the wire(s) into the electrical connector's slots, place a suitable tool behind the wire terminal and push the wire into the connector until the retaining tab locks it into place.

Rear

1. If equipped with a rear wiper switch, it will be located in the center of the dash.
2. Disconnect the negative battery cable. Using a small prybar, pry the rear wiper switch from the center of the dash.
3. Disconnect the electrical connector from the rear of the switch.
4. To install, reverse the removal procedures.

Instrument Cluster

REMOVAL AND INSTALLATION

Pick-Up and 4Runner

1. Disconnect the negative battery terminal from the battery.
2. Remove the upper and lower steering column covers.
3. Remove the instrument trim panel screws and the panel.
4. Disconnect the speedometer cable from the speedometer.
5. Remove the instrument panel screws and pull the panel forward. Disconnect the electrical connectors from the back of the panel and remove the panel.
6. To install, reverse the removal procedures.

Land Cruiser

1. Disconnect the negative battery terminal from the battery.
2. Disconnect the speedometer cable. Remove the instrument panel screws.
3. Loosen the steering column clamp by removing the attaching bolts.
4. Pull out the instrument panel and the speedometer, disconnect the electrical connectors and remove the panel.
5. To install, reverse the removal procedures.

Previa

1. Disconnect the negative battery cable.
2. Remove the cluster finish panel by removing the 2 screws and prying on the left side with a prybar. Be

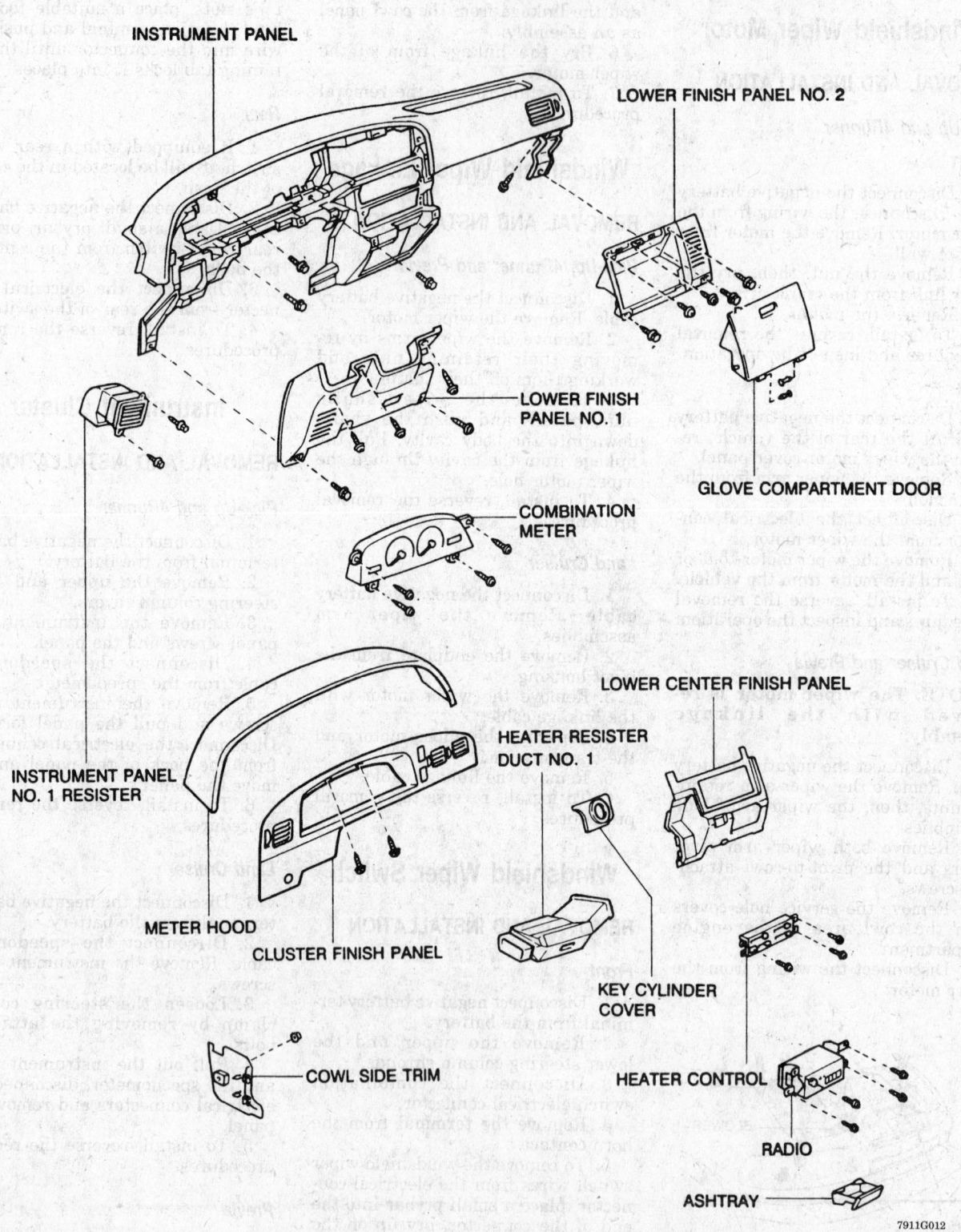

INSTRUMENT PANEL

LOWER FINISH PANEL NO. 2

LOWER FINISH PANEL NO. 1

GLOVE COMPARTMENT DOOR

COMBINATION METER

LOWER CENTER FINISH PANEL

INSTRUMENT PANEL NO. 1 RESISTER

HEATER RESISTER DUCT NO. 1

METER HOOD

CLUSTER FINISH PANEL

KEY CYLINDER COVER

COWL SIDE TRIM

HEATER CONTROL

RADIO

ASHTRAY

7911G012

Typical instrument cluster and panel assembly — Pick-Up and 4Runner

careful not to damage the plastic components.

3. Remove the 4 screws and disconnect the cable from the automatic transmission indicator. Remove the cable from the roller and cluster.

4. Disconnect the electrical connectors and remove from the vehicle.

5. To install, reverse the removal procedures.

Speedometer Cable

REMOVAL AND INSTALLATION

1. Disconnect the negative battery cable. Remove the instrument cluster and disconnect the cable from the speedometer.

2. Disconnect the other end of the speedometer cable from the transmission extension housing and pull the cable from its jacket at the transmission end.

NOTE: If the cable is being replaced because it is broken, be sure to remove both pieces of the broken cable.

3. Using graphite, lubricate the new speedometer cable and insert it into the cable jacket at the lower end.

4. Connect the speedometer cable to the transmission, then, to the instrument cluster.

5. To complete the installation, reverse the removal procedures.

Headlight/Dimmer Switch

REMOVAL AND INSTALLATION

1. Disconnect the negative battery terminal from the battery.

2. Remove the upper and lower steering column covers.

3. Disconnect the electrical connector from the combination switch.

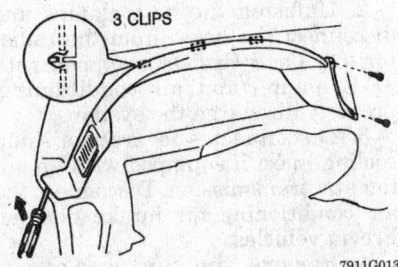

Instrument cluster finish panel removal — Previa

4. Remove the headlight switch-to-combination switch screws and the headlight switch from the combination switch.

5. To install, reverse the removal procedures.

Turn Signal Switch

REMOVAL AND INSTALLATION

1. Disconnect negative battery terminal.

2. Remove the upper and the lower steering column shrouds.

3. Disconnect the combination switch electrical connector.

4. At the left-rear of the combination switch, remove the mounting screws and the turn signal switch.

5. If necessary to the remove the turn signal switch wires from the electrical connector, place a small prybar into the end of the connector, pry up on the retaining tab and pull the wire(s) from the connector.

6. To install, place the wire(s) into the electrical connector's slots, place a prybar behind the wire terminal and push the wire into the connector until the retaining tab locks it into place.

7. To complete the installation, reverse the removal procedures.

Combination Switch

REMOVAL AND INSTALLATION

The combination switch is composed of the turn signal, the headlight control, the dimmer, the hazard, the wiper and the washer switches.

1. Disconnect the negative battery cable. Remove the steering wheel.

2. Remove the upper and lower steering column shroud screws and the shrouds.

3. Remove the combination switch screws and the switch from the column.

4. Disconnect the electrical connector from the combination switch. To remove the wires from the electrical connector, perform the following procedures.

   a. Using a small prybar, insert it into the open end between the locking lugs and the terminal.

   b. Pry the locking lugs upward and pull the terminal out from the rear.

   c. To install the terminals, simply push them into the connector until they lock securely in place.

5. To complete the installation, reverse the removal procedures.

Ignition Lock/Switch

REMOVAL AND INSTALLATION

The ignition lock/switch is located behind the combination switch on the steering column.

1. Disconnect the negative battery terminal.

2. Remove the upper and lower steering column covers.

3. Disconnect the ignition switch from the electrical connector.

4. Using the key in the ignition switch, turn it to the **ACC** position.

5. Using a thin rod, place it into the hole of the cylinder lock housing. Pushing down on the thin rod, pull out the cylinder lock.

6. Remove the unlock warning switch-to-combination switch screws and the unlock warning switch.

7. Remove the ignition switch-to-combination switch screw and the ignition switch.

8. To install, push the ignition switch into the housing and install the screw. Using the key, install cylinder lock into the housing until the retaining tab locks it in place.

9. To complete the installation, reverse the removal procedures.

Stoplight Switch

REMOVAL AND INSTALLATION

1. Disconnect the negative battery cable.

2. Remove the electrical connector from the switch at the brake pedal.

3. Remove the mounting nut and remove the switch from the bracket.

4. Installation is the reverse of the removal procedure.

Clutch Switch

REMOVAL AND INSTALLATION

1. Disconnect the negative battery cable.

2. Remove the electrical connector from the switch at the clutch pedal.

3. Remove the mounting nut and remove the switch from the bracket.

4. Installation is the reverse of the removal procedure.

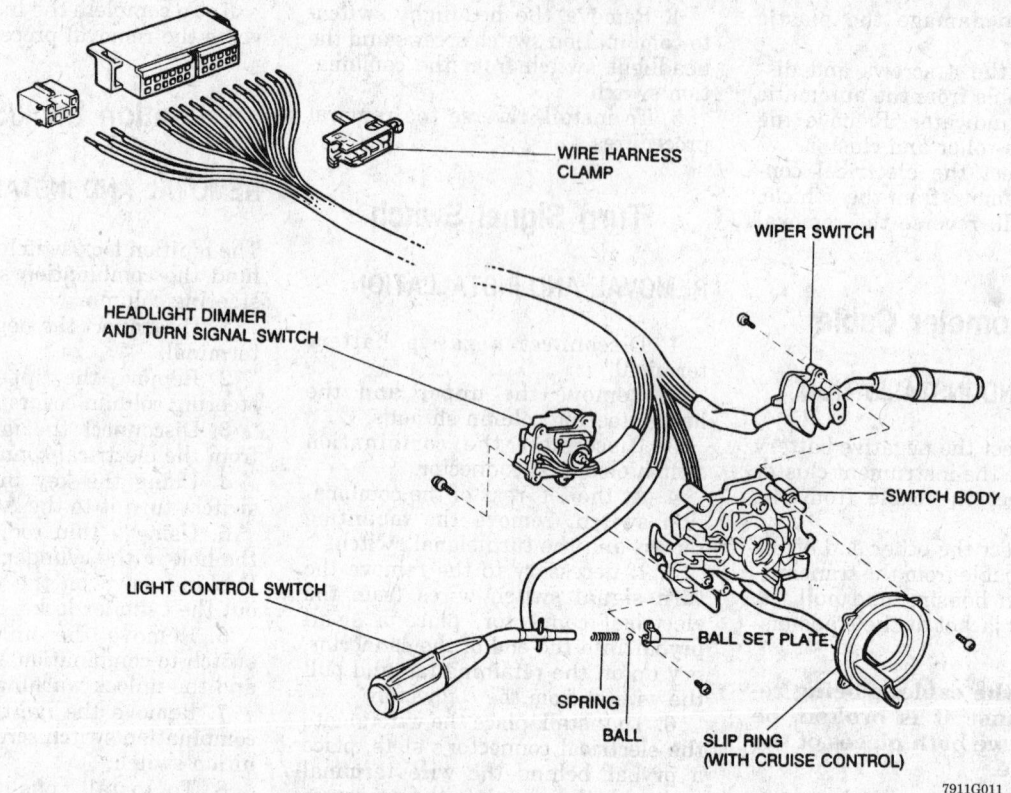

WIRE HARNESS CLAMP

WIPER SWITCH

HEADLIGHT DIMMER AND TURN SIGNAL SWITCH

SWITCH BODY

LIGHT CONTROL SWITCH

BALL SET PLATE

SPRING

BALL

SLIP RING (WITH CRUISE CONTROL)

7911G011

Typical combination switch assembly

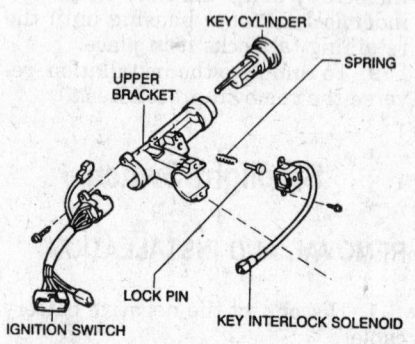

KEY CYLINDER

SPRING

UPPER BRACKET

LOCK PIN

KEY INTERLOCK SOLENOID

IGNITION SWITCH

7911G014

Ignition lock assembly

Fuses, Circuit Breakers and Relays

LOCATION

There are 3 fuse boxes on the Pick-Up, 4Runner and Land Cruiser. One is located in the engine compartment, 1 at the drivers side kick panel and 1 behind the glove box. The junction/relay and fuse block is located behind the heater controls, under the center instrument panel hood. Each fuse box has the fuse numbers and circuits protected on the lid of the box.

Computer

LOCATION

The ECU is located at the right kick panel for the Pick-Up and 4Runner, behind the glove compartment for the Land Cruiser, behind the trim panel or under the driver's seat for the Previa.

Flashers

The turn signal/hazard flasher is located under the instrument panel near the steering column for the Pick-Up, 4Runner and Previa. The flasher unit is located in the relay block at the left kick panel for the Land Cruiser.

Cruise Control

ADJUSTMENT

Pick-Up, 4Runner and Land Cruiser

1. Inspect that the control cable freeplay is less than 0.39 in. (10mm).
2. Connect the positive lead from the battery to terminals **1** and **2** and negative lead to terminal **3** of the actuator.

3. Slowly apply vacuum from 0–11.81 in. Hg. (0–300mm Hg), check that the control cable can be pulled smoothly and the cable stroke is at least 1.42 in. (36mm).

ENGINE COOLING

Radiator

REMOVAL AND INSTALLATION

1. Disconnect the negative battery cable. Drain the cooling system.
2. Unfasten the hose clamps and disconnect the hoses from the radiator. On Land Cruiser equipped with 3F-E engine and air conditioning, properly discharge the system.
3. Disconnect the transmission cooling lines, if equipped with an automatic transmission. Disconnect the air conditioning air intake duct on Previa vehicles.
4. Remove the fan shrouds, if equipped.
5. Remove the grille assembly and remove the hood lock from the radiator support. On Land Cruiser with

3F-E engine and air conditioning, remove the condenser to radiator bolts.

6. Remove the coolant recovery tank. Unbolt the radiator and remove it from the vehicle.

To install:

7. Install the radiator into position.

8. On Land Cruiser with air conditioning, install the condenser-to-radiator bolts.

9. Install the hood lock assembly and install the grille.

10. Connect the radiator hoses and the transmission cooler lines.

11. Connect the air conditioning intake duct on Previa vehicles.

12. Install the coolant recovery bottle. Refill the cooling system to the correct level.

13. Run the engine and check for leaks.

Heater Core

REMOVAL AND INSTALLATION

NOTE: If equipped with air conditioning, the heater and the air conditioner are completely separate units. Be certain when working under the dashboard that only the heater hoses are disconnected.

———— **CAUTION** ————
The air conditioning hoses are under pressure; if disconnected, the escaping refrigerant will freeze any surface with which it comes in contact, including skin and eyes.

Pick-Up, 4Runner and Previa

1. Disconnect the negative battery terminal from the battery.
2. Drain the cooling system.
3. Remove the glove box, the defroster hoses, the air damper, the air duct and the 2 side defroster ducts.
4. Remove the control unit from the instrument panel.
5. Disconnect the heater hoses from the core tubes.
6. Remove the retaining bolts and lift out the heater unit. At this point, the core may be pulled from the case.
7. To install, reverse the removal procedures. Refill the cooling system.

Land Cruiser

FRONT HEATER

NOTE: The entire heater unit must be removed to gain access to the heater core. This procedure requires almost complete disassembly of the instrument panel and lowering of the steering column.

1. Disconnect the negative battery terminal. Remove the glove box and the glove box door.
2. Remove the lower heater ducts. Remove the large heater duct from the passenger side of the heater unit.
3. Remove the ductwork from behind the instrument panel. Remove the radio.
4. Disconnect the wiring connector from the right-side inner portion of the glove opening.
5. Remove the instrument panel pad. Remove the hood release lever. Disconnect the hand throttle control cable.
6. Remove the retaining screw from the left-side of the fuse block.
7. Remove the steering column-to-instrument panel attaching nuts and carefully lower the steering column. Tag and disconnect the wiring as necessary in order to lower the column assembly.
8. Disconnect the electrical connector from the rheostat located to the left of the steering column opening.
9. Remove the center dual outlet duct which is attached to the upper portion of the heater unit.
10. Remove the lower instrument panel.
11. Tag and disconnect the hoses from the heater unit. Remove the heater unit-to-firewall fasteners and the heater unit.
12. Remove the heater core-to-heater unit pipe clamps and the heater core retaining clamp, then, withdraw the heater core from the heater unit.
13. To install, reverse the removal procedures. Torque the steering column-to-instrument panel fasteners to 14–15 ft. lbs. (18–20 Nm). Refill the cooling system.

REAR HEATER

1. Turn OFF the water valve and disconnect both hoses from the rear heater core.
2. Disconnect the wiring from the rear heater.
3. Remove the mounting bolts and lift out the core.
4. To install, reverse the removal procedures. Refill the cooling system.

Water Pump

REMOVAL AND INSTALLATION

22R-E Engine

1. Disconnect the negative battery cable. Drain the cooling system.
2. If equipped, remove the fan shroud bolts and the shroud.
3. Loosen the alternator adjusting link bolt and remove the drive belt, then, swing the alternator toward the engine.
4. If equipped with an air pump, air conditioning compressor or power steering pump drive belts, it may be necessary to loosen the adjusting bolt, remove the drive belt(s) and move the component(s) aside.
5. Remove the fan from the fluid coupling, the fluid coupling and pulley from the water pump, then, the water pump-to-engine bolts and the pump.
6. Clean the gasket mounting surfaces.
7. To install, use a new gasket, sealant and reverse the removal procedures. Adjust the drive belt(s) tension. Refill the cooling system.

3F-E Engine

1. Disconnect the negative battery cable.
2. Drain the engine coolant.
3. Remove the accessory drive belt. Loosen the power steering pump mount, idler pulley and adjusting bolts.
4. Disconnect the overflow tank hose.
5. Disconnect the radiator inlet hose and remove the fan shroud.
6. Remove the fan, fluid coupling and the water pump pulley.
7. Remove the alternator. Disconnect the hoses from the water pump.
8. Remove the water pump, power steering idler pulley and bracket as an assembly.
9. Installation is the reverse of the removal procedure. Torque the water pump mounting bolts to 27 ft. lbs. (37 Nm).

1FZ-FE Engine

1. Disconnect negative battery cable.
2. Drain engine coolant.
3. Disconnect the No. 3 water by-pass hose.
4. Disconnect the radiator inlet hose.
5. Loosen the water pump pulley mounting nuts.

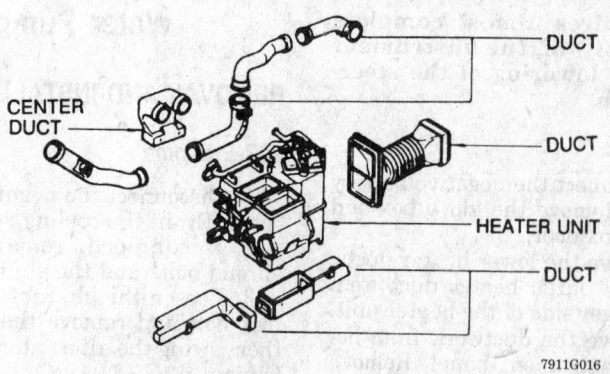

7911G016

Typical heater unit and ducts — Land Cruiser

6. Loosen the lock, pivot and adjusting bolts of the alternator. Remove the drive belts.

7. Remove the 2 bolts holding the fan shroud to the radiator. Remove the 4 water pump pulley mounting nuts.

8. Remove the fans with fluid coupling, water pump pulley and fan shroud.

9. Remove the 4 bolts, 2 nuts, water pump and gasket.

To install:

10. Install a new gasket and the water pump. Torque the 4 bolts and 2 nuts to 15 ft. lbs. (21 Nm).

11. Install the fan to the fluid coupling.

12. Install the fan with fluid coupling, water pump pulley and fan shroud.

13. Temporarily install the fan pulley mounting nuts. Install the fan shroud and tighten the 2 bolts.

14. Install the drive belts with the adjusting bolt and pivot bolt.

15. Adjust drive belts and tighten the 4 water pump pulley mounting nuts.

16. Connect the No. 3 water bypass hose and radiator inlet hose.

17. Fill the engine coolant.

18. Connect the negative battery cable. Start the engine and check for leaks.

3VZ-E Engine

1. Disconnect the negative battery cable.

2. Remove the timing belt assembly.

3. Remove the thermostat.

4. Remove the idler pulley.

5. Remove the water pump mounting bolts and remove the water pump.

To install:

6. Clean the mounting surface.

7. Use new seal packing on the water pump and install it in position on the engine.

8. Torque the bolts marked **A** to 13 ft. lbs. (18 Nm) and the bolts marked **B** to 14 ft. lbs. (20 Nm).

9. Install the thermostat and the idler pulley.

10. Install the timing belt assembly.

11. Connect the negative battery cable and refill the cooling system.

2TZ-FE Engine

1. Disconnect the negative battery cable and drain the engine coolant.

2. Raise the vehicle and support safely.

3. Disconnect the heater hose and radiator outlet hoses.

4. Remove the oil filter bracket.

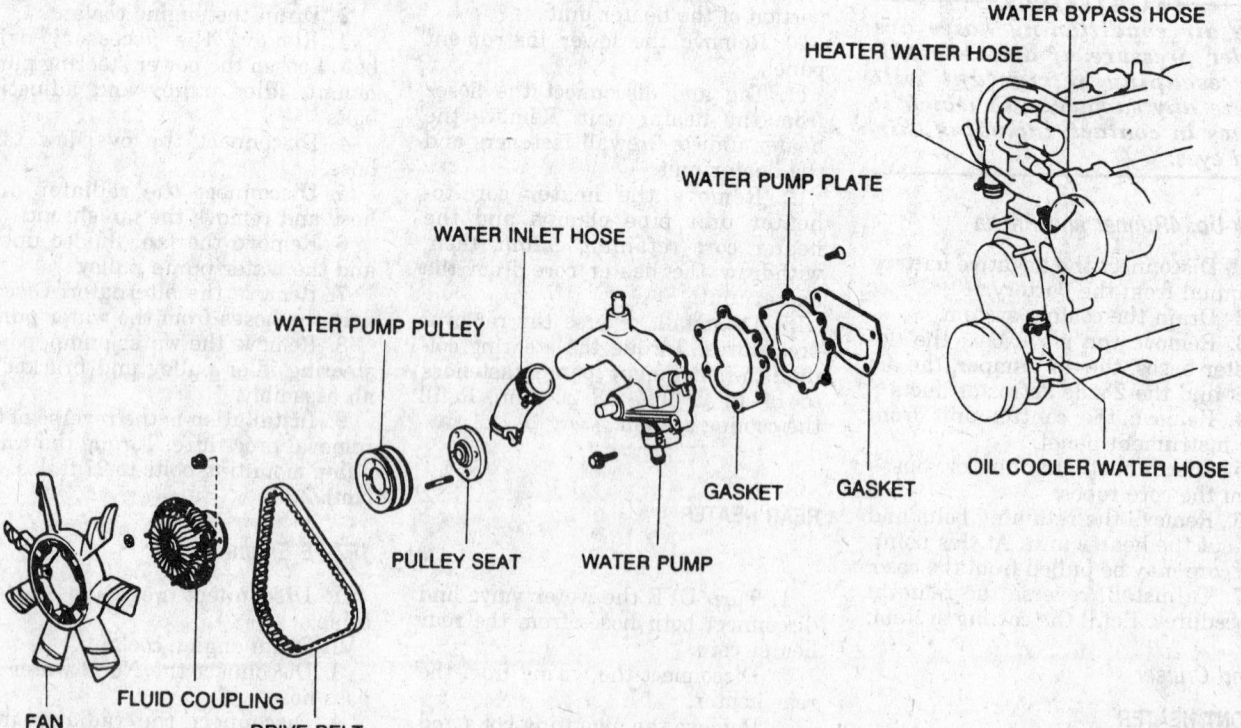

7911G018

Water pump assembly — 3F-E engine

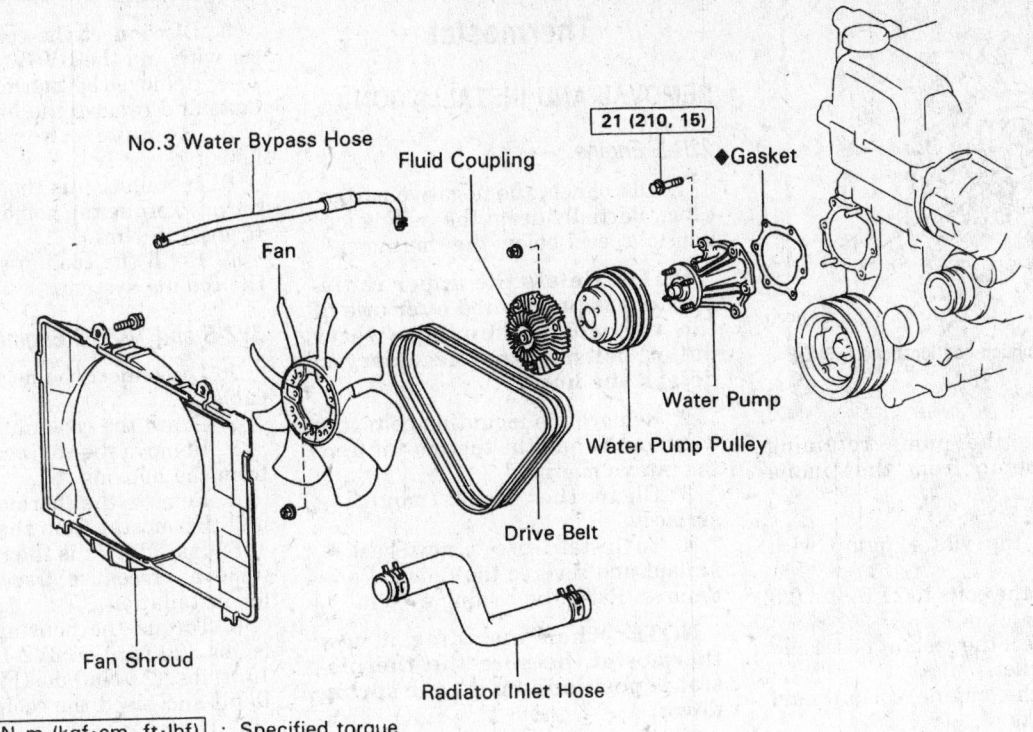

No.3 Water Bypass Hose
Fluid Coupling
21 (210, 15)
◆Gasket
Fan
Water Pump
Water Pump Pulley
Drive Belt
Fan Shroud
Radiator Inlet Hose

| N·m (kgf·cm, ft·lbf) | : Specified torque |
◆ Non-reusable part

8547C001

Water pump components — 1FZ-FE Engine

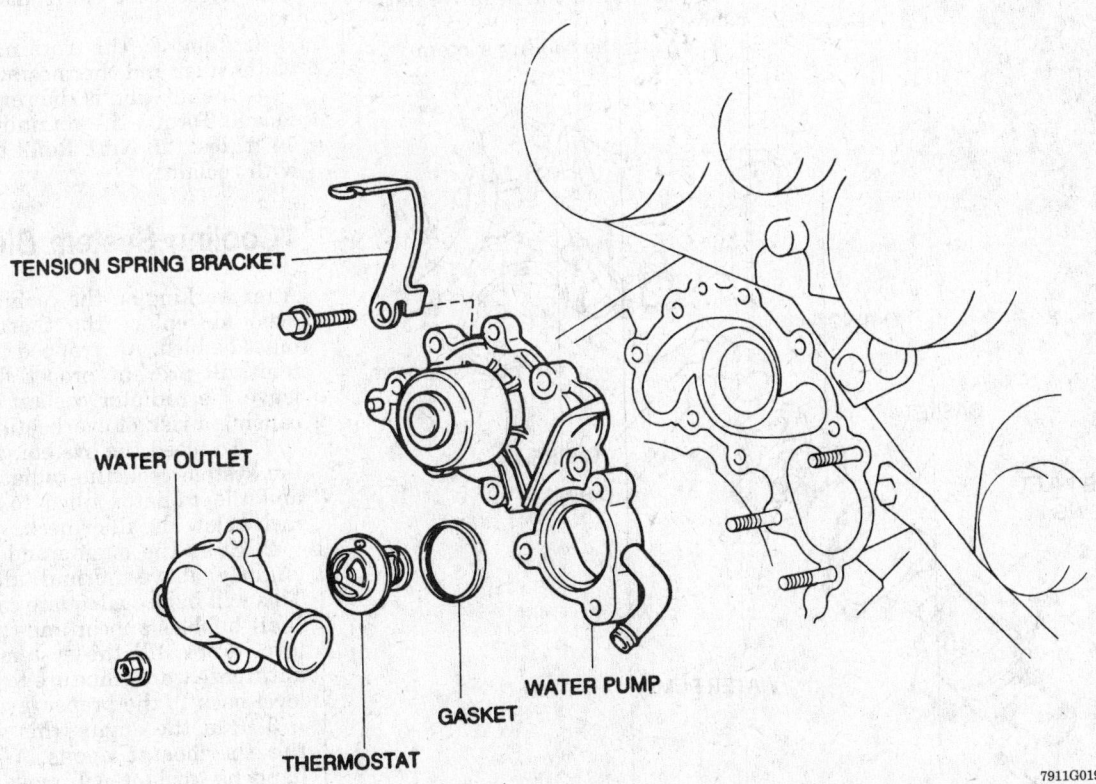

TENSION SPRING BRACKET

WATER OUTLET

WATER PUMP

GASKET

THERMOSTAT

7911G019

Water pump assembly — 3VZ-E engine

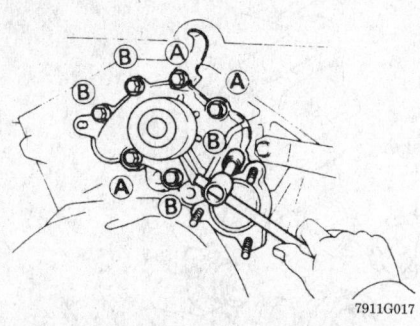

Water pump mounting bolt locations — 3VZ-E engine

5. Remove the pump retaining bolts and pump from the timing cover.

To install:

6. Install the water pump with new O-rings.

7. Torque the bolts to 21 ft. lbs. (28 Nm).

8. Reconnect the coolant hoses and oil filter bracket.

9. Refill the engine coolant and check for leaks.

Thermostat

REMOVAL AND INSTALLATION

22R-E Engine

1. Disconnect the negative battery cable. Partially drain the cooling system to a level below the thermostat.

NOTE: Unless the upper radiator hose is positioned over one of the thermostat housing (water outlet) bolts, it is not necessary to detach the hose.

2. Remove the mounting bolts, the water outlet and the thermostat from the intake manifold.

3. Clean the gasket mounting surfaces.

4. To install, use a new gasket, sealant and reverse the removal procedures. Refill the cooling system.

NOTE: When installing a new thermostat, be sure the thermostat is positioned with the spring down.

5. Bleed the cooling system.

3F-E Engine

1. Disconnect the negative battery cable.

2. Drain the cooling system.

3. Disconnect the cold start injector wire and the BVSV vacuum lines.

4. Remove the thermostat housing bolts and remove the housing.

5. Remove the thermostat housing.

6. Installation is the reverse of removal. Torque the housing bolts to 13 ft. lbs. (18 Nm).

7. Refill the cooling system. Bleed the cooling system.

3VZ-E and 1FZ-FE Engines

1. Disconnect the negative battery cable.

2. Drain the coolant.

3. Remove the radiator outlet hose from the housing.

4. Remove the thermostat housing and thermostat from the engine.

5. Installation is the reverse of the removal procedure. Use a new gasket for installation.

6. Torque the housing bolts to 14 ft. lbs. (20 Nm) on 3VZ-E engine and 15 ft. lbs. (21 Nm) on 1FZ-FE engine. Refill and bleed the cooling system.

2TZ-FE Engine

1. Raise the vehicle and support safely. Drain the engine coolant.

2. Disconnect the radiator outlet hose.

3. Remove the retaining bolts, water inlet and thermostat.

4. Installation is the reverse of removal. Torque the retaining bolts to 14 ft. lbs. (20 Nm). Refill the engine with coolant.

Cooling System Bleeding

After working on the cooling system, even to replace the thermostat, it must be bled. Air trapped in the system will prevent proper filling and leave the radiator coolant level low, causing a risk of overheating.

1. To bleed the system, start with the system cool, the radiator cap off and the radiator filled to about an inch below the filler neck.

2. Start the engine and run it at slightly above normal idle speed. This will insure adequate circulation. If air bubbles appear and the coolant level drops, fill the system with an antifreeze/water mixture to bring the level back to the proper level.

3. Run the engine this way until the thermostat opens. When this happens, coolant will move abruptly across the top of the radiator and the temperature of the radiator will suddenly rise.

4. At this point, air is often expelled and the level may drop quite a

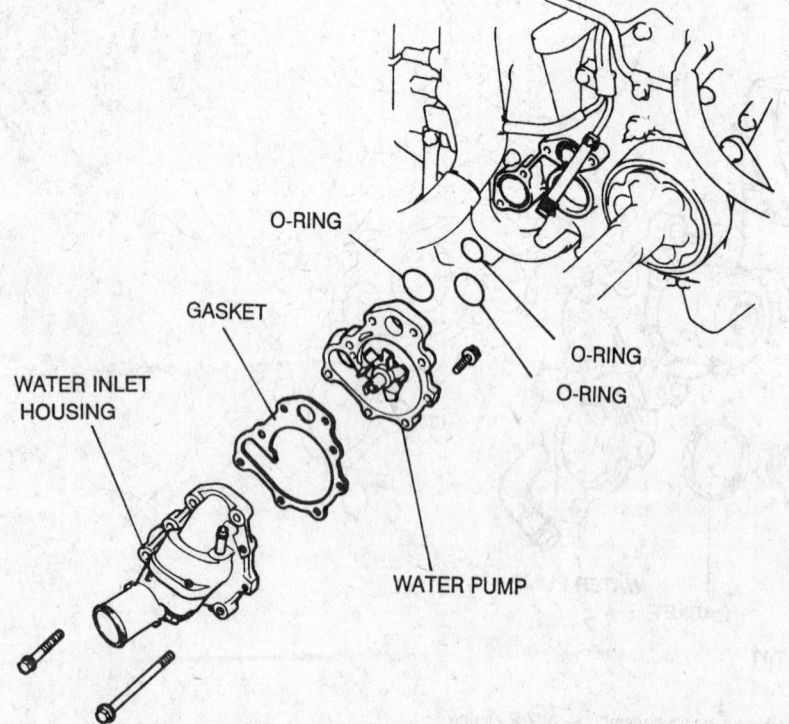

Water pump assembly — 2TZ-FE engine

WATER INLET HOUSING

GASKET

O-RING

O-RING

O-RING

WATER PUMP

bit. Keep refilling the system until the level is near the top of the radiator and remains constant.

5. If the vehicle has an overflow tank, fill the radiator right up to the filler neck. Replace the radiator filler cap.

FUEL SYSTEM

Fuel System Service Precaution

When working with the fuel system certain precautions should be taken; always work in a well ventilated area, keep a dry chemical (Class B) fire extinguisher near the work area. Always disconnect the negative battery cable and do not make any repairs to the fuel system until all the necessary steps for repair have been reviewed.

RELIEVING FUEL SYSTEM PRESSURE

1. Disconnect the negative battery terminal from the battery.
2. Allow the system enough time to bleed off the fuel pressure through the fuel return line.
3. Before disconnecting any fuel line component, place a rag under the item to catch any excess fuel.
4. After installation, install the negative battery terminal, turn **ON** the ignition switch and check for fuel leaks.

Fuel Tank

REMOVAL AND INSTALLATION

1. Disconnect the negative battery cable. Relieve the fuel pressure.
2. This procedure should be done with the tank less than 1/4 full. Place a suitable drain pan under fuel tank and remove the drain plug. If the tank is more than 1/4 full, use an approved siphon to remove the fuel from the tank.
3. Disconnect all hoses, wiring and tubes that can be accessed at this point.
4. Place a jack under the tank and remove the tank protector.
5. Remove the tank straps or retaining bolts.

6. Lower the tank far enough to disconnect the remaining hoses, wiring and tubes. Be careful not to damage the nylon fuel lines when removing the tank.
7. Drain the remaining fuel from the tank.
   To install:
8. Raise the tank and connect the hoses, wiring and tubes.
9. Install the retaining bolts or straps and torque to 29 ft. lbs. (39 Nm).
10. Connect the remaining hoses or wiring.
11. Refill the fuel tank and check for leaks.
12. Check the battery cable and check operation.

Fuel Filter

REMOVAL AND INSTALLATION

The fuel filter is located in the engine compartment, at the inlet line to the fuel rail.

1. Disconnect the negative battery cable.
2. Relieve the fuel system pressure.
3. Disconnect and plug the inlet and outlet lines from the filter.
4. Remove the filter retaining bolts and remove the filter.
5. Installation is the reverse of the removal procedure.
6. Use new O-rings and tighten the lines to 22 ft. lbs. (29 Nm).
7. Connect the negative battery cable. Run the engine and check for leaks.

Electric Fuel Pump

An electric fuel pump is used on all fuel injected engines. The fuel pump is wired into the ignition switch and oil pressure switch circuits. In the event of an oil pressure loss, the fuel pump is turned **OFF** so the engine will stall, thus preventing engine damage due to the oil pressure loss. The fuel pump will operate only when the ignition switch is turned to the **START** position and when the oil pressure is normal.

OPERATION TESTING

1. Disconnect the electrical clip from the oil pressure switch.
2. Turn the ignition switch to the **ON** position; do not start the engine.
3. Short the **Fp** and the **+B** terminals of the check connector. Check

the cold start injector hose for pressure.
4. Check for a smooth flow of gasoline from the fuel filter outlet. If the pump is noisy, it is probably defective. If the pump does not run, check the pump resistor and relay.
5. Disconnect the jumper wire and reconnect the check connector. Turn the ignition switch **OFF**.

PRESSURE TESTING

1. Disconnect the negative battery terminal from the battery and the wiring connector from the cold start injector.
2. Place a container or a shop towel near the end of the delivery tube.
3. Slowly loosen the cold start injector union bolt, then, remove the bolt and the gaskets. Drain the fuel line.
4. Using pressure gauge tool 09268-45011 or equivalent, connect it in line with the cold start injector. Reconnect the battery cable.
5. Short the **Fp** and **+B** terminals of the check connector wire. Turn the ignition switch to the **ON** position and measure the fuel pump pressure. It should be as follows:
   22R-E, 2TZ-FE, 3VZ-E engines — 38–44 psi (265–304 kPa)
   3F-E engine — 37–46 psi (255–314 kPa)
6. Turn the ignition switch **OFF**.

NOTE: If the pressure is high, replace the pressure regulator; if the pressure is low, check the hoses, the connections, the fuel pump, the fuel filter or the pressure regulator.

7. Remove the jumper wire from the check connector. Start the engine. Disconnect and plug the vacuum sensing hose at the pressure regulator, then, measure the fuel pressure at idle. It should be as follows:
   22R-E, 2TZ-FE, 3VZ-E engines — 38–44 psi (265–304 kPa)
   3F-E engine — 37–46 psi (255–314 kPa)
8. Reconnect the vacuum sensing hose to the pressure regulator. The pressure should now be as follows; if not, check the vacuum hose and/or the pressure regulator.
   22R-E, 2TZ-FE, 3VZ-E engines — 33–38 psi (226–265 kPa)
   3F-E engine — 33–37 psi (226–265 kPa)
9. Stop the engine and check that the fuel pressure remains at 21 psi. for 5 minutes. If not, check the fuel

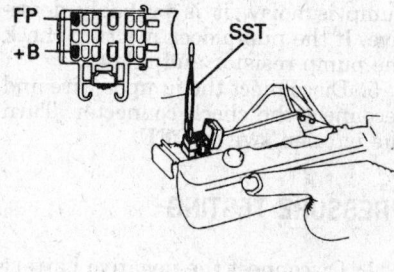

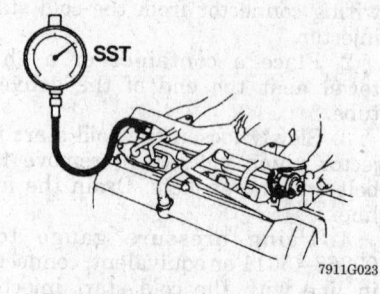

Testing the fuel pump pressure

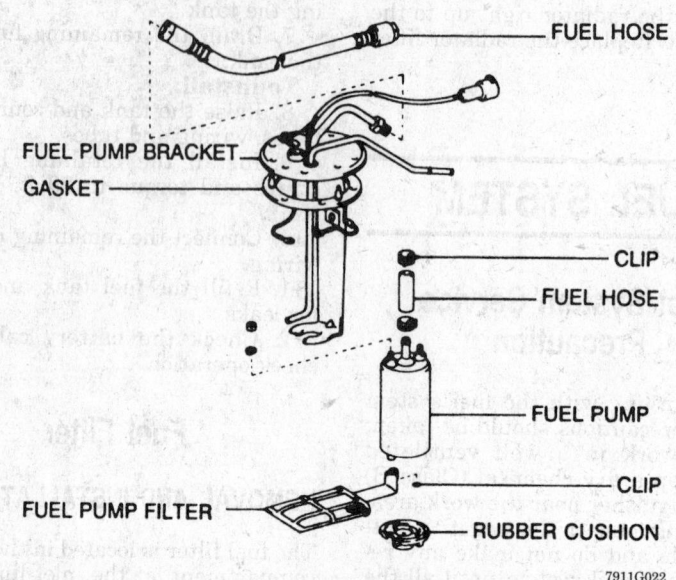

Typical electric fuel pump

pump, the pressure regulator and/or the injectors.

REMOVAL AND INSTALLATION

1. Disconnect the negative battery cable. Drain the fuel tank.

2. Disconnect the electrical connector and the fuel lines from the fuel tank.

3. Remove the inlet tube and mounting bolts/straps, then, the fuel tank from the vehicle.

4. Remove the access plate-to-fuel tank bolts, then, pull out the plate/fuel pump assembly.

5. Disconnect the electrical connectors from the fuel pump. Pull the bracket from the lower-side of the fuel pump, then, remove the fuel pump from the fuel hose.

6. Remove the rubber cushion, the clip and the fuel filter from the bottom of the fuel pump.

To install:

7. Install the fuel pump and use new gaskets.

8. Install the fuel tank and connect all electrical and fuel connections.

9. Torque the fuel pump bracket-to-fuel tank to 43 inch lbs. (5.3 Nm). Refill the fuel tank and check for leaks.

Fuel Injection

IDLE SPEED ADJUSTMENT

22R-E and 3VZ-E Engines

The engines are equipped with a computer activated, electronic fuel injection system. Prior to adjusting the idle speed, make sure the air cleaner is installed. All vacuum hoses are connected. All pipes and hoses in the air intake system are connected and in good condition. All fuel injection system wiring is connected and in good condition. The engine is at normal operating temperature. All accessories are **OFF**. Transmission selector lever in **N**.

1. Connect the tachometer positive (+) lead to the coil's (-) negative terminal or to the igniter's service connector, if provided.

2. Run the engine at 2500 rpm for 2 minutes.

3. Run the engine at idle and turn the idle speed adjusting screw to obtain the correct idle speed.

4. Disconnect and remove the tachometer.

3F-E, 2TZ-FE and 1FZ-FE Engines

These engines are equipped with electronic fuel injection. The idle speed is controlled by an Idle Speed Control (ISC) valve. The idle speed is preset at the factory and requires no adjustment. There are no idle speed adjusting screws.

3F-E engine: check that there is a clicking sound immediately after stopping the engine. Check the valve using an ohmmeter. Measure the resistance between the terminals.

• Terminals B1–S1 or S3 — 10–30 ohms

• Terminals B2–S2 or S4 — 10–30 ohms

1. If not within specifications, replace the ISC valve.

2. 2TZ-FE engine: using an ohmmeter, measure the resistance between terminals **B+** and the other 2. The resistance should be 18.8–22.8 ohms.

3. If the valve checks OK, remove the valve and clean the mounting area with carburetor cleaner. Install new gaskets and valve

IDLE MIXTURE ADJUSTMENT

The idle mixture adjustment is preset at the factory and controlled by the electronic control unit. There is no adjustment necessary or possible.

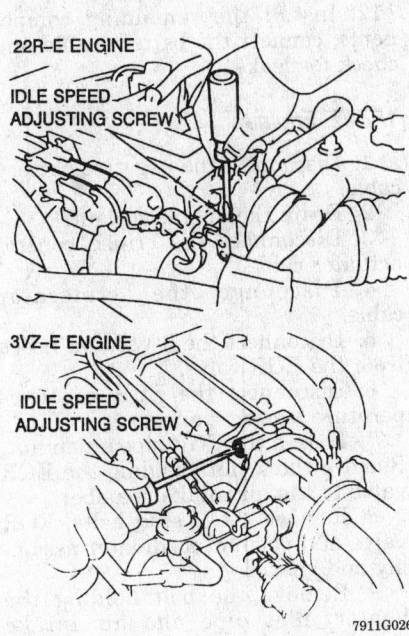

Idle speed adjusting screw — 22R-E and 3VZ-E engines

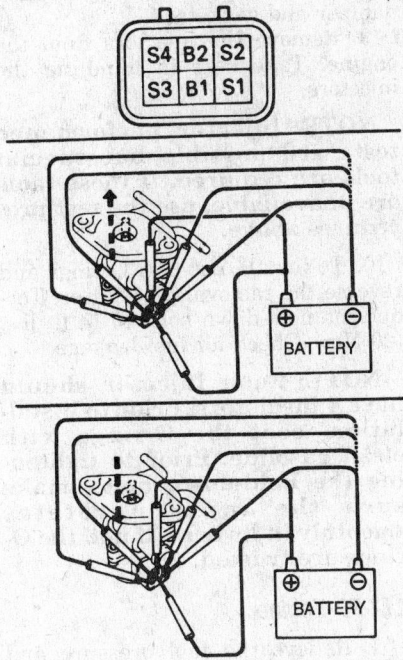

Checking ISC valve — 3F-E engine

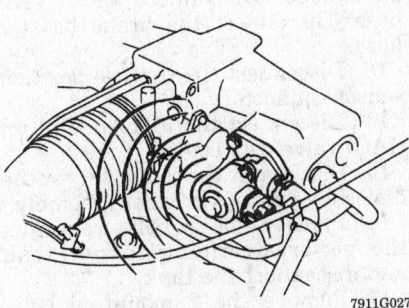

Checking Idle Speed Control (ISC) valve — 3F-E engine

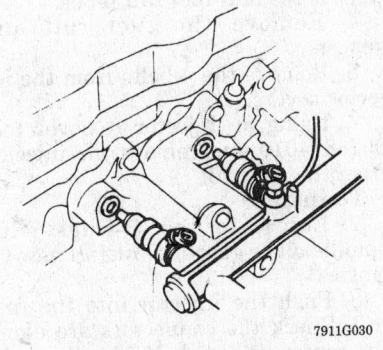

Removing the fuel delivery pipe

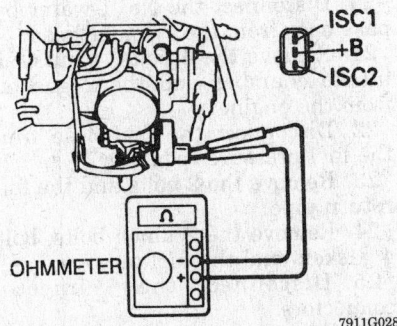

Checking ISC valve — 2TZ-FE engine

Cold Start Injector

The EFI engines have a cold start injector located in the intake air chamber which aids in cold weather starting.

REMOVAL AND INSTALLATION

1. Disconnect the negative battery cable and the cold start injector wire.
2. Place a shop towel or a container under the fuel delivery pipe and drain the fuel from the pipe.
3. Disconnect the fuel pipe from the cold start injector.

4. Remove the mounting bolts and the cold start injector from the intake air chamber.
5. To install, use new gaskets and reverse the removal procedures. Torque the injector bolts to 44–60 inch lbs. (5.4–6.8 Nm).

Fuel Pressure Regulator

The fuel pressure regulator is located on the fuel delivery pipe of the fuel system; it maintains a constant fuel pressure in the injection system.

REMOVAL AND INSTALLATION

1. Relieve the fuel pressure. Disconnect the vacuum sensing hose from the pressure regulator.

NOTE: On the 22R-E engines, remove the No. 1 EGR pipe.

2. Place a shop towel or a container under the fuel hose connection and disconnect the fuel return hose from the regulator.
3. Remove the locknut for 22R-E, and 3F-E engines, the mounting bolts for 3VZ-E engines and the pressure regulator from the fuel delivery pipe.
4. To install, reverse of removal. Torque the locknut to 22 ft. lbs. (30 Nm) for 22R-E, and 3F-E engines, bolts to 44–60 inch lbs. (5.4–6.8 Nm) for 3VZ-E engines, or bolts to 14 ft. lbs. (20 Nm) for 1FZ-FE engines. Start the engine and check for fuel leaks.

Fuel Injector

TESTING

Except 2TZ-FE and 1FZ-FE Engines

Each injector may be tested for operation while on the engine, in 2 ways.
1. Listen for a clicking at the injector.
2. Using an ohmmeter, check the continuity at each injector's terminal; the resistance should be 1.5–3.0 ohms.

1FZ-FE Engine

1. Remove the throttle body.
2. Disconnect the injector connectors.
3. Using an ohmmeter, check the continuity at each injector's terminal; the resistance should be 12–16 ohms.
4. Reconnect the injector connectors and install the throttle body.

REMOVAL AND INSTALLATION

Except 2TZ-FE and 1FZ-FE Engines

1. Disconnect the negative battery terminal from the battery and the ground strap from the rear side of the engine.
2. Disconnect the accelerator wire. If equipped with an automatic transmission, disconnect the throttle cable from the bracket and the clamp.
3. Disconnect the No. 1 and No. 2 PCV hoses.
4. Disconnect the following items:
   a. Brake power booster hose
   b. Air control valve hoses
   c. Vacuum Switching Valve (VSV)
   d. Evaporative emission control hose
   e. EGR vacuum hose and modulator
   f. Pressure regulator hose for 2WD
   g. Fuel pressure-up (VSV) and hose
   h. No. 1 and No. 2 air valve hose from the throttle body
   i. No. 2 and No. 3 water bypass hoses from the throttle body
   j. Cold start injector wire
   k. Throttle position wire
5. Remove the following items:
   a. Cold start injector-to-plenum chamber bolt.
   b. No. 1 EGR pipe-to-plenum chamber bolts.
   c. Manifold stay-to-plenum chamber bolts.
   d. Fuel hose clamp, 4 bolts, 2 nuts and the bond strap.
   e. The plenum chamber with the throttle body and gaskets.
6. Disconnect the fuel return hose.
7. Disconnect the following wires:
   a. Auxiliary air valve wire
   b. Knock sensor wire
   c. Oil pressure sender gauge/switch
   d. Starter wire (terminal 50)
   e. Transmission wires
   f. Air conditioning compressor wires
   g. Injector wires
   h. Water temperature sender gauge wire
   i. Overdrive temperature switch wire (air conditioning)
   j. Oxygen sensor and igniter wire
   k. Vacuum Switching Valve (VSV) wire (air conditioning)
   l. Cold start injector time switch wire
   m. Water temperature sensor wire

8. Disconnect the fuel hose from the delivery pipe with the pulsation damper and gaskets.
9. Remove the injectors from the engine. Take care in handling the injectors.

NOTE: Injector performance tests are possible but special tools are required. If these tools are unavailable, use the test procedures above.

10. To install, use new O-rings and reverse the removal procedures. Torque the hold-down bolts to 14 ft. lbs. (20 Nm). Check for fuel leakage.

NOTE: Each injector should have 4 insulators. Prior to installation, coat the O-rings with clean gasoline. Prior to tightening the hold-down bolts, make sure the injector rotates smoothly in its bore. If not, the O-rings are twisted.

2TZ-FE Engine

1. Relieve the fuel pressure and disconnect the negative battery cable.
2. Remove the right engine service hole.
3. Disconnect the PCV hose, engine wiring harness-to-injectors, vacuum hoses and fuel rail pipes.
4. Remove the fuel rail and spacers.
5. Remove the 4 bolts from the injector covers.
6. Using an injector remover tool 0926874010 and remove the injector from the fuel rail.
To install:
7. Lubricate the O-rings with spindle oil or gasoline. Install new O-rings.
8. Push the injector into the fuel rail. Check the connectors are along the center line of the fuel rail.
9. Install the insulator onto each injector.
10. Install the injector covers and fuel rail onto the engine.

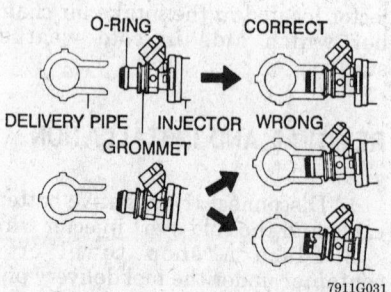

Injector installation into delivery pipe

1FZ-FE Engine

1. Disconnect the negative battery cable.
2. Drain the engine coolant.
3. Disconnect the cruise control actuator cable.
4. Disconnect the accelerator cable.
5. Disconnect the 3 vacuum hoses from the EGR valve.
6. Disconnect the EGR gas temperature sensor connector.
7. Loosen the EGR pipe union nut. Remove the 2 nuts holding the EGR valve to the air intake chamber.
8. Remove the 2 stud bolts, EGR valve and vacuum modulator assembly and gasket.
9. Remove the bolt holding the heater inlet pipe and air intake chamber.
10. Disconnect the air cleaner hose. Disconnect the No. 1 and No. 2 PCV hoses.
11. Disconnect the vacuum hoses.
12. Disconnect the No. 2 water bypass hose. Disconnect the EVAP hose. Disconnect the brake booster hose.
13. Disconnect the throttle position sensor connector.
14. Disconnect the Idle Air Control (IAC) valve connector.
15. Disconnect the connector for the emission control valve set assembly.
16. Remove the 3 bolts retaining the power steering reservoir tank and disconnect the tank.
17. Remove the 2 mounting bolts from the engine oil dipstick guide. Pull out the dipstick with the dipstick guide. Remove the O-ring from the dipstick guide.
18. Disconnect the ground strap.
19. Disconnect the 2 vacuum hoses from the TVV.
20. Disconnect the No. 1 water bypass hose from the cylinder head.
21. Remove the 4 bolts, 4 nuts, air intake chamber and the 2 gaskets from the engine.
22. Disconnect the fuel hose from the fuel pressure regulator.
23. Remove the 2 bolts and the fuel return pipe.
24. Remove the 2 union bolts, bolt, 4 gaskets and the fuel pipe.
25. Disconnect the 6 injector connectors.
26. Remove the 3 bolts and the delivery pipe together with the 6 injectors.

11. Torque the fuel rail retaining bolts to 14 ft. lbs. (20 Nm).
12. Install the remaining components, connect the battery cable and check for leaks.

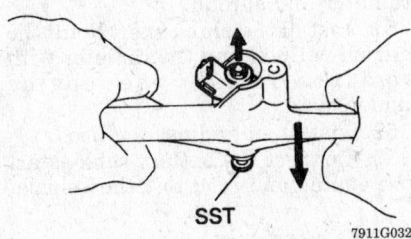

SST

7911G032

Injector removal — 2TZ-FE engine

27. Remove the 6 insulators and 3 spacers from the intake manifold.

28. Remove the 6 injectors from the delivery pipe.

29. Remove the O-ring and grommet from each injector.

To install:

30. Install an O-ring and grommet to each injector.

31. Install the injectors to the delivery pipe.

32. Install the 3 spacers and 6 insulators to the intake manifold.

33. Install the 6 injectors with the delivery pipe. Torque the 3 bolts to 15 ft. lbs. (21 Nm).

34. Connect the 6 injector connectors.

35. Install the fuel pipe and 4 gaskets. Torque the 2 union bolts to 22 ft. lbs. (29 Nm) and the bolt to 14 ft. lbs. (20 Nm).

36. Install the fuel return pipe and tighten the 2 bolts to 14 ft. lbs. (20 Nm).

37. Connect the fuel hose to the fuel pressure regulator.

38. Install the air intake chamber and 2 gaskets. TIghten the 4 bolts and 4 nuts to 15 ft. lbs. (21 Nm).

39. Connect the No. 1 water bypass hose to the cylinder head.

40. Connect the 2 vacuum hoses to the TVV.

41. Connect the ground strap.

42. Install a new O-ring to the oil dipstick guide and install the guide and dipstick. Tighten the 2 mounting bolts to 14 ft. lbs. (20 Nm).

43. Install the power steering reservoir tank and tighten the 3 bolts to 13 ft. lbs. (18 Nm).

44. Connect the connector for the emission control valve set assembly.

45. Connect the Idle Air Control (IAC) valve connector.

46. Connect the throttle position sensor connector.

47. Connect the brake booster hose.

48. Connect the EVAP hose and the No. 2 water bypass hose.

49. Connect the vacuum hoses.

50. Connect the No. 1 and No. 2 PCV hoses.

51. Connect the air cleaner hose.

52. Install the bolt holding the heater inlet pipe and the air intake chamber. Torque bolt to 14 ft. lbs. (20 Nm).

53. Temporarily install a new gasket and the EGR valve and vacuum modulator assembly. Torque the 2 stud bolts to 8 ft. lbs. (10 Nm)

54. Install the 2 nuts holding the EGR valve to the air intake chamber. Torque nuts to 14 ft. lbs. (19 Nm).

55. Tighten union nut of the EGR pipe to 47 ft. lbs. (64 Nm).

56. Connect the EGR gas temperature sensor connector.

57. Connect the 3 vacuum hoses to the EGR valve.

58. Connect the accelerator cable.

59. Connect the cruise control actuator cable.

60. Fill engine coolant.

61. Connect the negative battery cable.

ENGINE MECHANICAL

NOTE: Disconnecting the negative battery cable on some vehicles may interfere with the functions of the on board computer systems and may require the computer to undergo a relearning process, one the negative battery cable is reconnected.

Engine Assembly

REMOVAL AND INSTALLATION

22R-E Engine

1. Disconnect the negative battery cable.

2. Remove the engine undercover.

3. Disconnect the windshield washer hose and then remove the hood. Scribe matchmarks around the hinges for easy installation.

4. Drain the engine oil. Drain the engine coolant from the radiator and the cylinder block.

5. Drain the automatic transmission fluid on models so equipped.

6. Disconnect the air cleaner hose and then remove the air cleaner.

7. Remove the radiator and shroud.

8. Remove the coupling fan.

9. Disconnect the heater hoses at the engine.

10. If equipped with automatic transmissions, disconnect the accelerator and throttle cables at their bracket.

11. Disconnect the following:
   a. No. 1 and No. 2 PCV hoses
   b. Brake booster hose
   c. Air control valve hoses
   d. EVAP hose at the canister
   e. Actuator hose on vehicles with cruise control
   f. Vacuum modulator hose at the EGR valve
   g. Air valve hoses at the throttle body and chamber
   h. Two water bypass hoses at the throttle body
   i. Air control valve hose at the actuator
   j. Pressure regulator hose at the chamber
   k. Cold start injector pipe
   l. BVSV hose.

12. Tag and disconnect the cold start injector wire and the throttle position sensor wire.

13. Remove the EGR valve from the throttle chamber.

14. Disconnect the throttle chamber at the stay. Remove the chamber-to-intake manifold mounting bolts and lift off the throttle chamber.

15. Tag and disconnect the following wires:
   a. Cold start injector time switch wire
   b. Water temperature sensor wire
   c. If equipped with air conditioning: VSV and air conditioning compressor wires
   d. OD temperature switch wire (with automatic transmission)
   e. Injector wires
   f. Knock sensor connector
   g. Air valve wire
   h. Oil pressure switch wire
   i. Starter wire.

16. Remove the power steering pump from its bracket, if equipped. Disconnect the ground strap from the bracket.

17. If equipped with air conditioning, loosen the drive belt and remove the air conditioning compressor. Position it aside with the refrigerant lines attached.

18. Disconnect the engine ground straps at the rear and right side of the engine.

19. If equipped with a manual transmission, remove the shift lever from inside the vehicles.

20. Raise and safely support the vehicle. Drain the engine oil. Remove the rear driveshaft.

21. If equipped with automatic transmission, disconnect the manual shift linkage at the neutral start switch. On 4WD vehicles with automatic transmission, disconnect the transfer shift linkage.

22. Disconnect the speedometer cable. Be sure not to lose the felt dust protector and washers.

23. Remove the transfer case undercover on 4WD vehicles.

24. Remove the stabilizer bar on 4WD vehicles.

25. Remove the front driveshaft on 4WD vehicles.

26. Remove the No. 1 frame crossmember.

27. Disconnect the front exhaust pipe at the manifold and tail pipe and remove the exhaust pipe.

28. If equipped with manual transmission, remove the clutch release cylinder and its bracket from the transmission.

29. Remove the No. 1 front floor heat insulator and the brake tube heat insulator on 4WD vehicles.

30. On 2WD vehicles, remove the rear engine mount bolts, raise the transmission slightly with a floor jack and then remove the support member mounting bolts.

31. On 4WD vehicles, remove the 4 rear engine mount bolts, raise the transmission slightly with a floor jack and then remove the bolts from the side member and remove the No. 2 frame crossmember.

32. Lower the vehicle. Attach an engine hoist chain to the lifting brackets on the engine. Remove the engine mount nuts and bolts and slowly lift the engine/transmission from the vehicle.

To install:

33. Slowly lower the engine assembly into the engine compartment.

34. Raise the transmission onto the crossmember with a floor jack.

35. Align the holes in the engine mounts and the frame, install the bolts and then remove the engine hoist chain.

36. On 2WD vehicles, raise the transmission slightly and align the rear engine mount with the support member and tighten the bolts to 9 ft. lbs. (13 Nm). Lower the transmission until it rests on the extension housing and then tighten the bracket mounting bolts to 19 ft. lbs. (25 Nm).

37. On 4WD vehicles, raise the transmission slightly and tighten the No. 2 frame crossmember-to-side frame bolts to 70 ft. lbs. (95 Nm). Lower the transmission and tighten the rear engine mount bolts to 9 ft. lbs. (13 Nm).

38. On 4WD vehicles, install the brake tube and front floor heat insulators.

39. Install the clutch release cylinder and its bracket to the manual transmission. Tighten the bracket bolts to 29 ft. lbs. (39 Nm) and the cylinder bolts to 9 ft. lbs. (13 Nm).

40. Reconnect the exhaust pipe. Install the No. 1 frame crossmember.

41. On 4WD vehicles, install the front driveshaft, stabilizer bar and the transfer case undercover.

42. Connect the speedometer cable. Connect the transfer shift linkage on 4WD vehicles with automatic transmission.

43. Connect the manual shift linkage to the neutral start switch (automatic transmission only).

44. Install the rear driveshaft. Install the shift lever for manual transmission only.

45. Connect the engine ground straps. Install the air conditioning compressor.

46. Install the power steering pump and connect the ground strap.

47. Connect all of the following wires:
    a. Cold start injector time switch wire
    b. Water temperature sensor wire
    c. If equipped with air conditioning: VSV and air conditioning compressor wires
    d. OD temperature switch wire for automatic transmission
    e. Injector wires
    f. Knock sensor connector
    g. Air valve wire
    h. Oil pressure switch wire
    i. Starter wire

48. Connect all of the following parts:
    a. No. 1 and No. 2 PCV hoses
    b. Brake booster hose
    c. Air control valve hoses
    d. EVAP hose at the canister
    e. Actuator hose on vehicles with cruise control
    f. Vacuum modulator hose at the EGR valve
    g. Air valve hoses at the throttle body and chamber
    h. Two water bypass hoses at the throttle body
    i. Air control valve hose at the actuator
    j. Pressure regulator hose at the chamber
    k. Cold start injector pipe
    l. BVSV hose.

49. Connect the accelerator and throttle cables to the bracket for automatic transmission only.

50. Connect the heater hoses and install the coupling fan. Install the radiator and shroud.

51. Install the air cleaner. Refill the engine with oil and the radiator with coolant. Install the engine undercover.

52. Install and adjust the hood.

53. Connect the battery cable, start the engine and road test the vehicle.

3F-E and 1FZ-FE Engines

1. Disconnect the negative battery cable. Drain the engine coolant.

2. Scribe matchmarks around the hood hinges and then remove the hood.

3. Remove the battery and its tray.

4. Disconnect the accelerator and throttle cables.

5. Remove the air intake hose, air flow meter and air cleaner assembly.

6. Remove the coolant reservoir tank.

7. Remove the radiator.

8. Tag and disconnect the following wires and connectors:
    a. Oil pressure connector
    b. High tension cord at the coil
    c. Neutral start switch and transfer connectors near the starter
    d. Front differential lock connector
    e. Starter wire and connector
    f. Starter ground strap
    g. O_2 sensor connectors
    h. Alternator wire and connector
    i. Cooling fan connector
    j. Check connector.

9. Disconnect the following hoses:
    a. Heater hoses
    b. Fuel hoses
    c. Transfer case hose
    d. Brake booster hose
    e. Air injection hoses
    f. Distributor hose
    g. Emission control hoses

10. Remove the glove box, pull out the 4 connectors and then pull the EFI wiring harness from the cowl.

11. Unbolt the power steering pump and position it aside with the hoses still connected.

12. Do the same with the air conditioning compressor.

13. Raise the vehicle and remove the transfer case undercover. Drain the engine oil.

14. Remove the front and rear driveshafts.

15. Disconnect the speedometer cable.

16. Disconnect the engine ground strap.

17. Disconnect the 2 vacuum hoses at the diaphragm cylinder under the transfer case.

18. Remove the clip and pin and then disconnect the shift rod at the transfer case. Remove the nut, disconnect the washers and the shift lever at the shift rod.

19. Disconnect the transmission control rod.

20. Disconnect the exhaust pipe at the manifold.

21. With a floor jack under the transmission, remove the bolts and nuts that attach the frame crossmember and then remove the crossmember. Lower the vehicle.

22. Attach an engine hoist to the lifting brackets on the engine. Remove the engine mount nuts and bolts and slowly lift the engine/transmission from the vehicle.

To install:

23. Slowly lower the engine assembly into the engine compartment.

24. Raise the transmission onto the crossmember with a floor jack.

25. Align the holes in the engine mounts and the frame, install the bolts and then remove the engine hoist chain.

26. Raise the transmission slightly and tighten the frame crossmember-to-chassis bolts to 29 ft. lbs. (39 Nm). Tighten the 2 nuts to 43 ft. lbs. (59 Nm).

27. Install the exhaust pipe with a new gasket and tighten the nuts to 46 ft. lbs. (62 Nm).

28. Connect the transmission control rod. Connect the transfer case shift lever.

29. Connect the engine ground strap. Connect the speedometer cable.

30. Install the front and rear driveshafts. Tighten the nuts to 65 ft. lbs. (88 Nm).

31. Install the transfer case undercover. Install the air conditioning compressor. Install the power steering pump and tighten the pulley nut to 35 ft. lbs. (47 Nm).

32. Connect the EFI wiring harness at the ECU. Connect all of the following hoses:
   a. Heater hoses
   b. Fuel hoses
   c. Transfer case hose
   d. Brake booster hose
   e. Air injection hoses
   f. Distributor hose
   g. Emission control hoses.

33. Connect all of the following the wires and connectors:
   a. Oil pressure connector
   b. High tension cord at the coil
   c. Neutral start switch and transfer connectors near the starter
   d. Front differential lock connector
   e. Starter wire and connector
   f. Starter ground strap
   g. Oxygen sensor connectors
   h. Alternator wire and connector
   i. Cooling fan connector
   j. Check connector

34. Install the radiator and the coolant reservoir tank.

35. Install the air intake hose, air flow meter and air cleaner. Connect the accelerator and throttle cables.

36. Refill the engine with oil and the radiator with coolant. Install the engine undercover. Install the battery.

37. Install and adjust the hood.

38. Install the battery, start the engine and road test the vehicle.

3VZ-E Engine

1. Disconnect the battery cables and remove the battery.

2. Remove the engine undercover.

3. Disconnect the windshield washer hose and then remove the hood. Scribe matchmarks around the hinges for easy installation.

4. Drain the engine coolant from the radiator and the cylinder block.

5. Raise and safely support the vehicle. Drain the engine oil. Drain the automatic transmission fluid, if equipped.

6. Lower the vehicle. Disconnect the air cleaner hose and then remove the air cleaner.

7. Remove the radiator.

8. Remove all drive belts and then remove the fluid coupling and fan pulley.

9. Tag and disconnect the following wires and connectors:
   a. Left side and rear ground straps
   b. Alternator connector and wire
   c. Igniter connector
   d. Oil pressure switch connector
   e. ECU connectors
   f. VSV connectors
   g. Starter relay connector for manual transmission only
   h. Solenoid resistor connector
   i. Check connector
   j. Air conditioning compressor connector

10. Tag and disconnect the following hoses:
   a. Power steering hoses at the gas filter and air pipe
   b. Brake booster hose
   c. Cruise control vacuum hose, if equipped
   d. Charcoal canister hose at the canister
   e. VSV vacuum hoses.

11. Disconnect the accelerator, throttle and cruise control cables where applicable.

12. Unbolt the power steering pump and position it aside with the hydraulic lines still connected.

13. Properly discharge the air conditioning system. Remove the air conditioning compressor if equipped.

14. Disconnect the clutch release cylinder hose for manual transmission only.

15. Disconnect the 2 heater hoses.

16. Disconnect and plug the fuel inlet and outlet lines.

17. Remove the shift levers for manual transmission only.

18. Raise and safely support the vehicle. Remove the rear driveshaft.

19. Disconnect the manual shift linkage for automatic transmission only.

20. Disconnect the speedometer cable, don't lose the felt dust protector and washers.

21. Remove the transfer case undercover. Remove the stabilizer bar.

22. Remove the front driveshaft. Remove the front exhaust pipe.

23. Remove the No. 1 front floor heat insulator and the brake tube heat insulator.

24. Remove the rear engine mount bolts, raise the transmission slightly with a floor jack and then remove the 4 bolts from the side member and remove the No. 2 frame crossmember. Lower the vehicle.

25. Attach an engine hoist chain to the lifting brackets on the engine. Remove the engine mount nuts and bolts and slowly lift the engine/transmission from the vehicle.

To install:

26. Slowly lower the engine assembly into the engine compartment.

27. Raise the transmission onto the crossmember with a floor jack.

28. Align the holes in the engine mounts and the frame, install the bolts and then remove the engine hoist chain.

29. Raise the transmission slightly and tighten the No. 2 frame crossmember-to-side frame bolts to 70 ft. lbs. (95 Nm). Lower the transmission and tighten the 4 rear engine mount bolts to 9 ft. lbs. (13 Nm).

30. Install the brake tube and front floor heat insulators. Reconnect the exhaust pipe.

31. Install the No. 1 frame crossmember. Install the front driveshaft, stabilizer bar and the transfer case undercover.

32. Connect the speedometer cable. Connect the manual shift linkage for automatic transmission only.

33. Install the rear driveshaft. Install the shift levers for manual transmission only.

34. Install the fuel inlet and outlet lines. Connect the heater hoses.

35. Connect the clutch release cylinder hose. Install the air conditioning compressor.

36. Install the power steering pump and connect the ground strap.

37. Connect the throttle, cruise control and accelerator cables.

38. Connect the following hoses:
   a. Power steering hoses at the gas filter and air pipe
   b. Brake booster hose
   c. Cruise control vacuum hose, if equipped
   d. Charcoal canister hose at the canister
   e. VSV vacuum hoses.

39. Install the fan pulley, belt guide, fluid coupling and drive belt. Connect the following wires:
   a. Left side and rear ground straps
   b. Alternator connector and wire
   c. Igniter connector
   d. Oil pressure switch connector
   e. ECU connectors
   f. VSV connectors
   g. Starter relay connector for manual transmission only
   h. Solenoid resistor connector
   i. Check connector
   j. Air conditioning compressor connector

40. Install the air conditioning belt. Install the power steering pump and connect the ground strap.

41. Install the radiator and shroud. Install the air cleaner. Refill the engine with oil and the radiator with coolant.

42. Install the engine undercover. Install the battery. Install and adjust the hood.

43. Install the battery, start the vehicle and road test it.

2TZ-FE Engine

1. Disconnect the negative battery cable and drain the engine coolant and oil.

2. Raise the vehicle and support safely. Remove the engine under covers.

3. Remove the accessory drive belt and service bolts and nut at the front end of the driveshaft. Matchmark and disconnect the equipment driveshaft from the crankshaft pulley.

4. Label and disconnect all hoses, electrical connectors, vacuum lines and cables from the engine and position aside.

5. Disconnect the front driveshaft for 4WD only.

6. Remove the air intake connector and disconnect the engine wiring from the floor pan.

7. Remove the exhaust pipe from the manifold and disconnect the oxygen sensor connector.

8. Remove the rear driveshaft.

9. Place a engine/transmission jack under the engine and remove the engine and transmission mount bolts.

10. With the vehicle on a hoist, lower the engine with the transmission from the bottom of the vehicle.

To install:

11. Raise the engine/transmission into the vehicle and torque the mount bolts and nuts to 27 ft. lbs. (34 Nm).

12. Connect all electrical connectors, vacuum hoses, coolant hoses and cables to the engine.

13. Install the exhaust pipe and torque to 32 ft. lbs. (43 Nm).

14. Install the front (4WD) and rear driveshafts and torque to 14 ft. lbs. (21 Nm).

15. Install the equipment driveshaft to the pulley and torque the bolts to 38 ft. lbs. (54 Nm). Install the belt and adjust.

16. Refill the engine with oil and coolant.

17. Connect the battery cable, start the engine and check for leaks.

Engine Mounts

REMOVAL AND INSTALLATION

1. Raise the vehicle and support safely.

2. Remove the engine-to-mount bolt or nut.

3. Position a suitable jack under the engine block.

4. Raise the engine far enough to take the weight off the mount. Wedge a piece of wood between the engine and chassis in case the engine jack slips.

5. Remove the mount-to-body bolts and remove the mount.

To install:

6. Install the mount and torque the bolts to 34 ft. lbs. (46 Nm).

7. Remove the wood and lower the jack to engage the mount.

8. Torque the mount nut to 25 ft. lbs. (34 Nm).

9. Lower the vehicle and check for proper operation.

Cylinder Head

REMOVAL AND INSTALLATION

22R-E Engine

1. Relieve the fuel system pressure. Disconnect the negative battery cable.

2. Drain the coolant from the radiator and the cylinder block. Raise and safely support the vehicle. Drain the engine oil.

3. Disconnect and remove the air cleaner hose on the 22R-E engine.

4. Disconnect the oxygen sensor wire. Remove the nuts attaching the manifold to the exhaust pipe and then separate them.

5. Remove the oil dipstick. Remove the distributor with the spark plug leads attached.

6. Disconnect the upper radiator hose and the heater hoses where they attach to the engine and then position them aside.

7. Disconnect the actuator cable, the accelerator cable and the throttle cable for the automatic transmission at their bracket.

8. Tag and disconnect the following:
   a. Both PCV vacuum hoses
   b. Brake booster hose
   c. Actuator hose, if equipped with cruise control
   d. Air control valve hoses
   e. Air control valve.

9. Tag and disconnect the EGR vacuum modulator hoses and then remove the modulator itself along with the bracket.

10. Tag and disconnect the following:
   a. Green and brown BVSV hoses
   b. Vacuum advance hoses
   c. The 2 air valve hoses; one at the throttle body, the other at the air chamber
   d. Air control valve hose, if equipped with air conditioning
   e. Pressure regulator hose at the air chamber
   f. Cold start injector pipe and wire
   g. Throttle position sensor wire

11. Remove the bolt holding the EGR valve to the air chamber. Disconnect the chamber from the stay. Remove the air chamber-to-intake manifold bolts and then lift off the chamber with the throttle body.

12. Disconnect the fuel return hose.

13. Tag and disconnect the following:
   a. Water temperature sender gauge wire
   b. Temperature sensor wire

c. Start injection time switch wire

d. Fuel injector wires.

14. Remove the pulsation damper. Remove the bolt holding the fuel hose to the delivery pipe and then disconnect and remove the fuel hose.

15. Disconnect the wire and hose and then remove the air valve from the intake manifold.

16. Disconnect the bypass hose at the intake manifold on the 22R-E engine.

17. If equipped with power steering, remove the pump and position it aside without disconnecting the hydraulic lines.

18. Remove the 4 nuts and then remove the cylinder head cover.

19. Remove the rubber camshaft seals. Turn the crankshaft until the No. 1 piston is at TDC of its compression stroke. Matchmark the timing sprocket to the timing chain and then remove the semi-circular plug. Using a 19mm wrench, remove the camshaft sprocket bolt. Slide the distributor drive gear and spacer off the camshaft and wire the cam sprocket in place.

20. Remove the timing chain cover bolt in front of the cylinder head.

NOTE: This must be done before the cylinder head bolts are removed.

21. Remove the cylinder head bolts gradually, in 2–3 stages, in the correct order.

22. Using prybars applied evenly at the front and rear of the rocker arm assembly, pry the assembly off its mounting dowels.

23. Lift the cylinder head off its mounting dowels.

To install:

24. Apply liquid sealer to the front corners of the block and install the head gasket.

25. Lower the head over the locating dowels. Do not attempt to slide it into place.

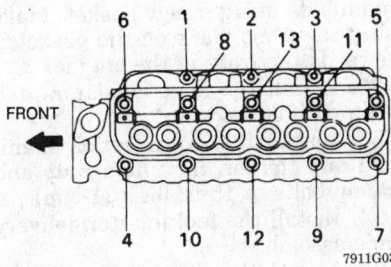

Cylinder head bolt removal sequence — 22R-E engine

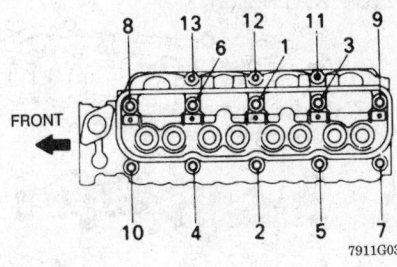

Cylinder head bolt installation sequence — 22R-E engine

26. Rotate the camshaft so the sprocket aligning pin is at the top. Remove the wire and hold the cam sprocket. Manually rotate the engine so the sprocket hole is also at the top. Wire the sprocket in place.

27. Install the rocker arm assembly over its positioning dowels.

28. Tighten the cylinder head bolts evenly, in 3 stages and in the correct order.

29. Install the timing chain cover bolt and tighten it to 7–11 ft. lbs. (11–15 Nm).

30. Remove the wire and fit the sprocket over the camshaft dowel. If the chain won't allow the sprocket to reach, rotate the crankshaft back and forth, while lifting up on the chain and sprocket.

31. Install the distributor drive gear and tighten the crankshaft bolt to 51–65 ft. lbs. (68–88 Nm).

32. Set the No. 1 piston at TDC of its compression stroke and adjust the valves.

33. After completing valve adjustment, rotate the crankshaft 352 degrees, so the 8 degree BTDC mark on the pulley aligns with the pointer.

34. Install the distributor.

35. Install the spark plugs and leads.

36. Make sure the oil drain plug is installed. Fill the engine with oil after installing the rubber cam seals. Pour the oil over the distributor drive gear and the valve rockers.

37. Install the rocker cover and tighten the bolts to 8–11 ft. lbs. (11–15 Nm).

38. Connect all the vacuum hoses and electrical leads which were removed during disassembly. Install the spark plug lead supports. Fill the cooling system. Install the air cleaner.

39. Tighten the exhaust pipe-to-manifold flange bolts to 25–33 ft. lbs. (34–45 Nm).

40. Reconnect the battery. Start the engine and allow it to reach normal operating temperature. Check and adjust the timing and valve clearance. Adjust the idle speed and mixture. Road test the vehicle.

3F-E Engine

1. Drain the coolant.

2. Disconnect the negative battery cable.

3. Scribe matchmarks around the hood hinges and then remove the hood.

4. Disconnect the accelerator and throttle cables.

5. Remove the air intake hose, air flow meter and air cleaner cap.

6. Unbolt the power steering pump and position it aside without disconnecting the hydraulic lines.

7. Unbolt the air conditioning compressor and position it aside without disconnecting the refrigerant lines.

8. Remove the power steering pump and air conditioning compressor brackets.

9. Disconnect the high tension leads from the spark plugs and the coil.

10. Disconnect and remove the heater water (oil cooler) pipe.

11. Disconnect the upper radiator hose.

12. Disconnect and plug the fuel lines.

13. Disconnect the exhaust pipe at the manifold.

14. Remove the air pump.

15. Remove the fuel delivery pipe along with the fuel injectors.

16. Remove the air injection manifold.

17. Remove the intake and exhaust manifolds.

18. Disconnect the water bypass hose at the water outlet and then remove the outlet.

19. Remove the spark plugs.

20. Remove the cylinder head cover and its gasket.

21. Loosen the bolts and nuts that attach the rocker shaft assembly in several stages and then remove the rocker shaft.

22. Remove the pushrods.

23. Remove the cylinder head bolts in the reverse of the tightening sequence. Remove the air pump bracket and engine hanger.

24. Lift the cylinder head off its mounting dowels.

To install:

25. Install the cylinder head on the cylinder block using a new gasket.

26. Lightly coat the threads of the cylinder head bolts with engine oil and then install them into the head.

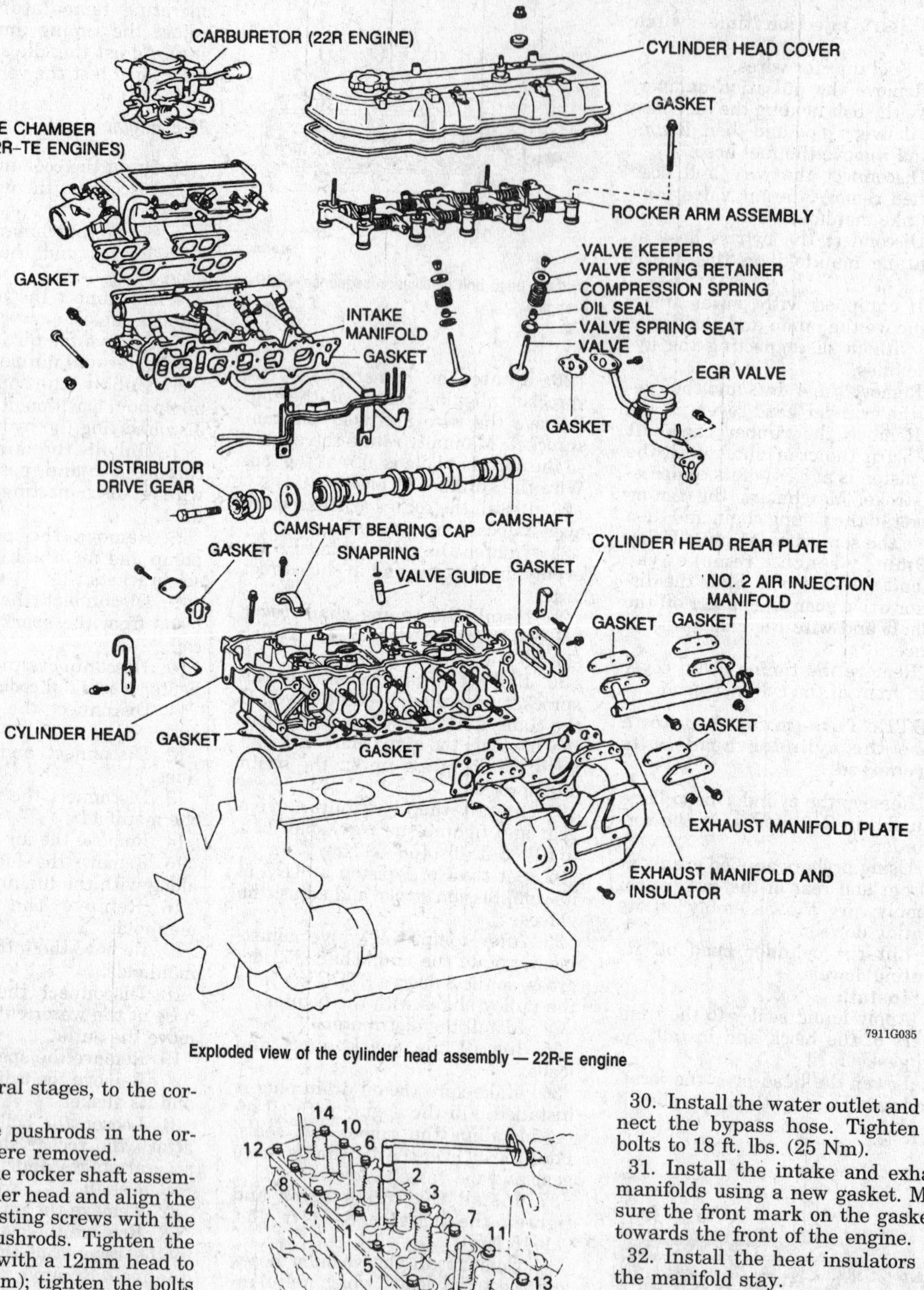

CARBURETOR (22R ENGINE)

CYLINDER HEAD COVER

GASKET

AIR INTAKE CHAMBER
(22R-E, 22R-TE ENGINES)

ROCKER ARM ASSEMBLY

GASKET

VALVE KEEPERS
VALVE SPRING RETAINER
COMPRESSION SPRING
OIL SEAL
VALVE SPRING SEAT
VALVE

INTAKE
MANIFOLD
GASKET

EGR VALVE

GASKET

DISTRIBUTOR
DRIVE GEAR

CAMSHAFT BEARING CAP   CAMSHAFT
GASKET   SNAPRING
                VALVE GUIDE   GASKET

CYLINDER HEAD REAR PLATE

NO. 2 AIR INJECTION
MANIFOLD
GASKET   GASKET

CYLINDER HEAD   GASKET

GASKET

GASKET

EXHAUST MANIFOLD PLATE

EXHAUST MANIFOLD AND
INSULATOR

7911G035

Exploded view of the cylinder head assembly — 22R-E engine

Tighten in several stages, to the correct torque.

27. Install the pushrods in the order that they were removed.

28. Position the rocker shaft assembly on the cylinder head and align the rocker arm adjusting screws with the heads of the pushrods. Tighten the mounting bolts with a 12mm head to 17 ft. lbs. (24 Nm); tighten the bolts with a 14mm head to 25 ft. lbs. (33 Nm).

29. Adjust the valve clearance and install the spark plugs. Install the cylinder head cover and tighten the cap nuts to 78 inch lbs. (8.8 Nm).

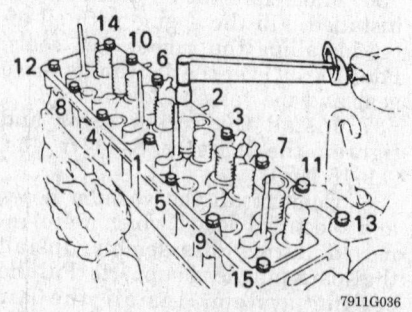

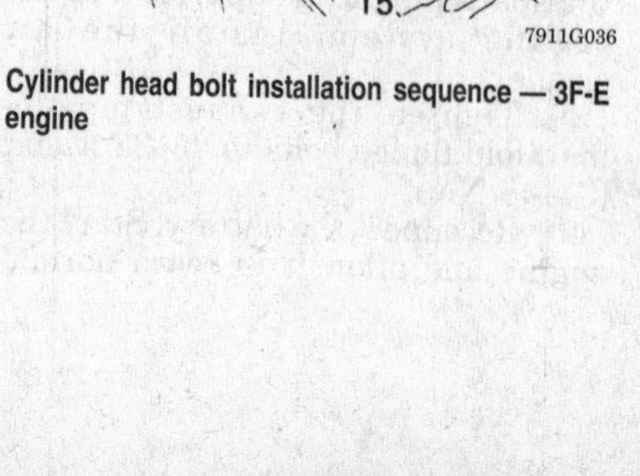

7911G036

Cylinder head bolt installation sequence — 3F-E engine

30. Install the water outlet and connect the bypass hose. Tighten the bolts to 18 ft. lbs. (25 Nm).

31. Install the intake and exhaust manifolds using a new gasket. Make sure the front mark on the gasket is towards the front of the engine.

32. Install the heat insulators and the manifold stay.

33. Install the air injection manifold and tighten the union nuts and clamp bolts to 15 ft. lbs. (21 Nm).

34. Install the fuel injector/delivery pipe assembly.

35. Install the air pump and connect the air hose.

36. Connect the exhaust pipe to the manifold. Use a new gasket and

tighten the bolts to 46 ft. lbs. (62 Nm).

37. Connect the fuel lines and the upper radiator hose.

38. Install the heater water pipe.

39. Connect the high tension cords.

40. Install the air conditioning compressor and the power steering pump. Remember to adjust the belt tension later.

41. Install the air intake hose, the air flow meter and the air cleaner cap.

42. Connect and adjust the accelerator and throttle cables.

43. Connect the battery cable, fill the engine with coolant, start the engine and check for any leaks. Road test the vehicle.

1FZ-FE Engine

1. Drain the coolant. Disconnect the negative battery cable. Remove the battery. Disconnect the ground strap and remove battery tray.

2. Disconnect the cruise control actuator cable. Disconnect the accelerator cable. Disconnect the volume air flow meter connector and wire clamp.

3. Loosen the air cleaner hose clamp. Loosen the No. 2 air hose clamp and disconnect the hose.

4. Remove the wing nut and loosen the 3 clips from the air cleaner. Remove the air cleaner cap, volume air flow meter and resonator.

5. Disconnect the engine ground straps. Disconnect the 3 vacuum hoses from the EGR valve. Disconnect the EGR gas temperature sensor connector.

6. Loosen the EGR pipe union nut. Remove the 2 nuts holding the EGR valve to the air intake chamber. Remove the 2 stud bolts, EGR valve and vacuum modulator assembly and gasket.

7. Remove the bolt holding the heater inlet pipe and air intake chamber. Disconnect the air cleaner hose. Disconnect the No. 1 and No. 2 PCV hoses.

8. Remove the 2 bolts and disconnect the heater valve. Remove the 2 bolts and disconnect the engine wire and ground strap. Remove the 4 bolts and remove the No. 2 and No. 3 cylinder head covers.

9. Disconnect the vacuum hoses.

10. Remove the 2 mounting bolts of the No. 1 and No. 2 spark plug cord clamps.

11. Disconnect the high tension cords at the rubber boot. Disconnect the high tension cord from the igni-tion coil. Disconnect the distributor connector.

12. Remove the distributor hold-down bolt and remove the distributor. Disconnect the No. 2 water by-pass hose. Disconnect the EVAP hose. Disconnect the brake booster hose.

13. Remove the alternator and the alternator bracket. Remove the 2 nuts, water outlet and the gasket. Disconnect the throttle position sensor connector. Disconnect the Idle Air Control (IAC) valve connector.

14. Disconnect the connector for the emission control valve set assembly. Remove the throttle body assembly. Remove the 3 bolts retaining the power steering reservoir tank and disconnect the tank.

15. Remove the 2 mounting bolts from the engine oil dipstick guide. Pull out the dipstick with the dipstick guide. Remove the O-ring from the dipstick guide.

16. Remove the 2 mounting bolts from the transmission oil dipstick guide. Pull out the dipstick with the dipstick guide. Remove the O-ring from the dipstick guide.

17. Disconnect the ground strap. Disconnect the 2 vacuum hoses from the TVV. Disconnect the No. 1 water bypass hose from the cylinder head.

18. Remove the 4 bolts, 4 nuts, air intake chamber and the 2 gaskets from the engine. Disconnect the fuel hose from the fuel pressure regulator.

19. Remove the 2 bolts and the fuel return pipe. Remove the 2 union bolts, bolt, 4 gaskets and the fuel pipe. Disconnect the 6 injector connectors.

20. Remove the 3 bolts and the de-livery pipe together with the 6 injectors. Remove the 6 insulators and 3 spacers from the intake manifold.

21. Remove the 6 injectors from the delivery pipe. Remove the O-ring and grommet from each injector.

22. Disconnect the following connectors:

   a. ECT sender gauge connector
   b. ECT cut switch connector
   c. ECT sensor connectors
   d. 2 knock sensor connectors
   e. Heated oxygen sensor connector and clamps
   f. 4 connectors from the transmission
   g. Starter connector
   h. Oil level sensor connector

23. Remove the bolt and disconnect the engine wire from the intake man-ifold. Remove the 2 bolts and disconnect the engine wire from the engine block. Disconnect the engine wire clamp.

24. Remove the 3 bolts and disconnect the engine wire from the cylinder head and intake manifold.

25. Remove the 2 bolts, 2 nuts, heater pipe and gasket. Remove the 2 bolts, 6 nuts, air pipe and 3 gaskets. Remove the 2 bolts and the PAIR reed valve.

26. Remove the 6 bolts, No. 1 heat insulator and the No. 2 heat insulator from the exhaust manifolds. Remove the 13 nuts, No. 1 exhaust manifold, No. 2 exhaust manifold and gaskets.

27. Remove the 2 bolts from the No. 1 engine hanger and remove the hanger. Remove the 2 bolts from the No. 2 engine hanger and remove the hanger.

28. Remove the 13 bolts from the cylinder head cover, remove the head cover and the gasket. Remove the spark plugs.

29. Set the No. 1 cylinder to TDC of the compression stroke. Remove the 2 nuts, chain tensioner and the gasket from the engine.

30. Remove the semi-circular plug from the camshaft timing gear. Place matchmarks on the camshaft timing gear and the timing chain. Remove the bolt from the intake camshaft and remove the distributor gear.

31. Remove the exhaust camshaft.

   a. Turn the exhaust camshaft with wrench until the service bolt hole of the subgear can be secured.

   b. Secure the exhaust camshaft subgear with a service bolt to the main gear.

   c. Set the timing mark of the camshaft driven gear to 35 degrees by turning the hexagon wrench head portion of the intake camshaft with a wrench.

   d. Lightly push the camshaft to-wards the rear without applying excessive force.

   e. Loosen and remove the No. 1 bearing cap bolts, alternately loos-ening the left and right bolts uniformly.

   f. Loosen and remove the No. 2, No. 7, No. 3 and No. 5 bearing cap bolts, in that order, in the same manner. Remove the bearing caps.

   g. Alternately and uniformly loosen and remove the No. 4 and No. 6 bearing cap bolts. Be sure the camshaft is being lifted out level and straight.

   h. Remove the bearing caps and remove the exhaust camshaft.

32. Remove the intake camshaft.

   a. Set the timing mark of the camshaft drive gear to 25 degrees by turning the hexagon wrench

head portion of the intake camshaft with a wrench.

b. Lightly push the intake camshaft towards the front without applying excessive force.

c. Loosen and remove the No. 1 bearing cap bolts, alternately loosening the left and right bolts uniformly.

d. Loosen and remove the No. 7, No. 3, No. 6 and No. 4 bearing cap bolts, in that order, in the same manner. Remove the bearing caps.

e. Alternately and uniformly loosen and remove the No. 2 and No. 5 bearing cap bolts. Be sure the camshaft is being lifted out level and straight.

f. Remove the bearing caps and remove the exhaust camshaft.

33. Remove the 2 bolts in front of the head.

34. Using SST 09011-38121 or equivalent, uniformly loosen and remove the 14 head bolts, in several passes.

35. Lift the cylinder head from the dowels on the cylinder block. Place the head on wooden blocks.

To install:

36. Install the cylinder head.

a. Apply seal packing to the forward corners of the cylinder head.

b. Install a new cylinder head gasket on the cylinder block.

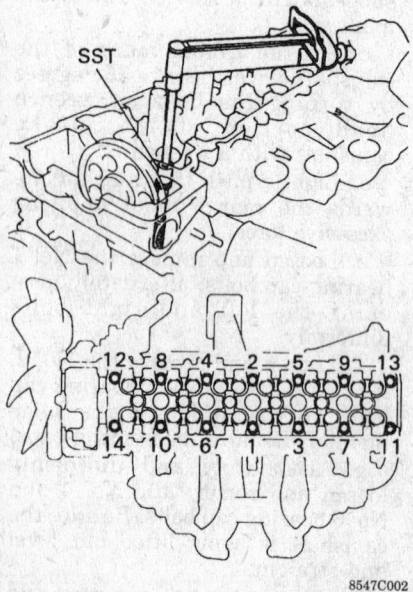

Cylinder head bolt loosening pattern — 1FZ-FE Engine

c. Place the cylinder head into position on the cylinder head gasket.

37. Install the 14 cylinder head bolts and plate washers. Tighten uniformly to 29 ft. lbs. (39 Nm).

38. Retighten the cylinder head bolts uniformly 90 degrees. Retighten the cylinder head bolts uniformly an additional 90 degrees.

39. Install the 2 front mounting bolts. Torque the bolts to 15 ft. lbs. (21 Nm).

40. Install the intake camshaft.

a. Apply engine oil to the thrust portion of the intake camshaft.

b. Lightly place the camshaft on top of the cylinder head at a 25 degree angle so the No. 1 and No. 4 lobes face downward.

c. Lightly push the camshaft towards the front.

d. Place the No. 2 and No. 5 bearing caps in place.

e. Temporarily tighten the bearing cap bolts uniformly and alternatively in several passes until the bearing caps are snug.

f. Place the No. 3, No. 4, No. 6 and No. 7 bearing caps in place.

g. Temporarily tighten the bearing cap bolts uniformly and alternatively in several passes until the bearing caps are snug.

h. Place the No. 1 bearing cap in place.

i. Temporarily tighten the bearing cap bolts alternatively in several passes until the bearing caps are snug.

j. Uniformly tighten the 14 bearing cap bolts in several passes. Torque the bolts to 12 ft. lbs. (16 Nm).

41. Install the exhaust camshaft.

a. Set the timing mark of the camshaft drive gear at 35 degrees by turning the hexagon wrench head portion of the intake camshaft with a wrench.

b. Apply engine oil to the thrust portion of the exhaust camshaft.

c. Align the camshafts by matching the timing marks on the gears.

d. Roll the exhaust camshaft onto the bearing journals while engaging gears with each other.

e. Lightly push the camshaft towards the front.

f. Place the No. 4 and No. 6 bearing caps in place.

g. Temporarily tighten the bearing cap bolts uniformly and alternatively in several passes until the bearing caps are snug.

h. Place the No. 2, No. 3, No. 5 and No. 7 bearing caps in place.

i. Temporarily tighten the bearing cap bolts uniformly and alternatively in several passes until the bearing caps are snug.

j. Place the No. 1 bearing cap in place.

k. Temporarily tighten the bearing cap bolts alternatively in several passes until the bearing caps are snug.

l. Uniformly tighten the 14 bearing cap bolts in several passes. Torque the bolts to 12 ft. lbs. (16 Nm).

42. Set the No. 1 cylinder to TDC of the compression stroke. Be sure the dots on the camshafts are in line.

43. With the matchmarks of the camshaft timing gear and the timing chain aligned, place the gear over the straight pin of the intake camshaft.

44. Align the straight pin of the intake camshaft gear with the straight pin of the distributor gear.

45. Install and torque the bolt on the intake camshaft to 54 ft. lbs. (74 Nm). Install a new gasket and the chain tensioner. Install the spark plugs.

46. Install a new gasket and the cylinder head cover. Tighten the 13 bolts.

47. Install 3 O-rings tot he water bypass outlet and pipe. Install the water bypass outlet and pipe. Tighten the 2 bolts.

48. Install the No. 1 engine hanger and the No. 2 engine hanger. Tighten the bolts.

49. Install new gaskest with the No. 1 exhaust manifold and No. 2 exhaust manifold and tighten the 13 nuts.

50. Install the No. 1 and No. 2 heat insulators to the exhaust manifolds. Tighten the 6 bolts.

51. Install the PAIR reed valve and tighten the 2 bolts. Install the air pipe with 3 new gaskets and tighten the 2 bolts and 6 nuts.

52. Install the heater pipe with a new gasket and tighten the 2 bolts and 2 nuts. Install the engine wire to the cylinder head and intake manifold. Tighten the 3 bolts.

53. Connect the engine wire clamp. Connect the engine wire to the engine block and tighten the 2 bolts. Connect the engine wire to the intake manifold and tighten the bolt.

54. Connect the following connectors:

a. ECT sender gauge connector

b. ECT cut switch connector

c. ECT sensor connectors

d. 2 knock sensor connectors

e. Heated oxygen sensor connector and clamps

f. 4 connectors from the transmission

g. Starter connector

h. Oil level sensor connector

55. Install an O-ring and grommet to each injector. Install the injectors to the delivery pipe. Install the 3 spacers and 6 insulators to the intake manifold.

56. Install the 6 injectors with the delivery pipe. Torque the 3 bolts to 15 ft. lbs. (21 Nm). Connect the 6 injector connectors.

57. Install the fuel pipe and 4 gaskets. Torque the 2 union bolts to 22 ft. lbs. (29 Nm) and the bolt to 14 ft. lbs. (20 Nm).

58. Install the fuel return pipe and tighten the 2 bolts to 14 ft. lbs. (20 Nm). Connect the fuel hose to the fuel pressure regulator.

59. Install the air intake chamber and 2 gaskets. Tighten the 4 bolts and 4 nuts to 15 ft. lbs. (21 Nm).

60. Connect the No. 1 water bypass hose to the cylinder head. Connect the 2 vacuum hoses to the TVV. Connect the ground strap.

61. Install a new O-ring to the transmission oil dipstick guide and install the guide and dipstick. Tighten the 2 mounting bolts to 14 ft. lbs. (20 Nm).

62. Install a new O-ring to the engine oil dipstick guide and install the guide and dipstick. Tighten the 2 mounting bolts to 14 ft. lbs. (20 Nm).

63. Install the power steering reservior tank and tighten the 3 bolts to 13 ft. lbs. (18 Nm).

64. Install the throttle body assembly and tighten the bolts to 15 ft. lbs. (21 Nm).

65. Connect the connector for the emission control valve set assembly. Connect the Idle Air Control (IAC) valve connector. Install the alternator bracket and the alternator.

66. Install a new gasket with the water outlet and tighten the 2 nuts. Connect the throttle position sensor connector.

67. Connect the brake booster hose. Connect the EVAP hose and the No. 2 water bypass hose.

68. Align and install the distributor and tighten the hold-down bolt. Connect the distributor connector. Connect the high tension cord to the ignition coil. Connect the high tension cords to the spark plugs.

69. Tighten the 2 mounting bolts to the No. 1 and No. 2 cord clamps. Connect the vacuum hoses. Connect the No. 1 and No. 2 PCV hoses. Connect the air cleaner hose.

70. Install the No. 2 and No. 3 cylinder head covers. Tighten the 4 bolts.

71. Install the engine wire and ground strap and tighten the 2 bolts. Install the heater valve and tighten the 2 bolts.

72. Install the bolt holding the heater inlet pipe and the air intake chamber. Torque bolt to 14 ft. lbs. (20 Nm).

73. Temporarily install a new gasket and the EGR valve and vacuum modulator assembly. Torque the 2 stud bolts to 8 ft. lbs. (10 Nm)

74. Install the 2 nuts holding the EGR valve to the air intake chamber. Torque nuts to 14 ft. lbs. (19 Nm).

75. Tighten union nut of the EGR pipe to 47 ft. lbs. (64 Nm). Install the engine ground straps.

76. Connect the EGR gas temperature sensor connector. Connect the 3 vacuum hoses to the EGR valve.

77. Install the air cleaner cap, volume air flow meter and resonator. Install the 3 clips and tighten the wing nut.

78. Connect the No. 2 air hose and tighten the clamp. Tighten the air cleaner hose clamp. Connect the volume air flow meter connector and wire clamp.

79. Connect the accelerator cable. Connect the cruise control actuator cable.

80. Fill engine coolant. Connect the negative battery cable.

3VZ-E Engine

1. Disconnect the negative battery cable.

2. Remove the air cleaner hose and case.

3. Drain the engine coolant.

4. Remove the radiator.

5. Unbolt the power steering pump and position it aside with the hoses still attached.

6. Remove all drive belts and then remove the fluid coupling and fan pulley.

7. Tag and disconnect all wires and connectors that will interfere with cylinder head removal.

8. Disconnect the following hoses:

a. Power steering air hoses

b. Brake booster hose

c. Cruise control vacuum hose

d. Charcoal canister has at the canister

e. VSV vacuum hose.

9. Disconnect the accelerator, throttle and cruise control cables.

10. Disconnect the clutch release cylinder hose for manual transmission only.

11. Disconnect the heater hoses and the fuel lines.

12. Remove the left side scuff plate and disconnect the O_2 sensor and then remove the front exhaust pipe.

13. Remove the timing belt.

14. Remove the distributor with the spark plug leads attached; position it aside.

15. Remove the air intake chamber.

16. Disconnect the connectors and then remove the engine wire.

17. Remove the Nos. 2 and 3 fuel pipes.

18. Remove the No. 4 timing belt cover.

19. Remove the No. 2 idler pulley and the No. 3 timing belt cover.

20. Disconnect the hose and remove the water bypass outlet.

21. Remove the intake manifold.

22. Remove the exhaust crossover pipe.

23. For the right side, remove the following:

a. Remove the reed valve with the No. 1 air injection manifold.

b. Remove the water bypass pipe mounting bolt.

c. Remove the cylinder head cover.

d. Remove the camshaft.

e. Loosen the cylinder head bolts in several stages, in the opposite order of the tightening sequence. Remove the air pump bracket and engine hanger.

f. Lift the cylinder head off its mounting dowels, do not pry it off.

24. For the left side, remove the following:

a. Remove the alternator.

b. Remove the oil dipstick guide tube.

c. Remove the cylinder head cover.

d. Remove the camshaft.

e. Loosen the cylinder head bolts in several stages, in the opposite order of the tightening sequence. Remove the air pump bracket and engine hanger.

f. Lift the cylinder head off its mounting dowels, do not pry it off.

To install:

25. Install the cylinder head on the cylinder block using a new gasket.

26. Lightly coat the threads of the cylinder head bolts with engine oil and then install them into the head. Tighten them in several stages, in the correct order. After the initial tightening, mark the front side the the top of the bolt with paint. Tighten the bolts an additional 90 degrees (¼ turn) and check that the mark is now facing the side of the head. Tighten the bolts an additional 90 degrees

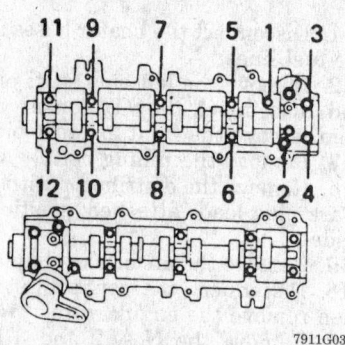

Camshaft bearing cap loosening sequence — 3VZ-E engine

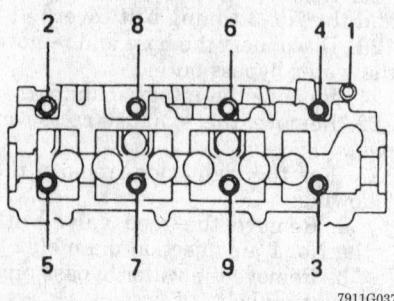

Cylinder head bolt removal sequence — 3VZ-E engine

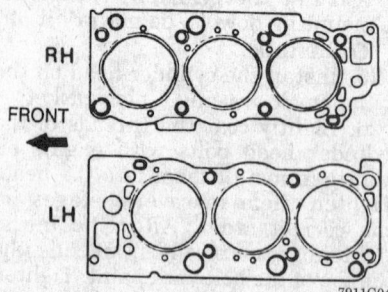

Cylinder head gasket installation — 3VZ-E engine

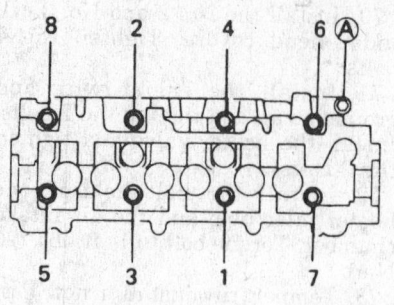

Cylinder head bolt tightening sequence — 3VZ-E engine

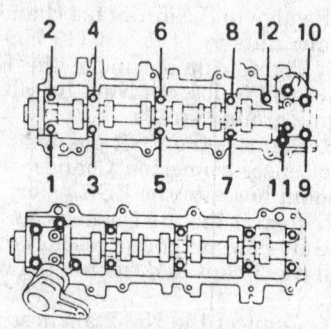

Camshaft bearing cap bolt tightening sequence — 3VZ-E engine

and check that the mark is now facing the rear of the head. Install the bolt (A) and tighten it to 27 ft. lbs. (37 Nm).

27. Install the camshaft.

28. Install the alternator and the water bypass pipe mounting bolt.

29. Install the reed valve with the No. 1 injection manifold.

30. Install the oil dipstick tube.

31. Install the crossover pipe and tighten it to 29 ft. lbs. (39 Nm).

32. Connect the oxygen sensor wire.

33. Install the intake manifold with new gaskets and tighten the mounting bolts to 29 ft. lbs. (39 Nm).

34. Install the water bypass outlet and tighten the bolts to 13 ft. lbs. (18 Nm).

35. Install the fuel delivery pipes and injectors.

36. Install the No. 2 idler pulley. Install the Nos. 3 and 4 timing belt covers and tighten the bolts to 74 inch lbs. (8.3 Nm).

37. Install the fuel pipes and tighten the union bolts to 22 ft. lbs. (29 Nm).

38. Install the timing belt. Install the cylinder head covers.

39. Install the air intake chamber and tighten the nuts and bolts to 13 ft. lbs. (18 Nm).

40. Install the EGR valve and connect all hoses and lines. Install the distributor and the front exhaust pipe.

41. Connect the fuel lines and heater hoses. Connect the clutch release cylinder hose.

42. Install the power steering pump. Connect and adjust all cables, hoses and wires previously removed.

43. Install the fan pulley, fluid coupling and drive belts. Install the radiator.

44. Install the air cleaner hose, refill the engine with coolant and connect the battery cable.

2TZ-FE Engine

1. Disconnect the negative battery cable.

2. Remove the engine/transmission assembly from the vehicle.

3. Remove the engine wiring from the engine and move aside.

4. Remove the No. 2 valve cover.

5. Mark the spark plug wires and disconnect. Matchmark the distributor, rotor and cylinder head. Remove the distributor and disconnect the wiring.

6. Remove the EGR valve.

7. Remove the fuel rail and water outlet.

8. Remove the intake and exhaust manifold assembly.

9. Remove the exhaust manifold heat insulator and oil return pipe.

10. Remove the No. 1 valve cover.

11. Place matchmarks on the timing sprocket and chain. Hold the camshaft with a wrench and remove the sprocket bolt.

12. Remove the chain tensioner and gasket.

13. Remove the No. 6 camshaft bearing cap.

14. Set the knock pin hole of the exhaust camshaft at the 5–30 degree BTDC. Uniformly loosen the camshaft bearing caps and remove the exhaust camshaft from the head.

15. Set the knock pin hole of the intake camshaft at the 75–100 degree BTDC. Uniformly loosen the camshaft bearing caps and remove the exhaust camshaft from the head.

16. Remove the 2 bolts in front of the head before removing the cylinder head retaining bolts.

17. Using a 12 sided socket wrench, remove the 10 cylinder head retaining bolts in sequence and remove the head from the engine.

To install:

18. Clean the gasket mating surfaces and check for warpage.

19. Install the head gasket and install the cylinder head.

20. Oil the bolts and torque in 3 steps, in sequence. If any of the bolts break, deform or do not meet the torque specification replace them.

21. Install and torque the 2 front bolts to 15 ft. lbs. (21 Nm).

22. Grease to all camshaft journals and caps.

23. Place the intake camshaft at 75–100 degrees BTDC. Install the bearing caps with the marking arrows facing forward. Uniformly torque the bearing cap bolts to 12 ft. lbs. (16 Nm).

24. Apply sealant to the bearing cap next to the timing chain sprocket.

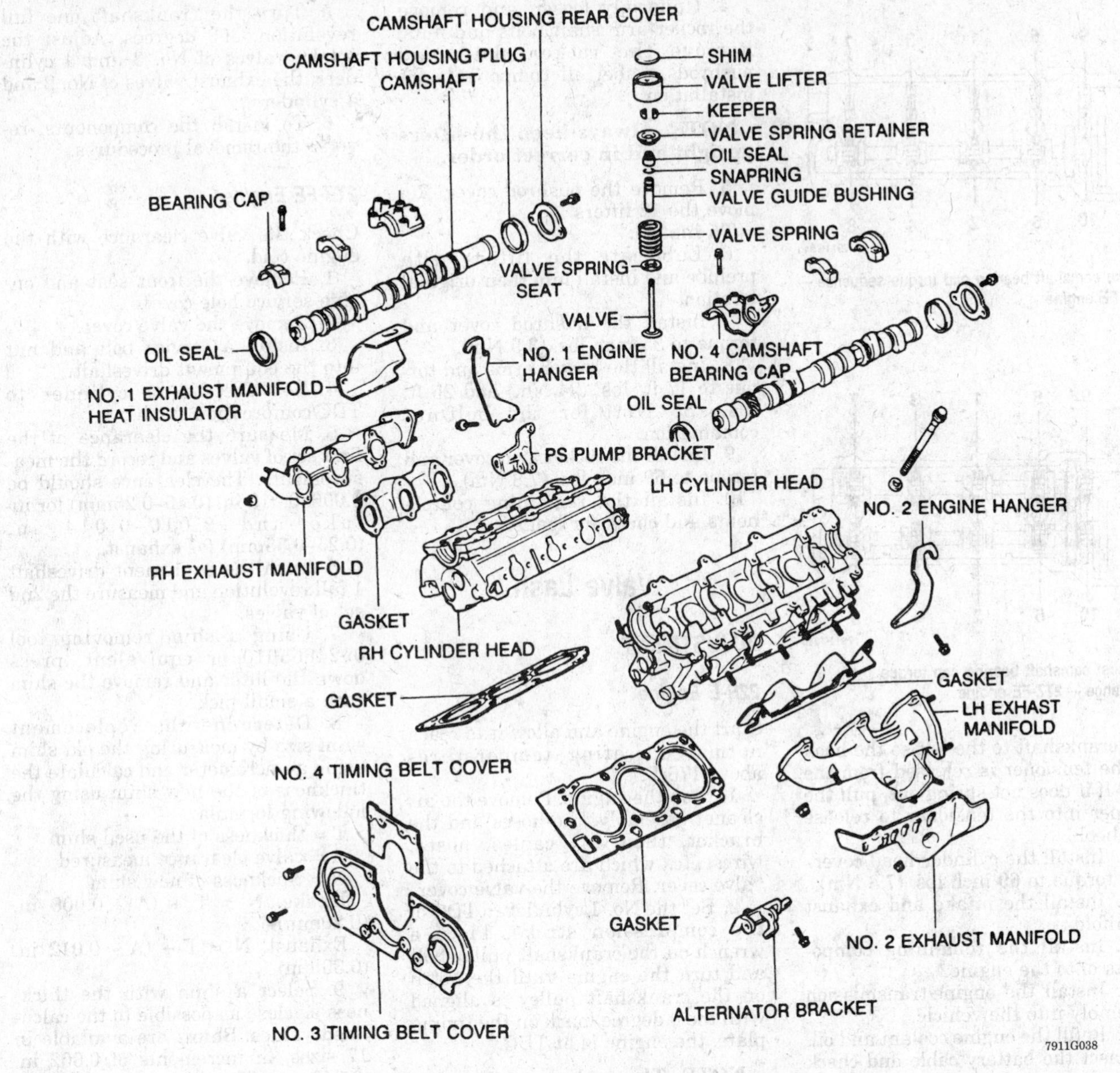

CAMSHAFT HOUSING REAR COVER

CAMSHAFT HOUSING PLUG
CAMSHAFT

SHIM
VALVE LIFTER
KEEPER
VALVE SPRING RETAINER
OIL SEAL
SNAPRING
VALVE GUIDE BUSHING

BEARING CAP

VALVE SPRING

VALVE SPRING SEAT

VALVE

OIL SEAL

NO. 1 ENGINE HANGER

NO. 4 CAMSHAFT BEARING CAP

OIL SEAL

NO. 1 EXHAUST MANIFOLD HEAT INSULATOR

PS PUMP BRACKET

LH CYLINDER HEAD

NO. 2 ENGINE HANGER

RH EXHAUST MANIFOLD

GASKET

RH CYLINDER HEAD

GASKET

GASKET

LH EXHAST MANIFOLD

NO. 4 TIMING BELT COVER

GASKET

GASKET

NO. 2 EXHAUST MANIFOLD

NO. 3 TIMING BELT COVER

ALTERNATOR BRACKET

7911G038

Exploded view of the cylinder head assembly — 3VZ-E engine

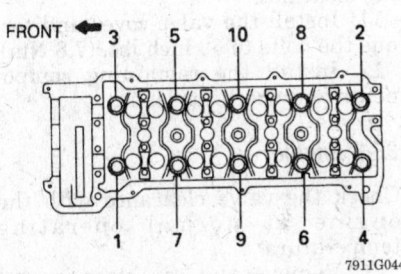

FRONT → 3 5 10 8 2
1 7 9 6 4

7911G044

Cylinder head loosening sequence — 2TZ-FE engine

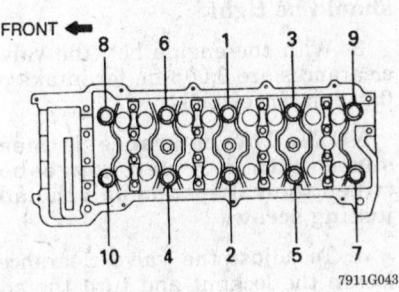

FRONT → 8 6 1 3 9
10 4 2 5 7

7911G043

Cylinder head torque sequence — 2TZ-FE engine

Place the intake camshaft at 5–30 degrees BTDC. Install the bearing caps with the marking arrows facing forward. Uniformly torque the bearing cap bolts to 12 ft. lbs. (16 Nm). Make sure the exhaust and intake camshaft gear alignment marks are facing each other. The one gear has 2 dots and the other has 1 dot.

25. Install the timing chain sprocket and torque the bolt to 54 ft. lbs. (74 Nm).

26. Release the ratchet pawl and fully push the plunger and apply the hook on the tensioner so it cannot spring out.

27. Install the tensioner and torque the bolts to 15 ft. lbs. (21 Nm). Turn

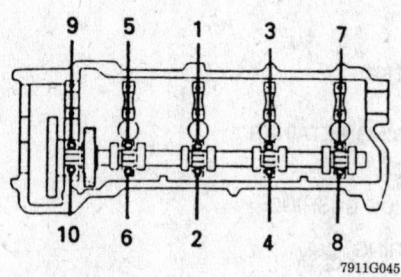

Intake camshaft bearing cap torque sequence — 2TZ-FE engine

7911G045

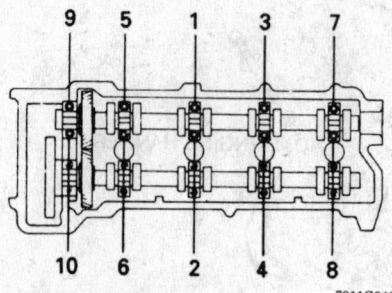

Exhaust camshaft bearing cap torque sequence — 2TZ-FE engine

7911G046

the crankshaft to the left so the hook of the tensioner is released from the pin. If it does not spring out, pull the slipper into the tensioner to release the hook.

28. Install the cylinder head covers and torque to 69 inch lbs. (7.8 Nm).

29. Install the intake and exhaust manifolds.

30. Install the remaining components onto the engine.

31. Install the engine/transmission assembly into the vehicle.

32. Refill the engine coolant and oil. Connect the battery cable and check for leaks.

Valve Lifters

REMOVAL AND INSTALLATION

Always replace the camshaft and lifters as a set. If not replacing, label all components for exact reinstallation.

3F-E Engine

1. Disconnect the negative battery cable.

2. Remove the spark plugs and tubes.

3. Remove the valve cover.

4. Uniformly loosen and remove the rocker arm shaft bolts and nuts. Remove the rocker shaft and pushrods. Label all components for installation.

NOTE: Always keep the lifters upright and in correct order.

5. Remove the pushrod cover. Remove the 12 lifters.

To install:

6. Lubricate the lifters with prelube and install into their original location.

7. Install the pushrod cover and torque to 35 inch lbs. (3.9 Nm).

8. Install the rocker arms and torque to 17 ft. lbs. (24 Nm) and 25 ft. lbs. (33 Nm) for the bolt/nut combination.

9. Install the rocker arm cover and torque to 69 inch lbs. (7.8 Nm).

10. Install the remaining components and check for leaks.

Valve Lash

ADJUSTMENT

22R-E Engine

Start the engine and allow it to reach normal operating temperatures above 175°F.

1. Stop the engine. Remove the air cleaner assembly, the hoses and the bracket, then any cables, hoses, wires, etc., which are attached to the valve cover. Remove the valve cover.

2. Set the No. 1 cylinder to TDC of the compression stroke. Place a wrench on the crankshaft pulley bolt and turn the engine until the notch on the crankshaft pulley is aligned with the 0 degree mark on the timing plate; the engine is at TDC.

NOTE: The rocker arms on cylinder No. 1 should be loose and the rocker arms on cylinder No. 4 should be tight.

3. With the engine hot, the valve clearances are 0.008 in. for intake or 0.012 in. for exhaust.

NOTE: The clearance is measured with a feeler gauge between the valve stem and the adjusting screw.

4. To adjust the valve clearance, loosen the locknut and turn the adjusting screw until the specified clearance is obtained. Tighten the locknut and check the clearance again. Adjust the intake valves of No. 1 and 2 cylinders; the exhaust valves of No. 1 and 3 cylinders.

5. Turn the crankshaft one full revolution, 360 degrees. Adjust the intake valves of No. 3 and 4 cylinders; the exhaust valves of No. 2 and 4 cylinders.

6. To install the components, reverse the removal procedures.

2TZ-FE Engine

Check the valve clearance with the engine cold.

1. Remove the front seat and engine service hole cover.

2. Remove the valve cover.

3. Install a service bolt and nut into the equipment driveshaft.

4. Set the No. 1 cylinder to TDC/compression stoke.

5. Measure the clearance of the first set of valves and record the measurements. The clearance should be 0.006–0.010 in. (0.15–0.25mm) for intake and 0.010–0.014 in. (0.25–0.35mm) for exhaust.

6. Turn the equipment driveshaft 1 full revolution and measure the 2nd set of valves.

7. Using a shim removing tool 0924855010 or equivalent, press down the lifter and remove the shim with a small pick.

8. Determine the replacement shim size by measuring the old shim using a micrometer and calculate the thickness of the new shim using the following formula:

T = thickness of the used shim
A = valve clearance measured
N = thickness of new shim

Intake: $N = T + (A - 0.008$ in. $(0.20mm)$

Exhaust: $N = T + (A - 0.012$ in. $(0.30mm)$

9. Select a shim with the thickness as close as possible to the calculated values. Shims are available in 17 sizes, in increments of 0.002 in. (0.050mm). The thickness is stamped on the shim.

10. Install the shims and recheck the clearance.

11. Install the valve cover and torque the bolts to 69 inch lbs. (7.8 Nm).

12. Install the remaining components and check for leaks.

3F-E Engine

Check the valve clearance with the engine at normal operating temperature.

1. Remove the air cleaner and valve cover.

2. Set the No. 1 cylinder to TDC. Make sure the No. 1 rocker arms are loose and the No. 6 are tight. If not, turn the crankshaft 1 turn and align the timing marks to 0.

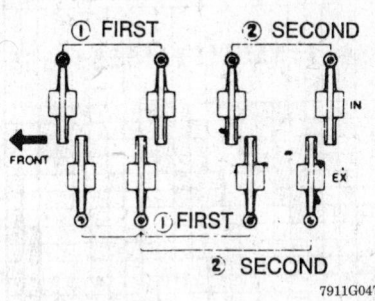

Valve adjustment sequence — 22R-E engine

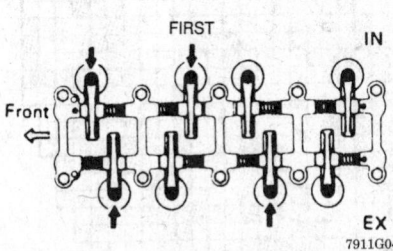

First step of the valve adjustment procedure — 22R-E engine

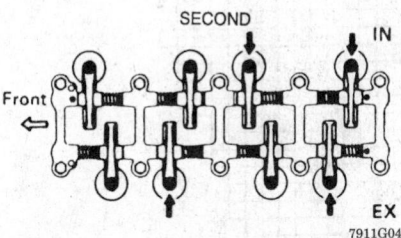

Second step of the valve adjustment procedure — 22R-E engine

3. Adjust the first set of valves to 0.008 in. (0.20mm) for intake and 0.014 in. (0.35mm) for exhaust valves.

4. After tightening the locknut, recheck the valve clearance.

5. Install the valve cover and air cleaner.

3VZ-E Engine

Check the valve clearance with the engine cold.
1. Remove the valve cover.

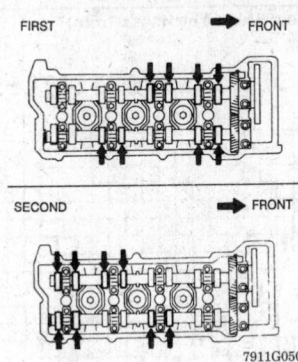

Valve clearance check — 2TZ-FE engine

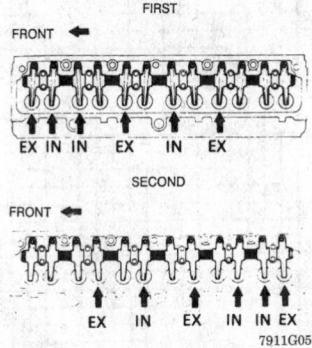

Adjusting valve clearance — 3F-E engine

2. Set the No. 1 cylinder to TDC/compression.

3. Measure the clearance of the lifters with the camshaft lobe at the base circle and record the measurements. The clearance should be as follows: 0.007–0.011 in. (0.18–0.28mm) intake; 0.009–0.013 in. (0.22–0.32mm) exhaust

4. Using a shim removing tool 0924855010 or equivalent, press down the lifter and remove the shim with a small pick.

5. Determine the replacement shim size by measuring the old shim using a micrometer and calculate the thickness of the new shim using the following formula:

T = thickness of the used shim
A = valve clearance measured
N = thickness of new shim
Intake: N = T + (A - 0.0091 in. (0.23mm)
Exhaust: N = T + (A - 0.0126 in. (0.32mm)

6. Select a shim with the thickness as close as possible to the calculated values. Shims are available in 25 sizes, in increments of 0.002 in.

(0.050mm). The thickness is stamped on the shim.

7. Install the shims and recheck the clearance.

8. Install the valve cover and torque the bolts to 69 inch lbs. (7.8 Nm).

9. Install the remaining components and check for leaks.

Rocker Arm Shafts

REMOVAL AND INSTALLATION

22R-E Engine

1. Remove the valve cover.

2. Remove the timing chain sprocket and secure the sprocket and chain to the engine with wire to ensure correct valve timing.

3. Uniformly loosen the 10 shaft bolts in the opposite sequence of tightening.

4. Remove the rocker arm shaft assembly from the cylinder head. Keep the assembly together for installation.

To install:
5. Install the rocker arm shaft assembly and torque the bolts in 3 steps, in sequence to 58 ft. lbs. (78 Nm).

6. Install the chain cover bolt and torque to 9 ft. lbs. (13 Nm).

7. Install timing chain sprocket, distributor drive gear and thrust plate. Torque the bolt to 58 ft. lbs. (78 Nm).

8. Adjust the valve clearance.

9. Install the valve cover and torque to 69 ft. lbs. (7.8 Nm).

10. Install the remaining components and check for leaks.

3F-E Engine

1. Remove the valve cover.

2. Uniformly loosen the shaft bolts starting from the ends and working inward.

3. Remove the rocker arm shaft assembly from the cylinder head. Keep the assembly together for installation.

To install:
4. Install the rocker arm shaft assembly and torque the bolts in 3 steps, start in the middle and move to the ends and torque in sequence to 17 ft. lbs. (24 Nm) and 25 ft. lbs. (33 Nm) for the bolt and nut combination.

5. Adjust the valve clearance.

6. Install the valve cover and torque to 69 ft. lbs. (7.8 Nm).

7. Install the remaining components and check for leaks.

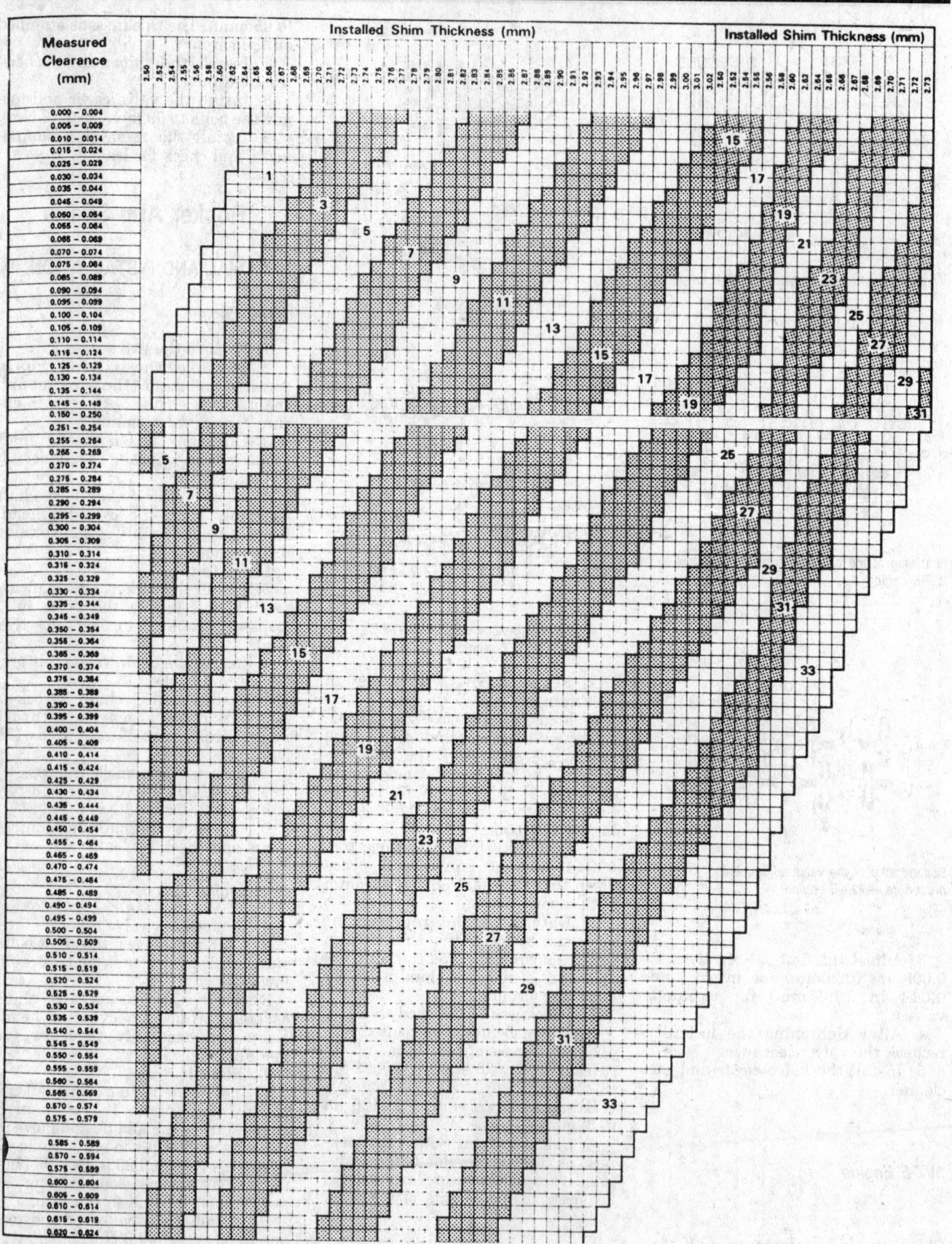

Intake shim selection chart — 2TZ-FE engine

7911G052

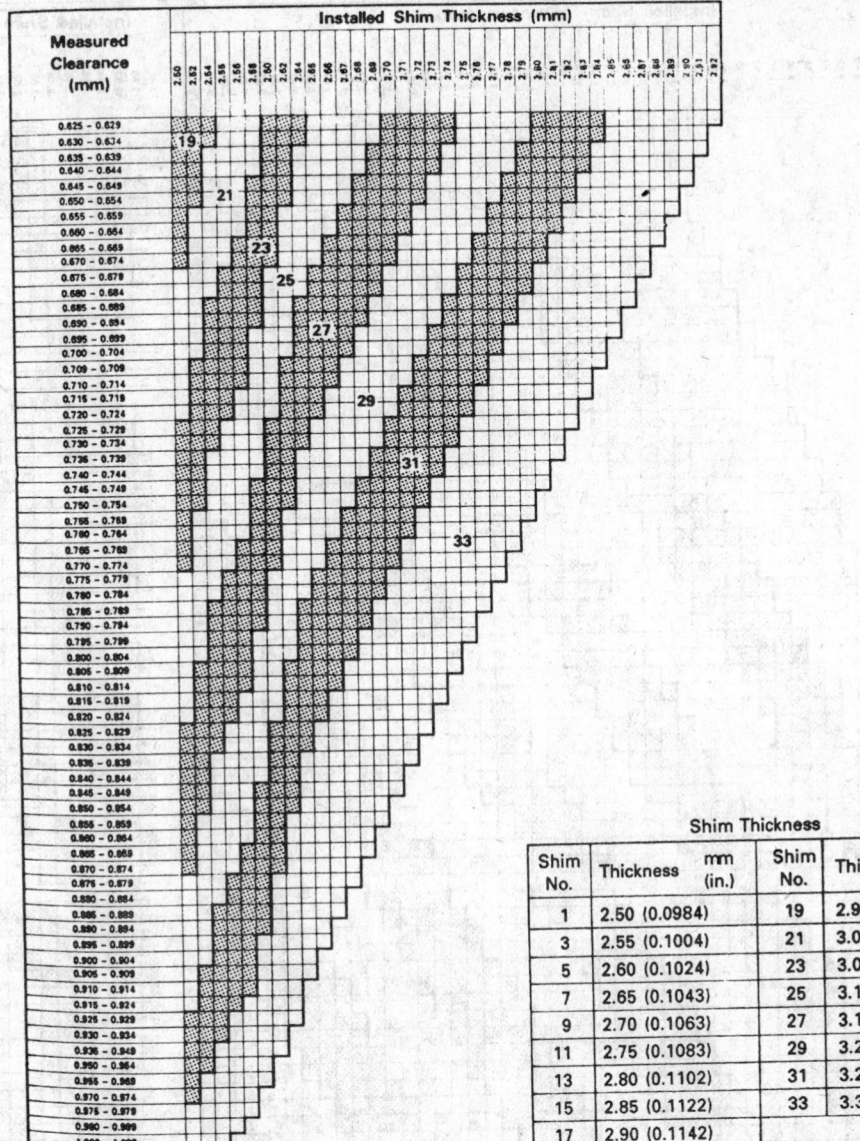

Intake shim selection chart (cont) — 2TZ-FE engine

Shim Thickness

Shim No.	Thickness mm (in.)	Shim No.	Thickness mm (in.)
1	2.50 (0.0984)	19	2.95 (0.1161)
3	2.55 (0.1004)	21	3.00 (0.1181)
5	2.60 (0.1024)	23	3.05 (0.1201)
7	2.65 (0.1043)	25	3.10 (0.1220)
9	2.70 (0.1063)	27	3.15 (0.1240)
11	2.75 (0.1083)	29	3.20 (0.1260)
13	2.80 (0.1102)	31	3.25 (0.1280)
15	2.85 (0.1122)	33	3.30 (0.1299)
17	2.90 (0.1142)		

7911G053

Intake Manifold

REMOVAL AND INSTALLATION

22R-E Engine

1. Relieve the fuel system pressure. Disconnect the negative battery cable.

2. Drain the cooling system.

3. Disconnect the air intake hose from both the air cleaner assembly on one end and the air intake chamber on the other.

4. Tag and disconnect all vacuum lines attached to the intake chamber and manifold.

5. Tag and disconnect the wires to the cold start injector, throttle position sensor and the water hoses from the throttle body.

6. Remove the EGR valve from the intake chamber.

7. Tag and disconnect the actuator cable, accelerator cable and throttle valve cable, if equipped, from the cable bracket on the intake chamber.

8. Unbolt the air intake chamber from the intake manifold and remove the chamber with the throttle body attached.

9. Disconnect the fuel hose from the fuel delivery pipe.

10. Tag and disconnect the air valve hose from the intake manifold.

11. Make sure all hoses, lines and wires are tagged for later installation and disconnected from the intake manifold. Unbolt the manifold from the cylinder head, removing the delivery pipe and injection nozzle with the manifold.

To install:

12. Clean the gasket mating surfaces and check for warpage.

13. Install the gasket and manifold. Torque the bolts to 13 ft. lbs. (18 Nm) starting from the middle and move outward.

14. Install the remaining components and check for leaks.

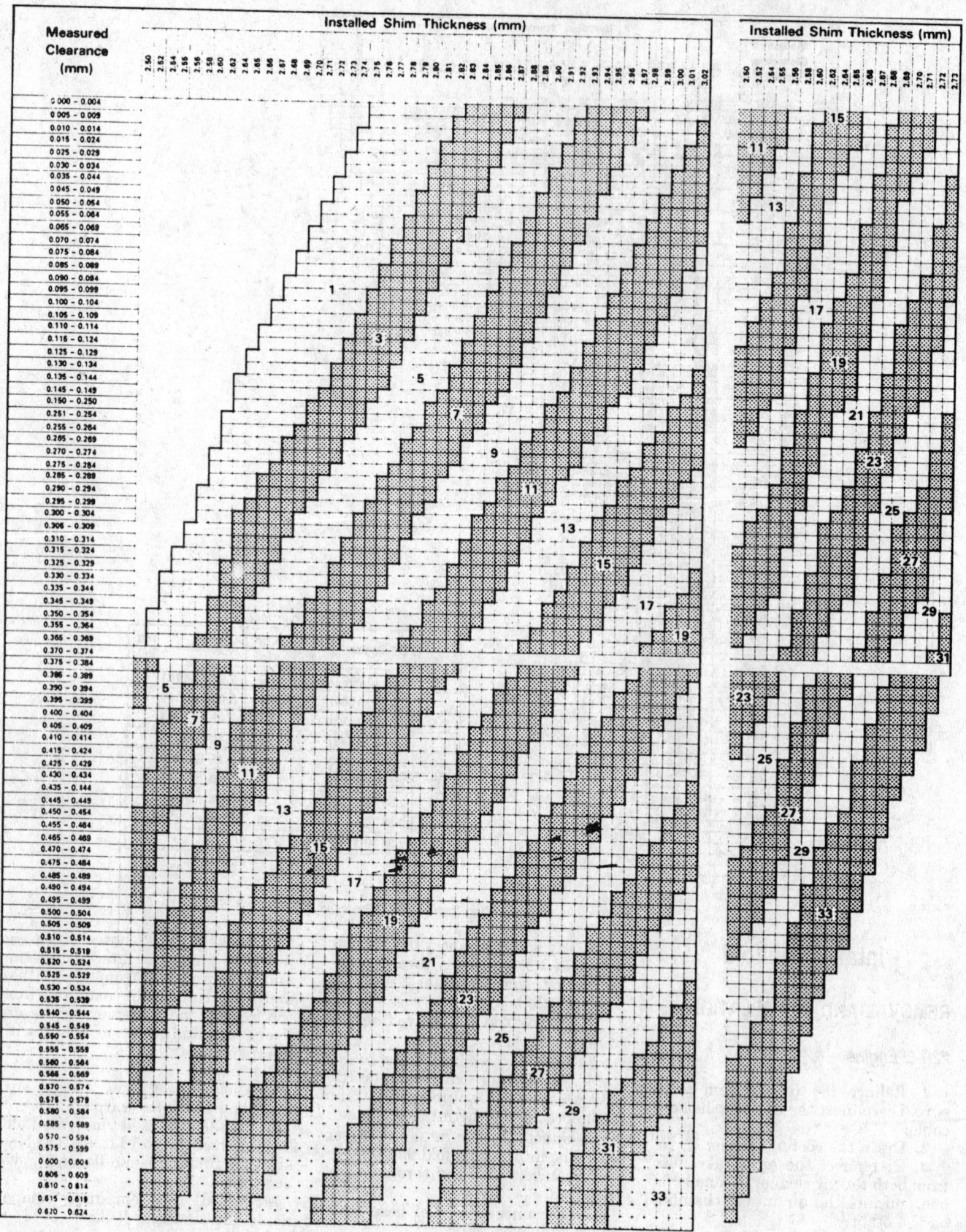

Exhaust shim selection chart (cont) — 2TZ-FE engine

7911G054

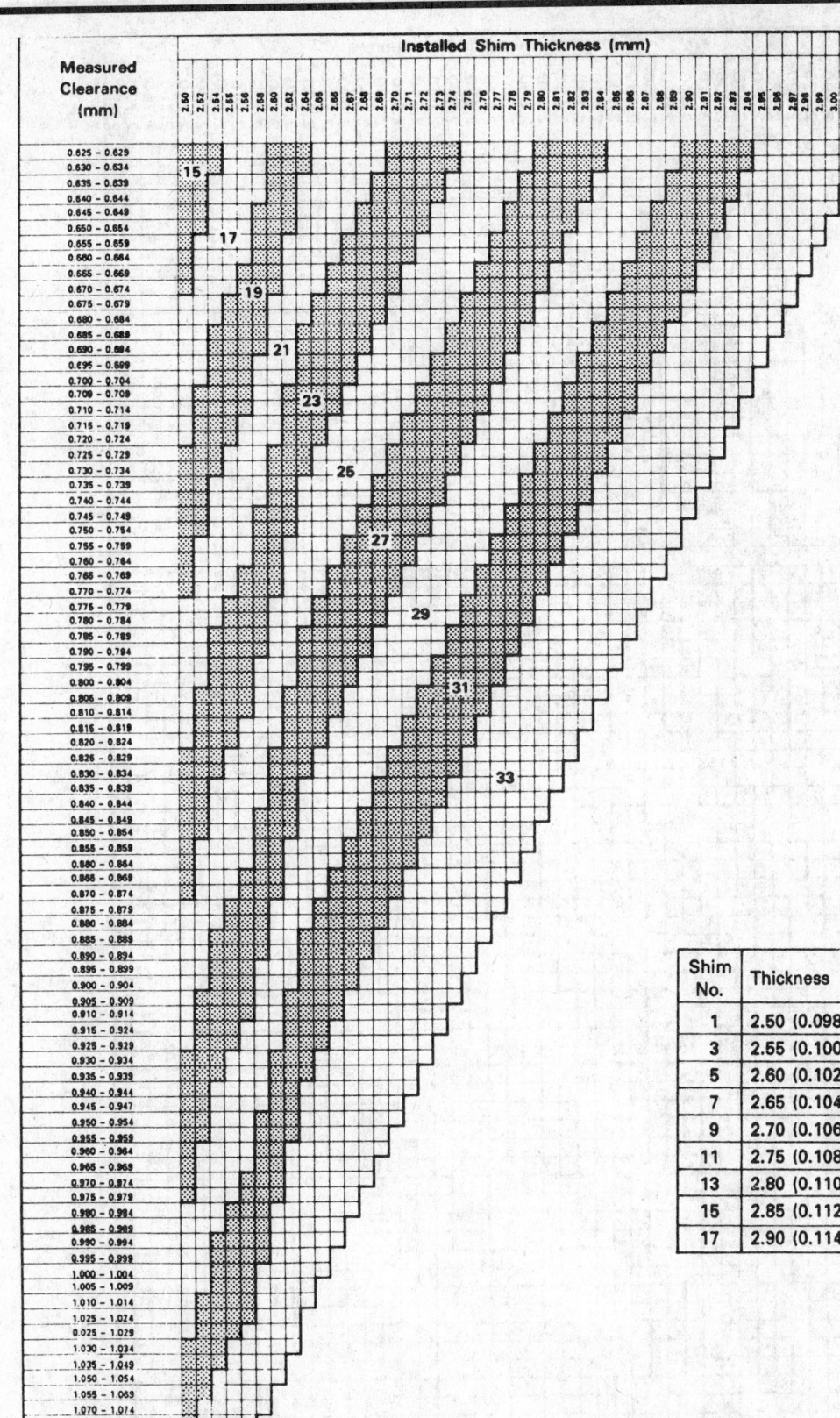

Shim Thickness

Shim No.	Thickness mm (in.)	Shim No.	Thickness mm (in.)
1	2.50 (0.0984)	19	2.95 (0.1161)
3	2.55 (0.1004)	21	3.00 (0.1181)
5	2.60 (0.1024)	23	3.05 (0.1201)
7	2.65 (0.1043)	25	3.10 (0.1220)
9	2.70 (0.1063)	27	3.15 (0.1240)
11	2.75 (0.1083)	29	3.20 (0.1260)
13	2.80 (0.1102)	31	3.25 (0.1280)
15	2.85 (0.1122)	33	3.30 (0.1299)
17	2.90 (0.1142)		

7911G055

Exhaust shim selection chart (cont) — 2TZ-FE engine

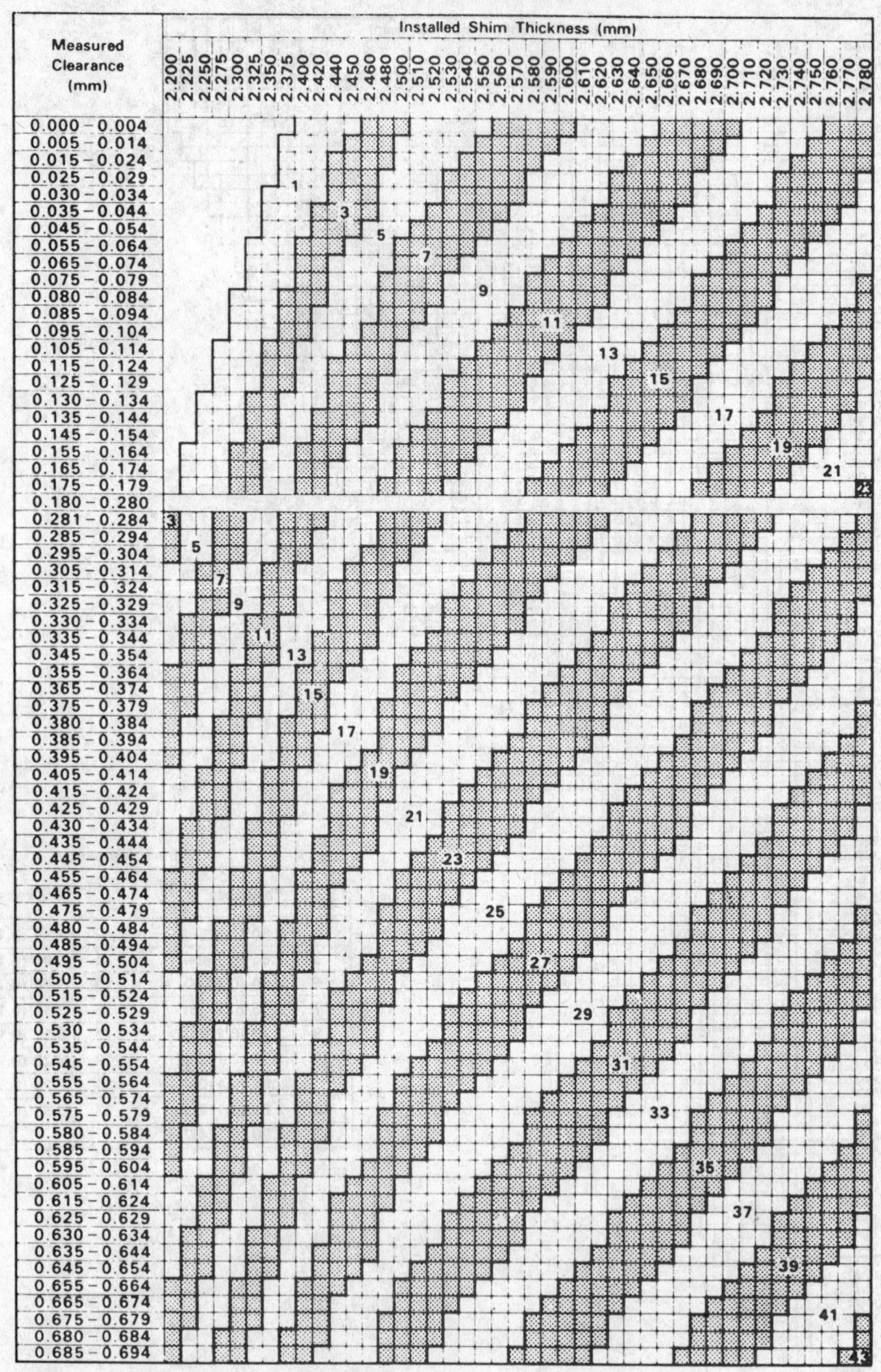

Intake shim selection chart — 3VZ-E engine

7911G058

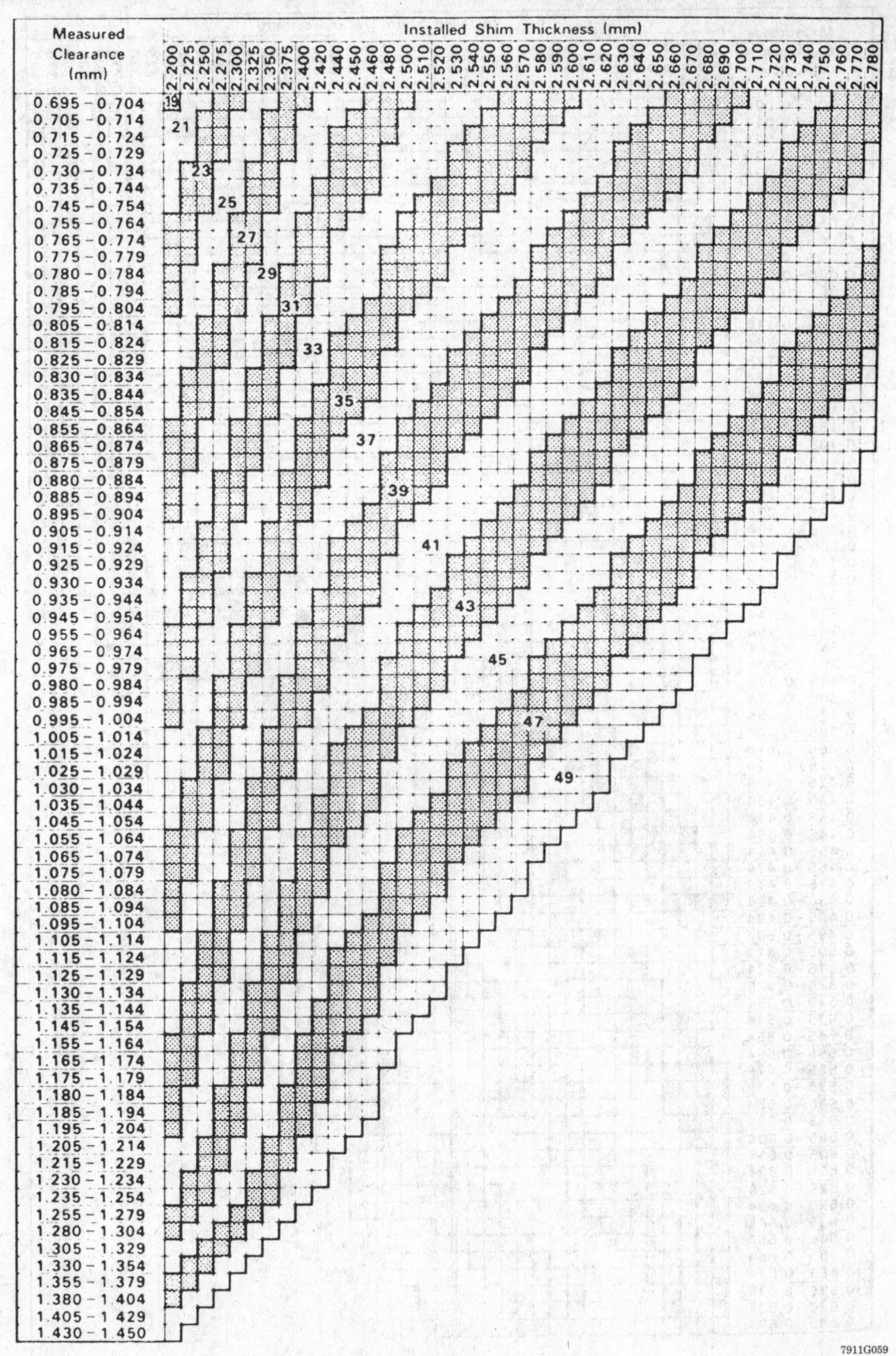

Intake shim selection chart (cont) — 3VZ-E engine

7911G059

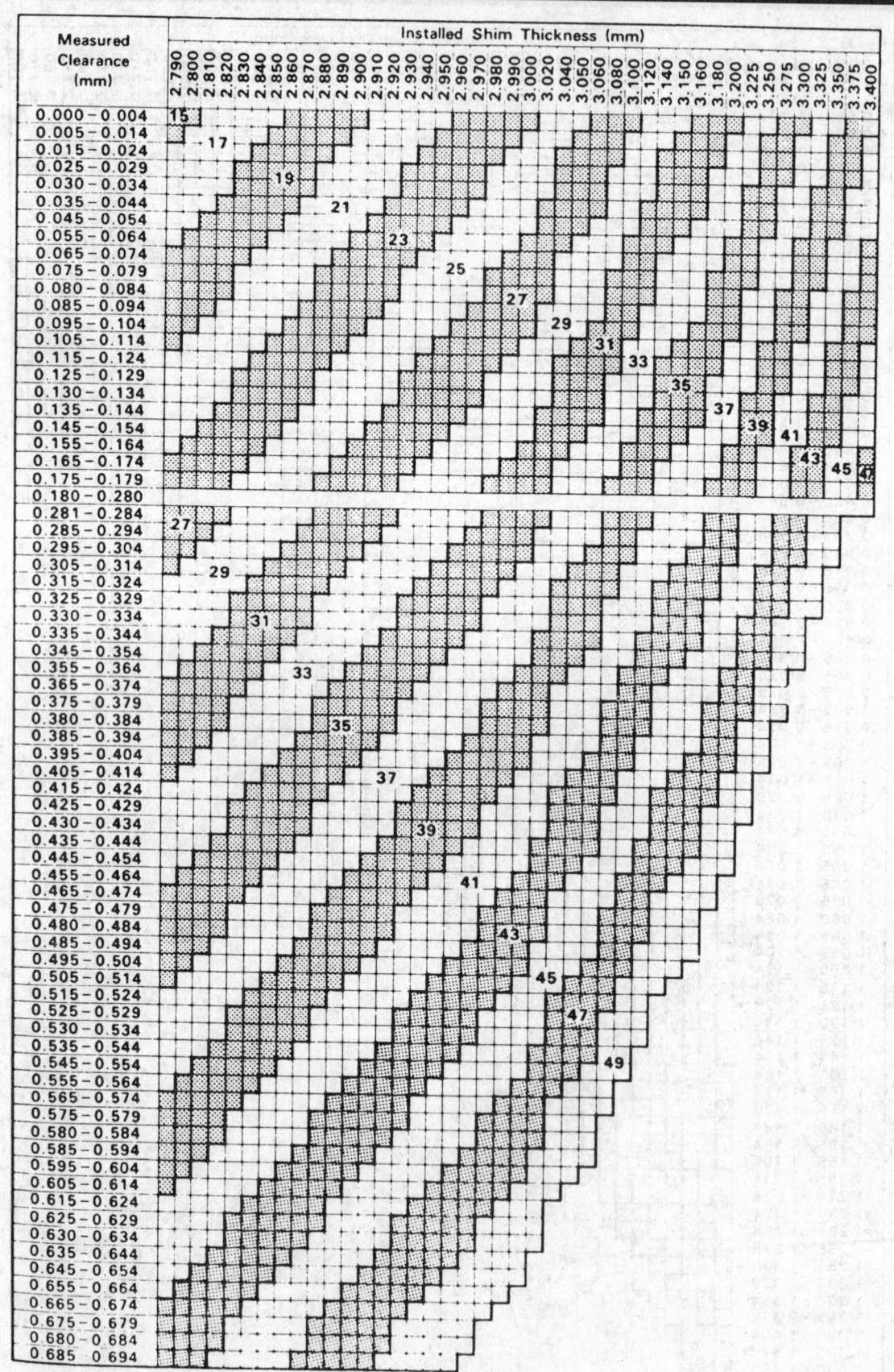

Intake shim selection chart (cont) — 3VZ-E engine

7911G060

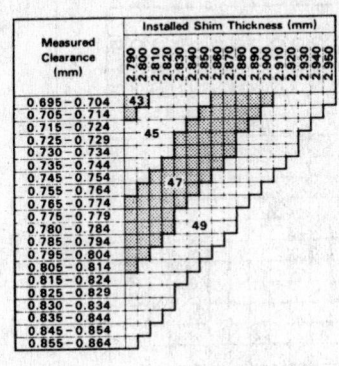

Shim Thickness

Shim No.	Thickness mm (in.)	Shim No.	Thickness mm (in.)
01	2.20 (0.0866)	27	2.85 (0.1122)
03	2.25 (0.0886)	29	2.90 (0.1142)
05	2.30 (0.0906)	31	2.95 (0.1161)
07	2.35 (0.0925)	33	3.00 (0.1181)
09	2.40 (0.0945)	35	3.05 (0.1201)
11	2.45 (0.0965)	37	3.10 (0.1220)
13	2.50 (0.0984)	39	3.15 (0.1240)
15	2.55 (0.1004)	41	3.20 (0.1260)
17	2.60 (0.1024)	43	3.25 (0.1280)
19	2.65 (0.1043)	45	3.30 (0.1299)
21	2.70 (0.1063)	47	3.35 (0.1319)
23	2.75 (0.1083)	49	3.40 (0.1339)
25	2.80 (0.1102)		

7911G061

Intake shim selection chart (cont) — 3VZ-E engine

3VZ-E Engine

1. Relieve the fuel system pressure. Disconnect the negative battery cable.

2. Drain the cooling system.

3. Disconnect the air intake hose from both the air cleaner assembly on one end and the air intake chamber on the other.

4. Tag and disconnect all vacuum lines attached to the intake chamber and manifold.

5. Disconnect the throttle position sensor connector at the air chamber. Disconnect the PCV hose at the union.

6. Disconnect the No. 4 water bypass hose at the manifold. Remove the No. 5 bypass hose at the water bypass pipe.

7. Disconnect the cold start injector and the vacuum hose at the fuel filter.

8. Remove the union bolt and gaskets, then remove the cold start injector tube.

9. Disconnect the EGR gas temperature sensor and the EGR vacuum hoses from the air pipe and the vacuum modulator.

10. Remove the EGR valve.

11. Disconnect the No. 1 air hose at the reed valve.

12. Remove the air intake chamber and then remove the engine wire.

13. Remove the union bolts and then remove the No. 2 and 3 fuel pipes.

14. Remove the No. 4 timing belt cover. Remove the the No. 2 idler pulley and the No. 3 timing belt cover.

15. Remove the fuel delivery pipes with their injectors.

16. Remove the water bypass outlet and then remove the intake manifold.

To install:

17. Install the intake manifold with new gaskets and tighten the mounting bolts to 29 ft. lbs. (39 Nm).

18. Install the water bypass outlet and tighten the 2 bolts to 13 ft. lbs. (18 Nm).

19. Install the fuel delivery pipes and injectors.

20. Install the No. 2 idler pulley. Install the No. 3 and 4 timing belt covers and tighten the bolts to 74 inch lbs. (8.3 Nm).

21. Install the fuel pipes and tighten the union bolts to 22 ft. lbs. (29 Nm).

22. Install the engine wire.

23. Install the air intake chamber and tighten the nuts and bolts to 13 ft. lbs. (18 Nm).

24. Install the EGR valve and connect all hoses and lines.

25. Install the air cleaner hose, refill the engine with coolant and connect the battery cable.

2TZ-FE Engine

1. Disconnect the negative battery cable.

2. Remove the engine from the vehicle.

3. Disconnect the fuel pipes and remove the fuel rail.

4. Label and disconnect all hoses, wiring and cables from the intake manifold.

5. Remove the water outlet and disconnect the PCV hose.

6. Remove the intake manifold stays.

7. Remove the retaining bolts, intake manifold and gasket.

To install:

8. Clean the gasket mating surfaces and check for warpage.

9. Install the gasket, manifold and bolts. Torque the bolts to 15 ft. lbs. (21 Nm), starting from the inside and work outward.

10. Install the manifold stays and torque the bolts to 27 ft. lbs. (37 Nm).

11. Connect the water bypass pipe and fuel rail.

12. Reconnect all wiring, hoses and cables to the manifold.

13. Install the engine into the vehicle.

14. Install the remaining components and check for leaks.

1FZ-FE Engine

1. Disconnect the negative battery cable.

2. Drain the engine coolant.

3. Disconnect the cruise control actuator cable.

4. Disconnect the accelerator cable.

5. Disconnect the 3 vacuum hoses from the EGR valve.

6. Disconnect the EGR gas temperature sensor connector.

7. Loosen the EGR pipe union nut. Remove the 2 nuts holding the EGR valve to the air intake chamber.

8. Remove the 2 stud bolts, EGR valve and vacuum modulator assembly and gasket.

9. Remove the bolt holding the heater inlet pipe and air intake chamber.

10. Disconnect the air cleaner hose. Disconnect the No. 1 and No. 2 PCV hoses.

11. Disconnect the vacuum hoses.

12. Disconnect the No. 2 water bypass hose. Disconnect the EVAP hose. Disconnect the brake booster hose.

13. Disconnect the throttle position sensor connector.

14. Disconnect the Idle Air Control (IAC) valve connector.

15. Disconnect the connector for the emission control valve set assembly.

16. Remove the 3 bolts retaining the power steering reservoir tank and disconnect the tank.

17. Remove the 2 mounting bolts from the engine oil dipstick guide. Pull out the dipstick with the dipstick guide. Remove the O-ring from the dipstick guide.

18. Disconnect the ground strap.

19. Disconnect the 2 vacuum hoses from the TVV.

20. Disconnect the No. 1 water bypass hose from the cylinder head.

21. Remove the 4 bolts, 4 nuts, air intake chamber and the 2 gaskets from the engine.

22. Disconnect the fuel hose from the fuel pressure regulator.

23. Remove the 2 bolts and the fuel return pipe.

24. Remove the 2 union bolts, bolt, 4 gaskets and the fuel pipe.

25. Disconnect the 6 injector connectors.

26. Remove the 3 bolts and the delivery pipe together with the 6 injectors.

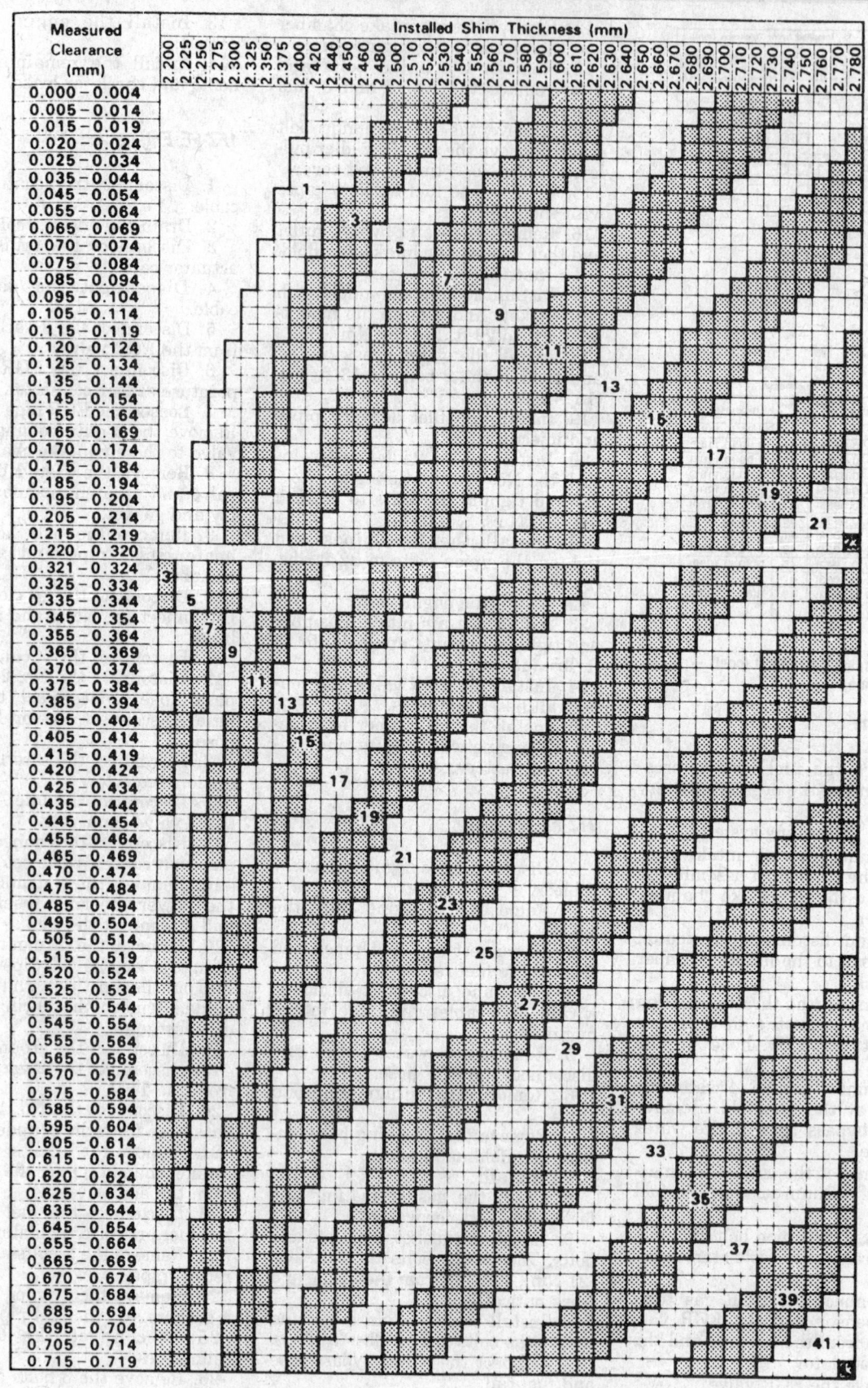

Exhaust shim selection chart — 3VZ-E engine

7911G062

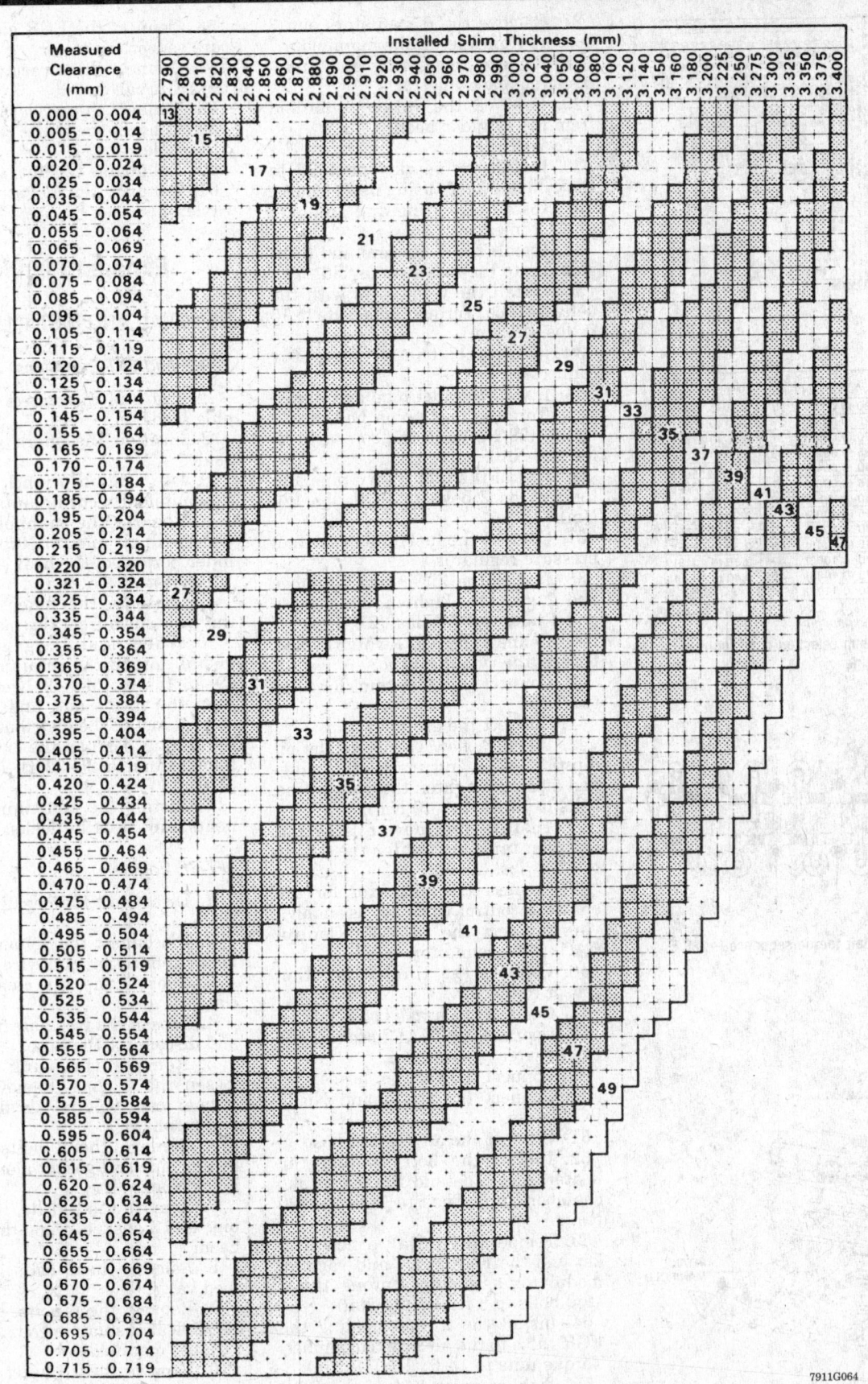

Exhaust shim selection chart (cont) — 3VZ-E engine

7911G064

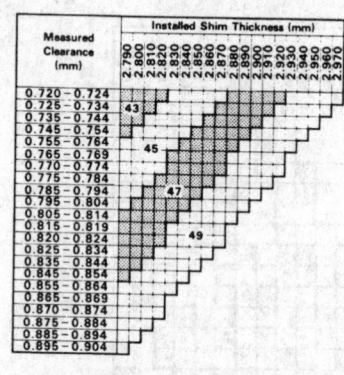

Exhaust shim selection chart (cont) — 3VZ-E engine

Measured Clearance (mm)	Installed Shim Thickness (mm)
0.720–0.724	
0.725–0.734	43
0.735–0.744	
0.745–0.754	45
0.755–0.764	
0.765–0.769	
0.770–0.774	47
0.775–0.784	
0.785–0.794	
0.795–0.804	49
0.805–0.814	
0.815–0.819	
0.820–0.824	
0.825–0.834	
0.835–0.844	
0.845–0.854	
0.855–0.864	
0.865–0.869	
0.870–0.874	
0.875–0.884	
0.885–0.894	
0.895–0.904	

(Installed Shim Thickness column headers: 2.790, 2.800, 2.810, 2.820, 2.830, 2.840, 2.850, 2.860, 2.870, 2.880, 2.890, 2.900, 2.910, 2.920, 2.930, 2.940, 2.950, 2.960, 2.970)

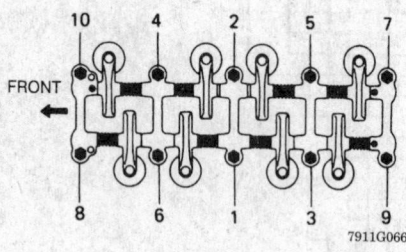

Shim Thickness

Shim No.	Thickness mm (in.)	Shim No.	Thickness mm (in.)
01	2.20 (0.0866)	27	2.85 (0.1122)
03	2.25 (0.0886)	29	2.90 (0.1142)
05	2.30 (0.0906)	31	2.95 (0.1161)
07	2.35 (0.0925)	33	3.00 (0.1181)
09	2.40 (0.0945)	35	3.05 (0.1201)
11	2.45 (0.0965)	37	3.10 (0.1220)
13	2.50 (0.0984)	39	3.15 (0.1240)
15	2.55 (0.1004)	41	3.20 (0.1260)
17	2.60 (0.1024)	43	3.25 (0.1280)
19	2.65 (0.1043)	45	3.30 (0.1299)
21	2.70 (0.1063)	47	3.35 (0.1319)
23	2.75 (0.1083)	49	3.40 (0.1339)
25	2.80 (0.1102)		

7911G065

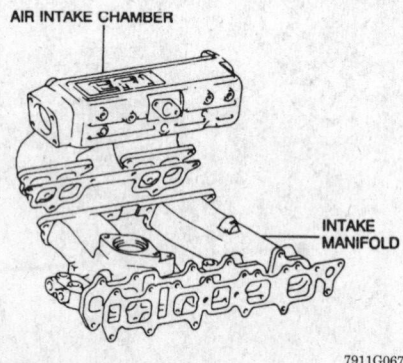

Rocker arm shaft torque sequence — 22R-E engine

7911G066

AIR INTAKE CHAMBER

INTAKE MANIFOLD

7911G067

Intake manifold assembly — 22R-E engine

27. Remove the 6 insulators and 3 spacers from the intake manifold.

28. Remove the O-ring and grommet from each injector.

29. Remove the intake manifold from the cylinder head.

To install:

30. Install the intake manifold to the cylinder head, using new gaskets.

31. Install an O-ring and grommet to each injector.

32. Install the 3 spacers and 6 insulators to the intake manifold.

33. Install the 6 injectors with the delivery pipe. Torque the 3 bolts to 15 ft. lbs. (21 Nm).

34. Connect the 6 injector connectors.

35. Install the fuel pipe and 4 gaskets. Torque the 2 union bolts to 22 ft. lbs. (29 Nm) and the bolt to 14 ft. lbs. (20 Nm).

36. Install the fuel return pipe and tighten the 2 bolts to 14 ft. lbs. (20 Nm).

37. Connect the fuel hose to the fuel pressure regulator.

38. Install the air intake chamber and 2 gaskets. TIghten the 4 bolts and 4 nuts to 15 ft. lbs. (21 Nm).

39. Connect the No. 1 water bypass hose to the cylinder head.

40. Connect the 2 vacuum hoses to the TVV.

41. Connect the ground strap.

42. Install a new O-ring to the oil dipstick guide and install the guide and dipstick. Tighten the 2 mounting bolts to 14 ft. lbs. (20 Nm).

43. Install the power steering reservior tank and tighten the 3 bolts to 13 ft. lbs. (18 Nm).

44. Connect the connector for the emission control valve set assembly.

45. Connect the Idle Air Control (IAC) valve connector.

46. Connect the throttle position sensor connector.

47. Connect the brake booster hose.

48. Connect the EVAP hose and the No. 2 water bypass hose.

49. Connect the vacuum hoses.

50. Connect the No. 1 and No. 2 PCV hoses.

51. Connect the air cleaner hose.

52. Install the bolt holding the heater inlet pipe and the air intake chamber. Torque bolt to 14 ft. lbs. (20 Nm).

53. Temporarily install a new gasket and the EGR valve and vacuum modulator assembly. Torque the 2 stud bolts to 8 ft. lbs. (10 Nm)

54. Install the 2 nuts holding the EGR valve to the air intake chamber. Torque nuts to 14 ft. lbs. (19 Nm).

55. Tighten union nut of the EGR pipe to 47 ft. lbs. (64 Nm).

56. Connect the EGR gas temperature sensor connector.

57. Connect the 3 vacuum hoses to the EGR valve.

58. Connect the accelerator cable.

59. Connect the cruise control actuator cable.

60. Fill engine coolant.

61. Connect the negative battery cable.

Exhaust Manifold

REMOVAL AND INSTALLATION

22R-E and 3VZ-E Engines

1. Tag and disconnect the spark plug leads.

2. Position the spark plug wires aside.

3. Use a 14mm wrench to remove the manifold securing nuts.

4. Remove the manifold(s), complete with air injection tubes and the inner portion of the heat stove.

To install:

5. Separate the inner portion of the heat stove from the manifold.

6. When installing the manifold(s), torque the retaining nuts to 29–36 ft. lbs. (41–49 Nm), working from the inside out, and in several stages. Install the distributor and set the timing. Tighten the exhaust pipe flange nuts to 25–32 ft. lbs. (34–45 Nm).

7. Install the remaining components and check for leaks.

1FZ-FE Engine

1. Disconnect the negative battery cable.

2. Disconnect the volume air flow meter connection and wire clamp.

3. Loosen the air cleaner hose clamp.

4. Loosen the No. 2 air hose clamp and disconnect the hose.

5. Remove the wing nut and loosen the 3 clips. Remove the air cleaner cap, volume air flow meter and resonator.

6. Remove the 2 bolts, 2 nuts, heater pipe and gasket along the cylinder head.

7. Remove the 2 bolts, 6 nuts, air pipe and 3 gaskets along the cylinder head.

8. Remove the 2 bolts and PAIR reed valve.

9. Remove the 6 bolts, No. 1 and No. 2 heat insulators from above the exhaust manifolds.

10. Remove the 13 nuts, No. 1 exhaust manifold, No. 2 exhaust manifold and 2 gaskets.

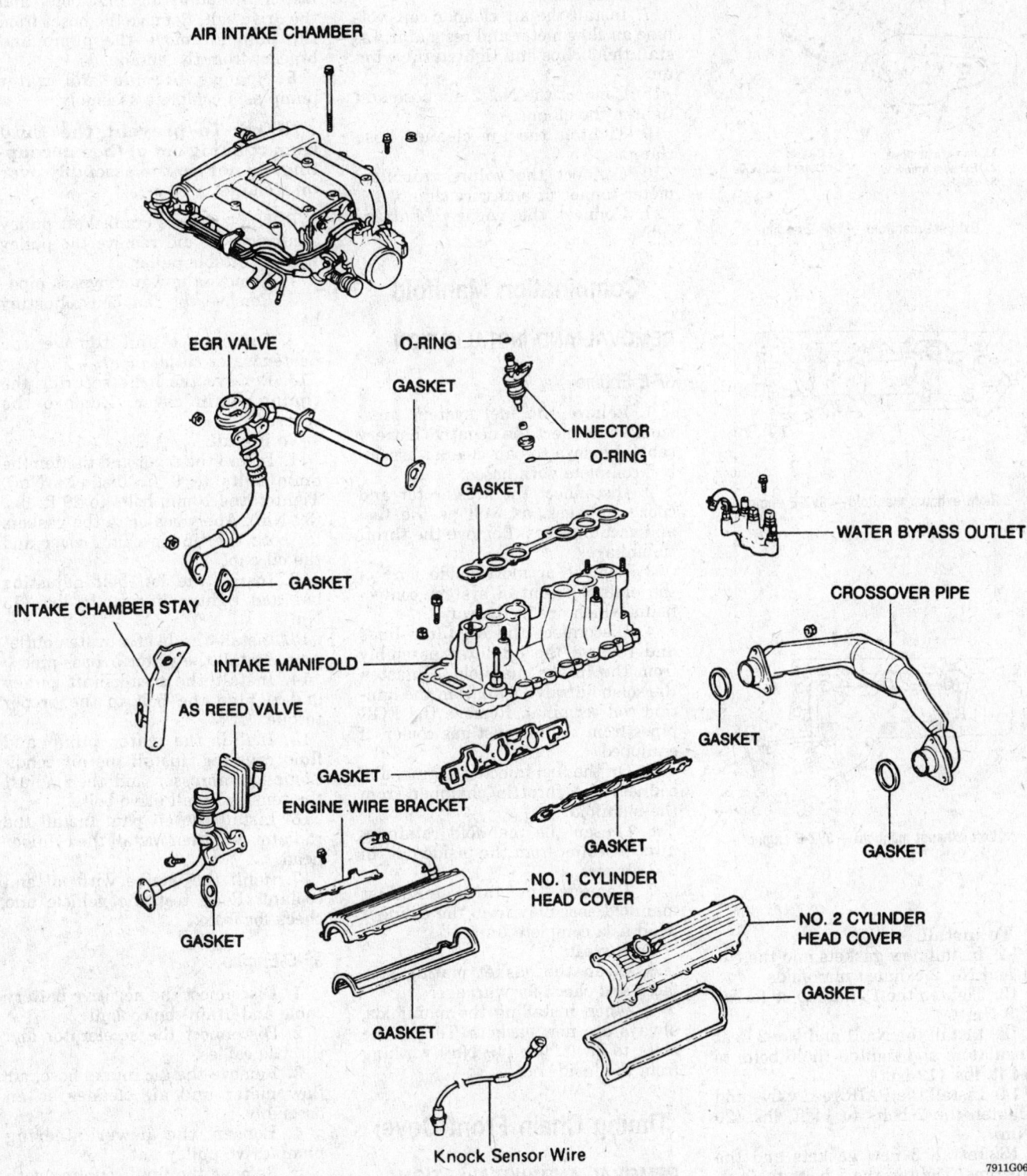

AIR INTAKE CHAMBER

EGR VALVE

O-RING

GASKET

INJECTOR

O-RING

GASKET

WATER BYPASS OUTLET

GASKET

CROSSOVER PIPE

INTAKE CHAMBER STAY

INTAKE MANIFOLD

AS REED VALVE

GASKET

GASKET

ENGINE WIRE BRACKET

GASKET

NO. 1 CYLINDER HEAD COVER

NO. 2 CYLINDER HEAD COVER

GASKET

GASKET

GASKET

GASKET

Knock Sensor Wire

7911G068

Intake manifold assembly — 3VZ-E engine

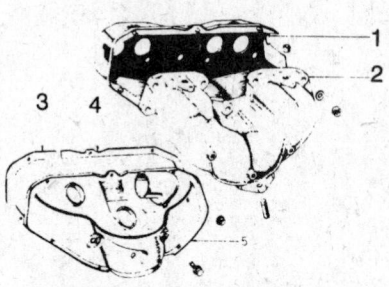

1. Inner heat stove
2. Exhaust manifold
3. Gasket
4. Gasket
5. Outer heat stove

7911G069

Exhaust manifold — 22R-E engine

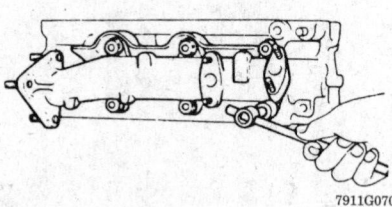

7911G070

Right exhaust manifold — 3VZ-E engine

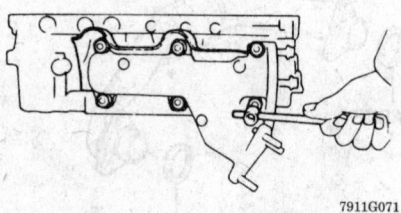

7911G071

Left exhaust manifold — 3VZ-E engine

To install:

11. Install new gaskets and the No. 1 and No. 2 exhaust manifolds.

12. Tighten the 13 nuts to 29 ft. lbs. (39 Nm).

13. Install the No. 1 and No. 2 heat insulators and tighten the 6 bolts to 14 ft. lbs. (19 Nm).

14. Install the PAIR reed valve and tighten the 2 bolts to 14 ft. lbs. (20 Nm).

15. Install 3 new gaskets and the air pipe. Tighten the 2 bolts to 14 ft. lbs. (20 Nm) and the 6 nuts to 15 ft. lbs. (21 Nm).

16. Install a new gasket and the heater pipe. Tighten the 2 bolts to 14 ft. lbs. (20 Nm) and the 6 nuts to 15 ft. lbs. (21 Nm).

17. Install the air cleaner cap, volume air flow meter and resonator. Install the 3 clips and tighten the wing nut.

18. Connect the No. 2 air hose and tighten the clamp.

19. Tighten the air cleaner hose clamp.

20. Connect the volume air flow meter connector and wire clamp.

21. Connect the negative battery cable.

Combination Manifold

REMOVAL AND INSTALLATION

3F-E Engine

1. Relieve the fuel system pressure. Disconnect the negative battery cable. Remove the air cleaner assembly, complete with hoses.

2. Disconnect the accelerator and choke linkages, as well as the fuel and vacuum lines. Remove the throttle linkage.

3. Remove or move aside, any of the emission control system components which are in the way.

4. Disconnect the oil filter lines and remove the oil filter assembly from the intake manifold. Unfasten the solenoid valve wire from the ignition coil terminal. Remove the EGR pipes from the exhaust gas cooler, if equipped.

5. On the fuel injected engine, disconnect the throttle chamber from the manifold.

6. Loosen the manifold retaining nuts, working from the inside out, in 2–3 stages.

7. Remove the intake/exhaust manifold assembly from the cylinder head as a complete unit.

To install:

8. Clean the gasket mating surfaces and check for warpage.

9. When installing the manifolds, always use new gaskets. Torque the bolts to 36 ft. lbs. (49 Nm) working from the inside out.

Timing Chain Front Cover

REMOVAL AND INSTALLATION

22R-E Engine

1. Disconnect the negative battery cable. Remove the cylinder head.

2. Remove the radiator.

3. Remove the alternator. Remove the oil pan.

4. If equipped with air pumps, unfasten the adjusting link bolts and the drive belt. Remove the hoses from the pump; remove the pump and bracket from the engine.

5. Remove the fan and water pump as a complete assembly.

NOTE: To prevent the fluid from running out of the fan coupling, do not tip the assembly over on its side.

6. Unfasten the crankshaft pulley securing bolt and remove the pulley with a suitable puller.

7. Remove the water bypass pipe.

8. Remove the fan belt adjusting bar.

9. Disconnect and remove the heater water outlet pipe.

10. Remove the bolts securing the timing chain cover. Remove the cover.

To install:

11. Install the cover and tighten the 8mm bolts to 9 ft. lbs. (13 Nm). Tighten the 10mm bolts to 29 ft. lbs. (39 Nm). Apply sealer to the gaskets for both the timing chain cover and the oil pan.

12. Install the fan belt adjusting bar and tighten it to 9 ft. lbs. (13 Nm).

13. Install the heater water outlet pipe. Install the water bypass pipe.

14. Install the crankshaft pulley and tighten the bolt to the proper torque.

15. Install the water pump and fluid coupling. Install the air conditioning compressor and then adjust the tension on all drive belts.

16. Install the oil pan. Install the radiator and then install the cylinder head.

17. Refill the engine with oil and coolant. Road test the vehicle and check for leaks.

3F-E Engine

1. Disconnect the negative battery cable and drain the coolant.

2. Disconnect the accelerator and throttle cables.

3. Remove the air intake hose, air flow meter and air cleaner as an assembly.

4. Loosen the power steering pump drive pulley nut.

5. Remove the fluid coupling with the fan and water pump pulley.

6. Remove the power steering pump and the air conditioning compressor. Remove their brackets. Remove the power steering pump idler pulley and its bracket.

7. Remove the cylinder head cover. Remove the rocker shaft assembly.

8. Remove the distributor.

9. Remove the pushrod cover and then remove the valve lifters. Be certain that they are kept in order.

10. Loosen the 6 bolts and then slide the power steering pump pulley off the crankshaft.

11. Using special tool 09213-58011 or equivalent, and a 46mm socket wrench, remove the crankshaft pulley bolt. Remove the pulley.

12. Remove the oil cooler pipe and its hose.

13. Remove the timing gear cover and gasket.

To install:

14. There are 3 sizes of timing gear cover bolts. Apply adhesive to the two **A** bolts. Install a new gasket and then position the cover. Finger-tighten all bolts. Align the crankshaft pulley set key with the groove of the pulley; gently tap the pulley onto the crankshaft. Tighten the cover bolts marked **A** to 18 ft. lbs. (25 Nm). Tighten those marked **B** or **C** to 43 inch lbs. (5 Nm). Tighten the pulley bolt to 253 ft. lbs. (343 Nm).

15. Position the power steering pulley on the crankshaft and tighten the bolts to 13 ft. lbs. (18 Nm).

16. Insert the valve lifters into their bores and install the pushrod cover. Tighten the bolts to 35 inch lbs. (4 Nm). Make sure the valve lifters are installed in the same bore that they were removed from.

17. Install the rocker shaft assembly, the cylinder head cover and the distributor.

18. Install the water pump pulley, fluid coupling and fan.

19. Install the power steering pump idler pulley and bracket. Install the power steering pump and air conditioning compressor. Adjust the drive belts.

20. Install the air cleaner assembly and then connect and adjust the accelerator and throttle cables.

21. Fill the engine with coolant and connect the battery cable. Start the engine and check for leaks. Check the ignition timing.

2TZ-FE Engine

1. Disconnect the negative battery cable.

2. Remove the engine from the vehicle.

3. Remove the cylinder head from the engine.

4. Remove the crankshaft pulley bolt by using a holding tool 0921358012 and 0933000021 or equivalent. Using a pulley pulling

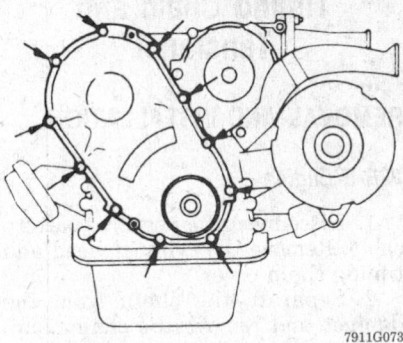

7911G073

Timing chain cover removal — 3F-E engine

tool 0995020017 or equivalent, remove the crankshaft pulley.

5. Remove the left engine mounting.

6. Remove the oil pressure switch and engine ventilation case.

7. Remove the oil pan using a pan removing tool 0903200100 or equivalent. Remove the oil baffle.

8. Remove the 3 bolts and oil filter bracket from the timing cover.

9. Remove the 12 bolts, 2 nuts and timing cover; 3 bolts are in the back of the cover. Be careful not to damage the mating surfaces during removal.

To install:

10. Clean the gasket surfaces and check for warpage.

11. Install new gaskets and torque the (A) bolts to 14 ft. lbs. (21 Nm), (B) bolts to 21 ft. lbs. (28 Nm) and the (C) bolts to 32 ft. lbs. (43 Nm).

12. Install the oil filter bracket and torque to 14 ft. lbs. (21 Nm).

13. Install the crankcase baffle plate, oil pan and ventilation case.

14. Install the oil pressure switch and left engine mount.

15. Install the crankshaft pulley and torque the bolt to 192 ft. lbs. (260 Nm).

16. Install the cylinder head and engine assembly into the vehicle.

17. Install the remaining components and check for leaks.

1FZ-FE Engine

1. Disconnect the negative battery cable.

2. Drain the engine cooling system.

3. Drain the engine oil.

4. Remove the engine under cover.

5. Remove the radiator.

6. Loosen the idler pulley nut and adjusting bolt. Remove the drive belt.

7. Remove the 4 mounting bolts. Disconnect the compressor from the bracket.

8. Remove the 5 bolts and the air conditioning compressor bracket.

9. Disconnect the No. 2 radiator hose from the water inlet.

10. Remove the 2 nuts and radiator pipe.

11. Remove the 4 bolts, 2 nuts, water pump and gasket.

12. Remove the cylinder head.

13. Disconnect the oil cooler pipe bracket from the No. 1 oil pan.

14. Remove the 4 bolts and the oil level sensor.

15. Remove the gasket from the oil level sensor.

16. Remove the 4 bolts holding the No. 1 oil pan to the transmission housing.

17. Remove the 17 bolts and 2 nuts holding the No. 2 oil pan and remove the pan.

18. Remove the 21 mounting bolts and 2 nuts and remove the No. 1 oil pan.

19. Remove the crankshaft pulley.

20. Remove the drive belt idler pulley.

21. Remove the 9 mounting bolts, 2 mounting nuts and the drive belt adjusting bar.

22. Remove the oil pump by prying the portions between the cylinder block and the oil pump apart.

23. Remove the oil pump O-rings and gasket.

24. Remove the timing chain cover.

25. Remove the timing chain and camshaft timing gear.

To install:

26. Install the timing chain and camshaft timing gear.

27. Install the timing chain cover.

28. Install the oil pump O-rings and gasket.

29. Install the oil pump.

30. Install the 9 mounting bolts, 2 mounting nuts and the drive belt adjusting bar.

31. Install the drive belt idler pulley.

32. Install the crankshaft pulley.

33. Install the No. 1 oil pan and tighten 21 mounting bolts and 2 nuts.

34. Install the No. 2 oil pan and tighten 17 bolts and 2 nuts.

35. Install the 4 bolts holding the No. 1 oil pan to the transmission housing.

36. Install the gasket and the oil level sensor. Tighten the 4 bolts.

37. Connect the oil cooler pipe bracket to the No. 1 oil pan.

38. Install the cylinder head.

39. Install the water pump and gasket. Tighten the 4 bolts and 2 nuts.

40. Install the radiator pipe. Tighten the 2 nuts.

41. Connect the No. 2 radiator hose to the water inlet.

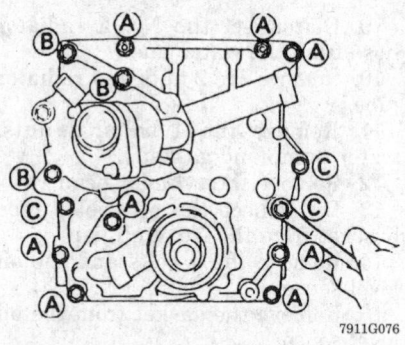

Timing chain cover torque sequence — 2TZ-FE engine

7911G076

42. Install the air conditioning compressor bracket. Tighten the 5 bolts.
43. Connect the compressor from the bracket. Tighten 4 mounting bolts.
44. Install the drive belt. Tighten the idler pulley nut and adjusting bolt.
45. Install the radiator.
46. Install the engine under cover.
47. Fill crankcase.
48. Connect the negative battery cable.
49. Fill and bleed the engine cooling system.

Front Cover Oil Seal

REPLACEMENT

22R-E Engine

1. Disconnect the negative battery cable. Remove the crankshaft pulley.
2. Using a small prybar, pry the oil seal from the oil pump housing.
3. Using the appropriate seal installer, drive the new seal into the oil pump housing. Apply multi-purpose grease to the lip of the new seal.
4. To complete the installation, reverse the removal procedures.

3F-E Engine

1. Disconnect the negative battery cable. Remove the crankshaft pulley.
2. Using a small prybar, pry the oil seal from the front cover.
3. Using the appropriate seal installer, drive the new seal into the front cover. Apply multi-purpose grease to the lip of the new seal.
4. To complete the installation, reverse the removal procedures.

Timing Chain and Tensioner

REMOVAL AND INSTALLATION

22R-E Engine

1. Disconnect the negative battery cable. Remove the cylinder head and timing chain cover.
2. Separate the chain from the damper and remove the chain, complete with the camshaft sprocket.
3. Remove the crankshaft sprocket and the oil pump drive with a puller.
4. Inspect the chain for wear or damage. Replace it if necessary.
5. Inspect the chain tensioner for wear. If it measures less than 11mm, replace it.
6. Check the dampers for wear. If their measurements are below the following specifications, replace them. The specification for the upper damper is 5.0mm and the lower damper is 4.5mm.
To install:
7. Rotate the crankshaft until its key is at TDC. Slide the sprocket in place over the key.
8. Place the chain over the sprocket so its single bright link aligns with the mark on the camshaft sprocket.
9. Install the cam sprocket so the timing mark falls between the two bright links on the chain.
10. Fit the oil pump drive spline over the crankshaft key.
11. Install the timing cover gasket on the front of the block.
12. Rotate the camshaft sprocket counterclockwise to remove the slack from the chain.
13. Install the timing chain cover and cylinder head.

2TZ-FE Engine

1. Remove the timing chain cover. There are 3 bolts in back of the cover.
2. Remove the cylinder head assembly.
3. Remove the chain slipper, damper and oil nozzle.
4. Remove the oil pump drive chain and idle gear.
5. Remove the crankshaft sprocket using a puller 0921336020 or equivalent.
To install:
6. Install the crankshaft sprocket using an installer tool 0960806040 or equivalent.
7. Install the idle sprocket, chain and tensioner. Torque the bolts to 14 ft. lbs. (21 Nm).

8. Check the spring is operating normally against the chain guide by pressing on the chain with a finger and then release. With the guide against the chain, torque the tensioner bolt to 14 ft. lbs. (20 Nm).
9. Install the oil nozzle and torque to 13 ft. lbs. (18 Nm).
10. Install the timing chain damper and slipper. Torque the bolts to 20 ft. lbs. (26 Nm).
11. Place the timing chain on the camshaft sprocket so the timing mark is between the bright chain links and is at 12 o'clock.
12. Place the timing chain on the crankshaft sprocket with the single bright link indicated aligned with the timing mark on the crankshaft sprocket at 6 o'clock.
13. Turn the camshaft sprocket counterclockwise to take the slack out of the chain.
14. Tie the timing chain with a cord.
15. Install the timing chain cover and cylinder head.
16. Install the remaining components and check for leaks.

1FZ-FE Engine

1. Disconnect the negative battery cable.
2. Drain the engine cooling system.
3. Drain the engine oil.
4. Remove the engine under cover.
5. Remove the radiator.
6. Loosen the idler pulley nut and adjusting bolt. Remove the drive belt.
7. Remove the 4 mounting bolts. Disconnect the compressor from the bracket.
8. Remove the 5 bolts and the air conditioning compressor bracket.
9. Disconnect the No. 2 radiator hose from the water inlet.
10. Remove the 2 nuts and radiator pipe.
11. Remove the 4 bolts, 2 nuts, water pump and gasket.
12. Remove the cylinder head.
13. Disconnect the oil cooler pipe bracket from the No. 1 oil pan.
14. Remove the 4 bolts and the oil level sensor.
15. Remove the gasket from the oil level sensor.
16. Remove the 4 bolts holding the No. 1 oil pan to the transmission housing.
17. Remove the 17 bolts and 2 nuts holding the No. 2 oil pan and remove the pan.
18. Remove the 21 mounting bolts and 2 nuts and remove the No. 1 oil pan.
19. Remove the crankshaft pulley.

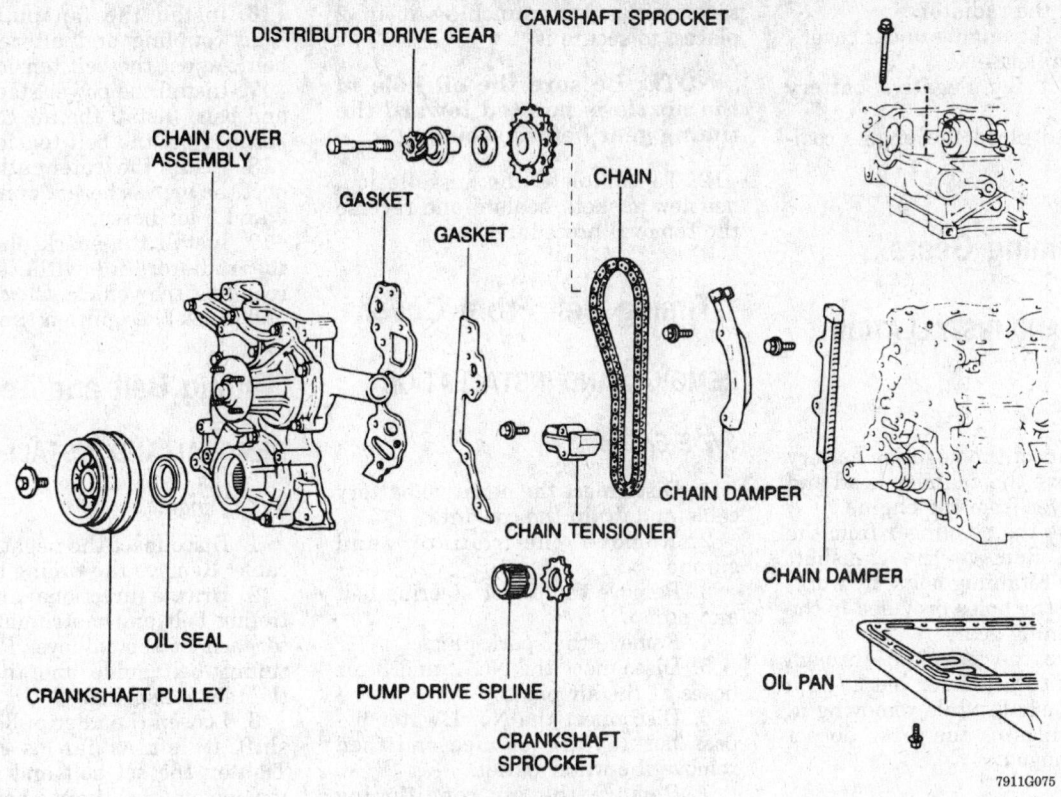

Timing chain and sprockets — 22R-E engine

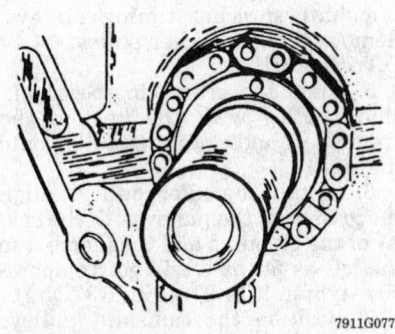

Aligning the crankshaft gear with the single bright link of the timing chain — 22R-E engine

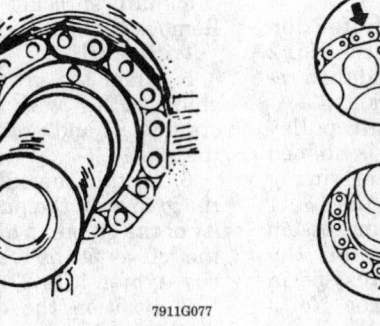

Timing chain alignment marks — 2TZ-FE engine

Aligning the camshaft sprocket mark between the 2 bright links of the timing chain — 22R-E engine

20. Remove the drive belt idler pulley.

21. Remove the 9 mounting bolts, 2 mounting nuts and the drive belt adjusting bar.

22. Remove the oil pump by prying the portions between the cylinder block and the oil pump apart.

23. Remove the oil pump O-rings and gasket.

24. Remove the timing chain cover.

25. Remove the timing chain and camshaft timing gear.

To install:

26. Install the timing chain and camshaft timing gear.

27. Install the timing chain cover.

28. Install the oil pump O-rings and gasket.

29. Install the oil pump.

30. Install the 9 mounting bolts, 2 mounting nuts and the drive belt adjusting bar.

31. Install the drive belt idler pulley.

32. Install the crankshaft pulley.

33. Install the No. 1 oil pan and tighten 21 mounting bolts and 2 nuts.

34. Install the No. 2 oil pan and tighten 17 bolts and 2 nuts.

35. Install the 4 bolts holding the No. 1 oil pan to the transmission housing.

36. Install the gasket and the oil level sensor. Tighten the 4 bolts.

37. Connect the oil cooler pipe bracket to the No. 1 oil pan.

38. Install the cylinder head.

39. Install the water pump and gasket. Tighten the 4 bolts and 2 nuts.

40. Install the radiator pipe. Tighten the 2 nuts.

41. Connect the No. 2 radiator hose to the water inlet.

42. Install the air conditioning compressor bracket. Tighten the 5 bolts.

43. Connect the compressor from the bracket. Tighten 4 mounting bolts.

44. Install the drive belt. Tighten the idler pulley nut and adjusting bolt.

45. Install the radiator.
46. Install the engine under cover.
47. Fill crankcase.
48. Connect the negative battery cable.
49. Fill and bleed the engine cooling system.

Timing Gears

REMOVAL AND INSTALLATION

3F-E Engine

1. Disconnect the negative battery cable. Remove the cylinder head and the front cover from the engine.
2. Remove the oil slinger from the crankshaft. Remove the camshaft thrust plate retaining bolts, by working through the holes provided in the camshaft timing gear.
3. Remove the camshaft through the front of the cylinder block. Support the camshaft while removing it, so the bearings or the lobes do not become damaged.

NOTE: The timing gear is a press-fit and cannot be removed without removing the camshaft.

4. Inspect the crankshaft timing gear. Replace it if it has worn or damaged teeth.
5. Remove the sliding key, then, pull the crankshaft timing gear from the crankshaft with a gear puller.
6. Use a large piece of pipe to drive the timing gear onto the crankshaft. Lightly and evenly tap the end of the pipe until the gear is in its original position.
To install:
7. Apply a coat of engine oil to the camshaft journals and bearings, then, insert the camshaft into the block.
8. Align the mating marks on the timing gears. Slip the camshaft into position. Torque the camshaft thrust plate bolts to 14.5 ft. lbs. (20 Nm).
9. Using a feeler gauge, check the gear backlash, inserted between the crankshaft and the camshaft timing gears. The maximum backlash should be 0.002–0.005 in.; if it exceeds this, replace one or both of the gears, as required.
10. Using a dial indicator, check the gear run-out. Maximum run-out, for both gears, is 0.008 in.; if not, replace the gear.
11. Install the oil nozzle, if removed, by screwing it in place with a

screwdriver and punching it in 2 places, to secure it.

NOTE: Be sure the oil hole in the nozzle is pointed toward the timing gear before securing it.

12. To complete the installation, use new gaskets, sealant and reverse the removal procedures.

Timing Belt Front Cover

REMOVAL AND INSTALLATION

3VZ-E Engine

1. Disconnect the negative battery cable and drain the coolant.
2. Remove the radiator and shroud.
3. Remove the power steering belt and pump.
4. Remove the spark plugs.
5. Disconnect the No. 2 and 3 air hoses at the air pipe.
6. Disconnect the No. 1 water bypass hose at the air pipe and then remove the water outlet.
7. Remove the air conditioning belt. Remove the alternator drive belt, fluid coupling, guide and fan pulley.
8. Disconnect the high tension cords and their clamps at the No. 2 (upper) timing belt cover and then remove the cover and its gaskets.
9. Rotate the crankshaft pulley until the groove on its lip is aligned with the **0** on the No. 1 (lower) timing belt cover, this should set the No. 1 cylinder at TDC of its compression stroke. The matchmarks on the camshaft timing pulleys must be in alignment with those on the No. 3 (upper rear) timing cover. If not, rotate the engine 360 degrees (1 complete revolution).
10. Remove the crankshaft pulley using a puller.
11. Remove the fan pulley bracket and then remove the No. 1 timing belt cover.
To install:
12. Install the No. 1 cover with the 2 gaskets and tighten the bolts to 48 inch lbs. (5.4 Nm).
13. Install the fan pulley bracket and tighten it to 30 ft. lbs. (41 Nm).
14. Install the No. 2 cover and tighten the bolts 48 inch lbs. (5.4 Nm).
15. Position the crankshaft pulley so the groove in the pulley is aligned with the Woodruff key in the crankshaft. Tighten the bolt to 181 ft. lbs. (245 Nm).

16. Install the fan pulley, guide, fluid coupling and alternator drive belt. Adjust the belt tension.
17. Install the power steering pump and belt. Install the air conditioning belt. Adjust the belt tension.
18. Install the water outlet and connect the bypass hose. Connect the No. 2 and 3 air hoses.
19. Install the spark plugs. Install the radiator, fill with coolant and road test the vehicle. Check for leaks and check the ignition timing.

Timing Belt and Tensioner

REMOVAL AND INSTALLATION

3VZ-E Engine

1. Disconnect the negative battery cable. Remove the timing belt covers.
2. Draw a directional arrow on the timing belt and matchmark the belt to each of the pulleys. Remove the timing belt guide and then remove the tension spring.
3. Loosen the idler pulley bolt and shift it left as far as it will go. Tighten the set bolt and relieve the tension on the timing belt. Remove the belt.
4. Remove the crankshaft and camshaft sprocket timing pulleys. Remove the No. 1 idler pulley.
To install:
5. Align the groove in the crankshaft pulley with the key on the crankshaft and press the pulley onto the shaft.
6. Install the idler pulley. Align the groove on the pulley with the cavity of the oil pump and force it to the left as far as it will go. Temporarily tighten it to 27 ft. lbs. (37 Nm).
7. Position the camshaft pulleys on the camshafts so the match holes in each pulley are in alignment with those on the No. 3 (upper rear) timing cover. Align the pulley matchmark with the one on the cover.

NOTE: Do not install the match pin. Check that the bolt head is not touching the pulley.

8. Install the timing belt around the timing pulleys. If reusing the old belt, make sure the arrow and matchmarks all line up with those made earlier on the pulleys.
9. Move the idler pulley to the right as far as it will go. Install the tension spring and then loosen the pulley bolt until the pulley moves lightly with the tension spring force.
10. Check the valve timing and belt tension by turning the crankshaft 2 complete revolutions clockwise.

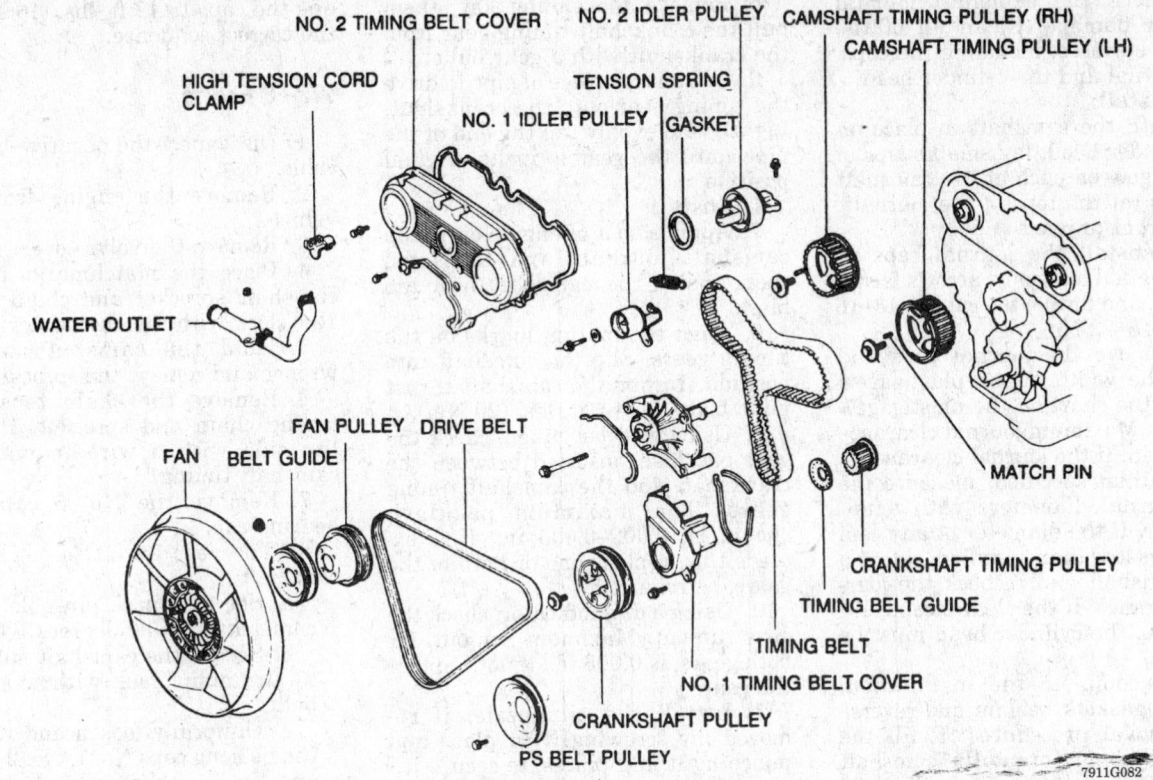

Timing belt components — 3VZ-E engine

Check that each pulley aligns with its timing marks. Retighten the idler pulley bolt to 27 ft. lbs. (37 Nm).

11. Remove the camshaft timing pulley bolts and align the match pin hole with the match pin hole in the camshaft. Install the pin and bolt and tighten to 80 ft. lbs. (108 Nm).

12. Remove the crankshaft timing pulley bolt and position the belt guide over the crankshaft pulley so the cupped side is out.

13. Install the timing covers. Connect the negative battery cable.

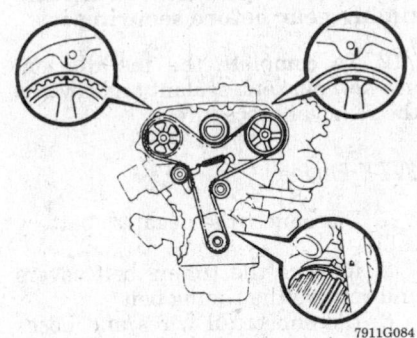

Rechecking the sprocket alignment — 3VZ-E engine

OIL SEAL REPLACEMENT

Remove the crankshaft pulley, timing belt cover and pry the seal from the retainer. Be careful not to damage the crankshaft. Install the seal with a seal installer 0930937010 or equivalent.

Camshaft

REMOVAL AND INSTALLATION

22R-E

1. Disconnect the negative battery cable. Remove the cylinder head cover.

2. Remove the rocker arm assembly from the cylinder head.

NOTE: It may be necessary to use a small prybar to lift the rocker arm assembly from the cylinder head.

3. Using a feeler gauge, measure the thrust bearing clearance at the front of the camshaft; the standard clearance is 0.003–0.007 in., it should not exceed 0.0098 in.

4. Remove the camshaft bearing caps and lift out the camshaft. Keep the bearings in order so they may be installed in their original position.

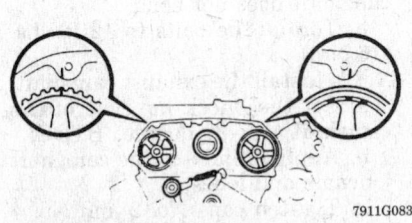

Aligning the timing marks with the rear cover — 3VZ-E engine

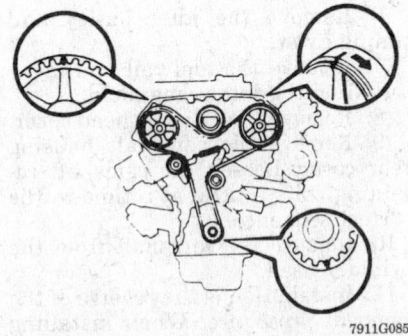

Installing the timing belt — 3VZ-E engine

5. Check the camshaft journal caps for damage. Clean all of the bearing surfaces, including the caps, cam journal and the cylinder head.

To install:

6. With the camshaft in place on the cylinder head, lay small strips of plastigage® on each of the camshaft journals (at the tops of the journals, facing front-to-rear).

7. Reinstall the journal caps in their original locations, arrows facing forward, and torque the caps to 13–16 ft. lbs. (18–22 Nm).

8. Remove the journal caps and gauge the width of the plastigage® against the chart on the plastigage® package. Maximum journal clearance is 0.004 in. If the journal clearance is greater than specified, measure the cam journal diameters with a micrometer. If the diameter of any cam journal is less than specified, obtain a new camshaft and recheck the journal clearance. If the clearance is still excessive, the cylinder head must be replaced.

9. To complete the installation, use new gaskets, sealant and reverse the removal procedures. Refill the cooling system. Torque the camshaft bearing cap bolts to 14 ft. lbs. (19 Nm), the cylinder head-to-engine block to 58 ft. lbs. (79 Nm), the timing chain cover-to-cylinder head bolt to 9 ft. lbs. (12 Nm), the camshaft sprocket-to-camshaft bolt to 58 ft. lbs. (79 Nm), the intake manifold bolts to 14 ft. lbs. (19 Nm), the exhaust manifold bolts to 33 ft. lbs. (45 Nm) and the rocker arm cover to 7–12 ft. lbs. (10–15 Nm). Replace the cooling system fluid and the engine oil. Adjust the valves, the drive belts, then, check and/or adjust the timing.

NOTE: If a new cam is installed, use an assembly lube on the cam lobes and engine oil on the journals. Change the engine oil and filter.

3F-E Engine

1. Disconnect the negative battery cable. Remove the cylinder head and the front cover from the engine.

2. Remove the oil slinger from the crankshaft. Remove the camshaft thrust plate retaining bolts, by working through the holes provided in the camshaft timing gear.

3. Remove the camshaft through the front of the cylinder block. Support the camshaft while removing it, so the bearings or the lobes do not become damaged.

4. Inspect the crankshaft timing gear. Replace it if it has worn or damaged teeth.

5. Remove the sliding key, then, pull the crankshaft timing gear from the crankshaft with a gear puller.

6. Use a large piece of pipe to drive the timing gear onto the crankshaft. Lightly and evenly tap the end of the pipe until the gear is in its original position.

To install:

7. Apply a coat of engine oil to the camshaft journals and bearings, then, insert the camshaft into the block.

8. Align the mating marks on the timing gears. Slip the camshaft into position. Torque the camshaft thrust plate bolts to 14.5 ft. lbs. (20 Nm).

9. Using a feeler gauge, check the gear backlash, inserted between the crankshaft and the camshaft timing gears. The maximum backlash should be 0.002–0.005 in.; if it exceeds this, replace one or both of the gears, as required.

10. Using a dial indicator, check the gear run-out. Maximum run-out, for both gears, is 0.008 in.; if not, replace the gear.

11. Install the oil nozzle, if removed, by screwing it in place and punching it in 2 places, to secure it.

NOTE: Be sure the oil hole in the nozzle is pointed toward the timing gear before securing it.

12. To complete the installation, use new gaskets, sealant and reverse the removal procedures.

3VZ-E Engine

1. Disconnect the negative battery cable.

2. Remove the timing belt covers and remove the timing belt.

3. Disconnect all wires and hoses to the air intake chamber.

4. Remove the bolts retraining the air intake chamber and remove the air intake chamber from the intake manifold.

5. Remove the rear timing belt cover.

6. Remove the idler pulley and timing cover.

7. Remove the fuel rail and injectors from the intake manifold.

8. Remove the cylinder head cover.

9. Remove the camshaft housing rear cover. Loosen the camshaft retaining bolts a little at a time in the correct sequence.

10. Remove the camshaft from the cylinder head.

11. Installation is the reverse of the removal procedure. When installing the bearing caps, make sure the arrow faces the front of the engine. Torque the caps to 12 ft. lbs. (16 Nm) in the correct sequence.

2TZ-FE Engine

1. Disconnect the negative battery cable.

2. Remove the engine from the vehicle.

3. Remove the valve cover.

4. Place the matchmarks on the camshaft sprocket and chain facing 12 o'clock with the engine upright.

5. Hold the camshaft with a wrench and remove the sprocket bolt.

6. Remove the chain tensioner, timing chain and sprocket. Hold to the side with a wire to maintain camshaft timing.

7. Remove the No. 6 camshaft bearing cap.

8. To remove the exhaust camshaft:

   a. Set the knock pin hole of the camshaft at 5–30 degrees BTDC.

   b. Secure the camshaft sub-gear to the main gear with a service bolt.

   c. Uniformly loosen and remove the bearing caps No. 1, No. 2, No. 3 and No. 5., in that order. Leave No. 4 tight.

   d. Loosen and remove the No. 4 bearing cap.

9. To remove the intake camshaft:

   a. Set the knock pin hole of the camshaft at 75–100 degrees BTDC.

   b. Uniformly loosen and remove the bearing caps No. 1, No. 2, No. 4 and No. 5., in that order. Leave No. 3 tight.

   c. Loosen and remove the No. 3 bearing cap.

To install:

10. To install the intake camshaft:

   a. Set the knock pin hole of the camshaft at 75–100 degrees BTDC.

   b. Apply prelube to the camshaft journals and lobes.

   c. Tighten caps No. 1 and No. 3 to draw the camshaft to the cylinder head.

   d. Uniformly torque the bearing caps in several steps to ensure the camshaft does not bend.

   e. Torque the bolts to 12 ft. lbs. (16 Nm).

11. To install the exhaust camshaft:

   a. Set the knock pin hole of the camshaft at 5–30 degrees BTDC.

   b. Apply prelube to the camshaft journals and lobes.

   c. Tighten caps No. 2 and No. 4 to draw the camshaft to the cylinder head.

   d. Uniformly torque the bearing caps in several steps to ensure the camshaft does not bend.

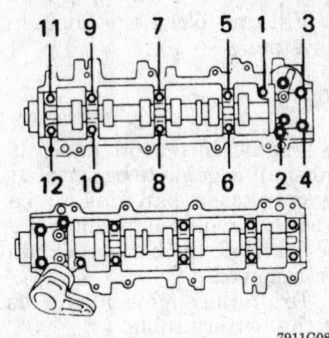

7911G086

Removing the camshaft bearing bolts — 3VZ-E engine

e. Torque the bolts to 12 ft. lbs. (16 Nm).

12. Apply sealer to the bottom of No. 6 bearing cap and install. Torque the cap to 12 ft. lbs. (16 Nm).

13. Install the camshaft sprocket and chain. Torque the bolt to 54 ft. lbs. (74 Nm).

14. Release the chain tensioner ratchet pawl. Fully push in the plunger and apply the hook to the pin so the plunger can not spring out and install the tensioner. Torque the bolts to 15 ft. lbs. (21 Nm).

15. Set the tensioner by pulling back on the slipper to release the hook.

16. Check the valve clearances.

17. Install the remaining components and check for leaks.

Piston and Connecting Rod

POSITIONING

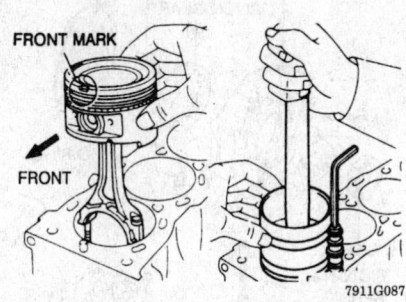

7911G087

Piston and connecting rod positioning — 22R-E and 3F-E engines

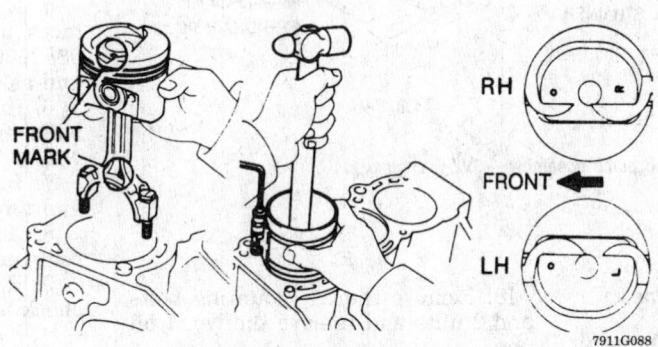

7911G088

Piston and connecting rod positioning — 3VZ-E engine; 2TZ-FE similar

ENGINE LUBRICATION

Oil Pan

REMOVAL AND INSTALLATION

Pick-Up and 4Runner

1. Raise the hood and disconnect the negative battery cable.

2. Raise and safely support the vehicle.

3. Drain the engine oil.

4. Remove the steering relay rod and the tie rods from the idler arm, pitman arm, and steering knuckles.

5. Remove the engine stiffening plates.

6. Remove the splash pans from under the engine.

7. Position a floor jack under the transmission and raise the engine/transmission assembly slightly.

8. Remove the front motor mount attaching bolts.

9. Remove the oil pan bolts and remove the oil pan.

10. Scrape the cylinder block and oil pan mating surfaces clean of any old sealing material. Apply gasket sealer to the oil pan when installing a new gasket. If equipped with the 22R-E engine, apply 5mm bead of gasket sealer; if equipped with the 3F-E or 3VZ-E engine, use 3mm bead. The parts should be installed within 5 minutes of applying the sealer.

11. The oil pan bolts should be tightened to 9 ft. lbs. (12 Nm) on the 22R-E engines; 6 ft. lbs. (10 Nm) (bolt), 52 inch lbs. (70 Nm) for the 3F-E or 3V-ZE engines. Tighten the bolts in a circular pattern, starting in the middle of the pan and working out towards the ends.

12. Lower the engine and tighten the motor mount bolts. Install the splash shields and stiffening plates.

13. Install any steering arms removed in Step 4 and then lower the vehicle; tighten all suspension com-

ponents and the motor mounts to their final torque with the vehicle resting on the ground.

14. Fill the engine with oil, road test the vehicle and check for leaks.

Land Cruiser Without 1FZ-FE Engine

1. Raise and safely support the vehicle. Remove the engine skid plates.

2. Remove the flywheel side cover and skid plate.

3. Disconnect the front driveshaft from the engine.

4. Drain the engine oil.

5. Remove the bolts which secure the oil pan. Remove the pan and its gasket.

6. Scrape away any old gasket material and then apply gasket sealer to the cylinder block mating surface and the No. 1 and No. 4 main bearing caps.

7. Install the oil pan and tighten the bolts to 69 inch lbs. (7.8 Nm). Always use a new pan gasket.

8. Connect the driveshaft, skid plate and flywheel side cover.

9. Lower the vehicle, fill the engine with oil and check for any leaks.

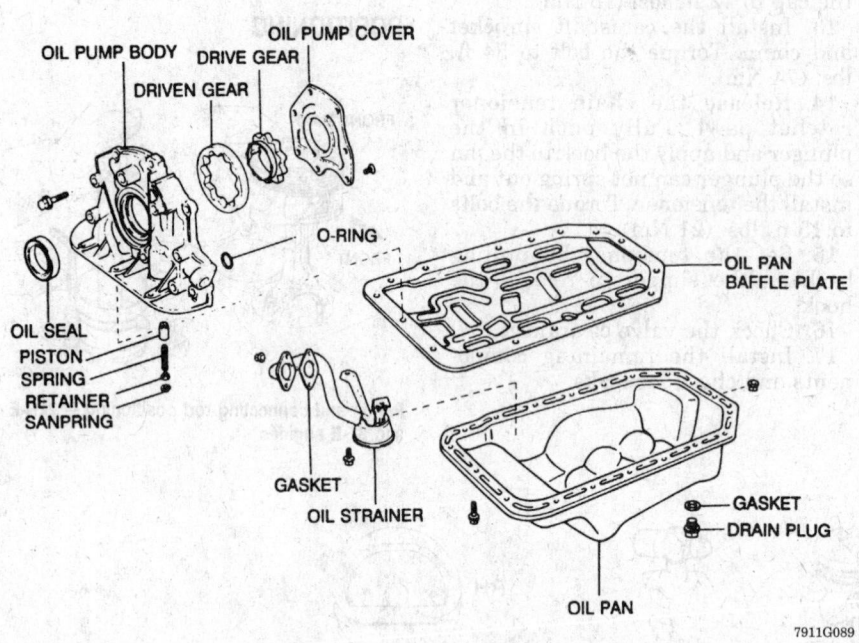

OIL PUMP BODY
DRIVE GEAR
OIL PUMP COVER
DRIVEN GEAR
OIL SEAL
PISTON
SPRING
RETAINER
SANPRING
O-RING
GASKET
OIL STRAINER
OIL PAN
BAFFLE PLATE
GASKET
DRAIN PLUG
OIL PAN

7911G089

Oil pan and pump assembly — 3VZ-E engine

Land Cruiser With 1FZ-FE Engine

1. Disconnect the negative battery cable.
2. Drain the engine cooling system.
3. Drain the engine oil.
4. Remove the engine under cover.
5. Remove the radiator.
6. Loosen the idler pulley nut and adjusting bolt. Remove the drive belt.
7. Remove the 4 mounting bolts. Disconnect the compressor from the bracket.
8. Remove the 5 bolts and the air conditioning compressor bracket.
9. Disconnect the No. 2 radiator hose from the water inlet.
10. Remove the 2 nuts and radiator pipe.
11. Remove the 4 bolts, 2 nuts, water pump and gasket.
12. Remove the cylinder head.
13. Disconnect the oil cooler pipe bracket from the No. 1 oil pan.
14. Remove the 4 bolts and the oil level sensor.
15. Remove the gasket from the oil level sensor.
16. Remove the 4 bolts holding the No. 1 oil pan to the transmission housing.
17. Remove the 17 bolts and 2 nuts holding the No. 2 oil pan and remove the pan.

18. Remove the 21 mounting bolts and 2 nuts and remove the No. 1 oil pan.

To install:

19. Install the No. 1 oil pan and tighten 21 mounting bolts and 2 nuts.
20. Install the No. 2 oil pan and tighten 17 bolts and 2 nuts.
21. Install the 4 bolts holding the No. 1 oil pan to the transmission housing.
22. Install the gasket and the oil level sensor. Tighten the 4 bolts.
23. Connect the oil cooler pipe bracket to the No. 1 oil pan.
24. Install the cylinder head.
25. Install the water pump and gasket. Tighten the 4 bolts and 2 nuts.
26. Install the radiator pipe. Tighten the 2 nuts.
27. Connect the No. 2 radiator hose to the water inlet.
28. Install the air conditioning compressor bracket. Tighten the 5 bolts.
29. Connect the compressor from the bracket. Tighten 4 mounting bolts.
30. Install the drive belt. Tighten the idler pulley nut and adjusting bolt.
31. Install the radiator.
32. Install the engine under cover.
33. Fill crankcase.
34. Connect the negative battery cable.

35. Fill and bleed the engine cooling system.

Previa

This engine has 2 oil pans. If the crankshaft is going to be serviced, the side crankcase pan has to be removed. If the oil pump sump is going to be serviced, the bottom oil pan has to be removed.

1. Drain the engine oil and disconnect the battery cable.
2. Remove the oil level sensor and gasket. Be careful not to drop the sensor when removing.
3. Remove the 14 bolts and 2 nuts.
4. Using a pan removing tool 0903200100 or equivalent, pry the pan from the engine, being careful not to damage the flange.

To install:

5. Clean the gasket mating surfaces and apply gasket sealer No. 0882600080 or equivalent, to the pan and assembly within 5 minutes.
6. Install the pan and torque the bolts and nuts to 48 inch lbs. (5.4 Nm).
7. Install the gasket, oil sensor and torque to 9 ft. lbs. (13 Nm).
8. Install the remaining components.
9. Refill the engine with oil and check for leaks.

Oil Pump

REMOVAL AND INSTALLATION

22R-E Engine

1. Raise and safely support the vehicle. Drain the oil, and remove the oil pan and the oil strainer and pick-up tube.
2. Remove the drive belts from the crankshaft pulley.
3. Remove the crankshaft bolt, and remove the pulley with a gear puller.
4. Remove the 5 bolts from the oil pump and remove the oil pump assembly.
5. Inspect the drive spline, driven gear, pump body, and timing chain cover for excessive wear or damage. If necessary, replace the gears or pump body or cover. Unbolt the relief valve (the vertical bolt on the pump body) when attached to the engine) and check the pistons, oil passages, and sliding surfaces for burrs or scoring. Inspect the crankshaft front oil seal and replace if worn or damaged.
6. When installing, use a new O-ring if necessary.

7. Apply a sealer to the upper bolt and install the 5 bolts.

8. Install the crankshaft pulley and use a new gasket on the oil strainer and oil pan. Be sure to apply sealer to the corners of the oil pan gasket before installing the pan.

3F-E Engine

1. Disconnect the negative battery cable. Raise and safely support the vehicle. Remove the oil pan.

2. Remove the oil strainer and unfasten the union nuts on the oil pump pipe.

3. Remove the lock wire and the oil pump retaining bolt and pipe from the engine.

4. Remove the oil pump cover and inspect the following parts for nicks, scoring, grooving, etc.:

   a. Pump cover
   b. Drive and driven gears
   c. Pump body

5. Replace either the damaged parts or the complete pump if damage is excessive.

To install:

6. Install the oil pump so the slot in the oil pump shaft is in alignment with the protrusion on the governor shaft of the distributor. Tighten the mounting bolts to 13 ft. lbs. (18 Nm).

7. Install the outlet pipe and tighten the union bolt to 33 ft. lbs. (44 Nm); use new gaskets.

8. Install the oil pan, fill the engine with oil and check for leaks.

NOTE: Be sure to check all of the gaskets and replace if necessary.

3VZ-E Engine

1. Disconnect the negative battery cable.

2. Remove the timing belt.

3. Raise and safely support the vehicle. Remove the engine under cover.

4. Remove the front differential.

5. Drain the oil.

6. Remove the crankshaft timing pulley.

7. Raise the engine slightly and remove the oil pan.

8. Remove the oil strainer. Insert a drift between the cylinder block and the oil pan baffle plate, cut off the sealer and remove the baffle plate.

NOTE: When removing the baffle plate with the drift, do not damage the baffle plate flange.

9. Remove the oil pump and O-ring.

To install:

10. Apply sealer to the oil pump mating surface running the bead on the inside of the bolts holes. Position a new O-ring in the groove in the cylinder block and install the pump so the spline teeth of the drive gear engage the large teeth on the crankshaft. Tighten the mounting bolts to 14 ft. lbs. (20 Nm).

11. Remove any old sealer and install the baffle plate with new sealer.

12. Install the oil strainer and tighten the bolts to 61 inch lbs. (7 Nm).

13. Install the oil pan, crankshaft pulley and the timing belt.

14. Install the front differential and the undercovers.

15. Fill the engine with oil and check for leaks.

2TZ-FE Engine

1. Remove the oil level sensor. Be careful not to drop the sensor when removing.

2. Remove the pan retaining bolts and pry the pan from the engine using a prying tool 0903200100 or equivalent. Be careful not to damage the flange.

To install:

3. Clean the gasket mating surfaces with a scraper and solvent.

4. Apply a bead of sealer 0882600080 or equivalent to the pan surface and install within 5 minutes.

5. Torque the pan bolts and nuts to 48 inch lbs. (5.4 Nm).

6. Install the oil sensor and torque the bolts to 9 ft. lbs. (13 Nm).

7. Install the remaining components and refill the with engine oil.

1FZ-FE Engine

1. Disconnect the negative battery cable.

2. Drain the engine cooling system.

3. Drain the engine oil.

4. Remove the engine under cover.

5. Remove the radiator.

6. Loosen the idler pulley nut and adjusting bolt. Remove the drive belt.

7. Remove the 4 mounting bolts. Disconnect the compressor from the bracket.

8. Remove the 5 bolts and the air conditioning compressor bracket.

9. Disconnect the No. 2 radiator hose from the water inlet.

10. Remove the 2 nuts and radiator pipe.

11. Remove the 4 bolts, 2 nuts, water pump and gasket.

12. Remove the cylinder head.

13. Disconnect the oil cooler pipe bracket from the No. 1 oil pan.

14. Remove the 4 bolts and the oil level sensor.

15. Remove the gasket from the oil level sensor.

16. Remove the 4 bolts holding the No. 1 oil pan to the transmission housing.

17. Remove the 17 bolts and 2 nut holding the No. 2 oil pan and remove the pan.

18. Remove the 21 mounting bolts and 2 nuts and remove the No. 1 oil pan.

19. Remove the crankshaft pulley.

20. Remove the drive belt idler pulley.

21. Remove the 9 mounting bolts, 2 mounting nuts and the drive belt adjusting bar.

22. Remove the oil pump by prying the portions between the cylinder block and the oil pump apart.

23. Remove the oil pump O-rings and gasket.

To install:

24. Install the oil pump O-rings and gasket.

25. Install the oil pump.

26. Install the 9 mounting bolts, 2 mounting nuts and the drive belt adjusting bar.

27. Install the drive belt idler pulley.

28. Install the crankshaft pulley.

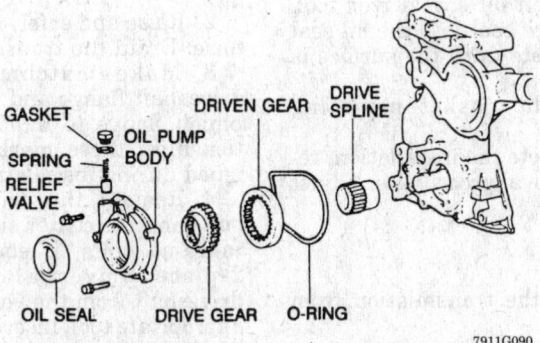

GASKET   OIL PUMP BODY   DRIVEN GEAR   DRIVE SPLINE

SPRING

RELIEF VALVE

OIL SEAL   DRIVE GEAR   O-RING

7911G090

Oil pump assembly — 22R-E engine

29. Install the No. 1 oil pan and tighten 21 mounting bolts and 2 nuts.

30. Install the No. 2 oil pan and tighten 17 bolts and 2 nuts.

31. Install the 4 bolts holding the No. 1 oil pan to the transmission housing.

32. Install the gasket and the oil level sensor. Tighten the 4 bolts.

33. Connect the oil cooler pipe bracket to the No. 1 oil pan.

34. Install the cylinder head.

35. Install the water pump and gasket. Tighten the 4 bolts and 2 nuts.

36. Install the radiator pipe. Tighten the 2 nuts.

37. Connect the No. 2 radiator hose to the water inlet.

38. Install the air conditioning compressor bracket. Tighten the 5 bolts.

39. Connect the compressor from the bracket. Tighten 4 mounting bolts.

40. Install the drive belt. Tighten the idler pulley nut and adjusting bolt.

41. Install the radiator.

42. Install the engine under cover.

43. Fill crankcase.

44. Connect the negative battery cable.

45. Fill and bleed the engine cooling system.

Rear Main Bearing Oil Seal

REMOVAL AND INSTALLATION

22R-E Engine

1. Raise and safely support the vehicle. Remove the transmission and the clutch assembly, if equipped. Remove the transfer case, if equipped.

2. Remove the flywheel or the flexplate from the crankshaft. Remove the cover plate from the rear of the engine.

3. Remove oil pan-to-oil seal retaining plate bolts, the oil seal retaining plate-to-engine bolts and oil seal retaining plate.

4. Carefully pry or drive the old seal from the retaining plate. Be careful not to damage the retaining plate.

5. Using an oil seal driver tool, drive the new seal into the oil seal retaining plate, until the surface is flush.

6. Lubricate the lips of the seal with multi-purpose grease.

7. Clean the gasket mounting surfaces.

8. To install, use new gaskets and reverse the removal procedures. Adjust the clutch.

3F-E Engine

1. Raise and safely support the vehicle. Remove the transfer case, the transmission and the clutch assembly.

2. Remove the flywheel from the crankshaft.

3. Using a small prybar, carefully pry the oil seal from the rear of the crankshaft.

4. Lubricate the lips of the seal with multipurpose grease.

5. Using an oil seal driver tool, drive the new seal into the rear of the crankshaft.

6. Clean the gasket mounting surfaces.

7. To install, reverse the removal procedures. Adjust the clutch.

3VZ-E Engine

1. Raise and safely support the vehicle. Remove the transmission and the clutch assembly, if equipped. Remove the transfer case, if equipped.

2. Remove the flywheel or the flexplate from the crankshaft. Remove the cover plate from the rear of the engine.

3. To replace the oil seal with the retaining plate removed:

   a. Remove oil pan-to-oil seal retaining plate bolts, the oil seal retaining plate-to-engine bolts and oil seal retaining plate.

   b. Carefully pry or drive the old seal from the retaining plate. Be careful not to damage the retaining plate.

   c. Using an oil seal driver tool, drive the new seal into the oil seal retaining plate, until the surface is flush.

   d. Lubricate the lips of the seal with multipurpose grease.

4. To replace the oil seal with the retaining plate installed:

   a. Cut off the oil seal lip.

   b. Using a small prybar, pry the oil seal from the retaining plate.

   c. Apply multi-purpose grease to the new oil seal.

   d. Using an oil seal driver tool, drive the new seal into the oil seal retaining plate until the surface is flush.

5. Clean the gasket mounting surfaces.

6. To complete the installation, reverse the removal procedures. Adjust the clutch.

2TZ-FE Engine

1. Remove the transmission from the vehicle.

2. Separate the transmission from the engine.

3. Remove the flywheel or flexplate.

4. Using a knife, cut off the lip of the oil seal.

5. Using a suitable prybar, pry the seal from the seal carrier. Be careful not to damage the crankshaft.

To install:

6. Clean the seal mating surfaces with solvent.

7. Apply grease to the seal lip.

8. Using an installer tool 0922356010 or equivalent, install the seal. Make sure the seal is seated properly. If not, the seal will leak and the engine will have to be removed again.

9. Install the engine/transmission assembly.

10. Install the remaining components and check for leaks.

MANUAL TRANSMISSION

Transmission Assembly

REMOVAL AND INSTALLATION

2WD Pick-Up

Disconnect the negative battery terminal.

1. Perform the following:

   a. Remove the center floor console, if equipped.

   b. Remove the shift lever handle, then the floor mat or carpet along with the shift lever boot in order to gain access to the shift lever.

   c. Using an shift lever removal tool, remove the shift lever.

NOTE: On the Pick-Up, remove the boot and the shift lever from inside the vehicle.

2. Raise and safely support the vehicle. Drain the transmission fluid.

3. Make matchmarks on the driveshaft flange and the differential pinion flange to indicate their relationships; these marks must be aligned during installation.

4. Remove the driveshaft flange bolts and the center support bearing-to-frame bolts, if equipped with a 2-piece driveshaft. Lower the driveshaft from the vehicle. Using an appropriate tool, insert it into the end of the transmission to prevent oil leakage.

5. Disconnect the back-up lamp switch electrical connector and the speedometer cable from the transmission, then tie the cable aside.

6. Disconnect the wiring at the starter. Remove the starter mounting bolts and lower the starter from the vehicle.

7. Remove the exhaust pipe clamp and the exhaust pipe.

8. If the hydraulic line from the clutch release cylinder is clamped to the frame, remove the clamp retaining bolt. Remove the release cylinder mounting bolts and the fork spring, if equipped. Tie the release cylinder aside.

NOTE: It is not necessary to disconnect the hydraulic line from the release cylinder.

9. On column shift vehicles, disconnect the shift selector linkage at the transmission and remove the transmission cross shafts.

10. Support the rear of the transmission with a jack and remove the transmission-to-crossmember bolts, the crossmember-to-frame bolts and the crossmember from the vehicle.

NOTE: When removing the crossmember, raise the rear of the transmission, just enough to take the weight off the crossmember.

11. Place a support under the engine with a wooden block (³⁄₄ in. thick) between the support and the engine oil pan.

NOTE: The wooden block and support should be no more than about ¼ in. away from the engine so when the engine is lowered, damage will not occur to any underhood components. If possible, shim the support so the wooden block touches the engine.

12. Remove the transmission-to-engine bolts, draw the transmission rearward and down, away from the engine.
To install:
13. Raise the transmission into position under the vehicle.
14. Install the transmission-to-engine bolts.
15. Torque transmission-to-engine bolts to 53 ft. lbs. (70 Nm), the stiffener plate bolts to 27 ft. lbs. (38 Nm), the transmission mount/bracket bolts to 19 ft. lbs. (28 Nm), the rear engine mount bracket-to-crossmember bolts to 9 ft. lbs. (12 Nm).
16. Connect the exhaust pipes and brackets. Install the starter and the clutch release cylinder.

17. Tighten the exhaust pipe-to-manifold bolts to 29 ft. lbs. (40 Nm), the upper exhaust pipe bracket-to-clutch housing bolts to 27 ft. lbs. (38 Nm), the lower exhaust pipe bracket-to-clutch housing bolts to 51 ft. lbs. (68 Nm), the lower starter bolt/release cylinder tube bracket bolt to 29 ft. lbs. (41 Nm), the clutch release cylinder bolts to 9 ft. lbs. (12 Nm).
18. Connect the remaining linkages and connect the driveshaft, aligning the matchmarks made during removal.
19. Refill the transmission to the correct level.
20. Install the shift lever and the center console.
21. Connect the negative battery cable.

4WD Pick-Up and 4Runner

1. Disconnect the negative battery terminal. Remove the starter upper mounting bolt.
2. Working inside the vehicle, pull up the shift lever boot and pull out the shift lever. If equipped with a 22R-E engine, pull up the shift lever boot, then, remove the mounting bolts and pull out the shift lever.
3. Using needle-nose pliers, remove the transfer case shift lever snapring and the shift lever.
4. Raise and safely support the vehicle.
5. Drain the lubricant from both the transmission and the transfer case.
6. Make matchmarks on the driveshaft flanges and the differential pinion flanges to indicate their relationships. These marks must be aligned during installation.
7. Remove the driveshaft mounting bolts and remove the front driveshaft assembly.

NOTE: Do not disassemble the front driveshaft to remove it.

8. Using a piece of chalk, place matchmarks on the rear driveshaft and the slip yoke to indicate their relationships; these marks must be aligned during installation.
9. Remove the mounting bolts from the rearward flange of the rear driveshaft. Lower the driveshaft from the vehicle. Remove the mounting bolts from the slip yoke flange, then, remove the flange and yoke assembly.
10. Unbolt the clutch release cylinder and tie it aside.

NOTE: It is not necessary to disconnect the hydraulic line from the clutch release cylinder.

11. Disconnect the starter motor electrical connectors. Remove the starter bolts and lower the starter from the vehicle.
12. At the transfer case, disconnect the speedometer cable (tie it aside), the back-up light switch connector and the 4WD indicator switch connector.
13. Disconnect the exhaust pipe clamp and the exhaust pipe from the transmission housing.
14. Remove the clutch release cylinder and the tube bracket, then, move the cylinder aside.

NOTE: When removing the clutch release cylinder, do not disassemble the hydraulic line from the cylinder.

15. Remove the crossmember-to-transfer case mounting bolts. Using a jack, raise the transmission and transfer case assembly off the crossmember. Remove the crossmember-to-frame attaching bolts and remove the crossmember.
16. Place a support under the engine oil pan, with a wooden block (³⁄₄ in. thick) between the support and the engine oil pan.

NOTE: The wooden block and support should be no more than about ¼ in. away from the engine so when the engine is lowered, damage will not occur to any underhood components. If possible, shim the support so the wooden block touches the engine.

17. Lower the jack until the engine rests on the support.
18. Remove the exhaust pipe bracket and the stiffener plate bolts.
19. Remove the transmission-to-engine bolts, draw the transmission/transfer case assembly rearward and down away from the engine.
20. Remove the transmission-to-transfer case adapter bolts and pull the transfer case from the transmission.
To install:
21. Raise the transmission into position under the vehicle.
22. Install the transmission-to-engine bolts.
23. Torque transmission-to-engine bolts to 53 ft. lbs. (73 Nm), the stiffener plate bolts to 27 ft. lbs. (38 Nm), the transmission mount/bracket bolts to 19 ft. lbs. (27 Nm), the rear engine mount bracket-to-crossmember bolts to 9 ft. lbs. (12 Nm).
24. Connect the exhaust pipes and brackets. Install the starter and the clutch release cylinder.
25. Tighten the exhaust pipe-to-manifold bolts to 29 ft. lbs. (40 Nm),

the upper exhaust pipe bracket-to-clutch housing bolts to 27 ft. lbs. (38 Nm), the lower exhaust pipe bracket-to-clutch housing bolts to 51 ft. lbs. (69 Nm), the lower starter bolt/release cylinder tube bracket bolt to 29 ft. lbs. (40 Nm), the clutch release cylinder bolts to 9 ft. lbs. (12 Nm).

26. Connect the remaining linkages and connect the driveshaft, aligning the matchmarks made during removal.

27. Refill the transmission to the correct level.

28. Install the shift lever and the center console.

29. Connect the negative battery cable.

Previa

1. Disconnect the negative battery cable and drain the transmission fluid.

2. Raise the vehicle and support safely.

3. Remove the starter motor. Matchmark the driveshafts-to-flange and remove the front (4WD) and rear driveshafts.

4. Remove the clutch release cylinder, hose and bracket.

5. Remove the exhaust pipe and bracket.

6. Disconnect the control cables/bracket and speed sensor connector.

7. Remove the engine-to-transmission stiffener plate.

8. Place a suitable transmission jack under the transmission.

9. Remove the engine rear mounting bolts and raise the rear side of the engine.

10. Remove the engine-to-transmission bolts, pull the transmission toward the rear and remove.

To install:

11. Align the input shaft with the clutch disc and push the transmission fully into position.

12. Install the transmission bolts and torque to 53 ft. lbs. (72 Nm).

13. Install the rear engine mounts and stiffener plate. Torque the bolt to 27 ft. lbs. (37 Nm).

14. Connect the speed sensor and control cables.

15. Install the exhaust pipe and torque the bracket to 37 ft. lbs. (51 Nm).

16. Install the clutch release cylinder, starter and driveshafts. Torque the starter to 41 ft. lbs. (56 Nm) and driveshaft bolts to 20 ft. lbs. (25 Nm).

17. Lower the vehicle.

18. Connect the battery cable and refill with transmission fluid.

CLUTCH

Clutch Assembly

REMOVAL AND INSTALLATION

1. Raise and safely support the vehicle. Remove the transmission from the vehicle.

2. Make matchmarks on the clutch cover and flywheel, indicating their relationship.

3. Loosen the clutch cover-to-flywheel retaining bolts a turn at a time. The pressure on the clutch disc must be released gradually.

4. Remove the clutch cover-to-flywheel bolts. Remove the clutch cover and the clutch disc.

5. If the clutch release bearing is to be replaced, perform the following:

a. Remove the bearing retaining clip(s), the bearing and hub.

b. Remove the release fork and the boot.

c. The bearing is press fitted to the hub.

d. Clean all parts and lightly grease the input shaft splines and all of the contact points.

e. Install the bearing/hub assembly, the fork, the boot and the retaining clip(s) in their original locations.

To install:

6. Inspect the flywheel surface for cracks, heat scoring (blue marks) and warpage. Replace or resurface the flywheel, if any damage is present.

NOTE: Before installing any new parts, make sure they are clean. During installation, do not get grease or oil on any of the components, as this will shorten clutch life considerably.

7. Using an clutch alignment tool, position the clutch disc against the flywheel. The raised center section of the disc faces the transmission.

8. Install the clutch cover over the disc and install the bolts loosely. Align the pressure plate-to-flywheel matchmarks. If a new or rebuilt clutch cover assembly is installed, use the matchmark on the old cover assembly as a reference. Torque the pressure plate-to-flywheel bolts to 14 ft. lbs. (19 Nm), using a criss-cross pattern.

9. Install the transmission into the vehicle.

PEDAL HEIGHT/FREE-PLAY ADJUSTMENT

The pedal height measurement is gauged from the angled section of the floorboard to the center of the clutch pedal pad. The correct pedal height is 6.12 in. for Pick-Up and 4Runner or 6.46 in. for Previa. If necessary, adjust the pedal height by loosening the locknut and turning the pedal stop bolt which is located above the pedal towards the driver's seat. Tighten the locknut after the adjustment.

Clutch Master Cylinder

REMOVAL AND INSTALLATION

Pick-Up and 4Runner

1. Disconnect the negative battery cable. Disconnect the master cylinder pushrod pin from the top of the clutch pedal.

2. Remove the hydraulic line from the master cylinder, being careful not to damage the compression fitting.

3. Remove the master cylinder-to-cowl nuts/ bolts.

4. To install, reverse the removal procedures. Partially tighten the hydraulic line before tightening the master cylinder mounting nut(s). Torque the nuts/bolts to 9 ft. lbs. (12 Nm). Bleed the clutch system. Adjust the pushrod play clearance.

Previa

1. Disconnect the negative battery cable.

2. Remove the instrument panel lower finish panel and steering column cover.

3. Remove the clip and clevis pin.

4. Disconnect the reservoir hose and clutch union line.

5. Remove the mounting bolts and pull out the master cylinder.

6. Installation is the reverse of removal. Torque the mounting bolts to 9 ft. lbs. (12 Nm).

7. Bleed the clutch hydraulic system.

8. Connect the battery cable and check operation.

PUSHROD ADJUSTMENT

The pedal pushrod play is the distance between the clutch master cylinder piston and the pedal pushrod located above the pedal towards the firewall. Since it is nearly impossible to measure this distance at the source, it must be measured at the pedal pad, preferably with a dial indi-

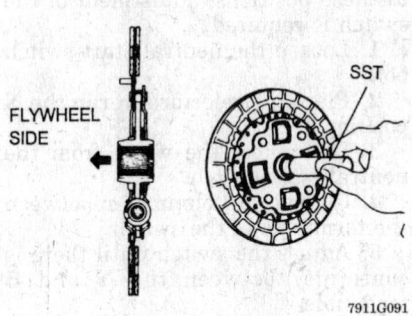

FLYWHEEL SIDE

SST

7911G091

Clutch disc installation

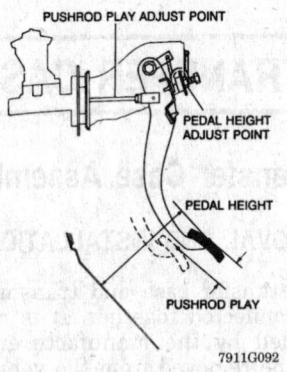

PUSHROD PLAY ADJUST POINT

PEDAL HEIGHT ADJUST POINT

PEDAL HEIGHT

PUSHROD PLAY

7911G092

Clutch pedal adjustment points

cator gauge. The pushrod play specification is: 0.040–0.200 in. for Land Cruiser and Previa or 0.039–0.197 in. for Pick-Ups and 4Runner. If necessary, adjust the pedal play by loosening the pedal pushrod locknut and turning the pushrod. Tighten the locknut after the adjustment.

FREE-PLAY ADJUSTMENT

The free-play measurement is the total travel of the clutch pedal from the fully released position to where resistance is felt as the pedal is pushed downward. The free-play specification is: 0.20–0.59 in. for all vehicles.

Clutch Slave Cylinder

REMOVAL AND INSTALLATION

1. Raise and safely support the vehicle.
2. If equipped, remove the tension spring on the clutch fork.
3. Remove the hydraulic line from the release cylinder. Be careful not to damage the fitting.
4. Turn the release cylinder pushrod in sufficiently to gain clearance from the fork.

5. Remove the mounting bolts and withdraw the cylinder.
6. To install, reverse the removal procedures. Bleed the clutch system. Adjust the fork tip clearance.

Hydraulic Clutch System Bleeding

1. Fill the master cylinder reservoir with brake fluid.
2. Remove the cap and loosen the bleeder screw on the clutch release cylinder. Cover the hole with a finger.
3. Pump the clutch pedal several times. Take the finger off the hole while the pedal is being depressed so the air in the system can be released. Put a finger back on the hole and release the pedal.
4. When fluid pressure can be felt tighten the bleeder screw.
5. Place a short length of hose over the bleeder screw and the other end in a jar ½ full of clean brake fluid.
6. Depress the clutch pedal and loosen the bleeder screw. Allow the fluid to flow into the jar.
7. Tighten the plug, then release the clutch pedal.
8. Repeat this procedure until no air bubbles are visible in the bleeder tube.
9. When there are no more air bubbles in the system, tighten the plug fully with the pedal depressed. Replace the plastic cap.
10. Refill the master cylinder to the correct level with brake fluid. Check the system for leaks.

AUTOMATIC TRANSMISSION

Transmission Assembly

REMOVAL AND INSTALLATION

1. Disconnect the negative battery terminal from the battery. On the Pick-Up and 4Runner, remove the air cleaner assembly.
2. Disconnect the transmission throttle cable from the throttle body.
3. Raise and safely support the vehicle. Drain the transmission fluid.
4. Disconnect the wiring connectors (near the starter) for the neutral start switch and the back-up light switch. If equipped, disconnect the

solenoid (overdrive) switch wiring at the same location. Disconnect the oil level gauge for Previa.
5. Disconnect the starter wiring at the starter. Remove the mounting bolts and the starter from the engine.
6. Make matchmarks on the rear driveshaft flange and the differential pinion flange. These marks must be aligned during installation.
7. Unbolt the rear driveshaft flange. If the vehicle has a 2 piece driveshaft, remove the center bearing bracket-to-frame bolts. Remove the driveshaft from the vehicle.
8. Disconnect the speedometer cable (tie it aside) and the shift linkage from the transmission.
9. Disconnect the transmission oil cooler lines at the transmission.
10. Disconnect the exhaust pipe clamp and remove the oil filler tube.
11. Support the transmission, using a jack with a wooden block placed between the jack and the transmission pan. Raise the transmission, just enough to take the weight off the rear mount.
12. On the Pick-Up and 4Runner, remove the rear engine mount with the bracket and the engine under cover, to gain access to the engine crankshaft pulley. Remove the stiffener plates on 2WD Previa.
13. Place a wooden block (or blocks) between the engine oil pan and the front frame crossmember.
14. Slowly, lower the transmission until the engine rests on the wooden block.
15. Remove the rubber plug(s) from the service holes located at the rear of the engine in order to gain access to the torque convertor bolts.
16. Rotate the crankshaft (to remove the torque convertor bolts) to access the bolts through the service holes.
17. Obtain a bolt of the same dimensions as the torque convertor bolts. Cut the head off the bolt and hacksaw a slot in the bolt opposite the threaded end.

NOTE: This modified bolt is used as a guide pin. Two guides pins are needed to properly install the transmission.

18. Thread the guide pin into one of the torque convertor bolt holes. The guide pin will help keep the convertor with the transmission.
19. Remove the stiffener plates from the transmission.
20. Remove the transmission-to-engine bolts, then carefully move the transmission rearward by prying on the guide pin through the service hole.

21. Pull the transmission rearward and lower it (front end down) from the vehicle.

To install:

22. Apply a coat of multi-purpose grease to the torque convertor stub shaft and the corresponding pilot hole in the flywheel.

23. Install the torque convertor into the front of the transmission. Push inward on the torque convertor while rotating it to completely couple the torque convertor to the transmission.

24. To make sure the convertor is properly installed, measure the distance between the torque convertor mounting lugs and the front mounting face of the transmission. The proper distance is 0.080 in.

25. Install guide pins into 2 opposite mounting lugs of the torque converter.

26. Raise the transmission to the engine, align the transmission with the engine alignment dowels and position the convertor guide pins into the mounting holes of the flywheel.

27. Install and tighten the transmission-to-engine mounting bolts. Torque the bolts to 47 ft. lbs. (63 Nm).

28. Remove the convertor guide pins and install the convertor mounting bolts. Rotate the crankshaft as necessary to gain access to the guide pins and bolts through the service holes. Evenly, tighten the convertor mounting bolts to 13 ft. lbs. (17 Nm). Install the rubber plugs into the access holes.

29. Install the engine undercover. Raise the transmission slightly and remove the wood block(s) from under the engine oil pan.

30. Install the transmission crossmember. Torque the crossmember-to-frame bolts to 26–36 ft. lbs. (34–48 Nm).

31. Lower the transmission onto the crossmember and install the transmission mounting bolts. Torque the bolts to 19 ft. lbs. (26 Nm).

32. Install the oil filler tube and connect the exhaust pipe clamp.

33. Connect the oil cooler lines to the transmission and torque the fittings to 25 ft. lbs. (34 Nm).

34. To complete the installation, reverse the removal procedures. Adjust the transmission throttle cable. Refill the transmission with Dexron®II fluid. Road test the vehicle and check for leaks.

SHIFT LINKAGE ADJUSTMENT

1. Loosen the adjustment nut on the transmission shift cable.

2. Push the manual lever of the transmission fully rearward except for Previa, or downward for Previa.

3. Move the manual lever back 2 notches, which is the **N** position except for Previa or 3 notches for Previa.

4. Set the gearshift selector lever in the **N** position.

5. Apply a slight amount of forward pressure on the selector lever and tighten the shift cable adjustment nut.

THROTTLE LINKAGE ADJUSTMENT

1. Remove the air cleaner assembly.

2. Push the accelerator to the floor and check that the throttle valve opens fully; if not, adjust the accelerator link, so it does.

3. Push back the rubber boot from the throttle cable which runs down to the transmission. Loosen the throttle cable adjustment nuts so the cable housing can be adjusted.

4. Fully open the throttle by pressing the accelerator all the way to the floor.

5. Adjust the cable housing so, with the throttle wide open, the distance between the outer cable end rubber cap to the inner cable stopper is 0–0.04 in. (0–1mm).

6. Tighten the nuts and double check the adjustment. Install the rubber boot and the air cleaner.

NEUTRAL START SWITCH ADJUSTMENT

The neutral safety switch prevents the vehicle from starting unless the gearshift selector is in either the **P** or **N** positions. If the vehicle will start

in these positions, adjustment of the switch is required.

1. Loosen the neutral start switch bolt.

2. Place the selector lever in the **N** position.

3. Disconnect the wires from the neutral start switch.

4. Connect an ohmmeter between the terminals of the switch.

5. Adjust the switch until there is continuity between the **N** and **B** terminals.

6. Reconnect the wires. Torque the bolt to 48 inch lbs. (65 Nm).

TRANSFER CASE

Transfer Case Assembly

REMOVAL AND INSTALLATION

The transfer case and transmission are connected together. It is recommended by the manufacturer that they be removed from the vehicle as an assembly and then separated for repairs.

DRIVE AXLE

Front Halfshaft

REMOVAL AND INSTALLATION

4WD Pick-Up and 4Runner

Remove the 4WD hub (with the flange) from the axle hub.

1. Raise and safely support the vehicle. Remove the wheel and tire assembly.

2. Disconnect and plug the brake line from the caliper. Remove the caliper from the axle hub.

3. Using a drift punch and a hammer, drive the lock washer tabs away from the locknut.

4. Remove the locknut from the halfshaft. Remove the lock washer, the adjusting nut, the thrust washer, the outer bearing and the axle hub/disc assembly from the vehicle.

5. Remove the knuckle spindle bolts, the dust seal and the dust cover. Using a brass bar and a hammer, tap the steering spindle from the steering knuckle.

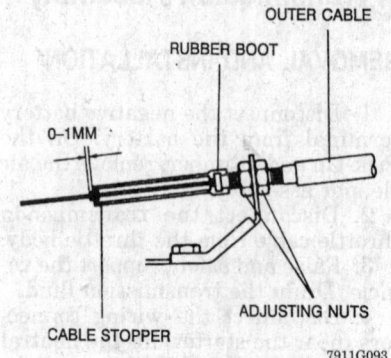

OUTER CABLE

RUBBER BOOT

0–1MM

ADJUSTING NUTS

CABLE STOPPER

7911G093

Throttle linkage adjustment

6. Turn the halfshaft until a flat spot on the outer shaft is in the upper position, then pull the halfshaft from the steering knuckle.

7. Using a slide hammer, pull the oil seal from the axle housing.

8. Using a clean shop towel, wipe the grease from inside the steering knuckle housing and the halfshaft.

To install:

9. Using an oil seal installation tool, drive a new oil seal into the axle housing until it seats.

10. Install the halfshaft into the axle housing.

11. Using multi-purpose grease, fill the steering knuckle cavity to about ¾ full.

12. To complete the installation, use new seals/gaskets and reverse the removal procedures.

13. Torque the steering spindle-to-steering knuckle bolts to 38 ft. lbs. (52 Nm), the axle hub adjusting nut to 18 ft. lbs. (25 Nm), the axle hub locknut to 33 ft. lbs. (44 Nm), the free wheel/locking hub nuts to 23 ft. lbs. (33 Nm) and the brake caliper to 65 ft. lbs. (88 Nm).

NOTE: To install the wheel bearings with the axle hub, torque the adjusting nut to 43 ft. lbs. (58 Nm), turn the axle hub (back and forth, several times), loosen the nut and retorque the adjusting nut to 18 ft. lbs. (24 Nm).

14. Install the wheel and tire assembly. Lower the vehicle.

4WD Previa

1. Raise and safely support the vehicle. Remove the wheel and tire assembly.

2. Using a drift punch and a hammer, drive the lock washer tabs away from the locknut.

3. Remove the locknut from the halfshaft. Remove the lock washer, the adjusting nut and the thrust washer.

4. Using a tie rod remover 0962810011 or equivalent, remove the tie rod end from the knuckle.

5. Remove the 6 bolts from the inner shaft joint.

6. Disconnect the knuckle from the lower ball joint by removing the 2 bolts.

7. Remove the halfshaft by pulling the knuckle outward and remove the halfshaft from the wheel hub. If the outer shaft will not come out of the hub, soak the splines with penetrating lube, install the nut and tap on the halfshaft with a soft hammer. Be careful not to damage the shaft threads.

To install:

NOTE: Coat the halfshaft splines with anti-seize compound to prevent spline seizure. This will help for future halfshaft removal.

8. Connect the lower ball joint and torque the bolts to 94 ft. lbs. (127 Nm).

9. Install the inner halfshaft joint-to-drive axle and torque the bolts to 51 ft. lbs. (61 Nm).

10. Install the tie rod end, torque the nut to 36 ft. lbs. (49 Nm) and install a new cotter pin.

11. Install the halfshaft nut and torque to 76 ft. lbs. (103 Nm).

12. Install the remaining components and check operation.

CV-Boot

REMOVAL AND INSTALLATION

Inner Boot

1. Remove the halfshaft from the vehicle.

2. Clean the halfshaft with soap and water. Remove the 2 inner boot clamps and slide the inner boot off the the joint.

3. Place matchmarks on the inner joint outer race and shaft. Remove the outer race from the shaft. Some joints have a large snapring on the inner side of the race that has to be removed.

4. Remove the snapring from the end of the inner joint. Pull the inner joint and boot from the shaft splines.

To install:

5. Install the boot, inner joint and snapring.

6. Fill the boot and joint with special CV-boot grease. The grease usually comes with replacement boot kits.

7. Slide the boot into position and install the clamps.

Outer Boot

1. Remove the inner joint and boot from the shaft.

2. Tape the inner splines to protect the boots.

3. Remove the 2 outer boot clamps and slide the outer boot off the the joint.

4. Installation is the reverse of removal. Clean the outer joint from all old grease and repack with special CV-boot grease.

Driveshaft and U-Joints

REMOVAL AND INSTALLATION

4WD Vehicles, Except Long Bed Pick-Up

REAR

1. Raise and safely support the vehicle and place a drain pan under the transmission.

2. Paint a mating mark on the halves of the rear universal joint flange.

3. Remove the bolts which hold the rear flange together.

4. Remove the splined end of the driveshaft from the transmission. The Previa rear shaft is bolted at both ends.

NOTE: Plug the end of the transmission with a rag or dummy flange to avoid losing transmission oil.

5. Remove the driveshaft from under the vehicle.

6. To install, reverse the removal procedures. Grease the splined end of the shaft before installing. Torque bolts to 31 ft. lbs. (42 Nm) for Previa or 54 ft. lbs. (75 Nm) for Pick-up and 4Runner.

All 4WD Vehicles

FRONT

1. Raise and safely support the vehicle.

2. Matchmark the driveshaft flange at the front axle housing and the transfer case.

3. On Previa, remove the center support bracket.

4. On Pick-Up and 4Runner, remove the flange dust cover.

5. Remove the bolts retaining the driveshaft and remove the driveshaft from the vehicle.

6. Install the driveshaft by aligning the matchmarks made during removal.

7. Torque the retaining bolts to 54–58 ft. lbs. (74–78 Nm). Torque the center support bracket bolts to 35 ft. lbs. (48 Nm). Make sure the drain hole is facing downward.

2WD Long Bed Pick-Up

REAR

1. Raise and safely support the vehicle.

2. Paint mating marks on all 6 flange halves.

3. Remove the bolts attaching the rear universal joint flange to the drive pinion flange.

4. Drop the rear section of the shaft slightly and pull the unit out of the center bearing sleeve yoke.

5. Remove the center bearing support from the crossmember.

6. Unbolt the driveshaft flange from the rear of the transmission and remove driveshaft along with center bearing support.

7. To install, align the matchmarks and reverse the removal procedures. Torque the flange bolts to 54 ft. lbs. (75 Nm).

Front Axle Shaft

REMOVAL AND INSTALLATION

Land Cruiser

1. Raise and safely support the vehicle. Remove the wheel and tire assembly.

2. Plug the brake master cylinder reservoir to prevent brake fluid leakage from the disconnected brake flexible hose.

3. Remove the outer axle shaft flange cap for automatic locking hub, the hub cover bolts and the cover for free wheel locking hub and the shaft snapring from the axle hub.

4. Remove the outer axle shaft flange for automatic locking hub or the hub ring-to-axle hub bolts, then alternately, screw 2 service bolts into the shaft flange or hub ring and remove the shaft flange or the hub ring with it's gasket.

5. Remove the caliper and disc.

6. Straighten the lock washer and remove the front wheel bearing adjusting nuts with front wheel adjusting nut wrench or similar tool.

7. Remove the front axle hub together with its claw washer, bearings and oil seal.

8. Remove the clip and disconnect the brake flexible hose from the brake tube.

9. Cut and remove the lock wire.

10. Using a soft mallet, lightly, tap the steering knuckle spindle and remove the spindle with it's gasket.

NOTE: When removing the steering knuckle spindle, if equipped with the ball joint type axle shaft joint, be prepared for the disconnection of the outer axle shaft from the joint. Prevent the shaft joint ball from falling from the joint.

11. If equipped with the ball type axle shaft joint, slide the inner front axle shaft from the axle housing. If equipped with the Birfield constant velocity joint type of axle shaft joint, remove the entire axle shaft assembly from the axle housing.

12. Using a bearing puller, remove the bushing from inside of knuckle spindle and the axle housing oil seal. Using a metal tube as a seating tool, drive oil seal into the axle housing and the new bushing into the knuckle spindle.

NOTE: If equipped with the ball joint type axle joint, install the inner axle with its proper spacer in position until the splines are fully meshed with the differential. If equipped with the Birfield constant velocity joint axle joint, install the axle into the housing and rotate the axle shaft until its splines mesh with the differential. Fill the steering knuckle about ¾ full with grease and place the joint ball on the inner shaft end.

13. To complete the installation, reverse the removal procedures. Adjust the wheel bearing preload.

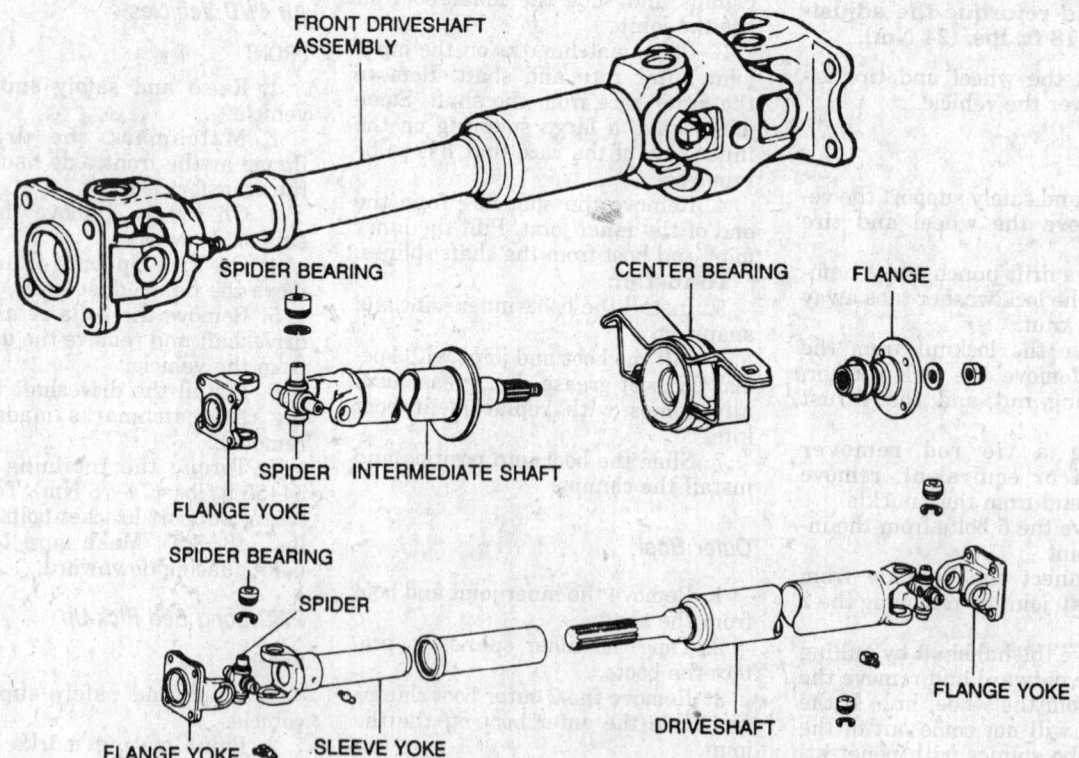

FRONT DRIVESHAFT ASSEMBLY

SPIDER BEARING

SPIDER   INTERMEDIATE SHAFT

FLANGE YOKE

CENTER BEARING   FLANGE

SPIDER BEARING

SPIDER

FLANGE YOKE

FLANGE YOKE   SLEEVE YOKE   DRIVESHAFT

FLANGE YOKE

7911G094

Driveshaft assemblies — Pick-Up and 4Runner

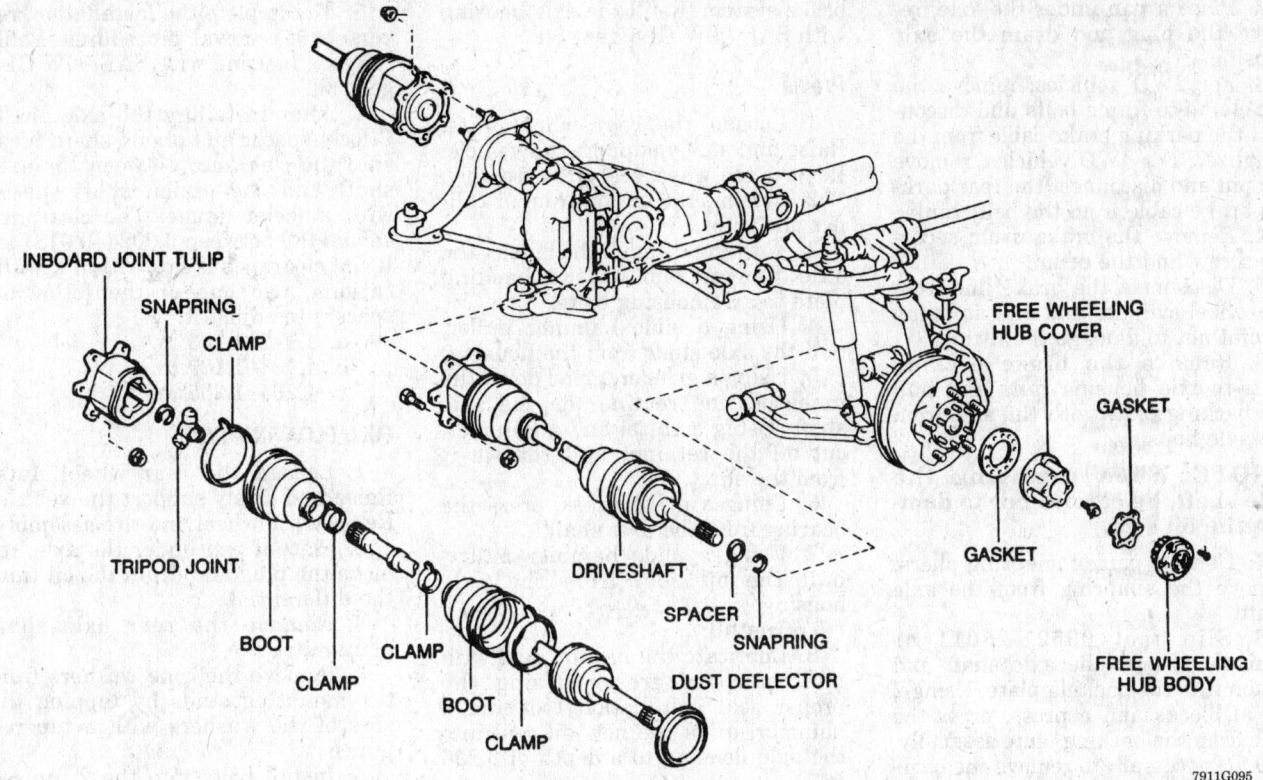

INBOARD JOINT TULIP
SNAPRING
CLAMP
TRIPOD JOINT
BOOT
CLAMP
CLAMP
BOOT
CLAMP
DRIVESHAFT
SPACER
SNAPRING
DUST DEFLECTOR
FREE WHEELING HUB COVER
GASKET
GASKET
FREE WHEELING HUB BODY

7911G095

Front drive axle assembly — Pick-Up and 4Runner

Front Axle Bearing

REMOVAL AND INSTALLATION

Except 4WD Previa

1. Raise and safely support the vehicle. Remove the 4WD hubs.
2. Using a small prybar, pry the grease seal from the rear of the disc/hub assembly, then remove the inner bearing from the assembly.
3. Using a shop cloth, wipe the grease from inside the disc/hub assembly.
4. Using a brass drift, drive the outer bearing races from each side of the disc/hub assembly.
5. Using solvent, clean all of the parts and blow dry with compressed air.
To install:
6. Using a bearing installation tool, drive the outer races into the disc/hub assembly until they seat against the shoulder.
7. Using multi-purpose grease, coat the area between the races and pack the bearings.
8. Place the inner bearing into the rear of the disc/hub assembly. Using a bearing installation tool, drive a new grease seal into the rear of the disc/hub assembly until it is flush with the housing.

9. Install the disc/hub assembly onto the axle shaft, the outer bearing, the thrust washer and the adjusting nut.
10. To adjust the bearing preload, perform the following:
    a. Torque the adjusting nut to 43 ft. lbs. (58 Nm).
    b. Turn the disc/hub assembly 2–3 times, from the left to the right.
    c. Loosen the adjusting nut until it can be turned by hand.
    d. Retorque the adjusting nut to 18 ft. lbs. (25 Nm).
    e. Install the lock washer and the locknut. Torque the locknut to 33 ft. lbs. (44 Nm).
    f. Check that the bearing has no play.
    g. Using a spring gauge, connect it to a wheel stud, the gauge should be held horizontal, then measure the rotating force, it should be 6–12 lbs. (8–15 Nm).
11. Lower the vehicle.

4WD Previa

1. Remove the steering knuckle from the vehicle. Place the assembly in a vise.
2. Using a hub remover tool (slide hammer) 0952000031 or equivalent,

remove the wheel hub from the knuckle.
3. Remove the bearing from the hub using a press and arbor tool 0955010012 or equivalent.
4. Remove the dust protector and oil seal.
5. Remove the bearing snapring from the knuckle and press the inner bearing from the knuckle.
To install:
6. Using a press and arbor tool 0960810010 or equivalent, press the bearing into the knuckle.
7. Install the outer oil seal and dust cover.
8. Press the axle hub onto the knuckle.
9. Install the knuckle assembly onto the vehicle.

Rear Axle Shaft and Bearings

REMOVAL AND INSTALLATION

Pick-Up and 4Runner

1. Loosen the rear wheel lug nuts, then raise and safely support the vehicle. Remove the wheel and tire assembly.

2. Place a pan under the axle, remove the plug and drain the axle housing.

3. For 2WD vehicles, remove the clip/clamp-to-frame bolts and disconnect the parking brake cable from the equalizer. For 4WD vehicles, remove the pin and disconnect the rear parking brake cable from the bell crank.

4. Remove the brake drum securing screw and the drum.

5. Disconnect the brake line from the wheel cylinder and plug it, being careful not to damage the fitting.

6. Remove the brake backing plate-to-axle housing nuts and pull the backing plate with the axle from the axle housing.

NOTE: When removing the axle shaft, be careful not to damage the oil seal.

7. Using a pair of snapring pliers, remove the snapring from the axle shaft.

8. Slip tool 09521-25011 or equivalent, over the axle shaft and fasten it to the backing plate. Using 2 metal blocks and a press, press the axle from the backing plate assembly.

9. If necessary to remove the bearing from backing plate, perform the following:

    a. Remove the brake spring, the retracting spring clamp bolt, the lower springs, the shoe strut, the brake shoes and the parking brake lever.

    b. Using a slide hammer puller, pull the outer oil seal from the backing plate.

    c. Press the bearing from the backing plate.

    d. Using the proper installation tools, press the new bearing into the backing plate.

    e. Using the proper seal installation tool, press the new oil seal into the backing plate.

    f. Reassemble the brake components to the backing plate.

10. Using a slide hammer, pull the oil seal from the axle housing.

To install:

11. Using the installation tool and a hammer, drive a new oil seal into the axle housing.

12. Using a press, press the axle shaft into the backing plate and the bearing retainer. Using snapring pliers, install the snapring onto the axle shaft.

13. Clean the gasket mounting surfaces.

14. To complete the installation, reverse the removal procedures. Torque the backing plate-to-axle housing nuts to 51 ft. lbs. (69 Nm). Adjust the brake shoe clearance and bleed the

brake system. Refill the axle housing with SAE 90W GL5 gear oil.

Previa

1. Loosen the rear wheel nuts. Raise and safely support the vehicle. Remove the wheel and tire assembly.

2. Remove the brake drum or caliper and rotor.

3. Working through the hole in the axle flange, remove the backing plate-to-axle housing bolts.

4. Using a slide hammer puller, pull the axle shaft from the housing.

5. Using a grinder, grind down the inner bearing retainer on the axle shaft. Using a chisel and a hammer, cut off the retainer and remove it from the shaft.

6. Using a arbor press, press the bearing from the axle shaft.

7. Using a slide hammer puller, pull the oil seal from the axle housing.

To install:

8. Lubricate the new oil seal with multi-purpose grease. Using the proper seal installation tool and a hammer, drive the new oil seal into the axle housing to a depth of 0.236 in.

9. To install, use new gaskets and reverse the removal procedures. Torque the axle retainer-to-housing bolts to 48 ft. lbs. (65 Nm).

Land Cruiser

SEMI-FLOATING TYPE

1. Loosen the rear wheel nuts. Raise and safely support the vehicle. Remove the wheel and tire assembly.

2. Place a pan under the axle, remove the plug and drain the oil from the differential.

3. Remove the brake drum and related parts, as follows:

    a. Remove the cover from the back of the differential housing.

    b. Remove the pin from the differential pinion shaft.

    c. Withdraw the pinion shaft and it's spacer from the case.

    d. Use a mallet to tap the rear axle shaft toward the differential, then remove the C-lock from the axle shaft.

    e. Withdraw the axle shaft from the housing.

4. Using a bearing puller, remove axle bearing and oil seal together from the axle housing. Using a metal tube and a hammer, drive the bearing and the seal into the housing until they seat.

NOTE: Do not mix the parts of the left and right axle shaft assemblies.

5. To complete the installation, reverse the removal procedures. Refill the axle housing with SAE 90W GL5 gear oil.

6. After installing the axle shaft, C-lock, spacer and pinion shaft, measure the clearance between the axle shaft and the pinion shaft spacer with a feeler gauge. The clearance should fall between 0.0024–0.0181 in. If the clearance is not within specifications, use one of the following spacers to adjust it:

    a. 1.172–1.173 in.
    b. 1.188–1.189 in.
    c. 1.204–1.205 in.

FULL FLOATING TYPE

1. Loosen the rear wheel nuts. Raise and safely support the vehicle. Remove the wheel and tire assembly.

2. Place a pan under the axle, remove the plug and drain the oil from the differential.

3. Remove the rear axle shaft plate nuts.

4. Remove the cone washers from the mounting studs by tapping the slits of the washers with a tapered punch.

5. Install bolts into the 2 unused holes of the axle shaft plate.

6. Tighten the bolts to draw the axle shaft assembly from the housing.

7. To install, use a new gasket, sealant and reverse the removal procedures. Torque the axle shaft nuts to 21–25 ft. lbs. (27–34 Nm).

Front Wheel Hub, Knuckle and Bearing

REMOVAL AND INSTALLATION

2WD Pick-Up

1. Raise and safely support the vehicle. Remove the wheel and tire assembly.

2. Remove the brake caliper. Do not disconnect the brake hose from the caliper. Suspend it on a wire.

3. Remove axle hub dust cap, the cotter pin, the nut lock, the adjusting nut, the thrust washer and the outer bearing, then pull the hub/disc assembly from the axle spindle.

4. Remove the backing plate cotter pins and the mounting nuts or bolts, then the backing plate.

5. Remove steering knuckle arm from the back of the steering knuckle.

6. Remove the nuts, the retainers and the bushings, then the shock absorber from the lower control arm.

7. Support the lower arm with a jack and raise to put pressure on spring.

NOTE: Be careful not to unbalance vehicle support stands when jacking up lower arm.

8. Remove cotter pins, then the upper and lower ball joint nuts. Using a ball joint removal tool, separate the ball joints from the steering knuckle.

9. Remove the steering knuckle from the vehicle.

NOTE: Whenever the hub/disc assembly is removed from the vehicle, it is good practice to replace the grease seal.

10. To install, reverse the removal procedures. Torque the upper ball joint nut to 80 ft. lbs. (109 Nm) for Pick-Up, the lower ball joint nut to 105 ft. lbs. (142 Nm) for Pick-Up or 76 ft. lbs. (109 Nm), the steering knuckle arm-to-steering knuckle bolts to 80 ft. lbs. (109 Nm) for Pick-Up, the shock absorber-to-lower control arm nuts to 19 ft. lbs. (27 Nm) and the backing plate-to-steering knuckle bolts to 80 ft. lbs. (109 Nm) for Pick-Up. Adjust the wheel bearing.

4WD Vehicles

1. Remove the front axle shaft assembly from the vehicle.

2. Remove the oil seal retainer and the oil seal set from the rear of the steering knuckle.

3. At the drag link end of the steering knuckle arm, remove the cotter pin. Using the proper tool, remove the plug from the drag link, then disconnect the drag link from the steering knuckle arm.

4. Remove the tie rod-to-steering knuckle, cotter pin and nut. Using the proper ball joint removal tool, separate the tie rod from the steering knuckle arm.

5. Remove the steering knuckle arm-to-steering knuckle (top) nuts and the steering knuckle-to-bearing cap (bottom) nuts. Using a tapered punch, tap the cone washers slits and remove the washers.

NOTE: Do not mix or lose the upper and lower bearing cap shims.

6. Using a bearing removal tool (without a collar), press the steering knuckle arm with the shims from the steering knuckle.

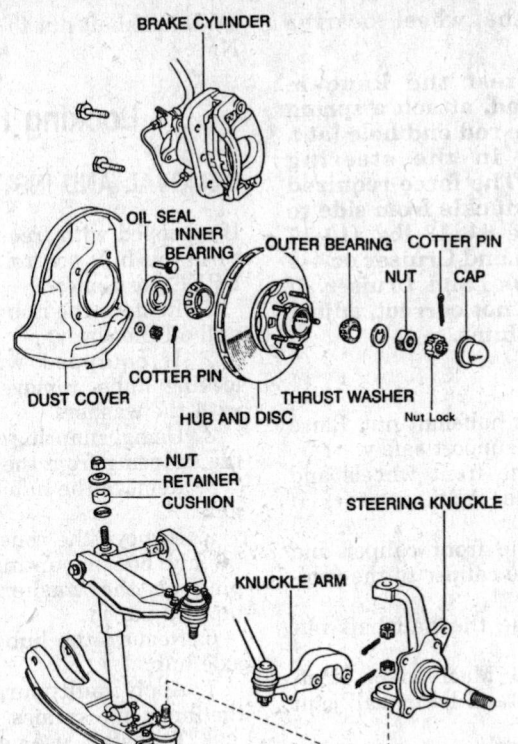

Front hub and steering knuckle — typical 2WD vehicle

7. Using a bearing removal tool (without a collar), press the bearing cap with the shims from the steering knuckle.

8. Remove the steering knuckle from the vehicle.

To install:

9. To install the steering knuckle, use a suitable tool to support the upper inner bearing. Using a hammer, tap the steering knuckle arm into the bearing inner race.

10. Using the proper tool, support the lower bearing inner race. Using a hammer, tap the bearing cap into the bearing inner race.

NOTE: When installing the drag link-to-steering knuckle arm, torque the plug all the way, then loosen it 1⅓ turns and secure it with the cotter pin.

11. To install, use gaskets, seals, pack the steering knuckle with multipurpose grease and reverse the removal procedures for the Land Cruiser.

a. Torque the steering knuckle arm-to-steering knuckle nuts to 71 ft. lbs. (95 Nm).

b. Torque the bearing cap-to-steering knuckle nuts to 71 ft. lbs. (95 Nm).

c. Torque the tie rod-to-steering knuckle arm nut to 67 ft. lbs. (91 Nm).

d. Torque the axle spindle-to-steering knuckle bolts to 38 ft. lbs. (51 Nm).

12. To install, reverse the removal procedures for the Pick-Up and 4Runner.

a. Torque the upper ball joint nut to 80 ft. lbs. (109 Nm) for Pick-Up and 4Runner.

b. Torque the lower ball joint nut to 105 ft. lbs. (142 Nm) for Pick-Up and 4Runner.

c. Torque the steering knuckle arm-to-steering knuckle bolts to 80 ft. lbs. (109 Nm) for Pick-Up and 4Runner.

d. Torque the shock absorber-to-lower control arm nuts to 19 ft. lbs. (27 Nm).

e. Torque the backing plate-to-steering knuckle bolts to 80 ft. lbs. (109 Nm) for Pick-Up and 4Runner.

13. Adjust the wheel bearing preload.

NOTE: To test the knuckle bearing preload, attach a spring scale to the tie rod end hole (at a right angle) in the steering knuckle arm. The force required to move the knuckle from side to side should be 6.6–13 lbs. (10–17 N) except for Land Cruiser or 4–5 lbs. (5–7 N) for Land Cruiser. If the preload is not correct, adjust by replacing shims.

Previa

1. Loosen the halfshaft nut. Raise the vehicle and support safely.
2. Remove the front wheels and disconnect the ABS sensor, if equipped.
3. Remove the front caliper and rotor. Secure the caliper to the vehicle with wire.
4. Remove the the halfshaft nut for 4WD.
5. Remove the MacPherson strut-to-knuckle bolts and lower ball joint bolts.
6. Separate the tie rod end using a remover tool 0962810011 or equivalent.
7. Make sure the halfshaft splines are loose and remove the halfshaft from the knuckle.
8. Remove the steering knuckle/hub assembly.
9. 2WD only, remove the grease cap. Using a chisel, release the nut stake and nut.
10. Using a hub remover tool (slide hammer) 0952000031 or equivalent, remove the wheel hub from the knuckle.
11. Remove the bearing from the hub using a press and arbor tool 0955010012 or equivalent.
12. Remove the dust protector and oil seal.
13. Remove the bearing snapring from the knuckle and press the inner bearing from the knuckle.
To install:
14. Using a press and arbor tool 0960810010 or equivalent, press the bearing into the knuckle.
15. Install the outer oil seal and dust cover.
16. Press the axle hub onto the knuckle.
17. 2WD only, install the locknut and torque to 147 ft. lbs. (199 Nm). Stake the nut and install the dust cover.
18. Install the knuckle assembly onto the vehicle. Torque the tie rod ends to 36 ft. lbs. (49 Nm), strut bolts to 231 ft. lbs. (314 Nm), lower ball joint bolts to 94 ft. lbs. (147 Nm) and

4WD halfshaft nut to 137 ft. lbs. (186 Nm).

Locking Hubs

REMOVAL AND INSTALLATION

If equipped with free-wheeling hubs, turn the hub control handle to the **FREE** position.
1. Remove the hub cover bolts and pull off the cover.
2. If equipped with automatic locking hubs, remove the axle bolt with the washer.
3. Using snapring pliers, remove the snapring from the axle shaft.
4. Remove the hub body mounting nuts.
5. Remove the cone washers from the hub body mounting studs by tapping on the washer slits with a tapered punch.
6. Remove the hub body from the axle hub.
7. Apply multi-purpose grease to the inner hub splines.
8. To install, use new gaskets and reverse the removal procedures. Torque the hub body-to-axle hub nuts to 23 ft. lbs. (31 Nm), the plate washer/bolt to 13 ft. lbs. (17 Nm) for auto. locking hub and the hub cover-to-hub body bolts to 7 ft. lbs. (10 Nm).

NOTE: To install the snapring onto the axle shaft, install a bolt into the axle shaft, pull it out and install the snapring.

Pinion Seal

REMOVAL AND INSTALLATION

1. Raise and safely support the vehicle.
2. Matchmark and remove the driveshaft.
3. Remove the companion flange from the differential.
4. Using puller 09308-10010 or equivalent, remove the oil seal from the housing.
5. Remove the oil slinger.
6. Remove the bearing and spacer.
To install:
7. Install the bearing spacer and bearing.

NOTE: Lubricate the seal lips with multi-purpose grease before installing it.

8. Install the oil slinger and using seal installer 09554-30011 or equivalent, install the oil seal.
9. Drive the seal into place, to a depth of 0.59 in below the housing lip

for 7.5 in. axles and 0.39 in. below the lip for 8 in. axles.
10. Install the companion flange and install the driveshaft.
11. Lower the vehicle.

Differential Carrier

REMOVAL AND INSTALLATION

Rear and Land Cruiser Front

1. Raise and safely support the vehicle. Drain the lubricant from the differential.
2. Remove the axle shafts from the axle housing.
3. Matchmark the driveshaft flange to the differential flange. Remove the mounting bolts and separate the driveshaft from the differential.
4. Remove the differential retaining nuts and pull the assembly from the differential housing.
5. Place matchmarks on the bearing caps, carrier housing and adjusting nuts.
6. Remove the 4 bolts and bearing caps. Lift the carrier assembly with the side bearings from the housing. Tag the parts to show the location for reassembly.
To install:
7. Place the bearing outer races on their respective bearings. Install the carrier into the differential housing.
8. Install the bearing adjusting nuts, bearing caps and bolts to original position. Torque the cap bolts to 58 ft. lbs. (78 Nm).
9. Use new gaskets and reverse the removal procedures. Torque the differential-to-axle nuts to 23 ft. lbs. (31 Nm) and the driveshaft flange-to-differential flange nuts/bolts to 31 ft. lbs. (43 Nm). Refill the axle with 80W-90 gear oil to a level of 1/4 in. below the fill hole.

NOTE: Before installing the carrier, apply a thin coat of liquid or silicone sealer to the carrier housing gasket and to the carrier side face of each carrier retaining nut.

Front

1. Raise and safely support the vehicle. Drain the lubricant from the differential.
2. Remove the front axle shafts or halfshafts from the axle housing.
3. Matchmark the front driveshaft flange to the differential flange. Remove the mounting bolts and separate the driveshaft from the differential.

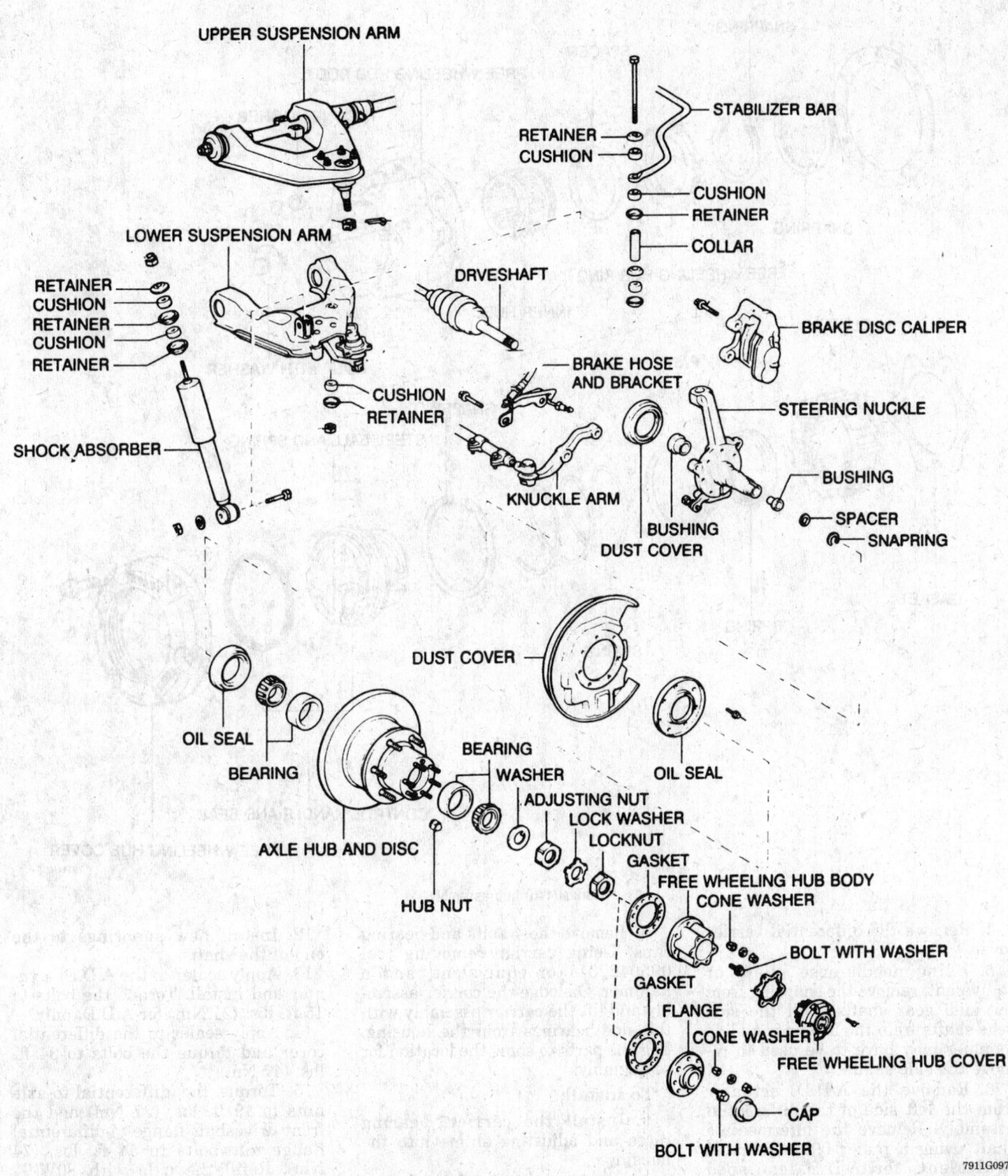

UPPER SUSPENSION ARM

STABILIZER BAR

RETAINER
CUSHION

CUSHION
RETAINER
COLLAR

LOWER SUSPENSION ARM

DRVESHAFT

BRAKE DISC CALIPER

RETAINER
CUSHION
RETAINER
CUSHION
RETAINER

BRAKE HOSE
AND BRACKET

STEERING NUCKLE

CUSHION
RETAINER

BUSHING

SHOCK ABSORBER

SPACER
SNAPRING

KNUCKLE ARM

BUSHING
DUST COVER

DUST COVER

OIL SEAL

BEARING

OIL SEAL

BEARING

BEARING
WASHER

ADJUSTING NUT
LOCK WASHER
LOCKNUT
GASKET

AXLE HUB AND DISC

FREE WHEELING HUB BODY
CONE WASHER

HUB NUT

BOLT WITH WASHER

GASKET

FLANGE

CONE WASHER

FREE WHEELING HUB COVER

CAP

BOLT WITH WASHER

7911G097

Front hub and steering knuckle — typical 4WD vehicle

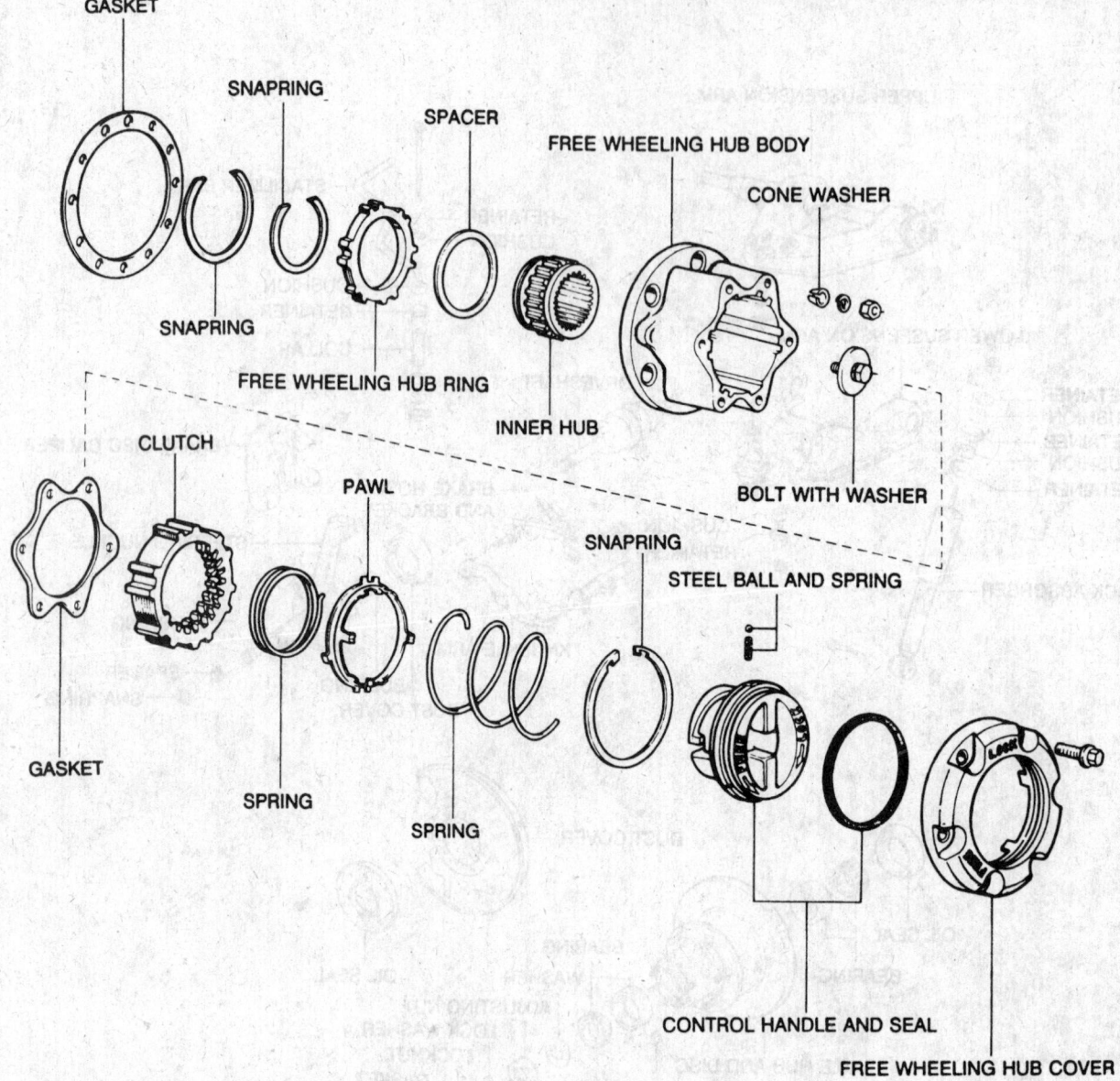

GASKET

SNAPRING

SPACER

FREE WHEELING HUB BODY

CONE WASHER

SNAPRING

FREE WHEELING HUB RING

INNER HUB

BOLT WITH WASHER

CLUTCH

PAWL

SNAPRING

STEEL BALL AND SPRING

GASKET

SPRING

SPRING

CONTROL HANDLE AND SEAL

FREE WHEELING HUB COVER

7911G098

Manual 4WD hub assembly

4. Remove the differential carrier cover.

5. Using needle-nose pliers or equivalent, remove the snapring from the side gear shafts. Pull the side gear shafts from the housing. A slide hammer may have to be used to remove the side shafts.

6. Remove the A.D.D. actuator from the left side of the differential assembly. Remove the intermediate shaft using a puller 0935020015 or equivalent, for A.D.D. equipped vehicles.

7. Place matchmarks on the bearing caps, carrier housing and adjusting nuts.

8. Remove the 4 bolts and bearing caps. Using carrier removing tool 0950422011 or equivalent, and a hammer. Dislodge the carrier assembly and lift the carrier assembly with the side bearings from the housing. Tag the parts to show the location for reassembly.

To install:

9. Install the carrier, bearing races and adjusting shims into the housing.

10. Install the bearing caps and torque the bolts to 58 ft. lbs. (78 Nm).

11. Install the side gear shaft oil seals and side shafts.

12. Install new snaprings to the end of the shafts.

13. Apply sealer to the A.D.D. actuator and install. Torque the bolts to 15 ft. lbs. (21 Nm) for A.D.D. only.

14. Apply sealer to the differential cover and torque the bolts to 34 ft. lbs. (47 Nm).

15. Torque the differential-to-axle nuts to 19 ft. lbs. (27 Nm) and the front driveshaft flange-to-differential flange nuts/bolts to 54 ft. lbs. (74 Nm). Refill the axle with 80W-90 gear oil to a level of ¼ in. below the fill hole.

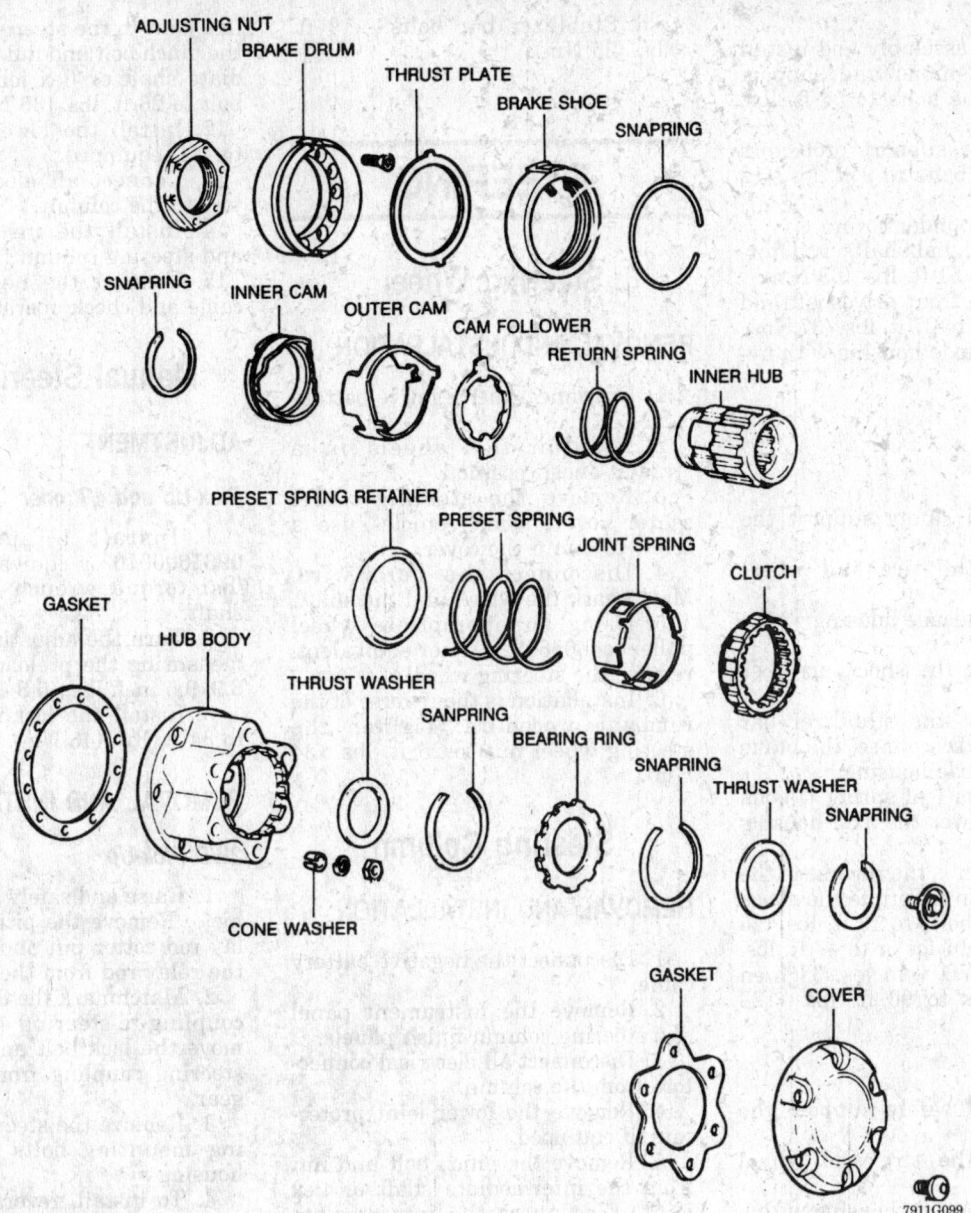

Automatic 4WD hub assembly

Axle Housing

REMOVAL AND INSTALLATION

Front

4WD VEHICLES, EXCEPT PREVIA

1. Raise and safely support the vehicle.

2. Matchmark and remove the front driveshaft.

3. Disconnect the axle shafts from the axle assembly.

4. Disconnect vacuum hoses, if equipped with automatic locking hubs.

5. Disconnect the 4WD indicator. Remove the front differential mounting bolt.

6. Support the axle housing with an suitable jack and remove the rear mounting bolts.

To install:

7. Install the differential in position under the vehicle.

8. Install the rear mounting bolts and torque to 123 ft. lbs. (167 Nm).

9. Install the front mounting bolt and torque to 108 ft. lbs. (147 Nm).

10. Connect vacuum hoses and the 4WD indicator.

11. Install the axle shafts and the driveshaft, aligning matchmarks made during removal.

12. Refill the axle with the correct oil and lower the vehicle.

4WD PREVIA

1. Raise the vehicle and safely support it and drain the axle housing.

2. Disconnect the driveshaft and halfshafts. Hang the shafts aside with wire. Be careful not to damage the rubber shaft boots.

3. Remove the left engine undercover and differential support protectors.

4. Place a jack under the axle housing and remove the 3 support bolts and 6 cushions. Lower the jack and remove the assembly.

To install:

5. Raise the assembly and install the collars, cushions and support bolts. Torque the bolts to 54 ft. lbs. (73 Nm).

6. Install the support protectors and torque the bolts to 9 ft. lbs. (12 Nm).

7. Install the under cover.

8. Install the halfshafts and torque the bolts to 51 ft. lbs. (69 Nm).

9. Install the front driveshaft and torque the bolts to 27 ft. lbs. (37 Nm).

10. Refill the axle housing with hypoid gear oil.

Rear

EXCEPT PREVIA

1. Raise and safely support the vehicle.

2. Remove the tire and wheel assemblies.

3. Support the axle housing with a suitable jack.

4. Disconnect the shock absorber lower bolts.

5. Disconnect the stabilizer bar and lateral rod. Disconnect the brake lines from the axle housing.

6. Remove the leaf spring U-bolts and carefully lower the axle housing from the vehicle.

7. Installation is the reverse of the removal procedure. Torque the shock absorber lower bolts to 19 ft. lbs. (25 Nm) on 2WD vehicles or to 47 ft. lbs. (64 Nm) on 4WD vehicles. Tighten the U-bolt nuts to 90 ft. lbs. (123 Nm).

PREVIA

1. Raise and safely support the vehicle.

2. Remove the tire and wheel assemblies.

3. Support the axle housing with a suitable jack.

4. Disconnect the shock absorber lower bolts.

5. Disconnect the stabilizer bar and lateral rod. Also, disconnect the upper and lower control arms.

6. Remove the brake lines from the axle housing.

7. Slowly lower the axle housing from the vehicle.

8. Installation is the reverse of the removal procedure. Observe the following torques:

   a. Shock absorber bottom bolts — 27 ft. lbs. (37 Nm) for 2WD or 94 ft. lbs. (127 Nm) for 4WD vehicles.

   b. Upper control arm bolts — 105 ft. lbs. (142 Nm).

   c. Lower control arm bolts — 105 ft. lbs. (142 Nm).

d. Stabilizer bar bolts — 19 ft. lbs. (25 Nm).

STEERING

Steering Wheel

REMOVAL AND INSTALLATION

1. Disconnect the negative battery cable.

2. Position the wheels in a straight-ahead position.

3. Remove the steering wheel center cover, some vehicles use a screw to retain the cover.

4. Disconnect the horn wire. Matchmark the wheel and the shaft.

5. Using an appropriate wheel puller tool 0960920011 or equivalent, remove the steering wheel.

6. Installation is the reverse of the removal procedure. Tighten the steering wheel nut to 25 ft. lbs. (34 Nm).

Steering Column

REMOVAL AND INSTALLATION

1. Disconnect the negative battery cable.

2. Remove the instrument panel and steering column finish panels.

3. Disconnect all electrical connectors from the column.

4. Remove the lower joint protectors, if equipped.

5. Remove the pinch bolt and nut from the intermediate shaft or flex joint. Disconnect the intermediate shaft from the column shaft or disconnect the flex joint from the steering gear.

6. Remove the column bracket-to-instrument panel nuts.

7. Remove the floor boot retainers and pull the boot away from the floor.

8. Remove the column from the vehicle. Do not hammer on the shaft.

To install:

9. Install the column into the vehicle. Make sure the plastic retainers are properly aligned. Torque the column-to-instrument panel nuts to 18 ft. lbs. (25 Nm).

10. Install the floor boot and retainers. Make sure the boot is sealed from water. Use sealer between the floor and boot.

11. Connect the intermediate shaft to the column shaft or connect the flex joint to the steering gear. Install the pinch bolt and nut to the intermediate shaft or flex joint. Torque the bolt to 26 ft. lbs. (35 Nm).

12. Install the lower joint protectors, if equipped.

13. Connect all electrical connectors to the column.

14. Install the instrument panel and steering column finish panels.

15. Connect the negative battery cable and check operation.

Manual Steering Gear

ADJUSTMENT

Pick-Up and 4Runner

1. Install a special socket 0961600010 or equivalent, and inch lbs. torque wrench on the worm shaft.

2. Turn the adjusting screw while measuring the preload. It should be 6.9–9.5 inch lbs. (0.8–1.1 Nm).

3. Install the locknut and torque to 34 ft. lbs. (46 Nm).

REMOVAL AND INSTALLATION

2WD Pick-Up

1. Raise and safely support the vehicle. Remove the pitman arm-to-relay rod cotter pin and nut. Separate the relay rod from the pitman arm.

2. Matchmark the flexible steering coupling-to-steering gear, then remove the lock bolt and separate the steering coupling from the steering gear.

3. Remove the steering gear housing mounting bolts and the gear housing.

4. To install, reverse the removal procedures. Torque the housing-to-frame bolts to 48 ft. lbs. (62 Nm), the pitman arm-to-relay rod nut 67 ft. lbs. (93 Nm) and the steering gear-to-coupling yoke to 15–20 ft. lbs. (20–27 Nm).

4WD Pick-Up and 4Runner

1. Raise and safely support the vehicle. Remove the stone shield from the gear housing, if equipped.

2. Matchmark the intermediate shaft-to-steering gear and disconnect them.

3. Remove the cotter pin and plug from the drag link.

4. Disconnect the drag link from the pitman arm.

5. Remove the pitman arm nut. Using a puller tool, separate the pitman arm from the steering gear.

6. Remove the steering gear housing-to-frame bolts and the gear housing.

7. To install, reverse the removal procedures. Torque the steering gear-to-frame bolts to 42 ft. lbs. (56 Nm), the steering gear-to-intermediate bolts to 29 ft. lbs. (40 Nm), the pitman arm-to-steering gear nut to 127 ft. lbs. (170 Nm).

NOTE: When installing the drag link to the pitman arm, tighten the plug completely and loosen it 1¹⁄₃ turns.

Land Cruiser

1. Raise and safely support the vehicle. Remove the worm yokes from the worm and the mainshaft.

2. Remove the intermediate shaft assembly.

3. Remove the pitman arm from the sector shaft.

4. Remove the steering gear-to-frame bolts and the steering gear from the vehicle.

5. To install, reverse the removal procedures. Torque the pitman arm to 119–141 ft. lbs. (163–190 Nm).

NOTE: The intermediate shaft must be installed with the wheels in a straight-ahead position and the steering wheel straight-ahead.

Power Steering Gear

ADJUSTMENT

Pick-Up and 4Runner

1. Install a special socket 0961600010 or equivalent, and inch lbs. torque wrench on the worm shaft.

2. Turn the adjusting screw while measuring the preload. It should be 2.6–4.8 inch lbs. (0.3–0.5 Nm).

3. Install the locknut and torque to 34 ft. lbs. (46 Nm).

Previa

1. Loosen the locknut and torque the rack guide spring cap to 18 ft. lbs. (25 Nm).

2. Return the cap 30 degrees.

3. Turn the control valve shaft right and left 1 or 2 times. Loosen the spring cap until the rack guide compression spring is not functioning.

4. Using an inch lbs. torque wrench on the worm shaft, tighten the rack guide cap until the preload is within 6.1–11.3 inch lbs. (0.7–1.3 Nm).

5. Torque the locknut to 41 ft. lbs. (56 Nm).

Land Cruiser

1. Turn the worm shaft in both directions to determine the exact center.

2. Install special socket 0961600010 or equivalent, and an inch lbs. torque wrench to the worm shaft.

3. Turn the adjusting screw while measuring the preload. It should be 6.5–9.5 inch lbs. (0.7–1.1 Nm).

4. Install a new seal and torque the locknut to 34 ft. lbs. (46 Nm).

REMOVAL AND INSTALLATION

2WD Pick-Up

1. Raise and safely support the vehicle. Disconnect and plug the pressure line clamp bolts at the steering gear.

2. Matchmark the intermediate shaft-to-steering gear, then, remove the coupling bolt and separate the intermediate shaft from the steering gear.

3. Remove the pitman arm-to-steering gear and the pitman arm-to-relay rod nuts.

4. Using a puller tool, separate the pitman arm from the relay rod and the pitman arm from the steering gear.

5. Remove the steering gear-to-frame bolts and the steering gear from the vehicle.

6. To install, reverse the removal procedures. Torque the steering gear-to-frame bolts to 48 ft. lbs. (66 Nm), the pitman arm-to-steering gear nut to 90 ft. lbs. (122 Nm), the pitman arm-to-relay rod nut to 67 ft. lbs. (92 Nm), the intermediate shaft-to-steering gear bolt to 19 ft. lbs. and the pressure line nuts to 33 ft. lbs. (45 Nm). Bleed the power steering system.

4WD Pick-Up and 4Runner

1. Remove the battery and the engine lower gravel shield.

2. Raise and safely support the vehicle. Disconnect and plug the pressure lines at the steering gear.

3. Remove the steering gear stone shield.

4. Matchmark the intermediate shaft-to-steering gear, then remove coupling bolt and the intermediate shaft from the steering gear.

5. Remove the pitman arm-to-steering gear nut. Using a puller tool, separate the pitman arm from the steering gear.

6. Remove the gear housing-to-frame bolts and the steering gear from the vehicle.

7. To install, reverse the removal procedures. Torque the steering gear-to-frame bolts to 42 ft. lbs. (57 Nm), the pitman arm-to-steering gear nut to 127 ft. lbs. (172 Nm), the intermediate shaft-to-steering gear bolt to 29 ft. lbs. (41 Nm) and the pressure line union nuts to 33 ft. lbs. (44 Nm). Bleed the power steering system.

Land Cruiser

1. Raise and safely support the vehicle. Disconnect the pressure lines from the steering gear.

2. Remove the intermediate shaft-to-steering gear bolt and the steering column-to-firewall bolts.

3. Loosen the steering column-to-dash bolts. Remove the pitman arm-to-steering gear nut.

4. Using a puller, separate the relay rod from the pitman shaft and the pitman arm from the steering gear.

5. Pull the steering column towards the passenger compartment to uncouple the steering shaft from the steering gear.

6. Remove the steering gear-to-frame bolts and the steering gear from the vehicle.

7. To install, reverse the removal procedures. Torque the steering gear-

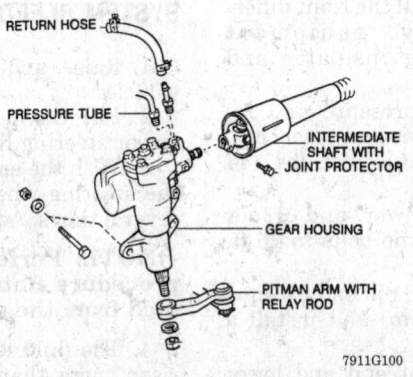

7911G100

Power steering gear assembly — all models

to-frame bolts to 40–63 ft. lbs. (54–86 Nm), the pitman arm-to-steering gear nut to 120–141 ft. lbs. (163–190 Nm), the intermediate shaft-to-steering gear bolt to 22–32 ft. lbs. (29–43 Nm), the pressure hose fitting to 29–36 ft. lbs. (40–48 Nm) and the return hose fitting to 24–30 ft. lbs. (35–41 Nm). Bleed the power steering system.

NOTE: During installation of the hydraulic lines, position each line clear of any surrounding components, then tighten the fittings.

Previa

1. Raise the vehicle and support safely.
2. Disconnect the tie rod ends using a separator tool 0961112010 or equivalent.
3. Place matchmarks on the universal joint and shaft. Remove the lower and upper joint bolts and slide the joint upward to disconnect.
4. Disconnect the pressure and return pipes using flarenut wrenches.
5. On 4WD, remove the front differential assembly, equipment driveshaft housing insulator and drive housing stay.
6. Remove the bracket bolts and grommets. Turn the housing toward the back side and slide the housing to the right side. Put the left tie rod end in the body panel. Pull the housing out through the opening in the left lower side of the body.

To install:

7. Install the gear housing and torque the mounting bolts to 56 ft. lbs. (76 Nm).
8. On 4WD, install the front differential assembly, equipment driveshaft housing insulator and drive housing stay.
9. Connect the pressure and return pipes using flarenut wrenches. Torque the fittings to 33 ft. lbs. (44 Nm).
10. Install the lower and upper joint bolts. Torque the bolts to 26 ft. lbs. (35 Nm).
11. Connect the tie rod ends, torque to 36 ft. lbs. (49 Nm) and install a new cotter pin.
12. Align the front end and lower the vehicle.

Power Steering Pump

REMOVAL AND INSTALLATION

Pick-Up, Land Cruiser and 4Runner

NOTE: Disconnect the air hoses from the air control valve and the high tension wires from the distributor.

1. Disconnect the negative battery cable. Loosen the power steering pump pulley nut.

NOTE: Use the drive belt as a brake to keep the pulley from rotating.

2. Place a container under the pump. Disconnect the return line and the pressure tube, then drain the fluid into the container.
3. Loosen the idler pulley nut and the adjusting bolt, then remove the drive belt.
4. Remove the drive pulley and the Woodruff key from the pump shaft.
5. Remove the mounting bolts and the power steering pump from the vehicle.
6. To install, reverse the removal procedures. Torque the pump pulley mounting bolt to 29 ft. lbs. (40 Nm), the pump pulley nut to 32 ft. lbs. (42 Nm) and the pressure hoses to 33 ft. lbs. (45 Nm). Adjust the drive belt tension. Bleed the power steering system.

BELT ADJUSTMENT

Use a belt tension gauge and make sure the tension is 105 lbs. (140 N) for new or 85 lbs. (115 N) for an old belt. Loosen the air pump mounting and adjust the pump until the proper tension is obtained. Tighten the mounting brackets and check operation.

SYSTEM BLEEDING

1. Raise and safely support the vehicle.
2. Fill the pump reservoir with power steering fluid.
3. With the engine running, rotate the steering wheel from lock to lock several times. Add fluid as necessary.

NOTE: Perform the bleeding procedure until all of the air is bled from the system.

4. The fluid level should not have risen more than 0.2 in.; if it does, check the pump.

Tie Rod Ends

REMOVAL AND INSTALLATION

1. Raise and safely support the vehicle.
2. Remove the wheel and tire assembly. Remove the cotter pin and nut.
3. Using a tie rod end puller, disconnect the tie rod from the relay rod.
4. Using a tie rod end puller remove the tie rod from the steering knuckle.
5. Remove the tie rod end from the vehicle.
6. Installation is the reverse of the removal procedure. Tighten the clamp nuts to 19 ft. lbs. (25 Nm) and the knuckle-to-arm nuts to 67 ft. lbs. (90 Nm). Always install a new cotter pin.

BRAKES

Master Cylinder

REMOVAL AND INSTALLATION

1. Disconnect the negative battery cable. Using a syringe, remove the brake fluid from the master cylinder.
2. Disconnect and plug the hydraulic lines at the master cylinder.
3. If equipped, disconnect the level warning switch connector from the master cylinder.
4. Remove the master cylinder-to-power booster nuts and the master cylinder assembly from the power brake unit.
5. To install, reverse the removal procedures. Torque the master cylinder mounting bolts to 9 ft. lbs. (12 Nm) and the brake lines-to-master cylinder to 11 ft. lbs. (15 Nm). Refill the master cylinder with new brake fluid and bleed the brake system.

Load Sensing Proportioning Valve

REMOVAL AND INSTALLATION

1. Raise and safely support the vehicle, so it is level.
2. Disconnect the No. 2 shackle from the bracket.
3. Disconnect and plug the brake lines from the load sensing valve.

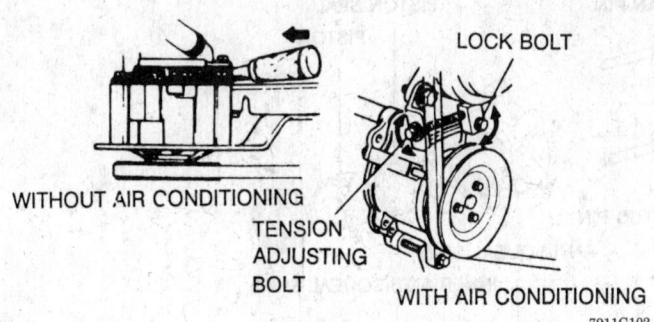

WITHOUT AIR CONDITIONING

LOCK BOLT

TENSION ADJUSTING BOLT

WITH AIR CONDITIONING

7911G102

Drive belt adjustment

4. Remove the load sensing valve bracket from the frame.

5. To install, reverse the removal procedures. Torque the load sensing valve-to-frame bolts to 14 ft. lbs. (18 Nm) and the brake tubes to 11 ft. lbs. (15 Nm). Bleed the brake system.

ADJUSTMENT

Except Previa

1. Adjust the load sensing valve and the rear axle load.

2. Check and/or adjust the length of the No. 2 shackle for distance from the center of the No. 2 shackle-to-shackle bracket bolt to the center of the No. 1 shackle-to-spring bolt, 3.07 in. for 2WD Pick-Up and Land Cruiser, 4.72 in. for 4WD Pick-Up and 4Runner or 1.18 in. for Previa.

3. Shortening the **A** length raises the pressure to the rear brakes and lengthening lowers the pressure. One turn will adjust the pressure to the rear brakes 28–51 psi (196–353 kPa).

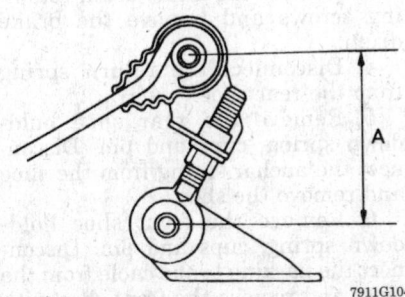

7911G104

Load sensing proportioning valve adjustment — Except Previa

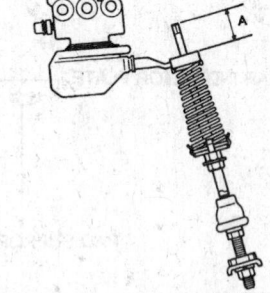

7911G105

Load sensing proportioning valve adjustment — Previa

Power Brake Booster

REMOVAL AND INSTALLATION

1. Disconnect the negative battery cable. Separate the master cylinder from the power brake booster.

2. Remove the vacuum hose form the power brake booster.

3. Working under the instrument panel, remove the brake pedal-to-brake booster rod clevis pin. Remove the power brake booster mounting bolts and the booster from the vehicle.

4. To install, reverse the removal procedures. Torque the power brake booster nuts to 9 ft. lbs. (12 Nm).

5. Adjust the length of the booster pushrod. Install the master cylinder gasket on the booster. Set the measurement tool 0973700010 or equivalent, so the pin slightly touches the piston.

6. Turn the tool upside down and measure the clearance between the

booster pushrod and pin head. The clearance should be **0**.

NOTE: When installing a new booster, make sure there is a little clearance between the pushrod end and the master cylinder piston.

Brake Caliper

REMOVAL AND INSTALLATION

1. Raise and safely support the vehicle.

2. Remove the wheel and tire assembly.

3. Remove the 2 wire clips at the ends of the brake pad pins.

4. Pull out the pads and anti-rattle springs.

5. Lift out the anti squeal shims.

6. Plug the vent hole on the master cylinder cap, to prevent fluid leakage. Disconnect and plug the brake line from the caliper.

7. Remove the 2 caliper mounting bolts and remove the caliper.

To install:

8. Position the caliper and install the mounting bolts. Tighten the caliper mounting bolts to 18 ft. lbs. (25 Nm) on Previa, 29 ft. lbs. (41 Nm) on 2WD vehicles or to 90 ft. lbs. (122 Nm) on 4WD vehicles.

9. Install the brake pads. Install the wheel and tire assembly and lower the vehicle.

10. Road test the vehicle.

Disc Brake Pads

REMOVAL AND INSTALLATION

2WD Vehicle

1. Raise and safely support the vehicle.

2. Remove the wheel and tire assembly.

3. Remove the bottom caliper retaining bolt and loosen the top bolt.

4. Pivot the caliper upward and suspend it with wire, do not disconnect the brake line.

5. Remove the anti-squeal springs, brake pads, anti-squeal shims, wear indicator plates and the 4 pad support plates.

6. Installation is the reverse of the removal procedure. Compress the caliper piston into the bore using a C-clamp. Torque the caliper bolts to 29 ft. lbs. (39 Nm).

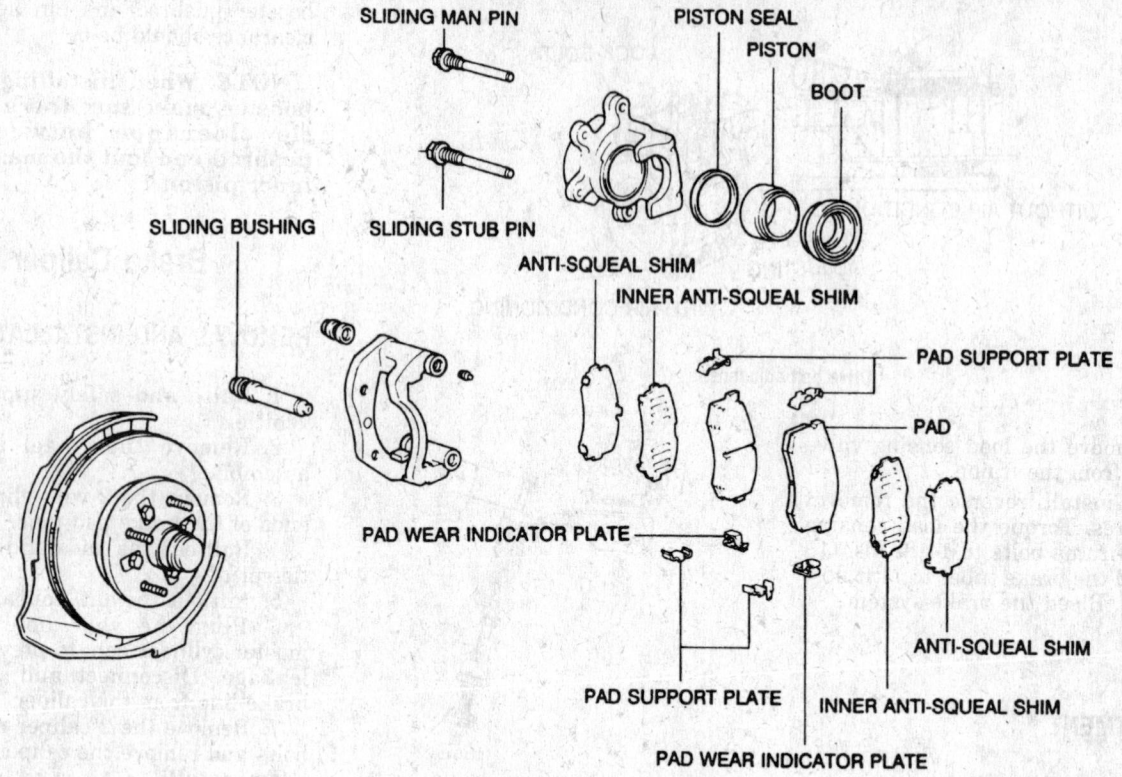

SLIDING MAN PIN PISTON SEAL PISTON BOOT
SLIDING BUSHING SLIDING STUB PIN
ANTI-SQUEAL SHIM INNER ANTI-SQUEAL SHIM
PAD SUPPORT PLATE PAD
ANTI-SQUEAL SHIM INNER ANTI-SQUEAL SHIM
PAD WEAR INDICATOR PLATE
PAD SUPPORT PLATE
PAD WEAR INDICATOR PLATE

7911G106

Front brake assembly — typical 2WD vehicle

4WD Vehicle

1. Raise and safely support the vehicle.

2. Remove the wheel and tire assembly.

3. Remove the brake pad retaining clips, 2 locating pins, anti-rattle spring, brake pads and anti-squeal shims.

4. Installation is the reverse of the removal procedure. Compress the caliper piston into the bore using a C-clamp. Torque the caliper bolt to 27 ft. lbs. (36 Nm).

Brake Rotor

REMOVAL AND INSTALLATION

1. Raise and safely support the vehicle.

2. Remove the wheels and tires.

3. Remove the caliper and brake pads. Hang from the suspension with a wire.

4. Remove the brake torque plate.

5. On 2WD vehicles except Previa, remove the grease cap, cotter pin and nut from the hub.

6. On 4WD vehicles, remove the bolt retaining the locking hub assembly and lift it off the hub. Remove the

nuts and washer from the inside of the hub.

7. Remove the rotor from the vehicle. Be careful not to drop the bearings from the hub.

To install:

8. Install the rotor. Be careful not to drop the bearings from the hub.

9. On 4WD vehicles, install the hub bolts.

10. On 2WD vehicles, install the grease cap, cotter pin and nut to the hub. Adjust the bearing preload.

11. Install the brake torque plate and torque the bolts to 77 ft. lbs. (104 Nm).

12. Install the caliper and brake pads.

13. Install the wheels and tires.

14. Bleed the brake system.

Brake Drums

REMOVAL AND INSTALLATION

1. Raise and safely support the vehicle.

2. Remove the wheel and tire assemblies.

3. Remove the brake drum retaining screws.

4. Remove the drum from the vehicle. If the drum is difficult to re-

move, release the brake adjusters from behind the drum.

5. Install the drum on the vehicle and install the retaining screws.

6. Install the wheel and tire assemblies.

7. Lower the vehicle. Check the operation of the brakes and adjust as needed.

Brake Shoes

REMOVAL AND INSTALLATION

1. Raise and safely support the vehicle.

2. Remove the wheel and tire assemblies.

3. Remove the brake drum retaining screws and remove the brake drum.

4. Disconnect the return spring from the rear shoe.

5. Remove the rear shoe hold-down spring, cups and pin. Disconnect the anchor spring from the shoe and remove the shoe.

6. Remove the front shoe hold-down spring, cups and pin. Disconnect the parking brake cable from the lever and remove the front shoe with the adjuster.

7. Remove the adjuster from the front shoe.

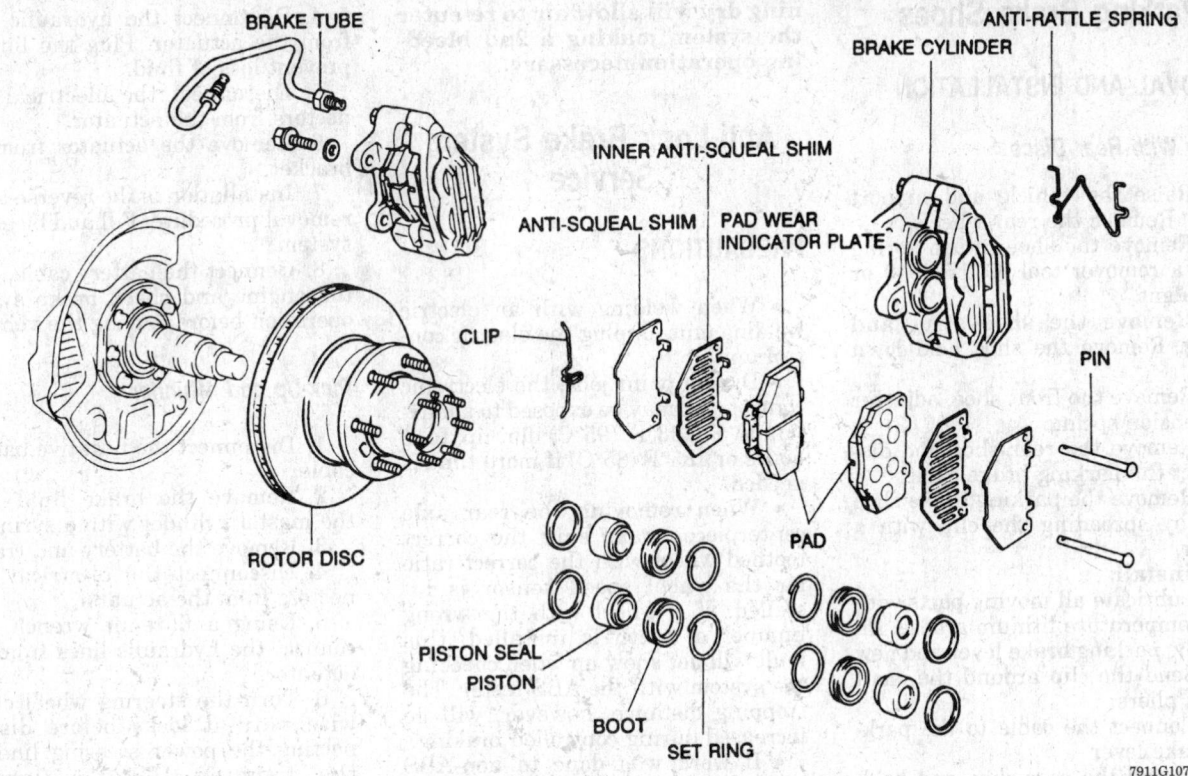

Front brake assembly — typical 4WD vehicle

8. Installation is the reverse of the removal procedure.

9. Adjust the brake shoes after the drum is installed. Once the vehicle is lowered, pump the brakes several times to seat the shoes.

Wheel Cylinder

REMOVAL AND INSTALLATION

1. Raise and safely support the vehicle.

2. Remove the wheel and tire assemblies.

3. Remove the brake drum and the brake shoes.

4. Disconnect and plug the brake line from the wheel cylinder.

5. Remove the wheel cylinder mounting bolts and remove the wheel cylinder from the vehicle.

6. Installation is the reverse of the removal procedure. Torque the mounting bolts to 7 ft. lbs. (10 Nm).

7. Bleed the brake system after installation.

Parking Brake Cable

ADJUSTMENT

2WD Pick-Up

1. Working under the vehicle, tighten the adjusting nut at the equalizer until the travel is within limits and there is no drag at the rear shoes.

2. Apply the parking brake several times and again check that there is no drag with the brake released.

4WD Pick-Up and 4Runner

1. Working under the vehicle, tighten the bellcrank stopper screw until the play at the rear brake links is gone, then loosen the nut 1 full turn. Tighten the locknut.

2. Tighten 1 of the adjusting nuts on the intermediate lever while loosening the other, until the travel is correct. Tighten the locknuts.

3. Confirm that the bellcrank is in contact with the backing plate.

Previa

REAR DRUMS

1. Raise and safely support the rear of the vehicle.

2. Remove the shift knob and the console box.

3. At the parking brake handle, loosen the cable locknut. Pull the hand brake upward about 4–5 clicks.

4. Turn the adjust nut until the rear wheels can no longer be turned, then, tighten the locknut.

5. Install the console and the shift knob.

REAR DISCS

1. Raise the vehicle and support safely. Remove the rear wheel.

2. Temporarily install lug nuts and remove the plug hole in the rotor.

3. Turn the adjuster and expand the shoes until the rotor disc locks.

4. Back off the adjuster 8 notches and install the hole plug.

5. Make sure there is no excessive drag on the parking brake.

6. Install the wheel and lower the vehicle.

7. Loosen the 2 adjusting nuts under the vehicle and adjust the parking brake No. 1 cable until the parking brake lever clicks 4–5 times.

Parking Brake Shoes

REMOVAL AND INSTALLATION

Previa With Rear Discs

1. Raise the vehicle and support safely. Remove the rear wheels.
2. Remove the shoe return spring using a remover tool 0971720010 or equivalent.
3. Remove the shoe strut and spring. Remove the shoe hold-down cups.
4. Remove the front shoe, adjuster and tension spring.
5. Remove the rear shoe and disconnect the parking brake cable.
6. Remove the parking brake shoe lever by spreading the clip with a prybar.

To install:

7. Lubricate all moving parts with high temperature lithium grease. Install the parking brake lever and new clip. Bend the clip around the shaft with a pliers.
8. Connect the cable to the parking brake lever.
9. Install the rear shoe and hold-down.
10. Install the front shoe, tension spring and adjuster.
11. Install the strut with spring and shoe return springs.
12. Install the rotor and remaining components.
13. Adjust the parking brake and lower the vehicle.

Bleeding the Brake System

1. Fill reservoir to the maximum fill mark.
2. Bleed the brakes in the following sequence: right rear, left rear, right front, left front and load sensing proportioning valve.
3. Attach a bleed hose to the caliper or wheel cylinder being bled, immerse the end of the bleed hose in a glass container partially filled with brake fluid.
4. Have a helper apply brake pedal to pressurize the system. Open the bleed screw ½ turn. Close the bleed screw when the fluid entering the glass container is free of bubbles.
5. Check the reservoir fluid level and add fluid to the **MAX** fill mark.
6. Repeat bleeding operations at remaining wheels.

NOTE: Do not allow the master cylinder reservoir to run dry while bleeding the brakes. Run- ning dry will allow air to re-enter the system making a 2nd bleeding operation necessary.

Anti-Lock Brake System Service

PRECAUTIONS

- When welding with an electric welding unit, unplug the electric control unit.
- During paint jobs, the electronic control unit may be exposed to a maximum of 203°F (95°C) for up to 2 hours or 185°F (85°C) if more time is needed.
- When removing the rear axle centerpiece, make sure the correct toothed wheel with the correct ratio for the wheel speed sensor is installed. If a wheel with the wrong number of teeth is installed, this fault will not show up when checking the system with the ABS tester. The stopping distance, however, will be increased during controlled braking.
- If work was done to non-ABS brake components, a simple operational test will be sufficient. This means that after driving about 5 mph, the warning light on the instrument panel should go out if the ABS system is intact.
- If ABS components have been replaced, the entire system should be checked using the appropriate tester in combination with brake test bench or an adaptor in combination with a multimeter.

RELIEVING ANTI-LOCK BRAKE SYSTEM PRESSURE

Pump the brake pedal at least 20 times with the ignition key in the **OFF** position. Place a shop rag around the hydraulic line fitting and wear safety glasses when disconnecting the hydraulic lines.

Anti-Lock Brake Actuator

REMOVAL AND INSTALLATION

Previa

1. Disconnect the negative battery cable.
2. Remove the brake fluid from the master cylinder with a syringe.
3. Remove the plastic cover from the actuator.

4. Disconnect the hydraulic lines from the actuator. Plug the lines to prevent loss of fluid.
5. Disconnect the electrical connectors from the actuator.
6. Remove the actuator from the bracket.
7. Installation is the reverse of the removal procedure. Fill and bleed the system.
8. Connect the battery cable, start the engine and check brake system operation before driving the vehicle.

Pick-Up and 4Runner

1. Disconnect the negative battery cable.
2. Remove the brake fluid from the master cylinder with a syringe.
3. Remove the battery and tray.
4. Disconnect the electrical connectors from the actuator.
5. Using a flarenut wrench, disconnect the hydraulic lines from the actuator.
6. Turn the steering wheel clockwise until it locks before disconnecting the power steering lines at the actuator. Using a flarenut wrench, disconnect the power steering lines from the actuator.
7. Remove the actuator and bracket.

To install:

8. Install the actuator and torque the bolts to 21 ft. lbs. (28 Nm).
9. Connect the hydraulic lines and torque to 11 ft. lbs. (15 Nm) and the power steering lines to 34 ft. lbs. (47 Nm).
10. Connect the electrical connectors and install the remaining components.
11. Bleed the brake system.

ABS Electronic Control Unit (ECU)

REMOVAL AND INSTALLATION

1. Disconnect the negative battery cable.
2. On Pick-up and 4Runner, remove the glove compartment assembly, disconnect the ECU and remove. The unit is located above the engine ECU.
3. On Previa, remove the audio power amplifier, if equipped.
4. Remove the ABS ECU and disconnect the wiring.
5. Installation is the reverse of removal.

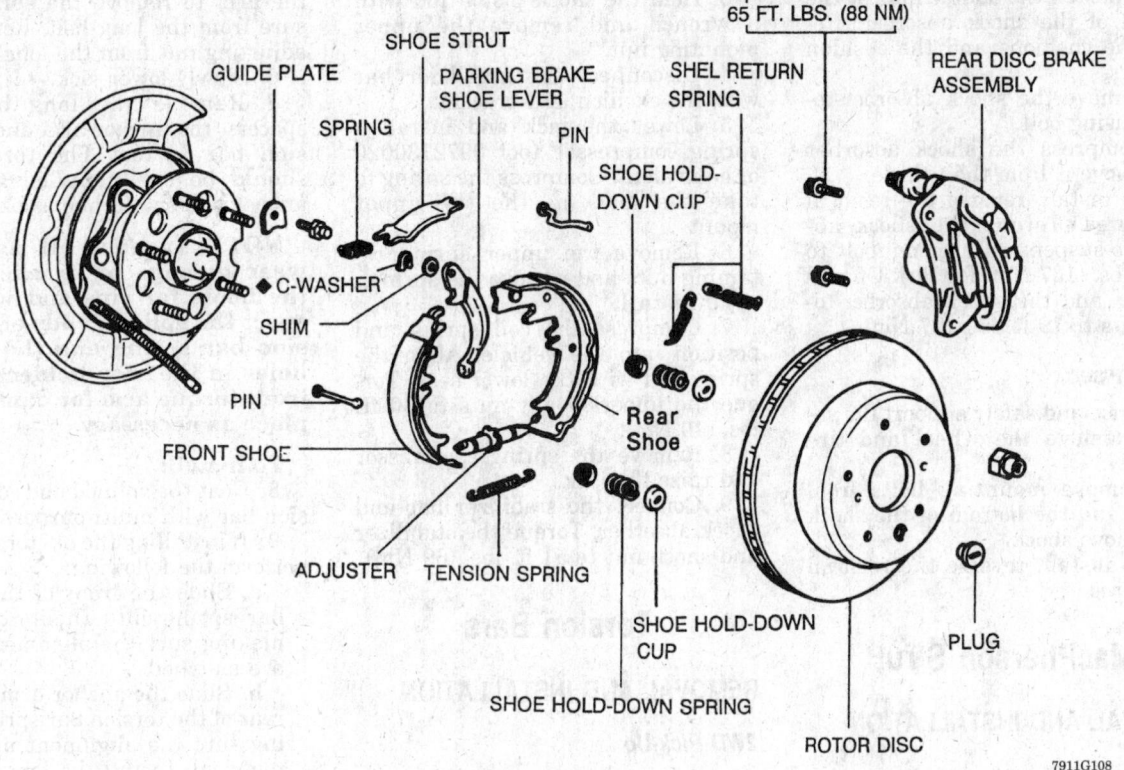

65 FT. LBS. (88 NM)

GUIDE PLATE
SHOE STRUT
PARKING BRAKE SHOE LEVER
SHEL RETURN SPRING
REAR DISC BRAKE ASSEMBLY
SPRING
PIN
SHOE HOLD-DOWN CUP
◆ C-WASHER
SHIM
Rear Shoe
PIN
FRONT SHOE
ADJUSTER
TENSION SPRING
SHOE HOLD-DOWN CUP
SHOE HOLD-DOWN SPRING
ROTOR DISC
PLUG

7911G108

Parking brake shoes — Previa with rear disc brakes

ANTI-LOCK BRAKE SYSTEM BLEEDING

Previa

Use the conventional brake system bleeding procedure.

Pick-Up and 4Runner

Use the conventional brake system bleeding procedure unless the power steering hoses are disconnected from the brake actuator.

1. Bleed the power steering system using the conventional method.
2. Bleed the brake system with the engine running.
3. Bleed the brake system with the engine not running.
4. Disconnect the connector from the actuator and solenoid relay.
5. Connect an actuator tester tool 0999000150 and 0999099205 or equivalent, to the actuator solenoid relay and body side of the wiring harness through a sub-wire.
6. Connect the red cable of the tester to the battery positive terminal and the black wire to the negative terminal.
7. Start the engine and run at idle.
8. Turn the selector switch on the tester to **AIR BLEED**.

9. Strongly depress the brake pedal and hold.
10. Push **ON** and release the ON/OFF switch, 3 seconds each for 5 times.
11. Release the switch and brake pedal.
12. Check the power steering fluid level and add Dexron®II fluid.
13. Remove the tester and reconnect the actuator and solenoid.

TO BODY
ACTUATOR
SST
SOLENOID RELAY
TO BODY
SUB WIRE HARNESS (SST)

7911G109

Brake system bleeding when the power steering system is disconnected at the actuator — Pick-Up and 4Runner with ABS

FRONT SUSPENSION

Shock Absorbers

REMOVAL AND INSTALLATION

2WD Pick-Up

1. Raise and safely support the vehicle. Remove the wheel and tire assembly.
2. Unfasten the double nuts at the top end of the shock absorber. Remove the cushions and the cushion retainers.
3. Remove the shock absorber-to-lower control arm bolts.
4. Compress the shock absorber and remove it from the vehicle.
5. To install, reverse the removal procedures. Torque the shock absorber-to-lower control arm bolts to 13 ft. lbs. (18 Nm) and the shock absorber-to-body nuts to 19 ft. lbs. (26 Nm).

4WD Pick-Up and 4Runner

1. Raise and safely support the vehicle. Remove the wheel and tire assembly.

2. Unfasten the double nuts at the top end of the shock absorber. Remove the cushions and the cushion retainers.

3. Remove the shock absorber-to-axle housing bolt.

4. Compress the shock absorber and remove it from the vehicle.

5. To install, reverse the removal procedures. Torque the shock absorber-to-suspension arm nut/bolt to 101 ft. lbs. (137 Nm) for Pick-Up and 4Runner and the shock absorber-to-body nuts to 19 ft. lbs. (27 Nm).

Land Cruiser

1. Raise and safely support the vehicle. Remove the wheel and tire assembly.

2. Remove mounting bolts from the top and the bottom of the shock and remove shock.

3. To install, reverse the removal procedures.

MacPherson Strut

REMOVAL AND INSTALLATION

Previa

1. Raise the vehicle and support safely.

2. Remove the halfshaft cotter pin and nut for 4WD only.

3. Disconnect the brake hose from the strut by removing the clips.

4. Loosen the 2 strut-to-knuckle bolts, do not remove.

5. Remove the stabilizer bar from the strut.

6. Remove the 3 upper strut mount nuts and remove the strut from the vehicle.

To install:

7. Install the strut and torque the upper nuts to 47 ft. lbs. (64 Nm).

8. Install the strut-to-knuckle bolts and torque to 231 ft. lbs. (314 Nm).

9. Install the stabilizer bar and torque the bolt to 76 ft. lbs. (103 Nm).

10. Install the halfshaft nut and torque to 136 ft. lbs. (187 Nm). Install a new cotter pin.

11. Install the remaining components and align the front end.

Coil Springs

REMOVAL AND INSTALLATION

Land Cruiser

1. Raise the vehicle and support the body and frame.

2. Raise the front axle assembly.

3. Hold the shock piston rod with a wrench and remove the upper mounting nut.

4. Disconnect the stabilizer bar with the cushion and bracket.

5. Lower the jack and install a spring compressor tool 0972730020 or equivalent. Compress the spring to take the load off the the upper mount.

6. Remove the upper spring retaining nuts and remove the spring.

To install:

7. Compress the coil spring and position into the vehicle. Align the spring end with the lower seat. Torque the upper mount nuts to 30 ft. lbs. (40 Nm).

8. Remove the spring compressor and raise the jack.

9. Connect the stabilizer bar and shock absorber. Torque the stabilizer and shock nut to 51 ft. lbs. (69 Nm).

Torsion Bars

REMOVAL AND INSTALLATION

2WD Pick-Up

The vehicles are equipped with torsion bar front springs.

NOTE: Great care must be taken to make sure springs are not mixed after removal. It is strongly suggested that before removal, each spring be marked with paint, showing front and rear of spring and from which side of the vehicle it was taken. If the springs are installed backwards or on the wrong sides of the vehicle, they could fracture. If replacing the springs, it is not necessary to mark them.

1. Raise and safely support the front of the vehicle.

2. Slide the boot from the rear of torsion bar spring, then paint an alignment mark from the torsion bar spring onto the anchor arm and the torque arm. There are right and left identification marks on the rear end of the torsion bar springs.

3. On the rear torsion bar spring holder, there is a long bolt that passes through the arm of the holder and up through the frame crossmember. Remove the locking nut only from this bolt.

4. Using a small ruler, measure the length from the bottom of the remaining nut to the threaded tip of the bolt and record this measurement.

5. Place a jack under the rear torsion bar spring holder arm and raise

the arm to remove the spring pressure from the long bolt. Remove the adjusting nut from the long bolt.

6. Slowly lower jack.

7. Remove the long bolt, the spacers, the anchor arm and the torsion bar spring. The torsion bar should be easily pulled from the anchor and the torque arms.

NOTE: Inspect all parts for wear damage or cracks. Check the boots for rips and wear. Inspect the splined ends of the torsion bar spring and the splined holes in the rear holder and the front torque arm for damage. Replace as necessary.

To install:

8. Coat the splined ends of the torsion bar with multi-purpose grease.

9. If installing the old torsion bars, perform the following:

a. Slide the front of the torsion bar spring into the torque arm, making sure the alignment marks are matched.

b. Slide the anchor arm onto the rear of the torsion bar spring, making sure the alignment marks are matched. Install the long bolt and it's spacers.

c. Tighten the adjusting nut so it is the same length as it was before removal.

NOTE: Do not install the locknut.

10. When installing a new torsion bar spring, perform the following:

a. Raise the front of the vehicle, replace the wheel and tire assembly, place a wooden block (7½ in. high) under the front tire. Lower the jack until the clearance between the spring bumper (on the lower control arm) and the frame is ½ in.

b. Slide the front of the torsion bar spring into the torque arm.

c. Install the anchor arm into the rear of the torsion bar spring, then the long bolt and the spacers. the distance from the top of the upper spacer to the tip of the threaded end of bolt is 0.310–1.100 in. for ½ ton vehicles or 0.430–1.220 in. for ¾ ton vehicles.

NOTE: Make sure the bolt and bottom spacer are snugly in the holder arm while measuring.

d. Remove the wooden block and lower the vehicle until it rests on the jackstands.

e. Install and tighten the adjusting nut until the distance from the bottom of the nut to the tip of the

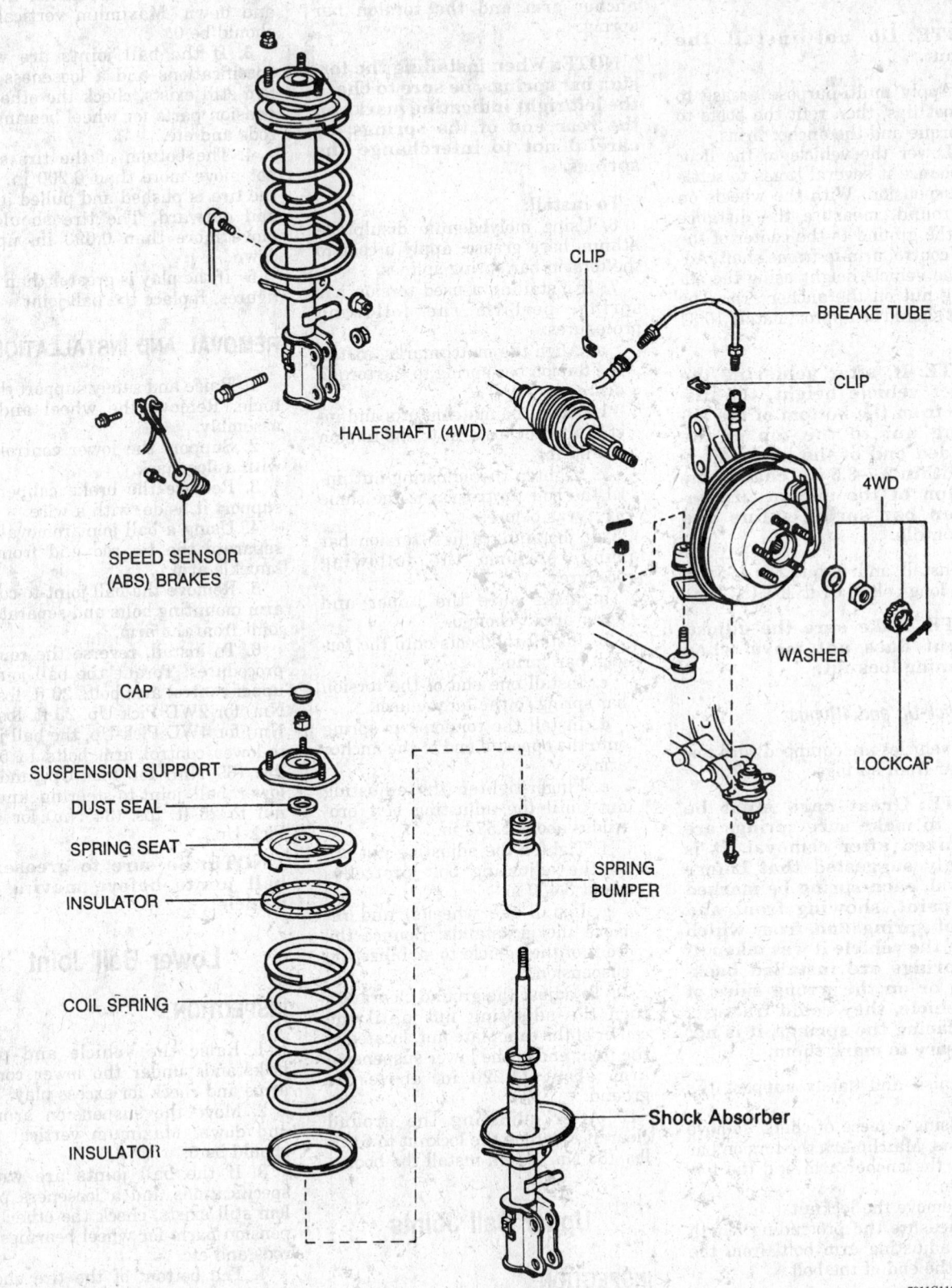

CLIP

BREAKE TUBE

CLIP

HALFSHAFT (4WD)

4WD

SPEED SENSOR
(ABS) BRAKES

WASHER

CAP

SUSPENSION SUPPORT

DUST SEAL

SPRING SEAT

INSULATOR

LOCKCAP

SPRING
BUMPER

COIL SPRING

Shock Absorber

INSULATOR

7911G110

Front suspension components — Previa

threaded end of the bolt is 2.7–3.5 in.

NOTE: Do not install the locknut.

11. Apply multi-purpose grease to the boot lips, then refit the boots to the torque and the anchor arms.

12. Lower the vehicle to the floor and bounce it several times to settle the suspension. With the wheels on the ground, measure the distance from the ground to the center of the lower control arm-to-frame shaft. Adjust the vehicle height using the adjusting nut on the anchor arm. The height should be approximately 10.31 in.

NOTE: If, after achieving the correct vehicle height, the distance from the bottom of the adjusting nut to the top of the threaded end of the long bolt is not within 2.7–3.5 in., change the position of the anchor arm-to-tension bar spring spline and reassemble.

13. Install and torque the locknut on the long bolt to 61 ft. lbs. (83 Nm).

NOTE: Make sure the adjusting nut does not move when tightening locknut.

4WD Pick-Up and 4Runner

These vehicles are equipped with torsion bar front springs.

NOTE: Great care must be taken to make sure springs are not mixed after removal. It is strongly suggested that before removal, each spring be marked with paint, showing front and rear of spring and from which side of the vehicle it was taken. If the springs are installed backwards or on the wrong sides of the vehicle, they could fracture. If replacing the springs, it is not necessary to mark them.

1. Raise and safely support the vehicle.

2. Using a piece of chalk, remove the boots. Matchmark the torsion bar spring, the anchor arm and the torque arm.

3. Remove the locknut.

4. Measure the protruding length of the adjusting arm bolt, from the nut to the end of the bolt.

NOTE: The adjusting arm bolt measurement is used as a reference to establish the chassis ground clearance.

5. Remove the adjusting nut, the anchor arm and the torsion bar spring.

NOTE: When installing the torsion bar springs, be sure to check the left/right indicating marks on the rear end of the springs; be careful not to interchange the springs.

To install:

6. Using molybdenum disulphide lithium base grease, apply a coat to the torsion bar spring splines.

7. If installing a used torsion bar spring, perform the following procedures:

 a. Align the matchmarks, install the torsion bar spring to the torque arm.

 b. Align the matchmarks and install the anchor arm to the torsion bar spring.

 c. Tighten the adjusting nut until the bolt protrusion is the same as it was before.

8. If installing a new torsion bar spring, perform the following procedures:

 a. Make sure the upper and lower arms rebound.

 b. Install the boots onto the torsion bar spring.

 c. Install one end of the torsion bar spring to the torque arm.

 d. Install the torsion bar spring onto the opposite end of the anchor arm.

 e. Finger-tighten the adjusting nut until the adjusting bolt protrudes about 1.570 in.

 f. Tighten the adjusting nut until the adjusting bolt protrudes about 3.430 in.

 g. Install the wheel(s) and remove the jackstands. Bounce the front of the vehicle to stabilize the suspension.

9. To adjust the ground clearance, turn the adjusting nut until the center of the cam plate nut, located of the front end of the lower suspension arm, about 11.220 in. above the ground.

10. After adjusting the ground clearance, torque the locknut to 61 ft. lbs. (83 Nm), then, install the boots.

Upper Ball Joints

INSPECTION

1. Raise the vehicle and place jackstands under the lower control arms and check for excess play.

2. Move the suspension arm up and down. Maximum vertical play should be 0.

3. If the ball joints are within specifications and a looseness problem still exists, check the other suspension parts for wheel bearings, tie rods and etc.

4. The bottom of the tire should not move more than 0.200 in. when the tire is pushed and pulled inward and outward. The tire should not move more than 0.090 in. up and down.

5. If the play is greater than these figures, replace the ball joint.

REMOVAL AND INSTALLATION

1. Raise and safely support the vehicle. Remove the wheel and tire assembly.

2. Support the lower control arm with a floor jack.

3. Remove the brake caliper and support it aside, with a wire.

4. Using a ball joint removal tool, separate the tie rod end from the knuckle arm.

5. Remove the ball joint-to-control arm mounting bolts and separate the joint from the arm.

6. To install, reverse the removal procedures. Torque the ball joint-to-upper control arm bolts 20 ft. lbs. (27 Nm) for 2WD Pick-Up, 25 ft. lbs. (34 Nm) for 4WD Pick-Up, the ball joint-to-lower control arm bolts to 51 ft. lbs. (69 Nm) for Pick-Up, and the lower ball joint-to-steering knuckle nut to 25 ft. lbs. (34 Nm) for 4WD Pick-Up.

NOTE: Be sure to grease the ball joints before moving the vehicle.

Lower Ball Joint

INSPECTION

1. Raise the vehicle and place jackstands under the lower control arms and check for excess play.

2. Move the suspension arm up and down. Maximum vertical play should be 0.

3. If the ball joints are within specifications and a looseness problem still exists, check the other suspension parts for wheel bearings, tie rods and etc.

4. The bottom of the tire should not move more than 0.200 in. when the tire is pushed and pulled inward and outward. The tire should not move more than 0.090 in. up and down.

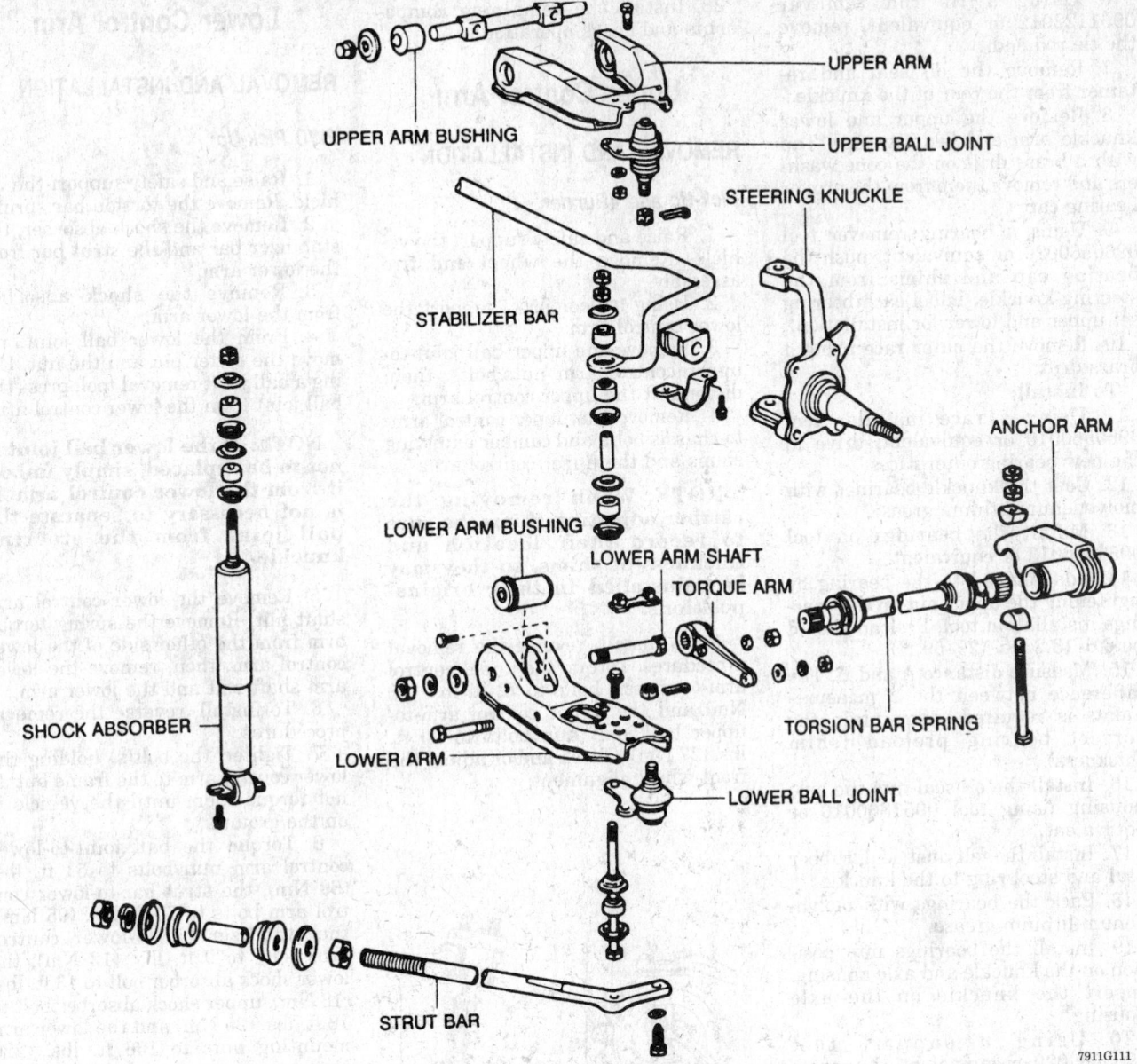

UPPER ARM

UPPER ARM BUSHING

UPPER BALL JOINT

STEERING KNUCKLE

STABILIZER BAR

ANCHOR ARM

LOWER ARM BUSHING

LOWER ARM SHAFT

TORQUE ARM

SHOCK ABSORBER

TORSION BAR SPRING

LOWER ARM

LOWER BALL JOINT

STRUT BAR

7911G111

Front suspension components — 2WD vehicle

5. If the play is greater than these figures, replace the ball joint.

REMOVAL AND INSTALLATION

1. Raise and safely support the vehicle. Remove the wheel and tire assembly.
2. Support the lower control arm with a floor jack.
3. Remove the brake caliper and support it aside, with a wire.
4. Using a ball joint removal tool, separate the tie rod end from the knuckle arm.
5. Using a ball joint removal tool, separate the upper ball joint from the steering knuckle.

6. Remove the ball joint-to-control arm mounting bolts and separate the joint from the arm.
7. To install, reverse the removal procedures. Torque the ball joint-to-upper control arm bolts 20 ft. lbs. (27 Nm) for 2WD Pick-Up, 25 ft. lbs. (34 Nm) for 4WD Pick-Up, the upper ball joint-to-steering knuckle nut to 80 ft. lbs. (122 Nm) for 2WD Pick-Up or 105 ft. lbs. (140 Nm) for 4WD Pick-Up.

NOTE: Be sure to grease the ball joints before moving the vehicle.

Knuckle Joint Bearings

REMOVAL AND INSTALLATION

Land Cruiser

1. Raise the vehicle and support safely. Remove the front wheels.
2. Remove the caliper, axle hub and rotor.
3. Remove the spindle mounting bolts, dust seal and cover.
4. Using a brass drift, tap the spindle off the steering knuckle. Tap around the side to dislodge.
5. Position 1 flat part of the outer shaft upward and pull out the axle shaft.

6. Using a tie rod remover 0961122012 or equivalent, remove the tie rod end.

7. Remove the oil seal and retainer from the rear of the knuckle.

8. Remove the upper and lower knuckle arm and bearing caps. Tap with a brass drift on the cone washers and remove them from the arm or bearing cap.

9. Using a bearing remover tool 0960660020 or equivalent, push the bearing cap and shims from the steering knuckle. Label each bearing set upper and lower for installation.

10. Remove the outer race using a brass drift.

To install:

11. Using a race installer tool 0960560010 or equivalent, drive in the new bearing outer races.

12. Coat the knuckle bearings with molybdenum lithium grease.

13. Mount the bearings on tool 0963460013 or equivalent.

14. Add preload to the bearing by tightening the upper nut on the bearings installation tool. Preload should be 6.6–13.2 lbs. (29–59 N).

15. Measure distance **A** and **B**. The difference between the 2 measurements is required to maintain the correct bearing preload (shim thickness).

16. Install the oil seal into the axle housing using tool 0951860010 or equivalent.

17. Install the felt dust seal, rubber seal and steel ring to the knuckle.

18. Pack the bearings with molybdenum lithium grease.

19. Install the bearings into position on the knuckle and axle housing. Insert the knuckle on the axle housing.

20. Using a support tool 0960660020 or equivalent, to support the bearings. Install the knuckle over the shims that were originally used or selected in the adjustment operation.

21. Using a hammer, tap the knuckle arm into the bearing inner races.

22. Install the bearing cap over the shims and tap with a hammer.

23. Install the cone washers and torque the nuts to 71 ft. lbs. (96 Nm).

24. Install the tie rod end and torque to 67 ft. lbs. (91 Nm). Install a new cotter pin.

25. Install the seal set to the knuckle.

26. Install the axle shaft and pack with grease.

27. Install the spindle dust cover and axle hub.

28. Install the remaining components and check operation.

Upper Control Arm

REMOVAL AND INSTALLATION

Pick-Up and 4Runner

1. Raise and safely support the vehicle. Remove the wheel and tire assembly.

2. Using a floor jack, support the lower control arm.

3. Remove the upper ball joint-to-upper control arm nuts/bolts, then, disconnect the upper control arm.

4. Remove the upper control arm-to-chassis bolts and camber adjusting shims and the upper control arm.

NOTE: When removing the camber adjusting shims, be sure to record their location and thickness of shims, so they may be reinstalled in their original positions.

5. To install, reverse the removal procedures. Torque the upper control arm-to-chassis bolts to 72 ft. lbs. (96 Nm) and the upper control arm-to-upper ball joint nuts/bolts to 20 ft. lbs. (27 Nm). Check and/or adjust the front wheel alignment.

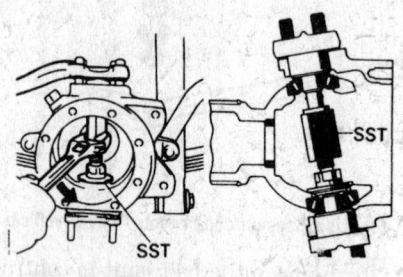

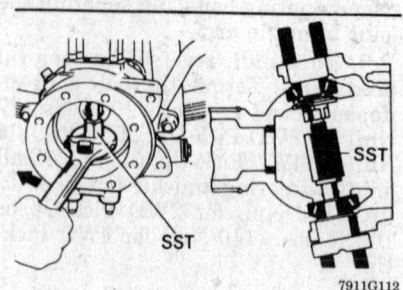

7911G112

Knuckle joint bearings — Land Cruiser

Lower Control Arm

REMOVAL AND INSTALLATION

2WD Pick-Up

1. Raise and safely support the vehicle. Remove the torsion bar spring.

2. Remove the shock absorber, the stabilizer bar and the strut bar from the lower arm.

3. Remove the shock absorber from the lower arm.

4. From the lower ball joint, remove the cotter pin and the nut. Using a ball joint removal tool, press the ball joint from the lower control arm.

NOTE: If the lower ball joint is not to be replaced, simply unbolt it from the lower control arm. It is not necessary to separate the ball joint from the steering knuckle.

5. Remove the lower control arm shaft nut. Remove the spring torque arm from the other side of the lower control arm, then, remove the lower arm shaft bolt and the lower arm.

6. To install, reverse the removal procedures.

7. Tighten the bolt(s) holding the lower control arm to the frame but do not torque them until the vehicle is on the ground.

8. Torque the ball joint-to-lower control arm nuts/bolts to 51 ft. lbs. (69 Nm), the strut bar-to-lower control arm bolts to 70 ft. lbs. (95 Nm), the stabilizer bar-to-lower control arm bolts to 9 ft. lbs. (12 Nm), the lower shock absorber bolt to 13 ft. lbs. (18 Nm), upper shock absorber bolt to 18 ft. lbs. (25 Nm) and the lower arm mounting nuts to 166 ft. lbs. (220 Nm).

9. Check and/or adjust the front end alignment.

NOTE: Do not torque the control arm bolts fully until the vehicle is lowered and bounced several times; if the bolts are tightened with the control arm(s) hanging, excessive bushing wear will result.

4WD Pick-Up and 4Runner

1. Raise and safely support the vehicle. Remove the shock absorber.

2. Disconnect the stabilizer bar from the lower suspension arm.

3. Remove the lower ball joint-to-lower control arm bolts, then, separate the control arm from the ball joint.

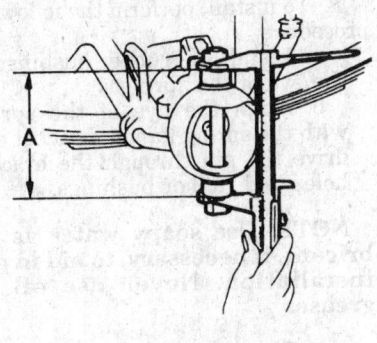

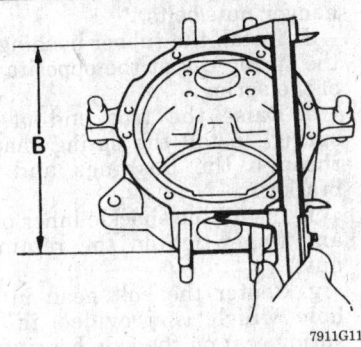

7911G113

Knuckle bearing preload — Land Cruiser

4. Using a piece of chalk, place matchmarks on the front/rear adjusting cams.

5. Remove the nuts and adjusting cams and the lower control arms.

6. To install, reverse the removal procedures. Torque the lower ball joint-to-lower control arm bolts to 20 ft. lbs. (27 Nm), the stabilizer bar-to-lower control arm bolts to 19 ft. lbs. (26 Nm), the shock absorber-to-lower control arm nut/bolt to 101 ft. lbs. (137 Nm).

7. Lower the vehicle to the ground, bounce it a few times, align the matchmarks and torque the adjusting cam nuts to 203 ft. lbs. (270 Nm). Check and/or adjust the front wheel alignment.

Land Cruiser

1. Raise the vehicle and support safely.

2. Support the frame and body. Support the axle assembly with a floor jack.

3. Remove the lower control arm-to-frame bolt.

4. Remove the 2 bolts and nuts from the axle housing and remove the control arm.

To install:

5. Install the control and bolts loosely. Do not tighten at this time.

6. Install the front wheels and lower the vehicle. Bounce the front end to stabilize the front suspension.

7. Torque the retaining bolts to 127 ft. lbs. (171 Nm).

Previa

1. Raise the vehicle and support safely. Remove the front wheel.

2. Remove the under cover and disconnect the lower ball joint from the knuckle.

3. Remove the 2 bolts and lower arm bracket, nut and arm shaft and lower control arm with ball joint.

To install:

4. Install the lower arm and retainers. Do not tighten at this time.

5. Connect the lower ball joint and torque to 94 ft. lbs. (127 Nm).

6. Install the front wheels and lower the vehicle.

7. Bounce the suspension up and down several times.

8. Raise the vehicle and support under the control arms with jackstands.

9. Torque the lower arm retainers to 121 ft. lbs. (164 Nm).

10. Install the remaining components and lower the vehicle.

Sway Bar

REMOVAL AND INSTALLATION

1. Raise the vehicle and support safely.

2. Remove the under covers.

3. Disconnect the sway bar links-to-control arms.

4. Disconnect the sway bar-to-frame bolts and remove the sway bar.

5. Installation is the reverse of removal. torque the frame bracket bolts to 14 ft. lbs. (19 Nm) and the link nuts to 76 ft. lbs. (103 Nm).

Front Wheel Bearings

REMOVAL AND INSTALLATION

NOTE: This procedure applies to RWD vehicles only. Refer to drive axle instructions for 4WD vehicles.

Pick-Up

1. Raise the vehicle and support safely. Remove the front wheel.

2. Remove the brake caliper and suspend with a wire.

3. Remove the bearing cap, cotter pin, nut and outer bearing. Do not drop the bearing.

4. Remove the rotor/hub assembly.

5. Pry the inner grease seal from the hub and remove the inner bearing.

6. Clean the grease from the hub using shop rags and compressed air. Do not use solvent to remove grease.

7. Using a brass drift and hammer, drive out the bearing outer races. Do not use old races with new bearings.

NOTE: Grind the outer circumference of the old bearing race with a grinder. Use this race to press in the new race.

8. Install the outer race into the hub using a press. If the new race gets damaged, replace with a new one.

9. Pack the bearings with high temperature bearing grease and install inner bearing.

10. Install the grease seal with tool 0960804100 or equivalent.

11. Install the rotor, outer bearing, washer, nut and nut lock.

12. Torque the nut to 25 ft. lbs. (34 Nm). Loosen the nut until it can be turned by hand.

13. Using a spring tension gauge attached to a lug bolt.

14. Tighten the nut until the bearing preload is 0.9–2.2 lbs. (3.9–9.8 N) for dual wheel vehicles or 1.3–4.0 lbs. (5.9–17.7 N) for single wheel vehicles.

15. Install nut lock, new cotter pin and grease cap.

16. Install the remaining components and check operation.

2WD Previa

1. Remove the steering knuckle from the vehicle. Place the assembly in a vise.

2. Remove the grease cap and locknut. Remove the spacer or speed sensor rotor.

3. Using a hub remover tool (slide hammer) 0952000031 or equivalent, remove the wheel hub from the knuckle.

4. Remove the bearing from the hub using a press and arbor tool 0955010012 or equivalent.

5. Remove the dust protector and oil seal.

6. Remove the bearing snapring from the knuckle and press the inner bearing from the knuckle.

To install:

7. Using a press and arbor tool 0960810010 or equivalent, press the bearing into the knuckle.

8. Install the outer oil seal and dust cover.

9. Press the axle hub onto the knuckle.

10. Install the new nut and torque to 147 ft. lbs. (199 Nm). Stack the nut using a chisel. Install the grease cap.
11. Install the knuckle assembly onto the vehicle.

REAR SUSPENSION

Shock Absorbers

REMOVAL AND INSTALLATION

Pick-Up, 4Runner and Land Cruiser

1. Raise and safely support the vehicle.
2. Remove the upper shock absorber retaining bolts from the upper frame member.
3. Remove the lower end bolt of the shock absorber from the spring seat.
4. Remove the shock absorber from the vehicle.

NOTE: Inspect the shock for wear, leaks or other signs of damage.

5. To install, reverse the removal procedures. Torque the upper bolt to 19 ft. lbs. (25 Nm) for 2WD vehicle or 47 ft. lbs. (63 Nm) for 4WD vehicle and the lower bolt to 19 ft. lbs. (25 Nm) for 2WD vehicle or 47 ft. lbs. (63 Nm) for 4WD vehicle.

Previa

1. Raise the vehicle and support safely.
2. Support the axle housing with a jack.
3. Disconnect the shock from the lower control arm. Hold the shaft with a suitable tool and remove the nut.
4. Remove the upper mount bolt and shock absorber.
To install:
5. Install the shock and torque the upper mount to 27 ft. lbs. (37 Nm) and tighten the lower mount nut until the shaft protrudes 0.0059 in. (1.5mm).
6. Lower the vehicle and check operation.

Coil Spring

REMOVAL AND INSTALLATION

Previa

1. Raise and safely support the vehicle. Support the axle housing with a floor jack. Remove the wheel and tire assembly.
2. Remove the shock absorber-to-axle housing bolt.
3. Remove the stabilizer-to-axle housing bar bushing bracket bolts.
4. Remove the lateral control arm-to-axle housing nut and disconnect the lateral control arm.
5. Lower the floor jack, then remove the coil spring(s) and the insulators.

NOTE: While lowering the axle housing, be careful not to snag the brake line of the parking brake cable.

6. To install, reverse the removal procedures. Torque the shock absorber bolt to 27 ft. lbs. (34 Nm), the lateral control arm-to-axle housing nut to 43 ft. lbs. (60 Nm) and the stabilizer-to-axle housing bolts to 27 ft. lbs. (34 Nm).

NOTE: Before tightening the lateral control arm and the stabilizer nuts/bolts, bounce the vehicle to stabilize the suspension.

Leaf Springs

REMOVAL AND INSTALLATION

1. Raise and safely support the vehicle. Support the axle housing with a floor jack. Remove the wheel and tire assembly.
2. Lower the floor jack to take the tension off the spring. Remove the shock absorber mounting nuts/bolts and the shock absorber.
3. Remove the cotter pins and the nuts from the lower end of the stabilizer link. Detach the link from the axle housing.
4. Remove the spring-to-axle housing U-bolt nuts, the spring bumper and the U-bolt.
5. At the front of the spring, remove the hanger pin bolt. Disconnect the spring from the bracket.
6. Remove the spring shackle retaining nuts and the spring shackle inner plate, then carefully pry out the spring shackle with a prybar.
7. Remove the spring from the vehicle.

To install:
8. To install, perform the following procedure:
   a. Install the rubber bushings in the eye of the spring.
   b. Align the eye of the spring with the spring hanger bracket and drive the pin through the bracket holes and rubber bushings.

NOTE: Use soapy water as lubricant, if necessary, to aid in pin installation. Never use oil or grease.

   c. Finger-tighten the spring hanger nuts/bolts.
   d. Install the rubber bushings in the spring eye at the opposite end of the spring.
   e. Raise the free end of the spring. Install the spring shackle through the bushings and the bracket.
   f. Install the shackle inner plate and finger-tighten the retaining nuts.
   g. Center the bolt head in the hole which is provided in the spring seat on the axle housing.
   h. Fit the U-bolts over the axle housing. Install the lower spring seat for 2WD vehicle or spring bumper for 4WD vehicle and the nuts.
9. To complete the installation, reverse the removal procedures. Torque the U-bolt nuts to 90 ft. lbs. (122 Nm), the hanger pin-to-frame nut to 67 ft. lbs. (90 Nm), the shackle pin nuts to 67 ft. lbs. (90 Nm), the shock absorber bolts to 47 ft. lbs. (65 Nm) for 4WD vehicle.

NOTE: When installing the U-bolts, tighten the nuts so the length of the bolts are equal.

Rear Control Arms

REMOVAL AND INSTALLATION

Previa

1. Raise and safely support the vehicle. Place a floor jack under the axle housing to support it.
2. Remove the upper control arm-to-body bolt, the upper control arm-to-axle housing bolt and the upper control arm from the vehicle.
3. Disconnect the brake line from the lower control arm.
4. Remove the lower control arm-to-body bolt, the lower control arm-to-axle housing bolt and the lower control arm from the vehicle.

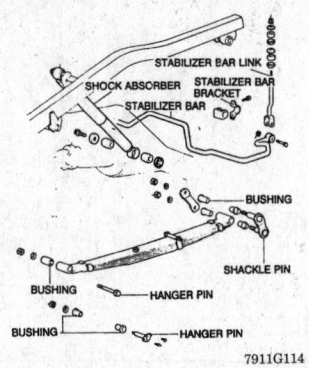

Rear suspension — except Previa

To install:

5. Install the upper control arm to the body and to the axle housing with the nuts. Do not tighten the nuts.

6. Install the lower control arm to the body and to the axle housing with the nuts. Do not tighten the nuts.

7. Remove the jack and the supports from under the vehicle. Bounce the vehicle to stabilize the suspension.

8. Using the floor jack under the axle housing, raise the vehicle. Place jackstands under the frame but do not let them touch the frame.

9. To complete the installation, torque the upper control arm-to-body bolt to 105 ft. lbs. (140 Nm), the upper control arm-to-axle housing bolt to 105 ft. lbs. (140 Nm), the lower control arm-to-body bolt to 130 ft. lbs. (176 Nm) and the lower control arm-to-axle housing bolt to 105 ft. lbs. (140 Nm).

Lateral Control Rod

REMOVAL AND INSTALLATION

Previa

1. Raise and safely support the vehicle. Place a floor jack under the axle housing and support it.

2. Remove the lateral control rod-to-axle housing nut.

3. Remove the lateral control rod-to-body nut and the control rod from the vehicle.

To install:

4. Raise the axle housing until the frame is just free of the jack.

5. Install the lateral control rod-to-body with the nut. Do not tighten the nut.

6. Install the lateral control rod-to-axle housing in the following order: washer, bushing, spacer, lateral control rod, bushing, washer and nut. Do not tighten the nut.

7. Remove the jack, lower the vehicle to the floor and bounce it to stabilize the suspension.

8. Using the floor jack under the axle housing, raise the vehicle. Torque the lateral control rod-to-body nut to 81 ft. lbs. (110 Nm) and the lateral control rod-to-axle housing nut to 43 ft. lbs. (58 Nm).

FIRING ORDERS

NOTE: To avoid confusion, always replace spark plug wires one at a time.

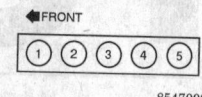

◄FRONT

85470002

2.5L Engine
Engine Firing Order:
1–2–3–4–5
Distributorless Ignition
System

ENGINE ELECTRICAL

NOTE: If equipped with a theft protected radio, obtain the security reset code before disconnecting the negative battery cable. EuroVans may have the battery either under the driver's seat or in the engine compartment.

Distributor

REMOVAL

EuroVan

1. Disconnect negative battery cable.
2. Turn the engine to the TDC of the cylinder No. 1. Remove the distributor cap and mark the position of the rotor to the distributor body and the distributor body to the engine block. This allows for easier installation.
3. Remove the distributor hold-down bolt and remove the distributor.

INSTALLATION

EuroVan

1. Adjust flywheel until the engine is at TDC.

2. Align the mark on the camshaft sprocket with the marking on the rear of the toothed belt guard.
3. Turn the rotor of the distributor so that it points to the marking for the No. 1 cylinder.
4. Insert the distributor into the engine, avoiding any nearby components.
5. Clean and inspect distributor cap. Install cap to the distributor and wires.
6. Check ignition timing and adjust if necessary.

Ignition Timing

ADJUSTMENT

EuroVan

1. Run the engine to normal operating temperature, stop engine and connect a tachometer and timing light according to the manufacturer's instructions.
2. With the ignition **ON**, engine not running, verify that the idle stabilizer valve hums or buzzes. Do not disconnect any vacuum lines from the distributor.
3. Start the engine. Disconnect the blue coolant temperature sensor plug.
4. Turn off all electrical equipment and set the idle speed.
5. Remove the timing mark cover from the top of the bell housing at the flywheel end of the engine and with the engine running, shine the timing light at the marks on the flywheel. If adjustment is required, loosen the distributor clamp bolt and rotate the distributor as needed to align the correct timing marks.
6. Stop the engine and reconnect the plugs.

Alternator

PRECAUTIONS

Several precautions must be observed with alternator equipped vehicles to avoid damage to the unit.

• If the battery is removed for any reason, make sure it is reconnected with the correct polarity. Reversing the battery connections may result in damage to the one-way rectifiers.
• When utilizing a booster battery as a starting aid, always connect the positive to positive terminals and the negative terminal from the booster battery to a good engine ground on the vehicle being started.

• Never use a fast charger as a booster to start vehicles.
• Disconnect the battery cables when charging the battery with a fast charger.
• Never attempt to polarize the alternator.
• Do not use test lights of more than 12 volts when checking diode continuity.
• Do not short across or ground any of the alternator terminals.
• The polarity of the battery, alternator and regulator must be matched and considered before making any electrical connections within the system.
• Never separate the alternator on an open circuit. Make sure all connections within the circuit are clean and tight.
• Disconnect the battery ground terminal when performing any service on electrical components.
• Disconnect the battery if arc welding is to be done on the vehicle.

BELT TENSION ADJUSTMENT

EuroVan

The Alternator V-belt on the EuroVan has a belt tensioner and does not need to be adjusted.

REMOVAL AND INSTALLATION

EuroVan

1. Disconnect the negative battery cable.
2. Remove the drive belt.
3. Disconnect the electrical connector from the alternator.
4. Remove the 2 alternator mounting bolts.
5. Remove the alternator.
To install:
6. Install the alternator and tighten the 2 mounting bolts.
7. Connect the electrical connectors.
8. Install and adjust the drive belt.
9. Connect the negative battery cable.

Starter

REMOVAL AND INSTALLATION

EuroVan

1. Disconnect negative battery cable.
2. Remove the plastic cap from solenoid switch.

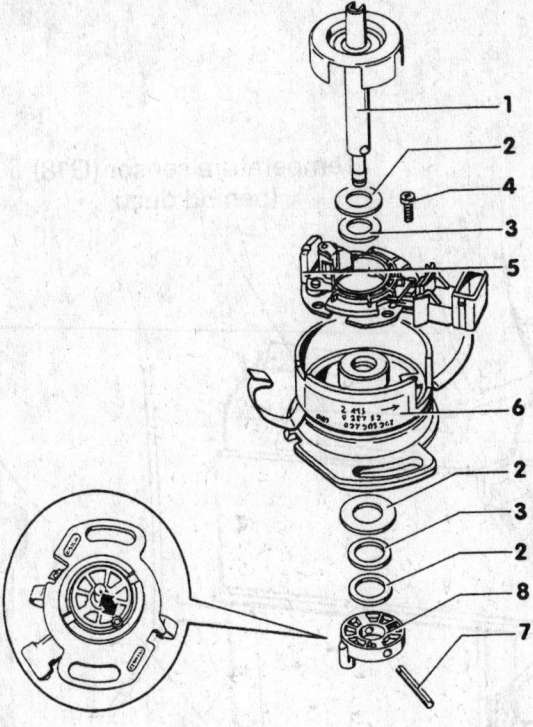

1 Ignition distributor shaft
2 Washers
3 Plastic spacer
4 Bolt 3 Nm (27 inch lb)
5 Hall sender
6 Ignition distributor housing
7 Pin
8 Coupling

85470056

Distributor assembly — EuroVan

3. Unlatch and disconnect the electrical connector at terminal **50**.

4. Disconnect the wiring at terminal **30**.

5. Remove the three mounting bolts on the starter and remove the starter.

To install:

6. Install starter and tighten the three mounting bolts to 15 ft. lbs. (20 Nm).

7. Connect electrical connector to terminal **30** and tighten nut to 9.6 ft. lbs. (13 Nm).

8. Connect and latch electrical connector at terminal **50**.

9. Replace black plastic cap to solenoid switch.

10. Connect negative battery cable.

CHASSIS ELECTRICAL

Heater Blower Motor

REMOVAL AND INSTALLATION

EuroVan

1. Disconnect the negative battery cable.

2. Remove the light inside of the glove compartment and disconnect the electrical connector.

3. Remove the seven screws retaining the glove compartment and remove the glove compartment.

4. Unclip the right air vent. Remove the screw holding the duct and remove the duct.

5. Disconnect the electrical harness connector from the fresh air blower series resistance.

6. Disengage the retaining tab at the bottom of the blower and turn the fresh air blower clockwise.

7. Move the fresh air blower to the center of the instrument panel and remove the blower.

To install:

8. Insert the blower into the heater box assembly.

9. Turn the fresh air blower counter-clockwise until the retaining tab clicks into place.

10. Connect the electrical harness connector to the fresh air blower series resistance.

11. Install the duct on the right air vent and install the screw to hold the duct. Clip the right air vent into place.

12. Place the glove compartment into the instrument panel and install the seven screws retaining the glove compartment.

13. Connect the electrical connector to the light inside of the glove compartment and install the light.

14. Connect the negative battery cable.

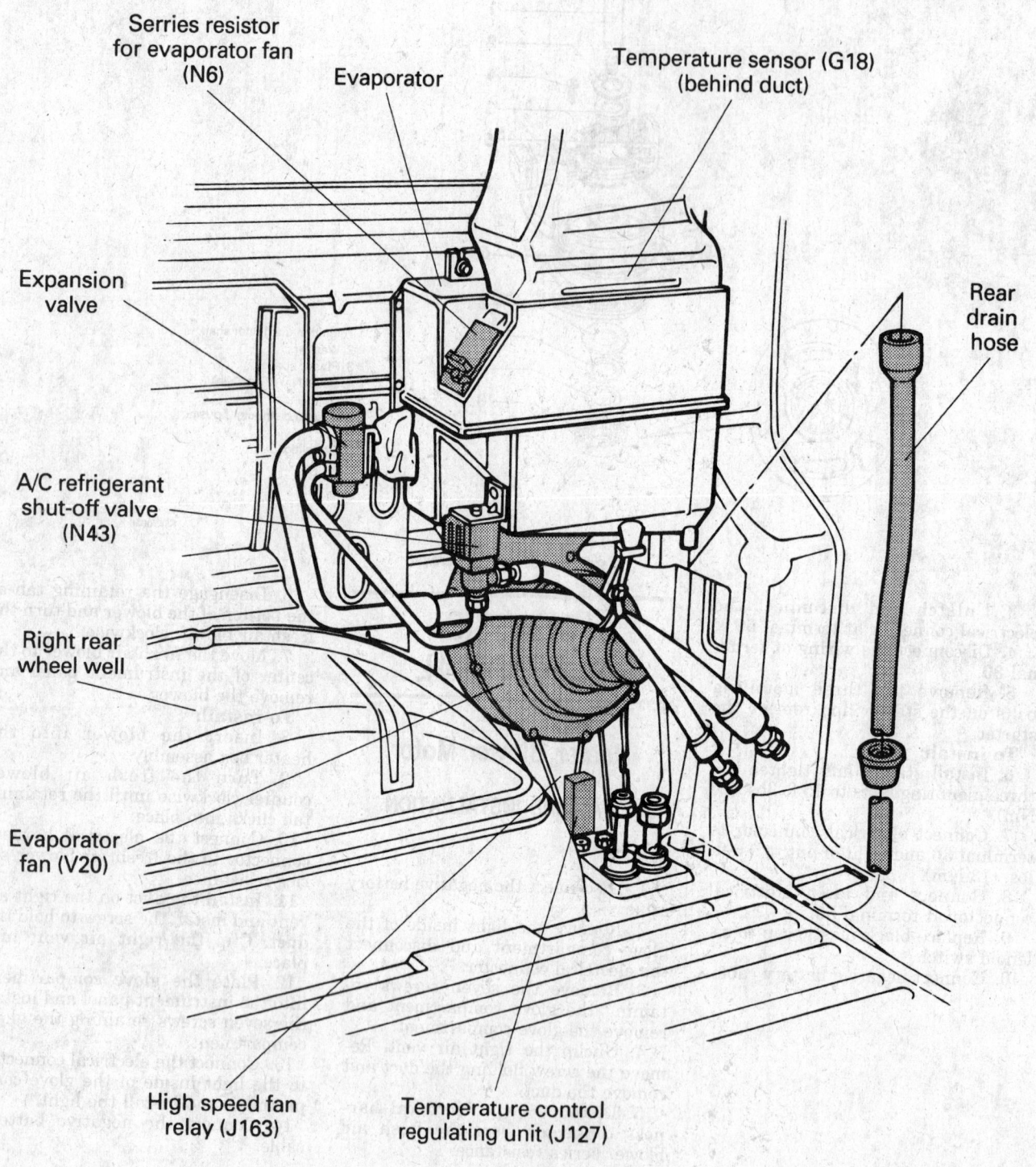

Serries resistor for evaporator fan (N6)

Evaporator

Temperature sensor (G18) (behind duct)

Rear drain hose

Expansion valve

A/C refrigerant shut-off valve (N43)

Right rear wheel well

Evaporator fan (V20)

High speed fan relay (J163)

Temperature control regulating unit (J127)

85470066

View of the rear air conditioning assembly — EuroVan

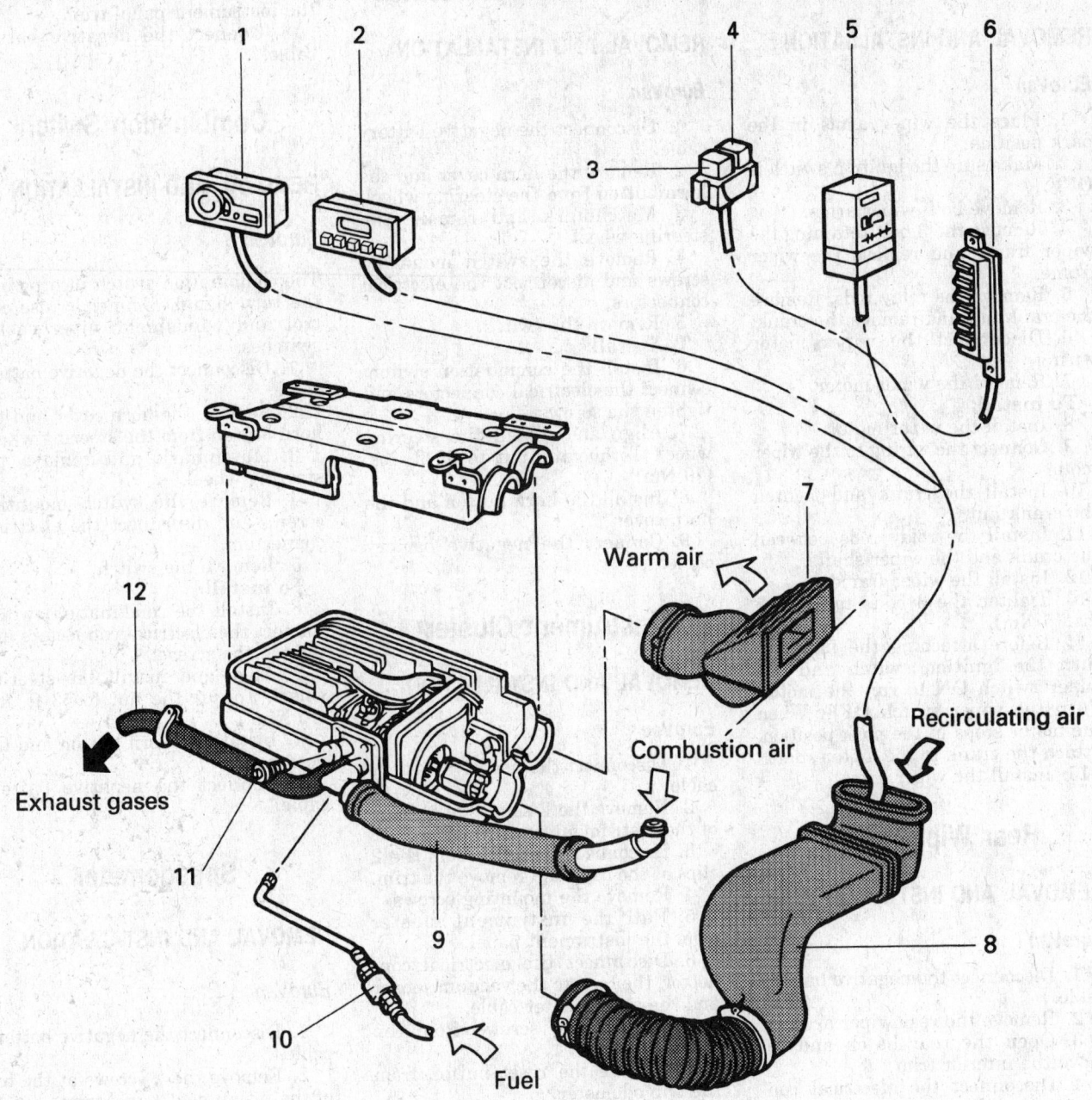

Warm air

Combustion air

Recirculating air

Exhaust gases

Fuel

1 Control panel with temperature control
   switch E13
2 Timer E111
3 Relay J116 for resistance lead
4 Relay J195 for glow plug
5 Control module J65
6 Fuse holder

7 Air vent
8 Intake duct
9 Combustion air hose
10 Fuel pump G23
11 Glow plug Q6
12 Exhaust pipe

85470067

Exploded view of the heating and ventilation assembly — EuroVan

Windshield Wiper Motor

REMOVAL AND INSTALLATION

EuroVan

1. Place the wiper arms in the park position.
2. Make sure the ignition switch is **OFF**.
3. Remove both wiper arms.
4. Remove the 3 bolt retaining the wiper frame and remove the wiper frame.
5. Remove the relay rods. Remove the crank nut and remove the crank.
6. Disconnect the wiper motor wiring.
7. Remove the wiper motor.
To install:
8. Install the wiper motor.
9. Connect the wiring to the wiper motor.
10. Install the crank and tighten the crank nut.
11. Install the relay rods between the crank and the wiper shafts.
12. Install the wiper frame.
13. Tighten the 3 bolts to 44 inch lbs. (5 Nm).
14. Before attaching the linkages, turn the ignition switch and the wiper switch **ON** to run the motor. Turn the wiper switch **OFF**. When the motor stops in the park position, attach the crank to the motor shaft.
15. Install the wiper arms.

Rear Wiper Motor

REMOVAL AND INSTALLATION

EuroVan

1. Disconnect the negative battery cable.
2. Remove the rear wiper arm.
3. Open the rear hatch and remove the interior trim.
4. Disconnect the electrical connector from the wiper motor.
5. Remove the wiper motor bracket.
6. Remove the wiper motor from the bracket.
To install:
7. Install the wiper motor. Tighten the bolts to 44 inch lbs. (5 Nm).
8. Install the wiper motor bracket.
9. Connect the electrical connector to the wiper motor.
10. Install the interior trim to the rear hatch.
11. Close rear hatch and install the wiper arm.
12. Connect the negative battery cable.

Windshield Wiper Switch

REMOVAL AND INSTALLATION

EuroVan

1. Disconnect the negative battery cable.
2. Remove the horn cover and the horn button from the steering wheel.
3. Matchmark and remove the steering wheel.
4. Remove the switch mounting screws and disconnect the electrical connectors.
5. Remove the switch.
To install:
6. Install the combination switch, connect the electrical connectors and tighten the screws.
7. Align and install the steering wheel. Torque the nut to 53 ft. lbs. (70 Nm).
8. Install the horn button and the horn cover.
9. Connect the negative battery cable.

Instrument Cluster

REMOVAL AND INSTALLATION

EuroVan

1. Disconnect the negative battery cable.
2. Remove the 2 screws at the top of the instrument panel trim.
3. Disconnect the trim from the 2 clips at the base and remove the trim.
4. Remove the mounting screws.
5. Pull the instrument cluster from the instrument panel.
6. Disconnect the electrical connector, the hose to the vacuum sensor and the speedometer cable.
7. Remove the screws from the front frame.
8. Remove the reset button from the trip odometer.
9. Pull out front frame from the instrument cluster.
To install:
10. Install the front frame to the instrument cluster.
11. Install the reset button to the trip odometer.
12. Install the screws to the front frame.
13. Install the hose to the vacuum sensor. Install the speedometer cable and the electrical connector.
14. Place the instrument cluster into the instrument panel.
15. Install the mounting screws.
16. Install the trim panel and clip the 2 clips.

17. Install the 2 screws at the top of the instrument panel trim.
18. Connect the negative battery cable.

Combination Switch

REMOVAL AND INSTALLATION

EuroVan

The combination switch incorporates the turn signal, dimmer, cruise control and windshield wiper/washer switches.

1. Disconnect the negative battery cable.
2. Remove the horn cover and the horn button from the steering wheel.
3. Matchmark and remove the steering wheel.
4. Remove the switch mounting screws and disconnect the electrical connectors.
5. Remove the switch.
To install:
6. Install the combination switch, connect the electrical connectors and tighten the screws.
7. Align and install the steering wheel. Torque the nut to 53 ft. lbs. (70 Nm).
8. Install the horn button and the horn cover.
9. Connect the negative battery cable.

Speedometer

REMOVAL AND INSTALLATION

EuroVan

1. Disconnect the negative battery cable.
2. Remove the 2 screws at the top of the instrument panel trim.
3. Disconnect the trim from the 2 clips at the base and remove the trim.
4. Remove the mounting screws.
5. Pull the instrument cluster from the instrument panel.
6. Disconnect the electrical connector, the hose to the vacuum sensor and the speedometer cable.
7. Remove the screws from the front frame.
8. Remove the reset button from the trip odometer.
9. Pull out front frame from the instrument cluster.
10. Remove the 4 screws retaining the speedometer and remove the speedometer.

To install:

11. Install the speedometer to the instrument cluster and tighten the 4 screws.

12. Install the front frame to the instrument cluster.

13. Install the reset button to the trip odometer.

14. Install the screws to the front frame.

15. Install the hose to the vacuum sensor. Install the speedometer cable and the electrical connector.

16. Place the instrument cluster into the instrument panel.

17. Install the mounting screws.

18. Install the trim panel and clip the 2 clips.

19. Install the 2 screws at the top of the instrument panel trim.

20. Connect the negative battery cable.

Ignition Lock/Switch

REMOVAL AND INSTALLATION

1. Disconnect negative battery cable.

2. Remove the steering wheel, steering column covers and the windshield wiper/combination switch assembly.

3. Use a ⅛ in. (3mm) drill to carefully drill a hole into the cylinder housing at the intersection of lines **A** and **B**. Dimension **A** is 0.472 in. (12mm); dimension **B** is 0.394 in. (10mm).

4. Carefully insert a punch into the hole and push in on the spring loaded detent.

5. With the key in the cylinder and turned to the **ON** position, pull the lock cylinder out.

To install:

6. Insert the key in the cylinder and push the cylinder into place. Make sure the pin engages correctly and that the retainer fits easily in place. Do not force any parts together. When they are correctly aligned, they will fit easily into place.

7. Install the windshield wiper/combination switch assembly.

8. Install the steering column covers and the steering wheel.

9. Connect the negative battery cable.

Stoplight Switch

REMOVAL AND INSTALLATION

EuroVan

The stoplight switch is located above the brake pedal.

1. Disconnect the negative battery cable.

2. Disconnect the electrical connector from the brake switch.

3. Remove the brake switch.

To install:

4. Pull the plunger of the switch out.

5. Guide the switch in through the mounting hole. Turn the switch 90 degrees to secure in place.

6. Connect the electrical connector.

7. Connect the negative battery cable.

Neutral Safety Switch

ADJUSTMENT

1. The combination neutral start and back-up light switch is mounted inside the shifter housing.

2. The engine should start in **P** or **N** only and the back-up lights should be on only in **R**.

3. Adjust the switch by loosening the screws and moving it on it's mounts.

4. After any adjustment or replacement, check that the engine starts only with the switch in **P** or **N** and the back-up lights come on only in **R**.

Fuses and Circuit Breakers

LOCATION

The fuse relay panel is located under the left side of the instrument panel, to the left side of the steering column.

Computers

LOCATIONS

The control module for the Digifant fuel system is on the left side of the engine compartment, mounted on the front of the fenderwell. The automatic transaxle control module is located to the right of the instrument panel, at the base of the "A" pillar. The control module for the ABS system is to the left of the instrument panel, at the base of the "A" pillar.

Flashers

LOCATIONS

The flasher unit on the EuroVan is on the fuse relay panel, under the left side of the instrument panel. On the fuse relay panel, the emergency flasher is the fourth relay down on the right side.

Cruise Control

ADJUSTMENT

EuroVan

1. Hold the accelerator pedal in the idle position and be careful not to depress it.

2. Move the adjusting sleeve with the linkage toward the vacuum servo unit, until resistance is felt.

3. Turn the adjusting sleeve to lock it.

4. Check that the accelerator pedal moves freely.

ENGINE COOLING

NOTE: Before disconnecting the negative battery cable, be sure to have the radio security code. Also, disconnecting the negative battery cable may interfere with the functions of the on board computer systems and may require the computer to undergo a relearning process, once the negative battery cable is reconnected.

Radiator

REMOVAL AND INSTALLATION

EuroVan

1. Disconnect the negative battery cable.

2. Remove the securing bolts from the left and right side of the grille.

3. Hinge the radiator and lock the carrier forward.

4. Disconnect the cooling fan and thermoswitch.

5. Drain the cooling system.

6. Disconnect all coolant hoses from the radiator.

7. Drive the pins out of the right and left side radiator bracket expanding clips.

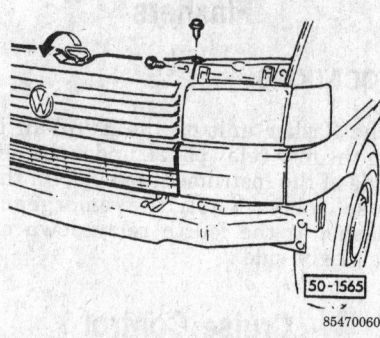

50-1565

85470060

Remove screws to unlatch the grille/radiator assembly — EuroVan

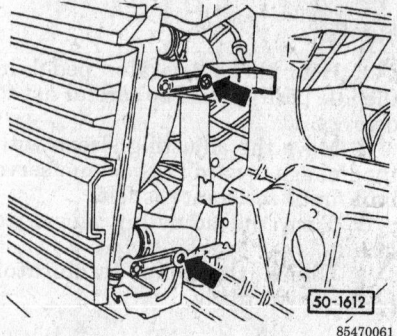

50-1612

85470061

Pull grille assembly out and lock carrier forward — EuroVan

8. Remove the radiator assembly complete with the hood-lock carrier and coolant hoses.

To install:

9. Install the radiator assembly into place.

10. Install the pins into the right and left side radiator bracket expanding clips.

11. Connect the coolant hoses to the radiator.

12. Connect the cooling fan and thermoswitch.

13. Push the radiator carrier back into place.

14. Install the securing bolts to the left and right sides of the grille.

15. Connect the negative battery cable. Fill and bleed the cooling system.

Electric Cooling Fan

REMOVAL AND INSTALLATION

EuroVan

1. Disconnect the negative battery cable.

2. Remove the securing bolts from the left and right side of the grille.

3. Hinge the radiator and lock the carrier forward.

4. Disconnect the cooling fan.

5. Remove the cooling fan retaining bolts and remove the cooling fan.

To install:

6. Install the cooling fan and torque the retaining bolts to 7 ft. lbs. (10 Nm).

7. Connect the cooling fan.

8. Push the radiator carrier back into place.

9. Install the securing bolts to the left and right sides of the grille.

10. Connect the negative battery cable.

Heater Core

REMOVAL AND INSTALLATION

EuroVan

FRONT

1. Disconnect the negative battery cable.

2. Drain the cooling system.

3. Remove the glove compartment.

4. Unclip the right air vent. Remove the screw holding the duct and remove the duct.

5. Remove the 3 screws retaining the air intake duct on the left side of the firewall, inside the engine compartment. Remove the duct.

6. Unclip the center air outlet vents. Remove the 2 screws retaining the center air outlet duct and remove the duct.

7. Remove the heater control cables from the heater box housing.

8. Disconnect the electrical harness connector from the fresh air blower series resistance.

9. Remove the 3 screws from the footwell air outlet cover and remove the cover.

10. Remove the 4 screws from the footwell air outlet console. Detach and remove the console.

11. Disconnect the coolant hoses from the heater core and plug the connections.

12. Remove the cable at the heater control valve.

13. Remove the 2 retaining screws from the heater box.

14. Remove the heater box housing.

15. Remove the 2 retaining screws and remove the heater core.

To install:

16. Install the heater core to the heater box.

17. Install the heater box and tighten the retaining screws.

18. Install the cable at the heater control valve.

19. Connect the coolant hoses to the heater core.

20. Install the footwell air outlet cover and console.

21. Connect the harness connector to the fresh air blower series resistance.

22. Install the cables to the heater/fresh air control.

23. Install the center air outlet and center air duct.

24. Install the air intake duct on the fire wall.

25. Install the right air duct and the glover compartment.

26. Connect the negative battery cable. Fill and bleed the cooling system.

REAR

1. Disconnect the negative battery cable.

2. Drain the cooling system.

3. Disconnect the wire harness connector from the rear heater.

4. Remove the coolant return hose and the coolant supply hose from the heater core.

5. Remove the 2 screws and unsnap the upper air outlet vent. Remove the 4 screws and remove the lower air outlet vent.

6. Remove the screws and remove the rear heater.

7. Remove the 2 retaining screws and remove the heater core.

To install:

8. Install the heater core and tighten the screws.

9. Install the rear heater and tighten the screws.

10. Install the lower air outlet vent and tighten the 4 screws.

11. Snap the upper air outlet vent into place and tighten the 2 screws.

12. Install the coolant return and supply hoses to the heater core.

13. Connect the wire harness to the rear heater.

14. Connect the negative battery cable.

15. Fill and bleed the cooling system.

Water Pump

REMOVAL AND INSTALLATION

EuroVan

1. Disconnect the negative battery cable.

2. Drain the cooling system.

3. Remove the securing bolts from the left and right side of the grille.

4. Hinge the radiator and lock the carrier forward.

5. Disconnect the harness connector to the water pump.

6. Remove the bolts retaining the water pump to the coolant pipe.

7. Remove the hoses from the water pump and remove the water pump.

To install:

8. Install the water pump to the coolant hose and connect the hoses.

9. Connect the harness connector to the water pump.

10. Push the radiator carrier back into place.

11. Install the securing bolts to the left and right sides of the grille.

12. Connect the negative battery cable.

13. Fill and bleed the cooling system. Run the engine and check for leaks.

Thermostat

REMOVAL AND INSTALLATION

On the Eurovan, the thermostat is located on the side of the engine, below the No. 1 and No. 2 spark plugs.

1. Disconnect the negative battery cable.

2. Drain the cooling system.

3. Remove the hoses from the thermostat housing.

4. Remove the housing top retaining bolts and remove the top of the housing.

5. Remove the thermostat from the housing.

To install:

6. Replace the O-ring in the top of the thermostat housing.

7. Install the thermostat in position and install the top of the housing.

8. Tighten the retaining bolts to 7 ft. lbs. (10 Nm) on the EuroVan. Connect the hoses and refill the cooling system.

9. Connect the negative battery cable and bleed the cooling system.

Cooling System Bleeding

NOTE: G11 antifreeze and coolant additives marked "in accordance with TL VW 774 A" are recommended. Anti-freeze other than the ones specified may cause corrosion of the cooling system.

1. Set the heater control to **MAX** heat.

2. If equipped, open the control valve for the auxiliary heater in the rear of the vehicle.

3. Open the breather screw in the hose to the heater core.

4. Fill the coolant expansion tank until the tank is full.

5. Start the engine. Increase the engine speed to 2000 rpm and continue to fill the tank until coolant flows from the bleeder or breather screw. Wait until coolant is flowing free of bubbles.

6. Add more coolant until the tank is full. Close the tank cap.

7. Turn the engine **OFF**. Restart the engine after 20 seconds.

8. At 2000 rpm, open the expansion cap.

9. Close the bleeder or breather screw when coolant flows out. Add coolant if necessary and close the tank cap.

FUEL SYSTEM

Fuel System Service Precautions

When working with the fuel system certain precautions should be taken; always work in a well ventilated area, keep a dry chemical (Class B) fire extinguisher near the work area. Always disconnect the negative battery cable and do not make any repairs to the fuel system until all necessary steps for repair have been reviewed.

Relieving Fuel System Pressure

The Digifant fuel injection system used in these vehicles will maintain a residual pressure up to 36 psi (2.5 bar) for 10–30 minutes after the ignition is switched OFF. If the system is working properly, the pressure is generated any time the ignition is switched ON, with or without the engine running. The fuel pump stops running after about 2 seconds if the engine is not turning over, but this is enough time to build pressure. To relieve the system pressure, locate the Tee fitting near the distributor and loosen the bolt to open the fitting. Cover the fitting with a shop rag to catch the fuel spray and dispose of the rag properly.

Fuel Tank

REMOVAL AND INSTALLATION

1. Disconnect the negative battery cable.

2. Raise and safely support the vehicle. Empty the fuel tank.

3. Disconnect the filler pipe. Label and disconnect the vent hose, supply hose and return hose.

4. Remove the splash shield from under the body.

5. Remove the fuel tank.

To install:

6. Install the fuel tank.

7. Install the splash shield.

8. Connect the vent hose, supply hose and return rose.

9. Connect the filler pipe.

10. Lower the vehicle.

11. Connect the negative battery cable.

Fuel Filter

REMOVAL AND INSTALLATION

On the EuroVan, the fuel filter is located under the right side of the vehicle, just ahead of the fuel tank. Some vehicles also have a small in-line filter before the fuel pump.

1. Disconnect the negative battery cable.

2. Relieve the fuel pressure.

3. Raise and safely support the vehicle.

4. Disconnect the fuel lines from the filter.

5. Remove the filter bracket retaining bolt and remove the filter.

6. Install the new filter in position, note the direction of the arrows for fuel flow.

7. Reconnect the fuel lines and lower the vehicle.

8. Connect the negative battery cable. Run the engine and check for leaks.

Electric Fuel Pump

PRESSURE TESTING

1. Connect tool VW-1318 or equivalent, 0–60 psi (4 bar) gauge to the Tee fitting next to the distributor. Locate the fuel pressure regulator near the center of the intake manifold.

2. Run the engine at idle and check the pressure reading. The pressure should be 29 psi (2 bar) with the vacuum line connected to the regula-

tor or 36–42 psi (2.5–3 bar) with the vacuum line disconnected.

3. Stop the engine and wait 10 minutes, the pressure should not drop below 29 psi (2 bar). If the pressure is not maintained;

a. Run the engine again to build pressure, then stop the engine.

b. Check the fuel pump check valve by clamping off the line from the fuel pump to the regulator and observing the gauge.

c. Check the pressure regulator by clamping off the return line to the fuel tank and observing the gauge.

d. Check the injectors by clamping the lines between the injectors and the regulator.

4. If the pressure drop stops or slows down, the problem is in the unit tested by clamping the line.

FLOW RATE TESTING

1. Disconnect the fuel return hose from the pressure regulator and plug the hose.

2. Attach a hose to the pressure regulator and place the other end into a measuring container.

3. Locate and remove the fuel pump relay in the separate box near the main ECU. When terminals 4 of relay J17 and a positive battery connection are jumpered on the Eurovan, the fuel pump will run.

4. Run the pump for 30 seconds and measure the fuel flow. The minimum specification is 17 oz. (500cc) in 30 seconds. If the flow is less and no other leak is found, replace the pump.

REMOVAL AND INSTALLATION

EuroVan

1. Disconnect the negative battery cable. Relieve the fuel system pressure.

2. Pull up the carpeting around the perforation to the right of the handbrake lever.

3. Remove the cover plate.

4. Disconnect the electrical harness connector from the fuel pump.

5. Disconnect the supply and return pipes from the flange on the fuel tank.

6. If equipped with an auxiliary heater, disconnect the fuel line between the supply and return lines.

7. Loosen the union nut.

8. Pull the flange and sealing ring out of the fuel tank opening.

9. Loosen the fuel pump unit from the bayonet connection by twisting to the left.

10. Remove the fuel pump from the fuel tank.

To install:

11. Install the fuel pump to the fuel tank. The fuel pump is installed at a 30 degree angle.

12. Tighten the bayonet connection to the right.

13. Lubricate the flange and install the flange and sealing ring to the fuel tank opening. Align the marks on the flange with the mark on the fuel tank.

14. Tighten the union nut.

15. Install the supply line, the return line and the fuel line between the supply and return lines, if equipped.

16. Connect the electrical harness connector.

17. Install the cover plate.

18. Install the carpeting by gluing or with Velcro.

19. Connect the negative battery cable.

Fuel Injection

IDLE SPEED AND MIXTURE ADJUSTMENT

1. Run the engine until it reaches normal operating temperature.

a. Turn **OFF** all electrical accessories and take readings when the radiator fan is not running.

b. Check that the throttle valve switch on the throttle body is in the closed position at idle.

c. The crankcase breather hose should be removed from the oil vent and plugged.

d. Check to see that the idle stabilizer is operating properly. With the ignition turned **ON**, the valve should hum or vibrate.

2. With the ignition **OFF**, connect a tachometer and timing light to the engine. Power is available at the alternator output terminal. Connect the tachometer to terminal **1** of the ignition coil for the rpm signal.

3. Connect the CO meter to the sample tap on the left side exhaust pipe.

4. With the ignition switch **OFF**, disconnect the oxygen sensor connector and the idle stabilizer control valve connector.

5. Start the engine and run it at idle speed. After 2 minutes, adjust as necessary by turning the adjusting screw on the throttle valve housing.

The idle speed should be 830–930 rpm.

6. Check the CO reading on the exhaust analyzer; the CO should be 0.3–1.1 percent. If the vehicle has an emissions information sticker in the engine compartment, use the CO specification on the sticker. The CO is set at the factory and controlled by the ECU, which is able to adapt to various altitudes and engine conditions to maintain correct air/fuel mixture. If the CO value is not correct, look for other problems with the engine, such as a vacuum leak or poor electrical connection, before adjusting the air/fuel mixture.

7. If the air/fuel mixture must be adjusted, the seal must be removed from the CO adjustment screw.

a. Center punch the sheet metal plug in the CO adjusting hole. Drill a 3/32 in. (2.5mm) hole in the center of the plug. Keep the area clean of metal shavings.

b. Screw a sheet metal screw into the plug.

c. Remove the plug by pulling straight out on the screw with pliers.

8. Start the engine and alternately turn the adjusting screws to obtain the correct CO and idle speed specifications.

9. Reconnect the oxygen sensor connector and idle stabilizer connector. Let the engine idle for approximately 2 minutes. Check the CO, idle speed and ignition timing and correct, if necessary, by repeating the above procedure.

10. Stop the engine. Install a new plug over the air/fuel mixture screw until it is flush with the housing.

Fuel Injector

REMOVAL AND INSTALLATION

EuroVan

1. Disconnect the negative battery cable.

2. Remove the air cleaner housing and the air cleaner element.

3. Remove the intake hose.

4. Disconnect the main fuel injector harness connector at the fuel rail.

5. Disconnect the crankcase breather hose.

6. Disconnect the fuel supply and return lines at the fuel rail.

7. Disconnect the vacuum hose from the fuel pressure regulator.

8. Remove the fuel rail mounting screws.

9. Remove the fuel rail assembly with the fuel injectors.

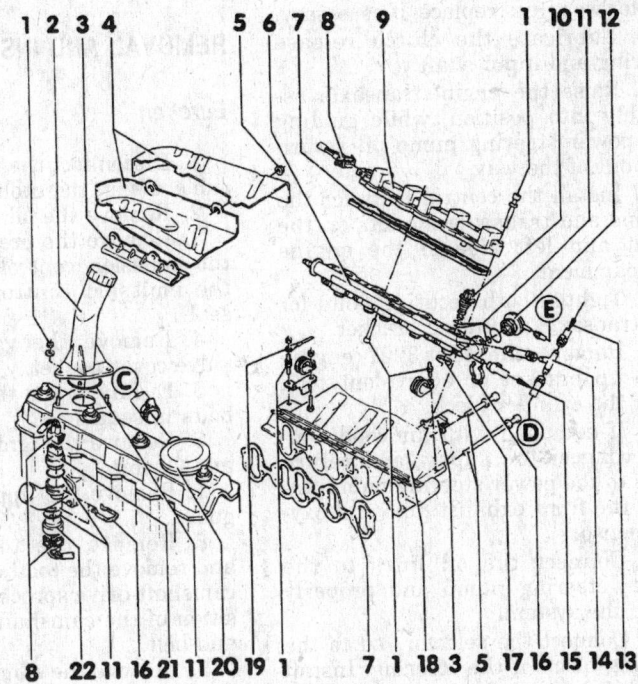

1 Nut 10 Nm (7 ft lb)
2 Oil filler pipe
3 Bracket
4 Hot air stove
5 Bolt 25 Nm (18 ft lb)
6 Lower section fuel rail
7 Gasket
8 Harness connector for
  fuel injectors
9 Upper section fuel rail
10 Fuel injectors
   (N 30, N 31, N 32, N 33, N 83)
11 O-ring
12 Fuel pressure regulator
13 Fuel supply line
14 T-connector
15 Fuel return line
16 Retaining clip
17 O-ring seal
18 Intake manifold
19 Ground connection
20 Emission control valve
21 Engine coolant temperature
22 Overheat fuse (F 51) and
   engine coolant temperature
   (ECT) sensor (G 2)

85470057

Fuel injection components — EuroVan

10. Remove the top screw and pry off the fuel rail upper section from the fuel rail lower section.

11. Press out injectors.

To install:

12. Replace sealing rings, O-rings and gaskets.

13. Place the gasket on the upper section of the fuel rail.

14. Lubricate the fuel injector O-rings with oil.

15. Insert the fuel injectors into the upper fuel rail section.

16. Press the upper fuel rail section, with the fuel injectors, into the lower fuel rail section.

17. Tighten the top screw to 7 ft. lbs. (10 Nm).

18. Place the fuel rail on the intake manifold and tighten the mounting screws to 7 ft. lbs. (10 Nm).

19. Connect the vacuum hose to the fuel pressure regulator.

20. Connect the fuel supply and return hoses.

21. Connect the main fuel injector harness connector at the fuel rail.

22. Connect the crankcase breather hose and attach to the oil filler pipe.

23. Install the suction hose and air cleaner assembly, with element.

24. Connect the negative battery cable.

EMISSION CONTROLS

Emission Warning Lamps

RESETTING

The emission systems incorporates a mileage counter which activates the oxygen sensor warning light on the instrument panel. The counter will illuminate the light at 60,000 mile intervals. The oxygen sensor must be replaced when the light comes ON. The light can reset by pushing the button on the mileage counter with a pencil. Locate the counter under the left front of the instrument panel, in line with the speedometer cable.

ENGINE MECHANICAL

NOTE: If equipped with a theft protected radio, obtain the reset security code before disconnecting the negative battery cable.

Engine

REMOVAL AND INSTALLATION

EuroVan

NOTE: The engine must be removed, with the transaxle, from below the vehicle.

1. Disconnect the negative battery cable. Drain the engine cooling system.

2. Support the upper control arms by fitting VW 3250 left and right support wedges or equivalent tool, to the upper wishbones.

3. Remove the noise damping pan.

4. Remove the cap on the coolant expansion tank.

5. Remove the securing bolts from the left and right side of the grille.

6. Hinge the radiator and lock the carrier forward.

7. Disconnect the cooling fan and thermoswitch.

8. Drain the cooling system.

9. Disconnect all coolant hoses from the radiator.

10. Drive the pins out of the right and left side radiator bracket expanding clips.

11. Remove the radiator assembly complete with the hood-lock carrier and coolant hoses.

12. Disconnect the speedometer drive at the connection point.

13. Detach the accelerator cable at the throttle body and support bracket.

14. Disconnect the clutch cable or slave cylinder.

15. Disconnect and push aside the engine, transaxle, alternator and starter wiring.

16. Disconnect all cooling, vacuum and intake hoses from the engine.

17. Disconnect the fuel supply line at the T-piece and the return line at the fuel rail.

18. Disconnect the gearshift from the transaxle:

  a. Remove the clevis mount of the selector rod.

  b. Pry up the shift lever at the front from the gear control lever.

  c. Disconnect the selector rod from the bearing block.

19. Disconnect oil lines from the power steering pump and allow the hydraulic fluid to drain.

20. If equipped with air conditioning, remove left-hand drive shaft and detach the right-hand drive shaft from the transaxle.

21. Remove the front exhaust pipe with the oxygen sensor.

22. Disconnect the supply and return lines from the power steering pump.

23. Bolt VW 3227 engine take up bracket or equivalent tool, to the cylinder block and torque to 15 ft. lbs. (20 Nm).

24. Raise the engine and transaxle slightly using VAG 1383A engine/transaxle lifter or equivalent tool.

25. Remove both securing bolts from the transaxle mounting bracket.

26. Remove the central bolts for the engine and transaxle mounts on the right and left side of the engine compartment.

27. Remove the engine/transaxle assembly downwards while guiding the power steering pump oil return line away.

To install:

28. Check the clutch release bearing for wear and replace, if necessary.

29. Lubricate the clutch release bearing and input shaft.

30. Raise the engine/transaxle assembly into position, while guiding the power steering pump oil return line out of the way.

31. Install the central bolts for the engine and transaxle mounts on the right and left side of the engine compartment.

32. Tighten both securing bolts for the transaxle mounting bracket.

33. Remove the VW 3227 engine take up bracket or equivalent tool, from the cylinder block.

34. If equipped with air conditioning, connect the supply and return lines to the power steering pump. Install the front exhaust pipe and oxygen sensor.

35. Connect the oil lines to the power steering pump and properly bleed the system.

36. Connect the selector rod to the bearing block of the steering. Install the shift lever at the front of the gear control lever. Install the clevis mount to the selector.

37. Connect the black fuel supply line at the T-piece and the blue return line at the fuel rail.

38. Connect all coolant, vacuum and intake hoses to the engine.

39. Connect the engine, transaxle, alternator and starter wiring.

40. Connect the clutch cable or slave cylinder.

41. Connect and adjust the accelerator cable to the throttle body.

42. Connect the speedometer cable at the connection point.

43. Install the radiator assembly into place.

44. Install the pins into the right and left side radiator bracket expanding clips.

45. Connect the coolant hoses to the radiator.

46. Connect the cooling fan and thermoswitch.

47. Push the radiator carrier back into place.

48. Install the securing bolts to the left and right sides of the grille.

49. Install the coolant expansion tank cap

50. Install the noise damping pan.

51. Remove VW 3250 left and right support wedges or equivalent tools, from the upper wishbones.

52. Connect the negative battery cable. Fill and bleed the cooling system.

Cylinder Head

REMOVAL AND INSTALLATION

EuroVan

1. Disconnect the negative battery cable. Drain the cooling system.

2. Remove the oil filler pipe.

3. Remove the breather hose from the emission control valve. Remove the emission control valve and oil seal.

4. Remove the valve cover and valve cover gasket.

5. Evenly loosen the cylinder head bolts in sequence.

6. Remove the ignition distributor and O-ring.

7. Remove the upper toothed belt guard.

8. Remove the tensioner pulley and remove the toothed belt from the camshaft drive sprocket. Note the position of the camshaft drive sprocket and belt.

9. Remove the camshaft drive pulley. Remove the rear toothed belt guard.

10. Disconnect the hoses from the cylinder head.

11. Remove the intake manifold from the cylinder head.

12. Remove the engine mount bracket from the cylinder head.

13. Remove the cylinder head.

To install:

14. Install a new cylinder head gasket to the engine block.

15. Install the cylinder head to the engine block.

16. Install the engine mount bracket to the cylinder head. Torque the bolt to 15 ft. lbs. (20 Nm).

17. Install the intake manifold to the cylinder head.

18. Connect the hoses to the cylinder head.

19. Install the rear toothed belt guard. Install the camshaft drive pulley.

20. Properly line up the toothed belt and the camshaft drive pulley. Torque the bolts labeled 8.8—63 ft. lbs. (85 Nm) and the bolts labeled 10.9—74 ft. lbs. (100 Nm).

21. Torque the bolt for the tensioner pulley to 15 ft. lbs. (20 Nm).

22. Install the tensioner pulley.

23. Install the upper toothed belt guard.

24. Install ignition distributor and O-ring. Replace O-ring, if damaged.

25. Evenly tighten the cylinder head bolts in sequence. Torque the head bolts to 30 ft. lbs. (40 Nm), then torque to 44 ft. lbs. (60 Nm). Turn

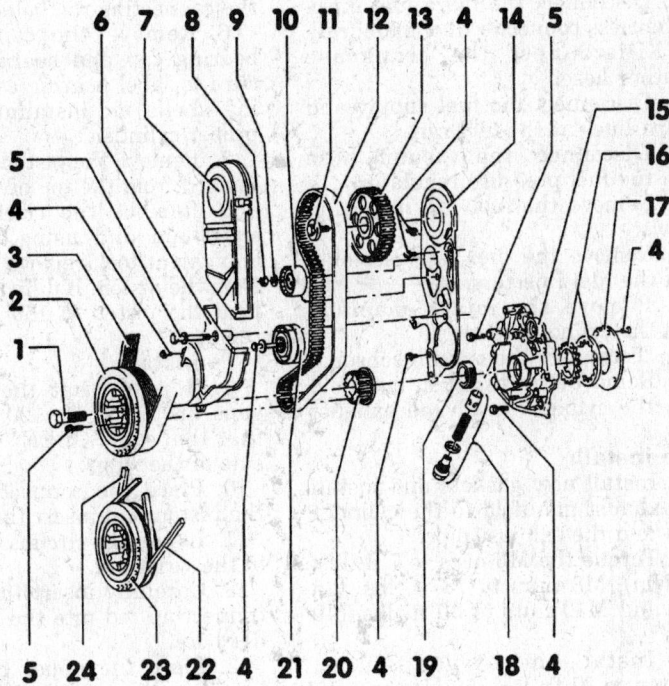

1	Bolt 460 Nm (339 ft lb)
2	Vibration damper for ribbed belt pulley
3	Ribbed belt
4	Bolt 10 Nm (7 ft lb)
5	Bolt 20 Nm (15 ft lb)
6	Lower toothed belt guard
7	Upper toothed belt guard
8	Washer 15 Nm (11 ft lb)
9	Washer
10	Tensioner pulley
11	Camshaft drive sprocket mounting screw
12	Toothed belt
13	Camshaft drive sprocket
14	Rear toothed belt guard
15	Oil pump
16	Oil pump gears
17	Cover
18	Oil pressure relief valve
19	Gasket
20	Crankshaft toothed belt drive sprocket
21	Idler pulley
22	Not for US vehicles
23	Not for US vehicles
24	Not for US vehicles

85470058

Belts and pulleys — EuroVan

Valve Lifters

REMOVAL AND INSTALLATION

EuroVan

1. Disconnect the negative battery cable.

2. Remove the valve cover and gasket.

3. Remove the upper toothed belt guard.

4. Remove the tensioner pulley and remove the toothed belt from the camshaft drive sprocket. Note the position of the camshaft drive sprocket and belt.

5. Remove the camshaft drive pulley. Remove the rear toothed belt guard.

6. Evenly remove the bearing caps.

7. Remove the camshaft. Note the position of the lobes.

8. Remove the hydraulic lifters.

To install:

9. Install the hydraulic lifters. Lubricate all contacting surfaces. Do not interchange lifters.

10. Replace the oil seal and install the camshaft.

11. Install the bearing caps. Tighten the bearing cap nuts evenly. Torque nuts to 15 ft. lbs. (20 Nm).

each bolt an additional ¼ turn, then another ¼ turn.

26. Install the valve cover.

27. Install the emission control valve and oil seal. Replace the oil seal, if damaged.

28. Connect the breather hose from the emission control valve.

29. Install the oil filler pipe. Torque the bolts to 7 ft. lbs. (10 Nm).

30. Connect the negative battery cable. Fill and bleed the cooling system.

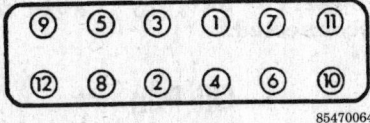

85470064

Cylinder head bolt installation sequence — EuroVan

12. Install the rear toothed belt guard. Install the camshaft drive pulley.

13. Properly line up the toothed belt and the camshaft drive pulley. Torque the bolts labeled 8.8–63 ft. lbs. (85 Nm) and the bolts labeled 10.9–74 ft. lbs. (100 Nm).

14. Torque the bolt for the tensioner pulley to 15 ft. lbs. (20 Nm).

15. Install the tensioner pulley.

16. Install the upper toothed belt guard.

17. Install the valve cover.

18. Install the emission control valve and oil seal. Replace the oil seal if damaged.

19. Connect the breather hose from the emission control valve.

20. Install the oil filler pipe. Torque the bolts to 7 ft. lbs. (10 Nm).

21. Connect the negative battery cable.

Intake Manifold

REMOVAL AND INSTALLATION

EuroVan

1. Disconnect the negative battery cable.

2. Remove the air cleaner housing and the air cleaner element.

3. Remove the intake hose.

4. Disconnect the main fuel injector harness connector at the fuel rail.

5. Disconnect the crankcase breather hose.

6. Disconnect the fuel supply and return lines at the fuel rail.

7. Disconnect the vacuum hose from the fuel pressure regulator.

8. Remove the fuel rail mounting screws.

9. Remove the fuel rail assembly with the fuel injectors.

10. Remove the intake manifold from the cylinder head.

To install:

11. Install new gasket and intake manifold and tighten bolts to 18 ft. lbs. (25 Nm).

12. Lubricate the fuel injector O-rings with oil.

13. Place the fuel rail on the intake manifold and tighten the mounting screws to 7 ft. lbs. (10 Nm).

14. Connect the vacuum hose to the fuel pressure regulator.

15. Connect the fuel supply and return hoses.

16. Connect the main fuel injector harness connector at the fuel rail.

17. Connect the crankcase breather hose and attach to the oil filler pipe.

18. Install the suction hose and air cleaner assembly, with element.

19. Connect the negative battery cable.

Exhaust Manifold

REMOVAL AND INSTALLATION

EuroVan

1. Disconnect the negative battery cable.

2. Remove the air cleaner housing and the air cleaner element.

3. Remove the intake hose.

4. Disconnect the main fuel injector harness connector at the fuel rail.

5. Disconnect the crankcase breather hose.

6. Disconnect the fuel supply and return lines at the fuel rail.

7. Disconnect the vacuum hose from the fuel pressure regulator.

8. Remove the fuel rail mounting screws.

9. Remove the fuel rail assembly with the fuel injectors.

10. Remove the intake manifold from the cylinder head.

11. Remove the heat shield/stove and the bracket.Disconnect the negative battery cable.

12. Remove the air cleaner housing and the air cleaner element.

13. Remove the intake hose.

14. Disconnect the main fuel injector harness connector at the fuel rail.

15. Disconnect the crankcase breather hose.

16. Disconnect the fuel supply and return lines at the fuel rail.

17. Disconnect the vacuum hose from the fuel pressure regulator.

18. Remove the fuel rail mounting screws.

19. Remove the fuel rail assembly with the fuel injectors.

20. Remove the intake manifold from the cylinder head.

21. Disconnect the oxygen sensor.

22. Remove the exhaust manifold from the cylinder head and exhaust pipe.

To install:

23. Install new gaskets and install the exhaust manifold to the cylinder head and the exhaust pipe.

24. Torque the M6 nuts to 7 ft. lbs. (10 Nm), M8 nuts to 18 ft. lbs. (25 Nm) and M10 nuts to 30 ft. lbs. (40 Nm).

25. Install the oxygen sensor. Tighten to 37 ft. lbs. (50 Nm).

26. Install the heat shield/stove bracket and the heat shield/stove.

27. Install new gasket and intake manifold and tighten bolts to 18 ft. lbs. (25 Nm).

28. Lubricate the fuel injector O-rings with oil.

29. Place the fuel rail on the intake manifold and tighten the mounting screws to 7 ft. lbs. (10 Nm).

30. Connect the vacuum hose to the fuel pressure regulator.

31. Connect the fuel supply and return hoses.

32. Connect the main fuel injector harness connector at the fuel rail.

33. Connect the crankcase breather hose and attach to the oil filler pipe.

34. Install the suction hose and air cleaner assembly, with element.

35. Connect the negative battery cable.

Pistons and Connecting Rods

REMOVAL AND INSTALLATION

EuroVan

1. Place the engine on a work stand.

2. Remove the cylinder head and gasket.

3. Remove the oil pan and gasket.

4. Label each piston and connecting rod for installation in the proper cylinder.

5. Front under the engine, remove the connecting rod bolts.

6. Remove the connecting rod bearing cap and bearing shells. Be sure to label bearing caps and bearing shells for installation into the proper cylinder.

7. Remove the piston and connecting rod from the top of the engine.

8. Remove the circlip from the wrist pin and using VW 222a or equivalent tool, remove the wrist pin from the piston. If difficult to remove, heat the piston to 150°F (60°C) and remove.

To install:

9. Be sure that the piston ring gaps are offset by 120 degrees and that the word "OBEN" is on the top side of the rings.

10. Place the connecting rod into the piston and insert the wrist pin.

11. Install the circlips on both sides of the wrist pin.

12. Carefully insert the piston and connecting rod into the proper cylinder bore.

13. Place the upper bearing shell between the crankshaft and the connecting rod. Place the lower bearing shell in the bearing cap and install on the crankshaft. Torque the new connecting rod bolts to 22 ft. lbs. (30 Nm), then turn the bolts an additional ¼ turn.

14. Install the oil pan with a new gasket.

15. Install the cylinder head and a new gasket.

ENGINE LUBRICATION

NOTE: Before disconnecting the negative battery cable, be sure to have the radio security code. Also, disconnecting the negative battery cable may interfere with the functions of the on board computer systems and may require the computer to undergo a relearning process, once the negative battery cable is reconnected.

Oil Pan

REMOVAL AND INSTALLATION

Eurovan

1. Place the engine in a work stand.

2. Remove the retaining bolts.

3. Remove the oil pan and the oil pan gasket from the cylinder block.

4. Installation is the reverse of the removal. Replace the oil pan gasket. Do not install the gasket with adhesive. Install M8 bolts with hex head on the transaxle side. Torque the bolts to 15 ft. lbs. (20 Nm).

Oil Pump

REMOVAL AND INSTALLATION

EuroVan

1. Disconnect the negative battery cable. Drain the engine oil.

2. Remove the upper toothed belt guard.

3. Remove the tensioner pulley and remove the toothed belt from the camshaft drive sprocket. Note the position of the camshaft drive sprocket and belt.

4. Remove the camshaft drive pulley. Remove the rear toothed belt guard.

5. Remove the crankshaft toothed pulley.

6. Remove the oil pressure relief valve.

7. Remove the bolts and remove the oil pump.

To install:

8. Install the oil pump and torque the bolts to 15 ft. lbs. (20 Nm).

9. Install the oil pressure relief valve. Torque to 30 ft. lbs. (40 Nm).

10. Install the crankshaft toothed pulley.

11. Install the rear toothed belt guard. Install the camshaft drive pulley.

12. Properly line up the toothed belt and the camshaft drive pulley. Torque the bolts labeled 8.8–63 ft. lbs. (85 Nm) and the bolts labeled 10.9–74 ft. lbs. (100 Nm).

13. Torque the bolt for the tensioner pulley to 15 ft. lbs. (20 Nm).

14. Install the tensioner pulley.

15. Install the upper toothed belt guard.

16. Connect the negative battery cable. Fill the engine oil and run the engine to check for leaks.

Flywheel Oil Seal

REMOVAL AND INSTALLATION

1. Remove the engine from the vehicle and support it in a suitable holding fixture. Remove the clutch, if equipped.

2. Remove the flywheel or torque converter driveplate.

3. Once the flywheel is removed, inspect the surface on the flywheel joining flange where the seal makes contact. If there is a deep grove or any other damage, the flywheel must be replace.

4. Remove the oil seal by prying it out of it's bore. Note the position of the the shims so they can be installed in the proper order.

5. Before installing a new seal, clean the crankcase oil seal recess and lubricate the new seal. Install the crankshaft endplay shims in the correct order.

6. Use an appropriate installation tool to press the seal in evenly. Be sure the seal rests squarely on the bottom of its recess. Make sure the correct side of the lip of the seal is facing inward, toward the crankcase.

7. Reinstall the flywheel after coating the oil seal contact surface with oil. Be careful not to damage the seal when sliding the flywheel into place. On the EuroVan torque the flywheel bolts to 22 ft. lbs. (30 Nm), then turn and additional ¼ turn.

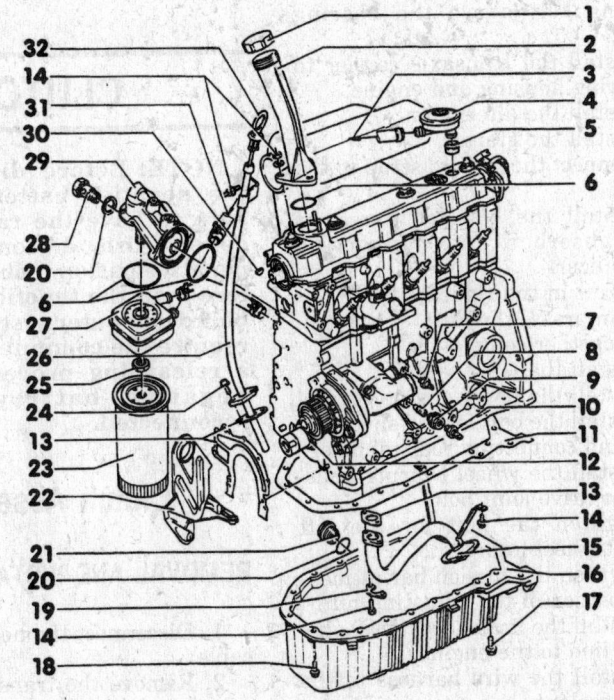

1	Screw cap
2	Oil filler pipe
3	To intake hose
4	Emission control valve
5	Oil seal
6	O-ring
7	0.3 bar oil pressure switch
8	Oil pressure retaining valve
9	Adaptor
10	1.8 bar oil pressure switch
11	Oil pan gasket
12	Drive dog for oil pump
13	Gasket
14	Bolt 10 Nm (7 ft lb)
15	Intake pipe
16	Oil pan
17	Bolt 20 Nm (15 ft lb)
18	Bolt 10 Nm (7 ft lb)
19	Locking plate
20	Oil seal
22	Baffle
23	Oil filter
24	Bolt 20 Nm (15 ft lb)
25	Nut 25 Nm (18 ft lb)
26	Guide tube
27	Oil cooler
28	Bolt 70 Nm (52 ft lb)
29	Oil filter bracket
30	Woodruff key
31	Dipstick
32	Hose

85470059

Lubrication system components — EuroVan

MANUAL TRANSAXLE

NOTE: Before disconnecting the negative battery cable, be sure to have the radio security code. Also, disconnecting the negative battery cable may interfere with the functions of the on board computer systems and may require the computer to undergo a relearning process, once the negative battery cable is reconnected.

Transaxle Assembly

REMOVAL AND INSTALLATION

EuroVan

1. Disconnect the negative battery cable.
2. Disconnect the clutch cable at the holder.
3. Remove the screws from the radiator and tilt forward.
4. Disconnect the electrical connectors from the transaxle and starter. Loosen the wire holder on the coolant hoses.
5. Unscrew the swivel head linkage connector on the transaxle.
6. Remove the front gear selector rod from the transaxle shift lever.
7. Unscrew the slave cylinder from the transaxle, set aside and secure with a wire.
8. Remove the holder for the input shaft/speedometer from the transaxle.
9. Remove the pipe for coolant, from the expansion tank to the water pump, from the starter.
10. Remove the wire harness from the pipe.
11. Remove the brake booster/engine vacuum line from the engine.
12. Release the tension on the torsion bar after measuring the position of the adjusting nut.
13. Loosen the bolt for the left halfshaft/wheel hub with the vehicle bearing on its road wheels.
14. Remove the wheel bearing housing/lower drive joint bolt. Support the drive joint.
15. Remove the bolt for the shock absorber and connecting rod/stabilizer.
16. Remove the lower engine cover.
17. Unscrew the left halfshaft from the transaxle.

18. Compress the shock absorber together completely.
19. Remove the left halfshaft.
20. Unscrew the right halfshaft and tie up.
21. Remove the bolt for the right shock absorber and connecting rod/stabilizer.
22. Disconnect the ground strap from the gearbox.
23. Remove the starter.
24. Remove the alternator.
25. Remove the transaxle carrier from the bearing housing and engine.
26. Remove the engine/transaxle mounting bolt above the bearing housing.
27. Without opening the air conditioning system, unbolt and move the compressor.
28. Remove the mounting bolts for the bonded rubber bushing.
29. Remove the drive shaft for the speedometer.
30. Using catching fixture 3184 or equivalent tool, remove the transaxle from the vehicle.

To install:

31. Install the transaxle to the vehicle.
32. Install the drive shaft for the speedometer.
33. Install the mounting bolts for the bonded rubber bushing.
34. Install air conditioning compressor.
35. Install the engine/transaxle mounting bolt above the bearing housing.
36. Install the transaxle carrier to the bearing housing and engine.
37. Install the alternator.
38. Install the starter.
39. Connect the ground strap to the gearbox.
40. Install the bolt for the right shock absorber and connecting rod/stabilizer.
41. Screw in the right halfshaft.
42. Compress the left shock absorber together completely.
43. Install the left halfshaft.
44. Install the lower engine cover.
45. Install the bolt for the shock absorber and connecting rod/stabilizer.
46. Install the wheel bearing housing/lower drive joint bolt.
47. Tighten the bolt for the left halfshaft/wheel hub.
48. Tighten the torsion bar at measured position of the adjusting nut.
49. Install the brake booster/engine vacuum line to the engine.
50. Install the wire harness to the pipe for coolant.
51. Install the pipe for coolant, from the expansion tank to the water pump, to the starter.

52. Install the holder for the input shaft/speedometer to the transaxle.
53. Install the slave cylinder to the transaxle.
54. Install the front gear selector rod to the transaxle shift lever.
55. Install the swivel head linkage connector on the transaxle.
56. Connect the electrical connectors to the transaxle and starter.
57. Return the radiator to its normal position and install the screws.
58. Connect the clutch cable at the holder.
59. Connect the negative battery cable.

LINKAGE ADJUSTMENT

EuroVan

1. Place the transaxle in neutral.
2. Loosen the clamp to allow free movement of the gate selector rod/gear shift console connect.
3. Remove the gear lever know and cover. Remove the frame with the rubber gaiter.
4. Insert the gauge 3258 or equivalent, as far as the stop. Tightening the knurled head screw.
5. Align the gate selector rod/gear shift console to be free of tension and tighten the clamp to 15 ft. lbs. (20 Nm).

CLUTCH

NOTE: Before disconnecting the negative battery cable, be sure to have the radio security code. Also, disconnecting the negative battery cable may interfere with the functions of the on board computer systems and may require the computer to undergo a relearning process, once the negative battery cable is reconnected.

Clutch Assembly

REMOVAL AND INSTALLATION

1. Disconnect the negative battery cable.
2. Remove the transaxle from the vehicle.
3. Remove the pressure plate securing bolts a turn at a time until all spring pressure is released.

4. Remove the bolts and remove the clutch assembly.

NOTE: Note which side of the clutch disc faces the flywheel and install the new disc in the same direction.

5. Before installing the new clutch, check the condition of the flywheel. It should not have excessive heat cracks and the friction surface should not be scored or warped. Check the condition of the throw out bearing. If the bearing is worn, replace it.

To install:

6. Lubricate the pilot bearing in the end of the crankshaft with grease.

7. Insert a pilot shaft, used for centering the clutch disc, through the clutch disc and place the disc against the flywheel. The pilot shaft will hold the disc in place.

NOTE: Make sure the correct side of the clutch disc is facing outward. The disc will rub the flywheel if it is incorrectly positioned.

8. After making sure the pressure plate aligning dowels will fit into the pressure plate, tighten the bolts a turn at a time until the plate is pulled into place. Torque the bolts to 15 ft. lbs. (20 Nm) on the EuroVan.

9. Remove the pilot shaft and install the transaxle.

10. Bleed the clutch system. Connect the negative battery cable. Check for proper operation of the clutch.

PEDAL HEIGHT ADJUSTMENT

1. The clutch pedal should have a free-play of 0.20–0.28 in. (5–7mm) and a 7 in. (178mm) total travel. If either of the above are not to specifications, adjust the master cylinder as follows.

2. Loosen the master cylinder pushrod locknut and shorten the pushrod length slightly.

3. Loosen the master cylinder bolts and push the cylinder as far forward as it will go. Retighten the bolts.

4. Remove the rubber cap from the clutch pedal stop screw and adjust distance to 0.89 in. (22mm). Install the rubber cap.

5. Lengthen the pushrod as necessary to obtain a pedal freeplay of 0.20–0.28 in. (5–7mm). Tighten the pushrod locknut.

6. Road test the vehicle to insure proper clutch operation.

Clutch Master Cylinder

REMOVAL AND INSTALLATION

1. Disconnect the negative battery cable.

2. Siphon the hydraulic fluid from the clutch master cylinder reservoir.

3. Pull back the carpeting from the pedal area and place some absorbent rags under the reservoir.

4. Pull the elbow connection from the top of the clutch master cylinder.

5. Disconnect and plug the pressure line from the rear of the master cylinder.

6. Remove the master cylinder mounting bolts and remove the cylinder from the rear.

7. Installation is the reverse of the removal procedure. Bleed the clutch system when finished.

Clutch Slave Cylinder

REMOVAL AND INSTALLATION

1. Locate the slave cylinder on the bell housing.

2. Disconnect and plug the pressure line from the slave cylinder.

3. Disconnect the return spring from the pushrod.

4. Remove the retaining circlip from the boot and remove the boot.

5. Remove the circlip and slide the slave cylinder rearwards from its mount.

6. Remove the spring clip from the mount.

7. Installation is the reverse of the removal procedure. Bleed the system and check the operation of the clutch.

Bleeding Hydraulic Clutch System

NOTE: Use brake fluid that meets DOT 3 or DOT 4 specifications.

1. Fill the clutch fluid reservoir and make sure the cap vent is open.

2. Locate the slave cylinder bleed nipple and remove all dirt and grease from the valve. Attach a hose to the nipple and submerge the other end of the hose in a glass jar containing clean brake fluid.

3. Have an assistant operate the clutch pedal. Depress the clutch pedal slowly to the floor, open the bleeder valve 1 turn. Hold the pedal on the floor until the bleeder valve is closed. Repeat this operation several times until no air bubbles are emitted from the tube.

NOTE: During the procedure, check the fluid level in the fluid reservoir. Never let the level fall below the ½ full mark.

4. After bleeding, discard the old fluid and top up the reservoir.

AUTOMATIC TRANSAXLE

NOTE: Before disconnecting the negative battery cable, be sure to have the radio security code. Also, disconnecting the negative battery cable may interfere with the functions of the on board computer systems and may require the computer to undergo a relearning process, once the negative battery cable is reconnected.

Transaxle Assembly

REMOVAL AND INSTALLATION

1. Disconnect the negative battery cable.

2. Remove the 3 torque converter-to-flywheel bolts through the hole in the top of the transaxle housing. Rotate the crankshaft to bring each bolt into position. Remove the top transaxle-to-engine bolts.

3. On the EuroVan, remove the screws and pull the radiator out on its hinges.

4. Raise and safely support the vehicle.

5. On the EuroVan, disconnect the front exhaust pipe and transaxle electrical connectors.

6. Disconnect both halfshafts from the transaxle, support them aside.

7. Disconnect the starter wiring and remove the starter.

8. Loosen the transaxle fluid dipstick tube.

9. Disconnect the accelerator linkage and accelerator cable.

10. Remove the circlip from the selector lever.

11. Support the engine with a suitable support bar.

12. Remove the ground strap and selector lever cable. Remove the side mounting bracket.

13. Support the transaxle with a suitable lifting device. Remove the rear transaxle support.

14. Remove the lower transaxle-to-engine bolts. Slowly lower the transaxle out of the vehicle. Use care not to drop the torque converter from the input shaft.

To install:

15. Make sure the torque converter is properly mounted on the one-way clutch and firmly seated into place. If the torque converter slips out of place when installing the transaxle, the oil pump driveshaft could be pulled out of the pump. This will cause serious damage when bolting the transaxle to the engine.

16. Raise the transaxle into position and start the bolts. Keep checking that the torque converter turns freely when tightening the bolts. If there is any binding, the torque converter has slipped off the clutch support and must be re-installed.

17. When the transaxle is fully in place against the engine, torque the lower bolts to 22 ft. lbs. (30 Nm).

18. Install the rear transaxle support.

19. Install the ground strap and selector lever cable. Install the side mounting bracket.

20. Remove the engine support bar and connect the selector lever.

21. Connect the accelerator cable and linkage. Attach the dipstick tube.

22. Install the starter and connect the wiring.

23. Connect the halfshafts and tighten the bolts to 33 ft. lbs. (45 Nm).

24. Install the upper transaxle bolts, tighten to 22 ft. lbs. (35 Nm).

25. On the EuroVan, connect the front exhaust pipe and the transaxle electrical connectors.

26. Lower the vehicle and install the torque converter bolts. Tighten to 22 ft. lbs. (35 Nm).

27. On the EuroVan, place the radiator back and tighten the screws.

28. Adjust the linkage as required. Connect the negative battery cable and check the operation of the transaxle.

SHIFT LINKAGE ADJUSTMENT

1. Make sure the shift cable is not kinked or bent and that the linkage and cable are properly lubricated.

2. Move the gear shift lever to the **P** position.

3. Loosen the shift rod bolt at the bottom of the selector, under the floor of the EuroVan.

4. Operate the transaxle control by hand to make sure it is in park.

5. Push the shift rod towards the rear and tighten the bolt.

DRIVELINE

Halfshaft

REMOVAL AND INSTALLATION

EuroVan

WITH MANUAL TRANSAXLE

1. Install the support tool 3250 or equivalent, to support the upper control arm.

2. Loosen the halfshaft bolt with the wheels on the ground.

3. Raise and safely support the vehicle.

4. Remove the bolts securing the wheel bearing housing to lower ball joint.

5. Remove the bolt for the shock absorber/stabilizer link rod.

6. Remove the axle shaft from the drive flange of the transaxle.

7. Compress the shock absorber completely and remove the halfshaft.

To install:

8. Compress the shock absorber completely and install the halfshaft. Release the shock absorber.

9. Install the axle shaft to the drive flange of the transaxle. Torque to 41 ft. lbs. (55 Nm).

10. Install the bolt for the shock absorber/stabilizer link rod.

11. Install the bolt securing the wheel bearing housing to the lower ball joint. Torque to 41 ft. lbs. (55 Nm).

12. Lower the vehicle and tighten the halfshaft bolt. Torque to 148 ft. lbs. (200 Nm).

WITH AUTOMATIC TRANSAXLE

1. Install the support tool 3250 or equivalent, to support the upper control arm on the left and right sides.

2. Loosen the half shaft with the wheels on the ground.

3. Raise and safely support the vehicle.

4. Remove the left shock absorber from the lower control arm and compress.

5. Remove the bolts and separate the wheel bearing housing/lower ball joint.

6. Remove the plug from the multi-function switch.

7. Remove the halfshaft from transaxle drive flange.

To install:

8. Install the halfshaft to the transaxle drive flange. Torque to 41 ft. lbs. (55 Nm).

9. Install the plug from the multi-function switch.

10. Install the wheel bearing housing/lower ball joint and tighten the bolts to 41 ft. lbs. (55 Nm).

11. Install the left shock absorber to the lower control arm and compress. Torque to 118 ft. lbs. (160 Nm).

12. Lower the vehicle.

13. Tighten the halfshaft with the wheels on the ground. Torque to 148 ft. lbs. (200 Nm).

Front Wheel Bearing and Seal

REMOVAL AND INSTALLATION

EuroVan

1. Install the support 3250 or equivalent tool, on both sides.

2. Loosen the axle shaft with the vehicle on all 4 wheels.

3. Remove the wheel. Raise and safely support the vehicle.

4. Remove the link rod bolt.

5. Remove the brake caliper and hang to the body with a wire.

6. Remove the brake disc and splash shield.

7. Press the rod off the steering arm.

8. Remove the bolts securing the wheel bearing housing/lower ball joint.

9. Mark the position of the eccentric bushing to the wheel bearing housing.

10. Separate the wheel bearing housing/upper ball joint.

11. Remove the wheel bearing housing.

12. Using tools 3253/1, 40-105, and VW408a or equivalents, press the wheel hub out of the wheel bearing housing.

13. Using tools 3253/1, VW442 and VW407 or equivalents, press the wheel bearing out of the housing.

To install:

14. Carefully press the new bearing into the housing. Be sure to press only on the outer race or the bearing will be damaged. Install the circlip.

15. Lubricate and install the new seals. Make sure they are installed evenly and fully seated in place.

16. When pressing the hub into the bearing, be sure to properly support the inner bearing race or the bearing will be damaged.

17. Install the wheel bearing housing.

18. Install the wheel bearing at the upper ball joint.

19. Install the wheel bearing at the lower ball joint and tighten the bolts.

20. Attach the rod to the steering arm.

21. Install the splash shield and the brake disc. Install the brake caliper.

22. Install the link rod bolt.

23. Install the wheel. Lower the vehicle.

24. Tighten the axle shaft to 199 ft. lbs. (270 Nm).

STEERING

NOTE: Before disconnecting the negative battery cable, be sure to have the radio security code. Also, disconnecting the negative battery cable may interfere with the functions of the on board computer systems and may require the computer to undergo a relearning process, once the negative battery cable is reconnected.

Steering Wheel

REMOVAL AND INSTALLATION

EuroVan

1. Disconnect the negative battery cable

2. Unclip the horn pad.

3. Remove the steering wheel nut.

4. Mark the steering wheel for reference when reinstalling. Remove the steering wheel.

To install:

5. Install the steering wheel, lining up the marks.

6. Tighten nut to 52 ft. lbs. (70 Nm).

7. Install horn pad.

Steering Column

REMOVAL AND INSTALLATION

1. Disconnect the negative battery cable.

2. Remove the steering wheel.

3. Remove the combination switch assemblies.

4. Disconnect the upper steering column from the lower steering column.

5. Disconnect the steering column from the column support.

6. Remove the steering column.

To install:

7. Install the steering column to the lower steering column and replace the bolts.

8. Connect the steering column to the support.

9. Install the combination switches.

10. Install the steering wheel.

11. Connect the negative battery cable.

Power Steering Gear

REMOVAL AND INSTALLATION

1. Raise and safely support the vehicle.

2. On the EuroVan, remove the heat shield.

3. Detach the connecting shaft from the coupling disc.

4. Remove both tie rod end nuts and separate the tie rod ends from the wheel bearing housings.

5. At the steering gear pinion, remove the universal joint clamp bolt.

6. Disconnect and plug the power steering lines from the steering gear housing. Place a drain pan under the power steering pump suction hose to catch the fluid when removing the power steering lines, then discard the fluid.

7. Remove the clamps from the subframe and remove the steering gear assembly.

To install:

8. Install the steering gear assembly and install the clamps to the subframe. Use new self-locking nuts on the clamps.

9. Torque the clamp bolts to 24 ft. lbs. (33 Nm) on the EuroVan.

10. Connect the steering gear pinion and the universal joint clamp bolt.

11. Install the tie rod ends to the wheel bearings and replace the nuts. Tighten the nuts to 30 ft. lbs. (40 Nm).

12. Connect the connecting shaft to the coupling disc.

13. Connect the hydraulic hose, using new O-rings.

14. Lower the vehicle.

15. Refill the system and bleed the power steering unit.

16. Check and adjust the front wheel alignment.

Power Steering Pump

REMOVAL AND INSTALLATION

1. Disconnect the negative battery cable. Place a pan under the power steering pump when draining the fluid.

2. On the Eurovan, remove the screws from the radiator and pull the radiator out on its hinges.

3. Remove the suction hose and pressure line from the pump, then drain the fluid into the pan.

4. Remove the V-belt pulley. Do not remove the pump bracket.

5. Remove the pump mounting bolts and remove the pump from the vehicle.

To install:

6. Install the pump and tighten the mounting bolts. Torque to 15 ft. lbs. (20 Nm).

7. Install the V-belt and pulley. Torque the bolts to 15 ft. lbs. (20 Nm).

8. Install the hoses using new O-rings.

9. Fill the reservoir with approved power steering fluid and bleed the system.

SYSTEM BLEEDING

1. Fill the power steering reservoir to **MAX** with Dexron® II automatic transmission fluid.

2. Raise and safely support the vehicle.

3. With the engine off, rotate the steering wheel from lock to lock.

4. Fill the reservoir to the **MAX** mark.

5. Start the engine several times, turning it off immediately after the engine starts. Add fluid as necessary, maintaining the level at the **MAX** mark.

NOTE: Never let the reservoir run out of fluid. Damage to the pump and/or steering gear may result.

6. When the fluid level no longer drops, start and run the engine. Rotate the steering wheel lock to lock several times. Check that no bubbles appear in the reservoir and that the level remains steady.

7. If air bubbles appear, repeat the procedure until the fluid is clear.

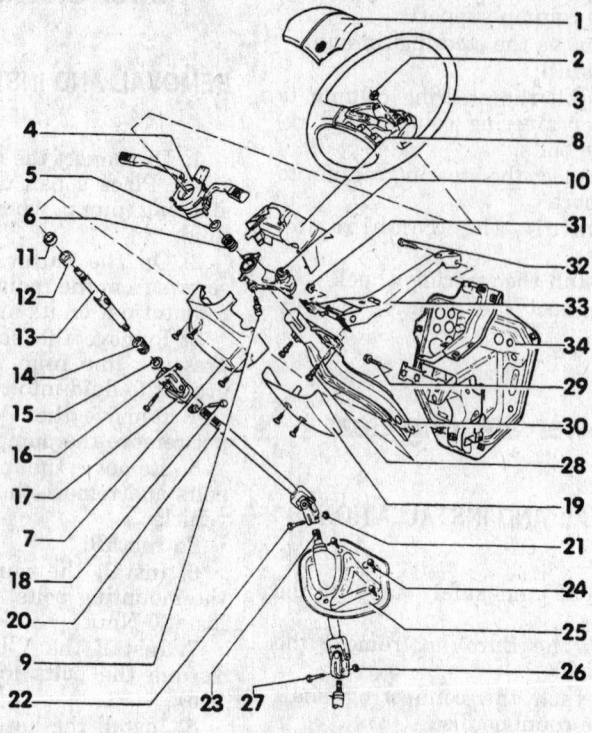

1 Cover
2 Nut 70 Nm (52 ft lb)
3 Steering wheel
4 Steering column switch
5 Clamping washer
6 Upper spring
7 Lower cover
8 Upper cover
9 Shear bolt
10 Steering lock housing
11 Support ring
12 Spacer bush
13 Upper steering column
14 Lower spring
15 Washer
16 Nut 30 Nm (22 ft lb)
17 Universal joint
18 Bolt 30 Nm (22 ft lb)
19 Cover
20 Center Steering column
21 Nut 30 Nm (22 ft lb)
22 Bolt
23 Lower steering column
24 Bolt 20 Nm (15 ft lb)
25 Relay plate with locating pin
26 Nut 30 Nm (22 ft lb)
27 Bolt
28 Shear bolt
29 Bolt 20 Nm (15 ft lb)
30 Column tube with lower bearing
   for steering column
31 Nut 16 Nm (12 ft lb)
32 Bolt 20 Nm (15 ft lb)
33 Crumble support
34 Mounting plate

85470062

Steering column assembly — EuroVan

Tie Rod Ends

REMOVAL AND INSTALLATION

1. Raise and safely support the vehicle.
2. Remove the cotter pins and nuts and separate the tie rod ends from the wheel bearing housing.
3. Loosen the locknut at the inner end and count the number of turns required to remove the tie rod end.
4. Installation is the reverse of the removal procedure. Be sure to install the tie rod end the same number of turns into the tie rod, then tighten the nut.
5. Install the tie rod end into the wheel bearing housing. Torque the tie rod end nut to 30 ft. lbs. (40 Nm).
6. Check and adjust the toe-in when finished.

BRAKES

NOTE: Before disconnecting the negative battery cable, be sure to have the radio security code. Also, disconnecting the negative battery cable may interfere with the functions of the on board computer systems and may require the computer to undergo a relearning process, once the negative battery cable is reconnected.

Master Cylinder

REMOVAL AND INSTALLATION

EuroVan

1. Disconnect the negative battery cable.
2. Disconnect the electrical connector.
3. Disconnect, tag and plug the brake lines at the master cylinder.
4. Remove the master cylinder mounting nuts.
5. Lift the master cylinder and reservoir out of the vehicle.

NOTE: Do not depress the brake pedal while the master cylinder is removed.

To install:

6. Position the master cylinder and reservoir assembly onto the mounting studs and install the washers and nuts. tighten the nuts.

7. Remove the plugs and connect the brake lines to the master cylinder.
8. Connect the wiring to master cylinder.
9. Connect the negative battery cable.
10. Fill the master cylinder and bleed the brake system.

Power Brake Booster

REMOVAL AND INSTALLATION

EuroVan

The brake booster is part of the master cylinder.

Disc Brake Pads

REMOVAL AND INSTALLATION

1. Raise and support the vehicle safely. Remove the wheel and tire assembly.
2. Using a 3/32 in. (2.4mm) drift pin, carefully drive the brake pad retaining pins inward.
3. Remove the brake pads.
4. Push the caliper piston into the caliper until it bottoms out.

To install:

5. Install the new brake pads and retaining pins. Check that the pins are fully seated in the caliper.

6. Install the wheel and tire assembly.

7. Repeat the procedure for the opposite side. Check the brake fluid level in the reservoir when finished.

8. Depress the brake pedal several times until pressure is felt before moving the vehicle.

Brake Rotor

REMOVAL AND INSTALLATION

EuroVan

1. Raise and safely support the vehicle. Remove the wheel and tire assembly.

2. Remove the brake pads and pins.

3. Without disconnecting the hydraulic hose, remove the brake caliper from the wheel bearing housing and support it out of the way. Do not let it hang by the hose.

4. Remove the screws and pull the rotor off the hub.

5. Installation is the reverse of the removal procedure. Torque the caliber bolts to 66 ft. lbs. (90 Nm).

Brake Drums

REMOVAL AND INSTALLATION

1. Raise and safely support the vehicle.

2. Remove the wheel and tire assembly.

3. Remove the drum retaining screws.

4. Remove the brake drum. If the drum will come off easily, turn the adjuster through the hole near the top of the backing plate.

5. Installation is the reverse of the removal. Adjust the brakes as required.

Brake Shoes

REMOVAL AND INSTALLATION

1. Raise and safely support the vehicle.

2. Remove the wheel and tire assembly.

3. Remove the brake drum.

4. Remove the brake shoe hold-down springs and pins.

5. Unhook the parking brake lever at the leading brake shoe.

6. Remove the lower return spring and the adjuster spring.

7. Move the brake shoes out of the lower support and unhook the return springs.

8. Remove the brake shoes and the push/adjusting rod.

To install:

9. Make sure the adjuster turns easily. Install the return springs and adjuster/push rod on the brake shoes.

10. Install the shoes on the backing plate and into the lower support.

11. Pull the top of the brake shoes around the wheel cylinder.

12. Install the hold-down spring and the pins.

13. Install the adjuster spring.

14. Attach the parking brake lever. Install the lower return spring.

15. Turn the brake adjuster to pre-adjust the shoes so they are about 0.060 in. (1.5mm) smaller diameter than the inside diameter of the drum.

16. Install the brake drum. Install the wheel and tire assembly.

17. Check the adjustment of the brakes.

Wheel Cylinder

REMOVAL AND INSTALLATION

1. Raise and support the vehicle safely. Remove the wheel and tire assembly. Remove the brake drum and brake shoes.

2. Disconnect and plug the brake line on the rear of the wheel cylinder.

3. Remove the bolts and lockwashers that attach the wheel cylinder to the backing plate and remove the wheel cylinder.

4. Position the new wheel cylinder on the backing plate and install the attaching bolts and lockwashers.

5. Connect the brake line.

6. Install the brake drum, brake shoes, wheel and tire assembly. Bleed the wheel cylinder.

Parking Brake Cable

REMOVAL AND INSTALLATION

1. Disconnect the cables at the hand brake lever by removing the nuts which secure the cables to the lever. Pull the cables rearward to remove that end from the lever bracket.

2. Raise and support the vehicle safely. Remove the wheel and tire assemblies.

3. Remove the brake drum and detach the cable end from the lever attached to the rear brake shoe.

4. Remove the brake cable bracket from the backing plate and remove the cable from the vehicle.

5. Installation is the reverse of the removal procedure.

6. Adjust the parking brake.

ADJUSTMENT

EuroVan

1. Release the parking brake.

2. Remove both rear drums.

3. Tighten the parking brake adjusting nut until the brake lever moves 0.08 in. (2.0mm) away from the brake shoe.

4. Reinstall the brake drums.

5. Check if both wheels rotate freely.

Anti-Lock Brakes Module

REMOVAL AND INSTALLATION

EuroVan

The ABS control module is located near lower left A-pillar.

1. Disconnect the negative battery cable.

2. Remove cover from the relay panel.

3. Pull aside the carpeting at the left A-pillar.

4. Press the spring to release the control module connector.

5. Pull the control module connector off upwards.

6. Remove the control module mounting screws.

7. Remove the control module from bracket.

To install:

8. Install the control module to the bracket.

9. Install the control module mounting screws.

10. Connect the electrical connector.

11. Install the carpeting. Replace relay panel cover.

12. Connect the negative battery cable.

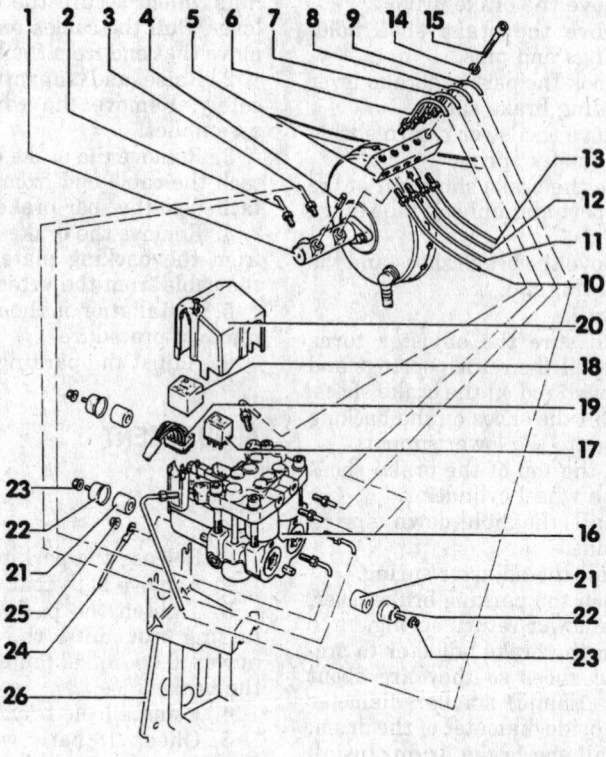

1. Tandem master cylinder
2. Secondary piston circuit brake line
3. Primary piston circuit brake line
4. Spring pin
5. Intermediate piece
6. Brake line "VR"
7. Brake line "HR"
8. Brake line "HL"
9. Brake line "VL"
10. Front right brake caliper line
11. Rear right wheel cylinder brake line
12. Rear left wheel cylinder brake line
13. Front left caliper brake line
14. Washer
15. Bolt 10 Nm (7 ft lb)
16. Hydraulic modulator (N 55)
17. Solenoid valve relay (J 106)
18. Return flow pump relay (J 105)
19. Wiring harness
20. Cover
21. Buffer
22. Mounting bushing
23. Nut
24. Ground wire
25. Nut
26. Console

85470063

Braking system with ABS — EuroVan

FRONT SUSPENSION

Shock Absorber

REMOVAL AND INSTALLATION

1. Raise and support the vehicle safely so the front suspension is hanging freely. Remove the wheel and tire assembly.

2. Support the lower control arm and remove the upper and lower shock absorber mounting bolts, nuts and washers.

3. Remove the shock absorber from the vehicle.

To install:

4. Install the shock absorber, rubber boot and stopper.

5. Tighten the upper shock absorber mounting nut until the rubber washer is compressed to the same width as the metal washer.

6. Raise the lower control arm and tighten the lower shock absorber mounting bolt to 118 ft. lbs. (160 Nm) on the EuroVan.

7. Install the wheel and tire assembly. Lower the vehicle.

Coil Spring

REMOVAL AND INSTALLATION

Upper Ball Joint

INSPECTION

1. Raise and support the vehicle safely so the front wheels are hanging freely.

2. Insert a prybar between the ball joint pinch bolt and the upper control arm.

3. Measure the distance of ball joint play.

4. If the play exceeds 0.1 in. (2.5mm), replace the ball joint.

REMOVAL AND INSTALLATION

EuroVan

1. Install support tool 3250 or the equivalent, on the right and left side.

2. Loosen the halfshaft bolt with the vehicle on the ground.

3. Remove the brake caliper and hang up with wire.

4. Remove the bolts and separate the lower ball joint and the wheel bearing housing.

5. Remove the bolt for the shock absorber and link rod/stabilizer.

6. Mark the position of the eccentric washer to the wheel bearing housing.

7. Remove the nut for upper ball joint.

8. Remove the mounting bolt for the eccentric washer from the wheel bearing housing.

9. Remove the wheel bearing housing.

10. Remove the eccentric bushing. Remove the circlip.

11. Press out ball joint.

To install:

12. Install the ball joint into the control arm. Install new circlip.

13. Install the eccentric bushing.

14. Bolt upper ball joint into the wheel bearing housing.

15. Install the wheel bearing housing.

16. Connect the shock absorber. Install the brake caliper.

17. Lower the vehicle and torque the halfshaft bolt to 148 ft. lbs. (200 Nm).

Lower Ball Joint

INSPECTION

1. Raise and safely support the vehicle so the front wheels are hanging freely.
2. Insert a prybar between the ball joint pinch bolt and the lower control arm.
3. Measure the distance of ball joint play.
4. If the play exceeds 0.1 in. (2.5mm), replace the ball joint.

REMOVAL AND INSTALLATION

EuroVan

1. The lower ball joint can be changed without removing the wheel bearing housing. Raise and safely support the vehicle and remove the wheel.
2. Install support tool 3250 or equivalent, on both sides.
3. Remove the bolt for the shock absorber and coupling rod/stabilizer.
4. Remove the bolts and separate the ball joint and the wheel bearing housing.
5. Press out the ball joint.
   To install:
6. Press the new ball joint into place.
7. Install the ball joint to the wheel bearing housing.
8. Connect the shock absorber and coupling rod/stabilizer and tighten bolt.
9. Check and adjust the front wheel alignment.

Upper Control Arms

REMOVAL AND INSTALLATION

1. Raise and support the vehicle safely. Remove the wheel and tire assembly.
2. Raise the lower control arm to place a slight load.
3. Disconnect the upper ball joint from the bearing housing.
4. Remove the upper control arm camber adjustment bolt and remove the control arm.
   To install:
5. Fit the control arm in place and install the long bolt with the eccentric washers.
6. On the EuroVan, torque the M14 bolts to 74 ft. lbs. (100 Nm).
7. Connect the upper ball joint and torque the bolts to 44 ft. lbs. (60 Nm).

8. Check and adjust the front wheel alignment.

Lower Control Arms

REMOVAL AND INSTALLATION

1. Raise and support the vehicle safely. Remove the wheel and tire assembly.
2. Remove the shock absorber and coil spring.
3. Disconnect the link rod from the control arm.
4. Remove the lower control arm bushing bolt and remove the control arm.
   To install:
5. Install the lower control arm in position, install the mounting bolt and torque to 118 ft. lbs. (160 Nm).
6. Install the link rod.
7. Install the shock and coil spring.
8. Install the wheel and tire. Check and adjust the front wheel alignment.

Torsion Bar

REMOVAL AND INSTALLATION

EuroVan

1. Disconnect the negative battery cable.
2. Remove the fuel tank.
3. Remove the exhaust system heat shield.
4. Mark the adjustment of the torsion bar on the thread of the stud.
5. Loosen the torsion bar.
6. Remove the bolts securing the torsion bar to the control arm and remove the torsion bar.
   To install:
7. Install the torsion bar and tighten the bolts.
8. Adjust the torsion bar to the marks on the studs.
9. Install the heat shield and the fuel tank.
10. Connect the negative battery cable.

REAR SUSPENSION

Shock Absorber

REMOVAL AND INSTALLATION

EuroVan

1. With the vehicle on its wheels, remove the behind the tire in the wheelwell.
2. Lift the vehicle to release the coil spring tension.
3. Hold the shock absorber with tool 3254 or equivalent, and remove from the control arm.
4. Installation is the reverse of the removal procedure.

Coil Springs

REMOVAL AND INSTALLATION

1. Raise and safely support the vehicle.
2. Remove the wheel and tire assembly.
3. Support the trailing arm or control arm and remove the shock absorber.
4. Lower the trailing arm or control arm slightly and remove the coil spring.
5. Installation is the reverse of the removal procedure.

Trailing Arms

REMOVAL AND INSTALLATION

—— CAUTION ——
Torque on the axle nut is very high and loosening it with a breaker bar may cause the vehicle to fall off the supports. Do not loosen or tighten this nut unless the vehicle is on all 4 wheels.

1. Raise and safely support the vehicle. Remove the wheel and tire.
2. Use a wheel puller to remove the hub.
3. Disconnect and plug the brake hydraulic line and disconnect the parking brake cable.
4. Remove the backing plate assembly from the trailing arm. The brake shoes do not need to be removed.
5. Disconnect the stabilizer bar.
6. Disconnect and remove the shock absorber and the coil spring.

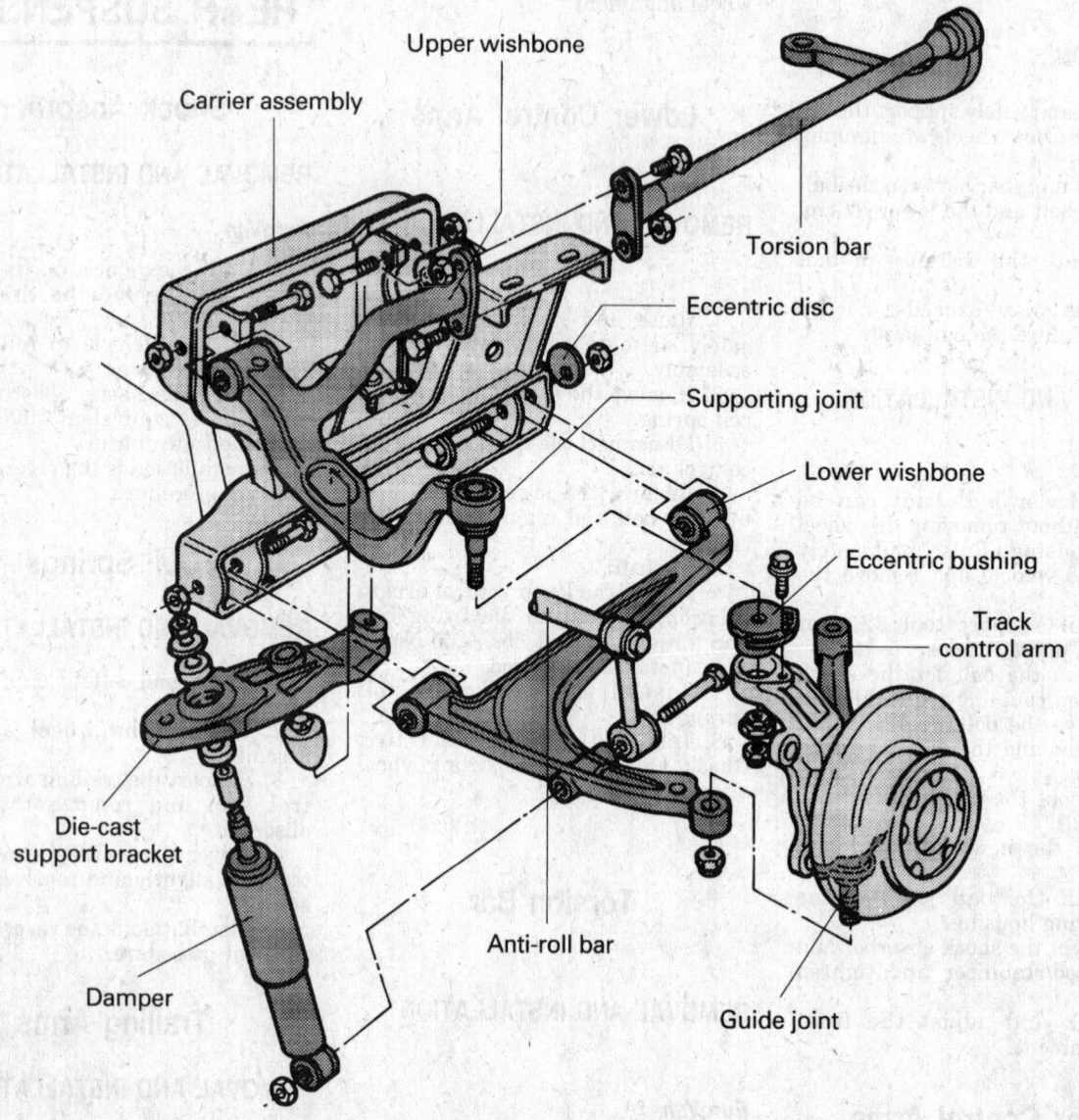

Upper wishbone

Carrier assembly

Torsion bar

Eccentric disc

Supporting joint

Lower wishbone

Eccentric bushing

Track control arm

Die-cast support bracket

Anti-roll bar

Damper

Guide joint

85470065

View of the front suspension assembly — EuroVan

7. Remove the trailing arm pivot bolt and lower the trailing arm from the vehicle.

To install:

8. Install the trailing arm in position and torque the pivot bolts to 74 ft. lbs. (100 Nm).

9. Install the shock absorber and the coil spring.

10. Connect the stabilizer bar. Torque bolt to 22 ft. lbs. (30 Nm).

11. Install the brake backing plate and torque the bolts 118 ft. lbs. (160 Nm). Connect the parking brake cable and the hydraulic line.

12. Install the hub and hand tighten the axle nut. Install the brake drum. Bleed and adjust the brakes as required.

Stabilizer Bar

REMOVAL AND INSTALLATION

EuroVan

1. Raise and safely support the vehicle.

2. Remove the wheel and tire assembly.

3. Remove the stabilizer bar linkage nuts on each side.

4. Remove the upper stabilizer bar brackets and bushings.

5. Remove the stabilizer bar from the vehicle.

To install:

6. Install the stabilizer in position. Install the brackets and bushings and torque the nuts or bolts to 18 ft. lbs. (25 Nm).

7. Install the stabilizer bar linkage and torque the nuts to 22 ft. lbs. (30 Nm).

Specifications

14

CHRYSLER CORPORATION

VEHICLE IDENTIFICATION CHART

		Engine Code					Model Year	
Code	Liters	Cu. In. (cc)	Cyl.	Fuel Sys.	Eng. Mfg.		Code	Year
K	2.5	153 (2507)	I4	TFI	Chrysler		N	1992
3	3.0	181 (2972)	V6	MFI	Mitsubishi		P	1993
R	3.3	201 (3300)	V6	MFI	Chrysler		R	1994
X	3.9	238 (3916)	V6	MFI	Chrysler		S	1995
Y	5.2	318 (5211)	V8	MFI	Chrysler		T	1996
8	5.9	359 (5882)	I6	DSL	Cummins			
5	5.9	360 (5899)	V8	TFI	Chrysler			
Z	5.9	360 (5899)	V8	TFI	Chrysler			
K	2.5	153 (2507)	I4	TFI	Chrysler			
3	3.0	181 (2972)	V6	MFI	Mitsubishi			
R	3.3	201 (3300)	V6	MFI	Chrysler			
X	3.9	238 (3916)	V6	MFI	Chrysler			
Y	5.2	318 (5211)	V8	MFI	Chrysler			
8	5.9	359 (5882)	I6	DSL	Cummins			
5	5.9	360 (5899)	V8	MFI	Chrysler			
Z	5.9	360 (5899)	V8	MFI	Chrysler			
K	2.5	153 (2507)	I4	TFI	Chrysler			
3	3.0	181 (2972)	V6	MFI	Mitsubishi			
R	3.3	201 (3300)	V6	MFI	Chrysler			
L	3.8	231 (3785)	V6	MFI	Chrysler			
X	3.9	238 (3916)	V6	MFI	Chrysler			
Y	5.2	318 (5211)	V8	MFI	Chrysler			
C	5.9	359 (5882)	I6	DSL	Cummins			
A	5.9	360 (5899)	V8	MFI	Chrysler			
5	5.9	360 (5899)	V8	MFI	Chrysler			
Z	5.9	360 (5899)	V8	MFI	Chrysler			
W	8.0	488 (7997)	V10	MFI	Chrysler			
G	2.5	153 (2507)	I4	TFI	Chrysler			
K	2.5	153 (2507)	I4	TFI	Chrysler			
3	3.0	181 (2972)	V6	MFI	Mitsubishi			
R	3.3	201 (3300)	V6	MFI	Chrysler			
L	3.8	231 (3785)	V6	MFI	Chrysler			
X	3.9	238 (3916)	V6	MFI	Chrysler			
Y	5.2	318 (5211)	V8	MFI	Chrysler			
C	5.9	359 (5882)	I6	DSL	Cummins			
5	5.9	360 (5899)	V8	MFI	Chrysler			
Z	5.9	360 (5899)	V8	MFI	Chrysler			
W	8.0	488 (7997)	V10	MFI	Chrysler			

DSL - Diesel
MFI - Multiport fuel injection
TFI - Throttle body fuel injection

ENGINE IDENTIFICATION

Year	Model	Engine Displacement Liters (cc)	Engine Series (ID/VIN)	Fuel System	No. of Cylinders	Engine Type
1992	Caravan	2.5 (2507)	K	TFI	4	SOHC
	Caravan	3.0 (2972)	3	MFI	6	SOHC
	Caravan	3.3 (3300)	R	MFI	6	OHV
	Dakota	2.5 (2507)	K	TFI	4	SOHC
	Dakota	3.9 (3916)	X	MFI	6	OHV
	Dakota	5.2 (5211)	Y	MFI	8	OHV
	Voyager	2.5 (2507)	K	TFI	4	SOHC
	Voyager	3.0 (2972)	3	MFI	6	SOHC
	Voyager	3.3 (3300)	R	MFI	6	OHV
	Town & Country	3.3 (3300)	R	MFI	6	OHV
	B150 Van	3.9 (3916)	X	MFI	6	OHV
	B150 Van	5.2 (5211)	Y	MFI	8	OHV
	B250 Van	3.9 (3916)	X	MFI	6	OHV
	B250 Van	5.2 (5211)	Y	MFI	8	OHV
	B250 Van	5.9 (5899)	Z	TFI	8	OHV
	B350 Van	5.2 (5211)	Y	MFI	8	OHV
	B350 Van	5.9 (5899)	Z	TFI	8	OHV
	D/W 150 Pick-up	3.9 (3916)	X	MFI	6	OHV
	D/W 150 Pick-up	5.2 (5211)	Y	MFI	8	OHV
	D/W 150 Pick-up	5.9 (5899)	Z	TFI	8	OHV
	D 250 Pick-up	3.9 (3916)	X	MFI	6	OHV
	D/W 250 Pick-up	5.2 (5211)	Y	MFI	8	OHV
	D/W 250 Pick-up	5.9 (5882)	8	DSL	6	OHV
	D/W 250 Pick-up	5.9 (5899)	Z	TFI	8	OHV
	D/W 350 Pick-up	5.9 (5882)	8	DSL	6	OHV
	D/W 350 Pick-up	5.9 (5899)	5	TFI	8	OHV
	Ramcharger	5.2 (5211)	Y	MFI	8	OHV
	Ramcharger	5.9 (5899)	Z	TFI	8	OHV
1993	Caravan	2.5 (2507)	K	TFI	4	SOHC
	Caravan	3.0 (2972)	3	MFI	6	SOHC
	Caravan	3.3 (3300)	R	MFI	6	OHV
	Dakota	2.5 (2507)	K	TFI	4	SOHC
	Dakota	3.9 (3916)	X	MFI	6	OHV
	Dakota	5.2 (5211)	Y	MFI	8	OHV
	Voyager	2.5 (2507)	K	TFI	4	SOHC
	Voyager	3.0 (2972)	3	MFI	6	SOHC
	Voyager	3.3 (3300)	R	MFI	6	OHV
	Town & Country	3.3 (3300)	R	MFI	6	OHV
	B150 Van	3.9 (3916)	X	MFI	6	OHV
	B150 Van	5.2 (5211)	Y	MFI	8	OHV
	B250 Van	3.9 (3916)	X	MFI	6	OHV
	B250 Van	5.2 (5211)	Y	MFI	8	OHV
	B250 Van	5.9 (5899)	Z	MFI	8	OHV
	B350 Van	5.2 (5211)	Y	MFI	8	OHV
	B350 Van	5.9 (5899)	Z	MFI	8	OHV
	D/W 150 Pick-up	3.9 (3916)	X	MFI	6	OHV
	D/W 150 Pick-up	5.2 (5211)	Y	MFI	8	OHV

ENGINE IDENTIFICATION

Year	Model	Engine Displacement Liters (cc)	Engine Series (ID/VIN)	Fuel System	No. of Cylinders	Engine Type
1993	D/W 150 Pick-up	5.9 (5899)	Z	MFI	8	OHV
	D 250 Pick-up	3.9 (3916)	X	MFI	6	OHV
	D/W 250 Pick-up	5.2 (5211)	Y	MFI	8	OHV
	D/W 250 Pick-up	5.9 (5882)	8	DSL	6	OHV
	D/W 250 Pick-up	5.9 (5899)	Z	MFI	8	OHV
	D/W 350 Pick-up	5.9 (5882)	8	DSL	6	OHV
	D/W 350 Pick-up	5.9 (5899)	5	MFI	8	OHV
	Ramcharger	5.2 (5211)	Y	MFI	8	OHV
	Ramcharger	5.9 (5899)	Z	MFI	8	OHV
1994	Caravan	2.5 (2507)	K	TFI	4	SOHC
	Caravan	3.0 (2972)	3	MFI	6	SOHC
	Caravan	3.3 (3300)	R	MFI	6	OHV
	Caravan	3.8 (3785)	L	MFI	6	OHV
	Dakota	2.5 (2507)	K	TFI	4	SOHC
	Dakota	3.9 (3916)	X	MFI	6	OHV
	Dakota	5.2 (5211)	Y	MFI	8	OHV
	Voyager	2.5 (2507)	K	TFI	4	SOHC
	Voyager	3.0 (2972)	3	MFI	6	SOHC
	Voyager	3.3 (3300)	R	MFI	6	OHV
	Voyager	3.8 (3785)	L	MFI	6	OHV
	Town & Country	3.8 (3785)	L	MFI	6	OHV
	B150 Van	3.9 (3916)	X	MFI	6	OHV
	B150 Van	5.2 (5211)	Y	MFI	8	OHV
	B250 Van	3.9 (3916)	X	MFI	6	OHV
	B250 Van	5.2 (5211)	Y	MFI	8	OHV
	B250 Van	5.9 (5899)	A	MFI	8	OHV
	B350 Van	5.2 (5211)	Y	MFI	8	OHV
	B350 Van	5.9 (5899)	A	MFI	8	OHV
	D 1500 Pick-up	3.9 (3916)	X	MFI	6	OHV
	D/W 1500 Pick-up	5.2 (5211)	Y	MFI	8	OHV
	D/W 1500 Pick-up	5.9 (5899)	Z	MFI	8	OHV
	D/W 2500 Pick-up	5.2 (5211)	Y	MFI	8	OHV
	D/W 2500 Pick-up	5.9 (5882)	C	DSL	6	OHV
	D/W 2500 Pick-up	5.9 (5899)	Z	MFI	8	OHV
	D/W 2500 Pick-up	8.0 (7997)	W	MFI	10	OHV
	D/W 3500 Pick-up	5.9 (5882)	C	DSL	6	OHV
	D/W 3500 Pick-up	5.9 (5899)	5	MFI	8	OHV
	D/W 3500 Pick-up	8.0 (7997)	W	MFI	10	OHV
1995-96	Caravan	3.0 (2972)	3	MFI	6	SOHC
	Caravan	3.3 (3300)	R	MFI	6	OHV
	Caravan	3.8 (3785)	L	MFI	6	OHV
	Dakota	2.5 (2507)	G	TFI	4	SOHC
	Dakota	3.9 (3916)	X	MFI	6	OHV
	Dakota	5.2 (5211)	Y	MFI	8	OHV
	Voyager	2.5 (2507)	K	TFI	4	SOHC
	Voyager	3.0 (2972)	3	MFI	6	SOHC
	Voyager	3.3 (3300)	R	MFI	6	OHV

ENGINE IDENTIFICATION

Year	Model	Engine Displacement Liters (cc)	Engine Series (ID/VIN)	Fuel System	No. of Cylinders	Engine Type
1995-96	Voyager	3.8 (3785)	L	MFI	6	OHV
	Town & Country	3.8 (3785)	L	MFI	6	OHV
	B150 Van	3.9 (3916)	X	MFI	6	OHV
	B150 Van	5.2 (5211)	Y	MFI	8	OHV
	B250 Van	3.9 (3916)	X	MFI	6	OHV
	B250 Van	5.2 (5211)	Y	MFI	8	OHV
	B250 Van	5.9 (5899)	Z	MFI	8	OHV
	B350 Van	5.2 (5211)	Y	MFI	8	OHV
	B350 Van	5.9 (5899)	Z	MFI	8	OHV
	D 1500 Pick-up	3.9 (3916)	X	MFI	6	OHV
	D/W 1500 Pick-up	5.2 (5211)	Y	MFI	8	OHV
	D/W 1500 Pick-up	5.9 (5899)	Z	MFI	8	OHV
	D/W 2500 Pick-up	5.2 (5211)	Y	MFI	8	OHV
	D/W 2500 Pick-up	5.9 (5882)	C	DSL	6	OHV
	D/W 2500 Pick-up	5.9 (5899)	Z	MFI	8	OHV
	D/W 2500 Pick-up	8.0 (7997)	W	MFI	10	OHV
	D/W 3500 Pick-up	5.9 (5882)	C	DSL	6	OHV
	D/W 3500 Pick-up	5.9 (5899)	5	MFI	8	OHV
	D/W 3500 Pick-up	8.0 (7997)	W	MFI	10	OHV

DSL - Diesel
MFI - Multiport fuel injection
TFI - Throttle body fuel injection
OHV - Overhead valve
SOHC - Single overhead camshaft

GENERAL ENGINE SPECIFICATIONS

Year	Engine ID/VIN	Engine Displacement Liters (cc)	Fuel System Type	Net Horsepower @ rpm	Net Torque @ rpm (ft. lbs.)	Bore x Stroke (in.)	Compression Ratio	Oil Pressure @ rpm
1992	K	2.5 (2507)	TFI	96@4400	133@2800	3.45x4.09	8.9:1	35-65@2000
	3	3.0 (2972)	MFI	143@5000	168@2500	3.59x2.99	8.9:1	30-80@3000
	R	3.3 (3300)	MFI	150@4800	185@3600	3.66x3.19	8.9:1	30-80@3000
	X	3.9 (3916)	MFI	175@4800	220@3200	3.91x3.31	9.1:1	30-80@3000
	Y	5.2 (5211)	MFI	170@4000	260@2000	3.91x3.31	9.2:1	30-80@3000
	8	5.9 (5882)	DSL	160@2500	400@1700	4.02x4.72	17.5:1	30-70@2500
	5	5.9 (5889)	TFI	193@4000	292@2400	4.00x3.58	8.1:1	30-80@3000
	Z	5.9 (5889)	TFI	193@4000	292@2400	4.00x3.58	8.1:1	30-80@3000
1993	K	2.5 (2507)	TFI	100@4800	135@2800	3.45x4.09	8.9:1	35-65@2000
	3	3.0 (2972)	MFI	143@5000	168@2500	3.59x2.99	8.9:1	30-80@3000
	R	3.3 (3300)	MFI	150@4800	185@3600	3.66x3.19	8.9:1	30-80@3000
	X	3.9 (3916)	MFI	175@4800	220@3200	3.91x3.31	9.1:1	30-80@3000
	Y	5.2 (5211)	MFI	230@4800	280@3200	3.91x3.31	9.1:1	30-80@3000
	8	5.9 (5882)	DSL	160@2500	400@1750	4.02x4.72	17.5:1	30-70@2500
	Z	5.9 (5899)	MFI	230@4000	325@2500	4.00x3.58	8.9:1	30-80@3000
	5	5.9 (5899)	MFI	230@4000	230@2800	4.00x3.58	8.9:1	30-80@3000
1994	K	2.5 (2507)	TFI	100@4800	135@2800	3.45x4.09	8.9:1	25-80@3000
	3	3.0 (2972)	MFI	143@5000	168@2500	3.59x2.99	8.9:1	30-80@3000
	R	3.3 (3300)	MFI	150@4800	185@3600	3.66x3.19	8.9:1	30-80@3000
	L	3.8 (3785)	MFI	162@4400	213@3300	3.78x3.43	9.0:1	30-80@3000
	X	3.9 (3916)	MFI	175@4800	220@3200	3.91x3.31	9.1:1	30-80@3000
	Y	5.2 (5211)	MFI	220@4400	300@3200	3.91x3.31	9.1:1	30-80@3000
	C	5.9 (5882)	DSL	160@2500 [1]	400@1600 [2]	4.02x4.72	17.5:1	30@2500
	A	5.9 (5899)	MFI	230@4000	330@3200	4.00x3.58	8.9:1	30-80@3000
	5	5.9 (5899)	MFI	230@4000	330@2800	4.00x3.58	8.9:1	30-80@3000
	Z	5.9 (5899)	MFI	230@4000	330@3200	4.00x3.58	8.9:1	30-80@3000
	W	8.0 (7997)	MFI	300@4000	450@2400	4.00x3.88	8.6:1	50-60@3000
1995-96	G	2.5 (2507)	TFI	100@4800	135@2800	3.45x4.09	8.9:1	25-80@3000
	K	2.5 (2507)	TFI	100@4800	135@2800	3.44x4.09	8.9:1	25-80@3000
	3	3.0 (2972)	MFI	143@5000	170@2800	3.59x2.99	8.9:1	30-80@3000
	R	3.3 (3300)	MFI	162@4800	194@3600	3.66x3.19	8.9:1	30-80@3000
	L	3.8 (3785)	MFI	162@4400	213@3300	3.78x3.43	9.0:1	30-80@3000
	X	3.0 (3916)	MFI	175@4800	220@3200	3.91x3.31	9.1:1	30-80@3000
	Y	5.2 (5211)	MFI	220@4400	300@3200	3.91x3.31	9.1:1	30-80@3000
	C	5.9 (5882)	DSL	160@2500 [1]	400@1600 [2]	4.02x4.72	17.5:1	30@2500
	5	5.9 (5899)	MFI	230@4000	330@2800	4.00x3.58	8.9:1	30-80@3000
	Z	5.9 (5899)	MFI	230@4000	330@3200	4.00x3.58	8.9:1	30-80@3000
	W	8.0 (7997)	MFI	300@4000	450@2400	4.00x3.88	8.6:1	50-60@3000

MFI - Multiport fuel injection
TFI - Throttle body fuel injection
DSL - Diesel
1 Manual transmission: 430@1600
2 Manual transmission: 175@2500

GASOLINE ENGINE TUNE-UP SPECIFICATIONS

Year	Engine ID/VIN	Engine Displacement Liters (cc)	Spark Plugs Gap (in.)	Ignition Timing (deg.) MT	Ignition Timing (deg.) AT	Fuel Pump (psi)	Idle Speed (rpm) MT	Idle Speed (rpm) AT	Valve Clearance In.	Valve Clearance Ex.
1992	K	2.5 (2507)	0.035	12B	12B	37-41	850	850	HYD	HYD
	3	3.0 (2972)	0.039-0.043	12B	12B	46-50	800	800	HYD	HYD
	R	3.3 (3300)	0.048-0.053	1	1	46-50	750	750	HYD	HYD
	X	3.9 (3916)	0.035	1	1	37-41	750	750	HYD	HYD
	Y	5.2 (5211)	0.035	1	1	37-41	700	700	HYD	HYD
	5	5.9 (5899)	0.035	10B	10B	13.5-15.5	700	700	HYD	HYD
	Z	5.9 (5899)	0.035	10B	10B	13.5-15.5	700	700	HYD	HYD
1993	K	2.5 (2507)	0.035	12B	12B	37-41	850	850	HYD	HYD
	3	3.0 (2972)	0.039-0.043	12B	12B	46-50	800	800	HYD	HYD
	R	3.3 (3300)	0.048-0.053	1	1	46-50	750	750	HYD	HYD
	X	3.9 (3916)	0.035	1	1	37-41	750	750	HYD	HYD
	Y	5.2 (5211)	0.035	1	1	37-41	700	700	HYD	HYD
	8	5.9 (5882)	0.035	1	1	35-45	700	700	HYD	HYD
	5	5.9 (5899)	0.035	1	1	35-45	700	700	HYD	HYD
	Z	5.9 (5899)	0.035	1	1	35-45	700	700	HYD	HYD
1994	K	2.5 (2507)	0.035	12B	12B	37-41	2	2	HYD	HYD
	3	3.0 (2972)	0.039-0.043	12B	12B	46-50	2	2	HYD	HYD
	R	3.3 (3300)	0.048-0.053	1	1	46-50	2	2	HYD	HYD
	L	3.8 (3785)	0.048-0.053	1	1	46-50	2	2	HYD	HYD
	X	3.9 (3916)	0.035	1	1	35-45	2	2	HYD	HYD
	Y	5.2 (5211)	0.035	1	1	35-45	2	2	HYD	HYD
	C	5.9 (5882)	0.035	1	1	35-45	2	2	HYD	HYD
	A	5.9 (5899)	0.035	1	1	35-45	2	2	HYD	HYD
	5	5.9 (5899)	0.035	1	1	35-45	2	2	HYD	HYD
	Z	5.9 (5899)	0.035	1	1	35-45	2	2	HYD	HYD
	W	8.0 (7997)	0.035	1	1	35-45	2	2	HYD	HYD
1995-96	G	2.5 (2507)	0.035	3	3	14.5	2	2	HYD	HYD
	K	2.5 (2507)	0.035	-	3	39	-	2	HYD	HYD
	3	3.0 (2972)	0.035	-	3	48	-	2	HYD	HYD
	R	3.3 (3300)	0.050	-	1	48	-	2	HYD	HYD
	L	3.8 (3785)	0.050	-	1	48	-	2	HYD	HYD
	X	3.9 (3916)	0.030	1	1	35-45	2	2	HYD	HYD
	Y	5.2 (5211)	0.030	1	1	35-45	2	2	HYD	HYD
	C	5.9 (5882)	0.030	1	1	35-45	2	2	HYD	HYD
	5	5.9 (5899)	0.030	1	1	35-45	2	2	HYD	HYD
	Z	5.9 (5899)	0.030	1	1	35-45	2	2	HYD	HYD
	W	8.0 (7997)	0.030	1	1	35-45	2	2	HYD	HYD

NOTE: The Vehicle Emission Control Information label often reflects specification changes made during production. The label figures must be used if they differ from those in this chart.

B - Before top dead center

HYD - Hydraulic

1 Ignition timing cannot be adjusted. Base engine timing is set at TDC during assembly

2 Refer to the Vehicle Emission Control Information (VECI) label for correct specification

3 Refer to the Vehicle Emission Control Information label for correct timing specification with a range of +/- 2.

DIESEL ENGINE TUNE-UP SPECIFICATIONS

Year	Engine ID/VIN	Engine Displacement cu. in. (cc)	Valve Clearance Intake (in.)	Valve Clearance Exhaust (in.)	Intake Valve Opens (deg.)	Injection Pump Setting (deg.)	Injection Nozzle Pressure (psi) New	Injection Nozzle Pressure (psi) Used	Idle Speed (rpm)	Cranking Compression Pressure (psi)
1992	8	5.9 (5882)	0.010	0.020	NA	1	3550	NA	2	NA
1993	8	5.9 (5882)	0.010	0.020	NA	1	3550	NA	2	NA
1994	C	5.9 (5882)	0.010	0.020	NA	1	3822	NA	2	NA
1995-96	C	5.9 (5882)	0.010	0.020	NA	1	3822	NA	3	NA

NOTE: The Vehicle Emission Control Information label often reflects specification changes made during production. The label figures must be used if they differ from those in this chart

NA - Not Available

1 Align marks on pump flange and gear housing

2 Automatic transmission with A/C - 700 rpm
Manual transmission with A/C: 750 rpm

3 Automatic transmission with A/C: 750-800 rpm
Manual transmission with A/C: 780 rpm

CAPACITIES

Year	Model	Engine ID/VIN	Engine Displacement Liters (cc)	Engine Oil with Filter (qts.)	Transmission (pts.) 4-Spd	Transmission (pts.) 5-Spd	Transmission (pts.) Auto.	Transfer Case (pts.)	Drive Axle Front (pts.)	Drive Axle Rear (pts.)	Fuel Tank (gal.)	Cooling System (qts.)
1992	Caravan	K	2.5 (2507)	4.5	-	4.8	1	2.4	-	4.0 2	3	9.5
	Caravan	3	3.0 (2972)	4.5	-	4.8	1	2.4	-	4.0 2	3	10.0
	Caravan	R	3.3 (3300)	4.5	-	4.8	1	2.4	-	4.0 2	3	10.0
	Dakota	K	2.5 (2507)	4.5	-	4.0	10.4	2.5	2.6	4	15.0 5	9.5
	Dakota	X	3.9 (3916)	4.5	-	6.6	10.4	2.5	2.6	4	15.0 5	14.0
	Dakota	Y	5.2 (5211)	4.5	-	6.6	10.4	2.5	2.6	4	15.0 5	14.3
	Voyager	K	2.5 (2507)	4.5	-	4.8	1	2.4	-	4.0 2	3	9.5
	Voyager	3	3.0 (2972)	4.5	-	4.8	1	2.4	-	4.0 2	3	10.0
	Voyager	R	3.3 (3300)	4.5	-	4.8	18.0	2.4	-	4.0 2	3	10.0
	Town & Country	R	3.3 (3300)	5.0	-	-	6	2.4	4.0	4.0	3	10.5
	B150 Van	X	3.9 (3916)	4.5	-	6.8	7	-	-	8	22.0 9	14.6 10
	B150 Van	Y	5.2 (5211)	4.5	-	6.8	7	-	-	8	22.0 9	16.5 10
	B250 Van	X	3.9 (3916)	4.5	-	6.8	7	-	-	8	22.0 9	14.6 10
	B250 Van	Y	5.2 (5211)	4.5	-	6.8	7	-	-	8	22.0 9	16.5 10
	B250 Van	Z	5.9 (5899)	4.5	-	6.8	7	-	-	8	35.0	15.0 10
	B350 Van	Y	5.2 (5211)	4.5	-	-	7	-	-	8	22.0 9	16.5 10
	B350 Van	Z	5.9 (5899)	4.5	-	-	7	-	-	8	35.0	15.0 10
	D/W 150 Pick-up	X	3.9 (3916)	4.5	-	8.0	7	11	12	13	22.0 14	15.1
	D/W 150 Pick-up	Y	5.2 (5211)	4.5	-	8.0	7	11	12	13	22.0 14	17.0
	D/W 150 Pick-up	Z	5.9 (5899)	4.5	-	8.0	7	11	12	13	30.0	15.5
	D 250 Pick-up	X	3.9 (3916)	4.5	-	8.0	7	-	12	13	22.0 14	15.1
	D/W 250 Pick-up	Y	5.2 (5211)	4.5	-	8.0	7	11	12	13	22.0 14	17.0
	D/W 250 Pick-up	8	5.9 (5882)	12.5	-	7.0	22.0	11	6.5	13	30.0	15
	D/W 250 Pick-up	Z	5.9 (5899)	4.5	-	8.0	7	11	12	13	30.0	15.5
	D/W 350 Pick-up	8	5.9 (5882)	12.5	-	7.0	22.0	11	6.5	13	30.0	15
	D/W 350 Pick-up	5	5.9 (5899)	4.5	-	8.0	7	11	12	13	30.0	15.5
	Ramcharger	Y	5.2 (5211)	4.5	-	8.0	7	11	12	13	34.0	17.0
	Ramcharger	Z	5.9 (5899)	4.5	-	8.0	7	11	12	13	34.0	15.5

CAPACITIES

Year	Model	Engine ID/VIN	Engine Displacement Liters (cc)	Engine Oil with Filter (qts.)	Transmission (pts.) 4-Spd	5-Spd	Auto.	Transfer Case (pts.)	Drive Axle Front (pts.)	Rear (pts.)	Fuel Tank (gal.)	Cooling System (qts.)
1993	Caravan	K	2.5 (2507)	4.5	-	4.8	[1]	2.4	-	4.0 [2]	[3]	9.5
	Caravan	3	3.0 (2972)	4.5	-	4.8	[1]	2.4	-	4.0 [2]	[3]	10.0
	Caravan	R	3.3 (3300)	4.5	-	4.8	[1]	2.4	-	4.0 [2]	[3]	10.0
	Dakota	K	2.5 (2507)	4.5	-	6.6	10.4	4.5	2.6	[16]	15.0 [5]	9.8
	Dakota	X	3.9 (3916)	4.5	-	6.6	10.4	4.5	2.6	[16]	15.0 [5]	14.0
	Dakota	Y	5.2 (5211)	5.0	-	6.6	10.4	4.5	2.6	[16]	15.0 [5]	14.3
	Voyager	K	2.5 (2507)	4.5	-	4.8	[1]	2.4	-	4.0 [2]	[3]	9.5
	Voyager	3	3.0 (2972)	4.5	-	4.8	[1]	2.4	-	4.0 [2]	[3]	10.0
	Voyager	R	3.3 (3300)	4.5	-	4.8	[1]	2.4	-	4.0 [2]	[3]	10.0
	Town & Country	R	3.3 (3300)	4.5	-	-	18.0	2.4	4.0	4.0	[2]	10.5
	B150 Van	X	3.9 (3916)	4.5	-	6.8	[7]	-	-	[8]	22.0 [9]	14.6 [10]
	B150 Van	Y	5.2 (5211)	4.5	-	6.8	[7]	-	-	[8]	22.0 [9]	16.5 [10]
	B250 Van	X	3.9 (3916)	4.5	-	6.8	[7]	-	-	[8]	22.0 [9]	14.6 [10]
	B250 Van	Y	5.2 (5211)	4.5	-	6.8	[7]	-	-	[8]	22.0 [9]	16.5 [10]
	B250 Van	Z	5.9 (5899)	4.5	-	6.8	[7]	-	-	[8]	35.0	15.0 [10]
	B350 Van	Y	5.2 (5211)	4.5	-	-	[7]	-	-	[8]	22.0 [9]	11.5 [10]
	B350 Van	Z	5.9 (5899)	4.5	-	-	[7]	-	-	[8]	35.0	15.0 [10]
	D/W 150 Pick-up	X	3.9 (3916)	4.5	-	8.0	[7]	[11]	[12]	[13]	22.0 [14]	15.1
	D/W 150 Pick-up	Y	5.2 (5211)	4.5	-	8.0	[7]	[11]	[12]	[13]	22.0 [14]	17.0
	D/W 150 Pick-up	Z	5.9 (5899)	4.5	-	8.0	[7]	[11]	[12]	[13]	30.0	15.5
	D250 Pick-up	X	3.9 (3916)	4.5	-	8.0	[7]		[12]	[13]	22.0 [14]	15.1
	D/W 250 Pick-up	Y	5.2 (5211)	4.5	-	8.0	[7]	[11]	[12]	[13]	22.0 [14]	17.0
	D/W 250 Pick-up	8	5.9 (5882)	12.5	-	7.0	22.0	[11]	6.5	[13]	30.0	[15]
	D/W 250 Pick-up	Z	5.9 (5899)	4.5	-	8.0	[7]	[11]	[12]	[13]	30.0	15.5
	D/W 350 Pick-up	8	5.9 (5882)	12.5	-	7.0	22.0	[11]	6.5	[13]	30.0	[15]
	D/W 350 Pick-up	5	5.9 (5899)	4.5	-	8.0	[7]	[11]	[12]	[13]	30.0	15.5
	Ramcharger	Y	5.2 (5211)	4.5	-	8.0	[7]	[11]	[12]	[13]	34.0	17.0
	Ramcharger	Z	5.9 (5899)	4.5	-	8.0	[7]	[11]	[12]	[13]	34.0	15.5
1994	Caravan	R	3.3 (3300)	4.5	-	4.6	18.0	2.4	-	4.0 [17]	[3]	10.5
	Caravan	L	3.8 (3785)	4.5	-	4.6	18.0	2.4	-	4.0 [17]	[3]	10.5
	Dakota	K	2.5 (2507)	4.5	-	[18]	[19]	2.5	3.0	[20]	15.0 [5]	9.8
	Dakota	X	3.9 (3916)	4.5	-	[18]	[19]	2.5	3.0	[20]	15.0 [5]	14.0
	Dakota	Y	5.2 (5211)	5.0	-	[18]	[19]	2.5	3.0	[20]	15.0 [5]	14.3
	Voyager	K	2.5 (2507)	4.5	-	4.6	18.0	-	-	-	18.0	9.5
	Voyager	3	3.0 (2972)	4.5	-	4.6	18.0	-	-	-	18.0	10.5
	Voyager	R	3.3 (3300)	4.5	-	4.6	18.0	2.4	-	4.0 [2]	[3]	10.5
	Voyager	L	3.8 (3785)	4.5	-	4.6	18.0	2.4	-	4.0 [2]	[3]	10.5
	Town & Country	L	3.8 (3785)	4.5	-	-	[3]	2.4	4.0	4.0 [4]	[2]	10.5
	B150 Van	X	3.9 (3916)	4.0	-	-	[21]	-	-	[22]	22.0 [9]	14.6
	B150 Van	Y	5.2 (5211)	4.5	-	-	[21]	-	-	[22]	22.0 [9]	16.5
	B250 Van	X	3.9 (3916)	4.5	-	-	[21]	-	-	[22]	22.0 [9]	14.6
	B250 Van	Y	5.2 (5211)	4.5	-	-	[21]	-	-	[22]	22.0 [9]	16.5
	B250 Van	A	5.9 (5899)	4.5	-	-	[21]	-	-	[22]	35.0	15.0 [23]
	B350 Van	Y	5.2 (5211)	4.5	-	-	[21]	-	-	[22]	22.0 [9]	16.5
	B350 Van	A	5.9 (5899)	4.5	-	-	[21]	-	-	[22]	35.0	15.0 [23]
	D 1500 Pick-up	X	3.9 (3916)	4.0	-	[18]	[19]	-	-	[26]	26.0 [9]	20.0

CAPACITIES

Year	Model	Engine ID/VIN	Engine Displacement Liters (cc)	Engine Oil with Filter (qts.)	Transmission (pts.) 4-Spd	5-Spd	Auto.	Transfer Case (pts.)	Drive Axle Front (pts.)	Rear (pts.)	Fuel Tank (gal.)	Cooling System (qts.)
1994	D/W 1500 Pick-up	Y	5.2 (5211)	5.0	-	18	19	24	25	26	26.0 [9]	20.0
	D/W 1500 Pick-up	Z	5.9 (5899)	5.0	-	18	19	24	25	26	26.0 [9]	20.0
	D/W 2500 Pick-up	Y	5.2 (5211)	5.0	-	18	19	24	25	26	26.0 [9]	20.0
	D/W 2500 Pick-up	C	5.9 (5882)	11.0	-	18	19	24	25	26	26.0 [9]	26.0
	D/W 2500 Pick-up	Z	5.9 (5899)	5.0	-	18	19	24	25	26	26.0 [9]	20.0
	D/W 2500 Pick-up	W	8.0 (7997)	7.0	-	18	19	24	25	26	26.0 [9]	24.0
	D/W 3500 Pick-up	C	5.9 (5882)	11.0	-	18	19	24	25	26	26.0 [9]	26.0
	D/W 3500 Pick-up	5	5.9 (5899)	5.0	-	18	19	24	25	26	26.0 [9]	20.0
	D/W 3500 Pick-up	W	8.0 (7997)	7.0	-	18	19	24	25	26	26.0 [9]	24.0
1995-96	Caravan	R	3.3 (3300)	4.5	-	-	18.0 [27]	2.4	-	4.0 [17]	3	10.5
	Caravan	L	3.8 (3785)	4.5	-	-	18.0 [27]	2.4	-	4.0 [17]	3	10.5
	Dakota	G	2.5 (2507)	4.5	-	18	19	2.5	3.0	20	15.0 [5]	9.8
	Dakota	X	3.9 (3916)	4.5	-	18	19	2.5	3.0	20	15.0 [5]	14.0
	Dakota	Y	5.2 (5211)	5.0	-	18	19	2.5	3.0	20	15.0 [5]	14.3
	Voyager	K	2.5 (2507)	4.5	-	-	1	-	-	-	20.0	9.5
	Voyager	3	3.0 (2972)	4.5	-	-	1	-	-	-	20.0	10.5
	Voyager	R	3.3 (3300)	4.5	-	-	1	2.4	-	4.0 [2]	3	10.5
	Voyager	L	3.8 (3785)	4.5	-	-	1	2.4	-	4.0 [2]	3	10.5
	Town & Country	L	3.8 (3785)	4.5	-	-	3	2.4	4.0	4.0 [4]	2	10.5
	B150 Van	X	3.9 (3916)	4.0	-	-	19	-	-	22	22.0 [9]	14.6
	B150 Van	Y	5.2 (5211)	5.0	-	-	19	-	-	22	22.0 [9]	16.5
	B250 Van	X	3.9 (3916)	4.0	-	-	19	-	-	22	22.0 [9]	14.6
	B250 Van	Y	5.2 (5211)	5.0	-	-	19	-	-	22	22.0 [9]	16.5
	B250 Van	Z	5.9 (5899)	5.0	-	-	19	-	-	22	35.0	15.0 [23]
	B350 Van	Y	5.2 (5211)	5.0	-	-	19	-	-	22	22.0 [9]	16.5
	B350 Van	Z	5.9 (5899)	5.0	-	-	19	-	-	22	35.0	15.0 [23]
	D 1500 Pick-up	X	3.9 (3916)	4.0	-	18	19	-	-	26	26.0 [9]	20.0
	D/W 1500 Pick-up	Y	5.2 (5211)	5.0	-	18	19	24	25	26	26.0 [9]	20.0
	D/W 1500 Pick-up	Z	5.9 (5899)	5.0	-	18	19	24	25	26	26.0 [9]	20.0
	D/W 2500 Pick-up	Y	5.2 (5211)	5.0	-	18	19	24	25	26	26.0 [9]	20.0
	D/W 2500 Pick-up	C	5.9 (5882)	11.0	-	18	19	24	25	26	26.0 [9]	26.0
	D/W 2500 Pick-up	Z	5.9 (5899)	5.0	-	18	19	24	25	26	26.0 [9]	20.0
	D/W 2500 Pick-up	W	8.0 (7997)	7.0	-	18	19	24	25	26	26.0 [9]	24.0
	D/W 3500 Pick-up	C	5.9 (5882)	11.0	-	18	19	24	25	26	26.0 [9]	26.0
	D/W 3500 Pick-up	5	5.9 (5899)	5.0	-	18	19	24	25	26	26.0 [9]	20.0
	D/W 3500 Pick-up	W	8.0 (7997)	7.0	-	18	19	24	25	26	26.0 [9]	24.0

1 Fleet vehicles: 19.0 pts.
Non-fleet vehicles: 18.0 pts.
2 Overrunning clutch: 0.78 pts.
3 FWD: 20.0 gals.
AWD: 18.0 gals.
4 With 7.25 in. rear: 2.5 pts.
With 8.25 in. rear: 4.4 pts.
5 Optional fuel tank: 22 gals.
6 A413: 17.8 pts.
A413 (fleet): 18.4 pts.
A413 (lock-up): 17.0 pts.
A604 (electronic): 18.2 pts.

7 A998/A999 and A727: 17.1 pts.
A500/A518: 20.4 pts.
8 Chrysler: 4.5 pts.
Dana 60: 6.25 pts.
9 Optional fuel tank: 35 gals.
10 With HD cooling or A/C, add one quart
11 NP205: 4.5 pts.
NP241: 6.0 pts.
12 Dana 44: 5.6 pts.
Dana 60: 6.5 pts.
13 Chrysler 8.25 in. and 9.25 in.: 4.5 pts.
Spicer and Dana 60: 6.0 pts.
Dana 70: 7.0 pts.
14 Optional fuel tank: 30 gals.

15 Manual transmission: 15.5 qts.
Automatic transmission: 16.5 qts.
16 With 7.25 in. rear: 3.0 pts.
With 8.25 in. rear: 4.4 pts.
17 Overrunning clutch: 0.75 pts.
18 NV3500: 4.2 pts.
NV4500: 8.0 pts.
AX15: 6.6 pts.
Getrag: 7.0 pts.
19 32RH: 17.0 pts.
36RH: 16.6 pts.
42RH: 20.2 pts.
46RH: 21.8 pts.
47RH: 30.8 pts.

CAPACITIES

Year	Model	Engine ID/VIN	Engine Displacement Liters (cc)	Engine Oil with Filter (qts.)	Transmission (pts.)			Transfer Case (pts.)	Drive Axle		Fuel Tank (gal.)	Cooling System (qts.)
					4-Spd	5-Spd	Auto.		Front (pts.)	Rear (pts.)		

20 7.25 in.: 2.9 pts.
   8.25 in.: 4.4 pts.
21 A998/A999 and A727: 17.2 pts.
   A500: 20.4 pts.
   A518: 21.4 pts.
22 Chrysler 8.25 in.: 4.4 pts.
   Chrysler 9.25 in.: 4.8 pts.
   Dana 60: 6.3 pts.
23 With rear heater: 16.0 qts.

24 NP231HD: 2.5 pts.
   NP241: 4.7 pts.
   NP241HD: 13 pts.
25 7.25 in.: 3 pts.
   Dana 44: 5.6 pts.
   Dana 60: 6.5 pts.

26 Chrysler 7.25 in.: 3 pts.
   Chrysler 8.25 in. and 9.25 in.: 4.8 pts.
   Spicer and Dana 60: 6.0 pts.
   Dana 70 and 80: 7.0 pts.
27 Overhaul fill capacity with torque converter empty

CAMSHAFT SPECIFICATIONS

All measurements given in inches.

Year	Engine ID/VIN	Engine Displacement Liters (cc)	Journal Diameter 1	2	3	4	5	Elevation In.	Ex.	Bearing Clearance	Camshaft End Play
1992	K	2.5 (2507)	1.375-1.376	1.375-1.376	1.375-1.376	1.375-1.376	1.375-1.376	NA	NA	NA	0.005-0.020
	3	3.0 (2972)	NA	NA	NA	NA	NA	[1]	[1]	NA	NA
	R	3.3 (3300)	1.997-1.999	1.980-1.982	1.965-1.967	1.949-1.952	-	0.400 [2]	0.400 [2]	0.001-0.005	0.005-0.012
	X	3.9 (3916)	1.982-1.983	1.967-1.968	1.951-1.952	1.561-1.562	-	0.373 [2]	0.0400 [2]	0.001-0.005	0.002-0.010
	Y	5.2 (5211)	1.998-1.999	1.982-1.983	1.967-1.968	1.951-1.952	1.561-1.562	0.373 [2]	0.400 [2]	0.001-0.005	0.002-0.010
	8	5.9 (5882)	2.125	2.125	2.125	2.125	-	1.852 [3]	1.841 [3]	0.001-0.005	0.006-0.010
	5	5.9 (5899)	1.998-1.999	1.982-1.983	1.967-1.968	1.951-1.952	1.561-1.562	0.410 [2]	0.410 [2]	0.001-0.005	0.002-0.010
	Z	5.9 (5899)	1.998-1.999	1.982-1.983	1.967-1.968	1.951-1.952	1.561-1.562	0.410 [2]	0.410 [2]	0.001-0.005	0.002-0.010
1993	K	2.5 (2507)	1.375-1.376	1.375-1.376	1.375-1.376	1.375-1.376	1.375-1.376	NA	NA	NA	0.005-0.013
	3	3.0 (2972)	NA	NA	NA	NA	NA	[1]	[1]	NA	NA
	R	3.3 (3300)	1.997-1.999	1.980-1.982	1.965-1.967	1.949-1.952	-	0.400 [2]	0.400 [2]	0.001-0.005	0.005-0.012
	X	3.9 (3916)	1.998-1.999	1.982-1.983	1.951-1.952	1.561-1.562	-	0.432 [2]	0.432 [2]	0.001-0.005	0.002-0.010
	Y	5.2 (5211)	1.998-1.999	1.982-1.983	1.967-1.968	1.951-1.952	1.561-1.562	0.432 [2]	0.432 [2]	0.001-0.005	0.002-0.010
	8	5.9 (5882)	2.125	2.125	2.125	2.125	-	1.852 [3]	1.841 [3]	0.001-0.005	0.006-0.010
	5	5.9 (5899)	1.998-1.999	1.982-1.983	1.967-1.968	1.951-1.952	1.561-1.562	0.410 [2]	0.410 [2]	0.001-0.005	0.002-0.010
	Z	5.9 (5899)	1.998-1.999	1.982-1.983	1.967-1.968	1.951-1.952	1.561-1.562	0.410 [2]	0.410 [2]	0.001-0.005	0.002-0.010

CAMSHAFT SPECIFICATIONS
All measurements given in inches.

Year	Engine ID/VIN	Engine Displacement Liters (cc)	Journal Diameter					Elevation		Bearing Clearance	Camshaft End Play
			1	2	3	4	5	In.	Ex.		
1994	K	2.5 (2507)	1.375-1.376	1.375-1.376	1.375-1.376	1.375-1.376	1.375-1.376	NA	NA	NA	0.005-0.013
	3	3.0 (2972)	NA	NA	NA	NA	NA	[1]	[1]	0.002-0.004	0.002-0.004
	R	3.3 (3300)	1.997-1.999	1.981-1.982	1.965-1.967	1.949-1.952	-	0.400	0.400	0.001-0.005	0.005-0.012
	L	3.8 (3785)	1.997-1.999	1.980-1.982	1.965-1.967	1.949-1.952	-	0.400	0.400	0.001-0.005	0.005-0.012
	X	3.9 (3916)	1.998-1.999	1.982-1.983	1.951-1.952	1.561-1.562	-	0.432 [2]	0.432 [2]	0.001-0.005	0.002-0.010
	Y	5.2 (5211)	1.998-1.999	1.982-1.983	1.967-1.968	1.951-1.952	1.561-1.562	0.432 [2]	0.432 [2]	0.001-0.005	0.002-0.010
	C	5.9 (5882)	2.125	2.125	2.125	2.125	-	1.398 [3]	1.398 [3]	0.001-0.005	0.006-0.010
	A	5.9 (5899)	1.998-1.999	1.982-1.983	1.967-1.968	1.951-1.952	1.561-1.562	0.410 [2]	0.410 [2]	0.001-0.005	0.002-0.010
	5	5.9 (5899)	1.998-1.999	1.982-1.983	1.967-1.968	1.951-1.952	1.561-1.562	0.410	0.410	0.001-0.005	0.002-0.010
	Z	5.9 (5899)	1.998-1.999	1.982-1.983	1.967-1.968	1.951-1.952	1.561-1.562	0.410	0.410	0.001-0.005	0.002-0.010
	W	8.0 (7997)	2.091-2.092	2.074-2.075	2.059-2.060	2.043-2.044	2.027-2.028 [4]	0.390	0.407	0.001-0.003	0.005-0.015
1995-96	G	2.5 (2507)	1.375-1.376	1.375-1.376	1.375-1.376	1.375-1.376	1.375-1.376	NA	NA	NA	0.005-0.013
	K	2.5 (2507)	1.375-1.376	1.375-1.376	1.375-1.376	1.375-1.376	1.375-1.376	NA	NA	NA	0.005-0.013
	3	3.0 (2972)	NA	NA	NA	NA	NA	[1]	[1]	0.002-0.004	0.002-0.004
	R	3.3 (3300)	1.997-1.999	1.981-1.982	1.965-1.967	1.949-1.952	-	0.400	0.400	0.001-0.005	0.005-0.012
	L	3.8 (3785)	1.997-1.999	1.980-1.982	1.965-1.967	1.949-1.952	-	0.400	0.400	0.001-0.005	0.005-0.012
	X	3.9 (3916)	1.998-1.999	1.982-1.983	1.951-1.952	1.561-1.562	-	0.432 [3]	0.432 [3]	0.001-0.005	0.002-0.010
	Y	5.2 (5211)	1.998-1.999	1.982-1.983	1.967-1.968	1.951-1.952	1.561-1.562	0.432 [3]	0.432 [3]	0.001-0.005	0.002-0.010
	C	5.9 (5882)	2.125	2..125	2.125	2.125	-	1.398 [3]	1.398 [3]	0.001-0.005	0.006-0.010
	5	5.9 (5899)	1.998-1.999	1.982-1.983	1.967-1.968	1.951-1.952	1.561-1.562	0.410	0.410	0.001-0.005	0.002-0.010
	Z	5.9 (5899)	1.998-1.999	1.982-1.983	1.967-1.968	1.951-1.952	1.561-1.562	0.410 [3]	0.410 [3]	0.001-0.005	0.002-0.010
	W	8.0 (7997)	2.091-2.092	2.074-2.075	2.059-2.060	2.043-2.044	2.027-2.028 [4]	0.390	0.407	0.001-0.003	0.005-0.015

NA - Not Available
1 Height of cam lobe: 1.604-1.624 in.
2 Lift at valve
3 Minimum diameter at peak of lobe
4 Journal No. 6: 1.917-1.918

CRANKSHAFT AND CONNECTING ROD SPECIFICATIONS

All measurements are given in inches.

Year	Engine ID/VIN	Engine Displacement Liters (cc)	Crankshaft				Connecting Rod		
			Main Brg. Journal Dia.	Main Brg. Oil Clearance	Shaft End-play	Thrust on No.	Journal Diameter	Oil Clearance	Side Clearance
1992	K	2.5 (2507)	2.3620-2.3630	0.0004-0.0028	0.002-0.007	3	1.968-1.969	0.0008-0.0034	0.005-0.013
	3	3.0 (2972)	2.3610-2.3620	0.0006-0.0020	0.002-0.010	3	1.968-1.969	0.0008-0.0028	0.001-0.004
	R	3.3 (3300)	2.5190	0.0004-0.0028	0.003-0.009	2	2.283	0.0008-0.0030	0.005-0.015
	R [1]	3.3 (3300)	2.5190	0.0007-0.0022	0.001-0.007	2	2.283	0.0008-0.0030	0.005-0.015
	X	3.9 (3916)	2.5000-2.5010 [2]		0.002-0.007	2	2.124-2.125	0.0005-0.0022	0.006-0.014
	Y	5.2 (5211)	2.4995-2.5005 [2]		0.002-0.007	3	2.124-2.125	0.0005-0.0022	0.006-0.014
	8	5.9 (5882)	3.2662 [3]	0.0047	0.005-0.012	6	2.714 [3]	0.0035	0.004-0.012
	5	5.9 (5899)	2.8095-2.8105 [2]		0.002-0.007	3	2.124-2.125	0.0005-0.0022	0.006-0.014
	Z	5.9 (5899)	2.8095-2.8105 [2]	[2]	0.002-0.007	3	2.124-2.125	0.0005-0.0022	0.006-0.014
1993	K	2.5 (2507)	2.3620-2.3630	0.0004-0.0028	0.002-0.007	3	1.968-1.969	0.0008-0.0034	0.005-0.013
	3	3.0 (2972)	2.3610-2.3620	0.0006-0.0020	0.002-0.010	3	1.968-1.969	0.0008-0.0028	0.001-0.004
	R	3.3 (3300)	2.5190	0.0004-0.0028	0.003-0.009	2	2.283	0.0008-0.0030	0.005-0.015
	R [1]	3.3 (3300)	2.5190	0.0007-0.0022	0.010-0.070	2	2.283	0.0008-0.0030	0.005-0.015
	X	3.9 (3916)	2.5000-2.5010 [2]		0.002-0.007	2	2.124-2.125	0.0005-0.0022	0.006-0.014
	Y	5.2 (5211)	2.4995-2.5005 [2]		0.002-0.007	3	2.124-2.125	0.0005-0.0022	0.006-0.014
	8	5.9 (5882)	3.2662 [3]	0.0047	0.005-0.012	6	2.714 [3]	0.0035	0.004-0.012
	5	5.9 (5899)	2.8095-2.8105 [2]		0.002-0.007	3	2.124-2.125	0.0005-0.0022	0.006-0.014
	Z	5.9 (5899)	2.8095-2.8105 [2]		0.002-0.007	3	2.124-2.125	0.0005-0.0022	0.006-0.014
1994	K	2.5 (2507)	2.3620-2.3630	0.0004-0.0028	0.002-0.007	3	1.968-1.969	0.0008-0.0034	0.005-0.013
	3	3.0 (2972)	2.3610-2.3620	0.0006-0.0020	0.002-0.010	3	1.968-1.969	0.0008-0.0028	0.001-0.004
	R	3.3 (3300)	2.5190	0.0004-0.0028	0.003-0.009	2	2.283	0.0008-0.0030	0.005-0.015
	L	3.8 (3785)	2.5190	0.0007-0.0030	0.004-0.012	2	2.283	0.0007-0.0030	0.005-0.015
	L [1]	3.8 (3785)	2.5190	0.0007-0.0022	0.003-0.009	2	2.283	0.0008-0.0030	0.005-0.015

CRANKSHAFT AND CONNECTING ROD SPECIFICATIONS

All measurements are given in inches.

Year	Engine ID/VIN	Engine Displacement Liters (cc)	Crankshaft				Connecting Rod		
			Main Brg. Journal Dia.	Main Brg. Oil Clearance	Shaft End-play	Thrust on No.	Journal Diameter	Oil Clearance	Side Clearance
1994	X	3.9 (3916)	2.5000-2.5010	[2]	0.002-0.007	2	2.124-2.125	0.0005-0.0022	0.006-0.014
	Y	5.2 (5211)	2.4995-2.5005	[2]	0.002-0.007	3	2.124-2.125	0.0005-0.0022	0.006-0.014
	C	5.9 (5882)	3.2662 [3]	0.0047	0.004-0.017	6	2.714 [3]	0.0035	0.004-0.012
	A	5.9 (5899)	2.8095-2.8105	[2]	0.002-0.007	3	2.124-2.125	0.0005-0.0022	0.006-0.014
	5	5.9 (5899)	2.8095-2.8105	[2]	0.002-0.007	3	2.124-2.125	0.0005-0.0022	0.006-0.014
	Z	5.9 (5899)	2.8095-2.8105	[2]	0.002-0.007	3	2.124-2.125	0.0005-0.0022	0.006-0.014
	W	8.0 (7997)	2.9995-3.0005	0.0002-0.0023	0.002-0.017	3	2.124-2.125	0.0002-0.0029	0.010-0.018
1995-96	G	2.5 (2507)	2.3620-2.3630	0.0003-0.0031	0.002-0.007	3	1.968-1.969	0.0008-0.0034	0.005-0.013
	K	2.5 (2507)	2.3620-2.3630	0.0004-0.0028	0.002-0.007	3	1.968-1.969	0.0008-0.0034	0.005-0.013
	3	3.0 (2972)	2.3610-2.3620	0.0006-0.0020	0.002-0.010	3	1.968-1.969	0.0006-0.0020	0.004-0.010
	R	3.3 (3300)	2.5190	0.0004-0.0028	0.003-0.009	2	2.283	0.0008-0.0030	0.005-0.015
	L	3.8 (3785)	2.5190	0.0007-0.0030	0.003-0.009	2	2.283	0.0007-0.0030	0.005-0.015
	L [1]	3.8 (3785)	2.5190	0.0007-0.0030	0.003-0.009	2	2.283	0.0008-0.0030	0.005-0.015
	X	3.9 (3916)	2.5000-2.5010	[2]	0.002-0.007	2	2.124-2.125	0.0005-0.0022	0.006-0.014
	Y	5.2 (5211)	2.4995-2.5005	[2]	0.002-0.007	3	2.124-2.125	0.0005-0.0022	0.006-0.014
	C	5.9 (5882)	3.2662 [3]	0.0047	0.004-0.017	6	2.714 [3]	0.0035	0.004-0.012
	5	5.9 (5899)	2.8095-2.8105	[2]	0.002-0.007	3	2.124-2.125	0.0005-0.0022	0.006-0.014
	Z	5.9 (5899)	2.8095-2.8105	[2]	0.002-0.007	3	2.124-2.125	0.0005-0.0022	0.006-0.014
	W	8.0 (7997)	2.9995-3.0005	0.0002-0.0023	0.003-0.012	3	2.124-2.125	0.0002-0.0029	0.010-0.018

1 Town & Country
2 0.0005-0.0015 on No. 1
  0.0005-0.0020 on Nos. 2-4
3 Maximum wear limit

VALVE SPECIFICATIONS

Year	Engine ID/VIN	Engine Displacement Liters (cc)	Seat Angle (deg.)	Face Angle (deg.)	Spring Test Pressure (lbs. @ in.)	Spring Installed Height (in.)	Stem-to-Guide Clearance (in.)		Stem Diameter (in.)	
							Intake	Exhaust	Intake	Exhaust
1992	K	2.5 (2507)	45	45	115@1.65	1.65	0.001-0.005	0.003-0.005	0.3124	0.3103
	3	3.0 (2972)	44.5	45.5	73@1.59	1.59	0.001-0.002	0.002-0.003	0.3130-0.3140	0.3120-0.3130
	R	3.3 (3300)	45	44.5	60@1.56	1.56	0.001-0.003	0.002-0.003	0.3110-0.3120	0.3110-0.3120
	R [1]	3.3 (3300)	45	44.5	60@1.56	1.56	0.001-0.003	0.002-0.006	0.3110-0.3120	0.3110-0.3120
	X	3.9 (3916)	44.25-44.75	43.25-43.75	[2]	[3]	0.001-0.002	0.002-0.004	0.3130	0.3130
	Y	5.2 (5211)	44.25-44.75	43.25-43.75	[2]	[3]	0.001-0.003	0.002-0.004	0.3130	0.3130
	8	5.9 (5882)	[4]	[4]	65@1.94 [4]	2.19	0.002-0.006	0.002-0.006	0.3130-0.3140	0.3130-0.3140
	5	5.9 (5899)	45	45	[5]	[3]	0.001-0.003	0.002-0.004	0.3720-0.3730	0.3710-0.3720
	Z	5.9 (5899)	45	45	[5]	[3]	0.001-0.003	0.002-0.004	0.3720-0.3730	0.3710-0.3720
1993	K	2.5 (2507)	45	45	115@1.65	1.65	0.001-0.005	0.003-0.005	0.3124	0.3103
	3	3.0 (2972)	44.5	45.5	73@1.59	1.59	0.001-0.002	0.002-0.003	0.3130-0.3140	0.3120-0.3130
	R	3.3 (3300)	45	44.5	95@1.57	1.62-1.68	0.001-0.003	0.002-0.006	0.3120-0.3130	0.3110-0.3120
	R [1]	3.3 (3300)	45	44.5	60@1.56	1.56	0.001-0.003	0.002-0.006	0.3110-0.3120	0.3110-0.3120
	X	3.9 (3916)	44.25-44.75	43.25-43.75	85@1.64	1.64	0.001-0.003	0.001-0.003	0.3110-0.3120	0.3110-0.3120
	Y	5.2 (5211)	44.25-44.75	43.25-43.75	85@1.64	1.64	0.001-0.003	0.001-0.003	0.3110-0.3120	0.3110-0.3120
	8	5.9 (5882)	[4]	[4]	65@1.94 [6]	2.19	0.002-0.006	0.002-0.006	0.3130-0.3140	0.3130-0.3140
	5	5.9 (5899)	44.25-44.75	43.25-43.75	85@1.64	1.64	0.001-0.003	0.002-0.004	0.3720-0.3730	0.3710-0.3720
	Z	5.9 (5899)	44.25-44.75	43.25-43.75	85@1.64	1.64	0.001-0.003	0.002-0.004	0.3720-0.3730	0.3710-0.3720
1994	K	2.5 (2507)	45	45	115@1.65	1.65	0.001-0.005	0.003-0.005	0.3124	0.3103
	3	3.0 (2972)	44.5	45.5	73@1.59	1.59	0.001-0.002	0.002-0.003	0.3130-0.3140	0.3120-0.3130
	R	3.3 (3300)	45	44.5	95@1.57	1.62-1.68	0.001-0.003	0.002-0.006	0.3120-0.3130	0.3110-0.3120
	L	3.8 (3785)	45	44.5	95@1.57	1.62-1.68	0.001-0.003	0.002-0.006	0.3120-0.3130	0.3110-0.3120
	L [1]	3.8 (3785)	45	44.5	60@1.56	1.56	0.001-0.003	0.003-0.005	0.3120-0.3130	0.3110-0.3120

VALVE SPECIFICATIONS

Year	Engine ID/VIN	Engine Displacement Liters (cc)	Seat Angle (deg.)	Face Angle (deg.)	Spring Test Pressure (lbs. @ in.)	Spring Installed Height (in.)	Stem-to-Guide Clearance (in.) Intake	Stem-to-Guide Clearance (in.) Exhaust	Stem Diameter (in.) Intake	Stem Diameter (in.) Exhaust
1994	X	3.9 (3916)	44.25-44.75	43.25-43.75	85@1.64	1.64	0.001-0.003	0.001-0.003	0.3110-0.3120	0.3110-0.3120
	Y	5.2 (5211)	44.25-44.75	43.25-43.75	85@1.64	1.64	0.001-0.003	0.001-0.003	0.3110-0.3120	0.3110-0.3120
	C	5.9 (5882)	4	4	81@1.94	2.36	0.002-0.006	0.002-0.006	0.3130-0.3140	0.3130-0.3140
	5	5.9 (5899)	44.25-44.75	43.25-43.75	85@1.64	1.64	0.001-0.003	0.002-0.004	0.3720-0.3730	0.3710-0.3720
	A	5.9 (5899)	44.25-44.75	43.25-43.75	85@1.64	1.64	0.001-0.003	0.002-0.004	0.3720-0.3730	0.3710-0.3720
	Z	5.9 (5899)	44.25-44.75	43.25-43.75	85@1.64	1.64	0.001-0.003	0.002-0.004	0.3720-0.3730	0.3710-0.3720
	W	8.0 (7997)	44.5	45	81-89@1.64	1.64	0.001-0.003	0.001-0.003	0.3110-0.3120	0.3110-0.3120
1995-96	G	2.5 (2507)	45	45	115@1.65	1.65	0.001-0.003	0.003-0.005	0.3124	0.3103
	K	2.5 (2507)	45	45	115@1.65	1.65	0.001-0.003	0.003-0.005	0.3124	0.3103
	3	3.0 (2972)	44.5	45.5	73@1.59	1.59	0.001-0.002	0.002-0.003	0.3130-0.3140	0.3120-0.3130
	R	3.3 (3300)	45	44.5	95@1.57	1.62-1.68	0.001-0.003	0.002-0.006	0.3120-0.3130	0.3110-0.3120
	L	3.8 (3785)	45	44.5	95@1.57	1.62-1.68	0.001-0.003	0.002-0.006	0.3120-0.3130	0.3110-0.3120
	X	3.9 (3916)	44.25-44.75	43.25-43.75	85@1.64	1.64	0.001-0.003	0.001-0.003	0.3110-0.3120	0.3110-0.3120
	Y	5.2 (5211)	44.25-44.75	43.25-43.75	85@1.64	1.64	0.001-0.003	0.001-0.003	0.3110-0.3120	0.3110-0.3120
	C	5.9 (5882)	4	4	81@1.94	2.36	0.002-0.006	0.002-0.006	0.3130-0.3140	0.3130-0.3140
	5	5.9 (5899)	44.25-44.75	43.25-43.75	85@1.64	1.64	0.001-0.003	0.002-0.004	0.3720-0.3730	0.3710-0.3720
	Z	5.9 (5899)	44.25-44.75	43.25-43.75	85@1.64	1.64	0.001-0.003	0.002-0.004	0.3720-0.3730	0.3710-0.3720
	W	8.0 (7997)	44.5	45	81-89@1.64	1.64	0.001-0.003	0.001-0.003	0.3110-0.3120	0.3110-0.3120

1 Town & Country
2 Intake: 78-88 at 1.69 in.
 Exhaust: 80-90 at 1.20 in.
3 Intake: 1.69
 Exhaust: 1.20

4 Intake: 30
 Exhaust: 45
5 Intake: 78-88 at 1.69 in.
 Exhaust: 80-90 at 1.48 in.
6 Minimum acceptable specification

PISTON AND RING SPECIFICATIONS

All measurements are given in inches.

Year	Engine ID/VIN	Engine Displacement Liters (cc)	Piston Clearance	Ring Gap			Ring Side Clearance		
				Top Compression	Bottom Compression	Oil Control	Top Compression	Bottom Compression	Oil Control
1992	K	2.5 (2507)	0.0005-0.0015	0.010-0.021	0.011-0.021	0.015-0.035	0.0015-0.0031	0.0002-0.0080	NA
	3	3.0 (2972)	0.0008-0.0015	0.012-0.018	0.010-0.016	0.012-0.035	0.0020-0.0035	0.0008-0.0020	NA
	R	3.3 (3300)	0.0009-0.0022	0.012-0.022	0.012-0.022	0.010-0.040	0.0012-0.0037	0.0012-0.0037	0.0005-0.0089
	X	3.9 (3916)	0.0005-0.0015	0.010-0.020	0.010-0.020	0.015-0.055	0.0015-0.0030	0.0015-0.0030	0.0020-0.0050
	Y	5.2 (5211)	0.0005-0.0015	0.010-0.020	0.010-0.020	0.015-0.055	0.0015-0.0030	0.0015-0.0030	0.0020-0.0050
	8	5.9 (5882)	NA	0.016-0.028	0.010-0.021	0.010-0.021	0.0030-0.0060	0.0030-0.0060	0.0020-0.0050
	5	5.9 (5899)	0.0005-0.0015	0.010-0.020	0.010-0.020	0.015-0.055	0.0015-0.0030	0.0015-0.0030	0.0020-0.0050
	Z	5.9 (5899)	0.0005-0.0015	0.010-0.020	0.010-0.020	0.015-0.055	0.0015-0.0030	0.0015-0.0030	0.0020-0.0050
1993	K	2.5 (2507)	0.0005-0.0015	0.010-0.020	0.011-0.021	0.015-0.055	0.0015-0.0031	0.0015-0.0037	NA
	3	3.0 (2972)	0.0012-0.0020	0.012-0.018	0.010-0.016	0.012-0.035	0.0020-0.0035	0.0008-0.0020	NA
	R	3.3 (3300)	0.0009-0.0022	0.012-0.022	0.012-0.022	0.010-0.040	0.0012-0.0037	0.0012-0.0037	0.0005-0.0089
	X	3.9 (3916)	0.0003-0.0008	0.010-0.020	0.010-0.020	0.010-0.050	0.0015-0.0030	0.0015-0.0030	0.0020-0.0080
	Y	5.2 (5211)	0.0003-0.0008	0.010-0.020	0.010-0.020	0.015-0.055	0.0015-0.0030	0.0015-0.0030	0.0020-0.0080
	8	5.9 (5882)	NA	0.016-0.028	0.010-0.021	0.010-0.021	0.0030-0.0060	0.0030-0.0060	0.0020-0.0050
	5	5.9 (5899)	0.0005-0.0015	0.010-0.020	0.010-0.020	0.015-0.055	0.0015-0.0030	0.0015-0.0030	0.0020-0.0080
	Z	5.9 (5899)	0.0005-0.0015	0.010-0.020	0.010-0.020	0.015-0.055	0.0015-0.0030	0.0015-0.0030	0.0020-0.0080
1994	K	2.5 (2507)	0.0005-0.0015	0.010-0.020	0.011-0.021	0.015-0.055	0.0015-0.0031	0.0015-0.0037	NA
	3	3.0 (2972)	0.0012-0.0020	0.012-0.018	0.018-0.024	0.008-0.024	0.0020-0.0035	0.0016-0.0033	NA
	3 [1]	3.0 (2972)	0.0012-0.0020	0.012-0.018	0.010-0.016	0.012-0.035	0.0020-0.0035	0.0008-0.0020	NA
	R	3.3 (3300)	0.0010-0.0022	0.012-0.022	0.012-0.022	0.010-0.040	0.0012-0.0037	0.0012-0.0037	0.0005-0.0089
	L	3.8 (3785)	0.0010-0.0022	0.012-0.022	0.012-0.022	0.010-0.040	0.0012-0.0037	0.0012-0.0037	0.0005-0.0089
	X	3.9 (3916)	0.0005-0.0015	0.010-0.020	0.010-0.020	0.010-0.050	0.0015-0.0030	0.0015-0.0030	0.0020-0.0080
	Y	5.2 (5211)	0.0005-0.0015	0.010-0.020	0.010-0.020	0.010-0.050	0.0015-0.0030	0.0015-0.0030	0.0020-0.0080

PISTON AND RING SPECIFICATIONS
All measurements are given in inches.

Year	Engine ID/VIN	Engine Displacement Liters (cc)	Piston Clearance	Ring Gap Top Compression	Ring Gap Bottom Compression	Ring Gap Oil Control	Ring Side Clearance Top Compression	Ring Side Clearance Bottom Compression	Ring Side Clearance Oil Control
1994	C	5.9 (5882)	NA	0.016-0.028	0.010-0.021	0.010-0.021	0.0030-0.0060	0.0030-0.0060	0.0020-0.0050
	A	5.9 (5899)	0.0005-0.0015	0.010-0.020	0.010-0.020	0.015-0.055	0.0016-0.0033	0.0016-0.0033	0.0020-0.0080
	5	5.9 (5899)	0.0005-0.0015	0.012-0.022	0.022-0.031	0.015-0.055	0.0016-0.0033	0.0016-0.0033	0.0020-0.0080
	Z	5.9 (5899)	0.0005-0.0015	0.012-0.022	0.010-0.020	0.015-0.055	0.0015-0.0030	0.0015-0.0030	0.0020-0.0080
	W	8.0 (7997)	0.0005-0.0015	0.010-0.020	0.010-0.020	0.015-0.055	0.0029-0.0038	0.0029-0.0038	0.0073-0.0097
1995-96	G	2.5 (2507)	0.0005-0.0015	0.010-0.020	0.011-0.021	0.015-0.055	0.0015-0.0031	0.0015-0.0037	NA
	K	2.5 (2507)	0.0005-0.0015	0.010-0.020	0.011-0.021	0.015-0.055	0.0015-0.0031	0.0015-0.0037	NA
	K [1]	2.5 (2507)	0.0005-0.0015	0.010-0.020	0.011-0.021	0.015-0.055	0.0015-0.0031	0.0015-0.0037	0.0020-0.0080
	3	3.0 (2972)	0.0012-0.0020	0.012-0.018	0.018-0.024	0.008-0.024	0.0020-0.0035	0.0016-0.0033	NA
	R	3.3 (3300)	0.0010-0.0022	0.012-0.022	0.012-0.022	0.010-0.040	0.0012-0.0037	0.0012-0.0037	0.0005-0.0089
	L	3.8 (3785)	0.0010-0.0022	0.012-0.022	0.012-0.022	0.010-0.040	0.0012-0.0037	0.0012-0.0037	0.0005-0.0089
	X	3.9 (3916)	0.0005-0.0015	0.010-0.020	0.010-0.020	0.010-0.050	0.0015-0.0030	0.0015-0.0030	0.0020-0.0080
	Y	5.2 (5211)	0.0005-0.0015	0.010-0.020	0.010-0.020	0.010-0.050	0.0015-0.0030	0.0015-0.0030	0.0020-0.0080
	C	5.9 (5882)	NA	0.016-0.028	0.010-0.021	0.010-0.021	0.0030-0.0060	0.0030-0.0060	0.0020-0.0050
	5	5.9 (5899)	0.0005-0.0015	0.012-0.022	0.022-0.031	0.015-0.055	0.0016-0.0033	0.0016-0.0033	0.0020-0.0080
	Z	5.9 (5899)	0.0005-0.0015	0.012-0.022	0.010-0.020	0.015-0.055	0.0015-0.0030	0.0015-0.0030	0.0020-0.0080
	W	8.0 (7997)	0.0005-0.0015	0.010-0.020	0.010-0.020	0.015-0.055	0.0029-0.0038	0.0029-0.0038	0.0073-0.0097

NA - Not Available
1 Voyager

TORQUE SPECIFICATIONS
All readings in ft. lbs.

Year	Engine ID/VIN	Engine Displacement Liters (cc)	Cylinder Head Bolts	Main Bearing Bolts	Rod Bearing Bolts	Crankshaft Damper Bolts	Flywheel Bolts	Manifold Intake	Manifold Exhaust	Spark Plugs	Lug Nut
1992	K	2.5 (2507)	1	2	3	50	70	17	17	26	95
	3	3.0 (2972)	80	60	38	110	70	17	17	20	95
	R	3.3 (3300)	4	2	3	40	70	17	17	30	95
	R 5	3.3 (3300)	4	2	3	50	70	17	17	26	95
	X	3.9 (3916)	105	85	45	135	55	45	6	30	7
	Y	5.2 (5211)	105	85	45	135	55	40	6	30	7
	8	5.9 (5882)	8	9	10	92	101	-	32	-	7
	5	5.9 (5899)	105	85	45	135	55	40	6	30	7
	Z	5.9 (5899)	105	85	45	135	55	40	6	30	7
1993	K	2.5 (2507)	1	2	3	50	70	17	17	26	95
	3	3.0 (2972)	80	60	38	110	70	17	17	20	95
	R	3.3 (3300)	4	2	3	40	70	17	17	30	95
	R 5	3.3 (3300)	4	2	3	50	70	17	17	26	95
	X	3.9 (3916)	105	85	45	135	55	45	6	30	7
	Y	5.2 (5211)	105	85	45	135	55	40	6	30	7
	8	5.9 (5882)	8	9	10	92	101	-	32	-	7
	5	5.9 (5899)	105	85	45	135	55	40	6	30	7
	Z	5.9 (5899)	105	85	45	135	55	40	6	30	7
1994	K	2.5 (2507)	1	2	3	85	70	17	17	20	95
	3	3.0 (2972)	80	60	38	112	70	15	16	20	95
	3 11	3.0 (2972)	80	60	38	112	70	17	17	20	95
	R	3.3 (3300)	1	2	3	40	70	17	17	20	95
	L	3.8 (3785)	1	2	3	40	70	17	17	20	95
	X	3.9 (3916)	16	85	45	135	55	12	25	30	13
	Y	5.2 (5211)	16	85	45	135	55	12	25	30	13
	C	5.9 (5882)	8	9	10	92	101	14	32	-	13
	5	5.9 (5899)	16	85	45	135	55	12	25	30	13
	A	5.9 (5899)	16	85	45	135	55	12	25	30	13
	Z	5.9 (5899)	16	85	45	135	55	12	25	30	13
	W	8.0 (7997)	16	85	45	135	55	16	16	30	13
1995-96	G	2.5 (2507)	1	2	3	85	70	17	17	20	95
	K	2.5 (2507)	1	2	3	85	70	17	17	20	95
	3	3.0 (2972)	80	60	38	112	70	15	16	20	95
	R	3.3 (3300)	1	2	3	40	70	17	17	20	95
	L	3.8 (3785)	1	2	3	40	70	17	17	20	95
	X	3.9 (3916)	16	85	45	135	55	12	25	30	13
	Y	5.2 (5211)	16	85	45	135	55	12	25	30	13
	C	5.9 (5882)	8	9	10	92	101	14	32	-	13
	5	5.9 (5899)	16	85	45	135	55	12	25	30	13
	Z	5.9 (5899)	16	85	45	135	55	12	25	30	13
	W	8.0 (7997)	16	85	45	135	55	16	16	30	13

1   Step 1: 45 ft. lbs.
    Step 2: 65 ft. lbs.
    Step 3: 65 ft. lbs.
    Step 4: Plus 1/4 turn

8   All bolts: 66 ft. lbs.
    Long bolts: 89 ft. lbs.
    All bolts and additional 1/4 turn

9   Step 1: 45 ft. lbs.
    Step 2: 88 ft. lbs.
    Step 3: 129 ft. lbs.

TORQUE SPECIFICATIONS
All readings in ft. lbs.

Year	Engine ID/VIN	Engine Displacement Liters (cc)	Cylinder Head Bolts	Main Bearing Bolts	Rod Bearing Bolts	Crankshaft Damper Bolts	Flywheel Bolts	Manifold Intake	Manifold Exhaust	Spark Plugs	Lug Nut

2 Step 1: 30 ft. lbs.
  Step 2: Plus 1/4 turn
3 Step 1: 40 ft. lbs.
  Step 2: Plus 1/4 turn
4 Step 1: 45 ft. lbs.
  Step 2: 65 ft. lbs.
  Step 3: 65 ft. lbs.
  Step 4: Plus 1/4 turn
  Torque small bolt in rear of head to 25 ft. lbs.
5 Town & Country
6 Bolts: 20 ft. lbs.
  Nuts: 15 ft. lbs.
7 1/2x20 stud with cone nut: 85-110 ft. lbs.
  5/8x18 stud with cone nut: 175-225 ft. lbs.
  5/8x18 stud with flanged nut: 300-350 ft. lbs.

10 Step 1: 26 ft. lbs.
   Step 2: 51 ft. lbs.
   Step 3: 73 ft. lbs.
11 Voyager
12 Step 1: Bolts 1-12: 6 ft. lbs. in sequence
   Step 2: Torque all bolts to 12 in. lbs. in alternating steps
   Step 3: Check that all bolts are tightened to 6 ft. lbs.
   Step 4: Tighten all bolts in sequence to 12 ft. lbs.
   Step 5: Check that all bolts are tightened to 12 ft. lbs.
13 5 stud wheel: 95 ft. lbs.
   8 stud wheel: 135 ft. lbs.
   8 stud dual wheel: 145 ft. lbs.
14 Intake manifold cover bolts: 18 ft. lbs.
15 50 ft. lbs. then 105 ft. lbs., in sequence
16 Lower intake: 40 ft. lbs.
   Upper intake: 16 ft. lbs.

BRAKE SPECIFICATIONS
All measurements in inches unless noted

Year	Model	Master Cylinder Bore	Brake Disc Original Thickness	Brake Disc Minimum Thickness	Brake Disc Maximum Runout	Brake Drum Diameter Original Inside Diameter	Brake Drum Diameter Max. Wear Limit	Brake Drum Diameter Maximum Machine Diameter	Minimum Lining Thickness Front	Minimum Lining Thickness Rear
1992	B150 Van	1.125	1.240	1.180	0.004	11.00	11.09	11.06	0.062	0.062
	B250 Van	1.125	1.240	1.180	0.004	11.00	11.09	11.06	0.062	0.062
	B350 Van	1.125	①	②	0.004	12.00	12.09	12.06	0.062	0.062
	Caravan	0.940	0.861	0.800	0.005	9.00	9.09	9.06	0.060	0.060
	Dakota	NA	0.861	0.810	0.004	9.00	9.09	9.06	0.060	0.060
	Dakota	NA	0.861	0.810	0.004	10.00	10.09	110.06	0.060	0.060
	D150 Pick-up	1.125	1.240	1.180	0.004	11.00	11.09	11.06	0.062	0.062
	D250 Pick-up	1.125	1.240	1.180	0.005	12.00	12.09	11.06	0.062	0.062
	D350 Pick-up	1.125	1.240	1.125	0.005	12.00	12.09	12.06	0.062	0.062
	Ramcharger	1.125	1.240	1.180	0.004	11.00	11.09	11.06	0.062	0.062
	Town & Country	0.940	0.861	0.800	0.005	9.00	9.09	9.06	0.062	0.062
	Voyager	0.940	0.861	0.800	0.005	9.00	9.09	9.06	0.060	0.060
	W150 Pick-up	1.125	1.240	1.180	0.004	11.00	11.09	11.06	0.062	0.062
	W250 Pick-up	1.125	①	②	0.005	12.00	12.09	12.06	0.062	0.062
	W350 Pick-up	1.125	1.180	1.125	0.005	12.00	12.09	12.06	0.062	0.062
1993	B150 Van	1.125	1.240	1.180	0.004	11.00	11.09	11.06	0.062	0.062
	B250 Van	1.125	1.240	1.180	0.004	11.00	11.09	11.06	0.062	0.062
	B350 Van	1.125	①	②	0.004	12.00	12.09	12.06	0.062	0.062
	Caravan	0.940	0.940	0.880	0.005	9.00	9.09	9.06	0.060	0.060
	Dakota	NA	0.861	0.810	0.004	9.00	9.09	9.06	0.060	0.060
	Dakota	NA	0.861	0.810	0.004	10.00	10.09	10.06	0.060	0.060
	D150 Pick-up	1.125	1.240	1.180	0.004	11.00	11.09	11.06	0.062	0.062
	D250 Pick-up	1.125	1.240	1.180	0.005	12.00	12.09	11.06	0.062	0.062
	D350 Pick-up	1.125	1.18	1.125	0.005	12.00	12.09	12.06	0.062	0.062
	Ramcharger	1.125	1.240	1.180	0.004	11.00	11.09	11.06	0.062	0.062
	Town & Country	0.940	0.861	0.800	0.005	9.00	9.09	9.06	0.062	0.062
	Voyager	0.940	0.940	0.880	0.005	9.00	9.09	9.06	0.060	0.060

BRAKE SPECIFICATIONS

All measurements in inches unless noted

Year	Model	Master Cylinder Bore	Brake Disc Original Thickness	Brake Disc Minimum Thickness	Brake Disc Maximum Runout	Brake Drum Diameter Original Inside Diameter	Brake Drum Diameter Max. Wear Limit	Brake Drum Diameter Maximum Machine Diameter	Minimum Lining Thickness Front	Minimum Lining Thickness Rear
1993	W150 Pick-up	1.125	1.240	1.180	0.004	11.00	11.09	11.06	0.062	0.062
	W250 Pick-up	1.125	1	2	0.005	12.00	12.09	12.06	0.062	0.062
	W350 Pick-up	1.125	1.180	1.125	0.005	12.00	12.09	12.06	0.062	0.062
1994	B150 Van	1.125	-	3	0.004	11.00	11.09	11.06	0.125	0.062 4
	B250 Van	1.125	-	3	0.004	11.00	11.09	11.06	0.125	0.062 4
	B350 Van	1.125	-	3	0.004	12.00	12.09	12.06	0.125	0.062 4
	Caravan	0.940	0.940	0.880	0.005	9.00	9.09	9.06	0.060	0.060 4
	Dakota	NA	0.861	0.810	0.004	9.00	9.09	9.06	0.060	0.060 4
	Dakota	NA	0.861	0.810	0.004	10.00	10.09	10.06	0.060	0.060 4
	D1500 Pick-up	1.125	1.260	3	0.004	11.00	11.09	11.06	0.062	0.062 4
	D2500 Pick-up	1.250	1.500	3	0.005	13.00	13.09	13.06	0.062	0.062 4
	D3500 Pick-up	1.250	1.500	3	0.005	13.00	13.09	13.06	0.062	0.062 4
	Town & Country	0.940	0.940	0.880	0.005	9.00	9.09	9.06	0.062	0.062 4
	Voyager	0.940	0.940	0.880	0.005	9.00	9.09	9.06	0.060	0.060 4
	W1500 Pick-up	1.125	1.260	3	0.004	11.00	11.09	11.06	0.062	0.062 4
	W2500 Pick-up	1.250	1.500	3	0.005	13.00	13.09	13.06	0.062	0.062 4
	W3500 Pick-up	1.250	1.500	3	0.005	13.00	13.09	13.06	0.062	0.062 4
1995-96	B150 Van	1.125	-	3	0.004	11.00	11.09	11.06	0.125	0.062 4
	B250 Van	1.125	-	3	0.004	11.00	11.09	11.06	0.125	0.062 4
	B350 Van	1.125	-	3	0.004	12.00	12.09	12.06	0.125	0.062 4
	Caravan	0.940	0.940	0.880	0.005	9.00	9.09	9.06	0.060	0.060 4
	Dakota	NA	0.861	0.810	0.004	9.00	9.09	9.06	0.060	0.060 4
	Dakota	NA	0.861	0.810	0.004	10.00	10.09	10.06	0.060	0.060 4
	D1500 Pick-up	1.125	1.260	3	0.004	11.00	11.09	11.06	0.062	0.062 4
	D2500 Pick-up	1.250	1.500	3	0.005	13.00	13.09	13.06	0.062	0.062 4
	D3500 Pick-up	1.250	1.500	3	0.005	13.00	13.09	13.06	0.062	0.062 4
	Town & Country	0.940	0.940	0.880	0.005	9.00	9.09	9.06	0.062	0.062 4
	Voyager	0.940	0.940	0.880	0.005	9.00	9.09	9.06	0.060	0.060 4
	W1500 Pick-up	1.125	1.260	3	0.004	11.00	11.09	11.06	0.062	0.062 4
	W2500 Pick-up	1.250	1.500	3	0.005	13.00	13.09	13.06	0.062	0.062 4
	W3500 Pick-up	1.250	1.500	3	0.005	13.00	13.09	13.06	0.062	0.062 4

1 Except 4000 lb. rear axle: 1.240 in.
  With 4000 lb. rear axle: 1.180 in.
2 With 3300 lb. or 3600 lb. rear axle: 1.180 in.
  With 4000 lb. rear axle: 1.125 in.
3 Minimum thickness indicated on rotor hub
4 For riveted brake shoes: 0.031

WHEEL ALIGNMENT

Year	Model		Caster Range (deg.)	Caster Preferred Setting (deg.)	Camber Range (deg.)	Camber Preferred Setting (deg.)	Toe-in (in.)	Steering Axis Inclination (deg.)
1992	Caravan	F	-	1 5/16P	1/8N-3/4P	5/16P	1/16P	12 3/16
		R	-	-	13/16N-7/16P	1/4P	0	-
	Dakota	F	1/2P-2 1/2P	1 1/2P	0-1P	1/2P	1/8P	NA
		R	-	-	1/16P-3/32P	1/32P	1/32P	NA
	Town & Country	F	-	1 5/16P	3/16N-13/16P	5/16P	1/16P	12 3/16
		R	-	-	13/16N-7/16P	3/16N	0	-
	Voyager	F	-	1 5/16P	1/8N-3/4P	5/16P	1/16P	12 3/16
		R	-	-	13/16N-7/16P	1/4P	0	-
	B150 Van		1 1/4P-3 3/4P	2 1/2P	5/8N-5/8P	0	0	NA
	B250 Van		1 1/4P-3 3/4P	2 1/2P	5/8N-5/8P	0	0	NA
	B350 Van		1 1/4P-3 3/4P	2 1/2P	5/8N-5/8P	0	0	NA
	D150 Pick-up		1N-2P	1/2P	0-1P	1/2P	1/8P	NA
	D250 Pick-up		1N-2P	1/2P	0-1P	1/2P	1/8P	NA
	D350 Pick-up		1N-2P	1/2P	0-1P	1/2P	1/8P	NA
	W150 Pick-up		1/2P-3 1/2P	2P	1/2P-1 1/2P	1P	1/8P	8 1/2 [1]
	W250 Pick-up		1/2P-3 1/2P	2P	1/2P-1 1/2P	1P	1/8P	8 1/2 [1]
	W350 Pick-up		1/2P-3 1/2P	2P	1/2P-1 1/2P	1P	1/8P	8 1/2 [1]
	Ramcharger		1N-2P	1/2P	0-1P	1/2P	1/8P	NA
	Ramcharger		1/2P-3 1/2P	2P	1/2P-1 1/2P	1P	1/8P	8 1/2 [1]
1993	Caravan	F	-	1 5/16P	1/4N-1P	3/4P	1/16P	12 3/16
		R	-	-	13/16N-7/16P	1/4P	0	-
	Dakota	F	1/2P-2 1/2P	1 1/2P	0-1P	1/2P	1/8P	NA
		R	-	-	1/16P-3/32P	1/32P	1/32P	NA
	Town & Country	F	-	1 5/16P	3/16N-13/16P	5/16P	1/16P	12 3/16
		R	-	-	13/16N-7/16P	3/16N	0	-
	Voyager	F	-	1 5/16P	1/4N-1P	3/4P	1/16P	12 3/16
		R	-	-	13/16N-7/16P	1/4P	0	-
	B150 Van		1 1/4P-3 3/4P	2 1/2P	5/8N-5/8P	0	0	NA
	B250 Van		1 1/4P-3 3/4P	2 1/2P	5/8N-5/8P	0	0	NA
	B350 Van		1 1/4P-3 3/4P	2 1/2P	5/8N-5/8P	0	0	NA
	D150 Pick-up		1N-2P	1/2P	0-1P	1/2P	1/4P	NA
	D250 Pick-up		1N-2P	1/2P	0-1P	1/2P	1/8P	NA
	D350 Pick-up		1N-2P	1/2P	0-1P	1/2P	1/8P	NA
	W150 Pick-up		1/2P-3 1/2P	2P	1N-1P	0	1/8P	8 1/2 [1]
	W250 Pick-up		1/2P-3 1/2P	2P	1N-1P	0	1/8P	8 1/2 [1]
	W350 Pick-up		1/2P-3 1/2P	2P	1N-1P	0	1/8P	8 1/2 [1]
	Ramcharger		1N-2P	1/2P	0-1P	1/2P	1/8P	NA
	Ramcharger		1/2P-3 1/2P	2P	1/2P-1 1/2P	1P	1/8P	8 1/2 [1]
1994	Caravan	F	-	1 5/16P	1/4N-3/4P	5/16P	1/16P	12 3/16
		R	-	-	13/16N-7/16P	1/4N	0	NA
	Dakota	F	1/2P-2 1/2P	1 1/2P	0-1P	1/2P	1/8P	NA
		R	-	-	0-1P	1/2P	1/8P	NA
	Town & Country	F	-	1 5/16P	1/4N-3/4P	5/16P	1/16P	12 3/16
		R	-	-	13/16N-7/16P	1/4P	0	-
	Voyager	F	-	1 5/16P	1/4N-3/4P	5/16P	1/16P	NA
		R	-	-	13/16N-7/16P	1/4P	0	NA

WHEEL ALIGNMENT

Year	Model		Caster Range (deg.)	Caster Preferred Setting (deg.)	Camber Range (deg.)	Camber Preferred Setting (deg.)	Toe-in (in.)	Steering Axis Inclination (deg.)
	B150 Van		1 1/4P-3 3/4P	2 1/2P	5/8N-5/8P	0	0	NA
	B250 Van		1 1/4P-3 3/4P	2 1/2P	5/8N-5/8P	0	0	NA
	B350 Van		1 1/4P-3 3/4P	2 1/2P	5/8N-5/8P	0	0	NA
	D1500 Pickup		2 3/4P-4 3/4P	3 3/4P	0-1P	1/2P	1/4P	NA
	D2500 Pick-up		2 1/2P-4 1/2P	3 1/2P	0-1P	1/2P	1/4P	NA
	D3500 Pick-up		2 1/4P-4 3/4P	3 1/4P	0-1P	1/2P	1/4P	NA
	W1500 Pick-up		2 1/2P-4 1/2P	3 1/2P	0-1P	1/2P	1/4P	NA
	W2500 Pick-up		2P-4P	3P	0-1P	1/2P	1/4P	NA
	W3500 Pick-up		2 1/4P-4 3/4P	3 1/4P	0-1P	1/2P	1/4P	NA
1995-96	Caravan	F	-	1 5/16P	1/4N-3/4P	5/16P	1/16P	12 3/16
		R	-	-	13/16N-7/16P	1/4N	0	NA
	Dakota	F	1/2P-2 1/2P	1 1/2P	0-1P	1/2P	1/8P	NA
		R	-	-	0-1P	1/2P	1/8P	NA
	Town & Country	F	-	1 5/16P	1/4N-3/4P	5/16P	1/16P	12 3/16
		R	-	-	13/16N-7/16P	1/4P	0	-
	Voyager	F	-	1 5/16P	1/4N-3/4P	5/16P	1/16P	12 3/16
		R	-	-	13/16N-7/16P	1/4N	0	-
	B150 Van		1 1/4P-3 3/4P	2 1/2P	5/8N-5/8P	0	0	NA
	B250 Van		1 1/4P-3 3/4P	2 1/2P	5/8N-5/8P	0	0	NA
	B350 Van		1 1/4P-3 3/4P	2 1/2P	5/8N-5/8P	0	0	NA
	D1500 Pick-up		2 3/4P-4 3/4P	3 3/4P	0-1P	1/2P	1/4P	NA
	D2500 Pick-up		2 1/2P-4 1/2P	3 1/2P	0-1P	1/2P	1/4P	NA
	D3500 Pick-up		2 1/4P-4 3/4P	3 1/4P	0-1P	1/2P	1/4P	NA
	W1500 Pick-up		2 1/2P-4 1/2P	3 1/2P	0-1P	1/2P	1/4P	NA
	W2500 Pick-up		2P-4P	3P	0-1P	1/2P	1/4P	NA
	W3500 Pick-up		2 1/4P-4 3/4P	3 1/4P	0-1P	1/2P	1/4P	NA

NA - Not Available
F - Front
R - Rear
1 King pin inclination

FORD MOTOR COMPANY

VEHICLE IDENTIFICATION CHART

Engine Code							Model Year	
Code	Liters	Cu. In. (cc)	Cyl.	Fuel Sys.	Eng. Mfg.		Code	Year
A	2.3	140 (2294)	4	MFI	Ford		N	1992
T	2.9	177 (2900)	6	MFI	Ford		P	1993
U	3.0	183 (2999)	6	MFI	Ford		R	1994
X	4.0	244 (3998)	6	MFI	Ford		S	1995
Y	4.9	300 (4916)	6	MFI	Ford		T	1996
N	5.0	302 (4949)	8	MFI	Ford			
H	5.8	351 (5752)	8	MFI	Ford			
M	7.3	445 (7292)	8	DSL	Ford			
G	7.5	460 (7538)	8	MFI	Ford			
A	2.3	140 (2294)	4	MFI	Ford			
U	3.0	183 (2999)	6	MFI	Ford			
X	4.0	244 (3998)	6	MFI	Ford			
Y	4.9	300 (4916)	6	MFI	Ford			
N	5.0	302 (4949)	8	MFI	Ford			
H	5.8	351 (5752)	8	MFI	Ford			
R	5.8	351 (5752)	8	MFI	Ford			
C	7.3	445 (7292)	8	IDI	Navistar			
M	7.3	445 (7292)	8	DSL	Navistar			
G	7.5	460 (7538)	8	MFI	Ford			
A	2.3	140 (2294)	4	MFI	Ford			
U	3.0	183 (2999)	6	MFI	Ford			
X	4.0	244 (3998)	6	MFI	Ford			
Y	4.9	300 (4916)	6	MFI	Ford			
N	5.0	302 (4949)	8	MFI	Ford			
H	5.8	351 (5752)	8	MFI	Ford			
R	5.8	351 (5752)	8	MFI	Ford			
F	7.3	445 (7292)	8	DI	Navistar			
K	7.3	445 (7292)	8	DSL	Navistar			
M	7.3	445 (7292)	8	DSL	Navistar			
G	7.5	460 (7538)	8	MFI	Ford			
A	2.3	140 (2294)	4	MFI	Ford			
U	3.0	183 (2999)	6	MFI	Ford			
4	3.8	231 (3785)	6	MFI	Ford			
X	4.0	244 (3998)	6	MFI	Ford			
Y	4.9	300 (4916)	6	MFI	Ford			
N	5.0	302 (4949)	8	MFI	Ford			
H	5.8	351 (5752)	8	MFI	Ford			
R	5.8	351 (5752)	8	MFI	Ford			
F	7.3	445 (7292)	8	DI	Navistar			
M	7.3	445 (7292)	8	DSL	Navistar			
G	7.5	460 (7538)	8	MFI	Ford			

MFI - Multiport fuel injection
DSL - Diesel

IDI - Indirect diesel injection
DI - Direct injection Turbo

ENGINE IDENTIFICATION

Year	Model	Engine Displacement Liters (cc)	Engine Series (ID/VIN)	Fuel System	No. of Cylinders	Engine Type
1992	Ranger	2.3 (2294)	A	MFI	4	SOHC
	Ranger	2.9 (2900)	T	MFI	6	OHV
	Ranger	3.0 (2999)	U	MFI	6	OHV
	Ranger	4.0 (3998)	X	MFI	6	OHV
	Aerostar	3.0 (2999)	U	MFI	6	OHV
	Aerostar	4.0 (3998)	X	MFI	6	OHV
	Explorer	4.0 (3998)	X	MFI	6	OHV
	Bronco	4.9 (4916)	Y	MFI	6	OHV
	Bronco	5.0 (4949)	N	MFI	8	OHV
	Bronco	5.8 (5752)	H	MFI	8	OHV
	E-150	4.9 (4916)	Y	MFI	6	OHV
	E-150	5.0 (4949)	N	MFI	8	OHV
	E-150	5.8 (5752)	H	MFI	8	OHV
	E-250	4.9 (4916)	Y	MFI	6	OHV
	E-250	5.0 (4949)	N	MFI	8	OHV
	E-250	5.8 (5752)	H	MFI	8	OHV
	E-250	7.3 (7292)	M	DDI	8	OHV
	E-250	7.5 (7538)	G	MFI	8	OHV
	E-350	4.9 (4916)	Y	MFI	6	OHV
	E-350	5.8 (5752)	H	MFI	8	OHV
	E-350	7.3 (7292)	M	DDI	8	OHV
	E-350	7.5 (7538)	G	MFI	8	OHV
	F-150	4.9 (4916)	Y	MFI	6	OHV
	F-150	5.0 (4949)	N	MFI	8	OHV
	F-150	5.8 (5752)	H	MFI	8	OHV
	F-250	4.9 (4916)	Y	MFI	6	OHV
	F-250	5.0 (4949)	N	MFI	8	OHV
	F-250	5.8 (5752)	H	MFI	8	OHV
	F-250	7.3 (7292)	M	DDI	8	OHV
	F-250	7.5 (7538)	G	MFI	8	OHV
	F-350	4.9 (4916)	Y	MFI	6	OHV
	F-350	5.8 (5752)	H	MFI	8	OHV
	F-350	7.3 (7292)	M	DDI	8	OHV
	F-350	7.5 (7538)	G	MFI	8	OHV
	F-Super Duty	7.3 (7292)	M	DDI	8	OHV
	F-Super Duty	7.5 (7538)	G	MFI	8	OHV
1993	Ranger	2.3 (2294)	A	MFI	4	SOHC
	Ranger	3.0 (2999)	U	MFI	6	OHV
	Ranger	4.0 (3998)	X	MFI	6	OHV
	Aerostar	3.0 (2999)	U	MFI	6	OHV
	Aerostar	4.0 (3998)	X	MFI	6	OHV
	Explorer	4.0 (3998)	X	MFI	6	OHV
	Bronco	4.9 (4916)	Y	MFI	6	OHV
	Bronco	5.0 (4949)	N	MFI	8	OHV
	Bronco	5.8 (5752)	H	MFI	8	OHV
	E-150	4.9 (4916)	Y	MFI	6	OHV
	E-150	5.0 (4949)	N	MFI	8	OHV

ENGINE IDENTIFICATION

Year	Model	Engine Displacement Liters (cc)	Engine Series (ID/VIN)	Fuel System	No. of Cylinders	Engine Type
1993	E-150	5.8 (5752)	H	MFI	8	OHV
	E-250	4.9 (4916)	Y	MFI	6	OHV
	E-250	5.0 (4949)	N	MFI	8	OHV
	E-250	5.8 (5752)	H	MFI	8	OHV
	E-250	7.3 (7292)	M	IDI	8	OHV
	E-250	7.5 (7538)	G	MFI	8	OHV
	E-350	4.9 (4916)	Y	MFI	6	OHV
	E-350	5.8 (5752)	H	MFI	8	OHV
	E-350	7.3 (7292)	M	IDI	8	OHV
	E-350	7.5 (7538)	G	MFI	8	OHV
	F-150	4.9 (4916)	Y	MFI	6	OHV
	F-150	5.0 (4949)	N	MFI	8	OHV
	F-150	5.8 (5752)	H	MFI	8	OHV
	F-250	4.9 (4916)	Y	MFI	6	OHV
	F-250	5.0 (4949)	N	MFI	8	OHV
	F-250	5.8 (5752)	H	EFI	8	OHV
	F-250	7.3 (7292)	M	IDI	8	OHV
	F-250	7.5 (7538)	G	EFI	8	OHV
	F-350	4.9 (4916)	Y	EFI	6	OHV
	F-350	5.8 (5752)	H	EFI	8	OHV
	F-350	7.3 (7292)	M	DDI	8	OHV
	F-350	7.5 (7538)	G	EFI	8	OHV
	Lightning Pick-up	5.8 (5752)	R	EFI	8	OHV
	F-Super Duty	7.3 (7292)	M	DDI	8	OHV
	F-Super Duty	7.5 (7538)	G	EFI	8	OHV
1994	Ranger	2.3 (2294)	A	MFI	4	SOHC
	Ranger	3.0 (2999)	U	MFI	6	OHV
	Ranger	4.0 (3998)	X	MFI	6	OHV
	Aerostar	3.0 (2999)	U	MFI	6	OHV
	Aerostar	4.0 (3998)	X	MFI	6	OHV
	Explorer	4.0 (3998)	X	MFI	6	OHV
	Bronco	5.0 (4949)	N	MFI	8	OHV
	Bronco	5.8 (5752)	H	MFI	8	OHV
	E-150	4.9 (4916)	Y	MFI	6	OHV
	E-150	5.0 (4949)	N	MFI	8	OHV
	E-150	5.8 (5752)	H	MFI	8	OHV
	E-250	4.9 (4916)	Y	MFI	6	OHV
	E-250	5.0 (4949)	N	MFI	8	OHV
	E-250	5.8 (5752)	H	MFI	8	OHV
	E-350	4.9 (4916)	Y	MFI	6	OHV
	E-350	5.8 (5752)	H	MFI	8	OHV
	E-350	7.3 (7292)	F	DI	8	OHV
	E-350	7.3 (7292)	K	IDI	8	OHV
	E-350	7.3 (7292)	M	IDI	8	OHV
	E-350	7.5 (7538)	G	MFI	8	OHV
	F-150	4.9 (4916)	Y	MFI	6	OHV
	F-150	5.0 (4949)	N	MFI	8	OHV

ENGINE IDENTIFICATION

Year	Model	Engine Displacement Liters (cc)	Engine Series (ID/VIN)	Fuel System	No. of Cylinders	Engine Type
1994	F-150	5.8 (5752)	H	MFI	8	OHV
	F-250	4.9 (4916)	Y	MFI	6	OHV
	F-250	5.0 (4949)	N	MFI	8	OHV
	F-250	5.8 (5752)	H	EFI	8	OHV
	F-250	7.3 (7292)	M	IDI	8	OHV
	F-250	7.5 (7538)	G	EFI	8	OHV
	F-350	4.9 (4916)	Y	EFI	6	OHV
	F-350	5.8 (5752)	H	EFI	8	OHV
	F-350	7.3 (7292)	F	DI	8	OHV
	F-350	7.3 (7292)	K	DDI	8	OHV
	F-350	7.3 (7292)	M	DDI	8	OHV
	F-350	7.5 (7538)	G	EFI	8	OHV
	Lightning Pick-up	5.8 (5752)	R	EFI	8	OHV
	F-Super Duty	7.3 (7292)	F	DI	8	OHV
	F-Super Duty	7.3 (7292)	K	IDI	8	OHV
	F-Super Duty	7.3 (7292)	M	DDI	8	OHV
	F-Super Duty	7.5 (7538)	G	EFI	8	OHV
1995-96	Ranger	2.3 (2294)	A	MFI	4	SOHC
	Ranger	3.0 (2999)	U	MFI	6	OHV
	Ranger	4.0 (3998)	X	MFI	6	OHV
	Aerostar	3.0 (2999)	U	MFI	6	OHV
	Aerostar	4.0 (3998)	X	MFI	6	OHV
	Explorer	4.0 (3998)	X	MFI	6	OHV
	Windstar	3.8 (3802)	4	MFI	6	OHV
	Bronco	5.0 (4949)	N	MFI	8	OHV
	Bronco	5.8 (5752)	H	MFI	8	OHV
	E-150	4.9 (4916)	Y	MFI	6	OHV
	E-150	5.0 (4949)	N	MFI	8	OHV
	E-150	5.8 (5752)	H	MFI	8	OHV
	E-250	4.9 (4916)	Y	MFI	6	OHV
	E-250	5.0 (4949)	N	MFI	8	OHV
	E-250	5.8 (5752)	H	MFI	8	OHV
	E-350	4.9 (4916)	Y	MFI	6	OHV
	E-350	5.8 (5752)	H	MFI	8	OHV
	E-350	7.3 (7292)	F	DI	8	OHV
	E-350	7.3 (7292)	K	IDI	8	OHV
	E-350	7.3 (7292)	M	IDI	8	OHV
	E-350	7.5 (7538)	G	MFI	8	OHV
	F-150	4.9 (4916)	Y	MFI	6	OHV
	F-150	5.0 (4949)	N	MFI	8	OHV
	F-150	5.8 (5752)	H	MFI	8	OHV
	F-250	4.9 (4916)	Y	MFI	6	OHV
	F-250	5.0 (4949)	N	MFI	8	OHV
	F-250	5.8 (5752)	H	MFI	8	OHV
	F-250	7.3 (7292)	M	IDI	8	OHV
	F-250	7.5 (7538)	G	MFI	8	OHV
	F-350	4.9 (4916)	Y	MFI	6	OHV

ENGINE IDENTIFICATION

Year	Model	Engine Displacement Liters (cc)	Engine Series (ID/VIN)	Fuel System	No. of Cylinders	Engine Type
1995-96	F-350	5.8 (5752)	H	MFI	8	OHV
	F-350	7.3 (7292)	K	IDI	8	OHV
	F-350	7.3 (7292)	F	DI	8	OHV
	F-350	7.3 (7292)	M	IDI	8	OHV
	F-350	7.5 (7538)	G	MFI	8	OHV
	Lightning Pick-up	5.8 (5752)	R	EFI	8	OHV
	F-Super Duty	7.3 (7292)	F	DI	8	OHV
	F-Super Duty	7.3 (7292)	M	DDI	8	OHV
	F-Super Duty	7.3 (7292)	K	IDI	8	OHV
	F-Super Duty	7.5 (7538)	G	EFI	8	OHV

MFI - Multiport fuel injection
DDI - Direct diesel injection
OHV - Overhead valve
SOHC - Single overhead camshaft

IDI - Indirect diesel injection
EFI - Electronic fuel injection
DI - Direct injection Turbo

GENERAL ENGINE SPECIFICATIONS

Year	Engine ID/VIN	Engine Displacement Liters (cc)	Fuel System Type	Net Horsepower @ rpm	Net Torque @ rpm (ft. lbs.)	Bore x Stroke (in.)	Compression Ratio	Oil Pressure @ rpm
1992	A	2.3 (2294)	MFI	100@4600	133@2600	3.78x3.13	9.2:1	40-60@2000
	T	2.9 (2900)	MFI	140@4600	170@2600	3.66x2.83	9.0:1	40-60@2000
	U	3.0 (2999)	MFI	145@4800	165@3600	3.50x3.14	9.3:1	40-60@2500
	X	4.0 (3998)	MFI	[1]	[2]	3.95x3.32	9.0:1	40-60@2000
	Y	4.9 (4916)	MFI	[1]	[2]	4.00x3.98	8.8:1	40-60@2000
	N	5.0 (4949)	MFI	185@3800	270@2400	4.00x3.00	9.0:1	40-60@2000
	H	5.8 (5752)	MFI	210@3800	315@2800 [3]	4.00x3.50	8.8:1	40-60@2000
	M	7.3 (7292)	DDI	180@3300 [4]	45@1400 [5]	11.00x4.18	21.5:1	40-70@2000
	G	7.5 (7538)	MFI	230@3600	390@2200	4.36x3.85	8.5:1	40-65@2000
1993	A	2.3 (2294)	EFI	100@4600	133@2600	3.78x3.13	9.2:1	40-60@2000
	U	3.0 (2999)	EFI	145@4800	165@3600	3.50x3.14	9.3:1	40-60@2500
	X	4.0 (3998)	EFI	[1]	[2]	3.95x3.32	9.0:1	40-60@2000
	Y	4.9 (4916)	EFI	[6]	[7]	4.00x3.98	8.8:1	40-60@2000
	N	5.0 (4949)	EFI	185@3800	270@2400	4.00x3.98	9.0:1	40-60@2000
	H	5.8 (5752)	EFI	200@3800	310@2800	4.00x3.50	8.8:1	40-65@2000
	R	5.8 (5752)	EFI	240@4200	340@3200	4.00x3.50	8.8:1	40-65@2000
	C	7.3 (7292)	IDI	190@3000	395@1400	4.11x4.18	21.5:1	40-70@2000
	M	7.3 (7292)	IDI	185@3000 [8]	360@400 [9]	4.11x4.18	21.5:1	40-70@2000
	G	7.5 (7538)	EFI	245@4000	400@2200	4.36x3.85	8.5:1	40-65@2000
1994	A	2.3 (2294)	EFI	100@4600	133@2600	3.78x3.13	9.2:1	40-60@2000
	U	3.0 (2999)	MFI	135@4600	160@2800	3.50x3.14	9.3:1	40-60@2500
	X	4.0 (3998)	EFI	160@4000	225@2500	3.95x3.32	9.0:1	40-60@2000
	Y	4.9 (4916)	EFI	[6]	[7]	4.00x3.98	8.8:1	40-60@2000
	N	5.0 (4949)	EFI	205@4000	275@3000	4.00x3.00	9.0:1	40-60@2000
	H	5.8 (5752)	EFI	210@3600	325@2800	4.00x3.50	8.8:1	40-65@2000
	R	5.8 (5752)	EFI	240@4200	340@3200	4.00x3.50	8.8:1	40-65@2000
	F	7.3 (7292)	DI	210@3000	425@2000	4.11x4.18	17.5:1	40-70@3000
	K	7.3 (7292)	IDI	190@3000	395@1400	4.11x4.18	21.5:1	40-70@2000
	M	7.3 (7292)	IDI	185@3000 [8]	360@1400 [9]	4.11x4.18	21.5:1	40-70@2000
	G	7.5 (7538)	EFI	245@4000	400@2200	4.36x3.85	8.5:1	40-88@2000

GENERAL ENGINE SPECIFICATIONS

Year	Engine ID/VIN	Engine Displacement Liters (cc)	Fuel System Type	Net Horsepower @ rpm	Net Torque @ rpm (ft. lbs.)	Bore x Stroke (in.)	Compression Ratio	Oil Pressure @ rpm
1995-96	A	2.3 (2294)	EFI	100@4600	133@2600	3.78x3.13	9.2:1	40-60@2000
	U	3.0 (2999)	MFI	135@4600	160@2800	3.50x3.14	9.3:1	40-60@2500
	4	3.8 (3802)	MFI	140@3800	215@2400	3.81x3.39	9.0:1	40-60@2500
	X	4.0 (3998)	EFI	160@4000	225@2500	3.81x3.39	9.0:1	40-60@2000
	Y	4.9 (4916)	EFI	145@3400 [10]	265@2000 [10]	4.00x3.98	8.8:1	40-60@2000
	N	5.0 (4949)	EFI	205@4000	275@3000	4.00x3.00	9.0:1	40-60@2000
	H	5.8 (5752)	EFI	210@3600	325@2800	4.00x3.50	8.8:1	40-65@2000
	R	5.8 (5752)	EFI	240@4200	340@3200	4.00x3.50	8.8:1	40-65@2000
	F	7.3 (7292)	DI	210@3000	425@2000	4.11x4.18	17.5:1	40-70@3000
	M	7.3 (7292)	IDI	185@3000 [8]	360@1400 [9]	4.11x4.18	21.5:1	40-70@2000
	G	7.5 (7538)	EFI	245@4000	400@2200	4.36x3.85	8.5:1	40-88@2000

MFI - Multiport fuel injection
DDI - Direct diesel injection
EFI - Electronic fuel injection
IDI - Indirect diesel injection
DI - Direct injection Turbo

1 Explorer and Aerostar: 155@4200
  Ranger: 160@4200
2 Aerostar: 215@2400
  Explorer: 220@2400
  Ranger: 225@2400
3 8500 lbs. GVWR-up: 310@2800
4 High altitude: 160@3300
5 High altitude: 305@1400

6 E-Series 3 speed automatic: 150@3400
  E-Series 4 speed OD automatic: 145@3400
  F-Series 5 speed manual or 4 speed OD automatic and 2.73 rear axle ratio: 145@3400
  F-Series 5 speed HD or 3 speed automatic: 150@3400
7 3 speed automatic: 260@2000
  4 speed OD automatic: 265@2000
  5 speed manual OD or 4 speed automatic OD: 265@2000
  5 speed manual HD or 3 speed automatic: 260@2000
8 High altitude: 165@3000
9 High altitude: 325@1600
10 Ratings are for E150-250 Van and regular Wagon with 4 speed automatic overdrive (E40D).
   Use 150hp@ 3400 rpm and 260 ft. lbs. @2000 rpm for all other applications

GASOLINE ENGINE TUNE-UP SPECIFICATIONS

Year	Engine ID/VIN	Engine Displacement Liters (cc)	Spark Plugs Gap (in.)	Ignition Timing (deg.) MT	Ignition Timing (deg.) AT	Fuel Pump (psi)	Idle Speed (rpm) MT	Idle Speed (rpm) AT	Valve Clearance In.	Valve Clearance Ex.
1992	A	2.3 (2294)	0.044	10B	10B	35-45	725	675	HYD	HYD
	T	2.9 (2900)	0.044	10B	10B	35-45	850	800	HYD	HYD
	U	3.0 (2999)	0.044	10B	10B	35-45	1	1	HYD	HYD
	X	4.0 (3998)	0.054	10B	10B	35-45	1	1	HYD	HYD
	Y	4.9 (4916)	0.044	10B	10B	50-60	700	575	HYD	HYD
	N	5.0 (4949)	0.044	10B	10B	35-45	775	675	HYD	HYD
	H	5.8 (5752)	0.044	10B	10B	35-45	775	675	HYD	HYD
	G	7.5 (7538)	0.044	10B	10B	35-45	775	675	HYD	HYD
1993	A	2.3 (2294)	0.044	10B	10B	35-45	725	675	HYD	HYD
	U	3.0 (2999)	0.044	10B	10B	35-45	1	1	HYD	HYD
	X	4.0 (3998)	0.054	10B	10B	35-45	1	1	HYD	HYD
	Y	4.9 (4916)	0.044	10B	10B	50-60	700	575	HYD	HYD
	N	5.0 (4949)	0.044	10B	10B	35-45	775	675	HYD	HYD
	H	5.8 (5752)	0.044	10B	10B	35-45	775	675	HYD	HYD
	R	5.8 (5752)	0.044	10B	10B	35-45	775	675	HYD	HYD
	G	7.5 (7538)	0.044	10B	10B	35-45	775	675	HYD	HYD

GASOLINE ENGINE TUNE-UP SPECIFICATIONS

Year	Engine ID/VIN	Engine Displacement Liters (cc)	Spark Plugs Gap (in.)	Ignition Timing (deg.)		Fuel Pump (psi)	Idle Speed (rpm)		Valve Clearance	
				MT	AT		MT	AT	In.	Ex.
1994	A	2.3 (2294)	0.044	10B	10B	35-45	725	675	HYD	HYD
	U	3.0 (2999)	0.044	10B	10B	35-45	1	1	HYD	HYD
	X	4.0 (3998)	0.054	10B	10B	35-45	1	1	HYD	HYD
	Y	4.9 (4916)	0.044	10B	10B	50-60	700	575	HYD	HYD
	N	5.0 (4949)	0.044	10B	10B	35-45	775	675	HYD	HYD
	H	5.8 (5752)	0.044	10B	10B	35-45	775	675	HYD	HYD
	R	5.8 (5752)	0.044	10B	10B	35-45	775	675	HYD	HYD
	G	7.5 (7538)	0.044	10B	10B	35-45	775	675	HYD	HYD
1995-96	A	2.3 (2294)	0.044	10B	10B	35-45	725	675	HYD	HYD
	U	3.0 (2999)	0.044	10B	10B	35-45	1	1	HYD	HYD
	4	3.8 (3802)	0.054	10B	10B	30-45	1	1	HYD	HYD
	X	4.0 (3998)	0.054	10B	10B	35-45	1	1	HYD	HYD
	Y	4.9 (4916)	0.044	10B	10B	50-60	700	575	HYD	HYD
	N	5.0 (4949)	0.044	10B	10B	35-45	775	675	HYD	HYD
	H	5.8 (5752)	0.044	10B	10B	35-45	775	675	HYD	HYD
	R	5.8 (5752)	0.044	10B	10B	35-45	775	675	HYD	HYD
	G	7.5 (7538)	0.044	10B	10B	35-45	775	675	HYD	HYD

NOTE: The Vehicle Emission Control Information label often reflects specification changes
changes made during production. The label figures must be used if they
differ from those in this chart.
B - Before top dead center
HYD - Hydraulic
1 Idle speed is electronically controlled and cannot be adjusted

DIESEL ENGINE TUNE-UP SPECIFICATIONS

Year	Engine ID/VIN	Engine Displacement cu. in. (cc)	Valve Clearance Intake (in.)	Exhaust (in.)	Intake Valve Opens (deg.)	Injection Pump Setting (deg.)	Injection Nozzle Pressure (psi) New	Used	Idle Speed (rpm)	Cranking Compression Pressure (psi)
1992	M	7.3 (7292)	HYD	HYD	-	8.5B 1	1875	1425	2	190-440
1993	C	7.3 (7292)	HYD	HYD	-	8.5B 1	1875	1425	2	190-440
	M	7.3 (7292)	HYD	HYD	-	8.5B 1	1875	1425	2	190-440
1994	M	7.3 (7292)	HYD	HYD	-	8.5B 1	1875	1425	2	3
	F	7.3 (7292)	HYD	HYD	-	4	NA	NA	2	3
	K	7.3 (7292)	HYD	HYD	-	4	NA	NA	2	3
1995-96	F	7.3 (7292)	HYD	HYD	-	4	1875	1425	2	3
	M	7.3 (7292)	HYD	HYD	-	8.5B 1	NA	NA	2	3

NOTE: The Vehicle Emission Control Information label often reflects specification
changes made during production. The label figures must be used if they
differ from those in this chart
HYD - Hydraulic
B - Before top dead center
NA - Not Available

1 At 2000 rpm
2 See underhood emission label
3 Compression pressure in the lowest cylinder must be at least
  75% of the highest cylinder
  Minimum pressure: 195 psi
  Maximum pressure: 440 psi
4 PCM controlled

CAPACITIES

Year	Model	Engine ID/VIN	Engine Displacement Liters (cc)	Engine Oil with Filter (qts.)	Transmission (pts.) 4-Spd	5-Spd	Auto.	Transfer Case (pts.)	Drive Axle Front (pts.)	Rear (pts.)	Fuel Tank (gal.)	Cooling System (qts.)
1992	Aerostar	U	3.0 (2999)	5.0	-	5.6	19.0	2.5	3.0	[1]	21.0	11.8
	Aerostar	X	4.0 (3998)	5.0	-	5.6	19.0	2.5	3.0	[1]	21.0	8.5
	Explorer	X	4.0 (3998)	5.0	-	5.6	19.0	3.0	[1]	[1]	21.0	8.5
	Ranger	A	2.3 (2294)	5.0	-	[2]	19.4	3.0	[1]	5.5	[3]	7.2
	Ranger	T	2.9 (2900)	5.0	-	3.0	[4]	[5]	[6]	[6]	[3]	7.5
	Ranger	U	3.0 (2999)	5.0	-	3.0	[4]	[5]	[6]	[6]	[3]	11.8
	Ranger	X	4.0 (3998)	5.0	-	3.0	[4]	[5]	[6]	[6]	[3]	8.5
	Bronco	Y	4.9 (4916)	6.0	7.0	7.0	24.0	[7]	5.5	5.5	32.0	14.0
	Bronco	N	5.0 (4949)	6.0	7.0 [8]	7.0	24.0	[7]	5.5	5.5	32.0	14.0
	Bronco	H	5.8 (5752)	6.0	7.0 [8]	7.0	24.0	[7]	5.5	5.5	32.0	15.0
	E-150	Y	4.9 (4916)	6.0	7.0	7.0	24.0	-	-	6.0 [9]	[10]	17.5
	E-150	N	5.0 (4949)	6.0	7.0 [8]	7.0	24.0	-	-	6.0 [9]	[10]	[11]
	E-150	H	5.8 (5752)	6.0	7.0 [8]	7.0	24.0	-	-	6.0 [9]	[10]	[12]
	E-250	Y	4.9 (4916)	6.0	7.0	7.0	24.0	-	-	6.0 [9]	[10]	17.5
	E-250	N	5.0 (4949)	6.0	7.0 [8]	7.0	24.0	-	-	6.0 [9]	[10]	[11]
	E-250	H	5.8 (5752)	6.0	7.0 [8]	7.0	24.0	-	-	6.0 [9]	[10]	[12]
	E-250	M	7.3 (7292)	10.0	7.0 [8]	7.0	24.0	-	-	6.0 [9]	[10]	31.0
	E-250	L	7.5 (7538)	6.0	7.0 [8]	7.0	24.0	-	-	6.0 [9]	[10]	28.0
	E-350	Y	4.9 (4916)	6.0	7.0	7.0	24.0	-	-	6.0 [9]	[10]	17.5
	E-350	H	5.8 (5752)	6.0	7.0 [8]	7.0	24.0	-	-	6.0 [9]	[10]	[12]
	E-350	M	7.3 (7292)	10.0	7.0 [8]	7.0	24.0	-	-	6.0 [9]	[10]	31.0
	E-350	L	7.5 (7538)	6.0	7.0 [8]	7.0	24.0	-	-	6.0 [9]	[10]	28.0
	F-150	Y	4.9 (4916)	6.0	7.0	7.0	24.0 [13]	[7]	6.0	6.0 [9]	19.0	14.0
	F-150	N	5.0 (4949)	6.0	7.0 [8]	7.0	24.0 [13]	[7]	6.0	6.0 [9]	19.0	14.0
	F-150	H	5.8 (5752)	6.0	7.0 [8]	7.0	24.0 [13]	[7]	6.0	6.0 [9]	19.0	15.0
	F-250	Y	4.9 (4916)	6.0	7.0	7.0	24.0 [13]	[7]	6.0 [9]	6.0 [9]	19.0	14.0
	F-250	N	5.0 (4949)	6.0	7.0 [8]	7.0	24.0 [13]	[7]	6.0 [9]	6.0 [9]	19.0	14.0
	F-250	H	5.8 (5752)	6.0	7.0 [8]	7.0	24.0 [13]	[7]	6.0 [9]	6.0 [9]	19.0	15.0
	F-250	M	7.3 (7292)	10.0	7.0 [8]	7.0	24.0 [13]	[7]	6.0 [9]	6.0 [9]	19.0	31.0
	F-250	L	7.5 (7538)	6.0	7.0 [8]	7.0	24.0 [13]	[7]	6.0 [9]	6.0 [9]	19.0	16.0
	F-350	Y	4.9 (4916)	6.0	7.0	7.0	24.0 [13]	[7]	6.0 [9]	6.0 [9]	19.0	17.5
	F-350	H	5.8 (5752)	6.0	7.0 [8]	7.0	24.0 [13]	[7]	6.0 [9]	6.0 [9]	19.0	15.0
	F-350	M	7.3 (7292)	10.0	7.0 [8]	7.0	24.0 [13]	[7]	6.0 [9]	6.0 [9]	19.0	31.0
	F-350	L	7.5 (7538)	6.0	7.0 [8]	7.0	24.0 [13]	[7]	6.0 [9]	6.0 [9]	19.0	16.0
1993	Aerostar	U	3.0 (2999)	5.0	-	5.6	19.0	2.5	3.0	[1]	21.0	11.8
	Aerostar	X	4.0 (3998)	5.0	-	5.6	19.0	2.5	3.0	[1]	21.0	8.5
	Explorer	X	4.0 (3998)	5.0	-	5.6	19.0	3.0	[1]	[1]	21.0	8.5
	Ranger	A	2.3 (2294)	5.0	-	[2]	19.4	3.0	[1]	5.5	[3]	7.2
	Ranger	U	3.0 (2999)	5.0	-	3.0	[4]	[5]	[6]	[6]	[3]	11.8
	Ranger	X	4.0 (3998)	5.0	-	3.0	[4]	[5]	[6]	[6]	[3]	8.5
	Bronco	Y	4.9 (4916)	6.0	7.0	7.0	24.0	[7]	5.5	5.5	32.0	14.0
	Bronco	N	5.0 (4949)	6.0	7.0 [8]	7.0	24.0	[7]	5.5	5.5	32.0	14.0
	Bronco	H	5.8 (5752)	6.0	7.0 [8]	7.0	24.0	[7]	5.5	5.5	32.0	15.0
	E-150	Y	4.9 (4916)	6.0	7.0	7.0	24.0	-	-	6.0 [9]	[10]	17.5
	E-150	N	5.0 (4949)	6.0	7.0 [8]	7.0	24.0	-	-	6.0 [9]	[10]	[11]
	E-150	H	5.8 (5752)	6.0	7.0 [8]	7.0	24.0	-	-	6.0 [9]	[10]	[12]

CAPACITIES

Year	Model	Engine ID/VIN	Engine Displacement Liters (cc)	Engine Oil with Filter (qts.)	Transmission (pts.)			Transfer Case (pts.)	Drive Axle		Fuel Tank (gal.)	Cooling System (qts.)
					4-Spd	5-Spd	Auto.		Front (pts.)	Rear (pts.)		
	E-250	Y	4.9 (4916)	6.0	7.0 [8]	7.0	24.0	-	-	6.0 [9]	10	17.5
	E-250	N	5.0 (4949)	6.0	7.0 [8]	7.0	24.0	-	-	6.0 [9]	10	[11]
	E-250	H	5.8 (5752)	6.0	7.0 [8]	7.0	24.0	-	-	6.0 [9]	10	[12]
	E-250	M	7.3 (7292)	10.0	7.0 [8]	7.0	24.0	-	-	6.0 [9]	10	31.0
	E-250	L	7.5 (7538)	6.0	7.0 [8]	7.0	24.0	-	-	6.0 [9]	10	28.0
	E-350	Y	4.9 (4916)	6.0	7.0 [8]	7.0	24.0	-	-	6.0 [9]	10	17.5
	E-350	H	5.8 (5752)	6.0	7.0 [8]	7.0	24.0	-	-	6.0 [9]	10	[12]
	E-350	C	7.3 (7292)	10.0	7.0 [8]	7.0	24.0	-	-	6.0 [9]	10	31.0
	E-350	M	7.3 (7292)	10.0	7.0 [8]	7.0	24.0	-	-	6.0 [9]	10	31.0
	E-350	L	7.5 (7538)	6.0	7.0 [8]	7.0	24.0	-	-	6.0 [9]	10	28.0
	F-150	Y	4.9 (4916)	6.0	7.0 [8]	7.0	24.0 [13]	7	6.0	6.0 [9]	19.0	14.0
	F-150	N	5.0 (4949)	6.0	7.0 [8]	7.0	24.0 [13]	7	6.0	6.0 [9]	19.0	14.0
	F-150	H	5.8 (5752)	6.0	7.0 [8]	7.0	24.0 [13]	7	6.0	6.0 [9]	19.0	15.0
	F-250	Y	4.9 (4916)	6.0	7.0 [8]	7.0	24.0 [13]	7	6.0	6.0 [9]	19.0	14.0
	F-250	N	5.0 (4949)	6.0	7.0 [8]	7.0	24.0 [13]	7	6.0	6.0 [9]	19.0	14.0
	F-250	H	5.8 (5752)	6.0	7.0 [8]	7.0	24.0 [13]	7	6.0	6.0 [9]	19.0	15.0
	F-250	C	7.3 (7292)	10.0	7.0 [8]	7.0	24.0 [13]	7	6.0	6.0 [9]	19.0	31.0
	F-250	M	7.3 (7292)	10.0	7.0 [8]	7.0	24.0 [13]	7	6.0	6.0 [9]	19.0	31.0
	F-250	L	7.5 (7538)	6.0	7.0 [8]	7.0	24.0 [13]	7	6.0	6.0 [9]	19.0	16.0
	F-350	Y	4.9 (4916)	6.0	7.0 [8]	7.0	24.0 [13]	7	6.0	6.0 [9]	19.0	17.5
	F-350	H	5.8 (5752)	6.0	7.0 [8]	7.0	24.0 [13]	7	6.0	6.0 [9]	19.0	15.0
	F-350	C	7.3 (7292)	10.0	7.0 [8]	7.0	24.0 [13]	7	6.0	6.0 [9]	19.0	31.0
	F-350	M	7.3 (7292)	10.0	7.0 [8]	7.0	24.0 [13]	7	6.0	6.0 [9]	19.0	31.0
	F-350	L	7.5 (7538)	6.0	7.0 [8]	7.0	24.0 [13]	7	6.0	6.0 [9]	19.0	16.0
	F-Superduty	C	7.3 (7292)	10.0	7.0 [8]	7.0	24.0 [13]	7	6.0	6.0 [9]	19.0	31.0
1994	Aerostar	U	3.0 (2999)	4.5	-	5.6	19.0	2.5	3.0	[1]	21.0	11.8
	Aerostar	X	4.0 (3998)	5.0	-	5.6	19.0	2.5	3.0	[1]	21.0	12.6
	Explorer	X	4.0 (3998)	5.0	-	5.6	[4]	3.0	[1]	[1]	19.3	[15]
	Ranger	A	2.3 (2294)	5.0	-	[2]	[4]	3.0	[1]	5.5	14	[16]
	Ranger	U	3.0 (2999)	4.5	-	5.6	[4]	5	6	6	14	[17]
	Ranger	X	4.0 (3998)	5.0	-	5.6	[4]	5	6	6	14	[15]
	Bronco	Y	4.9 (4916)	6.0	7.0	7.0	24.0	7	5.5	5.5	32.0	14.0
	Bronco	N	5.0 (4949)	6.0	7.0 [8]	7.0	24.0	7	5.5	5.5	32.0	14.0
	Bronco	H	5.8 (5752)	6.0	7.0 [8]	7.0	24.0	7	5.5	5.5	32.0	15.0
	E-150	Y	4.9 (4916)	6.0	7.0 [8]	7.0	24.0	-	-	6.0 [9]	10	14.0
	E-150	H	5.0 (4949)	6.0	7.0 [8]	7.0	24.0	-	-	6.0 [9]	10	15.0
	E-150	N	5.8 (5752)	6.0	7.0 [8]	7.0	24.0	-	-	6.0 [9]	10	14.0
	E-250	Y	4.9 (4916)	6.0	7.0 [8]	7.0	24.0	-	-	6.0 [9]	10	14.0
	E-250	N	5.0 (4949)	6.0	7.0 [8]	7.0	24.0	-	-	6.0 [9]	10	15.0
	E-250	H	5.8 (5752)	6.0	7.0 [8]	7.0	24.0	-	-	6.0 [9]	10	15.0
	E-250	M	7.3 (7292)	10.0	7.0 [8]	7.0	24.0	-	-	6.0 [9]	10	20.0
	E-250	L	7.5 (7538)	6.0	7.0 [8]	7.0	24.0	-	-	6.0 [9]	10	19.8
	E-350	Y	4.9 (4916)	6.0	7.0 [8]	7.0	24.0	-	-	6.0 [9]	10	17.5
	E-350	H	5.8 (5752)	6.0	7.0 [8]	7.0	24.0	-	-	6.0 [9]	10	15.0
	E-350	C	7.3 (7292)	10.0	7.0 [8]	7.0	24.0	-	-	6.0 [9]	10	20.0
	E-350	M	7.3 (7292)	10.0	7.0 [8]	7.0	24.0	-	-	6.0 [9]	10	20.0

CAPACITIES

Year	Model	Engine ID/VIN	Engine Displacement Liters (cc)	Engine Oil with Filter (qts.)	Transmission (pts.)			Transfer Case (pts.)	Drive Axle		Fuel Tank (gal.)	Cooling System (qts.)
					4-Spd	5-Spd	Auto.		Front (pts.)	Rear (pts.)		
	E-350	L	7.5 (7538)	6.0	7.0 [8]	7.0	24.0	-	-	6.0 [9]	[10]	19.8
	F-150	Y	4.9 (4916)	6.0	7.0 [8]	7.0	24.0 [13]	[7]	6.0	6.0 [9]	[10]	18
	F-150	N	5.0 (4949)	6.0	7.0 [8]	7.0	24.0 [13]	[7]	6.0	6.0 [9]	[10]	19
	F-150	H	5.8 (5752)	6.0	7.0 [8]	7.0	24.0 [13]	[7]	6.0	6.0 [9]	[10]	20
	F-250	Y	4.9 (4916)	6.0	7.0 [8]	7.0	24.0 [13]	[7]	6.0	6.0 [9]	[10]	18
	F-250	N	5.0 (4949)	6.0	7.0 [8]	7.0	24.0 [13]	[7]	6.0	6.0 [9]	[10]	18
	F-250	H	5.8 (5752)	6.0	7.0 [8]	7.0	24.0 [13]	[7]	6.0	6.0 [9]	[10]	20
	F-250	C	7.3 (7292)	10.0	7.0 [8]	7.0	24.0	-	-	6.0 [9]	[10]	20.0
	F-250	L	7.5 (7538)	6.0	7.0 [8]	7.0	24.0 [13]	[7]	6.0	6.0 [9]	19.0	19.8
	F-350	Y	4.9 (4916)	6.0	7.0 [8]	7.0	24.0 [13]	[7]	6.0	6.0 [9]	19.0	18
	F-350	H	5.8 (5752)	6.0	7.0 [8]	7.0	24.0 [13]	[7]	6.0	6.0 [9]	19.0	20
	F-350	C	7.3 (7292)	10.0	7.0 [8]	7.0	24.0 [13]	[7]	6.0	6.0 [9]	19.0	20.0
	F-350	M	7.3 (7292)	10.0	7.0 [8]	7.0	24.0 [13]	[7]	6.0	6.0 [9]	19.0	20.0
	F-350	L	7.5 (7538)	6.0	7.0 [8]	7.0	24.0 [13]	[7]	6.0	6.0 [9]	19.0	19.8
	F-Superduty	C	7.3 (7292)	10.0	7.0 [8]	7.0	24.0 [13]	[7]	6.0	6.0 [9]	19.0	20.0
1995-96	Aerostar	U	3.0 (2999)	4.5	-	5.6	19.0	2.5	3.0	[1]	21.0	11.8
	Aerostar	X	4.0 (3998)	5.0	-	5.6	19.0	2.5	3.0	[1]	21.0	12.6
	Explorer	X	4.0 (3998)	5.0	-	5.6	[4]	3.0	[1]	[1]	19.3	15
	Ranger	A	2.3 (2294)	5.0	-	[2]	[4]	3.0	[1]	5.5	14	16
	Ranger	U	3.0 (2999)	4.5	-	3.0	[4]	[5]	[6]	6	14	17
	Ranger	X	4.0 (3998)	5.0	-	3.0	[4]	[5]	[6]	6	14	15
	Windstar	4	3.8 (3802)	4.5	-	-	24.5	-	-	-	20.0	12.1
	Bronco	Y	4.9 (4916)	6.0	7.0	7.0	24.0	[7]	5.5	5.5	32.0	14.0
	Bronco	N	5.0 (4949)	6.0	7.0 [8]	7.0	24.0	[7]	5.5	5.5	32.0	14.0
	Bronco	H	5.8 (5752)	6.0	7.0 [8]	7.0	24.0	[7]	5.5	5.5	32.0	15.0
	E-150	Y	4.9 (4916)	6.0	7.0 [8]	7.0	24.0	-	-	6.0 [9]	[10]	14.0
	E-150	N	5.0 (4949)	6.0	7.0 [8]	7.0	24.0	-	-	6.0 [9]	[10]	15.0
	E-150	H	5.8 (5752)	6.0	7.0 [8]	7.0	24.0	-	-	6.0 [9]	[10]	14.0
	E-250	Y	4.9 (4916)	6.0	7.0 [8]	7.0	24.0	-	-	6.0 [9]	[10]	14.0
	E-250	N	5.0 (4949)	6.0	7.0 [8]	7.0	24.0	-	-	6.0 [9]	[10]	15.0
	E-250	H	5.8 (5752)	6.0	7.0 [8]	7.0	24.0	-	-	6.0 [9]	[10]	15.0
	E-250	M	7.3 (7292)	10.0	7.0 [8]	7.0	24.0	-	-	6.0 [9]	[10]	20.0
	E-250	L	7.5 (7538)	6.0	7.0 [8]	7.0	24.0	-	-	6.0 [9]	[10]	10.9
	E-350	Y	4.9 (4916)	6.0	7.0 [8]	7.0	24.0	-	-	6.0 [9]	[10]	17.5
	E-350	H	5.8 (5752)	6.0	7.0 [8]	7.0	24.0	-	-	6.0 [9]	[10]	15.0
	E-350	M	7.3 (7292)	10.0	7.0 [8]	7.0	24.0	-	-	6.0 [9]	[10]	20.0
	E-350	L	7.5 (7538)	6.0	7.0 [8]	7.0	24.0	-	-	6.0 [9]	[10]	19.8
	F-150	Y	4.9 (4916)	6.0	-7.0 [8]	7.0	24.0 [13]	[7]	6.0	6.0 [9]	[10]	18
	F-150	N	5.0 (4949)	6.0	7.0 [8]	7.0	24.0 [13]	[7]	6.0	6.0 [9]	[10]	19
	F-150	H	5.8 (5752)	6.0	7.0 [8]	7.0	24.0 [13]	[7]	6.0	6.0 [9]	[10]	20
	F-250	Y	4.9 (4916)	6.0	7.0 [8]	7.0	24.0 [13]	[7]	6.0	6.0 [9]	[10]	18
	F-250	N	5.0 (4949)	6.0	7.0 [8]	7.0	24.0 [13]	[7]	6.0	6.0 [9]	[10]	18
	F-250	H	5.8 (5752)	6.0	7.0 [8]	7.0	24.0 [13]	[7]	6.0	6.0 [9]	[10]	20
	F-250	L	7.5 (7538)	6.0	7.0 [8]	7.0	24.0 [13]	[7]	6.0	6.0 [9]	19.0	19.8
	F-350	Y	4.9 (4916)	6.0	7.0 [8]	7.0	24.0 [13]	[7]	6.0	6.0 [9]	19.0	18
	F-350	H	5.8 (5752)	6.0	7.0 [8]	7.0	24.0 [13]	[7]	6.0	6.0 [9]	19.0	20

CAPACITIES

Year	Model	Engine ID/VIN	Engine Displacement Liters (cc)	Engine Oil with Filter (qts.)	Transmission (pts.)			Transfer Case (pts.)	Drive Axle		Fuel Tank (gal.)	Cooling System (qts.)
					4-Spd	5-Spd	Auto.		Front (pts.)	Rear (pts.)		
	F-350	M	7.3 (7292)	10.0	7.0 [8]	7.0	24.0 [13]	7	6.0	6.0 [9]	19.0	20.0
	F-350	L	7.5 (7538)	6.0	7.0 [8]	7.0	24.0 [13]	7	6.0	6.0 [9]	19.0	19.8

1 Front axle Dana 28: 1.1 pts.
 Front axle Dana 35: 3.5 pts.
 Rear axle: 5.5 pts.
2 Mazda trans.: 3 pts.
 Mitsubishi trans.: 4.8 pts.
3 Short wheelbase: 17 gals.
 Long wheelbase: 17 or 21 gals.
 Ranger Supercab: 17 or 21 gals.
4 2WD: 19.4 pts.
 4WD: 20.0 pts.
5 BW 13-50 manual shift: 3.0 pts. Dextron II
 BW 13-50 electric shift: 6.5 pts. Dextron II
 BW 13-54 mechanical shift: 3.0 pts. Dextron II
 BW 13-50 contains no lubricant and none should be added
6 6.75" 6.75" ring gear: 3 pts.
 7.50" 7.50" ring gear: 5 pts.
7 New Process: 9 pts. Dextron II
 BW 1345: 6.5 pts. Dextron II
 BW 1356: 4 pts. Mercon
8 With OD: 4.5 pts.
9 Heavy duty: 7.5 pts.
10 124" Wheelbase: 18 gals.
 138", 158" and 176" Wheelbase and front-mounted tank: 22 gals.
 138", 158" and 176" Wheelbase and rear-mounted tank: 16 gals.
11 Manual trans.: 17.5 pts.
 Automatic trans.: 18.5 pts.

12 Manual trans.: 15 pts.
 Automatic trans.: 21 pts.
13 4WD: 27 pts.
14 Short wheelbase: 16.3
 Long wheelbase: 19.6
 Ranger Supercab: 19.6
15 4.0L without AC: 7.8 qts.
 4.0L with AC: 8.6 qts.
16 2.3L without AC: 6.5 qts.
 2.3L with AC: 7.2 qts.
17 3.0L without AC: 9.5 qts.
 3.0L with AC: 10.2 qts.
18 4.9L without AC: 13.0 qts.
 4.9L with AC or supercooling: 14.0 qts.
 4.9L with AC and supercooling: 15.6 qts.
19 5.0L with manual trans. and standard cooling system: 15.7 qts.
 5.0L with automatic trans. and standard cooling: 16.5 qts.
 5.0L with manual/automatic trans. and AC: 16.4 qts.
 5.0L with manual/automatic trans. with supercooling or supercooling and AC: 18.3 qts.
20 Manual trans. with standard cooling: 15.7 qts.
 Automatic trans. with standard cooling: 16.4 qts.
 Manual/automatic trans. with AC: 16.4 qts.
 Manual/automatic trans. with supercooling and AC: 18.0 qts.

CAMSHAFT SPECIFICATIONS
All measurements given in inches.

Year	Engine ID/VIN	Engine Displacement Liters (cc)	Journal Diameter					Elevation		Bearing Clearance	Camshaft End Play
			1	2	3	4	5	In.	Ex.		
1992	A	2.3 (2294)	1.7713-1.7720	1.7713-1.7720	1.7713-1.7720	1.7713-1.7720	NA	0.2380	0.2380	0.0010-0.0030	0.0010-0.0070
	T	2.9 (2900)	1.7285-1.7293	1.7135-1.7143	1.6985-1.6992	1.6835-1.6842	NA	0.3590	0.3700	0.0010-0.0030	0.0010-0.0040
	U	3.0 (2999)	2.0074-2.0084	2.0074-2.0084	2.0074-2.0084	2.0074-2.0084	NA	0.2600	0.2600	0.0010-0.0030	0.0070
	X	4.0 (3998)	1.9510-1.9520	1.9370-1.9380	1.9220-1.9230	1.9070-1.9080	NA	0.4020	0.4020	0.0010-0.0060	0.0090
	Y	4.9 (4916)	2.0170-2.0180	2.0170-2.0180	2.0170-2.0180	2.0170-2.0180	NA	0.2490-0.2470	0.2490-0.2470	0.0010-0.0030	0.0010-0.0070
	N	5.0 (4949)	2.0800	2.0650	2.0500	2.0350	2.0200	0.2370	0.2470	0.0010-0.0030	0.0010-0.0070
	H	5.8 (5752)	2.0810	2.0660	2.0510	2.0360	2.0210	0.2600	0.2600	0.0010-0.0030	0.0010-0.0070
	M	7.3 (7292)	2.0990-2.1000	2.0990-2.1000	2.0990-2.1000	2.0990-2.1000	2.0990-2.1000	NA	NA	0.0010-0.0030	0.0020-0.0090
	G	7.5 (7538)	2.1240-2.1250	2.1240-2.1250	2.1240-2.1250	2.1240-2.1250	2.1240-2.1250	0.2520	0.2780	0.0010-0.0030	0.0010-0.0060
1993	A	2.3 (2294)	1.7713-1.7720	1.7713-1.7720	1.7713-1.7720	1.7713-1.7720	NA	0.2380	0.2380	0.0010-0.0030	0.0010-0.0070
	U	3.0 (2999)	2.0074-2.0084	2.0074-2.0084	2.0074-2.0084	2.0074-2.0084	NA	0.2600	0.2600	0.0010-0.0030	0.0070
	X	4.0 (3998)	1.9510-1.9520	1.9370-1.9380	1.9220-1.9230	1.9070-1.9080	NA	0.4020	0.4020	0.0010-0.0060	0.0090
	Y	4.9 (4916)	2.0170-2.0180	2.0170-2.0180	2.0170-2.0180	2.0170-2.0180	NA	0.2490-0.2470	0.2490-0.2470	0.0010-0.0030	0.0010-0.0070
	N	5.0 (4949)	2.0800	2.0650	2.0500	2.0350	2.0200	0.2370	0.2470	0.0010-0.0030	0.0010-0.0070
	H	5.8 (5752)	2.0810	2.0660	2.0510	2.0360	2.0210	0.2780	0.2830	0.0010-0.0030	0.0010-0.0070
	R	5.8 (5752)	2.0810	2.0660	2.0510	2.0360	2.0210	0.2600	0.2780	0.0010-0.0030	0.0010-0.0070
	C	7.3 (7292)	2.0990-2.1000	2.0990-2.1000	2.0990-2.1000	2.0990-2.1000	2.0990-2.1000	NA	NA	0.0010-0.0030	0.0020-0.0090
	M	7.3 (7292)	2.0990-2.1000	2.0990-2.1000	2.0990-2.1000	2.0990-2.1000	2.0990-2.1000	NA	NA	0.0010-0.0030	0.0020-0.0090
	G	7.5 (7538)	2.1240-2.1250	2.1240-2.1250	2.1240-2.1250	2.1240-2.1250	2.1240-2.1250	0.2520	0.2780	0.0010-0.0030	0.0010-0.0060
1994	A	2.3 (2294)	1.7713-1.7720	1.7713-1.7720	1.7713-1.7720	1.7713-1.7720	NA	0.2380	0.2380	0.0010-0.0030	0.0010-0.0070
	U	3.0 (2999)	2.0074-2.0084	2.0074-2.0084	2.0074-2.0084	2.0074-2.0084	NA	0.2600	0.2600	0.0010-0.0030	0.0070
	X	4.0 (3998)	1.9510-1.9520	1.9370-1.9380	1.9220-1.9230	1.9070-1.9080	NA	0.4020	0.4020	0.0010-0.0060	0.0090

CAMSHAFT SPECIFICATIONS
All measurements given in inches.

Year	Engine ID/VIN	Engine Displacement Liters (cc)	Journal Diameter					Elevation		Bearing Clearance	Camshaft End Play
			1	2	3	4	5	In.	Ex.		
	Y	4.9 (4916)	2.0170-2.0180	2.0170-2.0180	2.0170-2.0180	2.0170-2.0180	NA	0.2490-0.2470	0.2490-0.2470	0.0010-0.0030	0.0010-0.0070
	N	5.0 (4949)	2.0800	2.0650	2.0500	2.0350	2.0200	0.2370	0.2470	0.0010-0.0030	0.0010-0.0070
	H	5.8 (5752)	2.0810	2.0660	2.0510	2.0360	2.0210	0.2780	0.2830	0.0010-0.0030	0.0010-0.0070
	R	5.8 (5752)	2.0810	2.0660	2.0510	2.0360	2.0210	0.2600	0.2780	0.0010-0.0030	0.0010-0.0070
	F	7.3 (7294)	2.1020-2.1050	2.1020-2.1050	2.1020-2.1050	2.1020-2.1050	2.1020-2.1050	NA	NA	0.0015-0.0120	0.0040-0.0120
	K	7.3 (7294)	2.1050-2.1025	2.1050-2.1025	2.1050-2.1025	2.1050-2.1025	2.1050-2.1025	NA	NA	0.0015-0.0035	0.0250-0.0090
	M	7.3 (7294)	2.1050-2.1025	2.1050-2.1025	2.1050-2.1025	2.1050-2.1025	2.1050-2.1025	NA	NA	0.0015-0.0035	0.0250-0.0090
	G	7.5 (7538)	2.1240-2.1250	2.1240-2.1250	2.1240-2.1250	2.1240-2.1250	2.1240-2.1250	0.2520	0.2780	0.0010-0.0030	0.0010-0.0060
1995-96	A	2.3 (2294)	1.7713-1.7720	1.7713-1.7720	1.7713-1.7720	1.7713-1.7720	NA	0.2380	0.2380	0.0010-0.0030	0.0010-0.0070
	U	3.0 (2999)	2.0074-2.0084	2.0074-2.0084	2.0074-2.0084	2.0074-2.0084	NA	0.2600	0.2600	0.0010-0.0030	0.0010-0.0070
	4	3.8 (3785)	2.0505-2.0515	2.0505-2.0515	2.0505-2.0515	2.0505-2.0515	2.0505-2.0515	0.2400-0.2450	0.2540-0.2590	0.0010-0.0030	0.0010-0.0060
	X	4.0 (3998)	1.9510-1.9520	1.9370-1.9380	1.9220-1.9230	1.9070-1.9080	NA	0.4020	0.4020	0.0010-0.0060	0.0090
	Y	4.9 (4916)	2.0170-2.0180	2.0170-2.0180	2.0170-2.0180	2.0170-2.0180	NA	0.2490-0.2470	0.2490-0.2470	0.0010-0.0030	0.0010-0.0070
	N	5.0 (4949)	2.0800	2.0650	2.0500	2.0350	2.0200	0.2370	0.2470	0.0010-0.0030	0.0010-0.0070
	H	5.8 (5752)	2.0810	2.0660	2.0510	2.0360	2.0210	0.2780	0.2830	0.0010-0.0030	0.0010-0.0070
	R	5.8 (5752)	2.0810	2.0660	2.0510	2.0360	2.0210	0.2600	0.2780	0.0010-0.0030	0.0010-0.0070
	F	7.3 (7294)	2.1020-2.1050	2.1020-2.1050	2.1020-2.1050	2.1020-2.1050	2.1020-2.1050	NA	NA	0.0015-0.0120	0.0040-0.0120
	M	7.3 (7294)	2.1050-2.1025	2.1050-2.1025	2.1050-2.1025	2.1050-2.1025	2.1050-2.1025	NA	NA	0.0015-0.0035	0.0250-0.0090
	G	7.5 (7538)	2.1240-2.1250	2.1240-2.1250	2.1240-2.1250	2.1240-2.1250	2.1240-2.1250	0.2520	0.2780	0.0010-0.0030	0.0010-0.0060

NA - Not Available

CRANKSHAFT AND CONNECTING ROD SPECIFICATIONS

All measurements are given in inches.

Year	Engine ID/VIN	Engine Displacement Liters (cc)	Crankshaft				Connecting Rod		
			Main Brg. Journal Dia.	Main Brg. Oil Clearance	Shaft End-play	Thrust on No.	Journal Diameter	Oil Clearance	Side Clearance
1992	A	2.3 (2294)	2.2051-2.2059	0.0008-0.0026	0.0040-0.0080	3	2.0462-2.0472	0.0008-0.0026	0.0040-0.0100
	T	2.9 (2900)	2.2433-2.2441	0.0008-0.0015	0.0040-0.0080	3	2.1252-2.1260	0.0006-0.0016	0.0040-0.0110
	U	3.0 (2999)	2.5190-2.5198	0.0010-0.0014	0.0040-0.0080	3	2.1253-2.1261	0.0010-0.0014	0.0060-0.0140
	X	4.0 (3998)	2.2433-2.2441	0.0005-0.0019	0.0120	3	2.1252-2.1260	0.0005-0.0022	0.0002-0.0025
	Y	4.9 (4916)	2.3982-2.3990	0.0009-0.0028	0.0040-0.0080	5	2.1228-2.1236	0.0009-0.0027	0.0060-0.0130
	N	5.0 (4949)	2.2482-2.2490	0.0008-0.0015	0.0040-0.0080	3	2.1228-2.1236	0.0008-0.0015	0.0100-0.0200
	H	5.8 (5752)	2.9994-3.0002	0.0008-0.0015	0.0040-0.0080	3	2.3103-2.3111	0.0008-0.0026	0.0100-0.0200
	M	7.3 (7292)	3.1228-3.1236	0.0018-0.0046	0.0250-0.0850	3	2.4980-2.4990	0.0011-0.0036	0.0120-0.0240
	G	7.5 (7538)	2.9994-3.0002	0.0008-0.00026	0.0040-0.0080	3	2.4992-2.5000	0.0008-0.0025	0.0100-0.0200
1993	A	2.3 (2294)	2.2051-2.2059	0.0008-0.0026	0.0040-0.0080	3	2.0462-2.0472	0.0008-0.0026	0.0040-0.0100
	U	3.0 (2999)	2.5190-2.5198	0.0010-0.0014	0.0040-0.0080	3	2.1253-2.1261	0.0010-0.0014	0.0060-0.0140
	X	4.0 (3998)	2.2433-2.2441	0.0005-0.0019	0.0120	3	2.1252-2.1260	0.0005-0.0022	0.0002-0.0025
	Y	4.9 (4916)	2.3982-2.3990	0.0009-0.0028	0.0040-0.0080	5	2.1228-2.1236	0.0009-0.0027	0.0060-0.0130
	N	5.0 (4949)	2.2482-2.2490	0.0008-0.0015	0.0040-0.0080	3	2.1228-2.1236	0.0008-0.0015	0.0100-0.0200
	H	5.8 (5752)	2.9994-3.0002	0.0008-0.0015	0.0040-0.0080	3	2.3103-2.3111	0.0008-0.0026	0.0100-0.0200
	R	5.8 (5752)	2.9994-3.0002	0.0008-0.0015	0.0040-0.0080	3	2.3103-2.3111	0.0008-0.0026	0.0100-0.0200
	C	7.3 (7292)	3.1228-3.1236	0.0018-0.0046	0.0250-0.0850	3	2.4980-2.4990	0.0011-0.0036	0.0120-0.0240
	M	7.3 (7292)	3.1228-3.1236	0.0018-0.0046	0.0250-0.0850	3	2.4980-2.4990	0.0011-0.0036	0.0120-0.0240
	G	7.5 (7538)	2.9994-3.0002	0.0008-0.0026	0.0040-0.0080	3	2.4992-2.5000	0.0008-0.0025	0.0100-0.0200
1994	A	2.3 (2294)	2.2051-2.2059	0.0008-0.0026	0.0040-0.0080	3	2.0462-2.0472	0.0008-0.0026	0.0040-0.0100
	U	3.0 (2999)	2.5190-2.5198	0.0010-0.0014	0.0040-0.0080	3	2.1253-2.1261	0.0010-0.0014	0.0060-0.0140
	X	4.0 (3998)	2.2433-2.2441	0.0005-0.0019	0.0120	3	2.1252-2.1260	0.0005-0.0022	0.0002-0.0025
	Y	4.9 (4916)	2.3982-2.3990	0.0009-0.0028	0.0040-0.0080	5	2.1228-2.1236	0.0009-0.0027	0.0060-0.0130

CRANKSHAFT AND CONNECTING ROD SPECIFICATIONS

All measurements are given in inches.

Year	Engine ID/VIN	Engine Displacement Liters (cc)	Crankshaft Main Brg. Journal Dia.	Main Brg. Oil Clearance	Shaft End-play	Thrust on No.	Connecting Rod Journal Diameter	Oil Clearance	Side Clearance
	N	5.0 (4949)	2.2482-2.2490	[1]	0.0040-0.0080	3	2.1228-2.1236	0.0008-0.0015	0.0100-0.0200
	H	5.8 (5752)	2.9994-3.0002	[1]	0.0040-0.0080	3	2.3103-2.3111	0.0008-0.0025	0.0100-0.0200
	R	5.8 (5752)	2.9994-3.0002	[1]	0.0040-0.0080	3	2.3103-2.3111	0.0008-0.0025	0.0100-0.0200
	F	7.3 (7292)	3.1228-3.1236	0.0018-0.0046	0.0025-0.0085	3	2.4980-2.4990	0.0011-0.0036	0.0120-0.0240
	K	7.3 (7292)	3.1228-3.1236	0.0018-0.0046	0.0025-0.0085	3	2.4980-2.4990	0.0011-0.0036	0.0120-0.0240
	M	7.3 (7292)	3.1228-3.1236	0.0018-0.0046	0.0025-0.0085	3	2.4980-2.4990	0.0011-0.0036	0.0120-0.0240
	G	7.5 (7538)	2.9994-3.0002	0.0008-0.0025	0.0040-0.0080	3	2.4992-2.5000	0.0008-0.0025	0.0100-0.0200
1995-96	A	2.3 (2294)	2.2051-2.2059	0.0008-0.0026	0.0040-0.0080	3	2.0462-2.0472	0.0008-0.0026	0.0040-0.0100
	U	3.0 (2999)	2.5190-2.5198	0.0010-0.0014	0.0040-0.0080	3	2.1253-2.1261	0.0010-0.0014	0.0060-0.0140
	4	3.8 (3802)	2.5190-2.5198	0.0010-0.0014	0.0040-0.0080	3	2.3103-2.3111	0.0009-0.0027	0.0047-0.0140
	X	4.0 (3998)	2.2433-2.2441	0.0005-0.0019	0.0120	3	2.1252-2.1260	0.0005-0.0022	0.0002-0.0025
	Y	4.9 (4916)	2.3982-2.3990	0.0009-0.0028	0.0040-0.0080	5	2.1228-2.1236	0.0009-0.0027	0.0060-0.0130
	N	5.0 (4949)	2.2482-2.2490	0.0008-0.0015	0.0040-0.0080	3	2.1228-2.1236	0.0008-0.0015	0.0100-0.0200
	H	5.8 (5752)	2.9994-3.0002	0.0008-0.0015	0.0040-0.0080	3	2.3103-2.3111	0.0008-0.0026	0.0100-0.0200
	R	5.8 (5752)	2.9994-3.0002	0.0008-0.0015	0.0040-0.0080	3	2.3103-2.3111	0.0008-0.0026	0.0100-0.0200
	F	7.3 (7292)	3.1228-3.1236	0.0018-0.0046	0.0025-0.0085	3	2.4980-2.4990	0.0011-0.0036	0.0120-0.0240
	M	7.3 (7292)	3.1228-3.1236	0.0018-0.0046	0.0025-0.0085	3	2.4980-2.4990	0.0011-0.0036	0.0120-0.0240
	G	7.5 (7538)	2.9994-3.0002	0.0008-0.0026	0.0040-0.0080	3	2.4992-2.5000	0.0008-0.0025	0.0100-0.0200

1 No. 1 bearing: 0.0001-0.0015
All others: 0.0005-0.0015

VALVE SPECIFICATIONS

Year	Engine ID/VIN	Engine Displacement Liters (cc)	Seat Angle (deg.)	Face Angle (deg.)	Spring Test Pressure (lbs. @ in.)	Spring Installed Height (in.)	Stem-to-Guide Clearance (in.)		Stem Diameter (in.)	
							Intake	Exhaust	Intake	Exhaust
1992	A	2.3 (2300)	45	44	149@1.12	1.53-1.59	0.0010-0.0027	0.0015-0.0032	0.3416-0.3423	0.3411-0.3418
	T	2.9 (2900)	45	44	143@1.22	1.58-1.61	0.0008-0.0025	0.0018-0.0035	0.3159-0.3167	0.3149-0.3156
	U	3.0 (2999)	45	44	185@1.16	1.58-1.61	0.0010-0.0027	0.0015-0.0032	0.3126-0.3134	0.3121-0.3129
	X	4.0 (3998)	45	44	138@1.22	1.58-1.61	0.0008-0.0025	0.0018-0.0035	0.3159-0.3167	0.3149-0.3156
	Y	4.9 (4916)	45	44	192@1.18	[1]	0.0010-0.0027	0.0010-0.0027	0.3415-0.3420	0.3415-0.3420
	N	5.0 (4949)	45	44	200@1.35	[2]	0.0010-0.0027	0.0015-0.0032	0.3415-0.3420	0.3415-0.3420
	H	5.8 (5752)	45	44	200@1.20	[3]	0.0010-0.0027	0.0015-0.0032	0.3415-0.3420	0.3415-0.3420
	M	7.3 (7292)	[4]	[4]	80@1.83	[5]	0.0055	0.0055	0.3716-0.3723	0.3716-0.3723
	G	7.5 (7538)	45	44	220@1.33	1.83	0.0010-0.0027	0.0015-0.0032	0.3415-0.3420	0.3415-0.3420
1993	A	2.3 (2300)	45	44	149@1.12	1.53-1.59	0.0010-0.0027	0.0015-0.0032	0.3416-0.3423	0.3411-0.3418
	U	3.0 (2999)	45	44	185@1.16	1.58-1.61	0.0010-0.0027	0.0015-0.0032	0.3126-0.3134	0.3121-0.3129
	X	4.0 (3998)	45	44	138@1.22	1.58-1.61	0.0008-0.0025	0.0018-0.0035	0.3159-0.3167	0.3149-0.3156
	Y	4.9 (4916)	45	44	192@1.18	[1]	0.0010-0.0027	0.0010-0.0027	0.3415-0.3420	0.3415-0.3420
	N	5.0 (4949)	45	44	200@1.35	[2]	0.0010-0.0027	0.0015-0.0032	0.3415-0.3420	0.3415-0.3420
	H	5.8 (5752)	45	44	200@1.20	[3]	0.0010-0.0027	0.0015-0.0032	0.3415-0.3420	0.3415-0.3420
	R	5.8 (5752)	45	44	200@1.20	[3]	0.0010-0.0027	0.0015-0.0032	0.3415-0.3420	0.3415-0.3420
	C	7.3 (7292)	[4]	[4]	80@1.83	[5]	0.0055	0.0055	0.3716-0.3723	0.3716-0.3723
	M	7.3 (7292)	[4]	[4]	80@1.83	[5]	0.0055	0.0055	0.3716-0.3723	0.3716-0.3723
	G	7.5 (7538)	45	44	220@1.33	1.83	0.0010-0.0027	0.0010-0.0027	0.3415-0.3420	0.3415-0.3420
1994	A	2.3 (2300)	45	44	126-142@1.12	1.53-1.59	0.0010-0.0027	0.0015-0.0032	0.3416-0.3423	0.3411-0.3418
	U	3.0 (2999)	45	44	185@1.16	1.58-1.61	0.0010-0.0027	0.0015-0.0032	0.3126-0.3134	0.3121-0.3129
	X	4.0 (3998)	45	44	138@1.22	1.58-1.61	0.0008-0.0025	0.0018-0.0035	0.3159-0.3167	0.3149-0.3156
	Y	4.9 (4916)	45	44	[7]	[1]	0.0010-0.0027	0.0010-0.0027	0.3415-0.3423	0.3415-0.3423

VALVE SPECIFICATIONS

Year	Engine ID/VIN	Engine Displacement Liters (cc)	Seat Angle (deg.)	Face Angle (deg.)	Spring Test Pressure (lbs. @ in.)	Spring Installed Height (in.)	Stem-to-Guide Clearance (in.)		Stem Diameter (in.)	
							Intake	Exhaust	Intake	Exhaust
	N	5.0 (4949)	45	44	200@1.20	6	0.0010-0.0027	0.0015-0.0032	0.3415-0.3423	0.3415-0.3418
	H	5.8 (5752)	45	44	200@1.20	3	0.0010-0.0027	0.0010-0.0027	0.3415-0.3420	0.3415-0.3420
	R	5.8 (5752)	45	44	200@1.20	3	0.0010-0.0027	0.0010-0.0027	0.3415-0.3420	0.3415-0.3420
	F	7.3 (7292)	4	4	200@1.38	5	0.0055	0.0055	0.3119-0.3126	0.3119-0.3126
	K	7.3 (7292)	4	4	200@1.38	5	0.0055	0.0055	0.3717-0.3724	0.3717-0.3724
	M	7.3 (7292)	4	4	200@1.40	5	0.0055	0.0055	0.3716-0.3723	0.3716-0.3723
	G	7.5 (7538)	45	44	220@1.33	1.83	0.0010-0.0027	0.0010-0.0027	0.3415-0.3423	0.3415-0.3423
1995-96	A	2.3 (2300)	45	44	126-142@1.12	1.53-1.59	0.0010-0.0027	0.0015-0.0032	0.3416-0.3423	0.3411-0.3418
	U	3.0 (2999)	45	44	185@1.16	1.58-1.61	0.0010-0.0027	0.0015-0.0032	0.3126-0.3134	0.3121-0.3129
	4	3.8 (3802)	44.5	45.8	220@1.18	1.97	0.0010-0.0028	0.0015-0.0033	0.3423-0.3415	0.3418-0.3410
	X	4.0 (3998)	45	44	138@1.22	1.58-1.61	0.0008-0.0025	0.0018-0.0035	0.3159-0.3167	0.3149-0.3156
	Y	4.9 (4916)	45	44	8	1	0.0010-0.0027	0.0010-0.0027	0.3415-0.3423	0.3415-0.3423
	N	5.0 (4949)	45	44	200@1.20	6	0.0010-0.0027	0.0015-0.0032	0.3415-0.3423	0.3415-0.3423
	H	5.8 (5752)	45	44	200@1.20	3	0.0010-0.0027	0.0010-0.0027	0.3415-0.3420	0.3415-0.3420
	R	5.8 (5752)	45	44	200@1.20	3	0.0010-0.0027	0.0010-0.0027	0.3415-0.3420	0.3415-0.3420
	F	7.3 (7292)	4	4	200@1.38	5	0.0055	0.0055	0.3119-0.3126	0.3119-0.3126
	M	7.3 (7292)	4	4	200@1.40	5	0.0055	0.0055	0.3716-0.3723	0.3716-0.3723
	G	7.5 (7538)	45	44	220@1.33	1.83	0.0010-0.0027	0.0010-0.0027	0.3415-0.3423	0.3415-0.3423

1 Intake: 1.64 in.
  Exhaust: 1.47 in.
2 Intake: 1.68 in.
  Exhaust: 1.59 in.
3 Intake: 1.78 in.
  Exhaust: 1.59 in.
4 Intake: 30
  Exhaust: 37.5

5 Intake: 1.767 in.
  Exhaust: 1.833 in.
6 Intake: 1.75-1.81 in.
  Exhaust: 1.59 in.
7 Intake: 166@1.240
  Exhaust: 166@1.070
8 Intake: 166-184@1.240
  Exhaust: 1.66-184@1.070

PISTON AND RING SPECIFICATIONS

All measurements are given in inches.

Year	Engine ID/VIN	Engine Displacement Liters (cc)	Piston Clearance	Ring Gap			Ring Side Clearance		
				Top Compression	Bottom Compression	Oil Control	Top Compression	Bottom Compression	Oil Control
1992	A	2.3 (2294)	0.0014-0.0022	0.0100-0.0200	0.0100-0.0200	0.0150-0.0550	0.0020-0.0040	0.0020-0.0040	SNUG
	T	2.9 (2900)	0.0011-0.0019	0.0150-0.0230	0.0150-0.0230	0.0150-0.0230	0.0020-0.0033	0.0020-0.0033	SNUG
	U	3.0 (2999)	0.0012-0.0023	0.0100-0.0200	0.0100-0.0200	0.0100-0.0490	0.0016-0.0037	0.0016-0.0037	SNUG
	X	4.0 (3998)	0.0008-0.0019	0.0150-0.0230	0.0150-0.0550	0.0150-0.0550	0.0020-0.0033	0.0020-0.0033	SNUG
	Y	4.9 (4916)	0.0014-0.0022	0.0100-0.0200	0.0100-0.0200	0.0100-0.0350	0.0019-0.0036	0.0020-0.0040	SNUG
	N	5.0 (4949)	0.0018-0.0026	0.0100-0.0200	0.0100-0.0200	0.0100-0.0350	0.0020-0.0040	0.0020-0.0040	SNUG
	H	5.8 (5752)	0.0022-0.0030	0.0100-0.0200	0.0100-0.0200	0.0150-0.0350	0.0019-0.0036	0.0020-0.0040	SNUG
	M	7.3 (7292)	0.0055-0.0085	0.0130-0.0450	0.0600-0.0800	0.0100-0.0240	0.0020-0.0040	0.0020-0.0040	0.0010-0.0030
	G	7.5 (7538)	0.0022-0.0300	0.0100-0.0200	0.0100-0.0200	0.0100-0.0350	0.0025-0.0045	0.0025-0.0045	SNUG
1993	A	2.3 (2294)	0.0014-0.0022	0.0100-0.0200	0.0100-0.0200	0.0150-0.0550	0.0020-0.0040	0.0020-0.0040	SNUG
	U	3.0 (2999)	0.0012-0.0023	0.0100-0.0200	0.0100-0.0200	0.0100-0.0490	0.0016-0.0037	0.0016-0.0037	SNUG
	X	4.0 (3998)	0.0008-0.0019	0.0150-0.0230	0.0150-0.0550	0.0150-0.0550	0.0020-0.0033	0.0020-0.0033	SNUG
	Y	4.9 (4916)	0.0014-0.0022	0.0100-0.0200	0.0100-0.0200	0.0100-0.0350	0.0019-0.0036	0.0020-0.0040	SNUG
	N	5.0 (4949)	0.0014-0.0022	0.0100-0.0200	0.0180-0.0280	0.0100-0.0400	0.0020-0.0040	0.0020-0.0040	SNUG
	H	5.8 (5752)	0.0018-0.0026	0.0100-0.0200	0.0100-0.0200	0.0150-0.0350	0.0019-0.0036	0.0020-0.0040	SNUG
	R	5.8 (5752)	0.0015-0.0023	0.0100-0.0200	0.0180-0.0280	0.0100-0.0400	0.0020-0.0040	0.0013-0.0033	SNUG
	C	7.3 (7292)	0.0055-0.0085	0.0130-0.0450	0.0600-0.0800	0.0100-0.0240	0.0020-0.0040	0.0020-0.0040	0.0010-0.0030
	M	7.3 (7292)	0.0055-0.0085	0.0130-0.0450	0.0600-0.0800	0.0100-0.0240	0.0020-0.0040	0.0020-0.0040	0.0010-0.0030
	G	7.5 (7538)	0.0022-0.0300	0.0100-0.0200	0.0100-0.0200	0.0100-0.0350	0.0025-0.0045	0.0025-0.0045	SNUG
1994	A	2.3 (2294)	0.0024-0.0034	0.0100-0.0200	0.0100-0.0200	0.0150-0.0550	0.0016-0.0033	0.0016-0.0033	SNUG
	U	3.0 (2999)	0.0012-0.0023	0.0100-0.0200	0.0100-0.0200	0.0100-0.0490	0.0016-0.0037	0.0016-0.0037	SNUG
	X	4.0 (3998)	0.0008-0.0019	0.0150-0.0230	0.0150-0.0230	0.0150-0.0550	0.0020-0.0033	0.0020-0.0033	SNUG
	Y	4.9 (4916)	0.0010-0.0018	0.0100-0.0200	0.0100-0.0200	0.0100-0.0350	0.0019-0.0036	0.0020-0.0040	SNUG

PISTON AND RING SPECIFICATIONS

All measurements are given in inches.

Year	Engine ID/VIN	Engine Displacement Liters (cc)	Piston Clearance	Ring Gap			Ring Side Clearance		
				Top Compression	Bottom Compression	Oil Control	Top Compression	Bottom Compression	Oil Control
	N	5.0 (4949)	0.0014-0.0022	0.0100-0.0200	0.0180-0.0280	0.0100-0.0400	0.0013-0.0033	0.0013-0.0033	SNUG
	H	5.8 (5752)	0.0018-0.0026	0.0100-0.0200	0.0100-0.0200	0.0150-0.0350	0.0019-0.0036	0.0020-0.0040	SNUG
	R	5.8 (5752)	0.0015-0.0023	0.0100-0.0200	0.0180-0.0280	0.0100-0.0400	0.0013-0.0033	0.0013-0.0033	SNUG
	F	7.3 (7292)	0.0036-0.0487	0.0140-0.0240	0.0620-0.7200	0.0120-0.0240	0.0020-0.0040	0.0020-0.0040	SNUG
	K	7.3 (7292)	0.0055-0.0085	0.0130-0.0450	0.0600-0.0850	NA	0.0020-0.0040	0.0020-0.0040	SNUG
	M	7.3 (7292)	0.0055-0.0085	0.0130-0.0450	0.0600-0.0800	0.0100-0.0240	0.0020-0.0040	0.0020-0.0040	0.0010-0.0030
	G	7.5 (7538)	0.0014-0.0022	0.0100-0.0150	0.0100-0.0200	0.0100-0.0300	0.0012-0.0022	0.0012-0.0022	SNUG
1995-96	A	2.3 (2294)	0.0024-0.0034	0.0100-0.0200	0.0100-0.0200	0.0150-0.0550	0.0016-0.0033	0.0016-0.0033	SNUG
	U	3.0 (2999)	0.0012-0.0023	0.0100-0.0200	0.0100-0.0200	0.0100-0.0490	0.0016-0.0037	0.0016-0.0037	SNUG
	4	3.8 (3802)	0.0014-0.0032	0.0110-0.0120	0.0010-0.0020	0.0150-0.0583	0.0016-0.0034	0.0016-0.0034	SNUG
	X	4.0 (3998)	0.0008-0.0019	0.0150-0.0230	0.0150-0.0230	0.0150-0.0550	0.0020-0.0033	0.0020-0.0033	SNUG
	Y	4.9 (4916)	0.0010-0.0018	0.0100-0.0200	0.0100-0.0200	0.0100-0.0350	0.0019-0.0036	0.0020-0.0040	SNUG
	N	5.0 (4949)	0.0014-0.0018	0.0100-0.0200	0.0180-0.0280	0.0100-0.0400	0.0013-0.0033	0.0013-0.0033	SNUG
	H	5.8 (5752)	0.0018-0.0026	0.0100-0.0200	0.0100-0.0200	0.0150-0.0350	0.0019-0.0036	0.0020-0.0040	SNUG
	R	5.8 (5752)	0.0015-0.0023	0.0100-0.0200	0.0180-0.0280	0.0100-0.0400	0.0013-0.0033	0.0013-0.0033	SNUG
	F	7.3 (7292)	0.0036-0.0049	0.0140-0.0240	0.0620-0.0720	0.0120-0.0240	0.0020-0.0040	0.0020-0.0040	SNUG
	M	7.3 (7292)	0.0055-0.0085	0.0130-0.0450	0.0600-0.0800	0.0100-0.0240	0.0020-0.0040	0.0020-0.0040	0.0010-0.0030
	G	7.5 (7538)	0.0014-0.0022	0.0100-0.0150	0.0100-0.0200	0.0100-0.0300	0.0012-0.0022	0.0012-0.0022	SNUG

NA - Not Available

TORQUE SPECIFICATIONS

All readings in ft. lbs.

Year	Engine ID/VIN	Engine Displacement Liters (cc)	Cylinder Head Bolts	Main Bearing Bolts	Rod Bearing Bolts	Crankshaft Damper Bolts	Flywheel Bolts	Manifold Intake	Manifold Exhaust	Spark Plugs	Lug Nut
1992	A	2.3 (2294)	[1]	[1]	[2]	100-120	56-64	14-21	14-21	5-10	[3]
	T	2.9 (2900)	[4]	65-75	19-24	85-96	47-52	18	25	15-18	[3]
	U	3.0 (2999)	[5]	65-81	[6]	141-169	54-64	18	25	8-10	[3]
	X	4.0 (3998)	[7]	66-77	19-24	[8]	59	[9]	19	10-15	[3]
	Y	4.9 (4916)	[10]	60-70	40-45	130-150	75-85	22-32	22-32	10-15	[11]
	N	5.0 (4949)	[12]	95-105	19-24	70-90	75-85	23-25	18-24	10-15	[11]
	H	5.8 (5752)	[12]	60-70	19-24	70-90	75-90	23-25	20-24	-	[11]
	M	7.3 (7292)	[13]	[14]	[15]	90	47	23-25	20-24	-	[11]
	G	7.5 (7538)	[12]	95-105	45-50	70-90	75-85	22-32	28-33	5-10	[11]
1993	A	2.3 (2294)	[1]	[1]	[2]	100-120	56-64	14-21	14-21	5-10	[3]
	U	3.0 (2999)	[5]	65-81	[6]	141-169	54-64	18	[9] 19	8-10	[3]
	X	4.0 (3998)	[7]	66-77	19-24	[8]	59	[9]	19	10-15	[3]
	Y	4.9 (4916)	[10]	60-70	40-45	130-150	75-85	22-32	22-32	10-15	[11]
	N	5.0 (4949)	[12]	95-105	19-24	70-90	75-85	23-25	18-24	10-15	[11]
	H	5.8 (5752)	[12]	60-70	19-24	70-90	75-90	23-25	20-24	10-15	[11]
	R	5.8 (5752)	[12]	60-70	19-24	70-90	75-90	23-25	20-24	-	[11]
	C	7.3 (7292)	[13]	[14]	[15]	90	47	23-25	20-24	-	[11]
	M	7.3 (7292)	[13]	[14]	[15]	90	47	23-25	20-24	-	[11]
	G	7.5 (7538)	[16]	95-105	95-105	70-90	75-85	22-32.	28-33	5-10	[11]
1994	A	2.3 (2294)	51	75-85	30-36	103-133	56-64	19-28	14-21	5-10	[3]
	U	3.0 (2999)	[18]	60	26	107	54-64	24	25	8-10	[3]
	X	4.0 (3998)	[7]	66-77	19-24	[8]	59	[9]	19	10-15	[3]
	Y	4.9 (4916)	[10]	60-70	40-45	130-150	75-85	22-32	22-32	10-15	[11]
	N	5.0 (4949)	[19]	60-70	19-24	70-90	75-85	23-25	18-24	10-15	[11]
	H	5.8 (5752)	[20]	95-105	40-45	70-90	75-90	23-25	20-24	10-15	[11]
	R	5.8 (5752)	[20]	95-105	40-45	70-90	75-90	23-25	20-24	10-15	[11]
	F	7.3 (7292)	[21]	95	70	90	89	18	45	-	-
	K	7.3 (7292)	[22]	[23]	[24]	90	[17]	24	-	-	[11]
	M	7.3 (7292)	[21]	[23]	[24]	90	47	23-25	20-24	-	[11]
	G	7.5 (7538)	[14]	95-105	45-50	70-90	[17]	22-32	28-33	5-10	[11]
1995-96	A	2.3 (2294)	51	75-85	30-36	103-133	54-64	19-28	14-21	5-10	[3]
	U	3.0 (2999)	[18]	60	26	107	54-64	24	25	8-10	[3]
	4	3.8 (3802)	[26]	65-81	31-36	103-132	54-64	[25]	19	8-10	85-105
	X	4.0 (3998)	[7]	66-77	19-24	[8]	59	[9]	19	10-15	[3]
	Y	4.9 (4916)	[10]	60-70	40-45	130-150	75-85	22-32	22-32	10-15	[11]
	N	5.0 (4949)	[19]	60-70	19-24	70-90	75-85	23-25	18-24	10-15	[11]
	H	5.8 (5752)	[20]	95-105	40-45	70-90	75-90	23-25	20-24	10-15	[11]
	R	5.8 (5752)	[20]	95-105	40-45	70-90	75-90	23-25	20-24	10-15	[11]
	F	7.3 (7292)	[21]	95	70	90	89	18	45	-	-
	M	7.3 (7292)	[21]	[23]	[24]	90	47	23-25	20-24	-	[11]
	G	7.5 (7538)	[27]	95-105	45-40	70-90	75-85	22-32	28-33	5-10	[11]

1 Step 1: 50-60 ft. lbs.
Step 2: 80-90 ft. lbs.
2 Step 1: 25-30 ft. lbs.
Step 2: 30-36 ft. lbs.
3 Aerostar, Explorer and Ranger: 100 ft. lbs.

11 E-F100, E-F150, E-F250: 90 ft. lbs.
E-F350 with single rear wheels: 135 ft. lbs.
F350 with dual rear wheels: 210 ft. lbs.
12 Step 1: 55-65 ft. lbs.
Step 2: 65-72 ft. lbs.

20 Step 1: 95-105 ft. lbs.
Step 2: 105-112 ft. lbs.
21 Step 1: 65 ft. lbs.
Step 2: 85 ft. lbs.
Step 3: 105 ft. lbs.

TORQUE SPECIFICATIONS

All readings in ft. lbs.

Year	Engine ID/VIN	Engine Displacement Liters (cc)	Cylinder Head Bolts	Main Bearing Bolts	Rod Bearing Bolts	Crankshaft Damper Bolts	Flywheel Bolts	Manifold Intake	Manifold Exhaust	Spark Plugs	Lug Nut

4 Step 1: 22 ft. lbs.
Step 2: 51-55 ft. lbs.
Step 3: Turn 90 degrees
5 Step 1: 48-54 ft. lbs.
Step 2: 63-80 ft. lbs.
6 Step 1: 20-28 ft. lbs.
Step 2: Back off a minimum of two turns
Step 3: 20-25 ft. lbs.
7 Tighten cylinder head bolts to 44 ft. lbs.
Tighten intake manifold bolts to 3-6 ft. lbs.
Tighten cylinder head bolts to 59 ft. lbs.
Tighten intake manifold bolts to 6-11 ft. lbs.
Tighten cylinder head bolts 85 degrees
Tighten intake manifold bolts to 11-15 ft. lbs.
Tighten intake manifold bolts to 15-18 ft. lbs.
8 Step 1: 30-37 ft. lbs.
Step 2: Turn 90 degrees
9 Step 1: 3-6 ft. lbs.
Step 2: 6-11 ft. lbs.
Step 3: 11-15 ft. lbs.
Step 4: 15-18 ft. lbs.
10 Step 1: 55 ft. lbs.
Step 2: 65 ft. lbs.
Step 3: 85 ft. lbs.

13 Step 1: 65 ft. lbs.
Step 2: 90 ft. lbs.
Step 3: 100 ft. lbs.
14 Step 1: 75 ft. lbs.
Step 2: 95 ft. lbs.
15 Step 1: 38 ft. lbs.
Step 2: 50-55 ft. lbs.
16 Step 1: 80 ft. lbs.
Step 2: 110 ft. lbs.
Step 3: 130-140 ft. lbs.
17 Step 1: 47 ft. lbs.
Step 2: Plus 45 degrees
18 Step 1: 37 ft. lbs.
Step 2: 68 ft. lbs.
19 5.0L with flanged head bolts:
Step 1: 25-35 ft. lbs.
Step 2: 40-55 ft. lbs.
Step 3: Turn an additional 1/4 turn
5.0L with hex head bolts:
Step 1: 55-65 ft. lbs.
Step 2: 65-72 ft. lbs.
Step 1: 55-65 ft. lbs.
Step 2: 65-72 ft. lbs.

22 Step 1: 65 ft. lbs.
Step 2: 90 ft. lbs.
Step 3: 110 ft. lbs.
23 Step 1: 95 ft. lbs.
Step 2: Plus 45 degrees
24 Step 1: 38 ft. lbs.
Step 2: 51 ft. lbs.
25 Lower intake manifold:
Step 1: 13 ft. lbs.
Step 2: 16 ft. lbs.
Upper intake manifold:
Step 1: 8 ft. lbs.
Step 2: 15 ft. lbs.
Step 3: 24 ft. lbs.
26 Step 1: 15 ft. lbs.
Step 2: 29 ft. lbs.
Step 3: 37 ft. lbs.
Step 4: Loosen each bolt one at a time
Step 5: Long bolts to 11-19 ft. lbs. plus 1/4 turn
Step 6: Short bolts to 7-15 ft. lbs. plus 1/4 turn
27 Step 1: 70-80 ft. lbs.
Step 2: 100-110 ft. lbs.
Step 3: 130-140 ft. lbs.

BRAKE SPECIFICATIONS

All measurements in inches unless noted

Year	Model		Master Cylinder Bore	Brake Disc Original Thickness	Brake Disc Minimum Thickness	Brake Disc Maximum Runout	Brake Drum Diameter Original Inside Diameter	Brake Drum Diameter Max. Wear Limit	Brake Drum Diameter Maximum Machine Diameter	Minimum Lining Thickness Front	Minimum Lining Thickness Rear
1992	Aerostar	1	NA	0.850	0.810	0.003	9.00	9.09	9.06	0.030	0.030
	Aerostar	2	NA	0.850	0.810	0.003	10.00	10.09	10.06	0.030	0.030
	Bronco		NA	1.160	1.120	0.003	11.03	11.09	11.06	0.030	0.030
	Explorer	1	0.938	0.850	0.810	0.003	9.00	9.09	9.06	0.030	0.030
	Explorer	3	0.938	0.850	0.810	0.003	10.00	10.09	10.06	0.030	0.030
	Explorer	4	0.975	0.850	0.810	0.003	10.00	10.09	10.06	0.030	0.030
	Ranger	1	0.938	0.850	0.810	0.003	9.00	9.09	9.06	0.030	0.030
	Ranger	3	0.938	0.850	0.810	0.003	10.00	10.09	10.06	0.030	0.030
	Ranger	4	0.975	0.850	0.810	0.003	10.00	10.09	10.06	0.030	0.030
	E-150		NA	1.160	1.120	0.003	11.03	11.09	11.06	0.030	0.030
	E-250		NA	1.220	1.180	0.003	12.00	12.09	12.06	0.030	0.030
	E-350		NA	1.220	1.180	0.003	12.00	12.09	12.06	0.030	0.030
	F-150		NA	1.160	1.120	0.003	11.03	11.09	11.06	0.030	0.030
	F-250		NA	1.220	1.180	0.003	12.00	12.09	12.06	0.030	0.030
	F-350		NA	1.220	1.180	0.003	12.00	12.09	12.06	0.030	0.030
	F-Superduty		NA	1.220	1.180	0.008	12.00	12.09	12.06	0.030	0.030

BRAKE SPECIFICATIONS

All measurements in inches unless noted

Year	Model		Master Cylinder Bore	Brake Disc Original Thickness	Brake Disc Minimum Thickness	Brake Disc Maximum Runout	Brake Drum Diameter Original Inside Diameter	Brake Drum Diameter Max. Wear Limit	Brake Drum Diameter Maximum Machine Diameter	Minimum Lining Thickness Front	Minimum Lining Thickness Rear
1993	Aerostar	1	NA	0.850	0.810	0.003	9.00	9.09	9.06	0.030	0.030
	Aerostar	2	NA	0.850	0.810	0.003	10.00	10.09	10.06	0.030	0.030
	Bronco		NA	1.160	1.120	0.003	11.03	11.09	11.06	0.030	0.030
	Explorer	1	0.938	0.850	0.810	0.003	9.00	9.09	9.06	0.030	0.030
	Explorer	3	0.938	0.850	0.810	0.003	10.00	10.09	10.06	0.030	0.030
	Explorer	4	0.975	0.850	0.810	0.003	10.00	10.09	10.06	0.030	0.030
	Ranger	1	0.938	0.850	0.810	0.003	9.00	9.09	9.06	0.030	0.030
	Ranger	3	0.938	0.850	0.810	0.003	10.00	10.09	10.06	0.030	0.030
	Ranger	4	0.975	0.850	0.810	0.003	10.00	10.09	10.06	0.030	0.030
	E-150		NA	1.160	1.120	0.003	11.03	11.09	11.06	0.030	0.030
	E-250		NA	1.220	1.180	0.003	12.00	12.09	12.06	0.030	0.030
	E-350		NA	1.220	1.180	0.003	12.00	12.09	12.06	0.030	0.030
	F-150		NA	1.160	1.120	0.003	11.03	11.09	11.06	0.030	0.030
	F-250		NA	1.220	1.180	0.003	12.00	12.09	12.06	0.030	0.030
	F-350		NA	1.220	1.180	0.003	12.00	12.09	12.06	0.030	0.030
	F-Superduty		NA	1.220	1.180	0.008	12.00	12.09	12.06	0.030	0.030
1994	Aerostar	1	0.938	0.850	0.810	0.003	9.00	9.09	9.06	0.030	0.030
	Aerostar	2	0.938	0.850	0.810	0.003	10.00	10.09	10.06	0.030	0.030
	Bronco		1.000	1.160	1.120	0.003	11.03	11.09	11.06	0.030	0.030
	Explorer	1	0.938	0.850	0.810	0.003	9.00	9.09	9.06	0.030	0.030
	Explorer	3	0.938	0.850	0.810	0.003	10.00	10.09	10.06	0.030	0.030
	Explorer	4	0.938	0.850	0.810	0.003	10.00	10.09	10.06	0.030	0.030
	Ranger	1	0.938	0.850	0.810	0.003	9.00	9.09	9.06	0.030	0.030
	Ranger	3	0.938	0.850	0.810	0.003	10.00	10.09	10.06	0.030	0.030
	Ranger	4	0.938	0.850	0.810	0.003	10.00	10.09	10.06	0.030	0.030
	E-150		1.000	1.160	1.120	0.003	11.03	11.09	11.06	0.030	0.030
	E-250	5		1.220	1.180	0.003	12.00	12.09	12.06	0.030	0.030
	E-350		NA	1.220	1.180	0.003	12.00	12.09	12.06	0.030	0.030
	F-150		1.000	1.160	1.120	0.003	11.03	11.09	11.06	0.030	0.030
	F-250	5		1.220	1.180	0.003	12.00	12.09	12.06	0.030	0.030
	F-350		1.125	1.220	1.180	0.003	12.00	12.09	12.06	0.030	0.030
	F-Superduty	F	NA	1.220	1.180	0.008	-	-	-	0.030	-
	F-Superduty	R	-	NA	1.430	0.008	-	-	-	-	0.030
1995-96	Aerostar	1	0.938	0.850	0.810	0.003	9.00	9.09	9.06	0.030	0.030
	Aerostar	2	0.938	0.850	0.810	0.003	10.00	10.09	10.06	0.030	0.030
	Bronco		1.000	1.160	0.960	0.003	11.03	11.09	11.06	0.030	0.030
	Explorer	1	0.938	0.850	0.810	0.003	9.00	9.09	9.06	0.030	0.030
	Explorer	3	0.938	0.850	0.810	0.003	10.00	10.09	10.06	0.030	0.030
	Explorer	4	0.938	0.850	0.810	0.003	10.00	10.09	10.06	0.030	0.030
	Ranger	1	0.938	0.850	0.810	0.003	9.00	9.09	9.06	0.030	0.030
	Ranger	3	0.938	0.850	0.810	0.003	10.00	10.09	10.06	0.030	0.030
	Ranger	4	0.938	0.850	0.810	0.003	10.00	10.09	10.06	0.030	0.030
	E-150		1.000	1.160	1.120	0.003	11.03	11.09	11.06	0.030	0.030
	E-250	5		1.220	1.180	0.003	12.00	12.09	12.06	0.030	0.030
	E-350		NA	1.220	1.180	0.003	12.00	12.09	12.06	0.030	0.030
	F-150		1.000	1.160	0.960	0.003	11.03	11.09	11.06	0.030	0.030

BRAKE SPECIFICATIONS

All measurements in inches unless noted

Year	Model		Master Cylinder Bore	Brake Disc Original Thickness	Brake Disc Minimum Thickness	Brake Disc Maximum Runout	Brake Drum Diameter Original Inside Diameter	Brake Drum Diameter Max. Wear Limit	Brake Drum Diameter Maximum Machine Diameter	Minimum Lining Thickness Front	Minimum Lining Thickness Rear
1995-96	F-250		5	1.220	6	0.003	12.00	12.09	12.06	0.030	0.030
	F-350		1.125	1.220	6	7	12.00	12.09	12.06	0.030	0.030
	F-Superduty	F	NA	1.220	1.180	0.008	-	-	-	0.030	-
	F-Superduty	R	-	NA	1.430	0.008	-	-	-	-	0.030
	Windstar		NA	1.020	0.097	0.003	9.84	NA	9.90	0.040	0.590

NOTE: Due to changes made during production, refer to manufacturer's specifications if they differ from those in this chart

NA - Not Available
F - Front
R - Rear
1 With 9 inch brakes
2 With 10 inch brakes
3 4x2 with 10 inch brakes
4 4x4 with 10 inch brakes
5 Under 6900 GVW: 1.062
  Over 6900 GVW: 1.125
6 4x2: 1.100 in.
  4x4: 1.120 in.
7 0.003 in. except F-350 4x2 with dual rear wheel and 2-piece rotor/hub: 0.010 in.

WHEEL ALIGNMENT

Year	Model	Ride Height (in.)	Caster Range (deg.)	Caster Preferred Setting (deg.)	Camber Range (deg.)	Camber Preferred Setting (deg.)	Toe-in (in.)
1992	Aerostar	1	2 1/2P-4 1/2P	3 1/2P	5/16N-11/16P	3/16P	1/32
	Bronco	3 1/4-3 1/2	6P-8P	2	1 3/4N-1/4N	1N	1/32
		3 1/2-3 3/4	5P-7P	2	3/4N-3/4P	0	1/32
		4-4 1/4	4P-6P	2	1/4P-1 3/4P	1 1/4P	1/32
		4 1/4-4 1/2	3P-5P	2	1 1/4P-2 3/4P	1 3/4P	1/32
	Explorer 4x2	1 1/2-2	12P-14P	3	5 1/8N-3 1/8N	3	0
		2-2 1/2	10P-12P	3	3 1/2N-1 1/2N	3	0
		2 1/2-3	8P-10P	3	2 1/2N-1/2N	3	0
		3-3 1/2	6 1/4P-8 1/4P	3	1 1/2N-1/2P	3	0
		3 1/2-4	5 1/4P-7 1/4P	3	1/2N-1 1/2P	3	0
		4-4 1/2	3 3/4P-5 3/4P	3	1/2N-2 1/2P	3	0
		4 1/2-5	2 1/4P-4 1/4P	3	1 1/2P-3 1/2P	3	0
	Explorer 4x4	1 1/2-2	10P-12P	3	5 3/4N-3 3/4N	3	0
		2-2 1/2	8P-10P	3	4 1/2P-2 1/2N	3	0
		2 1/2-3	6P-8P	3	3N-1N	3	0
		3-3 1/2	4 1/2P-6 1/2P	3	1N-1P	3	0
		3 1/2-4	3 1/4P-5 1/4P	3	1/2P-2 1/2P	3	0
		4-4 1/2	2 3/4P-4 3/4P	3	1 3/4P-3 3/4P	3	0
		4 1/2-5	1/2P-2 1/2P	3	3 1/2P-5 1/2P	3	0
	Ranger 4x2	3 1/4-3 1/2	6 1/8P-8 3/4P	3	1 1/2N-1P	3	0
		3 1/2-3 3/4	5 1/2P-8 1/8P	3	1N-1 3/4P	3	0
		3 3/4-4	4 5/8P-7 1/2P	3	1/4N-2 3/8P	3	0
		4-4 1/4	3 3/4P-6 5/8P	3	3/8P-3P	3	0
		4 1/4-4 1/2	3 1/4P-5 3/4P	3	1P-4P	3	0
		4 1/2-4 3/4	2 1/2P-5 1/4P	3	2P-4 5/8P	3	0

WHEEL ALIGNMENT

Year	Model	Ride Height (in.)	Caster Range (deg.)	Caster Preferred Setting (deg.)	Camber Range (deg.)	Camber Preferred Setting (deg.)	Toe-in (in.)
1992	Ranger 4x4	3 1/4-3 1/2	4P-6 1/2P	3	7/8n-1 3/4p	3	0
		3 1/2-3 3/4	3 1/4P-6P	3	1/4N-2 3/8P	3	0
		4-4 1/4	1 7/8P-4 5/8P	3	7/8P-3 1/2P	3	0
	E-150	4-4 1/2	7 1/2P-9 1/2P	2	1 1/4N-1/4P	2	1/32
		4 1/2-5	6 1/4P-8 1/4P	2	1/8N-1 1/4P	2	1/32
		5-5 1/2	5P-7P	2	7/8P-2 1/4P	2	1/32
		5 1/2-5 3/4	3 1/4P-5 1/4P	2	1 3/4P-3 1/4P	2	1/32
	E-250	3 3/4-4	7 5/8P-9 5/8P	2	3/4N-1/2P	2	1/32
		4 1/4-4 1/2	6 1/4P-8 1/4P	2	1/4P-1 1/2P	2	1/32
		4 3/4-5	5P-7P	2	1 1/4P-2 1/2P	2	1/32
		5 1/4-5 1/2	3 3/4P-5 3/4P	2	2 1/4P-3 1/2P	2	1/32
	E-350	3 3/4-4	7 5/8P-9 5/8P	2	3/4N-1/2P	2	1/32
		4 1/4-4 1/2	6 1/4P-8 1/4P	2	1/4P-1 1/2P	2	1/32
		4 3/4-5	5P-7P	2	1 1/4P-2 1/2P	2	1/32
		5 1/4-5 1/2	3 3/4P-5 3/4P	2	2 1/4P-3 1/2P	2	1/32
	F-150 4x2	3 1/4-3 1/2	5P-7P	2	3/4N-3/4P	0	1/32
		3 1/2-4	4P-6P	2	1/4N-1 1/4P	1P	1/32
		4-4 1/4	3 1/4P-5 1/4P	2	1/2P-2P	1P	1/32
		4 1/4-4 3/4	2 1/2P-4 1/2P	2	2P-3 1/2P	2 1/2P	1/32
		4 3/4-5	1 1/2P-3 1/2P	2	3P-4 1/2P	3 1/2P	1/32
	F-150 4x4	3 1/4-3 1/2	6P-8P	4	1 3/4N-1/4N	1N	1/32
		3 1/2-3 3/4	5P-7P	4	3/4N-3/4P	0	1/32
		4-4 1/4	4P-6P	4	1/4P-1 3/4P	1 1/4P	1/32
		4 1/4-4 1/2	3P-5P	4	1 1/4P-2 3/4P	1 3/4P	1/32
	F-250 4x2	2 1/2-2 3/4	5 1/4P-7 1/4P	4	1N-1/2P	0	1/32
		2 3/4-3	5P-7P	4	1/2N-3/4P	0	1/32
		3 1/4-3 1/2	4 1/2P-6 1/2P	4	1/8N-1 1/4P	3/4P	1/32
		3 3/4-4	4P-7P	4	1/2P-1 3/4P	1P	1/32
		4-4 1/4	3 1/2P-5 1/2P	4	3/4P-2 1/4P	1 1/2P	1/32
	F-250 4x4	5-5 1/5	3P-5P	5	1 3/4N-1/4N	1N	1/32
		5 1/2-5 3/4	3 1/8P-5 1/8P	5	3/4N-3/4P	0	1/32
		6-6 1/4	3 1/4P-5 1/4P	5	1/2P-2P	1P	1/32
		6 1/4-6 1/2	3 3/8P-5 3/8P	5	1 1/2P-3P	2P	1/32
		6 3/4-7	3 1/2P-5 1/2P	5	2 1/2P-4P	3P	1/32
	F-350 4x2	2 1/2-2 3/4	5 1/4P-7 1/4P	4	1N-1/2P	0	3/32
		2 3/4-3	5P-7P	4	1/2N-3/4P	0	3/32
		3 1/4-3 1/2	4 1/2P-6 1/2P	4	1/8N-1 1/4P	3/4P	3/32
		3 3/4-4	4P-7P	4	1/2P-1 3/4P	1P	3/32
		4-4 1/4	3 1/2P-5 1/2P	4	3/4P-2 1/4P	1 1/2P	3/32
	F-350 4x4	5-5 1/5	3P-5P	5	1 3/4N-1/4N	1N	1/32
		5 1/2-5 3/4	3 1/8P-5 1/8P	5	3/4N-3/4P	0	1/32
		6-6 1/4	3 1/4P-5 1/4P	5	1/2P-2P	1P	1/32
		6 1/4-6 1/2	3 3/8P-5 3/8P	5	1 1/2P-3P	2P	1/32
		6 3/4-7	3 1/2P-5 1/2P	5	2 1/2P-4P	3P	1/32

WHEEL ALIGNMENT

Year	Model		Ride Height (in.)	Caster Range (deg.)	Caster Preferred Setting (deg.)	Camber Range (deg.)	Camber Preferred Setting (deg.)	Toe-in (in.)
1993	Aerostar		1	2 1/4P-4 1/2P	3 1/4P	1/32N-11/16P	3/16P	1/32
	Bronco		1	2P-6P	-	-	1/4P	1/32
	Explorer 4x2		1	3P-8P	6	1/4N-3/4P	1/4P	1/32
	Explorer 4x4		1	2P-7P	6	1/4N-3/4P	1/4P	1/32
	Ranger 4x2		1	3P-8P	6	1/4N-3/4P	1/4P	1/32
	Ranger 4x4		1	2P-7P	6	1/4N-3/4P	1/4P	1/32
	E-150		1	2P-7 1/2P	-	1/4P-1/2P	1/4P	1/32
	E-250		1	2P-7 1/2P	-	0-1/2P	1/4P	1/32
	E-350		1	2P-7 1/2P	-	0-1/2P	1/4P	1/32
	F-150 4x2		1	2P-6P	-	-	1/4P	1/32
	F-150 4x4		1	2P-6P	-	1/4P-1/2P	1/4P	1/32
	F-250 4x2		1	2P-6P	-	-	1/4P	1/32
	F-250 4x4		1	2P-6P	-	-	1/4P	1/32
	F-350 4x2	7	1	2P-6P	-	-	1/2P	1/32
	F-350 4x2	8	1	2P-4 1/2P	-	-	1/2P	1/32
	F-350 4x4		1	2P-4 3/4P	-	1/4N-1/4P	0	1/32
	F-Superduty 4x2	9	1	2P-5P	3P	-	0	1/32
	F-Superduty 4x4	10	1	2P-5 1/2P	3P	-	5/8P	1/32
1994	Aerostar		1	2P-6P	3 1/2P	1/4N-3/4P	1/4P	1/16
	Bronco		1	2P-6P	4P	1/4N-3/4P	1/4P	1/16
	Explorer		1	2P-7P	4 1/2P	1/4N-3/4P	1/4P	1/16
	Ranger		1	2P-6P	4P	1/4N-3/4P	1/4P	1/16
	E-150		1	2P-7 1/2P	4 3/4P	1/4N-1/2P	1/4P	1/16
	E-250		1	2P-7 1/2P	4 3/4P	0-1P	1/4P	1/16
	E-350		1	2P-7 1/2P	4 3/4P	0-1P	1/4P	1/16
	F-150		1	2P-6P	4P	1/4N-1/2P	1/4P	1/16
	F-250		1	2P-6P	4P	1/4N-1/2P	1/4P	1/16
	F-350 4x2	7	1	2P-6P	4P	0-1P	1/2P	1/16
	F-350 4x2	8	1	1P-4 1/2P	2 3/4P	0-1P	1/2P	1/16
	F-350 4x4		1	2P-4 3/4P	3 3/8P	1/2N-1/2P	0	1/16
	F-Superduty 4x2	9	1	2P-5P	3 1/2P	1/32N-1/32P	0	1/16
	F-Superduty 4x4	10	1	2P-5 1/2P	3 3/4P	1/32N-1/32P	0	1/16
1995-96	Aerostar		1	2P-6P	3 1/2P	1/4N-3/4P	1/4P	1/32
	Bronco		1	2P-6P	4P	1/4N-3/4P	1/4P	1/16
	Explorer		1	2P-7P	4P	1/4N-3/4P	1/4P	1/16
	Ranger		1	2P-6P	4P	1/4N-3/4P	1/4P	1/16
	E-150		1	2P-7 1/2P	4 3/4P	1/2N-1/2P	0	1/16
	E-250		1	2P-7 1/2P	4 3/4P	0-1.00P	1/2P	1/16
	E-350		1	2P-7 1/2P	4 3/4P	0-1.00P	1/2P	1/16
	F-150		1	2P-6P	4P	1/4N-3/4P	1/4P	1/16
	F-250		1	2P-6P	4P	1/4N-3/4P	1/4P	1/16
	F-350 4x2	7	1	2P-6P	4P	0-1P	1/2P	1/16
	F-350 4x2	8	1	1P-4 1/2P	2 3/4P	0-1P	1/2P	1/16
	F350 4x4		1	2P-4 3/4P	3 3/8P	1/2N-1/2P	0	1/16
	Super Duty 4x2	9	1	2P-5P	3 1/2P	1/32N-1/32P	0	1/16
	Super Duty 4x4	10	1	2P-5 1/2P	3 3/4P	1/32N-1/32P	0	1/16

WHEEL ALIGNMENT

Year	Model	Ride Height (in.)	Caster Range (deg.)	Caster Preferred Setting (deg.)	Camber Range (deg.)	Camber Preferred Setting (deg.)	Toe-in (in.)
1995-96	F-150 4x4	1	2P-6P	4P	1/2N-3/4P	1/4P	1/16
	F-250 4x4	1	2P-6P	4P	1/4N-3/4P	1/4P	1/16
	Windstar	NA	- 11		-	12	13

NOTE: F150-250 4x4, F150-350 4x2, E150-350, Bronco: Caster and camber adjustments are possible with interchangeable sleeves located at the upper ball joint stud.

F250-350 with leaf spring suspension: Caster is adjustable by interchangeable sleeves or shims between the spring and axle.

F350, F-Superduty monobeam axles: Not Adjustable

1 Normal riding attitude with no more than 5/8 in. front and 3/4 in. rear side-to-side clearance

2 Not adjustable

3 Caster and camber adjustment is possible with installation of service adjusters

4 Adjusted by placing shims between leaf springs and front axle

5 Adjusted by placing shims between leaf springs and front axle, except with monobeam front suspension

6 Caster and camber adjustment is possible with installation of service adjusters

7 With single rear wheel

8 With dual rear wheel

9 Without stripped chassis

10 With stripped chassis

11 Caster, left wheel: 2 35/64P-4 3/64P (3 19/64P preferred)
Caster, right wheel: 3 3/64P-4 35/64P (3 51/64P preferred)

12 Camber, front: 3/4N-1/4P (1/4N preferred)
Camber, rear: 25/64N-25/64P (0 preferred)

13 Toe, front: 3/32N
Toe, rear: 1/16P

GENERAL MOTORS CORPORATION

VEHICLE IDENTIFICATION CHART

Engine Code						Model Year	
Code	Liters	Cu. In. (cc)	Cyl.	Fuel Sys.	Eng. Mfg.	Code	Year
4	2.2	134 (2189)	4	MFI	CPC	N	1992
A	2.5	151 (2474)	4	TFI	CPC	P	1993
R	2.8	173 (2835)	6	TFI	CPC	R	1994
D	3.1	191 (3130)	6	TFI	CPC	S	1995
L	3.8	231 (3785)	6	MFI	CPC	T	1996
W	4.3	263 (4293)	6	TFI	CPC		
Z	4.3	263 (4293)	6	TFI	CPC		
Z	4.3	263 (4293)	6	MFI	CPC		
Z	4.3	263 (4293)	6	MFI Turbo	CPC		
H	5.0	305 (4999)	8	TFI	CPC		
K	5.7	350 (5735)	8	TFI	CPC		
K	5.7	350 (5735)	8	MFI	CPC		
C	6.2	379 (6210)	8	DSL	CPC		
J	6.2	379 (6210)	8	DSL	CPC		
F	6.5	395 (6473)	8	DSL	CPC		
P	6.5	395 (6473)	8	DSL	CPC		
S	6.5	395 (6473)	8	DSL	CPC		
Y	6.5	395 (6473)	8	DSL	CPC		
N	7.4	454 (7440)	8	TFI	CPC		

TFI - Throttle body fuel injection
MFI - Multiport fuel injection
DSL - Diesel
CPC - Chevrolet/Pontiac/Canada

ENGINE IDENTIFICATION

Year	Model	Engine Displacement Liters (cc)	Engine Series (ID/VIN)	Fuel System	No. of Cylinders	Engine Type
1992	Astro/Safari	4.3 (4293)	W	TFI	6	OHV
	Astro/Safari	4.3 (4293)	Z	TFI	6	OHV
	Blazer	5.7 (5735)	K	TFI	8	OHV
	Lumina APV/Silhouette/Trans Sport	3.1 (3130)	D	TFI	6	OHV
	Lumina APV/Silhouette/Trans Sport	3.8 (3785)	L	MFI	6	OHV
	S10 Blazer/S15Jimmy/Bravada	4.3 (4293)	W	MFI	6	OHV
	S10 Blazer/S15Jimmy/Bravada	4.3 (4293)	Z	TFI	6	OHV
	S10 Pick-up/Sonoma	2.5 (2474)	A	TFI	4	OHV
	S10 Pick-up/Sonoma	2.8 (2835)	R	TFI	6	OHV
	S10 Pick-up/Sonoma	4.3 (4293)	W	MFI	6	OHV
	S10 Pick-up/Sonoma	4.3 (4293)	Z	TFI	6	OHV
	Suburban	5.7 (5735)	K	TFI	8	OHV
	Suburban	7.4 (7440)	N	TFI	8	OHV
	Syclone	4.3 (4293)	Z	MFI-Turbo	6	OHV

ENGINE IDENTIFICATION

Year	Model	Displacement Liters (cc)	Engine Series (ID/VIN)	Engine Fuel System	No. of Cylinders	Engine Type
1992	Typhoon	4.3 (4293)	Z	MFI-Turbo	6	OHV
	C1500	4.3 (4293)	Z	TFI	6	OHV
	C1500	5.0 (4999)	H	TFI	8	OHV
	C1500	5.7 (5735)	K	TFI	8	OHV
	C1500	6.2 (6210)	C	DSL	8	OHV
	C1500	6.2 (6210)	J	DSL	8	OHV
	C1500	7.4 (7440)	N	TFI	8	OHV
	C2500	4.3 (4293)	Z	TFI	6	OHV
	C2500	5.0 (4999)	H	TFI	8	OHV
	C2500	5.7 (5735)	K	TFI	8	OHV
	C2500	6.2 (6210)	C	DSL	8	OHV
	C2500	6.2 (6210)	J	DSL	8	OHV
	C2500	6.5 (6473)	F	DSL	8	OHV
	C2500	7.4 (7440)	N	TFI	8	OHV
	C3500	5.0 (4999)	H	TFI	8	OHV
	C3500	5.7 (5735)	K	TFI	8	OHV
	C3500	6.2 (6210)	C	DSL	8	OHV
	C3500	6.2 (6210)	J	DSL	8	OHV
	C3500	6.5 (6473)	F	DSL	8	OHV
	C3500	7.4 (7440)	N	TFI	8	OHV
	G10/G1500	4.3 (4293)	Z	TFI	6	OHV
	G10/G1500	5.0 (4999)	H	TFI	8	OHV
	G10/G1500	5.7 (5735)	K	TFI	8	OHV
	G20/G2500	4.3 (4293)	Z	TFI	6	OHV
	G20/G2500	5.0 (4999)	H	TFI	8	OHV
	G20/G2500	5.7 (5735)	K	TFI	8	OHV
	G30/G3500	4.3 (4293)	Z	TFI	6	OHV
	G30/G3500	5.7 (5735)	K	TFI	8	OHV
	G30/G3500	6.2 (6210)	C	DSL	8	OHV
	G30/G3500	6.2 (6210)	J	DSL	8	OHV
	G30/G3500	7.4 (7440)	N	TFI	8	OHV
	K1500	4.3 (4293)	Z	TFI	6	OHV
	K1500	5.0 (4999)	H	TFI	8	OHV
	K1500	5.7 (5735)	K	TFI	8	OHV
	K1500	6.2 (6210)	C	DSL	8	OHV
	K1500	6.2 (6210)	J	DSL	8	OHV
	K1500	7.4 (7440)	N	TFI	8	OHV
	K2500	4.3 (4293)	Z	TFI	6	OHV
	K2500	5.0 (4999)	H	TFI	8	OHV
	K2500	5.7 (5735)	K	TFI	8	OHV
	K2500	6.2 (6210)	C	DSL	8	OHV
	K2500	6.2 (6210)	J	DSL	8	OHV
	K2500	6.5 (6473)	F	DSL	8	OHV
	K2500	7.4 (7440)	N	TFI	8	OHV
	K3500	5.0 (4999)	H	TFI	8	OHV
	K3500	5.7 (5735)	K	TFI	8	OHV
	K3500	6.2 (6210)	C	DSL	8	OHV
	K3500	6.2 (6210)	J	DSL	8	OHV
	K3500	6.5 (6473)	F	DSL	8	OHV

ENGINE IDENTIFICATION

Year	Model	Displacement Liters (cc)	Engine Series (ID/VIN)	Engine Fuel System	No. of Cylinders	Engine Type
1992	K3500	7.4 (7441)	N	TFI	8	OHV
	P30	4.3 (4293)	Z	TFI	6	OHV
	P30	5.7 (5735)	K	TFI	8	OHV
	P30	6.2 (6210)	J	DSL	8	OHV
	P30	7.4 (7440)	N	TFI	8	OHV
1993	Astro/Safari	4.3 (4293)	W	MFI	6	OHV
	Astro/Safari	4.3 (4293)	Z	TFI	6	OHV
	Blazer/Yukon	5.7 (5735)	K	TFI	8	OHV
	Lumina APV/Silhouette/Trans Sport	3.1 (3097)	D	TFI	6	OHV
	Lumina APV/Silhouette/Trans Sport	3.8 (3785)	L	MFI	6	OHV
	S10 Blazer/S15Jimmy/Bravada	4.3 (4293)	W	MFI	6	OHV
	S10 Blazer/S15Jimmy/Bravada	4.3 (4293)	Z	TFI	6	OHV
	S10 Pick-up/Sonoma	2.5 (2474)	A	TFI	4	OHV
	S10 Pick-up/Sonoma	2.8 (2835)	R	TFI	6	OHV
	S10 Pick-up/Sonoma	4.3 (4293)	W	MFI	6	OHV
	Suburban	5.7 (5735)	K	TFI	8	OHV
	Suburban	7.4 (7440)	N	TFI	8	OHV
	Typhoon	4.3 (4293)	Z	MFI-Turbo	6	OHV
	C1500	4.3 (4293)	Z	TFI	6	OHV
	C1500	5.0 (4999)	H	TFI	8	OHV
	C1500	5.7 (5735)	K	TFI	8	OHV
	C1500	6.2 (6210)	C	DSL	8	OHV
	C1500	6.2 (6210)	J	DSL	8	OHV
	C1500	7.4 (7440)	N	TFI	8	OHV
	C2500	4.3 (4293)	Z	TFI	6	OHV
	C2500	5.0 (4999)	H	TFI	8	OHV
	C2500	5.7 (5735)	K	TFI	8	OHV
	C2500	6.2 (6210)	C	DSL	8	OHV
	C2500	6.2 (6210)	J	DSL	8	OHV
	C2500	6.5 (6505)	F	DSL	8	OHV
	C2500	7.4 (7440)	N	TFI	8	OHV
	C3500	4.3 (4293)	Z	TFI	6	OHV
	C3500	5.0 (4999)	H	TFI	8	OHV
	C3500	5.7 (5735)	K	TFI	8	OHV
	C3500	6.2 (6210)	C	DSL	8	OHV
	C3500	6.2 (6210)	J	DSL	8	OHV
	C3500	6.5 (6505)	F	DSL	8	OHV
	C3500	7.4 (7440)	N	TFI	8	OHV
	G10/G1500	4.3 (4293)	Z	TFI	6	OHV
	G10/G1500	5.0 (4999)	H	TFI	8	OHV
	G10/G1500	5.7 (5735)	K	TFI	8	OHV
	G10/G1500	6.2 (6210)	C	DSL	8	OHV
	G10/G1500	6.2 (6210)	J	DSL	8	OHV
	G10/G1500	7.4 (7440)	N	TFI	8	OHV
	G20/G2500	4.3 (4293)	Z	TFI	6	OHV
	G20/G2500	5.0 (4999)	H	TFI	8	OHV
	G20/G2500	5.7 (5735)	K	TFI	8	OHV
	G20/G2500	6.2 (6210)	C	DSL	8	OHV

ENGINE IDENTIFICATION

Year	Model	Displacement Liters (cc)	Engine Series (ID/VIN)	Engine Fuel System	No. of Cylinders	Engine Type
1993	G20/G2500	6.2 (6210)	J	DSL	8	OHV
	G20/G2500	7.4 (7440)	N	TFI	8	OHV
	G30/G3500	4.3 (4293)	Z	TFI	6	OHV
	G30/G3500	5.0 (4999)	H	TFI	8	OHV
	G30/G3500	5.7 (5735)	K	TFI	8	OHV
	G30/G3500	6.2 (6210)	C	DSL	8	OHV
	G30/G3500	6.2 (6210)	J	DSL	8	OHV
	G30/G3500	7.4 (7440)	N	TFI	8	OHV
	K1500	4.3 (4293)	Z	TFI	6	OHV
	K1500	5.0 (4999)	H	TFI	8	OHV
	K1500	5.7 (5735)	K	TFI	8	OHV
	K1500	6.2 (6210)	C	DSL	8	OHV
	K1500	6.2 (6210)	J	DSL	8	OHV
	K1500	7.4 (7440)	N	TFI	8	OHV
	K2500	4.3 (4293)	Z	TFI	6	OHV
	K2500	5.0 (4999)	H	TFI	8	OHV
	K2500	5.7 (5735)	K	TFI	8	OHV
	K2500	6.2 (6210)	C	DSL	8	OHV
	K2500	6.2 (6210)	J	DSL	8	OHV
	K2500	6.5 (6505)	F	DSL	8	OHV
	K2500	7.4 (7440)	N	TFI	8	OHV
	K3500	4.3 (4293)	Z	TFI	6	OHV
	K3500	5.0 (4999)	H	TFI	8	OHV
	K3500	5.7 (5735)	K	TFI	8	OHV
	K3500	6.2 (6210)	C	DSL	8	OHV
	K3500	6.2 (6210)	J	DSL	8	OHV
	K3500	6.5 (6505)	F	DSL	8	OHV
	K3500	7.4 (7441)	N	TFI	8	OHV
	P30	4.3 (4293)	Z	TFI	6	OHV
	P30	5.7 (5735)	K	TFI	8	OHV
	P30	6.2 (6210)	J	DSL	8	OHV
	P30	7.4 (7440)	N	TFI	8	OHV
1994	Astro/Safari	4.3 (4293)	W	TFI	6	OHV
	Astro/Safari	4.3 (4293)	Z	TFI	6	OHV
	Blazer/Yukon	5.7 (5735)	K	MFI	8	OHV
	Blazer/Yukon	6.5 (6505)	S	DSL	8	OHV
	Lumina APV/Silhouette/Trans Sport	3.1 (3097)	D	TFI	6	OHV
	Lumina APV/Silhouette/Trans Sport	3.8 (3785)	L	MFI	6	OHV
	S10 Blazer	4.3 (4293)	Z	TFI	6	OHV
	S10 Blazer/S15Jimmy/Bravada	4.3 (4293)	W	MFI	6	OHV
	S10 Pick-up/Sonoma	2.2 (2189)	4	MFI	4	OHV
	S10 Pick-up/Sonoma	4.3 (4293)	W	MFI	6	OHV
	S10 Pick-up/Sonoma	4.3 (4293)	Z	MFI	6	OHV
	Suburban	5.7 (5735)	K	TFI	8	OHV
	Suburban	6.5 (6505)	F	DSL	8	OHV
	Suburban	7.4 (7440)	N	TFI	8	OHV
	C1500	4.3 (4293)	Z	TFI	6	OHV
	C1500	5.0 (4999)	H	TFI	8	OHV
	C1500	5.7 (5735)	K	TFI	8	OHV

ENGINE IDENTIFICATION

Year	Model	Displacement Liters (cc)	Engine Series (ID/VIN)	Engine Fuel System	No. of Cylinders	Engine Type
1994	C1500	6.5 (6505)	P	DSL	8	OHV
	C1500	6.5 (6505)	S	DSL	8	OHV
	C2500	4.3 (4293)	Z	TFI	6	OHV
	C2500	5.0 (4999)	H	TFI	8	OHV
	C2500	5.7 (5735)	K	TFI	8	OHV
	C2500	6.5 (6505)	F	DSL	8	OHV
	C2500	6.5 (6505)	P	DSL	8	OHV
	C2500	6.5 (6505)	S	DSL	8	OHV
	C2500	7.4 (7440)	N	TFI	8	OHV
	C3500	5.0 (4999)	H	TFI	8	OHV
	C3500	5.7 (5735)	K	TFI	8	OHV
	C3500	6.5 (6505)	F	DSL	8	OHV
	C3500	6.5 (6505)	S	DSL	8	OHV
	G20/G2500	4.3 (4293)	Z	TFI	6	OHV
	G20/G2500	5.0 (4999)	H	TFI	8	OHV
	G20/G2500	5.7 (5735)	K	TFI	8	OHV
	G20/G2500	6.5 (6505)	P	DSL	8	OHV
	G30/G3500	4.3 (4293)	Z	TFI	6	OHV
	G30/G3500	5.7 (5735)	K	TFI	8	OHV
	G30/G3500	6.5 (6505)	Y	DSL	8	OHV
	G30/G3500	7.4 (7440)	N	TFI	8	OHV
	K1500	4.3 (4293)	Z	TFI	6	OHV
	K1500	5.0 (4999)	H	TFI	8	OHV
	K1500	5.7 (5735)	K	TFI	8	OHV
	K1500	6.5 (6505)	P	DSL	8	OHV
	K1500	6.5 (6505)	S	DSL	8	OHV
	K1500	7.4 (7440)	N	TFI	8	OHV
	K2500	4.3 (4293)	Z	TFI	6	OHV
	K2500	5.0 (4999)	H	TFI	8	OHV
	K2500	5.7 (5735)	K	TFI	8	OHV
	K2500	6.5 (6505)	P	DSL	8	OHV
	K2500	6.5 (6505)	S	DSL	8	OHV
	K2500	6.5 (6505)	F	DSL	8	OHV
	K2500	7.4 (7440)	N	TFI	8	OHV
	K3500	5.7 (5735)	K	TFI	8	OHV
	K3500	6.5 (6505)	F	DSL	8	OHV
	K3500	7.4 (7440)	N	TFI	8	OHV
	P30	4.3 (4293)	Z	TFI	6	OHV
	P30	5.7 (5735)	K	TFI	8	OHV
	P30	6.5 (6505)	F	DSL	8	OHV
	P30	6.5 (6505)	Y	DSL	8	OHV
	P30	7.4 (7440)	N	TFI	8	OHV
1995-96	Astro	4.3 (4293)	W	TFI	6	OHV
	Astro	4.3 (4293)	Z	TFI	6	OHV
	Lumina APV/Silhouette/Trans Sport	3.1 (3097)	D	TFI	6	OHV
	Lumina APV/Silhouette/Trans Sport	3.8 (3785)	L	MFI	6	OHV
	S10 Blazer	4.3 (4293)	Z	TFI	6	OHV
	S10 Blazer/S15 Jimmy	4.3 (4293)	W	MFI	6	OHV

ENGINE IDENTIFICATION

Year	Model	Displacement Liters (cc)	Engine Series (ID/VIN)	Engine Fuel System	No. of Cylinders	Engine Type
1995-96	S10 Pick-up/Sonoma	2.2 (2189)	4	MFI	4	OHV
	S10 Pick-up/Sonoma	4.3 (4293)	W	MFI	6	OHV
	S10 Pick-up/Sonoma	4.3 (4293)	Z	MFI	6	OHV
	Suburban	5.7 (5735)	K	TFI	8	OHV
	Suburban	6.5 (6505)	F	DSL	8	OHV
	Suburban	7.4 (7440)	N	TFI	8	OHV
	Tahoe/Yukon	5.7 (5735)	K	MFI	8	OHV
	Tahoe/Yukon	6.5 (6505)	S	DSL	8	OHV
	C1500	4.3 (4293)	Z	TFI	6	OHV
	C1500	5.0 (4999)	H	TFI	8	OHV
	C1500	5.7 (5735)	K	TFI	8	OHV
	C1500	6.5 (6505)	P	DSL	8	OHV
	C1500	6.5 (6505)	S	DSL	8	OHV
	C2500	4.3 (4293)	Z	TFI	6	OHV
	C2500	5.0 (4999)	H	TFI	8	OHV
	C2500	5.7 (5735)	K	TFI	8	OHV
	C2500	6.5 (6505)	F	DSL	8	OHV
	C2500	6.5 (6505)	P	DSL	8	OHV
	C2500	6.5 (6505)	S	DSL	8	OHV
	C2500	7.4 (7440)	N	TFI	8	OHV
	C3500	5.0 (4999)	H	TFI	8	OHV
	C3500	5.7 (5735)	K	TFI	8	OHV
	C3500	6.5 (6505)	F	DSL	8	OHV
	C3500	6.5 (6505)	S	DSL	8	OHV
	C3500	7.4 (7440)	N	TFI	8	OHV
	G20/G2500	4.3 (4293)	Z	TFI	6	OHV
	G20/G2500	5.0 (4999)	H	TFI	8	OHV
	G20/G2500	5.7 (5735)	K	TFI	8	OHV
	G20/G2500	6.5 (6505)	P	DSL	8	OHV
	G30/G3500	4.3 (4293)	Z	TFI	6	OHV
	G30/G3500	5.7 (5735)	K	TFI	8	OHV
	G30/G3500	6.5 (6505)	Y	DSL	8	OHV
	G30/G3500	7.4 (7440)	N	TFI	8	OHV
	K1500	4.3 (4293)	Z	TFI	6	OHV
	K1500	5.0 (4999)	H	TFI	8	OHV
	K1500	5.7 (5735)	K	TFI	8	OHV
	K1500	6.5 (6505)	P	DSL	8	OHV
	K1500	6.5 (6505)	S	DSL	8	OHV
	K1500	7.4 (7440)	N	TFI	8	OHV
	K2500	4.3 (4293)	Z	TFI	6	OHV
	K2500	5.0 (4999)	H	TFI	8	OHV
	K2500	5.7 (5735)	K	TFI	8	OHV
	K2500	6.5 (6505)	P	DSL	8	OHV
	K2500	6.5 (6505)	S	DSL	8	OHV
	K2500	6.5 (6505)	F	DSL	8	OHV
	K2500	7.4 (7440)	N	TFI	8	OHV
	K3500	5.7 (5735)	K	TFI	8	OHV
	K3500	6.5 (6505)	F	DSL	8	OHV

ENGINE IDENTIFICATION

Year	Model	Displacement Liters (cc)	Engine Series (ID/VIN)	Engine Fuel System	No. of Cylinders	Engine Type
	K3500	7.4 (7440)	N	TFI	8	OHV
	P30	4.3 (4293)	Z	TFI	6	OHV
	P30	5.7 (5735)	K	TFI	8	OHV
	P30	6.5 (6505)	F	DSL	8	OHV
	P30	6.5 (6505)	Y	DSL	8	OHV
	P30	7.4 (7440)	N	TFI	8	OHV

TFI - Throttle body fuel injection
MFI - Multiport fuel injection

DSL - Diesel
OHV - Overhead valve

GENERAL ENGINE SPECIFICATIONS

Year	Engine ID/VIN	Engine Displacement Liters (cc)	Fuel System Type	Net Horsepower @ rpm	Net Torque @ rpm (ft. lbs.)	Bore x Stroke (in.)	Compression Ratio	Oil Pressure @ rpm
1992	A	2.5 (2474)	TFI	105@4800	135@3200	4.00x3.00	8.3:1	41@2000
	R	2.8 (2835)	TFI	125@4800	150@2200	3.56x3.04	8.5:1	50@2000
	D	3.1 (3130)	TFI	120@4400	175@2200	3.50x3.30	8.9:1	15@1100
	L	3.8 (3785)	MFI	165@4300	220@3200	3.80x3.40	8.5:1	60@1850
	W	4.3 (4293)	TFI	200@4500	260@3600	4.00x3.48	9.1:1	18@2000
	Z	4.3 (4293)	TFI	1	2	4.00x3.48	9.3:1	18@2000
	H	5.0 (4999)	TFI	165@4400	240@2000	3.74x3.48	9.0:1	18@2000
	K	5.7 (5735)	TFI	3	4	4.00x3.48	8.5:1	18@2000
	C	6.2 (6210)	DSL	130@3600	240@2000	3.98x3.80	21.3:1	35@2000
	J	6.2 (6210)	DSL	135@3600	240@2000	3.98x3.80	21.3:1	350@2000
	F	6.5 (6473)	DSL	5	6	4.05x3.80	21.0:1	40-45@2000
	N	7.4 (7440)	TFI	230@3600	385@1600	4.25x4.00	8.0:1	40@2000
1993	A	2.5 (2474)	TFI	105@4800	135@3200	4.00x3.00	8.3:1	41@2000
	R	2.8 (2835)	TFI	125@2800	150@2200	3.56x3.04	8.5:1	50@2000
	D	3.1 (3130)	TFI	120@4400	175@2200	3.50x3.30	8.9:1	15@1100
	L	3.8 (3785)	MFI	165@4300	220@3200	3.80x3.40	8.5:1	60@1850
	W	4.3 (4293)	TFI	200@4500	260@3600	4.00x3.48	9.1:1	18@2000
	Z	4.3 (4293)	TFI	1	2	4.00x3.48	9.3:1	18@2000
	H	5.0 (4999)	TFI	165@4400	240@2000	3.74x3.48	9.0:1	18@2000
	K	5.7 (5735)	TFI	3	4	4.00x3.48	8.5:1	18@2000
	C	6.2 (6210)	DSL	130@3600	240@2000	3.98x3.80	21.3:1	35@2000
	J	6.2 (6210)	DSL	135@3600	240@2000	3.98x3.80	21.3:1	35@2000
	F	6.5 (6473)	DSL	5	6	4.05x3.80	21.0:1	40-45@2000
	N	7.4 (7440)	TFI	230@3600	385@1600	4.25x4.00	8.0:1	40@2000
1994	4	2.2 (2189)	MFI	118@5200	130@2800	3.50x3.46	9.0:1	56@3000
	D	3.1 (3130)	TFI	120@4400	175@2200	3.50x3.30	8.9:1	15@1100
	L	3.8 (3785)	MFI	165@4300	220@3200	3.80x3.40	8.5:1	60@1850
	W	4.3 (4293)	TFI	200@4500	260@3600	4.00x3.48	9.1:1	18@2000
	Z	4.3 (4293)	MFI	1	2	4.00x3.48	9.1:1	18@2000
	Z	4.3 (4293)	TFI	1	2	4.00x3.48	9.1:1	18@2000
	H	5.0 (4999)	TFI	175@4200	265@2800	3.74x3.48	9.0:1	18@2000
	K	5.7 (5735)	MFI	3	4	4.00x3.48	9.1:1	18@2000

GENERAL ENGINE SPECIFICATIONS

Year	Engine ID/VIN	Engine Displacement Liters (cc)	Fuel System Type	Net Horsepower @ rpm	Net Torque @ rpm (ft. lbs.)	Bore x Stroke (in.)	Compression Ratio	Oil Pressure @ rpm
	K	5.7 (5735)	TFI	3	4	4.00x3.48	9.1:1	18@2000
	F	6.5 (6473)	DSL	5	6	4.05x3.80	21.5:1	40-45@2000
	P	6.5 (6473)	DSL	190@3400	385@1700	4.06x3.82	21.5:1	40-45@2000
	S	6.5 (6473)	DSL	190@3400	275@1700	4.06x3.82	21.5:1	40-45@2000
	Y	6.5 (6473)	DSL	7	8	4.06x3.82	21.5:1	40-45@2000
	N	7.4 (7440)	TFI	230@3600	385@1600	4.25x4.00	8.0:1	40@2000
1995-96	4	2.2 (2189)	MFI	118@5200	130@2800	3.50x3.46	9.0:1	56@3000
	D	3.1 (3130)	TFI	120@4400	175@2200	3.50x3.30	8.9:1	15@1100
	L	3.8 (3785)	MFI	165@4300	220@3200	3.80x3.40	8.5:1	60@1850
	W	4.3 (4293)	TFI	200@4500	260@3600	4.00x3.48	9.1:1	18@2000
	Z	4.3 (4293)	MFI	1	2	4.00x3.48	9.1:1	18@2000
	Z	4.3 (4293)	TFI	1	2	4.00x3.48	9.1:1	18@2000
	H	5.0 (4999)	TFI	175@4200	265@2800	3.74x3.48	9.0:1	18@2000
	K	5.7 (5735)	MFI	3	4	4.00x3.48	9.1:1	18@2000
	K	5.7 (5735)	TFI	3	4	4.00x3.48	9.1:1	18@2000
	F	6.5 (6473)	DSL	5	6	4.05x3.80	21.5:1	40-45@2000
	P	6.5 (6473)	DSL	190@3400	385@1700	4.06x3.82	21.5:1	40-45@2000
	S	6.5 (6473)	DSL	190@3400	275@1700	4.06x3.82	21.5:1	40-45@2000
	Y	6.5 (6473)	DSL	7	8	4.06x3.82	21.5:1	40-45@2000
	N	7.4 (7440)	TFI	230@3600	385@1600	4.25x4.00	8.0:1	40@2000

TFI - Throttle body fuel injection
MFI - Multiport fuel injection
DSL - Diesel

1   S10, C/K Pick-up: 160@4000
    C/K HD Pick-up: 155@4000
    G Van: 150@4000
2   S10: 230@2800
    C/K Pick-up: 235@2400
    C/K HD Pick-up and G Van: 230@2400
3   Below 8500 GVWR: 210@4000
    Above 8500 GVWR: 190@4000

4   Below 8500 GVWR: 300@2800
    Above 8500 GVWR: 300@2400
5   Below 15,000 GVWR: 180@3400
    Above 15,000 GVWR: 190@3400
6   Below 15,000 GVWR: 380@1700
    Above 15,000 GVWR: 360@1700
7   Below 8500 GVWR: 155@3600
    Above 8500 GVWR: 160@3600
8   Below 8500 GVWR: 275@1700
    Above 8500 GVWR: 290@1700

GASOLINE ENGINE TUNE-UP SPECIFICATIONS

Year	Engine ID/VIN	Engine Displacement Liters (cc)	Spark Plugs Gap (in.)	Ignition Timing (deg.) MT	Ignition Timing (deg.) AT	Fuel Pump (psi)		Idle Speed (rpm) MT	Idle Speed (rpm) AT	Valve Clearance In.	Valve Clearance Ex.
1992	A	2.5 (2474)	0.060	1	1	9-13		1	1	HYD	HYD
	R	2.8 (2835)	0.040	1	1	9-13		1	1	HYD	HYD
	D	3.1 (3130)	0.045	1	1	9-13		1	1	HYD	HYD
	L	3.8 (3785)	0.060	1	1	41-47	2	1	1	HYD	HYD
	W	4.3 (4293)	0.035	1	1	9-13		1	1	HYD	HYD
	Z	4.3 (4293)	0.035	1	1	9-13		1	1	HYD	HYD
	H	5.0 (4999)	0.045	1	1	9-13		1	1	HYD	HYD
	K	5.7 (5735)	0.045	1	1	9-13		1	1	HYD	HYD
	N	7.4 (7440)	0.045	1	1	9-13		1	1	HYD	HYD
1993	A	2.5 (2474)	0.060	1	1	9-13		1	1	HYD	HYD
	R	2.8 (2835)	0.040	1	1	9-13		1	1	HYD	HYD
	D	3.1 (3130)	0.045	1	1	9-13		1	1	HYD	HYD
	L	3.8 (3785)	0.060	1	1	41-47	2	1	1	HYD	HYD
	W	4.3 (4293)	0.035	1	1	9-13		1	1	HYD	HYD
	Z	4.3 (4293)	0.035	1	1	9-13		1	1	HYD	HYD
	H	5.0 (4999)	0.045	1	1	9-13		1	1	HYD	HYD
	K	5.7 (5735)	0.045	1	1	9-13		1	1	HYD	HYD
	N	7.4 (7440)	0.045	1	1	9-13		1	1	HYD	HYD
1994	4	2.2 (2189)	NA	1	1	9-13		1	1	HYD	HYD
	D	3.1 (3130)	0.045	1	1	9-13		1	1	HYD	HYD
	L	3.8 (3785)	0.060	1	1	41-47	2	1	1	HYD	HYD
	W	4.3 (4293)	0.035	1	1	9-13		1	1	HYD	HYD
	Z	4.3 (4293)	0.035	1	1	9-13		1	1	HYD	HYD
	H	5.0 (4999)	0.045	1	1	9-13		1	1	HYD	HYD
	K	5.7 (5735)	0.045	1	1	9-13		1	1	HYD	HYD
	N	7.4 (7440)	0.045	1	1	9-13		1	1	HYD	HYD
1995-96	4	2.2 (2189)	NA	1	1	9-13		1	1	HYD	HYD
	D	3.1 (3130)	0.045	1	1	9-13		1	1	HYD	HYD
	L	3.8 (3785)	0.060	1	1	41-47	2	1	1	HYD	HYD
	W	4.3 (4293)	0.035	1	1	9-13		1	1	HYD	HYD
	Z	4.3 (4293)	0.035	1	1	9-13		1	1	HYD	HYD
	H	5.0 (4999)	0.045	1	1	9-13		1	1	HYD	HYD
	K	5.7 (5735)	0.045	1	1	9-13		1	1	HYD	HYD
	N	7.4 (7440)	0.045	1	1	9-13		1	1	HYD	HYD

NOTE: The Vehicle Emission Control Information label often reflects specification changes made during production. The label figures must be used if they differ from those in this chart.

HYD - Hydraulic

1   Refer to underhood label for exact setting

2   With key on and engine off

DIESEL ENGINE TUNE-UP SPECIFICATIONS

Year	Engine ID/VIN	Engine Displacement cu. in. (cc)	Valve Clearance Intake (in.)	Valve Clearance Exhaust (in.)	Intake Valve Opens (deg.)	Injection Pump Setting (deg.)	Injection Nozzle Pressure (psi) New	Injection Nozzle Pressure (psi) Used	Idle Speed (rpm)	Cranking Compression Pressure (psi)
1992	C	6.2 (6210)	HYD	HYD	2	1	1600	1500	2	NA
	J	6.2 (6210)	HYD	HYD	2	1	1600	1500	2	NA
	F	6.5 (6473)	HYD	HYD	2	2	1600	1500	2	NA
1993	C	6.2 (6210)	HYD	HYD	2	1	1600	1500	2	NA
	J	6.2 (6210)	HYD	HYD	2	1	1600	1500	2	NA
	F	6.5 (6473)	HYD	HYD	2	2	1600	1500	2	NA
1994	F	6.5 (6473)	HYD	HYD	2	2	1600	1500	2	NA
	P	6.5 (6473)	HYD	HYD	2	2	1800	1700	2	NA
	S	6.5 (6473)	HYD	HYD	2	2	1800	1700	2	NA
	Y	6.5 (6473)	HYD	HYD	2	2	1600	1500	2	NA
1995-96	F	6.5 (6473)	HYD	HYD	2	2	1600	1500	2	NA
	P	6.5 (6473)	HYD	HYD	2	2	1800	1700	2	NA
	S	6.5 (6473)	HYD	HYD	2	2	1800	1700	2	NA
	Y	6.5 (6473)	HYD	HYD	2	2	1600	1500	2	NA

NOTE: The Vehicle Emission Control Information label often reflects specification changes made during production. The label figures must be used if they differ from those in this chart

HYD - Hydraulic

NA - Not Available

1 Set by aligning marks on top of engine front cover and injection pump flange

2 Refer to underhood label

CAPACITIES

Year	Model	Engine ID/VIN	Engine Displacement Liters (cc)	Oil with Filter (qts.)	Engine Transmission (pts.) 4-Spd	Engine Transmission (pts.) 5-Spd	Engine Transmission (pts.) Auto.	Transfer Case (pts.)	Drive Axle Front (pts.)	Drive Axle Rear (pts.)	Fuel Tank (gal.)	Cooling System (qts.)
1992	Astro/Safari	W	4.3 (4293)	5.0	-	4.4	10.0	-	-	3.8	27.0	13.5 3
	Astro/Safari	Z	4.3 (4293)	5.0	-	4.4	10.0	-	-	3.8	27.0	13.5 3
	Blazer	K	5.7 (5735)	5.0	-	-	2	10.0	4.0	4	25.0 5	18.0
	Bravada	Z	4.3 (4293)	4.5	-	-	10.0	3.2	3.5	3.5	20.0	12.0
	Lumina APV/Silhouette/Trans Sport	D	3.1 (3130)	4.5	-	-	8.0	-	-	-	20.0	13.4
	Lumina APV/Silhouette/Trans Sport	L	3.8 (3785)	4.5	-	-	12.0	-	-	-	20.0	13.4
	S10 Blazer/S15 Jimmy	W	4.3 (4293)	4.5	-	-	10.0	-	3.5	3.5	20.0	12.0
	S10 Blazer/S15 Jimmy	Z	4.3 (4293)	5.0	-	4.4	10.0	4.6	3.5	3.5	20.0	12.1
	S10 Pick-up/Sonoma	A	2.5 (2474)	4.0	-	4.4	10.0	2.2	3.5	3.5	13.0 13	11.5
	S10 Pick-up/Sonoma	Z	2.8 (2835)	4.0	-	4.4	10.0	2.2	3.5	3.5	13.0 13	10.5
	S10 Pick-up/Sonoma	R	4.3 (4293)	5.0	-	4.4	10.0	2.2	3.5	3.5	20.0	12.1
	Suburban	K	5.7 (5735)	5.0	-	-	2	10.0	4.0	4	25.0 14	18.0
	Suburban	N	7.4 (7440)	6.0	-	-	2	10.0	4.0	4	25.0 14	24.5
	Syclone	Z	4.3 (4293)	4.5	-	-	10.0	3.2	3.5	3.5	20.0	13.5
	Typhoon	Z	4.3 (4293)	4.5	-	-	10.0	3.2	3.5	3.5	20.0	13.5
	C1500	Z	4.3 (4293)	5.0	-	1	2	-	-	4	6	11.0
	C1500	H	5.0 (4999)	5.0	-	1	2	-	-	4	6	18.0
	C1500	K	5.7 (5735)	5.0	-	1	2	-	-	4	6	18.0
	C1500	C	6.2 (6210)	7.0	-	1	2	-	-	4	6	25.0
	C1500	J	6.2 (6210)	7.0	-	1	2	-	-	4	6	25.0
	C1500	N	7.4 (7440)	6.0	-	1	2	-	-	4	6	25.0
	C2500	Z	4.3 (4293)	5.0	-	1	2	-	-	4	6	11.0

CAPACITIES

Year	Model	Engine ID/VIN	Engine Displacement Liters (cc)	Oil with Filter (qts.)	Engine Transmission (pts.)			Transfer Case (pts.)	Drive Axle		Fuel Tank (gal.)	Cooling System (qts.)
					4-Spd	5-Spd	Auto.		Front (pts.)	Rear (pts.)		
1992	C2500	H	5.0 (4999)	5.0	-	1	2	-	-	4	6	18.0
	C2500	K	5.7 (5735)	5.0	-	1	2	-	-	4	6	18.0
	C2500	C	6.2 (6210)	7.0	-	1	2	-	-	4	6	25.0
	C2500	J	6.2 (6210)	7.0	-	1	2	-	-	4	6	25.0
	C2500	F	6.5 (6473)	7.0	-	1	2	-	-	4	6	26.5
	C3500	H	5.0 (4999)	5.0	-	1	2	-	-	4	6	18.0
	C3500	K	5.7 (5735)	5.0	-	1	2	-	-	4	6	18.0
	C3500	C	6.2 (6210)	7.0	-	1	2	-	-	4	6	25.0
	C3500	J	6.2 (6210)	7.0	-	1	2	-	-	4	6	25.0
	C3500	F	6.5 (6473)	7.0	-	1	2	-	-	4	6	26.5
	C3500	N	7.4 (7440)	6.0	-	1	2	-	-	4	6	25.0 [7]
	G10/G1500	Z	4.3 (4293)	5.0	-	-	2	-	-	4	22.0 [8]	11.0 [9]
	G10/G1500	H	5.0 (4999)	5.0	-	-	2	-	-	4	22.0 [8]	17.0 [9]
	G10/G1500	K	5.7 (5735)	5.0	-	-	2	-	-	4	10	18.0 [9]
	G20/G2500	Z	4.3 (4293)	5.0	-	-	2	-	-	4	22.0 [8]	11.0 [9]
	G20/G2500	H	5.0 (4999)	5.0	-	-	2	-	-	4	22.0 [8]	17.0 [9]
	G20/G2500	K	5.7 (5735)	5.0	-	-	2	-	-	4	10	18.0 [9]
	G30/G3500	Z	4.3 (4293)	5.0	-	-	2	-	-	4	22.0 [8]	11.0 [9]
	G30/G3500	K	5.7 (5735)	5.0	-	-	2	-	-	4	10	18.0 [9]
	G30/G3500	C	6.2 (6210)	7.0	-	-	2	-	-	4	22.0 [8]	24.0 [9]
	G30/G3500	J	6.2 (6210)	7.0	-	-	2	-	-	4	22.0 [8]	24.0 [9]
	G30/G3500	N	7.4 (7440)	6.0	-	-	2	-	-	11	12	24.5 [9]
	K1500	Z	4.3 (4293)	5.0	-	1	2	-	-	4	6	11.0
	K1500	H	5.0 (4999)	5.0	-	1	2	-	-	4	6	18.0
	K1500	K	5.7 (5735)	5.0	-	1	2	-	-	4	6	18.0
	K1500	C	6.2 (6210)	7.0	-	1	2	-	-	4	6	25.0
	K1500	N	7.4 (7440)	6.0	-	1	2	-	-	4	6	25.0 [7]
	K2500	Z	4.3 (4293)	5.0	-	1	2	-	-	4	6	11.0
	K2500	H	5.0 (4999)	5.0	-	1	2	-	-	4	6	18.0
	K2500	K	5.7 (5735)	5.0	-	1	2	-	-	4	6	18.0
	K2500	C	6.2 (6210)	7.0	-	1	2	-	-	4	6	25.0
	K2500	J	6.2 (6210)	7.0	-	1	2	-	-	4	6	25.0
	K2500	N	7.4 (7440)	6.0	-	1	2	-	-	4	6	25.0 [7]
	K3500	K	5.7 (5735)	5.0	-	1	2	-	-	4	6	18.0
	K3500	N	7.4 (7440)	6.0	-	1	2	-	-	4	6	25.0 [7]
	K3500	J	6.2 (6210)	7.0	-	1	2	-	-	4	6	25.0
	P30	Z	4.3 (4293)	5.0	-	4.4	10.0	4.6	2.6	3.8	18.0	13.4
	P30	K	5.7 (5735)	5.0	-	3.6	2	-	-	4	10	18.0
	P30	J	6.2 (6210)	7.0	-	3.6	2	-	-	11	12	25.0
	P30	N	7.4 (7440)	5.0	-	3.6	2	-	-	4	10	18.0
1993	Astro/Safari	W	4.3 (4293)	5.0	-	4.4	10.0	-	-	3.8	27.0	13.5 [3]
	Astro/Safari	Z	4.3 (4293)	5.0	-	4.4	10.0	-	-	3.8	27.0	13.5 [3]
	Blazer/Yukon	K	5.7 (5735)	5.0	-	-	2	10.0	4.0	4	25.0 [5]	18.0
	Bravada	Z	4.3 (4293)	4.5	-	-	10.0	3.2	3.5	3.5	20.0	12.0
	Lumina APV/Silhouette/Trans Sport	D	3.1 (3130)	4.5	-	-	8.0	-	-	-	20.0	13.4
	Lumina APV/Silhouette/Trans Sport	L	3.8 (3785)	4.5	-	-	12.0	-	-	-	20.0	13.4
	S10 Blazer/S15 Jimmy	W	4.3 (4293)	4.5	-	-	10.0	-	3.5	3.5	20.0	12.0
	S10 Blazer/S15 Jimmy	Z	4.3 (4293)	5.0	-	4.4	10.0	4.6	3.5	3.5	20.0	12.1
	S10 Pick-up/Sonoma	A	2.5 (2474)	4.0	-	4.4	10.0	4.6	3.5	3.9	13.0 [13]	11.5
	S10 Pick-up/Sonoma	R	2.8 (2835)	4.0	-	4.5	10.0	4.6	3.5	3.9	13.0 [13]	10.5
	S10 Pick-up/Sonoma	W	4.3 (4293)	4.5	-	4.4	10.0	4.4	2.6	3.9	20.0 [14]	12.1
	Typhoon	Z	4.3 (4293)	4.5	-	-	10.0	3.2	3.5	3.5	20.0	13.5
	C1500	Z	4.3 (4293)	5.0	-	1	2	-	-	4	6	11.0

CAPACITIES

Year	Model	Engine ID/VIN	Engine Displacement Liters (cc)	Oil with Filter (qts.)	Engine Transmission (pts.)			Transfer Case (pts.)	Drive Axle		Fuel Tank (gal.)	Cooling System (qts.)
					4-Spd	5-Spd	Auto.		Front (pts.)	Rear (pts.)		
1993	C1500	H	5.0 (4999)	5.0	-	1	2	-	-	4	6	18.0
	C1500	K	5.7 (5735)	5.0	-	1	2	-	-	4	6	18.0
	C1500	C	6.2 (6210)	7.0	-	1	2	-	-	4	6	25.0
	C1500	J	6.2 (6210)	7.0	-	1	2	-	-	4	6	25.0
	C1500	N	7.4 (7440)	6.0	-	1	2	-	-	4	6	25.0
	C2500	Z	4.3 (4293)	5.0	-	1	2	-	-	4	6	11.0
	C2500	H	5.0 (4999)	5.0	-	1	2	-	-	4	6	18.0
	C2500	K	5.7 (5735)	5.0	-	1	2	-	-	4	6	18.0
	C2500	C	6.2 (6210)	7.0	-	1	2	-	-	4	6	25.0
	C2500	J	6.2 (6210)	7.0	-	1	2	-	-	4	6	25.0
	C2500	F	6.5 (6473)	7.0	-	1	2	-	-	4	6	26.5
	C3500	H	5.0 (4999)	5.0	-	1	2	-	-	4	6	18.0
	C3500	K	5.7 (5735)	5.0	-	1	2	-	-	4	6	18.0
	C3500	C	6.2 (6210)	7.0	-	1	2	-	-	4	6	25.0
	C3500	J	6.2 (6210)	7.0	-	1	2	-	-	4	6	25.0
	C3500	F	6.5 (6473)	7.0	-	1	2	-	-	4	6	26.5
	C3500	N	7.4 (7440)	6.0	-	1	2	-	-	4	6	25.0 [7]
	G10/G1500	Z	4.3 (4293)	5.0	-	-	2	-	-	4	22.0 [8]	11.0 [9]
	G10/G1500	H	5.0 (4999)	5.0	-	-	2	-	-	4	22.0 [8]	17.0 [9]
	G10/G1500	K	5.7 (5735)	5.0	-	-	2	-	-	4	15	18.0 [9]
	G10/G1500	C	6.2 (6210)	7.0	-	-	2	-	-	4	22.0 [8]	24.0 [9]
	G10/G1500	J	6.2 (6210)	7.0	-	-	2	-	-	4	22.0 [8]	24.0 [9]
	G20/G2500	Z	4.3 (4293)	5.0	-	-	2	-	-	4	22.0 [8]	11.0 [9]
	G20/G2500	H	5.0 (4999)	5.0	-	-	2	-	-	4	22.0 [8]	17.0 [9]
	G20/G2500	K	5.7 (5735)	5.0	-	-	2	-	-	4	15	18.0 [9]
	G20/G2500	C	6.2 (6210)	7.0	-	-	2	-	-	4	22.0 [8]	24.0 [9]
	G20/G2500	J	6.2 (6210)	7.0	-	-	2	-	-	4	22.0 [8]	24.0 [9]
	G30/G3500	Z	4.3 (4293)	5.0	-	-	2	-	-	4	22.0 [8]	11.0 [9]
	G30/G3500	K	5.7 (5735)	5.0	-	-	2	-	-	4	15	18.0 [9]
	G30/G3500	C	6.2 (6210)	7.0	-	-	2	-	-	4	22.0 [8]	24.0 [9]
	G30/G3500	J	6.2 (6210)	7.0	-	-	2	-	-	4	22.0 [8]	24.0 [9]
	G30/G3500	N	7.4 (7440)	6.0	-	-	2	-	-	11	12	24.5 [9]
	K1500	Z	4.3 (4293)	5.0	-	1	2	-	-	4	6	11.0
	K1500	H	5.0 (4999)	5.0	-	1	2	-	-	4	6	18.0
	K1500	K	5.7 (5735)	5.0	-	1	2	-	-	4	6	18.0
	K1500	C	6.2 (6210)	7.0	-	1	2	-	-	4	6	25.0
	K1500	N	7.4 (7440)	6.0	-	1	2	-	-	4	6	25.0 [7]
	K2500	Z	4.3 (4293)	5.0	-	1	2	-	-	4	6	11.0
	K2500	H	5.0 (4999)	5.0	-	1	2	-	-	4	6	18.0
	K2500	K	5.7 (5735)	5.0	-	1	2	-	-	4	6	18.0
	K2500	C	6.2 (6210)	7.0	-	1	2	-	-	4	6	25.0
	K2500	J	6.2 (6210)	7.0	-	1	2	-	-	4	6	25.0
	K2500	F	6.5 (6473)	7.0	-	1	2	-	-	4	6	26.5
	K2500	N	7.4 (7440)	6.0	-	1	2	-	-	4	6	25.0 [7]
	K3500	H	5.0 (4999)	5.0	-	1	2	-	-	4	6	18.0
	K3500	K	5.7 (5735)	5.0	-	1	2	-	-	4	6	18.0
	K3500	C	6.2 (6210)	7.0	-	1	2	-	-	4	6	25.0
	K3500	J	6.2 (6210)	7.0	-	1	2	-	-	4	6	25.0
	K3500	F	6.5 (6473)	7.0	-	1	2	-	-	4	6	26.5
	K3500	N	7.4 (7440)	6.0	-	1	2	-	-	4	6	25.0 [7]
	P30	Z	4.3 (4293)	5.0	-	4.4	10.0	4.6	2.6	3.8	18.0	13.4
	P30	K	5.7 (5735)	5.0	-	3.6	2	-	-	4	15	18.0
	P30	J	6.2 (6210)	7.0	-	3.6	2	-	-	11	12	25.0
	P30	N	7.4 (7440)	5.0	-	3.6	2	-	-	4	15	18.0

CAPACITIES

Year	Model	Engine ID/VIN	Engine Displacement Liters (cc)	Oil with Filter (qts.)	Engine Transmission (pts.) 4-Spd	5-Spd	Auto.	Transfer Case (pts.)	Drive Axle Front (pts.)	Rear (pts.)	Fuel Tank (gal.)	Cooling System (qts.)
1994	Astro/Safari	W	4.3 (4293)	5.0	-	4.4	10.0	-	-	3.8	27.0	13.5 3
	Astro/Safari	Z	4.3 (4293)	5.0	-	4.4	10.0	-	-	3.8	27.0	13.5 3
	Blazer/Yukon	K	5.7 (5735)	5.0	-	-	2	10.0	4.0	4	25.0 5	18.0
	Blazer/Yukon	F	6.5 (6473)	7.0	-	1	2	-	-	4	6	26.5
	Bravada	Z	4.3 (4293)	4.5	-	-	10.0	3.2	3.5	3.5	20.0	12.0
	Lumina APV/Silhouette/Trans Sport	D	3.1 (3130)	4.5	-	-	8.0	-	-	-	20.0	13.4
	Lumina APV/Silhouette/Trans Sport	L	3.8 (3785)	4.5	-	-	12.0	-	-	-	20.0	13.4
	S10 Blazer/S15 Jimmy	W	4.3 (4293)	4.5	-	-	10.0	-	3.5	3.5	20.0	12.0
	S10 Blazer/S15 Jimmy	Z	4.3 (4293)	5.0	-	4.4	10.0	4.6	3.5	3.5	20.0	12.1
	S10 Pick-up/Sonoma	4	2.2 (2189)	4.0	-	4.4	10.0	4.6	3.5	3.5	13.0 13	11.5
	S10 Pick-up/Sonoma	W	4.3 (4293)	4.5	-	4.4	10.0	4.6	3.5	3.5	20.0	12.0
	S10 Pick-up/Sonoma	Z	4.3 (4293)	5.0	-	4.4	10.0	4.6	3.5	3.5	20.0	12.0
	Suburban	K	5.7 (5735)	5.0	-	-	2	10.0	4.0	4	25.0 14	18.0
	Suburban	P	6.5 (6505)	7.0	-	1	2	-	-	4	6	25.0
	Suburban	S	6.5 (6505)	7.0	-	1	2	-	-	4	6	25.0
	Suburban	N	7.4 (7440)	6.0	-	-	2	10.0	4.0	4	25.0 14	24.5
	C1500	Z	4.3 (4293)	5.0	-	1	2	-	-	4	6	11.0
	C1500	H	5.0 (4999)	5.0	-	1	2	-	-	4	6	18.0
	C1500	K	5.7 (5735)	5.0	-	1	2	-	-	4	6	18.0
	C1500	F	6.5 (6473)	7.0	-	1	2	-	-	4	6	26.5
	C1500	N	7.4 (7440)	6.0	-	1	2	-	-	4	6	25.0
	C2500	Z	4.3 (4293)	5.0	-	1	2	-	-	4	6	11.0
	C2500	H	5.0 (4999)	5.0	-	1	2	-	-	4	6	18.0
	C2500	K	5.7 (5735)	5.0	-	1	2	-	-	4	6	18.0
	C2500	P	6.5 (6473)	7.0	-	1	2	-	-	4	6	26.5
	C2500	S	6.5 (6473)	7.0	-	1	2	-	-	4	6	26.5
	C3500	H	5.0 (4999)	5.0	-	1	2	-	-	4	6	18.0
	C3500	K	5.7 (5735)	5.0	-	1	2	-	-	4	6	18.0
	C3500	F	6.5 (6473)	7.0	-	1	2	-	-	4	6	26.5
	C3500	P	6.5 (6473)	7.0	-	1	2	-	-	4	6	26.5
	C3500	S	6.5 (6473)	7.0	-	1	2	-	-	4	6	26.5
	C3500	N	7.4 (7440)	6.0	-	1	2	-	-	4	6	25.0 7
	G10	Z	4.3 (4293)	5.0	-	1	2	-	-	4	22.0 8	11.0 9
	G10	H	5.0 (4999)	5.0	-	1	2	-	-	4	22.0 8	17.0 9
	G10	K	5.7 (5735)	5.0	-	1	2	-	-	4	16	18.0 9
	G10	P	6.5 (6505)	7.0	-	1	2	-	-	4	22.0 8	24.0 9
	G10	S	6.5 (6505)	7.0	-	1	2	-	-	4	22.0 8	24.0 9
	G20	Z	4.3 (4293)	5.0	-	1	2	-	-	4	22.0 8	11.0 9
	G20	H	5.0 (4999)	5.0	-	1	2	-	-	4	22.0 8	17.0 9
	G20	K	5.7 (5735)	5.0	-	1	2	-	-	4	16	18.0 9
	G20	P	6.5 (6505)	7.0	-	1	2	-	-	4	22.0 8	24.0 9
	G20	Y	6.5 (6505)	7.0	-	1	2	-	-	4	22.0 8	24.0 9
	G30	Z	4.3 (4293)	5.0	-	1	2	-	-	4	22.0 8	11.0 9
	G30	K	5.7 (5735)	5.0	-	1	2	-	-	4	16	18.0 9
	G30	P	6.5 (6505)	7.0	-	1	2	-	-	4	22.0 8	24.0 9
	G30	Y	6.5 (6505)	7.0	-	1	2	-	-	4	22.0 8	24.0 9
	G30	N	7.4 (7440)	6.0	-	1	2	-	-	4	12	24.5 9
	K1500	Z	4.3 (4293)	5.0	-	1	2	-	-	4	6	11.0
	K1500	H	5.0 (4999)	5.0	-	1	2	-	-	4	6	18.0
	K1500	K	5.7 (5735)	5.0	-	1	2	-	-	4	6	18.0
	K1500	F	6.5 (6505)	7.0	-	1	2	-	-	4	6	25.0
	K1500	N	7.4 (7440)	6.0	-	1	2	-	-	4	6	25.0 7
	K2500	Z	4.3 (4293)	5.0	-	1	2	-	-	4	6	11.0
	K2500	H	5.0 (4999)	5.0	-	1	2	-	-	4	6	18.0

CAPACITIES

Year	Model	Engine ID/VIN	Engine Displacement Liters (cc)	Oil with Filter (qts.)	Engine Transmission (pts.)			Transfer Case (pts.)	Drive Axle		Fuel Tank (gal.)	Cooling System (qts.)
					4-Spd	5-Spd	Auto.		Front (pts.)	Rear (pts.)		
1994	K2500	K	5.7 (5735)	5.0	-	1	2	-	-	4	6	18.0
	K2500	P	6.5 (6505)	7.0	-	1	2	-	-	4	6	25.0
	K2500	S	6.5 (6505)	7.0	-	1	2	-	-	4	6	25.0
	K2500	F	6.5 (6473)	7.0	-	1	2	-	-	4	6	26.5
	K2500	N	7.4 (7440)	6.0	-	1	2	-	-	4	6	25.0 7
	K3500	H	5.0 (4999)	5.0	-	1	2	-	-	4	6	18.0
	K3500	K	5.7 (5735)	5.0	-	1	2	-	-	4	6	18.0
	K3500	P	6.5 (6505)	7.0	-	1	2	-	-	4	6	25.0
	K3500	S	6.5 (6505)	7.0	-	1	2	-	-	4	6	25.0
	K3500	F	6.5 (6473)	7.0	-	1	2	-	-	4	6	26.5
	K3500	N	7.4 (7440)	6.0	-	1	2	-	-	4	6	25.0 7
	P30	Z	4.3 (4293)	5.0	-	4.4	10.0	4.6	2.6	3.8	18.0	13.4
	P30	K	5.7 (5735)	5.0	-	3.6	2	-	-	4	16	18.0
	P30	F	6.5 (6505)	7.0	-	3.6	2	-	-	11	12	25.0
	P30	N	7.4 (7440)	5.0	-	3.6	2	-	-	4	16	18.0
1995-96	Astro/Safari	W	4.3 (4293)	5.0	-	4.4	10.0	-	-	3.8	27.0	13.5 3
	Astro/Safari	Z	4.3 (4293)	5.0	-	4.4	10.0	-	-	3.8	27.0	13.5 3
	Lumina APV/Silhouette/Trans Sport	D	3.1 (3130)	4.5	-	-	8.0	-	-	-	20.0	13.4
	Lumina APV/Silhouette/Trans Sport	L	3.8 (3785)	4.5	-	-	12.0	-	-	-	20.0	13.4
	S10 Blazer/S15 Jimmy	W	4.3 (4293)	4.5	-	-	10.0	-	3.5	3.5	20.0	12.0
	S10 Blazer/S15 Jimmy	Z	4.3 (4293)	5.0	-	4.4	10.0	4.6	3.5	3.5	20.0	12.1
	S10 Pick-up/Sonoma	4	2.2 (2189)	4.0	-	4.4	10.0	4.6	3.5	3.5	13.0 13	11.5
	S10 Pick-up/Sonoma	W	4.3 (4293)	4.5	-	4.4	10.0	4.6	3.5	3.5	20.0	12.0
	S10 Pick-up/Sonoma	Z	4.3 (4293)	5.0	-	4.4	10.0	4.6	3.5	3.5	20.0	12.0
	Suburban	K	5.7 (5735)	5.0	-	-	2	-	-	4	6	18.0
	Suburban	P	6.5 (6505)	7.0	-	1	2	-	-	4	6	25.0
	Suburban	S	6.5 (6505)	7.0	-	1	2	-	-	4	6	25.0
	Suburban	N	7.4 (7440)	6.0	-	-	2	10.0	4.0	4	25.0 14	24.5
	Tahoe/Yukon	K	5.7 (5735)	5.0	-	-	2	10.0	4.0	4	25.0 5	18.0
	Tahoe/Yukon	F	6.5 (6473)	7.0	-	1	2	-	-	4	6	26.5
	C1500	Z	4.3 (4293)	5.0	-	1	2	-	-	4	6	11.0
	C1500	H	5.0 (4999)	5.0	-	1	2	-	-	4	6	18.0
	C1500	K	5.7 (5735)	5.0	-	1	2	-	-	4	6	18.0
	C1500	F	6.5 (6473)	7.0	-	1	2	-	-	4	6	26.5
	C1500	N	7.4 (7440)	5.0	-	1	2	-	-	4	6	25.0
	C2500	Z	4.3 (4293)	5.0	-	1	2	-	-	4	6	11.0
	C2500	H	5.0 (4999)	5.0	-	1	2	-	-	4	6	18.0
	C2500	K	5.7 (5735)	5.0	-	1	2	-	-	4	6	18.0
	C2500	P	6.5 (6473)	7.0	-	1	2	-	-	4	6	26.5
	C2500	S	6.5 (6473)	7.0	-	1	2	-	-	4	6	26.5
	C3500	H	5.0 (4999)	5.0	-	1	2	-	-	4	6	18.0
	C3500	K	5.7 (5735)	5.0	-	1	2	-	-	4	6	18.0
	C3500	F	6.5 (6473)	7.0	-	1	2	-	-	4	6	26.5
	C3500	P	6.5 (6473)	7.0	-	1	2	-	-	4	6	26.5
	C3500	S	6.5 (6473)	7.0	-	1	2	-	-	4	6	26.5
	C3500	N	7.4 (7440)	6.0	-	1	2	-	-	4	6	25.0 7
	G10	Z	4.3 (4293)	5.0	-	1	2	-	-	4	22.0 8	11.0 9
	G10	H	5.0 (4999)	5.0	-	1	2	-	-	4	22.0 8	17.0 9
	G10	K	5.7 (5735)	5.0	-	1	2	-	-	4	10	18.0 9
	G10	P	6.5 (6505)	7.0	-	1	2	-	-	4	22.0 8	24.0 9
	G10	S	6.5 (6505)	7.0	-	1	2	-	-	4	22.0 8	24.0 9
	G20	Z	4.3 (4293)	5.0	-	1	2	-	-	4	22.0 8	11.0 9
	G20	H	5.0 (4999)	5.0	-	1	2	-	-	4	22.0 8	17.0 9

CAPACITIES

Year	Model	Engine ID/VIN	Engine Displacement Liters (cc)	Oil with Filter (qts.)	Engine Transmission (pts.)			Transfer Case (pts.)	Drive Axle		Fuel Tank (gal.)	Cooling System (qts.)
					4-Spd	5-Spd	Auto.		Front (pts.)	Rear (pts.)		
1995-96	G20	K	5.7 (5735)	5.0	-	1	2	-	-	4	16	18.0 9
	G20	P	6.5 (6505)	7.0	-	1	2	-	-	4	22.0 8	24.0 9
	G20	Y	6.5 (6505)	7.0	-	1	2	-	-	4	22.0 8	24.0 9
	G30	Z	4.3 (4293)	5.0	-	1	2	-	-	4	22.0 8	11.0 9
	G30	K	5.7 (5735)	5.0	-	1	2	-	-	4	16	18.0 9
	G30	P	6.5 (6505)	7.0	-	1	2	-	-	4	22.0 8	24.0 9
	G30	Y	6.5 (6505)	7.0	-	1	2	-	-	4	22.0 8	24.0 9
	G30	N	7.4 (7440)	6.0	-	1	2	-	-	4	12	24.5 9
	K1500	Z	4.3 (4293)	5.0	-	1	2	-	-	4	6	11.0
	K1500	H	5.0 (4999)	5.0	-	1	2	-	-	4	6	18.0
	K1500	K	5.7 (5735)	5.0	-	1	2	-	-	4	6	18.0
	K1500	F	6.5 (6505)	7.0	-	1	2	-	-	4	6	25.0
	K1500	N	7.4 (7440)	6.0	-	1	2	-	-	4	6	25.0 7
	K2500	Z	4.3 (4293)	5.0	-	1	2	-	-	4	6	11.0
	K2500	H	5.0 (4999)	5.0	-	1	2	-	-	4	6	18.0
	K2500	K	5.7 (5735)	5.0	-	1	2	-	-	4	6	18.0
	K2500	P	6.5 (6505)	7.0	-	1	2	-	-	4	6	25.0
	K2500	S	6.5 (6505)	7.0	-	1	2	-	-	4	6	25.0
	K2500	F	6.5 (6473)	7.0	-	1	2	-	-	4	6	26.5
	K2500	N	7.4 (7440)	6.0	-	1	2	-	-	4	6	25.0 7
	K3500	H	5.0 (4999)	5.0	-	1	2	-	-	4	6	18.0
	K3500	K	5.7 (5735)	5.0	-	1	2	-	-	4	6	18.0
	K3500	P	6.5 (6505)	7.0	-	1	2	-	-	4	6	25.0
	K3500	S	6.5 (6505)	7.0	-	1	2	-	-	4	6	25.0
	K3500	F	6.5 (6473)	7.0	-	1	2	-	-	4	6	26.5
	K3500	N	7.4 (7440)	6.0	-	1	2	-	-	4	6	25.0
	P30	Z	4.3 (4293)	5.0	-	4.4	10.0	-	-	3.8	18.0	13.4
	P30	K	5.7 (5735)	5.0	-	3.6	2	-	-	4	16	18.0
	P30	F	6.5 (6505)	7.0	-	3.6	2	-	-	11	12	18.0
	P30	N	7.4 (7440)	5.0	-	3.6	2	-	-	4	16	18.0

1 New Venture Gear 4500: 8.0 pts.
   New Venture Gear 5LM60: 4.4 pts.
2 350C trans.: 6.3 pts.
   THM400 and 4L80 trans.: 9.0 pts.
   THM700 R4 and 4L60 trans.: 10.0 pts.
3 16.5 qts. with rear heater
4 8.5" ring gear: 4.2 pts.
   9.5" ring gear: 6.5 pts.
   9.75" ring gear: 6.0 pts.
   10.5" ring gear: 6.5 pts.
5 Available with optional 31 gallon tank
6 Std. available with 25 and 34 gallon tanks
   Chassis cab available with 22, 30 and 34 gallon tanks
7 3500HD: 28.5 qts. capacity
8 Available 32 and 41 gallon tanks

9 3 qts. with rear heater
10 Short bed: 16 gals.
    Long bed: 20 gals.
11 8.5" ring gear: 4.2 pts.
    9.5" ring gear: 6.5 pts.
    Chevrolet 10.5" ring gear: 6.5 pts.
    Dana 9.75" ring gear: 6.0 pts.
    Rockwell 12" ring gear: 12.5 pts.
12 Available with a variety of fuel tanks
13 Available with 20 gallon tank
14 Available 31 and 40 gallon tanks
15 Short bed: 20 gals.
    Long bed: 34 gals.
16 Short bed: 26 gals.
    Long bed: 34 gals.

CAMSHAFT SPECIFICATIONS

All measurements given in inches.

Year	Engine ID/VIN	Engine Displacement Liters (cc)	Journal Diameter					Elevation		Bearing Clearance	Camshaft End Play
			1	2	3	4	5	In.	Ex.		
1992	A	2.5 (2474)	1.8690	1.8690	1.8690	1.8690	1.8690	0.2510	0.2510	0.0007-0.0027	0.0015-0.0050
	R	2.8 (2835)	1.8680-1.8700	1.8680-1.8700	1.8680-1.8700	1.8680-1.8700	1.8680-1.8700	0.2620	0.2730	0.0010-0.0040	NA
	D	3.1 (3130)	1.8680-1.8820	1.8680-1.8820	1.8680-1.8820	1.8680-1.8820	NA	0.2310	0.2620	0.0010-0.0040	NA
	L	3.8 (3785)	1.7850-1.7860	1.7850-1.7860	1.7850-1.7860	1.7850-1.7860	NA	0.2500	0.2550	0.0005-0.0035	NA
	W	4.3 (4293)	1.8682-1.8692	1.8682-1.8692	1.8682-1.8692	1.8682-1.8692	NA	0.2800	0.2940	NA	0.0010-0.0090
	Z	4.3 (4293)	1.8682-1.8692	1.8682-1.8692	1.8682-1.8692	1.8682-1.8692	NA	0.2340	0.2570	0.0010-0.0030	0.0040-0.0120
	H	5.0 (4999)	1.8682-1.8692	1.8682-1.8692	1.8682-1.8692	1.8682-1.8692	1.8682-1.8692	0.2336	0.2565	NA	0.0040-0.0120
	K	5.7 (5735)	1.8682-1.8692	1.8682-1.8692	1.8682-1.8692	1.8682-1.8692	1.8682-1.8692	0.2565	0.2690	NA	0.0040-0.0120
	C	6.2 (6210)	2.1633-2.1642	2.1633-2.1642	2.1633-2.1642	2.1633-2.1642	2.0067-2.0089	0.2808	0.2808	0.0010-0.0040	0.0020-0.0120
	J	6.2 (6210)	2.1633-2.1642	2.1633-2.1642	2.1633-2.1642	2.1633-2.1642	2.0067-2.0089	0.2808	0.2808	0.0010-0.0040	0.0020-0.0120
	F	6.5 (6473)	2.1642-2.1663	2.1642-2.1663	2.1642-2.1663	2.1642-2.1663	2.0067-2.0089	0.2808	0.2808	1	0.0020-0.0120
	N	7.4 (7440)	1.9482-1.9492	1.9482-1.9492	1.9482-1.9492	1.9482-1.9492	1.9482-1.9492	0.2341-0.2345	0.2529-0.2531	NA	NA
1993	A	2.5 (2474)	1.8690	1.8690	1.8690	1.8690	1.8690	0.2510	0.2510	0.0007-0.0027	0.0015-0.0050
	R	2.8 (2835)	1.8680-1.8700	1.8680-1.8700	1.8680-1.8700	1.8680-1.8700	1.8680-1.8700	0.2620	0.2730	0.0010-0.0040	NA
	D	3.1 (3130)	1.8680-1.8820	1.8680-1.8820	1.8680-1.8820	1.8680-1.8820	NA	0.2310	0.2620	0.0010-0.0040	NA
	L	3.8 (3785)	1.7850-1.7860	1.7850-1.7860	1.7850-1.7860	1.7850-1.7860	NA	0.2500	0.2550	0.0005-0.0035	NA
	W	4.3 (4293)	1.8682-1.8692	1.8682-1.8692	1.8682-1.8692	1.8682-1.8692	NA	0.2880	0.2940	NA	0.0010-0.0090
	Z	4.3 (4293)	1.8682-1.8692	1.8682-1.8692	1.8682-1.8692	1.8682-1.8692	NA	0.2340	0.2570	0.0010-0.0030	0.0040-0.0120
	H	5.0 (4999)	1.8682-1.8692	1.8682-1.8692	1.8682-1.8692	1.8682-1.8692	1.8682-1.8692	0.2336	0.2565	NA	0.0040-0.0120
	K	5.7 (5735)	1.8682-1.8692	1.8682-1.8692	1.8682-1.8692	1.8682-1.8692	1.8682-1.8692	0.2565	0.2690	NA	0.0040-0.0120
	C	6.2 (6210)	2.1633-2.1642	2.1633-2.1642	2.1633-2.1642	2.1633-2.1642	2.0067-2.0089	0.2808	0.2808	0.0010-0.0040	0.0020-0.0120
	J	6.2 (6210)	2.1633-2.1642	2.1633-2.1642	2.1633-2.1642	2.1633-2.1642	2.0067-2.0089	0.2808	0.2808	0.0010-0.0040	0.0020-0.0120
	F	6.5 (6473)	2.1642-	2.1642-	2.1642-	2.1642-	2.0067-	0.2808	0.2808	1	0.0020-

CAMSHAFT SPECIFICATIONS

All measurements given in inches.

Year	Engine ID/VIN	Engine Displacement Liters (cc)	Journal Diameter 1	2	3	4	5	Elevation In.	Ex.	Bearing Clearance	Camshaft End Play
			2.1663	2.1663	2.1663	2.1663	2.0089				0.0120
	N	7.4 (7440)	1.9482-1.9492	1.9482-1.9492	1.9482-1.9492	1.9482-1.9492	1.9482-1.9492	0.2341-0.2345	0.2529-0.2531	NA	NA
1994	4	2.2 (2189)	1.8690	1.8690	1.8690	1.8690	1.8690	0.2510	0.2510	0.0007-0.0027	0.0015-0.0050
	D	3.1 (3130)	1.8680-1.8820	1.8680-1.8820	1.8680-1.8820	1.8680-1.8820	NA	0.2310	0.2620	0.0010-0.0040	NA
	L	3.8 (3785)	1.7850-1.7860	1.7850-1.7860	1.7850-1.7860	1.7850-1.7860	NA	0.2500	0.2550	0.0005-0.0035	NA
	W	4.3 (4293)	1.8682-1.8692	1.8682-1.8692	1.8682-1.8692	1.8682-1.8692	NA	0.288	0.294	NA	0.0010-0.0090
	Z	4.3 (4293)	1.8682-1.8692	1.8682-1.8692	1.8682-1.8692	1.8682-1.8692	NA	0.234	0.257	0.0010-0.0030	0.0040-0.0120
	H	5.0 (4999)	1.8682-1.8692	1.8682-1.8692	1.8682-1.8692	1.8682-1.8692	1.8682-1.8692	0.2336	0.2565	NA	0.0040-0.0120
	K	5.7 (5735)	1.8682-1.8692	1.8682-1.8692	1.8682-1.8692	1.8682-1.8692	1.8682-1.8692	0.2565	0.2690	NA	0.0040-0.0120
	F	6.5 (6473)	2.1642-2.1663	2.1642-2.1663	2.1642-2.1663	2.1642-2.1663	2.0067-2.0089	0.2808	0.2808	1	0.0020-0.0120
	P	6.5 (6473)	2.1642-2.1663	2.1642-2.1663	2.1642-2.1663	2.1642-2.1663	2.0067-2.0089	0.2808	0.2808	1	0.0020-0.0120
	S	6.5 (6473)	2.1642-2.1663	2.1642-2.1663	2.1642-2.1663	2.1642-2.1663	2.0067-2.0089	0.2808	0.2808	1	0.0020-0.0120
	Y	6.5 (6473)	2.1642-2.1663	2.1642-2.1663	2.1642-2.1663	2.1642-2.1663	2.0067-2.0089	0.2808	0.2808	1	0.0020-0.0120
	N	7.4 (7440)	1.9482-1.9492	1.9482-1.9492	1.9482-1.9492	1.9482-1.9492	1.9482-1.9492	0.2341-0.2345	0.2529-0.2531	NA	NA
1995-96	4	2.2 (2189)	1.8690	1.8690	1.8690	1.8690	1.8690	0.2510	0.2510	0.0007-0.0027	0.0015-0.0050
	D	3.1 (3130)	1.8680-1.8820	1.8680-1.8820	1.8680-1.8820	1.8680-1.8820	NA	0.2310	0.2620	0.0010-0.0040	NA
	L	3.8 (3785)	1.7850-1.7860	1.7850-1.7860	1.7850-1.7860	1.7850-1.7860	NA	0.2500	0.2550	0.0005-0.0035	NA
	W	4.3 (4293)	1.8682-1.8692	1.8682-1.8692	1.8682-1.8692	1.8682-1.8692	NA	0.2880	0.2940	NA	0.0010-0.0090
	Z	4.3 (4293)	1.8682-1.8692	1.8682-1.8692	1.8682-1.8692	1.8682-1.8692	NA	0.2340	0.2570	0.0010-0.0030	0.0040-0.0120
	H	5.0 (4999)	1.8682-1.8692	1.8682-1.8692	1.8682-1.8692	1.8682-1.8692	1.8682-1.8692	0.2336	0.2565	NA	0.0040-0.0120
	K	5.7 (5735)	1.8682-1.8692	1.8682-1.8692	1.8682-1.8692	1.8682-1.8692	1.8682-1.8692	0.2565	0.2690	NA	0.0040-0.0120
	F	6.5 (6473)	2.1642-2.1663	2.1642-2.1663	2.1642-2.1663	2.1642-2.1663	2.0067-2.0089	0.2808	0.2808	1	0.0020-0.0120
	P	6.5 (6473)	2.1642-2.1663	2.1642-2.1663	2.1642-2.1663	2.1642-2.1663	2.0067-2.0089	0.2808	0.2808	1	0.0020-0.0120

CAMSHAFT SPECIFICATIONS

All measurements given in inches.

Year	Engine ID/VIN	Engine Displacement Liters (cc)	Journal Diameter					Elevation		Bearing Clearance	Camshaft End Play
			1	2	3	4	5	In.	Ex.		
1995-96	S	6.5 (6473)	2.1642-2.1663	2.1642-2.1663	2.1642-2.1663	2.1642-2.1663	2.0067-2.0089	0.2808	0.2808	1	0.0020-0.0120
	Y	6.5 (6473)	2.1642-2.1663	2.1642-2.1663	2.1642-2.1663	2.1642-2.1663	2.0067-2.0089	0.2808	0.2808	1	0.0020-0.0120
	N	7.4 (7440)	1.9482-1.9492	1.9482-1.9492	1.9482-1.9492	1.9482-1.9492	1.9482-1.9492	0.2341-0.2345	0.2529-0.2531	NA	NA

NA - Not Available
1 Journals 1-4: 0.0010-0.0046
Journal 5: 0.0008-0.0044

CRANKSHAFT AND CONNECTING ROD SPECIFICATIONS

All measurements are given in inches.

Year	Engine ID/VIN	Engine Displacement Liters (cc)	Crankshaft				Connecting Rod		
			Main Brg. Journal Dia.	Main Brg. Oil Clearance	Shaft End-play	Thrust on No.	Journal Diameter	Oil Clearance	Side Clearance
1992	A	2.5 (2474)	2.3000	0.0005-0.0022	0.0035-0.0085	5	2.000	0.0005-0.0026	0.0060-0.0020
	R	2.8 (2835)	1	0.0016-0.0032	0.0024-0.0083	3	8	0.0014-0.0037	0.0063-0.0252
	D	3.1 (3130)	2.6473-2.6483	0.0012-0.0027	0.0024-0.0083	3	1.9983-1.9994	0.0011-0.0032	0.0140-0.0270
	L	3.8 (3785)	2.4988-2.4998	0.0008-0.0022	0.0030-0.0110	3	2.2487-2.2499	0.0008-0.0022	0.0030-0.0150
	W	4.3 (4293)	9	3	0.0020-0.0060	3	2.2487-2.2497	0.0013-0.0035	0.0060-0.0140
	Z	4.3 (4293)	2	3	0.0020-0.0060	3	2.2487-2.2497	0.0013-0.0035	0.0060-0.0140
	H	5.0 (4999)	2	3	0.0020-0.0060	5	2.0988-2.0998	0.0013-0.0035	0.0060-0.0140
	K	5.7 (5735)	2	3	0.0020-0.0060	5	2.0988-2.0998	0.0013-0.0035	0.0060-0.0140
	C	6.2 (6210)	4	5	0.0020-0.0070	3	2.3980-2.3990	0.0017-0.0039	0.0070-0.0240
	J	6.2 (6210)	4	5	0.0020-0.0070	3	2.3980-2.3990	0.0017-0.0039	0.0070-0.0240
	F	6.5 (6473)	4	5	0.0020-0.0070	3	2.3980-2.3990	0.0017-0.0039	0.0070-0.0240
	N	7.4 (7440)	6	7	0.0060-0.0100	5	2.1990-2.2000	0.0009-0.0025	0.0130-0.0230
1993	A	2.5 (2474)	2.3000	0.0005-0.0022	0.0035-0.0085	5	2.0000	0.0005-0.0026	0.0060-0.0020
	R	2.8 (2835)	1	0.0016-0.0032	0.0024-0.0083	3	8	0.0014-0.0037	0.0063-0.0252

CRANKSHAFT AND CONNECTING ROD SPECIFICATIONS

All measurements are given in inches.

Year	Engine ID/VIN	Engine Displacement Liters (cc)	Crankshaft				Connecting Rod		
			Main Brg. Journal Dia.	Main Brg. Oil Clearance	Shaft End-play	Thrust on No.	Journal Diameter	Oil Clearance	Side Clearance
1993	D	3.1 (3130)	2.6473-2.6483	0.0012-0.0027	0.0024-0.0083	3	1.9983-1.9994	0.0011-0.0032	0.0140-0.0270
	L	3.8 (3785)	2.4988-2.4998	0.0008-0.0022	0.0030-0.0110	3	2.2487-2.2499	0.0008-0.0022	0.0030-0.0150
	W	4.3 (4293)	9	3	0.0020-0.0070	3	2.2487-2.2497	0.0013-0.0035	0.0060-0.0140
	Z	4.3 (4293)	2	3	0.0020-0.0060	3	2.2487-2.2497	0.0013-0.0035	0.0060-0.0140
	H	5.0 (4999)	2	3	0.0020-0.0060	3	2.2487-2.2497	0.0013-0.0035	0.0060-0.0140
	K	5.7 (5735)	2	3	0.0020-0.0060	3	2.2487-2.2497	0.0013-0.0035	0.0060-0.0140
	C	6.2 (6210)	4	5	0.0020-0.0070	3	2.3980-2.3990	0.0017-0.0039	0.0070-0.0240
	J	6.2 (6210)	4	5	0.0020-0.0070	3	2.3980-2.3990	0.0017-0.0039	0.0070-0.0240
	F	6.5 (6473)	4	5	0.0020-0.0070	3	2.3980-2.3990	0.0017-0.0039	0.0070-0.0240
	N	7.4 (7440)	6	7	0.0060-0.0100	5	2.1990-2.2000	0.0009-0.0025	0.0130-0.0230
1994	4	2.2 (2189)	2.4945-2.4954	0.0006-0.0019	0.0020-0.0070	5	1.9983-1.9994	0.0098-0.0031	0.0039-0.0149
	D	3.1 (3130)	2.6473-2.6483	0.0012-0.0027	0.0024-0.0083	3	1.9983-1.9994	0.0011-0.0032	0.0140-0.0270
	L	3.8 (3785)	2.4988-2.4998	0.0008-0.0022	0.003-0.011	3	2.2487-2.2499	0.0008-0.0022	0.0030-0.0150
	W	4.3 (4293)	10	3	0.0020-0.0070	3	2.2487-2.2497	0.0013-0.0035	0.0060-0.0140
	Z	4.3 (4293)	2	3	0.0020-0.0060	3	2.2487-2.2497	0.0013-0.0035	0.0060-0.0140
	H	5.0 (4999)	2	3	0.0020-0.0060	5	2.0988-2.0998	0.0013-0.0035	0.0060-0.0140
	K	5.7 (5735)	2	3	0.0020-0.0060	5	2.0988-2.0998	0.0013-0.0035	0.0060-0.0140
	F	6.5 (6473)	11	12	0.0040-0.0098	3	2.3980-2.3990	0.0017-0.0039	0.0070-0.0240
	P	6.5 (6473)	11	12	0.0040-0.0098	3	2.3980-2.3990	0.0017-0.0039	0.0070-0.0240
	S	6.5 (6473)	11	12	0.0040-0.0098	3	2.3980-2.3990	0.0017-0.0039	0.0070-0.0240
	Y	6.5 (6473)	11	12	0.0040-0.0098	3	2.3980-2.3990	0.0017-0.0039	0.0070-0.0240
	N	7.4 (7440)	13	7	0.006-0.010	5	2.1990-2.2000	0.0009-0.0025	0.0130-0.0230

CRANKSHAFT AND CONNECTING ROD SPECIFICATIONS

All measurements are given in inches.

Year	Engine ID/VIN	Engine Displacement Liters (cc)	Crankshaft				Connecting Rod		
			Main Brg. Journal Dia.	Main Brg. Oil Clearance	Shaft End-play	Thrust on No.	Journal Diameter	Oil Clearance	Side Clearance
1995-96	4	2.2 (2189)	2.4945-2.4954	0.0006-0.0019	0.0020-0.0070	5	1.9983-1.9994	0.0098-0.0031	0.0039-0.0149
	D	3.1 (3130)	2.6473-2.6483	0.0012-0.0027	0.0024-0.0083	3	1.9983-1.9994	0.0011-0.0032	0.0140-0.0270
	L	3.8 (3785)	2.4988-2.4998	0.0008-0.0022	0.0030-0.0110	3	2.2487-2.2499	0.0008-0.0022	0.0030-0.0150
	W	4.3 (4293)	10	3	0.0020-0.0070	3	2.2487-2.2499	0.0013-0.0035	0.0060-0.0140
	Z	4.3 (4293)	2	3	0.0020-0.0060	3	2.2487-2.2499	0.0013-0.0035	0.0060-0.0140
	H	5.0 (4999)	2	3	0.0020-0.0060	5	2.0988-2.0998	0.0013-0.0035	0.0060-0.0140
	K	5.7 (5735)	2	3	0.0020-0.0060	5	2.0988-2.0998	0.0013-0.0035	0.0060-0.0140
	F	6.5 (6473)	11	12	0.0040-0.0098	3	2.3980-2.3990	0.0017-0.0039	0.0070-0.0240
	P	6.5 (6473)	11	12	0.0040-0.0098	3	2.3980-2.3990	0.0017-0.0039	0.0070-0.0240
	S	6.5 (6473)	11	12	0.0040-0.0098	3	2.3980-2.3990	0.0017-0.0039	0.0070-0.0240
	Y	6.5 (6473)	11	12	0.0040-0.0098	3	2.3980-2.3990	0.0017-0.0039	0.0070-0.0240
	N	7.4 (7440)	13	7	0.0060-0.0100	5	2.1990-2.2000	0.0009-0.0025	0.0130-0.0230

1 Three dots: 2.6478-2.64759
   Two dots: 2.64759-2.64790
   One dot: 2.64790-2.64822
2 No.1: 2.4484-2.4493
   Nos. 2-3: 2.4481-2.4490
   No. 4: 2.4479-2.4488
3 No. 1: 0.0008-0.0020
   Nos. 2-3: 0.0011-0.0023
   No. 4: 0.0017-0.0032
4 Nos. 1-4: 2.9495-2.9504
   No. 5: 2.9493-2.9502
5 Nos. 1-4: 0.0083
   No. 5: 0.0055-0.0093
6 Nos. 1-4: 2.7481-2.7490
   No. 5: 2.7476-2.7486
7 Nos. 1-4: 0.0013-0.0025
   No. 5: 0.0024-0.0040
8 Two dots: 1.9983-1.9989
   One dot: 1.9989-1.9994

9 No. 1: 2.4488-2.4495
   Nos. 2-3: 2.4485-2.4494
   No. 4: 2.4480-2.4489
10 No. 1: 2.2448-2.4495
   Nos. 2-3: 2.4485-2.4494
   No. 4: 2.4480-2.4489
11 Blue Nos. 1-4: 2.9495-2.9498
   Blue No. 5: 2.9493-2.9496
   Orange or red Nos. 1-4: 2.9498-2.9501
   Orange or red No. 5: 2.9496-2.9500
   White Nos. 1-4: 2.9501-2.9328
   White No. 5: 2.9500-2.9502
12 Nos. 1-4: 0.0017-0.0033
   No. 5: 0.0022-0.0037
13 Nos. 1-4: 2.7481-2.7490
   No. 5: 2.7476-2.7486

VALVE SPECIFICATIONS

Year	Engine ID/VIN	Engine Displacement Liters (cc)	Seat Angle (deg.)	Face Angle (deg.)	Spring Test Pressure (lbs. @ in.)	Spring Installed Height (in.)	Stem-to-Guide Clearance (in.)		Stem Diameter (in.)	
							Intake	Exhaust	Intake	Exhaust
1992	A	2.5 (2474)	46	45	1.58-1.70@ 1.04	1.44	0.0010-0.0025	0.0013-0.0030	0.3133-0.3138	0.3128-0.3135
	R	2.8 (2835)	46	45	88@1.57	1.57	0.0010-0.0027	0.0010-0.0027	0.3410-0.3417	0.3410-0.3417
	D	3.1 (3130)	46	45	82@1.58	1.57	0.0010-0.0027	0.0010-0.0027	NA	NA
	L	3.8 (3785)	46	45	210@1.315	1.69-1.71	0.0015-0.0035	0.0015-0.0032	NA	[1]
	W	4.3 (4293)	46	45	194-206@ 1.25	1.69-1.71	0.0011-0.0027	0.0011-0.0027	NA	NA
	Z	4.3 (4293)	46	45	194-206@ 1.25	1.72	0.0010-0.0027	0.0010-0.0027	NA	NA
	H	5.0 (4999)	46	45	76-84@1.70	1.72	0.0010-0.0027	0.0010-0.0027	NA	NA
	K	5.7 (5735)	46	45	76-84@1.70	1.72	0.0010-0.0027	0.0010-0.0027	NA	NA
	C	6.2 (6210)	46	45	230@1.39	1.81	0.0010-0.0027	0.0010-0.0027	NA	NA
	J	6.2 (6210)	46	45	230@1.39	1.81	0.0010-0.0027	0.0010-0.0027	NA	NA
	F	6.5 (6473)	46	45	230@1.39	1.81	0.0010-0.0027	0.0010-0.0027	NA	NA
	N	7.4 (7440)	46	45	74-86@1.80	1.80	0.0010-0.0027	0.0012-0.0029	NA	NA
1993	A	2.5 (2474)	46	45	1.58-1.70@ 1.04	1.44	0.0010-0.0025	0.0013-0.0030	0.3133-0.3138	0.3128-0.3135
	R	2.8 (2835)	46	45	88@1.57	1.57	0.0010-0.0027	0.0010-0.0027	0.3410-0.3417	0.3410-0.3417
	D	3.1 (3130)	46	45	82@1.58	1.57	0.0010-0.0027	0.0010-0.0027	NA	NA
	L	3.8 (3785)	46	45	210@1.32	1.69-1.72	0.0015-0.0035	0.0015-0.0032	NA	[1]
	W	4.3 (4293)	46	45	194-206@ 1.25	1.69-1.71	0.0011-0.0027	0.0011-0.0027	NA	NA
	Z	4.3 (4293)	46	45	194-206@ 1.25	1.72	0.0010-0.0027	0.0010-0.0027	NA	NA
	H	5.0 (4999)	46	45	76-84@1.70	1.72	0.0010-0.0027	0.0010-0.0027	NA	NA
	K	5.7 (5735)	46	45	76-84@1.70	1.72	0.0010-0.0027	0.0010-0.0027	NA	NA
	C	6.2 (6210)	46	45	230@1.39	1.81	0.0010-0.0027	0.0010-0.0027	NA	NA
	J	6.2 (6210)	46	45	230@1.39	1.81	0.0010-0.0027	0.0010-0.0027	NA	NA
	F	6.5 (6473)	46	45	230@1.39	1.81	0.0010-0.0027	0.0010-0.0027	NA	NA

VALVE SPECIFICATIONS

Year	Engine ID/VIN	Engine Displacement Liters (cc)	Seat Angle (deg.)	Face Angle (deg.)	Spring Test Pressure (lbs. @ in.)	Spring Installed Height (in.)	Stem-to-Guide Clearance (in.)		Stem Diameter (in.)	
							Intake	Exhaust	Intake	Exhaust
	N	7.4 (7440)	46	45	74-86@1.80	1.80	0.0010-0.0027	0.0012-0.0029	NA	NA
1994	4	2.2 (2189)	46	45	228@1.28	1.71	0.0010-0.0020	0.0010-0.0030	NA	NA
	D	3.1 (3130)	46	45	82@1.58	1.57	0.0010-0.0027	0.0010-0.0027	NA	NA
	L	3.8 (3785)	46	45	210@1.32	1.69-1.72	0.0015-0.0035	0.0015-0.0032	NA	[1]
	W	4.3 (4293)	46	45	194-206@1.25	1.69-1.71	0.0011-0.0027	0.0011-0.0027	NA	NA
	Z	4.3 (4293)	46	45	194-206@1.25	1.72	0.0010-0.0027	0.0010-0.0027	NA	NA
	H	5.0 (4999)	46	45	76-84@1.70	1.72	0.0010-0.0027	0.0010-0.0027	NA	NA
	K	5.7 (5735)	46	45	76-84@1.70	1.72	0.0010-0.0027	0.0010-0.0027	NA	NA
	F	6.5 (6473)	46	45	230@1.39	1.81	0.0010-0.0027	0.0010-0.0027	NA	NA
	P	6.5 (6473)	46	45	230@1.39	1.81	0.0010-0.0027	0.0010-0.0027	NA	NA
	S	6.5 (6473)	46	45	230@1.39	1.81	0.0010-0.0027	0.0010-0.0027	NA	NA
	Y	6.5 (6473)	46	45	230@1.39	1.81	0.0010-0.0027	0.0010-0.0027	NA	NA
	N	7.4 (7440)	46	45	74-86@1.80	1.80	0.0010-0.0027	0.0012-0.0029	NA	NA
1995-96	4	2.2 (2189)	46	45	228@1.28	1.71	0.0010-0.0020	0.0010-0.0030	NA	NA
	D	3.1 (3130)	46	45	82@1.58	1.57	0.0010-0.0027	0.0010-0.0027	NA	NA
	L	3.8 (3785)	46	45	210@1.32	1.69-1.72	0.0015-0.0035	0.0015-0.0032	NA	[1]
	W	4.3 (4293)	46	45	194-206@1.25	1.69-1.71	0.0011-0.0027	0.0011-0.0027	NA	NA
	Z	4.3 (4293)	46	45	194-206@1.25	1.72	0.0010-0.0027	0.0010-0.0027	NA	NA
	H	5.0 (4999)	46	45	76-84@1.70	1.72	0.0010-0.0027	0.0010-0.0027	NA	NA
	K	5.7 (5735)	46	45	76-84@1.70	1.72	0.0010-0.0027	0.0010-0.0027	NA	NA
	F	6.5 (6473)	46	45	230@1.39	1.81	0.0010-0.0027	0.0010-0.0027	NA	NA
	P	6.5 (6473)	46	45	230@1.39	1.81	0.0010-0.0027	0.0010-0.0027	NA	NA
	S	6.5 (6473)	46	45	230@1.39	1.81	0.0010-0.0027	0.0010-0.0027	NA	NA

VALVE SPECIFICATIONS

Year	Engine ID/VIN	Engine Displacement Liters (cc)	Seat Angle (deg.)	Face Angle (deg.)	Spring Test Pressure (lbs. @ in.)	Spring Installed Height (in.)	Stem-to-Guide Clearance (in.) Intake	Stem-to-Guide Clearance (in.) Exhaust	Stem Diameter (in.) Intake	Stem Diameter (in.) Exhaust
1995-96	Y	6.5 (6473)	46	45	230@1.39	1.81	0.0010-0.0027	0.0010-0.0027	NA	NA
	N	7.4 (7440)	46	45	74-86@1.80	1.80	0.0010-0.0027	0.0010-0.0027	NA	NA

NA - Not Available
1 Upper: 0.3129-0.3137
Lower: 0.3118-0.3126

PISTON AND RING SPECIFICATIONS

All measurements are given in inches.

Year	Engine ID/VIN	Engine Displacement Liters (cc)	Piston Clearance	Ring Gap Top Compression	Ring Gap Bottom Compression	Ring Gap Oil Control	Ring Side Clearance Top Compression	Ring Side Clearance Bottom Compression	Ring Side Clearance Oil Control
1992	A	2.5 (2474)	0.0015-0.0035	0.010-0.015	0.010-0.020	0.015-0.055	0.0015-0.0030	0.0015-0.0032	0.0050-0.0070
	R	2.8 (2835)	0.0007-0.0017	0.010-0.020	0.010-0.020	0.010-0.050	0.0010-0.0030	0.0015-0.0037	0.0080 MAX
	D	3.1 (3130)	0.0009-0.0022	0.010-0.020	0.020-0.028	0.010-0.030	0.0020-0.0035	0.0020-0.0035	0.0080 MAX
	L	3.8 (3785)	0.0004-0.0022 1	0.010-0.025	0.010-0.025	0.015-0.055	0.0013-0.0031	0.0013-0.0031	0.0011-0.0081
	W	4.3 (4293)	0.0007-0.0017	0.010-0.020	0.018-0.026	0.015-0.055	0.0014-0.0032	0.0014-0.0032	0.0014-0.0032
	Z	4.3 (4293)	0.0007-0.0017	0.010-0.020	0.010-0.025	0.015-0.055	0.0012-0.0032	0.0012-0.0032	0.0020-0.0070
	H	5.0 (4999)	0.0007-0.0017	0.010-0.020	0.018-0.026	0.010-0.030	0.0012-0.0032	0.0012-0.0032	0.0020-0.0070
	K	5.7 (5735)	0.0007-0.0017	0.010-0.020	0.018-0.026	0.010-0.030	0.0012-0.0032	0.0012-0.0032	0.0020-0.0070
	C	6.2 (6210)	2	0.012-0.022	0.030-0.039	0.010-0.020	0.0030-0.0070	0.0300-0.0400	0.0020-0.0040
	J	6.2 (6210)	2	0.012-0.022	0.030-0.039	0.010-0.020	0.0030-0.0070	0.0300-0.0400	0.0020-0.0040
	F	6.5 (6473)	2	0.010-0.020	0.030-0.039	0.010-0.023	0.0030-0.0070	0.0300-0.0400	0.0020-0.0040
	N	7.4 (7440)	0.0030-0.0042	0.010-0.018	0.016-0.024	0.010-0.030	0.0012-0.0029	0.0012-0.0029	0.0050-0.0065
1993	A	2.5 (2474)	0.0015-0.0035	0.010-0.015	0.010-0.020	0.015-0.055	0.0015-0.0030	0.0015-0.0032	0.0050-0.0070
	R	2.8 (2835)	0.0007-0.0017	0.010-0.020	0.010-0.020	0.010-0.050	0.0010-0.0030	0.0015-0.0037	0.0080 MAX
	D	3.1 (3146)	0.0009-0.0023	0.007-0.016	0.020-0.028	0.010-0.030	0.0020-0.0035	0.0020-0.0035	0.0080 MAX
	L	3.8 (3785)	0.0004-0.0022 1	0.010-0.025	0.010-0.025	0.015-0.055	0.0013-0.0031	0.0013-0.0031	0.0011-0.0081

PISTON AND RING SPECIFICATIONS

All measurements are given in inches.

Year	Engine ID/VIN	Engine Displacement Liters (cc)	Piston Clearance	Ring Gap			Ring Side Clearance		
				Top Compression	Bottom Compression	Oil Control	Top Compression	Bottom Compression	Oil Control
1993	W	4.3 (4293)	0.0007-0.0017	0.010-0.020	0.018-0.026	0.015-0.055	0.0014-0.0032	0.0014-0.0032	0.0014-0.0032
	Z	4.3 (4293)	0.0007-0.0017	0.010-0.020	0.010-0.025	0.015-0.055	0.0012-0.0032	0.0012-0.0032	0.0020-0.0070
	H	5.0 (4999)	0.0007-0.0021	0.010-0.020	0.018-0.026	0.010-0.030	0.0012-0.0032	0.0012-0.0032	0.0020-0.0070
	K	5.7 (5735)	0.0007-0.0021	0.010-0.020	0.018-0.026	0.010-0.030	0.0012-0.0032	0.0012-0.0032	0.0020-0.0070
	C	6.2 (6210)	3	0.010-0.020	0.030-0.039	0.010-0.020	5	0.0015-0.0030	0.0015-0.0035
	J	6.2 (6210)	3	0.010-0.020	0.030-0.039	0.010-0.020	5	0.0015-0.0030	0.0015-0.0035
	F	6.5 (6473)	4	0.010-0.020	0.030-0.039	0.010-0.020	5	0.0015-0.0030	0.0015-0.0035
	N	7.4 (7440)	0.0003-0.0042	0.010-0.018	0.016-0.024	0.010-0.030	0.0012-0.0029	0.0012-0.0029	0.0050-0.0065
1994	4	2.2 (2189)	0.0007-0.0017	0.010-0.020	0.010-0.020	0.010-0.050	0.0019-0.0027	0.0019-0.0027	0.0019-0.0082
	D	3.1 (3146)	0.0009-0.0023	0.007-0.016	0.020-0.028	0.010-0.030	0.0020-0.0035	0.0020-0.0035	0.008 MAX
	L	3.8 (3785)	0.0004-0.0022 [1]	0.010-0.025	0.010-0.025	0.015-0.055	0.0013-0.0031	0.0013-0.0031	0.0011-0.0081
	W	4.3 (4293)	0.0007-0.0017	0.010-0.020	0.018-0.026	0.015-0.055	0.0014-0.0032	0.0014-0.0032	0.0014-0.0032
	Z	4.3 (4293)	0.0007-0.0017	0.010-0.020	0.010-0.025	0.015-0.055	0.0012-0.0032	0.0012-0.0032	0.0020-0.0070
	H	5.0 (4999)	0.0007-0.0021	0.010-0.020	0.018-0.026	0.010-0.030	0.0012-0.0032	0.0012-0.0032	0.0020-0.0070
	K	5.7 (5735)	0.0007-0.0021	0.010-0.020	0.018-0.026	0.010-0.030	0.0012-0.0032	0.0012-0.0032	0.0020-0.0070
	F	6.5 (6473)	4	0.010-0.020	0.030-0.039	0.010-0.020	5	0.0015-0.0030	0.0015-0.0035
	P	6.5 (6473)	4	0.010-0.020	0.030-0.039	0.010-0.020	5	0.0015-0.0030	0.0015-0.0035
	S	6.5 (6473)	4	0.010-0.020	0.030-0.039	0.010-0.020	5	0.0015-0.0030	0.0015-0.0035
	Y	6.5 (6473)	4	0.010-0.020	0.030-0.039	0.010-0.020	5	0.0015-0.0030	0.0015-0.0035
	N	7.4 (7440)	0.0018-0.0030	0.010-0.018	0.016-0.024	0.010-0.030	0.0012-0.0029	0.0012-0.0029	0.0050-0.0065
1995-96	4	2.2 (2189)	0.0007-0.0017	0.010-0.020	0.010-0.020	0.010-0.050	0.0019-0.0027	0.0019-0.0027	0.0019-0.0082
	D	3.1 (3146)	0.0009-0.0023	0.007-0.016	0.020-0.028	0.010-0.030	0.0020-0.0035	0.0020-0.0035	0.0080 MAX
	L	3.8 (3785)	0.0004-0.0022 [1]	0.010-0.025	0.010-0.025	0.015-0.055	0.0013-0.0031	0.0013-0.0031	0.0011-0.0081

PISTON AND RING SPECIFICATIONS

All measurements are given in inches.

Year	Engine ID/VIN	Engine Displacement Liters (cc)	Piston Clearance	Ring Gap			Ring Side Clearance		
				Top Compression	Bottom Compression	Oil Control	Top Compression	Bottom Compression	Oil Control
1995-96	W	4.3 (4293)	0.0007-0.0017	0.010-0.020	0.018-0.026	0.015-0.055	0.0014-0.0032	0.0014-0.0032	0.0014-0.0032
	Z	4.3 (4293)	0.0007-0.0017	0.010-0.020	0.010-0.025	0.015-0.055	0.0012-0.0032	0.0012-0.0032	0.0020-0.0070
	H	5.0 (4999)	0.0007-0.0021	0.010-0.020	0.018-0.026	0.010-0.030	0.0012-0.0032	0.0012-0.0032	0.0020-0.0070
	K	5.7 (5735)	0.0007-0.0021	0.010-0.020	0.018-0.026	0.010-0.030	0.0012-0.0032	0.0012-0.0032	0.0020-0.0070
	F	6.5 (6473)	4	0.010-0.020	0.030-0.039	0.010-0.020	5	0.0015-0.0030	0.0015-0.0035
	P	6.5 (6473)	4	0.010-0.020	0.030-0.039	0.010-0.020	5	0.0015-0.0030	0.0015-0.0035
	S	6.5 (6473)	4	0.010-0.020	0.030-0.039	0.010-0.020	5	0.0015-0.0030	0.0015-0.0035
	Y	6.5 (6473)	4	0.010-0.020	0.030-0.039	0.010-0.020	5	0.0015-0.0030	0.0015-0.0035
	N	7.4 (7440)	0.0018-0.0030	0.010-0.018	0.016-0.024	0.010-0.030	0.0012-0.0029	0.0012-0.0029	0.0050-0.0065

1 Measured 44mm from top of piston
2 Bohn piston Nos. 1-6: 0.0035-0.0045
  Bohn piston Nos. 7-8: 0.0040-0.0050
3 Bore Nos. 1-6: 0.0025-0.0035
  Bore Nos. 7-8: 0.0030-0.0040
4 Bore Nos. 1-6: 0.0037-0.0047
  Bore Nos. 7-8: 0.0042-0.0052
5 Keystone type ring

TORQUE SPECIFICATIONS

All readings in ft. lbs.

Year	Engine ID/VIN	Engine Displacement Liters (cc)	Cylinder Head Bolts	Main Bearing Bolts	Rod Bearing Bolts	Crankshaft Damper Bolts	Flywheel Bolts	Manifold		Spark Plugs	Lug Nut
								Intake	Exhaust		
1992	A	2.5 (2474)	1	70	32	160	2	25	3	7-15	90
	R	2.8 (2835)	4	70	39	70	52	15	25	22	90
	D	3.1 (3130)	4	72	39	75	45	5	24	18	100
	L	3.8 (3785)	6	7	8	9	10	7	38	12	100
	W	4.3 (4293)	65	75	11	70	75	35	12	22	90
	Z	4.3 (4293)	65	75	11	70	75	35	12	22	90
	H	5.0 (4999)	65	14	45	70	75	35	12	15	13
	K	5.7 (5735)	65	14	45	70	75	35	12	15	13
	C	6.2 (6210)	15	16	48	200	66	31	26	-	13
	J	6.2 (6210)	15	16	48	200	66	31	26	-	13
	F	6.5 (6473)	15	16	48	200	66	31	26	-	13
	N	7.4 (7440)	80	100	48	85	65	40	40	22	13

TORQUE SPECIFICATIONS
All readings in ft. lbs.

Year	Engine ID/VIN	Engine Displacement Liters (cc)	Cylinder Head Bolts	Main Bearing Bolts	Rod Bearing Bolts	Crankshaft Damper Bolts	Flywheel Bolts	Manifold		Spark Plugs	Lug Nut
								Intake	Exhaust		
1993	A	2.5 (2474)	1	70	32	160	2	25	3	7-15	90
	R	2.8 (2835)	70	70	39	70	52	15	25	22	90
	D	3.1 (3130)	4	17	37	76	52	18	24	19	100
	L	3.8 (3785)	6	7	8	9	10	7	38	12	100
	W	4.3 (4293)	65	75	11	70	75	35	12	22	90
	Z	4.3 (4293)	65	75	11	70	75	35	12	22	90
	H	5.0 (4999)	65	14	45	70	75	35	12	15	13
	K	5.7 (5735)	65	14	45	70	75	35	12	15	13
	C	6.2 (6210)	15	16	48	200	66	31	26	-	13
	J	6.2 (6210)	15	16	48	200	66	31	26	-	13
	F	6.5 (6473)	15	16	48	200	66	31	26	-	13
	N	7.4 (7440)	80	100	48	85	65	40	40	22	13
1994	4	2.2 (2189)	20	70	38	77	55	24	10	19	100
	D	3.1 (3130)	21	17	37	76	52	18	25	19	100
	L	3.8 (3785)	6	7	8	9	10	7	38	11	100
	W	4.3 (4293)	65	75	11	70	75	35	12	22	90
	Z	4.3 (4293)	65	75	11	70	75	35	12	11	90
	H	5.0 (4999)	65	14	45	70	75	35	12	15	23
	K	5.7 (5735)	65	14	45	70	75	35	12	15	23
	F	6.5 (6473)	22	16	48	200	66	31	26	-	23
	P	6.5 (6473)	22	16	48	200	66	31	26	-	23
	S	6.5 (6473)	22	16	48	200	66	31	26	-	23
	Y	6.5 (6473)	22	16	48	200	66	31	26	-	23
	N	7.4 (7440)	80	100	48	85	65	35	40	22	23
1995-96	4	2.2 (2189)	20	70	38	77	55	24	10	19	100
	D	3.1 (3130)	21	17	37	76	52	18	25	19	100
	L	3.8 (3785)	6	7	8	9	10	7	38	11	100
	W	4.3 (4293)	65	75	11	70	75	35	12	22	90
	Z	4.3 (4293)	65	75	11	70	75	35	12	11	90
	H	5.0 (4999)	65	14	45	70	75	35	12	15	23
	K	5.7 (5735)	65	14	45	70	75	35	12	15	23
	F	6.5 (6473)	22	16	48	200	66	31	26	-	23
	P	6.5 (6473)	22	16	48	200	66	31	26	-	23
	S	6.5 (6473)	22	16	48	200	66	31	26	-	23
	Y	6.5 (6473)	22	16	48	200	66	31	26	-	23
	N	7.4 (7440)	80	100	48	85	65	35	40	22	23

1 Step 1: Tighten all head bolts to 18 ft. lbs.
  Step 2: Tighten all bolts to 26 ft. lbs., except No. 9
  Retorque No. 9 to 18 ft. lbs.
  Step 3: Tighten all an additional 90 degrees
2 Automatic trans.: 55 ft. lbs.
  Manual trans.: 65 ft. lbs.
3 Center bolts: 36 ft. lbs.
  Outer bolts: 26 ft. lbs.
4 Coat threads with sealer
  Tighten all bolts to 40 ft. lbs.
  Tighten all an additional 90 degrees (1/4 turn)
5 Tighten all bolts to 13 ft. lbs.
  Retorque to 19 ft. lbs.
6 Tighten bolts to 35 ft. lbs. then rotate 130 degrees
  Tighten four center bolts an additional 30 degrees

7 26 ft. lbs. plus 50 degrees
8 20 ft. lbs. plus 50 degrees
9 110 ft. lbs. plus 76 degrees
10 11 ft. lbs. plus 50 degrees
11 20 ft. lbs plus 60 degrees
12 Two center bolts: 26 ft. lbs.
  All others: 20 ft. lbs.
13 All 5 & 6 stud single rear wheels: 110 ft. lbs.
  All 8 stud single rear wheels: 120 ft. lbs.
  All 8 stud dual rear wheels: 140 ft. lbs.
  All 10 stud dual wheels: 175 ft. lbs.
14 Outer bolts on caps 2-4: 70 ft. lbs.
  All others: 80 ft. lbs.

TORQUE SPECIFICATIONS
All readings in ft. lbs.

Year	Engine ID/VIN	Engine Displacement Liters (cc)	Cylinder Head Bolts	Main Bearing Bolts	Rod Bearing Bolts	Crankshaft Damper Bolts	Flywheel Bolts	Manifold		Spark Plugs	Lug Nut
								Intake	Exhaust		

15 Coat threads with sealant
Tighten all bolts to 20 ft. lbs.
Retorque to 50 ft. lbs.
Tighten all bolts an additional 90 degrees (1/4 turn)

16 Outer bolts: 100 ft. lbs.
Inner bolts: 111 ft. lbs.

17 37 ft. lbs. plus 77 degrees

18 Tighten bolts to 13 ft. lbs.
Retorque to 22 ft. lbs.

19 1st-time installation (new head): 22 ft. lbs.
All other installations: 11 ft. lbs.

20 Short bolts: 43 ft. lbs. plus 90 degrees
Long bolts: 46 ft. lbs. plus 90 degrees

21 Coat threads with sealer
Tighten all bolts to 33 ft. lbs.
Tighten all an additional 90 degrees (1/4 turn)

22 Coat threads with sealant
Tighten all bolts to 20 ft. lbs.
Retorque to 50 ft. lbs.

23 All 5 & 6 stud single rear wheels: 110 ft. lbs.
All 8 stud single rear wheels: 120 ft. lbs.
All 8 stud dual rear wheels: 175 ft. lbs.

BRAKE SPECIFICATIONS
All measurements in inches unless noted

Year	Model	Master Cylinder Bore	Brake Disc Original Thickness	Minimum Thickness	Maximum Runout	Brake Drum Diameter Original Inside Diameter	Max. Wear Limit	Maximum Machine Diameter	Minimum Lining Thickness Front	Rear
1992	Astro/Safari	NA	1	2	0.004	9.50	9.59	9.56	0.030	0.030
	Blazer	NA	1.500	1.480	0.004	5	6	7	0.030	0.030
	Lumina APV/Silhouette/Trans Sport	0.944	1.043	0.972	0.004	8.86	8.91	8.88	0.030	0.030
	P30	NA	1.245	1.230	0.004	13.00	13.09	13.06	0.030	0.030
	S10 Blazer/S15 Jimmy/Bravada	NA	1.040	0.980	0.004	9.50	9.59	9.56	0.030	0.030
	S10 Pick-up/Sonoma	NA	1.040	0.980	0.004	9.50	9.59	9.56	0.030	0.030
	Suburban	NA	1.500	1.480	0.004	5	6	7	0.030	0.030
	Syclone	NA	1.040	0.980	0.004	9.50	9.59	9.56	0.030	0.030
	Typhoon	NA	1.040	0.980	0.004	9.50	9.59	9.56	0.030	0.030
	C1500	NA	1.250	1.230	0.004	5	6	7	0.030	0.030
	C2500	NA	1.500	1.480	0.004	5	6	7	0.030	0.030
	C3500	NA	1.500	1.480	0.004	5	6	7	0.030	0.030
	G10/G1500	NA	3	4	0.004	5	6	7	0.030	0.030
	G20/G2500	NA	3	4	0.004	5	6	7	0.030	0.030
	G30/G3500	NA	3	4	0.004	5	6	7	0.030	0.030
	K1500	NA	1.500	1.480	0.004	5	6	7	0.030	0.030
	K2500	NA	1.500	1.480	0.004	5	6	7	0.030	0.030
	K3500	NA	1.500	1.480	0.004	5	6	7	0.030	0.030
1993	Astro/Safari	NA	1	2	0.004	9.50	9.59	9.56	0.030	0.030
	Blazer/Yukon	NA	1.500	1.480	0.004	5	6	7	0.030	0.030
	Lumina APV/Silhouette/Trans Sport	0.944	1.043	0.972	0.004	8.86	8.91	8.88	0.030	0.030
	S10 Blazer/S15 Jimmy/Bravada	NA	1.040	0.980	0.004	9.50	9.59	9.56	0.030	0.030
	S10 Pick-up/Sonoma	NA	1.040	0.980	0.004	9.50	9.59	9.56	0.030	0.030
	Suburban	NA	1.500	1.480	0.004	5	6	7	0.030	0.030
	Typhoon	NA	1.040	0.980	0.004	9.50	9.59	9.56	0.030	0.030
	C1500	NA	1.250	1.230	0.004	5	6	7	0.030	0.030
	C2500	NA	1.500	1.480	0.004	5	6	7	0.030	0.030

BRAKE SPECIFICATIONS

All measurements in inches unless noted

Year	Model	Master Cylinder Bore	Brake Disc			Brake Drum Diameter			Minimum Lining Thickness	
			Original Thickness	Minimum Thickness	Maximum Runout	Original Inside Diameter	Max. Wear Limit	Maximum Machine Diameter	Front	Rear
1993	C3500	NA	1.500	1.480	0.004	5	6	7	0.030	0.030
	G10/G1500	NA	3	4	0.004	5	6	7	0.030	0.030
	G20/G2500	NA	3	4	0.004	5	6	7	0.030	0.030
	G30/G3500	NA	3	4	0.004	5	6	7	0.030	0.030
	K1500	NA	1.500	1.480	0.004	5	6	7	0.030	0.030
	K2500	NA	1.500	1.480	0.004	5	6	7	0.030	0.030
	K3500	NA	1.500	1.480	0.004	5	6	7	0.030	0.030
	P30	NA	1.245	1.230	0.004	13.00	13.09	13.06	0.030	0.030
1994	Astro/Safari	NA	1	2	0.004	9.50	9.59	9.56	0.030	0.030
	Blazer/Yukon	NA	1.500	1.480	0.004	5	6	7	0.030	0.030
	Lumina APV/Silhouette/Trans Sport	0.944	1.043	0.972	0.004	8.86	8.91	8.88	0.030	0.030
	S10 Blazer/S15 Jimmy/Bravada	NA	1.040	0.980	0.004	9.50	9.59	9.56	0.030	0.030
	S10 Pick-up/Sonoma	NA	1.040	0.980	0.004	9.50	9.59	9.56	0.030	0.030
	Suburban	NA	1.500	1.480	0.004	5	6	7	0.030	0.030
	C1500	NA	1.250	1.230	0.004	5	6	7	0.030	0.030
	C2500	NA	1.500	1.480	0.004	5	6	7	0.030	0.030
	C3500	NA	1.500	1.480	0.004	5	6	7	0.030	0.030
	G10/G1500	NA	3	4	0.004	5	6	7	0.030	0.030
	G20/G2500	NA	3	4	0.004	5	6	7	0.030	0.030
	G30/G3500	NA	1.280	1.230	0.004	11.00	11.09	11.06	0.030	0.030
	K1500	NA	1.500	1.480	0.004	5	6	7	0.030	0.030
	K2500	NA	1.500	1.480	0.004	5	6	7	0.030	0.030
	K3500	NA	1.500	1.480	0.004	5	6	7	0.030	0.030
1995-96	Astro/Safari	NA	1	2	0.004	9.50	9.59	9.56	0.030	0.030
	Lumina APV/Silhouette/Trans Sport	0.944	1.043	0.972	0.004	8.86	8.91	8.88	0.030	0.030
	S10 Blazer/S15 Jimmy	NA	1.040	0.980	0.004	9.50	9.59	9.56	0.030	0.030
	S10 Pick-up/Sonoma	NA	1.040	0.980	0.004	9.50	9.59	9.56	0.030	0.030
	Suburban	NA	1.500	1.480	0.004	5	6	7	0.030	0.030
	Tahoe/Yukon	NA	1.500	1.480	0.004	5	6	7	0.030	0.030
	C1500	NA	1.250	1.230	0.004	5	6	7	0.030	0.030
	C2500	NA	1.500	1.480	0.004	5	6	7	0.030	0.030
	C3500	NA	1.500	1.480	0.004	5	6	7	0.030	0.030
	G10/G1500	NA	3	4	0.004	5	6	7	0.030	0.030
	G20/G2500	NA	3	4	0.004	5	6	7	0.030	0.030
	G30/G3500	NA	1.280	1.230	0.004	11.00	11.09	11.06	0.030	0.030
	K1500	NA	1.500	1.480	0.004	5	6	7	0.030	0.030
	K2500	NA	1.500	1.480	0.004	5	6	7	0.030	0.030
	K3500	NA	1.500	1.480	0.004	5	6	7	0.030	0.030

NA - Not Available
1 Available with 1.040" and 1.250" rotors
2 1.040" rotors: 0.980
  1.250" rotors: 1.230
3 Available with 1.28" and 1.54" discs
4 1.280" disc: 1.230
  1.540" disc: 1.480

5 Available with 10", 11.15" and 13" drums
6 10" drums: 10.05
  11.15" drums: 11.24
  13" drums: 13.09
7 10" drums: 10.09
  11.15" drums: 11.21
  13" drums: 13.06

WHEEL ALIGNMENT

Year	Model		Caster Range (deg.)	Caster Preferred Setting (deg.)	Camber Range (deg.)	Camber Preferred Setting (deg.)	Toe-In (in.)	Steering Axis Inclination (deg.)
1992	Astro/Safari	1	1 11/16P-3 11/16P	2 11/16P	0-1 19/32P	13/16P	3/32P	NA
	Astro/Safari	2	2 1/16P-4 1/16P	3 1/16P	0-1 3/4P	7/8P	3/32P	NA
	Blazer		-	3	3/4P-2P	1 1/2P	1/8P	NA
	Lumina APV/Silhouette/Trans Sport		11/16P-2 11/16P	1 11/16P	1/2N-1/2P	0	0	NA
	S10 Blazer/S15 Jimmy/ Bravada		1P-3P	2P	0-1 5/8P	13/16P	1/8P	NA
	S10 Pick-up/Sonoma		1P-3P	2P	0-1 5/8P	13/16P	1/8P	NA
	Suburban		6	7	3/4P-2P	1 1/2P	0	NA
	Syclone		1P-3P	2P	0-1 5/8P	13/16P	1/8P	NA
	Typhoon		1P-3P	2P	0-1 5/8P	13/16P	1/8P	NA
	C1500		3 3/4P-5 3/4P	4 3/4P	0-1P	1/2P	1/8P	NA
	C2500		3 3/4P-5 3/4P	4 3/4P	0-1P	1/2P	1/8P	NA
	C3500		3 3/4P-5 3/4P	4 3/4P	0-1P	1/2P	1/8P	NA
	G10/G1500		-	4	1/4N-1 1/4P	1/2P	3/16P	NA
	G20/G2500		-	4	1/4N-1 1/4P	1/2P	3/16P	NA
	G30/G3500		-	4	1/2N-1P	1/4P	3/16P	NA
	K1500		1P-5P	3P	0-1P	1/2P	1/4P	NA
	K2500		1P-5P	3P	0-1P	1/2P	1/4P	NA
	K3500		1P-5P	3P	0-1P	1/2P	1/4P	NA
	P30		-	5	1/2N-7/8P	3/16P	3/16P	NA
1993	Astro/Safari	1	1 11/16P-3 11/16P	2 11/16P	0-1 19/32P	13/16P	3/32P	NA
	Astro/Safari	2	2 1/16P-4 1/16P	3 1/16P	0-1 3/4P	7/8P	3/32P	NA
	Blazer/Yukon		6	7	3/4P-2P	1 1/2P	0	NA
	Lumina APV/Silhouette/Trans Sport		11/16P-2 11/16P	1 11/16P	1/2N-1/2P	0	0	NA
	S10 Blazer/S15 Jimmy/ Bravada		1P-3P	2P	0-1 5/8P	13/16P	1/8P	NA
	S10 Pick-up/Sonoma		1P-3P	2P	0-1 5/8P	13/16P	1/8P	NA
	Suburban		6	7	3/4P-2P	1 1/2P	0	NA
	Typhoon		1P-3P	2P	0-1 5/8P	13/16P	1/8P	NA
	C1500		3 3/4P-5 3/4P	4 3/4P	0-1P	1/2P	1/8P	NA
	C2500		3 3/4P-5 3/4P	4 3/4P	0-1P	1/2P	1/8P	NA
	C3500		3 3/4P-5 3/4P	4 3/4P	0-1P	1/2P	1/8P	NA
	G10/G1500		-	4	1/4N-1 1/4P	1/2P	3/16P	NA
	G20/G2500		-	4	1/4N-1 1/4P	1/2P	3/16P	NA
	G30/G3500		-	4	1/2N-1P	1/4P	3/16P	NA
	K1500		1P-5P	3P	0-1P	1/2P	1/4P	NA
	K2500		1P-5P	3P	0-1P	1/2P	1/4P	NA
	K3500		1P-5P	3P	0-1P	1/2P	1/4P	NA
	P30		-	5	1/2N-7/8P	3/16P	3/16P	NA
1994	Astro/Safari	1	1 11/16P-3 11/16P	2 11/16P	0-1 19/32P	13/16P	3/32P	NA
	Astro/Safari	2	2 1/16P-4 1/16P	3 1/16P	0-1 3/4P	7/8P	3/32P	NA
	Blazer/Yukon		6	7	3/4P-2P	1 1/2P	0	NA
	Lumina APV/Silhouette/Trans Sport		11/16P-2 11/16P	1 11/16P	1/2N-1/2P	0	0	NA
	S10 Blazer/S15 Jimmy/ Bravada		1P-3P	2P	0-1 5/8P	13/16P	1/8P	NA
	S10 Pick-up/Sonoma		1P-3P	2P	0-1 5/8P	13/16P	1/8P	NA
	Suburban		6	7	3/4P-2P	1 1/2P	0	NA
	C1500		3 3/4P-5 3/4P	4 3/4P	0-1P	1/2P	1/8P	NA
	C2500		3 3/4P-5 3/4P	4 3/4P	0-1P	1/2P	1/8P	NA

WHEEL ALIGNMENT

Year	Model		Caster		Camber		Toe-in (in.)	Steering Axis Inclination (deg.)
			Range (deg.)	Preferred Setting (deg.)	Range (deg.)	Preferred Setting (deg.)		
	C3500		3 3/4P-5 3/4P	4 3/4P	0-1P	1/2P	1/8P	NA
	G10/G1500		-	4	1/4N-1 1/4P	1/2P	3/16P	NA
	G20/G2500		-	4	1/2N-1P	1/2P	3/16P	NA
	G30/G3500		-	5	1/2N-7/8P	3/16P	3/16P	NA
	K1500		1P-5P	3P	0-1P	1/2P	1/4P	NA
	K2500		1P-5P	3P	0-1P	1/2P	1/4P	NA
	K3500		1P-5P	3P	0-1P	1/2P	1/4P	NA
1995-96	Astro/Safari [1]		1 11/16P-3 11/16P	2 11/16P	0-1 19/32P	13/16P	3/32P	NA
	Astro/Safari [2]		2 1/16P-4 1/16P	3 1/16P	0-1 3/4P	7/8P	3/32P	NA
	Lumina APV/Silhouette/Trans Sport		11/16P-2 11/16P	1 11/16P	1/2N-1/2P	0	0	NA
	S10 Blazer/S15 Jimmy		1P-3P	2P	0-1 5/8P	13/16P	1/8P	NA
	S10 Pick-up/Sonoma		1P-3P	2P	0-1 5/8P	13/16P	1/8P	NA
	Suburban		6	7	3/4P-2P	1 1/2P	0	NA
	Tahoe/Yukon		6	7	3/4P-2P	1 1/2P	0	NA
	C1500		3 3/4P-5 3/4P	4 3/4P	0-1P	1/2P	1/8P	NA
	C2500		3 3/4P-5 3/4P	4 3/4P	0-1P	1/2P	1/8P	NA
	C3500		3 3/4P-5 3/4P	4 3/4P	0-1P	1/2P	1/8P	NA
	G10/G1500		-	4	1/4N-1 1/4P	1/2P	3/16P	NA
	G20/G2500		-	4	1/2N-1P	1/2P	3/16P	NA
	G30/G3500		-	5	1/2N-7/8P	3/16P	3/16P	NA
	K1500		1P-5P	3P	0-1P	1/2P	1/4P	NA
	K2500		1P-5P	3P	0-1P	1/2P	1/4P	NA
	K3500		1P-5P	3P	0-1P	1/2P	1/4P	NA

NA - Not Available

1 2WD
2 4WD
3 With ride height 2 1/2-4, caster should be 8
4 Ride height and preferred camber settings:
   1 1/2": 3 3/8P
   2": 3P
   2 1/2": 2 11/16P
   3": 2 5/16P
   3 1/2": 2P
   3 3/4": 1 3/16P
   4": 1 11/16P

5 Ride height and preferred camber settings:
   2 1/2: 2 5/16 degrees
   3: 1 11/16 degrees
   3 1/2: 1 3/16 degrees
   3 3/4: 15/16 degrees
   4: 5/8 degrees
6 2WD: 3 3/4P-5 3/4P
   4WD: 2P-4P
7 2WD: 4 1/4P
   4WD: 3P
NA - Not Available

JEEP

VEHICLE IDENTIFICATION CHART

Engine Code						Model Year	
Code	Liters	Cu. In. (cc)	Cyl.	Fuel Sys.	Eng. Mfg.	Code	Year
P	2.5	150 (2458)	4	MFI	Chrysler	N	1992
S	4.0	242 (3966)	6	MFI	Chrysler	P	1993
P	2.5	150 (2458)	4	MFI	Chrysler	R	1994
S	4.0	242 (3966)	6	MFI	Chrysler	S	1995
Y	5.2	318 (5211)	8	MFI	Chrysler	T	1996
P	2.5	150 (2458)	4	MFI	Chrysler		
S	4.0	242 (3966)	6	MFI	Chrysler		
Y	5.2	318 (5211)	8	MFI	Chrysler		
P	2.5	150 (2458)	4	MFI	Chrysler		
S	4.0	242 (3966)	6	MFI	Chrysler		
Y	5.2	218 (5211)	8	MFI	Chrysler		
P	2.5	150 (2458)	4	MFI	Chrysler		
S	4.0	242 (3966)	6	MFI	Chrysler		
Y	5.2	218 (5211)	8	MFI	Chrysler		

MFI - Multiport fuel injection

ENGINE IDENTIFICATION

Year	Model	Engine Displacement Liters (cc)	Engine Series (ID/VIN)	Fuel System	No. of Cylinders	Engine Type
1992	Cherokee	2.5 (2458)	P	MFI	4	OHV
	Cherokee	4.0 (3966)	S	MFI	6	OHV
	Comanche	2.5 (2458)	P	MFI	4	OHV
	Comanche	4.0 (3966)	S	MFI	6	OHV
	Wrangler	2.5 (2458)	P	MFI	4	OHV
	Wrangler	4.0 (3966)	S	MFI	6	OHV
1993	Cherokee	2.5 (2458)	P	MFI	4	OHV
	Cherokee	4.0 (3966)	S	MFI	6	OHV
	Wrangler	2.5 (2458)	P	MFI	4	OHV
	Wrangler	4.0 (3966)	S	MFI	6	OHV
	Grand Cherokee	4.0 (3966)	S	MFI	6	OHV
	Grand Cherokee	5.2 (5211)	Y	MFI	8	OHV
	Grand Wagoneer	5.2 (5211)	Y	MFI	8	OHV
1994	Cherokee	2.5 (2458)	P	MFI	4	OHV
	Cherokee	4.0 (3966)	S	MFI	6	OHV
	Wrangler	2.5 (2458)	P	MFI	4	OHV
	Wrangler	4.0 (3966)	S	MFI	6	OHV
	Grand Cherokee	4.0 (3966)	S	MFI	6	OHV
	Grand Cherokee	5.2 (5211)	Y	MFI	8	OHV
1995-96	Cherokee	2.5 (2458)	P	MFI	4	OHV
	Cherokee	4.0 (3966)	S	MFI	6	OHV
	Wrangler	2.5 (2458)	P	MFI	4	OHV
	Wrangler	4.0 (3966)	S	MFI	6	OHV
	Grand Cherokee	4.0 (3966)	S	MFI	6	OHV
	Grand Cherokee	5.2 (5211)	Y	MFI	8	OHV

MFI - Multiport fuel injection
OHV - Overhead valve

GENERAL ENGINE SPECIFICATIONS

Year	Engine ID/VIN	Engine Displacement Liters (cc)	Fuel System Type	Net Horsepower @ rpm	Net Torque @ rpm (ft. lbs.)	Bore x Stroke (in.)	Compression Ratio	Oil Pressure @ rpm
1992	P	2.5 (2458)	MFI	123@5250 [1]	139@3250 [2]	3.88x3.19	9.1:1	37@1600 [4]
	S	4.0 (3966)	MFI	180@4750	220@2500 [3]	3.88x3.44	8.8:1	37@1600 [4]
1993	P	2.5 (2458)	MFI	130@5250	139@3250 [2]	3.88x3.19	9.1:1	37@1600 [4]
	S	4.0 (3966)	MFI	180@4750	220@2500 [3]	3.88x3.44	8.8:1	37@1600 [4]
	Y	5.2 (5211)	MFI	220@4800	285@3600	3.91x3.31	9.1:1	30@3000 [4]
1994	P	2.5 (2458)	MFI	130@5250	139@3250 [5]	3.88x3.19	9.1:1	37@1600 [4]
	S	4.0 (3966)	MFI	180@4750	220@4000 [6]	3.88x3.44	8.8:1	37@1600 [4]
	Y	5.2 (5211)	MFI	220@4800	285@3600	3.91x3.31	9.1:1	30@3000 [4]
1995-96	P	2.5 (2458)	MFI	130@5250	139@3250 [5]	3.88x3.19	9.1:1	37@1600 [8]
	S	4.0 (3966)	MFI	180@4750 [7]	220@4000 [6]	3.88x3.44	8.7:1	37@1600 [8]
	Y	5.2 (5211)	MFI	220@4400	285@3600	3.91x3.31	9.1:1	30@3000 [8]

MFI - Multiport fuel injection
1 Cherokee and Comanche: 130@5250
2 Cherokee and Comanche: 149@3250
3 Cherokee, Comanche and Grand Wagoneer :225@4000
4 Above 3000 rpm, pressure can vary to a maximum of 80 psi.
5 Cherokee: 149@3250
6 Cherokee and Grand Wagoneer: 225@4000
7 Cherokee and Grand Cherokee: 190@4750
8 Above 3000 rpm, pressure can vary to a maximum of 75 psi, except on 5.2L.
  On 5.2L, pressure can vary to 80 psi maximum

GASOLINE ENGINE TUNE-UP SPECIFICATIONS

Year	Engine ID/VIN	Engine Displacement Liters (cc)	Spark Plugs Gap (in.)	Ignition Timing (deg.) MT	AT	Fuel Pump (psi)	Idle Speed (rpm) MT	AT	Valve Clearance In.	Ex.
1992	P	2.5 (2458)	0.035	[1]	[1]	39-41	[1]	[1]	HYD	HYD
	S	4.0 (3966)	0.035	[1]	[1]	39-41	[1]	[1]	HYD	HYD
1993	P	2.5 (2458)	0.035	[1]	[1]	39-41	[1]	[1]	HYD	HYD
	S	4.0 (3966)	0.035	[1]	[1]	39-41	[1]	[1]	HYD	HYD
	Y	5.2 (5211)	0.035	[1]	[1]	39-41	[1]	[1]	HYD	HYD
1994	P	2.5 (2458)	0.035	[1]	[1]	39-41	[1]	[1]	HYD	HYD
	S	4.0 (3966)	0.035	[1]	[1]	39-41	[1]	[1]	HYD	HYD
	Y	5.2 (5211)	0.035	[1]	[1]	39-41	[1]	[1]	HYD	HYD
1995-96	P	2.5 (2458)	0.035	[1]	[1]	39-41 [2]	[1]	[1]	HYD	HYD
	S	4.0 (3966)	0.035	[1]	[1]	39-41 [2]	[1]	[1]	HYD	HYD
	Y	5.2 (5211)	0.035	[1]	[1]	39-41 [2]	[1]	[1]	HYD	HYD

NOTE: The Vehicle Emission Control Information label often reflects specification changes made during production. The label figures must be used if they differ from those in this chart.

HYD - Hydraulic
1 Not adjustable
2 With the vacuum line disconnected from the fuel pressure regulator (if equipped).
  Fuel pressure is measured at the test port pressure fitting on fuel rail.

CAPACITIES

Year	Model	Engine ID/VIN	Engine Displacement Liters (cc)	Engine Oil with Filter	Transmission (pts.)			Transfer Case (pts.)	Drive Axle		Fuel Tank (gal.)	Cooling System (qts.)
					4-Spd	5-Spd	Auto.		Front (pts.)	Rear (pts.)		
1992	Cherokee	P	2.5 (2458)	4.0	-	7.4 [1]	17.0	3.0 [2]	2.5	2.5 [3]	20.2	10.5
	Cherokee	S	4.0 (3966)	6.0	-	6.7	17.0	3.0 [2]	2.5	2.5 [3]	20.2	12.0
	Comanche	P	2.5 (2458)	4.0	7.0	7.4 [1]	17.0	2.2	2.5	2.5 [3]	18.5 [4]	10.0
	Comanche	S	4.0 (3966)	6.0	7.0	6.7	17.0	2.2	2.5	2.5 [3]	18.5 [4]	12.0
	Wrangler	P	2.5 (2458)	4.0	-	7.4 [1]	16.0	3.3	2.5	2.5 [3]	15.0 [5]	9.0
	Wrangler	S	4.0 (3966)	6.0	-	6.7	16.0	3.3	2.5	2.5 [3]	15.0 [5]	10.0
1993	Cherokee	P	2.5 (2458)	4.0	-	7.4 [1]	17.0	3.0 [2]	2.5	2.5 [3]	20.2	10.0
	Cherokee	S	4.0 (3966)	6.0	-	6.7	17.0	3.0 [2]	2.5	2.5 [3]	20.2	12.0
	Wrangler	P	2.5 (2458)	4.0	-	7.4 [1]	16.0	3.3	2.5	2.5 [3]	15.0 [5]	9.0
	Wrangler	S	4.0 (3966)	6.0	-	6.7	16.0	3.3	2.5	2.5 [3]	15.0 [5]	10.5
	Grand Cherokee	S	4.0 (3966)	6.0	-	6.5	17.0	3.2 [6]	3.1	3.4	23.0	9.3
	Grand Cherokee	Y	5.2 (5211)	5.0	-	6.5	17.0	3.2 [6]	3.1	3.4	23.0	14.9
	Grand Wagoneer	Y	5.2 (5211)	5.0	-	-	17.0	3.2 [6]	3.1	3.4	23.0	14.9
1994	Cherokee	P	2.5 (2458)	4.0	-	7.4 [1]	17.0	3.0 [2]	2.5	2.5 [3]	20.2	10.0
	Cherokee	S	4.0 (3966)	6.0	-	6.7	17.0	3.0 [2]	2.5	2.5 [3]	20.2	12.0
	Wrangler	P	2.5 (2458)	4.0	-	7.4 [1]	16.0	3.3	2.5	2.5 [3]	15.0 [5]	9.0
	Wrangler	S	4.0 (3966)	6.0	-	6.7	16.0	3.3	2.5	2.5 [3]	15.0 [5]	10.5
	Grand Cherokee	S	4.0 (3966)	6.0	-	6.5	17.0	3.2 [6]	3.1	3.4	23.0	12.0
	Grand Cherokee	Y	5.2 (5211)	5.0	-	6.5	17.0	3.2 [6]	3.1	3.4	23.0	14.9
1995-96	Cherokee	P	2.5 (2468)	4.0	-	6.6 [7]	17.0	3.0 [2]	3.1	3.5 [8]	20.2	10.0
	Cherokee	S	4.0 (3966)	6.0	-	6.6	17.0	3.0 [2]	3.1	3.5 [8]	20.2	12.0
	Wrangler	P	2.5 (2468)	4.0	-	6.6	17.5	[9]	3.7	3.5 [8]	15.0 [5]	9.0
	Wrangler	S	4.0 (3966)	6.0	-	6.6	17.5	[9]	3.7	3.5 [8]	15.0 [5]	10.5
	Grand Cherokee	S	4.0 (3966)	6.0	-	6.5	17.0	3.2 [10]	3.1	3.4	23.0	12.0
	Grand Cherokee	Y	5.2 (5211)	5.0	-	6.5	19.5	3.2 [10]	3.1	3.4	23.0	14.9

1 2WD - 7.4 pts.
2 Command-Trac - 2.2 pts.
3 Heavy Duty - 3.0 pts.
4 Long Bed - 23.5 gals.
5 Optional - 20 gal.
6 NP242: 2.9
  NP249: 3.0
7 2WD: 7.0 pts.
8 8 1/4 axle: 4.4 pts.
  When equipped with TRAC-LOK, include 2 oz. of friction modifier additive
9 Command-Trac:
  Automatic: 2.2 pts.
  Manual: 3.3 pts.
10 NP242: 2.9
  NP249: 2.5

CAMSHAFT SPECIFICATIONS

All measurements given in inches.

Year	Engine ID/VIN	Engine Displacement Liters (cc)	Journal Diameter					Elevation		Bearing Clearance	Camshaft End Play
			1	2	3	4	5	In.	Ex.		
1992	P	2.5 (2548)	2.0300-2.0290	2.0200-2.0190	2.1000-2.0090	2.0000-1.9990	-	0.2650	0.2650	0.0010-0.0030	-
	S	4.0 (3966)	2.0300-2.0290	2.0200-2.0190	2.1000-2.0090	2.0000-1.9990	-	0.2530	0.2530	0.0010-0.0030	-
1993	P	2.5 (2458)	2.0300-2.0290	2.0200-2.0190	2.1000-2.0090	2.0000-1.9990	-	0.2650	0.2650	0.0010-0.0030	-
	S	4.0 (3966)	2.0300-2.0290	2.0200-2.0190	2.1000-2.0090	2.0000-1.9990	-	0.2530	0.2530	0.0010-0.0030	-
	Y	5.2 (5211)	1.9990-1.9980	1.9830-1.9820	1.9680-1.9670	1.9520-1.9510	1.5615-1.5605	NA	NA	0.0010-0.0030	0.0020-0.0100
1994	P	2.5 (2458)	2.0300-2.0290	2.0200-2.0190	2.0100-2.0090	2.0000-1.9990	-	0.2650	0.2650	0.0010-0.0030	-
	S	4.0 (3966)	2.0300-2.0290	2.0200-2.0190	2.0100-2.0090	2.0000-1.9990	-	0.2530	0.2530	0.0010-0.0030	-
	Y	5.2 (5211)	1.9990-1.9980	1.9830-1.9820	1.9680-1.9670	1.9520-1.9510	1.5615-1.5605	NA	NA	0.0010-0.0030	0.0020-0.0100
1995-96	P	2.5 (2458)	2.0300-2.0290	2.0200-2.0190	2.0100-2.0090	2.0000-1.9990	-	0.2650	0.2650	0.0010-0.0030	-
	S	4.0 (3966)	2.0300-2.0290	2.0200-2.0190	2.0100-2.0090	2.0000-1.9990	-	0.2530	0.2530	0.0010-0.0030	-
	Y	5.2 (5211)	1.9990-1.9980	1.9830-1.9820	1.9680-1.9670	1.9520-1.9510	1.5615-1.5605	NA	NA	0.0010-	0.0020-0.0100

NA - Not Available

CRANKSHAFT AND CONNECTING ROD SPECIFICATIONS

All measurements are given in inches.

Year	Engine ID/VIN	Engine Displacement Liters (cc)	Crankshaft				Connecting Rod		
			Main Brg. Journal Dia.	Main Brg. Oil Clearance	Shaft End-play	Thrust on No.	Journal Diameter	Oil Clearance	Side Clearance
1992	P	2.5 (2458)	2.4996-2.5001	0.0010-0.0025	0.0015-0.0065	2	2.0934-2.0955	0.0010-0.0025	0.0100-0.0190
	S	4.0 (3966)	2.4996-2.5001	0.0010-0.0025	0.0015-0.0065	3	2.0934-2.0955	0.0010-0.0025	0.0100-0.0190
1993	P	2.5 (2458)	2.4996-2.5001	0.0010-0.0025	0.0015-0.0065	2	2.0934-2.0955	0.0010-0.0025	0.0100-0.0190
	S	4.0 (3966)	2.4996-2.5001	0.0010-0.0025	0.0015-0.0065	3	2.0934-2.0955	0.0010-0.0025	0.0100-0.0190
	Y	5.2 (5211)	2.4995-2.5005	[1]	0.0020-0.0100	3	2.1240-2.1250	0.0005-0.0022	0.0060-0.0140
1994	P	2.5 (2458)	2.4996-2.5001	0.0010-0.0025	0.0015-0.0065	2	2.0934-2.0955	0.0010-0.0025	0.0100-0.0190
	S	4.0 (3966)	[2]	0.0010-0.0025	0.0015-0.0065	2	2.0934-2.0955	0.0010-0.0025	0.0100-0.0190
	Y	5.2 (5211)	2.4995-2.5005	[1]	0.0020-0.0100	3	2.1240-2.1250	0.0005-0.0022	0.0060-0.0140
1995-96	P	2.5 (2458)	2.4996-2.5001	0.0010-0.0025	0.0015-0.0065	2	2.0934-2.0955	0.0010-0.0025	0.0100-0.0190
	S	4.0 (3966)	2.4996-.2.5001	0.0010-0.0025	0.0015-0.0065	2	2.0934-2.0955	0.0010-0.0025	0.0100-0.0190
	Y	5.2 (5211)	2.4995-2.5005	[1]	0.0020-0.0100	3	2.1240-2.1250	0.0005-0.0022	0.0060-0.0140

1 No. 1: 0.0005-0.0015
Except No. 1: 0.0005-0.0025
2 No. 7: 2.4980-2.4995
Except No.7: 2.4996-2.5001

VALVE SPECIFICATIONS

Year	Engine ID/VIN	Engine Displacement Liters (cc)	Seat Angle (deg.)	Face Angle (deg.)	Spring Test Pressure (lbs. @ in.)	Spring Installed Height (in.)	Stem-to-Guide Clearance (in.)		Stem Diameter (in.)	
							Intake	Exhaust	Intake	Exhaust
1992	P	2.5 (2458)	44.5	45	200@1.216	1.640	0.0010-0.0030	0.0010-0.0030	0.3110-0.3120	0.3110-0.3120
	S	4.0 (3966)	44.5	45	210@1.200	1.625	0.0010-0.0030	0.0010-0.0030	0.3110-0.3120	0.3110-0.3120
1993	P	2.5 (2458)	44.5	45	200@1.216	1.640	0.0010-0.0030	0.0010-0.0030	0.3110-0.3120	0.3110-0.3120
	S	4.0 (3966)	44.5	45	210@1.200	1.625	0.0010-0.0030	0.0010-0.0030	0.3110-0.3120	0.3110-0.3120
	Y	5.2 (5211)	44.25-44.75	43.25-43.75	200@1.212	1.640	0.0010-0.0030	0.0010-0.0030	0.3110-0.3120	0.3110-0.3120
1994	P	2.5 (2458)	44.5	45	200@1.216	1.640	0.0010-0.0030	0.0010-0.0030	0.3110-0.3120	0.3110-0.3120
	S	4.0 (3966)	44.5	45	200@1.216	1.640	0.0010-0.0030	0.0010-0.0030	0.3110-0.3120	0.3110-0.3120
	Y	5.2 (5211)	44.25-44.75	43.25-43.75	200@1.212	1.640	0.0010-0.0030	0.0010-0.0030	0.3110-0.3120	0.3110-0.3120
1995-96	P	2.5 (2458)	44.5	45	200@1.216	1.640	0.0010-0.0030	0.0010-0.0030	0.3110-0.3120	0.3110-0.3120
	S	4.0 (3966)	44.5	45	200@1.216	1.640	0.0010-0.0030	0.0010-0.0030	0.3110-0.3120	0.3110-0.3120
	Y	5.2 (5211)	44.25-44.75	43.25-43.75	200@1.212	1.640	0.0010-0.0030	0.0010-0.0030	0.3110-0.3120	0.3110-0.3120

PISTON AND RING SPECIFICATIONS

All measurements are given in inches.

Year	Engine ID/VIN	Engine Displacement Liters (cc)	Piston Clearance	Ring Gap			Ring Side Clearance		
				Top Compression	Bottom Compression	Oil Control	Top Compression	Bottom Compression	Oil Control
1992	P	2.5 (2458)	0.0013-0.0021	0.0100-0.0200	0.0100-0.0200	0.0150-0.0550	0.0010-0.0032	0.0010-0.0032	0.0010-0.0021
	S	4.0 (3966)	0.0009-0.0017	0.0100-0.0200	0.0100-0.0200	0.0100-0.0250	0.0017-0.0032	0.0017-0.0032	0.0010-0.0080
1993	P	2.5 (2458)	0.0013-0.0021	0.0100-0.0200	0.0100-0.0200	0.0150-0.0550	0.0010-0.0032	0.0010-0.0032	0.0010-0.0021
	S	4.0 (3966)	0.0013-0.0017	0.0100-0.0200	0.0100-0.0200	0.0100-0.0250	0.0017-0.0032	0.0017-0.0032	0.0010-0.0080
	Y	5.2 (5211)	0.0005-0.0015	0.0100-0.0200	0.0100-0.0200	0.0100-0.0500	0.0015-0.0030	0.0015-0.0030	0.0020-0.0080
1994	P	2.5 (2458)	0.0013-0.0021	0.0100-0.0200	0.0100-0.0200	0.0150-0.0550	0.0010-0.0032	0.0010-0.0032	0.0010-0.0085
	S	4.0 (3966)	0.0013-0.0017	0.0100-0.0200	0.0100-0.0200	0.0100-0.0250	0.0017-0.0032	0.0017-0.0032	0.0010-0.0095
	Y	5.2 (5211)	0.0005-0.0015	0.0100-0.0200	0.0100-0.0200	0.0100-0.0500	0.0015-0.0030	0.0015-0.0030	0.0020-0.0080

PISTON AND RING SPECIFICATIONS

All measurements are given in inches.

Year	Engine ID/VIN	Engine Displacement Liters (cc)	Piston Clearance	Ring Gap			Ring Side Clearance		
				Top Compression	Bottom Compression	Oil Control	Top Compression	Bottom Compression	Oil Control
1995-96	P	2.5 (2458)	0.0013-0.0021	0.0100-0.0200	0.0100-0.0200	0.0150-0.0550	0.0010-0.0032	0.0010-0.0032	0.0010-0.0085
	S	4.0 (3966)	0.0013-0.0017	0.0100-0.0200	0.0100-0.0200	0.0100-0.0250	0.0017-0.0032	0.0017-0.0032	0.0010-0.0095
	Y	5.2 (5211)	0.0005-0.0015	0.0100-0.0200	0.0100-0.0200	0.0100-0.0500	0.0015-0.0030	0.0015-0.0030	0.0020-0.0080

TORQUE SPECIFICATIONS

All readings in ft. lbs.

Year	Engine ID/VIN	Engine Displacement Liters (cc)	Cylinder Head Bolts	Main Bearing Bolts	Rod Bearing Bolts	Crankshaft Damper Bolts	Flywheel Bolts	Manifold		Spark Plugs	Lug Nut
								Intake	Exhaust		
1992	P	2.5 (2458)	[1]	80	33	80	[3]	[4]	30	27	80-110
	S	4.0 (3966)	[2]	80	33	80	105	[5]	[5]	27	80-110
1993	P	2.5 (2458)	[1]	80	33	80	[3]	[4]	30	27	80-110
	S	4.0 (3966)	[2]	80	33	80	105	[5]	[6]	27	80-110
	Y	5.2 (5211)	[6]	85	45	135	105	[7]	20	30	80-110
1994	P	2.5 (2458)	[1]	80	33	80	105	[5]	[5]	27	80-110
	S	4.0 (3966)	[2]	80	33	80	105	[6]	[6]	27	80-110
	Y	5.2 (5211)	[6]	85	45	135	105	[7]	20	30	80-110
1995-96	P	2.5 (2458)	[1]	80	33	80	105	[5]	[5]	27	80-110
	S	4.0 (3966)	[2]	80	33	80	105	[8]	[8]	27	80-110
	Y	5.2 (5211)	[6]	85	45	135	105	[7]	20	30	80-110

1 Step 1: 22 ft. lbs.
Step 2: 45 ft. lbs.
Step 3: Bolts 1-6: 110 ft. lbs.
Step 4: Bolt 7: 100 ft. lbs.
Step 5: Bolts 8-10: 110 ft. lbs.

2 Step 1: 22 ft. lbs.
Step 2: 45 ft. lbs.
Step 3: Bolts 1-10 and 12-14: 110 ft. lbs.
Step 4: Bolt 11: 100 ft. lbs.

3 Step 1: 50 ft. lbs.
Step 2: Plus 60 degrees

4 Bolts 1, 6 & 7: 30 ft. lbs.
Bolts 2-5: 23 ft. lbs.

5 Bolt 1: 30 ft. lbs.
Bolts 2-7: 23 ft. lbs.

6 Step 1: 50 ft. lbs.
Step 2: 105 ft. lbs.

7 Step 1: Torque bolts 1-4 to 72 in. lbs.
Step 2: Torque bolts 5-12 to 72 in. lbs.
Step 3: Torque all bolts to 12 ft. lbs.

8 Bolts 1-5 and 8-11: 24 ft. lbs.
Bolts 6-7: 23 ft. lbs.

BRAKE SPECIFICATIONS
All measurements in inches unless noted

Year	Model	Master Cylinder Bore	Brake Disc			Brake Drum Diameter			Minimum Lining Thickness	
			Original Thickness	Minimum Thickness	Maximum Runout	Original Inside Diameter	Max. Wear Limit	Maximum Machine Diameter	Front	Rear
1992	Comanche	0.937	NA	NA[1]	0.003	NA	[2]	NA	NA	NA
	Wrangler	0.937	NA	NA[1]	0.003	NA	[2]	NA	NA	NA
	Cherokee	0.937	NA	NA[1]	0.003	NA	[2]	NA	NA	NA
1993	Wrangler	NA	NA	0.890	0.005	NA	[2]	NA	NA	NA
	Cherokee	NA	NA	0.890[3]	0.005	NA	[2]	NA	NA	NA
	Grand Cherokee	NA	NA	0.890[4]	0.005	-	-	-	NA	NA
	Grand Wagoneer	NA	NA	0.890[4]	0.005	-	-	-	NA	NA
1994	Wrangler	NA	0.940	0.890	0.005	9.00	[2]	9.06	0.030	0.030
	Cherokee	NA	0.940	0.890	0.005	9.00	[2]	9.06	0.030	0.030
	Grand Cherokee	0.990	0.940[5]	0.890[4]	0.005	-	-	-	0.030	0.030
1995-96	Wrangler	NA	0.940	0.890	0.005	9.00	[2]	9.06	0.030	0.030
	Cherokee	NA	0.940	0.890	0.005	9.00	[2]	9.06	0.030	0.030
	Grand Cherokee	0.990	0.940[5]	0.890[6]	0.005	-	-	-	0.030	0.030

NA - Not Available
1 Minumum useable thickness is either cast or stamped on rotor hub face
2 Maximum diameter is listed on outside of drum
3 2WD - 0.866 inch
4 Rear rotors have minimum allowable thickness listed on edge of parking brake drum
5 Rear rotor original thickness: 0.440
6 Rear rotors have minimum allowable thickness listed 0.370

WHEEL ALIGNMENT

Year	Model	Caster		Camber		Toe-in (in.)	Steering Axis Inclination (deg.)
		Range (deg.)	Preferred Setting (deg.)	Range (deg.)	Preferred Setting (deg.)		
1992	Comanche	5P-9P	6P	3/4N-1/2P	0	0	NA
	Wrangler	[1]	[2]	1/2N-1/2P	0	0	NA
	Cherokee	5P-9P	6P	3/4N-1/2P	0	0	NA
1993	Wrangler	[1]	[2]	1/2N-1/2P	0	0	NA
	Cherokee	5P-9P	6P	3/4N-1/2P	0	0	NA
	Grand Cherokee	6 1/2P-7 1/2P	7P	3/4N-1/2P	1/4N	0-1/4P	NA
	Grand Wagoneer	6 1/2P-7 1/2P	7P	3/4N-1/2P	1/4N	0-1/4P	NA
1994	Wrangler	[1]	[2]	1/2N-1/2P	0	0	NA
	Cherokee	5 1/4P-8P	7P	3/4N-1/2P	1/4N	0	NA
	Grand Cherokee	6 1/2P-7 1/2P	7P	3/4N-1/2P	1/4N	0-1/4P	NA
1995-96	Wrangler	[1]	[2]	1/2N-1/2P	0	0	NA
	Cherokee	5 1/4P-8P	7P	3/4N-1/2P	1/4N	0	NA
	Grand Cherokee	6 1/2P-7 1/2P	7P	3/4N-1/2P	1/4N	0-1/4P	NA

NA - Not Available
N - Negative
P - Positive
1 With manual transmission: 6 1/2P-9P
   With automatic transmission: 5 1/4P-7 1/4P
2 With manual transmission: 6 1/2P
   With automatic transmission: 8P

CHRYSLER IMPORTS

ENGINE IDENTIFICATION

Year	Model	Engine Displacement Liters (cc)	Engine Series (ID/VIN)	Fuel System	No. of Cylinders	Engine Type
1992	D-50	2.4 (2350)	W	MFI	4	SOHC
	D-50	3.0 (2972)	S	MFI	6	SOHC
1993	D-50	2.4 (2350)	W	MFI	4	SOHC
	D-50	3.0 (2972)	N	MFI	6	SOHC

MFI - Multiport fuel injection
SOHC - Single overhead camshaft

GENERAL ENGINE SPECIFICATIONS

Year	Engine ID/VIN	Engine Displacement Liters (cc)	Fuel System Type	Net Horsepower @ rpm	Net Torque @ rpm (ft. lbs.)	Bore x Stroke (in.)	Compression Ratio	Oil Pressure @ rpm
1992	W	2.4 (2350)	MFI	116@5000	132@3500	3.41x3.94	8.5:1	40-85@3000
	S	3.0 (2972)	MFI	140@4800	170@2800	3.59x2.99	8.8:1	30-80@3000
1993	W	2.4 (2350)	MFI	116@5000	132@3500	3.41x3.94	8.5:1	40-85@3000
	N	3.0 (2972)	MFI	140@4800	170@2800	3.59x2.99	8.9:1	30-80@3000

MFI - Multiport fuel injection

GASOLINE ENGINE TUNE-UP SPECIFICATIONS

Year	Engine ID/VIN	Engine Displacement Liters (cc)	Spark Plugs Gap (in.)	Ignition Timing (deg.) MT	Ignition Timing (deg.) AT	Fuel Pump (psi)	Idle Speed (rpm) MT	Idle Speed (rpm) AT	Valve Clearance In.	Valve Clearance Ex.
1992	W	2.4 (2350)	0.039-0.043	5B	5B	46-50	750	750	HYD	HYD
	S	3.0 (2972)	0.039-0.043	12B	12B	46-50	800	800	HYD	HYD
1993	W	2.4 (2350)	0.039-0.043	5B	5B	46-50	750	750	HYD	HYD
	N	3.0 (2972)	0.039-0.043	12B	12B	46-50	800	800	HYD	HYD

NOTE: The Vehicle Emission Control Information label often reflects specification
changes made during production. The label figures must be used if they
differ from those in this chart.
B - Before top dead center
HYD - Hydraulic

CAPACITIES

Year	Model	Engine ID/VIN	Engine Displacement Liters (cc)	Engine Oil with Filter (qts.)	Transmission (pts.)			Transfer Case (pts.)	Drive Axle		Fuel Tank (gal.)	Cooling System (qts.)
					4-Spd	5-Spd	Auto.		Front (pts.)	Rear (pts.)		
1992	D-50	W	2.4 (2350)	1	-	5.0	14.4	4.6 2	2.7	2.7	3	4
	D-50	S	3.0 (2972)	5.2	-	5.0	14.4	4.6 2	2.7	2.7	3	8.8
1993	D-50	W	2.4 (2350)	5.1	-	5.0	15.4	4.6	2.4	3.2	5	6.4
	D-50	N	3.0 (2972)	5.0	-	5.0	15.4	4.6	2.4	5.4	5	8.8

1 2WD: 4.1 qts.
   4WD: 5.2 qts.
2 Fill to bottom edge of fill plug hole
3 2WD standard body: 14 gals.
   2WD long body: 18 gals.
   4WD standard body: 16 gals.
   4WD long body: 20 gals.
4 2WD: 6.4 qts.
   4WD: 8.8 qts.
5 2WD standard body: 14 gals.
   2WD long body: 16 gals.
   4WD standard body: 16 gals.
   4WD long body: 20 gals.

CAMSHAFT SPECIFICATIONS

All measurements given in inches.

Year	Engine ID/VIN	Engine Displacement Liters (cc)	Journal Diameter					Elevation		Bearing Clearance	Camshaft End Play
			1	2	3	4	5	In.	Ex.		
1992	W	2.4 (2350)	1.34	1.34	1.34	1.34	1.34	1.650-1.670	1.650-1.670	0.002-0.004	0.004-0.016
	S	3.0 (2972)	1.34	1.34	1.34	1.34	-	1.624	1.624	0.002-0.004	0.004-0.016
1993	W	2.4 (2350)	1.34	1.34	1.34	1.34	1.34	1.650-1.670	1.650-1.670	0.002-0.004	0.004-0.016
	N	3.0 (2972)	1.34	1.34	1.34	1.34	-	1.624	1.624	0.002-0.004	0.004-0.008

CRANKSHAFT AND CONNECTING ROD SPECIFICATIONS

All measurements are given in inches.

Year	Engine ID/VIN	Engine Displacement Liters (cc)	Crankshaft				Connecting Rod		
			Main Brg. Journal Dia.	Main Brg. Oil Clearance	Shaft End-play	Thrust on No.	Journal Diameter	Oil Clearance	Side Clearance
1992	W	2.4 (2350)	2.2440	0.0008-0.0020	0.0020-0.0100	3	1.772	0.0008-0.0020	0.0040-0.0100
	S	3.0 (2972)	2.3610-2.3620	0.0006-0.0020	0.0020-0.0100	3	1.968-1.969	0.0008-0.0028	0.0010-0.0040
1993	W	2.4 (2350)	2.2440	0.0008-0.0020	0.0020-0.0100	3	1.772	0.0008-0.0020	0.0040-0.0100
	N	3.0 (2972)	2.3620	0.0008-0.0020	0.0020-0.0098	3	1.968	0.0008-0.0020	0.0039-0.0098

14 SPECIFICATIONS

VALVE SPECIFICATIONS

Year	Engine ID/VIN	Engine Displacement Liters (cc)	Seat Angle (deg.)	Face Angle (deg.)	Spring Test Pressure (lbs. @ in.)	Spring Installed Height (in.)	Stem-to-Guide Clearance (in.) Intake	Stem-to-Guide Clearance (in.) Exhaust	Stem Diameter (in.) Intake	Stem Diameter (in.) Exhaust
1992	W	2.4 (2350)	44-44.5	45-45.5	73@1.59	1.59	0.0012-0.0039	0.0020-0.0060	0.310	0.310
	S	3.0 (2972)	44.5	45.5	73@1.59	1.59	0.0010-0.0020	0.0020-0.0030	0.313-0.314	0.312-0.313
1993	W	2.4 (2350)	44-44.5	45-45.5	73@1.59	1.59	0.0008-0.0039	0.0020-0.0060	0.310	0.310
	N	3.0 (2972)	44-45.5	45-45.5	74@1.59	1.59	0.0012-0.0039	0.0020-0.0059	0.313-0.314	0.312-0.313

PISTON AND RING SPECIFICATIONS

All measurements are given in inches.

Year	Engine ID/VIN	Engine Displacement Liters (cc)	Piston Clearance	Ring Gap Top Compression	Ring Gap Bottom Compression	Ring Gap Oil Control	Ring Side Clearance Top Compression	Ring Side Clearance Bottom Compression	Ring Side Clearance Oil Control
1992	W	2.4 (2350)	0.0008-0.0016	0.0100-0.0310	0.0080-0.0310	0.0080-0.0390	0.0010-0.0040	0.0010-0.0040	NA
	S	3.0 (2972)	0.0008-0.0015	0.0120-0.0180	0.0100-0.0160	0.0120-0.0350	0.0020-0.0035	0.0008-0.0020	NA
1993	W	2.4 (2350)	0.0008-0.0016	0.0100-0.0310	0.0080-0.0310	0.0080-0.0390	0.0010-0.0040	0.0010-0.0040	NA
	N	3.0 (2972)	0.0008-0.0016	0.0118-0.0177	0.0098-0.0157	0.0079-0.0276	0.0012-0.0035	0.0008-0.0024	NA

NA - Not Available

TORQUE SPECIFICATIONS

All readings in ft. lbs.

Year	Engine ID/VIN	Engine Displacement Liters (cc)	Cylinder Head Bolts	Main Bearing Bolts	Rod Bearing Bolts	Crankshaft Damper Bolts	Flywheel Bolts	Manifold Intake	Manifold Exhaust	Spark Plugs	Lug Nut
1992	W	2.4 (2350)	1	37-39	33-35	80-94	95	11-14	11-14	18-20	51-57
	S	3.0 (2972)	80	60	38	110	70	17	17	20	95
1993	W	2.4 (2350)	1	37-39	33-35	80-94	95	11-14	11-14	18-20	51-57
	N	3.0 (2972)	80	60	38	110	70	17	17	20	95

1 Hot engine: 73-79 ft. lbs.
Cold engine: 65-72 ft. lbs.

BRAKE SPECIFICATIONS

All measurements in inches unless noted

Year	Model	Master Cylinder Bore	Brake Disc		Maximum Runout	Brake Drum Diameter			Minimum Lining Thickness	
			Original Thickness	Minimum Thickness		Original Inside Diameter	Max. Wear Limit	Maximum Machine Diameter	Front	Rear
1992	D-50	0.940	0.861	0.800	0.006	10.00	10.09	10.06	0.060	0.060
1993	D-50	0.940	1.020	0.800	0.006	10.00	10.09	10.06	0.060	0.060

WHEEL ALIGNMENT

Year	Model		Caster		Camber		Toe-in (in.)	Steering Axis Inclination (deg.)
			Range (deg.)	Preferred Setting (deg.)	Range (deg.)	Preferred Setting (deg.)		
1992	D-50	1	2P-4P	3P	1/8P-1 1/8P	3/4P	1/16P	NA
		2	1P-3P	2P	1/2P-1 1/2P	1P	1/16P	NA
1993	D-50	1	2P-4P	3P	1/8P-1 1/8P	3/4P	1/16P	NA
		2	1P-3P	2P	1/2P-1 1/2P	1P	1/16P	NA

NA - Not Available
1 2WD
2 4WD

GEO

ENGINE IDENTIFICATION

Year	Model		Engine Displacement Liters (cc)	Engine Series (ID/VIN)	Fuel System	No. of Cylinders	Engine Type
1992	Tracker		1.6 (1590)	U	TFI	4	SOHC
1993	Tracker		1.6 (1590)	U	TFI	4	SOHC
1994	Tracker		1.6 (1590)	U	TFI	4	SOHC
	Tracker	1	1.6 (1590)	U	MFI	4	SOHC
1995-96	Tracker		1.6 (1590)	U	TFI	4	SOHC
	Tracker	1	1.6 (1590)	U	MFI	4	SOHC

TFI - Throttle body fuel injection
MFI - Multiport fuel injection
SOHC - Single overhead camshaft
1 California and New York models

GENERAL ENGINE SPECIFICATIONS

Year	Engine ID/VIN		Engine Displacement Liters (cc)	Fuel System Type	Net Horsepower @ rpm	Net Torque @ rpm (ft. lbs.)	Bore x Stroke (in.)	Compression Ratio	Oil Pressure @ rpm
1992	U		1.6 (1590)	TFI	80@5400	94@3000	2.95x3.54	8.9:1	51-62@3000
1993	U		1.6 (1590)	TFI	80@5400	94@3000	2.95x3.54	8.9:1	51-62@3000
1994	U		1.6 (1590)	TFI	80@5400	94@3000	2.95x3.54	8.9:1	47-61@3000
	U	1	1.6 (1590)	MFI	95@5600	98@4000	2.95x3.54	8.9:1	47-61@3000
1995-96	U		1.6 (1590)	TFI	80@5400	94@3000	2.95x3.54	8.9:1	47-61@3000
	U	1	1.6 (1590)	MFI	95@5600	98@4000	2.95x3.54	8.9:1	47-61@3000

TFI - Throttle body fuel injection
MFI - Multiport fuel injection
1 California and New York models

GASOLINE ENGINE TUNE-UP SPECIFICATIONS

Year	Engine ID/VIN		Engine Displacement Liters (cc)	Spark Plugs Gap (in.)	Ignition Timing (deg.) MT	Ignition Timing (deg.) AT	Fuel Pump (psi)	Idle Speed (rpm) MT	Idle Speed (rpm) AT	Valve Clearance In.	Valve Clearance Ex.
1992	U		1.6 (1590)	0.030	8B	8B	34-40	800	800	0.0090- 1 0.0110	0.0102- 0.0118
1993	U		1.6 (1590)	0.030	8B	8B	34-40	800	800	0.0090- 1 0.0110	0.0102- 0.0118
1994	U		1.6 (1590)	0.030	8B	8B	34-40	800	800	0.0090- 1 0.0110	0.0102- 0.0118
	U	2	1.6 (1590)	0.030	8B	8B	36-43	800	800	0.0050- 0.0070	0.0050- 0.0070
1995-96	U		1.6 (1590)	0.030	8B	8B	34-41	800	800	0.0090- 1 0.0110	0.0102- 0.0118
	U	2	1.6 (1590)	0.030	8B	8B	36-43	800	800	0.0050- 0.0070	0.0050- 0.0070

NOTE: The Vehicle Emission Control Information label often reflects specification changes made during production. The label figures must be used if they differ from those in this chart.
B - Before top dead center
HYD - Hydraulic

1 Specifications for hot engine. Cold adjustment set valve lash:
Intake: 0.0051-0.0067
Exhaust: 0.0063-0.0073
2 California and New York models

CAPACITIES

Year	Model	Engine ID/VIN	Engine Displacement Liters (cc)	Engine Oil with Filter (qts.)	Transmission (pts.)			Transfer Case (pts.)	Drive Axle		Fuel Tank (gal.)	Cooling System (qts.)
					4-Spd	5-Spd	Auto.		Front (pts.)	Rear (pts.)		
1992	Tracker	U	1.6 (1590)	4.5	-	3.2	9.8 [1]	3.6	4.6	2.1	11.1	[2]
1993	Tracker	U	1.6 (1590)	4.5	-	3.2	10.2 [1]	3.6	3.6	2.2	11.1	[2]
1994	Tracker	U	1.6 (1590)	4.5	-	3.2	10.2 [1]	3.6	3.6	2.2	11.1	[3]
1995-96	Tracker	U	1.6 (1590)	4.5	-	3.2	10.2 [1]	3.6	3.6	2.2	11.1	[3]

1 Automatic transmission - Specification is after complete overhaul. Drain and fill will be less

2 Manual transmission: 5.6 qts.
Automatic transmission: 5.5 qts.

3 Manual transmission: 5.6 qts.
Automatic transmission: 11.1 qts.

CAMSHAFT SPECIFICATIONS

All measurements given in inches.

Year	Engine ID/VIN	Engine Displacement Liters (cc)	Journal Diameter					Elevation		Bearing Clearance	Camshaft End Play
			1	2	3	4	5	In.	Ex.		
1992	U	1.6 (1590)	1.7372-1.7381	1.7451-1.7460	1.7530-1.7539	1.7609-1.7618	1.7687-1.7697	1.4763-1.4724	1.4749-1.4724	0.0020-0.0036	0.0039
1993	U	1.6 (1590)	1.7372-1.7381	1.7451-1.7460	1.7530-1.7539	1.7609-1.7618	1.7687-1.7697	1.4763-1.4724	1.4749-1.4724	0.0020-0.0036	0.0039
1994	U	1.6 (1590)	1.7372-1.7381	1.7451-1.7460	1.7530-1.7539	1.7609-1.7618	1.7687-1.7697	1.4763-1.4724	1.4749-1.4724	0.0020-0.0036	0.0039
	U [1]	1.6 (1590)	1.1000-1.1008	1.1000-1.1008	1.1000-1.1008	1.1000-1.1008	1.1000-1.1008	1.4241-1.4303	1.4314-1.4376	0.0020-0.0036	0.0039
1995-96	U	1.6 (1590)	1.7372-1.7381	1.7451-1.7460	1.7530-1.7539	1.7609-1.7618	1.7687-1.7697	1.4763-1.4724	1.4749-1.4724	0.0020-0.0036	0.0039
	U [1]	1.6 (1590)	1.1000-1.1008	1.1000-1.1008	1.1000-1.1008	1.1000-1.1008	1.1000-1.1008	1.4241-1.4303	1.4314-1.4376	0.0020-0.0036	0.0039

1 GSi model

CRANKSHAFT AND CONNECTING ROD SPECIFICATIONS

All measurements are given in inches.

Year	Engine ID/VIN	Engine Displacement Liters (cc)	Crankshaft				Connecting Rod		
			Main Brg. Journal Dia.	Main Brg. Oil Clearance	Shaft End-play	Thrust on No.	Journal Diameter	Oil Clearance	Side Clearance
1992	U	1.6 (1590)	2.0465-2.0472	0.0012-0.0023	0.0100-0.0149	3	1.7316-1.7323	0.0008-0.0031	0.0039-0.0078
1993	U	1.6 (1590)	2.0465-2.0472	0.0012-0.0023	0.0100-0.0149	3	1.7316-1.7323	0.0008-0.0031	0.0039-0.0078
1994	U	1.6 (1590)	2.0465-2.0472	0.0008-0.0016	0.0010-·0.0049	3	1.7316-1.7323	0.0008-0.0019	0.0039-0.0078
1995-96	U	1.6 (1590)	2.0465-2.0472	0.0008-0.0016	0.0010-0.0049	3	1.7316-1.7323	0.0008-0.0019	0.0039-0.0078

VALVE SPECIFICATIONS

Year	Engine ID/VIN	Engine Displacement Liters (cc)	Seat Angle (deg.)	Face Angle (deg.)	Spring Test Pressure (lbs. @ in.)	Spring Installed Height (in.)	Stem-to-Guide Clearance (in.)		Stem Diameter (in.)	
							Intake	Exhaust	Intake	Exhaust
1992	U	1.6 (1590)	45	45	54.7-64.3@1.63	1.91	0.0008-0.0019	0.0014-0.0025	0.2742-0.2748	0.2737-0.2742
1993	U	1.6 (1590)	45	45	54.7-64.3@1.63	1.91	0.0008-0.0019	0.0014-0.0025	0.2742-0.2748	0.2737-0.2742
1994	U	1.6 (1590)	45	45	50.2-64.3@1.63	1.63	0.0008-0.0019	0.0014-0.0025	0.2742-0.2748	0.2737-0.2742
	U [1]	1.6 (1590)	45	45	23.6-27.5@1.24	1.24	0.0008-0.0018	0.0018-0.0028	0.2152-0.2157	0.2142-0.2148
1995-96	U	1.6 (1590)	45	45	50.2-64.3@1.63	1.63	0.0008-0.0019	0.0014-0.0025	0.2742-0.2748	0.2737-0.2742
	U [1]	1.6 (1590)	45	45	23.6-27.5@1.24	1.24	0.0008-0.0018	0.0018-0.0028	0.2152-0.2157	0.2142-0.2148

1 California and New York models

PISTON AND RING SPECIFICATIONS

All measurements are given in inches.

Year	Engine ID/VIN	Engine Displacement Liters (cc)	Piston Clearance	Ring Gap			Ring Side Clearance		
				Top Compression	Bottom Compression	Oil Control	Top Compression	Bottom Compression	Oil Control
1992	U	1.6 (1590)	0.0008-0.0015	0.0079-0.0137	0.0079-0.0137	0.0079-0.0275	0.0012-0.0027	0.0008-0.0023	NA
1993	U	1.6 (1590)	0.0008-0.0015	0.0079-0.0137	0.0079-0.0137	0.0079-0.0275	0.0012-0.0027	0.0008-0.0023	NA
1994	U	1.6 (1590)	0.0008-0.0015	0.0079-0.0129	0.0079-0.0137	0.0079-0.0275	0.0012-0.0027	0.0008-0.0023	NA
1995-96	U	1.6 (1590)	0.0008-0.0015	0.0079-0.0129	0.0079-0.0137	0.0079-0.0275	0.0012-0.0027	0.0008-0.0023	NA

NA - Not Available

TORQUE SPECIFICATIONS

All readings in ft. lbs.

Year	Engine ID/VIN	Engine Displacement Liters (cc)	Cylinder Head Bolts	Main Bearing Bolts	Rod Bearing Bolts	Crankshaft Damper Bolts	Flywheel Bolts	Manifold		Spark Plugs	Lug Nut
								Intake	Exhaust		
1992	U	1.6 (1590)	54	39	26	81 [1]	58	17	17	18	87
1993	U	1.6 (1590)	54	39	26	81 [1]	58	17	17	18	87
1994	U	1.6 (1590)	52 [2]	40	26	81 [1]	58	17	17	18	87
1995-96	U	1.6 (1590)	52 [2]	40	26	81 [1]	58	17	17	18	87

1 Crankshaft timing belt sprocket
2 Tighten in three steps

BRAKE SPECIFICATIONS

All measurements in inches unless noted

Year	Model	Master Cylinder Bore	Brake Disc			Brake Drum Diameter			Minimum Lining Thickness	
			Original Thickness	Minimum Thickness	Maximum Runout	Original Inside Diameter	Max. Wear Limit	Maximum Machine Diameter	Front	Rear
1992	Tracker	NA	0.394	0.315	0.006	8.66	8.74	8.74	0.236 [1]	0.210 [1]
1993	Tracker	NA	0.394	0.315	0.006	8.66	8.74	8.74	0.236 [1]	0.210 [1]
1994	Tracker	NA	0.394	0.315	0.006	8.66	8.74	8.74	0.236 [1]	0.210 [1]
1995-96	Tracker	NA	0.394	0.315	0.006	8.66	8.74	8.74	0.236 [1]	0.210 [1]

NA - Not Available

[1] Minimum lining thickness includes pad/shoe backing

WHEEL ALIGNMENT

Year	Model	Caster		Camber		Toe-in (in.)	Steering Axis Inclination (deg.)
		Range (deg.)	Preferred Setting (deg.)	Range (deg.)	Preferred Setting (deg.)		
1992	Tracker	1 1/2P-2 1/2P	2P	1/2N-1 1/2P	1/2P	5/64P-1/4P	31
1993	Tracker	1 1/2P	2P	1/2N-1 1/2P	1/2P	5/64P-1/4P	31
1994	Tracker	1/2P-2 1/2P	1 1/2P	1/2N-1 1/2P	1/2P	5/64P-1/4P	31
1995-96	Tracker	1/2P-2 1/2P	1 1/2P	1/2N-1 1/2P	1/2P	5/64P-1/4P	31

P - Positive
N - Negative

ISUZU

VEHICLE IDENTIFICATION CHART

Engine Code						Model Year	
Code	Liters	Cu. In. (cc)	Cyl.	Fuel Sys.	Eng. Mfg.	Code	Year
L	2.3	137 (2254)	4	2BC	Isuzu	N	1992
E	2.6	156 (2559)	4	MFI	Isuzu	P	1993
Z	3.1	189 (3098)	6	TFI	Isuzu	R	1994
V	3.2	193 (3165)	6	MFI	Isuzu	S	1995
W	3.2	193 (3165)	6	MFI	Isuzu	T	1996
L	2.3	137 (2254)	4	2BC	Isuzu		
E	2.6	156 (2559)	4	MFI	Isuzu		
Z	3.1	189 (3098)	6	TFI	Isuzu		
V	3.2	193 (3165)	6	MFI	Isuzu		
W	3.2	193 (3165)	6	MFI	Isuzu		
L	2.3	137 (2254)	4	1	Isuzu		
E	2.6	156 (2559)	4	MFI	Isuzu		
Z	3.1	189 (3098)	6	TFI	Isuzu		
V	3.2	193 (3165)	6	MFI	Isuzu		
W	3.2	193 (3165)	6	MFI	Isuzu		
L	2.3	137 (2254)	4	MFI	Isuzu		
E	2.6	156 (2559)	4	MFI	Isuzu		
V	3.2	193 (3165)	6	MFI	Isuzu		
W	3.2	193 (3165)	6	MFI	Isuzu		

BC - Barrel carburetor
MFI - Multiport fuel injection
TFI - Throttle body fuel injection

1 Federal: 2 barrel carburetor
California: Multiport fuel injection

ENGINE IDENTIFICATION

Year	Model	Engine Displacement Liters (cc)	Engine Series (ID/VIN)	Fuel System	No. of Cylinders	Engine Type
1992	Amigo	2.3 (2254)	4ZD1	2BC	4	SOHC
	Amigo	2.6 (2559)	4ZE1	MFI	4	SOHC
	Pick-up	2.3 (2254)	4ZD1	2BC	4	SOHC
	Pick-up	2.6 (2559)	4ZE1	MFI	4	SOHC
	Pick-up	3.1 (3098)	CPC	TFI	6	OHV
	Rodeo	2.6 (2559)	4ZE1	MFI	4	SOHC
	Rodeo	3.2 (3165)	6VD1	MFI	6	SOHC
	Trooper	3.2 (3165)	6VD1	MFI	6	SOHC
	Trooper	3.2 (3165)	6VD1	MFI	6	DOHC
1993	Amigo	2.3 (2254)	4ZD1	2BC	4	SOHC
	Amigo	2.6 (2559)	4ZE1	MFI	4	SOHC
	Pick-up	2.3 (2254)	4ZD1	2BC	4	SOHC
	Pick-up	2.6 (2559)	4ZE1	MFI	4	SOHC
	Pick-up	3.1 (3098)	CPC	TFI	6	OHV
	Rodeo	2.6 (2559)	4ZE1	MFI	4	SOHC

ENGINE IDENTIFICATION

Year	Model	Engine Displacement Liters (cc)	Engine Series (ID/VIN)	Fuel System	No. of Cylinders	Engine Type
1993	Rodeo	3.2 (3165)	6VD1	MFI	6	SOHC
	Trooper	3.2 (3165)	6VD1	MFI	6	SOHC
	Trooper	3.2 (3165)	6VD1	MFI	6	DOHC
1994	Amigo	2.6 (2559)	4ZE1	MFI	4	SOHC
	Pick-up	2.3 (2254)	4ZD1	2BC	4	SOHC
	Pick-up	2.3 (2254)	4ZD1	MFI	4	SOHC
	Pick-up	2.6 (2559)	4ZE1	MFI	4	SOHC
	Pick-up	3.1 (3098)	CPC	TFI	6	OHV
	Rodeo	2.6 (2559)	4ZE1	MFI	4	SOHC
	Rodeo	3.2 (3165)	6VD1	MFI	6	SOHC
	Trooper	3.2 (3165)	6VD1	MFI	6	SOHC
	Trooper	3.2 (3165)	6VD1	MFI	6	DOHC
1995-96	Pick-up	2.3 (2254)	4ZD1	MFI	4	SOHC
	Pick-up	2.6 (2559)	4ZE1	MFI	4	SOHC
	Rodeo	2.6 (2559)	4ZE1	MFI	4	SOHC
	Rodeo	3.2 (3165)	6VD1	MFI	6	SOHC
	Trooper	3.2 (3165)	6VD1	MFI	6	SOHC
	Trooper	3.2 (3165)	6VD1	MFI	6	DOHC

MFI - Multiport fuel injection
BC - Barrel carburetor
TFI - Throttle body fuel injection

DOHC - Double overhead camshaft
SOHC - Single overhead camshaft
OHV - Overhead valve

GENERAL ENGINE SPECIFICATIONS

Year	Engine ID/VIN	Engine Displacement Liters (cc)	Fuel System Type	Net Horsepower @ rpm	Net Torque @ rpm (ft. lbs.)	Bore x Stroke (in.)	Compression Ratio	Oil Pressure @ rpm
1992	4ZD1	2.3 (2254)	2BC	96@4600	123@2600	3.52x3.54	8.3:1	57@3000
	4ZE1	2.6 (2559)	MFI	120@4600	150@2600	3.65x3.74	8.6:1	57-71@4000
	CPC	3.1 (3098)	TFI	120@4400	165@2800	3.50x3.31	8.5:1	30-55@2000
	6VD1 [1]	3.2 (3165)	MFI	175@5200	188@4000	3.67x3.03	9.3:1	57-80@3000
	6VD1 [2]	3.2 (3165)	MFI	190@5600	195@3800	3.67x3.03	9.3:1	57-80@3000
1993	4ZD1	2.3 (2243)	2BC	96@4600	123@2600	3.52x3.54	8.3:1	57@3000
	4ZE1	2.6 (2559)	MFI	120@4600	150@2600	3.65x3.74	8.6:1	57-71@4000
	CPC	3.1 (3098)	TFI	120@4400	165@2600	3.50x3..31	8.5:1	30-55@2000
	6VD1 [1]	3.2 (3165)	MFI	175@5200	188@4000	3.67x3.03	9.3:1	57-80@3000
	6VD1 [2]	3.2 (3165)	MFI	190@5600	195@3800	3.67x3.03	9.3:1	57-80@3000
1994	4ZD1	2.3 (2254)	2BC	96@4600	123@2600	3.52x3.54	8.3:1	57@3000
	4ZD1	2.3 (2254)	MFI	100@4600	125@2600	3.52x3.54	8.3:1	57@3000
	4ZE1	2.6 (2559)	MFI	120@4600	150@2600	3.65x3.74	8.6:1	57-71@4000
	CPC	3.1 (3098)	TFI	120@4400	165@2800	3.50x3.31	8.5:1	30-55@2000
	6VD1 [1]	3.2 (3165)	MFI	175@5200	188@4000	3.67x3.03	9.3:1	57-80@3000
	6VD1 [2]	3.2 (3165)	MFI	190@5600	195@3800	3.67x3.03	9.3:1	57-80@3000
1995-96	4ZD1	2.3 (2254)	MFI	100@4600	125@2600	3.52x3.54	8.3:1	57@3000
	4ZE1	2.6 (2559)	MFI	120@4600	150@2600	3.65x3.74	8.6:1	57-71@4000
	6VD1 [1]	3.2 (3165)	MFI	175@5200	188@4000	3.67x3.03	9.3:1	57-80@3000
	6VD1 [2]	3.2 (3165)	MFI	190@5600	195@3800	3.67x3.03	9.8:1	57-80@3000

BC - Barrel carburetor
MFI - Multiport fuel injection
TFI - Throttle body fuel injection

1 Single overhead camshaft
2 Double overhead camshaft

GASOLINE ENGINE TUNE-UP SPECIFICATIONS

Year	Engine ID/VIN	Engine Displacement Liters (cc)	Spark Plugs Gap (in.)	Ignition Timing (deg.) MT	AT	Fuel Pump (psi)	Idle Speed (rpm) MT	AT	Valve Clearance In.	Ex.
1992	4ZD1	2.3 (2254)	0.040	6B	6B	3.5	850	950	0.006	0.010
	4ZE1	2.6 (2559)	0.040	12B	12B	35	850	950	0.008	0.008
	CPC	3.1 (3098)	0.040	10B	10B	9-13	800	800	1	1
	6VD1	3.2 (3165)	0.040-0.043	5B	5B	41-46	750	750	NA	NA
1993	4ZD1	2.3 (2254)	0.040	6B	6B	3.5	850	950	0.006	0.010
	4ZE1	2.6 (2559)	0.040	12B	12B	35	850	950	0.008	0.008
	CPC	3.1 (3098)	0.040	10B	10B	9-13	800	800	1	1
	6VD1	3.2 (3165)	0.040-0.043	5B	5B	41-46	750	750	NA	NA
1994	4ZD1	2.3 (2254)	0.040	2	2	3	850	950	4	4
	4ZE1	2.6 (2559)	0.040	12B	12B	35	850	950	0.008	0.008
	CPC	3.1 (3098)	0.040	10B	10B	9-13	800	800	1	1
	6VD1	3.2 (3165)	0.040-0.043	5B	5B	41-46	750	750	NA	NA
1995-96	4ZD1	2.3 (2254)	0.040	12B	-	35	850	950	0.008	0.008
	4ZE1	2.6 (2559)	0.040	12B	12B	35	850	950	0.008	0.008
	6VD1	3.2 (3165)	0.040-0.043	5B	5B	41-46	750	750	NA	NA

NOTE: The Vehicle Emission Control Information label often reflects specification changes made during production. The label figures must be used if they differ from those in this chart.

B - Before top dead center

HYD - Hydraulic

NA - Non-adjustable

1 Zero lash, plus 1 1/4 turns

2 Carbureted: 6B
  Fuel-injected: 12B

3 Carbureted: 3.5 psi
  Fuel-injected: 35 psi

4 Carbureted, Intake: 0.006
  Carbureted, Exhaust: 0.010
  Fuel-injected: 0.008

CAPACITIES

Year	Model	Engine ID/VIN	Engine Displacement Liters (cc)	Engine Oil with Filter (qts.)	Transmission (pts.)			Transfer Case (pts.)	Drive Axle		Fuel Tank (gal.)	Cooling System (qts.)
					4-Spd	5-Spd	Auto.		Front (pts.)	Rear (pts.)		
1992	Amigo	4ZD1	2.3 (2254)	4.2	-	3.2				3.2	21.9	9.5
	Amigo	4ZE1	2.6 (2559)	5.2	-	6.2				3.8	21.9	9.5
	Pick-up	4ZD1	2.3 (2254)	4.2	-	3.2				3.2	1	9.5
	Pick-up	4ZE1	2.6 (2559)	5.2	-	6.2				3.8	1	9.5
	Pick-up	CPC	3.1 (3098)	4.5	-	6.2				3.8	21.9	11.4
	Rodeo	4ZE1	2.6 (2559)	5.8	-	2				3.9	21.9	9.5
	Rodeo	6VD1	3.2 (3165)	6.2	-	2				3.9	21.9	3
	Trooper	6VD1	3.2 (3165)	6.3	-	6.2				3.9	22.5	4
	Trooper	6VD1	3.2 (3165)	6.3	-	6.2				3.9	22.5	4
1993	Amigo	4ZD1	2.3 (2254)	4.2	-	3.2				3.2	21.9	9.5
	Amigo	4ZE1	2.6 (2559)	5.2	-	6.2				3.8	21.9	9.5
	Pick-up	4ZD1	2.3 (2254)	4.2	-	3.2				3.2	1	9.5
	Pick-up	4ZE1	2.6 (2559)	5.2	-	6.2				3.8	1	9.5
	Pick-up	CPC	3.1 (3098)	4.5	-	6.2				3.8	21.9	11.4
	Rodeo	4ZE1	2.6 (2559)	5.8	-	2				3.9	21.9	9.5
	Rodeo	6VD1	3.2 (3165)	6.2	-	2				3.9	21.9	3
	Trooper	6VD1	3.2 (3165)	6.3	-	6.2				3.9	22.5	4
	Trooper	6VD1	3.2 (3165)	6.3	-	6.2				3.9	22.5	4
1994	Amigo	4ZE1	2.6 (2559)	5.2	-	6.2				3.8	21.9	9.5
	Pick-up	4ZD1	2.3 (2254)	4.2	-	3.2				3.2	1	9.5
	Pick-up	4ZE1	2.6 (2559)	5.2	-	6.2				3.2	1	9.5
	Pick-up	CPC	3.1 (3098)	4.5	-	6.2				3.2	21.9	11.4
	Rodeo	4ZE1	2.6 (2559)	5.8	-	2				3.9	21.9	9.5
	Rodeo	6VD1	3.2 (3165)	6.2	-	2				3.9	21.9	3
	Trooper	6VD1	3.2 (3165)	6.3	-	6.2				3.9	22.5	4
	Trooper	6VD1	3.2 (3165)	6.3	-	6.2				3.9	22.5	4
1995-96	Pick-up	4ZD1	2.3 (2254)	3.7	-	3.2				3.2	1	9.5
	Pick-up	4ZE1	2.6 (2559)	4.4	-	6.2				3.8	1	9.5
	Rodeo	4ZE1	2.6 (2559)	4.4	-	2				5	21.9	9.5
	Rodeo	6VD1	3.2 (3165)	6.2	-	2				5	21.9	3
	Trooper	6VD1	3.2 (3165)	5.7	-	6.2				3.8	22.5	4
	Trooper	6VD1	3.2 (3165)	5.7	-	6.2				3.8	22.6	4

1 Standard bed: 14.0
Spacecab and long bed: 19.8
2 MUA transmission: 6.2
Borg-Warner transmission: 4.8
3 Manual transmission: 9.7
Automatic transmission: 9.3

4 Manual transmission: 9.3
Automatic transmission: 9.0
5 Saginaw: 4.0
Dana: 3.8

CAMSHAFT SPECIFICATIONS
All measurements given in inches.

Year	Engine ID/VIN	Engine Displacement Liters (cc)	Journal Diameter					Elevation		Bearing Clearance	Camshaft End Play
			1	2	3	4	5	In.	Ex.		
1992	4ZD1	2.3 (2254)	1.3310-1.3390	1.3310-1.3390	1.3310-1.3390	1.3310-1.3390	1.3310-1.3390	1.4320-1.4560	1.4320-1.4560	0.0033-0.0051	0.0002-0.0059
	4ZE1	2.6 (2559)	1.3310-1.3390	1.3310-1.3390	1.3310-1.3390	1.3310-1.3390	1.3310-1.3390	NA	NA	0.0026-0.0043	0.0080 [5]
	CPC	3.1 (3098)	1.8670-1.8810	1.8670-1.8810	1.8670-1.8810	1.8670-1.8810	NA	0.2300-0.2670	0.2300-0.2670	0.0010-0.0040	NA
	6VD1 [1]	3.2 (3165)	1.7634-1.7701	1.7634-1.7701	1.7634-1.7701	1.7634-1.7701	NA	[3]	[3]	0.0016-0.0197	0.0028-0.0098
	6VD1 [2]	3.2 (3165)	1.0555-1.0618	1.0555-1.0618	1.0555-1.0618	1.0555-1.0618	NA	[4]	[4]	0.0019-0.0059	0.0020-0.0079
1993	4ZD1	2.3 (2254)	1.3310-1.3390	1.3310-1.3390	1.3310-1.3390	1.3310-1.3390	1.3310-1.3390	1.4320-1.4560	1.4320-1.4560	0.0033-0.0051	0.0002-0.0059
	4ZE1	2.6 (2559)	1.3310-1.3390	1.3310-1.3390	1.3310-1.3390	1.3310-1.3390	1.3310-1.3390	NA	NA	0.0026-0.0043	0.0080 [5]
	CPC	3.1 (3098)	1.7634-1.7701	1.7634-1.7701	1.7634-1.7701	1.7634-1.7701	NA	[3]	[3]	0.0016-0.0197	0.0028-0.0098
	6VD1 [1]	3.2 (3165)	1.0555-1.0618	1.0555-1.0618	1.0555-1.0618	1.0555-1.0618	NA	[4]	[4]	0.0019-0.0059	0.0020-0.0079
	6VD1 [2]	3.2 (3165)	1.0500-1.0510	1.0500-1.0510	1.0500-1.0510	1.0500-1.0510	1.0500-1.0510	1.5030	1.5030	0.0011-0.0031	0.0020-0.0060
1994	4ZD1	2.3 (2254)	1.3310-1.3390	1.3310-1.3390	1.3310-1.3390	1.3310-1.3390	1.3310-1.3390	1.4320-1.4560	1.4320-1.4560	0.0033-0.0051	0.0002-0.0059
	4ZE1	2.6 (2559)	1.3310-1.3390	1.3310-1.3390	1.3310-1.3390	1.3310-1.3390	1.3310-1.3390	NA	NA	0.0026-0.0043	0.0080
	CPC	3.1 (3098)	1.8670-1.8810	1.8670-1.8810	1.8670-1.8810	1.8670-1.8810	NA	0.2300-0.2670	0.2300-0.2670	0.0010-0.0040	NA
	6VD1 [1]	3.2 (3165)	1.7634-1.7701	1.7634-1.7701	1.7634-1.7701	1.7634-1.7701	NA	[3]	[3]	0.0016-0.0197	0.0028-0.0098
	6VD1 [2]	3.2 (3165)	1.0555-1.0618	1.0555-1.0618	1.0555-1.0618	1.0555-1.0618	NA	[4]	[4]	0.0019-0.0059	0.0020-0.0079
1995-96	4ZD1	2.3 (2254)	1.3310-1.3390	1.3310-1.3390	1.3310-1.3390	1.3310-1.3390	1.3310-1.3390	1.4320-1.4560	1.4320-1.4560	0.0033-0.0051	0.0002-0.0059
	4ZE1	2.6 (2559)	1.3307-1.3386	1.3307-1.3386	1.3307-1.3386	1.3307-1.3386	1.3307-1.3386	1.4311-1.4331	1.4311-1.4331	0.0033-0.0059	0.0020-0.0079
	6VD1 [1]	3.2 (3165)	1.7634-1.7701	1.7634-1.7701	1.7634-1.7701	1.7634-1.7701	1.7634-1.7701	1.3480-1.3500	1.4638-1.4658	0.0016-0.0197	0.0028-0.0098
	6VD1 [2]	3.2 (3165)	1.0555-1.0618	1.0555-1.0618	1.0555-1.0618	1.0555-1.0618	1.0555-1.0618	1.3437-1.3457	1.3437-1.3457	0.0019-0.0059	0.0020-0.0079

NA - Not Available
1 Single overhead camshaft
2 Double overhead camshaft
3 Intake or exhaust: 1.6732-1.6870
4 Intake: 1.7441-1.7579
Exhaust: 1.7429-1.7567
5 Limit

CRANKSHAFT AND CONNECTING ROD SPECIFICATIONS

All measurements are given in inches.

Year	Engine ID/VIN	Engine Displacement Liters (cc)	Crankshaft Main Brg. Journal Dia.	Crankshaft Main Brg. Oil Clearance	Crankshaft Shaft End-play	Thrust on No.	Connecting Rod Journal Diameter	Connecting Rod Oil Clearance	Connecting Rod Side Clearance
1992	4ZD1	2.3 (2254)	2.1819-2.2016	0.0009-0.0047	0.0024-0.0118	3	1.9065-1.9262	0.0012-0.0470	0.0078-0.0130
	4ZE1	2.6 (2559)	2.1819-2.2016	0.0009-0.0047	0.0024-0.0118	3	1.9065-1.9262	0.0012-0.0470	0.0078-0.0130
	CPC	3.1 (3098)	2.6473-2.6483	0.0012-0.0027	0.0024-0.0083	3	1.9983-1.9994	0.0011-0.0032	0.0140-0.0267
	6VD1	3.2 (3165)	2.5165-2.5170	0.0010-0.0050	0.0020-0.0120	3	2.2434-2.2441	0.0010-0.0047	0.0060-0.0160
1993	4ZD1	2.3 (2254)	2.1819-2.2016	0.0009-0.0047	0.0024-0.0118	3	1.9065-1.9262	0.0012-0.0470	0.0078-0.0130
	4ZE1	2.6 (2559)	2.1819-2.2016	0.0009-0.0047	0.0024-0.0118	3	1.9065-1.9262	0.0012-0.0470	0.0078-0.0130
	CPC	3.1 (3098)	2.6473-2.6483	0.0012-0.0027	0.0024-0.0083	3	1.9983-1.9994	0.0011-0.0032	0.0140-0.0267
	6VD1	3.2 (3165)	2.5165-2.5170	0.0010-0.0050	0.0020-0.0120	3	2.2434-2.2441	0.0010-0.0047	0.0060-0.0160
1994	4ZD1	2.3 (2254)	2.1819-2.2016	0.0009-0.0047	0.0024-0.0118	3	1.9065-1.9262	0.0012-0.0470	0.0078-0.0130
	4ZE1	2.6 (2559)	2.1819-2.2016	0.0009-0.0047	0.0024-0.0118	3	1.9065-1.9262	0.0012-0.0470	0.0078-0.0130
	CPC	3.1 ((3098)	2.6473-2.6483	0.0012-0.0027	0.0024-0.0083	3	1.9983-1.9994	0.0011-0.0032	0.0140-0.0267
	6VD1	3.2 (3165)	2.5165-2.5170	0.0010-0.0050	0.0020-0.0120	3	1.2434-2.2441	0.0010-0.0047	0.0060-0.0160
1995-96	4ZD1	2.3 (2254)	2.2016-2.2022	0.0009-0.0047	0.0024-0.0118	3	1.9262-1.9268	0.0012-0.0470	0.0079-0.0130
	4ZE1	2.6 (2559)	2.2016-2.2022	0.0009-0.0047	0.0024-0.0118	3	1.9262-1.9268	0.0012-0.0470	0.0079-0.0130
	6VD1	3.2 (3165)	2.5165-2.5170	0.0010-0.0047	0.0023-0.0094	3	2.1229-2.1235	0.0010-0.0047	0.0063-0.0157

VALVE SPECIFICATIONS

Year	Engine ID/VIN	Engine Displacement Liters (cc)	Seat Angle (deg.)	Face Angle (deg.)	Spring Test Pressure (lbs. @ in.)	Spring Installed Height (in.)	Stem-to-Guide Clearance (in.)		Stem Diameter (in.)	
							Intake	Exhaust	Intake	Exhaust
1992	4ZD1	2.3 (2254)	45	45	49-56@1.61	1.61	0.0009-0.0080	0.0015-0.0098	0.3102-0.3134	0.3091-0.3124
	4ZE1	2.6 (2559)	45	45	49-56@1.61	1.61	0.0009-0.0080	0.0015-0.0098	0.3102-0.3134	0.3091-0.3124
	CPC	3.1 (3098)	46	45	82@1.58	1.58	0.0010-0.0027	0.0010-0.0027	0.3410-0.3420	0.3410-0.3420
	6VD1	3.2 (3165)	45	45	45-55@1.54	1.54	0.0009-0.0078	0.0012-0.0078	0.2323-0.2346	0.2323-0.2350
1993	4ZD1	2.3 (2254)	45	45	49-56@1.61	1.61	0.0009-0.0080	0.0015-0.0098	0.3102-0.3134	0.3091-0.3124
	4ZE1	2.6 (2559)	45	45	49-56@1.61	1.61	0.0009-0.0080	0.0015-0.0098	0.3102-0.3134	0.3191-0.3124
	CPC	3.1 (3098)	46	45	82@1.58	1.58	0.0010-0.0027	0.0010-0.0027	0.3410-0.3420	0.3410-0.3420
	6VD1	3.2 (3165)	45	45	45-55@1.54	1.54	0.0009-0.0078	0.0012-0.0078	0.2323-0.2346	0.2323-0.2350
1994	4ZD1	2.3 (2254)	45	45	49-56@1.61	1.61	0.0009-0.0080	0.0015-0.0098	0.3102-0.3134	0.3091-0.3124
	4ZE1	2.6 (2559)	45	45	49-56@1.61	1.61	0.0009-0.0080	0.0015-0.0098	0.3102-0.3134	0.3191-0.3124
	CPC	3.1 (3098)	46	45	82@1.58	1.58	0.0010-0.0027	0.0010-0.0027	0.3410-0.3420	0.3410-0.3420
	6VD1	3.2 (3165)	45	45	45-55@1.54	1.54	0.0009-0.0078	0.0012-0.0078	0.2323-0.2346	0.2323-0.2350
1995-96	4ZD1	2.3 (2254)	45	45	49-56@1.61	1.61	0.0009-0.0080	0.0015-0.0098	0.3102-0.3134	0.3091-0.3124
	4ZE1	2.6 (2559)	45	45	45-55@1.61	1.61	0.0009-0.0080	0.0015-0.0098	0.3102-0.3134	0.3091-0.3124
	6VD1	3.2 (3165)	45	45	45-55@1.54	1.54	0.0009-0.0078	0.0012-0.0078	0.2323-0.2353	0.2323-0.2350

PISTON AND RING SPECIFICATIONS

All measurements are given in inches.

Year	Engine ID/VIN	Engine Displacement Liters (cc)	Piston Clearance	Ring Gap			Ring Side Clearance		
				Top Compression	Bottom Compression	Oil Control	Top Compression	Bottom Compression	Oil Control
1992	4ZD1	2.3 (2254)	0.0008-0.0016	0.0120-0.0180	0.0240-0.0280	0.0080-0.0280	0.0010-0.0024	0.0008-0.0022	NA
	4ZE1	2.6 (2559)	0.0010-0.0018	0.0120-0.0180	0.0240-0.0280	0.0080-0.0280	0.0010-0.0024	0.0008-0.0022	NA
	CPC	3.1 (3098)	0.0009-0.0022	0.0100-0.0200	0.0200-0.0280	0.0100-0.0300	0.0020-0.0035	0.0020-0.0035	NA
	6VD1	3.2 (3165)	0.0016-0.0023	0.0138-0.0185	0.0177-0.0236	0.0059-0.0177	0.0006-0.0015	0.0006-0.0015	NA
1993	4ZD1	2.3 (2254)	0.0008-0.0016	0.0120-0.0180	0.0240-0.0280	0.0080-0.0280	0.0010-0.0024	0.0008-0.0022	NA
	4ZE1	2.6 (2559)	0.0010-0.0018	0.0120-0.0180	0.0240-0.0280	0.0080-0.0280	0.0010-0.0024	0.0008-0.0022	NA
	CPC	3.1 (3098)	0.0009-0.0022	0.0100-0.0200	0.0200-0.0280	0.0100-0.0300	0.0020-0.0035	0.0020-0.0035	NA
	6VD1	3.2 (3165)	0.0016-0.0023	0.0138-0.0185	0.0177-0.0236	0.0059-0.0177	0.0006-0.0015	0.0006-0.0015	NA
1994	4ZD1	2.3 (2254)	0.0008-0.0016	0.0120-0.0180	0.2400-0.0280	0.0080-0.0280	0.0010-0.0024	0.0008-0.0022	NA
	4ZE1	2.6 (2559)	0.0010-0.0018	0.0120-0.0180	0.2400-0.0280	0.0080-0.0280	0.0010-0.0024	0.0008-0.0022	NA
	CPC	3.1 (3098)	0.0009-0.0022	0.0100-0.0200	0.0200-0.0280	0.0100-0.0300	0.0020-0.0035	0.0020-0.0035	NA
	6VD1	3.2 (3165)	0.0016-0.0023	0.0138-0.0185	0.0177-0.0236	0.0059-0.0177	0.0006-0.0015	0.0006-0.0015	NA
1995-96	4ZD1	2.3 (2254)	0.0008-0.0016	0.0118-0.0177	0.0236-0.0283	0.0079-0.0276	0.0010-0.0024	0.0008-0.0022	NA
	4ZE1	2.6 (2559)	0.0010-0.0018	0.0118-0.0177	0.0236-0.0283	0.0079-0.0276	0.0010-0.0024	0.0008-0.0022	NA
	6VD1	3.2 (3165)	0.0016-0.0023	0.0138-0.0185	0.0177-0.0236	0.0059-0.0177	0.0006-0.0015	0.0006-0.0015	NA

NA - Not Available

TORQUE SPECIFICATIONS
All readings in ft. lbs.

Year	Engine ID/VIN	Engine Displacement Liters (cc)	Cylinder Head Bolts	Main Bearing Bolts	Rod Bearing Bolts	Crankshaft Damper Bolts	Flywheel Bolts	Manifold Intake	Manifold Exhaust	Spark Plugs	Lug Nut
1992	4ZD1	2.3 (2254)	[1]	72	43	87	40	16	16	14	[2]
	4ZE1	2.6 (2559)	[1]	72	43	87	40	16	16	14	[2]
	CPC	3.1 (3098)	[3]	72	39	70	52	19	25	14	[2]
	6VD1	3.2 (3165)	[4]	29	39	123	40	17	42	13	87
1993	4ZD1	2.3 (2254)	[1]	72	43	87	40	16	16	14	[2]
	4ZE1	2.6 (2559)	[1]	72	43	87	40	16	16	14	[2]
	CPC	3.1 (3098)	[3]	72	39	70	52	19	25	14	[2]
	6VD1	3.2 (3165)	[4]	29	49	123	40	17	42	13	87
1994	4ZD1	2.3 (2254)	[1]	72	43	87	40	16	16	14	[2]
	4ZE1	2.6 (2559)	[1]	72	43	87	40	16	16	14	[2]
	CPC	3.1 (3098)	[3]	72	39	70	52	19	25	14	[2]
	6VD1	3.2 (3165)	[4]	29	49	123	40	17	42	13	87
1995-96	4ZD1	2.3 (2254)	[1]	72	43	87	40	16	16	14	[2]
	4ZE1	2.6 (2559)	[1]	72	43	87	40	16	16	14	[2]
	6VD1	3.2 (3165)	[4]	29	40	123	40	17	42	13	87

1 Step 1: 58 ft. lbs.
Step 2: 72 ft. lbs.
2 Steel wheels: 58-72 ft. lbs.
Aluminum wheels: 80-94 ft. lbs.
3 Step 1: 41 ft. lbs.
Step 2: Turn an additional 90 degrees
4 8x1.25 bolts: 15 ft. lbs.
11x1.5 bolts: 47 ft. lbs.

BRAKE SPECIFICATIONS
All measurements in inches unless noted

Year	Model	Master Cylinder Bore	Brake Disc Original Thickness	Brake Disc Minimum Thickness	Brake Disc Maximum Runout	Brake Drum Diameter Original Inside Diameter	Brake Drum Diameter Max. Wear Limit	Brake Drum Diameter Maximum Machine Diameter	Minimum Lining Thickness Front	Minimum Lining Thickness Rear
1992	Amigo	1.000	[3]	[4]	0.005	8.27 [5]	8.32 [5]	NA	0.039	0.039 [6]
	Pick-up	0.938	[7]	[8]	[9]	10.01 [5]	10.06	NA	0.039	[10]
	Rodeo [1]	1.000	0.866	[11]	0.005	10.00	10.06	NA	0.039	[10]
	Rodeo [2]	1.000	[12]	[13]	0.005	8.27 [5]	8.32 [5]	NA	0.039	0.039
	Trooper	1.000	[12]	[13]	0.005	8.27 [5]	8.27 [5]	NA	0.039	0.039 [6]
1993	Amigo	1.000	[3]	[4]	0.005	8.27 [5]	8.32 [5]	NA	0.039	0.039 [6]
	Pick-up	0.938	[7]	[8]	[9]	10.01	10.06	NA	0.039	[10]
	Rodeo [1]	1.000	0.866	[11]	0.005	10.00	10.06	NA	0.039	[10]
	Rodeo [2]	1.000	[12]	[13]	0.005	8.27 [5]	8.32 [5]	NA	0.039	0.039
	Trooper	1.000	[12]	[13]	0.005	8.27 [5]	8.27 [5]	NA	0.039	0.039 [6]
1994	Amigo	1.000	[3]	[4]	0.005	8.27 [5]	8.32 [5]	NA	0.039	0.039 [6]
	Pick-up	0.938	[7]	[8]	[9]	10.01	10.06	NA	0.039	[10]
	Rodeo [1]	1.000	0.866	[11]	0.005	10.00	10.06	NA	0.039	[10]
	Rodeo [2]	1.000	[12]	[13]	0.005	8.27 [5]	8.32 [5]	NA	0.039	0.039
	Trooper	1.000	[12]	[13]	0.005	8.27 [5]	8.27 [5]	NA	0.039	0.039 [6]
1995-96	Pick-up	0.938	[7]	[8]	[9]	10.01	10.06	10.06	0.039	[10]
	Rodeo [1]	1.000	0.866	[6]	0.005	10.00	10.06	10.06	0.039	
	Rodeo [2]	1.000	[3]	[13]	0.005	8.27 [5]	8.32 [5]	8.32 [5]	0.039	0.039
	Trooper	1.000	[3]	[13]	0.005	8.27 [5]	8.32 [5]	8.32 [5]	0.039	0.039 [6]

NA - Not Available
1 2.6L engine
2 3.2L engine

BRAKE SPECIFICATIONS

All measurements in inches unless noted

Year	Model	Master Cylinder Bore	Brake Disc			Brake Drum Diameter			Minimum Lining Thickness	
			Original Thickness	Minimum Thickness	Maximum Runout	Original Inside Diameter	Max. Wear Limit	Maximum Machine Diameter	Front	Rear

3 Front: 1.026
  Rear: 0.709
4 Front: 0.970
  Rear: 0.654 (Minimum machine diameter: 0.668)
5 Emergency brake drum surface
6 Specification includes disc pads and parking brake shoes
7 Front: 0.886
  Rear: 0.472
8 Front: 0.811
  Rear: 0.417 (Minimum machine diameter: 0.417)

9 Front: 0.0050
  Rear: 0.0051
10 Disc: 0.040
  Drum: 0.039
11 0.811 (Minimum machine diameter: 0.826)
12 Front: 1.020
  Rear: 0.710
13 Front: 0.969 (Minimum machine diameter: 0.983)
  Rear: 0.654 (Minimum machine diameter: 0.668)

WHEEL ALIGNMENT

Year	Model		Caster		Camber		Toe-in (in.)	Steering Axis Inclination (deg.)
			Range (deg.)	Preferred Setting (deg.)	Range (deg.)	Preferred Setting (deg.)		
1992	Amigo		1 3/4P-3 1/4P	2 1/2P	1/2N-1 1/2P	1/2P	0-3/16P	10
	Pick-up	1	7/8P-2 3/8P	1 5/8P	1/2N-1 1/2P	1/2P	0-3/16P	10
	Pick-up	2	1 1/8P-2 5/8P	1 7/8P	1/2N-1 1/2P	1/2P	0-3/16P	10
	Pick-up	3	1 3/16P-2 11/16P	1 15/16P	1/2N-1 1/2P	1/2P	0-3/16P	10
	Pick-up	4	1 7/16P-2 15/16P	2 3/16P	1/2N-1 1/2P	1/2P	0-3/16P	10
	Rodeo		1 9/16P-2 1/16P	2 1/3P	1/2N-1 1/2P	1/2P	0-3/16P	10
	Trooper	5	1 1/4P-2 3/4P	2P	1/2N-1/2P	0	3/32N-3/16P	12
	Trooper	6	1 7/16P-2 15/16P	2 3/16P	1/2N-1/2P	0	3/32N-3/32P	12
1993	Amigo		1 3/4P-3 1/4P	2 1/2P	1/2N-1 1/2P	1/2P	0-3/16P	10
	Pick-up	1	7/8P-2 3/8P	1 5/8P	1/2N-1 1/2P	1/2P	0-3/16P	10
	Pick-up	2	1 1/8P-2 5/8P	1 7/8P	1/2N-1 1/2P	1/2P	0-3/16P	10
	Pick-up	3	1 3/16P-2 11/16P	1 15/16P	1/2N-1 1/2P	1/2P	0-3/16P	10
	Pick-up	4	1 7/16P-2 15/16P	2 3/16P	1/2N-1 1/2P	1/2P	0-3/16P	10
	Rodeo		1 9/16P-2 1/16P	2 1/3P	1/2N-1 1/2P	1/2P	0-3/16P	10
	Trooper	5	1 1/4P-2 3/4P	2P	1/2N-1/2P	0	3/32N-3/16P	12
	Trooper	6	1 7/16P-2 15/16P	2 3/16P	1/2N-1/2P	0	3/32N-3/32P	12
1994	Amigo		1 3/4P-3 1/4P	2 1/2P	1/2N-1 1/2P	1/2P	0-3/16P	10
	Pick-up	1	7/8P-2 3/8P	1 5/8P	1/2N-1 1/2P	1/2P	0-3/16P	10
	Pick-up	2	1 1/8P-2 5/8P	1 7/8P	1/2N-1 1/2P	1/2P	0-3/16P	10
	Pick-up	3	1 3/16P-2 11/16P	1 15/16P	1/2N-1 1/2P	1/2P	0-3/16P	10
	Pick-up	4	1 7/17P-2 15/16P	2 3/16P	1/2N-1 1/2P	1/2P	0-3/16P	10
	Rodeo		1 9/16P-2 1/16P	2 1/3P	1/2N-1 1/2P	1/2P	0-3/16P	10
	Trooper	5	1 1/4P-2 3/4P	2P	1/2N-1/2P	0	3/32P-3/16P	12
	Trooper	6	1 7/16P-2 15/16P	2 3/16P	1/2N-1/2P	0	3/32P-3/16P	12
1995-96	Pick-up	1	7/8P-2 3/8P	1 5/8P	1/2N-1 1/2P	1/2P	0-3/16P	10
	Pick-up	2	1 1/8P-2 5/8P	1 7/8P	1/2N-1 1/2P	1/2P	0-3/16P	10
	Pick-up	3	1 3/16P-2 11/16P	1 15/16P	1/2N-1 1/2P	1/2P	0-3/16P	10
	Pick-up	4	1 7/16P-2 15/16P	2 3/16P	1/2N-1 1/2P	1/2P	0-3/16P	10
	Rodeo		1 9/16P-3 3/32P	2 11/32P	1/2N-1 1/2P	1/2P	0-3/16P	10
	Trooper	5	1 1/4P-2 3/4P	2P	1/2N-1/2P	0	3/32N-3/32P	12
	Trooper	6	1 7/16P-2 15/16P	2 3/16P	1/2N-1/2P	0	3/32N-3/32P	12

NA - Not Available
1 2WD short wheelbase
2 2WD long wheelbase
3 4WD short wheelbase
4 4WD long wheelbase
5 2 door
6 4 door

MAZDA

ENGINE IDENTIFICATION

Year	Model	Engine Displacement Liters (cc)	Engine Series (ID/VIN)	Fuel System	No. of Cylinders	Engine Type
1992	B2200	2.2 (2184)	F2	EFI	4	SOHC
	B2200	2.2 (2184)	F2	2BC	4	SOHC
	B2600i	2.6 (2606)	G6	EFI	4	SOHC
	MPV	2.6 (2606)	G6	EFI	4	SOHC
	MPV	3.0 (2954)	JE	EFI	6	SOHC
	Navajo	4.0 (4016)	X	EFI	6	OHV
1993	B2200	2.2 (2184)	F2	2BC	4	SOHC
	B2200	2.2 (2184)	F2	EFI	4	SOHC
	B2600i	2.6 (2606)	G6	EFI	4	SOHC
	MPV	2.6 (2606)	G6	EFI	4	SOHC
	MPV	3.0 (2954)	JE	EFI	6	SOHC
	Navajo	4.0 (4016)	X	EFI	6	OHV
1994	B2300	2.3 (2298)	A	EFI	4	SOHC
	B3000	3.0 (2968)	V	EFI	6	OHV
	B4000	4.0 (4016)	X	EFI	6	OHV
	MPV	2.6 (2606)	G6	EFI	4	SOHC
	MPV	3.0 (2954)	JE	EFI	6	SOHC
	Navajo	4.0 (4016)	X	EFI	6	OHV
1995-96	B2300	2.3 (2298)	A	EFI	4	SOHC
	B3000	3.0 (2968)	U	EFI	6	OHV
	B4000	4.0 (4016)	X	EFI	6	OHV
	MPV	3.0 (2954)	JE	EFI	6	SOHC

EFI - Electronic fuel injection
BC - Barrel carburetor
SOHC - Single overhead camshaft
DOHC - Double overhead camshaft
OHV - Overhead valve

GENERAL ENGINE SPECIFICATIONS

Year	Engine ID/VIN	Engine Displacement Liters (cc)	Fuel System Type	Net Horsepower @ rpm	Net Torque @ rpm (ft. lbs.)	Bore x Stroke (in.)	Compression Ratio	Oil Pressure @ rpm
1992	F2	2.2 (2184)	EFI	110@4700 [1]	130@3000 [2]	3.39x3.70	8.6:1	43-57@3000
	F2	2.2 (2184)	2BC	85@4500	118@2500	3.39x3.70	8.6:1	43-57@3000
	JE [3]	3.0 (2954)	EFI	195@5750	200@3500	3.54x3.05	9.2:1	46-71@3000
	JE [4]	3.0 (2954)	EFI	150@5000	165@4000	3.54x3.05	8.5:1	53-75@3000
	G6	2.6 (2606)	EFI	121@4600	149@3500	3.62x3.86	8.4:1	45-58@3000
	X	4.0 (4016)	EFI	160@4500	225@2500	3.95x3.32	9.1:1	40-60@2000
1993	F2	2.2 (2184)	EFI	145@4300	190@3500	3.39x3.70	7.8:1	43-57@3000
	F2	2.2 (2184)	2BC	110@4700	130@3000	3.39x3.70	8.6:1	43-56@3000
	JE [3]	3.0 (2954)	EFI	195@5750	200@3500	3.54x3.05	9.2:1	53-75@3000
	G6	2.6 (2606)	EFI	121@4600	149@3500	3.62x3.86	8.4:1	45-58@3000
	X	4.0 (4016)	EFI	160@4500	[5]	3.94x3.31	9.0:1	40-60@2000
	JE [4]	3.0 (2954)	EFI	150@5000	165@4000	3.54x3.05	8.5:1	53-75@3000
1994	A	2.3 (2298)	EFI	98@4600	130@2600	3.78x3.13	9.2:1	40-60@2000
	G6	2.6 (2606)	EFI	121@4600	149@3500	3.60x3.90	8.4:1	45-58@3000
	JE	3.0 (2954)	EFI	155@5000	169@4000	3.50x3.00	8.5:1	53-75@3000
	U	3.0 (2968)	EFI	140@4800	160@3000	3.50x3.14	9.3:1	40-60@2500
	X	4.0 (4016)	EFI	160@4500	[6]	3.95x3.32	9.1:1	40-60@2000
1995-96	A	2.3 (2298)	EFI	112@4800	135@2400	3.78x3.13	9.2:1	36-71@3000
	JE	3.0 (2954)	EFI	155@5000	169@4000	3.50x3.00	8.5:1	53-75@3000
	U	3.0 (2968)	EFI	145@4800	165@3000	3.50x3.14	9.3:1	36-71@3000
	X	4.0 (4016)	EFI	160@4200	220@3000	3.95x3.32	9.0:1	36-71@3000

EFI - Electronic fuel injection
BC - Barrel carburetor
[1] B2200 models: 91@4500
[2] B2200 models: 118@2000
[3] Double overhead camshaft
[4] Single overhead camshaft
[5] Manual transmission: 220@2500
Automatic transmission: 220@2200
[6] Automatic transmission: 220@2800
Manual transmission: 225@2500

GASOLINE ENGINE TUNE-UP SPECIFICATIONS

Year	Engine ID/VIN	Engine Displacement Liters (cc)	Spark Plugs Gap (in.)	Ignition Timing (deg.) MT	AT	Fuel Pump (psi)	Idle Speed (rpm) MT	AT	Valve Clearance In.	Ex.
1992	F2	2.2 (2184)	0.041	6B [1]	6B [1]	30-38 [2,3]	750 [4]	750 [5]	HYD	HYD
	F2 [6]	2.2 (2184)	0.041	9B	9B	30-38 [2]	750	750	HYD	HYD
	G6	2.6 (2606)	0.041	5B [7]	5B [7]	30-38 [2]	750 [8]	770 [8]	HYD	HYD
	JE	3.0 (2954)	0.041	11B [7]	11B [7]	30-38 [2]	800 [8]	800 [8]	HYD	HYD
	X	4.0 (4016)	0.052-0.056	10B [9]	10B [9]	35-45 [2]	[10]	[10]	HYD	HYD
1993	F2	2.2 (2184)	0.039-0.043 [11]	5-7B [1]	5-7B [1]	30-38 [2,12]	730-770 [1,13]	750-790 [1,13]	HYD	HYD
	G6	2.6 (2606)	0.039-0.043	4-6B [1]	4-6B [1]	30-38 [2]	730-770 [1]	750-790 [1]	HYD	HYD
	JE	3.0 (2954)	0.039-0.043	10-12B [1]	10-12B [1]	30-38 [2]	780-820	780-820	HYD	HYD
	X	4.0 (4016)	0.052-0.056	10B [1]	10B [1]	35-45 [2]	780-820	780-820	HYD	HYD
1994	A	2.3 (2298)	0.042-0.046	8-12B [14]	8-12B [14]	30-45 [2]	475-575	475-575	HYD	HYD
	G6	2.6 (2606)	0.039-0.043	4-6B [1]	4-6B [1]	30-38 [2]	750-800	750-800	HYD	HYD
	JE	3.0 (2954)	0.039-0.043	10-12B [1]	10-12B [1]	30-38 [2]	780-820	780-820	HYD	HYD
	U	3.0 (2968)	0.042-0.046	8-12B [14]	8-12B [14]	30-45 [2]	[15]	[15]	HYD	HYD
	X	4.0 (4016)	0.052-0.056	8-12B [9]	8-12B [9]	30-45 [2]	[15]	[15]	HYD	HYD
1995-96	A	2.3 (2298)	0.042-0.046	8-12B [14,9]	8-12B [14,9]	35-45 [2]	475-575	475-575	HYD	HYD
	JE	3.0 (2954)	0.039-0.043	-	10-12B [18]	30-37 [2]	-	780-820 [16]	HYD	HYD
	U	3.0 (2968)	0.042-0.046	8-12B [14]	8-12B [14]	35-45 [2]	[17]	[17]	HYD	HYD
	X	4.0 (4016)	0.052-0.056	8-12B [14,9]	8-12B [14,9]	35-45 [2]	[17]	[17]	HYD	HYD

NOTE: The Vehicle Emission Control Information label often reflects specification changes made during production. The label figures must be used if they differ from those in this chart.

B - Before top dead center

HYD - Hydraulic

1 Data link connector terminal 10 grounded
2 Pressure indicated is with gauge in-line, regulator vacuum hose connected and engine idling
3 Canadian carbureted models:
Manual transmission: 3.4-4.7
Automatic transmission: 2.8-3.6
4 Canadian B2200 models: 800-850 rpm
5 B2200 models with automatic transmission: 770 rpm
6 Turbo

7 Plus or minus 1 degree
8 Plus or minus 20 rpm
9 Base timing, not adjustable
10 Not adjustable
11 Carbureted models: 0.028-0.033
12 Carbureted models with manual transmission: 3.7 to 4.7
Carbureted models with automatic transmission: 2.8 to 3.6
13 Carbureted models: 800-850 rpm
14 With "SPOUT" shorting bar disconnected
15 Automatically adjusted
16 Data link connector terminal 10 grounded and transmission in park
17 Not adjustable

CAPACITIES

Year	Model	Engine ID/VIN	Engine Displacement Liters (cc)	Engine Oil with Filter (qts.)	Transmission (pts.) 4-Spd	5-Spd	Auto.	Transfer Case (pts.)	Drive Axle Front (pts.)	Rear (pts.)	Fuel Tank (gal.)	Cooling System (qts.)
1992	B2200	F2	2.2 (2184)	4.3	-	4.2	15.8 [1]	-	-	2.6	14.8 [2]	7.9
	B2600i	G6	2.6 (2606)	5.0	-	[3]	15.8 [1]	4.2	3.2	3.6	15.9	7.2
	MPV	G6	2.6 (2606)	5.0	-	6.0	15.8 [4]	-	-	3.2	16.3 [6]	[5]
	MPV	JE	3.0 (2954)	5.0	-	6.0	15.8 [4]	3.2	3.6	3.2	19.3	[7]
	Navajo	X	4.0 (4016)	5.0	-	5.6	20.0	2.5	3.5	5.3	19.3	7.8 [4]
1993	B2200	F2	2.2 (2184)	4.3	-	4.2	15.8 [1]	-	-	2.6	14.8 [2]	7.9
	B2600i	G6	2.6 (2606)	5.0	-	[3]	15.8 [1]	4.2	3.2	3.6	15.9	7.6
	MPV	G6	2.6 (2606)	5.0	-	-	15.8 [4]	-	-	3.2	19.6 [6]	10.3
	MPV	JE	3.0 (2954)	5.0	-	-	15.8 [4]	3.2	3.6	3.2	19.3	7.8 [4]
	Navajo	X	4.0 (4016)	5.0	-	5.6	20.0	2.5	3.5	5.3	19.3	8.0
1994	B2300	A	2.3 (2298)	5.0	-	3.6	19.4	-	-	5.0 [8]	16.3 [9]	11.8
	B3000	U	3.0 (2968)	4.5	-	3.6	[10]	2.5	5.0	5.0 [8]	16.3 [9]	8.1 [11]
	B4000	X	4.0 (4016)	5.0	-	3.6	[10]	2.5	5.0	3.2	19.6	7.6
	MPV	G6	2.6 (2606)	5.0	-	-	15.8 [4]	-	-	3.2	19.6 [6]	10.3
	MPV	JE	3.0 (2954)	5.0	-	-	15.8 [4]	3.2	3.6	3.2	19.3	8.0
	Navajo	X	4.0 (4016)	5.0	-	5.6	20.0	2.5	3.5	5.3	19.3	7.2
1995-96	B2300	A	2.3 (2298)	5.0	-	5.6	19.4	2.5	3.5	5.0	16.3 [12]	[13]
	B3000	U	3.0 (2968)	5.0	-	5.6	[10]	2.5	3.5	5.0	16.3 [12]	[14]
	B4000	X	4.0 (4016)	5.0	-	5.6	[10]	2.5	3.5	5.0	[16]	[15]
	MPV	JE	3.0 (2954)	5.0	-	-	18.2	3.2	3.6	3.2		10.3

1 Electronically-controlled transmission: 18.2 pts.
2 Long bed: 17.4 gals.
3 2WD: 6.0 pts.
  4WD: 6.8 pts.
4 With AC: 8.6 qts.
5 Automatic transmission: 7.6 qts.
  Manual transmission: 7.2 qts.
6 With 4 wheel drive: 19.8 gals.
7 Manual transmission: 10.1 qts.
  Automatic transmission: 10.3 qts.
8 Limited slip differential: 5.0 to 5.3 pts. plus four oz. of friction modifier
9 Long bed and cab plus: 19.6 gals.
10 2WD: 19.4 pts.
   4WD: 20.0 pts.
11 With AC super cool and automatic transmission: 8.5 qts.
12 Long bed and Supercab: 19.6 gals.
13 Without A/C: 6.5 qts.
   With A/C: 7.2 qts.
14 Without A/C: 9.5 qts.
   With A/C: 10.2 qts.
15 Without A/C: 7.8 qts.
   Wtih A/C: 8.6 qts.
16 2WD: 19.6 gals.
   4WD: 19.8 gals.

CAMSHAFT SPECIFICATIONS
All measurements given in inches.

Year	Engine ID/VIN	Engine Displacement Liters (cc)	Journal Diameter 1	2	3	4	5	Elevation In.	Ex.	Bearing Clearance	Camshaft End Play
1992	F2	2.2 (2184)	1.2575-1.2584	1.2563-1.2572	1.2563-1.2572	1.2563-1.2572	1.2575-1.2584	1.4905-1.4984	1.4905-1.4984	1	0.0030-0.0080
	G6	2.6 (2606)	1.1788-1.1797	1.1776-1.1786	1.1776-1.1786	1.1776-1.1786	1.1788-1.1797	1.6344-1.6423	1.6452-1.6531	1	0.0059-0.0080
	JE [2]	3.0 (2954)	1.9261-1.9267	1.9258-1.9266	1.9258-1.9266	1.9261-1.9267	NA	1.6084-1.6163	1.6178-1.6257	3	0.0020-0.0080
	JE [4]	3.0 (2954)	1.1787-1.1797	1.1776-1.1785	1.1776-1.1785	1.1787-1.1797	NA	1.5800-1.5874	1.5794-1.5873	5	0.0012-0.0080
	X	4.0 (4016)	1.9510-1.9520	1.9370-1.9380	1.9220-1.9230	1.9070-1.9080	NA	0.4024	0.4024	0.0010-0.0026	0.0040-0.0080
1993	F2	2.2 (2184)	1.2575-1.2584	1.2563-1.2572	1.2563-1.2572	1.2563-1.2572	1.2575-1.2584	1.4905-1.4984	1.4905-1.4984	1	0.0030-0.0080
	KL	2.5 (2496)	6	1.0201-1.0209	1.0201-1.0209	1.0201-1.0209	1.0213-1.0220	1.7067-1.7145	1.7067-1.7145	7	0.0020-0.0056
	G6	2.6 (2606)	1.1788-1.1797	1.7776-1.1786	1.7776-1.1786	1.7776-1.1786	1.1788-1.1797	1.6344-1.6423	1.6452-1.6531	1	0.0059-0.0080
	JE [4]	3.0 (2954)	1.9261-1.9267	1.9258-1.9266	1.9258-1.9266	1.9261-1.9267	NA	1.6084-1.6163	1.6178-1.6257	3	0.0020-0.0080
	JE [2]	3.0 (2954)	1.1787-1.1797	1.1776-1.1785	1.1776-1.1785	1.1787-1.1797	NA	1.5800-1.5874	1.5794-1.5873	5	0.0012-0.0080
	X	4.0 (4016)	1.9510-1.9520	1.9370-1.9380	1.9220-1.9230	1.9070-1.9080	NA	0.4024	0.4024	0.0010-0.0026	0.0004-0.0008
1994	A	2.3 (2299)	1.7713-1.7720	1.7713-1.7720	1.7713-1.7720	1.7713-1.7720	NA	0.2381	0.2381	0.0010-0.0070	0.0010-0.0090
	G6	2.6 (2606)	1.1788-1.1797	1.1776-1.1786	1.1776-1.1786	1.1776-1.1786	1.1788-1.1797	1.6344-1.6423	1.6452-1.6531	1	0.0059-0.0080
	JE [4]	3.0 (2954)	1.1788-1.1795	1.1776-1.1783	1.1776-1.1783	1.1788-1.1795	NA	1.5800 1.5874	1.5794 1.5873	5	0.0012-0.0080
	JE [2]	3.0 (2954)	1.9261-1.9267	1.9258-1.9266	1.9258-1.9266	1.9261-1.9267	NA	1.6084-1.6163	1.6178-1.6257	3	0.0020-0.0080
	U	3.0 (2968)	2.0074-2.0084	2.0074-2.0084	2.0074-2.0084	2.0074-2.0084	2.0074-2.0084	0.2550	0.2550	0.0010-0.0030	0.0001
	X	4.0 (4016)	1.9510-1.9520	1.9370-1.9380	1.9220-1.9230	1.9070-1.9080	NA	0.4024	0.4024	0.0010-0.0026	0.0004-0.0008
1995-96	A	2.3 (2299)	1.7713-1.7720	1.7713-1.7720	1.7713-1.7720	1.7713-1.7720	-	0.2163	0.2163	0.0010-0.0060	0.0010-0.0090
	JE-ZE	3.0 (2954)	1.1788-1.1795	1.1776-1.1783	1.1776-1.1783	1.1788-1.1795	-	1.5800-1.5874	1.5794-1.5873	5	0.0012-0.0080
	JE	3.0 (2954)	1.9261-1.9267	1.9258-1.9266	1.9258-1.9266	1.9261-1.9267	-	1.6084-1.6163	1.6178-1.6257	3	0.0020-0.0080
	U	3.0 (2968)	2.0074-2.0084	2.0074-2.0084	2.0074-2.0084	2.0074-2.0084	2.0074-2.0084	0.2600	0.2600	0.0010-0.0030	0.0070
	X	4.0 (4016)	1.9510-1.9520	1.9370-1.9380	1.9220-1.9230	1.9070-1.9080	-	0.4024	0.4024	0.0010-0.0060	0.0250-0.0640

NA - Not Available
1 Nos. 1 and 5: 0.0014-0.0033
5 Nos. 1 and 4: 0.0016-0.0060
Nos. 2 and 3: 0.0028-0.0060

CAMSHAFT SPECIFICATIONS

All measurements given in inches.

Year	Engine ID/VIN	Engine Displacement Liters (cc)	Journal Diameter					Elevation		Bearing Clearance	Camshaft End Play
			1	2	3	4	5	In.	Ex.		

Nos. 2, 3, 4: 0.0026-0.0045

2 SOHC engine

3 Nos. 1 and 4: 0.0031-0.0044
Nos. 2 and 3: 0.0031-0.0047

4 DOHC engine

6 Right exhaust and left intake: 1.0213-1.0220
Right intake and left exhaust: 1.1801-1.1811

7 Nos. 1 and 5: 0.0016-0.0047
Nos. 2, 3, 4: 0.0028-0.0059

CRANKSHAFT AND CONNECTING ROD SPECIFICATIONS

All measurements are given in inches.

Year	Engine ID/VIN	Engine Displacement Liters (cc)	Crankshaft				Connecting Rod		
			Main Brg. Journal Dia.	Main Brg. Oil Clearance	Shaft End-play	Thrust on No.	Journal Diameter	Oil Clearance	Side Clearance
1992	F2	2.2 (2184)	2.3597-2.3604	①1	0.0031-0.0120	3	2.0055-2.0061	0.0011-0.0039	0.0040-0.0120
	G6	2.6 (2606)	2.3597-2.3604	0.0010-0.0031	0.0031-0.0118	4	2.0055-2.0061	0.0011-0.0039	0.0043-0.0120
	JE	3.0 (2954)	2.4385-2.4392	0.0010-0.0031	0.0031-0.0118	4	2.0842-2.0848	0.0009-0.004	0.0070-0.0160
	X	4.0 (4016)	2.2433-2.2441	0.0005-0.0019	0.0160-0.0126	3	2.1252-2.1260	0.0003-0.0024	0.0002-0.0025
1993	F2	2.2 (2184)	2.3597-2.3604	①1	0.0032-0.0118	3	2.0056-2.0060	0.0011-0.0039	0.0040-0.0120
	G6	2.6 (2606)	2.3598-2.3604	0.0010-0.0031	0.0032-0.0118	4	2.0055-2.0060	0.0011-0.0039	0.0044-0.0120
	JE	3.0 (2954)	2.4385-2.4392	0.0010-0.0031	0.0031-0.0118	4	2.0842-2.0848	0.0009-0.004	0.0070-0.0160
	X	4.0 (4016)	2.2433-2.2441	0.0005-0.0019	0.0160-0.0126	3	2.1252-2.1260	0.0003-0.0024	0.0002-0.0025
1994	A	2.3 (2299)	2.2059-2.2051	0.0008-0.0026	0.0040-0.0120	3	2.0462-2.0472	0.0008-0.0026	0.0035-0.0140
	G6	2.6 (2606)	2.3598-2.3604	0.0010-0.0031	0.0032-0.0118	3	2.0055-2.0060	0.0011-0.0039	0.0044-0.0120
	JE	3.0 (2954)	2.4385-2.4392	0.0010-0.0031	0.0032-0.0118	4	2.0847-2.0848	0.0009-0.004	0.0070-0.0160
	U	3.0 (2954)	2.5190-2.5198	0.0005-0.0023	0.0040-0.0080	4	2.1253-2.1261	0.0007-0.0027	0.0060-0.0140
	X	4.0 (4016)	2.2433-2.2441	0.0005-0.0019	0.0160-0.0126	3	2.1252-2.1260	0.0003-0.0024	0.0000-0.0020
1995-96	A	2.3 (2299)	2.2051-2.2059	0.0008-0.0026	0.0040-0.0120	3	2.0462-2.0472	0.0008-0.0026	0.0035-0.0140
	JE	3.0 (2954)	2.4385-2.4392	0.0010-0.0031	0.0032-0.0118	4	2.0843-2.0849	0.0009-0.0040	0.0070-0.0160
	U	3.0 (2968)	2.5190-2.5198	0.0005-0.0023	0.0040-0.0080	4	2.1253-2.1261	0.0007-0.0027	0.0060-0.0140
	X	4.0 (4016)	2.2433-2.2441	0.0005-0.0019	0.0020-0.0126	3	2.1252-2.1260	0.0003-0.0024	0.0002-0.0025

1 Nos. 1, 2, 4 and 5: 0.0010-0.0031
No. 3: 0.0012-0.0031

VALVE SPECIFICATIONS

Year	Engine ID/VIN	Engine Displacement Liters (cc)	Seat Angle (deg.)	Face Angle (deg.)	Spring Test Pressure (lbs. @ in.)	Spring Installed Height (in.)	Stem-to-Guide Clearance (in.)		Stem Diameter (in.)	
							Intake	Exhaust	Intake	Exhaust
1992	F2 [1]	2.2 (2184)	45	45	[2]	[3]	0.0010-0.0024	0.0012-0.0026	0.3161-0.3167	0.3159-0.3165
	G6	2.6 (2606)	45	45	0.069	1.970	0.0010-0.0024	0.0012-0.0026	0.2744-0.2750	0.2742-0.2748
	JE [4]	3.0 (2954)	45	45	0.060	1.720	0.0010-0.0024	0.0012-0.0026	0.2350-0.2356	0.2348-0.2354
	JE [5]	3.0 (2954)	45	45	[6]	[7]	0.0010-0.0024	0.0012-0.0026	0.2744-0.2750	0.3159-0.3165
	X	4.0 (4016)	45	44	0.078	1.910	0.0008-0.0025	0.0018-0.0035	0.3159-0.3167	0.3149-0.3156
1993	F2 [1]	2.2 (2184)	45	45	[2]	[3]	0.0010-0.0024	0.0012-0.0026	0.3162-0.3167	0.3160-0.3165
	G6	2.6 (2606)	45	45	0.069	1.963	0.0010-0.0023	0.0012-0.0025	0.2744-0.2749	0.2743-0.2748
	JE [4]	3.0 (2954)	45	45	0.060	1.720	0.0010-0.0024	0.0012-0.0026	0.2350-0.2356	0.2348-0.2354
	JE [5]	3.0 (2954)	45	45	[6]	[7]	0.0010-0.0023	0.0012-0.0025	0.2745-0.2750	0.3160-0.3165
	X	4.0 (4016)	45	44	0.078	1.910	0.0008-0.0025	0.0018-0.0035	0.3159-0.3167	0.3149-0.3156
1994	A	2.3 (2299)	45	44	0.078	1.877	0.0010-0.0055	0.0015-0.0055	0.3416-0.3423	0.3411-0.3418
	G6	2.6 (2606)	45	45	0.069	1.963	0.0010-0.0023	0.0012-0.0025	0.2744-0.2749	0.2743-0.2748
	JE [4]	3.0 (2954)	45	45	0.060	1.720	0.0010-0.0024	0.0012-0.0026	0.2350-0.2356	0.2348-0.2354
	JE [5]	3.0 (2954)	45	45	[6]	[7]	0.0010-0.0023	0.0012-0.0025	0.2745-0.2750	0.3160-0.3165
	U	3.0 (2968)	44	44	-	1.840	0.0010-0.0027	0.0015-0.0032	0.3134-0.3126	0.3129-0.3121
	X	4.0 (4016)	45	44	0.078	1.910	0.0008-0.0025	0.0018-0.0035	0.3159-0.3167	0.3149-0.3156
1995-96	A	2.3 (2299)	45	44	0.078	1.540-1.580 [1]	0.0010-0.0027	0.0015-0.0032	0.2746-0.2754	0.2736-0.2744
	JE	3.0 (2954)	45	45	[2]	[3]	0.0010-0.0023	0.0012-0.0025	0.2745-0.2750	0.3160-0.3165
	U	3.0 (2968)	45	44	-	1.736-1.650 [4]	0.0010-0.0027	0.0015-0.0032	0.3134-0.3126	0.3129-0.3121
	X	4.0 (4016)	45	44	0.078	1.910 [5]	0.0008-0.0025	0.0018-0.0035	0.3159-0.3167	0.3149-0.3156

1 B2200
2 Inner: 0.060 Outer: 0.070
3 Inner: 1.681 Outer: 1.984
4 DOHC engine
5 SOHC engine
6 Intake - Inner: 0.063, Outer: 0.071
Exhaust - Inner: 0.073, Outer: 0.080
7 Intake - Inner: 1.56, Outer: 1.73
Exhaust - Inner: 1.59, Outer: 1.77

PISTON AND RING SPECIFICATIONS

All measurements are given in inches.

Year	Engine ID/VIN	Engine Displacement Liters (cc)	Piston Clearance	Ring Gap			Ring Side Clearance		
				Top Compression	Bottom Compression	Oil Control	Top Compression	Bottom Compression	Oil Control
1992	F2	2.2 (2184)	0.0017-0.0024	0.0080-0.0130	0.006-0.011	0.008-0.027	0.0012-0.0027	0.0012-0.0027	NA
	G6	2.6 (2606)	0.0023-0.0029	0.0080-0.0140	0.010-0.016	0.008-0.027	0.0012-0.0028	0.0012-0.0028	NA
	JE	3.0 (2954)	0.0009-0.0020	0.0080-0.0140	0.006-0.012	0.008-0.028	0.0012-0.0028	0.0012-0.0028	NA
	X	4.0 (4016)	0.0008-0.0019	0.0150-0.0230	0.015-0.023	0.015-0.055	0.0020-0.0033	0.0020-0.0033	NA
1993	F2	2.2 (2184)	0.0017-0.0024	0.0080-0.0130	0.006-0.011	0.008-0.027	0.0012-0.0027	0.0012-0.0027	NA
	G6	2.6 (2606)	0.0023-0.0029	0.0080-0.0130	0.010-0.015	0.008-0.027	0.0012-0.0027	0.0012-0.0027	NA
	JE	3.0 (2954)	0.0010-0.0020	0.0080-0.0130	0.006-0.012	0.008-0.027	0.0012-0.0027	0.0012-0.0027	NA
	X	4.0 (4016)	0.0008-0.0019	0.0150-0.0230	0.015-0.023	0.015-0.055	0.0020-0.0033	0.0020-0.0033	NA
1994	A	2.3 (2299)	0.0024-0.0034	0.0100-0.0200	0.010-0.020	0.015-0.049	0.0016-0.0033	0.0016-0.0033	NA
	G6	2.6 (2606)	0.0023-0.0029	0.0080-0.0130	0.010-0.015	0.008-0.027	0.0012-0.0027	0.0012-0.0027	NA
	JE	3.0 (2954)	0.0010-0.0020	0.0080-0.0130	0.006-0.012	0.008-0.027	0.0012-0.0027	0.0012-0.0027	NA
	U	3.0 (2968)	0.0012-0.0023	0.0100-0.0200	0.010-0.020	0.010-0.049	0.0016-0.0037	0.0016-0.0037	NA
	X	4.0 (4016)	0.0008-0.0019	0.0150-0.0230	0.015-0.023	0.015-0.055	0.0020-0.0033	0.0020-0.0033	NA
1995-96	A	2.3 (2299)	0.0010-0.0020	0.0080-0.0016	0.013-0.019	0.010-0.030	0.0016-0.0033	0.0016-0.0033	NA
	JE	3.0 (2954)	0.0010-0.0020	0.0080-0.0130	0.006-0.013	0.008-0.027	0.0012-0.0027	0.0012-0.0027	NA
	U	3.0 (2968)	0.0012-0.0022	0.0100-0.0200	0.010-0.020	0.010-0.049	0.0016-0.0037	0.0016-0.0037	NA
	X	4.0 (4016)	0.0008-0.0019	0.0150-0.0230	0.015-0.023	0.015-0.055	0.0020-0.0033	0.0020-0.0033	NA

NA - Not Available

TORQUE SPECIFICATIONS
All readings in ft. lbs.

Year	Engine ID/VIN	Engine Displacement Liters (cc)	Cylinder Head Bolts	Main Bearing Bolts	Rod Bearing Bolts	Crankshaft Damper Bolts	Flywheel Bolts	Manifold Intake	Manifold Exhaust	Spark Plugs	Lug Nut
1992	F2	2.2 (2184)	59-64	61-65	48-51	116-123	71-76	14-22	25-36	11-17	65-87
	G6	2.6 (2606)	1	61-65	48-51	130-145	67-72	14-19	16-21	11-17	65-87
	JE	3.0 (2954)	2	3	4	116-123	76-81	14-19	16-21	11-17	65-87
	X	4.0 (4016)	5	66-77	18-24	30-37	59	5	18	11-17	100
1993	F2	2.2 (2184)	59-64	61-65	48-51	116-123	71-76	14-22	25-36	11-17	100
	G6	2.6 (2606)	1	61-65	48-51	130-145	67-72	14-19	16-21	11-17	65-87
	JE	3.0 (2954)	2	3	4	116-123	76-81	14-19	16-21	10-13	65-87
	X	4.0 (4016)	5	66-77	18-24	30-37	59	5	18	11-17	100
1994	A	2.3 (2298)	6	7	30-36	15-22	60	19-28	8	7-15	100
	G6	2.6 (2606)	1	61-65	48-51	130-145	67-72	14-19	16-21	11-17	100
	JE	3.0 (2954)	2	3	4	116-123	76-81	14-19	16-21	10-13	65-87
	U	3.0 (2968)	9	59	23-28	24	59	10	18	7-15	100
	X	4.0 (4016)	5	66-77	18-24	30-37	59	5	18	11-17	100
1995-96	A	2.3 (2298)	11	8	30-36	103-133	56-64	19-28	7	7-15	100
	JE	3.0 (2954)	12	13	14	116-122	76-81	14-19	16-21	10-13	65-87
	U	3.0 (2968)	15	55-62	23-28	92-122	54-64	16	15-22	7-14	100
	X	4.0 (4016)	17	66-77	18-24	30-37	59	19	18	7-15	100

1 Step 1: 59-64 ft. lbs.
  Step 2: Tighten two bolts nearest gear 12-17 ft. lbs.

2 Step 1: 14 ft. lbs.
  Step 2: Turn each bolt 90 degrees
  Step 3: Repeat Step 2

3 Step 1: 14 ft. lbs.
  Step 2: Plus 90 degrees
  Step 3: Plus 45 degrees

4 Step 1: 22 ft. lbs.
  Step 2: Turn each nut 40 degrees

5 Step 1: Tighten cylinder head to 44 ft. lbs.
  Step 2: Tighten intake manifold to 3-6 ft. lbs.
  Step 3: Tighten cylinder head to 59 ft. lbs.
  Step 4: Tighten intake to 6-11 ft. lbs.
  Step 5: Tighten cylinder head 80 to 85 degrees
  Step 6: Tighten intake manifold 11-15 ft. lbs., then 15-18 ft. lbs.

6 Step 1: 51-59 ft. lbs.
  Step 2: 80-89 ft. lbs.

7 Step 1: 15-22 ft. lbs.
  Step 2: 45-59 ft. lbs.

8 Step 1: Tighten by hand until seated
  Step 2: 50-60 ft. lbs.
  Step 3: 75-85 ft. lbs.

9 Step 1: 59 ft. lbs.
  Step 2: Back off one full turn
  Step 3: 37 ft. lbs.
  Step 4: 68 ft. lbs.

10 Step 1: 11 ft. lbs.
   Step 2: 19 ft. lbs.

11 Step 1: 51 ft. lbs.
   Step 2: Plus 90-100 degrees

12 Step 1: 12.7-16.2 ft. lbs.
   Step 2: Turn each bolt, in sequence, 90 degrees
   Step 3: Repeat Step 2

13 Step 1: 12.7-16.2 ft. lbs.
   Step 2: Turn each bolt, in sequence, 90 degrees
   Step 3: Turn each bolt, in sequence, 45 degrees

14 Step 1: 20-23.5 ft. lbs.
   Step 2: Plus 90 degrees

15 Step 1: 33-41 ft. lbs.
   Step 2: 63-73 ft. lbs.

16 Step 1: 11 ft. lbs.
   Step 2: 19-24 ft. lbs.

17 Step 1: 22-26 ft. lbs.
   Step 2: 52-56 ft. lbs.
   Step 3: Plus 90 degrees

18 Step 1: 9-11 ft. lbs.
   Step 2: 50-55 ft. lbs.

19 Step 1: 6 ft. lbs.
   Step 2: 11 ft. lbs.
   Step 3: 16 ft. lbs.

BRAKE SPECIFICATIONS

All measurements in inches unless noted

Year	Model	Master Cylinder Bore	Brake Disc Original Thickness	Brake Disc Minimum Thickness	Brake Disc Maximum Runout	Brake Drum Diameter Original Inside Diameter	Brake Drum Diameter Max. Wear Limit	Brake Drum Diameter Maximum Machine Diameter	Minimum Lining Thickness Front	Minimum Lining Thickness Rear
1992	B2200	0.875	1	2	0.006	10.24	10.30	NA	0.118	0.040
	B2600	0.875	1	2	0.006	10.24	10.30	NA	0.118	0.040
	MPV	0.940	3	4	0.004	10.24	10.30	NA	0.080	0.040
	Navajo	NA	NA	0.810	0.010	NA	5	0.06	NA	NA
1993	MPV	0.940	3	4	0.004	10.24	10.30	NA	0.080	0.040
	B2200	0.875	1	2	0.006	10.24	10.30	NA	0.118	0.040
	B2600	0.875	1	2	0.006	10.24	10.30	NA	0.118	0.040
	Navajo	NA	NA	0.810	0.010	NA	5	0.06	NA	NA
1994	MPV	0.940	3	4	0.004	10.24	10.30	NA	0.080	0.040
	B2300	NA	NA	0.810	0.003	NA	5	0.003	0.012	0.003
	B3000	NA	NA	0.810	0.003	NA	5	0.003	0.012	0.003
	B4000	NA	NA	0.810	0.003	NA	5	0.003	0.012	0.003
	Navajo	NA	NA	0.810	0.010	NA	5	0.060	NA	NA
1995-96	B2300	NA	NA	0.810	0.003	NA	5	0.003	0.012	0.003
	B3000	NA	NA	0.810	0.003	NA	5	0.003	0.012	0.003
	B4000	NA	NA	0.810	0.003	NA	5	0.003	0.012	0.003
	MPV	0.940	6	7	0.004	-	-	-	0.080	0.080

NA - Not Available
1 4x2: 0.790
  4x4: 0.870
2 4x2: 0.710
  4x4: 0.790
3 4x2: 1.180
  4x4: 1.100
4 4x2: 1.100
  4x4: 1.020

5 Refer to the maximum diameter stamped on drum
6 Front 4x2: 1.180
  Front 4x4: 1.100
  Rear: 0.710
7 Front 4x2: 1.100
  Front 4x4: 1.020
  Rear: 0.630

WHEEL ALIGNMENT

Year	Model		Caster Range (deg.)		Caster Preferred Setting (deg.)	Camber Range (deg.)	Camber Preferred Setting (deg.)	Toe-in (in.)	Steering Axis Inclination (deg.)
1992	B2200		0-1 2/3P	3	1 5/16P	1/3P-1 1/3P	3/4P	0-1/4P	NA
	B2200		0-1 2/3P	3	1 5/16P	1/3P-1 1/3P	3/4P	0-1/4P	NA
	B2600	1	0-1 2/3P	3	1 5/16P	1/3P-1 1/3P	3/4P	0-1/4P	NA
	B2600	2	0-1 2/3P	4	1 5/6P	1/3P-1 1/2P	1P	0-1/4P	NA
	MPV	1	4 1/16P-5 9/16P		4 13/16P	1/8N-7/8P	3/8P	5/16P	NA
	MPV	2	4 5/16P-5 13/16P		6 1/16P	5/16N-11/16P	3/16P	5/16P	NA
	Navajo		2 1/2P-6P		-	3/4N-1 1/4P	-	1/8N-1/8P	NA
1993	B2200		0-1 2/3P	3	1 5/16P	1/3P-1 1/3P	3/4P	0-1/4P	NA
	B2600	1	0-1 2/3P	3	1 5/16P	1/3P-1 1/3P	3/4P	0-1/4P	NA
	B2600	2	0-1 2/3P	4	1 5/16P	1/3P-1 1/2P	1P	0-1/4P	NA
	MPV	1	4 1/16P-5 9/16P		4 13/16P	7/8N-7/8P	3/8P	5/16P	NA
	MPV	2	4 5/16P-5 13/16P		5 1/16P	5/16N-11/16P	3/16P	5/16P	NA
	Navajo		2 1/2P-6P		-	3/4N-1 1/4P	-	1/8N-1/8P	NA
1994	B2300		2P-6P		4P	1/4N-3/4P	1/4P	1/32	-
	B3000		2P-6P		4P	1/4N-3/4P	1/4P	1/32	-
	B4000	1	2P-6P		4P	1/4N-3/4P	1/4P	1/32	-
	B4000	2	2P-7P		5P	1/4N-3/4P	1/4P	1/32	-
	MPV	1	4 1/6P-5 9/16P		4 13/16P	1/8N-7/8P	3/8P	5/16P	NA
	MPV	2	4 5/16P-5 13/16P		5 1/16P	5/16N-11/16P	3/16P	5/16P	NA
	Navajo		2 1/2P-6P		-	3/4N-1/14P	-	1/8N-1/8P	NA
1995-96	B2300		2P-6P		4P	1/4N-3/4P	1/4P	1/32P	-
	B3000		2P-6P		4P	1/4N-3/4P	1/4P	1/32P	-
	B4000	1	2P-6P		4P	1/4N-3/4P	1/4P	1/32P	-
		2	2P-7P		4 1/2P	1/4N-3/4P	1/4P	1/32P	-
	MPV	1	4 1/16P-5 9/16P		4 13/16P	1/8N-7/8P	3/8P	5/32P	12 15/16
		2	4 5/16P-5 13/16P		5 1/16P	5/16N-11/16P	3/16P	5/32P	11 13/16

NA - Not Available
F - Front
R - Rear
1 2WD
2 4WD
3 If equipped with Power Steering: 1 1/3P-2 1/8P
4 If equipped with Power Steering: 2 3/4P

MITSUBISHI

VEHICLE IDENTIFICATION CHART

Engine Code						Model Year	
Code	Liters	Cu. In. (cc)	Cyl.	Fuel Sys.	Eng. Mfg.	Code	Year
D	1.8	112 (1834)	4	MFI	Mitsubishi	N	1992
W	2.4	147 (2350)	4	MFI	Mitsubishi	P	1993
S	3.0	181 (2972)	6	MFI	Mitsubishi	R	1994
C	1.8	112 (1834)	4	MFI	Mitsubishi	S	1995
G	2.4	147 (2350)	4	MFI	Mitsubishi	T	1996
H	3.0	181 (2972)	6	MFI	Mitsubishi		
C	1.8	112 (1834)	4	MFI	Mitsubishi		
G	2.4	147 (2350)	4	MFI	Mitsubishi		
H	3.0	181 (2972)	6	MFI	Mitsubishi		
M	3.5	213 (3497)	6	MFI	Mitsubishi		
C	1.8	112 (1834)	4	MFI	Mitsubishi		
G	2.4	147 (2350)	4	MFI	Mitsubishi		
H	3.0	181 (2972)	6	MFI	Mitsubishi		
M	3.5	213 (3497)	6	MFI	Mitsubishi		

MFI - Multiport fuel injection

ENGINE IDENTIFICATION

Year	Model	Engine Displacement Liters (cc)	Engine Series (ID/VIN)	Fuel System	No. of Cylinders	Engine Type
1992	Expo	1.8 (1834)	4G93	MFI	4	SOHC
	Expo	2.4 (2350)	4G64	MFI	4	SOHC
	Truck	2.4 (2350)	4G64	MFI	4	SOHC
	Truck	3.0 (2972)	6G72	MFI	6	SOHC
	Montero	3.0 (2972)	6G72	MFI	6	SOHC
1993	Expo	1.8 (1834)	4G93	MFI	4	SOHC
	Expo	2.4 (2350)	4G64	MFI	4	SOHC
	Truck	2.4 (2350)	4G64	MFI	4	SOHC
	Truck	3.0 (2972)	6G72	MFI	6	SOHC
	Montero	3.0 (2972)	6G72	MFI	6	SOHC
1994	Expo	1.8 (1834)	4G93	MFI	4	SOHC
	Expo	2.4 (2350)	4G64	MFI	4	SOHC
	Truck	2.4 (2350)	4G64	MFI	4	SOHC
	Truck	3.0 (2972)	6G72	MFI	6	SOHC
	Montero	3.0 (2972)	6G72	MFI	6	SOHC
	Montero	3.5 (3497)	6G74	MFI	6	DOHC
1995-96	Expo	1.8 (1834)	4G93	MFI	4	SOHC
	Expo	2.4 (2350)	4G64	MFI	4	SOHC
	Mighty Max	2.4 (2350)	4G64	MFI	4	SOHC
	Montero	3.0 (2972)	6G72	MFI	6	SOHC
	Montero	3.5 (3497)	6G74	MFI	6	DOHC

MFI - Multiport fuel injection
SOHC - Single overhead camshaft
DOHC - Double overhead camshaft

GENERAL ENGINE SPECIFICATIONS

Year	Engine ID/VIN		Engine Displacement Liters (cc)	Fuel System Type	Net Horsepower @ rpm		Net Torque @ rpm (ft. lbs.)		Bore x Stroke (in.)	Compression Ratio	Oil Pressure @ rpm
1992	4G93		1.8 (1834)	MFI	113@6000		116@4500		3.19x3.50	9.5:1	41@2000
	4G64	1	2.4 (2350)	MFI	116@5000		136@3500		3.41x3.94	8.5:1	41@2000
	4G64	2	2.4 (2350)	MFI	136@5500		145@4250		3.41x3.94	9.5:1	41@2000
	6G72		3.0 (2972)	MFI	151@5000		174@4000		3.59x2.99	8.9:1	30-80@2000
1993	4G93		1.8 (1834)	MFI	113@6000		116@4500		3.19x3.50	9.5:1	41@2000
	4G64	1	2.4 (2350)	MFI	116@5000		136@3500		3.41x3.94	8.5:1	41@2000
	4G64	2	2.4 (2350)	MFI	136@5500		145@4250		3.41x3.94	9.5:1	41@2000
	6G72		3.0 (2972)	MFI	151@5000		174@4000		3.59x2.99	8.9:1	30-80@2000
1994	4G93		1.8 (1834)	MFI	113@6000		116@4500		3.19x3.50	9.5:1	41@2000
	4G64	1	2.4 (2350)	MFI	116@5000		136@3500		3.41x3.94	8.5:1	41@2000
	4G64	2	2.4 (2350)	MFI	136@5500		145@4250		3.41x3.94	9.5:1	41@2000
	6G72		3.0 (2972)	MFI	151@5000		174@4000		3.59x2.99	8.9:1	30-80@2000
	6G74		3.5 (3496)	MFI	215@5500		228@3000		3.66x3.38	9.5:1	30-80@2000
1995-96	4G93		1.8 (1834)	MFI		3	116@4500		3.19x3.50	9.5:1	41@2000
	4G64		2.4 (2350)	MFI		4	148@3000		3.41x3.94	9.5:1	41@2000
	6G72	5	3.0 (2972)	MFI		6		7	3.59x2.99	9.0:1	30-80@2000
	6G74		3.5 (3497)	MFI	214@5000		228@3000		3.66x3.38	9.5:1	30-80@2000

MFI - Multiport fuel injection
1 2 valves per cylinder
2 4 valves per cylinder
3 California: 111@6000
  Except California: 113@6000
4 California: 138@5500
  Except California: 141@5500

5 Montero SOHC, 4 valves per cylinder
6 California: 168@5500
  Except California: 177@5500
7 California: 183@4500
  Except California: 188@4500

GASOLINE ENGINE TUNE-UP SPECIFICATIONS

Year	Engine ID/VIN		Engine Displacement Liters (cc)	Spark Plugs Gap (in.)	Ignition Timing (deg.)		Fuel Pump (psi)	Idle Speed (rpm)		Valve Clearance	
					MT	AT		MT	AT	In.	Ex.
1992	4G93		1.8 (1834)	0.039-0.043	5B	5B	38	750 [1]	750 [1]	0.008	0.012
	4G64	2	2.4 (2350)	0.039-0.043	5B	5B	38	750	750	HYD	HYD
	4G64	3	2.4 (2350)	0.039-0.043	5B	5B	38	800	800	HYD	HYD
	6G72	2	3.0 (2972)	0.039-0.043	5B	5B	38	700	700	HYD	HYD
	6G72	3	3.0 (2972)	0.039-0.043	5B	5B	38	700	700	HYD	HYD
1993	4G93		1.8 (1834)	0.039-0.043	5B	5B	38	750 [1]	750 [1]	0.008	0.012
	4G64	2	2.4 (2350)	0.039-0.043	5B	5B	38	750	750	HYD	HYD
	4G64	3	2.4 (2350)	0.039-0.043	5B	5B	38	800	800	HYD	HYD
	6G72	2	3.0 (2972)	0.039-0.043	5B	5B	38	700	700	HYD	HYD
	6G72	3	3.0 (2972)	0.039-0.043	5B	5B	38	700	700	HYD	HYD
1994	4G93		1.8 (1834)	0.039-0.043	5B	5B	38	750	750	0.008	0.012
	4G64	2	2.4 (2350)	0.039-0.043	5B	5B	38	750	750	HYD	HYD
	4G64	3	2.4 (2350)	0.039-0.043	5B	5B	38	800	800	HYD	HYD
	6G72	2	3.0 (2972)	0.039-0.043	5B	5B	38	700	700	HYD	HYD
	6G72	3	3.0 (2972)	0.039-0.043	5B	5B	38	700	700	HYD	HYD
	6G74		3.5 (3496)	0.039-0.043	5B	5B	38	700	700	HYD	HYD
1995-96	4G93		1.8 (1834)	0.039-0.043	5B	5B	38	750	750	0.008 [4]	0.012 [4]
	4G64		2.4 (2350)	0.039-0.043	5B	5B	38	800	800	HYD [4]	HYD [4]
	6G72		3.0 (2972)	0.039-0.043	5B	5B	38	700	700	HYD [4]	HYD [4]
	6G72		3.0 (2972)	0.039-0.043	5B	5B	38	700	700	HYD [4]	HYD [4]
	6G74		3.5 (3497)	0.039-0.043	5B	5B	38	700	700	HYD [4]	HYD [4]

NOTE: The Vehicle Emission Control Information label often reflects specification changes made during production. The label figures must be used if they differ from those in this chart.
B - Before top dead center
HYD - Hydraulic

1 California: 700
2 Single overhead camshaft
3 Double overhead camshaft
4 Hot engine

CAPACITIES

Year	Model	Engine ID/VIN	Engine Displacement Liters (cc)	Engine Oil with Filter (qts.)	Transmission (pts.)			Transfer Case (pts.)	Drive Axle		Fuel Tank (gal.)	Cooling System (qts.)
					4-Spd	5-Spd	Auto.		Front (pts.)	Rear (pts.)		
1992	Expo	4G93	1.8 (1834)	4.0	-	[1]	[2]	1.2	-	1.5	14.5	6.3
	Expo	4G64	2.4 (2350)	4.0	-	4.8	[2]	1.2	-	1.5	15.9	6.8
	Truck	4G64	2.4 (2350)	4.2	-	4.9	14.8	-	-	3.2	[3]	[4]
	Truck	6G72	3.0 (2972)	5.0	5.3	5.3	-	4.7	2.4	5.5	15.9	8.9
	Montero	6G72	3.0 (2972)	5.5	5.3	5.3	15.2	4.8	2.6	5.5	24.3	10.0
1993	Expo	4G93	1.8 (1834)	4.0	-	[1]	[2]	1.2	-	1.5	14.5	6.3
	Expo	4G64	2.4 (2350)	[5]	-	4.8	[2]	1.2	-	1.5	15.9	6.8
	Truck	4G64	2.4 (2350)	4.2	-	4.9	14.8	-	-	3.2	[3]	[4]
	Truck	6G72	3.0 (2972)	5.0	-	5.3	-	4.7	2.4	5.5	15.9	8.9
	Montero	6G72	3.0 (2972)	5.5	-	5.3	15.2	4.8	2.6	5.5	24.3	10.0
1994	Expo	4G93	1.8 (1834)	4.0	-	[1]	[2]	1.2	-	1.5	14.5	6.3
	Expo	4G64	2.4 (2350)	[5]	-	4.8	[2]	1.2	-	1.5	15.9	6.8
	Truck	4G64	2.4 (2350)	4.2	-	4.9	14.8	-	-	3.2	[3]	[4]
	Truck	6G72	3.0 (2972)	5.0	-	5.3	-	4.7	2.4	5.5	15.9	8.9
	Montero	6G72	3.0 (2972)	5.5	-	5.3	15.2	4.8	2.6	5.5	24.3	10.0
	Montero	6G74	3.5 (3497)	5.5	-	5.3	15.2	5.2	2.6	5.5	24.3	10.0
1995-96	Expo	4G93	1.8 (1834)	4.0	-	[1]	[2]	1.2	NA	1.5	14.5	6.3
	Expo	4G64	2.4 (2350)	[5]	-	4.8	[2]	1.2	NA	1.5	15..9	6.8
	Mighty Max	4G64	2.4 (2350)	4.2	-	4.9	14.8	NA	NA	3.2	13.7	6.3
	Montero	6G72	3.0 (2972)	5.1	-	5.3	15.2	4.8	2.6	5.5	24.3	10.0
	Montero	6G74	3.5 (3497)	5.1	-	5.3	15.2	5.2	2.6	5.5	24.3	10.0

NA - Not Available
1 FWD: 3.8 pts.
  AWD: 4.8 pts.
2 FWD: 12.8 pts.
  AWD: 13.8 pts.
3 Std. body: 13.7 gals.
  Long body: 18.2 gals.

4 Manual transmission: 6.3 qts.
  Automatic transmission: 6.4 qts.
5 8 valve: 4.1 qts.
  16 valve: 4.5 qts.

CAMSHAFT SPECIFICATIONS
All measurements given in inches.

Year	Engine ID/VIN	Engine Displacement Liters (cc)	Journal Diameter					Elevation		Bearing Clearance	Camshaft End Play
			1	2	3	4	5	In.	Ex.		
1992	4G93	1.8 (1834)	1.769	1.769	1.769	1.769	1.769	1.487 [1]	1.500	0.0020-0.0040	0.002-0.008
	4G64	2.4 (2350)	1.339	1.339	1.339	1.339	1.339	[1]	[1]	0.0020-0.0040	0.002-0.008
	6G72	3.0 (2972)	1.339	1.339	1.339	1.339	-	1.374	1.374	0.0020-0.0040	0.002-0.008
1993	4G93	1.8 (1834)	1.769	1.769	1.769	1.769	1.769	1.487	1.500	0.0020-0.0040	0.002-0.008
	4G64 [2]	2.4 (2350)	1.339	1.339	1.339	1.339	1.339	1.669	1.669	0.0020-0.0040	0.002-0.008
	4G64 [3]	2.4 (2350)	1.769	1.769	1.769	1.769	1.769	1.472	1.475	0.0020-0.0040	0.002-0.008
	6G72 [3]	3.0 (2972)	1.339	1.339	1.339	1.339	-	1.374	1.374	0.0020-0.0040	0.002-0.008
1994	4G93	1.8 (1834)	1.769	1.769	1.769	1.769	1.769	1.487	1.500	0.0020-0.0040	0.002-0.008
	4G64 [2]	2.4 (2350)	1.339	1.339	1.339	1.339	1.339	1.669	1.669	0.0020-0.0040	0.002-0.008
	4G64 [3]	2.4 (2350)	1.769	1.769	1.769	1.769	1.769	1.472	1.475	0.0020-0.0040	0.002-0.008
	6G72 [3]	3.0 (2972)	1.339	1.339	1.339	1.339	-	1.374	1.374	0.0020-0.0040	0.002-0.008
	6G74	3.5 (3497)	1.022	1.022	1.022	1.022	-	1.366	1.355	0.0020-0.0040	0.002-0.008
1995-96	4G93	1.8 (1834)	1.769	1.769	1.769	1.769	1.769	1.487	1.500	0.0020-0.0040	0.002-0.008
	4G64 [4]	2.4 (2350)	1.339	1.339	1.339	1.339	1.339	1.669	1.669	0.0020-0.0040	0.002-0.008
	4G64 [5]	2.4 (2350)	1.769	1.769	1.769	1.769	1.769	1.472	1.480	0.0020-0.0040	0.002-0.008
	6G72 [6]	3.0 (2972)	1.339	1.339	1.339	1.339	1.339	1.620	1.620	0.0020-0.0040	0.002-0.008
	6G72 [7]	3.0 (2972)	1.769	1.769	1.769	1.769	1.769	1.480	1.450	0.0020-0.0040	0.002-0.008
	6G74	3.5 (3497)	1.022	1.022	1.022	1.022	1.022	1.370	1.350	0.0020-0.0040	0.002-0.008

1 ID mark D: 1.669
  ID mark AR: 1.753
2 8 valve single overhead camshaft
3 16 valve single overhead camshaft

4 8 valve SOHC
5 16 valve SOHC
6 12 valve SOHC
7 24 valve SOHC

CRANKSHAFT AND CONNECTING ROD SPECIFICATIONS

All measurements are given in inches.

Year	Engine ID/VIN	Engine Displacement Liters (cc)	Crankshaft Main Brg. Journal Dia.	Main Brg. Oil Clearance	Shaft End-play	Thrust on No.	Connecting Rod Journal Diameter	Oil Clearance	Side Clearance
1992	4G93	1.8 (1834)	1.969	0.001-0.002	0.002-0.010	3	1.772	0.001-0.002	0.004-0.010
	4G64	2.4 (2350)	2.244	0.001-0.002	0.002-0.007	3	1.772	0.001-0.002	0.004-0.010
	6G72	3.0 (2972)	2.362	0.001-0.002	0.002-0.010	3	1.969	0.001-0.002	0.004-0.010
1993	4G93	1.8 (1834)	1.969	0.001-0.002	0.002-0.010-	3	1.772	0.001-0.002	0.004-0.010
	4G63	2.0 (1997)	2.244	0.001-0.002	0.002-0.007	3	1.772	0.001-0.002	0.004-0.010
	4G64	2.4 (2350)	2.244	0.001-0.002	0.002-0.007	3	1.772	0.001-0.002	0.004-0.010
	6G72	3.0 (2972)	2.362	0.001-0.002	0.002-0.010-	3	1.969	0.001-0.002	0.004-0.010
1994	4G93	1.8 (1834)	1.969	0.001-0.002	0.002-0.010	3	1.772	0.001-0.002	0.004-0.010
	4G64	2.4 (2350)	2.244	0.001-0.002	0.002-0.007	3	1.772	0.001-0.002	0.004-0.010
	6G72	3.0 (2972)	2.362	0.001-0.002	0.002-0.010	3	1.969	0.001-0.002	0.004-0.010
	6G74	3.5 (3496)	2.520	0.001-0.002	0.002-0.010	3	2.165	0.001-0.002	0.004-0.010
1995-96	4G93	1.8 (1834)	1.969	0.001-0.002	0.002-0.010	3	1.772	0.001-0.002	0.004-0.010
	4G64	2.4 (2350)	2.244	0.001-0.002	0.002-0.007	3	1.772	0.001-0.002	0.004-0.010
	6G72	3.0 (2972)	2.362	0.001-0.002	0.002-0.010	3	1.969	0.001-0.002	0.004-0.010
	6G74	3.5 (3497)	2.520	0.001-0.002	0.002-0.010	3	2.165	0.001-0.002	0.004-0.010

VALVE SPECIFICATIONS

Year	Engine ID/VIN	Engine Displacement Liters (cc)	Seat Angle (deg.)	Face Angle (deg.)	Spring Test Pressure (lbs. @ in.)	Spring Installed Height (in.)	Stem-to-Guide Clearance (in.)		Stem Diameter (in.)	
							Intake	Exhaust	Intake	Exhaust
1992	4G93	1.8 (1834)	44-44.5	45-45.5	49@1.74	1.74	0.0010-0.0020	0.0010-0.0020	0.236	0.236
	4G64	2.4 (2350)	44-44.5	45-45.5	73@1.59	1.59	0.0010-0.0020	0.0020-0.0040	0.315	0.311
	6G72	3.0 (2972)	44-44.5	45-45.5	72.5@1.59	1.59	0.0010-0.0020	0.0020-0.0040	0.315	0.311
1993	4G93	1.8 (1834)	44-44.5	45-45.5	49@1.74	1.74	0.0010-0.0020	0.0010-0.0020	0.236	0.236
	4G64 [1]	2.4 (2350)	44-44.5	45-45.5	73@1.59	1.59	0.0010-0.0020	0.0020-0.0040	0.315	0.311
	4G64 [2]	2.4 (2350)	44-44.5	45-45.5	60@1.74	1.74	0.0010-0.0020	0.0020-0.0030	0.236	0.232
	6G72 [1]	3.0 (2972)	44-44.5	45-45.5	72.5@1.59	1.59	0.0010-0.0020	0.0020-0.0040	0.315	0.311
1994	4G93	1.8 (1834)	44-44.5	45-45.5	49@1.74	1.74	0.0010-0.0020	0.0010-0.0020	0.236	0.236
	4G64 [1]	2.4 (2350)	44-44.5	45-45.5	73@1.59	1.59	0.0010-0.0020	0.0020-0.0040	0.315	0.311
	4G64 [2]	2.4 (2350)	44-44.5	45-45.5	60@1.74	1.74	0.0010-0.0020	0.0020-0.0030	0.236	0.232
	6G72 [1]	3.0 (2972)	44-44.5	45-45.5	72.5@1.59	1.59	0.0010-0.0020	0.0020-0.0040	0.315	0.311
	6G74	3.5 (3497)	44-44.5	45-45.5	52.9@1.49	1.49	0.0010-0.0020	0.0020-0.0040	0.260	0.256
1995-96	4G93	1.8 (1834)	44-44.5	45-45.5	49@1.74	1.74	0.0010-0.0020	0.0012-0.0024	0.236	0.236
	4G64 [1]	2.4 (2350)	44-44.5	45-45.5	73@1.59	1.59	0.0010-0.0020	0.0020-0.0035	0.315	0.311
	4G64 [2]	2.4 (2350)	44-44.5	45-45.5	60@1.74	1.74	0.0010-0.0020	0.0010-0.0020	0.236	0.232
	6G72 [3]	3.0 (2972)	44-44.5	45-45.5	72.5@1.59	1.59	0.0010-0.0020	0.0020-0.0035	0.315	0.311
	6G72 [4]	3.0 (2972)	44-44.5	45-45.5	60@1.74	1.74	0.0010-0.0020	0.0016-0.0028	0.236	0.236
	6G74	3.5 (3497)	44-44.5	45-45.5	52.9@1.49	1.49	0.0010-0.0020	0.0020-0.0035	0.260	0.256

1 8 valve SOHC
2 16 valve SOHC
3 12 valve SOHC
4 24 valve SOHC

PISTON AND RING SPECIFICATIONS

All measurements are given in inches.

Year	Engine ID/VIN	Engine Displacement Liters (cc)	Piston Clearance	Ring Gap Top Compression	Bottom Compression	Oil Control	Ring Side Clearance Top Compression	Bottom Compression	Oil Control
1992	4G93	1.8 (1834)	0.0010-0.0020	0.0100-0.0160	0.0160-0.0220	0.0080-0.0240	0.0010-0.0030	0.0010-0.0020	NA
	4G64	2.4 (2350)	0.0010-0.0020	0.0100-0.0160	0.0180-0.0240	0.0080-0.0240	0.0010-0.0030	0.0010-0.0020	NA
	6G72	3.0 (2972)	0.0010-0.0020	0.0120-0.0180	0.0180-0.0240	0.0080-0.0240	0.0010-0.0030	0.0010-0.0020	NA
1993	4G93	1.8 (1834)	0.0010-0.0020	0.0100-0.0160	0.0160-0.0220	0.0080-0.0240	0.0010-0.0030	0.0010-0.0020	NA
	4G64 [1]	2.4 (2350)	0.0010-0.0020	0.0100-0.0160	0.0180-0.0240	0.0080-0.0240	0.0010-0.0020	0.0010-0.0020	NA
	4G64 [2]	2.4 (2350)	0.0010-0.0020	0.0100-0.0140	0.0180-0.0280	0.0040-0.0160	0.0010-0.0020	0.0010-0.0020	NA
	6G72	3.0 (2972)	0.0010-0.0020	0.0120-0.0180	0.0180-0.0240	0.0080-0.0240	0.0010-0.0030	0.0010-0.0020	NA
1994	4G93	1.8 (1834)	0.0010-0.0020	0.0100-0.0160	0.0160-0.0220	0.0080-0.0240	0.0010-0.0030	0.0010-0.0020	NA
	4G64 [1]	2.4 (2350)	0.0010-0.0020	0.0100-0.0160	0.0180-0.0240	0.0080-0.0240	0.0010-0.0020	0.0010-0.0020	NA
	4G64 [2]	2.4 (2350)	0.0010-0.0020	0.0100-0.0140	0.0180-0.0280	0.0040-0.0160	0.0010-0.0020	0.0010-0.0020	NA
	6G72	3.0 (2972)	0.0010-0.0020	0.0120-0.0180	0.0180-0.0240	0.0080-0.0240	0.0010-0.0030	0.0010-0.0020	NA
	6G74	3.5 (3496)	0.0010-0.0020	0.0120-0.0180	0.0180-0.0240	0.0040-0.0140	0.0010-0.0030	0.0010-0.0020	NA
1995-96	4G93	1.8 (1834)	0.0008-0.0016	0.0098-0.0157	0.0157-0.0217	0.0079-0.0236	0.0012-0.0028	0.0008-0.0024	NA
	4G64 [1]	2.4 (2350)	0.0004-0.0012	0.0098-0.0157	0.0157-0.0236	0.0079-0.0236	0.0012-0.0028	0.0012-0.0028	NA
	4G64 [2]	2.4 (2350)	0.0010-0.0020	0.0098-0.0138	0.0157-0.0236	0.0079-0.0236	0.0012-0.0028	0.0012-0.0028	NA
	6G72	3.0 (2972)	0.0010-0.0020	0.0118-0.0177	0.0177-0.0236	0.0079-0.0236	0.0012-0.0028	0.0008-0.0024	NA
	6G74	3.5 (3497)	0.0010-0.0020	0.0118-0.0177	0.0177-0.0236	0.0039-0.0137	0.0012-0.0028	0.0008-0.0024	NA

1 8 valve SOHC
2 16 valve SOHC

TORQUE SPECIFICATIONS
All readings in ft. lbs.

Year	Engine ID/VIN	Engine Displacement Liters (cc)	Cylinder Head Bolts	Main Bearing Bolts	Rod Bearing Bolts	Crankshaft Damper Bolts	Flywheel Bolts	Manifold Intake	Manifold Exhaust	Spark Plugs	Lug Nut
1992	4G93	1.8 (1834)	[1]	[2]	[3]	134	72	14	[4]	18	65-80
	4G64	2.4 (2350)	80	38	14	87	98	13	13	18	[5]
	6G72	3.0 (2972)	80	57	38	136	54	10	14	18	[6]
1993	4G93	1.8 (1834)	[1]	[2]	[3]	134	72	14	[4]	18	65-80
	4G64	2.4 (2350)	[1]	[2]	[3]	87	98	13	13	18	65-80
	6G72	3.0 (2972)	80	57	38	136	54	10	14	18	[6]
1994	4G93	1.8 (1834)		[2]	[3]	134	72	14	[4]	18	65-80
	4G64	2.4 (2350)	[1]	[2]	[3]	87	98	13	13	18	65-80
	6G72	3.0 (2972)	80	57	38	136	54	10	14	18	[6]
	6G74	3.5 (3496)	80	54	38	136	54	10	14	18	72-87
1995-96	4G93	1.8 (1834)	[1]	[2]	[3]	134	72	14	[4]	18	65-80
	4G64	2.4 (2350)	[1]	[2]	[3]	87	98	13	13	18	87-101
	6G72 [7]	3.0 (2972)	80	47	38	136	54	10	14	18	72-87
	6G72 [8]	3.0 (2972)	80	67	38	134	54	16	22	18	72-87
	6G74	3.5 (3497)	80	54	NA	134	54	10	33	18	72-87

1 Step 1: 54 ft. lbs.
Step 2: 14.5 ft. lbs. plus 1/4 turn
Step 3: Plus an additional 1/4 turn
2 Step 1: 18 ft. lbs.
Step 2: Plus 1/4 turn
3 Step 1: 14.5 ft. lbs.
Step 2: Plus 1/4 turn
4 M10: 22 ft. lbs.
M8: 13 ft. lbs.
8 24 valve, SOHC

5 Expo: 65-80 ft. lbs.
Truck: 87-101 ft. lbs.
6 Truck: 87-101 ft. lbs.
Montero: 72-87 ft. lbs.
7 12 valve, SOHC
8 24 valve, SOHC

BRAKE SPECIFICATIONS
All measurements in inches unless noted

Year	Model	Master Cylinder Bore	Brake Disc Original Thickness	Brake Disc Minimum Thickness	Brake Disc Maximum Runout	Brake Drum Diameter Original Inside Diameter	Brake Drum Diameter Max. Wear Limit	Brake Drum Diameter Maximum Machine Diameter	Minimum Lining Thickness Front	Minimum Lining Thickness Rear
1992	Expo	0.938 [1]	[2]	[3]	0.003	[4]	[5]	-	0.079	0.079 [6]
	Montero	0.938	[7]	[3]	0.003	-	7.80	-	0.079	0.079 [8]
	Truck	0.938	0.866	0.803	0.006	10.00	10.08	-	0.079	0.039
1993	Expo	0.938 [1]	[2]	[3]	0.003	[4]	[5]	-	0.079	0.079 [6]
	Montero	0.938	[7]	[3]	0.003	-	7.80	-	0.079	0.079 [8]
	Truck	0.938	0.866	0.866	0.006	10.00	10.08	-	0.079	0.079 [8]
1994	Expo	0.938 [1]	[2]	[3]	0.003	[4]	[5]	-	0.079	0.039
	Montero	0.938	[7]	[3]	0.003	-	7.80	-	0.079	0.079 [6]
	Truck	0.938	0.866	0.803	0.006	10.00	10.08	-	0.079	0.039
1995-96	Expo	0.938 [1]	[2]	[3]	0.003	-	-	-	0.079	0.079 [6]
	Mighty Max	0.938	0.866	0.803	0.006	10.00	10.08	-	0.079	0.039
	Montero	0.938	[7]	[3]	0.003	-	7.80	-	0.079	0.079 [6]

1 With ABS: 1.000
2 Front: 0.940
Rear: 0.390
3 Front: 0.880
Rear: 0.330
4 8 inch drum: 8.00
9 inch drum: 9.00
5 8 inch drum: 8.10
9 inch drum: 9.10
6 Drum shoe: 0.040
7 Front: 0.940
Rear: 0.710
8 Drum shoe: 0.177

WHEEL ALIGNMENT

Year	Model			Caster Range (deg.)	Caster Preferred Setting (deg.)	Camber Range (deg.)	Camber Preferred Setting (deg.)	Toe-in (in.)	Steering Axis Inclination (deg.)
1992	Expo	1	F	1°30'P-2°50'P	2°10'P	0°10'N-0°50'P	0°20'P	0°	NA
	Expo	2	F	1°25'P-2°45'P	2°05'P	0°10'P-1°10'P	0°40'P	0°	NA
	Expo		R	-		1°N-0	0°30'N	0.19P	NA
	Montero		F	2°P-4°P	3°P	0°10'P-1°10'P	0°40'P	0.14P	NA
	Montero		R	-	-	NA	0°	0°	NA
	Truck	3	F	1°30'P-3°30'P	2°30'P	0°10'P-1°10'P	0°40'P	0.08P	NA
	Truck	4	F	1°P-3°P	2°P	0°30'P-1°30'P	1°P	0.08P	NA
	Truck		R	-	-	NA	0°	0°	NA
1993	Expo	1	F	1°30'P-2°50'P	2°10'P	0°10'N-0°50'P	0°20'P	0°	NA
	Expo	2	F	1°25'P-2°45'P	2°05'P	0°10'P-1°10'P	0°40'P	0°	NA
	Expo		R	-		1°N-0	0°30'N	0.19P	NA
	Montero		F	2°P-4°P	3°P	0°10'P-1°10'P	0°40'P	0.14P	NA
	Montero		R	-	-	NA	0°	0°	NA
	Truck	3	F	1°30'P-3°30'P	2°30'P	0°10'P-1°10'P	0°40'P	0.08P	NA
	Truck	4	F	1°P-3°P	2°P	0°30'P-1°30'P	1°P	0.08P	NA
	Truck		R	-	-	NA	0°	0°	NA
1994	Expo	1	F	1°30'P-2°50'P	2°10'P	0°10'N-0°50'P	0°20'P	0°	NA
	Expo	2	F	1°25'P-2°45'P	2°05'P	0°10'P-1°10'P	0°40'P	0°	NA
	Expo		R	-	-	1°N-0	0°30'N	0.19P	NA
	Montero		F	2°P-4°P	3°P	0°10'P-1°10'P	0°40'P	0.14P	NA
	Montero		R	-	-	NA	0°	0°	NA
	Truck	3	F	1°30'P-3°30'P	2°30'P	0°10'P-1°10'P	0°40'P	0.08P	NA
	Truck	4	F	1°P-3°P	2°P	0°30'P-1°30'P	1°P	0.08P	NA
	Truck		R	-	-	NA	0°	0°	NA
1995-96	Expo	1	F	1°50'P-2°84'P		0°17'N-0°83'P	0°33'P	0.12P	NA
	Expo	2	F	1°41'P-2°75'P		0°17'P-1°17'P	0°67'P	0.12P	NA
	Expo		R	-	-	1N-0	0°50'N	0.08P	NA
	Mighty Max		F	1°50'P-3°50'P	2°50'P	0°17'P-1°17'P	0°67'P	0.08P	NA
	Mighty Max		R	-	-	NA	0°	0°	NA
	Montero		F	2°P-4°P	3°P	0°17'P-1°17'P	0°67'P	0.14P	NA
	Montero		R	-	-	0°	0°	0°	NA

NA - Not Available
F - Front
R - Rear
1 FWD
2 AWD
3 2WD
4 4WD

NISSAN

ENGINE IDENTIFICATION

Year	Model	Engine Displacement Liters (cc)	Engine Series (ID/VIN)	Fuel System	No. of Cylinders	Engine Type
1992	Pick-up	2.4 (2389)	KA24E	MFI	4	SOHC
	Pick-up	3.0 (2960)	VG30E	MFI	6	SOHC
	Pathfinder	3.0 (2960)	VG30E	MFI	6	SOHC
1993	Pick-up	2.4 (2389)	KA24E	MFI	4	SOHC
	Pick-up	3.0 (2960)	VG30E	MFI	6	SOHC
	Quest	3.0 (2960)	VG30E	MFI	6	SOHC
	Pathfinder	3.0 (2960)	VG30E	MFI	6	SOHC
1994	Pick-up	2.4 (2389)	KA24E	MFI	4	SOHC
	Pick-up	3.0 (2960)	VG30E	MFI	6	SOHC
	Quest	3.0 (2960)	VG30E	MFI	6	SOHC
	Pathfinder	3.0 (2960)	VG30E	MFI	6	SOHC
1995-96	Pick-up	2.4 (2389)	KA24E (S)	MFI	4	SOHC
	Pick-up	3.0 (2960)	VG30E (H)	MFI	6	SOHC
	Quest	3.0 (2960)	VG30E (W)	MFI	6	SOHC
	Pathfinder	3.0 (2960)	VG30E (H)	MFI	6	SOHC

MFI - Multiport fuel injection
SOHC - Single overhead camshaft

GENERAL ENGINE SPECIFICATIONS

Year	Engine ID/VIN	Engine Displacement Liters (cc)	Fuel System Type	Net Horsepower @ rpm	Net Torque @ rpm (ft. lbs.)	Bore x Stroke (in.)	Com-pression Ratio	Oil Pressure @ rpm
1992	KA24E	2.4 (2389)	MFI	134@5200	154@3600	3.50x3.78	8.6:1	60@3000
	VG30E	3.0 (2960)	MFI	153@4800	180@4000	3.43x3.27	9.0:1	53@3200
1993	KA24E	2.4 (2389)	MFI	134@5200	154@3600	3.50x3.78	8.6:1	60@3000
	VG30E	3.0 (2960)	MFI	153@4800	180@4000	3.43x3.27	9.0:1	53@3200
1994	KA24E	2.4 (2389)	MFI	134@5200	154@3600	3.50x3.78	8.6:1	60@3000
	VG30E	3.0 (2960)	MFI	153@4800	180@4000	3.43x3.27	9.0:1	53@3200
1995-96	KA24E	2.4 (2389)	MFI	134@5200	154@3600	3.50x3.78	8.6:1	60@3000
	VG30E	3.0 (2960)	MFI	153@4800	180@4000	3.43X3.27	9.0:1	53@3200

MFI - Mutliport fuel injection

GASOLINE ENGINE TUNE-UP SPECIFICATIONS

Year	Engine ID/VIN	Engine Displacement Liters (cc)	Spark Plugs Gap (in.)	Ignition Timing (deg.) MT	Ignition Timing (deg.) AT	Fuel Pump (psi)	Idle Speed (rpm) MT	Idle Speed (rpm) AT	Valve Clearance In.	Valve Clearance Ex.
1992	KA24E	2.4 (2389)	0.033	10B	10B	33 ①	750	750 ②	HYD	HYD
	VG30E	3.0 (2960)	0.041	15B	15B	33 ①	750	750 ②	HYD	HYD
1993	KA24E	2.4 (2389)	0.033	10B	10B	33 ①	800	800 ②	HYD	HYD
	VG30E	3.0 (2960)	0.041	15B	15B	33 ①	750	750 ②	HYD	HYD
1994	KA24E	2.4 (2389)	0.033	10B	10B	33 ①	800	800 ②	HYD	HYD
	VG30E	3.0 (2960)	0.041	15B	15B	33 ①	750	750 ②	HYD	HYD
1995-96	KA24E	2.4 (2389)	0.033	10B	10B	36 ①	800	800 ②	HYD	HYD
	VG30E	3.0 (2960)	③	15B	15B	34 ①	750	750 ②	HYD	HYD

NOTE: The Vehicle Emission Control Information label often reflects specification changes made during production. The label figures must be used if they differ from those in this chart.
B - Before top dead center
HYD - Hydraulic

① System pressure at idle with vacuum hose connected
Should increase to 43 psi when disconnected
② Automatic transmission in neutral
③ Quest: 0.033
Pick-up and Pathfinder: 0.041

CAPACITIES

Year	Model	Engine ID/VIN	Engine Displacement Liters (cc)	Engine Oil with Filter (qts.)	Transmission (pts.) 4-Spd	Transmission (pts.) 5-Spd	Transmission (pts.) Auto.	Transfer Case (pts.)	Drive Axle Front (pts.)	Drive Axle Rear (pts.)	Fuel Tank (gal.)	Cooling System (qts.)
1992	Pick-up	KA24E	2.4 (2389)	①	-	2	3	-	4	5	16.0	6
	Pick-up	VG30E	3.0 (2960)	7	-	8	3	-	9	5.8	21.0 ⑩	11
	Pathfinder	VG30E	3.0 (2960)	7	-	8	3	-	9	5.8	21.0	11
1993	Pick-up	KA24E	2.4 (2389)	①	-	2	3	-	4	5	16.0	6
	Pick-up	VG30E	3.0 (2960)	7	-	8	3	-	9	5.8	21.0 ⑩	11
	Pathfinder	VG30E	3.0 (2960)	7	-	8	3	-	9	5.8	20.0	11
	Quest	VG30E	3.0 (2960)	4.0	-	-	20.0	-	-	-	20.0	12
1994	Pick-up	KA24E	2.4 (2389)	①	-	2	16.8	-	4	5	16.0	6
	Pick-up	VG30E	3.0 (2960)	7	-	8	3	-	11.0	5.8	21.0 ⑩	11
	Pathfinder	VG30E	3.0 (2960)	7	-	8	3	-	11.0	5.8	20.0	12
	Quest	VG30E	3.0 (2960)	4.0	-	-	20.0	-	-	-	20.0	11
1995-96	Pick-up	KA24E	2.4 (2389)	①	-	13	-	-	14	15	15.9	6
	Pick-up	VG30E	3.0 (2960)	7	-	13	17	2.4	14	15	21.1	16
	Pathfinder	VG30E	3.0 (2960)	7	-	13	17	2.4	14	15	20.4	16
	Quest	VG30E	3.0 (2960)	4.3	-	-	20.0	-	-	-	20.0	12

1 2WD: 4.1 qts.; 4WD: 3.5 qts.
2 2WD: 4.25 pts.; 4WD: 8.50 pts.
3 2WD: 16.75 pts.; 4WD: 18.0 pts.
4 Front differential: 2.75 pts.
Transfer case: 4.62 pts.
5 2WD: 3.12 pts.; 4WD: 2.75 pts.
6 2WD: 8.6 qts.; 4WD: 9.5 qts.
7 2WD: 4.25 pts.; 4WD: 3.60 qts.
8 2WD: 5.1 pts.; 4WD: 7.6 pts.
9 Front differential: 3.12 pts.
Transfer case: 4.62 pts.
10 SE models: 16 gals.
11 2WD: 11.4 qts.; 4WD: 12.4 qts.

12 With rear heater: 12.75 qts.
Without rear heater: 11.3 qts.
13 2WD KA24DE: 4.3 pts.
4WD KA24DE: 8.5 pts.
2WD VG30DE: 5.1 pts.
4WD VG30DE: 7.6 pts.
14 R180A: 2.75 pts.
R200A: 3.1 pts.
15 H190A: 3.1 pts.
C200: 2.75 pts.
H233B: 5.9 pts.
16 2WD: 11.4 qts.; 4WD: 12.4 qts.
17 2WD: 8.4 pts.; 4WD: 9.0 pts.

CAMSHAFT SPECIFICATIONS
All measurements given in inches.

Year	Engine ID/VIN	Engine Displacement Liters (cc)	Journal Diameter					Elevation		Bearing Clearance	Camshaft End Play
			1	2	3	4	5	In.	Ex.		
1992	KA24E	2.4 (2389)	1.2967-1.2974	1.2967-1.2974	1.2967-1.2974	1.2967-1.2974	1.2967-1.2974	1.765-1.773	1.765-1.773	1	0.002-0.005
	VG30E	3.0 (2960)	2	2	2	2	2	1.557-1.564	1.557-1.564	1	0.001-0.002
1993	KA24E	2.4 (2389)	1.2967-1.2974	1.2967-1.2974	1.2967-1.2974	1.2967-1.2974	1.2967-1.2974	1.765-1.773	1.765-1.773	1	0.002-0.005
	VG30E	3.0 (2960)	2	2	2	2	2	3	3	1	0.001-0.002
1994	KA24E	2.4 (2389)	1.2967-1.2974	1.2967-1.2974	1.2967-1.2974	1.2967-1.2974	1.2967-1.2974	1.765-1.773	1.765-1.773	1	0.002-0.005
	VG30E	3.0 (2960)	2	2	2	2	2	3	3	1	0.001-0.002
1995-96	KA24E	2.4 (2389)	1.2967-1.2974	1.2967-1.2974	1.2967-1.2974	1.2967-1.2974	1.2967-1.2974	1.765-1.773	1.765-1.773	4	0.002-0.005
	VG30E	3.0 (2960)	2	2	2	2	2	3	3	4	0.003-0.006

1 Clearance: 0.0017-0.0038
Limit: 0.005
2 Left camshaft, rear journal: 1.6732-1.6742
Left camshaft, middle three journals: 1.8504-1.8514
Left camshaft, front journal: 1.8898-1.8907
Right camshaft, rear journal: 1.6732-1.6742
Right camshaft, other journals: 1.8504-1.8514

3 Pick-up and Pathfinder: 1.557-1.564
Quest: 1.533-1.541
4 Clearance limit: 0.0018-0.0034
Limit: 0.0047

CRANKSHAFT AND CONNECTING ROD SPECIFICATIONS

All measurements are given in inches.

Year	Engine ID/VIN	Engine Displacement Liters (cc)	Crankshaft Main Brg. Journal Dia.	Crankshaft Main Brg. Oil Clearance	Crankshaft Shaft End-play	Crankshaft Thrust on No.	Connecting Rod Journal Diameter	Connecting Rod Oil Clearance	Connecting Rod Side Clearance
1992	KA24E	2.4 (2389)	[1]	0.0008- 0.0019 [2]	0.002- 0.007	3	2.3603- 2.3612	0.0004- 0.0014 [2]	0.008- 0.016
	VG30E	3.0 (2960)	[3]	0.0011- 0.0022 [4]	0.002- 0.007	4	1.9667- 1.9675	0.0006- 0.0021 [4]	0.008- 0.014
1993	KA24E	2.4 (2389)	[1]	0.0008- 0.0019 [2]	0.002- 0.007	3	2.3603- 2.3612	0.0004- 0.0014 [2]	0.008- 0.016
	VG30E	3.0 (2960)	[3]	0.0011- 0.0022 [4]	0.002- 0.007	4	1.9667- 1.9675	0.0006- 0.0021 [4]	0.008- 0.014
1994	KA24E	2.4 (2389)	[1]	0.0008- 0.0019 [2]	0.002- 0.007	3	2.3603- 2.3612	0.0004- 0.0014 [2]	0.008- 0.016
	VG30E	3.0 (2960)	[3]	0.0011- 0.0022 [4]	0.002- 0.007	4	1.9667- 1.9675	0.0006- 0.0021 [4]	0.008- 0.014
1995-96	KA24E	2.4 (2389)	[5]	0.0008- 0.0019 [2]	0.002- 0.007	3	2.3603- 2.3612	0.0004- 0.0014 [2]	0.008- 0.016
	VG30E	3.0 (2960)	[3]	0.0011- 0.0022 [4]	0.002- 0.007	4	1.9667- 1.9675	0.0006- 0.0021 [4]	0.008- 0.014

1 Grade 0: 2.3609-2.3612
  Grade 1: 2.3606-2.3609
  Grade 2: 2.3603-2.3606
2 Wear limit: 0.0040
3 Grade 0: 2.4790-2.4793
  Grade 1: 2.4787-2.4790
  Grade 2: 2.4784-2.4787

4 Wear limit: 0.0035
5 Grade 0: 2.5057-2.5060
  Grade 1: 2.5060-2.5064
  Grade 2: 2.5064-2.5068

VALVE SPECIFICATIONS

Year	Engine ID/VIN	Engine Displacement Liters (cc)	Seat Angle (deg.)	Face Angle (deg.)	Spring Test Pressure (lbs. @ in.)	Spring Installed Height (in.)	Stem-to-Guide Clearance (in.)		Stem Diameter (in.)	
							Intake	Exhaust	Intake	Exhaust
1992	KA24E	2.4 (2389)	45	45.5	[1]	NA	0.0008-0.0021	0.0016-0.0028	0.2742-0.2748	0.3129-0.3134
	VG30E	3.0 (2960)	45	45.25-45.75	[2]	[3]	0.0008-0.0021	0.0016-0.0029	0.2742-0.2748	0.3136-0.3138
1993	KA24E	2.4 (2389)	45	45.5	[1]	NA	0.0008-0.0021	0.0016-0.0028	0.2742-0.2748	0.3129-0.3134
	VG30E	3.0 (2960)	45	45.25-45.75	[2]	NA	0.0008-0.0021	0.0016-0.0029	0.2742-0.2748	0.3136-0.3138
1994	KA24E	2.4 (2389)	45	45.5	106@1.026	NA	0.0008-0.0021	0.0016-0.0028	0.2742-0.2748	0.3129-0.3134
	VG30E	3.0 (2960)	45	45.25-45.75	[1]	NA	0.0008-0.0021	0.0016-0.0029	0.2742-0.2748	0.3136-0.3138
1995-96	KA24E	2.4 (2389)	45	45.5	[1]	NA	0.0008-0.0021	0.0016-0.0028	0.2742-0.2748	0.3129-0.3134
	VG30E	3.0 (2960)	45	45.25-45.75	[2]	NA	0.0008-0.0021	0.0016-0.0029	0.2742-0.2748	0.3136-0.3138

NA - Not Available

[1] Intake:
Inner: 63.9 @ 1.28
Outer: 135.2 @ 1.48
Exhaust:
Inner: 74 @ 1.15
Outer: 144 @ 1.34

[2] Inner: 57.3 @ 0.984
Outer: 117.7 @ 1.181

[3] Inner: 1.378; Outer: 1.575

PISTON AND RING SPECIFICATIONS

All measurements are given in inches.

Year	Engine ID/VIN	Engine Displacement Liters (cc)	Piston Clearance	Ring Gap			Ring Side Clearance		
				Top Compression	Bottom Compression	Oil Control	Top Compression	Bottom Compression	Oil Control
1992	KA24E	2.4 (2389)	0.0008-0.0016	0.011-0.020	1	0.008-0.027	0.002-0.003	0.001-0.003	NA
	VG30E	3.0 (2960)	0.0006-0.0014	0.008-0.017	0.007-0.017	0.008-0.030	0.002-0.003	0.001-0.003	0.001-0.007
1993	KA24E	2.4 (2389)	0.0008-0.0016	0.011-0.020	0.018-0.027	0.008-0.027	0.002-0.003	0.001-0.003	NA
	VG30E	3.0 (2960)	0.0006-0.0014	0.008-0.017	0.007-0.017	0.008-0.030	0.002-0.003	0.001-0.003	0.001-0.007
1994	KA24E	2.4 (2389)	0.0008-0.0016	0.011-0.020	0.018-0.027	0.008-0.027	0.002-0.003	0.001-0.003	0.003-0.005
	VG30E	3.0 (2960)	0.0006-0.0014	0.008-0.017	0.007-0.017	0.008-0.030	0.002-0.003	0.001-0.003	0.001-0.007
1995-96	KA24E	2.4 (2389)	0.0008-0.0016	0.011-0.021	0.018-0.027	0.008-0.027	0.002-0.003	0.001-0.003	0.003-0.005
	VG30E	3.0 (2960)	0.0006-0.0014	0.008-0.017	0.007-0.017	0.008-0.030	0.002-0.003	0.001-0.003	0.001-0.007

NA - Not Available

1 Grade 1 (R or T): 0.018-0.027

Grade 2 (N): 0.022-0.028

TORQUE SPECIFICATIONS
All readings in ft. lbs.

Year	Engine ID/VIN	Engine Displacement Liters (cc)	Cylinder Head Bolts	Main Bearing Bolts	Rod Bearing Bolts	Crankshaft Damper Bolts	Flywheel Bolts	Manifold Intake	Manifold Exhaust	Spark Plugs	Lug Nut
1992	KA24E	2.4 (2389)	[1]	34-38	[2]	105-112	[3]	14	14	18	[4]
	VG30E	3.0 (2960)	[5]	67-74	[2]	90-98	72-80	[6]	15	18	[4]
1993	KA24E	2.4 (2389)	[1]	34-38	[2]	105-112	[3]	14	14	18	[4]
	VG30E	3.0 (2960)	[5]	67-74	[2]	90-98	72-80	[6]	15	18	[4]
1994	KA24E	2.4 (2389)	[1]	34-38	[2]	105-112	[3]	14	14	18	[7]
	VG30E	3.0 (2960)	[5]	67-74	[2]	90-98	72-80	[6]	15	18	[7]
1995-96	KA24E	2.4 (2389)	[1]	34-38	[8]	87-116	[3]	14	14	18	[9]
	VG30E	3.0 (2960)	[10]	67-74	[8]	90-98	72-80	[11]	15	18	[9]

1 Step 1: 22 ft. lbs.
  Step 2: 58 ft. lbs.
  Step 3: Loosen completely then retorque to 22 ft. lbs.
  Step 4: 58 ft. lbs. or an additional 80-85 degrees
2 12 ft. lbs. then an additional 60-65 degrees
3 Manual transmission: 105-112 ft. lbs.
  Automatic transmission: 69-76 ft. lbs.
4 Pick-up and Pathfinder with single wheel: 87-108 ft. lbs.
  Dual wheel: 166-203 ft. lbs.
5 Step 1: 22 ft. lbs.
  Step 2: 43 ft. lbs.
  Step 3: Loosen completely then retorque to 22 ft. lbs.
  Step 4: 40-47 ft. lbs. or an additional 60-65 degrees
6 Nuts: 18 ft. lbs. in two steps
  Bolts: 13 ft. lbs. in two steps

7 Pick-up with single wheel: 87-108 ft. lbs.
  Pick-up with dual wheel: 166-203 ft. lbs.
8 10-12 ft. lbs. plus 60-65 degrees or 28-33 ft. lbs.
9 Quest: 80 ft. lbs.
  Pick-up with single wheels: 87-108 ft. lbs.
  Pick-up with dual wheels: 166-203 ft. lbs.
10 Step 1: 22 ft. lbs.
   Step 2: 43 ft. lbs.
   Step 3: Loosen completely and retorque to 22 ft. lbs.
   Step 4: Torque to 40-47 ft. lbs. or an additional 60-65 degrees
11 Step 1: Tighten nuts and bolts to 3 ft. lbs.
   Step 2: Tighten bolts to 12-14 ft. lbs.; nuts to 17-20 ft. lbs.
   Step 3: Repeat Step 2

BRAKE SPECIFICATIONS
All measurements in inches unless noted

Year	Model	Master Cylinder Bore	Brake Disc			Brake Drum Diameter			Minimum Lining Thickness	
			Original Thickness	Minimum Thickness	Maximum Runout	Original Inside Diameter	Max. Wear Limit	Maximum Machine Diameter	Front	Rear
1992	Pick-up	[1]	NA	[2]	0.003	NA	-	[3]	0.079	[4]
	Pathfinder	[1]	NA	[5]	0.003	NA	-	[6]	0.079	[4]
1993	Quest	1.000	NA	0.945	0.003	NA	-	9.90	0.079	0.079
	Pick-up	1.000	NA	[2]	0.003	NA	-	[3]	0.079	[4]
	Pathfinder	1.000	NA	[5]	0.003	NA	-	[7]	0.079	[4]
1994	Quest	1.000	NA	0.945	0.003	NA	-	9.90	0.079	0.079
	Pick-up	1.000	NA	[2]	0.003	NA	-	[3]	0.079	[8]
	Pathfinder	1.000	NA	[5]	0.003	NA	-	[7]	0.079	[8]
1995-96	Quest	1.000	1.020	0.945	0.003	9.84	NA	9.90	0.079	0.079
	Pick-up	1.000	[9]	[10]	0.003	[11]	NA	[3]	0.079	0.059
	Pathfinder	1.000	[12]	[5]	0.003	[13]	NA	[7]	0.079	0.059

NA - Not Available

1 With ABS: 1.000
  Without ABS: 0.938
2 2WD, KA24 engine:
  Front: 0.787; Rear: 0.630
  VG30E engine:
  Front: 0.945; Rear: 0.630
3 2WD: 10.30
  4WD: 11.67
  Rear disc parking brake drum: 7.52
4 Disc brake: 0.079
  Drum brake: 0.059
5 Front: 0.945
  Rear: 0.630
6 Rear disc parking brake drum: 7.52

7 Rear drum brake: 10.30
  Rear disc parking brake drum: 7.52
8 Disc brake: 0.079
  Drum brake: 0.059
9 2WD KA24E: 0.870
  2WD VG30E: 1.020
  4WD: 1.020
10 2WD KA24E: 0.787
  2WD/4WD VG30E: 0.945
11 2WD: 10.24
  4WD: 11.61
12 Front: 1.020
  Rear: 0.710
13 Rear drum: 10.24
  Parking drum: 7.48

WHEEL ALIGNMENT

Year	Model		Caster Range (deg.)	Caster Preferred Setting (deg.)	Camber Range (deg.)	Camber Preferred Setting (deg.)	Toe-in (in.)		Steering Axis Inclination (deg.)
1992	Pick-up 2WD	F	0°23'N-1°07'P	0°22'P	0°20'N-1°10'P	0°25'P	0.12P	1	NA
	Pick-up 4WD	F	0°33'P-2°03'P	1°18'P	0°05'N-1°25'P	0°40'P	0.06P	1	NA
	Pathfinder	F	0°33'P-2°03'P	1°18'P	0°05'N-1°25'P	0°40'P	0.06P	1	NA
1993	Quest	F	0°03'P-1°33'P	0°48'P	0°27'N-1°03'P	0°48'N	0.12P		NA
	Quest	R	-	-	0°15'N-0°15'P	0	0		NA
	Pick-up 2WD	F	0°23'N-1°07'P	0°22'P	0°20'N-1°10'P	0°25'P	0.12P	1	NA
	Pick-up 4WD	F	0°33'P-2°03'P	1°18'P	0°05'N-1°25'P	0°40'P	0.16P	1	NA
	Pathfinder	F	0°33'P-2°03'P	1°18'P	0°05'N-1°25'P	0°40'P	0.16P	1	NA
1994	Quest	F	0°03'P-1°33'P	0°48'P	0°27'N-1°03'P	0°48'N	0.12P		NA
	Quest	R	-	-	0°15'N-0°015'P	0	0		NA
	Pick-up 2WD	F	0°23'N-1°07'P	0°22'P	0°20'N-1°10'P	0°25'P	0.12P	1	NA
	Pick-up 4WD	F	0°33'P-2°03'P	1°18'P	0°05'N-1°25'P	0°40'P	0.16P	1	NA
	Pathfinder	F	0°33'P-2°03'P	1°18'P	0°05'N-1°25'P	0°40'P	0.16P	1	NA
1995-96	Quest	F	3.00P-1.58P	2.29P	0.42N-1.08P	0.33N	0.12P		NA
		R	-	-	0.25N-0.25P	0	0		NA
	Pick-up 4WD	F	0.42N-1.08P	0.33P	0.33N-1.17P	0.42P	0.12P	1	NA
	Pathfinder	F	0.58P-2.08P	1.33P	0.08N-1.42P	0.67P	0.16P	1	NA
	Pathfinder	F	0.58P-2.08P	1.33P	0.08N-1.42P	0.67P	0.16P	1	NA

NA - Not Available
F - Front
R - Rear
1 With radial tires

SUZUKI

ENGINE IDENTIFICATION

Year	Model		Engine Displacement Liters (cc)	Engine Series (ID/VIN)	Fuel System	No. of Cylinders	Engine Type
1992	Samurai		1.3 (1298)	3	EFI	4	SOHC
	Sidekick		1.6 (1590)	0	EFI	4	SOHC
	Sidekick	1	1.6 (1590)	0	MFI	4	SOHC
1993	Samurai		1.3 (1298)	3	EFI	4	SOHC
	Sidekick		1.6 (1590)	0	EFI	4	SOHC
	Sidekick	1	1.6 (1590)	0	MFI	4	SOHC
1994	Samurai		1.3 (1298)	3	TFI	4	SOHC
	Sidekick		1.6 (1590)	0	TFI	4	SOHC
	Sidekick	2	1.6 (1590)	0	MFI	4	SOHC
1995-96	Samurai		1.3 (1298)	3	TFI	4	SOHC
	Sidekick		1.6 (1590)	0	TFI	4	SOHC
	Sidekick	2	1.6 (1590)	0	MFI	4	SOHC

EFI - Electronic fuel injection
MFI - Multiport fuel injection
TFI - Throttle body fuel injection

SOHC - Single overhead camshaft
1 4 door
2 16 valve engine

GENERAL ENGINE SPECIFICATIONS

Year	Engine ID/VIN		Engine Displacement Liters (cc)	Fuel System Type	Net Horsepower @ rpm	Net Torque @ rpm (ft. lbs.)	Bore x Stroke (in.)	Compression Ratio	Oil Pressure @ rpm
1992	3	1	1.3 (1298)	EFI	66@6000	76@3500	2.91x2.97	9..5:1	43-60@3000
	0		1.6 (1590)	EFI	80@5400	94@3000	2.95x3.54	8.9:1	51-63@3000
	0	2	1.6 (1590)	MFI	95@5600	98@4000	2.95x3.54	9.5:1	47-61@3000
1993	3	1	1.3 (1298)	EFI	66@6000	76@3500	2.91x2.97	9.5:1	43-60@3000
	0		1.6 (1590)	EFI	80@5400	94@3000	2.95x3.54	8.9:1	51-63@3000
	0	2	1.6 (1590)	MFI	95@5600	98@4000	2.95x3.54	9.5:1	47-61@3000
1994	3	1	1.3 (1298)	TFI	66@6000	76@3500	2.91x2.97	9.5:1	43-60@3000
	0		1.6 (1590)	TFI	80@5400	94@3000	2.95x3.54	8.9:1	51-63@3000
	0	3	1.6 (1590)	MFI	95@5600	98@4000	2.95x3.54	9.5:1	47-61@3000
1995-96	3	1	1.3 (1298)	TFI	66@6000	76@3500	2.91x2.97	9.5:1	43-60@3000
	0		1.6 (1590)	TFI	80@5400	94@3000	2.95x3.54	8.9:1	51-63@3000
	0	3	1.6 (1590)	MFI	95@5600	98@4000	2.95x3.54	9.5:1	47-61@3000

EFI - Electronic fuel injection
MFI - Multiport fuel injection
TFI - Throttle body fuel injection

1 Samurai
2 Sidekick 4 door
3 Sidekick 16 valve engine

GASOLINE ENGINE TUNE-UP SPECIFICATIONS

Year	Engine ID/VIN	Engine Displacement Liters (cc)	Spark Plugs Gap (in.)	Ignition Timing (deg.) MT	AT	Fuel Pump (psi)	Idle Speed (rpm) MT	AT	Valve Clearance In.	Ex.
1992	3	1.3 (1298)	0.029	8B	NA	34-40	800	NA	0.009-0.011 [1]	0.010-0.012 [1]
	0	1.6 (1590)	0.029	8B	8B	34-40	800	800	0.009-0.011 [1]	0.010-0.011 [1]
1993	3	1.3 (1298)	0.029	8B	NA	34-40	800	NA	0.009-0.011 [1]	0.010-0.012 [1]
	0	1.6 (1590)	0.029	8B	8B	34-40	800	800	0.009-0.011 [1]	0.010-0.011 [1]
1994	3	1.3 (1298)	0.029	8B	NA	34-40	800	NA	0.009-0.011 [1]	0.010-0.012 [1]
	0	1.6 (1590)	0.029	8B	8B	34-40	800	800	0.009-0.011 [1]	0.010-0.012 [1]
1995-96	3	1.3 (1298)	0.029	8B	NA	34-40	800	NA	0.009-0.011	0.010-0.012
	0	1.6 (1590)	0.029	5B	5B	34-40	800	800	0.009-0.011	0.010-0.012

NOTE: The Vehicle Emission Control Information label often reflects specification changes made during production. The label figures must be used if they differ from those in this chart.
B - Before top dead center

NA - Not Available
HYD - Hydraulic
1 Specifications for hot engine
Cold engine: Intake: 0.005-0.007; Exhaust: 0.006-0.008

CAPACITIES

Year	Model	Engine ID/VIN	Engine Displacement Liters (cc)	Engine Oil with Filter (qts.)	Transmission (pts.) 4-Spd	5-Spd	Auto.	Transfer Case (pts.)	Drive Axle Front (pts.)	Rear (pts.)	Fuel Tank (gal.)	Cooling System (qts.)
1992	Samurai	3	1.3 (1298)	3.7	-	2.7	-	1.7	4.2	3.2	10.6	5.1
	Sidekick	0	1.6 (1590)	4.5	-	3.2	10.8	3.6	2.1	4.6	11.1	1
1993	Samurai	3	1.3 (1298)	3.7	-	2.7	-	1.7	4.2	3.2	10.6	5.1
	Sidekick	0	1.6 (1590)	4.5	-	3.2	10.8	3.6	2.1	4.6	11.1	1
1994	Samurai	3	1.3 (1298)	3.7	-	2.8	-	1.7	4.2	3.2	10.6	5.1
	Sidekick	0	1.6 (1590)	4.4	-	2	3	3.6	2.2	4.6	4	1
1995-96	Samurai	3	1.3 (1298)	3.7	-	2.8	-	1.7	4.2	3.2	10.6	5.1
	Sidekick	0	1.6 (1590)	4.4	-	2	3	3.6	2.2	4.6	4	1

1 With automatic transmission: 5.5 qts.
  With manual transmission: 5.6 qts.
2 2WD: 4.0 pts.
  4WD: 3.2 pts.

3 2 door: 6.0 pts.
  4 door: 5.3 pts.
4 2 door: 11.1 gals.
  4 door: 14.5 gals.

CAMSHAFT SPECIFICATIONS

All measurements given in inches.

Year	Engine ID/VIN	Engine Displacement Liters (cc)	Journal Diameter					Elevation		Bearing Clearance	Camshaft End Play
			1	2	3	4	5	In.	Ex.		
1992	3	1.3 (1298)	1.7372-1.7381	1.7451-1.7460	1.7530-1.7539	1.7609-1.7618	1.7687-1.7697	1.4763-1.4724	1.4763-1.4724	0.0020-0.0036	0.0039
	0	1.6 (1590)	1.7372-1.7381	1.7451-1.7460	1.7530-1.7539	1.7609-1.7618	1.7687-1.7697	1.4763-1.4724	1.4763-1.4724	0.0020-0.0036	0.0039
	0 ¹	1.6 (1590)	1.1000-1.1008	1.1000-1.1008	1.1000-1.1008	1.1000-1.1008	1.1000-1.1008	1.4551-1.4557	1.4328-1.4334	0.0016-0.0032	0.0039
1993	3	1.3 (1298)	1.7372-1.7381	1.7451-1.7460	1.7530-1.7539	1.7609-1.7618	1.7687-1.7697	1.4763-1.4724	1.4763-1.4724	0.0020-0.0036	0.0039
	0	1.6 (1590)	1.7372-1.7381	1.7451-1.7460	1.7530-1.7539	1.7609-1.7618	1.7687-1.7697	1.4763-1.4724	1.4763-1.4724	0.0020-0.0036	0.0039
	0 ¹	1.6 (1590)	1.1000-1.1008	1.1000-1.1008	1.1000-1.1008	1.1000-1.1008	1.1000-1.1008	1.4551-1.4557	1.4328-1.4334	0.0016-0.0032	0.0039
1994	3	1.3 (1298)	1.7372-1.7381	1.7451-1.7460	1.7530-1.7539	1.7609-1.7618	1.7687-1.7697	1.4763-1.4724	1.4763-1.4724	0.0020-0.0036	0.0039
	0	1.6 (1590)	1.7372-1.7381	1.7451-1.7460	1.7530-1.7539	1.7609-1.7618	1.7687-1.7697	1.4763-1.4724	1.4763-1.4724	0.0020-0.0036	0.0039
	0 ¹	1.6 (1590)	1.1000-1.1008	1.1000-1.1008	1.1000-1.1008	1.1000-1.1008	1.1000-1.1008	1.4241-1.4303	1.4314-1.4376	0.0016-0.0032	0.0039
1995-96	3	1.3 (1298)	1.7372-1.7381	1.7451-1.7460	1.7530-1.7539	1.7609-1.7618	1.7687-1.7697	1.4763-1.4724	1.4763-1.4724	0.0020-0.0036	0.0039
	0	1.6 (1590)	1.7372-1.7381	1.7451-1.7460	1.7530-1.7539	1.7609-1.7618	1.7687-1.7697	1.4763-1.4724	1.4763-1.4724	0.0020-0.0036	0.0039
	0 ¹	1.6 (1590)	1.1000-1.1008	1.1000-1.1008	1.1000-1.1008	1.1000-1.1008	1.1000-1.1008	1.4241-1.4303	1.4314-1.4376	0.0016-0.0032	0.0039

1 Sidekick 16 valve engine

CRANKSHAFT AND CONNECTING ROD SPECIFICATIONS

All measurements are given in inches.

Year	Engine ID/VIN	Engine Displacement Liters (cc)	Crankshaft				Connecting Rod		
			Main Brg. Journal Dia.	Main Brg. Oil Clearance	Shaft End-play	Thrust on No.	Journal Diameter	Oil Clearance	Side Clearance
1992	3	1.3 (1298)	1	0.0008-0.0016	0.0044-0.0122	3	1.7710-1.7716	0.0012-0.0019	0.0039-0.0078
	0	1.6 (1590)	2	0.0008-0.0023	0.0044-0.0149	3	1.7316-1.7323	0.0008-0.0031	0.0039-0.0137
1993	3	1.3 (1298)	1	0.0008-0.0016	0.0044-0.0122	3	1.7710-1.7716	0.0012-0.0019	0.0039-0.0078
	0	1.6 (1590)	2	0.0008-0.0023	0.0044-0.0149	3	1.7316-1.7323	0.0008-0.0031	0.0039-0.0137
1994	3	1.3 (1298)	1	0.0008-0.0016	0.0044-0.0122	3	1.7710-1.7716	0.0012-0.0019	0.0039-0.0078
	0	1.6 (1590)	2	0.0008-0.0023	0.0044-0.0149	3	1.7316-1.7323	0.0008-0.0031	0.0039-0.0137
1995-96	3	1.3 (1298)	1	0.0008-0.0016	0.0044-0.0122	3	1.7710-1.7716	0.0012-0.0019	0.0039-0.0078
	0	1.6 (1590)	2	0.0008-0.0023	0.0044-0.0149	3	1.7316-1.7323	0.0008-0.0031	0.0039-0.0137

1 No. 1: 1.7714-1.7716
No. 2: 1.7712-1.7714
No. 3: 1.7710-1.7712

2 No. 1: 2.0470-2.0472
No. 2: 2.0468-2.0470
No. 3: 2.0465-2.0468

VALVE SPECIFICATIONS

Year	Engine ID/VIN		Engine Displacement Liters (cc)	Seat Angle (deg.)	Face Angle (deg.)	Spring Test Pressure (lbs. @ in.)	Spring Installed Height (in.)	Stem-to-Guide Clearance (in.)		Stem Diameter (in.)	
								Intake	Exhaust	Intake	Exhaust
1992	3		1.3 (1298)	45	45	55-64@1.63	1.941	0.0008-0.0019	0.0014-0.0025	0.2742-0.2748	0.2737-0.2742
	0		1.6 (1590)	45	45	55-64@1.63	1.907	0.0008-0.0019	0.0014-0.0025	0.2742-0.2748	0.2737-0.2742
	0	1	1.6 (1590)	45	45	24-28@1.24	1.450	0.0008-0.0018	0.0018-0.0028	0.2152-0.2157	0.2142-0.2148
1993	3		1.3 (1298)	45	45	55-64@1.63	1.941	0.0008-0.0019	0.0014-0.0025	0.2742-0.2748	0.2737-0.2742
	0		1.6 (1590)	45	45	55-64@1.63	1.987	0.0008-0.0019	0.0014-0.0025	0.2742-0.2748	0.2737-0.2742
	0	1	1.6 (1590)	45	45	24-28@1.24	1.450	0.0008-0.0018	0.0018-0.0028	0.2152-0.2157	0.2142-0.2148
1994	3		1.3 (1298)	45	45	55-64@1.63	1.941	0.0008-0.0019	0.0014-0.0025	0.2742-0.2748	0.2737-0.2742
	0		1.6 (1590)	45	45	55-64@1.63	1.987	0.0008-0.0019	0.0014-0.0025	0.2742-0.2748	0.2737-0.2742
	0	1	1.6 (1590)	45	45	24-28@1.24	1.450	0.0008-0.0018	0.0018-0.0028	0.2152-0.2157	0.2142-0.2148
1995-96	3		1.3 (1298)	45	45	55-64@1.63	1.941	0.0008-0.0019	0.0014-0.0025	0.2742-0.2748	0.2737-0.2742
	0		1.6 (1590)	45	45	55-64@1.63	1.987	0.0008-0.0019	0.0014-0.0025	0.2742-0.2748	0.2737-0.2742
	0	1	1.6 (1590)	45	45	24-28@1.24	1.450	0.0008-0.0018	0.0018-0.0028	0.2152-0.2157	0.2142-0.2148

1 Sidekick 16 valve engine

PISTON AND RING SPECIFICATIONS

All measurements are given in inches.

Year	Engine ID/VIN	Engine Displacement Liters (cc)	Piston Clearance	Ring Gap			Ring Side Clearance		
				Top Compression	Bottom Compression	Oil Control	Top Compression	Bottom Compression	Oil Control
1992	3	1.3 (1298)	0.0008-0.0015	0.0079-0.0129	0.0079-0.0137	0.0079-0.0275	0.0012-0.0027	0.0008-0.0023	NA
	0	1.6 (1590)	0.0008-0.0015	0.0079-0.0137	0.0079-0.0137	0.0079-0.0275	0.0012-0.0027	0.0008-0.0023	NA
1993	3	1.3 (1298)	0.0008-0.0015	0.0079-0.0129	0.0079-0.0137	0.0079-0.0275	0.0012-0.0027	0.0008-0.0023	NA
	0	1.6 (1590)	0.0008-0.0015	0.0079-0.0137	0.0079-0.0137	0.0079-0.0275	0.0012-0.0027	0.0008-0.0023	NA
1994	3	1.3 (1298)	0.0008-0.0015	0.0079-0.0129	0.0079-0.0137	0.0079-0.0275	0.0012-0.0027	0.0008-0.0023	NA
	0	1.6 (1590)	0.0008-0.0015	0.0079-0.0137	0.0079-0.0137	0.0079-0.0275	0.0012-0.0027	0.0008-0.0023	NA
1995-96	3	1.3 (1298)	0.0008-0.0015	0.0079-0.0275	0.0079-0.0275	0.0079-0.0275	0.0012-0.0027	0.0008-0.0023	NA
	0	1.6 (1590)	0.0008-0.0015	0.0079-0.0137	0.0079-0.0137	0.0079-0.0275	0.0012-0.0027	0.0008-0.0023	NA

NA - Not Available

TORQUE SPECIFICATIONS

All readings in ft. lbs.

Year	Engine ID/VIN	Engine Displacement Liters (cc)	Cylinder Head Bolts	Main Bearing Bolts	Rod Bearing Bolts	Crankshaft Damper Bolts	Flywheel Bolts	Manifold		Spark Plugs	Lug Nut
								Intake	Exhaust		
1992	3	1.3 (1298)	51-54	36-41	24-26	76-83 [1]	41-47	13-20	13-20	14-21	58-80
	0	1.6 (1590)	51-54	36-41	24-26	76-83 [1]	55-58	13-20	13-20	14-21	58-80
1993	3	1.3 (1298)	51-54	36-41	24-26	76-83 [1]	41-47	13-20	13-20	14-21	58-80
	0	1.6 (1590)	51-54	36-41	24-26	76-83 [1]	55-58	13-20	13-20	14-21	58-80
1994	3	1.3 (1298)	51-54	36-41	24-26	76-83 [1]	41-47	13-20	13-20	14-21	58-80
	0	1.6 (1590)	48-51	36-41	24-26	76-83 [1]	55-58	13-20	13-20	14-21	58-80
1995-96	3	1.3 (1298)	51-54	36-41	24-26	76-83 [1]	50-52	13-20	13-20	15-22	36-50
	0	1.6 (1590)	48-51	36-41	24-26	76-83 [1]	55-58	13-20	13-20	14-21	58-80

1 Specification shown is for crankshaft timing sprocket bolt

BRAKE SPECIFICATIONS

All measurements in inches unless noted

| Year | Model | Master Cylinder Bore | Brake Disc | | | Brake Drum Diameter | | | Minimum Lining Thickness | |
			Original Thickness	Minimum Thickness	Maximum Runout	Original Inside Diameter	Max. Wear Limit	Maximum Machine Diameter	Front	Rear
1992	Samurai	NA	0.394	0.334	0.006	8.66	8.74	8.74	0.236	0.120
	Sidekick	NA	0.394	0.315	0.006	8.66	8.74	8.74	0.315	0.120
	Sidekick [1]	NA	0.669	0.591	0.006	10.00	10.07	10.07	0.315	0.120
1993	Samurai	NA	0.394	0.334	0.006	8.66	8.74	8.74	0.236	0.120
	Sidekick	NA	0.394	0.315	0.006	8.66	8.74	8.74	0.315	0.120
	Sidekick [1]	NA	0.669	0.591	0.006	10.00	10.07	10.07	0.315	0.120
1994	Samurai	NA	0.394	0.334	0.006	8.66	8.74	8.74	0.236	0.120 [2]
	Sidekick	NA	0.669	0.591	0.006	10.00	10.07	10.07	0.315	0.120 [2]
1995-96	Samurai	NA	0.394	0.394	0.006	8.66	8.74	8.74	0.236	0.120 [2]
	Sidekick	NA	0.669	0.591	0.006	10.00	10.07	10.07	0.100	0.120 [2]

NA - Not Available
1 4 door
2 Measurement is for lining and backing

WHEEL ALIGNMENT

| Year | Model | Caster | | Camber | | Toe-in (in.) | Steering Axis Inclination (deg.) |
		Range (deg.)	Preferred Setting (deg.)	Range (deg.)	Preferred Setting (deg.)		
1992	Samurai	2.50P-4.50P	3.50P	0.25P-1.75P	1P	0.15P-0.47P	9
	Sidekick	0.50P-2.50P	1.50P	0.50N-1.50P	0.50P	0.31P-0.25P	NA
1993	Samurai	2.50P-4.50P	3.50P	0.25P-1.75P	1P	0.15P-0.47P	9
	Sidekick	0.50P-2.50P	1.50P	0.50N-1.50P	0.50P	0.31P-0.25P	NA
1994	Samurai	2.50P-4.50P	3.50P	0.25P-1.75P	1P	0.16P-0.47P	NA
	Sidekick	0.50P-2.50P	1.50P	0.50N-1.50P	0.50P	0.08P-0.24P	NA
1995-96	Samurai	2.50P-4.50P	3.50P	0.25P-1.75P	1P	0.16P-0.47P	NA
	Sidekick	0.50P-2.50P	1.50P	0.50N-1.50P	0.50P	0.08P-0.24P	NA

NA - Not Available
N - Negative
P - Positive

TOYOTA

ENGINE IDENTIFICATION

Year	Model	Engine Displacement Liters (cc)	Engine Series (ID/VIN)	Fuel System	No. of Cylinders	Engine Type
1992	Previa	2.4 (2438)	2TZ-FE	EFI	4	DOHC
	4Runner	2.4 (2366)	22R-E	EFI	4	SOHC
	4Runner	3.0 (2959)	3VZ-FE	EFI	6	SOHC
	Pick-up	2.4 (2366)	22R-E	EFI	4	SOHC
	Pick-up	3.0 (2959)	3VZ-FE	EFI	6	SOHC
	Land Cruiser	4.0 (3956)	3F-E	EFI	6	OHV
1993	Previa	2.4 (2438)	2TZ-FE	EFI	4	DOHC
	4Runner	2.4 (2366)	22R-E	EFI	4	SOHC
	4Runner	3.0 (2959)	3VZ-E	EFI	6	SOHC
	Pick-up	2.4 (2366)	22R-E	EFI	4	SOHC
	Pick-up	3.0 (2959)	3VZ-E	EFI	6	SOHC
	T100	3.0 (2959)	3VZ-E	EFI	6	SOHC
	Land Cruiser	4.5 (4477)	1FZ-FE	EFI	6	DOHC
1994	Previa 1	2.4 (2438)	2TZ-FE	EFI	4	DOHC
	4Runner	2.4 (2366)	22R-E	EFI	4	SOHC
	4Runner	3.0 (2959)	3VZ-E	EFI	6	SOHC
	Pick-up	2.4 (2366)	22R-E	EFI	4	SOHC
	Pick-up	3.0 (2959)	3VZ-E	EFI	6	SOHC
	T100	2.7 (2693)	3RZ-FE	EFI	4	DOHC
	T100	3.0 (2959)	3VZ-E	EFI	6	SOHC
	Land Cruiser	4.5 (4477)	1FZ-FE	EFI	6	DOHC
1995-96	Previa	2.4 (2438)	2TZ-FE	EFI	4	DOHC
	Previa 1	2.4 (2438)	2TZ-FE	EFI	4	DOHC
	4Runner	2.4 (2366)	22R-E	EFI	4	SOHC
	4Runner	3.0 (2959)	3VZ-E	EFI	6	SOHC
	Pick-up	2.4 (2366)	22R-E	EFI	4	SOHC
	Pick-up	3.0 (2959)	3VZ-E	EFI	6	SOHC
	Tacoma	2.4 (2438)	2RZ-FE	EFI	4	DOHC
	Tacoma	2.7 (2693)	3RZ-FE	EFI	4	DOHC
	Tacoma	3.4 (3378)	5VZ-FE	EFI	6	DOHC
	T100	2.7 (2693)	3RZ-FE	EFI	4	DOHC
	T100	3.4 (3378)	5VZ-FE	EFI	6	DOHC
	Land Cruiser	4.5 (4477)	1FZ-FE	EFI	6	DOHC

EFI - Electronic fuel injection
SOHC - Single overhead camshaft
DOHC - Double overhead camshaft

OHV - Overhead valve
1 Supercharged

GENERAL ENGINE SPECIFICATIONS

Year	Engine ID/VIN	Engine Displacement Liters (cc)	Fuel System Type	Net Horsepower @ rpm	Net Torque @ rpm (ft. lbs.)	Bore x Stroke (in.)	Compression Ratio	Oil Pressure @ rpm
1992	2TZ-FE	2.4 (2438)	EFI	138@5000	154@4000	3.74x3.39	9.1:1	36-71@3000
	22R-E	2.4 (2366)	EFI	116@4800	140@2800	3.62x3.50	9.3:1	36-71@3000
	3VZ-FE	3.0 (2959)	EFI	185@5200	195@4400	3.44x3.23	9.6:1	4.3 [1]
	3F-E	4.0 (3956)	EFI	154@4000	220@3000	3.70x3.74	8.1:1	36-71@4000
1993	2TZ-FE	2.4 (2438)	EFI	138@5000	154@4000	3.74x3.39	9.1:1	36-71@3000
	22R-E	2.4 (2366)	EFI	116@4800	140@2800	3.62x3.50	9.3:1	36-71@3000
	3VZ-E	3.0 (2959)	EFI	150@4800	180@3400	3.44x3.23	9.0:1	36-71@4000
	1FZ-FE	4.5 (4477)	EFI	212@4600	275@3200	3.94x3.74	9.0:1	36-71@3000
1994	2TZ-FE	2.4 (2438)	EFI	161@5000	201@3000	3.74x3.39	8.9:1	36-71@3000
	2TZ-FE	2.4 (2438)	EFI	138@5000	154@4000	3.74x3.39	9.1:1	36-71@3000
	22R-E	2.4 (2366)	EFI	116@4800	140@2800	3.62x3.50	9.3:1	36-71@3000
	3RZ-FE	2.7 (2693)	EFI	150@4800	177@4000	3.74x3.74	9.5:1	36-71@3000
	3VZ-E	3.0 (2959)	EFI	150@4800	180@3400	3.44x3.23	9.0:1	36-71@4000
	1FZ-FE	4.5 (4477)	EFI	212@4600	275@3200	3.94x3.64	9.0:1	36-71@3000
1995-96	2TZ-FE	2.4 (2438)	EFI	161@5000	201@3000	3.74x3.39	8.9:1	36-71@3000
	2TZ-FE	2.4 (2438)	EFI	138@5000	154@4000	3.74x3.39	9.1:1	36-71@3000
	22R-E	2.4 (2366)	EFI	116@4800	140@2800	3.62x3.50	9.3:1	36-71@3000
	2RZ-FE	2.4 (2438)	EFI	142@5000	160@4000	3.74x3.38	9.5:1	36-71@3000
	3RZ-FE	2.7 (2693)	EFI	150@4800	177@4000	3.74x3.74	9.5:1	36-71@3000
	3VZ-E	3.0 (2959)	EFI	150@4800	180@3400	3.44x3.23	9.0:1	36-71@3000
	5VZ-FE	3.4 (3378)	EFI	190@4800	220@3400	3.68x3.23	9.6:1	4.3 [1]
	1FZ-FE	4.5 (4477)	EFI	212@4600	275@3200	3.94x3.64	9.0:1	36-71@3000

EFI - Electronic fuel injection
1 At idle

GASOLINE ENGINE TUNE-UP SPECIFICATIONS

Year	Engine ID/VIN	Engine Displacement Liters (cc)	Spark Plugs Gap (in.)	Ignition Timing (deg.) MT	AT	Fuel Pump (psi)	Idle Speed (rpm) MT	AT	Valve Clearance In.	Ex.
1992	22R-E	2.4 (2366)	0.031	5B	5B	38-44	750	850	0.008	0.012
	2TZ-FE	2.4 (2438)	0.043	5B	5B	38-44	700	750	1	2
	3VZ-FE	3.0 (2952)	0.043	10B	10B	38-44	650-750	650-750	0.005-0.009	0.011-0.015
	3F-E	4.0 (3956)	0.031	-	7B	37-46	650	650	0.008	0.014
1993	22R-E	2.4 (2366)	0.031	5B	5B	38-44	750	850	0.008	0.012
	2TZ-FE	2.4 (2438)	0.043	5B	5B	38-44	700	750	1	2
	3VZ-E	3.0 (2959)	0.041	10B	10B	38-44	800	800	3	4
	1FZ-FE	4.5 (4477)	0.031	-	3B	38-44	-	600-700	0.006-0.010	0.010-0.014
1994	22R-E	2.4 (2366)	0.031	5B	5B	38-44	750	850	0.008	0.012
	2TZ-FE	2.4 (2438)	0.043	5B	5B	38-44	-	750	1	2
	3RZ-FE	2.7 (2693)	0.031	5B	-	38-44	750	-	0.008	0.012
	3VZ-E	3.0 (2959)	0.031	10B	10B	38-44	800	800	3	4
	1FZ-FE	4.5 (4477)	0.031	-	3B	38-44	-	600-700	0.006-0.010	0.010-0.014
1995-96	22R-E	2.4 (2366)	0.031	5B	5B	38-44	750	850	0.008	0.012
	2TZ-FE	2.4 (2438)	0.043	5B	5B	38-44	-	750	1	2
	2RZ-FE	2.4 (2438)	0.031	5	5	38-44	650-750	650-750	0.006-0.010	0.010-0.014
	3RZ-FE	2.7 (2693)	0.031	5	5	38-44	750	-	0.008	0.012
	3VZ-E	3.0 (2959)	0.031	10B	10B	38-44	800	800	3	4
	5VZ-FE	3.4 (3378)	0.043	6	6	38-44	650-750	650-750	0.006-0.009	0.011-0.014
	1FZ-FE	4.5 (4477)	0.031	-	3B	38-44	-	600-700	0.006-0.010	0.010-0.014

NOTE: The Vehicle Emission Control Information label often reflects specification changes made during production. The label figures must be used if they differ from those in this chart.
B - Before top dead center
1 Intake: 0.006-0.010 (cold)

2 Exhaust: 0.010-0.014 (cold)
3 Intake: 0.007-0.011 (cold)
4 Exhaust: 0.009-0.013 (cold)
5 5B at idle, with terminal TE1 and E1 connected of DLC1
6 10B at idle, with terminal TE1 and E1 connected of DLC1

CAPACITIES

Year	Model	Engine ID/VIN	Engine Displacement Liters (cc)	Engine Oil with Filter (qts.)	Transmission (pts.) 4-Spd	5-Spd	Auto.	Transfer Case (pts.)	Drive Axle Front (pts.)	Rear (pts.)	Fuel Tank (gal.)	Cooling System (qts.)
1992	Previa	2TZ-FE	2.4 (2438)	6.1	-	1	5.0	3.0	2.2	3.2	19.8	12.3
	Pick-up	22R-E	2.4 (2366)	4.5	-	2	3	4	5	6	7	8
	Pick-up	3VZ-E	3.0 (2959)	4.8	-	2	3	4	5	6	7	9
	4Runner	22R-E	2.4 (2366)	4.5	-	2	3	4	5	6	10	8
	4Runner	3VZ-E	3.0 (2959)	4.8	-	2	3	4	5	6	10	9
	Land Cruiser	3F-E	4.0 (3956)	8.2	-	-	12.6	4.4	6.0	6.8	25.1	11
1993	Previa	2TZ-FE	2.4 (2438)	6.1	-	1	5.0	3.0	2.2	3.2	19.8	12.3
	Pick-up	22R-E	2.4 (2366)	4.5	-	12	13	14	5	15	16	17
	Pick-up	3VZ-E	3.0 (2959)	4.8	-	12	13	14	5	15	16	18
	4Runner	22R-E	2.4 (2366)	4.5	-	12	13	14	5	15	16	17
	4Runner	3VZ-E	3.0 (2959)	4.8	-	12	13	14	5	15	16	18
	T100	3VZ-E	3.0 (2959)	4.8	-	6.4	13	2.4	5	15	16	18
	Land Cruiser	1FZ-FE	4.5 (4477)	7.8	-	-	12.6	19	20	6.8	25.1	14.8
1994	Previa	2TZ-FE	2.4 (2438)	6.1	-	-	5.0	3.0	2.2	3.2	19.8	13.0
	Previa	2TZ-FZE	2.4 (2438)	6.1	-	-	5.0	3.0	2.2	3.2	19.8	13.0
	Pick-up	22R-E	2.4 (2366)	4.5	-	12	13	14	5	15	16	17
	Pick-up	3VZ-E	3.0 (2959)	4.8	-	12	13	14	5	15	16	18
	4Runner	22R-E	2.4 (2366)	4.5	-	12	13	14	5	15	16	17
	4Runner	3VZ-E	3.0 (2959)	4.8	-	12	13	14	5	15	16	18
	T100	3RZ-FE	2.7 (2693)	5.6	-	2.7	-	-	-	3.8	19.8	9.2
	T100	3VZ-E	3.0 (2959)	4.8	-	6.4	13	2.4	5	15	16	18
	Land Cruiser	1FZ-FE	4.5 (4477)	7.8	-	-	12.6	19	20	6.8	25.1	14.8
1995-96	Previa	2TZ-FE	2.4 (2438)	6.1	-	-	5.0	3.0	2.2	3.2	19.8	13.0
	Previa	2TZ-FZE	2.4 (2438)	6.1	-	-	5.0	3.0	2.2	3.2	19.8	13.0
	Pick-up	22R-E	2.4 (2366)	4.5	-	12	21	14	5	22	16	17
	Pick-up	3VZ-E	3.0 (2959)	4.8	-	12	21	14	5	22	16	23
	4Runner	22R-E	2.4 (2366)	4.5	-	12	21	14	5	22	16	23
	4Runner	3VZ-E	3.0 (2959)	4.8	-	12	21	14	5	22	16	23
	Tacoma	2RZ-FE	2.4 (2438)	5.8	-	24	25	2.2	26	2.9	15.1	28
	Tacoma	3RZ-FE	2.7 (2693)	5.8	-	24	25	2.2	26	27	18.0	28
	Tacoma	5VZ-FE	3.4 (3378)	29	-	24	25	2.2	26	27	18.0	30
	T100	3RZ-FE	2.7 (2693)	5.6	-	2.7	-	-	-	3.8	19.8	9.2
	T100	5VZ-FE	3.4 (3378)	31	32	21	2.4	3.9	22		24.0	23
	Land Cruiser	1FZ-FE	4.5 (4477)	7.8	-	-	12.6	19	20	6.8	25.1	14.8

1 2WD: 4.6; 4WD: 5.4
2 2WD with W56: 5.0
  4WD with W56: 6.4
  4WD with G58: 8.2
  4WD with R150F: 6.4
3 2WD with A340E: 3.4
  4WD: with A340H: 9.6
  4WD: with A340F: 4.2
4 Counter gear type: 2.4
  Planetary gear type: 2.4
  A340H: 1.8
5 Standard: 3.4; ADD: 4.0
6 2WD with 7.5" differential: 2.8
  2WD with 8.0" differential: 3.8
  4WD: 4.6
7 Short bed: 13.7
  Long bed: 17.2
  4WD long bed: 19.3

13 2WD: 3.4
  4WD with A340H: 9.6
  4WD with A340F: 4.2
14 Except 3VZ-E AT (VF1A type): 2.4
  3VZ-E AT (A340H): 1.6
15 2WD: 3.8; 4WD: 4.6
16 With standard tires: 17.2
  With optional 31x10.5 tires: 18.8
17 With rear heater: 9.2
  Without rear heater: 8.9
18 2WD manual transmission: 11.0
  2WD automatic tranmission: 10.8
  4WD manual transmission: 11.1
  4WD automatic transmission: 10.9
19 With ABS: 2.8
  Without ABS: 3.6
20 With differential lock: 5.6
  Without differential lock: 5.8

24 W59:
  2WD: 5.4
  4WD: 5.2
  R150, R150F:
  2WD: 5.4
  4WD: 4.6
25 A43D: 5.0
  A340E: 3.4
  A340F: 4.2
26 Without ADD: 2.32
  With ADD: 2.44
27 Extra long: 4.4
  All others: 5.4
28 2WD with manual transmission: 8.5
  2WD with automatic transmission: 8.2
  4WD with manual transmission: 8.8
  4WD with automatic transmission: 8.7
29 2WD: 5.7

CAPACITIES

Year	Model	Engine ID/VIN	Engine Displacement Liters (cc)	Engine Oil with Filter (qts.)	Transmission (pts.)			Transfer Case (pts.)	Drive Axle		Fuel Tank (gal.)	Cooling System (qts.)
					4-Spd	5-Spd	Auto.		Front (pts.)	Rear (pts.)		

8 Except 4WD automatic transmission: 8.9
  4WD automatic transmission: 9.6
9 Manual tranmission: 11.1
  Automatic transmission: 10.9
10 Standard: 17.2; Optional: 19.3
11 With rear heater: 20.6
  Without rear heater: 18.5
12 G58: 8.2
  R150F: 6.4

21 Drain and refill:
  A340E: 3.4
  A340F: 4.2
22 2WD: 4.4
  4WD: 4.3
23 2WD with manual transmission: 10.6
  2WD with automatic transmission: 10.5
  4WD with manual transmission: 10.6
  4WD with automatic transmission: 10.8

4WD: 5.5
30 With manual transmission: 10.7
  With automatic transmission: 10.5
31 2WD: 5.5
  4WD: 5.0
32 2WD: 5.4
  4WD: 4.6
  All others: 5.4

CAMSHAFT SPECIFICATIONS
All measurements given in inches.

Year	Engine ID/VIN	Engine Displacement Liters (cc)	Journal Diameter					Elevation		Bearing Clearance	Camshaft End Play
			1	2	3	4	5	In.	Ex.		
1992	2TZ-FE	2.4 (2438)	1.0614-1.0620	1.0614-1.0620	1.0614-1.0620	1.0614-1.0620	NA	1.7839-1.7878	1.7740-1.7779	0.0010-0.0031	0.0016-0.0047
	22R-E	2.4 (2366)	1.2984-1.2992	1.2984-1.2992	1.2984-1.2992	1.2984-1.2992	NA	1.6783-1.6819	1.6807-1.6842	0.0004-0.0024	0.0031-0.0071
	3VZ-E	3.0 (2959)	1.0610-1.0616	1.0610-1.0616	1.0610-1.0616	1.0610-1.0616	NA	1.6598-1.6638	1.6520-1.6559	0.0014-0.0028	0.0013-0.0031
	3F-E	4.0 (3956)	1.8880-1.8888	1.8289-1.8297	1.7699-1.7707	1.7108-1.7116	NA	1.5102-1.5142	1.5059-1.5098	0.0010-0.0030	0.0079-0.0103
1993	2TZ-FE	2.4 (2438)	1.0614-1.0620	1.0614-1.0620	1.0614-1.0620	1.0614-1.0620	NA	1.7839-1.7878	1.7740-1.7779	0.0010-0.0031	0.0016-0.0047
	22R-E	2.4 (2366)	1.2984-1.2992	1.2984-1.2992	1.2984-1.2992	1.2984-1.2992	NA	1.6783-1.6819	1.6807-1.6842	0.0004-0.0024	0.0031-0.0071
	3VZ-E	3.0 (2959)	1.0610-1.0616	1.0610-1.0616	1.0610-1.0616	1.0610-1.0616	NA	1.6598-1.6638	1.6520-1.6559	0.0014-0.0028	0.0013-0.0031
	1FZ-FE	4.5 (4477)	1.0614-1.0620	1.0614-1.0620	1.0614-1.0620	1.0614-1.0620	NA	1.9925-1.9965	1.9925-1.9965	0.0010-0.0024	0.0012-0.0031
1994	2TZ-FE	2.4 (2438)	1.0614-1.0620	1.0614-1.0620	1.0614-1.0620	1.0614-1.0620	NA	1.7839-1.7878	1.7740-1.7779	0.0010-0.0031	0.0016-0.0047
	22R-E	2.4 (2366)	1.2984-1.2992	1.2984-1.2992	1.2984-1.2992	1.2984-1.2992	NA	1.6783-1.6819	1.6807-1.6842	0.0004-0.0024	0.0031-0.0071
	3RZ-FE	2.7 (2693)	1.0614-1.0620	1.0614-1.0620	1.0614-1.0620	1.0614-1.0620	NA	1.7839-1.7878	1.7740-1.7779	0.0010-0.0031	0.0016-0.0047
	3VZ-E	3.0 (2959)	1.0610-1.0616	1.0610-1.0616	1.0610-1.0616	1.0610-1.0616	NA	1.6598-1.6638	1.6520-1.6559	0.0014-0.0028	0.0013-0.0031
	1FZ-FE	4.5 (4477)	1.0614-1.0620	1.0614-1.0620	1.0614-1.0620	1.0614-1.0620	NA	1.9925-1.9965	1.9925-1.9965	0.0010-0.0024	0.0012-0.0031

CAMSHAFT SPECIFICATIONS

All measurements given in inches.

Year	Engine ID/VIN	Engine Displacement Liters (cc)	Journal Diameter					Elevation		Bearing Clearance	Camshaft End Play
			1	2	3	4	5	In.	Ex.		
1995-96	2TZ-FE	2.4 (2438)	1.0614-1.0620	1.0614-1.0620	1.0614-1.0620	1.0614-1.0620	NA	1.7839-1.7878	1.7740-1.7779	0.0010-0.0031	0.0016-0.0047
	22R-E	2.4 (2366)	1.2984-1.2992	1.2984-1.2992	1.2984-1.2992	1.2984-1.2992	NA	1.6783-1.6819	1.6807-1.6842	0.0004-0.0024	0.0031-0.0071
	2RZ-FE	2.4 (2438)	1.0614-1.0620	1.0614-1.0620	1.0614-1.0620	1.0614-1.0620	1.0614-1.0620	1.7839-1.7878	1.7740-1.7779	0.0010-0.0024	0.0016-0.0037
	3RZ-FE	2.7 (2693)	1.0614-1.0620	1.0614-1.0620	1.0614-1.0620	1.0614-1.0620	1.0614-1.0620	1.7839-1.7878	1.7740-1.7779	0.0010-0.0031	0.0016-0.0047
	3VZ-E	3.0 (2959)	1.0610-1.0616	1.0610-1.0616	1.0610-1.0616	1.0610-1.0616	NA	1.6598-1.6638	1.6520-1.6559	0.0014-0.0028	0.0013-0.0031
	5VZ-FE	3.4 (3378)	1.0610-1.0616	1.0610-1.0616	1.0610-1.0616	1.0610-1.0616	NA	1.6657-1.6697	1.6520-1.6559	0.0014-0.0028	0.0013-0.0031
	1FZ-FE	4.5 (4477)	1.0614-1.0620	1.0614-1.0620	1.0614-1.0620	1.0614-1.0620	NA	1.9925-1.9965	1.9925-1.9965	0.0010-0.0024	0.0012-0.0031

NA - Not Available

CRANKSHAFT AND CONNECTING ROD SPECIFICATIONS

All measurements are given in inches.

Year	Engine ID/VIN	Engine Displacement Liters (cc)	Crankshaft Main Brg. Journal Dia.	Main Brg. Oil Clearance	Shaft End-play	Thrust on No.	Connecting Rod Journal Diameter	Oil Clearance	Side Clearance
1992	2TZ-FE	2.4 (2438)	2.3617-2.3622	0.0009-0.0019	0.0008-0.0087	3	[1]	0.0012-0.0023	0.0063-0.0123
	22R-E	2.4 (2366)	2.3616-2.3622	0.0010-0.0022	0.0008-0.0087	3	2.0861-2.0866	0.0010-0.0022	0.0008-0.0087
	3VZ-FE	3.0 (2959)	2.5191-2.5197	0.0011-0.0022	0.0008-0.0087	3	2.1648-2.1654	0.0011-0.0026	0.0059-0.0130
	3F-E	4.0 (3956)	[2]	0.0008-0.0017	0.0024-0.0063	3	2.1252-2.1260	0.0008-0.0024	0.0043-0.0091
1993	2TZ-FE	2.4 (2438)	2.3617-2.3622	0.0009-0.0019	0.0008-0.0087	3	[1]	0.0012-0.0023	0.0063-0.0123
	22R-E	2.4 (2366)	2.3616-2.3622	0.0010-0.0022	0.0008-0.0087	3	2.0861-2.0866	0.0010-0.0022	0.0008-0.0087
	3VZ-E	3.0 (2959)	2..5195-2.5197	0.0009-0.0017	0.0008-0.0098	3	2.1648-2.1654	0.0009-0.0021	0.0059-0.0130
	1FZ-FE	4.5 (4477)	2.7158-2.7165	0.0016-0.0032	0.0008-0.0087	3	[3]	0.0013-0.0020	0.0063-0.0103
1994	2TZ-FE	2.4 (2438)	2.3617-2.3622	0.0009-0.0019	0.0008-0.0087	3	[1]	0.0012-0.0023	0.0063-0.0123
	22R-E	2.4 (2366)	2.3616-2.3622	0.0010-0.0022	0.0008-0.0087	3	2.0861-2.0866	0.0010-0.0022	0.0008-0.0087
	3RZ-FE	2.7 (2693)	2.3617-2.3622	0.0009-0.0019	0.0008-0.0087	3	2.0861-2.0866	0.0012-0.0023	0.0063-0.0123
	3VZ-E	3.0 (2959)	2.5195-2.5197	0.0009-0.0017	0.0008-0.0098	3	2.1648-2.1654	0.0009-0.0021	0.0059-0.0130
	1FZ-FE	4.5 (4477)	2.7158-2.7165	0.0016-0.0032	0.0008-0.0087	3	[3]	0.0013-0.0020	0.0063-0.0103
1995-96	2TZ-FE	2.4 (2438)	2.3617-2.3622	0.0009-0.0019	0.0008-0.0087	3	[1]	0.0012-0.0023	0.0063-0.0123
	22R-E	2.4 (2366)	2.3616-2.3622	0.0010-0.0022	0.0008-0.0087	3	2.0861-2.0866	0.0010-0.0022	0.0008-0.0087
	2RZ-FE	2.4 (2438)	[4]	[5]	0.0008-0.0087	3	[6]	0.0012-0.0022	0.0063-0.0123
	3RZ-FE	2.7 (2693)	[4]	[5]	0.0008-0.0087	3	[6]	0.0012-0.0022	0.0063-0.0123
	3VZ-E	3.0 (2959)	2.5195-2.5197	0.0009-0.0017	0.0008-0.0098	3	2.1648-2.1654	0.0009-0.0021	0.0059-0.0130
	5VZ-FE	3.4 (3378)	2.5195-2.5197	0.0009-0.0017	0.0008-0.0087	3	2.1648-2.1654	0.0009-0.0021	0.0059-0.0130
	1FZ-FE	4.5 (4477)	2.7158-2.7165	0.0016-0.0032	0.0008-0.0087	3	[3]	0.0013-0.0020	0.0063-0.0103

[1] No. 1: 2.2047-2.2050
No. 2: 2.2051-2.2053
No. 3: 2.2054-2.2057
[2] No. 1: 2.6367-2.6376
No. 2: 2.6957-2.6967
No. 3: 2.7548-2.7557
No. 4: 2.8139-2.8148
[3] There are five sizes of standard connecting rod bearings, marked 2, 3, 4, 5 and 6 accordingly.
Replace with one having the same number (located on outside of bearing end). If the bearing

[4] No. 3: 2.2615-2.3620
Others: 2.3617-2.3622
[5] No. 3: 0.0012-0.0022
All others: 0.0009-0.0019
[6] Mark 4: 2.2047-2.2050
Mark 5: 2.2050-2.2052
Mark 6: 2.2052-2.2054

CRANKSHAFT AND CONNECTING ROD SPECIFICATIONS

All measurements are given in inches.

		Engine		Crankshaft				Connecting Rod		
Year	Engine ID/VIN	Displacement Liters (cc)	Main Brg. Journal Dia.	Main Brg. Oil Clearance	Shaft End-play	Thrust on No.	Journal Diameter	Oil Clearance	Side Clearance

number cannot be determined, select correct bearing by adding together the numbers
imprinted on connecting rod and crankshaft, then selecting the bearing with the same
number as the total   EXAMPLE: Connecting rod 3 + Crankshaft 1= 4. Use bearing 4.

VALVE SPECIFICATIONS

Year	Engine ID/VIN	Engine Displacement Liters (cc)	Seat Angle (deg.)	Face Angle (deg.)	Spring Test Pressure (lbs. @ in.)	Spring Installed Height (in.)	Stem-to-Guide Clearance (in.) Intake	Stem-to-Guide Clearance (in.) Exhaust	Stem Diameter (in.) Intake	Stem Diameter (in.) Exhaust
1992	2TZ-FE	2.4 (2438)	45 1	44.5	57-63	1.406	0.0010-0.0024	0.0012-0.0026	0.2350-0.2356	0.2348-0.2354
	22R-E	2.4 (2366)	45 1	44.5	66.1	1.594	0.0010-0.0024	0.0012-0.0026	0.3138-0.3144	0.3136-0.3142
	3VZ-FE	3.0 (2952)	45	44.5	38-42	1.311	0.0010-0.0024	0.0012-0.0026	0.2350-0.2356	0.2348-0.2354
	3F-E	4.0 (3956)	45	44.5	71.6	1.693	0.0012-0.0024	0.0016-0.0028	0.3140	0.3137
1993	2TZ-FE	2.4 (2438)	45 1	44.5	57-63	1.406	0.0010-0.0024	0.0012-0.0026	0.2350-0.2356	0.2348-0.2354
	22R-E	2.4 (2366)	45 1	44.5	66.1	1.594	0.0010-0.0024	0.0012-0.0026	0.3138-0.3144	0.3136-0.3142
	3VZ-E	3.0 (2959)	45 1	44.5	54-57	1.575	0.0010-0.0024	0.0012-0.0026	0.3138-0.3144	0.3136-0.3142
	1FZ-FE	4.5 (4477)	45	44.5	53.4	1.437	0.0010-0.0024	0.0012-0.0026	0.2744-0.2750	0.2742-0.2748
1994	2TZ-FE	2.4 (2438)	45 1	44.5	57-63	1.406	0.0010-0.0024	0.0012-0.0026	0.2350-0.2356	0.2348-0.2354
	22R-E	2.4 (2366)	45 1	44.5	66.1	1.594	0.0010-0.0024	0.0012-0.0026	0.3138-0.3144	0.3136-0.3142
	3RZ-FE	2.7 (2693)	45 1	44.5	57-63	1.406	0.0010-0.0024	0.0012-0.0026	0.2350-0.2356	0.2348-0.2354
	3VZ-E	3.0 (2959)	45 1	44.5	54-57	1.575	0.0010-0.0024	0.0012-0.0026	0.3138-0.3144	0.3136-0.3142
	1FZ-FE	4.5 (4477)	45	44.5	53.4	1.437	0.0010-0.0024	0.0012-0.0026	0.2744-0.2750	0.2742-0.2748
1995-96	2TZ-FE	2.4 (2438)	45 1	44.5	57-63@ 1.406	1.406	0.0010-0.0024	0.0012-0.0026	0.2350-0.2356	0.2348-0.2354
	22R-E	2.4 (2366)	45 1	44.5	66.1@1.594	1.594	0.0010-0.0024	0.0012-0.0026	0.3138-0.3144	0.3136-0.3142
	2RZ-FE	2.4 (2438)	45 1	44.5	40-46@ 1.406	1.406	0.0010-0.0024	0.0012-0.0026	0.2350-0.2356	0.2348-0.2354
	3RZ-FE	2.7 (2693)	45 1	44.5	57-63@ 1.406	1.406	0.0010-0.0024	0.0012-0.0026	0.2350-0.2356	0.2348-0.2354

VALVE SPECIFICATIONS

Year	Engine ID/VIN	Engine Displacement Liters (cc)	Seat Angle (deg.)	Face Angle (deg.)	Spring Test Pressure (lbs. @ in.)	Spring Installed Height (in.)	Stem-to-Guide Clearance (in.)		Stem Diameter (in.)	
							Intake	Exhaust	Intake	Exhaust
1995-96	3VZ-E	3.0 (2959)	45 [1]	44.5	54-57@ 1.575	1.575	0.0010-0.0024	0.0012-0.0026	0.3138-0.3144	0.3136-0.3142
	5VZ-FE	3.4 (3378)	45	44.5	41.9-46.3@ 1.311	1.311	0.0010-0.0024	0.0012-0.0026	0.2350-0.2356	0.2348-0.2354
	1FZ-FE	4.5 (4477)	45	44.5	53.4@1.437	1.437	0.0010-0.0024	0.0012-0.0026	0.2744-0.2750	0.2742-0.2748

1 Blend seat with 30 and 60 degree cutters to center the 45 degree portion on valve face

PISTON AND RING SPECIFICATIONS

All measurements are given in inches.

Year	Engine ID/VIN	Engine Displacement Liters (cc)	Piston Clearance	Ring Gap			Ring Side Clearance		
				Top Compression	Bottom Compression	Oil Control	Top Compression	Bottom Compression	Oil Control
1992	2TZ-FE	2.4 (2438)	0.0012-0.0020	0.0118-0.0169	0.0177-0.0236	0.0051-0.0150	0.0008-0.0028	0.0012-0.0028	SNUG
	22R-E	2.4 (2366)	0.0008-0.0016	0.0098-0.0185	0.0236-0.0323	0.0079-0.0224	0.0012-0.0028	0.0012-0.0028	SNUG
	3VZ-FE	3.0 (2959)	0.0031-0.0039	0.0091-0.0327	0.0150-0.0366	0.0059-0.0354	0.0012-0.0028	0.0012-0.0028	0.0012-0.0028
	3F-E	4.0 (3956)	0.0011-0.0019	0.0079-0.0165	0.0197-0.0283	0.0079-0.0323	0.0012-0.0028	0.0020-0.0035	SNUG
1993	2TZ-FE	2.4 (2438)	0.0012-0.0020	0.0118-0.0169	0.0177-0.0236	0.0051-0.0150	0.0008-0.0028	0.0012-0.0028	SNUG
	22R-E	2.4 (2366)	0.0008-0.0016	0.0098-0.0185	0.0236-0.0323	0.0079-0.0224	0.0012-0.0028	0.0012-0.0028	SNUG
	3VZ-E	3.0 (2959)	0.0031-0.0039	0.0091-0.0327	0.0150-0.0366	0.0059-0.0354	0.0012-0.0028	0.0012-0.0028	SNUG
	1FZ-FE	4.5 (4477)	0.0016-0.0024	0.0118-0.0205	0.0177-0.0264	0.0059-0.0205	0.0016-0.0031	0.0012-0.0028	SNUG
1994	2TZ-FE	2.4 (2438)	0.0012-0.0020	0.0118-0.0169	0.0177-0.0236	0.0051-0.0150	0.0008-0.0028	0.0012-0.0028	SNUG
	22R-E	2.4 (2366)	0.0008-0.0016	0.0098-0.0185	0.0236-0.0323	0.0079-0.0224	0.0012-0.0028	0.0012-0.0028	SNUG
	3RZ-FE	2.7 (2693)	0.0019-0.0024	0.0118-0.0157	0.0157-0.0194	0.0157-0.0194	0.0008-0.0028	0.0012-0.0028	0.0019-0.0024
	3VZ-E	3.0 (2959)	0.0031-0.0039	0.0091-0.0327	0.0150-0.0366	0.0059-0.0354	0.0012-0.0028	0.0012-0.0028	0.0012-0.0028
	1FZ-FE	4.5 (4477)	0.0016-0.0024	0.0118-0.0205	0.0177-0.0264	0.0059-0.0205	0.0016-0.0031	0.0012-0.0028	SNUG

PISTON AND RING SPECIFICATIONS

All measurements are given in inches.

Year	Engine ID/VIN	Engine Displacement Liters (cc)	Piston Clearance	Ring Gap			Ring Side Clearance		
				Top Compression	Bottom Compression	Oil Control	Top Compression	Bottom Compression	Oil Control
1995-96	2TZ-FE	2.4 (2438)	0.0012-0.0020	0.0118-0.0169	0.0177-0.0236	0.0051-0.0150	0.0008-0.0028	0.0012-0.0028	SNUG
	22R-E	2.4 (2366)	0.0008-0.0016	0.0098-0.0185	0.0236-0.0323	0.0079-0.0224	0.0012-0.0028	0.0012-0.0028	SNUG
	2RZ-FE	2.4 (2438)	0.0022-0.0031	0.0118-0.0157	0.0157-0.0197	0.0051-0.0150	0.0008-0.0028	0.0012-0.0028	SNUG
	3RZ-FE	2.7 (2693)	0.0019-0.0024	0.0118-0.0157	0.0157-0.0194	0.0051-0.0150	0.0008-0.0028	0.0012-0.0028	0.0019-0.0024
	3VZ-E	3.0 (2959)	0.0031-0.0039	0.0091-0.0327	0.0150-0.0366	0.0059-0.0354	0.0012-0.0028	0.0012-0.0028	0.0012-0.0028
	5VZ-FE	3.4 (3378)	0.0053-0.0060	0.0118-0.0197	0.0157-0.0236	0.0059-0.0217	0.0016-0.0031	0.0012-0.0028	0.0012-0.0028
	1FZ-FE	4.5 (4477)	0.0016-0.0024	0.0118-0.0205	0.0177-0.0264	0.0059-0.0205	0.0016-0.0031	0.0012-0.0028	SNUG

TORQUE SPECIFICATIONS

All readings in ft. lbs.

Year	Engine ID/VIN	Engine Displacement Liters (cc)	Cylinder Head Bolts	Main Bearing Bolts	Rod Bearing Bolts	Crankshaft Damper Bolts	Flywheel Bolts	Manifold		Spark Plugs	Lug Nut
								Intake	Exhaust		
1992	2TZ-FE	2.4 (2438)	1	2	3	192	4	15	36	11-15	-
	22R-E	2.4 (2366)	53-63	69-83	40-47	120-130	73-86	13-19	26-36	11-15	-
	3VZ-FE	3.0 (2959)	5	6	7	176-186	63-67	11-15	25-33	11-15	-
	3F-E	4.0 (3956)	87-93	8	40-46	247-259	60-68	9	9	11-15	-
1993	2TZ-FE	2.4 (2438)	1	2	3	192	4	15	36	11-15	-
	22R-E	2.4 (2366)	53-63	69-83	40-47	120-130	73-86	13-19	26-36	11-15	-
	3VZ-E	3.0 (2959)	5	6	7	176-186	63-67	11-15	25-33	11-15	-
	1FZ-FE	4.5 (4477)	10	11	11	304	-	15	29	15	-
1994	2TZ-FE	2.4 (2438)	1	2	3	192	4	15	36	11-15	-
	22R-E	2.4 (2366)	53-63	69-83	40-47	120-130	73-86	13-19	26-36	11-15	--
	3RZ-FE	2.7 (2693)	10	10	14	192	6	22	36	14	-
	3VZ-E	3.0 (2959)	5	6	7	176-186	63-67	11-15	25-33	11-15	-
	1FZ-FE	4.5 (4477)	10	11	12	304	-	15	29	15	-
1995-96	2TZ-FE	2.4 (2438)	1	2	3	192	4	15	36	11-15	-
	22R-E	2.4 (2366)	53-63	69-83	40-47	120-130	73-86	13-19	26-36	11-15	-
	2RZ-FE	2.4 (2438)	1	13	14	193	65	22	36	14	83
	3RZ-FE	2.7 (2693)	1	13	14	15	15	°22	36	14	-
	3VZ-E	3.0 (2959)	5	6	7	176-186	63-67	11-15	25-33	11-15	-
	5VZ-FE	3.4 (3378)	5	7	15	176-186	63-67	11-15	25-33	11-15	76
	1FZ-FE	4.5 (4477)	10	11	12	304	-	15	29	15	-

TORQUE SPECIFICATIONS
All readings in ft. lbs.

Year	Engine ID/VIN	Engine Displacement Liters (cc)	Cylinder Head Bolts	Main Bearing Bolts	Rod Bearing Bolts	Crankshaft Damper Bolts	Flywheel Bolts	Manifold Intake	Manifold Exhaust	Spark Plugs	Lug Nut

1 Step 1: 29 ft. lbs.
Step 2: 90 degree turn
Step 3: 90 degree turn
2 Step 1: 20 ft. lbs.
Step 2: 35 ft. lbs.
Step 3: 58 ft. lbs.
3 Step 1: 22 ft. lbs.
Step 2: 90 degree turn
4 Manual transmission: 65 ft. lbs.
Automatic transmission: 54 ft. lbs.
5 Step 1: 27 ft. lbs.
Step 2: 33 ft. lbs.
Step 3: 90 degree turn
Step 4: 90 degree turn
6 Step 1: 18 ft. lbs.
Step 2: 90 degree turn
7 Step 1: 45 ft. lbs.
Step 2: 90 degree turn

8 17mm bolts: 85 ft. lbs.
19mm bolts: 99 ft. lbs.
9 14mm bolts: 37 ft. lbs.
17mm bolts: 51 ft. lbs.
Nuts: 41 ft. lbs.
10 Step 1: 27 ft. lbs.
Step 2: 90 degree turn
Step 3: 90 degree turn
11 Step 1: 54 ft. lbs.
Step 2: 90 degree turn
12 Step 1: 35 ft. lbs.
Step 2: 90 degree turn
13 Step 1: 29 ft. lbs.
Step 2: 90 degree turn
14 Step 1: 33 ft. lbs.
Step 2: 90 degree turn
15 Step 1: 19 ft. lbs.
Step 2: 90 degree turn

BRAKE SPECIFICATIONS
All measurements in inches unless noted

Year	Model	Master Cylinder Bore	Brake Disc Original Thickness	Brake Disc Minimum Thickness	Maximum Runout	Brake Drum Diameter Original Inside Diameter	Max. Wear Limit	Maximum Machine Diameter	Minimum Lining Thickness Front	Minimum Lining Thickness Rear
1992	Previa	NA	1	2	0.0028	10.00	-	10.08	0.039	0.039
	Pick-up	NA	3	4	5	6	-	7	0.039	0.039
	4Runner	NA	0.984	0.906	0.0035	11.61	-	11.69	0.059	0.039
	Land Cruiser	NA	0.984	0.906	0.0059	11.61	-	11.69	0.059	0.059
1993	Previa	NA	1	2	0.0028	10.00	-	10.08	0.039	0.039
	Pick-up	NA	3	8	5	6	-	7	0.039	0.039
	4Runner	NA	0.984	0.906	0.0035	11.61	-	11.69	0.059	0.039
	Land Cruiser	NA	1.260 9	1.181 10	0.0059	11.61	-	11.69	0.059	11
1994	Previa	NA	1	2	0.0028	10.00	-	10.08	0.039	0.039
	Pick-up	NA	12	13	0.0035	6	-	7	14	0.039
	4Runner	NA	0.984	0.906	0.0035	11.61	-	11.69	0.059	0.039
	Land Cruiser	NA	1.260 9	1.181 10	0.0059	11.61	-	11.69	0.059	11
1995-96	Previa	NA	1	2	0.0028	10.00	-	10.08	0.039	0.039
	Pick-up	NA	12	13	0.0035	6	-	7	14	0.039
	4Runner	NA	0.984	0.906	0.0035	11.61	-	11.69	0.059	0.039
	Land Cruiser	NA	1.260 9	1.181 10	0.0059	11.61	-	11.69	0.059	
	Tacoma	NA	0.866	0.787	0.0028	6	-	7	0.039	0.039 15

NA - Not Available

1 Front with rear drum brake: 0.984
Front with rear disc brake: 0.866
Rear disc brake: 0.709
2 Front with rear drum brake: 0.906
Front with rear disc brake: 0.787
Rear disc brake: 0.669

6 2WD: 10.00; 4WD: 11.61
7 2WD: 10.08; 4WD: 11.69
8 2WD (PD60 type disc): 0.906
2WD (PD66 type disc): 1.102
2WD (FS17, 18 type disc): 0.787
4WD (S12+12 type disc): 0.709
9 Rear disc: 0.630

BRAKE SPECIFICATIONS
All measurements in inches unless noted

Year	Model	Master Cylinder Bore	Brake Disc			Brake Drum Diameter			Minimum Lining Thickness	
			Original Thickness	Minimum Thickness	Maximum Runout	Original Inside Diameter	Max. Wear Limit	Maximum Machine Diameter	Front	Rear

    3 2WD (PD60 type disc): 0.984
       2WD (PD66 type disc): 1.181
       2WD (FS17, 18 type disc): 0.866
       4WD (S12+12 type disc): 0.787
    4 2WD (PD60 type disc): 0.787
       2WD (PD66 type disc): 1.102
       2WD (FS17, 18 type disc): 0.787
       4WD (S12+12 type disc): 0.709
    5 PD60, FS17, FS18, S12+12 type discs: 0.0035

    10 Rear disc: 0.709
    11 Brake shoe lining: 0.059
        Disc pad lining: 0.039
    12 2WD: 0.866; 4WD: 0.787
    13 2WD: 0.787; 4WD: 0.709
    14 2WD: 0.059; 4WD: 0.039
    15 Brake shoe lining: 0.059
        Disc pad lining: 0.039

WHEEL ALIGNMENT

Year	Model		Caster		Camber		Toe-in (in.)	Steering Axis Inclination (deg.)
			Range (deg.)	Preferred Setting (deg.)	Range (deg.)	Preferred Setting (deg.)		
1992	Pick-up 2WD	1,2	0-1 1/2P	3/4P	1/4N-1 1/4P	1/2P	1/32N-5/32N	10
	Pick-up 2WD	1,3	1/16N-1 71/6P	11/16P	5/16N-1 3/16P	7/16P	1/32N-5/32N	10
	Pick-up 2WD	1,4	7/32P-1 23/32P	31/32P	5/16N-1 3/16P	7/16P	0-3/16N	10 1/32
	Pick-up 2WD	1,5	1/2P-2P	1 1/4P	3/8N-1 1/8P	3/8P	1/32N-7/32N	10 1/32
	Pick-up 2WD	1,6	3/16N-1 5/16P	9/16P	1/4N-1 1/4P	1/2P	1/8N-5/16N	10
	Pick-up 2WD	1,7	3/16N-1 5/16P	9/16P	1/4N-1 1/4P	1/2P	3/32N-9/32N	10
	Pick-up 2WD	1,8	1P-2 1/2P	1 3/4P	1/4N-1 1/4P	1/2P	3/32N-9/32N	10
	Pick-up 2WD	1,9	7/16P-1 15/16P	1 3/16P	3/8N-1 1/8P	3/8P	1/32N-7/32N	10 3/32
	Pick-up 2WD	1,10	7/16P-1 15/16P	1 3/16P	5/16N-1 3/16P	7/16P	1/32N-7/32N	10 1/16
	Pick-up 2WD	1,11	1P-2 1/2P	1 3/4P	1/4N-1 1/4P	1/2P	1/8N-5/16N	10
	Pick-up 4WD		2P-3P	2 1/2P	1/4P-1 1/4P	3/4P	0-1/16N	11 13/16
	4-Runner		2P-3P	2 1/2P	1/4P-1 1/4P	3/4P	1/32N-3./32N	11 13/16
	Land Cruiser	12	11/16P-2 11/16P	1 11/16P	1/4P-1 3/4P	1P	0-3/16N	13
	Land Cruiser	13	2P-4P	3P	1/4P-1 3/4P	1P	0-3/16N	13
	Previa 2WD		4 3/4P-6 1/4P	5 1/2P	21/32N-27/32P	3/32P	0-3/16N	10 19/32
	Previa 4WD		4 19/32P-6 3/32P	5.11/32P	1/2N-1P	1/4P	1/32N-7/32N	10 19/32
1993	Pick-up 2WD	14	0-1 1/2P	3/4P	1/4N-1 1/4P	1/2P	0.03N-0.13P	9 1/4
	Pick-up 2WD	15	0-1 1/2P	3/4P	1/4N-1 1/4P	1/2P	0.02N-0.14P	9 1/4
	Pick-up 2WD	16	1/4P-1 3/4P	1P	1/4N-1 1/4P	1/2P	0-0.16P	9 1/4
	Pick-up 2WD	17	1/2P-2P	1 1/4P	1/4N-1 1/4P	1/3P	0.05N-0.20P	9 1/4
	Pick-up 2WD	18	1/4N-1 1/4P	1/2P	1/4N-1 1/4P	1/2P	0.14N-0.30P	9 1/4
	Pick-up 2WD	19	1P-2 1/4P	1 3/4P	1/4N-1 1/4P	1/2P	0.14N-0.30P	9 1/4
	Pick-up 2WD	20	1/2P-2P	1 1/4P	1/4N-1 1/4P	1/3P	0.05N-0.20P	9 1/4
	Pick-up 2WD	21	1P-2 1/2P	1 3/4P	1/4N-1 1/4P	1/2P	0.014N-0.30P	9 1/4
	Pick-up 4WD		1 3/4P-3 1/4P	2 1/2P	0-1 1/2P	3/4P	0.04N-0.012P	11
	4-Runner		1 3/4P-3 1/4P	2 1/2P	0-1 1/2P	3/4P	0.04N-0.012P	11
	Land Cruiser		2P-4P	3P	1/4P-1 3/4P	1P	0-016P	12 1/4
	Previa		4 3/4P-6 1/4P	5 1/2P	3/4N-3/4P	0	0-016P	9 3/4
	T100 2WD	22	1 3/4P-3 1/4P	2 1/2P	1/4N-1 1/4P	1/2P	0.04N-0.20P	9 1/4
	T100 2WD	23	2 1/4P-3 3/4P	3P	0-1 1/2P	1/2P	0.27N-0.43P	8 3/4
	T100 4WD		3/4P-2 1/4P	1 1/2P	0-1 1/2P	3/4P	0.04N-0.20P	11

WHEEL ALIGNMENT

Year	Model		Caster Range (deg.)	Caster Preferred Setting (deg.)	Camber Range (deg.)	Camber Preferred Setting (deg.)	Toe-in (in.)	Steering Axis Inclination (deg.)
1994	Pick-up 2WD	24	0-1 1/2P	3/4P	1/4N-1 1/4P	1/2P	0.03N-0.13P	9 1/4
	Pick-up 2WD	25	1/2P-2P	1 1/4P	1/4N-1 1/4P	1/3P	0.05N-0.20P	9 1/4
	Pick-up 4WD		1 3/4P-3 1/4P	2 1/2P	0-1 1/2P	3/4P	0.04N-0.12P	11
	4-Runner		1 3/4P-3 1/4P	2 1/2P	0-1 1/2P	3/4P	0.04N-0.12P	11
	Land Cruiser		2P-4P	3P	1/4P-1 3/4P	1P	0-0.16P	12 1/4
	Previa 2WD		4 3/4P-6 1/4P	5 1/2P	3/4N-3/4P	0	0-0.16P	9 3/4
	Previa 4WD		4 3/4P-6 1/4P	5 1/2P	1/2N-1P	1/4P	0.04N-0.20P	9 3/4
	T100 2WD	9	1 3/4P-3 1/4P	2 1/2P	1/4N-1 1/4P	1/2P	0.04N-0.20P	9 3/4
	T100 2WD	10	2 1/4P-3 3/4P	3P	0-1 1/2P	1/2P	0.27N-0.43P	8 3/4
	T100 4WD		3/4P-2 1/4P	1 1/2P	0-1 1/2P	3/4P	0.04N-0.20P	11
1995-96	Pick-up 2WD	1	0-1 1/2P	3/4P	1/4N-1 1/4P	1/2P	0.03N-0.13P	9 1/4
	Pick-up 2WD	2	1/2P-2P	1 1/4P	1/4N-1 1/4P	1/3P	0.05N-0.20P	9 1/4
	Pick-up 4WD		1 3/4P-3 1/4P	2 1/2P	0-1 1/2P	3/4P	0.04N-0.12P	11
	4Runner		1 3/4P-3 1/4P	2 1/2P	0-1 1/2P	3/4P	0.04N-0.12P	11
	Land Cruiser		2P-4P	3P	1/4P-1 3/4P	1P	0-0.16P	12 1/4
	Previa 2WD		4 3/4P-6 1/4P	5 1/2P	3/4N-3/4P	0	0-0.16P	9 3/4
	Previa 4WD		4 3/4P-6 1/4P	5 1/2P	1/2N-1P	1/4P	0.04N-0.20P	9 3/4
	Tacoma 2WD		1 1/3P-2 1/3P	1 5/6P	1/2N-1/2P	0	0.04N-0.04P	10
	Tacoma 4WD		2 1/3P-3 1/3P	2 5/6P	1/2N-1/2P	0	0.08N-0.08P	10 3/4
	T100 2WD	9	1 3/4P-3 1/4P	2 1/2P	1/4N-1 1/4P	1/2P	0.04N-0.20P	9 3/4
	T100 2WD	10	2 1/4P-3 3/4P	3P	0-1 1/2P	1/2P	0.04N-0.20P	9 3/4
	T100 4WD		3/4P-2 1/4P	1 1/2P	0-1 1/2P	3/4P	0.27N-0.43P	8 3/4
								11

1 NOTE: Front end alignment specifications are given according to the Vehicle Identification Number. Before using this information, verify that this number is correct for the alignment data used.
2 RN80L-TRSD, RN80L-TRMD
3 RN80L-TRMR
4 RN85L-TRMD, RN85L-TRSD
5 RN90L-CRSD, RN90L-CRMD
6 VZN85L-THMD
7 ZVN85L-THSD
8 VZN85L-TWMR, VZN85L-TWSR
9 VZN90L-CRMD, VZN90L-CRSD
10 VZN90L-CRMG, VZN90L-CRPG
11 VZN95L-TWMR, VZN95L-TWSR
12 With 10.5R tire
13 Without 10.5R tire

14 RN80L-TRSDEA, RN80L-TRSDEK, RN80L-TRMDEA, RN80L-TRMDEK
15 RN80L-TRMREA, RN80L-TRMREK
16 RN85L-TRMDEA, RN85L-TRMDEK, RN85L-TRSDEA, RN85L-TRSDEK
17 RN90L-CRSDEA, RN90L-CRSDEK, RN90L-CRMDEA, RN90L-CRMDEK
18 VZN85L-THMDEA, VZN85L-THSDEA
19 VZN85L-TWMREA6, VZN85L-TWSREA6
20 VZN90L-CRMDEA, VZN90L-CRMDEK, VZN90L-CRSDEA, VZN90L-CRSDEK, VZN90L-CRMGEA, VZN90L-CRPGEA
21 VZN95L-TWMREA6, VZN95L-TWSREA6, VZN95L-TWSREK6
22 1/2 ton
23 1 ton
24 RN80L-TRSDEA, RN80L-TRMDEA, RN80L-TRMREA, RN80L-TRMREK
25 RN90L-CRSDEA, RN90L-CRMDEA, RN90L-CRSDEK, RN90L-CRMDEK, VZN90L-CRMDEA, VZN90L-CRMDEK, VZN90L-CRSDEA, VZN90L-CRSDEK, VZN90L-CRMGEA, VZN90L-CRPGEA

VOLKSWAGEN

ENGINE IDENTIFICATION

Year	Model	Engine Displacement Liters (cc)	Engine Series (ID/VIN)	Fuel System	No. of Cylinders	Engine Type
1993	Eurovan	2.5 (2459)	AAF	Digifant	5	SOHC

SOHC - Single overhead camshaft

GENERAL ENGINE SPECIFICATIONS

Year	Engine ID/VIN	Engine Displacement Liters (cc)	Fuel System Type	Net Horsepower @ rpm	Net Torque @ rpm (ft. lbs.)	Bore x Stroke (in.)	Compression Ratio	Oil Pressure @ rpm
1993	AAF	2.5 (2459)	Digifant	109@4500	140@2200	3.19x3.76	8.5:1	28@2000

GASOLINE ENGINE TUNE-UP SPECIFICATIONS

Year	Engine ID/VIN	Engine Displacement Liters (cc)	Spark Plugs Gap (in.)	Ignition Timing (deg.) MT	Ignition Timing (deg.) AT	Fuel Pump (psi)	Idle Speed (rpm) MT	Idle Speed (rpm) AT	Valve Clearance In.	Valve Clearance Ex.
1993	AAF	2.5 (2459)	NA	NA	NA	NA	NA	NA	HYD	HYD

NOTE: The Vehicle Emission Control Information label often reflects specification changes made during production. The label figures must be used if they differ from those in this chart.
NA - Not Available
HYD - Hydraulic

CAPACITIES

Year	Model	Engine ID/VIN	Engine Displacement Liters (cc)	Engine Oil with Filter (qts.)	Transmission (pts.) 4-Spd	Transmission (pts.) 5-Spd	Transmission (pts.) Auto.	Transfer Case (pts.)	Drive Axle Front (pts.)	Drive Axle Rear (pts.)	Fuel Tank (gal.)	Cooling System (qts.)
1993	Eurovan	AAF	2.5 (2459)	5.9	-	NA	NA	-	NA	NA	21.1	12.2

NA - Not Available

CAMSHAFT SPECIFICATIONS

All measurements given in inches.

Year	Engine ID/VIN	Engine Displacement Liters (cc)	Journal Diameter					Elevation		Bearing Clearance	Camshaft End Play
			1	2	3	4	5	In.	Ex.		
1993	AAF	2.5 (2459)	NA	NA	NA	NA	NA	NA	NA	NA	NA

NOTE: Bearing clearances and end play specifications are wear limits
NA - Not Available

CRANKSHAFT AND CONNECTING ROD SPECIFICATIONS

All measurements are given in inches.

Year	Engine ID/VIN	Engine Displacement Liters (cc)	Crankshaft				Connecting Rod		
			Main Brg. Journal Dia.	Main Brg. Oil Clearance	Shaft End-play	Thrust on No.	Journal Diameter	Oil Clearance	Side Clearance
1993	AAF	2.5 (2459)	NA	NA	NA	NA	NA	NA	NA

NA - Not Available

VALVE SPECIFICATIONS

Year	Engine ID/VIN	Engine Displacement Liters (cc)	Seat Angle (deg.)	Face Angle (deg.)	Spring Test Pressure (lbs. @ in.)	Spring Installed Height (in.)	Stem-to-Guide Clearance (in.)		Stem Diameter (in.)	
							Intake	Exhaust	Intake	Exhaust
1993	AAF	2.5 (2459)	NA	NA	NA	NA	NA	NA	NA	NA

NA - Not Available

PISTON AND RING SPECIFICATIONS

All measurements are given in inches.

Year	Engine ID/VIN	Engine Displacement Liters (cc)	Piston Clearance	Ring Gap			Ring Side Clearance		
				Top Compression	Bottom Compression	Oil Control	Top Compression	Bottom Compression	Oil Control
1993	AAF	2.5 (2459)	NA	NA	NA	NA	NA	NA	NA

NA - Not Available

TORQUE SPECIFICATIONS

All readings in ft. lbs.

| Year | Engine ID/VIN | Engine Displacement Liters (cc) | Cylinder Head Bolts | Main Bearing Bolts | Rod Bearing Bolts | Crankshaft Damper Bolts | Flywheel Bolts | Manifold | | Spark Plugs | Lug Nut |
								Intake	Exhaust		
1993	AAF	2.5 (2459)	NA	NA	NA	NA	NA	NA	NA	NA	NA

NA - Not Available

BRAKE SPECIFICATIONS

All measurements in inches unless noted

| Year | Model | Master Cylinder Bore | Brake Disc | | | Brake Drum Diameter | | | Minimum Lining Thickness | |
			Original Thickness	Minimum Thickness	Maximum Runout	Original Inside Diameter	Max. Wear Limit	Maximum Machine Diameter	Front	Rear
1993	Eurovan	NA	NA	NA	NA	NA	NA	NA	NA	NA

NA - Not Available

WHEEL ALIGNMENT

| Year | Model | Caster | | Camber | | Toe-in (in.) | Steering Axis Inclination (deg.) |
		Range (deg.)	Preferred Setting (deg.)	Range (deg.)	Preferred Setting (deg.)		
1993	Eurovan	NA	NA	NA	NA	NA	NA

NA - Not Available

Brakes **15**

DOMESTIC
BRAKE SYSTEM
SERVICE

HYDRAULIC BRAKE SYSTEM TROUBLE DIAGNOSIS

Condition	Possible Cause	Correction
Insufficient brakes	1. Improper brake adjustment. 2. Worn lining. 3. Sticking brakes. 4. Brake valve pressure low. 5. Master cylinder low on brake fluid.	1. Adjust brakes. 2. Replace brake lining and adjust brakes. 3. Lubricate brake pivots and support platforms. 4. Inspect for leaks and obstructed brake lines. 5. Fill master cylinder and inspect for leaks.
Brakes apply slowly	1. Improper brake adjustment or lack of lubrication. 2. Excessive leakage with brakes applied. 3. Restriction in brake line or hose.	1. Adjust brakes and lubricate linkage. 2. Inspect all fittings and lines for leaks and repair as necessary. 3. Clean or replace brake line or hose.
Spongy pedal	1. Air in hydraulic system. 2. Swollen rubber parts due to contaminated brake fluid. 3. Improper brake shoe adjustment. 4. Brake fluid with low boiling point. 5. Brake drums ground excessively.	1. Fill and bleed hydraulic system. 2. Clean hydraulic system and recondition wheel cylinders and master cylinder. 3. Adjust brakes. 4. Flush hydraulic system and refill with proper brake fluid. 5. Replace brake drums.
Erratic brakes	1. Linings soaked with grease or brake fluid. 2. Primary and secondary shoes mounted in wrong position.	1. Correct the leak and replace brake lining. 2. Match the primary and secondary shoes and mount in proper position.
Chattering brakes	1. Improper adjustment of brake shoes. 2. Loose front wheel bearings. 3. Hard spots in brake drums. 4. Out-of-round brake drums. 5. Grease or brake fluid on lining.	1. Adjust brakes. 2. Clean, pack and adjust wheel bearings. 3. Grind or replace brake drums. 4. Grind or replace brake drums. 5. Correct leak and replace brake lining.
Squealing brakes	1. Incorrect lining. 2. Distorted brakedrum. 3. Bent brake support plate. 4. Bent brake shoes. 5. Foreign material embedded in brake lining. 6. Dust or dirt in brake drum. 7. Shoes dragging on support plate. 8. Loose support plate. 9. Loose anchor bolts. 10. Loose lining on brake shoes or improperly ground lining.	1. Install correct lining. 2. Grind or replace brake drum. 3. Replace brake support plate. 4. Replace brake shoes. 5. Replace brake shoes. 6. Use compressed air and blow out drums and support plate and shoes. 7. Sand support plate platforms and lubricate. 8. Tighten support plate attaching nuts. 9. Tighten anchor bolts. 10. Replace brake shoes and cam-grind lining.
Brakes fading	1. Improper brake adjustment. 2. Improper brake lining. 3. Improper type of brake fluid. 4. Brake drums ground excessively.	1. Adjust brakes correctly. 2. Replace brake lining. 3. Drain, flush and refill hydraulic system. 4. Replace brake drums.

HYDRAULIC BRAKE SYSTEM TROUBLE DIAGNOSIS

Condition	Possible Cause	Correction
Dragging brakes	1. Improper brake adjustment. 2. Distorted cylinder cups. 3. Brake shoe seized on anchor bolt. 4. Broken brake shoe return spring. 5. Loose anchor bolt. 6. Distorted brake shoe. 7. Loose wheel bearings. 8. Obstruction in brake line. 9. Swollen cups in wheel cylinder or master cylinder. 10. Master cylinder linkage improperly adjusted.	1. Correct adjust brakes. 2. Recondition or replace cylinder. 3. Clean and lubricate anchor bolt. 4. Replace brake shoe return spring. 5. Adjust and tighten anchor bolt. 6. Replace defective brake shoes. 7. Lubricate and adjust wheel bearings. 8. Clean or replace brake line. 9. Recondition wheel or master cylinder. 10. Correctly adjust master cylinder linkage.
Hard pedal	1. Incorrect brake lining. 2. Incorrect brake adjustment. 3. Frozen brake pedal linkage. 4. Restricted brake line or hose.	1. Install matched brake lining. 2. Adjust brakes and check fluid. 3. Free up and lubricate brake linkage. 4. Clean out or replace brake line hose.
Wheel locks	1. Loose or torn brake lining. 2. Incorrect wheel bearing adjustment. 3. Wheel cylinder cups sticking. 4. Saturated brake lining.	1. Replace brake lining. 2. Clean, pack and adjust wheel bearings. 3. Recondition or replace the wheel cylinder. 4. Reline front, rear or all four brakes.
Brakes fade (high speed)	1. Improper brake adjustment. 2. Distorted or out of round brake drums. 3. Overheated brake drums. 4. Incorrect brake fluid (low boiling temperature). 5. Saturated brake lining.	1. Adjust brakes and check fluid. 2. Grind or replace the drums. 3. Inspect for dragging brakes. 4. Drain, flush and refill and bleed the hydraulic brake system. 5. Reline brakes as necessary.

General Information

Servicing the hydraulic brake system is chiefly a matter of adjustments, replacement of worn or damaged parts and correcting the damage caused by grit, dirt or contaminated brake fluid. Always make sure the brake system is clean and tightly sealed when a brake job is completed and that only approved heavy duty brake fluid is used.

Approved heavy duty brake fluid keeps the correct consistency throughout the widest temperature range, will not affect rubber parts, helps protect metal parts and assures long, trouble free brake operation.

Never use brake fluid from a container that has been used for any other liquid. Mineral oil, alcohol, antifreeze or cleaning solvents, even in very small quantities, will contaminate brake fluid. Contaminated brake fluid will cause piston cups and the valve(s) in the master cylinder to swell and deteriorate.

Brake fluid will also absorb moisture from the air. Over time, brake fluid stored for long periods, and fluid inside the brake system will be affected by this moisture. Rust, corrosion and pitting of system components result.

Some fleet managers change the brake fluid in their vehicles every year or two to avoid brake system problems caused by moisture.

Use extreme care when using brake fluid. It will damage painted surfaces.

The hydraulic braking system consists of a master cylinder, sometimes a power booster depending on application, hydraulic line and hoses, control valves and calipers and/or wheel cylinders. Newer models incorporate a computer controlled wheel antilock system. When the brake pedal is depressed, the master cylinder forces brake fluid to the calipers and/or cylinders. Sliding rubber seals contain the fluid and prevent leakage.

Return springs in the master cylinder help the brake pedal return to the unapplied position. Check valves, in most cases regulate the return flow of the fluid to the master cylinder. Other valves, such as the metering valve, proportioning valve, or combination valve, regulate the flow of fluid to the caliper/wheel cylinder, to achieve efficient braking.

Dual braking systems were introduced on many light trucks and vans during the late 1960's. The main difference is the use of a tandem master cylinder which is essentially two master cylinders in one. Two separate pistons share one bore and two fluid reservoirs are built into one housing. Dual brake lines split the calipers and/or wheel cylinders into two groups, each actuated by its own, separate master cylinder piston. In the event of failure of one of the dual systems, the other should provide enough braking to safely stop the vehicle. The development of dual braking systems is an improvement over the older single systems where a leak anywhere would allow the fluid to escape resulting in loss of braking.

The dual system usually includes some type of warning light on the instrument panel, activated by a pressure differential valve. The valve reacts to loss of hydraulic pressure that might result from failure on either side of the system.

Vehicles are generally equipped with either a front/rear wheel split or a diagonally split system. On front/rear systems, the front wheels are connected to one circuit while the rear wheels are connected to the other circuit. These systems are the most popular ever since front disc brakes were introduced. Since a greater amount of

brake fluid is moved in a disc brake system, one chamber of the the the master cylinder feeds the front discs, while the other chamber feeds the rear wheel cylinders.

Diagonally split systems have diagonally opposite wheels connected to each circuit.

Because of the differences in pressure and the amount of fluid required to operate disc brakes and drum brakes, a control valve, often called a proportioning valve or combination valve is installed between the master cylinder and the rest of the system. This valve has several sections and functions.

The metering, or hold off section of the valve limits the pressure to the front disc brakes until a predetermined front input pressure is reached, enough to overcome the rear shoe retractor springs. The is generally no restriction to the inlet pressures below about 3 psi to allow for pressure equalization during the no apply periods.

Another section of the valve proportions, or measures out the outlet pressure to the rear brakes after a predetermined rear input pressure has been reached. This is done to prevent rear wheel lockup on vehicles with light rear wheel loads.

Yet another section of the valve is

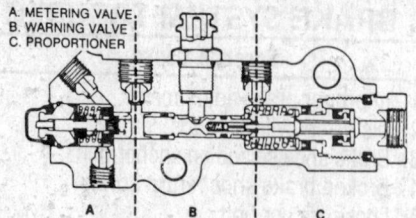

A. METERING VALVE.
B. WARNING VALVE.
C. PROPORTIONER

Brake proportioning valve — typical

designed to constantly compare front and rear brake pressure from the master cylinder and will turn on a warning light in the event of a front or rear system malfunction. On some systems, after repairs are made, and the system properly bled, the valve will center itself and the warning lamp will shut off. On other systems, the switch will latch so the warning light will stay on until a repair is made, and the switch manually reset, generally be one or two firm brake applications.

These valves are also designed with a bypass feature which assures full system pressure to the rear brakes in the event of a front brake system malfunction, and full front pressure is retained in the event of a rear malfunction.

These valves are not to be disassembled for repair. Replace defective valves.

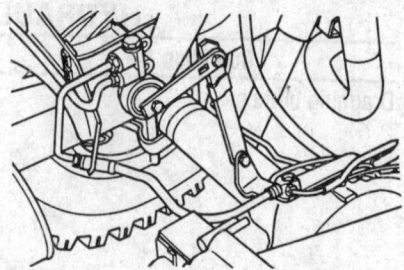

General Motors Corporation height sensing valve — typical

Most light trucks have some sort of height sensing valve. The vehicle braking force is distributed to the front and rear wheels as determined be either a light or heavy payload. The valve is usually mounted on the frame and a linkage connects the valve to a bracket mounted on the axle.

Adding suspension accessories or other equipment (such as load leveling kits, lift kits, extra springs, etc.) or making modifications that will change the distance between the axle and frame without changing the load will provide a false reading to the sensing valve. This could result in unsatisfactory brake performance which could result in an accident and possibly personal injury.

GM CORPORATION BRAKE DIAGNOSIS

DIAGNOSIS OF THE BRAKE SYSTEM

Problem	Possible Cause	Correction
Uneven brake action (brakes pull)	1. Incorrect tire pressure.	1. Inflate evenly on both sides to specifications.
	2. Front end out of alignment.	2. Check and align to specifications.
	3. Loose suspension parts.	3. Check all the suspension mountings.
	4. Worn out brake linings.	4. Replace with lining of the correct material.
	5. Incorrect lining material.	5. Replace with linings of the correct material.
	6. Malfunctioning caliper assembly.	6. Check for frozen or sluggish pistons and the lubrication of the retainer bolts. Caliper should slide.
	7. Loose calipers.	7. Check and torque.
	8. Contaminated brake linings.	8. Repair as necessary. Replace the linings in complete axle sets.
	9. Malfunctioning rear brakes.	9. Check for inoperative self adjusters. Weak return springs. Leaking wheel cylinders.
	10. Leaking wheel or piston cylinder seal.	10. Repair as necessary.
	11. Restricted brake tubes or hoses.	11. Check for collapsed rubber hoses or damaged lines. Repair as necessary.
	12. Unmatched tires on the same axle.	12. Same style tires with about the same tread should be used on the same axle.
Slow pedal return	Compensating (peripheral) holes in the quick take-up valve are clogged.	Replace the master cylinder.

DIAGNOSIS OF THE BRAKE SYSTEM

Problem	Possible Cause	Correction
Brakes squeak	1. Worn out linings.	1. Replace the linings.
	2. Glazed brake linings.	2. Replace the linings.
	3. Heat spotted rotors or drums.	3. Check per instructions. If within specifications, machine the rotor or drum.
	4. Weak or incorrect brake shoe retention springs.	4. Replace with new retention springs.
	5. Contaminated brake linings.	5. Repair as necessary. Replace the linings in complete axle sets.
	6. Incorrect lining material.	6. Replace with linings of correct material.
	7. Brake assembly attachments missing or loose.	7. Repair as necessary.
	8. Excessive brake lining dust.	8. Clean the dust from the brake assembly.
Brake pedal pulsates	1. Excessive rotor lateral runout.	1. Check per instructions. If within specifications, machine the rotor.
	2. Rear drums out of round.	2. Check per instructions. If within specifications, machine the drum.
	3. Heat spotted rotors or drums.	3. Check per instructions. If within specifications, machine the drum.
	4. Incorrect wheel bearing adjustments.	4. Repair as necessary.
	5. Out of balance wheel assembly.	5. Repair as necessary.
	6. Brake assembly attachments missing or loose.	6. Repair as necessary.
Excessive pedal effort	1. Leaking vacuum system.	1. Repair as necessary.
	2. Malfunctioning power brake unit.	2. Repair as necessary.
	3. Worn out linings.	3. Replace the linings.
	4. Malfunctioning proportioning valve.	4. Replace the combination valve.
	5. Incorrect lining material.	5. Replace with linings of the correct materials.
	6. Incorrect wheel cylinder.	6. Replace with the correct size wheel cylinder.
	7. Center orifice in quick take-up valve clogged.	7. Replace the master cylinder.
Brakes drag	1. Malfunctioning caliper assembly.	1. Check for frozen or sluggish pistons and the lubrication of the retainer bolts. Caliper should slide.
	2. Contaminated or improper brake fluid.	2. Repair as necessary.
	3. Improperly adjusted parking brake.	3. Adjust as necessary.
	4. Restricted brake tube or hoses.	4. Check for collapsed rubber hoses or damaged lines. Repair as necessary.
	5. Malfunctioning proportioning valve.	5. Replace the combination valve.
	6. Malfunctioning self adjusters.	6. Repair as necessary.
	7. Malfunctioning master cylinder.	7. Repair as necessary.
	8. Improperly adjusted master cylinder pushrod.	8. Adjust pushrod length.

Brake warning light comes on	1. Air in the brake system.	1. Check the fluid level. Check for leaks in the lines, wheel cylinders, or master cylinder. Bleed the system.
	2. Malfunctioning master cylinder.	2. Check for malfunctioning or leaking metering valve. Repair as necessary.
	3. Contaminated or improper brake fluid.	3. Repair as necessary.
	4. Parking brake on or not fully released.	4. Check the parking brake. Repair as necessary.
	5. Worn out brake lining.	5. Replace the linings.
	6. Incorrect wheel bearing adjustment.	6. Repair as necessary.
	7. Malfunctioning self adjusters.	7. Repair as necessary.
	8. Brake assembly attachments missing or loose.	8. Replace or repair as necessary.
	9. Improperly adjusted master cylinder pushrod.	9. Adjust the pushrod length.
	10. RWAL system malfunction.	**10. Refer to REAR WHEEL ANTILOCK BRAKE SYSTEM**
Excessive pedal travel	1. Fluid level low in the master cylinder reservoir.	1. Fill the reservoir with approved brake fluid. Check for leaks and air in the system. Check the warning light.
	2. Air in the brake system.	2. Check for leaks in the lines, wheel cylinders, or master cylinder. Bleed the system.
	3. Malfunctioning self adjusters.	3. Repair as necessary.
	4. Master cylinder.	4. Replace or repair as necessary.
	5. Incorrect wheel bearing adjustment.	5. Repair as necessary.
	6. Improperly adjusted master cylinder pushrod.	6. Adjust the master cylinder pushrod.
	7. Fluid bypassing quick take-up valve to the reservoir.	7. Replace the master cylinder.
	8. Leaking brake line or connection.	8. Repair as necessary.
	9. Leaking wheel cylinder or caliper.	9. Repair as necessary.

General Diagnosis

LOW PEDAL

Normal brake lining wear reduces pedal reserve. Low pedal reserve may also be caused by the lack of brake fluid in the master cylinder. This means a brake adjustment is required. Check fluid level in the master cylinder and add as required.

FLUID LOSS

If the master cylinde00requires constant addition of brake fluid, fluid may be leaking past the piston cups in the master cylinder, calipers or wheel cylinders, the brake lines or hoses, or through loose connections. Brake hoses often have copper sealing washers which may need to be replaced. Replace worn or damaged components, refill and bleed the system.

FLUID CONTAMINATION

To determine if contamination exists in the brake fluid as indicated by swollen, deteriorated rubber parts like wheel cylinder cups, the following tests can be made.

Place a small amount of the drained brake fluid into a clear glass bottle. Separation of the fluid into distinct layers will indicate mineral oil content. Be safe and discard the old brake fluid that has been bled from the system since it may contain dirt and other contamination and should not be reused.

BRAKE ADJUSTMENT

Self adjusting brakes usually do not require manual adjustment. When installing new brake shoes, it may be advisable to make the initial adjustment manually to speed up adjusting time.

AUTOMATIC ADJUSTER CHECK

On most vehicles, drum brakes appear only on the rear axle. Brake adjustments are automatic and are made during reverse brake applications.

Raise and safely support the vehicle, have a helper in the driver's seat to apply brakes. Remove the plug from the adjustment slot to observe the star wheel (some models are adjusted through the face of the brake drum others through the backing plate). Tighten the adjusting star wheel screw until the wheel can just be turned by hand. The brake drag should be equal at both wheels. Back off the adjusting star wheel about 30-35 notches. The brakes should have no drag after the adjuster has been backed off about 15 notches. If heavy drag is present, the parking brake likely needs service and/or adjustment.

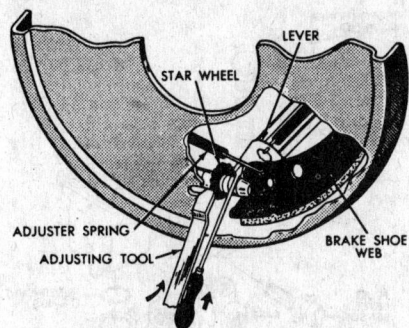

Brake adjustment—typical

NOTE: It will be necessary to carefully insert a small, stiff wire or thin tool to hold the automatic adjustment lever away from the star wheel to allow backing off the adjustment. Install adjusting hole cover in backing plate. Check parking brake adjustment.

HYDRAULIC LINE REPAIR

Steel tubing is used for the hydraulic lines, and special flexible hoses connect moving parts such as front calipers which turn with the steering, and the connection between the body and rear axle.

When replacing steel lines or flexible brake hose, use only exact replacements, in both size and quality.

NOTE: Never use copper tubing for hydraulic brake lines because copper is subject to fatigue cracking and corrosion which could result in brake failure. Use specially made steel brake lines only. Tighten all connections securely.

After replacement, bleed the brake system at each wheel and at the booster, if equipped with a bleeder screw.

Flexible hoses should be inspected for any signs of road damage, cracks or chafing any of which requires immediate hose replacement. Hoses feeding front brake calipers are often equipped with a copper washer for a seal. This should also be replaced when hoses are renewed. After hose installation, make sure the hose is not twisted. Many hoses have a painted stripe on them to help the technician determine if the hose is twisted.

If a length of steel brake line tubing must be replaced and the end flared, a special double flaring tool must be used. Always inspect newly formed flares for defects. Double lap flaring tools must be used. Single flares cannot hold the high pressures in the brake system and tend to crack. When bending brake tubing to fit the frame or rear axle contours, be careful not to

crack or kink the tube. Always clean the inside of even new brake tube with clean isopropyl alcohol.

GENERAL MOTORS CORPORATION

Master Cylinder Service

In addition to standard master cylinder functions, a quick take-up feature in included on most models. This provides a large volume of fluid to the wheels at low pressure with the initial brake application. This large volume of fluid is needed to overcome the clearance created by the seals retracting the pistons into the front calipers and the spring retraction of the rear brake shoes.

NOTE: General Motors Corporation does not recommend honing the bores of either cast iron or composite master cylinders. When the brake master cylinder is overhauled, it is recommended that the cylinder body be replaced rather than attempting to clean up a scuffed cylinder by honing the bore. The master cylinder has a hard, highly polished surface which is produced by diamond boring followed by ball or roller burnishing under heavy pressure. Honing will destroy this surface which will cause rapid wear of rubber cups. Do not use kerosene, gasoline or other solvents for cleaning or flushing master cylinder and components. The use of these solvents or any other with a trace of mineral oil, will damage rubber parts.

DELCO CAST IRON MASTER CYLINDER

Disassembly and Assembly

1. Remove cover, rubber diaphragm and drain reservoir.
2. Remove snapring and primary piston assembly.
3. Plug rear port and apply low pressure air to front port. Secondary piston will pop out. Use shop cloth to catch piston. Use caution. The piston may come out with considerable force. Remove seals from secondary piston.
4. If tube seats must be replaced,

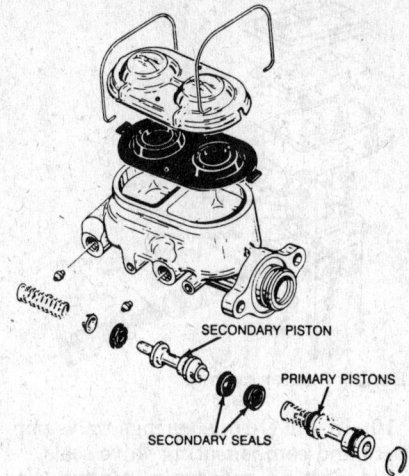

GM cast iron master cylinder

thread in self-tapping screw into seat, remove with locking pliers.

5. Clean all metal parts in denatured alcohol, the rubber parts in brake fluid.
6. A stained or discolored bore may be cleaned with fine crocus cloth. Do not attempt to hone the bore.
7. Lube all seals and the bore with clean brake fluid. Install seals on pistons and assemble.
8. Push primary piston with smooth rounded end tool and install snapring.
9. If tube seats are replaced, seat with spare brake tube nut.
10. Install diaphragm into cover and install cover.

BENDIX MASTER CYLINDER

Disassembly and Assembly

1. Remove cover, rubber diaphragm and drain reservoir.
2. Locate and remove the reservoir to body bolts and remove reservoir.
3. Remove the seals, poppet valves and springs from cylinder body.
4. Remove snapring and primary piston.
5. Plug rear port and apply low pressure air to front port. Secondary piston will pop out. Use shop cloth to catch piston. Use caution. The piston may come out with considerable force. Remove seals from secondary piston.
6. Clean all metal parts in denatured alcohol, the rubber parts in brake fluid.
7. A stained or discolored bore may be cleaned with fine crocus cloth. Do not attempt to hone the bore.
8. Lube all seals and the bore with clean brake fluid. Install seals on pistons and assemble.
9. Push primary piston with smooth rounded end tool and install snapring.

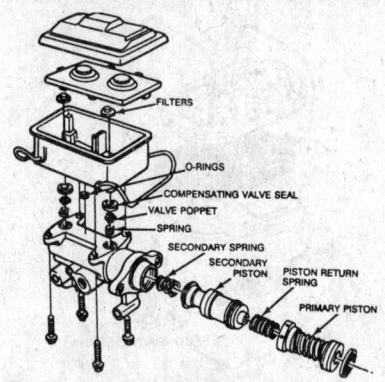

Bendix master cylinder

10. Install O-ring, springs, valve poppets and compensating valve seals.
11. Bolt on reservoir, replace diaphragm and cover.

DELCO COMPOSITE MASTER CYLINDER

Disassembly and Assembly

EXCEPT LUMINA APV, SILHOUETTE AND TRANS SPORT

1. Remove cover, rubber diaphragm and drain reservoir.
2. Clamp mounting flange of cylinder in vise and pry reservoir off. Remove reservoir grommet.
3. Remove snapring and primary piston.
4. Plug rear port and apply low pressure air to front port. Secondary piston will pop out. Use shop cloth to catch piston. Use caution. The piston may come out with considerable force. Remove seals from secondary piston.
5. Clean all metal parts in denatured alcohol, the rubber parts in brake fluid.
6. A stained or discolored bore may be cleaned with fine crocus cloth. Do not attempt to hone the bore.
7. Lube all seals and the bore with clean brake fluid. Install seals on pistons and assemble.
8. Push primary piston with smooth rounded end tool and install snapring.
9. Install grommets and press reservoir on with rocking motion. Install diaphragm and cover.

LUMINA APV, SILHOUETTE AND TRANS SPORT

1. Remove cover, rubber diaphragm and drain reservoir.
2. Remove fluid level sensor switch using needle nose pliers to compress switch locking tabs at the inboard side of master cylinder.
3. Remove proportioner valve assemblies by unscrewing cap assemblies, removing the O-rings and

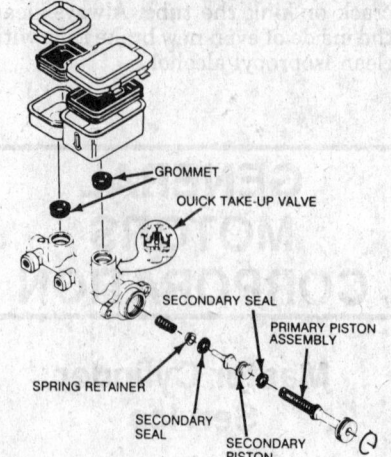

GM composite master cylinder

springs. Remove pistons with needle nose pliers. Use care. Do not scratch piston stems.
3. Remove snapring and primary piston.
4. Apply low pressure air into upper outlet port at blind end of bore. Plug all other ports. Secondary piston will pop out. Use shop cloth to catch piston. Use caution. The piston may come out with considerable force. Remove seals from secondary piston.
5. To remove reservoir, clamp flange (never the body) of master cylinder in vise. Drive out spring pins with 1/8 in. punch. Pull reservoir straight up and remove O-rings from grooves in reservoir.
6. Clean all metal parts in denatured alcohol, the rubber parts in brake fluid.
7. Inspect the bore for scoring or corrosion. If noted, replace master cylinder. No abrasives should be used in bore. Do not attempt to hone the bore.
8. Install new seals on reservoir, press into cylinder body and install spring pins.
9. Lube all seals and the bore with clean brake fluid. Install seals on pistons and assemble.
10. Push primary piston with smooth rounded end tool and install snapring.
11. Install proportioner valve assemblies and fluid level sensor, making sure locking tabs snap into place.
12. Install diaphragm and cover.

Brake Booster Service

Three types of brake boosters are used: a single diaphragm, a tandem diaphragm and a hydraulic booster (Hydro-Boost).

The vacuum boosters may have a vacuum switch to activate a brake warning light in case of low booster vacuum or vacuum pump malfunc-

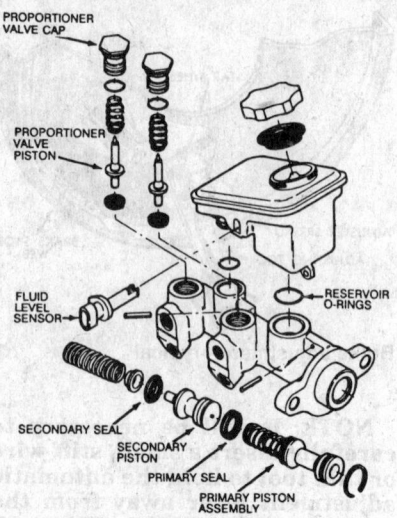

Lumina APV master cylinder

tion. Under normal operating conditions, with brakes released, a vacuum suspended booster operates with vacuum on both sides of its diaphragm (or both diaphragms in a tandem diaphragm unit). When the brakes are applied, air at atmospheric pressure is admitted to one side of the diaphragm (or both diaphragms in a tandem diaphragm unit) to provide the power assist.

The hydraulic brake booster (Hydro-Boost) uses a hydraulic pump to power the system and a pneumatic accumulator as a reserve system. In this system no special fluids are used. However, care must be taken to use the correct fluids. The master cylinder and brake system operate on standard brake fluid. The hydraulic pump, which is driven by pressure from the power steering pump, uses power steering fluid.

VACUUM DIAPHRAGM BRAKE BOOSTERS

Disassembly and Assembly

SINGLE DIAPHRAGM BOOSTER

NOTE: A special brake booster disassembly tool is recommended for this procedure.

1. With the booster unit off the vehicle, and the master cylinder removed from the booster, take off the boot and silencer disc from the booster's mounting (rear) side. Remove the vacuum check valve, grommet and the front housing seal from the face side.
2. Scribe a mark across the front and rear housings to aid assembly.
3. Clamp the base in a vise with the power section facing up. Separate the front and rear housings by pressing down (using the special disassembly

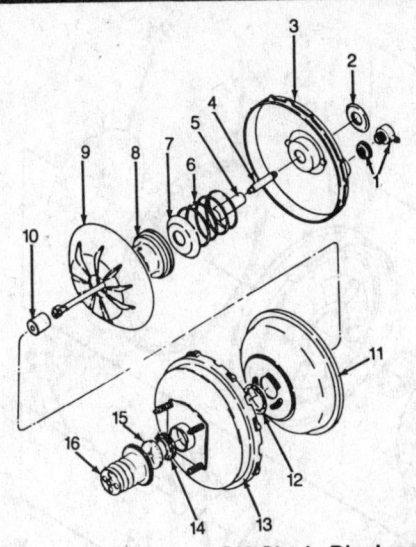

1. Check valve and grommet
2. Front housing seal
3. Front housing
4. Piston rod
5. Reaction retainer
6. Return springs
7. Reaction body retainer
8. Power piston and pushrod assembly
9. Diaphragm support
10. filter
11. Diaphragm
12. Diaphragm retainer
13. Rear housing
14. Power piston bearing
15. Silencer disc
16. Boot

GM Single Diaphragm Booster

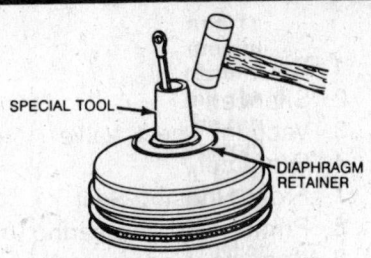

Installing diaphragm retainer with pipe driver

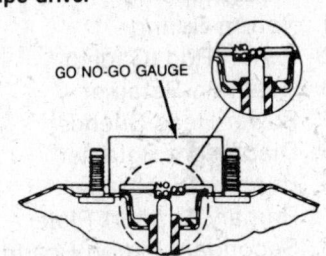

Using special GO NO-GO gauge to check pushrod

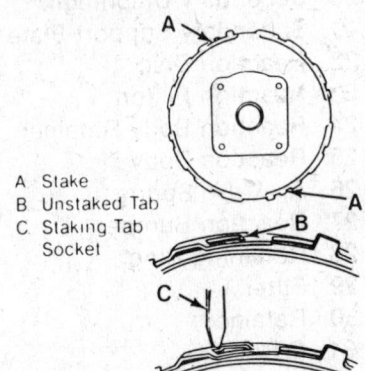

A. Stake
B. Unstaked Tab
C. Staking Tab Socket

Staking the booster tabs

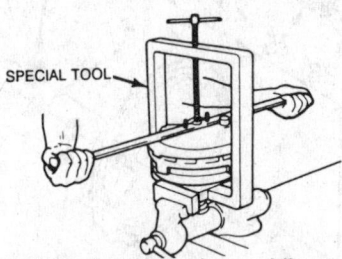

Special tool presses down while housing is turned

tool, if available) and rotating the housing counterclockwise to the unlocked position. Loosen carefully as it is spring loaded.

4. Remove the large return spring and the power piston which will likely still have the pedal pushrod attached.

5. Remove the power piston bearing from the rear housing.

6. Remove the reaction body retainer, the master cylinder piston rod, and reaction retainer.

7. Remove the filter with an awl or similar tool.

8. Separate the power piston and pedal pushrod. To do this, grasp the outside edge of the diaphragm support and diaphragm. Hold the pushrod down against a hard surface and use slight force to dislodge the diaphragm retainer.

9. Remove the diaphragm from the diaphragm support.

10. Inspect all parts for corrosion, nicks, cracks, cuts, scoring, distortion or excessive wear. Replace as required. Clean all parts in denatured alcohol, but do not immerse the power piston and pushrod assembly in alcohol. Dry with compressed air.

11. Lubricate the inside diameter of the diaphragm lip with a thin layer of silicone grease and install the diaphragm into its support.

12. Install the diaphragm and support onto the power piston and push-

rod assembly. Use a new retainer and install with a pipe-like driver.

13. Install filter, reaction retainer, piston rod, and reaction body retainer.

14. Install the reaction body retainer disc. Lubricate the inside and outside of the power piston bearing with silicone grease and install in rear housing.

15. Install power piston group into rear housing, put in the return spring and assemble front housing to rear housing. Align mating marks made before disassembly.

16. Apply pressure in clockwise direction to lock housings together. Stake the housing at two tabs 180 degrees apart. Do not stake a tab that has been previously staked.

17. Lubricate the check valve grommet with silicone grease and install it and the check valve in the front cover.

18. Install the front housing seal, silencer disc, and boot.

19. The piston rod should be checked with a special GO, NO-GO gauge. If not within limits, replace the rod.

TANDEM DIAPHRAGM BOOSTER

NOTE: A special brake booster disassembly tool is recommended for this procedure.

1. With the booster unit off the vehicle, and the master cylinder removed from the booster, take off the boot and silencer disc from the booster's mounting (rear) side. Remove the vacuum check valve, grommet and the front housing seal from the face side.

2. Scribe a mark across the front and rear housings to aid assembly.

3. Clamp the base in a vise with the power section facing up. Separate the front and rear housings by pressing down (using the special disassembly tool, if available) and rotating the housing counterclockwise to the un-

locked position. Loosen carefully as it is spring loaded.

4. Remove the large return spring and the power piston which will likely still have the pedal pushrod attached.

5. Remove the power piston bearing from the rear housing.

6. Remove the piston rod, reaction retainer and power head silencer ring.

7. Remove the power piston assembly and pushrod. Grasp the assembly at the outside edge of the housing divider and both diaphragms. Hold the pushrod down against a hard surface. Tap to dislodge diaphragm retainer.

8. Remove the primary diaphragm (rear) and primary support plate from the housing divider and separate the primary diaphragm from its support plate.

9. Remove the secondary diaphragm (front) and secondary support plate from the housing divider. Remove the secondary piston bearing from the center of the housing divider and separate the secondary diaphragm from its support plate.

10. Remove the reaction plate retainer, reaction body, reaction disc, and reaction piston from the reaction body.

1. Boot
2. Silencer
3. Vacuum Check Valve
4. Grommet
7. Front Housing Seal
8. Primary Piston Bearing
9. Rear Housing
10. Front Housing
11. Return Spring
12. Piston Rod (Gaged)
13. Reaction Retainer
14. Power Head Silencer
15. Diaphragm Retainer
16. Primary Diaphragm
17. Primary Support Plate
18. Secondary Piston Bearing
19. Housing Divider
20. Secondary Diaphragm
21. Secondary Support Plate
22. Reaction Disc
23. Reaction Piston
24. Reaction Body Retainer
25. Reaction Body
26. Air Valve Spring
27. Reaction Bumper
28. Retaining Ring
29. Filter
30. Retainer
31. O-Ring
32. Air Valve Push Rod Assembly
33. Power Piston

Tandem diaphragm vacuum booster components

11. Remove the air valve spring and reaction bumper from the end of the pushrod. Carefully remove the retaining ring from the pushrod, and remove the pushrod by inserting a suitable tool through the eyelet end and pulling straight out. Considerable force will be required.

12. Remove the filter, retainer and O-ring from the pushrod assembly.

13. Inpect all parts for corrosion, nicks, cracks, cuts, scoring, distortion or excessive wear. Replace as required. Clean all parts in denatured alcohol, but do not immerse the power piston and pushrod assembly in alcohol. Dry with compressed air.

14. Using silicone grease, lubricate the O-ring for the pushrod and install the pushrod into the power piston, then install the retainer and seat.

15. Install the filter over the pushrod eyelet and into the power piston and install the retaining ring.

16. Assemble the reaction bumber, air valve spring, reaction piston and reaction disc into the reaction body. Install the reaction body retainer.

17. Using silicone grease, lubricate the inside diameter of both the primary and secondary diaphragm as well as the secondary piston bearing.

18. Assemble the secondary diaphragm to its support plate and slide the assembly over the power piston/pushrod assembly.

19. Install the secondary piston bearing into the housing divider. The flat surface of the bearing goes on the same side as the six raised lugs on the divider. Install this assembly over the power piston/pushrod assembly.

20. Assemble the primary diaphragm to its support plate, by folding the diaphragm up, away from the support plate and slide the assembly over the power piston/pushrod assembly. Fold the primary diaphragm back into position and pull the outside edge of the diaphragm over the formed flange of the housing divider.

NOTE: Check that the beads on the secondary diaphragm are seated evenly around the complete circumference.

21. Install a new diaphragm retainer and install with a pipe-like driver.

22. Install the silencer ring, reaction retainer and piston rod.

23. Lubricate the inside and outside diameters of the primary piston bearing with silicone grease and install into the rear housing.

24. Install the power piston assembly into the rear housing.

25. Install the return spring and assemble front housing to rear housing. Align mating marks made before disassembly.

26. Apply pressure in clockwise direction to lock housings together. Stake the housing at two tabs 180 degrees apart. Do not stake a tab that has been previously staked.

27. Lubricate the check valve grommet with silicone grease and install it and the check valve in the front cover.

28 Install the front housing seal, silencer disc, and boot.

29. The piston rod should be checked with a special GO, NO-GO gauge. If not within limits, replace the rod.

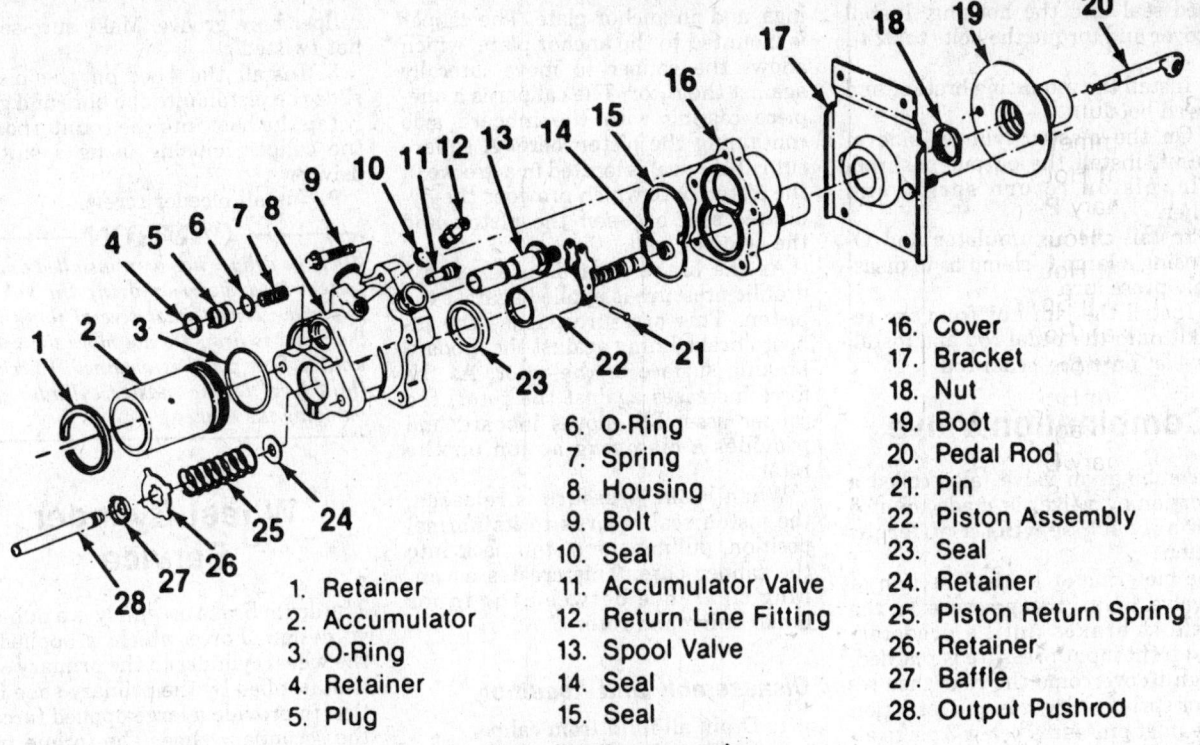

16. Cover
17. Bracket
18. Nut
19. Boot
20. Pedal Rod
21. Pin
22. Piston Assembly
23. Seal
24. Retainer
25. Piston Return Spring
26. Retainer
27. Baffle
28. Output Pushrod

6. O-Ring
7. Spring
8. Housing
9. Bolt
10. Seal
11. Accumulator Valve
12. Return Line Fitting
13. Spool Valve
14. Seal
15. Seal

1. Retainer
2. Accumulator
3. O-Ring
4. Retainer
5. Plug

Hydro-Boost components

HYDRO-BOOST

The Bendix Hydro-Boost uses the hydraulic pressure supplied by the power steering pump to provide a power assist to brake application. It has identifying information stamped into the housing near the inlet line. When servicing this unit, there are some special tools that are recommended for these procedures.

Disassembly and Assembly

——— CAUTION ———

This system uses an accumulator that contains compressed gas. Do not apply heat to the accumulator. Use caution or personal injury may result. Do not attempt to repair a defective accumulator. Always replace with a new unit. Dispose of an inoperative accumulator by drilling a 1/16 in. diameter hole through the end of the accumulator can opposite the O-ring.

1. Remove the accumulator. Note that an adapter (a piece of strap metal with a hole drilled to accommodate a mounting stud) is used along with a C-clamp. Depress the accumulator with the C-clamp, insert a punch into the hole on the housing and remove the snapring retainer. Release the C-clamp, remove the accumulator and O-ring.

2. Remove the retainer from the small port above the mounting flange and remove the plug, O-ring and spring.

3. Remove the star-shaped retainer from the mounting flange bore and remove the output pushrod, baffle, piston return spring and inner retainer.

4. Remove the pedal rod boot and mounting bracket, if installed. On some installations it may be necessary to saw off the eyelet of the pedal rod. Make sure exact replacements or the replacement parts kit is available before cutting the original part.

5. Remove the cover bolts and separate the cover from the housing. Remove the seals (a large figure-eight shaped seal and a smaller seal on the end of the piston assembly).

6. Remove the piston assembly and the O-ring seal on the housing side of the piston.

7. Remove the spool valve.

8. Remove the accumulator valve. It may be necessary to fish this small valve out with a thin wire hook.

9. Remove the return line fitting and seal.

10. Clean all parts in power steering fluid. Inspect the spool valve for corrosion, nicks and scoring. If found, replace the complete booster. Discoloration of the spool or bore is not harmful and is no cause for replacement. Check all components for damage or wear, especially the tube seat in the housing. This seat can be removed with a Easy-Out type remover, and its replacement installed by tapping gently into place.

11. Lubricate all seals and friction

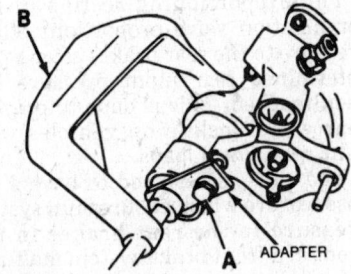

A. Nut
B. C-clamp
Removing the accumulator

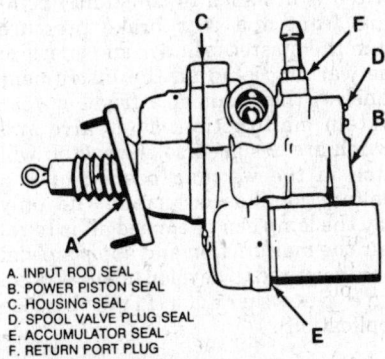

A. INPUT ROD SEAL
B. POWER PISTON SEAL
C. HOUSING SEAL
D. SPOOL VALVE PLUG SEAL
E. ACCUMULATOR SEAL
F. RETURN PORT PLUG
Hydro-Boost seal leak areas

metal parts with power steering fluid.

12. Install the return line fitting and seal.

13. Install the accumulator valve and spool valve.

14. Install the seal and piston assembly, place the small seal on the piston assembly end and the figure eight

shaped seal into the housing. Install the cover and torque the bolts to 22 ft. lbs.

15. Install the mounting bracket and pushrod boot.

16. On the master cylinder side of the unit, install the output pushrod, baffle, piston return spring and retainer.

17. Install the accumulator and O-ring using a large C-clamp as in disassembly procedure.

18. Install the jam nut from the repair kit onto the pedal rod and install the eyelet onto the pedal rod.

Combination Valve

The combination valve (also called a proportioning valve) is made up of 3 sections, each serving a different function.

The metering or hold-off section of the valve limits the pressure to the front disc brakes until a predetermined front input pressure is reached, enough to overcome the rear shoe retractor springs. There is no restriction to the inlet pressures below 3 psi to allow for pressure equalization during no-apply periods.

The proportioning section of the combination valve proportions outlet pressure to the rear brakes after a predetermined rear input pressure has been reached. This is done to prevent rear wheel lockup on vehicles with light rear wheel loads.

The valve is designed to have a by-pass feature which ensures full system pressure to the rear brakes in the event of a front brake system malfunction. Full front pressure is retained in the event of rear malfunction.

The pressure-differential warning switch is designed to constantly compare front and rear brake pressure from the master cylinder and energize the warning lamp on the instrument panel in the event of a front or rear system malfunction. The valve and switch are designed so the switch will latch in the warning postion once a malfunction has occurred. The only way the lamp can be turned off is to repair the malfunction and apply a pedal force required to develop about 450 psi line pressure (a firm brake application).

Valve Overhaul

The combination valve is not repairable and must be replaced as a complete assembly.

Caliper Service

The disc brake assembly consists of a caliper and piston assembly, rotor, lin-

ings, and an anchor plate. The caliper is mounted to the anchor plate, which allows the caliper to move laterally against the rotor. The caliper is a one-piece casting with the inboard side containing the piston bore. A square cut rubber seal is located in a groove in the piston bore which provides the hydraulic seal between the piston and the cylinder wall.

As the brake pedal is pressed, hydraulic pressure is applied against the piston. This pressure pushes the inboard brake lining against the inboard braking surface of the rotor. As the force increases against the rotor, the caliper assembly moves inboard and provides a clamping action on the rotor.

When brake pressure is released, the piston seal returns to its normal position, pulling the piston back into the caliper bore. This creates a running clearance between the inner brake lining and rotor.

Disassembly and Assembly

1. Drain all fluid from caliper.
2. Pad interior of caliper with clean shop towels and use just enough compressed air to ease the piston out of the bore.

─── **CAUTION** ───

Do not place fingers in front of piston to try to catch piston or protect it when applying compressed air. This could result in serious injury. Use just enough air to ease the piston out. If piston is blown out, even with padding, it may be damaged.

3. Remove boot, being careful not to scratch bore.
4. Remove square cut seal from caliper bore groove.
5. Remove bleeder valve.
6. Clean all parts with denatured alcohol, blow dry with compressed air. Inspect all parts for scoring, corrosion or damage to chrome plating on piston. Replace if damaged. Fine crocus cloth can be used to polish out any light corrosion.
7. Lubricate the new piston seal, caliper bore and piston with clean brake fluid and install the seal in the

caliper bore groove. Make sure seal is not twisted.

8. Install the boot on the piston, slide the piston into the bore and gently tap the boot into the counterbore of the caliper housing using a suitable driver.
9. Install bleeder screw.

─── **CAUTION** ───

After the caliper has been installed and the system bled, before moving the vehicle, pump the brake pedal several times until the pedal is firm. Do not move the vehicle until a firm pedal is obtained. Check the fluid level in the master cylinder after pumping the brakes.

Wheel Cylinder Service

The drum brake assembly is a duo-servo design. Force which is applied by the wheel cylinder to the primary shoe is multiplied by the primary shoe friction to provide a large applied force to the secondary shoe. The torque from the brake shoes is transferred to the anchor pin and through the backing plate, the the axle flange. Brake adjustments are automatic and are made during reverse brake applications.

Wheel cylinders may need reconditioning or replacement whenever the brake shoes are replaced or when required to correct a leak condition. In some cases, the wheel cylinders can be disassembled without removing them from the backing plate. On others, the cylinder must be removed before being disassembled.

Leaks which coat the boot and the cylinder with fluid, or result in a dropped reservoir fluid level, or dampen and stain the brake linings are dangerous. Such leaks can cause the brakes to grab or fail and should be immediately corrected. A leakage, not immediately apparent, can be detected by pulling back the cylinder boot. A small amount of fluid seepage dampening the interior of the boot is normal. However, a dripping boot is not. Unless other conditions causing a brake to pull, grab or drag become obvious, the wheel cylinder is suspect and should be included in general reconditioning.

Cylinder binding may be caused by rust, deposits, grime, or swollen cups due to fluid contamination, or by a cup wedged into an excessive piston clearance.

Hydraulic system parts should not be allowed to come into contact with oil or grease, neither should those be handled with greasy hands. Even a trace of any petroleum based product

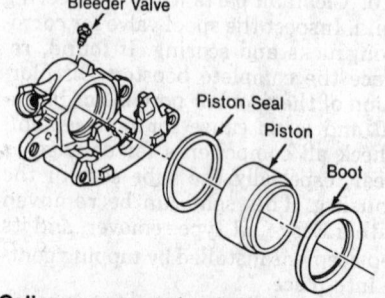

Caliper components – typical

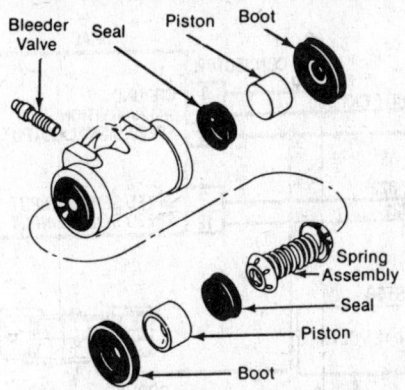

Bleeder Valve • Seal • Piston • Boot

Spring Assembly

Seal

Piston

Boot

Wheel cylinder components – typical

is sufficient to cause damage to the rubber parts.

Disassembly and Assembly

1. Remove the brake bleeder screw.
2. Remove the dust boots, allow any brake fluid to drain out.
3. Remove the pistons, seals and inner spring.
4. Inspect the bore for scoring and corrosion. The inside of the bore may be cleaned with fine crocus cloth. If bore is scored, replace cylinder. Clean the cylinder with brake fluid.
5. Lubricate the seals with brake fluid and install. Cup lips should always face inward. Install the spring assembly and seals.
6. Carefully install the pistons and dust boots.
7. Install the bleeder screw.

Anti-Lock Braking Systems

Despite advances in brake design over the years, even the best systems in use can still lock up during certain road conditions, such as wet road surfaces. When the brakes lock up, the driver can lose control of the vehicle, because a locked wheel cannot absorb any cornering or lateral forces, and steering is lost. It is impossible to brake to a maximum and at the same time steer the vehicle when the front wheels are locked. If the back wheels are locked the vehicle will become unstable and start to slide.

While many different ways have been tried over the years to solve this problem, mechanical sensors could not provide sufficient information about wheel rotation speed and mechanical control units could not operate the brakes fast enough to prevent brake lockup.

The growth of the electronics industry has allowed small computers (microprocessors) to be reduced in both size and cost. Coupled with fast reacting electronic sensors, anti-lock braking has become more reliable with widespread application.

REAR WHEEL ANTI-LOCK BRAKE SYSTEM

General Motors Corporation's system is called Rear Wheel Antilock System (RWAL) and its application is on selected 2WD models. It is designed to reduce the occurrence of the rear wheel lockup during a severe brake application.

The system functions by regulating the rear hydraulic brake line pressure. The pressure regulation is accomplished by a control valve which is located under the master cylinder. The control valve is made up of 2 valves, a dump valve which releases pressure into an accumulator, and an isolation valve which maintains rear brake pressure. The valve is controlled by a microcomputer which is part of the Electronic Control Unit (ECU). The ECU is mounted next to the master cylinder. In a severe brake application as pressure is applied to the brake pedal, the ECU is designed to permit the valve to do one of three functions or a combination of all three. The ECU will allow the valve to either maintain the same amount of hydraulic pressure, release hydraulic pressure through the dump valve into the accumulator, or increase the pressure by pulsing the isolation valve.

The ECU operates by receiving signals from the speed sensor which is located in the transmission and the brake lamp switch. The speed sensor sends its signal to the digital ratio adapter which is part of the instrument cluster. If the axle ratio or tire size is changed, it will be necessary to recalibrate the digital ratio adapter.

The RWAL system is connected to the existing brake warning lamp located on the dash. An indication of the RWAL operation is a bulb check performed each time the ignition is turned ON. The warning lamp will remain on for about two seconds. A RWAL system malfunction is indicated by a brake warning lamp.

To aid in diagnosing problems, trouble codes are produced by the system. Trouble codes are available at the ALDL (Assembly Line Diagnostic Link) the twelve terminal connector wired to the Electronic Control Module and located under the instrument panel in the passenger compartment. These codes are read by jumping terminal A (which is ground) of the ALDL

● - - - - **ELECTRIC**
●——— **HYDRAULIC**

A. To Front Brakes
1. Master Cylinder
2. Brake Light Switch
3. Instrument Cluster
4. Digital Ratio Adapter
5. Speed Sensor
6. Transmission
7. Isolation/Dump Valve
8. RWAL Control Module
9. Brake Warning Light
10. Combination Valve

General Motors Rear Wheel Antilock Brake System (RWAL)

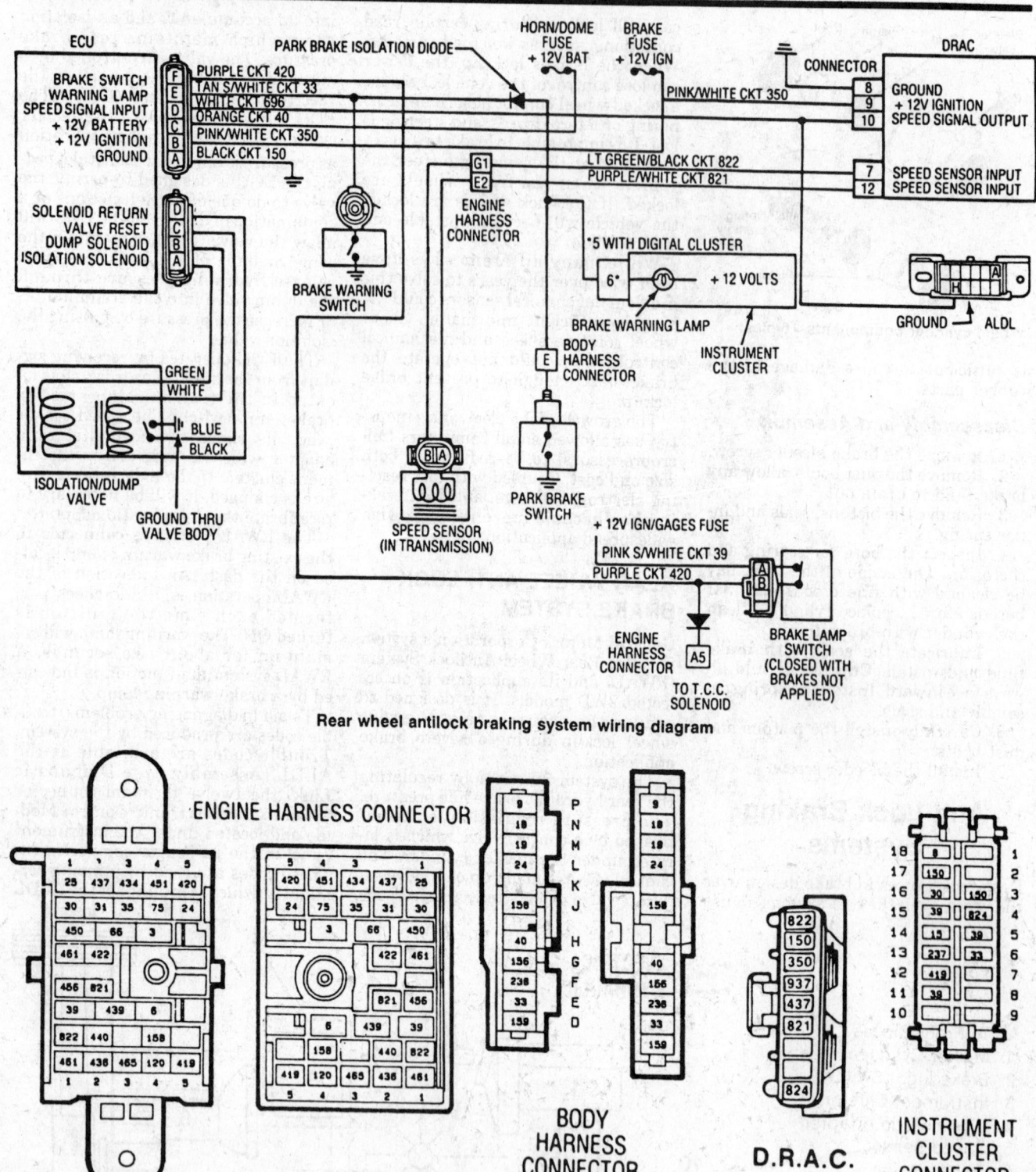

Rear wheel antilock braking system wiring diagram

ENGINE HARNESS CONNECTOR

BODY HARNESS CONNECTOR

D.R.A.C.

INSTRUMENT CLUSTER CONNECTOR

Rear wheel antilock connectors

to terminal H of the ALDL and observing the flashing of the brake warning light. The terminals must be jumped for about 20 seconds before the code will begin to flash. In counting code pulses, count the number of short flashes starting from the long flash. Include the long flash as a count.

NOTE: Sometimes the first count sequence will be short. However, subsequent counts will be accurate. If there is more than one failure, only the first recognized failure code will be retained and flashed.

To clear trouble codes, with the igni-tion OFF, remove the brake fuse, wait five seconds, and then reinstall fuse.

Circuit Maintenance and Repair

All electrical connections must be kept clean and tight. Make sure that connectors are properly seated and all of the sealing rings on weather-proof

REAR WHEEL ANTILOCK BRAKE SYSTEM DIAGNOSTIC CODES

CODE	SYSTEM PROBLEM
CODE 1	Electronic control unit malfunction
CODE 2	Open isolation valve or faulty ECU
CODE 3	Open dump valve or faulty ECU
CODE 4	Grounded antilock valve switch
CODE 5	Excessive actuations of dump valve during an antilock stop
CODE 6	Erratic speed signal
CODE 7	Shorted isolation valve or faulty ECU
CODE 8	Shorted dump valve or faulty ECU
CODE 9	Open circuit to the speed signal
CODE 10	Brake lamp switch circuit
CODE 11	Electronic control unit malfunction
CODE 12	Electronic control unit malfunction
CODE 13	Electronic control unit malfunction
CODE 14	Electronic control unit malfunction
CODE 15	Electronic control unit malfunction

Trouble codes are available at the ALDL (Assembly Line Diagnostic Link), the twelve terminal connector wired to the Electronic Control Module and located under the instrument panel in the passenger compartment. These codes are ready by jumping terminal A (which is ground) of the ALDL to terminal H of the ALDL and observing the flashing of the brake warning light.

connections are in place. With the low current and voltage levels found in some circuits, it is important that all connections be the best possible. Special tools are required for servicing GM's Weather-Pack connectors. This special tool is required to remove the pin and sleeve terminals. If removal is attempted with an ordinary pick, there is a good chance that the terminal will be bent or deformed. These terminals cannot be straightened once they are bent.

Use care when probing the connections or replacing terminals in them. It is possible to short between opposite terminals. If this happens to the wrong terminal part, it is possible to damage certain components. Always use jumper wires between connectors for circuit checking. Never probe through Weather-Pack seals.

When diagnosing for possible open circuits, it is often difficult to locate them by sight because oxidation or terminal misalignment are hidden by the connectors. Merely wiggling a connector on a sensor or in the wiring harness may correct the open circuit condition. This should always be considered when an open circuit is indicated while troubleshooting. Intermittent problems may also be caused by oxidized or loose connections.

Removal and Installation

RWAL ELECTRONIC CONTROL UNIT

The RWAL Electronic Control Unit (ECU) is not serviceable. It should be replaced when diagnosis shows it to be malfunctioning.

NOTE: Do not touch the electrical connections and pins or allow them to come into contact with brake fluid as this will damage the RWAL ECU.

1. Disconnect the electrical connectors.
2. Remove the RWAL ECU by prying the tab at the rear of the ECU and pulling it forward toward the front of the vehicle.
3. To install, simply slide the RWAL ECU into its bracket on the master cylinder until the tab locks into the hole.
4. Install the electrical connectors. If brake fluid has gotten on the connectors, clean then with water followed by isopropyl alcohol.

ISOLATION/DUMP VALVE

The Isolation/Dump valve is not serviceable. It should be replaced when diagnosis shows it to be malfunctioning.

NOTE: Do not touch the electrical connections and pins or allow them to come into contact with brake fluid as this will damage the RWAL ECU.

1. Disconnect the brake line fittings and remove the bolts holding the valve to the bracket.
2. Disconnect the electrical connector from the RWAL ECU. Do not allow the valve to hang by the pigtail.
3. Remove the valve from the vehicle.
4. When installing replacement valve, torque bolts to 21 ft. lbs, brake line fittings to 18 ft. lbs.
5. Install the electrical connectors.

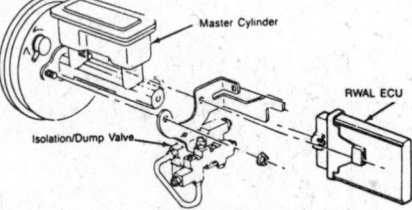

RWAL ECU and Isolation/Dump Valve

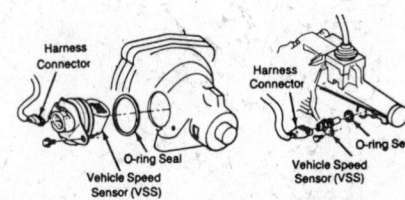

Transmission speed sensor installation

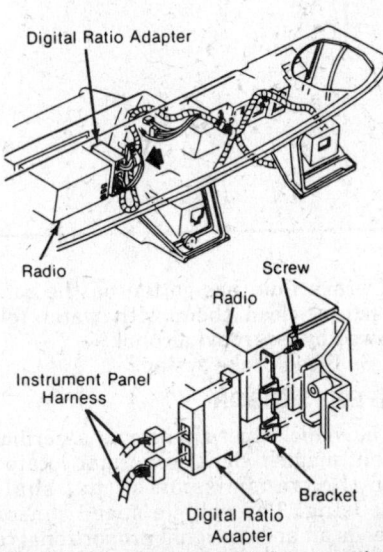

Digital ratio adapter controller mounting

DIAGNOSIS OF THE VEHICLE SPEED SENSOR
AND DIGITAL RATIO ADAPTER CONTROLLER

Problem	Possible Cause	Correction
Speedometer and odometer are inaccurate	Incorrect digital ratio adapter.	Check for the correct digital ratio adapter.
Speedometer and odometer do not operate properly	1. Inoperative digital ratio adapter.	1. Disconnect the digital ratio adapter, and place the ignition in run. Check for voltage between the pink/black wire in the harness and a good chassis ground. If the voltage is less than the battery voltage, check for an open or short in the pink/black wire.
	2. Poor ground path from the digital ratio adapter.	2. Check for voltage between the pink/black wire in the harness and the black/white wire. If the voltage is less than battery voltage, check for an open or short in the black/white wire.
	3. No signal from the vehicle speed sensor.	3. Raise and support the vehicle, start the engine, and place the transmission in drive. Check for AC voltage that changes with the engine rpm between the purple/white wire, and the light green/black wire at the digital ratio adapter. If there is not AC voltage at these wires, check for opens in the purple/white wire and the light green wire. If there are not shorts or opens, replace the vehicle speed sensor.
	4. Inoperative digital ratio adapter (speedometer output).	4. Raise and support the vehicle, start the engine, and place the transmission in drive. Check for AC voltage that changes with the engine rpm between the light blue/black and the black/white wires at the digital ratio adapter connector (connector attached) if AC voltage varies with RPM, replace the digital ratio adapter.
	5. Inoperative digital ratio adapter (cruise output).	5. Raise and support the vehicle, start the engine, and place the transmission in drive. Check for AC voltage that changes with the engine rpm between the yellow and the black/white wires at the digital ratio adapter connector (connector attached) if AC voltage varies with rpm, replace the digital ratio adapter.
	6. Inoperative instrument cluster.	6. Refer to DIAGNOSIS OF THE ELECTRONIC INSTRUMENT CLUSTER.

If brake fluid has gotten on the connectors, clean them with water followed by isopropyl alcohol.

6. Bleed brake system.

SPEED SENSOR

The vehicle speed sensor is a permanent magnet signal generator located on the transmission output shaft housing. The vehicle speed sensor sends an analog signal proportional to the propeller shaft speed. This signal goes to the Digital Ratio Adapter Controller (DRAC) which is used to change the speed sensor signal to a digital signal for the electronic instrument cluster.

The speed sensor is not serviceable. It should be replaced when necessary. The sensor is located in the left rear of the transmission on 2WD models and on the transfer case of 4WD models.

The resistance of the speed sensor should be 900-2000 ohms.

1. Remove the electrical connector.
2. Most applications will use a bolt retainer which is removed. Pull the speed sensor out of transmission housing. Have container ready to catch transmission fluid.
3. Always use new O-ring seal when installing speed sensor. Coat the seal with a thin film of transmission fluid.
4. Install retainer bolt if used and connect electrical harness.

NOTE: The speedometer must recalibrated when rear axle ratio or tire size is changed.

FOUR WHEEL ANTI-LOCK BRAKE SYSTEM

In 1990, selected G.M. models with All Wheel Drive (AWD) could be equipped with a Four Wheel Antilock System (4WAL). It too is designed to to reduce wheel lockup during severe braking. Like the Rear Wheel Antilock system, it works by regulating hyrdaulic brake line pressure. An Electro-Hydraulic Control Unit valve (EHCU), located under the master cylinder, is made up of two types of valves. Isolation valves maintain pressure to each front wheel separately and to the rear wheels combined. Dump valves dump pressure to each front wheel separately and to the rear wheels combined. The valves are controlled by a microcomputer which is part of the EHCU valve. Under severe braking, the EHCU valve will al-

low the valves to either maintain the same hydraulic pressure, release hydraulic pressure through the dump valves into the accumulator, or increase pressure.

The EHCU valve operates by receiving signals from the speed sensors, located at each wheel and the brake lamp switch. The speed sensors are connected directly to the EHCU valve through the 8 pin connector.

The 4WAL system is connected to the ANTILOCK warning lamp in the instrument panel. An indication of 4WAL operation and a bulb check is performed each time the ignition is turned ON. The warning lamp will remain on for about 2 seconds. A 4WAL system malfunction is indicated by the ANTILOCK warning light.

To aid in diagnosing problems, trouble codes are produced by the system. Trouble codes are available at the Assembly Line Diagnostic Link (ALDL) the twelve terminal connector wired to the Electronic Control Module and located under the instrument panel in

the passenger compartment. These codes are read by jumping terminal A of the ALDL to terminal H of the ALDL and observing the flashing of the ANTILOCK. The terminals must be jumped for a few seconds before the code will begin to flash. The ANTILOCK light will flash in a manner similar to the SERVICE ENGINE SOON light for the fuel and emissions system.

In counting code pulses, count the number of short flashes starting from the long flash. Include the long flash as a count.

ALDL Connector

G.M. FOUR WHEEL ANTILOCK BRAKE SYSTEM DIAGNOSTIC CODES

CODE	SYSTEM PROBLEM
CODE 21	Right front speed sensor or circuit open
CODE 22	Missing right front speed signal (set with vehicle in motion)
CODE 23	Erratic right front speed sensor
CODE 25	Left front speed sensor or circuit open
CODE 26	Missing left front speed signal (set with vehicle in motion)
CODE 27	Erratic left front speed sensor
CODE 28	Erratic speed sensor signal (two drop-outs above 20 mph)
CODE 29	Simultaneous drop-out of all four sensors (at speeds above 8 mph)
CODE 31	Right rear speed sensor or circuit open
CODE 32	Missing right rear speed signal (set with vehicle in motion)
CODE 33	Erratic right rear speed sensor
CODE 35	Left rear speed sensor or circuit open
CODE 36	Missing left rear speed signal (set with vehicle in motion)
CODE 37	Erratic left rear speed sensor
CODE 38	Wheel speed error (set with vehicle in motion)
CODES 41 thru 66 and 71 thru 74	4WAL control unit
CODE 67	Open motor circuit or shorted ECU output
CODE 68	Locked motor or shorted motor circuit
CODES 68, 43, 44, 47, 48, 53 and 54	Loss of power ground
CODE 81	Brake switch circuit shorted or open
CODE 85	Open antilock warning lamp
CODE 86	Shorted antilock warning lamp
CODE 88	Shorted brake warning lamp

FOUR WHEEL ANTILOCK WIRING DIAGRAM

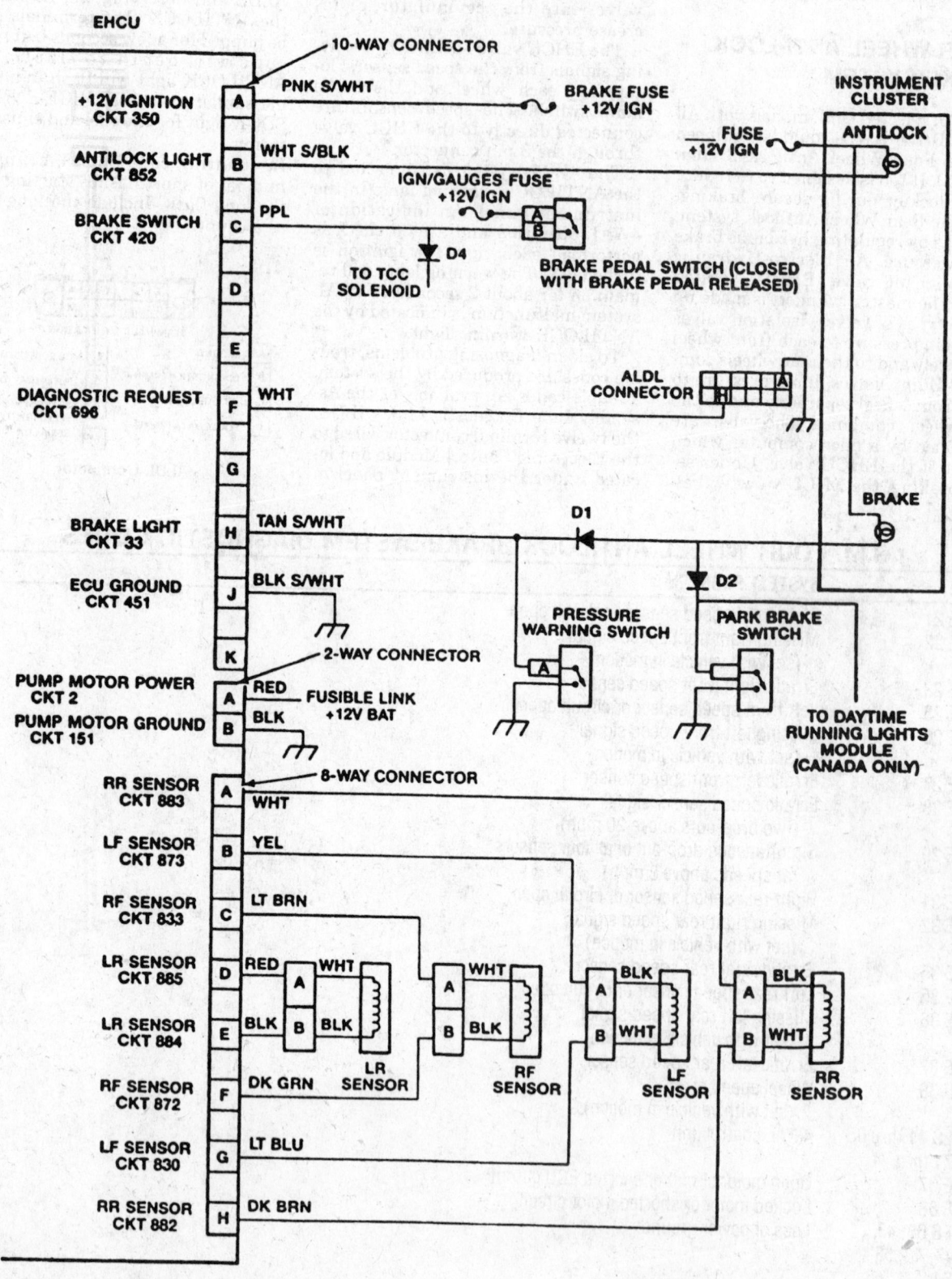

FOUR WHEEL ANTILOCK BRAKE SYSTEM

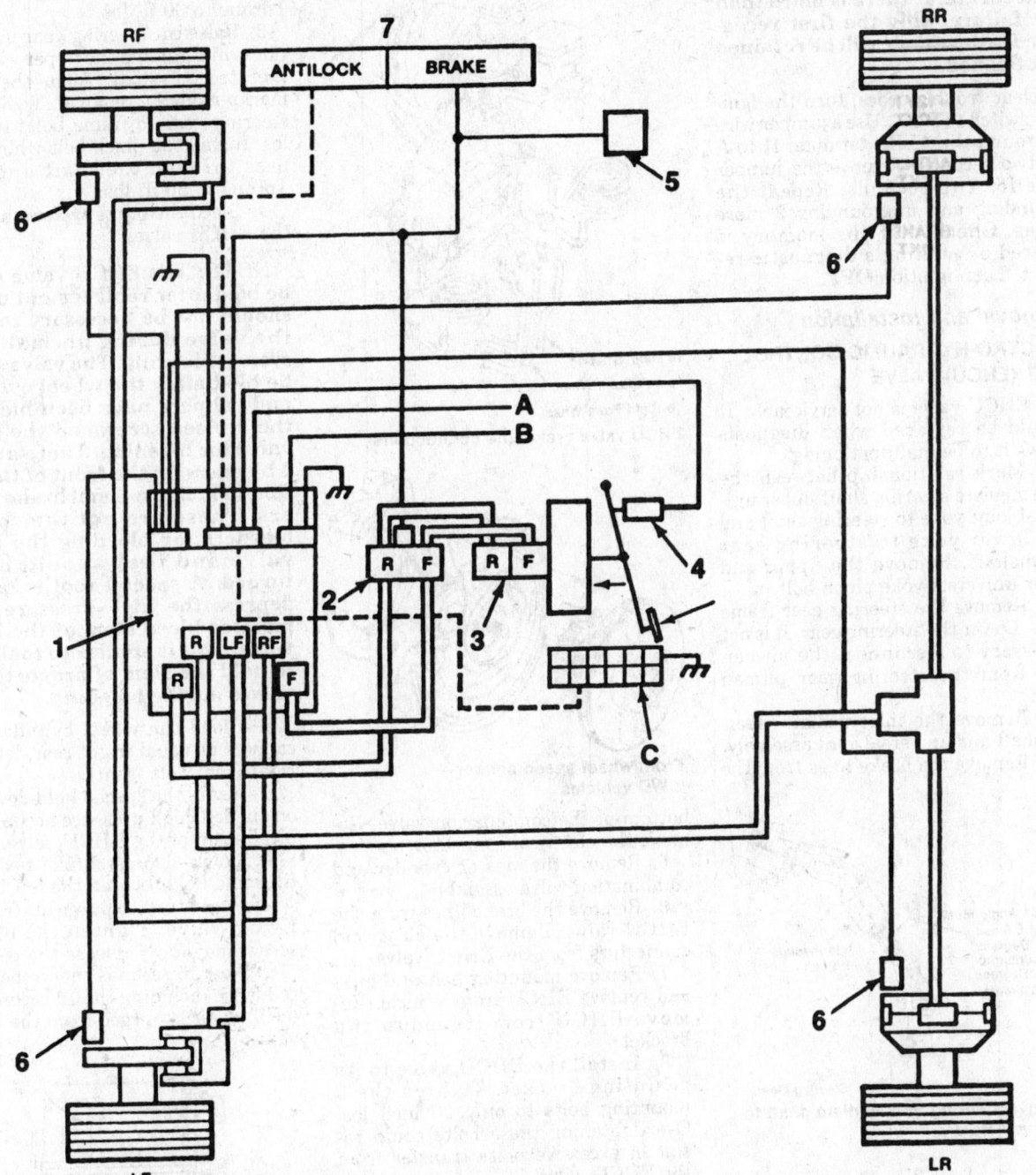

A. To Ignition Switch (B+)
B. To Battery (B+)
C. ALDL
1. 4WAL EHCU Valve
2. Combination Valve
3. Master Cylinder
4. Brake Pedal Switch
5. Park Brake Switch
6. Wheel Speed Sensors
7. Warning Lamps

NOTE: Sometimes the first count sequence will be short. However, subsequent counts will be accurate. If there is more than one failure, only the first recognized failure code will be retained and flashed.

To clear trouble codes, turn the ignition switch to RUN. Use a jumper wire to ground the ALDL terminal H to A for two seconds. Remove the jumper wire for two seconds. Repeat the grounding and ungrounding 2 more times. Check that the memory is cleared by making a diagnostic request. Turn ignition OFF.

Removal and Installation

ELECTRO-HYDRAULIC CONTROL UNIT (EHCU) VALVE

The EHCU valve is not serviceable. It should be replaced when diagnosis shows it to be malfunctioning.

1. Mark relationship between the intermediate steering shaft upper universal joint yoke to steering shaft and the lower yoke to steering gear wormshaft. Remove the upper and lower universal yoke pinch bolt.

2. Remove the steering gear frame bolts. Lower the steering gear. It is not necessary to disconnect the pitman arm from the steering gear pitman shaft.

3. Remove the intermediate steering shaft and universal joint assembly.

4. Remove the brake lines from the

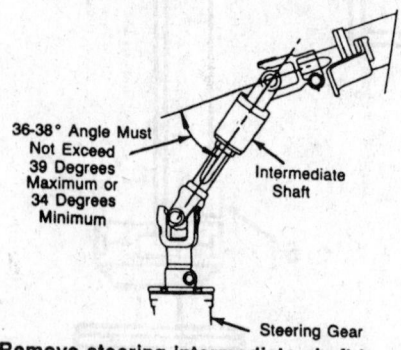

36-38° Angle Must Not Exceed 39 Degrees Maximum or 34 Degrees Minimum

Intermediate Shaft

Steering Gear

Remove steering intermediate shaft to remove EHCU

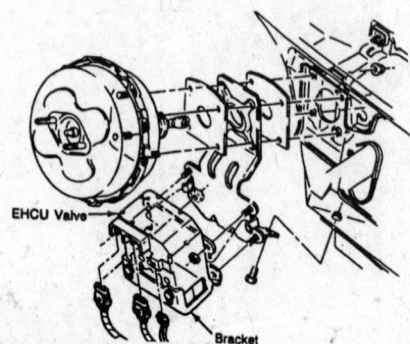

EHCU Valve

Bracket

EHCU valve mounting

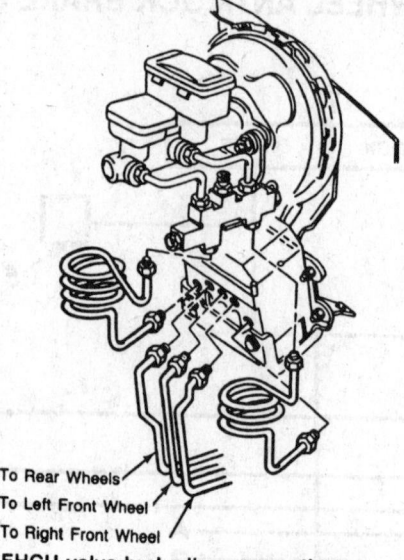

To Rear Wheels
To Left Front Wheel
To Right Front Wheel

EHCU valve brake line connections

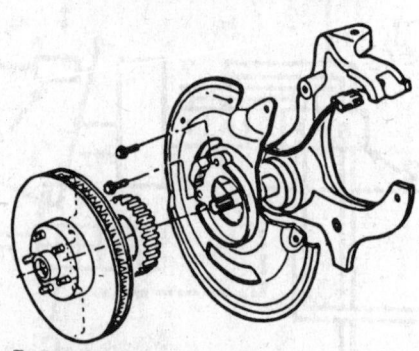

Front wheel speed sensor— 2 WD vehicles

bottom of the combination valve. Remove the electrical connector.

5. Remove the master cylinder and combination valve assembly.

6. Remove the brake lines from the EHCU valve. Remove the electrical connectors from the EHCU valve.

7. Remove mounting bolt and nuts and remove EHCU from vehicle. Remove EHCU from its mounting bracket.

8. Install the EHCU valve to its mounting bracket. Tighten the 6 mounting bolts to only 60 inch lbs. Overtightening these bolts could result in excessive noise transfer from the EHCU valve.

9. Install the EHCU valve and bracket assembly into the vehicle and install the fasteners. Torque the bolt to 33 ft. lbs., the nuts to 20 ft. lbs.

10. Install the electrical connectors and the brake lines to the EHCU valve.

11. Install the master cylinder and combination valve assembly. Connect the electrical connector and the brake lines to the combination valve.

12. Install the steering intermediate shaft. Start by placing the lower yoke onto the steering gear wormshaft.

Align the match marks made at removal. Install the pinch bolt which must pass through the shaft undercut. Torque to 30 ft. lbs.

13. Raise the steering gear into position while guiding the upper yoke onto the steering shaft. Align the match marks made at removal. Tighten the steering gear to frame bolts to 55 ft. lbs. Install the pinch bolt which must pass through the shaft undercut. Torque to 30 ft. lbs.

14. Bleed the brake system including the EHCU valve.

NOTE: The EHCU valve should be bled after replacement only. It should not be necessary to bleed the valve during normal brake system bleeding. The valve should be bled after the wheel cylinders and calipers have been bled. Use the 2 bleed screws on the EHCU valve for bleeding. There are also 2 bleeders on the front of the unit that look like normal brake bleeders. These are not the correct bleeders for bleeding the EHCU valve and they should not be turned. A special tool is used to depress the high pressure accumulator bleed stem of the EHCU valve. This is similar to tools used to hold the stem of proportioning valves during bleeding.

15. Bleed the wheel cylinders and calipers as usual (right rear, left rear, right front, left front).

16. Install the special hold-down tool on the left high pressure accumulator bleed stem of the EHCU valve.

17. Slowly depress brake pedal one time and hold. Loosen the left bleeder screw ¼–½ turn to purge air from the EHCU valve. Tighten the bleeder screw and slowly release the pedal.

18. Wait 15 seconds then repeat this sequence including the 15 second wait until all air is purged from the EHCU valve.

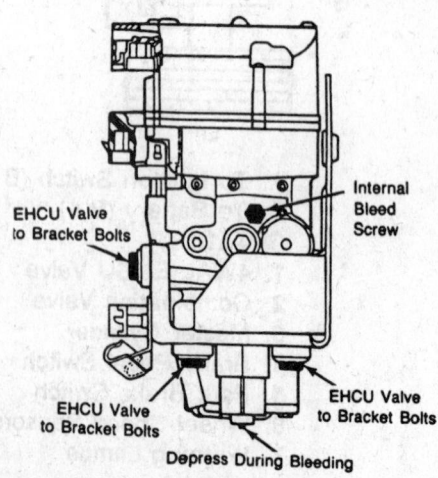

EHCU Valve to Bracket Bolts

Internal Bleed Screw

EHCU Valve to Bracket Bolts

EHCU Valve to Bracket Bolts

Depress During Bleeding

EHCU valve bleeders

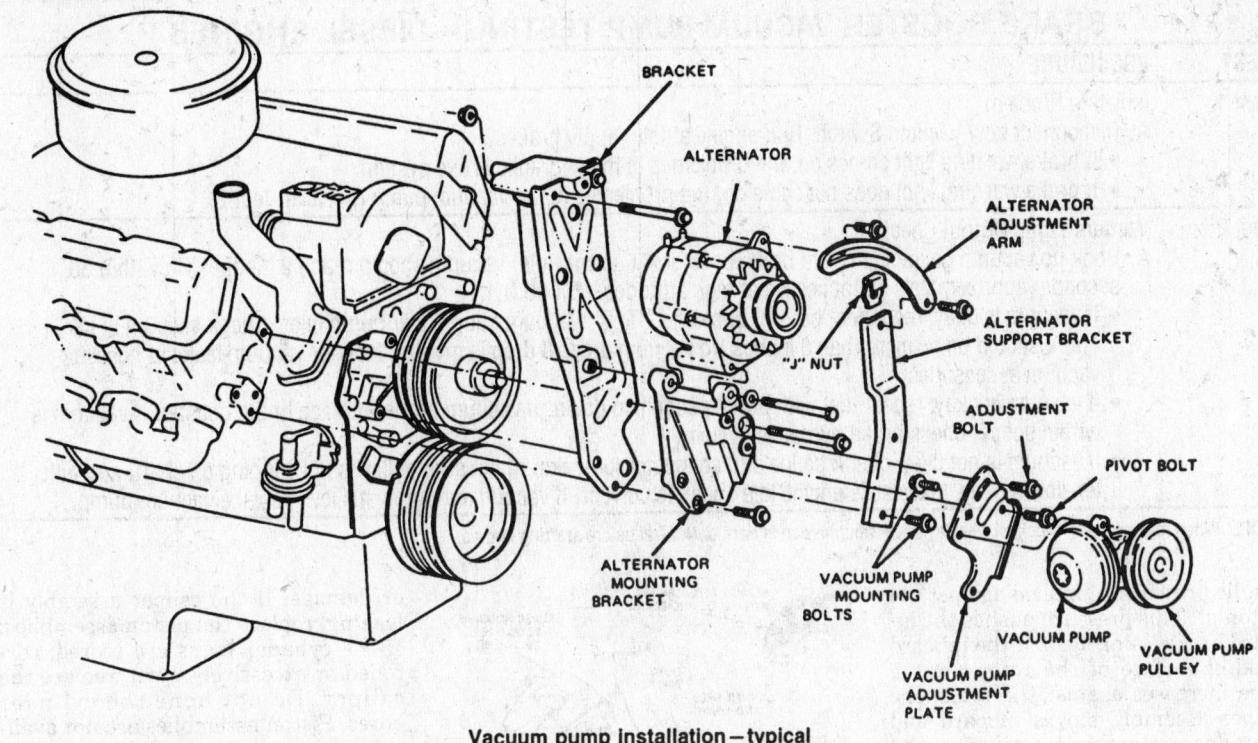

Vacuum pump installation—typical

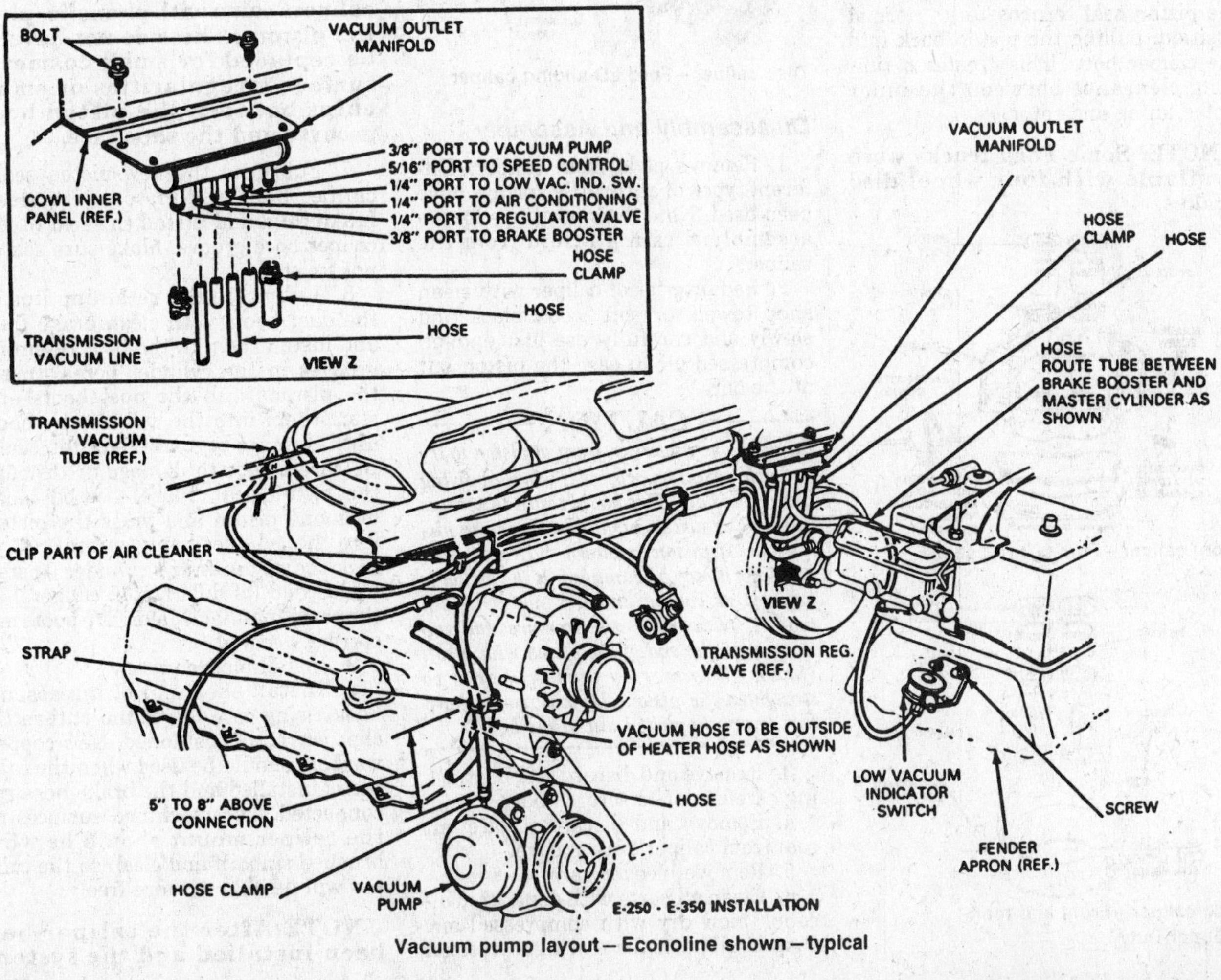

BRACKET

ALTERNATOR

ALTERNATOR ADJUSTMENT ARM

ALTERNATOR SUPPORT BRACKET

"J" NUT

ADJUSTMENT BOLT

PIVOT BOLT

ALTERNATOR MOUNTING BRACKET

VACUUM PUMP MOUNTING BOLTS

VACUUM PUMP ADJUSTMENT PLATE

VACUUM PUMP

VACUUM PUMP PULLEY

BOLT

VACUUM OUTLET MANIFOLD

COWL INNER PANEL (REF.)

3/8" PORT TO VACUUM PUMP
5/16" PORT TO SPEED CONTROL
1/4" PORT TO LOW VAC. IND. SW.
1/4" PORT TO AIR CONDITIONING
1/4" PORT TO REGULATOR VALVE
3/8" PORT TO BRAKE BOOSTER

HOSE CLAMP

HOSE

HOSE

TRANSMISSION VACUUM LINE

VIEW Z

TRANSMISSION VACUUM TUBE (REF.)

CLIP PART OF AIR CLEANER

STRAP

5" TO 8" ABOVE CONNECTION

HOSE CLAMP

VACUUM PUMP

TRANSMISSION REG. VALVE (REF.)

VACUUM HOSE TO BE OUTSIDE OF HEATER HOSE AS SHOWN

HOSE

VACUUM OUTLET MANIFOLD

HOSE CLAMP   HOSE

HOSE ROUTE TUBE BETWEEN BRAKE BOOSTER AND MASTER CYLINDER AS SHOWN

VIEW Z

LOW VACUUM INDICATOR SWITCH

SCREW

FENDER APRON (REF.)

E-250 - E-350 INSTALLATION

Vacuum pump layout—Econoline shown—typical

BRAKE BOOSTER VACUUM PUMP TESTING—DIESEL ENGINES

TEST	PROCEDURE
Test 1	**Isolating Problem** A. Disconnect Low Vacuum Switch. Run engine at idle, apply brakes. • If brake warning light comes on, the problem is in the hydraulic brake system. • If brake warning light does not come on, the problem is in the vacuum pump (perform Test 2).
Test 2	**Vacuum Pump Output Check** A. Hook up vacuum gauge to hose at brake booster. At normal idle, vacuum should reach 21 inches Hg within 30 seconds (approximately 16 inches Hg at high altitudes—5,000 ft.). • If vacuum is okay, reconnect booster base and "TEE" vacuum gauge near pump inlet. Check vacuum at idle. There should be no more than 3 inches Hg vacuum drop. If drop is greater, look for vacuum leaks at hoses or vacuum accessories. • If vacuum is okay, repeat test with brake pedal held down. If vacuum drops, replace brake booster. If vacuum is within specs, check brake hydraulic system. • If vacuum is not okay, check gauge and connector for leaks. Make sure pulley is not slipping on shaft, and belt tension is okay. Make sure engine idle speed is correct. If vacuum output is still low, replace vacuum pump.

NOTE: When making tests, block all wheels, place transmission in Park or Neutral before starting engine.

draulic pressure is applied against the piston(s). This pressure pushes the inboard brake lining against the inboard braking surface of the rotor. As the force increases against the rotor, the caliper assembly moves inboard and provides a clamping action on the rotor.

When brake pressure is released, the piston seal returns to its normal position, pulling the piston back into the caliper bore. This creates a running clearance between the inner brake lining and rotor.

NOTE: Some Ford trucks were available with four wheel disc brakes.

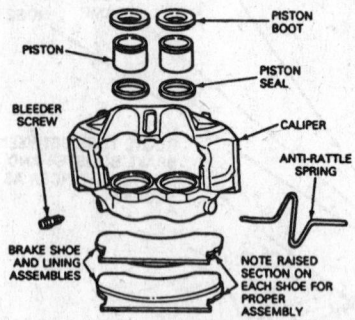

Front caliper—Ford HD rail slider

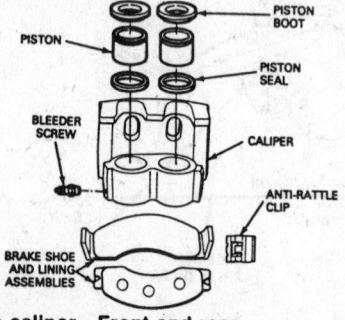

Disc caliper—Front and rear,
F-Super Duty

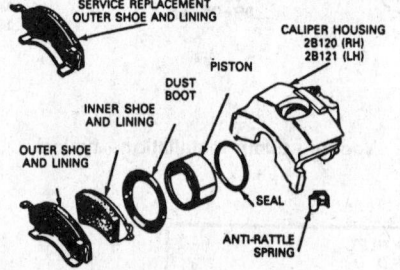

Disc caliper—Ford LD sliding caliper

Disassembly and Assembly

1. Remove pads from caliper. Different types of anti-rattle springs have been used. Note their positions for reassembly. Drain all fluid from the caliper.

2. Pad interior of caliper with clean shop towels or soft wood block and slowly and carefully use just enough compressed air to ease the piston out of the bore.

— CAUTION —

Do not place fingers in front of piston to try to catch piston or protect it when applying compressed air. This could result in serious injury. Use just enough air to ease the piston out. If piston is blown out, even with padding, it may be damaged. If the piston is jammed or cocked and will not come out readily, release the air pressure and tap sharply on the end of the piston with a soft (brass) hammer or plastic mallet to straighten the piston. Do not use a sharp tool to pry the piston out of the bore.

3. Remove and discard seal boot, being careful not to scratch bore.

4. Remove and discard square cut seal from caliper bore groove.

5. Remove bleeder valve.

6. Clean all parts with denatured alcohol, blow dry with compressed air. Inspect all parts for scoring, corrosion

or damage. If the caliper assembly is leaking, replace the piston assemblies. If the cylinder bores are scored, corroded or excessively worn, replace the caliper. Do not hone the cylinder bores. Piston assemblies are not available for oversize bores.

NOTE: Some versions of Ford calipers came with phenolic (plastic) pistons. These do not have to be replaced for small cosmetic surface irregularities or small chips between the piston boot grooves and the shoe face.

7. Lubricate the new piston seals, caliper bore and piston with clean brake fluid and install the seal in the caliper bore groove. Make sure seal is not twisted.

8. Lubricate the retaining lips of the dust boots with clean brake fluid and install them in the boot retaining grooves in the cylinder bores. Insert the pistons into the dust boots and start them into the cylinder by hand until they are beyond the piston seals. Be careful not to damage or dislodge the piston seal. Place a wood block over one piston and press the piston into the cylinder being careful not to cock the piston in the cylinder. Install the second (of dual piston calipers) in the same manner. Make sure boots are correctly seated.

9. Install bleeder screw.

10. Install shoe and lining assemblies, using care to get the anti-rattle clips correctly positioned. New copper washers should be used when the caliper is installed and the brake hose reconnected. The machined surfaces of the caliper mount should be wire brushed smooth and clean so the caliper will be able to more freely.

NOTE:After the caliper has been installed and the system

bled, before moving the vehicle, pump the brake pedal several times until the pedal is firm. Do not move the vehicle until a firm pedal is obtained. Check the fluid level in the master cylinder after pumping the brakes.

Wheel Cylinder Service

The rear brakes are drum type with internal expanding shoes. The rear brakes are of the single anchor type, mounted to the same anchor and actuated by one wheel cylinder. The wheel cylinder has 2 pistons. Brake adjustments are automatic and are made during reverse brake applications.

Wheel cylinders may need reconditioning or replacement whenever the brake shoes are replaced or when required to correct a leak condition. Leaks which coat the boot and the cylinder with fluid, or result in a dropped reservoir fluid level, or dampen and stain the brake linings are dangerous. Such leaks can cause the brakes to grab or fail and should be immediately corrected. A leakage, not immediately apparent, can be detected by pulling back the cylinder boot. A small amount of fluid seepage dampening the interior of the boot is normal. However, a dripping boot is not. Unless other conditions causing a brake to pull, grab or drag become obvious, the wheel cylinder is suspect and should and should be included in general reconditioning.

Cylinder binding may be caused by rust, deposits, grime, or swollen cups due to fluid contamination, or by a cup wedged into an excessive piston clearance.

Hydraulic system parts should not be allowed to come into contact with oil or grease, neither should those be handled with greasy hands. Even a trace of any petroleum based product is sufficient to cause damage to the rubber parts.

Disassembly and Assembly

1. Remove the brake bleeder screw.
2. Remove the dust boots, allow any, brake fluid to drain out.
3. Remove the pistons, seals and inner spring.
4. Inspect the bore for scoring and corrosion. The inside of the bore may be cleaned with fine crocus cloth. If bore is scored, replace cylinder. Clean the cylinder with brake fluid.
5. Lubricate the seals with brake fluid and install. Cup lips should always face inward. Install the spring assembly and seals.

6. Carefully install the pistons and dust boots.
7. Install the bleeder screw.

Anti-Lock Braking Systems

Despite advances in brake design over the years, even the best systems in use can still lock up during certain road conditions, such as wet road surfaces. When the brakes lock up, the driver can lose control of the vehicle, because a locked wheel cannot absorb any cornering or lateral forces, and steering is lost. It is impossible to brake to a maximum and at the same time steer the vehicle when the front wheels are locked. If the back wheels are locked the vehicle will become unstable and start to slide.

While many different ways have been tried over the years to solve this problem, mechanical sensors could not provide sufficient information about wheel rotation speed and mechanical control units could not operate the brakes fast enough to prevent brake lockup.

The growth of the electronics industry has allowed small computers (microprocessors) to be reduced in both size and cost. Coupled with fast reacting electronic sensors, anti-lock braking has become more reliable with widespread application.

REAR WHEEL ANTI-LOCK BRAKE SYSTEM

Ford Motor Company's Rear Antilock Brake System (RABS) continually monitors rear wheel speed with a sensor mounted on the rear axle. When the teeth on an exciter ring, mounted inside the rear axle on the differential gear case, pass the sensor pole piece, an AC voltage is induced in the sensor circuit with a frequency proportional to the average rear wheel speed. In the event of an impending lockup condition during braking, the RABS modulates hydraulic pressure to the rear brakes. This inhibits rear wheel lockup.

When the brake pedal is applied, the RABS module senses the drop in rear wheel speed. If the rate of deceleration is too great, indicating the wheel lockup is going to occur, the RABS module activates the electro-hydraulic valve causing isolation valve to close. With the isolation valve closed, the rear wheel cylinders are isolated from the master cylinder and the rear brake pressure cannot increase. If the rate of deceleration is still too great, the RABS module will energize the dump solenoid with a series of rapid pulses to

bleed off rear wheel cylinder fluid into an accumulator built into the RABS valve. This will reduce the rear wheel cylinder pressure and allow the rear wheels to spin back up to vehicle speed. Continuing under RABS module control, the dump and isolation solenoids will be pulsed in a manner that will keep the rear wheels rotating while still maintaining high levels of deceleration during braking.

At the end of the stop, when the operator releases the brake pedal, the isolation valve de-energizes and any fluid in the accumulator is returned to the master cylinder. Normal brake operation is resumed.

System Self Test

The RABS module performs system tests and self-tests during startup and normal operation. The valve, sensor, and fluid level circuits are monitored for proper operation. If a fault is found the RABS will be deactivated and the REAR ANTILOCK light will be illuminated. Most faults will cause the light to stay illuminated until the ignition is turned **OFF**. While the light is illuminated a diagnostic flashout code may be obtained. However, there are certain faults (those associated with the fluid level switch or loss of power to the module) that will cause the system to be deactivated and the REAR ANTILOCK light to be illuminated but will not provide a diagnostic flashout code will be available.

Warning Lights

The RABS uses both the BRAKE and REAR ANTILOCK instrument panel warning lights to alert the driver to a system malfunction. Both lights must be working properly to assist in problem diagnosis. The red BRAKE warning light is used to indicate a low fluid level condition, parking brake applied condition or, for vehicles equipped with diesel engines, a low vacuum condition. To check this light, turn the key to START. The light should glow in this position. If it fails to glow, service of the electrical system is required.

NOTE: If the red light continues to glow after the key is in the RUN position, repair the brake system as required. If the brake system checks out OK, troubleshooting will be required to diagnose the RABS problem.

The yellow REAR ANTILOCK warning light is used to indicate an RABS malfunction and a deactivation of the RABS. To check this light, turn the key to **ON** or **START**. The light should perform a self-check, glowing for about 2 seconds. If the light fails to

glow or continues to glow after two seconds, troubleshooting of the warning lights is required.

A diode/resistor is located on the main trunk of the instrument panel wiring harness where the RABS module connector pigtail intersects the main trunk. The diode/resistor isolates the RABS module from the parking brake switch and the low vacuum switch (diesel engines). If the diode/resistor did not prevent voltage from reaching the RABS module, the yellow REAR ANTILOCK lamp would turn on and the system would be shut down whenever the parking brake was applied or the low vacuum switch was closed.

Flashout Codes

Whenever the yellow REAR ANTILOCK light comes on during normal operation, a flashout code may be obtained to aid in problem diagnosis. If the vehicle is shut off before the code is read, the code will be lost. In some cases the code may reappear when the vehicle is restarted. In other cases, the vehicle may have to be driven to reproduce the problem and, if the problem was associated with an intermittent condition, it may be difficult to reproduce. Therefore, whenever possible, it is recommended that the code be read before the vehicle is shut off.

NOTE: Place blocks behind the rear wheels and in front of the front wheels to prevent the vehicle from moving while the flashout code is being taken. If the BRAKE light is also on, due to a grounding of the fluid level cir-

cuit (perhaps low brake fluid), no flashout code will be flashed and the REAR ANTILOCK light will remain on steadily. If there is more than one system fault only the first recognized flashout code may be obtained.

Obtaining the Flashout Code

A flashout code may be obtained only when the yellow REAR ANTILOCK light is ON. No code will be flashed if the system is operating properly.

Before obtaining the flashout code, drive the vehicle to a level area, and place the shift lever in **P** for automatic transmissions and neutral for manual transmissions.

Notice whether the red BRAKE light is on or not (for future reference) and then apply the parking brake. Keep the ignition ON so that the code will not be lost.

NOTE: Place blocks behind the rear wheels and in front of the front wheels to prevent the vehicle from moving while the flashout code is being taken.

To obtain the flashout code, locate the RABS diagnostic connector (with the black/orange wire) and attach a jumper wire to it. Momentarily ground it to the chassis. When the ground is made and then broken the REAR ANTILOCK light should begin to flash.

NOTE: If the red BRAKE light was on (as noticed before the parking brake was applied) the problem may be with the low fluid level circuit and, in this case, no

flashout code will be flashed and the light will remain on steadily.

The code consists of a number of short flashes and ends with a long flash. Count the short flashes and include the following long flash in the count to obtain the proper code number. For example, three short flashes followed by one long flash indicates Flashout Code Four. The code will continue to repeat itself until the key is turned off. It is recommended that the code be verified by reading it several times. In addition, the first code flashed may be too short because it may have been started in the middle. It should be ignored.

COMPONENT LOCATION

F SERIES AND BRONCO

The RABS consists of the following components:

1. RABS module located in the cab to the right of the brake pedal under the upper dash panel.

2. RABS valve (dual solenoid electro-hydraulic) is located on the left frame rail just behind the number one crossmember.

3. RABS speed sensor located on the rear axle housing and the exciter ring is located inside on the gear carrier.

4. Yellow REAR ANTILOCK warning light is in the instrument cluster.

5. RABS diagnostic connector is located in the cab and clipped on the main instrument panel wiring harness about six inches from the firewall near the parling brake pedal.

6. Diode/resistor element is located

FORD REAR WHEEL ANTILOCK BRAKE SYSTEM DIAGNOSTIC CODES
Codes Are Yellow REAR ANTILOCK Light Flashing—Count Flashes

CODE	SYSTEM PROBLEM
CODE 1	This code is not used and should not occur
CODE 2	Open isolate circuit
CODE 3	Open dump circuit
CODE 4	Check RABS valve
CODE 5	Check RABS valve/4 × 4 indicator switch (4WD)
CODE 6	Check sensor for loose connections, chips, bad exciter ring
CODE 7	No isolate valve self test
CODE 8	No dump valve self test
CODE 9	Check sensor wiring for high resistance
CODE 10	Check sensor wiring for low resistance (shorted)
CODE 11	Check stop lamp switch
CODE 12	Check for low fluid level, bad brake light wiring
CODE 13	RABS module failure—replace
CODE 14	RABS module failure—replace
CODE 15	RABS module failure—replace
CODE 16	This code is not used and should not occur

NOTE: CODES 1 and 16 are not used. When checking resistance in the antilock brake system, always disconnect the battery. Improper resistance readings will occur with the vehicle battery connected.

Component Location F-150—F-350, Bronco

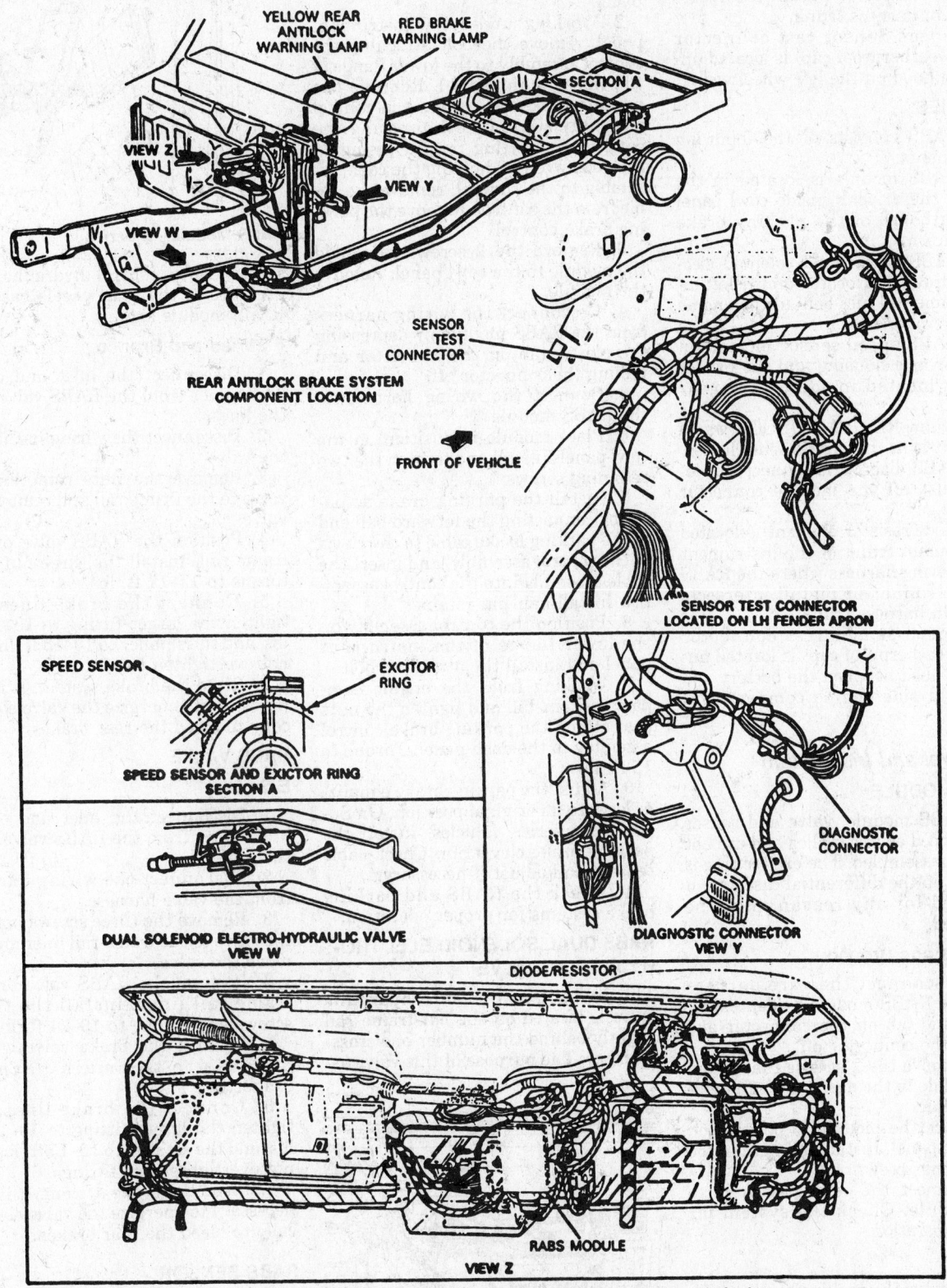

YELLOW REAR
ANTILOCK
WARNING LAMP

RED BRAKE
WARNING LAMP

SECTION A

VIEW Z

VIEW Y

VIEW W

REAR ANTILOCK BRAKE SYSTEM
COMPONENT LOCATION

SENSOR
TEST
CONNECTOR

FRONT OF VEHICLE

SENSOR TEST CONNECTOR
LOCATED ON LH FENDER APRON

SPEED SENSOR

EXCITOR
RING

SPEED SENSOR AND EXICTOR RING
SECTION A

DUAL SOLENOID ELECTRO-HYDRAULIC VALVE
VIEW W

DIAGNOSTIC
CONNECTOR

DIAGNOSTIC CONNECTOR
VIEW Y

DIODE/RESISTOR

RABS MODULE

VIEW Z

RABS Component Location—F Series, Bronco shown—typical

on the main trunk of the instrument panel wiring harness where the RABS module connector pigtail intersects the main harness trunk.

7. Speed Sensor test connector (with weatherproof cap) is located under the hood on the left wheel well.

E SERIES

The RABS consists of the following components:

1. RABS module is located in the cab on the driver's inside cowl panel just outboard of the parking brake mechanism.

2. RABS valve (dual solenoid electro-hydraulic) is located on the left inside frame rail just behind the engine mount crossmember.

3. RABS speed sensor located on the rear axle housing and the exciter ring is located inside on the gear carrier.

4. Yellow REAR ANTILOCK warning light is in the instrument cluster.

5. RABS diagnostic connector is located just off the module connector harness.

6. Diode/resistor element is located on the main trunk of the instrument panel wiring harness where the RABS module connector pigtail intersects the main harness trunk.

7. Speed sensor test connector (with weatherproof cap) is located under the hood between the battery and the right side engine compartment wall.

Removal and Installation

RABS MODULE

The RABS module, valve and sensor are serviced as assemblies and are not to be disassembled. The exciter ring is pressed on the differential case and, if removed for any reason, must be discarded.

F Series and Bronco

1. Disconnect the wire harness from the RABS module by depressing the plastic tab on the connector and pulling the connector off.

2. Remove the 2 screws that retain the module to the dash panel. Remove the module.

3. Place the module in position on the dash panel. Install and tighten the 2 retaining screws.

4. Connect the wiring harness to the module. Check the system for proper operation.

E Series

1. Remove the parking brake actuator assembly. Start by loosening the adjusting nut at the equalizer. On F-Super Duty series vehicles remove the clevis pin at the parking brake. Working from the engine compartment, re-

move the nuts attaching the parking brake control assembly to the dash panel.

2. Working under the instrument panel, remove the bolt attaching the control assembly to the lower flange of the instrument panel. Remove the parking brake cable from the control assembly clevis by compressing the conduit end fitting prongs (using ½ inch box wrench) holding the cable assembly to the control, remove the cable from the control. Remove the parking brake control.

3. Remove the 2 screws that hold the module to the cowl panel. Remove the module.

4. Disconnect the wiring harness from the RABS module by depressing the plastic tab on the connector and pulling the connector off.

5. Connect the wiring harness to the RABS module.

6. Place module in position on the cowl panel. Install and tighten the two retaining screws.

7. Install the parking brake actuator by connecting the forward ball end of the parking brake cable to the clevis of the control assembly, and insert the cable assembly into the control assembly. Install hair pin retainer.

8. Position the control assembly on the lower flange of the instrument panel and install the attaching bolt.

9. Working from the engine compartment, install and tighten the nuts that attach the parking brake control assembly to the dash panel. Torque to 15 ft. lbs.

10. Adjust the parking brake equalizer lever to its original position. On Super Duty series vehicles, install the parking brake clevis pin. Check cable tension and adjust if necessary.

11. Check the RABS and parking brake systems for proper operation.

RABS DUAL SOLENOID ELECTRO-HYDRAULIC VALVE

The dual solenoid electro-hydraulic valve is located on the left frame rail slightly behind the number one crossmember. The purpose of this valve as-

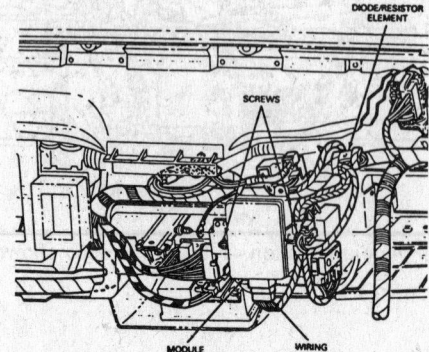

RABS Module – F Series, Bronco

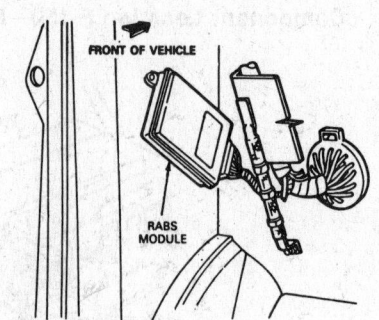

RABS Module – E Series

sembly is to control hydraulic fluid pressure to the rear wheels based on RABS module signals.

F Series and Bronco

1. Disconnect the inlet and outlet brake lines from the RABS valve. Cap the lines.

2. Disconnect the wiring harness to the valve.

3. Remove the nuts retaining the valve to the frame rail and remove the valve.

4. Position the RABS valve on the frame rail. Install the three nuts and torque to 12–17 ft. lbs.

5. Connect the brake lines and tighten the larger fitting to 10–17 ft. lbs. and the smaller to 10–15 ft. lbs. Do not overtighten the fittings.

6. Bleed the brake system. It is not necessary to energize the valve electrically to bleed the rear brakes.

RABS VALVE

E Series

1. Disconnect the inlet and outlet brake lines from the RABS valve. Cap the lines.

2. Disconnect the wiring harness from the valve harness.

3. Remove the three screws holding the valve to the frame rail liner and remove the valve.

4. Position the RABS valve on the frame rail liner, install the three screws and torque to 19–24 ft. lbs.

5. Connect the brake valve wiring harness to the main harness connector.

6. Connect the brake lines and tighten the larger fitting to 10–17 ft. lbs. and the smaller to 10–15 ft. lbs. Do not overtighten the fittings.

7. Bleed the brake system. It is not necessary to energize the valve electrically to bleed the rear brakes.

RABS SENSOR

1. The RABS sensor is located on the rear axle housing. Remove the wiring connector.

2. Remove the sensor hold-down bolt and remove the sensor from the axle housing.

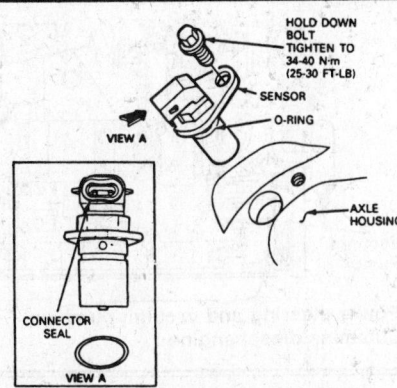

Speed sensor mounts to rear axle housing

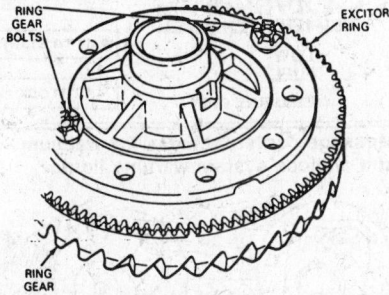

Exciter ring for speed sensor is pressed on gear carrier

3. When installing, clean the axle mounting surface. Use care to keep dirt from entering the axle housing.

4. Inspect and clean the magnetized sensor pole piece to ensure that it is free from loose metal particles which could cause erratic system operation. Inspect the sensor O-ring for damage and replace if necessary.

5. Lightly lubricate the sensor O-ring with motor oil, align the sensor bolt hole and install. Do not apply force to the plastic sensor connector. The sensor flange should slide to the mounting surface. This will insure the air gap setting is between 0.005–0.045 in.

6. Inspect the blue sensor connector seal and replace it if missing or damaged. Push the connector on the sensor.

NOTE: The clearance between the sensor and the excitor ring should be no greater than 0.050 inches. To measure, remove the sensor from the axle carrier, and measure the height of the pole piece from the mounting face of the flange. Sensor pole should be 1.07–1.08 in. Measure the depth from axle housing mounting surface to the top of the exciter teeth. Subtract the two measurements to get the sensor gap.

EXCITER RING

The exciter ring is pressed onto the differential case. To inspect it, remove the sensor from the axle housing.

View the exciter ring teeth through the sensor hole. Rotate the rear axle and check the exciter ring teeth for damage or breakage. Dented or broken teeth could cause the RABS system to function when not required. To replace the exciter ring, the differential case must be removed from the axle housing and the exciter ring pressed off the case. Upon removal, the exciter ring must be discarded. It is not to be reused.

FUSES

Three replaceable fuses are involved with RABS. The fuses are located in the fuse box. A 20 amp fuse protects the total RABS. A 15 amp fuse protects the red BRAKE and yellow REAR ANTILOCK warning lights. Another 15 amp fuse protects the four-way stop lamp cluster.

CHRYSLER CORPORATION

Master Cylinder Service

Chrysler Corporation uses a dual master cylinder which contains a double hydraulic cylinder with two fluid reservoirs and primary and secondary hydraulic pistons. On most models, the master cylinder is assisted by a vacuum booster. The unit is mounted on a 90 degree bracket on some models, directly to the dashboard on others. Hydraulic rear drum brakes with automatic adjusters and self-adjusting front disc brakes are standard on all models.

The front outlet tube of the master cylinder is connected to the hydraulic system control valve and then to the rear brakes. This is referred the secondary system. The rear outlet tube is connected to the control valve and to the front brakes. This system is referred to as the primary system. No residual pressure valves are used in the master cylinder outlets.

During normal operation, the fluid level in the master cylinder will rise during brake operation and fall during release. It is also expected that the fluid level will decrease with brake pad wear. In addition, a trace of brake fluid on the booster shell below the master cylinder mounting flange will often be found as a result of the normal lubricating action of the master cylinder

bore and seal. All of these conditions are considered normal and are not indications the master cylinder needs service.

Two types of master cylinders were used by Chrysler Corporation; 1) a cast iron master cylinder with built-in reservoir and separate proportioning valve and, 2) a master cylinder with a pressed on plastic reservoir. The body of the two-piece master cylinder is made of anodized aluminum and the reservoir is made of nylon. Both compartments of the reservoir are interconnected to permit equalization of the fluid level. However, a sufficient quantity of fluid is retained in the reservoir of the unaffected system to permit operation of that half of the master cylinder even if the other half of the reservoir is drained due to a hydraulic leak.

Use extra care when servicing aluminum master cylinders not to cross thread brake line fittings and do not overtighten any threaded connection.

In the event of a front brake system malfunction the proportioning valve with a bypass feature allows full hydraulic pressure to the rear brake system.

Disassembly and Assembly

The manufacturer does not recommend that either the cast iron or the aluminum master cylinder be overhauled, but replaced only. Do not attempt to hone the bore of the aluminum master cylinder or the hard anodized surface will be removed.

On the aluminum master cylinders, the plastic reservoir may be replaced using the following procedure:

1. Clean the outside of the master cylinder and remove the caps. Drain and discard remaining brake fluid.

2. Hold the master cylinder in a soft-jaw vise and grasp the plastic reservoir. Firmly rock reservoir from side to side to and remove it from the master cylinder housing. Don't pry the reservoir off with a tool that could damage the plastic body.

3. Remove and discard the reservoir grommets from the master cylinder body.

4. To install, lubricate the new

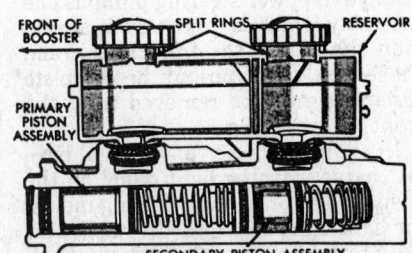

Chrysler aluminum master cylinder

Removing plastic reservoir from master cylinder housing

grommets with brake fluid and install in the master cylinder body.

5. Place the reservoir in position. Make sure it is positioned properly and that the lettering can be read from the left side of the master cylinder. Install by rocking the reservoir while pressing down. Seat the reservoir until the bottom of the reservoir touches the top of the grommets.

Brake Booster Service

Chrysler Corporation models covered here are equipped with vacuum boosters.

Under normal operating conditions, with brakes released, a vacuum suspended booster operates with vacuum on both sides of its diaphragm (or both diaphragms in a tandem diaphragm unit). When the brakes are applied, air at atmospheric pressure is admitted to one side of the diaphragm (or both diaphragms in a tandem diaphragm unit) to provide the power assist.

Brake boosters used by Chrysler Corporation are not repairable and if defective, the booster must be replaced as a unit, including the check valve. Do not remove the check valve.

Brake Booster Vacuum Pump

On gasoline engine vehicles, engine vacuum is used to power the vacuum booster brake. On diesel engines, there is not enough vacuum available for vacuum booster brake operation.

On diesel engine vehicles, vacuum is supplied from a pump. On Chrysler Corporation vehicles equipped with Cummins Turbo Diesels, the vacuum pump and power steering pump is one assembly which is driven from a common shaft from the front gear train. To service either pump, the complete assembly must be removed from the front gear housing.

In addition, these vehicles will have an engine warning light panel on the dash which contains 5 warning indicator lights: Brake, Water In Fuel, Wait To Start, Anti-Lock and Low Fuel. The Brake light is connected to a sen-

sor that monitors vacuum in the brake booster system. The Brake light when lit indicates low vacuum. If this light comes on, the brake system must be serviced.

NOTE: The brake light will also be activated when the parking brake is on or there is a hydraulic brake failure.

The vacuum pump provides vacuum for the brake booster and dash controllers. The vacuum sensor is mounted under the left hood hinge in the engine compartment. Vacuum is supplied by a hose Teed off the check valve in the brake booster. The sensor will activate the brake light on the warning light panel in 10 seconds or less when the vacuum drops to 8.5 in. Hg or less in the brake system.

Removal and Installation

1. Remove the vacuum pump and power steering pump assembly by removing the 2 bolts which should need an 18mm wrench.
2. Clean the gasket from the engine rear cover.
3. Install the pump assembly with a new gasket. Torque the bolts to 57 ft. lbs.

Disassembly and Assembly

1. Before starting pump disassembly, make a pin 2 in. long and 0.312 in. diameter. Use an 8mm bolt or a piece of drill rod. This pin must be hard so make it from a 10.9 grade metric bolt or at least an SAE Grade 8 capscrew.
2. Insert the pin into the pump shaft and screw a M14-2mm threaded capscrew in against the pin.
3. Tighten the capscrew against the pin to draw off the gear/eccentric/bearing assembly off of the power steering pump shaft.
4. Inspect the gear for excessive wear or damage. If the gear/eccentric is not damaged, do not separate them. If the gear is damaged, use a press to press the eccentric out of the gear. Use a flat plate over the new gear and press it onto the eccentric until it bottoms.
5. Inspect the bearing, turning it by hand. If the bearing looks good, and feels smooth to turn, do not separate them. If the bearing/eccentric is bad, press the eccentric out of the bearing, using the appropriate size socket or tool that will press only on the inner race of the bearing. Press it on until it bottoms.
6. With a 15mm wrench, remove the 4 nuts and separate the power steering pump from the vacuum pump housing. Remove the two short pushrods from the housing. Inspect the pushrods. They should move smoothly, but should not move side to side.

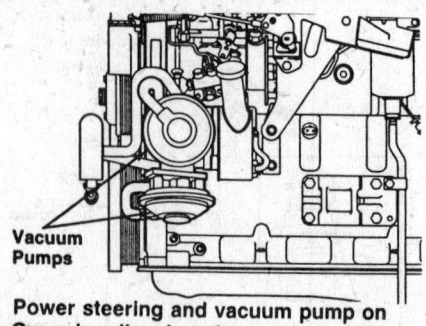

Power steering and vacuum pump on Cummins diesel engine

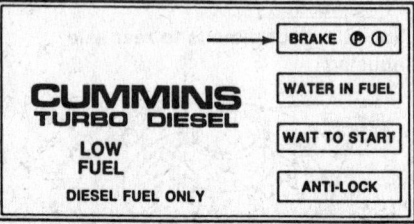

Message center includes low vacuum and antilock system warning lights

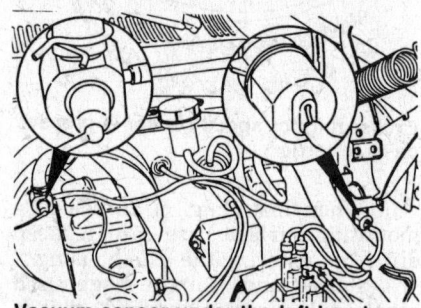

Vacuum sensor under the left hood hinge is supplied by line from booster check valve

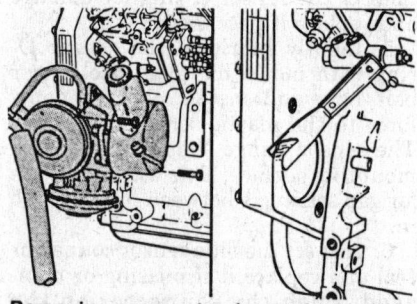

Removing power steering and vacuum pump assembly from engine's gear drive

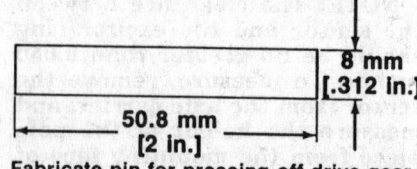

Fabricate pin for pressing off drive gear

7. With a 10mm wrench, remove the diaphragm assemblies from the housing. If the diaphragms are bad, they must be replaced as a unit. Remove and discard the O-rings from the center bore and push rod bores.

8. Clean all parts and dry with compressed air.

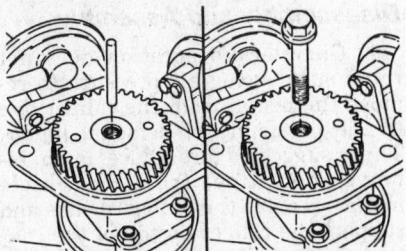

Insert pin, tighten capscrew against pin to draw gear assembly from pump shaft

9. Install the two spacers on the studs on the back of the power steering pump.

10. Install the vacuum pump housing onto the power steering pump using a new O-ring lubricated with engine oil. Install the four retaining nuts and with a 15mm wrench, torque to 18 ft. lbs.

11. Install the gear/eccentric/bearing assembly by pulling it onto the power steering shaft with a ⅜–18 thread capscrew with a flat washer threaded into the power steering pump shaft. Pull it on until it bottoms. Remove capscrew and washer.

NOTE: This is a press fit and will require a minimum of SAE Grade 8 capscrew for thread strength.

12. Lubricate the pushrods with engine oil and install then in the housing. Install new O-rings, also lubricated with engine oil.

13. With a 10mm wrench, install the

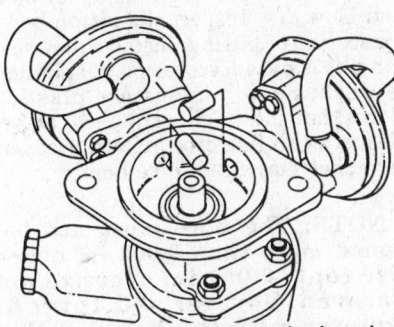

Remove the pushrods from the housing

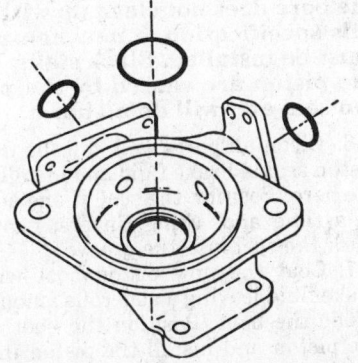

Remove vacuum diaphragm assemblies, then O-rings

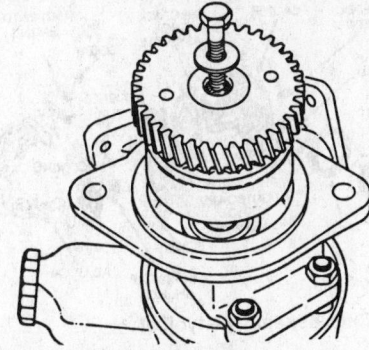

Use ⅜-18 Grade 8 capscrew to draw assembly onto pump shaft

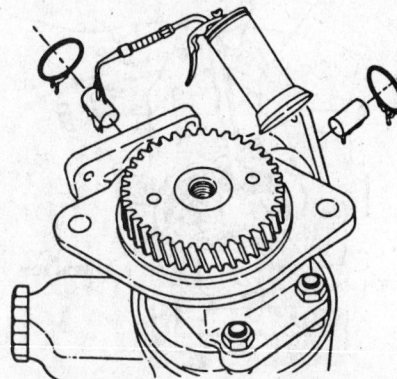

Lube pushrods and O-rings with engine oil at assembly

diaphragm assemblies. Torque to 7 ft. lbs.

14. Install the assembly to the engine with new gaskets. Torque bolts to 57 ft. lbs.

Combination Valve

All models have a hydraulic system control valve in the brake system. The valve is usually mounted on the frame rail below the master cylinder. The control valve assembly in B-150 and B-250 models combines a brake warning switch with a hold-off and proportioning valve assembly. A brake warning switch and hold-off valve assembly are combined and used on B-350 models. Hold-off and Proportioning valves are used because of different braking characteristics between disc and drum brakes.

A height sensing proportioning valve regulates the front to rear braking balance based upon vehicle load conditions. The valve senses vehicle loads through variations in rear suspension height. With a light load on the rear axle, the valve reduces hydraulic pressure to the rear brakes. As the load increases, more hydraulic pressure is released to the rear brakes.

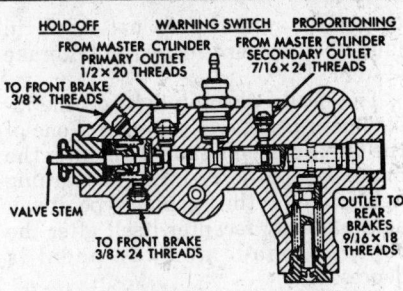

Combination warning switch/hold-off/proportioning valve assembly—Typical

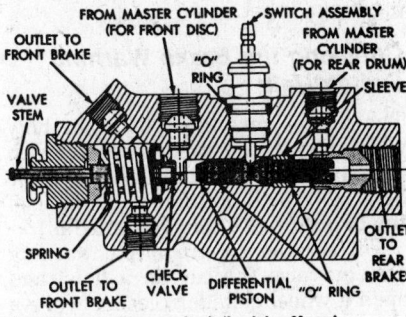

Brake warning switch/hold-off valve

HOLD-OFF VALVE

The hold-off valve section of the combination valve holds off pressure to the front disc brakes to allow the rear drum brake shoes to overcome the return springs and begin to contact the drums. This valve keeps the output pressure to the front brakes in the 3–30 psi range until the hold-off pressure is reached (117 psi) and then blends back to give full output pressure to the front brakes under heavy brake applications. This feature helps keep the front brakes from locking under light pedal applications when driving on icy surfaces. The hold-off valve has no effect on front brake pressure during hard stops.

Checking the Hold-Off Valve

A visual check will show that the valve stem extends slightly when the brakes are applied and retracts when the brakes are released.

In case of a hold-off valve malfunction, remove the valve and install a new combination valve assembly.

BRAKE WARNING SWITCH

The hydraulic brake system is split. The front brakes are part of one system and the rear brakes are part of the other. Both systems are routed through, but hydraulically separated by the pressure differential swicth. The function of this switch is to alert the driver to a malfunction in one of the hydraulic systems. Since the brake system is split, a failure in one part of

the brake system does not result in failure of the entire hydraulic brake system.

The brake warning light on the instrument panel will come on if one of the brake systems should fail after the brake pedal is depressed. The warning light switch is the latching type. It will automatically recenter itself after the repair is made and the pedal is depressed.

The instrument panel bulb can be checked each time the ignition switch is turned to **ON, START** or the parking brake is set.

Checking the Brake Warning Switch Unit

The brake warning light is lit only when the parking brake is applied with the ignition key turned **ON**. The same light will also illuminate should one of the two service brake systems fail.

To test the service brake warning system, raise the car on a hoist and open a wheel cylinder bleeder while a helper depresses the brake pedal and watches the warning light. If the light fails to light, check for a burned out bulb, disconnected socket, or a broken or disconnected wire at the switch. If the bulb is not burned out and the wire continuity is uninterupted check the service brake warning switch operation with a test lamp between the switch terminal and a voltage source.

If the light still fails to light, disconnect the brake tubes from the valve assembly and install a new valve assembly. If a new is installed, bleed the system. The warning switch is not serviced separately. Do not remove the swicth or attempt to repair.

After repairing and bleeding the brake system applying the brakes with moderate force will hydraulically recenter the valve's piston and automatically turn off the warning light. Do not disassemble to reset the piston.

Caliper Service

Chrysler Corporation calipers are one-piece castings with the inboard side containing the piston bore. A square cut rubber seal is located in a groove in the piston bore which provides the hydraulic seal between the piston and the cylinder wall.

As the brake pedal is pressed, hydraulic pressure is applied against the piston. This pressure pushes the inboard brake lining against the inboard braking surface of the rotor. As the force increases against the rotor, the caliper assembly moves inboard and provides a clamping action on the rotor.

When brake pressure is released,

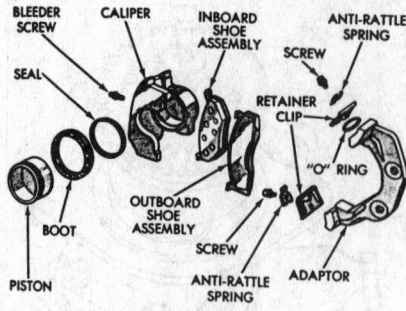

Caliper assembly—typical

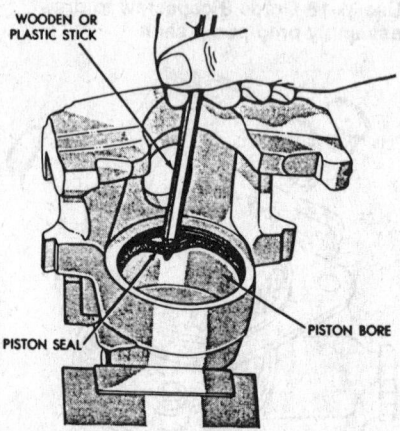

Remove piston seal without scratching bore

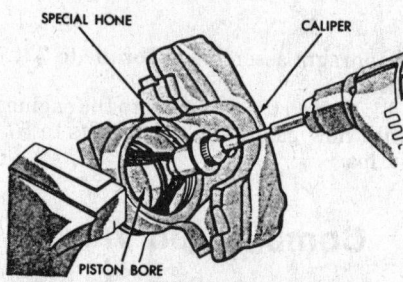

Clean up bore with light honing

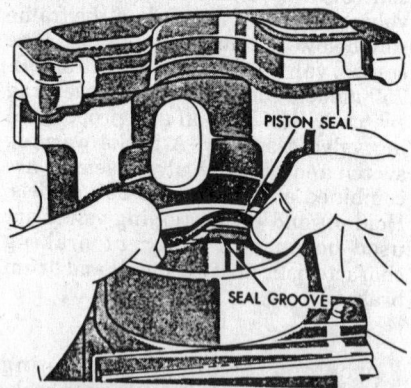

Lubricate piston seal with brake fluid and install

the piston seal returns to its normal position, pulling the piston back into the caliper bore. This creates a running clearance between the inner brake lining and rotor.

Disassembly and Assembly

1. Chrysler Corporation does not recommend using air pressure to remove the piston from the caliper due to the possibility of personal injury. Their suggested procedure is to remove the caliper from its vehicle mount, remove the outboard shoe and support the caliper on top of the control arm on shop towels to absorb brake fluid. Carefully depress the brake pedal and allow hydraulic pressure to push the piston out of the bore.

NOTE: The brake pedal will fall away when the piston has passed the bore opening. Prop the brake pedal to any position below the first inch of pedal travel to prevent loss of brake fluid. If both front caliper pistons are to be removed, disconnect the flexible brake line at the frame bracket after removing the first piston. Plug the brake line to remove the piston from the opposite caliper.

2. Remove the flexible brake line from the caliper.

3. Mount the caliper in a soft-jaw vise. Do not use too much pressure or the bore will be distorted and the piston will bind.

4. Remove the dust boot and, using a small, pointed wooden stick, work the piston seal out of its groove in the caliper bore. Do not use any metal tool which might nick or scratch the bore. Discard the seal.

5. Clean all parts well using alcohol and blow dry. Inspect the piston bore for scoring or pitting. Install a new piston if it is pitted, scored or the plating is worn. Some pistons are plastic. Bores that show light scratches can be cleaned with fine crocus cloth. Deeper scratches may need to be hones.

NOTE: The bore must not be honed more than 0.002 in. over-size (only 0.001 in. oversize on Caravan, Voyager and Town & Country models). Measure the bore accurately before honing. If the bore does not clean up within this specification, a new housing must be installed. Black stains on the piston are caused by the piston seal and will do no harm.

6. Clean all parts well, dip the new piston seal in brake fluid and install in the bore. Position the seal at one area at a time and, using fingers, gently work the seal into the groove.

7. Coat the new piston boot with brake fluid leaving a generous amount inside the boot. Position the boot on the piston and install the piston into the bore, pushing it past the piston seal until it bottoms in the bore.

8. Position the dust boot and with a circular driver, seal into the caliper.

9. Install the flexible brake hose with new seals.

Wheel Cylinder Service

The rear brakes are drum type with internal expanding shoes. The rear brakes are of the single anchor type, mounted to the same anchor and actuated by 1 wheel cylinder. The wheel cylinder has 2 pistons. Brake adjustments are automatic and are made during reverse brake applications.

Wheel cylinders may need reconditioning or replacement whenever the brake shoes are replaced or when required to correct a leak condition. Leaks which coat the boot and the cylinder with fluid, or result in a dropped reservoir fluid level, or dampen and stain the brake linings are dangerous. Such leaks can cause the brakes to grab or fail and should be immediately corrected. A leakage, not immediately apparent, can be detected by pulling back the cylinder boot. A small amount of fluid seepage dampening the interior of the boot is normal. However, a dripping boot is not. Unless other conditions causing a brake to pull, grab or drag become obvious, the wheel cylinder is suspect and should and should be included in general reconditioning.

Cylinder binding may be caused by rust, deposits, grime, or swollen cups due to fluid contamination, or by a cup wedged into an excessive piston clearance.

Hydraulic system parts should not be allowed to come into contact with oil or grease, neither should those be handled with greasy hands. Even a trace of any petroleum based product is sufficient to cause damage to the rubber parts.

Disassembly and Assembly

1. Remove the brake bleeder screw.
2. Remove the dust boots, allow any brake fluid to drain out.
3. Remove the pistons, seals and inner spring.
4. Inspect the bore for scoring and corrosion. The inside of the bore may be cleaned with fine crocus cloth. If bore is scored, replace cylinder. Black stains on the cylinder walls are caused by the piston cups and will not impair operation of the cylinder. Clean the cylinder with alcohol or brake fluid.
5. Lubricate the seals with brake fluid and install. Cup lips should always face inward. Install the spring assembly and seals.

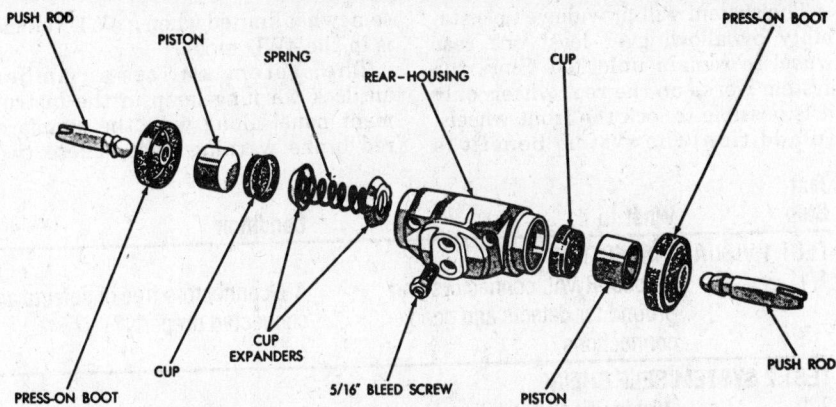

Rear wheel cylinder for 11 and 12 inch brakes—typical

6. Carefully install the pistons and dust boots.
7. Install the bleeder screw.

Anti-Lock Braking Systems

Despite advances in brake design over the years, even the best systems in use can still lock up during certain road conditions, such as wet road surfaces. When the brakes lock up, the driver can lose control of the vehicle, because a locked wheel cannot absorb any cornering or lateral forces, and steering is lost. It is impossible to brake to a maximum and at the same time steer the vehicle when the front wheels are locked. If the back wheels are locked the vehicle will become unstable and start to slide.

While many different ways have been tried over the years to solve this problem, mechanical sensors could not provide sufficient information about wheel rotation speed and mechanical control units could not operate the brakes fast enough to prevent brake lockup.

The growth of the electronics industry has allowed small computers (microprocessors) to be reduced in both size and cost. Coupled with fast reacting electronic sensors, anti-lock braking has become more reliable with widespread application.

REAR WHEEL ANTI-LOCK BRAKE SYSTEM

Chrysler Corporation's Rear Wheel Antilock brake system (RWAL) is designed to prevent rear wheel lockup under heavy braking conditions. Antilock braking allows a vehicle to stop without locking the wheels and therefore maintains directional stability.

The RWAL system uses a standard master cylinder and booster arrangement with a vertical split hydraulic circuit. An electronic control module,

rear wheel speed sensor, and a dual solenoid control valve (hydraulic valve) are the major components added to this system. No hydraulic pumps are used. Braking pressure comes directly from pushing on the brake pedal.

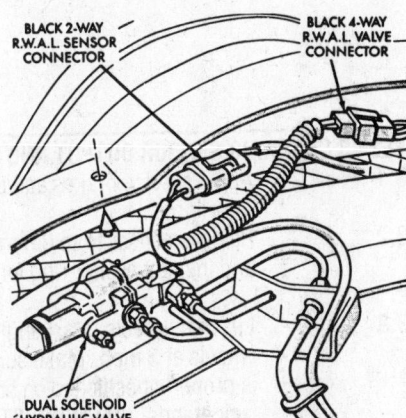

RWAL connection locations—typical

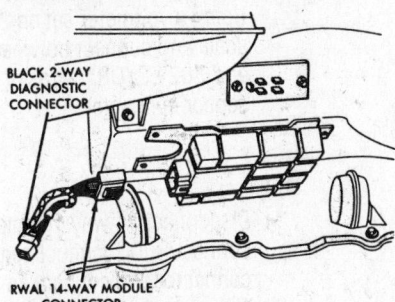

RWAL electronic brake control module—typical

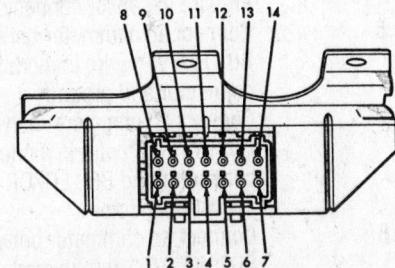

RWAL electronic brake control module pin locations

The system will provide vehicle stability by allowing at least one rear wheel to remain unlocked. Since the system works on the rear wheels only it is possible to lock the front wheels. In addition, the system benefit is somewhat limited when a 4WD vehicle is in the 4WD mode.

The system utilizes an amber antilock warning lamp in the instrument panel along with the standard red brake warning light. These two lights work together to notify the driver the driver that the system is working correctly. These lamps are also used to blink fault codes for system diagnosis.

Test Step	What to do	Condition	Yes	No
TEST 1 VISUAL INSPECTION				
1.1	Inspect RWAL connectors and ground for defects and good connections	Are connectors free of defects and connected properly?	Go to Test 2	Repair or connect terminals as required
TEST 2 SYSTEM SELF CHECK				
2.1	Turn ignition switch to run position	Both lamps illuminate for 2 seconds then go out as system performs self check	Go to Test 3	Choose another condition
		Antilock and brake lamp stay on	Go to Test 6	Choose another condition
		Antilock lamp off and will not self check, brake lamp checked OK	Go to Test 7	Choose another condition
		Brake lamp on, antilock lamp off and does self check	Go to Test 8	Choose another condition
		Antilock and brake lamps flashing	Go to Test 9	Choose another condition
		Brake lamp off, antilock lamp on, antilock lamp does self check	Go to Test 10	Choose another condition
TEST 3 CHECKING SENSOR OUTPUT AND PHYSICAL CONDITION				
3.1	Apply service brakes and check stop lights	Stop lamps illuminate	Go to Test 3.2	Repair stop lamp circuit
3.2	Remove sensor from differential and inspect exciter ring for damage	Exciter ring in good condition	Reinstall sensor. Go to Test 3.3	Replace exciter ring and retest system
3.3	Lift rear wheels, start engine, run wheels at 5 mph. Make sure vehicle is properly positioned on hoist or jack stands. **WARNING: STAY CLEAR OF ROTATING WHEELS.** Using a voltmeter set on 2 volt AC scale and connect between B01 PK and B02 LG/OR* wires of the sensor connector	Is voltage 650 MV (RMS) or greater?	Go to Test 5	Go to Test 3.4
3.4		Has sensor been replaced?	Go to Test 3.5	Replace sensor and go to Test 3.3
3.5	Disconnect 14 way module connector. Disconnect sensor connector and connect an ohmmeter between B01 RD/VT* wire in module connector and B01 PK wire in sensor connector	Is there continuity?	Go to Test 3.6	Repair open circuit
3.6	Connect an ohmmeter between B01 RD/VT* wire in module connector and ground	Is there continuity?	Repair circuit for a short to ground	Go to Test 3.7
3.7	Connect an ohmmeter between B02 WT/VT* wire in module connector and B02 LG/OR wire in sensor connector	Is there continuity?	Repair circuit for an open circuit	Go to Test 3.8
3.8	Connect an ohmmeter between B02 WT/VT* wire in module connector and ground	Is there a short to ground?	Repair circuit for short to ground	Go to Test 4

Test Step	What to do	Condition	Yes	No
TEST 4 CHECKING SENSOR GAP				
4.1	Remove sensor from differential. Measure height of sensor pole piece from mounting face of sensor (should be 1.07″–1.08″). Measure top of exciter ring teeth from sensor mounting face on differential (should be 1.085″–1.12″). Subtract measurements as shown to obtain sensor gap. Gap must be a minimum of 0.005″ and a maximum of 0.05″	Was gap within specifications?	Go to Test 5	Go to Test 4.2
4.2	Look at sensor measurement from Test 4.1 (should be 1.07″–1.08″)	Was sensor measurement within specifications?	Repair differential and retest system	Replace sensor and retest system
TEST 5 CHECKING FOR BRAKE MECHANICAL PROBLEMS				
5.1	Check rear brakes for mechanical problems such as grabbing, locking or pulling	Are the rear brakes functioning properly?	Replace module and retest system	Repair mechanical problem and retest system
TEST 6 CHECKING THE DIAGNOSTIC CONNECTOR GROUND				
6.1	Locate the black 2-way diagnostic connector below RWAL module. Connect a jumper wire between the diagnostic connector and ground	Is there a flashout code?	Go to Test 11	Go to 6.2
6.2	Turn ignition off. Disconnect 14-way connector from module and connect an ohmmeter between the BK* in the 14-way connector and the BK* in the 2-way diagnostic connector	Is there continuity?	Go to Test 6.3	Repair open circuit and retest system
6.3	Check brake fluid level in master cylinder reservoir	Is brake fluid level correct?	Go to Test 6.4	Find and repair leak and retest system
6.4	Reconnect 14-way module connector. Disconnect connector from the pressure differential switch. Turn ignition to run position	Do both antilock lamp and brake lamp stay on?	Go to Test 6.5	Check brake system for air in lines or mechanical damage
6.5		Does the vehicle have a diesel engine?	Go to Test 6.6	Go to Test 6.7
6.6	Disconnect harness connector from vacuum warning switch. Turn the ignition switch to the run position	Do both lamps stay on?	Go to Test 6.7	Check complete vehicle vacuum system, repair as required and retest system
6.7	Disconnect 14-way module connector. Turn ignition switch to the run position	Are both antilock lamp and brake lamp off?	Go to Test 6.8	Choose another condition
		Antilock lamp on, brake lamp off	Repair AT1 orange wire for short to ground between module and antilock lamp	Repair short to ground in differential switch sensor wiring, B01 PK and B02 LG/OR
6.8	Remove and inspect antilock fuse	Is fuse open?	Check and repair all circuits fuse is protecting. Replace fuse	Go to Test 6.9

Test Step	What to do	Condition	Yes	No
TEST 6 CHECKING THE DIAGNOSTIC CONNECTOR GROUND				
6.9	Connect a voltmeter between pin 3 RD/YL wire of 14-way module connector and ground	Is voltage greater than 9 volts?	Go to Test 6.10	Repair the D1 RD/YL wire for an open
6.10	Remove and inspect the stop lamp fuse.	Is the fuse open?	Check and repair all circuits fuse is protecting for shorts and replace fuse	Go to Test 6.11
6.11	Connect a voltmeter between pin 9 of the 14-way module connector and ground	Is voltage greater than 9 volts?	Replace module and retest system	Repair the D3B PK/DB* wire for open circuit.
TEST 7 CHECKING MODULE GROUND AND POWER				
7.1	Make sure module connector is fully-plugged into module	Is connector plugged in?	Go to Test 7.2	Plug connector in and retest system
7.2	Disconnect battery and 14-way module connector. With an ohmmeter set on 200 ohm scale, check resistance between pin 10 BK/LG wire on the 14-way harness connector and ground	Is resistance less than 1 ohm?	Go to Test 7.3	Repair H40 BK/LG for an open or damaged circuit
7.3	Remove and inspect antilock lamp fuse	Is fuse open?	Check and repair all circuits fuse is protecting for shorts and replace fuse	Go to Test 7.4
7.4	Connect battery and turn ignition to run position. With a voltmeter set on 20 volt DC scale, check voltage between Pin 2 Orange wire of the 14-way module connector and ground	Is voltage less than 9 volts?	Go to Test 7.5	Replace the module and retest system
7.5	Check antilock bulb	Is bulb open?	Replace bulb and retest system	Repair AT1 orange wire for open circuit between pin 2 and fuse
TEST 8 CHECKING PARKING SYSTEM AND MODULE				
8.1	Turn ignition to run position. Pull lever to release parking brake	Does the brake lamp go off?	Disregard failure, retest antilock and brake lamp for 2 second self check	Go to Test 8.2
8.2	Pull park brake release lever with one hand and pull pedal up with other hand	Did brake lamp go off	Repair park brake mechanism or switch	Go to Test 8.3
8.3	Disconnect black 1-way park brake switch connector	Did brake lamp go off	Adjust or replace park brake switch and retest system	Go to Test 8.4
8.4	Disconnect 14-way module connector	Did brake lamp go off?	Replace module and retest system	Repair P5 BK/GY wire for a short to ground

Test Step	What to do	Condition	Yes	No
TEST 9 CHECKING FOR INTERMITTENT PROBLEMS				
9.1	Disconnect 14-way module connector. With a voltmeter set on 20 volt DC scale, check voltage between pin 3 RD/YL wire on the 14-way module connector and ground. Turn ignition to run position and shake the instrument panel harness	Is voltage steady at 9 volts?	Go to Test 9.2	Repair D1 RD/YL for open circuit
9.2	Disconnect battery, set ohmmeter on 200 scale and connect between pin 12 BK wire of the 14-way module connector and ground, then shake the instrument panel harness	Is resistance 100K or greater and steady?	Go to Test 9.3	Repair DK/BK/* wire for a short to ground
9.3	With ohmmeter set on 200 ohm scale, connect between Pin 10 BK/LG wire of the 14-way module connector and ground, then shake instrument panel harness.	Is resistance steady at 1 ohm?	Replace module and retest system	Repair open circuit in H40 BK/LG
TEST 10 CHECKING FOR OPEN OR DISCONNECTED PARK BRAKE SWITCH CONNECTOR				
10.1	Make sure the P5 BK/GY wire at the park brake switch is connected	Is P5 wire connected to park brake switch?	Go to Test 10.2	Connect and retest system
10.2	Disconnect park brake switch connector. Disconnect message center black 6-way connector. Connect an ohmmeter between P5 BK/BY wire in both connectors	Is there continuity?	Go to Test 10.3	Repair P5 BK/GY wire for open circuit
10.3	Inspect instrument cluster printed circuit board for damage	Is printed circuit board damaged?	Replace printed circuit board	Replace brake warning lamp bulb
TEST 11 FLASHCODES				
11.1	Connect a jumper wire between the diagnostic connector and ground. Count the flashes including the long flash that starts the flash code count. Choose the proper condition	Antilock lamp and brake lamp flash 1 time	Go to Test 12	
		Antilock lamp and brake lamp flash 2 times.	G to Test 13	
		Antilock lamp and brake lamp flash 3 times.	G to Test 14	
		Antilock lamp and brake lamp flash 4 times.	G to Test 15	
		Antilock lamp and brake lamp flash 5 times.	G to Test 16	
		Antilock lamp and brake lamp flash 6 times.	G to Test 17	
		Antilock lamp and brake lamp flash 7 times.	G to Test 18	
		Antilock lamp and brake lamp flash 8 times.	G to Test 19	
		Antilock lamp and brake lamp flash 9 times.	G to Test 20	
		Antilock lamp and brake lamp flash 10 times.	G to Test 21	
		Antilock lamp and brake lamp flash 11 times.	G to Test 22	

Test Step	What to do	Condition	Yes	No
TEST 11 FLASHCODES				
		Antilock lamp and brake lamp flash 12 times.	G to Test 23	
		Antilock lamp and brake lamp flash 13 times.	G to Test 24	
		Antilock lamp and brake lamp flash 14 times.	G to Test 25	
		Antilock lamp and brake lamp flash 15 times.	G to Test 26	
		Antilock lamp and brake lamp flash 16 times.	G to Test 27	
TEST 12 ONE FLASH				
12.1	One flash code should not occur. Perform flashcode procedure several times	Are you still getting code 1?	Go to Test 5	Go to Test 11
TEST 13 TWO FLASHES				
13.1	Disconnect battery and 14-way module connector. Set an ohmmeter on 200 ohm scale and connect between pin 1 LG wire of the 14-way module connector and ground	Does the circuit have over 6 ohms?	Go to test 13.2	Replace the module and retest system
13.2	Disconnect valve harness connector from valve connector. Connect an ohmmeter between B09 GY/WT of harness connector and ground	Is resistance greater than 1 ohm?	Repair B09 GY/WT wire for an open circuit or high resistance. Check for contaminated or loose connector pins and retest system	Go to Test 13.3
13.3	Connect an ohmmeter between IS1 LG/* and B09 GY/WT wires in the 4-way black valve connector	Does circuit have over 6 ohms?	Replace antilock valve and retest system	Repair the IS1 LG/* for open circuit from valve to computer module and retest system
TEST 14 THREE FLASHES				
14.4	Disconnect battery. Remove 14-way module harness connector from module. Set ohmmeter on 200 ohm scale and connect to pin 8 DS1 WT/BR and ground	Does circuit have over 3 ohms?	Go to Test 14.2	Replace module and retest system
14.2	Disconnect the 4-way valve harness connector. Connect an ohmmeter between DS1 WT and B09 GY/NT wires in valve connector	Does circuit have over 3 ohms?	Replace antilock valve and retest system	Repair DS1 WT wire for open between module connector and valve connector

Test Step	What to do	Condition	Yes	No
TEST 15 FOUR FLASHES				
15.1	Disconnect the 4-way valve harness connector from valve connector. Set ohmmeter on 20K scale and connect between VS1 LB wire in valve body and ground	Is resistance greater than 10K ohms?	Go to Test 15.2	Replace the antilock valve and retest system
15.2	Connect an ohmmeter between VS1 LB and B09 GY/WY wires in the valve connector	Is resistance greater than 10K ohms?	Go to Test 15.3	Replace the antilock valve and retest system
15.3	Disconnect battery. Disconnect the 14-way module harness connector from module. Set ohmmeter on 200K scale and connect to pin 11, VS1 LB of 14-way connector and ground	Is resistance greater than 100K ohms?	Replace module and retest system	Repair VS1 LB wire for a short to ground between valve and module. Retest system
TEST 16 FIVE FLASHES				
16.1	Did the failure occur in 2 wheel drive mode?		Go to Test 16.2	Go to Test 16.3
16.2	Disconnect 14-way module connector from module to deactivate antilock system. Drive the vehicle in 2 wheel drive mode and make normal and safe stops to determine the condition of the rear brakes	Are the brakes functioning normally?	Replace the antilock valve and retest system	Repair rear brakes and retest system
16.3	Disconnect 14-way module connector from module. Turn ignition key to run position. Shift into 4 wheel drive. Set a voltmeter to 20 vdc and connect between pin 4, X4 LG/BR wire and ground	Is voltage greater than 1 volt?	Repair X4 wire for an open or 4 wheel drive indicator switch. Retest system	Replace antilock valve and retest system
TEST 17 SIX FLASHES				
17.1	Recheck flashcode after driving vehicle	Antilock light and brake light flash 6 times	Go to Test 17.2	Go to Test 11
17.2	Disconnect battery. Disconnect 14-way module connector. Set ohmmeter on 200 ohm scale and connect between pin 13, B02 WT/VT and pin 14, B01 RD/VT of harness connector. Shake antilock wiring harness from differential to module	Is resistance constant at 1000–2000 ohms?	Go to Test 17.3	Repair circuit. Retest system
17.3	Remove sensor from the differential and inspect for build up of metal chips on sensor pole piece	Are metal chips present?	Drain and clean differential. Check exciter ring for broken or chipped teeth. Retest system	Go to Test 17.4
17.4	Look into sensor hole in differential and rotate exciter ring and check for damage (missing or bent teeth)	Is exciter ring intact?	Go to 17.5	Replace exciter ring. Retest system
17.5	Reinstall sensor. Disconnect 2-way RWAL sensor connector. With a voltmeter on 2 volt scale, connect between B01 PK and B2 LG/OR wires of sensor connector. Raise rear wheels off floor and run at 5 mph. **WARNING: STAY CLEAR OF ROTATING WHEELS**	Is voltage greater than 650 MV and steady?	Replace module. Retest system	Replace sensor. Recheck sensor output. Retest system

Test Step	What to do	Condition	Yes	No
TEST 18 SEVEN FLASHES				
18.1	Disconnect 4-way valve harness connector from valve connector. Connect an ohmmeter between IS1 LG/* and B09 GY/WT wire in valve connector	Is resistance less than 3 ohms?	Replace antilock valve. Retest system	Go to Test 18.2
18.2	Disconnect battery. Disconnect 4-way valve harness connector from valve connector. Disconnect 14-way module harness connector from module. Set ohmmeter on 20K ohms scale and connect between Pin 1, IS1 LG/* wire in harness connector and ground	Is resistance greater than 20K ohms?	Replace module. Retest system	Repair IS1 LG/* for a short between antilock valve and module. Retest system
TEST 19 EIGHT FLASHES				
19.1	Disconnect 4-way valve harness from valve connector. Set ohmmeter on 200 ohm scale and connect between DS1 WT and B09 GY/WT wires in valve connector	Is resistance less than 1 ohm?	Replace antilock valve. Retest system	Go to Test 19.2
19.2	Disconnect battery. Disconnect 4-way valve connector. Disconnect 14-way module connector. Set ohmmeter on 20K ohm scale and connect between pin 8, DS1 WT/BR and ground	Is resistance greater than 20K ohms?	Replace module	Repair DS1 WT/BR for a short to ground between antilock valve and module. Retest system
TEST 20 NINE FLASHES				
20.1	Disconnect 2-way sensor harness connector from sensor on differential housing. Set ohmmeter on 20K scale and connect to B01 PK and B02 LG/OR wire on sensor	Is resistance greater than 2500 ohms?	Replace sensor. Recheck resistance. **Make sure seal is in place between sensor and connector.** Retest system	Go to Test 20.2
20.2	Reconnect sensor harness **making sure seal is in place.** Disconnect battery. Disconnect 14-way module connector. Connect an ohmmeter between pin 13, B02 WT/VT and pin 14, B01 RD/VT wires in module harness connector	Is resistance greater than 2500 ohms?	Repair B02 WT/VT and B01 RD/VT for open circuits between the module and sensor. Retest system	Replace computer module. When reconnecting sensor, **make sure seal is in place.** Retest system
TEST 21 TEN FLASHES				
21.1	Set ohmmeter on 20K ohm scale. Disconnect 2-way sensor connector from sensor on differential. Connect an ohmmeter between B01 PK and B02 LG/OR wires on sensor	Is resistance less then 1000 ohms?	Replace sensor. Recheck resistance. **Make sure seal is in place between sensor and connector.** Retest system	Go to Test 21.2

Test Step	What to do	Condition	Yes	No
TEST 21 TEN FLASHES				
21.2	Disconnect battery. Disconnect 14-way module. Connect an ohmmeter between pin 14, B01 RD/VT and ground	Is resistance greater than 20K ohms?	Go to Test 21.3	Repair B01 RD/VT circuit between the module and sensor. When reconnecting sensor, **make sure seal is in place.** Retest system
21.3	Connect an ohmmeter between pin 13, B02 WT/VT and pin 14 B01 RD/VT wire in module harness connector	Is resistance greater than 20K ohms?	Replace module. Retest system.	Repair B01 RD/VT and B02 WT/VT circuit. When reconnecting sensor, **make sure seal is in place.** Retest system
TEST 22 ELEVEN FLASHES				
22.1	Recheck flash code after driving vehicle at 35 mph or greater.	Antilock light and brake light flash 11 times	Go to Test 22.1	Go to Test 11
22.2	Apply vehicle service brakes and check vehicle stop lights	Are stop lights operating correctly?	Go to Test 22.3	Repair the stop lamp circuit. Retest system
22.3	Turn ignition switch off. Disconnect 14-way module connector from module. Connect a voltmeter between pin 7, D4 WT of harness connector and ground while stepping on brake pedal	Is voltage less than 9 volts?	Repair D4 WT for open circuit between stop light switch and module. Retest system	Check 4-way flasher, directional wiring, and feedback through stop light circuit. Also check for proper operation of cruise control. Recheck antilock and brake lights for proper 2 second bulb check
TEST 23 TWELVE FLASHES				
23.1	This code should not occur. Read flashcodes several times	Are 12 flashes still present?	Replace module. Retest system	Go to Test 11
TEST 24 THIRTEEN FLASHES				
24.1	Read flashcode	Are 13 flashes present?	Replace module. Retest system	Go to Test 11
TEST 25 FOURTEEN FLASHES				
25.1	Read flashcode	Are 14 flashes present?	Replace module. Retest system	Go to Test 11
TEST 26 FIFTEEN FLASHES				
26.1	Read flashcode	Are 15 flashes present?	Replace module. Retest system	Go to Test 11
TEST 27 SIXTEEN OR MORE FLASHES				
27.1	Read flashcode	Are 16 or more flashes present?	Replace module. Retest system	Go to Test 11

Major Components

The system continually monitors rear wheel speed with a sensor mounted on the rear axle. A toothed exciter ring is press fit onto the differential case next to the differential ring gear and provides a signal for the sensor. When the teeth on the exciter ring pass the sensor pole piece, an AC voltage is induced in the sensor circuit with a frequency proportional to the average rear wheel speed. In the event of an impending lockup condition during a braking, the RWAL modulates hydraulic pressure to the rear brakes. This inhibits rear wheel lockup.

The electronic brake control module is located behind the glove box on most models. The control module monitors the rear wheel speed and controls the dual solenoid valve.

The control module determines if the rear wheels are decelerating too quickly and sends a signal to the dual solenoid hydraulic valve to prevent rear wheel lockup. The control module also performs a system self check every time the ignition key is turned **ON**.

The dual solenoid hydraulic valve is located between the rear brakes and the proportioning valve and is attached on the left frame rail near the rear axle.

Under normal conditions, the valve will allow brake fluid to flow freely between the master cylinder and the rear brakes. Once antilock braking begins the control module will trigger the valve to either isolate or reduce pressure to the rear wheels.

The electronic control module has the capability of generating and storing fault codes. Only one code can be stored and shown at any one time. Also, if a fault code is generated the electronic control module will retain the code even after a key **OFF** condition.

If a problem is detected the electronic control module will illuminate the amber antilock brake warning lamp and set a fault code. When a fault code is set the red brake warning lamp will also be lit. To determine what the fault code is, momentarily ground the RWAL diagnostic connector and count the flashes of the amber antilock warning lamp. The initial flash will be a long flash followed by a number of short flashes. The long flash indicates the beginning of the fault number sequence and the short flashes are a continuation of that sequence. Count the long flash with the short flashes to have an accurate fault code count.

To clear a fault code disconnect the control module connector from the module or disconnect the battery for at least five seconds. During system re-

test, wait 30 seconds to make sure the fault code does not reappear.

Removal and Installation
RWAL SPEED SENSOR

1. Raise and safely support vehicle.
2. Remove sensor hold down-bolt.
3. Remove sensor shield and sensor from differential by pulling sensor out of differential.
4. Disconnect wiring from sensor.
5. To install, connect wiring to sensor. Be sure the seal is in place between the sensor and wiring connector.
6. Install the sensor into the differential housing with a new O-ring.
7. Install sensor shield.
8. Install sensor hold down bolt. Torque to 170–230 inch lbs.
9. Lower vehicle.

ELECTRONIC BRAKE CONTROL MODULE

1. Remove the right side sill plate.
2. Remove the right side cowl cover.
3. Remove the three screws that attach electronic brake control module to side cowl.
4. Disconnect the wiring from the module.
5. When installing, connect the wiring first, then install the three mounting screws.
6. Install the right side cowl cover and sill plate.

DUAL SOLENOID HYDRAULIC VALVE

1. Raise and safely support vehicle.
2. Remove the brake lines from the valve.
3. Remove the 2 nuts that hold the valve to the frome.
4. Remove the valve from the frame and disconnect the wiring.
5. When installing, connect the wiring first, then install the valve. Torque the hold-down nuts to 16–25 ft. lbs.
6. Bleed the solenoid valve and the rear brakes.
7. Lower hoist.

JEEP

Master Cylinder Service

Jeep uses a dual master cylinder which contains a double hydraulic cylinder with 2 fluid reservoirs and primary and secondary hydraulic pistons. The master cylinder is assisted by a vacuum booster. Hydraulic rear drum brakes with automatic adjusters and

self-adjusting front disc brakes are standard on all models.

The front outlet tube of the master cylinder is connected to the hydraulic system control valve and then to the rear brakes. This is referred the secondary system. The rear outlet tube is connected to the control valve and to the front brakes. This system is referred to as the primary system. No residual pressure valves are used in the master cylinder outlets.

During normal operation, the fluid level in the master cylinder will rise during brake operation and fall during release. It is also expected that the fluid level will decrease with brake pad wear. In addition, a trace of brake fluid on the booster shell below the master cylinder mounting flange will often be found as a result of the normal lubricating action of the master cylinder bore and seal. All of these conditions are considered normal and are not indications the master cylinder needs service.

Two types of master cylinders were used; 1) a cast iron master cylinder with built-in reservoir and separate proportioning valve and, 2) a master cylinder with a pressed on plastic reservoir. The body of the two-piece master cylinder is made of anodized aluminum and the reservoir is made of nylon. The two compartments of the reservoir are interconnected to permit equalization of the fluid level. However, a sufficient quantity of fluid is retained in the reservoir of the unaffected system to permit operation of that half of the master cylinder even if the other half of the reservoir is drained due to a hydraulic leak. There is another type of master cylinder used on vehicles equipped with anti-lock brakes. See anti-lock section.

Use extra care when servicing aluminum master cylinders not to cross thread brake line fittings and do not overtighten any threaded connection.

In the event of a front brake system malfunction the proportioning valve with a bypass feature allows full hydraulic pressure to the rear brake system.

Disassembly and Assembly

While the manufacturer does give overhaul procedures for the master cylinder, the manufacturer does not permit that either the cast iron or aluminum master cylinder be honed in an attempt to restore the surface. Replace the cylinder if the bore is corroded or if doubt exists about cylinder bore condition.

CAST IRON MASTER CYLINDER – EXCEPT ANTI-LOCK

1. Remove the cover and drain fluid. Examine cover seal for damage.

2. Mount cylinder in vise and press in primary piston. Remove snapring.

3. Remove the primary piston and discard. It is serviced only as an assembly.

4. Apply a small amount of compressed air to secondary outlet while covering small ports at bottom of rear reservoir to ease secondary piston from bore.

5. Disassemble secondary piston. Discard seals, spring and retainer.

6. Inspect bore carefully, clean and dry with compressed air. Do not hone bore if scored. Replace the assembly.

7. Coat the cylinder bore and new piston assemblies with clean brake fluid. Assemble the secondary piston, making sure the seals are facing the proper direction. Assemble the retainer and return spring and insert assembly into the cylinder bore.

8. Install the primary piston into the bore, push in and install the snapring.

9. Bench-bleed the master cylinder before installation.

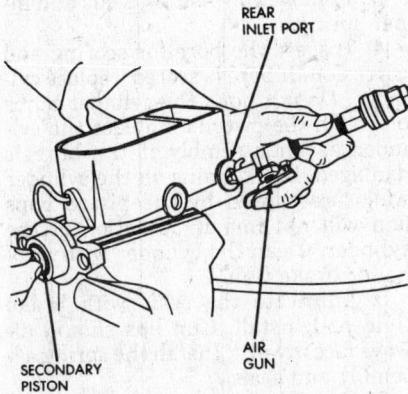

Use air pressure to remove secondary piston

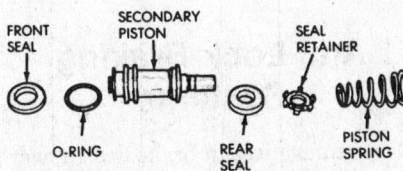

Secondary piston components

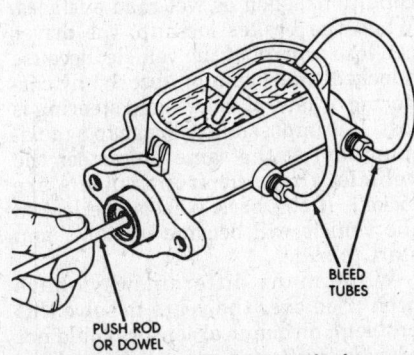

Bleeding master cylinder—typical

ALUMINUM MASTER CYLINDER— EXCEPT ANTI-LOCK

1. Remove the reservoir cover, seal and drain fluid.

2. Mount the cylinder in a vise. Clamp vise jaws on one of the mounting ears so cylinder bore not be distorted.

3. Remove reservoir with a rocking motion. Remove the seal grommets.

4. Remove the cylinder snapring.

5. Remove the primary piston and discard. It is serviced only as an assembly.

6. Apply a small amount of compressed air to secondary outlet to ease secondary piston from bore.

7. Disassemble secondary piston. Discard seals, spring and retainer.

8. Inspect the cylinder check valve. Remove the valve snapring and replace the valve if necessary. The tube seats can also be replaced. Remove by forced a hardened self-tapping screw, then pry upwards using the proper tools to remove the seat.

9. Inspect bore carefully, clean and dry with compressed air. Do not hone bore if scored. Replace the assembly.

10. Coat the cylinder bore and new piston assemblies with clean brake fluid. Assemble the secondary piston, making sure the seals are facing the proper direction. Assemble the retainer and return spring and insert assembly into the cylinder bore.

11. Install the primary piston into the bore, push in and install the snapring.

12. Install new reservoir grommets into the cylinder body.

13. Turn reservoir upside down and place on flat surface. Press the master cylinder onto the reservoir with a rocking motion. Be sure it is fully seated.

14. Bench bleed the master cylinder before installation.

Brake Booster Service

Jeep models covered are equipped with vacuum boosters, except those equipped with the anti-lock brake system. Anti-lock master cylinder/power brake booster units are not repairable and must be replaced as a complete assembly.

Under normal operating conditions, with brakes released, a vacuum suspended booster operates with vacuum on both sides of its diaphragm (or both diaphragms in a tandem diaphragm unit). When the brakes are applied, air at atmospheric pressure is admitted to one side of the diaphragm (or both diaphragms in a tandem diaphragm unit) to provide the power assist.

Brake boosters used by Jeep are not repairable and if defective, the booster

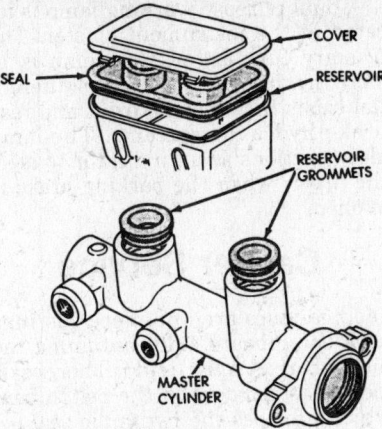

Aluminum master cylinder

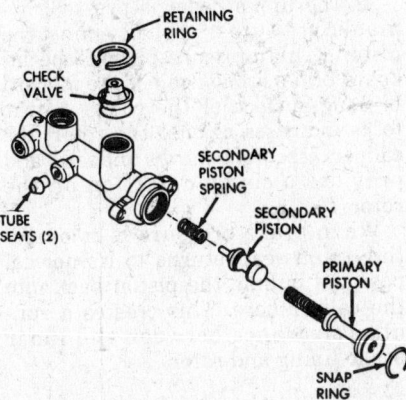

Aluminum master cylinder components

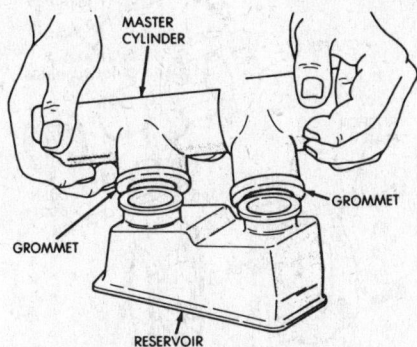

Installing the reservoir to the master cylinder body

must be replaced as a unit. The brake boosters used on different models of Jeeps are different sizes and are not interchangeable.

Combination Valve

All models have a hydraulic system control valve in the brake system. A combination proportioning valve/pressure differential switch is used on all models. Comanche series pickup trucks are equipped with a rear brake height sensing proportioning valve. The valve adjusts front-rear brake proportioning to maintain brake balance when the vehicle is loaded.

A dual purpose warning lamp is located in the instrument cluster. The primary function of this lamp is to alert the driver if a pressure differential exists between the front and rear brake hydraulic systems. The lamp also functions as an indicator to alert the driver when the parking brake is applied.

Caliper Service

Jeep calipers are one-piece castings with the inboard side containing the piston bore. A square cut rubber seal is located in a groove in the piston bore which provides the hydraulic seal between the piston and the cylinder wall.

As the brake pedal is pressed, hydraulic pressure is applied against the piston. This pressure pushes the inboard brake lining against the inboard braking surface of the rotor. As the force increases against the rotor, the caliper assembly moves inboard and provides a clamping action on the rotor.

When brake pressure is released, the piston seal returns to its normal position, pulling the piston back into the caliper bore. This creates a running clearance between the inner brake lining and rotor.

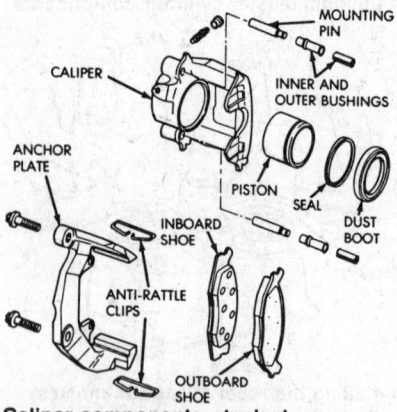

Caliper components – typical

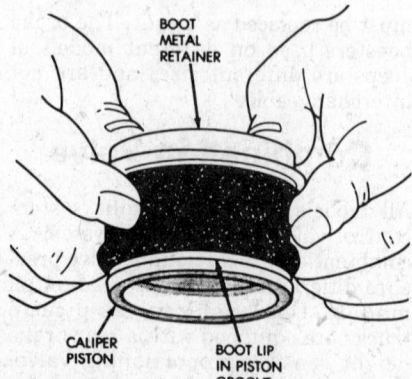

Install dust boot on piston, then fold into place

Disassembly and Assembly

1. Place shop towels under the caliper piston to protect it during removal. Apply a little compressed air to slowly ease the piston out of the bore.

2. Remove the dust boot and, using a small, pointed wooden stick, work the piston seal out of its groove in the caliper bore. Do not use a screwdriver or metal tool which might nick or scratch the bore. Discard the seal.

3. Clean all parts well using alcohol and blow dry. Inspect the piston bore for scoring or pitting. Install a new piston if it is pitted, scored or the plating is worn. Jeep does not recommend honing calipers or using any type of abrasives on the basis that abrasives will ruin the piston plating and cause it to corrode and bind. Replace the piston if damaged in any way.

4. Clean all parts well, dip the new piston seal in brake fluid and install in the bore. Position the seal at one area at a time and, using fingers, gently work the seal into the groove.

5. Slide the metal retainer part of the new dust boot over the open end of the piston. Pull the retainer rearward until the boot lip seats in the groove at the end of the piston. Push the metal retainer part of the boot forward until flush with the rim at the open end of the piston. Then snap boot folds in place. Finally, install the piston in the caliper bore with a twisting motion being careful not to unseal the piston seal.

6. Seal the metal retainer part of the dust boot in the caliper with a circular driver.

7. Install new mounting bushings in the caliper as required. Install bleeder screw if removed.

8. Install the flexible brake hose with new seals.

Wheel Cylinder Service

The rear brakes are drum type with internal expanding shoes. The rear brakes are of the single anchor type, mounted to the same anchor and actuated by one wheel cylinder. The wheel cylinder has two pistons. Brake adjustments are automatic and are made during reverse brake applications.

Wheel cylinders may need reconditioning or replacement whenever the brake shoes are replaced or when required to correct a leak condition. Leaks which coat the boot and the cylinder with fluid, or result in a dropped reservoir fluid level, or dampen and stain the brake linings are dangerous. Such leaks can cause the brakes to grab or fail and should be immediately corrected. A leakage, not immediately

apparent, can be detected by pulling back the cylinder boot. A small amount of fluid seepage dampening the interior of the boot is normal. However, a dripping boot is not. Unless other conditions causing a brake to pull, grab or drag become obvious, the wheel cylinder is suspect and should be included in general reconditioning.

Cylinder binding may be caused by rust, deposits, grime, or swollen cups due to fluid contamination, or by a cup wedged into an excessive piston clearance.

Hydraulic system parts should not be allowed to come into contact with oil or grease, neither should those be handled with greasy hands. Even a trace of any petroleum based product is sufficient to cause damage to the rubber parts.

Disassembly and Assembly

1. Remove the brake bleeder screw.
2. Remove the dust boots, allow any brake fluid to drain out.
3. Remove the pistons, seals and inner spring.
4. Inspect the bore for scoring and corrosion. If bore is scored, replace cylinder. Do not hone the cylinder bores or polish the pistons. Replace the cylinder as an assembly if the bore is damaged. Black stains on the cylinder walls are caused by the piston cups and will not impair operation of the cylinder. Clean the cylinder with alcohol or brake fluid.
5. Lubricate the seals with brake fluid and install. Cup lips should always face inward. Install the spring assembly and seals.
6. Carefully install the pistons and dust boots.
7. Install the bleeder screw.

Anti-Lock Braking Systems

Despite advances in brake design over the years, even the best systems in use can still lock up during certain road conditions, such as wet road surfaces. When the brakes lock up, the driver can lose control of the vehicle, because a locked wheel cannot absorb any cornering or lateral forces, and steering is lost. It is impossible to brake to a maximum and at the same time steer the vehicle when the front wheels are locked. If the back wheels are locked the vehicle will become unstable and start to slide.

While many different ways have been tried over the years to solve this problem, mechanical sensors could not provide sufficient information about

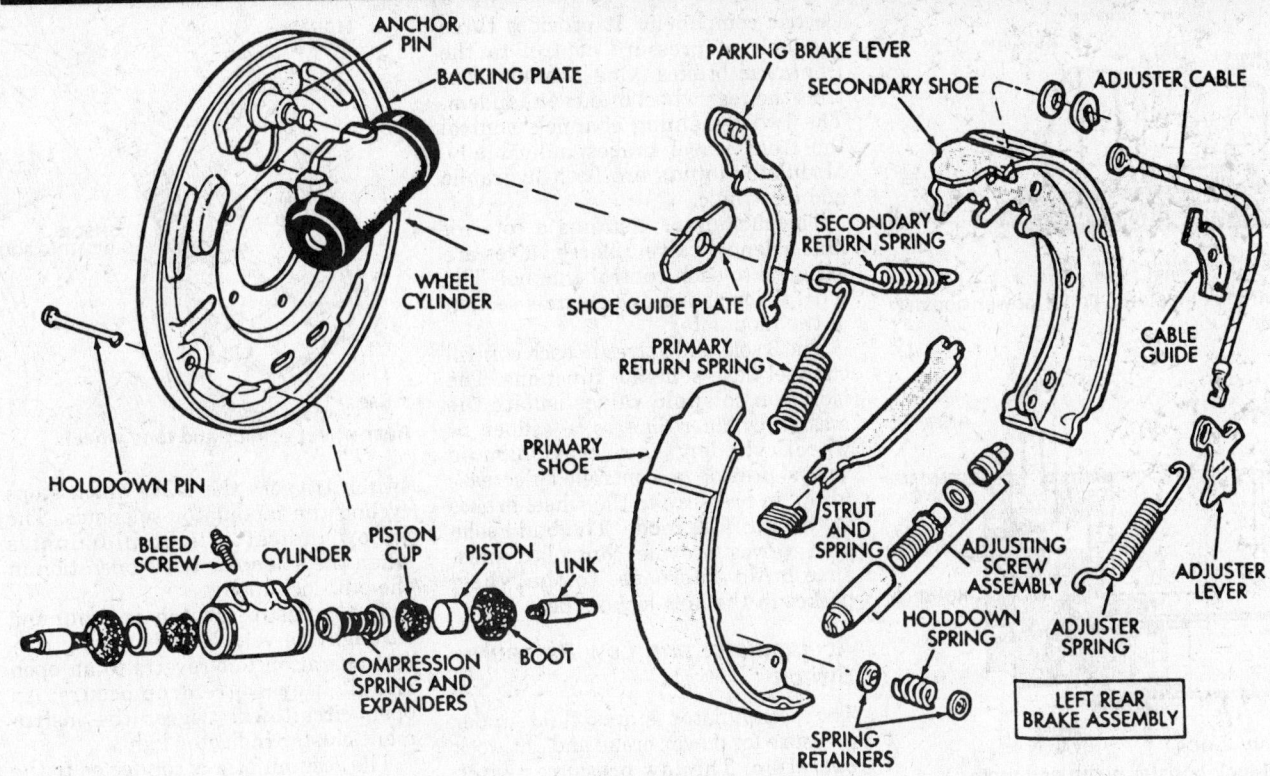

ANCHOR PIN

BACKING PLATE

PARKING BRAKE LEVER

SECONDARY SHOE

ADJUSTER CABLE

WHEEL CYLINDER

SECONDARY RETURN SPRING

SHOE GUIDE PLATE

CABLE GUIDE

PRIMARY RETURN SPRING

HOLDDOWN PIN

PRIMARY SHOE

STRUT AND SPRING

ADJUSTING SCREW ASSEMBLY

ADJUSTER LEVER

BLEED SCREW

CYLINDER

PISTON CUP

PISTON

LINK

HOLDDOWN SPRING

ADJUSTER SPRING

COMPRESSION SPRING AND EXPANDERS

BOOT

SPRING RETAINERS

LEFT REAR BRAKE ASSEMBLY

Rear drum brakes—Comanchee, Cherokee, Wrangler shown—typical

wheel rotation speed and mechanical control units could not operate the brakes fast enough to prevent brake lockup.

The growth of the electronics industry has allowed small computers (microprocessors) to be reduced in both size and cost. Coupled with fast reacting electronic sensors, anti-lock braking has become more reliable with widespread application.

Jeep's antilock brake system is available on 70 Series (Cherokee/Wagoneer Sport trucks) models with Select-Track four wheel drive. It is an electronically operated, power assisted, all wheel brake control system. The system is designed to retard wheel lockup during periods of high wheel slip when braking. Retarding wheel lockup is accomplished by modulating fluid pressures to the wheel brake units.

The 70 Series anti-lock system is a 3 channel design. The front wheel brakes are controlled individually and the rear wheel brakes in tandem.

System pressure is modulated according to wheel speed, degree of wheel slip and rate of deceleration. A sensor at each wheel converts wheel speed into electronic signals. The signals are transmitted to the brake system control unit for processing and determination of deceleration rate and wheel slip.

Basic system components include wheel sensors, fluid level and pressure switches, a pressure modulator, an accumulator, an electric booster pump, a master cylinder/power boost unit and an electronic control unit. Two instrument cluster indicator lights (one red, one yellow) are used to signal system condition and operating status.

The anti-lock electronic control system is separate from other electrical circuits in the vehicle. A specially programmed ECU is used for operational control.

The accumulator tank and the small accumulator on the booster pump both contain high pressure gas charges which assist in maintaining boost pressure. Do not puncture or attempt to disassemble either of these components at any time.

When servicing the anti-lock system, keep system components clean. Do not allow any dirt or foreign material to enter the system. Clean the reservoir cap and exterior thoroughly before removing the cap to add fluid. Dirt or foreign material in the system could result in poor brake system performance and possible component failure.

The manufacturer recommends Mopar brake fluid or equivalent meeting DOT 3 standards only. Never use reclaimed fluid or fluid from an open container that has been allowed to stand for any length of time.

> **CAUTION**
>
> *The normal working pressure of the anti-lock boost system is 1650–2050 psi. System pressure must be pumped down before any pressure lines are loosened or disconnected. Failure to do so could result in personal injury. To reduce system pressure, turn the ignition key OFF. They apply the brakes 45–50 times (until pedal is firm) to reduce fluid pressure in the accumulator, booster, pump and lines. Wear safety goggles when disconnecting fluid lines.*

MAJOR COMPONENTS

Master Cylinder/Power Booster Unit

The master cylinder and power booster pistons are located in a single, cast aluminum, cylinder body. A fluid reservoir is attached to the body with rubber seals.

The fluid reservoir is internally separated into 3 sections by bulkheads. A common fluid fill is used for the 3 sections.

The power booster is a demand type component. Power assist occurs only when the brakes are applied. Power assist is from high pressure brake fluid supplied by the electric motor driven booster pump. The pump is connected to the system accumulator. The accumulator is connected to the booster unit in the master cylinder.

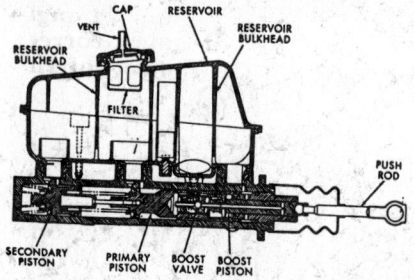

Anti-lock master cylinder/power booster unit

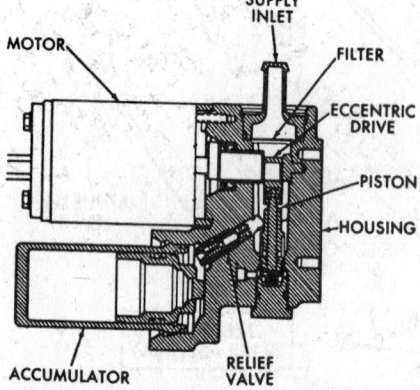

Anti-lock booster pump and motor assembly

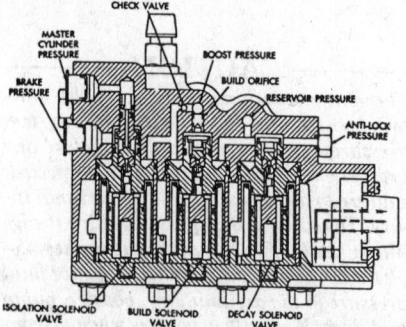

Pressure modulator channel—typical

Pump and Motor Assembly

The booster pump is powered by an electric motor. The motor and pump are combined in a common housing. The pump piston operates off an eccentric drive. An internal relief valve and a pressure switch control pump output. The housing contains a small accumulator which operates in tandem with the main accumulator.

The pump supplies fluid boost pressure for both standard and anti-lock brake operation. Pump operating pressure range is 1650–2050 psi. The pump motor is equipped with a thermal fuse which stops the pump if operating temperatures approach overheat range. The fuse does not reset once it is tripped.

Pressure Modulator

The pressure modulator is a hydro-

electric component. It provides three channels of pressure control to the front/rear brakes. One channel controls the rear wheel brakes in tandem. The two remaining channels control the front wheel brakes individually. Modulator inputs are both hydraulic and electronic.

The modulator contains a total of nine solenoid valves. Three valves are assigned to each control channel. The illustration shows one channel section of the modulator.

The 3 solenoid valves in each control channel have separate functions. The isolation solenoid valves isolate the master cylinder line to a caliper or wheel cylinder. The decay solenoid valves provide a controlled decrease (drop) in pressure to the wheel brakes in the anti-lock mode. The build solenoid valves provide controlled pressure build (increase) to the wheel brakes in the anti-lock mode.

Accumulator and Low Pressure Switch

The accumulator stores fluid under pressure for power brake and anti-lock operation. The low pressure switch monitors fluid pressure and is connected to the ECU.

If pressure falls below a minimum value of approximately 1050 psi, the

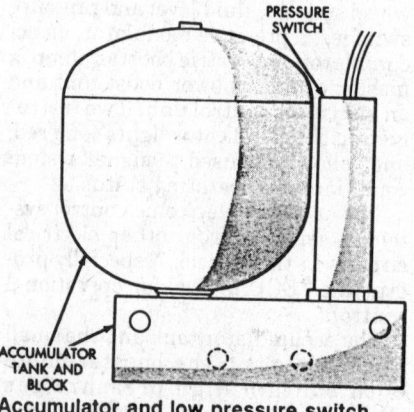

Accumulator and low pressure switch

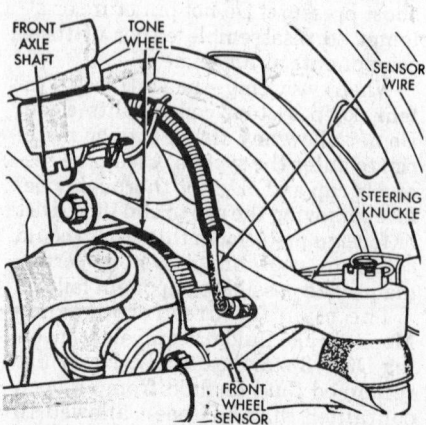

Front wheel sensor and tone wheel

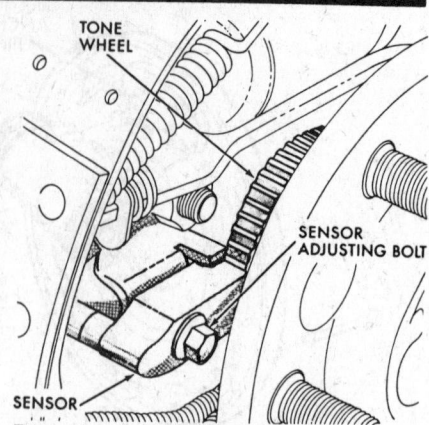

Rear wheel sensor and tone wheel

switch triggers the ECU which stops cycling the modulator solenoids. The yellow indicator light illuminates when the solenoids cease operation in the anti-lock mode.

The pressure switch is grounded through the vehicle body during normal operation but reverts to an open circuit if pressure drop occurs. An open circuit will trigger the instrument cluster indicator lights.

The accumulator is connected to the pump and power booster unit respectively.

Wheel Sensors

A sensor is used at each wheel. The sensors convert wheel speed into an electronic signal which is transmitted to the anti-lock ECU. A toothed-type tone wheel serves as the trigger mechanism for each sensor. The tone wheels are mounted at the outboard ends of the front and rear axle shafts.

Boost Pressure Differential Switch

The boost pressure differential switch is mounted in the pressure modulator. The switch checks the pressure differential between modulated boost pres-

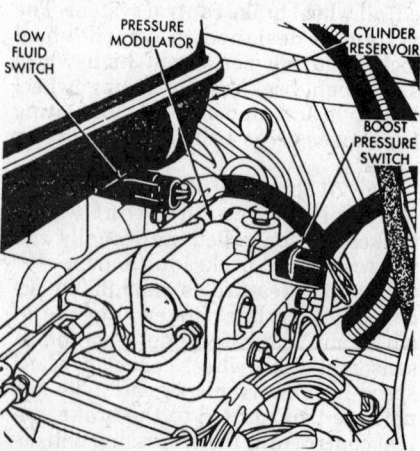

Boost pressure differential and low fluid switch locations

sure and the master cylinder primary system pressure.

The switch is in circuit with the ECU and instrument panel indicator lights. The switch is open when pressure differential is normal. The switch will ground (through the vehicle body) if a pressure differential problem is detected. Once grounded, the switch signals the ECU to illuminate the indicator lights.

Fluid Level Switch

A fluid level switch is located in the master cylinder reservoir. The switch activates the red indicator light if the fluid level falls below the required level. The yellow light also comes on if the vehicle speed is above approximately 2.5 mph.

Electronic Control Unit

A separate electronic control unit (ECU) is used to monitor and control the entire anti-lock system. The ECU is attached to a bracket located under the rear seat. The power up voltage source for the ECU is through the ignition switch in the ON or RUN position.

The anti-lock ECU is separate from the other vehicle electronic systems. It contains a self-diagnostic program

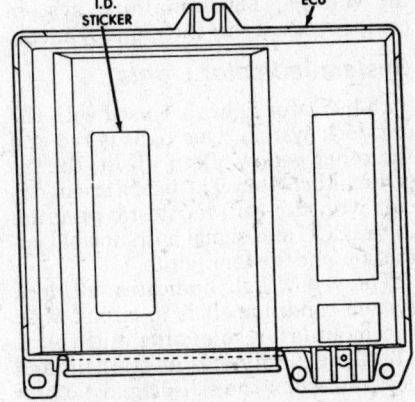

Anti-lock electronic control unit

which triggers the indicator lights when a system fault is detected. Faults are stored in a diagnostic program memory. Faults remain in memory until cleared. However, if the battery is disconnected, stored faults are erased.

The ECU is also equipped with a mercury switch. The switch monitors the degree of vehicle deceleration to determine what type of surface the vehicle is on. The switch provides input to the ECU for improved operation in the 4WD mode on low traction (slippery) road surfaces.

NOTE: Proper mounting angle of the ECU is critical to correct and accurate operation of the mercury switch.

System Relays

There are 3 system relays. The yellow indicator light and modulator power relays are located on the driver side inner fender panel. The relay wires are in the engine compartment wire harness.

The pump/motor relay is part of the pump motor harness and is located at the passenger side of the engine compartment.

The modulator power relay is connected to the pressure modulator solenoids and the ECU. When the system is powered up, the ECU supplies the operating voltage (12 volts) to the solenoids through the relay.

The indicator light relay is connected to the modulator solenoid relay and the indicator light. The relay turns the yellow light on when the modulator power relay is off. The yellow light is turned off when the modulator power relay is energized.

The pump motor relay starts/stops the pump motor when signaled by the pump switch.

Anti-lock modulator/indicator light relays and harness location

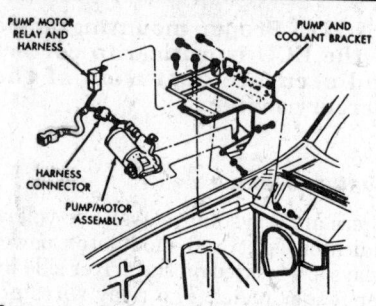

Pump motor relay and harness

Ignition Switch

The anti-lock ECU and indicator lights are in the standby mode with the ignition switch in the **OFF** or **ACCESSORY** position. No operating voltage is supplied.

In the **ON** and **RUN** positions, the switch supplies the ECU, pump motor and indicator lights with a 12 volt power supply.

In the **START** position, only the indicator lights are supplied with operat-ing voltage. The remaining system components are in the standby mode.

System Indicator Lights

Two indicator lights are used with the anti-lock system. One light is red and the other yellow. Both are in the instrument cluster. The lights are in circuit with the self diagnostic program in the ECU and signal both normal operation and system faults.

The yellow light indicates anti-lock system condition. It is in circuit with the modulator solenoids and relay. The light illuminates at start-up and goes out when the self-diagnostic program determines system operation is normal.

If a fault occurs, the yellow light remains on until the fault is either corrected, the battery is disconnected, or the ignition switch is cycled (turned **OFF** and then **ON**). Cycling the ignition switch may not turn the light off after some faults.

The yellow light illuminates in tan-dem with the red warning light to indicate certain types of faults. The pressure modulator solenoids are in circuit with the yellow indicator light. When the yellow light is on (system fault occurred), the solenoids are disabled.

The red light serves as the system warning light (low fluid, parking brake on, system pressure differential, etc.). The light illuminates in tandem with the yellow anti-lock light when certain system faults occur.

There are time delays built into indicator light illumination. These delays are provided as a means of identifying some system faults.

Proportioning Valve

The combination front/rear brake pressure switch and proportioning valve is connected between the master cylinder and modulator. The switch and valve operate normally in the standard braking mode. In the anti-lock mode, the proportioning valve is

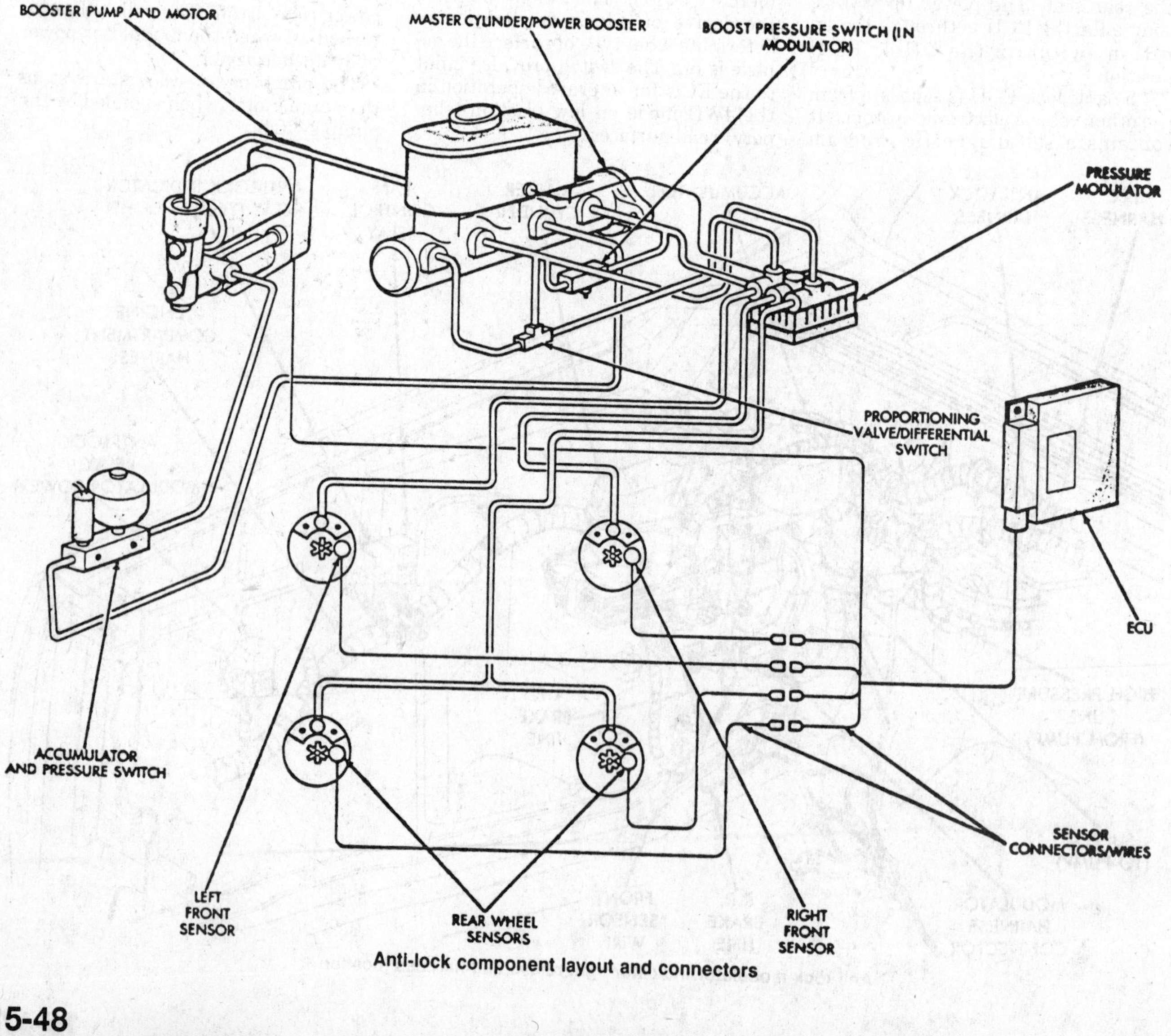

Anti-lock component layout and connectors

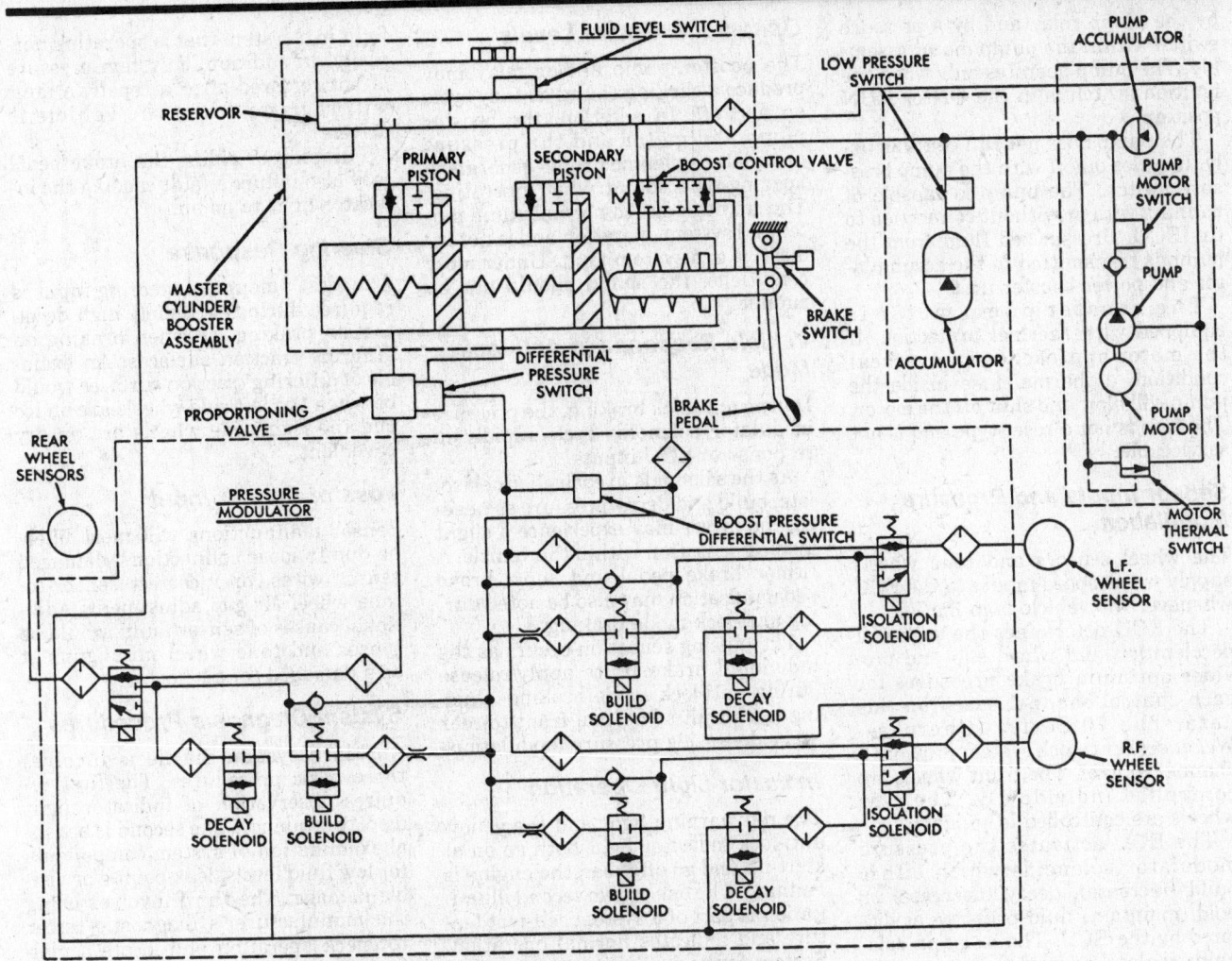

Anti-lock three channel schematic

isolated to enable brake pressure modulation during anti-lock system operation. The pressure differential switch is only activated by a difference in pressure between the front and rear (primary and secondary) brake circuits.

Parking Brake Switch

The switch is connected to the ECU low fluid circuit. When the switch is activated, the red indicator light illuminates. If vehicle speed is above approximately 2.5 mph, the yellow light will also illuminate.

SYSTEM OPERATION

Component Connections

The booster pump and accumulator provide the fluid pressure needed for power assist. The accumulator is connected to the pump by a high pressure feed line. A second high pressure line connects the accumulator to the booster section of the master cylinder. A low

pressure supply line connects the reservoir to the booster pump.

Fluid from the master cylinder is channeled to the calipers and wheel cylinders through the pressure modulator. The 3 solenoid valves (isolation—decay—build) in each modulator control channel are contained within the modulator body.

The wheel sensors are connected directly to the ECU. The sensor triggering devices (tone wheels), are mounted on the axle shafts.

System Power Up

The anti-lock system is in standby mode with the ignition switch in **OFF** or **ACCESSORY** position. When the switch ismoved to the **START** position, voltage through the switch activates the indicator lights only. The ECU and other system components are still the standby mode.

The indicator lights illuminate as part of the self test feature and remain on until the switch is in the **RUN** position.

In the **ON** and **RUN** position, 12 volts are supplied through the ignition

switch to power up the ECU and system components.

When the vehicle is motionless (no wheel speed inputs) and the ignition switch is in the **ON** or **RUN** position, the modulator solenoids are activated and briefly exercised. This serves two purposes: It checks solenoid function as part of the self diagnostic feature and ensures proper solenoid operation after periods of inactivity.

Boost Pressure and Fluid Supply

The system main fluid supply is contained in the master cylinder reservoir and the accumulator. Additional fluid is also contained in the booster pump accumulator. The pump and main accumulator provide the reserve fluid pressure needed for power brake assist.

Fluid stored in the accumulator is at normal working pressure of 1650–2050 psi. The accumulator contains enough pressurized fluid for 25–30 power assisted brake applications if a pump fault should occur.

Pump motor operation is controlled

by the pump relay and by a pressure switch within the pump/motor assembly. The pump operates only when the ignition switch is in the **ON** or **RUN** position.

The pump does not run continuously. It cycles on/off with the pump pressure switch. The pump is capable of running with or without connection to the ECU. Pressurized fluid from the pump is transmitted to the accumulator and power booster unit.

The booster pump motor is equipped with thermal protection. If the motor approaches an overheat condition, a thermal fuse inside the pump will blow and shut off the motor. The fuse is not a reset-type and is not serviceable.

Sensor Inputs and Pressure Modulation

The wheel sensors and tone wheels supply wheel speed inputs to the ECU whenever the vehicle is in motion.

The ECU determines the degree of deceleration and wheel slip and provides optimum brake pressures for each control channel based on this data. The 70 Series (Cherokee/Wagoneer) anti-lock system provides 3 channel control. The front wheels are controlled individually. The rear wheels are controlled in tandem.

The ECU activates the pressure modulator solenoids which either build (increase), decay (decrease) or hold (maintain) fluid pressure as dictated by the ECU. The isolation solenoids isolate normal fluid pressure from the master cylinder to the rear wheels or to the left or right front wheel as needed. Wheel brake isolation occurs prior to build/decay solenoid operation.

Solenoid operation is not entirely constant in the anti-lock mode. Operation occurs in brief, rapid cycles front-to-rear and side-to-side. Rapid changes in input data will produce equally rapid changes in pressure modulation. The isolation, decay, and build functions are capable of function changes and cycle times measured in milliseconds.

SERVICE DIAGNOSIS

Wheel/Tire Size and Input Signals

Anti-lock system operation is dependent on signals from the wheel sensors. The vehicle wheels and tires must all be the same size and type in order to generate accurate signals. Variations in wheel/tire size will produce inaccurate input signals resulting in incorrect pressure modulation.

Operational Sound Levels

The booster pump and/or relay may produce a clicking sound as they cycle on and off. In addition, the booster pump and motor and the pressure modulator solenoids may generate a buzzing-type sound when operating. The sound is due to normal pump motor and system operation and is not indicative of a system fault. Under most conditions, the sound should not be audible.

Vehicle Response in Anti-lock Mode

During anti-lock braking, the pressure modulator solenoids cycle rapidly in response to ECU inputs.

As the solenoids in each channel isolate, build and decay pressure as needed, the driver may experience a slight pulsing sensation within the vehicle. A firmer brake pedal and some brake pedal pulsation may also be noted during anti-lock mode braking.

The pulsing sensation occurs as the individual brake units apply/release during anti-lock mode braking. Pulsing is a result of normal front-to-rear and side-to-side pressure modulation.

Indicator Light Operation

The red warning light and the yellow anti-lock indicator light both go on at start-up and go off when the engine is running. The one or two second illumination is part of a system self-test feature and indicates normal operation. System faults are indicated when one or both of the lights illuminate after initial start-up system check.

Driver Induced System Faults

Some driving or operational situations can induce faults in an anti-lock system that is actually operating correctly.

Induced faults are not true faults; a component malfunction as not actually occurred. Instead, they are a result of driver actions recognized by the diagnostic program as improper operation.

Improper parking brake use can induce faults in the self-diagnostic program. If a driver attempts to move the vehicle with the parking brakes applied, a system fault will register. Or, if the parking brake is applied while the vehicle is in motion, a system fault will also register. One or both indicator lights will illuminate in either situation. The red light illuminates for parking brake faults. The yellow light illuminates if a fault is sensed.

Faults can be induced in the system through excessive wheel spin. Wheel spin due to low traction surfaces or high speed acceleration can induce a

fault in a system that is operating normally. In addition, if system pressure is not restored after a repair, a fault will register when the vehicle is driven.

Pumping or riding the brake pedal may also induce a fault causing the indicator light to go on.

Steering Response

A modest amount of steering input is required during extremely high deceleration braking, or when braking on differing traction surfaces. An example of differing traction surfaces would be when the left side wheels are on ice and the right side wheels are on dry pavement.

Loss of Sensor Input

Sensor malfunctions will most likely be due to loose connections, damaged sensor wires, or incorrect sensor-to-tone wheel air gap adjustment. Additional causes of sensor faults would be sensor and tone wheel misalignment or a damaged tone wheel.

System Diagnosis Procedures

Anti-lock system diagnosis involves three basic procedures. The first requires observation of indicator light display sequence. The second is a visual examination of system components for low fluid levels, leak points, or visible damage. The third involves using the manufacturer's diagnostic tester to check operation and locate a malfunctioning circuit.

The two indicator lights will illuminate separately, simultaneously, or with varying delays depending on the fault. The lights signal low fluid levels, pressure drops and other hydro-electrical faults. The service diagnosis charts for indicator light display can be used when a fault is detected.

COMPONENT SERVICEABILITY

The master cylinder/power booster unit, pressure modulator, accumulator, pump/motor and proportioning valve are not repairable components. If diagnosis indicates a malfunction has occurred, these components are to be replaced as a complete assembly.

The fluid level switch in the master cylinder and the boost pressure switch in the modulator are also not serviceable. The switches cannot be removed from their respective components.

The electrical harnesses, pump bracket, pump high pressure and supply hose, system relays and wheel sensors can be serviced individually.

The tone wheels are permanently attached to the axle shafts and are not

SERVICE DIAGNOSIS

SYSTEM FAULT	POSSIBLE CAUSE	INDICATOR LIGHT DISPLAY
LOW FLUID	SYSTEM LEAK. ACCUMULATOR CHARGE LOW OR LOST.	RED LIGHT ON. YELLOW LIGHT ON WITHIN 1/2 SECOND WHEN VEHICLE SPEED EXCEEDS 2.5 MPH.
PARKING BRAKES APPLIED	PARKING BRAKES NOT RELEASED BEFORE DRIVING VEHICLE.	RED LIGHT ON. YELLOW LIGHT ON IF VEHICLE SPEED EXCEEDS 2.5 MPH.
PRESSURE DROP AT ACCUMULATOR	ACCUMLATOR GAS CHARGE LOST. SYSTEM LEAK. PUMP/MOTOR MALFUNCTION. PROLONGED STOP ON ICY SURFACE WITH TRANSMISSION IN GEAR.	YELLOW LIGHT ON. RED LIGHT WILL ALSO COME ON WITHIN 20 SECONDS.
DIFFERENTIAL PRESSURE SWITCH (IN PROPORTIONING VALVE) ACTUATED	SYSTEM LEAK. MASTER CYLINDER MALFUNCTION (SECONDARY PISTON). AIR IN SYSTEM.	RED LIGHT ON. YELLOW LIGHT COMES ON AT VEHICLE SPEED OF 3 MPH.
PRESSURE DROP AT BOOST PRESSURE SWITCH AND PRESSURE DIFFERENTIAL SWITCH	MASTER CYLINDER MALFUNCTION (PRIMARY PISTON). SYSTEM LEAK. AIR IN SYSTEM.	RED LIGHT ON. YELLOW LIGHT COMES ON AT VEHICLE SPEED OF 3 MPH.
WHEEL SENSOR FAULT (FRONT ONLY)	SENSOR-TO-TONE WHEEL SPACING INCORRECT (SPACE TOO LARGE). DAMAGED SENSOR WIRE, SENSOR, OR TONE WHEEL. SENSOR AND TONE WHEEL MISALIGNED. SENSOR DISCONNECTED.	YELLOW LIGHT ON. (AFTER 15 MPH)
WHEEL SENSOR FAULT (FRONT OR REAR ONE OR TWO MISSING SIGNALS)	DAMAGED SENSOR, WIRE, OR CONNECTOR. SENSOR DISCONNECTED. EXCESSIVE WHEEL SPIN. MISALIGNED OR DAMAGED TONE WHEEL. OPEN SENSOR OR WIRE.	YELLOW LIGHT ON AT 15 MPH IF FAULT OCCURRED <u>BEFORE</u> VEHICLE DRIVE-OFF. OR, ORANGE LIGHT ON AT 8 MPH IF FAULT OCCURRED <u>AFTER</u> VEHICLE DRIVE-OFF.
EXCESSIVE DECAY SOLENOID OPERATION	MODULATOR/SOLENOID FAULT. WHEEL SENSOR FAULT. EXTREMELY LOW AMBIENT TEMPERATURES. VEHICLE ON ICE COVERED SURFACE. TIRES HYDROPLANING ON WATER COVERED ROAD SURFACE.	YELLOW LIGHT ON WITHIN 1-2 SECONDS.
PRESSURE MODULATOR SOLENOID FAULT	SOLENOID SHORTED OR OPEN. DECAY AND BUILD SOLENOID ON AT SAME TIME. OPEN/SHORT IN MODULATOR HARNESS.	YELLOW LIGHT ON.
PUMP/MOTOR RUN-ON	EXCESSIVE RUN TIME. RELAY SHORTED, MOTOR SWITCH SHORTED.	RED LIGHT ON IF PUMP RUNS MORE THAN 4 MINUTES WITH NO BRAKE.
PUMP/MOTOR INOPERATIVE	PUMP RELAY FAULT. NO VOLTAGE TO MOTOR. DAMAGED PUMP OR MOTOR. PUMP GAS CHARGE LOST.	YELLOW LIGHT ON. RED LIGHT ON AFTER 20 SECONDS.
LOW VOLTAGE	SYSTEM VOLTAGE BELOW 9V. SHORT, OPEN IN FEED WIRES OR RELAY. FUSE BAD. POOR GROUND. LOOSE, DISCONNECTED WIRE IN SYSTEM. BATTERY LOW OR DISCHARGED	YELLOW LIGHT ON.
NO BRAKE SIGNAL	SYSTEM LEAK. MASTER CYLINDER MALFUNCTION. PUMP/MOTOR MALFUNCTION. ACCUMULATOR OR MODULATOR FAULT.	RED LIGHT ON DURING BRAKING.
RELAY FAULT	RELAY SHORTED OR OPEN.	YELLOW LIGHT ON.
ECU SELF DIAGNOSTIC FEATURE INOPERATIVE (SOLENOIDS NOT TEST-EXERCISED AT START-UP)	IGNITION SWITCH IN OFF POSITION. PARKING BRAKES ON (NOT RELEASED AT DRIVE-OFF). SYSTEM COMPONENT HAS MALFUNCTIONED. LOW FLUID LEVEL/LEAK IN SYSTEM.	YELLOW LIGHT ON.

Jeep Anti-lock diagnosis chart

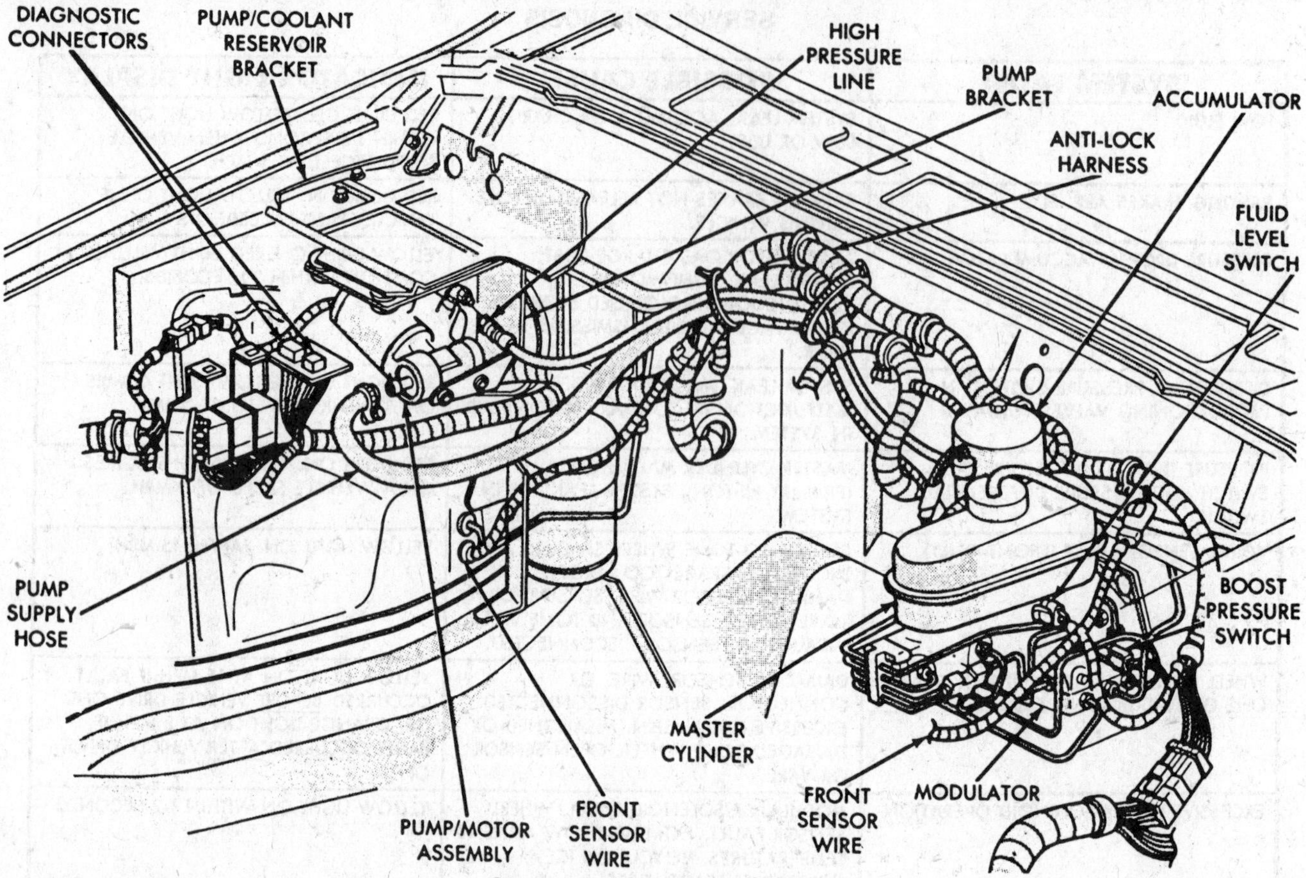

DIAGNOSTIC
CONNECTORS

PUMP/COOLANT
RESERVOIR
BRACKET

HIGH
PRESSURE
LINE

PUMP
BRACKET

ACCUMULATOR

ANTI-LOCK
HARNESS

FLUID
LEVEL
SWITCH

PUMP
SUPPLY
HOSE

BOOST
PRESSURE
SWITCH

MASTER
CYLINDER

FRONT
SENSOR
WIRE

MODULATOR

PUMP/MOTOR
ASSEMBLY

FRONT
SENSOR
WIRE

System components and location

replaceable. If a tone wheel becomes damaged, it will be necessary to replace the tone wheel and axle shaft as an assembly.

The wheel brake components such as calipers, brakeshoes, wheel cylinders, rotors and drums are all serviced the same as standard brake system components.

Wheel Sensors

The wheel sensors have a polyethylene spacer strip attached to the sensor contact face. When installing a sensor, be very sure this spacer strip actually touches the tone wheel. The strips are made in the exact thickness needed for correct sensor-to-tone wheel spacing (air gap). If the spacing (air gap) is too great, the sensors will not transmit accurate speed signals to the ECU. If the spacer strip is missing from an original, or not provided on a replacement sensor, the correct sensor-to-tone wheel air gap will have to be established with a brass feeler gauge. A brass feeler gauge must be used to avoid disrupting sensor polarity

If the sensor strip is missing from a reuseable sensor, set the sensor-to-tone wheel air gap as follows:

Set front sensor air gap to 0.013–0.019 in.

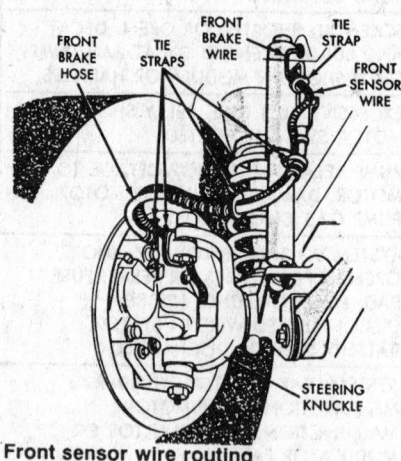

FRONT
BRAKE
HOSE

FRONT
BRAKE
WIRE

TIE
STRAPS

TIE
STRAP

FRONT
SENSOR
WIRE

STEERING
KNUCKLE

Front sensor wire routing

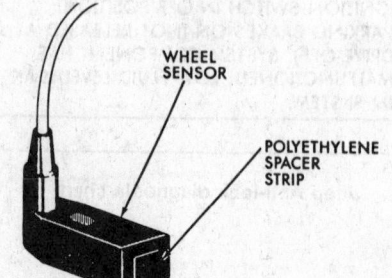

WHEEL
SENSOR

POLYETHYLENE
SPACER
STRIP

Sensor spacer strip

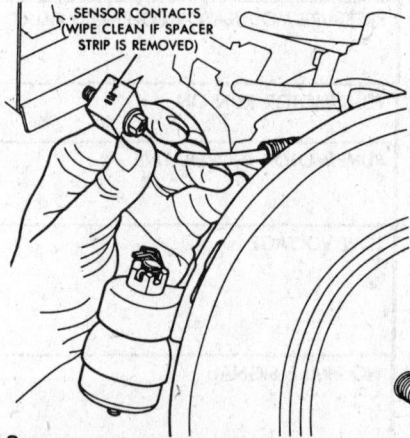

SENSOR CONTACTS
(WIPE CLEAN IF SPACER
STRIP IS REMOVED)

Sensor contacts (spacer strip removed)

Set rear sensor air gap to 0.030–0.036 in.

Removal and Installation
FRONT WHEEL SENSOR

1. Raise and safely support vehicle and turn wheel outward for easier access tosensor.

2. Note the sensor wire routing for installation reference. Cut the tie straps holding wire to steering knuckle and brake line.

3. If sensor is covered with heavy

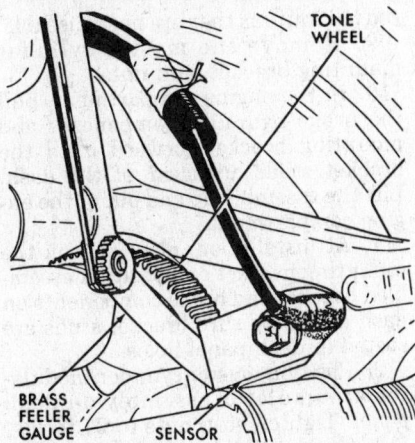

Adjusting sensor-to-wheel air gap

accumulations of dirt or mud, clean the sensor and surrounding area before proceeding. This is necessary to avoid possible damage when removing the sensor.

4. Remove the sensor attaching screw and remove the sensor from the steering knuckle.

5. Unseat the grommet holding the sensor wire in the wheel house panel.

6. In the engine compartment, disconnect the sensor wire connector at the anti-lock harness plug. Remove sensor and wire.

7. Before installing a new or reinstalling an original front wheel sensor, note the condition of the spacer strip. If the strip is securely attached and in good condition, a spacing (air gap) adjustment will not be needed. However, if the strip is loose or damaged, the correct air gap will have to be established with a brass feeler gauge.

8. To install a new sensor, route the wire through the wheelhouse grommet hole and connect the sensor to the harness plug. Seat the grommet.

9. Position the sensor on the steering knuckle and install the bolt fingertight.

10. If the sensor strip was in good condition and securely attached, lightly press the sensor against the tone wheel and tighten the bolt to 11 ft. lbs.

11. If the sensor spacer strip is missing, loose or damaged and the sensor contacts are exposed, perform the following steps:

   a. Remove the spacer strip if completely loose or torn. Wipe sensor contacts clean with a shop towel.

   b. Set sensor-to-tone wheel air gap to 0.013–0.019 in. with a brass feeler gauge.

   c. Tighten the sensor bolt to 11 ft. lbs. and recheck spacing.

12. Secure the sensor wire to the brake line and steering knuckle with new tie straps.

REAR WHEEL SENSOR REMOVAL

1. Raise and fold the rear seat forward for access to the rear sensor connectors. They are located near the ECU. Separate both sensor connections.

2. Push the sensor grommets and sensor wires through the floorpan.

3. Raise and safely support the vehicle and remove the wheel and brake drum.

4. Cut and remove the tie straps securing the sensor wires to the axle and rear brake hose.

5. Unseat the sensor backing plate grommet, remove the sensor attach bolt and remove the sensor by pulling the wire through the grommet hole in the backing plate.

6. Before installing a new or reinstalling an original rear wheel sensor, note the condition of the spacer strip. If the strip is securely attached and in good condition, a spacing (air gap) adjustment will not be needed. However, if the strip is loose or damaged, the correct air gap will have to be established with a brass feeler gauge.

7. If the sensor spacer strip is missing, loose or damaged and the sensor contacts are exposed, perform the following steps:

   a. Remove the spacer strip if completely loose or torn. Wipe sensor contacts clean with a shop towel.

   b. Set sensor-to-tone wheel air gap to 0.030–0.036 in. with a brass feeler gauge.

   c. Tighten the sensor bolt to 11 ft. lbs. and recheck spacing.

8. Route the sensor wires to the rear seat area, feed the wires through the access holes and seat the grommets in the floorpan.

9. Secure the sensor wire with wire ties to the rear brake hose and axle. Make sure the wire is clear or rotating components.

10. Install the brake drum and wheel then lower vehicle.

11. Connect the sensors to the harness connects, reposition carpet and fold down rear seat.

BOOSTER PUMP AND MOTOR

——— CAUTION ———

The normal working pressure of the anti-lock boost system is 1650–2050 psi. System pressure must be pumped down before any pressure lines are loosened or disconnected. Failure to do so could result in personal injury. To reduce system pressure, turn the ignition key OFF. Then apply the brakes 45–50 times (until pedal is firm) to reduce fluid pressure in the accumulator, booster, pump and lines. Wear safety goggles when disconnecting fluid lines.

1. Turn the ignition switch to the **OFF** position and apply the brakes

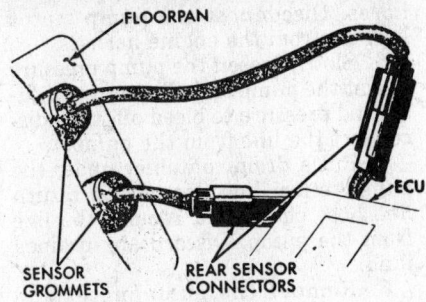

Rear sensor connectors

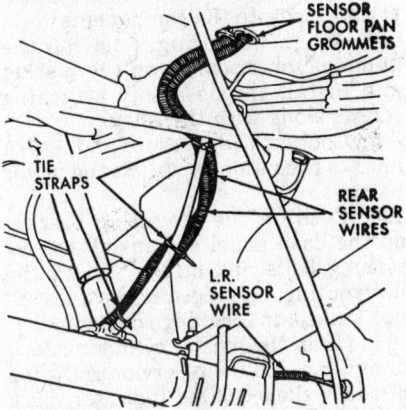

Rear sensor wire routing and attachment

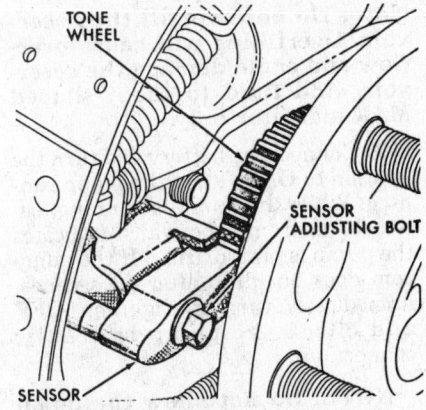

Rear sensor installation

(pump pedal) 45–50 times (until pedal is firm on initial apply) to reduce system fluid pressure.

NOTE: When the reserve pressure is depleted, the reservoir fluid level will rise above the MAX fill mark but will not overflow unless the reservoir was overfilled to begin with.

2. Disconnect the battery negative cable.

3. Remove the coolant pressure bottle retaining strap and move the reservoir aside. It is not necessary to disconnect the bottle hoses, just move the bottle aside for working clearance.

4. Remove the bolts holding the two-piece mounting bracket to the dash and inner fender panels. Rotate the bracket and pump/motor assembly to one side for access to the wires and

hoses. Disconnect the pump motor harness from the engine harness.

5. Slowly loosen the pump pressure line at the pump and allow any residual fluid pressure to bleed off, then disconnect the line from the pump.

5. Put a drain container under the pump return line, loosen the return line hose clamp and remove the line from the pump. Discard any drained fluid.

6. Remove the pump/motor and bracket as an assembly.

7. Remove the relay from the bracket and separate the components.

8. When installing, position the pump/motor assembly on the bracket and install the assembly attaching screws along with the relay.

9. Connect the pressure and return lines to the pump as well as the motor harness.

10. Position the mounting bracket on the dash panel and install the attaching bolts and screws. Check the line routing, making sure the lines are not kinked or touching the engine.

11. Clean the master cylinder exterior and cap. Fill the reservoir to the top of the V-shaped MAX indicator mark with DOT 3 rated brake fluid.

Note: Do not overfill the reservoir. Overfilling will cause overflow and could damage the reservoir. Add fluid to the V-shaped MAX indicator only.

12. Connect the battery and turn the ignition to **ON** to start the pump running. While the pump is running, listen for an rpm drop which indicates the pump is pressurizing. If the pump rpm does not drop after 20 seconds, immediately turn the ignition **OFF** and check the pump hydraulic connections.

NOTE: Do not allow the pump to run if it does not pressurize. If the pump rpm does not drop after 20 seconds run time, turn the ignition OFF immediately to avoid pump damage.

13. Add fluid to master cylinder reservoir if necessary.

MASTER CYLINDER

The master cylinder, modulator and accumulator are serviced as an assembly only. Do not attempt to disassemble or repair these components.

———— CAUTION ————

CAUTION: The normal working pressure of the anti-lock boost system is 1650–2050 psi. System pressure must be pumped down before any pressure lines are loosened or disconnected. Failure to do so could result in personal injury. To reduce system pressure, turn the ignition key OFF. Then apply

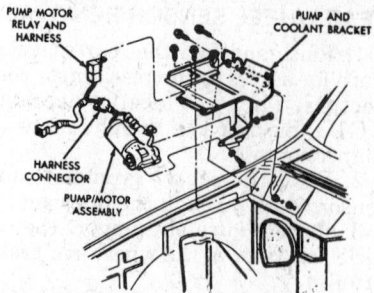

Pump motor harness and relay

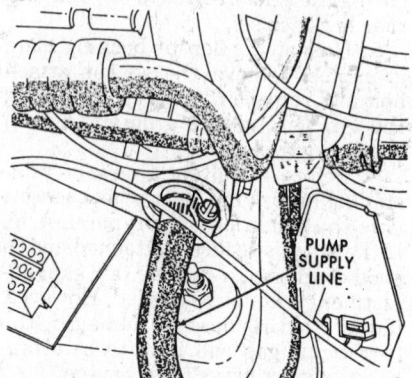

Pump pressure and supply line connections

the brakes 45–50 times (until pedal is firm) to reduce fluid pressure in the accumulator, booster, pump and lines. Wear safety goggles when disconnecting fluid lines.

1. Pump system pressure down by turning the ignition **OFF** and applying the brake pedal 45–50 times until the pedal becomes firm.

2. Disconnect the battery. Remove the windshield washer fluid reservoir attaching screrws, disconnect the hoses and wires and remove the reservoir.

3. Remove the air cleaner assembly, disconnect the ECU harness wire connectors at the pressure modulator and disconnect the wires at the proportioning valve differential switch.

4. Disconnect the high pressure line at the accumulator block. Cap the line to keep out dirt.

5. Disconnect the supply line at the reservoir. Cap the line to keep out dirt. Discard any fluid that drains from the line.

6. Disconnect the low pressure switch wires, and the wires at the modulator boost pressure and fluid level switches.

7. Disconnect the front brakelines at the outboard side of the pressure modulator.

8. In the passenger compartment, remove the instrument panel lower trim cover for access to the brake pedal. Disconnect the brakelight switch wires, remove the master cylinder pushrod bolt and disconnect the pushrod from the pedal. Discard the push-

rod bolt nuts as they are not reuseable.

9. Remove the master cylinder mounting bracket stud nuts.

10. In the engine compartment, pull the brake hydraulic components and mounting bracket forward until the bracket studs are clear of the dash. Lift the assembly up and out of the engine compartment.

11. At installation, place pad on the mounting bracket assembled bracket and brake components on dash panel. Be sure bracket studs are seated in dash panel holes.

12. Position master cylinder/modulator/accumulator assembly on dash panel. Tighten stud nuts to 27 ft. lbs.

13. Connect the harness wires to the modulator, low pressure switch, differential switch and the low fluid and boost pressure switches.

14. In the passenger compartment, install the nuts of the mounting studs and torque to 31 ft. lbs.

15. Align the brake pedal, brakelight switch, master cylinder push rod and install the pushrod bolt.

NOTE: The pushrod bolt must be installed correctly to avoid interference with the dash bracket. The bolt must be installed with the bolt head at the left side of the pedal.

16. Install new nuts on the push rod bolt. Tighten the inner lock nut to 25 ft. lbs. and the outer jam nut to only 75 in. lbs. Connect the brake light switch wires and install the lower trim panel.

17. In the engine compartment, connect the brake lines to the proportioning valve and connect the pressure and return lines to the accumulator.

18. Install the air cleaner assembly, connect the hoses and wires to the washer reservoir and install the reservoir to the fender panel.

19. Clean the master cylinder exterior and cap. Fill the reservoir to the top of the V-shaped MAX indicator mark with DOT 3 rated brake fluid.

20. Connect the battery and turn the ignition to ON to start the pump running. While the pump is running, listen for an rpm drop which indicates the pump is pressurizing. If the pump rpm does not drop after 20 seconds, immediately turn the ignition OFF and check the pump hydraulic connections.

NOTE: Do not allow the pump to run if it does not pressurize. If the pump rpm does not drop after 20 seconds run time, turn the ignition OFF immediately to avoid pump damage.

21. Add fluid to master cylinder reservoir if necessary.

22. Bleed the brake system.

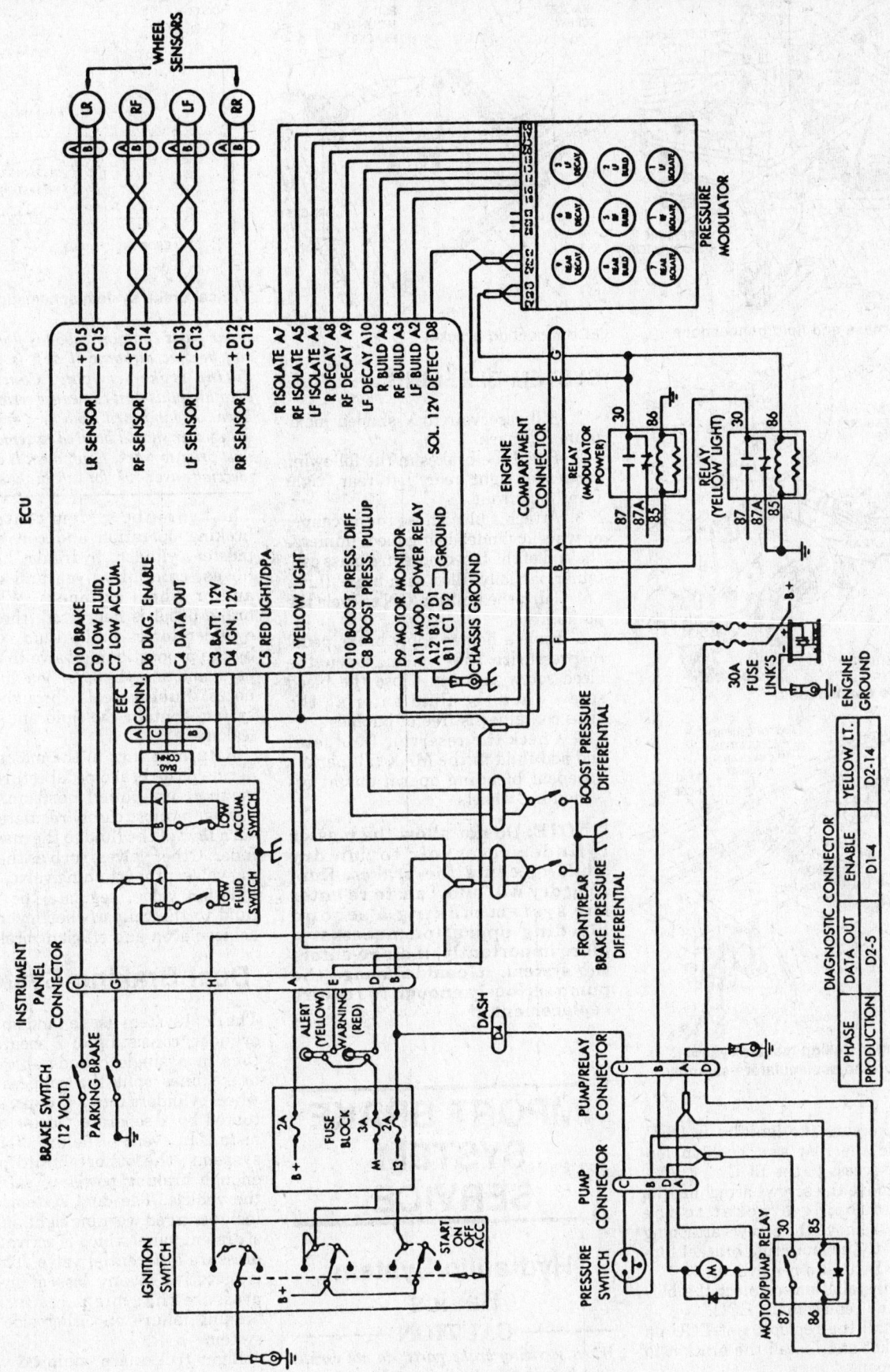

Anti-lock ECU wiring diagram

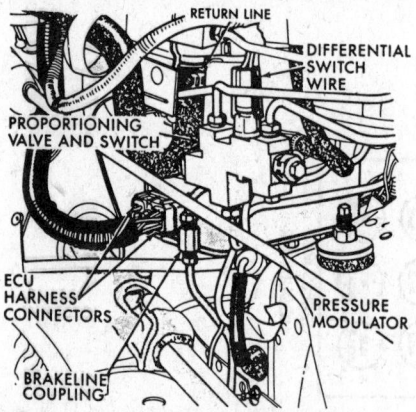
ECU harness and fluid connections

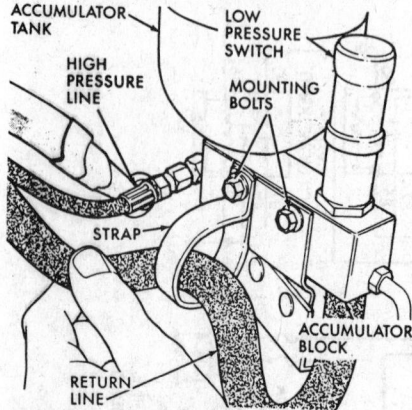
Fluid line connections

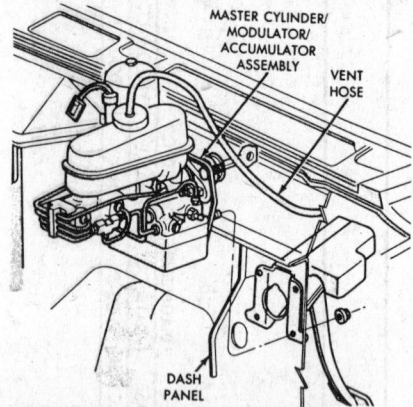
Removing/installing master cylinder, modulator and accumulator assembly

ECU

1. Make sure the ignition is **OFF**, then fold the rear seat cushion forward for access to the ECU.
2. Remove the screws attaching the ECU mounting bracket to the floorpan, remove the screws attaching the ECU to the mounting bracket, unplug the ECU and remove.
3. At installation, connect the harness of the replacement ECU.
4. Install the replacement ECU on the bracket and install the bracket to the floorpan.
5. Fold down rear seat.

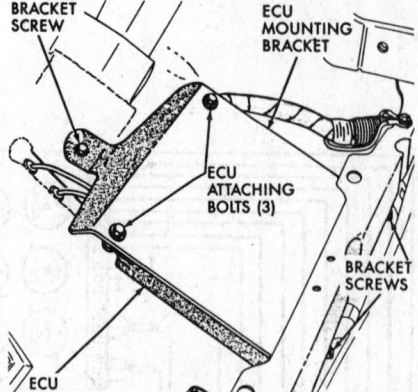
ECU mounting bracket

SYSTEM BLEEDING

1. Fill reservoir to V-shaped maximum fill mark.
2. Bleed the brakes in the following sequence: right rear, left rear, right front, left front.
3. Attach a bleed hose to the caliper or wheel cylinder being bled, immerse the end of the bleed hose in a glass container partially filled with brake fluid.
4. Turn the ignition **ON** to cycle the pump.
5. Have a helper apply brake pedal to pressurize the system. Open the bleed screw ½ turn. Close the bleed screw when the fluid entering the glass container is free of bubbles.
6. Check the reservoir fluid level and add fluid to the **MAX** fill mark.
7. Repeat bleeding operations at remaining wheels.

NOTE: Do not allow the master cylinder reservoir to run dry while bleeding the brakes. Running dry will allow air to re-enter the system making a second bleeding operation necessary. More importantly, if air re-enters the system, it could damage the pump seriously enough to require replacement.

IMPORT BRAKE SYSTEM SERVICE

Hydraulic System Basics

——— CAUTION ———

When servicing brake parts, do not create dust by grinding the linings or by blowing them clean with compressed air. Many

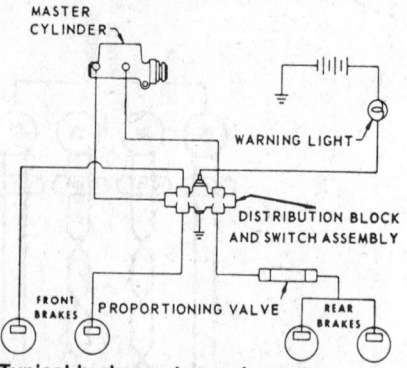
Typical brake system schematic

brake parts contains asbestos fibers which can become airborne if dust is generated during brake servicing. Continuously breathing this dust can cause serious bodily harm. A dampened cloth or a spray bottle with water should be used to remove brake dust prior to work. Equipment is also commercially available for safe brake servicing.

The hydraulic system controls the braking operation and consists of a master cylinder, hydraulic lines and hoses, control valves and calipers and/or wheel cylinders. When the brake pedal is depressed, the master cylinder forces brake fluid regulated by the proportioning valve to the calipers and/or cylinders, via lines and hoses. Rubber seals throughout the system contain the fluid and prevent leakage.

Return springs in the master cylinder help the brake pedal return to the original unapplied position. Check valves (in most cases) regulate the return flow of the fluid to the master cylinder. Other valves, such as the metering valve, proportioning valve, or combination valve, regulate the flow of fluid to the caliper/wheel cylinder, to achieve even and efficient braking.

Dual Braking Systems

The dual system uses a tandem master cylinder, consisting of 2 separate pistons in a single cylinder bore. Dual brake lines split the calipers and/or wheel cylinders into 2 groups, each actuated by a separate master cylinder piston. In event of failure of 1 of the systems, the other should provide enough braking power to safely stop the vehicle. The dual system usually includes a red warning light on the instrument panel which is activated by a pressure differential valve. The valve is sensitive to any loss of hydraulic pressure that might result from a braking failure on either side of the system.

Light trucks are equipped with either a front/rear wheel split or a diagonally split system. On front/rear sys-

tems, the front wheels are connected to one circuit while the rear wheels are connected to the other circuit. Diagonally split systems have diagonally opposite wheels connected to each circuit.

Brake Fluid

Approved DOT3 heavy duty type brake fluid retains the correct consistency throughout the widest range of temperature variation, will not affect rubber cups or seals, helps protect the metal parts of the brake system against failure and has a high boiling point to assure long trouble free brake operation when properly maintained.

Never use brake fluid from a container that has been used for any other liquid. Mineral oil, alcohol, antifreeze, or cleaning solvents, even in very small quantities, will contaminate brake fluid. Contaminated brake fluid will cause rubber parts within the hydraulic system to swell or deteriorate. Always return the cap to the fluid container after using the brake fluid. This will prevent the fluid from absorbing moisture from the surrounding air, which will lower its boiling point. Do not use brake fluid that has been sitting in an unopened container for an extending amount of time.

Hydraulic Line Repair

Steel tubing is used for the hydraulic lines between any 2 parts that do not move independant of one another, like the master cylinder and the front brake tube connector, or along the axle tubes between the brake tee and the rear brake cylinders. Brake hoses provide a flexible connection between the tube and a part that moves independantly, like the hose that connects the brake tube to the front brake calipers or the tube that runs along the body of the vehicle conneted by hose down to the axle.

BRAKE TUBING

If a section of the brake tube becomes damaged, the entire section should be replaced with tubing of the same type, size, shape, and length. Copper tubing should not be used in the hydraulic system. When bending brake tubing to fit the frame or axle contours, be careful not to kink or crack the tube.

All brake tubing should be double flared to provide good leak proof connections. Always clean the inside of a new brake tube with clean isopropyl alcohol before installing.

BRAKE HOSE

All flexible brake hoses should be carefully inspected often. They should be replaced if they show any signs of softening, cracking, swelling or other damage.

When installing a new brake hose, make sure it is not twisted and is positioned to avoid contact with other vehicle components under any suspension condition.

Hydraulic Control Valves

PRESSURE DIFFERENTIAL VALVE

The valve activates a panel warning lamp in event of pressure loss failure. As pressure fails in one split system, the other system's normal pressure causes a piston in the switch to compress a spring and move until an electrical circuit is completed lighting the dash lamp. Normally, the spring balanced piston automatically recenters when the brake pedal is released, thus flashing the warning lamp only during brake application and will re-center automatically after repairs are successfully completed and the system is properly bled.

METERING VALVE

Often used on vehicles equipped with front disc and rear drum brakes, the metering valve improves braking balance during light brake applications by preventing application of the front disc brakes unitl the pressure to the rear brakes overcomes the tension of the rear brake shoe return springs. Thus, when the front brake pads contact the rotor the rear brakes shoes move outward to contact the brake drum at approximately the same time.

The metering valve should be inspected whenever the brakes are serviced. A slight amount of moisture inside the boot does not indicate a defective valve, however a great deal of fluid indicates a faulty valve and replacement is recommended. Make sure to install the brake lines in the correct ports when installing a new valve, crossed lines will cause the hydraulic system to malfunction.

PROPORTIONING VALVE

The proportioning valve is used to transmit full inoput pressure to the rear brakes up to a certain point (the split point). Beyond the split point, it reduces the amount of pressure to the rear brakes according to a certain ratio, which is built into the valve. On light pedal applications, equal braking pressure is transmitted to to the front and rear brakes. During heavier brake applications, however, the pessure delivered to the rear brakes is lower than that at the front brakes to prevent rear wheel lockup and skidding.

Whenever the brakes are serviced, the valve should be inspected. To check valve operation, install hydraulic gauges ahead of and behind the valve and determine that it has an operative transition point above which rear brake pressure is proportioned. If the valve is leaking replacement is required.

COMBINATION VALVE

A valve combining two or three functions (metering, proportioning, and/or brake warning) may be used. The combination valve is usually mounted under the hood close to the master cylinder, where the brake lines can be easily routed to the front and rear wheels. The combination valve is a non-serviceable unit, and if found to be malfunctioning, must be replaced as a unit.

Disc Brakes

CALIPERS

Caliper disc brakes can be divided into 3 types: dual piston floating caliper, single piston floating caliper and single piston sliding caliper. On the floating caliper types, the inner pad is hydraulically pushed into contact with the disc, while the reaction force generated is used to pull the outer pad into contact with the other side of the disc, made possible by allowing the caliper to move slightly along the axle's center line. Two pistons may be used to accomodate more severe braking requirements on heavier vehicles. All disc brake systems are self-adjusting and have no provision for amnual adjustment.

With the sliding caliper type, the caliper assembly slides along the smooth and lubricated surface of a key or stopper (nomenclature varies between manufacturers) which is held stationary by cotter pins or retaining bolts. The caliper is held against the key or stopper with 1 or 2 support springs.

One of the recent developments in brake equipment materials includes the use of aluminum calipers for the purpose of saving weight. A vast array of anti-rattle springs, clips and anti-squeal pads and shims are used by manufacturers to prevent the pads from making any undesirable noises.

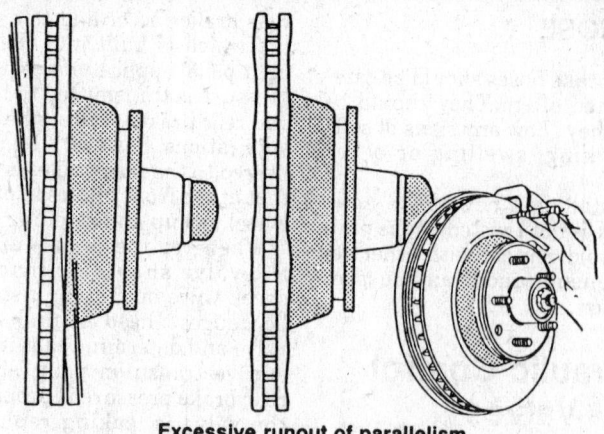

Excessive runout of parallelism

Wobble pump action resulting from a warped rotor

In addition, most brake pads are comprised of semi-metallic materials for improved stopping power. Unfortunately, these pads often produce an annoying brake squeal as they are used, but the squeal itself should not reduce the stopping ability of the pads. If the pad kit includes plates or shims, use them when servicing the disc brakes. Aftermarket spreads and sprays are also available to quiet noisy pads. It is always a good idea to replace calipers in pairs.

ROTORS

Rotors provide the surface upon which the brake pads stop the vehicle. It is important to inspect the rotor carefully. Manufacturers differ some on permissable runout (warpage) of the rotor, but excessive runout can usually be felt as a pulsation at the brake pedal regardless of the specification. A wobble pump effect is created when the rotor is not perfectly flat and the pad hits a high spot forcing fluid back into the master cylinder. This alternating pressure causes a pulsation which is felt at the pedal when the brakes are applied. An excessive amount of runout can cause the pads to be out of adjustment because they cannot hold themselves against the rotor at all times. It is always a good idea to replace rotors in pairs.

To check the actual runout of the ro-

tor, fist tighten the spindle nut to remove all endplay. Fasten a dial indicator on the suspension on a convenient location so the pin contacts the rotor surface about 1 in. from its outer edge. Set the dial at 0 and check the runout while turning the rotor 1 full revolution. If the rotor is warpe beyond limits, the rotor should be replace. Rotors the are not warped beyond the specification can be resurfaced, as long as the final thickness is not below the minumum thickness requirement of the rotor.

Lateral Runout: The wobbly movement of the rotor from side to side as it rotates. Excessive lateral runout causes the rotor faces to knock bask the pads and can cause brake chatter, shudder or vibration.

Parallelism (lack of): This refers to the amount of variation in the thickness of the rotor. Excessive variation of parallelism can cause a pulsating pedal, front end vibrations or grabbing condiions; a condition comparable to an out-of-round brake drum. Check parallelism with a micrometer. Measure the thickness of the rotor a 8 or more equally spaced locations on the rotor, equally distant from the outer edge, preferably at the mid-point of the braking surface. A lack of parallelism results if the difference between the highest and lowest measurement is beyond the parallelism specification.

Surface or Micro-inch finish, flatness and smoothness: These terms all refer to the degree of perfection of the flat surfaces on each side fo the rotor. Visually inspecting the rotor, the machined surface should have a fine ground polish with a swirling pattern to reduce brake squeal.

DISC BRAKE PADS

The brake pads are the tools that the vehicle uses to stop, so they should be inspected very carefully. Pads should be replaced only in sets (both sides of

the same axle) if any of the pads is damaged, cracked, burnt, or separated from the plate that it is glued or riveted to. Replace the pads if any of their lining is worn down to $\frac{1}{16}$ in. thickness. If the lining is allowed to wear beyond this point, severe and costly damage to the rotor may result. Note that individual state inspection guidelines take precedence over these general recommendation.

Floating caliper type disc brake pads may wear at an angle; the measurement should always be taken at the narrowest end of the taper. Tapered lining should be replaced if the amount of tapering exceeds $\frac{1}{8}$ in. from end to end and the cause of the taper should be investigated and repaired, if possible.

To prevent potentially costly paint damage, remove some brake fluid from the master fluid reservoir and install the reservoir cover before servicing the pads. When installing new pads, the caliper piston is forced back into its bore and fluid is pushed back into the master cylinder. The fluid could spill and remove paint from any painted surface that it comes in contact with.

When the caliper is removed from its mouning adaptor, do not allow it to dangle by the brake hose. This can damage the hose and create a dangerous situation. Always rest the caliper on a suspensiion member of suspent it from the frame with a wire or rope.

Drum Brakes

WHEEL CYLINDERS

The wheel cylinder performs in response to the master cylinder. It receives fluid from the hydraulic tube through its inlet port. As the pressure increases, the wheel cylinder cups and pistons are forced apart. As a result, the hydraulic pressure is converted into mechanical force acting on the brake shoes. The variation in wheel cylinder size (diameter) is one of the factors controlling the distribution of braking force in a vehicle. Bleeder screws are provided to remove air or vapor trapped in the system.

Wheel cylinders may need reconditioning or replacement whenever the brake shoes are replaced or when required to correct a leak condition. On many designs, the wheel cylinders can be diassembled without removing them from the backing plate. On some designs, however, the cylinder is mounted in an indention in the backing plate or a cylinder piston stop is welded to the backing plate. When servicing brakes of this type, the cylinder must be removed from the backing plate before being disassembled.

Leaks which coat the boot and the cylinder with fluid, or result in a dropped reservoir fluid level, or dampen and stain the brake linings are dangerous. Such leaks can cause the brakes to grab or fail and should be immediately corrected. A leakage, not immediately apparent, can be detected by pulling back the cylinder boot. A small amount of fluid seepage dampening the interior of the boot is normal, however a dripping boot is not. Unless other conditions causing a brake to pull, grab, or drag becomes obvious, the wheel cylinder is a suspect and should be included in general reconditioning. It is always a good idea to service wheel cylinders in pairs.

Cylinder binding may be caused by rust, deposits, grime, or swollen cups due to fluid contamination, or by a cup wedged into an excessive piston clearance. If the clearance between the pistons and the bore wall exceeds allowable values, a condition called heel drag may exist. It can result in rapid cup wear and can cause the pistons to retract very slowly when the brakes are released. A ring of a hard, crystal like substance is sometimes noticed in the cylinder bore where the piston stops after the brakes are released.

BRAKE DRUMS

The condition of the brake drum surface is equally as important as the surface of the lining. All drum braking surfaces should be clean, smooth, free of hark spots, heat damage, scoring and forign material embedded in the braking surface. The drum should not be out-of-round, bell mouthed or barrel shaped. Drums should be checked with a drum micrometer before resurfacing to see if it within over-size limits. If the drum is within safe limints, it should be machined to true the drum surface and to remove any contamination in the surface from previous linings and road matter. Too much metal removed from the drum is unsafe and may result in brake fade due to the thin drum not being able to absorb the heat generated, vibration from ensuing drum distortion and generally unsafe conditions.

Brake drum runout should not exceed 0.005 in. Drums machined to more than 0.060 in. oversize are unsafe and should be replaced. It is always good practice to replace drums on both whels at the same time to ensure even braking.

If the drums are in good condition, smooth up any slight scoring by sanding with coarse sand paper, then polishing with emery cloth. If deep scores or grooves are present, machine the drums to restore them to good operating condition.

DRUM BRAKE SHOES

The brake shoes should also be inspected very carefully. Shoes should be replaced only in sets (both sides of the same axle) if any of the shoes are bent, damaged, cracked, burnt, or separated from the plate that it is glued or riveted to. Replace the shoes if any of their lining is worn down to $1/16$ in. thickness. If the lining is allowed to wear beyond this point, severe and costly damage to the drum may result. Note that individual state inspection guidelines take precedence over these general recommendation.

Rear brakes with weak return springs may create a bell-mouthed condition which causes the shoes to wear at an angle; if so the measurement should always be taken at the narrowest end of the taper. Tapered linings should be replaced if the amount of tapering is excessive and the cause of the taper should be investigated and repaired, if possible.

Disassemble and assemble one side at a time to prevent improper assembly. This will also provide a model that can be refered if the installation doen not look right. Always complete the brake shoe adjustment with the wheels installed and adjust the parking brake cable last.

STAR AND SCREW ADJUSTER

Star and screw self-adjusters are used on most late-model vehicles. This system requires manual adjustment only when the shoes have been replaced, when the star wheel has been disturbed or when the star wheel is not operating properly. As the star wheel is turned, it expands or contracts the shoes accordingly.

In most cases, the brakes can be initially adjusted by removing the drum, measuring the internal diameter of the drum and setting the shoes to slightly less than that measurement. Normally, the brakes will self-adjust when the vehicle is backed up and the brakes are firmly applied.

CHRYSLER IMPORTS/ MITSUBISHI

NOTE: When cleaning brake system components, use only brake fluid or denatured isopropyl alcohol. Never use a mineral-based solvent such as gasoline or paint thinner; these fluids will leave a residue that may swell and deteriorate rubber parts within the system. All alcohol must be removed from the system when the work is done because alcohol mixed with brake fluid lowers its boiling point.

Do not hone any aluminum bores. There is a hard anodized coating on the aluminum which will be removed if honed. This will allow the aluminum to wear quickly and will damage the component.

Master Cylinder Service

Disassembly and Assembly

1. Remove the brake fluid reservoir retainer screw, if equipped and remove the reservoir and seals or remove the reservoir unions and seals.
2. Push the primary piston in and remove the stopper bolt and gasket.
3. Hold the pistons in and remove the snapring.

NOTE: Do not disassemble either piston assembly as the individual parts are not serviceable.

4. Let the primary piston spring out and remove the primary piston assembly.
5. Remove the secondary piston assembly. This may be accomplished by carefully blowing low pressure compressed air through the secondary side outlet port if it does not come out easily.
6. Remove the brake line connector block and washers.
To assemble:
7. Coat the master cylinder bore and secondary and primary piston seals liberally with brake fluid.
8. Install both assemblies to the master cylinder.
9. Push the pistons in and install a new snapring.
10. Hold the pistons in and install the stopper bolt with a new gasket.
11. Install the brake fluid reservoir or unions with new seals. Install the reservoir retaining screw, if equipped.
12. Install the connector block with new washers.

Brake Booster Service

The brake boosters installed on these vehicles are not serviceable. If the unit is defective, replace the entire assembly.

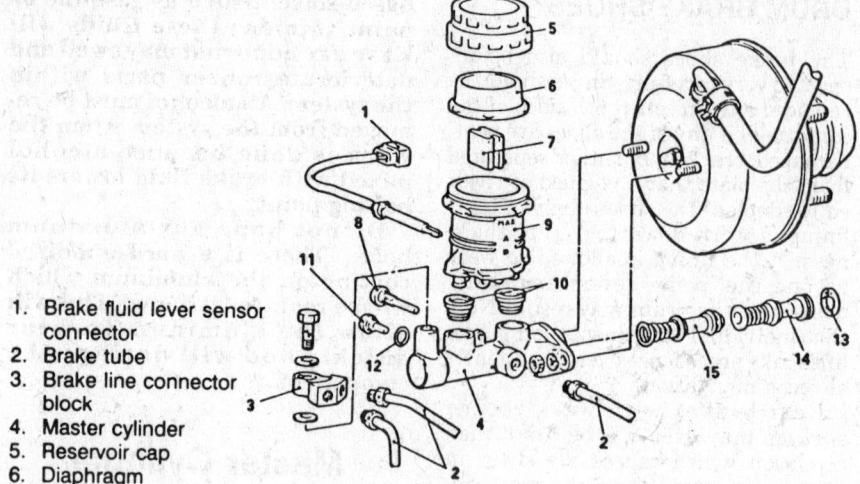

1. Brake fluid lever sensor connector
2. Brake tube
3. Brake line connector block
4. Master cylinder
5. Reservoir cap
6. Diaphragm
7. Float
8. Reservoir retainer screw
9. Reservoir
10. Reservoir seals
11. Piston stopper bolt
12. Gasket
13. Snapring
14. Primary piston assembly
15. Secondary assembly

Chrysler/Mitsubishi master cylinder

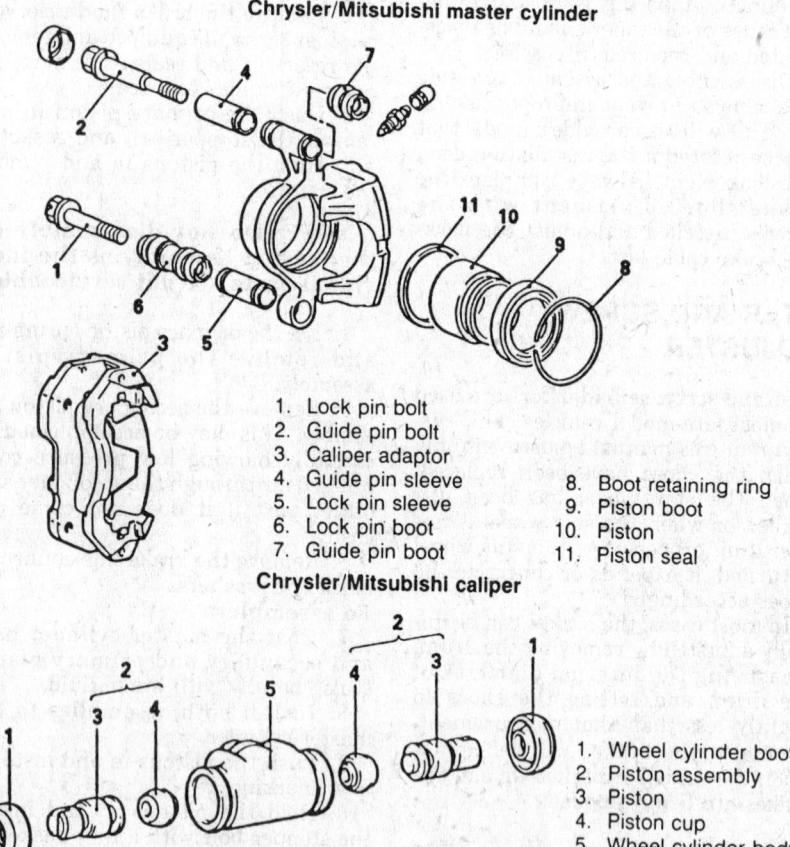

1. Lock pin bolt
2. Guide pin bolt
3. Caliper adaptor
4. Guide pin sleeve
5. Lock pin sleeve
6. Lock pin boot
7. Guide pin boot
8. Boot retaining ring
9. Piston boot
10. Piston
11. Piston seal

Chrysler/Mitsubishi caliper

1. Wheel cylinder boot
2. Piston assembly
3. Piston
4. Piston cup
5. Wheel cylinder body

Chrysler/Mitsubishi wheel cylinder

Caliper Service

Disassembly and Assembly

1. Remove the bleeder screw.
2. Drain the brake fluid from the caliper.
3. Remove the dust boot ring and the dust boot.
4. Position a shop rag opposite the top of the piston. Apply low pressure compressed air to the fluid inlet and carefully blow the piston out of the bore.

—— **CAUTION** ——

Do not put fingers where the piston will land when it is blown out of the caliper. The force of the piston can crush fingers and cause personal injury.

5. Remove the piston seal from inside the bore.

To assemble:

6. Blow out all fluid passages with low pressure compressed air.
7. Slight corrosion or rust can be removed with commutator paper or crocus cloth. Replace pistons that are pitted, scored, peeling or otherwise damaged.
8. Lubricate the caliper bore with brake fluid. Lubricate the seal and install it in the groove.
9. Lubricate the piston and install it to the bore until it bottoms. If the piston will not go in by hand, it is probably cocked. Remove it and reinstall.
10. Apply lubricant to the dust boot mounting groove and install the boot. Install the retaining ring.
11. Apply rust penetrant to the bleeder screw threads and install to the caliper. Tighten it until it is just snug against its seat.

Wheel Cylinder Service

Disassembly and Assembly

1. Remove the bleeder screw, if equipped.
2. Remove both rubber boots.
3. Remove the piston assemblies, each consisting of the piston and cup.
4. Remove the piston cups from the pistons, being careful not to scratch the piston.
5. Remove the return spring.
6. Hone the cylinder bore if it is not damaged, to provide a smooth sealing surface. Wash and dry the bore after honing.

To assemble:

7. Lubricate the cylinder bore with brake fluid.
8. Lubricate the new piston cups and install them to the pistons, with their lips facing upward. Install the assemblies to the cylinder.
9. Apply lubricant to the boot mounting groove and install the boot.
10. Apply rust penetrant to the bleeder screw threads and install to the wheel cylinder. Tighten it until it is just snug against its seat.

ISUZU

NOTE: When cleaning brake system components, use only brake fluid or denatured isopropyl alcohol. Never use a mineral-based solvent such as gasoline or paint thinner; these fluids will leave a residue that may swell and deteriorate rubber parts within

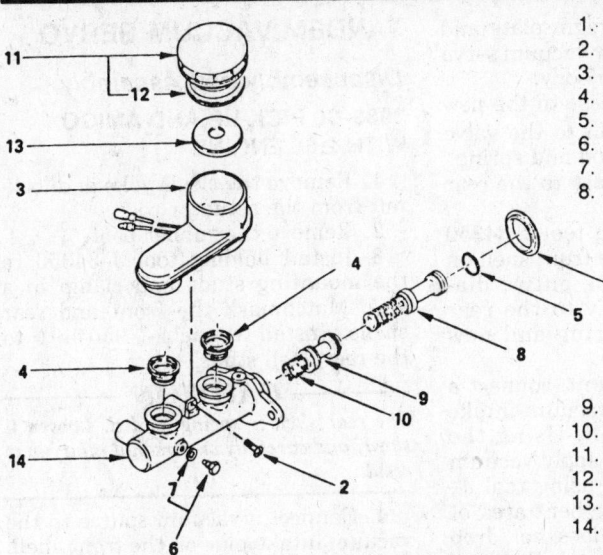

1. Dust seal
2. Screw
3. Brake fluid reservoir
4. Grommet
5. Snapring
6. Stopper bolt
7. Gasket
8. Primary piston assembly

9. Secondary assembly
10. Secondary piston spring
11. Reservoir cover
12. Seal
13. Float magnet
14. Cylinder body

Isuzu master cylinder

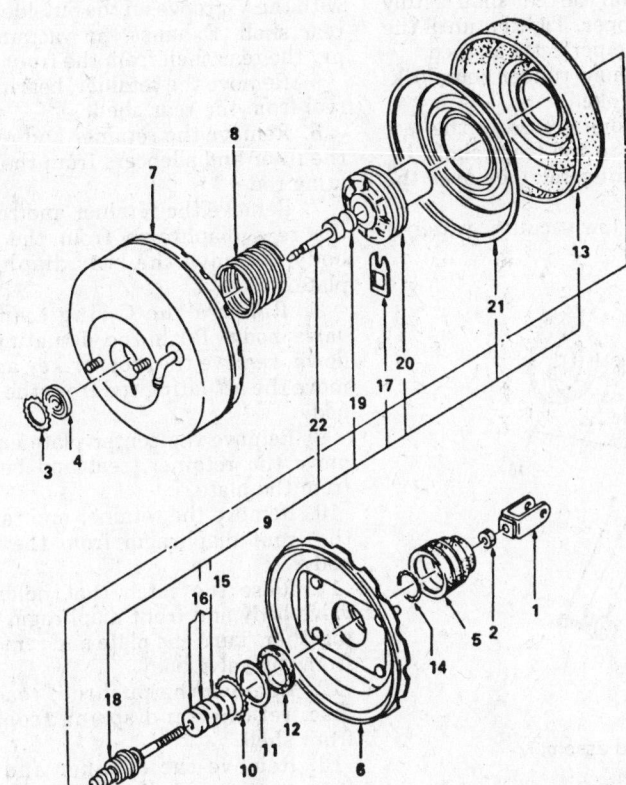

1. Clevis yoke
2. Locknut
3. Servo retainer
4. Seal
5. Rubber boot
6. Rear shell assembly
7. Front shell assembly
8. Servo spring
9. Diaphragm plate assembly
10. Servo retainer
11. Servo bearing

12. Valve body seal
13. Vacuum servo diaphragm
14. Servo retainer
15. Vacuum filter
16. Vacuum silencer
17. Actuating rod stopper key
18. Actuating rod
19. Reaction disc
20. Valve body
21. Diaphragm plate
22. Pushrod assembly

Isuzu single vacuum servo booster

the system. All alcohol must be removed from the system when the work is done because alcohol mixed with brake fluid lowers its boiling point.

Do not hone any aluminum bores. There is a hard anodized coating on the aluminum which will be removed if honed. This will allow the aluminum to wear quickly and will damage the component.

Master Cylinder Service

Disassembly and Assembly

1. Remove the brake fluid reservoir retainer screw.
2. Remove the reservoir and seals.
3. Remove the dust seal from the end of the master cylinder.
4. Push the primary piston in and remove the stopper bolt and gasket.
5. Hold the pistons in and remove the snapring.

NOTE: Do not disassemble either piston assembly as the individual parts are not serviceable.

6. Let the primary piston spring out and remove the primary piston assembly and end washer, if equipped.
7. Remove the secondary piston assembly. This may be accomplished by carefully blowing low pressure compressed air through the secondary side outlet port if it does not come out easily.

To assemble:

8. Coat the master cylinder bore and secondary and primary piston seals liberally with brake fluid. Install both assemblies to the master cylinder.
9. Push the pistons in and install a new snapring.
10. Hold the pistons in and install the stopper bolt with a new gasket.
11. Install the brake fluid reservoir with new seals. Install the reservoir retaining screw.

Brake Booster Service

SINGLE VACUUM SERVO

Disassembly and Assembly

EXCEPT 1988–90 PICK-UP AND AMIGO WITH 2.6L ENGINE AND 1988–90 TROOPER II

1. Remove the clevis yoke and locknut from the actuator rod. Remove the low vacuum switch (diesel only).
2. Pry out the servo retainer and seal from the front of the shell.
3. Remove the rubber boot.

CAUTION
The rear shell is spring loaded. Loosen it slowly and carefully or personal injury may result.

4. Matchmark the front and rear shells. Using wrench J–9504–01 and holder J–34250, separate the 2 shells slowly. Remove the servo spring.

5. Remove the entire diaphragm plate assembly.

6. Pry out the servo retainer, bearing and valve body seal from the rear shell.

7. Using a knife, cut the vacuum servo diaphragm and remove. Make sure not to damage the valve body when cutting.

8. Remove the servo retainer from the valve body.

9. Remove the vacuum filter and silencers from the valve body.

10. Push in the actuating rod and remove the rod stopper key. Remove the actuating rod assembly.

11. Remove the reaction disc, valve body, diaphragm plate and pushrod assembly.

To assemble:

12. Install the new actuating rod assembly to the valve body. Push the rod in and install the rod stopper key.

13. Install the new vacuum silencers and filter.

14. Install the new retainer to the rear shell.

15. Install the diaphragm plate and carefully attach the new vacuum servo diaphragm to the valve body.

16. Apply silicone grease to the new reaction disc and install to the valve body. Install the pushrod and spring.

17. Apply silicone grease to the rear shell seal and install.

18. Mount the holding tool J–34350 in a vise and mount the front shell on the tool. Assemble the entire diaphragm plate assembly to the rear shell. Install the bearing and new retainer.

19. To assemble the unit, connect a vacuum source to the vacuum intake pipe on the front shell. Using the matchmarks as guides, apply vacuum and assemble the unit using tool J–9504–01. Make sure the bent area of the of the diaphragm does not drop against the front and rear shell engaging areas.

20. Rotate the rear shell clockwise until the notch on the rear shell is fully against the stopper. Tighten until the matchmarks are perfectly aligned.

21. Install the new rubber boot, locknut and clevis yoke.

22. Apply silicone grease to the last seal and install to the front shell. Install the remaining retainer over the seal.

23. Install the low vacuum switch, if equipped.

TANDEM VACUUM SERVO

Disassembly and Assembly

1988–90 PICK-UP AND AMIGO WITH 2.6L ENGINE

1. Remove the clevis yoke and locknut from the actuator rod.

2. Remove the rubber boot.

3. Install holding tool J–34350 to the mounting studs and clamp in a vise. Matchmark the front and rear shells. Install wrench J–9504–01 to the rear shell studs.

CAUTION
The rear shell is spring loaded. Loosen it slowly and carefully or personal injury may result.

4. Connect a vacuum source to the vacuum intake pipe on the front shell. Rotate the lever counterclockwise slightly (about 1/20 turn). The front shell caulking tab must be aligned with the V-groove on the outside of the rear shell. Exhaust the vacuum and pry the rear shell from the front shell.

5. Remove the retainer, bearing and seal from the rear shell.

6. Remove the retainer and remove the filter and silencers from the actuating rod.

7. Remove the retainer and remove the rear diaphragm from the valve body. Remove the rear diaphragm plate.

8. Remove the C-ring from the valve body. Push the actuating rod down, remove the stopper key and remove the actuating rod from the valve body.

9. Remove the center plate and remove the retainer, seal and bearing from the plate.

10. Remove the retainer and remove the front diaphragm from the valve body.

11. Raise the catch that holds the valve body and front diaphragm plate together. Turn the plate and remove it from the valve body.

12. Remove the pushrod, reaction disc, retainer and spring from the front shell.

13. Remove the retainer and seal from the front shell.

To assemble:

14. Apply silicone grease to the seal and install to the front shell and install the retainer over the seal. Lubricate the diaphragm sliding surfaces on the inside of the shell with the same grease.

15. Lubricate the pushrod stem and install to the hub reaction disc.

16. Lubricate and install a new O-ring to the valve body. Set the diaphragm plate on the valve body and rotate it to install. Install the new front diaphragm and retainer.

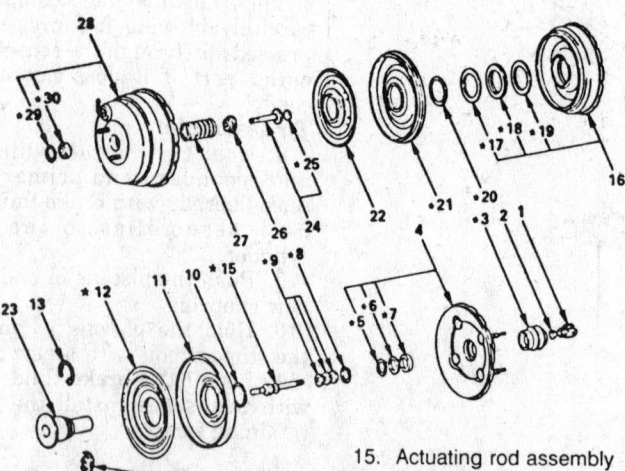

1. Clevis yoke	15. Actuating rod assembly
2. Locknut	16. Center plate
3. Rubber boot	17. Retainer
4. Rear shell	18. Seal
5. Retainer	19. Bearing
6. Bearing	20. Retainer
7. Valve body seal	21. Front diaphragm
8. Retainer	22. Front diaphragm plate
9. Filter and silencer	23. Valve body and O-ring
10. Retainer	24. Pushrod
11. Rear diaphragm	25. Reaction disc
12. Rear diaphragm plate	26. Retainer
13. C-ring	27. Spring
14. Stopper key	28. Front shell
	29. Retainer
	30. Plate and seal

Isuzu tandam vacuum servo— Pick-Up and Amigo with 2.6L engine

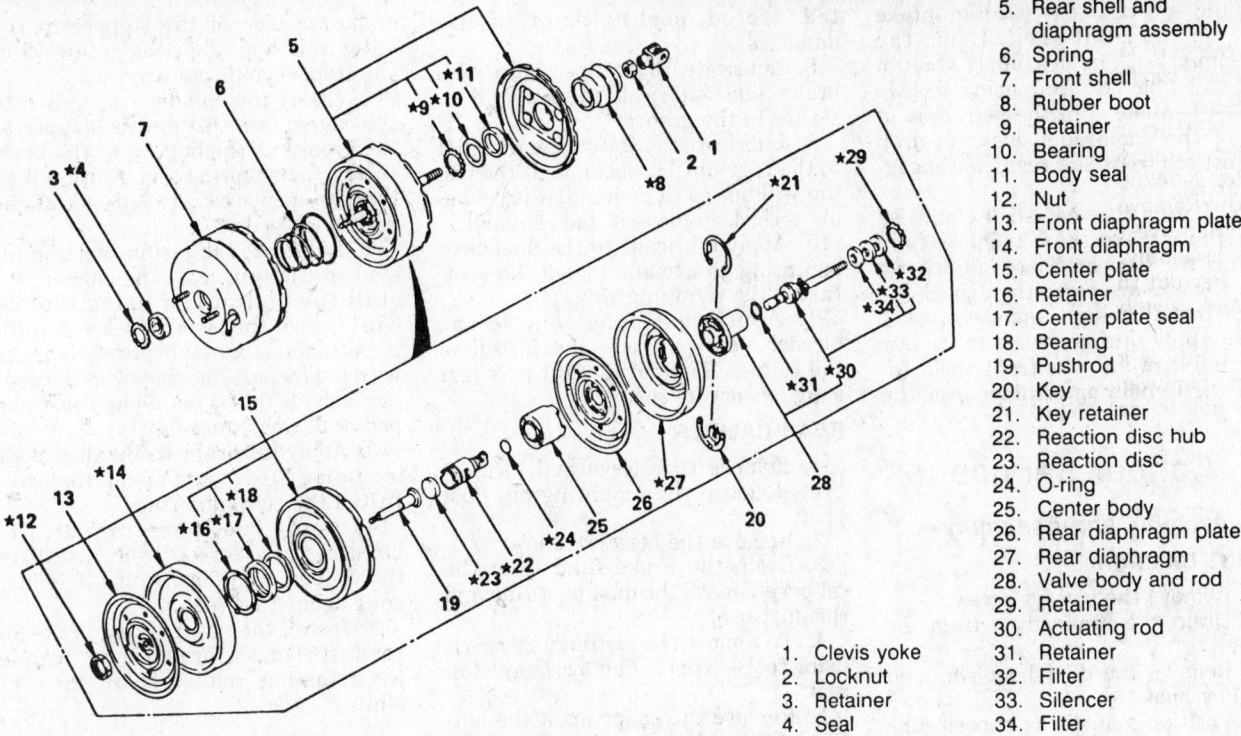

5. Rear shell and
   diaphragm assembly
6. Spring
7. Front shell
8. Rubber boot
9. Retainer
10. Bearing
11. Body seal
12. Nut
13. Front diaphragm plate
14. Front diaphragm
15. Center plate
16. Retainer
17. Center plate seal
18. Bearing
19. Pushrod
20. Key
21. Key retainer
22. Reaction disc hub
23. Reaction disc
24. O-ring
25. Center body
26. Rear diaphragm plate
27. Rear diaphragm
28. Valve body and rod
29. Retainer
30. Actuating rod
31. Retainer
32. Filter
33. Silencer
34. Filter

1. Clevis yoke
2. Locknut
3. Retainer
4. Seal

★ REPAIR KIT

Isuzu tandam vacuum servo—   Trooper II

17. Lubricate and install the bearing, seal and retainer to the center plate.

18. Use installer J-38595 to install the center plate assembly to the valve body.

19. Align the arrow mark on the rear diaphragm plate with the mark on the valve body and install the plate with a tilting motion. Install a new retainer to the front diaphragm.

20. Lubricate and install the actuating rod to the valve body and install the C-ring. Push the actuating rod and install the stopper key.

21. Install the first filter, the silencer then the second filter to the valve body and install the new retainer.

22. Lubricate and install the seal, bearing and retainer to the rear shell.

23. Mount the holding tool J-34350 in a vise and mount the front shell on the tool. Assemble the entire center plate assembly to the rear shell.

24. To assemble the unit, connect a vacuum source to the vacuum intake pipe on the front shell. Using the matchmarks as guides, apply vacuum and assemble the unit using tool J-9504-01. Make sure the bent area of the of the diaphragm does not drop against the front and rear shell engaging areas.

25. Rotate the rear shell clockwise until the notch on the rear shell is fully against the stopper. Tighten until the matchmarks are perfectly aligned.

26. Install the new rubber boot, locknut and clevis yoke.

27. Adjust the pushrod length to 0.7 in. (18.2mm) from the base of the front shell.

1988–90 TROOPER/TROOPER II

1. Remove the clevis yoke and locknut from the actuator rod.

2. Pry out the servo retainer and seal from the front of the shell.

─── **CAUTION** ───

The rear shell is spring loaded. Loosen it slowly and carefully or personal injury may result.

3. Matchmark the front and rear shells. Using wrench J-9504-01 and holder J-34250 (holes elongated to fit), separate the 2 shells slowly. Remove the servo spring.

4. Remove the rubber boot.

5. Remove the retainer, bearing and seal from the rear shell.

6. To disassemble the diaphragm assembly, remove the large nut with a 1½ in. wrench.

7. Remove the front diaphragm plate, front diaphragm and center plate.

8. Remove the retainer, center plate seal and bearing from the center plate.

9. Remove the pushrod and carefully pry the key out of the valve body. Remove the key retainer.

10. Rotate the reaction disc hub 90 degrees and release it from the center body. Remove the reaction disc and O-ring.

11. Remove the center body and diaphragm from the rear diaphragm plate.

12. Remove the valve body assembly. Remove the retainer and remove the actuating rod.

13. Remove the retainer and remove the filters and silencer from the rod.

To assemble:

14. Install the valve body to the rear diaphragm plate. Install the retainer with the cutouts to the valve body lugs and install the actuating rod.

15. Install the new rear diaphragm.

16. Install the center body and new lubricated O-ring. Set the retainer against the outer pawl of the reaction and rotate the reaction disc 90 degrees to install.

17. Install the key retainer, push in the actuating rod and install the stopper key.

18. Install the new filter, silencer, second filter and retainer.

19. Install the reaction disc (with the stepped side inward) and pushrod.

20. Lubricate and install the bearing, center plate seal and retainer to the center plate.

21. Install the front diaphragm to its plate and install 1½ in. nut.

22. Lubricate and install the seal, bearing and retainer to the rear shell. Install the new rubber boot.

23. Mount the holding tool J-34350 in a vise and mount the front shell on the tool. Assemble the entire diaphragm assembly, spring and the rear shell.

24. To assemble the unit, connect a

vacuum source to the vacuum intake pipe on the front shell. Using the matchmarks as guides, apply vacuum and assemble the unit using tool J–9504–01. Make sure the bent area of the of the diaphragm does not drop against the front and rear shell engaging areas.

25. Rotate the rear shell clockwise until the notch on the rear shell is fully against the stopper. Tighten until the matchmarks are perfectly aligned.

26. Install locknut and clevis yoke.

27. Apply silicone grease to the last seal and install to the front shell. Install the remaining retainer over the seal.

Caliper Service

Disassembly and Assembly

FRONT CALIPER

1. Remove the bleeder screw.
2. Drain the brake fluid from the caliper.
3. Remove the dust boot ring and the dust boot.
4. Position a shop rag opposite the top of the piston. Apply low pressure compressed air to the fluid inlet and carefully blow the piston out of the bore.

CAUTION

Do not put fingers where the piston will land when it is blown out of the caliper. The force of the piston can crush fingers and cause personal injury.

---

5. Remove the piston seal from inside the bore.

To assemble:

6. Blow out all fluid passages with low pressure compressed air.
7. Slight corrosion or rust can be removed with commutator paper or crocus cloth. Replace pistons that are pit-

ted, scored, peeling or otherwise damaged.

8. Lubricate the caliper bore with brake fluid. Lubricate the seal and install it in the groove.
9. Lubricate the piston and install it to the bore until it bottoms. If the piston will not go in by hand, it is probably cocked. Remove it and reinstall.
10. Apply lubricant to the dust boot mounting groove and install the boot. Install the retaining ring.
11. Apply rust penetrant to the bleeder screw threads and install to the caliper. Tighten it until it is just snug against its seat.

REAR CALIPER

1. Remove the sleeve and its dust boot. Remove the mounting pin dust boot.
2. Remove the bleeder screw.
3. Drain the brake fluid from the caliper. Remove the dust boot ring and the dust boot.
4. To remove the piston, unscrew it using tool J–37617. Remove the piston seal.
5. Remove the snapring at the bottom of the caliper bore. Pull out the pad adjusting spindle along with the retainer, spring, spring plate and stopper. Remove the O-ring from the spindle.
6. Remove the parking brake link from the bottom of the caliper bore.
7. Remove the parking brake lever, spring and dust boot.
8. Remove the return spring and dust boot.

To assemble:

9. Apply brake system compatible grease to the parking brake link and install.
10. Lubricate and install the new O-ring to the pad adjusting spindle. Attach the stopper, spring plate, spring and retainer to the spindle. Turn the

embossed side of the stopper to the outer side and align the cutaways of the stopper and retainer.

11. Insert the spindle assembly into the caliper bore fitting the stopper to the groove at the bottom of the bore. Install the snapring and position it so that the open area between ends aligns with the bleeder.
12. Lubricate the piston seal and install to the groove in the caliper. Install the piston and using tool J–37617, turn the piston clockwise until it bottoms. Align the piston cutouts with the inspection window in the caliper body. If this is not done, the brake pads will wear unevenly.
13. Apply lubricant to the dust boot mounting groove and install the boot. Install the retaining ring.
14. Apply rust penetrant to the bleeder screw threads and install to the caliper. Tighten it until it is just snug against its seat.
15. Install the new parking brake lever dust boot, spring and lever. Torque the retaining bolt to 35 ft. lbs. (47 Nm).

Wheel Cylinder Service

Disassembly and Assembly

1. Remove the bleeder screw.
2. Remove both rubber boots.
3. Remove the pistons from the cylinder.
4. Remove the piston cups.
5. Remove the return spring.
6. Hone the cylinder bore if it is not damaged, to provide a smooth sealing surface. Wash and dry the bore after honing.

To assemble:

7. Lubricate the cylinder bore with brake fluid. Install the return spring.
8. Lubricate the new piston cups and install them to the cylinder. Lubricate and install the pistons.
9. Apply lubricant to the boot mounting groove and install the boot.
10. Apply rust penetrant to the bleeder screw threads and install to the wheel cylinder. Tighten it until it is just snug against its seat.

MAZDA

NOTE: When cleaning brake system components, use only brake fluid or denatured isopropyl alcohol. Never use a mineral-based solvent such as gasoline or paint thinner; these fluids will leave a residue that may swell and deteriorate rubber parts within

1. Sleeve
2. Sleeve dust boot
3. Guide pin dust boot
4. Bleeder and cap
5. Dust seal ring
6. Dust seal
7. Piston
8. Piston seal
9. Caliper body

Isuzu front caliper

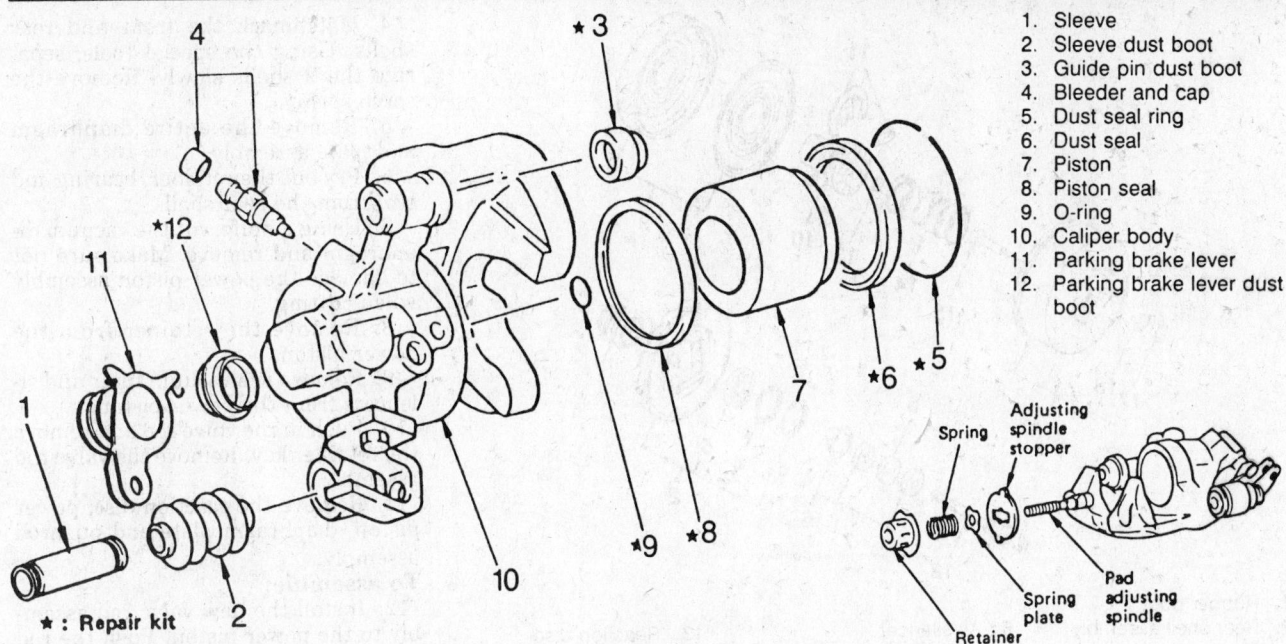

1. Sleeve
2. Sleeve dust boot
3. Guide pin dust boot
4. Bleeder and cap
5. Dust seal ring
6. Dust seal
7. Piston
8. Piston seal
9. O-ring
10. Caliper body
11. Parking brake lever
12. Parking brake lever dust boot

★ : Repair kit

Isuzu rear caliper

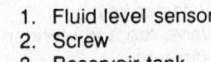

the system. All alcohol must be removed from the system when the work is done because alcohol mixed with brake fluid lowers its boiling point.

Do not hone any aluminum bores. There is a hard anodized coating on the aluminum which will be removed if honed. This will allow the aluminum to wear quickly and will damage the component.

Master Cylinder Service

Disassembly and Assembly

1. Remove the brake fluid reservoir retainer screw.
2. Remove the reservoir and seals.
3. Remove the dust seal from the end of the master cylinder.
4. Push the primary piston in and remove the stopper bolt and gasket.
5. Hold the pistons in and remove the snapring.
6. Let the primary piston spring out and remove the primary piston assembly and end washer, if equipped.
7. Remove the secondary piston assembly. This may be accomplished by carefully blowing low pressure compressed air through the secondary side outlet port if it does not come out easily.

To assemble:

8. Assemble the secondary piston assembly, if it was disassembled. Coat the master cylinder bore and secondary and primary piston seals liberally with brake fluid. Install both assemblies to the master cylinder.

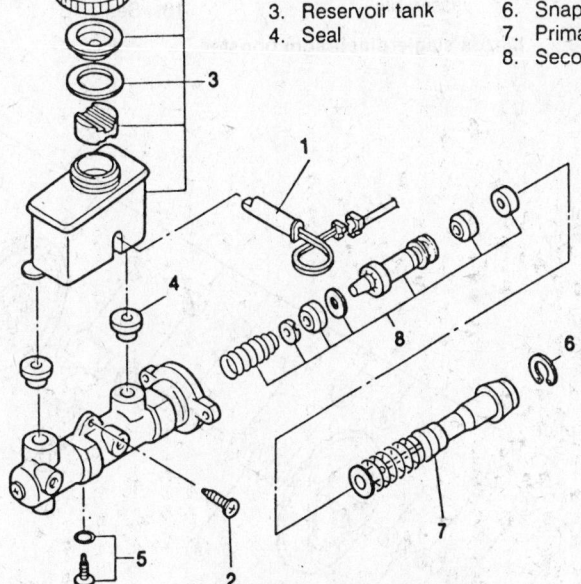

1. Fluid level sensor
2. Screw
3. Reservoir tank
4. Seal
5. Stopper screw and O-ring
6. Snapring
7. Primary piston assembly
8. Secondary assembly

Mazda master cylinder

9. Push the pistons in and install a new snapring.
10. Hold the pistons in and install the stopper bolt with a new gasket.
11. Install the brake fluid reservoir with new seals. Install the reservoir retaining screw.

Brake Booster Service

The brake booster on the MPV is not serviceable. If the unit is defective, replace the entire assembly.

SINGLE DIAPHRAGM

Disassembly and Assembly

2WD PICK-UP

1. Remove the clevis yoke and locknut from the actuator rod.
2. Pry out the servo retainer and seal from the front of the shell.
3. Remove the rubber boot.

— **CAUTION** —

The rear shell is spring loaded. Loosen it slowly and carefully or personal injury may result.

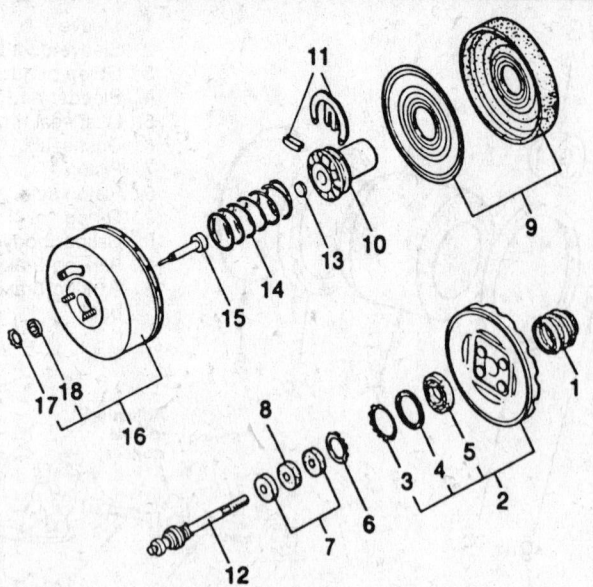

4. Matchmark the front and rear shells. Using the special tools, separate the 2 shells slowly. Remove the servo spring.

5. Remove the entire diaphragm and plate assembly.

6. Pry out the retainer, bearing and seal from the rear shell.

7. Using a knife, cut the vacuum diaphragm and remove. Make sure not to damage the power piston assembly when cutting.

8. Remove the retainer from the power piston.

9. Remove the vacuum filter and silencers from the power piston.

10. Push in the valve rod and remove the retainer key. Remove the valve rod assembly.

11. Remove the reaction disc, power piston, diaphragm plate and pushrod assembly.

To assemble:

12. Install the new valve rod assembly to the power piston. Push the rod in and install the retainer key.

13. Install the new vacuum silencers and filter.

14. Install the new retainer to the rear shell.

15. Install the diaphragm plate and

1. Rubber boot
2. Rear shell assembly
3. Retainer
4. Bearing
5. Dust seal
6. Retainer
7. Air filter
8. Air silencer
9. Diaphragm and plate
10. Power piston assembly
11. Retainer key
12. Valve rod and plunger assembly
13. Reaction disc
14. Spring
15. Pushrod
16. Front shell assembly
17. Retainer
18. Seal

Mazda single diaphragm booster

1. Clevis
2. Nut
3. Rear shell assembly
4. Front shell assembly
5. Boot
6. Rear shell
7. Retainer
8. Bearing
9. Seal
10. Locknut
11. Front diaphragm
12. Front diaphragm plate
13. Center plate
14. Retainer
15. Seal
16. Bearing
17. Stopper and key
18. Retainer
19. Retainer
20. Air filter
21. Air silencer
22. Valve rod and plunger assembly
23. Valve body
24. O-ring
25. Reaction disc hub
26. O-ring
27. Reaction disc
28. Rear diaphragm
29. Rear diaphragm plate
30. Spring
31. Pushrod
32. Front shell
33. Retainer
34. Seal

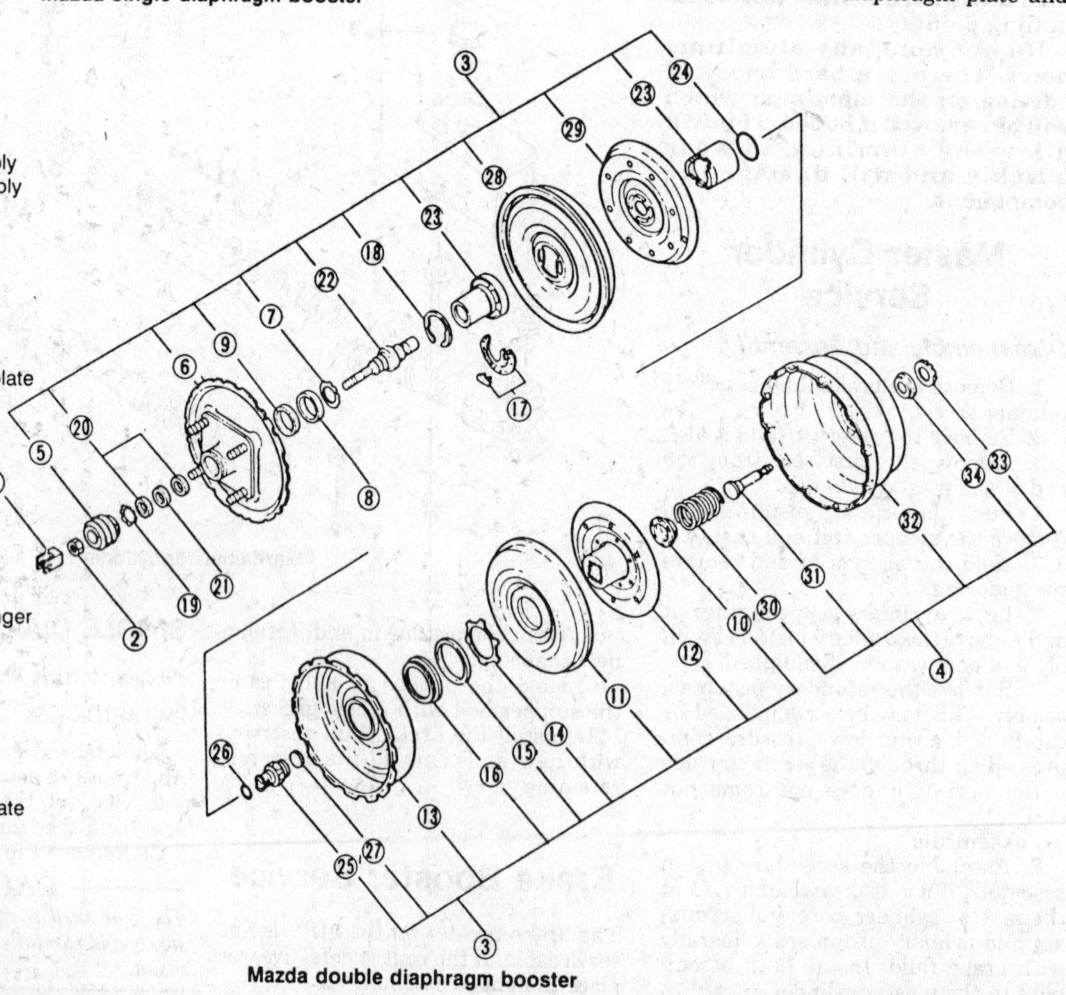

Mazda double diaphragm booster

carefully attach the new vacuum diaphragm to the power piston.

16. Apply silicone grease to the new reaction disc and install to the power piston. Install the pushrod and spring.

17. Apply silicone grease to the rear shell seal and install.

18. Mount the front shell in a vise. Assemble the entire diaphragm plate assembly to the rear shell. Install the bearing and new retainer.

19. To assemble the unit, connect a vacuum source to the vacuum intake pipe on the front shell. Using the matchmarks as guides, apply vacuum and assemble the unit using the special tool. Make sure the bent area of the of the diaphragm does not drop against the front and rear shell engaging areas.

20. Rotate the rear shell clockwise until the notch on the rear shell is fully against the stopper. Tighten until the matchmarks are perfectly aligned.

21. Install the new rubber boot, locknut and clevis yoke.

22. Apply silicone grease to the last seal and install to the front shell. Install the remaining retainer over the seal.

DOUBLE DIAPHRAGM

Disassembly and Assembly

4WD PICK-UP

1. Remove the clevis yoke and locknut from the actuator rod.

2. Pry out the servo retainer and seal from the front of the shell.

— CAUTION —

The rear shell is spring loaded. Loosen it slowly and carefully or personal injury may result.

3. Matchmark the front and rear shells. Using the special tools, separate the shells. Remove the rubber boot.

4. Clamp holding tool 49-U043-002 in a vise and mount the rear shell assembly to the tool. Uncrimp the reaction disc hub. Remove the locknut using wrench 49-U043-001.

5. Remove the retainer, bearing and seal from the rear shell.

6. Remove the front diaphragm plate, front diaphragm and center plate.

7. Remove the retainer, center plate seal and bearing from the center plate.

8. Remove the pushrod and carefully pry the key out of the valve body.

9. Remove the key retainer.

10. Rotate the reaction disc hub 90 degrees and release it from the center body. Remove the reaction disc and O-ring.

11. Remove the center body and diaphragm from the rear diaphragm plate.

12. Remove the valve body assembly. Remove the retainer and remove the actuating rod.

13. Remove the retainer and remove the filters and silencer from the rod.

To assemble:

14. Install the valve body to the rear diaphragm plate. Install the retainer with the cutouts to the valve body lugs and install the actuating rod.

15. Install the new rear diaphragm.

16. Install the center body and new lubricated O-ring. Set the retainer against the outer pawl of the reaction and rotate the reaction disc 90 degrees to install.

17. Install the key retainer, push in the actuating rod and install the stopper key.

18. Install the new filter, silencer, second filter and retainer.

19. Install the reaction disc (with the stepped side inward) and pushrod.

20. Lubricate and install the bearing, center plate seal and retainer to the center plate.

21. Install the front diaphragm to its plate and install locknut using the special wrench. Crimp the reaction disc hub in the 2 notched grooves of the locknut.

22. Lubricate and install the seal, bearing and retainer to the rear shell. Install the new rubber boot.

23. Align the notches of the rear shell and center plate. Make sure the bent area of the of the diaphragm does not drop against the front and rear shell engaging areas.

24. Push down and rotate the rear shell clockwise until the notch on the rear shell is fully against the stopper. Tighten until the matchmarks are perfectly aligned.

25. Install locknut and clevis yoke.

26. Apply silicone grease to the last seal and install to the front shell. Install the remaining retainer over the seal.

Caliper Service

Disassembly and Assembly

1. Remove the bleeder screw.

2. Drain the brake fluid from the caliper.

3. Remove the dust boot.

4. Position a shop rag opposite the top of the piston. Apply low pressure compressed air to the fluid inlet and carefully blow the piston out of the bore.

— CAUTION —

Do not put fingers where the piston will land when it is blown out of the caliper. The force of the piston can crush fingers and cause personal injury.

5. Remove the piston seal from inside the bore.

To assemble:

6. Blow out all fluid passages with low pressure compressed air.

7. Slight corrosion or rust can be removed with commutator paper or crocus cloth. Replace pistons that are pitted, scored, peeling or otherwise damaged.

8. Lubricate the caliper bore with brake fluid. Lubricate the seal and install it in the groove.

9. Lubricate the piston and install it to the bore until it bottoms. If the piston will not go in by hand, it is probably cocked. Remove it and reinstall.

10. Apply lubricant to the dust boot mounting groove and install the boot.

11. Apply rust penetrant to the bleeder screw threads and install to the caliper. Tighten it until it is just snug against its seat.

Wheel Cylinder Service

Disassembly and Assembly

1. On the left side, remove the bleeder screw and check ball.

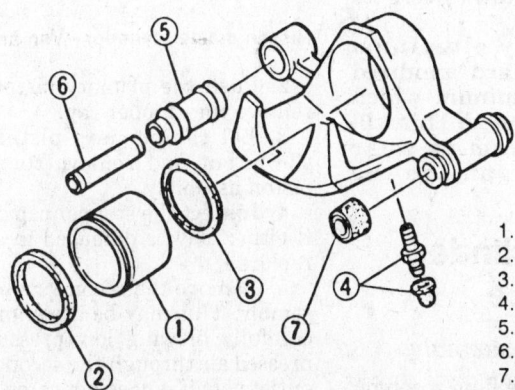

1. Piston
2. Dust seal
3. Piston seal
4. Bleeder and cap
5. Pin boot
6. Pin
7. Bushing

Mazda caliper

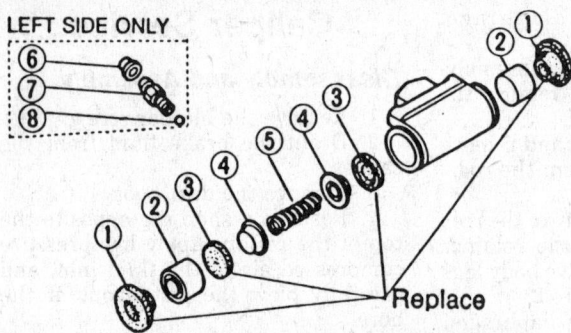

LEFT SIDE ONLY
6
7
8

1. Dust boots
2. Pistons
3. Piston rubber cups
4. Piston cups
5. Spring
6. Rubber cap
7. Bleeder
8. Steel ball

Replace

Mazda wheel cylinder

2. Remove both dust boots.
3. Remove the pistons.
4. Remove the piston cups.
5. Remove the return spring.
6. Hone the cylinder bore if it is not damaged, to provide a smooth sealing surface. Wash and dry the bore after honing.

To assemble:

7. Lubricate the cylinder bore with brake fluid. Install the return spring.
8. Lubricate the new piston cups and install them to the cylinder. Lubricate and install the pistons.
9. Apply lubricant to the boot mounting groove and install the boot.
10. Apply rust penetrant to the bleeder screw threads and install it with the check ball to the wheel cylinder. Tighten until just snug.

NISSAN

NOTE: When cleaning brake system components, use only brake fluid or denatured isopropyl alcohol. Never use a mineral-based solvent such as gasoline or paint thinner; these fluids will leave a residue that may swell and deteriorate rubber parts within the system. All alcohol must be removed from the system when the work is done because alcohol mixed with brake fluid lowers its boiling point.

Do not hone any aluminum bores. There is a hard anodized coating on the aluminum which will be removed if honed. This will allow the aluminum to wear quickly and will damage the component.

Master Cylinder Service

Disassembly and Assembly

1. Remove the brake fluid reservoir and seals or hoses.

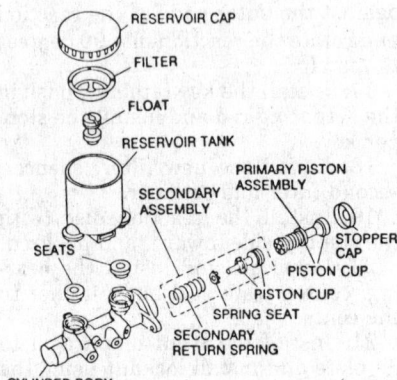

Nissan master cylinder—Pick-Up and Pathfinder

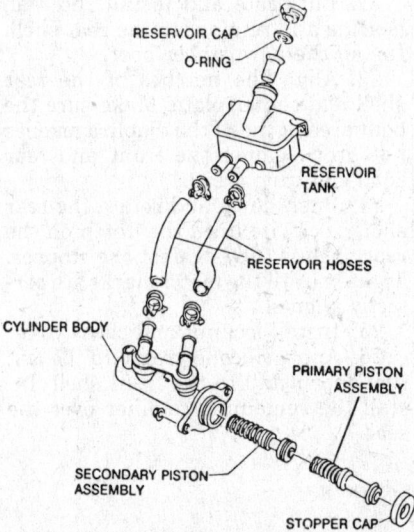

Nissan master cylinder—Van and Axxess

2. Push the primary piston in and remove the stopper cap.
3. Let the primary piston spring slowly out and remove the primary piston assembly.
4. Inspect the stopper cap carefully. If either claw is damaged in any way, replace it.
5. Remove the secondary piston assembly. This may be accomplished by carefully blowing low pressure compressed air through the secondary side outlet port if it does not come out easily. Disassemble the secondary piston

on Pick-Up and Pathfinder only. The secondary pistons on Axxess and Van are not serviceable.

To assemble:

6. Assemble the secondary piston assembly, if it was disassembled. Coat the master cylinder bore and secondary and primary piston seals liberally with brake fluid. Install both assemblies to the master cylinder.
7. Push the pistons in and install the stopper cap.
8. Install the fluid reservoir and seals, if equipped.

Brake Booster Service

The brake boosters installed on these vehicles are not serviceable. If the unit is defective, replace the entire assembly.

Caliper Service

SINGLE PISTON TYPE

Disassembly and Assembly

1. Remove the bleeder screw.
2. Drain the brake fluid from the caliper.
3. Remove the dust seal ring (rear caliper only) and the dust seal.
4. Position a shop rag opposite the top of the piston. Apply low pressure compressed air to the fluid inlet and carefully blow the piston out of the bore.

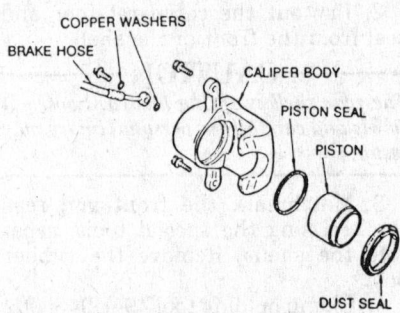

Nissan single piston front caliper

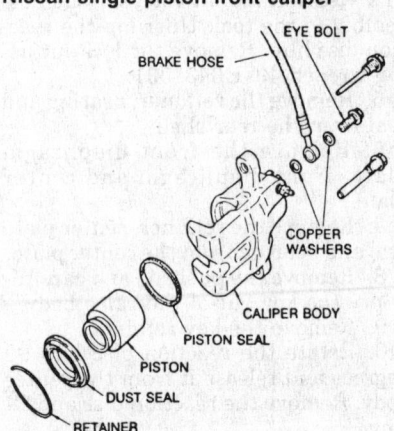

Nissan rear caliper

———— CAUTION ————

Do not put fingers where the piston will land when it is blown out of the caliper. The force of the piston can crush fingers and cause personal injury.

5. Remove the piston seal from inside the bore.

To assemble:

6. Blow out all fluid passages with low pressure compressed air.

7. Slight corrosion or rust can be removed with commutator paper or crocus cloth. Replace pistons that are pitted, scored, peeling or otherwise damaged.

8. Lubricate the caliper bore with brake fluid. Lubricate the seal and install it in the groove.

9. Lubricate the piston and install it to the bore until it bottoms. If the piston will not go in by hand, it is probably cocked. Remove it and reinstall.

10. Apply lubricant to the dust seal mounting groove and install the seal. Install the retaining ring, if equipped.

11. Apply rust penetrant to the bleeder screw threads and install to the caliper. Tighten it until it is just snug against its seat.

DOUBLE PISTON TYPE

Disassembly and Assembly

1. Remove the bleeder screw.
2. Drain the brake fluid from the caliper.
3. Remove the dust covers.
4. Position a shop rag opposite the top of the piston. Apply low pressure compressed air to the fluid inlet and carefully blow the pistons out of their bores. If both pistons do not come out, install the extracted piston back into its bore just enough to seal; then hold it place with a suitable spacer. Blow out the remaining piston.

———— CAUTION ————

Do not put fingers where the piston will land when it is blown out of the caliper. The force of the piston can crush fingers and cause personal injury.

5. Remove the piston seals from inside the bore.

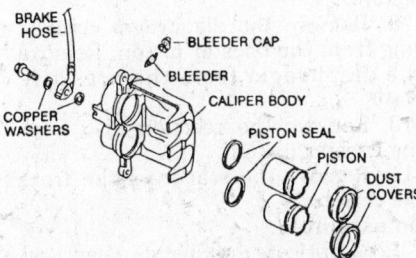

Nissan double piston caliper

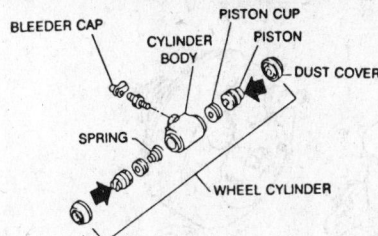

Nissan wheel cylinder

To assemble:

6. Blow out all fluid passages with low pressure compressed air.

7. Slight corrosion or rust can be removed with commutator paper or crocus cloth. Replace pistons that are pitted, scored, peeling or otherwise damaged.

8. Lubricate the caliper bore with brake fluid. Lubricate the seals and install in the grooves.

9. Lubricate the pistons and install them to the bores until they bottom. If either piston will not go in by hand, it is probably cocked. Remove it and reinstall.

10. Apply lubricant to the dust seal mounting grooves and install the seals.

11. Apply rust penetrant to the bleeder screw threads and install to the caliper. Tighten it until it is just snug against its seat.

Wheel Cylinder Service

Disassembly and Assembly

1. Remove the bleeder screw.
2. Remove both dust covers.
3. Remove the pistons.
4. Remove the piston cups.
5. Remover the return spring.
6. Hone the cylinder bore if it is not damaged, to provide a smooth sealing surface. Wash and dry the bore after honing.

To assemble:

7. Lubricate the cylinder bore with brake fluid. Install the return spring.

8. Lubricate the new piston cups and install them to the cylinder. Lubricate and install the pistons.

9. Apply lubricant to the dust cover mounting groove and install the cover.

10. Apply rust penetrant to the bleeder screw threads and install to the wheel cylinder. Tighten it until it is just snug against its seat.

SUZUKI/GEO

NOTE: When cleaning brake system components, use only

brake fluid or denatured isopropyl alcohol. Never use a mineral-based solvent such as gasoline or paint thinner; these fluids will leave a residue that may swell and deteriorate rubber parts within the system. All alcohol must be removed from the system when the work is done because alcohol mixed with brake fluid lowers its boiling point.

Do not hone any aluminum bores. There is a hard anodized coating on the aluminum which will be removed if honed. This will allow the aluminum to wear quickly and will damage the component.

Master Cylinder Service

Disassembly and Assembly

1. Remove the brake fluid reservoir screw of roll pin and remove the reservoir. Remove the seals.

2. Push the primary piston in and remove the snapring.

3. Let the primary piston spring slowly out and remove piston stopper, cups and the primary piston assembly.

4. Remove the secondary piston stopper bolt.

5. Remove the secondary piston assembly. This may be accomplished by carefully blowing low pressure compressed air through the secondary side outlet port if it does not come out easily. Disassemble the secondary piston.

To assemble:

6. Assemble the secondary piston assembly. Coat the master cylinder bore and secondary and primary piston seals liberally with brake fluid. Install both assemblies to the master cylinder.

7. Install the cups and stoppers. Install the snapring.

8. Push the pistons in and install the stopper bolt.

9. Install the fluid reservoir and seals.

Brake Booster Service

SINGLE DIAPHRAGM TYPE

SAMURAI

1. Remove the piston rod from the booster.

2. Remove the pushrod clevis and locknut.

3. Mount the booster on the holding tool set 09950–88210. Do not tighten the 2 outer nuts to more than 30 inch lbs. or the booster may become deformed.

4. Turn the special tool bolt clock-

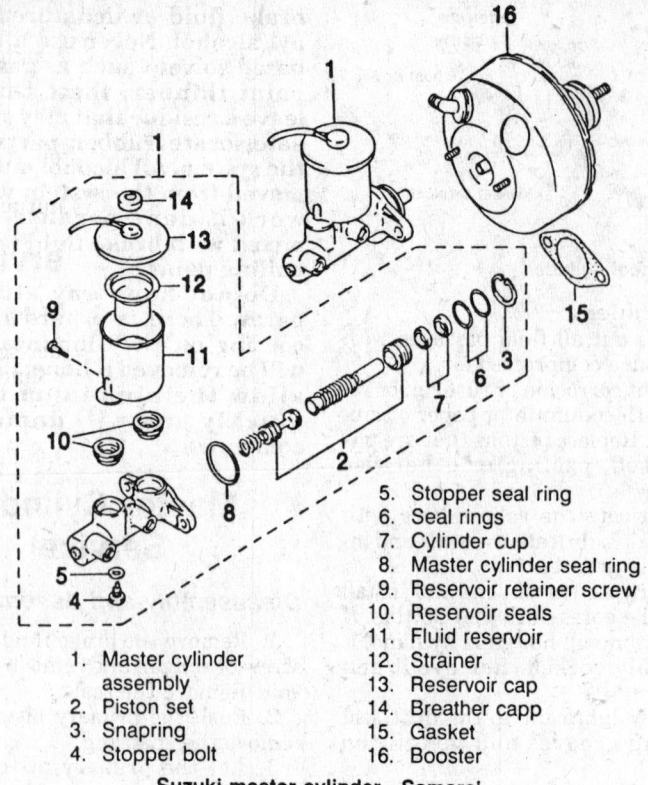

5. Stopper seal ring
6. Seal rings
7. Cylinder cup
8. Master cylinder seal ring
9. Reservoir retainer screw
10. Reservoir seals
11. Fluid reservoir
12. Strainer
13. Reservoir cap
14. Breather capp
15. Gasket
16. Booster

1. Master cylinder
   assembly
2. Piston set
3. Snapring
4. Stopper bolt

Suzuki master cylinder—Samarai

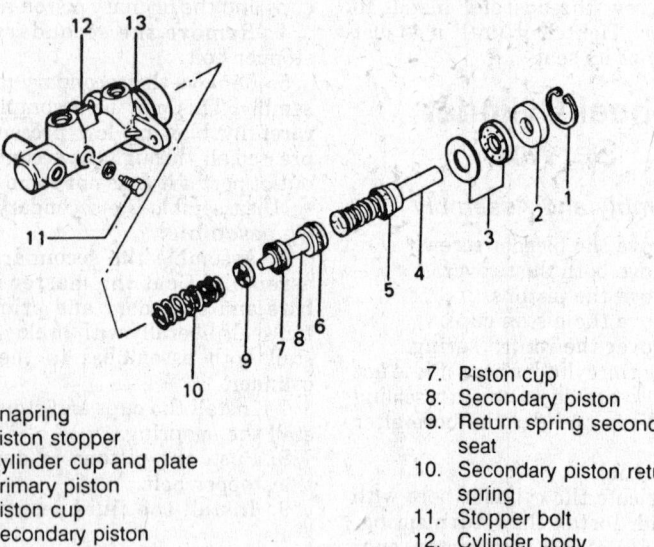

1. Snapring
2. Piston stopper
3. Cylinder cup and plate
4. Primary piston
5. Piston cup
6. Secondary piston
   pressure cap

7. Piston cup
8. Secondary piston
9. Return spring secondary
   seat
10. Secondary piston return
    spring
11. Stopper bolt
12. Cylinder body
13. Seal

Suzuki/Geo master cylinder—Sidekick and Tracker

wise until the projection and depression in the bodies match. Matchmark the bodies at that location.

5. Remove the booster from the tool and separate the bodies.

— CAUTION —

The rear body is spring loaded. Loosen it slowly and carefully or personal injury may result.

6. Remove the boot, air cleaner elements and air cleaner separator from the rear body.

7. Turn the booster piston counterclockwise and remove from the rear body.

8. Push the air valve down and remove the stopper key. Remove the air valve assembly from the booster piston.

9. Remove the diaphragm from the pressure plate.

10. Remove the reaction disc from the booster piston.

11. Remove the seal from the from the rear body.

To assemble:

12. Lubricate and install a new seal to the rear body.

13. Lubricate and install the booster air valve to the booster piston.

14. Compress the valve and install the stopper key.

15. Install the new diaphragm to the pressure plate. Make sure the diaphragm is seated securely in its groove in the pressure plate.

16. Lubricate the face and install the reaction disc to the booster piston.

17. Install the booster piston to the rear body by turning it clockwise into place.

18. Install the new air cleaner separator and elements to the air valve rod.

19. Install the boot to the rear body.

20. Place the front body on the special tool and place the return spring on it large end up.

21. Place the assembled rear body on the return spring and compress. Turn the special bolt counterclockwise until the projection and depression line up.

22. Install the piston rod into the booster piston.

23. Install the locknut and clevis.

SIDEKICK AND TRACKER

1. Remove the pushrod clevis.

2. Remove the locknut.

3. Mount the booster on the holding tool set 09950–88210. Do not tighten the 2 outer nuts to more than 30 inch lbs. or the booster may become deformed.

4. Turn the special tool bolt clockwise until the projection and depression in the bodies match. Matchmark the bodies at that location.

5. Remove the booster from the tool and separate the bodies.

— CAUTION —

The rear body is spring loaded. Loosen it slowly and carefully or personal injury may result.

6. Remove the piston rod, boot, air cleaner elements and air cleaner separator from the rear body.

7. Remove the valve stopper key cushion.

8. Push the air valve down and remove the stopper key. Remove the air valve assembly from the booster piston.

9. Remove the diaphragm circular ring from the booster piston. Remove the diaphragm from the pressure plate.

10. Remove the reaction disc from the booster piston.

11. Remove the seal from the from the rear body.

To assemble:

12. Lubricate and install a new seal to the rear body.

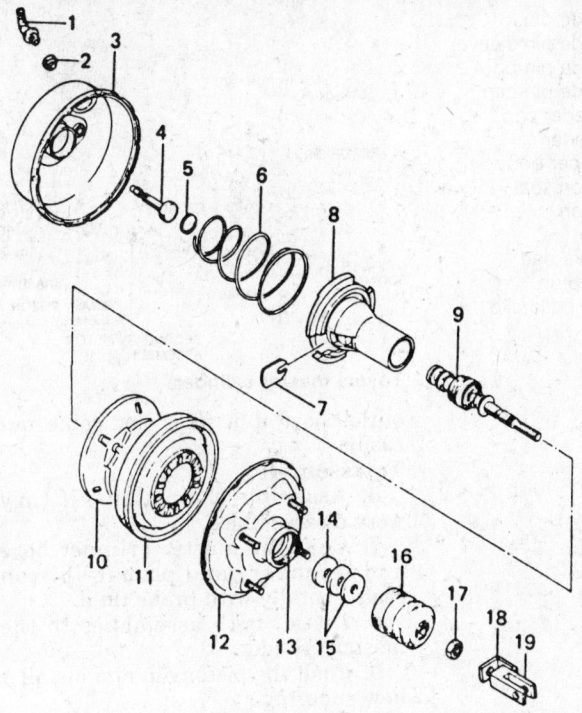

1. Vacuum check valve
2. Grommet
3. Front body
4. Piston rod
5. Reaction disc
6. Booster piston return spring
7. Valve stopper key
8. Booster piston
9. Booster air valve assembly
10. Pressure plate
11. Diaphragm
12. Rear body
13. Seal
14. Air cleaner separator
15. Air cleaner element
16. Rubber boot
17. Nut
18. Bracket
19. Pushrod clevis

Suzuki single diaphragm booster—Samarai

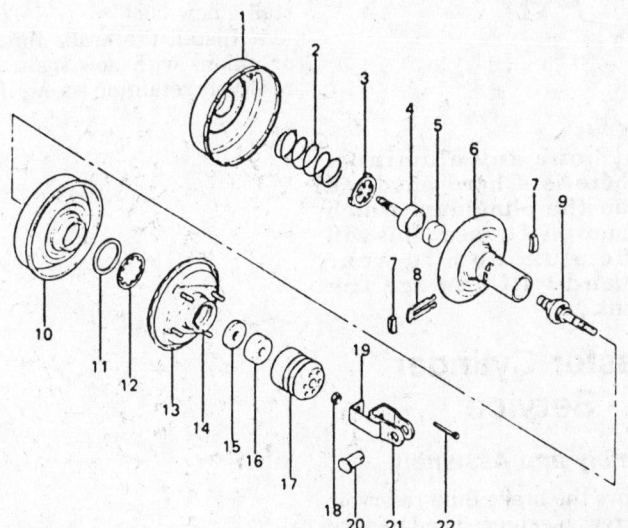

1. Front body	8. Valve stopper key	15. Air cleaner separator
2. Booster piston return spring	9. Booster air valve assembly	16. Air cleaner element
3. Piston rod retainer	10. Diaphragm	17. Rubber boot
4. Piston rod	11. Diaphragm retainer	18. Nut
5. Reaction disc	12. Retainer	19. Bracket
6. Booster piston	13. Rear body	20. Clevis pin
7. Key cushion	14. Seal	21. Pushrod clevis
		22. Cotter pin

Suzuki/Geo single diaphragm booster—Sidekick and Tracker

13. Install the retainer to the diaphragm. Install the diaphragm to the booster piston and install the new diaphragm circular ring.

14. Lubricate and install the booster air valve to the booster piston. Compress the valve and install the stopper key. Install the cushion to the notch in the stopper.

15. Install the booster piston to the rear body.

16. Install the new air cleaner separator and elements to the air valve rod.

17. Install the boot to the rear body.

18. Lubricate the face and install the reaction disc to the booster piston.

19. Place the front body on the special tool and place the return spring,

rod retainer and piston rod on it.

20. Place the assembled rear body on the return spring and compress. Turn the special bolt counterclockwise until the projection and depression line up.

21. Install the piston rod into the booster piston.

22. Install the locknut and clevis.

Caliper Service

Disassembly and Assembly

1. Remove the bleeder screw.
2. Drain the brake fluid from the caliper.
3. Remove the cylinder boot.
4. Position a shop rag opposite the top of the piston. Apply low pressure compressed air to the fluid inlet and carefully blow the piston out of the bore.

— **CAUTION** —

Do not put fingers where the piston will land when it is blown out of the caliper. The force of the piston can crush fingers and cause personal injury.

5. Remove the piston seal from inside the bore.

To assemble:

6. Blow out all fluid passages with low pressure compressed air.
7. Slight corrosion or rust can be removed with commutator paper or crocus cloth. Replace pistons that are pitted, scored, peeling or otherwise damaged.
8. Lubricate the caliper bore with brake fluid. Lubricate the seal and install it in the groove.
9. Lubricate the piston and install it to the bore until it bottoms. If the piston will not go in by hand, it is probably cocked. Remove it and reinstall.
10. Apply lubricant to the cylinder boot mounting groove and install.
11. Apply rust penetrant to the bleeder screw threads and install to the caliper. Tighten it until it is just snug against its seat.

Wheel Cylinder Service

Disassembly and Assembly

1. Remove the bleeder screw, if equipped.
2. Remove both rubber boots.
3. Remove the piston assemblies, each consisting of the piston and cup.
4. Remove the piston cups from the pistons, being careful not to scratch the piston.
5. Remove the return spring.
6. Hone the cylinder bore if it is not damaged, to provide a smooth sealing

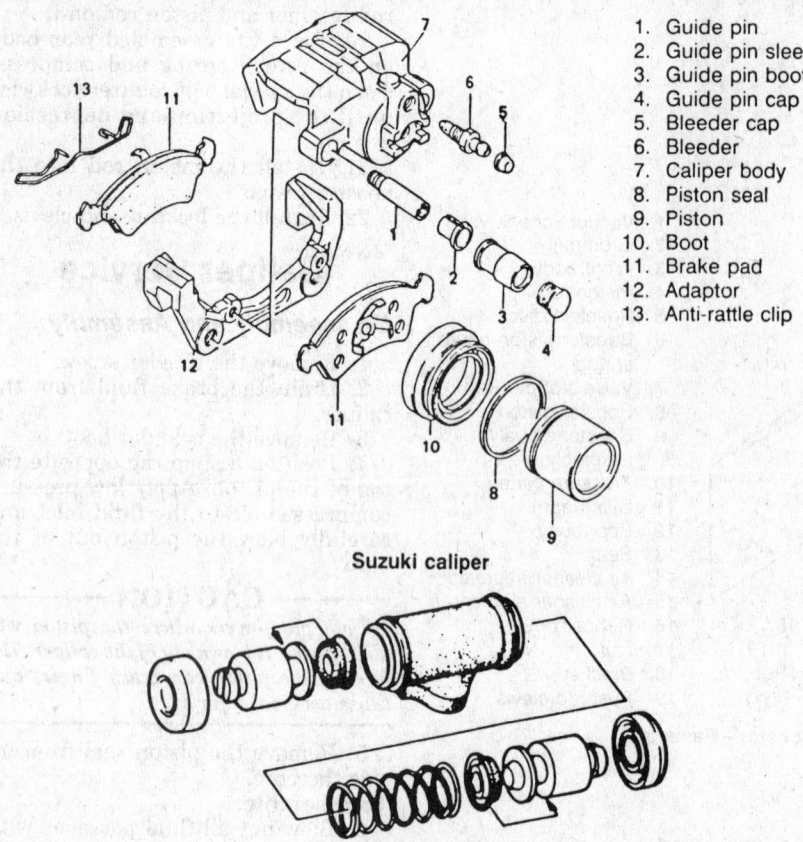

1. Guide pin
2. Guide pin sleeve
3. Guide pin boot
4. Guide pin cap
5. Bleeder cap
6. Bleeder
7. Caliper body
8. Piston seal
9. Piston
10. Boot
11. Brake pad
12. Adaptor
13. Anti-rattle clip

Suzuki caliper

Suzuki wheel cylinder

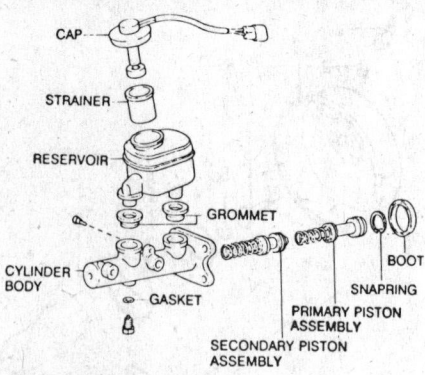

Toyota master cylinder

surface. Wash and dry the bore after honing.

To assemble:

7. Lubricate the cylinder bore with brake fluid.

8. Lubricate the new piston cups and install them to the pistons, with their lips facing upward. Install the assemblies to the cylinder.

9. Apply lubricant to the boot mounting groove and install the boot.

10. Apply rust penetrant to the bleeder screw threads and install to the wheel cylinder. Tighten until it is just snug against its seat.

TOYOTA

NOTE: When cleaning brake system components, use only brake fluid or denatured isopropyl alcohol. Never use a mineral-based solvent such as gasoline or paint thinner; these fluids will leave a residue that may swell and deteriorate rubber parts within the system. All alcohol must be removed from the system when the work is done because alcohol mixed with brake fluid lowers its boiling point.

Do not hone any aluminum bores. There is a hard anodized coating on the aluminum which will be removed if honed. This will allow the aluminum to wear quickly and will damage the component.

Master Cylinder Service

Disassembly and Assembly

1. Remove the brake fluid reservoir retainer screw, if equipped and remove the reservoir and seals or remove the reservoir unions and seals.

2. Remove the boot. Push the primary piston in and remove the stopper bolt and gasket.

3. Hold the pistons in and remove the snapring.

NOTE: Do not disassemble either piston assembly on the Pick-Up and 4Runner. The individual parts are not serviceable.

4. Let the primary piston spring out and remove the primary piston assembly.

5. Remove the secondary piston assembly. This may be accomplished by carefully blowing low pressure compressed air through the secondary side

outlet port if it does not come out easily.

To assemble:

6. Assemble the pistons, if they were disassembled.

7. Coat the master cylinder bore and secondary and primary piston seals liberally with brake fluid.

8. Install both assemblies to the master cylinder.

9. Push the pistons in and install a new snapring.

10. Hold the pistons in and install the stopper bolt with a new gasket. Install a new boot.

11. Install the brake fluid reservoir or unions with new seals. Install the reservoir retaining screw, if equipped.

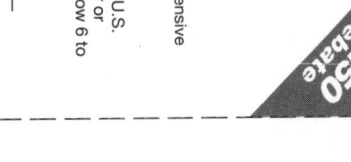
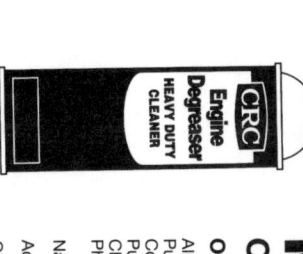

HERE'S HOW TO GET YOUR CASH

1. Purchase any of the selected quality AC products on the front of the coupon from your local AC-Delco retailer during the rebate period through December 31, 1996.
2. Circle the price of your AC product on your store receipt (dated during the rebate period) and clip the "AC" brand name and part number from each package as proof of purchase.
3. Complete this coupon and mail it with your receipts and proof of purchase to:

AC-Delco Rebate, P.O. Box 5970, Kalamazoo, MI 49003-5970

This rebate request must be received by Jan. 31, 1997. Good only in USA.

Number of AC Spark Plugs/Glow Plugs	x $ .35 = $		(Excludes AC RAPIDFIRE Spark Plugs.)
Number of AC Oil Filters	x $1.25 = $		
Number of AC Air Filters	x $1.75 = $		
	TOTAL REBATE $		

Name _____

Address _____

City _____ State ___ Zip ___

Make/Model/Year of Vehicle _____ Mileage ___ Engine ___ Cylinders ___

AC Products Used _____

NOTE: Please allow up to 90 days for you rebate. Offer effective through December 31, 1996. Coupon must be received by January 31, 1997. Rebate limited to a maximum of 32 AC Spark Plugs/Glow Plugs (AC RAPIDFIRE Spark Plug is not eligible for this rebate), 4 AC Oil Filters, 4 AC Air Filters per household. Reproduction of coupon not accepted. Offer good only in U.S.A. Void where prohibited. Not available to clubs, groups or other organizations or to AC-Delco direct or indirect retailers.

Valvoline $3.00 Cash-Back Offer on DURABLEND™

To receive your Valvoline® DuraBlend™ check good for cash, complete this special order form and send it with your proof-of-purchase* to the address below. **REBATE REQUESTS MUST BE MAILED WITHIN 30 DAYS OF CASH REGISTER RECEIPT DATE.**

DuraBlend™ $3.00 Cash-Back • 400 Benigno Blvd. • Bellmawr, NJ 08031

* Proof-of-Purchase includes:

Your original dated sales receipt for Valvoline® DuraBlend™ Motor Oil; AND One of the following (check one):

___ UPC code from bottom of one six-pack case containers of Valvoline® Semi-Synthetic DuraBlend™ Motor Oil.

___ Tamper-proof rings from up to six 1 quart bottles of Valvoline® DuraBlend™ Motor Oil.

Rebate requests must be made on this special order form and may not be mechanically reproduced. Offer Good October 1, 1995 to December 31, 1996. Limit of one Valvoline® DuraBlend™ check per household, address or organization. Maximum rebate of $3.00 allowed. Requests in excess of the limit will not be acknowledged or returned. Offer good only in the USA and Puerto Rico. Offer void where prohibited, taxed or otherwise restricted by law. May not be used in conjunction with any other Valvoline offer. Allow 8 weeks for delivery of your Valvoline® DuraBlend™ Check. Rebate check must be cashed within 90 days of issue. (Rebate checks will not be sent to a post box number.)
PLEASE COMPLETE THE FOLLOWING INFORMATION. PLEASE PRINT, NO ADDRESS LABELS ACCEPTED.

Name _____

Address _____ Apt.# ___

City _____ State ___ Zip ___

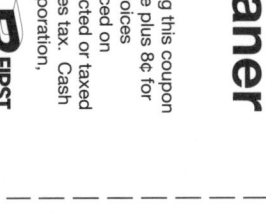
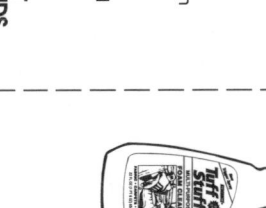